The Dictionary of Art

32

Varnish

TO

Wavere

GROVE

The Dictionary of Art

edited by JANE TURNER, in thirty-four volumes, 1996

This edition is distributed within the United Kingdom and Europe
by Macmillan Publishers Limited, London, and within the United States and Canada by
Grove's Dictionaries Inc., New York.

Text keyboarded by Wearset Limited, Sunderland, England
Database management by Pindar plc, York, England
Imagesetting by William Clowes Limited, Suffolk, England
Printed in the United States of America by RR Donnelley & Sons Company, Willard, Ohio

British Library Cataloguing in Publication Data	*Library of Congress Cataloging in Publication Data*

The dictionary of art
  1. Art - Dictionaries 2. Art - History -
    Dictionaries
I. Turner, Jane
703
 	
ISBN 1-884446-00-0
	The dictionary of art / editor, Jane Turner.
	  p. cm.
	  Includes bibliographical references and index.
	  Contents: 1. A to Anckerman
	  ISBN 1-884446-00-0 (alk. paper)
	  1. Art—Encyclopedias.
	  I. Turner, Jane, 1956–
	N31.D5 1996 96–13628
	703—dc20 CIP

The Dictionary of Art · volume thirty-two

Contents

List of Colour Illustrations   vi

General Abbreviations   vii

A Note on the Use of the Dictionary   xiii

The Dictionary, Volume Thirty Two:
Varnish–Wavere   1

Illustration Acknowledgements   926

List of Colour Illustrations

PLATE I. **Wall painting**

1. Wall painting of a garden, from the tomb of Nebamun, Thebes, Egypt, *c.* 1400 BC (London, British Museum/Photo: Trustees of the British Museum)

2. Wall painting of a garden scene (detail), from the Villa of Livia, Prima Porta, late 1st century BC (Rome, Museo Nazionale Romano delle Terme/Photo: AKG Ltd, London/Eric Lessing)

PLATE II. **Wall painting**

1. Wall painting of the *Anastasis* ('Harrowing of Hell'; early 14th century), in the apse of the parekklesion of the church of Christ the Saviour in Chora, Istanbul (Photo: Ancient Art and Architecture Collection, London)

2. Wall painting by Simone Martini: *Maestà* (1312–15), Sala del Mappamondo, Palazzo Pubblico, Siena (Photo: Scala, Florence)

PLATE III. **Wallpaper**

Great Indian Tiger Hunt (detail), wallpaper by Joseph Dufour & Cie, Paris, colour printed from woodblocks, 2.27 × 1.60 m, from the series *Views of India*, 1815 (Manchester, University of Manchester, Whitworth Art Gallery/Photo: Whitworth Art Gallery)

PLATE IV. **Wallpaper**

1. Arabesque wallpaper panel by Jean-Baptiste Réveillon, colour printed from woodblocks, from near Paris, *c.* 1785–8 (Paris, Musée des Arts Décoratifs/Photo: Musée des Arts Décoratifs)

2. Wallpaper with pattern of lace, ribbons and roses, colour printed from woodblocks on satin ground with flocking, 640 × 500 mm, from France, *c.* 1850 (Uxbridge, Arthur Sanderson and Sons Ltd/Photo: Arthur Sanderson and Sons Ltd)

3. Wallpaper frieze of drapery by Zuber & Cie, colour printed from woodblocks with flocking and overprinting, 490 × 690 mm, from Paris, 1826 (Rixheim, Musée du Papier Peint/Photo: © Zuber & Cie, Rixheim)

PLATE V. **Wallpaper**

1. Wallpaper design by Walter Crane, printed by Jeffrey and Co., colour printed from woodblocks, frieze of *Fruit*, 546 × 1010 mm, and detail of filling of *Orange Tree*, 1.57 × 1.06 m, from London, 1902–3 (Manchester, University of Manchester, Whitworth Art Gallery/Photo: Whitworth Art Gallery)

2. *Roma*, wallpaper frieze by William Shand Kydd, colour printed and stencilled on Japanese grasspaper, 740 × 1204 mm, *c.* 1900 (Manchester, University of Manchester, Whitworth Art Gallery/Photo: Whitworth Art Gallery)

3. *Provence*, wallpaper designed by Lucienne Day, printed by John Line and Sons Ltd, colour screenprint, 200 × 255 mm, 1951 (London, Middlesex University, Silver Studio Collection)

PLATE VI. **Wallpaper**

Chinese export wallpaper, tempera, 2.44 × 1.22 m, second half of the 18th century (London, Victoria and Albert Museum/Photo: Board of Trustees of the Victoria and Albert Museum)

PLATE VII. **Watercolour**

1. Anthony van Dyck: *Wood near a Harbour*, watercolour and gouache, over some pen and brown ink, 189 × 267 mm, *c.* 1635–41 (Birmingham, University of Birmingham, Barber Institute of Fine Arts/Photo: Barber Institute of Fine Arts)

2. Eugène Delacroix: *Woman Bathing and her Moorish Servant*, watercolour over graphite, 160 × 183 mm, 1832 (Cambridge, MA, Fogg Art Museum/Photo: Harvard University Art Museums, Bequest of Grenville L. Winthrop)

PLATE VIII. **Watercolour**

1. J. M. W. Turner: *The Rhine at Reichenau*, watercolour, 244 × 311 mm, *c.* 1841 (London, Tate Gallery/Photo: Tate Gallery)

2. Paul Klee: *Abstraction: Coloured Circles Joined by Bands of Colour*, watercolour, 117 × 172 mm, 1914 (Berne, Kunstmuseum, Paul Klee Stiftung/Photo: Paul Klee Stiftung, Inv. F8/© DACS, 1996)

General Abbreviations

The abbreviations employed throughout this dictionary, most of which are listed below, do not vary, except for capitalization, regardless of the context in which they are used, including bibliographical citations and for locations of works of art. The principle used to arrive at these abbreviations is that their full form should be easily deducible, and for this reason acronyms have generally been avoided (e.g. Los Angeles Co. Mus. A. instead of LACMA). The same abbreviation is adopted for cognate forms in foreign languages and in most cases for plural and adjectival forms (e.g. A.= Art, Arts, Arte, Arti etc). Not all related forms are listed below. Occasionally, if a name, for instance of an artists' group or exhibiting society, is repeated within the text of one article, it is cited in an abbreviated form after its first mention in full (e.g. The Pre-Raphaelite Brotherhood (PRB) was founded...); the same is true of archaeological periods and eras, which are abbreviated to initial letters in small capitals (e.g. In the Early Minoan (EM) period...). Such abbreviations do not appear in this list. For the reader's convenience, separate full lists of abbreviations for locations, periodical titles and standard reference books and series are included as Appendices A–C in vol. 33.

A.	Art, Arts	Anthropol.	Anthropology	Azerbaij.	Azerbaijani
A.C.	Arts Council	Antiqua.	Antiquarian, Antiquaries	B.	Bartsch [catalogue of Old Master prints]
Acad.	Academy	app.	appendix		
AD	Anno Domini	approx.	approximately	b	born
Add.	Additional, Addendum	AR	Arkansas (USA)	BA	Bachelor of Arts
addn	addition	ARA	Associate of the Royal Academy	Balt.	Baltic
Admin.	Administration			bapt	baptized
Adv.	Advances, Advanced	Arab.	Arabic	BArch	Bachelor of Architecture
Aesth.	Aesthetic(s)	Archaeol.	Archaeology	Bart	Baronet
Afr.	African	Archit.	Architecture, Architectural	Bask.	Basketry
Afrik.	Afrikaans, Afrikaner	Archv, Archvs	Archive(s)	BBC	British Broadcasting Corporation
A.G.	Art Gallery				
Agrar.	Agrarian	Arg.	Argentine	BC	Before Christ
Agric.	Agriculture	ARHA	Associate of the Royal Hibernian Academy	BC	British Columbia (Canada)
Agron.	Agronomy			BE	Buddhist era
Agy	Agency	ARIBA	Associate of the Royal Institute of British Architects	Beds	Bedfordshire (GB)
AH	Anno Hegirae			Behav.	Behavioural
A. Inst.	Art Institute	Armen.	Armenian	Belarus.	Belarusian
AK	Alaska (USA)	ARSA	Associate of the Royal Scottish Academy	Belg.	Belgian
AL	Alabama (USA)			Berks	Berkshire (GB)
Alb.	Albanian	Asiat.	Asiatic	Berwicks	Berwickshire (GB; old)
Alg.	Algerian	Assist.	Assistance	BFA	Bachelor of Fine Arts
Alta	Alberta (Canada)	Assoc.	Association	Bibl.	Bible, Biblical
Altern.	Alternative	Astron.	Astronomy	Bibliog.	Bibliography, Bibliographical
a.m.	ante meridiem [before noon]	AT&T	American Telephone & Telegraph Company	Biblioph.	Bibliophile
Amat.	Amateur	attrib.	attribution, attributed to	Biog.	Biography, Biographical
Amer.	American	Aug	August	Biol.	Biology, Biological
An.	Annals	Aust.	Austrian	bk, bks	book(s)
Anatol.	Anatolian	Austral.	Australian	Bkbinder	Bookbinder
Anc.	Ancient	Auth.	Author(s)	Bklore	Booklore
Annu.	Annual	Auton.	Autonomous	Bkshop	Bookshop
Anon.	Anonymous(ly)	Aux.	Auxiliary	BL	British Library
Ant.	Antique	Ave.	Avenue	Bld	Build
Anthol.	Anthology	AZ	Arizona (USA)	Bldg	Building

vii

Bldr	Builder	Chin.	Chinese	Cur.	Curator, Curatorial, Curatorship
BLitt	Bachelor of Letters/Literature	Christ.	Christian, Christianity	Curr.	Current(s)
BM	British Museum	Chron.	Chronicle	CVO	Commander of the [Royal] Victorian Order
Boh.	Bohemian	Cie	Compagnie [French]		
Boliv.	Bolivian	Cinema.	Cinematography	Cyclad.	Cycladic
Botan.	Botany, Botanical	Circ.	Circle	Cyp.	Cypriot
BP	Before present (1950)	Civ.	Civil, Civic	Czech.	Czechoslovak
Braz.	Brazilian	Civiliz.	Civilization(s)	$	dollars
BRD	Bundesrepublik Deutschland [Federal Republic of Germany (West Germany)]	Class.	Classic, Classical	*d*	died
		Clin.	Clinical	d.	denarius, denarii [penny, pence]
		CO	Colorado (USA)		
Brecons	Breconshire (GB; old)	Co.	Company; County	Dalmat.	Dalmatian
Brez.	Brezonek [lang. of Brittany]	Cod.	Codex, Codices	Dan.	Danish
Brit.	British	Col., Cols	Collection(s); Column(s)	DBE	Dame Commander of the Order of the British Empire
Bros	Brothers	Coll.	College		
BSc	Bachelor of Science	collab.	in collaboration with, collaborated, collaborative	DC	District of Columbia (USA)
Bucks	Buckinghamshire (GB)			DDR	Deutsche Demokratische Republik [German Democratic Republic (East Germany)]
Bulg.	Bulgarian	Collct.	Collecting		
Bull.	Bulletin	Colloq.	Colloquies		
bur	buried	Colomb.	Colombian	DE	Delaware (USA)
Burm.	Burmese	Colon.	Colonies, Colonial	Dec	December
Byz.	Byzantine	Colr	Collector	Dec.	Decorative
C	Celsius	Comm.	Commission; Community	ded.	dedication, dedicated to
C.	Century	Commerc.	Commercial	Democ.	Democracy, Democratic
c.	*circa* [about]	Communic.	Communications	Demog.	Demography, Demographic
CA	California	Comp.	Comparative; compiled by, compiler	Denbs	Denbighshire (GB; old)
Cab.	Cabinet			dep.	deposited at
Caerns	Caernarvonshire (GB; old)	Concent.	Concentration	Dept	Department
C.A.G.	City Art Gallery	Concr.	Concrete	Dept.	Departmental, Departments
Cal.	Calendar	Confed.	Confederation	Derbys	Derbyshire (GB)
Callig.	Calligraphy	Confer.	Conference	Des.	Design
Cam.	Camera	Congol.	Congolese	destr.	destroyed
Cambs	Cambridgeshire (GB)	Congr.	Congress	Dev.	Development
can	canonized	Conserv.	Conservation; Conservatory	Devon	Devonshire (GB)
Can.	Canadian	Constr.	Construction(al)	Dial.	Dialogue
Cant.	Canton(s), Cantonal	cont.	continued	diam.	diameter
Capt.	Captain	Contemp.	Contemporary	Diff.	Diffusion
Cards	Cardiganshire (GB; old)	Contrib.	Contributions, Contributor(s)	Dig.	Digest
Carib.	Caribbean	Convalesc.	Convalescence	Dip. Eng.	Diploma in Engineering
Carms	Carmarthenshire (GB; old)	Convent.	Convention	Dir.	Direction, Directed
Cartog.	Cartography	Coop.	Cooperation	Directrt	Directorate
Cat.	Catalan	Coord.	Coordination	Disc.	Discussion
cat.	catalogue	Copt.	Coptic	diss.	dissertation
Cath.	Catholic	Corp.	Corporation, Corpus	Distr.	District
CBE	Commander of the Order of the British Empire	Corr.	Correspondence	Div.	Division
		Cors.	Corsican	DLitt	Doctor of Letters/Literature
Celeb.	Celebration	Cost.	Costume	DM	Deutsche Mark
Celt.	Celtic	Cret.	Cretan	Doc.	Document(s)
Cent.	Centre, Central	Crim.	Criminal	Doss.	Dossier
Centen.	Centennial	Crit.	Critical, Criticism	DPhil	Doctor of Philosophy
Cer.	Ceramic	Croat.	Croatian	Dr	Doctor
cf.	confer [compare]	CT	Connecticut (USA)	Drg, Drgs	Drawing(s)
Chap., Chaps	Chapter(s)	Cttee	Committee	DSc	Doctor of Science/Historical Sciences
Chem.	Chemistry	Cub.	Cuban		
Ches	Cheshire (GB)	Cult.	Cultural, Culture	Dut.	Dutch
Chil.	Chilean	Cumb.	Cumberland (GB; old)	Dwell.	Dwelling
				E.	East(ern)

EC	European (Economic) Community	figs	figures	Heb.	Hebrew
Eccles.	Ecclesiastical	Filip.	Filipina(s), Filipino(s)	Hell.	Hellenic
Econ.	Economic, Economies	Fin.	Finnish	Her.	Heritage
Ecuad.	Ecuadorean	FL	Florida (USA)	Herald.	Heraldry, Heraldic
ed.	editor, edited (by)	*fl*	*floruit* [he/she flourished]	Hereford & Worcs	Hereford & Worcester (GB)
edn	edition	Flem.	Flemish	Herts	Hertfordshire (GB)
eds	editors	Flints	Flintshire (GB; old)	HI	Hawaii (USA)
Educ.	Education	Flk	Folk	Hib.	Hibernia
e.g.	*exempli gratia* [for example]	Flklore	Folklore	Hisp.	Hispanic
Egyp.	Egyptian	fol., fols	folio(s)	Hist.	History, Historical
Elem.	Element(s), Elementary	Found.	Foundation	HMS	His/Her Majesty's Ship
Emp.	Empirical	Fr.	French	Hon.	Honorary, Honourable
Emul.	Emulation	frag.	fragment	Horiz.	Horizon
Enc.	Encyclopedia	Fri.	Friday	Hort.	Horticulture
Encour.	Encouragement	FRIBA	Fellow of the Royal Institute of British Architects	Hosp.	Hospital(s)
Eng.	English	FRS	Fellow of the Royal Society, London	HRH	His/Her Royal Highness
Engin.	Engineer, Engineering			Human.	Humanities, Humanism
Engr., Engrs	Engraving(s)	ft	foot, feet	Hung.	Hungarian
		Furn.	Furniture	Hunts	Huntingdonshire (GB; old)
Envmt	Environment	Futur.	Futurist, Futurism	IA	Iowa
Epig.	Epigraphy	g	gram(s)	ibid.	*ibidem* [in the same place]
Episc.	Episcopal	GA	Georgia (USA)	ICA	Institute of Contemporary Arts
Esp.	Especially	Gael.	Gaelic		
Ess.	Essays	Gal., Gals	Gallery, Galleries	Ice.	Icelandic
est.	established	Gaz.	Gazette	Iconog.	Iconography
etc	*etcetera* [and so on]	GB	Great Britain	Iconol.	Iconology
Ethnog.	Ethnography	Gdn, Gdns	Garden(s)	ID	Idaho (USA)
Ethnol.	Ethnology	Gdnr(s)	Gardener(s)	i.e.	*id est* [that is]
Etrus.	Etruscan	Gen.	General	IL	Illinois (USA)
Eur.	European	Geneal.	Genealogy, Genealogist	Illum.	Illumination
Evangel.	Evangelical	Gent.	Gentleman, Gentlemen	illus.	illustrated, illustration
Exam.	Examination	Geog.	Geography	Imp.	Imperial
Excav.	Excavation, Excavated	Geol.	Geology	IN	Indiana (USA)
Exch.	Exchange	Geom.	Geometry	in., ins	inch(es)
Excurs.	Excursion	Georg.	Georgian	Inc.	Incorporated
exh.	exhibition	Geosci.	Geoscience	inc.	incomplete
Exp.	Exposition	Ger.	German, Germanic	incl.	includes, including, inclusive
Expermntl	Experimental	G.I.	Government/General Issue (USA)	Incorp.	Incorporation
Explor.	Exploration			Ind.	Indian
Expn	Expansion	Glams	Glamorganshire (GB; old)	Indep.	Independent
Ext.	External	Glos	Gloucestershire (GB)	Indig.	Indigenous
Extn	Extension	Govt	Government	Indol.	Indology
f, ff	following page, following pages	Gr.	Greek	Indon.	Indonesian
		Grad.	Graduate	Indust.	Industrial
F.A.	Fine Art(s)	Graph.	Graphic	Inf.	Information
Fac.	Faculty	Green.	Greenlandic	Inq.	Inquiry
facs.	facsimile	Gr.-Roman	Greco-Roman	Inscr.	Inscribed, Inscription
Fam.	Family	Gt	Great	Inst.	Institute(s)
fasc.	fascicle	Gtr	Greater	Inst. A.	Institute of Art
fd	feastday (of a saint)	Guat.	Guatemalan	Instr.	Instrument, Instrumental
Feb	February	Gym.	Gymnasium	Int.	International
Fed.	Federation, Federal	h.	height	Intell.	Intelligence
Fem.	Feminist	ha	hectare	Inter.	Interior(s), Internal
Fest.	Festival	Hait.	Haitian	Interdiscip.	Interdisciplinary
fig.	figure (illustration)	Hants	Hampshire (GB)	intro.	introduced by, introduction
Fig.	Figurative	Hb.	Handbook	inv.	inventory

Inven.	Invention	m	metre(s)	Moldov.	Moldovan
Invest.	Investigation(s)	m.	married	MOMA	Museum of Modern Art
Iran.	Iranian	M.	Monsieur	Mon.	Monday
irreg.	irregular(ly)	MA	Master of Arts; Massachusetts (USA)	Mongol.	Mongolian
Islam.	Islamic			Mons	Monmouthshire (GB; old)
Isr.	Israeli	Mag.	Magazine	Montgoms	Montgomeryshire (GB; old)
It.	Italian	Maint.	Maintenance	Mor.	Moral
J.	Journal	Malay.	Malaysian	Morav.	Moravian
Jam.	Jamaican	Man.	Manitoba (Canada); Manual	Moroc.	Moroccan
Jan	January	Manuf.	Manufactures	Movt	Movement
Jap.	Japanese	Mar.	Marine, Maritime	MP	Member of Parliament
Jav.	Javanese	Mason.	Masonic	MPhil	Master of Philosophy
Jew.	Jewish	Mat.	Material(s)	MS	Mississippi (USA)
Jewel.	Jewellery	Math.	Mathematic	MS., MSS	manuscript(s)
Jord.	Jordanian	MBE	Member of the Order of the British Empire	MSc	Master of Science
jr	junior			MT	Montana (USA)
Juris.	Jurisdiction	MD	Doctor of Medicine; Maryland (USA)	Mt	Mount
KBE	Knight Commander of the Order of the British Empire			Mthly	Monthly
		ME	Maine (USA)	Mun.	Municipal
KCVO	Knight Commander of the Royal Victorian Order	Mech.	Mechanical	Mus.	Museum(s)
		Med.	Medieval; Medium, Media	Mus. A.	Museum of Art
kg	kilogram(s)	Medic.	Medical, Medicine	Mus. F.A.	Museum of Fine Art(s)
kHz	kilohertz	Medit.	Mediterranean	Music.	Musicology
km	kilometre(s)	Mem.	Memorial(s); Memoir(s)	N.	North(ern); National
Knowl.	Knowledge	Merions	Merionethshire (GB; old)	*n*	refractive index of a medium
Kor.	Korean	Meso-Amer.	Meso-American	n.	note
KS	Kansas (USA)			N.A.G.	National Art Gallery
KY	Kentucky (USA)	Mesop.	Mesopotamian	Nat.	Natural, Nature
Kyrgyz.	Kyrgyzstani	Met.	Metropolitan	Naut.	Nautical
£	libra, librae [pound, pounds sterling]	Metal.	Metallurgy	NB	New Brunswick (Canada)
		Mex.	Mexican	NC	North Carolina (USA)
l.	length	MFA	Master of Fine Arts	ND	North Dakota (USA)
LA	Louisiana (USA)	mg	milligram(s)	n.d.	no date
Lab.	Laboratory	Mgmt	Management	NE	Nebraska; Northeast(ern)
Lancs	Lancashire (GB)	Mgr	Monsignor	Neth.	Netherlandish
Lang.	Language(s)	MI	Michigan	Newslett.	Newsletter
Lat.	Latin	Micrones.	Micronesian	Nfld	Newfoundland (Canada)
Latv.	Latvian	Mid. Amer.	Middle American	N.G.	National Gallery
lb, lbs	pound(s) weight	Middx	Middlesex (GB; old)	N.G.A.	National Gallery of Art
Leb.	Lebanese	Mid. E.	Middle Eastern	NH	New Hampshire (USA)
Lect.	Lecture	Mid. Eng.	Middle English	Niger.	Nigerian
Legis.	Legislative	Mid Glam.	Mid Glamorgan (GB)	NJ	New Jersey (USA)
Leics	Leicestershire (GB)	Mil.	Military	NM	New Mexico (USA)
Lex.	Lexicon	Mill.	Millennium	nm	nanometre (10^{-9} metre)
Lg.	Large	Min.	Ministry; Minutes	nn.	notes
Lib., Libs	Library, Libraries	Misc.	Miscellaneous	no., nos	number(s)
Liber.	Liberian	Miss.	Mission(s)	Nord.	Nordic
Libsp	Librarianship	Mlle	Mademoiselle	Norm.	Normal
Lincs	Lincolnshire (GB)	mm	millimetre(s)	Northants	Northamptonshire (GB)
Lit.	Literature	Mme	Madame	Northumb.	Northumberland (GB)
Lith.	Lithuanian	MN	Minnesota	Norw.	Norwegian
Liturg.	Liturgical	Mnmt, Mnmts	Monument(s)	Notts	Nottinghamshire (GB)
LLB	Bachelor of Laws			Nov	November
LLD	Doctor of Laws	Mnmtl	Monumental	n.p.	no place (of publication)
Lt	Lieutenant	MO	Missouri (USA)	N.P.G.	National Portrait Gallery
Lt-Col.	Lieutenant-Colonel	Mod.	Modern, Modernist	nr	near
Ltd	Limited	Moldav.	Moldavian		

Nr E.	Near Eastern
NS	New Style; Nova Scotia (Canada)
n. s.	new series
NSW	New South Wales (Australia)
NT	National Trust
Ntbk	Notebook
Numi.	Numismatic(s)
NV	Nevada (USA)
NW	Northwest(ern)
NWT	Northwest Territories (Canada)
NY	New York (USA)
NZ	New Zealand
OBE	Officer of the Order of the British Empire
Obj.	Object(s), Objective
Occas.	Occasional
Occident.	Occidental
Ocean.	Oceania
Oct	October
8vo	octavo
OFM	Order of Friars Minor
OH	Ohio (USA)
OK	Oklahoma (USA)
Olymp.	Olympic
OM	Order of Merit
Ont.	Ontario (Canada)
op.	opus
opp.	opposite; opera [pl. of opus]
OR	Oregon (USA)
Org.	Organization
Orient.	Oriental
Orthdx	Orthodox
OSB	Order of St Benedict
Ott.	Ottoman
Oxon	Oxfordshire (GB)
oz.	ounce(s)
p	pence
p., pp.	page(s)
PA	Pennsylvania (USA)
p.a.	per annum
Pak.	Pakistani
Palaeontol.	Palaeontology, Palaeontological
Palest.	Palestinian
Pap.	Paper(s)
para.	paragraph
Parag.	Paraguayan
Parl.	Parliament
Paroch.	Parochial
Patriarch.	Patriarchate
Patriot.	Patriotic
Patrm.	Patrimony
Pav.	Pavilion
PEI	Prince Edward Island (Canada)
Pembs	Pembrokeshire (GB; old)

Per.	Period
Percep.	Perceptions
Perf.	Performance, Performing, Performed
Period.	Periodical(s)
Pers.	Persian
Persp.	Perspectives
Peru.	Peruvian
PhD	Doctor of Philosophy
Philol.	Philology
Philos.	Philosophy
Phoen.	Phoenician
Phot.	Photograph, Photography, Photographic
Phys.	Physician(s), Physics, Physique, Physical
Physiog.	Physiognomy
Physiol.	Physiology
Pict.	Picture(s), Pictorial
pl.	plate; plural
Plan.	Planning
Planet.	Planetarium
Plast.	Plastic
pls	plates
p.m.	post meridiem [after noon]
Polit.	Political
Poly.	Polytechnic
Polynes.	Polynesian
Pop.	Popular
Port.	Portuguese
Port.	Portfolio
Posth.	Posthumous(ly)
Pott.	Pottery
POW	prisoner of war
PRA	President of the Royal Academy
Pract.	Practical
Prefect.	Prefecture, Prefectural
Preserv.	Preservation
prev.	previous(ly)
priv.	private
PRO	Public Record Office
Prob.	Problem(s)
Proc.	Proceedings
Prod.	Production
Prog.	Progress
Proj.	Project(s)
Promot.	Promotion
Prop.	Property, Properties
Prov.	Province(s), Provincial
Proven.	Provenance
Prt, Prts	Print(s)
Prtg	Printing
pseud.	pseudonym
Psych.	Psychiatry, Psychiatric
Psychol.	Psychology, Psychological
pt	part

Ptg(s)	Painting(s)
Pub.	Public
pubd	published
Publ.	Publicity
pubn(s)	publication(s)
PVA	polyvinyl acetate
PVC	polyvinyl chloride
Q.	quarterly
4to	quarto
Qué.	Québec (Canada)
R	reprint
r	*recto*
RA	Royal Academician
Radnors	Radnorshire (GB; old)
RAF	Royal Air Force
Rec.	Record(s)
red.	reduction, reduced for
Ref.	Reference
Refurb.	Refurbishment
reg	*regit* [ruled]
Reg.	Regional
Relig.	Religion, Religious
remod.	remodelled
Ren.	Renaissance
Rep.	Report(s)
repr.	reprint(ed); reproduced, reproduction
Represent.	Representation, Representative
Res.	Research
rest.	restored, restoration
Retro.	Retrospective
rev.	revision, revised (by/for)
Rev.	Reverend; Review
RHA	Royal Hibernian Academician
RI	Rhode Island (USA)
RIBA	Royal Institute of British Architects
RJ	Rio de Janeiro State
Rlwy	Railway
RSA	Royal Scottish Academy
RSFSR	Russian Soviet Federated Socialist Republic
Rt Hon.	Right Honourable
Rur.	Rural
Rus.	Russian
S	San, Santa, Santo, Sant', São [Saint]
S.	South(ern)
s.	solidus, solidi [shilling(s)]
Sask.	Saskatchewan (Canada)
Sat.	Saturday
SC	South Carolina (USA)
Scand.	Scandinavian
Sch.	School
Sci.	Science(s), Scientific
Scot.	Scottish
Sculp.	Sculpture

SD	South Dakota (USA)	suppl., suppls	supplement(s), supplementary	Urb.	Urban
SE	Southeast(ern)	Surv.	Survey	Urug.	Uruguayan
Sect.	Section	SW	Southwest(ern)	US	United States
Sel.	Selected	Swed.	Swedish	USA	United States of America
Semin.	Seminar(s), Seminary	Swi.	Swiss	USSR	Union of Soviet Socialist Republics
Semiot.	Semiotic	Symp.	Symposium		
Semit.	Semitic	Syr.	Syrian	UT	Utah
Sept	September	Tap.	Tapestry	*v*	*verso*
Ser.	Series	Tas.	Tasmanian	VA	Virginia (USA)
Serb.	Serbian	Tech.	Technical, Technique	V&A	Victoria and Albert Museum
Serv.	Service(s)	Technol.	Technology	Var.	Various
Sess.	Session, Sessional	Territ.	Territory	Venez.	Venezuelan
Settmt(s)	Settlement(s)	Theat.	Theatre	Vern.	Vernacular
S. Glam.	South Glamorgan (GB)	Theol.	Theology, Theological	Vict.	Victorian
Siber.	Siberian	Theor.	Theory, Theoretical	Vid.	Video
Sig.	Signature	Thurs.	Thursday	Viet.	Vietnamese
Sil.	Silesian	Tib.	Tibetan	viz.	*videlicet* [namely]
Sin.	Singhala	TN	Tennessee (USA)	vol., vols	volume(s)
sing.	singular	Top.	Topography	vs.	versus
SJ	Societas Jesu [Society of Jesus]	Trad.	Tradition(s), Traditional	VT	Vermont (USA)
Skt	Sanskrit	trans.	translation, translated by; transactions	Vulg.	Vulgarisation
Slav.	Slavic, Slavonic			W.	West(ern)
Slov.	Slovene, Slovenian	Transafr.	Transafrican	w.	width
Soc.	Society	Transatlant.	Transatlantic	WA	Washington (USA)
Social.	Socialism, Socialist	Transcarpath.	Transcarpathian	Warwicks	Warwickshire (GB)
Sociol.	Sociology	transcr.	transcribed by/for	Wed.	Wednesday
Sov.	Soviet	Triq.	Triquarterly	W. Glam.	West Glamorgan (GB)
SP	São Paulo State	Tropic.	Tropical	WI	Wisconsin (USA)
Sp.	Spanish	Tues.	Tuesday	Wilts	Wiltshire (GB)
sq.	square	Turk.	Turkish	Wkly	Weekly
sr	senior	Turkmen.	Turkmenistani	W. Midlands	West Midlands (GB)
Sri L.	Sri Lankan	TV	Television		
SS	Saints, Santi, Santissima, Santissimo, Santissimi; Steam ship	TX	Texas (USA)	Worcs	Worcestershire (GB; old)
		U.	University	Wtrcol.	Watercolour
SSR	Soviet Socialist Republic	UK	United Kingdom of Great Britain and Northern Ireland	WV	West Virginia (USA)
St	Saint, Sankt, Sint, Szent			WY	Wyoming (USA)
Staffs	Staffordshire (GB)	Ukrain.	Ukrainian	Yb., Y.-b.	Yearbook, Year-book
Ste	Sainte	Un.	Union	Yem.	Yemeni
Stud.	Study, Studies	Underwtr	Underwater	Yorks	Yorkshire (GB; old)
Subalp.	Subalpine	UNESCO	United Nations Educational, Scientific and Cultural Organization	Yug.	Yugoslavian
Sum.	Sumerian			Zamb.	Zambian
Sun.	Sunday	Univl	Universal	Zimb.	Zimbabwean
Sup.	Superior	unpubd	unpublished		

A Note on the Use of the Dictionary

This note is intended as a short guide to the basic editorial conventions adopted in this dictionary. For a fuller explanation, please refer to the Introduction, vol. 1, pp. xiii–xx.

Abbreviations in general use in the dictionary are listed on pp. vii–xii; those used in bibliographies and for locations of works of art or exhibition venues are listed in the Appendices in vol. 33.

Alphabetization of headings, which are distinguished in bold typeface, is letter by letter up to the first comma (ignoring spaces, hyphens, accents and any parenthesized or bracketed matter); the same principle applies thereafter. Abbreviations of 'Saint' and its foreign equivalents are alphabetized as if spelt out, and headings with the prefix 'Mc' appear under 'Mac'.

Authors' signatures appear at the end of the article or sequence of articles that the authors have contributed; in multipartite articles, any section that is unsigned is by the author of the next signed section. Where the article was compiled by the editors or in the few cases where an author has wished to remain anonymous, this is indicated by a square box (□) instead of a signature.

Bibliographies are arranged chronologically (within a section, where divided) by order of year of first publication and, within years, alphabetically by authors' names. Abbreviations have been used for some standard reference books; these are cited in full in Appendix C in vol. 33, as are abbreviations of periodical titles (Appendix B). Abbreviated references to alphabetically arranged dictionaries and encyclopedias appear at the beginning of the bibliography (or section).

Biographical dates when cited in parentheses in running text at the first mention of a personal name indicate that the individual does not have an entry in the dictionary. The presence of parenthesized regnal dates for rulers and popes, however, does not necessarily indicate the lack of a biography of that person. Where no dates are provided for an artist or patron, the reader may assume that there is a biography of that individual in the dictionary (or, more rarely, that the person is so obscure that dates are not readily available).

Cross-references are distinguished by the use of small capital letters, with a large capital to indicate the initial letter of the entry to which the reader is directed; for example, 'He commissioned LEONARDO DA VINCI . . .' means that the entry is alphabetized under 'L'.

V

[continued]

Varnish. Coating material consisting of resin dissolved in a liquid, which dries to form a transparent film. Drying may result from the evaporation of a SOLVENT vehicle to leave a glassy residue of resin, or from a combination of solvent evaporation and chemical reaction between resin molecules to form larger molecular units (polymerization). Traditionally, varnish films have a high gloss, but, by varying the varnish constituents and the method of application, it is possible to vary the degree of gloss as well as the hardness, toughness and flexibility of the film. Varnishes may be colourless or tinted by the addition of dyes or pigments. The word 'varnish' is derived from the medieval (*c.* 8th century) Latin *veronix* or *vernix*, itself related to the Greek *berenice*, then apparently used for amber. By extension, *vernix* came to be used for sandarac resin, sometimes confused with amber and a common ingredient in medieval varnish recipes. By the 15th or 16th centuries *vernix* also denoted juniper resin. The word 'varnish' only acquired its modern meaning around the late 16th century; before this time the liquid coating material was known by such names as the Italian *vernice liquida.*

See also LACQUER, §I, 3 and 4 and RESIN, §1.

1. Materials and techniques. 2. Uses. 3. Conservation.

1. MATERIALS AND TECHNIQUES.

(i) Natural resin varnishes.

(a) Oil-based. In Europe the earliest varnishes consisted of natural resins (*see* RESIN, §1) dissolved in hot linseed oil, and oil varnishes of this type remained the standard coating material for a wide range of applications until well into the 20th century. Some very early recipes are extremely complicated: one cited in the early 9th-century collection known as the *Compositiones variae* (Lucca, Bib. Capitolare, MS. 490) includes eight different resins, two of which are the gum-resins myrrh and frankincense. Other ingredients can probably be identified as Chios turpentine, galbanum, larch turpentine (i.e. Venice turpentine), mastic, sandarac and pine resin (colophony). Later varnish recipes, such as those described by Theophilus in *De diversis artibus* (*c.* 1140), are essentially very similar to 19th- or 20th-century recipes. The ingredients consisted typically of one or more insoluble or 'hard' resins such as sandarac (*see*

RESIN, §1) and a 'boiled' oil, generally linseed. For the resin to dissolve in the oil it was necessary to melt or 'run' it by heating it to about 300°C; the oil was heated separately to about 240–260°C and added gradually to the liquid resin. The mixture was then 'boiled' until the varnish could be drawn out to form a string, at which point it was allowed to cool. After the time of Theophilus driers (e.g. lead salts) were frequently incorporated during the heating process. In the 19th and 20th centuries a varnish thus prepared was diluted with oil of turpentine (in earlier recipes there is frequently no indication that the mixture was diluted) and it would probably have been necessary to warm the varnish for use.

Apart from sandarac, juniper resin and the highly insoluble fossil resin amber, pine resin (rosin or colophony), the solid residue left after the distillation of turpentine oil, was probably also used. It is more readily soluble in hot oil than the generally recommended 'hard' resins, although the resultant varnish is rather less hard wearing. It is still in use, either directly or in a modified form. Venice turpentine, from the European larch, mentioned in 17th-century varnish recipes, for example, makes a less satisfactory varnish, although it has been used as an ingredient in paint media. 'Hard' resins used have included the African and South American copals and mastic; as well as being widely used as a varnish, the latter was an ingredient in oil-varnish paint media such as megilp (*see* PAINT, §I, 2(ii)). The use of such media is documented from the late 17th century, but they appear to have been used increasingly from the latter part of the 18th (*see* PAINTING MEDIUM). Before the invention of synthetic resin varnishes copal-oil varnishes were widely used in the 19th century and early 20th as a varnish not only for paintings but also for, for example, woodwork (*see* LACQUER, §I, 3). The 'semi-fossil' kauri resin was also imported into Europe from New Zealand in the 19th century for varnish preparation.

Varnishes prepared from oil and natural resins tend to be rather dark in colour in bulk; the more they are heated, the darker they become, although their drying properties are improved. After the initial evaporation of any volatile diluent, they harden and dry principally by the formation of cross-linkages between the triglyceride molecules of the drying oil and become increasingly insoluble, producing very tough, quite hard-wearing films. An aged varnish of

1

this type may be difficult to remove (*see* §3 below). Although a thin film of the fresh varnish may have little perceptible colour, it will darken with age. An oil varnish used as a medium for easel painting may cause such defects as cracking and wrinkling of the paint film.

(b) Spirit-based. Spirit, or solvent-type, varnishes consist of a natural resin dissolved in a rapidly evaporating solvent such as alcohol or oil of turpentine; they were unknown in Europe much before the early 16th century and are still used today. Materials used have included the balsamic resin benzoin, from the Styracaceae family (from Sumatra and Thailand), dissolved in alcohol, but in the 19th and 20th centuries mastic or dammar resins dissolved in turpentine were generally used. Dammars appear in varnish preparation in Europe *c.* 1830, although they would have been widely used for many purposes in the areas around the Indian Ocean (e.g. Malaysia, Indonesia and the Indian subcontinent) where the species of tree producing them occurs. Solvent-type varnishes dry by evaporation of the solvent, leaving a film of the resin; they may be brushed or sprayed on to the object. As natural resins oxidize and yellow with age, the films discolour; they also become brittle and fragile and are usually only suitable for use on objects that do not receive much wear and tear.

(c) Other organically based varnishes. A variety of other naturally occurring materials may be used as varnishes. Beaten egg-white gives a sheen to the surface of paintings to which it is applied, and it was sometimes used as a temporary varnish before the final varnish could be applied. An aqueous solution of gum arabic, which gives a fairly glossy surface, can be used similarly, particularly in manuscript illumination; also known as gum acacia, it was used in ancient Egypt. Frescoes and marble sculptures were sometimes given a thin protective coating of wax in the early Middle Ages. Shellac, which is secreted by insects of the family Tachardiidae found throughout the Indian subcontinent and in parts of Burma and Thailand (*see* LACQUER, §I, 2), has been used as a coating on furniture— so-called French polish (*see* WOOD (i), §III, 5)—small decorative objects, metal items and scientific instruments. It can be applied either in alcoholic solution or as the melted material. Japanese lacquer (*urushi*) is a thick, milky, water-in-oil emulsion produced by the sumac tree *Rhus vernicifera*, which grows in Japan and China, and it has been used from very early times (*see* LACQUER, §I, 1).

(ii) Synthetic resin varnishes. In the 20th century synthetic resin varnishes largely superseded those prepared from natural resins (*see* RESIN, §2). Some, such as rosin derivatives, alkyds and certain phenolic and epoxy resins, can be modified with unsaturated oils; others, such as polyvinyl acetate and the polyacrylate and cyclohexanone resins widely used in conservation (*see* §3 below), may be applied in solvents in the same way as dammar and mastic. For any particular class of polymer, by varying the starting materials and conditions it is possible to obtain a product with the desired physical properties of hardness, flexibility and solubility. The glass transition temperature, the temperature at which a polymer changes from a glassy to a flaccid state, determines the mechanical properties of the polymer. Other properties, such as refractive index, may also alter around this temperature. It indicates the softness of a resin: if a varnish resin is too soft, the varnish may pick up dirt; if too hard, it may lack flexibility and crack. The molecular weight of the resin (natural or synthetic) has an influence on such properties as the viscosity of the varnish. The refractive index of the resin to some extent influences the effect the varnish film has on the appearance of the object. Polyvinyl acetate (formed from vinyl acetate), first available in the 1930s, is very stable but little used as a varnish for conservation purposes as it is only soluble in relatively polar solvents. Far more important from the point of view of conservation are certain polyacrylate resins—Paraloid B–72 and Paraloid B–67—which have slightly different physical properties and are both widely used. Alkyds are perhaps the most widely used group of synthetic coating materials. Alkyd resins closely resemble drying oils, which may indeed be incorporated into the resin molecule; varying the ingredients and careful control of the reaction give products with a range of properties (such as gloss and flexibility) suitable for many different purposes, including varnishes for wood. Polyurethane resins are extremely tough, hard, inert varnishes used, for example, for floors. Similarly durable products may be obtained from certain formulations of epoxy resins, although these tend to darken. Cyclohexanone or ketone resins have properties rather similar to dammar and mastic and are widely used in the conservation of paintings.

BIBLIOGRAPHY

C. L. Eastlake: *Materials for a History of Oil Painting* (London, 1847/*R* New York and London, 1960), i, pp. 229–54

R. Mayer: *Artist's Handbook* (1941, rev. 4/1982), pp. 180–213, 715–17

R. L. Feller, N. Stolow and E. H. Jones: *On Picture Varnishes and their Solvents* (Oberlin, 1959, rev. Cleveland, OH, 1971/*R* Washington, DC, 1985), pp. 119–45

Surface Coatings, i: *Raw Materials and their Usage,* Oil and Colour Chemists' Association (Kensington, New South Wales, 1974, rev. London, 1983), pp. 45–56, 65–74, 77–9, 84, 88–90, 96, 99–115, 144–52

C. V. Horie: *Materials for Conservation: Organic Consolidants, Adhesives and Coatings* (London, 1987), pp. 92–6, 103–12, 116–17, 145–53, 165–70

J. S. Mills and R. White: *The Organic Chemistry of Museum Objects* (London, 1987, 2/1994), pp. 35–6, 42–3, 95–128, 132–40, 179–84

Cleaning, Retouching and Coatings: Technology and Practice for Easel Paintings and Polychrome Sculpture: Preprints of the Contributions to the IIC Congress: Brussels, 1990, esp. pp. 63–80, 131–3

2. USES. Varnishes are used as protective or decorative coatings. The choice of varnish depends on the hardness, inertness, flexibility, durability, resistance to darkening and solubility required. The highly durable but insoluble coatings such as polyurethane and epoxy-resin varnishes are particularly suitable where the coating is intended to be both permanent and hard-wearing (e.g. on furniture or wood floors); they are not appropriate for temporary use. Some varnish formulations, such as those of certain alkyd resins, can be baked to form a durable coating with high gloss; these are suitable for enamels, for example.

The varnishes used as protective coatings on easel paintings do not need to be so resilient, and solvent-based types are used. The colours of a painting will appear more saturated if the varnish resin has a high refractive index, but other factors should also be taken into account, for example the surface gloss, how well the varnish wets the paint surface and the extent to which it penetrates the paint. A varnish gives visual unity to a painted surface, providing depth as well as the desired degree of gloss. A matt surface, often considered more appropriate for paintings in tempera, may be obtained by using a resin constituent of high viscosity, by adjusting the spraying conditions, or by incorporating a matting agent such as microcrystalline wax or beeswax. Varnishes may penetrate the paint film to some extent; in the case of a freshly painted picture this is not desirable, and many authorities, including Cennino Cennini, writing in the 1390s and referring to paintings in tempera, have advised against varnishing a painting too soon after it has been finished. In the past, temporary egg-white varnishes, which did not penetrate vulnerable fresh paint and which could be removed by washing a short while later, were often suggested as an interim measure.

Tinted varnishes were widely used as a decorative coating over metal leaf in interior decoration and for furniture, picture frames, mirrors and sculpture. They also appear in easel painting, wall painting and on other painted surfaces. Tinted red, green or yellow, they are used over gold leaf to simulate jewels. Yellow-tinted varnishes have a long history of use over silver or tin leaf in imitation of the more expensive gold leaf, or to intensify the colour of gold leaf (*see* GILDING, §I). Varnishes have also been used as a paint medium, such as the unctuous gelled megilp medium of the late 18th century and the 19th (*see* PAINT, §I). The proportion of varnish in these mixtures was quite high, as much as 1:1 mastic varnish to linseed oil; as a result the paint medium retained a degree of solubility even when aged. The paint was also liable to crack or discolour. However, in slightly earlier times a very little varnish might be added to oil paint to give desired properties of flow, gloss or richness to particular colours or passages of paint (*see* GLAZE and OIL PAINTING, §I). The addition of a proportion of pine-resin varnish to oil paint was suggested in late 17th-century painters' and decorators' manuals to give increased gloss and improved weather resistance to the final coating. Retouching varnishes are used during oil painting to bring out the full colour of passages that have sunk or dried matt and to lessen the absorbency of an area where painting is to be continued, allowing subsequent layers of paint to flow on easily. The use of isolating varnishes over a recently dried painted area allows work to be continued or corrected without affecting the paint beneath.   Various types of varnish materials are used to protect untouched, or lightly etched areas on copper or zinc plates during additional etching bites; such varnishes are generally based on wax and asphaltum and are known as 'stopping-out' varnishes (*see* ETCHING, §I). They may also be used to paint the design on to a prepared, grounded aquatint plate before etching. The fixatives used on pastel or charcoal drawings to prevent the pigment being brushed away, for example dilute aqueous gum arabic and alcoholic solutions of cellulose nitrate, are in effect very dilute varnish solutions. Mastic or shellac solutions are often used for charcoal drawings but are unsuitable for pastel drawings as they affect the colour.

BIBLIOGRAPHY

C. Cennini: *Il libro dell'arte* (MS.; *c.* 1390); trans. and notes by D. V. Thompson jr (1933), pp. 99–100

R. Mayer: *Artist's Handbook* (1941, rev. 4/1982), pp. 174–5, 184–6, 217–27, 325–7, 427, 533–7

Surface Coatings, Oil and Colour Chemists' Association, Australia, i: *Raw Materials and their Usage* (Kensington, New South Wales, 1974, rev. London, 1983); ii: *Paints and their Applications* (Kensington, New South Wales, 1974, rev. London, 1984)

3. CONSERVATION. Varnishes that serve a decorative purpose rather than, or as well as, a protective function and those used as painting media are examples of varnish for which conservation treatment may be considered appropriate. In these circumstances, the varnish is considered and treated in a manner comparable with that accorded to a paint. The criteria taken into account before, or during, treatment to paint are similar in the case of varnishes, bearing in mind the fact that some varnishes may be rather more soluble than a normal oil paint film of equivalent age and so require a careful choice of cleaning method. A varnish that acts solely as a protective coating is less likely to be conserved, unless there is some particular reason: for example, the varnish is of considerable age and therefore of historical interest. In other cases when a protective varnish deteriorates it is usually removed, if possible, and replaced. Removal of dark yellowish varnish from Velázquez's *Toilet of Venus* ('Rokeby *Venus*', *c.* 1651; London, N.G.; *see* VELÁZQUEZ, DIEGO, fig. 8) revealed delicate luminous colour and bold brushwork. Since the 19th century, attempts have been made to 'reform' deteriorated varnish or paint films, essentially by exposing the painting to vapours of a suitable solvent; the effects are often only temporary. One of the earliest reforming procedures was the Pettenkofer process, patented by its inventor Max von Pettenkofer in Bavaria in 1863, whereby paintings were exposed to alcohol vapour and copaiva balsam.

The role of varnishes in conservation is of fundamental importance. For conservation purposes the ideal varnish should be colourless, transparent and without physical or chemical effect on any property (such as colour of paint) of the artefact, either initially or as the result of any alteration in its own physical or chemical properties. It should not discolour and should retain sufficient flexibility to accommodate any normal movement in the varnished surface caused by fluctuations in atmospheric conditions. The composition of the varnish ingredients should be known and should not include ingredients such as plasticizers, which might migrate into paint or the fabric of the object. It should remain easily removable (even after deterioration) without damage to the object, as reversibility is one of the most important attributes of any conservation treatment. It should not have any deleterious effect on the health of the conservator (many solvents in common use have vapours that are toxic or flammable). The resin component should preferably dissolve in relatively mild, non-polar solvents such as white spirit, reducing the risk that the artefact will be adversely affected by the solvent. The varnishes used in conservation are usually based on thermoplastic synthetic resins (e.g. polyacrylates and cyclohexanones) and also, to some extent, natural resins (e.g. dammar); certain hydrogenated hydrocarbon resins have also been suggested for use.

However closely varnishes may meet the required specifications when first applied, changes may take place with time. The materials used may be subject to deterioration, often caused by the reaction of a varnish component with oxygen, frequently catalysed by light or heat. As a result the polymer chains may break down, causing the varnish film to weaken or become brittle; or they may cross-link, rendering it less soluble. Yellowing of the varnish film and an increased polarity of the resin used also result from chemical reactions of this type. The increased polarity necessitates the use of a more polar solvent to remove the varnish than that in which it was applied, thus increasing the risk of damage to the artefact itself.

It is often felt that dammar varnish gives a more satisfactory result when used on a picture surface than many synthetic resin varnishes: the relatively low molecular weight and high refractive index of the resin give a varnish that makes the pigments appear saturated in colour. However, it has certain disadvantages: it tends to wrinkle and to 'bloom' under certain circumstances. ('Bloom' gives the surface of the varnish a white or misty appearance; mastic and other varnishes are also affected. There are a number of possible causes.) It also becomes brittle and yellows in a relatively short time (*c.* 20 years), although the addition of an antioxidant to the varnish reduces yellowing. Partial removal of varnish from Sassoferrato's *Virgin and Child Embracing* revealed the freshness of its colours (see fig.). However, research has shown that the addition of light stabilizing chemicals to the varnish film and the elimination of ultraviolet radiation result in an increase in the useful life of dammar varnish; it may thus be made more suitable for conservation purposes. Varnishes prepared from mastic, which deteriorates in a rather similar manner to dammar, and certain cyclohexanone resin varnishes commonly used in conservation, which tend to become brittle, have similarly been stabilized by these means under laboratory conditions.

BIBLIOGRAPHY

R. L. Feller, N. Stolow and E. H. Jones: *On Picture Varnishes and their Solvents* (Oberlin, 1959, rev. Cleveland, OH, 1971/*R* Washington, DC, 1985)

H. Ruhemann: *The Cleaning of Paintings: Problems and Potentialities* (London, 1968), pp. 269–79

C. V. Horie: *Materials for Conservation: Organic Consolidants, Adhesives and Coatings* (London, 1987)

E. R. de la Rie and A. M. Shedrinsky: 'The Chemistry of Ketone Resins and the Synthesis of a Derivative with Increased Stability and Flexibility', *Stud. Conserv.*, xxxiv/1 (1989), pp. 9–19 [with bibliog. refs]

E. R. de la Rie and C. W. McGlinchey: 'Stabilized Dammar Picture Varnish', *Stud. Conserv.*, xxxiv/3 (1989), pp. 137–46 [with bibliog.]

Cleaning, Retouching and Coatings: Technology and Practice for Easel Paintings and Polychrome Sculpture: Preprints of the Contributions to the IIC Congress: Brussels, 1990, pp. 81–4, 158–76, 160–64, 168–73

JO KIRBY

1. Varnish partially removed from the *Virgin and Child Embracing* by Sassoferrato, oil on canvas, 972×740 mm, 1660–85 (London, National Gallery); photograph taken during the cleaning process, 1983

Varnucci, Bartolomeo di Antonio (*b* Florence, 1410; *d* Florence, 1479). Italian illuminator and stationer. He is documented from 1440, when he enrolled in the Arte de Medici e Speziali, and began to work for the Badia in Florence with his brother Giovanni. When the latter died, Bartolomeo entered the bottega of his younger brother, Chimenti. Bartolomeo was not an innovator and was of second rank compared to such skilled illuminators as Francesco d'Antonio del Chierico, Gherardo di Giovanni di Miniato del Foro, Monte di Giovanni di Miniato del Foro and Attavante degli Attavanti. His handling of volume, the sculptural quality of his scrolls and his use of large, densely hatched areas in landscapes, beards and hair, are reminiscent of contemporary sculpture; the influence of Donatello's low reliefs is especially evident in Bartolomeo's use of the 'heroic putto' (e.g. initial S, Florence, Bib. Medicea-Laurenziana, MS. S Marco 616, fol. 4*r*). Bartolomeo worked mainly on liturgical manuscripts and Books of Hours, sometimes in collaboration with other artists. For example he came into contact with Battista di Niccolò da Padova and Ser Ricciardo di Nanni while working on the four-volume Lectionary (Florence, Bib. Medicea-Laurenziana, MSS Edili 141–7) for Florence Cathedral. Among his large-scale works are two Missals (Florence, Bib. Medicea-Laurenziana, MSS Edili 103–4), also commissioned by the cathedral authorities, in June 1456 and March 1458, respectively. His other patrons included the Stamperia (press) di Ripoli, for which between 1474 and 1480 he produced four *Libri di compagnia*, two copies of the *Life of St Catherine* and a Psalter written by Frate Matteo da Pistoia. In his Books of Hours the repetitiveness of certain compositional schemes marks Bartolomeo as a conservative artist; nonetheless, his works do not lack original illustrative ideas (e.g. Catania, Bib. Reg. U., MS. F. 109, fol. 56*r*; Rome, Bib. Casanatense, MS. 244, fol. 155*r*).

BIBLIOGRAPHY

M. Levi d'Ancona: *Miniatura e miniatori a Firenze dal XIV al XVI secolo* (Florence, 1962), pp. 29–37

A. Garzelli: *Miniatura fiorentina del Rinascimento, 1440–1525: Un primo censimento*, i (Florence, 1985), pp. 29–31

PATRIZIA FERRETTI

Varo, Remedios (*b* Anglés, nr Girona, Spain, 16 Dec 1908; *d* Mexico City, 8 Oct 1966). Spanish painter, active in Mexico. She began her studies at the Real Academia de San Fernando in Madrid in 1934 and even in her earliest work showed a tendency to work from the imagination. In 1937, while living in Paris, she married the French poet Benjamin Péret (*b* 1899) and through him became involved in the activities of the Surrealists. The influence of Surrealism is apparent in early works such as *Vegetal Puppets* (1938; priv. col., see Kaplan, p. 62), in which the elongated floating figures are formed out of wax dripped on to an unprimed wooden surface. After the occupation of France by Germany, Varo and Péret fled in 1942 to Mexico, where many exiled Surrealists, notably Leonora Carrington and Wolfgang Paalen, were already active.

Varo did not begin to paint full-time until 1953, and her most characteristic work dates from this period. She was greatly influenced by André Breton in her cultivation of dream-like moods, but she rejected an unswerving reliance on the subconscious in favour of deliberate fantasies. Her painstaking technique suggests a direct debt to medieval art, for example to the Romanesque frescoes of her native Catalonia, especially in the treatment of architectural elements. In typical early works such as *Useless Science or the Alchemist* (1955; priv. col., see Kaplan, p. 126) buildings, objects and clothing take on a life of their own, undergoing a metamorphosis linked to the theme of a spiritual journey; the natural environment, often shown as threatening, is populated with male and female figures who resemble the artist herself. Humorous touches help to dissipate the otherwise solemn mood of these claustrophobic spaces. Another characteristic painting, *Hairy Locomotion* (oil on hardboard, 1960; Mexico City, Márgara Garza priv. col., see Kaplan, p. 157), exemplifies both the artist's command of line and the unrestrained imagination by which everyday objects and events undergo mutations into unusual things. Three men, identified by the artist as detectives, appear to float within a labyrinthine architecture as they steer their way through corridors on enormous beards that are considerably longer than their bodies. She remained faithful to such dream-like atmospheres and perplexing narratives in the works painted over the last few years of her life.

BIBLIOGRAPHY

O. Paz, R. Callois and J. González: *Remedios Varo* (Mexico City, 1966)
E. Jaguer: *Remedios Varo* (Mexico City, 1980)
Remedios Varo, 1913–1963 (exh. cat., Mexico City, Mus. A. Mod., 1983)
J. A. Kaplan: *Unexpected Journeys: The Art and Life of Remedios Varo* (New York and London, 1988)

MARGARITA GONZÁLEZ ARREDONDO

Varotari, Alessandro. *See* PADOVANINO.

Vartu. *See* VERTUE.

Vasa. Swedish family of rulers, patrons and collectors.

(1) Gustav I [Gustav Eriksson], King of Sweden (*b* 12 May 1496; *reg* 1523–60; *d* 29 Sept 1560). Patron. He had an important role in introducing foreign, particularly Flemish, artists to Sweden: for example the Flemish sculptor Willem Boy created a wooden relief portrait of *King Gustav I* (Mariefred, Gripsholm Slott, Stat. Porträttsaml.) and later produced the tomb of *Gustav I* and his two wives (1560–70; Uppsala Cathedral; *see* SWEDEN, fig. 12). Gustav also hired Flemish tapestry-weavers, such as Paul de Buche (*d* 1565). For reasons of security, Gustav strengthened the existing royal castles and built new ones at Gripsholm, Vadstena and Uppsala.

□

(2) Sigismund [Zygmunt] **III**, King of Poland [Sigismund, King of Sweden] (*b* Gripsholm, 20 June 1566; *reg* in Poland 1587–1632; *reg* in Sweden 1594–9; *d* Warsaw, 30 April 1632). Patron, collector and amateur painter, goldsmith and wood-carver, grandson of (1) Gustav I. He was the son of John III, King of Sweden (*reg* 1568–92), and Catherine Jagiellon (1526–83), daughter of Sigismund I (Sigismund the Old), King of Poland; he became the elected King of Poland in 1587 and in 1594 also became hereditary King of Sweden. Educated at the court in Stockholm by the Swede Nils Rasch, the Livonian Arnold Grothus (*c.* 1522–99) and the Polish Jesuit Pakosz Bernard Gołyński (1546–99), Sigismund was a learned man and spoke several languages. Initially he had his court in Kraków, but by 1611 he had moved to Warsaw. In 1592 he married Grand Duchess Anna (1573–98), daughter of Charles (*reg* 1564–90), the Habsburg ruler of Styria (now part of Austria), and after her death, in 1605 he married her sister Constance (1588–1631).

Sigismund's patronage reflected his profound religious devotion: the arts and artists he promoted were representative of the Baroque style and of Catholic ideology, and were influenced primarily by Italian and Flemish art. Buildings, both sacred and secular, were modelled on the austere early Baroque architecture of Rome. Interior decoration in Italian and local marble was characteristic for the period. Sigismund employed many Italian and Swiss-Italian architects: Jacopo Rotondo from Scuol in 1598–1606, then from 1603 Giovanni Trevano, Matteo Castello from Melide from 1614 to before 1632, and Giovanni Battista Gisleni from Rome in the years 1630–32. The King's major ecclesiastical foundations were the Jesuit church of SS Peter and Paul in Kraków (1596–1635; designed by Giuseppe Britius [Brizzi] and Trevano), the Royal Chapel of St Casimir (1624–36; by Constante Tencalla) at Vilnius Cathedral and the Sigismund Chapel (1598; built ?1605–76; designed by Gisleni) at Wawel Cathedral (*see* KRAKÓW, §IV, 2(ii)). Sigismund presented chapels and churches with devotional objects that he imported from abroad or made himself. Silver sculptures for the altars at the Vilnius Chapel, as well as those for the chapel of the Black Madonna at Jasna Góra Monastery in Częstochowa, were commissioned by the King in Augsburg. The silver coffin of St Stanislav (destr. 1655) for Wawel Cathedral in Kraków was also provided by the King. Sigismund both undertook new building projects and rebuilt some of the existing royal residences in Kraków and Warsaw. In Warsaw works concentrated on three buildings: the Royal Castle (before 1619; *see* WARSAW, §V, 1), the Kazimierzowski Palace and the Ujazdów Castle. In

Kraków, the Wawel Castle was rebuilt after the fire of 1598 in the new Baroque style (*see* KRAKÓW, §IV, 1).

Sigismund III brought together an outstanding collection of works of art, of which little has survived. It was particularly rich in Italian and Flemish paintings and Flemish and oriental tapestries. The few books with embossed royal ex-libris that are preserved in Sweden indicate the richness of Sigismund's library. No inventory has survived of the collections, but they are known from contemporary accounts which confirm Sigismund's love for the arts. 'His Majesty . . . is awaiting the paintings with great joy, it is strange how much he loves the beautiful things he possesses', Gołyński wrote in 1588 to Father Stanisław Reszka (1544–1600), who from the late 1580s acted in Rome as one of the King's artistic agents, sending over Italian paintings, tapestries and curiosities for the royal *Kunstkammer*. Ruggiero Salomoni acted as an agent in Naples around 1619.

Mythological and allegorical scenes (destr.) painted by Antonio Vassilacchi and Palma Giovane (e.g. *Virgin and Child with SS John the Baptist and Stanislav*; destr. 1944) were sent over from Venice. Tommaso Dolabella, a pupil of Vassilacchi, became court painter, and decorated the royal residences with large-scale historic and military scenes. Sefer Muratowicz (*d* 1610) was sent to Persia in 1601 to commission tapestries, tents and arms for the King. Around 1620 Piotr Żeroński contacted Peter Paul Rubens and Jan Breughel the elder on behalf of the King, and in the following year Breughel wrote to Cardinal Federico Borromeo: 'I have sent many paintings to the King of Poland who likes our work'. Pieter Claesz. Soutman was appointed as court portraitist in 1624, but his portraits of *Sigismund III* and *Queen Constance* in coronation robes are known only from copies (1624 and 1642 respectively; Munich, Alte Pin.) and from a print by Jonas Suyderhoef. Several of Emperor Rudolf II's court painters, including Hans von Aachen, Aegidius Sadeler II and Herman Hahn, also worked for Sigismund III, as did the portrait painter Marcin Kober from Wrocław and Krzysztof Boguszewski (*d* 1635), who painted devotional scenes influenced by Flemish art.

Works of art ascribed to Sigismund himself include several devotional paintings, for example the *Allegory of Suppression of Heresy* (Munich, Alte Pin.) and portraits of his family (e.g. a miniature portrait of *Constance of Habsburg*; Kraków, Czartoryski Found.). As a goldsmith, Sigismund III produced a number of liturgical and other objects often with the help of a Venetian goldsmith named ?Redura. They include a reliquary incorporating earlier plaques and jewels for the head of St Jacek [Hiacynthus] (1621; Kraków, Dominican Monastery), a silver wine cup with turquoises and old coins (Vienna, Ksthist. Mus.) and a salt-cellar (Munich, Bayer. Nmus.). One of Sigismund's tools is preserved at the National Museum in Warsaw. The King presented various individuals with self-portrait medals hung on chains that he forged himself. One such medal is depicted on the portrait engraved in 1629 by Jan Engelhart (*b* 1585) of *Andrzej Bobola*, the King's chamberlain. Sigismund also set gems and hardstones in rings and made clocks and watches.

The art collections assembled by Sigismund III were subsequently enlarged by his sons (3) Vladislav IV and (4)

John II, but later dispersed and partly destroyed. Some of these objects, together with other items from the royal collections, were taken in 1642 to Bavaria in the dowry of Princess Anne Catherine Constance (1619–80; now partly in Munich, Residenz and Bayer. Staatsgemäldesammlungen). Another part of the collection was taken in 1669 by John II to Paris.

BIBLIOGRAPHY
J. Lipski: *Oratio funebris D. D. Sigismundi* (Kraków, 1633)
C. Lechicki: *Mecenat Zygmunta III* [The patronage of Sigismund III] (Warsaw, 1932)
W. Tomkiewicz: 'Mecenat artystyczny i kolekcjonerstwo Zygmunta III' [Sigismund III as patron and collector], *Z dziejów polskiego mecenatu artystycz nego w wieku XVII* [From the history of artistic patronage in Poland in the 17th century] (Warsaw, 1952), pp. 11–29
J. Białostocki: 'Weneckie zamó ienia Zygmunta III' [The Venetian Orders of Sigismund III], *Biul. Hist. Sztuki*, xvi/1 (1954), pp. 162–4
J. Ruszczycówna: 'Portrety Zygmunta III i jego rodziny' [The portraits of Sigismund III and his family], *Rocz. Muz. N. Warszaw./Annu. Mus. N. Varsovie*, xiii/1 (1969), pp. 151–270
Sztuka dworu Wazów w Polsce [The arts at the Vasa court in Poland] (exh. cat., ed. J. T. Petrus; Kraków, Wawel Castle, 1976)
H. Wisner: *Zygmunt III Waza* [Sigismund III Vasa] (Warsaw, 1984)
M. Karpowicz: *Królewski zamek Wazów w Warszawie* [The Royal Castle of the Vasas in Warsaw] (Warsaw, 1987)
J. A. Chrościcki: 'Czy można nazwać mecenasami polskich Wazów?' [Can the Polish Vasas be called patrons?], *Tryumfy i porażki* [Triumphs and defeats] (Warsaw, 1989), pp. 183–201

(3) Vladislav [Ladislas; Władysław] **IV**, King of Poland (*b* Łobzów, nr Kraków, 9 June 1595; *reg* 1632–48; *d* Merecz, Lithuania, 20 May 1648). Collector and patron, son of (2) Sigismund III. His mother was Sigismund III's first wife, Anne of Habsburg. In 1632 Vladislav IV was elected King of Poland (not to be confused with the earlier Vladislav IV, of the Piast dynasty; *reg* 1320–33), and he was also heir to the Swedish throne and the Grand Duchy of Moscow. In 1624, when still Prince Royal, he was sent on a year-long journey around Europe as part of his education. What began as a pilgrimage to Loreto and Rome turned into an artistic journey, during which he visited many important collections of art and artists' studios, making purchases and commissions to enrich the collections established by his father. On 5 and 12 October 1624 contracts with the Brussels weaver Jacob Geubels the younger (*fl* 1624–7) were concluded for ten tapestries depicting scenes from *The Odyssey*, together with ten landscape tapestries. These tapestries were brought to Poland at the end of 1632 and were used to decorate the presbytery of Wawel Cathedral in Kraków, during Vladislav's coronation ceremony. While in Antwerp, the Prince Royal visited the studios of Rubens and Jan Breughel the elder. A portrait of the *Prince Royal*, mentioned in the writings of Giovanni Pietro Bellori and Jean Le Laboureur, the French ambassador to Brussels, was painted by Rubens in September 1624 (untraced). An engraving by Jacob van der Heyden and two studio versions of the portrait survive (New York, Met.; Genoa, Pal. Durazzo Pallavicini). The Prince Royal also visited the Bolognese studio of Guido Reni, from whom he had earlier commissioned the *Rape of Europa* (London, priv. col.). *Prince Vladislav in his 'Kunstkammer'* (Warsaw, Royal Castle), painted by Etienne de La Hyre (*c.* 1583–1643) in 1626 in Warsaw, provides an interesting insight into the Prince's collection at this early stage. The works on display include, among others, *Mary Magdalene* by Hans von Aachen, the *Rape of the*

Sabine Women by Giambologna, *St Peter* and *St Paul* by Rubens, and a drawing by Hendrik Goudt from 1608, based on Adam Elsheimer's *Tobias and the Angel* (probable original, Frankfurt am Main, Städel. Inst. & Städt. Gal.).

Vladislav continued embellishing the Kazimierzowski Palace and the Royal and Ujazdów castles in Warsaw, where works concentrated on the interiors and surrounding parks, and the chapel of St Casimir in Vilnius, all begun by Sigismund III, and made creative contributions to architectural and urban projects. Vladislav was also an outstanding patron of the opera. From 1637 most performances were held in the newly built 1000-seat, two-tiered theatre in the southern wing of the Royal Castle in Warsaw. Augustyn Locci the elder and GIOVANNI BATTISTA GISLENI provided stage designs, which were often engraved by Willem Hondius (*b* after 1597; *d* 1658). Vladislav commissioned Gisleni to design the Marble Room at the Royal Castle (*see* WARSAW, fig. 5), in which dynastic assertions were expressed by heraldic cartouches in gilded stucco and by ceiling paintings by Tommaso Dolabella, representing the King's military victories, as well as by 22 royal portraits by Pieter Danckerts de Rij (*see* DANCKERTS DE RIJ), incorporated in marble panelling of the walls (1640–43; destr.; restored 1980s in its 18th-century form; four portraits now in Warsaw, Royal Castle). On the square laid out by Locci in front of the castle, Vladislav erected the Sigismund III Column (1624–44; *in situ*), the first free-standing monument in Warsaw. The column was designed by Constante Tencalla (*see* TENCALLA, (1)), the statue of the King represented as *miles christianus* was made by Clemente Molli (*d* 1678) and cast in bronze by Daniel Tym (*fl* 1627–55). Vladislav also employed military engineers, among others Krzysztof Arciszewski (1592–1656), and sent them to study in Holland. He improved the fortification system in Poland by fortifying strategic sites and by building new arsenals in Lwów (now L'viv) and Warsaw. Despite these efforts, the royal buildings were destroyed during the Swedish invasions of 1655–60, works of art were either destroyed or pillaged, and the flourishing centre of arts and music created by Vladislav in Warsaw ceased to exist.

BIBLIOGRAPHY
W. Tomkiewicz: 'Zbiory artystyczne Władysława IV' [The art collection of Vladislav IV], *Z dziejów polskiego mecenatu artystycznego w wieku XVII* [From the history of artistic patronage in Poland in the 17th century] (Warsaw, 1952), pp. 30–46 [Pol. and Fr. text]
A. Przyboj, ed.: *Die Reise des Kronprinzen Władysław* (Munich, 1988)

(4) John [Jan] **II (Kasimir)** [Casimir; Kazimierz], King of Poland (*b* Kraków, 22 March 1609; *reg* 1648–68; *d* Nevers, France, 16 Dec 1672). Patron and collector, son of (2) Sigismund III. John was educated at his father's court in Warsaw, and in 1649 he married Queen Maria Louisa Gonzaga (1612–67), the widow of his brother (3) Vladislav IV. He inherited his father's and brother's collections of art, which he enriched with works he acquired during foreign trips in the 1630s and 1640s. He continued works undertaken by Sigismund III and Vladislav IV (e.g. the Sigismund Chapel, Wawel Cathedral, Kraków; completed 1676) and employed some of their artists, including Giovanni Battista Gisleni. Daniel Schulc and Giovanni Francesco Rossi also worked for him; the latter carved busts of the royal couple (e.g. Stockholm,

Livrustkam.). Together with his wife, John brought the Sisters of the Visitation of Our Lady to Poland from France and founded a convent in Warsaw in 1654–66. After his abdication in 1668, John left Poland for Paris, taking part of his collection with him. He spent the rest of his life as abbot of St Germain-des-Prés. His monument in the church was erected by Balthazard de Marsy (1628–74) and Gaspard de Marsy (1624/5–81); it incorporates a kneeling figure of *John Casimir* and a bronze relief by Jean Thibaut, showing the *Victory over the Turks at Beresteczko*. The inventory compiled in Paris after the death of John included a *St Peter* (New York, priv. col.) by Rubens and an *Actaeon* and a *Bathing Diana* by Rembrandt, pictures by Herri met de Bles, Jan Breughel the elder, Frans Francken II, as well as Flemish tapestries, ceremonial crowns and reliquaries. Part of the collection was purchased by the French king Louis XIV.

BIBLIOGRAPHY
W. Tomkiewicz: 'Pośmiertny inwentarz zbiorów Jana Kazimierza' [The inventory compiled after the death of John Casimir], *Z dziejów polskiego mecenatu artystycznego w wieku XVII* [From the history of artistic patronage in Poland in the 17th century] (Warsaw, 1952), pp. 62–258 [Pol. text]
J. A. Chrościcki: *Kościół Wizytek* [The church of the Sisters of the Visitation] (Warsaw, 1973)

JULIUSZ A. CHROŚCICKI

(5) Christina, Queen of Sweden (*b* Stockholm, 8 Dec 1626; *reg* 1632–54; *d* Rome, 19 April 1689). Collector and patron, great-granddaughter of (1) Gustav I. Emancipated and unconventional, intellectual and cosmopolitan, she was called 'the Minerva of the North' for her avid interest in the sciences and her acquisition of 'all sorts of beautiful and curious objects'. As long as she reigned in Sweden, she had the financial means, and the power, to satisfy her appetite for art acquisitions; after her abdication, she was often hampered by lack of money.

1. COLLECTING AND PATRONAGE. The nucleus of Queen Christina's celebrated collection was acquired when the Swedish army stormed Prague in 1648, seizing for her the collections of the Holy Roman Emperor Rudolf II. Although many of the titles and descriptions of works listed in the 1652–3 inventory of Christina's collection are too scanty to allow certain identification of its *c.* 40,000 items, 33,000 were coins and medals; of the 750 paintings, 470 came from Prague. There were works by Dürer and other leading German artists, but the Queen's particular taste was for Italian pictures, especially those of Raphael. She presented her Swedish entourage and various other recipients in Europe with many of Rudolf II's northern European works of art; among them were Pieter Bruegel the elder's *Dulle Griet* ('Mad Meg'; 1562; Antwerp, Mus. Mayer van den Bergh; *see* BRUEGEL, (1), fig. 2) and *The Cripples* (*c.* 1568; Paris, Louvre), Holbein's *Fountain of Life* (1519; Lisbon, Mus. N. A. Ant.) and Dürer's *Adam and Eve* (1504; Madrid, Prado).

When Queen Christina abdicated (1654) and settled in Rome (1655), most of the northern works still in her collection (many of which did not come from Prague) remained in Stockholm Castle, where some were destroyed when it burnt down in 1697; others are now in the Nationalmuseum, including Lucas Cranach I's *The Payment* (1532), Jan Massys's *Venus Cytherea* (1561) and

Psyche Carried by Cupids (*c.* 1593) by Adriaen de Vries. The Queen took with her only *c.* 20 portraits and *c.* 40 works by Italian masters. This initial Italian ensemble she enriched in Rome with taste and discrimination and with the assistance of such eminent artists as Bernini and connoisseurs including Giovanni Pietro Bellori, who became her antiquarian. Her residence, the Palazzo Riario on the Via della Lungara (now partly demolished and partly integrated in the Palazzo Corsini), became a veritable private museum, finally displaying *c.* 270 paintings. More than twenty were by, or attributed to, Titian, among them the *Death of Actaeon* (*c.* 1562; London, N.G.), the *Three Ages of Man* (*c.* 1510–15; *see* TITIAN, fig. 2) and *Venus Anadyomene* (*c.* 1525; both Mertoun Gardens, Borders, on loan to Edinburgh, N.G.), fourteen by Veronese, including *Hermes, Aglauros and Herse* (*c.* 1576; Cambridge, Fitzwilliam) and six large *Allegories* (*c.* 1570s; four in London, N.G.; two in New York, Frick), and Correggio's *Leda* (*c.* 1527–30; Berlin, Gemäldegal.) and *Danaë* (*c.* 1527–30; Rome, Gal. Borghese). Among the works she managed to assemble by her favourite painter, Raphael, were five small predella panels (London, N.G.; two in London, Dulwich Pict. Gal.; Boston, MA, Isabella Stewart Gardner Mus.; New York, Met.) that she bought from a monastery in Perugia in 1663. Rubens's Italian production was also well represented, with, for instance, *Hercules and Omphale* (*c.* 1605; Paris, Louvre) and *Tomyris* (1620; Boston, MA, Mus. F.A.).

The Queen cared little for contemporary artists, with the exception of Bernini. Almost all the paintings and sculptures she owned by Bernini have disappeared, but the *Salvator mundi* sculpture that he bequeathed to her has recently been rediscovered (1679–80; Norfolk, VA, Chrysler Mus.). They were on friendly terms, and Bernini once declared that she was able to appreciate his sculptures 'into their very finest points'. Giovanni Battista Gaulli similarly related how judicious the Queen was in her views about art and how much he profited from every visit to the Palazzo Riario. Contemporary sculptors, including Ercole Ferrata, were commissioned mainly with restorations and completions of Queen Christina's collection of about 160 antique statues, busts and other sculpture (mainly Madrid, Prado) that she assembled in Italy. They were handsomely presented against a background of mural landscapes or *verdure* tapestries from Delft. Particularly admired was the Stanza delle Muse on the ground-floor of the Palazzo Riario, where statues of eight *Muses* (Madrid, Prado), restored works from Villa Adriana, were placed together with a modern *Apollo* (1662) by Francesco Maria Nocchieri. Another main piece, now known as the *San Ildefonso* group (?1st century BC; Madrid, Prado), probably from the school of Pasiteles, depicts two young men.

Queen Christina drew moral as well as aesthetic instruction from the art of antiquity: 'The great painters and great sculptors study antiques not only to copy them but to make their own originals the more perfect. Princes should study the heroes of bygone days in the same way. It is a matter of being not a copy but an original.' The Queen wanted to make her Roman residence into a work of art in itself and her library into a sanctuary of all human knowledge. Artists, scholars and dilettanti were always

welcome to visit and study her treasures. Carlo Maratti copied Correggio; the Benedictines Jean Mabillon and Bernard de Montfaucon examined medieval manuscripts; Jean Vaillant (1632–1726) studied the carefully selected numismatic collection; and others the drawings by Michelangelo, Raphael, Hendrick Goltzius, Claude Lorrain, Bernini and other masters.

2. DISPERSAL OF COLLECTIONS. After Queen Christina's death, her collections were soon dispersed. She had bequeathed them to her close friend Cardinal Decio Azzolino, but he died shortly afterwards, whereupon almost everything was sold by his nephew and heir to Livio Odescalchi, the Duca di Bracciano. When he died in 1713, the antique works were acquired by Philip V, King of Spain, in 1721, and 259 paintings by Philippe II, Duc d'Orléans, in 1724. These paintings remained in the Palais Royal in Paris until 1792, when the Orléans collection was sold, and mostly passed into distinguished British collections. In 1690 Queen Christina's library was sold to Pope Alexander VIII (*reg* 1689–91), who donated the *c.* 900 medieval manuscripts (*Codices reginensis*) to the Biblioteca Apostolica Vaticana. Her gems (untraced) were purchased by Prince Charles Alexander of Lorraine (1712–80) and some of her most valuable drawings by the Teylers Foundation, Haarlem, in 1790 (Haarlem, Teylers Mus.). Other drawings had been disposed of earlier (for example, 100 of them came into the possession of Pierre Crozat), but as the contents of her albums were rarely specified in her inventories there is much uncertainty still about their scope and their fate. In 1794 Pope Pius VI bought Queen Christina's older medals (Rome, Vatican, Cabinet of Coins and Medals; Paris, Bib. N.). Taken together, however, the inventories of 1652–3 (Stockholm, Kun. Bib.), 1656 (Antwerp, Stadsarchf; see Denucé) and 1676 (Stockholm, Riksarkv) and, above all, the *post-mortem* inventory of 1689 (Rome, Archv. Cent. Stato; see Granberg) present one of the most remarkable private collections of the Baroque era.

BIBLIOGRAPHY

O. Granberg: *Drottning Kristinas tafvelgalleri på Stockholms slott och i Rom, dess uppkomst och dess öden ända till våra dagar* [Queen Christina's picture gallery in Stockholm Castle and in Rome, its origin and destiny up to today] (Stockholm, 1896; abridged Fr. ed. *La Galerie de tableaux de la reine Christine de Suède*, Stockholm, 1897)

J. Denucé: *De Antwerpsche 'Konstkamers' fronnen voor de geschiednis van de geschiednis van de Vlaamsche kunst* [The Antwerp Kunstkamer's sources for the history of Flemish art] (Antwerp, 1932)

Analecta reginensia, 3 vols (Stockholm, 1966) [vol. i: documents and studies; vol. ii: *Les Dessins italiens de la reine Christina de Suède* (exh. cat. by J. Q. van Regteren Altena, Stockholm, Nmus., 1966)]

Christina Drottning av Sverige (exh. cat., Stockholm, Nmus., 1966; Eng. trans.)

Queen Christina of Sweden at Rome, 1655–1689 (exh. cat., Rome, Vatican, Bib. Apostolica, 1989)

PONTUS GRATE

Vasanzio [Vansanzio; Van Zanten], **Giovanni** [Fiammingo, Giovanni; Sanctis, Giovanni de; Santen, Giovanni van] (*b* Utrecht, ?1550; *d* Rome 21 Aug 1621). Dutch architect and cabinetmaker, active in Italy. He may already have been resident in Rome *c.* 1583, but he is first recorded there in 1600 as a 'camerlengo' (officer) of the brotherhood of S Maria in Camp Santo. He initially ran a cabinetmaker's workshop in the Via Giulia, specializing in desks with inlay work ('studiuoli': hence his nickname 'Giovanni degli Studiuoli'). In 1611 he is mentioned as 'architetto delle fontane'; in this capacity he worked with Domenico Fontana (iii) on numerous fountains in Rome, including the Fontana di Ponte Sisto (1613), consisting of a single triumphal arch; the Fontana dell' Aquila (1614), Vatican Gardens; the Fontana di Velo and di Poggia (1615–16), Quirinal Gardens; and the Fontana della Galera (1620), Vatican Gardens.

After the death in 1613 of Flaminio Ponzio, whom he had served as an assistant, Vasanzio was given the post of architect for the papal palaces. By then he was involved in many building projects but continued to work as a cabinetmaker, especially for the Borghese family. On the instructions of Pope Paul V he continued the architectural work on the Palazzo Quirinale, begun by Ponzio; in 1614 he took part with Carlo Maderno in deliberations about the Tiber harbour on the Ripetta and in 1617–18, with Martino Ferrabosco, he erected the clock-tower (destr. mid-17th century during the building of Bernini's colonnades) above the entrance to the Vatican Palace. For the Pope's nephew, Cardinal Scipione Borghese, Vasanzio continued other works begun by Ponzio: he completed the façade, which Ponzio had raised to cornice level, of the church of S Sebastiano fuori le Mura, the wooden roof of which Vasanzio himself had made in 1612, and he was responsible for further work on the Villa Borghese, particularly the façade (c. 1616). From 1615 he extended the Villa Mondragone in Frascati by a connecting wing, erected a beautiful courtyard loggia there and installed the Fontana dei Draghi and the nymphaeum on the terrace. He supervised the construction of the connecting wing between the two old palaces and the new building of the Osteria on Scipione Borghese's country estate Montefortino (now called Artena), and restored the Casale Cecchignola, where he also laid out the grounds (1618–19). Also in 1618 Vasanzio renovated the cathedral of Monte Porzio, designed a small church for the country estate of Molara and began renovating the titular church of S Crisogono in Rome (continued after Vasanzio's death by Giovanni Battista Soria). Like his predecessor Ponzio, Vasanzio was also occasionally assisted by Carlo Maderno; as a result of this teamwork it is difficult in the case of some of Cardinal Scipione Borghese's schemes to determine the question of attribution. Between 1611 and 1614 Vasanzio and Maderno collaborated on the Ripetta wing of the Palazzo Borghese in the Campo Marzio: while Maderno provided the overall idea, Vasanzio was responsible for the detailed execution. The same applies to the palace in the Piazza Montecavallo on the Quirinal (now the Palazzo Pallavicini-Rospigliosi). Here, Vasanzio's contribution is presumed to lie in the architecture of the Casino dell' Aurora, in the balustrades and the fishpond within the grounds, while Maderno's role encompassed structural as well as artistic aspects, since Vasanzio, with his training as a cabinetmaker, had insufficient technical knowledge.

Vasanzio's work as an independent architect is difficult to document. The façade of the Villa Borghese on the Pincio (as shown in old views), covered in Mannerist fashion with niches, recesses, Classical statuary and reliefs, in contrast, for example, with the restraint of Baldassare Peruzzi's Villa Farnesina (1505–11), and the window-frames on the inner façade of S Crisogono, which must have been one of his last designs, show Vasanzio to have been a pupil of Ponzio, whose forms he took over, inlaid like marquetry and decorated with stucco ornamentation, to produce an effect similar to applied wood-carving.

BIBLIOGRAPHY

G. Baglione: *Vite* (1642); ed. V. Mariani (1935)
J. A. F. Orbaan: *Documenti sul barocco a Roma* (Rome, 1920)
——: 'Florentijnsche gegevens (Jan van Santen)', *Oud-Holland*, xliii (1926), pp. 277–88
G. J. Hoogewerff: 'Giovanni van Santen: Architetto della Villa Borghese', *Roma*, iv (1928), pp. 1–12, 49–64
J. Mandl: 'Jan van Santen in Artena und Cecchignola: Beiträge zur Bautätigkeit des Cardinals Scipione Borghese', *Meded. Ned. Hist. Inst. Rome*, xviii (1938), pp. 127–36
——: 'De Bouwmeester Jan van Santen en zijn Tijdgenossen', *Meded. Ned. Hist. Inst. Rome*, i (1942), pp. 89–106
——: 'Giovanni Vasanzio fra gli architetti del tempo di Paolo V', *Palladio*, vi (1942), pp. 49–56
G. J. Hoogewerff: 'Architetti durante il pontificato di Paolo V Borghese', *Archv. Soc. Romana Stor. Patria*, lxvi (1943), pp. 135–47
H. Hibbard: *The Architecture of the Palazzo Borghese* (Rome, 1962)
C. H. Heilmann: 'Die Entstehungsgeschichte der Villa Borghese in Rom', *Münchn. Jb. Bild. Kst*, xxiv (1973), pp. 97–158
B. Ringbeck: *Giovanni Battista Soria: Architekt Scipione Borgheses* (diss., Münster, Westfäl. Wilhems-U., 1987)

BIRGITTA RINGBECK

Vasarely, Victor (*b* Pecs, Hungary, 9 April 1908). French painter and printmaker of Hungarian birth. He was one of the leading figures in the development of geometrical abstraction known as Op art, which acquired widespread popularity in Europe and the USA during the 1960s. He studied in Budapest at the Academy of Painting (1925–7) and under Alexander Bortnyk (1893–1977) at the 'Mühely' Academy, also known as the Budapest Bauhaus (1929–30). In 1930 he moved to Paris and worked as a graphic designer for the next decade. He was thus able to commit himself seriously to the task of devising a new pictorial language only in the period following World War II. After what he regarded as a false start in 1944–6, he began the process of lengthy and methodical abstraction from particular features of his environment that resulted in his pure and individual style of the 1960s.

At the Budapest Bauhaus, Vasarely had become aware of the formal and geometrical language that masters of the original Bauhaus (Vasily Kandinsky, Paul Klee and László Moholy-Nagy) had employed in their courses for artists and designers. His work during the 1930s shows a sophisticated grasp of the techniques of applied art that can clearly be traced to this source. Vasarely's development from 1947, however, shows that he was by no means satisfied with these technical applications. At a period when Parisian art was dominated by Tachism, he returned to the geometric abstraction pioneered by such artists as Piet Mondrian and Kazimir Malevich. His repeated studies of specific environments, including the Breton island of Belle-Isle (1947), were designed to produce a new and rigorous system that could be applied universally by artists.

The effect of Vasarely's research was first evident in the series entitled *Homage to Malevich* (1952–8), in which the Suprematist painter's famous black square on a white ground is quoted and also transformed: by being turned round on a notional axis, it is, in Vasarely's words, 'dynamized'. Vasarely had realized that the use of illusory effects like this could transform the relatively stable structures preferred by earlier masters into shimmering and vibrant configurations that dazzled the eye of the spectator, even though their basis lay in simple abstract forms. He demonstrated this particularly well in the version of *Homage to Malevich*, termed an 'outdoor mural movement', for the Housing Centre of the University of Caracas, Venezuela (ceramics, *c.* 100 sq. m.). In his *Planetary Folklore* series (1960–64), this aim came to complete fruition. Each work was composed of an aggregate of 'plastic units' (geometric shapes of varying types and colours superimposed on an overall grid): a high degree of regularity was thus combined with a brilliant optical effect (see Vasarely, 1978, nos 24–9).

Vasarely's claim that his work had a significance that went beyond his individual career found a justification in the 1960s through his influence on groups of younger artists such as the Groupe de Recherche d'Art Visuel (GRAV), as well as through the widespread diffusion of his designs by way of posters, fabric patterns and other images in mass circulation. He believed that his research could provide design prototypes for architectural and urban schemes on a vast scale and completed several such projects at such sites as the Gare Montparnasse, Paris. He opened a museum about his own work (*c.* 1970) at the château de Gordes, near Avignon, and in 1975 he inaugurated the more ambitious, purpose-built Fondation Vasarely on the land of the Jas-de-Bouffon, near Aix-en-Provence, previously owned by Cézanne, which had been placed at his disposal. At the foundation, showcases display the different stages and periods of his work, their layout a pattern in itself.

WRITINGS

Vasarely: La grande monographie, 4 vols, intro. M. Joray (Neuchâtel, 1965–78)
Plasticité (Paris, 1969)
Vasarely (Paris, 1978) [incl. excerpts from his 'Notes brutes']

BIBLIOGRAPHY

F. Popper: *Origins and Development of Kinetic Art* (London, 1968), pp. 96–101
G. Diehl: *Vasarely* (Lugano, 1972)

STEPHEN BANN

Vasari. Italian family of artists and writers. As a prototype of the intellectual artist, (1) Giorgio Vasari, more than any other, determined the shape taken by court display and church decoration in Rome and Florence in the late Renaissance. As the author of the *Vite* ('Lives'), he founded critical art historiography. He was also one of the earliest collectors of Old Master drawings, which he mounted in his famous *Libro de' disegni*. His nephew (2) Giorgio Vasari *il giovane*, an expert in mathematics, perspective, military architecture and cosmography, is best known for his work as an essayist and for organizing his uncle's private papers.

(1) Giorgio Vasari (*b* Arezzo, 30 July 1511; *d* Florence, 27 June 1574). Painter, draughtsman, architect, writer and collector.

I. Life and work. II. Working methods and technique. III. Writings. IV. Collection. V. Character and personality.

I. *Life and work.*

1. Training and early works, before 1537. 2. First major commissions, 1537–53. 3. Years of maturity, 1553–74.

1. TRAINING AND EARLY WORKS, BEFORE 1537. From a family of potters (*vasaio*, hence Vasari), Giorgio was the son of Antonio Vasari (*d* 1527) and Maddalena Tacci (*d* 1558). Information on his training should be treated with caution, as it is based almost exclusively on his autobiography. From 1520 to 1524 he was taught Latin, and probably ancient mythology and religion, by Antonio da Saccone, otherwise unknown, and Giovanni Pollastra (1465–1540), who undoubtedly shaped his literary inclinations. Giorgio's predilection for learned, allegorical subjects in his paintings and his ability to express himself in writing were unusual for a painter of his time. He received his first training as a painter in Arezzo from Guillaume de Marcillat, who had been employed in Rome at the Vatican and knew the works there by Michelangelo and Raphael. Vasari's accomplishments attracted the attention of the Cardinal of Cortona, Silvio Passerini (1470–1529), the tutor of Alessandro and Ippolito de' Medici, and he took Vasari with him to Florence in 1524. There he was taught with the two Medici by Pierio Valeriano (1477–1558). Vasari continued his artistic training in Florence in the workshops of Andrea del Sarto and Baccio Bandinelli, working with Francesco Salviati.

The expulsion of the Medici in 1527 ended Vasari's first stay in Florence. He returned to Arezzo, where he met Rosso Fiorentino, who provided him with a drawing for a painting of the *Resurrection* (untraced). In 1529 Vasari was again in Florence; he joined the workshop of Raffaello da Brescia (again with Salviati) and began an apprenticeship as a goldsmith with Vittorio Ghiberti (ii). In October he went to Pisa to paint a fresco (untraced) and met the Olivetan monk Don Miniato Pitti, who was later of great importance to him. In 1530 he returned to Arezzo by way of Modena and Bologna, where he collaborated on the decorations for the coronation of Charles V. A year later, at the invitation of Cardinal Ippolito de' Medici, he went to Rome, where he entered his service in January 1532. With Salviati, he studied works of ancient and contemporary Roman art and architecture. It was at this time that he met Paolo Giovio, who was later to obtain important commissions for him and to encourage him to write his *Vite*.

In the summer of 1532 Vasari returned to Florence, where he offered his services to Alessandro and Ottaviano de' Medici. Vasari's earliest surviving work, the *Entombment* (Arezzo, Mus. Casa Vasari), was painted for Ippolito in this period. It shows clearly the influence of Rosso and of northern graphic art as well as Bandinelli's style of drawing. The painting earned Vasari the admiration of the Duke of Florence, Alessandro de' Medici, through whom he received further commissions, many arranged by Ottaviano, including portraits of *Lorenzo il Magnifico* (see fig. 1) and *Alessandro de' Medici* (both 1534; Florence, Uffizi). These portraits are important particularly for the use of complicated symbolism. In the portrait of *Lorenzo il Magnifico*, for which a drawing by Vasari (the earliest known) has survived (Florence, Uffizi), a number of inscriptions allude to the virtue of the sitter, an idea no doubt devised by a literary adviser, probably Giovio. In the portrait of *Alessandro de' Medici*, on the other hand, the symbolic meaning is conveyed by objects alluding to the aims and ambitions of the Duke. The complex meaning of the work would not have been fully comprehensible without the explanation given by Vasari in a letter to Ottaviano, the first of many such accounts.

In 1535 Ippolito de' Medici died. Since Vasari's new patron, Alessandro de' Medici, was mainly interested in fortifications, the artist now began to study architecture. The first result of these studies was the organ base (*in situ*) for the cathedral of Arezzo, in which he mixed 15th-century motifs with those from the architecture of Michelangelo. In 1536 Vasari collaborated on the temporary decorations for the entry of Charles V into Florence. He executed this large commission quickly, with the aid of many assistants, demonstrating a talent for organization that he put to good use later in his career, when he was in charge of large-scale projects for his court patrons. The following year he produced several works for Arezzo, including a *Deposition* (Arezzo, SS Annunziata), again influenced by Rosso, and frescoes for S Rocco (detached; Arezzo, Gal. & Mus. Med. & Mod.; Monte San Savino, S Chiara). These earliest surviving frescoes show Vasari's virtuoso technique; they have a freshness and lightness often lacking in his panel paintings.

2. First major commissions, 1537–53.

(i) 1537–40. With the murder of Alessandro de' Medici in 1537, Vasari lost his second princely patron. He decided to give up the precarious existence of the court artist and earn his living from art alone. Through his former teacher Pollastra, he went to work for the monks at Camaldoli. There he painted a *Virgin and Child with SS John the Baptist and Jerome* (1537; *in situ*), frescoes (destr.) and an altarpiece of the *Nativity* (1538; *in situ*), a night scene of which the lighting effects were much admired. He interrupted the works at Camaldoli by a journey to Rome made in early 1538, accompanied by his assistant Giovanni Battista Cungi. A year earlier he had expressed the wish to return to Rome, where, as he wrote in a letter, the study of ancient and modern works had brought contemporary art to perfection, an idea he developed later, in the *Vite*. Vasari stated that he executed more than 300 drawings in Rome, many in the newly excavated villa of Nero, the Domus Aurea (*see* ROME, §V, 5). He claimed that this trip influenced his painting of the *Assumption* for S Agostino in Monte San Savino (1538–9; *in situ*), but the work is, in fact, based on elements from two paintings of the subject by Andrea del Sarto (both Florence, Pitti). The combining of his own pictorial ideas with those of others remained characteristic of Vasari's oeuvre.

In 1539, through Don Miniato Pitti, Vasari was commissioned to execute works for S Michele in Bosco, near Bologna: *Abraham and the Three Angels* (untraced), *Christ in the House of Mary and Martha* (*in situ*), the *Feast of St Gregory* (with Cristofano Gherardi; Bologna, Pin. N.) and frescoes with scenes from the *Apocalypse* (*in situ*), after

1. Giorgio Vasari: *Lorenzo il Magnifico*, oil on panel, 0.90×0.72 m, 1534 (Florence, Galleria degli Uffizi); posthumous portrait

Dürer. In Bologna he studied works by Parmigianino and also Raphael's *St Cecilia* (Bologna, Pin. N.), from which he did a drawing of a *Standing Man* (Florence, Uffizi). The influence of his stay in Bologna is evident in a stylistic change in his painting, which lost its hard, metallic quality and gained a new elegance and ornamental refinement.

In 1540 Vasari painted the high altar at Camaldoli, depicting the *Descent from the Cross* (1540; Camaldoli, SS Donato e Ilariano; see fig. 2). While there, he met Bindo Altoviti, who commissioned from him a painting for his chapel in SS Apostoli, Florence. As Vasari hoped this work would aid his return to Florence, he prepared it with great care. The painting, an *Immaculate Conception* (*in situ*; see fig. 3), was derived from a composition by Rosso. The success of Vasari's composition is indicated by the large fee he received and by the numerous replicas. His treatment of the theme became an iconographic model followed in central Italian art until the early 17th century. The popularity of such paintings illustrating learned programmes is also attested by Vasari's *Penitent St Jerome*, first executed for Ottaviano de' Medici in 1541 and repeated several times for other patrons (Chicago, A. Inst.; Florence, Pitti; Leeds, C.A.G.; Vincigliata, Graetz priv. col.). Apart from the didactic paintings on Christian or allegorical subjects for which he is known, Vasari also painted works with more frivolous, mainly erotic, themes. Most are untraced, but there are echoes in some individual

2. Giorgio Vasari: *Descent from the Cross*, oil on panel, 2.10×3.11 m, 1540 (Camaldoli, SS Donato e Ilariano)

figures in the later decorations in the Quartiere degli Elementi of the Palazzo Vecchio.

(ii) 1541–5. At the invitation of Pietro Aretino, Vasari went to Venice in 1541. On the journey he viewed art and visited fellow artists in a number of north Italian cities. In Mantua he visited Giulio Romano, and in Ferrara he stayed with Garofalo. In Venice in 1542 (with Cungi, Gherardi and others) he painted the stage-set for Aretino's *La talanta* and decorated the walls of the room in which it was performed. This work was crucial in the development of his interior decorations. Through Michele Sanmicheli, he was commissioned to do nine ceiling paintings in the Palazzo Corner Spinelli in Venice (dispersed). For his host, Francesco Leoni, he painted a *Holy Family with St Francis* (Los Angeles, CA, Co. Mus. A.), his most lavish and perhaps his best version of the subject.

On his return to Tuscany, Vasari began decorating the house he had acquired in Arezzo in 1541 (*see* ARTIST'S HOUSE, fig. 1). In the autumn of 1542 he went to Rome, where he painted a *Deposition* for Bindo Altoviti (untraced; drawing Paris, Louvre; replica Siena, Col. Chigi-Saracini). The painting earned Michelangelo's approval; it also brought Vasari into contact with Cardinal Alessandro Farnese, and in early 1543 he painted *Justice* (Naples, Capodimonte) for the Cardinal's Rome residence, the Palazzo della Cancelleria. This learned allegory was clearly

intended to catch the attention of the Cardinal and indeed opened the way for the commission of the Cancelleria frescoes in 1546. In the meantime, Vasari painted, among other works, a *Deposition* for S Agostino (Rome, Gal. Doria-Pamphili), a variant of the Camaldoli composition, showing the influence of Michelangelo and Salviati.

In 1544 Vasari went to Naples, where, again for the Olivetans, he painted the *Presentation of Christ*, for the high altar of S Anna dei Lombardi (Naples, Capodimonte), and, with Raffaello dal Colle and others, decorated their refectory, with dazzling white stucco and colourful grotesques (*in situ*), which clearly owe much to Venetian influences. Vasari painted many other works in Naples, including the *Crucifixion* for S Giovanni a Carbonara (*in situ*). The powerful religious expressiveness of this work, unique in his oeuvre, clearly reflects the wishes of the patron, the theologian Girolamo Seripando (1493–1563). In October 1545 Vasari returned to Rome, where he executed the remaining Neapolitan commissions: 18 panels with scenes from the *Old Testament* and the *Life of St John the Baptist* for the sacristy of S Giovanni a Carbonara, and the organ doors for Naples Cathedral (*in situ*). During this period Titian was in Rome, and Vasari accompanied him to places of interest.

(iii) 1546–53. In March 1546 Vasari received from Alessandro Farnese the commission for the decoration of

3. Giorgio Vasari: *Immaculate Conception*, oil on panel, 3.45×2.37 m, 1541 (Florence, SS Apostoli)

a hall in the Cancelleria. These frescoes were completed in an extremely short time (100 days), hence the name of the room, Sala dei Cento Giorni. Vasari was therefore obliged to use a large number of assistants, and he was not satisfied with the result; but this first large court fresco cycle did give him useful experience for later commissions. The cycle depicts the *Deeds of Pope Paul III*, the Cardinal's grandfather, in a complex setting of fictive architecture, the most striking elements of which are the staircases leading the eye from the room into each scene.

According to Vasari's own account, it was during this period, and encouraged by Giovio, that he began writing the *Vite*, although he must have begun collecting material long before. In the months after his return to Florence in autumn 1546, he worked primarily on the *Vite*, probably completing the text by the autumn of 1547. In October he went to Rimini, to paint the *Adoration of the Magi* for S Maria di Scolca (main panel, Rimini, S Fortunato). He also painted the *Stigmatization of St Francis* for S Francesco there (1548; *in situ*) and a *Deposition* for the Camaldolese abbey of Classe, near Ravenna (Ravenna, Accad. B.A.). Also in 1548 he visited Urbino, where he probably saw the ducal collection.

In the summer of the same year Vasari completed the decoration of his house in Arezzo, begun in 1542. It is characteristic of his self-confidence that he lavished as much effort on his own house as on those of his patrons.

This may also reflect the influence of the elaborately decorated houses of Andrea Mantegna and Giulio Romano, which he had seen in Mantua in 1541. On the ceiling of the Sala della Fama, he painted the figure of *Fame*, surrounded by personifications of the arts: *Poetry*, *Painting*, *Sculpture* and *Architecture*. It was a pictorial expression of the equality of the arts, an idea he elaborated later in a letter to Benedetto Varchi on the PARAGONE, and in the introduction to the *Vite*. His ideas on art theory were also reflected in the decoration of the other rooms. The Sala del Trionfo della Virtù, painted in 1548, includes monochrome frescoes illustrating well-known anecdotes about artists recorded by Pliny. Also in 1548 Vasari's work for Cardinal Giovanni Maria del Monte (later Pope Julius III) began with plans for a country house near Monte San Savino (probably never executed).

At the end of 1549 Vasari married Nicolosa Bacci (1536–84) from Arezzo. The match was negotiated by his friend Vincenzo Borghini, the prior of the Ospedale degli Innocenti. In April 1550 the first edition of the *Vite* was published. By this time Vasari was again in Rome, working with Bartolomeo Ammanati on the design of the del Monte Chapel in S Pietro in Montorio, commissioned by Julius III. Other works of the time include the *Beheading of St John the Baptist* for S Giovanni Decollato (*in situ*), designs for the Villa Giulia, frescoes (destr.) for the loggia of the Villa Altoviti, frescoes (Rome, Pal. Venezia) for the

4. Giorgio Vasari: *Study for the Ceiling of the Sala di Cosimo il Vecchio, Palazzo Vecchio, Florence,* pen and brown ink, 320×440 mm, 1556 (Paris, Musée du Louvre)

loggia of the Palazzo Altoviti, and a painting of *Patience* (Florence, Pitti) for Bernardo Minerbetti, Bishop of Arezzo (1507–74). At Minerbetti's request, Vasari used in this work a motif from Michelangelo, a variation of a figure from the *Crucifixion of St Peter* (Rome, Vatican, Pauline Chapel). Numerous copies of this 'invention' testify to its success.

3. YEARS OF MATURITY, 1553–74. In 1553 Vasari designed decorations for the façade and interior (*in situ*) of the palazzo of Sforza Almeni (*d* 1566), aide to Cosimo I, who played an important role in the negotiations that brought Vasari back to the service of the Medici in 1554, a post that he retained until the end of his life. These frescoes were executed mainly by Gherardi, after a programme by Cosimo Bartoli (Davis, 1980). Vasari and Gherardi collaborated on another major fresco decoration in these years, for the Compagnia del Gesù in Cortona (*in situ*). Vasari's activities during 1554 also included plans and a wooden model for the completion of S Maria Nuova in Cortona, begun in 1550.

(i) Palazzo Vecchio. (ii) Other architectural commissions and ephemeral decorations. (iii) Other painted works.

(i) Palazzo Vecchio. Vasari's first major task for Cosimo was the remodelling of the Palazzo Vecchio in Florence as a ducal residence. His work there, as architect and painter, occupied a large part of his creative energy from 1555 to 1572. It was the most extensive palace decoration executed to a coherent programme in 16th-century Italy and the prototype for the residence of an absolute ruler. In many cases Vasari only produced designs (see fig. 4), and the execution of the paintings was left largely to his

5. Giorgio Vasari: *Apotheosis of Cosimo I* (1565), oil on panel, ceiling of the Salone del Cinquecento, Palazzo Vecchio, Florence

numerous assistants. The programmes, devised with Bartoli and Borghini, were so complex that by 1558 Vasari decided to produce a written explanation of the decoration, the *Ragionamenti* (*see* §III, 2 below). Works began in 1555, in the Quartiere degli Elementi on the second floor and in the Quartiere di Leone X on the first, with collaborators including Gherardi and Joannes Stradanus.

The *Genealogy of the Gods* was chosen as the theme for the Quartiere degli Elementi; the Quartiere di Leone X was to illustrate the *History of the House of Medici*, with individual rooms devoted to depictions of the deeds of important family members (for illustration *see* MEDICI, DE', (2) and (14)). The programme was without parallel in earlier history paintings, and in his *Ragionamenti* Vasari further emphasized the encomiastic theme, pointing out that everything depicted in the rooms devoted to the gods had its counterpart in the rooms below, in the deeds of the Medici. These links were not represented visually, however, and may have been an interpretation after the event.

The choice of subject for the Quartiere di Leone X differed fundamentally from the historical themes represented in Italian family palazzi. Feats of arms were largely ruled out as a theme for the Medici, but, as Vasari had learnt in the Cancelleria, acts of patronage were also suitable for pictorial representation. In 1550, in the *Vite*, he had already stressed the special role of the Medici in the rebirth of the arts. It is not surprising, therefore, that scenes illustrating this idea appear in most of the rooms. Vasari's interpretation of the history of the Medici remained the model until the 17th century. From about 1562, work began on the decorations of the Quartiere del Duca Cosimo (largely destr.) and the Quartiere di Eleonora, the paintings for which were executed mainly by Stradanus.

The first phase of work in the Palazzo Vecchio culminated in the remodelling and decoration of the Salone del Cinquecento, the great hall built by Cronaca in 1495. In 1560 Vasari submitted a model for the project to Michelangelo, who suggested raising the ceiling. Work began in 1563 and was completed in 1571. The general theme of the decoration is the history of Florence from its foundation in 70 BC. Scenes of the wars against Pisa and Siena occupy two side walls and the major part of the ceiling. The subject for the central ceiling panel, originally a personification of Florence in Glory, was changed to the *Apotheosis of Cosimo I* (see fig. 5); the Grand Duke thus appears as the culmination of the whole of Florentine history. Vasari executed the 42 panels of the ceiling with many collaborators, including Prospero Fontana, Giovan Battista Naldini, Stradanus and Jacopo Zucchi.

(ii) Other architectural commissions and ephemeral decorations. Vasari received his three largest architectural commissions in 1559–62: the Uffizi in Florence, buildings for the Order of the Cavalieri di S Stefano in Pisa, which involved the remodelling of the town centre, and the dome of the Madonna dell'Umiltà in Pistoia. The Uffizi, a building to house the offices of 13 administrative authorities then scattered about Florence, was an expression of the political unity that Cosimo I had imposed on his state. The plans for the project, documented from 1559, were possibly

6. Giorgio Vasari: the Uffizi, Florence, 1560–1580s

based on a sketch by Cosimo. Vasari designed two long wings, stretching from the Piazza della Signoria to the river, where they terminate in a linking wing (see fig. 6). Each authority was provided with a complex of rooms on the ground-floor, the mezzanine and the main floor, with direct access from the portico. The arrangement of the offices is reflected in the articulation of the façade, divided into units of three bays. On the ground-floor the entrance to each unit is marked by pairs of Doric columns, flanked by piers; on the main floor the central window of the unit is emphasized by a segmental pediment. The upper floor (loggia), which was not connected to the rooms below, was probably originally intended for the use of the Duke. It was given a new function in 1565, as part of the passage (Corridoio Vasariano) linking the Palazzo Vecchio to the Palazzo Pitti across the river. Construction of the Uffizi began in 1560, but it was still unfinished when Vasari died. The building was completed in the 1580s by Bernardo Buontalenti.

In 1561 Vasari was given the house he occupied in Borgo Santa Croce by Cosimo. His many projects for the Duke at this time left him little opportunity for other work and he had to decline an invitation to decorate the Sala Regia in the Vatican in the same year. In this year he also began planning the buildings in Pisa for the Order of the Cavalieri di S Stefano, founded by Cosimo, and the remodelling of the town centre. These projects, mainly concerned with rebuilding older palazzi, were intended to eradicate traces of the governmental seat of the Republic of Pisa. Work began in 1562 with the remodelling of the Palazzo dei Cavalieri, for which Vasari designed a *sgraffito* façade (*see* FAÇADE DECORATION, fig. 4). He also designed the church of S Stefano (1565–9) and its interior decoration; later he painted its altarpiece. The Canonica and the Palazzo dell'Orologio, planned and begun by Vasari, were completed in the 17th century.

Vasari's third great architectural project, and technically the most difficult, was the dome of the Madonna dell'Umiltà in Pistoia (1563–8). One of the largest domes in 16th-century Italy, it is a double-shell construction with a complex system of internal ribs.

Other architectural commissions in this period included building the passage linking the Palazzo Vecchio, the Uffizi and the Palazzo Pitti and, not least, the radical remodelling of S Maria Novella and Santa Croce in Florence. In 1566 Vasari designed a magnificent ciborium for Santa Croce. Vasari's work for the Medici court also involved temporary decorations, notably for the wedding in 1565 of Francesco I de' Medici to Joanna of Austria (1547–78) and for the baptism of their daughter Eleonora de' Medici in 1568.

7. Giorgio Vasari: *Apelles and the Shoemaker* (*c.* 1569), fresco, Casa Vasari, Florence

(iii) Other painted works. Owing to the quantity of projects, during these years Vasari made increasing use of collaborators, even for works for himself, such as the family altar in the parish church of Arezzo. For the main panel of this altarpiece he used the *Calling of SS Peter and Andrew*, originally painted for Julius III in 1551 (Arezzo, Badia); the side panels were left to Stradanus and Poppi. From at least 1561 he was collecting material for the new edition of the *Vite*, the first volume of which was printed in 1564; the second and third volumes were delayed until 1568. He made two journeys in connection with his revisions. In May 1563 he went to Arezzo, Cortona, Assisi, Loreto, Ancona and Venice. On a second, longer trip, in April and May 1566, he visited numerous towns in central and northern Italy, including Parma, where he saw works by Correggio. In Cremona he stayed with the family of Sofonisba Anguissola, and in Venice he visited Titian.

In early 1567 Vasari was again in Rome, to deliver to Pius V the *Adoration of the Magi* he had ordered for Santa Croce in Bosco Marengo. The Pope then commissioned the *Last Judgement* for the high altar there (both *in situ*). The same year Vasari began frescoing the walls of the *salone* in the Palazzo Vecchio. He took on so many other commissions as well that in December 1568 Borghini felt called on to write to him: 'It has sometimes seemed to your friends that you take on too many jobs, which are

then not done by your hand and cannot bring you the glory befitting you' (Frey, ii, p. 411). Works of these years also included the *Forge of Vulcan* (Florence, Uffizi) for Francesco de' Medici, the *Coronation of the Virgin* for the parish church of Arezzo (Arezzo, Badia), the *Assumption* (Florence, S Maria Assunta), the *Standard of St Roch* (Arezzo, Gal. & Mus. Med. & Mod.) and the *Last Supper* (Figline, Ospedale Serristori). He also produced a series of altarpieces for S Maria Novella and Santa Croce in Florence, remodelled by him in 1565, and, some time after 1569, he frescoed the *salone* of his house in Florence (see fig. 7). Here, as at his house in Arezzo, he depicted ancient legends about artists, but he was now emphasizing the role of *disegno*, which he had defined as the father of the three sister arts in the 1568 edition of his *Vite* (see §III, 1(ii) below), by representing him in the centre of the main fresco as a three-headed figure on the threshold between the realms of nature and of art. He was obliged to use assistants to help him in this work.

Vasari went to Rome in February 1570 to see three chapels in the Vatican that Pius V had commissioned him to decorate. On his return to Florence, he worked with Borghini on the plans for a small room, the *studiolo*, in the Palazzo Vecchio for Cosimo's son Francesco (see STUDIOLO, fig. 2). His painting for the *studiolo*, *Perseus Freeing Andromeda* (see fig. 8), reflects the cheerful sensuality of his earlier works. Other projects included the plans for decorating the dome of Florence Cathedral, for which again Borghini drew up the programme. Vasari returned to Rome in December to begin decorating the Vatican chapels. The frescoes in all three chapels (*in situ*) were largely executed by collaborators such as Zucchi and Alessandro Fei, while Vasari painted the altarpieces: a *Coronation of the Virgin* for the chapel of S Michele (main panel Livorno, S Caterina) and the *Martyrdom of St Stephen* (Rome, Pin. Vaticana) and the *Death of St Peter Martyr* (Vienna, Ksthist. Mus.) for the chapels dedicated to these saints.

In 1571, after completing the chapels, Vasari was awarded a knighthood by the Pope. He returned to Florence, where he completed the frescoes in the Salone del Cinquecento in the Palazzo Vecchio and prepared to decorate the cathedral dome. At the end of 1571 he painted the *Battle of Lepanto* in the Sala Regia (Vatican). Returning briefly to Florence in May, he began the frescoes in the cathedral dome and designed the Loggia in Arezzo. By November he was continuing his work in the Sala Regia, where he painted a second scene of the *Battle of Lepanto*, the *Massacre of the Huguenots*, the *Return of Gregory XI* and *Gregory IX Excommunicating Frederick II*, assisted by Lorenzo Sabatini, Giacomo Coppi and Denys Calvaert. He also designed frescoes (some destr.) for the staircases of the Vatican Palace, executed by Donato da Formello. Another project in the Vatican, however, Vasari's design for the ceiling of the Pauline Chapel, was rejected by Gregory XIII. Back in Florence in 1573, Vasari continued the decoration of the cathedral dome, which was incomplete at his death. He was buried in the family chapel in Arezzo parish church.

II. Working methods and technique.

Vasari could manage his immense workload only with the aid of assistants; the large number of painters who worked for him contributed significantly to the dissemination of his style. For most of his paintings and frescoes he provided drawings (which he regarded as the real creative process); the contribution of the workshop was limited mainly to the execution, with little scope for initiative. This working method emphasized the importance of drawing, or design (*disegno*). In the introduction to the *Vite*, he described at length the stages of the design process, and there are examples of each stage in his work: sketches capturing an initial idea; carefully executed drawings (see fig. 9) and full-scale cartoons, which only needed to be traced on to the work surface. He appears to have kept the drawings and cartoons in his workshop for repeated use. There are numerous examples in his oeuvre of the repetition of single figures and of compositions. The drawing of a *Standing Man* (Florence, Uffizi) was used in Camaldoli and in the Cancelleria; the composition of his drawing of *St Michael* (1541; Munich, Alte Pin.) was repeated exactly, nearly 30 years later, on the ceiling of the chapel of S Michele in the Vatican; the allegories created for the refectory of Monteoliveto reappear in the Cancelleria and the Palazzo Vecchio. This economical reuse of drawings was another factor that contributed to Vasari's ability to complete large commissions quickly.

8. Giorgio Vasari: *Perseus Freeing Andromeda* (1570), oil on slate, 1.17×1.00 m, *studiolo* of Francesco I, Palazzo Vecchio, Florence

9. Giorgio Vasari: *Prudence*, pen and brown ink and brown wash, heightened in white, on blue paper, 345×260 mm, *c.* 1544–5 (Paris, Institut Néerlandais)

III. *Writings.*

1. The *Vite.* 2. Other writings.

1. THE 'VITE'.

(i) First edition. (ii) Second edition. (iii) Critical reception.

(i) First edition.

(a) Introduction. (b) Classification. (c) *Disegno* and other central themes.
(d) Technique. (e) Sources.

(a) Introduction. Vasari's *Vite* (*Le vite de più eccellenti architetti, pittori, et scultori . . .*) was published, amid widespread interest, in 1550, by the Florentine printer Lorenzo Torrentino (*d* 1563). The work, two volumes with more than a thousand pages, was dedicated to Cosimo I de' Medici. It contains a general preface (*proemio*), an introduction to architecture, sculpture and painting, and three parts consisting of artists' biographies, each with its own *proemio*. The first part comprises 28 lives (from Cimabue to Lorenzo di Bicci), the second 54 (from Jacopo della Quercia to Pietro Perugino), the third 51 (from Leonardo da Vinci to Michelangelo, the only living artist included). As Vasari also discussed pupils and assistants in many of the lives, however, the number of artists mentioned is considerably higher. The work ends with remarks addressed to 'artists and readers', and there are several indices, which give access to the contents in unusual detail.

Vasari's fame rests principally on this book, of which the second, enlarged edition, published in 1568, was the basis of all subsequent editions and translations. For this work Vasari is considered the father of art history (*see* ART HISTORY, §I, 2). The *Vite* is more than just a chronological sequence of biographies (as had already existed), it is the first critical history of artistic style. History for Vasari was more than the mere compiling of annals or chronicles: just as general historians aimed to teach men wisdom in conducting their lives, he wished 'to be of service to art'; he wanted not merely to 'say what has been produced and achieved, but to distinguish the better from the good, the excellent from the highly competent, and to describe with some care the ways in which artists and sculptors conceive, depict and treat their subjects, as well as their inventions and fancies'.

Vasari's view of the past was not impartial. It is the view of an artist who has learnt that perfection in art cannot be taken for granted: once achieved it can be lost again. He described the process of the rebirth of art, the *rinascita*, to make clear to his readers the value of artistic heritage. Many of his statements need to be understood in the light of this concern for the survival of art. He thought that, although art is the responsibility of the artist, it is nevertheless not his burden alone. He knew from experience how capricious patrons could be and was too conscious of their influence on the practical conditions of artists' lives to omit them from his book. The *Vite* was addressed to anyone interested in art and its history, as collector, patron or artist. This viewpoint, far removed from that of today, should be borne in mind when considering Vasari's achievement, which consisted in compiling, classifying and evaluating a copious amount of material.

Vasari's influential division of the history of art into epochs was based on a biological concept of history familiar since antiquity: the comparison between the ages of a human being and the development of a state. Vasari used it to present his history of the rebirth of the arts since Cimabue in three periods. These are defined in the introductions to the three biographical parts of the *Vite*: art had risen slowly to the height of perfection in antiquity and then declined gradually from the time of Constantine on, through the invasions of the barbarians, the Goths, and then was destroyed completely. The Goths determined the subsequent forms taken by art, in particular architecture, which Vasari therefore called 'German' or 'Gothic'. He and his contemporaries saw little of merit in the Gothic style. For him, it was only with Cimabue, Giotto and other artists of the 14th century that there was a rebirth of art, an art 'wholly and principally an imitation of nature'. This first phase, *primi lumi*, was followed by the period of growth and improvement (*augumento*) and was finally succeeded by the third epoch, which extended to Vasari's own time, the time of perfection (*perfezione*), attained with Michelangelo. The idea of the perfecting of art through its increased resemblance to nature was not an invention of Vasari's; it too was found in antiquity, for example in a passage of Cicero's *Brutus* that Vasari used almost verbatim (without acknowledgement).

(b) Classification. Vasari applied this model to the art of his own age and also used it as a means of classifying the art of the past. In his view and that of his contemporaries, the art of Raphael and Michelangelo had equalled and even surpassed that of antiquity. Thus artists of earlier times could be judged and classified in terms of their closeness to this ideal, to the *perfetta regola*. Vasari was aware that this classification did not automatically coincide with an order based on date; for example, he observed that Donatello, although of the second period chronologically, could be regarded as belonging to the third on the basis of his achievements.

In addition to the absolute criterion, the *perfetta regola dell'arte*, Vasari posited as a second, relative standard the peculiarity of time, *la qualità de' tempi*. In this way, earlier art, which could only be described as imperfect if judged by the criteria of the present, could nevertheless be praised. He justified this procedure in the second part of the *Vite*, where he wrote of the works of Andrea Pisano and others: 'anyone who pays regard to the abilities of that time . . . will consider them not only beautiful . . . but admirable and will feel an infinite satisfaction at the sight of these first beginnings, these sparks of the good that began to glow in works of painting and sculpture.' Here too he pointed to his general principle of historiography, that one should take account of time, place, circumstances and persons in judging historical facts.

Vasari's commitment to judging art from a relative historical standpoint is shown by his return to this point in his concluding remarks to artists in the edition of 1568:

> I may seem to have been over generous in praising some older or more recent masters .... I can only reply that I believe I have not praised such artists unconditionally, but always conditionally, with due regard to place, time and other

such considerations. In truth, although Giotto was undoubtedly very praiseworthy in his own day, I do not know what people would have said about him and other old masters had they lived at the time of Michelangelo. What is also worth noting is that the artists of our century, who have attained the highest degree of perfection, would not be in the position they hold today had not those who came before us been what they were.

After its clumsy beginnings, which Vasari excused because of the lack of knowledge and good examples, art was perfected in the second phase according to his classification, corresponding roughly to the 15th century. In this epoch 'all things are done better, with more invention and design, with a more beautiful style and greater industry.' Vasari used the three concepts of style (*maniera*), invention (*invenzione*) and design (*disegno*) to describe the progress of art of this time. He also borrowed the concepts of rule, order and measure (*regola*, *ordine*, *misura*) from the theory of architecture and applied them to the other arts. In the third epoch, according to Vasari, art attained perfection; until then it had been dry and pedantic, lacking lightness, grace and an indefinable quality that could not be gained by study. The impetus to surpass the second stylistic stage came, he wrote, from the contemporary discovery of antique statues. He maintained, however, that the achievements of 15th-century art, which he saw as founded entirely on study, deliberation and calculation, were still valid. He attempted to express this

10. Giorgio Vasari: *Self-portrait*, woodcut, 200×135 mm; from the *Vite* (2/1568)

in a famous statement: 'What rule lacks is a certain freedom (*licenzia*), which, without itself being a rule, is governed by rule and can exist without creating confusion or disrupting order.' This abstract definition becomes more comprehensible if it is read with a passage from his life of Michelangelo, who had made in the new sacristy of S Lorenzo 'fine cornices, capitals, pedestals, doors, tabernacles' that were 'entirely different from that which people had earlier respected as measure, order and rule, according to general custom.' Michelangelo had thereby broken the chains that had caused 'everyone to continue always along the habitual road'. Freedom, however, was not arbitrary; it was restricted by the judgement of the eye (*giudizio dell'occhio*); the eye thus assumed the function of the rule, becoming the ultimate authority.

In the biographies of individual artists the theme of artistic development gives way to an emphasis on the individuality of the artist, his personal style, his works and his character. The same interest in the individual was given visual expression by the portraits at the beginning of each *vita*, already planned for the 1550 edition but realized only in 1568 (see fig. 10).

(c) Disegno *and other central themes.* The developmental model and the individual biographies are, however, only a framework for Vasari's discussion of the artists' works. To understand these properly, the reader needed to know how they were made and to be aware of the possibilities and aims of the various artistic genres. To improve the reader's awareness of these, in his first preface Vasari discussed a theme popular in his day: the comparison (*paragone*) of sculpture with painting (*see* PARAGONE). He was not concerned with proving that one was superior to the other (although his sympathy clearly lay with painting), rather, he had other objectives. First, he wanted to introduce *disegno* (*see* DISEGNO E COLORE), the fundamental concept of the whole of the *Vite*, the common 'father' of all the arts, which he defined fully in the second edition of 1568 (*see* §(ii) below). With the concept of *disegno* Vasari not only set aside the rivalry between the three visual arts, but found for the first time a viable basis for uniting them and allowing them to be discussed on equal terms. Equally important for Vasari, however, were the arguments brought forward in this debate, through which he was able to present a series of points that could be used not to demonstrate the superiority of this or that art, but to assert the importance of visual art as a whole, and so justify the subject of his book.

Another theme that runs through the whole work is the relationship between artist and patron. Vasari contrasted, for example, the covetousness of contemporary patrons with the generous attitudes of patrons in antiquity. As an artist, he was all too aware of the essential role of patrons, and he repeatedly emphasized their influence in fostering or obstructing artists and therefore art:

in our age greater and much better works would be achieved than in antiquity, if the endeavours of artists were granted their just reward. But the fact that the masters of art have to struggle more to escape hunger than to achieve fame, this fact oppresses their spirits and deprives them (shame and disgrace on those who could help but do not care!) of the opportunity to make themselves known.

Vasari contrasted these complaints with the role he ascribed to the Medici in the development of the *rinascita*. Indeed, one of the themes underlying the whole of the *Vite*, from the life of Giotto to that of Michelangelo, is the support given to art by the members of this family.

(d) Technique. Vasari also considered that knowledge of the technical or craft aspects of the three arts was essential for judging works. Without this, it was not possible to appreciate an artist's achievement properly. In the *Vite* the introductions to the three arts, known as the *teoriche*, are devoted to setting out this technical knowledge. The work is not a technical manual like that of Cennino Cennini. For example, at the beginning of the section on architecture Vasari explained that technical details had been omitted, since Vitruvius and Leon Battista Alberti had already written on them at length; he proposed instead to discuss how beautiful buildings should be constituted. He then sketched briefly the range of artistic skills perfected in his day, from architecture to painting, from bronze-casting to mosaic, from the techniques of vaulting to stained-glass windows. The reader should have knowledge of the difficulties and terminology of these techniques in order to understand, while reading the ensuing historical survey, how the perfection of artistic skill had been achieved. By placing this summary of artistic activities before the historical account, Vasari showed from the very beginning the goal towards which the artists' efforts were leading. This goal was the artistic practice of his own time. Thus it is clear that Vasari by no means intended, as is sometimes suggested, to present the epoch of art history he was describing as already complete. Also apparent here is his concern not to become tedious or pedantic, but to offer something of value to both layman and artist. In the discussion of the five architectural orders, for example, Vasari defined them only briefly before going on to characterize in detail Gothic architecture as an aberration.

Simultaneously in the introductions Vasari developed a number of aesthetic categories, thus establishing the criteria by which well-made art was to be recognized and judged. Each of the three *teoriche* contains a section in which the components of good architecture, sculpture or painting are discussed. He was not providing a complete system of aesthetics or art theory; his account was based on the statements of Leon Battista Alberti and other earlier theoreticians. However, by combining sections devoted to the judgement of the eye with others describing the technical aspects of art, Vasari offered a new perspective to the reader, especially to one who was not an artist. Like the production of art, the judging of art follows rules that can be learnt. These rules not only help in the recognition of good or perfect contemporary art but also help to assess the degree to which earlier art approached perfection and so to classify it. Vasari also implied that an account of earlier art was not a task merely for the chronicler, but one requiring the application of aesthetic, specifically art-historical, criteria. He implied the same when he remarked that he did not simply follow his written sources but was always careful to check their observations against the evidence of his own eyes.

(e) Sources. Little is known of Vasari's sources for the first edition. In the text he mentioned Vitruvius and Cesare di Lorenzo Cesariano, the architectural treatises of Alberti and Sebastiano Serlio, Lorenzo Ghiberti's *Commentari* and unspecified writings by Raphael and Domenico Ghirlandaio. Other works available to him included Antonio Manetti's life of Filippo Brunelleschi, Francesco Albertini's guide to Florence (*Memoriale di molte statue e pitture . . . di Florentia*; Florence, 1510), Pietro Aretino's letters, Antonio Billi's *Libro* and a lost source that was also used by Anonimo Magliabechiano and by Giovanni Battista Gelli.

(ii) Second edition. The references to sources in the second edition of the *Vite* are more plentiful than in the first and are supplemented by the author's correspondence. He made extensive use of the histories of Paulus Diaconus (*b* *c.* AD 720–24; *d* 799), the chronicle by Giovanni Villani (*d* 1348) and Matteo Villani (*d* 1363), as well as other local chronicles, Antonio Filarete's architectural treatise and much more. In Michelangelo's *vita* he incorporated excerpts from Ascanio Condivi's life of the artist of 1553 without acknowledgement. He drew extensively on inscriptions and obtained further details from his friends and correspondents, such as Fra Marco de' Medici in Verona, G. B. Grassi, Danese Cattaneo, Bartoli and, above all, Borghini, but little has survived in written form.

This second edition, published by Giunti in three volumes in 1568, was much larger than the first: about 1500 pages, two thirds devoted to the third epoch alone, with about 30 new biographies. Some of the new chapters hardly deserve the title of biography since they are mainly accounts of the history of particular artistic genres. For example, there is a history of gem-cutting in the life of Valerio Belli, and the life of Marcantonio Raimondi has a short history of prints and engravings. Such passages permitted Vasari to give information about a number of artists to whom he did not devote biographies of their own. The discussion of artists in terms of a common technique in the 1568 edition was not completely new but developed out of an idea already present in the first edition, which gave a summary of the history of oil painting in the *teoriche*. The fact that in the second edition these digressions are not in the technical introductions—the logical place for them—but appear later was due to the process of revision. For the first edition Vasari had delivered a largely complete manuscript to the printer, but the first parts of the second edition were already being published (1564) while other sections were still being revised.

The broadening of Vasari's range of interests is undoubtedly connected to his position at the Medici court, where he was responsible for all kinds of artistic activities. This probably prompted the long descriptions of temporary decorations in the second edition. A detailed description of the wedding festivities of 1565–6, written by Giovan Battista Cini (1528–86), was printed at the end of the new chapter on the members of the Accademia del Disegno. Such events, and the decoration of the Palazzo Vecchio, required the most diverse artistic skills; this may account for the references in the second edition to many artistic genres hardly mentioned in 1550.

Where links through common techniques were not possible, Vasari grouped artists according to national, regional or local affiliations. There are sections on Italian and Netherlandish artists and on those from Friuli, northern Italy, Verona etc. These classifications signalled a change in structure from the first edition of the *Vite*, although the title was retained. This change was required to incorporate the enormously increased volume of information. Vasari had been considering organizing the work into these 'collective' lives from as early as 1550. Also new were the references to private collections, especially to the drawings in Vasari's own *Libro de' disegni* (*see* §IV below). He was aware that such collections illustrated his conception of art history as a history of style. Underlying this is the increased importance of the concept of *disegno* in the second edition. He defined it, at the start of the essay on painting, as follows:

> Seeing that Design, the parent of our three arts, Architecture, Sculpture, and Painting, having its origin in the intellect, draws out from many single things a general judgement, it is like a form or idea of all the objects in nature, most marvellous in what it compasses, for not only in the bodies of men and of animals but also in plants, in buildings, in sculpture and in painting, design is cognizant of the proportion of the whole to the parts and of the parts to each other and to the whole. Seeing too that from this knowledge there arises a certain conception and judgement, so that there is formed in the mind that something which afterwards, when expressed by the hands, is called design, we may conclude that design is not other than a visible expression and declaration of our inner conception and of that which others have imagined and given form to in their idea. … What design needs, when it has derived from the judgement the mental image of anything, is that the hand, through the study and practice of many years, may be free and apt to draw and to express correctly, with the pen, the silver-point, the charcoal, the chalk, or other instrument, whatever nature has created. For when the intellect puts forth refined and judicious conceptions, the hand which has practised design for many years, exhibits the perfection and excellence of the arts as well as the knowledge of the artist. (trans. Maclehose)

The second edition contains a wealth of new data, and errors from the first edition were corrected, although new ones were added (Kallab). The moving spirit behind the revisions and the collection of new material was Borghini. While the first edition owed much to Paolo Giovio's rhetorical model of historiography, the second edition bears the stamp of Borghini's factual approach. Borghini wanted Vasari to write a general history of Italian painting and sculpture. According to Borghini, Vasari's efforts should not concentrate on biographical details of the artists, but on the discussion of their works, including detailed information on their location and subject. Vasari's journey of 1566 may have been in response to Borghini's request. Vasari also supplied details on medieval architecture; moreover, the famous definition of *disegno* of 1568 was probably also developed in discussion with Borghini, if not actually edited by him. Borghini's influence should not be overestimated, however, as the essential ideas and opinions in the second edition remain Vasari's own. Many of the changes follow directions already indicated in the first edition, but the framework of the first edition is still visible in the second. It is significant that Vasari made virtually no changes to the introductions.

The inclusion of living artists is often cited as the most important new feature in the second edition, but such an extension was already contemplated in the first edition. It is not so much the inclusion of living artists that significantly distinguishes the second edition from the first, but the problem of concluding the historical narrative. The first edition ended with Michelangelo as the living embodiment of perfection in art; art history had reached its climax but not its end. With the master's death in 1564, Vasari had to formulate a future for art or concede that art history had indeed come to an end. The author was almost forced to look round for alternatives. The solution was to distinguish between the means of art—*disegno*, perfected by Michelangelo—and the constant goals of art (Alpers). This is illustrated by a passage inserted in the *vita* of Raphael in 1568. Vasari argued that Raphael realized he could not equal Michelangelo in the depiction of the naked body, i.e. in *disegno*, but that progress in painting was nevertheless possible in *invenzione*, the narrative element in art. Thus Raphael had given up imitating Michelangelo in *disegno* and striven to excel him in other areas, a practice Vasari endorsed: 'artists who devoted themselves solely to studying Michelangelo … created a harsh, difficult manner without charm or colour and with little invention, whereas, had they striven to develop and perfect the other parts of their art, they would have done themselves and the world a service.'

This more critical view can be found in Michelangelo's *vita* of the second edition; in it Vasari argued that while the master wanted to paint only the human body, artists who chose the other way, based on the charm of colours or new *invenzioni*, were also among the masters of the first rank. This new attitude to Michelangelo and the emphasis on tendencies embodied by Raphael and Titian clearly reveals the influence of Pietro Aretino and Lodovico Dolce (Roskill). In a separate, revised edition of the life of Jacopo Sansovino, published in 1570, Vasari conceded that Sansovino had surpassed Michelangelo in some respects (Davis, 1981 exh. cat., p. 295).

Vasari departed from his original concept of the *Vite* only in some parts of the second edition; elsewhere he intensified his criticism of the Venetians' lack of mastery of *disegno*. He also acceded only partially to Borghini's desire that he write a general history of art. His Tuscan bias is clearly discernible, and this became a target for critics of the next generation. Despite the defects and errors of detail for which Vasari can be criticized, his achievement as an art historian cannot be overestimated. The *Vite* remains a fundamental work of art history, the essential source for the study of the Italian Renaissance.

(iii) Critical reception. Vasari's enduring reputation is based far more on the *Vite* than on his own artistic works. In the 16th century its worth was recognized by writers such as Raffaele Borghini and Giovanni Battista Armenini, but it also became a focus for criticism. Gian Paolo Lomazzo, for example, felt called on to defend Vasari against the accusation of partisanship, a charge repeated in 1573 by Johann Fischart (*c.* 1545–1589/90), who took exception to Vasari's disparaging account of German art (evidence of how quickly and widely the *Vite* were disseminated).

Criticism of the *Vite*, mainly by the Venetians and Bolognese, reached a peak in the 17th century, in the works of Conte Carlo Malvasia and Giulio Cesare Gigli.

The interest with which Vasari's work was read and the controversy that it engendered are demonstrated by the marginal notes in copies of the *Vite* by such artists as Federico Zuccaro, Annibale Carracci, Francisco de Holanda and El Greco, or by connoisseurs such as Sebastiano Resta. The strongest evidence of its impact, however, is provided by the many editions published and the numerous histories of art modelled on it in the following century, including the *Schilder-boeck* ([1603]–1604) of Karel van Mander I, Francisco Pacheco's *Arte de la pintura* (1649) and the *Teutsche Academie* (1675) of Joachim von Sandrart. Few of these matched Vasari for originality or critical intelligence.

2. OTHER WRITINGS. Vasari's other writings are less significant, although they do contain important information about his own art. His letter to Varchi concerning the *paragone* has been mentioned. The *Ragionamenti*, his explanation of the paintings in the Palazzo Vecchio, was published posthumously by his nephew (2) Giorgio Vasari *il giovane*, in 1588, from a non-autograph manuscript (Florence, Uffizi). This text was known in Vasari's lifetime, however, and is mentioned several times in the *Vite*. It is the first of a series of similar descriptions of complex palazzo decorations published by artists or their advisers in the last quarter of the 16th century. Vasari may have been influenced by the tradition of published descriptions of festivities—he himself published a description of this kind, concerning the baptism of Eleonora de' Medici in 1568 (*see* §I, 3(ii) above)—or he may have been continuing his old habit of explaining his paintings on profane subjects in detailed letters to his patrons.

Vasari's letters, some of which are of considerable literary quality, were part of an extensive body of writings that has survived only in part (Arezzo, Mus. Casa Vasari; New Haven, CT, Yale U. Lib.). These writings, which include his *Ricordanze* as well as the *Zibaldone* (a collection of notes mainly about his paintings but also the *Vite*), offer a wealth of information, not yet fully explored, on Vasari's own works and the artistic life of his time.

IV. Collection.

Vasari collected, to some extent systematically, examples of the art both of his predecessors and of his contemporaries. This collection was confined largely to drawings, which he assembled and mounted in his famous *Libro de' disegni* (of which there were probably at least seven volumes). Since the *disegno* represented for Vasari the true intellectual achievement of the artist, first formed in the mind and then transferred to the paper, it was only natural for him to acquire examples of this direct expression of artistic achievement. He began the collection during his apprenticeship (1528–9) with Vittorio Ghiberti (ii), who gave him a group of drawings by Lorenzo Ghiberti and artists of the 14th century, probably from Lorenzo's collection. The value Vasari placed on his drawings is shown by the care with which he mounted them in the *Libro* (*see* MOUNTING, fig. 4), with woodcut portraits from

the *Vite* and fanciful marginal drawings. The collection began to be dispersed soon after Vasari's death: one volume was given to Francesco I de' Medici, others later came into the possession of Niccolò Gaddi. In the 17th century the volumes began to be broken up. Today most of the pages are in the Louvre, Paris, and the Uffizi, Florence, while others are in Oxford, Stockholm and other collections. In cases where Vasari's marginal drawings have been removed from the pages (as in the Uffizi), their provenance from his collection is hardly provable.

The rest of Vasari's collecting was more haphazard. Apart from a plaster statue of *Venus* by Bartolomeo Ammanati (Arezzo, Mus. Casa Vasari), his most important pieces were: a terracotta head of the emperor *Galba* (Arezzo, Mus. Casa Vasari) by Andrea Sansovino; Rosso Fiorentino's *modello*, owned by Pollastra, for the ceiling decoration proposed for SS Annunziata in Arezzo (untraced); a painting of the *Virgin and Child* by Parmigianino, bought in Bologna in 1540 (untraced); the head and an arm of Michelangelo's large model for the statue of *St Cosmas* in the New Sacristy (Florence, S Lorenzo); and Niccolò Tribolo's terracotta copy (London, V&A) of Michelangelo's *Night*, also from the New Sacristy.

V. Character and personality.

Passages in Vasari's letters and in the *Vite* reveal much of his character. In the earliest surviving letter, written on his visit to Rome in 1532, he expressed his desire to be one of those who receive pensions and other rewards for their art. He devoted much of his energy to this end, with considerable success. Giovio described him, in 1543, as a capable, efficient painter able to take quick decisions, qualities that must have commended him to impatient patrons such as Alessandro Farnese (and later to the Medici). Vasari's negotiations with Francesco Bacci, the father of his future wife, are particularly illuminating about his ambitions. Clearly reluctant to be tied to provincial Arezzo by his wife or her parents, Vasari instructed his intermediary, Borghini, to make clear to the Bacci family that it was essential for his professional life for him to work away from home. This craving for fame and money was criticized by contemporaries, including Ottaviano de' Medici and Borghini.

Vasari's pride in his success and in the social status his work had brought him is clear from an episode he related in the *Vite*. When the painter Jacone (*d* 1553) asked him in a provocative manner how he was, Vasari replied:

> I am well, my dear Jacone. I used to be poor like all of you, and now I have three thousand scudi and more. You used to think me foolish, but now the monks and priests consider me an excellent man. I used to serve you and now this servant serves me and leads my horse. I used to wear the clothes poor artists wear, and now I am dressed in velvet. I used to go on foot and now I ride on horseback. So, my dear Jacone, I really am well, may God preserve you.

Not surprisingly his ambition aroused the envy of some artists (e.g. Benvenuto Cellini); but he was on friendly terms with a greater number, notably Michelangelo, Gherardi, Salviati and Fontana. The fact that on several occasions he produced drawings for Fontana's paintings suggests that for all his ambition he was also capable of selfless friendship.

WRITINGS

Le vite de più eccellenti architetti, pittori, et scultori italiani, da Cimabue insino a' tempi nostri: Descritte in lingua Toscana, da Giorgio Vasari pittore aretino. Con una sua utile & necessaria introduzzione a le arti loro (Florence, 1550)

Descrizione dell'apparato fatto nel Tempio di S. Giovanni di Fiorenza per lo battesimo della Signora prima figliuola dell'Illustrissimo, et Eccellentissimo S. Principe di Fiorenza, et Siena Don Francesco Medici [. . .] (Florence, 1568)

Le vite de' più eccellenti pittori, scultori, e architettori [. . .] (Florence, 1568)

Ritratti de' più eccellenti pittori, scultori et architetti contenuti nelle vite di M. Giorgio Vasari [. . .] (Florence, 1568) [very rare edition of portraits from the *Vite*; see C. Davis in 1981 exh. cat., pp. 257–9]

Vita del Gran Michelagelo Buonarroti [. . .] (Florence, 1568) [rare edition of the *Vita* of Michelangelo; see U. Procacci in 1981 exh. cat., pp. 284ff]

Vita di M. Iacopo Sansovino scultore & architetto eccellentissimo della Serenissima Repubblica di Venetia (?Venice, 1570) [see C. Davis in 1981 exh. cat., pp. 293–5]

Ragionamenti [. . .] sopra le inventioni [. . .] dipinte in Firenze nel Palazzo di loro Altezze Serenissime [. . .] (Florence, 1588)

K. Frey and H. W. Frey, eds: *Der literarische Nachlass Giorgio Vasaris*, 3 vols (Munich, 1923–40/*R* Hildesheim, 1982)

A. del Vita, ed.: *Lo Zibaldone di Giorgio Vasari* (Rome, 1937)

MODERN EDITIONS OF THE 'VITE'

G. Vasari: *Opere*; ed. G. Milanesi, 9 vols (Florence, 1878–85, 2/1906/*R* 1981) [incl. *Vite* of 1568, *Ragionamenti* and letters; superseded by later edns, but often cited; useful notes]

——: *La vita di Michelangelo nelle redazioni del 1550 e del 1568*; ed. P. Barocchi, 5 vols (Milan and Naples, 1962–7) [definitive edn; comprehensive commentary]

——: *Le Vite [. . .]*; ed. P. della Pergola, L. Grassi and G. Previtali, 9 vols (Milan 1962–6) [reliable edn of *Vite* of 1568]

——: *Le vite de' più eccellenti pittori, scultori e architettori nelle redazioni del 1550 e 1568*; ed. R. Bettarini and P. Barocchi, 6 vols [text] (Florence, 1966–87) [crit. edn, only one containing complete texts of both edns, including original indices; *Commento secolare* assembles notes from most older edns]

——: *Le vite de' più eccellenti architetti, pittori, et scultori italiani da Cimabue insino a' tempi nostri nell'edizione per i tipi di Lorenzo Torrentino Firenze 1550*; ed. L. Bellosi and A. Rossi (Turin, 1986) [reliable edn of *Vite* of 1550]

TRANSLATIONS

L. Schorn and E. Förster, trans.: *Leben der ausgezeichnetsten Maler, Bildhauer und Baumeister von Cimabue bis zum Jahre 1567*, 6 vols in 8 parts (Stuttgart and Tübingen, 1832–49/*R* Worms, 1983)

L. Maclehose, trans.: *Vasari on Technique*, ed. G. B. Brown (London, 1907/*R* New York, 1960)

G. du C. de Vere, trans.: *Lives of the Most Eminent Painters, Sculptors and Architects*, 10 vols (London, 1912–15/*R* New York, 1979)

A. Chastel, ed. and trans.: *Les Vies des meilleurs peintres, sculpteurs et architectes*, 12 vols (Paris, 1981–9) [detailed notes include latest res.; xii, *Vasari illustré*, illustrates 205 works mentioned in the *Vite* and many drgs from Vasari's *Libro*]

BIBLIOGRAPHY

EARLY SOURCES

G. Gaye, ed.: *Carteggio inedito d'artisti dei secoli XIV, XV, XVI*, ii (Florence, 1840), pp. 502–18 [Vasari's will]

G. degli Azzi and A. del Vita: 'Documenti vasariani', *Il Vasari*, iv (1931), pp. 216–31

N. V. Palli D'Addario: 'Documenti vasariani nell'Archivio Guidi', *Convegno 1981*, pp. 363–89

R. Williams: 'Notes by Vincenzo Borghini on Works of Art in San Gimignano and Volterra: A Source for Vasari's *Lives*', *Burl. Mag.*, cxxvii (1985), pp. 17–21

R. G. Babcock and D. J. Ducharne: 'A Preliminary Inventory of the Vasari Papers in the Beinecke Library', *A. Bull.*, lxxi (1989), pp. 300–04

P. J. Jacks: 'The Composition of Giorgio Vasari's *Ricordanze*: Evidence from an Unknown Draft', *Ren. Q.*, xlv (1992), pp. 739–84

MONOGRAPHS

[No single work encompasses the full range of Vasari's activity]

Studi vasariani. Atti del convegno internazionale per il IV centenario della prima edizione delle 'Vite' del Vasari: Firenze, 1950 [cited as *Atti: 1950*]

Il Vasari storiografo e artista. Atti del congresso internazionale nel IV centenario della morte, Arezzo: Firenze, 1974 [cited as *Atti: 1974*]

T. S. R. Boase: *Giorgio Vasari: The Man and the Book* (Princeton, 1979); review by M. Baxandall in *TLS* (Feb 1980), p. 111

Giorgio Vasari: Principi, letterati e artisti nelle carte di Giorgio Vasari. Pittura vasariana dal 1532 al 1554 (exh. cat., Arezzo, Casa Giorgio Vasari; Arezzo, S Francesco; 1981) [cited as 1981 exh. cat.; detailed bibliog.; separate appendices; *Indici, con aggiunte e revisioni*, ed. C. Davis and M. D. Davis (Florence, 1982)]

Giorgio Vasari tra decorazione ambientale e storiografia artistica. Convegno di studi: Arezzo, 1981 [cited as *Convegno: 1981*]

P. Barocchi: *Studi vasariani* (Milan, 1984)

ILLUSTRATIONS

A. Paolucci and A. M. Maetzke: *La casa del Vasari in Arezzo* (Florence, 1988)

L. Corti: *Vasari: Catalogo completo dei dipinti* (Florence, 1989) [not complete cat. rais.; not all works illus.]

U. Muccini: *Il Salone del Cinquecento in Palazzo Vecchio* (Florence, 1990)

U. Muccini and A. Cecchi: *Le Stanze del Principe in Palazzo Vecchio* (Florence, 1991)

PAINTINGS

P. Barocchi: *Vasari pittore* (Milan, 1964) [suppl.: 'Complementi al Vasari pittore', *Atti & Mem. Accad. Tosc. Sci. & Lett., 'La Colombaria'*, xiv (1963–4), pp. 251–309]

E. A. Carroll: 'Lappoli, Alfani, Vasari and Rosso Fiorentino', *A. Bull.*, xlix (1967), pp. 297–304

N. Rubinstein: 'Vasari's Painting of *The Foundation of Florence* in the Palazzo Vecchio', *Essays in the History of Architecture Presented to Rudolf Wittkower* (London, 1967), pp. 64–73

E. Pillsbury: 'Three Unpublished Paintings by Giorgio Vasari', *Burl. Mag.*, cxii (1970), pp. 94–101

M. Guillaume: 'Vasari au Musée de Dijon', *Mém. Acad. Sci., A. & B.-Lett. Dijon*, cxxi (1970–72), pp. 277–84

P. Fehl: 'Vasari's *Extirpation of the Huguenots*', *Gaz. B.-A.*, lxxxiv (1974), pp. 157–284

H. Röttgen: 'Zeitgeschichtliche Bildprogramme der katholischen Restauration unter Gregor XIII., 1572–1589', *Münchn. Jb. Bild. Kst*, xxvi (1975), pp. 85–122

U. Davitt Asmus: *Corpus Quasi Vas. Beiträge zur Ikonographie der italienischen Renaissance* (Berlin, 1977), pp. 41–113

C. Davis: 'The Pitfalls of Iconology, or How it Was that Saturn Gelt his Father', *Stud. Iconog.*, iv (1978), pp. 79–84

——: 'Per l'attività del Vasari nel 1553: Incisioni degli affreschi di Villa Altoviti e la Fontanalia di Villa Giulia', *Mitt. Ksthist. Inst. Florenz*, xxiii (1979), pp. 197–224

E. Allegri and A. Cecchi: *Palazzo Vecchio e i Medici* (Florence, 1980) [best general work on the Palazzo Vecchio, incl. drgs and docs]

C. Davis: 'Frescoes by Vasari for Sforza Almeni, "Coppiere" to Duke Cosimo I', *Mitt. Ksthist. Inst. Florenz*, xxiv (1980), pp. 127–202

——: 'New Frescoes by Vasari: *Colore* and *Invenzione* in Mid-16th-century Florentine Painting', *Pantheon*, xxxviii (1980), pp. 153–7

M. Campbell: 'Il ritratto del *Duca Alessandro de' Medici* di Giorgio Vasari: Contesto e significato', *Convegno: 1981*, pp. 339–61

P. L. De Castris: 'Napoli 1544: Vasari e Monteoliveto', *Boll. A.*, lxvi (1981), pp. 59–88

E. McGrath: '*Il senso nostro*: The Medici Allegory Applied to Vasari's Mythological Frescoes in the Palazzo Vecchio', *Convegno: 1981*, pp. 117–34

E. Parma Armani: 'Fonti per il *Convito per le nozze di Ester e Assuero* di Giorgio Vasari in Arezzo', *Stud. Stor. A., U. Genova, Ist. Stor. A.*, iii (1981), pp. 61–75

P. Tinagli Baxter: 'Rileggendo i *Ragionamenti*', *Convegno: 1981*, pp. 83–93

F. H. Jacobs: 'Vasari's Vision of the History of Painting: Frescoes in the Casa Vasari, Florence', *A. Bull.*, lxvi (1984), pp. 399–416

R. Roani Villani: 'Un'eco della rafaellesca *Incoronazione della Vergine* de Monteluce in un dipinto del Vasari nella Badia aretina', *Paragone*, xxxv/407 (1984), pp. 57–62

D. L. Clark: 'Vasari's *Temptation of St Jerome* Paintings: Artifacts of his Camaldoli Crisis', *Stud. Iconog.*, x (1984–6), pp. 97–118

L. D. Cheney: 'Vasari's *Chamber of Abraham*: A Religious Painted Ceiling in the Casa Vasari of Arezzo', *16th C. J.*, xviii (1987), pp. 355–80

——: 'Vasari's Depiction of Pliny's *Histories*', *Explor. Ren. Cult.*, xv (1989), pp. 97–120

V. Markova: 'Un *Baccanale* ritrovato di Giorgio Vasari, proveniente dalla Galleria Gerini', *Kunst des Cinquecento in der Toskana* (Munich, 1992), pp. 237–41

R. Starn and L. Partridge: *Arts of Power: Three Halls of State in Italy, 1300–1600* (Berkeley, 1992), pp. 203–12

J. Kliemann: *Gesta dipinte: La grande decorazione nelle dimore italiane dal quattrocento al seicento* (Cinisello Balsamo, 1993) [Cancelleria, pp. 37–51; Palazzo Vecchio, pp. 69–78]

ARCHITECTURE, EPHEMERAL DECORATION AND APPLIED ARTS

G. Capovilla: 'Giorgio Vasari e gli edifici dell'Ordine Militare di S Stefano in Pisa (1562–1571) (con lettere inedite del Vasari)', *Stud. Stor.*, xvii (1908), pp. 305–79; xviii (1909), pp. 581–602; xix (1910), pp. 27–55, 147–226

P. Barocchi: 'Il Vasari architetto', *Atti Accad. Pontaniana*, vi (1958), pp. 113–36

V. Cazzato: 'Vasari e Carlo V: L'ingresso trionfale a Firenze del 1536', *Atti: 1974*, pp. 179–204

M. Fossi: 'Il Vasari e la basilica dell'Umiltà di Pistoia', *Atti: 1974*, pp. 127–141

J. Lessmann: *Studien zu einer Baumonographie der Uffizien Giorgio Vasaris in Florenz* (diss., U. Bonn, 1975)

M. T. Bartoli: 'La Badia delle SS Flora e Lucilla in Arezzo', *Stud. & Doc. Archit.*, vi (1976), pp. 27–37

E. Pillsbury: 'Vasari's Staircase in the Palazzo Vecchio', *Collaboration in Italian Renaissance Art: In Memoriam Charles Seymour, Jr* (New Haven and London, 1978), pp. 125–42

M. B. Hall: *Renovation and Counter-Reformation: Vasari and Duke Cosimo in Sta Maria Novella and Sta Croce, 1565–1577* (Oxford, 1979)

E. Codini Karwacka: 'Piazza dei Cavalieri ed edifici adiacenti', *Livorno e Pisa: Due città e un territorio nella politica dei Medici* (exh. cat. by M. Mirri and others, Pisa, Arsenale Galee, Arsenale Mediceo, 1980), pp. 223–41

A. Nova: 'The Chronology of the Del Monte Chapel in S Pietro in Montorio in Rome', *A. Bull.*, lxvi (1984), pp. 150–54

R. Lunardi: 'La ristrutturazione vasariana di Santa Maria Novella: I documenti ritrovati', *Mem. Domenicane*, n. s. 19 (1988), pp. 403–19

A. Nova: *The Artistic Patronage of Pope Julius III (1550–1555): Profane Imagery and Buildings for the Del Monte Family in Rome*, Outstanding Diss. F.A. (New York and London, 1988)

P. Roselli: 'La vicenda costruttiva delle Logge Vasari ad Arezzo', *QUASAR*, i (1989), pp. 31–42

J. von Henneberg: 'The Church of Santo Stefano dei Cavalieri in Pisa: New Drawings', *Ant. Viva*, xxx/1–2 (1991), pp. 29–42

——: 'Of Altars and Drawings: Vasari's Projects for S Stefano dei Cavalieri in Pisa (?)', *Master Drgs*, xxx (1992), pp. 201–9

C. Conforti: *Giorgio Vasari architetto* (Milan, 1993)

L. Satkowski: *Giorgio Vasari, Architect and Courtier* (Princeton, 1993)

DRAWINGS

G. Thiem: 'Vasaris Entwürfe für Gemälde in der Sala Grande des Palazzo Vecchio zu Florenz', *Z. Kstgesch.*, xxiii (1960), pp. 97–135

Mostra di disegni del Vasari e della sua cerchia (exh. cat., ed. P. Barocchi; Florence, Uffizi, 1964)

G. Thiem: 'Neuentdeckte Zeichnungen Vasaris und Naldinis für die Sala Grande des Palazzo Vecchio in Florenz', *Z. Kstgesch.*, xxxi (1968), pp. 143–50

The Age of Vasari (exh. cat., ed. M. Milkovich and D. A. Porter; Notre Dame, IN, Snite Mus. A.; Binghamton, SUNY; 1970)

C. Monbeig-Goguel: *Maîtres toscans nés après 1500, morts avant 1600: Vasari et son temps* (1972), i of *Inventaire général des dessins italiens du Louvre* (Paris, 1972–)

G. Thiem: 'Neue Funde zu Vasaris Dekorationen im Palazzo Vecchio', *Atti: 1974*, pp. 267–73

E. Pillsbury: 'The Sala Grande Drawings by Vasari and his Workshop: Some Documents and New Attributions', *Master Drgs*, xiv (1976), pp. 127–46

A. Cecchi: 'Borghini, Vasari, Naldini e la *Giuditta* del 1564', *Paragone*, xxviii/323 (1977), pp. 100–07

——: 'Nuove acquisizioni per un catalogo dei disegni di Giorgio Vasari', *Ant. Viva*, xvii/1 (1978), pp. 52–61

J. Kliemann: 'Zeichnungsfragmente aus der Werkstatt Vasaris und ein unbekanntes Programm Vincenzio Borghinis für das Casino Mediceo in Florenz: Borghinis *invenzioni per pitture fatte*', *Jb. Berlin. Mus.*, xx (1978), pp. 157–208

C. Monbeig-Goguel: 'Chronique vasarienne', *Rev. A.*, lvi (1982), pp. 65–80

——: 'Drawings by Vasari and his Circle in the Collection of the Louvre: An Examination and New Findings', *Drawing*, xi/1 (1989), pp. 1–6

A. Cecchi: 'Disegni inediti o poco noti di Giorgio Vasari', *Kunst des Cinquecento in der Toskana* (Munich, 1992), pp. 242–8

A. Nova: 'Salviati, Vasari and the Reuse of Drawings in their Working Practice', *Master Drgs*, xxx (1992), pp. 83–108

VASARI AS HISTORIAN, WRITER AND COLLECTOR

W. Kallab: *Vasaristudien* (Vienna and Leipzig, 1908) [fundamental study of Vasari's sources]

J. Schlosser Magnino: *Die Kunstliteratur* (Vienna, 1924); rev. as *La letteratura artistica*, ed. O. Kurz (Florence, 1964/*R* 1979), pp. 287–346

E. Panofsky: 'Das erste Blatt aus dem *Libro* Giorgio Vasaris: Eine Studie über die Beurteilung der Gotik in der italienischen Renaissance', *Städel-Jb.*, vi (1930), pp. 25–72 [Eng. trans. in E. Panofsky: *Meaning in the Visual Arts* (New York, 1955), pp. 169–235]

P. Barocchi: 'Il valore dell'antico nella storiografia vasariana', *Il mondo antico nel rinascimento. Atti del V Convegno internazionale di studi sul rinascimento: Firenze, 1956* (Florence, 1958), pp. 217–36

J. Rouchette: *La Renaissance que nous a léguée Vasari* (Bordeaux, 1959)

S. Alpers: 'Ekphrasis and Aesthetic Attitudes in Vasari's *Lives*', *J. Warb. & Court. Inst.*, xxiii (1960), pp. 190–215

E. H. Gombrich: 'Vasari's *Lives* and Cicero's *Brutus*', *J. Warb. & Court. Inst.*, xxiii (1960), pp. 309–11

W. Prinz: 'Vasaris Sammlung von Künstlerbildnissen', *Mitt. Ksthist. Inst. Florenz*, xii (1966) [suppl.]

E. H. Gombrich: 'The Leaven of Criticism in Renaissance Art', *Art, Science and History in the Renaissance*, ed. C. S. Singleton (Baltimore, 1967), pp. 3–42

M. W. Roskill: *Dolce's 'Aretino' and Venetian Art Theory of the Cinquecento* (New York, 1968), pp. 63–5

R. Bettarini: 'Vasari scrittore: Come la Torrentiniana diventò Giuntina', *Atti: 1974*, pp. 485–500

W. Kemp: 'Disegno: Beiträge zur Geschichte des Begriffes zwischen 1547 und 1607', *Marburg. Jb. Kstwiss.*, xix (1974), pp. 219–40

L. Ragghianti Collobi: *Il 'Libro de' disegni' del Vasari*, 2 vols (Florence, 1974)

Z. Ważbiński: 'L'idée de l'histoire dans la première et la seconde édition des *Vies* de Vasari', *Atti: 1974*, pp. 1–25

C. Goldstein: 'Vasari and the Florentine Accademia del Disegno', *Z. Kstgesch.*, xxxviii (1975), pp. 145–52

G. Dalli Regoli: 'Sul *Libro de' disegni* di Giorgio Vasari', *Crit. A.*, xli/146 (1976), pp. 39–43

L. Ragghianti Collobi: 'Aggiunte per il *Libro de' disegni* del Vasari', *Crit. A.*, n. s. 23, cliv–vi (1977), pp. 165–86

P. Barocchi: 'Storiografia e collezionismo dal Vasari al Lanzi', *Stor. A. It.*, ii (1979), pp. 5–82

C. Monbeig-Goguel: 'A propos de Vasari, historien et collectionneur: Giulio Romano et Giorgio Vasari, le dessin de la *Chute d'Icare* retrouvé', *Rev. Louvre*, xxix (1979), pp. 273–6

L. Riccò: *Vasari scrittore: La prima edizione del libro delle 'Vite'* (Rome, 1979)

M. Cristofani: 'Vasari e le antichità', *Prospettiva*, xxxiii–vi (1983–4), pp. 367–9

M. Winner: 'Il giudizio di Vasari sulle prime tre stanze di Raffaello in Vaticano', *Raffaello in Vaticano* (exh. cat., Rome, Musei Vaticani, 1984), pp. 179–93

P. De Vecchi: 'Raffaello nelle *Vite* del Vasari', *A. Crist.*, lxxiii (1985), pp. 258–62

H. Wohl: 'The Eye of Vasari', *Mitt. Ksthist. Inst. Florenz*, xxx (1986), pp. 537–68

R. Le Mollé: *Georges Vasari et le vocabulaire de la critique d'art dans les 'Vite'* (Grenoble, 1988)

P. Rubin: 'What Men Saw: Vasari's Life of Leonardo da Vinci and the Image of the Renaissance Artist', *A. Hist.*, xiii (1990), pp. 34–46

J. Kliemann: 'Giorgio Vasari: Kunstgeschichtliche Perspektiven', *Kunst und Kunsttheorie, 1400–1900*, ed. P. Ganz and others (Wiesbaden, 1991), pp. 29–74

A. Conti: 'Osservazioni e appunti sulla *Vita* di Leonardo di Giorgio Vasari', *Kunst des Cinquecento in der Toskana* (Munich, 1992), pp. 26–36

D. Cast: 'Reading Vasari Again: History, Philosophy', *Word & Image*, ix (1993), pp. 29–38

H. Maginnis: 'Giotto's World through Vasari's Eyes', *Z. Kstgesch.*, lvi (1993), pp. 385–408

CRITICAL RECEPTION AND REPUTATION OF THE 'VITE'

R. Dos Santos: 'Un Exemplaire de Vasari annoté par Francisco de Olanda', *Atti: 1950*, pp. 91ff

G. L. Pinette: 'Über deutsche Kunst und Künstler (Fischarts Kritik an Vasari)', *Jb. Vorarlberg. Landesmusver.* (1966), pp. 9–21

X. De Salas: 'Un Exemplaire des *Vies* de Vasari annoté par le Gréco', *Gaz. B.-A.*, lxix (1967), pp. 176–80

M. Capucci: 'Dalla biografia alla storia: Note sulla formazione della storiografia artistica nel seicento', *Stud. Seicent.*, ix (1968), pp. 81–125

L. Puppi: 'La fortuna delle *Vite* nel Veneto dal Ridolfi al Temanza', *Atti: 1974*, pp. 405–37

R. Salvini: 'L'eredità del Vasari storiografo in Germania: Joachim von Sandrart', *Atti: 1974*, pp. 759–71

H. Belting: 'Vasari und die Folgen: Die Geschichte der Kunst als Prozess?', *Historische Prozesse*, ed. K.-G. Faber and C. Meier (Munich, 1978), pp. 98–126

M. Fanti: 'Le postille carraccesche alle *Vite* del Vasari: Il testo originale', *Il Carrobbio*, v (1979), pp. 147–64

X. De Salas: 'Las notas del Greco a la *Vida de Tiziano* de Vasari', *Bol. Mus. Prado*, iii (1982), pp. 78–86

——: 'Las notas del Greco a la *Vida de Tiziano* de Vasari', *El Greco: Italy and Spain*, ed. J. Brown and J. M. Pita Andrade, Stud. Hist. A., xiii (Washington, 1984), pp. 161–9

S. A. Vosters: 'Lampsonio, Vasari, van Mander y Pacheco', *Goya*, clxxxix (1985), pp. 130–39

C. Dempsey: 'The Carracci *postille* to Vasari's *Lives*', *A. Bull.*, lxviii (1986), pp. 72–6

M. Hochmann: 'Les Annotations marginales de Federico Zuccaro à un exemplaire des *Vies* de Vasari: La Réaction anti-vasarienne à la fin du XVIe siècle', *Rev. A.*, lxxx (1988), pp. 64–71

E. Grasman: 'La controversia fra il Vasari ed il Malvasia nella letteratura artistica del settecento', *Il luogo ed il ruolo della città di Bologna tra Europa continentale e mediterranea: Atti del Colloquio C.I.H.A.: Bologna, 1990*, ed. G. Perini (Bologna, 1992), pp. 529–38

G. Perini, ed.: *Gli scritti dei Carracci* (Bologna, 1990) [intro. C. Dempsey]

P. L. Rubin: *Giorgio Vasari: Art and History* (New Haven and London, 1995)

JULIAN KLIEMANN

(2) Giorgio Vasari, il giovane (*b* Arezzo, 6 Nov 1562; *d* Florence, 17 Nov 1625). Essayist and architect, nephew of (1) Giorgio Vasari. He obtained Florentine citizenship in 1591 and was subsequently given numerous high-ranking posts within the Medici administration. In Arezzo, where he was appointed ambassador in 1614 to Cosimo II de' Medici, Grand Duke of Florence, he built a monastery, possibly to the commission of Bishop Usimbardi. After Bartolomeo Ammanati's death, he worked on the church of S Maria in Gradi, for which he designed the main altar (1607). In Florence he produced plans (not executed) for the façade of the cathedral, a pulpit in the church of Santo Spirito and the chapel of S Lorenzo (1604). Vasari il giovane admired the serenity of Filippo Brunelleschi's works and in his own designs showed considerable graphic and structural ingenuity.

In the extensive collection of Vasari's building plans (Florence, Uffizi) a clear attempt may be seen to reduce the whole field of ancient and modern architecture to a single modular system. His plan for an ideal city, while not based on any social doctrine, reveals a strong desire for order and centralization: the main streets follow the directions of the eight winds and converge in a single piazza dominated by the prince's palazzo and the law courts. The plan is a coherent representation of Medici absolutism (although this is not expressly stated by Vasari), with its public buildings—churches, monasteries, hospitals, centres of civil and ecclesiastical authority, multiple dwellings, a university, an arsenal and a port—all part of a heliocentric city dominated by the prince, of whom the architect is a faithful functionary.

UNPUBLISHED SOURCES

Florence, Bib. Riccardiana [MS. of *Libro di fortificatione . . .*(1570); MS. of *Studio di varii instrumenti per misurare la vista* (1600)]

WRITINGS

Città ideale . . . disegnata l'anno 1598 (1598; Florence, Uffizi, MS. 4529–4594); ed. V. Stefanelli (Rome, 1970)

Piante di chiese, palazzi e ville di Toscana e d'Italia . . . (1598; Florence, Uffizi, MS. 4715–4944); ed. V. Stefanelli (Rome, 1970)

Porte e finestre di Firenze e di Roma (Florence, Uffizi, MS. 4715A–4944A); ed. F. Borsi and C. Acidini in *Il disegno interrotto: Trattati medicei d'architettura* (Florence, 1980), pp. 295–321

BIBLIOGRAPHY

R. Klein: 'L'Urbanisme utopique de Filarte à Valentin Andrae', *La Forme et l'intelligible: Ecrits sur la Renaissance et l'art moderne* (Paris, 1970), pp. 310–26; Eng. trans. (New York, 1979), pp. 89–101

L. Olivato: 'Profilo di Giorgio Vasari il Giovane', *Riv. Ist. N. Archeol. & Stor. A.*, n. s., xvii (1970), pp. 181–229

——: 'Testimonianze della cultura architettonica spagnola (e araba) nel Rinascimento italiano: Alcuni disegni di Giorgio Vasari il Giovane', *Actas del XXIII Congreso internacional de historia del arte: Granada, 1976–8*, ii, pp. 378–84 [Contains the drawings (Florence, Uffizi) of buildings in Spain and Tunis, including the Cathedrals of Seville and Toledo and the Alcazar at Toledo]

ANTONIO MANNO

Vasaro, Giovanni [Zoan] **Maria** (*b* ?Faenza; *fl c.* 1475–1550). Italian ceramics painter. Although he was probably a native of Faenza, as his decorative repertory would suggest, he was active at the beginning of the 16th century in Castel Durante. His most famous signed work, a goblet (1508; ex-Met., New York), was made in honour of Pope Julius II. From this and other works that can be attributed to him on stylistic grounds, it is evident that he specialized in symmetrical compositions for plates, with a border of grotesques, trophies and musical instruments surrounding a central cavetto. Although his life and work are poorly documented, a survey of the maiolica of this period indicates that his work was very influential on maiolica artists who worked around Castel Durante during the first half of the 16th century.

BIBLIOGRAPHY

B. Rackham: 'Der Majolikmaler Giovanni Maria von Casteldurante', *Pantheon*, i (1928), pp. 435–45; ii (1929), pp. 88–92

CARMEN RAVANELLI GUIDOTTI

Vasconcelos, Constantino de (*b* Braga; *d* Lima, 22 Aug 1668). Portuguese architect and engineer, active in Peru. He was educated in the Renaissance humanist tradition, studying philosophy, theology, mathematics, cosmography, perspective and architecture after Vitruvius. Vasconcelos went to the Spanish Viceroyalty of Peru in 1629 with Don Hernando de Vera y Zúñiga, Archbishop of Santo Domingo, who had been transferred to a new seat in Cuzco. To celebrate the arrival of the new archbishop, in 1630 Vasconcelos designed a gold medal, which was sent to Spain. He then worked as an engineer in mines at Oruro, Potosí and Huancavelica. Vasconcelos took part as a cosmographer and military engineer in the 1645 expedition to Valdivia in Chile, where he drew a topographical map of the port and a design for its fortifications. His architectural masterpiece was the church of S Francisco (1657–74), Lima, largely built under the supervision of his assistant Manuel de Escobar (1639–93). Here Vasconcelos employed the anti-seismic *quincha* form of construction, using plastered reeds on a wooden frame, which was adopted in Lima and elsewhere on the Peruvian coast. The façade (begun 1669) features two towers with military rustication, banded at the lower levels, which embrace a retablo-type entrance bay, delicately detailed in striking contrast. The cloister elevations use overlapping

Serlianas at first-floor level, the side openings partially filled in to display oval apertures.

BIBLIOGRAPHY

M. Suárez de Figueroa: *Templo de N. grande patriarca San Francisco de la provincia de los doce apóstoles de el Perú en la ciudad de los reyes* (Lima, 1675)

B. Gento Sanz: *San Francisco de Lima* (Lima, 1945)

G. Lohmann Villena: *Las minas de Huancavelica en los siglos XVI y XVII* (Seville, 1949), pp. 292, 315–36, 338–41, 343–5, 396

D. Angulo Iñiguez and others: *Historia del arte hispanoamericano*, ii (Barcelona, 1950), pp. 136, 142–4

H. Rodríguez-Camilloni: 'El conjuncto monumental de San Francisco de Lima en los siglos XVII y XVIII', *Bol. Cent. Invest. Hist. & Estét. U. Caracas*, (1972), pp. 31–60

——: 'The Retablo-façade as Transparency: A Study of the Frontispiece of San Francisco, Lima', *An. Inst. Invest. Estét.* (1991), pp. 111–22

HUMBERTO RODRÍGUEZ-CAMILLONI

Vasconcelos, Félix Machado da Silva Castro e. *See* MACHADO DA SILVA CASTRO E VASCONCELOS, FÉLIX.

Vasconcelos, Joaquim de (*b* Oporto, 10 Feb 1849; *d* Oporto, 2 Mar 1936). Portuguese critic and art historian. He studied music and fine arts in Germany (1859–65), and after touring Europe he settled in 1869 in Oporto, where he began researching into Portuguese art. The results of this were published in a variety of newspapers and periodicals, as he had no official post or support. His work, however, which showed great integrity, erudition and critical insight, laid the foundation for the first school of Portuguese art history. In 1871 he discovered in Vienna a portrait of *John I* (*reg* 1385–1433; Lisbon, Mus. N. A. Ant.) and in 1882 he found in the monastery of S Vicente de Fora in Lisbon the famous panels (Lisbon, Mus. N. A. Ant.) by Nuno Gonçalves, the exceptional quality of which, in the context of European art of the 15th century, he at once recognized. He was also an authority on, among other Renaissance artists, the work of Francisco de Holanda and published many of his writings as well as the first major study of the artist (1899). He emphasized the cultural links between the architecture and art of Portugal and that of Northern Europe (especially Flanders), the importance of van Eyck's visit to Portugal of 1428–9, the influence of Dürer, and also the relationship of the Manueline style to Late Gothic architecture in Europe. He gave great importance to the Romanesque and to the persistence of popular and indigenous elements in the art of northern Portugal. He also wrote on the decorative arts (gold- and silverwork, ceramics) and crafts.

WRITINGS

Albert Dürer e a sua influência na Península (Oporto, 1877)

ed.: F. de Holanda: *Da fábrica que falece à cidade de Lisboa: Da ciência do desenho* (Oporto, 1879) [edn of MS. of 1571]

Da architectura manuelina (Coimbra, 1885)

ed.: F. de Holanda: *Da pintura antigua* (Oporto, 1890–92, rev. 1918, 1930) [edn of MS. of 1548]

'Relação da viagem de João Van Eyck a Portugal: Subsídio para a história da pintura em Portugal no século XIV', *Rev. Soc. Martins Sarmento*, xiv (1897) [and as offprint]

Francisco de Holanda: Vier Gespräche über die Malerei geführt zu Rom 1538 (Vienna, 1899)

A arte e a natureza em Portugal (Oporto, 1902–8)

Arte românica em Portugal (Oporto, 1918)

BIBLIOGRAPHY

Grande enciclopédia portuguesa e brasileira (Lisbon and Rio de Janeiro, 1936–60), xxxiv, pp. 293–5

A. Cruz: *Joaquim de Vasconcelos: O homem e a obra* (Oporto, 1950)

LUCILIA VERDELHO DA COSTA

Vasconi, Claude (*b* Rosheim, 24 June 1940). French architect. He was trained as an architect at the Ecole Nationale Supérieure des Arts et Industries in Strasbourg and first worked for the new town of Cergy-Pontoise. There he was responsible for the layout of the Centre Urbain around the Préfecture and was involved in the design of several commercial and public buildings such as the cultural centre and the Hôtel de Ville (1974–9). He opened his own office in 1973 and worked on a number of housing projects in new towns. He also designed the Forum des Halles (1973–9; with Georges Pancreac'h) in the centre of Paris; this is a multi-storey, high-tech, commercial centre, partially below ground level, whose recessed, glazed arcades echo the buttresses of the nearby church of St Eustache. Another major project was his appointment by the Régie Renault to plan for the future development of its long-established industrial site at Boulogne-Billancourt, immediately to the west of Paris. Here Vasconi built the 57 Métal workshop (1981–2) that was reminiscent of some expressionist factories by Hans Poelzig; its powerful massing was based on the rhythm of huge sheds. This building was a remarkable achievement in a country where industrial architecture is underrated, and Vasconi was awarded the Grand Prix National d'Architecture in 1982 as a result. His work in the 1990s included the World Trade Centre Tower (1991–5) for the Euralille development, a cultural centre (1993) in Mulhouse, and a congress centre (1994) in Reims, all modernist compositions in metal and glass.

BIBLIOGRAPHY

Claude Vasconi: Projets et réalisations, 1972–1982 (Paris, 1983)

'Claude Vasconi: Du Forum au Corum', *Tech. & Archit.*, 374 (1987), pp. 109–26

P. Joffroy: *Claude Vasconi, 1980–1990* (Paris and Milan, 1990)

ISABELLE GOURNAY

Vase painters. This article covers Greek and South Italian vase painters of the 7th–3rd century BC. Vase painters distinguished by small capital letters have separate biographical entries within this article.

I. Attribution.

Ancient Greek vases can be classified by period, place of production, fabric, shape, technique and decoration. It is also possible to identify styles of individual artists when sufficient vases have been preserved from a single area of production over a significant period and when these display similar decorative figures and patterns. Most Greek vase painters so far identified were active either in Athens during the 6th to 4th centuries BC or in 4th- and 3rd-century BC South Italy. The painters have been more often identified than the potters, partly because scholars have tended to concentrate on vase decoration rather than shape.

Greek vase painting is actually line drawing on the curved surfaces of clay vases made for particular functions to which the figure scenes sometimes allude. Patterns are an integral part of the decoration and remain important even when figures occupy the major part of the painted surface. The rendering of patterns and figures on individual Athenian vases is usually so consistent that one artist must normally have been responsible for both. Since human figures dominate most scenes, it is often assumed that stylistic elements in their execution should be the primary basis for determining attribution. This is, however, incorrect: examination of the figures is only the final stage in the process of attribution. Initially the shape must be examined, then the technique of decoration, the patterns, the iconography and the overall design of the painted elements. None of these can be assessed in isolation, and attribution remains subjective, although when many features can be taken into account and many contemporary vases are available for comparison this mode of classification is greatly strengthened. Few other art forms, in effect, offer such copious material for attribution.

Greek vases are rarely signed by either painter or potter, and no artist whose signature survives is mentioned in contemporary sources. Greek vase painting is wholly undocumented, and most artists' signatures occur on Athenian 6th- and 5th-century BC Black-figure and Red-figure vases. Painters signed with the verb *egrapsen* ('painted'), potters with the verb *epoiesen* ('made'). Makers may have fashioned the vase or simply supervised its production, and they appear to have been senior to painters. Using these two types of signature, the significance of which was not then fully understood, some later 19th-century scholars began to attribute signed Athenian vases to individual artists. Results were, however, inconclusive or misleading. Then, from 1911, J. D. BEAZLEY began to publish attributions of unsigned vases to unknown artists whom he named, often after museums housing their work (e.g. the Berlin Painter) or after a favourite subject (e.g. the Gorgon Painter). Over a period of more than 50 years he assigned more than 50,000 vases to over 1000 artists, classes and groups, publishing these attributions in what have become the standard reference works on the subject (Beazley, 1942, 1956 and 1971). Beazley left approximately the same number of vases unassigned.

Beazley's method was undoubtedly influenced by Giovanni Morelli's work on Renaissance painters, popularized in England by Bernard Berenson *c.* 1900. Morelli's system depended on detailed scrutiny of draughtsmanship, especially of the human body, and he particularly recommended the study of drawings, since these reveal use of lines more clearly than paintings. As line drawing involving human figures, Greek vase painting was admirably suited to Morellian morphological analysis. Beazley supplemented this approach with careful study of the features peculiar to Greek vases. In doing this he created his own method of attribution, which was subsequently applied to Corinthian vases by his pupil H. G. G. Payne, to Greek vases of South Italy by A. D. Trendall, and to various Archaic Greek vases by other scholars.

BIBLIOGRAPHY

H. G. G. Payne: *Necrocorinthia: A Study of Corinthian Art in the Archaic Period* (Oxford, 1931)
J. D. Beazley: 'Citharoedus', *J. Hell. Stud.*, xxii (1942), pp. 70–98
——: *Red-figure* (1942, 2/1963)
——: *Black-figure* (1956)
——: *Paralipomena* (1971)
C. M. Robertson: 'Beazley and After', *Münchn. Jb. Bild. Kst*, xxvii (1976), pp. 29–46
D. C. Kurtz: 'Beazley and the Connoisseurship of Greek Vases', *Greek Vases in the J. Paul Getty Museum*, iii (Malibu, 1986), pp. 237–50
D. C. Kurtz, ed.: *Lectures on Greek Vases by J. D. Beazley* (Oxford, 1989)
A. D. Trendall: *Red Figure Vases of South Italy and Sicily* (London, 1989)

D. C. KURTZ

II. Painters.

Acheloos Painter (*fl c.* 525–*c.* 500 BC). Greek vase painter. His name vase was a Black-figure neck amphora (untraced; ex-Berlin, Antikensamml.; see *Corp. Vasorum Ant.*, Berlin v, pl. 26.1) showing Herakles fighting the river god Acheloos. He is one of the few members of the LEAGROS GROUP (see below) with a large enough oeuvre to be given a separate list of attributions by Beazley, who viewed him as a genuine member of the group but suggested that his different outlook set him apart from the others. His choice of the larger vase shapes—mainly amphorae and hydria—is conventional for the group, but he also painted a number of smaller vases that appear on stylistic grounds to be later. His choice of subject-matter also differs in emphasis from the rest of the Leagros group: he liked to paint scenes with Herakles but not Troy, and he deliberately chose comic episodes. His other favourite subjects were symposia and the associated dancing; his revellers are usually middle-aged and corpulent, not the more normal elegant youths, and he frequently burlesqued the conventions of such scenes.

His style of drawing and composition is clearly that of the Leagros group: his scenes are large and dark, his figures big and long-legged, with a distinctive trunklike nose, especially in his comic scenes. All his work is Black-figure with little added colour. He shows less interest than the rest of the Leagros Group in the observation of anatomical detail and generally composed his scenes with fewer figures and less overlap. His interest was in behaviour, and his best painting includes his revellers, large, confident women (e.g. Cambridge, Fitzwilliam, GR 125, 1864) and some attractive animals: a frightened bull, a dog reaching for food from a table when his owner's attention is distracted (Moignard), a Kerberos behaving like any nervous dog. The Acheloos Painter's most important characteristic is his talent for comedy, most distinctively illustrated by his painting on a vase described by Beazley (1951): Herakles, a hulking, messy figure, is not always in control of what is happening; the boar is escaping from him. On the other side of the same vase Herakles is not sure that he will get away with the apples of the Hesperides. The hero is shown at his most human and least successfully heroic. In this aspect of his work the Acheloos Painter foreshadows later tendencies to use serious mythological figures for comic effect.

See also GREECE, ANCIENT, §V, 5(ii)(d).

BIBLIOGRAPHY

J. D. Beazley: 'Attic Black-figure: A Sketch', *Proc. Brit. Acad.*, xiv (1928), pp. 28, 46–7, pls 14–15
E. Langlotz: *Griechische Vasen in Würzburg* (Munich, 1932), pls 41, 52
J. D. Beazley: *Development of Black-figure* (1951, 3/1986), pp. 86–7, 116, pls 42–3
D. von Bothmer: 'Attic Black-figured Pelikai', *J. Hell. Stud.*, lxxi (1951), pp. 40–42
J. D. Beazley: *Black-figure* (1956), pp. 382–7, 696

——: *Paralipomena* (1971), pp. 168–70

J. Boardman: *Athenian Black Figure Vases: A Handbook* (London, 1974), p. 111, figs 209–11

L. Burn and R. Glynn: *Beazley Addenda: Additional References to* ABV, ARV2 *and* Paralipomena (Oxford, 1982, rev. T. H. Carpenter, 2/1989)

E. A. Moignard: 'The Acheloos Painter and Relations', *Annu. Brit. Sch. Athens*, lxxi (1982), pp. 201–11, pls 7–14

ELIZABETH MOIGNARD

Achilles Painter [Meletos Painter] (*fl c.* 470–*c.* 425 BC). Greek vase painter. He is named after an Attic Red-figure amphora depicting *Achilles* (see GREECE, ANCIENT, fig. 112). He studied under the BERLIN PAINTER late in the latter's career and apparently took over the commission for Black-figure Panathenaic amphorae from his workshop. However, the vast majority of some 300 vases ascribed to him are either Red-figure or, slightly more often, White-ground works. He was the greatest White-ground lekythos painter, and his simple, balanced compositions with quiet, emotionless figures parallel the High Classical style of the Parthenon sculptures. In Red-figure he favoured Nolan amphorae and lekythoi, though he also decorated a few larger shapes, such as neck amphorae, loutrophoroi, kraters and stamnoi, as well as a skyphos, a dinos, a pointed amphora, pelikai, hydriai and oinochoai. Among his specialities were squat lekythoi decorated with a bust above a line in added white that ran around the lower body of the vase.

Beazley originally assigned many of the Achilles Painter's early Red-figure works (*c.* 470–*c.* 450 BC) to a 'Meletos Painter' until he realized that the two painters were the same man. At first his drawing style was tentative and similar to that of the Berlin Painter, whose preferred later subjects, such as fleeing women and gods pursuing their lovers, he also shared. However, the Achilles Painter's fine, steady line and his excellent draughtsmanship are already evident on several early vases including a large bell krater with a man and a realistically depicted old warrior, perhaps *Tereus and Pandion* (New York, Met., 07.286.81).

During the Achilles Painter's middle and late career (*c.* 450–*c.* 430 BC) his drawing style matured and stabilized, though his Red-figure works vary in quality. Several are rather summary and repetitious depictions of his favourite scenes, such as *Eos Pursuing Kephalos or Tithonos*, and a youth leaving home, while many of the figures on the backs of his Nolan amphorae, pelikai and small kraters are almost identical. However, some of his Red-figure vases are extremely fine and apparently influenced by monumental art. *Achilles* on the artist's name-piece recalls the *Doryphoros* of POLYKLEITOS, while the *Amazonomachy* on a large calyx krater (Ferrara, Mus. N. Archeol., 2890 T 1052) seems to have been inspired by wall painting, for in this work the painter abandoned his usual simple, static scenes for one with many figures caught up in the turmoil of combat. What inspired the masterpiece on a calyx krater (Malibu, CA, Getty Mus., 77.AE.44.1) with *Herakles Giving his Bow and Arrows to Philoktetes* is uncertain. However, these vases are all distinguished by dilute glaze colouring and sometimes shading, great attention to detail and extremely careful drawing. His final works, on the other hand, suggest a decline in the artist's powers.

The Achilles Painter's White-ground lekythoi are more uniformly excellent, and he clearly led the development of such vases. Many White-ground lekythoi by contemporary artists such as the Bird Painter and Thanatos Painter follow his compositions and figure types. As on his early Red-figure, the drawing on his early White-ground vases (*c.* 460–*c.* 450 BC) is stiff, and the themes and composition are restricted. Two women are normally depicted facing each other, both standing or one standing and one sitting. Their exposed skin is emphasized in applied white. Dromippos, son of Dromokleidos, and Diphilos, son of Melanopos, are the kalos names he used most frequently in this period. During his middle career (*c.* 450–*c.* 435 BC) scenes with two women continued, but two figures on either side of a tomb also became a common subject. Applied white was no longer used, while golden dilute glaze replaced brown dilute glaze for the outlines. Hygiainon and Axiopeithes, son of Alkimachos, were the preferred names in his kalos inscriptions. One masterpiece (Berlin, Antikenmus., 1983.1) with a warrior and an old man grieving at a tomb is a transitional piece with characteristics of both early and middle periods. Two other masterpieces from his middle career, a lekythos with *Two Muses at Mt Helikon* (Munich, Staatl. Antikensamml., ex-Schoen 80) and another with a warrior and a woman (Athens, N. Archaeol. Mus., 1818; *see* CERAMICS, colour pl. II, fig. 1), have the serene atmosphere, simple, relaxed figures and balanced composition typical of his High Classical work. Finally, on a few of his last lekythoi the artist used matt paint instead of golden dilute glaze for the outlines.

The Achilles Painter had several students, the most important being the PHIALE PAINTER. They shared the same workshop with some lesser Red-figure artists such as the Dwarf Painter, the Persephone Painter and the Clio Painter. Several important contemporary artists, such as the KLEOPHON PAINTER and the Painter of Munich 2335, also had contact with this workshop and were influenced by the Achilles Painter. On one loutrophoros (Philadelphia, U. PA, Mus., 30.4.1) the Achilles Painter drew the main frieze, while the Sabouroff Painter decorated the less important area. These contacts reflect the fact that the Achilles Painter was the most important and influential Classical vase painter and one of the best ancient draughtsmen.

BIBLIOGRAPHY

J. D. Beazley: 'The Master of the Achilles Amphora in the Vatican', *J. Hell. Stud.*, xxxiv (1914), pp. 179–236

S. B. Luce: 'The Diphilos-Dromippos Lecythi, and their Relation to Mr. Beazley's "Achilles Master"', *Amer. J. Archaeol.*, xxiii (1919), pp. 19–32

J. D. Beazley: *Attic White Lekythoi* (Oxford, 1938), pp. 13–16

——: *Red-figure* (1942, 2/1963), ii, pp. 986–1004, 1676–7, 1708

P. E. Arias and M. Hirmer: *Tausend Jahre griechischer Vasenkunst* (Munich, 1960); Eng. trans. rev. B. B. Shefton as *A History of Greek Vase Painting* (London, 1962), pp. 359–64

D. C. Kurtz: *Athenian White Lekythoi* (Oxford, 1975), pp. 41–8

I. Wehgartner: *Ein Grabbild des Achilleusmalers* (Berlin, 1985)

J. H. Oakley: *The Achilles Painter* (in preparation)

JOHN H. OAKLEY

Painter of Acropolis 606 (*fl c.* 575–*c.* 550 BC). Greek vase painter. The artist is named after a large Attic Black-figure dinos (*see* GREECE, ANCIENT, fig. 98), and six other vases or fragments are attributed to him. Like his contemporaries NEARCHOS and LYDOS he painted large vases in the monumental tradition of the NETTOS PAINTER. His name piece has large, boldly arranged figures, while the Corinthianizing animal friezes favoured by his miniaturist predecessors are relegated to subsidiary zones. Its vivid battle scene captures the moment of greatest suspense, with chariots clashing fiercely over the body of a fallen warrior. Muscular fighters with twisted moustaches and bright clothing and armour aim their spears at each other, while trim charioteers lean intently forward to control their rearing horses. The corpse sprawls in a grotesque pose, with one twisted arm at its side, the other wrapped round its neck, ending in a raised claw like hand. The figure rivals some of Homer's evocations of the horrors of war and anticipates some of Picasso's.

The artist's other works convey the same vehemence, grandeur and disdain for dainty miniaturism. Thus, a pair of moustached warriors on rearing horses fills each of the panels of a majestic amphora (Berlin, Antikenmus., 4823), and each side of the neck of a cruder neck amphora (Geneva, Mus. A. & Hist., MF 153) bears a thick-set male head with a twirled moustache. Three fragmentary figures of boxers (Athens, Acropolis Mus., 633) also express this artist's staunch championing of Athenian monumentality.

BIBLIOGRAPHY

J. D. Beazley: 'Attic Black-figure: A Sketch', *Proc. Brit. Acad.*, xiv (1928), pp. 13–14
——: *Development of Black-figure* (1951, 3/1986), pp. 35–6
——: *Black-figure* (1956), p. 81
——: *Paralipomena* (1971), p. 30

JODY MAXMIN

Affecter (*fl* second half of the 6th century BC). Greek vase painter. This Attic Black-figure artist's name derives from the distinctive mannered appearance of his figures. Most of the 132 vases attributed to him are well preserved due to having been buried in Etruscan tombs. Indeed, almost all were apparently produced for export, which perhaps partly explains his idiosyncratic style. Black-figure work tends naturally towards formalism, as is apparent in little-master cups and works by the AMASIS PAINTER. However, the Affecter's emphasis on the decorative effects created by his silhouette figures is unique, and contrasts with the general trend of his time towards stressing the narrative element in paintings. His compositions involve small-headed figures in loose drapery spattered with ornamental dots, whose long limbs create angular gestures and poses. The themes are highly repetitive (e.g. scenes of pederastic pursuit, a *God Enthroned with Hermes, Soldiers Arming, Dionysos and his Followers, Theseus and the Minotaur, Men on Horseback*), and he produced few interesting mythological scenes. The Affecter specialized in decorating amphorae but chose unconventional types, again apparently in a search for stylistic effect. Both as potter of his own vessels and as painter he employed old-fashioned forms (e.g. ovoid neck amphorae, low picture friezes, figures on the necks, double rays above the foot) but combined them imaginatively with inventions of his own. With his meticulous draughtsmanship he did achieve true masterpieces, of old-fashioned but incontestable elegance.

BIBLIOGRAPHY

J. D. Beazley: *Black-figure* (1956), pp. 238–48, 690–91
——: *Paralipomena* (1971), pp. 110–12, 524
H. Mommsen: *Der Affecter: Forschungen zur antiken Keramik II Reihe, Kerameus 1*, 2 vols (Mainz, 1975)

J. H. Oakley: 'A Fragmentary Skyphos by the Affecter', *Hesperia*, xlviii (1979), pp. 393–6
D. von Bothmer: 'The Affecter Amphora', *J. Walters A.G.*, xxxviii (1980), pp. 94–107
L. Burn and R. Glynn: *Beazley Addenda: Additional References to ABV, ARV2 and Paralipomena* (Oxford, 1982, rev. T. H. Carpenter, 2/1989), pp. 60–64
H. A. Shapiro: 'Poseidon and the Tuna', *Ant. Class.*, lviii (1989), pp. 32–43

HEIDE MOMMSEN

Aison (*fl c.* 440–*c.* 420 BC). Greek vase painter. Although *c.* 50 works have been attributed to him, his signature survives only on a fine Red-figure kylix (Madrid, Mus. Arqueol. N., 11265) decorated with the *Exploits of Theseus*. Six episodes are competently but routinely depicted on the outside of the kylix, but the culmination of the cycle, the *Defeat of the Minotaur*, is treated more lavishly in the tondo. With his patron goddess Athena by his side, the hero drags the dead Minotaur from its labyrinth, which is represented by a fine Ionic building bordered at its right-hand edge by a suitably labyrinthine vertical meander stripe. The scene is skilfully conceived and executed. The circular ground is elegantly criss-crossed by a balanced composition of vertical and diagonal lines, while the three figures are pointedly contrasted by their poses and appearance: the aloof and dignified goddess, the athletic, straining hero, and the grotesque, limp torso of the Minotaur.

This work has strong links with the Theseus cup (London, BM, E 84) of the KODROS PAINTER, and the two artists were surely contemporaries, though the Kodros Painter was perhaps slightly older. Another close contemporary was the ERETRIA PAINTER. It has also been suggested (Knigge) that the vases generally ascribed to the MEIDIAS PAINTER were actually late works by Aison. Some aspects of the styles of the two painters are indeed extraordinarily similar: the often slightly down-turned heads, with their long, straight noses and large eyes; the hair of the male figures, which tends to straggle round the neck; the musculature of the naked males, particularly the unusual long double line marking the median division of the abdomen. Yet there are also significant differences: whereas Aison generally depicted lively scenes, and strongly favoured chiastic movement, the Meidias Painter's scenes are generally peaceful and static. Thus Knigge's theory has not been widely accepted, and scholars prefer to regard the Meidias Painter as Aison's pupil.

Aison was a competent and occasionally excellent artist. His painting was careful and precise, his patternwork neat. He decorated many shapes besides cups: squat lekythoi, a head kantharos, oinochoai, hydriai, loutrophoroi, a neck amphora, pelikai and two pyxides. His subjects were also varied, ranging from many commonplace scenes of athletes and of youths leaving home to more unusual themes. Theseus is shown in three other scenes, twice in Amazonomachies, and once leaving home. A small pyxis (Boston, MA, Mus. F.A., 04.18) depicts a very rare scene, *Odysseus' Encounter with Nausikaa*. Also of considerable interest are two allusions to the cult of Adonis, only introduced to Athens in about 440 BC and rarely depicted in contemporary vase paintings. On a squat lekythos (Paris, Louvre, MNB 2109) the seated Adonis is waited upon by Aphrodite and other women, while an acorn lekythos (Athens, Acropolis Mus. 6471) depicts the *Gardens of Adonis*.

BIBLIOGRAPHY

C. Dugas: *Aison et la peinture céramique à Athènes à l'époque de Périclès* (Paris, 1930)

J. D. Beazley: *Red-figure* (1942, 2/1963)

W. Real: *Die Entwicklung der Vasenmalerei im ausgehenden 5. Jahrhundert v. Chr.* (Aschendorff, 1973), pp. 13–19

U. Knigge: 'Aison, der Meidiasmaler? Zu einer rotfigurigen Oionchoe aus dem Kerameikos', *Mitt. Dt. Archäol. Inst.: Athen. Abt.*, xc (1975), pp. 123–43

D. Cramers: *Aison en de Meidias-schilder* (diss., Leuven, U. Catholique, 1980)

LUCILLA BURN

Amasis Painter (*fl c.* 560–*c.* 515 BC). Greek vase painter. He is named after eight Attic Black-figure vases decorated by one artist and signed by the potter Amasis. These signatures only appeared, however, from *c.* 550 BC, a decade after his earliest attributed work, the alabastron from the Athenian Agora (Athens, Agora Mus., P 12628). The Amasis Painter was a prolific artist, and over 130 examples of his work survive. He decorated numerous shapes, ranging from one-piece amphorae and neck amphorae, often with unusual details, to small, exquisite pieces, such as oinochoai, lekythoi, cups and rare shapes such as the aryballos and the mastoid.

The Amasis Painter's earliest vases are sometimes rather conservatively decorated, good examples being four lekythoi (Paris, Louvre, F 71 and F 192; Philadelphia, U. PA, Mus., MS 4849; Tübingen, Eberhard-Karls-U., Antikensamml., 7434), an alabastron (Athens, Agora Mus., P 12628) and a cup (Mainz, Johannes Gutenberg-U., 88). However, the drawing is sure and strong and sometimes clearly influenced by KLEITIAS. Nonetheless, the Amasis Painter's mature work (*c.* 550–*c.* 515 BC) is his most famous, for example the amphora in Würzburg (U. Würzburg, Wagner-Mus., L 265), the two neck amphorae in Boston, MA (Mus. F.A., 01.8026 and 01.8027) or the neck amphora in Paris, (Bib. N., 222), the splendid cup in the Norbert Schimmel collection (Kings Point, New York: see von Bothmer, pp. 217–19), the oinochoe in London (BM, B 471) and the two lekythoi in New York (Met., 31.11.10 and 56.11.1). On these the painter's crisp, precise incision skilfully defines the individual figures, and he embellishes their garments, resulting in a rich tapestry-like effect that balances the carefully chosen ornaments articulating the vases' various parts.

The Amasis Painter's subject-matter and approach successfully reveal certain aspects of his personality. His sense of humour is reflected in the playful scene of *Satyrs Making Wine* on the Würzburg amphora, while representations of Dionysos and his companions (e.g. on Würzburg 265 and Paris, Bib. N., 222) imply a wider interest in the Dionysiac revels. Some other scenes are difficult to identify; thus the scene of *Athena Confronting Poseidon* on one side of Paris, Bibliothèque Nationale 222, perhaps represents the contest to become the patron deity of Athens, while the scenes of horse-training on a lekythos (St Petersburg, Hermitage, 2635) and an aryballos (New York, Met., 62.11.11) and of courtship on an olpe (New York, Met., 59.11.17) are less easy for the modern viewer to interpret in a specific way. However, the artist also depicted well-known myths, such as *Herakles Choking the Lion* on an oinochoe (Paris, Louvre, F 37), the *Young Achilles Receiving his Armour* (with the figures labelled to avoid ambiguity) and *Herakles and Apollo Struggling for the Delphic Tripod* (Boston, Mus. F.A., 01.8027). On the Schimmel cup the two sides are linked thematically: one shows the *Stable of Poseidon*, the other *Poseidon with Heroes*. The subject is unique and is based on the *Iliad* (XIII.10–31), where Poseidon's grooms harness his team and Poseidon descends to the Trojan plain to encourage the Greek forces.

The Munich amphora (Staatl. Antikensamml., 8763) graphically depicts a splendid cavalcade at full gallop, and the Amasis Painter also painted scenes of daily life, the most famous being on the two lekythoi in New York. One (Met., 56.11.1) provides the fullest pictorial record of an Attic rural wedding. It shows the groom's mother inside his house with the wedding party arriving by cart. The other (Met., 31.11.10) depicts women weighing, spinning and weaving wool, then folding the finished cloth.

The Amasis Painter's vases are distinctive, and he showed great versatility in invariably coordinating shape, ornament and figural decoration. His figures are often small but never fussy; his compositions are often full but never cluttered.

BIBLIOGRAPHY

J. D. Beazley: *Development of Black-figure* (1951, 3/1986), pp. 52–7

——: *Black-figure* (1956), pp. 150–58, 687–8, 714

——: *Paralipomena* (1971), pp. 62–7

D. von Bothmer: *The Amasis Painter and his World: Vase-painting in Sixth-century B.C. Athens* (Malibu, 1985)

MARY B. MOORE

Analatos Painter (*fl* Athens, *c.* 705–*c.* 680 BC). Greek vase painter. His name piece is the Early Proto-Attic hydria (Athens, N. Archaeol. Mus., 313) found at Analatos, a modern suburb of Athens. He was a pioneer of the Orientalizing movement in Attic vase painting (*see* GREECE, ANCIENT, §V, 4). His style evolved from the Late Geometric II (*c.* 735–*c.* 700 BC) workshop of the PAINTER OF ATHENS 894, especially from its Stathatou hand. On his earliest known vase, a hydria in Melbourne (N.G. Victoria, D23/1982), a funerary *prothesis* (laying out) scene on the neck has links with the Geometric past. Male and female dancers occupy the same position on the Analatos hydria, showing the painter's style in the making. For the first time on an Athenian vase, Orientalizing curvilinear plant ornament fills the main body zone, flanked on one side by rampant lions. The dancers, although still in Geometric silhouette, have beaky facial features and reserved dotted eyes; massed dots cover the women's skirts, and the painter's own favourite trefoil plant ornament is often placed in the field.

An amphora in Paris (Louvre, CA 2985, *c.* 690 BC) bears a mixed dance on the neck, with a characteristically Analatan face, square and craggy, drawn in outline; typical are the heavily circled eye, fleshy nose, small mouth and pointed beard swinging in a sharp curve from the cheek, as are the sphinxes above, with their scaly wings. Incision is used experimentally for minor details in the chariot frieze below but abandoned in the chariots on a later krater (Munich, Staatl. Antikensamml., 6077), remarkable for the painter's individual lions with spotted jowls. In his latest major work, on two high-footed cauldrons made for an aristocratic funeral (Mainz, Johannes Gutenberg U., 153, 156), he experimented with the Black-and-white style, which became standard in the Middle Proto-Attic phase of vase painting (*c.* 670–*c.* 630 BC).

See also GREECE, ANCIENT, §V, 4(iii).

BIBLIOGRAPHY

J. M. Cook: 'Protoattic Pottery', *Annu. Brit. Sch. Athens*, xxxv (1934–5), pp. 172–6
R. Hampe: *Ein frühattischer Grabfund* (Mainz, 1960), pp. 30–35, 77–8
E. T. H. Brann: *Late Geometric and Protoattic Pottery, Mid 8th to Late 7th Century BC* (1962), viii of *The Athenian Agora* (Princeton, 1953–), pp. 10, 19–20
J. M. Cook: 'A Painter and his Age', *Mélanges A. Varagnac* (Paris, 1971), pp. 167–76

NICOLAS COLDSTREAM

Andokides Painter (*fl c.* 525–*c.* 515/510 BC). Greek vase painter. He was named after the potter Andokides, by whom he was employed, and he was the first great practitioner, and probably the inventor, of Attic Red-figure. His works survive on fewer than 20 vases (all either amphorae or cups), almost half of which are bilingual. Their Black-figure pictures are probably attributable to another artist, the LYSIPPIDES PAINTER, who began as a pupil of the Black-figure master EXEKIAS. The Andokides Painter's earliest works, by contrast, are on Red-figure amphorae (New York, Met., 63.11.6; Berlin, Antikenmus. 2159; Paris, Louvre, G 1) and closer in style (e.g. the treatment of energetic, full-bodied figures and stacked drapery folds) and subject-matter (e.g. *Herakles and Apollo Struggling for the Tripod*) to sculptural decoration from the Siphnian Treasury (*see* DELPHI, §2), than to Black-figure paintings.

In the Andokides Painter's early works the Red-figure silhouettes are not yet emphasized by contour stripes of black glaze, while relief lines only appear sporadically. Incision is restricted to areas (e.g. hair contours) that were difficult to reserve. Globules of glazed clay give a relief effect to details such as hair and grapes. The painter experimented on a belly amphora with white slip for female flesh (Paris, Louvre, F 203) and represented the human body in complicated positions, though at the expense of anatomical precision (e.g. his wrestlers and satyrs on two belly amphorae (Berlin, Antikenmus., 2154, and Orvieto, Mus. Etrus. Faina, 64, respectively). He used hooked lines for collarbones and knee joints and often drew bony protuberances at wrist, elbow and heel. His early works include loose compositions depicting daily activities such as athletics, musical contests and women (possibly Amazons) bathing.

The Andokides Painter's unusual partnership with the Lysippides Painter began halfway through his career. On one bilingual amphora (*see* GREECE, ANCIENT, fig. 108) Achilles and Ajax appear on both sides, but only the Red-figure heroes have a monumentality and a liveliness that transcend the Exekian tradition. On another bilingual amphora (Boston, MA, Mus. F.A., 99.538) the two artists painted the same composition, *Herakles Driving a Bull to Sacrifice*, in different techniques. In one case the division of labour was particularly clever: shields of fallen Black-figure warriors on the exterior of a bilingual eye cup (Palermo, Mus. Reg., V650) are in Red-figure. On the Andokides Painter's contemporary Red-figure amphora

with *Herakles Fighting the Amazons* (Orvieto, Mus. Etrus. Faina, 64) the profusion of incision, added colour and patterns display a new influence of Black-figure.

The Andokides Painter's latest Red-figure pictures are all on bilingual amphorae. In these the figure contours are more natural and the compositions more effectively structured. The artist's favourite hero, Herakles, recurs in vivid and original compositions, for example crouching to coax Kerberos on a belly amphora (Paris, Louvre, F 204) or wrestling with the Nemean lion, which has vaulted on to his shoulders on another (London, BM, B 193). Herakles is invariably attended by a figure of Athena resembling a sculpted kore from the Acropolis. The Andokides Painter depicted a cheerful, lively world with infectious enthusiasm, and his richly dressed figures evoke the aristocratic sophistication of Peisistratid Athens.

BIBLIOGRAPHY

R. Norton: 'Andokides', *Amer. J. Archaeol.*, xi (1896), pp. 1–41
E. Langlotz: *Zur Zeitbestimmung der strengrotfigurigen Vasenmalerei und der gleichzeitigen Plastik* (Leipzig, 1920), pp. 18–31
W. Technau: 'Eine Amphora des Andokidesmalers in der Sammlung des Conte Faina zu Orvieto', *Corolla Ludwig Curtius* (Stuttgart, 1937), pp. 132–41
J. D. Beazley: *Red-figure* (1942, 2/1963), i, pp. 2–5; iii, p. 1617
P. E. Arias and M. Hirmer: *Tausend Jahre griechischer Vasenkunst* (Munich, 1960); Eng. trans. rev. B. B. Shefton as *A History of Greek Vase Painting* (London, 1962), pp. 316–17
H. Marwitz: 'Zur Einheit des Andokidesmalers', *Jhft. Österreich. Archäolog. Inst. Wien*, xlvi (1961–3), pp. 73–104
E. R. Knauer: *Die Berliner Andokides-Vase* (Stuttgart, 1965)
D. von Bothmer: 'Andokides the Potter and the Andokides Painter', *Bull. Met.*, xxiv (1965–6), pp. 201–12
J. D. Beazley: *Paralipomena* (1971), pp. 320–21
J. Boardman: *Athenian Black Figure Vases: A Handbook* (New York, 1974), p. 105
——: *Athenian Red-figure Vases: The Archaic Period* (London, 1975), pp. 15–17
B. Cohen: *Attic Bilingual Vases and their Painters* (New York, 1978), pp. 1–8, 105–93
L. Burn and R. Glynn: *Beazley Addenda: Additional References to ABV, ARV2 and Paralipomena* (Oxford, 1982; rev. T. H. Carpenter, 2/1989)

BETH COHEN

Antimenes Painter (*fl c.* 530–*c.* 510 BC). Greek vase painter. He is named after a kalos inscription praising Antimenes on a hydria (Leiden, Rijksmus. Oudhd., PC 63). He was one of the most prolific Black-figure artists in Athens in the 6th century BC, and *c.* 140 of his pieces are extant. He decorated mainly standard neck amphorae and hydriai, though also a few bell amphorae and pseudo-Panathenaic amphorae, a dinos, a psykter and a calyx krater. Most were found in Etruria, especially at Vulci.

The Antimenes Painter began his career in the workshop of two pupils of EXEKIAS, the potter Andokides and the LYSIPPIDES PAINTER, though he does not seem to have been formally the latter's pupil. Stylistic similarities with PSIAX encouraged Beazley to call him Psiax' 'brother'. The Antimenes Painter's style is in fact plainer than that of either the Lysippides Painter or Psiax; his figures are large and powerful, and he avoided overlaps whenever possible. His painting is not always accurate, though even his small pictures are rendered in great detail; for example those on the shoulders and predellas of his hydriai, or on the neck of an amphora (Paris, Louvre, F 201). Similarities in the subject-matter and composition, in the predellas and in ornamentation, suggest that all three artists collaborated within a single workshop complex.

The Antimenes Painter's work comprised three phases. The first is characterized by frequent repetition of the same themes, with the influence of the Lysippides Painter evident in both subject-matter and composition. During the second, the Antimenes Painter led a workshop whose production included more unusual shapes such as dinoi, calyx kraters and psykters. The third phase represents the zenith of the painter's career. Though it has yielded fewer vases, these are painted in meticulous detail. A few groups briefly carried on the Antimenes Painter's style but gradually merged into the workshop of the KLEOPHRADES PAINTER.

The Antimenes Painter depicted many subjects, and he also introduced new details into earlier themes or gave them an idyllic slant, as in the two scenes on neck amphorae of *Herakles Greeting Pholos* (London, BM, B 226) and *Herakles with Kerberos* (Paris, Louvre, F 228). Herakles was the painter's favourite hero (*see* GREECE, ANCIENT, fig. 163); fountain-house scenes also occur frequently. His innovative pictures include one on his name-piece of men and youths at a bathhouse surrounded by trees, and two on amphorae showing the olive harvest (London, BM, B 226 and Berlin, Antikensamml., F 1855), which also respect the relative proportions of men and trees. The *Beheading of Medusa* on a neck amphora (Munich, Staatl. Antikensamml., 1555) and the battle scene from the *Little Iliad* on a hydria (Basle, Antikenmus.) are impressively dramatic and attest to the painter's particular success in rendering these narrative scenes. The Antimenes Painter was probably also the first to use the White-ground technique on the necks of amphorae and hydriai, and to decorate these two shapes with frontal Dionysos masks derived from eye cups. Thus, though he showed a certain conservatism in adhering to Black-figure when his contemporaries were adopting Red-figure, his innovations suggest a deliberate effort to keep Black-figure competitive.

See also GREECE, ANCIENT, fig. 101.

BIBLIOGRAPHY
J. D. Beazley: *Black-figure* (1956), pp. 266–76
——: *Paralipomena* (1971), pp. 161–72
J. Burow: 'Der Antimenesmaler', *Forsch. Ant. Ker.: Kerameus*, 7 (1989) [whole issue; with illus. of works discussed above]

JOHANNES BUROW

Arkesilaos Painter (*fl c.* 565–*c.* 555 BC). Greek vase painter. A Lakonian Black-figure artist, he is named after a cup from Vulci (Paris, Bib. N., Cab. Médailles, 189; *see* GREECE, ANCIENT, fig. 103) showing King Arkesilaos of Cyrene (probably Arkesilaos II, *reg c.* 565–560 BC) watching the weighing and packing of a white substance (?silphion), a precious plant used as a medicine which was the monopoly of the kings of Cyrene. The subject of this cup was used by early scholars to support the mistaken view that Lakonian vases were in fact Cyrenean. The career of the Arkesilaos Painter was short and few works by him—most of them cups—have survived. Two of his cups are decorated with mythological scenes: one (Rome, Villa Giulia) shows *Herakles Pursuing Two Amazons*; the other (Rome, Vatican, Mus. Gregoriano Etrus., 16592) depicts *Atlas* and the *Torture of Prometheus*. He also favoured

symposium scenes. The Arkesilaos Painter was not a first-rate draughtsman; his style is rather naive and his figures stiff. He does, however, display a liking for narrative and his scenes are lively and expressive. His choice and treatment of subjects make him perhaps the most original of the 6th-century BC Lakonian vase painters.

BIBLIOGRAPHY
E. A. Lane: 'Lakonian Vase-painting', *Annu. Brit. Sch. Athens*, xxxiv (1933–4), pp. 140–41
P. Pelagatti: 'Kylix laconica con Eracle e le Amazzoni', *Bull. Corr. Hell.*, lxxxii (1958), pp. 482–94
P. E. Arias and M. Hirmer: *Tausend Jahre griechischer Vasenkunst* (Munich, 1960); Eng. trans. and rev. by B. Shefton as *A History of Greek Vase Painting* (London, 1962), pp. 309–10
C. M. Stibbe: *Lakonische Vasenmaler des sechsten Jahrhunderts v. Chr.*, 2 vols (Amsterdam and London, 1972), pp. 107–19

MARIA PIPILI

Athena Painter (*fl c.* 490–*c.* 480 BC). Greek vase painter. He belonged to the last generation of Attic Black-figure vase painters, who now painted only small vessels such as lekythoi and oinochoai. He decorated both shapes, but specialized in lekythoi (about 150 are attributed to him) and employed both red and white grounds: occasionally he used the outline technique for the attributes of his conventional black silhouette figures (e.g. Athens, N. Archaeol. Mus., 1809; see Kurtz, pl. 60/2). He drew simply, but well: his figures are large and powerful, while careful incision gives them an appearance of animation. His name derives from his numerous portrayals of Athena. In addition to typical Late Archaic subjects (stories of gods and heroes, Dionysiac revels, battles, animals), he also painted some unusual scenes, such as *Satyrs Performing a War Dance* (Athens, N. Archaeol. Mus., 18567) or *Hyakinthos Escaping across the Sea on a Swan* (Berlin, Pergamonmus., 30852).

The Athena Painter's workshop mainly produced numerous White-ground oinochoai, though the form and ornamentation of a few Red-figure lekythoi show that they were also made there. They are ascribed to the Red-figure Bowdoin Painter, but stylistic similarities suggest that they were decorated by the same painter as their Black-figure counterparts, so that the Bowdoin Painter and the Athena Painter were in fact probably the same person: the difference in subject-matter between the Black- and Red-figure lekythoi (the latter mainly depicting women) perhaps simply reflects a difference of function in the vases.

BIBLIOGRAPHY
C. H. E. Haspels: *Attic Black-figured Lekythoi* (Paris, 1936)
J. D. Beazley: *Black-figure* (1956), pp. 522–4, 704–5
——: *Paralipomena* (1971), pp. 260–62
D. C. Kurtz: *Athenian White Lekythoi* (Oxford, 1975)

BETTINA JESKE

Painter of Athens 894 (*fl c.* 720–*c.* 700 BC). Greek vase painter. An inventive and influential artist active in Athens, he worked at the close of the Late Geometric style (*c.* 760–*c.* 700 BC); his silhouette figure drawing follows the tradition of the DIPYLON MASTER (*see* below) but in a more cursive and relaxed manner. His name piece, the slim neck-handled amphora in Athens (*see* GREECE, ANCIENT, fig. 86), represents the leading figured shape of the day, of which over 30 examples come from his workshop; the attached terracotta serpents indicate their funerary purpose. The neck panel on these vessels often portrays a condensed *prothesis* (laying out) scene, in which female mourners are distinguished by long hair and latticed skirts. Main body zones often bear chariot processions showing more sense of movement than do those of the Dipylon Master, and files of foot-soldiers carrying round shields with blazons. Subsidiary zones may contain animal friezes with grazing deer or hounds chasing a hare or, less frequently, bulls, centaurs or prowling lions of Near Eastern inspiration. Geometric ornament here plays only a subordinate part.

Other shapes from this painter's prolific workshop include hydriae with scenes of dancing women, one-piece rounded (i.e. unarticulated) oinochoai with animals on the shoulder, and shallow skyphoi with figured decoration inside, influenced by metal bowls from the Levant (*see* PHOENICIAN, §6).

Several of the later vessels from the Athens 894 workshop are attributable to the mannered and fastidious hand of the amphora in the Stathatou collection (Athens, N. Archaeol. Mus., St 222); this artist appears to have been the teacher of the ANALATOS PAINTER, the leading personality of the Early Proto-Attic phase (*c.* 700–*c.* 670 BC).

See also GREECE, ANCIENT, §V, 3(ii).

BIBLIOGRAPHY
J. M. Cook: 'Athenian Workshops around 700', *Annu. Brit. Sch. Athens*, xlii (1947), pp. 146–9
J. M. Davison: 'Attic Geometric Workshops', *Yale Class. Stud.*, xvi (1961), pp. 41–5
J. N. Coldstream: *Greek Geometric Pottery* (London, 1968), pp. 58–64
NICOLAS COLDSTREAM

Baltimore Painter (*fl c.* 330–*c.* 310 BC). Vase painter, active in Apulia. He may have worked near Canosa, where many of his vases have been found, though there is some connection with the UNDERWORLD PAINTER, who was probably from Tarentum. He is named after a monumental volute krater in Baltimore, MD (Walters A.G., 48.86), possibly depicting *Hermes and Persephone in the Underworld*. There are many other mythological subjects in his unusually large oeuvre, though they lack the originality of his near contemporary, the DARIUS PAINTER, probably also from Tarentum. A characteristic example of the Baltimore Painter's slightly coarse but vivid style is provided by another volute krater (Ruvo di Puglia, Mus. Jatta, 424), with an agitated representation of the *Death of the Children of Niobe*. In addition to large numbers of minor vases mostly decorated with a single painted female head, his workshop produced many volute kraters with scenes at grave shrines. The figures in the shrines, representing the deceased and members of their family, are sometimes painted with various colours (red, orange–yellow and white). In his multi-figured compositions the painter often depicted objects of various types scattered all over the ground, the most characteristic being a hydria with one visible M-shaped handle. The Baltimore Painter was not a meticulous draughtsman: his lines tend to be thick, but his rapid brush movements add a touch of character. The early works of his successor, the White Saccos Painter, are extremely close to those of the Baltimore Painter.

BIBLIOGRAPHY
A. D. Trendall and A. Cambitoglou: *The Red-figured Vases of Apulia*, ii (Oxford, 1982), pp. 856–81
——: *The Red-figured Vases of Apulia: Supplement 1* (London, 1983), pp. 146–62
A. D. Trendall: *Red Figure Vases of South Italy and Sicily* (London, 1989), pp. 97–9
A. D. Trendall and A. Cambitoglou: *The Red-figured Vases of Apulia: Supplement 2* (London, 1992), pp. 268–88
MARGOT SCHMIDT

Beldam Painter (*fl* second quarter of the 5th century BC). Greek vase painter. He was the last painter of large Attic Black-figure lekythoi and the first artist to adorn this shape with burial scenes (e.g. Athens, N. Archaeol. Mus., 1982), foreshadowing the tomb-lekythoi of Classical times. He was also the first to paint false-bottomed lekythoi, of which his name vase (Athens, N. Archaeol. Mus., 1129) is the oldest preserved example (*c.* 475 BC). He favoured unusual subjects and dramatic effects, as in his depictions of *Satyrs Tormenting a Woman* (the 'Belle Dame' of his name vase) and *Pirates Drowning Bound Men* (both Athens, N. Archaeol. Mus., 1129 and 487). He also painted smaller lekythoi of inferior quality (chimney-mouthed lekythoi) which are typical mass-produced vases with little variation in form and decoration. The figures on these are small and sketchy; paired lines were often incised into the clay beneath the picture while it was still wet.

The workshop of the Beldam Painter specialized in pattern lekythoi, with ivy, meshwork and chessboard designs, and palmette lekythoi. These were exported in large quantities throughout the Mediterranean area and even copied (e.g. in South Italy). The use of purely ornamental designs was adopted by other workshops for kantharoi, skyphoi and cups. The Beldam Painter probably also produced at least one Red-figure lekythos (Copenhagen, Nmus., 1941).

BIBLIOGRAPHY
C. H. E. Haspels: *Attic Black-figured Lekythoi* (Paris, 1936), pp. 170–91, 266–71
J. D. Beazley: *Red-figure* (1942, 2/1963), i, pp. 750–52
——: *Black-figure* (1956), pp. 586–7, 709
——: *Paralipomena* (1971), pp. 292–4
D. C. Kurtz: *Athenian White Lekythoi* (Oxford, 1975), pp. 18–20, 84–7, 153–5
BETTINA JESKE

Berlin Painter (*fl c.* 500–*c.* 460s BC). Greek vase painter. He is named after a large Type A amphora (Berlin, Antikenmus., 2160) and was among the finest Attic Red-figure vase painters. His paintings often suit the shapes of their vases so beautifully that he probably also made the vases themselves. During his long career he attracted many influential followers.

The exceptional number of works (almost 300) assigned to the Berlin Painter is partly explained by the artist's productivity, but also by his consistent and easily recognizable style. Most of the vases of known provenance come from Italy, especially Vulci, but some fine specimens were found in Athens, including a White-ground plate depicting the goddess *Athena* (Athens, Acropolis Mus., 427). This is the only White-ground piece firmly assigned to the Berlin Painter but, since his pupils often used the technique, he probably produced other similar works. He may also have held the commission for Black-figure

Panathenaic amphorae; a series (e.g. Athens, Acropolis Mus., 981 and Berlin, Antikenmus., 1832) painted in the 460s BC resembles his work but also that of his pupil the ACHILLES PAINTER. At the same time the Berlin Painter used silhouette for a funerary cavalcade beneath the principal, Red-figure scene on his loutrophoros (U. Erlangen, bib., 526). In Attica this type of vase was used exclusively in the practice of cleansing the body before marriage and at death. Hermonax, his pupil, painted many, and the Achilles Painter at least one.

The Berlin Painter decorated many shapes. Amphorae, kraters of various types, pelikai, hydriai and stamnoi are the most common types of his larger pots; among the smaller are oinochoai, Nolan neck amphorae and lekythoi. A pair of phialai (Malibu, CA, Getty Mus., 76.AE.16.1–2) were identified as late as 1976. He may also have decorated cups; one very early and very fine cup (Athens, Agora Mus., P24 113) was assigned to him but may be by a contemporary. It is the only piece possibly associated with the painter that bears a signature, that of the potter Gorgos.

Identifying the earliest work of the Berlin Painter can be difficult, since his style was still developing and the influence of his likely teachers, PHINTIAS and EUTHYMIDES was still strong. Initially, very early vases were assigned to a Nereus Painter and a Vienna Painter. The same problem arises less markedly with the Berlin Painter's late work, which often resembles that of his pupils. At first Beazley (1911) considered these late vases to be 'schoolpieces', but he subsequently apportioned many between the master and his pupils. A quaint and somewhat old-fashioned aspect of his later style also resembles the Mannerism of the young PAN PAINTER. Three of the Berlin Painter's pupils were particularly important: the Providence Painter, whose style was the most Archaic; Hermonax, who was either younger or more Classical; and the Achilles Painter. With their preference for Nolan amphorae and lekythoi, the Providence and Achilles Painters, and the latter's pupil the PHIALE PAINTER, perpetuated the Berlin Painter's influence for nearly a century.

The Berlin Painter's career began when Black-figure was still flourishing, although mainly on smaller vases, including neck amphorae of various types (Panathenaic, large versions with twisted handles, Nolans and doubleens) and lekythoi, and he apparently collaborated with artists specializing exclusively in Black-figure. He also either decorated non-figural black-painted vases with Red-figure patterns or strongly influenced others who did, such as the Group of the Floral Nolans. He frequently accentuated the glossy black backgrounds of his vases by restricting his figures and patterns. His lekythoi sometimes have black bodies and figured shoulders, like those of the Achilles and Phiale Painters, or a single figure overlapping a black shoulder on the Nolan principle. His larger vases rarely have multi-figure friezes but often focus on a single figure or closely-knit group. This spotlight effect is particularly characteristic of the artist, who applied it effectively, even to very large vases, using his figures, poses, gestures, drapery or accoutrements to create interesting and varied silhouettes.

The Berlin Painter apparently also introduced a staple motif of later Red-figure vase painting, the mantle figure or motionless draped male, reproduced with monotonous regularity and great facility on the reverse of the vases. Such figures persisted throughout the 5th century BC, generally grouped in pairs or threes, and they were inherited by South Italian Red-figure artists. The Berlin Painter's following was large because some of his stylistic devices were easily copied. Even the master himself apparently succumbed to something like mass production, judging by the profusion and poor quality of his later work. At the highest point of his career he generally gave more attention to the patterns created by his figures than to the story they told. This too made his style easier to imitate than that of his great contemporary the KLEO-PHRADES PAINTER, who apparently had no following. Despite its grace, the Berlin Painter's work, in contrast to that of the Kleophrades Painter, lacks feeling.

The Berlin Painter often depicted deities; their aloofness and grandeur suited his style (see GREECE, ANCIENT, fig. 110). He also painted athletes and satyrs, but even the latter generally look refined and well-mannered. In his later years he introduced motifs that became popular with his successors: the warrior leaving home and the two-figure pursuit. A few early vases have kalos inscriptions praising youths, and Beazley's original name for the artist, the Socrates Master, derived from one. The artist's best works belong to his early phase, when large shapes predominated: amphorae, neck amphorae, kraters, stamnoi and hydriai, the earliest being of Black-figure type. The draughtsmanship of details of figures and patterns ranges from careful to very fine, even on modest vases. In his middle phase the range of shapes apparently became more restricted and the style of decoration looser. By his late phase Nolans and lekythoi predominated, with some stamnoi and hydriai. The patterns were stereotyped and sometimes careless, and the figures became more angular with less lively contours and sometimes scant detail. The painter's finest work is illustrated by his namepiece, a Type A amphora depicting *Hermes and the Satyr Oreimachos* (see fig.). His teachers, Phintias and Euthymides, had painted the same shape, but quite differently. Here the figures are grouped almost as one and highlighted against the background, which is markedly unrestricted by the patterned frame. The figures float freely on the glossy black surface, supported only by a short decorative band and surmounted by another running around the neck, both with unusual patterns complementing the atypical grouping, in which Hermes extends both arms, holding a jug in one hand and a large kantharos and his staff in the other. He looks ahead as he strides forward, while a fawn noses toward the kantharos, brushing between his legs and those of the satyr, Oreimachos. The names of both are neatly incised beside their heads. As the satyr turns he looks back at his arched tail, which amplifies the contours of Hermes' cloak, and extends his right arm in the same direction while clasping a lyre under his left. The whole design is perfectly suited and subordinated to the vase's shape.

BIBLIOGRAPHY

J. D. Beazley: 'The Master of the Berlin Amphora', *J. Hell. Stud.*, xxxi (1911), pp. 276–95
——: *Der Berliner Maler* (Berlin, 1930; Eng. trans., Melbourne, 1964)
——: *Red-figure* (1942, 2/1963), ii, pp. 1633–5, 1700–01
D. M. Robertson: 'The Gorgos Cup', *Amer. J. Archaeol.*, lxii (1958), pp. 55–66

Berlin Painter: Type A amphora depicting *Hermes and the Satyr Oreimachos*, h. 690 mm, Attic Red-figure, *c.* 480 BC (Berlin, Antikenmuseum)

J. D. Beazley: *Paralipomena* (1971)
J. Boardman: *Athenian Red Figure Vases: The Archaic Period* (London, 1975), pp. 91–5, 111
L. Burn and R. Glynn: *Beazley Addenda: Additional References to* ABV, ARV2 *and* Paralipomena (Oxford, 1982, rev. T. H. Carpenter, 2/1989)
D. C. Kurtz: *The Berlin Painter* (Oxford, 1983)

D. C. KURTZ

Boreads Painter (*fl c.* 575–*c.* 565 BC). Greek vase painter. He was influenced by Corinthian work and was among the earliest Lakonian Black-figure vase painters (*see* GREECE, ANCIENT, §V, 5(iii)), and apparently established the canonical decorative scheme for Lakonian cups, which have an exergue under the main scene in the interior and patterned bands on the exterior with horizontal palmettes by the handles. His surviving output is limited to cups, and these, though numerous, are mostly fragmentary. Most come from Samos, Naukratis and Olympia, none from Sparta. He is named after a vase (Rome, Villa Giulia) depicting *The Boreads Pursuing the Harpies*. Unlike his contemporary the NAUKRATIS PAINTER, he was a narrative artist whose simply painted, lively scenes would have been better suited to long friezes than they were to their constricted cup tondi. In addition to several paintings of the Boreads he depicted *Bellerophon and the Chimaera*, the *Introduction of Herakles to Olympos*, and, more than once, *Herakles and the Hydra* and *Achilles' Ambush of Troilos*. The decoration surrounding the tondi almost always consists of pomegranates. His work was imitated by later Lakonian artists, including his pupil the RIDER PAINTER and the ARKESILAOS PAINTER, and influenced cups from Samos and Chios.

BIBLIOGRAPHY
E. A. Lane: 'Lakonian Vase-painting', *Annu. Brit. Sch. Athens*, xxxiv (1933–4), pp. 130–34
M. Moretti: 'Coppa laconica da Caere', *Archeol. Class.*, iv (1952), pp. 10–13
C. M. Stibbe: *Lakonische Vasenmaler des sechsten Jahrhunderts v. Chr.*, 2 vols (Amsterdam and London, 1972), pp. 87–106

MARIA PIPILI

Brygos Painter (*fl c.* 490–*c.* 470 BC). Greek vase painter. Active in Athens, he was one of the finest Red-figure cup painters of the Late Archaic period. He is named from the potter signature of Brygos, and the potter and painter may in fact have been the same person. His teacher was ONESIMOS, whose influence is apparent in the Brygos Painter's depiction of individualized male figures with hairy chests or receding hairlines, in his portrayal of twisting poses with foreshortened limbs, as well as in the general qualities of liveliness and energy that characterize his work. The Brygos Painter, however, went beyond his teacher in infusing his figures with passion, and in his accomplished rendition of the different stages of human life, from children (e.g. cup, Rome, Vatican, Mus. Gregoriano Etrus., 16582; skyphos, Boston, MA, Mus. F.A., 10.176) to the old and regal (e.g. cup, Paris, Louvre, G 152; skyphos, Vienna, Ksthist. Mus., 3710). His personal hallmarks, such as faces with narrow eyes and expressive mouths and his predilection for dilute glaze washes, were adopted by a large circle of followers.

The Brygos Painter's vases seldom bear inscriptions, and these are often misspelt and include nonsense inscriptions, also found on vases by members of his circle.

Besides the potter signatures on five cups, some individual figures are labelled, or words may be shown issuing from their mouths. *Kalos* names are rare. The Brygos Painter's preferred border for tondo scenes was the stopt meander, often interrupted by cross-squares or chequer-squares. The exterior of the vessel may also have such a border, or simply two reserved lines under the figural scene. The space beneath the handles may be decorated with palmettes or animals such as dogs. The Brygos Painter was an acute observer, and most of his cups depict scenes from daily life: revels, symposia, athletes, warriors with horses, men and youths courting, and erotic scenes. All of these often include lively, inquisitive dogs. Like those of Onesimos, these pictures sometimes have an unsavoury element, but the well-known tondo scene of a youth vomiting, presumably after the party depicted on the cup's exterior, nevertheless has a gentle quality (U. Würzburg, Wagner-Mus., 479; *see* GREECE, ANCIENT, fig. 111). The Brygos Painter's mythological scenes, which are among his finest mature works, are often unusual and inventive, both in terms of the moment depicted and in the composition (e.g. a kantharos depicting *Zeus Pursuing Ganymede*, Boston, MA, Mus. F.A.; *see* GREECE, ANCIENT, fig. 73). A strong interest in suggesting spatial effects is apparent, from the overlapping cattle in the story of the baby Hermes (cup, Rome, Vatican, Mus. Gregoriano Etrus., 16582), or the chariot of Selene seen head-on (cup, Berlin, Schloss Charlottenburg, 2293), to the frequent inclusion of architectural elements, or the indication of roundness and volume with dilute glaze shading.

Like Onesimos and others of his contemporaries, the Brygos Painter also worked in the White-ground technique, producing an oinochoe, an alabastron and several cups including one containing the beautiful Maenad Tondo (Munich, Mus. Ant. Kleinkst, 2645). He was one of the first to distinguish female flesh by the use of a second white. Shapes other than cups decorated by the Brygos Painter include an early kantharos (Boston, MA, Mus. F.A., 95.36), the masterly skyphoi of his mature period depicting revellers (Paris, Louvre, G 156) or the *Ransom of Hektor* (Vienna, Ksthist. Mus., 3710) and the unusual late kalathoid vase showing *Sappho and Alkaios* (Munich, Mus. Ant. Kleinkst, 2416). Other late works include two dozen lekythoi (e.g. Oxford, Ashmolean, 318) and several animal-head rhyta (e.g. in the form of a donkey's head; Paris, Louvre, C 11741).

The Brygos Painter's masterpieces are the cups of his mature period. By contrast, his late work is weak, with elongated figures lacking structure or a sense of energy and individuality. It is hard to tell where the Brygos Painter's oeuvre ends and that of his school begins. His most important followers were the Dokimasia Painter, to whom several vases listed by Beazley as the Brygos Painter's have been attributed, the Briseis Painter and the Foundry Painter.

BIBLIOGRAPHY
J. D. Beazley: *Attic Red-figured Vases in American Museums* (Cambridge, MA, 1918), pp. 89–93
——: *Red-figure* (1942, 2/1963), i, pp. 368–85; ii, pp. 1649, 1701
——: 'Brygan Symposia', *Studies Presented to David Moore Robinson* (St Louis, MO, 1953), pp. 74–83

P. E. Arias and M. Hirmer: *Tausend Jahre griechischer Vasenkunst* (Munich, 1960); Eng. trans. and rev. by B. Shefton as *A History of Greek Vase Painting* (London, 1962), pp. 336–9

A. Cambitoglou: *The Brygos Painter* (Sydney, 1968)

J. D. Beazley: *Paralipomena* (1971), pp. 365–8, 512

M. Wegner: *Brygosmaler* (Berlin, 1973)

J. Boardman: *Athenian Red Figure Vases: The Archaic Period* (London, 1975), pp. 135–7

E. Simon, M. Hirmer and A. Hirmer: *Die griechischen Vasen* (Munich, 1976), pp. 111–16

J. R. Mertens: *Attic White-ground* (New York, 1977), pp. 168–9

L. Burn and R. Glynn: *Beazley Addenda: Additional References to* ABV, ARV2 *and* Paralipomena (Oxford, 1982, rev. T. H. Carpenter, 2/1989), pp. 224–9

D. Williams: 'An Oinochoe in the British Museum and the Brygos Painter's Work on White Ground', *Jb. Berlin. Mus.*, xxiv (1982), pp. 17–40

I. Wehgartner: *Attische weissgründige Keramik* (Mainz, 1983), pp. 56, 58, 85

H. R. Immerwahr: *Attic Script* (Oxford, 1990), pp. 88–9

M. Robertson: *The Art of Vase Painting in Ancient Athens* (Cambridge, 1992), pp. 93–100

DIANA BUITRON

C Painter (*fl c.* 575–*c.* 555 BC). Greek vase painter and potter. Active in Athens, the C Painter (C for Corinthianizing) is the earliest known painter of the Siana cup (named after a village in Rhodes where the cups were first found), as well as of the lip-cup (with high-stemmed foot and offset lip) and the Merrythought cup (with nearly hemispherical bowl and knobbed wishbone handles). His work also includes skyphoi, lekanides, tripod-kothons and votive plates (for vase shapes *see* GREECE, ANCIENT, §V, 1(ii)(a) and fig. 71). Siana cups, however, formed his main production: about 140 cups and fragments have been attributed to him.

In his early period (*c.* 575–*c.* 570 BC) he painted mainly winged female figures in the tondos of his cups; borders were usually a band of tongues and one dotted band. On the outside he depicted combats, cavalcades and symposia, and the heroes Achilles and Troilos. The figures are thickset, with meticulous incision.

In his middle period (*c.* 570–*c.* 565 BC) the C Painter's tondos usually depicted running warriors and sometimes mythological figures; the borders were bands of tongues with one or two dotted bands. Subjects on the outside of his cups included the usual early-period motifs and such new ones as heroic fights and gatherings, and mythological scenes of pursuit. The style is ornate, with ornamental fillings in the field, elaborate incision and an abundance of added colours. There is a greater freedom of composition compared with other periods. Based on their style of drawing and painting, the C Painter's Merrythought cup in Würzburg (U. Würzburg; Wagner-Mus., L 451) and two double-decker Siana cups (London, BM, B380, and Athens, N. Archaeol. Mus., 531) must date to this period, as well as skyphoi, lekanis lids, tripod-kothons and votive plates. The finest examples of his oeuvre are found among these works, particularly his tripod-kothons and lekanis lids.

The cups attributed to his late period (*c.* 565–*c.* 560 BC) are larger than earlier ones. Apart from the familiar designs, the tondos often feature a winged youth who may be interpreted as the male counterpart of Nike, the messenger of victory gained in games. Borders are mainly a band of tongues either alone or combined with a single dotted band. Sporting scenes are depicted in great numbers on the outside of the cups: horse races replace the earlier military cavalcades, and gatherings of riders or of men and youths (return of the victorious athletes and jockeys) are common. This interest in sport may have been occasioned by Peisistratos' reorganization of the Panathenaic games in *c.* 566 BC. In other scenes, mythological escapes replace scenes of pursuit, and symposion scenes virtually disappear; heroic fights are replaced by scenes of ordinary combat. Added colours are used much less than in the middle period, and the incisions are more casual.

In his final period (*c.* 560–*c.* 555 BC), the C Painter produced very large cups showing mainly animals in the tondos and a single band of tongues for the border. The painter reverted to familiar subjects—symposia, komos scenes, combats. Some of the cups from this phase have an undecorated exterior, and little use is made of added colours; black is often thinly applied, giving a brownish effect, and the incisions are faint.

The C Painter was the master of a Siana-cup workshop that existed in Athens for some 30 years. At least ten artisans from the workshop can be distinguished. The eldest, the Cassandra Painter, worked from *c.* 570 to *c.* 565 BC. The Taras Painter (referred to by Beazley as the Shadow of the C Painter) and the Malibu Painter joined the workshop in the mid-560s; the latter worked there for some 15 years and the former until the very end of the workshop in *c.* 540 BC. The Vintage Painter, the Adelph Painter, the Double-palmette Painter and the Omobono Painter worked from *c.* 560 BC to *c.* 555 BC; the Painter of the Burgon Sianas and the Epignote Painter joined the workshop in the 550s.

See also GREECE, ANCIENT, §V, 5(ii)(b).

BIBLIOGRAPHY

H. A. G. Brijder: *Siana Cups I and Komast Cups*, Allard Pierson Series, iv (Amsterdam, 1983)

Corp. Vasorum Ant., Athens, National Museum, iii (1986), pls 7–11

H. A. G. Brijder: 'C Painter', *Siana Cups II: The Heidelberg Painter*, Allard Pierson Series viii (Amsterdam, 1991), p. 513

——: 'Simply Decorated, Black Siana Cups by the Taras Painter and Cassel Cups', *Bull. Ant. Besch.*, lxviii (1993), pp. 129–45

H. A. G. BRIJDER

Chicago Painter (*fl c.* 460–*c.* 450 BC). Greek vase painter. He is named after an Attic stamnos depicting preparations for a Dionysiac ritual (Chicago, IL, A. Inst., 89.22). He was a pupil of the VILLA GIULIA PAINTER (*see* below), and painted all his vases in the Red-figure technique, preferring large pots, especially stamnoi, kraters and hydriai. He also decorated smaller shapes, including pelikai, oinochoai, a lekythos, a pyxis and a cup. Nearly 50 vases by him are known.

The Chicago Painter clearly based his style on that of his teacher, who generally painted stock figures in unimaginative compositions. However, his own figures are less stiff and interact more successfully. Many appear too tall and thin, while the tops of their heads are exaggeratedly rounded and heavy. They are often active and gesture expressively with their hands. The artist's favourite subject was maenads making ready for a Dionysiac festival, perhaps the Lenaia, though it is confined to stamnoi, such as his name-piece. He also favoured departure and pursuit scenes, while the most noteworthy of his few mythological pictures, on a pelike (Lecce, Mus. Prov. Sigismondo Castromediano, 570), shows *Polyneikes Bribing Eriphyle with the Necklace of Harmonia.*

BIBLIOGRAPHY
J. D. Beazley: *Red-figure* (1942, 2/1963), i, pp. 628–32; ii, pp. 1662–3
G. M. A. Richter: *Attic Red-figured Vases* (New Haven, 1946, 2/1958), pp. 105–6
B. Philippaki: *The Attic Stamnos* (Oxford, 1967), pp. 110–19

JOHN H. OAKLEY

Darius Painter (*fl c.* 340–*c.* 330 BC). Vase painter, active in Apulia. Possibly active in Tarentum, he was the leading artist in his field of his time, exercising a strong influence on late Apulian vase painting in general (*see also* UNDER-WORLD PAINTER below). The Darius Painter is named after his monumental volute krater in Naples (h. 1.3 m; Mus. Archeol. N., 81947) depicting the Persian king Darius, who is identified by an inscription, and his entourage listening to a messenger. This elaborate, multi-figured scene may relate to an historical event at the beginning of the Ionian Revolt in 499 BC (i.e. more than 150 years before the painter's own time), which was reported by Herodotos (*Histories* V.cv–cvii). The rare or unique subjects of many of his other works, which are sometimes identified by inscriptions accompanying the main characters, also evince his surprising erudition. Unusually, instead of always depicting heroes, he frequently chose myths involving well-known heroines, such as Andromeda, Antigone, Antiope and Kreousa, and more obscure female figures such as Rhodope (calyx krater; Basle, Antikenmus., S34) and the daughters of the Delian king Anios, who actually occur twice (calyx krater, Miami, priv. col.; loutrophoros, Naples, priv. col.).

Like most late Apulian vases, those by the Darius Painter with known provenances were discovered in tombs. Their subjects may therefore contain some funerary symbolism, but, unlike many of his colleagues, the Darius Painter rarely adopted the more explicitly funerary scenes centred on grave monuments.

His monumental volute kraters, such as the Darius Krater and its companion piece from the same chamber tomb at Canosa representing the *Funeral of Patroklos* (h. 1.42 m; Naples, Mus. Archeol. N., 81393; *see* GREECE, ANCIENT, fig. 119), provide excellent examples of the artist's characteristic multi-figured compositions. These are arranged in several horizontal registers, with subtle correspondences and interactions between the different elements, apparently designed to stress the causes and consequences of human or divine actions. More aesthetically appealing are some of his medium-sized compositions on calyx kraters and bell kraters. Here the figures are normally disposed in two registers, the upper one being often reserved for the gods, who appear to be contemplating the mythological scenes enacted below. The reverses often depict scenes of Dionysos and his companions, perhaps an allusion to the bliss of the afterlife, given their funerary context. Minor vases, notably pelikai, from the Darius Painter's workshop often depict bridal preparations.

The Darius Painter was a gifted draughtsman. The details of his figures are painted in fine and fluid lines, while stronger and bolder strokes emphasize their different poses. Though, like his forerunners, he used stock figures and conventional poses, he conveyed the dramatic spirit of his sources, drawn from mythology, and possibly more indirectly, from Greek drama. Moreover, despite the heterogeneity of his models, he succeeded in developing an individualistic style. Among his finest achievements was the use of the three-quarter view to express a wide range of emotions, from quiet grief to fury and frenzy. His apparent interest in physiognomy is demonstrated in his masterly rendering of the agitated countenance of Oedipus, absorbed in the crucial dialogue with the blind Teiresias on a small oinochoe (Basle, Antikenmus., BS 473). Rather than aiming at psychological realism, he developed pictorial formulae (e.g. the shape of brows, lips etc) to express and define emotion and pathos. In evolving what might be termed his grammar of physiognomy, he may have explored to some extent the possibilities inherent in contemporary theoretical treatises (for discussion of these *see* GREECE, ANCIENT, §VI, 3). The vases from his mature period, which may date as late as *c.* 320 BC, evince fuller use of added colours, such as purple-red and yellowish white.

BIBLIOGRAPHY
M. Schmidt: *Der Dareiosmaler und sein Umkreis* (Münster, 1960)
A. D. Trendall and A. Cambitoglou: *The Red-figured Vases of Apulia*, ii (Oxford, 1982), pp. 482–508
——: *The Red-figured Vases of Apulia: Supplement 1* (London, 1983), pp. 73–80
A. D. Trendall: *Red Figure Vases of South Italy and Sicily* (London, 1989)
A. D. Trendall and A. Cambitoglou: *The Red-figured Vases of Apulia: Supplement 2* (London, 1992), pp. 145–54

MARGOT SCHMIDT

Dipylon Master (*fl c.* 760–*c.* 735 BC). Greek vase painter. His work belongs to the first stage of the Late Geometric (LG) style, and he is named after the Dipylon cemetery in Athens, for which he and his workshop made many huge funerary vessels (*see* GREECE, ANCIENT, fig. 85). These vases were used to mark aristocratic graves and to receive libations for the dead (belly-handled amphorae for female burials, pedestalled kraters for male). All such monumental vessels are decorated with a *prothesis* scene in which the bier of the deceased is surrounded by mourners. On kraters, the *prothesis* includes a following of armed warriors and chariot teams; battle scenes, either on land or at sea, may occur elsewhere on the vase. Subsidiary zones contain rectilinear geometric ornament, with the key meander as an important motif. Amphorae may also be decorated with friezes of goats and deer, adapted from Levantine ivories and metal bowls. Most of the Dipylon vases were excavated in the late 19th century and are now in either Athens (N. Archaeol. Mus.) or Paris (Louvre). Some 50 vases have been attributed to the Dipylon Master's workshop, and fine examples of the Dipylon Master's own work include an amphora in Athens (N. Archaeol. Mus., 804) and a krater in Paris (Louvre, A 517). His career marks a sudden flourishing of large-scale figural drawing after the Dark Age, when representational motifs on pottery had been extremely rare.

The Dipylon Master is the first recognizable artistic personality in Greek vase painting with a consistent figural style. His humans, in dark silhouette, are hardly less 'geometric' than the abstract ornament surrounding them, and his figures of mourners tearing their hair are especially characteristic: the thorax and raised arms form a tall isosceles triangle, with angles at waist and elbows; the head and lower body are in profile, and curves are minimal. Overlapping figures are avoided, and the viewpoint is varied so that every limb is visible. Thus, however elaborate the scene, the function of each figure, whether mourner, warrior, archer, charioteer or rower, is clearly defined. Foot-soldiers carry the 'Dipylon shield', its sides cut back to reveal the warrior's arms. This may represent a contemporary shield type, or a 'heroic' reminiscence of the Minoan–Mycenaean figure-of-eight shield at a time when epic poetry was already in circulation. The Dipylon Master's rendering of animals and inanimate objects is equally clear, simple and conceptual. In *prothesis* scenes, the chequered shroud is lifted to reveal the deceased on the bier. Chariots are shown with their two wheels side by side, although the box is in profile. In manned warships, both sides of the ship are shown so that all rowers may be visible. Animals, always in silhouette, are distinguished by pose as well as by anatomical details: chariot horses stand facing forwards, deer graze, goats recline looking backwards. Within the figural fields, light filling ornaments occupy the background, softening the contrast between bold silhouette figures and hatched geometric ornament elsewhere on the vessel.

Several different painters within the workshop can be distinguished from variations in the figure drawing, especially in the 'Dipylon shields'. Sometimes the work of two artists occurs on the same krater. Vases from the workshop's later stage, exemplified by a krater in Paris (Louvre, A 552), depict only the *prothesis* with retinue, with no battle scenes. In addition to the monumental vessels with funerary scenes, the Dipylon Master's workshop also produced large round-mouthed pitchers, neck-handled amphorae, oinochoai, tankards and high-rimmed bowls, decorated with animal friezes or with linear ornament alone.

BIBLIOGRAPHY

F. Villard: *Corp. Vasorum Ant.*, France fascicle 18, Louvre fascicle 11, (Paris, 1954)

J. M. Davison: *Attic Geometric Workshops*, Yale Class. Stud. xvi (New Haven, 1961), pp. 21–36, 133–40

J. N. Coldstream: *Greek Geometric Pottery* (London, 1968), pp. 29–41

NICOLAS COLDSTREAM

Douris (*fl c.* 500–*c.* 460 BC). Greek vase painter and potter. Active in Athens, he worked in the Red-figure technique, and his exceptionally long career extended from the end of the Archaic period until late in the Early Classical period. Of his extensive output (at least 280 vases are attributed to him by Beazley), he signed some 40, most as the painter, though some as potter. However, this does not mean that he established his own workshop only later in his career, since his signatures as a potter occur on early vases, and painting was clearly his principal activity. He evidently also had a considerable school from early in his career. Douris must have been well known among other vase painters, for his name regularly occurs in their work. The picture on the inside of a cup by Onesimos (from Cerveteri; Brunswick, ME, Bowdoin Coll. Mus. A., 1930.1) shows a woman with a skyphos clearly signed by Douris. His name appears quite frequently in the work of the Cartellino Painter, and a cup by the Triptolemos Painter (from Cerveteri; Berlin, Staatl. Museen Preuss. Kultbes., 2286), who must have been his pupil, is signed with his name, possibly to increase its value.

Beazley divided Douris' work into four phases, corresponding to alterations in both the ornamentation and the *kalos* names used in inscriptions (*see* GREECE, ANCIENT, §V, 1(vi)(c)). In the first phase Douris experimented with matching the painted decoration to the form of the vessel, still largely employing the Late Archaic repertory. He created some superb pieces notable for the fineness of their draughtsmanship, including a signed aryballos depicting a youth and a young woman (from Athens; Athens, N. Archaeol. Mus., T.E. 556). Ornamentation is rich and there are impressive compositions, particularly in the tondo pictures inside cups, which may even have additional friezes round the inner rim. The second phase is marked by greater simplicity, with the proportions of the figures becoming more compact, especially in sporting scenes. Douris adopted the hooked representation of the collarbone that other painters had abandoned long before. In the third phase his characteristic style appears not only in the composition but also in such details as thick hems on garments and clusters of brushstrokes in the narrow parallel folds, and in such ornaments as the alternating meander squares and crossed panels framing his pictures. There is greater richness of ornament, in contrast to the generally routine quality of these pieces. Banquet scenes are more frequent, with back views demonstrating Douris' adoption of the most recent developments in perspective, if in a rather schematized way. The fourth phase is largely a continuation of the third, not least in the increasingly rich decoration, though it is differentiated by such details as the doubling of the meander squares in the inside frames. Besides cups, which constitute 90% of his output, other shapes were introduced, including the skyphos, rhyton, oinochoe, kantharos and psykter. His lekythoi include some fine white-ground examples, painted in great detail. None of these late pieces is signed.

Of the subjects treated, everyday scenes account for over half; the rest are mostly fighting scenes, some of them mythological. The mythological scenes are particularly interesting and include *Eos Carrying the Dead Memnon* (*see* GREECE, ANCIENT, fig. 81), the *Fight for Achilles' Weapons*, the *Gigantomachy*, the *Amazonomachy*, the *Exploits of Theseus*, and several versions of the *Fight between Peleus and Thetis*. A unique variant of the story of Jason is depicted inside a cup (from Cerveteri; Rome, Vatican), showing Jason hanging out of the dragon's mouth in the presence of Athena, and a psykter (London, BM, E 768) with *Satyrs at Play* is particularly outstanding.

BIBLIOGRAPHY

E. Pottier: *Douris et les peintres de vases grecs* (Paris, 1907)

J. C. Hoppin: *A Handbook of Attic Red-figured Vases*, i (Cambridge, MA, 1919), pp. 208–91

J. D. Beazley: *Red-figure* (1942, 2/1963), i, pp. 425–53, ii, pp. 1651–3, 1701

M. Wegner: *Duris: Ein künstlermonographischer Versuch* (Münster, 1968)

J. D. Beazley: *Paralipomena* (1971), pp. 374–6, 521

J. Boardman: *Athenian Red Figure Vases: The Archaic Period* (London, 1975), pp. 137–40

D. M. Buitron: *Douris* (diss., New York U., 1976)

L. Burn and R. Glynn: *Beazley Addenda: Additional References to* ABV, ARV2 *and* Paralipomena (Oxford, 1982, rev. T. H. Carpenter, 2/1989), pp. 235–42

D. Buitron-Oliver: *Douris: A Master-painter of Athenian Red-figure Vases*, Kerameus, i (Mainz, 1995)

REINHARD STUPPERICH

Epiktetos (*fl c.* 520–*c.* ?480 BC). Greek vase painter. Active in Athens, he was one of the major artists of the first generation of Attic Red-figure vase painters, and he signed his name on over 40 vases, often misspelling the accompanying verb. Over 112 vases by him survive: most are cups, but larger shapes include calyx kraters, a volute krater, skyphoi, kantharoi and an oinochoe. Some of his finest work is on plates.

Epiktetos' earliest vase, also one of the earliest known examples of the shape, is a calyx krater (Rome, Villa Giulia), signed on the foot by Andokides as potter. Epiktetos may well have begun his career in the workshop of Andokides, but the painter with whom in general he had most affinity, sharing a similar delicacy and precision of line, was Psiax, who also collaborated with the potter Andokides. Epiktetos' earliest cups were bilingual eye-cups, painted first for Nikosthenes' workshop and soon after for Hischylos': like Oltos, he appears to have changed workshops frequently. Epiktetos' Black-figure work is confined to the tondi of these early eye-cups, which carried figures in action, such as revellers, warriors or animals. Between the eyes of the Red-figure exteriors, figures in action also occur, for example the squatting, frontal satyr on a cup in Würzburg University (Wagner-Mus., 468). This early example of a favoured motif shows that, almost from the start of his career, Epiktetos had an interest in rendering complex poses, an interest taken up by the Pioneer Group. This early work also includes a kantharos signed by Nikosthenes as potter (Odessa, A. Mus.). Epiktetos' early style is characterized by a slight awkwardness; the figures are stiff, with outsized heads. The borders of the hair are incised, whereas in later examples the contour is reserved.

The interiors of the cups painted for Hischylos show Epiktetos' Black-figure style at its finest. The figures are elegant and the compositions skilful. The cups' Red-figure exteriors are initially rougher, as Epiktetos continued his exploration of figures in motion, but a degree of accomplishment equal to his Black-figure work soon appears, reaching a great facility in drawing combined with graceful energy. To this phase also belong his Red-figure palmette eye-cups painted for Pamphaios, and the series of signed plates, which particularly demonstrate his superb balance of sinuous line and control of the circular field. Three of these (London, BM, E 135–7) show respectively an archer, a warrior with a horse, and two revellers. No kalos inscriptions appear in Epiktetos' early works, but Hipparchos is praised on a series of Red-figure cups of his mature period. These are decorated on both interior and exterior with mythological subjects, such as *Theseus and the Minotaur*, *Herakles and Busiris* and *Achilles and Ajax*, and with scenes from daily life, such as revels or symposia (e.g. a cup-skyphos depicting *Serving the Wine*; Oxford, Ashmolean; *see* GREECE, ANCIENT, fig. 72). Together these scenes show Epiktetos' predilection for swift, graceful action and succinct characterization, along with his developing ability

to show the body in unusual poses. His cups of this period have palmettes at the handles, the most elaborate of which is on a cup (London, BM, E 38) signed by the potter Python, who also worked extensively with the painter Douris.

Epiktetos continued to paint bilingual eye-cups into his mature phase, but his greater freedom of drawing style conflicted with the old-fashioned decorative format, and he soon abandoned it. He experimented with coral red on at least two cups and collaborated on two others with the Euergides Painter, who painted the Red-figure exteriors. In his late period Epiktetos collaborated with Pistoxenos, who signed as potter on a skyphos (London, BM, E 139). Epiktetos' later work shows the influence of the Pioneer Group in the depiction of complex or unusual poses. However, though his long career spanned the transition from Archaic to Classical art, he never abandoned his essentially Archaic drawing style.

BIBLIOGRAPHY

J. D. Beazley: *Attic Red-figured Vases in American Museums* (Cambridge, MA, 1918), pp. 14–18

W. Kraiker: 'Epiktetos: Eine Studie zur archaischen attischen Malerei', *Jb. Dt. Archäol. Inst.*, xliv (1929), pp. 141–97

J. D. Beazley: *Red-figure* (1942, 2/1963), i, pp. 70–79; ii, pp. 1623–4, 1705

P. Arias and M. Hirmer: *Tausend Jahre griechischer Vasenkunst* (Munich, 1960); Eng. trans. by B. Shefton as *A History of Greek Vase Painting* (London, 1962), pp. 319–20

A. MacSweeney: 'A Red Figured Eye-cup by Epiktetos and Pamphaios', *Allen Mem. A. Mus. Bull.*, xxv/3 (1968), pp. 104–13

J. D. Beazley: *Paralipomena* (1971), pp. 328–9

J. Boardman: *Athenian Red Figure Vases: The Archaic Period* (London, 1975), pp. 57–9

M. Robertson: 'Beazley and After', *Münchn. Jb. Bild. Kst*, xxvii (1976), pp. 29–46

E. Simon, M. Hirmer and A. Hirmer: *Die griechischen Vasen* (Munich, 1976), pp. 96–7

H. Giroux: *Corp. Vasorum. Ant.*, Fr. fasc. 28, Louvre fasc. 19 (Paris, 1977), pp. 14, 21, 24

B. Cohen: *Attic Bilingual Vases and their Painters* (New York, 1978), pp. 400–38

K. Schefold: *Götter- und Heldensagen der Griechen in der spätarchaischen Kunst* (Munich, 1978), pp. 65, 134–5, 151

L. Burn and R. Glynn: *Beazley Addenda: Additional References to* ABV, ARV2 *and* Paralipomena (Oxford, 1982, rev. T. H. Carpenter, 2/1989), pp. 166–9

H. R. Immerwahr: *Attic Script* (Oxford, 1990), pp. 61–3

M. Robertson: *The Art of Vase Painting in Classical Athens* (Cambridge, 1992), pp. 16–18

DIANA BUITRON

Eretria Painter (*fl c.* 440–*c.* 415 BC). Greek vase painter. He was among the most prolific and original Classical Athenian Red-figure artists and was named after an epinetron from Eretria (Athens, N. Archaeol. Mus., 1629). Almost 150 vases painted by him survive, of which about 90 are cups, the rest including various shapes of pots and two epinetra. Of the cups, 80 come from one workshop, which also employed three lesser artists, the Calliope Painter, the Disney Painter and the Painter of the Naples Hydriskai. When depicting athletes and youths the Eretria Painter usually adhered to standard workshop designs. However, he devised his own compositions for dancing satyrs and Amazons (cups, Taranto, Mus. N., 8720; Naples, Mus. Archeol. N., H 2613). He produced unusual depictions of the deeds of Theseus and used inscriptions to transform a common departure scene into an episode from the Trojan War, one of his favourite subjects (cup, Ferrara, Mus. N. Archeol., T 128). He probably also portrayed the Thessalians who arrived to support Athens early in the Peloponnesian War (cup, Malibu, CA, Getty Mus., 85.AE.474).

Although the Eretria Painter apparently painted mainly cups, his best work is on pots, which he decorated for at least six different workshops. Early in his career he painted a pair of large oinochoai showing *King Pandion Leaving his Family* (Palermo, Mus. Reg., L.N.I.484) and *Herakles Attacking the Sacred Hind* (Agrigento, Mus. Reg. Archeol., V 1568). On these vases his style is close to that of the KODROS PAINTER, as also on a cup with *Athletes and Trainers* (Paris, Louvre, G 457). On one early and one late rare Type D kantharos (Paris, Bib. N., R 851; Taranto, Mus. N.), depicting respectively *Achilles and Patroklos Leaving Phthia* and *Menelaos and Odysseus Waiting at Troy after Requesting the Return of Helen*, he shows a preference for finely drawn, miniature figures and for Trojan themes.

Another one of the Eretria Painter's favourite subjects was women. Thus a pyxis (London, BM, E 774) depicts *Women Bringing Gifts to a Bride on the Morning after her Wedding*. By adding the names of Nereids he transformed the scene into a mythic sphere, as he did on his namepiece, which has three scenes connected with marriage. In one, Harmonia prepares for her wedding under the supervision of Aphrodite and her attendants. In another Peleus and Thetis wrestle, symbolizing the physical union of man and woman. In the third Alkestis receives her female friends and relatives on the day after her wedding to Admetos. Few other vase painters combined three related scenes so artfully on a single vase; the Eretria Painter did so again on his tallboy lekythos (New York, Met., 31.11.13). This depicts women in corresponding scenes, but connected with death, and combines two Redfigure friezes with a White-ground frieze, the technique for funerary vases.

The Eretria Painter also produced some unique Dionysiac scenes. Thus two choes (Athens, Vlasto priv. col., see Lezzi-Hafter, ii, pls 136–7) depict scenes from the Anthesteria, the springtime festival of Dionysos at Athens, while the Dionysiac revel labelled with island names (cup, Warsaw, N. Mus., 142458) may represent a lost comedy.

On choes and lekythoi, the Eretria Painter worked with AISON and the MEIDIAS PAINTER, whereas on a ram's head rhyton (Ferrara, Mus. N. Archeol., T 5) he took up the tradition of the SOTADES PAINTER. However, because he worked in different workshops, the Eretria Painter left no true successor, despite his long career.

BIBLIOGRAPHY

A. Furtwängler: *Vasen*, i of *Die Sammlung Sabouroff* (Berlin, 1883), pp. 4–8, text to pl. LV

J. D. Beazley: *Red-figure* (1942, 2/1963), ii, pp. 1247–55, 1688, 1704–5, 1708

B. Schweitzer: *Mythische Hochzeiten*, vi of *Sitzungsberichte der Heidelberger Akademie der Wissenschaften Philosophisch-historische Klasse* (Heidelberg, 1961)

J. D. Beazley: *Paralipomena* (1971), pp. 469–70, 522

I. Jucker: 'Kephalos im Göttergarten', *Beiheft Ant. Kst*, ix (1973), pp. 63–8

A. Lezzi-Hafter: *Der Eretria-Maler*, 2 vols (Mainz, 1988)

Data courtesy of the Beazley Archive, Oxford University.

ADRIENNE LEZZI-HAFTER

Euphronios (*fl c.* 520–*c.* 500 BC). Greek vase painter and potter. He signed eight Attic vases as painter, while two of his calyx kraters (New York, Met., 1972.11.10 and Paris, Louvre, G 33) are signed by the potter Euxitheos and two of his cups (Munich, Staatl. Antikensamml., 2620 and Paris, Louvre, Cp 11981) by the potter Kachrylion. All date from before 500 BC. Thereafter, the artist apparently concentrated exclusively on making pots: he signed at least 12 cups decorated by other painters, the latest (*c.* 470 BC; Berlin, Antikenmus., 2282) being by the Pistoxenos Painter, while an inscription on a pillar monument that Euphronios dedicated on the Athenian Acropolis (see A. Raubitschek: *Dedications from the Athenian Akropolis*, Cambridge, MA, 1949, pp. 255–8, no. 225) calls him 'the Potter'.

Euphronios was undoubtedly the most talented of the Red-figure Pioneer group (*see also* EUTHYMIDES and PHINTIAS). Not only was he the best draughtsman, but he was also the first painter to use dilute glaze lines and relief contours to produce rich decorative compositions, and his successful technical experiments profoundly influenced the work of his immediate successors, particularly the BERLIN PAINTER and the KLEOPHRADES PAINTER.

Euphronios was the first painter to favour the calyx krater, whose shape was probably invented by EXEKIAS, and they rank among his best works. He also painted a volute krater, stamnoi, neck amphorae, neck pelikai (a rare variant), a hydria, psykters, several cups and a fragmentary plate. His style was monumental and best suited to large surfaces. However, he also successfully decorated smaller formats such as cups (e.g. Munich, Staatl. Antikensamml., 2620). His compositions often contain many figures with considerable overlapping and foreshortening. Good examples occur on three calyx kraters (Dallas, TX, priv. col., see Vermeule, pp. 34–9; New York, Met., 1972.11.10; Paris, Louvre, G 103) and on his volute krater (Arezzo, Mus. Archeol. Mecenate, 1465). All attest to his particular interest in anatomy.

Euphronios' paintings generally depict heroic scenes or scenes of Athenian daily life. His depictions of Herakles are especially memorable. Louvre G 103 shows *Herakles Wrestling with Antaeus*. His right arm is under the giant's left armpit, his left around his neck, hands gripped together tightly. Euphronios has brilliantly contrasted the hero's neat hair and beard and tense profile with the giant's dishevelled hair and beard, bared teeth and helpless frontal pose, probably deliberately juxtaposing Herakles' straining right foot with Antaeus' limp right hand. At the same time, the drama is heightened by three women rushing about, gesturing excitedly. The hero's declawed lion skin, bow and quiver complete the composition.

Herakles is also depicted on Arezzo 1465, this time as *Herakles Fighting the Amazons*. Though three confront him, they seem to have little chance as he strides forward, bow outstretched, brandishing his club. A fourth Amazon has sunk down wounded while another is about to be slain by Telamon. On the other side of the vase four more Amazons run up, presumably as reinforcements. The splendid calyx krater in Dallas shows *Herakles Killing Kyknos* (the son of Ares who robbed Apollo of sacrificial victims on their way to Delphi). Kyknos falls backwards, his face frontal and contorted in pain as blood pours from his wounds, while Athena moves in to keep Ares at bay with her aegis over her outstretched arm.

Finally, *Herakles Stealing the Cattle of Geryon* appears on the exterior of a cup (Munich, Staatl. Antikensamml., 2620), the cattle on one side, the fight on the other. One of Geryon's three monstrous bodies is wounded, as is his herdsman Eurytion, while his guard dog, Orthos, lies dead.

The New York calyx krater has a rare but memorable scene from the Trojan War: *The Rescue of the Body of Sarpedon*, the Lycian king killed by Patroklos (*see* GREECE, ANCIENT, fig. 109). Sarpedon's youthful body extends almost across the whole width of the vase as Sleep and Death lift it to take it away for burial. Blood pours from his wounds, while his one visible heavily lashed eye is closed and his teeth are clenched. Hermes stands behind the group ready to guide them, while they are flanked by Laodamos and Hippolytos.

Euphronios' scenes of daily life are also among his best. One of the most important is the *Symposion* (drinking party) on the fragmentary calyx krater in Munich (Staatl. Antikensamml., 8935) where one of the participants is labelled *Smikros*, probably Euphronios' fellow Pioneer of that name. The scene extends over both sides of the vase, showing the symposiasts singing and drinking to the accompaniment of a female flute player. A smaller symposion scene appears on each side of the neck of a neck amphora (Paris, Louvre, G 30), showing one youth playing kottabos (flicking the dregs of his wine), another accompanying himself on the lyre. Finally, a variant symposion scene, involving nude women, occurs on a psykter (St Petersburg, Hermitage, 644). Meanwhile, the reverse of the Antaeus krater depicts a *Musical Contest* with a youth stepping up to the podium, flutes in hand, in front of three youths. Athletes occur on each side of the small calyx krater (Berlin, Antikenmus., 2180) in poses that have an almost photographic quality of 'frozen moments', testifying to Euphronios' powers of observation. Several are boldly foreshortened, like many of Euphronios' other figures. Other scenes of daily life appear on the pelike in the University of Chicago and the Villa Giulia, Rome (Beazley, 1963): on one side a boy ties a man's sandal; on the other a youth plays with a marten, while the reverse of the New York calyx krater shows young men arming for battle and the inside of the Munich cup shows a youthful horseman in a Thracian cloak.

Euphronios was the first Red-figure painter to exploit the new technique, and though his extant output is rather small, his influence on the next generation of artists was pervasive. His amply proportioned figures, large-scale compositions and technical brilliance opened up an entirely new approach to the decoration of Greek vases.

BIBLIOGRAPHY

J. D. Beazley: *Red-figure* (1942, 2/1963), i, pp. 13–17
E. Vermeule: 'Fragments of a Symposium by Euphronios', *Ant. Kst*, viii (1965), pp. 34–9
J. D. Beazley: *Paralipomena* (1971), pp. 321–2
D. von Bothmer: 'Der Euphronioskrater in New York', *Archäol. Anz.*, 91 (1976), pp. 485–512
J. Frel: 'Euphronios and his Fellows', *Ancient Greek Art and Iconography*, ed. W. G. Moon (Madison, 1983), pp. 147–58

Euthymides (*fl c.* 515–*c.* 500 BC). Greek vase painter. Euthymides signed eight Athenian vases, six as painter, the other two as potter, one of which, an oinochoe (New York, Met., 1981.11.9), he clearly did not paint. Like EUPHRONIOS (*see* above) and PHINTIAS (*see* below), Euthymides was a member of the Pioneer group of artists who explored the possibilities of the recently invented Red-figure technique. His inscription *Euphronios never did anything this good* on the back of a Type A amphora (Munich, Staatl. Antikensamml., 2307) is probably a playful challenge to the younger artist rather than a taunt and clearly implies that painters were aware of each other's work.

Euthymides favoured Type A amphorae and kalpides, but he also painted three neck amphorae, including one (Warsaw, N. Mus., 142332) with twisted handles (a new feature), a pelike, a volute krater, a psykter, a cylindrical stand, a plate and two cups. His compositions are simple and legible, with big bold figures that rarely overlap. However, he delighted in foreshortening. His subjects range from mythological scenes to scenes of everyday life. His cylindrical stand (Athens, Agora Mus., P 4683) depicts a moment of tranquillity among the gods, with Apollo holding his lyre and standing between Leto and Artemis, while the contrasting *Gigantomachy* on a fragmentary cup (Athens, Acropolis Mus., 211) attests to Olympian unity in the face of an external threat. Dionysiac scenes appear on three hydriai, two with Dionysos sitting between satyrs and/or maenads (St Petersburg, Hermitage, 624 (St. 1624) and Orvieto, Mus. Etrus. Faina, 68), the third with a satyr creeping up on two nude women at a fountain (ex-Frankfurt am Main; see Beazley, 1971). The komasts on Munich 2307 are in a similar spirit. The most famous heroic scene is the *Arming of Hektor* on Munich 2307 where Hektor's parents gaze at him with an intensity that seems to be a premonition of his death. A similar but less dramatic composition occurs in the *Arming of Thorykion* on a Type A amphora (Munich, Staatl. Antikensamml., 2308). On another Type A amphora (Munich, Staatl. Antikensamml., 2309), Theseus carries off Helen, who is wrongly labelled as Korone. The powerful drawing and bold foreshortening in this scene show Euthymides at the height of his powers. A large painting of *Herakles Fighting the Amazons* occurs on the neck of the volute krater in Serra Orlando (Morgantina Mus.), a rugged composition possibly inspired by the *Amazonomachy* on Euphronios' volute krater in Arezzo (Mus. Archeol. Mecenate, 1465). Finally, Euthymides' scenes of Athenian daily life include the athletes with their trainer on Munich 2308, also depicted on his psykter in Turin (Mus. Civ. A. Ant., 4123), and the youth pouring wine from a pointed amphora and the symposia on his volute krater in Serra Orlando and on the hydria in Bonn (Rhein. Friedrich-Wilhelms-U., 70).

BIBLIOGRAPHY

J. D. Beazley: *Red-figure* (1942, 2/1963), i, pp. 26–9
——: *Paralipomena* (1971), pp. 323–4, 520

Exekias (*fl c.* 540–*c.* 520 BC). Greek vase painter. He signed two Attic Black-figure vases as potter and painter and eleven simply as potter. Only about 40 pieces by him survive. His drawing style is sure, his line elegant and refined and his human and animal figures always have a noble look. His sensitivity to the intricate relationship between a vase's shape and its decoration was equalled only by his contemporary, the AMASIS PAINTER.

Exekias' favourite shapes were the neck amphora and the panel amphora. His early neck amphora (*c.* 540 BC; Berlin, Antikenmus., 1720), signed as both potter and painter, looks rather old-fashioned compared with a mature specimen (London, BM, B 210), signed only as potter, since the latter has the taller, more ovoid form standard from *c.* 530 BC. Exekias' masterpiece (Rome, Vatican, Mus. Gregoriano Etrus., 344), signed as both potter and painter, is another mature work and the earliest canonical Type A amphora, with flanged handles decorated with ivy and a foot in two degrees, consisting of a base fillet above a torus. Equally famous is another work signed by Exekias as potter (Munich, Staatl. Antikensamml., 2044), probably the earliest Type A eye cup, with a deep bowl sharply offset from the stem and a pair of apotropaic eyes on each side of the exterior. Exekias' latest vase (Athens, Agora Mus., P 1044) was also a new shape, the calyx krater, and on his signed dinos (Rome, Villa Giulia, 50599) Exekias pioneered a new decorative scheme limiting figural decoration to the inside of the mouth instead of setting it in friezes on the outside. This system became standard for Attic Black-figure dinoi from *c.* 530 BC.

Exekias probably deliberately signed his more innovative works. His unsigned shapes include a Panathenaic amphora of *c.* 540 BC (Karlsruhe, Bad. Landesmus., 65.45), which is contemporary with an exquisite pyxis (Brauron Mus.) praising Stesagoras; the miniature figures of the latter resemble those on the shoulders of two neck amphorae (Boston, MA, Mus. F.A., 89.273 and New York, Met., 17.230.14). Other mature works are the splendid funerary plaques of *c.* 530 BC (Berlin, Antikenmus., 1811–26 and Athens, N. Archaeol. Mus., 2414–17).

Exekias' ability to render complicated themes in subtle, memorable ways was unsurpassed, and while some mythological scenes, such as his *Herakles Choking the Nemean Lion* (Berlin, Antikenmus., 1720), conform with the conventions of Archaic Greek art, he excelled at inventing new subjects or reinterpreting old ones. His favourite themes were episodes from the Trojan cycle, the most famous being the scene on a Type A amphora of *Ajax and Achilles Playing a Board Game* (Rome, Vatican, Mus. Gregoriano Etrus., 344; see fig.). The splendidly dressed pair sit opposite each other intent on the game, with their shields framing the picture. Inscriptions provide their names and the results of their throws (Achilles 4, Ajax 3), but, even without these, it is clear that Achilles will win. Thus, while the bare-headed Ajax hunches forward tensely, gripping his two spears tightly together, Achilles sits up straighter and seems grander in his tall, plumed helmet. The subject was new and Exekias' version was copied by his contemporaries and immediate successors.

Although *Achilles' Spearing of Penthesilea* was normally incorporated into large battle scenes, on two neck amphorae (London, BM, B209 and B210) Exekias concentrated solely on the two protagonists, emphasizing the poignancy of the moment. Sometimes, for other subjects, he presented a fuller picture, as in the now fragmentary representation of the harnessing of Achilles' chariot team (H. Cahn priv. col., on loan to Antikenmus., Basle, HC 300) or the depiction of a war chariot with a wounded trace horse fallen to its side, while the rest of the team scrambles to safety (Zurich, priv. col.; ex-Roš priv. col., Baden, see Moore, 1982, pl. 76, fig. 1). This latter scene may represent the *Death of Pedasos*, the one mortal horse in Achilles' otherwise invincible team. Exekias was also the first to depict the *Fight for the Body of Patroklos* (on his calyx krater; Athens, Agora Mus., A-P 1044), showing the youthful corpse lying on the ground, eyes closed, while the Greeks and Trojans continue to attack each other ferociously. The scene's identity would be uncertain without its accompanying inscriptions. A similar scene, without inscriptions, appears beneath one handle of Exekias' Munich cup (Staatl. Antikensamml., 2044).

Two of Exekias' scenes of Ajax are particularly noteworthy. On one side of a Type A amphora (Philadelphia, U. PA, Mus., MS 3442) he brilliantly depicted Ajax' efforts to lift the dead Achilles. Ajax bends over the corpse with a tight grip on each arm, but Achilles' head hangs down heavily, with the end of the helmet crest trailing on the ground. On two neck amphorae (Berlin, Antikenmus., 1718 and Munich, Staatl. Antikensamml., 1470) Exekias completely reworked traditional scenes of *Ajax Carrying the Body of Achilles Back to the Greek Camp*. Thus, while earlier artists showed Achilles' body stripped of armour and Ajax hardly burdened, he depicted both Achilles and Ajax in full armour, including their heavy shields. The effect is of slow, deliberate motion. Interestingly, Ajax moves to the left, the direction usually associated with losers in Archaic Greek art, perhaps alluding to the quarrel between Ajax and Odysseus over Achilles' armour, which led to Ajax' suicide. Exekias' version of this scene was also adopted by other Black-figure painters.

Exekias' treatment of the *Suicide of Ajax* itself was unique. Vase scenes from the 7th century BC onwards had shown the hero already impaled on his sword. However, on his Type B amphora (Boulogne, Mus. Mun., 558) Exekias chose the moment before Ajax threw himself on the weapon. Ajax crouches, patting down the soil around his sword to plant it firmly in the ground. His furrowed brow expresses his final moments of anguish, while his nudity and bare-headedness suggest vulnerability and the wispy palm tree emphasizes his solitude. Exekias' version recalls Sophokles' *Ajax* (815–22) where Ajax muses on the irony whereby the sword Hektor gave him and the belt he gave to Hektor both helped to bring about their owners' deaths; and surely both painter and poet drew on the same source.

Other mythological themes also attest to Exekias' inventiveness. The scene of Dionysos sailing in his boat accompanied by dolphins, inside Exekias' cup (Munich, Staatl. Antikensamml., 2044), is especially important. It may recall the Homeric *Hymn of Dionysos* (VII. 35–44, 51–3) in which the sailors who had kidnapped the god become terrified when he makes a vine grow as high as the ship's mast; they consequently jump into the sea and turn into dolphins. However, it may also reflect Dionysos' mission to spread viticulture throughout Greece. Equally memorable is the *Homecoming of the Dioskouroi* on a Type A amphora (Rome, Vatican, Mus. Gregoriano Etrus., 344), a quiet scene that reflects the feelings between family members that do not need to be spoken. So too are the painting on Berlin 1720 of *Damophon and Akamas Leading*

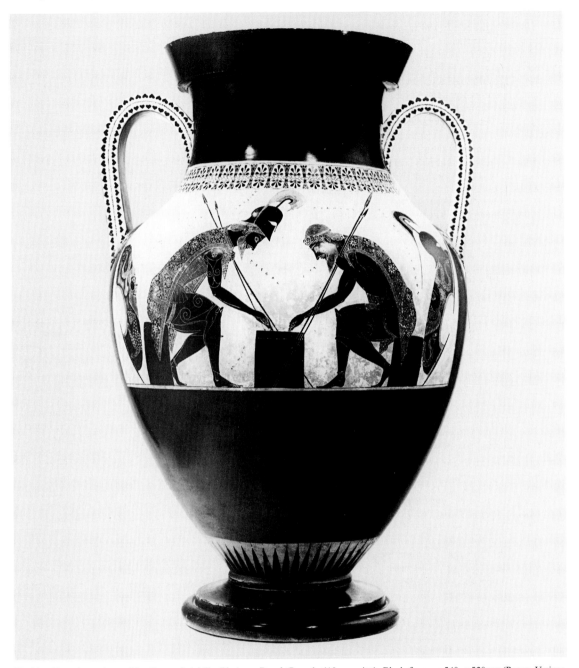

Exekias: Type A amphora with *Ajax and Achilles Playing a Board Game*, h. 610 mm, Attic Black-figure, *c.* 540–*c.* 520 BC (Rome, Vatican, Museo Gregoriano Etrusco)

Their Horses and, on an amphora (Orvieto, Mus. Etrus. Faina, 187), the *Introduction of Herakles*, both with the chariot of Athena. Herakles is also shown on a calyx krater (Athens, Agora Mus., A-P 1044), and on another amphora, sitting with the Olympian gods (Orvieto, Mus. Etrus. Faina, 78). Interestingly, Exekias only once depicted, on a neck amphora (Budapest, Mus. F.A., 50.189) the *Dionysiac Revels*, a subject that clearly interested the Amasis Painter.

Exekias also painted scenes of daily life, though they were never popular in Attic Black-figure before *c.* 520 BC.

His pyxis (Brauron Mus.) shows a victor in a chariot race holding a palm branch, followed by his unharnessed horses each led by a groom, and a fragmentary amphora (Philadelphia, PA, Mus. A., 4873) depicts a man quietly grazing his horses. Exekias' fragmentary funerary plaques with scenes of mourning and burial (Athens, N. Archaeol. Mus., 2414, 2417; Berlin, Antikenmus., 1811–26) reveal his sensitivity to the tragic side of human experience.

Exekias showed greater originality than any other Black-figure painter and many Red-figure ones. Moreover, on the rare occasions when he used stock motives or standard compositions, the result was far superior to other treatments of the same themes. He often reduced the number of figures in his compositions to those essential for the narrative. He was a serious painter who could convey moods and psychological states despite the limitations of the Black-figure technique. He preferred scenes displaying tension in subtle ways and occasionally focused on the moment just before an event as the one most pregnant with meaning. His work is characterized by simple compositions and tempered action, with no redundant figures or gestures. These features link him more closely to artists of the high Classical period than to his 6th-century contemporaries.

BIBLIOGRAPHY

J. D. Beazley: *Development of Black-figure* (1951, 3/1986), pp. 58–68
——: *Black-figure* (1956), pp. 143–6, 686–7, 714
——: *Paralipomena* (1971), pp. 59–61
J. Boardman: 'Exekias', *Amer. J. Archaeol.*, lxxxii (1978), pp. 11–25
H. Mommsen: 'Achill und Aias pflichtvergessen?', *Tainia Roland Hampne zum 70. Geburtstag* (Mainz, 1980), pp. 139–52
M. B. Moore: 'Exekias and Telamonian Ajax', *Amer. J. Archaeol.*, lxxxiv (1980), pp. 417–34
——: 'The Death of Pedasos', *Amer. J. Archaeol.*, lxxxvi (1982), pp. 578–81
——: 'Athena and Herakles on Exekias' Calyx-krater', *Amer. J. Archaeol.*, xc (1986), pp. 35–9

MARY B. MOORE

Ganymede Painter (*fl c.* 330–*c.* 320 BC). Vase painter, active in Apulia. He seems to have worked in close collaboration with a slightly older colleague, the Patera Painter, and was active in Tarentum or the area of Canosa. He is named for the scene on the neck of a volute krater (Switzerland, priv. col.) showing Ganymede carried off by Zeus in the guise of a swan (as was usual on Apulian vases) instead of an eagle. Presumably a representation of apotheosis (given the context and the elaborate floral setting of the scene), it may hold a message of funerary symbolism. Indeed most of the Ganymede Painter's vases, including many volute kraters with mascarons on the handles and characteristically elaborate neck decoration, were evidently destined for funerary use. Among his subjects, scenes depicting grave shrines (*naiskoi*) predominate, for example the main scene on his name vase. The idea of death is also present in his few other representations of mythological subjects, as on another volute krater (Switzerland, priv. col.), with *Amphiaraos Welcomed to the Underworld*; on a hydria (U. Zurich, Archäol. Inst.), with *Niobe Mourning at the Tomb of her Children*; and a situla (Bloomington, IN, U. A. Mus.), with the *Metamorphosis of Actaeon*. On an amphora (Basle, Antikenmus., S 40), Orpheus himself appears in a grave shrine visiting a man holding a small papyrus roll (possibly the deceased as an Orphic initiate). Among beautiful tendrils and colourful flowers on the necks of the painter's volute kraters there often appears a female head painted in white and golden-yellow, perhaps a goddess. These colours as well as a lively red are skilfully used for the modelling of secondary objects, for example offerings, such as cuirasses and shields, in the funerary scenes. Gradual transitions from white to golden-yellow often emphasize the highlights and shadows.

BIBLIOGRAPHY

A. D. Trendall and A. Cambitoglou: *The Red-figured Vases of Apulia*, ii (Oxford, 1982), pp. 793–803, pls 294–8
A. D. Trendall: *Red Figure Vases of South Italy and Sicily* (London, 1989), pp. 95–6, figs 238–42
A. D. Trendall and A. Cambitoglou: *The Red-figured Vases of Apulia: Supplement 2* (London, 1992)

MARGOT SCHMIDT

Gorgon Painter (*fl c.* 600–*c.* 580 BC). Greek vase painter. The Gorgon Painter is named after a dinos with stand (Paris, Louvre, E 874) showing the Gorgons chasing Perseus after he has decapitated their sister Medusa. He decorated only *c.* 35 extant vases, but these take many shapes; some, such as his namepiece, are large, as are the standed kraters and amphorae, others are smaller, such as oinochoai. One of his lekythoi is of the rare round-bodied type (London, Russell priv. col.; see Beazley, 1956). He was also the first Attic Black-figure artist to decorate plates, and some splendid examples survive. Almost all his vases with known provenances come from Attica, with a few from Naukratis, since at this time Greek vases were not generally exported to Italy.

The Gorgon Painter's style exhibits some of the boldness of the NETTOS PAINTER, but he preferred smaller formats, often with the figure or figures in a panel. This use of panels was an innovation and probably explains his liking for amphorae and oinochoai. He probably also introduced horse-head amphorae, which have panels on each side containing the head of a horse. The earliest examples (*c.* 600 BC) closely resemble the heads of the chariot horses on his namepiece and on one of his standed kraters (Athens, Acropolis Mus., 474). So far, however, no horse-head amphora has been securely attributed to the Gorgon Painter, and caution is necessary in crediting him with the invention of this restrained and rather sombre series of vases, probably intended as grave markers.

The Gorgon Painter generally painted animals, either singly as on his oinochoai, in opposed pairs as on the amphorae, or in friezes as in the secondary zone of his namepiece and on his plates. His namepiece represents his main contribution to the depiction of mythological subjects, while a standard krater (Athens, Acropolis Mus., 474) shows a frontal chariot, perhaps with mythological connotations, as well as a figure of Hermes in an animal frieze.

BIBLIOGRAPHY

J. D. Beazley: *Development of Black-figure* (1951, 3/1986), pp. 15–16
——: *Black-figure* (1956), pp. 8–10
——: *Paralipomena* (1971), pp. 6–7

□

Group E (*fl* mid-6th century BC). Greek vase painters. Approximately 100 Attic Black-figure vases are attributed to this group, which J. D. Beazley, its creator, described as 'large and compact' (Beazley, 1931/2). The 'E' stands for 'Exekianizing', because the Group's work anticipated EXEKIAS. Beazley's three lists of Group E vases differ, however, in their degree of 'connection with Exekias'. The first (1931/2) contains 42 examples, many so coherent in shape, subject-matter and style that they may be by one man. The most popular vases are Type B amphorae, large vessels with panels depicting the Group's recurrent themes: *Herakles and the Lion, Theseus and the Minotaur,* the *Birth of Athena* and scenes with chariots in frontal view. Most of the paintings are in a style that, though sober and technically competent, is rather loose and sketchy. Some of the finer paintings, however, combine technical control with an elegance and restraint that clearly anticipate Exekias. The finest of these is a well-shaped amphora (Paris, Louvre, F53), painted with an exacting, almost Exekian touch. Its chariot scene features horses with a bearing and style foreshadowing those of Exekias, and two have names that Exekias gave to his thoroughbreds. Though the reverse of the vase was actually signed by Exekias as potter, and the whole piece surpasses the rest in technical refinement and proximity to Exekias, Beazley was cautious about attribution of the paintings. He concluded simply that most of the first list was by one painter and that Louvre F53 'and group E or part of it' might eventually prove to be 'early work of Exekias himself'. In Beazley's second list (1956) of 71 Group E vases some of the new examples clearly resemble Exekias' work; others do so only vaguely. Finally, many of the newcomers on Beazley's third list (1971) of 90 vases have no significant ties with Exekias at all. Several of these (e.g. the pointed neck amphora; Beazley, 1971, p. 57, no. 58ter) are so unlike Exekias' work that Beazley may simply have been using Group E as a repository for unattributed mid-6th-century BC vases. Two works ascribed to the group since Beazley's death do, however, vindicate his early hopes. On an amphora (Toledo, OH, Mus. A., 80.1022) signed by Exekias as potter, one of the careering chariots is driven by Anchippos, which is the name of the mounted hoplite on Louvre F53, and the other's exquisite horses include one named Kalliphoras, as on Louvre F53 and on several vases painted by Exekias. An eye cup (New York, Met., L.1981.145) is still more evocative of Exekias, foreshadowing his famous Dionysos cup (Munich, Staatl. Antikensamml., 2044), with its decorative eyes, nose and eyebrows on either side, and battling warriors around the handles.

BIBLIOGRAPHY
J. D. Beazley: 'Groups of Mid-sixth-century Black-Figure', *Annu. Brit. Sch. Athens*, xxxii (1931/2), pp. 1–22
——: *Development of Black-figure* (1951, 3/1986), pp. 63–4
——: *Black-figure* (1956), pp. 133–8
M. B. Moore: 'Horses by Exekias', *Amer. J. Archaeol.*, lxxii (1968), pp. 357–68
J. D. Beazley: *Paralipomena* (1971), pp. 54–7

JODY MAXMIN

Group of the Huge Lekythoi (*fl c.* 410–*c.* 400 BC). Greek vase painters. The five White-ground lekythoi painted with matt colours attributed to this 'group' apparently come from the same Athenian workshop and represent the work of one artist rather than several, since their technical and stylistic peculiarities set them apart from all other examples of this shape. These features include: huge size (h. 680–1100 mm), which gives the group its name; a separate mouth; the absence of a bottom; a White ground even on areas normally painted black; a modified system of ornamentation (no maeander above the picture); and different patterns (e.g. a wreath of leaves) on the shoulder. They suggest that the vases imitate the marble lekythoi being produced in Athens at that time as funerary monuments.

The principal art-historical importance of the Group of the Huge Lekythoi is the manner in which their pictures are painted: the pictures are richly polychromatic and show some attempt to depict objects in perspective, but a further peculiarity is the use of shading, albeit partial and imperfect. While female bodies are painted white and left unshaded, male bodies are painted reddish brown and shaded with a hatching composed of fine dark strokes. However, there is no use of highlights. These lekythoi nevertheless constitute important early examples of shadow painting (*skiagraphia*) in Greek art, which is known from literary sources to have been developed at the end of the 5th century BC. The iconography of the pictures is traditional (the visit to the grave, the *prothesis*). The pictures are close in style to those on GROUP R lekythoi, but without the same quality in line and expression.

BIBLIOGRAPHY
J. D. Beazley: *Red-figure* (1942, 2/1963), ii, p. 1390
F. Brommer: 'Ein Lekythos in Madrid', *Madrid. Mitt.*, x (1969), pp. 155–71
D. C. Kurtz: *Athenian White Lekythoi* (Oxford, 1975), pp. 68–73
L. Burn and R. Glynn: *Beazley Addenda: Additional References to* ABV, ARV2 *and* Paralipomena (Oxford, 1982, rev. T. H. Carpenter, 2/1989)

Group R (*fl c.* 420–*c.* 410 BC). Greek vase painters. The output of this group consists of largish White-ground lekythoi. Their shape, ornamentation, painting technique and colouring (red contour lines, blackish grey ornamentation and matt blue or green drapery) show that they are from the same workshop as the lekythoi of the REED PAINTER, hence the label 'Group R' (short for 'Reed Painter'). According to J. D. Beazley (1938), these works may have been produced by more than one painter, but the two most famous and best-preserved lekythoi in the group (Athens, N. Archaeol. Mus., 1816 and 1817) are definitely by the same hand. All the Group R lekythoi exhibit extremely meticulous and subtle outline drawing, particularly apparent in the figures' eloquent hands: the lively contours and twisting bodies give an impression of plasticity and depth. The faces frequently have melancholy expressions with slightly lowered eyes surrounded by lashes and are often seen in three-quarter view; this melancholy is also reflected in the figural poses. Some are bent or slumped forwards, leaning languidly on a stick or a lance; heads are generally bowed, and the hands often hang limply. Almost all the pictures show grave scenes with three figures, with the deceased person sitting at the centre in front of a broad funerary stele, with a male or female figure standing on either side. Female mourners hold the traditional offerings for the dead (baskets of fillets and oil flasks) and occasionally weapons. Their hair is nearly always short as a sign of mourning, not tied up in a chignon as often in works by the Reed Painter. They make none of the usual gestures of mourning, such as tearing the hair or beating the breast: the grief is internalized.

The paintings of Group R have long been associated with PARRHASIOS, a famous panel painter. Ancient descriptions of his skills and techniques tally remarkably well with the characteristics of Group R pictures, but the different requirements of vase and panel painting must be borne in mind.

BIBLIOGRAPHY

J. D. Beazley: *Attic White Lekythoi* (London, 1938), pp. 24–5
——: *Red-figure* (1942, 2/1963), ii, pp. 1383–4, 1692
S. Papaspyridi-Karusu: 'Scherbe einer attischen weissgrundigen Lekythos', *Ant. & Abendland*, v (1956), pp. 71–4
J. D. Beazley: *Paralipomena* (1971), p. 486
D. C. Kurtz: *Athenian White Lekythoi* (Oxford, 1975), pp. 58–68
L. Burn and R. Glynn: *Beazley Addenda: Additional References to* ABV, ARV2 *and* Paralipomena (Oxford, 1982, rev. T. H. Carpenter, 2/1989)
I. Wehgartner: *Attische weissgrundige Keramik* (Mainz, 1983), p. 29

IRMA WEHGARTNER

Heidelberg Painter (*fl c.* 560–*c.* 540 BC). Greek vase painter. With the C PAINTER and the Griffin Bird Painter he was the most prolific painter of Athenian Black-figure Siana cups, decorating some 125 extant specimens, which he probably also made, as well as a skyphos, a panel amphora and a kantharos.

The Heidelberg Painter was not a meticulous draughtsman: his incision is usually rather coarse, his best work occurring on double-deckers of his middle period such as his name vases (Heidelberg, Ruprecht-Karls-U., Samml. Ant. Kleinkst Archäol. Inst.). He was a shorter-lived contemporary of the AMASIS PAINTER, and each influenced the other, favouring fringed garments and static, symmetrical compositions around central figures. Herakles was his favourite tondo figure, depicted with the lion, the boar, Nereus, Nessos and an Amazon. Two opposed figures also occur frequently, especially those of Dionysos, Aphrodite and Ariadne, and the cups' exteriors were decorated using both the overlap and double-decker systems. The subjects on these exteriors cover mythology, warfare, sport and Dionysiac revels. The Heidelberg Painter was the first to establish the iconographic repertory involving Dionysos and Herakles.

BIBLIOGRAPHY

J. D. Beazley: 'Amasea', *J. Hell. Stud.*, li (1931), pp. 275–82
——: *Development of Black-figure* (1951, 3/1986), pp. 46–8
——: *Black-figure* (1956), pp. 63–7, 682
——: *Paralipomena* (1971), pp. 26–7
J. Boardman: *Athenian Black Figure Vases: A Handbook* (London, 1974), p. 33
L. Burn and R. Glynn: *Beazley Addenda: Additional References to* ABV, ARV2 *and* Paralipomena (Oxford, 1982, rev. T. H. Carpenter, 2/1989)
H. A. G. Brijder: *Siana Cups I and Komast Cups*, Allard Pierson Series, iv (Amsterdam, 1983)
——: 'Changing the Subject: Evidence on Siana Cups', *Ancient Greek and Related Pottery: Proceedings of the International Vase Symposium in Amsterdam, 12–15 April 1984*, pp. 248–51
——: 'A Pre-dramatic Performance of a Satyr Chorus by the Heidelberg Painter', *Enthousiasmos: Essays Presented to J. M. Hemelrijk* (Amsterdam, 1986), pp. 879–91
A. Blair Brownlee: 'Attic Black-figure from Corinth, I', *Hesperia*, lvi (1987), pp. 73–95, nos 14 and 25
H. A. G. Brijder: *Siana Cups II: The Heidelberg Painter* (Amsterdam, 1991)

H. A. G. BRIJDER

Hirschfeld Painter (*fl c.* 750–*c.* 730 BC). Greek vase painter. He was active in Athens during the first phase of the Late Geometric style (LGI). He is named after a monumental pedestalled krater (Athens, N. Archaeol. Mus., 990), published in 1872 by G. Hirschfeld shortly after its discovery in the Dipylon cemetery. Like several other more fragmentary kraters by the same vase painter, it is decorated with funerary imagery and was designed to mark an aristocratic male burial. The main scene shows the *ekphora* ceremony, in which the dead man on the bier is conveyed by waggon to the grave, attended by mourners. A retinue of chariots, driven by armed warriors, fills the zone below. As on other important vases by this painter or from his workshop, geometric ornament plays only a subsidiary part in the decoration. The Hirschfeld krater is contemporary with the later monumental vases from the Dipylon Master's workshop, but the style of the figures in silhouette is quite different. Female mourners are distinguished by short strokes for breasts; their heads are in profile, with beaky noses, and eyes reserved and dotted. As they tear their hair, their bent arms and broad shoulders form a rectangle; their chests are frontal, forming concave equilateral triangles. The legs are shown with calves in profile but frontal thighs, thus appearing bow-legged. Chariot horses have a stiff and frozen look, with insubstantial bodies, trumpet-shaped muzzles and elongated cannon bones. Other vases from the Hirschfeld Painter's workshop depict goats equally idiosyncratically; these are either standing or kneeling, but always looking to the front with large, inquiring eyes. Among the filling ornaments, dotted motifs prevail.

BIBLIOGRAPHY

J. M. Davison: *Attic Geometric Workshops*, Yale Classical Studies, xvi (New Haven, 1961), pp. 36–40, 141–2
J. N. Coldstream: *Greek Geometric Pottery* (London, 1968), pp. 41–4

NICOLAS COLDSTREAM

Hunt Painter (*fl c.* 565–*c.* 530 BC). Greek vase painter. His name derives from two cups (Florence, Mus. Archeol., 85118; Leipzig, Karl-Marx-U., Archäol. Inst., T 302; Paris, Louvre, E 670) showing a boar hunt, possibly the legendary Kalydonian one. He had a long career, and many of his vases survive. His range of subject-matter and quality of drawing make him one of the most important Lakonian vase painters. Unlike the earlier Naukratis Painter and Boreads Painter, whose work shows Corinthian influence, the Hunt Painter owed more to Attic vase painting for both his drawing style and his iconography. Apart from cups, which were widely exported, he painted a hydria found on Rhodes (Rhodes, Archaeol. Mus., 15373) and a few lakainai, which come from Sparta itself. He probably invented a new shape of cup, the Lakonian droop cup (e.g. Oxford, Ashmolean, 1935.192; Taranto, Mus. N., 52847), similar to the contemporary Attic droop cup, though it is not known which variety was developed first, and he apparently produced more inscribed vases than any other Lakonian vase painter. The Hunt Painter favoured narrative scenes and had a rich mythological repertory, often using episodes from the story of Herakles. He also painted such everyday scenes as fighting, hunting and revelling. Both of the hunting scenes after which he is named are porthole compositions, with part of the image cut off by the frame of the tondo, a characteristic device employed several times by the Hunt Painter.

See also GREECE, ANCIENT, §V, 5(iii).

BIBLIOGRAPHY

E. A. Lane: 'Lakonian Vase-painting', *Annu. Brit. Sch. Athens*, xxxiv (1933/4), pp. 141–3
B. B. Shefton: 'Three Laconian Vase-painters', *Annu. Brit. Sch. Athens*, xlix (1954), pp. 306–8
C. M. Stibbe: *Lakonische Vasenmaler des sechsten Jahrhunderts v. Chr.*, 2 vols (Amsterdam and London, 1972), pp. 121–50, pls 68–87

MARIA PIPILI

Kadmos Painter (*fl c.* 420–*c.* 400 BC). Greek vase painter. About 40 Attic Red-figure vases, all large, have been attributed to the Kadmos Painter, whose work is similar but superior to that of the Pothos Painter; there also seem to have been connections with the MEIDIAS PAINTER. Active in Athens, most of his paintings are on bell kraters, but the finer work occurs on calyx and column kraters, hydriai and pelikai, and on the one volute krater attributed to him (Ruvo di Puglia, Mus. Jatta, 1093), a vase of monumental proportions. His more modestly sized name vase (Berlin, Pergamonmus., 2634) is one of a pair of elegant hydriai. It is finely potted, with immaculate and unusual floral decoration; its figure scene does not show the actual struggle between Kadmos and the serpent, but a static assembly of participants and observers. The Kadmos Painter favoured elaborate, multi-figured and often unusual mythological scenes. The contest between Apollo and Marsyas occurs six times; another frequent subject was Dionysos, who was depicted not only in conventional compositions with satyrs and maenads but also banqueting with Herakles, greeting Apollo at Delphi and approaching the abandoned Ariadne on Naxos. Other rare themes include Theseus' visit to the seabed and Herakles on the pyre. The scenes quite frequently include a tripod, possibly indicating the influence of dithyrambs. The Kadmos Painter was a competent draughtsman, but his compositions are weak; the multi-figure scenes, with characters set at different levels, are stiffly and rather symmetrically arranged, with little interaction between the figures.

BIBLIOGRAPHY

Enc. A. Ant.: 'Cadmo, Pittore di'
J. D. Beazley: *Red-figure* (1942, 2/1963), ii, pp. 1184–7
H. Sichtermann: *Griechische Vasen in Unteritalien aus der Sammlung Jatta in Ruvo* (Tübingen, 1966), pp. 20–21
H. Froning: *Dithyrambos und Vasenmalerei in Athen* (Würzburg, 1971), pp. 29–51
W. Real: *Studien zur Entwicklung der Vasenmalerei im ausgehenden 5. Jahrhundert v. Chr.* (Münster, 1973), pp. 75–83

LUCILLA BURN

Kleitias (*fl c.* 570–*c.* 560 BC). Greek vase painter. He signed five Attic vases as painter, always in collaboration with the potter Ergotimos. The most famous of these is a volute krater, the so-called François Vase (Florence, Mus. Archeol., 4209); the others are smaller vessels—a standlet (New York, Met., 31.11.4) and three Gordion cups, only one of which (Berlin, Antikenmus., 4604) has figural decoration. Other paintings attributed to him are on drinking vessels (skyphoi or kantharoi), mainly from excavations on the Athenian Acropolis and in fragmentary condition.

Kleitias' drawing style is crisp and precise. Though his figures are usually small, they are vigorous and robust, and he was a master at balancing colourful and decorative elements with simple and plain ones. He almost always identified his figures with inscriptions, as on the François Vase. This vase brilliantly exemplifies Kleitias' delight in narrative, and the dignified procession of Olympian gods attending the marriage of Peleus and Thetis is especially memorable. The striking figure of Dionysos looks straight out, as if inviting the viewer to join the festivities. Peleus and Thetis were Achilles' parents; hence, no doubt, the

positioning directly below the wedding scene of a scene from the Trojan War with Achilles pursuing Troilos. Most poignant here is the startled reaction of Troilos' father, Priam, when Antenor reports his son's impending death. Other scenes on this magnificent vase are: the *Kalydonian Boar Hunt*, in which the deaths of a hunter and a dog are especially vividly portrayed; the *Victory Dance of Theseus after the Killing of the Minotaur* (see also two fragments in Athens, Acropolis Mus., 596 and 598), in which one of Theseus' shipmates sees the celebration and throws up his arms in joy while another swims to shore with long powerful strokes; the rarely depicted *Funeral Games of Patroklos*; *Ajax Carrying the Body of Achilles*, a Trojan episode that appears on the back of each handle; a humorous depiction of the *Return of Hephaistos to Olympos*, with a glum Hera stuck to her throne, a triumphant-looking Dionysos and Athena taunting Ares for his failure to persuade Hephaistos to return to Olympos; and finally, on the foot, the amusing scene of *Pygmies Fighting Cranes*. One often overlooked detail is the running Gorgon on the downward curve of each handle just above the rim: when the vase was filled with wine, the Gorgons would appear to run over the sea, as they did when chasing Perseus. Kleitias' other mythological scenes are fragmentary but nevertheless attest to his ability to convey the essence of the subject. They include a fragment depicting the *Birth of Athena* (Athens, Acropolis Mus., 597), in which the goddess springs fully armed from the head of her father Zeus (the earliest known painting of this subject), and a neck fragment from a volute krater with *Odysseus Escaping from the Cave of Polyphemos* (Basle, Herbert Cahn priv. col., 1418), which joins another fragment illustrating *Perseus and the Gorgons* (Moscow, Pushkin Mus. F.A., 2986; see von Bothmer).

Kleitias was not only a master of Attic Black-figure technique but also one of the first artists to demonstrate its expressive potential. He paved the way for the narrative achievements of his successors of the mid-6th century BC.

For further discussion *see* GREECE, ANCIENT, §V, 5(ii).

BIBLIOGRAPHY

J. D. Beazley: *Development of Black-figure* (1951, 3/1986), pp. 24–34
——: *Black-figure* (1956), pp. 76–8, 682
P. E. Arias and M. Hirmer: *Tausend Jahre griechischer Vasenkunst* (Munich, 1960); Eng. trans. and rev. by B. Shefton as *A History of Greek Vase Painting* (London, 1962), pp. 286–92
J. D. Beazley: *Paralipomena* (1971), p. 29
M. Cristofani: 'Il cratere François nella storia dell'archeologia "romantica"', *Boll. A.*, special ser., i (1980), pp. 11–23 [good illus.]
D. von Bothmer: 'A New Kleitias Fragment from Egypt', *Ant. Kst* [Basle], xxiv (1981), pp. 66–7

MARY B. MOORE

Kleophon Painter (*fl c.* 440–*c.* 420/410 BC). Greek vase painter. He is named after a kalos inscription praising the youth Kleophon on an Attic Red-figure stamnos (St Petersburg, Hermitage, B 2353). He was initially a member of the workshop of POLYGNOTOS, but also worked with the ACHILLES PAINTER, as a Nolan amphora (Angers, Mus. Turpin de Crissé, 13), lekythos (New York, Met., 22.139.189) and pelike (London, BM, E 392) attest, and he eventually taught the Dinos Painter. The attribution to him of the White-ground work of the Bosanquet Painter and Thanatos Painter (Felten) is unconvincing. However,

a Black-figure Panathenaic amphora (Copenhagen, Ny Carlsberg Glyp., 3606) may be his.

The Kleophon Painter mainly decorated large pots, particularly kraters, stamnoi, pelikai and loutrophoroi, but also a few small vases, including a cup, lekythos and skyphos. His draughtsmanship is among the best of its time and reflects the style of the Parthenon sculptures. His figures' poses are often simple, solemn and majestic. Their tilted heads suggest emotion, and their rapt expressions have a certain nobility. Their intense, well-drawn eyes, and the two parallel strokes which often occur at the centre of the ear, are characteristic. Many figures in the procession in honour of Apollo on one side of a volute krater (Ferrara, Mus. N. Archeol., 44894) seem to be copied from the Parthenon frieze, and, significantly, one of the artist's vases, a calyx krater, was found in the workshop of the sculptor PHEIDIAS at Olympia (Olympia, Archaeol. Mus.).

The painter frequently repeated the same scenes, occasionally with almost the same compositions and poses, as illustrated by two stamnoi with his favourite scene, the departure of a warrior (St Petersburg, Hermitage, B 1148; Munich, Staatl. Antikensamml., 2415). Other scenes from daily life that he repeated frequently include revels, sacrifice and women in their quarters. His myth scenes are rare, and their iconography is derived from vases produced in Polygnotos' workshop. Again they are often repetitive: Amazonomachies are the most common, while the *Return of Hephaistos* and the *Contest between Apollo and Marsyas* each occur on two vases. The latter illustrates the Kleophon Painter's interest in musical performances, also attested by one of his most important vases, a bell krater (Copenhagen, Nmus., 13817) depicting a dithyrambic chorus. Stock figures of mantled youths often decorate the backs of his vases.

The painter's style deteriorated towards the end of his career. His later figures, such as those on a loutrophoros with an interesting scene of warriors at a tomb (Athens, N. Archaeol. Mus., 1700), are more sketchily drawn, have less anatomical detail and often have rather puffy musculature. The drapery is more detailed, but lacks its earlier fluency.

BIBLIOGRAPHY

J. D. Beazley: *Red-figure* (1942, 2/1963), ii, pp. 1143–51, 1684, 1703, 1707
G. Gualandi: 'Le ceramiche del pittore di Kleophon rinvenute a Spina', *A. Ant. & Mod.*, xvii (1962), pp. 227–60
——: 'Il pittore di Kleophon', *A. Ant. & Mod.*, xvii (1962), pp. 341–83
K. F. Felten: *Thanatos- und Kleophonmaler: Weissgrundige und rotfigurige Vasenmalerei der Parthenonzeit* (Munich, 1971)
C. Isler-Kerényi: 'Chronologie und "Synchronologie" attischer Vasenmaler der Parthenonzeit', *Ant. Kst*, suppl. ix: *Festschrift für H. Bloesch* (1973), pp. 29–30, 32–3
M. Halm-Tisserant: *Le Peintre de Cléophon* (diss., U. Strasbourg, 1984)

JOHN H. OAKLEY

Kleophrades Painter (*fl c.* 505–*c.* 475 BC). Greek vase painter. He produced some of the finest examples of Attic Red-figure vase painting (*see* GREECE, ANCIENT, §V, 6(i)), but, since none of his preserved works is signed, he is named after the potter Kleophrades, son of Amasis, whose signature appears on an early, exceptionally large Red-figure cup (Paris, Bib. N., 535, 699). The signature 'Epiktetos' on a late pelike (Berlin, Antikenmus., 2170) is a modern forgery. Nonsense inscriptions appear on his

early vases, and for long afterwards he generally only wrote either *kalos* or *kale* (never specifying a love name), or standard inscriptions on Panathenaic amphorae. Later, however, he began to label mythological characters, sometimes alluding to literary sources.

Though scholars once believed that the Kleophrades Painter was not Athenian, his juvenilia (e.g. a hydria, Salerno, Mus. Civico, 1371; psykters, Compiègne, Mus. Vivenel, 1068; Paris, Louvre, G 57), as well as the general robustness of his style, derive from the Pioneer group of Attic Red-figure artists. EUTHYMIDES has been called his teacher, but he must also have learnt early from EUPHRONIOS. The Kleophrades Painter was among the last great Attic vase painters to use the Black-figure technique for works other than Panathenaic amphorae. He applied it to neck amphorae and lids, as well as to subsidiary friezes on Red-figure pots (e.g. an amphora, Munich, Staatl. Antikensamml., 2305; a loutrophoros, Paris, Louvre, CA 453). The Athenas on his Panathenaic amphorae have pegasos shield devices, and the sports most commonly depicted are chariot races and foot races (e.g. New Haven, CT, Yale U. A.G., 1909.12, 1909.13; Paris, Louvre, F 277).

Most of the nearly 150 vases and fragments attributed to the Kleophrades Painter are large shapes, often decorated in special ways. His liking throughout his career for impressive Red-figure calyx kraters (e.g. New York, Met., 08.258.58; Tarquinia, Pal. Vitelleschi, RC 4196) and kalpides (e.g. Rouen, Mus. Ant., 25; Munich, Staatl. Antikensamml., 2426) probably reflects the early influence of Euphronios. On these shapes, however, the Kleophrades Painter sometimes ran the figural friezes all the way round, as on his unusual, decorated, pointed amphorae (Berlin, Antikenmus., 1970.5; Munich, Antikensamml., 2344). Since his early output included psykters, which normally bore continuous friezes, the scheme may have been borrowed from them. During his prime, the Kleophrades Painter produced a series of vases without framed panels, which simply had single or paired statuesque red figures on meander bases on each side. He employed this format on neck amphorae (e.g. New York, Met., 13.233; London, BM, E 270) and amphorae of Panathenaic shape (e.g. Leiden, Rijksmus. Oudhd., PC 80; Basle, Antikenmus.), and later on a Type A amphora (U. Würzburg, Wagner-Mus., 508), at least one bell krater (Basle, Antikenmus.) and several pelikai (e.g. Berlin, Antikenmus., 2170). The Kleophrades Painter rivalled the supreme exponent of this decorative mode, his contemporary, the BERLIN PAINTER. His bold stamnoi (e.g. Paris, Louvre, C 10748 and G 55) and simplified, more pedestrian pelikai (e.g. Copenhagen, Nmus., 149; Berlin, Antikenmus., 2170) were produced only later in his career as his powers began to wane. He evidently also decorated significant quantities of cups and small vases, but only a few survive, most of which are either early or late works (e.g. cups, Paris, Bib. N., 535, 699; London, BM, E 73; a skyphos, Florence, Mus. Archeol., 4218).

The Kleophrades Painter consistently chose particular forms of ornament: simple key patterns; more complex meanders, often interrupted by black or cross-filled squares (especially for lower borders); egg patterns, especially for rims and lower panel-borders on hydriai; palmettes in both horizontal picture-borders and independent friezes; net patterns for vertical borders, especially on hydriai and pelikai; and tongues just beneath the junction of body and neck, on psykters and stamnoi. Significantly, the patterns on his earliest works are black (e.g. a hydria, Salerno; amphorae, Rome, Vatican, Mus. Gregoriano Etrus.; Munich, Antikensamml., 2305) or bilingual ornament (e.g. an amphora, U. Würzburg, Wagner-Mus., 507; calyx kraters, Paris, Louvre, G 48; Tarquinia, Pal. Vitelleschi, RC 4196). Similarly several of his Red-figure vases adhere to Black-figure decorative schemes: for example the volute krater with figural friezes only on the neck (Malibu, CA, Getty Mus., 77.AE.11 and 76.AE.132.1B) and the cup with a decorated zone around the tondo (London, BM, E 73).

Several distinctive characteristics mark the Kleophrades Painter's style. He usually incised hair contours rather than reserving them in standard Red-figure fashion, and he often left loose strands along the lower edges of women's hair and sometimes rendered all the hair strand by strand, rather than as a solid black mass. His early figures have ear lobes that project forwards, and other features that continued to occur, including the depiction of the pupil and iris detailed as dot within circle, often in dilute glaze; aquiline noses with a rounded nostril indicated by a black relief line; lips bordered above and below by black lines; back views with a black line representing the spine; broad frontal knees; hooks for ankles and frontal feet with circular toes. He repeatedly depicted satyrs and centaurs with expressive frontal faces (e.g. a calyx krater, Cambridge, MA, Sackler Mus., 1960.236; a skyphos, Florence, Mus. Archeol., 4218) and produced some of the first

three-quarter-view human faces (a stamnos, London, BM, E 441). Later in his career he used a black line for the *linea alba* and treated collarbones as a single, long line with a semicircular depression at the centre. The Kleophrades Painter's masterly drawing is enhanced by nuances of texture and colour: glazed clay dots for curls and grapes; dilute glaze for light hair and animals' hides; red for minor objects such as wreaths, flowers and thongs; and even white, as for the hair of old men.

The Kleophrades Painter's subjects are fairly typical of the early 5th century BC, including themes from everyday life as well as myth and legend. He drew musicians, amorous youths, athletes and trainers, and warriors arming or leaving home, along with heroes such as Herakles, Theseus and Achilles. Scenes of Dionysos and of satyrs and maenads featured on important works throughout his career. The continuous frieze on an early calyx krater (Cambridge, MA, Sackler Mus., 1960.236) depicts *The Return of Hephaistos*, and the figures are still based on the elegant, simple silhouettes of Euthymides, though the composition is more monumental. There is great variety in the figures' poses and attributes, and vitality in the satyrs. The Kleophrades Painter's individual style is more developed in the continuous frieze on a pointed amphora (Munich, Staatl. Antikensamml., 2344) depicting Dionysos with his entourage. Here the scene is enlivened by washes of dilute glaze, as on the god's metal kantharos, animal skins and snakes, and made more intense by the painter's psychological insight, as in the depiction of the blonde maenad with her head tossed back in Dionysiac ecstasy. A later *Return of Hephaistos* depicted around a calyx krater

Kleophrades Painter (attrib.): Kalpis (detail) depicting *Phineus and the Harpies*, h. 390 mm, diam. 150 mm, Attic Red-figure, *c.* 480 BC (Malibu, J. Paul Getty Museum)

from his mature period (Paris, Louvre, G 162) is unusual in including Hera ensnared in the trick throne. The procession here is led by Hermes, and the scene has some unexpected details, such as Hephaistos in a workman's cap riding his mule side-saddle, and Dionysos drunkenly trailing behind, supported by a satyr. Eyes are shown in different positions in their sockets and indicate the mood or physical condition of an individual or the relationships between figures.

The mature works of the Kleophrades Painter often avoid intense action, instead focusing on the prelude or aftermath of an event, anticipating Classical Greek drama. A neck amphora with twisted handles (c. 490–c. 480 BC; New York, Met., 13.233) has a magnificently drawn Herakles turning expectantly as he flees with the Delphic tripod, pursued by the elegant figure of Apollo on the other side of the vase. A later Type A amphora with unframed decoration (U. Würzburg, Wagner-Mus., 508) shows the *Exchange of Gifts between Ajax and Hector*. The heroes appear on opposite sides of the vase, here restrained by wise elders, Phoinix and probably Priam, and the opposed pairs are almost mirror images.

Representations of the aged regularly appear on the Kleophrades Painter's mature works. In the panel of a late kalpis, *Phineus and the Harpies* (85.AE.316; see fig.), three unusually charming, flying harpies steal loaves of bread and meat from Phineus' table. The blind prophet Phineus, King of Thrace, is a study of old age and infirmity. His sagging profile is topped by sparse hair shaved close to the skull, while his blind eye is rendered by a single curved black line. His hands, outstretched in protest, flail ineffectually at the air. The result is a mixture of the poignant and the playful characteristic of the Kleophrades Painter.

The Kleophrades Painter's most famous composition occurs in a long frieze around another kalpis, the Vivenzio Hydria (Naples, Mus. Archeol. N., 2422), and depicts events and images from the fall of Troy: *Aeneas Carrying Anchises*, fallen warriors, the *Rape of Cassandra, Trojan Women Lamenting*, the *Death of Priam*, a scene in which ?Andromache is shown attacking a Greek warrior with a pestle, and the *Rescue of Aithra by her Grandsons*. This extraordinary panorama of death, despair, valour and hope was perhaps inspired by the Persian invasion of Athens in 480 BC and may be the finest extant vase painting of the Trojan saga. The Kleophrades Painter's brilliant innovations in composition and his rendering of human mental and physical states foreshadowed the work of the great muralist Polygnotos of Thasos. His style evolved from the experiments of the Pioneer group and approached the developed forms of Early Classical times.

See GREECE, ANCIENT, fig. 75.

BIBLIOGRAPHY

J. D. Beazley: 'Kleophrades', *J. Hell. Stud.*, xxx (1910), pp. 38–68
——: *Der Kleophrades-Maler* (Berlin, 1933; Eng. trans., Mainz, 1974)
G. M. A. Richter: 'The Kleophrades Painter', *Amer. J. Archaeol*, xl (1936), pp. 100–15
J. D. Beazley: *Red-figure* (1942, 2/1963), i, pp. 181–93; ii, pp. 1631–3
L. Schnitzler: 'Vom Kleophrades-Maler', *Opscula Atheniensia*, ii (1955), pp. 47–60
J. D. Beazley: *Black-figure* (1956), pp. 404–6, 696, 715
R. Lullies: *Die Spitzamphora des Kleophrades-Malers* (Bremen, 1957)
A. H. Ashmead: 'Fragments by the Kleophrades Painter from the Athenian Agora', *Hesperia*, xxxv (1966), pp. 20–36
J. D. Beazley: *Paralipomena* (1971), pp. 175–6, 340–41
A. Greifenhagen: *Neue Fragmente des Kleophradesmalers* (Heidelberg, 1972)
J. Boardman: 'The Kleophrades Painter's Cup in London', *Getty Mus. J.*, i (1974), pp. 7–13
——: 'The Kleophrades Painter at Troy', *Ant. Kst*, xix (1976), pp. 3–18
J. Frel: 'The Kleophrades Painter in Malibu', *Getty Mus. J.*, iv (1977), pp. 63–76
B. Cohen: 'Paragone: Sculpture Versus Painting, Kaineus and the Kleophrades Painter', *Ancient Greek Art and Iconography*, ed. W. G. Moon (Madison, 1983), pp. 171–92
M. Robertson: 'Fragments of a Dinos and a Cup Fragment by the Kleophrades Painter', *Occas. Pap. Ant.: Gr. Vases Getty Mus.*, i/1 (1983), pp. 51–4
S. Matheson: 'Panathenaic Amphorae by the Kleophrades Painter', *Occas. Pap. Ant.: Gr. Vases Getty Mus.*, v/4 (1989), pp. 95-112
E. Kunze-Götte: *Der Kleophrades-Maler unter Malern schwarzfiguriger Amphoren: Eine Werkstattstudie* (Mainz, 1992)

BETH COHEN

Kodros Painter (*fl c.* 445–*c.* 430 BC). Greek vase painter. He is named after a scene in the tondo of a fine Attic Red-figure cup (Bologna, Mus. Civ. Archeol., PU 273), in which the heroic Kodros, last king of Athens, sets out for battle. On the outside of the cup are two further scenes of heroes departing: *Theseus and Phorbas*, and *Ajax with Menestheus*. In both cases the leave-takings are watched by figures closely associated with Athens; Aigeus, Athena, Melite and Lykos. This cup was painted in the 430s BC, in the years preceding the Peloponnesian War (431–404 BC) when many Athenians were themselves setting out for battles.

As a Late Classical artist the Kodros Painter was one of the last vase painters to specialize in decorating cups, which had had their greatest vogue in late Archaic times. He was probably a slightly older contemporary of the ERETRIA PAINTER and AISON, and stylistically he had much in common with them both. His floruit dates coincided with the construction of the Parthenon, and his style and temperament recall its sculptures. Over 52 cups or fragments of cups are attributed to him, and his work is distinctive. Anatomical details are lightly but convincingly rendered, with small, neat facial features and characteristically convoluted shell-like ears. He skilfully depicted his figures in various poses; in profile or three-quarter back view, crouching, or even flying through the air. The palmettes under the handles of his cups and the patterned borders of the tondi are also consistently neat and elegant.

The Kodros Painter's subject-matter is varied and interesting. Athletic scenes predominate, and, while many of these are unexceptional, some are *tours de force*; for example a cup (London, BM, E 94) on which one wrestler throws another in the 'flying mare' position. There are also vivid glimpses of athletes off the field, as on another cup (London, BM, E 83) where one athlete helps another wash his hair. Other cups show youths and warriors leaving home, and there are a few satyr scenes, notably one in which satyrs carrying a curious assortment of objects, including a heron, accost a youth on his way to a music lesson (Cambridge, Fitzwilliam, 2–1977). This scene may derive from a satyr play, but it also reflects Athenian street life. The Kodros Painter's work also includes mythological episodes, some of which are traditional and heroic, such as the *Kalydonian Boar Hunt* (Berlin, Antikenmus., 25381) or the *Symposion of the Gods* (London, BM, E 82), while others are enlivened by idiosyncratic touches. On a cup in London (BM, E 84), for example, the same six exploits of Theseus are represented around the tondo and on the outside, but the hero's pose is reversed, so that when seen in front view inside he is in back view outside, a playful three-dimensional effect. Of especial interest are the Kodros Painter's depictions of Attic mythology, for example the *Birth of Erichthonios* (Berlin, Antikenmus., 2537) and the complex, obscure myth of *Telamon and Eriboia* (Basle, Antikenmus., BS 432), as well as his name-piece, the *Departure of Kodros*. This emphasis on Athenian themes makes him a significant forerunner of such important late 5th-century BC artists as the MEIDIAS PAINTER.

BIBLIOGRAPHY

J. D. Beazley: *Red-figure* (1942, 2/1963), ii, pp. 1268–72
E. Paribeni: 'Pittore di Kodros', *Enc. A. Ant.* (Rome, 1958–73), iv, pp. 378–80
E. Berger: 'Zur Deutung einer neuen Schale des Kodrosmalers', *Ant. Kst*, xi (1968), pp. 125–36
W. Real: *Studien zur Entwicklung der Vasenmalerei im ausgehenden 5. Jahrhundert v. Chr.* (Münster, 1973)
L. Burn: 'A Heron on the Left, by the Kodros Painter', *Proceedings of the Third Symposium on Ancient Greek and Related Pottery: Copenhagen, 1987*, pp. 99–106
T. Seki: 'London E 84: A Trick Cup?', *Proceedings of the Third Symposium on Ancient Greek and Related Pottery: Copenhagen, 1987*, pp. 585–91

LUCILLA BURN

Kuban Painter (*fl c.* 410–*c.* 400 BC). Greek vase painter. He decorated the most important of a group of Panathenaic amphorae made in Athens, named the Kuban Group from the Kuban region in southern Russia, where the name-vase was found. All the vases are Black-figure amphorae that, filled with olive oil, were awarded as prizes in the contests associated with the quadrennial Athenian festival, the Great Panathenaia. The nucleus of the Kuban Group consists of three amphorae (St Petersburg, Hermitage, 17553; London, BM, B605 and B606). On stylistic grounds Beazley associated with these a slightly earlier amphora (London, BM, 1903. 2-17.1) and two fragments (Thessaloniki, Archaeol. Mus., 34.352; Oxford, Ashmolean, 1966.935). He also related other fragments now in Oxford and Thessaloniki to the Kuban Group (Beazley, 1956, pp. 411–12). Further attributions have been made of fragments from the Theban Kabeirion and the Athenian Agora (Braun and Haevernick; Moore and Philippides) and from the excavations in the Athenian Kerameikos (J. Frel; unpublished).

The Kuban Group amphorae have melon-shaped bodies and a heavy appearance. Of the four complete vases, three are of normal height (670–730 mm), but the slightly earlier amphora is smaller than usual (570 mm). The painter decorated them with a scheme that is normal for Panathenaic vases, with the reverse showing the contest for which the amphora was awarded, painted in the slick manner of the time. St Petersburg 17553 depicts the final moment of a boxing match, London B605 a youth testing his javelin, and London B606 a four-horse chariot at full speed. Most interesting is the picture on London 1903.2-17.1: two youths on horseback cast javelins at a shield fixed to a post. This is the earliest occurrence of an event, the quintain, which seems to have been added to the Panathenaia in the late 5th century BC. On all four vases

the obverse represents the conventional image of *Athena*, armed with spear and shield and striding to the left, flanked by Doric columns surmounted by cocks. The cocks of the Kuban Group are tall, emaciated birds. The figure of Athena is distinctly elongated, with a small head in relation to its height, and drawn in a somewhat archaizing style. The garments are richly adorned with white and red decorations, including dot-rosettes, stars, waves, zigzags, lotus and palmettes, and an olive wreath. The hem of the *chiton* is particularly elaborate: on London B606 it has a row of diminutive female dancers that have been connected with the 'Lakonian Dancers' group by the sculptor Kallimachos (Tiverios). The different white blazons used on Athena's shield include a *nike*, gorgon-heads surrounded by rays, and a famous Early Classical statue group, the *Tyrannicides*. The latter sculpture represented Harmodios and Aristogeiton, who slew Hipparchos at the Panathenaia in 514 BC, and it was set up in the Agora in 477/6 BC to serve as a symbol of liberty and democracy. This group was used as a shield-device not only on London B605 but also on two Panathenaic amphorae now in Hildesheim (Pelizaeus Mus., 1254 and 1253), and all three vases were presumably made in the same year, probably late 403 BC, after the Athenian democrats had overthrown the oligarchy of the Thirty and before the Great Panathenaia of 402 BC. In the same year the Ionic alphabet was officially adopted at Athens: it was employed for the traditional inscription on all three amphorae with the *Tyrannicides* shield-blazon.

BIBLIOGRAPHY

K. Peters: *Studien zu den panathenäischen Preisamphoren* (Berlin, 1942)
J. D. Beazley: 'Panathenaica', *Amer. J. Archaeol.*, xlvii (1943), pp. 441–5
—: *Black-figure* (1956)
J. Frel: *Panathenaic Prize Amphoras* (Athens, 1973)
B. A. Sparkes: 'Quintain and the Talcott Class', *Ant. Kst*, xx (1977), pp. 8–25
K. Braun and T. E. Haevernick: *Bemalte Keramik und Glas* (1981), iv of *Das Kabirenheiligtum bei Theben* (Berlin, 1940–)
M. Tiverios: '"Saltantes Lacaenae"', *Archaiol. Ephemeris* (1981), pp. 25–37
N. Eschbach: *Statuen auf panathenäischen Preisamphoren des 4. Jahrhunderts v. Chr.* (Mainz, 1986)
M. B. Moore and M. Z. P. Philippides: *Attic Black-figured Pottery* (1986), xxiii of *The Athenian Agora* (Princeton, 1953–)
P. D. Valavanis: 'Säulen, Hähne, Niken und Archonten auf panathenäischen Preisamphoren', *Archäol. Anz.* (1987), pp. 467–80

IAN McPHEE

Leagros group (*fl c.* 525–*c.* 500 BC). Greek vase painters. The group is named after five hydriai with kalos inscriptions praising Leagros. Its artists formed the last major group of Athenian Black-figure painters of large vases; they generally favoured shapes with broad surfaces suiting their large-scale compositions. Thus, of more than 400 vases attributed to them, about half are large hydriai with flat shoulders, or neck amphorae, the remainder mainly being other amphorae and kraters, as well as lekythoi. Like most contemporary artists, the Leagros group painters framed their compositions on large vases with patterned borders. However, they abandoned the hitherto common animal frieze below the body pictures of hydriai, replacing it with palmettes framed in scrollwork or loops, an already established Red-figure pattern. Indeed they sometimes even replaced the ivy trails, which commonly flanked paintings on contemporary Black-figure hydriai, with palmettes.

Although Beazley identified some individual artists within the group, its members' styles resemble each other so closely that further subdivision is difficult. The Painter of Louvre F314 appears to have specialized almost exclusively in stamnoi, while some Leagros group artists decorated other types of vases. The little that is known of the pot making of the Leagros group suggests that the vessels were made in the same workshop as pots of the Red-figure Pioneer group (*see* PHINTIAS, EUPHRONIOS and EUTHYMIDES). Leagros group work certainly shows the Pioneers' influence. Thus, while Black-figure artists generally painted few figures, avoided overlap, used colour and surface pattern to improve definition and shunned complex poses and anatomical studies, the Leagros group broke all these conventions. Instead, they produced strikingly complex scenes, with overlapping figures distinguished by very bold, clear incision, in emulation of the Pioneers' technical experiments. Leagros group painters also used little added colour, reflecting Red-figure practice, and minimal incised surface pattern. Their figures are large and take up almost the whole scene, while trees with trailing branches often fill the larger spaces producing a dark and crowded effect. The action sometimes overlaps its borders, occasionally with, presumably unintended, comic results, as when half a chariot emerges from the side of the picture. This tendency again reflects occasional Red-figure practice, particularly in the tondos of cups. Many of the group's vases also show figures twisting or bending, with an attention to details of musculature that clearly echoes the Pioneers' interest in anatomy and foreshortening. A favourite Leagran pose involves a head in profile, a frontal torso, and one leg frontal, one in profile.

The Leagros group's subjects are generally mythological. The *Adventures of Herakles* and the Trojan cycle are the most frequent and often incorporate new features, such as the prominence given to the dying Eurytion in *Herakles' Battle with Geryon* (on a hydria; London, BM, B310), or new episodes, such as *Herakles' Fight with Antaeus* (e.g. on a belly amphora; Munich, Staatl. Antikensamml., 1417), a subject also painted in Red-figure by Euphronios. The scenes from the Trojan cycle are strikingly brutal, for example on three hydriai showing *Troilos Killed by Achilles* (Munich, Staatl. Antikensamml., 1700), the *Sack of Troy and Murder of Priam* (*see* GREECE, ANCIENT, fig. 102) and the *Sacrifice of Polyxena* (Berlin, Pergamonmus., 1902). Bold depictions of established themes also occur, such as Ajax carrying Achilles' body over his shoulder (on a hydria; Munich, Staatl. Antikensamml., 1712). At the same time, a few vases reflect the growing interest in rendering everyday life apparent in Red-figure work: for example a rare scene of a potter's workshop on a hydria (*see* GREECE, ANCIENT, fig. 74), repeated scenes of departing warriors (e.g. on a hydria; London, BM, B314) and a cooking scene on an olpe (Berlin, Antikenmus., 1915). Some mythological scenes compress several episodes of a story; thus a hydria (Boston, MA, Mus. F.A., 63.473) merges the dragging of Hector's body away from the walls of Troy, the dragging of Hector's body around Patroklos' tomb,

and Iris summoning Priam to ransom Hector's body. Similar complex iconographic presentations feature on many of the group's most important vases.

The Leagros group's significance lies mainly in its attempt to compete with the then established Red-figure medium by stretching Black-figure to its technical limits. Ironically, despite their many successes, these painters clearly demonstrated the limitations of Black-figure and so contributed to its demise.

BIBLIOGRAPHY
J. D. Beazley: 'Attic Black-figure: A Sketch', *Proc. Brit. Acad.*, xiv (1928), pp. 26–8, 43–6, pl. 14
C. H. E. Haspels: *Attic Black-figured Lekythoi* (Paris, 1936), pp. 52, 59
J. D. Beazley: *Development of Black-figure* (1951, 3/1986), pp. 54, 74–80, 81, 86; pls 84–7
——: *Black-figure* (1956), pp. 354–91, 665, 695–6, 715, 716
E. T. Vermeule: 'The Vengeance of Achilles', *Bull. Mus. F.A., Boston*, lxiii (1965), pp. 35–52
J. D. Beazley: *Paralipomena* (1971), pp. 161–72
J. Boardman: *Athenian Black Figure Vases: A Handbook* (London, 1974), pp. 110–11; figs 199–207
L. Burn and R. Glynn: *Beazley Addenda: Additional References to* ABV, ARV2 *and* Paralipomena (Oxford, 1982, rev. T. H. Carpenter, 2/1989), pp. 95ff

ELIZABETH MOIGNARD

Lydos (*fl c.* 565–*c.* 535 BC). Greek vase painter. Active in Athens, he was among the finest Black-figure vase painters, and more than 130 vases of various shapes and sizes are attributed to him, though only two are signed. One is a lebes from the Acropolis (Athens, N. Archaeol. Mus., no. 607), the other a Type B amphora (Paris, Louvre, F 29). On both vases the artist's name has a definite article: 'the Lydian' was clearly his nickname, indicating some direct or indirect connection with Lydia. The inscription on the lebes further suggests that Lydos was a potter too. However, he also decorated vases for other potters, including Nikosthenes, Kolchos, Epitimos, and probably Amasis and Sotes. His style owed something to the workshop of the Ptoon Painter, to Kleitias and to the painter of Acropolis 606.

Lydos' career coincided with the period when Attic vases had a virtual monopoly of international markets, and his works have been found as far afield as the Black Sea, Ampurias (Emporiae) in Spain, and Tamassos in Cyprus. Among the most important works of his first period, painted when the early Black-figure decorative tradition of bands of animals and monsters was still strong, are a hydria depicting *Herakles and Geryon* (Rome, Villa Giulia, M 430) and a Tyrrhenian amphora depicting the *Judgement of Paris* and *Revellers at a Symposion* (Florence, Mus. Archeol., 70995). Characteristic works of his second period, during which his individual painting style developed fully, are a kylix with the *Deification of Herakles* (Taranto, Mus. N., 20137), the signed lebes depicting a *Gigantomachy*, an amphora with the *Pursuit of Troilos* and the *Sack of Troy* (Berlin, Pergamonmus., 1685), a column krater with the *Return of Hephiastos* (New York, Met., 31.11.11.), a plate with the *Arming of Achilles* (Athens, N. Archaeol. Mus., 507), and an amphora-psykter depicting *Dionysos and his Followers* and *Theseus and the Minotaur* (London, BM, B148). Towards the end of his career, when he had exhausted the possibilities offered by Black-figure, Lydos began to experiment with other forms of expression, such as the use of outline drawing, as on an important work from his late period, an oinochoe-psykter depicting *Herakles and Kyknos* (Berlin, Pergamonmus., 1732).

Lydos chose his subjects from both mythology and everyday life. Stories of Herakles, Dionysos and his followers, and the Trojan War were frequent themes in his work, while his characteristic everyday subjects were athletes, warriors and erotic scenes. Movement and symmetry clearly attracted him, and, while his drawing was always precise, the restraint of his early works later gave way to exuberance. His human figures are distinguished by their clear outlines and correct proportions. However, his style of depicting animals and monsters is less easily attributable, since it was imitated by his two closest pupils, the Painter of Vatican 309 and the Painter of Louvre F 6.

BIBLIOGRAPHY

A. Rumpf: *Sakonides* (Leipzig, 1937)
J. D. Beazley: *Development of Black-figure* (1951, 3/1986), pp. 38–45
——: *Black-figure* (1956), pp. 107–13, 684–5, 714
——: *Paralipomena* (1971), pp. 43–6
D. Callipolitis-Feytmans: *Les Plats attiques à figures noires* (Paris, 1974), pp. 87–110
M. A. Tiverios: *O Ludos kai to ergo tou* [Lydos and his oeuvre] (Athens, 1976)
L. Burn and R. Glynn: *Beazley Addenda: Additional References to* ABV, ARV2 *and* Paralipomena (Oxford, 1982, rev. T. H. Carpenter, 2/1989), pp. 29–33

M. A. TIVERIOS

Lysippides Painter (*fl c.* 530–*c.* 510 BC). Greek vase painter. An Attic Black-figure artist active during the transition from Black-figure to Red-figure, he is named after a kalos inscription on a neck amphora (London, BM, B 211) praising the youth Lysippides; some 30 vases, including amphorae, hydriae and cups, are ascribed to him. His most discussed works are Black-figure paintings on seven bilingual vases: a cup bearing the potter Andokides' signature and six amphorae, with Red-figure pictures attributed to the ANDOKIDES PAINTER, the probable inventor of the new Red-figure technique. The collaboration of two painters on the same vase was uncommon, so that some scholars believe that the Andokides Painter and the Lysippides Painter are the same artist. However, the conventional nature of the Black-figure paintings seems out of keeping for a brilliant innovator. Although he was the major follower of EXEKIAS, the Lysippides Painter's pictures are often derivative and not of the highest quality. His Exekian style was at first awkward (e.g. amphora, Rome, Villa Giulia, 24998), then refined (e.g. eye cup, Palermo, Mus. Reg., V 650) and finally sketchy and somewhat overblown (e.g. belly amphora, London, BM, B 193).

The Lysippides Painter was fond of horses and chariots (e.g. amphora, New York, Met., 58.32; hydria, Paris, Louvre, F 294) and favoured front views of the latter (e.g. neck amphorae, Oxford, Ashmolean, 208; Munich, Staatl. Antikensamml., 1575). He employed interlocking hooks for horses' hocks and knees, and curved lines and hooks for men's kneecaps and ankles respectively. He depicted Herakles wrestling the Nemean lion (e.g. amphorae, Prégny, Baron E. de Rothschild, priv. col.; Bologna, Mus. Civ. Archeol., 151), fighting Kyknos (cup, Cambridge, Fitzwilliam, 37.12), with the boar (oinochoe, London, BM, B 492), playing the cythara (Rome, Villa Giulia, 24998; Munich, Staatl. Antikensamml., 1575), in chariot scenes,

and also fighting Geryon and the Amazons on his masterpiece, the largest extant Black-figure eye cup (London, BM, B 426). This has a chariot and horseman depicted inside, around a Dionysiac tondo.

Like the bilingual version in Palermo, the Lysippides Painter's Black-figure eye cups (e.g. Brussels, Mus. Royaux A. and Hist., A3645; Munich, Staatl. Antikensamml., 2080) were probably produced in Andokides' pottery. Indeed, the Lysippides Painter may be identifiable with Andokides, since the potter also followed Exekias. The bilingual amphorae must also have come from Andokides' workshop. Some have the same subjects on both sides (e.g. *Achilles and Ajax Playing*, Boston, MA, Mus. F.A., 01.8037; *Herakles Banqueting*, Munich, Staatl. Antikensamml., 2301), while others feature different ones on either side (e.g. London, BM, B 193, with *Achilles and Ajax* in Black-figure and *The Nemean Lion* in Red-figure). In both cases the artist's Black-figure painting is characteristically old-fashioned. Thus, on the bilingual amphora (Paris, Louvre, F 204) he depicted a standard Black-figure Dionysos accompanied by a maenad (possibly Ariadne) and satyrs, opposite the Andokides Painter's unusual Herakles and Kerberos. His mature works are more complex, due to the inspiration of the Andokides Painter, and he even adapted the latter's Kerberos scene for a late Black-figure amphora (Moscow, Pushkin Mus. F.A., 70), inserting his favourite god, Hermes. However, the drawing is finicky, the composition crowded and the mood solemn, showing how far removed his literal, traditional nature was from the fresh sensibility of his Red-figure colleague.

BIBLIOGRAPHY

R. Norton: 'Andokides', *Amer. J. Archaeol.*, xi (1896), pp. 1–41
J. D. Beazley: 'Attic Black-figure: A Sketch', *Proc. Brit. Acad.*, xiv (1928), pp. 24–5
——: *Red-figure* (1942, 2/1963), i, p. 2
——: *Development of Black-figure* (1951, 3/1986), pp. 70–71, 85, 103
R. Lullies: 'Eine Schale des Andokides-Malers in München', *Z. Ges. Keramikfreunde*, i (1953), pp. 15–20
J. D. Beazley: *Black-figure* (1956), pp. 254–65
H. Marwitz: 'Zur Einheit des Andokidesmalers', *Jhft. Österreich. Archäolog. Inst. Wien*, xlvi (1961–3), pp. 73–104
J. D. Beazley: *Paralipomena* (1971), pp. 113–16
J. Boardman: *Athenian Black Figure Vases: A Handbook* (London, 1974), p. 105
——: *Athenian Red Figure Vases: The Archaic Period* (London, 1975), pp. 15–17
B. Cohen: *Attic Bilingual Vases and their Painters* (New York, 1978), pp. 1–104
L. Burn and R. Glynn: *Beazley Addenda: Additional References to* ABV, ARV2 *and* Paralipomena (Oxford, 1982, rev. T. H. Carpenter, 2/1989), pp. 65–7

BETH COHEN

Macmillan Painter [Chigi Painter] (*fl c.* 660–*c.* 640 BC). Greek vase painter. Active in Corinth, he is named after the aryballos (*see* GREECE, ANCIENT, fig. 89) found there and presented by Malcolm Macmillan in 1889 to the British Museum. He is also known as the Chigi Painter after the Chigi Jug (Rome, Villa Giulia, 22679), which was exported to Veii in Etruria. He was a leading painter in the Proto-Corinthian style (*see* GREECE, ANCIENT, §V, 4(ii)), specializing in the decoration of ovoid aryballoi (containers of perfumed oil). Despite the small size of these vessels (average h. 70 mm), there are several zones of surface decoration on the body, including an

Orientalizing floral design on the shoulder, solid rays round the base, a main figured central zone and one or more subsidiary figured friezes below. The main scene exploits to the utmost the newly devised Black-figure technique of incised silhouette, which allowed the overlapping of figures in closely knit compositions without any loss of clarity (*see* GREECE, ANCIENT, §V, 5). Often he varies the usual colour scheme by applying different shades of brown for human flesh and body armour, in addition to the purplish-red normally used for minor details.

This painter's aryballoi belong to the second half of the Middle Proto-Corinthian phase (mid-7th century BC), and the earliest examples bear mythical representations. On one vase, Berlin 2686 (Berlin, Antikenmus.), four centaurs collapse under a shower of arrows from Herakles' bow. Another (Boston, Mus. F.A., 95.10) shows Bellerophon with Pegasus, flying through the air to assail the fire-breathing Chimaira. The paintings on both these vases are rendered with vigour and *joie de vivre*; their backgrounds are packed with varied filling ornaments, which on the painter's more mature work are thinned out or omitted altogether. On later vases the scenes are confined to purely human conflict; tense battle scenes are wrapped round the main zones, with 18 hoplites (armed foot soldiers) on the Macmillan Aryballos and 21 on Berlin 3773 (Berlin, Antikenmus.); the warriors are equipped with the newly invented hoplite panoply. In both scenes, many different designs are emblazoned on the warriors' overlapping shields, as they endeavour to keep their ranks.

On three aryballoi the decoration breaks into the third dimension. The mouth of the Macmillan aryballos is modelled as a lion's head after the Neo-Hittite prototype: cubic, pug-like and benign. Similarly, three human heads in the Daedalic sculptural style, with Orientalizing layered wigs, surmount an aryballos in Taranto (Mus. N., 4173). Both leonine and human heads are combined on Berlin 3773, for which a tiny rampant lion serves as the handle.

The Macmillan Painter's latest work appears on a larger type of vessel, the olpe, the baggy, round-mouthed jug introduced in the Late Proto-Corinthian phase (*c.* 650–*c.* 640 BC). On the Chigi Vase, his finest work, the body carries two broad zones. Above, hoplite ranks are piped into battle by a child; the extraordinary realism of the drawing makes this scene an indispensable document for our understanding of early hoplite warfare. Below, several themes are juxtaposed: a sadly fragmentary scene of the *Judgement of Paris*, in which painted inscriptions name the figures; a double-bodied sphinx; a procession of horsemen, sometimes shown two abreast and distinguished by different colours; and a lion hunt in which the Assyrian type of lion, with heavy body, massive mane and a muzzle more pointed than in the Neo-Hittite examples, makes its first appearance in Greek vase painting.

The painter's subsidiary scenes are among his liveliest creations, showing him to be a virtuoso in miniature vase painting. Breaking away from conventional animal friezes, he specialized in horse races and hunts, brilliantly executed with a sense of rapid movement and an astonishing variety of detail, often in fields less than 10 mm high.

BIBLIOGRAPHY

K. F. Johansen: *Les Vases sicyoniennes* (Paris, 1923), pp. 98–9
J. L. Benson: *Die Geschichte der korinthischen Vasen* (Basle, 1953), pp. 18–19
T. J. Dunbabin and C. M. Robertson: 'Some Protocorinthian Vase-painters', *Annu. Brit. Sch. Athens*, xlviii (1953), pp. 179–80

NICOLAS COLDSTREAM

Makron (*fl* early 5th century BC). Greek vase painter. He has been ascribed over 350 vases, more than any other Athenian painter in the Red-figure technique. However, only one is certainly signed by him. Makron worked consistently with the potter Hieron, and of more than 30 signed works by Hieron almost all are painted by Makron. Most of the vessels are cups on tall stands, and the pictures inside these are always framed with a simple meander.

Like most vase painters, Makron may also have worked as a potter. Despite the large number of vases attributed to him, his work displays great unity. The *kalos* names correspond with those on later vases by DOURIS, suggesting that Makron worked prolifically over a short period, though a certain development can be perceived in his output.

Makron's drawing is generally less fine than Douris', but it developed rapidly, becoming richer and more decorative, more fluid and skilful, particularly in the representation of human proportions, especially in the case of women. A few pieces, mainly with mythological subjects, were thoughtfully composed and drawn in great detail. Typical features include heads with a flat skull-pan and deep eyebrows, and garments with carefully drawn and variably disposed drapery. There is sometimes a suggestion of fair hair in single locks, as well as rich figural decoration on clothing and other objects. Though Makron represented clothing with increasing virtuosity, the outlines of the body were always clearly stated—in the case of female figures in the transparently drawn chiton—forming the basis for the pictures. The composition of the tondi inside cups generally shows a unified conception and the outside decoration, made up of multi-figured friezes based on groups of two, has a balanced rhythm, with dancing and Dionysiac celebrations as frequent subjects. The outside and inside pictures are generally related thematically. Mythology does not feature largely in Makron's work: his preferred subjects were sport, banquets, dancing, scenes of Dionysiac revelry or worship, and erotic scenes, of which there are a great many, primarily rows of courting couples, more often both male than of mixed sex. Among the mythological scenes, those involving the Trojans and their allies are prominent. Herakles also figures, as do Peleus and Thetis. Makron's masterpieces include a cup with the *Judgement of Paris* (Berlin, Antikenmus.) and two exceptionally fine skyphoi, one showing *Helen with Paris* (and on the other side *Helen with Menelaus*), which carries the only unequivocal signature by Makron (Boston, MA, Mus. F.A.), and the other showing *Triptolemos among the Eleusinian Gods* (London, BM). Of the non-mythological pieces, an aryballos depicting *Children with Toy Chariots* (Oxford, Ashmolean) deserves special mention.

Pupils of Makron in the second quarter of the 5th century BC probably included the Clinic Painter and the Telephos Painter. Their pictures are sometimes rather mannered, but they are more often humorous in effect than those of their teacher.

BIBLIOGRAPHY

F. Leonard: *Über einige Vasen aus der Werkstatt des Hieron* (diss., U. Greifswald, 1912)

J. C. Hoppin: *A Handbook of Attic Red-figured Vases*, ii (Cambridge, MA, 1919), pp. 38–110

J. D. Beazley: *Red-figure* (1942, 2/1963), i, pp. 458–82; ii, 1654–5, 1706

L. D. Caskey and J. D. Beazley: *Attic Vase Paintings in the Museum of Fine Arts, Boston*, iii (London, 1963), pp. 30–31

J. D. Beazley: *Paralipomena* (1971), pp. 377–9

J. Boardman: *Athenian Red Figure Vases: The Archaic Period* (London, 1975), p. 140

G. Nachbaur: *Schalen des Makron aus der Werkstatt des Hieron* (diss., Graz, Karl-Franzens-U., 1978)

D. von Bothmer: 'Notes on Makron', *The Eye of Greece*, ed. J. Boardman and D. Kurtz (Cambridge, 1982), pp. 13–26

L. Burn and R. Glynn: *Beazley Addenda: Additional References to* ABV, ARV2 *and* Paralipomena (Oxford, 1982, rev. T. H. Carpenter, 2/1989), pp. 243–7

M. Denouelles: 'Macron au Louvre', *Rev. Louvre*, 41 (1991), no. 5–6, pp. 13–26

REINHARD STUPPERICH

Mannerist Workshop (5th century BC). Greek vase painters. This group of over 15 Attic Red-figure vase painters, including the PAN PAINTER, worked throughout the 5th century BC, mainly decorating column kraters, hydriai and pelikai. Their rather affected style is characterized by tall, slender figures with small heads, and by the perpetuation of Archaic features. The latter include stacked pleats and groups of folds in garments, hanging lotus-bud chains and framed pictures on pelikai and the shoulders of hydriai, as well as subjects such as the *Draped Apollo Playing a Lyre* (e.g. on a column krater; Tarquinia, Pal. Vitelleschi, 684) and *Ajax and Achilles Playing a Board Game* (e.g. on a column krater; Berlin, Pergamonmus. 3199).

The group frequently depicted revels and symposia and, later, domestic scenes. Some of their mythological scenes are unparalleled in Athenian vase painting: for example the *Madness of Salmoneus* (Chicago, IL, A. Inst., 89.16) and the *Death of Prokris* (London, BM, E 477), both on column kraters. On a pelike (Naples, Mus. Archeol. N., ex-Spinelli 2041) *Io* was depicted for the first time with a human body, under the influence of contemporary theatre.

The earliest members of the group, such as the Pig Painter and the Leningrad Painter, were taught by MYSON; it was later influenced by, among others, the NIOBID PAINTER and POLYGNOTOS and his group, the KLEOPHON PAINTER and the KADMOS PAINTER. One artist's signature survives, on an amphora (London, BM, E 284), revealing that a late group member, the Nausikaa Painter, was also called Polygnotos.

BIBLIOGRAPHY

J. D. Beazley: *Red-figure* (1942, 2/1963), i, pp. 562–88, ii, pp. 1106–25

J. Boardman: *Athenian Red Figure Vases: The Archaic Period* (London, 1975)

L. Burn and R. Glynn: *Beazley Addenda: Additional References to* ABV, ARV2 *and* Paralipomena (Oxford, 1982, rev. T. H. Carpenter, 2/1989)

THOMAS MANNACK

Marsyas Painter (*fl* mid-4th century BC). Greek vase painter. He is among the better known of the KERCH STYLE painters (*see* above) and a late but accomplished practitioner of Attic Red-figure. His tall, slender figures combine frontal with three-quarter views and other parts of the body in profile, giving an impression of three-dimensionality. This is illustrated by a pelike showing *Peleus Abducting Thetis* (*see* GREECE, ANCIENT, fig. 115), which also includes a three-quarter back view of a naked nymph running into the background, creating a sense of depth that was new to vase painting at the time. He is named after the depiction on a pelike (St Petersburg, Hermitage, KEK 8) of *Marsyas Awaiting his Fate*. The characteristic crispness and plasticity of the drapery of the Marsyas Painter's clothed figures may have been inspired by sculpture. Like many of his contemporaries he used white highlighting to emphasize certain figures and objects or to focus or balance his compositions. He also occasionally employed other colours, notably blue and red, to enhance clothing and erotes' wings, with gold for jewellery, erotes' wings and any details in relief. His fine, precise drawing recalls works by such predecessors as the Jena Painter, and his stylistic innovations contributed to the final flowering of Attic Red-figure.

BIBLIOGRAPHY

K. Schefold: *Untersuchungen zu den Kertscher Vasen* (Berlin, 1934), pp. 127–31

J. D. Beazley: *Red-figure* (1942, 2/1963), ii, pp. 1474–76

E. Simon: *Die griechischen Vasen* (Munich, 1976, 2/1981), pp. 157–60

A. Lebel: *The Marsyas Painter and Some of his Contemporaries* (diss., Oxford U., 1989)

A. LEBEL

Meidias Painter (*fl c.* 420–*c.* 400 BC). Greek vase painter. He is named after the potter's signature on a large Red-figure hydria (*see* GREECE, ANCIENT, fig. 114) and was one of the last great Athenian vase painters. His teacher was probably AISON (*see* above), but the style and subject-matter of his work suggest that he was also influenced by the older KODROS PAINTER and ERETRIA PAINTER. The Meidias Painter himself later attracted an important following, including Aristophanes, the Painter of the Carlsruhe Paris and the Painter of the Athens Wedding. Over 250 vases are attributed to the group. Some of these artists decorated large vases, especially hydriai, but most of them favoured smaller shapes, such as choes, pyxides, squat lekythoi and lekanides. The Meidian style and its iconography have a distinctive extravagance (Beazley) and evoke a sensual, leisured and luxurious world that is the visual counterpart to the poetry of the contemporary tragedian Agathon, represented in Plato's *Symposion* as a master of the flowery phrase.

Meidian compositions are densely packed with figures, mostly female, clustered into affectionate groups of two or three. They are generally 'Polygnotan' (*see* POLYGNOTOS OF THASOS) in having no single ground line. Instead, the figures are set at various levels and are occasionally only partly visible. White lines suggest irregularities in the terrain, while trees, shrubs and scattered flowers contribute to the outdoor effect. The Meidias Painter himself was adept at using vase shapes and compositions that complemented each other. On his name-piece, for example, the outward-facing chariot teams of the Dioskouroi lead the eye towards the projecting handles, but the focus then moves back along the horses' bodies to the central scene of the Dioskouroi and their brides, and on to Aphrodite, watching from below.

Meidian figures have distinctive faces. Noses are long and straight, eyes large, mouths small, chins heavy and rounded, and heads are often shown in three-quarter view.

Women are slim and long-legged, men plump and effeminate. Both sexes have elegant hands and feet, with long, tapering fingers and toes. The women are always elaborately attired. Their often transparent, multi-pleated drapery clings tightly to the body or swirls away in exaggerated flourishes, and is sometimes decorated with stars, palmettes or wave patterns. Hair styles vary: several types of richly patterned headdress occur, but the hair sometimes hangs loose in prolific curls and ringlets. Gold earrings, necklaces, bracelets and hair ornaments are worn, while girdles are also tipped with gold.

The Meidias Painter and his associates worked during the Peloponnesian War (431–404 BC), yet their subjects were almost exclusively peaceful. Aphrodite was their favourite deity, occasionally accompanied by her consort Adonis, the dying god whose vegetation cult had recently been introduced to Athens. Thus, one of a fine pair of hydriai in Florence (Mus. Archeol., 81948) depicts Adonis lying back against Aphrodite's knees, while the other (81947) depicts his mortal counterpart Phaon, the Lesbian ferryman on whom Aphrodite bestowed eternal youth and irresistible charm. On both vases, as often elsewhere, Aphrodite is attended by a retinue of personified abstractions in the form of Eunomia (Good Order), Eukleia (Good Repute), Eudaimonia (Happiness) and Eutychia (Good Fortune). Despite subsidiary political, religious and philosophical connotations, the main function of these figures was probably to create an atmosphere of peace, harmony and beauty, as a form of escapism from the horrors of war. Other favourite Meidian figures include the legendary musicians Mousaios and Thamyris, always attended by Muses and other women. They too occur in peaceful scenes, but even ostensibly violent subjects were generally transformed into gentle idylls. On the painter's name-piece, the *Rape of the Leukippidai* was refined into a peaceful elopement. Similarly, Herakles is depicted not battling with the Hydra or with Geryon, but contemplating the beauty of his wife, Deianeira (on a pelike, New York, Met., 37.11.23), or, as on the name vase, sitting at ease in the Garden of the Hesperides, watched by an amiable serpent and plied with golden fruit by the nymphs. Such escapist scenes were often endowed with a specifically Athenian character by the inclusion of Athenian tribal heroes. For example Akamas, Oineus, Hippothoon and Antiochos relax with Herakles in the Garden of the Hesperides, enjoying the sort of existence for which their descendants might happily have exchanged their wearisome lives. They embody the nostalgic mood of contemporary Athenian thought, as does another popular Meidian subject, the birth from the ground of Erichthonios.

BIBLIOGRAPHY

H. Nicole: *Meidias et le style fleuri* (Paris, 1908)
J. D. Beazley: *Attic Red-figured Vases in American Museums* (Cambridge, MA, 1918), p. 185
W. Hahland: *Vasen um Meidias* (Berlin, 1930)
G. Becatti: *Meidias: Un manierista antico* (Florence, 1947)
W. Real: *Studien zur Entwicklung der Vasenmalerei im ausgehenden 5. Jahrhundert v. Chr.* (Münster, 1973)
U. Knigge: 'Aison, der Meidiasmaler? Zu einer rotfigurigen Oinochoe aus dem Kerameikos', *Mitt. Dt Archäol. Inst.: Athen. Abt.*, xc (1975), pp. 123–43
L. Burn: *The Meidias Painter* (Oxford, 1987)

LUCILLA BURN

Myson (*fl* first quarter of 5th century BC). Greek vase painter. His name is given by the Greek inscription, 'Myson painted and made [me]', on a small Attic Red-figure column krater (Athens, N. Archaeol. Mus., Acropolis 806). His importance lies in his influence on his milieu and on the craft itself. He is best known for his picture of *Kroisos on his Pyre* on an amphora (Paris, Louvre, G 197). This and other early work show ambition and indicate an apprenticeship among the Pioneers. Crossing paths with the Eucharides Painter, the Göttingen Painter and the Chairippos Painter, he then specialized in column kraters, the first in Athens to do so in quantity. Of some 90 vases attributed to him, most are column kraters, usually with a single figure on each side, a style made popular by his contemporary the BERLIN PAINTER. Myson combined a certain grace with a heavy line; his style tightened, then grew flabby. Details in his later work often parallel work of much earlier artists. His preferred subjects were revellers, athletes and Dionysiac scenes; the exceptions are often interesting or unusual. Myson taught the earliest members of the MANNERIST WORKSHOP, which was active for over 50 years.

BIBLIOGRAPHY

E. Pottier: 'Deux silènes démolissant un tertre funéraire', *Mnmt & Mém.: Fond. Piot*, xxix (1927–8), pp. 149–92
J. D. Beazley: *Red-figure* (1942, 2/1963), i, pp. 237–44; ii, pp. 1592, 1638
A. B Follmann: *Der Pan-Maler* (Bonn, 1968), pp. 70–74 [relationship with Pan Painter]
J. D. Beazley: *Paralipomena* (1971), pp. 349, 510
J. Boardman: *Athenian Red Figure Vases: The Archaic Period* (London, 1975/R 1983), p. 112
L. Burn and R. Glynn: *Beazley Addenda: Additional References to* ABV, ARV2 *and* Paralipomena (Oxford, 1982, rev. T. H. Carpenter, 2/1989)
L. Berge: *Myson: A Craftsman of Attic Red-figured Vases* (Chicago, 1994)

L. BERGE

Naukratis Painter (*fl c.* 575–*c.* 550 BC). Greek vase painter. Together with the BOREADS PAINTER, he represents the 'old generation' in Lakonian Black-figure. His name vase, a cup from Naukratis, Egypt (London, BM, B 4), depicts a standing female figure holding a plant and surrounded by winged daemons. This has been interpreted as the nymph Kyrene but is more likely to be the vegetation deity Artemis Orthia. Such representations of single divine or daemonic figures, outside any narrative context, were favoured by the Naukratis Painter. Two cups attributed to him (Paris, Louvre, E 668; Taranto, Mus. N., IG 4988) show a seated *Zeus* with an eagle flying towards him, and a cup from Cerveteri (Mus. N. Cerite, 90287) depicts *Poseidon Riding a Hippokampos*. The interiors of other cups variously show a daemon (a sphinx, a Gorgon, a Boread, or Pegasos), and there are also some symposion scenes with winged daemons surrounding the diners (e.g. cup, Paris, Louvre, E667). The Naukratis Painter may have invented the characteristic high foot of the Lakonian cup, and he also worked on other shapes including lakainai, kraters and hydriai. He was a good draughtsman and produced fine decorative friezes and rich floral patterns. From Corinthian vase painting he borrowed such designs as the animal frieze, which he used on both small and larger vases.

The Naukratis Painter had a strong influence on all the later important Lakonian vase painters, and his manner was also imitated by lesser followers until the end of the 6th century BC.

See also GREECE, ANCIENT, §V, 5(iii).

BIBLIOGRAPHY

E. A. Lane: 'Lakonian Vase-painting', *Annu. Brit. Sch. Athens*, xxxiv (1933/4), pp. 139–40
B. B. Shefton: 'Three Laconian Vase-painters', *Annu. Brit. Sch. Athens*, xlix (1954), pp. 303–6
C. M. Stibbe: *Lakonische Vasenmaler des sechsten Jahrhunderts v. Chr.*, 2 vols (Amsterdam and London, 1972), pp. 45–85, pls. 1–26

MARIA PIPILI

Nearchos (*fl c.* 560–*c.* 550 BC). Greek vase painter and potter. His signature appears on seven Attic Black-figure pots and one clay plaque, once as potter and painter, otherwise, as far as preserved, only as potter. His significance as a potter is hard to assess because of the fragmentary state of his vases. His four early lip cups have exceptionally thin sides, while his two signed kantharoi dedicated on the Acropolis were unusually large (estimated h. 500 mm; Athens, N. Archaeol. Mus., Acropolis 611, 612). Five of Nearchos' signed works were painted by him, while the remaining three cups bear so little painting that this cannot be attributed. Finally, fragments of a further kantharos have been ascribed to Nearchos on stylistic grounds.

Nearchos' status as a master of Attic Black-figure is based mainly on the fragments of the only vase he signed as painter: a kantharos showing *Achilles with his Chariot* (Athens, N. Archaeol. Mus., Acropolis 611). This painting does not illustrate any specific scene from the *Iliad*. Instead, Nearchos created his own image of the hero setting out for battle by linking two complementary scenes that otherwise only occur separately: the *Nereids Bearing Achilles' Weapons* and the *Harnessing of Achilles' Chariot*. The names of the horses and of the charioteer are not those traditionally associated with Achilles. Nonetheless, the depiction of the hero gently fitting a bridle on one of his steeds suggests the intimate relationship between Achilles and Xanthos, the divine horse who foretold his death (*Iliad*, XIX.400–24). Meanwhile, Achilles' attitude of calm dignity and the scene's general evocation of solemnity and foreboding make Nearchos a forerunner of the artists of the full Classical period (*c.* 450–*c.* 400 BC).

The pictures on Nearchos' kantharoi are painted in the Black-figure technique, but are unusually colourful and give some idea of the lost wall paintings of the period: one of the horses is completely red, another white with black outlines, while the tongue pattern above the pictures is painted on a white ground. Nearchos was the first Attic artist to depict the harnessing of a chariot team, a theme that became highly popular in the second half of the 6th century BC, and he was also the first to represent *Herakles and Atlas* (inside a cup; Berne, priv. col.). In addition, he signed a remarkable aryballos (New York, Met., 26.49) with delicate comic pictures around the mouth and on the handle which show his talent as a miniaturist. Nearchos' two sons TLESON and Ergoteles were also miniaturists, and, since both their signatures included their father's name, Nearchos may have remained in charge of their workshop in his old age. This conjecture is supported by Nearchos' dedication of a marble statue by the well-known

sculptor ANTENOR on the Acropolis at a time (*c.* 520 BC) when he can no longer have been active as a painter or potter. At any rate the dedication testifies to the continuing commercial success of the pottery workshop.

BIBLIOGRAPHY

G. M. A. Richter: 'An Aryballos by Nearchos', *Amer. J. Archaeol.*, xxxvi (1932), pp. 272–5
J. D. Beazley: *Development of Black-figure* (1951, 3/1986), pp. 37–8
——: *Black-figure* (1956), pp. 82–3, 347, 682
D. von Bothmer: 'Five Attic Black-figure Lip-cups', *Amer. J. Archaeol.*, lxvi (1962), pp. 255–8
J. D. Beazley: *Paralipomena* (1971), pp. 30–31, 70, 523
H. Jucker: 'Herakles und Atlas auf einer Schale des Nearchos in Bern', *Festschrift für Frank Brommer* (Mainz, 1977), pp. 191–9
I. Scheibler: 'Griechische Künstlervotive der archaischen Zeit', *Münchn. Jb. Bild. Kst*, xxx (1979), pp. 9–10
L. Burn and R. Glynn: *Beazley Addenda: Additional References to* ABV, ARV2 *and* Paralipomena (Oxford, 1982, rev. T. H. Carpenter, 2/1989), p. 23

HEIDE MOMMSEN

Nettos Painter (*fl c.* 620–*c.* 600 BC). Greek vase painter. The Nettos Painter is named from the Attic spelling of the Centaur Nessos, who is depicted in the episode of *Herakles Slaying Nessos* on the neck of the splendid Attic Black-figure neck amphora, the artist's masterpiece (*see* GREECE, ANCIENT, fig. 95). He is the earliest Attic Black-figure vase painter to have left sufficient vases (about 30) for it to be possible to chart his chronology and to interpret his artistic personality. Most of these vases were found in Attica, where they served as grave markers or tomb furnishings. Four vases formerly ascribed to the Chimaera Painter were recognized by Beazley as examples of his early work.

The Nettos Painter preferred to decorate large shapes, chiefly amphorae and skyphos–kraters, though he also painted some lekanides and a plaque. The best examples of his large-scale work are his name piece, three skyphos–kraters from the cemetery at Vari (Athens, N. Archaeol. Mus., 16382, 16383, 16384), a fragmentary amphora (Aigina, Archaeol. Mus., 585) and two well-preserved amphorae (Athens, Agora Mus., P 1247, and Eleusis Mus., Z 21). The lekanides from Vari (Athens, N. Archaeol. Mus., 16363–16369, 16414 and 16416e) bear good examples of his smaller paintings.

Early works by the Nettos Painter generally depict single figures occupying most of the available surface (e.g. the sphinx on Eleusis Mus., Z 21) or, more often, pairs of animals, such as the sphinxes on the stand of Athens 16382 or the two felines attacking a bull depicted on its bowl. (This theme has a long history in both sculpture and painting.) Similarly, a skyphos–krater (Athens, Kerameikos Mus., 154) presents a powerful version of the confrontation between Bellerophon and the Chimaira, and an amphora (Athens, Agora Mus., P 1247) shows a sphinx on each side, probably intended as guardians of a tomb since the vase is weathered. A skyphos–krater of his middle phase (Athens 16383) has a vivid scene of a galloping cavalcade, and this is also the time when his sequence of lekanides begins. He decorated these smallish bowls with friezes of animals, a scheme inherited from Corinth. His louterion (Berlin, Pergamonmus., 1682; destr. during World War II, see Beazley, 1971) may have been of a later date. It was decorated with two panels. One depicted Harpies, the other Perseus, and the figures were labelled, as are those of Herakles and Nessos on the artist's namepiece, where Herakles is shown killing Nessos, who had tried to ravish his wife, Deianeira, while carrying her across the River Evenus. The stumbling centaur raises both hands in supplication, and his long, shaggy beard and coarse features contrast sharply with the trim beard and refined features of Herakles. This deliberate contrast between man and monster later became a frequent theme in Attic vase painting. On the body of the vase, Medusa's two sisters fly over a 'sea' of wave-like spirals surmounted by a frieze of leaping dolphins. On the viewer's far left Medusa sinks down on one knee, blood spilling from her severed neck. Perseus himself is omitted, but his presence is clearly felt. Equally ambitious is the scene on a skyphos–krater (Athens, N. Archaeol. Mus., 16384) of *Herakles Freeing Prometheus from the Eagle*. Prometheus is shown still fettered, while Herakles, who has already wounded the bird in the neck, is drawing his bow and aiming another arrow. On the stand of the same vase a dignified procession of four women depicts a quieter moment from this artist's repertory. Each woman is holding a palmette, and a Doric column, perhaps representing a temple, flanks the scene at each side. This is the first appearance in Attic Black-figure of an architectural element. Equally dignified is the lyre player on the fragmentary plaque (Athens, Agora Mus., A–P 1085).

The Nettos Painter's flexibility makes him one of the masters of Attic Black-figure. Despite his preference for large vessels and his manner of letting his figures extend unrestrained over their surfaces, he was also adept at painting smaller vessels with figural friezes framed above and below by ornamental bands. Similarly, while he preferred to depict mythical monsters, he also produced some unforgettable narrative scenes, including those on Athens, National Archaeological Museum, 1002 and 16384, and Kerameikos Museum, 154. His drawing style is for the most part expansive and bold, with sure and competent incision, and the black glaze is often enlivened by skilful application of additional white or red. He was the first Attic painter to master the Black-figure technique and to break completely with Proto-Attic style, thus opening the way for later painters.

BIBLIOGRAPHY
J. D. Beazley: *Development of Black-figure* (1951, 3/1986), pp. 13–15
——: *Black-figure* (1956), pp. 4–6, 679
A. Boegehold: 'The Nessos Amphora: A Note on the Inscription', *Amer. J. Archaeol.*, lxvi (1962), pp. 405–6
S. Karouzou: *Angeia tou Anagyrountou* [Pots from Anagyrous] (Athens, 1963)
J. D. Beazley: *Paralipomena* (1971), pp. 1–5

Nikias Painter (*fl c.* 420–*c.* 400 BC). Greek vase painter. Active in Athens, he was a contemporary of the MEIDIAS PAINTER (*see above*) and is named after the potter Nikias, who signed one of his bell kraters (London, BM, 1898.7-16.6). There are 37 vases or fragments attributed to him, primarily bell kraters but also some hydriai and oinochoai and one rhyton. He frequently depicted athletes, revellers, symposia and sacrifice scenes; the reverse sides of his bell kraters almost always bear the same three draped youths. Among his more unusual themes are *Leda and the Egg*, armed runners casting lots at a statue of Athena and two

scenes with crouching dancers. His hydriai carry typical Meidian subjects: two show the *Judgement of Paris*, while three others depict brides accompanied by divinities and women. The artist's name vase shows the end of a torch-race, with Nike flying up to the winning runner with the sash of victory; a wreathed old man leaning on a staff stands behind the altar. This may be the god or hero, perhaps Prometheus, in whose honour the race was run; the inscription on the wreath of the victor identifies him as the tribal hero Antiochos. The scene seems to represent simultaneously both mythical and contemporary torch races. The Nikias Painter's style is casual rather than precise: the facial features recall works by AISON (*see above*) and the Meidias Painter, but the musculature is sketchy; the drapery, though fussy and elaborate, bears very little correspondence to either the forms or the movements of the limbs beneath it.

BIBLIOGRAPHY
J. D. Beazley: *Red-figure* (1942, 2/1963), ii, pp. 1333–5
W. Johannowsky: 'Due vasi del Pittore di Nicia al Museo Nazionale di Napoli', *Boll. A.*, n. s. 3, xlv (1960), pp. 202–12
W. Real: *Studien zur Entwicklung der Vasenmalerei im ausgehenden 5. Jahrhundert v.Chr.* (Münster, 1973), pp. 37–40

LUCILLA BURN

Niobid Painter (*fl c.* 470–*c.* 445 BC). Greek vase painter and potter. He is named after a scene on an Attic calyx krater depicting the *Killing of the Niobids* (Paris, Louvre, G 341), and some 130 vases and fragments have been attributed to him. He was trained in the workshop of the BERLIN PAINTER, but *c.* 470 BC he set up his own workshop along with the Altamura Painter and the Blenheim Painter. This specialized in producing large vases and was subsequently taken over by his pupil POLYGNOTOS.

The Niobid Painter's work reflects the transition from the Archaic style of Red-figure vase painting to the Classical style. His early compositions, figures and drapery were stiff and simple (e.g. lekanis, Naples, Mus. Archeol. N., 2638). Subsequently, however, his compositions became more complex, his figures began to interact, and his drapery became softer and more substantial with increasingly sharply differentiated details, culminating around 450 BC in works such as his name vase. His draughtsmanship was always careful and assured. His figures are tall and slender and have broad heads with idealized profiles and clearly differentiated features. Their ears are elongated and their eyes wide open and surmounted by a long flat brow, while the eye socket is suggested by a second line on the upper eyelid. The mouths have downturned corners and full bottom lips, while the chins are heavy and prominent. The men's bodies are muscular and their garments substantial.

The Niobid Painter followed the Berlin Painter's tastes in vase shapes and ornament. Thus he favoured kraters, neck amphorae, hydriai and pelikai, generally decorating them with an edging consisting of a meander interrupted by crosses in squares, with a band of lotus palmettes round the mouth and lyre palmettes and palmette trees near the handles. The ornament is distinguished by its varied and meticulously drawn tendrils and leaves.

The Niobid Painter's commonest scenes are of lovers pursuing each other, sacrifices, the *Departure of Triptolemos* and great battles involving Amazons, centaurs, giants or Trojans. The depictions of sacrifices generally consist of three figures, and are skilfully composed to suggest the emotional bonds between them and give a sense of timeless universality. The artist also seems to have been intent on glorifying Athens. Thus he preferred the Athenian hero Theseus to the more generally Greek hero Herakles and drew inspiration from Athens' role in the recent Persian wars, while using Triptolemos, originally an Eleusinian hero, to embody Athens' claim to be the cultural and political centre of Greece.

Many scenes by the Niobid Painter and his followers may reflect lost wall paintings by Polygnotos of Thasos or Mikon. The most famous (on his name vase, on the opposite side to the *Killing of the Niobids*) was originally thought to depict the Argonauts but probably represents the gathering of the Athenian heroes before the Battle of Marathon (490 BC). In it the artist abandoned the single ground line usual in vase painting to create an illusion of depth. However, while this device was almost certainly borrowed from murals, the style of painting was adapted to suit the smaller field provided by the vases.

See also GREECE, ANCIENT, figs 70 and 113.

BIBLIOGRAPHY

T. B. L. Webster: *Der Niobidenmaler* (Leipzig, 1935)
J. D. Beazley: *Red-figure* (1942, 2/1963), i, pp. 598–608
E. Simon: 'Polygnotan Painting and the Niobid Painter', *Amer. J. Archaeol.*, lxvii (1963), pp. 43–62
P. E. Arias: 'Problemi stilistici, iconologici e cronologici sul Pittore dei Niobidi', *Atti Pont. Accad. Romana Archeol.*, liii–liv (1984), pp. 145–79
S. Bonomi: 'Una nuova pelike del Pittore dei Niobidi', *Archäol. Anz.*, (1985), pp. 29–47
M. Prange: *Der Niobidenmaler und seine Werkstatt* (Frankfurt am Main, 1991)

MATHIAS PRANGE

Oltos (*fl c.* 525–*c.* 500 BC). Greek vase painter. He was an important early Athenian Red-figure artist. He apparently trained in the workshop of NIKOSTHENES and initially specialized in bilingual eye cups, decorating more extant specimens than any other artist. Indeed, most of his over 150 surviving works are cups, including the two potted by Euxitheos that bear Oltos' painter-signature (Berlin, Pergamonmus., 2269; Tarquinia, Pal. Vitelleschi, RC 6848). He was particularly influenced by the earliest Red-figure artists, the ANDOKIDES PAINTER and PSIAX, while his Black-figure output recalls Psiax in motif and the ANTIMENES PAINTER in style. Oltos employed Black-figure exclusively for scenes on eye-cup tondos, such as the *Running Dionysos Carrying a Rhyton and Vine* (Rome, Vatican, Mus. Gregoriano Etrus. 498) or the *Spear-bearing Trumpeters* (Rome, Vatican, Mus. Gregoriano Etrus., 46; Bryn Mawr Coll., PA, Riegal Mem. Mus.), using fine incision and substantial added red. Between the large eyes on the cups' exteriors he painted Red-figure trumpeters, warriors, athletes, women, beasts, plants or inanimate objects. The genre suited his forthright, repetitive style.

Oltos' characteristic kalos inscriptions praising Memnon first appeared on the hastily painted bilingual vases and Red-figure palmette-eye cups of his middle period. The various potters' signatures on his works (e.g. Nikosthenes, Pamphaios, Chelis, Kachrylion and Euxitheos) attest to the late Archaic painter's mobility between workshops. The mature Oltos learnt much from the younger artist EUPHRONIOS, whom he surely met at the potteries of Kachrylion and Euxitheos. Thus, his stately *Assembly of Gods* on the exterior of a Red-figure cup (Tarquinia, Pal. Vitelleschi, RC 6848) rivals works of the Pioneer group in its intricately detailed composition and sure draughtsmanship. Oltos, however, always remained more interested in elegant decoration than in naturalism. Contact with the Pioneers may also explain why his masterpieces occur on unusual or innovative shapes. Thus, he painted special Red-figure Nikosthenic amphorae (Paris, Louvre, G 2, G 3) and a special Red-figure stamnos (London, BM, E 437) potted by Pamphaios, placing Red-figure palmettes at the handles of both, as he generally did on his Red-figure cups.

The pictures on his two psykters (wine coolers) typify his style and personality with their deceptively simple figures drawn with a supple relief line over the vessels' sharply curving surfaces. Athletes and their trainers encircle one (New York, Met., 10.20.18): as usual, the figures have downturned lips, hands in affected gestures and long feet, and are drawn in profile but without great anatomical detail. On the other (New York, Met., 1989.281.69) the frieze of singing warriors mounted on dolphins is a clever creation for a vessel designed to float within a krater. Oltos was an energetic and enterprising painter whose long career extended from the early development of Red-figure to the experiments of the Pioneers.

BIBLIOGRAPHY

F. P. Johnson: 'Oltos and Euphronios', *A. Bull.*, xix (1937), pp. 537–60
J. D. Beazley: *Red-figure* (1942, 2/1963), i, pp. 53–67, ii, pp. 1622–3, 1700
A. Bruhn: *Oltos and Early Red-figure Vase Painting* (Copenhagen, 1943)
P. E. Arias and M. Hirmer: *Tausend Jahre griechischer Vasenkunst* (Munich, 1960): Eng. trans. and rev. by B. Shefton as *A History of Greek Vase Painting* (London, 1962), pp. 320–22
J. D. Beazley: *Paralipomena* (1971), pp. 326–8
J. Boardman: *Athenian Red Figure Vases: The Archaic Period* (London, 1975)
B. Cohen: *Attic Bilingual Vases and their Painters* (New York, 1978)
L. Burn and R. Glynn: *Beazley Addenda: Additional References to* ABV, ARV2 *and* Paralipomena (Oxford, 1982, rev. T. H. Carpenter, 2/1989), pp. 162–6

BETH COHEN

Onesimos (*fl c.* 505–*c.* 480 BC). Greek vase painter. Active in Athens, he specialized in decorating cups, mostly of Type B, and his work evinces a lively, energetic personality. His name is known from the signature on a cup (Paris, Louvre, G 105) also signed by EUPHRONIOS as potter. At least 10 other cups painted by him bear Euphronios' signature, and others have been attributed on the basis of the potting style.

Onesimos worked in steady collaboration with Euphronios, who also profoundly influenced his drawing style. His preferred kalos name was 'Panaitios', which led to his also being called the Panaitios Painter, sometimes identified as a different and earlier artist. J. D. Beazley listed vases attributed to the Panaitios Painter (Beazley, 1942), but these are all now usually considered the work of Onesimos. In addition, some of the vases attributed by Beazley to the Eleusis Painter or Proto-Panaetian Group probably represent Onesimos' earliest work. Besides the kalos inscription 'Panaitios', Onesimos frequently praised Athenodotos and, less often, Leagros on his early cups.

Later, the names Erothemis, Boukolos, Lykos and Aristarchos occur: the first two are unique to Onesimos, the second two also occur on the vases of his pupil the Antiphon Painter. Onesimos' early work is marked by large tondi with big, boldly drawn figures in complex action poses, often with frontal limbs or heads, for example the satyr in the tondo of a cup (10.179) in the Museum of Fine Arts, Boston, MA. Satyrs and maenads occur especially often in his early work, as do themes drawn from the legends of Troy, Theseus or Medea, for which Onesimos invented new and unusual compositions, often filling his tondi with figures, as on a kylix depicting Theseus visiting Amphitrite accompanied by Athena and a small triton (Paris, Louvre, G 104).

With his associates in Euphronios' workshop, the BRYGOS PAINTER, DOURIS and the Antiphon Painter, Onesimos experimented with less familiar techniques, such as White-ground or coral-red. He sometimes used White-ground for the entire interior of a cup, as on early fragments from Eleusis (Eleusis Mus., 518 and 519), or, unusually, only in the zone around the tondo. He also painted a Red-figure zoned cup with a *Gigantomachy* surrounding the picture of *Selene* in the tondo (Athens, First Ephoria Store). Among the ornamental motifs he employed were a variety of meander types. He came to prefer the stopt meander as a border for tondi, and one or two reserved lines for the ground-line on the exterior. Though he specialized in cups, Onesimos also decorated a few small vases, an alabastron and several kyathoi.

In his mature work Onesimos turned from mythological subjects to those taken from daily life. Scenes involving athletes, lovers or party guests gave scope for his mastery of foreshortening and zest for lively action with twisting back views and various unsavoury poses. He noted realistic details, such as hairy male bodies, receding hairlines or sagging female breasts (*see* DRESS, fig. 1). He also painted genre scenes, for example a school scene, a fisher boy, a boy reading or a negro groom. Several of these cups carry inscriptions. Some have 'spoken' inscriptions, such as the lovers in the tondo of a cup in the Museum of Fine Arts, Boston, MA (65.873). Onesimos' later work is distinguished by smaller, more graceful figures with quieter, almost introspective attitudes. He was one of the most forceful representatives of the generation of vase painters that followed the Pioneer Group, continuing their experiments in the representation of the human body. He had a discernible influence on his contemporaries, and his style was carried on by several pupils, including the Brygos Painter.

BIBLIOGRAPHY

J. D. Beazley: *Attic Red-figured Vases in American Museums* (Cambridge, MA, 1918), pp. 14–18
——: *Red-figure* (1942, 2/1963), i, pp. 313–30; ii, pp. 1645–6, 1701, 1706
——: 'Some Fragments by the Panaitios Painter', *Amer. J. Archaeol.*, lxvi (1962), pp. 235–6
——: *Paralipomena* (1971), pp. 358–61, 511
D. Williams: 'The Ilioupersis Cup in Berlin and the Vatican', *Jb. Berlin. Mus.*, xviii (1976), pp. 9–23
M. Ohly-Dumm: 'Medeas Widderzauber auf einer Schale aus der Werkstatt des Euphronios', *Getty Mus. J.*, ix (1981), pp. 5–21
L. Burn and R. Glynn: *Beazley Addenda: Additional References to* ABV, ARV2 *and* Paralipomena (Oxford, 1982, rev. T. H. Carpenter, 2/1989), pp. 166–9
I. Wehgartner: *Attische weissgrundige Keramik* (Mainz, 1983), pp. 81–4
B. A. Sparkes: 'Aspects of Onesimos', *Greek Art: Archaic into Classical*, ed. C. Boulter (Leiden, 1985), pp. 18–39
H. R. Immerwahr: *Attic Script* (Oxford, 1990), pp. 84–5
M. Robertson: *The Art of Vase Painting in Classical Athens* (Cambridge, 1992), pp. 43–51

DIANA BUITRON

Pan Painter (*fl c.* 480–*c.* 450 BC). Greek vase painter. Active in Attica, he was associated with the MANNERIST WORKSHOP (*see* above) and named by Beazley after the picture on the obverse of a Red-figure bell krater (Boston, MA, Mus. F.A., 10.185) showing *Pan in Pursuit of a Young Goatherd*. More than 160 vases have been attributed to him, one of the earliest being a psykter in Munich (Staatl. Antikensamml., 2417), usually thought to date from the 480s BC, although dates as late as 460 BC have been suggested. The end of his career is represented by a bell krater (Palermo, Mus. Reg., V778) and some other vases with less generous use of relief lines.

The Pan Painter's drawing style is distinctive. The heads of his figures are round, with rounded and heavy chins and thick necks in which the musculature is sometimes indicated by one or two brown lines. White hair is usually indicated by reserved areas. His rendering of male anatomy relates to that of MYSON (*see* above), with two divisions of the abdominal muscles rather than the usual three. The arms are strong, with upper muscles sometimes shown by brown-glaze opposed semicircles and lower ones by a brown-glaze line running diagonally from the inside of the elbow to the wrist. Frontal feet are common, occasionally with more than five toes, which are drawn as small arcs. Boots, elegant high leather shoes and sandals strapped to the calves also occur often, as on works by the Mannerists, the Niobid Painter and others. Rocks, sometimes covered with a yellow wash and with stylized cracks, are another distinctive feature. Garments fall in straight folds, frequently grouped in fours, and stacked pleats. The *chiton* often forms a bolster either side of the waist when belted.

Some of the Pan Painter's compositions are outstanding. On a pelike (Athens, N. Archaeol. Mus., 9683) Herakles is shown holding an Egyptian by his feet, with a group of two other Egyptians forming a dynamic triangular composition around a centrally placed altar. The range of vase shapes is exceptionally wide, including cups; hydriai; oinochoai; loutrophoroi; both neck and belly amphorae; bell, calyx and volute kraters; lebetes; stamnoi; alabastra; a kantharos and a psykter. His favoured shapes, however, appear to have been lekythoi, including two White-ground examples, column kraters, pelikai and Nolan amphorae, nearly all with triple handles. With the exception of those on two of his pelikai, his pictures, even on large vases, are unframed. Eight small pelikai seem to come from the same potter's workshop, and most of these have a distinctive pattern of ovolos with blackened centres on the neck. The Pan Painter's patterns are usually simple: keys or broken stopt meanders in pairs or threes, alternating with saltires, sometimes with dots, or crosses in squares.

The Pan Painter's subjects are equally varied, including gods, heroes and scenes of daily life, often with unusual touches. The psykter in Munich shows *Apollo Fighting Idas for the Love of Marpessa*, a subject also depicted by the Triptolemos Painter, with whose workshop he seems to have had connections. Two vases depict *Artemis Turning*

Actaeon's Dogs against their Master. On the earlier, a volute krater (Athens, N. Archaeol. Mus., Akr. 760) the scene alludes conventionally to Actaeon's metamorphosis into a deer by dressing him in a deerskin, but on the reverse of the later vase (the artist's name-piece; see above) no transformation is suggested. Two paintings depict scenes from the *Iliad*, with *Achilles Slaying Penthesilea* on a calyx krater (Cambridge, Fitzwilliam, GR 3.1971), and the *Ransom of Hector* on a stamnos (Paris, Louvre, C108221). The former also shows *Herakles with Syleus*, and two vases depict *Herakles Killing the Egyptian King Busiris* (Athens, N. Archaeol. Mus., 9683; Leipzig, Karl-Marx-U., Archäol. Inst., T651). On the vase in Athens, a pelike, the detail is remarkable. The Egyptians, who have negroid features, are correctly shown as being circumcised. The altar is adorned with mouldings, palmettes and volutes. A rare depiction of the *Infant Herakles Killing the Snakes in his Cradle* (a cup; Leipzig, Karl-Marx-U., Archäol. Inst., T3365) is also by the Pan Painter. *Theseus Fighting the Minotaur* occurs on a skyphos (New York, Met., X.22.25 (GR85)), and both this and the *Infant Herakles* were subjects popular with the other Mannerists. So too were the *Death of Kaineus* (column krater; London, BM, E473), *Triptolemos Bringing Man the Gift of Corn* (pelike; Ferrara, Mus. N. Archeol., 83(42)) and *Perseus and Medusa* (hydria; London, BM, E181). Scenes of daily life include sacrifices and musical and domestic scenes, and often depict herms.

The Pan Painter was possibly a pupil of Myson (Beazley, 1963), but some scholars consider his teacher to have been a colleague of Peithinos and the Sosias Painter (Follmann) or the Berlin Painter (Sourvinou-Inwood). There are certainly connections between the works of the BERLIN PAINTER and the Pan Painter, since the former decorated an equally wide range of shapes, but also favoured lekythoi and Nolan amphorae. His preference for single, grand figures can be paralleled in the Pan Painter's work, as can his choice of ornament. The Pan Painter's treatment of male anatomy does, however, suggest that Myson taught him and that he was only later influenced by the Berlin Painter. Myson was the founder of a Mannerist workshop that lasted to the end of the 5th century BC, but, while the Pan Painter can be classed as a Mannerist, he differed from the others in quality and character, and his style is in fact 'subarchaic' (Beazley, 1944): both his early and later vases tend to be more elaborately decorated, while the figures are more slender, posing rather than acting, and the drapery shows decorative rather than realistic treatment.

No pupils of the Pan Painter are known, though his influence has been noted in the scenes of revellers by the Cleveland Painter, the Alkimachos Painter and the earlier Mannerists. There is no known example of the Pan Painter's signature. The word *kalos* (Gr.: 'beautiful') occurs on two of his vases, though without the customary named youth, while a vase from his circle praises Hippon.

BIBLIOGRAPHY

J. D. Beazley: 'The Master of the Boston Pan-Krater', *J. Hell. Stud.*, xxxii (1912), pp. 354–69
——: *Red-figure* (1942, 2/1963), i, pp. 550–61
——: *The Pan Painter* (Oxford, 1944)
A. B. Follmann: *Der Pan-Maler* (diss., U. Bonn, 1968)
C. Sourvinou-Inwood: 'Who Was the Teacher of the Pan Painter?', *J. Hell. Stud.*, xcv (1975), pp. 107–21
M. Robertson: 'Two Pelikai by the Pan Painter', *Greek Vases in the J. Paul Getty Museum*, iii (Malibu, 1986), pp. 71–90

THOMAS MANNACK

Paseas [Cerberus Painter] (*fl c.* 520–*c.* 510 BC). Greek vase painter. Formerly called the Cerberus Painter (after a plate, Boston, MA, Mus. F.A., 01.8025, showing *Herakles Leading Kerberos*), he was a minor Athenian Red-figure painter, primarily of plates and small vases (e.g. cups, an alabastron and a standlet); he also decorated several votive plaques of Athena (Athens, N. Archaeol. Mus., Acropolis 2583–5, 2587–9, 2591) in Black-figure on white ground. On some, flesh is emphasized by outline as well as a second white, while one preserves his unique signature: 'one of the paintings of Paseas'.

Paseas' energetic figures, with over-large heads and simple bodies, derive from the ANDOKIDES PAINTER, but also recall OLTOS and the Pioneers: in several techniques his skill recalls PSIAX. He commonly reserved hair borders and used red inscriptions, yet his style remained naively old-fashioned. His subjects include *Theseus* (Paris, Louvre, G 67), *Dionysos* (New Haven, CT, Yale U. A.G., 170) and male athletes (U. Amsterdam, Pierson Sticht., 2474; London, BM, E 138), all on plates; female dancers on a standlet (London, BM, E 809); and charming erotica such as a woman with phallus bird on a chalicup (Rome, Villa Giulia; Heidelberg, Ruprecht-Karls-U., 20). A plate depicting an *Archer on Horseback* (Oxford, Ashmolean, 310) carries a kalos inscription praising Miltiades, while Paseas' masterpieces, the *Kerberos* scene and a touching *Rape of Kassandra* (New Haven, CT, Yale U. A.G., 169), are also on plates.

BIBLIOGRAPHY

C. Roebuck: 'White-ground Plaques by the Cerberus Painter', *Amer. J. Archaeol.*, xliii (1939), pp. 467–73
J. D. Beazley: *Red-figure* (1942, 2/1963), i, pp. 163–4, ii, p. 1630
J. Boardman: 'A Name for the Cerberus Painter?', *J. Hell. Stud.*, lxxv (1955), pp. 154–5
J. D. Beazley: *Black-figure* (1956), pp. 352–3, 399–400
——: *Paralipomena* (1971), pp. 160, 174, 337
J. Boardman: *Athenian Black Figure Vases: A Handbook* (New York, 1974)
——: *Athenian Red Figure Vases: The Archaic Period* (London, 1975)
J. R. Mertens: *Attic White-ground: Its Development on Shapes Other than Lekythoi* (New York and London, 1977)
L. Burn and R. Glynn: *Beazley Addenda: Additional References to ABV, ARV2 and Paralipomena* (Oxford, 1982, rev. T. H. Carpenter, 2/1989), pp. 95, 104, 182

BETH COHEN

Phiale Painter (*fl c.* 450–*c.* 425 BC). Greek vase painter. He is named after an Attic Red-figure phiale depicting a *Dancing School* (Boston, MA, Mus. F.A., 97.371), and he is attributed with a further 202 extant vases, all but seven of which are also Red-figure. These few White-ground works are his best, and include some genuine masterpieces.

Although he also decorated other shapes, the Phiale Painter preferred Nolan amphorae and lekythoi. His deployment of two rows of pictures on calyx kraters and of shoulder figures on his lekythoi is unusual but characteristic. Though he was a pupil of the ACHILLES PAINTER, his vigorous figures, painted with rapid, sketchy lines, contrast with the static, precisely drawn figures of his teacher. His medium-sized figures are the most successful, the larger ones being somewhat sparsely drawn and the smaller ones poorly proportioned.

The Phiale Painter's range of subjects is remarkable, and some of his mythological scenes seem inspired by Greek tragedy. His hydriai with *Thamyras and the Muses* (Rome, Vatican, Mus. Gregoriano Etrus., 16549: Naples, Mus. Archeol. N., 81531) may reflect Sophocles' *Thamyras*, and the scenes on his White-ground calyx kraters of *Perseus and Andromeda* (Agrigento, Mus. Reg. Archeol.) and *Hermes Bringing the Infant Dionysos to Papposilenos and the Nymphs of Nysa* (Rome, Vatican, Mus. Gregoriano Etrus., 16586) may derive from Sophocles' *Andromeda* and *Dionysiskos* respectively. Rare subjects also occur, such as *Perseus and the Graiai* on a fragment (Delos, Archaeol. Mus.) and *Bendis* on a cup (Verona, Mus. Archeol. Teat. Romano, 52). There are also some unusual scenes from daily life—for example the *Unveiling of the Bride* on a loutrophoros (Boston, MA, Mus. F.A., 10.223) and a chorus of muffled dancers on a double-register calyx krater (Rome, Vatican, Mus. Gregoriano Etrus., Astarita 42)—while recurrent scenes include a youth or god pursuing a woman, a dancing girl and mistress, *Europa and the Bull* and women in domestic settings.

The subject-matter of his White-ground work and its intense treatment often distinguish it from that of his contemporaries. On a lekythos (Munich, Staatl. Antikensamml., 6248) Hermes, leader of souls on their last journey, beckons gently to a woman standing in front of a tomb and adjusting a wreath on her head before departing for the underworld. On another (Athens, N. Archaeol. Mus., 19355), a woman stands to the left of a tomb, holding a pet hare, while an old maidservant kneels wailing at the other side.

The Red-figure paintings vary more in quality. Some have a certain monumentality, for example the scene on a stamnos (Warsaw, N. Mus., 142465) depicting women preparing for a Dionysiac ritual. Others, especially on Nolan amphorae and lekythoi, are less carefully drawn, though their compositions still give an attractive impression of unrestrained movement which contrasts with the works of many contemporary painters, notably the Achilles Painter, who seem to have been more profoundly influenced by the serenity of the Parthenon sculptures.

BIBLIOGRAPHY

J. D. Beazley: *Red-figure* (1942, 2/1963), ii, pp. 1014–26, 1678
G. M. A. Richter: *Attic Red-figured Vases* (New Haven, 1946, 2/1958), pp. 122–3
P. E. Arias and M. Hirmer: *Tausend Jahre griechischer Vasenkunst* (Munich, 1960), trans. and rev. by B. Shefton as *A History of Greek Vase Painting* (London, 1962), pp. 364–5, 367, 374
D. C. Kurtz: *Athenian White Lekythoi* (Oxford, 1975), pp. 48–50
J. H. Oakley: *The Phiale Painter*, Kerameus, viii (Mainz, 1990)
——: 'Attische rotfigurige Pelike des Phiale Malers und weitere Addenda', *Archäol. Anz.* (in preparation)

JOHN H. OAKLEY

Phintias (*fl c.* 520–*c.* 500 BC). Greek vase painter and potter. Phintias signed six vases as painter and three, which he did not paint, as potter. The spelling of his name varies, suggesting that he was not highly literate. Altogether, less than 20 vases ascribed to him survive, but these display considerable variety of shape, including Type A amphorae, a pelike, a volute krater, calyx kraters, both kalpis and shoulder-type hydriai, a psykter and drinking cups.

Phintias was one of the so-called Pioneer group of vase painters (which also included the more gifted Euthymides and Euphronios), who explored and developed the new, Red-figure technique (*see* GREECE, ANCIENT, §V, 6(i)). His drawing is bold and simple and avoids over-embellishment of garments and armour. He was, however, attentive to detail, as in his careful drawing on an amphora (Paris, Louvre, G 42) of the soles of Leto's sandals. Like other Pioneers, he mastered the art of bold anatomical foreshortening, a good example being the figure of Apollo on an amphora (Tarquinia, Pal. Vitelleschi, RC 6843). His compositions seldom contain many figures, usually only three or four, and spread comfortably over the surface of the vase.

Phintias' subjects vary considerably and do not reveal particular preferences for specific myths or scenes of daily life. Among his most impressive paintings is *Herakles and Apollo Struggling for the Delphic Tripod* (on Tarquinia, Pal. Vitelleschi, RC 6843). It shows a youthful-looking Herakles firmly grasping one leg of the tripod and threatening Apollo with his club. The other side of the amphora shows *Satyrs with Maenads in the Presence of Dionysos*. A satyr depicted full-face and a close-knit group comprising a satyr and maenad recall similar groups in the work of the Amasis Painter, and the figure of Tityos carrying off Leto probably derives from such groups as the wrestlers on an amphora by the Andokides Painter (Berlin, Antikenmus., 2159). On Phintias' pelike (Paris, Louvre, Cp 10784) a satyr and a maenad make music and dance while Dionysos looks on. The scenes of revelling on the body of a hydria (Munich, Staatl. Antikensamml., 2422) are in a similar vein, and the shoulder of this vase depicts *Satyrs Molesting a Deer*. Other mythological scenes painted by Phintias involve heroes and their exploits. One side of a cup (Munich, Staatl. Antikensamml., 2590 (J401)) shows *Herakles Wrestling with the Giant Alkyoneus*; the other depicts *Herakles and Apollo Struggling for the Delphic Tripod*. A calyx krater (St Petersburg, Hermitage, 1843) shows *Theseus Struggling with a Beast* (probably the bull of Marathon), and a fragment (Limenas Mus.) depicts *Achilles Fighting Memnon*. An amphora (Paris, Louvre, G 42) and a psykter (Boston, MA, Mus. F.A., 01.8019) both show scenes of youthful athletes with their trainers. Other images of daily life include a *Music Lesson* on another hydria (Munich, Staatl. Antikensamml., 2421) and *Youths at a Fountain* and *A Boy Buying a Vase* on a cup (Baltimore, MD, Mus. A.). Symposia are depicted on the shoulders of two hydriai (London, BM, E 159 and Munich, Staatl. Antikensamml., 2421).

BIBLIOGRAPHY

J. D. Beazley: *Red-figure* (1942, 2/1963), i, pp. 23–25
——: *Paralipomena* (1971), pp. 323, 507, 509

□

Polion (*fl c.* 430–*c.* 410 BC). Greek vase painter. About 21 vases or fragments have been ascribed to him, ranging from kraters to oinochoai and lekythoi. Active in Athens, his name is known from the signature on a large Red-figure volute krater (New York, Met., 27.122.8) depicting *Apollo Preparing to Mount his Chariot*. The scene covers both sides of the vase, showing Apollo taking his lyre from Leto, while Artemis, holding the reins, looks back at him.

Hermes stands at the horses' heads, Athena behind them, and Zeus, Hera, Dionysos, Poseidon and Herakles are also present. The figures are statuesque and rather static, and are arranged along a single ground-line. Most are swathed in drapery, with their bodies and legs in three-quarter view and their heads in profile. The painting is careful, the effect dignified, yet both subject and composition seem unenterprising. Polion was apparently aware of new advances in composition though not altogether comfortable with them. This impression is confirmed by scenes on a second large volute krater (Ferrara, Mus. N. Archeol., T. 127) showing *Thamyris Playing his Lyre before the Muses* and the *Return of Hephaistos*. Here, though the figures are not set on a single ground-line, they are not dispersed freely over the field in the more progressive manner of the Meidias Painter and other contemporaries. Instead they are simply arranged on two discrete levels. While Polion's subjects are often conventional, some are more unusual. The scene of Thamyris is remarkable for its representation of the *xoana* (wooden statues) of the Muses and may show the influence of a dithyramb, as may a scene on a bell krater (New York, Met., 25.78.66) depicting comic silenoi dancing and strumming their lyres below an inscription referring to the Athenian festival of the Panathenaia.

BIBLIOGRAPHY
Enc. A. Ant.
J. D. Beazley: *Red-figure* (1942, 2/1963), ii, pp. 1171–3
W. Real: *Studien zur Entwicklung der Vasenmalerei im ausgehenden 5. Jahrhundert v. Chr.* (Münster, 1973), pp. 28–34

LUCILLA BURN

Polygnotos (*fl c.* 450–*c.* 425 BC). Greek vase painter. He was a prolific Athenian Red-figure artist of the High Classical period (*c.* 450–*c.* 400 BC), who was trained in the workshop of the NIOBID PAINTER, from whom he derived his monumental style. This was apparently based on Early Classical wall paintings, notably by MIKON and POLYGNOTOS OF THASOS, after whom this vase painter was probably named, and is characterized by the use of an uneven ground-line to suggest landscape, as on Polygnotos' early pelike showing *Apollo Attacking Tityos* (Paris, Louvre, G 375).

Like other vase painters in Periclean Athens, Polygnotos modelled some of his figures on the sculptures designed by PHEIDIAS for the Parthenon. Thus the two horsemen on his stamnos (Oxford, Ashmolean, 1916.68) echo the riders on the Parthenon frieze (442–438 BC), while many of his other figures recall the frieze in their stateliness or in more specific details.

Polygnotos decorated large pots, primarily amphorae, stamnoi and kraters, and depicted an unusually wide variety of subjects for his time. He favoured combat scenes, including ones from epic poetry, such as *Greeks Fighting Amazons*, *Kaineus and the Centaurs*, *Apollo and Tityos*, *Perseus and Medusa*, *Ajax and Kassandra* and the *Death of Laios*. He also portrayed quieter traditional subjects, including *Triptolemos*, scenes of lovemaking, symposia, sacrifices and departing warriors. Five vases signed by Polygnotos survive, among them two stamnoi (Brussels, Musées Royaux A. & Hist., A 134; London, BM 96.7–16.5), and nearly 70 more have been attributed to him, mostly by Beazley, who also regarded him as having

supervised a large workshop, including the Peleus Painter and KLEOPHON PAINTER.

BIBLIOGRAPHY
J. D. Beazley: *Red-figure* (1942, 2/1963), ii, pp. 1027–33
P. E. Arias and M. Hirmer: *Tausend Jahre griechischer Vasenkunst* (Munich, 1960), Eng. trans. and rev. by B. Shefton as *A History of Greek Vase-painting* (London, 1962)
S. B. Matheson: 'Polygnotos: An *Iliupersis* Scene at the Getty Museum', *Greek Vases in the J. Paul Getty Museum*, iii (Malibu, 1986)

SUSAN B. MATHESON

Polyphemos Painter (*fl c.* 670–*c.* 650 BC). Greek vase painter. He was active either in Athens or on the island of Aegina in the Saronic Gulf. An imaginative innovator in mythical representation on a grand scale, he was named after the Middle Proto-Attic amphora from Eleusis (Eleusis Mus.) showing the intoxicated Polyphemos blinded by Odysseus (*see* GREECE, ANCIENT, fig. 90). His early work owes something to the Early Proto-Attic (*c.* 700–*c.* 670 BC) Mesogeia Painter (*see* GREECE, ANCIENT, §V, 4(iii)), who was perhaps his teacher. On the Eleusis amphora his style is mature, exploiting black and white paint equally. His human figures are in silhouette, except for outlined faces; heads are rounded above, with receding forehead and chin, and bull neck. Minimal use is made of incision, and figures do not overlap. On the neck the giant Polyphemos, blinded while asleep, holds a wine cup to explain his misfortune. On the body Perseus, having beheaded Medusa, escapes from her two enraged Gorgon sisters, protected by Athena; uniquely, the Gorgons' faces are portrayed as Near Eastern metal cauldrons with serpents appended. The confronting lion and boar on the shoulder of the vase bare their teeth, typically aggressive specimens of this painter's animal repertory.

A krater stand (ex-Pergamonmus., Berlin; see Corp. Vasorum Ant., Berlin i, pp. 24–5, pls 31–3), a later work of this painter, shows, among an assembly of chieftains, a figure named, in Aiginetan script, Menelas (Menelaos). The stand, like several other works by this hand, is from Aigina but made of Attic clay; Aiginetan clay is unsuitable for the production of fine painted pottery. It follows either that the Polyphemos Painter was an Aiginetan resident in Athens, or that he worked on Aigina in the Proto-Attic tradition.

BIBLIOGRAPHY
Corp. Vasorum Ant., Berlin, i
G. E. Mylonas: *Ho Protoattikos amphoreus tis Eleusinos* [The Protoattic amphora, from Eleusis] (Athens, 1957)
E. T. H. Brann: *Late Geometric and Protoattic Pottery, Mid 8th to Late 7th Century BC* (1962), viii of *The Athenian Agora* (Princeton, 1953–), pp. 11, 23–4
S. P. Morris: *The Black and White Style: Athens and Aigina in the Orientalizing Period* (New Haven, 1984), pp. 37–51

NICOLAS COLDSTREAM

Priam Painter (*fl c.* 515–*c.* 500 BC). Greek vase painter. He is named after a Black-figure hydria (Madrid, Mus. Arqueol. N., 10920) depicting *Priam Setting out to Ransom the Body of Hector*. The nearly 60 vases attributed to him cover an unusually wide variety of subjects, which are sometimes accompanied by narrative inscriptions. There is compositional balance between decorated and undecorated areas, costumes and accessories are often elaborate and exotic, and horses are small and fine-boned, with little or no indication of musculature. This refinement recalls works by the ANTIMENES PAINTER and by PSIAX, who may have been his teacher: the RYCROFT PAINTER was apparently a workshop colleague. Women are frequently depicted in scenes greatly animated by their gestures and poses: in an orchard, bathing in a grotto or fetching water at a fountain. Chariot scenes and depictions of Herakles and other heroes departing are also common, while his *Herakles Fighting Alkyoneus* and *Aeneas Carrying his Father* are among the earliest examples of these scenes. These works are related iconographically to the ANDOK-IDES PAINTER and his circle, and both iconographically and compositionally to paintings by the LEAGROS GROUP. Sometimes the frame of the decorative panel interrupts the narrative elements; conversely figures sometimes overlap the frame, a device apparently designed to create elementary spatial relationships and to compete with the innovations of Red-figure painting.

BIBLIOGRAPHY

W. G. Moon: 'The Priam Painter: Some Iconographic and Stylistic Associations', *Ancient Greek Art and Iconography* (Madison, 1983), pp. 97–118

WARREN G. MOON

Pronomos Painter (*fl c.* 410–*c.* 390 BC). Greek vase painter. He was an exponent of the florid style of Athenian vase painting of the late 5th century BC and early 4th, and he is named after the flute player Pronomos (*fl c.* 400–*c.* 380 BC) depicted on a large volute krater (Naples, Mus. Archeol. N., 3240). The Pronomos Painter may have been a pupil of both the Dinos Painter and the Kadmos Painter, and his style is particularly close to that of the Painter of Louvre G 433, with whom he collaborated on one vase (Berlin, Staatliche Museen, 2642). The Painter of Vienna 1089 must have been his pupil. The Pronomos Painter decorated at least one volute krater, two bell kraters and a squat lekythos, and his later works probably included a pelike (Athens, N. Archaeol. Mus., 1333), a calyx krater (Genoa, Mus. Osp. Civ., 1911.163) and a hydria (San Simeon, CA, State Historical Monument). His subject-matter can be mythological, Dionysiac or even theatrical, for his name-vase shows the actors, chorus and poet of a satyr-play. The florid style in which he worked is exemplified by the depiction of garments richly ornamented with enscrolled palmettes, rosettes or asterisks and by the considerable use of white and golden dilute glaze. His treatment of the male torso in three-quarter view and of the head in profile is also characteristic.

BIBLIOGRAPHY

A. Furtwängler and K. Reichhold, eds: *Griechische Vasenmalerei*, iii (Munich, 1932), pp. 132–50 [contribution by E. Buschor]
J. D. Beazley: *Red-figure* (1942, 2/1963), ii, pp. 1336–7
F. Brommer: 'Zur Deutung der Pronomosvase', *Archäol. Anz.* (1964), pp. 109–14
E. Simon: 'Die "Omphale" des Demetrios', *Archäol. Anz.* (1971), pp. 199–206
W. Real: *Studien zur Entwicklung der Vasenmalerei im ausgehenden 5. Jahrhundert v. Chr.* (Münster, 1973)
I. McPhee: 'Turin 4122 and the Pronomos Painter', *Amer. J. Archaeol.*, lxxxii (1978), pp. 551–3
M. Robertson: *The Art of Vase Painting in Classical Athens* (Cambridge, 1992), pp. 255–9

IAN McPHEE

Psiax [Menon Painter] (*fl c.* 525–*c.* 510 BC). Greek vase painter. He played an important role in the transition from Attic Black-figure to Red-figure. Formerly called the Menon Painter, after the potter's signature on a Red-figure amphora (Philadelphia, U. PA, Mus., 5349), he signed two Red-figure alabastra as painter, both of which bear the signature of the potter Hilinos (Karlsruhe, Bad. Landesmus., 242 (B 120) and Odessa, A. Mus.).

Psiax was an experimenter who mastered several vase-painting techniques, including Black-figure, and variants with White-ground or coral-red glaze, Six's technique and Red-figure. Fewer than 50 works are attributed to him, and these include large vases (e.g. amphorae, hydriai and calyx kraters) and small vases (cups, an aryballos, alabastra, a lekythos, kyathoi, a mastos and plates).

His attractive miniatures recall Black-figure work by the AMASIS PAINTER, who may have been his teacher. Signatures of the potter Andokides on two of his amphorae (London, BM; Madrid, Mus. Arqueol. N.) attest to his connection with the workshop that produced the earliest Red-figure and bilingual vases, and where Psiax must have worked beside the ANDOKIDES PAINTER. He clearly painted both the Red-figure and Black-figure monumental compositions on his stiffly formal bilingual amphora (Munich, Staatl. Antikensamml., 2302 (J. 373)). The Red-figure scene shows *Dionysos Reclining Between a Dancing Maenad and Satyr*; the Black-figure one, *Iolaos Steadying Herakles' Chariot*. The latter has a kalos inscription praising Hippokrates, and elsewhere Psiax praised Aischis, Karystios and Smikrion. Unusually in Red-figure, Psiax's inscriptions are always incised.

He favoured Dionysiac subjects, as on his Black-figure kyathos (Milan, Mus. Poldi Pezzoli, 482), and the exploits of Herakles, for example *Herakles and the Nemean Lion* (Black-figure amphora, Brescia, Mus. Civ. Età Romana), *Herakles with Amazons* (Red-figure aryballos, ex-Bologna, Mus. Civ. Archeol., PU 322), or *Herakles with a Horse of Diomedes* (coral-red cup, St Petersburg, Hermitage). Horses appear in Psiax's best large compositions. Two amphorae, in Brescia and Philadelphia (U. PA, Mus., 5399), show *Horses Led by Youths in Thracian Dress*. The stately chariot-harnessing scene on a hydria (destr.; see Beazley, 1978, p. 293) was Psiax's monumental, Black-figure masterpiece. A similar, but livelier, hydria scene (Hartford, CT, Wadsworth Atheneum) recalls the ANTI-MENES PAINTER, whom J. D. Beazley termed 'Psiax's brother'.

Psiax's paintings on both Red-figure and Black-figure small vases share the same imagery and delicate, sinuous, vivid draughtsmanship. He combined fine design with sensitivity to colour, as on the perfectly composed tondo of his Red-figure cup showing *A Young Archer in Scythian Dress Grasping the Reins of a Red-maned Horse* (New York, Met., 14.146.1). The warriors' spears on the outside are white with black incised heads. Elsewhere Psiax even added objects in clay relief, and he was among the first Red-figure painters to reserve hair contours. The anatomy of the warriors on his New York cup is detailed, with limbs twisting, shields shown in profile and three-quarter view, and one warrior falling in back view. This interest in anatomy and space anticipates the Pioneer group, and indeed, PHINTIAS and EUPHRONIOS may have been his pupils. Archer, trumpets and warrior recur on Black-figure plates (London, BM) where Psiax retreated to a charmingly old-fashioned decorative realm.

BIBLIOGRAPHY

H. R. W. Smith: *New Aspects of the Menon Painter* (Berkeley, 1929)
G. M. A. Richter: 'The Menon painter = Psiax', *Amer. J. Archaeol.*, xxxviii (1934), pp. 547–54
J. D. Beazley: *Red-figure* (1942, 2/1963), i, pp. 6–8; ii, pp. 1617–18
——: *Black-figure* (1956), pp. 292–5, 692
P. E. Arias and M. Hirmer: *Tausend Jahre griechischer Vasenkunst* (Munich, 1960); Eng. trans. and rev. by B. Shefton as *A History of Greek Vase Painting* (London, 1962), pp. 304–5
J. D. Beazley: *Paralipomena* (1971), pp. 127–8, 321
J. Boardman: *Athenian Black Figure Vases: A Handbook* (London, 1974), p. 106
——: *Athenian Red Figure Vases: The Archaic Period* (London, 1975), pp. 17–18
B. Cohen: *Attic Bilingual Vases and their Painters* (New York, 1978), pp. 194–239, 276–87
J. R. Mertens: 'Some New Vases by Psiax', *Ant. Kst*, xxii (1979), pp. 22–37
L. Burn and R. Glynn: *Beazley Addenda: Additional References to* ABV, ARV2 *and* Paralipomena (Oxford, 1982, rev. T. H. Carpenter, 2/1989), pp. 76–7, 150–51

BETH COHEN

Ram Jug Painter (*fl c.* 665–*c.* 640 BC). Greek vase painter. He is named after the scene on the Middle Proto-Attic Black-and-white-style jug (Aigina, Archaeol. Mus., 566), in which Odysseus' comrades escape from Polyphemos under rams' bellies. The Aiginetan provenance of many vessels attributed to this painter has prompted a view that he worked on Aigina rather than in Athens. He was schooled in the tradition of the Early Proto-Attic (*c.* 700–*c.* 670 BC) style of the ANALATOS PAINTER, and his earliest work may be seen in the Kerameikos Mug group, showing chariot teams, hoplite warriors and mourning women. The ovoid krater in Berlin (ex-Pergamonmus., A32; see Corp. Vasorum Ant., Berlin i, pp. 19–20, pls 19–21) has also been attributed to his early stage, portraying Apollo, Artemis and a scene identified by some as Orestes slaying Aigisthos.

His mature figure style appears on the Ram Jug and on the fragmentary amphora showing Peleus handing over his infant son Achilles to the care of the centaur Cheiron, who returns from the chase (Berlin, Antikenmus., A9). The squarish human faces are in outlined profile, with a gentle curve on the upper contour; characteristic are the sloping almond eye under a long brow, the large aquiline nose, the short mouth and the curved line of the chin carried up to the ear. The painter's animals have similar eyes; their bodies are in silhouette, sometimes with touches of incision or white paint. An olpe (wine jug) with a large lion head in outline (Athens, Agora Mus., P 22550) is a fine specimen of the painter's late style of animal drawing, which reveals a delight in resilient curves.

See also GREECE, ANCIENT, §V, 4(iii).

BIBLIOGRAPHY

J. M. Cook: 'Protoattic Pottery', *Annu. Brit. Sch. Athens*, xxxv (1934–5), pp. 193–4
S. Papaspyridi-Karouzou: 'Archaika mnemeia tou Ethnikou Mouseiou' [Archaic objects from the National Museum], *Archaiol. Ephimeris* (1952), pp. 149–66
E. T. H. Brann: *Late Geometric and Protoattic Pottery, Mid 8th to Late 7th Century BC* (1962), viii of *The Athenian Agora* (Princeton, 1962), pp. 11, 23–4

S. P. Morris: *The Black and White Style: Athens and Aigina in the Orientalizing Period* (New Haven, 1984), pp. 51–9

NICOLAS COLDSTREAM

Reed Painter (*fl c.* 420–*c.* 410 BC). Greek vase painter. He mainly decorated small or medium-sized Attic White-ground lekythoi, exclusively in matt paint, and is named after the reeds that he often depicted. His output was large, but monotonous both in its subject-matter and in its individual motifs. He usually depicted only two figures: generally a youth and a woman, less often two women, on either side of a broad funerary stele; or Charon waiting in his boat among the reeds to ferry the deceased, normally a woman, across the Styx. His more unusual pictures, which include several depicting three figures, battles or horse-riding, and one depicting a prothesis, mostly occur on a few larger lekythoi.

The patternwork invariably consists of meanders with saltire squares above the picture and palmettes and scrolls on the shoulder. A few palmette leaves are red, otherwise all the elements are dark grey. The figures have striking red outlines. The figure drawing is competently executed with a sweeping line, but perfunctory and lacking in expression. Bodies are often in three-quarter view, creating some impression of depth, but heads are always in profile. The pictures give an impression of sketchiness, owing to the disappearance of the short-lived matt paint that originally coloured the cloaks and shawls revealing incomplete outlines (*see* GREECE, ANCIENT, §V, 7). Similarities in patternwork, colour scheme and painting technique suggest that the Reed Painter shared a workshop with GROUP R (*see* above).

BIBLIOGRAPHY

J. D. Beazley: *Red-figure* (1942, 2/1963), ii, pp. 1376–82, 1692, 1704
——: *Paralipomena* (1971), pp. 485–6
D. C. Kurtz: *Athenian White Lekythoi* (Oxford, 1975)
L. Burn and R. Glynn: *Beazley Addenda: Additional References to* ABV, ARV2 *and* Paralipomena (Oxford, 1982, rev. T. H. Carpenter, 2/1989)

IRMA WEHGARTNER

Rider Painter (*fl c.* 570–*c.* 535 BC). Greek vase painter. He was the least important of the five major Lakonian Black-figure vase painters of the 6th century BC, and his work was never innovative. The Rider Painter was a pupil of the BOREADS PAINTER and later imitated in turn the work of the Naukratis Painter, the Arkesilaos Painter and the Hunt Painter. He is named from the scenes of a rider accompanied by small winged daemons on three cups (St Petersburg, Hermitage, 183; London, BM, B1; Paris, Louvre, E 665), which may be imitations of a lost work by the Naukratis Painter. The least talented of his colleagues, he had a dry, careless style, particularly on his latest vases, and the only interesting aspect of his work is his predilection for lively narrative scenes, often given unusual and humorous renderings. His various mythological subjects include the heroes Herakles, Bellerophon, Achilles and Odysseus, and he also painted such everyday scenes as revels and symposia. Many scenes, however, suffer from clumsy and vague execution, which makes them difficult to interpret. Thus, a scene on a cup depicting a seated figure with an eagle (Tocra, Archaeol. Mus., 932) presumably imitates the Naukratis Painter's scenes of Zeus (e.g. on a cup; Paris, Louvre, E 668), but it in fact looks more like Prometheus bound. A cup that appears to show an unidentified warrior attacking a snake at a fountain (Paris, Louvre, E 669) resembles depictions of Achilles' ambush of Troilos, though it is certainly a different event, possibly Apollo and Python, or Kadmos and the Dragon.

See also GREECE, ANCIENT, §V, 5(iii).

BIBLIOGRAPHY
C. Rolley: 'Le Peintre des cavaliers', *Bull. Corr. Hell.*, lxxxiii (1959), pp. 275–84, pl. 12
C. M. Stibbe: *Lakonische Vasenmaler des sechsten Jahrhunderts v. Chr.*, 2 vols (Amsterdam and London, 1972), pp. 151–75, pls 93–112

MARIA PIPILI

Rycroft Painter (*fl c.* 510 BC). Greek vase painter. He painted in the Black-figure style at a time when most of his contemporaries were turning to Red-figure, and intimations of the new outline technique may be seen in his figures. Beazley associated him with Psiax and the Priam Painter, and Boardman compared his work with the Pioneer Group of Attic Red-figure painters. His name vase (Oxford, Ashmolean, 1965.118), a belly amphora of Type A, bears a scene of *Leto Mounting a Chariot* with Apollo, Artemis and Hermes in attendance; indeed, chariot scenes occur more often than any other theme in his work. Several amphorae and hydriae show wedding scenes with chariots, and they also occur in some of his Dionysiac scenes, another favourite theme. In addition to vases, a plaque from the Acropolis at Athens is attributed to him, painted with a scene of *Athena Watching the Vintage*.

BIBLIOGRAPHY
J. D. Beazley: *Black-figure* (1956), pp. 335–8
——: *Paralipomena* (1971), pp. 148–9
J. Boardman: *Athenian Black Figure Vases: A Handbook* (London, 1974), p. 113

Sophilos (*fl c.* 600–*c.* 570 BC). Greek vase painter. Like other contemporary Athenian Black-figure artists, he imitated the Corinthian animal style, decorating his vases mainly or entirely with mixed processions of wild, tame and mythological creatures. Such friezes were easily copied, so that it is often difficult to ascribe them to specific artists. However, between 40 and 46 large pots or fragments are attributed to Sophilos. His animal friezes are executed in a lively and careless style, so that his importance is due to his rarer many-figured friezes depicting mythological subjects. These are more ambitious and more detailed than any earlier pictures of myths, and several are signed by the artist, making Sophilos the first Greek vase painter whose real name is known.

Sophilos' best-preserved mythological frieze occurs on the shoulder of the Erskine Dinos (London, BM, 1971.11–1.1; *see* GREECE, ANCIENT, fig. 96). It occupies a rather higher band than the conventional animal friezes beneath it and depicts the *Procession of Gods at the Marriage of Peleus and Thetis*. Peleus is shown standing in front of his house, holding a kantharos for a libation, and greeting a procession of 41 deities in brightly coloured robes arriving on foot or in carriages, led by their messenger Iris. All the figures are labelled with inscriptions, and some are also identified by special attributes. Sophilos has used his uninhibited drawing style imaginatively to create an animated festive scene with Apollo singing and playing the lyre and a muse playing Pan-pipes. This figural frieze is made to stand out from the animal friezes beneath it by various means: female figures and some horses are drawn in outline instead of silhouette; female clothing is depicted in white paint applied directly on to the clay and outlined in red and decorated with red animal friezes and ornaments; and the inscriptions too are in red paint. Fragments of a similar dinos dedicated by Sophilos on the Athenian Acropolis also survive (Athens, N. Archaeol. Mus., Acropolis 587). Slightly later, KLEITIAS tackled the *Wedding of Peleus and Thetis* in a strikingly similar way on his famous calyx krater (Florence, Mus. Archeol., 4209) though in a more sophisticated miniaturistic style. Whether he modelled his work directly on that of Sophilos, or whether both artists shared a common source, is uncertain.

Fragments of a third dinos signed by Sophilos (Athens, N. Archaeol. Mus., 15499) depict the *Funeral Games of Patroklos*. The scene has two unique features: an inscription recording its subject, and a representation of a grandstand packed with wildly gesticulating spectators urging on a four-horse chariot. Achilles was also depicted, but only his name and the fingertips of one hand survive. Sophilos also decorated the first extant *lebes gamikos* (Izmir, Archaeol. Mus. 3332), a cult vessel for the bridal bath. His choice of scene was also new: the *Wedding of Helen and Menelaos*, with the bride and groom in one carriage and a second carriage carrying Helen's brothers, the Dioscuri (Castor and Pollux). Only a few other fragments of mythological friezes by Sophilos remain. However, he also produced clay funerary plaques (Athens, Vlasto Col.; see Bakir, p. 69–71). These depicted the bewailing of the dead and were destined to decorate tombs.

BIBLIOGRAPHY
J. D. Beazley: *Black-figure* (1956), pp. 37–43, 681, 714
——: *Paralipomena* (1971), pp. 18–19
G. Bakir: *Sophilos: Ein Beitrag zu seinem Stil* (Mainz, 1981)
L. Burn and R. Glynn: *Beazley Addenda: Additional References to* ABV, ARV2 *and* Paralipomena (Oxford, 1982, rev. T. H. Carpenter, 2/1989), p. 10–12
D. Williams: 'Sophilos in the British Museum', *Greek Vases in the J. Paul Getty Museum*, i (Malibu, 1983), pp. 9–34

HEIDE MOMMSEN

Sotades Painter (*fl c.* 470–*c.* 450 BC). Greek vase painter. Active in Athens, he was among the finest Early Classical vase painters. Like the best of his late Archaic predecessors, he suited his style to his medium, yet he was apparently also influenced by developments in large-scale painting. He is named after the potter's signature on some of his vases, though the decoration often complements the crafting of these so well that potter and painter may have been the same man.

The Sotades Painter was a master of both the Red-figure and White-ground techniques. He was essentially a miniaturist, painting either small vases or vases with only a small field for decoration. His White-ground work appears in the tondi of three small, delicate cups in London (BM, D 5–7), while his Red-figure work includes cups, a skyphos, a kantharos and several rhyta of various forms ranging from conventional animal heads to black boys being eaten by crocodiles (e.g. London, BM, E 789) and a camel flanked by two figures, one Persian and one black

(Paris, Louvre, CA 3825), which display the virtuosity of the potter Sotades. Another vase, so far unparalleled, is shaped like a knucklebone (London, BM, E 804). It is decorated on all four sides with a Red-figure scene of a bald-headed man apparently instructing several girl dancers. While three dancers have their feet on the ground, the rest appear to float, and the scene may show Aiolos directing the dance of the clouds. The skilful adaptation of the scene to the shape of the vase typifies works by Sotades and the Sotades Painter. The man stands by the vase's opening, its curved edge suggesting a cave, while the fluid movements of the dancers are accentuated by the vessel's alternately swelling and contracting contours.

The Sotades Painter's figures are neat and precise, and their drapery appears transparent, revealing the forms of the bodies beneath. Their features are small and sometimes quite idiosyncratic, and, despite the miniature scale of the work, the detail is such that, when transparencies of the painter's White-ground scenes are projected on a screen, they resemble genuine murals, suggesting that he had an interest in larger-scale contemporary painting. In his White-ground works particularly, he tries to convey texture by liberally applying extra layers of painted, or perhaps gilded, clay, and experimenting with shading to suggest the feel of a snake's scales or animal fur.

The Sotades Painter's range of subject-matter is wide and interesting. Satyrs occur frequently, as actors or with maenads or animals. There are also several rarer mythological subjects, including *Pandora* on a sphinx rhyton (London, BM, E 788). The camel rhyton (see above) depicts, in Red-figure, a *Combat Between a Greek and a Persian*: most unusually, the Persian is shown winning. Especially intriguing are the subjects of three White-ground cups (London, BM, D 5–7), found together in an Athenian tomb. The scene on D 7, with a rustic, an enormous snake and a recumbent woman, may represent Orion, about to be punished by a serpent for assaulting the goddess Artemis, Kadmos and the Theban serpent, or the beekeeper Aristaios, with Eurydice and the snake that killed her as she fled from his advances. The two girls picking apples on D 6 may represent the Hesperides, and D 5 depicts Glaukos and Polyeidos, perfectly illustrating the Sotades Painter's ability to evoke an entire story in a single scene.

BIBLIOGRAPHY

E. Buschor: *Das Krokodil des Sotades* (Munich, 1919)
L. Curtius: 'Der Astragal des Sotades', *Sber. Heidelberg. Akad. Wiss.*, iv (1923)
J. D. Beazley: *Red-figure* (1942, 2/1963), i, pp. 763–73
L. Kahil: 'Un Nouveau Vase plastique du potier Sotadès au Musée du Louvre', *Rev. Archéol.* (1972), pp. 271–84
M. Robertson: *A History of Greek Art* (Cambridge, 1975), pp. 263–6
L. Burn: 'Honey Pots: Three White-ground Cups by the Sotades Painter', *Ant. Kst*, xxviii (1985), pp. 93–105
A. Griffiths: '"What Leaf-fringed Legend?": A Cup by the Sotades Painter in London', *J. Hell. Stud.*, cvi (1986), pp. 58–70
A. Collinge: 'Aristaios, or his Father-in-law?', *Ant. Kst*, xxxi (1988), p. 9
H. Hoffmann: 'Aletheia: The Iconography of Death/Rebirth in Three Cups by the Sotades Painter', *Res*, 17–18 (1989), pp. 68–88

LUCILLA BURN

Swing Painter (*fl* c. 540–c. 520 BC). Greek vase painter. He is named after an Athenian Black-figure amphora (Boston, MA, Mus. F.A., 98.918) depicting a demure lady on a swing observed by two men on either side. The painting's spirit and style typify the artist's prime. Abandoning the solemn themes and meticulousness of his mentors, he preferred loose compositions of charming half-pious, half-sheepish yokels with large flat feet, slouching posture and drooping heads who 'all look like geese' (Beazley, 1931/2). These scenes are often unusual or humorous (e.g. men walking on stilts or naked and beset by bees); others, however, are more conventional (e.g. warriors preparing for battle or fighting, or Herakles or Athena with their adversaries), though even here the warriors' sweet demeanour makes their warfare unconvincing. The artist's earlier paintings were much closer to the mainstream tradition of such mid-6th-century BC masters as EXEKIAS (*see above*). They contain dense and intricate compositions, heavy with horses and muscular warriors, in which sombre men and women gather round departing chariots. Though they are often excellent technically, their appeal is evanescent; the artist's fame derives from his later modest, colloquial style and quirky subjects. Though only a lesser painter, the Swing Painter was prolific, decorating over 150 extant pieces (e.g. in Paris, Louvre; Rome, Villa Giulia; St Petersburg, Hermitage; London, BM; Munich, Staatl. Antikensamml.).

BIBLIOGRAPHY

J. D. Beazley: 'Groups of Mid-sixth-century Black-figure', *Annu. Brit. Sch. Athens*, xxxii (1931–2), pp. 1–22
——: *Black-figure* (1956), pp. 304–10
——: *Paralipomena* (1971), pp. 132–5
E. Böhr: *Der Schaukelmaler* (Mainz, 1982)
——: 'Weitere Werke des Schaukelmalers', *Praestant Interna: Festschrift für Ulrich Hausmann* (Tübingen, 1982), pp. 213–20

JODY MAXMIN

Talos Painter (*fl* c. 410–c. 390 BC). Greek vase painter. He is named after a large Attic Red-figure volute krater (Ruvo di Puglia, Mus. Jatta, 1501) depicting a rarely illustrated episode from the voyage of the Argonauts, the *Death of the Bronze Giant Talos*. The artist seems to have preferred such large vases, which he decorated with big figures in a florid style, employing much added white paint. The figures' garments have elaborate patterns, favourite motifs including linked black palmettes, long black rays and waves; some vases have figural borders depicting battle scenes, Nikai, four-horse chariots and sphinxes. Musculature is carefully delineated and often shaded with dilute glaze to produce a strong sense of volume, while some heads are shown in three-quarter view. Garments are sometimes finely pleated in a mannered fashion. Beazley attributed only seven vases to the painter, but he apparently decorated at least four other extant specimens (U. Würzburg, Wagner-Mus., H 5708 a–e; Naples, Mus. Archeol. N., 2883; Rome, Villa Giulia, 2382; Potenza, Mus. Archeol. Prov., 54622). Apart from the story of Talos, the painter's subject-matter includes *Dionysos and Hephaistos Reclining under a Pergola*, the *Apotheosis of Herakles*, *Theseus and Peirithoos Sacrificing in the Presence of Helen*, a remarkable *Gigantomachy* and warriors fighting on foot and on horseback: some scenes seem to be inspired by contemporary megalographic wall paintings (*see* GREECE, ANCIENT, §VI, 2). The artist's own background is unclear, though his style may owe something to the Dinos Painter and the KADMOS PAINTER.

BIBLIOGRAPHY

J. D. Beazley: *Red-figure* (1942, 2/1963), ii, pp. 1338–9
——: *Paralipomena* (1971), p. 481
E. Simon: 'Dionysos und Hephaistos auf einem Kelchkrater des Talos-malers', *Pantheon*, xxxvi (1978), pp. 199–206
G. Greco: 'Un cratere del pittore di Talos da Serra di Vaglio', *Riv. Ist. N. Archeol. & Stor. A.*, n. s. 2, viii–ix (1985–6), pp. 5–35

IAN McPHEE

Tleson (*fl c.* 555–*c.* 535 BC). Greek vase painter. He was the son of NEARCHOS. He has been judged the 'most typical of the [Attic Black-figure] Little Masters' (Beazley, 1986), and he apparently combined potting and painting, mainly producing lip cups which he signed as potter between the handle palmettes, but also band cups (*see* GREECE, ANCIENT, §V, 1(ii)). His drawing was at its most refined and accurate early in his career, when he also added abundant red and white: later his figures became more repetitive and slipshod. Tleson's lip-cup tondi usually contain birds, animals or compound creatures such as centaurs, sirens, sphinxes or Pegasus. The finest, however, have human figures (e.g. the *Returning Hunter*, London, BM, B 421; *Eris*, Berlin, Pergamonmus., F 1775; *Theseus and the Minotaur*, Toledo, OH, Mus. A., 1958.70), the mythological ones being labelled. Some lip cups have no external decoration; others have the usual miniature figures at the centre of the lip on either side, generally winged compound creatures (e.g. sphinxes and sirens), poultry or quadrupeds, but in one case masturbating satyrs (London, BM, B 410). Tleson's band cups have the same animals or mythical creatures arranged in groups of three or four, the commonest scheme being two opposed cocks between two hens on one side and a stag, goat or ram between two sirens on the other. His animal decoration was carelessly imitated by several minor painters.

BIBLIOGRAPHY

J. C. Hoppin: *A Handbook of Greek Black-figured Vases* (Paris, 1924), pp. 365–405
J. D. Beazley: 'Little Master Cups', *J. Hell. Stud.*, lii (1932), pp. 172–96
——: *Development of Black-figure* (1951, 3/1986), pp. 50, 55
——: *Black-figure* (1956), pp. 178–83
——: *Paralipomena* (1971), pp. 74–6
J. Boardman: *Athenian Black Figure Vases: A Handbook* (London, 1974), p. 60
L. Burn and R. Glynn: *Beazley Addenda: Additional References to* ABV, ARV2 *and* Paralipomena (Oxford, 1982, rev. T. H. Carpenter, 2/1989), pp. 50–51
J. T. Haldenstein: *Little Master Cups: Studies in Sixth-century Attic Black-figure Vase Painting* (diss., U. Cincinnati, 1982; microfilm, Ann Arbor), pp. 70–78
Corp. Vasorum Ant., Germany, lviii, Munich 1 (1988), pp. 23–30
Corp. Vasorum Ant., Germany, lviii, Munich 2 (1989), pp. 16–18
Corp. Vasorum Ant., Netherlands, Amsterdam 2 (in preparation), pls 92, 93.1

H. A. G. BRIJDER

Underworld Painter (*fl c.* 330–*c.* 310 BC). Vase painter, active in Apulia. He is named after a famous monumental volute krater found at Canosa (Munich, Staatl. Antikensamml., 3297), with a multi-figured composition showing *Pluto and Persephone in their Palace* surrounded by figures of the Underworld. This is among the most important of a group of late Apulian vases attributed to various painters that show Underworld scenes. What sets the Underworld Painter clearly apart and justifies his name is his individualistic treatment of the Underworld theme and his particular interest in the fate of Orpheus. For example, on a

volute krater (Naples, Mus. Archeol. N., SA 709) he showed Orpheus not alone but standing with Eurydice before Hades, whereas other painters tended to neglect the love story. Another volute krater (Munich, Staatl. Antikensamml., 3296), the companion to his name-piece, bears an impressive representation of *Medea Slaughtering One of her Children* in the presence of the horrified ghost of her father and the demon Oistros, all the main figures being identified by inscriptions. Among the Underworld Painter's most interesting vases are unique representations of mythological twins, as on the masterful volute krater (Geneva, Mus. A. & Hist.) depicting a *Herdsman Returning Melanippe's Babies*, another scene in which the figures are identified by inscriptions. The vivid depiction of emotions expressed on the astonished faces of the family who had abandoned the babies almost equals that of the mature works of the DARIUS PAINTER. An outstanding earlier work on a tall lekythos (h. 950 mm; Richmond, VA, Mus. F.A., 80.162) represents multiple twins: the *Dioskouroi Raping the Leukippidai* (against the protest of their former bridegrooms who were also twins or at least brothers).

The Underworld Painter was evidently inspired directly or indirectly by literary sources: his rather early volute krater showing *Hector's Farewell to Andromache and his Infant Son Astyanax* (Berlin, Antikenmus., 1984.45) was probably based on the tragedy *Hector* by his contemporary, the poet Astydamas, while the story represented in the Melanippe painting may go back to Euripides. The Underworld Painter's earlier works testify more clearly to the strong influence of the Darius Painter, but his artistic temperament seems always to have been rather different: there is an element of violence in his drawing style; his lines tend to be thicker, with the physiognomies coarser, though still expressive; and subsidiary objects such as pieces of furniture are rendered with much less detail and elaboration.

BIBLIOGRAPHY

A. D. Trendall and A. Cambitoglou: *The Red-figured Vases of Apulia*, ii (Oxford, 1982), pp. 531–40
——: *The Red-figured Vases of Apulia: Supplement 1* (London, 1983), pp. 83–6
A. D. Trendall: *Red Figure Vases of South Italy and Sicily* (London, 1989), pp. 90–91
A. D. Trendall and A. Cambitoglou: *The Red-figured Vases of Apulia: Supplement 2* (London, 1992), pp. 161–5

MARGOT SCHMIDT

Villa Giulia Painter (*fl c.* 470–*c.* 440 BC). Greek vase painter. The Master of the Villa Giulia Calyx krater, to give him his full name, has been attributed with *c.* 120 surviving vases. Most of these are large—kraters, stamnoi, pelikai and kalpides—though he also painted smaller shapes, including alabastra, leythoi, pyxides, rhyta and cups (*see* GREECE, ANCIENT, fig. 71). The cups and the large pots are iconographically dissimilar and must be anchored in different traditions. His figures are normally tall and solemn and are frequently shown pouring a libation, as in the gathering of gods on a cylindroid (Cambridge, Fitzwilliam X13). He added a personal touch to traditional themes: a young satyr appears in the procession of adult satyrs and maenads on a calyx krater (Karlsruhe, Bad. Landesmus. 208); the infant Dionysos is shown in the lap of Hermes on a calyx krater in Moscow (Pushkin Mus.

F.A. 16732); and on an alabastron (Providence, RI, Sch. Des., Mus. A. 25.088) he painted a mother or nurse with two boys, one asleep on her shoulder, the other holding tight to her chiton. He must also have been fond of animals: a fawn looks up at Apollo on the replica pelikai at Malibu, CA (Getty Mus. 77. AE.12.1–2; see Frel); a heron stalks through a *gynaikeion* (women's quarters) on a kalpis (Switzerland, priv. col.; sold Basel, Münzen und Medaillen AG, 19 Feb 1980, no. 105); and he frequently painted horsemen. His mythological themes include Perseus sneaking up to the Gorgon on a bell-krater in Madrid (Mus. Arqueol. N. 11010), the daughters of Pelias hatching mischief on a kalpis (Cambridge, Fitzwilliam 12.17), and, on another kalpis (Rome, Vatican, Mus. Gregoriano Etrus. 16509), the sleeping Herakles being robbed by satyrs, a scene which must have been inspired by a satyr play. More than half of his preserved stamnoi depict the Lenaia, a festival celebrating the new wine and the rebirth of Dionysos. Athenian women appear as maenads, though a parasol on one stamnos (Boston, MA, Mus. F.A. 90.155) reveals their true origins.

On his name piece (Rome, Villa Giulia 909) a dozen maidens hold each other's hands and dance to the sound of a flute. The frieze continues without interruption around the krater, though the painter normally distinguishes between front and back. One fragmentary vase is an example of a double-register krater (see Beazley, 1942, 2/1963, 619, 13); other krater fragments are covered with white slip (e.g. Reggio Calabria, Mus. N.; Palermo, Mus. Reg.), a technique he also used on lekythoi and alabastra. His stamnoi and kalpides are of two distinct shapes, the latter decorated on the shoulder or belly.

Most of the cups attributed to the Villa Giulia Painter depict youths, grown men and athletes, one of whom is shown as a victor, wearing sashes (Rome, Villa Giulia 5993). On a cup in St Petersburg (Hermitage B1535) a hetaira plays with balls, and a youth is shown wearing female headgear; another has dancing maenads with winged sleeves (Basle, priv. col.; sold Basle, Kunst und Antiquitätenmesse, 1979, no. 93). Since Beazley's latest list of the Villa Giulia Painter's known vases in 1971, three more White-ground cups have been attributed to him; one of these, an early work, shows Apollo revealing himself to a Muse (Boston, MA, Mus. F.A. 00356; see Beazley, 1942, 2/1963, 741 middle; for others see Vickers, pl. 17.18 ab and Bothmer). Stylistically, the Villa Giulia Painter has several roots. With his cups he follows the workshop tradition of the Brygos Painter; with some of the closed vases he might have learnt from the Berlin Painter's late school, forming—together with the Chicago and the Methyse painters—an 'academic' wing of that tradition. The period of his activity is reflected in the development of his figures from sturdy early Classical forms to slim and elegant high Classical styles.

BIBLIOGRAPHY

J. D. Beazley: 'The Master of the Villa Giulia Calyx-Krater', *Mitt. Dt. Archäol. Inst.: Röm. Abt.*, xxvii (1912), pp. 286–97
——: *Red-figure* (1942, 2/1963), i, pp. 618–26; ii, 1662
——: *Paralipomena* (1971), pp. 398, 514
M. J. Vickers: 'A New Cup by the Villa Giulia Painter', *J. Hell. Stud.*, xciv (1974), pp. 177–9
J. Frel: *Paintings on Vases in Ancient Greece* (Los Angeles, 1979), nos 30–31

D. von Bothmer: 'Greek and Roman Art', *Bulletin of the Metropolitan Museum of Art: Notable Acquisitions* (1979–80), pp. 14–15
L. Burn and R. Glynn: *Beazley Addenda: Additional References to* ABV, ARV2 *and* Paralipomena (Oxford, 1982, rev. T. H. Carpenter, 2/1989), pp. 270–71
D. L. Wieland: 'Achill verabschiedet sich von seinen Eltern. Ein rotfiguriger Kelchkrater des Villa Giulia-Malers', *Archäol. Samml. U. Zürich*, xv (1989), pp. 6–14
Data courtesy of the Beazley Archive, Oxford University.

ADRIENNE LEZZI-HAFTER

Vasi, Giuseppe (*b* Corleone, Sicily, 27 Aug 1710; *d* Rome, 16 April 1782). Italian engraver and painter. After completing a classical education, he trained as a printmaker in Palermo, possibly at the Collegio Carolino, which was founded by the Jesuit Order in 1728 and at which the etcher Francesco Ciché (*fl* before 1707; *d* Palermo, 1742) was a teacher. Vasi was already an accomplished engraver when, in 1736, he contributed to the illustration of *La reggia in trionfo* by Pietro La Placa, which described the festivities held in Palermo to mark the coronation of Charles VII of Naples (the future Charles III of Spain). That same year Vasi moved to Rome, where, as a Neapolitan subject, he was immediately afforded the protection of the ambassador, Cardinal Troiano Aquaviva d'Aragona (1694–1747). In Rome he met other artists who worked for the same patron: Sebastiano Conca, Luigi Vanvitelli and Ferdinando Fuga. It is against this background that Vasi's work in Rome, when he was in residence at the Palazzo Farnese, should be considered: his monopoly as the engraver of the Roman records of the monarch, the plates for the festivals of the 'Chinea' and the triumphal arches erected in front of the Palatine gardens on the occasion of temporal sovereignty over Rome.

About 1741–3 Vasi conceived the idea of a collection of views of Rome and published his *Vedute del Tevere*, which preceded the great work of his life, the ten volumes of *Delle magnificenze di Roma antica e moderna* (1747–61). This extraordinary collection of more than 250 plates offers a lively and detailed panorama of contemporary Rome, classified by subject, including city gates, squares, churches, convents, palaces, bridges and villas. The gigantic *Prospetto dell'alma città di Roma* was dedicated in 1765 to Charles III, then King of Spain. In addition to engraving the 437 plates, Vasi wrote several accompanying texts, often of some length. He also produced a guidebook, the *Itinerario istruttivo . . . di Roma*, which was first published in 1763 and repeatedly updated during his lifetime. After his death further editions were published by his son Mariano (*b* Rome, 15 Aug 1744; *d* Rome, 26 Nov 1820), who was also an engraver. Giuseppe Vasi's most important pupil was Piranesi, whom he taught the technique of single-cut engraving in the early 1740s.

BIBLIOGRAPHY

Thieme–Becker
H. Millon: 'Vasi–Piranesi–Juvarra', *Piranèse et les Français: Colloque tenu à la villa Medicis, 1976*, ed. G. Brunel (Rome, 1978), pp. 345–62
O. Michel: 'L' "Accademia"', *Le Palais Farnèse: Ecole française de Rome*, i (Rome, 1981), pp. 597–602
L. Scalabroni: *Giuseppe Vasi, 1710–1782* (Rome, 1981)

OLIVIER MICHEL

Vasiliki. Site in eastern Crete on low hills flanking the north–south route across the Ierapetra Isthmus, inhabited *c*. 3500–*c*. 1050 BC. First investigated by R. B. Seager

(1903–6), it has been substantially reinterpreted by A. Zoïs (from 1970). Although there are traces of Early Minoan (EM) I (*c.* 3500/3000–*c.* 2900/2600 BC) pottery, the first clear signs of habitation are of early EM II (*c.* 2900/2600–*c.* 2200 BC) date. Buildings belonging to several phases had covered the main hilltop by Middle Minoan (MM) IA (*c.* 2050–*c.* 1900 BC). The main surviving structures are two buildings of early EM II date and, to their south, two of late EM II. The settlement was destroyed in a great conflagration towards the end of EM II. The southern pair (now the Red/East and West houses) were regarded by Seager as a single 'House on the Hill'. Zoïs showed that they were separate buildings, which somewhat weakens earlier theories that Vasiliki anticipated features of Minoan palatial architecture (*see* MINOAN, §II). Even so, they are large and relatively complex and their layout differs from the agglutinative approach of contemporary MYRTOS (Phournou Koriphi). Larger rooms, one with a well, faced on to a central space and perhaps had some communal function; smaller ones in groups and rows behind show clear differentiation of purpose. A substantial courtyard lies to the west, with other yards to the north.

Decorative features of these houses include early instances of the typical Minoan use of red-painted plaster on walls and floors. Furniture and equipment recovered are relatively meagre: a sophisticated bronze mould for double axes (Herakleion, Archaeol. Mus.) may date from this phase; otherwise there are only two broken metal axes and a few stone objects, including Cycladic-style figurines. The most important remains are of pottery. The site has given its name to a distinctive handmade ware typical of EM II (*see* MINOAN, §III, 3(ii)). It is represented in a full range of tablewares.

MM I (*c.* 2050–*c.* 1800 BC) buildings have been found only at the periphery of the hilltop, though they are thought to extend down the east slope. Seager excavated two (his Houses A and B), Zoïs parts of three others. One contained five stone lamps (Herakleion, Archaeol. Mus.). The structures vary in quality, and though their foundations were more solidly constructed than those of their predecessors, perhaps to counter earthquakes, the site was severely damaged by a tremor in MM II (*c.* 1800–*c.* 1650 BC).

In Neo-Palatial times (MM III to Late Minoan (LM) I, *c.* 1675–*c.* 1425 BC), the whole hilltop was built over and parts of five or so structures are known. The most complete, house M, lies to the north-east, and, though not so large or well equipped as the town houses and villas of TYLISSOS or AMNISOS, it is a substantial village dwelling that compares well with any at GOURNIA. Later Minoan occupation is barely represented, though a species of 'fortification' wall is broadly dated to LM III (*c.* 1390–*c.* 1050 BC). Burials in the vicinity of the settlement include a MM enclosure and cemetery of pithoi interments to the south, and, further uphill to the west, a LM IIIB–C (*c.* 1335–*c.* 1180 BC) tholos.

BIBLIOGRAPHY

R. B. Seager: 'Excavations at Vasiliki, 1904', *Trans. Dept Archaeol., Free Mus. Sci. & A., U. PA*, i (1905), pp. 207–21

——: 'Report of Excavations at Vasiliki, Crete, in 1906', *Trans. Dept Archaeol., Free Mus. Sci. & A., U. PA*, ii (1907), pp. 111–32

A. Zoïs: 'Vasiliki, Hierapetra', *Ergon Archaiol. Etaireias* (1972), pp. 113–18; (1974), pp. 107–12; (1975), pp. 189–93; (1976), pp. 195–200; (1977), pp. 195–9; (1982), pp. 48–51

——: *Vasiliki 1*, Edition of the Archaeological Society, lxxxiii (Athens, 1976)

——: 'Excavations at Vasiliki, Hierapetra', *Praktika Athen. Archaiol. Etaireias* (1976), pp. 440–59

A. Kanta: *The Late Minoan III Period in Crete: A Survey of Sites, Pottery and their Distribution*, Stud. Medit. Archaeol., lviii (Göteborg, 1980)

A. Zoïs: 'Vasiliki', *The Aerial Atlas of Ancient Crete*, ed. J. W. Myers, E. E. Myers and G. Cadogan (Berkeley, 1992), pp. 274–9

D. EVELY

Vasil'yev, Fyodor (Aleksandrovich) (*b* Gatchina, nr St Petersburg, 22 Feb 1850; *d* Yalta, 6 Oct 1873). Russian painter. The son of a post-office employee, he did not receive any regular training in art, but in ?1863 he attended the school of drawing of the Society for the Encouragement of Artists in St Petersburg. He worked with the landscape painter Ivan Shishkin on the island of Valaam in Lake Ladoga in 1867, and his friendship with Ivan Kramskoy greatly influenced the formation of his creative identity, as did his private study of the techniques of masters of Russian and foreign art, notably from the Düsseldorf and the Barbizon schools. Vasil'yev's first original works date from 1866–7. By 1870 he was already widely known in the artistic circles of St Petersburg and Moscow as a highly poetic, unusually gifted landscape painter, and he gradually became noted for his naturalism. His paintings *The Return of the Herd* (1868) and the more mature *The Thaw* (1871; both Moscow, Tret'yakov Gal.), among others, received the highest awards in competitions held by the Society for the Encouragement of Artists.

A trip to the Volga in summer 1870 with the artists Il'ya Repin and Ye. Makarov (1842–84) was important for Vasil'yev. In response to the landscape of the Volga his pictures became more spacious, with greater depth and spiritual power, as in *Volga Lagoons* (1870; Moscow, Tret'yakov Gal.) and *View of the Volga: Barges* (1870; St Petersburg, Rus. Mus.). Vasil'yev contracted tuberculosis, however, and was compelled to move to Yalta in summer 1871. Here, he worked harder and more fruitfully; in less than two years he completed a great number of carefully worked studies, several large paintings, some unfinished, including *The Wet Meadow* (1872) and *In the Crimean Mountains* (1873; both Moscow, Tret'yakov Gal.), and many drawings (e.g. *Evening*, sepia; Moscow, Tret'yakov Gal.). In Vasil'yev's work, nature motifs took on an unprecedented, disturbed psychologism, a tense emotional quality, which makes it (like the paintings of Aleksey Savrasov) an important link between the Russian Romantic–realist landscape and the 'mood landscapes' of Levitan in harmony with the Art Nouveau era.

BIBLIOGRAPHY

Fyodor Aleksandrovich Vasil'yev, 1850–1873 (exh. cat.; Moscow, Tret'yakov Gal.; St Petersburg, Rus. Mus., 1975)

F. S. Mal'tseva: *Fyodor Aleksandrovich Vasil'yev: Zhizn' i tvorchestvo* [Fyodor Aleksandrovich Vasil'yev: life and work] (Moscow, 1984)

L. I. IOVLEVA

Vasil'yev, Grigory. *See* SOROKA, GRIGORY.

Vasil'yev, Nikolay (Vasil'yevich) (*b* Pogorelki, Yaroslavl' province, 8 Dec 1875; *d* Finland, ?1941). Russian architect. He studied at the Institute of Civil Engineers, St Petersburg, from 1896 to 1901 and then from 1901 to 1904 at the Academy of Arts with Leonty Benois. He was a talented and original exponent of the northern European version of Art Nouveau (Rus. *stil' modern*), and he influenced many architects in St Petersburg. His work also parallels attempts in Finland and the Baltic states to develop a National Romantic style in architecture. This is evident in the combination of functional expediency, emotional quality, direct expression of construction methods and materials and the realization of vernacular traditions. In the Savitsky Mansion (1904–6) in Tsarskoye Selo (now Pushkin) and the residential building (1906–7), with Aleksey Bubyr' (1876–1919), at Stremyannaya Street 11, St Petersburg, the intense dynamics of the façades are underlined by contrasting natural and artificial materials. Similar sculptural effects are seen in his buildings in Tallinn (formerly Reval). In the mosque (1910–20) that he designed for St Petersburg, with S. S. Krichinsky (1874–1923) and Aleksandr Gogen (1856–1914), the stylized forms of the ancient architecture of Central Asia are supplemented by the characteristic traits of the *modern* style: severe, powerful masses and granite facing. Other works are more innovative and appear to anticipate functionalism: for example with E. F. Virrikh (1860–1927) he planned the department store of the Guards' Economic Society (1908–9), Zhelyabov Street (now Bol'shaya Konnyushennaya) 21–3, St Petersburg, the largest commercial building in the city, with a monolithic, reinforced concrete frame. In the commercial arcades (1912) at 57 Liteyny Prospect in St Petersburg the large, flat planes of the glazing and the granite facing of the vertical supporting elements expose the frame structure. From 1923 Vasil'yev worked in the USA for Warren & Wetmore in New York. He also designed a house for Fyodor Chaliapin in Biarritz and took part in international competitions, including that for the Palace of Soviets (1931) in Moscow.

BIBLIOGRAPHY

V. G. Lisovsky: 'Master shkoly natsional'nogo romantizma' [Master of the school of National Romanticism], *Stroitel'stvo & Arkhit. Leningrada*, iv (1975), pp. 42–4

B. L. Vasil'yev and B. M. Kirikov: 'Tvorcheskiye svyazi finskikh i peterburgskikh zodchikh v nachala XX veka: Arkhitektura "severnogo moderna"' [Creative links between Finnish and St Petersburg architects at the beginning of the 20th century: 'northern Art Nouveau' architecture], *Skand. Sborn.*, xxvi (1981), pp. 186–206

B. M. KIRIKOV

Vasio Vocontiorum [now Vaison-la-Romaine]. Site of a Roman city (*fl* mid-1st century AD–*c*. 475). It originated as a native settlement of the Vocontii and occupied hillsides north of the River Ouvèze, southern France, over which a single-span Roman bridge still stands. The theatre (1st century AD) is the main surviving public building. Its *cavea*, cut into the north side of the Puymin Hill, has been extensively restored. The stage building was of western type with doors set in curved and rectangular exedrae. In front of it, rock-cut shafts contained the curtain mechanism. Statues of emperors and local dignitaries from the theatre are displayed in the nearby Musée Archéologique. The excavated town houses are the best-preserved in France, notable for their Hellenistic peristyle courtyards. Among those on the southern slopes of the Puymin Hill, the House of the Messii (2nd century AD) had at the east end large rooms paved in *opus sectile* facing the peristyle; the marble head of Apollo (formerly mistakenly called the

Venus of Vaison; ?1st or 2nd century AD; Vaison-la-Romaine, Mus. Archaéol.) was found there. At the west end smaller rooms, including a kitchen and baths, surrounded three enclosed courtyards. In the area of La Villasse to the south-west, a street on a different alignment from those on the Puymin Hill had shops on both sides, a marble-paved and frescoed basilican hall on the east (1st century AD), and opposite, the entrance to the House of the Silver Bust, named after the bust of a man in a toga (?3rd century AD; Vaison-la-Romaine, Mus. Archéol.). This, the largest of the houses at Vaison, had three main elements: a columned vestibule leading from the street to a peristyle courtyard and a large reception room; beyond, and at right angles to that axis, a larger peristyle and two covered reception rooms with a hall or open courtyard between them; and finally a much larger trapezoidal peristyle garden with a suite of baths to the north, originally perhaps a separate establishment. To the west, the House of the Dolphins was built in the Augustan period (27 BC–AD 14) as a Hellenistic peristyle house; in the late 1st century AD the addition of an atrium beyond the tablinum gave the layout a more Roman character.

BIBLIOGRAPHY

J. Sautel: *Vaison dans l'antiquité*, 3 vols (Avignon, 1941–2)

C. Goudineau: *Les Fouilles de la Maison au Dauphin: Recherches sur la romanisation de Vaison* (Paris, 1979)

T. F. C. BLAGG

Vasnetsov. Russian family of artists.

(1) Viktor (Mikhaylovich) Vasnetsov (*b* Lop'yal, Vyatka province [now Kirov region], 15 May 1848; *d* Moscow, 23 July 1926). Painter, designer and graphic artist. He played a leading role in the evolution of Russian art from 19th-century realism towards Art Nouveau with a national historical slant. The son of a priest, he studied at a theological seminary in Vyatka (1862–7); then, developing a passion for drawing, he entered the drawing school of the Society for the Encouragement of the Arts, St Petersburg, and studied under Ivan Kramskoy in 1867–8. He perfected his skills at the Academy of Arts, St Petersburg, in 1869–75 and joined the WANDERERS in 1878.

Vasnetsov's extraordinarily rich and varied work divides clearly into two major periods. In the first he adhered to the principles of Critical Realism epitomized by the work of the Wanderers. The heroes of these paintings are most often the St Petersburg poor, for example a poverty-stricken old couple moving to a new dwelling in *From Lodging to Lodging* (1876; Moscow, Tret'yakov Gal.). Vasnetsov showed himself to be a sly humorist in the picture *Préférence* (1879; Moscow, Tret'yakov Gal.), which pokes ironic fun at the spiritual poverty and emptiness of petit-bourgeois life. These pictures are based on the traditions of genre painting, detailed and full of subtle psychological nuances, derived from older Dutch painting, and the works of William Hogarth and Pavel Fedotov. Here irony and compassion merge into a lively unity. From impressions gained during a stay in Paris (1876–7) Vasnetsov produced a large canvas, *Fairground Booths in Paris* (1876–7; Moscow, Tret'yakov Gal.), which is thematically related to Honoré Daumier's 'clowns'.

A decisive change occurred in Vasnetsov's work under the Old Russian Revival, a powerful upsurge of public interest in the ancient national past, which developed in the final decades of the 19th century, and he became the founder and major representative of this movement in the fine arts. Dealing with subjects from national mythology, he radically reformed the Russian historical genre, combining genuine historical details reproduced with archaeological accuracy with the stirring atmosphere of legend. Among his masterpieces of this period are *After Prince Igor's Battle with the Polovtsy* (1880), on a subject from the 12th-century *Slova o polku Igoreve* ('Lay of the host of Igor'), *Alyonushchka* (1881), with the young heroine of folktales embodying the bitter lot of the orphan, and *Ivan the Terrible* (1897; all Moscow, Tret'yakov Gal.). His *Bogatyrs* (see fig.), with the majestic figures of the bogatyrs (folk heroes), the mounted warrior knights, guarding the frontiers of their country, became one of the most popular classic images from national painting. The entire structure of his canvases also changed appreciably. His compositions grew in scale, his handling of colour gained monumentality, and the psychological vignettes of his early work gave way to symbolic epic. Many works of the second period, for example the *Three Princesses of the Underground Kingdom* (1881; Moscow, Tret'yakov Gal.), already contain all the typological traits of the decorative picture panels of the Art Nouveau style. Vasnetsov's painting was acclaimed abroad, particularly by Rainer Maria Rilke, as an expression of the 'new Russian style'.

Vasnetsov also worked successfully in the fields of portrait painting, book illustration and stage design. His sketches for the settings for Aleksandr Ostrovsky's play *Snegurochka* ('The Snow-maiden'; watercolour, 1881–2; Abramtsevo, Mus.–Estate), staged in the private theatre of the patron SAVVA MAMONTOV, and for Nikolay Rimsky-Korsakov's opera of the same name (watercolour and gouache, 1885; Moscow, Tret'yakov Gal.), staged at Mamontov's private Russian Opera in Moscow, represent an innovation in Russian stage design. These works lovingly re-create the medieval decorative motifs that Vasnetsov had learnt by studying Old Russian applied art. Vasnetsov showed himself, further, to be a considerable master of monumental painting with his panel *The Stone Age* (1883–5), painted for the Historical Museum in Moscow and depicting the ancient forebears of the Slavs. But his most ambitious monumental works were his murals for the cathedral of St Vladimir in Kiev (oil on plaster, 1885–96) in which he sought to overcome both traditional Byzantine artistic canons and abstract academicism. Vasnetsov intensified the lyrical element in religious images and framed them in folk ornament. His contribution to the history of architecture is also substantial. He saw in the Old Russian Revival style not simply a pretext for stylized reconstruction, but also a vehicle for the embodiment of such central qualities of Old Russian architecture as organic unity and decorative richness of form. A church in the spirit of the medieval tradition of Pskov and Novgorod (1881–2) and the 'Hut on hen's legs' (1883) from the playful fairy-tale 'Izbushka na Kur'ikh Nozhkakh' were built at Abramtsevo

Viktor Vasnetsov: *Bogatyrs*, oil on canvas, 2.95×4.46 m, 1881–98 (Moscow, Tret'yakov Gallery)

from his sketches. He also designed the decorative composition for the façade of the Tret'yakov Gallery in Moscow (1906). His house, built to his design in 1894, was turned into the V. M. Vasnetsov House-Museum in 1953.

WRITINGS

Pis'ma, dnevniki, vospominaniya, suzhdeniya sovremennikov [Letters, diaries, reminiscences, judgements of his contemporaries] (Moscow, 1987)

BIBLIOGRAPHY

N. Morgunov and N. Morgunova-Rudnitskaya: *V. M. Vasnetsov* (Moscow, 1962)

V. A. Vasnetsov: *Stranitsy proshlogo: Vospominaniya o khudozhnikakh brat'yakh Vasnetsovykh* [Pages from the past: reminiscences about the artists the Vasnetsov brothers] (Leningrad, 1976)

N. Shanina: *V. Vasnetsov* (Leningrad, 1979)

V. M. Vasnetsov (1848–1926) [exh. cat., Moscow, Tret'yakov Gal., 1990]

M. N. SOKOLOV

(2) Apollinary (Mikhaylovich) Vasnetsov (*b* Ryabovo, Vyatka province [now Kirov region], 6 Aug 1856; *d* Moscow, 23 Jan 1933). Painter and teacher, brother of (1) Viktor Vasnetsov. He received his early artistic training from his brother. Apollinary lived in St Petersburg from 1872 to 1875 and was influenced by the realist works of Il'ya Repin and Vasily Polenov. From 1878 he lived in Moscow, but he also travelled extensively in Russia and abroad. His first mature paintings document and celebrate the beauties of the Russian landscape. In *My Native Land* (1886; Moscow, Tret'yakov Gal.) the expansive, rural scene is filled with a golden light. His best, large-scale landscapes, such as *The Russian North* (St Petersburg, Rus. Mus.), capture the great distances, untouched forests and spectacular sunsets of Siberia.

Like several of his contemporaries, Vasnetsov responded in the 1890s to the growing interest in national history. He concentrated on representations of the architecture of old Moscow, using archaeological evidence. *Mid-seventeenth-century Moscow: The Moskvoretsky Bridge and Water Gates* (1900; Moscow, Tret'yakov Gal.) is a typical example, combining an accurate reconstruction of the architecture with invented scenes from everyday life. Vasnetsov's twin interests in landscape painting and archaeology are reflected in his later career: from 1901 to 1918 he taught landscape painting at the Moscow School of Painting, Sculpture and Architecture, and from 1918 to 1929 he was Chairman of the Commission for the Study of Old Moscow.

WRITINGS

Khudozhestvo: Opyt analiza ponyatiy, opredelyayushikh iskusstva zhivopisi [Artistic skill: an attempt to analyse concepts determining the art of painting] (Moscow, 1908)

'Oblik staroy Moskvy' [The appearance of old Moscow], *Istoriya' russkogo iskusstva* [The history of Russian art], ii, ed. I. Grabar' (Moscow and St Petersburg, 1910)

BIBLIOGRAPHY

'Pictures of Old Moscow by A. Vasnetzoff', *Int. Studio*, xlvi/184 (1912), pp. 273–9 [illus.]

E. Vasnetsova: *Apollinary Vasnetsov* (Moscow, 1980) [with Eng. summary; many colour illus.]

MARIAN BURLEIGH-MOTLEY

Vaso puerperalo. *See under* DESCHO DA PARTO.

Vásquez, Dagoberto (*b* Guatemala City, 2 Nov 1922). Guatemalan sculptor and painter. After studying at the Academia de Bellas Artes in Guatemala City (1937–44), he received a grant that enabled him to continue his studies from 1945 to 1949 at the Escuela de Artes Aplicadas of the Universidad de Chile in Santiago, Chile. He was part of a generation of artists who revitalized art in Guatemala after World War II; like Guillermo Grajeda Mena, Roberto González Goyri and, later, Efraín Recinos, he was associated with the efforts of several architects to integrate the arts in their new buildings.

As both a sculptor and a painter Vásquez maintained a consistent artistic line without obvious changes, achieving a personal synthesis of expressionism and abstraction with a great simplicity of form. His sculptures were made of a variety of materials, including marble, bronze, clay, sheet brass, wood and concrete. Among his most important works, all in Guatemala City, are the *Origins of Life* (7.5×2.5 m, 1951), a mosaic at the Instituto de Nutrición de Centroamérica y Panamá (INCAP); two concrete reliefs cast *in situ*, *Song for Guatemala* (10×6 m, 1957; Guatemala City, Pal. Mun.) and *Economy and Culture* (40×7 m, 1964; Guatemala City, Banco de Guatemala); and bronzes such as *Christ* (h. 1.7 m, 1974) for the Capilla San Ignacio and *Fire* (h. 1.7 m, 1980) for the Organización Eléctrica Guatemalteca.

BIBLIOGRAPHY

Dagoberto Vásquez (exh. cat., Guatemala City, Gal. El Túnel, 1983)

JORGE LUJÁN-MUÑOZ

Vásquez Brito, Ramón (*b* Porlamar, 29 Aug 1927). Venezuelan painter and teacher. He studied from 1943 to 1947 at the Escuela de Artes Plásticas in Caracas, where he then taught from 1947 to 1973. His painting, which evolved from Cubism through geometric abstraction to lyrical landscape painting, shows his attraction to coastal light and to open spaces. The colours are limited to shades of blue, green, grey and white. Vásquez Brito represented Venezuela in the 31st Venice Biennal in 1962 and during his career received numerous national awards, including the CONAC Prize at the 11th Biennale of Visual Arts (1983) at the Museo de Arte Contemporáneo de Caracas.

ANA TAPIAS

Vassal de Saint-Hubert, Jean-Antoine-Hubert (*b* Montpellier, 2 Aug 1741; *d* Paris, 7 Sept 1782). French financier and collector. His collection comprised Dutch, French and a few Italian paintings, mounted engravings and drawings and a major collection of sculpture. Some of these works came from famous collections, including those of the Mariette and Crozat families. The large number of Dutch paintings in the collection consisted principally of 17th-century genre scenes and landscapes but also included works attributed to Rembrandt, Adam Elsheimer and Frans Hals. The French paintings included works by 17th- and 18th-century artists such as Simon Vouet, Eustache Le Sueur (*Death of the Virgin*; St Petersburg, Hermitage; now attributed to Charles Poërson), Laurent de La Hyre, Sébastien Bourdon (five works), Claude Lorrain, Nicolas Poussin and Nicolas de Largillierre (*Self-portrait*, 1711; Versailles, Château). Vassal's interest in both historical and genre painting and in the most recent work of the French school was apparent not only in his paintings but also in his collection of drawings, which also contained many 16th- and 18th-century Italian works, including those of Correggio, Pietro da Cortona, Andrea Sacchi, Carlo Maratta, Rosalba Carriera, Sebastiano Ricci and Gaspare Vanvitelli. The collection of sculptures included an important group of terracottas by François Du Quesnoy. Sales in 1774, 1779 and 1783 dispersed Vassal's collection.

BIBLIOGRAPHY
Thieme–Becker
C. Blanc: *Le Trésor de la curiosité*... (Paris, 1857); i, pp. 447ff; ii, p. 77
Les Vieux Hôtels de Paris, xviii (Paris, 1928), p. 16, no. 43
L. Dermigny: *La Chine et l'Occident: Le Commerce à Canton au XVIIIe siècle, 1789–1833* (Paris, 1963), pp. 349–51

□

Vassallettus [Bassallectus; Bassallettus]. Italian family of marble workers, sculptors and architects. Several generations of the family are documented between 1154 and 1260. The main emphasis of their work was sculptural, more so than was the case with other Roman marble-working families (*see* COSMATI), but they also produced a large quantity of costly showpiece architectural work with ornamentation close to antique models. Between 1220 and 1260 members of the Vassallettus family were the most prominent and successful of the Roman marble workers. Their works in Rome, the cloister of S Giovanni in Laterano and the portico of S Lorenzo fuori le mura, are the most visible expression of the papal ambitions that were pursued from the time of Innocent III (1198–1216).

Records of the first Vassallettus are a little equivocal: the signature of one 'Romanus Basiletti' (i.e. Vassallettus) was once noted near the tomb of a cardinal of *c*. 1150 in the temple of Romulus at SS Cosma e Damiano. Fragments of the raised wall tomb with a baldacchino supported by columns and an architrave using simple antique forms have survived. Petrus Vassallettus must belong to the next generation. Fragments bearing his signature survive from the destroyed interior furnishings of Segni Cathedral (1185), and he signed with NICOLAUS DE ANGELO the monumental paschal candlestick (*c*. 1200) in S Paolo fuori le mura. The *Passion* reliefs on the shaft show a knowledge of Early Christian sarcophagus reliefs that is exceptional for medieval Rome, where sculpture remained almost exclusively apotropaic in nature. Finally, as Petrus Bassallettus, he signed the ciborium of S Pietro in Cori (destr.) with his otherwise unknown brother Johannes.

All the authenticated 13th-century works are signed only with the family name Vassallettus (spelt in a variety of ways), but several individual artists may be disguised under this name. One of their earliest known works came from Old St Peter's and was signed MAGISTRI VASSALETTI; it must have been the former marble paschal candlestick (destr.), which was very large. The base of another paschal candlestick with two lion sculptures dated 1220 survived into the 19th century but is now untraced. The splendid lion signed BASSALLECTUS in the portico of SS Apostoli in Rome was also a holder for a paschal candlestick; it is modelled on the Egyptian granite lions that stood in front of the Pantheon in the Middle Ages.

The rood screens and some other liturgical furniture in S Saba, Rome, bore the signature MAGISTER BASSALLET-TUS. Other works, the nature of which is uncertain, are known from signed fragments in the Roman churches of Santa Croce in Gerusalemme and S Pudenziana. Only a

few fragments testify to the magnificence of the interior decoration of the collegiate church of Lanuvio (1240), signed by both Vassallettus and Drudus de Trivio. Finally a tabernacle in S Francesco, Viterbo, bears a signed inscription.

More substantial works by Vassallettus survive in Anagni Cathedral. The papal throne with its superb lion sculptures (*c*. 1260) is signed VASALETO DE ROMA on the inlaid marble disc at the back of the throne. This and the ornate paschal candlestick, which is borne by lions and sphinxes and crowned by a half-naked Atlas figure, are among the last Vassallettus works to have survived. According to Winckelmann the name ASSALECTUS was inscribed on the base of an antique statue of Asklepios.

The family's reputation has been largely derived from the magnificent polychrome architecture of the cloister of S Giovanni in Laterano. It can be deduced from the pretentious inscription (NOBILIT[ER] DOCT[US] HAC VAS-SALECTVS I[N] ARTE CV[M] PATRE CEPIT OPVS Q[VO]D SOL[VS] PERFICIT IP[S]E) that the work was begun by the father and finished by the son. The construction of the cloister was underway in 1227 and must have been completed before the 1230s. The oriental splendour of the coloured and gold mosaic overlay is applied to an architectural system that conforms strictly to antique models. All the entrances are guarded by pairs of fine, animated beasts: sphinxes to the south and, on the east and west, lions based on antique models. The sculptor's inventiveness found an outlet in the spandrel decoration and the masks along the cornices. On the basis of their similarity with the frieze decoration, the portico and the nave capitals of S Lorenzo fuori le mura (*c*. 1216–40; canons' benches dated 1254) have been attributed plausibly to the same workshop (Giovannoni). The sculptors who worked on the Lateran cloister were also probably responsible for the north wing of the equally magnificent cloister of S Paolo fuori le mura, which was built later and in a more lavish style than the other wings.

BIBLIOGRAPHY
J. Winckelmann: *Sämtliche Werke*, ed. J. Eiselein, i (Donaueschingen, 1825) p. 270
G. B. De Rossi: 'Del cosi detto opus alexandrinum e dei marmorarii romani in S Maria di Castello, Tarquinia', *Bull. Archeol. Crist.* (1875), pp. 110–31
A. L. Frothingham: 'Scoperta dell'epoca precisa della costruzione del chiostro presso la Basilica lateranense', *Bull. Archeol. Crist.*, iii (1892), pp. 145–9
G. Giovannoni: 'Opere dei Vassalletti', *L'Arte*, xi (1908), pp. 262–83
A. Galieti: 'Memorie della chiesa medievale di Città Lavinia', *L'Arte*, xii (1909), pp. 349–58
M. E. Cannizzaro and J. C. Gavini: 'Sulla ricostruzione della "schola cantorum" di S Saba', *Boll. A.*, ix (1915), pp. 129–35
A. Sibilia: *Guido storico-artistica della cattedrale di Anagni* (Anagni, 1936)
P. Gianfrotta: 'Un Giovanni Vassalletto ignoto', *Boll. Ist. Stor. A. Lazio Merid.*, viii (1975), pp. 63–70
D. F. Glass: *Studies on Cosmatesque Pavements*, Brit. Archaeol. Rep. (Oxford, 1980)
E. Bassan: 'Il candelabro di S Paolo fuori le mura: Note nella scultura a Roma tra XII e XIII secolo', *Stor. A.*, xlv (1982), pp. 117–31
I. Herklotz: '*Sepolcra*' e '*monumenta*' del medioevo: Studi nell'arte sepolcrale in Italia (Rome, 1985)
P. C. Claussen: *Magistri Dectissimi Romani: Die römischen Marmorkünstler des Mittelalters*, Forsch. Kstgesch. & Christ. Archäol., xiv (Wiesbaden, 1987)

For further bibliography *see* COSMATI.

P. C. CLAUSSEN

Vassallo, Antonio Maria (*b* Genoa, *c.* 1620; *d* Milan, *c.* 1664–72). Italian painter and etcher. He was from a wealthy family and received a good education before starting his training as an artist with the Flemish painter Vincent Malo (in Genoa in 1634; *d* Venice, 1649). Despite his rather brief artistic career, his oeuvre is comparatively large. Most of his pictures exhibit the same figure style, brownish colour scheme and technique, and, judging from the dates of *SS Francis, Clare, Agnes and Catherine* (1648; Genoa, Gal. Pal. Bianco) and the *Martyrdom of Marcello Mastrilli* (1664, formerly read as 1637; ex-convent of Carignano; see Belloni, 1978), Vassallo remained active for a number of years. He is best known for his skill in painting rustic pastorals and mythological subjects loaded with still-life elements and animals. His expertise in this genre was partly due to his study under Malo and was further stimulated by the presence of many northern artists in Genoa who pursued this speciality, among them the de Wael brothers, Jan Roos (1591–1638) and Pieter Boel. The art of northern Europe was popular in Genoa, and Sinibaldo Scorza, Giovanni Benedetto Castiglione, Niccolo Cassana and Antonio Travi painted similar subjects. Vassallo's style in such works as *Orpheus Charming the Animals* (Moscow, Pushkin Mus. F.A.) and the *Finding of Cyrus* (St Petersburg, Hermitage) is close to that of Castiglione. This affinity is again apparent in the turbaned figures, wooded landscape and romantic fragments of classical sculpture in the *Leto* (Genoa, Pal. Reale) and in the crosshatching of Vassallo's early etching of *Diogenes* (Rome, Gab. N. Stampe). It is also evident in *The Kitchen* (Washington, DC, N.G.A.), in which the animals and still-life are richly coloured and painted with a loaded brush in a style reminiscent of that of Bernardo Strozzi. Vassallo's work is, however, distinguished from Castiglione's by the slighter proportions of the animals and figures, the clearer compositions and more restrained movement and light effects.

Vassallo's many religious paintings (12 of which are listed in inventories of 1641 and 1658) are less well known. In their brownish palette, *sfumato* and undulating draperies they adhere generally to the northern tradition of Malo and parallel the style of Giovanni Bernardo Carbone, which was inspired by the work of Anthony van Dyck. Vassallo's two lunettes, *St Simone Stock Receiving the Cloak from the Virgin* and the *Virgin Appearing to the Pope* (before 1654; Genoa, S Anna), have the sulphur colouring of Castiglione's paintings of the 1650s and display Vassallo's skill in portraiture and in the fine definition of flowers and decorative objects in landscape. Other paintings, such as the *Miracle of Blessed Andrea da Spello* (Genoa, Pal. Gal. Bianco), a smaller version of this work (Genoa, Accad. Ligustica) and the signed *Penitent Magdalene* (Genoa, Pal. Gal. Bianco, storage), also include poetic landscapes. Vassallo was also known as a portrait painter, and a portrait of *Marcantonio Grillo in the Guise of Rinaldo Holding Armida* is recorded in an inventory of 1679.

BIBLIOGRAPHY

R. Soprani: *Vite* (1674), pp. 227–9; ed. C.G. Rath (1768), pp. 332–9
O. Grosso: 'A. M. Vassallo e la pittura d'animali nei primi del '600 a Genova', *Dedalo*, ii–iii (1922–3), pp. 502–22
G. V. Castelnovi: 'La pittura nella prima metà del seicento: Dall'Ansaldo a Orazio de Ferrari', *La pittura a Genova e in Liguria*, ii (Genoa, 1971, rev. 1987), pp. 112–13, 145–6
V. Belloni: *Pittura genovese del seicento*, ii (Genoa, 1974), pp. 84–6
——: 'Un po' di chiaro sul pittore Anton Maria Vassallo', *La Squilla*, iv (1978), pp. 18–19
Disegni genovese dal XVI al XVIII secolo (exh. cat. by M. Newcome Schleier, Florence, Uffizi, 1989), cat. no. 56
Genova nell' età' barocca (exh. cat., ed. E. Gavazza and G. R. Terminiello; Genoa, Pal. Spinola and Pal. Reale, 1992)
Kunst in der Republik Genua, 1528–1815 (exh. cat., Frankfurt am Main, Schirn Ksthalle, 1992)

M. NEWCOME

Vassé, Louis-Claude (*b* Paris, 1716; *d* Paris, 30 Oct 1772). French sculptor. Son and pupil of the decorative sculptor François-Antoine Vassé (1681–1736), he entered Edme Bouchardon's workshop, becoming his favourite pupil. In 1739 he won the Prix de Rome with a bas-relief representing *Jezebel Devoured by Dogs* (untraced), and the following year he went to the Académie de France in Rome, returning to Paris in 1745. He was approved (*agréé*) by the Académie Royale in 1748 and received (*reçu*) as a full member in 1751 on presentation of a statuette of a *Sleeping Shepherd* (marble; Paris, Louvre). In 1761 he was made professor at the Académie Royale, and he was appointed Dessinateur de l'Académie des Inscriptions in 1762. From 1748 he exhibited at the Salon, notably a plaster model of a tomb (1748; untraced) comprising a woman weeping over an urn veiled with her draperies, the type of funerary monument in which he was to specialize in both free-standing and relief formats. In 1750 he exhibited a bust of *Benedict XIV*, a model of a *Weeping Virgin* and terracotta sketch models of *Daedalus* and *Nessus* as well as a proposal for a public square with an equestrian statue of *Louis XV* (all untraced).

Vassé was ambitious, and he was aided in his desire for a prestigious career by the collector and antiquary the Comte de Caylus, who in turn hoped through Vassé to bring about a return to Classical ideals in French sculpture. Consequently Vassé took his inspiration primarily from Classical Antiquity but undertook commissions for less high-minded work if they benefited his career, casting a relief in bronze of the *Entombment* (1752; untraced), modelled by his father for the high altar of Notre-Dame, Paris, and providing a stone statue (*La Jardinière*, 1753; destr.) for Mme de Pompadour's dairy at Crécy. In 1755 Vassé executed a marble statue of *Cupid Seated on the Seashore Rounding up his Doves* (Paris, Louvre, see *Rev. Louvre*, i (1987), p. 41), a classicizing work of Alexandrian grace, for the collector Ange-Laurent de Lalive de Jully. Further examples of Vassé's work in this genre of refined and erotic sculpture, which was particularly popular with contemporary collectors, are *Venus Targeting Cupid's Arrows* (marble, 1758; Versailles, Château), given by Louis XV to Mme Du Barry in 1761, and the statue of *Diana* commissioned by Frederick II of Prussia for Schloss Sansssouci, Potsdam (marble, 1769; *in situ*).

Although Vassé's decorations for Gothic churches such as St Germain-l'Auxerrois, Paris, and the cathedrals of Auxerre and Bourges have largely disappeared, much of his funerary sculpture survives, including the classicizing relief personifying *Sorrow* for Caylus's tomb (marble, *c.* 1765; Paris, Louvre) and his most accomplished and ambitious work in this field, the tomb of *Stanislav Leszczynski*, King of Poland and Duc de Lorraine (marble, begun 1768; Nancy, Notre-Dame de Bonsecours), consisting of statues of Stanislav, Lorraine and Charity arranged in a triangular composition against a pyramid of black marble. He was also a creditable portrait sculptor, as shown by his five retrospective busts of famous citizens of Troyes (marble; Troyes, Mus. B.-A. & Archéol.), as well as his busts of children.

Contemporaries criticized Vassé for his often unscrupulous ambition, but he was nevertheless one of the most gifted sculptors of Louis XV's reign. Although often somewhat programmatic in his approach to Classicism, he was also capable of great delicacy of modelling and a certain charm. He continued the efforts of Bouchardon to reintroduce purity and simplicity into French sculpture and trained many pupils, including Félix Lecomte (1737–1817), Martin-Claude Monot (1733–1803), François-Nicolas Delaistre and Yves-Eloi Boucher (1738–82).

BIBLIOGRAPHY

Lami; Thieme–Becker

L. Réau: 'Un Sculpteur oublié du XVIIIe siècle, Louis-Claude Vassé', *Gaz. B.-A.*, n.s. 5, ii (1930), pp. 31–56

F. Souchal: 'A Statue by L.-C. Vassé: The Nymph of Dampierre', *Apollo*, cvi (1977), pp. 408–10

B. Black: *Vassé's 'Bambinelli': The Child Portraits of an 18th-century French Sculptor* (London, 1994)

FRANÇOIS SOUCHAL

Vassilacchi, Antonio [Aliense] (*b* Melos, 1556; *d* Venice, 15 April 1629). Italian painter of Greek descent. He arrived in Venice not later than 1571, when his father was supplying provisions to the Venetian fleet. It is unlikely that he had received any artistic training in Greece; probably his first teacher was Paolo Veronese, in whose workshop in Venice he was involved in the copying of drawings and paintings. In 1574, together with Veronese and Jacopo Tintoretto, he was employed decorating the triumphal arch (destr.) erected on the Venice Lido, after designs by Andrea Palladio, for the arrival of Henry III, King of France. He worked with Benedetto Caliari on the frescoes in the bishop's residence at Treviso (*c.* 1579) and, with Dario Varotari, on the decoration of the Villa Emo Capodilista at Montecchia, near Padua. In these works he adopted the dramatic chiaroscuro effects of Tintoretto, rather than following the painterly effects of his master, Veronese; of all Venetian Mannerists he followed Tintoretto most closely.

In 1584 Vassilacchi first worked in the Doge's Palace, painting a series of *Virtues* and some grisailles on the ceiling of the Sala dello Scrutinio, the most interesting of these being *Pietro Ziani Rejecting the Office of Doge* and the *Death of Ordelafo Falier during the Battle of Zara*, in which he emphasized the violence of the scenes by highlighting anatomy and using dramatic contrasts of light and shade.

A vivid *Resurrection* (Venice, S Marziale) dates from 1586; equally melodramatic is the *Punishment of the Serpents* (1588; Venice, S Angelo Raffaele), in which the serpentine figures, agitated drapery and the dramatic use of light reveal his debt to Tintoretto. In 1591–2 Vassilacchi collaborated with Tintoretto and his son Domenico on the decoration of the Scuola dei Mercanti; Vassilacchi's surviving works from this commission are a *Visitation* (Venice, Semin. Patriarcale) and an *Adoration of the Shepherds* (Loreo, parish church). In this last work his style

is more tranquil; the intimacy of the pastoral scene is probably influenced by the work of Jacopo Bassano.

In 1593–4 Vassilacchi worked on a series of 11 canvases of the *Life of Christ* and the *Passion* for S Pietro, Perugia, which constitutes his masterpiece. The large, theatrical compositions are inspired by Tintoretto's works for the Scuola di S Rocco in Venice: the light is intensely expressive, particularly in the nocturnal scenes; the compositions display considerable spatial complexity; and the uncompromising realism demonstrates his interest in the work of Flemish painters.

An *Adoration of the Magi* was painted *c.* 1600 for the Sala del Consiglio dei Dieci in the Doge's Palace. In his later works Vassilacchi softened the Mannerist tension, perhaps under the influence of Domenico Tintoretto and Palma Giovane, with whom he collaborated on the decoration (1602–5) of Salò Cathedral. He also worked with Antonio Foler on the frescoes (before 1616) of the Villa Barbarigo, Noventa Vicentina. His late works, such as the *Portrait of Federico Contarini* (1613; Venice, Le Zitelle) and the *Birth of the Virgin* (1623; Padua, S Maria in Vanzo), show him to have abandoned the dynamic movement of Mannerism and adopted the quieter mood in painting promoted after the Council of Trent.

BIBLIOGRAPHY

Thieme–Becker

G. Boccassini: 'Profilo dell'Aliense', *A. Veneta*, xii (1958), pp. 111–25

R. Pallucchini: *La pittura veneziana del seicento*, i (Milan, 1981), pp. 44–6

Da Tiziano a El Greco: Per la storia del manierismo a Venezia, 1540–1590 (exh. cat., ed. R. Pallucchini; Venice, Doge's Palace, 1981), p. 231

MASSIMO GEMIN

Vassilakis, Panayiotis. *See* TAKIS.

Vassilieff [Vasiliyev], **Danila (Ivanovich)** (*b* Kagal'nitskaya, nr Rostov-on-Don, 16 Dec 1897; *d* Melbourne, 22 March 1958). Australian painter and sculptor of Russian birth. He had no early formal art training, attending instead the Technical Artillery School in St Petersburg before serving in the Russian army (1917–18). He fled Russia, travelled overland through Asia and arrived in Australia in 1923. In 1929 he went to France to study art and then worked as an artist in Brazil, the West Indies, England, Spain and Portugal. In 1935 he returned to Australia where he began painting street scenes of the inner suburbs of Sydney and Melbourne, for example a *Street in Fitzroy* (1937; Mr and Mrs John Reed priv. col., see St John Moore, p. 48). Vassilieff's direct and expressive painting with its graphic spontaneity and free use of colour was opposed to the influence of French formal abstraction on Australian art. The roots of his art lie as much in the folk art of his Cossack heritage as in the work of such artists as Vincent van Gogh, Maurice de Vlaminck and Chaïm Soutine, whom he admired.

In 1939 Vassilieff moved to semi-rural Warrandyte, near Melbourne, where he taught art at the Koornong Experimental School. His house, Stonygrad, became a meeting-place for a group of younger artists that included Albert Tucker, Sidney Nolan, Arthur Boyd and John Perceval. By the late 1940s his painting became more ambitious and increasingly concerned with representing the psychological traumas of his life allegorically. At this time he also began carving figures using a variety of local stone; between 1947 and 1952 sculpture dominated his output. The highly polished and simplified figures, for example *Stenka Razin* (Lilydale marble, 1953; Canberra, N. G.), reflect the influence of Henry Moore's work but possess a vitality that is the stamp of Vassilieff's character. He spent his last years in north-eastern Victoria, where he returned to teaching and to painting. Vassilieff's volatile and vital presence and the earthy humanism of his art were a powerful influence on Australian Expressionism in the 1940s.

BIBLIOGRAPHY
F. St John Moore: *Vassilieff and his Art* (Melbourne, 1982)

RICHARD HAESE

Vassiliou, Spyros (*b* Galaxidi, 27 April 1902; *d* Athens, 22 March 1985). Greek painter, printmaker, illustrator and stage designer. He studied painting at the Higher School of Fine Arts in Athens from 1921 to 1927 and had his first one-man show in Athens in 1929. In the years that followed he had numerous one-man shows in almost all the capital cities of Europe and participated in 80 group exhibitions internationally. In 1930 he received an Academy of Athens award for his fresco designs for the church of St Dionysios the Areopagite in Athens (1930–39), the first of many ecclesiastical commissions in Greece, including St Vlassios of Xylokastro (1936–45), St Charalambos in Akrata and St Nicholas in Pefkakia. In 1935 he won commissions to design and execute the frescoes in SS Constantine and Helen, Detroit, MI. During and immediately after World War II he made illustrated manuscripts and woodcuts of Greek patriotic subjects. He was one of the founder-members of the Stathmi group in 1949. In the 1950s and 1960s he became a highly fashionable and prolific artist. He produced many illustrations for literary publications and periodicals, and designed a large number of prints for the Greek National Tourist Organization. For many years he taught stage design at the Greek National School of Drama in Athens, and he designed sets and costumes for over 150 plays, operas and films, among them Molière's *Malade imaginaire* at the Olympia Theatre in Athens (1933) and Carlo Goldoni's *Servant of Two Masters* at the New Drama Scene, Athens (1938). In terms of subject-matter, his paintings present familiar objects in unusual juxtapositions against backgrounds that never vary: always the bright blue sea and the reflected glare of the sun. He used the techniques of Byzantine art in some of his secular paintings.

BIBLIOGRAPHY
Spyros Vassiliou (exh. cat. by L. Finer, intro. by D. Papastamos, Athens, N.G., 1975)

FANI-MARIA TSIGAKOU

Vassilyov, Ivan (Tsokov) (*b* Oriakhovo, near Russe, 28 Feb 1893; *d* Sofia, 6 June 1979). Bulgarian architect and urban planner. He studied painting (1913–16) at the Akademie der Bildenden Künste, Munich, and graduated in architecture (1919) at the Technische Hochschule, Karlsruhe. On returning to Bulgaria he established a partnership with Dimiter Tsolov (1896–1970) until 1948. Their early designs include a number of accomplished private houses in Sofia, such as the Chaprashikoff House, 29 Oborishte Street (1930). Their public projects in Sofia

represent a synthesis of contemporary artistic trends with an emphasis on sculptural decoration, as at the Farmers' Bank (1925), which reveals Secessionist elements, with sculptural ornament and a cartouche above the door, and the University Library (1934), which is in the Neo-classical style, with bronze lions sculpted by Lyouben Dimitrov (*b* 1904). Vassilyov's most significant work is the Bulgarian National Bank (1934–9), Sofia, where the strongly decorated façade, including a sculpted figure of *St Nicholas*, is matched by the ornamented details of the interior, such as the ventilation gratings and the capitals of the colonnade in the second-floor hall. A sculpture of a lion by Michaylo Parashchuk (1878–1963) and stained-glass windows by Ivan Penkov (1897–1957) and Dechko Uzunov reflect the intention to achieve a synthesis of the arts, inspired by Secessionist examples. Vassilyov also designed the City Hall (1938–42) and the National Library of SS Cyril and Methodius (1942–54), both in Sofia, and in 1953 he helped plan the reconstruction of the city centre.

BIBLIOGRAPHY
N. Paskalev: *Ivan Vassilyov* (Sofia, *c.* 1978)

JULIANA NEDEVA-WEGENER

Vatagin, Vasily (Alekseyevich) (*b* Moscow, 1 Jan 1884; *d* Moscow, 31 May 1969). Russian sculptor, illustrator and painter. He studied in the Department of Natural Sciences at Moscow University (1902–7), from 1899 also with N. A. Martynov, and in 1904–6 with Konstantin Yuon. In 1903–13 he travelled throughout western and southern Europe, India and Ceylon (now Sri Lanka), and ancient Indian culture was especially influential on his work. The most accomplished 20th-century Russian animal artist, Vatagin combined an intense feeling for appearance and habits with a mystical approach to nature. The mythology of the transmigration of souls imparts an almost human individuality to his animals and provides a poetic background to his oeuvre. He used a late Symbolist style with Orientalist tendencies. His sculptures vary textural effects to suit the characteristics of the animal (e.g. *Walruses*, wood, 1909, and *Tiger*, bronze, 1925–6; both Moscow, Tret'yakov Gal.), and he depicted monkeys with particular frequency. He also produced book illustrations (e.g. for Rudyard Kipling's *Jungle Book* (*Mowgli*, lithographs, 1926)). From the 1930s to the 1950s he decorated the Darwin Anthropology and Zoology Museums in Moscow, mostly with large painted panels containing accurate rather than poetic depictions.

WRITINGS
Vospominaniya, zapiski animalista, stat'i [Memoirs, notes of an animal artist, articles] (Moscow, 1980)

BIBLIOGRAPHY
A. Bakushinsky and A. Molodchikov: *V. A. Vatagin* (Moscow, 1933)
V. A. Tikhanova: *Ptitsy i zveri Vasiliya Vatagina* [The birds and animals of Vasily Vatagin] (Moscow, 1987)

M. N. SOKOLOV

Vatapi. *See* BADAMI.

Vathypetro. Large Late Minoan I (*c.* 1560–*c.* 1425 BC) country house a few kilometres south of Archanes and Knossos in northern central Crete. Excavated by SPYRIDON MARINATOS in 1949–51, it stands on a spur overlooking fertile country, dominated by Mt Juktas to the north-west, with its shrines. The house, which measures over 20×20 m, was apparently not part of a village or hamlet. Its few outbuildings include a kiln, while in the house itself are presses for olive oil and wine. Its architecture exemplifies the high quality of building of these large villas, which probably controlled large estates. Features include ashlar masonry, column bases of different stones, pillar basements, recesses for windows and a paved west court. On the east side of the building, opposite the entrance and across a small courtyard, is a tripartite shrine, with a central recess (possibly for a seat or statue) between two square masonry structures with hollow centres. These may have held flagstaff-like masts, as depicted on the peak-sanctuary chlorite and gold rhyton from KATO ZAKROS (Herakleion, Archaeol. Mus.), or they may be the bases of platforms. Vathypetro had at least two building phases, but, as the site has not been published fully, many details that would be important for the history of Minoan architecture and society are still unclear. It nevertheless remains an excellent illustration of the tendency, particularly marked in the Neo-Palatial period, for complex buildings to be erected in rural areas, to serve not only as lavish dwellings for local dignitaries, but as centres for farming, local administration and religion. (*See also* MINOAN, §II.)

BIBLIOGRAPHY

S. Marinatos: 'Anaskaphai Vathypetrou Archanon (Kritis)' [Excavations at Vathypetro, Archanai (Crete)], *Praktika Athen. Archaiol. Etaireias* (1949), pp. 100–09
——: 'Megaron Vathypetrou' [The megaron of Vathypetro], *Praktika Athen. Archaiol. Etaireias* (1950), pp. 242–57
——: 'Anaskaphi megarou Vathypetrou (Kritis)' [Excavation of the megaron at Vathypetro (Crete)], *Praktika Athen. Archaiol. Etaireias* (1951), pp. 258–72
——: 'Anaskaphai en Vathypetro (Kritis)' [Excavations at Vathypetro (Crete)], *Praktika Athen. Archaiol. Etaireias* (1952), pp. 592–610
S. Marinatos and M. Hirmer: *Crete and Mycenae* (London, 1960), pp. 137, 140
C. Davaras: *Guide to Cretan Antiquities* (Park Ridge, 1976), pp. 335–7
J. W. Shaw: 'Evidence for the Minoan Tripartite Shrine', *Amer. J. Archaeol.*, lxxxii (1978), pp. 429–48 (442–6)
G. C. Gesell: *Town, Palace and House Cult in Minoan Crete*, Stud. Medit. Archaeol., lxvii (Göteborg, 1985), pp. 20, 29–30, 136–7
B. Rutkowski: *The Cult Places of the Aegean* (New Haven and London, 1986), p. 34
G. Cadogan: 'Vathypetro', *The Aerial Atlas of Ancient Crete*, ed. J. W. Myers, E. E. Myers and G. Cadogan (Berkeley, 1992), pp. 280–83
J. Driessen and I. Sakellarakis: 'The Vathypetro-Complex: Some Observations on its Architectural History and Function', *The Function of the Minoan 'Villa': Proceedings of the Eighth International Symposium at the Swedish Institute* (Athens, 1992)

GERALD CADOGAN

Vaṭodaka. *See* BADOH.

Vau, Le. *See* LE VAU.

Vauban, Sébastien Leprestre [Le Prestre] **de** (*b* Saint-Léger-de-Foucheret [now Saint-Léger-Vauban], nr Avallon, Yonne, May 1633; *d* Paris, 30 March 1707). Marshal of France, engineer, architect and urban planner. He was responsible for the main phase in the building of bastioned strongholds in France, which was necessitated by Louis XIV's numerous wars. He was born into the lower ranks of the aristocracy and began his career in the regiment of Louis II, Prince of Condé, in 1651, moving into the King's service two years later. He became inspector-general of fortifications in 1673 and in 1703 a Marshal of France. From his first major project of military planning at Lille in 1667, he was responsible for more than 30 new defensive walls and citadels and for laying out over 100 fortified towns.

By turning to good account the experience of his predecessors, particularly Blaise de Pagan (1604–65), Vauban perfected methods of attacking and defending fortified towns by rationalizing their means of blockade, with the object of avoiding loss of life and reducing the length of a siege. He used parallel dugouts or trenches surrounding the besieged town, and set up batteries of artillery perpendicular to the defensive cannons, allowing gunfire to rake and ricochet. In thus modernizing the principles of attack, Vauban developed his basic assumptions on the subject of fortification. A fortified town, he believed, should dominate the surrounding land for purposes of observation and to prevent the enemy's firing from above. Defences should be thick and built out of large masses of ballast, strengthened and supported by stonework, to resist the besieger's cannons, while ramparts should be equipped with bastions at suitable intervals to block side-fire. Bastions, in their turn, should be protected by counterguards and other defences, and staggered to increase the number of obstacles to the assailant. Vauban worked to a single principle: adapt the fortification to the contours of the town. His innovations—bastioned towers with blockhouses, first employed at Besançon in 1687, the wall-line broken by ramparts and the doubling of the outer defences—were always used in accordance with the nature of the terrain. The citadel, reduced to the garrison, was—for example at Lille—placed at a distance from the town. Vauban's so-called 'three systems', according to doctrine established in France in the 18th and 19th centuries, belie the variety of his layouts. His genius lay in drawing all the logical consequences from the principles of attack and applying them to new or renovated fortifications.

In his concern to protect the frontiers of France, Vauban devised in 1678 a double line of fortified towns extending from Dunkerque to Metz (the *frontière de fer*) and around the perimeter of the kingdom: south to Entrevaux and Antibes, along the south coast to Perpignan and up to Camaret along the Bay of Biscay. This was the first time that France's defences had been treated as a whole; Vauban termed the area so enclosed the 'square meadow' (pré-carré). To defend the coast he developed a small fort for low-angled 'grazing-fire' on to water, with squat, semicircular batteries, as at Camaret (Finistère; 1694). He also gave much attention to the inland façades of maritime fortifications, for example at Blaye (Gironde; 1681), and recommended the installation of beacons consisting of a main tower and a stair turret. In mountainous terrain, notably at Briançon (Hautes-Alpes; 1692), he resorted to a more conventional layout for a bastioned fortification, with concentric surrounding walls in the medieval manner. On level terrain, the substitution of a bastioned fortification for a medieval wall involved an enlargement of the original town boundary, especially when, as at Verdun (1664–92), he used the river to improve his system of defence with a network of sluice-gates to produce artificial flooding. The addition of a citadel built at some distance from the town—Arras (Pas-de-Calais; 1668), Besançon

(Doubs; 1674–87) and Strasbourg (1681)—involved the creation of new districts, hence towns modernized by Vauban tended to expand in order to embrace all their defences within the same bastioned wall-line. An esplanade, where construction was prohibited, divided the citadel from the urban sector. Vauban created nine complete fortified towns for the defence of the French frontier. Of these, there remain today Sarrelouis (Sarre, Germany; 1680), Huningue (Haut-Rhin; 1679), Longwy (Meurthe-et-Moselle; 1679), Phalsbourg (Haut-Rhin; 1679), Neuf-Brisach (Bas-Rhin; 1698), Mont-Dauphin (Hautes-Alpes, south of Briançon; 1692) and Mont-Louis (south-west of Perpignan; 1681). The fortifications of Montroyal in Germany were built in 1692 and razed by Vauban ten years later, and the fortifications of Fort-Louis-du-Rhin (Bas-Rhin; 1687) were destroyed in 1794.

Vauban applied simple principles of construction and urban planning. The surrounding wall was as regular as possible: a notable example is the octagonal layout of Neuf-Brisach. The town's organization was based on military requirements, with a chequered ground-plan for the functional distribution of public buildings and private houses around a vast central square, intended for manoeuvres. The headquarters of military command were integrated harmoniously with such civil and religious buildings as the town hall, church and covered markets. Barracks, with wings for the officers at both ends, and gunpowder stores were built on the ramparts. In general, the boundaries of these fortified towns were marked by a final surrounding wall, and the building of military and public buildings followed an existing blueprint, with only the construction materials changing according to the region. The architecture of the houses was also governed by set patterns. A man of his time, Vauban was well acquainted with the aesthetic rigours of classical architecture; this is particularly evident in the town entrance-gates on which he set sculpted decorations glorifying the King.

To complement this work, Vauban made scale models of the fortified towns that he built or restructured. Built to a scale of 1/600, they carefully reproduced the physiognomy of a town and often included the projected work. These relief plans, of which about 30 survive, form a public collection, housed in the Musée des Plans–Reliefs, Paris.

Vauban was also engaged on civil projects, notably in the sphere of water management, in which he suggested ways of completing the Midi canal (1687–91). He also planned great works for Cherbourg, Saint-Malo, Saint-Servan (Ile-et-Vilaine) and even Quebec, then under French rule, with a view to improving trade between France and her colonies. No field of activity left him indifferent and he recorded his thoughts in the writings that he titled, not without humour, *Oisivetés, ou Pensées diverses d'un homme qui n'avait pas grand'chose à faire* (c. 1705). These memoirs, on a highly eclectic range of subjects, deal with everything from the cultivation of forests to the calculation of the population of Canada in the year 2000. They became known only after his death and were used by 18th-century encyclopedists. His last work, *Projet d'une dîme royale* (1707), proposed a total recasting of the taxation system and was condemned by the King. This profoundly affected Vauban, and he died a few weeks later.

For illustration of work *see* MILITARY ARCHITECTURE AND FORTIFICATION, fig. 11.

UNPUBLISHED SOURCES
Oisivetés, ou Pensées diverses d'un homme qui n'avait pas grand'chose à faire (Paris, c. 1705)

WRITINGS
Projet d'une dîme royale (Rouen, 1707)
Traité de l'attaque des places (Paris, 1737)

BIBLIOGRAPHY
A. M. Augoyat: *Aperçu historique sur les fortifications, les ingénieurs et le corps du génie en France*, 3 vols (Paris, 1860–64)
R. d'Aiglun: *Vauban, sa famille et ses écrits, ses Oisivetés et sa correspondance*, 2 vols (Paris, 1910/R Geneva, 1972)
R. L. Blomfield: *Sebastian Le Prestre de Vauban, 1633–1707* (London, 1938)
L. Grodecki: 'Vauban urbaniste', *Bull. Soc. Etud. XVIIe Siècle* (July–Oct 1957), pp. 329–59
M. Parent and J. Verroust: *Vauban* (Paris, 1971, rev. 1982)
A. Blanchard: *Les Ingénieurs du 'Roy' de Louis XIV à Louis XVI: Etude du corps des fortifications* (Montpellier, 1979)
C. Brisac: *Le Musée des plans-reliefs* (Paris, 1981)
Actes du colloque de l'Association Vauban: Vauban Réformateur: Paris, 1983
N. Faucherre: *Places fortes, bastions du pouvoir* (Paris, 1986)

CATHERINE BRISAC

Vaudoyer. French family of architects. (1) Antoine-Laurent-Thomas Vaudoyer was an influential administrator and teacher in post-Revolutionary Paris, his atelier producing some of the most important innovators in French architecture of the first half of the 19th century. His son (2) Léon Vaudoyer was one of the founders of the new Romantic movement in architecture, his theories embodied in his principal works—the Conservatoire des Arts et Métiers, Paris, and Marseille Cathedral. Léon's son Alfred Vaudoyer (*b* Paris, 13 March 1846; *d* Jouy-en-Josas, 1917), who trained with his father, helped complete Marseille Cathedral, but he worked principally in private practice, building numerous houses in a neo-Renaissance style in the western suburbs of Paris, especially around Jouy-en-Josas. He also designed several pavilions for the Expositions Universelles in Paris (1878, 1889, 1900). Alfred's son Georges Vaudoyer (*b* Jouy-en-Josas, 1877; *d* Paris, 1947) and grandson Jean-Laurent Vaudoyer (*b* Paris, 1902; *d* Paris, 1975) continued the family tradition into the 20th century; Georges was noted for innovative work in the design of public housing.

BIBLIOGRAPHY
Les Vaudoyer: Une dynastie d'architectes (exh. cat. by B. Bergdoll, Paris, Mus. d'Orsay, 1991)

(1) Antoine-Laurent-Thomas Vaudoyer (*b* Paris, 20 Dec 1756; *d* Paris, 27 May 1846). He was destined for a military career and served briefly in a cavalry regiment before entering the Académie d'Architecture, Paris, in 1778. His master was Antoine-François Peyre, whose office was from the late 1770s one of the most engaged in promoting architectural Neo-classicism; Charles Percier, Pierre-François-Léonard Fontaine and Louis-Pierre Baltard were among his pupils in the early 1780s when Vaudoyer entered the studio. While Peyre encouraged a refined understanding of antique models and prepared his students for archaeological research as a foundation for their design solutions, the students were also captivated by Etienne-Louis Boullée's quest for a 'natural' architecture of emotive effects. Julien-David Le Roy, a professor of architecture at the Académie and pioneer explorer of Greek antiquity, was also a formative influence.

Vaudoyer won the Prix de Rome in 1783 and spent the years 1784–8 at the Académie de France in Rome. His restoration study of the Theatre of Marcellus (published in 1812) was one of the first of those detailed archaeological studies that became a requirement of architectural students at the Ecole des Beaux-Arts until the early 20th century. Vaudoyer also explored the limits of symbolism and pure geometric form in architecture in a series of private sketches, most notably in his famous design for a *Maison d'un cosmopolite*, which, in the spirit of Boullée's famous design for a cenotaph to Newton (for illustration *see* BOULLÉE, ETIENNE-LOUIS), was designed in the form of a sphere, or globe, unadorned except for the patterns of the constellations pierced in its surface to light the interior spaces. This was an essay in architectural symbolism of the sort Léon Vaudoyer later labelled *architecture parlante* (*Magasin pittoresque*, 1859), a term coined in sceptical satire of his father's generation's search for an architecture that could communicate through symbol and sensational effects, and in support of his own belief that all architectural form acquires meaning through historical evolution, not wilful invention.

Vaudoyer's return to Paris on the eve of the Revolution could scarcely have been less auspicious; he soon found his potential clients in exile and the Académie in turmoil. He accepted posts as architect of the Dépôt de Guerre and as an assessor in the administration of *biens nationaux*, charged with the valuation of confiscated ecclesiastical and aristocratic properties. In 1795 he joined the newly created Conseil des Bâtiments Civils, where for the next three decades he oversaw the maintenance, expansion and re-creation of some of the most prestigious educational and artistic institutions of the capital, including the Collège des Quatres Nations, which he adapted (1806–20) to serve as the Institut de France. Projects for completing the Madeleine (1806) as a Temple of Glory for the Napoleonic armies and for a new Ecole des Beaux-Arts (1811) near the Champs de Mars remained unexecuted. The only completely new public building built to his designs was the Marché des Carmes (1811–24; destr.) on the Place Maubert. Although he undertook considerable private work, mostly interiors, such as the splendid apartments (1809–11) for the Prince de Salm-Dyck in the Rue du Bac, Paris, Vaudoyer's mark was made principally as an administrator and teacher, and here his importance for the first two generations of 19th-century academic architects in France was enormous.

Vaudoyer had begun teaching shortly after his return from Rome when, taking advantage of a liberalization of admission to the Académie's architectural school that permitted some unsponsored pupils to participate in academic competitions, he opened the first *atelier libre*. This was the prototype for the teaching ateliers that became the lynchpin of the Ecole des Beaux-Arts, which had grown from the small private school of architecture set up by Julien-David Le Roy after the abolition of the *académies* in 1793. Until 1795, when the school received official

recognition, Vaudoyer, like Le Roy, organized competitions and rewarded students with books, drawing instruments and engravings taken from his own collection. Vaudoyer conceived the project of publishing the winning designs in large folio volumes of engravings, the first published in 1806, and these volumes were a key to the tremendous influence of the Ecole.

Vaudoyer's atelier, shared with his nephew Louis-Hippolyte Lebas after 1819 and taken over by his son Léon Vaudoyer in 1832, remained one of the most prominent throughout the first half of the century; it produced a first or second Grand Prix every year between 1824 and 1830, during which period it became a seedbed of the Romantic movement in architecture as some of Vaudoyer's students sought to respond to the Romantic historiography and contemporary political implications of the teachings of François Guizot and Jacques-Nicolas-Augustin Thierry (1795–1856). The challenge to the academic doctrine of idealist Neo-classicism in favour of an historically relative view of architectural forms and style (*see* §(2) below) was spearheaded by Henri Labrouste who, together with his brother Théodore, had studied alongside Léon Vaudoyer in the atelier.

UNPUBLISHED SOURCES

Paris, Bib. N., MS. Fr. 12340 [*Dissertation sur l'architecture*, 1832]
London, RIBA, MS. fol. 1823 [another version of the above]

WRITINGS

Idées d'un citoyen français sur le lieu destiné à la sépulture des hommes illustres de la France (Paris, 1791)
Projet de restauration des piliers du dôme du Panthéon français an VI (Paris, 1798)
'Plan d'un projet de restauration de l'église de la Madeleine, dans la forme du Panthéon de Rome, par M. Vaudoyer, architecte', *Annales du Musée*, vii (1803), pp. 25–8
with H.-P.-D. Allais and A. Detournelle: *Projets d'architecture et autre productions de cet art, qui ont merités les grands prix* (Paris, 1806)
Plan, coupe et élévation du Palais de l'Institut Impérial de France, suivant sa nouvelle restauration (Paris, 1811)
Description du théâtre de Marcellus à Rome rétablis dans son état primitif d'après les vestiges qui en reste encore (Paris, 1812)
'Les Monuments sous le Premier Empire d'après le journal inédit de Vaudoyer . . . notices sur différents objets concernant l'architecture et les arts', *Amis Mnmts & A.*, viii (1901), pp. 91–117, 194–205, 226–74; ix (1902), pp. 5–10, 145–51

BIBLIOGRAPHY

C. Landon: 'Maison d'un cosmopolite', *Annales du Musée*, ii (1802), pp. 123–8
C. Daly: 'Notices nécrologiques: MM. Vaudoyer et Baltard', *Rev. Gén. Archit.*, vi (1845–6), pp. 547–52
H. Ottomeyer: 'Autobiographies d'architectes parisiens, 1759–1811', *Bull. Soc. Hist. Paris & Ile-de-France* (1971), pp. 141–206
A. Friedman: 'Academic Theory and A.-L.-T. Vaudoyer's *Dissertation sur l'architecture*', *A. Bull.*, 67 (1985), pp. 110–23

(2) Léon Vaudoyer (*b* Paris, 7 June 1803; *d* Paris, 9 Feb 1872). Son of (1) Antoine-Laurent-Thomas Vaudoyer. He enrolled at the Ecole des Beaux-Arts in 1819 as a pupil of his father and his cousin, Louis-Hippolyte Lebas. In 1826 he joined the growing numbers of Grand Prix winners from the atelier with a project (Rome, Pal. Farnese) for *Une Académie de France à Rome* and travelled to Rome to join FÉLIX DUBAN, Henri Labrouste (*see* LABROUSTE, (2)) and LOUIS DUC, the three previous winners who were already engaged in studying the antiquities of Rome from a new and challenging point of view. Vaudoyer had earlier won an unusual open competition (1825) for a public monument and tomb to *General Foy*, a hero of the Napoleonic Wars and one of the most gifted orators of the liberal opposition in the early 1820s. Vaudoyer's design was executed in collaboration with the sculptor DAVID D'ANGERS, whose life-size statue took the guise of a classical orator continuing to harangue the masses from the miniature Doric temple Vaudoyer designed on the highest point of the Père Lachaise cemetery, Paris. This reinforced the young Vaudoyer's belief in the possibility of a socially and politically engaged architecture.

At the Villa Medici in Rome Vaudoyer formed a close association with his fellow students, together known as the band of four or the 'romantics'; they studied architectural monuments in Italy and Sicily as records of political, historical and social evolution, and they ranged more widely than previous generations, studying also Etruscan, early medieval and Byzantine monuments. Vaudoyer became interested in the historical theories and social agenda of Saint-Simonism, especially after the July Revolution (1830), and he returned to Paris in 1832 determined that architecture could be an instrument of social reform. Through his friendships with Léonce Reynaud and Hippolyte Fortoul, Vaudoyer was drawn into the circles of a splinter group of Saint-Simonians led by Jean Reynaud (Léonce's brother) and Pierre Leroux. He contributed frequently to their innovative publication projects aimed at creating a popular press, particularly the *Magasin pittoresque*, France's first sustained illustrated magazine.

During this period Vaudoyer began his rise through the state architectural profession, serving first as building Inspecteur under Jacques Lacornée (1782–1856) on the completion of the great administrative building on the Quai d'Orsay (1833–41; destr.) for the Cours des Comptes and the Conseil d'Etat. Vaudoyer's own ideas were explored in a competition project (1836–7; unexecuted) for a new town hall for Avignon; in decorations for a series of ceremonies and festivals, most notably with Duc for the funeral (1835) for the victims of the Fieschi plot to assassinate King Louis-Philippe; and in historical studies of French medieval and Renaissance architecture for the newly founded Commission des Monuments Historiques. He travelled frequently with Fortoul, to England (1837) and Germany (1839), acting as architectural adviser for Fortoul's *De l'art en Allemagne* (Paris, 1840–41), one of the clearest expositions of the Romantics' historical ideas, in which Fortoul coined the phrase that became Vaudoyer's motto: 'L'architecture est la véritable écriture des peuples'.

Vaudoyer's first opportunity to put these historical theories into practice came in 1838, when he was appointed architect of the Conservatoire des Arts et Métiers, housed since 1798 in the former monastery of St Martin-des-Champs, Paris. Unlike his predecessors, who had sought to mask the historical diversity of this complex, Vaudoyer sought to give a narrative clarity to the different epochs represented there by restoration, infill and new construction, rendering a walk through the site a lesson in the development of French architectural style and technique. He first created a monumental entrance court, reorientating the buildings to face the Rue St Martin by refacing the 18th-century central building and adding a great formal entrance and exterior staircase. This was reached from a *porte-cochère* on the Rue St Martin, with twin caryatids of

'Art' and 'Science' flanking the entrance. The great entrance court was flanked on the right by the medieval refectory, restored as the Conservatoire's library (see fig. 1), and a pendant on the left—Vaudoyer's first new building—in which he took up the themes of the Gothic refectory. In the 1850s he restored the Early Gothic church for the display of the large steam engines, adding rich polychromatic decoration, and began work on the French Renaissance-inspired wings along the Rue St Martin to house laboratories and classrooms. The whole was an historical panorama in which the new was didactically shown to have emerged from the inherent logic of the old.

Vaudoyer's rise to prominence was assured when Fortoul became Ministre de l'Instruction Publique et des Cultes (1851). The two men worked together for the next five years until Fortoul's death (*see* FORTOUL, HIPPOLYTE), and Vaudoyer was one of three inspecteurs in the Service des Edifices Diocésains, formed in 1853 to oversee all construction and restoration in France's ecclesiastical buildings. Their most extravagant project was the construction of a monumental new cathedral for Marseille, dramatically poised over the new ports and docks. Vaudoyer was first involved in 1845 in the selection of a site; he then presented a design in 1852, which was considerably modified before construction began (1855). Vaudoyer's project (see fig. 2), its green-and-white marble banding one of the first major exercises in structural polychromy

1. Léon Vaudoyer: Conservatoire des Arts et Métiers, Paris, 1838–72

2. Léon Vaudoyer: Marseille Cathedral, 1855–72, consecrated 1893

in 19th-century France, was a demonstration of his historicist theory of architecture as 'an unbroken chain of continual progress'. In the cathedral, a synthesis of Roman, Byzantine, medieval and Renaissance forms, he wove together spatial, structural and decorative elements from the succession of architectural styles that had superseded each other both in Marseille and in the development of the French cathedral; its plan combined the basilica, a domed Greek cross and an ambulatory with radiating chapels reminiscent of a medieval pilgrimage church. Vaudoyer died before either of his great projects was completed. Work at the Conservatoire continued under the direction of Gabriel Auguste Ancelet (1829–95), and the cathedral was completed by Vaudoyer's most loyal pupil Henri-Jacques Espérandieu and by Henri-Antoine Révoil (1820–1900), who drew up revised schemes for the sculptural and mosaic decoration of both the façade and the interior, left incomplete when the cathedral was belatedly consecrated in 1893. Much of the furnishings of the chapels and sacristies was completed after 1900 by his son Alfred Vaudoyer.

WRITINGS
with A. Lenoir: 'Etudes d'architecture en France', *Mag. Pittoresque*, pp. 7–20 (1839–52)
contributions to: *Encyclopédie nouvelle: Dictionnaire philosophique, scientifique, litéraire et industriel*, ed. P. Leroux and J. Reynaud, (1840); 'Basilique', ii (1836), pp. 463–70; 'Cirque', iii (1840), pp. 626–30

Instruction sur les moyens de prévenir ou de faire cesser les effets de l'humidité dans les bâtiments (Paris, 1844)
'Histoire de l'architecture en France', *Patria*, ed. E. Charton, ii (Paris, 1846), pp. 2113–200
'Colonnes monumentales de la barrière du Trône', *Mag. Pittoresque*, 16 (1848), pp. 195–7
'Les Bizarreries de Ledoux', *Mag. Pittoresque*, 27 (1859), pp. 27–9

BIBLIOGRAPHY
C. Blanc: 'Léon Vaudoyer et l'exposition de son oeuvre à l'Ecole des Beaux-arts', *Le Temps* (27 & 28 April 1873)
G. Davioud: 'Notice biographique sur Léon Vaudoyer', *Rev. Gén. Archit.*, 30 (1873), pp. 67–72
H. Revoil: 'Biographie des architectes contemporains: Léon Vaudoyer', *Moniteur Architectes*, n. s. 7 (May 1873)
P. Sédille: 'Exposition des oeuvres de Léon Vaudoyer, architecte, à l'Ecole des Beaux-arts', *Chron. A.* (March 1873), pp. 77–9
F. P. Cockerell: 'Biographical Notices of Deceased Foreign Members: Léon Vaudoyer', *Sess. Pap. RIBA* (1875–6), pp. 215–18
C. Blanc: *Les Artistes de mon temps* (Paris, 1876), pp. 225–48
E. Parrocel: *L'Art dans le Midi* (Marseille, 1881–4)
B. Bergdoll: *Historical Reasoning and Architectural Politics: Léon Vaudoyer and the Development of French Historicist Architecture* (diss., New York, Columbia U., 1986)
D. Van Zanten: *Designing Paris: The Architecture of Duban, Labrouste, Duc and Vaudoyer* (Cambridge, MA, 1987)
B. Bergdoll: 'Les Projets de Léon Vaudoyer pour une reconstruction sous le second empire: L'Historicisme didactique', *La Sorbonne et sa reconstruction*, ed. P. Rivé (Paris, 1987), pp. 54–64
——: 'La Cathédrale de Marseille: Fonctions politiques d'un monument éclectique', *Bull. Soc. Hist. A. Fr.* (1988), pp. 129–43
——: 'L'Architecture religieuse', *Marseille au XIXième: Rêves et triomphes* (exh. cat., Marseille, Mus. B.-A., 1991), pp. 184–211

——: 'La Nouvelle Major et le 'mythe de Marseille' sous le second empire', *Marseille: La Passion des contrastes*, ed. M. Culot and D. Droucourt (Liège, 1991), pp. 266–85
——: *Léon Vaudoyer: Historicism in the Age of Industry* (New York, 1994)

BARRY BERGDOLL

Vaudremer, (Joseph-Auguste-)Emile (*b* Paris, 6 Feb 1829; *d* Paris, 7 Feb 1914). French architect, teacher and writer. He studied (from 1847) at the Ecole des Beaux-Arts, Paris, in the studios of Guillaume Abel Blouet and E.-J. Gilbert, winning the competition for the Prix de Rome jointly with Paul Bonnet in 1854. His entry was a 'building intended for the sepulchre of the rulers of a great empire', and his design combined the interior and plan of the 17th-century chapel of the Hôtel des Invalides, Paris, with an exterior on the thoroughly Neo-classical theme of the Mausoleum of Halikarnassos. In Rome, Vaudremer's contemporaries included Honoré Daumet, Edmond-Jean-Baptiste Guillaume (1826–94) and later Ernest-George Coquart, a generation of architects whose work was somewhat overshadowed by the achievements of such older men as Henri Labrouste and (Jacques-)Félix Duban. Vaudremer's dispatches from Rome show a fascination for funeral monuments, and he sketched the Castel Sant'Angelo, built as the Emperor Hadrian's mausoleum, later writing a full archaeological report on the building with a suggested reconstruction. Returning to Paris in 1858, he was appointed deputy inspector of works under Duban on the new Quai Malaquais wing of the Ecole des Beaux-Arts. In 1860 he began teaching at the Ecole des Beaux-Arts, where his studio included such students as Louis Sullivan before he closed it in 1880. Also in 1860 Vaudremer benefited from the expansion of the boundaries of Paris, being appointed architect to the 13th and 14th arrondissements on the recommendation of Victor Baltard.

Vaudremer's promotion earned him the important commission (1862) of a large prison (1865–85) in the Rue de la Santé. His design adapted the ideas expounded by Blouet in his *Instruction et programmes pour la construction de maisons d'arrêt et de justice* (Paris, 1841) with additional designs by Romain Harou (1796–1858) and Hector Horeau, ideas embodied in the unexecuted prison project (1839–40) for Alessandria, Italy, by Henri Labrouste, and at the Prison Mazas (1843–50; destr. 1898), Paris, by E.-J. Gilbert. At the Prison de la Santé, the cells were built on a radial plan with a central rotunda; the building is a rational structure without any concession to academicism and is dominated by the coupled chimneys of the furnaces, which flank the rotunda.

In 1864 Vaudremer began his major work, the new church of St Pierre de Montrouge, Paris (see fig.). Built on a triangular site like Baltard's St Augustin, Paris, St Pierre (completed 1870) combines French Romanesque with Early Christian and Italian Romanesque styles derived from the cathedrals of Ravenna, Palermo and Monreale, and the church of S Miniato al Monte, Florence. At the west end is a porch tower, and over the crossing is a rectangular lantern. The construction is influenced by Labrouste (the terracotta gutters, for example, are modelled on those of the latter's Bibliothèque Sainte-Geneviève) and followed the recommended practice of the

Emile Vaudremer: St Pierre de Montrouge, Paris, 1864–70

Service des Edifices Diocésains under Paul Abadie, in that the visible wall-surfaces comprise large ashlar blocks, while the infilling is of much smaller squared stones. Austere, powerful and with a dramatically lit interior, the church was soon acknowledged as an important work. After 1870 Vaudremer drew closer to the Service des Edifices Diocésains and became one of its leading architects. In 1873 he was given charge of the diocese of Beauvais and in that capacity built the bishops' palace there. In 1876, following a reorganization of the architecture departments of the city of Paris, he headed the religious buildings section, designing the church of Notre-Dame d'Auteuil (1876–80), influenced by Abadie's Poitiers Romanesque manner.

In 1878 Vaudremer was a judge at the Exposition Universelle, Paris, and the following year he succeeded Louis Duc as a member of both the Académie des Beaux-Arts and the Commission des Bâtiments Scolaires. Vaudremer became a prolific designer of school buildings, in which he was keenly interested. In preparation for the Exposition Universelle of 1889, he designed a model building, the Lycée Buffon (1885–90, 1895–9) on the Boulevard Pasteur, as well as the Lycée Molière (*c*. 1885) at Passy, both in Paris, and subsequently schools at Grenoble (1885–8) and Montauban (1885–6). They are sober designs combining yellow brick and white stone with huge windows and arcaded galleries laid out as covered walkways opening on to courtyards or gardens, with corner pavilions of Renaissance inspiration. The chief merits of his schools are the quality of their design, the sober materials and the sheer logic of their form, which derives from the earlier work of Eugène Train, particularly the Collège Chaptal (1866–76), Paris. This talent for sobriety and refinement may be found also in the few private houses he designed and in two further religious buildings, the Protestant Temple de Belleville (1877–80) in the Rue Julien-Lacroix and the admirable Greek Orthodox church (1890–95) in the Rue Georges-Bizet.

WRITINGS
Monographie de la maison d'arrêt et de correction pour hommes, construite à Paris par Emile Vaudremer (Paris, 1871)
Exposition Universelle du 1878: Sur la section d'architecture (Paris, 1880) [extracted from the general report on the Exposition]

BIBLIOGRAPHY
Macmillan Enc. Architects
L. Magne: *L'Architecture française du siècle* (Paris, 1889)
'M. Emile Vaudremer', *Constr. Mod.*, x (1895), pp. 337–9
J. Hermant: 'Emile Vaudremer', *Architecture* [Paris], xxvii (1914), pp. 65–8
A. Drexler, ed.: *The Architecture of the Ecole des Beaux-Arts* (Cambridge, MA, 1977)

FRANÇOIS LOYER

Vaudreuil, Comte de [Paule de Rigaud, Joseph-Hyacinthe-François de] (*b* Santo Domingo, French Antilles, 2 March 1740; *d* Paris, Jan 1817). French courtier, patron and collector. He was the son of the governor-general of Santo Domingo, French Antilles, and his noble ancestry and vast income derived from the colonies led to an introduction to the court of Louis XVI. He acquired his first paintings, which included Adriaen van de Velde's *Beach at Scheveningen* (1660; Paris, Louvre), in 1779. Guided by Jean-Baptiste-Pierre Le Brun, he collected Italian, French and northern Old Master paintings and became the most important patron and collector of French art in late 18th-century Paris, building a chronological and representative collection of French paintings from the 17th and 18th centuries. These included Poussin's *Holy Family on the Steps* (1648; Washington, DC, N.G.A.), Watteau's *Halt during the Chase* (*c*. 1720; London, Wallace), Le Nain's *Blacksmith's Shop* (Paris, Louvre) and David's *Oath of the Horatii* (1784; Paris, Louvre). Vaudreuil was Elisabeth-Louise Vigée Le Brun's most important private patron during the 1780s and may have been her lover. In November 1784, facing financial ruin, Vaudreuil sold all but his French paintings through Jean-Baptiste-Pierre Le Brun; the royal collection thus acquired many of the best northern paintings that he owned, including Rembrandt's *Philosopher* (1632) and van Dyck's *President Richardot* (*c*. 1618–19; both Paris, Louvre). In 1787 he shared the disgrace of Charles-Alexandre de Caloune and went into exile; many of his works of art were dispersed in a further sale. Returning to Paris after the collapse of the First Empire, he was appointed lieutenant-general of the army and governor of the Tuileries, with apartments in the Palais Royal.

BIBLIOGRAPHY
P. G. Le Roy: *La Famille de Rigaud de Vaudreuil* (Paris, 1938)
C. B. Bailey: 'The Comte de Vaudreuil: Aristocratic Collecting on the Eve of the Revolution', *Apollo*, cxxx (1989), pp. 19–26, 68–9

☐

Vaughan, (John) Keith (*b* Selsey Bill, Sussex, 23 Aug 1912; *d* London, 4 Nov 1977). English painter and writer. He abandoned a career in advertising in 1939 to pursue painting. From 1941 to 1944 he served in the Pioneer Corps. His drawings of army life, however, such as *Breakfast in the Marquee* (1942; see Vaughan, p. 49), attracted attention and he entered the circle of Peter Watson in London. From 1946 to 1952 he shared a studio with John Minton. As a younger generation Neo-Romantic he was heavily influenced by Graham Sutherland, Henry Moore and William Blake, seen for example in *Apocalyptic Figure* (1942; Cardiff, N. Mus.). During the 1950s Paul Cézanne and Henri Matisse were major influences, but most important was that of Nicolas De Stael, who enabled him to reconcile figurative and abstract elements. He was essentially a painter of figure compositions that attempted to balance male nudes with abstract environments, exemplified by his nine *Assemblies* begun in 1952 (e.g. *Second Assembly of Figures*, oil on board, 1953; see Yorke, p. 277).

After 1945 Vaughan travelled in the Mediterranean, North Africa, Mexico and the USA, where he was resident artist at Iowa State University in 1959. He taught in London at Camberwell School of Art (1946–8) and the Central School of Arts and Crafts (1948–57) and was a visiting teacher at the Slade School of Fine Art (1959–77). His remarkable journal (1939–77), inspired by André Gide, reveals the tension in his life and work between intellectual puritanism and unrepressed sensuality. His work can be regarded as an expression of his feelings about the male body. Despite considerable success, including the award of a CBE in 1965, he became increasingly melancholic and reclusive.

WRITINGS
Keith Vaughan: Journal and Drawings, 1939–1965 (London, 1966)

BIBLIOGRAPHY
A Paradise Lost: The Neo-Romantic Imagination in Britain, 1935–55 (exh. cat., ed. D. Mellor; London, Barbican A.G., 1987)
M. Yorke: *The Spirit of the Place: Nine Neo-Romantic Artists and their Times* (London, 1988), pp. 225–84, *passim*

VIRGINIA BUTTON

Vaughan, Robert (*b c.* 1600; *d* before 8 Jan 1664). ?Welsh engraver, active in England. He was a versatile line engraver, producing portraits, maps, bookplates, series of prints (e.g. the *Nine Modern Worthies of the World* of 1622) and the occasional broadsheet. His portraits range from national heroes of recent history, such as *Sir Francis Drake* (n.d.) to influential contemporaries, including the lawyer *Sir George Croke* (n.d.). His work, generally far less coarse than that of many of his English contemporaries, shows a steady craftsmanlike approach, dull and unimaginative at its worst, but at its best having a simple honesty and clarity. His letter of 22 June 1650 (Aberystwyth, N. Lib. Wales) to Sir Owen Wynn of Gwydir reveals that Vaughan had a working knowledge of heraldry and shared the current enthusiasm for antiquarianism. He may also have been interested in alchemical magic: Elias Ashmole's *Theatrum chemicum Britannicum* (1652), an anthology of poems on alchemy, is illustrated with Vaughan's engravings, and among those Welsh writers with whom Vaughan was associated throughout his working life were the alchemist poet Thomas Vaughan, whose *Lumen de lumine* (1651) incorporated an illustrative design by the engraver. Thomas's brother, Henry Vaughan, was a major religious poet whose *Olor Iscanus* (1651), a selection of poems and translations, carried an engraved title-page by Robert Vaughan showing a swan on a river, alluding to the 'Swan of Usk' of the book's title. The year these two books appeared the engraver, a royalist supporter during the civil wars, was indicted by the Commonwealth authorities for publishing a portrait print of the recently executed King, Charles I. Examples of his work are in the British Museum, London.

BIBLIOGRAPHY

A. M. Hind: *The Reign of Charles I*, ed. M. Corbett and M. Norton (1955), iii of *Engraving in England in the Sixteenth and Seventeenth Centuries* (Cambridge, 1952–64), pp. 48–91

R. T. Godfrey: *Printmaking in Britain: A General History from its Beginnings to the Present Day* (Oxford, 1979), p. 18

CHRISTOPHER FOLEY

Vaughan-Richards, Alan (Kenneth Hamer) (*b* Maidenhead, 1925; *d* London, 29 May 1989). English architect. He went to Lagos, Nigeria, to work and there married Ayo Vaughan (1928–93), daughter of a prominent Lagos family. A student at the London Polytechnic from 1945 to 1950, he graduated with a Diploma in Architecture in 1950. After two years of apprenticeship in Britain, he worked in northern Iraq with the Iraqi Development Board. In 1954 he enrolled in the Tropical Course at the Architectural Association, London, under the direction of Maxwell Fry, who was to have a far-reaching impact in shaping the idiom of contemporary architecture in Nigeria. In 1956 Vaughan-Richards went to Nigeria to work in the Lagos office of Architects Co-Partnership (ACP). Back in their London office in 1957, he designed the award-winning (RIBA Bronze) undergraduate accommodation for St John's College, Oxford. As the scheme was structured around the hexagonal dormitory space and rest-room facilities, it was affectionately nicknamed the 'Beehive'. In 1958–61 he was the ACP associate partner in the Lagos office, and in 1961, when ACP withdrew from Nigeria, he opened his own one-man practice. During the period 1961–70, he produced for the University of Lagos a series of elegant buildings, notable for their sensitive siting, discreet entries and daring use of local material. The six-storey University Flat (1964) is perhaps the most dramatic, with the geometry of the spaces reinforced by the orientation inducing strong ventilation. *Building Lagos* (1976), co-authored with the journalist and historian Kunle Akinsemoyin, is a beautiful testimony to the culture and architectural history of Lagos and confirms Vaughan-Richards's pre-eminent role in the Historical Buildings and Monuments project in Lagos State (1985–7). In several of his projects, he collaborated with Nigerian artists: for example Felix Ibudor (1928–91) contributed sculpture to his Investment House (1959) and mosaic murals to the Bristol Hotel (1957), while Ben Enwonwu (1921–94) produced sculpture and Bruce Onobrakpeya painted murals for the temporary complex (1962) for the University of Lagos, Idi Araba. In 1970, Vaughan-Richards and Roye Ibru (*b* 1935) merged their practice. The Ibru, Vaughan-Richards Partnership was responsible for several major institutional projects including the master-plans for the universities of Benin (1971) and Lagos (1980). Vaughan-Richards was a member of the NIA and a Fellow of the RIBA.

For general discussion of modern Nigerian architecture *see also* LAGOS and NIGERIA, §IV.

WRITINGS

'The New Generation: A View of the Future of Building Design', *W. Afr. Bldr & Architect*, vii/1 (1967), pp. 2–15; vii/2 (1967), pp. 24–49

with K. Akinsemoyin: *Building Lagos* (Lagos, 1976)

DAVID ARADEON

Vault. Usually a roof or ceiling in stone, concrete or some other material, constructed upon the principle of the arch. It may be semicircular or segmental in profile, or be made up of arches and segments of arches in various combinations. A vault will commonly have stones or blocks arranged concentrically in such a manner as to support each other in compression. The purpose of a vault is to provide a weather-proof and fireproof covering, even when surmounted by a wooden roof, and vaults are usually built in non-combustible materials, although they may sometimes be made of wood. Vaults have also had a deep symbolic significance: the emperor's canopy in Imperial Rome, the Vault of Heaven in a Christian church, or simply as a demonstration of the financial power and status of a patron.

Because masonry vaults are especially difficult to construct over a wide span or at a great height, they are found only in more advanced architectural technologies. True masonry vaults occur in ancient Egypt, Assyria and in Western architecture since Classical times. Under Western influence the vault has been adopted in many parts of the world: North and South America, Africa, and most of Asia.

There follows an alphabetical listing and descriptions of vault types. Types of rib-vaulting (curving, jumping, lierne, net, pendant, ploughshare, quadripartite, reticulated, sexpartite, stalactite, star, tierceron, triradial) are listed under the heading for 'Rib'. Cross-references within this article are indicated in the form 'see *Trough* above or below'; cross-references to other articles in the *Dictionary* are in the usual form '*see* MASONRY'.

Annular. Vaulted passage rather than a vault type, being a corridor arranged in a ring-plan, usually about an apse, and covered by a barrel vault (see fig. 1a). Concrete annular vaults were built by the Romans in the Sanctuary of Fortuna Primigenia, Praeneste (now Palestrina), in the 2nd century BC, and they are found in the substructures of Roman semicircular theatres and circular or elliptical amphitheatres, for example in the Colosseum (*c.* AD 80), Rome, where the ground level has a continuous annular-vaulted ambulatory. Some circular, centrally planned, Early Christian churches, such as S Costanza (*c.* 350), Rome, have annular vaults covering the ambulatory.

The term annular is specifically applied to a barrel-vaulted, curving passage within the apse of an Early Christian church, which often supports raised tiers of seats similarly arranged in a semicircular plan, such as the 5th-century Mastichari Basilica (Kos, Greece), or the 6th-century Hagia Eirene (now Aya Irini Kilisesi, Istanbul, Turkey).

Originally such vaulted annular passages were purely functional, but a new role was created, probably at Old St Peter's, Rome, around the year 600, when a vaulted annular passage was built within the earlier apse, giving access to

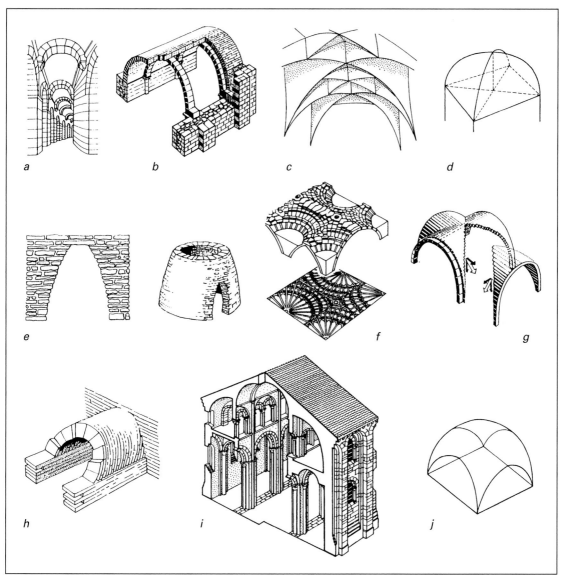

1. Types of vault: (a) annular; (b) barrel; (c) cellular; (d) cloister; (e) corbelled; (f) fan; (g) groin; (h) pitched-brick; (i) quadrant barrels (over galleries); (j) sail

another passage leading to the saint's tomb beneath the altar. The idea was adapted in many churches, for example All Saints (8th century) at Brixworth, Northants, Clermont-Ferrand Cathedral (*c.* 950), France, St Michael (*c.* 1000) in Hildesheim, Germany, and Chartres Cathedral (*c.* 1020), France. The annular vault is little known after *c.* 1050.

Barrel [tunnel]. Vault based on the repeated arch, with a semicircular or pointed profile (see fig. 1b). The thrust and weight of the vault are uniform throughout its length. The earliest barrel vaults are found in Egyptian mud-brick buildings, such as the Ramesseum (*c.* 1250 BC), Thebes. Stone barrel vaults occur *c.* 800 BC, at Medinet Habu, Middle Egypt, by which time barrel vaults are also found

in Assyrian architecture. Many early examples employ pitched-brick technique (see below), and thus could be built without supporting centering.

Arched vaults appeared in Greek architecture in, for example, the stair passages of the Temple of Apollo (*c.* 330 BC) at Didyma, Turkey, but the Romans built many stone and brick barrel vaults from an early date, for example the 2nd-century BC Cloaca Maxima, Rome, and the 1st-century BC concrete barrel vaults over the market-hall at Ferentino, Italy. Barrel vaults are found in AD 64–8 in the Domus Aurea, Rome (*see* ROME, ANCIENT, §II, 1(ii)(c)), which also has segmental, or less than semicircular barrel vaults, and other, very depressed, segmental concrete barrel vaults occur in the 2nd-century AD House of the Charioteers, Ostia, Italy.

Stone and rubble barrel vaults are common in many post-Roman styles, either as very broad arches supporting domes, as in Hagia Eirene (6th century) in Istanbul, and Aachen Cathedral (c. 800), Germany, or covering main spaces such as S Maria de Naranco (842–50) in Oviedo, Spain, or Cluny Abbey (c. 1010), France. The loss of Roman concrete technology restricted the span of such barrel vaults to a fraction of their Imperial prototypes.

Medieval builders were loath to pierce the walls beneath barrel vaults and thus create weaknesses in the structure. In early Islamic architecture, such as the audience hall at Qusayr 'Amra, Jordan, barrel vaults were set transversely in sequence, so that windows could be cut in the end walls. A similar solution was tried at St Philibert (?early 12th century), Tournus, France, where a sequence of short barrel vaults was set transversely across the interior space. Another, tried (c. 1090) at Cluny Abbey, was the pointed barrel-vault profile, which changed the dynamics, with the two arcs leaning inwards. Pointed barrel vaults became particularly characteristic of Cluniac and Cistercian buildings in the 12th century. Some Romanesque barrel vaults have openings cut into their haunches, as at Payerne Abbey church (c. 1080), Switzerland—a technique later revived in England, where vaults were occasionally constructed as rammed-rubble barrels stiffened with ribs, and with large pierced openings for clerestory lighting, as at Tewkesbury Abbey (1320s) and Gloucester Abbey (now Cathedral; c. 1337). Barrel vaults in the Roman style were revived in the Italian Renaissance (e.g. the 15th-century churches of S Andrea, Mantua, and the Badia, S Domenico di Fiesole, nr Florence).

Cellular [crystal]. Type of vault with no structural ribs and panels but multiple, individual folded 'cells', giving a prismatic display of angular diamond-plan folds (see fig. 1c). They ignore strict bay divisions, being composed of a pattern of repeated units, but, unlike net vaults (see under *Rib* below), their essential structure results in a dramatically uneven surface. The cellular vault derives its strength from the rigidity of the 'folded' web. An embryonic example of the structural principle exists at Heisterbach Abbey (c. 1202–37), Germany.

Late medieval cellular vaults probably imitate Islamic design, where cellular vaults were commonly employed within the pendentives or squinches of domes, as at the Muradiye Camii (1424–6) in Bursa, Turkey. They are usually brick-built, plastered, with painted geometrical designs. Emphatically folded cellular vaults became very common in 15th-century European Late Gothic, especially in the Germanic regions, for example at the Franciscan church (after 1408) in Salzburg, Austria, the Great Hall of the Albrechtsburg (1471) in Meissen, Germany, the Jagiellonian University (1492–7) at Kraków, Poland, and the parish church of Blatná (1515), Bohemia.

Cloister [coved; domical]. See also *Trough* below. A cloister vault is formed when equal-sized, pointed barrel vaults intersect (see fig. 1d), as in the Mausoleum of S Aquilino (late 4th century) at S Lorenzo, Milan. Cloister vaults can be formed by the intersection of four or six barrel vaults, resulting in eight- or twelve-sided structures; Filippo Brunelleschi's dome on Florence Cathedral can be interpreted as such. In post-Renaissance architecture cloister vaults were occasionally employed to cover square-plan rooms, as in the Porcelain Room (1754–9; now Naples, Capodimonte) from the Palazzo Reale at Pórtici.

Corbelled. In that a corbelled vault is not based on the technology of the arch this is not true vaulting. A corbel is a horizontal bracket, well seated into a wall. A series of corbels of increasing projection, each using the support of the one below, builds up a diagonal cove, and a corbelled arch is created when two opposing coves meet (see fig. 1e). If this is repeated in the form of a tunnel, or above a circular-planned structure, a stone 'vault' results. Corbelled vaults have severe limitations. Their span is restricted by the mass of the required stabilizing masonry, and the centre, whether a tunnel or a dome, is liable to collapse. The main advantage is that, as each course is laid horizontally, corbelled vaults may be built without recourse to wooden centering. The earliest form of corbelled vaulting exists within the Great Pyramid of Cheops (c. 2400 BC) at Giza, Egypt, where the walls of the stairway (h. 9 m) are corbelled almost from floor level, the last metre spanned by single blocks. Such vaults remained rare in Egyptian architecture.

The most famous early corbelled vaults occur in Mycenaean architecture. The tomb known as the Treasury of Atreus (c. 1300–1250 BC) at Mycenae, Greece, has a corbelled vault (h. 13.2 m) with a span of 14.5 m. The structure has a 'beehive' profile, with 33 courses of corbelled masonry springing from the floor level. Corbelled vaults occur in many architectural styles, such as the Gallarus Oratory (?8th–?12th century AD), Ireland, and the Toltec-Maya structures (?10th century AD) at Chichén Itzá, Mexico.

Coved. See *Cloister* above.

Cross. See *Groin* below.

Domical. Alternative term for a cloister vault (see above) and, in American usage, for a sail vault (see below).

Fan. An English speciality, a shell technology based on inverted, cut-stone cones (see MASONRY, §III, 3(iii)). True fan vaults consist entirely of shaped blocks with no conventional ribs and panels. The quarter- or semicircular cones butt against each other, creating a central zone of inward pressure sufficient to suspend an almost flat cut-stone ceiling or sculptured boss (see fig. 1f). In the earliest fan vaults on a monumental scale, in the cloister of Gloucester Abbey (now Cathedral; see GLOUCESTER (i), fig. 2), the rib pattern is merely inscribed upon the visible underside of the cones, flowing freely from bay to bay without interruption, placing fan vaults in the same class as net vaults (see under *Rib: Net*). The surface of each cone is subdivided into wedge-shaped panels by slender ribs, all of the same length and girth. There are no specific diagonals, although some fan vaults reinstate the concept of bay division by stressing the transverse, as at King's College Chapel (1512–15) in Cambridge. The panel heads usually contain cusped arches imitating tracery; indeed, fan vaulting can be seen as the extension to the ceiling of a traceried elevation. In early fan vaults, the ribs terminate at a semicircular 'bounding' rib that defines the cone, but in some 15th-century vaults, a distinction between 'major' and 'minor' ribs was established, the major ribs continuing to a central feature, as in Bell Henry tower (1504–9) at Canterbury Cathedral. The extensive centering required for fan vaults makes them difficult to erect across wide spans, but they are ideal for small-scale chapels or cloisters, for example Bishop Alcock's chantry chapel (c. 1488) at Ely Cathedral. Some larger-scale vaults incorporate a degree of traditional rib and panel construction and are thus not true fan vaults (e.g. Henry VII's Chapel, 1503–9 in Westminster Abbey).

Flat-topped. Vault with a horizontal cap. This might be achieved by various means, as in the corbel-vaulted stair-hall of the Great Pyramid at Giza (see *Corbelled*) and the side chambers of the domed octagonal room in the Domus Aurea, Rome (AD 64–8), which have flat concrete vaults. The creation of truly flat vaults is difficult in any medium other than concrete, and even then there is a natural limit to the possible dimensions. Some flat vaults utilize sub-arches or struts to support their weak centres. The substructure of the basilica in the agora (c. AD 180) at Izmir, Turkey, has radial arches supporting a marble floor. Similarly underpinned flat-topped vaults occur in England in the Berkeley Chapel, Bristol Cathedral, and the pulpitum (c. 1320–30) of Southwell Minster, Notts, and in the contemporary so-called Tonsur chapel in the cloister of Magdeburg Cathedral, Germany. The north porch of St Mary's, Bury St Edmunds (Suffolk), has a flat-topped vault of c. 1450.

Groin [cross]. One of the commonest of all vault types, consisting of two barrel vaults intersecting at right angles, folding the shell into two crossing diagonals (groins; see fig. 1g). Much of the weight and thrust of the vault is transmitted down the groins, relieving considerable lengths of the wall from the burden of support. The resulting lunette spaces are relatively free for windows or other openings. The disadvantages include the degree of wall buttressing required at the supporting points and the difficulty of constructing groin vaults on other than square plans.

The Romans were first to develop groin vaults, for example at the Baths of Titus (AD 80; destr.) in Rome. They built them in concrete, often with embedded brick diagonal ribs for extra strength, as at the Baths of Diocletian (c. AD 300) in Rome. The ease with which the Romans vaulted vast spaces with concrete groin vaults, such as the diagonals (l. 35 m) of the groin vaults of the Basilica of Maxentius (c. 310) in Rome, was to be a constant challenge to later builders, bereft of Roman concrete technology. Brick groin vaults also occur in the 6th-century praetorium at Zenobia (now Halabiyeh, Iraq), and cut-stone groins were employed in the Mausoleum of Theodoric (c. 525) in Ravenna, Italy.

Groin vaults based on simpler, rammed–rubble techniques continued in many post-Roman architectural styles, for example at the Carolingian Cathedral of Aachen (c. 800), but inadequate technology imposed limits upon their span, which was generally 6–8 m, although Speyer Cathedral (c. 1080) has rubble groin vaults more than 13 m wide. From c. 1100, with the development of rib vaults (see below), groin vaults were quickly superseded in western Europe, although cut-stone groin vaults continued

in the eastern Mediterranean, for example in the Islamic Towers (c. 1190) at Baalbek, Lebanon, and the Crusader castle of Saone (c. 1200), Syria. Groin vaults, with their Roman connotations, were frequently revived in the Renaissance and later, as in the chapel (1699–1707) of the château of Versailles, France, and the Benedictine church (1718–25) in Rohr, Germany.

Guastavino. Form of vault of Catalan origin extensively used in the USA from the late 19th century (see GUASTA-VINO, RAFAEL).

Pendentive. See *Sail* below.

Pitched-brick. Technical term for a particular way of laying the individual bricks or stones in a barrel or groin vault. In a pitched-brick vault the bricks are laid upright with their long sides in a curve or semicircle (see fig. 1h). Pitched-brick vaults were used in Mesopotamia from the 3rd millennium BC onwards. The Egyptians used the method for their mud-brick barrel vaults, for example the Ramesseum (c. 1250 BC) in Thebes. The vaults are constructed in individual arcs pressed one against the other, often slumped over at an angle thus removing the need for wooden centering as a support. This was an advantage, since the technique was used predominantly in areas where wood was scarce. The largest vault of this type, the iwan (h. 35 m) of the Sasanian empire (AD 224–651) known as Taq-i Kisra, still stands near Baghdad in Iraq. The Romans also used pitched-bricks in barrel vaults, for example in the substructure of the basilica (late 3rd century AD) at Aspendos, Turkey, where the haunches have coursed voussoirs, while the central section is probably pitched. From c. 300 the technique was frequently employed in Byzantine architecture around the Aegean, for example in the groin vaults above the Yerebatan Cistern (6th century) in Istanbul; the domes of Hagia Sophia (after 532) are built in a related fashion. The technique is found in other brick traditions, such as the Mahabodhi temple (c. 750 and later) at Bodhgaya, India.

Quadrant. Half-barrel vault, usually with a quarter-circle profile, though occasionally more or less. Developed in early Romanesque architecture, quadrant vaults lean inwards across an aisle, usually to support a full barrel vault (see fig. 1i), as, for example, at Sant Pere de Rodes (c. 1022), Spain, and in the west block (? before 1056) at St Philibert, Tournus, France, where rubble quadrant vaults spanning the aisles support continuous barrels over the main vessel. In the second half of the 11th century quadrant vaults became widespread; examples can be found in Normandy at St Etienne (original state c. 1065) in Caen, and Cerisy-la-Forêt Abbey (c. 1080), Payerne Abbey church (c. 1080), Switzerland, Gloucester Abbey (now Cathedral; c. 1087), and in most of the pilgrimage churches of southern France and Spain, such as Ste Foy, Conques. The pilgrimage churches have quadrants in the galleries butting directly against the thrust of the high barrel vault. Quadrant vaults were so successful in supporting high barrel vaulting that they long remained popular in southern Europe, where the absence of clerestory lighting was not significant, but the continuous linear support afforded by quadrant vaults was unnecessary in Gothic technology, and they quickly disappeared from northern Europe.

Rib. Vault with visible diagonal cross-arches of stone or brick, on which a lightweight webbing rests during construction. For assembling large-scale concrete groin vaults, the Romans often employed brick ribs as self-supporting crossing arches that were used to assist in building the shell, and acted as stiffening for the completed vault (*see* ROME, ANCIENT, §II, 2(i)(g)). They were buried within the concrete and became invisible once the plaster finish was applied. The principle behind the new rib-vaulting technique, developed (*c.* 1100) at Durham Cathedral, England, involved larger stone diagonal arches that would act as a permanent scaffolding for the webbing while providing a stiffened, cut-stone centre for the vault. The web or shell of the rib vault remains distinct from its supporting ribs. The coursed-stone webs rest upon the topside or extrados of the masonry ribs and, if the stones are sufficiently well cut so as to interlock one with the next, the completed webs continue to stand even if the ribs are removed, as was clearly demonstrated when several French cathedrals were bombarded in World War I, the vault ribs often collapsing but the webs remaining secure. The idea of rib vaulting was probably suggested by the type of temporary wooden CENTERING employed in northern Europe, with two intersecting wooden arches forming the frame for the lighter shuttering.

The advantages of the rib vault over its predecessors were many. Most important was ease of construction: the two diagonal arches needed minimal centering and once built were virtually self-supporting. By making the ribs of sufficient girth, much of the shuttering for the web construction could be supported by the ribs, which also acted as the 'foundation' for the webs. Once built, a rib vault has specialized elements. In a groin vault the whole shell acts in unison, each section having multiple functions: covering, supporting and transmitting weight and thrust. While the folded form of the shell directs much of the weight and thrust to particular points, the entire structure takes part in that transmission (*see* MASONRY, §III, 3(iii)). In a rib vault, however, the web provides the stone canopy and hence the fire and weather protection. It rests almost entirely upon the diagonal ribs and, where present, the transverse arches, but most of the weight and dynamics of each section of the web are transferred to the ribs and carried down towards the springing point of the vault. This specialization enables the entire structure to be relatively lightweight as the webs have only to support themselves. The precision cutting of many 13th-century French vault webs led to the lightest possible coverings. Like a groin vault, the major thrust of a rib vault is outwards and downwards, more keenly so owing to the concentrated mass of the ribs; but, with sufficient exterior buttressing, the elevational wall plays a minimal supporting role and may be safely pierced.

There follows an alphabetical listing and descriptions of rib-vault types.

Curving [curvilinear]. Late Gothic type, with rib plans based not on straight lines intersecting at angles but flowing lines merging one into the next, creating decorative patterns apparently unconnected to the requirements of engineering (see fig. 2a). They are most common in Germany and Bohemia, occasionally appearing in England, as in the nave aisles (*c.* 1340) of St Mary Redcliffe, Bristol, and the Beauchamp Chapel (*c.* 1440) at St Mary's, Warwick. Discreet curves occur (*c.* 1415) in St Bartholomäus, Frankfurt am Main, and (*c.* 1439) in St Stephan, Braunau am Inn, Austria, but the first large-scale curving vaults exist under the gallery of SS Ulrich and Afra (1492), Augsburg. In some examples, the ribs are of dubious structural value, the vault webs being cut-stone ceilings on a shallow arc, sometimes called 'shells', and held up by tension provided by external means. The ribs merely act to enliven and adorn the surface; some are totally detached from the ceiling, free to wander at the architect's whim. On occasion the curving ribs are even disguised as tree branches or other vegetable matter, as on the Vladislav II gallery (1493) in Prague Cathedral. Model analysis reveals that the ribs of some curving vaults closely reflect isostatic lines of pressure within the shell, although this may not have been known to their builders.

Curving vaults were part of the general trend towards fantasy evident in much north European Late Gothic architecture, and were particularly popular in hall churches, where the aisles of equal height permitted the rib patterns to flow freely throughout the whole interior, treating the supporting piers as mere interruptions to their progress, or, as at St Barbara (*c.* 1512), Kutná Hora, Bohemia, where the gallery ceilings are the same height as the main vessel (for illustration *see* KUTNÁ HORA).

Jumping [Ger. *Springewölbe*]. Jumping vaults are characterized by the absence of visible springing points, the ribs bursting abruptly as if escaping from within the wall or pier (see fig. 2b). Jumping vaults were most popular in late medieval Germany, although possibly originating in France. The east end of St Nazaire (*c.* 1270), Carcassonne, has vaults with a geometric springing point lying theoretically somewhere within the interior of the slender piers. At the parish church (*c.* 1280) of Bad Wimpfen, Germany, the diagonal ribs jump abruptly from the wall, as do all the ribs in the north porch (*c.* 1325) of St Mary Redcliffe, Bristol. There are, however, more than stylistic reasons for the creation of jumping vaults. As buttressing technology improved, vaults became flatter and less in need of the long ribs running from springer to apex. Tight, four-centred and flatter vaults were awkward both visually and technically: it was far better to snip off the unwanted lower sections of the vault profile. St Mary's (*c.* 1390) in Warwick, presents the classic compromise, with a segmental jumping vault underpinned by openwork struts correcting the geometry. Most of the late examples are German: the Heiliggeistkirche (1407) in Landshut, St Georg (1448–92) at Dinkelsbühl, Schwäbisch Gmünd Cathedral and the late 15th-century choir of Freiburg im Breisgau Cathedral.

Lierne. Vault pattern in which the major ribs are connected by small, secondary ribs known as liernes (see fig. 2c). Technically, liernes do not arise from the springing point of the vault, but branch from diagonals, tiercerons or transverse ribs. They appeared first in France (e.g. Airvault, *c.* 1200), although the English became their greatest exponents. The earliest known English liernes occur in the crypt (1290s; rest.) of St Stephen's Chapel,

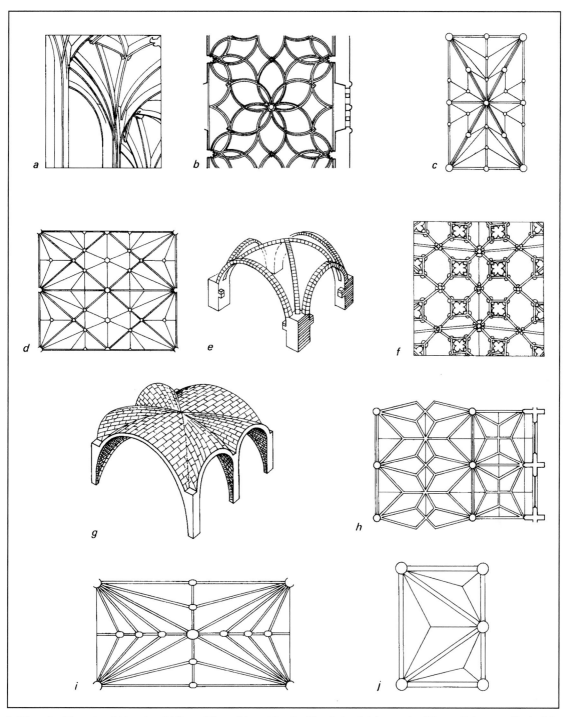

2. Rib vaults: (a) curving; (b) jumping; (c) lierne; (d) net; (e) quadripartite; (f) reticulated; (g) sexpartite; (h) star; (i) tierceron; (j) triradial

Palace of Westminster, and Pershore Abbey (*c.* 1290). They spread quickly to the cathedrals of Wells and Bristol (early 14th century) and Ely (*c.* 1330), reappearing in Europe about 1400 at Ulm Cathedral and St Martin, Landshut. Lierne vaults are essential ingredients of all European Late Gothic styles, for example at St Mary's (*c.* 1390) in Stargard Szczeciński, Poland, and Seville Cathedral (*c.* 1500), Spain.

Although liernes were decorative in origin, they soon played an essential role in the structure of many English vaults. The English had taken advantage of their tierceron vaults (see below), laying short webbing stones like planks across the narrow spans; but as the ribs diverged and the gaps became wider, liernes were often employed to subdivide the panels, thus facilitating the web construction. The nave vault (c. 1465) of Norwich Cathedral is a good example of this.

Net. Vault pattern deployed on a grid, ignoring bay divisions. It rejects both the rigid geometry and the structure of rectangular-plan rib vaults, with their pattern of intersecting diagonals, in favour of a repeated overlapping mesh design, commonly based on long ribs traversing two or more bays (see fig. 2d), or bypassing any geometrical centre and terminating on the line of a transverse arch, for example in the choir (c. 1385) of Prague Cathedral. Net vaults created a single design for the whole roof, abandoning the rhythmic repetition of a standard rib vault. The earliest net vaults occurred in 13th-century France at Toussaints Church, Angers. They were developed in English lierne vaults, for example in the aisles of Bristol Cathedral (from 1298), the pulpitum vault (c. 1317) at Exeter Cathedral and, most notably, the nave (1321) of Tewkesbury Abbey, with its syncopated overlay of diagonals, some intersecting normally in the middle of each bay but others crossing at the apexes of the transverse arches. In many net vaults the structure is a barrel or shell, stiffened by a supporting cellular mesh of the ribs, and pierced by low lunettes for clerestory windows. Net vaults are most common in Germany and Bohemia, occurring in Prague Cathedral (1385) and St Martin (c. 1390) at Landshut. They appear in many Late Gothic European styles, for example at S Juan de los Reyes (c. 1480) in Toledo, Spain, and St Martin (16th century) at Mastaing, France. See also *Reticulated* below.

Pendant. Vault with a suspended stone spar descending from its apex for decorative effect. Pendants are created by the downward extension of a voussoir, but have little if any structural value. Their inspiration is Islamic (*see* MUQARNAS). Their earliest use may have been in the St Catherine chapel (c. 1340; destr.) at Strasbourg Cathedral, and they were later employed by Peter Parler at Prague Cathedral (e.g. the Sacristy, 1356–62). Pendants commonly terminate with foliate bosses, which occasionally provide ledges for the springing of skeletal ribs, as in the south porch (c. 1370) of Prague Cathedral, or complete cones of ribs. Pendants belong to the fantasy world of late medieval architecture and may be found in the Stephansdom (1396) in Vienna, in England at Oxford Cathedral (c. 1480) and Westminster Abbey (1502–12), and in the south porch (c. 1500) of Albi Cathedral, France.

Ploughshare. The technique of twisting the web of a rib vault beyond 90° in order to create larger clerestory openings. The problem arose before the development of flying buttresses (c. 1175), with vaults springing from the base of the clerestory in order to utilize supporting elements beneath the aisle or tribune roof. The consequent vault lunette restricted the size of the clerestory opening, but if the web were splayed back at an acute angle from the diagonal rib, a greater clerestory area could be revealed. Even after fliers enabled the vault to spring clear of the clerestory base line, ploughsharing remained in use so that the largest possible clerestory openings could be inserted

as, for example, at Chartres Cathedral (c. 1200). The technique survived longest in England, where flying buttresses were little used and vault springing levels remained low, as at St Saviour's Cathedral (c. 1225) in Southwark. One method developed to assist in the extreme turning of the web was the introduction of tiercerons at Lincoln Cathedral (c. 1200). The extra ribs facilitated the curve of the webbing to an extent that the vaults almost appear detached from the wall, for example in the retrochoir of Ely Cathedral (begun 1236) and Exeter Cathedral (c. 1290).

Quadripartite. The earliest and most common form of rib vault. Quadripartite vaults consist of two diagonal arches intersecting within a rectangular bay (see fig. 2e). They were first used in Durham Cathedral (c. 1100) over the choir aisles and probably in the high vaults (destr.). Quadripartite vaults occur in the transepts at Winchester Cathedral (revaulted c. 1105) and at Lessay Abbey (c. 1110), Normandy. The quadripartite vault was the most popular form in Gothic architecture, unchallenged in French Gothic from c. 1200 to c. 1400. Its simplicity of form and rhythmic articulation especially complemented the vertical emphasis of the High Gothic and Rayonnant styles, which were exported widely across Europe. The Italians built giant quadripartite vaults in brick, for example at S Petronio (c. 1400) in Bologna, but the English, Spanish and Germans eventually found the form too dull and, perhaps, too difficult, developing the more elaborate lierne and other decorative vaults.

Reticulated. A term loosely applied to various types of net (see above), grid or mesh vaults. More particularly, it might indicate a net vault incorporating various elements drawn from window tracery, such as cusping, and straight-sided lozenges (see fig. 2f). Cusping was first applied to rib vaults in England, as at Bristol Cathedral (c. 1310), Wells Cathedral and Ottery St Mary collegiate church (c. 1335), Devon, and demonstrates the English obsession with tracery forms and excessive decoration. The south nave aisle (c. 1340) of St Mary Redcliffe, Bristol, has straight-sided diamond lozenge motifs with internal cusping, drawn from reticulated tracery, used in an attempt to unify elevation and vault. Neither form found much favour in European Gothic, the earliest use of tracery vaults being in Frankfurt am Main parish church (c. 1415). A small group of tracery vaults occurred in Germany in the mid-15th century, for example the Fürstenkapelle of Meissen Cathedral and the castle chapel at Altenburg; the Abbot's Chapel (c. 1490) in the Hôtel de Cluny (now the Musée de Cluny), Paris, has traceried infill between the ribs. See also *Net* above.

Sexpartite. Six-part rib vaults based on the geometry of the square. Most medieval church plans have oblong bays, the arcade wall being half the width of the main span. In Romanesque quadripartite vaults employing semicircular arches, the transverse arches are longer and higher than the elevational wall arches, causing visual and structural problems, which were eventually solved by using pointed arches of variable width, but the Normans developed sexpartite vaults as an alternative. Two adjoining bays were treated as one, the twin oblongs forming a square on plan (see fig. 2g). Hence, the wall and transverse arches could be equal, although the diagonals became even longer and higher. In order to denote the mid-point bay division, an additional transverse arch intersected the diagonals at the apex, forming the 'six-part' rib pattern, as at St Etienne and La Trinité (*c.* 1120), both in Caen. The main structural benefit, one peculiarly important to the Normans, was that the diagonal thrust approached the wall at 45°, and was more easily absorbed within the Norman THICK-WALL STRUCTURE than a quadripartite vault arriving at a more oblique angle.

The sexpartite vault was used in many early Gothic buildings, for example Laon Cathedral (*c.* 1157), where substantial buttressing under the aisle roofs provided an alternative support to the Norman thick wall. Once thin walls with external, exposed buttressing became feasible with the invention of flying buttresses (*c.* 1175), the advantages of sexpartite vaulting were reduced. Flying buttresses require the diagonal thrusts to approach as near the transverse line as possible, for which narrow single bays of quadripartite vaulting are ideal. The wider spread of the sexpartite vault buckled the thin clerestory wall, now lifted clear of under-roof support, and the wide angle between diagonal and flier threatened to topple the structure. Thus the elevational solution of Chartres Cathedral (from 1194) marked the end of sexpartite vaults. Although some later examples exist in less technically 'Gothic' structures, for example S Francesco (*c.* 1250) in Bologna, sexpartite vaults are rare after *c.* 1220.

Stalactite. Hanging, decorative protrusions suspended beneath vaults of various constructions (*see* MUQARNAS and see *Pendant* above).

Star [stellar]. See also *Triradial* below. Vaults with star patterns created from liernes and tiercerons, but usually without continuous diagonal ribs (see fig. 2h). They first appeared in early 14th-century England soon after the introduction of the lierne. The choir aisle vaults at Wells Cathedral (*c.* 1330) may be the earliest, with twin, truncated tiercerons from each springing point, producing liernes that join to sprout short diagonals crossing at the centre of the bay. The star pattern arises from the overlay of the cross-plan of the resulting lozenges and the diagonal tiercerons. The nave (*c.* 1340) of St Mary Redcliffe, Bristol, and the vault over the Hall staircase (*c.* 1385) at New College, Oxford, have similar stellar patterns, while the choir vaults of Ely Cathedral (*c.* 1335) combine both quadripartite and six-pointed star vaults, a common practice in later English Perpendicular vaults, for example the nave aisles of Canterbury Cathedral (*c.* 1390). Some English vaults are difficult to categorize, with complex combinations of stellar patterns, net vaults and shell structures; the Lady Chapel (*c.* 1320) of Wells Cathedral has a form of stellar-vaulted ribbed dome.

Star vaults are also found in northern Germany *c.* 1310, but in triradial form (see below). Star vaults on the English model appeared during the 1390s in the St Catherine's Chapel of the Heiliggeistkirche at Landshut, after which the pattern is common in German lands in varying vault technologies, as in the rib vaults of Steyr parish church (before 1443), Austria, and in the cellular vaulting of the Franciscan church, Salzburg.

Tierceron. Vault pattern created by the use of secondary ribs, tiercerons, added to a standard diagonal or quadripartite vault, rising from the main vault springing-point but terminating at a ridge (see fig. 2i), or cross-axial ridge rib. The tierceron, an early 13th-century English invention, was not decorative but structural in origin. The English avoided the thin-walled constructional system of French Gothic, with its reliance upon exterior flying buttresses to sustain the vault, continuing to use the thick-wall structure for this purpose, with additional buttressing concealed beneath the aisle roofs, thereby severely restricting the clerestory zone. In order to increase the clerestory lighting, the vault webs were folded back behind the angle of the diagonal ribs in the ploughshare technique (see above). The fold of the web was sometimes so extreme that extra ribs (tiercerons) were applied to support the twisting web and to facilitate its abrupt change of direction: the nave of Lincoln Cathedral (*c.* 1235) is an early and important example. Tierceron vaults were very common in England by *c.* 1300, when so many tiercerons were being added to vaults that they appear to be cones of ribs, almost detached from the wall, as at Exeter Cathedral presbytery (*c.* 1290s) and Ely Cathedral choir (*c.* 1335). From tierceron patterns were developed lierne and star vaults (see above), and the notion of a vault made predominantly of clusters of stone ribs was important to the development of the all-stone fan vault (see above).

Tierceron vaults were rare in Europe before *c.* 1280, even in those areas where ridge ribs were used, such as Poitiers Cathedral (*c.* 1200). Tiercerons first appeared in Germany in the form of triradial vaults (see below) and 'English' tierceron vaults occur in France from *c.* 1380, as in the La Grange chapels of Amiens Cathedral. In some late medieval rib vaults, diagonals were abandoned altogether in favour of paired tiercerons, for example in the choir of Prague Cathedral (*c.* 1380).

Triradial. Rib vaults where the web segments are enriched with three-pronged rib motifs, connected either to the springing points or to the central boss of each bay (see fig. 2j). The characteristic triple ribs are not liernes in the English manner, which never arise from the vault springing points, but rather bifurcated diagonals or tiercerons. Triradials evolved in square-ended, twin-aisled buildings where at the east wall the vault design had to be divided between three windows: hence four springing points sent ribs to one central support. The corner angles became difficult to vault, but triradials eased the problem by acting as 'sub-vaults'. Triradials soon assumed decorative significance, and additional springing points were provided.

The earliest examples occur in eastern Europe, for example at the Marienkirche (1280s) in Lübeck, Germany, St James (*c.* 1310) in Toruń, Poland, and Malbork Castle chapter house (*c.* 1320), Poland, where an oblong vault, resting upon a row of three columns, springs from 22 points. Triradials occurred later in south-west Germany, for example at Maulbronn Abbey (*c.* 1340) and in Peter Parler's Sacristy at Prague Cathedral (*c.* 1360). They were not common in England, although they can occasionally be found in the miniature canopy vaults of niches, for example in the west tower of St Michael Coslany (*c.* 1425) in Norwich, and the pulpitum at Canterbury Cathedral (*c.* 1452). See also *Star* above.

Sail [pendentive; domical]. Vault based on the principle of the dome, and sometimes called a saucer dome or, in the USA, a domical vault. It has concentric courses laid at an angle, but differing from a true dome in its flatter profile and square plan (see fig. 1j above). Where a sail vault is constructed above arched openings, as in the aisle of a church, the apex is always higher than the supporting apexes, giving the effect of a shallow, upturned bowl. Sail vaults occur in brick, as in the 11th- or 12th-century Karakgümrük Cistern, Istanbul, or with brick strengthening ribs, as at S Ambrogio (*c.* 1120) in Milan, and in stone with diagonal ribs, as in the cathedrals of Angers and Le Mans (*c.* 1150), France, and in Germany at Münster Cathedral (*c.* 1220). Late medieval sail vaults occur in England, where there was a revival of several primitive vault forms, as in the Lady Chapel of Wells Cathedral (before 1326). Sail vaults were revived in Renaissance Italy by Brunelleschi in Florence for the Ospedale degli Innocenti (1419), S Lorenzo (1420s) and Santo Spirito (1436).

Segmental. Barrel or shell of less than semicircular profile. The essential tension is maintained either by lateral resistance or dead-weight. Segmental vaults were used in Roman architecture, as in the Domus Aurea of Nero (AD 64–8), and were revived by Donato Bramante in the crypt of Pavia Cathedral, Italy, in the 1490s.

Trough. Term for an extended cloister vault, resembling an upturned animal feeding-trough, either flat-topped or pointed, with a coved profile to the long sides, and hipped ends. The vault type is rare but is found in some early Renaissance buildings in Italy, for example the throne room of the Ducal Palace (1464) in Urbino, and the Libreria Sansoviniana (1537) in Venice. The form was occasionally employed in Rococo buildings, such as the Wallfahrtskirche (1745–50) in Birnau, Germany, and a later, flat-topped example may be seen over the Grande Salle of the Opéra (1861), Paris. See also *Cloister* above.

Tunnel. See *Barrel* above.

Wooden. Wooden vaults are not technically vaults but imitations, sometimes referred to as 'false-work'. Carpentry vaults have quite different properties from masonry structures, especially in their dynamics and weight distribution. As most wooden vaults have been destroyed by fire or rot it is not possible to detect their precise origin. In addition, it is sometimes difficult to determine whether the underside of a pitched wooden roof that has been 'dressed' to resemble a stone vault, such as the refectory (perhaps 11th century) in the Great Lavra, Mt Athos, Greece, can really represent a serious attempt to deceive the onlooker. St Hilaire, Poitiers, is said to have been covered with a wooden barrel vault (*c.* 1050; destr.) and barrel–vaulting appears to have been the favoured wooden form before the mid-13th century, for example at Byland Abbey (*c.* 1185; destr.), N. Yorks, and the cloisters of Mont-Saint-Michel Abbey (*c.* 1220), Normandy.

Wooden vaults seem to have been most common in medieval England, where stone vaults are less frequent than in Europe. Both Lichfield Cathedral and St George's Chapel, Windsor Castle, had carpentry rib vaults *c.* 1240, the royal association of the latter lending respectability to the form. Many English buildings appear to have been designed specifically to receive wooden vaults, including Lincoln Cathedral's cloister (*c.* 1280), York Minster (*c.* 1220–*c.* 1390), the upper chapel (*c.* 1340) of St Stephen's, Palace of Westminster, and the Octagon at Ely Cathedral (*c.* 1340). The decision in favour of wooden vaults seems to have been quite conscious in a country where the art of roof carpentry was very advanced. In Europe wooden vaults are rare and tend to be found only in minor ecclesiastical or secular buildings, such as the Town Hall (*c.* 1380) of Bruges, Belgium.

BIBLIOGRAPHY

R. Willis: 'On the Construction of Vaults in the Middle Ages', *Trans. RIBA*, i/11 (1842), pp. 1–69; also in *Architectural History of Some English Cathedrals*, 2 vols (Chicheley, 1972)
E.-E. Viollet-le-Duc: 'Voûte', *Dictionnaire raisonné de l'architecture française du XIe au XVIe siècle*, 10 vols (Paris, 1858–68), ix, pp. 464–550
A. French and I. Chaplin: *Stereotomy* (New York, 1911)
A. K. Porter: *The Construction of Lombard and Gothic Vaults* (New York, 1911)
P. Séjourné: *Grandes Voûtes*, 3 vols (Bourges, 1913–16)
E. Lefèvre-Pontalis: 'Les Voûtes en berceau et d'arêtes sans doubleaux', *Bull. Mnmtl*, lxxx (1921), pp. 71–85
H. du Ranquet and E. du Ranquet: 'Origine française du berceau roman', *Bull. Mnmtl*, xc (1931), pp. 3–28
M. Aubert: 'Les Plus Anciennes Croisées d'ogives: Leur rôle dans la construction', *Bull. Mnmtl*, xciii (1934), pp. 5–67, 137–237
J. Kalinka: 'Monolithic Concrete Construction for Hangars', *Mil. Engin.*, xxxii (1940), pp. 54–6
K. Schulze: *Die Gewölbesysteme im spätgotischen Kirchenbau in Schwaben von 1440–1520* (Reutlingen, 1940)
K. Conant: 'Observations on the Vaulting Problems of the Period 1088–1211', *Gaz. B.-A.*, xxvi (1944), pp. 127–34
G. Kubler: 'A Late Gothic Computation of Rib Vault Thrust', *Gaz. B.-A.*, xxvi (1944), pp. 135–48
F. Hess: *Steinverbände und Gewölbebau aus künstlichen Steinen* (Munich, 1948)
M. Salvador: 'Thin Shells', *Archit. Rec.*, cxvi (1954), pp. 173–9
K. H. Clasen: *Deutsche Gewölbe der Spätgotik* (Berlin, 1958)
J. Fitchen: *The Construction of Gothic Cathedrals* (Chicago, 1961)
F. W. Fisher: *Die spätgotische Kirchenbaukunst am Mittelrhein, 1410–1520* (Heidelberg, 1962)
P. Frankl: *Gothic Architecture*, Pelican Hist. A. (Harmondsworth, 1962)
J. Heyman: 'Spires and Fan Vaults', *Int. J. Solids & Structures*, iii (1967), pp. 243–57
H. Kubach: *Romanesque Architecture* (New York, 1975)
J. Heyman: *Equilibrium of Shell Structures* (Oxford, 1977)
J. B. Ward-Perkins: *Roman Architecture* (New York, 1977)
P. Crossley: 'Wells, the West Country and Central European Gothic', *British Archaeological Association Conference Transactions IV. Medieval Art and Architecture in Wells and Glastonbury: Wells, 1978*, pp. 81–109
J. Harvey: *The Perpendicular Style* (London, 1978)
J. Bony: *The English Decorated Style* (Oxford, 1979)
W. Leedy: *Fan Vaulting: A Study of Form, Technology and Meaning* (London, 1980)
R. Mark: *Experiments in Gothic Structure* (Cambridge, MA, 1982)
W. Taylor and R. Mark: 'The Technology of Transition: Sexpartite to Quadripartite Vaulting in High Gothic Architecture', *A. Bull.*, lxiv (1982), pp. 579–87
R. Bezenval: *Technologie de la voûte dans l'orient ancien*, Editions Recherche sur les Civilisations, 'Synthèse', xv (Paris, 1984)

FRANCIS WOODMAN

Vauquer [Vauquier], **Jean** [Jacques] (*b* Blois, 11 Oct 1621; *d* Blois, 31 Aug 1686). French etcher, draughtsman and gold-engraver. He came from a family of clockmakers in Reims. His oeuvre consists of more than 130 prints, made with a fine, delicate line, after his own compositions and those of Jean-Baptiste Monnoyer, his master and kinsman. Apart from a few biblical subjects on black ground for medals, snuff-boxes or watch-cases, he mostly represented flowers in bouquets or in vases, baskets, garlands or friezes. These were published by Nicolas Langlois (1640–1703) or François de Poilly (1623–93), often grouped in series: *Livre de fleurs* (10 pls); *Vases de fleurs propre pour les peintres, brodeurs et dessinateurs* (40 pls); *Livres de fleurs propre pour les orfèvres et graveurs* (8 pls, signed V. F. with the annotation *à Blois*). According to Mariette, Vauquer was skilled in drawing flowers and particularly excelled in engraving flowers and other decorations on jewellery. His brother Robert Vauquer (1625–70) was an enamel painter.

BIBLIOGRAPHY

Mariette

D. Guilemard: *Les Maîtres ornemanistes* (Paris, 1880), p. 85

VÉRONIQUE MEYER

Vautier, Benjamin. *See* BEN.

Vautier, (Louis) Benjamin, the elder (*b* Morges, Switzerland, 27 April 1829; *d* Düsseldorf, 25 April 1898). Swiss painter. He was apprenticed to an enameller in Geneva and took drawing lessons from Jules Hébert (1812–97). From 1850 to 1853 he lived in Düsseldorf, where he was taught by Carl Ferdinand Sohn and Rudolf Jordan. The naturalistic and discursive painting *Village Church with Congregation* (1856; Worms, Ksthaus Heylshof) was based on his ethnographic studies in the Bernese Oberland and stresses psychological characterization through individual facial expressions at the cost of narrative.

In 1857 Vautier settled permanently in Düsseldorf and began to paint the peasant scenes from the Black Forest and Alsace-Lorraine that became his standard subjects. *Sewing Class* (1859; Düsseldorf, Gal. Paffrath) exemplifies his mature approach to genre painting. The scene, although naturalistic, is theatrically staged and decisively lit, drawing together individual characters within the unifying narrative context of a common activity. He applied this formula repeatedly, avoiding social comment or unpleasant subjects such as abject poverty or menial toil. His late work *Homecoming* (1881; Milwaukee, WI, A. Mus.) depicts Swabian peasant life and shows that his style did not change appreciably during his successful career. Muted local colours, theatrical gestures and drama, and particularized settings characterize his static country idylls.

BIBLIOGRAPHY

A. Rosenberg: *Vautier* (Leipzig, 1897)

Die Düsseldorfer Malerschule (exh. cat., Düsseldorf, Kstmus., 1979)

The René von Schleinitz Collection at the Milwaukee Art Center (exh. cat. by R. Bisanz, Madison, WI, A. Cent., 1980)

RUDOLF M. BISANZ

Vaux, Calvert (*b* London, 20 Dec 1824; *d* Bensonhurst, NY, 19 Nov 1895). American architect and landscape designer of English birth. He was apprenticed (?1840–45) to the architect Lewis Nockalls Cottingham in London. In 1846 he and George Truefitt (1824–1902) toured Europe and afterwards helped found the Architectural Association in London.

In 1850 Vaux accepted the offer of A. J. DOWNING to work in Newburgh, NY, and in 1851 the two formed a partnership. Vaux became involved in an expanding ar-

chitectural and landscape design business extending from New England to Washington, DC. After Downing's death (1852), Vaux collected the partnership's house plans and his own designs done alone or with FREDERICK CLARKE WITHERS and published them as *Villas and Cottages* (1857). This became the principal vehicle for transmitting Downing's distinctly American planning idioms to builders and the architectural profession. Opposed to Revivalism, Vaux was probably the era's first architectural author to abandon style-based design titles. Believing that all styles have the 'self-same geometry' he urged that they all be studied, but only for the appropriate ideas, not 'authority'. Having been naturalized in 1856, in 1857 he helped found the American Institute of Architects.

Vaux wished to use architecture and landscape design as a means to implement social improvement, and his work included hospitals (the first being Sheppard Asylum, Baltimore, planned in 1861), museums (the original parts of the Metropolitan Museum of Art, New York, 1874–80, with JACOB WREY MOULD, and the Museum of Natural History, New York, 1874–7), planned suburban residential communities (Riverside, IL, 1868–70, with FREDERICK LAW OLMSTED), charitable institutions (11 buildings for New York City's Children's Aid Society) and numerous public parks. For Central Park (begun 1858), the result of a competition instigated by the board of Park Commissioners, Vaux collaborated with Olmsted. Their plan, Greensward, became the model for urban American parks and established the profession of landscape architect (Vaux's term). Vaux was eventually appointed Landscape Architect to the Department of Parks in New York City.

Vaux was technically as well as aesthetically progressive, creating many significant innovations. With the ventilation expert Lewis W. Leeds (?1829–96) he obtained several patents for heating devices. In 1857 he became the first architect to advocate apartment houses for New York City. The 'parkway' concept of urban planning was developed from Vaux's plan for Prospect Park (from 1865), Brooklyn. Vaux's polychromatic stonework was considered equal to that of Mould by the contemporary critic Schuyler.

Vaux wrote the entry on 'Landscape Gardening' for the *Encyclopedia Britannica* (1866). The London *Builder* featured his designs from 1856 (Bank of New York) to 1873 (proposed Philadelphia Centennial Building). His New York town house (1881–4) for Governor Samuel J. Tilden was illustrated in both the Parisian *L'Architecture américaine* (1886) and the *American Architect and Building News* (5 Sept 1891). Vaux worked in partnership, at various times, with Withers, Leeds, Olmsted, George K. Radford (*b* 1826; *fl* 1900) and Samuel Parsons jr (1844–1923). His English-born assistant Thomas Wisedell (1846–84) went on to become New York's 'leading theatrical architect' (*NY Times*, 1884). His pupils included Parsons, his son Downing Vaux (1856–1926), Robert W. Gardner (1866–1937) and Charles Francis Osborne (1855–1913), later a professor of architecture at Cornell University and the University of Pennsylvania. He also influenced H. H. Richardson in his bold use of stone in the landscape architecture of Central Park.

WRITINGS

Villas and Cottages (New York, 1857/*R* 1968, rev. 2/1864/*R* 1970)
Regular contributions to the London *Builder* (1856–73)

BIBLIOGRAPHY

Macmillan Enc. Architects
[M. Schuyler]: 'Recent Building in New York', *Harper's Mthly*, lxvii (1883), p. 573
S. Giedion: *Space, Time and Architecture* (Cambridge, MA, 1941, rev. 5/1982), p. 360, figs 217–18
J. D. Single: 'Bibliography of the Life and Works of Calvert Vaux', *Amer. Assoc. Archit. Bibliog.: Pap.*, v (1968), pp. 71–93
W. Alex: *Calvert Vaux: Architect and Planner* (New York, 1994)

ARTHUR CHANNING DOWNS JR

Vauxcelles, Louis [Mayer, Louis] (*b* Paris, 1 Jan 1870). French critic. He is now best known for having invented the term 'les fauves' to describe Matisse and his colleagues in 1905. This has contributed to the impression that he was an opponent of modern art. In fact, although he did consistently decry Cubism and related avant-garde tendencies, he was a staunch defender of anti-academic painting and sculpture throughout his career. He began writing on art in the 1890s and quickly established himself as a lively and industrious recorder of the Parisian art scene. By 1914 he was probably the best-known and most widely read critic of the time: he was art correspondent for *Excelsior* and *Gil Blas* and wrote regularly in many other papers and periodicals. He was also a member of the executive committee of the Salon d'Automne and had personal contacts with many artists and dealers. In 1916, while maintaining his column on *Le Carnet de la semaine* (under the name Pinturicchio), which he continued for many years, he set up his own review, *Le Carnet des artistes*, with the backing of the same publisher, Albert Dubarry. After World War I he was able to found a more substantial periodical, *L'Amour de l'art*, which he edited from 1920 to 1923.

Vauxcelles himself once observed that 'art critics age badly', and it is the case that his artistic sympathies and principles were established at the turn of the century. His overall goal was to establish the primacy of the individualist, 'progressive' tradition in modern French art over the academic school. One reason why he attacked Cubism was that he saw it as a return to doctrinal, rule-bound art as opposed to a practice based on individual sensibility. The other was that he could not accept the idea of non-representational art. When Braque, after 1918, made his work easier to decipher and asserted his personal style, Vauxcelles began to acknowledge his work as a worthy continuation of the French tradition.

WRITINGS

Le Fauvisme (Geneva, 1959)

BIBLIOGRAPHY

M. Gee: *Dealers, Critics and Collectors of Modern Painting* (New York and London, 1981), pp. 101–53
C. Green: *Cubism and its Enemies* (London, 1987), pp. 121–218

MALCOLM GEE

Vaux-le-Vicomte, château of. French château *c.* 6 km north-east of Melun, in the département of Seine-et-Marne. It was built in 1656–61 for NICOLAS FOUQUET, Louis XIV's Surintendant des Finances, by Louis Le Vau (*see* LE VAU, (1), §3 and fig. 4) with the assistance of Charles Le Brun (*see* LE BRUN, CHARLES, §1(ii)(b)). The gardens were laid out by André Le Nôtre under Le Vau's guidance. The forerunner of Versailles, it is the most important château built in France in the mid-17th century; it was here that Le Vau, Le Brun and Le Nôtre learnt to work as a team and to produce the unity of architecture, interior decoration and garden layout that distinguishes the Louis XIV style.

1. BUILDINGS. Built in creamy limestone, the main block of the château is of compact design and sits in splendid isolation, surrounded by a moat and with an inner forecourt without flanking wings. The entrance front is a series of recessed planes with two-bay outer pavilions with tall roofs overlapping two-bay inner pavilions with mansard roofs that provide a necessary intermediary between the lower roof of the main block (see fig.). The outer forecourt beyond the moat is flanked by two vast courtyards of stables and service buildings in brick and stone, providing the architectural overture to the château and the huge formal gardens beyond. The château and courtyards are visually related by the use of tall roofs on the pavilions nearest the château and mansard roofs on those nearest the entrance gates. On the garden side of the château the composition is dominated by an oval dome, a feature first introduced by Le Vau at Le Raincy (begun 1643; destr.) All these elements were hurriedly assembled by Le Vau (the outer shell of the building was completed in a single year, with 18,000 workmen simultaneously employed), which probably explains why the elevations are not well marshalled: the projecting oval Salon in particular does not harmonize with the rest of the garden façade.

Inside the château, Le Vau placed the main apartments on the ground floor, thus obviating the need for a grand staircase. A triple archway motif links the front entrance, the rectangular entrance hall, the domed oval Salon beyond and in turn the door on to the perron overlooking the gardens. To the left of the Salon are the rooms intended for the King, while to the right are those of Fouquet. The interior decoration was entrusted to Le Brun, who designed the paintings, stuccowork and tapestries, thereby giving the interiors a noble unity of style. Originally there were 143 tapestries, many woven at the factory established by Fouquet at the nearby village of Maincy (*see* FRANCE, §XI, 1(iv)). Some of the interior statuary, notably in the Grand Salon, was by François Girardon, who also executed the elaborate stucco decoration in conjunction with Nicolas Legendre. The ceilings at Vaux-le-Vicomte are of particular interest. That of the first vestibule (now the dining-room) to the right of the entrance hall retains the tradition of exposed and delicately painted beams, which is typically French. In the Chambre du Roi the ceiling is an elaborate composition of allegorical paintings, ornate mouldings and figures in full relief, which is typically Italian and probably based on Pietro da Cortona's work in the Pitti Palace, Florence. The decorations were almost complete, with the notable exception of the painting of the interior of the dome, for the famous celebrations on 17 August 1661, when Fouquet entertained Louis XIV and the Court, three weeks before his arrest and disgrace. His arch-enemy Jean-Baptiste Colbert wasted no time in appropriating Fouquet's team of artists and craftsmen to

Château of Vaux-le-Vicomte by Louis Le Vau, begun 1656; engraving by Israel Sylvestre, 430×725 mm, 17th century (Paris, Bibliothèque Nationale)

the service of the King and removing the finest statues and rarest trees in the park to Versailles.

2. GARDENS. The gardens at Vaux-le-Vicomte were the first great work of André Le Nôtre (*see* LE NÔTRE, ANDRÉ, fig. 1). One of the objects of his extensive layout was to present a number of 'pictures' of the house. In his own plan of the gardens he showed the avenue running north from the entrance gates to a *rond-point*, from which only the central block of the château is visible. This avenue is intersected by another at exactly the point at which not only the château but also its flanking archways are included in the picture. The underlying principles of the layout were that the formality of the château required a corresponding formality in its immediate surroundings and that the landscape should be the creation of human reason, making use of all that perspective, proportion and a subtle touch of optical illusion could confer. Le Nôtre built his design along a central axis 800 m long from the windows of the Salon to the once-gilded colossal copy of the Farnese *Hercules* by Michel Anguier, which marks the horizon to the south. Anguier was the major provider of outdoor sculpture at Vaux-le-Vicomte. The first impression is one of symmetry, but this is soon perceived to contain a refreshing note of variety. The land gently dips towards the small valley of the Anqueuil, a slope that has been cleverly used to conceal a number of features, notably the Grandes Cascades, which overlook the canalized stream and are answered by the grotto on the opposite bank. To the east the ground rises sufficiently to enable walks at two different levels and some impressive flights of stone steps, in particular the Grille d'Eau at the end of the first transverse alley, which served as an outdoor theatre for

Molière. The gardens were reconstructed in the early 20th century by M. Alfred Sommier, omitting only the Allée d'Eau, which formed an avenue of fountains linking the first and second transverse alleys. It was described by Madeleine de Scudéry (1607–1701) as 'une balustrade de crystal'.

See also GARDEN, §VIII, 4(ii).

BIBLIOGRAPHY

U. Châtelain: *Le Surintendant Nicolas Foucquet, protecteur des lettres, des arts et des sciences* (Paris, 1905)
A. France and J. Cordey: *Le Château de Vaux-le-Vicomte* (Paris, 1924)
E. de Ganay: *André Le Nostre, 1613–1700* (Paris, 1962)
F. H. Hazlehurst: *Gardens of Illusion: The Genius of André Le Nostre* (Nashville, 1980)
K. Woodbridge: *Princely Gardens: The Origins and Development of the French Formal Garden* (London, 1986)

IAN DUNLOP

Vayreda y Vila, Joaquín (*b* Girona, 23 May 1843; *d* Olot, Girona, 31 Oct 1894). Spanish painter, draughtsman and etcher. He studied at the Escuela de Bellas Artes de S Jorge in Barcelona and in the workshops of Martí Alsina and Narciso Pascual Colomer. He was politically involved as a supporter of Don Carlos, the claimant to the throne, and in 1872, during the Second Carlist War, he was forced to emigrate to France with his friend, the painter José Berga y Boix (1837–1914). There he met Corot and various artists of the Barbizon school, who decisively affected his style. On his return to Spain, Vayreda y Vila opened a workshop in Catalonia and became the initiator of the school of landscape painting in Olot. Here he founded the Centro Artístico, which was joined by such painters as Antonio Caba (1838–1907), Modesto Urgell (1839–1919) and Berga y Boix. Some 250 oils by Vayreda y Vila survive, mainly views of Olot and figure compositions from his early period, as well as numerous drawings and etchings. He was awarded numerous international prizes, and at the Exposició Internacional, Barcelona, in 1929 a large retrospective exhibition of his work was organized.

BIBLIOGRAPHY

R. Benet: *Joaquín Vayreda: Antecedents, l'ambient, l'home, l'artista* (Barcelona, 1922)

J. Campdevila: *Vayreda* (Barcelona, 1926)

R. Benet: *La figura patricia y el arte de Joaquín Vayreda* (Barcelona, 1943)

JOSÉ LUIS MORALES Y MARÍN

Vaz, Gaspar (*b* Viseu, *fl* 1490; *d* ?Viseu, 1569). Portuguese painter. He was probably first taught in Viseu by Vasco Fernandes, and in 1514–15 he was a pupil in Lisbon of Jorge Afonso, court painter to Manuel I. After his return to Viseu in 1515, he frequently worked with Fernandes. In spite of the differences in style between the Lisbon and regional workshops, Vaz was successful in blending the two manners, although the influence of Viseu predominates. The polyptych of *Nossa Senhora da Glória* (*c.* 1542; Tarouca, S João) can be securely attributed to Vaz; evidence of his apprenticeship is apparent in the angels of the central panel, which show a transition in style from the Renaissance to early Mannerism. His use of elements taken from Fernandes is seen in the panel of the *Adoration of the Magi*, in which he copied a figure from the great *Calvary* by Fernandes (*c.* 1535–40; Viseu, Mus. Grão Vasco). It is possible that the two artists collaborated on the *St Michael* (*c.* 1535–42; Tarouca, S João), the composition of which, with its swirling drapery and the twisting serpentine figure of the archangel, is more Mannerist in style.

BIBLIOGRAPHY

L. Reis-Santos: *Vasco Fernandes e os pintores de Viseu do século XVI* (Lisbon, 1946)

A. Gusmão: *Os primitivos e a renascença in arte portuguesa: Pintura* (Lisbon, 1950), pp. 236–9

DAGOBERTO L. MARKL

Vaz, João (*b* Setúbal, 9 March 1859; *d* Lisbon, 15 Feb 1931). Portuguese painter. Between 1872 and 1878 he attended the Academia de Belas-Artes, Lisbon, where he was a pupil of Tomás José da Anunciação and António Silva Porto. In 1878 he travelled in Spain and France. When he returned to Lisbon he became one of the founders of the Grupo do Leão (1881–89), where he exhibited from 1882. His work was shown at the Sociedade Promotora de Belas-Artes in 1880 and 1884 and at the Grémio Artístico (Artistic Guild) from 1891 to 1899.

Vaz was a naturalistic landscape and scene painter and an excellent colourist whose main work was devoted to depicting the River Tagus and the Sado, the river at Setúbal. His fine riverine landscapes, with their reflections of light on water, sometimes show picturesque scenes of boats whose shadows are mirrored on the water surface, as in *On the Tagus* (1897) and *Boats* (both Lisbon, Mus. N. A. Contemp.). He was a sensitive painter of seascapes, as is seen in his coastal views, such as *Aloes* and *Rocks, Setúbal* (both Lisbon, Mus. N. A. Contemp.). These scenes are painted in a transparent and luminous blue, with the blurred outlines of distant houses, or they depict the dense forms of rocks. His paintings have a poetic quality,

landscapes that capture the silence of tranquil waters or scenes that evoke the quiet seclusion of cloisters and church interiors with soft, filtered golden light, as in the *Choir, Igreja da Madre de Deus, Lisbon* (*c.* 1917; Lisbon, Mus. N. A. Contemp.).

Vaz's work evolved around the Grupo do Leão, led by Silva Porto, who was a leading influence in its activities. From 1884 Vaz taught at the Xabregas Industrial School in Lisbon, becoming its Director in 1889. He was made an *académico de mérito* in 1897, and his work was featured from 1901 in the Salons of the Sociedade Nacional de Belas-Artes and in Rio de Janeiro and São Paulo. His work was also shown in international exhibitions from 1896. In 1932 a retrospective exhibition of his work was held in Lisbon.

BIBLIOGRAPHY

D. de Macedo and A. Ramalho: *João Vaz: Um retratista, um marinhista* (Lisbon, 1954)

J.-A. França: *A arte em Portugal no século XIX*, ii (Lisbon, 1966), pp. 52–3

Soleil et ombre: L'Art portugais du XIXème siècle (exh. cat., ed. J.-A. França; Paris, Petit Palais, 1987–8), pp. 255–8 and cover

LUCÍLIA VERDELHO DA COSTA

Vazcardo, Juan (*b* Caparroso, Navarre, 1584; *d* Caparroso, 1653). Spanish sculptor. He was the leading sculptor of the early Baroque period in the Navarre, Rioja and the Basque region, where his activity over a wide area was based on his workshop at Cabredo (Navarre). His art is characterized by a certain dry realism within forms derived from the classicism of Juan de Ancheta, whose pupil Pedro González de San Pedro was Vazcardo's father-in-law and with whom Vazcardo collaborated. The progressive dryness of his models recalls the work of Gregorio Fernández in the angularity of his draperies, which he could have learnt from works by Fernández in the Basque country, or from one of his followers such as Pedro Jiménez, with whom he collaborated in 1624 on the high altar and four side altars in the parish church of Oyón (Álava).

The late classicism of Vazcardo's work is seen in the design of the retables he made. Among his most notable works, all with fine relief carving, are the ciborium, with a relief of the *Resurrection* (1614; *in situ*), and the *retablo mayor*, all in Santa María de los Reyes, Laguardia, Álava. After 1630 he was assisted by his son-in-law Diego Jiménez II on retables at the parish churches of Briones (1630); Lapuebla de Labarca, Álava (1638); Fuenmayor, La Rioja; and Páganos, Álava, which contains a fine group of the *Assumption*.

BIBLIOGRAPHY

S. Andrés Ordax: *La escultura romanista en Álava* (Vitoria, 1973)

J. J. Martín González: *Escultura barroca en España, 1600–1770* (Madrid, 1983), pp. 304–6

SALVADOR ANDRÉS ORDAX

Vaz Dourado, Fernñão (*b* India, 1520–30; *d* India, *c.* 1581). Portuguese cartographer. He has been considered the most eminent Portuguese cartographer of the 16th century. He was the son of a nobleman, Francisco Dourado, a courtier (*moço de câmara*) to Manuel I of Portugal who embarked for the East in an armada that sailed in 1513; his mother was an Indian woman. He must have been a youth when he took part in the second siege of Diu in Arakan (1546). He sailed in the eastern oceans, and it is known from the tombstone of his daughter, who died in Goa in 1571, that he was a *fronteiro-mor* (captain of a frontier fortress), as he states in the frontispieces of two of his atlases dated 1568 and 1580. It is possible that he learnt cartography from Diego Botelho Pereira, who worked in India. A tide-table in Vaz Dourado's *Atlas of the Universe* of 1575 (London, BL) relating to the west coast of the Iberian peninsula suggests that he was in Portugal at this date, and this is likely because the volume is dedicated to King Sebastian. In the atlas of 1580 (Munich) he describes himself as 'frontier captain in Indian lands' (*fronteiro das partes da India*), which indicates that he returned to the East after a short stay in Europe.

Vaz Dourado's maps were among the finest examples produced in his time and are outstanding both for the care that he gave to the finishing touches as well as for the quality of his drawing. He enriched his maps with innumerable details of interest, such as various types of sailing ships and the appropriate flora and fauna of the various land areas. He used elegant engraving for the illuminated lettering of his titles and for the navigational information in his atlases, and he adorned his maps with beautiful borders and decorative devices based on the designs of Sebastiano Serlio, including escutcheons garlanded with flowers or fruits and cartouches surrounded with fantastic figures and arranged symmetrically on the page. In addition he was a skilled colourist; in this respect Vaz Dourado's maps are unequalled among those by Portuguese cartographers of the 16th century.

The seven known works by Vaz Dourado are: *Atlas of the Universe* (1568; Madrid, Pal. Liria, Col. Duke of Alba), which consists of fourteen maps and five folios with cosmographical and navigational information and contains the first known detailed maps of Japan and Ceylon; *Map of the Western Indian Ocean* (?*c*. 1568; London, BL); *Atlas of the Universe* (1570; San Marino, CA, Huntington Lib.), which has seventeen maps and three folios with cosmographical information relevant to navigation and a map of Brazil that shows for the first time (incorrectly) the course of the River Maranhão linked to that of the Amazon; *Atlas of the Universe* (1571; Lisbon, Arquiv. N.), with fifteen maps and three folios; *Atlas of the Universe* (1575; London, BL), which has seventeen maps and three folios of cosmographical information relevant to navigation and is dedicated to King Sebastian of Portugal; *Atlas of the Universe* (1576; Lisbon, Bib. N.), with seventeen maps and three folios of cosmographical information; and *Atlas of the Universe* (1580; Munich, Bayer. Staatsbib.), with fifteen maps and three folios of navigational information for pilots.

BIBLIOGRAPHY

A. Cortesão: *Cartografia e cartógrafos portugueses dos séculos XV e XVI*, ii (Lisbon, 1935), pp. 7–104

——: *Portugaliae monumenta cartographica*, iii (Lisbon, 1960), pp. 3–28

LUIS DE ALBUQUERQUE

Vázquez. Spanish family of engravers. Bartolomé Vázquez (*b* Córdoba, 1749; *d* Madrid, 1802) was also a silversmith. He was self-taught in the art of engraving and studied engravings by Francesco Bartolozzi. From 1782 he began working in stipple engraving (pointillé). His first works using this method were devotional engravings, including a *Mater dolorosa*, after Anton Raphael Mengs, and an *Ecce homo*, after Ramón Bayeu (both 1785). The same year he was made an Académico de mérito at the Real Academia de S Fernando, Madrid. He also engraved Raphael's *Madonna della Sedia* in 1789 and some portraits in the series *Hombres ilustres* (Madrid, 1789). His skill in using colour is seen in the *Rielves Mosaic* (1788). His son José Vázquez (*b* Córdoba, 1768; *d* Madrid, 1804) was his pupil and collaborator. In 1787 José received the prize for engraving from the Real Academia de S Fernando, Madrid, and he was made an academician in 1799.

BIBLIOGRAPHY

Conde de la Viñaza: *Adiciones al diccionario* (1889–94)

F. Esteve Botey: *Historia del grabado* (Barcelona, 1935), p. 307

A. Gallego: *Historia del grabado* (Madrid, 1979), pp. 261–2

E. Páez Ríos: *Repertorio* (1981–3)

A. Tomás and M. S. Silvestre: *Estampas y planchas de la Real Academia en al Museo de Bellas Artes de Valencia* (Valencia, 1982)

J. Carrete, F. Checa and V. Bozal: *El grabado en España: Siglos XV al XVIII*, Summa A., xxxi (Madrid, 1987), pp. 514–17, 523–4, 569–71

BLANCA GARCÍA VEGA

Vázquez, Alonso (*b* Ronda, *c*. 1565; *d* Mexico City, *c*. 1608). Spanish painter. He probably trained either with Luis de Vargas or with his pupil Antonio de Arjián in Seville, where Vázquez worked from 1588 until his departure for New Spain in 1603. Influenced by the work of northern Renaissance masters such as Marten de Vos and Maarten van Heemskerck, Vázquez's art is a good example of late 16th-century Mannerism in Seville. The sculpturesque quality of his forms, interest in detail and taste for exaggerated gestures and contorted poses reflect both Italian and Flemish influences. Vázquez earned a reputation for his virtuoso treatment of still-lifes in his paintings, as in *Lazarus and the Rich Man* (1588–1603; untraced, see Brown, p. 131), painted for Fernando Enríquez de Ribera, 3rd Duque de Alcalá. The *Last Supper* (1588–1603; Seville, Mus. B.A.) combines Flemish motifs taken from prints by or after van Heemskerck and de Vos. The theatrical composition contains still-life objects depicted with great care and attention to detail. Vázquez's earliest dated work, the *Resurrection* (1590; Seville, S Ana), is in the Roman tradition; it shows strong draughtsmanship, daring foreshortening and is powerfully expressive.

In 1600 Vázquez collaborated with Francisco Pacheco on the scenes from the *Life of St Peter Nolasco* and from the *Life of St Raymund Nonnatus* in the great cloister of the Mercedarian Convent, Seville. The *Death of St Hermengild* (begun 1603; Seville, Mus. B.A.) was one of the first large-scale canvases to be painted in Seville. It was left unfinished on Vázquez's departure for New Spain and was completed by Juan de Uceda Castroverde. The composition, divided into earthly and heavenly zones, anticipates 17th-century Baroque art in Seville. Vázquez's work in New Spain is undocumented, but attribution to him on stylistic grounds is almost certain for *St Michael Casting out the Devil* and *St Michael Protecting a Noble Boy against a Naked Temptress and a Horned Satan* (both 1603–8; Mexico City, Mus. S Carlos). He helped to establish the types and compositions that were influential in Mexico in the first half of the 17th century.

BIBLIOGRAPHY

F. Pacheco: *Arte* (1649); ed. F. J. Sánchez Cantón (1956), ii, pp. 14, 19, 37, 53–4, 84, 109, 126

A. A. Palomino de Castro y Velasco: *Museo pictórico* (1715–24)

G. Kubler and M. Soria: *Art and Architecture in Spain and Portugal and their American Dominions, 1500–1800*, Pelican Hist. A. (Harmondsworth, 1959)

J. M. Serrera: 'Pinturas y pintores del siglo XVI en la catedral de Sevilla', *La Catedral de Sevilla* (Seville, 1985), pp. 395–7

E. Valdivieso: *Historia de la pintura sevillana: Siglos XIII al XX* (Seville, 1986), pp. 96–102

J. Brown: *The Golden Age of Painting in Spain* (New Haven and London, 1991), pp. 118–19, 126

☐

Vázquez, Juan Bautista, *el viejo* (*b* Pelayos, Salamanca, *c.* 1510; *d* Llerena, Badajoz, 12 June 1588). Spanish sculptor and engraver. The elegant Mannerism and refinement of his works, and the anatomical correctness of the figures, indicate that he may have trained in Italy. He had a workshop in Ávila until 1554, when he settled in Toledo. While there he executed carvings for the cathedral and worked on the wooden altarpiece of the parish church of Almonacid de Zorita (1554–6; partly destr. 1936; remains, Torrelaguna, collegiate church, and Oropesa, convent of the Oblates) and on that of S Maria la Blanca, Toledo (1556), among others.

In 1561 Vázquez was called to Seville to complete an altarpiece started by Isidro Villoldo for the Cartuja de las Cuevas, Seville. He was also asked to complete the altarpiece started by Nufro Ortega (1516–75) in 1559 in the church of the Asunción, Carmona, but this was not finished until 1569. Among the many works Vázquez executed in Seville were the wooden *Virgin of the Fiebres* (1561; Seville, Magdalena), the marble tomb of *Antonio Corro* (1564; San Vicente de la Barquera, Nuestra Señora de los Angeles) and the wooden altarpiece (1575–7) for the church of S Maria, Medina Sedonia. During this period Vázquez's figures evolved and became rounder, as in his wooden *Virgin of the Piña* (1577; Lebrija, S Maria de la Oliva).

Vázquez also made models to be cast in bronze, possibly including one for the *Giraldillo* (h. 4 m) cast by Bartolomé Morel in 1568 for the Giralda Tower, Seville. He decorated the Royal Galley for Don John of Austria, the victor of Lepanto, and may have made the copy (1554) of Michelangelo's *Pietà* in Ávila Cathedral. He was also a skilled engraver (e.g. *Juan de Malara*, Madrid, Bib. N., see Estella, 1990, fig. 21), signing his work *B. V.*, and may have been a painter as well.

BIBLIOGRAPHY

Ceán Bermúdez; Thieme–Becker

Conde de la Viñaza: *Adiciones al diccionario* (1889–94)

M. Gómez Moreno: *La escultura del renacimiento en España* (Barcelona, 1931)

G. Weise: *Spanische Plastik aus sieben Jahrhunderten*, iv (Tübingen, 1939)

J. Hernández Diaz: *Imaginería hispalense del bajo renacimiento* (Seville, 1951)

J. M. Azcarate: *Escultura del siglo XVI*, A. Hisp., xiii (Madrid, 1958)

A. Carrasco Garcia: *Escultores, pintores y plateros del bajo renacimiento en Llerena* (Badajoz, 1982)

J. M. Palomero Paramo: 'Bautista Vázquez el viejo y la portada del Colegio de Doncellas nobles de Toledo', *Bol. Semin. Estud. A. & Arqueol.* (1983), pp. 464–74

——: *El retablo sevillano del renacimiento: Análisis y evolución (1560–1629)* (Seville, 1983)

M. Estella: 'Juan Bautista Vázquez el viejo y el Museo Lázaro', *Goya*, 193–5 (1986), pp. 120–25

J. M. Palomero Paramo: 'Juan Bautista Vázquez el viejo y el retablo de la *Virgen de la Piña* de Lebrija', *Archv Hispal.* (1986), pp. 161–3

M. Estella: *Juan Bautista Vázquez el viejo en Castilla y América* (Madrid, 1990)

M. I. Rodríguez Quintana: '1559, un año para el aguafuerte español: La compañía Vázquez-Montoya', *Archv Esp. A.*, lxv (1992), pp. 119–221

MARGARITA ESTELLA

Vázquez, Pedro Ramírez. *See* RAMÍREZ VÁZQUEZ, PEDRO.

Vázquez (de Segovia), Lorenzo (*b c.* 1450; *d* before 1515). Spanish architect. He appears to have been trained in the Late Gothic tradition established by Juan Guas and Enrique Egas, and he was the first to introduce Renaissance motifs into Spanish architecture. There is, however, no evidence that he trained in Italy, or that he travelled to Florence and Rome with the Embassy of Iñigo López de Mendoza, 2nd Conde de Tendilla, as has been suggested. Italian elements in Vázquez's work could have been derived from information provided by clients, for instance in the form of drawings. Vázquez is first documented in Valladolid (1490); his patron was Pedro González de Mendoza, the Cardinal of Santa Cruz. In 1491 he became Master of Works to the Cardinal (working with Alberto de Carvajal, who was in Valladolid from 1488 to 1493). Vázquez planned the chapel altarpiece for the Cardinal's foundation, the Colegio Mayor de Santa Cruz, Valladolid, before June 1494. Parts of the foundation building were designed in the Italian style and have been attributed to Vázquez, for example the central bay of the dressed-stone façade, the main portal, the cornice, the balustrade and the buttresses decorated with pairs of pilasters. The correct use of certain details compared with the errors usually found in Vázquez's work suggests, however, that the building was not the work of a single architect.

When Mendoza died in 1495, Vázquez maintained his ties with the Cardinal's family. In 1496 he surveyed works carried out on the house of González de Mendoza in the city of Guadalajara. In 1502, while in the service of Juan de la Cerda II, Duque de Medinaceli, he surveyed work on the castle of Cihuela. This activity supports the theory that he designed the palace of Cogolludo (*c.* 1492–5), Guadalajara, for Luis de la Cerda, Duque de Medinaceli, a building with Gothic elements as well as pseudo-Corinthian column supports for the patio, and a dressed-stone façade without towers. Its Late Gothic windows and ornamental crenellations detract from the Italian quality of the façade, which was otherwise similar to that of the Colegio at Valladolid. The monastery of S Antonio (1489–1509), Mondéjar (Guadalajara), founded by the 2nd Conde de Tendilla, is also similar in style to the Colegio; Vázquez is documented as directing the building work. The basic structure of the church is Gothic, but much of the detailing is Italian in inspiration, for example the portal, with its candelabra decorations, the triangular pediment combined with a curved tympanum, and the greatly elongated pilasters, with unorthodox capitals supporting the ribbed vaults.

The last records of Vázquez are dated 1508/9. At this time he was a virtual prisoner in the castle of La Calahorro, Granada, where he was working (1506–12) for Rodrigo Díaz de Vivar y de Mendoza, 1st Marqués del Zenete. It is possible that Vázquez had designed the castle itself, including the lower storey of the central courtyard, using Composite orders based on a drawing in the *Codex Escurialensis* (which contained examples of architecture and ornament from 15th-century Italy, and which was brought from Rome by the Marqués *c.* 1506). Vázquez may also have designed the unusual staircase built around an open well. The palace of Pedro Fajardo (1506–16) in Vélez Blanco, Almería, built for the 1st Marqués de los Vélez, has recently been ascribed to Vázquez, but without foundation.

BIBLIOGRAPHY

M. Gomez-Moreno: 'Sobre el Renacimiento en Castilla: Hacia Lorenzo Vázquez', *Archv Esp. A. & Arqueol.*, i (1925), pp. 1–40
F. de B. San Roman: 'Las obras y los arquitectos del Cardenal Mendoza', *Archv Esp. A. & Arqueol.*, v (1931), pp. 153–61
F. Chueca Goitia: *Arquitectura del siglo XVI*, A. Hisp. (Madrid, 1953), pp. 35–6, 51–2
H. W. Kruft: 'Un cortile rinascimentales italiano nella Sierra Nevada: La Calahorra', *Ant. Viva*, viii (1969), pp. 35–51
——: 'Ancora sulla Calahorra: Documenti', *Ant. Viva*, xi (1972), pp. 35–45
L. Cervera Vera: *Arquitectura del Colegio Mayor de Santa Cruz en Valladolid* (Valladolid, 1982)

FERNANDO MARÍAS

Vázquez Díaz, Daniel (*b* Riotinto, nr Nerva, Huelva, 15 Jan 1882; *d* Madrid, 17 March 1969). Spanish painter and etcher. He moved to Madrid in 1903, becoming friendly with Juan Gris and copying paintings in the Museo del Prado. In 1906, on his way to Paris, he held his first one-man exhibition in San Sebastián and visited Fuenterrabía, near Irún, which subsequently became an inexhaustible source of artistic inspiration. In Paris he lived through the birth of Cubism, which gave his work a lasting legacy of solid, rigorously constructed planes. He took part in the Salon des Indépendants and the Salon d'Automne on several occasions and struck up friendships with Picasso and the Nicaraguan poet Rubén Darío.

On his return to Spain in 1918, Vázquez Díaz settled permanently in Madrid, where he continued to paint and began teaching, first in his own studio and later as professor of mural painting at the Escuela de Bellas Artes de S Fernando, introducing his pupils to the new art forms. In 1925 he took part in the *Exposición de artistas ibéricos* held in Madrid in the Parque del Retiro. His prolific output continued, concentrating on portraiture (e.g. *Eva*, Madrid, Mus. A. Contemp.), still-lifes and landscape; he also produced a series of murals on the *Discovery of America* (1927–30) for the Franciscan monastery of La Rábida near Huelva. Vázquez Díaz had numerous exhibitions and won several awards, such as the Grand Prize at the Bienal Hispanoamericana de Arte in Madrid (1951) and the Medal of Honour at the Exposición Nacional de Bellas Artes in 1954. He was elected an academician of the Real Academia de Bellas Artes de San Fernando in 1949.

BIBLIOGRAPHY

E. Lafuente Ferrari: *Vázquez Díaz y su vida* (Madrid, 1962)
A. Benito Jaén: *Vázquez Díaz, vida y pintura* (Madrid, 1971)
F. Garfias: *Vida y obra de Vázquez Díaz* (Madrid, 1972)

PALOMA ALARCÓ CANOSA

Veau, Louis Le. *See* LE VAU, (1).

Vecchi, Giovanni (Liso) de' [Giovanni dal Borgo] (*b* Borgo San Sepolcro, 1536/7; *d* Rome, 13 April 1615). Italian painter. Often classified as an Italian Mannerist, he may have been a disciple of the painter Raffaello dal Colle in Rome. It is likely that he worked alongside Giuseppe Ceracchi at the Palazzo Belvedere in the Vatican in Rome during the early 1560s, and he may have been closely associated there with Santi di Tito between *c.* 1562 and 1564. He was almost certainly the painter called 'Giovanni dal Borgo' who worked at the Villa d'Este in Tivoli in 1568. He is first documented in Rome as a member of the Accademia di S Luca in 1570 and during the first half of that decade was employed on two enterprises initiated by Alessandro Farnese: the religious decoration of the oratory of the Gonfalone in Rome, and the secular work at the Villa Farnese at Caprarola, where he worked within the ambience of Federico Zuccaro and Jacopo Bertoia. According to Giovanni Baglione, de' Vecchi executed frescoes at Caprarola in the Sala del Mappamondo (*c.* 1574) and in the Sala degli Angeli (*c.* 1575–6). There is little doubt that he designed the frescoes in both rooms. In the Sala del Mappamondo he certainly executed most of the allegorical figures (e.g. *Asia* and *Africa*) and the ornamentation, while in the Sala degli Angeli he probably executed the decorative and allegorical lunettes. The ceiling fresco there, the *Fall of the Angels*, was formerly also attributed to him.

De' Vecchi painted religious subjects, primarily in fresco, in churches throughout Rome, for example the *Adoration of the Shepherds* (fresco, 1574–5; S Eligio degli Orefici; *in situ*). In 1578 he became a member of the Congregazione dei Virtuosi al Pantheon, but during this period he appears to have returned intermittently to Borgo San Sepolcro. Among his few surviving pictures there are two oil paintings dating from the first half of the 1580s: the *Nativity of the Virgin* and the *Presentation in the Temple* (both Sansepolcro, Mus. Civ.). Both pictures display an acute and artificial manipulation of pictorial space, a capriciousness in details of gesture and expression, and a vivacious colouring that suggests the influence of early 16th-century Venetian art. These, together with the frescoes at Caprarola, exemplify de' Vecchi's Mannerist style.

In 1578 he was commissioned to paint a fresco cycle of the *Legend of the Cross* at the oratory of the Crocifisso di S Marcello, Rome. Although he executed only part of this programme, his first painting, *St Helena Ordering the Search for the True Cross* (*c.* 1580; see fig.), which is perhaps somewhat old-fashioned in its conception, is notable for showing a tentative abandonment of Mannerist principles and a new inclination towards greater psychological depth and naturalism. De' Vecchi's most important commission of the 1580s was for frescoes, begun in 1583, depicting the *Four Doctors of the Latin Church* on the vault pendentives at Il Gesù in Rome. He may also have designed a fresco for the cupola. His work was overpainted (1675–6) by Giovanni Battista Gaulli, but two of the pendentives were recorded in a painting of *Urban VIII Visiting Il Gesù during the Centenary Celebrations of the Jesuit Order, 1639* (oil on canvas, 1641; Rome, Pal. Braschi), executed by Andrea Sacchi, Jan Miel and Filippo Gagliardi (*d* 1659).

During the 1580s and 1590s de' Vecchi participated in the decoration of a number of chapels and executed a

Giovanni de' Vecchi: *St Helena Ordering the Search for the True Cross* (*c.* 1580), fresco, oratory of the Crocifisso di S Marcello, Rome

series of frescoed altars in Rome, including *St Francis Receiving the Stigmata*. His mature style is embodied in one of his last major paintings, *Pope Gregory the Great's Procession with the Miraculous Icon of the Virgin Mary during the Plague of 590* (oil on slate; S Maria in Aracoeli; *in situ*). This picture has an intense mystical quality, expressed by concentrated chiaroscuro and heightened colour. Much of the artist's previous use of descriptive incident and detail has been eliminated, and the sentiment of the picture is substantially more sombre and meditative than decorous or rhetorical. This is perhaps the most pious work of de' Vecchi's late career and may support suggestions that he became increasingly responsive to the mood of the Counter-Reformation.

BIBLIOGRAPHY

G. Baglione: *Vite* (1642); ed. V. Mariani (1935), pp. 25, 96, 104, 121–8, 155

R. Roli: 'Giovanni de' Vecchi', *A. Ant. & Mod.*, 29 and 31–2 (1965), pp. 45–56, 324–34

S. J. Freedberg: *Painting in Italy, 1500–1600*, Pelican Hist. A. (Harmondsworth, 1970), pp. 443–4, 447–8

A. Pinelli: 'Pittura e controriforma: "Convenienza" e misticismo in Giovanni de' Vecchi', *Ric. Stor. A.*, 6 (1977), pp. 49–64

J. Heideman: 'A New Dating of De' Vecchi's "Procession" Painting in Santa Maria in Aracoeli in Rome', *Paragone*, xxxix/455 (1988), pp. 51–61

□

Vecchia, Pietro della (*b* Venice or Vicenza, 1602/3; *d* Venice, 6 Sept 1678). Italian painter. Until 1984 he was

mentioned as Pietro Muttoni, called della Vecchia. However, this description was founded on a misunderstanding created by Lanzi, who in his *Storia pittorica della Italia* confused the name of the artist with the name of a collection, Muttoni, in which he had seen one of his paintings. In fact, Pietro was from the well-known Venetian family, the della Vecchia. His earliest known works, two representations of *St Francis*, which have survived in many versions (e.g. Modena, Gal. Estense; Rovigo, Accad. Concordi), and a *Crucifixion* (1633; Venice, S Lio) are so heavily influenced by Carlo Saraceni and his student and collaborator Jean Leclerc as to suggest that della Vecchia trained with them. Certain Caravaggesque elements, which remained in his work for some time to come, suggest that he spent some time in Rome after Leclerc had left Venice, in 1621 or 1622. The influence of Alessandro Varotari or Padovanino, who is described by sources (e.g. Orlandini) as della Vecchia's teacher, is only noticeable in dated works from 1635 onwards. Della Vecchia probably worked in Padovanino's studio *c.* 1625–6, after his trip to Rome, and from the latter he derived his great interest in 16th-century painting in Venice and the Veneto. His monumental *Crucifixion* (1637; Venice, Fond. Cini), in which the composition harks back to the 16th century while the figures derive from Caravaggio, is characteristic of this phase. Around 1640 the influence of Bernardo Strozzi is apparent in his work, as in the *Angel Offering a Skull to St Giustina, Who Stands between St Joseph and St John* (1640; Venice, Accad.), painted for the church of S Giustina. Also in 1640 he began to design cartoons for the mosaics in S Marco, on which he worked until 1673.

In the 1650s della Vecchia's style became more dramatic, and he again sought inspiration in Caravaggio. This is especially evident in paintings dating from 1652–5: the series of seven canvases, mainly of martyrdoms, for the church of S Teonisto in Treviso (five in Treviso, Mus. Civ. Bailo; others destr.) and two monumental paintings, the *Martyrdom of SS Gervasio and Protasio* and the *Discovery of the Bodies of SS Gervasio and Protasio*, in the choir of the parish church of Carpenedo. A high point in this development are two extant paintings, the *Conversion of Francesco Borgia* (Brest, Mus. Mun.) and the *Jesuit Marco Gussoni* (untraced), from the series of seven painted between 1664 and 1674 for the second court of the Jesuit monastery in Venice. A macabre light, a narrow, suffocating space and highly theatrical gestures distinguish these impressive works. Nevertheless, it was his paintings on secular subjects, almost without exception undated, that made della Vecchia famous. He was able to absorb the styles of 16th-century artists with astonishing ease, and imitated the manner of Giorgione, Titian, Palma Vecchio, Lorenzo Lotto and Romanino with such skill that even today some of these works are considered to be 16th-century originals. Apart from character heads (e.g. *Soldier with Plumed Hat*, St Petersburg, Hermitage), half-length warriors (e.g. *Man Drawing his Dagger*, Vienna, Ksthist. Mus.), soldiers playing dice, and musical parties (e.g. *The Concert*, Berlin, Gemäldegal.), he also painted themes, as in *Socrates and two Pupils* (Madrid, Prado), that reflect the interests of the literary Accademia degli Incogniti. In the wide range of his commissions, official and private—including some for libertine members of the Incogniti—this talented artist reflected many aspects of 17th-century Venetian taste.

BIBLIOGRAPHY

DBI [with full bibliog.]

M. Boschini: *La carta del navegar pittoresco* (Venice, 1660); ed. A. Pallucchini (Venice and Rome, 1966), p. 536

P. A. Orlandi: *Abecedario pittorico nel quale compendiosamente sono descritte le patrie, i maestri, ed i tempi . . .* (Bologna, 1704/R Geneva, 1973), p. 319

A. M. Zanetti: *Della pittura veneziana* (Venice, 1771), pp. 387–90

L. Lanzi: *Storia pittorica della Italia dal risorgimento delle belle arti fin presso al fin del XVIII secolo* (Bassano, 1795–6, rev. 3, 1809)

N. Ivanoff: 'Il grottesco nella pittura veneziana del seicento: Pietro il Vecchia', *Emporium*, 99 (1944), pp. 85–94

L. Gambarin: 'Il Vecchia cartonista in San Marco', *A. Ven.*, xv (1961), pp. 250–52

R. Pallucchini: *La pittura veneziana del seicento* (Milan, 1981), i, pp. 172–8; ii, figs 500–538

B. Aikema: 'Pietro Vecchia e i gesuiti', *Studi barocchi, 2: Le ricche minere della pittura veneziana*, ed. V. Sgarbi (Rome, 1982), pp. 121–35

——: 'Pietro della Vecchia, a Profile', *Saggi & Mem. Stor. A.*, xiv (1984), pp. 79–100

E. Bordignon Favero: 'La bottega di Pietro Vecchia a Venezia', *Atti & Mem. Accad. Patavina Sci., Lett. & A.*, cxvii (1984–5)

B. Aikema: *De schilder Pietro della Vecchia en de erfenis van de Renaissance in Venetië* (Nijmegen, 1986)

——: *Pietro della Vecchia and the Heritage of the Renaissance in Venice* (Florence, 1990)

BERNARD AIKEMA

Vecchietta [Lorenzo di Pietro di Giovanni] (*bapt* Siena, 11 Aug 1410; *d* Siena, 6 June 1480). Italian painter, sculptor, goldsmith and architect.

1. BEFORE *c.* 1465. He was formerly believed to have been born *c.* 1412 in the Tuscan town of Castiglione d'Orcia, but del Bravo has identified him with the Lorenzo di Pietro di Giovanni who was baptized in Siena in 1410. His name appears in a list of the members of the Siena painters' guild in 1428. From the evidence of later works he is generally supposed to have been apprenticed to Sassetta, but his early work has not been identified. Between *c.* 1435 and 1439 he executed for Cardinal Branda Castiglione (1350–1443) a series of frescoes at Castiglione Olona, near Varese in Lombardy. He has been considered an assistant of MASOLINO DA PANICALE in this enterprise, but the scenes of the martyrdoms of SS Lawrence and Stephen in the apse of the Collegiata, below Masolino's vault frescoes, show that Vecchietta's closely packed compositional style was already fully formed. He also painted the frescoes (partially published by Bertelli) in the chapel of the Cardinal's palace in the town, depicting the Evangelists (vault) and friezes of male and female saints (side walls). Although abraded and fragmentary, they nevertheless indicate the naturalistic effects of atmospheric lighting and foreshortening that, more than any other Sienese painter of his day, he had learnt from Masolino and the Florentine painters. In 1439, aided by Sano di Pietro, he painted the figures of a wooden *Annunciation* group (untraced) for the high altar of Siena Cathedral.

Vecchietta's earliest surviving documented work is the *Allegory of the Blessed Sorore and the Education of the Foundlings* (1441) in the Ospedale di S Maria della Scala, Siena; it is the only fresco to be preserved of four he painted there, and the first of several major commissions for the hospital (*see* SIENA, §III, 2). It contrasts with the neighbouring frescoes by Domenico di Bartolo in its orderly and rational approach to the architectural setting (in which a Roman triumphal arch is set in front of an aisled nave) and in its subtly graded coloration. In 1442, styled for the first time by his nickname, he is documented as carving and painting a *Risen Christ* (untraced) for the high altar of Siena Cathedral. Although his paintings and sculpture are usually considered separately, the two functions reinforced each other throughout his remaining career. For example, the measured approach to monumentality in his fresco of the *Lamentation* (1.90×2.08 m, 1445–8; Monteriggioni, Mus. Semin. Arcivescovile), formerly in the Martinozzi Chapel in S Francesco, Siena, is also evident in the contemporary painted wood *Pietà* (h. 960 mm) at S Donato, Siena, which has a similar composition.

Vecchietta worked in both miniature and monumental styles, so that works carried out in the same years for the sacristy of the Ospedale di S Maria della Scala, Siena, show differing forms of expression. The painted panels of the sacristy's reliquary cabinet (2.73×1.87 m with doors closed, 1445–9; Siena, Pin. N.) are by at least two artists, but those on the exterior bearing local Sienese saints are closer to Vecchietta's style: *Blessed Agostino Novello* and *Blessed Catherine of Siena* are certainly autograph panels. The *Passion* scenes on the interior are by a gifted miniaturist in his workshop. Although damaged, the frescoes of 1446–9 show a contrasting spaciousness. Christ blessing, Evangelists, Doctors of the Church and Prophets are depicted on the vault of the sacristy, while on the walls are Old and New Testament scenes and the *Last Judgement*; van Os (1974) has shown how the imagery is employed to illustrate the articles of faith in the Creed. This is also the subject of the ceiling frescoes of the baptistery in Siena (1450–53), which revert to an ostensibly miniaturist precision of placement, but cleaning has revealed that the brushwork was carried out with remarkable freedom. Tawny russet hues predominate. Benvenuto di Giovanni, recorded in 1483 as working in the baptistery, may have executed the frescoes of the *Miracles of St Anthony of Padua*.

The lunette fresco of the *Madonna of Mercy* (mid-1450s) in the Ufficio del Sale, Palazzo Pubblico, Siena, again shows a free brushstroke deployed to characterize a number of figures. A delicate range of pinks now predominates, but otherwise this fresco has a grave overall expression in common with the altarpiece of the *Virgin and Child with Saints* (see fig. 1) from the Villa Monselvoli, Siena. The restraint of these iconic works co-exists with a fresher approach to narrative in such smaller-scale paintings as the *biccherna* panel of the *Coronation of Pius II* (590×405 mm, 1460; Siena, Pal. Piccolomini, Archv Stato), the pope who was to be Vecchietta's next main patron, and the predella of the altarpiece of the *Virgin and Child with Saints* (*c.* 1461–2; now Pienza, Mus. Cattedrale) from S Niccolò a Spedaletto, Pienza. An especially delightful *plein-air* quality permeates the predella panel of monks building a church, a scene from the *Life of St Benedict* (295×450 mm; Sant'Anna in Camprena, Monastery).

Bellosi, possibly referring to a record from 1460 of a debt owed by 'Master Lorenzo di Pietro and Benvenuto and Francesco, painters', has divided responsibility for a group of lively predella panels among three artists, claiming the *Miracle of St Louis of Toulouse* (Rome, Pin. Vaticana)

1. Vecchietta: *Virgin and Child with Saints*, tempera on panel, 1.56×2.30 m, 1457 (Florence, Galleria degli Uffizi)

for Vecchietta, the *Miracle of St Anthony of Padua* (Munich, Alte Pin.) for Benvenuto di Giovanni and the *Sermon of St Bernardino of Siena* (Liverpool, Walker A.G.) for the young Francesco di Giorgio Martini. The style of all three scenes, in which the painstaking perspective established in the Pellegrinaio fresco appears again, is, however, that of Vecchietta, whose self-portrait is discernible in the Liverpool panel (he also appears in the *Madonna of Mercy* fresco and in his late altarpiece in Siena; see §2 below). Panels assumed to be from the same predella, two representing flagellants (Ajaccio, Mus. Fesch, and Bayonne, Mus. Bonnat) and two embodying Franciscan allegories (both Munich, Alte Pin.), are also more likely to be by Vecchietta than by Francesco di Giorgio.

The brilliant modulation of light and shade and the perfect integration of figure and setting that characterize the fresco of *St Catherine of Siena* (Doc. 1460 but dated 1461, the year of Catherine's canonization) in the Sala del Mappamondo in the Palazzo Pubblico, Siena, and the signed triptych of the *Assumption of the Virgin with Four Saints* (*c.* 1462) in Pienza Cathedral can be attributed chiefly to Vecchietta's growing experience of sculpture. His grave and even bleak marble niche figures of *SS Peter and Paul* (1458–62) on the Loggia della Mercanzia, Siena, show strong influence of Donatello, the *St Paul* being based on Donatello's *St Mark* for Orsanmichele, Florence. The taut play of line in these statues, however, is entirely Vecchietta's own.

2. AFTER *c.* 1465. Vecchietta's work became increasingly diversified. As early as 1460 he had travelled to Rome to obtain Pius's approval for the model of his design for the Piccolomini Loggia in Siena. He served as a fortifications expert throughout the Sienese territories (1467–70) and provided Siena Cathedral with silver reliquary busts of saints (1472–6; all untraced). This technical agility was best realized in the production of large-scale bronze sculptures, the chief undertakings of his late career, which necessitated numerous assistants. The tomb effigy of the humanist and jurist *Mariano Sozzini* (*d* 1467) for S Domenico, Siena (now Florence, Bargello; Bellosi attributes the work to Francesco di Giorgio), shows an unflinching naturalism in the shrivelled face and crinkly drapery; a 16th-century source ascribes the *Sozzini* to Vecchietta, and Bellosi is unconvincing in reattributing it to Francesco di Giorgio Martini. Vecchietta's most elaborate work in bronze is the multi-figured ciborium (1467–72; transferred to the high altar of Siena Cathedral in 1506, replacing Duccio's *Maestà*) made for the high altar of S Maria della Scala, Siena. Supported on a stem embellished with putti and music-making angels, the tempietto-shaped body of the ciborium is in the form of the Holy Sepulchre in Jerusalem. It is topped by a statuette of the *Risen Christ*, superb in contrapposto and balancing precariously on a chalice. Pfeiffer explained the whole as a Dominican apologetic of the veneration due to the Holy Blood. A painted model for the ciborium survives (Siena, Pin. N.). In the highly detailed, signed bronze relief of the *Resurrection* (543×412 mm, 1472; New York, Frick), Vecchietta drew on his experiences as a painter. The piece is both too richly worked and too weighty to have served as a tabernacle door as is sometimes claimed.

Vecchietta's signed wood figures of *St Anthony Abbot* (dated 1475; *in situ*) and *St Bernardino of Siena* (Florence, Bargello) were both made for Narni Cathedral. While the latter is relatively restrained, the former, well over life-size, is at once brooding and familiar, a massive volumetric study like most of his late works.

In 1477 Vecchietta succeeded in his petition of the previous year to build a burial chapel to his own design for himself and his wife in S Maria della Scala, Siena. On the altar was placed the great bronze figure of the *Risen Christ* (see fig. 2), which now adorns the high altar of the church. Behind hung his panel of the *Virgin and Child with SS Peter, Paul, Lawrence and Francis* (Siena, Pin. N.), the two last being the name-saints of Vecchietta and his wife Francesca. It is remarkable that he signed the bronze as painter and the panel as sculptor, in a way that proclaims his mastery of both media and also their inter-reliance. Despite the damaged condition of the painting, the original splendour of the figures grouped harmoniously within their golden apse can still be estimated. Vecchietta's final commission (1480) was for painted wood reliefs of the *Death of the Virgin* and *Assumption of the Virgin* (Lucca, Villa Guinigi), but he lived to execute only the first, the *Assumption* being completed by Neroccio de' Landi. This is a final instance of how Vecchietta helped to mould two generations of Sienese artists, but his greatest legacies were the works for his own chapel. It has been noted that the unprecedented, life-size bronze figure must have lingered in Michelangelo's mind when he planned the *Risen Christ* in S Maria sopra Minerva, Rome.

BIBLIOGRAPHY

Thieme–Becker

G. Vasari: *Vite* (1550, rev. 2/1568); ed. G. Milanesi (1878–85), iii, pp. 69–81

G. Milanesi: *Documenti per la storia dell'arte senese*, 3 vols (Siena, 1854–6)

C. del Bravo: *Scultura senese del quattrocento* (Florence, 1970), pp. 60–91

H. W. van Os: *Vecchietta and the Sacristy of the Siena Hospital Church: A Study in Renaissance Religious Symbolism* (The Hague, 1974)

A. Pfeiffer: *Das Ciborium im Sieneser Dom: Untersuchungen zur Bronzeplastik Vecchiettas* (diss., Marburg, Philipps-U., 1975)

H. W. van Os: 'Vecchietta and Blessed Sorore: A Vexed Question in the Iconography of the Saints in Sienese Painting', *Festschrift Wolfgang Braunfels* (Tübingen, 1977), pp. 281–7

——: 'Vecchietta and the Persona of the Renaissance Artist', *Studies in Late Medieval and Renaissance Painting in Honor of Millard Meiss*, i (New York, 1977), pp. 445–54

P. Torriti: *La Pinacoteca Nazionale di Siena: I dipinti dal XII al XV secolo* (Genoa, 1977), pp. 351–63

I. Lavin: 'The Sculptor's "Last Will and Testament"', *Allen Mem. A. Mus. Bull.*, xxxv (1977–8), pp. 4–16

E. Carli: *Gli scultori senesi* (Milan, 1980), pp. 42–4, pls 264–82

Pienza e La Val d'Orcia: Opere d'arte restaurate dal XIV al XVII secolo (exh. cat., ed. A. Bagnoli and L. Martini; Pienza, Pal. Piccolomini, 1984), pp. 42–50

S. Hansen: *Die Loggia della Mercanzia in Siena* (Worms, 1987)

Scultura dipinta: Maestri di legname e pittori a Siena, 1250–1450 (exh. cat., ed. A. Bagnoli and R. Bartalini; Siena, Pin. N., 1987), pp. 172–80

C. Bertelli: 'La cappella del Palazzo Branda Castiglioni', *Arte in Lombardia tra gotico e rinascimento* (exh. cat., Milan, Pal. Reale, 1988), pp. 297–303

Painting in Renaissance Siena, 1420–1500 (exh. cat. by K. Christiansen and C. B. Strehlke, New York, Met., 1988), pp. 15–18, 258–63

Francesco di Georgio e il rinascimento a Siena, 1450–1500 (exh. cat., ed. L. Bellosi, Siena, Sant'Agostino, 1993)

JAMES DAVID DRAPER

2. Vecchietta: *Risen Christ*, bronze, h. 1.83 m, 1476 (Siena, S Maria della Scala)

Vecchietti, Bernardo (*b* Florence, 31 March 1514; *d* Florence, 20 Dec 1590). Italian patron and collector. His father, Giovanni di Bernardo Vecchietti, had enriched the family and bought a country seat, the Villa Il Riposo, near Florence. Bernardo's main claim to fame was his discovery of Giambologna. He was host to Giambologna for about 14 years (1552–66) and introduced him to Prince Francesco de' Medici. He played an important role in spreading an awareness of Giambologna's small bronzes, created first for Vecchietti himself and then for a large Florentine and international clientele; he also secured Medici commissions for the sculptor for monumental works in Florence.

Vecchietti embarked on his career as a diplomat under Cosimo I de' Medici, and made frequent visits to Venice (those of 1554–5 and 1557 are recorded), where he bought jewellery for the Medici court, and to Rome (1570), where he purchased several antiques. He acquired a specialist knowledge of jewellery, and played an increasingly prominent role as artistic adviser in the reign of Francesco I de' Medici, who in 1578 made him a senator. He organized the decoration of the cupola of Florence Cathedral, promoting Federico Zuccaro, to whom the commission was awarded in 1575. He was instrumental in the enrichment of Florence by monumental sculptures, among them Giambologna's *Rape of a Sabine* (1583; Florence, Loggia Lanzi; *see* GIAMBOLOGNA, fig. 2) and an equestrian statue of *Cosimo I de' Medici* (1587–93; Florence, Piazza della Signoria). He transformed the medieval family residence at 2 Via de' Vecchietti into a Renaissance palazzo (using Giambologna's designs from 1578), and enriched the Villa Il Riposo, where he employed Giambologna, Gregorio Pagani and, after 1584, Santi di Tito. He gave paintings to the family church of S Donato (destr.), and was granted the rights of patronage to a chapel in S Maria Novella, which was modernized (1575) by the Medici. This suggests the closeness of his relationship to the court, and his support for the Medici interest in the new religious art of the Counter-Reformation. In 1587, on the recommendation of Ferdinand I de' Medici, he organized the funeral of Francesco I.

At the Villa Il Riposo, Vecchietti created a rich art collection; Giambologna contributed to its development as a studio and museum from 1552 to 1566, and after 1584. The collection was rich in small sculptures. Vecchietti was particularly attracted by the sculptor's models and ensured the survival of a large number of Giambologna's sketch models in wax and clay (e.g. *Hercules and the Hydra*, c. 1579; Florence, Pal. Vecchio). He also had a collection of celebrated Old Master drawings, cartoons and pictures, among them a cartoon for Leonardo da Vinci's *Leda* (destr.) and Michelangelo's cartoon for the *Battle of Cascina* (destr.). Raffaele Borghini, in a dialogue entitled *Il riposo* (1584), described the collections and recorded the discussions on art that took place at the villa. The Villa Il Riposo was important in the history of collecting, and Borghini described not only its contents but also the didactic aims of its creator. Many of the sculptor's models were bought by William Locke of Norbury Park in the late 18th century, and were admired by English artists and collectors in the early 19th (for the later history of the Vecchietti collection, see Avery, 1987, p. 241).

BIBLIOGRAPHY

R. Borghini: *Il Riposo* (Florence, 1584); facs., ed. M. Rosci (Milan, 1967), 2 vols
S. Platt: *Villa Il Riposo: The Concept and the Reality*, Pius XII Institute, Rosary College, River Forest, IL (Oct 1968), p. 9
C. Avery: 'Bernardo Vecchietti and the Wax Models of Giambologna', *La Ceroplastica nella scienza e nell'arte: Atti del congresso internazionale: Firenze, 1975*, pp. 461–76
D. Heikamp: 'The Grotto of the Fata Morgana and Giambologna Marble Gorgon', *Ant. Viva*, xx (1981), pp. 12, 30, n. 2
A. Natali: 'Candior Animus', *Ant. Viva*, xx/4 (1981), pp. 22–31
M. Bury: 'Bernardo Vecchietti, Patron of Giambologna', *I Tatti Stud.*, i (1985), pp. 13–56
C. Avery: *Giambologna* (Oxford, 1987)

Z. WAŹBIŃSKI

Vecchio Bolognese, il. *See* AIMO, DOMENICO.

Vecellio. Italian family of artists. They came from Pieve di Cadore and can be traced back to the 13th century. The family, which included numerous notaries, magistrates and mayors, became wealthy and prominent locally. There were artists in two branches, one descended from Conte Vecellio, a notary who served as the town mayor, military leader and ambassador to Venice, and one from his brother Giovanni Antonio Vecellio (*d* 1497). The son of Conte Vecellio, Gregorio Vecellio (*c.* 1455–1530), who was a civic official in Cadore, had two sons who were painters. The elder, (1) Francesco Vecellio, trained as a painter in Venice, where the family name was linked with the timber trade. He was joined there by his younger brother Tiziano Vecellio (*see* TITIAN), who became the leading painter in Venice and one of the most important artists in Italy in the 16th century. Titian trained his second son, (2) Orazio Vecellio, who painted in his father's style. (3) Cesare Vecellio belonged to the branch of the family descended from Giovanni Antonio. He trained in Titian's workshop and remained there until the latter's death in 1576, when he began to work independently. His younger brother, Fabrizio Vecellio (*b* early 1520s), was also a painter. (4) Marco Vecellio, the son of Titian's second cousin, was a mediocre follower of the master's style, as was Marco's son Tiziano Vecellio, or 'Tizianello' (1570–1650), who wrote a biography of Titian (*La vita del insigne Tiziano Vecellio*, 1622). Tommaso Vecellio (1576–*c.* 1629), Marco's nephew, who worked in Pieve di Cadore, was another mediocre follower of Titian. Francesco, Cesare, Orazio and Marco were the family members allowed to use the appellation 'di Tiziano'. Titian's assistant GIROLAMO DENTI was also permitted to use this signature.

BIBLIOGRAPHY

G. Vasari: *Vite* (1550, rev. 2/1568); ed. G. Milanesi (1878–85)
S. Ticozzi: *Vite dei pittori Vecelli di Cadore* (Milan, 1817)
J. A. Crowe and G. B. Cavalcaselle: *Life and Times of Titian* (London, 1877, rev. 2/1881)
Mostra dei Vecellio (exh. cat. by F. Valcanover, Belluno, Mus. Civ., 1951)
R. Pallucchini: *Tiziano* (Florence, 1969)
G. Fabbiani: 'Artisti cadorini', *Archv Stor. Belluno, Feltre & Cadore*, 190 (1970)
F. Heinemann: 'La bottega di Tiziano', *Tiziano e Venezia. Atti del convegno: Venezia, 1976*
M. Roy Fisher: *Titian's Assistants During the Later Years* (New York and London, 1977)

(1) Francesco Vecellio (*b* Pieve di Cadore, 1475; *d* Pieve di Cadore, 1559–60). Painter. He trained in Venice in the workshop of Giovanni Bellini, whose influence is evident in the altarpiece he painted for Santa Croce, Belluno, the *Virgin and Child Enthroned with Saints* (Berlin). He served in the Venetian army *c.* 1508–9, and when he returned to painting he came under the influence of his brother Titian, with whom he began to collaborate on, for example, the frescoes (1511) in the Scuola di S Antonio in Padua and the polyptych of the *Virgin and Child Enthroned* (central panel, Sédico, parish church). The Sédico altarpiece may have been planned by Titian, but was certainly executed by Francesco and is his best work. He did not develop further artistically, however, and his later work continued to reflect Titian's early style, often with poorly assimilated influences from other artists. This conservative tendency is clear in his altarpiece of the *Virgin and Child Enthroned with Saints* (1524; S Vito di Cadore, parish church), with its echoes of Palma Vecchio. Even more regressive is the *Noli me tangere* (Oriago, S Maria Maddalena), derived from Jacopo Bassano. In his organ shutters (*c.* 1530) for S Salvatore, Venice (*Transfiguration, Resurrection, St Augustine, St Theodore*), he attempted, somewhat awkwardly, more dramatic compositions of a Mannerist type. He left Venice in 1534 to look after the family's affairs in Pieve di Cadore, where he continued to execute such modest local commissions as the *Virgin and Child Enthroned* (Venas di Cadore, parish church).

BIBLIOGRAPHY
G. Fiocco: 'Profilo di Francesco Vecellio', *A. Ven.*, vii (1953), pp. 39–44
F. Valcanover: 'Il polittico Vecelliano di Sédico', *Archv Stor. Belluno, Feltre & Cadore*, 130 (1955), pp. 25–31
M. Lucco: 'Francesco Vecellio', *Proposte di restauro* (Castelfranco, 1978), pp. 49–52, 119–20

(2) Orazio Vecellio (*b c.* 1515; *d* Venice, before 23 Nov 1576). Painter, nephew of (1) Francesco Vecellio. The second son of Titian, he trained in his father's workshop and accompanied him to Rome in 1545 and to Augsburg in 1548. Vasari mentioned him favourably, particularly his portrait of the musician *Battista Ceciliano* (untraced), executed in Rome. Other sources and his few surviving works suggest, however, that he was an inadequate painter, perhaps with a talent for adapting or copying his father's works, as in, for example, a *Venus and Adonis* (untraced). In the 1550s he painted the polyptych in S Andrea, Serravalle (Vittorio Veneto), representing the *Virgin and Child Enthroned with SS Andrew and Peter*, the *Annunciation*, and the *Coronation of the Virgin*. The *Assumption of the Virgin* in Sargnano parish church (Belluno) can also be ascribed to him, but the donor is a later addition. Titian held Orazio in high esteem, and in 1564, certainly owing to his father's influence, he competed successfully against Jacopo Tintoretto and Paolo Veronese for the commission to paint the *Battle of Castel Sant'Angelo* (destr. 1577) for the Sala del Gran Consiglio in the Doge's Palace in Venice. His limitations as a painter are obvious both in the congested altarpiece (*c.* 1559) in the church at Sorisole (Bergamo) and in the reliquary shutters in S Biagio, Calàlzo (Belluno), painted in 1566, which are stiff compositions, probably adapted from models by Titian and Jacopo Bassano. Works executed in collaboration with his father include the large *Flight from Egypt* (St Petersburg, Hermitage) and the *Mystic Marriage of St Catherine* (London, Hampton Court, Royal Col.).

BIBLIOGRAPHY
G. Vasari: *Vite* (1550, rev. 2/1568); ed. G. Milanesi (1878–85), vi, p. 588
G. Cadorin: *Dello amore ai veneziani di Tiziano Vecellio* (Venice, 1833)
J. A. Crowe and G. B. Cavalcaselle: *Life and Times of Titian* (London, 1877, rev. 2/1881)

(3) Cesare Vecellio (*b* Pieve di Cadore, 1521; *d* Venice, 2 March 1601). Painter and engraver, relative of (1) Francesco Vecellio. He was also a distant relation of Titian. Probably after training in Cadore with Francesco, he joined Titian's workshop in Venice. He travelled with Titian, visiting Augsburg in 1548, and remained in the shop until Titian's death in 1576. His independent works showed great decorative skill, particularly his scenes from the *Life of the Virgin* (1577) and the *Deposition*, both for S Maria Assunta, Lentiai (Belluno; *in situ*). In these paintings, he seemed to turn away from Titian and to look towards the work of Andrea Schiavone and Jacopo Tintoretto. Apart from occasional visits to Venice, he was active mainly in Cadore and Belluno, where he decorated a room in the Palazzo Piloni with the *Four Seasons*. Probably his most successful work in terms of style and the use of colour is the altarpiece of the *Virgin and Child with SS Sebastian and Gregory the Great, and Giovanni Loredan* (1584; Belluno Cathedral). Here, with his usual Mannerist themes, he demonstrated an unusual awareness of the real world, both in his use of light and in the disposition and depiction of figures. His gift for portraiture is also shown in other works, such as the altarpieces in Tarzo (Treviso) and Borgo Valsugana (Trento), in which the naturalistic effects are worthy of Leandro Bassano at his best. For the parish church of Pieve di Cadore he executed an important painting, the *Surrender of Cadore to Venice* (1599). He also painted the shutters of the old organ there (*St Peter, St Paul*, the *Annunciation*) and a lavish, but lifeless altarpiece of the *Last Supper*, which is dominated by a background of classical architecture inspired by Andrea Palladio. Many other works are in churches of the Cadore region and there is a *Trinity* in Milan (Brera). Cesare also worked as an engraver, producing, for example, the *Adoration of the Name of Jesus* (*c.* 1575). He published the first illustrated costume book, *De gli habiti antichi et moderni di diverse parti del mondo* (Venice, 1590), with 450 woodcuts by Cristoforo Guerra, based on drawings by Vecellio (*see* FASHION PLATE AND COSTUME BOOK). The edition of 1598 has 503 prints, but there are fewer illustrations in later editions (Madrid, 1794; Paris, 1856–9). He also published a book on embroidery and lacemaking, the *Corona delle nobili et virtuose donne* (Venice, 1591), which was reissued in many editions, as late as 1891.

BIBLIOGRAPHY
F. Vergerio: *La chiesa monumentale di Santa Maria di Lentiai* (Alassio, 1931)
L. Alpago Novello: *Gli incisori bellunesi* (Venice, 1939–40)
G. Fiocco: 'Note su Cesare Vecellio', *Lettere ed arti* (1946)
F. Valcanover: *Le venti tavole del soffitto di S. M. Assunta di Lentiai di Cesare Vecellio* (Belluno, 1956)
M. Lucco: 'Cesare Vecellio', *Arte del '600 nel Bellunese* (Padua, 1981)

(4) Marco Vecellio (*b* Pieve di Cadore, 1545; *d* Venice, 1611). Painter, relative of (3) Cesare Vecellio. He too was distantly related to Titian and worked in his shop in Venice. He gained Titian's respect and permission to use the denomination 'di Tiziano' with which he signed his numerous works after Titian's death in 1576. In 1566, using cartoons by Titian, he collaborated with Girolamo Denti and Emanuele d'Augusta on the frescoes of the *Life of the Virgin and Christ* (destr.) in the arch-diaconal church of Pieve di Cadore. Until *c.* 1600 he was active chiefly in Cadore and the Veneto, producing repetitive works in dull, monotonous colours in a debased version of Titian's style. It is unlikely, therefore, that he painted the colourful and lively polyptych at SS Addolorata, Pieve di Zoldo, which has been attributed to him. He was on good terms with Doge Leonardo Donà (*reg* 1606–12), and in the early 17th century he executed many works in important Venetian churches (e.g. the *Annunciation*, S Giacomo a Rialto), and the votive painting of *Doge Donà* (S Giovanni Elemosinaro). For the Doge's Palace, Venice, he painted vast canvases including *Pope Clement VII and the Emperor Charles V* in the Sala del Consiglio dei Dieci, the *Masters of the Mint* in the Sala del Senato, the *Virgin and Child with St Mark and Doge Donà* in the Sala della Bussola, and the *Naval Battle at Cape Maleo* in the Sala dello Scrutinio. He also executed a series of portraits of members of the Querini family (Venice, Fond. Querini-Stampalia).

BIBLIOGRAPHY

M. Boschini: *Le minere della pittura veneziana* (Venice, 1664)

D. M. Federici: *Memorie trevigiane sulle opere di disegno* (Venice, 1803)

M. Dazzi and E. Merkel: *Catalogo della Fondazione Scientifica Querini-Stampalia* (Venice, 1979)

SERGIO CLAUT

Vecsei [née Hollo], **Eva** (*b* Vienna, 21 Aug 1930). Canadian architect of Hungarian descent. She studied architecture at the University of Technical Sciences, Budapest, and was an assistant professor at the School of Architecture there in 1952–3. She was involved with housing projects in Hungary before she and her husband, architect Andrew Vecsei, went to Montreal in the aftermath of the Hungarian uprising of 1956. She became a naturalized Canadian citizen in 1962. Vecsei was involved in some of the largest developments of the period in Montreal. From 1964 to 1970 she was an associate with the firm Affleck, Desbarats, Dimakopoulos, Lebengold, Sise, where she was a designer on the Place Bonaventure (1964–8). This huge multi-use complex, which covers six acres in eastern downtown Montreal, is constructed in a largely Modernist idiom; its appearance is stark and cubical, yet it has a monumental presence. A more complex articulation characterizes the seven-acre complex La Cité (1973–7), Montreal, Vecsei's first project as head of her own firm (from 1973). Built in a climate of hostility to high-rise developments and, at times, daunting financial constraints (which made it necessary to redesign the project several times), Vecsei successfully integrated a network of high-rise buildings (three apartment blocks, an office tower and hotel) and underground structures (shops, restaurants and circulation areas). The L-shaped apartment towers rise gradually in steps away from the street that divides them, responding to the scale of the surrounding churches and rows of town houses. Vecsei believed in the intellectual integrity of Modernist architecture—its focus on geometry, simplicity and repetition and its harmony of structure, plan and materials—yet felt that these could lead to a bland lack of creativity and inventiveness. She therefore advocated bold surface treatment and the use of decoration, and this approach distinguishes La Cité from Place Bonaventure.

BIBLIOGRAPHY

Contemp. Architects

Z. Kosa: *History of Modern Architecture* (Budapest, 1975)

M. F. Schmertz: 'La Cité', *Archit. Rec.*, clxiii/1 (1978), pp. 111–16

WALTER SMITH

Vedat [Vedat Bey; Vedat Tek] (*b* Istanbul, 1873; *d* Istanbul, 1942). Turkish architect and teacher. After completing his secondary education at the Ecole Nonge in Paris, he studied painting at the Académie Julian and civil engineering at the Ecole Centrale, and then trained as an architect at the Ecole des Beaux-Arts, completing his studies in 1897. On returning to Istanbul in 1899, he was employed by the Municipality, becoming chairman of the Supervising Committee for Public Works and later the chief architect. In 1900 he also became the first Turk to teach architectural history at the Fine Arts Academy in Istanbul. Like his contemporary, Kemalettin Bey, he played an important role in the development of a revivalist Turkish idiom in architecture, known as the First National Architectural Style. Vedat's first major work, the Central Post Office (1909) in Sirkeci, Istanbul, employed such features of traditional Ottoman architecture as depressed or pointed arches and glazed tiles (*see* ISLAMIC ART, §II, 7(i)) and had a small mosque attached to the rear of the building in the revivalist style. The general massing of the building, however, including the use of semi-circular pilasters with Corinthian capitals at the upper levels and the large central hall with an iron and glass roof, derived from Vedat's Beaux-Arts training. At about the same time he designed the Imperial Offices of the Land Registry, a large building on the Atmeydan in Istanbul that combined a similar mixture of features. In 1923, when Ankara became the capital of the new Turkish republic, Vedat was recruited from Istanbul to build two important buildings: the new National Assembly (1924), a symmetrical two-storey rectangular building with exterior rubble walls of pink-coloured local stone, and the Ankara Palace Hotel, begun in 1924 and completed by Kemalettin Bey in 1927.

BIBLIOGRAPHY

S. Özkan: 'Mimar Vedat Tek, 1873–1942', *Mimarlık*, xi–xii (1973), pp. 45–51

R. Holod and A. Evin, eds: *Modern Turkish Architecture* (Philadelphia, 1984), pp. 12–15, 41–5, 53–8

S. J. VERNOIT

Vedder, Elihu (*b* New York, 26 Feb 1836; *d* Rome, 29 Jan 1923). American painter, illustrator, sculptor and writer. He studied under Tompkins Harrison Matteson in Shelbourne, NY, and went to Paris in March 1856. After eight months in the studio of François-Edouard Picot, he settled in Florence until the end of 1860. There he learnt drawing from Raffaello Bonaiuti, became interested in the Florentine Renaissance and attended the free Accademia Galli. A more significant artistic inspiration came from the Italian artists at the Caffè Michelangiolo: Telemaco Signorini, Vincenzo Cabianca (1827–1902) and especially Nino Costa (1827–1902). This group sought new and untraditional pictorial solutions for their compositions and *plein-air* landscapes and were particularly interested in the experiences of Gustave Courbet and the Barbizon painters. They became known as Macchiaioli for their use of splashes (*macchia*) of light and shadows and for their revolutionary (*maquis*) attitude to prevailing styles. Among Vedder's most notable Florentine landscapes are *Mugnone Torrent near Fiesole* (Detroit, MI, Inst. A.) and *Le Balze, Volterra* (Washington, DC, N. Mus. Amer. A.); he also made many sketches, drawings and pastels of the Tyrrhenian coast, Lake Trasimene, the Roman Campagna, Egypt and Capri, which exemplify the realistic approach to landscape practised by the artists of the Macchiaioli.

Vedder returned to New York and supported himself during the American Civil War (1861–5) as an illustrator for *Vanity Fair* and *Leslie's Illustrated News*. He also began painting such works as the *Questioner of the Sphinx* (1863; Boston, MA, Mus. F.A.), the *Lair of the Sea Serpent* (1864; Boston, MA, Mus. F.A.) and the *Lost Mind* (1864–5; New York, Met.), which evoke a melancholy atmosphere that presages European Symbolism. In 1865 he returned to Paris and joined William Morris Hunt and Charles Caryl Coleman (1840–1928) for painting in Brittany in the summer. After another visit to Rome in 1866, Vedder returned to New York in 1868, where he sold his landscape and genre paintings to Boston patrons and married Caroline Rosekrans who settled with him in Rome in October 1869. His works of this period include the tiny drawings of the *Soul of the Sunflower* (1868; priv. col., see exh. cat., fig. 142) and the *Sea Princess* (1868; priv. col., see exh. cat., fig. 143). A visit to London in 1870 resulted in contact with the Pre-Raphaelites and other English artists. Works such as the *Cumaean Sibyl* (1876; Detroit, MI, Inst. A.), *Greek Girls Bathing* (1877; New York, Met.) and *Head of Medusa* (1878; San Diego, CA, Mus. A.; see fig.) reveal the classical subject-matter and stylistic linearity more commonly associated with Edward Burne-Jones, Frederic Leighton and Lawrence Alma-Tadema.

During the 1880s Vedder returned almost every year to America, where he was active in the decorative arts, designing stained-glass windows for Louis Comfort Tiffany and illustrating five covers for *The Century Illustrated* (1881). His 56 drawings for Edward FitzGerald's translation of *The Rubáiyát of Omar Khayyám* (Washington, DC, N. Mus. Amer. A.) are some of the earliest examples of Art Nouveau in America, and this edition (pubd 1884) opened an era in American art publishing; these drawings also inspired Vedder to paint such works as the *Cup of Death* (1881; Washington, DC, N. Mus. Amer. A.) and *The Pleiads* (1885; New York, Met.). At the turn of the century he received many important commissions for mural painting, including those for the Walker Art Building (1892) at Bowdoin College, Brunswick, ME, Collis P. Huntington's dining-room (1893; New York) and the five panels *Government* (1896–7; Washington, DC, Lib. Congr.). He also produced designs for small sculptural objects, including bell-pulls and door-knockers. His only large-scale work was *The Boy* (1900–02; Chicago, IL, A. Inst.), a fountain cast in bronze by Charles Keck.

After 1900 Vedder painted little, spending many months at his villa in Capri and writing his humorous, whimsical autobiography, *The Digressions of 'V'* (Boston, 1910), as well as two volumes of verse. Edgar P. Richardson compared Vedder's art to a visit to the Etruscan museum in the Villa Giulia, Rome, where, bursting through the cold order of Roman art is a weird and haunting imagination, a fantastic invention that disconcerts and fascinates (see Soria, 1970, p. 6).

BIBLIOGRAPHY

R. Soria: *Elihu Vedder: American Visionary Artist in Rome (1836–1923)*, intro. E. P. Richardson (Cranbury, NJ, 1970)

Elihu Vedder: *Head of Medusa*, oil on paper attached to canvas, 282×304 mm, 1878 (San Diego, CA, San Diego Museum of Art)

Perceptions and Evocations: The Art of Elihu Vedder (exh. cat., Washington, N. Mus. Amer. A., 1979)

R. Soria: *Dictionary of Nineteenth-century American Artists in Italy, 1760–1914* (Cranbury, NJ, 1982)

REGINA SORIA

Vedisā. *See* BESNAGAR.

Vedova, Emilio (*b* Venice, 9 Aug 1919). Italian painter and printmaker. He was the son of an artisan and was essentially self-taught as an artist. In his early drawings, inspired by Venetian churches, for example *San Moisè* (1937–8; artist's col., see Schulz-Hoffmann and others, fig. 1), the artist investigated the dynamics of space, concentrating his attention on bands of lines and coagulated structures; in his studies based on the work of Old Masters, for example *Moses Making Water Spring from the Rock (after Tintoretto)* (1942; Florence, Col. della Ragione), the figures are intended to be energy nuclei in their own right or in virtual expansion. It is above all in his encounter with the dense colour of Georges Rouault and Maurice de Vlaminck, however, that he expanded the neo-Baroque quality of his works into new imaginary realms.

Vedova participated in the activities of the CORRENTE group in 1942 and signed the manifesto 'Oltre Guernica' in May 1946 and that of the FRONTE NUOVO DELLE ARTI in October 1946; he was also a member of Fronte's successor, the GRUPPO DEGLI OTTO PITTORI ITALIANI. These groups adopted an anti-19th-century style of painting that rejected aesthetic indulgence and demanded the spectator's participation. Inspired by the moral and aesthetic position expressed in Picasso's *Guernica* (Madrid, Prado), Vedova attempted to remain faithful to the sense of disinterested moral involvement that he regarded as the basis of each work of art. He reposed the geometric strictness of Cubism in modern terms and tempered its tonal harshness with a sense of emotional involvement. The painting style developed by Vedova required the will to experiment and a great expenditure of physical energy. It is, therefore, no coincidence that his early studies give the impression of feverishness or convulsion.

From 1948 Vedova began producing series that are either dynamic themselves or structured to exploit the dynamic qualities of light, including the *Cycles of Nature* (e.g. *Cycle of Nature No. 3, Palmaria*; Utrecht, W. Hoogendijk priv. col.), *Cycles of Protest* (e.g. *Cycle of Protest 1958 No. 1*, ex-Hamburg, Gal. Neuendorf) and *Clashes of Circumstances* (e.g. *Clash of Circumstances '59– 1*, ex-Hamburg, Gal. Neuendorf). In 1959 he created large polyptychs, sometimes asymmetrical and L-shaped, consisting of a number of works on the same theme, for example the series *Clashes of Circumstances*, which filled one room at the exhibition *Vitalità nell'arte* in the Palazzo Grassi in Venice. In 1961 he designed the setting and costumes for Luigi Nono's *Intolleranza '60*, staged at the Teatro La Fenice in Venice: it was a triumphant display of the possibilities of light, an example of the 'theatre of harsh realities' involving the spectators. In the same year Vedova began his series of *Multiples*, paintings with a new type of structure, constructed on different levels and interlocking planes and offering a wide variety of visual possibilities. Here he strove to identify painting, theatrical space and spectator: the dynamic space is unpredictable, aggressive and stimulating, and the spectator experiences the figurative process in an onslaught of alarming signals, appeals and symbols. This investigation, which relies ever more heavily on a discourse between the spectator and the artist's 'presence' in the work, evolved in the reliefs initiated in 1963 (e.g. *Berlin 1939*, 1964; artist's col., see Schulz-Hoffmann and others, fig. 30) and the massive *Space-multiple-light* (53×24×16 m, 1965; shown at *Expo 67* in Montreal, see Schulz-Hoffmann and others, pp. 66–7 and 70–74), in which sophisticated projectors and electronic instruments created unusual effects with moving, superimposed and continuous light. This complex structure was followed by other cycles of works with the same or similar titles, including *Lacerations* (1975–8; e.g. *Lacerations Cycle 77/78 – 2 – Binary 4*, 1977–8; artist's col., see Schulz-Hoffmann and others, pp. 74–5), the monochrome series *De America* (1976; e.g. *De America '76– 1*; artist's col., see Schulz-Hoffmann and others, p. 78) and the polyptychs *Co-presences* (1977–83; e.g. *Cycle '81 – Co-presences – 6 –*, 1981; artist's col., see Schulz-Hoffmann and others, p. 56) and *Registrations* (1977–83; e.g. *Registration '81 – 5*, 1981; artist's col., see Schulz-Hoffmann and others, p. 55). His series of *Multiples* were groups of works created using the most diverse techniques, placed in spatial relationships on platforms (*Binaries*) of wood and steel, sometimes enhanced by monotone electronic sounds, as in *Venezia Revenice* (1978; exh. Venice, Pal. Grassi, 1978). Among his most important creations during the 1980s were the light effects for Luigi Nono's *Prometheus* (Venice, Teat. La Fenice, 1984), which represented the sum of Vedova's experiences, and his *Disks* (1985; exh. Madrid, Caja Pensiones, see Schulz-Hoffmann and others, pp. 8–16), pictorial complexes in round or oval form, presented from several viewpoints (vertical,

suspended, slanting, touching etc), which display an original reappropriation of space and can produce a sense of vertigo.

In his later creations Vedova continued to pursue his investigations into physical space independently of any prejudged attitudes towards balance, logic and behaviour; awareness of man's destiny and of his tendency to break rules also shows itself in his contributions to various discussions and international debates. By making use of the latest technological materials and discoveries, Vedova appears to be attempting a 'total art' dreamt of by the Futurists in 1913, with the difference that his spectacular, centralized creations are not a hymn to modern times, but rather a confirmation of the feelings of alarm and distress that pervade contemporary society. Criticism of this Abstract Expressionist work has emphasized the emotional aspect, but it is always sustained by strict formal considerations.

BIBLIOGRAPHY

G. Marchiori: *Emilio Vedova* (Venice, 1951)
W. Haftmann: *Malerei im 20. Jahrhundert* (Munich, 1954)
M. Brion: *Art abstrait* (Paris, 1956)
W. Haftmann: *Emilio Vedova* (Munich, 1960)
M. Tapié: *Morphologie autre* (Turin, 1960)
G. C. Argan and M. Calvesi: *Vedova: Compresenze, 1946–1981* (Milan, 1981)
G. Celant: 'Gli artisti nel loro studio', *Vogue Italia Speciale*, 10 (1985)
M. Wechsler: 'Emilio Vedova', *Wolkenkratzer A. J.* (1985)
C. Schulz-Hoffmann and others: *Emilio Vedova* (Munich, 1986)

PIERO PACINI

Veduta [It.: 'view']. Term applied to a painting, drawing or print representing a landscape or town view that is largely topographical in conception, as opposed to the fantasy view or CAPRICCIO. Artists who produced *vedute* are known as *vedutisti*. The *veduta* or souvenir view, with its origins in pilgrimage images of Rome from the later 16th century onwards, reached its peak as a genre in Italy during the era of the GRAND TOUR. Benefiting from such technical aids as the CAMERA OBSCURA, particularly at the hand of Canaletto in Venice, it was also to reflect an increasing concern with the specifics of the observed natural world characteristic of the Enlightenment. During the latter half of the 18th century, with the revolutionary vision of Piranesi in Rome, the *veduta* was transformed into a vehicle for emotional responses to the visible world, especially of the surviving remains of antiquity. In this respect it contributed to the emergence of Romanticism in the visual arts and was finally extinguished as a significant art form with the invention of photography.

For a discussion of the *veduta* in the context of related art forms *see* ARCHITECTURAL PICTURES, §§2 and 3; TOWNSCAPE; and URBAN LIFE.

1. Development and peak. 2. Decline.

1. DEVELOPMENT AND PEAK.

(i) Venice. (ii) Rome.

(i) Venice. Venice, that most densely urban of environments, was the birthplace of the *veduta* and home of its main innovators. The city, with its intensely introspective character, had a long tradition of self-scrutiny, as manifested in topographical incidents within the religious pictures of the Bellini family and Vittore Carpaccio, as

well as in the backgrounds of early Renaissance portraits. While during the 16th and 17th centuries Rome had seen the production of engraved souvenir views of the pilgrimage sites and prominent monuments by Antoine Lafrery, Alessandro Specchi and Giovanni Battista Falda, the first important advances in the genre appeared in Venice, where there was a demand for recording state ceremonies and festivals.

Significantly, the earliest *vedutisti* in Venice came from northern Europe, with its long-standing preoccupations with observed fact in painting stretching back to 15th-century Flemish art. At a time when native Venetian painting was at a low ebb in the early 17th century, the first view painters there included Joseph Heintz (ii) from Germany and Gustav Richter (1665–1745) from Sweden. Heintz, active in Venice by 1625, concentrated on documenting festivals, such as that shown in his picture of the Patriarch's procession to S Pietro di Castello (Venice, Correr), with its frenzied plethora of doll-like figures and accumulated incidents. An artist of far higher calibre, however, was Gaspar van Wittel (Vanvitelli), who had arrived from Rome by 1697, the date of a *veduta* of Venice, now in the Prado, Madrid. As the true founder of the school of *vedutisti* in Venice, Vanvitelli's influence is seen in the work of the first native view painter, Luca Carlevaris. Although born in Udine, the son of an architect, he made Venice his adopted city and it provided the setting for a number of ambitious paintings recording ceremonies and state functions with a panoramic range of detail. His sizeable canvas recording the ambassadorial procession of Charles Montagu, 4th Earl of Manchester, before the Palazzo Ducale in 1707 (for illustration *see* CARLEVARIS, LUCA) was painted for this patron, who took it back to his Northamptonshire seat, Kimbolton Castle. Surviving oil sketches of genre detail and a sketchbook of figure studies (London, V&A) indicate the fastidious care taken by Carlevaris to construct these elaborate anthologies of civic ritual. Other such works recorded the regatta in honour of Frederick IV of Denmark (1707) and the Imperial embassy of Count Colloredo (1727), both of which were engraved. In 1703 when Carlevaris published a book of etched views expressly, as its title page indicates, to celebrate the splendours of the Venetian Republic, he created prototypes, if rather mechanical in style, for a range of graphic *vedute*. These mass-produced works were to make the genre both attractively commercial as well as widely diffused in the growing Grand Tour market.

The career and prolific output of Canaletto over some four decades of activity, however much according to legend it eclipsed the work of Carlevaris, are part of a far larger phenomenon as the Grand Tour reached its peak of demand for 'ricordi' during the middle decades of the 18th century. Patronage by the 'milordi inglesi' was to make the *veduta* the most popular contemporary art form next to the commemorative portrait, while the genre spread to other key centres such as Rome, Florence and Naples. Canaletto met the demand with skills of an exceptional order, grounded in his early training in stage design, and an entrepreneurial capacity to use formula compositions (assisted by annotated record drawings on site) and an increasing studio assistance.

A key factor in the success of Canaletto and the *veduta* market in Venice was the patronage of the businessman and later British Consul Joseph Smith. During the 1720s and 1730s Smith not only acted as an intermediary but himself commissioned works, including 12 outstanding paintings of the Grand Canal. These works, including the *Grand Canal from the Salute towards the Carità* (*see* TOWNSCAPE, fig. 2), were to enter the British royal collection when Smith sold his pick of Canalettos to George III in 1762. Such masterpieces of precise observation were highly contrived to include the maximum of information. Canaletto exploited the devices of theatrical perspective and the services of the camera obscura to compress a formidable quantity of topographical detail into a setting that was also filled with enlivening genre detail and acutely perceived effects of light on a range of building materials. Perhaps never before had specific architecture been so accurately depicted, so much so that historians of Venice can still date the minutiae of urban change from these visual documents. The scale of Canaletto's production for a single client is demonstrated by an entire room of 22 companion views of Venice at Woburn Abbey, Beds, produced for John Russell, 4th Duke of Bedford (1710–71), sometime after 1732. This fashion of devoting a room arrangement to displaying *vedute* from the Grand Tour is paralleled on a more modest level in the Cabinet at Felbrigg Hall, Norfolk, with its original hang of 26 gouache views by Giovanni Battista Busiri, bought in Rome around 1739–40 by William Windham (1717–61).

In 1735, with Smith's encouragement, Canaletto published a collection of his 12 views of the Grand Canal, as well as two festival compositions, engraved by Antonio Visentini, as *Prospectos magni canalis venetiarum* (a second edition with 24 additional *vedute* appeared in 1742). These works exercised a considerable influence on the demand for and standards of engraved *vedute* elsewhere. Around 1744 Canaletto issued a sequence of his own etchings, dedicated in homage to Smith, not only incorporating subjects on the River Brenta but also fantasy views, or '*vedute ideate*', which served to raise the *veduta* formula to a higher imaginative level (*see* CAPRICCIO). Owing to a decline in the tourist market during the War of the Austrian Succession, from 1746 Canaletto spent some ten years in England, based mainly in London. There his topographical paintings included a pair of superlative *vedute* of the Thames and of Whitehall respectively, as seen from Richmond House, commissioned in 1747 for Charles Lennox, 2nd Duke of Richmond (now at Goodwood House, W. Sussex). These and a selection of views of London and such stately homes as Badminton House, Glos, and Alnwick Castle, Northumb., exercised an important influence on English topographical art, as exemplified by such artists as Samuel Scott (e.g. *An Arch of Westminster Bridge*; for illustration *see* SCOTT, SAMUEL) and William Marlow (e.g. *Capriccio: St Paul's and a Venetian Canal*, London, Tate).

While Canaletto's ambitious commemorative *vedute*, epitomized by the '*Bucintoro' Returning to the Molo on Ascension Day* (versions, Milan, Crespi Col., and Windsor Castle, Berks, Royal Col.; see fig. 1) were never surpassed, recognition of the *veduta* as a genre in the academic hierarchy was slow. It was not until 1763 that Canaletto

1. Canaletto: *'Bucintoro' Returning to the Molo on Ascension Day*, oil on canvas, 0.76×1.17 m, 1730 (Windsor Castle, Berks, Royal Collection)

was admitted to the Venetian Accademia, and even then his reception piece was an architectural capriccio (Venice, Accademia). By that time the *veduta* in Venice had such outstanding exponents as the tragically short-lived Michele Giovanni Marieschi (who published a series of 21 etched *vedute* of Venice in 1741) and Canaletto's nephew Bernardo Bellotto. The latter left Venice at the age of 27, carrying the art form to northern Europe. He was based at Dresden from 1747 as painter to Frederick Augustus II. There he painted such *vedute* as *Dresden from the Right Bank of the Elbe* (1748; *see* BELLOTTO, BERNARDO, fig. 1). From Dresden he visited and recorded Vienna and Munich before settling in Poland in 1767, where he worked for the remainder of his life in Warsaw for King Stanislas II Augustus Poniatowski.

The career and output as a *vedutista* of Francesco Guardi, in marked contrast to Bellotto's stylistic dependence on his uncle, was from the early 1760s to invest the *veduta* with a greater interpretative range of expression. Never as popular as Canaletto with visitors to Venice, his name was rarely mentioned in contemporary accounts despite 30 years as a *vedutista*. For him topography in terms of record took second place to the aim of evoking atmosphere, so that the frenetic and animated figurative detail in, for example, his view of the *Piazza S Marco* (*see* GUARDI, (2), fig. 2) virtually takes priority over the architecture as subject-matter. Significantly, it was the later 19th-century collectors who relished the vibrancy of brushstroke and vivacity of subject-matter in Guardi's canvases (understandably, the capriccio became his ideal outlet for expression). This belated recognition of his genius is demonstrated by four major works in the Wallace Collection, London, and two complementary views of the

Basin of S Marco on an exceptionally large scale in the Rothschild Bequest at Waddesdon Manor, Bucks.

(ii) Rome. In Rome during the 18th century an equally avid need for *vedute* as that in Venice had developed from a long-standing tradition of pilgrimage souvenirs and topographical works, from Lafrery and Etienne Dupérac in the 16th century to Falda in the 17th and Specchi in the early 18th. As with Venice, the presence in Rome towards the end of the 17th century of such northern artists as Jacob de Heusch (1656–1701), Hendrik Frans van Lint (1684–1763), Jan Frans van Bloemen and, above all, Gaspar van Wittel (Vanvitelli), laid the foundations of a local school of *vedutisti*. Van Wittel, born and trained in Holland, was working in Rome by the Jubilee of 1675 and produced dated *vedute* in 1681 (e.g. Rome, Pal. Barberini and Pal. Colonna; *see* WITTEL, GASPAR VAN). Apart from his influential visit to Venice in or just before 1697 and one to Naples in 1700, he was active in Rome until *c.* 1730. Thomas Coke, the future 1st Earl of Leicester and builder of Holkham Hall, Norfolk, acquired at least seven views from van Wittel during his Grand Tour in 1715/16 (including one of *Venice from the Bacino*), still in the Holkham collection.

The most important Italian artist to take these developments further in Rome and to dominate the Grand Tour market for the painted *veduta* was the Emilian decorative painter Giovanni Paolo Panini. Apart from a considerable quantity of views commissioned by foreign visitors, including *Interior of St Peter's* (London, N.G.), Panini showed outstanding ability to record ceremonial events incorporating portraits and lively genre incidents.

Major commissions were received from the French ambassador to the Holy See, Cardinal Melchior de Polignac, in 1729–30, representing the festival in Piazza Navona commemorating the birth of the Dauphin, son of Louis XV (*see* PANINI, GIOVANNI PAOLO, fig. 2), and the Cardinal's visit to St Peter's (both Paris, Louvre). Panini's early training in stage design furnished him, like Canaletto, with advanced skills in perspective that made his panoramic views particularly attractive to patrons who required their Roman experiences to be compressed into a single canvas, often incorporated, back in England, into a decorative setting such as an overmantel. Not surprisingly, Panini's greatest achievements were to be spectacular *vedute ideate*, cappricci rather than *vedute*, in which individual works of architecture (and sculpture) were accurately delineated within an imaginary setting. Paralleling Panini's pictorial output in the field of engraved views was the work of the Sicilian Giuseppe Vasi, who between 1747 and 1760 published the main sights of the city in a sequence of 250 plates gathered together in the 10 books of his *Delle magnificenze di Roma antica e moderna*. Apart from several ambitious large-scale plates of the interior of St Peter's and of the Aventine Hill during the 1770s, Vasi's greatest achievement was a magisterial engraved panorama of the Eternal City from the Janiculum (*Prospetto dell'alma città di Roma*) issued in 1765 that measures 1.00×2.56 m (e.g. London, RIBA and BM).

Almost certainly assisting Vasi in the early stages of his panoramic *veduta* was Giovanni Battista Piranesi, the artist who was to transform the engraved view from a tourist souvenir into a sophisticated vehicle for scholarly communication and highly charged emotional responses. Piranesi's collection of early *vedute*, produced as small illustrations for guidebooks shortly after his arrival from Venice in the 1740s, proved a test-bed for daring experiments with the genre. Apart from his training in architecture, engineering and stage design, he pushed the medium of topographical etching to a pitch whereby effects of light and atmosphere invested the engraved view with new levels of meaning. By 1747 he was ready to adapt these ideas to a far larger format of plate in his celebrated series the *Vedute di Roma*. Over the next 30 years until his death in 1778, he produced individually or in groups some 135 plates (including two frontispieces) surveying the main ancient and modern monuments of Rome and its environs. Since these images reflected Piranesi's current preoccupations, the plates produced during the heat of the Greco-Roman quarrel in the 1760s, such as that of the *Basilica of Maxentius* (see fig. 2), use the full rhetoric of exaggerated scale and histrionic lighting to defend the engineering prowess of imperial Rome against its Philhellene detractors. Owing to Piranesi's acute business sense and his organization of an efficient printmaking establishment, the rapid diffusion of these powerful images acquired by visitors to Rome spread an indelible impression of 'Romanità' that has not diminished with time. The powerful impact of these plates still stands out on the walls of surviving 18th-century print rooms devised in country

2. Giovanni Battista Piranesi: *Basilica of Maxentius*, etching, 485×705 mm, *c.* 1775; from his series *Vedute di Roma* (Rome, *c.* 1748–78)

houses to accommodate the graphic souvenirs of the Grand Tour, such as those at Woodhall Park, Herts, and Blickling Hall, Norfolk.

2. DECLINE. The legacy of Canaletto, Panini and Piranesi as outstanding exponents of the *veduta* continued into the early 19th century—in Venice with such painters as Giovanni Migliara, in Rome with the topographical engraver Luigi Rossini (1790–1857) and in Naples with the German painter Philipp Hackert. By then the decline of the Grand Tour and the rise of Romanticism, when interpretation rather than depiction began to transform topography into a more personal vision, gradually rendered the *veduta* obsolescent. Such was the mood expressed by the Swiss painter Henry Fuseli in a lecture to students of the Royal Academy in London, when he referred to the genre as 'that last branch of uninteresting subjects, that kind of landscape which is entirely occupied with the tame delineation of a given spot' (*Lecture IV on Painting*, London, 1805, p. 217). It remained for the invention of the camera to deliver the coup de grâce to the *veduta*.

BIBLIOGRAPHY

K. T. Parker: *The Drawings of Canaletto at Windsor Castle* (London, 1948)
J. Byam Shaw: *The Drawings of Francesco Guardi* (London, 1951)
M. Pittaluga: *Acquafortisti veneziani del settecento* (Florence, 1953)
E. K. Waterhouse: *Painting in Britain, 1530–1790*, Pelican Hist A. (Harmondsworth, 1953, rev. 4/1978)
Paesisti e vedutisti a Roma nel '600 e nel '700 (exh. cat. by N. di Carpegna, Rome, Pal. Barberini, 1956)
M. Levey: *Painting in 18th-century Venice* (London, 1959, rev. 1980)
F. Arisi: *Giovanni Paolo Pannini* (Piacenza, 1961)
W. G. Constable: *Canaletto, Giovanni Antonio Canal*, 2 vols (Oxford, 1962); ed. J. G. Links (Oxford, 1989)
G. Briganti: *Gaspar van Wittel e l'origine della veduta settecentesca romana* (Rome, 1966)
Vedutisti veneziani del settecento (exh. cat. by P. Zampetti, Venice, Accad., 1967)
A. Morassi: *Guardi: Antonio e Francesco Guardi* (Venice, 1973)
R. Bromberg: *Canaletto's Etchings* (London, 1974, rev. San Francisco, 2/1993)
J. G. Links: *Canaletto and his Patrons* (London, 1977)
J. Wilton-Ely: *The Mind and Art of Piranesi* (London, 1978)
——: *Giovanni Battista Piranesi: The Complete Etchings*, 2 vols (San Francisco, 1994)
The Glory of Venice: Art in the 18th Century (exh. cat., ed. J. Martineau and A. Robison; London, RA, 1994)

JOHN WILTON-ELY

Veen [Vaenius; Venius], **Otto van** (*b* Leiden, *c.* 1556; *d* Brussels, 6 May 1629). Flemish painter and draughtsman of Dutch birth. Although born in Holland, he is regarded as an artist of the Catholic southern Netherlands, where he spent most of his active life. He seems to have been acquainted with most of the Netherlandish scholars of his time, and his works testify to his broad humanistic learning. This and his prominent role in the early manifestations of the Counter-Reformation in Antwerp may have led Rubens to choose him as a teacher. Van Veen's importance as an artist has often been compared to the career of his famous pupil, for whom he was certainly the most important exemplar of the *pictor doctus* or learned painter. Van Veen obviously represents the older generation's more classicizing and conservative response to the Counter-Reformation. For him, the return to the spiritual values of the past also implied a recovery of the pictorial style of the High Renaissance, with its deliberate borrowings from the paintings of such artists as Raphael and

Correggio. By contrast, Rubens became the driving force behind the development of the full Flemish Baroque.

1. EARLY CAREER, BEFORE *c.* 1604. He came from a patrician family that claimed aristocratic descent. His father Cornelis held high offices in Leiden, for example that of burgomaster of the city in 1565. Otto's education was divided between the Latin school and his apprenticeship as a painter with Isaac Claesz. van Swanenburgh, a former pupil of Frans Floris in Antwerp. Van Veen's father, because of his political position and his Catholic faith, left Leiden with his family in October 1572. After a stay in Antwerp of a few months, he applied on 17 February 1573 for a passport to travel to Aachen, allegedly for health reasons. Shortly afterwards Otto went to Liège and entered the service of Prince-Bishop Gerard de Groesbeeck as a page. At the same time he continued his studies as a painter with Dominicus Lampsonius (1532–99), the Prince-Bishop's secretary, and with Jean Ramey. This period in his life assured him the lifelong protection of the Catholic hierarchy, which served him often in his later career. Lampsonius, a prolific writer but not a very gifted painter himself, further encouraged van Veen's interest in literature.

In 1574 or 1575 van Veen travelled to Italy, where he stayed for at least five years (seven according to van Mander), apparently most of the time in Rome, where Cardinal Cristoforo Madruzzo, until his death in 1578, was his patron. No paintings, drawings or documentary references have survived from this period, and although Sandrart recorded that van Veen was a pupil of Federico Zuccaro in Rome (and on stylistic grounds this is not

1. Otto van Veen: *Mystic Marriage of St Catherine*, oil on panel, 1.84×1.46 m, 1589 (Brussels, Musée d'Art Ancien)

impossible), it is probable that Sandrart misread van Mander's remark that van Veen's teacher, Lampsonius, had in his youth had contacts with such artists as Taddeo and Federico Zuccaro in Rome.

Around 1580 van Veen left Italy. According to van Mander, he spent some time at the court of Emperor Rudolf II in Prague and that of William V of Bavaria in Munich before returning to the Netherlands. Van Veen returned to Liège, where, probably in the early 1580s, he became court painter to Ernest of Bavaria (*d* 1612), who became Prince-Bishop of Liège in 1581 and Elector of Cologne in 1583. A visit to Leiden in 1583–4 is attested by several dated entries—one by the Classical scholar Justus Lipsius (1547–1606)—in van Veen's *Liber Amicorum* (Brussels, Bib. Royale Albert 1er) and by his portrait of the *Van Veen Family* (Paris, Louvre), also dated 1584.

Ambitious to be attached to a more important court, van Veen next joined Alessandro Farnese, 3rd Duke of Parma and Governor of the southern Netherlands, in Brussels, succeeding as court painter Joos van Winghe, who had left for Germany in 1584. While in the Duke's service, van Veen painted several portraits of his patron (e.g. Brussels, Mus. A. Anc.), but Farnese's frequent absences on military campaigns left him little occasion for artistic patronage. On, or shortly before, Farnese's death in 1592, van Veen settled in Antwerp, but his earliest known altarpiece, the *Mystic Marriage of St Catherine* (1589; Brussels, Mus. A. Anc.; see fig. 1), was commissioned in Brussels, for the city's church of the Capucines. This work and the altarpieces for Brussels Cathedral and the Dominican church in Leuven show van Veen to have been influenced by Correggio and Parmigianino in style and colouring.

In 1593 van Veen became a master in the Antwerp Guild of St Luke and shortly afterwards married Maria Loots, the daughter of an affluent patrician family. His continuous presence in Antwerp until 1615 is attested by many documents and by the important commissions from ecclesiastical and political authorities. Between 1594 and 1599 he painted the *Martyrdom of St Andrew* for the high altar of the St Andrieskerk, and several guilds and fraternities commissioned altarpieces for their chapels in the cathedral: the wardens of the chapel of the Holy Sacrament (1593–4), the Guild of St Luke itself (1601) and the Mercers (1607). For the decoration of the chapel of the town hall he painted an *Assumption of the Virgin* (1602). The city magistrates had already commissioned him to execute the designs for a series of tapestries depicting the *Victories of Archduke Albert* (1597; designs untraced; tapestries, Madrid) and to design the decorations for the triumphal entry of Archduke Albert and Archduchess Isabella into the city in 1599.

Van Veen ran a busy and productive studio with numerous pupils, the most famous being Rubens, who was with him from *c.* 1594 to *c.* 1600. For many years van Veen's studio was one of the leading production centres in Antwerp. He was elected dean of the Guild of St Luke in 1602 and dean of the Romanists in 1606. In a letter to Archduke Albert of 1619, van Veen stated that at the same period his fame was such that he had had offers of employment from such patrons as the Archbishop of Salzburg and the King of France.

2. LATER CAREER AND DECLINE, *c.* 1604 AND AFTER. Although the Archduke and Archduchess did not appoint van Veen as their court painter, he was in Albert's service by 1604 as engineer at the Antwerp Citadel, and in 1612 was surveyor of the Brussels Mint. His court commissions as a painter were few, although he executed portraits of the Archduke and Archduchess (e.g. copies, Brussels, Mus. A. Anc.); in 1609 he was paid 600 livres for three paintings commissioned by his patrons, and in 1615 Isabella ordered a triptych with *St George and the Dragon* for the Guild of the Crossbowmen of Brussels. Two paintings for the convent of the Discalced Carmelites at Marlagne, near Namur, were his last commission from the Archduke and Archduchess, executed in 1620–21.

From the first decade of the 17th century onwards van Veen became increasingly involved in writing and illustrating books; the most famous are his emblem books *Quinti Horatii Flacci emblemata* (Antwerp, 1607), *Amorum emblemata* (Antwerp, 1608) and *Amoris divini emblemata* (Antwerp, 1615; *see* EMBLEM BOOK), for which numerous grisaille drawings have survived (e.g. 103 for the first book in New York, Pierpont Morgan Lib.; see fig. 2). He also wrote texts on a number of theoretical issues. After Rubens's return from Italy in 1608, van Veen gradually disappeared from the Antwerp art scene. In 1611 master and pupil competed (both unsuccessful at the time) for a commission for the high altar in the church of Onze-Lieve-Vrouw. But by 1615 van Veen was complaining to Archduke Albert that he had not been offered any important commissions by him for a long time. Antwerp patrons seem likewise to have abandoned him. A series of

2. Otto van Veen: *Virtus inconcussa (Unshaken Virtue)*, grisaille oil sketch on paper, 203×165 mm, before or in 1607 (New York, Pierpont Morgan Library); preparatory design for engraving in his *Quinti Horatii Flacci emblemata* (Antwerp, 1607), p. 9

12 paintings of the *Romans and the Batavians* (*c.* 1612; Amsterdam, Rijksmus.) and another of 6 panels of the *Triumph of the Church* (*c.* 1615–20; Munich, Alte Pin.) are among the last examples of his work as a painter. In 1615 the artist moved to Brussels and apparently in straitened circumstances continued to petition his patrons for financial support, which was granted; his widow even received help from Isabella after the artist's death.

BIBLIOGRAPHY

BNB; Meissner

F. Sweertius: *Athenae Belgicae* (Antwerp, 1628), pp. 590–91
J. van den Gheyn: *Album Amicorum de Otto Venius: Reproduction intégrale en fac-similé avec introduction, traductions, notes* (Brussels, 1911)
M. de Maeyer: 'Otto Venius en de tapijtreeks *De veldslagen van Aartshertog Albrecht*' [Otto Venius and the tapestry series *The Battles of Archduke Albert*], *A. Textiles*, ii (1955), pp. 105–11
J. Müller Hofstede: *Otto van Veen: Der Lehrer des P. P. Rubens* (diss., U. Freiburg im Breisgau, 1959)
——: 'Zum Werke des Otto van Veen, 1590–1600', *Mus. Royaux B.-A. Belgique: Bull.*, vi (1957), pp. 127–74
J. R. Judson: 'Van Veen, Michelangelo and Zuccari', *Essays in Honor of Walter Friedländer* (New York, 1965), pp. 100–110
F. Baudouin: 'Een jeugdwerk van Rubens, *Adam en Eva* en de relatie van Veen en Rubens', *Antwerpen* (1968), pp. 45–61
T. Wilberg Vignau-Schuurman: 'Joris Hoefnagels Groteskenserie en de *Amorum Emblemata* van Otto van Veen', *Opstellen voor H. van de Waal* (Leiden, 1970), pp. 214–32
I. Gerards-Nelissen: 'Otto van Veen's *Emblemata Horatiana*', *Simiolus*, v (1971), pp. 20–63
L. van Looveren: '*Venationum novem archtype*: Negen allegorische jachttaferelen door Otto van Veen' [*Venationum novem archtype*: Nine allegorical hunting paintings by Otto van Veen], *Gulden Passer*, lii (1974), pp. 151–75 [issue dedicated to Louis Lebeer]
J. Müller Hofstede: '*Ut pictura poesis*: Rubens und die humanistische Kunsttheorie', *Internationaal Rubenscolloquium: Antwerpen, 1977*; also in *Gent. Bijd. Kstgesch. & Oudhdknd.*, xxiv (1976–8), pp. 171–89
L. Seth: 'Vermeer och van Veens *Amorum Emblemata*', *Ksthist. Tidskr.*, xlix (1980), pp. 17–40
H. Vlieghe: 'Rubens and van Veen in Contest: A Marginal Note', *Studia Ioanni Bialostocki* (Warsaw, 1981), pp. 477–82
L. Forster: 'Die *Emblemata Horatiana* des Otho Vaenius', *Wolfenbüttel. Forsch.* (1981), pp. 117–28
J. Foucart: 'Quelques inédits d'Otho Vaenius', *Rubens and his World* (Antwerp, 1985), pp. 97–108
E. Larsen: *Seventeenth-century Flemish Painting* (Freren, 1985), pp. 58–60
N. Walch: 'Deux eaux-fortes anonymes en relation avec le tableau d'Otto van Veen *Le Christ mort soutenu par un ange*', *Gulden Passer*, lxi–lxiii (1985), pp. 629–43 [issue devoted to Léon Voet]
P. Verhoeven: 'Civilis en zijn Bataven: Symbool van Hollands patriotisme', *Hermeneus*, lviii (1986), pp. 32–40
A. Vogl: *Der Bilderzyklus 'Der Triumph der Kirche' von Otto van Veen* (Munich, 1987)
Van Bruegel tot Rubens: De Antwerpse schilderschool, 1550–1650 (exh. cat. Antwerp, Kon. Mus. S. Kst., 1992), pp. 320–21

CARL VAN DE VELDE

Veerendael [Verendael], **Nicolaes** [Nicolaas] **van** (*b* Antwerp, 1626, *bapt* 19 Feb 1640; *d* Antwerp, *bur* 11 Aug 1691). Flemish painter. He was taught by his father, Willem van Veerendael, and was a member of the Antwerp Guild of St Luke by 1657. Apart from some allegorical scenes with monkeys in the style of Jan Breughel I and David Teniers (ii) (e.g. Brussels, Mus. A. Anc.), van Veerendael painted flower-pieces. Initially these were small, bright, graceful bouquets in tall, narrow vases, or cartouches and garlands surrounding a religious scene, sometimes by another artist, such as the *Cartouche with the Virgin Surrounded by a Floral Wreath* (Berlin, Gemäldegal.), in which the central grisaille is by Erasmus Quellinus. In his early work van Veerendael was influenced by Daniel Seghers, but he worked with more glaze and stronger and

more contrasting colours. The bouquets from the 1670s are more informal, and insects and *vanitas* elements are sometimes included, indicating his debt to the work of Jan Davidsz. de Heem, with whom he collaborated on a flower still-life (Munich, Alte Pin.). After 1680 van Veerendael painted much more freely and briskly and used fewer glazes (e.g. *Flowers and Fruit*, Evansville, IN, Mus. A. & Sci.). Despite his susceptibility to outside influences, he did achieve a recognizable style and can be seen as a forerunner of 18th-century Flemish flower painting.

BIBLIOGRAPHY

A Fruitful Past: A Selection of Dutch and Flemish Seventeenth-century Paintings (exh. cat. by S. Segal, New York, Gal. Naumann, 1983), pp. 86–93
Flowers and Nature: Netherlandish Flower Painting of Four Centuries (exh. cat. by S. Segal, Osaka, Nabio Mus.; Tokyo, Station Gal.; Sydney A.G. NSW; 1990), pp. 214–15

ELS VERMANDERE

Vega, de. Spanish family of architects.

(1) Luis de Vega (*d* Madrid, 10 Nov 1562). He lived in Madrid where he worked for the University of Alacalá (1520) and as Maestro Mayor (Supervising Architect) until his death. He built a palace (1524) in Valladolid for Francisco de los Cobos, the Secretary of Emperor Charles V, which Philip III transformed into a royal palace (1601). It was constructed around a rectangular courtyard, with galleries on two floors, supported by columns with depressed arches, spandrels with medallions, a balustrade and a corner design that abuts two columns at an angle. The composition derives from the Gothic style and has Classical elements, but Vega's treatment of the orders is clumsy, as is the overall composition. This part of Luis de Vega's design remains intact, but the façade, originally articulated with a composition of large halls between two towers, was modified by Francisco de Mora (1602) and at the beginning of the 20th century underwent a disastrous transformation. In 1534, on the orders of Charles V, Vega enlarged the building, adding a lateral courtyard in the form of a trapezoid. Known as the Galería de Saboya, this curiously planned courtyard has long corridors forming two superimposed galleries placed above columns and semi-circular arches.

In Medina del Campo, Vega constructed a palace (1528) for Diego Beltrán, later purchased by the banker Rodrigo de Dueñas. It is built around a rectangular courtyard on two storeys, with columns and three-centred arches, balustrades and spandrels with medallions. Vega's mastery of the Classical style is more evident than in the earlier Valladolid palace; at Medina del Campo he made use of an entablature, and the corner is turned on a single column. The cloistral open-well staircase is one of the most spectacular and inventive of the period. The front elevation of the palace consists of a single tower with a corner window, while the portal combines a Gothic structure with Renaissance elements.

For Archbishop Alonso de Fonseca y Acevedo, Vega designed a wing of the Colegio de Santiago Alfeo (1529; destr.) in Salamanca and also drew up plans (1545; not executed) for the Hospital de la Sangre in Seville. Charles V, however, was Vega's principal patron. Vega travelled to Granada to see the city and Pedro Machuca's designs for the Imperial Palace at the Alhambra (1528). Appointed as his Majesty's Maestro Mayor, together with Alonso de Covarrubias (Valladolid, 21 December 1537), he worked on the Alcázar of Seville (1550), where the elevated gallery of the Patio de las Doncellas is attributed to him. He was consultant for the Alcázar of Toledo where Covarrubias was works architect. His main activity, however, was in Madrid, where he supervised the construction of the Alcázar (1536; destr. 1734) to designs by Alonso de Covarrubias.

Vega initiated the conversion of the fortress of Simancas, outside Valladolid, into archives (1539). He also designed and built the Palacio del Pardo and Torre de la Parada (1543) on the outskirts of Madrid, creating a square block with four towers in the corners and a central courtyard, restored the Alcázar of Segovia (1544) and worked on the gardens and old palace of Aranjuez (1551). He designed the palace of Valsaín (1552), outside La Granja, now in ruins, and acquired the Casa de Campo for Philip II (1561), adding an impressive stretch of greenery and woodland, which linked the Madrid Alcázar with the hunting grounds of the Pardo by means of the royal gardens.

BIBLIOGRAPHY
E. Llaguno y Amírola and J. A. Ceán-Bermúdez: *Noticias de los arquitectos y arquitectura de España desde su restauración*, ii (Madrid, 1829, R/1977)
E. García Chico: *Medina del Campo* (1961), iii of *Catálogo monumental de la Provincia de Valladolid*
J. J. Martín González: 'El Palacio de "El Pardo" en el Siglo XVI', *Bol. Semin. Estud. A. & Arqueol.*, xxxvi (1970), pp. 5–41
J. Rivera Blanco: *El Palacio Real de Valladolid (Capitanía General de la VII Región Militar)* (Valladolid, 1981)
J. Urrea: 'El arquitecto Luis de Vega (h. 1495–1562)', *A introdução da arte da Renascença na Península Ibérica* (Coimbra, 1981), pp. 147–68
A. Bustamante García: *La arquitectura clasicista del foco vallisoletano (1561–1640)* (Valladolid, 1983)
F. Marías: *La arquitectura del renacimiento en Toledo (1541–1631)*, i (Toledo, 1983)
A. Martínez Martínez: 'Proceso arquitectónico del Palacio Real de "El Pardo" en el siglo XVI', *Reales Sitios: Rev. Patrm. N.*, 76 (1983), pp. 11–16
V. Gerard: *De castillo a palacio: El Alcázar de Madrid en el siglo XVI* (Bilbao, 1984)
J. Rivera Blanco: *Juan Bautista de Toledo y Felipe II: La implantación del clasicismo en España* (Valladolid, 1984)
E. E. Rosenthal: *The Palace of Charles V in Granada* (Princeton, 1986)

A. BUSTAMANTE GARCÍA

(2) Gaspar de Vega (*fl* 1546; *d* before 31 Aug 1576). Nephew of (1) Luis de Vega. A follower of his uncle, in 1552 he became Maestro Mayor of the new organization of royal building works, the Junta de Obras y Bosques, created under Prince Philip (later Philip II), who had a deep interest in architecture. Vega's role was principally technical, and no work or design can be directly attributed to him. Between 1552 and 1554 he was an assistant to Alonso de Covarrubias at the Alcázar, Toledo; his work on the palace of Valsaín (begun 1552; ruined), outside La Granja, included towers and verandahs in a Flemish manner, as instructed by Philip II. He also made a design for Charles V for the palace at Yuste (1554; destr. *c.* 1814), which, in its mixture of cloistered monastery and royal palace, prefigured the design of the Escorial. In 1554 he accompanied Prince Philip to England, returning via Flanders and France; he made a report critical of French royal palaces (1556). He was then required to make progress reports on all the royal sites and gardens. In 1559,

following the orders of Philip II, he replaced the flat lead roofs on the Alcázar in Toledo with Flemish pitched slate roofs, a practice that became widespread in Spain. His work, in the Flemish manner, at the palaces of El Pardo (1562–65), Madrid, Casa de Campo (begun ?1556), Madrid, and the Armería (?1556–64), Madrid, is no longer extant; while that at the convent of Uclés (begun ?1556), Cuenca, has been submerged by later work. After the appointment of Juan Bautista de Toledo as royal architect in 1561, Vega's role as technical administrator diminished; however, as Toledo was not only ill, but unfamiliar, after his sojourn in Italy, with technical practices in Spain, Vega was called in February 1566 to advise on the practicality of Toledo's proposals for the Escorial.

WRITINGS
Informe de Gaspar Vega sobre los palacios de Francia, que vió a su vuelta de Inglaterra, y acerca de las obras reales (16 May 1556; Segovia); ed. F. Iñiguez Almech in *Casas reales y jardines de Felipe II* (Madrid, 1952)

BIBLIOGRAPHY
E. Llaguno y Amirola: *Noticias* (1829), ii
F. Chueca Goitia: *Arquitectura del siglo XVI*, A. Hisp. xi (Madrid, 1953)
G. Kubler: *Building the Escorial* (Princeton, 1986)
F. Marías: *La arquitectura del renacimiento en Toledo, 1541–1631*, ii (Toledo, 1986)
J. Miguel Morán Turina and F. Checa Cremades: *Las casas del rey, casas de campo, cazaderos y jardines, siglos XVI y XVII* (Madrid, 1986)

Vega, Eduardo (*b* Cuenca, 13 June 1938). Ecuadorean ceramicist. He studied from 1958 to 1960 at the Real Academia de S Fernando and in the studio of Eduardo Peña in Madrid. He attended the Brixton School of Building, London, from 1960 to 1961 and went on to study ceramics at the Ecole des Beaux-Arts et des Arts Appliqués à l'Industrie in Bourges with Jean Lerat and Jacqueline Lerat between 1967 and 1968. On returning to Cuenca, a region with a strong pottery tradition, he created one of his most outstanding murals, the *Land of El Dorado* (1969; Cuenca, Hotel El Dorado). At the time he was the only artist in the country extensively involved in producing ceramic murals. His large-format works, in terracotta and decorated with slip, emphasize volume by creating sharp contrasts of light and shade. His depiction of tropical abundance and of historical and mythical characters and other stylized local details combine to produce optical labyrinths. By incorporating international styles his works bring together the vocabulary of Pre-Columbian ceramics and 20th-century pottery to create a very personal language. In 1973 Vega set up the ceramics business Artesa en Cuenca, for which he designed hundreds of decorative and utilitarian pieces, which bore the trademark *Vega* and were exported worldwide. Notable later works included *Of the Three Moons* (1985–7; Quito, Banco Ecuatoriano de la Vivienda), and *The Totems* (1991, Cuenca, Redrigio Crespo and Unidad Nacional Arennes), a monumental ensemble of concrete and clay.

BIBLIOGRAPHY
A. Kennedy: 'Los geográficos murales de Eduardo Vega', *Trama*, 47 (1988), pp. 69–72
J. Dávila: 'Eduardo Vega: El misterio de la arcilla', *Rev. Diners*, 84 (1989), pp. 44–8
A. Kennedy Troya: 'La cerámica artística actual', *Historia de la cerámica en el Ecuador: Síntesis* (Cuenca, 1992), pp. 44–5

ALEXANDRA KENNEDY TROYA

Vega, Francisco Preciado de la. *See* PRECIADO DE LA VEGA, FRANCISCO.

Vega, Jorge de la (*b* Buenos Aires, 27 March 1930; *d* Buenos Aires, 26 Aug 1971). Argentine painter. He studied architecture for six years before devoting himself to painting. His first works were sensitive geometric abstractions. In 1961 he took part in the exhibition *Otra figuración* at the Galería Peuser in Buenos Aires with Ernesto Deira, Rómulo Macció and Luis Felipe Noé, working in a style derived from the Cobra group; this was a milestone in the renewal of Argentine figurative painting. The Surrealist elements visible in his early work disappeared during the two years that he lived in the USA from 1965, first to teach painting at Cornell University in Ithaca, NY, and then on a Fulbright fellowship. On his return to Argentina he began to paint psychologically penetrating pictures of male and female faces and body parts, such as *Jigsaw Puzzle* (1967; see Glusberg, p. 76), in a bold graphic style reminiscent of poster designs. Capturing expressions full of feeling and emotion but picturing them in a style at once ironic and dramatic, de la Vega wanted his art to be as natural and free from limitations as life itself. During the last years of his life he also wrote and sang popular protest songs.

BIBLIOGRAPHY
C. Córdova Iturburu: *80 años de pintura argentina* (Buenos Aires, 1978), pp. 152, 175–6, 193, 218–19
J. Glusberg: *Del Pop-art a la Nueva Imagen* (Buenos Aires, 1985), pp. 74–6

JORGE GLUSBERG

Vega, José Gutiérrez de la. *See* GUTIÉRREZ DE LA VEGA, JOSÉ.

Vega, Luis Fernández de la. *See* FERNÁNDEZ DE LA VEGA, LUIS.

Vehap'ar's Gospels. Armenian illuminated Gospel book (320×245 mm; Erevan, Matenadaran Inst. Anc. Armen. MSS, MS. 10780) written in uncials on parchment and comprising 269 folios in 33 gatherings of mostly 8 leaves. The principal colophon is missing, but the manuscript has several inscriptions that help to trace its history from the date of its first restoration in 1088 to 1978, when it was presented by Katholikos Vehap'ar to the Matenadaran Library. From 1437 to 1466 it was in the library of Tat'ev Monastery, and from 1481 to 1609 in the church of the village of K'iwrlar, where it remained until 1720. Various other owners have added their inscriptions, dated 1729, 1765, 1766 and 1780.

The full-page illustrations include the elaborately decorated borders of the Letter of Eusebios to Karpianos (fol. 1*r*) and of the canon tables (fols 1*v*–4*r*), a *Group Portrait of the Owners* (fol. 5*r*), the *Old Testament* (fol. 5*v*) and the *Evangelist Portraits* each preceding the corresponding Gospel (fols 21*v*, 79*v*, 128*v* and 210*v*). Some 64 narrative miniatures are placed in the text close to the stories they illustrate, as in the *Betrayal of Christ* and *Peter Cutting the Ear of Malchus* (*see* ARMENIA, fig. 5). This cycle of miniatures is matched in Armenian manuscripts only by that of the eight artists who decorated a 13th-century Gospel book (Erevan, Matenadaran Inst. Anc. Armen. MSS, MS. 7651). Even among Greek manuscripts (*see* EARLY CHRISTIAN AND BYZANTINE ART, §V, 2) the only earlier instance of a Gospel book with text interrupted by narrative miniatures is the Sinope fragment (probably 6th century; Paris, Bib. N., MS. suppl. gr. 1286).

The miniatures and canon tables in the Vehap'ar's Gospels bear a close resemblance to those in the Matenadaran MS. 6201, which was copied in 1038. The palaeography and style of the iconography suggest that the Gospels were made during the first half of the 11th century in the vicinity of Sebastia in Cappadocia (Turkey). They also contain many of the Syriac features that characterize the Melitene group of manuscripts (e.g. Erevan, Matenadaran Inst. Anc. Armen. MSS, MS. 6201), such as the placing of the narrative miniatures and *Evangelist Portraits* at a right angle to the text. In general the figures are short and stocky, and painted on to the plain parchment (e.g. fols 117*r* and 122*r*). The most interesting iconographic feature is the depiction of Christ and the Apostles in clerical stoles (fols 99*r*, 108*r* and 117*r*). In two other Melitene group manuscripts, one of 1018 (Erevan, Matenadaran Inst. Anc. Armen. MSS, MS. 4801) and the other of 1064 (Jerusalem, Gulbenkian Lib., MS. 1924, e.g. fol. 6), the Evangelists also wear stoles.

BIBLIOGRAPHY
A. S. Mat'evosyan: 'Vehap'ari Avetarane' [Vehap'ar's Gospels], *Êdjmiadzin*, v (1978), pp. 34–51
T. Izmailova: 'Quelques miniatures de l'évangile du Katholikos (Vehap'ar)', *IV International Symposium on Armenian Art: Thesis of Reports: Erevan, 1985*
A. S. Mat'evosyan: 'Erkou arzhek'avor jeragrer S. Mesrop Mashtosi anvan Matenadanarin' [Two precious manuscripts presented to St Mesrop Mashtots Institute of Ancient Manuscripts (Matenadaran)], *Êdjmiadzin*, xii (1986), pp. 45–51

VREJ NERSESSIAN

Vehicle [binding medium]. Liquid in which dry pigments are dispersed to make paint. The vehicle may modify the appearance of the pigments, as in oil acrylic and encaustic paints. In watercolour and casein paints, the vehicle has little visual effect and serves only to bind the pigments into a film and to adhere them to the support.

RUPERT FEATHERSTONE

Veiga Guignard, Alberto da. *See* GUIGNARD, ALBERTO DA VEIGA.

Veii [Gr. Ventia; It. Veio]. Etruscan site *c.* 20 km north of Rome, set on a triangular tufa plateau bounded by two streams and accessible only from the north-west. Veii was apparently the largest city of the Etruscan twelve-city league, with an extensive territory and control of the River Tiber to the south. Excavations at Veii began in the 18th century, and the site has now been systematically explored. The earliest, small settlements on the site were Early Iron Age, and these villages later combined to form a substantial centre. The necropoleis contain chamber tombs, mostly for cremation burials, but, as elsewhere in Etruria, inhumation became more common in the Orientalizing period and rock-cut tombs under large tumuli were constructed. The Tomb of the Ducks (*c.* 675–*c.* 650 BC) contains probably the oldest known Etruscan wall painting, and the Campana Tomb (*c.* 600 BC) also predates any of the painted tombs at Tarquinia (*see* ETRUSCAN, §V, 5(i)).

Dating from the 6th century BC there are remains of city walls (11 km in circuit) and several temple complexes. Finds from the small temple in the Piazza d'Armi include terracotta plaques from a relief frieze depicting a military parade (*c.* 600–*c.* 550 BC). The Portonaccio Temple, just south of the city, is famous for its Archaic terracotta acroterial sculptures representing Apollo and other divine figures (all *c.* 515–*c.* 490 BC; Rome, Villa Giulia; see fig.; *see also* ETRUSCAN, §III, 1). These are among the most impressive works of Archaic Etruscan art, and may have composed a narrative group ranged along the roof-ridge of the temple (for reconstruction *see* ETRUSCAN, fig. 10). Some scholars consider the Portonaccio Group to be the work of the Veientine sculptor Vulca, mentioned in later literary sources. He may also have produced work for the Capitoline Temple at Rome (Pliny: *Natural History*

Veii, terracotta statue of *Apollo*, from the Portonaccio Temple, *c.* 515–*c.* 490 BC (Rome, Museo Nazionale di Villa Giulia e Soprinten-denza alle Antichità per l'Etruria Meridionale)

XXXV.157) and is notable as the only important Etruscan artist whose name survives.

There are relatively few archaeological remains of 5th-century BC date, but these may include a megaron-type house on the north side of the city. This has walls of tufa ashlar and a door with tapering jambs resembling Etruscan tomb doors. The late 5th-century BC Malavolta Head (Rome, Villa Giulia) formed part of a votive statue of a young man in the Sanctuary of Minerva and is another fine example of Veientine terracotta sculpture. During much of the 5th century BC Veii was engaged in conflict with Rome, relating to control of the River Tiber, and in 396 BC Roman forces under the dictator Furius Camillus conquered the city. Veii was destroyed and the cult of Uni (Juno) transferred to Rome. Julius Caesar later established a colony on the site, and, under Augustus, Veii became a *municipium* (free town) in 1 BC. Remains of Imperial date suggest that it was a town of respectable size, but Roman Veii did not flourish and its name continued to be used by Roman writers as a byword for decay and ruin.

BIBLIOGRAPHY

J. B. Ward-Perkins: 'Veii: The Historical Topography of the Ancient City', *Pap. Brit. Sch. Rome*, xvi (1961), pp. 1–17

A. Kahane, L. M. Threipland and J. B. Ward-Perkins: 'The Ager Veientanus, North and East of Veii', *Pap. Brit. Sch. Rome*, xxiii (1968), pp. 1–28

MARCO RENDELI

Veit, Philipp (*b* Berlin, 13 Feb 1793; *d* Mainz, 18 Dec 1877). German painter. The stepson, from 1804, of Friedrich von Schlegel, he studied (1808–11) at the Akademie in Dresden under Friedrich Matthäi (1777–1845) and Caspar David Friedrich. He showed talent in drawing but, on moving to Vienna in 1811, had difficulties with painting in oil, and turned to watercolour. Through Schlegel, Veit came to know many of the leading Romantics in Vienna, such as the poet and novelist Joseph von Eichendorff. In 1813–14 Veit took part in the campaign against Napoleon and returned briefly to Berlin. In 1815 he completed a votive picture, the *Virgin with Christ and St John*, for the church of St James in Heiligenstadt, Vienna (*in situ*), inspired by the work of Pietro Perugino and Raphael. In 1815 Veit left for Italy where he stayed until 1830. In Rome he joined the circle around Friedrich Overbeck and Peter Cornelius, becoming a leading Nazarene (*see* NAZARENES). With these artists he took part in providing fresco decorations (1816–17) for the Casa Bartholdy (now the Bibliotheca Hertziana): Veit painted the scene of *Joseph and Potiphar's Wife* and a decorative lunette allegory, the *Seven Years of Plenty* (both now Berlin, Staatl. Mussen, N.G.). In 1818 Veit was commissioned to paint the fresco of the *Triumph of Religion* in the Museo Chiaramonti in the Vatican, one of a series of murals recording the services of Pope Pius VII to science and art. Veit also took part in the decoration of the Casino Massimo in Rome (1818–24), painting the ceiling of the Dante Room with the *Heavens of the Blessed* and the *Empyrean* (*in situ*). In these frescoes and in his *Maria Immaculata* in Trinità dei Monti (1829–30; *in situ*) Veit proved himself the finest colourist of the Nazarene artists. While in Rome, Veit also painted some excellent portraits, notably a *Self-portrait* (*c.* 1816; Mainz, Landesmus.; see fig.). He also

Philipp Veit: *Self-portrait*, oil on canvas, 530×450 mm, *c.* 1816 (Mainz, Landesmuseum)

produced a fine series of pencil drawings of his fellow German artists in Rome (e.g. Mainz, Landesmus.).

In 1830 Veit returned to Germany to take up the post of Director at the Städelsches Kunstinstitut in Frankfurt am Main. He was responsible for the enlargement of the gallery collection as well as the education of students. Among those who studied under Veit were Alfred Rethel and Eduard Jakob von Steinle. About 1832 Veit painted allegorical murals for the Kunstinstitut; these alluded to the contents of the collection and embodied the theories of art and history embraced by Veit and Schlegel. Veit's pictorial programme culminated in the three-part fresco of the *Introduction of the Arts to Germany through Christendom* (1832–6; *in situ*; other murals destr.). Veit produced several religious pictures while in Frankfurt, the most successful of these being the *Two Marys at Christ's Grave* (several versions, e.g. 1846; Berlin, Staatl. Mussen, N.G.). In these he avoided sentimentality through fragmented local colours and the monumentality of the two female figures in a sparse landscape. Veit initiated the collaborative project of the decoration of the Kaisersaal (Council Chamber) in the Frankfurt Römer: he painted four portraits of emperors (*Otto I, Frederick II, Henry VII* and *Charlemagne; in situ*). Veit abandoned his earlier bright palette in favour of a more reticent coloration, using tones often mixed with grey and brown. Working on a more intimate scale too, he produced some excellent portraits of women, for example that of *Marie von Bernus* (1838; Frankfurt am Main, Städel. Kstinst.). In 1843, after lengthy disagreements with the Städelsches Kunstinstitut administration, Veit resigned the office of Director and moved, with his students, into studios in the Deutschordenshaus

in Sachsenhausen, Frankfurt. In 1853 he moved to Mainz, in order to decorate the cathedral, providing designs and cartoons (Berlin, Altes Mus., and Mainz, Landesmus.) that his students executed in encaustic (from 1861) on the cathedral walls; only the cycle showing the *Life of Christ*, over the arches of the nave, survives. Veit did not succeed in linking either this work or his oil paintings to the achievements of his early years in Frankfurt. He returned to the theme of the Martyrdom of St Sebastian for the altarpiece for the church of St Stephan in Mainz in 1866 (destr.). His remarkable *Self-portrait* of 1873 (Mainz, Landesmus.) reveals, with its veiled greens and browns and loose brushstrokes, that Veit was aware of the new tendencies in painting in France and Munich.

WRITINGS
Zehn Vorträge über Kunst (Cologne, 1891)

BIBLIOGRAPHY
Thieme–Becker
M. Spahn: *Philipp Veit* (Bielefeld and Leipzig, 1901)
H. Weizsäcker and A. Dessoff: *Kunst und Künstler in Frankfurt am Main im neunzehnten Jahrhundert* (Frankfurt am Main, 1907–9)
W. Veit: 'Erinnerungen an den Historienmaler Philipp Veit', *Alte & Neue Welt*, x–xi (1910), pp. 377–83, 417–20
Philipp Veit. Porträts (exh. cat., Mainz, Landesmus., 1977–8)
N. Suhr: *Christian Lotsch, Philipp Veit und Eduard von Steinle. Zur Künstlerkarikatur des 19. Jahrhunderts* (Worms, 1985)
——: *Philipp Veit (1793–1877): Leben und Werk eines Nazareners* (Weinheim, 1991)

NORBERT SUHR

Veitshöchheim. Village in Bavaria, 7 km north-east of Würzburg, Germany. The garden at Veitshöchheim is the best-preserved Rococo garden in Germany. It was created in several stages between 1702 and 1776 as the pleasure-ground of the Prince–Bishops of Würzburg, who had had a summer residence with a pheasantry at Veitshöchheim since 1680 (*see* GARDEN, fig. 54). In the first phase after 1702, under Prince–Bishop Johann Philipp von Greiffenklau, the basic layout was established; the final, luxurious elaboration, with ornaments, sculptures and waterworks, was executed in 1763–8 under Adam Friedrich von Seinsheim; it was planned by Johann Philipp Geigel (1757–1800), with sculptures by Ferdinand Tietz, Johann Wolfgang von der Auwera and Johann Peter Wagner. The garden (270×475 m) consists of two parts of different sizes, each with its own axis of symmetry. The smaller part is related symmetrically to the castle (designed by Heinrich Zimmer, 1680–82; extended by Balthasar Neumann, 1749–53; the far larger part lying to one side of it to the south; its east–west main axis is parallel to that of the palace garden. The large, transverse, rectangular garden, laid out with trees and hedges, is divided in the longitudinal (north–south) direction into three zones of unequal widths, each representing iconographically distinct spheres. The narrow wooded strip to the east with animal figures points to the realm of nature; the somewhat broader strip next to it with deciduous trees, hedges and stone figures of cavaliers, court ladies and playing children addresses the sphere of courtly culture; while the broad strip to the west embellished with two lakes represents the world of gods and the arts. Mount Parnassus with a grotto base (1765–66 by Tietz) rises steeply from the large lake, which lies symmetrically on the main axis; it is crowned by the winged horse Pegasus, and around the lake are arranged statues of the Olympian gods and the seasons. Only the large lake provides a fairly large open space, formerly flanked by a cascade (destr. in World War II); otherwise the park is intimate, labyrinthine and full of playful surprises.

BIBLIOGRAPHY

H. Kreisel: *Der Rokokogarten zu Veitshöchheim* (Munich, 1953)
W. Tunk: *Veitshöchheim: Schloss und Garten* (Munich, 1962, 5/1986)

REINHARD ZIMMERMANN

Veken, Nicolas [Nicholas; Nicolaas] **van der** (*b* Mechelen, 1637; *d* Mechelen, 1709). Flemish sculptor. He was a pupil of Maximilaan Labbé (*fl c.* 1629) and Lucas Faydherbe and became a master sculptor of the Mechelen Guild of St Luke in 1662. He worked almost entirely in wood and, unusually, coloured his own figures, which perhaps accounts for their exceptional synthesis and unity. He is best known for his confessionals, including those in SS Pieter en Pauwelkerk (1683–4), St Janskerk (1692) and St Katelijnekerk, all in Mechelen, and for his many refined yet powerful depictions of *Christ as a Man of Sorrows* in both stone (e.g. *c.* 1688; Mechelen Cathedral) and oak (e.g. early 1690s; Antwerp, Klooster van de Zusters Apostelinnen). His small ivory crucifixes with elegant elongated figures of Christ in attenuated poses recall those by Faydherbe. He is documented as the teacher of Cornelis van der Veken (*c.* 1657–1740; presumably a relation) in 1671 and of Frans de Leenheer and Frans Dielen in 1684.

BIBLIOGRAPHY

C. Poupeye: 'Nicolas van der Veken, sculpteur malinois du XVIIe siècle', *Annales du XXIIe congrès archéologique et historique de Belgique: Mechelen, 1911*, ii, pp. 261–325
——: 'Nicholas van der Veken, sculpteur malinois du XVIIe siècle', *Bull. Cerc. Archéol., Litt., & A. Malines*, xxi (1911), pp. 65–131
W. Godenne: 'Christ de pitié: Sculptures diverses', *Hand. Kon. Kring Oudhdknd., Lett. & Kst Mechelen/Bull. Cerc. Archéol., Litt. & A. Malines*, lxxiv (1970), pp. 115–23
G. Geens: 'Nicolaas van der Veken', *De beeldhouwkunst in de eeuw van Rubens* [Sculpture in the century of Rubens] (Brussels, 1977), pp. 216–18

CYNTHIA LAWRENCE

Vela, Vincenzo (*b* Ligornetto, Ticino, 3 May 1820; *d* Mendrisio, Ticino, 3 Oct 1891). Swiss sculptor. He worked first in Besazio and Viggiù as an apprentice doing rough carving, then in Milan at the cathedral workshops as a stone-dresser. While in Milan he attended the Accademia di Brera and also worked in the studio of Benedetto Cacciatori (1794–1871). Like many of his generation of sculptors, Vela was early on in his career profoundly impressed by the works of Lorenzo Bartolini, especially the *Trust in God* (marble, 1836; Milan, Mus. Poldi Pezzoli). The influence of this statue of a kneeling, nude girl is evident in Vela's *Morning Prayer* (Milan, priv. col.). This work, commissioned in 1846 by Conte Giulio Litta, is a clear tribute to the purist tendency of Milanese sculpture during the 1840s.

In 1847 Vela went to Rome, where he associated with Adamo Tadolini, Pietro Tenerani and Giovanni Dupré. The naturalism prevalent in this circle induced him to address new themes with a new plastic vigour, as in his statue of *Spartacus* (original plaster, Ligornetto, Mus. Vela); this was begun in 1847 in Rome and sent to Milan to be shown in the annual Brera Exhibition, but the marble version (Geneva, Mus. A. & Hist.) for the Duca Antonio Litta was not completed until 1850, a delay caused by

Vela's service in the Swiss Sonderbund War in 1848. The statue, which represents the Thracian slave who led a revolt against Republican Rome in the moment after he has broken his chains, is a strongly stated polemical work, characterized by a rough realism. In the context of Lombardy's subjection to Austria, this was a provocative work, and Vela decided to take refuge temporarily in Ligornetto. In 1852 he produced the statue *Desolation* (Lugano, Villa Ciani) for the exiled Ciani brothers; its naturalism is more moderate, approaching a neo-Renaissance idealization in the smoothness of the surfaces and in the definition of volumes. To this phase of Vela's career belongs the marble group of the *Queens Maria Theresa and Maria Adelaide* (1861; Turin, Consolata Church), remarkable for its minutely detailed rendering of the lace collars and trimmings; the tomb of *Antonio Rosmini* (*c.* 1857; Stresa, SS Crocefisso), in which the interplay between Vela's realistic tendency and abstract composition becomes more evident; and the monuments to *Gaetano Donizetti* (1855; Bergamo, S Maria Maggiore) and to *Tommaso Grossi* (Milan, Brera). These works established in Italy the type of Realist portrait statue that was enormously popular in the celebratory monuments of the second half of the 19th century; similarly, Vela's nearly 100 portrait busts (e.g. *Massimo d'Azeglio*, orignal plaster, *c.* 1860–65; Ligornetto, Mus. Vela) epitomize the *verismo* style.

In 1852 Vela went to Turin, where in 1856 he became professor of sculpture at the Accademia Albertina; he remained in this post until 1867. His *Last Days of Napoleon* (Versailles, Château), a marble seated statue of the dying Emperor, was produced in Turin in 1866 and exhibited, with clamorous success, at the 1867 Exposition Universelle in Paris. A crucial work, it combines an uncompromising realism with an abstract type of figure, thus encapsulating not only Vela's strengths but also his defects. The minute attention to detail, though not so refined as in the group of the *Queens*, co-exists with a movement of planes and an undulation of surfaces that seems to presage the best work of Giuseppe Grandi. On the other hand, some of Vela's marble female nudes, at once solid and delicate, seem close to contemporary figures by Antonio Tantardini (1829–79) and Francesco Barzaghi (1839–92). These include *Flora* (1857–8; Padua, Mus. Civ.), the *Naiad Rising from a Shell* (Turin, Pal. Arnaboldi) and two versions of *Spring* (Trieste, priv. col.; Milan, Gal. A. Mod.), in which the flowering shrub that accompanies the figure is minutely described, bud by bud. A very different figurative solution emerged in Vela's work during the 1880s in the *Ecce homo* (marble, Verate Brinza, Varese, funeral chapel of the Giulini Della Porta family). As with *Spartacus*, Vela succeeded in giving a strongly dramatic thrust to the subject, with pictorial effects created by the play of light and shadow over the broad surfaces.

After leaving Turin to settle permanently in Ligornetto, Vela created one of the most intense works of his career, and one of the most important sculptures of 19th-century Italian social realism. This is the monumental high-relief entitled *Victims of Labour* (bronze, 1882–3; Rome, G.N.A. Mod.; see fig.), commemorating the workers who died during the construction of the St Gotthard railway tunnel. Vela executed the work in the hope that it would be placed

Vincenzo Vela: *Victims of Labour*, bronze, 2.39×3.23 m 1882–3 (Rome, Galleria Nazionale d'Arte Moderna)

at the entrance of the tunnel, but the message was unpopular with the authorities and a cast was not installed until 1932. In this sculpture every canon of ideal beauty is violently repudiated, and all academic modes are negated: under a leaden vault, barely lit by lanterns, a group of miners pass with grim faces, heads sunk in hunched shoulders, carrying a crude stretcher with the body of one of their comrades. In its pitiless exploration of human types and in its setting, it carries an ideological and aesthetic message that again embodies Vela's uncompromising realism.

BIBLIOGRAPHY
Thieme–Becker
E. Lavagnino: *L'arte moderna*, ii (Turin, 1956), pp. 628–33
E. Piceni and M. Cinotti: 'La scultura a Milano dal 1815 al 1915', *Stor. Milano*, xv (Milan, 1962), pp. 594–7
D. Bacile: *Arte e socialità in Italia dal realismo al simbolismo, 1865–1915* (Milan, 1979), pp. 217–19
H. W. Janson: *Nineteenth-century Sculpture* (London, 1985), pp. 156–8

VALERIO TERRAROLI

Velamendi, Juan Miguel de. *See* VERAMENDI, JUAN MIGUEL DE.

Velarde, Pablita [*Tse Tsan*: 'Golden Dawn'] (*b* Santa Clara Pueblo, NM, 19 Sept 1918). Native North American painter. She was educated at local Catholic schools, where she was given the name Pablita, and studied under Dorothy Dunn and TONITA PENA at the Indian Art School in Santa Fe (*see* NATIVE NORTH AMERICAN ART, §IV, 2). An extended tour in 1938 with Western writer–artist Ernest Thompson Seton showed her new directions and suggested a role for her in Native North American art. She taught briefly at Santa Clara Day School, but left to pursue a full-time art career. She built the first truly professional studio in the Pueblos. She married Herbert O. Hardin, an Anglo policeman, and had two children: Herbert Hardin jr and Helen Hardin. Velarde worked in casein, tempera, oil and acrylic, and produced many murals and paintings portraying the familiar scenes of her Pueblo world. By 1950 she was the most important woman painter in the Pueblos and enjoyed international recognition. In 1956 she adopted a new technique using fine hand-ground earth pigments. Her awards included the Palmes d'Académiques (1954), the Waite Phillips Trophy (1968) and the New Mexico Governor's Award (1977). Her work appeared in many publications, notably in her own prize-winning volume on Pueblo folk tales: *Old Father, the Story Teller* (Santa Fe, 1989). The meteoric rise of her daughter, HELEN HARDIN, caused an unfortunate rift in their relationship, and for a period affected the careers of both women.

BIBLIOGRAPHY
M. C. Dillon: *Pablita Velarde* (Santa Fe, n.d.)
T. LeViness, 'Pablita Velarde, Pueblo Painter', *Amer. Artist* (April 1965), pp. 40–45

FREDERICK J. DOCKSTADER

Velasco, José María (*b* Temascalcingo, Mexico, 6 July 1840; *d* Mexico City, 27 Aug 1912). Mexican painter. As a landscape painter he was the most representative figure of Mexican academic painting in the 19th century. He produced a large body of work, in which the main theme was the spectacular natural scenery of his own country, interpreted according to his own singular vision. Stylistic unity and meticulously high standards of production characterize his work.

Velasco was from a small village in the provinces and from a family with no artistic tradition, but he began attending evening drawing classes at the Academia de Bellas Artes de S Carlos in Mexico City in 1858. He worked briefly in the studio of the Catalan painter Pelagrín Clavé but felt unhappy with the style imposed on him and completed his training from 1860 in the studio of Eugenio Landesio. Landesio's method lay in the faithful representation of nature, in careful drawing, in a thorough knowledge of colouring technique and above all in perspective. Velasco assimilated all that Landesio taught him, eventually surpassing him but without losing the classical composition, measured colour, accurate drawing and absence of drama with which his academic training had imbued him: he never painted a storm in his landscapes.

Velasco was objective by temperament, an observer of nature in its most minute details, and it was thus that he painted rocks, foliage, waterfalls and the shapes of clouds. He began teaching at the academy in 1868 but without creating a school of painting, his students imitating him but never surpassing him. His work was removed from that of contemporary European landscape painters, from the naturalism of Gustave Courbet and the symbolism of German artists such as Caspar David Friedrich. Instead he kept to what he had learnt from Landesio.

Velasco's early paintings, such as *Rustic Bridge at San Angel* (1862; Mexico City, Mus. N. A.), centre on landscapes in the vicinity of Mexico City. Landesio's influence is clearly evident in an *Outing in the Surroundings of Mexico City* (1866; Mexico City, Mus. N. A.). In 1874 Velasco and his family settled in Villa Guadalupe, high up on the northern outskirts of Mexico City. The landscape of the Valley of Mexico, seen from a high vantage point and with its grandeur and the special light peculiar to high places, became his main subject. Between 1873 and 1877 he created some of his most important landscapes, capturing for the first time the valley's extraordinary scale. The *Valley of Mexico* (1875; Mexico City, Mus. N. A.; see fig.) reveals his command of perspective, the vastness of the setting emphasized by the insertion of tiny human figures; the transparency of the atmosphere is indicated by the snowy caps of the volcanoes. Another major landscape of this period, entitled simply *Mexico* (1877; Mexico City, Mus. N. A.), is a symbolic work that subtly incorporates the eagle of the national coat of arms.

From the end of the 1870s Velasco broadened the range of themes treated in his paintings. Landscape sometimes served as a pretext for treating history and archaeology, as in *Pyramids at Teotihuacán* (1878; Mexico City, priv. col., see Fernández, 1983, pl. 122) and *Netzahualcoyotl's Bath in Texcoco* (1878; Mexico City, Mus. N. A.). Both the

José María Velasco: *Valley of Mexico*, oil on canvas, 465×620 mm, 1875 (Mexico City, Museo Nacional de Arte)

natural sciences and positivism interested Velasco, leading him on occasion to represent foliage and trees with botanical precision, as in the *Bridge at Metlac* (1881; Mexico City, priv. col., see Fernández, 1983, pl. 126). In the large pictures on the theme of evolution that he painted in 1904 for the Instituto Geológico (Mexico City, U.N. Autónoma), he demonstrated his knowledge of the evolution of the species on earth and in water. Such scientific concerns were also manifested in several paintings in which he showed Halley's Comet passing across the Mexican sky in 1910.

Velasco often painted the peaks of volcanoes such as Popocatepetl and Ixtaccihuatl, as well as Citlaltepetl or Pico de Orizaba, which are such salient characteristics of the Mexican landscape; an original view of the first two can be found in *Volcanoes Seen from Atlixco, Puebla* (1887; Mexico City, Banco N. de México). In one version of *Citlaltepetl* (1892; Mexico City, priv. col.) the composition is divided into two sections: the lower band contains the tropical vegetation of Veracruz, while the upper section represents the volcano amidst the arid landscape and the cold light of the peaks. Velasco painted *Citlaltepetl* again in a curious canvas in which he included a train (1897; Mexico City, Mus. N. A.) as a symbol of progress, which some of his critics had accused him of ignoring.

Velasco visited Paris in 1889 as head of the Mexican mission to the Exposition Universelle, where he exhibited 68 paintings. The influence of the Impressionists can be seen in several small sketches such as *Landscape: Europe* (1889; Mexico City, priv. col., see Fernández, 1983, pl. 138). However, on his return to Mexico after travelling through England, Germany, Italy and Spain, Velasco again centred his work on the Valley of Mexico, now frequently depicting it from a lower viewpoint. *Chimalpa Hacienda* (1893; Mexico City, Mus. N. A.), depicting the distant farm set in a large valley with volcanoes in the background, exemplifies the classical, descriptive style maintained by Velasco until his death.

BIBLIOGRAPHY
J. de la Encina: *El paisajista José María Velasco* (Mexico City, 1943)
J. Fernández: *El arte del siglo XIX en México* (Mexico City, 1952, rev. 2/1967/R 1983), pp. 85–104
C. Pellicer: *José María Velasco: Pinturas, dibujos, acuarelas* (Mexico City, 1970)

XAVIER MOYSSÉN

Velasco, Juan Fernández de. *See* FERNÁNDEZ DE VELASCO, JUAN.

Velasco, Luis de (*b* Toledo, *c.* 1550; *d* Toledo, 1 March 1606). Spanish painter. He was one of the most significant painters in Toledo in the late 16th century. His style, based on Italian aesthetics, is characterized by simplicity of composition and monumentality of form, qualities typical of painting in Toledo at that time. The work of artists engaged at the monastery and church of the Escorial influenced his painting, and echoes of El Greco can also be seen in some pieces. From 1571 he was a painter for Toledo Cathedral, executing the triptych of the *Virgin of Grace* (1584) for the cloister. Still preserved in the cathedral precincts, the central section depicts the *Virgin and Child Enthroned with Fernando de Antequera and SS Blaise and Anthony Abbot*, while the side panels show *SS Philip and*

James and *SS Cosmas and Damian*. The latter two panels display a conception clearly derived from the pictures of pairs of saints in the basilica church at the Escorial by such artists as Alonso Sánchez Coello and Juan Fernández de Navarrete. Between 1592 and 1600 he painted an altarpiece for San Blas Chapel in Toledo Cathedral, consisting of five panels, the central one of which (now in Toledo, Archv & Bib. Capitulares) is dedicated to the saint of the chapel and the remaining four (now in the sacristy) to the Evangelists. He also painted *Cardinal Quiroga* (1594) and *Cardinal García de Loaysa* (1599), two portraits in the series of Toledan prelates, located in the chapter house. Few of his works remain outside the cathedral precincts, one exception being the altarpiece (1574–83) for the church of Sonseca, near Toledo. His son Cristóbal de Velasco (1578–1627) was also a painter and a pupil of his father.

BIBLIOGRAPHY
Ceán Bermúdez
F. Pérez Sedano and M. R. Zarco del Valle: *Datos documentales inéditos para la historia del arte español, I: Notas del archivo de la catedral de Toledo*, 2 vols (Madrid, 1914–16)
A. Sánchez-Palencia: 'Los retablos de la capilla de San Blas de la catedral de Toledo', *Archv Esp. A.*, xlvii (1974), pp. 407–10
El Greco of Toledo (exh. cat., Madrid, Prado, 1982), pp. 144, 161

TRINIDAD DE ANTONIO SAÉNZ

Velasco, Pedro Fernández de, 2nd Conde de Haro (*b c.* 1425; *d* Castile, before 20 Aug 1492). Spanish noble officer and patron. He was the son of Beatriz Manrique and Pedro Fernández de Velasco, 1st Conde de Haro (1399–1470), who played a leading role in the civil unrest in the reigns of John II (1406–54) and Henry IV (1454–74). In 1473 the 2nd Conde became Constable of Castile, the first of his line. He enhanced his political position by his marriage with Mencia de Mendoza, the sister of Cardinal Mendoza, as well as by supporting the Catholic monarchs Ferdinand and Isabella in the wars against Portugal and Granada. He founded the chapel of Purification in Burgos Cathedral, now known as the chapel of the Condestable, in 1482 (*see* BURGOS, §2). A series of great craftsmen, Gil de Siloe, Simón de Colonia (*see* COLONIA, (2)) and Diego de Siloe, were employed on its construction, but it is hard to say how many of them were chosen by the Constable since the building reached completion only in the years 1523–32, long after his death and that of his wife (1500). Innocent VIII, however, when he gave it his papal blessing in 1486, recorded that 4000 gold ducats had by then been spent on it. The chapel is richly decorated, and the marble tombs of the founder and his wife lie in the centre. In 1487 the Constable also endowed a chest of 200,000 maravedises to be placed in the chapel for the redemption of captives or, failing that, for the endowment of dowries for unmarried girls. He was assisted in this by the Catholic monarchs, who granted him 100,000 maravedises for the purpose.

Pedro Fernández de Velasco also built in Burgos a town palace with corner towers, the Casa del Cordón, towards the end of the 15th century. The master carpenter was a converted Moor, Ali de Francia, who became Juan de Francia (*fl* late 15th century). On the exterior, rectangular labels, like an alfiz, were used to frame the doors and windows with a knotted cord, which symbolized the girdle of St Francis.

BIBLIOGRAPHY
B. Bevan: *History of Spanish Architecture* (London, 1938)
L. Torres Balbás: *Arquitectura Gótica*, A. Hisp.: Hist. Univl A. Hisp., vii (Madrid, 1952)

J. R. L. HIGHFIELD

Velathri. *See* VOLTERRA.

Velázquez Bosco, Ricardo (*b* Burgos, 1843; *d* Madrid, 31 July 1923). Spanish architect and art historian. He was one of the best-qualified exponents of late 19th-century architecture in Spain. Although his training had a historical bias, he was influenced by contemporary developments in European architecture. His work had links with that of the Belgian Joseph Poelaert, and he also assimilated aspects of the aesthetic of John Ruskin, introducing into his architecture red brick, with its various hues, and strips of polychrome ceramic, generally fabricated by Daniel Zuloaga (1852–1921). He was also acquainted with the Dutch architecture of the school of P. J. H. Cuypers. He drew extraordinarily well, and it was for this reason that he took part in the expedition to the Far East of the frigate *Arapiles*. His merits were soon recognized, and he was to become the favourite architect for state projects. In 1881 he obtained the chair of history of art in the Escuela de Arquitectura in Madrid, becoming a director of this centre from 1910 to 1918, the year in which he retired. His interest in medieval art and architecture, in which he undertook significant research, also became apparent in his considerable restoration work, working, for example, on the convent of S María in La Rábida in Huelva, the Mezquita in Córdoba and other buildings in the city that had been erected by the caliphs. He undertook the first excavations of the old courtly city of Madinat al-Zahra, near Córdoba. The elevations of these edifices, however, never influenced his own architecture.

His first important constructions were to be distinguished by the use of iron, as for the Palacio de Cristal (1887), built in the park of the Buen Retiro in Madrid for the Exposición de Filipinas, and iron combined with brick, as in the pavilion (1883) built in the Retiro for the Exposición de Minería and now known as the 'Pabellón Velázquez'. The division of the façade into five sections, a characteristic of this architect's work derived from French traditional architecture, reappears in one of his best constructions, the Escuela de Minas (1886–93) in Madrid, which has a rectangular ground-plan around a large courtyard. His most classic work was the west façade of the Casón del Buen Retiro (1886), while his most ostentatious edifice was the Ministerio de Fomento (1893–7; now Ministerio de Agricultura). Here brick and stone combine with Zuloaga's ceramics and Agustín Querol y Subirats's sculptures to endow the façade with a grandiose appearance. The central section of the façade stands out, forming a portico, and is flanked by two side wings, a typical feature of his work. Its style underlines, better than any of his other works, the monumental nature of late 19th-century eclectic architecture throughout Europe. On 24 May 1894 he became a member of the Reale Academia de Bellas Artes de S Fernando in Madrid, with 'Architecture in the Middle Ages' as his inaugural speech. Velázquez

Bosco was also an outstanding town-planner, helping to draw up plans (1902; Seville, Archv Admin. Mun., Obras Pub.) to enlarge the elegant district of La Palmera in Seville.

WRITINGS
El arte del califato de Córdoba (Madrid, 1912)

BIBLIOGRAPHY
J. A. Gaya: *Arte del siglo XIX* (Madrid, 1966)
P. Navascués: *Arquitectura y arquitectos madrileños del siglo XIX* (Madrid, 1973)
P. Navascués and others: *Del neoclasicismo al modernismo* (Madrid, 1979)
Guía de arquitectura y urbanismo de Madrid (Madrid, 1982–3), pp. 21, 29, 91, 173, 177, 178, 186, 193
M. Gómez-Morán: 'Arquitectura del siglo XIX', *Historia de la arquitectura española* (Barcelona, 1987)

ALBERTO VILLAR MOVELLÁN

Velázquez, Diego (Rodríguez de Silva y) (*b* Seville, *bapt* 6 June 1599; *d* Madrid, 7 Aug 1660). Spanish painter. He was one of the most important European artists of the 17th century, spending his career from 1623 in the service of Philip IV of Spain. His early canvases comprised *bodegones* and religious paintings, but as a court artist he was largely occupied in executing portraits, while also producing some historical, mythological and further religious works. His painting was deeply affected by the work of Rubens and by Venetian artists, especially Titian, as well as by the experience of two trips (1629–31 and 1649–51) to Italy. Under these joint influences he developed a uniquely personal style characterized by very loose, expressive brushwork. Although he had no immediate followers, he was greatly admired by such later painters as Goya and Manet.

I. Life and work. II. Working methods and technique. III. Character and personality. IV. Critical reception and posthumous reputation.

I. Life and work.

1. Early years in Seville, 1599–1623. 2. Madrid and first visit to Italy, 1623–31. 3. Madrid, 1631–49. 4. Second visit to Italy, 1649–51. 5. Final years in Madrid, 1651–60.

1. EARLY YEARS IN SEVILLE, 1599–1623. His father's family (de Silva) was of Portuguese origin and his mother's was from Seville. Athough he later tried (without much success) to prove that his family was of noble origin, it is probable that they were hidalgos (gentry) of moderate means. In 1609, according to Palomino, Velázquez spent several months in the studio of Francisco de Herrera the elder, a prestigious young painter whose disagreeable character soon drove Velázquez to leave, and in December 1610 he entered the studio of FRANCISCO PACHECO, with whom he signed a contract for a six-year apprenticeship on 17 September 1611. Velázquez became a close friend of Pacheco and his family, and without doubt this enabled him to gain introductions to the most cultivated members of Sevillian society who met at Pacheco's studio, which resembled an academy. Velázquez learnt from his master the techniques and practices of painting and gained a knowledge of Christian iconography, in which Pacheco was an expert; in addition, his involvement with Pacheco's circle of friends provided the younger man with a literary grounding more extensive than usual for a Spanish artist of the period. Pacheco's studio offered his pupils (among whom was also Alonso Cano) an informal atmosphere

and, in contrast with the old-fashioned style of Pacheco, the young artists soon turned towards the new tenebrist naturalism in the manner of Caravaggio, who was known through works that came from Italy. Pacheco recounted how Velázquez hired a villager as a model, whom he used for studies of different moods and poses.

On 14 May 1617, at the end of his apprenticeship, Velázquez was examined by the Alcaldes Veedores (overseers of the art of painting), Pacheco and Juan de Uceda Castroverde, and granted a licence to work as an independent painter, take on apprentices and open a shop, in accordance with the guild rules then operating in Spain and particularly in Seville. In the following year he married Pacheco's daughter Juana. Two daughters were born, one in 1619 and one in 1621, and an apprentice (Diego de Melgar) entered his studio in 1620.

Most of Velázquez's earliest work was of religious subjects, treated in a traditional manner, as was normal for Spanish artists of the time. Such works as the *Immaculate Conception* or *St John the Evangelist on Patmos* (both *c.* 1618; London, N.G.), the *Adoration of the Magi* (1619; Madrid, Prado) and what remains of a dispersed group of *Apostles*, with their strong individual characterization (*St Paul*, Barcelona, Mus. A. Cataluna; and *St Thomas*, Orléans, Mus. B.-A.), are iconographically close to contemporary works by Zurbarán or the young Cano; however, Velázquez's work has a greater expressive strength, greater sense of volume and a more violent intensity of illumination. He also produced a number of *bodegones*, or genre paintings (*see* BODEGÓN), and two compositions that, although they appear on one level to be genre works, containing abundant still-life, are in fact religious paintings, although this element is confined to the background. In both the *Christ in the House of Martha and Mary* (*c.* 1618; London, N.G.) and the *Supper at Emmaus* ('*La Mulata*'; Dublin, N.G.) Velázquez seems to have been inspired by engravings of the work of such Flemish artists as PIETER AERTSEN and JOACHIM BEUCKELAER, but he reinterpreted them in a tenebrist tone and has made the representation even more ambiguous. These works are deliberately confusing: by placing the religious element in the background, the artist has made it unclear whether a real event is occurring in another room seen through a gap or a doorway, or whether there is a painting hung on the wall, or even whether there is an image reflected in a mirror of an event that is happening in the spectator's space.

There are, however, several *bodegones* of a less complex kind in which the artist interprets his subject-matter with implacable objectivity. The *Old Woman Frying Eggs* (Edinburgh, N.G.; *see* BODEGÓN, fig. 1), *The Concert* (Berlin, Gemäldegal.), the two versions of *Men around a Table* (Budapest, Mus. F.A.; St Petersburg, Hermitage) and the *Youths Eating* (London, Apsley House) were all painted between 1617 and 1619; this series of *bodegones* culminates in the superb *Waterseller of Seville* (London, Apsley House; see fig. 1). It seems clear in these works, as in certain of his religious paintings, especially the *Apostles*, that Velázquez must have known some of the earliest works (1613–15) of Jusepe de Ribera (e.g. *Smell*; Madrid, D. Juan Abelló priv. col.), which could already have arrived in Seville and impressed him with their naturalism. From

1. Diego Velázquez: *Waterseller of Seville*, oil on canvas, 1.06×0.82 m, *c.* 1617–19 (London, Apsley House)

very early on, however, it seems that Velázquez's principal preoccupation was with portrait painting, for which he was extraordinarily gifted. The two signed portraits of *Mother Jerónima de la Fuente* (1620; Madrid, Prado; Madrid, Fernández Araoz priv. col., see Brown, p. 32) are particularly intense. With the accession to the throne of Philip IV (*see* HABSBURG, §II, (7)) in 1621, who was served by the statesman Gaspar de Guzmán y Pimentel, Conde de OLIVARES (soon after Conde-Duque), who had lived in Seville, many Sevillian intellectuals hoped for preferment in Madrid. Velázquez, encouraged no doubt by Pacheco, travelled to the court in 1622, where he made useful contacts in the Conde-Duque's circle and began to gain a reputation for his skills as a portrait painter, although he did not then receive any royal commission.

2. MADRID AND FIRST VISIT TO ITALY, 1623–31. In the summer of 1623, through the good offices of Pacheco's friends, Velázquez was called to Madrid to paint a portrait of the young King (untraced). The great success of this first royal portrait and the recent death (1622) of Rodrigo de Villandrando led to Velázquez's immediate appointment as Pintor del Rey (6 October 1623). Still newly arrived at court, he executed a number of portraits for private clients, for which he was paid, but from then on would work only for the King and aimed to forget all commercial associations of his activity, which were regarded as 'low and servile' in Spain. Many years later, in connection with his ennoblement, he would affirm that he had never painted except 'by order of his Majesty and

in order to please him'. His position as Pintor del Rey allowed him direct access to the royal collections, and it is clear that he closely studied the portraits by Antonis Mor, Alonzo Sánchez Coello and Juan Pantoja de la Cruz. Velázquez's first portraits of the young king *Philip IV* (New York, Met.; Madrid, Prado), that of *Infante Carlos* (Madrid, Prado) as well as those of the *Conde-Duque de Olivares* (São Paulo, Mus. A. Assis Châteaubriand; New York, Hisp. Soc. America Mus.), follow these 16th-century models, particularly Coello, who in his time had been able to blend the minutely detailed objectivity of Flemish painting typical of his own master, Mor, with the atmospheric vibrancy of the world of Titian. Velázquez moved in that direction, progressively lightening the backgrounds, especially around the heads of his subjects, and modifying the positions of the legs in search of a more elegant silhouette. The portrait of *Philip IV* (*c.* 1626; Madrid, Prado) with a petition in his hand shows how he first composed the King standing with his legs apart in the traditional manner, only to rework it later, with the legs almost together, in search of a 'bobbin'-shaped outline.

Between the years 1623 and 1629, when he left for Italy, Velázquez attentively studied the Venetian paintings in the royal collections, especially those by Titian, of whom he would always remain a fervent admirer. The two most important canvases painted by Velázquez during those years, and warmly praised by his contemporaries, have

been lost: the equestrian portrait of *Philip IV* (1625), probably inspired by Titian's portrait of *Charles V* (Madrid, Prado), and the *Expulsion of the Moriscos* (1627). In March 1627 Velázquez had been appointed Ujier de Cámara, a position in the royal household that brought with it not only a salary but accommodation and other benefits. That year, and in reply to accusations made by other artists that he was only capable of painting portraits, he executed a canvas, in competition with other court painters (Vicente Carducho, Eugenio Cajés and Angelo Nardi), taking as his subject a recent event (1609), the *Expulsion of the Moriscos*. The painting was elected the best by a jury comprising Father Juan Bautista Maíno and Giovanni Battista Crescenzi and was hung in the Salón Grande of the palace, where it was destroyed in the fire of 1734.

In 1628 Peter Paul Rubens arrived in Madrid on a difficult diplomatic mission from London. He remained at the court for nearly a year and Velázquez was deeply impressed by the character of the great Flemish artist, who was then at the height of his fame and creative powers. He accompanied him on his visit to the Escorial, and it is likely that the many paintings executed by Rubens during his stay in Madrid were done in the studio of Velázquez, who shared his taste for Venetian painting, especially that of Titian, some of whose works he copied in Madrid. Velázquez's only work of complex composition extant

2. Diego Velázquez: *Joseph's Coat Presented to Jacob*, oil on canvas, 2.17×2.85 m, *c.* 1629–30 (Madrid, El Escorial)

from the period 1623–9 is the *Feast of Bacchus* ('*The Drunkards*', 1628–9; Madrid, Prado), which follows the trend of giving a contemporary interpretation to mythological subject-matter in a manner analogous to the Counter-Reformation paintings of the Life of Christ or the saints. Thus, the group around Bacchus are ordinary peasants, interpreted with harsh realism; the whole is close in spirit to his first Sevillian works, which also influenced the dense colouring and strong, luminous contrasts of the main group, as well as the taste for still-life details. The inclusion of the landscape, depicted with light and transparent tones, is an indication of the way in which his style would develop.

In June 1629, shortly after the departure of Rubens, Velázquez sought and obtained permission to go to Italy. He was provided with letters of recommendation and introduction to various Italian courts, and the ambassadors of Parma, Tuscany and Venice notified their respective masters of the visit; all of them emphasized his familiarity with the King and the Conde-Duque. This unusual honour even led the ambassador of Parma to suspect that the journey was being made with the intention of spying. The details of the journey were recorded by Pacheco, who described it as a true study-trip. Velázquez left from Barcelona with the cortège of Ambrogio Spinola, Marqués de los Balbases, and he visited Venice, Ferrara, Cento, Loreto, Bologna and Rome, where he spent a year staying with the Spanish ambassador Manuel de Acevedo y Zúñiga, Conde de Monterrey. In 1630 the artist travelled to Naples to paint the portrait of Philip IV's sister María (who was staying there on the way to Hungary for her wedding), where he must have met Ribera.

The journey to Italy was, without doubt, definitive in orientating the direction of Velázquez's development and in establishing fertile contact with contemporary Italian artists. Not only was his love of Venice and Titian confirmed, but he also met Guercino and Ribera and absorbed the artistic trends in Rome, including the influence of such artists as Andrea Sacchi. The two great compositions painted in Rome and taken to Spain on his return, the *Forge of Vulcan* (Madrid, Prado) and *Joseph's Coat Presented to Jacob* (Madrid, Escorial; see fig. 2), are perfect examples of his synthesis of the expressive world of Roman Bolognese classicism, with the almost academic treatment of the nude, a concern with the expression of emotion and the successful treatment of space, based (especially in *Joseph's Coat*) on a sober use of geometric perspective.

3. MADRID, 1631–49. In January 1631 Velázquez returned to Madrid and to his duties at the palace, painting a portrait of the Infante Baltasar Carlos (possibly that in Boston, Mus. F.A.), who had been born during his absence. In the following years he continued to enjoy royal protection and was granted new positions and conditions of pay; in 1634 he even transferred the post of Ujier de Cámara to his son-in-law Juan Bautista Martínez del Mazo, who had married his daughter Francisca in 1633. Some of the works painted immediately after his return to Madrid (e.g. *St Thomas Receiving the Girdle*, Orihuela, Mus. A. Sacro; *Christ Contemplated by the Christian Soul*, London, N.G.) are close in style and display similar preoccupations to the works executed in Italy. Their composition is austere, but they are executed with a technique that is increasingly loose and Venetian, and yet at the same time constrained. They are perhaps the last great religious works by the artist, who concentrated thereafter almost exclusively on portraiture and on allegorical or historical compositions. The 1630s and 1640s were his most productive years, during which his Italian experience was fully realized and his individual language became increasingly defined. The royal commissions for the Palacio del Buen Retiro (Madrid; mostly destr.) and the Torre de la Parada (a hunting-lodge in the grounds of EL PARDO, nr Madrid) were, without doubt, the most important of his activities, and in them the transformation of his style and his significance in Madrid can clearly be seen.

In 1636 Velázquez was given the title of Ayuda de Guarda Ropa and *c.* 1635–6 he worked on canvases for the Palacio del Buen Retiro; this was being built for the King at the behest of Olivares and was to be lavishly decorated (*see* MADRID, §IV, 1). For the great Salón de Reinos, Velázquez painted a series of equestrian portraits (Madrid, Prado) glorifying the Habsburg dynasty. These continue the series begun by Titian with his *Charles V at Mühlberg* and by Rubens, whose *Philip II* (both Madrid, Prado) Velázquez would certainly have seen being painted in Madrid. The new portraits of *Philip III* and his wife *Margaret of Austria*, as well as that of *Isabella of Bourbon*, the wife of Philip IV, seem to have been prepared by another artist in a style close to that of Bartolomé González, but Velázquez repainted them almost entirely with surprisingly free touches, giving them a vivacity and luminous expressiveness that were completely new. *Philip IV on Horseback* (Madrid, Prado; see fig. 3) and the heir,

3. Diego Velázquez: *Philip IV on Horseback*, oil on canvas, 3.01×3.18 m, *c.* 1635 (Madrid, Museo del Prado)

4. Diego Velázquez: *Surrender of Breda* (*'The Lances'*), oil on canvas, 3.07×3.70 m, 1635 (Madrid, Museo del Prado)

Infante Baltasar Carlos on Horseback, are entirely autograph and already show the masterly way in which Velázquez fused the figure with the surrounding space. The background landscapes, painted in silvery tones, faithfully capture the Sierra de Guadarrama on the outskirts of Madrid, and movement is portrayed with surprising vivacity, although the postures of the horses were almost certainly based on engraved models. The *Surrender of Breda* (*'The Lances'*, 1635; Madrid, Prado; see fig. 4) was painted for the same room and forms part of the series of 12 battle scenes on which Vincente Carducho, Eugenio Cajés, Félix Castello, Jusepe Leonardo, Juan Bautista Maino, Francisco de Zurbarán and Antonio de Pereda also worked. Velázquez's ambitious composition is resolved with an extraordinary classical equilibrium, in which the groups of Spanish victors and defeated Dutchmen, led by their generals, are carefully balanced. The surrender, symbolized by the key being given to Spinola, is conducted with dignity and humanity and contrasts with the traditional heroic depiction of an apotheosis of the victor and the humiliation of the vanquished.

For the hunting-lodge at the Torre de la Parada, which was to house the great series of paintings based on Ovid's

Metamorphoses executed by Rubens and his workshop, as well as Frans Snyders's hunting scenes and still-lifes, Velázquez painted a series of portraits of members of the royal family (*Philip IV*, *Prince Baltasar Carlos* and the *Cardinal-Infante Ferdinand*; all Madrid, Prado). They are shown in hunting dress, accompanied by their dogs. Set against an open landscape of clear luminosity, they are depicted with extraordinary simplicity, without any courtly trappings, and with great vitality. Also for the Torre de la Parada, Velázquez painted the figures of *Menippus* and *Aesop* (*c.* 1636–40; both Madrid, Prado); they are depicted with lively expressiveness as beggars in a similar vein to Ribera's interpretation of the ancient philosophers, but in a technique very different from that of Velázquez's early years, when it is possible to detect his relationship with models of the most rigorous tenebrism. The seated figure of *Mars* (Madrid, Prado), while seeming to suggest the *Ares Ludovisi* (Rome, Mus. N. Romano) in his attitude of defeat and weariness, has also been seen as a melancholy meditation on the arms of Spain in decline.

In the same decade he executed a large number of court portraits, ranging from royalty to the court dwarfs and jesters. Of similar date to the canvases in the Buen Retiro (*c.* 1635–6) must be the equestrian portrait of the *Conde-Duque de Olivares* (Madrid, Prado), a work with a theatrical emphasis somewhat different from his usual controlled style, and the bust of *Francisco I d'Este, Duke of Modena* (1638; ex-Gal. & Mus. Estense, Modena, 1989), which is executed with a very loose technique and is profoundly expressive of the sitter's inner life. The fall of Olivares in 1643 meant that the King took direct control of state affairs for a while, and he joined the military campaign against France in Aragón and Catalonia, during which Velázquez portrayed him in military dress in the city of Fraga (1644; New York, Frick; for illustration *see* HABSBURG, §II(7)). Another work from 1644 is the portrait of *Don Diego de Acedo* (Madrid, Prado), the court midget, one of a series of portraits of disfigured men treated with extraordinary sensitivity. Outstanding among them are *Francisco de Lezcano* ('*Niño de Vallecas*') and *Sebastián de Morra* (or *Juan Calabazas*, sometimes known as the '*Bobo de Coria*') (both Madrid, Prado). Of similar date are standing portraits of other court fools (*hombres de placer*), in which the subjects are depicted with an ever-freer technique, and in which the admiration and knowledge of Titian and the Venetians is abundantly clear (e.g. *Don Juan of Austria*; Madrid, Prado). In the portrait of *Pablillos de Valladolid* (Madrid, Prado; see fig. 5) the background space is defined wholly in terms of light and shade, which gives the figure a powerful expressiveness. A number of portraits of women must also belong to the late 1640s. The intimacy of tone suggests that the sitters may have been drawn from the artist's own family circle. They include the *Lady with a Fan* (London, Wallace), the *Portrait of a Young Woman* (Chatsworth, Derbys) and the *Woman Sewing* (Washington, N.G.A.), all of which are executed with extraordinary restraint. There are very few religious works from these years: apart from the *Crucifixion* (Madrid, Prado), which was a royal commission for the convent of S Plácido and a work of severe classicism that still shows Italian influences, there is *SS Anthony Abbot and Paul the Hermit* (Madrid, Prado), painted for one of the hermitages of the Buen Retiro, the extensive landscape of which links the work to the hunting portraits in the Torre de la Parada. The *Coronation of the Virgin* (Madrid, Prado), painted for the Queen's oratory in the Alcázar, displays a sober elegance and a Venetian richness of colouring.

In January 1643 Velázquez had been appointed Ayuda de Cámara, an important promotion, and in June he was made superintendant of the palace works (under the authority of the Marqués de Malpica). This post suggests a knowledge of architecture that had not been recognized before by some of his colleagues. Nevertheless, in 1647 he was successively appointed overseer and accountant for the works in the Octagonal Room, a new luxurious salon that was being built in the palace. His power and influence in courtly life had grown considerably, and the transformation of the old Alcázar into a more modern palace with private rooms, enfilades and fresco decoration was next entrusted to the painter. Lacking experience of the technique of fresco painting, and anxious to augment the royal collections, Velázquez requested a trip to Italy to purchase works of art and to contract painters capable of decorating the vaults of the renovated Alcázar.

5. Diego Velázquez: *Pablillos de Valladolid*, oil on canvas, 2.09×1.25 m, *c.* 1645 (Madrid, Museo del Prado)

4. SECOND VISIT TO ITALY, 1649–51. The second trip to Italy led to the culmination of Velázquez's art and allowed him to affirm his absolute mastery in Rome itself. The portraits that he executed in Rome were regarded even then as exceptional works and created a profound impression on subsequent Roman portraiture. The only certain and extant self-portrait (Valencia, Mus. B.A.) dates from this trip and shows all the serious and lordly detachment noted by contemporary writers. The artist left Málaga in January 1649 as part of the official suite that was travelling to Italy to receive the King's new wife, his niece the Archduchess Mary Anne of Austria. They landed at Genoa and went on to Milan to await the Austrian retinue, but Velázquez then travelled to Venice, where he acquired some important works by Veronese (e.g. *Venus and Adonis*) and Tintoretto (e.g. *Purification of the Booty of the Midianite Virgins*), which are still in the Prado. While he was there he met Marco Boschini, who noted the artist's preference for Venice and its art. Velázquez then went to Bologna, Modena and Parma, passed through Florence— which he had not visited on his first trip—and

arrived in Rome. He later travelled to Naples to make some payments on behalf of the King.

Velázquez remained in Rome until 1651, integrating himself easily into the Roman artistic environment. The first work from the trip is the portrait of his servant and pupil *Juan de Pareja* (New York, Met.), which, in its powerful intensity of expression, caused universal astonishment when it was exhibited in the Pantheon in 1650 (*see* PAREJA, JUAN DE). Velázquez's position as painter to the King enabled him to frequent the Vatican and to paint *Innocent X* (Rome, Gal. Doria-Pamphili; see fig. 6), a work of exceptional strength and liveliness; the likeness of the portrait impressed everybody, and it is even said that the Pope commented that it was 'too truthful'. Although the composition follows traditional papal portraits, its expressiveness is achieved by a confident use of a range of reds. These works, and the portraits of other Roman personalities, opened the doors of the Accademia di San Luca and of the Congregazione dei Virtuosi at the Pantheon to the artist. Other portraits painted during this period (e.g. *Camillo Massimi*, Kingston Lacy, Dorset, NT; *Cardinal Camillo Astalli-Pamphili*, New York, Hisp. Soc. American Mus.) confirm the degree of perfection and simplicity that his technique had attained, although they failed to reach the superb quality of *Juan de Pareja* and *Innocent X*. The two small landscapes of the Villa Medici in Rome (both Madrid, Prado; see fig. 7) must also date from this second trip to Italy. The *Toilet of Venus* (the Rokeby *Venus*; London, N.G.; see fig. 8) is recorded in the inventory of the 7th Marqués del Carpio y Heliche in 1651, and must have been painted in Italy and sent to Spain before the

7. Diego Velázquez: *Garden of the Villa Medici*, oil on canvas, 487×426 mm, *c.* 1650–51 (Madrid, Museo del Prado)

painter returned there. It is the first known female nude in Spanish painting (they were extremely rare for religious and moral reasons). While clearly influenced by Titian's Venuses, Velázquez replaced the full sensual opulence of the Venetian model with an intensely personal nervous vitality and youthful grace.

In Rome, Velázquez enjoyed respect and prestige. Although his means of acquiring works of art (often by pressuring owners to give them away as 'gifts') brought adverse comments, even among the Spanish, he was at ease in Italy and repeatedly delayed his return, despite the constant requests of the King that he return 'by sea and not by land' so as not to prolong his absence further. His arrangement for engaging Pietro da Cortona in the service of the King failed, as the painter did not wish to leave Italy, but Velázquez was able to establish positive contacts with the Bolognese artists Agostino Mitelli and Angelo Michele Colonna, who accepted the invitation, although they did not arrive in Madrid until 1658.

5. FINAL YEARS IN MADRID, 1651–60. In 1651, more than two years after his departure, Velázquez returned to Spain and once again took up his work on the decoration of the Alcázar. In March 1652 he was appointed Aposentador Mayor de Palacio, a position of importance and responsibility that signified a decisive advance in his career but which in turn greatly limited the amount of time he could dedicate to painting. This, in turn, meant the greater involvement of his son-in-law del Mazo in the production of official copies of his royal portraits. The Baroque scheme of decoration in the Alcázar consisted of complex themes, mainly drawn from Classical mythology and rare in Spanish art. Velázquez painted four rectangular canvases for the overdoors of the Salón de los Espejos. Three

6. Diego Velázquez: *Innocent X*, oil on canvas, 1.40×1.20 m, *c.* 1650–51 (Rome, Galleria Doria-Pamphili)

(*Venus and Adonis, Psyche and Cupid, Apollo and Marsyas*) were lost in the fire at the Alcázar in 1734; the fourth (*Mercury and Argus*) is now in the Prado. The composition of the latter, with the slumped body of Argus overcome by sleep as Mercury moves nearer to surprise him, has a striking immediacy and realism achieved by a freedom of execution using almost spongy brushstrokes. The figure of Argus recalls that of the *Dying Gaul* (Rome, Mus. Capitolino), which Velázquez must have known in Rome.

Another work of mythological subject-matter, like the Rokeby *Venus*, may be related to Velázquez's stay in Italy. *Las hilanderas* ('The Weavers'; Madrid, Prado; see fig. 9), which depicts the fable of Arachne, was also, like the *Venus*, painted for a private collector, Don Pedro de Arce, and is perhaps the most complex of Velázquez's mythological compositions. In a manner that is analogous with some of his earliest religious work (e.g. *Christ in the House of Martha and Mary*) the main action—the moment at which Minerva curses Arachne, whom she turns into a spider for having dared to challenge her—is relegated to the background and set against Arachne's tapestry. In the foreground, a weaver's workshop is so accurately depicted that in the 19th century it was believed that the picture was no more than a large genre scene. The atmosphere of the illuminated interior, the rapid spinning of the wheel, the ambiguous treatment of the story, which is derived of rhetorical emphasis and presented as an ordinary event, make this one of the most personal and significant of the artist's works. Here too can be detected homage by

Velázquez to Italian artists; the *contrapposto* of the two figures in the foreground seems to be derived from one of Michelangelo's pairs of *ignudi* on the ceiling of the Sistine Chapel, and the background tapestry depicting Ovid's *Rape of Europa* pays tribute to Titian, whose painting of the same subject (Boston, MA, Isabella Stewart Gardner Mus.; *see* TITIAN, fig. 8) was then in the Alcázar Real.

During the last years of his activity, when his extensive palace duties left him with less time for painting, Velázquez focused almost exclusively on the execution of royal portraits, and these late portrait busts of *Philip IV* (Madrid, Prado; London, N.G.) show, with acute psychological depth, the transformation of the sensual young man into the tired and embittered man that the King had become in his last years. The portraits of the young queen *Mary Anne of Austria* (Madrid, Prado; Paris, Louvre), who arrived in Madrid while Velázquez was in Rome, and whom he must have painted *c.* 1652, the portrait of *Princess María Teresa* (*c.* 1653; Vienna, Ksthistmus.) and, above all, those of the royal children born during that period, *Infanta Margarita María* and *Infante Felipe Próspero*, present a portrait gallery of unequalled images of children. The portraits of the *Infanta Margarita María* (Vienna, Ksthistmus.) include one of her aged two wearing a pink dress (*c.* 1653), another aged five, with a pink and silver dress (*c.* 1655) and another, in blue, with an older guardian, at the age of nine (1659). The portrait of *Infante Felipe Próspero* (1659; Vienna, Ksthistmus.), who was born in

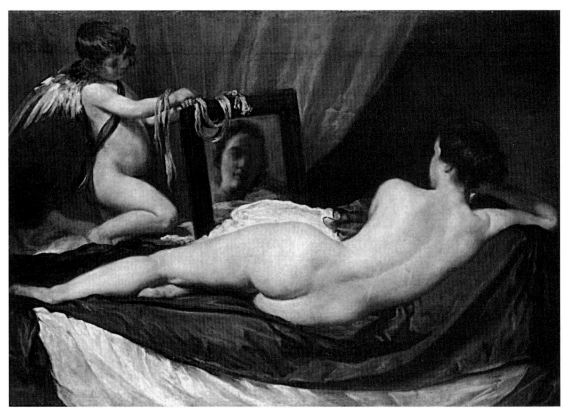

8. Diego Velázquez: *Toilet of Venus* (the Rokeby *Venus*), oil on canvas, 1.23×1.77 m, *c.* 1651 (London, National Gallery)

9. Diego Velázquez: *Las hilanderas* ('*The Weavers*'), oil on canvas, 2.23×2.93 m, *c.* 1656 (Madrid, Museo del Prado)

1657 and who died as a child in 1661, shows him with a little dog. Despite the demands of etiquette, the formality of gestures and the stiffness of their dress, the artist was able to evoke with remarkable delicacy the spirit of childhood and subtle changes in physiognomy.

In 1656 Velázquez was responsible for hanging in the Escorial some of the paintings acquired in Italy and others bought at the auction in England of Charles I's collection. His role as Aposentador was in this case also that of museologist, and this is made clear in the 'memoria' (untraced) in which Velázquez describes the works and their installation. In that same year he painted what is his masterpiece, *Las meninas* (1656; Madrid, Prado; see fig. 10), known in its time as the *Portrait of the Family*, and which Luca Giordano called the 'theology of painting'. It represents the culmination of the painter's dual approach of combining the immediate truth of what is seen with the enigmatic richness of the concept. The canvas depicts the Princess Margarita María, surrounded by her maids of honour (*meninas*), her servants, dwarfs and clowns, in an austere room in the Alcázar. To one side Velázquez has included a self-portrait, showing him at work on a large canvas, of which we see only part of the back. He faces out towards the viewer, whose position is that of the artist's subject. On the rear wall, however, a heavily framed ebony mirror reflects the image of Philip IV and his wife Mary Anne, who are thus both the models that Velázquez paints and the viewers of the painting. The royal couple become the protagonists of the canvas, endowing it with complex political significance, while at the same time the

painter and his art also acquire special importance. In the treatment of atmosphere, of the intervening spaces and the aerial perspective, *Las meninas* is the culmination of Velázquez's art and a major work of universal importance.

In 1658 Velázquez was granted the title of Knight of Santiago. As a high-ranking functionary of the palace, his last official role was to organize the meeting between Philip IV and Louis XIV of France at which the latter received as his bride the King's daughter, the Infanta María Teresa. The ceremony took place in June 1660 on the Franco-Spanish border, on the Isla de los Faisanes in the Bidassoa River, and with it the Peace of the Pyrenees was sealed, ending the war between Spain and France. On his return to Madrid, Velázquez fell ill and died; seven days later his wife also died.

II. Working methods and technique.

The art of Velázquez developed in a coherent fashion, with a clear evolution from the early work done in Seville, which is marked by an intense tenebrist naturalism, to the final works, which display fleeting brushwork and boldness in the treatment of the strokes of paint that are absolutely exceptional. As a young artist he seems to have been preoccupied with mastering reality and expression, using a very intense light to accentuate volume, outline and the particular nature of objects. In the early works executed in Seville his colours, applied in a thick, malleable paste, are dark in range with earthy tones predominating—

10. Diego Velázquez: *Las meninas*, oil on canvas, 3.21×2.81 m, 1656 (Madrid, Museo del Prado)

browns and deep reds, with bronze-coloured skin-tones. In these works his draughtsmanship is careful, the details shown with great precision. The intense luminosity accentuates areas of shade and further underlines the effect of volume, by delineating the forms against very dark backgrounds. From 1622, however, following his first journey to Madrid, his technique began to change: his palette lightened, especially in the backgrounds, which became greyer, and at the same time he began to simplify the minutely detailed treatment of faces, without losing their expressive intensity or psychological truth; the portrait of the poet *Luis de Góngora* (1622; Boston, MA, Mus. F.A.), painted in Madrid, is a good example of this.

Velázquez's first trip to Rome (1629–31) marks a change in his art. In the two paintings from that visit—the *Forge of Vulcan* and *Jacob's Coat* (see §I, 2 above)—the range of colours is already much clearer and more luminous, and the loose and vibrant brushstrokes, especially in the background of *Jacob's Coat*, are produced with new freedom. In the great *Surrender of Breda*, which he painted later in Madrid, all trace of the dark modelling of his early works has disappeared, and the subject is drenched with light and radiates naturalism. The free brushwork, independent of the drawing, suppresses form, producing a purely visual effect that is complete only when the spectator is at a distance from the work. Velázquez generally worked directly on to the canvas, altering the design as he progressed. In the artist's remarkable portraits of court dwarfs and jesters his technique of using strokes of paint without line lends intense life to the faces and expressions of the figures, conveying their disturbed

mental states with great delicacy, as in the portrait of the jester *Pablillos de Valladolid*. The bravura portrait of *Innocent X* (see §I, 4 above), although traditional in format and displaying Titian's tonal harmonies, takes to hitherto unknown extremes the daring and visible use of brushstrokes and the mastery of the difficult harmonization of various tones of red juxtaposed with white and gold. The two small landscapes (almost oil sketches) of the Villa Medici gardens, executed at the same time, display an absolute freedom of touch and a profound lyricism that seem to anticipate the effects of the Impressionists in the 19th century. Velázquez used the exposed weave of the canvas to create the illusion of brickwork, and the movement of the eye between these passages and the different layers of paint gives the works a strong sense of three-dimensionality.

On his return from Rome, Velázquez's style had again subtly altered. In such works as *Mercury and Argus* (see §I, 5 above), which is of course meant to be viewed from a distance, a close inspection reveals an almost incoherent mass of brushstrokes that composes itself when seen from a few metres. Velázquez has here devised a range of colour using the most refined greys and mauves. The final portraits of the King show the culmination of this process, and a comparison with the earlier royal portraits reveals the transformation from terse brushstrokes, which seem to model the rounded forms of the face, into softer and more open brushwork, composed of light, juxtaposed touches. The late portraits of the royal children are a testimony to the artist's sensitivity to their personality, whose melancholy grace is conveyed in a remarkable fashion, and to his intensely personal sense of colour, with pearly greys, cold greens, salmon pink and violet carmine, flecked with dazzling touches of silver. At the same time, the technique with which he portrays the richness of their clothing became increasingly light and intangible, with free brushstrokes that could almost be qualified as Impressionist and that subsequently greatly impressed 19th-century French artists.

III. Character and personality.

Velázquez was a reserved man, often accused of arrogance by his contemporaries; indeed, the King himself remarked on the element of indolent superiority in the artist's character that distanced him from routine work. His career as an artist was bound up with his desire to better himself and break out of the social and economic ties associated with his profession in Spain at that period. The confidence and obvious appreciation of the King certainly aided his exceptional rise, and his position aroused envy and slander at court. On the other hand, it freed him from dependency on religious commissions, which was the lot of other Spanish artists, and even gave him a measure of independence from private patrons. Crucially, his post at court gave him the chance to study the royal collections and the works of Titian and Rubens, which were to be central to his development as an artist.

While on his second visit to Italy, Velázquez made contact with high-ranking members of the Curia, and even the Pope, who would support his petition for nobility and the membership of the Order of Santiago. On his return to Madrid, he intensified his campaign and openly requested his preferment; in 1658 he achieved his wish.

Contrary to the view of the Consejo de Ordenes, who failed to agree that the candidate possessed the required 'nobility and qualities', the King, after obtaining an exceptional papal bull, granted Velázquez the title of Knight of Santiago, something previously reserved for the nobility.

Despite abundant documentation of Velázquez's career, little is known of his private life, apart from some documents dating from 1652. These reveal that the reason for his delay in returning to Spain after his second visit to Italy was the birth of an illegitimate son in Rome, whose welfare and nursing costs were met by the Spanish ambassador. The inventory drawn up after Velázquez's death reveals that he led a comfortable, even luxurious life for a Spanish painter. He had a notable library containing numerous books on architectural theory, mathematics, astronomy and astrology, philosophy and ancient history, as well as substantial works of poetry in Spanish, Italian and Latin. There was, however, a surprising lack of religious works, which generally predominated in the collections of his contemporaries. The posthumous accusation by his enemies that he had defrauded the Crown was proved unfounded, and Velázquez was exempted from all imputation.

IV. Critical reception and posthumous reputation.

The work of Velázquez, whose position in the history of European painting was exceptional, did not have the repercussions on Spanish painting of the time that might be expected. With his production limited to the immediate environment of the court, only those who had easy access to the Alcázar knew his work and could learn from it, in particular from the portraits, as was the case with Juan de Miranda Carrexo or Claudio Coello. Most of the art produced in Madrid after Velázquez was of a religious nature and bore little relation to his work. His principal pupil and collaborator, Juan Bautista Martínez del Mazo, was responsible for many of the copies of Velázquez's official portraits, although some of the portraits originally attributed to del Mazo were, in fact, executed by painters whose work in this genre is otherwise unknown, for example Francisco de Burgos Mantilla and Francisco de Palacios (c. 1622–52). Juan de Pareja, who was Velázquez's servant and who executed a number of sober portraits in his manner, departed from his master's style in his religious paintings. Nothing remains of the work of other artists who passed through Velázquez's studio (e.g. Diego de Melgar, who entered the workshop as an apprentice in 1620, or Tomás de Aguilar, who was painting in 1660). Velázquez's work in Italy, however, was influential on portraiture there, in particular in Rome and Genoa, where his use of a dark ground was taken up by a number of artists (some of Bernini's paintings were even attributed to Velázquez).

In the 18th century the art of Velázquez, which was highly praised by theoreticians, including Anton Raphael Mengs, had a decisive influence on Goya, who engraved a number of works by the Sevillian painter and who owed much of his own technique to him. In the 19th century Velázquez was a definitive model in Spain for such artists as Eduardo Rosales Gallina. During the Peninsular War (1808–14) a number of works by Velázquez arrived in northern Europe and with the 'discovery' of Spain and the opening of the Prado to the public, his fame began to spread. The first modern biography was written by Stirling-Maxwell in 1855. In 1865 Manet visited Madrid and was deeply impressed by 'the painter of painters' and copied some of his work. Other artists working at the end of the 19th century such as James McNeil Whistler and John Singer Sargent were also influenced by a knowledge of Velázquez's work. In the 20th century Picasso painted a series of works based on *Las meninas* (see PICASSO, PABLO, fig. 9).

BIBLIOGRAPHY

In 1960, on the centenary of his death, documents, notices and texts referring to Velázquez were compiled: *Varia Velazqueña II* (Madrid, 1960); a monumental bibliographical compilation (1814 titles) to 1961 can be found in J. A. Gaya Nuño: *Bibliografía crítica y antológica de Velázquez* (Madrid, 1963)

EARLY SOURCES

L. Díaz del Valle: *Epílogo y nomenclatura de algunos artífices* (MS.; 1647); partly pubd in *Varia Velazqueña II* (Madrid, 1960), pp. 59–62
F. Pacheco: *Arte* (1649); ed. F. Sánchez Cantón (1956)
J. Martínez: *Discursos practicables del nobilísimo arte de la pintura* (MS. c. 1675); ed. V. Carderera (Madrid, 1866)
A. A. Palomino de Castro y Velasco: *Museo pictórico* (1715–24)

MONOGRAPHS AND EXHIBITION CATALOGUES

W. Stirling-Maxwell: *Velázquez and his Works* (London, 1855)
C. B. Curtis: *Velázquez and Murillo* (New York and London, 1883)
G. Cruzada Villaamil: *Anales de la vida y las obras de D. Diego de Silva Velázquez* (Madrid, 1885)
K. Justi: *Diego Velázquez und sein Jahrhundert* (Bonn, 1888; Eng. trans., London, 1889)
A. de Beruete: *Velázquez* (Paris, 1898; Eng. trans., London, 1906)
J. Octavio Picón: *Vida y obra de Velázquez* (Madrid, 1899)
W. Gensel: *Velázquez: Der Meisters Gemälde*, Klass. Kst Gesamtausgeben (Stuttgart and Leipzig, 1905; rev. by J. Allende Salazar, Berlin, 1925)
J. Moreno Villa: *Velázquez* (Madrid, 1920)
A. L. Mayer: *Velázquez: A Catalogue Raisonné of the Pictures and Drawings* (London, 1936)
E. Lafuente Ferrari: *Velázquez: Complete Edition* (London and New York, 1943)
E. du Gué Trapier: *Velázquez* (New York, 1948)
B. de Pantorba: *La vida y la obra de Velázquez: Estudio biográfico y crítico* (Madrid, 1955)
K. Gerstenberg: *Diego Velázquez* (Munich and Berlin, 1957)
Velázquez y lo Velazqueño (exh. cat. by V. de Sambricio, Madrid, Prado, 1960–61)
J. López Rey: *Velázquez: A Catalogue Raisonné of his Oeuvre* (London, 1963)
J. Camón Aznar: *Velázquez* (Madrid, 1964)
J. López Rey: *Velázquez: Work and World* (London, 1968)
J. Gudiol: *Velázquez, 1599–1660* (Barcelona, 1973; Eng. trans., London, 1974)
J. López Rey: *Velázquez: The Artist as a Maker* (Lausanne and Paris, 1979)
E. Harris: *Velázquez* (Oxford, 1982)
J. Brown: *Velázquez: Painter and Courtier* (New Haven and London, 1986)
Velázquez (exh. cat. by J. Gállego, A. Dominguez Ortiz and A. E. Pérez Sánchez, New York, Met; Madrid, Prado; 1989–90)

TECHNIQUE

G. McKim-Smith, G. Andersen-Bergdoll and R. Newman: *Examining Velázquez* (London and New Haven, 1988)
M. C. Garrido Pérez: *Velázquez: Técnica y evolución* (Madrid, 1992)
G. McKim-Smith and R. Newman: *Ciencia e historia del arte: Velázquez en el Prado* (Madrid, 1993)

SPECIALIST STUDIES

J. Ortega y Gasset: *Papeles sobre Velázquez y Goya* (Madrid, 1950)
J. A. Maravall: *Velázquez y el espíritu de la modernidad* (Madrid, 1960)
M. Foucault: *Les Mots et les choses* (Paris, 1966)
R. Gaya: *Velázquez: Pájaro solitario* (Barcelona, 1969, rev. 1984)
L. Díez del Corral: *Velázquez: La monarquía e Italia* (Madrid, 1979)

B. Wind: *Velázquez's bodegones: A Study in Seventeenth-century Spanish Genre Painting* (Fairfax, 1987)
J. F. Moffit: *Velázquez: Prática e idea. Estudios dispersos* (Málaga, 1991)

ALFONSO E. PÉREZ SÁNCHEZ

Velázquez, González. *See* GONZÁLEZ VELÁZQUEZ.

Velázquez, Héctor. *See under* TORRES & VELÁZQUEZ.

Velc. *See* VULCI.

Velde, van. Dutch family of artists, active in France.

(1) Bram van Velde (*b* Zoeterwoude, nr Leiden, 19 Oct 1895; *d* Grimaud, France, 28 Dec 1981). Painter and printmaker. Born into a humble family, he was apprenticed at the age of 12 to a firm of decorators. He soon developed an interest in painting and was encouraged by his employer to devote himself to it. He therefore moved to Germany, briefly staying in Munich before settling in the artists' colony at Worpswede, near Bremen. While there he painted brightly coloured Expressionist works such as *Yellow Nude* (1922–4; Paris, priv. col., see Putman, pl. 4) as well as making his first lithographs.

Leaving Germany in 1924, van Velde settled in Paris where he became acquainted with the work of van Gogh, Cézanne and the Impressionists, as well as contemporary French art. In Paris he painted mainly landscapes and still-lifes such as *The Moon* (1930; Paris, Jacques Putman priv. col., see Putman, pl. 20), which showed him combining the flattened space of Cubism and the bright colouring of Fauvism. He moved to Corsica in 1930, where the cost of living was less, returning to Paris in 1931. He moved to Cala Ratjada in Mallorca in 1932 for the same reason. At this time his paintings showed an increasing simplification of forms towards abstraction, though as yet they remained essentially figurative, as in *Still-life* (1932–5; Saint-Etienne, Mus. A. & Indust.). At the outbreak of the Spanish Civil War in 1936 he was forced to leave the island, returning to Paris. There his brother, (2) Geer van Velde, introduced him to the playwright Samuel Beckett, who was to be one of his earliest and most energetic supporters. Works of this period, such as the gouache *Untitled* (1936–41; Paris, Jacques Putman priv. col., see Putman, pl. 30), were richly coloured, the semi-abstract forms charged with a primitive violence. In 1938, after failing to renew his residency papers, he was arrested and jailed at Bayonne for four weeks, an experience that profoundly affected him. While imprisoned he produced a number of ink drawings reflecting his misery. Prevented from returning to the Netherlands, from 1941 until 1945 he remained in Paris suffering such loneliness that he was unable to paint.

In 1945 van Velde had his first one-man show at the Galerie Mai in Paris. He was given a five-year contract by the Galerie Maeght in 1947, and in 1948 an exhibition of his work was held there, although it was a critical and commercial failure. His exhibition at the Kootz Gallery in New York in 1948 was also a failure, although it influenced American artists such as de Kooning. By the late 1940s his style had matured into abstraction. Characterized by expressive, often triangular forms, as in *Untitled* (1948; Paris, Gal. Maeght, see Putman and Juliet, pl. 45), the works are nevertheless figuratively suggestive. From the

1950s onwards gouache and lithography became increasingly important media in his output, leading to such works as the gouache *Untitled* (1951; Saint-Paul-de-Vence, Fond. Maeght) or the lithograph *Untitled* (1955; Geneva, Mus. A. & Hist.). After years of virtual neglect he began to acquire an international reputation in the late 1950s. In 1958 he lived in Fox, Haute-Provence, and then returned briefly to Paris before settling in 1959 in Geneva, where he remained until 1977.

Van Velde's style remained basically constant from this time onwards while becoming increasingly fluid and spontaneous, leading to works such as *Untitled* (1966; Paris, Cent. N. A. Contemp.), in which paint drips are prominent. This expressive spontaneity earned him the admiration of Cobra artists such as Pierre Alechinsky and Asger Jorn. He had produced lithographic illustrations since the 1940s, as in those for Beckett's *Le Calmant* (Paris, 1941), but he worked increasingly in this area in the 1970s, illustrating, for example, Friedrich Hölderlin's *L'Unique* (Paris, 1973). In 1977 van Velde left Geneva for Paris and in 1980 moved to Grimaud where he remained until his death. Throughout his life he retained a great scepticism towards both the world and his own work, and it was from this consequent inner torment that his work resulted. He himself stated: 'The world is a mystery that my painting helps me to penetrate. What I feel is too strange, too violent for me to capture it in a word or thought. It demands to appear and I paint' (1968 exh. cat., p. 13).

BIBLIOGRAPHY
S. Beckett, G. Duthuit and J. Putman: *Bram van Velde* (Paris, 1958)
J. Putman: *Bram van Velde* (Turin, 1960)
Bram van Velde: Paintings, 1957–1967 (exh. cat. by S. Beckett and F. Meyer, New York, Knoedler's; Buffalo, NY, Albright-Knox A.G.; 1968)
Bram van Velde: Oeuvre lithographié, 1923–1973 (exh. cat. by R. M. Mason and J. Putman, Geneva, Mus. A. & Hist., 1974)
J. Putman and C. Juliet: *Bram van Velde* (Paris, 1975)
C. Juliet: *Rencontres avec Bram van Velde* (Montpellier, 1984)

(2) Geer van Velde (*b* Lisse, 5 April 1898; *d* Cachan, nr Paris, 5 March 1977). Painter, brother of (1) Bram van Velde. He was self-taught as a painter. From 1904 until 1924 he lived in The Hague, where he was apprenticed to the decorating firm of Kramer. In his spare time he painted subjects from nature. In 1925 he followed his brother to Paris. Influenced by Marc Chagall he painted abstract motifs in a clear colouring, adapted from his environment, for example *Palette and Brushes* (1925–30; Paris, Pompidou). After 1930 he experimented extensively, developing a painting style characterized by a systematic relationship between large shapes. In 1937 van Velde met the playwright Samuel Beckett. In the year of his first one-man exhibition, at the Guggenheim Jeune Gallery in London (1939), he settled in Cagnes-sur-Mer, where he created works that became the basis for his post-war development: a progression from recognizable imagery towards abstract–geometric paintings, which was preceded by changes in his drawings and gouaches.

In 1944 van Velde moved to Cachan and became friends with Pierre Bonnard. In 1946 he had an exhibition at Galerie Maeght in Paris. By this time he was known as a painter of abstract compositions and was considered a member of the Ecole de Paris. Works such as *View*

Overlooking the Sea (1946; Paris, Pompidou) were characterized by their emphasis on colour, light and space, which he saw as metaphysical entities. During the 1950s he increasingly sought to express silence, harmony and controlled emotion through subjects observed in the studio. Critics looked upon him as a typical 'northern' painter, despite the fact that his work was included in such major exhibitions of French painting as *Painting in France, 1900–1967* (1968; Washington, DC, N.G.A.; New York, Met.). His paintings convey an admiration for the work of Piet Mondrian, Pieter Saenredam and Johannes Vermeer.

BIBLIOGRAPHY
Geer van Velde–Bram van Velde (exh. cat., text by S. Beckett; New York, Kootz Gal., 1948)
Geer van Velde, 1898–1977: Schilderijen en tekeningen [Geer van Velde, 1898–1977: paintings and drawings] (exh. cat., The Hague, Gemeentemus., 1981)

JOHN STEEN

Velde, van de [den] **(i).** Dutch family of artists. (1) Esaias van de Velde was the second son of Cathalyne van Schorle and the painter and art dealer Hans van den Velde (1552–1609), a Protestant who fled religious persecution in Antwerp and settled in Amsterdam in 1585. On his father's death, Esaias, a painter, draughtsman and etcher, moved to Haarlem with his mother, and the same year he married Katelyna Maertens, with whom he had four children: Jan (*b* 1614), Esaias the younger (*b* 1615), Anthonie the younger (1617–72) and a daughter, Jacquemijntgen (*b* 1621). Both Esaias the younger and Anthonie the younger became artists, the latter a still-life painter named after his uncle, the Antwerp painter Anthonie van den Velde the elder (*b c.* 1557). Esaias's older brother, Jan van de Velde I (1568–1623), was a famous calligrapher, who moved from Antwerp to Rotterdam after his marriage in 1592. His eldest son, (2) Jan van de Velde II, was a painter, draughtsman and printmaker, like his uncle. He had a son, Jan van de Velde III (1619/20–62), who became a still-life painter. Both (1) Esaias and (2) Jan played an important role in the development of naturalistic Dutch landscapes in the 17th century.

(1) Esaias [Esias] **van de Velde** (*b* Amsterdam, *bapt* 17 May 1587; *d* The Hague, *bur* 18 Nov 1630). Painter, draughtsman and etcher. He probably received his earliest training from his father. It is also possible that he studied with the Antwerp painter Gillis van Coninxloo, who moved to Amsterdam in 1595 (ten years after Esaias's father). He may also have trained with David Vinckboons, whose work shows similarities with that of Esaias. Esaias became a member of the Haarlem Guild of St Luke in 1612, the same year as Willem Buytewech and the landscape painter Hercules Segers. During this Haarlem period Esaias had two pupils, Jan van Goyen and Pieter de Neijn (1597–1639), but by 1618 he had moved with his family

1. Esaias van de Velde: *Riders in a Landscape*, oil on panel, 250×325 mm, 1614 (Enschede, Rijksmuseum Twenthe)

to The Hague, where he joined the Guild of St Luke in October of that year.

1. PAINTINGS. Esaias left an extensive painted oeuvre of over 180 pictures, 117 of which are landscapes. He signed his paintings in two different ways: in the early period (*c.* 1614–16) *E Van Den Velde*; in the later period simply *E. V. Velde*. However, a clear chronological dividing line between the use of the two signatures cannot be drawn.

(i) Landscapes. The work of Esaias's predecessors Coninxloo, Vinckboons and Roelandt Savery represents the last of the Mannerist tradition, in which landscapes were constructed in a fantastic and unrealistic manner, showing turbulent and hilly scenes from a low point of view so that the sky or the horizonline almost disappears. The German painter Adam Elsheimer, whose work became known in Holland through reproductive prints, offered a new alternative: simple compositions—often with a strong diagonal—and a tighter conception of the individual forms achieved by means of clear outlines and the use of chiaroscuro. Such a concept of landscape was truer to nature and became the point of departure for Esaias's own landscapes. The earliest known examples, *Winter Landscape* (1614; Cambridge, Fitzwilliam) and *Riders in a Landscape* (see fig. 1), were executed in Haarlem and already show his characteristic low horizon, a landscape articulated by a diagonal river course, vertical framing groups of trees and horizontal elements. The colouration is tonal, uniform and undramatic; Esaias's striving after a realistic recreation of the Dutch landscape in all its monotony can already be clearly sensed in this early picture.

The incidental character of that early landscape is even more evident in the *View of Zierikzee* (1618; Berlin, Gemäldegal.), in which the silhouette of the city of Zierikzee is captured as a play of masses and outlines under an open sky, without framing devices on either side. The bold realism of this little picture from the beginning of Esaias's Hague period is unmatched in his oeuvre. The colouring, with a series of fine greenish, blueish and brownish tones, composed from myriad tiny flecks of paint, foreshadows the dissolution of form that was to be the most important innovation of Dutch landscape painting later in the 17th century: the effect of the ambient air on the appearance of objects.

In the 1620s Esaias occupied himself primarily with three types of landscape: the dune and coastal landscape,

2. Esaias van de Velde: *Dune Panorama*, oil on panel, 180×225 mm, 1629 (Amsterdam, Rijksmuseum)

the river landscape and the hilly or fantasy landscape. Only the coastal landscapes build on the accomplishments of the earlier Haarlem pictures, for example *Dune Panorama* (see fig. 2). His river landscapes show the most compositional experimentation: the idyllic central composition of *The Ferry* (1622; Amsterdam, Rijksmus.) depicts a gently bending river framed in the foreground by trees. The drawing *Boat Moored before a Walled Farm* (1623; Brighton, A.G. & Mus.) shows a variation of this theme, in which the river course is pushed to one side of the picture. The extensive use of chiaroscuro to define the composition is a new development in the art of the Dutch landscape. Jan van Goyen took up this compositional principle and made it the foundation of his own work. Esaias's third type of landscape picture, the so-called 'hilly landscape', represents the most traditional and academic aspects of his work.

The imaginary landscape is fundamentally un-Dutch in character and originates in part from the works of Coninxloo and the Frankenthal school artists. The contemporary academic definition of landscape derived from van Mander's *Schilder-boek* (1604), where landscape was defined as an autonomous pictorial genre for the first time (Bengtsson). The work of Savery and the Dutch Italianates must also be considered when assessing Esaias's fantasy landscapes. These are best represented as three types: a cliff landscape untouched by civilization (e.g. *Path to the Left of Cascade Falls*, 1625; Riga, Mus. Foreign A.); a mountain landscape with distant fortifications or circular Roman temples (e.g. *Hilly Landscape*, 1624; Prague, N.G., Šternberk Pal.); and the panoramic landscape, which is in part developed out of the second type (e.g. *Hilly Country*, 1627; Copenhagen, Stat. Mus. Kst).

(ii) Subject pictures. Esaias also painted genre and sacred scenes, most of which are set within a landscape. Genre paintings, such as the outdoor parties (*buitenpartijen*), date from the years 1614–24 and reflect the influence of Mannerism (e.g. *Garden Party before a Palace*, 1614; The Hague, Mauritshuis). Many of these banquet pictures are also intended to be read as moralizing representations of the Prodigal Son, or the theme of love for sale may be intended. The iconography of the Five Senses also plays a role in the composition. Often the landscape in these works dwarfs the foreground figures, even those with religious content; the figures become purely staffage before a landscape that is sometimes fantastic, sometimes purely Dutch (e.g. *Christ and the Canaanite Woman*, 1617; New York, S. P. Steinberg priv. col., see Keyes, pl. 76). These pictures also frequently have the character of an interior scene, with the narrative action pushed sharply into the foreground with an enveloping coulisse of trees, recalling the work of Elsheimer (cf. the *Preaching of John the Baptist*, 1618; Karlsruhe, Staatl. Ksthalle; and the version of *c.* 1622; Vienna, Ksthist. Mus.).

In the 1620s Esaias is documented as collaborating with the architectural painter BARTHOLOMEUS VAN BASSEN, for whose interior scenes Esaias painted the figures and also the representations of 'pictures within the picture'. Together they worked on licentious genre subjects but also on ostentatious interiors with religious themes or ecclesiastical interiors. A rich interior that is typical of van Bassen's collaboration with Esaias is found in the painting *Sumptuous Interior with Banqueters* (Amsterdam, Rijksmus.), which shows a room with exceptionally rich furnishings including a coffered ceiling, marble-tiled floor and leather wall-hangings. Esaias's figures enliven these grandiose interiors and present a parallel to the garden parties and banqueting scenes in their selection of *dramatis personae*. The moral content of the interior scenes is underlined through the choice of the pictures within the picture, which are to be understood as providing a contrast to the loose conduct of the characters. Esaias also peopled van Bassen's magnificent church interiors, and here as well the actions of the figures are not casual, but carefully composed and subordinated to a higher didactic content (e.g. *Interior of a Renaissance Church*, 1626; The Hague, Mauritshuis).

The pictures produced by van de Velde and van Bassen were highly prized in their time: the collector Cornelis Cornelisz. van Leuwen of Delft, for whom an entire series of such pictures was painted, paid between 100 and 160 guilders per work. About 30 or so paintings survive from this collaboration. Esaias also provided the staffage for landscape paintings by other artists.

2. DRAWINGS AND PRINTS. Esaias's graphic work is as extensive as his paintings, with over 200 secure attributions recognized today; its development mirrors that found in his paintings. Drawings from his Haarlem years, such as the *View of Spaarnewoude* (Amsterdam, Rijksmus.), have a rigid construction with sharply outlined forms, whereas landscape drawings produced after his move to The Hague, for instance *River Landscape with a Ferry* (*c.* 1625; Chantilly, Mus. Condé), are experimental in nature, with the river no longer the centre of the composition, but to one side.

Esaias was also active as an engraver and etcher, and *c.* 120 prints by him are known (e.g. *Farmhouse in the Vicinity of Haarlem*, *c.*1614; *see* PRINTS, fig. 4). In these works the strokes are short and straight, and changes in direction are conveyed in short breaks and intervals rather than curves; often a few strokes firmly laid down suffice to achieve the desired painterly effect. In the place of the older, more volumetric mode of representation, Esaias employed a planar, painterly mode as the decisive means of expression.

BIBLIOGRAPHY

A. Houbraken: *De groote schouburgh* (1718–21), i, p. 275

K. Zoege von Manteuffel: *Die Künstlerfamilie van de Velde* (Bielefeld and Leipzig, 1927)

W. Stechow: 'Esaias van de Velde and the Beginning of Dutch Landscape Painting', *Ned. Ksthist. Jb.* (1947), pp. 83–94

A. Bengtsson: *Studies on the Rise of Realistic Landscape Painting in Holland, 1610–1625*, Figura, iii (Stockholm, 1952)

W. Stechow: *Dutch Landscape Painting of the 17th Century* (London, 1966), pp. 19–23, 51–6, 84–8

L. J. Bol: *Holländische Maler des 17. Jahrhunderts neben den grossen Meistern* (Brunswick, 1967), pp. 135–6

T. Gerszi: 'Zur Zeichenkunst Esaias van de Veldes', *Acta Hist. A. Acad. Sci. Hung.*, xxiv (1978), pp. 273–7

E. Spickernagel: 'Holländische Dorflandschaften im frühen 17. Jahrhundert, *Städel-Jb.*, n. s. vii (1979), pp. 133–48

Esaias van de Velde, schilder, 1590/91–1630: Jan van Goyen, tekenaaer, 1596–1656 (exh. cat., Amsterdam, Ksthandel Gebr. Douwes; 1981)

Dutch Figure Drawing from the Seventeenth Century (exh. cat. by P. Schatborn, Amsterdam, Rijksmus.; Washington, DC, N.G.A.; 1981), pp. 24, 43, 62, 74, 144

G. S. Keyes: *Esaias van de Velde (1587–1630)* (Doornspijk, 1984)
Masters of 17th-century Dutch Landscape Painting (exh. cat., ed. P. C. Sutton; Amsterdam, Rijksmus.; Boston, MA, Mus. F.A.; Philadelphia, PA, Mus. A.; 1987–8), pp. 497–502

IRENE HABERLAND

(2) Jan van de Velde II (*b* Rotterdam or Delft, *c.* 1593; *d* Enkhuizen, Nov 1641). Draughtsman, printmaker, painter and print publisher, nephew of (1) Esaias van de Velde. In 1613 he was apprenticed to the draughtsman-engraver Jacob Matham in Haarlem and was registered there as a master in 1614. In the years following he made several series of landscape prints, some of which he published himself, others with the addresses of Claes Jansz. Visscher, Robert de Baudous (1574–after 1656) and Hendrick Hondius the elder. Although a number of views of Rome and a large *Panorama of Naples* have been attributed to Jan II, it seems unlikely that he actually went to Italy but rather based his southern landscapes on the drawings and prints of colleagues who had been there. Together with Willem Buytewech and Claes Jansz. Visscher, Jan van de Velde made important innovations in Dutch landscape art. His landscape drawings and prints are characterized by simple compositions and fluent hatching and had an enormous influence on the work of other artists, including Rembrandt.

In 1618 van de Velde married Stintje Fredericksdr. Non in Enkhuizen and then went to live in Haarlem, where in 1635 he became commissioner for the Guild of St Luke. There he produced *c.* 480 prints, not only landscapes but also portraits and genre scenes, as well as illustrations for Bredero's *Groot liedboek* ('Large book of songs'; 1622), Samuel Ampzing's *Beschrijvinge ende lof der stad Haerlem* ('Description and praise of the city of Haarlem'; 1628) and other works.

Initially van de Velde worked after his own designs, but later he mostly based his etchings and engravings on drawings by other artists, including Buytewech, Pieter Saenredam, Moses van Uyttenbroeck, Pieter de Molijn, (1) Esaias van de Velde and Jan Martsen the younger.

Jan's night scenes in the manner of Adam Elsheimer and Hendrick Goudt are famous. Some of his portrait prints were inspired by paintings of Frans Hals, for example his engraving after Hals's *Jacobus Zaffius* (Haarlem, Frans Halsmus.), which shows that the painting was later considerably reduced in size.

A small oval panel, *Winter Landscape*, with the monogram I.V.V. (Amsterdam, Rijksmus.), confirms that van de Velde was also a painter. On the basis of this work, a group of six paintings has been ascribed to him, including a *Winter Landscape* (Paris, Fond. Custodia, Inst. Neer.). His drawn oeuvre comprises *c.* 100 sheets, mostly executed in pen and brown ink in a distinctive linear style. Occasionally a drawing is finished with watercolour or gouache or given broad washes with a brush (e.g. *Landscape with Trees and Farms*; Rotterdam, Mus. Boymans–van Beuningen; see fig.).

This technique can also be seen in a number of market scenes, which were very much influenced by drawings by Buytewech. Jan van de Velde's pupils are thought to have included Willem Outgersz. Ackersloot, Cornelis van Kittenstein (1598–1652), Claes Pouwelsz. and Simon Poelenburch (1591–after 1625). By 5 July 1641 he and his wife were again living in Enkhuizen.

BIBLIOGRAPHY
Hollstein, *Dut. & Flem.*; Thieme–Becker
D. Franken and J. P. van der Kellen: *L'Oeuvre de Jan van de Velde, graveur hollandais, 1593–1641* (Amsterdam, 1883, rev. 1968)
J. G. van Gelder: *Jan van de Velde, 1593–1641: Teekenaar–schilder* [Jan van de Velde, 1593–1641: draughtsman-painter] (The Hague, 1933)
——: 'Jan van de Velde, 1593–1641: Teekenaar-schilder, Addenda 1, *Oud-Holland*, lxx (1955), pp. 21–40
——: 'Drawings by Jan van de Velde', *Master Drgs*, v (1967), pp. 39–42
Dawn of the Golden Age: Northern Netherlandish Art, 1580–1620 (exh. cat., Amsterdam, Rijksmus., 1993–4), pp. 320–21, 658–62

GER LUIJTEN

Velde, van de (ii). Dutch family of painters and draughtsmen of Flemish origin.

Jan van de Velde II: *Landscape with Trees and Farms*, pen and brown ink with blue wash, *c.* 1620–30 (Rotterdam, Museum Boymans–van Beuningen)

I. Introduction. II. Marine artists. III. Collections. IV. Studio organization. V. Posthumous reputation.

I. Introduction.

The family came from Oostwinkel, near Ghent in East Flanders, the birthplace of the seaman Willem van de Velde, who was for a time master of a transport vessel. By 1631 his son, the marine painter (1) Willem van de Velde I, had moved to Leiden, where he married Judith van Leeuwen, whom he divorced in 1662. Two of their sons became painters: (2) Willem van de Velde II, born in Leiden, and ADRIAEN VAN DE VELDE, born after the family moved to Amsterdam *c.* 1633–6. Willem II was a marine artist like his father; the two worked closely together and moved to England in the winter of 1672–3. By contrast, Adriaen was primarily a landscape painter, influenced by Jan Wijnants and Philips Wouwerman; he died shortly before his father and brother emigrated to England.

The reasons for Willem the elder and Willem the younger's move are not fully documented, but no doubt the principal cause was the politically unsettled and dangerous state of the northern Netherlands following the French invasion in May 1672. A letter from Pieter Blauw to Cardinal Leopoldo de' Medici of June 1674 clearly states that Willem I had departed for England more than 18 months before, 'seeing that he, as a result of the bad condition here during these wars, cannot do his work'. Many other Dutch artists, engravers and craftsmen had likewise fled to England from Holland, encouraged to do so by Charles II's declaration of 1 June 1672. The move proved particularly beneficial for the van de Veldes because both Charles and his brother James, Duke of York (later James II), were yachtsmen and took a keen interest in maritime affairs. Charles provided them with a house in East Lane, Greenwich, allowed them the use of the Queen's House as a studio and on 12 January 1674 issued a royal warrant which ordered:

> the Salary of One hundred pounds p. Annm unto William Van de Velde the Elder for taking and making Draughts of sea fights, and the like Salary of One Hundred pounds p. Annm unto William Van de Velde the Younger for putting the said Draughts into Colours for our particular use.

In 1691 the van de Velde family moved from Greenwich to Westminster, London, where both Willem I and Willem

II died. They are buried alongside each other in the church of St James, Piccadilly, London. Willem II's sons, Willem van de Velde III (*b* Amsterdam, *bapt* 4 Sept 1667; *d* ?London, after 1708) and Cornelis van de Velde (*fl* 1699–1729), about whom little is known, were both marine painters in London. Certain paintings, once thought to be inferior works by the hand of Willem II, are often assigned to Willem III.

II. Marine artists.

(1) Willem [William] van de Velde I [*de oude*; the elder] (*b* Leiden, 1611; *d* London, Dec 1693). His training and early activity in Leiden and Amsterdam is not well documented, but he spent his entire working life drawing ships and small craft. His drawings provided him with the raw material for his grisailles (*penschilderingen* or 'pen paintings' drawn in ink on a prepared white canvas or oak panel). He was constantly at sea with the Dutch fleet, sometimes as an independent observer, sometimes in an official capacity. He was present at the Battle of Scheveningen in 1653 and made drawings from the deck of his galliot (a small Dutch sailing vessel). He witnessed the Battle of the Sound in 1658, which is recorded in a grisaille (London, N. Mar. Mus.), and the defeat of the Dutch fleet at the Battle of Lowestoft in 1665. In 1666 he made a sequence of drawings recording every stage of the epic Four Days' Battle off Dunkirk, with the approval and protection of Admiral de Ruyter. For the next six years he was at home in Amsterdam working on his grisailles. On the outbreak of the Third Anglo-Dutch War in 1672 he rejoined the Dutch fleet and made on-the-spot drawings of the Battle of Sole Bay.

One of Willem I's first commissions in England was the design of a series of tapestries commemorating the Battle of Sole Bay (five tapestries in London, Hampton Court, Royal Col.; one in London, Queen's House). In 1673 he was at sea again, in a vessel provided for him by the Duke of York, making drawings of the first and second battles of Schooneveld. The King would not allow him to risk his life again, however, and so he missed the second battle of the Texel. During the ensuing years of peace, he recorded royal embarkations and arrivals in the Thames estuary. He was still drawing ships and painting grisailles in his seventies.

Willem I's drawings, mostly carried out in pen and grey wash, provide an extraordinarily complete record of the

Willem van de Velde I: *The Ship 'Mordaunt'*, pencil and wash, 162×525 mm, *c.* 1681 (London, National Maritime Museum)

ships and small craft of Holland and England in the late 17th century. The complex forms of men-of-war are drawn from all angles with a thorough understanding of ship construction. Particular attention is always paid to such details as figureheads, stern carvings and gunports, which differentiate one ship from another. Some of the drawings are tightly controlled and carefully worked, whereas others, such as his portrait of *The Ship 'Mordaunt'* (*c.* 1681; London, N. Mar. Mus.; see fig.), are executed with a dashing freedom of touch. The fluidity of his best drawings contrasts markedly with his grisaille paintings, which have a curiously static appearance. The waves are stylized and follow the conventions of earlier engravers. The elegantly drawn groups of figures often introduced in the foreground are humorously observed, but curiously frozen in appearance. Only the ships seem to come to life. In the large grisaille painting of *The Dutch Ship 'Oosterwijk' under Sail near the Shore* (London, N. Mar. Mus.) he showed an absolute mastery of form and detail in his drawing of the elaborately decorated hull, the sails, rigging and flags of the principal ship. His battle scenes combine acute observation of ships in action with a regard for the decorative appearance of the picture as a whole. The *Battle of the Sound* (London, N. Mar. Mus.) and the *Battle of Scheveningen* (Amsterdam, Rijksmus.) are good examples. Although his fame rests on his grisailles and his drawings, van de Velde the elder occasionally produced oil paintings in his later years. Most of these are ship portraits, and

though useful as historical documents, they lack the vigour and assurance of his son (2) Willem van de Velde II's work in this medium.

(2) Willem [William] **van de Velde II** [*de jonge*; the younger] (*b* Leiden, 1633; *d* London, 6 April 1707). Son of (1) Willem van de Velde I. Around 1648 Willem II moved to Weesp to study under Simon de Vlieger, whose sombre and atmospheric seascapes were a foil to the more prosaic realism of his father's work. In 1652 he was back in Amsterdam, where he married Petronella le Maine. The marriage was dissolved a year later. He took up work in his father's studio, and his earliest paintings were signed by van de Velde the elder as head of the studio. In 1666 Willem II married Magdalena Walraven in Amsterdam. His domestic life and his character remain a mystery.

Willem II had precocious gifts as an artist, and many of his celebrated calm scenes with shipping were painted while he was still in his twenties. The *States Yacht in a Fresh Breeze Running down towards a Group of Dutch Ships* (1673; London, N. Mar. Mus.; see fig. 1) shows many of the qualities that brought him fame: exquisitely drawn ships, a careful regard for the placing of each vessel to create a satisfying composition and an atmosphere of serene tranquillity. During the next ten years he painted a succession of calms. These usually depict Dutch fishing boats at low tide among the mud banks of Holland's northern coast. One of the finest examples of these, *Calm:*

1. Willem van de Velde II: *States Yacht in a Fresh Breeze Running down towards a Group of Dutch Ships*, oil on canvas, 0.75×1.08 m, 1673 (London, National Maritime Museum)

A Wijdschip and a Kaag in an Inlet close to a Sea Wall (or *Dutch Vessels close Inshore at Low Tide*; London, N.G.; for illustration *see* MARINE PAINTING), has a sky of breathtaking beauty comparable with those of Jacob van Ruisdael and John Constable. Willem the younger was still only 32 when he painted *Calm: Dutch Ships Coming to Anchor* (London, Wallace), regarded by many as his masterpiece. In this picture he demonstrated that he was as capable of working on a large scale as he was on the much smaller scale of the cabinet picture. The picture was commissioned by Admiral Cornelis Tromp and shows the *Liefde*, Tromp's flagship, at the Battle of Lowestoft in 1665.

The subject-matter of van de Velde's paintings underwent a marked change during the 1670s, after his removal to England. Instead of groups of anonymous fishing boats, he tended to paint portraits of particular ships, such as royal yachts and men-of-war, while storm and shipwreck subjects replace the calms of the 1660s. One reason for this change in mood may have been the influence of Ludolf Bakhuizen, who specialized in dramatic storm scenes. He had settled in Amsterdam in 1649 and soon became a serious rival to the van de Veldes. However the talents of van de Velde the younger were more than equal to the challenge, and in his celebrated *The English Ship 'Resolution' in a Gale* (London, N. Mar. Mus.) he showed that he could paint storms with the same mastery he had brought to calms.

Apart from several paintings depicting the Four Days' Battle of 1666, Willem II painted few sea battles before coming to England. From 1672 they became a major preoccupation, as both the Duke of York and the King commissioned depictions of English naval actions. After the end of the Anglo-Dutch wars in 1674, he also painted sea battles for Dutch patrons (for further discussion and illustration *see* BATTLE PICTURES AND MILITARY SCENES, §2(ii) and fig. 1). The greatest of his battle pieces, *The 'Gouden Leeuw' at the Battle of the Texel* (1686; London, N. Mar. Mus.), was commissioned by Admiral Tromp (1629–91), almost certainly for display in Trompenburg, his recently built château near Hilversum.

Unlike his father, Willem II did not make a regular practice of sailing with the Dutch or the English fleets, and the only action of the Anglo-Dutch wars that he is likely to have witnessed was the Four Days' Battle. All his other battle pictures were painted from sketches made by his father. His working method seems to be illustrated in Michiel van Musscher's amusing portrait of *Willem van de Velde the Younger in his Studio* (*c.* 1665–7; England, Lord Northbrook priv. col., see *The Treasure Houses of Britain* (exh. cat., ed. G. Jackson-Stops; Washington, DC, N.G.A., 1985), no. 305), in which the artist is shown seated at his easel with drawings of ships scattered on the floor for reference. After the death of his father in 1693, however, it became necessary for van de Velde the younger to be present himself at important maritime events, and an order from the English Admiralty dated 18 May 1694 indicates his official role. Soon afterwards he joined the fleet commanded by Admiral Russell and spent a year in the Mediterranean.

No longer subject to his father's obsession with accuracy, Willem II adopted a freer approach in his later work.

2. Willem van de Velde II: *Cannon Shot*, oil on canvas, 785×670 mm, *c.* 1660 (Amsterdam, Rijksmuseum)

His brushwork became fluid and open, and some of his smaller pictures have something of the immediacy of oil sketches, in contrast to the highly finished state of his earlier works. His last major work was the *Calm: The 'Royal Sovereign' at Anchor* (1703; London, N. Mar. Mus.). Less dramatic than the similar, though more celebrated *Cannon Shot* (*c.* 1660; Amsterdam, Rijksmus.; see fig. 2), it shows no weakening of the artist's power. The drawing of the principal ship is as masterful as ever, the smaller vessels are grouped with his usual skill, and the great expanse of cloudy sky is painted with the utmost subtlety.

III. Collections.

The major collections of paintings by the two marine artists are divided between England and the Netherlands. Some of the finest oil paintings by van de Velde the younger are in the British Royal Collection, the Wallace Collection and the National Gallery in London. The National Maritime Museum, Greenwich, London, has the largest collection of van de Velde drawings, numbering over 1400 sheets, together with an impressive selection of paintings and grisailles by both the elder and the younger.

In the Netherlands the major collection of drawings is in the Boymans–van Beuningen Museum, Rotterdam, while the Rijksmuseum, Amsterdam, has a comprehensive collection of grisailles and paintings. The Mauritshuis in The Hague has several fine works, and the Amsterdam Historisch Museum has one of van de Velde the younger's masterpieces, *The 'Gouden Leeuw' off Amsterdam*, a sweeping view of shipping on the River IJ painted for the City of Amsterdam in 1686.

IV. Studio organization.

The huge quantity of paintings and drawings that the van de Veldes produced has caused considerable problems of attribution. Apart from the fact that Willem I assisted his son by supplying him with detailed drawings, evidence suggests that the van de Veldes employed a number of studio assistants who collaborated with van de Velde the younger on many of his pictures. These included Joris van der Haagen and Willem II's son Cornelis, who married van der Haagen's daughter. Willem II's other son, also called Willem, also worked in the studio for a time. The fame of the van de Veldes also attracted a number of Dutch and English followers, many of whom produced versions and imitations of van de Velde compositions. Peter Monamy and Robert Woodcock (*c.* 1691–1728) in England and Jacob Knyff (1639–81) and Isaac Sailmaker (*c.* 1633–1721) in the Netherlands were among the most talented of these.

V. Posthumous reputation.

Willem II's work continued to influence several generations of English marine artists throughout the 18th century and into the 19th. Samuel Scott, who owned some van de Velde pictures, was heavily influenced by him in his early years. Charles Gore (1729–1807) painted charming watercolours in the van de Velde manner. Charles Brooking, Dominic Serres and Nicholas Pocock are all known to have copied van de Velde compositions. J. M. W. Turner regarded van de Velde as one of the great masters, and his famous Bridgewater sea-piece, *Dutch Boats in a Gale: Fishermen Endeavouring to Put their Fish on Board* (exh. RA 1801; Duke of Sutherland priv. col., see *Turner, 1775–1851* (exh. cat. by M. Butlin and A. Wilton, London, Tate; London, RA; 1984–5), no. 71), was a deliberate challenge to van de Velde's *Kaag Close-hauled in a Fresh Breeze* (Toledo, OH, Mus. A.). Constable admired van de Velde and copied his work, and so did the two most gifted English marine artists of the Victorian period, Clarkson Stanfield and E. W. Cooke.

BIBLIOGRAPHY

E. Michel: *Les van de Velde* (Paris, 1892)
C. Hofstede de Groot: *Holländischen Maler* (1907–28), vii, pp. 1–171
K. Zoege von Manteuffel: *Die Künstlerfamilie van de Velde* (Bielefeld, 1927)
H. P. Baard: *Willem van de Velde de oude, Willem van de Velde de jonge* (Amsterdam, 1942)
M. S. Robinson: *Van de Velde Drawings in the National Maritime Museum*, 2 vols (Cambridge, 1958–74)
R. E. J. Weber: 'Willem van de Velde de oude als topograaf van onze zeegaten' [Willem van de Velde the elder as topographer of Dutch seaways], *Oud-Holland*, xc/2 (1976), pp. 115–31
P. D. Fraser: 'Charles Gore and the Willem van de Veldes', *Master Drgs*, xv/4 (1977), pp. 375–87
M. S. Robinson and R. E. J. Weber: *The Willem van de Velde Drawings in the Boymans–van Beuningen Museum, Rotterdam*, 3 vols (Rotterdam, 1979)
R. E. J. Weber: 'The Artistic Relationship between the Ship Draughtsman Willem van de Velde the Elder and his Son the Marine Painter in the Year 1664', *Master Drgs*, xvii/2 (1979), pp. 152–61
Willem van de Velde de oude, 1611–1693: Scheepstekenaar [Willem van de Velde the elder: ship draughtsman] (exh. cat. by A. W. F. M. Meij, Rotterdam, Boymans–van Beuningen, 1980)
Zeichner der Admiralität: Marine-Zeichnungen und -Gemälde von Willem van de Velde dem Älteren und dem Jüngeren (exh. cat., ed. G. Kauffman; Hamburg, Altonaer Mus.; London, N. Mar. Mus.; 1981–2)
E. H. H. Archibald: 'The Willem van de Veldes: Their Background and Influence on Maritime Painting in England', *J. Royal Soc. A.*, cxxx/5310 (1982), pp. 347–60
The Art of the van de Veldes (exh. cat. by D. Cordingly and W. Percival-Prescott, London, N. Mar. Mus., 1982)
M. S. Robinson: *The Paintings of the Willem van de Veldes* [cat. rais.], 2 vols (London, 1990)

DAVID CORDINGLY

Velde, Adriaen van de (*bapt* Amsterdam, 30 Nov 1636; *bur* Amsterdam, 21 Jan 1672). Dutch painter, draughtsman and etcher, son of Willem van de Velde I (*see* VELDE (ii), VAN DE, (1)). According to Houbraken, he first studied in Amsterdam with his father; however, unlike his father and his brother, Willem van de Velde II, Adriaen did not incline towards marine painting, so he was sent to Haarlem to complete his training with the landscape painter Jan Wijnants. By 1657 Adriaen had settled in Amsterdam, where various documents regularly record his presence until his death. During a career of less than two decades, van de Velde produced an extensive and varied body of paintings, drawings and prints. Meadows and Italianate views with herdsmen and their cattle make up the bulk of his oeuvre, although—as far as is known—he never travelled to Italy. He also painted beaches, dunes, forests, winter scenes, portraits in landscape settings, at least one genre piece (*Woman Drinking*, 1662; ex-Gemäldegal. Alte Meister, Dresden, see Zoege van Manteuffel, pl. 58) and a few historical pictures. His earliest known works are six etchings of 1653, and dated paintings survive for every year from 1654 to 1671. Pastures with cattle and herders predominate in his work of 1653–8. The paintings and prints of these years reveal no trace of Wijnants's influence. Instead, the young van de Velde emulated the art of Paulus Potter and, to a lesser extent, that of Karel Dujardin.

1. PAINTINGS. Potter's example informs not only Adriaen's choice of the cattle-piece as his preferred subject, but also his depiction of the meadow landscape, the tight, precise technique he employed to paint grass, foliage and fur, and the hard, cool sunlight that pervades pictures of the mid-1650s, such as *Two Cows* (1656; Wanas, Sweden, Wachtmeister priv. col., see Hofstede de Groot, no. 234). Warmer hues and a softer, yellower sunlight—a response to the works of the Italianate painters Dujardin, Nicolaes Berchem and Jan Asselijn—entered van de Velde's pictures about 1658, and, at the same time, he began to engage a broader range of landscape subjects. A farmyard (London, N.G.) and two forest scenes (London, N.G., and Frankfurt am Main, Städel. Kstinst. & Städt. Gal.), all conspicuously indebted to Potter, date from this year, as does the *Riding School* (Raleigh, NC Mus. A.), based on similar depictions of equestrian subjects by Dujardin.

Also from 1658 is the brilliant *Beach at Scheveningen* (Kassel, Schloss Wilhelmshöhe), the most original and harmonious of van de Velde's rare beach scenes. Unlike the monochromatic atmosphere of most contemporary views of the Dutch coast, van de Velde suffused the entire scene with a warm sunlight that deepens the shadows and catches the figures' vivid colours against the rich browns of the sand and greys of the sea. This luminosity and pronounced local colour, adapted from the Italianate painters' evocation of Mediterranean light, eventually

Adriaen van de Velde: *Landscape with Cattle and Figures*, oil on canvas, 1257×1670 mm, 1664 (Cambridge, Fitzwilliam Museum)

extended to Adriaen's pictures of Dutch pastures, woods and dunes, as well as to his own Italianate views.

In 1659 van de Velde painted *The Ferry* (Schwerin, Staatl. Mus.), the first of his landscapes in which the large scale and the individuality of the figures transcend the function of mere staffage. The prominence of the meticulously drawn figures and animals in his landscapes constitutes another essential ingredient in van de Velde's mature style of the late 1650s. A life study in red chalk (Leiden, Rijksuniv., Prentenkab.) for one of the boatmen in *The Ferry* affirms that this crucial element in van de Velde's work depended on his practice of drawing from the model in the studio and from cattle in the fields (*see* §2 below). The stylistic innovations of 1658–9 laid the foundation for van de Velde's remarkable development during the 1660s, which culminated in such works as the *Migration of Jacob* (1663; London, Wallace), with its numerous large-scale and painstakingly individualized figures. This is also apparent in pastoral and Italianate scenes dominated by relaxing shepherds and grazing cattle, for instance the *Landscape with Cattle and Figures* (see fig.), which epitomizes the type of pastoral scene that constituted van de Velde's favourite subject during the last decade of his short life. Its idyllic Italianate setting, congenial herders surrounded by various farm animals, warm light, intensely green, feathery foliage (turned blue in places due to pigment changes), majestic fair-weather sky and immense foreground tree with a truncated crown are recurring elements in his mature works.

Due to his skill in painting figures and animals, van de Velde was frequently employed to add staffage to pictures by fellow landscape artists, including Jacob van Ruisdael, Meindert Hobbema (*see* HOBBEMA, MEINDERT, fig. 1), Jan Wijnants, Jan van der Heyden and Frederik de Moucheron. As early as 1664 an inventory lists paintings by Wijnants and Moucheron 'gestofferd door Adriaen van de Velde', and Adriaen's contribution to these collaborative efforts demonstrably increased their market value.

Besides the *Migration of Jacob*, van de Velde's rare history paintings include a group of biblical and allegorical works set in interiors. Among the latter are a Passion series executed for the Augustinian *schuilkerk* (clandestine church) 'De Ster' in Amsterdam (1664; Nijmegen, Augustinian Friars; see Hofstede de Groot, nos 11, 14–16 and 18), an *Allegory* (1663; Moscow, Pushkin Mus. F.A.) and an *Annunciation* (1667; Amsterdam, Rijksmus.). The style he adapted for these large-scale figural paintings derives from the classicizing manner practised in Amsterdam and Haarlem during the 1650s and 1660s by such artists as Dujardin and Jan de Bray.

2. DRAWINGS. One of the most gifted and versatile 17th-century Dutch draughtsmen, van de Velde is also one of the few landscape painters of the period whose

method of design can to some degree be reconstructed. His numerous surviving drawings include landscapes sketched from nature, compositional ideas for paintings and prints, cattle drawn from life and nudes and other figures executed from studio models. Van de Velde used three types of preparatory study for his paintings. He began with a preliminary compositional sketch, in which he summarily jotted down the broad outlines of the design. From this first idea he produced a second, fully resolved and detailed drawing of the whole composition. Although not transferred directly to the canvas or panel, this second design served as the model for the finished work. In addition, he made chalk studies from life for the principal figures and animals in his pictures.

3. ETCHINGS. Van de Velde's activity as a printmaker was concentrated in the years 1653, 1657–9 and 1670. Most of his 28 etchings depict farm animals. The finest are distinguished by their forceful draughtsmanship and the masterful evocation of strong light and deep shadows on the solid flanks of grazing and resting cows. While the subject-matter and design of his prints was suggested by the work of other etchers of animal subjects (e.g. Potter, Dujardin and Berchem), van de Velde's brilliant use of the etching needle at once emulates and surpasses Dujardin's technique.

BIBLIOGRAPHY
Hollstein: *Dut. & Flem.*; Thieme–Becker
A. Houbraken: *De groote schouburgh* (1718–21), iii, pp. 90–91
A. D. de Vries: 'Biografische aanteekeningen betreffende voornamelijk Amsterdamsche schilders, plaatsnijders, enz.', *Oud-Holland*, iv (1886), pp. 143–4
C. Hofstede de Groot: *Holländischen Maler*, iv (1911), pp. 475–608
K. Zoege van Manteuffel: *Die Künstlerfamilie van de Velde* (Bielefeld and Leipzig, 1927), pp. 55–83
W. Stechow: *Dutch Landscape Painting of the Seventeenth Century* (London, 1966), pp. 31–2, 60–61, 80, 98–9, 107–9, 160–62
W. Robinson: 'Preparatory Drawings by Adriaen van de Velde', *Master Drgs*, xvii (1979), pp. 3–23
——: 'Some Studies of Nude Models by Adriaen van de Velde', *Donum Amlcorum: Essays in Honour of Per Bjurström* (Stockholm, 1993), pp. 53–66
WILLIAM W. ROBINSON

Velde, Henry Van de. *See* VAN DE VELDE, HENRY.

Velden, Petrus van der (*b* Rotterdam, 5 May 1837; *d* Auckland, New Zealand, 11 Nov 1913). Dutch painter. Originally trained as a lithographer, he ran a lithographic printing works in Rotterdam around the years 1858–67, and then studied at the academies in Rotterdam and Berlin. After a stay on the island of Marken (1871–3) he lived in or near The Hague until 1888. During this period he painted mainly genre scenes such as *Dutch Funeral* (1872; Christchurch, NZ, McDougall A.G.) and the *Old Cellist* (1887; The Hague, Gemeentemus.); he also produced some landscapes, for example *Snow on the Sand Dunes* (1889–90; Wellington, Mus. NZ, Te Papa Tongarewa). His work of this Dutch period displays a tension between Naturalism and Romantic Realism in the style of Jozef Israels. In 1890 van der Velden moved to Christchurch in New Zealand, where he painted rather monochromatic impressionistic landscapes. Important works from this period include *Rock Study, Sumner* (*c.* 1890; Wellington, Mus. NZ, Te Papa Tongarewa) and *Mountain Stream, Otira Gorge* (1891; Dunedin, NZ, Pub. A.G.). From 1898

to 1904 he lived in Australia, returning to New Zealand permanently in 1904. The few works painted during these later years reveal an increased vibrancy of colour and a looser, more expressive technique. With such works as the colourful *Aim of All Existence* (*c.* 1907; Christchurch, NZ, J. F. Hutchinson priv. col.) and watercolours such as *Trees* (*c.* 1909; priv. col., see Wilson, 4.1.2.7) he finally distanced himself from the dark tonalities of Israels.

BIBLIOGRAPHY
Van der Velden: Paintings and Drawings in the Collection of the National Art Gallery, Wellington (Wellington, NZ, N.A.G., 1968)
T. L. R. Wilson: *Petrus van der Velden (1837–1913)*, 2 vols (Sydney, 1979)
ANNEMIEKE HOOGENBOOM

Vélez, José Miguel (*b* Cuenca, July 1829; *d* Cuenca, 1 Dec 1892). Ecuadorean sculptor. He received his training in the workshop of the Cuencan painter Eusebio Alarcón (*fl* 1835–64). From a young age he was interested in polychromed wood-carving on religious themes, a medium that was greatly esteemed by the Quito school during the colonial period. Vélez, however, transformed the former Baroque language into Neo-classicism, inspired by imported examples and incorporating the academic teachings brought so late into Ecuador. Especially worthy of mention are his Crucifixes (e.g. *Holy Christ*; church of Señor de las Aguas, Girón, Azuay), as well as his images of the Infant Christ and Calvary, which were sought after by collectors, religious communities and museums throughout the country. Together with Gaspar de Sangurima (1787–*fl* 1833), his disciple Daniel Alvarado (*c.* 1867–1953) and other local engravers, Vélez managed to make Cuenca the most important centre of 19th-century sculpture in the country. His portraiture was also significant, and he created a series of busts of public figures in wood and marble, including that of the celebrated Franciscan journalist *Fray Vicente Solano* (Cuenca, Colegio Semin.).

BIBLIOGRAPHY
F. J. M. Vargas: *El arte religioso en Cuenca* (Quito, 1967)
J. T. León: *Biografías de artistas y artesanos del Azuay* (Cuenca, 1969)
Saluat: *Historia del arte ecuatoriano*, iii (Quito and Barcelona, 1977), pp. 237–9
ALEXANDRA KENNEDY TROYA

Vélez Blanco Castle. Spanish castle situated in Almería. It is one of a series of fortresses (together with those of Mula, Murcia and Cuevas de Almanzora in Almería) built at the beginning of the 16th century by Pedro Fajardo y Chacón, first Marqués de los Vélez (1484–1540) and Governor of the kingdom of Murcia. The fortress has an elongated ground-plan and is crowned on the north front by a keep. The most important part of the ensemble is the square courtyard, which was removed from Spain in 1904 and is now in New York (Met.), with the position of the east and west galleries reversed.

According to an inscription in the courtyard, the castle was built between 1506 and 1515 after Fajardo received the lordship of the town from Ferdinand II and Isabella (1503), took up residence there (1505) and was given the title of Marqués (1507) by Ferdinand, who was then regent. The heraldry of the principal areas of the castle, including the coat of arms of his second wife, Mencía de la Cueva, belongs to this period. However, that of his third wife, Catalina de Silva, whom he married in 1518, is evident in other parts of the castle. A bronze door, signed *Luis* by the artisan who made it, is dated 1515 (Mexico City, priv. col.).

The fortified areas of the castle, particularly the defences and the Late Gothic east gallery of the courtyard, are examples of late 15th-century Spanish art. Attempts have been made to link this building with the chapel of the Vélez family in Murcia Cathedral (completed in 1507), which is also Gothic. By contrast, the three other galleries of the courtyard have columns, arches and windows with Italian Renaissance detailing and sculpture. The castle was one of the first buildings in Spain to present this style, which reflected the Italianate education of the Marqués de los Vérez (a disciple of the humanist Pietro Martire d'Anghiera), who is portrayed in a frieze as accompanying the Emperor Titus on his triumphal entry into Rome. All of these elements were carved in local marble, and each of the three decorated galleries has a different composition. The gallery at the south entrance, beside the staircase which leads up two flights, has two levels of arcading. The east side has a gallery only on the upper floor, and the west side has two triple sets of superimposed openings. The layout appears to have been influenced by an earlier courtyard in the Spanish style, which would have made it necessary to use low arches. The marble carved elements cannot be precisely dated, and there is no documentary evidence on the identity of the artists responsible. The carved work has been attributed to Martín Milanés and Francisco Florentín, who were active in Granada in 1520, the master sculptor Egidio della Verda, who contributed in 1511 to LA CALAHORRA castle, and, more cautiously, to a workshop of Tuscan and Ligurian sculptors. The castle itself has been implausibly attributed to Lorenzo Vázquez de Segovia on the grounds that both La Calahorra Castle and Vélez Blanco Castle derive from models in the *Codex Escurialensis*, but Vázquez de Segovia's use of Italianate elements in La Calahorra differs considerably from Vélez Blanco. At La Calahorra the detailing of the windows and the incorrect mouldings and curves of the arches indicate the presence of Italian craftsmen working under a Spanish architect unused to the contemporary forms of architecture in Rome.

Like La Calahorra Castle, though less perfectly, Vélez Blanco Castle is a good example of the early application of Italian stylistic elements in Spain at the beginning of the 16th century. They are subordinated here to Spanish structural traditions without really transforming them, at the instance of a member of the Spanish nobility with humanist and antiquarian interests.

BIBLIOGRAPHY

M. Gómez-Moreno: 'Sobre el renacimiento en Castilla: Notas para un discurso preliminar I: Hacia Lorenzo Vázquez', *Archv Esp. A. & Arqueol.*, i (1925), pp. 1–40
B. G. Proske: *Castilian Sculpture, Gothic to Renaissance* (New York, 1951)
F. Chueca Goitia: *Arquitectura del siglo XVI*, xi: *Ars hispaniae* (Madrid, 1953)
J. A. Tapia Garrido: *Vélez Blanco* (Vélez Blanco, 1959)
G. Marañón: *Los tres Vélez* (Madrid, 1960)
O. Raggio: 'The Velez Blanco Patio', *Bull. Met.*, xxiii (1964), pp. 141–76; Sp. trans. in *Anales de la Universidad de Murcia*, xxvi/2 and 3 (1967–8), pp. 231–61
E. Cooper: *Castillos señoriales de Castilla de los siglos XV y XVI*, 2 vols (Madrid, 1980)
M. Fernández: 'Hacia una recuperación del palacio de Vélez Blanco (Almería): Los ordenes en la arquitectura del protorrenacimiento', *Fragmentos*, viii–ix (1986), pp. 78–89

FERNANDO MARÍAS

Vélez de Guevara y Tassis, Iñigo. *See* OÑATE Y DE VILLAMEDIANA, Conde de.

Velho, Bartolomeu (*b* Lisbon, *fl c.* 1560; *d* France, 20 Feb 1568). Portuguese cartographer, active in France. He was probably the son of the illuminator Diogo Fernandes, and the little that is known about Velho concerns his last days after he had moved to France around 1567 to serve the king. The five known examples of Velho's work are a fusiform map (*c.* 1560; Paris, Bib. N., Rés. Ge. D 7824); a world atlas with sixteen maps and two pages depicting cosmographic elements (*c.* 1560; San Marino, CA, Huntington Lib.); a set of four maps of the world (Florence, Accad. B.A. & Liceo A.); *Cosmographia* (1568; Paris, Bib. N., Rés. Ge. EE 266); and a map (Paris, Bib. N., Rés. Ge. B 1148) attributed to him by Teixeira da Mota (1960) on stylistic grounds. His works have little artistic interest except for the *Cosmographia*, in which the depiction of the allegorical figures representing the known planets is particularly fine. These include the sun, which was thought at the time to be a planet. The folio devoted to the *Figuration of the Celestial Bodies* consists of a planisphere divided into two circles.

BIBLIOGRAPHY

S. Viterbo: *Trabalhos náuticos dos portugueses dos séculos XVI e XVII*, i (Lisbon, 1898), pp. 310–22
A. Teixeira da Mota: *Portugaliae monumenta cartographica* (Lisbon, 1960), ii, pp. 89–92; v, p. 185

LUIS DE ALBUQUERQUE

Velho, Tomé (*b* Lamarosa, nr Tentúgal, *c.* 1550; *d* Tentúgal, 1632). Portuguese architect and sculptor. He moved *c.* 1570 to Coimbra, where he joined the group of sculptors working around João de Ruão, who then dominated Portuguese sculpture. It was there that Velho first encountered architectural forms based on classical models and a decorative style, originating in northern Europe, in which Mannerist ornament was superimposed on classical structures.

Numerous extant documents refer to the activities of Tomé Velho and to his civic life. His first important assignment was in 1576, when he worked in collaboration with João de Ruão on the construction of the church of Bouças, Matosinhos, near Oporto. João de Ruão was then old and unable to travel to the north of the country, and he left his assistant to complete the work. In 1582 Tomé Velho was in charge of the construction, decoration and sculpture of the chapel of S Teotónio in the chapter room of the Augustinian monastery of Santa Cruz, Coimbra. While adopting a hybrid architectural style, he remained faithful to the northern taste for minutely detailed decoration and the use of Flemish strapwork in a version of the Renaissance style of decoration as practised by João de Ruão after 1530. This taste for decoration and for the picturesque is evident in the structure of the chapel of S Teotónio, in which Velho copied the chapel of the Holy Sacrament of the Sé Velha, Coimbra, built by João de Ruão in 1566. In 1583 Velho was commissioned, with Duarte de Melo, to build a chapel (Capela do Mestre

Escola) and altarpiece dedicated to St Catherine at Coimbra Cathedral.

In 1589 Tomé Velho was responsible for the construction and carving of the altarpiece in the chancel of the parish church of Cantanhede. In the same year he was working on the convent of Our Lady of Mount Carmel, Tentúgal, where he was responsible for the nuns' quarters and private chapel, with its fine vault, and where he was influenced by the style of the 16th-century colleges of the University of Coimbra.

BIBLIOGRAPHY

P. Quintino Garcia: *Artistas de Coimbra* (Coimbra, 1923)
A. Nogueira Gonçalves: *Inventário artístico de Portugal: Distrito de Coimbra* (Lisbon, 1952)
——: 'Tomé Velho artista coimbrão na passagem dos séculos XVI e XVII', *Ocidente*, lxxxiii (1972), pp. 219–36

PEDRO DIAS

Veli Can [Valī Jān] (*b* Tabriz; *fl* Istanbul, *c*. 1580–*c*. 1600). Ottoman painter. According to the Ottoman chronicler Mustafa 'Ali, he was a student of the Safavid court painter SIYAVUSH and came to the Ottoman court at Istanbul *c*. 1580. Mustafa 'Ali claimed that, despite Veli Can's gifts as a draughtsman, his style did not progress and his work remained the same throughout his career. His name appears in the registers of the corporation of Ottoman artists for 1595–6 and 1596–7 with a daily salary of seven *akče*, a mediocre sum, which bears out Mustafa 'Ali's assessment. The large number of dubious attributions to the artist had made the definition of his style impossible until Denny discovered a tiny hidden signature on a drawing (Istanbul, Topkapı Pal. Lib., H. 2836). From this drawing, depicting a bird and a grotesque head in foliage, he has convincingly assigned three other drawings (Istanbul, Topkapı Pal. Lib., H. 2147, fol. 23*v* and H. 2162, fol. 8*v*; Paris, Mus. Jacquemart-André, MS. 261) to the artist. The rounded serrations of the leaf edges and bold, black sweeping lines that form the spines of the leaves place these drawings squarely in the *saz*, or non-historical Ottoman court style of the late 16th century (*see* ISLAMIC ART, §III, 4(vi)(e)). The grotesque head in Veli Can's signed drawing, however, is clearly borrowed from the style of his mentor.

BIBLIOGRAPHY

Mustafa 'Ali: *Manāqib-i hunarvarān* [Wonderful deeds of the artists], ed. Ibn al-Amin Mahmud Kamal (Istanbul, 1926)
I. Stchoukine: *La Peinture turque* (Paris, 1971), pp. 34–5
W. B. Denny: 'Dating Ottoman Turkish Works in the Saz Style', *Muqarnas*, i (1983), pp. 103–21

SHEILA R. CANBY

Veličković, Vladimir (*b* Belgrade, 11 Aug 1935). Serbian painter and printmaker. Graduating from the Faculty of Architecture in Belgrade, he worked as assistant in the workshop of Krsto Hegedušić in Zagreb (1962–3). He lived in Paris after 1966 and taught at the Ecole Nationale Supérieure des Beaux-Arts after 1983. He first belonged to the Painters' Circle of Belgrade, which was strongly influenced by local Surrealist tradition. His pictures of this period represent fantastic, decaying or crippled figures, painted in a very expressive style.

In Paris, Veličković's painting became more Baroque under the influence of exponents of social criticism and such painters as Robert Rauschenberg and Francis Bacon.

His subject was invariably the tortured, mutilated, wounded human figure. He began to introduce various implements of torture, changing them increasingly into measuring or optical devices similar to those used by Eadweard Muybridge in his shots of moving people or animals. The *Man Jumping Up and Down Over Muybridge* (1973; Rotterdam, Boymans–van Beuningen) is an example of his work in the 1970s. In this period he began to incorporate into his pictures concrete scenes of animals and people from the photographs by Muybridge, which grew progressively more monochrome.

BIBLIOGRAPHY

J.-L. Ferrier: *Veličković* (Paris, 1976)
M. Le Bot: *Vladimir Veličković* (Paris, 1979)
A. Gutherc and others: *Veličković* (Paris, 1983)
M. B. Protić and others: *Vladimir Veličković* (Ljubljana, 1986)

JURE MIKUŽ

Veliki Preslav. *See* PRESLAV.

Veliko Turnovo [formerly Tărnovo]. Town in northern Bulgaria on the River Yantra, situated on two hills known as Tsarevets and Trapesitsa in a naturally fortified location. Excavations have revealed that the earliest remains date from the 3rd millennium BC. Fortification walls dating from the 1st to the 7th century AD have been discovered on Tsarevets; the Slavs settled here in the 6th century AD. The First Bulgarian Kingdom fell to the Byzantine empire in 971, and remained under Byzantine domination until 1188, when Tărnovo became the capital of the Second Bulgarian Kingdom. In 1393 it finally fell to the Ottomans; from 1235 it was also the seat of the Bulgarian patriarchate. The royal palace and the remains of the patriarchal palace, each with their own churches and protected by their own walls, are situated on Tsarevets. Some 20 churches have been found here, and over 18 on Trapesitsa; they were destroyed by the Turks at the time of the conquest in 1393. In a residential area between the two hills in the Assenova Mahala quarter are the late 12th-century church of St Dimiter, the ruins of the mid-13th-century church of the Forty Martyrs Monastery, and the 13th-century church of SS Peter and Paul (rebuilt 1980).

Most of the 13th–14th-century churches on Tsarevets have domed cruciform plans, while single-nave churches prevail on Trapesitsa. The walls of both types are made of alternating bands of brick and stone and articulated with rows of niches, the arches of which are also of stone and brick surmounted by curved rows of ceramic roundels and rosettes: brick ornamentation decorates the tympana of the niches. All these features are characteristic of the decoration of contemporary church buildings at NESEBĂR.

The earliest surviving wall paintings on Tsarevets date to the end of the 12th century or the beginning of the 13th and were found in Church No. 9; they show faces and ornaments in the late Komnenian style. The wall paintings in the church of the Forty Martyrs Monastery are thought to be contemporary with the column of Tsar Ivan Assen II (*reg* 1218–41) commemorating his victory in 1230 over Despot Theodore Angellos Dukas Komnenos (ruler of Epeiros from 1215; Emperor of Thessaloniki 1224–30), which was placed in the church. The wall paintings preserved today are on the western wall of the narthex; until the earthquake of 1913 the eastern wall of the narthex also survived and it bore scenes from the Old Testament and the *Dormition of the Virgin*. The earliest known wall-painted church calendar (menologion) was also in the narthex, with scenes of *May* and *June* on the destroyed eastern wall and *March*, *July* and *August* on the western wall. In the lunettes there are images of the *Virgin*, *St Anne* and *St Elizabeth* suckling their infants. The iconographic schemes follow those of 11th–12th-century Byzantine miniatures and icons. They are realized in a late Komnenian style, with a softening of the outline and drapery, and an enrichment of the colour scheme, and they employed a mixed technique consisting of fresco finished with tempera once the original painting was dry. Paintings, which may date from later in the 13th century, discovered on the outer side of the western wall of the narthex include the *Source of the Wisdom of St John Chrysostom*, the *Prophet Elijah Fed by a Raven* and *St Antony the Great Visiting St Paul of Thebes*, as well as four figures of monastic saints. The wall-painting fragments in Churches Nos 10 and 13 on Trapesitsa are similar in style, depicting numerous warrior saints in a variety of postures, as well as ornamental motifs. The wall paintings in the church of SS Nicholas and Panteleimon at BOYANA are often thought to derive from this school.

There were, however, other styles of painting at Tărnovo, as is evident in the wall paintings in the church of the monastery of SS Peter and Paul founded at Assenova Mahala by Tsar Ivan Assen II's queen Anna-Maria (*reg* 1221–37). Here, in the space below the western arches under the dome, medallions have been found from the original painting scheme showing images of martyrs. They bear the features of the new Picturesque style, which was characteristic of the 13th century, and resemble the frescoes in the church of the Ascension (1234–5) at MILEŠEVA in Serbia and in the church of the Acheiropoietos in Thessaloniki. From 1416 until 1872 the Bulgarian Church was under the control of the patriarch of Constantinople. The church of SS Peter and Paul was repainted *c.* 1450, probably by painters from Constantinople, and works showing the *Tree of Jesse* and the *Oecumenical Councils* in the narthex are particularly worthy of note. Scenes from the menologion were painted in the exonarthex *c.* 1600. The wall paintings with Greek inscriptions in the church of St George date from the 17th century.

Tărnovo was also a major centre of literary output. Among its productions were the earlier Greek *Chronicle of Manasses* (1344–5; Rome, Vatican, Bib. Apostolica, MS. Slav. 2), the *Tetraevangelium* (1356; London, BL, Add. MS. 39627) of Tsar Ivan Alexander (*reg* 1331–71) and the Tomich Psalter (1360s; Moscow, Hist. Mus., MS. 2752), all copied and illustrated at Tărnovo.

A number of buildings survive from the 'Revival' period in Bulgarian art and architecture (18th–19th century), such as the church of SS Konstantin and Elena (1873) and the Hadji Nikoli Inn (1858; *see* BULGARIA, fig. 3) built by Nikola Fichev (*b* 1836).

BIBLIOGRAPHY

A. Grabar: *La Peinture religieuse en Bulgarie* (Paris, 1928)
B. Filow: *Geschichte der altbulgarischen Kunst* (Berlin, 1930)
A. Dzhurova: *Hiliada godini bălgarska răkopisna kniga* [One thousand years of Bulgarian manuscripts] (Sofia, 1981)
L. Mavrodinova: 'L'Ecole de peinture de Turnovo à la lumière de recherches récentes', *Akten des XVI Internationaler Byzantinistenkongress: Wien, 1981*, ii/5, pp. 225–9

LILIANA MAVRODINOVA

Veliky Ustyug [Rus.: 'Great Ustyug']. Town in Russia on the River Sukhona *c.* 300 km north-west of Kirov. The original settlement of Gleden grew up between the 8th and 10th centuries, 3 km south of today's city centre. By the time of the first documentary reference to Veliky Ustyug in chronicles in 1212 the population had moved to the present location on the opposite bank of the Sukhona. Its position at the junction of the water routes from Moscow to Arkhangel'sk and Siberia made it a great trade and industrial centre in the 16th and 17th centuries.

Ustyug was an early centre of icon painting. Other crafts that flourished included silver filigree work, enamelling, engraving, birchbark-carving and painting on wood. Ustyug caskets with secret locks and tin-plated 'musical chimes' covered with designs recalling frost patterns were especially sought after and exported to other parts of Russia and to Iran, China and India. In the 18th century Ustyug silversmiths developed the distinctive Northern school of niello art (Tula work), the daintiness of which is closely related to contemporary engraving and book illustration. It is also noted for the unusually strong bond between the niello compound and the silver. The technical and stylistic peculiarities of Ustyug niello spread to Vologda, Vyatka, Arkhangel'sk, Tobol'sk and Yakutsk. Craftsmen from Ustyug even taught the subtleties of this intricate art to artists in Moscow. Between 1761 and 1776 the factory belonging to the Popov merchants produced silver mounts for church books, church vessels, caskets, powder cases, snuff-boxes and scent bottles. Although diverse in form and design, these were decorated with similar ornamental or narrative designs in low relief set against recessed matt backgrounds. Brass and copper items, many of them enamelled, were also produced in

Veliky Ustyug, Trinity Cathedral (1699), Gledensky monastery of the Trinity, founded 12th century

quantity. In the 19th century nielloed objects were covered with representations of towns, geographical maps and vegetable ornament. By the early 20th century trade had declined, but a workshop for the production of various items of nielloed silver was opened in 1929. This later formed the basis for the Severnaya Chern (Northern niello) cooperative (1933) and finally a factory (1960).

The town contains many monuments of architectural interest, including the church of the Ascension (1648), built in the 'ornamental architecture' style and with its façades decorated in patterns made from brick and coloured tiles. The monastery of the Archangel Michael (founded 1212) has a cathedral (1653), a tent-roofed bell-tower, a single-piered refectory, the gate-church of St Vladimir and the monks' cells (1736–7). Trinity Cathedral (1699) within the Gledensky monastery of the Trinity (see fig.) contains an 18th-century, five-tiered, carved wooden openwork iconostasis. Other churches include the cathedral of the Assumption (1619–59), the church of St Prokopy (1668), the Summer (1689–96) and Winter (1725–30) churches of the Transfiguration and the churches of Dmitri Solunsky (1700–08) and Sergey of Radonezh (1739–47). Important secular buildings include the Baroque Shilov and Zakharov houses (1787–91) and the Local History Museum, built in a Neo-classical style.

BIBLIOGRAPHY

T. T. Gol'dberg: *Chernevoye serebro Velikogo Ustyuga* [Nielloed silver from Veliky Ustyug] (Moscow, 1952)
M. P. Lukin and N. M. Davydova: *Narodnoye iskusstvo ustyuzhan* [Folk art from Ustyug] (Vologda, 1971)
P. A. Tel'tevsky: *Veliky Ustyug* (Moscow, 1977)
G. Bocharov and V. Vygolov: *Sol'vychegodsk, Veliky Ustyug Tot'ma* (Moscow, 1983)
S. I. Maslenitsyn: 'Master Ustyuzhskoy cherni M. P. Chirkov' [M. P. Chirkov, master of Ustyug niello], *Narodnyye mastera, traditsi Shkoly* (Moscow, 1985), pp. 89–97
V. P. Shil'nikovskaya: *Veliky Ustyug* (Moscow, 1987)

ALEKSANDR U. GREKOV

Vellert [Felaert; Vellaert; Staren, van], **Dirk** [Dieric] (**Jacobsz.**) [Theodoricus Iacobi] (*b* ?Amsterdam, *c.* 1480–85; *d* Antwerp, after 30 Dec 1547). South Netherlandish stained-glass designer, printmaker and glasspainter. Guicciardini referred to him as one of the three leading glass painters in Flanders, along with Aerdt Ortkens and Theodore Stas. Until 1901, when Glück identified him with the Monogrammist D✕V, he appeared in the literature as 'Dirk van Staren'. Glück associated a woodcut device of the Antwerp Guild of St Luke, signed with this monogram and dated 1526, with a reference in the guild records stating that Vellert executed a device for the guild the second year he was dean (1526).

1. Life. 2. Works. 3. Influence.

1. LIFE. Vellert is probably the glazier 'Theodoricus Iacobi Amstelredamus' mentioned by Gerardus Geldenhauer in his journal of 1522. It has been suggested that his father was a priest living in Amsterdam named Jacob Vellert. However, Jacob Vellert was apparently dead by 1460, too early to be Dirk's father, although it is possible that the artist was related to him. It has also been claimed that Dirk Vellert received his early training in Mechelen *c.* 1508–10, but the only works ascribed to this putative Mechelen period are a group of drawings no longer accepted as Vellert's (London, BM; Paris, Fond. Custodia, Inst. Néer.; and Amsterdam, Rijksmus.). (Likewise, most of the drawings published by Beets as early works should not be included in the artist's oeuvre.)

Vellert was inscribed as a master in the Guild of St Luke in 1511, and he registered six apprentices between 1512 and 1530. He is always referred to in the guild records as a glazier. He was dean of the guild in 1518 and 1526. The accounts for Antwerp Cathedral in 1539–40 record that his assistants were paid a tip for the delivery of a stained-glass window, which was inserted above the pulpit (destr.). A document in the Antwerp archives dated 30 December 1547 records that he granted a procuration to two lawyers in Amsterdam to manage his legal affairs; he probably died shortly thereafter.

2. WORKS. Vellert was primarily active as a designer of stained glass, and his reputation in this field was international. His most important surviving work is the design of parts of the 24 stained-glass windows at King's College Chapel, Cambridge, commissioned by King Henry VIII. Vellert may have been involved with this project from its beginning (*c.* 1517) until the 1540s. Besides designs for monumental glass, Vellert also made small-scale painted glass roundels, an extremely popular form of window decoration in the 16th century, and drew designs for roundels. Vellert also made prints and very likely panel paintings as well.

(*i*) *Monumental windows.* Friedländer was the first to suggest that the Master D✕V was the designer of some of the windows at King's College Chapel. This suggestion, accepted by later writers, was confirmed in 1964 when Boon discovered a preparatory drawing by Vellert (Brunswick, ME, Bowdoin Coll. Mus. A.) for the three scenes of *Christ Appearing to the Apostles*, *Peter and John Healing the Lame Man at the Gate of the Temple* and the *Death of Ananias*. It is not clear whether Vellert painted the glass himself or if, in fact, he ever travelled to England. The artist is not named in the contracts, where others are mentioned as the glaziers. According to Wayment, Vellert's hand is to be discerned in the most sensitively painted parts of the windows. For other sections, Vellert probably provided full-scale cartoons to be used by the other glaziers. The programme of the windows presents Old and New Testament scenes that are related typologically. There are numerous compositional borrowings, for instance from the work of Pieter Coecke van Aelst.

Vellert was also apparently responsible for the design of a window (1516–21; destr. 1942) in the Marienkirche at Lübeck, which displayed two five-pointed stars similar to the one employed in his monogram. Judging from photographs, the window seemed close to Vellert's style. In 1532 the city of Leiden commissioned from Vellert a stained-glass window as a gift to the president of the grand council in Mechelen, but unfortunately there is no trace of this window.

(*ii*) *Small-scale roundels and drawings.* Vellert's earliest known works are two painted glass roundels, which probably formed part of a series of the six Petrarchian *Triumphs*: the *Triumph of Time* (see fig. 1), the only work signed with the artist's full name, dated 21 April 1517, and the *Triumph of Faith*, signed with the monogram and dated May 1517 (Amsterdam, Rijksmus.). Both are executed with brown paint on clear glass and measure 230 mm, a standard size for such roundels. In the first glass, the figure of Time is borrowed from an anonymous Florentine engraving, and two other figures are derived from prints after Andrea Mantegna's *Triumph of Caesar*. Vellert's later roundels, such as the monogrammed *Abraham Prostrate before God* and the *Judgement of Cambyses* (both Amsterdam, Rijksmus.), the latter monogrammed and dated 1542, employ grisaille and silver-stain instead of brown paint.

The next known dated work after the early roundels of 1517 is a monogrammed drawing of the *Trinity* (9 May 1520; Paris, Edmond de Rothschild priv. col.), possibly a study for an altarpiece or a print. The ornamental architecture and elongated proportions of the figures are reminiscent of the Antwerp Mannerists, but the figures already display the rotund muscularity of Vellert's later works. Possibly earlier than the *Trinity* is an undated drawing of the *Consecration of St Myra* (Rotterdam, Mus. Boymans–van Beuningen), which, according to Boon, is a preliminary study for a window by Vellert made between 1516 and 1521 (destr. 1533) for the altar of St Nicholas in Antwerp Cathedral.

About 50 of Vellert's designs for small-scale roundels are preserved, most signed with the monogram and dated with the day, month and year. The dated designs were made within a nine-year period (1523–32), but several undated drawings can be placed later. The year 1523 was extremely productive: the artist dated 14 drawings in that year, and others can be added on the basis of style. Most of the roundels were apparently conceived as parts of various series. For instance, seven compositions are known for a set of the *Life of the Virgin*, two for the Petrarchian *Triumphs* and four for a *Life of Abraham*.

The prints of Albrecht Dürer were one of Vellert's most important sources for his designs. Dürer mentioned Vellert three times in the diary of his trip to the Netherlands (1520–21), noting that he gave Vellert a set of the *Apocalypse* woodcuts and later referring to a banquet that the glazier held on 12 May 1521. A set of drawings of the *Apocalypse*, probably designs for glass, signed with Vellert's monogram but not dated (c. 1523–5; Berlin, Kupferstichkab.; Paris, Edmond de Rothschild priv. col.), is based on some of these woodcuts. In many cases Vellert devoted a separate drawing to different episodes that Dürer had combined in one composition. For instance, Vellert represented the four horsemen of the Apocalypse on four sheets, while Dürer depicted them on one. A proportion study by Dürer (London, BM) is thought to have been the inspiration behind Vellert's drawing of a *Nude Bather* (Paris, Louvre), sometimes called the first nature study of a nude in Flemish art.

Dürer's woodcuts of the *Life of the Virgin* provided the source for Vellert's series of medallions of the subject known from autograph drawings and glass roundels painted by the workshop. The whole series is dated on the basis of the monogrammed drawing of the *Adoration of the Magi* (1532; Vienna, Albertina). Four of the drawings

1. Dirk Vellert: *Triumph of Time*, painted glass roundel, diam. 230 mm, 1517 (Brussels, Musées Royaux d'Art et d'Histoire)

are apparently unfinished, giving some idea of Vellert's working method (the *Birth of the Virgin* and the *Adoration of the Child*, both Weimar, Schlossmus.; and the *Presentation in the Temple* and the *Marriage of the Virgin*, both London, BM). In these drawings the composition was first drawn with pen and brown ink, either by the artist himself or by an assistant, and then it was gone over by Vellert with thicker, darker lines of brown ink. In this second stage, the artist repeatedly changed the poses of the figures and motifs and even rearranged the composition. This same technique can be seen in Vellert's later drawings, for instance the three sheets of the *Life of Abraham* (c. 1535, London, BM).

(iii) Prints. With one late exception, Vellert's prints were all executed from 1522 to 1526, and almost all are dated with the day of the month and the year. He was one of the first Antwerp artists to make engravings and etchings, and he may have done so following the example of Dürer and Lucas van Leyden. Vellert made small intaglio prints of religious, mythological and secular subjects, reminiscent of those of the German Little Masters, as well as larger religious prints and several woodcuts, notably the device of the Guild of St Luke (Hollstein, no. 21) and a *Schoolroom* (1526; Hollstein, no. 20; one known impression, London, BM), which may have been intended to be pressed into a book. He frequently combined the etching and engraving techniques, creating rich textures with hatching and stippling. Vellert's prints often show the influence of Lucas van Leyden in the figure type, for instance in the figure of the saint in the *St Elizabeth of Hungary* (1524; B. 10). The *Temptation of Christ* (1523; B. 5) depends closely on Lucas's engraving of the subject (1518; B. 41), especially the figure of the devil.

2. Dirk Vellert: *The Flood*, engraving and etching, 281×302 mm, 1544 (London, British Museum)

In only one case does a preparatory drawing exist for a print, the *Calling of SS Peter and Andrew* (1523; B. 3; Amsterdam, Rijksmus.). The drawing, in reverse and traced for transfer, is in a different technique from Vellert's designs for glass. Instead of pen and ink on cream paper, it employs brush and brown ink on brown prepared paper. The drawing is dated two years earlier than the print (1525).

Vellert's love of ornament and his use of Italianate grotesquerie are evident in his engravings of the *Vision of St Bernard* of 1524 (B. 8) and *St Luke Painting the Virgin* of 1526 (B. 9), the latter the same year he was dean of the guild. This Italianate ornamentation is contrasted in some of the prints with remarkably naturalistic landscape backgrounds, for instance in the *Vision of St Bernard*. These landscapes may have been influenced by Dürer's prints.

There is only one print by Vellert known from after 1526, the large mixed engraving and etching of *The Flood* (B. 2; see fig. 2), his last known work. Beets suggested that this print was designed in the late 1520s, but this is not convincing. The deep recession, with figures gradually receding in the distance, is different from the earlier prints and has been compared to the mature works of Bernard van Orley. Several figures in the print seem to have been inspired by Marcantonio Raimondi's *Massacre of the Innocents*. Beets tried to attribute to Vellert the ornamental engravings of Master GJ, but Popham has convincingly disputed this proposal.

(iv) Panel paintings. The core works of the group of panel paintings attributed to Vellert by Glück, Baldass and Friedländer are a triptych of the *Adoration of the Magi* (Rotterdam, Mus. Boymans–van Beuningen), a panel of the same subject (Lille, Mus. B.-A.), a triptych of the *Ecce homo* (Brussels, Mus. Assist. Pub.) and a *Holy Family* (Kremsmünster, Stiftsgal.). None of these panels is signed or dated, but they show similarities with Vellert's documented works in the proportions of the figures and in the facial types. These panels form a stylistically coherent group characterized by quivering draughtsmanship, bright colours and fluid brushwork, which reveals some of the underdrawing. The figures are often bulky and elongated, and the gestures of the hands are expressively exaggerated. In their subjects, compositions and use of Italianate ornament these paintings are related to the works of the Antwerp Mannerists. Wayment doubted that the triptych with the *Adoration of the Magi* is by Vellert, and by the 1990s further study was needed to determine whether these panels are indeed by the artist. The suggestion that they are early works of Jan Gossart is not convincing.

3. INFLUENCE. Vellert's influence has been seen in contemporary stained glass, for instance in the large-scale windows of Léon d'Oultres (Liège workshop, 1530) in the cathedral of St Paul, Liège, and the windows (1528–33) painted by Claes Mathyssen at the church of St Catherine at Hoogstraeten. These windows show similarities in

composition and figure type to the glass at King's College and Lübeck. Although Vellert's prints did not have the enormous impact of those of either Dürer or Lucas van Leyden, they were often copied by artists such as the Master S and Allaert Claez. They were also frequently used as patterns for glass roundels, and a stained-glass window in the church of Conches, near Evreux, is based on the *Vision of St Bernard*.

BIBLIOGRAPHY

Hollstein: *Dut. & Flem.*
L. Guicciardini: *Descrittione di . . . tutti i Paesi Bassi* (1567), p. 146
A. von Bartsch: *Le Peintre-graveur* (1803–21) [B.]
G. Glück: 'Beiträge zur Geschichte der Antwerpner Malerei in XVI Jahrhundert', *Jb. Ksthist. Samml. Allhöch. Ksrhaus.*, xxii (1901), pp. 10–34
N. Beets: 'Dirick Jacobsz. Vellert: Schilder van Antwerpen', *Onze Kst*, x (1906), pp. 137–53; xi (1907), pp. 109–22; xiii (1908), pp. 165–88; xx (1912), pp. 133–52; xl (1922), p. 85
L. Baldass: 'Dirk Vellert als Tafelmaler', *Belvedere*, i (1922), pp. 162–7
A. E. Popham: 'The Engravings and Woodcuts of Dirick Vellert', *Prt Colr Q.*, xii (1925), pp. 343–68
M. J. Friedländer: *Die altniederländischen Malerei* (Berlin, 1924–37), xii (1935), pp. 42–51; Eng. trans. as *Early Netherlandish Painting* (Leiden, 1967–76), xii, pp. 27–31
K. G. Boon: 'Two Designs for Windows by Dierick Vellert', *Master Drgs*, ii (1964), pp. 153–6
H. Wayment: *The Windows of King's College Chapel, Cambridge*, Corp. Vitrearum Med. Aevi, GB, Suppl. vol., i (London, 1972)
The Age of Bruegel: Netherlandish Drawings in the Sixteenth Century (exh. cat. by J. Hand and others; Washington, DC, N.G.A.; New York, Pierpont Morgan Lib.; 1986–7), pp. 288–93

ELLEN KONOWITZ

Vellore. Town with an imposing fort in North Arcot District, Tamil Nadu, India. Though modified in later times, much of the fort's fabric dates to the 16th century AD, when it was reinforced by Chinna Bomma, the local governor of the NAYAKA dynasty. The circular bastions and turrets overlook a substantial moat. There is a single entrance on the east side.

The Jalakanteshvara Temple inside the fort is a well-preserved complex, mostly dating to the 16th century. It is surrounded by a double enclosure (Skt *prākāra*) of high walls broken on the south by a *gopura* (towered gateway), the two lowest (granite) storeys of which are decorated with mouldings, delicately ornamented pilasters and niches, now empty. The renovated pyramidal tower has six diminishing storeys with projections in the middle of each long side. The crowning roof has arched ends with monster masks. The principal temple is typical of the VIJAYANAGARA period, although its towers are modern renovations. It consists of a *liṅga* shrine on the west and a Nataraja shrine on the north, opening off a common hall with sculpted columns (*see* INDIAN SUBCONTINENT, fig. 85). The inner doorway of the main shrine is flanked by large guardian figures. Immediately east of the hall a lamp column and an image of Shiva's bull, Nandi, demarcate the major axis, although there is no doorway, just a pierced stone window. Images of the Shaiva saints (south), Ganesha (west) and a fire altar (north) are set in colonnades along the side walls. A minor shrine for the goddess is positioned in the north-west corner.

In the south-west part of the outer enclosure is a free-standing pillared hall (*maṇḍapa*) renowned for its sculptures, equalled only by those at SRIRANGAM. The outer piers are carved almost in the round to represent riders on rearing lion-like monsters (*yāḷi*s) and richly bridled horses. Subsidiary themes include warriors, hunters and mythical beasts. The base is adorned with panels of warriors. Some of the interior columns have panels with miniature figures and ornamental motifs, while others have attached colonnettes. The ceilings are also elaborate, with the central panel carved as a flower surrounded by parrots. The raised dais within the hall has an exquisitely carved base with friezes of animals and serpents. A less ornamented hall is at the south-east corner.

Located about 1.2 km east of the fort are tombs associated with Tipu Sultan (*reg* 1782–99), ruler of Mysore, whose family was detained in Vellore following his unsuccessful uprising against English forces in 1799.

BIBLIOGRAPHY

S. Toy: *The Fortified Cities of India* (London, 1966)
Jaffer Adam Ayub Khan: 'The Vellore Fort', *Inside Outside* (June–July, 1987), pp. 136–43 [incl. temple plan]

GEORGE MICHELL

Vellum. Skin of a calf, which is treated for use as a fine quality writing or drawing support. Vellum is sometimes used incorrectly as a substitute for the generic term PARCHMENT, which refers to any animal skin, including also that of kids and lambs.   ☐

Velten, Georg Friderick. *See* FEL'TEN, YURY.

Velzna. *See* ORVIETO.

Venado Beach. Pre-Columbian site on the Gulf of Panama, just west of the Panama Canal and *c.* 16 km from the 16th-century settlement of Old Panama in the Canal Zone. It is noted for its large number of burials and their accompanying grave goods. The site was discovered in 1948 and excavated in 1951 by Neville A. Harte, Samuel K. Lothrop and the Peabody Museum of Archaeology and Ethnology, Harvard University, where the finds are held. Further excavations were directed by Thelma Bull in 1958. The excavations recovered 369 bodies in both individual and group graves. Lothrop described some of these as 'bathtub' burials, with the bodies placed in the grave floors either in an extended or a flexed position. More important people were buried in side chambers cut into the rock. In some cases, infants had been placed in urns and buried with an adult. Lothrop believed these bodies represented natural deaths, suicides and sacrificial victims. Many had obviously been mutilated by decapitation, amputation or dismemberment. According to Claude Baudez, this differential treatment of the dead suggests a stratified society.

There is a general agreement that the polychrome ceramics found at Venado Beach belong to the Early Coclé phase or the Santa María phase (*see also* COCLÉ). More common was a polished brown ware with incised and modelled decoration. Gordon Willey suggested that Venado Beach acted as a meeting ground for two distinct ceramic traditions: the incised and modelled wares of Darien and Colombia and the polychrome ware of central Panama. According to Olga Linares, most of the ceramics from this site contain motifs identical to those of Coclé, but instead of being painted they are modelled, stamped and incised. She concluded that this similarity indicates a cultural link between these areas. Despite the general agreement regarding the nature of these ceramics, the two radiocarbon dates of *c.* AD 210 and *c.* 960 may not be accurate. Thus the dating of the site is somewhat difficult: Linares proposes a date of *c.* AD 300–*c.* 500 to *c.* AD 800, while Wolfgang Haberland suggests *c.* AD 650–*c.* 920. As well as ceramics, the Venado Beach burials contained stone celts, pendants, beads and discs of stone, shell, bone, gold and *tumbaga* (an alloy of gold and copper). Most of the gold objects appear to be related to the area of Darien in eastern Panama, not to Coclé.

For discussion of Pre-Columbian Panama *see also* SOUTH AMERICA, PRE-COLUMBIAN, §II.

BIBLIOGRAPHY

S. K. Lothrop: 'Suicide, Sacrifice and Mutilations in Burials at Venado Beach, Panama', *Amer. Ant.*, xix (1954), pp. 226–34

T. H. Bull: 'Excavations at Venado Beach, Canal Zone', *Panama Archaeologist*, i (1958), pp. 6–14

G. R. Willey: *An Introduction to American Archaeology*, ii (Englewood Cliffs, 1971)

O. F. Linares: *Ecology and the Arts in Ancient Panamá: On the Development of Social Rank and Symbolism in the Central Provinces*, Studies in Pre-Columbian Art and Archaeology, xvii (Washington, DC, 1977)

W. Haberland: 'Lower Central America', *Chronologies in New World Archaeology*, ed. R. E. Taylor and C. W. Meighan (New York, 1978), pp. 395–430

C. F. Baudez: 'Cultural Development in Lower Central America', *Aboriginal Cultural Development in Latin America: An Interpretive Review*, ed. B. Meggers and C. Evans (Washington, DC, 1983), pp. 45–54

JOAN K. LINGEN

Vēnāḍu. *See* TRAVANCORE.

Venda. Group of Bantu-speaking peoples of diverse origins living in the north-eastern Transvaal, South Africa, and south-eastern Zimbabwe. From the early 18th century to the late 19th these peoples formed a large empire composed of an immigrant Shona/Rozwi group and mixed Sotho and Shona inhabitants of the Zoutpansberg district. The Venda language is distinct from that of their neighbours, the Sotho Tswana in the south and west, the Tsonga in the east and the Shona in the north, but they share many cultural traits with both the Shona and the Sotho. Venda are known particularly for their wood-carving arts, although they also have interesting architectural and ceramic traditions. They are known to have smelted iron ore in the past and to have made objects out of it, although their uses and meanings are obscure and the tradition itself is defunct.

1. ARCHITECTURE. Stone-walled settlements related to those of GREAT ZIMBABWE are scattered across Venda territory, from the confluence of the Shashe and Limpopo in the north-west to the town of Tzaneen in the south-east. The first-known capital (*c.* 1700) of the Venda empire at Dzata in the Nzhelele Valley consists of circular stone enclosures at the top and bottom of a fortified hill. Similar complexes continued to be built into the late 20th century by Venda chiefs on the upper reaches of the southern slopes of the Soutpansberg. In the past, monoliths were placed on the walls to commemorate the ancestors, and the traditions continue but with wooden staves. The use of both stone walling and staves is the prerogative of chiefs of the royal lineage. Within the walls, dwellings of mud-and-thatch construction are erected according to a set hierarchy. In the past, the capital of a chief could have up to 5000 inhabitants, with the chief and his wives occupying the highest point in the settlement.

2. WOOD-CARVING. Much of the wood-carving produced by Venda artists was made for chiefs and used only in their capitals. Most important were large, monoxylous doors (*ngwenya;* the word for crocodile), drums (*ngoma*) and xylophones (*mbila*). All these objects were decorated, mainly with interlacing chevrons, forming triangles and diamonds, interspersed with concentric circles. The composition of these designs is interpreted by Venda as representing the crocodile and the serpent, both of which are important in Venda cosmogony. The crocodile is a particularly important and frequently used symbol for the chief: doors bearing such designs were reserved exclusively for the entrance to the chief's own sleeping hut, and, as signs of chiefship, they were important in succession rites. Large hemispherical drums, embellished with similar designs on the panels of the drum's upper body, between their four handles, acted as magical repositories of the chief's power to make rain. Xylophones with decorated keys were played at court, especially on important ritual occasions.

Another object type intimately linked to the courts but not owned by chiefs were the divination bowls used by healers to detect witches (see fig.). These were shallow, hemispherical vessels the wide, flat rims of which were embellished with designs in relief depicting the emblems of kinship groups and symbols of gender. A crocodile and various other symbols of chiefship were carved in the

Venda divination bowl, wood, diam. 312 mm (London, British Museum)

bottom of the bowl. Filled with water, the bowls represented Lake Fundudzi, the only natural lake in the area, which is regarded as the home of the spirits and therefore sacred. Maize pips floating but touching the sides indicated which kinship groups harboured a witch. The undersides of the bowls also carried designs, similar in shape and meaning to those on chiefs' doors. Small bone tablets (*thangu*), also used in divination, are carved with designs similar to those on the rims of divination bowls.

Also linked with courts are the wooden figures used during the third and final stage of female initiation (Blacking, 1969). Such figures have continued to be used to instruct young women in their social and sexual duties as Venda wives. Ethnic identity is emphasized in this instruction and is evident in the morphology of the figures. Hence, most represent physical ideals of Venda men and women, although some depict Tsonga and other 'foreigners'. Generally not more than 250 mm high, the figures have shortened proportions, with smoothly rounded body forms, spatulate hands and domed feet. From the late 1930s the numbers of these figures in use increased dramatically.

3. OTHER ARTS. Clay figures were used in the first and third stages of initiation. Made by women, these figures are more innovative in style than those in wood. They are not baked and are destroyed after each initiation school. They are used in conjunction with the telling of picaresque tales. Women potters also make hemispherical and almost spherical vessels in a variety of sizes, usually with geometric motifs in a band around the belly of the pot. The designs are engraved on the surface of the red clay and picked out in graphite. Women also trace decorative patterns in the mud and dung floors of courtyards and, more recently, on courtyard walls. Beaded waistbands and small front aprons are made and worn by females. After puberty these are hidden under salempore cloth-and-hide aprons.

BIBLIOGRAPHY

H. A. Stayt: *The Bavenda* (London, 1931)
N. J. Van Warmelo, ed.: *Contributions towards Venda History, Religion and Tribal Ritual*, Union of South Africa, Department of Native Affairs, Ethnological Publications, iii (Pretoria, 1932)
J. Blacking: 'Songs, Dances, Mimes and Symbolism of Venda Girls' Initiation Schools', *Afr. Stud.*, xxviii (1969), pp. 3–35, 69–118, 149–99, 215–66
J. Walton: 'Art and Magic in the Southern Bantu Vernacular Architecture', *Shelter, Sign and Symbol*, ed. P. Oliver (London, 1975), pp. 117–34
D. N. Beach: *The Shona and Zimbabwe, 900–1850: An Outline of Shona History* (London, 1980)
A. Nettleton: 'The Venda Model Hut', *Afr. A.*, xviii/3 (1985), pp. 87–90, 98
T. N. Huffman: 'Iron Age Settlement Patterns and the Origins of Class Distinction in Southern Africa', *Adv. World Archaeol.*, v/2 (1986), pp. 291–338

ANITRA NETTLETON

Vendramin, Andrea (*b* Venice, ?1565; *d* Venice, 18 Nov 1629). Italian collector. He lived in a palazzo on the Grand Canal near S Gregorio. Although he was descended from a branch of the family of GABRIELE VENDRAMIN, there was no connection between the two collections. Andrea's represents one of the most significant examples of the cabinet of curiosities in Venice at the beginning of the 17th century. Illustrated catalogues of it survive today (London, BM; see Jacobs), showing the high quality of

the pieces, his taste for the marvellous and his encyclopedic interests: he claimed, in particular, to possess the tomb of Aristotle. Vincenzo Scamozzi in his *Idea dell'architettura universale* (1615) mentioned that the collection contained antiquities, minerals, petrified material and seven statues by Alessandro Vittoria in a *scrittorio* in ebony and olive-wood, as well as essentially Venetian paintings, and that, as was fashionable, it was directed towards the art of the past. The paintings, mainly from the late 15th century and the 16th, included works by Vincenzo Catena, Vittore Carpaccio, Palma Vecchio, Pordenone, Andrea Schiavone and Tintoretto.

After Andrea's death, his collection passed into the hands of the brothers Gerard and Jan REYNST; probably almost all the pieces went to Amsterdam. Two-thirds of the items in the Reynsts' catalogue of antiquities come from Andrea's collection. The Reynst collection was progressively dispersed after Gerard died in 1658. The works were appraised by the art dealer Gerrit Uylenburgh, a cousin of Rembrandt's wife, Saskia, which probably explains why the painter knew this collection: it has been suggested that Rembrandt's paintings of *Hendrickje at the Window* (Berlin, Gemäldegal.) and *Alexander the Great* (Lisbon, Mus. Gulbenkian) were both inspired by pictures illustrated in the Vendramin catalogue. During a voyage to The Hague in 1660, the newly restored English King Charles II received as a present from the city of Amsterdam 12 antique statues and 24 Italian paintings from the Reynst collection, including Cariani's *Venus* (London, Hampton Court, Royal Col.).

Subsequently the antiquities were acquired in part by Jan Six, and in the mid-18th century some were in the possession of Gerard Papenbroek (1673–1743), whose collections, and thus also a good part of Vendramin's antiquities, form the core of the Rijksmuseum van Oudheden, Leiden. Other pieces were acquired by Gerrit Uylenburgh, who sold them in 1670.

It is possible now to identify only a small number of paintings from Andrea's collection, among them a *Virgin and Child* from the school of Giovanni Bellini (Cambridge, MA, Fogg) and a *Judgement of Paris* and an *Apollo and Marsyas* by Andrea Schiavone, which were sold by the Soviet government and which in 1932 were in the possession of R. Neumann in Berlin.

BIBLIOGRAPHY

V. Scamozzi: *L'idea dell'architettura universale* (Venice, 1615), p. 305
T. Borenius: *The Picture Gallery of Andrea Vendramin* (London, 1923)
E. Jacobs: 'Das Museo Vendramin und die Sammlung Reynst', *Repert. Kstwissen.*, xlvi (1925), pp. 15–39
T. Borenius: 'More about the Vendramin Collection', *Burl. Mag.*, lx (1932), pp. 140–44
A. M. S. Logan: *The 'Cabinet' of the Brothers Gerard and Jan Reynst* (Amsterdam, Oxford and New York, 1979)
K. Pomian: 'Antiquari e collezionisti', *Stor. Cult. Ven.*, iv/1 (1983), pp. 493–547
I. Favaretto: *Arte antica e cultura antiquaria nelle collezioni venete al tempo della Serenissima* (Rome, 1990), pp. 143–51

Vendramin, Gabriele (*b* Venice, 1484; *d* Venice, 15 March 1552). Italian collector. A Venetian nobleman, he was descended from Doge Andrea Vendramin (*reg* 1476–8) and was related to Doge Andrea Gritti (*reg* 1523–38). His wealth came from trade in soap and from land revenues. His palazzo in the parish of S Fosca was frequented by *virtuosi*, and his contacts included many learned patricians. He was the brother-in-law of Taddeo Contarini and knew two other great collectors, Antonio Pasqualino and Michele Contarini. Enea Vico and Hubertus Goltzius praised his collection of medals (Vico, 1555), and Antonio Francesco Doni in *I marmi* described a visit to his collection, where Vendramin showed him an ancient bronze lion, among many rare pieces. Sebastiano Serlio mentioned him as a connoisseur of architecture, and Marcantonio Michiel visited and described his collection in 1530. Vendramin was appointed to his only public office, the minor role of Consigliere della Città, in 1550. His will, a codicil of which was witnessed by Titian, placed his collection in trust.

After Vendramin's death, the collection remained in the Palazzo S Luca in the care of his eldest nephew, Luca. After family disputes about the sale of coins to Venetian merchants, inventories were finally drawn up in 1567–9. The paintings were appraised by Jacopo Tintoretto and Titian's son Orazio Vecellio, and the antiquities by Alessandro Vittoria, Jacopo d'Antonio Tatti Sansovino and Tomaso da Lugano (*fl c.* 1556). Guglielmo Gonzaga, 3rd Duke of Mantua, tried unsuccessfully to acquire some of the antiquities through the mediation of Titian in 1570 and against a background of further conflicts between the heirs and other descendants of Vendramin. These prolonged disputes resulted in a new inventory of the collection in 1601. In 1615 Vincenzo Scamozzi reported that the collection was preserved under seal in the Palazzo S Luca, but it was progressively dispersed during the 17th century, and certain paintings were acquired by Nicolas Régnier. The two inventories of 1567–9 and 1601 permit identification of some of the pieces from Vendramin's collection: the most famous are *La vecchia* and *The Tempest* by Giorgione (both *c.* 1506–10; Venice, Accad.; for the latter *see* GIORGIONE, fig. 3); the *Vendramin Family* by Titian (1547; London, N.G.), which shows Gabriele, his brother Andrea, and the latter's sons kneeling before a reliquary of the True Cross, which was involved in two miracles and was given by a mid-14th century ancestor; and Jacopo Bellini's book of drawings (London, BM; *see* BELLINI, (1), fig. 3). He also possessed important Netherlandish paintings: a diptych attributed to Jan Gossart (Rome, Gal. Doria-Pamphili) and a portrait of a man, then believed to be a self-portrait, by Dürer (perhaps that in Genoa, Pal. Rosso).

UNPUBLISHED SOURCES

Venice, Casa Goldoni, Archivio Vendramin [1567–9 and 1601 inventories]

BIBLIOGRAPHY

M. Michiel: *Notizia d'opere di disegno* (MS.; *c.* 1520–40); ed. G. Frizzoni (Bologna, 1884); Eng. trans. by P. Mussi, ed. G. C. Williamson, as *The Anonimo* (London, 1903/*R* New York, 1969)

S. Serlio: *Il terzo libro* (Venice, 1540)

A. F. Doni: *I Marmi*, iii (Venice, 1552), fol. 40

E. Vico: *Discorsi sopra le medaglie de gli antichi* (Venice, 1555), pp. 16, 88

H. Goltzius: *C. Julius Caesar, sive historiae imperatorum Caesarumque Romanorum ex antiquis numismatibus restituatae* (Bruges, 1563)

V. Scamozzi: *L'idea dell'architettura universale* (Venice, 1615)

A. Rava: 'Il "camerino delle anticaglie" di Gabriele Vendramin', *Nuo. Archv Ven.*, xxxix (1920), pp. 155–81

D. Battilotti and M. T. Franco: 'Regesti di committenti e dei primi collezionisti di Giorgione', *Ant. Viva*, xvii/4–5 (1978), pp. 64–8

S. Settis: *La 'Tempesta' interpretata, i committenti, il soggetto* (Turin, 1978), pp. 129–33

J. Anderson: 'A Further Inventory of Gabriel Vendramin's Collection', *Burl. Mag.*, cxxi (1979), pp. 639–48 [incl. 1601 inventory]

I. Favaretto: *Arte antica e cultura antiquaria nelle collezioni venete al tempo della serenissima* (Rome, 1990), pp. 79–82

MICHEL HOCHMANN

Vendramini, Giovanni [John] (*b* Roncade, nr Bassano, 1769; *d* London, 8 Feb 1839). Italian stipple-engraver, active in England. He was a pupil and assistant to Francesco Bartolozzi in London. His early work included five of the *Cries of London* after Francis Wheatley, published (1793–7) by Colnaghi's. For the publisher John P. Thompson he engraved several large plates after Robert Ker Porter, such as the *Death of Sir Ralph Abercromby* (1804). Vendramini was in Russia in 1805–7, and on his return he concentrated on producing large stipple-plates of Italian Old Masters. However, he also engraved and published prints of contemporary interest, such as a set of 16 portraits of the European leaders who visited London in 1814–15.

BIBLIOGRAPHY

DNB; Thieme–Becker

Obituary, *A.-Un.*, i (1839), p. 61

DAVID ALEXANDER

Veneer. Thin sheets of decorative material, usually wood, but also occasionally ivory, tortoiseshell or brass, used to cover the surface of furniture constructed of coarser and cheaper wood (*see* AUSTRIA, fig. 29; BOULLE, ANDRÉ-CHARLES; MARQUETRY, §1; and WOOD (i), §III, 1).

☐

Venegas, Francisco (*fl* 1578; *d* ?1594). Spanish painter, goldsmith and wood-carver, active in Portugal. According to da Costa, he was first trained as a goldsmith. He was apprenticed in Seville in the workshop of Luis de Vargas (1506–68), studying the early Roman Mannerists and being especially influenced by the work of Perino del Vaga, who had taught Vargas in Rome and Naples. It is not known exactly when Venegas went to Portugal, though it was before the annexation of the Portuguese crown in 1580, as his elegant drawing of the *Last Judgement* (Lisbon, Mus. N.A. Ant.) is dedicated to King Henry, which must date it to *c.* 1578. This drawing, in an agitated Mannerist style, contains figures that are mainly copies after Michelangelo's fresco in the Sistine Chapel. It is not known whether Venegas ever visited Rome or if the drawing derives from his studies in Vargas's studio.

In 1582 Venegas supervised a large allegorical fresco decoration (destr. 1601) in the Hospital Real, Todos-os-Santos, Lisbon. He was appointed court painter to Philip II (Philip I of Portugal) in 1583. In 1590 he received the commission, in competition with Nicolau de Frias, to design the retable of the Misericórdia Church, Oporto, which was painted by Diogo Teixeira in the following year. He designed a retable for the high altar in the church of S Vicente de Fora, Lisbon, which was begun in 1582 by Juan de Herrera and Filippo Terzi but never completed (drawing, Lisbon, Mus. N. A. Ant.).

Venegas's most important works are the signed panels for the high altar of Nossa Senhora da Luz, Carnide (Lisbon), perhaps the finest example of a Mannerist retable in Portugal, with its Italianate style, elongated proportions and elegant carved design composed of corbels, angels, garlands and fruit. The design of the wooden frame may also be by Venegas after the patterns of Sebastiano Serlio, with three stages containing eight panel paintings; it is effectively integrated with the architecture of the chancel, which is by Jerónimo de Ruão.

Of the eight panels painted in collaboration with Teixeira, Venegas contributed the *Coronation of the Virgin*, the *Annunciation*, the *Immaculate Conception*, all signed, and the *Presentation of the Virgin in the Temple* (all *c.* 1585–90). They are in the same style, showing his free gradation of rather cold colours, broad brushstrokes, serpentine outlines of figures and richly textured depiction of fabrics. This is apparent especially in the central panel, formerly entitled *Adoration of Our Lady of Light* and now shown to be an allegory of the *Immaculate Conception*, a subject previously painted by Vargas in his altarpiece in the chapel of the Conception, Seville Cathedral (1561). Venegas's panel demonstrates his inventiveness in the handling of the effects of moonlight, which illuminates the composition, and the Neo-Platonic beauty of the naked Eve in the foreground.

Venegas's drawings show considerable skill and fine modelling, as in *Pentecost* (study for a panel in the Madre de Deus Monastery, Lisbon; see fig.), *Ascension, Triumph of the Eucharist, Allegory of Religion* (study for ceiling medallions) and *Virtuous Love Chastising Profane Love* (all *c.* 1578–90; Lisbon, Mus. N.A. Ant.). The last, showing an eroticism equalled in contemporary Portuguese culture only by Canto IX of Luís de Camões's *Lusiads* (1572), may have been a study for an untraced private commission from a more enlightened patron interested in Italian culture.

Venegas is regarded as the leading representative of Mannerism in Portugal, where Mannerist art for the most part confined itself to conventional solutions following the decrees of the Council of Trent. Although he surpassed such contemporaries as Gaspar Dias, António Campelo, Fernão Gomes and Teixeira in the boldness and sophistication of his art, he had no following.

Francisco Venegas: *Pentecost*, pen and brown ink and brown wash, 225×247 mm, 1578–90 (Lisbon, Museu Nacional de Arte Antiga)

BIBLIOGRAPHY

F. da Costa: *Antiguidade da arte da pintura* (MS.; 1696); ed. G. Kubler (New Haven and London, 1967), p. 266

A. de Gusmão: *Diogo Teixeira e seus colaboradores* (Lisbon, 1955), pp. 12–13, 15

D. L. Markl and V. Serrão: 'Ós tectos maneiristas da igreja do Hospital Real de Todos-os-Santos e os seus autores', *Bol. Cult. Assembl. Distr. Lisboa*, lxxxvi (1980), pp. 161–215

V. Serrão: *A pintura maneirista em Portugal* (Lisbon, 1982), pp. 64–70

——: *O maneirismo e o estatuto social dos pintores portugueses* (Lisbon, 1983), pp. 252–3, 364–7

J. A. Seabra: 'Francisco Venegas e o seu painel da Imaculada na igreja de Nossa Senhora da Luz em Carnide', *Vértice*, iii (1988), pp. 31–90

VITOR SERRÃO

Veneroni, Giannantonio [Gianantonio; Giovanni Antonio] (*b* Pavia, 1683–6; *d* Broni, 18 April 1749). Italian architect. He trained from 1700 to 1707 with the Milanese architect Giuseppe Quadrio and successfully completed his studies to become 'engineer and architect'. His first assignments were as land surveyor for the Collegio Borromeo in Pavia and various commissions for the local aristocracy and religious orders. He also taught architecture in Pavia for a long time. Veneroni's only consistently acknowledged work is the Palazzo Mezzabarba (1726–32; now the town hall), Pavia, which was erected for the counts Giuseppe and Gerolamo Mezzabarba. The building is in the form of a long parallelepiped, with two separate entrances on the front; a wide staircase is situated in a block that juts out at right angles to the rear. Thoenes suggested that the original project was organized around two courts corresponding to the twin entrances and that this scheme was not fully realized. The façade is distinguished by the elegant ornament at the windows and the symmetrical portals, surmounted by wide balconies. One of the portals leads to a scenographic entrance hall with three aisles, the other to a blind wall. A giant order of pilasters divides a rhythmical sequence of round-headed windows. These forms are reminiscent of the work of Francesco Borromini, and their unexpected presence in Lombardy has led to speculation as to their source. Both Arslan and Thoenes suggested that they were derived from Roman prototypes, although Wittkower classed the Palazzo Mezzabarba as a work of the Italian Rococo. In 1733–4 Veneroni built the Mezzabarba Chapel, known as the Oratory of SS Quirico e Siro, at right angles to the main elevation of the palace; this is an oval chamber with the entrance and altar on the long axis.

Other works attributed to Veneroni include the façade of S Marco (1712–38), Pavia, erected for the Minim Friars; it lies in the middle of a conventual building and is curved inwards in the manner of Borromini's Oratory of S Filippo Neri, Rome. Projects for the bishop's palace and S Filippo, Lodi, have also been ascribed to Veneroni owing to their stylistic resemblance to the works in Pavia and to the patronage of Ambrogio Mezzabarba, Bishop of Lodi (*reg* 1725–42), who was the brother of Giuseppe and Gerolamo Mezzabarba. Veneroni was probably responsible for the restoration (1735) of the castle at Montalto Pavese for the Belcredi family. He also executed the façade (*c.* 1737) of the parish church of San Genesio, near Pavia, which resembles that of S Marco; the original trilobate plan for the church was never realized (Zatti).

Thieme–Becker

BIBLIOGRAPHY

F. Bartoli: *Notizia delle pitture, sculture ed architetture delle città d'Italia* (Venice, 1777), ii, pp. 12, 35
E. Arslan: 'Per l'architettura lombarda del primo settecento: A proposito di una chiesa dell'oltrepò pavese', *Boll. Soc. Pavese Stor. Patria*, vii (1944), pp. 81–94
C. Thoenes: 'Un architetto pavese del settecento', *Atti VIII convegno nazionale di storia dell'architettura: Caserta, 1953*, pp. 179–92
R. Wittkower: *Art and Architecture in Italy, 1600 to 1750*, Pelican Hist. A. (Harmondsworth, 1958), p. 242
S. Colombo: 'Contributo per G. A. Veneroni, architetto', *Commentari*, xiv/2–3 (1963), pp. 186–203
L. Grassi: *Provincie del barocco e del rococo* (Milan, 1966), pp. 443–75 [many pls]
S. Zatti: 'Novità per Gio. Antonio Veneroni, architetto pavese del settecento', *Boll. Soc. Pavese Stor. Patria*, n. s., xli (1989), pp. 119–37

ANNA MENICHELLA

Venetian empire. Lands controlled by the Republic of Venice from the 11th century until the late 18th. As an imperial power, Venice expanded both overseas (the *stato di mar*; see fig. 1) and in Italy (the *stato di terra*). The former was largely in lands once ruled by the Byzantine empire in Istria, Dalmatia, Albania and the Peloponnese, as well as islands in the Ionian, Aegean and eastern Mediterranean seas. The *stato di terra* was the product of acquisitions in the modern regions of the Veneto, Lombardy and the Romagna.

1. HISTORY. The Republic's territorial ambitions were first directed overseas and stemmed from links with Byzantium and growing maritime trade. Venice tried to achieve an ascendancy over Istria and Dalmatia from the 11th century, but her ambitions emerged more clearly in the Fourth Crusade (1202–4), which led to the dismemberment of the Byzantine empire. The Republic, however, found it impossible to make good all her gains: Durrazzo (now Durrës), for example, was held from 1205 to 1213 only. Moreover, Venetian acquisitions aroused the enmity of other powers: in 1358 Venice was forced to abandon Ragusa (now Dubrovnik) and all her other Dalmatian holdings to Hungary. Yet the disasters afflicting the Christian powers of the Balkans in the face of Ottoman expansion contributed to a temporary revival in imperial fortunes *c.* 1400, until Ottoman strength began to outclass Venetian resources. From the later 15th century the *stato di mar* began to shrink, although the decline was both slow and at times reversed. Gains on the Italian mainland came later, mostly in the first half of the 15th century, although its frontiers were pushed back by the Habsburgs and the papacy in the 16th century. In 1797, when the city was taken by Napoleon, the Republic still retained a large mainland state and ruled much of Istria, the Dalmatian coast and the Ionian Islands.

The subject territories were variously acquired: by conquest, purchase, spontaneous or induced surrender, after periods of ascendancy or by infiltration. The nature of these territories also varied, from coastal stations with slight resources of their own and no independent political tradition (e.g. Methoni and Koroni, Greece) to substantial cities with extensive territory, active commerce and industries and a history of self-government (e.g. Padua and Verona). Variety also characterized the empire's geography

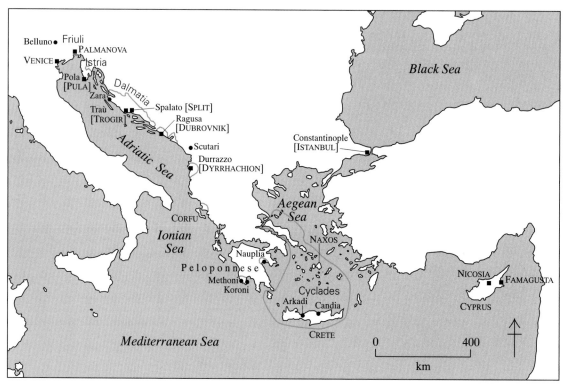

1. Map of the *stato di mar*, late 15th century; those areas with separate entries in this dictionary are distinguished by CROSS-REFERENCE TYPE

and climate, race, language and religion: subjects of the Republic included Italians, Slavs, Albanians, Greeks and Jews. By contrast, the Republic's initial aims were relatively few, seeking to protect and extend her commerce, to defend previous gains and even Venice from attack, and to pre-empt rivals. Subsequently other goals emerged: taxation, raw materials, and naval and military assistance. Venetians as private citizens looked for opportunities in commerce, ecclesiastical and secular office, and acquisition of land.

In some areas, such as Friuli, Albania and the Cyclades, Venice ruled indirectly over vassal or client lords, but the Republic's general goal was a highly centralized empire, with sovereign authority concentrated in Venice. Only Venetian nobles were appointed to key offices. Officials were appointed for short terms, issued with minute rules of conduct, rarely reappointed and liable to investigation *in situ* and at home. Proto-mercantilist policies were introduced to favour the Venetian economy. Centralization was, however, less burdensome in practice than in theory. The corps of officials in any 'posting' was small, often inexperienced and rarely supported by an effective garrison (only in Crete was there extensive colonial settlement). The central government faced problems in communicating orders and collecting information, but it finally realized the wisdom of earning its subjects' acceptance by respecting local customs and leaving the social order and distribution of wealth substantially unaltered: even though imperial subjects were excluded from all but local administration, they could attain partial Venetian citizenship and found the Republic open to petition.

This did not mean that Venetian government escaped criticism and revolt. The native aristocracy on Crete, for example, put up a long resistance, while Venetian settlers on the island resented being treated as second-class citizens. Local élites disliked being used as agents of the Republic's rule, especially in such matters as taxation. Yet, if loyalty was rarely as deep-rooted as the Republic's propagandists claimed, it is remarkable that such a far-flung and disparate empire was maintained for so long. The reasons are various. Venice could appear as a shield for its Christian—especially its Roman Catholic—subjects from the Turkish menace. Its policies were imbued with pragmatism and tempered by indifference, ignorance and inefficiency. For the most part it was not a colonial empire, and if an imperial ideology existed it recognized the need to afford justice, protection and economic opportunity to the subject populations.

2. ART. From the above it should be clear why the artistic influence of Venice as an imperial power was relatively slight. The Venetian presence can be detected in the ubiquitous Lion of St Mark sculpted on many buildings, and in the painted and carved coats of arms of Venetian officials on, for example, the public buildings in the Piazza dei Signori, Verona. On a larger scale it can be seen in the bastioned fortifications built from the 16th century, notably in the designs of Michele Sanmicheli and his followers in Crete, Cyprus and in Dalmatia at Spalato (now Split; see fig. 2) and Zara (now Zadar). The elaborate geometric fortifications of Nicosia (from 1567) and PALMANOVA (from 1593) designed by the Friulian engineer Giulio

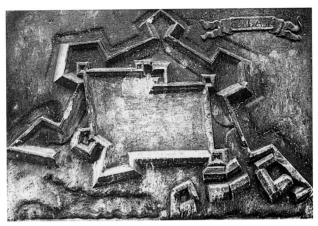

2. Venetian fortifications shown on relief map of Split, from the façade of S Maria Zobenigo, Venice, *c.* 1683

Savorgnano (1516–95) are good surviving examples. Venetian rule also led to the construction and enlargement of such administrative buildings as the Palazzo dei Rettori, Belluno (1491–1536), largely to the designs of the Venetian Giovanni Candi (1440–1506). As well as working on the defences of Famagusta from 1558 to 1562, Giovanni Girolamo Sanmicheli redesigned the government palace. The Republic's representatives also sponsored the construction of aqueducts and fountains, as in 1627 at Candia (now Herakleion) under the rule of Francesco di Pietro Morosini (*see* CRETE, §5). More generally, Venetian influence can be detected in the ornate Gothic decoration of doors and windows in late medieval public and private buildings in Istria, Dalmatia and mainland Italy.

In the east, for example on Naxos, Venetian settlers had to fortify their country residences, whereas on the mainland the growing taste for country life among the Venetian nobility encouraged the evolution of a style of villa architecture closely associated with Andrea Palladio (e.g. Villa Rotonda, near Vicenza). On the mainland Venetian patronage of the Church was active and sustained, but in the largely Orthodox east it was generally confined to the cities (e.g. Ayios Markos, Candia, 1239); the Baroque monastery of Arkadi on Crete (1657) is something of an exception. The negative aspect of the Venetian impact can be seen in the damage to the cultural life of Crete caused by the appropriation of the Orthodox Church's wealth and the introduction of a foreign, largely absentee and Roman Catholic episcopate.

The revival of icon and wall painting in 15th- and 16th-century Crete, however, was not untouched by Venetian and Italian influences, and Venetian rule by no means stifled artistic activity throughout the empire, at least in the larger centres and richer provinces. Candia, especially after the fall of Constantinople in 1453, became an important centre for the production of and trade in icons, Venetian merchants participating in their extensive export in the Orthodox world and beyond. Again, if some Dalmatian artists trained in Venice, such as the 15th-century sculptor and architect Giorgio da Sebenico, if a few Venetians worked in the region, as did Carlo Crivelli, who was made a citizen of Zara in 1465, and if a general

Venetian influence can be detected in Dalmatian painting and sculpture, many workshops flourished in the 15th century and a distinct, non-derivative, school can be identified in the work of such artists as the painter Biagio di Giorgia de Traù, working between 1412 and 1450.

The impact of the empire on the artistic life of the capital is also hard to define. Venice was traditionally dependent on the immigration of craftsmen and the import of raw materials (e.g. Istrian stone and Veronese marble) from the Adriatic region, Italy and further afield. The Republic's involvement in the eastern Mediterranean had exposed her to Byzantine influence before the *stato di mar* was formed. The taste for detailed landscapes evident in the work of Venetian painters *c.* 1500 may have been stimulated by a growing familiarity with the mainland provinces. Artists from subject territories, such as Pisanello from Verona, Giulio Clovio from Croatia and El Greco from Crete, were attracted to Venice, but they were not necessarily monopolized by it.

Spoils of empire were, however, gathered in the city, even if plans in the early 16th century to rebuild on the Lido the Roman amphitheatre at Pola (now Pula) went unfulfilled. The bronze horses looted from Constantinople in 1204 were set up on the façade of S Marco *c.* 1250; stone lions of various dates brought back from a campaign in the Peloponnese in 1684 were placed round the gate of the Arsenal. Artists and architects were commissioned to celebrate the achievements of empire: S Marco, obviously Byzantine in both design and decoration, has been interpreted (at least in part) as an expression of the Republic's self-image as heir to the Eastern empire. In the Doge's Palace generations of painters were employed to commemorate triumphs in east and west. For example, on the walls of the Sala del Maggior Consiglio, the Venetian role in the Fourth Crusade was celebrated in canvases by Andrea Vincentino (1539–1617), Tintoretto and Palma Giovane. Panels on the ceiling record Venetian campaigns against the Turks and in defence of the *stato di terra*, for example that by Palma Giovane depicting Andrea Gritti's recapture of Padua in 1510.

Occasionally monuments were put up to outstanding military commanders, for example the equestrian statue of the mercenary captain *Bartolomeo Colleoni* (1481–8; Venice, Campo SS Giovanni e Paolo; *see* VERROCCHIO, ANDREA DEL, fig. 4). Venetian families and individuals with imperial connections could be similarly celebrated: reliefs on the tomb of *Caterina Cornaro, Queen of Cyprus* (1580–86; Venice, S Salvadore), the work of Bernardino di Francesco Contino (*d* before 1597), record her role in securing Cyprus for Venice in 1489. The tomb of *Francesco Morosini* ('il Peloponnesiaco'; doge 1688–94; Venice, S Stefano), attributed to Filippo Parodi, commemorates his wars against the Turks, including the bombardment and capture of the Acropolis of Athens in 1687.

Lastly, the Republic's claim to be the protector of its subjects probably encouraged immigration, particularly after Turkish pressure on Dalmatia, Albania, Greece and the islands. The contribution of scribes and scholars from Crete is well known in the history of humanism and printing, notably the publication of Greek texts in Venice by Aldus Manutius. S Giorgio dei Greci was begun by Sante Lombardo in 1539 for the city's large Greek community; the Scuola di S Nicolò dei Greci was built near by to designs by Baldassare Longhena from 1678. Earlier, the Albanian community received permission to found a confraternity (*scuola*) in 1442. The construction of its meeting-house began in 1489; reliefs and inscriptions record Venetian efforts to defend Scutari (now Shkodër) from the Turks in 1474 and 1479. In 1502 the Albanians commissioned a cycle of canvases (dispersed) devoted to the *Life of the Virgin* from the workshop of Vittore Carpaccio. In 1516 Carpaccio executed a Lion of St Mark for the Sala della Volte in the Doge's Palace: the paws of this symbol of Venetian power rest on both land and sea. In their various ways, such works illustrate the rich cosmopolitan character of the culture of the Venetian empire.

BIBLIOGRAPHY

E. A. Freeman: *Subject and Neighbouring Lands of Venice* (London, 1881)
G. Gerola: *Monumenti veneti nell'isola di Creta*, 4 vols (Venice, 1905–32)
W. Miller: *The Latins in the Levant* (London, 1908)
H. Brown: *Dalmatia* (London, 1925)
F. Thiriet: *La Roumanie vénitienne au moyen âge* (Paris, 1959)
D. S. Chambers: *The Imperial Age of Venice* (London, 1970)
F. C. Lane: *Venice: A Maritime Republic* (Baltimore and London, 1973)
A. Pertusi, ed.: *Venezia e il Levante*, 2 vols (Florence, 1973–4)
H. G. Beck and others: *Venezia: Centro di mediazione tra oriente e occidente* (Florence, 1977)
F. Thiriet: *Etudes sur la Romanie greco-vénitienne* (London, 1977)
J. Morris: *The Venetian Empire* (London, 1980)
G. Cozzi and M. Knapton: *Storia della Repubblica di Venezia dalla guerra di Chioggia alla rinconquista della terraferma*, Storia d'Italia, xii/1 (Turin, 1986)
From Byzantium to El Greco: Greek Frescoes and Icons (exh. cat., ed. M. Acheimastou-Potamianou; London, RA, 1987)
J. E. Law: 'Il quattrocento a Venezia', *Storia della società italiana*, ed. G. Cherubini and others, viii (Milan, 1988), pp. 233–312
B. Arbel and others: *Latins and Greeks in the Eastern Mediterranean after 1204* (London, 1989)
Biagio di Giorgio da Traù (exh. cat., Venice, S Bartolomeo, 1989)
G. Cozzi, M. Knapton and G. Scarabello: *La Repubblica di Venezia nell'età moderna, dal 1517 alla fine della Repubblica*, Storia d'Italia, xii/2 (Turin, 1992)

JOHN LAW

Veneto, Bartolomeo. *See* BARTOLOMEO VENETO.

Veneto-Saracenic. Term applied to a large group of 15th- and 16th-century metal wares, primarily in European collections, once attributed to Muslim craftsmen working in Venice. The objects concerned—they include covered bowls with a rounded base or cylindrical form, spherical incense burners, candlesticks, buckets and salvers—are domestic in character. Made of brass (or bronze), they are inlaid with geometric or arabesque motifs in silver, with occasional traces of gold and frequent additions of a black compound, the widely differing designs being organized concentrically, centrifugally or centripetally. The term is sometimes loosely applied to objects decorated with figural ornament and Western coats of arms. None of the objects is dated, although a salver in Vienna (Mus. Angewandte Kst, GO.81) bears the date 1550 and the signature of Nicolo Rugina Greco da Corfu incised on the back; this inscription was probably added after the salver had been imported into the West. A number of pieces are signed by the masters Mahmud al-Kurdi and Zayn al-Din, and many bear European coats of arms, notably a group of small candlesticks with a truncated conical base and straight shaft (e.g. three in Venice, Correr, with the arms of the Malipiero family).

The identification of these objects as 'Veneto-Saracenic' was popularized by Lavoix (1862), who believed that Muslim metalworkers had worked in Venice and trained Italian craftsmen in the Islamic style. The latter signed themselves 'Ageminius' and described their work as *all gemina* or *alla gemina*, terms thought to be derived from the Arabic *'ajamī* ('Persian'; cf. later Venetian dialect *azzimina*). Although based only on circumstantial evidence, Lavoix's thesis was widely accepted until 1970, when Huth questioned whether guild laws would have allowed the presence of foreign craftsmen on Venetian territory. Huth also noted the difficulty of distinguishing whether a piece was an Islamic original or a close Western copy. No documentary evidence to support or disprove either contention has been discovered. The division of Veneto-Saracenic metalwork into more precise categories was begun by Melikian-Chirvani, who dated one subgroup to the late Mamluk period (*c.* 1400–1517). Many of the objects in this sub-group have a Western shape, and Melikian-Chirvani suggested that they were fashioned in the West and exported to the Middle East for decoration before being reimported into Venice. He thought that the Western coats of arms indicated that the objects had been made on commission. Allan suggested Mamluk Damascus, Cairo or the Jazira as a provenance for another sub-group, while Auld has tentatively divided 280 of the objects into three categories: Turkoman, Mamluk and Western.

The identification of the Turkoman sub-group of over a hundred pieces is based on the eleven pieces signed by Mahmud al-Kurdi (three in London, BM; two in U. London, Courtauld Inst. Gals; one each in London, V&A; Cividale del Friuli, Mus. Archeol. N.; Madrid, Mus. Galdiano; Bologna, Mus. Civ. Med.; Paris, Louvre; and St Petersburg, Hermitage; other objects attributed to al-Kurdi by Mayer can be excluded on stylistic grounds). This master is thought to have worked in eastern Anatolia or western Iran in the late 15th century, when these areas were ruled by the Turkoman confederation of the AQQOYUNLU. The objects he made are decorated with centrifugal designs of cusped ogees, lime-shaped medallions and cruciform motifs inlaid in silver in both spatial and linear techniques (i.e. using small sheets of metal or metal wire) against a minutely incised arabesque ground. Their decoration displays affinities with that on metalwork made during the same period for the Timurid dynasty in eastern Iran and Central Asia and the Mamluk rulers of Egypt and Syria (*see* ISLAMIC ART, §IV, 3(i)(b) and (iii)(b)), but Mahmud al-Kurdi had an added interest in drama and colour. His reliance on Timurid precedent can be seen on a salver in the British Museum (1878.12–30.705; see fig.), especially in the centrifugal design and individual motifs of the border and in the use of a crosshatched ground. Mamluk motifs were also adopted: the signature contained within the central field of blazon-like roundels, and the cross-petalled lotus blossoms on the outside rim, for example. The same exuberant eclecticism is found on objects that Allan (p. 142) has attributed to Turkoman patronage, and this variety of motifs may be the result of the conquests of the Aqqoyunlu sovereign Uzun Hasan (*reg* 1453–78) at the expense of his Qaraqoyunlu and

'Veneto-Saracenic' brass salver by Mahmud al-Kurdi, engraved with arabesque designs and inlaid with silver, diam. 290 mm, from eastern Anatolia or western Iran, late 15th century (London, British Museum)

Timurid neighbours. Uzun Hasan had diplomatic links with Venice from 1463 to 1475, and a covered bowl by Mahmud al-Kurdi (U. London, Courtauld Inst. Gals) bears an inscription in Arabic together with a transliteration of it in Latin script; the bowl may have been intended as a diplomatic gift. Mahmud al-Kurdi's work is also linked stylistically to Aqqoyunlu manuscript illumination. A Koran dated 1483 (Dublin, Chester Beatty Lib., MS. 1502), for example, shares both individual motifs and Mahmud al-Kurdi's approach to design. Six pieces in a related style were signed by the master Zayn al-Din (Baltimore, MD, Walters A.G.; Paris, Louvre; Venice, Correr; London, BM; London, V&A; sold London, Christie's, 11 June 1986, lot 430). They bear motifs not found in Mahmud al-Kurdi's work: a subdivided split palmette and a type of arabesque common in Ottoman metalwork, ceramics and architectural ornament of the 16th century. Zayn al-Din may have been among the metalworkers removed from Tabriz to Istanbul in 1514 as a result of the conquest of the former Aqqoyunlu capital by the Ottoman sultan Selim I. A piece by Zayn al-Din in the Bargello, Florence, a fine round-bottomed box and cover, is known to have been in the collection of Ferdinand I de' Medici from 1589 and was formerly displayed in the Sala della Tribuna of the Uffizi Palace, Florence, evidence of the respect paid to Islamic inlaid metalwork in the High Renaissance.

The second sub-group, which includes the bulk of the Veneto-Saracenic pieces, is related to late 15th-century Mamluk metalwork: designs are organized centripetally or in concentric bands, and the motifs are typically Mamluk. These last include geometric interlacing; alternating knots, twisted ropes and trefoiled trelliswork derived from calligraphy; and roundels within plain or cusped fillet borders that are linked to the fillet strips between concentric bands of decoration. A typical piece is a spherical incense burner (Washington, DC, Freer, 39.58) composed of identical hemispheres. Each has a central roundel of knotwork that is repeated in a broad band on the walls. Both the knotted roundel and band have a narrow border of running stems bearing small trefoils, and the four areas are delineated by narrow fillet frames. The ground is coarsely engraved with scrolls, and the incisions are filled with a black organic compound. None of the objects in this group is signed, but many bear north Italian (and specifically Venetian) coats of arms. Although these are too general or too incomplete to provide precise information about ownership, they are nonetheless visual evidence of the close diplomatic and commercial links between the Mamluk and Venetian states.

The third sub-group consists of objects apparently made in the West, probably in northern Italy, in imitation of Islamic wares. Individual motifs were copied accurately, but there is a basic misunderstanding of the rules of Islamic proportion and a disregard for any relationship between positive and negative shape. An example (London, U. Courtauld Inst. Gals), indisputably Western because of the inclusion of tiny birds, masks and grotesques among the foliage, displays the characteristic disharmony between the width and the breadth of the cartouches. These do, however, rely on Islamic prototypes for their trefoil finials and for the way in which they are cut short at the border by the rim. Other Western characteristics are found in the arabesque infill, which is broken up to fill each individual area, and the strict division between the bands of the concentric arrangement. In Islamic design the arabesque ground would have continued uninterrupted, as the space they fill would have been seen not as contained but as infinite.

BIBLIOGRAPHY

M. Boni: *Notizia di una casettina geografica opera di commessi d'oro e argento all'agemina* (Venice, 1800)

D. Francesconi: *Illustrazione di una urnetta lavorata d'oro e di vari altri metalli all gemina coll'iscriptione 'Paulus Ageminius Faciebat'* (Venice, 1800)

H. Lavoix: 'Les Azziministes', *Gaz. B.-A.*, xii (1862), pp. 64–74

——: 'Les Arts musulmans: De l'ornementation arabe dans les oeuvres des maîtres italiens', *Gaz. B.-A.*, xvi (1877), pp. 15–29

S. Lane-Poole: 'A Venetian Azzimina of the 16th Century', *Mag. A.* (1886), pp. 450–53

W. L. Hildburgh: 'Dinanderie Ewers with Venetian-Saracenic Decorations', *Burl. Mag.*, lxxix (1941), pp. 17–22

L. A. Mayer: *Islamic Metalworkers and their Works* (Geneva, 1959)

B. W. Robinson: 'Oriental Metalwork in the Gambier Parry Collection', *Burl. Mag.*, cix (1967), pp. 169–73

U. Scerrato: *Arte islamica a Napoli* (Naples, 1967)

H. Huth: '"Sarazenen" in Venedig?', *Festschrift für Heinz Ladendorf* (Cologne, 1970), pp. 58–68

M. S. Melikian-Chirvani: 'Venise, entre l'orient et l'occident', *Bull. Etud. Orient.*, xxvii (1974), pp. 109–26

M. Spallanzani: 'Metalli islamici nelle collezioni medicee dei secoli XV–XVI', *Le arti del principato mediceo* (Florence, 1980), pp. 95–117

G. Curatola and M. Spallanzani: *Metalli islamici dalle collezioni granducali* (Florence, 1981)

E. Atıl, W. T. Chase and P. Jett: *Islamic Metalwork in the Freer Gallery of Art* (Washington, DC, 1985)

M. Spallanzani: 'Il piatto islamico Venier-Molin del Bargello', *Renaissance Studies in Honor of Craig Hugh Smyth*, ii (Florence, 1985), pp. 465–72

J. W. Allan: *Metalwork of the Islamic World: The Aron Collection* (London, 1986)

S. Auld: '*Veneto-Saracenic' Metalwork: Objects and History* (diss., U. Edinburgh, 1989)

R. Ward, S. La Niece, D. Hook and R. White: '"Veneto-Saracenic" Metalwork: An Analysis of the Bowls and Incense Burners in the British Museum', *Post-med. Archaeol.*, xxviii (1994)

SYLVIA AULD

Venetsianov, Aleksey (Gavrilovich) (*b* Moscow, 18 Feb 1780; *d* Safonkovo, 16 Dec 1847). Russian painter, printmaker and teacher. The son of a reasonably well-to-do merchant, he studied in a private boarding-school in Moscow. He worked as a draughtsman in Moscow and then as a land surveyor in St Petersburg, where he probably studied with the portraitist Vladimir Borovikovsky in the first decade of the 19th century. However, he received no formal training. In 1808 he made several etchings for the *Zhurnal karikatur,* a satirical publication he hoped to bring out regularly; but they were banned by the censor and destroyed. In the first two decades of the 19th century Venetsianov was active primarily as a portrait painter, often working in pastel. His early portraits can be sentimental and romantic, but later ones are marked by simplicity and authenticity and succeed in conveying both the character of the model and nature of his or her usual surroundings.

In 1815 Venetsianov acquired a small estate near the village of Safonkovo in the province of Tver' and began to spend the summer months there, increasingly taking peasant life as the main subject of his paintings. Little stylistic change was evident at first, but in 1822 he was prompted to take a more poetic approach to the realistic portrayal of rural life when he remarked the treatment of light in a painting by the French artist François Granet, an *Interior View of the Choir of the Church of the Capuchin Monastery in Rome,* which was shown at the Hermitage in 1821. From then on Venetsianov sought to follow nature rather than any particular model in earlier painting. The first results of this change of attitude were paintings on themes from rural life: *Peeling Beetroot* (not later than 1822), the *Threshing Floor* (1821–3), the *Morning of the Lady of the Manor* (1823) and *Sleeping Shepherd* (1823–4; all St Petersburg, Rus. Mus.). In the first of these, Venetsianov kept some traditional features, but in the *Threshing Floor* he interpreted nature more directly. When planning this picture, he ordered his serfs to saw out the end wall of a barn; he then placed his peasants in appropriate poses inside the opening created and then recorded this scene on to the canvas. Despite the relative naivety of this first experiment in painting directly from nature, it was an important step for Venetsianov towards an early form of realism, a term that can be used to characterize his work as a whole.

Venetsianov's early paintings lacked a poetic foundation, but this soon made its appearance, becoming the basic distinguishing quality of all his mature works. The poetry of everyday life permeates the *Morning of the Lady of the Manor* and *Sleeping Shepherd.* The first shows the interior of a room in the landowner's house with the lady (the artist's wife) explaining to two peasant girls their tasks for the day. Light falls through the open window, enveloping the figures, the folding screen, the table and other objects in the room and also uniting the interior with the landscape outside. While similar to much German and Scandinavian Biedermeier painting, Venetsianov's interiors were of a kind new to Russia. With this painting Venetsianov initiated a long line of interior scenes executed by both his pupils and other painters.

In *Sleeping Shepherd* the main figure is placed in the foreground against a landscape painted with remarkable

Aleksey Venetsianov: *In the Ploughed Field: Spring*, oil on canvas, 512×655 mm, early 1820s (Moscow, Tret'yakov Gallery)

directness and lack of artifice: a stream lying motionless between its banks, a fisherman standing stock-still at its edge, a woman carrying buckets of water in the field beyond. The painting demonstrates Venetsianov's conviction that nature possessed an essentially poetic character of its own that the painter had merely to detect and record.

In his mature paintings Venetsianov also emerged as the precursor of later Russian genre painting. During the 18th century genre scenes had appeared only sporadically, and the isolated examples that occurred were not part of a coherent line of development and were without any consistency. Genre painting appeared in Russia rather belatedly and, because of this, assimilated features characteristic of other picture types such as the landscape, the portrait and the still-life. Elements of landscape and portrait painting can be seen in both *Sleeping Shepherd* and the *Morning of the Lady of the Manor*. Influences from still-life painting reveal themselves in almost all of Venetsianov's work: Venetsianov always paid great attention to detail, to the individual object, however lowly. Another characteristic of Venetsianov's genre painting is the fact that it does not contain any clearly defined action and is devoid of dramatic conflict. It presents the viewer with illustration rather than anecdote. Venetsianov's most successful works, of the 1820s, display these qualities.

Two paintings, *In the Ploughed Field: Spring* (early 1820s; see fig.) and *At the Harvest: Summer* (mid-1820s; both Moscow, Tret'yakov Gal.), are rightfully considered to be Venetsianov's finest achievements. It is possible that they were intended to form part of a cycle of the four seasons. In the painting *In the Ploughed Field* Venetsianov used a very simple motif: a woman leads by the bridle a pair of horses harnessed to a harrow, while at the edge of the field a child sits playing. This unsophisticated scene reveals the grandeur of a simple world: an ordinary Russian landscape with a field and a high sky acquires a new significance. In the small canvas *At the Harvest*, the action is equally simple: a woman has interrupted her work and is sitting on a raised platform in the foreground to suckle a baby who has been brought to her from home. Here Venetsianov treated the same themes of motherhood, the land and the peasant's work on the land. Sunlight drenches the whole rye field, and bold areas of local colour are combined with subtle gradations of shading. Despite the vertical format of the painting, there is a strong sense of the horizontal. Venetsianov was the first Russian painter to convey such a sense of space in the Russian countryside and he achieved this, in part, by removing classical framing devices. Above all, Venetsianov saw the land as the place where human beings live and work every day.

A large number of portrait sketches of peasants, which testify to the artist's attentive and affectionate attitude towards his models, date from the 1820s and 1830s, for example *Two Peasant Boys with a Kite* (1820s; St Petersburg, Rus. Mus.). In the 1830s his work underwent more fundamental changes: subjects were taken from the canon of academic art, as in *The Bather* (early 1830s; St Petersburg, Rus. Mus.) or *Bacchante* (*c.* 1832; Moscow, Tret'yakov Gal.). Some genre paintings of the late 1830s acquire narrative traits and a didactic character.

From the 1820s Venetsianov was also active as a teacher. His pupils (among them many of his serfs, some of whom were emancipated at Venetsianov's insistence) received their instruction from the artist in St Petersburg and on his estate at Safonkovo. He had his own teaching methods: he gave preference to working from nature, permitting the copying of the works of Old Masters only in the last stages of training, and setting his pupils to draw and paint the simplest household objects. He gave equal prominence to different genres. Among his most significant pupils were Aleksandr Alekseyev (1811–78), Aleksey Tyranov (1808–59), Lavr Plakhov (1810–81) and Grigory Soroka.

As a whole Venetsianov's work can be seen as a blend of different stylistic principles. He combined classical notions of the unchanging character of everyday life with an understanding of the beauty of the world uncluttered by preconceptions. At the same time, there are elements in his paintings, and particularly in his portraits, of both sentimentality and Romanticism, and he was one of the first Russian artists to turn directly to realism.

WRITINGS

A. V. Kornilova, ed.: *A. G. Venetsianov: Stati, pis'ma, vospominaniya o khudozhnika* [A. G. Venetsianov: articles, letters, recollections about the artist] (Leningrad, 1980)

BIBLIOGRAPHY

A. N. Savinov: *A. G. Venetsianov: Zhizn' i tvorchestvo* [A. G. Venetsianov: life and work] (Moscow, 1955)

G. Smirnov: *Venetsianov i yego shkola* [Venetsianov and his school] (Leningrad, 1973) [with Eng., Fr. and Ger. summary and colour illus.]

T. V. Alekseyeva: *Khudozhniki shkoly Venetsianova* [Artists of the school of Venetsianov] (Moscow, 1982)

A. G. Venetsianov: Vystavka proizvedeniy k 200-letiyu so dnya rozhdeniya [A. G. Venetsianov: an exhibition of his works on the 200th anniversary of his birth] (exh. cat., St Petersburg, Rus. Mus., 1983)

D. V. SARAB'YANOV

Veneziano, Agostino. *See* MUSI, AGOSTINO DEI.

Veneziano, Antonio. *See* ANTONIO VENEZIANO.

Veneziano, Baptista. *See* FRANCO, BATTISTA.

Veneziano, Bonifazio. *See* PITATI, BONIFAZIO DE'.

Veneziano, Carlo. *See* SARACENI, CARLO.

Veneziano, Domenico. *See* DOMENICO VENEZIANO.

Veneziano, Jacometto. *See* JACOMETTO VENEZIANO.

Veneziano, Lorenzo. *See* LORENZO VENEZIANO.

Veneziano, Paolo. *See* PAOLO VENEZIANO.

Veneziano, Sebastiano. *See* SEBASTIANO DEL PIOMBO.

Venezuela, Republic of. South American country, bordered by the Caribbean Sea to the north, Brazil to the south, Guyana to the east and Colombia to the west (see fig. 1). Its name, meaning 'little Venice', was given to it in 1499 by the Italian explorer Amerigo Vespucci, who compared the indigenous people's dwellings, which were built on water, to those of the Italian city. The country is divided into twenty states, two federal territories, one federal district and the insular territories. The capital is CARACAS (founded 1567). The majority of the country's *c.* 20 million inhabitants live along the coast. More than 60% of the population are of mixed ethnic origin, 20% Caucasian, 9% of African descent and *c.* 2% Amerindian. The country's topography and location provide it with a variety of climates. The west, lying at the tip of the Andes, has fertile valleys: the two most important Andean cities are Mérida and San Cristóbal. Maracaibo, Venezuela's great oil city to the north, has a hot, dry climate; the other major city on the Venezuelan gulf, Coro, founded in 1528, has a well-preserved historic district. On the central plains large cattle ranches extend along the Apure, Arauca and Capanaparo, and in the south and east are the rainforest, the Amazon and Amacuro territories and the Orinoco River, one of the longest in the world. The north-eastern area of Venezuela has developed a strong tourist industry, centred on Puerto de la Cruz and Barcelona on the Caribbean coast; Barcelona, Cumaná, Clarines and Araya have remained virtually unchanged since Independence (1821) and are renowned for their colonial splendour. The remains of Nueva Cádiz, one of the oldest Spanish settlements on the continent, are preserved at Cubagua island.

This article discusses the arts and architecture in the region from Spanish colonization onwards. For a discussion of Pre-Columbian culture in this region, which was limited owing to its isolation from the great Andean cultures of the south, *see* SOUTH AMERICA, PRE-COLUMBIAN, §§II, V, and VII, 1.

I. Introduction. II. Indigenous culture. III. Architecture. IV. Painting, graphic arts and sculpture. V. Gold and silver. VI. Textiles. VII. Patronage, collecting and dealing. VIII. Museums. IX. Art education. X. Art libraries and photographic collections.

I. Introduction.

When Columbus arrived in the area comprising modern Venezuela on his third voyage in 1498, the profuse vegetation and immense rivers convinced him he had reached paradise, and so he called the region Isla de Gracia. The following year the Italian explorer Amerigo Vespucci reached the Coquivacoa Gulf (now the Gulf of Maracaibo). During the colonial period the province was administered by the Audiencia of Santo Domingo and the Viceroyalty of Nueva Granada. The settlement of Nueva Cádiz was first established by the Spanish *c.* 1510, and colonization continued in 1514 with a settlement of Dominican friars on the eastern coast of Cumaná, but the major territorial conquests took place on the western coast. From Coro (founded 1528) the Spanish launched their conquest of Venezuela, using Coro and El Tocuyo (founded 1547) as political and administrative centres. The major cities were founded by colonists farming cacao

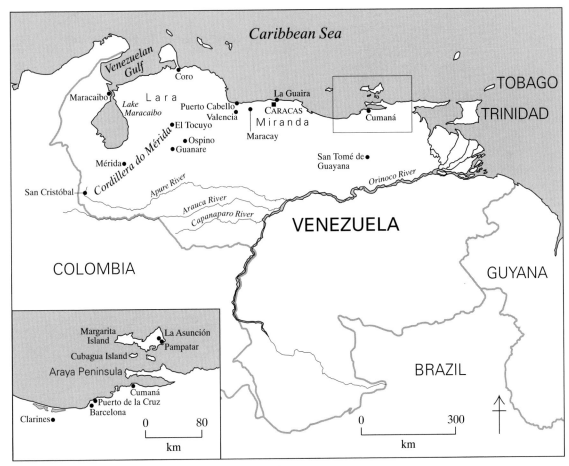

1. Map of Venezuela; the site CARACAS has a separate entry in this dictionary

and tobacco using African and indigenous labour, based on the *encomienda* system, whereby Indians were granted as slaves to the conquerors.

The exploitation of minerals and agriculture quickly led to a feudal production system based on export, and during the 17th century the province's expanding economy created a wealthy Creole upper class, commonly called 'los grandes cacaos'; with the Church, some of these wealthy figures were patrons of the arts. Prosperity increased further when Venezuela became a Capitanía General in 1777. The economic and political conflicts between the conspicuous colonial class and their Spanish rulers, however, eventually led in 1806 to Venezuela's long and bloody revolutionary war, led by Francisco de Miranda and Simón Bolívar; independence was achieved in 1821, two years after the formation by Bolívar of Gran Colombia, comprising Venezuela, Ecuador and Panama. In 1830 Gran Colombia was divided, and General José Antonio Paez became Venezuela's political and military figurehead. His control profoundly marked the evolution of the country's centralized power structure in the 19th century and early 20th. Political and economic instability followed Paez's defeat in 1846, with the liberals and conservatives vying for power without instigating any substantial reforms.

Antonio Guzmán Blanco led the country through constant political turmoil from 1870 to 1890, but some important social advances were made during this time, and Guzmán was a strong supporter of the arts. It is often said ironically that Venezuela did not enter the 20th century until 1936, following the death (1935) of the dictator Juan Vicente Gómez, but Gómez was succeeded by other equally repressive military governments. Oil meanwhile became the government's largest source of income and significantly improved the country's economy, financing the foundation of artistic institutions but also highlighting the unequal distribution of wealth.

After overthrowing Venezuela's first democratic government (1945–8), in 1948 Marcos Pérez Jiménez took power and curtailed all political freedom. A national uprising in 1958 overthrew Jiménez, and in 1961 Venezuela's first democratic constitution was adopted. In the 1970s and 1980s the international oil crisis benefited Venezuela, but this sudden increase in national wealth created a false illusion of splendour, permitting large-scale construction and investment in heavy industry, social services and education but also encouraging political corruption, which intensified social inequalities. The economic crisis of the late 1980s led to further social upheaval and to several futile military coups, which threatened South America's oldest and most stable democracy.

BIBLIOGRAPHY
J. F. Acevedo Mijares: *Historia del arte en Venezuela* (Caracas, 1951)
A. Boulton: *Historia de la pintura en Venezuela*, 3 vols (Caracas, 1964–72)
Venezuela, 1498–1810, Sociedad Amigos del Museo de Bellas Artes (Caracas, 1965)
G. Moron: *Historia de Venezuela*, 5 vols (Caracas, 1971)
E. Armitano, ed.: *Diccionario biográfico de las artes plásticas en Venezuela: Siglos XIX y XX* (Caracas, 1973)
J. Calzadilla: *El arte en Venezuela* (Caracas, 1976)
Arte de Venezuela, Consejo Municipal del Distrito Federal (Caracas, 1977)
Diccionario manual de Venezuela: Geográfico histórico y biográfico (Caracas, 1982)

II. Indigenous culture.

When Amerigo Vespucci reached the Coquivacoa Gulf, he marvelled at the skill of the indigenous inhabitants, whose homes, known locally as *palafitos*, were built on water. When the Spaniards arrived, different regions of the country showed diverse stages of cultural development. Most of the flatlands, the jungle and central mountain range were occupied by Carib peoples; some were nomadic hunters, while others settled in the fertile valleys or beside rivers. Their dwellings were built from compressed mud and reeds with palm roofs, and they produced carved tools and weapons, musical instruments and sophisticated ceramics. In the Andean region most Pre-Columbian peoples were related to the Chibcha nation (one of the major Andean cultures) and were known as Timoto-Cuicas. They had sophisticated agricultural systems and produced a wide range of ceramics, textiles, gold ornaments, religious artefacts and stone or obsidian tools; these peoples made their dwellings from stone, adobe and other local materials.

Indigenous building forms, materials and techniques were adapted by the colonists, who incorporated new architectural elements such as doors, large windows, patios and courtyards into the religious, governmental and private buildings of the 15th and 16th centuries (*see* §III below). Spanish crafts were introduced by the colonists, and their workshops employed indigenous labour for the most rudimentary tasks. In the absence of Spanish labour, *mestizos* or *pardos* (men of mixed racial origin), however, gradually acquired the full range of skills as carpenters, gilders, metal-casters and painters of religious icons and idols, continuing indigenous craft traditions but adding European techniques and materials to create a unique phenomenon of transculturation. During the first half of the 18th century the mestizo artist Juan Pedro López (1724–87) was an exemplary figure, being a gifted sculptor of religious images as well as an excellent portrait painter.

Important elements of indigenous crafts remain in the contemporary production of textiles in Quibor valley in the state of Lara. These items are a direct legacy of the Arawak peoples who occupied the valley at the time of the Spanish settlers. Hammocks (*chinchorros*) are made principally in Zulia, Apure and Mérida, and different types of basket are produced in the coastal regions, notably by family-run workshops on the island of Margarita, as well as along the eastern coast and in the region of Coro in the west.

Ceramics, both utilitarian and artistic, are made in a number of different styles depending on the region and

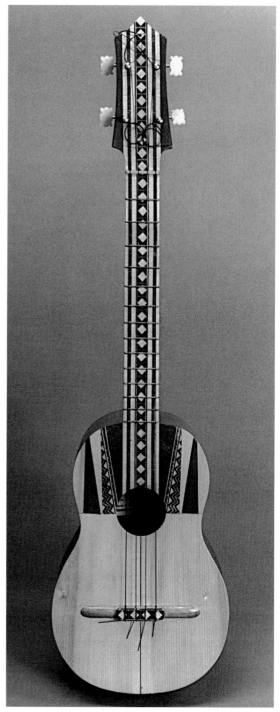

2. *Cuatro* made by Cruz Quinal of Cumanacoa Sucre State, l. 0.70 m, 1980s (London, Horniman Museum and Library)

local influence. In the Andean states the ceramics are still handmade, almost exclusively by women, and they are sometimes painted in vibrant colours with abstract designs. A very refined pottery painted with white abstract figures is produced in the states of Lara and Yaracuy in the mid-west of the country by individuals and workshops.

Another strong tradition of contemporary indigenous culture is the production of musical instruments. Influenced by Pre-Columbian, African or Spanish models, craftsmen produce chord instruments such as guitars and *cuatros* (small guitar-like instruments; see fig. 2) in Carora and Barquisimeto in the state of Lara, and in the state of Sucre. In Barlovento in the central region drums are made from hollowed trunks to obtain different tones. Maracas, also Pre-Columbian in origin, are created in various parts of the country.

Traditional dances with Pre-Columbian influences such as the *mare-mare* and the *sebucan* on the eastern coast are still performed, and the feast of Los diablos de Yare, which is African in influence, is celebrated in Miranda: during the feast the frenzied dancers sing while wearing masks representing the Devil. A number of traditional dances and religious festivals such as the Cruz de Mayo in the Caribe region demonstrate the way in which Pre-Columbian and African cults are interwoven with Christian beliefs and iconography.

During the 20th century many artists were strongly influenced by indigenous art forms, including ARMANDO REVERÓN, whose works challenged the traditional separation between academic and non-academic art; naive art, produced by artists who have not had traditional academic training, often used as its subject-matter such popular events as religious celebrations. Indigenous artistic production continued to exist alongside this.

Perhaps the most noteworthy 20th-century indigenous artist was JUAN FÉLIX SÁNCHEZ, whose work encompassed painting, sculpture, architecture, textile design and other forms of arts and crafts. Produced in an isolated site high in the Andes in Mérida, Sánchez's output represents an Andean tradition of self-taught artists whose work defies the boundaries between the utilitarian and the artistic and the sacred and the secular. Near his home he created from 1952 a complex of architecture, sculpture and outdoor furniture using local materials such as stone, gravel and wood arranged on a series of terraces on the mountainside; the whole symbolizes the passion and agony of Christ. Sánchez also used unique three-heddle frames instead of the traditional two-heddle frames for weaving textile designs with abstract patterns in subtle colours, characteristics that relate his work to that of Venezuelan kinetic artists, especially Carlos Cruz-Diez. Despite its variety, Sánchez's work has an integrity binding together his religious and aesthetic ideas, the natural environment in which he lived and his country's history.

BIBLIOGRAPHY

M. Acosta Saignes: *Estudios en antropología, sociología, historia y Foclor* (Caracas, 1980)
F. Vegas: *Venezuelan Vernacular* (Princeton, 1985)
G. Gasparini: *Arquitectura popular de Venezuela* (Caracas, 1986)

MARIO ELOY VALERO

III. Architecture.

1. 1514–1821. 2. 1821–*c.* 1900. 3. After *c.* 1900.

1. 1514–1821.

(i) Religious. It has been estimated that of *c.* 130 extant churches of the colonial period, only 10 originated in the 16th and 17th centuries (Bayón and Marx, p. 32). Although the Gothic style was still prevalent in Spain when that country launched itself into the conquest of the New World, the style failed to put down roots in Venezuela; it is, however, probable that traces of Gothic were evident in the two ephemeral churches of Cubagua and in the earliest stone houses erected by the Spanish. The first churches were built by Dominican and Franciscan missionaries along the coast; indeed the humble church erected by Fray Francisco de Córdova and Fray Juan Garcés when they arrived in Cumaná in 1514, was perhaps the earliest, but by 1515 nothing remained of it. In early 1517 another Franciscan expedition arrived, and within a couple of years the missionaries built two churches and two houses and opened schools and a home for indigenous children. This attempt at peaceful colonization (which also provided the first formal education in Venezuela) was cut short by a fire that destroyed the buildings in September 1520, and no new attempt was made for some time. It seems that in 1537 the church of Santiago may have been inaugurated on the desert island of Cubagua, but already by the following year the local inhabitants began to leave the island, and in 1540 the Cabildo and royal officials moved to Cabo de la Vela.

Since barely any trace remains of the earliest Spanish buildings in Venezuela, the origins of religious architecture there must be sought in the contemporary and almost identical cathedrals of Coro and La Asunción on the island of Margarita. These churches established a scheme of construction that underwent few significant variations until well into the 19th century: a rectangular floor-plan was divided into three naves by masonry arcades, usually Tuscan columns with round arches, the spandrel walls of which directly supported the open timber rafters of collar-beam roofs. This system perhaps has its immediate precedent in Tenerife, although the panelled roof is a characteristic variant of the Venezuelan style. Construction of the church of La Asunción (now the cathedral) began in 1570, but by the end of the century only the main chapel (which collapsed in 1667), sacristy and tower had been erected. A double-pitched roof was expressed externally in a simple gable, unadorned but for a portal with a marked Renaissance flavour: a round arch surmounted by a decorated frieze and pediment carried on short columns that rise from the impost of the arch. Work on Coro Cathedral began in 1583 and was completed in 1617; the 'maestro' Francisco Ramirez from Margarita worked on the presbytery and sacristies in 1608–13. The city had been built as an episcopal see in 1531, and the first 11 bishops in Venezuela came from Coro; in 1637 the see was transferred to Caracas. The church's interior has taller columns and five nave-arches, instead of six, in a length equal to that of La Asunción, producing a loftier space, covered with a single-pitched open roof: a simple bell-tower was added by 'maestro' Bartolomé de Naveda in 1630. It has undergone many restorations, the first in 1775 and the latest in 1958.

The monastery of S Francisco was founded in Caracas in 1572; an early adobe church was replaced in 1593 with a more permanent structure designed by Antonio Ruiz

3. Francisco Andrés Meneses: façade of Caracas Cathedral, 1711–13

Ullán, which was notable for having a plain rear wall and a nave and aisles separated by two series of piers, without arches, that held cross-pieces on their lintels. (The plan is preserved in the Archivo General de Indias, Seville.) Destroyed in the earthquake of 1641, the church was succeeded initially by a more modest one with one aisle and side chapels, but in 1745 Fray Mateo Veloz returned the church to its original three-aisle form. Remodelling in 1887, however, destroyed its unity: the robust pillars were exchanged for lighter ones, the choir was modified, the wooden tribunes were removed, and the *Mudéjar* panelled ceiling was covered by a smooth wooden ceiling; fortunately the original ceiling was uncovered again in 1942.

The first cathedral in Caracas (begun in 1614) was not extant for long, as it was destroyed in the earthquake of 17 June 1641. In the mid-1660s the first steps were taken towards erecting a new larger, five-nave cathedral (by Juan de Medina), the construction of which was to take ten years, although the complementary works continued until 1713. The same constructional method was used: the nave arcades were carried on octagonal columns, and the walls above the arches were pierced with relieving arches to reduce superimposed load. The rendered brick façade (1711–13) has been attributed to Francisco Andrés Meneses (see fig. 3). In 1766 another violent earthquake caused new damage to the stricken cathedral, though mostly to the tower, which had been built in three parts; the earthquake of 1812 left the upper part damaged, and

it was then permanently removed, leaving just the lower parts. The earthquakes, however, were arguably not the worst affliction suffered by the cathedral, which underwent subsequent remodellings and restorations. In January 1866 work began on reforms that totally altered the floor-plan: the aisles were lengthened to locate the canonical choir behind the main altar, and to this effect the sacristy was demolished, and the precious retable of carved, gilded wood with the tabernacle in silver relief was removed. As part of the remodelling of 1932 the original octagonal stone columns and the open-rafter roof were all concealed. Of particular interest, however, are the chapels on the epistle side: in the chapel of the Most Holy Trinity lie the remains of Simon Bolívar's parents; its ceiling is panelled and coffered, and the whole is beautifully gilded.

The prosperity enjoyed by Venezuela in the 18th century, fuelled by the creation of the Real Compañía Guipuzcoana in Caracas (which in 1728 won the right to monopolize the import of European goods) and the liberal administration of the Bourbons in Spain, was reflected in architecture, and although no monuments of great distinction were built, there was considerable building activity that included many interesting, if comparatively modest, churches. In the valleys around Caracas notable examples included the churches at Petare (Miranda), begun in 1704 but built slowly over more than half a century, and at Turmero (Aragua), under construction in 1781. Both were built to the usual Venezuelan scheme, with three-storey façades divided by pilaster grids characteristic of the simplified rhythmic Venezuelan Baroque. To the west, at El Tocuyo (Lara), founded in 1545, churches had vaulted presbyteries, lateral chapels and domed crossings. Well-known examples included Nuestra Señora de la Concepción (1766), the façade of which replicated that of Caracas Cathedral; S Francisco (after 1776) with domed side chapels; and S Domingo (1766), which had entablature blocks between the columns and arches of the nave arcades, after the contemporary church of La Concepción de la Orotava, Tenerife. Gasparini pointed to the absence of exuberant decoration in 18th-century Venezuelan architecture typical of Latin American Baroque elsewhere. Columns were generally cylindrical and wooden, with a Roman Doric base and Tuscan capital; the solomonic column was little used in Venezuela, and instead the *estípite* was favoured, notably among retable designers. The arch took various forms: the lightly flared semicircular arch is found in Caracas Cathedral and in S Francisco in El Tocuyo; the flat arch, which is neither moulded nor flared, was used in the façades of S Francisco, Guanare, and the parish church of Ospino; and in the last third of the 18th century lobate and mixtilinear arches appeared. In Caracas the churches of Altagracia, Las Mercedes and Santísima Trinidad (now the Panteón Nacional) suffered severely in the earthquake of 1812; they were, however, rebuilt later in the century.

(ii) Military and domestic. The broad coastline of Venezuela, constantly exposed to invasion from the Caribbean, had to be protected by military fortifications at strategic points. The ruins of the most important fortress are on the Araya peninsula opposite Cumaná. Work began there in 1622 under Juan Bautista Antonelli the younger (*c.* 1585–1649)

and was completed around mid-century by the engineer Jerónimo de Soto. The fortress's trapezoid plan is earthquake-resistant, and the whole structure is built from blocks of stone. On the island of Margarita stand the forts of S Carlos Borromeo (1664–84) in Pampatar and of S Rosa in La Asunción. The castle of S Carlos in Maracaibo, protecting access to the lake, was completed in 1682 by Francisco Ricardo and was enlarged and modified in 1784 by the engineer Casimiro Isava. Beside the city of San Tomé de Guayana, but later moved to Angostura, the fort of S Francisco was built in 1678–81 to defend the Orinoco River. Construction of the fort of Puerto Cabello was begun in 1732 principally to protect the interests of the Real Compañía Guipuzcoana; designed by Juan Amador Courten in the shape of a fan open to the sea, it was completed in 1741 by Juan Gayangos.

The origins of the Venezuelan colonial house can be found above all in southern Andalusia, Spain, and perhaps also in the Canary Islands, where climatic conditions are similar. The Andalusian-style patio, suited to the new environment, is found in numerous houses in Venezuela's principal cities and towns. In the early years of colonization, however, indigenous materials and techniques were often used. The most notable colonial houses are to be found in the interior. Generally in Caracas and towns in the interior the houses are of one storey for fear of earthquakes, and the rooms enclose a patio on two or three sides; some houses have more than one internal patio. In the commercial coastal cities such as La Guaira and Puerto Cabello buildings with two storeys are found; those houses on the coast most worthy of mention include the house of the Real Compañía Guipuzcoana (now the customs house) in La Guaira, which has sturdy Tuscan columns on the ground floor of the patio directly supporting elegant timber balconies above; while in Coro there is an admirable group of colonial houses in Calle Azamora.

2. 1821–*c*. 1900. Following Independence (1821) the few civil buildings that the Republican government inherited included the houses of the Real Compañía Guipuzcoana in La Guaira and Puerto Cabello. When the religious orders withdrew, numerous convents also passed into government hands, and these were used for various civil and military purposes, such as universities and barracks. A clearly defined architectural profession still did not exist at this point, and nor did it for the duration of the 19th century. The Colegio de Ingenieros was founded in 1861 in Caracas, and the architects' role was filled by engineering graduates such as Olegario Meneses (*c*. 1810–60), who designed the southern part of the Universidad Central de Venezuela (1840s) in Caracas, the first important architectural project in Republican Venezuela. The design included a patio open to the street formed by two-storey arcades of Tuscan and Ionic half columns on pilasters. When a cholera epidemic hit Caracas in 1855, Meneses designed the Hijos de Dios cemetery in the north of the city, which conformed with his markedly Neo-classical style. Another engineer active during this period in the field of architecture was Alberto Lutowski (1809–71), who was responsible for the extensive arcaded market in Valencia (1845–8), the first of its type and size in Venezuela, and the S Jacinto

market (1853) in Caracas, which comprised three pavilions each of three storeys. He also built two churches: that of Nuestra Señora del Rosario in Antímano and the Nuevo Templo de S José in Puerto Cabello; both were built in stone in 1857.

The coming to power in 1870 of Antonio Guzmán Blanco was a mixed blessing for Venezuelan architecture. On the one hand his presidency gave a vigorous boost to construction, while on the other he sanctioned the destruction of a number of notable historic buildings. Luciano Urdaneta (1825–99), the son of the distinguished figure Rafael Urdaneta, and a graduate engineer from the Ecole Nationale Supérieure d'Arts et Métiers in Paris, planned the Palacio Legislativo (the first part of the Capitolio) in Caracas in 1872. Despite the fact that the south façade does not reflect the building's true dimensions, the central pediment being no more than a decorative feature over the entrance, the sobriety of the Tuscan columns and the rhythm and proportion of the windows make the building an accomplished example of Neo-classical architecture. The Palacio Federal in Caracas, completed in 1877 in collaboration with Roberto García (1841–1936), is much

4. Luciano Urdaneta and Roberto García: entrance façade of the Palacio Federal, the Capitolio, Caracas, completed 1877

more Baroque, as much in the tense line of its front, with its Corinthian columns and caryatids (see fig. 4), as in its oval dome; it was here that the ministries and government officials were to be based, and it was the most important building erected under Guzmán Blanco. Throughout the whole ensemble of the Capitolio extensive use is made of columns, railings and iron grilles imported from England. Also by Urdaneta was the design for the Parque de El Calvario (1873) in Caracas.

The most prolific architect employed by Guzmán Blanco was Juan Hurtado Manrique (1837–96), who applied with fluency formal repertoires from different sources. He designed the collegiate Gothic Revival façade of the Universidad (1876), Caracas, in a curious classical arrangement of Gothic elements that included a balustrade with crocketted finials, as well as Gothic-style buildings for the Museo Nacional (see also §VIII below) and the Santa Capilla (both 1883); the last, built on the site of the church of S Jacinto (demolished by Guzmán Blanco), is modelled on the 13th-century Sainte-Chapelle in Paris (see PARIS, fig. 34). Indeed, the architectonic quality of the Gothic Revival style generally in Venezuela in the 19th century reflected French models and was formal and structurally modest. Hurtado Manrique achieved better results in the basilica of S Teresa (1876; for illustration see CARACAS), the most attractive and monumental of 19th-century Venezuelan churches in terms of both its scale, with its two Neo-classical façades, and its spaciousness, enhanced by multiple cupolas in the side chapels. The Neo-colonial arcades in the patios of the Casa Amarilla de la Cancillería (rebuilt 1891), a two-storey townhouse on the Plaza Bolívar, and the Arco de la Federación, both Caracas, are other derivations from French architecture. Antonio Malaussena (1853–1919), an architect of French origin, designed the column in the Plaza Bolívar commemorating the Battle of Carabobo of 1821; he went on to design the Teatro Municipal (1890), a sumptuous neo-Baroque work for which, despite the reduction in scale, the Opéra in Paris appears to have been the model. Several works from the era of Guzmán Blanco were undertaken under the supervision of the Minister for Public Works, Jesús Múñoz Tebar (1847–1909), who alone was responsible for the Hospital Vargas (1891), an imposing ensemble based on French hospital design, although with an unusual reworking of Gothic forms adapted to the tropical climate.

At the end of the century President Joaquín Crespo built his two residences in Caracas, a villa at Santa Inés and the Palacio de Miraflores. The first, initially Neo-classical but later covered with a form of decoration similar to Art Nouveau that made abundant use of plaster reliefs, wall paintings and different types of glass, was executed under the Spanish Catalan architect Juan Salas, who brought to Caracas a group of craftsmen from Spain, including wood-carvers, carpenters and plasterers. This decorative style was sometimes referred to as the 'crespista style' and was influential on houses in Caracas during that period and into the first years of the 20th century, creating eclectic examples of architecture.

3. AFTER c. 1900. Urban dwellings during the 20th century, particularly in Caracas, retained the simplified forms of the colonial house, though reduced to more modest proportions with, at the front, a door and two windows. The hall and patio were retained, and in the more sumptuous houses these were enclosed by columns; in others fretted wooden screens and stained glass were used. The influence of Dutch architecture, transmitted via the Antilles, can be seen in Maracaibo. Architecture during the régime (1899–1908) of Cipriano Castro was, in its use of a formal vocabulary, a continuation of the 19th century. Its major representative was Alejandro Chataing (1874–1928), who, even in the aftermath of the economic and political crisis of 1902, designed between 1904 and 1912 a large number of public buildings in Caracas; these included the neo-Baroque Teatro Nacional (1904), with coupled columns, a giant Composite order and ornate sculptural groups; the Second Empire-style Palacio de la Gobernación y de Justicia (1905); the Academia Militar (1905), planned around a spacious parade-ground in the Beaux-Arts tradition and raised on a great podium on a hilly site; the Museo Bolivariano (1911); the Archivo General de la Nación (1912); and a number of banks, cinemas and churches in Caracas. In 1904 he also designed Villa Zoila as a residence for the President, and in 1912 he designed the house of the Boulton family; both buildings were in the Paraíso district of Caracas and gave rise there to a new type of dwelling for the capital. Chataing used the widest variety of formal repertories, largely borrowed from French architecture, which included steeply pitched roofs of varied forms covered with flat tiles, with double columns, dressed stone walls and entrance halls sheltered by metal-framed glass roofs; no Venezuelan architect was as prolific, and none used with such freedom all manner of formal themes.

Eclecticism, both successful and unsuccessful stylistically, endured through the 27 years of government by Juan Vicente Gómez (1908–35), both in the construction of private houses in Caracas and in public buildings. Examples of the latter are found throughout Venezuela: the Hotel Jardín (1915) and large hotels designed by Ricardo Razetti (1864–1932) in Maracay; and Palacio de Gobierno at San Cristóbal, together with the annexed houses with their Art Nouveau façades; and in Maracaibo the Egyptian Revival prison (1908) designed by Luis Múñoz Tebar. Simplified industrial forms lent an air of modernism to the salt depositories by Rafael Seijas Cook (1887–1969). The young Spanish Catalan architect Manuel Mujica (1897–1963) who arrived in Caracas in 1927 continued the trend for Neo-colonial architecture in the numerous houses he designed for the first residential suburbs of Caracas. He subsequently changed to a more Modernist style with notable results, including, among others, his own house in Campo Alegre (1936).

The International Style was introduced to Caracas by the French urban planner Maurice Rotival c. 1936. Carlos Raúl Villanueva, who had studied at the Ecole des Beaux-Arts and the Institut d'Urbanisme in Paris and was a member of Rotival's team, had designed the Modernist residence of La Florida (1934) in Caracas, despite returning to a form of neo-classicism for the Museo de Ciencias Naturales and the Museo de Bellas Artes (both begun in 1935), both in Caracas. He returned to Modernism in his design for the Escuela Gran Colombia (1939), Caracas, one of many designs for school buildings backed by the

5. Carlos Gómez de Llarenas: Teatro Teresa Carreño, Caracas, completed 1983

government of Eleazar López Contreras. In 1940 Villanueva redeveloped the residential area of El Silencio in Caracas, marking a new era in Venezuelan architecture with his concept of interconnected residential blocks giving on to a central open area, including an arcaded main plaza. Also from his practice, which was to train the next generation of young architects, were the projects for the Urbanización General Rafael Urdaneta (1943), Maracaibo, the Cerro Piloto (1953) and the imposing residential group 23 de Enero (1955–7), Caracas. In 1944, the practice began the celebrated project for the Ciudad Universitaria, Caracas, freeing itself gradually from its initial classicism to arrive finally at the most accomplished blend of styles in Venezuelan architecture in the Aula Magna (1952; for illustration see VILLANUEVA, CARLOS RAÚL) and the central ensemble of the Universidad Central; the buildings and open spaces between were further embellished by the inclusion of works of art by leading international artists such as Henri Laurens and Fernand Léger.

From the examples set by Manuel Mujica there emerged in parallel a trend that attempted to give value to certain elements of popular Venezuelan architecture, such as tiled roofs, timber structures and whitewashed walls. The principal protagonists of this trend were Tomás José Sanabria (b 1922) and Fruto Vivas (b 1928), whose series of houses in the environs of Caracas began with his own at Altamira (1954). Between 1952 and 1954, however, the Centro Simón Bolívar was built around the Plaza Bolívar in Caracas by Cipriano Domínguez, and two of the International Style administrative buildings around the square have towers of over 30 storeys; the whole ensemble

reflects the influence of Le Corbusier and was to have a considerable effect on future constructions in the capital's centre. New generations of architects went on to erect some notable buildings in Caracas: they included the Banco Central (1959–63) by Tomás José Sanabria; the Edificio Polar (1952–3; with Pacheco Martin Vegas, b 1920) and the Banco Metropolitano (1957) by José Miguel Galia (b 1919), who also built the Seguros Orinoco building (1976); the building of the Corporación Venezolana de Guayana (1967–70) by Jesús Tenreiro (b 1936); the new Ateneo (1974–82) by Gustavo Legorburo (b 1930); and the commercial centres by Antonio Pizani (b 1937).

One of the most significant buildings of the late 20th century was the Teatro Teresa Carreño (completed 1983) by Carlos Gómez de Llarenas (b 1939), in which modern materials such as plastic, aluminium and opaque glass, combined with concrete, were used to notable effect (see fig. 5). Also by Gómez de Llarenas is the Torre Europa, in which dark glass is set against pre-cast cladding. The gigantic residential ensemble of Parque Central (1983), Caracas, by Enrique Sisco (b 1940) and Daniel Fernández Shaw (b 1939) is an expression of the same tendency with its 50-storey glass towers. In the sphere of popular housing numerous suburbs were built in the late 20th century, leading to a spectacular growth in the area and increased population of Venezuelan cities. Although the building of housing was anticipated, the cities' infrastructure was not taken into consideration, and retrospective solutions have been sought. The metro system in Caracas was developed in an attempt to solve the problem of transportation from suburban areas. In the interior of the country numerous housing projects were also undertaken, but these are lamentably uniform in design and fail to take into account the climatic and cultural differences of each region.

BIBLIOGRAPHY

D. Anguló Iñiguez, E. Marco Dorta and J. M. Buschiazzo: *Historia del arte hispano-americano*, 3 vols (Barcelona, 1945–56), i, pp. 532–3, 538–9; iii, pp. 165–222

C. R. Villanueva: *La Caracas de ayer y de hoy, su arquitectura colonial y la reurbanización de El Silencio* (Paris, 1950)

G. Gasparini: *La casa colonial venezolana* (Caracas, 1962)

——: *La arquitectura colonial en Venezuela* (Caracas, 1965)

F. Bullrich: *New Directions in Latin American Architecture* (London, 1969), pp. 20–27, 69–83

G. Gasparini: *Restauración de templos coloniales en Venezuela* (Caracas, 1969)

G. Gasparini and J. P. Posani: *Caracas a través de su arquitectura* (Caracas, 1969)

E. Pardo Stolk: *Las casas de los caraqueños* (Caracas, 1969)

G. Gasparini: *Temples coloniales en Venezuela* (Caracas, 1976)

D. Bayón and P. Gasparini: *The Changing Shape of Latin American Architecture* (New York, 1979)

A. Leszek Zawisza: *Anuario de arquitectura, Venezuela 1981* (Caracas, 1981)

——: *Arquitectura y obras públicas en Venezuela, siglo XIX*, 3 vols (Caracas, 1984)

G. Gasparini and L. Margolies: *Arquitectura popular en Venezuela* (Caracas, 1986)

D. Bayón and M. Marx: *A History of South American Colonial Art and Architecture* (New York, 1989), pp. 32–7, 130–36, 364

J. F. Liernur: *America Latina: Architettura, gli ultimi vent'anni* (Milan, 1990), pp. 180–96

ELIDA SALAZAR

IV. Painting, graphic arts and sculpture.

1. 1514–1821. 2. 1821–*c.* 1900. 3. After *c.* 1900.

1. 1514–1821. The country's geographical location in the north of South America and the fact that its most important towns were almost all built near the coast influenced its artistic development during Spanish rule, as the cities traded principally with the Viceroyalty of Mexico, the islands of Puerto Rico and Cuba, and Spain. The earliest artistic activity took place in the second half of the 16th century, after the establishment of the first towns. Inspired by European examples, local art evolved slowly in parallel with the gradual growth of the cities. From 1637, however, with the transfer of civil and religious authority from Coro to Caracas, there grew an artistic centre that in time became the most important in the country; by the 18th century there were *c.* 130 artists active in Caracas, often working in several genres.

Initially the majority of artists were white, while the remainder were so-called *pardos libres* or mestizos. The white artists of European descent provided instruction based on models from Spain or the Canary Islands, while the second group developed the skills to provide the religious art demanded by the Church and commissioned by some wealthy individuals. In Caracas a close network of artists developed, owing to frequent marriages between members of artistic families, and these close bonds created a continuity of style in their work that survived the progressive succession of Baroque, Rococo and Neoclassical styles.

Unlike other Latin American countries, in Venezuela there were no artists' guilds with fixed sets of rules, so that many artists—either separately or in groups—practised painting, sculpture, gilding, silver-plating and ornamentation. Artists began their apprenticeships between the ages of eight and twelve in the workshop of a master craftsman, who would teach them the trade in five years (although this could be extended up to eight); the master also undertook to feed and clothe the apprentice and to teach him the Catholic faith. During the 17th century the development of the arts was, however, very limited, owing to the poverty of the people and a series of disasters—plagues and epidemics, earthquakes, pirate raids—that destroyed or severely damaged the towns that were in the process of formation; thus, although several artists achieved some renown, their work has disappeared.

Much more remains, however, of the work of 18th-century artists. Francisco José de Lerma (*fl* 1719–53) was a brilliant painter who displayed a knowledge of European works gained via Flemish, Sevillian or Italian prints; his *Our Lady of Mercy* (Caracas, Mus. A. Colon.) was inspired by an engraving by Gian Marco Cavalli. Certain similarities with the work of the Mexican Juan Correa suggest Lerma may have been familiar with the latter's paintings. In his palette Lerma combined sepias with dark grey, yellow and red, and occasionally emerald green, sky blue and white. His contemporaries, who used a limited range of austere colours, included Fernando Alvarez Carneiro (1696–1744), who is known for his two large paintings of the *Life of St Francis of Assisi* (Caracas, S Francisco); and José Lorenzo Zurita (1695–1753), who produced two portraits of *Don Juan Mijares de Solórzano* and one of *Bishop José Félix Valverde* (Caracas, Mus. A. Colon.). The sculptor Enrique Antonio Hernández Prieto (*fl* 1742–5) carved the clothed statue of *St Peter* in Caracas Cathedral, which is impressive for its vigour and realism.

In the second half of the 18th century there was a change from the rather austere tradition that had dominated since the 17th century: the arrival of several artists from the Canary Islands revived the arts at the same time as prosperity increased. The dominant figure of this period was Juan Pedro López (1724–87), the son of Canary Islanders, a painter, sculptor and gilder who produced an extensive body of work. Judging by his style, López's apprenticeship may well have taken place in the workshop of a fellow Canary Islander who had settled in Caracas, and his work had considerable impact on other artists in the city. The wood-carver and sculptor Domingo Gutiérrez (1709–93) used the Rococo style in the altarpieces and frames he made for López's paintings. The compositions used by López also drew their inspiration from European engravings and reflect his ability as a sculptor. His style is related to that of certain Mexican painters, such as Miguel Cabrera, and his use of colour was, like that of Cabrera, marked predominantly by the yellows, ochres, pinks and blues characteristic of the Rococo style. Outstanding in López's vast production were the *Virgin of the Carmelites Protecting the Carmelite Nuns* (*c.* 1774; see fig. 6) and the works painted in 1755 for the altarpiece of the main sacristy of Caracas Cathedral, and his sculptures include the *Statue of Faith*, cast in bronze for the cathedral tower in 1769.

Influenced in part by the works of López, but also informed by realist tendencies, a group of *pardos libres* formed what was effectively a school under the guidance

6. Juan Pedro López: *Virgin of the Carmelites Protecting the Carmelite Nuns*, oil on canvas, 1.47×1.06 m, *c.* 1774 (Caracas, Asociación Venezolana, Amigos del Arte Colonial)

of Antonio José Landaeta, but which in the late 18th century fell increasingly under the influence of the Puerto Rican artist José de Campeche y Rivafrecha and the Mexicans José de Páez and José de Alzibar. The intensity of the colours of their paintings gradually diminished, and they became affected and sugary. Although often similar in appearance, the works of the sculptor of religious images José Francisco Rodríguez (1747–1808), known as 'El Tocuyano', included the excellent carved group representing the *Coronation of the Virgin* (Caracas, S Francisco). Other artists active at the end of the 18th century included the portrait painter José Antonio Peñaloza (*fl* 1776–1803), Francisco Contreras (*fl* 1767–1819) and Francisco Lovera (*fl* 1795). Painting also developed to an extent in the cities of El Tocuyo and Mérida, both situated in the west of the country. These centres, much smaller than Caracas, developed special features that distinguished them, although their overall production was generally uniform, characterized by the use of brilliant colours in paintings executed on wood, using a technique based on a mixture of tempera and oil.

An earthquake in 1812, which destroyed the main cities, and the War of Independence that followed, ending in 1821, effectively halted artistic development. Only two painters succeeded in continuing the tradition they had inherited from the Hispanic past: the former student of Antonio José Landaeta JUAN LOVERA (who became the portrait painter of the national heroes of Independence), and Hilarión Ibarra (*fl* 1798–1854), whose works reveal a

naivety and lack of academic knowledge; the sculptor José de la Merced Rada (*fl* 1797–1855) produced religious images that had a certain charm. These artists contributed to the shift that eventually took place towards greater national pride and the celebration of the heroes and battles of the Independence movement.

CARLOS F. DUARTE

2. 1821–*c.* 1900. At the time of independence (1821) Venezuela was still fundamentally an agricultural nation, and it was not until the 20th century that the more diverse economy was strong enough to sustain a broad range of artistic institutions. The Republic had been constituted in 1811 but 20 years of wars had paralysed all other activity in the country. Juan Lovera, one of the most significant painters of this transitional phase, created an important body of portraits of the principal leaders of independence; the first lithographic press in Caracas was also housed in his workshop.

In 1835 the Academia de Dibujo y Pintura was founded, the only formal establishment of its kind in Caracas at the time (*see also* §IX below). In 1849 a painting class was begun there, and the name was changed to the Academia de Bellas Artes; the first director was Antonio José Carranza (1817–93), an accomplished portrait painter. During the same period foreign scientists and artists began to arrive in Venezuela, just as they did in other newly liberated countries in South America, to explore and depict the tropical landscape. One of the first among these 'traveller–reporter' artists was the German painter Ferdinand Bellermann (1814–89), who lived in the country from 1841 to 1844 and travelled through a substantial part of it, making records in pencil and on canvas (e.g. *View of La Guaira*, 1842–6; Caracas, priv. col.). The Englishman Lewis B. Adams (1809–53) was considered the best painter in Caracas, where he died in 1853; a prolific portrait painter, he had a significant influence on the young artists of the period. Other foreign visitors included the Danish artist Fritz Georg Melbye (1826–96) and the young Camille Pissarro, who travelled with him in 1852–4. These two artists assembled an important body of pictures, significant not only for their artistic value but also as a reflection of the social customs of the time and as a record of the environment (e.g. Pissarro's *View of La Guaira*, watercolour, 1851; priv. col.); Melbye remained a further ten years after Pissarro's departure.

During the second half of the 19th century foreign artists and scientists continued to visit the country, but the degree of political stability under the presidency (1870–90) of Antonio Guzmán Blanco also stimulated artistic activity on the part of native inhabitants. Of particular note was MARTÍN TOVAR Y TOVAR. A pupil of León Cogniet in Paris from 1851 to 1855, he was dedicated principally to portraiture and epic themes. His greatest work was the *Battle of Carabobo*, executed in Paris and first exhibited in Caracas in 1888 and hung in the Salón Elíptico of the Palacio Federal in Caracas; measuring 26×13 m it is believed to have been the largest picture in Latin America at the time. Tovar also executed the *Signing of the Independence Act* (Caracas, Col. Concejo Mun.), for which he won first prize in the Exposición Nacional in 1883; it was he who initiated the academic style in

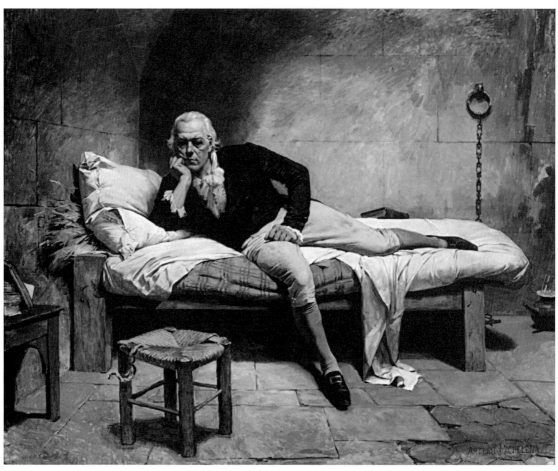

7. Arturo Michelena: *Miranda in La Carraca*, oil on canvas, 1896 (Caracas, Galería de Arte Nacional)

Venezuela, based principally on the epic theme of the history of the country's independence. ARTURO MICHELENA, at the age of only 16, set up a school of painting with his father Juan Antonio Michelena in Valencia, Venezuela, and went on in 1885 to study painting in Paris in the studio of Jean-Paul Laurens at the Académie Julian. He was awarded the gold medal in the second class of the official Salon in Paris in 1887 for his painting *Sick Child* (untraced; copy in Caracas, Gal. A. N.) when he was only 24; this was quite a distinction, considering not only his youth but also the fact that he was a foreign artist. Further success came in the Exposition Universelle in Paris in 1887, when he entered his painting of *Charlotte Corday* (Caracas, Gal. A.N.) and won a gold medal in the first class. His skill was matched by his thematic versatility. He depicted religious and mythological subjects as well as epic and historical ones (e.g. *Miranda in La Carraca*, 1896; Caracas, Gal. A.N.; see fig. 7).

CRISTÓBAL ROJAS was equally skilful. Like the others, he studied in Paris, in the studio of Jean-Paul Laurens, but his brief career prevented a fuller development. His principal works generally treated the realist themes that were fashionable at the end of the century: scenes of poverty, destitution and death (e.g. *Misery*, 1886; Caracas,

Gal. A.N.), but he painted equally magnificent canvases on other themes, including still-lifes, mythological subjects and one historical painting, the *Death of Girardot in Bárbula* (1883; Caracas, Gal. A.N.). In Venezuela, as happened frequently in other Latin American countries, political instability often prevented the harmonious equilibrium that could encourage the arts, and for this reason there are frequent interruptions in the production of some Venezuelan artists. The three figures discussed above, however, demonstrated a degree of artistic accomplishment that had never previously been reached in the country, and their work stimulated a high standard of production in their successors, some of whom went on to achieve international renown.

3. AFTER *c.* 1900 The modern period in Venezuelan painting began with Tito Salas (1888–1974), who studied in Paris from 1905 and who mastered a wide stylistic range, being influenced particularly by Impressionism but also by academic painting. He attended the Académie Julian under Laurens, as well as the Académie des Beaux-Arts under Lucien Simon and the Académie de la Grande Chaumière, where he encountered the work of the Spaniards Joaquín Sorolla y Bastida and Ignacio Zuloaga. At

the age of 19 he won a gold medal at the Paris Salon (1907) with the painting of the '*S Genaro*', which was the first demonstration of a new pictorial style in Venezuelan painting. A recurring subject was the leader of the independence movement, Simón Bolívar, and many of Salas's paintings are housed in the Casa Natal del Libertador, Caracas.

Venezuela's proximity to the great sailing routes of the Caribbean and the Atlantic has historically been of great cultural value to the country, making information from Europe speedily available. Indeed, in the first decade of the 20th century the names of Cézanne, Monet and Renoir were already known in Caracas. In 1912 a group of young artists including MANUEL CABRÉ and ANTONIO EDMONDO MONSANTO set up the Círculo de Bellas Artes in Caracas in open rebellion against the academic tradition represented by the Director of the Academia de Bellas Artes, ANTONIO HERRERA TORO, and with a desire to make landscape painting more popular; it is ironic that Herrera Toro had himself studied in Paris, bringing with him a fairly free and well-developed stylistic language that served in the training of the very group that now opposed him, but their dissatisfaction indicated the degree to which Venezuela was receptive to the most up-to-date European trends. This spirit of intellectual renewal affected not only painting but also collecting, generating a higher level of interest in the work of young artists and marking the beginning of an era of greater artistic activity in the visual arts. This was despite the fact that Caracas scarcely had 120,000 inhabitants, and the political and economic situation in the country at large was still rather unstable.

Under the direct influence of French Impressionism, Venezuelan visual arts, led spiritually by the Círculo de Bellas Artes, acquired a new stylistic sense and new subjects, as much in conceptual as in figurative terms. Social and epic themes were replaced initially by landscape painting, which was given a stylistic and colouristic treatment that differed from the sketches of the 19th-century traveller–reporter artists. A particularly influential early figure was EMILIO BOGGIO, who had lived in Paris and was inspired by the Impressionists. ARMANDO REVERÓN developed a supremely advanced technique for depicting the effects of changing light on figurative subjects through a chromatic process, surpassing any realistic representation. This approach was at its most effective during his 'White Period' of the mid-1920s to mid-1930s, when he used only white paint and kept patches of the canvas bare. Other notable figures active during the same period included FEDERICO BRANDT, who studied in Paris and the Netherlands and specialized in Dutch-inspired interior scenes and *bodegones*. LUIS ALFREDO LÓPEZ MÉNDEZ produced landscapes in the tradition of the Círculo de Bellas Artes, while Manuel Cabré was the most distinguished contemporary landscape painter, depicting the mountains of Caracas in a vigorous style and with strong colourist ability; RAFAEL MONASTERIOS was an acutely sensitive and subtle painter in the same tradition, producing such works as *Caricuao Turret* (1930; Caracas, Gal. A.N.); his contributions to the genre earned him the Premio Nacional de Pintura in 1941. Also of note were MARCOS CASTILLO, an accomplished painter of portraits and still-lifes, and the sculptor and painter FRANCISCO

NARVÁEZ, who distinguished himself in both fields by winning national prizes in each.

In 1936 the Academia de Bellas Artes changed its name to the Escuela de Artes Plásticas y Aplicadas; at this point some of the most accomplished artists of the time entered its staff. Not long after, in 1945, a new (but all too short) phase in the political life of Venezuela began, with a three-year period of democracy, during which pedagogic ideas were revised and brought up to date. This new wealth from Venezuela's exploitation of its oil altered the fundamental bases of social structures, and this in turn had repercussions on the arts, notably in the creation of institutions and increased financial assistance for students (*see also* §§VII and VIII below). A new group of young artists set off to complete their studies in the USA, Paris, Mexico and Chile, and some of these went on to achieve international renown. Among them HÉCTOR POLEO, the first Venezuelan painter to explore Surrealism, and JACOBO BORGES, whose paintings developed from an early Cubism to an Expressionist style used to convey social criticism, are particularly notable. LUIS GUEVARA MORENO moved from abstraction to figuration in his paintings and engravings, as did OSWALDO VIGAS (see fig. 8), whose paintings, sculptures and pottery were inspired by Pre-Columbian art. MERCEDES PARDO, who studied in Paris and Chile, worked through abstraction and *Art informel* towards geometric abstraction in her paintings and prints. The sculptor MARISOL was born in Paris and studied painting there before changing to sculpture, adopting a Pop art style and using it as a means of expressing the position of women in society.

While others did not study abroad, their work often showed the influence of European or North American styles: RAMÓN VÁSQUEZ BRITO worked initially in a Cubist

8. Oswaldo Vigas: *Imposing Symbol*, oil on canvas, 800×800 mm, 1956 (Washington, DC, Museum of Modern Art of Latin America)

style before going on to produce landscapes; RÉGULO PÉREZ was particularly influential and over a 20-year period belonged to some of the most significant Venezuelan artists' groups, including the avant-garde Taller Libre de Arte (1948–52), whose members were interested in the history and culture of Venezuela, Los Disidentes (who promoted geometric abstraction), Pez Dorado and Presencia 70. The printmaker and painter LUISA PALACIOS was an important figure in the promotion of graphic art through her presidency (1975) of the Centro de Enseñanza Gráfica (CEGRA) and her role in founding the Taller de Artes Gráficas (TAGA, 1976). ALIRIO PALACIOS also pursued graphic art, studying engraving in China, where he was inspired to produce largely black-and-white images; and VÍCTOR LUCENA, in addition to his work as a painter and installation artist, produced notable book designs. The more local genre of naive art was explored by such figures as BÁRBARO RIVAS, a self-taught painter whose works are distinguished by their rich treatment of colour and by their multifocal effect.

Three figures deserve special attention for their innovative contributions to art internationally. JESÚS SOTO was a key figure in the development of kinetic art, having exhibited in Paris in 1955 in the exhibition *Le Mouvement*, in which the art form made its first public appearance; in works based on geometric patterns, Soto explored such factors as the distance that separates the spectator from the object and the vibration that takes place on the surface of the picture when the spectator moves. It was as part of this quest to investigate the importance of space as a conceptual material in the work of art that Soto created the *Penetrables* (e.g. 1968; Berne, Ksthalle), in which the spectator was able to move between suspended nylon threads. Similarly, CARLOS CRUZ-DIEZ explored the reactions of colour to vibration, with optical elements that simultaneously fuse, mix and change, creating, with the movement of the spectator, a range of colours that interweave and disappear and a great mobile space that changes, builds, disappears and becomes real at the moment when the spectator is in front of the work (e.g. his series *Physichromy*, begun 1959).

ALEJANDRO OTERO, another graduate of the Escuela de Artes Plásticas, arrived in Paris in 1946 and, after briefly being influenced by Picasso, he reached such an acute purification of the image that it virtually disappeared, leaving only visual references as an original point of departure. In the mid-1950s he further revised the concepts of form and colour, based on a new visual rhythm, in his *Colourhythms*, in which a group of vertical bands interweave and yet simultaneously maintain visual unity (e.g. *Colourhythm 1*, 1955; New York, MOMA). In later years Otero's work was based on large metallic structures in which the movement within the actual work was the principal function of the structure. Around 1986 he built *Sun Tower*, a 50 m-high structure of steel and rust-proof aluminium, in the large Raúl Leoni reservoir in Guri, a mining region of Venezuela. The structure is composed of two large discs spinning in opposite directions, movements governed by the wind; it constitutes one of the most outstanding symbols of artistic production in contemporary Venezuela.

ALFREDO BOULTON

BIBLIOGRAPHY

J. Semprum: *Estudios críticos* (Caracas, 1938)
J. Nucete Sardi: *Notas sobre la pintura y la escultura en Venezuela* (Caracas, 1940, 3/1957)
Tres siglos de pintura venezolana (exh. cat. by E. Planchart, Caracas, Mus. B.A., 1948)
M. Picón-Salas: *La pintura en Venezuela* (Caracas, 1954)
E. Planchart: *La pintura en Venezuela* (Caracas, 1956)
Veinte años del Salon a través de sus premios (exh. cat., Caracas, Mus. B.A., 1959)
J. Calzadilla: *El abstraccionismo en Venezuela* (Caracas, 1961)
——: *Pintores venezolanos* (Caracas, 1963)
A. Boulton: *Historia de la pintura en Venezuela*, 3 vols (Caracas, 1964–72)
J. Calzadilla: *El arte en Venezuela* (Caracas, 1967)
P. Briceño: *La escultura en Venezuela* (Caracas, 1969)
L. A. López Méndez: *El Círculo de Bellas Artes* (Caracas, 1969)
A. Boulton: *Historia de la pintura en Venezuela*, iii (Caracas, 1972)
C. F. Duarte: 'Historia y origen de varias obras atribuídas a Juan Pedro López', *Bol. Hist. Fund. John Boulton* (1972), no. 30
C. F. Duarte and G. Gasparini: *Arte colonial en Venezuela* (Caracas, 1974)
J. Calzadilla and R. Montero Castro: *Visión de la pintura en Venezuela* (Caracas, 1975)
C. F. Duarte: 'Visión de las artes durante el período colonial', *Bol. Hist. Fund. John Boulton* (1975), no. 39
P. Erminy and J. Calzadilla: *El paisaje como tema en la pintura venezolana* (Caracas, 1975)
J. Calzadilla: *El arte en Venezuela* (Caracas, 1976)
Las artes plásticas en Venezuela, Consejo Nacional de la Cultura (Caracas, 1976)
J. Calzadilla: *Movimientos y vanguardia en el arte contemporáneo en Venezuela* (Caracas, 1978)
C. F. Duarte: *Pintura e iconografía popular de Venezuela* (Caracas, 1978)
——: *Historia de la escultura en Venezuela: Época colonial* (Caracas, 1979)
B. Rodríguez: *Breve historia de la escultura contemporánea en Venezuela* (Caracas, 1979)
Gráfica venezolana: Aguatinta, intaglio, serigrafía, litografía (exh. cat., Caracas, Mus. B.A., 1979)
Arte constructivo venezolano, 1945–1965 (exh. cat., Caracas, Gal. A.N., 1979–80)
A. Boulton: *La pintura en Venezuela* (Caracas, 1987)

ALFREDO BOULTON, CARLOS F. DUARTE

V. Gold and silver.

As early as 1519, ten silver chalices are recorded as having been supplied to the Venezuelan missions by the Sevillian silversmith Juan de Oñate (1549–1624), but it was not until 1557 that another Sevillian, Cristobal del Espinar, arrived in Venezuela to establish a workshop, probably in the settlement of Coro. A Portuguese silversmith, Francisco de Acosta, was established in Caracas (founded in 1568) by 1572, but, unlike in Peru and Mexico, the lack of significant natural resources of precious metals meant that most gold and silver objects were imported. At the end of the 17th century and throughout the 18th, however, there was a great increase in the activity of goldsmiths in Caracas. Juan Picón's great monstrance (1678; Caracas Cathedral), set with numerous gemstones, shows his confident use of the Baroque style. A silver sepulchre by Sebastian de Ochoa Montes (1725–8; Caracas, S Francisco) incorporates some Indian influences, reflecting de Ochoa's mestizo origins; most Venezuelan silverwork, however, is thoroughly Spanish in style. More original is the work of Domingo Vicente Nuñez (1703–65); his monumental tabernacles (e.g. Caracas, S Teresa), which made use of the *estípite* type of column, were extremely influential. The work of Pedro Ignacio Ramos (*fl* 1739–81) represents the mature Venezuelan Baroque style in silver. His antependium of *c.* 1755, now in the church of Nuestra Señora de

Altagracia, Caracas, shows his ability to mix Rococo ornament with Baroque forms.

Monstrances encrusted with gemstones, for example that made by an unknown goldsmith for the church of S Lucía, Miranda, in 1761, represent the wealth of mineral resources in Nueva Granada. One made by Francisco de Landaeta (*fl* 1740–1802) for the church of S Francisco, Caracas, is totally Baroque in style, while another, also made by him for Macaray Cathedral at the end of his career, shows confident use of Neo-classical ornament. The work of his contemporary, Pedro Fermín Arias (1753–1814), also shows a gradual transition from Baroque to Neo-classical styles.

With the establishment of a siversmiths' guild in the second half of the 18th century, a system of assaying and hallmarking was used. A small number of pieces from this period are struck with the name of the silversmith, while some are also stamped with CARACAS in a rectangular punch. After independence in 1830 there were few important ecclesiastical commissions, and silversmiths made only such functional domestic objects as salvers, candlesticks, dishes and cups, which are indistinguishable from Spanish examples.

BIBLIOGRAPHY

G. Gasparini and C. F. Duarte: *Los retablos del período colonial en Venezuela* (Caracas, 1971)

C. F. Duarte: *El orfebre Pedro Ignacio Ramos* (Caracas, 1974)

——: *El maestro de oro y plata Francisco de Landaeta* (Caracas, 1977)

——: *El arte de la platería en Venezuela: Período hispánico* (Caracas, 1988)

CHRISTOPHER HARTOP

VI. Textiles.

The manufacture of rugs in Venezuela began at the end of the 16th century. It is known that by *c.* 1605 there were various textile mills operating in the cities of Mérida and Trujillo. Rugs were also made in Barquisimeto and El Tocuyo and, later, in Caracas.

The Spanish constructed cotton mills in the Andean region, as cotton was produced in abundance in Pueblo Llano, San Juan, Lagunillas and El Egido. Blankets and rugs were later made in these mills using wool and hair from the llama. Herds of sheep and llama were very common in the region, especially in the villages along the Valle de las Piedras and in Timotes. The colours white, black and brown were found in their natural state, and additional colours were produced from vegetable dyes. Intense shades of red, blue, yellow and green were used, at times mixed with one another to achieve a larger number of colours.

High-warp, vertical looms were used. In rugs made in Mérida, the warp threads were made up of three thin strands of cotton twisted together. The weft threads were much thicker, made up of between 12 and 20 strands twisted together to make one thread. This technical detail was peculiar to the weavers in this region, as in other rugs the warp and weft threads were usually of the same thickness. The different-coloured knots that constituted the decoration were inserted into the weave and covered the weft as well as the warp. The type of knot used was a Spanish knot, a simple knot around one thread. For this reason the knots appeared in a zigzag form, and in those designs composed of straight lines they were not easily

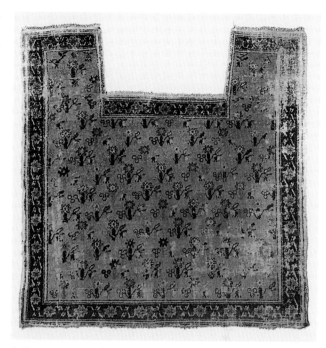

9. Altar rug, cotton and wool, 1.82×1.82 m, from Mérida, 2nd half of the 18th century (Caracas, Asociación Venezolana, Amigos del Arte Colonial Colección: on loan to Caracas, Museo de Arte Colonial de Caracas)

distinguishable. Depending on the distance between the warp threads, there could be between 4 and 20 knots per square centimetre. The nap was cut over the entire surface after the rug had been finished, in the Spanish fashion.

The designs of the four examples that survive from the vast production at Mérida are loose, abstract compositions of infinite variety (see fig. 9). A link is evident with designs from Cuenca and Alcaraz, which were in turn derived from the Turkish 'garden' rug that had a central area surrounded by a bordered strip with a further outer border. The decorative repertory includes such birds as ducks and herons, as well as various stylized flowers, some of which resembled the *fraile jón*, a plant of the Andean plateau. The manufacture of rugs in Mérida, where the most renowned mills were those of the Jesuits, continued until the end of the 19th century. Very little is known of production in Caracas, since all material evidence has disappeared, and the only graphic documents that exist, relating to one item manufactured at the end of the 18th century, give information only on the design and colour; these are derived from the European Neo-classical style and are perhaps inspired by the designs of the Adam brothers in England. From the few written documents that exist, it is known that although there was a preference for the colour green, rugs in a variety of colours were also made. It is thought that rugs continued to be produced in Caracas after the War of Independence.

The manufacture of cloth was an industry that achieved a reasonably high level of development, and it contributed in large part to stimulating the economy in the new cities at the end of the 16th century. A variety of articles was made, for example altarcloths, napkins, towels, sheets, pillow-cases, tablecloths and painting canvases, using the 'linen of the earth' as the fabrics produced were called. From a very early date cotton and linen fabrics were made in Caracas, Chacao, Aragua, El Tocuyo, Mérida and Trujillo. In Caracas, for example, there was 'a mill where linen is woven' that belonged to Francisco de Castillo and was mentioned in his estate inventory of 1621. It is recorded that in 1636 Diego Vásquez Escobedo gave 200 reales to Francisco de Guadalupe to bring him two pieces of 'Aragua linen', indicating that this type of manufacture was in full production and that the name was already known in Caracas. The linen of El Tocuyo also achieved great fame, to the extent that even in the late 20th century certain fabrics produced in some areas of South America are known by the name of that city.

BIBLIOGRAPHY

C. F. Duarte: *Historia de la alfombra en Venezuela* (Caracas, 1979)
——: *Historia del traje durante la época colonial venezolana* (Caracas, 1984)

CARLOS F. DUARTE

VII. Patronage, collecting and dealing.

During the colonial era in Venezuela there was little patronage of the arts other than that offered by the Church. The first collections were created in the mid-17th century and comprised locally produced religious images commissioned by the Church. The artists who produced such works generally remained anonymous and received meagre payment for their work. Some private families supported artists by commissioning paintings for oraria, chapels and church altars. The nobility and upper middle classes also imported images of devotional saints or dedications to the Virgin from New Spain (Mexico) or from Europe, or else commissioned portraits from Spanish painters established in the newly created colonies. The possession of numerous paintings in the houses of land-owners and distinguished figures was a measure of status: the more objects and images there were, the greater one's wealth, standing and religious devotion. This type of collecting therefore fulfilled a function of snobbery, and collectors blindly followed the dictates of fashion without taking account of the aesthetic or historical value of works.

Information on collecting during this period has been gathered largely through the efforts of Alfredo Boulton, who conducted extensive research into the wills of these noblemen and ecclesiastical figures, who can be defined as the first true collectors of art in Venezuela. It is known, for example, that Diego Fernández de Araujo owned a variety of paintings on religious themes, and this type of research has made it possible to assess how limited the knowledge of painting was at the time. Noblemen typically commissioned full-length portraits of themselves and their wives; an inscription at the foot of the work identified the subjects, listing their titles and including a picture of their escutcheon; these works often remained anonymous, however. This situation continued during the 18th century, as art continued to contribute solely to raising the importance of the Church and indicating the status of the powerful.

The tumultuous events surrounding the achievement of independence in 1821, however, and the rapid changes in society that ensued were to have a profound effect on the tradition of collecting in Venezuela. While the Spanish colonial empire was dismantled and destroyed as fast as possible, art nevertheless constituted an important witness to the political process. Patriotic and allegorical portraits of the life and work of the liberators and paintings commemorating the major battles were commissioned for government palaces, and new academic styles emerged. Some private collections were renewed with commissioned works showing naturalistic details, such as landscapes and family portraits, but collecting generally was still not widespread. In the second half of the 19th century, during the government (1870–90) of General Antonio Guzmán Blanco, the State began to promote the arts actively. By granting protection to the painters Martín Tovar y Tovar, Arturo Michelena and Cristóbal Rojas the State helped to raise the status and quality of painting in Venezuela. Among others who benefited was Antonio Herrera Toro, who at the end of the century received financial assistance from the government for his studies in France. Tito Salas (1888–1974) was likewise assisted by the government (1899–1908) of Cipriano Castro in his studies in France and Spain.

In the 20th century landscapes and still-lifes helped establish a realist tradition, which, in its evocations of everyday life, attracted the attention of the potential collector. Arístides Rojas was the first important collector in Venezuela, and the fact that he collected not only antique objects, stylish furniture and works in gold but also works by Venezuelan artists helped raise the status of the latter. Successive dictatorships, however, disrupted the cultural development of the country, and it was only after the death of General Juan Vicente Gómez in 1935 that Venezuela achieved a renaissance of sorts in the field of literature and the arts. The inauguration in Caracas in 1938 of the Museo de Bellas Artes and the building in 1944–5 of the Ciudad Universitaria, also in Caracas and both by Carlos Raúl Villanueva, signified Venezuela's embracing of modernity, underlined by Villanueva's invitation to the most important international artists of the period to create works for the university campus and buildings. In the mid-1940s an important group of pupils from the Escuela de Artes Plásticas y Aplicadas, Caracas, was given grants to study in Chile, Mexico, the USA and France. In 1944 the private sector instituted various painting prizes, and some individuals even contributed towards the cost of European studies for some artists.

The country's intellectual and economic élite began to collect works of international art based on knowledge and historical awareness, rather than in response to fashion. The collection of Cubist works made by Pedro Vallenilla Echeverría was outstanding, containing works by Picasso, Braque, André Lhote, Juan Gris, Robert Delaunay and Auguste Herbin, among others; the dedication of José Luis Plaza's collection to the work of Giorgio Morandi makes it one of the most important in the world; the Boulton collection, begun by Alfredo Boulton's ancestor Arístides Rojas, contains not only fundamental works of painting but also coins and medals, furniture and porcelain; and the collection of José R. Urbaneja, donated to the Museo de Bellas Artes, contains pieces of china and heraldic porcelain from the 18th century that greatly enriched the heritage of the museum. It was through private collectors that the collections of corporations and financial institutions were started, as wealthy businessmen had greater power to purchase works as well as the facilities to exhibit and preserve them. Examples of such collections include those of the Banco Central de Venezuela, Seguros Carabobo, the Fundación Polar, the Banco Mercantil and the Banco Consolidado.

The fluctuating socio-political and economic situation in Venezuela has affected the quality and quantity of art collections throughout the 20th century. Interest has grown, as much on the part of public institutions as privately, in collecting contemporary Latin-American art; this is due largely to the professionalization of the Museo de Bellas Artes as well as to the appearance of new museums, such as the Galería de Arte Nacional (founded in 1975) and the Museo de Arte Contemporáneo de Caracas Sofía Imber (founded 1974), which carry out educational and promotional work. The Federación de Fundaciones Privadas comprises 112 institutions dedicated to helping to cover the costs of studying in various different professional disciplines, including the arts. In the 1990s Venezuelan collectors recognized worldwide included Gustavo and Patricia Cisneros, with their important collection of contemporary Latin-American art, and Miguel Angel Capriles, the owner of the most important collection of modern Latin-American art in the South American continent.

The first galleries aimed at stimulating and encouraging the commercialization of art in Venezuela appeared mid-century. Small-scale art dealers appeared first, functioning as traders entrusted by collectors to update their old-fashioned collections, and this gave rise to the first commercial galleries established by private foundations and connoisseurs of modern art (e.g. Fundación Eugenio Mendoza, Galería Clara Sujo, Galería Adler-Castillo). In the 1980s a significant number of new galleries began to emerge in major Venezuelan cities, responding to a new interest among young people and the professional middle class. Art auctions were first held in Venezuela on the initiative of the Fundación Eugenio Mendoza, which, from the first in 1953, held the only important and respected auctions in the country. Other sporadic auctions are held for charitable or fund-raising purposes, such as that held in 1991 to raise funds for the rebuilding of the Casa Amarilla de la Cancillería.

BIBLIOGRAPHY

A. Rojas: *Obras escogidas de Arístides Rojas* (Paris, 1907)

20 obras de la Colección Pedro Vallenilla Esheverría: Primera exposición de un ciclo dedicado a las colecciones privadas en Venezuela (exh. cat., Caracas, Mus. B.A., 1959)

A. Boulton: *Historia de la pintura en Venezuela*, i (Caracas, 1964)

Donación Miguel Otero Silva: Obras de la colección de pintores venezolanos destinadas al Museo de Bellas Artes de Caracas y al Museo Regional de Barcelona (exh. cat., Caracas, Mus. B.A., 1965)

A. Boulton: *Historia de la pintura en Venezuela*, ii (Caracas, 1968)

G. Gasparini and C. Duarte: *Los retablos del período colonial en Venezuela* (Caracas, 1971)

Los 80: Panorama de las artes visuales en Venezuela (exh. cat., Caracas, Gal. A.N., 1989)

ALFREDO BOULTON, ZULEIVA VIVAS

VIII. Museums.

As in many other Latin American countries, museums in Venezuela did not develop until later in the country's history, partly because of the lack of a substantial middle class with available leisure time and resources to promote the study and cultivation of the fine arts. The oil boom of the 1940s gave rise to an impressive and dramatic growth in the number and comprehensiveness of art museums. The most important examples are in Caracas. The institution with the oldest continuous history is the Museo de Bellas Artes, which forms part of a cultural complex in the heart of the city. It was founded in 1874 as the Museo Nacional, by the culturally minded Antonio Guzmán Blanco (President, 1870–90). The architect Juan Hurtado Manrique (1837–96) designed a Gothic Revival structure for the museum, which was erected and opened in 1875. Like many 19th-century museums, it was a general cultural institution containing not only paintings but also a mineral collection, stuffed birds and handicrafts made by indigenous artists. In 1917 the museum was relocated and its name changed to the Museo de Bellas Artes. It acquired the collection of the Academia de Bellas Artes, which included important works by various colonial and 19th-century Venezuelan artists. Construction of the present building in the Parque los Caobos did not begin until July 1935. Venezuela's most renowned and influential architect of the period, CARLOS RAÚL VILLANUEVA, chose the site and drew up plans for the museum, making the most of the park and its vegetation. Opened in 1938, the new building houses some of the best works by past and present Venezuelan artists as well as works by various foreign artists whose influence had been felt in Venezuela. In 1952 the museum was enlarged in a project again undertaken by Villanueva.

Another major institution in Caracas is the Museo de Arte Contemporáneo, founded in 1974. Its mission was to create and maintain a permanent collection of works by late 20th-century Venezuelan and foreign artists. Built mainly of reinforced concrete, iron and glass, the building was constructed in two stages, with the first storey finished in 1974 and the second in 1982. The museum now consists of five floors, three of which are devoted to exhibition space. The institution's library of *c.* 17,500 volumes is one of the largest fine arts libraries in the country (*see also* §X below). In the selection of works by foreign artists, Sofía Imber de Rangel, former Director of the museum, was particularly influential as she had lived in Europe and had made contact with many of the leading artists of the post-World War II period. The Museo de Arte Colonial, in a late 18th-century house at the Quinta de Anauco, Caracas, is the best example in Venezuela of a museum devoted to the fine and decorative arts of the Spanish colonial period. The institution was founded by Don Juan Javier Mijares de Solorzano. In 1958 the 'Anauco' house was donated to the nation by the Eraso family as a permanent seat of colonial art. The building is typical of a Venezuelan *estancia* and possesses an impressive internal patio. The various corridors are lined with pillars of the Tuscan order supporting a wooden roof; flat plaster ceilings are lined by simple mouldings in accordance with late 18th-century taste.

A number of smaller museums exist that are devoted to the arts and crafts of the colonial period, to the period of the Wars of Independence (1806–21) or to later in the

19th century. Since Venezuela's national hero and liberator, Simón Bolívar, is still treated with great reverence, it is not surprising that two museums are devoted to him: the Museo Cuadra de Bolívar and the Museo Bolivariano, both in Caracas. The former contains murals by Tito Salas portraying incidents during the revolutionary war, while the latter contains historical paintings and portraits of Bolívar and his contemporaries. One museum of note outside Caracas is the Fundación Museo de Arte Moderno 'Jesús Soto' in Ciudad Bolívar, which is also an international research centre for constructivist, geometric and kinetic art. Three individuals were responsible for championing the idea of the museum: Soto himself, who wanted his native town to have a fine arts centre, the architect Villanueva and the governor of the state. Inaugurated in 1973, the museum manifests the influence and taste of Soto, not only in the various works by him in the collection but also in the paintings and graphic works by other contemporary artists, acquired by Soto when he was in Paris. The museum, containing works by over 200 artists, has six large exhibition halls and an enclosed garden patio.

BIBLIOGRAPHY
Catálogo del Museo de Bellas Artes (Caracas, 1958)
M. G. Arroyo and R. Lozano: *El Museo de Bellas Artes de Caracas y algunas de sus obras* (Caracas, 1978)
C. F. Duarte: *Museo de Arte Colonial de Caracas, 'Quinta de Anauco'* (Caracas, 1979)
H. Lassalle: 'Ciudad Bolívar's Museum of Modern Art: The Soto Foundation Museum', *Museum*, xxxvii/3 (1985), pp. 156–62
J. M. Salvador: 'The Caracas Museum of Contemporary Art', *Museum*, xxxvii/1 (1985), pp. 41–5
——: *Obras ejemplares del Museo de Arte Contemporáneo de Caracas* ([Caracas], 1985)

ANTHONY PÁEZ MULLAN

IX. Art education.

During the initial stages of the Spanish colonization of Venezuela, art objects were imported from Spain and later from Mexico and Peru, and it was only in the 17th century that Spanish artists came to the colony to aid in the production of religious images. It was thus in a rather unstructured manner that the teaching of drawing, painting and sculpture to the indigenous people, those of African descent and creoles began; they were also taught European methods of construction by being involved in erecting ecclesiastical buildings. Artists were apprenticed between the ages of eight and twelve in the workshop of a master craftsman and would remain there between five and eight years, learning the master's trade. There was virtually no other artistic education in Venezuela for two centuries, although an informal school was established by Antonio José Landaeta in the late 18th century, and in 1818 an elementary school was run in Caracas by Vicente Méndez; drawing was taught there by the painter Juan Lovera.

It was only with the rise of the Venezuelan republican state in the 1820s that institutionalized, government-backed art education was established. The Sociedad Económica de Amigos del País, created in 1829 by José Antonio Páez to stimulate economic, political, social and cultural development, sanctioned the creation of a drawing school, which, with the name of Academia de Dibujo y Pintura and under the direction of Joaquín Sosa, began functioning in Caracas in 1835. In November 1838, by resolution of the Diputación Provincial de Caracas, the Escuela Normal de Dibujo was established; this opened in 1839 with 39 pupils and was directed by the painter and lithographer Celestino Martínez. In 1849 the Diputación Provincial changed the Academia de Dibujo y Pintura to the Academia de Bellas Artes, and painting and music were added to its teaching; Antonio José Carranza (1817–93) directed the arts department. In 1852 the same Diputación founded the Instituto Provincial de Bellas Artes.

The Academia de Bellas Artes remained in existence for almost a century, led by the most representative artists of the period, who followed the precepts and methodology of European academic institutions. The presidency (1870–90) of Antonio Guzmán Blanco continued to favour the arts and education, and students at the Academia began to benefit from grants enabling them to study in Europe. In its final period the Academia was directed by ANTONIO HERRERA TORO, an austere, conservative man opposed to changes in methods of study. In 1912 a group of rebel students founded an independent workshop in Caracas called the Círculo de Bellas Artes. This action initiated a process of reforms to art education in Venezuela that remains incomplete.

In 1936 the Academia de Bellas Artes was reconstituted as the Escuela de Artes Plásticas y Aplicadas, under the directorship of ANTONIO EDMUNDO MONSANTO, and the period of domination by the Academia was thus ended. In 1949 the school began to call itself the Escuela de Artes Plásticas y Artes Aplicadas Cristóbal Rojas; later it became the Escuela de Artes Plásticas Cristóbal Rojas, and finally the Escuela de Artes Visuales Cristóbal Rojas. In 1958, after the fall of the dictatorship of Marcos Pérez Jiménez, the students and a number of teachers asked the Ministerio de Educación to nominate a commission to reorganize the education system. One of their requests was that professional artistic training should be included in general education; another, that artistic training be divided into basic, intermediate and higher levels. These hopes were finally realized only in 1991, when the Consejo Nacional de la Cultura supported the Ministerio de Educación in renovating the entire system of art education, creating the Instituto Universitario de Estudios Superiores de Artes Plásticas Armando Reverón, whose curriculum is based on an integral conception of culture and art. Within the framework of this inter-institutional agreement a new curriculum was approved for the Escuela de Artes Visuales Cristóbal Rojas; this pilot scheme, if successful, was to be applied subsequently to all the other art schools nationally. With regard to graphic arts, the Centro de Enseñanza Gráfica (CEGRA) and the Taller de Artes Gráficas (TAGA) were both established in 1976 by MANUEL ESPINOZA, LUISA PALACIOS and others.

BIBLIOGRAPHY
J. Nucete Sardi: *Notas sobre la pintura y la escultura en Venezuela* (Caracas, 1940, rev. 1950)
R. de la Plaza: *Ensayos sobre el arte en Venezuela* (Caracas, 1977)
A. Madriz: *La enseñanza de la educación artística en Venezuela* (Caracas, 1985)

MANUEL ESPINOZA

X. Art libraries and photographic collections.

Among the most important art libraries in Venezuela is the library of the Museo de Bellas Artes in Caracas, which contains *c.* 6000 volumes on art from the prehistoric period to the present. The museum's research department also has an important journal and slide library, covering art in general but specializing in Latin American and Venezuelan art; this material has been undergoing classification since 1978. The Biblioteca Pública de Arte Sofía Imber, attached to the Museo de Arte Contemporáneo in Caracas, was founded in 1974 and holds *c.* 7500 monographs as well as 10,000 national and foreign exhibition catalogues, 17,000 transparencies, videos and audio-visual material on art from prehistoric times onwards. Also of significance is the Centro de Información y Documentación Nacional de las Artes Plásticas (CINAP), part of the Galería de Arte Nacional in Caracas, created in 1976. Its documentary material includes books and journals on Venezuelan art, and it also has a slide library with black-and-white photographs, transparencies, videos and a 'verbal archive' (comprising artists' interviews recorded on cassettes and in script form). The Biblioteca Carlos Manuel Muller, part of the Museo de Arte Colonial at the Quinta Anauco, Caracas, specializes in colonial (particularly Venezuelan) Latin American art. The architecture faculty of the Universidad Central de Venezuela in Caracas has an important documentation centre containing books and journals on architecture.

Documentary photographic archives on themes related to art can also be found in a number of institutions in Venezuela. The archive of the education ministry's División de Tecnología Educativa possesses 800,000 negatives on political, social and cultural events in Venezuela and has transparencies, videos and 16-mm films on art; it is used essentially as a teaching aid by schools and universities, but is also open to the general public. The Archivo Audiovisual de Venezuela, which forms part of the Biblioteca Nacional, holds many 19th- and 20th-century photographic collections as well as an oral-history archive and

specializes in national history and art. It holds the Exposición Anual de Fotografía Documental, as well as workshops and seminars, and has an important cartographical and iconographical collection with over 43,000 images. Noteworthy among private collections are the Fundación Boulton in Caracas, with 19th- and 20th-century photographs and documentation, and the collection of Carlos Eduardo Misle, which specializes in 19th-century photographs. Other noteworthy audiovisual institutions include the Museo Audiovisual in Caracas and Artevisión at the Universidad Simón Bolívar, which produces art documentaries for television; various oil companies and banks also have slide libraries and documentary archives and sponsor documentary videos and art books.

SUSANA BENKO

Venice [It. Venezia]. Capital of the Veneto region of Italy. The city is built on an archipelago of about 100 islets in the centre of the extensive Venetian lagoon (see fig. 1). It has been renowned since the Middle Ages for its art and architecture and it owes the survival of much of its historic fabric to its isolated position.

I. History and urban development. II. Art life and organization. III. Centre of production. IV. Buildings. V. Scuole.

I. History and urban development.

1. Before 1180. 2. 1180–1453. 3. 1454–1797. 4. After 1797.

1. BEFORE 1180. Venice was founded in the 7th century AD by inhabitants of cities in the Roman Empire, who were fleeing barbarian invasions on the mainland. The earliest settlement was only one of a confederation of twelve similar settlements in the lagoons that once stretched from the Po Delta around the Gulf of Venice to modern Trieste. The first capital of this confederation was Heraclea and the second Malamocco, the latter within the

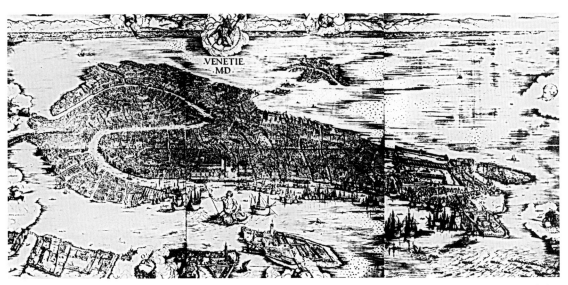

1. *Map of Venice* by Jacopo de' Barbari, woodcut in six blocks, 1.35×2.82 m, *c.* 1500 (Venice, Biblioteca Nazionale Marciana); aerial view showing the Grand Canal with the Rialto Bridge, the Piazza S Marco (lower centre), the Arsenal (far right), the Isola S Giorgio (bottom centre), SS Giovanni e Paolo (right of the Rialto Bridge)

Venetian lagoon. Internecine strife and frequent flooding led to a final transfer of the government of the confederation to Rivo Alto (Rialto) in AD 810, with a chapel to the patron saint, firstly S Todaro. Nineteen years later, the body of the Evangelist St Mark was brought to Rivo Alto from Alexandria; his immediate adoption as the new patron saint confirmed that Rivo Alto was to be the new permanent capital, and his symbol, the winged lion, became that of Venice. Gradually, Venice grew to eclipse all other members of the confederation, although the closest ones (TORCELLO, Murano and Chioggia) benefited from their proximity to the capital.

The archipelago on which the city was to grow measured about 1.5×5 km. Initial settlement was scattered, although gradually two nuclei, Rialto and S Marco, emerged to form the centre of the city. Rialto developed market functions very early as a result of its location in the centre of the archipelago and of the lagunar network of deep channels. S Marco was settled because it guarded the entrance to the Grand Canal and commanded a great natural harbour with direct access to the sea. A new chapel dedicated to S Marco was begun immediately after 839, but there were two subsequent rebuildings before the present church was begun *c.* 1063; it was structurally complete by the end of the century (*see* §IV, 1(i) below). The seat of government first took the form of a fortified castle, destroyed by fire in 976, but immediately rebuilt on a larger scale.

Other islets settled in this early period included S Pietro di Castello, where the cathedral was established; S Zaccaria, where a monastery was founded in the 9th century; SS Apostoli, an important centre containing the fortified house of an early doge; and S Giorgio Maggiore, where a Benedictine monastery was founded in 982. Other island-parishes were founded in all parts of the archipelago in the 9th, 10th and 11th centuries, many of them along the Grand Canal. As the city grew in the 11th century, some parishes became important local centres, with their own markets and the houses (later palaces) of their leading families, the core of the patriciate. By 1200 there were over 70 parishes, each centred on its own *campo* (field or square), with a well for fresh water. Two distinct communications networks developed. The commercial one was formed by the natural watercourse of the Grand Canal, the city's main artery, and by the dozens of subsidiary canals (*rii*) and the navigable channels of the lagoon. The terrestrial network, consisting of the parish squares, their surrounding streets (*calli*) and timber bridges linking the islets allowed land communication on horseback or on foot.

The Venetians had little access to building materials; the first structures were of timber, their roofs thatched with osiers from the lagunar margins. Since these buildings were light, foundations were not a significant consideration. Later, though, as the city grew, more permanent materials were necessary. Bricks were first obtained from the nearby ruins of Roman Altinum and then from brickfields near Mestre. Timber was originally cut from the coastal forests, but these stocks were soon depleted, and it was then obtained from further afield, chiefly from the forests of the Friuli and the colony of Istria. From the latter also came Istrian limestone, an essential complement to the local brick, while a richer effect was achieved by using Verona or Carrara marble, or Greek marble from ancient ruins. With the building of more substantial structures, timber rafts became necessary as foundations.

By the 10th century Venice had established important commercial links with Constantinople (now Istanbul) and in the 10th and 11th centuries was granted trading privileges by Byzantine emperors. The important shipbuilding industry was taken under state control at the Arsenal (founded 1104) and greatly expanded. These factors facilitated the Republic's subsequent powerful commercial and territorial expansion eastwards (*see* VENETIAN EMPIRE). Venice's growth as capital of a great trading empire is inseparable from the growth of S Marco as its spiritual and political centre, and that of Rialto as its commercial heart. At the former, there was initially a square in front of the church and a small inlet, adjacent to the palace of government, for mooring ships. The key period in the development of this civic focus was the reign of Doge Sebastiano Ziani (*reg* 1172–78), who transformed the area: the inlet was reclaimed from the lagoon to form the Piazzetta S Marco, and Ziani erected two monolithic columns to form a symbolic gateway to the city from the sea. The space in front of S Marco was then greatly enlarged by the filling in of a narrow canal and the rebuilding of S Geminiano further west, to form a square the same length as that of today. After 1172 the palace was rebuilt in a more substantial form that survived until the building of the south wing of the present Doge's Palace in the mid-14th century. At about the same time the first timber bridge was built at Rialto, connecting S Marco with the markets, which had been moved to the other bank of the Grand Canal in 1097 to facilitate expansion.

2. 1180–1453. By 1200 Venice had a population of around 100,000 and was one of the largest cities in western Europe; it comprised a constellation of island-parishes from Mendigola in the west to S Pietro in the east. A further boost to development followed the taking of Constantinople (1204) during the Fourth Crusade; as a result, a vast booty of sculptures and artefacts was brought back to Venice, including the four horses of S Marco (*see* §IV, 1(ii) below). Rialto was well established by this time as the hub of Venice's retail and commercial trade. Bulk goods were unloaded at the adjacent quays, some of which had specialist functions indicated by their present names: Riva del Vin (wine); Riva del Ferro (iron and steel); Riva del Carbon (coal). Banks and insurance offices were centred on the little square in front of S Giacomo; gold and jewellery were worked in the adjacent Ruga degli Orefici, while near by were the fruit, fish and vegetable markets. The focal role of the area around S Marco was considerably enhanced in the 13th century; in 1264 the piazza was paved for the first time, and in 1277 the Zecca (Mint) was moved here from Rialto, so that all major offices of state were concentrated here. In 1310 great granaries were built near by to house the city's emergency grain supplies.

The structure of the Venetian constitution was largely established by the end of the 13th century. The doge, elected by a complex procedure designed to avoid nepotism, stood at the head of several councils (including the

Senato, Collegio and Consiglio dei Dieci) whose members were selected for short terms of office from the Maggior Consiglio. The latter was an assembly of several hundred Venetians eligible for election. In the *Serrata* or 'closing' of this council in 1297 its membership was restricted to the nobles, who thus gained the right to lifelong and hereditary participation in governing the state. The growth of the government institutions and the increasing international importance of Venice necessitated substantial rebuilding of the Doge's Palace; the south wing was begun *c.* 1340, but was not complete until *c.* 1400, when the central window was installed (see fig. 23 below). The rebuilding of the Piazzetta wing then followed, and finally the Porta della Carta was built, the climax of this long programme of civic works (for further discussion *see* §IV, 6(i) below).

In the east of the city, the Arsenal developed as another specialized zone (see fig. 2). It was centred on the original basin of the Arsenale Vecchio, but by 1300 even this large basin was inadequate, and a great new extension was begun, the Arsenale Nuovo, completed *c.* 1325. This became Venice's great naval base and shipbuilding quarter, surrounded by high walls and defensive towers. It was highly organized and rigidly specialized and by the mid-15th century it was probably the largest industrial complex in Europe, employing several thousand men on a rationalized production-line system. Completed ships were fitted out in the Arsenale Vecchio before entering the Bacino and then the Adriatic.

The plan (*c.* 1350; Venice, Bib. N. Marciana) by Paolino da Venezia provides the earliest clear representation of the city; about 100 parish and monastic churches are shown, as well as the important satellite islands of Giudecca and Murano and many monastery-islets in the lagoon. Venice was by this time a true metropolis, with every major feature of its urban form clearly established, with the six urban districts (*sestieri*). A hierarchy of settlement within the city had developed, with such important secondary focuses as S Polo and SS Apostoli. Even the lesser islets between the established parishes were now built up, and all were linked by bridges with ramped steps for horses. Beyond Murano there were further satellites, such

2. Venice, the Arsenal, aerial view showing (above centre) the small rectangular basin of the Arsenale Vecchio (founded 1104), with canal access to the lagoon, and to its right the larger basins of the Arsenale Nuovo (completed *c.* 1325) and Arsenale Nuovissimo (early 16th century), which were joined together to form one large body of water *c.* 1914

as Burano and Torcello. The entire lagoon now formed an extension of the city, and many of these further satellites had specialized functions: Torcello was a religious centre and seat of a bishopric; Chioggia produced salt and was the headquarters of the sea-fishing fleet; Murano produced glass (*see* §III, 3 below). The lesser islands produced fruit, vegetables and wine, all of which were sold at Rialto.

Fourteenth-century expansion, which included the acquisition of Treviso in 1339, was abruptly halted by the plague, the Black Death, of *c.* 1348, which killed up to half the city's population. It was followed by war (1378–80) against Venice's great rival, Genoa, culminating in the siege of Chioggia, which brought Venice for the first (and only) time to the brink of violent conquest. The Genoese were repulsed, and there was a long period of recovery, which continued until the mid-15th century. After 1400, the Republic expanded on the Italian mainland, occupying much of the Po plain and the present Veneto, including VICENZA in 1404, PADUA and VERONA in 1405 and Ravenna in 1442. By the 1420s Venice was once again the wealthiest city in western Europe and capital of a trading empire that embraced much of the eastern Mediterranean.

Many public works were undertaken to improve the metropolis. The department of the Piovego, in particular, had responsibility for building and maintaining bridges, quays and canals and for enforcing building codes. Many new wells were built to alleviate water shortages, and a long programme of paving all principal streets and squares was begun. Building techniques became more refined and specialized as experience with larger and higher structures grew. By the late 14th century, larger palaces were often supported on timber piles driven into the underlying clay (e.g. the south wing of the Doge's Palace). Two vital constructional principles needed to be followed by Venetian architects: the load of a building had to be minimized and it had to be spread as evenly as possible on the foundations. Brick remained the basic building material, with widespread use of white Istrian stone for almost all detailing, especially of windows, balconies and doorways. Floors and roofs were of timber, and vaults were rarely constructed owing to the dangers of settlement. For the same reason, campanili often collapsed or had to be rebuilt. The increased population led to higher buildings and acute land shortages in the city centre. Many streets were extremely narrow, but additional space was gained on upper floors by jetties (*barbacani*) and by building over streets (*sottoporteghi*). The frequent fires led to the development of the characteristic Venetian chimney-pot, incorporating a cinder-trap.

Several specialized building types evolved, of which the *palazzo-fondaco* (or *fontego*) of the merchant noble is the most distinctive and widespread. The *fondaco* element was a warehouse with adjacent offices: it was typically centred on a long hall, the *androne*, which usually ran the entire depth of the building and was directly accessible from the canal. On the first floor was the apartment of the noble and his family; the plan reflected that of the ground floor, with a great hall or *portego* above the *androne*. The earliest surviving examples are Byzantine in style and date from the 13th century—they include the two Donà palaces near Rialto, the Ca' da Mosto and the Fondaco dei Turchi (heavily restored in the 19th century). An indigenous

Gothic style gradually developed and became universal by about 1300. Its characteristic features are a symmetrical façade with a central water-gate for unloading goods and a group of large windows on the *piano nobile* admitting light to the great hall. As land became scarce, older two-storey palaces were replaced by new ones on three or four floors, with servants' rooms and kitchens usually located in the attic. Towards the rear of the palace there was a courtyard containing a well, and an external stair giving direct access to the living accommodation above. Many such palaces lined the Grand Canal but they were also built in parish squares throughout the city. Early Gothic examples include the two Soranzo houses at S Polo and Palazzo Gritti. Among 15th-century examples is the Ca' d'Oro (1421–40), the most richly decorated of all. The many foreign communities also had their own *fondachi* combining the function of warehouse with that of lodgings for local representatives and travelling merchants. The Fondaco dei Tedeschi was the largest, but Arabs, Greeks and Turks also had their own warehouses.

The two other chief building types are the Scuole Grandi (*see* §V below) and churches. Vaulting was particularly difficult, and Gothic vaults were commonly reinforced with timber or iron ties. Most of the early medieval churches have been lost owing to successive rebuildings, but elements survive at S Nicolò dei Mendicoli and at S Giacomo, Rialto. The chief surviving Gothic churches are monastic in origin and include the two great Dominican and Franciscan houses of SS Giovanni e Paolo and S Maria Gloriosa dei Frari, founded by Doge Jacopo Tiepolo (*reg* 1229–49; *see* §IV, 3 and 4 below). Both are typically Venetian brick basilicas, with wide bays, tripartite façades and fine stone porticos. S Stefano (14th century, completed *c.* 1430) is similar, while the Madonna dell'Orto (early to mid-15th century) is a fine later Gothic example.

3. 1454–1797. Venice's period of greatest prosperity survived the fall of Constantinople in 1453 to continue into the later 15th century, although there was an outbreak of plague in 1478; in the 16th century, although expansion continued, Venice was beset by crises, notably a fire on the Rialto in 1514 (see below) and further epidemics, particularly severe in 1527 and 1575. There was, however, considerable building activity in all spheres. Much of the work was done by foreigners, of whom the most notable after *c.* 1470 were Pietro Lombardo and Mauro Codussi. Lombardo brought an idiosyncratic Renaissance style to Venice, while Codussi developed a more classical, monumental version. The definitive picture of Venice in this period is Jacopo de' Barbari's extraordinarily detailed woodcut of *c.* 1500 (see fig. 1 above). The city centre was now densely built up; beyond was a slightly less dense secondary zone, while only at the perimeter was there open space, chiefly orchards and monastic gardens.

In the 1480s a great era of new works began at S Marco with the rebuilding of the east wing of the Doge's Palace, after a fire in 1483 had destroyed the ducal apartments. These works were begun by Antonio Rizzo and included his Scala dei Giganti, the ceremonial stair from which new doges were proclaimed (see fig. 24 below). In the Piazza S Marco the Procuratie Vecchie were built in the 1490s to replace the earlier procurators' apartments; at the same

3. Venice, Piazza S Marco, showing the Procuratie Vecchie (1490s) to the left, S Marco (begun *c.* 1063) and the campanile centre and the Procuratie Nuove (late 16th century to mid-17th) to the right

time the Torre dell'Orologio was built, forming a gateway where the Merceria, the chief business street, enters the piazza (for further discussion *see* BUON (ii)).

The early, decorative Lombard style is exemplified by such buildings as the Palazzo Dario (1487), the Scuola Grande di S Giovanni Evangelista (*c.* 1478–81), the façade of the Scuola Grande di S Marco, rebuilt after a fire in 1485 (begun by Lombardo but completed by Codussi in the early 1490s; *see* §V, 3 and fig. 27 below), and S Maria dei Miracoli (*c.* 1489) by Lombardo (for illustration *see* LOMBARDO, (1)). Codussi introduced a more disciplined approach, and his S Michele in Isola (*c.* 1468–77) is the first fully Renaissance structure in the lagoons. His later work, such as S Maria Formosa (begun 1492) and S Giovanni Crisostomo (begun 1497), exhibits an elegant vocabulary and a mastery of interior spaces, while his Palazzo Corner Spinelli (*c.* 1490) and Palazzo Loredan (later Vendramin Calergi; begun *c.* 1502; *see* CODUSSI,

MAURO, fig. 2) show his development towards a monumental, self-assured style in which a traditional plan is faced with a Roman, classical façade.

The Piazzetta was transformed in the early 16th century; the old markets were removed, and Jacopo Sansovino's magnificent Libreria Marciana was built (*see* §IV, 7 below), to balance the Doge's Palace situated opposite. By setting the library back from the campanile, Sansovino considerably widened this end of the piazza, establishing its final shape and dimensions (see fig. 3). Sansovino also designed the adjacent Zecca (Mint), begun *c.* 1537. This building, with its strong modelling and rustications symbolic of its function, marked a further stage in the aggrandizement of the S Marco area. Sansovino's third work at S Marco is the Loggetta (*c.* 1537–42; *see* SANSOVINO, JACOPO, fig. 3) at the base of the campanile, built as a meeting-place for the nobility. In 1574 and 1577 serious fires destroyed most of the interior of the south and east wings of the Doge's

Palace, necessitating an extensive programme of internal rebuilding. The last in this long series of civic works were Vincenzo Scamozzi's procurators' houses, the Procuratie Nuove (*see* SCAMOZZI, (2); completed after 1640 by Baldassare Longhena), which followed the new corner of the piazza established by Sansovino and continued Sansovino's elevation along the south side of the square. Thus by 1600 the piazza had assumed its definitive form; the Prigioni Nuove (new prisons), connected to the Doge's Palace by the Ponte dei Sospiri (1603), were built at about the same time.

Rialto, the city's financial heart, was almost entirely destroyed in a disastrous fire in 1514, and only S Giacomo escaped serious damage. The urgent necessity to rebuild quickly in order to avoid disruption to trade meant that there were no urbanistic innovations, and the old street-pattern was retained. Several buildings were completely rebuilt by Antonio Scarpagnino, including the Fabbriche Vecchie (*c.* 1520) and the Palazzo dei Dieci Savi (1521). A little later, Sansovino's Fabbriche Nuove followed (1552–5), and finally in 1588 a competition was held for a new stone Rialto Bridge. Despite proposals by Palladio and Sansovino, the winner was Antonio da Ponte, whose daring single-span arch of 28 m was completed in 1591 (see fig. 4). In the early 16th century there was further expansion of the Arsenal, with the enclosure of the great Arsenale Nuovissimo (see fig. 2 above), later developed as shipbuilding yards. Many other works from 1539 to 1583 modernized and rationalized ship production.

Sixteenth-century development directly reflected population patterns. In 1500 Venice was still one of Europe's largest cities, with nearly 150,000 inhabitants. There was further expansion until the disastrous plague of 1575, which killed up to 40% of the population. Attempts were made to increase land by reclamation around the perimeter of the city; the Zattere quays were built in 1519, but the major expansion was to the north and west. To the north,

the Fondamente Nuove were built after 1589, extending the city 200 m into the lagoon. In this period, too, northern Cannaregio was further developed with palaces, houses and terraces. To the west, an even larger zone was reclaimed by 1600, between Santa Croce and the Mendigola peninsula. This land, the Terreni Nuovi, was developed with a regular arrangement of parallel canals and rectangular islets. By 1700 more than half of the zone was built up, mostly with long terraces of houses or apartments for rent. Much housing in the 16th and 17th centuries took a similar form and was built by wealthy patricians, by the Scuole Grandi or the procurators of S Marco, all extensive landowners. Such development was to a high density, with apartment blocks up to five or six storeys high.

The Jewish Ghetto, established by decree in 1526, was the first in Europe. By 1600 it was one of the most notable seats of Jewish culture, with 5000 inhabitants. Initially confined to a single islet, isolated at night, it spread over two adjacent islands as numbers grew. Housing densities became the highest in the city, with houses of up to eight storeys. Five synagogues represented Jews of diverse origins. Other foreign communities also retained their identity in the city, notably the Greeks, with their own church, S Giorgio dei Greci (begun 1539). Later, the Armenians made a spiritual and cultural base at S Lazzaro in the lagoon.

The city's satellite communities, including Murano and the Giudecca, were rapidly developed by the nobility after 1500. Suburban villas were built on these islands, often with large gardens for which there was no space in the city centre. This early *villeggiatura* grew in importance as the patriciate increasingly left the city in the summer for these villas. Palazzo Trevisan (*c.* 1556) at Murano is one of the few surviving examples of such houses; similar buildings with extensive gardens lined the northern shore of the Giudecca. After mid-century, though, the nobility turned

4. Venice, Rialto Bridge, by Antonio da Ponte, completed 1591

5. Venice, Ca' Rezzonico, designed by Baldassare Longhena, façade, 1649–62

to the mainland, acquiring great country estates and building much larger villas. The first ones lined the Brenta Canal, between the lagoon and Padua; among them was Palladio's Villa Foscari ('La Malcontenta'), begun *c.* 1558. Dozens were built throughout the 16th and 17th centuries, culminating in such palatial houses as Villa Pisani at Stra (*c.* 1730–60).

Sebastiano Serlio's architectural treatise (*see* SERLIO, SEBASTIANO), first published in Venice 1537–47, had a great impact on his own and succeeding generations, notably on Jacopo Sansovino, whose first major palace, Palazzo Dolfin (begun 1538), reflects this influence. The later Palazzo Corner at S Maurizio (begun 1545) marks the culmination of this stage of the monumental Venetian Renaissance. These palaces are characterized by imposing stone façades with superimposed Classical orders and are paralleled by such works as Michele Sanmicheli's Palazzo Corner at S Polo (*c.* 1550) and his Palazzo Grimani (1556; *see* SANMICHELI, MICHELE, fig. 2), one of the finest in the city. Many other palaces were built in the 16th century, and although several were clad with stone, none was as monumental as these. The façades usually followed more traditional forms; Palazzo Balbi (*c.* 1582–9) is a prominent example, with Baroque influence already visible.

Important churches of the early 16th century include Giorgio Spavento's masterpiece, S Salvatore (begun 1506), still early Renaissance in style and with a noble, imposing interior. A little later, Sansovino's ecclesiastical works included S Martino (1553), much of S Francesco della

Vigna (1534) and S Giuliano (1553), and he also worked on the vast Scuola Grande della Misericordia, which was never completed. His contemporary, Scarpagnino, worked on the Scuola Grande di S Rocco (for illustration *see* SCARPAGNINO, ANTONIO) and rebuilt the Fondaco dei Tedeschi after its destruction by fire in 1505. The two most notable later 16th-century churches are Palladio's S Giorgio Maggiore and Il Redentore (*see* PALLADIO, ANDREA, fig. 7). The former was a reconstruction of a former monastery, and Palladio's work included the cloister and refectory as well as the church, while the latter was built to commemorate the end of the plague of 1575. Both interiors are essays in the manipulation of light and space, while the façades, with their giant orders and superimposed pediments, develop Palladio's façade of 1562 at S Francesco della Vigna.

Venice's mercantile empire declined in relative importance from the mid-17th century, as other colonial powers established trade routes all over the world, and the Republic's political power waned throughout the 18th century. Venice now derived much of its wealth from its mainland empire and from cultural activities: it was an important centre of the Grand Tour, and its Carnival and the great festival of Ascension Day attracted great numbers of visitors. Considerable building activity continued despite the political setbacks. Two great houses, both begun by Baldassare Longhena, dominated the Baroque period: Ca' Rezzonico (see fig. 5) and Ca' Pesaro. Neither of these sumptuous palaces was completed before Longhena's death, but they mark the final stage of Venetian palace-building on such a scale. By this time such houses were more important as places of entertainment than as nuclei of a great trading empire, as the ballroom at Ca' Rezzonico attests. Among the few important later houses, Palazzo Grassi (1748) by Giorgio Massari is a fine Neo-classical example.

Church design in the Baroque period was also dominated by Longhena. His great votive church, S Maria della Salute (see ITALY, fig. 19), was begun after the plague of 1630. Its dome closes the vista down the Grand Canal, while the interior develops Palladio's vocabulary into a centralized space with radiating chapels. Longhena's other works include the church of the Scalzi, S Maria di Nazareth (1649–59) and the Ospedaletto (1667–78). Many other Baroque and Rococo works confirm the vigour with which the styles were adopted: S Maria del Giglio (c. 1678) by Giuseppe Sardi (fl 1630–99); S Maria della Fava (after 1705) by Antonio Gaspari (1658/9–1738); S Moisè (1668) by Alessandro Tremignon, perhaps the most richly ornamented church façade in the city; and finally the more restrained Neo-classicism of Andrea Tirali (c. 1660–1737) at S Nicolò da Tolentino (1706–14). Some new building types emerged in the 17th and 18th centuries, notably the theatre, of which there were seven by 1700, although none survives. The most important, the Teatro La Fenice (destr. 1996; for illustration see SELVA, GIOVANNI ANTONIO), was built in 1792 by Giovanni Antonio Selva, but rebuilt in replica internally after a fire. In the 18th century there was also a proliferation of *ridotti* (gaming-houses) and coffee-houses, two of which, Florian and Quadri, survive in Piazza S Marco.

4. AFTER 1797. The domestic economy stagnated after the fall of the Republic to Napoleon in 1797. The city was first ceded to Austria (until 1806), then to France (until 1814) and finally back to Austria, until the Venetians' popular insurrection under Daniele Manin in 1848. This turbulent era ended with the cession of the former Republic's mainland territories to a unified Italy in 1866, when Venice, too, joined the new state. The Napoleonic dissolution of the monasteries resulted in the demolition of several foundations including Santa Croce and various parish churches, including S Baseggio, S Provolo and S Angelo. In the city, many works were undertaken after 1800. Clearances east of the Arsenal provided the first public gardens, the Giardini Pubblici (c. 1810), and the second, the Papadopoli Gardens, were created in 1836 on the site of Santa Croce. Piazza S Marco achieved its present appearance with Napoleon's destruction of the west end (including S Geminiano) and its replacement by the Ala Napoleonica, intended to complete his Palazzo Reale in the former Procuratie Nuove. The granaries were also demolished to lay out the adjacent Giardinetto Reale. A little later Lorenzo Santi built the Palazzo Patriarcale (c. 1837–50; see SANTI, LORENZO) in the Piazzetta dei Leoni to the north of S Marco, the first Neo-classical building in the vicinity of the basilica.

The construction of a railway connection (1841–6) with the mainland ended centuries of isolation and had a very significant effect on the city's structure. The monastery of S Lucia was demolished to build a new terminus, and several other works improved communications within the city. Two new bridges were built across the Grand Canal, the Accademia Bridge (1854) and the Ferrovia (Railway) Bridge in 1858. Soon afterwards, clearances in the city included the creation of the Strada Nova (c. 1870) to improve communications between S Marco and the station and Calle XXII Marzo, near S Marco. In 1872 the first *vaporetto* (water-bus) service was begun, succeeded in 1905 by a comprehensive lagunar ferry network. Tourism had been much encouraged by the writings of John Ruskin, particularly *The Stones of Venice* (1851–3). He visited Venice 11 times between 1835 and 1888, recording the architecture in drawings and daguerreotypes and became increasingly alarmed by what he saw as incompetent restoration being undertaken in response to the tourist boom. With others, he opposed a proposed restoration of the façade of S Marco, and from 1880 opinion turned against the complete rebuilding of Venetian masterpieces. Promoted by Ruskin, G. E. Street and Viollet-le-Duc, Venetian polychrome Gothic enjoyed a high international reputation.

There were attempts to revive industry, concentrated at Murano (with new glassworks) and the Giudecca, culminating in the vast Gothic Revival Stucky Mill of 1883 by Ernest Wullekopf; but the most notable growth after 1900 was in tourism, particularly on the Lido. The Grand Hotel des Bains (1900) and the Excelsior (1908) formed the catalyst for rapid growth of that island, firstly as a resort, and then as a 'garden suburb'. In 1933 a new road bridge was built parallel to the rail causeway, terminating at Piazzale Roma, with large multi-storey carparks and a bus terminus. To further facilitate communications with the city centre, the Rio Nuovo was cut, directly linking the Grand Canal at Ca' Foscari with Piazzale Roma. After 1945 acute overcrowding led to the building of large new housing estates, notably at S Elena and Sacca Fisola on the Giudecca. The city's population declined dramatically in the second half of the 20th century, and there was increased migration to Mestre, the former mainland satellite, which became larger and more populous than Venice. The rapid growth of the industrial complex on the lagoon shore at Marghera resulted in air and water pollution, and the lowering of the water-table led to increasingly frequent flooding; permanent flood-barriers were planned as a long-term solution to this problem. Mass tourism also put great stress on local infrastructures, with traffic congestion on the causeway and overcrowding in the city centre.

BIBLIOGRAPHY

E. R. Trincanato: *Venezia minore* (Milan, 1948)
J. McAndrew: *Venetian Architecture of the Early Renaissance* (Cambridge, MA, 1960)
S. Muratori: *Studi per una operante storia urbana di Venezia* (Rome, 1960)
P. Maretto: *L'edilizia gotica veneziana* (Rome, 1961)
E. Arslan: *Venezia gotica* (Milan, 1970; Eng. trans., London, 1972)
G. Perocco and A. Salvadori: *Civiltà di Venezia*, 3 vols (Venice, 1973–6)
W. Wolters: *La scultura veneziana gotica, 1300–1460*, 2 vols (Venice, 1976)
D. Howard: *The Architectural History of Venice* (London, 1980)
G. Bellavitis and G. Romanello: *Venezia*, Le città nella storia d'Italia (Rome, 1985)
P. Maretto: *La casa veneziana nella storia della città* (Venice, 1986)
R. J. Goy: *Venetian Vernacular Architecture: Traditional Housing in the Venetian Lagoon* (Cambridge, 1989)

—: *The House of Gold: Building and Palace in Medieval Venice* (Cambridge, 1992)

RICHARD J. GOY

II. Art life and organization.

1. Before 1350. 2. 1350–1453. 3. 1454–1599. 4. 1600–1797. 5. After 1797.

1. BEFORE 1350. Although a small number of 9th- and 10th-century stone-carvings, probably from the original building of S Marco (destr. 976; *see* §IV, 1(ii) below), have been incorporated in the present basilica, the earliest significant Venetian work dates from after 1000. An 11th-century well-head (Venice, Correr) exemplifies the mixture of styles characteristic of Venetian art of this period, combining the linear vegetal or animal motifs of Lombard art with more classical Byzantine forms, including such architectural elements as columns and arches (*see* ROMANESQUE, §III, 1(vi)(d)). The most ambitious sculptural programme during the 12th century was the decoration of S Marco, although this relied heavily on reusing antique and Early Christian works. Venetian sculptors did, however, produce significant works for S Marco, which began to reflect the Romanesque style of Benedetto Antelami from the late 12th century. Nonetheless, much of the basilica's sculpture was executed in a Byzantine style, as can be seen from the 13th-century carvings of *Christ Blessing* and the *Virgin in Prayer* in the central portal. Byzantine influences were intensified after the sack of Constantinople (1204), when the Venetians brought back many important artefacts (*see* §IV, 1(iv) below), including four ancient Greek or Roman horses (Venice, Mus. S Marco), made from gilded bronze, which were formerly installed on the west façade of S Marco (copies *in situ*).

During the Middle Ages the work at S Marco dominated the city's art life, attracting Greek as well as local craftsmen. The magnificent mosaics, mostly created between the late 11th century and the end of the 13th, reflect typically Venetian imagery, such as that of the city's patron St Mark, while adopting a basically Byzantine style (*see* §IV, 1(iii) below). The mosaics are closely related to those in the apse of Torcello Cathedral (for discussion and illustration *see* TORCELLO, §1) and indicate that Venetian art was strongly influenced by developments in Torcello, which did not decline until the later Middle Ages, and other neighbouring communities.

During the 14th century artists continued to maintain the traditional qualities of Venetian art, while assimilating the new Gothic style. In 1342–5 for example, Doge ANDREA DANDOLO, an important patron who was also responsible for new mosaics in the basilica, commissioned a reconstruction in the Gothic style of the Pala d'Oro altarpiece in S Marco (*see* §IV, 1(v) below and fig. 20 below). The remade altarpiece also incorporated a wooden cover (Venice, Mus. S Marco) painted with scenes from the *Life of St Mark* by Paolo Veneziano. The latter belonged to a family of artists, and his work exemplifies the Venetian combination of Byzantine and Gothic elements, as is displayed in his polyptych of the *Coronation of the Virgin* (1340s; Venice, Accad.; *see* PAOLO VENEZIANO, fig. 2). Although he may have had the status of official painter to the Republic of Venice, he also received commissions from many parts of northern Italy and

Dalmatia, anticipating the enormous international popularity that Venetian artists were to gain in the following centuries.

BIBLIOGRAPHY

L. Testi: *La storia della pittura veneziana*, i (Bergamo, 1909)

R. Pallucchini: *La pittura veneziana del trecento* (Venice and Rome, 1965)

F. Brunello: *Arti e mestieri a Venezia nel medioevo e nel rinascimento* (Vicenza, 1981)

B. Bertoli, ed.: *I mosaici di S Marco: Iconografia dell'Antico e del Nuovo Testamento* (Milan, 1986)

T. Pignatti: *Venezia: Mille anni d'arte* (Venice, 1989)

2. 1350–1453. During this period Venice was conservative in its social and economic structures. The chief patrons were the state (e.g. the decoration of S Marco and the Doge's Palace; *see* §IV, 1 and 6 below), religious communities and churches, the confraternities (*scuole*; *see* §V below) and private individuals. Important areas of artistic production in this period were in manuscripts and ceramics (*see* §III, 1 and 2 below), while painting was revived around the mid-14th century under the Republic's official painter PAOLO VENEZIANO, whose work, although strongly founded in a Byzantine idiom, was increasingly influenced by Gothic forms. GENTILE DA FABRIANO, who came to Venice in 1408, initiated the Late Gothic phase in Venetian painting that was continued by such artists as JACOBELLO DEL FIORE, MICHELE GIAMBONO, Antonio Vivarini (*see* VIVARINI, (1)) and Jacopo Bellini (*see* BELLINI, (1)); in the work of the latter, an increasingly Renaissance character is evident.

For the most part artists were not distinguished from craftsmen, but in the latter half of the period there were some, for example Jacopo Bellini and Jacobello del Fiore, who aspired to a higher status. Painters, stone-carvers and wood-carvers were artisans who were obliged to belong to guilds, and who typically carried on business in family partnerships. Painters formed one branch of their guild, the Arte dei Dipintori, which also included leather gilders, painters of curtains and wooden chests, and decorators of playing cards. In documents, painters were often referred to as 'pittori di santi', as their main activity was painting altarpiece panels with figures of the Virgin and saints, both for churches and private houses. Wood-carvers ('intagliatori di legno') belonged to another, separate guild, and there were many disputes over demarcation between the two. Wood-carvers produced altarpieces and frames for painted panels, statues of saints, choir-stalls and many other objects. Their work was usually painted and gilded. All craftsmen working and trading in stone and marble belonged to the Arte dei Tagliapietre. The guild statutes made no distinction between trading in stone and marble, stonemasonry and stone-carving, and a single family partnership might combine all these activities, as did that of Giovanni Buon and his son Bartolomeo Buon, who were in partnership between 1423 and 1443, even though individual members of the workshop might specialize in one activity.

In this period the painters', stone-carvers' and wood-carvers' guilds laid down few regulations on apprenticeship and entry to the guild. The length of apprenticeship for painters varied, but the stone-carvers' guild stipulated a period of at least five years in 1449. There were no mastership tests before the 16th century, and an apprentice who had finished his term and paid a fee was admitted as a master. The ease of entry to the guild reflects the short supply of skilled artisans following the Black Death of *c*. 1348. Paintings were not permitted to be sold in Venice except from the shops of members of the Arte dei Dipintori. The exception to this was the fair at Ascension, which was a free market to which foreigners both brought their wares and came to buy, and at which works of art and antiques changed hands. Neither painters' nor sculptors' workshops were in any particular area of Venice. A stone-carver's workshop was a yard attached to his house; stone-carvers tended to work to order and did not stock finished articles for sale in the same way as a painter. In Venice family partnerships were the usual type of business association both for merchants and artisans, and it is noticeable that the practice of painting and sculpting ran in families: the Bellini, Vivarini and del Fiore (painters), dalle Masegne and Buon (sculptors); the Gruato family produced five generations of sculptors (documented between 1350 and 1478). The guild dues were lower for the sons of existing members, and premises, tools, stocks and drawings were passed on from father to son. Workshops were not large, with probably no more than two or three family members and a few apprentices and other assistants. Slaves might work at their master's craft, and women may also have helped; they are mentioned in some guild statutes, although not in the painters' or sculptors'.

The government of Venice regulated guilds and craftsmen. In order to promote the growth of crafts and industries in the city, it encouraged skilled craftsmen to settle in Venice and took measures to keep Venetian masters in the city. In 1381 a law was passed threatening anyone who persuaded a master craftsman to leave Venice with six years' imprisonment. Care was taken that there were always master mosaicists in the city to repair the mosaics in S Marco and add to them. When the last remaining mosaic master, Jacobello della Chiesa, died in 1424, the Senate sent to Genoa to fetch his former colleague back to Venice. The gold and more brilliantly coloured tesserae were made in the glass furnaces of Murano (*see* §III, 3 below). There was no Venetian school of fresco painting in the 14th century and, conscious of the high prestige of the medium in the rest of Italy, the Venetian government commissioned the Paduan Guariento to paint a large fresco of *Paradise* (now in the Sala dell' Armamento) for the newly built Sala del Maggior Consiglio, the largest council-chamber in the Doge's Palace. He was required to train two Venetian apprentices while he carried out the work from 1365–68. Although many foreign craftsmen (e.g. painters from Florence and stone-carvers from Florence and north Italy) came to work in Venice between 1400 and 1450, there was no significant opposition to them from the guilds.

BIBLIOGRAPHY
P. Paoletti: *L'architettura e la scultura del rinascimento in Venezia*, 3 vols (Venice, 1893)
L. Testi: *La storia della pittura veneziana*, 2 vols (Bergamo, 1909)
M. Muraro: *Pitture murali nel Veneto e tecnica dell'affresco* (Venice, 1960), pp. 25–32
E. Favaro: *L'arte dei pittori in Venezia e i suoi statuti*, Università di Padova, Pubblicazioni della Facoltà di Lettere e Filosofia, lv (Florence, 1975)
W. Wolters: *La scultura veneziana gotica, 1300–1460*, 2 vols (Venice, 1976)
D. Rosand: *Painting in Cinquecento Venice: Titian, Veronese, Tintoretto* (New Haven and London, 1982), pp. 1–46
S. Connell: *The Employment of Sculptors and Stonemasons in Venice in the Fifteenth Century*, Outstanding Diss. F.A. (New York and London, 1988)

SUSAN CONNELL

3. 1454–1599.

(i) Painting. (ii) Sculpture. (iii) Patronage.

(i) Painting. During the later 15th century a distinct school of painting developed in Venice. It was characterized by the exploration of colour and light and by the sensuous rendering of surface texture. As in the preceding period, painters continued to be organized in the Arte dei Pittori, and many of them were also in family workshops. During the second half of the 15th century the leading artists working in this way were the VIVARINI and the BELLINI families, while during the 16th century TITIAN, Jacopo Tintoretto (*see* TINTORETTO, (1)), PAOLO VERONESE and Francesco Bassano the elder (*see* BASSANO) were all working with members of their families. Some painters gained considerable social status: members of the Bellini family held offices in the Scuola Grande di S Marco, and Jacopo Tintoretto was granted membership of the Scuola Grande di S Rocco as part of his remuneration. Gentile and Giovanni Bellini and, later, Titian were appointed official painters of the Republic. Both Gentile and Titian were knighted.

Many artists who were not native Venetians made a significant contribution to the city's art. For example, the decade (1443–53) spent by Donatello in nearby Padua played a pivotal role for Venetian sculptors and painters. In the second half of the 15th century the most influential painters from outside Venice were Andrea Mantegna, who was working in Padua in the 1450s, and the Sicilian Antonello da Messina, who was in Venice in 1475–6. Although Giovanni Bellini had probably experimented with oil paint before Antonello's visit, it was the latter's use of this medium that determined the Venetian's subsequent development. As head of the local school Bellini influenced many painters, including Cima da Conegliano, Francesco Bissolo and Giovanni Mansueti. His art also affected the German Albrecht Dürer, who visited Venice in 1495 and 1505–7. In the early 16th century Palma Vecchio was the leading member of a colony of Lombard artists in Venice that also included Giovanni Cariani and Giovanni Girolamo Savoldo. Around 1540 Giorgio Vasari and other Florentines visited the city, and in the 1560s the young El Greco spent several years in the workshops of Titian and Tintoretto.

Initially, predominantly religious paintings were produced, mainly altarpieces for Venice's churches, votive pictures and devotional images for private use. Formats of altarpieces varied, but the medieval polyptych was gradually replaced by the Renaissance *pala*, usually representing a *Sacra conversazione*, as in Giovanni Bellini's S Giobbe Altarpiece (Venice, Accad.; *see* BELLINI, (3), fig. 3). This format was established in the 1470s, but polyptychs continued to be produced throughout the 16th century. Votive pictures usually represented donors kneeling in front of a saint or the Virgin (e.g. *see* BELLINI, (3), fig. 1). Large numbers of devotional images, mostly half-length representations of the Virgin and Child, were executed in workshops, not necessarily to commission. According to statistics of *c.* 1600 practically every Venetian household owned such pictures. Religious images were produced by all painters throughout the period, and such variations of the *Sacra conversazione* as Titian's Pesaro *Madonna* (1519–26; Venice, S Maria dei Frari) remained popular. Increasingly, altarpieces also depicted narrative events, the most influential example being Titian's *Death of St Peter Martyr* (1526–30; Venice, SS Giovanni e Paolo; destr. 1867). During the late 15th century and the early 16th, however, narrative themes were predominantly represented on canvas in large-scale cycles. The most prominent of these was the series of historical–political paintings for the Sala del Maggior Consiglio in the Doge's Palace, begun by Gentile Bellini in 1474. Other council chambers were given similar decorative schemes, as part of a campaign that continued for almost a century and involved all major Venetian painters. When many of the paintings were destroyed by fires in 1574 and 1577 they were immediately replaced, either by Veronese and Tintoretto and their workshops, or by painters of a younger generation, including Palma Giovane, the leading painter of his day (*see* §IV, 6(ii) and fig. 25 below).

The *scuole* (*see* §V below) modelled themselves on the patrician government in organization and artistic taste. The wealthy *scuole grandi*, in particular, decorated their assembly halls with narrative sequences similar to those of the Doge's Palace, preferring to commission artists previously employed by the state, but focusing on religious–social subjects related to their own social function. Around 1500 Gentile Bellini, Vittore Carpaccio and others were meticulously illustrating contemporary life, as shown by the canvases for the Scuola Grande di S Giovanni Evangelista (1494–1506; Venice, Accad.; see fig. 26 below). Other schemes, for example Carpaccio's cycle of the mid-1490s for the Scuola di S Orsola (Venice, Accad.; *see* CARPACCIO, (1), fig. 4), were painted for the *scuole piccole*. From the 1540s such programmes often also included lavishly carved and gilded compartmentalized ceilings with paintings. All the leading painters produced ceiling paintings for private, public and religious buildings. Paolo Veronese was particularly renowned for his canvases in the Doge's Palace (1553 and later; *see* VERONESE, PAOLO, fig. 1) and in S Sebastiano (*c.* 1555). The largest cycle of narrative paintings, comprising approximately 60 canvases, was executed by Tintoretto (*see* TINTORETTO, (1)) and his workshop for the Scuola Grande di S Rocco (1565–88). In the second half of the 16th century these paintings had their counterparts in frescoes of allegorical and mythological subjects that were painted in villas on the Venetian mainland. Many of them, for example those of *c.* 1561 in the Villa Barbaro at Maser, were produced by Veronese (*see* VERONESE, PAOLO, fig. 3 and ILLUSIONISM, colour pl. IV) and his compatriot Giambattista Zelotti. In Venice itself frescoes were also common and were painted by such artists as PORDENONE, but they deteriorated quickly in the lagoon's damp climate. It is probable that young artists painted frescoes on façades in order to advertise their art, and Giorgione and Titian's work at the Fondaco dei Tedeschi may be an example of this.

In the late 15th century the private portrait gained popularity, in addition to the already established official state portrait. The Bellini are usually credited with its introduction, but Netherlandish portraits, several of which were held in Venetian collections, were also influential. During the 16th century portraits increased in size, and three-quarter or even full-length representations were favoured, in proportion to the sitter's growing sense of self-importance. Titian and LORENZO LOTTO created the psychologically most intense likenesses (e.g. *see* TITIAN, fig. 9), both of single sitters and of groups. The numerous portraits (including self-portraits) of painters in this period demonstrate their changing status from that of craftsmen to artists (see fig. 6). The increasing popularity of the private portrait led to the development of a fashion for representations of imaginary semi-nude female sitters; these in turn led to the theme of the Reclining Venus. Such erotic subjects, reserved for private viewing, had been introduced by Giorgione in the *Sleeping Venus* (?1508–10; Dresden, Gemäldegal. Alte Meister; *see* GIORGIONE, fig. 5) and were elaborated by many painters, most notably Palma Vecchio. Similarly, landscape became increasingly prominent in Venetian painting. Initially used as a backdrop in paintings by Giovanni Bellini, for example in his *Agony in the Garden* (*c.* 1465; London, N.G.; *see* LANDSCAPE PAINTING, fig. 3), and, above all, CIMA DA CONEGLIANO, landscape later played a major role in the pastorals and *poesie* of the 16th century, as can be seen in Titian's *Rape of Europa* (*c.* 1560; Boston, MA, Isabella Stewart Gardner Mus.). Giorgione's *Tempest* (Venice,

6. Palma Giovane: *Self-portrait*, oil on canvas, 1.28×0.96 m, *c.* 1590 (Milan, Accademia di Belle Arti di Brera)

Accad.; *see* GIORGIONE, fig. 3) is an outstanding example of this new genre. From the second quarter of the 16th century mythological narratives, often in a landscape setting, quickly gained popularity. Working in Venice, Titian supplied numerous mythologies to such princely patrons as Alfonso I d'Este and Philip II of Spain.

Preparatory drawings appear to have played a minor role in Venice, and they were not necessarily regarded as part of the process of making a picture. This led Vasari to accuse Venetian artists of 'not being capable of making designs'. On the other hand, as Venice was a leading centre of the early printing industry, prints, woodcuts and engravings were produced in large numbers (*see* §III, 1 below). The prints were mostly reproductions of paintings, frescoes and drawings, which could thereby reach a wide audience. Prints by German artists were particularly popular. Closely connected to the Germans was Jacopo de' Barbari (see fig. 1 above), who at the end of the 15th century improved engraving techniques and was able to pull many impressions from one plate. He inspired younger engravers, including Giulio and Domenico Campagnola.

(ii) Sculpture. Most sculptors in Venice of this period were also active as architects (and vice versa). Although some specialized in figure carving, all were members of the masons' guild, the Arte dei Tagliapietra. In 1460 masons were in such demand that the Venetian government attracted foreign craftsmen by granting them citizens' status. By 1491, however, local craftsmen felt threatened by the predominance of foreign (mostly Lombard) masons and complained about foreign competition, mentioning as many as 126 non-Venetian masters and their 50 apprentices as opposed to only 40 Venetian masters. The leading Lombards were Pietro Lombardo and his sons Antonio Lombardo and Tullio Lombardo. Numerous other sculptors were active in the city, but few works are signed or documented, and many projects were workshop productions. Among the identifiable sculptors of the early 16th century are Giovanni Buora (before 1450–1513), Giovanni Battista and Lorenzo Bregno, Antonio Minello and GIOVANNI MARIA MOSCA PADOVANO, whose work was related to the style of the Lombardo family, and Bartolomeo di Francesco Bergamasco (*d* 1527/8). Throughout the period, sculpture in Venice was made largely by non-Venetians: Jacopo Sansovino and DANESE CATTANEO came from Tuscany, and Nicolò Roccatagliata (*fl* 1593–1636) was from Genoa. Others came from the Venetian mainland: Antonio Rizzo and Girolamo Campagna were from Verona, Andrea Riccio and TIZIANO ASPETTI from Padua, and Alessandro Vittoria was from Trent. Like painters, many sculptors and masons (e.g. the Lombardo and the Bregno families) worked in family businesses. Some workshops were of an impressive size: Pietro Lombardo employed 25 masons (including stonecutters and sculptors) on at least one occasion. Workshops were located all over the city, often near a canal to facilitate the transport of stone. Temporary workshops were set up on site for larger undertakings. At times, projects necessitated the collaboration of sculptors and painters. In 1476 Antonio Rizzo carved a pulpit with reliefs (destr. 1485) for the Scuola Grande di S Marco, after designs by Gentile Bellini. During the late 16th century Alessandro Vittoria

and the painter Palma Giovane, who were close friends, collaborated on several occasions, for example on the altar of the Merciai (the mercers' guild; *c.* 1584; Venice, S Giuliano; *see* VITTORIA, ALESSANDRO, fig. 2).

Venetian sculpture remained essentially Gothic until the death (*c.* 1464–7) of Bartolomeo Buon, when the Renaissance style was introduced by ANTONIO RIZZO in such works as the altars of St Paul and St James (1465–9; Venice, S Marco). Although numerous sculpted altarpieces decorated Venice's churches, the major genre of Venetian sculpture developing during the late 15th century was the ducal tomb. The first monument of the period was produced by members of the Bregno family for *Doge Francesco Foscari* (*c.* 1460; Venice, S Maria Gloriosa dei Frari; for illustration *see* BREGNO, (1)). It is still a predominantly Gothic work, but a new type emerged in the 1470s, combining Roman triumphal arch motifs with traditional elements. During the late 15th century and the early 16th most ducal tombs were produced in the Lombardo workshop, the foremost example being Tullio Lombardo's monument to *Doge Andrea Vendramin* (*c.* 1488–94; Venice, SS Giovanni e Paolo; *see* LOMBARDO, §II(2), fig. 1). Tullio's avid pursuit of the Antique reflects Venetian artistic taste of *c.* 1500, when the interest in Classical art had become widespread. In 1504 Pomponius Gauricus published his treatise *De sculptura*, in which he praised Tullio Lombardo as the leading artist–sculptor of his day. The vogue for *all'antica* sculpture manifested itself in many small bronzes and reliefs but, paradoxically, it found its most rigorous expression in Tullio Lombardo's marble relief altarpiece of the *Coronation of the Virgin* (*c.* 1500–02) in S Giovanni Crisostomo.

Sculptural monuments embellished many of Venice's public spaces. One of the most outstanding examples is the bronze equestrian statue of *Bartolomeo Colleoni* (commissioned 1480; *see* VERROCCHIO, ANDREA DEL, fig. 4) in the Campo SS Giovanni e Paolo. It was designed by the Florentine Andrea del Verrocchio and completed after his death (1488) by the Venetian Alessandro Leopardi. Leopardi also contributed to the sculptural decoration of the Piazza S Marco and its surrounding: the three bronze flag staff bases (1505–6, Venice, Piazza S Marco; for illustration *see* LEOPARDI, ALESSANDRO) and the two giant *Moors* (1497–9) on the clock tower, which are possibly by Leopardi, are part of a complex programme designed to express Venice's glory. Moreover, they attest to the status of bronze as the most prestigious material for sculpture, a view also endorsed by Gauricus. In the wake of Donatello's activity, Padua developed an important bronze industry, led by Bartolomeo Bellano and, later, ANDREA RICCIO, who excelled in making small bronzes, mostly for humanists' collections. At the end of the 15th century such works also gained popularity in Venice. Monumental bronzes were also produced; the tomb and altar with life-size figures (1503–22) by Antonio Lombardo (*see* LOMBARDO, §II(3)) and PAOLO DI MATTEO SAVIN in the Zen Chapel, S Marco, were the largest bronze works in Venice of the early 16th century. The most important Venetian sculpture of Jacopo Sansovino, chief architect and sculptor of the Venetian Republic in the mid-16th century, was also executed in bronze. Under Sansovino the sculptural programme of the S Marco precinct was continued with four

7. Alessandro Vittoria: gilded stucco vault (detail; 1577–9), Scala d'Oro, Doge's Palace, Venice

bronze statues for the Loggetta of the Campanile and bronze reliefs as well as statues for the choir of S Marco. The sculptural decoration required for Sansovino's buildings was produced in his workshop, where the most gifted member was Alessandro Vittoria. Vittoria and, later, Girolamo Campagna were entrusted with prestigous state commissions. Vittoria introduced stucco for the vault decorations of Sansovino's staircase in the Doge's Palace (the Scala d'Oro; see fig. 7) and in the Libreria Marciana as well as the figures in the chapel of the Rosary in SS Giovanni e Paolo. Apart from marble and bronze he also used clay for numerous portrait busts, the counterparts to portraits from the workshops of Tintoretto or Palma Giovane. Campagna designed the bronze statuary for the high altars of two of Palladio's churches: Il Redentore (1589–90) and S Giorgio Maggiore (1592–3; see CAMPA-GNA, GIROLAMO, fig. 2).

(iii) Patronage. Although many Venetian artists worked for European courts, Venetian art itself was not centred around the taste of a court or one dominant family. The ideology of the state, however, influenced the pattern for corporate and private patronage. The central institutions responsible for state patronage were S Marco and the Doge's Palace (see §IV, 1 and 6 below). Many artists sought state patronage, as it increased their reputation and provided them with a pension. While it was customary for the doge (and other government officials) to commission a votive or devotional picture for the Doge's Palace, only a few doges, for example Agostino Barbarigo (see BARBA-RIGO) and ANDREA GRITTI, were major patrons in their own right. The example set by the patrician government at the Doge's Palace was followed by the *scuole* as well as

by several religious orders, including the Hieronymites at S Sebastiano. Occasionally, the state or corporate patrons organized competitions. The commission for the *Colleoni* monument (see §(iii) above) probably resulted from a competition, and in the 16th century the Scuola Grande di S Rocco launched two competitions: in 1516 for the high altar of S Rocco and in 1564 for the pictorial decoration of its assembly halls (see §V, 4 below).

Religious images were commissioned by all types of patrons, but most were made for laymen. From *c.* 1500 private individuals ordered an increasing number of secular paintings for domestic settings. Various private collections existed during the late 15th century and the early 16th. Several of these, including the well-known ones of Andrea Odoni and Gabriele Vendramin, were described by the patrician and connoisseur MARCANTONIO MICHIEL in the first half of the 16th century. Giorgione was among the first to work almost exclusively for this new market, executing paintings of ambiguous or erotic subject-matter. When at the end of the 15th century humanist schools were founded in Venice, patrons also became increasingly interested in works of Classical art. In 1523 Cardinal Domenico Grimani bequeathed his collection of antiquities to the state, and it was displayed in the Doge's Palace. When in 1593 Domenico's nephew Giovanni Grimani left 200 antique marble works to the Republic, the entire collection was moved to the Libreria Marciana, and the Statuario Pubblico was established in 1596 as the first public archaeological museum.

The guidebook of 1581, *Venetia città nobilissima et singolare*, by Francesco Sansovino (see SANSOVINO, (2)) is an invaluable source of information on the art life and organization of 16th-century Venice.

BIBLIOGRAPHY

Pomponius Gauricus: *De sculptura* (1504); ed. and Fr. trans. by A. Chastel and R. Klein (Geneva, 1969)
F. Sansovino: *Dialogo di tutte le cose notabili che sono in Venetia* (Venice, 1561)
——: *Venetia città nobilissima et singolare* (Venice, 1581); ed. G. Stringa (Venice, 1604); ed. G. Martinioni (Venice, 1663)
F. Frizzoni, ed.: *Anonimo Morelliano: Notizie d'opere di disegno* (Bologna, 1884) [notes of Marcantonio Michiel]
P. Paoletti: *L'architettura e la scultura del rinascimento a Venezia* (Venice, 1893)
P. Molmenti: *La storia di Venezia nella vita privata dalle origini alla caduta della Repubblica*, 3 vols (Bergamo, 1927–9)
J. Schulz: *Venetian Painted Ceilings of the Renaissance* (Berkeley and Los Angeles, 1968)
W. Stedman Sheard: *The Tomb of Doge Andrea Vendramin in Venice by Tullio Lombardo* (diss., New Haven, CT, Yale U., 1971)
O. Logan: *Culture and Society in Venice, 1470–1790: The Renaissance and its Heritage* (London, 1972)
M. Perry: 'The Statuario Pubblico of the Venetian Republic', *Saggi & Mem. Stor. A.*, viii (1972), pp. 75–253
G. Perocco and A. Salvadori: *Civiltà di Venezia*, 3 vols (Venice, 1974–6)
M. Maek-Gerard: 'Die "Milanexi" in Venedig', *Wallraf-Richartz-Jb.*, xli (1980), pp. 105–30
T. Pignatti, ed.: *Le scuole di Venezia* (Venice, 1981)
The Genius of Venice, 1500–1600 (exh. cat., ed. J. Martineau and C. Hope; London, RA, 1983)
N. Huse and W. Wolters: *Venedig: Die Kunst der Renaissance* (Munich, 1986; Eng. trans., 1988)
S. Connell: *The Employment of Sculptors and Stonemasons in Venice in the Fifteenth Century*, Outstanding Diss. F. A. (New York and London, 1988)
P. Fortini Brown: *Narrative Painting in the Age of Carpaccio* (New Haven, 1988)

D. Chambers and B. Pullan, eds: *Venice: A Documentary History, 1450–1630* (Oxford, 1992)

M. Hochmann: *Peintres et commandittaires à Venise (1540–1628)* (Rome, 1992)

P. Humfrey: *The Altarpiece in Renaissance Venice* (New Haven, 1993)

4. 1600–1797.

(i) Painting. (ii) Sculpture. (iii) Patronage.

(i) Painting. The great century of Venetian painting came to an end with the death of Jacopo Tintoretto (1594), and in the 17th century painting played a less significant role, especially in comparison with contemporary painting in Rome or Naples. The works of Domenico Tintoretto, Palma Giovane and PADOVANINO were on the whole less distinguished than the achievements of their predecessors. The leading painters in the early 17th century were non-Venetians and included the German JOHANN LISS, Domenico Fetti from Rome and BERNARDO STROZZI from Genoa. Around 1600 such artists as Peter Paul Rubens, HANS ROTTENHAMMER I and Adam Elsheimer visited Venice to study the masterpieces of the previous century and by *c.* 1650 it was one of the most visited cities in Italy. While some of the numerous foreign artists stayed for only short periods, others settled, either working to local commissions or sending their paintings to patrons abroad. During the middle of the 17th century comparatively few local artists were working in the city, although they were particularly active on the Venetian mainland; in Venice itself non-Venetian artists continued to dominate the field. The Neapolitan Luca Giordano, who visited the city several times after 1652, was among the most influential painters. His High Baroque history paintings and altar-pieces (e.g. *Assumption of the Virgin, c.* 1667; *Birth of the Virgin, c.* 1674 and *Presentation of the Virgin, c.* 1674; all S Maria della Salute) had a lasting impact on most painters of the late 17th century in Venice, including Antonio Zanchi from Este, the Genoese Giovanni Battista Langetti and the German Johann Carl Loth (in Venice from *c.* 1655). Among the other non-Venetians were the Florentine Sebastiano Mazzoni and, later, the Frenchman Louis Dorigny. In the last years of the 17th century, however, a local school of painting developed and was centred around a mid-17th-century generation of artists, most notably Andrea Celesti, Gregorio Lazzarini, Antonio Molinari, Luca Carlevaris, Antonio Balestra and Niccolò Bambini (1651–1736). In the 18th century Venetian painting gained world fame for a second time. As in earlier periods, Venetian painters were often working in family businesses. During the 18th century the most important were those of Sebastiano Ricci and his nephew Marco, Giambattista Tiepolo and his sons Giandomenico and Lorenzo (*see* TIEPOLO), Canaletto and his nephew Bernardo Bellotto, Domenico Guardi with his sons Giovanni Antonio and Francesco and the latter's son Giacomo (*see* GUARDI), Pietro Longhi and his son Alessandro (*see* LONGHI (iii)).

Altarpieces and other religious paintings remained central tasks, as the Church continued to play a leading role in Venetian society, although no new picture types developed in this field. As painters worked increasingly for a growing grand-bourgeois society and foreigners, other categories of painting, such as views and genre gained importance. View paintings (*see* VEDUTA) could either be exact topographical renderings or imaginary views (*see* CAPRICCIO). While views of Venice had already served as backdrops to Renaissance paintings, in the late 17th century they emerged as a separate genre, often representing such festive events as public receptions, processions, regattas and concerts. The *vedute* of LUCA CARLEVARIS were the first paintings of the period to consciously emphasize the grandeur of Venice. The recording of public ceremony became an important task for Venetian artists, and 18th-century Venice 'proliferated with forms of self-representation, wrapped in a fantasy existence in which it was still a proud and powerful republic' (Levey, 1959). Carlevaris's paintings were followed by the *vedute* of CANALETTO and Francesco Guardi (*see* GUARDI, (2)), the most outstanding view painters of the period. Pure landscapes, a minor category in Venice, were supplied by Marco Ricci (e.g. for illustration *see* RICCI, (2)), the Florentine Francesco Zuccarelli and Giuseppe Zais.

Pietro Longhi specialized in small-scale genre paintings and conversation pieces and recorded the everyday life of Venetian upper-class society as well as scenes of Venetian street life. On a larger scale genre scenes were represented in pictures by Giovanni Battista Piazzetta (e.g. *Idyll on the Seashore; c.* 1745; Cologne, Wallraf-Richartz-Mus.; *see* PIAZZETTA, GIOVANNI BATTISTA, fig. 2) and Giandomenico Tiepolo (e.g. *Peasants Eating Out of Doors*; 1757; Vicenza, Villa Valmarana; for illustration *see* TIEPOLO, (2)). Although official portraits continued to be made for the doges and other government officials (e.g. *see* PALMA, (3), fig. 2), portrait painting in Venice was not particularly distinguished. The pastel likenesses of ROSALBA CARRIERA, one of the very few women in a world dominated by male painters, were a notable exception. There was a revival of large-scale religious, historical and mythological narrative painting during the late 17th century, as can be seen in works by ANTONIO ZANCHI and GREGORIO LAZZARINI. Fresco painting played an important role in 18th-century Venice. The highly decorative manner of Paolo Veronese was rediscovered by such artists as Sebastiano Ricci (*see* RICCI (i), (1)), who painted the *Legends of St Martial* (before 1702; *in situ*) on the ceiling of S Marziale, and the development was brought to its climax by Giambattista Tiepolo and his son Giandomenico. Working both in fresco and canvas, Giambattista decorated villas on the Venetian mainland and produced such paintings as the *Apotheosis of the Pisani Family* (1761–2), a ceiling fresco in the Villa Pisani, Stra. He also painted church ceilings, for example the *Translation of the Santa Casa di Loreto* (1745; Venice, S Maria di Nazareth, destr. 1915) and decorated palaces in Venice itself. In the latter the Tiepolo often glorified patrons who had recently bought their way into Venetian nobility, as can be seen in the ballroom frescoes of *c.* 1745–50 in the Palazzo Labia and in the *Allegory of the Wedding of Ludovico Rezzonico and Faustina Savorgnan* (1758; Venice, Ca' Rezzonico).

The Venetian state planned to establish an Academy of Painting and Sculpture from 1724 following the foundation of similar institutions elsewhere, but this idea was not realized until 1750 under Giovanni Battista Piazzetta. Piazzetta, who never left Venice after 1711, attracted numerous pupils, and his workshop already functioned as a kind of private academy in the 1740s. The Venetian

Academy was officially acknowledged in 1756, with Giambattista Tiepolo as its president, but it played a marginal role in the artistic life of Venice and did not even organize exhibitions. Few official art exhibitions took place in Venice. Most paintings were still produced to commission, but many painters exhibited informally in Piazza S Marco. A more systematic outdoor art exhibition was held annually in front of the Scuola Grande di S Rocco on the feast day of its patron saint, as illustrated by Canaletto in *Venice: The Feast Day of St Roch* (*c.* 1735; London, N.G.; *see* EXHIBITION, fig. 2). Many Venetian painters did very little work for native patrons, and instead they travelled abroad to work at the European courts. Sebastiano and Marco Ricci, Canaletto and GIOVANNI ANTONIO PELLEGRINI spent several years in London, while the latter's sister-in-law Rosalba Carriera travelled to Paris and Vienna. The Tiepolo worked in Würzburg and Madrid, while Bernardo Bellotto was active in Dresden and Warsaw.

Venice continued to be an important centre of the printing industry. The best-known masterpieces of Venetian art were often reproduced in prints. Contemporary painters also produced pictures and, in particular, drawings that were primarily made to be reproduced in prints. Canaletto, for instance, executed 12 watercolours that were engraved by Giambattista Brustolon and used by Francesco Guardi for 12 of his best-known paintings. The leading Venetian engraver was ANTONIO VISENTINI and he produced a series of engravings after Canaletto's paintings for the English collector and patron Consul Joseph Smith.

(ii) Sculpture. Alessandro Vittoria's death (1608) left the field open to followers who lacked the earlier master's creative energy. With the exception of Girolamo Campagna, who lived until 1625, few sculptors of great note were active in Venice in the early and middle years of the 17th century. In general, sculpture played a subsidiary part, much of it being executed in architects' workshops as architectural decoration. As before, many local sculptors were organized in family workshops, the largest being those of the Comin, BONAZZA, Gai and MARINALI families. Although in the 17th century most masons would have specialized either as sculptors or as architects, the Arte dei Tagliapietra did not officially differentiate between the two until 1724. Before that date masons often produced architectural as well as sculptural work. The outstanding single work of sculpture of the late 17th century is the marble high altar (1670) of S Maria della Salute by the Flemish-born sculptor JOSSE DE CORTE (see fig. 8). Corte settled in Venice *c.* 1655 and was one of many immigrant sculptors active in the lagoon. In addition to numerous Italians there were other northerners, including the Fleming Heinrich Meyring (*fl* 1679–1714) and the German Melchior Barthel. Among the important sculptors of the 18th century were GIOVAN MARIA MORLAITER, Giovanni Marchiori, Antonio Gai, Antonio Corradini and Pietro Baratta (1659–1727). Although they produced much good work, little of it is outstanding. The most notable architectural sculpture was made for the exterior of S Maria della Salute (*see* ITALY, fig. 19). The sculpture of Antonio Canova belongs properly to the Napoleonic era, but he was nevertheless active in Venice before the fall of

8. Josse de Corte: *Queen of Heaven Expelling the Plague* (1670), marble high altar, S Maria della Salute, Venice

the Republic (e.g. *Daedalus and Icarus*, 1778; Venice, Correr). Several other church façades were given profuse sculptural decoration. Some of them were designed as memorials to individuals or families, for example S Moisè (1668), designed by Alessandro Tremignon (*fl* second half 17th century), with statues by Heinrich Meyring. S Maria del Giglio (1678–83), designed by Giuseppe Sardi (*c.* 1621–99), with an effigy of *Antonio Barbaro* by Josse de Corte is another example. Inside the churches monumental tombs, in particular those of the doges, continued to be carved in a tradition established during the late 16th century, as exemplified in S Maria Gloriosa dei Frari by the tomb of *Doge Giovanni Pesaro*, designed (1659–69) by Baldassare Longhena, and sculpted (1665–9) by Melchior Barthel. Some sculptors who specialized in wood carving are of interest: Francesco Pianta the younger (*fl c.* 1650–92) produced a series of wooden panels with allegorical figures for the large hall of the Scuola Grande di S Rocco, while ANDREA BRUSTOLON was renowned for his highly decorative Rococo furniture, which often took the form of gnarled tree trunks.

(iii) Patronage. The years between 1600 and 1797 were not a period of great political or economic upheaval in Venice, but rather a time of steady, if very slow, decline. While during the Renaissance state patronage had encompassed large-scale projects (*see* §3 above), little of the kind was carried out during the later period. The ambitions of wealthy individuals replaced the communal ideals of the

state. Throughout the 17th century and the first half of the 18th, the Venetian Church, and in particular the religious orders, were growing in wealth. Much secular property passed into clerical ownership, and donations were continuous in a city that possessed a large number of major Christian relics. In the prolonged wake of the Counter-Reformation the religious orders, backed by rich benefactors, vied with one another in securing works from Venice's leading artists. Sebastiano Ricci, Giambattista Tiepolo and Piazzetta were in greatest demand and such works as Ricci's *Virgin and Child with Saints*, (1708; Venice, S Giorgio Maggiore) and Piazzetta's *Virgin and Child Appearing to St Philip Neri* (1725–6; Venice, S Maria della Fava) resulted from this patronage. While the Church remained a leading patron of contemporary Venetian art, the role of confraternities, which were no longer of economic importance, was negligible. The Scuola Grande di S Maria dei Carmini was the notable exception, as it employed several leading artists of the period, above all Giambattista Tiepolo and Piazzetta.

As fewer old Venetian families remained wealthy, private art patronage shifted significantly from the established local patriciate to the newly wealthy nobility and rich foreigners. Art works commissioned by the new nobles were glorifications of the individual patrons and the families rather than expressions of homage to the Republic of Venice. As a result of these patrons' conservative taste, the more progressive Venetian painters found little employment; preference was given to those working in a 17th-century idiom, for example Antonio Zanchi, Gregorio Lazzarini, Antonio Balestra and Niccolò Bambini. The notable exception in the mid-18th century was Giambattista Tiepolo, who continued to express the glorification of the nobility—both new and old. All types of Venetian patrons, including the state, the nobility and the Church, tended to be conservative. Many Venetian collectors appear to have ignored contemporary artists and to have turned instead to the 16th-century masters. Beside the need for magnificent ceiling decoration there was no great local market for contemporary art, and the fame of 18th-century Venetian art is largely because many Venetian artists catered for the city's tourists. Innumerable topographical views were produced as 'large-scale picture postcards' for foreign visitors. The most prominent foreign collectors in the city were JOSEPH SMITH, who had a considerable collection of Venetian paintings, drawings and engravings, and the German JOHANN MATTHIAS SCHULENBURG, who was marshal of the Venetian armies between 1715 and 1747. Smith, Schulenburg and the Venetian patron and collector FRANCESCO ALGAROTTI were crucial to the creation of fashions in contemporary art.

As the fame of Venetian art increased, publications on the subject multiplied. Francesco Sansovino's Guidebook *Venetia città nobilissima et singolare* (1581) was updated for a first time in 1604 by Giovanni Stringa and for a second time in 1663 by Giustiniano Martinioni. In the 1660s and 1670s MARCO BOSCHINI published various guidebooks on Venetian painting, the most important of which, *Le ricche minere della pittura veneziana* (1674), was revised and republished by Anton Maria Zanetti the younger in 1733. In 1771 Zanetti published his own *Della pittura veneziana*

e delle opere pubbliche de' veneziani maestri (*see* ZANETTI, (2)). A similar account of Venetian sculptors and architects was written in 1778 by the architect and art historian Tommaso Temanza.

BIBLIOGRAPHY

M. Boschini: *Le ricche miniere della pittura veneziana* (Venice, 1674)
A. M. Zanetti: *Della pittura veneziana* (Venice, 1771)
T. Temanza: *Vite dei più celebri architetti, scultori, e pittori veneziani* (Venice, 1778)
P. Molmenti: *La storia di Venezia nella vita privata dalle origini alla caduta della Repubblica*, 3 vols (Bergamo, 1927–9)
C. Donzelli: *I pittori veneti del settecento* (Florence, 1957)
M. Levey: *Painting in XVIII Century Venice* (London, 1959)
R. Pallucchini: *La pittura veneziana del settecento* (Venice and Rome, 1960)
V. Branca, ed.: *Barocco europeo e barocco veneziano*, Civiltà europea e civiltà veneziana (Florence, 1962)
F. Haskell: *Painters and Patrons: A Study of the Relation between Italian Art and Society in the Age of the Baroque* (London, 1963, rev. New Haven, 4/1980)
C. Semenzato: *La scultura veneta del seicento e del settecento* (Venice, 1966) [comprehensive cat.]
C. Donzelli and G. M. Pilo: *I pittori del seicento veneto* (Florence, 1967)
Il Console Smith mercante e collezionista (Vicenza, 1971)
Venise au XVIII siècle (exh. cat. by F. Vivian, Paris, Mus. Orangerie, 1971)
G. Perocco and A. Salvadori: *Civiltà di Venezia*, 3 vols (Venice, 1974–6)
V. Branca, ed.: *Dall'età barocca all'Italia contemporanea*, Storia della civiltà veneziana, iii (Florence, 1979)
Venetian Seventeenth Century Painting (exh. cat. by H. Potterton, London, N.G., 1979)
R. Palluahini: *La pittura veneziana nel seicento* (Milan, 1981)
G. Arnaldi and M. Pastore Stocchi, eds: *Il settecento*, Storia della Cultura Veneta, v/1–2 (Vicenza, 1985)
The Glory of Venice: Art in the 18th Century (exh. cat., ed. J. Martineau and A. Robinson; London, RA, 1994)

JOACHIM STRUPP

5. AFTER 1797. The loss of Venetian independence and pride as a result of the French and Austrian occupations initially had a damaging effect on artistic activity in the city. The predominance of Neo-classicism among sculptors and architects is best represented by the monument to *Antonio Canova* (1827) in S Maria Gloriosa dei Frari. In the same church the later monument to *Titian* (1838–52) by Luigi Zandomeneghi (1778–1850) and Pietro Zandomeneghi (1806–66) shows the gradual decline in Neo-classical ideals. Venice was isolated from artistic developments abroad and this, combined with a severe economic recession in the 1820s and 1830s, inhibited a revival of the arts. An important consequence of Napoleon's policies was, however, the foundation of the Gallerie dell'Accademia in 1807. Based on the parts of the collections of FILIPPO FARSETTI that had been sold to the Academy in 1805, the gallery was opened to the public in 1817, largely thanks to the efforts of LEOPOLDO CICOGNARA, President of the Academy from 1808 to 1826. In 1830 Teodoro Correr (*see* CORRER, (2)) bequeathed to the city his collections of prints, paintings and antiques (now partly in the Museo Correr, interior redesigned 1960 by Carlo Scarpa).

During the early 19th century Venice was discovered by foreign artists, in particular the British. Lord Byron (1788–1824) had popularized the romantic decay of Venice in such works as the *Two Foscari*, *Ode on Venice* and *Childe Harold's Pilgrimage*; Turner, who first visited in 1819, developed the theme of a decaying civilization in such paintings as the *Sun of Venice Going to Sea* (1843; London, Tate). Richard Parkes Bonington visited Venice in 1826 and emphasized the eastern influences of the architecture and costumes. Other English visitors were Samuel Prout, Clarkson Stanfield and William Etty. The Venetian work of English artists was commercially successful and large runs of prints were issued to satisfy the growing demand from a new breed of tourists. At this time there was also a revival in the Venetian crafts of glassblowing and lace-making, which was sponsored by the government (*see* §III, 3(iv) and 4(ii) below).

Daniele Manin's revolt against the Austrians and the siege of Venice (1848–9) inspired a new sense of patriotism and artistic activity. The artist Ippolito Caffi took an active part in the revolt and painted such scenes of war as the *Nocturnal Bombardment of Marghera, 25th May 1849* (Venice, Mus. Risorgimento); for his activities he was persecuted by the Austrian police. The reunification of Venice to Italy in 1866 marked the beginning of an artistic Renaissance led by such artists as Giacomo Favretto, Guglielmo Ciardi (1843–1917), Ettore Tito (1859–1941), Pietro Fragiacomo (*b* 1856) and Luigi Nono (1850–1918). Ciardi had links with the Macchiaioli in Florence and brought a new sense of realism and light to Venetian art. Favretto painted Venetian genre scenes, which focus on social realities rather than panoramic backdrops. His *Vandalismo (Poveri antichi!)* (Milan, Brera; see fig. 9) is a comment on the restoration or destruction of a Tiepolo

ceiling. Nono painted the city's poor. History painting continued to thrive, in particular scenes from the death of Titian or the execution of Doge Falier (*reg* 1354–5), while Shakespearean themes were also popular; the 18th-century *il tempo felice* was nostalgically depicted as a golden era.

During the late 19th century there was an influx of foreign artists who stayed for long periods and became part of the artistic scene. James McNeill Whistler stayed during 1880, while John Singer Sargent and Walter Sickert returned frequently, mixing with Venetian society. The Palazzo Barbaro, owned by the Curtis family, American relations of Sargent, became a focal point for much artistic and literary activity. The international aspect of Venetian artistic life was reinforced by the establishment of the Biennale in 1895 under the guidance of Professor Antonio Fradeletto. The success of the original exhibition led to the building of a series of pavilions in the Giardini Pubblici, each devoted to one nation. Fradeletto's taste was conservative, but in 1910 Gustav Klimt was given a one-man show inaugurating a more progressive approach. In 1946 the avant-garde tendencies in Italian painting were brought together in the FRONTE NUOVO DELLE ARTI, which included such leading Venetian painters among its founding members as Giuseppe Santomoso and Emilio Vedova; they went on to form the GRUPPO DEGLI OTTO PITTORI ITALIANI in 1952 with other artists of a more abstracting inclination. The continuation of the Biennale, despite breaks during the war years, and the establishment of the Peggy Guggenheim Museum (1949) have ensured a place for Venice in the international art scene, even if the city has not established its own particular school or style.

BIBLIOGRAPHY
C. P. Brand: *Italy and the English Romantics* (Cambridge, 1957)
G. Perocco: *La pittura veneta dell'ottocento* (Milan, 1967)
Venezia nell'ottocento: Immagini e mito (exh. cat. by G. Pavenello and G. Romanini, Venice, Correr, 1983)
Venice: The American View, 1860–1920 (exh. cat. by M. Lovell, San Francisco, CA, F.A. Museums, 1984)
Visions of Venice (exh. cat. by M. Spender, London, Bankside Gal., 1990)
J. Halsby: *Venice: The Artist's Vision* (London, 1990)

JULIAN HALSBY

III. Centre of production.

1. Manuscripts, books and prints. 2. Ceramics. 3. Glass. 4. Textiles.

1. MANUSCRIPTS, BOOKS AND PRINTS. Illuminated manuscripts from Venice reflect its unique political structure as well as the nature of its institutions. The earliest examples date from the 13th century when Venice became a major European power after the conquest of Constantinople in 1204. Byzantine and western Romanesque traditions are combined in a distinctly Venetian idiom in the historiated initials of an early 13th-century giant Bible (Venice, Bib. N. Marciana, MS. lat. I, 1–4 [2108–2111]), those in an Antiphonary for S Marco (priv. col.) and in the Epistolary (Padua, Bib. Capitolare) written in 1259 by Giovanni da Gaibano for Padua Cathedral, to which can be linked a few other manuscripts in a similar style. Larger numbers of illuminated manuscripts survive from the second quarter of the 14th century, including three splendid liturgical books made for S Marco (Venice, Bib. N. Marciana, MSS lat. I, 100 [2089], I, 101 [2660] and III, 111 [211]), which may have been commissioned by Doge

9. Giacomo Favretto: *Vandalismo (Poveri antichi!)*, oil on canvas, 1000×660 mm, 1880 (Milan, Accademia di Belle Arti di Brera)

Andrea Dandolo to fit into older jewelled book covers brought from Constantinople. The initials in these books show the evolution of a specifically Venetian combination of Byzantine, Bolognese and other Gothic elements.

Venetian guilds and confraternities were closely scrutinized by the Republic, a situation reflected in the production of official manuscripts. The *mariegole*, containing guild regulations, open with images of patron saints or scenes relating to the organization. Although the earliest are Byzantine in style, by the mid-14th century the miniatures show the influence of Bolognese and French illumination. The first initial of the *Mariegola dei pelizeri de ovra vera* (1334; Venice, Correr, MS. IV, 18) shows *Christ Blessing* in a Byzantine style with a more naturalistically rendered worker holding up cloaks of vair below. The *ducali*, which record the vows (*promissioni*) of each newly elected doge and list the duties (*commissioni*) of Venetian governors of subject cities, open with images of the doge, St Mark, Venice personified or a patron saint. Other secular manuscripts from the Veneto include illustrated romances, chronicles of Venetian history and scientific treatises, for example the Carrara Herbal (*c.* 1400; London, BL, Egerton MS. 2020), made in Padua with many plants observed directly from nature.

In the late 14th century the reformed monastic orders, especially the Benedictines of S Giustina, Padua, and the Camaldolites of S Michele, Murano, commissioned new choir-books, which continued to be produced in the Veneto until the 16th century; they show styles ranging from extravagant Late Gothic to fully Renaissance compositions with classicizing decorative and figural components.

Manuscript illumination in Venice from 1400 to 1440 was dominated by CRISTOFORO CORTESE, who painted many religious, literary and Classical texts, including works by such authors as Cicero, Seneca and Terence, demonstrating the spread of humanism in the Veneto. Leonardo Bellini (*see* BELLINI, (4)) was prominent from the later 1450s to the 1480s. He executed *ducali*, including the *promissione* of Doge Cristoforo Moro (1463; London, BL, Add. MS. 15816), and humanist texts with noble Venetian coats of arms. His works incorporate Renaissance elements, while the *Old Testament* miniatures in the Hebrew ROTHSCHILD MISCELLANY (Jerusalem, Israel Mus., MS. 180/51) contain exceptional landscapes. More fully classicizing works were produced in Venice and Padua in the 1450s and 1460s under Mantegna's influence by such illuminators as the Tiptoft Master, the Master of the Victoria and Albert Petrarch, FRANCO DEI RUSSI, GIROLAMO DA CREMONA, the scribe BARTOLOMEO SANVITO and perhaps Mantegna himself. Frontispieces framed with Classical architecture and bearing faceted initials imitating Roman epigraphic letters appeared. Illusionistic effects were achieved through painting the area near the edge of the text to look like a torn piece of parchment with monuments and landscapes behind.

The arrival of printing in Venice in 1469 intensified the Classical Revival in Veneto–Paduan illumination, in part because Latin authors predominated in the earliest editions (see below). Generous spaces were left blank by the printers for initial letters to be added by hand. Some were completed by well-established illuminators such as Franco

dei Russi and Girolamo da Cremona, just as they would have illuminated manuscripts. Younger artists who matured in the 1470s, such as Giovanni Vendramini, the MASTER OF THE PUTTI (*see* MASTERS, ANONYMOUS, AND MONOGRAMMISTS, §I), the London Pliny Master (*fl* 1472–83), the Pico Master (*fl* 1469–94) and Antonio Maria da Villafora, specialized in decorating printed books, executing frontispieces with Classical architecture and mythical creatures. The compositions were frequently drawn in pen with only touches of wash for colour, harmonizing well with the printed page. Painted coats of arms often appear, but sometimes the shield is blank, suggesting that the decoration was prepared speculatively. In the 1490s the use of woodcuts presaged the end of the illuminator's trade. The great printer Aldus Manutius (*d* 1515), however, occasionally still printed on parchment, and copies of his editions were illuminated in the early 16th century. BENEDETTO BORDON painted a few ecclesiastical manuscripts and many *ducali* in these years, including the Evangeliary (1523–5; Dublin, Chester Beatty Lib., MS. 107) for S Giustina, Padua. Finally, from 1520 to 1570, there survive over 40 *ducali* showing the influence of Titian, from the workshop of an illuminator with the initials *T*. *Ve.*

The Venetian printing industry grew rapidly after printing with movable type arrived in Venice in 1469. By 1500 over 200 firms had printed at least one book, with more than 3000 editions, making Venice the greatest centre for printing in Europe. Venetian incunabula (books printed before the end of 1500) were distinguished by their large size, handsome layout and beautifully designed type. A Frenchman, Nicolas Jenson, was the most successful printer in the 1470s and set high standards for design, particularly in editions of Classical texts set with Roman type. A market for printed ecclesiastical and legal books soon developed, but these were usually set with Gothic types. Large woodcut initials and borders appeared in Venetian books printed in 1476–8 by the Germans Erhard Ratdolt (*fl* 1462–*c.* 1518), Bernard Mahler and Peter Löslein (*fl* 1476–8), but in general printers in Venice resisted illustrating books with figural woodcuts until *c.* 1490. In the transitional period, frontispieces and initials were left blank and individual copies were completed by illuminators (see above).

In the early 1490s there was a rapid increase in the number of Venetian books with woodcut frontispieces and narrative scenes. Initially these were simple outline woodcuts in two principal styles by artists designated the 'Popular Designer' and the 'Classical Designer' (Hind), who were probably illuminators and may perhaps be identified as the Pico Master (*fl* 1469–94) and Benedetto Bordon respectively. Elegant architectural frontispieces and vivacious vignettes by the Popular Designer appear in editions between 1489 and 1494, while after 1493 the style of the Classical Designer predominates. Initially 'Classical style' woodcuts were also simple outline cuts, although the figure style was more monumental and reminiscent of paintings by Mantegna. The culmination of this style is represented by the beautiful woodcuts in the HYPNEROTOMACHIA POLIPHILI (Venice, 1499) by Francesco Colonna, which have been attributed to a wide variety of artists, including Bordon. It was printed by Aldus Manutius, the most distinguished printer in Venice from the mid-1490s until his death in 1515. His fame rests on his many editions in Greek and on the handsome design of small volumes printed in innovative cursive types, now known as italic.

By the end of the 15th century artists in the Veneto were also producing woodcuts and engravings independent of printed books. Classicizing engravings of the 1470s and 1480s by ANDREA MANTEGNA, and woodcuts and engravings by Albrecht Dürer (*see* DÜRER, (1)) in the 1490s, profoundly influenced all subsequent printmakers in northern Italy. Both achieved volumetric effects by modelling figures with parallel strokes or with cross-hatching. Works continuing this style include the magnificent multi-block woodcut *Map of Venice*, designed by Jacopo de' Barbari (*c.* 1500; 12 extant copies, e.g. London, BM; original blocks in Venice, Correr; see fig. 1 above); a series of the *Triumph of Caesar* designed by Benedetto Bordon and cut by a German, Jacob of Strassburg (*fl* 1494–1530); and engravings by Giulio Campagnola, whose pastoral imagery additionally reflects the paintings of Giorgione.

Titian introduced a looser woodcut style after 1510, and woodcutters emulated the longer, broader lines of his drawings. His large multi-block woodcut of the *Crossing of the Red Sea* was published by Bernardino Benaglio, whose request for a privilege to print cites UGO DA CARPI as the cutter. Da Carpi in turn probably invented the chiaroscuro woodcut, using multiple blocks and colours of ink in imitation of wash drawings. Domenico Campagnola and Niccolò Boldrini also sometimes collaborated with Titian and spread his sweeping style in landscapes with religious or secular subjects.

Venice remained an important centre of fine printing throughout the 16th century. After 1500 illustrations in Venetian books also shifted from outline woodcuts to prints with fine modelling lines that heightened the three-dimensional qualities of figures and objects; engravings also occasionally replaced woodcuts for full-page illustrations. Title-pages with architectural elements, classicizing decorative motifs, allegorical figures and even narrative scenes in fictive reliefs became common. Illustrated technical treatises of high quality included the *De humani corporis fabrica libri septem* by the anatomist Andreas Vesalius, prepared in Italy but printed in Basle (1543) by Johannes Oporinus. It is not known who produced the accompanying woodcuts of partially dissected human figures set in landscapes, although the designs apparently originated in the circle of Titian, and his pupil Jan Steven van Calcar appears to be responsible for some of the illustrations. The woodcuts by Andrea Palladio illustrating Daniele Barbaro's translation of Vitruvius, *I dieci libri dell'architectura* (Francesco Marcolini, 1556), and Palladio's own *I quattro libri dell'architettura* (Domenico de' Franceschi, 1570) are impressive for their archaeological expertise and balanced designs. In literature, the elegant, Mannerist engravings for Ludovico Ariosto's *Orlando furioso* (Francesco de' Franceschi, 1584) by Girolamo Porro (*fl* 1574–1604) are among the most elaborate illustrations of any Venetian Renaissance book. These works epitomize the combined intellectual, artistic and entrepreneurial character of book and print production in Renaissance Venice.

BIBLIOGRAPHY

Prince d'Essling [V. Maséna]: *Les Livres à figures vénitiens de la fin du XVe siècle et du commencement du XVIe (1469–1525)*, 6 vols (Florence, 1907–14)

Catalogue of Books Printed in the XVth Century, London, BM cat., v (London, 1924) [with facs. of typefaces]

A. M. Hind: *An Introduction to a History of Woodcut* (London, 1935)

M. Sander: *Le Livre à figures italien depuis 1467 jusqu'à 1530*, 6 vols (New York, 1941–3)

R. Pallucchini: *La pittura veneziana del trecento* (Venice, 1964)

G. Mariani Canova: *La miniatura veneta del rinascimento* (Venice, 1969)

J. Schulz: 'The Printed Plans and Panoramic Views of Venice (1486–1797)', *Saggi & Mem. Stor. A.*, vii (1970), pp. 13–108

G. M. Zuccolo Padrono: 'Il Maestro "T". Ve' e la sua bottega: Miniature veneziane del XVIo secolo', *A. Ven.*, xxv (1971), pp. 53–71

Early Italian Engravings from the National Gallery of Art (exh. cat. by J. Levenson, K. Oberhuber, J. Sheehan, Washington, DC, N.G.A., 1976)

L. V. Gerulaitis: *Printing and Publishing in Fifteenth-century Venice* (Chicago, 1976)

Titian and the Venetian Woodcut (exh. cat., ed. D. Rosand and M. Muraro; Washington, DC, N.G.A., 1976)

M. Lowry: *The World of Aldus Manutius* (Ithaca, NY, 1979)

L. Armstrong: *Renaissance Miniature Painters and Classical Imagery: The Master of the Putti and his Venetian Workshop* (London, 1981)

G. Mariani Canova: 'La miniatura nei manoscritti liturgici della congregazione di S Giustina in area padana', *Riforma del convegno per il VI centenario della nascita di Ludovico Barbo, 1382–1443: Padova, Venezia, Treviso, 19–24 settembre 1982*

G. Dillon: 'Sull libro illustrato del quattrocento: Venezia e Verona', *La stampa degli incunaboli nel Veneto*, ed. N. Pozza (Vicenza, 1984), pp. 81–96

J. J. G. Alexander: 'Initials in Renaissance Illuminated Manuscripts: The Problem of the So-called "Litera Montiniana"', *Renaissance- und Humanistenhandschriften* (Oldenbourg, 1989), pp. 145–55

L. Armstrong: 'Il maestro di Pico: Un miniatore veneziano del tardo quattrocento', *Saggi & Mem. Stor. A.*, xvii (1990)

J. M. Massing: *The Triumph of Caesar* by Benedetto Bordone and Jacobus Argentoratensis', *Prt Q.*, vii (1990), pp. 11–39

M. Lowry: *Power, Print, Profit: Nicolaus Jenson and the Rise of Venetian Publishing in Renaissance Europe* (Cambridge, 1990)

G. Mariani Canova: 'La miniatura nei libri liturgici marciani', *Musica e liturgia a San Marco: Testi e melodie per la liturgia delle ore dal XII al XVII secolo: Dal graduale tropato del duecento ai graduali cinquecenteschi*, ed. G. Cattin, 4 vols (Venice, 1990–92), i, pp. 149–84

L. Armstrong: 'The Impact of Printing on Miniaturists in Venice after 1469', *Printing the Written Word: The Social History of Books, ca. 1450–1530*, ed. S. Hindman (Ithaca, NY, 1991), pp. 174–202

The Painted Page: Italian Renaissance Book Illumination, 1450–1550 (exh. cat., ed. J. J. G. Alexander; London, RA, 1994)

LILIAN ARMSTRONG

2. CERAMICS. Ceramic production flourished in Venice from the Middle Ages. The earliest wares were decorated with designs of Byzantine derivation. During the 14th century the already numerous craftsmen formed the *Fraglia* and decorated their wares with *sgraffito* designs of Middle Eastern origin. During the 15th century the ornamental repertory widened to include courtly designs, plant motifs and heraldic animals. Towards the end of the 15th century the so-called *graffito a fondo abbassato* was introduced, which involved removing slip from the ground in order to leave an image in relief. Wares decorated *alla porcellana* ('in the style of porcelain') and *alla damaschina* ('in the style of Damascus wares') showed the lasting influences of East Asian pottery imported into Venice. The technique of painting on a pale-blue ground (*berrettino*) is documented from the late 15th century. Venetian potters were in regular contact with potters from other Italian centres of production; their *sgraffito* work seems to imitate examples from Padua and Ferrara, while the maiolica resembles that of Faenza, partly because the

Faenzan potters enjoyed special concessions in the markets of the Veneto region.

The most important 16th-century Venetian workshops included those of Maestro Ludovico, Maestro Jacopo da Pesaro (*fl* 1507–46) and Maestro Domenico (*fl* 1540–68). Wares were decorated with medallions, coats of arms, mythological scenes, portraits, wreaths *alla porcellana* (e.g. plate, 1516; London, BM), arabesques and trophies. The palette was often very bright, with a rich use of yellow–orange, blue and green. Typical 16th-century Venetian wares include rounded, pot-bellied pharmaceutical jars known as *a palla* (ball-shaped). During the 17th century production continued, although the decorative schemes became more sober.

During the 18th century several important porcelain factories were established including the VEZZI PORCELAIN FACTORY, which operated briefly between 1720 and 1727. The few surviving examples of Vezzi porcelain are greatly valued for their original forms and their finely executed decoration, which was sometimes enriched with gold. The small factory established in 1761 by the Saxon potter Nathaniel Friedrich Hewelke (*fl* 1756–66) was active only until 1763, while the highly successful factory established *c.* 1764 by Geminiano Cozzi existed until 1812 (*see* COZZI PORCELAIN FACTORY). Craftsmen who had formerly worked for Giovanni Battista Antonibon (*d* 1739) at Nove, near Bassano, were employed at the factory, which produced fine maiolica and cream-coloured earthenware in the English style. Among the most popular decorative motifs, executed in a wide range of colours, were chinoiseries, village scenes, heraldic devices and floral garlands in a Rococo and, later, a Neo-classical style. The factory also produced groups of figures representing characters from the *commedia dell'arte* and figures in contemporary costume.

BIBLIOGRAPHY
A. Alverà Bortolotto: *Storia della ceramica a Venezia* (Milan, 1981)

LUCIANA ARBACE

3. GLASS.

(i) Before 1500. (ii) 1500–99. (iii) 1600–1797. (iv) After 1797.

(i) Before 1500. Various reasons have been proposed for the rise of glassmaking in Venice. Some historians have suggested that it may have been due to the presence of important late Roman centres in the Veneto; others have emphasized the presence of numerous monastic communities in Venice and on the islands in the lagoon that could initiate and promote vigorous experiments in glass technology. The widespread use of mosaic decoration in the Veneto also suggests that furnaces must have already been in operation in order to produce glass tesserae. Finally there were constant commercial, political and cultural relations between Venice and the Middle East, where the tradition of artistic glass manufacture had continued since Classical times with no breaks or periods of decline.

Between the 11th and 13th centuries the Venetian glassmakers were called *fioleri*, from *fiola*, a type of round-bellied bottle with a narrow neck. This indicates that during this period Venetian glass manufacture must have been mainly concerned with the production of objects for domestic use. On the nearby island of Murano there was already an established and rapidly expanding glass industry, the growing success of which helped to accelerate the process whereby the island became independent of Venice; in fact it had already obtained substantial guarantees of independence. The thriving industry needed an organizational structure, and from 1224 the glassmakers belonged to the Corporazione dei Vetrai, which in 1271 adopted a statute, the Capitulare de Fiolaris (also known as *Mariegole*), which was renewed in 1441. This strictly regulated apprenticeships, sales, imports and exports, and above all Venetian craftsmen were forbidden to move to other cities to establish or work in glasshouses for fear of creating rival centres of production. Yet although these rules were often reaffirmed, they were destined to be more and more easily evaded as the demand for Venetian glass increased in the rest of Italy and Europe. In 1291 an edict issued by the Magistrature of the Venetian Republic closed all the glasshouses in Venice and transferred them to Murano for fear of furnace fires. This also helped the guild's protectionist system and furthered Venice's monopoly of the production of blown glass.

From its origins, Venetian glass was of a sodaic type as the flux that was mixed with the silica (extracted from sand) was obtained from the ashes of vegetable materials. Depending on the chromatic effect desired, metallic oxides could be added to the frit, or manganese dioxide could be used as a decolourizing agent. Soda glass is a very ductile material, and the instruments used for working the metal were few and simple: apart from the blowpipe, moulds were sometimes used, as well as iron pincers for modelling details, and special scissors. The basic tools remained substantially unchanged, despite the increased complexity of the manufactured pieces.

The first datable pieces from the second half of the 15th century provide indisputable evidence of the high degree of technical perfection and the exquisite stylistic refinement achieved during the period by the Murano craftsmen. Most of the objects (goblets, cups, beakers, plates, bowls) were made of deep-blue, emerald-green or red glass, with rich and vivid polychrome enamelling and gilding. The style of decoration between 1460 and 1480 shows a clear relationship with, if not actually a derivation from, contemporary painting and manuscript illumination. The prevalence of brilliant colours and gold, as well as the recurrent friezes, with crowns, scrolled botanical motifs and medallions enclosing portraits, or even scenes of processions, Triumphs of Venus and Fountains of Love, were undoubtedly derived from manuscript illumination. The Barovier Cup (1470–80; Murano, Mus. Vetrario; *see* GLASS, colour pl. VIII, fig. 3), a wedding cup, is made in deep-blue glass and decorated with polychrome enamelling with portraits of the bride and groom enclosed in two medallions. The remaining space is occupied by scenes of the cavalcade towards the Fountain of Love and women bathing in the fountain. The figurative inventions, choice of subjects, stylistic solutions and the highly refined sense of colour can also be seen in relation to the Venetian school of painting and the intense activity in those years of such artists as Vittore Carpaccio and Giovanni Bellini. There was also a group of painters in Murano who must have had an influence on glass design. This was led by the circle of Bartolomeo Vivarini and his brother Alvise Vivarini together with Alvise's daughter Armenia Vivarini, who was perhaps also a painter; in the 16th century she entered the glassmaking trade and is thought to have invented a particular type of *acquereccia* (ornamental water jug), decorated with a miniature reproduction of a ship. Original sources and documents contain the names of many famous master glassmakers, but as the craftsmen of Murano did not sign their works, it is difficult to identify the maker of any piece with reasonable accuracy.

Techniques of glassmaking at Murano remained essentially the same until about 1450, when ANGELO BAROVIER invented a new type of transparent glass that used not only manganese dioxide as a decolourizing agent, which counteracted the impurities that had sullied the old glass, but also special preparations and processes. This colourless metal was very pure and so closely resembled rock crystal that it was called *cristallo*. The exceptional qualities of this product brought such fame to Barovier that he received insistent and flattering invitations to the courts of the Medici and Francesco Sforza, Duke of Milan. Very soon the method of producing the new glass became widely known and practised, and numerous other craftsmen joined the inventor in producing *cristallo* to supply the enormous demand. Enamelled decoration was also applied to articles made in the new glass in very brilliant colours, highlighted with gold. Rather than figurative subjects this ornamentation consisted of decorated bands with dots and scrolls in the form of vines, tiles or scales. Specific pieces were commissioned to commemorate important events in aristocratic families, the designs including noble coats of arms or heraldic symbols. The latter type of decoration can be seen in two gourd-shaped, *cristallo* pilgrim-flasks (see fig. 10), one of which presents the enamelled coat of arms of the Bentivoglio family, while the other bears the arms of the Sforza family. They were made in 1492 on the occasion of the marriage between Alessandro Bentivoglio and Ippolita Sforza. Another example is the *cesendello* (a cylindrical, hanging lamp) in *cristallo* decorated with small points and polychrome enamel and gold imbrication, bearing the coat of arms of the Tiepolo family (late 15th century or early 16th; Murano, Mus. Vetrario).

In the late 15th century the Murano craftsmen sought new technical solutions: typical of this period is 'chalcedony' glass (so called because of its likeness to the hardstone of that name). This glass is dull red in colour with polychrome venation obtained by adding metallic compounds to the vitreous mixture (e.g. pitcher, *c*. 1500; London, BM; *see* GLASS, colour pl. VIII, fig. 1). Numerous contemporary paintings provide ample pictorial evidence of the presence and use of such glass objects in Venice and elsewhere during this period. Since glass is a material that does not change significantly with age (which means the date of manufacture cannot be deduced from the state of the material) and the techniques and even the designs used by the Murano glassmakers remained almost unchanged over the centuries, such iconographic references assist with the identification and dating of glass articles.

(ii) 1500–99. At the end of the 15th century and the beginning of the 16th the production of *lattimo* (milk glass) became widespread. This white, opaque glass, already known to the ancient Romans, was often used to

10. Two glass pilgrim-flasks, with enamel and gilt decoration, showing the coats of arms of the Bentivoglio and Sforza families, Murano, 1492 (Bologna, Museo Civico)

imitate Chinese porcelain. In some documents it is referred to as *vetro porcellano* (porcelain glass). The decoration of *lattimo* was usually figurative and was clearly influenced by such contemporary painters as Giovanni Bellini, Vittore Carpaccio and Bartolomeo Montagna, with frequent representations of sacred subjects or portraits of men and women. *Lattimo* glass was also used for a different decorative effect, which was inspired by the ancient Roman practice of decorating glass with twisted, white canes applied to the edges of dishes and bowls. The Murano masters imbedded filaments of *lattimo* glass into the transparent molten glass to obtain a decoration of parallel streaks. As the technique developed it became possible to incorporate threads of *lattimo* glass that were rolled into spirals or woven, thus creating pieces decorated with *retortoli* (twists) or *reticelli* (nets). During the 16th century glassmakers using this technique, which by analogy with goldsmith's work was called *filigrana* (filigree) decoration, produced astonishing results in Murano. Numerous examples of this technique exist (see fig. 11).

During the 16th century the taste for rich polychrome decoration finally declined. Owing mainly to the discovery and spread of *cristallo* the Murano glassmakers began to produce works that gave more prominence to the material itself rather than the decoration. The finest pieces produced in the 16th century are undoubtedly represented by an important series of *cristallo* chalices and goblets. These are transparent, without any decoration, graceful with thin, blown or moulded pillar stems. The forms were no longer based on metal models but determined directly by the characteristics of the material and by the particular technical and executive procedures involved in working glass. The elegance of line is perfectly suited to the unrivalled transparency of the glass.

11. Glass pitcher with *reticello* decoration, h. 198 mm, Murano, 1550–1600 (Murano, Museo Vetrario)

In this period the main stylistic emphasis was on the line and harmony of form, and pictorial decoration was relegated to a very secondary role. It can be found, for example, on a few plates, inspired by subjects drawn from well-known engravings of the period (which in turn repeated themes depicted by such famous painters as Raphael). These were executed on the back surface using the technique of cold painting (with lacquer or oil paint) rather than enamelling. This form of decoration is extremely perishable, and it has often almost completely worn off. In the last decades of the 16th century colour appeared sporadically in the decoration of goblets, but this was limited to azure-blue edging or applied threading in wing-like designs on the stem. Another important product of 16th-century technical experimentation was 'ice glass', so called because of the cracked appearance of the material. The effect was obtained by immersing the white-hot metal in water while it was still being worked and blowing it, sometimes with the help of moulds, into simple forms such as goblets, fruit stands and baskets, which were sometimes decorated with applied masks or lions' heads (e.g. basket, 1550–1600; Murano, Mus. Vetrario). It was perhaps the emphasis on purity of line that favoured the introduction of another decorative technique using very light diamond-point engraving. The subjects included plant motifs, geometrical figures, arabesques, grotesques, satyrs and mythological figures. The pioneer of this technique was probably Vincenzo d'Angelo del Gallo, who c. 1550 obtained exclusive rights to the process.

The production of mirrors is closely related to the art of glassmaking and also dependent on it. Mirrors, in fact, were often adorned with delicate engravings either on the plate itself or on the frame (when the latter was not made in carved wood or in other forms of worked glass). While glass mirrors (*see* MIRROR, §VI, 1) were probably invented in Germany, the Del Gallo brothers obtained the patent in 1507, and it was thanks to the Venetians in the late 15th century and the early 16th that this type of product came into wide production and use. Glass mirrors were valued not only for their practical effectiveness but also for their high decorative quality. The practice of the glassmakers of Murano was to blow rough glass plates, which because of the technical difficulties were rather small, by the same method used for window panes. They were passed on to the *specchieri* (mirror-makers), who had their workshops in Venice itself. These craftsmen squared the plates, polished them and applied a thin coating of tin or mercury. Finished with precious carved-wood or engraved-glass frames, such mirrors became important elements in the furnishing of aristocratic homes.

Another thriving sector of Venetian glassmaking was in the production of glass beads, which were imitation pearls made of coloured vitreous paste, used for necklaces, for decoration of garments and for rosaries. They were produced in rough form in Murano and finished in Venice with the flame of a lamp, so that they were also called *perle a lume* (lamplight pearls).

(iii) 1600–1797. Despite the restrictions on the Venetian glassmakers, craftsmen emigrated from Murano to other centres in Italy and to European countries where Venetian products had enjoyed enormous success. The imitation of Muranese models began the so-called *à la façon de Venise*, in which the techniques and typologies were copied so faithfully that it is often difficult to establish the origin of a piece.

The uncontested success of Venetian glassware did not prevent the furnaces established in such countries as the Netherlands, Sweden, Denmark and England from being a serious threat to Venetian production. The goods that they could now produce locally no longer had to be imported at very high prices. In addition, north European taste influenced glass production in Murano. Although the designs of the 17th century followed the lines laid down in the preceding period, foreign influences favoured more complicated form and decoration and a greater chromatic and structural richness. This was also a consequence of changing times: the 16th century, with its emphasis on linearity and purity of form and the near or complete absence of polychrome elements, gave way to the new Baroque style with its predilection for vivid colours and unusual, often fussy designs. Wares produced during this period resemble those of the 16th century not only in form but also in technique and show a development of technical methods to an almost virtuosic level of skill: this is evident, for example, in *filigrana* glass, which became increasingly complex, and also in diamond-point engraved pieces. Another example of technical bravura can be seen in the applied, moulded masks (in clear or coloured glass), or the stems of goblets decorated with *alette* (wings) in the form of small crests, which became increasingly rich, elaborate and intricate. The influence of the style *à la façon de Venise* and the new Baroque taste is also evident in creations that were more specifically modern: a type of goblet in which the stem was made in the shape of a convoluted serpent, often in blue glass (e.g. wineglass, 17th century; London, V&A), and a whole series of other objects, which sometimes took the form of small lamps and were decorated with shells, birds, crustaceans and even human caricatures.

The Baroque taste for the unusual, the artificial and the bizarre is well exemplified in the book by Prince Luigi d'Este, *Il libro del Serenissimo Signore Luigi d'Este* (1617), which contains over 1000 drawings by an unknown designer. Examples of these pieces are displayed in the Museo Vetrario in Murano and the Museo Poldi Pezzoli in Milan. Another book, the *Bicchierografia* (1604) by Giovanni Maggi, illustrates some fantastic glass articles from the collection of Cardinal Del Monte, as well as others of his own design.

In the 17th century chalcedony glass was revived and to enhance its brilliance it was sometimes mixed with aventurine, a vitreous paste invented at the beginning of the century that contained copper particles that produced a scintillating effect (e.g. bowl, 17th century; Coburg, Veste Coburg). The effect looked very expensive and was therefore also suitable for jewellery, tobacco cases and buttons.

During this period external factors prevented the expansion of the Venetian market, which was in any case beginning to contract. Famine and plague decimated the ranks of the master glassmakers, while demand in both the domestic and foreign markets was reduced by the competition of such countries as Bohemia (which produced a luminous glass with added potassium), England (which produced lead glass) and France (where the minister Jean-Baptiste Colbert encouraged the production of large mirrors using innovative techniques). The artistic glassmakers of Murano responded at the beginning of the 18th century by revitalizing the traditional techniques, producing pieces of such exquisite refinement that they competed successfully with the north European glassmakers almost until the end of the century.

In 1708–9 Frederick IV of Denmark (1671–1730) was in Venice and acquired a collection of glass, some of which was a gift from the Senate of the Venetian Republic (Copenhagen, Rosenborg Pal.). The articles in clear or *filigrana* glass were enriched with polychrome, floral and animal motifs on the stems or as crests. Other examples show the return to favour of coloured vitreous pastes such as chalcedony, opalescent, malachite and aventurine glass. The technique of *lattimo* glass was also revived, both in *filigrana* work, which was no longer limited to white, but enriched with coloured strands in pink, blue or red, and in the use of its characteristic milky white quality to imitate Chinese porcelain. The forms of the so-called *porcellana contrafacta* in enamelled *lattimo* glass were inspired by such porcelain objects as cups, saucers and small jugs with polychrome or gold decoration. These objects found a wide market, and their production did not cease even when potters learnt to make hard- and soft-paste porcelains. *Lattimo* pieces are the only glass products that can be identified by marks or monograms, so it is possible to attribute them precisely to particular craftsmen, or more often to families of artists. One family famous for *porcellana contrafacta* were the Bertolini, active from the beginning of the 18th century; another was the Miotti family in the

second quarter of the century, who operated the Il Gesù glassworks in Murano and signed their works with the monogram IHS (see fig. 12). The Brussa family, from Murano, produced such utilitarian wares as beakers, carafes and bottles, in common transparent glass, enamelled with floral and animal motifs and sacred or profane figures. However, the volume of their output was not always matched by high-quality production.

A particularly outstanding 18th-century glassmaker was Giuseppe Lorenzo Briati (1686–1772), who played an important role not only in the propagation, but often the actual invention of some types of glass products that enabled the Venetian factories to meet foreign competition. Briati was famous for his table centrepieces called *deseri* or *trionfi*, which were perfectly suited to the late 18th-century taste for rich and magnificent furnishings.

12. *Lattimo*-glass sprinkler, h. 276 mm, attributed to the Miotti workshop, Murano, 1725–50 (Corning, NY, Museum of Glass)

These centrepieces adorned the banquets of doges and aristocrats on important ceremonial occasions. They were composed of numerous small pieces and represented miniature architectural complexes, gardens and fountains and were worked and decorated with *lattimo*, enamelling and coloured vitreous pastes. Briati was also famous for his chandeliers, called *ciocche*, in which the very slender metal armature was completely covered with glass branches set one within the other. These in turn were enriched with multicoloured floral bouquets, droplets and swags. Others were designed in a vaguely East Asian style. They created a remarkable scenographic effect that provided a perfect complement to the luxurious furnishings of the aristocratic dwellings of the time (e.g. of mid-18th century; Venice, Ca' Rezzonico). Briati was also probably responsible for an innovation in the design of mirrors, which enabled Venice to overcome the fierce French competition: the frames were no longer made of wood but entirely of glass, composed of many small pieces in varied forms and colours (e.g. of mid-18th century; Murano, Mus. Vetrario). The competition, however, particularly from Bohemia and England, increased, and Murano was forced to adopt new 'imported' techniques and typologies. Briati experimented with a type of glass based on potassium, similar to Bohemian crystal. The taste for engraved glass in the Bohemian style also spread, and Bohemian engravers came to live and work in Venice.

Such works inspired by foreign tastes, however, although justified by commercial considerations, never really became part of the deep-rooted inspiration of the Murano artists. They continued to produce wares that were tied to the old technical and stylistic tradition of Venetian glassmaking, with its usual passion for colour and its specific relationship with contemporary trends in painting and engraving. Through the 18th century the Venetian glass industry had found a way to prolong its great artistic flowering and international success. But the political events that overwhelmed the Republic, until it finally fell in 1797, created a crisis in the glassmaking sector that was intensified by the problems of foreign competition and by the necessary emphasis on quantity rather than aesthetic criteria in glass production. This decline marked the end of the European primacy of Murano.

(iv) After 1797. The grave crisis that the Venetian glass industry was passing through was confirmed in 1806 by the dissolution of the Corporazione dei Vetrai. Part of the problem was that in Murano the organization of the work was still based on the technical ability and inventiveness of individual craftsmen, in contrast with the modern industrial structure prevailing in such countries as England and Bohemia. But the crisis was also caused by the loss of real inspiration on the part of the Murano glassmakers, who produced pedestrian bottles, flasks and drinking vessels enamelled mostly in white. The glassmakers persisted in a sterile repetition of obsolete models and techniques.

However, in the 1840s the first signs of revival began to appear: Pietro Bigaglia (1786–1876) and Lorenzo Radi (1803–74), while remaining within the familiar technical and stylistic tradition, gave their creations an innovative flavour. Bigaglia made large Classical-style vases in green,

pink and blue opaque glass which resembled granite (e.g. of *c.* 1845; Murano, Mus. Vetrario). Bigaglia also produced the earliest *millefiori* paperweight *c.* 1845. Radi was responsible for the revival of chalcedony glass, and in 1854 the Fratelli Toso factory was established in Murano for the production of traditional, blown glassware.

As a result of this increased activity, there was a revival of European interest in Venetian glass. This may have partly inspired the initiative of Abbot Vincenzo Zanetti (1824–83), who in 1861 founded an archive in Murano for the documentation of the island's ancient art of glassmaking and the Museo Vetrario di Murano, where craftsmen could find ample material for inspiration and which in the late 20th century constitutes one of the world's richest and most important collections of glass. Later a school of design for glassmakers was established beside the museum; and in 1864 the first exhibition of contemporary Murano glass was held with great success. The enthusiasm of the glassmakers was thus revived, and several new factories were established by such artists as Antonio Salviati (1816–1900), who in 1866 founded the Venice & Murano Glass & Mosaic Co. Ltd with English capital. The new production was marked by an extremely high, often virtuosic level of technical skill, as well as by a systematic revival of styles. This recovery involved not only the production of Renaissance-style wares but also, in response to a growing interest in archaeology, the imitation of Roman glassware called murrhine (mosaic glass), for which Vincenzo Moretti (1835–1900) was largely responsible, and 'Corinth' glasses, which imitated antique ceramics, with chromatic effects that were speckled, blotched or made iridescent in various ways to suggest years of interment.

Although this kind of production conformed to the eclectic taste of the 19th century and had great success at the Expositions Universelles in Paris, it was still far removed from contemporary trends in European art. It was not until the 1920s that Murano again won full international success: the objects exhibited at the Exposition des Arts Décoratifs et Industriels of 1925 in Paris expressed the mature experience of an industry now autonomous in technique and style. While the traditional Murano factories continued to produce wares in eclectic 19th-century taste, others emerged under Vittorio Zecchin (1878–1947), Ercole Barovier (1889–1974) and Paolo Venini, who made glass in pure, simple, elegant forms, using hot techniques rather than cutting or engraving. The revival of Murano glassmaking was not interrupted even in the years after World War II, and post-war Venetian glass is distinguished by a vibrant palette and such free, asymetrical forms as Venini's 'Fazzoletto' vase (see fig. 13).

Blown glass does not, however, suit industrial processes or mass serial production. The traditional idea, still deeply rooted, of glass as a form of artistic and creative expression can survive only when the designer and executor are one; yet there have been attempts, with very interesting results, at collaboration between Murano glassmakers and such contemporary artists as Pablo Picasso, Hans Arp, Carlo Scarpa and Max Ernst, all of whom have designed models for glasshouses in Murano. This singular alliance between experience and inventiveness is bringing the art of Italian glassmaking again to the forefront of the contemporary art world.

BIBLIOGRAPHY

G. Lorenzetti: *Murano e l'arte del vetro soffiato* (Venice, 1953)

L. Zecchin: *Murano e l'arte del vetro, guida al Museo Vetrario di Murano* (Venice, 1953)

Glass from the Corning Museum of Glass (Corning, 1955, rev. 1974)

A. Gasparetto: *Il vetro di Murano* (Venice, 1958)

G. Mariacher: *Il vetro soffiato* (Milan, 1960)

——: *Vetri italiani del cinquecento* (Milan, 1963)

——: *Vetri italiani del seicento e del settecento* (Milan, 1965)

——: *L'arte del vetro dalle origini al rinascimento* (Milan, 1966)

——: *Vetri di Murano* (Milan and Rome, 1967)

——: *Specchiere italiane e cornici da specchio dal XV al XIX secolo* (Milan, 1969)

A. Dorigato: *Vetri di Murano del settecento* (Venice, 1981)

R. Barovier Mentasti: *Il vetro veneziano* (Milan, 1982)

Mille anni di arte del vetro a Venezia (exh. cat., Venice, Correr, 1982)

A. Dorigato: *Vetri: Rinascimento e barocco* (Novara, 1985)

——: *Vetri del settecento e dell'ottocento* (Novara, 1985)

PAOLO D'ALCONZO

4. TEXTILES.

(i) Tapestry. Because it was such a lively trading centre, Venice was one of the few Italian cities where independent tapestry workshops could prosper on a fairly continuous basis in post-medieval times. The earliest recorded workshop is that of the master weavers Giovanni of Bruges and Valentino of Arras in 1421. Many authors believe that this workshop, or another contemporary local one, wove the *Passion* cycle (*c.* 1420–30; Venice, Mus. S Marco; *see* ITALY, fig. 99) for the cathedral of S Marco from cartoons by Zanino di Pietro; more recently the cartoons have also been attributed to Niccolò di Pietro or his circle, although others believe the tapestries were woven north of the Alps. By the 1460s the weaver–merchant Rinaldo Boteram (pseud. di Gualtieri) from Brussels had also established a shop in Venice, apparently mainly to sell imported Flemish tapestries. Renaissance documents often mention Venice as a source of ready-made, probably mostly Flemish, tapestries, so there were most likely other shops in addition to that of Boteram.

Tapestry-weavers apparently continued to work in Venice almost continuously throughout the 16th and 17th centuries; *The Pentecost* (*c.* 1510–20) in S Maria della Salute in Venice may be one of their products. Cartoons for lost tapestries were designed by, among others, Titian (four *Theological Virtues* for Senator Carlo Zane, woven in 1562 by the Flemish master Lazzaro Canaam; *fl* 1562–72) and Domenico Tintoretto (an eight-piece *Life of St Lorenzo Giustiniani* for Caterino Malipiero, ordered from Girolamo de Bassi in 1596). Two families of weavers—Angelo di Battista Clemente from Friuli and his sons and the possibly Flemish Zinquevie—were active at this time. About 1677 Pietro Fevère's son, Filippo Fevère (*fl* 1648–after 1677), established a workshop in Venice. Nonetheless, tapestries continued to be ordered from other Italian cities and from abroad.

Two important tapestry workshops are documented in the 18th century, both of which received public funding as schools from the 1760s: the school of Pietro Davanzo (*b* late 17th century; *d* 1776) also taught textile design, while that of Antonio Dini (*b* early 18th century; *d* 1771) taught only tapestry-weaving. Dini's daughters Lucia Dini and Giuseppa Dini continued weaving tapestries until

13. Opaque-glass 'Fazzoletto' vase, h. 149 mm, made by Venini & C., Murano, *c.* 1950 (Vienna, Österreichisches Museum für Angewandte Kunst)

1798. About 1800 the embroiderer Bernardino Bussoni (*b c.* 1746; *d* 1817) also specialized in tapestry copies of paintings. There was then a hiatus in the production of tapestries in Venice until the mid-1950s, when the work and teaching of the artist–weaver Wanda Casaril (*b* 1933) began to encourage a revival of the art.

BIBLIOGRAPHY

M. Viale Ferrero: *Arazzi italiani del cinquecento* (Milan, 1963), pp. 14, 45

W. Wolters: 'Über die Wandteppiche von S Marco in Venedig und ihren Meister', *Pantheon*, xxiii (1965), pp. 75–83

R. Pallucchini and others: 'Arazzi dei secoli XV e XVI', *Il Tesoro e il Museo*, ed. H. R. Hahnloser, ii of *Il Tesoro di San Marco* (Florence, 1971), pp. 233–58

M. Stucky-Schürer: *Die Passionsteppiche von San Marco in Venedig* (Berne, 1972)

G. Delmarcel and J.-K. Steppe: 'Les Tapisseries du Cardinal Erard de la Marck, prince-évêque de Liège', *Rev. A.*, xxv (1974), pp. 43, 54

B. Boucher: 'Jacopo Sansovino and the Choir of St Mark's', *Burl. Mag.*, cxviii (1976), pp. 234–9

CANDACE J. ADELSON

(ii) Lace. The precise origins of lacemaking in Venice are unknown, but by the second half of the 16th century flourishing needle and bobbin lace industries existed and numerous pattern books were being published. Techniques and designs differed from those in Flanders, even though in the early 17th century forms of tape lace were invented to imitate Flemish designs. By the mid-17th century Venetian needle lace was developing into a highly successful luxury industry: beautiful Baroque designs of foliate scrolls, executed in a heavy relief technique in linen and sometimes in gold thread were popular throughout Europe. Towards the end of the century a lighter, frothy style emerged to satisfy changing tastes, but a dramatic decline then ensued as other centres and types of lace took over. Needle lace continued to be made for church use and light silk and linen laces were introduced in the 1750s, enabling the industry to linger on until the 19th-century revival. This was initiated in 1872 by the establishment on

the island of Burano of a needle-lace school, which soon developed a distinctive style, as well as producing much reproduction lace and remodelling antique lace. Parallel developments in bobbin lace were begun in Pellestrina and elsewhere by such Venetian entrepreneurs as Michelangelo Jesurum (*d* 1910), who also introduced a polychrome silk lace in the 1870s. The industry flourished until the 1930s, but declined thereafter. Venice played little part in the modern lace movement.

BIBLIOGRAPHY
R. Savio and L. Savio: 'L'organizzazione del lavoro femminile a Venezia nelle antiche istituzioni di ricovero e di educazione', *I pizzi: Moda e simbolo* (exh. cat., ed. A. Mottola Molfino and T. Binaghi Olivari; Venice, Pal. Grassi, 1977)
La Scuola dei merletti di Burano (exh. cat., Burano, 1981)
L. Bellodi Casanova: 'Venezia e Laguna', *Cinque secoli di merletti europei: I capolavori* (exh. cat., ed. D. Davanzo Poli; Burano, 1984), pp. 12–32
G. Mariacher and others: *Il merletto di Pellestrina* (Pellestrina, 1986) [bilingual text]

PATRICIA WARDLE

IV. Buildings.

1. S Marco. 2. S Giorgio Maggiore. 3. SS Giovanni e Paolo. 4. S Maria Gloriosa dei Frari. 5. S Maria della Salute. 6. Doge's Palace. 7. Libreria Marciana.

1. S MARCO. The cathedral of Venice since 1807, S Marco is the most important example of Veneto-Byzantine art, fusing Byzantine influence with Romanesque experiments and Gothic innovations in a highly original manner

14. Venice, S Marco, interior looking east, begun *c.* 1063

(see fig. 26 below). Despite centuries of rebuilding, alteration and superimposition, the building has retained its feeling of coherence, mainly owing to the rich mosaic covering, which is subsumed into the architecture, transfiguring the interior structure and redefining the space in terms of colour.

(i) Architecture. (ii) Sculpture. (iii) Mosaics. (iv) Treasury. (v) Pala d'Oro.

(i) Architecture. The church built to give the relics of St Mark (*see* §I, 1 above) a worthy burial place was the first of three successive buildings on the same site. It was begun by Doge Giustiniano Partecipazio (*reg* 827–9) as a ducal chapel, an integral part of the seat of government, and was consecrated in 832 under Doge Giovanni I Partecipazio (*reg* 829–36). Not even the ground-plan is known for certain. Scholars have maintained that it was an aisled basilica with an apse, crypt and portico, after the example of buildings in Ravenna; but studies by the excavator, Forlati, indicate that S Marco was a centrally planned, Greek-cross building from the start. The two Partecipazio doges had lived in Constantinople and could have been influenced by such buildings as Justinian's church of the Holy Apostles (destr.; *see* ISTANBUL, §IV, 9(i)), but the plan could equally have been inspired by western martyria. The first church may have been destroyed, but was more likely only damaged, by a fire in 976; it was immediately restored in an identical form by Doge Pietro I Orseolo (*reg* 976–8) and consecrated in 978. Some architectural and decorative elements of the two first churches were reused in the third church, which is essentially the extant building.

The present building was begun *c.* 1063 under Doge Domenico Contarini (*reg* 1043–71), who wished it to reflect the increased power and wealth of Venice. He preserved the earlier foundations and reused some of the outside walls and brickwork of the earlier building. At his death the church must have been well advanced, as it was completed by Doge Vitale Falier (*reg* 1084–96) and consecrated in 1094. Tradition states that Doge Falier found the body of St Mark (lost during Contarini's building works) and rebuilt the tomb, presbytery and crypt; this complex renovation was the start of the ceaseless process of renovation and addition that gives the basilica its unique character.

S Marco is built of brick with a marble facing. It is centrally planned, on a Greek cross, with an east–west axis of 76.5 m (including the later narthex), and has five hemispherical domes on pendentives, one at the centre and one on each of the four arms. The internal height of the central dome is 28.5 m. The domes rest on a double order of gigantic roundheaded arches, almost in the form of barrel vaulting, supported by four grouped piers at each corner (see fig. 14). Columns divide each cross arm into three aisles and support the galleries (now reduced to walkways) above the arches, which are enclosed by marble screens. The presbytery is raised over a crypt, which has three apses. The main eastern apse of the upper church is semicircular inside and polygonal outside, the exterior divided by a balcony and decorated with blind arcades and niches. The church was originally fronted at the west by a simple portico faced with exposed brickwork and must have looked very bare and austere. Venetian chroniclers state that Byzantine architects were summoned, again basing the church on the Holy Apostles (remodelled in the 9th century) at Constantinople. The origins of the architect have been much debated, but the building was probably a fusion of different regional ideas.

From the beginning of the 13th century the portico was replaced by a narthex that surrounded the whole western arm. In consequence, in about 1231 the domes were heightened, the original masonry being concealed under higher, lead-covered domes, curved over a spherical wooden framework and topped by onion-shaped cupolas. The narthex itself is divided into bays by lightly pointed arches and is topped by small domes (see fig. 3 above). A balcony divides the façade horizontally. The lower part, on two orders of superposed columns, has a series of deep, roundheaded containing arches, the central one being higher and deeper than those on the sides (*see* RUSKIN, JOHN, fig. 2). The portals are within the arches, the two outer ones topped by Arabic–Moorish cimatia, the intermediate by Gothic three-light windows and the central portal by reliefs within the arch. The upper, re-entrant storey has five arches corresponding to the lower ones; the central arch encloses a large semicircular window, the side ones have lunettes with mosaics. Above the arches rises the rich Gothic coping with what may be the earliest ogee arches (*c.* 1250) in Europe, spires, tabernacles and pinnacles. The north and south façades are slightly different, the north with two sets of four superposed arches, the south with half that number. Later additions to the building include the Cappella di S Isidoro, built and decorated (*see* §(iii)(d) below) by Doge ANDREA DANDOLO.

The detached campanile (now 98.6 m high; see fig. 3 above) seems to have been created from an ancient lookout tower, probably in the second half of the 12th century. Its structure was repeatedly altered; growing in height and impressiveness, the campanile soon became a central landmark not only relative to the Piazza S Marco but to the whole city. The upper part was seriously damaged by lightning in 1489, and after an earthquake in 1511 the pyramidal tiled roof was replaced by a high pyramidal pinnacle on a quadrangular drum. The campanile collapsed in 1902 and was faithfully rebuilt in 1912.

BIBLIOGRAPHY

R. Cattaneo: *L'Architecture en Italie du VI au XI siècle* (Venice, 1895)
P. Toesca: *Il medioevo* (Turin, 1927), vol. ii
D. Talbot Rice: *Byzantine Art* (Oxford, 1935)
S. Bettini: *L'architettura di S Marco: Origini e significato* (Padua, 1946)
G. Musolino: *La basilica di S Marco in Venezia* (Venice, 1955)
O. Demus: *The Church of S Marco in Venice: History, Architecture, Sculpture*, Dumbarton Oaks Studies, vi (Washington, DC, 1960) [with a contribution by F. Forlati]
S. Bettini: 'Un libro su San Marco', *A. Ven.*, xv (1961), pp. 263–77
R. Krautheimer: *Early Christian and Byzantine Architecture*, Pelican Hist. A. (Harmondsworth, 1965)
Venezia e Bisanzio (exh. cat., Venice, 1974)
F. Forlati: *La basilica di S Marco attraverso i suoi restauri* (Trieste, 1975)
U. Franzoi and D. di Stefano: *Le chiese di Venezia* (Venice, 1976)
J. Warren: 'The First Church of S Marco in Venice', *Antiqua. J.*, lxx/2 (1990), pp. 327–59

LIA DI GIACOMO

(ii) Sculpture. S Marco is very rich both in carved architectural decoration and in independent sculptural works. The architectural elements include those fixed to the exterior and interior walls and those that form part of the structure itself. Only a small part of this number of the carved architectural elements, which include capitals, bases, lintels, architraves and door frames, is contemporary with the architecture, stylistically related to it and is datable on the basis of it. Most of the sculpture consists of reused pieces of earlier date or of later additions. The overall decoration of the basilica thus results from the juxtaposition and contrast of very different sculptural elements. These are mainly reliefs, as sculpture in the round generally played a secondary role in post-Iconoclastic Byzantine art. Unlike other important Romanesque churches in Europe, there was never a clear iconographic programme at S Marco; each relief was conceived and treated individually with its own self-contained symbolic and decorative significance. While the basilica still had little sculptural decoration at the time of Doge Domenico Contarini, it was enriched in the 12th century by the addition of various elements that were reused in a manner typical of the Byzantine Empire. Even in the 13th century the sculptural decoration of architectural elements was limited to the arches over the façade portals and did not extend to the other parts of the church.

The relief sculpture at S Marco is usually classified into three main groups: pieces datable between the 5th and 12th centuries, those executed *ad hoc* in the 11th and 12th centuries, and cycles realized between the 13th and 15th centuries. The first group includes reused Early Christian material of white Greek marble. Among the most important examples are large *plutei* datable to the 6th century, with crosses or peacocks facing a central *chrismon*. Further examples, from the 7th–8th centuries, include *plutei* and sarcophagus fronts with delicate tracery and pointed acanthus leaves, as well as *plutei* with rhomboid or geometric motifs. Others, thought to survive from the earlier basilica (*c.* 832), are decorated with interwoven reeds more common in the architectural decoration of small pilasters and *plutei* in the west, or with the wide plaited ribbons typical of Balkan Middle Byzantine *plutei*. This group also comprises 10th-century circular panels with animal motifs, which reproduce in stone exarchal terracotta prototypes such as those in Pomposa Abbey (*see* ROMANESQUE, III, 1(vi)(c)).

Free-standing sculpture of antique origin includes the 3rd- or 4th-century porphyry group of the *Tetrarchs* (*see* ROME, ANCIENT, fig. 82) on the south-west corner of the Treasury façade, as well as the four alabaster columns supporting the ciborium of the high altar, decorated with reliefs and commonly ascribed to the 5th or 6th century, but in fact dating from the end of the 11th century (Polacco), and the four gilded bronze horses (Venice, Mus. S Marco; formerly on the façade but now replaced by copies), looted from Constantinople in 1204.

The second main group of sculpture includes the few works traceable to the period under Doge Contarini, in particular the *plutei* on the women's galleries (*matronei*), carved in a classicizing style with animal and plant motifs. These reflect more directly the courtly style of Constantinople, but they were probably carved in Venice by Eastern artists employed in the building of the basilica. There are numerous 11th- and 12th-century examples of woven reed and shoot motifs demonstrating the importance of the high-medieval tradition and of the Middle Byzantine

15. Relief-carvings (13th and 14th centuries) on the central portal, west front, S Marco, Venice

influence, both of which were very apparent in the Venetian workshops.

A separate, very small group of 12th-century sculpture shows the penetration of Lombard–Emilian Romanesque forms. At the end of that century and the beginning of the 13th, both works in the style of Benedetto Antelami and spoils from the Byzantine Empire were common, so that the sculpture produced by local artists reveals an assimilation and a singular mixture of Byzantine motifs with those derived from Antelami. This can be seen in the 13th- and much of the 14th-century architectural decoration of the façade of S Marco, for example in the arches of the central portal (see fig. 15), which are decorated with cycles of the *Months*, the *Virtues*, the *Beatitudes* and the *Trades*, juxtaposed with such carvings in the Byzantine style as *Christ Blessing* and the *Virgin in Prayer*. These styles merged in such late 14th-century reliefs as *St George* and *Hercules and the Boar* (both between the arches of the façade). The Late Gothic crowning elements and the freestanding statues of the early 15th century, especially those by Niccolò di Piero Lamberti and Piero di Niccolò Lamberti constitute the last significant cycle of architectural sculpture at S Marco, although independent works such as the marble iconostasis (1394) by Jacobello dalle Masegne and Pierpaolo dalle Masegne and several doges' tombs were also produced in the 14th and 15th centuries.

BIBLIOGRAPHY
O. Demus: *The Church of San Marco in Venice: History, Architecture, Sculpture* (Washington, DC, 1960), pp. 109–90

W. Wolters, ed.: *Die Skulpturen von San Marco in Venedig: Die figürlichen Skulpturen der Aussenfassaden bis zum 14. Jahrhundert* (Berlin, 1979)
R. Polacco: 'Le colonne del ciborio di S Marco', *Venezia A.*, i (1987), pp. 32–8

ROBERTO CORONEO

(iii) Mosaics. Executed over 200 years, from the late 11th century to the end of the 13th (with extensive later additions, replacements and repairs), the wall mosaics of S Marco constitute the most extensive and comprehensive mosaic programme in existence. While only about one-third of the surface is original, later restorers were generally faithful to the medieval compositions, and approximately three-quarters of the programme survives, at least indirectly. The work of successive groups of craftsmen, some Greek or Greek-trained, others local, the mosaics are nonetheless remarkably homogeneous. To a great extent, they reflect Venice's attempts to establish its political and ecclesiastic status.

Three principal phases can be discerned in the decorations: the central doorway and the main apse, with its emphasis on St Mark, represents the initial undertaking; a second phase comprises the vast 12th-century programme in the five domes and interior vaults; while the final phase includes the atrium decoration, carried out after the capture of Constantinople in 1204. Later work includes the decoration of the baptistery and various chapels.

(a) Central door and main apse. (b) Domes and interior vaults. (c) Narthex and façade. (d) Later work. (e) Pavement.

(a) Central door and main apse. The earliest surviving mosaics in the church, attributable to the last three decades

of the 11th century, decorate the arches above (*Virgin and Child* and *Apostles*) and at either side (the *Evangelists*) of the central door of the narthex. They seem to be the work of mosaicists from Constantinople who had been engaged in other projects in the Veneto, including perhaps the apse of Torcello Cathedral. The mosaics of the main apse of S Marco were also begun at this time. The conch bears *Christ Pantokrator*, a replacement of 1506 that may be a faithful copy of the original subject. Below are four Venetian patron saints whose relics were treasured in the church: the titular saint, Mark, portrayed in a frontal pose; St Peter, who according to legend had requested Mark to write his Gospel; St Hermagoras, the Evangelist's first disciple and the first bishop of Aquileia-Grado; and St Nicholas, the patron of the Venetian fleet. Although datable to the 11th century, the figures of SS Peter and

Nicholas are by a team from the Greek East, different from that responsible for the mosaics flanking the door. The other two figures were evidently executed by another mosaicist after the fire of 1106, and they show greater monumentality and softness of expression.

(b) Domes and interior vaults. The decorative programme of the main church was, like the architecture, based generally on Justinian's church of the Holy Apostles in Constantinople (destr.). The depiction of *Christ Pantokrator* in the apse rather than the apex of the central dome as in the Holy Apostles and most other Byzantine churches had repercussions throughout the interior that generally reinforced an overall shift of focus to the east end. *Christ Emmanuel* was introduced into the eastern dome, while the *Ascension* occupied the usual place of the

16. Mosaic of *Christ Emmanuel, the Virgin and Prophets* (12th century; rest. *c.* 1500), east dome, S Marco, Venice

17. Mosaic of *Venetians Praying for the Discovery of the Relics of St Mark* (1250s), west wall of the south transept, S Marco, Venice

Pantokrator in the central cupola, undoubtedly because the feast of the Ascension (the *sensa*) was the most important Venetian state celebration. *Pentecost* remained in the west dome over the nave, as in the Holy Apostles, with apostolic missionary activities depicted on the vaults below.

Work began in the east cupola but was interrupted at some stage after 1150 by a disaster, possibly an earthquake. The mosaics are therefore not homogeneous. The central medallion contains a half-length figure of *Christ Emmanuel* (mostly renewed *c*. 1500 after a fire) surrounded by standing figures in a radial arrangement, representing the Virgin and 12 prophets (see fig. 16). Four of the prophets (Jeremiah, Daniel, Obadiah and Habakkuk) continue the early 12th-century style of the main apse, although the Byzantine conventions have become exaggerated and infiltrated by such local features as hard, linear forms and juxtaposed contrasting colours. The Virgin and the other prophets are executed in the 'dynamic' style characteristic of the 1170s, with agitated drapery and intricate surface patterning; although they show familiarity with contemporary Byzantine art, they are distinctly Venetian in character.

The same style—a blend of Byzantine, Venetian and Western elements—is continued in the central dome of the *Ascension*, perhaps the most harmonious composition in the church. Although Byzantine in composition, the *Ascension* includes such Latin elements as SS Paul and

Mark among the Apostles and personifications of Virtues and Beatitudes between the windows.

The *Pentecost* dome has none of the rhythmical refinements of the *Ascension* and must date before the break in work in the mid-12th century. Its schematic interpretation of Byzantine sources, such as the monumental seated Apostles, suggests that it was the product of local workmen following Greek models. It is enlivened, however, by the interest in exotic types in the paired figures representing the Nations between the windows.

The programmes of the transept cupolas are independent of the main, Byzantine-derived scheme and belong instead to the imagery of their related chapels. The north dome, dedicated to St John the Evangelist, shows the Evangelist in prayer with five scenes from his life, while the south dome bears standing figures of SS Nicholas, Clement, Leonard and Blaise, all Venetian patron saints. Probably dating from the second quarter of the 12th century, the lateral cupolas reflect the more schematic style of local mosaicists.

Much the same Venetian transformation of Byzantine conventions can be detected in the slightly earlier decorations of the two choir chapels flanking the east dome, dedicated respectively to St Peter and St Clement. Planned together, these mosaics emphasize the roles of Church and State by focusing on two aspects of the legend of St Mark. The vaults and upper walls of the chapel of St Peter bear scenes from the *Life of St Mark*, beginning with his consecration by St Peter, the Prince of Apostles, and ending with his death and burial. Their counterparts in the south chapel trace the Venetian role in the story with the recovery of St Mark's relics in Muslim Alexandria and their translation to Venice.

Closely related in style to the mosaics of the St Peter Chapel are the scenes from the *Life of Christ* decorating the great arch separating the central and south domes. The modelling is more robust than in the choir chapel mosaics, however, and may reflect stronger Byzantine influence. The poorly preserved *Miracles of Christ* (some destr.) in and around the chapels of both north and south transept seem to have been produced during the second quarter of the 12th century. The mechanical, dull rendering of the *Life of the Virgin* and the *Infancy of Christ* in the western bays of the transepts are later, probably dating from the very end of the 12th century. A similar date probably also applies to the scenes showing a miracle and the death or burial of each of the 12 Apostles, appropriately depicted on the lateral vaults beneath the *Pentecost* dome (north side replaced 1619–24).

The removal of the galleries over the aisles of the cross arms rendered large flat surfaces visible from the ground; from the start of the 13th century, these were covered with mosaic. The spectacular *Agony in the Garden* on the south wall of the west arm was produced between 1215 and 1225. Although the mosaicists were probably Venetians, the panel reveals an acquaintance with the new, monumental style of Constantinople acquired either through travel or by means of model books in the period immediately after the conquest of the city. Despite many awkward, even rigid passages, the figures convey a monumental quality that is entirely lacking in the immediately preceding works. Although by different artists, the separate panels on the north and south walls of the west arm portraying Christ and the Virgin, each flanked by four prophets, were influenced by the *Agony in the Garden* and probably date from *c.* 1220–25. The *Venetians Praying for the Discovery of the Relics of St Mark* (see fig. 17) and the *Miraculous Appearance of the Relics in 1094* on the west wall of the south transept, dating from the 1250s, present a ceremonial portrait of the important figures in contemporary Venetian society. In the latest interior decoration, *Christ Enthroned between the Virgin and St Mark* above the main door of the west wall, Byzantine influence re-emerges, not only in the theme, which is based on the Deesis (Christ with the Virgin and St John the Baptist), but also in the emphatic modelling.

(c) Narthex and façade. The influx of wealth from occupied Constantinople, including 'much mosaic to adorn the church of S Marco' (Demus, ii, p. 229, n. 7), enabled the Venetians to decorate the narthex during the second and third quarters of the 13th century. The emphasis here is on historical narrative, in contrast to the hierarchical Byzantine schemes of the interior. Accented by portraits of prophets and saints and by other figures, the mosaics show over 125 episodes from Genesis and Exodus (see fig. 18). The programme may reflect a Venetian response to Old Testament cycles in both fresco and

18. Mosaic of *Noah Guiding the Birds into the Ark* (13th century), narthex, south vault of the entrance bay, S Marco, Venice

mosaic in the Early Christian basilicas of Rome and in the 12th-century Norman churches of Sicily, but the models were Greek. The images adhere closely to those in the late 5th-century COTTON GENESIS (partly destr.; London, BL, MS. Cotton Otho B. VI), although costumes and superficial details are updated. For the scenes from the *Life of Moses*, the mosaicists seem to have used a contemporary illuminated Byzantine Octateuch. The emphasis on Joseph and Moses in the cycle may reflect a desire to emphasize St Mark's connection with Egypt.

Soon after the narthex was completed, some of the mosaicists decorated the vaults of the south-west entrance hall (now Cappella Zen). The cycle dedicated to the *Life of St Mark* repeats episodes already represented in the north transept, but it amplifies the narrative to underscore Venice's divine right to the relics. The story was continued on the façade of the church: the *Translation of the Relics* was depicted in the lower lunettes and the *Deposition, Harrowing of Hell, Resurrection* and *Ascension* were shown in the upper ones. Only the first is preserved (north doorway); the other scenes can be glimpsed in Gentile Bellini's *Procession in Piazza San Marco* (1496; see fig. 26 below).

(d) Later work. Although the main programmes were completed by the end of the 13th century, work still continued in S Marco. In the 1340s the mosaics of the baptistery and chapel of S Isidoro were commissioned by Doge ANDREA DANDOLO. The former mostly bear scenes from the *Life of St John the Baptist* and show the influence of contemporary Venetian painting, while the latter depict events from the *Life of St Isidore* and the *Translation of his Relics to Venice*. From *c.*1430 to 1451 the north transept chapel of the Madonna dei Mascoli was decorated with mosaics depicting the *Life of the Virgin*, with designs prepared by Venetian and Tuscan artists, such as MICHELE GIAMBONO and ANDREA DEL CASTAGNO.

Fire necessitated extensive repairs as early as the 15th century, but restorations of this period, for example the *Christ Pantokrator* of the main apse (1506), were undoubtedly generally faithful to the medieval mosaics they replaced. The mosaics produced by the great Venetian painters such as Giuseppe Salviati, Jacopo Tintoretto, Titian and Veronese (e.g. north transept *Miracles of Christ*), on the other hand, were new creations; and many were commissioned explicitly to replace the older works, now considered ugly. The so-called restorations of the 18th and 19th centuries were almost as detrimental to the medieval works; and it was only during the 20th century that scientific techniques and research began to protect the mosaics and permit their study.

(e) Pavement. The fine polychrome mosaic pavement, largely composed of spolia (marble, porphyry etc), has been much restored, but it is essentially 12th century in date and is related to the pavement of SS Maria e Donato, Murano (1141). The emphasis is on geometric motifs, with some peacocks, heraldic animals in circles and confronted birds and beasts; foliate decoration is confined to the borders and isolated panels. The interlaced circles are of Byzantine derivation, but the other compositions and decorative motifs are closer to western sources.

BIBLIOGRAPHY

O. Demus: *The Mosaics of San Marco in Venice*, 4 vols (Chicago, 1984)
X. Barral i Altet: *Les Mosaïques de pavement médiévales de Venise, Murano, Torcello* (Paris, 1985)
O. Demus: *The Medieval Mosaics of San Marco, Venice: A Color Archive* (Chicago and London, 1986) [microfiche]

HERBERT L. KESSLER

(iv) Treasury. The collection of objects housed in the Treasury has its origins in the booty from the sack of Constantinople in 1204, although some of this must have been damaged or destroyed in a fire in 1230. Numerous items were later added to the Treasury's holdings and, despite the melting down of many precious objects in 1797, it still contains the most important assemblage of Byzantine work in precious metals in existence. The first inventory of the Treasury dates from 1283 and lists 41 items or groups of objects, including 8 relics; several of the textiles mentioned have not survived, such as the red flag of St Mark carried by the Doge on the *Bucentaur*, the state barge. The next inventory (1325) is much fuller and indicates a substantial increase in the number of acquisitions. Successive inventories from the 15th century also reflect the Treasury's continuing growth. The current catalogue (1971) contains 294 entries, including objects of ancient Egyptian (from the 3rd millennium BC onwards), Roman and Islamic origin, numerous works in precious metals made up to the 19th century, rock-crystal and glass, 3 painted polyptychs and a number of tapestries and other textiles.

The most highly prized items in the original group of objects from Constantinople would have been gold and

19. Venice, Treasury of S Marco, Byzantine icon of the *Archangel Michael*, gems, gold and enamel in relief, 460×350 mm, 11th century (with some later additions)

silver reliquaries containing some of the most venerated relics. That five of these survived the fire of 1230 is clear from their depiction in a 14th-century marble relief (see Hahnloser, pl. cxviii, no. 71) on the exterior. Other items in this group include gold or silver-gilt and enamel icons, chalices, book covers and a votive crown, as well as secular vessels of onyx, agate and glass (*see* EARLY CHRISTIAN AND BYZANTINE ART, fig. 79) and objects in rock-crystal and marble. Although looted from Constantinople, not all these items were made there, and it is evident that some were imported from elsewhere in the Mediterranean.

Among the most remarkable surviving Byzantine works in precious metal are the post-9th century icon of the *Virgin Nikopoia*, surrounded by a frame of 16 Byzantine enamels of later date; two gold and enamel icons in relief of the *Archangel Michael*, one full-length (see fig. 19) and one half-length (both 11th century, some later additions); ten chalices made from antique hardstone vessels with Byzantine silver-gilt and enamel mounts of the 10th–12th centuries, two of which have inscriptions referring to a Byzantine emperor named Romanos; gold and enamel book covers of the 9th, 10th and 14th centuries; and a votive crown (*see* EARLY CHRISTIAN AND BYZANTINE ART, fig. 89) belonging to Leo VI (*reg* 886–912) of silver-gilt and enamel, which is the only surviving example of a type otherwise known only from texts.

Besides Byzantine artefacts, the Treasury contains numerous examples of Venetian goldsmiths' work that reflect the development of artistic life in the Republic, including several items displaying gold filigree, which was applied to a variety of objects, such as a series of reliquaries (14th–19th centuries) and a silver-gilt antependium of Pope Gregory XII (1406–8). There are also many items made by goldsmiths from other parts of Italy and from France. In addition the Treasury contains 13 ancient Islamic objects: several, such as the chalice formed from a green glass bowl, have been converted to Christian use. Persian carpets and a number of 15th- and 16th-century north European tapestries are among the finest textiles in the Treasury.

BIBLIOGRAPHY

A. Pasini: *Il tesoro di San Marco in Venezia*, 2 vols (Venice, 1885–6)
E. Molinier: *Le Trésor de la basilique de Saint-Marc à Venise* (Venice, 1888)
R. Gallo: *Il tesoro di San Marco e la sua storia* (Venice and Rome, 1967)
H. R. Hahnloser, ed.: *Il tesoro e il museo* (1971), ii of *Il tesoro di San Marco* (Florence, 1965–71)

(*v*) *Pala d'Oro*. A uniquely rich altarpiece of 187 enamel plaques and 1927 gems mounted in a rectangular gilt frame (see fig. 20). The first Pala d'Oro of which there is documentary evidence was commissioned in 976 from workshops in Constantinople by Doge Pietro I Orseolo; it is uncertain which, if any, of the enamels now on the altarpiece survive from that work. The present altarpiece has a 14th-century inscription, according to which a second version was commissioned by Doge Ordelafo Falier (*reg* 1102–18) and completed in 1105; this in turn was renovated in 1209 under Doge Pietro Ziani (*reg* 1205–29). In 1342–5, under Doge Andrea Dandolo, the altarpiece was completely remade and given its present form. Gems are mentioned in the 1105 and 1345 renovations. At the same time a wooden cover (Venice, Mus. S Marco) was painted with scenes from the *Life of St Mark* by Paolo Veneziano. While the Gothic style of the last renovation is clear, no consensus has been reached as to which enamels relate to which renovation, nor even which were made especially for the altarpiece.

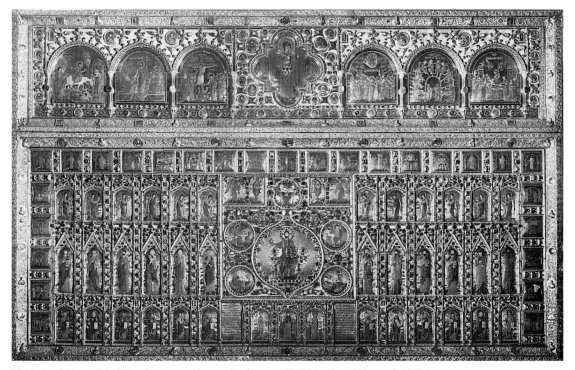

20. Venice, S Marco, Pala d'Oro altarpiece, gold, enamel and gems, 2.12×3.34 m, ? AD 976, remade 1342–5

The altarpiece is divided horizontally into two parts. The upper is the more simple in design and consists principally of six large arcuated enamels showing the last six scenes of the *Twelve Feasts*. These enamels clearly form part of a set and may have been taken from the templon of the church of the Pantokrator in Constantinople. They are placed symmetrically either side of a large quatrefoil enamel plaque of *St Michael the Archangel*; all seven plaques are certainly Byzantine work of the 12th century.

In the centre of the lower part is a large enamel of *Christ Enthroned*, surrounded by the four *Evangelists* and with the Hetoimasia and cherubim above; to either side are twelve tall rectangular plaques of standing *Apostles*, with twelve arcuated plaques of *Archangels* above them. Below, twelve plaques of standing *Prophets* are arranged either side of three figural plaques and two others with the 14th-century inscription. The three plaques include portraits of a Byzantine empress named in Greek as *Eirene*, probably the wife of Alexios I Komnenos (*reg* 1081–1118), and of a figure named in Latin as *Doge Ordelafo Falier*. These most probably came from the 1105 renovation, and if so there would also have been a portrait of Alexios I himself, which was probably removed in 1209. The top row of this lower part consists of seventeen square plaques of scenes from the *Life of Christ* flanked by standing portraits of six *Deacon Saints*. Ten square plaques with scenes from the *Life of St Mark* are distributed down each side of the frame. These, with the *Christological Scenes*, *Deacons* and several of the *Prophets*, all have Latin inscriptions. There are 101 further small plaques distributed over the whole altarpiece.

BIBLIOGRAPHY
H. R. Hahnloser, ed.: *Il tesoro di San Marco: La Pala d'Oro* (Florence, 1965) [full bibliog. and illus.]
G. Lorenzoni: *La Pala d'Oro di San Marco* (Florence, 1965)
J. de Luigi-Pomorisac: *Les Emaux byzantins de la Pala d'Oro de l'Eglise de Saint Marc à Venise*, 2 vols (Zurich, 1966)
R. Gallo: *Il tesoro di San Marco e la sua storia* (Venice and Rome, 1967)
J. Déer: 'Die Pala d'Oro in neuer Sicht', *Byz. Z.*, lxii (1969), pp. 308–44
M. Frazer: 'The Pala d'Oro and the Cult of St Mark in Venice', *Jb. Österreich. Byz. Ges.*, xxxii (1982), pp. 273–9

PAUL HETHERINGTON

2. S GIORGIO MAGGIORE. The Benedictine monastery, located opposite the Doge's Palace on the island of S Giorgio (see fig. 1 above), was founded in 982. The present church, begun by ANDREA PALLADIO in 1566, was the fifth on the site according to Francesco Sansovino, replacing one consecrated in 1419. When Venice was occupied by Napoleon in 1797 the monastery became a garrison for French, and later Austrian, troops whose tenure damaged the buildings. The library, archive and most portable works of art were removed from the island and never fully restituted. Restored to the Benedictines, the church was reconsecrated in 1808. The monastery has been physically rehabilitated through the benefaction of Conte Vittorio Cini, whose Fondazione Giorgio Cini, which supports the arts and humanities, was established in the monastery in 1951.

(i) Architecture. (ii) Decoration.

(i) Architecture. The main period of work on the monastic buildings was during the 16th century, although according to Vasari the first library (destr.) was constructed in 1433 by Michelozzo. The dormitory, completed by Giovanni Buora around 1513 and situated behind the east end of the old church, has a tripartite semicircular arched façade in the Lombard–Venetian style facing the Riva degli Schiavoni. The cloister of the Laurels was begun *c.* 1516 by Buora's son, Andrea (*d c.* 1556), and, with a new chapter house, was completed in the late 1530s. Work on a new refectory was initiated in the 1540s but was delayed until 1560 when Palladio's presence at the monastery was first recorded on 3 July. In two years Palladio had completed the structure, which was composed of an anteroom, stairway and barrel-vaulted hall including three large thermal windows (since blocked)

In 1565 Palladio made a wood model (untraced) for a new church. The cruciform plan incorporates a spacious barrel-vaulted nave with a domical crossing, an enlarged transept (to accommodate the participants in the rituals for the feast of St Stephen, co-titular saint of the church) and an elongated apsidal choir behind the presbytery. The interior elevation consists of a monumental Composite order of engaged columns and pilasters raised on pedestals, carrying an imposing entablature, applied to a brick fabric covered in white stucco and illuminated by thermal windows. The church, including the quadrangular space of the presbytery but not the apsidal choir, was completed under Palladio's supervision in 1575. A year after Palladio's death in 1580, the church was in use. Construction on the apsidal choir was in progress by 1583 and completed by 1589. It has been proposed that the elongated apse, separating the choir entirely from the presbytery, was the result of a new plan by Palladio for the church and monastery, coinciding with the 1579 initiation of the cloister of the Cypresses (Isermeyer). The relation of the executed façade (see fig. 21) to Palladio's designs has been the source of much discussion (Cooper). Istrian stone was first collected for the façade in 1597, and work was begun in 1599 but was not completed until 1610. A monumental

21. Venice, S Giorgio Maggiore, by Andrea Palladio, 1566–75; façade 1599–1610

Composite order on high pedestals supports a pediment crowning the nave; this is interlocked with a lower, horizontal temple front, which coincides with the aisles. Below this, single-storey Corinthian pilasters frame triangular pedimented aedicules containing sculptural decoration celebrating the history of the church.

(ii) Decoration. The principal decoration for the refectory, the monumental *Marriage at Cana* (6.69×9.90 m; Paris, Louvre), was commissioned in 1562 from Paolo Veronese and finished in 1563. An extensive campaign of decoration on the church was undertaken in the 1590s, employing some of the leading artists of Venice. Work on the two-tier ornamented, walnut choir-stalls was begun in 1594 by Gasparo de' Gatti. Forty-eight panels in high relief narrating the *Life and Miracles of St Benedict* are inscribed and dated 1598 by the Flemish sculptor Albert van der Brulle. The high altar (1592–4) by Girolamo Campagna, after a design by Antonio Vassilacchi, is a singular example for this date of a freestanding tabernacle with a bronze figural group (*God the Father on the Globe of the World Supported by the Four Evangelists; see* CAMPAGNA, GIROLAMO, fig. 2). It is flanked in the presbytery by two contemporary *laterali* (1590–4) by Jacopo Tintoretto, the *Gathering of the Manna* and the *Last Supper,* completing a eucharistic cycle. Jacopo, his son Domenico and their workshop completed a number of altarpieces that fill marble frames designed by Palladio, including the *Resurrection with St Andrew, Vincenzo Morosini and his Family* (accompanied by busts from the workshop of Alessandro Vittoria), the *Coronation of the Virgin with SS Benedict, Gregory, Maurus and Placidus* and the *Martyrdom of St Stephen,* as well as one of Jacopo's final works, the *Entombment* (1594) in the chapel of the Dead. One of the last works of Jacopo Bassano, the *Adoration of the Shepherds* (before 1592), is sited across the nave from his son Leandro's *Miracle of the Immobility of St Lucy* (1596). In the nave, Campagna's marble *Virgin and Child with Angels* faces a 15th-century polychrome wooden *Crucifixion,* which survives from the earlier church. Sebastiano Ricci's altarpiece of the *Virgin and Child with Saints* (1708) was a later addition. In the 17th century Baldassare Longhena headed major projects, which included several altars in the church, a monumental staircase (1643–5) and a new library (begun 1641) situated between the cloisters, for which the allegorical cycle of the *Triumph of Wisdom* (by 1664–8) was painted by Giovanni Coli and Filippo Gherardi.

BIBLIOGRAPHY

F. Sansovino: *Venetia, città nobilissima et singolare* (Venice, 1581; ed. G. Martinioni, Venice, 1663)

E. Cicogna: *Delle iscrizioni veneziane,* iv (Venice, 1834/R Bologna, 1969)

G. Damerini: *L'isola e il cenobio di San Giorgio Maggiore* (Venice, 1956)

C.-A. Isermeyer: 'Il primo progetto del Palladio per S Giorgio secondo il modello del 1565', *Boll. Cent. Int. Stud. Archit. Andrea Palladio,* xxii (1980), pp. 259–68

T. E. Cooper: *The History and Decoration of the Church of San Giorgio Maggiore in Venice* (diss., Princeton U., NJ, 1990) [extensive bibliog.]

TRACY E. COOPER

3. SS GIOVANNI E PAOLO. The principal Dominican church in Venice, also known as S Zanipolo. The Dominicans were granted a site in Venice in 1234 by Doge Jacopo Tiepolo (*reg* 1229–49). The first church, of which no trace survives, was constructed by 1293 and had already been

22. Venice, SS Giovanni e Paolo, begun 1333–4

chosen by several doges, including Ranier Zeno (*reg* 1253–68) and both Jacopo and Lorenzo Tiepolo (*reg* 1268–75), as their place of burial. In 1333–4 fund-raising began for a new church, which was consecrated in 1430. The building takes the form of a basilica, laid out on a Latin cross plan with a five-bay nave flanked by aisles, a domed crossing and five contiguous apsed chapels at the east end. Work had reached the crossing by 1368—the date inscribed on the transverse arch of the north transept.

As early as 1362 the tomb of *Doge Giovanni Dolfin* (*reg* 1356–61) was located on the south wall of the presbytery, followed by the adjacent tomb (*c.* 1368) of *Doge Marco Cornaro* (*reg* 1365–8), for which Nino Pisano carved a *Virgin and Child.* The most splendid of the presbytery monuments is that of *Doge Michele Morosini* (*reg* 1382), combining mosaic, sculpture and fresco. In 1390 the State contributed 10,000 ducats towards the building of the church and the construction of the chapel of S Domenico (now del Rosario). The church roof was complete by 1417, while between 1420 and 1430 the monks' choir and the organ loft (dismantled 1690) were raised in the fifth bay of the nave. The earliest side chapel, begun 1448, was that of S Lodovico Bertrando (now of the Addolorata), designed in an elegant Gothic style that is visible in the linear complexities of the windows and the terracotta ornament under the eaves. In 1458 the main portal was redesigned (see fig. 22), with the addition of a cluster of non-structural columns (purchased from the church of S Andrea di Torcello) in the manner of the portals of S Marco, or of the Arco Foscari at the Doge's Palace (see fig. 24 below). Bartolomeo Buon (i) supervised the work, which partly obscured the previous Gothic arcuated façade. Precocious classical elements such as a cornice and frieze, and volutes within the Gothic foliage of the capitals, indicate that carvers from both Florence and Milan were involved in the project, which was complete by 1464. Later in the decade Pietro Lombardo executed the tomb of *Doge Pasquale Malipiero,* followed by his masterpiece, the tomb of *Doge Pietro Mocenigo.* By the end of the century a further Renaissance element was added: the hemispherical dome over the crossing, already visible in Jacopo de' Barbari's aerial view of Venice of *c.* 1500 (see fig. 1 above).

In the first decade of the 16th century the decision was taken to designate SS Giovanni e Paolo a pantheon for the condottieri Dionigi Naldo da Brisighella, Nicolò Orsini and Leonardo da Prato, heroes of the League of Cambrai War (1508–16). The theme is echoed in the lowest register of the stained-glass window in the right transept, where the soldier saints Theodore and George are depicted, together with SS John and Paul. Although warriors' tombs (e.g. that of *Jacopo Cavalli, d* 1384) had existed in the church from the 14th century, Verrocchio's equestrian bronze statue of *Bartolomeo Colleoni* (*see* VERROCCHIO, ANDREA DEL, fig. 4), erected in 1494 in front of the church, may have provided a more immediate stimulus for this decision. The tradition of commemorating military heroes in this church was continued in the following centuries. In the same spirit, the sculptor and architect Alessandro Vittoria supervised the building and redecoration of the chapel of the Rosary (1582–1608) to honour the victory of the Battle of Lepanto (1571). The chapel, together with paintings by Vittoria's contemporaries and altarpieces by Titian and Giovanni Bellini, was burnt down in 1867 (reopened in 1959). Meanwhile massive late Renaissance tombs by Girolamo Grapiglia (*fl* 1572–1621) were built for the doges *Leonardo Loredan* and *Alvise Mocenigo* in the presbytery and on the west wall respectively.

The church and monastery underwent several alterations in the Baroque period. Lunette windows were inserted in the south aisle and façade. In 1639 the chapel of the Addolorata was redecorated. Between 1638 and 1663 the main altar was built by Baldassare Longhena, who later worked extensively at the monastery, redesigning the cloisters, dormitory, staircase (1664), library (opened 1683) and refectory (which contained Paolo Veronese's *Feast in the House of Levi*, 1573; Venice, Accad.; *see* VERONESE, PAOLO, fig. 4). Andrea Tirali (*c.* 1660–1737) built the chapel of S Domenico after 1705; it was sumptuously decorated by Giuseppe Mazza, Giovanni Battista Piazzetta and Francesco Bernardoni (*fl* early 18th century). In 1705–8 Tirali also built the massive *Valier* family monument in the south aisle.

In 1809 the monastery and the adjacent Scuola di S Marco were transformed into a military hospital during the second French occupation of Venice. Following Napoleon's suppression of such churches as S Marina and S Maria dei Servi, several monuments, including the tomb of *Doge Andrea Vendramin* by Tullio Lombardo (1488–94; for illustration *see* LOMBARDO, (2)), were relocated to SS Giovanni e Paolo. Various changes were made to the fenestration. The 17th-century lunettes in the south aisle were altered in the 19th century to neo-Gothic triple windows. In 1922, during repairs to the church after damage in World War I, the two small round windows were restored to the façade, while the present lateral windows (imitating the original two-light windows at clerestory level) were inserted along the aisle.

BIBLIOGRAPHY

F. Z. Boccazzi: *La basilica dei Santi Giovanni e Paolo in Venice* (Venice, 1965) [with bibliog.]

H. Dellwing: *Studien zur Baukunst der Bettelorden im Veneto* (Munich, 1970)

L. Puppi: *La grande vetrata della basilica di San Giovanni e Paolo* (Venice, 1985)

L. Moretti: 'Notizie e appunti su G. B. Piazzetta: Alcuni Piazzetteschi e G. B. Tiepolo', *Atti Ist. Ven. Sci., Lett. &A.*, cxlviii (1985–6), pp. 195–209

C. R. Puglisi: 'The Cappella di San Domenico in Santi Giovanni e Paolo', *A. Ven.*, xl (1986), pp. 230–8

PHILIP RYLANDS

4. S MARIA GLORIOSA DEI FRARI. The visually coherent Franciscan church belies a complex history of construction that spanned nearly 200 years. In the second quarter of the 13th century the Order received an abandoned Benedictine abbey from Doge Jacopo Tiepolo (*reg* 1229–49), who agreed to reconstruction and improvements on the site near the canal of the Frari ('brothers'). Despite three distinct building phases, the church and its two attached cloisters preserve the simplicity that is attributed to a design of Nicola Pisano (Vasari).

The building was begun in 1250; by 1280 the first Gothic structure, a hall church with an aisleless nave, suitable for preaching, was complete. Sixty years later, the prosperous Franciscans had so increased their following that they required a larger, more ambitious structure with arcaded aisles. In 1340, aided by patrons of the Gradenigo, Giustiani and Savelli families, they began a new church adjacent to the still functioning older building. Jacopo Celega (*d* before 30 March 1386), the architect of the imposing campanile, began work in 1361 and may have supervised the entire second construction. Records show that his son, Pietro Paolo (*d* 2 May 1417), was still working on the project in 1396 when the campanile, one of the highest in Venice, was completed and the lead roof installed. In the early 15th century, the friars engaged builders to complete the new church, in particular the last three bays towards the present entrance façade. With minor changes, the style and spirit of the 1340 design were continued. The older church was demolished in 1415 as the new one neared completion. At approximately the same time, large altars and sepulchral monuments were placed along the aisle walls between the windows, obliterating a wealth of 14th-century frescoes. The aesthetics of the interior also suffered from the inclusion of tie-beams across the nave and between the arcade arches; this distracting maze of wood was an essential addition to counter potential damage occasioned by the settling of the church's pilings in the lagoon mud.

The present cruciform church comprises a vaulted nave with massive columns dividing it from the aisles. Nearly all the window and door openings rise to pointed arches, with only a few openings in the upper parts indicating the later preference for round-headed arches. On the façade, small round windows, symmetrically placed, echo the large rose window. The original designer confined exterior decoration to discreet blind arcading at the upper edge of the brick walls. During the Renaissance phase, sections of ornamental brick serving to heighten the structure were added at the top of the façade, as were the three airy, decorative, finial forms placed above them. These find visual consonance with those above the left side entrance, a form that acts as a buttressing mass for the campanile. The later ornamental additions do not depart significantly from the style of the earlier church, thus ensuring the coherence of the exterior design.

One of the greatest architectural glories of the church is the octagonal apse with multi-level, bifurcated glass and carved, wooden altar screen, a rare inclusion in an Italian church. The large, round-arched opening of the screen frames the high altar, above which is the *Assumption of the Virgin* (1518) by Titian, a large, dramatic composition manifesting the theme of the church's name, which was commissioned by Father Germano, a prior of the Frari monastery. Carved stone sculptures by Pietro Lombardo complete the decorative programme of the apse. The vast transept area, of equal length to the nave, contains six unusually shaped chapels, three on either side of the main altar space. The plan of each chapel terminates in a point, thus creating a lively exterior line at the east end. Venetian confraternities and nobility hired artists to decorate individual chapels. In a left aisle chapel, the Pesaro family commissioned a painting by Titian, now known as the Pesaro *Madonna* (1519–26). In the nave, immediately preceding the transept, is a three-tiered wooden choir-stall carved in 1468 by the Venetian Marco Cozzi (*d* 1485), a commission of the Correr family. Among the other well-known monuments and works of art in the church are the tombs of *Titian* (1838–52) by Pietro and Luigi Zandomeneghi, of *Doge Francesco Foscari* by Antonio and Paulo Bregno (*c*. 1460; for illustration *see* BREGNO, (1)) and of *Doge Nicolò Tron* (*c*. 1476–80; for illustration *see* RIZZO, ANTONIO), a triptych (1488) by Giovanni Bellini and a wooden statue of *John the Baptist* (1438) by Donatello.

BIBLIOGRAPHY
J. White: *Art and Architecture in Italy*, Pelican Hist. A. (Harmondsworth, 1966)
U. Franzoi and D. di Stefano: *Le chiese di Venezia* (Venice, 1976)

PHILANCY N. HOLDER

5. S MARIA DELLA SALUTE. The principle Baroque church in Venice (*see* ITALY, fig. 19), the Salute is the magnum opus of architect BALDASSARE LONGHENA. A severe plague struck Venice in the summer of 1630 and led to a decree of the Venetian Senate on 22 October 1630 commissioning a votive church dedicated to the Virgin. Longhena, then aged 33, won the subsequent competition (1631) with a model that has not survived. On 9 November 1687, over five years after Longhena's death, the Salute was finally consecrated and the Festa della Salute (still celebrated today on 21 Nov) was instituted as a major religious festival, with important consequences for musical patronage. At a time of hostility between Venice and the Papacy, the scale of the Salute and its prominent site was an affirmation of the power and autonomy (the *salute*) of the Venetian Church.

The plan consists of a domed octagon, with an engaged chancel also covered by a dome followed by a rectangular choir—a combination probably derived from Michele Sanmicheli's Madonna di Campagna, Verona (begun 1559). The choice of a central plan recalls Palladio's first project for the earlier plague church in Venice, the Redentore (begun 1577). For the Salute, Longhena had in mind the metaphor of the Virgin's crown, identifying her as the Queen of Heaven. Accordingly, careful attention was paid to lighting in the church. One theatrical effect is

now lost: the admission of bright sunlight from a window (now closed) in the south wall of the choir behind the Virgin on the high altar where, in Josse de Corte's sculptural *tableau vivant*, she casts out the plague. Like Palladio, Longhena united distinct areas within the church by controlling the spectator's views, both down the axis (beginning with the view from the Grand Canal) and from the centre of the octagon. To this end, he designed wedge-shaped octagonal piers that align with the walls of the side chapels across the ambulatory. He also created sequences of columnar orders, round arches and coloured patterns in vistas. The spaces are thus revealed sequentially rather than instantaneously, an important distinction between the Baroque architecture of Venice and Rome. The scenographic element in the Salute, where the beholder's view is drawn through a succession of arches towards the spiritual centre of the church, together with other details, e.g. the choice of sculpture over the high altar and the absence of polychrome marble in favour of the simple contrast between plaster and stone, all derive from Palladio. So, too, does the rigid application of arithmetical proportions to the volumes and distances.

The exterior of S Maria della Salute owes its sculptural impact to the massing of forceful architectural components, e.g. the major and minor cupolas, the high twin towers, the huge main door and the massive whorls of the buttresses. The chapels which project at either side of the main entrance are treated as façades in their own right. Designed at a time when Bernini and Borromini were still at the beginning of their careers, the Salute ranks among Italy's earliest important Baroque buildings.

BIBLIOGRAPHY
G. Moschini: *La chiesa e il seminario di S Maria della Salute* (Venice, 1842)
V. Piva: *Il tempio della Salute eretto per voto della repubblica veneta* (Venice, 1930)
R. Wittkower: 'Santa Maria della Salute: Scenographic Architecture and the Venetian Baroque', *J. Soc. Archit. Historians*, xvi (1957), pp. 3–10
E. Bassi: *Architettura del sei e settecento a Venezia* (Naples, 1962)
C. Semenzato: *La scultura veneta nel seicento e settecento* (Venice, 1967)
M. Muraro: 'Iconografia e ideologia del tempio della Salute a Venezia', *Barocco fra Italia e Polonia*, ed. J. Slaski (Venice, 1974), pp. 71–9
R. Wittkower: *Studies in the Italian Baroque* (London, 1975), pp. 125–52
L. Puppi: *Longhena* (Milan, 1982)

PHILIP RYLANDS

6. DOGE'S PALACE.

(i) Architecture and sculpture. (ii) Painting and decoration.

(i) Architecture and sculpture. The palace, situated in the Piazzetta between S Marco and the Grand Canal, was rebuilt and remodelled repeatedly during its history, as is reflected in its mixture of Byzantine, Gothic and Renaissance features. The present building, constructed largely in the 14th and 15th centuries, replaced a 9th-century fortified castle on the same site. The new structure was to serve both as the official residence of the doge and as the seat of government, a dual purpose that influenced every aspect of the building, including the style and iconography of its decoration. In a city the very existence of which depended upon the balance of commercial and diplomatic ties with both the Near East and western Europe, the palace was designed to serve both practical and diplomatic purposes, by flattering and overwhelming its visitors and at the same time instructing them on the unique qualities of the city they were visiting. The unknown architects who

23. Venice, Doge's Palace, main façade, begun *c.* 1340

began the reconstruction of the building designed it as a replica of a Byzantine palace in order to impress visitors from Constantinople.

The Byzantine source of the design partly explains the strangely top-heavy structure, with a loggia and delicately traceried gallery appearing to support the solid walls of the upper storeys. The main façade facing the Grand Canal (begun *c.* 1340) has an arcade composed of 36 short, thick columns, above which 71 columns form a gallery (see fig. 23). The shapes of the arcade and gallery arches, as well as the tracery that originally decorated the windows, show the architects' attempt to combine Gothic elements with the eastern design. The wall above, covered with a diaper pattern of white Istrian stone and rose-coloured Verona marble, adds to the colourful exoticism of the building, as does the delicate crenellation that crowns this façade. Although constructed as late as the 15th century, the adjoining wing facing the Piazzetta was designed in a similar style, while the façade facing the Rio di Palazzo, begun *c.* 1484 by Antonio Rizzo and completed *c.* 1510 by Pietro Lombardo, is an odd, piecemeal structure, marked by an irregular fenestration and an uneven cornice. The diamond-patterned stonework at basement level is unusual in Venice and the idea was probably imported from the mainland, reflecting the city's increasing involvement with the rest of Italy at that time.

The sculptural decoration of the two principal façades is medieval in its encyclopedic character. Although some of the capitals are simply ornamental, most of them as well as the larger sculptures in this area are allegorical, designed to impress upon the city leaders their obligation to justice and virtue. The capital of the corner column by the Porta della Carta is decorated with an allegorical figure of *Justice*, while a larger 15th-century sculpture of the *Judgement of Solomon* appears above. On the other two corners 14th-century sculptures depicting the *Drunkenness of Noah* and *Adam and Eve* serve as reminders of human weakness. The column capitals (many of which have been replaced or are badly worn) were carved with such personifications of Virtue and Justice as *Moses*, *Solon*, *Aristotle* and *Numa Pompilius*, and images of the *Planets* and the *Months*, according to an iconographic programme derived from Gothic cathedrals.

The Porta della Carta, situated between the palace and S Marco, forms the main entrance to the courtyard and palace. It was begun by Giovanni Buon and his son Bartolomeo Buon in 1438, and with its mixture of Gothic and proto-Renaissance elements provides the most important surviving example of the Venetian style of that time (for illustration *see* BUON (i), (1)). Its present name refers to the government's practice of posting proclamations on the doorway, though it was originally referred to as the 'Golden Doorway' on account of its extensive gilding. Despite being stripped of its gold and polychromy the doorway remains rich in detail and iconography. Extending the iconography of the façade sculpture, a figure of *Justice* crowns the doorway, while *St Mark*, the patron saint of Venice, appears in a roundel below. In the canopied niches placed against the side pillars are statues of Virtues: *Prudence*, *Charity*, *Temperance* and *Fortitude*.

Immediately above the door a relief showing *Doge Francesco Foscari Kneeling before the Lion of St Mark* reproduces an earlier sculpture that was destroyed during the revolutionary turmoil of 1797. It symbolizes the divine approval of the Republic, a theme that was often represented inside the palace.

The Porta della Carta leads through a vaulted corridor known as the Porticato Foscari to the Arco Foscari (see fig. 24), which was built in the 15th century and embellished by later doges. The structure serves both as an impressive triumphal arch leading to the palace courtyard and as a transept façade for S Marco. Many of its important architectural elements, such as the two superimposed orders and the columns, pinnacles and figure sculpture above, are derived from the west façade of S Marco. Sculptures by Rizzo of *Adam* and *Eve* (replaced by copies) echo the religious tone of the basilica. Thus the Arco Foscari reveals two tendencies prominent in 15th-century Venetian civic architecture: the desire to establish richly decorated focal points along major visual and ceremonial axes, and the willingness to combine elements from different styles to achieve the greatest possible richness of colour and texture.

The courtyard was built in several stages from the late 15th century to the mid-16th. Its principal architect was Rizzo, who began to rebuild the courtyard after it was destroyed by fire in 1483, and who continued to work on it until 1498, when he fled the city after being found to have embezzled money from the palace workshop treasury. He was succeeded by Pietro Lombardo, who generally followed Rizzo's plan. Rizzo's structure, which is seen most clearly in the façade facing the Grand Canal, displays the Venetian Gothic interest in rich surface elaboration marked by irregular rhythms (caused in part by the need to work around the existing interior spaces and fenestration) and rich textural effects. However, it also shows Classical borrowings in many of its decorative elements such as garlands, arms, armour and inlaid roundels. The final result is a pleasing mixture of syncopated rhythms and richly varied textures, although the effect of his work has been somewhat obscured by sculpture added in the 16th and 17th centuries.

The courtyard served as a large gathering place for the citizens and provided an elegant setting for the impressive Scala dei Giganti (see fig. 24), built by Rizzo after the earlier staircase was destroyed in the fire of 1483. The structure fulfilled several functions, serving as the grand entrance to the palace, the site of major ceremonies such as the coronation of the doge and as the major sculptural

24. Venice, Doge's Palace, courtyard, showing the Arco Foscari (begun 15th century) in the centre and the Scala dei Giganti (begun after 1483) to the right

focus of the palace. Its role, therefore, was not only practical but also symbolic, as is apparent from the design. Rizzo deliberately emphasized the staircase by giving it a different scale and decoration in relation to the surrounding walls. The massive staircase leads into the palace through three arches of the first floor arcade, recalling a Roman triumphal arch. A small prison used to house traitors and enemies of the state was situated below the stairs, so that the doge could ceremonially tread on them as he entered and exited the palace. Colossal statues of *Mars* and *Neptune*, sculpted by Jacopo Sansovino and his pupils in the 16th century, crown the staircase on either side and proclaim the military and naval power of Venice (*see* SANSOVINO, (1) and fig. 4).

The staircase and the Arco Foscari separate the main courtyard from the Cortile dei Senatori, a small area built *c.* 1520 in which members of the Senate gathered during state ceremonies. Antonio Scarpagnino, the presumed architect of at least part of the internal façade, harmonized it with the main courtyard by repeating many of the forms found there. This audience area, together with the staircase and the rest of the courtyard, reflects the sense of theatre that characterized the Doge's Palace, where the city's major events were acted out.

Much of the palace was destroyed by fire in 1574 and 1577, and many influential citizens of Venice, including Palladio, proposed rebuilding it in a grandiose Renaissance style. Palladio found the building particularly hideous: 'The fabric was in a barbarous style because, to say nothing of the ugliness of the orders, it was very weak, having the solid part above the void, and the thick and heavy part above the narrow.' Jacopo Sansovino was the only leading Venetian architect to support the city leaders' decision to rebuild the palace in its original form.

BIBLIOGRAPHY

G. Fogolari: *Il Palazzo Ducale* (Milan, 1949)
G. Mariacher: *Il Palazzo Ducale* (Florence, 1950)
L. Serra: *The Doge's Palace* (Rome, 1951)
E. Bassi and E. Tricanato: *Il Palazzo Ducale nella storia e nell'arte di Venezia* (Milan, 1960)
D. Pincus: *The Arco Foscari: The Building of a Triumphal Gateway in Fifteenth Century Venice* (New York, 1976)
P. Lauritzen: *Palaces of Venice* (New York, 1978)
D. Howard: *The Architectural History of Venice* (New York, 1981)
H. Honour: *The Companion Guide to Venice* (Englewood Cliffs, 1983)

(ii) Painting and decoration. The decorative programme of the interior of the Doge's Palace was designed to represent the most illustrious moments in the history of the Venetian Republic and to impress its visitors with the splendour of the city. Though originally decorated in the 14th, 15th and early 16th centuries by leading artists from both the city and the mainland, including GUARIENTO, GENTILE DA FABRIANO, Pisanello, Giovanni Bellini (*see* BELLINI, (3)), Carpaccio and Titian, most of the existing decoration postdates the fire of 1577, which gutted the palace destroying most of the earlier masterpieces.

The Scala dei Giganti (*see* §(i) above) leads into a loggia, which in turn opens on to the Scala d'Oro that leads to the main halls of the palace. The latter staircase was completed in the mid-16th century and received its name from the rich gold stucco decoration on its vaulted ceiling. The decorative scheme was designed by Alessandro Vittoria and is a simplified version of the decoration planned

by Jacopo Sansovino for the bronze door of the sacristy of S Marco. The ceiling contains a profusion of decorative motifs—foliage, crowns, busts of heroes, philosophers, orators, and personifications of history, politics, religion, law and science—intended to overwhelm the visitor with a host of references to Venetian glories rather than to present a unified allegorical programme.

The staircase leads to a vestibule (the Atrio Quadrato) with a ceiling painting (*c.* 1654–5) by Jacopo Tintoretto showing Doge Girolamo Priuli (*reg* 1559–67) receiving the sword and balance, emblems of Venice, from Justice, while the Virgin and Priuli's patron saint, Jerome, pray for the prosperity of his reign. The theme of the painting echoes the emphasis on Justice seen in the palace's exterior decoration, while the heavenly setting of the scenes implies divine approval of the Venetian Republic. Beyond the vestibule is a succession of state rooms. The Sala delle Quattro Porte, which served first as the seat of the College and then as a vestibule of honour, was partially designed by Palladio. The decoration of the room, which includes a statue by Vittoria of *Vigilance*, illustrates the power and virtues of the Venetian Republic. The stuccoed ceiling was painted by Jacopo Tintoretto with an allegory of the *Triumph of Venice* (1577) surrounded by smaller compartments in which are depicted the regions and cities under Venetian control. On one wall is a canvas by Titian and his nephew Marco Vecellio showing *Doge Antonio Grimani Adoring Faith*, while Andrea Vicentino's *Entrance of Henry III into Venice in 1574* appears on another. An allegorical scene of *Neptune Offering Venice the Gifts of the Sea* (1745–50) was added by Giambattista Tiepolo.

The Sala dell'Anticollegio was given a particularly rich decoration in order to impress the foreign ambassadors who would wait here before an audience with the doge. The ceiling contains one of Veronese's finest works, *Venice Distributing Honours and Rewards*, painted in 1586–7. Four works painted by Tintoretto in 1577–8 in the vestibule were moved into this room in 1714: *Bacchus, Ariadne and Venus*, the *Three Graces and Mercury*, the *Forge of Vulcan* and *Minerva Rejecting Mars*. A fireplace by Vincenzo Scamozzi and Veronese's lavish *Rape of Europa* (1580) completed the decoration of this room.

Just beyond is the Sala del Collegio, the main audience hall, where the doge, six councillors, three chiefs of the Criminal Courts, the appointed sages of the Republic, and the three heads of the Council of Ten sat on state occasions. The ceiling is decorated with a series of paintings commissioned from Veronese in 1574 illustrating the power and virtues of Venice, including the large *Venice Enthroned with Justice and Peace* and a painting of *Mars and Neptune* symbolizing the military and naval power of the city. Smaller paintings of the *Virtues*, represented as richly dressed female figures, complete the painted decoration of the ceiling. On the walls below are illustrations by Veronese and Tintoretto of four 16th-century doges celebrating military victories or giving thanks to religious figures for their successes or, in one case, for deliverance of the city from the plague.

The Sala del Senato is similarly decorated with paintings illustrating divine protection of Venice and the development of her culture. The central compartment of the ceiling shows the *Triumph of Venice as Queen of the Sea*,

25. Venice, Doge's Palace, Sala del Maggior Consiglio, ceiling painting by Paolo Veronese: *Triumph of Venice*, oil on canvas, 1579–82

designed by Tintoretto and executed by his pupils. Another painting by Tintoretto's school portrays Doge Loredan praying to the Virgin for help in defeating the Turks and stopping the plague. A canvas over the door by Palma Giovane shows Doge Pasquale Cicogna asking Christ to save the city from famine and pestilence (*see* PALMA, (3), fig. 2), while yet another shows Venice's victorious battle against the League of Cambrai.

The Sala del Consiglio dei Dieci was the site of the meetings of the ten magistrates appointed to protect the city and its government from political enemies. It contained three paintings by Veronese dated 1553–4: *Jupiter Expelling the Vices* (Paris, Louvre; replaced *in situ* by 17th-century copy), an allegory of the justice meted out by the Council; *Juno Bestowing Gifts upon Venice*, suggesting the bounty the city enjoyed thanks to her conquest of vice; and *Youth and Age* (*see* VERONESE, fig. 2), also known as *Proserpina and Pluto*, an allegorical reference to the old and new domains of the Republic.

Other government chambers were also lavishly decorated in the 15th and 16th centuries, as were the doge's private rooms. The most monumental decoration was reserved, however, for the Sala del Maggior Consiglio, a vast room that could hold as many as 3000 people. This was the site of the legislative meetings of the lower house of the Venetian government, which numbered up to 1600 members; elections and banquets were also held here. After most of the 14th- and 15th-century masterpieces were destroyed in the fire of 1577, Veronese and Tintoretto were called in to redecorate the room with historical and mythological scenes illustrating the wars, victories and growth of Venice. On the ceiling are paintings showing *Venice, Queen of the Sea Presenting the Doge with an Olive Branch*, probably by Tintoretto and his pupils, and a *Triumph of Venice* (1579–82; see fig. 25) that was painted by Veronese. The walls are decorated with scenes of the 12th-century conflict between Emperor Frederick Barbarossa and Pope Alexander III, in which Venice achieved prestige as a diplomatic negotiator, as well as events of the Fourth Crusade (1204). Other battle scenes complete the wall decoration. Above is a frieze by Domenico Tintoretto depicting the first 76 doges of Venice. Only Marino Falier, who was executed for treason, is omitted. In his place is a black curtain, a reminder that even the most powerful man in Venice was subject to justice. All of these decorations are overpowered by Jacopo and Domenico Tintoretto's enormous (if not entirely compositionally satisfying) image of *Paradise* (1588–90), which gained fame as the largest painting on canvas (7.62×21.34 m) in the world. It filled the wall behind the thrones of the doge and the heads of government, and thus acted as a final, overwhelming reminder of the divinely privileged position the Venetians gave themselves.

BIBLIOGRAPHY

T. Pignatti: *The Golden Century of Venetian Painting* (New York, 1979)
H. Honour: *The Companion Guide to Venice* (Englewood Cliffs, 1983)
R. W. Rearick: *The Art of Paolo Veronese* (New Haven, 1986)
D. Rosand: *Painting in Cinquecento Venice: Titian, Veronese and Tintoretto* (New Haven, 1986)

For further bibliography *see* §(i) above.

JANE NASH MALLER

7. LIBRERIA MARCIANA. Located in the Piazzetta opposite the Doge's Palace, it was commissioned by the Procurators of S Marco following bequests to the Republic of two distinguished private libraries—Francesco Petrarch's in 1362 and Cardinal Bessarion's in 1468. In 1812 the building was requisitioned by Napoleon and much of its contents transferred to the Doge's Palace and never fully restituted. It was restored in 1929, with the Biblioteca Nazionale Marciana occupying the first floor as well as the adjacent Zecca and one wing of the Procuratie Nuove.

(i) Architecture. The library was designed by Jacopo Sansovino in the Roman Renaissance style and is noted for the pictorial quality of its Istrian stone façade as well as the festive character of its decoration, paralleling its civic role and scenographic position. Raised on a three-step podium, it has a two-storey, twenty-one bay façade employing a repeated Serlian motif, with a triple arcade at each end. Crowned by a balcony, the façade has an Ionic order superimposed over the Doric order of the ground-floor. Entrance to the library is through a monumental portal in the central bay, up a grand stairway to a square vestibule preceding a long, rectangular *salone* (reading room).

Construction began by 1537 at the corner by the campanile, following the initial demolition of hostelries and shops in the Piazzetta. The setting back of the library in relation to the campanile had a profound impact on the realignment of the public space of Piazza S Marco. In 1539 a competition was held for the design of the corner of the building according to Vitruvian principles, and Sansovino's model was judged victorious. His fortunes were reversed, however, when the vaulting he had insisted upon against local advice collapsed in the first bay of the *salone* in 1545. He was jailed, lost his salary and position for almost two years and was required to pay for repairs. A wood-beam ceiling was constructed instead, but the coved interior reflected Sansovino's original intention. Work under Sansovino halted early in 1556 with sixteen bays completed; in 1582 the last five bays and a subsequent programme of modification to its interior were entrusted to Vincenzo Scamozzi (*see* SCAMOZZI, (2)), who was also responsible for the Procuratie Nuove on the south side of the Piazza, next to the Libreria. Scamozzi, critical of the library's proportions and its juncture with the Zecca, urged the addition of a third storey, but his recommendations were rejected in 1588 and Sansovino's design was preserved. From 1588 to 1590 Scamozzi was occupied with work on the interior, and in 1591 he began the transformation of the vestibule from a patricians' school for humanistic studies to a museum housing the collection of Patriarch Giovanni Grimani's antiquities, bequeathed to the Republic in 1587 and installed in 1596.

(ii) Decoration. The allegorical and mythological decoration of the exterior was largely executed in the 1550s and continued the vein of politically charged allusions found in the nearby Loggetta (*see* SANSOVINO, JACOPO, fig. 3). The arcade, with its vaulting of interlocking framed compartments in gilded and painted stucco, came to serve as the patricians' afternoon meeting-place. Sansovino directed Bartolomeo Ammanati, Alessandro Vittoria, Danese Cattaneo and others in the execution of the

architectural sculpture. Vittoria and assistants were responsible for the *Feminone* (1553–5), two monumental caryatids flanking the entrance portal. The only one of the Olympian deities and heroes of the balustrade sculptures to be completed before Sansovino's death was Ammanati's *Neptune* (lost mid-18th century); the remainder were done under Scamozzi, including six by Girolamo Campagna (1549–by June 1625) between 1588 and 1591.

The interior decoration was begun in 1556 when seven painters, including Giuseppe Salviati, Andrea Schiavone and Paolo Veronese, were commissioned to paint the *salone* ceiling. Twenty-one tondi with allegorical subjects are framed in geometric compartments similar to the portico decoration; Veronese's *Music* was awarded a gold chain in a competition (1556) judged by Titian and Sansovino. The walls originally followed an architectural scheme of decorative pilaster enframements designed by Sansovino, with a painted series of philosophers in niches executed by artists already active in the *salone*, including Veronese. The majority, however, were by Jacopo Tintoretto, who had been excluded from the ceiling commissions. Ridolfi praised Tintoretto's 'stupendous figure' of *Diogenes*, 'so boldly coloured that he seems distinct from the niche where he is painted'.

Vittoria's contract of 1560 testifies to work begun on the stucco framework and reliefs of the stairway, which consists of two barrel-vaulted flights. The tripartite interlocking framework alternates rectangular compartments containing stuccos with simulated gold mosaic backgrounds and octagonal paintings by Battista Franco in the first flight, and by Battista del Moro (*c*. 1514–before 1574), in the second. Representations of astrological, mythological and allegorical figures and personifications of the natural sciences and liberal arts terminate with a stucco figure of *Vera Sapienza* at the entry to the vestibule. A fictive architectural soffit was painted (1559–60) in the vestibule by the Brescian *quadratura* specialists Cristoforo and Stefano Rosa. Titian subsequently painted the ceiling octagon, usually thought to represent an *Allegory of Wisdom*, although formerly identified as *History* (Ridolfi). Jacopo Tintoretto and Domenico Molin had executed four portraits of procurators and four paintings of philosophers by 1562, when they were commissioned to paint two more paintings each. These were accompanied by six fictive bronze chiaroscuro paintings and a frieze with putti and garlands. The vestibule lost its original character when it was remodelled as a museum in the 1590s.

BIBLIOGRAPHY

F. Sansovino: *Venetia, città nobilissima et singolare* (Venice, 1581); ed. G. Martinioni (Venice, 1663)

V. Scamozzi: *L'idea della architettura universale*, 2 vols (Venice, 1615/*R* Ridgewood, NJ, 1964)

C. Ridolfi: *Meraviglie* (1648); ed. D. von Hadeln, 2 vols (1914–24/*R* 1965)

G.-A. Moschini: *Guida per la città di Venezia*, 2 vols (Venice, 1815)

M. Zorzi: *La Libreria di San Marco* (Milan, 1987) [comprehensive history and bibliog.]

C. Hope: 'The Ceiling Paintings in the Libreria Marciana', *Nuovi studi su Paolo Veronese*, ed. M. Gemin (Venice, 1990), pp. 290–8

T. Hirthe: 'Zum Programm des Bibliothekssaals der Libreria Marciana in Venedig', *Iconographie der Bibliotheken* (Wiesbaden, 1992), pp. 107–58

TRACY E. COOPER

V. Scuole.

Religious confraternities, formed in the 13th century and dedicated to a patron saint, the *scuole* met for church services, for the funerals of their members and for their yearly banquets. Venice had a large number of these institutions, which took various forms: they included organizations attached to the city's trade guilds (*arti*), which acted for the benefit of practitioners of a particular trade; those formed for immigrant communities; for such groups as the lame or blind; or for specific purposes, for instance the accompaniment of condemned criminals. Income from fees, property and investment was used to aid members and their families. Most confraternities remained small in membership and restricted in function; the role of these *scuole piccole* in the patronage of Venetian art is not fully defined but was certainly less important than that of the *scuole grandi*, the largest, wealthiest and most prestigious of the *scuole*, which are discussed in detail below.

1. Introduction. 2. Scuola Grande di S Giovanni Evangelista. 3. Scuola Grande di S Marco. 4. Scuola Grande di S Rocco. 5. Scuola Grande di S Maria della Misericordia. 6. Scuola Grande di S Maria della Carità. 7. Scuola Grande di S Teodoro.

1. INTRODUCTION. Six *scuole grandi* were recognized by the middle of the 16th century: the Scuola di S Maria della Carità, the Scuola di S Marco and the Scuola di S Giovanni Evangelista were established in 1261 in the aftermath of the flagellant movement, which had swept Italy in the previous year; the Scuola di S Maria della Misericordia was established in 1308; the Scuola di S Rocco was recognized as a *scuola grande* in 1489; and the Scuola di S Teodoro was the last to be recognized, in 1552. Between the early 15th century and the late 16th, major sums were spent on the construction and decoration of their meeting-houses; after the Venetian government itself, these confraternities were probably the most important source of large-scale artistic commissions in Renaissance Venice. Their commissions greatly encouraged the development of a Venetian Renaissance artistic style, but the artistic productions were also closely related to the purpose and values of these religious brotherhoods.

Already by the 14th century, the *scuole grandi* had begun to outstrip other Venetian confraternities in size and prestige. The Scuola di S Marco, named after Venice's patron saint, was given an upper limit of 600 brothers; the others were allowed to enrol 550 members. That the large confraternities were able find well over 3000 men willing to pay the entrance fee and annual dues, as well as to participate in the various ceremonies is itself an indication of the prestige these institutions enjoyed in Venetian society. By the later 14th century the *scuole grandi* had developed a system of internal government. At the top were four major offices including the leader (*guardian grande*), his assistant (*vicario*), a record keeper (*scrivano*) and a master of the novices (*guardian da matin*); assisting them in maintaining contact with the brothers scattered across Venice were the deacons (*degani*), two of whom represented each of the six *sestieri* of Venice. The officers and deacons met regularly as a committee (*banca*) to discuss policy, to raise and allocate money, and later to commission works of art. At the beginning of the 15th century the offices had become important enough to be reserved by law to native-born citizens of Venice; in the 16th century, these positions conferred great prestige on those elected to serve their confraternities.

In the course of the 14th century, the *scuole grandi* began to shift their devotional emphasis away from personal devotions towards a more civic orientation. Much of their wealth was accumulated through gifts and bequests. Some of this was used to support the poorer brothers and their families through the distribution of alms or the provision of inexpensive housing to those on small incomes; to establish small hospitals, which provided physical and spiritual care for those without families; and to provide dowries to the daughters of poor brothers so that they could marry and live honourably. From the 14th century part of their wealth was used to acquire adequate meeting-houses. Originally the brothers had rented rooms from ecclesiastical establishments, but after 1300 they began to purchase vacant land or underused buildings. These early meeting-houses were probably fairly small, like the disused old meeting-house of the Scuola di S Maria della Misericordia in Cannaregio (*see* §5 below), but they included at least one large meeting-room (*sala*) to accommodate the whole brotherhood in general and religious meetings, often another large meeting-room (*androne*) for processions and flagellant sessions and usually also a small committee-room (*albergo*) for the meetings of the *banca*. The construction of meeting-houses forced the *scuole grandi* into fixed locations. The Scuola di S Giovanni Evangelista settled close to S Giovanni Evangelista in the *sestiere* of S Polo; the Scuola di S Marco, established first in the *sestiere* of Santa Croce, was after 1438 located next to SS Giovanni e Paolo in the *sestiere* of Castello; the Scuola di S Maria della Carità was established adjacent to the monastery of S Maria della Carità in the *sestiere* of Dorsoduro; the Scuola di S Maria della Misericordia was adjacent to S Maria della Misericordia Abbey in the *sestiere* of Cannaregio; the Scuola di S Rocco near S Maria Gloriosa dei Frari in the *sestiere* of S Polo after 1478; and the Scuola di S Teodoro opposite S Salvatore in the *sestiere* of S Marco.

From the early 15th century the *scuole grandi* began to enlarge and renovate their old meeting-houses, or to build large new ones as well as to decorate the rooms with splendid paintings. Some of the best architects in Venice worked to give the confraternities suitably magnificent meeting-houses, and some of the best painters decorated the walls with paintings illustrating biblical incidents or narratives appropriate to the brotherhoods. Most of the great commissions initiated by the *scuole grandi* occurred between the early 15th century and the later 16th, the period when they were especially wealthy and active as Christian institutions. Of the six, the Scuola di S Giovanni Evangelista, the Scuola di S Marco and the Scuola di S Rocco were most actively involved as patrons. Indeed, the two former were especially competitive in the building and decoration of their meeting-houses.

2. SCUOLA GRANDE DI S GIOVANNI EVANGELIS-TA. This *scuola* was pioneering in using art to reflect its growing status in Venetian society. In the first quarter of

the 15th century it carried out major structural renovations of its meeting-house, probably enlarging its main meeting-hall and decorating it with an ornate ceiling. Since it owned a famous, miracle-working relic of the True Cross, the confraternity decided in 1414 to commission a series of paintings commemorating the recent miracles of this relic; in 1421 it also commissioned a series of paintings illustrating scenes from the Old and New Testaments. These innovative projects may have acted as precedents, encouraging the other *scuole grandi* to increase their public profile.

In the second half of the 15th century the Scuola di S Giovanni Evangelista became involved in a form of artistic competition with the Scuola di S Marco. In the 1460s it commissioned from Jacopo Bellini, the most important painter in Venice at this time, paintings illustrating scenes from the New Testament, of which four have survived: the *Annunciation*, the *Birth of the Virgin* (both Turin, Gal. Sabauda), the *Marriage of the Virgin* and the *Epiphany* (both New York, Stanley Moss Col.). From the 1480s the *scuola*, responding to the innovative activities of the Scuola di S Marco (*see* §3 below), spent more money, first to create a new style of Renaissance meeting-house and then to decorate it. In 1481 Pietro Lombardo created a court-yard by erecting a marble screen with classicizing motifs to enclose the *calle* between the meeting-house and the nearby church. In the 1490s the confraternity greatly expanded its meeting-house. Mauro Codussi, architect to the Scuola di S Marco, supervised the raising of the floor and enlargement of the windows of its main meeting-room; a new entrance (1512) was added, together with a double-branched monumental staircase (1498) suitable for grand processions like that being built at the Scuola di S Marco. As a result, the confraternity's cramped medieval quarters were transformed into a spacious and elegant Renaissance meeting-house.

To complement these structural works, the Scuola di S Giovanni Evangelista commissioned equally rich pictorial decoration. For the walls of the Sala dell'Albergo, a number of leading painters in the emerging Venetian Renaissance style received commissions to paint a new series of large paintings (all Venice, Accad.). These illustrate the miracles of its relic and also celebrate the confraternity as an important institution in Venice. In 1494 Vittore Carpaccio painted the *Patriarch of Grado Curing a Demoniac*, while Giovanni Mansueti painted the *Miracle of the True Cross at the Campo di S Lio*. In 1496 Gentile Bellini was engaged to paint his celebrated *Procession of the True Cross in the Piazza S Marco* (see fig. 26), illustrating a great public procession and depicting the Piazza S Marco in minute detail as it appeared in the late 15th century; in 1500 he began the *Miracle of the True Cross at the Bridge of S Lorenzo*; and in 1501 he painted the *Miraculous Healing of Pietro dei Ludovici*. Lazzaro Bastiani painted the *Donation of the Relic of the True Cross* (*c.* 1495) commemorating the donation of the relic in 1369 by Philippe de Mézières, Chancellor of Cyprus, to Andrea Vendramin, *guardian grande* of the Scuola di S Giovanni Evangelista. In the early 1500s Benedetto Diana painted *A Child Fallen from a Ladder Is Miraculously Saved* and Giovanni Mansueti painted the *Miraculous Cure of the Daughter of Ser Benvegnudo da San Polo*, both glorifying the miracles worked by the relic while in the possession of the *scuola*, thus

26. Venice, Scuola Grande di S Giovanni Evangelista, *Procession of the True Cross in the Piazza S Marco* by Gentile Bellini, oil on canvas, 3.67×7.45 m, 1496 (Venice, Galleria dell'Accademia)

emphasizing the supernatural power in the confraternity's control. Also celebrated are the confraternity's officers, whose portraits appear in many of the paintings, and Venice itself, which is illustrated in great detail.

After *c.* 1510 the Scuola di S Giovanni Evangelista was less involved in major commissions of art, perhaps because it was largely satisfied with its meeting-house, or perhaps because it had little spare capital as a result of the growing fiscal demands of the state. In the 17th century it was engaged in making expensive repairs and modifications to its meeting-house and in commissioning new paintings, but the confraternity was no longer able to afford the work of leading artists.

3. SCUOLA GRANDE DI S MARCO. The confraternity began its institutional existence in the *sestiere* of Santa Croce but in 1438 moved to the north-east corner of the city, where it built a new meeting-house on a site located next to SS Giovanni e Paolo. The early form of this building is not known owing to its destruction by fire in 1485. In the 1460s, perhaps responding to innovations pioneered by the Scuola di S Giovanni Evangelista, the officers of the Scuola di S Marco commissioned for the main meeting-room a series of paintings illustrating scenes from the Old and New Testaments (all destr.): in 1466 a *Crucifixion* and *Christ Driving the Money-changers from the Temple* from Jacopo Bellini; the *Crossing of the Red Sea* and the *Passage through the Desert* from his son Gentile; in 1468 a painting from Bartolomeo Vivarini and Andrea da Murano, the subject of which is unclear; and in 1470 scenes from the *Story of David* and *Noah's Ark* from Giovanni Bellini, although his failure to complete the works eventually led to the withdrawal of the commission, which was given to Bartolomeo Montagna.

The fire of 1485 provided the *scuola* with the opportunity to rebuild and redecorate. Unlike the Scuola di S Giovanni Evangelista, which had to adapt an old building located on a circumscribed piece of land, the Scuola di S Marco could begin again and with more undeveloped land available to the rear of its first building. The first stage was the rebuilding of the meeting-house itself (begun 1487), but on a larger scale to ensure that the *scuola* retained its image of primacy in Venice. By 1490 the main construction work on the new meeting-house was sufficiently complete for the embellishment of the building to begin. Pietro Lombardo and Giovanni di Antonio Buora (1450–1513) directed the construction of the lower part of the façade (begun 1489; see fig. 27), incorporating some sculptures saved from the old meeting-house, while Pietro's son Tullio created the low-relief panels (1489–90) at street level, two containing the *Lions of St Mark* flanking the main door into the meeting-house, and two illustrating *St Mark Healing Anianus* and *St Mark Baptizing Anianus* (*see* LOMBARDO, §II(2)). Unique in the sculptural embellishment of the *scuole grandi*, the monumental and classicizing approach of these panels looked forward to the stylistic developments of the High Renaissance in Venice. Further innovations followed in the mid-1490s, when MAURO CODUSSI (who had become chief architect in 1490) pioneered the development of the type of ornate, double-branched monumental internal staircase (destr. 1812, reconstructed 1952), ideal for processions, connecting the ground-floor meeting-room with the Sala Grande. These innovations in scale and style represented a departure from the older conception of a meeting-house.

In the early 16th century, perhaps in response to the series of paintings of the True Cross in the Scuola di S Giovanni Evangelista, the Scuola di S Marco decided to decorate its Sala dell'Albergo. Capitalizing on the local importance of St Mark as Venice's patron saint and urged on by Gentile Bellini, the most famous Venetian painter of the time who was by then an officer in the confraternity, the *banca* chose as the theme of the paintings famous events from the *Life of St Mark*. In 1506 Gentile Bellini

27. Venice, Scuola Grande di S Marco, façade (1489–95); lower part by Pietro Lombardo and Giovanni di Antonio Buora, upper part by Mauro Codussi and sculptural reliefs by Tullio Lombardo

began the first painting, *St Mark Preaching in Alexandria* (Milan, Brera), which his brother Giovanni finished in 1507. In 1515 Giovanni Bellini signed a contract to paint the *Martyrdom of St Mark in Alexandria* (Venice, Accad., on dep. Osp. Civ.), which his pupil Vittore Belliniano finished in 1526. Three further paintings illustrating scenes in this series were executed *c.* 1518–26 by Giovanni Mansueti: *St Mark Healing Anianus* (Venice, Accad.), *St Mark Baptizing Anianus* (Milan, Brera) and *Episodes from the Life of St Mark* (Venice, Accad.). After a short hiatus large canvases, illustrating additional miracles performed by St Mark, were commissioned for the upstairs Sala Grande. Many leading Venetian artists were employed: in 1523–4 Palma Vecchio to paint *St Mark Saving Venice from the Ship of Demons* (*in situ*); in 1534 Paris Bordone to paint the *Presentation of the Ring to the Doge* (Venice, Accad.; *see* BORDONE, PARIS, fig. 1); and in 1548 Tintoretto to paint the *St Mark Rescuing the Slave* (Venice, Accad.; *see* TINTORETTO, (1), fig. 2), followed in 1562 by the *Finding of the Body of St Mark* (Milan, Brera; *see* TINTORETTO, (1), fig. 3), the *Removal of the Body of St Mark* (Venice, Accad.) and *St Mark Saving the Saracen* (Venice, Accad.). Other paintings followed, completing the decoration of the Sala Grande. The cycle celebrated the

apostolate and martyrdom of St Mark in Alexandria, the translation of his relics to Venice and some of the miracles he worked in Venice; they also reminded both the brothers and other Venetians of the civic religious power of the confraternity's and the city's patron saint. The portraits of many officers and visual representations of Venice in a number of paintings celebrated the importance of the *scuola grande* and created a vicarious link between the past and present united in the life and works of this saint.

In the 17th century the Scuola di S Marco completed the embellishment of its Sala Grande with many ornate panels and striking paintings. Although no longer a functioning confraternity (it is now the Ospedale Civile), the meeting-house remains as it appeared in the late 18th century, with the scenes from the *Life of St Mark* still *in situ* in the small committee meeting-room. The accumulated commissions represent a conscious investment in art as a means of venerating a patron saint and promoting the confraternity. Only one other *scuola* was able to follow its example: the Scuola Grande di S Rocco.

4. SCUOLA GRANDE DI S ROCCO. Founded in the aftermath of the plague of 1478, it rapidly gained the status of a *scuola grande*. Originally it had few resources, but

28. Venice, Scuola Grande di S Rocco, Sala dell'Albergo, *Crucifixion* by Tintoretto, oil on canvas, 5.36×12.24 m, 1565

veneration of St Roch and the fear generated by repeated visitations of the plague, notably those of 1478, 1527 and 1571, encouraged many Venetians to make bequests and gifts to it; by the end of the 16th century it was the richest of all Venice's *scuola grandi*. It was the only *scuola grande* to build its own church, S Rocco (begun 1489; consecrated 1508; rebuilt 18th century), which is located next to S Maria Gloriosa dei Frari. This was followed by the construction of a meeting-house on vacant land across the square from the church. Work was begun on this in 1517 and continued until the end of the 16th century. The early work was entrusted to Pietro Buon or possibly Bartolomeo Buon, who laid out the basic structure including the grand staircase and raised the first storey. From 1527 Antonio Scarpagnino continued the work, bringing a more classicizing style to the upper storey. The meeting-house is similar in its asymmetrical design to that of the Scuola di S Marco, but in a more flamboyant style, especially its richly carved façade (for illustration *see* SCARPAGNINO, ANTONIO).

After the mid-16th century the building was ready for work to begin on the decoration of the rooms. In 1565 the confraternity commissioned Tintoretto (*see* TINTORETTO, (1)) to paint a huge *Crucifixion* (see fig. 28) in the Sala dell'Albergo of the meeting-house; in 1566–7 he painted three more scenes from the Passion, *Christ before Pilate*, the *Way to Calvary* and a *Pietà*, as well as secondary works on the ceiling (all *in situ*). In 1575 Tintoretto began the decorative programme of the Salone Maggiore with ceiling paintings illustrating the various charitable functions of the brotherhood while the walls were covered with New Testament scenes, thus introducing the Passion narrative of the Sala dell'Albergo. Between 1583 and 1587 Tintoretto returned to the *scuola* to decorate the lower-level meeting-room with paintings illustrating the *Life of the Virgin*. Since Tintoretto painted the vast majority of the paintings, the rooms have a unity of style not found in the meeting-houses of the other *scuole grandi*. Still a functioning confraternity, the Scuola di S Rocco maintains

its meeting-house much as it was in its heyday around 1600.

5. SCUOLA GRANDE DI S MARIA DELLA MISERICORDIA. Founded in 1308, it was located well away from the centre of Venice on a severely circumscribed site in Cannaregio. In the 1440s, apparently in response to the innovations of the Scuola di S Marco, the Scuola della Misericordia enlarged its meeting-house by extending the

29. Venice, Scuola Grande di S Maria della Misericordia, *Madonna of Mercy* attributed to Bartolomeo Buon, marble, installed on the façade in 1451 (London, Victoria and Albert Museum)

front wall towards the Campo della Misericordia, and by adding a new façade decorated by a large *Madonna of Mercy* (London, V&A; see fig. 29), which is attributed to Bartolomeo Buon or to his workshop (*see* BUON (i), (1)). This building (the so-called Scuola Vecchio della Misericordia) is the best surviving example of a confraternity meeting-house dating from the early 15th century. The limitations of the site and lack of funds prevented further enlargements during the 15th century.

In 1509, having decided to erect a completely new meeting-house on its land on the other side of the canal, the confraternity commissioned Pietro and Tullio Lombardo to begin work, but the project was dogged by financial problems and administrative indecision and was never carried out. Only after the disasters of the War of the League of Cambrai and the plague of 1527 did the Scuola della Misericordia feel confident enough to consider beginning the project again. The *banca* wanted a large meeting-house and commissioned Jacopo Sansovino to build it, beginning in 1535. Sansovino planned a large building with many Roman stylistic details, an artistic coup against the other *scuole grandi*, but the confraternity did not have sufficient funds to sustain the project. The building work was repeatedly interrupted by the problems in Venice during the 16th century or by the changing ideas of the *banca*. In 1544, for instance, it rejected Sansovino's plan to have vaulted ceilings in the new meeting-house, preferring instead the traditional flat ceilings that could be decorated with paintings; the *banca* also opened a new competition for the structure and decorative details of the monumental, two-branched staircase, a sign that the confraternity had again rejected the advice of its architect. When Sansovino died in 1570, the brick walls had just been erected; only after many more tribulations and an embarrassing merger with the wealthy Scuola Piccola di S Maria dell'Orto, were the roof, the upper room and staircase set in place to allow the formal translation (1589) of the confraternity from its old to its new meeting-house.

This meeting-house, monumental in its conception, was clearly too expensive for the resources of the Scuola della Misericordia. There is no evidence to suggest that the confraternity ever commissioned a series of paintings to celebrate either of its meeting-houses with scenes from the life of its patron saint or miracles worked by a relic. Clearly, the resources at the disposal of the *scuola*, greatly diminished by demands made by the state and by the cost of supporting its poor brothers during the later 15th century and the 16th, were inadequate to meet the expense of erecting the largest meeting-house in the city, which remains unfinished and little decorated.

30. Venice, Scuola Grande di S Maria della Carità, *Virgin and Child with SS Jerome and Gregory, Ambrose and Augustine* by Antonio Vivarini and Giovanni d'Alemagna, oil on canvas, 3.44×4.77 m, 1446 (Venice, Galleria dell'Accademia)

6. SCUOLA GRANDE DI S MARIA DELLA CARITÀ. This was an ancient and wealthy *scuola grande* with a fine meeting-house close to the centre of the city. The state of the confraternity's archives and the many structural alterations to the building, most notably those in the early 19th century, when the meeting-house was altered to become Venice's Galleria dell'Accademia, make it very difficult to assess the confraternity's contribution as a patron. The *scuola* was located next to the monastery of S Maria della Carità, from which it first rented rooms and later purchased land and buildings. By 1343 it had two large meeting-rooms, one above the other, perhaps creating the original model of the *androne* or lower meeting-room and the *sala* or main meeting-room. Traces of fresco can still be seen near the cornice of the *sala*, which suggests that the room may originally have been decorated with frescoes.

Like the other *scuole grandi* in the mid-15th century, the Scuola della Carità improved its meeting-house, which was extended into the Campo della Carità in order to build an *albergo* for the meetings of the *banca*. This was decorated with a triptych by Antonio Vivarini and Giovanni d'Alemagna, the *Virgin and Child with SS Jerome and Gregory, Ambrose and Augustine* (1446; Venice, Accad.; see fig. 30), and a ceiling of elaborate panels. Possibly at this time the *scuola* erected the Gothic façade seen in the background of Canaletto's *Stonemason's Yard* (1726–7; London, N.G.; *see* CANALETTO, fig. 1). In the early 16th century the confraternity was considering further improvements, mainly decorations for its Sala dell'Albergo. In 1534 Titian was commissioned to paint a very large *Presentation of the Virgin* (1534–8; *in situ*), a work of complex design and symbolism, to cover one entire wall of the Sala dell'Albergo, where the *banca* usually distributed alms and made the annual selection of the young women who would receive the confraternity's dowry contributions; thus the subject-matter reflected the confraternity's charitable activities, reinforced by the many portraits of officers shown looking on as the young Virgin ascends the steps to the temple. Additions to the decoration of the room were Giampietro Silvio's *Marriage of the Virgin* (1540–3) and Girolamo Denti's *Annunciation* (1557–61; both Parish Church of Venice, Accad., on dep. Mason Vicentino). After the 1560s the *scuola* apparently did not make any more major additions to its meeting-house. Although it considered the possibility of constructing an ornate staircase like those of the other *scuole grandi*, this project was not begun until the mid-18th century when Giorgio Massari changed the façade and improved the *androne*, and Barnardino Maccaruzzi (*d* 1798) constructed the curved double staircase.

7. SCUOLA GRANDE DI S TEODORO. The old *scuola piccola* in honour of S Teodoro, traditionally Venice's patron saint alongside St Mark, was the last to be elevated to the status and responsibilities of a *scuola grande*, in 1552. It was successful in enrolling many new brothers from the rich merchants residing near the Rialto Bridge. In 1555, well after the other confraternities had set out the definitive Venetian style of a confraternity meeting-house, the Scuola di S Teodoro decided to erect a meeting-house, but it was not until 1576 that the necessary land opposite the newly

31. Venice, Scuola Grande di S Teodoro, staircase by Giuseppe Sardi and Baldassare Longhena, 1661

constructed S Salvador was acquired. Under the supervision of Simone Sorella, the meeting-house was gradually constructed following the established plan of a large meeting-room on the ground floor connected by a double-branched staircase to the vast and elegant upper meeting-room and committee room. In the 17th century, thanks to a very large bequest from a wealthy brother, Jacopo Galli, the *scuola* commissioned Giuseppe Sardi (*d* 1699) and Baldassare Longhena to provide a rich and elaborate classical façade (1649–55) for the meeting-house and to build the double-branched staircase (1661; see fig. 31). The surviving meeting-house is on a scale similar to those of the Scuola di S Giovanni Evangelista and the Scuola di S Marco. Inside, the decoration includes paintings with scenes from the *Life of St Theodore*, commissioned during the 17th and 18th centuries. Although the confraternity commissioned paintings from famous artists of the later 17th century and the early 18th, these works did not have the great cultural impact of the commissions of the other confraternities, and this confraternity never became as famous as the other five. The confraternity was dissolved during the Napoleonic occupation; the meeting-house is now used for exhibitions and concerts.

BIBLIOGRAPHY
P. Paoletti: *La Scuola Grande di San Marco* (Venice, 1929)
R. Gallo: 'La Scuola Grande di San Teodoro in Venezia', *Atti Ist. Ven. Sci., Lett. & A.*, cxx (1961–2), pp. 461–95
L. Sbriziolo: 'Le confraternite veneziane di devozione: Saggio bibliografico e premesse storiografiche', *Riv. Stor. Chiesa Italia*, xxi (1967), pp. 167–97
B. Pullan: *Rich and Poor in Renaissance Venice: The Social Institutions of a Catholic State to 1620* (Oxford, 1971)
P. L. Sohm: 'The Staircases of the Venetian Scuole Grandi and Mauro Coducci', *Architectura* [Milan], viii (1978), pp. 125–49

S. Gramigna and A. Perissa: *Scuole di arti, mestieri e devozione a Venezia* (Venice, 1981)

R. Maschio: 'Le scuole grandi a Venezia', *Storia della cultura veneta dal primo quattrocento al Concilio di Trento*, ed. G. Arnaldi and M. Pastore Stocchi, III/iii (Vicenza, 1981)

T. Pignatti, ed.: *Le scuole di Venezia* (Milan, 1981)

P. L. Sohm: *The Scuola Grande di San Marco, 1437–1550: The Architecture of a Venetian Lay Confraternity* (New York, 1981)

R. Mackenney: 'Devotional Confraternities in Renaissance Venice', *Voluntary Religion*, ed. W. Shiels and D. Wood, Stud. Church Hist. (Oxford, 1986), pp. 85–96

P. F. Brown: *Venetian Narrative Painting in the Time of Carpaccio* (New Haven, 1988)

WILLIAM B. WURTHMANN

Venius, Otto van. *See* VEEN, OTTO VAN.

Venne, Adriaen (Pietersz.) van de (*b* Delft, 1589; *d* The Hague, 12 Nov 1662). Dutch painter, draughtsman and poet.

1. Early training and Middelburg years, 1589–1624. 2. The Hague, 1625–62.

1. EARLY TRAINING AND MIDDELBURG YEARS, 1589–1624. De Bie's account (1661) is the only known source on van de Venne's youth and training. He was born of 'worthy' parents who had fled to Delft from the southern Netherlands to escape war and religious strife. Inspired by his early study of Latin to become an illustrator, he was partly self-taught but also received instruction in painting and illumination from the otherwise unrecorded Leiden goldsmith and painter Simon de Valck. His second teacher, Hieronymus van Diest (not the later marine artist), is equally obscure, but according to de Bie he painted grisailles, a technique that van de Venne later employed extensively.

Van de Venne's father, Pieter, and his elder brother, Jan (*bur* Middelburg, 3 May 1625), are recorded in Middelburg, Zeeland, in 1605 and 1608 respectively, and Adriaen is documented there from 1614 to 1624. His earliest dated paintings, *Summer* and *Winter* (both Berlin, Gemäldegal.) and *Fishing for Souls* (Amsterdam, Rijksmus.; see fig. 1), all from 1614, reveal a mature artist with a knowledge of landscapes done by local Middelburg painters and the Fleming Jan Breughel the elder; *Fishing for Souls* also displays the iconographic individuality that characterizes most of his work. An extensive, yet minutely detailed, panel, it is an allegory of the religious divisions in Europe set in the context of the Dutch war of independence from Roman Catholic Spain. Boats on a wide river are occupied by either Protestant or Catholic churchmen. Each faction attracts converts, the Protestants through the scriptures, the Catholics through music and other methods considered to be underhand. The two camps are also presented on each riverbank in a multitude of small portraits. The informal, vernacular language dispenses with the personifications and trumpeting angels that were standard in such allegorical works. This formula is repeated in van de Venne's three other major paintings, all completed during his Middelburg years. The *Allegory of the Twelve Years Truce* (1616; Paris, Louvre) again makes extensive use of portraits, this time to illustrate the benefits of peace that resulted from the ceasefire agreed in 1609 between the Dutch (under their Stadholder, Prince Maurice of Orange Nassau) and the Spanish-dominated southern Netherlands (under their regents, Albert and Isabella). *Prince Maurice and Frederick Henry Visiting the Horsefair at Valkenburg* (1618; Amsterdam, Rijksmus.) contains innumerable vignettes of the peasantry in the tradition of Pieter Bruegel I and the *View of the Harbour at Middelburg* (Amsterdam, Rijksmus.), said by Franken (1878) to have been dated 1625 but more probably painted *c.* 1616,

1. Adriaen van de Venne: *Fishing for Souls*, oil on panel, 0.98×1.89 m, 1614 (Amsterdam, Rijksmuseum)

apparently commemorates the visit of Elizabeth Stuart (the future 'Winter Queen') to the town in 1613.

Van de Venne produced other, more minor paintings in Middelburg but also embarked on his varied activities as a book illustrator, print designer, political propagandist and poet; in these he worked closely with his brother Jan, by then a well-known publisher and art dealer. Van de Venne's book illustrations usually concentrate on the human figure and are among his most successful works, combining a gift for narrative clarity with an informal compositional charm. They contributed greatly towards the popularity of Dutch emblem books in the 17th century, and his talents were employed by the leading writers of his day. His earliest illustrations were published in 1618 in the first works of the poet Jacob Cats (i): *Silenus Alcibiadis* or *Proteus*, later republished as *Sinne- en minnebeelden* ('Emblems of the mind and of love'), and *Maechden-plicht* ('Maids' duty'). Jan van de Venne was Cats's publisher until Jan's death in 1625, but Adriaen remained the poet's chief illustrator until at least 1656, when *Doot-kiste* ('Coffins') and *Aspasia* were published. In 1623 Jan published Constantijn Huygens's first two literary works: *Costelyck mal* ('Costly folly') and *Batava Tempe . . . Haagse Voorhout*, with plates designed by Adriaen. The illustrations had originally been intended for inclusion in the *Zeeusche nachtegael* ('Zeeland nightingale'), also published by Jan in 1623, a collection of writings in praise of Zeeland for which Adriaen again supplied the illustrations as well as much of the text. It was his first publication as a writer and is a landmark in the history of book design. He also produced the illustrations for Johannes de Brune's *Emblemata of zinnewerk* (Amsterdam, 1624), which are among his finest compositions.

From 1618 van de Venne designed several prints on a larger scale, most of them propagandist in intent. His portraits of the Stadholder *Prince Maurice* and of his successor *Frederick Henry* were engraved in 1618 by Willem Jacobsz. Delff (with a portrait of *William the Silent* added en suite in 1623 from a painting of 1621) and impressions were purchased by the States General, the ruling executive of the United Dutch Provinces. They and the municipality of Middelburg also acquired impressions of Delff's *Cavalcade of Nassau Princes*, made to van de Venne's design in 1621. A large engraving on four plates of the *Arrival of Frederick V, Elector Palatine, and his Bride, Elizabeth Stuart, in Flushing in 1613* appeared in 1618, the year in which his first political broadsheets were published. The engraving *The Righteous Sieve*, for which van de Venne's preparatory drawing survives (Rotterdam, Hist. Mus., 1388), defends Prince Maurice's overthrow of Johan van Oldenbarnevelt (the powerful Advocate of the States of Holland) and of the Remonstrant faction in the Dutch Calvinist church (see Royalton-Kisch, 1988, pp. 59–61). Other political prints appeared in the 1620s (and to a lesser extent later), always supporting the house of Orange Nassau or the cause of the 'Winter King and Queen', who from 1621 lived in exile in The Hague.

2. THE HAGUE, 1625–62. Evidence that van de Venne was ever directly employed by either the house of Orange Nassau or the court of the 'Winter King and Queen' is only circumstantial, but the nature of the first works he

2. Adriaen van de Venne: *'Winter King and Queen'*, watercolour and gouache heightened with gold, 96×152 mm, from an album of 102 miniatures, 1626 (London, British Museum, 1978-6-24-42, fol. 12)

produced in The Hague strongly supports the suggestion. Van de Venne is first documented there on 22 March 1625, the date of the copyright granted him for Cats's *Houwelyck* ('Marriage'), which he had also illustrated. This was the last book to be published by Jan van de Venne. Prince Maurice died on 23 April 1625, an event commemorated by Adriaen in several paintings (e.g. Amsterdam, Rijksmus.) and a propagandist print of his deathbed. Impressions of the latter were purchased by the States General on 21 July 1625. Four small, precisely detailed panels of the *Four Seasons* (Amsterdam, Rijksmus.) also date from 1625. The same year he must have begun work on the exquisite album of 105 miniatures (completed 1626; London, BM; see fig. 2), of which three are now missing. Internal evidence suggests that the album may have been commissioned by the 'Winter King' as a personal gift to the new Stadholder, Frederick Henry, celebrating the latter's assumption of power and his marriage in 1625 to Amalia von Solms, a maid of honour to the 'Winter Queen' and the daughter of the King's late chief steward. Entitled *tLants sterckte* ('Fortress and strength of the land'), the album eulogizes the Stadholder's rule, country and people at all levels of society. The nation's military prowess, its court, professions and major industries are illustrated, together with a section devoted to peasant 'drollery'. The drawings also depict a variety of topics emblematically, from the Stadholder's political aspirations to coarse sexual jokes. In its breadth of scope, purpose and technique, it is a unique production in Dutch art, distantly related to the German tradition of the *album amicorum*. It draws on every facet of van de Venne's wide artistic experience, and the small scale as well as the medium of brightly coloured bodycolour, often heightened in gold, provided him with a perfect vehicle for expression.

The album's dependence on an emblematic language and on peasant genre is repeated in most of van de Venne's numerous grisaille paintings. The earliest dated examples (Plokker, nos 1, 56 and 57) are from 1621, when he was still in Middelburg, but the overwhelming majority were executed in The Hague. In style and iconography these broadly executed works contrast sharply with the polychrome paintings of the Middelburg period. They concentrate on human (usually peasant) folly, the moral often being conveyed by an inscribed motto, such as *Armoe soeckt list* ('Poverty seeks cunning') or *Let op U selven* ('Observe yourself'). This combination of word and image allies them to the tradition of emblematic literature, but the motifs are usually unique to van de Venne. Also in grisaille are his large portrait of the *'Winter King and Queen' with Frederick Henry and Amalia von Solms* (1626; Amsterdam, Rijksmus.), based on a composition in the British Museum album of miniatures, the portrait of *Christian IV of Denmark as Pacifier* (1643; Helsingør, Kronborg Slot) and several religious paintings. Polychrome works executed in The Hague are not common, although in 1647–8 he designed a tapestry almost 8 m long depicting the *Battle of Nieuwpoort* (Brussels, Pal. B.-A.). The later works never repeat the precise touch of the Middelburg paintings, which is echoed only in his preparatory drawings for book illustrations, a large collection of which is in the Museum Catsianum (now in Leiden, Bib. Rijksuniv.). He also designed plates for Adrianum Valerium, Jacobus van Heemskerck, Philips van Lansbergen, Lieuwe van Aitzema, Jacob van Oudenhoven and others. Van de Venne seems never to have practised engraving, but employed numerous reproductive printmakers.

Van de Venne published his main literary works with his own illustrations during his years in The Hague, chief among them *Sinne-vonck op den Hollantschen turf* ('Spark of sense on Dutch peat') and *Wys-mal* ('Wise folly'), both from 1634, and *Tafereel van de belacchende werelt* ('Picture of the ridiculous world') of 1635. Highly imaginative books, they draw their inspiration from contemporary colloquial language and shun the imitation of antique models preferred by writers such as P. C. Hooft, Huygens and Joost van den Vondel. This attempt to formulate a new vernacular style in Holland is the one factor that unifies most of van de Venne's art, whatever the medium. His intensely felt and vivid response to contemporary life distinguishes him from other artists working in a similar vein, such as David Vinckboons, Hendrick Avercamp and Esaias van de Velde. Yet despite his apparent rejection of an international grand style, he did associate himself with the court on both a political and personal level. He also worked to improve the status of the artist in society, playing an active role in the Guild of St Luke in The Hague (member 1625; deacon 1631–2 and 1636–8; dean 1640). He was also a founder-member of Pictura, the artists' confraternity established in The Hague in 1656. At his death he was in debt. He married in 1614 and had two sons who were painters, Pieter van de Venne (1624–57), a still-life specialist, and Huybrecht van de Venne (1635–76 or later), who is said by de Bie to have followed his father's style, but none of whose works is known.

UNPUBLISHED SOURCES

Amsterdam, Rijksmus., MS. Rijksprentenkab. [D. Franken and F. G. Waller: *L'Oeuvre de Adriaen van de Venne, c.* 1910]

BIBLIOGRAPHY

Hollstein: *Dut. & Flem.*
C. de Bie: *Het gulden cabinet* (1661), pp. 234–6
D. Franken: *Adriaen van de Venne* (Amsterdam, 1878)
G. van Rijn, ed.: *Katalogus der historie . . . prenten . . . verzameld door A. van Stolk* (Amsterdam, 1895–7); *Index* (The Hague, 1933)
L. J. Bol: 'Adriaen Pietersz. van de Venne, schilder en teyckenaer', *Tableau*, v (1982–3), nos 2–6; vi (1983–4), nos 1–5 [with further bibliog.]
A. Plokker: *Adriaen Pietersz. van de Venne (1589–1662): De grisailles met spreukbanden* (Leuven, 1984)
M. Royalton-Kisch: 'The Tapestry of the *Battle of Nieuwpoort*', *Bull. Mus. Royaux A. & Hist.*, lviii (1987), pp. 63–78
——: *Adriaen van de Venne's Album in the British Museum* (London, 1988)
L. J. Bol: *Adriaen Pietersz. van de Venne: Painter and Draughtsman* (Doornspijk, 1989)

MARTIN ROYALTON-KISCH

Vennekool [Vennecool], **Steven** (*b* ?1657; *d* Amsterdam, *bur* 7 March 1719). Dutch architect. He was one of the most important architects of the final phase of Dutch classicism, known as the Severe style, which he used in his design for the town hall at Enkhuizen (1686), a detached, rectangular building with a sandstone façade. The barely projecting central bay is emphasized by a balcony above the entrance and an attic with sculptures and ornamental vases. Above the roof rises a polygonal domed tower. In 1695 Vennekool restored the château of Middachten (De Steeg), which had been destroyed by the French in 1672. He changed the rectangular courtyard into an oval stairwell with two sets of staircases along the walls, topped by a stuccoed dome-light. By contrast, in 1691 he had created a magnificent Baroque ensemble: the monumental triumphal arch (destr.; known through prints) erected on the occasion of William III's entry into The Hague after his coronation as King of England. The ornate construction consisted of two triumphal arches, which, with their freestanding columns, supported a large gateway crowned with a dome that bore an equestrian statue of *William III*. The whole was richly embellished with trophies, statues and panels with allegorical scenes.

BIBLIOGRAPHY

H. M. van den Berg: *De Nederlandse monumenten van geschiedenis en kunst* [Dutch monuments of history and art], viii (The Hague, 1955)
W. Kuyper: *Dutch Classicist Architecture* (Delft, 1980)

PAUL H. REM

Vent, Hans (*b* Weimar, 13 Feb 1934). German painter, draughtsman and graphic designer. Following an apprenticeship as a building painter in Weimar (1948–51), he attended the Fachschule für Ausbautechnik in Weimar in 1952 and graduated as a Meister der volkseigenen Industrie. In 1953 he worked as a restoration trainee in Gotha. From 1953 to 1958 he studied at the Kunsthochschule in Weissensee, Berlin. By the end of his course of study, essential characteristics of his art were already evident: the working of a theme in series and variations and his colourist sensitivity. His inclination towards landscapes and to the naked human body and to colour and light in atmospheric transparency may derive from the rural cocoon of Weimar where he grew up. Vent loved balance in his pictures and used paint to articulate the interchange between painting and reality.

Around 1963 Vent began to study the human figure in landscape. He developed a loose style of applying paint in pastel tones, and his first variations on *Bathers at the Sea* appeared. In 1965 he turned almost completely from oil painting and towards tempera, in which he gave expression to his desire for fluid, playful application of paint and arabesque outlines. *People on the Beach* was a major theme, of which he made numerous variations, working in both small and large format.

BIBLIOGRAPHY
Hans Vent (exh. cat., E. Berlin, Gal. Arkade, 1974)
A. Förster: *Hans Vent: Maler und Werk* (Dresden, 1976)
Hans Vent (exh. cat., E. Berlin, Pal. Ephraim, 1990)
CHRISTOPH TANNERT

Ventana Cave. Rock shelter in North America, in the Castle Mountains, AZ. It was occupied in Pre-Columbian times from *c.* 10,000 BC to *c.* AD 1300. Ventana Cave was excavated by the American archaeologist Emil Haury and the results were published by the University of New Mexico Press. The earliest layers of occupation contained crude, then more sophisticated, stone tools (including projectile points, of which the type—Clovis or Folsom—is disputed), a variety of faunal remains and shells from the Gulf of California, *c.* 160 km to the west. The inhabitants practised a hunting–gathering economy. Later layers contained artefacts of the Hohokam culture (*fl c.* 300 BC–AD 1300) of the US Southwest, including evidence of their agricultural way of life (*see also* SNAKETOWN), such as maize-grinding stones, pottery and remains of netting, cordage, basketwork, leather and feather objects and cotton textiles. The pottery is typical of early Hohokam styles, with red-on-buff decorations (*see also* NATIVE NORTH AMERICAN ART, §V, 1(i)): dots, hatched lines, interlocking scrolls and keys, patterns of wavy and straight lines, circles with projecting curved flanges and angular bird and human forms. Material excavated from the site is housed mainly in the university museums of New Mexico and Arizona.

BIBLIOGRAPHY
E. W. Haury and others: *The Stratigraphy and Archaeology of Ventana Cave, Arizona* (Albuquerque, 1950, rev. Tucson, 1975)
DAVID M. JONES

Ventanas, Las. *See* PEÑOL DE JUCHIPILA.

Ventia. *See* VEII.

Ventura di Andrea Vitoni. *See* VITONI, VENTURA DI ANDREA.

Venturi. Italian family of art historians, critics, museum officials and teachers.

(1) Adolfo Venturi (*b* Modena, 4 Sept 1856; *d* Santa Margherita Ligure, nr Genoa, 10 June 1941). He studied at the Istituto di Belle Arti, Modena, and in 1878 was appointed to the post of inspector at the Galleria e Museo Estense, Modena, the history of which he wrote. His research and publications were particularly concerned with Ferrarese Renaissance painting. In 1883 he was appointed a member of the Deputazione di Storia Patria in the province of Modena, serving under its president Giuseppe B. Campori. In 1885 he became a member of the Deputazione for Bologna. He contributed to many foreign journals, especially from Germany, completing the research on Ferrarese painting begun by Giovanni Morelli and Giovanni Battista Cavalcaselle. He also collaborated on an exhibition of Ferrarese painting held at the Burlington Fine Arts Club in London in 1894.

In 1888 Venturi was appointed to the Ministero della Pubblica Istruzione (Direzione Generale delle Antichità e Belle Arti) in Rome, where he catalogued art objects, advised on state acquisitions (e.g. the Galleria Borghese) and introduced measures to prevent the illicit removal of works of art. A record of his work is contained in the volumes of the *Gallerie nazionali italiane*, an annual account of the state collections modelled on similar works produced in Prussia and Vienna, in which he invited contributions from his most important colleagues in art administration, including Corrado Ricci, Giulio Cantalamessa (1846–1924) and Enrico Ridolfi. Also in 1888 Venturi co-founded the *Archivio storico dell'arte*, the first periodical in the Italian language specializing in the study of Italian art. He took over as director of the journal in 1898, renaming it *L'arte* and publishing in it articles by his most notable Italian and foreign colleagues, including Wilhelm von Bode and Emile Bertaux.

In 1890 Venturi began lecturing on art history at the Università degli Studi di Roma, 'La Sapienza', where in 1901 he was appointed professor, the first chair in art history at an Italian university. In 1895 he served on the jury to select the winner of the gold medal at the first Biennale in Venice. The following year Venturi founded a school of advanced study in art history, the Scuola di Perfezionamento negli Studi di Storia dell'Arte Medioevale e Moderna, at which many of the later experts in art education and administration in Italy were trained. During the last years of the century Venturi was also engaged in a series of conferences on and studies of aesthetic iconography, undertaking and presenting research on the representation of the life of the Virgin over the centuries. These were widely successful but led to conflicts between Venturi and scholars in such disciplines as philosophy and the history of religion.

In 1901 Venturi was appointed a member of the Académie Française and in the same year the publication began of his *Storia dell'arte italiana* on which he worked until the very end of his life. This project, which was originally planned as a compendium in seven volumes, was later expanded. It became the chief outlet for the research conducted by Venturi, occasionally with the help of his university students. Organized as a series of monographs on individual artists, it presents much of the historical research undertaken on painters, sculptors and architects of the 15th and 16th centuries.

In 1898 Venturi had been appointed Director of the Galleria Nazionale d'Arte Antica in Palazzo Corsini, Rome. He later became a member of the Consiglio Superiore di Antichità e Belle Arti, and in 1912 he organized the tenth Congresso Internazionale di Storia dell'Arte in Rome, at which he drew attention to the need for an edition of early sources for the study of the history of Italian art. In 1922 Venturi became head of the Istituto di Belle Arti of Modena, and in 1924 he received the honorific title Senator. In 1931 he retired as professor at the university; in 1939 he donated his own library to the Istituto Centrale per il Restauro in Rome. His collection of photographs is at the Università degli Studi di Roma, 'La Sapienza'.

UNPUBLISHED SOURCES
Pisa, Scu. Norm. Sup. [notebooks and letters]

WRITINGS
La R. Galleria Estense in Modena (Modena, 1882/*R* 1990 [anastatic edn]) with others: *Gallerie nazionali italiane* (Rome, 1894–1902)
La Madonna (Milan, 1900; Eng. trans., London, 1902)

Storia dell'arte italiana, 11 vols (Milan, 1901–40/*R* Nendeln, 1967)

Atti del X congresso internazionale di storia dell'arte: Rome, 1912, pp. 497–500

Memorie autobiografiche (Milan, 1927/*R* Turin, 1991)

Epoche e maestri dell'arte italiana (Turin, 1956) [anthology of writings]

BIBLIOGRAPHY

P. Toesca: *Adolfo Venturi* (Rome, 1941)

G. Nicodemi, ed.: 'Bibliografia di A. Venturi', *L'Arte*, xvi (July 1944–Dec 1946), pp. 25–102

Celebrazioni venturiane nel centenario della nascita di Adolfo Venturi, 1856–1956 (exh. cat., Modena, Gal. & Mus. Estense, 1957)

G. Agosti: 'La perizia dei quadri borghese documentata nell'Archivio della Galleria: Adolfo Venturi ed altri tra scienza dell'arte e interessi ministeriali', *Ric. Stor. A.*, 23 (1984), pp. 45–72

——: 'Giovanni Morelli e Adolfo Venturi: Alle origini dell'istituzione delle discipline storico-artistiche in Italia', *Giovanni Morelli e la cultura dei conoscitori. Atti del convegno: Bergamo, 1987*, i, pp. 253–77

G. Agosti, ed.: *Introduzione al carteggio di Adolfo Venturi*, 2 vols (Pisa, 1990–92)

(2) Lionello Venturi

(*b* Modena, 25 April 1885; *d* Rome, 14 Aug 1961). Son of (1) Adolfo Venturi. He took a degree in history at the Università degli Studi di Roma. After being Vice-Director of the Gallerie dell'Accademie in Venice (1909) and the Galleria Borghese in Rome (1909–10), in 1912 he became Director of the Pinacoteca of the Palazzo Ducale in Urbino. He studied 15th- and 16th-century Venetian art and the paintings of the school of Caravaggio, and from 1914 to 1931 he was Professor of Art History at the Università degli Studi di Torino. During the 1920s he began working on a revised history of art, in which he emphasized work such as that of the French Impressionists, Cézanne, Modigliani and the Gruppo Sei in opposition to that of the Novecento Italiano and the second wave of Futurism. He also proposed new methodological criteria for art criticism, derived mainly from the philosophy of Benedetto Croce. In 1925 he signed Giovanni Gentile's *Manifesto degli intellettuali fascisti*. In addition to his teaching and writing, he promoted the private collection of art assembled by the industrialist Riccardo Gualino, but these activities were interrupted in 1931 when he was forced to move to Paris as a result of his refusal to swear allegiance to the Fascist regime. During World War II he lived in the USA, where he was visiting professor at such institutions as Johns Hopkins University in Baltimore, MD (1940), and L'Ecole Libre des Hautes Etudes in New York (1943). From 1945 to 1960 he taught at the Università degli Studi di Roma, 'La Sapienza'. Many of his books were published by the Swiss company Skira, which was run by his son-in-law, Albert Skira. Venturi also actively promoted such important exhibitions of contemporary art as those of Picasso (1953) and Emilio Vedova (1952), as well as that of the GRUPPO DEGLI OTTO PITTORI ITALIANI at the Biennale in Venice in 1952.

WRITINGS

Pretesti di critica (Milan, 1929)

History of Art Criticism (New York, 1936)

Painters and Painting: How to Look at a Picture, from Giotto to Chagall (New York and London, 1946; It. trans., Rome, 1956)

Otto pittori italiani (Milan, 1952)

Regular contributions to *L'Arte* (1903–35) and *Commentari* (1950–61)

BIBLIOGRAPHY

E. Battisti, ed.: *Scritti di storia dell'arte in onore di Lionello Venturi* (Rome, 1956), pp. 319–35

N. Ponente: 'Bibliografia degli scritti di Lionello Venturi', *Commentari*, viii (July–Dec 1962), pp. 155–9

M. M. Lamberti: 'Lionello Venturi sulla via dell'impressionismo', *An. Scu. Norm. Sup. Pisa, Lett., Stor. & Filos.*, 3rd ser., i/1 (1971), pp. 257–77

G. C. Argan: 'Le polemiche di Lionello Venturi', *Stud. Piemont.*, i (1972), pp. 118–24

Lionello Venturi e l'avanguardia italiana (exh. cat. by C. F. Teodoro, Modena, 1991)

Da Cézanne all'arte astratta: Omaggio a Lionello Venturi (exh. cat. by S. Cortenate and R. Lambarelli, Milan, 1992)

GIACOMO AGOSTI

Venturi, Rauch & Scott Brown. American architectural, urban planning, exhibition and furniture design partnership formed in 1980 by Robert Venturi (*b* Philadelphia, 25 June 1925), John Rauch (*b* Philadelphia, 23 Oct 1930) and Denise Scott Brown [née Lakofski] (*b* Nkana, Northern Rhodesia [now Zambia], 3 Oct 1930). Venturi studied architecture at Princeton University, NJ (BA 1947, MFA 1950), and between 1950 and 1958 he worked in various offices including those of Oskar Stonorov, Eero Saarinen and Louis Kahn. He also spent a period (1954–6) as Fellow at the American Academy in Rome. In 1957 he joined the staff of the University of Pennsylvania, Philadelphia, the start of an extensive teaching career. He was then in partnership with Paul Cope and H. Mather Lippincott (1958–61), with William Short (1961–4) and from 1964 with Rauch, who graduated from the University of Pennsylvania in 1957. Denise Scott Brown studied at the University of the Witwatersrand, Johannesburg (1948–51), the Architectural Association, London (AA.Dip. 1956), and the University of Pennsylvania (MCity Planning 1960, MArch 1965). She worked with various firms in Johannesburg, London and Rome, and taught at several universities in the USA from 1960 to 1968. In 1967 she married Venturi and joined the practice of Venturi and Rauch as an architect and planner, making a significant theoretical contribution and bringing a profound concern for social planning to its work.

The partnership of Venturi, Rauch & Scott Brown, like all those in which Venturi was involved, pioneered a vision of architecture founded on a fundamental rethinking of the forms and ideas of Modernism. Two lines of inquiry dominated this process. The first was demonstrated in Venturi's book *Complexity and Contradiction in Architecture* (1966), which was derived from his teaching and became a seminal work in the search for alternatives to the uniformity of the International style. It involved the exploration of an expanded formal vocabulary based on such concepts as accommodation of the existing ambiguity of form and the 'messy vitality' of the ordinary. All were formal strategies drawn from a wide range of historical examples, including the work of such modernists as Louis Sullivan, Le Corbusier and Alvar Aalto, such modern traditionalists as Edwin Lutyens, and such Renaissance and Baroque masters as Michelangelo and Bernardo Antonio Vittone, as well as from the vernacular. The second line of inquiry was epitomized by *Learning from Las Vegas* (1972), written by Venturi, Scott Brown and their associate Steven Izenour, which stressed that architecture should have an intentionally symbolic dimension, as ironically revealed, for example, in the contrast between an elaborate roadside sign in Las Vegas and the banal casino building behind. The lesson to be learnt was not that a profound, contemporary building should be ordinary, but that it should represent ordinariness symbolically,

Venturi, Rauch & Scott Brown: Gordon Wu Hall, Butler College, Princeton University, New Jersey, 1980

using the history of architecture and the vernacular landscape as its means and expressing itself in a qualified, accommodating and ambiguous formal vocabulary.

The essential difference between the work of Venturi's office and the Modern Movement against which it reacted was thus the attempt to draw strength from the ordinary rather than the ideal. This tendency became apparent at least as early as the project for a beach house (1959; unexecuted): exaggeratedly tall chimney served as an emphatic gesture of human habitation rising above a house of which the interior was a balance of stylistic ambiguities. Purity of form was rejected in favour of complexity and contradiction of form and symbol. The house (1962) for Venturi's mother in Chestnut Hill, MD, is a *tour de force* of ambiguous formal composition: it combines echoes of the Italian Baroque in its split pediment, of Le Corbusier's Villa Stein (1927), Paris, in its spatial layering and ribbon windows, of Michelangelo's mannerist Porta Pia (1561–4), Rome, in the fireplace mass, and of the Philadelphia Shingle style of Wilson Eyre in its living hall and staircase. At the same time, at a symbolic level, it is humanistic and reflective rather than utopian and assertive.

Appreciation of the nobility of the ordinary is equally present in such later buildings as the Fire Station No. 4 (1966), Columbus, IN, with an urban street wall, prominent hose tower and big signs reflecting the dominance of the motor car in the environment, and the Best Products showroom (1977), Oxford Valley, PA, with its pattern of overscaled flowers. Both are symbolic expressions of the existing world that achieve a distance from the ordinary vernacular and allow the observer to see that world with a fresh perspective; in the words of *Learning from Las Vegas*, they are 'decorated sheds' or relatively simple buildings that have special architectural embellishment at points of particular public focus.

Other projects by Venturi explore the ordinariness of history more than that of the commercial vernacular, for example the Trubeck and Wislocki houses (1970), Nantucket Island, and such public buildings as the Gordon Wu Hall (1980; see fig.), Butler College, and the Molecular Biology building (1983), both at Princeton University. In each case Venturi referred to a different but 'ordinary' period of the past, one that was readily accessible to the American eye. Thus the ancient colonial shingled box is recalled in Nantucket, and the collegiate Gothic style in the buildings at Princeton, seen particularly in the heraldry device of the portal at Gordon Wu Hall.

The classical tradition was usually reserved by Venturi's office for the grandest public buildings and urban designs, whether in the discreet use of the Baroque in the competition entry (1979) for the new Parliament House, Canberra, Australia; the rhythms of the Laguna Gloria Art Museum (1983), Austin, TX, which echo the work of Lutyens; the suggestions of Frederick Law Olmsted's romantic classicism in the Westway Riverfront Park project (1978–85), New York; or the sophisticated and refined

Anglo-Italian classicism of the National Gallery extension (1987–91), London. In these projects a continuity exists with classicism, not because the classical ideal of man's perfectibility is still considered relevant (as it is for classical revivalists), but because the deforming impact of modern culture on this sense of the ideal is held to be of even greater value. This is the most profound level of the ordinary in Venturi's work, and it is what defines it as neither revivalist nor Modernist in the orthodox sense, but rather as a reformulated modernism appropriate to the late 20th century (*see also* POST-MODERNISM).

In the field of exhibition and furniture design, the work of Venturi, Rauch & Scott Brown reflects the philosophical preoccupations of their architectural work. They designed several large exhibitions at museums in various cities in the USA, including Washington, DC, New York and Philadelphia, and carried out industrial design projects such as furniture, fabrics and homeware for Alessi International, Milan (1983 and 1985), Formica Corporation, New York (1983), and Knoll International, New York (1984; *see* UNITED STATES OF AMERICA, §VI, 5).

WRITINGS
R. Venturi: *Complexity and Contradiction in Architecture* (New York, 1966)
R. Venturi, D. Scott Brown and S. Izenour: *Learning from Las Vegas* (Cambridge, MA, 1972)
R. Venturi and D. Scott Brown: *A View from the Campidoglio: Selected Essays, 1953–1984* (New York, 1984)

BIBLIOGRAPHY
V. Scully: *The Shingle Style Today or the Historian's Revenge* (New York, 1974)
R. Maxwell and R. A. M. Stern: *Venturi and Rauch* (London, 1978)
G. Pettena and M. Vogliazzo, eds: *Venturi, Rauch and Scott Brown* (Milan, 1981)
G. Macrae-Gibson: 'The Ironies of the Difficult Whole', *The Secret Life of Buildings: An American Mythology for Modern Architecture* (Cambridge, MA, 1985) pp. 142–69
A. Sanmartín, ed.: *Venturi, Rauch and Scott Brown* (Barcelona and London, 1986)
S. von Moos: *Venturi, Rauch and Scott Brown: Buildings and Projects* (New York, 1987)
C. Mead, ed.: *The Architecture of Robert Venturi* (Albuquerque, 1989)
GAVIN MACRAE-GIBSON

Venturini, Giovanni Francesco (*b* Rome, 1650; *d* Rome, after 1710). Italian printmaker. A pupil of Giovan Battista Galestruzzi, with whom he collaborated on a series of engravings after frescoes by Polidoro da Caravaggio, he is best known for his two series of engraved *vedute*: *Fontane ne' palazzi e ne' giardini di Roma* and *Fontane nel giardino estense in Tivoli*. These were printed by A. de Rossi in 1684, completing the famous work by Giovanni Battista Falda on the same subject. Venturini also contributed to other collections of Roman *vedute*, such as the *Insignium Romae Templorum Prospectus* (1684) and the *Disegni di vasi, altari e cappelle nelle chiese di Roma* (1690). On the whole he remained faithful to the style of his master Galestruzzi, which was analytical yet at the same time picturesque, whether in etching or engraving.

BIBLIOGRAPHY
B. Disertori: 'La regia calcografica: Antichi vedutisti e paesisti, IV', *Emporium*, lviii/339 (1923), pp. 148–68
P. Arrigoni and A. Bertarelli: *Piante e vedute di Roma e del Lazio conservate nella raccolta delle stampe e dei disegni* (Milan, 1939)
C. A. Petrucci: *Catalogo generale delle stampe tratte da rami incisi posseduti dalla Calcografia Nazionale* (Rome, 1953)
E. Coen Pirani: *Il libro illustrato italiano* (Rome, 1956)

C. A. Petrucci: *Il Caravaggio acquafortista ed il mondo calcografico romano* (Rome, 1956)
UGO RUGGERI

Venus de' Medici. Celebrated work of antique sculpture. It depicts a nude Venus, her head turned to the left, her hands covering her breasts and genitals (h. 1.53 m; Florence, Uffizi; *see* ANTIQUE, THE, fig. 2), and is perhaps the work of an Athenian follower of Praxiteles of the 1st century BC, probably based on a bronze original derived from the *Venus of Knidos*. On the base is an inscription attributing it to Kleomenes the Athenian. The inscription is certainly spurious but, as Ennio Quirino Visconti noted, it may have been copied from an original signature. The statue, which was in the Villa Medici in Rome perhaps from the end of the 16th century, is documented there with certainty in 1638 by the three plates that François Perrier devoted to it in his survey of the most beautiful statues of Rome (*Segmenta nobilium signorum et statuarum*). In 1677 Pope Innocent XI approved its transfer to Florence, where the following year it was exhibited in the Tribune of the Uffizi. In 1800 it was loaded on a ship for Palermo in an attempt to save it from the French, but after long diplomatic negotiations they managed to obtain it, and in 1803 the *Venus* was in Paris. It was returned in 1815 and from the following year was again displayed in the Tribune. The statue has been restored in numerous places. When it arrived in Florence from Rome it was given arms made by the sculptor Ercole Ferrata. The *Venus de' Medici* was the object of great admiration, which perhaps reached its peak during the struggle between the Florentines and the French. Luca Giordano had a celebrated passion for the statue, which he copied from every angle. Jonathan Richardson was famous for standing before it for ten hours without pause, and the English writer Joseph Spence visited it almost a hundred times. It was replicated in bronze for Charles I, King of England, and for the Duke of Marlborough. Numerous plaster casts and marble copies were made; the lead copies made in the 18th century for English gardens are famous.

BIBLIOGRAPHY
G. A. Mansuelli: *Le sculture* (1958), i of *Galleria degli Uffizi*, 4 vols (Rome, 1958–61), pp. 71–3
M. Robertson: *A History of Greek Art* (Cambridge, 1975), p. 549
F. Haskell and N. Penny: *Taste and the Antique: The Lure of Classical Sculpture, 1500–1900* (New Haven and London, 1981), pp. 325–8

Venus de Milo. Marble statue of a semi-nude Venus (h. 2.04 m; Paris, Louvre). Its twisting composition (*see* GREECE, ANCIENT, fig. 69) is probably the work of the Greek artist Alexandros of Antioch on the Meander, active in the 2nd century BC, who in turn was inspired by a pre-Hellenistic model. The artist's name was incised on a block of stone that was found together with the *Venus* but later lost. A few scholars in the past doubted the connection between the block and the statue and hence the attribution of the work to Alexandros. Some attributed the work to Praxiteles, and the loss of the inscribed block may have been engineered to support this theory. The statue was found in 1820 by a peasant on the island of Melos. When found it was in two pieces, along with other fragments. It was bought by the Marquis de Rivière, who donated it to Louis XVIII, King of France. The latter in turn donated it to the Musée du Louvre, where the sculpture has been on display since 1821. The *Venus* was repaired in haste, evidently in order to exhibit it quickly, so that in 1875 the work had to be done again. It has never been fully restored, perhaps because of the disparity of opinions regarding its original state. Some scholars thought it should be identified as a victorious Venus, in which case she would hold the apple of Paris in her hand. Others favoured the hypothesis that the statue was a sort of guardian divinity of the island, who would also be holding a fruit, perhaps an apple, as her attribute. Others proposed that she had held a shield or a lyre, or saw her as part of a group originally including Mars. The statue is one of the most famous sculptures in the world, although some have called attention to its coldness and suggested that its fame is disproportionate to its real artistic merits.

BIBLIOGRAPHY

W. Furtwängler: *Masterpieces of Greek Sculpture* (London, 1895), pp. 367–401

M. Robertson: *A History of Greek Art* (Cambridge, 1975), pp. 553–4

F. Haskell and N. Penny: *Taste and the Antique: The Lure of Classical Sculpture, 1500–1900* (New Haven and London, 1981), pp. 328–30

LUCA LEONCINI

Venusti, Marcello [Mantovano, Marcello] (*b* Como, ?1512–15; *d* Rome, 14 Oct 1579). Italian painter. Although he may have studied in Mantua, the earliest notices of the artist date from his participation in the workshop of Perino del Vaga in Rome in the 1540s. His first important commission, to copy Michelangelo's *Last Judgement* (Rome, Vatican, Sistine Chapel; *see* ROME, fig. 43), came from Cardinal Alessandro Farnese in 1548; the small-scale painting (Naples, Capodimonte) is a valuable document of the appearance of the fresco before Daniele da Volterra added draperies. It secured Venusti's reputation and began his long friendship with Michelangelo, who allowed him to execute numerous small-scale paintings based on his designs, usually of religious subjects. Venusti often added the settings to Michelangelo's figure studies and elaborated details to create devotional works with the intensity of miniature paintings. Among those recorded by Vasari and later sources are a large-scale *Annunciation* (Rome, S Giovanni in Laterano, sacristy), based on a Michelangelo drawing owned by Tommaso de Cavalieri (Florence, Uffizi, no. 229F), and an *Annunciation* for the Cesi Chapel in S Maria della Pace in Rome (replica, Rome, Pal. Barberini; Michelangelo's drawing, New York, Pierpont Morgan Lib.). A *St Jerome* was engraved in 1558 by Sebastiano da Reggio (*fl c.* 1550–60).

Numerous small paintings based on Michelangelo's 'presentation drawings' (highly finished drawings; for illustration *see* PRESENTATION DRAWING) have been attributed to Venusti, but his only signed and dated work is a *Holy Family* (1563; Leipzig, Mus. Bild. Kst.). Many Michelangelesque chalk drawings have been wrongly attributed to him; his own drawings, mostly in pen and wash, reveal a sweetness and suavity that distinguish him from the master and other imitators. Similar qualities are found in his independent paintings, among which are *Nativity with a Circle of Putti* (Rome, S Silvestro al Quirinale) and *St Bernard* (Rome, Vatican Mus.).

BIBLIOGRAPHY

G. Vasari: *Vite* (1550, rev. 2/1568); ed. G. Milanesi (1878–85), v, pp. 625, 632; vii, pp. 272–5

G. Mancini: *Considerazioni sulla pittura* (*c.* 1618); ed. A. Marucchi (Rome, 1956)

G. Baglione: *Vite* (1642); ed. V. Mariani (1935)

F. Scanelli: *Il microcosmo della pittura* (Cesena, 1657)

A. Bertolotti: *Artisti lombardi a Roma*, 2 vols (Milan, 1881)

A. Venturi: *Storia* (1901–40) IX, vi, pp. 475–94

C. de Tolnay: 'Marcello Venusti as Copyist of Michelangelo', *A. America*, xxviii (1940), pp. 169–76

F. Zeri: *Pittura e controriforma* (Turin, 1957)

J. Wilde: 'Cartonetti by Michelangelo', *Burl. Mag.*, ci (1959), pp. 370–80

P. Borland: 'A Copy by Venusti after Michelangelo', *Burl. Mag.*, ciii (1961), pp. 433–4

A. Perrig: 'Michelangelo und Marcello Venusti: Das Problem der Verkündigungs- und Olberg Konzeption Michelangelos', *Wallraf-Richartz-Jb.*, xxiv (1962), pp. 261–94

B. Davidson: 'Drawings by Marcello Venusti', *Master Drgs*, xi (1973), pp. 3–18

Quadri romani fra '500 e '600 (exh. cat., ed. C. Strinati; Rome, Pal. Venezia, 1979)

L. Russo: 'San Bernardo Schiaccia il Demonio', *Bull. Mnmt., Mus. & Gal. Pont.*, iv (1983), pp. 173–8

JANIS CALLEN BELL

Venuti, Ridolfino (*b* Cortona, 1705; *d* Rome, 1763). Italian antiquary and writer. He took his doctorate in civil and canon law in Rome, where he joined the entourage of Cardinal Alessandro Albani; he also began to study Classical art. His *Collectanea antiquitatum romanarum* (folio, 1736) was the first fruit of his Roman sojourn and of his friendship with other scholars and antiquaries, such as Antonio Francesco Gori, whose pupil he declared himself to be. This work, a catalogue of the collection of Antonio Borioni, was divided into 100 descriptive tables listing the objects represented in 100 corresponding engravings.

Venuti next applied himself to the study of the medals in Cardinal Albani's collection; the resulting catalogue was published in 1739. Venuti pursued his interest in numismatics with a philologist's passion and rigour, establishing the chronology of each subject and explaining its iconography. He went on to undertake a study of papal coins; about that time Pope Benedict XIV appointed him commissioner for the antiquities of Rome and custodian of the pontifical galleries. In 1744 Venuti published *Numismata romanorum pontificum*, a revised and corrected version of an earlier catalogue by Filippo Bonanni (1638–1725); it was arranged chronologically and gave some information about the coiners.

In the following years Venuti undertook the preparation of an extensive guidebook to Rome, published in 1766, and studied the antiquities possessed by the Mattei family in the Villa Celimontana (first volume, 1779). In 1762 his collection of *vedute* of Italy was published in London in three languages.

WRITINGS

Collectanea antiquitatum romanarum (Rome, 1736)

Numismata maximi moduli . . . ex museo Alexandri S.R.E. Card. Albani (Rome, 1739)

Numismata romanorum pontificum (Rome, 1744)

A Collection of Some of the Finest Prospects in Italy with Short Remarks on them (London, 1762) [text in Eng., Fr. and It.]

Accurata e succinta descrizione topografica e istorica di Roma moderna (Rome, 1766)

Monumenta vetera mattheiana, i (1779; completed and rev. G. C. Amaduzzi)

BIBLIOGRAPHY

G. de Lorenzi: 'Da Filippo Buonaiuti a Ridolfino Venuti: Alcune osservazioni sull'interesse per la medaglistica papale nella prima metà dell''700', *Annu. Accad. Etrus. Cortona*, xxi (1984), pp. 151–4

D. Gallo: 'Ridolfino Venuti: Antiquario illuminato', *L'Accademia Etrusca* (exh. cat., ed. P. Barocchi and D. Gallo; Cortona, Mus. Accad. Etrus., 1985), pp. 84–93

FRANCESCA CAPPELLETTI

Veraguas. Pre-Columbian culture of the Veraguas Province of central Panama. This area extends from the Caribbean Sea to the Pacific Ocean; it is bordered on the west by the Bocas del Toro and Chiriquí provinces and on the east by the Colon and Coclé provinces, and by the Azuero Peninsula provinces of Los Santos and Herrera. The extreme northern and southern parts consist of high mountains supporting a wet tropical climate, while the central area is dry. Veraguas culture was included by Richard Cooke as part of the central Panamanian cultural region, which exhibits cultural homogeneity through much of the archaeological record. More broadly, it is classed as part of the Intermediate area (*see* SOUTH AMERICA, PRE-COLUMBIAN, §II). Its earliest known site, Pueblo Nuevo on the Veraguas–Chiriquí border, has yielded a radiocarbon date of *c.* 230 BC, but the presence of iron tools in graves near Soná indicates the continuous use of the site into the 16th century AD. There are few published reports of excavations from Veraguas, and its cultural definition by Samuel Lothrop (1950) is based principally on the well-documented archaeological collection at the Peabody Museum of Archaeology and Ethnology at Harvard University, Cambridge, MA. Other sizeable collections are in the Museo Nacional de Panama and in the University Museum, University of Pennsylvania, Philadelphia.

There are no masonry structures known from Veraguas; it is best known for gold artefacts from graves. As in most of Panama, archaeological information comes mainly from grave contents. Similar to many in Costa Rica, Veraguas cemeteries consist of shaft-and-chamber tombs *c.* 3–6 m deep. From these have come elaborate *metates* (grinding stones), plain and painted ceramics and a variety of gold objects similar to those from SITIO CONTE and the COCLÉ culture.

1. METALWORK. Reports from Columbus's fourth voyage to the New World describe spectacular gold items worn by the indigenous population. Chiefs were said to be attired in golden helmets or headbands and chest-plates, arm- and leg-bands, and to have flat gold discs attached to their cloaks. Other items of jewellery included necklaces, pendants, earrings, earplugs and nose ornaments. All the major goldworking techniques were known (*see* SOUTH AMERICA, PRE-COLUMBIAN, §VIII, 5). Large items comprised thin sheets of hammered gold, embossed with human and animal motifs. Smaller objects, such as pendants and ear and nose ornaments, were cast using the lost-wax process into elaborate zoomorphic or anthropomorphic shapes. Cooke (1972) considered that the evidence indicated a fully developed goldworking technology, introduced to Panama from the SINÚ and Quimbaya regions of Colombia, although the iconography seems purely Panamanian. The typical animals portrayed were those native to the environment: monkeys, jaguars, frogs, snakes, crocodiles, owls, bats, eagles and long-beaked birds. As in Coclé society, these objects are interpreted as representative of rank and social status, and thus were symbols of élite power. Despite the visible similarity of the Veraguas and Coclé goldwork, the objects from Veraguas graves contain less gold. They were formed from tumbaga, an alloy of gold and copper, which was gilded on to the surface of an object using the *mise-en-couleur* technique (a process in which the gold is 'floated' to the surface with acids). That Veraguas goldwork was held in high esteem is attested by finds in distant locations, as far north as CHICHÉN ITZÁ in Mesoamerica.

2. POTTERY. The earliest ceramic remains from Pueblo Nuevo are typical of the early monochrome styles found throughout much of lower Central America. Known as Scarified ware, it is decorated with zones of simple engraved, incised or stamped geometric patterns. Other decorative techniques consist of small modelled and appliquéd designs of animals and human images and looped tripod legs on buff or red globular jars. Later developments of Veraguas pottery are typical of the rest of central Panama and include bichrome, trichrome and polychrome vessels from graves. Among those from the height of the Veraguas culture, in the 12th century AD, were bowls raised on tall, round pedestal bases or tripod supports. These were decorated with geometric designs of birds, monkeys, turtles or reptilian creatures. Grave contents also included typical Coclé-related ceramics, such as Conte and Macaracas polychromes, and even the latest styles of the Herrera phase (*see* COCLÉ), all probably imports from Coclé and further east.

3. SCULPTURE. A third group of artefacts consists of the numerous stone *metates* from Veraguas and the entire central Panama region. These are three-legged or four-legged types, with rectangular or oval plates. The crudest examples are boulder-like, with short, heavy legs and troughlike grinding plates, probably for ordinary, daily use. The most common utilitarian type encountered in Veraguas culture is extremely heavy, with tapered rectangular legs and a plate that may be slightly curved. According to Lothrop these were so common that three or four of them were often sunk into the earth to form the floor of a shaft grave. All of these *metates* probably belong to the 'classic Veraguas phase' dated *c.* AD 1100.

More elaborate *metates*, from both Veraguas and adjacent provinces, are carved in various ways (*see also* SOUTH AMERICA, PRE-COLUMBIAN, §II, 3). One type has sculpted undersides, semi-rectangular grinding plates and three tall, thin, undecorated conical legs. Attached to the undersides of the plates are zoomorphic or geometric shapes, some resembling birds. Another type, particularly common in the Veraguas culture, is known as the 'flying panel' *metate* or 'altar' (*see* SOUTH AMERICA, PRE-COLUMBIAN, fig. 10 and EASTERN AND CENTRAL COSTA RICA, fig. 1). Examples of this type have relatively flat plates, tapered cylindrical tripod supports and slightly raised rims. Attached to one leg and to the underside of the plate is a horizontal bar, popularly called a 'flying panel'. Also usually attached to the underside are from one to four human or animal images—monkeys, bats, snakes, felines and birds.

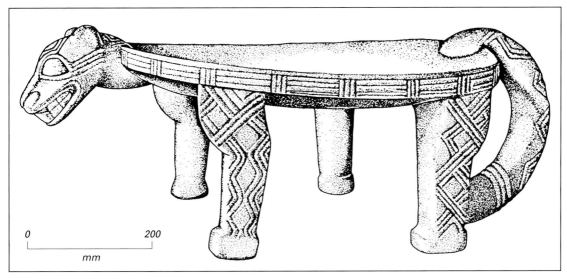

Veraguas, jaguar effigy *metate*, stone, 800×275 mm, from Las Palmas, *c.* 12th century AD (Cambridge, MA, Harvard U., Peabody Mus.); drawing

A third type of elaborate *metate* is the effigy *metate* (see fig.). This type has a relatively thin plate supported on four animal-shaped legs and, at the ends, a projecting feline head and a long curved tail. All examples are carved from volcanic stone and range in size from 0.25 to 1.20 m in length and from 0.10 to 0.40 m in height. All have well-delineated oval or circular eyes, erect ears and typical feline snouts with nostrils, and mouths with canine and other teeth exposed. Most have incised surface decoration of diagonal interlace, angular frets or diamond patterns. Veraguas effigy *metate*s are almost identical in size, shape and surface ornamentation to those from Costa Rica and the similarities are so strong as to suggest a single culture area, or a long-distance trade route from the Atlantic watershed of Costa Rica, through western Panama, to Veraguas Province.

BIBLIOGRAPHY

S. K. Lothrop: 'Archaeology of Southern Veraguas, Panama', *Mem. Peabody Mus. Archaeol. & Ethnol.*, ix (1950) [whole issue]
R. G. Cooke: *The Archaeology of the Western Coclé Province of Panama* (diss., U. London, 1972)
M. Helms: *Ancient Panama: Chiefs in Search of Power* (Austin, 1979)
R. G. Cooke: 'Archaeological Research in Central and Eastern Panama: A Review of Some Problems', *The Archaeology of Lower Central America*, ed. F. W. Lange and D. Z. Stone (Sante Fe, 1984), pp. 263–304

JOAN K. LINGEN

Veramendi [Velamendi], **Juan Miguel de** (*b* Viscaya Prov.; *fl* 1552–72). Spanish architect, active in Peru. He is documented as having worked in the cities of Cuzco and La Plata (now Sucre, Bolivia). In 1559 Veramendi was called upon by the Cabildo authorities of Cuzco Cathedral to supply plans for a new building. He signed the contract on 17 October 1559, agreeing to work as Maestro Mayor on the cathedral for an annual salary of 3000 pesos. Construction started to Veramendi's plans on 11 February 1560 but was never finished, and the scheme was superseded by a new design attributed to Francisco Becerra. Records (Cuzco Cathedral Archives, 'Actas capitulares', i, fol.114*r–v*) also indicate that another architect, Juan Correa, was engaged to work on the original design by Veramendi between 1561 and 1564. Veramendi's other major work was the first cathedral in La Plata, with a rib-vaulted transept and sanctuary, built from 1552 to 1572. In 1583 Francisco de Veramendi, possibly a relative of Juan Miguel, was engaged in the construction of a new chapel in this cathedral.

BIBLIOGRAPHY

R. Vargas Ugarte: *Ensayo de un diccionario de artífices de la América meridional* (Lima, 1947, 2/Burgos, 1968), pp. 107–9
H. E. Wethey: *Colonial Architecture and Sculpture in Peru* (Cambridge, MA, 1949, 2/1969), p. 40
J.M. Covarrubias Pozo: *Cuzco colonial y su arte* (Cuzco, 1958), pp. 13–14
E. Harth-Terré: 'La obra de Francisco Becerra en las catedrales de Lima y Cuzco', *An. Inst. A. Amer. & Inves. Estét.*, xiv (1961), pp. 18–57

HUMBERTO RODRÍGUEZ-CAMILLONI

Verandah [veranda]. Semi-enclosed space on one or more sides of a building, constructed either by extending the roof downwards and supporting it with pillars or by adding a separate pillared gallery to the side. The pillars may occasionally be linked by a balustrade or latticework. The verandah, particularly associated with European buildings in India (see fig.) and other colonial areas from the 18th century, has both social and climatic functions, providing a semi-private space and sheltering users and building from sun and rain.

The verandah is a typical feature of the dwellings of Europeans who moved from temperate zones to hotter climates and built houses designed to meet cultural expectations brought from their countries of origin. Even in elementary form, the verandah was not universally present in the indigenous building forms of those regions to which it was taken by European colonists. The term entered the English language from India (Hindi *varandā*), its origins probably either Spanish or Portuguese. The first recorded use is in 1498, in a Portuguese account of the voyage of Vasco da Gama to India (*Roteiro da viagem de Vasco da*

Hawkers on verandah at East-Parade Bungalow.

Verandah interior, Anglo-Indian colonial bungalow, Bangalore; from a photograph *c.* 1930

Gama em MCCCCXCVII (Lisbon, 1838)). The term and concept, native to the medieval building of northern Portugal and Spain, were introduced by the Portuguese to Brazil and India. Its first recorded use in English is in Charles Lockyer's *An Account of the Trade in India* (London, 1711), the frequency of references increasing from the mid-18th century, though all refer to an Indian context, as when William Hodges described a bungalow as being 'covered with one general thatch which comes low to each side; the spaces between...are viranders or open porticos' (*Travels in India, during the Years 1780, 1781, 1782, 1783* (London, 1793)).

The verandah was introduced into England in the context of colonialism and the increasing commercialization of agriculture at the close of the 18th century. With the fashion for creating Arcadian prospects on their country estates, landlords encouraged architects to produce picturesque cottage designs. John Plaw's *Sketches for Country Houses, Villas, and Rural Dwellings* (London, 1800) contains the earliest recorded use of the term in a specifically English context; Plaw, drawing on colonial knowledge from India, included a design for a cottage 'with a viranda in the manner of an Indian bungalow'.

In the first two decades of the 19th century the verandah became a fashionable feature of domestic architecture in Britain, both on the lodges of new country estates and, added in cast-iron form, on Regency terraces (see Harris and Lever, fig. 166). In 1807 Robert Southey (1774–1843) wrote, 'Here is a fashion lately introduced from better climates, of making verandahs, verandahs in a country where physicians recommend double doors, and double windows as a precaution against intolerable cold.'

A distinction needs to be made between the presence of the term and the independent existence of the feature it describes. In North America the feature, generally termed a 'piazza', existed from the late 17th century. In the early 18th century French colonists along the Mississippi built one-storey houses surrounded by a *gallerie*. Similar forms, although not the name, were known in the West Indies. The feature can be identified in illustrations of early Australian buildings in the 1790s, although the term is not known there before 1805, when it was also in use in South Africa. In the USA it was recorded in 1819, though the feature it describes was still usually called a piazza in the 19th century and subsequently a 'porch'. From the late 19th century the verandah became an increasingly popular feature for those forms of leisure building, such as the weekend cottage, bungalow, hotel or pavilion, which represented, in spatial terms, the surplus time and wealth of the industrialized market society.

See also VERNACULAR ARCHITECTURE, §IV and fig. 25.

BIBLIOGRAPHY
H. Yule and A. C. Burnell: *Hobson-Jobson: Being a Glossary of Anglo-Indian Colloquial Words and Phrases* (London, 1886, rev. 2/1903)
H. Morrison: *Early American Architecture* (New York, 1952)
J. Harris and J. Lever: *Illustrated Glossary of Architecture, 850–1830* (New York, 1966)
D. Batlin: *The Australian Verandah* (Sydney, 1976)
A. D. King: *The Bungalow: The Production of a Global Culture* (London, 1984)

ANTHONY D. KING

Verberchem. *See under* WITSEN, WILLEM.

Verberckt. Flemish family of artists, active also in France. (1) Jacques Verberckt went to Paris, became a naturalized French subject and was the principal ornamental sculptor for the Bâtiments du Roi during the Louis XV period. Jacques's brother (2) Michiel Verberckt and the latter's son (3) Jan Baptist Verberckt I and grandson Jan Baptist Verberckt II (*b* Antwerp, 17 Jan 1774; *d* Antwerp, 24 Oct 1838) remained in their native Antwerp, where they worked as silversmiths in the family workshop.

(1) Jacques [Jacob] **Verberckt** (*b* Antwerp, 24 Feb 1704; *d* Paris, 9 Dec 1771). Sculptor and ornamentalist. He studied in Antwerp with his uncle, Michiel van der Voort I, but left for Paris *c.* 1716 and by 1727 was working for the Bâtiments du Roi as an ornamental sculptor and virtuoso carver of wooden panelling and picture frames. He gained favour with the Premier Architecte du Roi, Jacques Gabriel V, and his son Ange-Jacques Gabriel and worked on many of the royal châteaux. He was approved (*agréé*) by the Académie Royale in 1733. He collaborated with Jules Degoullons (*c.* 1671–1737) on decorations at Versailles (e.g. the Chambre de la Reine, 1730; *in situ*), and for the apartments of the Dauphin and for the Petite Galerie of the king's apartments (both 1736; *in situ*). The style of this work, which accorded equal importance to the carving of the border mouldings and to the fields of the panels, later influenced the work of François de Cuvilliés I at the Munich Residenz and of Georg Wenzeslaus von Knobelsdorff at Schloss Charlottenburg, Berlin. Between 1735 and 1738 Verberckt executed, under Ange-Jacques Gabriel's supervision, further works in the king's apartments, subsequently providing decoration for other members of the king's family, for example carved panelling with trophies representing *Earth* and *Water* in the inner closet of the apartment of Mme Adélaïde (1752; *in situ*). He also worked at the châteaux of Fontainebleau (the king's bedchamber, 1752), La Muette, Choisy, Bellevue and Saint-Hubert. Among his few surviving free-standing sculptures are the Fontaine de la Douane at Bordeaux (completed 1740; drawing, Paris, Mus. A. Déc.) and two vases in marble (1742–7; one in Paris, Louvre) for the royal gardens at Choisy.

BIBLIOGRAPHY
Lami
M. Gallet and Y. Bottineau: *Les Gabriel* (Paris, 1982)
B. Pons: *De Paris à Versailles: Les Sculpteurs ornemanistes parisiens et l'art décoratif des Bâtiments du Roi* (Paris, 1986)
——: 'Jacques Verberckt (1704–71), sculpteur des Bâtiments du Roi', *Gaz. B.-A.*, 6th ser., cxix (1992), pp. 173–87

GUILHEM SCHERF

(2) Michiel (Jos) Verberckt (*b* Antwerp, 17 March 1706; *d* Antwerp, 10 Nov 1778). Silversmith, brother of (1) Jacques Verberckt. He was apprenticed in 1726 to Jan Carel II van Beughen and became a master in 1734. In the same year he married a daughter of the silversmith Jan Baptist Buijssens I. He was dean of the goldsmiths' guild (1740–42; 1758). Michiel Verberckt specialized in the production of silverwork for churches in Antwerp and the surrounding region but he also made some domestic silver, decorated with excellent chasing, first in the late Baroque style but later in a Neo-classical style.

(3) Jan Baptist Verberckt I (*b* Antwerp, 5 April 1735; *d* Antwerp, 9 March 1819). Silversmith, son of (2) Michiel Verberckt. He was an apprentice in his father's workshop, while at the same time taking lessons in modelling (1751–4) from the sculptor Cornelis d'Heur at the Academie. One of his earliest works is a signed chased silver font. From 1756 to 1761 he worked in the workshop of his uncle (1) Jacques Verberckt in Paris. He returned to Antwerp in 1761 and became a journeyman in his father's workshop but engraved his own signature on some objects. From 1762 to 1767 he attended lessons in drawing and sculpture at the Academie. In 1767 he became professor of modelling in plaster at the Academie and in 1771 a master silversmith.

Jan Baptist Verberckt took over his father's workshop in 1775. Under the French occupation he was appointed as dean of the goldsmiths' guild (1794) and commissioned to melt down confiscated silverwork. His workshop was taken over in 1811 by his son Jan Baptist Verberckt II.

The Verberckts's successful workshop produced monumental liturgical silver, as well as a great variety of domestic silverwork. His early work is in the Rococo style, but in later years he followed the pure French Neo-classical style of about 1800.

BIBLIOGRAPHY
Antwerps huiszilver 17e en 18e eeuw (exh. cat. by P. Baudouin and G. van Hemeldonck, Antwerp, Rubenshuis, 1988–9), nos. 121–3, 143–53, 172

PIET BAUDOUIN

Verboeckhoven. Belgian family of artists.

(1) Eugène(-Joseph) Verboeckhoven (*b* Warneton, nr Ypres, 18 June 1798; *d* Brussels, 19 Jan 1881). Painter and printmaker. Son of the sculptor Barthélemy Verboeckhoven (1759–1840), he began drawing as a young child. His initial desire to become a sculptor led him to produce a few models (e.g. *Lion and Tiger*; Ghent, Oudhdknd.

Mus. Bijloke). In 1815 his family moved to Ghent, where he attended the Academie from 1816 to 1818, supported by the sculptor Albert Voituron (1787–1847) and later by a Ghent patron, Ferdinand Van der Haegen. From 1818 he was a pupil of Balthasar-Paul Ommeganck, from whom he imbibed the classical landscape tradition that informed the best of his own work, such as *Landscape with Cattle and a Cowherd by a Tree* (1824; Amsterdam, Rijksmus.). Other works from this period, for example the *Halting Place* (1826; priv. col., see exh. cat., p. 318), heralded a new realism in Verboeckhoven's work. He abandoned the human figure in order to produce prosaic but popular pictures of sheep, cattle and donkeys; these animals take on human characteristics in his work and are reminiscent of bourgeois portraits of the time.

In 1827 Verboeckhoven moved to Brussels with his family, and the following year, while travelling through Germany and the Netherlands, he discovered the work of Paulus Potter, which was a turning-point in his career. Returning to Brussels, he was involved in the successful struggle for Belgian independence. He was made director of the Musée de Bruxelles by the provisional government, and, thanks to his initiative, the pictures in Antwerp Cathedral, including those by Peter Paul Rubens, were saved when the town came under fire in 1832. He became a teacher at the Académie Royale in Brussels in 1845, and his pupils there included Louis-Pierre Verwée (1807–77) and his son Alfred Jacques Verwée, and the brothers Charles Tschaggeny (1815–94) and Edmond Tschaggeny (1818–73). Aside from his own large body of work, Verboeckhoven frequently added staffage to landscapes by, among others, Jean-Baptiste De Jonghe, Henri Van Assche, Barend Cornelis Koekkoek and Louis-Pierre Verwée.

Verboeckhoven's work developed little after 1840, and his pictures clearly lack direct observation of nature. Sometimes he took more trouble than usual over royal commissions, such as the portrait of *Queen Louise's Dog* (Brussels, Mus. A. Anc.) or one of Leopold I's favourite animals (Brussels, Mus. Dynastie), and on occasion he produced striking, if improbable, scenes of feline combat against a theatrical backdrop, for example the *Ferocious Fight between the White Horse and the Roaring Lion* (1855; priv. col.; see *Du coq à l'âne: La Peinture animalière en Belgique au XIXe siècle* (exh. cat., ed. N. Hostyn and C. Delvoye; Brussels, Passage 44, 1982), p. 91).

Verboeckhoven produced some 53 etchings (e.g. *Joseph Prudhomme*) and, following a visit to London to see the royal menagerie, published *Animaux remarquables de la ménagerie* (1825).

BIBLIOGRAPHY
L. Alvin: 'Eugène Verboeckhoven', *Annu. Acad. Royale Sci., Lett. & B.-A. Belgique*, xlix (1883), pp. 341–88
P. Berko and V. Berko, eds: *Eugène Verboeckhoven* (Brussels, 1981)
1770–1830: Autour du néo-classicisme en Belgique (exh. cat., Brussels, Mus. Ixelles, 1985–6), pp. 283–4, 317–18

(2) Louis-Charles Verboeckhoven (*b* Warneton, nr Ypres, 5 Feb 1802; *d* Brussels, 25 Sept 1889). Painter, brother of (1) Eugène Verboeckhoven. He studied in Brussels under his father, Barthélemy, and his brother. He concentrated on marine painting, generally scenes from the North Sea, as in *Dutch Coast* (1840; Liège, Mus. B.-A.). Usually these scenes include a variety of boats, from humble fishing vessels to grand, two-masted brigs from foreign fleets, often shown in swelling or tempestuous seas, their sails billowing in the wind (e.g. *Rough Sea*, 1841; Kortrijk, Mus. S. Kst.). Verboeckhoven often collaborated with his brother, the latter filling in many of his compositions with figures and animals. His son, Louis Verboeckhoven (*d* 1884), lived in Ghent and painted landscapes, flower-pieces and still-lifes.

DOMINIQUE VAUTIER

Verbrugghen [Verbruggen; Verbrughen]. Flemish family of artists.

(1) Peeter Verbrugghen (i) (*b* Antwerp, *bapt* 5 June 1615; *d* Antwerp, 31 Oct 1686). Sculptor and stone merchant. He was apprenticed in 1626 to Simon de Neve (*d* before 1652). Later he worked under Erasmus Quellinus (i), and in 1641, the year he became a master sculptor, he married his master's daughter, Cornelia Quellinus. Through his collaboration with his brother-in-law Artus Quellinus (i), he absorbed the Quellinus family style, which he passed on to his 21 apprentices, among them Matheus van Beveren, Peter Scheemaeckers (i) and his own sons. From 1659 until 1661 he was Dean of the Antwerp Guild of St Luke. His major work was the furnishing of St Paul's, Antwerp, where he was responsible for the oak confessionals in 1657–9. In 1654 he made the oak organ case in collaboration with Artus Quellinus (i), and in 1670 he and his son (2) Peeter Verbrugghen (ii) were responsible for the high altar, also of oak. His own static, thick-set, hieratic sculptures belong to the Flemish High Baroque tradition.

(2) Peeter Verbrugghen (ii) (*b* Antwerp, *bapt* 17 Aug 1648; *d* Antwerp, 9 Oct 1691). Sculptor, stone merchant and etcher, son of (1) Peeter Verbrugghen (i). After his apprenticeship with his father, he went to Rome in 1674. While there he is known to have made drawings (untraced), presumably after Gianlorenzo Bernini and the Antique, which were used by his brother (3) Henricus-Franciscus Verbrugghen. In 1680 Peeter (ii) gained his mastership but remained in his father's workshop as a collaborator. In 1691 he became Dean of the Guild of St Luke. He was a fine craftsman rather than an original artist.

(3) Henricus-Franciscus [Hendrik-Frans] **Verbrugghen** (*b* Antwerp, *bapt* 30 April 1654; *d* Antwerp, *bur* 6 March 1724). Sculptor, architect and book illustrator, son of (1) Peeter Verbrugghen (i). He began his career under the book illuminator Jan Ruyselinck but became a master sculptor in 1682, the year he married Susanna Verhulst. He became Dean of the Guild of St Luke in 1689. Most of his work was done for churches. In 1684 he created two limewood side altars (h. 5 m) for the chapel of Our Lady of Good Will at Duffel. Here he introduced into the Netherlands a new motif, derived from the work of Bernini and consisting of an oval painting supported by two flying angels. His communion rails (l. 20 m; 1695) for St Walburgis, Bruges, are a highpoint of Flemish Baroque sculpture; the virtuoso handling of the marble makes them look as if modelled from wax. His tactile sense is best shown in the figure of *St Augustine* (h. 7 m; 1697), placed under the pulpit of St Augustine's, Antwerp, in which the grain of the wood is used to suggest the wrinkles of the saint's face and the texture of his clothes. In the highly original oak pulpit he made for the Jesuits of Leuven (1696–9; Brussels Cathedral), a narrative scene is included under the body of the pulpit, which is united in a curvilinear movement with the supporting beams and the sound-board. In 1713 Henricus-Franciscus went bankrupt, but he continued his work on the marble high altar (1713–19) of St Bavo, Ghent.

BIBLIOGRAPHY

BNB; Thieme–Becker
Tentoonstelling van teekeningen der Verbrugghen's [Exhibition of drawings of the Verbrugghens] (exh. cat., Antwerp, Stadsfestzaal, 1939)
C. van Herck: 'Hendrik-Frans Verbrugghen, Antwerps beeldhouwer, 1654–1724', *Jb. Antwerpens Oudhdknd. Kring*, xvi (1940), pp. 19–80
I. Kockelbergh: *De Antwerpse 'Meester Constbeldthouwer' Henricus-Franciscus Verbrugghen, 1654–1724* (diss., U. Ghent, 1986)

IRIS KOCKELBERGH

Verdier, François (*b* Paris, 1651; *d* Paris, *bur* 20 June 1730). French painter and draughtsman. He was the son of Louis Verdier, a court clockmaker. He studied (1668–71) at the Académie Royale and in 1668 and 1671 won prizes for drawing. In 1677 he received the commission to paint that year's 'May' for Notre-Dame in Paris, the *Raising of Lazarus* (Paris, St Germain-des-Prés). In 1678 he became a member of the Académie, which required him to paint *Hercules Slaying Geryon* (untraced) as his *morceau de réception*. In 1679 Verdier travelled to Rome, to continue his training until 1680 at the Académie de France.

In the years following his return to Paris he worked mainly on official commissions and under the guidance of Charles Le Brun, whose niece he married in 1685. For the Gobelins he painted cartoons (Fontainebleau, Château) for a series of tapestries of *The Months*, which were woven in 1687–8 for the Grand Trianon at Versailles and which depict Greek gods with their appropriate zodiacal signs. He assisted Le Brun in the decoration of the Galerie d'Apollon at the Louvre and painted 14 decorative mythologies (1688–98) for the Grand Trianon, his most important group of works. Although otherwise his work is heavily dependent on Le Brun, these paintings are idiosyncratic in their artificiality of colour and the extreme classicism of their forms. Verdier's commissions for the Grand Trianon included also a large Poussinesque altarpiece of the *Assumption of the Virgin* (1688; Versailles, Château).

In 1684 Verdier had been appointed a professor at the Académie, a post that he held until 1699. After this date he seems to have existed on his earnings as a draughtsman. Some of his numerous nude life studies (e.g. Paris, Louvre, Cab. Dessins) were engraved and published in 1747 by Nicolas de Poilly the younger (1675–1747) as *Recueil de plusieurs figures d'Académie, dessinées d'après nature par François Verdier, peintre ordinaire du Roy* (e.g. Paris, Bib. N., Cab. Est.).

BIBLIOGRAPHY

Mariette; Thieme–Becker
A.-N. Dézallier d'Argenville: *Abrégé de la vie des plus fameux peintres* (1745–52, 2/1762), iv, p. 138–9
A.-P.-F. Robert-Dumesnil: *Le Peintre-graveur français* (1835–71), viii, p. 280
P. M. Auzas: 'Les Grands Mays de Notre Dame de Paris', *Gaz. B.-A.*, xxxvi (1949), p. 177
A. Schnapper: 'L'*Assomption de la Vierge* de François Verdier', *Rev. Louvre*, xiv (1964), pp. 323–6

B. Lossky: 'Les Figures des dieux pour la tenture des mois arabesques', *Rev. Louvre*, xxiii (1973), pp. 169–72

V. Kaposy: 'Une Oeuvre de François Verdier', *Bull. Mus. N. Hong. B.-A.*, liii (1979), pp. 189–97

——: 'Remarques sur quelques oeuvres de François Verdier', *Acta His. A. Acad. Sci. Hung.*, xxvi (1980), pp. 75–91

CATHRIN KLINGSÖHR-LE ROY

Verdizotti [Verdezotti; Verdizzotti], **Giovanni** [Zuan] **Maria** (*b* Venice, 1525; *d* Venice, 1600). Italian printmaker, draughtsman and writer. He is mainly remembered for his friendship with Titian, who, in 1556, introduced him to Vasari. After the death in that year of Pietro Aretino, he probably became Titian's secretary. According to Ridolfi, Verdizotti specialized in painting small scenes of landscapes with tiny figures, but no painted work can be attributed with certainty to him. The most secure work in his rather obscure oeuvre is the signed drawing of *Cephalus and Procris* (pen and ink; Brunswick, Herzog Anton Ulrich-Mus.), which shows an intelligent adherence to Titian's graphic style as seen in the master's preparatory drawings (Berlin, Kupferstichkab.; Frankfurt am Main, Städel. Kstinst. & Städt. Gal.) for the *Resurrection* polyptych (1521–2; Brescia, SS Nazaro e Celso). He probably also executed the drawing of a *Bear Devouring a Rabbit in a Landscape* (pen and ink and wash; Florence, Uffizi), which carries the motto *naturam ars vincit*. This work is very similar in style to the woodcuts that illustrate his *Cento favole* (Venice, 1570). Similarly, the putative portrait of *Titian* (pen and ink; Haarlem, Teylers Mus.) is close to the Brunswick *Cephalus and Procris*. Another drawing with a plausible attribution to Verdizotti is the *Landscape with Houses* (pen and ink; Milan, Bib. Ambrosiana). In 1597 Verdizotti published his *Vite de' Santi Padri* in Venice, illustrating it with woodcuts of his own design. In the preface to this work it is mentioned that he had a canonry at Castelcucco, near Treviso. Among the large corpus of pen drawings inspired by Titian, the *Study of a Tree* (pen and ink; Madrid, Real Acad. S Fernando, Mus.) can be assigned to Verdizotti, but the *Study of Rocks and Trees* in the same collection does not appear to be his and is probably of a later date.

BIBLIOGRAPHY

G. Vasari: *Vite* (1550, rev. 2/1568); ed. G. Milanesi (1878–85), vii
L. Dolce: *Dialogo della pittura* (Venice, 1557); ed. M. W. Roskill (New York, 1968)
C. Ridolfi: *Meraviglie* (1648); ed. D. von Hadeln (1914–24), ii
N. L. Cittadella: 'Torquato Tasso e Giovanni Verdizzotti', *Ateneo Ven.*, v (1871), pp. 287–98
D. von Hadeln: *Die Zeichnungen des Tizian* (Berlin, 1924)
H. Tietze and E. Tietze-Conrat: *The Drawings of the Venetian Painters in the 15th and 16th Centuries* (New York, 1944)
G. Venturini: 'Giovanni Maria Verdizzotti, pittore e incisore, amico e discepolo di Tiziano', *Boll. Mus. Civ. Padova*, lix (1970), pp. 33–73
H. E. Wethey: *Titian and his Drawings with Reference to Giorgione and Some Close Contemporaries* (Princeton, 1987)

UGO RUGGERI

Verdun, Nicholas of. *See* NICHOLAS OF VERDUN.

Verdun, Richard of. *See* RICHARD OF VERDUN.

Verdussen, Jan Peeter (*b* Antwerp, *c.* 1700; *d* Avignon, 31 March 1763). Flemish painter and draughtsman. He came from a long line of Antwerp artists and apparently learnt the local tradition of landscape and battle painting from his father, Peeter Verdussen (1662–after 1710). Jan Peeter Verdussen went to Turin, where he entered the service of Charles-Emanuel III of Savoy, King of Sardinia, for whom he painted the great military feats of the reign, for example the *Defeat of the Imperial Forces by the Franco-Sardinian Army on 19 September 1734* (Turin, Gal. Sabauda). In 1744 Verdussen was recorded in Marseille, and in 1759 he presented his *morceau de réception*, the *Cavalry Charge* (Marseille, Mus. B.-A.), at the Académie de Marseille, of which he may later have served as director (although this is unconfirmed). Verdussen had considerable skill in composing cavalry battle scenes in the tradition of Philips Wouwerman, Adam Frans van der Meulen and the Chevalier (Karel) Breydel (1677–1733). Verdussen's drawings include the *Battle of Plaisance* (1746; Avignon, Mus. Calvet). He loved horses, an interest clearly evident in his work. Although he began as a painter of 'wars in lace' (e.g. the *Siege of Saint-Guilhain*, Versailles, Château; and the *Baggage-train of an Army Surprised by the Enemy*, Schleissheim, Neues Schloss), he increased his repertory to include more peaceful subjects (e.g. the *Horse Market* and the *Market in a Castle*, both Metz, Mus. A. & Hist.; and a *Mountainous Italianate Landscape with a Castle and Shepherd*, Karlsruhe, Bad. Landesmus.).

BIBLIOGRAPHY

Thieme–Becker; Wurzbach
F. J. Van den Branden: *Geschiedenis der Antwerpsche schilderschool* (Antwerp, 1883), p. 1080
P. Bautier: 'Les Peintres bataillistes Pierre et Jean-Pierre Verdussen', *An. Acad. Royale Archéol. Belgique*, ix (1921–2), p. 289
——: *La Peinture en Belgique au XVIIIe siècle* (Brussels, 1945), pp. 12–13

ALAIN JACOBS

Verein Berliner Künstler [Association of Berlin Artists]. German group of artists. It was founded in 1814 as the Berlinischer Künstler Verein (BKV) in response to the feeling that the end of the War of Liberation (1813) against France marked the beginning of a new era in art, requiring all forces to work together towards joint action. Initially there were 32 members; this number soon rose to 45. The moving force behind BKV was the architect Louis Catel (1776–1819), but its dominant personality was Johann Gottfried Schadow. Its purpose was 'friendly teaching, advice and conversation about art and art objects'. From the outset the association's activities also included social gatherings. A collection of over 600 drawings (Berlin, Berlin Mus.) documents the artistic activity at the weekly meetings. The BKV accepted younger members in the years that followed, but despite this in 1825 several of them banded together to form the Verein Jüngerer Berliner Künstler (which later included Adolph Menzel), where enjoyment and sociability were given much more emphasis. That group remained in existence until 1847.

The arrival in Berlin in 1841 of Peter Cornelius, on whom Wilhelm Hensel and some young, conservatively minded artists grouped around him pinned great hopes, led to the foundation in the same year of the Verein Berliner Künstler (VBK). The BKV gradually merged with it. The VBK, which initially had no eminent members, developed slowly at first. Its main purpose was to provide mutual support in the deteriorating economic situation. The twice-yearly parties played an important role in keeping the group together. The revolutions of 1848 strengthened the artists' self-confidence, but it was only after the foundation of the German Reich (1871) that the VBK developed into an institution whose impact on Berlin artistic life was on a par with that of the Akademie der Künste.

In 1866 the VBK had 145 members. By 1872 it had 274 ordinary and 98 extraordinary members. It endeavoured to increase state patronage of the arts and to gain influence over the purchasing policy of the Nationalgalerie. It organized its own exhibitions, including a permanent display, and supported its members through an emergency assistance fund. It built up a library and a collection of costumes and weaponry and organized a dispatch service for works of art. Above all, however, it improved commissions for artists by developing their relations with the rich middle classes. The *Gründerzeit* (1871–3), a period of rapid industrial expansion, promoted the formation of private collections of art; the imperial family were also patrons of the association.

The VBK reached the height of its influence in 1891 when it held an international exhibition to mark its 50th anniversary. From 1893 it collaborated with the Akademie in organizing the Grosse Berliner Kunstausstellung; it was now officially recognized as representing the artistic community of Berlin. Among the festivities it staged in this period was the Pergamonfest (1886), held to celebrate the successes of German archaeology in Pergamon and Olympia; imperial Germany saw itself as the heir to antiquity, as was demonstrated by the concurrence between contemporary art, tradition and science in official cultural and educational policies.

Anton von Werner (President, 1887–95, 1899–1901, 1906–7) was principally responsible for the VBK's powerful position. As early as 1892, however, deep divisions were manifested in a controversy between attitudes to official art and to modern, revolutionary art; this mirrored a general debate in society between conservative and liberal reforming forces. In 1892 Edvard Munch was invited to hold an exhibition, but his work was perceived as provocative, and a proposal by members that the exhibition should be closed down was carried by a narrow margin. This row led to the formation of the breakaway Freie Künstlervereinigung; even before this, in 1892, the 'Vereinigung der Elf' (also called 'Gruppe der Elf'), which included Max Liebermann, Walter Leistikow and Franz Skarbina, had called for a renewal of art and the acceptance of Impressionist ideas.

The Berliner Secession, founded in 1898, was the most significant of other generally short-lived artists' groups in opposing the conservative stance of the VBK (*see* SECESSION, §2). The construction of grand premises (inaugurated 1898) on Bellevuestrasse failed to stem the gradual decline in the power of the VBK; it chose not to oppose the absolutist art policy of William II (*reg* 1888–1918) and made the material welfare of artists its principal concern; such new concepts as Art Nouveau were accepted in moderation. After World War I the VBK opened up to the democratic structures of artistic life as well as to newer art movements, but it nonetheless continued to be strongly bound up with tradition, as the large exhibition *Hundert Jahre Berliner Kunst* (1929) showed. The association's opulent premises were vacated in 1930 in exchange for a more modest building in Lützowplatz, so that the proceeds could be used to honour social commitments. After 1933 the association's conservative stance helped it to remain in existence. It did not, however, comply totally with the demands of the Nazis.

The VBK's new offices were destroyed by bombing in World War II. In 1949 the association was granted permission to resume its activities, but it was confined to the western sector of Berlin. Its first post-war exhibition was held in 1950. The VBK moved to new premises, on Schöneberger Ufer, in 1964. Its most important task by the late 20th century was to exhibit members' work. When it celebrated its 150th anniversary in 1991, its membership consisted of 122 painters, sculptors and architects from a variety of artistic styles.

BIBLIOGRAPHY

L. Pietsch, ed.: *Verein Berliner Künstler: Festschrift zur Feier seines fünfzigjährigen Bestehens, 19 Mai 1891* (Berlin, 1891)
Hundert Jahre Berliner Kunst im Schaffen des Vereins Berliner Künstler (exh. cat. by G. J. Kern and M. Osborn, Berlin, Ver. Berlin. Kstler, 1929)
100 Jahre Verein Berliner Künstler (exh. cat., Berlin, Ver. Berlin. Kstler, 1941)
'. . . Und abends in Verein': Johann Gottfried Schadow und der berlinische Künstler-Verein, 1814–1840* (exh. cat., Berlin, Berlin Mus., 1983)
Verein Berliner Künstler: Versuch einer Bestandsaufnahme von 1841 bis zur Gegenwart (Berlin, 1991)

HELMUT BÖRSCH-SUPAN

Verelst. Dutch family of painters. Pieter Verelst (?1618–?86) was from Antwerp and a pupil of Gerrit Dou. He was the father of Harman Verelst (1641/2–99), a portrait painter, and (1) Simon Verelst, who was renowned for his flower paintings. Both brothers moved to London to practise. Harman's daughter (2) Maria Verelst followed in his footsteps and enjoyed success in England, while Harman's son Cornelis Verelst (1667–1734) was the father of (3) William Verelst, who was probably the most accomplished portrait painter in the family.

(1) Simon (Pietersz.) Verelst (*b* The Hague, 21 Aug 1644; *d* London, ?1721). He joined the Guild of St Luke at The Hague in 1666 and in 1669 went to London, where he was visited on 11 April by Samuel Pepys, to whom he tried to sell 'a little flower-pott of his doing' for £70. Verelst was certainly the finest flower painter to work in England until the arrival of Jean-Baptiste Monnoyer.

Many signed examples of Verelst's flower paintings are known, and his style is easily recognizable (e.g. *Group of Flowers*, Cambridge, Fitzwilliam; *Vase of Flowers with a Butterfly*, Oxford, Ashmolean). According to George Vertue, Verelst was encouraged to take up portrait painting by George Villiers, 2nd Duke of Buckingham, and he was soon receiving commissions from the Court, even providing competition for Peter Lely. Although his flower paintings, which continue to be esteemed, were within the realistic Dutch tradition, his portraits were influenced by the more superficial contemporary French taste. His subjects included *Charles II* (e.g. Parham House, W. Sussex) and several portraits of Mary of Modena, one of which includes a typical vase of flowers (Longleat House, Wilts). His portrait of *Louise de Kerouaille, Duchess of Portsmouth* (London, Hampton Court, Royal Col.) is one of several portraits of Charles II's mistresses. His main patron could have been Nell Gwyn, of whom a sequence of portraits survive (including a signed head in the National Portrait Gallery, London, no. 2476). Verelst 'grew very proud and conceited' and at some point was confined for insanity; it has been alleged that the madness caused him to paint roses and peonies hopelessly over scale. He died 'at a great age'; the date given varies between 1710 and 1721, although the later year seems to be more likely.

BIBLIOGRAPHY

S. Pepys: *Diary*; ed. R. Latham and W. Matthews, ix (London, 1976), p. 515
H. Walpole: *Anecdotes of Painting in England* (1762–71); ed. R. N. Wornum (1849)
'The Note-books of George Vertue', *Walpole Soc.*, xviii (1930); xx (1932); xxii (1934); xxiv (1936); xxvi (1938); xxix (1947) [index]
E. K. Waterhouse: *Painting in Britain, 1530–1790*, Pelican Hist. A. (London, 1953, rev. 4/1978), p. 145
E. Croft-Murray and P. Hulton: *British Museum Catalogue of British Drawings*, i (London, 1960), pp. 535–6
F. Lewis: *Simon Pietersz. Verelst: 'The God of Flowers'* (Leigh-on-Sea, 1979) [with a Verelst genealogy]

RICHARD JEFFREE

(2) Maria Verelst (*b* Vienna, 1680; *d* London, 1744). Niece of (1) Simon Verelst. When she was three years old she moved to London, where she later studied with (1) Simon Verelst and her father Harman Verelst. She became accomplished at finely detailed oil paintings and also as a languages teacher. According to anecdote, her success as a painter was due, at least in part, to her linguistic abilities. One night at the theatre some men near by were conversing at length in German and admiring Maria. She turned to them and, speaking in German, told them that to compliment her in such extravagant terms was no compliment. The men continued in Latin; when Maria then responded in Latin the men were impressed enough to make her acquaintance. Subsequently she painted a portrait of each, and as a result of the men's connections she built up a cultured clientele. A *Portrait of a Young Man* (Nuremberg, Ger. Nmus.) is attributed by some to Maria Verelst.

BIBLIOGRAPHY

C. Erskine Clement: *Women in the Fine Arts* (Boston and New York, 1904, 2/Cambridge, MA, 1905)
C. Petteys and others: *Dictionary of Women Artists* (Boston, MA, 1985)

(3) William [Willem] **Verelst** (*fl* London 1732–56). Nephew of (2) Maria Verelst. His major work is perhaps the *Georgia Council of 1734–5* (Wintherthur, DE, Dupont Mus.), but Verelst also produced a number of small-scale portraits and conversation pieces, including the fine *Gough Family* (1741; Elvetham Hall, Hants). His life-size portraits are usually distinguished by solid characterization and dramatic lighting, as in *John, 9th Earl of Rothes* (1732; Leslie House, Fife) and *Mrs Bamber* (1743; Hatfield House, Herts). Verelst also produced attractive three-quarter-length portraits of young women, for example *Kitty Clive* (1740; London, Garrick Club).

UNPUBLISHED SOURCES

London, NPG [typescript MS. by C. H. Collins Baker (n.d.)]

BIBLIOGRAPHY

Waterhouse: *18th Century*
E. K. Waterhouse: *Painting in Britain, 1530–1790*, Pelican Hist. A. (Harmondsworth, 1953, rev. 4/1978), pp. 145, 193
Manners and Morals (exh. cat. by E. Einberg, London, Tate, 1988), pp. 124–5, 247

RICHARD JEFFREE

Vereshchagin, Vasily (Vasil'yevich) (*b* Cherepovets, nr Vologda, 26 Oct 1842; *d* Port Arthur [now Lüshun], 13 April 1904). Russian painter. The most accomplished Russian 19th-century battle painter, he was the son of a landowner and was educated from 1850 to 1860 in the Cadet Corps in St Petersburg, finishing with the rank of naval cadet. He sailed in 1858 and 1859 on the frigate *Kamchatka*, and other vessels, to Denmark, France and England, and developed a love of travel. Abandoning the career of a naval officer, he entered the St Petersburg Academy of Arts in 1860. However, dissatisfied with the conservatism and idealistic conventions of the academic system of teaching and craving to create 'an art of great ideas', he left the academy early, in 1863. The 'Revolt of the 14 Artists', who were opposed to academic teaching and later formed the Wanderers, took place at this time. The Critical Realism of the Wanderers always elicited Vereshchagin's passionate sympathy, and he later took part in some of their exhibitions. In 1864, having travelled to Paris, Vereshchagin came under the influence of Jean-Léon Gérôme, visiting his studio at the Ecole des Beaux-Arts. Gérôme's compositional skill in his history paintings and his effective handling of detail made a great impression on Vereshchagin. He was also impressed by the Orientalist paintings of Gérôme and of the French painter Alexandre Bida (1813–95).

Vereshchagin travelled ceaselessly, across Russia and to Western Europe. He went twice to Turkestan (1867–8; 1869–70), where he took part in the military actions of the Russian armies moving south of the frontier of the Russian empire, and twice to India (1874–6; 1882). In 1877–8 he was wounded in the Russo-Turkish War. He also visited Syria and Palestine (1884), the USA (1888–9 and 1902), the Philippines (1901), Cuba (1902) and Japan (1903). He produced numerous sharply observed ethnographic and social studies from life, distilling his observations in the battle paintings that brought him great fame. A romantic contemplativeness and pleasure in the diverse beauty of the world are characteristic of his landscape and genre pictures (on Central Asian, Indian, Russian, Caucasian and other themes), but as a battle painter he embraced the principles of Critical Realism. His battle paintings responded to the transition in European late 19th-century history painting from classical and romantic heroization to a more critical representation of war as tragic error. His paintings stand out against this background for their monumental pathos and passionate declamation of pacifism. Although traditional, they nevertheless anticipate socially committed work of the 20th century.

In Vereshchagin's large-scale Turkestan series (1869–73), the colouring itself, yellow-brown and saturated with desert air, seems heavy with the tragedy of death. The best-known work of the series, the *Apotheosis of War* (1870–71; Moscow, Tret'yakov Gal., see fig.), which depicts a group of skulls against the background of a deserted horizon, bears a significant inscription on the frame: 'Dedicated to all great conquerors: past, present and future'. (The artist used inscriptions on frames on a number of occasions, reinforcing the declamatory style of his pictures.) The anti-war symbolism of this work encompasses several areas: Tamerlane (or Timur, the central Asian ruler of the 14th century; the original name for the

Vasily Vereshchagin: *Apotheosis of War*, oil on canvas, 1.27×1.97 m, 1870–71 (Moscow, Tret'yakov Gallery)

picture was *Apotheosis of Tamerlane*), gloomy reflections on Turkestan and the Franco-Prussian War (the picture was completed while newspaper reports were being received of the latter). After his journey across India, Vereshchagin began (mainly in 1876) the Indian series, which shows the colonial expansion of the English. In 1878–80 he created the Balkan series, devoted to the Russo-Turkish War. Although a pan-Slavist mood prevailed in Russian society at that time and there was a movement of solidarity with the Bulgarian people who were struggling against the yoke of the Ottoman empire, Vereshchagin still produced terrifying depictions of battles that have no trace of patriotic bias. The painting the *Conquered: Funeral* (1878–9; Moscow, Tret'yakov Gal.) produced an especially strong impression on his contemporaries.

Among Vereshchagin's next series, that on the theme of the war against the French in 1812 enjoyed the greatest popularity. The paintings in this huge series are not entirely free from the theatrical and the grandiose, but certain images are memorable because of their dramatic effects, for example *Keep Away, I'll Take Care of Him* (1887–95; Moscow, Hist. Mus.), which depicts the Russian partisans in an ambush, surrounded by the branches of a snow-covered forest. During the 1880s Vereshchagin also frequently returned to a more evangelical theme, depicted with the strict verism that is characteristic of all his work. From 1870 to 1890 exhibitions of Vereshchagin's work travelled throughout Europe and the USA, arousing strong reactions. By the turn of the century he had become the most popular Russian artist abroad. In his own country

too, his appeal for pacifism and his social concern attracted the sympathy of the liberally minded circles of society (e.g. the critic Vladimir Stasov and the writer V. M. Garshin, among others). Vereshchagin's work can be connected, through the tradition of anti-militarist protest, with such German Expressionists as Käthe Kollwitz and Otto Dix; the central motif of the *Apotheosis of War* has been repeated many times in 20th-century anti-war posters. Vereshchagin was killed in the Russo-Japanese war zone, in an explosion on the battleship *Petropavlovsk*.

WRITINGS

Na voyne v Azii i Evrope: Vospominaniya [At war in Asia and Europe: reminiscences] (Moscow, 1894)

Perepiska V. V. Vereshchagina i V. V. Stasova [The correspondence of V. V. Vereshchagin and V. V. Stasov], 2 vols (Moscow, 1950–51)

Perepiska V. V. Vereshchagina i P. M. Tret'yakova 1874–1898 [The correspondence of V. V. Vereshchagin and P. M. Tret'yakov 1874–1898] (Moscow, 1963)

Izbrannye pis'ma [Selected letters] (Moscow, 1981)

BIBLIOGRAPHY

A. K. Lebedev: *V. V. Vereshchagin: Zhizn' i tvorchestvo* [V. V. Vereshchagin: life and work] (Moscow, 1972)

V. Belentschikow: 'Krieg ohne Glorie', *Bild. Kst*, 29 (1981), pp. 314–16

V. V. Vereshchagin: Vospominaniya syna khudozhnika [V. V. Vereshchagin: reminiscences of the artist's son] (Leningrad, 1982)

E. V. Zavadskaya: *V. V. Vereshchagin* (Moscow, 1986)

A. K. Lebedev and A. V. Solodovnikov: *V. V. Vereshchagin* (Leningrad, 1987)

L. Demin: *S mol' bertom pozemnomu sharu: Mir glazami V. V. Vereshchagina* [Around the world with an easel: the world through the eyes of V. V. Vereshchagin] (Moscow, 1991)

Vereysky, Georgy (Semyonovich) (*b* Proskurov [now Khmel'nitsky], Ukraine, 30 July 1886; *d* Leningrad [now St Petersburg], 18 Dec 1962). Russian printmaker, draughtsman, watercolourist and museum curator of Ukrainian birth. He studied in St Petersburg in 1913–16 under Mstislav Dobuzhinsky, Boris Kustodiyev and Anna Ostroumova-Lebedeva. He was a member of the World of Art (Mir Iskusstva) society and took part in their exhibitions. He was an expert on ancient European drawing, and between 1918 and 1930 he was in charge of the department of drawing and engraving at the Hermitage, St Petersburg.

Vereysky represented a tendency in Russian art stemming from the traditions of the World of Art with its concern for technical mastery and its retrospective spirit. He used various techniques (lithography, etching, drawing and black watercolour), producing monochromes with a rich tonal range. He was primarily a master of the psychologically penetrating portrait, and he gradually moved from his early dry style to one that was freer and more pictorial. Among his most accomplished portrait series and lithographic albums are *Portraits of Russian Artists* (Petrograd, 1922, and Leningrad, 1927), *Russian Writers* (issues 1–2, Leningrad, 1927–9) and a series of portraits of Russian cultural figures (1944–61). He also turned to landscape, producing intimate, lyrical images.

BIBLIOGRAPHY

G. A. Chernova: *G. S. Vereysky* (Moscow, 1965)
G. S. Vereysky: Akvareli, risunki [G. S. Vereysky: watercolours, drawings] (Moscow, 1973)

M. N. SOKOLOV

Vergara. Spanish family of artists. Arnao de Vergara (*c*. 1490–1557) was master sculptor and glass painter for Burgos Cathedral from 1521 to 1525, then in Seville until 1538 and in Granada until 1557. Of his brothers, Arnao de Flandes (*b c*. 1490), a glass painter, worked with him in Seville Cathedral from 1534, and Nicolás de Vergara de Flandes (*fl* 1500–52), a sculptor and mason, worked at Burgos Cathedral. Arnao de Vergara had a son, (1) Nicolás de Vergara (i), who had two sons, (2) Nicolás de Vergara (ii) and Juan de Vergara (*d* 1588), who became a glass painter.

(1) Nicolás de Vergara (i) (*b* ?Toledo, *c*. 1517; *d* Toledo, 11 Aug 1574). Sculptor, painter and architect. He worked first as a sculptor and glass painter and was a master of both these crafts for Toledo Cathedral from 1542 until his death. From 1555 he worked with Juan Bautista Vázquez on retables for the church at Huéscar, Granada (1555), and for S María la Blanca in Toledo (1558) and on tombs at Almagro, Ciudad Real (1555), and Villagarcía, Badajoz (1560). He also designed important pieces in silver, such as the *arca* of S Eugenio (1569; Toledo Cathedral). His most outstanding sculpture (1564–74) decorates the choir-screen in Toledo Cathedral, but more individual are his works in bronze, such as the lecterns (1562–71) in Toledo Cathedral and the grille (1566–80) of the tomb (1518–21) of *Cardinal Francisco Jiménez de Cisneros* in the chapel of the University of Alcalá de Henares, which demonstrate his classical version of Alonso Berruguete's style. He provided the architectural decoration (1569) for the chapel of the Virgen de la Salud in S Leocadia, Toledo, and in 1573 he began the stucco decoration, painting and sculpture of the retable and chapel of S Gil in Toledo Cathedral (completed by (2) Nicolás de Vergara (ii)).

(2) Nicolás de Vergara (ii) (*b* Toledo, *c*. 1542; *d* Toledo, 11 Dec 1606). Architect, sculptor and painter, son of (1) Nicolás de Vergara (i). Although he succeeded his father as master sculptor and glass painter of Toledo Cathedral, he was especially concerned with architecture. He carved a marble figure of *St Eugenius* (*c*. 1575) for the Puerta Nueva de Bisagra, Toledo, and as architect was twice Maestro Mayor of Toledo Cathedral (1575–82 and 1587–1606). He worked first in the later style of Alonso de Covarrubias but then moved closer to the classical manner introduced by Juan de Herrera. He was, however, the most creative and individual of Herrera's followers, both in his treatment of wall surfaces (relying on the Classical orders and reducing the use of entablatures) and in his management of space and light. His most important works are the cloister of S Bernardo (1576), Toledo, the church and sacristy of the Hospital of S Juan Bautista (*c*. 1576), Tavera, the sacristy of S Pedro Mártir (1587), Toledo, both the chapel of S José and the church at the Hospital de la Caridad (1588), Illescas, the whole chapel of the Virgen del Sagrario (1591), Toledo Cathedral, the planning of the Plaza Mayor in both Talavera de la Reina and Toledo (1593), the Capilla de las Reliquias (1595) in the monastery of Guadalupe, the parish church of Noblejas (1598), Toledo, and S Pedro Mártir (1605), Toledo.

BIBLIOGRAPHY

F. Pérez Sedano: *Datos documentales inéditos para la historia del arte español: Notas del archivo de la catedral de Toledo* (Madrid, 1914)
M. R. Zarco del Valle: *Datos documentales para la historia del arte español: Documentos de la catedral de Toledo*, 2 vols (Madrid, 1916)
J. M. de Azcárate: *Escultura del siglo XVI*, A. Hisp., xiii (Madrid, 1958)
F. Portela Sandoval: 'Nicolás de Vergara, el Mozo', *Goya*, 112 (1973), pp. 208–13
F. Marías: *La arquitectura del Renacimiento en Toledo, 1541–1631*, 4 vols (Toledo and Madrid, 1983–6)
M. Estella Marcos: *Juan Bautista Vázquez el Viejo en Castilla y América: Nicolás de Vergara, su colaborador* (Madrid, 1990)

FERNANDO MARÍAS

Vergara, José (*b* Valencia, 2 June 1726; *d* Valencia, 9 March 1799). Spanish painter. He came from a Valencian family of sculptors and painters, including Francisco Vergara (the elder; 1681–1753) and Ignacio Vergara (the younger; 1715–76), both sculptors.

With his brother Ignacio, José Vergara was decisively involved in the creation of the Academia de S Bárbara, which in 1768, under the patronage of Charles III, became the Academia de S Carlos. Vergara was appointed the first Director of Painting in March 1765 and its first Director General (1779–81 and 1787–90). His teachings, and the large number of works that he did for religious orders in Valencia and the province of Valencia, as well as in Alicante and Castellón, proved crucial for the development and evolution of Valencian painting in the 18th century. His fresco compositions were much finer and fresher than his works on canvas or panel (see fig.), and he was, in his time, one of the leading fresco painters in Valencia. His style has a certain affinity with the work of Neapolitan artists and has been compared with that of Paolo de Matteis and, less appropriately, of Corrado Giaquinto. Vergara was also aware of the work of earlier artists such

José Vergara: *Self-portrait* (Madrid, Academia de S Fernando)

as Juan de Juanes and Francisco Ribalta, and he made copies after their works.

In 1744–5 Vergara received his first important commission, to paint the pendentives of the transept vault in the cathedral at Játiva, on which he depicted a fresco of biblical heroines (destr. 1886). His paintings in fresco for the church of S Rosa de Lima, Valencia (now Mus. Hist.; *in situ*), depict scenes from the *Life of St Rosa* (*c.* 1760). His canvases for the side altars include the *Mystic Marriage of St Catherine*, the *Martyrdom of St Catherine* and the *Presentation of the Virgin* (all 1760). For his paintings between the pilasters in the chapel of the Virgen de los Desamparados (Virgin of the Abandoned or Deserted) in the church of the same name in Valencia (*c.* 1765), he returned to the theme of biblical heroines. His painting on canvas for the altar depicted the bestowal of the habit on a member of the Brotherhood before an image of the Virgen de los Desamparados (*c.* 1765; *in situ*). Between about 1772 and 1781 he decorated the chapel of S Vincente Ferrer in the convent of S Domingo, Valencia, where he depicted the *Exaltation of St Vincent in Glory* on the vault of the apse; in the four pendentives, he painted miracles from the *Life of St Vincent Ferrer*; and for the canvas for the high altar his subject was *St Vincent Preaching on the Last Judgement*.

Vergara's most important and influential work was carried out in fresco and on canvas for the parish church of S Juan Bautista, Chiva, on which he worked intermittently (1769–90). The scheme began with the *Four Evangelists* (1769) for the pendentives of the transept. Between

1784 and 1787 he painted the *Gloria* in the chancel and in 1790 *St John the Baptist Preaching in the Desert* on canvas for the main altar. He resolved the scheme of decoration of the rear wall with figures of St Peter and St Paul flanking the main altar, in the same way that the Genoese painter Matarana (*fl* end of the 16th century) had previously treated the rear wall of the church of the Patriarch, Valencia.

Vergara's decoration in fresco for the archiepiscopal church of Villarreal, Castellón, was composed of scenes from the *Life of St James the Apostle* (1760–70) on the pendentives of the transept and scenes on a eucharistic theme for the chapel of the Comunión. From 1780 Vergara collaborated with José Camarón Melía at the monastery of El Puig on the decoration of the *camarín*, the space behind the altar.

Between 1782 and 1786 Vergara painted the decoration in fresco of the chapel of the Comunión in the church of S Juanes, Valencia, whose external iconographic programme on the theme of the Eucharist was drawn up by the artist. From the beginning of the 1790s until 1795 he worked on a commission from the chapter of Valencia Cathedral to paint canvases for various chapels, including that of the *Martyrdom of St Vincent Ferrer* on the epistle side.

Vergara was also significant as a man of letters and art critic, mostly producing works (none of them published) related to the fine arts, academic discourses and notes on the lives of Valencian artists, which Marcos Antonio de Orellana may have used for his own book on the same subject. Vergara also left explanations (all untraced) of some of the iconographic programmes in his own paintings.

BIBLIOGRAPHY

Ceán Bermúdez

'La familia Vergara', *Archv A. Valenc.*, iii/2 (1917), p. 151

M. A. Orellana: *Biografía pictórica valentina o vida de los pintores, arquitectos, escultores y grabadores valencianos* (Madrid, 1930, rev. Valencia, 2/1967)

ADELA ESPINÓS DÍAZ

Vergé, Jacques. *See* BERGÉ, JACQUES.

Verge, John (*b* Christchurch, Hants, 15 March 1782; *d* nr Kempsey, NSW, 9 July 1861). Australian architect of English birth. He came from a family whose members had worked in the building trade for generations. His father, Nicholas Verge, was a bricklayer, and Verge entered the family trade. About 1804 he went to London and worked there as a tradesman and builder, probably also acquiring experience of architecture. By 1828 he was an established builder and owned several properties in London, but in that year he moved to Sydney with the intention of farming, acquiring a large pastoral property on the Williams River, NSW. By 1830, however, financial constraints forced him to return to Sydney, where he quickly established a large and successful practice as an architect–builder, assisted from 1832 by John Bibb (1810–62), a trained architect. During the next seven years they reportedly produced more than a hundred buildings, mostly in a Neo-classical Georgian style, among which were some of the finest houses of the period in Sydney. Surviving examples include Tusculum (1831), Woolloomooloo, with an encircling verandah supported on cast-iron columns; Toxteth Park House (1831) and Lyndhurst (1833; both altered), Glebe; and Elizabeth Bay House (1835), Elizabeth Bay, built for the Colonial Secretary Alexander Macleay, which has a grand, elliptical, domed stair-hall, with a first-floor gallery opening through tall arches. Outside Sydney Verge designed Camden Park House (begun 1831), Camden, for William Macarthur, which has a columned porch on the entrance façade and a colonnade on the garden front; it also had the first bathroom—in reality a bath-house—in Australia. At Denham Court (1833), near Campbelltown, Verge's additions transformed the building into a small version of a building of the same name in Bucks, England, with two bow-fronted, single-storey wings abutting a new two-storey east front. All Verge's work was characterized by beautiful detailing, particularly in the cedar joinery, although his interior planning was often weak. Other commissions included the first Congregationalist and Baptist churches in Sydney and the addition of vestries to the east end of Francis Greenway's church of St James, Sydney, which were designed to match the original. Verge also designed the British Residency (1833–4; now the Treaty House) in Waitangi, New Zealand; prefabricated in Sydney, it was the first building in New Zealand to be designed by a practising architect. In 1837 Verge retired, leaving Bibb to take over the practice.

BIBLIOGRAPHY

M. Herman: *The Early Australian Architects and their Work* (Sydney, 1954, 2/1970)
W. G. Verge: *John Verge: Early Australian Architect* (Sydney, 1962)
R. Roxburgh: *Early Colonial Houses of New South Wales* (Sydney, 1974, 3/1980)
J. Broadbent, I. Evans and C. Lucas: *The Golden Decade of Australian Architecture: The Work of John Verge* (Sydney, 1978)

VALERIE A. CLACK

Vergelli, Tiburzio (*b* Camerino, 1555; *d* ?Loreto, 7 April 1610). Italian sculptor. He may have been trained as a bronze sculptor in Recanati at the Fonderia Recanatese and is first recorded in 1572 as an assistant of Girolamo Lombardo in Loreto. In 1576 he was paid for work on the frames and reliefs of the four bronze doors of the S Casa in the basilica of S Maria in Loreto. He assisted Antonio Calcagni in 1582 in casting bronzes for the Massilla–Rogati Chapel in the same church and collaborated with Antonio Lombardo II (*c.* 1564–between 1608 and 1610) in 1583 on the group of the *Virgin and Child* for the basilica's façade. In 1585 he was commissioned by the Camerino town council to execute a bronze seated statue of *Sixtus V* (completed 1589; Camerino, Piazza Cavour). The dull characterization of the Pope is relieved by Vergelli's attention to ornamental detail in the throne and the reliefs of female allegories decorating the base. In 1590 the Governatore of the S Casa allocated to Vergelli the north door of the basilica: it was inaugurated in 1598. This bronze door, divided into ten rectangular panels framed by scrolled foliage and oval reliefs, complements Antonio Calcagni's right door, both iconographically and stylistically. Although the decoration of the earlier doors of the S Casa by the Lombardo family is reminiscent of that of Lorenzo Ghiberti's Florentine Baptistery doors, Vergelli's use of oval reliefs containing statuettes of Virtues or low-relief scenes and his pictorial treatment of space and mass in the large reliefs are distinctive of his own more florid style. The richly ornamented font in the basilica, abundantly decorated with swags of fruit, reliefs, statuettes of Virtues, and angels, and surmounted by a group depicting the *Baptism*, was completed between 1600 and 1607 by Vergelli and his assistants. A bronze group of the *Virgin and Child with the Infant St John* (London, V&A) relates closely to the group of *Charity* on the font, suggesting a similar date.

BIBLIOGRAPHY

M. Santori: *Sisto V e la sua statua a Camerino* (Camerino, 1905)
G. Pauri: *I Lombardi–Solari e la scuola recanatese di scultura* (Recanati, 1915), pp. 53–4
C. Ricci: 'Statue e busti di Sisto V', *L'Arte*, xix (1916), pp. 163–74
A. Venturi: *Storia*, x, pt 2 (1936), pp. 735–46
K. Weil Garris: *The Santa Casa di Loreto: Problems in Cinquecento Sculpture*, 2 vols (New York and London, 1977), pp. 101, 348
A. Radcliffe: 'Tiburzio Vergelli, Giambologna, and a Rare Bronze Group from Recanati', *Antol. B.A.*, 24–27 (1984), pp. 21–5
P. Dal Poggetto, ed.: *Le arti nelle Marche al tempo di Sisto V* (Milan, 1992)

ANTONIA BOSTRÖM

Vergina. Village *c.* 64 km south-west of Thessaloniki, Greece, once the site of ancient Aigai, the first capital of the Macedonian dynasty. Excavations, begun in 1861 and recommenced in 1938, continued into the late 20th century; they have uncovered a prehistoric tumulus cemetery, a large Hellenistic palace, a theatre, a small temple, the city walls, remains of houses and eleven monumental vaulted tombs, of which four are royal burial vaults. The many important finds are now in the Archaeological Museum, Thessaloniki.

The palace (end of the 4th century BC) is one of the largest surviving buildings of the Hellenistic period (104.5×88.5 m). Its design is simple but impressive, with rooms arranged around a courtyard to form a harmonious architectural ensemble. The complex is divided by a central axis into two parts, north and south. Along the whole north side runs a long, narrow verandah facing northwards on to the Macedonian plain. The most formal room in the palace is a circular chamber, the 'tholos', in which the inscription 'to Herakles the ancestor' was found. The most luxurious rooms were in the south wing and had mosaic floors. Only one of these, with rich plant ornament, survives. The east wing, where the entrance was, had a second storey. All the surviving architectural elements bear witness to the care with which the palace was constructed. The theatre dates from the same period. It had stone seats in the first row only; the rest must have been wooden. The *orchestra* had a diameter of 28.44 m. It was in the theatre in 336 BC that Philip II was murdered and Alexander proclaimed King of Macedonia.

The great tombs found around Vergina are typical of the 'Macedonian' type (*see also* GREECE, ANCIENT, §II, 1(i)(d)). They have vaulted ceilings and monumental façades like those of temples or houses, with a marble door in the centre, half columns on either side and an entablature. The largest among them measure 8–10 m long, 5–8 m wide and 5–6 m high. Most were robbed in antiquity, but two royal tombs were found unplundered. The larger was almost certainly that of Philip II (*reg* 359–336 BC), while the second, the 'Prince's Tomb', contained the remains of a youth 12–14 years old, perhaps Alexander IV (*d* 310 BC), the son of Alexander the Great. Many of the numerous objects found in these two tombs are fine works of art: even the weapons, such as the unique iron breastplate and iron helmet, are examples of a highly developed technology and of exceptional artistic quality. Among the other objects, the silver vessels form the largest group and include the most elegant of all ancient Greek examples. Several are decorated with relief heads, undoubtedly by some great 4th-century BC masters of the embossed technique. A group of small ivory carvings must also be attributed to highly accomplished artists: they once decorated a wooden couch and throne, which have rotted, leaving no trace. Among the dozens of small heads is a marvellous portrait of Philip II (*see* GREECE, ANCIENT, fig. 166c) and another of Alexander the Great, the only extant contemporary portraits of these two kings. Among the gold objects the most precious are the two caskets that contained the cremated bones of Philip II and his queen. As works of art, however, the gold wreaths and the diadem are unique, the latter being arguably the most beautiful of all Greek gold ornaments.

The wall paintings in the tombs provide the first important examples of this genre from ancient Greece. Paintings survive from five of the tombs. The 'Prince's Tomb' has a narrow decorative frieze showing *Chariot Racing*. On the façade of an early 3rd-century BC tomb the deceased is depicted as a standing foot-soldier, with a spear in his right hand, while on his left a standing female figure holds out a gold wreath with which to crown him. On his right is a seated warrior. The three individual figures are well drawn and painted in a full range of colours. Although they cannot be considered great works, they are among the best Early Hellenistic examples of

painting. However, the wall paintings on the façade of Philip II's tomb and on the internal walls of a smaller chamber tomb are indisputably great works of the 4th century BC. On the façade of Philip's tomb is a frieze (1.16×5.56 m) depicting a *Hunt in a Wood*, in which men on horseback and on foot with dogs hunt wild animals in a landscape of trees, rocks and mountains. The drawing and compositional quality are exceptional, and the work may be attributable to PHILOXENOS OF ERETRIA. Of the same high quality, though in a different technique, is the *Rape of Persephone* (see fig.) inside a smaller tomb (Tomb II), which also contains some other, isolated female figures. Here the painter's preliminary sketch with incised lines in the fresh plaster has an inspired and dynamic quality, and this work may be attributable to NIKOMACHOS OF THEBES. A marble throne found in the largest known 'Macedonian' tomb (discovered in September 1987) bears a well-preserved painting of a four-horse chariot with the imposing figures of Hades and Persephone standing behind. The work dates from *c.* 340 BC, but the identity of the painter is uncertain.

BIBLIOGRAPHY
M. Andronicos: *Vergina: The Prehistoric Necropolis and the Hellenistic Palace*, Stud. Medit. Archaeol. (Lund, 1964)
——: *To nekrotapheion ton tymvon* [The cemetery of tombs], i of *Vergina* (Athens, 1969–)
N. G. L. Hammond: *A History of Macedonia*, i (Oxford, 1972)
M. Andronicos: 'The Finds from the Royal Tombs at Vergina', *Proc. Brit. Acad.*, lxv (1979), pp. 355–67
——: *Vergina: The Royal Tombs and the Ancient City* (Athens, 1984)
A. J. N. W. Prag, J. H. Musgrave and R. A. H. Neave: 'The Skull from Tomb II at Vergina', *J. Hell. Stud.*, civ (1984), pls ii–vii
M. Andronicos: 'Some Reflections on the Macedonian Tombs', *Annu. Brit. Sch. Athens*, lxxxii (1987), pp. 1–16
N. G. L. Hammond: 'The Royal Tombs at Vergina: Evolution and Identities', *Annu. Brit. Sch. Athens*, lxxxvi (1991), pp. 69–82
                                                    MANOLIS ANDRONICOS

Verhaecht [van Haecht; Verhaegt], **Tobias** (*b* Antwerp, 1561; *d* Antwerp, 1631). Flemish painter and draughtsman, active also in Italy. He spent much of his early life in Florence, where he won the favour of Francesco I, Grand Duke of Tuscany (*reg* 1574–87), and in Rome, where he earned a reputation as a painter of landscape frescoes. In 1590 he became a master in the Guild of St Luke, Antwerp. A year later he married Suzanna van Mockenborch, a distant relation of Rubens; she died in 1595, and he remarried the next year. Verhaecht was an active member of the rhetoricians' chamber, the Gillyflower, as his father had been, and he wrote a comedy for them in 1620 and donated two complete costumes for torch-bearers. In 1594 he was commissioned to design the decorations for the triumphal entry into Antwerp of Archduke Ernst of Hungary (1553–95). Verhaecht trained several pupils, including his son WILLEM VAN HAECHT II and, briefly, Rubens.

Despite the fact that Verhaecht lived in a period when Netherlandish landscape art was undergoing a great revolution and artists were beginning to depict the landscape of their own country, he continued to paint imaginary panoramic mountainous landscapes and broad prospects dominated by desolate rocky outcrops. His paintings and drawings are often fantastic landscapes constructed around

Vergina, wall painting depicting the *Rape of Persephone*, Tomb II, 4th century BC (*in situ*)

the juxtaposition of topographically interesting and unusual details. The stretched landscape, the high viewpoint and the distinctly fantastic aspects are all retardataire, and his work is closest in style to the set of 12 large engraved landscapes published by Hieronymus Cock after designs by Pieter Bruegel I. These prints were produced some 60 or 70 years before Verhaecht's dated works, which all fall within the period 1612 to 1623. Verhaecht was certainly aware of the work of his more progressive contemporaries such as Josse de Momper II and Gillis van Coninxloo III, and he borrowed elements from their works. A number of Verhaecht's landscapes were made into prints by Hans Collaert, Egbert van Panderen and Hendrik I Hondius (ii). Apart from landscapes, several paintings of the *Tower of Babel* by Verhaecht have survived, and these, like his landscapes, are characterized by a precise technique. The figures in these paintings are by such artists as Jan Breughel I, Frans Francken II and Sebastiaen Vrancx.

BIBLIOGRAPHY
Y. Thiery: *Le Paysage flamand au XVIIe siècle* (Paris and Brussels, 1953), pp. 61, 199
J. Van Roey: 'De eerste leermeester van P. P. Rubens: Tobias van Haecht [The first teacher of P. P. Rubens: Tobias van Haecht]', *De Rederijker* (Nov–Dec 1977)
HANS DEVISSCHER

Verhaegen, Arthur Théodore, Baron (*b* Brussels, 31 Aug 1847; *d* Brussels, 11 Sept 1917). Belgian architect, designer, engineer, writer and politician. After graduating as an engineer at the University of Ghent in 1870, he established himself in Charleroi before settling in Ghent on his marriage in 1872. Under the influence of JEAN-BAPTISTE-CHARLES-FRANÇOIS BETHUNE, he worked in the Belgian Gothic Revival style on architecture, furniture and wall paintings and in stained glass, gold, iron and embroidery. From 1875 to 1895 he directed the workshop for stained glass founded by Bethune. Verhaegen's most important building is the new Beguinage (1873) of Sint Amandsberg near Ghent, which conforms to the severe Gothic Revival ideals of Bethune and anticipates some of the features of garden-city designs. His churches and conventual buildings at Ghent (Poortakker, 1874; St Macharius, 1880–82), Hekelgem (abbey, 1880; church destr.), Paris (Oeuvre des Flamands Church, *c.* 1875) and Rome (Everlasting Adoration, 1885–6) and châteaux at Watermaal-Bosvoorde (1880–81) and Merelbeke (1884–5) were also in a severe Gothic Revival style. Among his successful restorations are churches at Soignies and Nivelles and the Pont des Trous at Tournai. He published monographs on Bruges Cathedral (1879), Byloke Abbey at Ghent (1889) and the Châteaux de Laerne (1891) and the Gerard Duivelsteen at Ghent (1894). At the end of his career he concentrated on politics and, as a co-founder of the Association Ouvrière Anti-Socialiste, the Ligue Démocratique Belge and the newspaper *Het Volk*, became one of the creators of the Belgian Christian Democratic movement.

BIBLIOGRAPHY
BNB
V. Fris: 'In memoriam Arthur Verhaegen', *Bull. Maatsch. Gesch. Oudhdknd. Gent*, xxiv/26 (1919), pp. 123–7
J. De Maeyer: *Arthur Verhaegen. Bijdrage tot de studie van het ultramontanisme: 1847–1884* (diss., Leuven, Katholieke U., 1976)
J. van Cleven: 'Tussen burgerlijke romantiek en grootstedelijke realiteit', *Gent en architectuur*, ed. N. Poulain (Bruges, 1985), pp. 104–5

——: 'Sint-Lucasateliers in de plastische kunsten en de toegepaste kunst', *De Sint-Lucasscholen en de neogotiek*, ed. J. De Maeyer (Leuven, 1988), pp. 303, 377–8
JEAN VAN CLEVEN

Verhaegen [Verhaeghen], **Theodoor** (*b* Mechelen, *bapt* 4 June 1700; *d* Mechelen, 21 April 1754). Flemish sculptor. He was the son of a joiner and was apprenticed to the sculptor Jan-Frans Boeckstuyns. He later worked in Antwerp with Michiel van der Voort I, Johannes Claudius von Cock and Willem Ignatius Kerricx. In 1720 he was in the Brussels workshop of Pieter-Denis Plumier. On returning to Mechelen after Plumier's death in 1721, he assisted van der Voort with the elaborate carved wooden pulpit (1721) for the monastery of Leliëndael; this pulpit (now Mechelen Cathedral) was to prove a decisive influence on his own pulpits.

Around 1732 Verhaegen worked for the Onze-Lieve-Vrouwekerk at Ninove, where his carved wooden panels of the *Life of St Cyprian* and the *Life of St Cornelius* show him to be a master of relief sculpture. His monumentally plastic Baroque confessional (1736) for the same church is the most remarkable of its kind in the southern Netherlands (for illustration *see* CONFESSIONAL). Similarly dramatic and sculptural in concept are Verhaegen's wooden pulpit for Onze-Lieve-Vrouw van Hanswijk, Mechelen, with a rockwork base and a sound-board covered with clouds, and the altar of St Nicholas (before 1755) for the parish church at Dendermonde, where the statue of the saint is almost smothered by its complicated baldacchino. Verhaegen's style in church furnishings was carried on by such pupils as Pieter Valckx.

BIBLIOGRAPHY
NBW; Thieme–Becker; Wurzbach
J. Immerzeel: *De levens en werken der Hollandsche en Vlaamsche kunstschilders, beeldhouwers, graveurs en bouwmeesters* [The lives and works of the Dutch and Flemish painters, sculptors, engravers and architects], iii (Amsterdam, 1843), pp. 172–3
C. Poupeye: *Théodore Verhaegen: Sculpteur malinois du XVIIIe siècle* (Brussels, 1914)
IRIS KOCKELBERGH

Verhaeren, Emile (Adolphe Gustave) (*b* Saint-Amand-sur-Escaut, Belgium, 21 May 1855; *d* Rouen, 27 Nov 1916). Belgian writer and critic. He initially studied law in Leuven but abandoned it for literature shortly after qualifying. He was the most important Belgian poet of the Symbolist movement; his works include *Les Flamandes* (Brussels, 1885) and *Les Forces tumultueuses* (Paris, 1902). He also produced a substantial body of prose, dominated by literary and art criticism. He took up criticism from 1880, writing for *L'Art moderne*, a journal founded by Edmond Picard (1836–1924). Verhaeren took over the exhibitions section, at the request of Octave Maus, from 1883 and later joined the journal's management committee. He also wrote on art and literature for numerous other publications, such as *La Jeune Belgique*, *Le Progrès*, *La Société nouvelle* and *L'Art libre*.

Verhaeren promoted modernist ideas and took a great interest in everything 'visual'; he defended Les XX and La Libre Esthétique and ardently supported Impressionism and Neo-Impressionism. He wrote *James Ensor* (Brussels, 1908) and also appreciations of Fernand Khnopff (in *L'Art moderne* in 1886 and 1887), who illustrated his *Soirs* trilogy of poems (1881–91), of Old Masters such as Rubens, Rembrandt and Grünewald, and of Blake and Delacroix. He associated with a wide circle of literary and artistic figures, including Théo Van Rysselberghe, Dario de Regoyos, Willy Schlobach (1864–1951), Georges Seurat and Constant Montald (1862–1944).

WRITINGS

James Ensor (Brussels, 1908/*R* 1974)
Impressions (Paris, 1926–8) [collected crit.]
Sensations (Paris, 1927) [collected crit.]

BIBLIOGRAPHY

A. Mabille de Poncheville: *Vie de Verhaeren* (Paris, 1953)
J.-M. Culot: *Bibliographie d'Emile Verhaeren* (Brussels, 1954)
Le Centenaire d'Emile Verhaeren (1855–1955), Académie Royale de Langue et de Littérature Françaises de Belgique (Brussels, 1956) [with add. bibliog.]
C. Maingon: *Emile Verhaeren: Critique d'art* (Paris, 1984)
J. Warmoes: 'Verhaeren: Critique d'art', *Dario de Regoyos* (exh. cat., Brussels, Banque-Lambert, 1985), pp. 29–51

DANIELLE DERREY-CAPON

Verhagen [Verhaegen], **Pierre-Joseph** (*b* Aarschot, 1728; *d* Leuven, 1811). Belgian painter. He was a late imitator of Rubens, and his entire career reflects his unwillingness to come to terms with the Neo-classicism of the late 18th century. At 18 he was in the studio of Balthazar Beschey in Antwerp. There he studied the work of Rubens and the Antwerp school. For the first 20 years of his career Verhagen received few commissions and supported himself with decorative work. His first important painting was the *Presentation of the Virgin* (Ghent, Mus. S. Kst.), and this large Baroque work brought him commissions (e.g. *St Stephen Receiving the Papal Legates*, Vienna, Ksthist. Mus.). Charles of Lorraine (1712–81) offered to finance Verhagen on a visit to Italy. Verhagen left for Italy in 1771 but found the Neo-classicism prevalent in Rome of little interest. He did, however, produce a few works in this period, for example the *Pilgrims to Emmaus* (Laxenburg, Altes Schloss). He left Rome in 1773 and returned to Leuven via Vienna. His later years were more successful for him. His works from this period show that although Verhagen may have adopted some Neo-classical subject-matter and occasionally included architectural details in his works, for example in the *Continence of Scipio* (1805; Leuven; Mus. Vander Kelen-Mertens) and the *Infant Moses Presented by his Mother to the Daughter of Pharoah* (1786; Leuven, Stadhuis), he was essentially a Rubéniste, given his emphasis on colour rather than line. However, his work is very uneven in quality, often careless and impetuous in execution, and he lacked Rubens's genius. Verhagen was regarded during the 19th century and the early 20th as a major 18th-century Belgian artist, but more latterly as a representative of an artistic movement at its nadir and an artist who clung to Baroque formulae that had lost their meaning.

BIBLIOGRAPHY

E. Van Even: *De schilder P. J. Verhaegen: Leven en werken* (Leuven, 1875)
1770–1830: Autour du Néo-classicisme en Belgique (exh. cat., Brussels, Mus. Ixelles, 1985–6), pp. 52–5

BERNADETTE THOMAS

Verhagen der Stomme [the Mute], **Hans** (*b* ?Mechelen, 1540–45; *fl* Antwerp, *c.* 1554–1600). Flemish painter, possibly active also in the northern Netherlands. A 'Hansken' or 'Hans Verhaghen' is mentioned in documents in 1554 and 1555 as an apprentice in Antwerp to the Mechelen *doek schilder* Anthoni Bessemers. In July 1572 a Hans Verhaghen married Janneken Aelbrechs in the church of Onze-Lieve-Vrouw in Antwerp. There was a painter by the name of Hans Verhaghen from Mechelen working around 1600 in Rotterdam and Delft, probably painting cartoons for the tapestry works. To what extent these items of information relate to the same person remains unresolved.

Four animal drawings in Vienna (Vienna, Österreich. Nbib., Cod. min. 42, fols 26, 116, 118, 121) carry an inscription in the hand of Joris Hoefnagel attributing the drawings to *Hans Verhagen den stommen van Antwerpen*. This attribution by a near-contemporary fellow citizen seems reliable, even if the place named may relate only to the place of origin of the work and not to the painter's native town. In addition to the four studies in the Vienna Codex, there are another twenty drawings by the same hand (Berlin, Kupferstichkab., KdZ 26213–32), which also portray animals, including the elephant that was on show in Antwerp in the autumn of 1563. The drawing of a sea eagle (KdZ 26226) was copied by Joris Hoefnagel in 1577 (Paris, Louvre, RF 38985).

Hans Verhagen der Stomme reveals himself in his drawings as an exceptionally exact observer of the animal world, which he set down on paper in what might be termed zoological teaching tablets, generally showing animals in their characteristic outline or in complementary views using opaque colours. He marked the beginning of scientific animal illustration in Antwerp. The zoological reliability with which native and foreign animals were recorded in Verhagen's drawings made a considerable impact on other artists, who repeatedly copied them. Hans Bol used them in his three volumes *Icones . . . animalium* (Copenhagen, Kon. Bib., Gamle Kon. Saml., 3471 I-III), as did Joris Hoefnagel in his four-volume manuscript of natural history miniatures (ex-Rosenwald priv. col.; Washington, DC, N.G.A.; including sheets that have been removed from the volumes), the Roman Missal of Archduke Ferdinand of Tyrol (Vienna, Nbib, Cod. 1784) and in such items as Giovanni Ambrogio Maggiori's ivory box (Stockholm, Kun. Slottet) made for a *Kunstkammer*. Other copies made by anonymous artists working in the later 16th century and the early 17th can be found in the Staatliche Graphische Sammlung in Munich, the Prentenkabinet of the Rijksmuseum in Amsterdam (the Lambert Lombard album), the Biblioteca Universitaria in Pisa (MS. 514) and elsewhere.

BIBLIOGRAPHY

M. L. Hendrix: *Joris Hoefnagel and the 'Four Elements': A Study in Sixteenth-century Nature Painting* (diss., Princeton U., NJ, 1984; microfilm, Ann Arbor, 1986), pp. 160–62 [attributing the Verhagen drgs to Hoefnagel]
Dürer und die Tier- und Pflanzenstudien der Renaissance (exh. cat. by F. Koreny, Vienna, Albertina, 1985), pp. 130–31, 276
P. Dreyer: 'Zeichnungen von Hans Verhagen dem Stummen von Antwerpen: Ein Beitrag zu den Vorlagen der Tierminiaturen Hans Bols und Georg Hoefnagels', *Jb. Ksthist. Samml. Wien*, lxxxii (1986), pp. 115–44
——: 'Zoological Animal Drawings and the Role of Hans Verhagen the Mute from Antwerp', *Drawing: Masters and Methods: Raphael to Redon* (London, 1992), pp. 38–49

PETER DREYER

Verhas. Belgian family of painters. Emmanuel Verhas (1799–1864) was art master for more than 20 years at the Dendermonde Academie, where he taught his sons, (1) Frans Verhas and (2) Jan Frans Verhas.

(1) Frans Verhas (*b* Dendermonde, 1832; *d* Schaerbeek, Brussels, 22 Nov 1897). Having trained with his father, he studied in Brussels before settling permanently at Schaerbeek in 1867. In Brussels he specialized almost exclusively in producing genre paintings of bourgeois subjects. His compositions were skilfully executed and he showed a keen eye for detail, portraying sumptuous interiors decorated with tapestries, satins, animal pelts and marble as a backdrop to playing children and elegant women dressed in crinolines, or striking aristocratic poses: for example *The Lion* (1874; Ghent, Mus. S. Kst.) and the *Inconsolable Woman* (1878; Antwerp, Kon. Mus. S. Kst.). He also painted historical subjects, which he treated with a powerful sense of realism (e.g. *Louis XIV before Dendermonde in 1667*, 1881; and the *League of Noblemen*; both Dendermonde, Stadhuis), and executed portraits (e.g. *Mariam Van Duyse*, 1852; Dendermonde, Vrouwekerk).

BIBLIOGRAPHY
Thieme–Becker

(2) Jan Frans Verhas (*b* Dendermonde, 9 Jan 1834; *d* Brussels, 31 Oct 1896). Brother of (1) Frans Verhas. Having trained with his father, he studied at the Antwerp Academie under Nicaise De Keyser and Jan Verschaeren (1803–63) from 1853 to 1860. He then went to Brussels and was placed second in the Prix de Rome in 1860. In Rome in 1862 he painted two works, commissioned by the Belgian government: *Velleda* and the *Battle of Callo, 20 June 1638* (Beveren, Gemeentelijk Mus.). On returning to Belgium from Italy (and after a period in Paris) he lived in Binche from 1864 to 1867 and was married there; one of his daughters later married the Belgian landscape painter Ghisbert Combaz (1869–1941).

In 1867 Verhas settled permanently in Brussels, where his distinguished and refined paintings were soon successful. He gave up historical subjects and religious themes in order to concentrate on salon pieces and portraits. He painted politicians, diplomats and artists, but his fame rests on his work as a painter of portraits of children, for example the *Choice, Interior with Young Girl* (1874; Dendermonde, Stadhuis), the *Painting Master* (1877; Ghent, Mus. S. Kst.) and the *Fisherman's Daughter* (Liège, Mus. B.-A.). He also applied his striking realist style to several large compositions of more public subjects, such as the *Review of the Schools on 23 August 1878* (1880; Brussels, Mus. A. Mod.) and the *Procession in Honour of Sir Polydor De Keyser, Lord Mayor of London* (1888; Dendermonde, Stadhuis), a series of canvases that brought together a large number of portraits of children and diverse public figures. Towards the end of his career he turned to painting lively views of Heyst beach, including his masterpiece *Donkey Rides on Heyst Beach* (1884; Antwerp Kon. Mus. S. Kst.).

BIBLIOGRAPHY
Het kind in onze kunst van 1800 tot heden (exh. cat., Brussels, ASLK, 1983–4), p. 113

ALAIN JACOBS

Verhelst, Egid [Aegid], **I** (*b* Antwerp, *bapt* 13 Dec 1696; *d* Augsburg, 19 April 1749). Flemish sculptor and stuccoist active in Germany. He was probably trained by his father Gillis Verhelst, and in 1718 went to Munich, presumably via Paris, where he entered the workshop of his fellow countryman, the leading court sculptor Guillielmus de Grof. After being resident in Ettal intermittently from 1726 to 1736, he settled in Augsburg in 1738. His earliest known work is a 60 mm-high head of a boy in ivory (1722; Munich, Bayer. Nmus.), a piece which prefigures his later cherubs. Of his works for Ettal Abbey 12 fairly crude over life-size marble figures (*c.* 1726–35) on the church façade and two charming wall fountains with lead figures (*c.* 1726–30) in the sacristy have been preserved. His chief work there, the high altar of the abbey church with a monumental *Assumption*, made either of wood or stucco with lead relief panels (from 1726), was destroyed by fire in 1744. Among Verhelst's other works are four side altars and other sculptures for the abbey church of Diessen am Ammersee (1738–40), the pulpit of the abbey church at Ochsenhausen (1741), four allegorical figures in the throne-room of the prince-abbot's residence at Kempten (*c.* 1742), a painted wood *Lamentation* group (*c.* 1745) in the pilgrimage church of Herrgottsruh at Friedberg, near Augsburg (see fig.), and figures or groups of the *Seasons* in cast lead in the Rijksmuseum in Amsterdam and in the Bayerisches Nationalmuseum in Munich. He worked predominantly in wood, the preferred material of the local sculptors, but he also used stone and, in emulation of de Grof, lead. He collaborated with various Augsburg goldsmiths, carving models for their figurative works. He brought ideas from his Flemish homeland and from his teacher de Grof into the Rococo ecclesiastical sculpture of Bavaria and Swabia, and exerted a particular influence on the Augsburg stucco modellers, above all Johann Georg Üblher. Verhelst's cherubs were also used for decades as models by other stuccoists of the Wessobrunn school. His

Egid Verhelst: *Lamentation over the Dead Christ*, wood and polychromy, h. 1.13 m, *c.* 1745 (Friedberg, Herrgottsruh)

sons Placidus Verhelst (1727–?78) and Ignaz Wilhelm Verhelst (1729–92) jointly continued the family workshop until 1774, when Placidus went to Moscow. They achieved a high standard of output, but are scarcely identifiable as separate creative individuals. A third son, Egid Verhelst II (1733–1818), was an engraver.

BIBLIOGRAPHY

D. Dietrich: *Aegid Verhelst, 1696–1749: Ein flämischer Bildhauer in Süddeutschland* (Weissenhorn, 1986)

PETER VOLK

Verheul, Johannes Dirkz. (*b* Rotterdam, 14 Feb 1860; *d* Rotterdam, ?19 Oct 1948). Dutch architect. He was trained in his father's business and attended evening classes at the Academie voor Beeldende Kunsten en Technische Wetenschappen in Rotterdam (1872–7). Then he went to the Polytechnische School in Delft, obtaining a diploma in 1882. His career immediately expanded once he was commissioned in 1883 to build Rotterdam Theatre (destr. 1940), which was in a Dutch Neo-Renaissance style, like many of the designs of his early period. He built the concert hall and auditorium De Kunstmin (1888–90) at St Jorisweg 76, Dordrecht, in the same style; it was rebuilt (1939–40) by Sybold van Ravesteyn. Verheul also designed the water-towers (1885; destr. 1925) at Schiedam in a more historicizing style. Later he felt more attracted to *Jugendstil*, specifically *Nieuwe Kunst*. One of his most important designs in this style was the building (1900–02; destr. 1974) in Utrecht for the insurance company 'De Utrecht'. One of Verheul's least characteristic buildings of this period is the Witte Huis (1899–1901) at Raadhuisstraat 6, Amsterdam, designed with his brother Cornelis Verheul for the Rotterdamsche Verzekering-Societeiten (Rotterdam Insurance Company). This fine surviving example of *Jugendstil* is distinguished by large glass surfaces in parabolic frames and white glazed brick. His style became more traditional from 1910.

BIBLIOGRAPHY

H. J. F. de Roy van Zuydewijn: *Amsterdamse bouwkunst, 1915–1940* (Amsterdam, n.d.)

E. C. Geesink: *De architect J. Verheul Dzn* (diss., Amsterdam, Vrije U., 1989)

E. MATTIE, M. DE MOOR

Verheyden, Isidore (*b* Antwerp, 24 Jan 1846; *d* Brussels, 1 Nov 1905). Belgian painter. His father was the painter Jean-François Verheyden, and he trained at the Académie Royale des Beaux-Arts in Brussels, where he was taught by Joseph Quinaux (1822–95). Quinaux, who took his pupils on long walks in the countryside around Brussels, first instilled a love of nature in Verheyden. In 1866 Verheyden entered the studio of Jean-François Portaels, where he met several artists, such as Edouard Agneesens and Emile Wauters, who were keen to break with academic tradition. Verheyden first exhibited in 1870 with a number of portraits.

    Between 1874 and 1884 Verheyden spent most of his time in Hoeylaert, near Brussels, where, isolated from other artistic influences, he developed a style of his own and produced such works as *The Harvest* (1880; Brussels, Pal. Royal). The nearby forest of Soignes was a favourite subject for many of Verheyden's paintings of this period. He exhibited successfully at the triennial Salons and in

1883 settled in Brussels. He was one of the first members of Les XX (*see* 〈VINGT〉, LES), but he remained aligned to the group's more conservative wing and resisted its more radical proposals. After three years he resigned from the group as a protest against what he saw as the excesses of Impressionism. He had nevertheless been influenced by Impressionism, and had briefly attempted to incorporate vibrant light effects into his painting, although his landscapes lacked the Impressionist lightness of touch. He claimed that he wished to 'paint without fixing contours'. After leaving Les XX, Verheyden spent much of his time in the Campine and Bas-Escaut areas of Belgium, producing works such as *Pilgrimage in Campine* (Antwerp; Kon. Mus. S. Kst.). He also experimented with more violently expressive painting techniques in a number of seascapes such as the *Rough Sea* (Brussels, Mus. Ixelles).

    As well as painting landscapes, Verheyden produced a few still-lifes and was a very successful portrait painter, adopting a more sculptural style using sombre colours, as in *Edouard Agneesens* (1867; Brussels, Mus. A. Mod.) and *Paul van den Eeckhoudt* (1900; Brussels, Mus. A. Mod.). In 1900 he was appointed professor at the Académie Royale des Beaux-Arts in Brussels, a post he held until his death.

BNB   BIBLIOGRAPHY

C. Lemonnier: *L'Ecole belge de peinture, 1830–1905* (Brussels, 1906)

P. Colin: *La Peinture belge depuis 1830* (Brussels, 1930)

P. Colin: 'La Vie artistique', *Nouv. J.* (21 Oct 1942)

Verheyden, Pieter [Peter]. *See* HEYDEN, PIETER VAN DER.

Verhulst, Mayken [Maaiken; Mayke; Meyken] [Bessemers, Marie de] (*b* Mechelen, *c.* 1520; *bur* Mechelen, 1 April 1600). Flemish painter, second wife of PIETER COECKE VAN AELST I. She was the daughter of a little-known painter in Mechelen but became famous during her lifetime. Best known for miniatures, she was described by Lodovico Guicciardini in 1567 as one of the five principal female painters in the Netherlands. Despite such acclaim, no extant signed works are known. She had three children with Pieter Coecke van Aelst: Paul, who became a painter, Katherine and Marie (or Mayken), who married Pieter Bruegel the elder. Verhulst was documented by Karel van Mander as the first person to teach watercolour painting to her grandson Jan Breughel the elder. She may also have taught Jan's brother Pieter Brueghel the younger. It was suggested by Bergmans that four works by the BRUNSWICK MONOGRAMMIST (*see* MASTERS, ANONYMOUS, AND MONOGRAMMISTS, §III) should be attributed to Verhulst.

BIBLIOGRAPHY

S. Bergmans: 'Le Problème de Jan van Hemessen, monogrammatiste de Brunswick', *Rev. Belge Archéol. & Hist. A./Belge Tijdschr. Oudhdknde & Kstgesch.*, xxiv (1955), pp. 133–57

G. Greer: *The Obstacle Race* (London, 1979), p. 26

C. Petteys and others: *Dictionary of Women Artists* (Boston, MA, 1985)

Verhulst, Rombout (*b* Mechelen, 15 Jan 1624; *d* The Hague, *bur* 27 Nov 1698). Flemish sculptor, active in the Netherlands. He studied in Mechelen with Rombout Verstappen (*d* 1636) and Frans van Loo (*fl* 1607–35) and perhaps also with Lucas Faydherbe. In 1646 he moved to Amsterdam, where he later worked under Artus Quellinus (i) (e.g. portrait bust, *Artus Quellinus*, Utrecht, Cent. Mus.) on the decoration of the Amsterdam Stadhuis (now Royal Palace); at some point between 1646 and 1654 he may have made a trip to Italy. For the Stadhuis, Verhulst executed the figure of *Venus* and reliefs of *Fidelity* and *Silence* (before 1658) for its galleries and produced terracotta studies (*c.* 1655; Amsterdam, Rijksmus.) for the *griffiersstoel* (bench of the court clerk) and bronze doors of the Vierschaar (tribunal). In 1658 Verhulst was living in Leiden, where he was involved in decorative projects for Pieter Post's Waag (Weighhouse), including the marble relief *The Butter-seller* (1662; *in situ*). By 1663 he had moved to The Hague, where he became a member of the Guild of St Luke in 1668 and of the Academy 'Pictura' in 1676.

After Quellinus's return to Antwerp in 1665, Verhulst became the most prominent sculptor working in the Netherlands; he produced portrait busts, funerary monuments, garden statuary and small-scale works in ivory. His portraits eloquently capture the personality of his sitters: especially notable are the naturalistic pair of busts of *Willem, Baron van Liere* and *Maria van Reygersberg* (terracotta, *c.* 1663–70; Amsterdam, Rijksmus.), while the bust of *Jacob van Reygersberg* (1671; Malibu, CA, Getty Mus.) is a good example of his marble-carving technique.

Verhulst created a number of important funerary monuments, including the marble table tombs with recumbent effigies of the scholar *Johan Polyander Kerkhoven* (1663; Leiden, St Peter) and of *Willem van Liere and Maria van Reygersberg* (1663; Katwijk aan den Rijn, Hervormde Kerk). His sensitive handling of physiognomy and graceful treatment of drapery also appear in his marble wall tombs for Dutch naval heroes, including those of *Maarten Harpertszoon Tromp* (1658; Delft, Oude Kerk; designed by Jacob van Campen; naval relief by Willem de Keyser), *Jan van Galen* (1654; designed by Artus Quellinus (i); naval relief by Willem de Keyser) and *Michiel Adriaanszoon de Ruyter* (1677–81; both Amsterdam, Nieuwe Kerk). Other works attributed to Verhulst include several garden statues, such as *Prudence* and *Destiny* (sandstone, *c.* 1660–65; Amsterdam, Rijksmus.) and ivory carvings such as the medallion *Portrait of a Young Man* (Amsterdam, Rijksmus., *see* NETHERLANDS, THE, fig. 61).

Although Verhulst owed a stylistic debt to Quellinus, he did not fully share Quellinus's classicizing tendencies; his works are conceived with greater warmth and executed with greater delicacy, exhibiting similarities to those of Antwerp sculptors in the circle of Rubens, including Hans van Mildert and Lucas Faydherbe. Verhulst's works in wood, stone, ivory and above all marble are admirable for their sensitive modelling and subtle rendering of textures, as well as for their skilful disposition of Baroque compositional devices. He is widely considered to be the foremost Flemish marble-carver of the 17th century.

BIBLIOGRAPHY

M. van Notten: *Rombout Verhulst, beeldhouwer 1624–1698: Een overzicht zijner werken* (The Hague, 1907)

E. Neurdenberg: *De zeventiende eeuwsche beeldhouwkunst in de Noordelijke Nederlanden: Hendrick De Keyser, Artus Quellien en Rombout Verhulst en tijdgenoten* (Amsterdam, 1948), pp. 210, 293

K. Fremantle: *The Baroque Town Hall of Amsterdam* (Utrecht, 1959)

J. Leeuwenberg and W. Halsema Kubes: *Beeldhouwkunst in het Rijksmuseum* (Amsterdam, 1973), pp. 234–42

F. T. Scholten: *Rombout Verhulst te Groningen* (Utrecht, 1983)

CYNTHIA LAWRENCE

Véri(-Raionard), Louis-Gabriel, Marquis de (*b* Séguret, nr Avignon, 28 March 1722; *d* Paris, 25 Jan 1785). French nobleman and collector. He came from an old but poor noble family, which was involved in municipal affairs in Séguret. In 1751 he moved to Paris. His brother, the Abbé Joseph-Alphonse de Véri (1724–99) travelled widely in Europe during the 1750s and lived in Rome for 10 years from 1762; it was he who controlled the family purse and paid Louis-Gabriel's many debts. Following his return to Paris in 1772 the brothers' fortunes changed dramatically, and they were able to rent jointly a hôtel particulier in the fashionable Faubourg St Germain. They probably frequented the same social circles, which included Mme Geoffrin, the Marquis de Marigny and Ange-Laurent de La Live de Jully. The Marquis's purchases may have been inspired and financed by his brother, who in the course of his travels had frequented the studios of famous artists but was probably not himself a collector. The collection, acquired directly from artists, at salons and through dealers and sales, included some Dutch and Italian paintings but was particularly remarkable for the number of very recent, fashionable paintings by contemporary French painters. The eight works by Fragonard included *Two Sisters* (?*c.* 1772; New York, Met.); the *Little Girl with the Marmot* (*c.* 1775; Moscow, Pushkin Mus. F.A.); and *The Bolt* (*c.* 1778; Paris, Louvre). Among the paintings by Greuze were the *Ungrateful Son* (1777), the *Punished Son* (1778; both Paris, Louvre) and a portrait of *Benjamin Franklin* (1777; priv. col.; see Sellers, fig. 1). The collection, which was assembled with unusual rapidity (primarily between 1775 and 1779), also contained works by Hubert Robert, Joseph Vernet and Jean-Baptiste Pierre. It included various genres and artists but no Neo-classical history paintings; it was probably accessible to artists and collectors. Véri bequeathed his estate to his brother, who sold his collection within the year (Paris, Alexandre-Joseph Paillet and C.-P. Boileau, 12–14 Dec 1785).

BIBLIOGRAPHY

J. de Witte, ed.: *Le Journal de l'abbé de Véri*, 2 vols (Paris, 1928–30)

C. C. Sellers: ' "La Noblesse d'une âme libre": The Franklin of Greuze and de Véri', *A. Q.* [Detroit], xxvi (1963), pp. 3–6

C. Bailey: 'Le Marquis de Véri: Collectionneur', *Bull. Soc. Hist. A. Fr.* (1983), pp. 67–83
☐

Verino, Benedetto. *See under* MASTERS, ANONYMOUS, AND MONOGRAMMISTS, §I: MASTER OF THE DIE.

Verino, Ugolino (*b* Florence, Jan 1438; *d* Florence, 10 May 1516). Italian humanist and poet. He was a pupil of Cristoforo Landino whose influence is apparent in such early works as *Flametta* (1458–64), a collection of 62 love elegies and epigrams, and *Paradisus* (undated), which blends classical culture with Christianity. In his later work, however, Verino rejected pagan influences and concentrated more straightforwardly on religious themes, as in the *Epigrammata*, seven books of religious poems written in 1485. Verino's writings contain numerous economiastic allusions to recent and contemporary artists and, although the favourable comparisons drawn with the ancients follow a standard formula, Verino appears to have been genuinely interested in the artistic developments of his time. In *Flametta* he praised the work of Apollonio di Giovanni and the patronage of Cosimo de' Medici. In his most important work, the epic *Carliades* (1480–93), in which Charlemagne is presented as a champion of the Church, Verino eulogized Botticelli, who is again singled out for praise in the short poem *De gloria urbis Florentina* (or *De illustratione urbis Florentiae*), the first version of which was written *c.* 1487 (published Paris, 1583), along with numerous other artists including Giotto, Leonardo (judged to have surpassed all others but criticized for underproduction), Domenico Ghirlandaio and Davide Ghirlandaio, Donatello and Brunelleschi. In similar vein, Verino also wrote an epigram *On the Painters and Sculptors of Florence who Can Be Equalled to the Ancient Greeks* (Florence, Bib. Medicea–Laurenziana, Plut. 39, Cod. 40. III, fol. 26 v.). Verino was influenced by the preaching of Girolamo Savonarola and in 1490 became a *piagnone*, or weeper, as the friar's followers were called, although he later turned against him.

WRITINGS
Flametta (MS.; 1458–64); ed. L. Mencaraglia (Florence, 1940)
Carmina; ed. F. Arnaldi in *Poeti latini del quattrocento* (Milan and Naples, 1964)

BIBLIOGRAPHY
A. Lazzari: *Ugolino e Michele Verino* (Turin, 1897)
G. Bottiglioni: 'La lirica latina in Firenze nella seconda metà del secolo XV', *An. Scu. Norm. Sup. Pisa*, xxv (1913), pp. 173–84
A. Chastel: *Marsile Ficin et l'art* (Geneva, 1954)
E. Gombrich: *Norm and Form* (London, 1966, rev. Oxford, 4/1985)

OLIMPIA THEODOLI

Veris da Milano, de. Italian family of painters. On the basis of one documented early 15th-century fresco, the *Last Judgement* (Campione, S Maria dei Ghirli), three other works have been attributed to Lanfranco de Veris da Milano and his son Filippolo de Veris da Milano. According to the inscription on the fresco (now illegible; transcribed by Gerspach and Toesca), in 1400 the students of S Maria dei Ghirli and other individuals from Campione, with alms raised by the church, commissioned the two painters to execute the work, which was completed on 23 June that year. The composition, painted on an exterior wall of the church, is divided into two zones. Owing to its obvious superiority, particularly in the figure drawing, the upper, larger zone of the *Last Judgement* has been attributed to the older, presumably more experienced Lanfranco, while the lower and smaller zone, traditionally assigned to Filippolo, depicts the tortures of Hell. At the far right is an unmistakably secular scene in which two men serenade a courtesan: one of the men, a fashionably dressed young aristocrat, stands directly in front of the woman and sings to her, while his grotesquely featured companion to the left plays the rebec and seems to beat time with his right foot. The characters' style of dress is close to that seen in works by Pisanello, but here tends to the comical rather than the elegantly fashionable. The figures have individualized features and expressions, the singing aristocrat's being especially charming. The drawing of hands, however, is less satisfactory. The colours of the *Last Judgement* tend towards pastel; they are dominated by a light lapis blue, rose–orange, blue–green, some brown and a great deal of pale yellow. The remarkable swirling angels have golden haloes.

Illustrations for the *Tacuinum sanitatis in medicina* reveal the interest in nature characteristic of Lombard illuminators. Folios 88*r*–95*v* of a copy in Vienna (Vienna, Österreich. Nbib., Codex Vindobonensis serie nova 2644) have been attributed to a Lombard artist akin to the de Veris (Toesca) but are probably by the de Veris themselves. The exaggeration of gestures and expressions separates these eight examples from the other 98 illustrations in the same volume. In the folio entitled *Oleum amygdolarum* (almond oil), the druggist, sporting a jaunty beret and beard with curly white highlights recalling those in the hair of the angels in the Campione *Last Judgement*, carefully pours medicine into a cup, while the patient, a thickset youth, presses his fist to his chest to still a coughing fit. This patient can be compared to the lute-player in the Campione *Last Judgement*, a brother in form and feature. Four pairs of angels frescoed around a tabernacle in S Maria a Campomorto, Siziano, near Pavia, have been added to the de Veris oeuvre (Gregori). The lyrical, rhythmic forms, spirited hairstyles and sharp profiles derive directly from the Campione *Last Judgement*. Because they display less of the expressionistic quality of the *Last Judgement*, the angels have been assigned to Filippolo, who may have survived his father by several decades, and a date in the second quarter of the 15th century has been proposed for them. The painter of the elegant *Virgin and Child with St Anthony Abbot and a Donor* (Lodi, S Francesco) worked in the most advanced Late Gothic style. The calligraphic rhythms of the drapery, flaming finials of the throne, faces of the Virgin and donor and the spiky trefoil motif surrounding the entire fresco are close to the Campione *Last Judgement*. Owing to certain affinities with the work of Michelino da Besozzo, the painting may possibly be assigned to Filippolo.

EWA

BIBLIOGRAPHY
E. Gerspach: 'Gli affreschi di Campione', *L'Arte*, v (1902), pp. 161–7
F. M. Valeri: 'Campione', *Rass. A.*, viii/10 (1908), pp. 167–74
P. Toesca: *La pittura e la miniatura nella Lombardia* (Milan, 1912)
M. Gregori: 'A proposito dei De Veris', *Paragone*, viii/87 (1957), pp. 43–5
S. Matalon and F. Mazzini: *Affreschi del tre e quattrocento in Lombardia* (Milan, 1958), pp. 17–18, 33
S. Matalon: 'Restauro di affreschi lombardi', *Boll. A.*, xlvii/2–3 (1962), pp. 268–72
F. Mazzini: *Affreschi lombardi del quattrocento* (Milan, 1965), pp. 419–20, pls 1–12 [incl. the only colour illustrations available]
G. Algeri: 'La pittura in Lombardia nel primo quattrocento', *La pittura in Italia: Il quattrocento*, ed. F. Zeri (Venice, 1986), i, pp. 53–71; ii, p. 617 [bibliog.]

ALEXANDRA HERZ

Verismo. Movement in Italy, primarily in Naples and Tuscany, from *c.* 1850 to 1900 that developed as a response to naturalism and realism in French art and literature. The principal visual artists were Antonio Mancini, FRANCESCO PAOLO MICHETTI and Vincenzo Gemito. In the early part of the century, which was dominated by Neo-classical idealism, an interest in the representation of the real world was confined to landscape painting (e.g. *Scuola di Posillipo*) and portrait painting, as practised by Andrea Appiani. One of the first Italian painters to observe nature systematically in a similar way to realist artists in France was FILIPPO PALIZZI. In his work *Vineyard with Priest* (Rome, G. N. A. Mod.), every detail is minutely depicted. Another form of realism is to be seen in the work of Domenico Morelli who, while breaking classical canons and working in tones and values rather than in contours, maintained the importance of imagination over observation. Thus in the *Christian Martyrs* (1855; Naples, Capodimonte) naturalistic light and colour enhance a religious theme. However, the MACCHIAIOLI, based in Tuscany, were the first group of Italian painters to show an overriding interest in the effects of natural light on form and to concentrate on contemporary subjects, whether political events, as in Michele Cammarano's battle scenes of the Risorgimento, or intimate interiors, as with the paintings of Adriano Cecioni and Odoardo Borrani (1834–1905). One of its members, Giovanni Fattori, wrote in 1903 that Verismo should be a means to 'show posterity our ways' (Maltese, p. 22). Towards the end of the century, particularly in Naples, the desire to capture the essence of contemporary life and to portray the world as it appeared became the dominant movement in both literature and art. A new awareness of popular culture, regional characteristics and local dialects was created by such authors as Giovanni Verga (1840–1922). Among the most prominent painters in this manner was Mancini who, while being close to Morelli stylistically, portrayed ordinary Neapolitans (e.g. *Street Urchin*, 1868; The Hague, Rijksmus. Mesdag) with a new and profound empathy. Equally, Michetti and Gioacchino Toma portrayed the poor with great fidelity. Although the most successful painter of the group, Michetti's flamboyant colour and painterly effects helped to divert the original intentions of Verismo towards sentimentality and overdramatization. In sculpture, Gemito was the most innovative and successful exponent of Verismo. His sculptures are the antithesis of Neo-classical works: each surface is depicted, every flicker of light and shade is suggested, and the poses are taken from ordinary attitudes emphasizing the three-dimensionality of form rather than the noble outline (e.g. *Little Fisherboy*; for illustration *see* GEMITO, VINCENZO). This approach was taken to its ultimate conclusion with Medardo Rosso's portrait heads, where form virtually dissolves.

Comanducci

BIBLIOGRAPHY

F. Bellonzi: *Verismo e tradizione in Antonio Mancini*, Atti della Accademia Nazionale di San Luca, vi/3 (Rome, 1963)

C. Maltese: *Realismo e verismo nella pittura italiana* (Milan, 1967)

Verity, Frank [Francis] **(Thomas)** (*b* London, 1867; *d* Bournemouth, Hants, 14 Aug 1937). English architect. He was the son of Thomas Verity (1837–91), a highly successful theatre architect and Surveyor of Theatres to the Lord Chamberlain from 1878 to 1891. After studying at the Architectural Association, London, in 1883 Verity was articled to his father and in 1887 entered the Royal Academy Schools under R. Phené Spiers (1838–1916). He went to Paris to the Atelier Blouet, then headed by Jean-Louis Pascal, and was attracted by emergent French Neoclassicism. In 1889 Verity returned to London, won the Tite Prize (for studies in Italianate architecture), became an Associate of the RIBA and a partner in his father's theatre-based practice. He worked on several projects with his father and after his death built five theatres, most notably The Empire (1893–1904), Leicester Square, London. In his theatre designs he reacted against the plush-and-gilt style of Frank Matcham, preferring 'correct' classical detailing and introducing the use of real marbles, bronze and French stuc (plaster jointed to imitate stone). In 1896 Verity designed the New Travellers' Club, 96–7 Piccadilly, which was highly praised by H. S. Goodhart Rendel. In 1912 he designed his first cinema, the New Gallery, 121A Regent Street (destr.) and went on to design at least 20 more in London, the English provinces and Paris. In 1924 he was awarded the London Architecture Medal for his Shepherd's Bush Pavilion (1923), west London, an enormous cinema with a severe brick exterior and classically detailed entrance. His influential cinema interiors were in a stripped classical style and pioneered the use of the great balcony and intimidating side wall. He was European adviser to the Paramount Cinema Company, and he followed his father as Surveyor of Theatres to the Lord Chamberlain.

Perhaps more influential than his theatres and cinemas, however, were Frank Verity's mansion flats, in which he reinterpreted French models in the setting of London. H. S. Goodhart-Rendel was enthusiastic in his praise of Verity's austere French style, attributing his own awakening to architecture to Verity's flats at 12 Hyde Park Place (1908). With few exceptions, Verity's mansion blocks were astylar. His Cleveland House (1905), Cleveland Row, is articulated with a boldly rusticated ground floor and slightly projecting rusticated pavilions; the street railings are unusual in being supported by extremely heavy stone posts. The ironwork is French in style and the building is given scale by a deep cornice with paired modillions. This style set a pattern for central London mansion blocks until the 1930s, not least because it was imitated by his successful former assistants, Albert E. Richardson and Charles Lovett Gill (1880–1960).

After Edward VII's accession to the throne (1901), he made alterations to the interior decoration of Buckingham Palace and appointed Verity to redecorate the State Apartments. From 1908 to 1911 Verity and Richardson designed the Regent Street Polytechnic (now University of Westminster) and St George's House, Regent Street, for the Raoul Shoe Company. These introduced a more distinctly French style to the rebuilding of Regent Street, although his design for a complete block remained unexecuted. In 1923 Verity took into partnership his son-in-law, Samuel Beverley (1896–1959), an Australian-trained architect who had entered Verity's office in 1922. Together they designed flats in Hyde Park Place (1928) and the Carlton Cinema (1928), Haymarket. On Verity's death Beverley continued the practice as Verity & Beverley.

WRITINGS

'Some Recent Mansion Flats in London', *Archit. Rev.* [London], xxiii (1908), pp. 286–95

'The Shepherd's Bush Pavilion', *Archit. Rev.* [London], lvi (1923), pp. 132–9

BIBLIOGRAPHY

A. T. Edwards: 'The Work of Frank T. Verity', *Architects' J.*, lxi/1566 (1925), pp. 36–59

[H. S. Goodhart-Rendel]: Obituary, *RIBA J.*, xliv (1937), pp. 1008–99, 1071

A. S. Gray: *Edwardian Architecture* (London, 1985)

DAVID PROUT

Verkade, Jan (*b* Zaandam, 18 Sept 1868; *d* Beuron, 19 July 1946). Dutch painter. He moved to Amsterdam in 1876. As a boy he was given drawing lessons by Hendrik Johannes Haverman. Between 1887 and 1890 he trained at the Rijksacademie voor Beeldende Kunsten in Amsterdam, under August Allebé. He continued his studies in Hattem in the province of Gelderland with his brother-in-law Jan Voerman. Verkade worked from models but also painted landscapes of the Ijssel river with cows in a simplified Realism. In 1890 he visited the exhibition of Les XX in Brussels.

Inspired by Joris-Karl Huysmans' *A rebours*, Verkade went to Paris in February 1890. Jacob Meyer de Haan introduced him to Gauguin and Paul Sérusier, through whom he came into contact with Maurice Denis. He joined the meetings of the Nabis at Paul Ranson's studio where he met Edouard Vuillard, Pierre Bonnard and Ker-Xavier Roussel. Because of his great height he was referred to in the group as the 'Nabi obélisqual'. At the banquet in honour of Gauguin's departure for Tahiti at the Café Voltaire in 1891, he met Mogens Ballin, with whom he travelled to Pont-Aven in Brittany. Sérusier joined them and they travelled to Huelgoat, also in Brittany. At Sérusier's recommendation he read *Les Grands Initiés* (1889) by Edouard Schuré. After a short stay in Pouldu, he returned to Paris and in October 1891 continued travelling to Amsterdam. At the beginning of 1891 Sérusier stayed with him for two weeks. Jan Verkade brought him into contact with friends from the academy, Richard Roland Holst and Jan Toorop. In February 1892 he returned to Paris with Sérusier.

Verkade's work *c.* 1892 showed similarities with that of Emile Bernard, Sérusier, Charles Filiger and Armand Séguin. He painted primarily Breton landscapes and still-lifes, for example *Decorative Landscape* (1891–2; Stockholm, Nmus.). With Sérusier, Denis, Bonnard, Vuillard and Ranson he submitted work to the eighth Salon des Indépendants. He also painted the backcloth for the puppet show *Les Sept Princesses* by Maurice Maeterlinck at the Théâtre d'Art, Paris, for which Sérusier had designed the set and Denis the costumes.

In April 1892 Verkade travelled to Brittany again, this time with Ballin to Saint-Nolff and later to Pouldu where he met with Filiger again. During this period he became a Catholic. In September he travelled with Ballin to Florence, Fiesole, Siena, Rome and Assisi. He also stayed in Florence during April and May 1893, where Sérusier joined him. Until November 1893 Verkade stayed in the monastery of Fiesole, where he painted two murals. He started a correspondence with Didier Lenz (1832–1928), a painter and Abbot of the Benedictine Monastery in Beuron, Germany, which he visited on his return to the Netherlands in November 1893. In February 1894 he travelled to Copenhagen, where he exhibited 40 drawings and study-heads from Brittany, and 25 oil sketches, landscapes, portraits and still-lifes.

In April 1894 Verkade travelled to Beuron. He painted there until his ordination into the Benedictine Order, after which he called himself Dom Willibrord Verkade. From 1895 until 1897 he painted St Gabriel's in Prague from designs by the German Desiderius Lenz. Between 1903 and 1905 he worked in the Benedictine Monastery of Monte Cassino. An exhibition of his drawings was held at the Larensche Kunsthandel in Amsterdam in December 1905. He painted the church in Aichhalden in the Black Forest in 1906, and he was visited by Toorop. From 1906 to 1908 he stayed in Munich, where he kept company with Alexei Jawlenski, visiting Denis and Sérusier in Paris in 1907. From 1909 until 1912 he stayed in Palestine. He painted little after 1915. Verkade published regularly in *Die Christliche Kunst*.

BIBLIOGRAPHY

Dom Willibrord Verkade: *In blijde gebondenheid* [In joyful restraint] ('s Hertogenbosch, 1934)

B. Dorival: 'Le Portrait de Dom Verkade par Maurice Denis', *Mus. France* (9 Nov 1948), pp. 244–6

L. Gans: 'Jan Verkade: Een bepaald aspect van zijn kunst uit de jaren 1891–1910' [Jan Verkade: a particular aspect of his art during the years 1891–1910], *Ned. Ksthist. Jb.*, vii (1956), pp. 219–44

Jan Verkade: Hollandse volgeling van Gauguin (exh. cat., Amsterdam, Rijksmus. van Gogh, 1988) [also Fr. and Ger. edn]

The Age of Van Gogh: Dutch Painting, 1880–1895 (exh. cat., ed. R. Bionda, C. Blotkump and others; Glasgow, Burrell Col.; Amsterdam, Rijksmus. van Gogh; 1990–91) [Dut. edn as *De schilders van tachtig: Nederlandse schilderkunst, 1880–1895*]

JOHN STEEN

Verkolje. Dutch family of painters, draughtsmen and mezzotint engravers. (1) Jan Verkolje I, the son of a locksmith, specialized in genre scenes set in richly furnished interiors, although he also painted mythological scenes and portraits. Among his followers were his two sons, (2) Nicolaas Verkolje and Jan Verkolje II (*d* 1760).

(1) Jan [Johannes] **Verkolje I** (*b* Amsterdam, 9 Feb 1650; *d* Delft, *bur* 8 May 1693). According to Houbraken, he spent six months as the pupil of Jan Andrea Lievens (1644–80), where he completed unfinished mythological and genre pictures by Gerrit Pietersz. van Zijl (1619–65). Verkolje married in Delft in 1672 and in the following year joined the city's Guild of St Luke, serving as its dean between 1678 and 1688.

Verkolje's genre scenes, for example the *Musical Company* (1673; Amsterdam, Rijksmus.), *The Messenger* (1674; The Hague, Mauritshuis) and the *Elegant Couple* (*c.* 1674; England, priv. col., see 1984 exh. cat., p. 335), were influenced by Gabriel Metsu, Gerard ter Borch (ii) and Caspar Netscher. Verkolje's portraits commanded high prices and were greatly valued for their outstanding finish, a style more polished than that of his predecessors. His work as a mezzotint engraver was equally appreciated and sought after. On the basis of a few mezzotints made between 1680 and 1684 after the work of English artists, it is generally supposed that Verkolje lived in London at that time, although this is unproven. As a draughtsman, he made precise, small cabinet pieces usually employing pen and ink with brown wash or watercolour heightened with white chalk. Houbraken mentioned Albertus van der Burgh (*b* 1672), Joan van der Spriet (*fl c.* 1700) and Willem Verschuuring (1657–1715), among others, as Verkolje's pupils.

BIBLIOGRAPHY

Hollstein: *Dut. & Flem.*; Thieme–Becker; Wurzbach

A. Houbraken: *De groote schouburgh* (1718–21), i, p. 236; ii, p. 196; iii, pp. 282–6

Printmaking in the Age of Rembrandt (exh. cat. by C. S. Ackley, Boston, MA, Mus. F.A.; St Louis, MO, A. Mus.; 1980–81), pp. 283–4

Masters of 17th-century Dutch Genre Painting (exh. cat. by P. C. Sutton and others, Philadelphia, PA, Mus. A.; Berlin, Gemäldegal.; London, RA; 1984), pp. 335–6

IRENE HABERLAND

(2) Nicolaas Verkolje (*b* Delft, 11 April 1673; *d* Amsterdam, 21 Jan 1746). Son of (1) Jan Verkolje I. He studied with his father and became, like Jan, a versatile artist, producing not only genre pieces but also mythological scenes, ceiling paintings and portraits. He was also an expert mezzotint artist, like his father. In 1700 Nicolaas settled in Amsterdam, where he remained until his death. He was commissioned in 1731 to make prints after seven paintings by Gérard de Lairesse in the town hall of The Hague. He occasionally painted figures in the work of Isaac de Moucheron.

Nicolaas Verkolje's work was clearly influenced by that of de Lairesse, Adriaen van der Werff and Gabriel Metsu. His changing use of styles and formats typifies his efforts to accommodate early 18th-century Dutch taste, as in, for example, his *Apotheosis of the East India Company* (Amsterdam, Rijksmus.), which is in the manner of a French academic painting, seen through the eyes of Adriaen van der Werff, but on a much-reduced scale. In *The Soothsayer* (Toledo, OH, Mus. A.), in contrast, there is no trace of a more sophisticated international style, the work being entirely in the manner of an early 17th-century Dutch painting. Verkolje's many-sided artistic production was highly popular with collectors, and his popularity continued after his death and until the end of the 18th century, as is confirmed by the demand for his portraits.

BIBLIOGRAPHY

J. W. Niemeijer: 'Notities bij de portretten van Nicolaas Verkolje', *Oud-Holland*, lxxvi (1961), pp. 209–11

Dutch Masterpieces from the Eighteenth Century: Paintings and Drawings, 1700–1800 (exh. cat. by E. R. Mandle and J. W. Niemeijer, Minneapolis, MN, Inst. A.; Toledo, OH, Mus. A.; Philadelphia, PA, Mus. A.; 1971–2), pp. 106–7

C. J. A. Wansink: 'Een teruggevonden schilderij van Nicolaas Verkolje (1673–1746)', *Oud-Holland*, ci (1987), pp. 86–8

TON GEERTS

Verlat, Charles [Karel] (*b* Antwerp, 24 Nov 1824; *d* Antwerp, 23 Oct 1890). Belgian painter and teacher. He studied at the Antwerp Academy and was admitted to Ary Scheffer's atelier at the Ecole des Beaux-Arts in Paris in 1850. He discovered Delacroix in the museums and studios of Paris, but he remained Flemish at heart, particularly admiring the colours of Rubens's Medici cycle in the Louvre. With his contemporary, Eugène Verboeckhoven, he became the heir to the Flemish tradition of genre painting in which animals were the main protagonists, capturing the subtle colour and texture of fur with great exactitude (e.g. *Pig and Ass*; Antwerp, Kon. Mus. S. Kst). He remained in Paris until 1868, and from 1869 to 1874 he taught at the Weimar Kunstschule.

Between 1875 and 1877 Verlat travelled to Egypt and Palestine to make studies for subsequent paintings of the life of Christ and the Virgin Mary. Back in Antwerp he exhibited religious subjects, landscapes and pictures of monuments in a realistic style marked by intense light and colour contrasts. He eventually reverted to a more subdued tonality. In later years he specialized in painting monkeys and portraits of European intellectual society. Between 1881 and 1882 he executed two large didactic panoramas (untraced), which combined painting and sculpture. In 1877 Verlat joined the Antwerp Akademie voor Schone Kunsten as a professor of painting and did much to reform its curriculum. He became its director in 1885. Among his pupils were Charles Mertens and Henry Van de Velde.

BIBLIOGRAPHY

V. Verlat and C. Verlat: *Ch. Verlat* (Antwerp, 1925)

W. Koninckx: *Trois peintres anversois: Ch. Verlat, P. Verhaert, Ch. Martens* (Brussels, 1944)

BERNADETTE THOMAS

Verly, François (*b* Lille, 9 March 1760; *d* Saint-Saulve, 24 Aug 1822). French architect and urban planner. He began his architectural education at the Académie des Arts in Lille, completed it at the Académie Royale d'Architecture in Paris and returned to Lille in 1786 to practise architecture. Projects in Lille, Arras and Saint-Omer quickly earned him regional recognition, for example the conversion of the church of St Laurent, Lille, into a 'Temple de la Raison' in 1793–4, but he achieved special prominence through a series of plans (1792–5; unexecuted) for the reconstruction of Lille after the French Revolution. The most visionary of these was one for a group of secular monuments comprising a public hall, belfry, baths and a theatre. Their design reflected the taste for large scale and for extensive, flat surfaces, simple geometry and novel formal juxtapositions that was exemplified in contemporary works in Paris by Jacques Gondoin, François-Joseph Belanger and Claude-Nicolas Ledoux—at least some of which Verly may have seen at first hand. Verly left Lille in 1801 for Antwerp, where he was named Municipal Architect in 1802. Until 1814, when he lost his position with the fall of the French Empire, Verly produced numerous plans (mostly unexecuted) for the improvement of Antwerp's waterfront and street system, in accordance with Napoleon's ambition to transform the city into a first-class port (e.g. warehouses built on the Scheldt River *c* 1815; destr.). Verly also designed many public and private buildings in a fairly severe Neoclassical style, for example the Palace of Justice, Amsterdam, only a few of which were actually carried out. One still extant is the private house built at St-Katelijnevest 15–16, Antwerp (1801). Leaving Antwerp, Verly settled in Brussels where, for several years, he enjoyed the favour of William I, King of the Netherlands, and many other prominent clients, including the painter Jacques-Louis David. Some of his latest works, of which there were few after 1818, were in the romantic style. Verly was not only an architect but also a talented draughtsman and engraver. Among his pupils were the architect Benjamin Dewarlez and the archaeologist Charles Verly (*b* 1794), his nephew.

BIBLIOGRAPHY

J.-J. Duthoy: 'Un Architecte néo-classique: François Verly, Lille, Anvers, Bruxelles', *Rev. Belge Archéol. & Hist. A.*, xli (1972), pp. 119–50

J. A. Leith: 'Projects for a Revolutionary Center: Verly's Plans for Lille', *Daidalos*, 7 (1983), pp. 56–63

P. Lombaerde: 'De stedebouwkundige werken van François Verly' [The urban planning work of François Verly], *Antwerpen tijdens het Franse*

Keizerrijk, 1804–1814 [Antwerp during the French Empire, 1804–1814], ed. P. Lombaerde (Antwerp, 1989), pp. 100–27
J. A. Leith: *Space and Revolution: Projects for Monuments, Squares and Public Buildings in France 1789–1799* (Montreal, 1991), pp. 232–7

ALFRED WILLIS

Vermeer, Johannes [Jan] (*b* Delft, *bapt* 31 Oct 1632; *d* Delft, *bur* 16 Dec 1675). Dutch painter. He is considered one of the principal Dutch genre painters of the 17th century. His work displays an unprecedented level of artistic mastery in its consummate illusion of reality. Vermeer's figures are often reticent and inactive, which imparts an evocative air of solemnity and mystery to his paintings.

I. Life and work. II. Working methods and technique. III. Iconography. IV. Critical reception and posthumous reputation.

I. Life and work.

Johannes Vermeer was the second and youngest child of Digna Baltens and Reynier Jansz. Vermeer (alias Vos), both Reformed Protestants. Vermeer's father was trained in Amsterdam to weave caffa (a fine, patterned fabric of satin, silk or velvet) and eventually became an innkeeper and picture dealer (a capacity in which he registered with the Delft Guild of St Luke in 1631). Reynier Jansz.'s activities as a picture dealer with contacts among local painters and collectors undoubtedly influenced the career choice of the young Vermeer, who presumably began his artistic training sometime in the mid-1640s.

In December 1653 Vermeer was admitted as a master to the Delft Guild of St Luke, an act that granted him the right to sell his work in Delft, take on pupils and even to sell paintings by other artists as his father had done before him, an occupation in which he would later engage. According to guild regulations, any painter who enrolled as a master had to serve at least six years as an apprentice with a recognized artist (or artists), either in Delft or elsewhere. The identity of Vermeer's teacher or teachers has long been debated. In one version of the frequently quoted poem by Arnold Bon published in Dirck van Bleyswijck's *Beschryvinge der stadt Delft* (1667), Vermeer is described as the artist who trod masterfully in the path of 'the Phoenix', Carel Fabritius. The poem alludes to the explosion of the Delft municipal arsenal in 1654, a catastrophe that levelled a large portion of the city, tragically claiming many victims, including Fabritius, an artist who had arrived in the city around 1650 and become its leading master. The poem has led to the misleading theory that Fabritius was Vermeer's teacher, even though Bon merely implied that Vermeer succeeded Fabritius as the foremost painter in Delft. Although the two artists' similar subjects and style, along with their common interest in perspective and optics, are adduced to support the theory, it is unlikely, since Fabritius enrolled in the Guild of St Luke only in October 1652 (one year before Vermeer).

Leonard Bramer also could have been Vermeer's teacher. When he returned to his native Delft after a long stay in Italy in 1628, he quickly established himself as one of the principal painters in the city. Given Bramer's prominence it is possible that he taught Vermeer, even if his surviving work consists largely of easel paintings depicting luminous, energetic figures sometimes posed within dark, cavernous settings, a style that has little in common with Vermeer's art. Whether or not Bramer was Vermeer's teacher, there is evidence that he was a friend of the artist's family. A document dated 5 April 1653 indicates that Bramer attempted to intervene on Vermeer's behalf in an effort to convince the latter's future mother-in-law to consent to his marriage to her daughter.

Montias (1989) hypothesized that Vermeer, after spending the first four years of his apprenticeship in Delft, concluded his training in Amsterdam or Utrecht, or possibly both cities in succession. The influence of painters from Amsterdam and Utrecht on Vermeer's early work and the fact that the Utrecht artist Abraham Bloemaert was a distant relative of his future wife's family support this theory.

On 20 April 1653, several months before enrolling in the guild, Vermeer married Catharina Bolnes (*b* 1631; *bur* 2 Jan 1688). Catharina's mother, Maria Thins (*b c.* 1593; *bur* 27 Dec 1680), initially objected to the marriage, possibly on social and financial grounds—Maria was descended from a distinguished family from Gouda—and also because she and her daughter were practising Roman Catholics. However, Vermeer must have converted to Catholicism sometime between the couple's betrothal and the wedding ceremony, since the latter occurred in a small, predominantly Catholic village outside Delft. Vermeer and his wife eventually had eleven children; this large family undoubtedly placed a tremendous economic strain on the artist.

The only undisputed, dated works by the artist are *The Procuress* (Dresden, Gemäldegal. Alte Meister) of 1656 and two others, *The Astronomer* (Paris, Louvre) of 1668 and *The Geographer* (Frankfurt am Main, Städel. Kstinst.) of 1669. (In the latter two cases the dates may be later additions based on the original ones.) Nevertheless, scholars agree on a general outline of the chronology of Vermeer's paintings, with only slight variations. Thirty-five paintings are considered genuine, although the authorship of three is debated: *St Praxedis* (priv. col.; see Wheelock, 1986), the *Woman with a Lute* (New York, Met.) and the *Girl with a Red Hat* (Washington, DC, N.G.A.). Vermeer's artistic career can be conveniently divided into three periods.

1. Early period, *c.* 1655–7. 2. Middle period, *c.* 1657–67. 3. Late period, *c.* 1667–75.

1. EARLY PERIOD, *c.* 1655–7. The early period of Vermeer's artistic career was devoted to experimentation in techniques and subject-matter. His earliest works are history paintings. Such paintings, illustrating episodes from the Bible, mythology or Classical and modern history, were most highly esteemed by contemporary art theorists. Clearly at this stage in his career, Vermeer aspired to be a history painter. *Christ in the House of Mary and Martha* (Edinburgh, N.G.) is perhaps his earliest surviving work, painted *c.* 1655. Like all of those produced during Vermeer's early period, it is much larger than most of his later paintings and includes large-scale figures placed in the foreground. It is a broadly painted work and reveals the artist's knowledge of contemporary developments in history painting in Amsterdam, for it is clearly dependent on

a painting of the same subject (Valenciennes, Mus. B.-A.) by the Fleming Erasmus Quellinus (i), an artist active in the decoration of the new town hall in Amsterdam. Quellinus's work resembles Vermeer's in motifs such as the open door in the background, and in the pose of Christ with Mary at his feet. The figure of Christ is also dependent on prototypes from Italian art. The sensitivity to light in this painting—its cool effects reminiscent of pictures by the Utrecht Caravaggisti—together with its colour scheme and such motifs as the Oriental rug on the table anticipate later developments in Vermeer's art. Vermeer's knowledge of contemporary trends in history painting in Amsterdam is also demonstrated in his only surviving mythological painting, *Diana and her Companions* (The Hague, Mauritshuis; see fig. 1). It was completed around the same time as *Christ in the House of Mary and Martha*. The figures were influenced by those in the background of a painting of the same subject (Berlin, Bodemus.) by the Amsterdam artist Jacob van Loo.

Despite Vermeer's early dependence on artistic developments in Amsterdam and to a lesser extent Utrecht, his work is somewhat distinctive: the rich palette and facture of *Diana and her Companions*—which differs markedly from *Christ in the House of Mary and Martha*—has long been compared to that of 16th-century Venetian paintings, particularly those by Titian; moreover, its composition derives from representations of *Diana and Acteon* by Titian and Rubens (see Blankert in 1980–81 exh. cat., no. 54).

Vermeer's ambitions to become a history painter may also explain his interest in Italian art. Since he presumably did not travel to Italy, his knowledge of Italian art was possibly acquired in Amsterdam, which had more important collections of Italian painting than did his native Delft. Johannes de Renialme, the owner of the *Visit to the Tomb* (untraced), was an important dealer–collector of Italian art who was primarily based in Amsterdam (but also active in Delft; Montias, 1980). Vermeer himself was

1. Johannes Vermeer: *Diana and her Companions*, 985×1050 mm, *c*. 1655 (The Hague, Koninklijk Kabinet van Schilderijen 'Mauritshuis')

eventually recognized as an expert in Italian art, for in May 1672 he was summoned to The Hague (along with several other painters) to appraise a collection of 12 Italian paintings that were at the source of a dispute between the art dealer Gerrit Uylenburgh and their prospective buyer, Frederick William, the Grand Elector of Brandenburg.

The controversial *St Praxedis* (priv. col.) also testifies to Vermeer's exposure to Italian art during the early stages of his career. This work, a copy of a painting by the contemporary Florentine master Felice Ficherelli (1605–?1669), is signed and dated 1655 in the lower left and also has an additional signature in the lower right: *Meer N*[aar] *R*[ip]*o*[s]*o*, 'Vermeer after Riposo', the latter being Ficherelli's nickname.

The last painting ascribed to Vermeer's early period is the signed and dated *Procuress* (1656; Dresden, Gemäldegal. Alte Meister), which shows continued links with the Amsterdam and Utrecht schools. The warm colours and chiaroscuro effects recall the paintings of Rembrandt and his pupils of the late 1640s and 1650s, for example Nicolaes Maes. The subject was probably inspired by pictures by the Utrecht Caravaggisti; Vermeer's mother-in-law owned a work of the same subject (Boston, MA, Mus. F.A.) by Dirck van Baburen, which later appeared in the background of two paintings by Vermeer. At first glance, *The Procuress* could be categorized as a genre painting. However, the anachronistic Burgundian costume of the smiling man on the left—a possible self-portrait of the artist—indicates that Vermeer intended it to be a history painting. It probably represents an episode from the New Testament parable of the prodigal son, in which

the unruly youth dissipates his inheritance, an episode often rendered in contemporary guise by Dutch artists.

2. MIDDLE PERIOD, *c.* 1657–67. *The Procuress* can be considered a crucial transitional work as its subject shares many features with genre paintings, the type of work that is most frequently associated with Vermeer. Most of the paintings of the middle period (along with those of the late period) are genre paintings, that is, scenes of everyday life.

Vermeer's first *genre pur* is his *Girl Asleep at a Table* (New York, Met.). Its comparatively large scale, spatial ambiguities and palette recall *The Procuress*, suggesting that it should be dated *c.* 1657. This and related works reflect Vermeer's response to the revolutionary formal and iconographic developments in Dutch genre painting around 1650. The raucous scenes painted in earlier decades (often of peasants and soldiers) declined in popularity in favour of subjects such as elegantly attired figures engaged in a wide variety of leisure activities. Accompanying this shift in subject-matter were stylistic changes as well: individual paintings exhibit reduced numbers of figures whose dimensions are enlarged in relation to overall space. The newer generation of artists, such as Gerard ter Borch (ii) and Pieter de Hooch, remained sensitive to the renderings of textures and stuffs but also focused on the subtle, natural evocations of light and shadow on figures and objects firmly planted within the confines of carefully constructed spaces. Their superbly balanced, dramatic works contrast strongly with the evenly lit, monochromatic interiors of their predecessors. Vermeer was certainly familiar with ter Borch's work and probably with the artist himself, even though the latter lived in Deventer: they both signed a notary document in Delft on 22 April 1653 (Montias, 1980).

The stimulus of de Hooch, who lived in Delft between *c.* 1652 and *c.* 1661, must explain Vermeer's growing interest in the placement of figures within solidly constructed, light-filled spaces. Vermeer's next four paintings, a closely related group, all differ considerably from the artist's previous work and reflect in varying degrees the influence of de Hooch. *Soldier with a Laughing Girl* (New York, Frick; *see* SCIENCE AND ART, fig. 4), *Girl Reading a Letter at an Open Window* (Dresden, Gemäldegal. Alte Meister), *The Milkmaid* (Amsterdam, Rijksmus.) and the *Glass of Wine* (Berlin, Gemäldegal.) were probably painted between 1658 and 1661. In contrast to the paintings of his early period, Vermeer reduced the size of the figures in relation to the overall space, and his application of paint became thicker as he modelled the figures and objects to display a tremendous tactility. He also paid scrupulous attention to the naturalistic effects of light within the interiors of these works.

The *Soldier with a Laughing Girl* is considerably accomplished in this respect: the superb rendition of the myriad effects of light and shadow within this brightly illuminated interior reveals Vermeer's great technical mastery and introduces a heretofore unseen level of realism in Dutch art. The distortions in size and scale between the soldier (silhouetted in stark *contre-jour* in the foreground) and the woman (seated in the middleground), along with the unfocused look of such motifs as the lion-headed finial on

2. Johannes Vermeer: *Woman with a Water Jug*, 457×406 mm, *c.* 1662–5 (New York, Metropolitan Museum of Art)

her chair, her hands and the wine glass she is holding, provide the earliest evidence of Vermeer's interest in optical devices (*see* §II below). Vermeer replicated the unfocused appearance of the motifs that he would have seen through an optical device by applying his famous *pointillés* (small dots of paint employed to yield the effect of broken contours and dissolved forms in light).

Pointillés are used in *The Milkmaid* to impart an extraordinary tactile reality to such objects as the chunks of bread. The chunks are encrusted with so many *pointillés* that these dots of paint seem to exist independently of the forms they describe. This tactility is also detected in other works of this phase: the carpets on the table of the *Girl Reading a Letter at an Open Window* and the *Glass of Wine* have a palpable knubby quality that is completely different from the broad, general planes of the carpet in the early *Christ in the House of Mary and Martha*.

Vermeer's rapid mastery of the depiction of forms in space probably stimulated his interest in townscape painting, a genre in which he produced at least three pictures, as is known from the catalogue of the auction in 1696 of Jacob Dissius's collection (*see* §IV below), which includes 'A view of a house standing in Delft', 'A view of some houses . . .' and 'The town of Delft in perspective, to be seen from the south . . .'. Two of them survive, the *Little Street* (*c.* 1658–60; Amsterdam, Rijksmus.; *see* NETHERLANDS, THE, fig. 18) and the famous *View of Delft* (*c.* 1661; The Hague, Mauritshuis; *see* DELFT, fig. 2). The titles in the old sale catalogue suggest that Vermeer might have done the three paintings in sequence, working from the simplest composition of a house in Delft to the most complicated one, a view of the city itself. Vermeer took liberties with the dimensions of buildings for aesthetic effect in his *View of Delft*, but it is nonetheless an extraordinary document of the 17th-century appearance of the city and a *tour de force* in the rendition of light and shadow.

Despite his comparative youth, Vermeer had reached great artistic heights by the early 1660s. His colleagues elected him headman of the Guild of St Luke in the autumn of 1662 (a two-year position to which he was re-elected in 1670). He was the youngest artist to be chosen for the post since the guild had been reorganized in 1611, a reflection certainly of the esteem of his fellow artists but also of the fact that by 1662 many other possible candidates had either died or left the city (Montias, 1989).

Vermeer continued to modify his style throughout the 1660s. A level of refinement that had hitherto been lacking was introduced in such works as *Woman with Two Men* (Brunswick, Herzog Anton Ulrich-Mus.), as well as the 'pearl pictures' (a group of paintings of women, usually dated between 1662 and 1665, that share a common motif of pearls and a luminous, silvery tonality), among which are the *Woman with a Water Jug* (New York, Met.; *see* fig. 2), *Woman Reading a Letter* (Amsterdam, Rijksmus.), *Woman with a Pearl Necklace* (Berlin, Gemäldegal.) and the *Woman Holding a Balance* (Washington, DC, N.G.A.). Vermeer no longer relied on pasty modelling with thick impasto, and his use of *pointillés* became less obtrusive. The paint surfaces are smoother, with less tactile detail, and the lighting effects, though at times retaining their brilliance, are generally less bold. Many of these works

exude an air of reticence and introspection that has been so highly esteemed in Vermeer's art in the 20th century.

Vermeer's stylistic shift towards greater refinement is best explained as a response to contemporary developments by the Leiden 'fine' painters, particularly the precision and sophistication characteristic of the work of Frans van Mieris (i). Vermeer's famous *Head of a Girl with a Pearl Earring* (*c.* 1665; The Hague, Mauritshuis; see fig. 3) also belongs to this period. All the contours of this small canvas are created with delicately modulated tones of paint in place of outlines. Even the bridge of the young woman's nose is delineated not by line but by a subtle, barely perceptible application of impasto. The edge of the nose is not even distinguishable from the right cheek; the two features simply blend together. The resultant optical effects are stunning, as the girl's features are refined and purified (in a manner far removed from the highly detailed figures painted by van Mieris) to the extent that it is difficult to identify this work as a portrait of a specific person.

During his middle period Vermeer also produced two paintings with deep spatial recessions: the *Music Lesson* (London, Buckingham Pal., Royal Col.) and *The Concert* (ex-Isabella Stewart Gardner Mus., Boston, MA; 1990; see fig. 4), which were probably painted slightly later than the 'pearl paintings'—perhaps 1665 or 1666. Although these pictures evolved from the earlier *Glass of Wine* and *Woman with Two Men*, they represent Vermeer's most spatially complex works to date. In both, the figures are placed in the background in an effort to exploit the volumetric qualities of the scene as a whole. The *Music Lesson*, possibly the later of the two, displays a rigorous

3. Johannes Vermeer: *Head of a Girl with a Pearl Earring*, oil on canvas, 460×400 mm, *c.* 1665 (The Hague, Koninklijk Kabinet van Schilderijen 'Mauritshuis')

4. Johannes Vermeer: *The Concert*, oil on canvas, 690×630 mm, *c.* 1665–6 (ex-Isabella Stewart Gardner Museum, Boston, MA, 1990)

5. Johannes Vermeer: *Love Letter*, oil on canvas, 440×385 mm, *c.* 1667 (Amsterdam, Rijksmuseum)

spatial construction with carefully orchestrated arrangements of light, colours and forms (for instance, the parallel beams of the ceiling and the white, grey and black pattern of the lozenge-shaped floor tiles).

The crowning achievement of Vermeer's middle period is the equally ambitious *Allegory of Painting* (*c.* 1666–7; Vienna, Ksthist. Mus.; *see* MODEL, ARTIST'S, fig. 2), a work still in the artist's possession at his death. In it, Vermeer harmoniously integrated a variety of exquisitely painted figures and objects within a carefully constructed, light-suffused room. The result is an unsurpassed masterpiece of luminosity and spatial illusion, one that is also characterized by the quintessential detachment and reticence so often associated with Vermeer's art.

3. LATE PERIOD, *c.* 1667–75. Various details in the *Allegory of Painting* anticipate the style that characterizes Vermeer's late period. The material lying on the table beside the mask is so unfocused and abstract that it resembles melted wax. The chandelier exhibits similar abstract qualities, its diffuseness enhanced by *pointillés* that, when compared to those in earlier pictures, have been reduced to small, flat rectangular planes. The abstraction evident in these motifs became a dominant feature in Vermeer's late paintings as he tended to focus on patterns of colours on objects at the expense of describing their textures. The increased stylization was not unique to him: such tendencies are seen in the art of many Dutch painters active in the 1670s and after. The long-desired goal of mastering the illusion of reality, which was finally achieved by painters, including Vermeer, who were active between 1650 and 1670, left many artists (particularly those of a younger generation) with few aesthetic alternatives save the introduction of mannered elegance and refinement into their work (Blankert, 1978).

The *Love Letter* (*c.* 1667; Amsterdam, Rijksmus.; see fig. 5) is Vermeer's first painting to display on a wide scale those stylistic features associated with his late style. The mistress and maid are viewed through a vestibule, an unusual device that was perhaps influenced by the work of the Dordrecht painter Samuel van Hoogstraten (Slatkes, 1981). The architectonic features of the vestibule and back room are sharply linear. Such details as the right door jamb in the vestibule are delineated by single, vertical strokes of light. This geometric purity extends to the figures themselves. Vermeer's earlier interest in the depiction of subtle nuances of light has disappeared in favour of crisp, clear divisions of light and shadow. These cold, refined features are especially strong in paintings executed around 1670–71. The same linear precision is displayed in works such as the *Lady Writing a Letter with her Maid* (Dublin, N.G.). The refinement and abstraction of forms towards geometric ends is complete. The garments of the maid looking out of the window are so sharply defined in terms of light and shadow that they actually resemble the fluting on Classical columns. Even the carpet on the table on which the mistress is writing shares these abstract features: unlike the carpet in the early *Christ in the House of Mary and Martha*, with its broad general planes, and the carpets in such middle period works as the *Glass of Wine*, with their knubby quality, it hangs in a most unnatural, boxlike manner.

The impression of abstraction and purity conveyed in the works produced *c.* 1670–71 increased in those painted during the artist's last years (1672–5), as in the *Allegory of Faith* (New York, Met.) and the *Guitar Player* (London, Kenwood House; see fig. 6). The composition of the *Guitar Player* is unusual, as the artist has placed the girl so far to the left that her arm is partly cut off. The forms are again crisply defined, and the girl's fingers, the head of the guitar and the frame of the picture on the wall in the background are highlighted with the *pointillés* of Vermeer's late period: extremely flat, geometric touches of impasto.

Perhaps there are links between Vermeer's style in these paintings and his circumstances at this time. His last three years were filled with great financial hardship, much of which was caused by the economic crisis that engulfed the Netherlands in the wake of the French invasion of 1672. In 1677 Vermeer's widow—still saddled with formidable debts—testified that during the ruinous war with France the artist could sell none of his paintings nor those by other masters in whose work he dealt. This turmoil undoubtedly affected the production and sale of art everywhere, but in Vermeer's case the problems were clearly exacerbated by his laborious approach to his craft.

II. Working methods and technique.

It has been observed that since the Renaissance no artist's fame has rested on so few pictures as has Vermeer's (Slatkes, 1981). He probably did not paint many more works than the 35 that survive; his total output has been estimated at between 43 and 60 paintings (Montias, 1989). Vermeer thus most likely produced on average about two to three paintings per year. The reasons for this are undoubtedly linked to his meticulous working methods. Laboratory analysis has revealed that the artist continually reworked his paintings to clarify compositional, spatial and iconographic relationships, as he did, for example, in the *Girl Asleep at a Table*. At various stages in its genesis, it included a dog in the doorway, a man entering the room, an additional chair or table at the middle right edge and grapes and grape leaves in a bowl on the table in the foreground (Ainsworth and others, 1982). Vermeer also adjusted the shapes of objects within the composition. For instance, in the *Music Lesson* he made the lid of the clavecin wider on the girl's right than on the left in order to reduce the viewer's visual propensity to connect the two halves of the lid through the girl, which, in effect, would have lessened the painting's convincing illusion of reality (Wheelock, 1981). Occasionally changes in Vermeer's paintings can be observed by the naked eye. The faint shadow of one of his lion-headed chair finials can be seen directly to the right of the lower edge of the window in the *Woman with a Water Jug*. As laboratory examination has confirmed, this is a vestige of a chair that Vermeer painted out of the composition (Wheelock, 1984). Similarly, a close inspection of the jug and hands of the servant in *The Milkmaid* reveals a number of pentiments, created as the artist struggled to depict them convincingly.

Vermeer was a fastidious artist who diligently strove to achieve the masterful harmony that is now associated with his paintings. That he achieved such extraordinary states of compositional equilibrium is all the more remarkable

6. Johannes Vermeer: *Guitar Player*, oil on canvas, 530×463 mm, *c.* 1672 (London, Kenwood House, Iveagh Bequest)

given that no preparatory drawings by him survive. In the *Allegory of Painting* the canvas on which the artist is working includes a white chalk outline of the figure of History; perhaps Vermeer worked in the same manner (though no evidence of this has been found).

Vermeer's application of paint was equally painstaking and complex. This is particularly true of the pictures produced during his middle period, in which he gradually abandoned the use of thick impasto in favour of an intricate application of opaque and semi-transparent paints and thin glazes. In the *Woman with a Water Jug* Vermeer applied a light ochre ground to provide a warm base for the overlying colours and to delineate shadows such as those on the right side of the girl's jacket. In the lower right a second ground layer (the imprimatura) of reddish-brown covers the first one; it enhances the reddish glow of the reflections on the brass basin and also serves as the base colour for the tablecloth. The rich pattern of the tablecloth is simply composed of freely but carefully brushed strokes of primary colours and oranges (Wheelock, 1981).

Vermeer's complex technique also accounts for the scumbled appearance of his paintings. For example, in the *Head of a Girl with a Pearl Earring* the contour of the young woman's face is blurred by a fine line of flesh-coloured glaze extended over the dark background (Wheelock, 1981). Vermeer achieved equally impressive visual effects by subtly changing the hues that define objects in relation to the amount of light that strikes them. In the *Music Lesson*, for instance, the inscribed letters on the cover of the clavecin are painted in ochre to the left of its player and in lilac to her right, where there is more shadow. Similar colour changes are seen in the windows at the left as Vermeer captured the play of sunlight and shadow on the glass (Wheelock, 1981).

The scumbled contours and subtle colour modulations of Vermeer's paintings demonstrate his unrivalled expertise in rendering optical effects, as do the objects that appear distorted and out of focus. He could not have seen these distortions with the naked eye, and it is now generally accepted that he observed them through a camera obscura, a device consisting of a darkened chamber with a small opening that receives an image and projects it with a lens, while retaining its natural appearance, on to a facing surface. Renaissance artists had used the camera obscura as an aid in rendering perspective, which probably explains Vermeer's initial interest in it as well. However, the general enthusiasm among Delft artists such as Bramer and Fabritius for optical phenomena may have prompted Vermeer to begin experimenting with the device. The camera obscura has a limited depth of field, and spatial and focal distortions are therefore intrinsic to the image it projects. Moreover, the device reduces the scale of objects but not the amount of colour or light that reflects off them, so colour accents and light contrasts gain in intensity. The difference between Vermeer's use of the camera obscura and that by earlier artists—as well as later ones, among them Canaletto—was that the others always corrected its inherent distortions. Vermeer, by contrast, seemed to revel in them, as he attempted to replicate the optical distortions seen through the apparatus. For instance, in the *Soldier with a Laughing Girl* (*c.* 1658)— probably Vermeer's first work created with the assistance of the camera obscura—there are discrepancies in scale between the two figures, along with diffuse highlights, particularly around the lion-headed chair finials and the girl's hands. Vermeer also applied *pointillés* to these motifs in order to duplicate the halations that were viewed through the device.

Vermeer frequently employed the camera obscura thereafter, which accounts for such unusual optical phenomena as the collapsed perspective in such paintings as the *View of Delft* or the sensuous halations and focal distortions of the *Girl with a Red Hat*. However, Vermeer's use of the device should not be overemphasized. There is no evidence, for example, that Vermeer either traced or copied his compositions directly from the projected image of the camera obscura. The enchanting optical effects produced by the apparatus no doubt stimulated his aesthetic interest to such an extent that he often imitated them in his art. Yet simultaneously Vermeer modified these effects to suit his artistic vision, often, surprisingly, exaggerating them. This is especially true of his *pointillés*. Although Vermeer first used *pointillés* to reproduce halations that are commonly seen through the camera obscura, he soon realized their independent aesthetic potential. It is unlikely, for instance, that he observed them on the bread depicted in *The Milkmaid* since the camera obscura will only cause halations on projected objects that reflect light (such as metal or polished wood). In the *View of Delft* Vermeer applied *pointillés* to the shadowy hulls of the boats moored along the Schie in an effort to suggest flickering reflections from the water. Had these boats been viewed through a camera obscura, reflections would not have been detected because they would be visible only in direct sunlight (Wheelock, 1981). It would thus be reductive to consider the *View of Delft*—or, for that matter, any painting by Vermeer—as a simple transcription of the image that the artist had seen through the camera obscura.

Vermeer's laborious working method apparently precluded his training students within a traditional studio setting, although it is possible that he trained one or more of his many children. The *Girl with a Flute* (Washington, DC, N.G.A.), once thought to be by Vermeer, is now ascribed to the artist's immediate circle; it may have been completed by one of his children, since there is no record of any students.

III. Iconography.

Like genre paintings by other Dutch artists, those by Vermeer do not reproduce value-free slices of daily life in Delft, for it is now known that Dutch 17th-century art was laden with meaning. Vermeer's art may be stunningly naturalistic and mysteriously solemn, but it is nevertheless symbolic. In other ways, however, he parted company with many of his colleagues' more traditional approaches to symbolism. Attempts to decipher the iconographic complexities of Vermeer's art have often proved elusive. Fortunately, our frustrations are more than adequately compensated for by the solemn beauty and mystery of his creations.

In many instances the rooms in Vermeer's paintings closely resemble one another (cf. the *Glass of Wine* and the *Woman with Two Men*; the *Girl Reading a Letter at an Open Window* and the *Soldier with a Laughing Girl*). This has led to unsuccessful attempts to identify the spaces depicted in the paintings with those that actually existed in his mother-in-law's house (into which Vermeer and his family had probably moved *c.* 1660; Swillens, 1950). Vermeer also resorted to an impressive array of 'studio props' ranging from paintings (which he reproduced so faithfully that their authorship can often be determined) to costumes, musical instruments, furniture and wall coverings, including maps, which are generally rendered with great fidelity (Welu, 1975). While many of these objects are identifiable (thanks to the artist's death inventory of 1676; van Peer, 1957), he continually varied their appearance along with that of the rooms in which they are depicted. The variations from painting to painting are seemingly inexhaustible: the famous chairs with lion-headed finials are often shown with different upholstery, the patterns of tiles on the floors change, the pictures on the walls vary in scale and have different frames, the placement of windows is altered with respect to the back walls etc. Vermeer's endless adjustments to existing objects and spaces in his work suggest that his paintings, like those of his contemporaries, are best understood as carefully orchestrated constructs of reality, created in the interests of meaning.

Scholars have addressed the question of meaning in Vermeer's art with only limited success, a reflection no doubt of the evocative yet enigmatic nature of his imagery. Vermeer's works are arresting for their general lack of narrative, for their eternalization of seemingly inconse-quential moments. On those occasions when there is a motif with an ostensibly unequivocal meaning, the ambi-guity of the overall context in which it appears invariably gives rise to contradictory interpretations. On the wall in the background of *The Concert* is a copy of Dirck van Baburen's *Procuress*, which is generally acknowledged to symbolize venal love. However, while some scholars have concluded that Vermeer represented an elegant brothel in this work (Gowing, 1952; Mirimonde, 1961), others, noting the subtle, understated character of the musical trio in combination with the landscapes elsewhere on the wall and on the lid of the harpsichord, have interpreted it in a more positive light, as a contrast to the group in Baburen's *Procuress* (Moreno, 1982; Goodman-Soellner, 1989).

In some cases, motifs that would have clarified the meaning seem to have been deliberately omitted or painted out. For example, in the *Girl Reading a Letter at an Open Window* Vermeer originally included a large roemer and, more significantly, a picture of Cupid holding up a card on the wall behind the woman (Mayer-Meintschel, 1978–9). If these motifs had remained, the significance of the woman's activity of reading a letter—often associated with love in 17th-century Dutch art—would have been appar-ent. In its final state, with Vermeer's deliberate removal of these motifs, the painting is mysteriously ambiguous, which undeniably contributes to its appeal.

The imagery of other paintings by Vermeer is far less allusive. The presence of a stained-glass medallion of Temperance within the mullioned window in the *Woman with Two Men* was clearly meant to be interpreted in relation to the potentially intemperate actions of the couple in the room (Klessman in 1978 exh. cat.). Similarly, the pose of the woman in the *Girl Asleep at a Table*, with her hand supporting her head, must be linked with traditional images of sloth (Kahr, 1972). The *Allegory of Painting* was once thought to be a self-portrait of Vermeer, but owing to the archaic costume of the artist, the presence of Clio (the muse of history) and such motifs as the masks on the table, it is now universally understood as an allegory of painting. In creating this picture, Vermeer, an artist with a respectable library, probably had recourse to the most famous iconographic handbook of the day, Cesare Ripa's *Iconologia*, available in a Dutch translation of 1644. This same book informs the ambitious *Allegory of Faith*, a painting probably commissioned by a wealthy Catholic patron (de Jongh, 1975–6). Its complex symbolism, expli-cating the mysteries of the Roman Catholic faith, was already recognized when it was auctioned at the end of the 17th century. The *Woman Holding a Balance* is ostensibly a genre scene, but it has also been convincingly interpreted as an allegory of truth (Gaskell, 1984).

IV. Critical reception and posthumous reputation.

Despite the mastery of Vermeer's art, it did not exert a lasting impact on other artists. Vermeer had no recorded pupils, and there are only isolated examples of his influence on other artists, such as Emanuel de Witte (Slatkes, 1981), Jan Steen, Pieter de Hooch and Gabriel Metsu. Yet he was a well-respected member of the Delft artistic community and enjoyed the patronage of contemporary collectors,

particularly those in his native town. This must have assured him, at least to some extent, of a regular income. Vermeer's principal patron, a man who possibly had first right of refusal over his paintings, was a wealthy Delft citizen, Pieter Claesz. van Ruijven (*bapt* 10 Dec 1624; *bur* 7 Aug 1674). Van Ruijven loaned Vermeer and his wife 200 guilders in 1657. According to Montias (1987), who has written extensively on Vermeer's possible patrons, this loan may have been an advance towards the purchase of one or more paintings. Vermeer possibly had more than a professional association with van Ruijven and his wife, Maria de Knuijt (*bur* 26 Feb 1681). In her section of the couple's last will and testament (1665), Maria de Knuijt instructed that 500 guilders be left to the painter, the only non-family member to be singled out for a special bequest. This is apparently a rare, if not unique, example of a 17th-century Dutch patron bequeathing money to an artist (Montias, 1987). The bulk of the van Ruijven estate—including the couple's collection of paintings—was inher-ited by their only surviving child, Magdelena (*bapt* 12 Oct 1655; *bur* 16 June 1682). Several months before the death of her mother, Magdelena had married Jacob Abrahamsz. Dissius (*bapt* 23 Nov 1653; *bur* 14 Oct 1695), who became the heir of the estate when Magdelena died childless in June 1682 (Montias 1987). In May 1696, seven months after Dissius's own death, his art collection, including 21 paintings by Vermeer, was auctioned. This sale is well documented, which led to the earlier, erroneous assump-tion that Dissius had been a patron of Vermeer. Despite the reasonably steady income that Vermeer could depend on from van Ruijven, this arrangement was also injurious. The fact that a significant proportion of Vermeer's works remained in the family collection until 22 years after van Ruijven's death probably limited the spread of the artist's reputation beyond his native city.

Hendrick van Buyten (*b* 1632; *d* July 1701) was another Delft citizen who owned a number of paintings by Vermeer. He was a baker by trade, though he accrued substantial wealth through a large inheritance (Montias, 1987). An inventory of his possessions, drawn up on the occasion of his second marriage in 1683, includes three paintings by Vermeer. Two of these paintings were ac-quired after Vermeer's death from his widow as collateral for a huge debt owed for bread. The other painting was already in van Buyten's possession by 1663, as is known from remarks made by the Frenchman Balthazar de Monconys in his diary (published in 1666). De Monconys visited Delft on 11 August 1663 in the company of a Catholic priest and a layman. The three men visited Vermeer's studio, but since there were no paintings to be seen—the artist was probably working on commission by this time—they were sent to the shop of a baker who owned one. This baker, undoubtedly Hendrick van Buyten, showed them his painting of a single figure by Vermeer, boasting that 600 livres (probably 600 guilders) had been paid for it. Van Buyten's quotation of such an exorbitant price might be construed as a feeble attempt to impress a well-to-do foreigner; de Monconys himself commented that he considered the painting overpaid for if it had been bought for 'six pistoles' (60 guilders).

Paintings by the artist also appear in collections in other Dutch cities. A 'face by Vermeer' was listed in the death inventory (4 Aug 1664) of the sculptor Jean Larson (*d* 1664), who lived in The Hague. A wealthy Amsterdam banking official named Hendrick van Swoll (1632–98) also owned a painting by Vermeer, which was auctioned in April 1699, along with other works in his collection. In the auction catalogue it is described as 'a seated woman with several meanings, representing the New Testament'. This painting, which fetched the high price of 400 guilders, can be identified as the *Allegory of Faith*. Outside the Dutch Republic, the Antwerp jeweller and banker Diego Duarte owned a large collection of paintings that included a work by Vermeer. In an inventory of July 1682, the picture was valued at 150 guilders and described as 'a piece with a lady playing the clavecin with accessories . . .'.

Despite Vermeer's connections with van Ruijven and the fact that his paintings appear in the inventories of collectors in Amsterdam, Antwerp and The Hague, references to Vermeer in the art literature of his day are scarce. He is mentioned twice in Dirck van Bleyswijck's *Beschryvinge der stadt Delft* (1667), once in van Bleyswijck's list of painters still working in Delft and then briefly in the poem by Arnold Bon (*see* §I above). That these references are cursory should not be construed negatively, since authors of Dutch city descriptions were traditionally most verbose about deceased artists or ones who no longer resided in the city in question. Van Bleyswijck's succinct reference to Vermeer is quoted verbatim in the first volume of Arnold Houbraken's *Groote schouburgh der Nederlantsche konstschilders en schilderessen* (1718). This extremely short entry might seem surprising, but Houbraken was only well informed about artists who had been active in his native Dordrecht or in his adopted city, Amsterdam. His dependence on van Bleyswijck as a source for information about Vermeer and other Delft artists merely testifies to his unfamiliarity with the artistic scene in that city.

Vermeer's works were not entirely forgotten in the 18th century, even if his name sometimes was. The major reason for the artist's partial fall into obscurity was the rather limited size of his oeuvre. Before the invention of photography, the degree of recognition of works by a particular artist often hinged on the quantity produced. Large numbers of paintings guaranteed familiarity, since these would appear with some frequency in private collections and at auctions. Thus such artists as Nicolaes Berchem and Philips Wouwerman enjoyed great prestige among 18th-century and early 19th-century connoisseurs, while the names of Vermeer and others with comparatively small outputs were often forgotten. It is not surprising, then, that paintings now known to be by Vermeer were earlier occasionally attributed to other, more widely known artists such as Rembrandt and Pieter de Hooch. Yet Vermeer's name did not entirely sink into oblivion: there is a reference to him in the *Mercure de France* of June 1727 by the connoisseur Dezallier d'Argenville, who advised aspiring collectors to include paintings by 'Vandermeer' in their collections (Wheelock, 1977). Further evidence of the high esteem in which the artist's paintings were held is provided by enthusiastic descriptions found in certain 18th-century auction catalogues (Blankert, 1978). Moreover, confusion over attributions worked both ways: paintings by Vermeer were misattributed, but his name was sometimes erroneously attached to the works of other artists.

The first engravings after paintings by Vermeer were produced towards the end of the 18th century. With the onset of the 19th century his reputation gradually rose. In van der Eynden and van der Willigen's *Geschiedenis der vaderlandsche schilderkunst* (1816) he is called 'the Titian of the modern painters of the Dutch school, for his strong colours and fluent brush technique' (Blankert, 1978). National admiration for Vermeer's art in the Netherlands in the early years of the 19th century culminated in 1822 with the purchase of the *View of Delft* by the Mauritshuis, the newly opened State Museum in The Hague, for the then exorbitant sum of 2900 guilders.

The revolutionary social and political developments that took place in Europe during the 1830s and 1840s led to renewed appreciation of many Dutch artists. The rise of the Realist school of painting in France coincided in particular with a growing interest in the works of 17th-century Dutch painters, whose views of daily life were mistakenly considered precedents for the socially and politically informed paintings of such realists as Gustave Courbet. Vermeer himself was rediscovered during the formative stages of the Impressionist movement, when followers of Courbet began to depict scenes of contemporary life with great sensational immediacy (Meltzoff, 1942). Naturally, Vermeer's art—with its bold display of tactile reality, its extraordinary optical fidelity and its eternalization of seemingly inconsequential moments—appealed greatly to these artists. Perhaps equally significant, Vermeer's art gained recognition at approximately the same time that photography was invented.

The first scientific analyses of Vermeer's art were published by Théophile Thoré (under the pseudonym Willem Bürger) in a number of books and journals in the late 1850s and 1860s, culminating with his lengthy study in 1866. Thoré's appreciation of Vermeer's art was indelibly linked to his political views; a radical republican, he had been exiled after the failed coup of May 1848. During his 13-year exile he travelled extensively in Switzerland, England, Belgium and the Netherlands, studying collections first-hand and refining his skills as an art critic and connoisseur. To Thoré, Vermeer's work embodied the purest expression of what he believed to be art's supreme purpose: to portray and ennoble the daily life of common man. Thoré's socio-political view of Vermeer and Dutch art in general is now seen as anachronistic. Yet despite this and many other shortcomings in his studies—most notably his erroneous attribution of some 40 paintings to Vermeer (*see* VREL, JACOBUS)—its impact was enormous. Studies by Henry Havard (1888), Cornelis Hofstede de Groot (1907) and Eduard Plietzsch (1911) followed in the wake of Thoré's as Vermeer rapidly acquired a reputation as one of the greatest Dutch artists of the 17th century. During the years in which these publications appeared, several wealthy American businessmen and socialites acquired the few remaining paintings by Vermeer available on the art market; their munificence accounts for the impressive number of works by the artist now in public collections in Boston, New York and Washington, DC.

Perhaps the most fantastic ramification of the veritable explosion of interest in Vermeer's art was the case of the forger HAN VAN MEEGEREN. Van Meegeren produced a number of forgeries of paintings by Vermeer and other 17th-century Dutch artists. One of these, the *Supper at Emmaus*, was purchased in 1937 by the Boymans Museum in Rotterdam for the enormous sum of 550,000 guilders. The attribution to Vermeer of this and other paintings produced by van Meegeren was not seriously doubted until 1945, when the forger, in order to exonerate himself from charges that he sold Dutch national treasures to the Nazis, claimed that he had painted the *Supper at Emmaus*. Subsequent scientific examination of the canvas, together with van Meegeren's demonstration to the court of his complicated method of creating convincing forgeries, proved that his claims were truthful. The *Supper at Emmaus*, with its distinct resemblance to the art of Caravaggio, was cleverly calculated to appeal to scholars who were desperately searching for early works by Vermeer. Clearly, the overwhelming enthusiasm for Vermeer's art at that time, which had completely outpaced cautious scholarship, had prejudiced the otherwise sound critical faculties of many noteworthy art historians. This is the only way to explain how forgeries that to the modern eye have such glaring weaknesses could have ever been considered authentic.

Scholarly interest in the art of Vermeer continued in the post-World War II era. Studies such as those by Gowing (1952), Blankert (1978, rev. in Blankert, Montias and Aillaud, 1986), Wheelock (1981), Slatkes (1981) and Montias (1989) have been characterized by an increasingly refined critical approach to his oeuvre.

BIBLIOGRAPHY

GENERAL

EWA
H. Havard: *L'Art et les artistes hollandais*, 4 vols (Paris, 1879–81)
——: *Van der Meer de Delft* (Paris, 1888)
C. Hofstede de Groot: *Holländischen Maler*, i (1907)
A. K. Wheelock: *Perspective, Optics and Delft Artists around 1650* (New York, 1977)
Die Sprache der Bilder: Realität und Bedeutung in der niederländischen Malerei des 17. Jahrhunderts (exh. cat., ed. R. Klessman; Brunswick, Herzog Anton Ulrich-Mus., 1978)
Gods, Saints and Heroes: Dutch Painting in the Age of Rembrandt (exh. cat. by Albert Blankert and others, Washington, DC, N.G.A.; Detroit, MI, Inst. A.; Amsterdam, Rijksmus.; 1980–81)
M. W. Ainsworth and others: *Art and Autoradiography: Insights into the Genesis of Paintings by Rembrandt, Van Dyck and Vermeer* (New York, 1982)
J. M. Montias: *Artists and Artisans in Delft: A Socio-economic Study of the Seventeenth Century* (Princeton, 1982)

MONOGRAPHS

W. Bürger [E. J. T. Thoré]: *Van der Meer de Delft* (Paris, 1866)
E. Plietzsch: *Vermeer van Delft* (Leipzig, 1911)
P. T. A. Swillens: *Johannes Vermeer: Painter of Delft, 1632–1675* (Utrecht, 1950)
L. Gowing: *Vermeer* (London, 1952; New York, 1970)
A. Blankert: *Vermeer of Delft* (Oxford, 1978)
L. J. Slatkes: *Vermeer and his Contemporaries* (New York, 1981)
A. K. Wheelock: *Jan Vermeer* (New York, 1981)
A. Blankert, J. M. Montias and G. Aillaud: *Vermeer* (Paris, 1986; Eng. trans., 1988)
J. M. Montias: *Vermeer and his Milieu: A Web of Social History* (Princeton, 1989)
D. Arasse: *Vermeer: Faith in Painting* (Princeton, 1994)

SPECIALIST STUDIES

S. Meltzoff: 'The Rediscovery of Vermeer', *Marsyas*, ii (1942), pp. 145–66
A. J. J. M. van Peer: 'Drie collecties schilderijen van Vermeer', *Oud-Holland*, lxxii (1957), pp. 92–103
A. P. de Mirimonde: 'Les Sujets musicaux chez Vermeer de Delft', *Gaz. B.-A.*, n. s. 6, lvii (1961), pp. 29–50
C. Seymour: 'Dark Chamber and Light-filled Room: Vermeer and the Camera Obscura', *A. Bull.*, xlvi (1964), pp. 323–31
A. J. J. M. van Peer: 'Jan Vermeer van Delft: Drie archiefvonsten', *Oud-Holland*, lxxxiii (1968), pp. 220–24
D. A. Fink: 'Vermeer's Use of the Camera Obscura: A Comparative Study', *A. Bull.*, liii (1971), pp. 493–505
M. Kahr: 'Vermeer's *Girl Asleep*: A Moral Emblem', *Met. Mus. J.*, vi (1972), pp. 115–32
J. Welu: 'Vermeer: His Cartographic Sources', *A. Bull.*, lvii (1975), pp. 529–47
E. de Jongh: 'Pearls of Virtue and Pearls of Vice', *Simiolus*, viii (1975–6), pp. 69–97
J. M. Montias: 'New Documents on Vermeer and his Family', *Oud-Holland*, xci (1977), pp. 267–87
A. Mayer-Meintschel: 'Die *Briefleserin* von Jan Vermeer van Delft: Zum Inhalt und zur Geschichte des Bildes', *Jb. Staatl. Kstsamml. Dresden*, xi (1978–9), pp. 91–9
J. M. Montias: 'Vermeer and his Milieu: Conclusion of an Archival Study', *Oud-Holland*, xciv (1980), pp. 44–62
I. L. Moreno: 'Vermeer's *The Concert*: A Study in Harmony and Contrasts', *Rutgers A. Rev.*, iii (1982), pp. 51–7
A. K. Wheelock and C. J. Kaldenbach: 'Vermeer's *View of Delft* and his Vision of Reality', *Artibus & Hist.*, iii (1982), pp. 9–35
I. Gaskell: 'Vermeer, Judgement and Truth', *Burl. Mag.*, cxxvi (1984), pp. 557–61
A. K. Wheelock: 'Pentimenti in Vermeer's Paintings: Changes in Style and Meaning', *Holländische Genremalerei im 17. Jahrhundert: Symposium, Berlin, 1984*, pp. 385–412
——: '*St Praxedis*: New Light on the Early Career of Vermeer', *Artibus & Hist.*, vii (1986), pp. 71–89
J. M. Montias: 'Vermeer's Clients and Patrons', *A. Bull.*, lxix (1987), pp. 68–76
E. Goodman-Soellner: 'The Landscape on the Wall in Vermeer', *Ksthist. Tidskr.*, lviii (1989), pp. 76–88
P. O. Elousson: 'The Geographer's Heart: A Study of Vermeer's Scientists', *Ksthist. Tidskr.*, lx (1991), pp. 17–25
G. J. M. Webber: 'Johannes Vermeer, Pieter Jansz. van Asch und das Problem der Abbildungstreue', *Oud-Holland*, cviii (1994), pp. 98–106
Johannes Vermeer (exh. cat by A. K. Wheelock and B.J.B. Broos, Washington, DC, N.G.A.; The Hague, Mauritshuis; 1995–6)

WAYNE FRANITS

Vermeersch, José (*b* Bissegem, 6 Nov 1922). Belgian ceramicist and painter. He studied from 1934 to 1941 at the drawing academy in Kortrijk, and from 1941 to 1943 at the Koninklijke Academie voor Schone Kunsten in Antwerp, where in 1944 he followed Constant Permeke's course. He established himself as a contractor for the installation of fireplaces and ceramic tiling. Vermeersch's artistic début was as a painter, but after achieving considerable success in the early 1970s he became regarded as one of the most important representatives of massive, figurative ceramic sculpture in Belgium. He usually modelled life-size figures in a romantic-expressionist style that was derived from the work of Constant Permeke and Marino Marini. His subjects were standing, kneeling or sitting figures, and dogs. Each of his characteristically misproportioned forms has heavy feet, torso and head, and scrawny limbs. As material he used various types of clay, more or less like a metalworker, rolling them out into layers to make the construction of the figures more rapid. Conceived frontally and built up from base to top, the figures were sometimes embellished with necklaces or with hair made from flax, obtaining a polychrome effect on the thin ceramic surface by using different clays and deliberately trying to produce handmade imperfections and accidental features. In 1973 and 1984 Vermeersch was chosen to represent Belgium at the Venice Biennale.

BIBLIOGRAPHY
M. Duchateau: *José Vermeersch* (Tielt, 1978)
M. Le Bof: *José Vermeersch* (Bruges, 1988)
José Vermeersch, Works in Terracotta (exh. cat., Stanford, CA, U. A.G. & Mus., 1989)

HERWIG TODTS

Vermeer [van der Meer; ver Meer] **van Haarlem.** Dutch family of artists. The history of this family from Haarlem is confusing since there were as many as five generations with the forename Jan. A Jan Vermeer (*fl* 1598–1612), whose occupation is not known, married Janneken Woutersd. Knyff, the sister of the painter Jacob Woutersz. Knyff. Their son, known as Jan Vermeer I (*b* Haarlem, *c.* 1600/1; *d* Haarlem, Feb 1670), was an art dealer, distiller and tobacco merchant; he is also said to have been a landscape painter, but this activity is not well documented. Two of Jan I's sons became landscape painters, (1) Jan Vermeer II and his lesser-known brother, Isaak Vermeer (*bapt* Haarlem, 19 Sept 1635; *d* after 1665). The artistic tradition continued with the two sons of Jan II, (2) Jan Vermeer III and his brother Barent Vermeer (*bapt* Haarlem, 20 March 1659; *d* 1690–1702), a still-life painter. Yet another minor painter of the same name, usually referred to as Jan Vermeer IV (*fl* 1694), is presumed to have been a descendant of the same family. 'Van Haarlem' is traditionally added to the surname to distinguish the family members from Johannes Vermeer of Delft.

(1) Jan [Johannes; Johannis] **Vermeer van Haarlem II** [the elder] (*b* Haarlem, 22 Oct 1628; *d* Haarlem, *bur* 25 Aug 1691). Painter. For ten years from 1638, Jan Vermeer II was a pupil of Jacob (Willemsz.) de Wet (1610–71/2), to whose Rembrandtesque manner he was evidently impermeable. He entered the Haarlem Guild of St Luke in 1654, the year of his marriage, and remained in Haarlem for the rest of his life. His early influences were fellow Haarlem landscape painters, especially Jacob van Ruisdael, and he continued to paint heavily wooded landscapes recalling the work of such followers of Ruisdael as Adriaen Verboom (1628–70) and Jan van Kessel (*c.* 1641–80) throughout his career. His late work, possibly influenced by Philips Koninck, is more panoramic: it includes such landscapes as *Dunes near Haarlem* (Paris, Louvre) and extensive views inland from the coastal dunes, which exploit the natural advantage of a high viewpoint. These paintings are predominantly yellow and dark green in tone, with strong shadows.

(2) Jan [Johan] **Vermeer van Haarlem III** [the younger] (*b* Haarlem, 29 Nov 1656; *d* Haarlem, 28 May 1705). Painter and draughtsman, son of (1) Jan Vermeer van Haarlem II. He was a pupil of his father and of Nicolaes Berchem. He probably visited Italy before entering the Haarlem Guild of St Luke in 1681. His pictures, for example *Landscape with Flock* (1677; ex-art market, Vienna, 1948; see Bernt, 1948, p. 720), display his father's heavy green and yellow tonality, but his subject-matter, shepherds and their flocks in Italianate, and sometimes mountainous, settings, derives from Berchem. His work, like that of his friend Simon van der Does (*c.* 1653–1718) and that of Dirk van Bergen, constitutes a dilution, rather than a development, of Berchem's style. He made numerous drawings, such as *Landscape with Flock and Castle*

beside a Lake (1704; Hamburg, Ksthalle), most of which include depictions of sheep. He drew in red or black chalk, often adding watercolour, and he usually signed and dated his work.

BIBLIOGRAPHY
Thieme–Becker
W. Bernt: *Niederländische Maler des 17. Jahrhunderts*, 3 vols (Munich, 1948, rev. 3/1969–70)
——: *Niederländische Zeichner des 17. Jahrhunderts* (Munich, 1957)

GEORGE GORDON

Vermehren, (Johan) Frederik [Frits] **(Nicolai)** (*b* Ringsted, 12 May 1823; *d* Copenhagen, 10 Jan 1910). Danish painter. He trained from 1844 at the Akademi for de Skønne Kunster in Copenhagen, where he was taught by C. W. Eckersberg. At the same time he also took lessons with the painter Jørgen Pedersen Roed, whom he had known since childhood. With artists such as Julius Exner (1825–1910) and Christian Dalsgaard (1824–1907), Vermehren was part of the National Romanticism movement of the mid-19th century, which was influenced by the Danish art historian N. L. Høyen. Artists were encouraged to go into the countryside to study the peasantry, and Vermehren went to Jutland where he painted *Jutland Shepherd on the Moors* (1855; Copenhagen, Stat. Mus. Kst.). The painting typifies his interest in depicting man in close contact with nature, particularly the more picturesque side of peasant life.

In 1855 Vermehren travelled to Italy, painting in the Sabine mountains like many other Danish artists of the 'Golden Age', for example *Street Scene in Gerano, Sabine Mountains* (1856, Nivå, Nivaagaards Malsaml.). He also painted a number of fine, psychologically searching portraits, particularly after 1870, such as *Portrait of Mrs (Karen Johanne Juliane) Wanscher* (1869; priv. col.). In 1865 he became a teacher at the Akademi in Copenhagen, and in 1874 he was appointed professor.

BIBLIOGRAPHY
T. Faaborg: *J. F. N. Vermehren*, 2 vols (Copenhagen, 1923–4)
M. Zenius: *Genremaleri og virkelighed* [Genre painting and reality] (Copenhagen, 1976)

ELISABETH CEDERSTRØM

Vermeulen, Jan. *See* MOLANUS, JOHANNES.

Vermexio, Andrea (*fl* 1594; *d* Syracuse, Dec 1643). Italian architect, of Spanish descent. He is known to have made substantial contributions to some of the most important buildings constructed in Syracuse during the period of renovation before the earthquake of 1693 (*see* SYRACUSE, §2). His best-known work is the Palazzo Vescovile (1618), notable for its harmonious proportions. The building's lack of surface decoration also enhances the refinement of its rusticated ashlar facing, the grading of the cornices and the detailed rustication. These characteristics make the Palazzo typical of building in Syracuse in the period of transition from the Renaissance to the Baroque. Other buildings executed by Vermexio include the church of S Benedetto (1619) and the church of Monte Vergini (1622–5), both of which reflect a more conventional Renaissance taste. He was also consulted on many other projects, a reflection of the privileged position that he enjoyed in the sphere of civic patronage in Syracuse. He is also known to have collaborated on several projects with his son Giovanni Vermexio, who designed the Palazzo del Senato in Syracuse.

BIBLIOGRAPHY

G. Agnello: *I Vermexio, architetti ispano–siculi del secolo XVII* (Florence, 1959)
——: 'L'architettura di Siracusa nel sei e settecento', *Palladio*, xviii (1968–9), pp. 111–32

LUCIA TRIGILIA

Vermeyen [Maius; Vermay; Vermey], **Jan** [Jehan] **Cornelisz.** [Mayo, Juan de] (*b* Beverwijk, *c.* 1500; *d* Brussels, *c.* 1559). Dutch painter, draughtsman, etcher and tapestry designer, active in Flanders and Spain. His early paintings show links with the work of Jan van Scorel, Jan Gossart and Bernard van Orley; it is thus assumed that he trained in the northern Netherlands, probably together with van Scorel in the workshop of Cornelis Willemsz. (*fl* 1481–?1552) in Haarlem or Jacob Cornelisz. van Oostsanen in Amsterdam. Vermeyen could also have worked briefly with Gossart after the latter had moved to the Utrecht area in 1517 and perhaps also with van Orley in Brussels before he started his own workshop in 1525. In that year he entered the service of Margaret of Austria in Mechelen. He travelled with her to Augsburg and Innsbruck, where he painted nineteen portraits of the imperial family, only one of which survives, that of *Cardinal Erard de La Marck* (*c.* 1528–9; Amsterdam, Rijksmus.); there are only workshop copies of the rest. Vermeyen's figures are rather stocky and swollen, and the influence of van Scorel and Gossart is clear. The most striking feature of these early portraits is the aggressively gesticulating hands with outstretched fingers.

After Margaret of Austria's death in 1530, Vermeyen entered the service of Mary of Hungary, for whom he copied works by Titian. The portraits painted between 1530 and 1544 create a calmer impression (e.g. *Felipe de Guevara*, 1531; Williamstown, MA, Clark A. Inst.). His early religious pictures with their cool colours and hard lines drawn from van Scorel's early work evolved to warmer scenes with dramatic lighting effects, as in the *Holy Family by the Fire* (*c.* 1532–3; Vienna, Ksthist. Mus.). A few etchings made by Nicolas Hogenberg in 1531 after lost paintings reveal Jan Cornelisz. Vermeyen's predilection for chiaroscuro.

In 1534 Vermeyen moved to Spain to work for Mary's brother, the Emperor Charles V, whose crusade to Tunis he joined in April 1535. During this time it seems that he sketched the various events of the journey and conquest, as well as the buildings, landscapes and people, and these he published as etchings soon afterwards. These exotic scenes were a great success and included the portrait of the moor *Mulay Ahmad* (*c.* 1535–6; Hollstein, no. 11) and the *Oriental Feast* (*c.* 1535–6; Hollstein, no. 5), which depicts Mulay Ahmad and his retinue at a meal. In these prints Vermeyen's etching technique is still strongly influenced by the art of engraving, but later he found a more expressive style of etching, as may be seen in his etched portrait of *Cardinal Erard de La Marck* (*c.* 1538; Hollstein, no. 10).

Vermeyen was in Toledo with Charles V in 1539 and in 1540 journeyed with him to the southern Netherlands. In Ghent Charles V had to intervene in an uprising against his taxation policies, and Vermeyen recorded this in a gouache drawing, the *Pardon of Ghent* (1540; Brussels,

Jan Cornelisz. Vermeyen: *Muster in Barcelona*, black chalk and watercolour on paper mounted on canvas, 3.85×6.62 m, cartoon for the *Conquest of Tunis* tapestry series, *c.* 1546–54 (Vienna, Kunsthistorisches Museum)

Bib. Royale Albert 1er). It could be that on the return journey from Tunis between 1535 and 1536 Vermeyen visited Italy with Charles V and his entourage, where he may have admired the work of Correggio and other masters. The clumsy and poorly assimilated Italian style of his religious pictures of the 1530s was replaced in the 1540s by a looser and more fluent manner of painting, perhaps influenced by Correggio, as is starkly manifest in the *Marriage at Cana* (c. 1540–41; Amsterdam, Rijksmus.). Vermeyen's etchings of this period are also free and expressive, such as *Virgin and Child with an Angel Playing a Guitar* (1545; Hollstein, no. 1), and his portraits are drawn more fluently, perhaps influenced by the many sketches done on the crusade, and coloured much more warmly. His figures are placed further into the background, and by abandoning the heavily gesturing hands he achieved greater expressiveness, as in the *Portrait of a Dignitary* (c. 1543; Karlsruhe, Staatl. Ksthalle). In the late 1540s the portraits became sketchier, cooler in colouring and more prosaic. Stylistically, his religious works became more classical. The most important picture of this period is the triptych with the *Raising of Lazarus* (c. 1548; Brussels, Mus. A. Anc.), with the donors, the Micault family, depicted on the side wings.

After 1545 Vermeyen's most important work comprised designs and cartoons, influenced by both Dürer and Raphael, for a series of 12 tapestries (5.22 m high) with scenes of the *Conquest of Tunis* (1546–54; for illustration *see* HABSBURG, §I(5)). Charles V commissioned the series as a lasting reminder of his successful occupation of the town, and Mary of Hungary supervised the work. The tapestries were woven by Willem de Pannemaker and his workshop, and in 1554 and 1559 two similar series were woven on a smaller scale based on smaller cartoons. Only one small fragment survives of the preparatory drawings (Amsterdam, Rijksmus.), but ten of the large cartoons have been preserved (see fig.). Each scene shows an event from the journey to Tunis and its occupation, with densely peopled scenes set in a North African landscape with many well-observed details.

Jan Vermeyen's son Hans Vermeyen (*d* 15 Oct 1606) was active as a goldsmith.

BIBLIOGRAPHY
Hollstein: *Dut. & Flem.* [H]; Wurzbach
A. E. Popham: 'Catalogue of Etchings by Jan Cornelisz. Vermeyen', *Oud-Holland*, xliv (1927), pp. 174–82
C. van den Bergen-Pantens: 'Le Triptyque Micault de J. C. Vermeyen', *Mus. Royaux B.-A. Belgique: Bull.* (1973), pp. 33–7
M. J. Friedländer: *Early Netherlandish*, xii (1975), pp. 85–90
H. J. Horn: 'The *Sack of Tunis* by Jan Cornelisz. Vermeyen: A Section of a Preliminary Drawing for his *Conquest of Tunis* Series', *Bull. Rijksmus.*, xxxii (1984), pp. 17–24
Art before Iconoclasm: North Netherlandish Art, 1525–1580 (exh. cat. by J. P. Filedt Kok, Q. Halsema-Kubes and W. T. Kloek, Amsterdam, Rijksmus., 1986), i, p. 33; ii, pp. 201–7

ELS VERMANDERE

Vermiculation [from Lat. *vermis*: 'worm']. Stonework decorated with random grooves that resemble worm tracks.

See also under MASONRY, §II.

□

Vermont, Hyacinthe Collin de. *See* COLLIN DE VERMONT, HYACINTHE.

Vernacular [Folk] **architecture.** Term used to describe informal, usually domestic, architecture that is rooted in local traditions and is generally produced by craftsmen with little or no formal academic training and whose identity is unrecorded. The vernacular architecture of any region may be characterized by the use of a particular material readily available in the area, by the prevalence of a particular building type related to the dominant local economic activities or by the use of a particular style, possibly derived from local materials and techniques. A comprehensive definition is impossible, however, since there is little agreement among scholars as to which is the essential quality by which an architectural work, technique or feature can be characterized as vernacular (*see* §I, 1 below).

For this reason, vernacular architecture is sometimes identified negatively, that is to say as comprising any building activity that does not form part of the academic, 'high-style' or 'polite' architectural tradition, of which the conventional aesthetic criteria are usually perceived as inappropriate when applied to the vernacular. Thus in regions where such a distinction between two sorts of tradition is unknown, such as sub-Saharan Africa and much of Asia, specific discussion of vernacular architecture has little meaning.

For the same reason, the identification and characterization of the vernacular is simplest in Europe, where the opposing formal or high-style tradition is most prominent and most easily recognizable. In North America, however, discussion of vernacular architecture is necessarily more complex, since vernacular forms, types and techniques have been introduced by different immigrant communities as well as evolving organically, while in Central and South America the assimilation by the indigenous communities of the styles and techniques of Spanish and Portuguese high-style (and especially religious) architecture can itself be said to constitute a distinct, if highly unusual, vernacular tradition. In the Islamic lands, on the other hand, it is more natural to identify the vernacular tradition in architecture with the rich and varied tradition of largely domestic building that has long existed alongside Islamic religious architecture.

Revivals in vernacular architecture of the late 19th century and the 20th are important, involving either a return to vernacular building methods or the application of vernacular motifs to modern building types. Some notable attempts have also been made by eminent architects in the Middle East and Latin America to draw on vernacular traditions in the creation of distinctively contemporary works.

Because it is less useful to identify a distinct vernacular tradition in such countries as China and Japan, discussion of their traditional domestic architecture is contained in the relevant country survey article rather than the regional surveys in §II below. Further discussion relevant to vernacular architecture may also be found in articles discussing aspects of structure, carpentry and stonework, in all of which vernacular and high-style architecture share a common vocabulary.

See also TIMBER STRUCTURE, MASONRY, MOULDING, BRICK and ROOF.

I. Introduction. II. Regional survey.

I. Introduction.

1. Problems of definition. 2. Historiography. 3. Research methods.

1. PROBLEMS OF DEFINITION. Although the term 'vernacular' has been applied to buildings since 1857, it only began to be used widely after the formation in England of the Vernacular Architecture Group in 1954 (see Hall, 1974). In Germany and Scandinavia the subject is described as *Hausforschung*, *byggeskik* or *byggnadskultur* ('building custom or culture'), while in France *la maison paysanne* is often used. Elsewhere, 'folk architecture' is a common description. As these terms imply, the study of vernacular architecture involves a social dimension as well as an interest in the purely technical aspects of construction. The nuances and ambiguities of the subject are illuminated by a series of antitheses between what is and what is not vernacular architecture. One crucial distinction is the threshold between vernacular and high-style or polite architecture (Brunskill, 1970, p. 25), in which the design inspiration is drawn not principally from tradition but from consciously chosen stylistic prototypes. The differentiation is not absolute, however. High-style features were frequently absorbed into vernacular traditions, especially in decoration. Ornamental moulded plaster in an English farmhouse in Devon does not take it across the polite threshold, even though it shares motifs with a nearby Palladian country house. Equally, the use of vernacular structural techniques, such as mud-walling in the service wing, does not make the Palladian house vernacular.

The short distances over which members of most historic communities made regular social contacts and the fine scale of variation in available building materials result in one of the fascinations of vernacular architecture: the small regions (sometimes only a few miles across) in which distinctive building traditions are found. Comparisons of vernacular buildings, particularly in the study of Western European vernacular architecture, are therefore generally on a local or regional scale, of 'polite' buildings on a national or international scale. This contrast of scale relates directly to the other major antithesis, that between vernacular and popular buildings. The latter are still the buildings of ordinary people, but their styles and designs are national rather than local. The inception of popular buildings can often be related to developing communications, especially canals and railways, facilitating the mass distribution of building materials.

Together with these non-traditional materials came novel plans, taken from pattern books or other publications, or from similar houses elsewhere. Although regional distinctions might still appear, these trends led to the dilution of vernacular traditions and the rapid homogenization of new buildings. Examples are as widely distributed as the workers' housing of early 19th-century Manchester, England, and the railroad towns of New Mexico, USA (built after the opening of the Atchison, Topeka and Santa Fe railroad in the 1880s).

The antithesis between vernacular and high-style architecture correlates with other characteristics that are sometimes used for definition but are really implied by it. Thus, the occupiers (and sometimes builders) of vernacular buildings are generally taken to be of lower rather than higher social status. For Western society, a line is sometimes drawn below gentry level, but Brunskill (1970) pointed out that the vernacular threshold moved with time. An 18th-century Danish herregård or manor house may be clearly supra-vernacular, but a 15th-century Scottish baron's tower is as firmly traditional.

Similarly, while domestic, agricultural and early industrial buildings may be vernacular, religious buildings are more often polite. Liturgical function and aesthetic expectations often led to the building of churches in styles and materials entirely different from those of the houses in the communities they served. The rare exceptions are informative. A timber-framed church built in 1799 in the French settlement at Cahokia, IL, USA, has the framing and roof structure found both in local houses and in their predecessors in Normandy. It demonstrates the limitations on materials and design capability available in this frontier community. A still weaker distinction, yet one worth making for northern Europe, is that vernacular buildings are more often of timber, polite ones of stone (Miłobędzki, 1989). There are inevitable exceptions, usually the result of sparse supplies of one or the other material. However, when both timber and stone could be obtained, stone was usually the more prestigious and expensive material, used for churches and defensive buildings such as castles surrounded by timber residential and agricultural buildings.

A contrast is sometimes suggested between vernacular building, covering historic buildings in industrialized countries, and primitive building, meaning contemporary ones elsewhere. Essentially, this differentiates living vernacular traditions from those that have been superseded by popular building styles. The distinction is of little value. The period at which traditional buildings cease to be constructed varies from one country, region, building type and social level to another, and the extent of industrialization is only one of many influences. It is perhaps more valid to mark a boundary between vernacular buildings and those that may be called sub-vernacular, so crude and simple that they lack any architectural character. However, even such buildings as this generally incorporate traditional features, whether consciously or unconsciously.

Rudofsky, in his influential description of vernacular architecture *Architecture without Architects* (1964), makes two valuable points, though he is misleading in one key respect. First, he shows that the architectural quality of vernacular buildings is always visible. Whether one considers the decorative framing of 16th-century German *fachwerk* or the carving of a Papuan spirit house, the buildings make architectural statements and are not simply functional. Secondly, the absence of an architect is axiomatic, at least insofar as the architect's task is seen as the conscious creation of a building following and developing declared stylistic criteria.

Nevertheless, it remains an important aspect of vernacular buildings that they are undoubtedly the creation of craftsmen who set out to demonstrate their technical skill and design ability (as well as their client's status in society). To overlook this is to ignore the individuals most responsible for vernacular architecture. The anonymity of these craftsmen reflects the wider social extent of vernacular building before the Renaissance. The differentiation of architects from craftsmen only became clear in Europe in the 16th century. Before then, the design and construction of major as well as minor building was undertaken by craftsmen trained in local traditions. Similar structural techniques and decoration were used in both. Only the size and plan distinguished high-style buildings from vernacular.

The ambiguities inherent in all definitions of vernacular architecture require them to be interpreted broadly. Rigid application of precise criteria is stultifying, leading only to barren arguments about the inclusion or exclusion of particular buildings.

2. HISTORIOGRAPHY. The earliest interest in traditional buildings was visual, expressed in the work of topographical artists such as John Buckler (1770–1851), whose sketchbooks (London, BL; Add. MSS 36353–36443) indiscriminately include English churches, manors and timber-framed barns and houses. Indeed, the landscapes of Albrecht Dürer, from the late 15th century and early 16th, show the same precise observation of German *fachwerk* buildings (e.g. *Wire-drawing Mill*; Berlin, Kupferstichkab.). Early descriptions of typical buildings are also found in 18th- and 19th-century reports on agricultural and social conditions; a notable example is the 1789 survey of Danish farmhouses (Lerche, 1987).

The systematic study of houses as historical entities began in Germany. In the 1850s Georg Landau described plan and structure as well as decoration. He identified the Saxon house, the large north German house combining both living quarters, barn and cow-stalling under one roof. Landau's work, viewing houses as expressions of folk culture, set the pattern for his many successors in Germany, Austria and Switzerland and dominated a century of German scholarship. However, interpretation of their excellent fieldwork was sometimes confused by the application of theories of ethnic origins and the development of complex plan typologies that attempted to link regional house types into common Germanic forms. Only the wholesale revision of dates through dendrochronology and the new political climate of the 1950s allowed an escape from this intellectual strait-jacket.

No other countries matched the intensity of this early German work. Study of the very different Scandinavian houses was stimulated in the 1880s by the foundation of the Swedish and Norwegian open-air museums at Skansen and Bygdøy, but few scholars carried on this early interest; S. Erixon, in his monumental study *Svensk byggnadskultur* (1945), is a notable exception. In England two pioneers, S. O. Addy (1898) and C. F. Innocent (1916), produced general studies. The first concentrated on documentary sources, the second on structural details; both emphasized cruck construction, thereby beginning a fascination with this technique, which dominates medieval peasant houses in much of England (Alcock, 1981). After Innocent, little of lasting significance appeared until Fox and Raglan's exemplary *Monmouthshire Houses* (1951–4) demonstrated an archaeological approach to a regional building tradition, setting the style for many later studies.

The second half of the 20th century saw a blossoming of interest in the subject. Most countries can now show the beginnings of a systematic study of their traditional architecture, whether arising from increasing national consciousness, from historical interests widening to include peasant material culture or simply from the influence of other workers. In some countries, national organizations (in England, for example, the Royal Commission on Historical Monuments) have been set up or have extended their interests to include vernacular buildings (Mercer, 1975). Groups and societies have also sprung up, most significantly the Arbeitskreis für Hausforschung (Germany, 1950), the Vernacular Architecture Group (England, 1954, publishing since 1970 the only international journal on the subject, *Vernacular Architecture*) and the Vernacular Architecture Forum (USA, 1979). They have stimulated recording work, leading to an explosion in vernacular architecture studies, nowhere more prominently than in the USA, where innumerable local traditions have been delineated, each one recognizable as the product of an immigrant group whose Old World building style was subtly transformed by its new environment and by contact with other cultural traditions (see §II, 4 below).

3. RESEARCH METHODS. Buildings are artefacts, the largest, least portable and most valuable objects found in pre-industrial societies. As such, they should be of major significance for understanding both culture and economy. To realize this importance, research on buildings needs to explore these wider aspects in object-driven studies. However, some of the few recent studies have been deeply flawed, based on simplistic theoretical models, such as the internationality of 'folk housing', whose validity derives from chance similarities between local vernacular traditions that vanish on more detailed examination. To achieve wider objectives it is essential first to understand the buildings themselves (object-oriented study).

Vernacular buildings pose special problems in comparison to high-style architecture, the most serious of these being the problem of dating. For high-style buildings, documentary evidence of date is frequently available, while decorative details allow close stylistic comparisons. Neither is generally useful for vernacular buildings. In some areas (e.g. Germany, England, Ireland), dendrochronology has begun to provide a framework of precise dates, but the technique is not always successful and can never be applied to every building. The ability to identify and date numerous stages of construction from the structure itself is therefore crucial. An English medieval open-hall house might first have gained an end bay, next a 16th-century hall chimney and upper floor and a 17th-century stair turret and parlour fireplace, and finally a symmetrical 18th-century façade; or it would have perhaps been divided into three cottages with the inclusion of additional stairs and partitions.

The essence of detailed building study lies in the unravelling of such complex sequences, identifying characteristic building plans and structural techniques. Procedures have gradually been developed involving a distinctive combination of architectural and archaeological recording, though without the latter's full rigour; the essential character of a roof truss is clearer in its original form rather than with every broken joint and distortion drawn in archaeological detail. The approach varies according to the aspect of the building under examination. For plans, the identification of primary walls is crucial, but secondary (perhaps modern) partitions may be omitted. The layout of upper floors is important, both in revealing house size and as evidence for attitudes to privacy. In considering structures, the questions depend on the materials. In carpenters' work, three aspects are vital: structural method (e.g. roof truss form, bracing pattern, frame articulation); decorative detail (e.g. arch-bracing, cusping, chamfers and chamfer stops); and technical detail (especially jointing (Hewett, 1980), but also timber conversion and utilization). In a building's finish, the nails used to attach panelling or plastering laths may be more significant than the iconography of the wall-paintings on the plaster. With stone, the same points are relevant in modest as in grand buildings: material and types of stonework; mouldings; wall thickness; straight joints and signs of alterations. In earth walling, the colour and the construction (with or without shuttering, in shallow or deep sections) can elucidate building sequences.

The intensification of interest in vernacular architecture is so recent that it has yet to be fully exploited as primary historical, economic and social evidence (but see Smith, 1992, and Alcock, 1993). The critical challenge in vernacular architecture studies is the application of its detailed evidence in wider contexts, especially in illuminating the differing mental attitudes of people to their environment through the interpretation of their domestic and working space.

BIBLIOGRAPHY
S. O. Addy: *The Evolution of the English House* (London, 1898, rev. 2/1933)
W. Pessler: *Das altsächsische Bauernhaus* (Brunswick, 1906, rev. Hildesheim, 1978)
C. F. Innocent: *The Development of English Building Construction* (Cambridge, 1916, rev. Newton Abbot, 1977)
S. E. Erixon: *Svensk byggnadskultur* (Stockholm, 1945, rev. 2/1982)
C. Fox and Lord Raglan: *Monmouthshire Houses*, 3 vols (Cardiff, 1951–4, rev. 1994)
B. Rudofsky: *Architecture without Architects* (New York, 1964; Albuquerque, 1987)
P. Oliver, ed.: *Shelter and Society* (London, 1969)
R. W. Brunskill: *Illustrated Handbook of Vernacular Architecture* (London, 1970, rev. 3/1986)
R. de Z. Hall: *A Bibliography on Vernacular Architecture* (Newton Abbot, 1972)
——: 'The Origins of the Vernacular Architecture Group', *Vern. Archit.*, v (1974), pp. 3–6
E. Mercer: *English Vernacular Houses: A Study of Traditional Farmhouses and Cottages* (London, 1975)
K. Bedal: *Historische Hausforschung* (Münster, 1978)
C. A. Hewett: *English Historic Carpentry* (London, 1980)
N. W. Alcock: *Cruck Construction: An Introduction and Catalogue* (London, 1981)
D. Upton: 'The Power of Things: Recent Studies in Vernacular Architecture', *Amer. Q.*, xxxv (1983), pp. 262–79
M. W. Barley: *Houses as History* (London, 1986)
G. Lerche: *Bøndergårde i Danmark, 1789–90* [Farmhouses in Denmark, 1789–90] (Copenhagen, 1987)
S. A. Miłobędzki: 'Architecture in Wood: Technology, Symbolic Content, Art', *Artibus & Hist.*, x/19 (1989), pp. 177–206
J. T. Smith: *English Houses: 1200–1800* (London, 1992)
N. W. Alcock: *People at Home* (Chichester, 1993)

N. W. ALCOCK

II. *Regional survey.*

1. Northern Europe. 2. Southern Europe. 3. Central and Eastern Europe. 4. North America. 5. Central and South America. 6. Australasia. 7. Islamic lands. 8. Indian subcontinent.

1. NORTHERN EUROPE.

(i) United Kingdom. (ii) France. (iii) Germany. (iv) The Netherlands. (v) Denmark. (vi) Norway, Sweden and Finland.

(i) United Kingdom. The presence of Europe's most varied topography and climate has brought lasting social and economic contrasts to the United Kingdom. These are reflected in the rich variety of vernacular buildings that survive in their thousands over much of the British countryside. Despite this great variety in use of materials and decorative treatment, these vernacular styles have one important factor in common. In each locality, at any given time, a single local style was commonly used to the exclusion of all others. Because this style might remain current for several generations, and because it depended on local circumstances that (for lack of documentation) are often not readily understood, vernacular buildings are often hard to date, and attempts are made harder still by centuries of accretion or adaptation.

(a) Social and cultural background. (b) Materials and techniques. (c) Planning.

(a) Social and cultural background. Vitally important in the development of this vernacular architecture has been the availability of good local materials and the skills of the local craftsmen in using them, but equally important was the broad cultural background of social, political and economic circumstances. In England, vernacular architecture can be said to begin at the point when the peasantry began to share in the local wealth hitherto monopolized by the Church and the aristocracy. Thus, vernacular buildings date from the early 13th century to the early 19th, when the gathering momentum of the Industrial Revolution increasingly imposed a national homogeneity of materials and design. Only in the rural areas of the far north of England and Scotland, which were relatively backward economically, did vernacular traditions linger until well into the 19th century.

The long-established concentration of wealth in the south and east of England led to the early development there of vernacular houses, as opposed to mere hovels. Largely through the patronage of the Church, building skills improved quickly in the 12th and 13th centuries, and their application filtered down from high-style projects, such as churches, to manor houses, barns and cottages. While most vernacular structures of this period were domestic, a few were agricultural, principally barns. The great stone barns built by monastic foundations in the south and west were architecturally on a level with their churches, but the timber-framed, aisled barns of the east and south-east, also often built for religious patrons, were built similarly to contemporary vernacular houses. One example is the Barley Barn (c. 1205–30) at Cressing Temple, Essex (Tyers and Hibbard, 1993). The end of the Middle Ages brought great economic and social changes that tended to benefit the lower classes. The inflation of the 16th century favoured peasant farmers or yeomen to

1. Vernacular houses at Chipping Campden, Gloucestershire, 15th–17th centuries

2. House at King's Stanley, Gloucestershire, 16th century

an even greater extent, and the buildings that these groups could afford to construct in the period from 1500 to 1700 marked the heyday of British vernacular architecture (see fig. 1).

Growing numbers of craftsmen, such as masons, carpenters, bricklayers, tilers, plasterers, thatchers and glaziers were available, and their knowledge of the capabilities of local materials (see §(b) below), combined with an awareness of architectural style derived from work on high-style buildings, helped to foster the endless variety of vernacular architecture. The need for economy meant that current national styles had to be adapted to local circumstances. As the cost of transporting materials any distance was high, vernacular architecture often demonstrated the craftsman's skill in executing in timber or brick what in a high-style building would be worked in fine stone. The craftsman's knowledge of high-style design was often limited and might extend only as far as a naive understanding of what old-fashioned national styles were like. A

hardy conservatism was of the essence, but this did not cramp the imagination.

(b) Materials and techniques. Vernacular styles depended on the availability of local materials as well as the craftsmen who could use them, and what gives many places their special architectural character, apart from style, is the homogeneity of local materials. The great divergence in availability of materials is a major factor in the strongly contrasting pattern of vernacular styles in the United Kingdom. The south-eastern counties of England have little good building stone, unlike the band of counties stretching diagonally from Dorset in the south to Lincolnshire and Yorkshire in the north-east, which have various limestones, excellent for building (see fig. 2). Further north and west, the building stone is variable both in type and quality. Many local sandstones are soft and weather badly. Other stones, particularly the carboniferous stones of the Pennines and lowland Scotland and the granites of the uplands of the West Country, North Wales, the Lake District and the Scottish Highlands, are practically indestructible but are so hard that they inhibit decoration.

Many regions without building stones have deposits of heavy clay soils, on which woodland and particularly oak grows well. This became the principal material for constructing timber-framed buildings. Although many of the first vernacular buildings were built of stone, timber came to dominate the development of vernacular architecture until *c.* 1600, because it was readily available in the areas where prosperity encouraged building. This is particularly apparent in Essex, where timber-framing developed rapidly from the 13th century, the West Midlands and the Welsh borders. When brick became fashionable, the heavy soils of these areas were ideal for brick-making. By the middle of the 17th century, brick was rapidly becoming cheaper than timber, a change reflected in the vernacular architecture of these areas. Another building material was cob, used in Devon, a surprisingly tough mixture of unbaked earth and a binding material such as straw or cowhair.

Even where the building material was the same, local craftsmen in different areas developed different methods of using it, which gives vernacular styles their character. Consequently, a timber-framed house in Kent is recognizably different from one built in Shropshire or Lancashire. In the south-east, decoration at first usually relied on large panels spanned by curved triangulating braces and was superseded by closely set studs, giving a pronounced vertical effect (see fig. 3). Although close studding became widespread in England and Wales, the variants on the earlier southern style in the west and north included chevron and herringbone patterning of the timbers, or the division of the façade into squares filled with cusping to produce a starry effect. A very decorative late 16th-century example of this is Top Farm, Knockin, Shropshire.

(c) Planning. The planning of most vernacular houses reflected the pattern set by housing of the upper classes. They were based on a central hall, with an open hearth, used as a communal space and flanked by private chambers and service rooms. Bayleaf Farm, an early 15th-century

example (extended, early 16th-century) from near Eden-bridge, Kent, has been reconstructed in its original form (Singleton, Weald & Downland Open Air Mus.). Variants of these hall-houses, depending on the taste and wealth of the builder and the materials available, are found in many parts of England and Wales. In many parts of the poorer west and north, where pastoral farming was dominant, a cattle-house took the place of the service rooms, to form what is known as a longhouse, a type developed from the late 15th century. From the early 16th century, developing ideas of comfort and the more ready availability of glass led to the division of the halls in hall-houses by floors, the substitution of fireplaces and chimneys for the old open hearths, and glazed windows. By the end of the century, more compact floor-plans were developing, moving away from the old single-pile plan. Such changes usually came at the same time as there was a change in the type of materials, i.e. from timber to brick.

The largest vernacular dwellings were the timber-framed houses of Kent, of which the finest examples built between the 14th and 16th centuries survive in such villages as Biddenden, Cranbrook, Headcorn and Staplehurst. The money that paid for these houses came from cattle farming and the domestic industry of weaving. By contrast, the far less profitable pastoral economy of Devon supported the much humbler longhouse, with its central doorway giving access to the shippon or cattle-house, as well as the domestic rooms of the inhabitants. Colliehole, Pizwell and Lettaford, all in Devon, are hamlets with surviving characteristic groups of longhouses.

In some parts of the Pennines, notably to the west of Halifax, W. Yorks, there is evidence that by the late 15th century yeomen were also starting to build more permanent houses. Although combined barns and cattle-houses (locally called laithes) were sometimes built on to the side of farmhouses, they lack common entrances. By the 17th century, timber for wall construction was being superseded by Pennine stone, whose hardness inhibited carving except over the entrances, which were often given wildly curving arches and other patterns (see fig. 4). Further north, in the counties adjacent to the borders of Scotland, sporadic warfare and endemic poverty discouraged vernacular architecture except for defensible small houses, known as bastles or pele-towers, where one or two rooms were built above cattle-houses. When peace followed the union of the two Crowns in 1603, more conventional longhouses were built. In the highlands of Scotland, a vernacular architecture hardly developed at all and was confined to very small houses built of unbaked earth or local stone comprising only one or two rooms built directly on the ground.

Of vernacular agricultural buildings, barns, granaries and warehouses were the most important and were simply large open buildings designed for storage. Barns usually had a central threshing floor with large doors on each side. Cattle-houses varied extensively from region to region in their arrangement of stalls, mangers and storage space for foodstuffs and as preferred methods for treating cattle changed. Other building types served the needs of sheep, pigs, poultry and pigeons, and ingenious solutions were found for combining all these functions within one building.

3. Cottage at Lynsted, Kent, 16th century

4. House in Bishopdale, North Yorkshire, 1640

By the middle of the 19th century, vernacular architecture in the United Kingdom was effectively dead. It was at this point that vernacular revival styles became popular, as architects sought to satisfy a popular longing for the rural elysium perceived to have existed before the Industrial Revolution. The best known was the Old English style, the most famous exponents of which were George Devey and Richard Norman Shaw. Highly debased forms of vernacular revival in the 20th century have been applied to much suburban housing and even to supermarkets, in order that large developments could be thinly disguised as 17th-century farm buildings.

BIBLIOGRAPHY

I. Peate: *The Welsh House: A Study of Folk Culture* (London, 1940, rev. 3/Liverpool 1946)
M. W. Barley: *The English Farmhouse and Cottage* (London, 1961)
A. Clifton-Taylor: *The Pattern of English Building* (London, 1972, rev. 1980)
P. Smith: *The Houses of the Welsh Countryside* (London, 1975)
C. A. Hewett: *English Historic Carpentry* (London, 1980)
A. Fenton and B. Walker: *The Rural Architecture of Scotland* (Edinburgh, 1981)

A. Gailey: *Rural Houses of the North of Ireland* (Edinburgh, 1984)
A. Quiney: *The Traditional Buildings of England* (London, 1990)
I. Tyers and H. Hibbard: 'The Barley Barn, Cressing Temple', *Vern. Archit.*, 24 (1993), pp. 50–51

ANTHONY QUINEY

(ii) France. Peasant economies and cultures were retained in rural France into the 20th century, and vernacular buildings were still being constructed in the 1920s and 1930s; traditional building skills survived World War II. The resulting legacy is the richest in Europe, although seriously affected by the social and economic changes in rural areas since 1945. Interest in vernacular architecture in France began among geographers in the 1920s, and ethnologists and architects became involved in the 1930s and 1940s. Since the 1960s considerable advances in recording and analysis have been made, with support from such bodies as the Inventaire Général des Monuments et des Richesses Artistiques de la France.

(a) Materials and techniques. (b) Planning.

(a) Materials and techniques. French vernacular architecture is particularly striking in the variety of available materials, particularly stone: granites, basalts, sandstones, schists, slates and limestones are all found in abundance. The choice of material reflected availability, cultural practice and technology; materials were rarely transported far, and changes in lithology are reflected in vernacular buildings. Fissile limestones of the south were in use for drystone corbelled structures from at least Neolithic times. Certain outcrops lend themselves to dressed stonework (e.g. the limestones of Caen and Vernon in Normandy); in areas of abundant high-quality stone such as the white *tuffeaux* of the Loire valley and black basalt in the Massif Central, even the most humble dwellings may be constructed of finely cut blocks. Much of this material was also used for rubble walling, set in a clay mortar, but with ashlar frequently used for doorway and window dressings.

Superficial deposits of sands and clays add further variety. Earth and brick are common materials; thousands of rural buildings have cob walls (*torchis, pisé*) of solid clay. Timber-framing is common in Normandy, the north-east, the Champagne, Burgundy, Berry, the Jura and Alpine areas as well as in other regions; log-cabin construction is found in the Vosges, the Alps and the Jura. The most striking differences in roofing material lie between the Roman tiles (*tuiles creuses*) of the low-pitched roofs of the south and the steeper-pitched northern roofs. Roofing of reed-, wheat- or rye-straw thatch was once very common, but slate or tile have generally replaced thatch since the 19th century. Stone slates are known in many parts of France and have been used at least since the Middle Ages in particular areas.

There is some evidence that in regions where stone-walled buildings are now universal there was once a thriving timber-frame tradition (*see* TIMBER STRUCTURE, §II, 2(ii)). Such was the case in Brittany before the great reconstruction in the 15th century of seigneurial buildings and in the 16th century of peasant houses. Aisled-hall construction (in which the roof is supported by a pair of timber or stone arcades dividing the plan into a central longitudinal nave and aisles) is widely found; surviving structures date from the 12th to the 17th century. It is still to be found in domestic buildings in south-west France (Landes, Basses-Pyrénées), in Champagne, the Alps and the Jura. This distribution suggests that it was probably once widespread and that regression has occurred; the fact that non-domestic aisled buildings survive elsewhere in France supports this view, for example the many aisled market halls such as those at Troussures (Oise), Richelieu (Indre-et-Loire), Saint-Pierre-sur-Dives (Calvados) and Questembert (Morbihan).

Of other roof structures, the king-post truss is by far the most common and is the only method of roof support in the vast majority of peasant buildings, as well as in

5. Single-storey *maison cauchoise*, La Queue du Chien, Blacqueville, Pays de Caux, Normandy, probably 17th century

larger domestic buildings, farm buildings and churches, from the medieval period onwards. It is found from the Pas-de-Calais to the Pyrenees and from the Cotentin to Provence; in Brittany it mingles with the cruck tradition. Two forms are found: the full king-post rising from the tie-beam (e.g. Le Fretay, Pancé, Ille-et-Vilaine); and the upper king-post rising from the collar (e.g. Moulin d'Haroult, Saint-M'Hervé, Ille-et-Vilaine). The short king-post is associated with the low-pitched roofs of southern France, from the Loire to the Mediterranean. Coupled- or trussed-rafter roofs are found in major churches of the 12th century (St Germain-des-Prés, Paris) and in major domestic buildings until the 16th century all over northern France (e.g. La Grand'Cour, Taden, Côtes-d'Armor). Collar-and-tie-beam trusses are known only in western Brittany, where they are confined to houses and farm buildings at the middle and lower ends of the social scale; spatial distribution is remarkably discrete and is bounded on the east by the limits of the Breton language. Cruck structures occur in Brittany (Penhap, Marzan, Morbihan), the Massif Central (Limousin), the Dordogne and the Pas-de-Calais (Canlers); cruck variants are more widely distributed, and the so-called upper-cruck truss is used for roofs of town houses from the 16th century. Many surviving examples are nevertheless late in date, and the origins and evolution of the type remain tantalizingly speculative.

(b) Planning. The common ground-floor hall, open to the roof and with a centrally placed open hearth, probably started to go out of fashion in France towards the end of the 13th century. It was generally replaced at upper social levels by two or more superimposed halls, each provided with adjoining chambers. Open halls with central hearths are now only known from excavation evidence, except for one example in a standing building near Rouen, discovered in 1993. In north-west France, at the level of the smaller manor house, such open halls, usually accompanied by a single seigneurial chamber over a kitchen or cellar, continued to be built until the 16th century, always with a gable hearth and chimney-stacks; a number survive. Chimney-stacks were well established in 12th-century France, although in the Morbihan a few open hearths survived at the lowest social level to the 1950s. The centrally placed hearths of the houses of Bresse, with their *cheminées sarrazines* (decorated earthenware chimney-pots with lateral openings), and those of the great aisled-hall houses of the Jura, with their *tuyés* (ground-floor chambers centrally placed in the house, with an open hearth; smoke rises by a wooden chimney-flue to ridge-level, where its escape is controlled by movable shutters), provide an echo of the once ubiquitous open hearth.

If France boasts a rich heritage of medieval buildings, representative of the noble lifestyle, its first 'permanent' vernacular houses generally date from the 16th century. The single-cell house is widely distributed, particularly in the north-west. It witnessed the complete life-cycle, for families with ten or more children, from birth to death. In Anjou, Brittany and Normandy the hearth is almost invariably in the gable, a doorway and a solitary window being provided in the façade. Some houses of this kind were free-standing, the homes of landless labourers, others formed part of a row. Such dwellings are not necessarily

6. Priest's first-floor hall house, Le Yaudet, Ploulec'h, Brittany, 16th century

to be associated with low social status; some were dower houses, others associated with noble residences. A single cell implies only the absence of need of specialist accommodation; under-developed specialization of room function is one of the persistent characteristics of French vernacular architecture.

The longhouse, a rectilinear building in which man and beast are housed at opposite ends under a single roof with entry by a common central doorway, has been recorded throughout Brittany, where it was until recent times the standard house-type on small farms with livestock (e.g. Kervaly, Plumergat and Morbihan). It has also been observed, either in pure or derivative versions, in Mayenne, Anjou and Normandy, where the *maison cauchoise* (see fig. 5), a house-type found in the Pays de Caux, east of the river Seine and north of Rouen, has every indication of being a longhouse derivative. Vernacular houses from Normandy to the Pas-de-Calais bear a strong resemblance to longhouse types that may once have been common up to the Flemish border. The more complex multi-cell houses of the Ardennes provide further evidence of the type, and there are also strong indications of 'longhouse form' on the western side of the Massif Central (département of Cantal). In the south-west, the Dordogne contains examples of house-and-byre under the same roof, the house in some cases separated from the byre by a *grange* or barn, with internal access throughout its length. In the Lozère there are longhouses in which kitchen and stable are separated only by a wooden partition, the common doorway leading into the byre as in Brittany. The pure longhouse has also been recorded in the Ariège region of the Pyrenees. Together with its derived forms, the longhouse is thus strongly represented across northern and western France. An interesting aspect of this distribution is that it accords well with that of known crucks and cruck-like forms.

The first-floor hall house exists throughout western Europe; the principal, and sometimes the only, room is at first-floor level, over an undercroft used as a store, wine-cellar, for trade or craft or for housing livestock. The type may be free-standing, or it may adjoin another house or farm building. It exists also in the elaborate multi-cellular

7. Aisled-hall house, Ville-du-Pont, Les Jarrans, Jura, probably 18th century

forms of the Mediterranean zone. At a much higher social level it is found in the castles and homes of the nobility (e.g. Kerandraou, Troguéry, Côtes-d'Armor), where it almost certainly originated during the Middle Ages. It was favoured by the clergy (see fig. 6), many of whom were recruited from noble families. Public buildings are often of this type, sometimes with several superimposed halls; examples are to be found in the towns, notably in the south-west (Cordes, Saint-Antonin-Noble-Val). Many such first-floor halls are now reinterpreted as 'chamber-blocks' originally associated with a ground-floor hall, either attached or free-standing. France is also rich in urban houses from the 12th and 13th centuries, almost all of which contain first-floor halls; Cluny in Burgundy, still effectively a Romanesque town, has well over 100 surviving houses of this kind, many hidden behind later façades. In the Mediterranean region the *maison-à-étage* has a long ancestry; it may well have been diffused along the western coastlands from the Mediterranean, adopted first by the nobility and bourgeoisie and later by others of lesser social status.

Aisled-hall houses are now confined to only a few parts of France, but the plan-form survives widely in barns, market halls and churches. Some of the finest examples are the market halls of medieval date (e.g. Saint-Pierre-sur-Dives, Calvados, 12th century), those of the 16th and 17th centuries (e.g. Questembert, Richelieu, Troussures) and barns. The houses of the Landes are of aisled construction, although the 'aisles' are often separated from the 'nave' by continuous arcades pierced only by doorways. Many examples have wooden aisle-posts; domestic accommodation together with storage facilities occupy the aisles, the nave being used for vehicles and implements. In all cases the tie-beam supports a king-post and ridge-piece. The Dordogne is a zone of cultural transition with the aisled house existing alongside longhouse derivatives as well as more complex southern forms. The Basque house

is still of the classic aisled form but more complex in its functional subdivision. Stone-walled and all-timber forms are known. While examples with a two-storey nave and aisles exist, others with two and even three full storeys are well known (e.g. the *maison labourdine*, found at Osses and Cambo-les-Bains, in the Labourd between the rivers Adour and Bidouze and the Pyrenees). Further evidence of the aisled house comes from the Champagne, where it exists in large numbers, and from eastern and south-eastern France. In the Jura, the smaller aisled houses, wholly constructed of pine, may have a central nave flanked by two aisles; the biggest farms have a double nave divided by massive king-post trusses rising from the ground and flanked by double aisles (see fig. 7). Such large buildings still house not only the family but also the cattle and hay for the winter; they may rise through three or four storeys. Numerous structures from the Ardennes to the Var carry strong hints of the tradition. There is abundant evidence of the survival of the aisled-hall house in south-western France and of its presence along the eastern zone from the Ardennes to Provence.

BIBLIOGRAPHY

Charpentes, maisons à pans de bois, beffrois de charpente (Paris, n.d.)
J. Brunhes: 'Les Types régionaux de maisons et carte générale des toits', *Histoire de la nation française* (1920), i of *Introduction générale: Géographie humaine de la France*, ed. G. A. A. Hanotaux (Paris, 1920–35), pp. 411–44
A. Demangeon: 'L'Habitation rurale en France: Essai de classification des principaux types', *An. Géog.*, xxix (1920), pp. 352–75
H. Deneux: 'L'Evolution des charpentes du XIe au XVIIIe siècle', *Architecte* (1927), pp. 19–89
Maisons paysannes de France (Paris, 1966–)
L'Architecture vernaculaire (Paris, 1977–)
G. I. Meirion-Jones: *La Maison traditionnelle: Bibliographie d'architecture vernaculaire en France* (Paris, 1978)
J.-C. Bans and P. G. Bans: 'Notes on the Cruck Truss in Limousin', *Vern. Archit.*, x (1979), pp. 22–9
C. Lhuisset: *L'Architecture rurale en Languedoc, en Roussillon* (Paris, 1980)
Etudes et recherches d'architecture vernaculaire (Paris, 1981–)

G. I. Meirion-Jones: 'The Seventeenth-century *greniers-à-sel* at Honfleur, Calvados', *Archaeol. J.*, cxxxviii (1981), pp. 248–58

——: *The Vernacular Architecture of Brittany: An Essay in Historical Geography* (Edinburgh, 1982)

——: 'The Vernacular Architecture of France: An Assessment', *Vern. Archit.*, xvi (1985), pp. 1–17

J.-M. Pesez: 'Le Foyer de la maison paysanne (XIe–XVe siècles)', *Archeol. Méd.*, xvi (1986), pp. 65–92

G. I. Meirion-Jones and M. C. E. Jones: *Wonderful Châteaux in Brittany* (Rennes, 1991)

G. I. Meirion-Jones and M. C. E. Jones, eds: *Manorial Domestic Buildings in England and Northern France*, Society of Antiquaries of London, xv (London, 1993) [occas. pap.]

GWYN MEIRION-JONES

(iii) Germany. Research in the second half of the 20th century into vernacular architecture in Germany has established the great age of many forms of houses and a sharp regional, social and typological differentiation from the late Middle Ages onwards. It has also revealed the often surprising quality of buildings of even the lower social strata in terms of building techniques, use of space and the treatment of coloured surfaces. Although few complete vernacular structures survive from as far back as the 12th century (e.g. the Romanisches Haus, 116; Münstereifel), reused elements in stone, generally cellars with vaulted roofs or beamed ceilings (e.g. houses at Freiburg im Breisgau of 1170), are not uncommon.

Although vernacular architecture survived in parts of Germany into the late 19th century, it succumbed, as elsewhere in Europe, to the advance of industrially produced building materials and the demands of modern heating, sanitation and insulation. Although these have reduced regional influences on house styles, the strength of vernacular architectural traditions is still such as to distinguish many modern housing types built in different parts of Germany.

(a) Materials and techniques. (b) Planning.

(a) Materials and techniques. Houses built in stone have survived from the 13th century onwards in most of the older German towns, particularly in Regensburg, Cologne, Konstanz and Trier. They were presumably built for the clergy and richer urban classes. Surprisingly, in the 14th and 15th centuries stone dwellings became less common than timber ones. Rural stone buildings in the Middle Ages were clearly a great rarity, although an exception is in the area around Regensburg, where one- and sometimes two-storey buildings are securely traceable as early as 1300, most probably connected with viniculture. Until the 18th century, the proportion of buildings with solid stone walls rose only gradually in south and west Germany (see fig. 8),

8. Stone houses in Klingengasse, Rothenburg ob der Tauber, Bavaria, 16th–17th centuries

9. Timber-framed houses on the Pegnitz, Nuremberg, 16th–17th centuries

and it was only after that date that stone finally established itself in most towns outside the brick-using areas. From the early 19th century, stone became characteristic of many rural areas such as the Eifel, the Saarland and parts of Brandenburg, Saxony and Bavaria. A longer tradition of rammed earth structures has so far only been traced in parts of Thuringia and Saxony. Fired clay materials (brick and tiles) were also used, and from *c.* 1230 buildings built entirely of brick displaced timber structures in the northern and eastern German coastal towns, a process that has been best investigated at Lübeck, which by 1300 was almost exclusively brick-built. In these areas, brick retained its dominance into the 20th century. The towns of southern Bavaria developed the use of brick at about the same period.

Timber is regarded as by far the most widespread and characteristic building material in German towns and villages. The earliest surviving evidence of timber-framed urban housing is mid-13th-century (houses of 1250 in Regensburg, 1261 in Esslingen, 1276 in Göttingen and 1289 in Limburg). The first recorded rural timber-framed buildings in Germany date from 1367 (re-erected; Bad Windsheim, Fränk. Freilandmus.). Medieval timber construction was generally plain and functional. Only towards

the end of the 15th century did it become more ostentatious, reaching its apogee in the late 16th century and the early 17th at almost all social levels throughout Germany (e.g. the Knochenhaueramthaus (1529; destr. 1945; rebuilt) in Hildesheim and the Salzhaus (1600; destr. 1944; rebuilt) in Frankfurt am Main). In this period timber-framed structures (see fig. 9) competed fully with the richest stone buildings, and they retained their popularity in rural areas, such as Hessen, into the 19th century. In the towns, however, timber-framing lost most of its appeal in the 18th century, giving way to plastered and brick buildings. Although oak was used predominantly for framing, softwood played a no less important role in southern and eastern regions of Germany.

A different, less widespread form of timber construction is log construction, for which softwood is almost always used. Although it can be traced to prehistoric times, hitherto few examples pre-1500 have been documented. It is confined to southern and eastern Bavaria but also occurs in the highlands east of the Saale. Unlike timber-framing, it is almost exclusively a rural form of building and is usually without decorative forms; only at the corners may the timbers be artistically joined. Outside southern Bavaria, log construction is often combined with the timber frame. A special form of this combination is the *Umgebinde*, numerous examples of which dating from the 17th–19th centuries have survived, especially in eastern Saxony. The timber-framed upper floor of the house is supported by an open frame of vertical beams, behind which is the statically independent log structure of the ground floor.

(b) Planning. The regional diversity of houses in Germany is extremely great. There is an undisputed contrast between the north, central and south German vernacular styles, even though this division is very crude and sometimes conceals common developments as well as obscuring the major differences within each of these areas. For a very long time the north and north-west German house was characterized by a large hall with an open fire in a hearth or fireplace, while the south German house had a smoke-free room with a stove. This applied equally to peasant and burgher houses. Houses with integral stables were predominant in almost all rural regions of Germany.

In north Germany, by no later than the 14th century, a highly impressive type of house developed, the *Niederdeutsches Hallenhaus* ('north German aisled-hall house'). This was a single structure with three sections, containing the threshing floor (hall), the stable and barn, and the living quarters. The size varied widely, from over 40×15 m (examples in Münsterland), down to scarcely 8 m square. Despite regional diversities, this form can be relatively easily defined geographically: it extends from the eastern Netherlands in the west through the northern Rhineland, Westphalia and Lower Saxony to Mecklenburg in the east; to the Mittelgebirge and sometimes beyond in the south; and almost to the Danish border in the north. The reasons for its emergence and dissemination are not yet fully understood, but the type derives from the living-and-stable halls or longhouses of the coastal region.

The form of the north German hall house, the oldest surviving examples of which were built *c.* 1500, reached its highpoint and most widespread use in the 16th and 17th centuries. Since the 18th century it has been either in decline or remodelled or replaced, usually by stone structures. Only in isolated cases have hall houses remained in unchanged use up to the mid-20th century. Other forms of vernacular architecture in north Germany are the *Gulfhaus*, traceable in east and north Friesland from the 16th century, a huge stable barn with appended living-quarters, and the narrow *Langhaus* in Schleswig, which is similar in principle to houses in Denmark (*see* §(v) below). Lower-Rhenish farmhouses with a similar internal frame of two rows of posts, but a different functional division of space, can be regarded as a transitional form of the north German hall house. In about the oldest surviving example (1476; reconstructed in Kommern, Rhein. Freilichtmus. & Landesmus. Vlksknd.) a large central hearth-room takes the place of the hall.

Unlike the relatively large north German farmhouses, in central Germany smaller houses predominate, although they usually have two storeys. Narrow, elongated buildings with the entrance on the long side are typical here. Clearly defined forms are difficult to distinguish, the characteristic element being a multiplicity of similar forms over large regions. While these buildings have predominantly three

or more zones of use, including stables as well as living-quarters with living room and kitchen, shorter buildings with two zones and no stable were also built, especially in the Rhineland. In the former type, the middle zone with the stove or fireplace is strikingly dominant, with no division in earlier times between hall and kitchen. The starting-point of development in western Germany was clearly houses with roof supports passing right up to the ridge-piece, which according to present research go back to the mid-15th century.

One of the best-researched regions of Germany is middle Franconia (the area around Nuremberg). Here a history of the rural house showing great continuity can be traced from the 14th century. The oldest surviving buildings show a highly differentiated plan of considerable size (*c.* 13×15 m), with living room, kitchen, bedroom and stable. This type differs from modern houses in the region by its tall internal framework, which can consist of two or three bays, and a thatched, hipped roof. It has close links to the urban house, both having clay-lined wooden walls in the living rooms or *Bohlenstuben* ('boarded rooms'), which are found invariably in most of south Germany from not later than the 13th century to the 16th. They reappear in vernacular architecture in Saxony and Thuringia in the 17th and 18th centuries. In general, the size of the house increased again towards the south of Germany, largely because, especially in south-west Germany (i.e. Upper Swabia and the Black Forest), the barn with its entrance and threshing floor was incorporated in the main house (*Mittertennhaus*), whereas almost everywhere else it was the largest and most important adjoining building. Forms of farmhouse can often be observed in south Germany in which the stables, cellar and other utility rooms take up the ground floor of the house, while the living rooms occupy the upper floor (stilted house). The main centre of such houses is Swabia, but other examples are documented far from there, and the form was certainly developed as early as the 15th century; here too a kinship with urban house designs is evident.

BIBLIOGRAPHY

J. Schepers: *Das Bauernhaus in Nordwestdeutschland* (Münster, 1943)

H. Schilli: *Das Scharzwaldhaus* (Stuttgart, 1953, 2/1965)

Das deutsche Bürgerhaus (Tübingen, 1959–)

J. Schepers: *Westfalen-Lippe*, ii of *Haus und Hof deutscher Bauern* (Münster, 1960)

T. Gebhard: *Der Bauernhof in Bayern* (Munich, 1975)

J. Hähnel: *Die Stube: Wort- und sachgeschichtliche Beiträge zur historischen Hausforschung* (Münster, 1975)

K. Bedal: *Ländliche Ständerbauten des 15. bis 17. Jahrhunderts in Holstein und im südlichen Schleswig* (Neümunster, 1977)

——: *Historische Hausforschung: Eine Einführung in Arbeitsweise, Begriffe und Literatur* (Münster, 1978)

V. Gläntzer: *Wohnen um 1800 in Deutschland* (Münster, 1978)

G. Eitzen: *Niederrheinische Bauernhäuser vom 15. bis zum Beginn des 18. Jahrhunderts* (Cologne, 1981)

K. Baumgarten: *Das deutsche Bauernhaus* (Berlin, 1982, 2/1985)

A. Wiedenau: *Katalog der romanischen Steinbauten in westdeutschen Städten und Siedlungen* (Tübingen, 1983)

K. Bedal and others: *Ein Bauernhaus aus dem Mittelalter* (Bad Windsheim, 1987)

Berichte zur Haus- und Bauforschung (Sobernheim, 1990–)

KONRAD BEDAL

(iv) The Netherlands. One of the most striking features of Dutch vernacular architecture is its variety. This applies particularly to farms, of which there are over 30 types,

10. Aisled-hall farm, Amersfoort, Utrecht, early 19th century

apparently differing in every possible way. Variations in size, shape, plan, constructional details, use of building materials and colouring are considerable, even within each region. There are, however, some general characteristics. Dutch farms are multi-purpose buildings, combining storage with cattle housing and working space. Living accommodation is attached to the working part of the farm or under the same roof. Timber-framing is used for the main structural elements. A series of box-frames, each consisting of two posts, one tie-beam and two braces, coupled by plates and wind braces (see TIMBER STRUCTURE, §II), bears the entire load of the roof. Finally, most farms are aisled. Despite their differences in other respects, all Dutch farms can be traced back to three house-groups of late medieval origins, each of which forms part of a larger European group. Through the continuous process of specialization and adaptation to local geographical, economic and social circumstances, farms within each group have developed a great many variations.

The farms in the central and largest part of the country, from the German border to the North Sea (Drenthe, Overijssel, Gelderland, Utrecht, Zuid-Holland and Brabant), belong to the German hall house-group (see §(iii) above). Here the box-frame construction is of the anchor-beam type, with the tie-beam lowered between the posts. The aisled-hall farm has a rectangular plan with low side walls and a steep hipped or gabled roof. In these compact buildings, cattle are housed in the aisles, heads to the open nave, which serves as a threshing-floor; crops are stored overhead. The front part of the building contains the living

accommodation. In a simple example of this type (see fig. 10) in the central part of the Netherlands, cowhouse, crop storage, dairy and living-quarters are all under the same roof. The chimney marks the separation between house and working part of the farm. Walls were originally timber-framed with wattle and daub infill, while roofs were thatched. From the early 16th century these local materials were gradually replaced by brick and pantiles. This development started in the affluent coastal provinces and ended as late as the second half of the 19th century in the sandy eastern regions inland. Some eastern areas also retained until the early 20th century the aisled-hall type in its simplest form: the *los hoes* ('open house'), where people, livestock and stored crops occupied the same space (examples from Beuningen, Overijssel; Harreveld, Gelderland; and Zeijen, Drenthe; all Arnhem, Rijksmus. Vlksknd. Ned. Openluchtmus.). Elsewhere, dwelling and working parts were generally divided by a fire-wall, which induced a separate development of both ends of the building (examples from Beltnim, Gelderland and Giethoorn, Overijssel; all Arnhem, Rijksmus. Vlksknd. Ned. Openluchtmus.).

Owing to its distribution over a large area with different economic and environmental conditions, the aisled-hall type developed a wide range of variations. In the fertile river areas, farms developed the L- or T-shaped plan through the sideward extension of the domestic end (example of an L-shaped plan farm from Varik, Gelderland; Arnhem, Rijksmus. Vlksknd. Ned. Openluchtmus.). In the western grassland regions, large dairy cellars with mezzanine rooms overhead were added to the house, while the wide, open nave was replaced by a narrow feeding passage. Elsewhere, the gradual increase of crops led to the introduction of ground-floor storage and a repositioning of the threshing floor (examples from Staphorst, Overijssel; and Budel, Noord-Brabant; all Arnhem, Rijksmus. Vlksknd. Ned. Openluchtmus.).

The provinces along the northern coastline (Friesland, Groningen and Noord-Holland) form part of the area (extending into northern Germany and Denmark) where the 'Frisian' house-group dominates. The main characteristics are the aisled box-frame construction with a superimposed tie-beam, the layout of the cowhouse with the cattle placed between partitions, heads to the wall, and the storage of crops at ground-floor level. The oldest type here is the longhouse, which contained only dwelling and cowhouse, while crops were stored outside. From the late 16th century this simple type was gradually replaced by huge buildings combining storage, housing for animals and working space. The nave is used for storage; one aisle contains working space, the other the cowhouse. The house part is attached to the working part and extends beyond the barn. This type, the *kophalsromp* ('head-neck-body')—named after its outline—is widespread in Friesland (example from Midlum, Friesland; Arnhem, Rijksmus. Vlksknd. Ned. Openluchtmus.) and Groningen. Another type, the *stelp* or *stolp* (example from Zuid-Scharwoude, Noord-Holland; Arnhem, Rijksmus. Vlksknd. Ned. Openluchtmus.), includes the living-quarters under the main roof, and variations of it are found in all the northern provinces. Although most of these farms have brick walls, weatherboarding is still found in large parts of Noord-Holland.

The third basic type is found in the southern, inland part of the country bordering Belgium and Germany (Limburg), the tail-end of a large Central European house-group. The main characteristics of these buildings are their single-span structures with high side walls and (originally) separate functional entities. The different elements of the farm are either strung into long structures or (particularly on the fertile loessial soils) placed in a square around an open courtyard (example from Krawinkel, Limburg; Arnhem, Rijksmus. Vlksknd. Ned. Openluchtmus.). Structurally, these buildings are either brick or stone or are timber-framed (anchor-beam box-frame) with brick or wattle and daub infill. In the extreme south of Limburg some quarried stone is available.

BIBLIOGRAPHY

R. C. Hekker: 'De ontwikkeling van de boerderijvormen in Nederland' [The development of farm types in the Netherlands], *Duizend jaar bouwen* [One thousand years of building history], ii (Amsterdam, 1957), pp. 197–316

De benaming van houtverbindingen en constructieve houten elementen bij oude boerderijen: Een poging tot systematisering [The naming of wood joints and constructional wooden elements in old farms: an attempt at systematizing] (Arnhem, 1973)

R. C. Hekker: *Historische boerderijtypen* [Historic farm types] (Arnhem, 1991)

E. L. van Olst: *Uilkema: Een historisch boerderij-onderzoek: Boerderij-onderzoek in Nederland, 1914–1934* [Uilkema: a historical farm research project: historic farm research in the Netherlands, 1914–1934] (Arnhem, 1991)

ELLEN VAN OLST

(v) Denmark. Vernacular town and manor houses survive in Denmark from the mid-16th century and farmhouses from the beginning of the 18th century. Earlier structures are known only from archival sources and archaeological work, which have not yet provided enough information to determine regional variations in building style. Regional differences that did develop after 1700 became blurred after *c.* 1870. The Danish farm consists of several ranges (dwelling, stable, barn and threshing-floor) grouped around a central farmyard (see fig. 11). The number of ranges was determined by the output of the farm. Only in Schleswig and on Bornholm were there longhouses, with accommodation shared between humans and livestock. The ranges, which were always single-storey, were joined together in east Denmark and were detached, but very close, in west Denmark. Three- and four-range farms were usual, but in east Schleswig, west Jutland and on the islands south of Fyn, a form with the house, stable and threshing-floor in a single range was widespread. Another form in west Jutland had parallel ranges containing house and farm buildings on an east–west alignment. An increase in farming output after 1800 caused the ranges to grow in size, and further increases in the 1880s led to the construction of standard brick buildings.

Houses generally contained three rooms, a living-room, a middle room and another large room, one of which ran the depth of the building. In east Denmark and north Jutland, the living-room was heated by an enclosed stove that was lit from the other side of the wall in the kitchen and scullery fireplace, which also contained a baking oven. Living-rooms in other regions had an open hearth, which was also used for cooking. The middle room also often contained both a stove and a scullery fireplace with a bread oven. The living-room was furnished with seats along the window wall and box beds opposite.

Half-timbering was the dominant method of construction until *c.* 1870, but in north-west Schleswig and central Jutland, timber was already a scarce resource by the 18th century, and there brick was used. Rubble was used in the 18th and 19th centuries, mostly in outbuildings. Roofs were usually thatched in straw or reed. On Zealand, Lolland and Falster, as well as in part of east Jutland, the thatch was secured by rods fastened to the battens, while

11. Farmhouse at Åstrup, Falster, Denmark, late 18th century

in the rest of Denmark the thatch was stitched to the battens with straw rope. The ridges were sealed with straw, turf or seaweed, secured with wooden collars or pegs. The half-timbering was filled with wattle and daub and, after *c.* 1800, with brick. The exterior was then plastered and limewashed. Until the early 19th century the posts and panelwork were generally white, but thereafter regional differences were established. In east Denmark and north Jutland, they remained white; on Funen the brick or plaster was painted white or yellowish white, while the timber-framing was picked out in red, brown or black; in east Jutland, the walls were yellow or red with black timber-framing.

Urban dwellings developed few regional characteristics. In the commercial centres, some merchants' houses were built in brick after the Dutch style, but stagnation set in from the mid-17th century after several unsuccessful wars against Sweden. The plots of ground in most towns were deep but relatively narrow, so that houses developed an L-shaped plan with the main block fronting the street and a narrower side wing behind. The main block contained two rooms, one at the front and one at the back, with the fireplace in the cross wall. Gabled houses predominated in south Jutland and were built in many places until the late 16th century. In southern Jutland and Funen, timbering was richly carved with rosette motifs on the short diagonal braces. The jetties and the eaves were carried on brackets, which could be carved either in the usual European way with volutes or acanthus or with local variations developed in the various larger towns.

BIBLIOGRAPHY

H. Zangenberg: *Danske bøndergårde: Grundplaner og konstruktioner* [Danish farms: plans and construction], *Dan. Flkeminder*, xxxi (1925)
Nmus. Arbejdsmk (1930), pp. 39–49
Nmus. Arbejdsmk (1947), pp. 11–20
H. Lund and K. Millech, eds: *Danmarks bygningskunst* [Danish architecture] (Copenhagen, 1963)
S. Jespersen: *Studier af Danmarks bønderbygninger* [Studies of Danish farm buildings] (Copenhagen, 1966)
B. Stoklund: *Bondegård og byggeskik, før 1850* [Farm and building styles, before 1850] (Copenhagen, 1969)
H. Lund, ed.: *Danmarks arkitektur* [Danish architecture] (Copenhagen, 1980)

JØRGEN GANSHORN

(vi) Norway, Sweden and Finland. The predominant occupation in Norway, Sweden and Finland until the second half of the 19th century was pastoral farming, supplemented by fishing and hunting, and later forestry. Rural habitation was therefore typically a farmstead, generally consisting of a group of small buildings owned and occupied by a single family. Each farm would have been self-supporting, and this often meant self-sufficient in house-building too, the skills being passed on from father to son. As a result it could take a relatively long time before technical developments or architectural innovations were accepted.

(a) Materials and techniques. (b) Planning.

(a) Materials and techniques. Although an abundant supply of building stone is available in all three countries, the ease in obtaining wood and using it for building has led to a total domination of timber architecture. Timber houses are also more hospitable in the harsh northern climate. Pine and spruce are both abundant, but pinewood

is a more durable building material and has therefore been used to a greater extent; previously it was also more widespread. Growing tall and straight, pine is particularly suitable for the type of construction that has traditionally been used for both human habitation and most farm buildings in this part of the world, i.e. the log building, the solid walls of which are made from horizontal logs notched together at the corners (*blockbau*). Internal cross walls are locked into long walls in the same way. The form and complexity of the notch and the decorative treatment of the projecting log-end display historical and regional variations. In the gables and at other unstable parts of the walls, the horizontal logs are pinned together with dowels.

In Scandinavian log architecture the logs are carefully trimmed to fit snugly together. There is a broad shallow groove running along the underside to help the log sit more firmly on the log below and to hold insulation material when necessary (dried moss is traditionally used). Formerly the logs were left exposed, but after the introduction *c.* 1500 of the water-powered saw, boards became more readily available, and cladding became common, spreading into rural districts from the towns. Both horizontal and vertical boarding are found, depending to some extent on location, and it may be restricted to the main façade. Details in the design also vary from district to district. Such embellishments as carved pediments, richly profiled mouldings and fretwork are found on houses both with and without cladding, the custom having spread from town to country and from high- to low-status dwellings.

Log architecture was probably introduced to Scandinavia from Russia during the Viking Age in the 9th or 10th century. Archaeological excavations have shown that a typical medieval urban property contained many separate buildings and that the dwelling house was a small house roofed with turf and heated by a central open hearth or a flueless stone-built oven in one corner. Wall-logs were of modest diameter and apparently unworked other than being stripped of bark, and corner-notching seems generally to have been of the simplest kind, a semicircular cut in the upper half of the log to receive the next log at right angles. There is also evidence for there having been upper storeys.

No medieval log-buildings are known from urban areas, but there are many still standing in rural districts, especially in Dalarna, Jämtland and Härjedalen in central Sweden and in Telemark in southern Norway. The greatest number are in Norway, where over 200 are known. In contrast to the remains recorded in urban excavations, the surviving rural examples are often structurally much more sophisticated. The logs in the ground-frame are usually trapezoidal in section, and the wall logs may be trimmed to give an oval or faceted cross-section. Intricate notching techniques are known from the 12th century. Logs of very large dimensions are used, especially from the 17th century on.

Simple log structures have no roof trusses. There are basically two types of roof contruction: the 'purlin-roof' with logs running parallel with the ridge-piece from gable to gable, and the less common 'rafter-roof', where squared timbers run from the top of the side walls up to a ridge-piece. In the latter construction there may also be tie-beams notched into the long walls. The roof consists of boards, the direction of which depends on the underlying construction. In parts of Sweden split logs are used instead of boards. In many cases the boards are covered with a water-resistant layer, traditionally birch bark, on which turf is laid; wooden shingles or stone slabs are also used. The earliest examples of slates and pantiles are from the 17th century.

As wall-openings lead to instability in this kind of structure, they have traditionally been kept to a minimum. Windows were at first merely small rounded openings between two logs or else non-existent: the only source of daylight would have been from the door or the smoke-vent in the roof. Glazing was not introduced until after the end of the Middle Ages, and the windows were fixed. Where openable, they are always of casement type, the lights occasionally hinged to the central post. Door- and window-openings are stabilized either by grooved uprights into which the chamfered log-ends are slotted or by vertical splines inserted into a continuous groove in the cut end of the logs. Both constructions allow the logs to settle without causing any distortion of the door or window frame.

Already in medieval times dwelling houses were often raised from the ground on stones, the gap between floor and wall being sealed by an internal earth-filled box-bench. There is early evidence for boarded floors, the boards resting on joists often not attached to the walls. Flagstone floors are also known. Log buildings can be dismantled and re-erected fairly easily, and until modern times it was not uncommon for rural builders to prefabricate the whole structure before transporting it to town and re-erecting on the purchaser's site. Similarly, the lower wall timbers, which are susceptible to rotting, can be removed and replaced by jacking up the building.

Although vernacular architecture is dominated by log-built structures, other types of construction occur, either for functional reasons, or because long straight softwood timbers were not available. Most famously there was 'stave' architecture in Norway (*see* NORWAY, §II, 1), which is really an extremely sophisticated version of the simple post-built structure that was usual for all kinds of buildings in both Norway and Sweden from prehistoric times until it was gradually superseded by log architecture. In south-west Norway there are a small number of unaisled barns, possibly medieval in date, whose construction is based on a row of braced post-and-tie-beam frames with the connecting wall plate lying on top of the tie-beams, in other words the 'reversed assembly' known in English medieval timber architecture.

'Slab' architecture is a term sometimes used to describe the other major type of construction involving solid horizontal-log walls that is found in both Norway and Sweden, and especially on Gotland. Upright posts are fixed to a ground frame at the four corners and at intervals along the walls and have vertical grooves into which the tapered ends of logs or thick planks are slotted. In this way shorter timbers can be used, for example of oak. The roof typically consists of main rafters running from the top of the wall to a ridge pole. The gables are filled with vertical boards. Timber-framed structures with brick infill

12. Storehouse from Søndre Tveito, Norway, *c.* 1300; reconstruction (Oslo, Norsk Folkemuseum)

are less common except in the south of Sweden. Sometimes planks are used between the studs in the manner described above.

Combinations of log and frame construction also occur. At one end of a log-built house the ground- and first-floor-level logs of the side walls extend beyond the end wall, terminating at a transverse log that is jointed to them in the traditional way. Upright posts at the two corners form a box-frame extension, which is filled with upright boards (see fig. 12). The upper storey is usually log-built for the full length, with dowelled log gables in the usual manner supporting a purlin roof.

(b) Planning. In the Middle Ages post-built longhouses with domestic quarters at one end and shelter for the farm animals at the other were replaced by log-built structures. Unless extensive use is made of scarfing, or internal cross walls can support a scarfed ridge pole, the size of a log-built structure will be governed by the length of timber available. The large multi-functional longhouse was therefore replaced by a number of small separate log-built structures, each fulfilling a different function. The typical farmhouse plan, consisting of one large room with two smaller chambers at one end, continued essentially in both urban and rural districts right up to the 20th century. It was often extended by the addition of a second large room so that the two small rooms lay in the centre of the building. Full upper storeys in dwelling houses became possible after the introduction of the chimney at the end of the Middle Ages. The fireplace was moved to the rear small room, which thus became a kitchen, while stairs in the front chamber or entrance hall gave access to upper rooms with windows in the gable walls. Latterly, the front central bay was sometimes heightened, causing a break in the slope of the roof, or it was given a pitched roof at right angles to the main roof.

13. Niemela tenant farm from Konginkangas, Finland, 18th century; reconstruction (Helsinki, Seurasaari Open-Air Museum)

After the farmhouse, the building that traditionally received most attention was a two-storey log building with a stateroom or guest chamber on the upper floor and storerooms below. There are several surviving medieval examples, especially in Telemark in southern Norway. The wall logs are often trimmed to an oval cross-section and the buildings richly decorated with carving. While the log-built core of the building continues up into the second storey, there is usually an external balcony or gallery, often partly enclosed, projecting on one or more sides at the upper level. The external staircase is placed in this narrow area below the overhanging gallery, partly protected from the weather. With an external stair, the storage area on the lower floor can be kept locked even when the guest chamber is in use. In the 18th century it became common to place the building on a timber substructure or tall stone-capped posts. In Karelia the area between the tall foundation posts might be enclosed with plank walls.

Other buildings on the farmstead traditionally included a combined bakehouse/brewery, byres, stalls, barns and other storehouses. Later there might also be a separate dwelling for use in the summer and a house for the retired parents of the current farmer. In Finland the bathhouse or *sauna* has always played a central role and was often the first permanent building to be erected. A stone-built stove was the usual means of heating, with the smoke finding its own way out through an open vent in the roof until chimneys became common there in the 18th century.

The traditional layout of the farmstead varies from region to region. In central and northern Norway farm buildings are often grouped around a rectangular court-yard, while in the south they are often arranged in two rows. Regional variations in Sweden range from the strict rectangular arrangement in the north to more loosely grouped buildings in central and southern districts. In Finland the farmstead generally forms an enclosed group, often around a rectangular courtyard (see fig. 13), but in the east the buildings were grouped more loosely and are more reminiscent of a traditional Russian farm layout. The traditional rural architecture of Karelia in south-east Finland is characterized by large multi-functional log-built buildings.

In the late 19th century, farm holdings that had become split up and scattered through generations of division through inheritance were regrouped and the farmsteads dispersed to give a more rational use of the land. In Dalarna in Sweden and in western Norway, however, many of the old townships containing several farmsteads have survived. Also during the last 100 years traditional rural architecture has suffered through the introduction of new agricultural techniques and the appearance of professional building contractors. Large standard multi-purpose buildings have replaced the many small functional buildings, which have often simply been abandoned. In northern Scandinavia the Saami continued for a long time to use traditional structures based on a framework of curved wood with walls of sods and turf, while nomadic reindeer herders used tents of wooden poles and skins.

Until the 19th century, urban vernacular architecture did not differ substantially from that on the farm, and two-storey log-built houses with board cladding are still found in most towns. The explosive growth of the urban population in the 19th century led to the appearance in the larger towns of brick-built apartment buildings in Neo-classical style and villas built of wood in the eclectic style of the day.

BIBLIOGRAPHY

S. E. Erixon: *Svensk byggnadskultur* (Stockholm, 1945, rev. 2/1982)
A. Berg: Norske gårdstun [Norwegian farmsteads] (Oslo, 1968)
C. Norberg-Schulz and G. Bugge: *Stav og laft* [Pole and log] (Oslo, 1969)
J. M. Richards: *800 Years of Finnish Architecture* (Newton Abbot, 1978)
J. Holan: *Norwegian Wood* (New York, 1990)

CLIFFORD D. LONG, OLA STORSLETTEN

2. SOUTHERN EUROPE.

(i) Introduction. (ii) Iberian peninsula. (iii) West Mediterranean islands. (iv) Italian peninsula. (v) Balkan peninsula.

(i) Introduction. In southern Europe vernacular buildings survive from many periods and display considerable variety of construction, plan and building materials. Deeply rooted in each local environment and culture, these buildings are a vital element of Mediterranean landscapes and heritage. No single set of factors can explain their character and diversity. Climate, local relief and building materials, ethnic differences, social organization, economic activities, demographic processes, defensive considerations and the muted influence of changing fashions in polite architecture have all helped to mould traditional building forms and diversify them locally and regionally. In the 20th century, however, and especially after World War II, rural life was profoundly changed by a number of factors: state rural reconstruction schemes, agricultural modernization, spreading urban influences, the decay of mountain communities and transhumance owing to depopulation, the drainage, reclamation and planned settlement of many lowland and coastal areas, improvement of communications and availability of new building materials, and the growth of mass tourism. Modernization and improved rural living standards led to much rebuilding in the countryside but broke the continuity of local building traditions. Increasingly, traditional houses have been replaced by buildings with little or no local flavour, in the form of standardized, functional dwellings or structures inspired by international, urban fashions.

Within southern Europe, areas characterized by either nucleated villages, hamlets, dispersed farms or distinctive combinations of these basic settlement types form a complicated, multi-causal spatial pattern. In many parts of the Mediterranean, defensive and other considerations frequently led in the past to concentration of the farming population in crowded, hilltop villages. Often the distinction between a substantial village and a town is rather arbitrary. Typical hilltop villages are compact and walled with close-set buildings and narrow alleys, a public open space (*plaza, piazza, place, platea*), churches, and houses of varied size and architectural pretensions. In general appearance and layout there is little to differentiate the villages of Spain, Italy or Mediterranean France: variations are chiefly local and regional rather than national. Besides the compact hill village, other distinctive village morphologies occur, such as the straggling linear forms in certain Alpine valleys, compact linear forms developed along routeways, or the numerous planned, grid-plan villages of the Danubian lowlands. Marked agglomeration shows some correlation with arid southern areas such as New Castile in Spain, southern Italy and Greece, while smaller villages, hamlets and dispersed farms are more characteristic of pluviose Spain, central Italy, the Po plain and the Alps.

House type and settlement form may have a recognizable organic unity, structural and aesthetic. In many of the compact hill villages and towns of, for example, the Aegean islands, Liguria and the Amalfi region in Italy, streets and alleys are built over, and the combined structures form an interacting organism or 'megastructure' rather than a mere accumulation of independent dwellings. The settlements are unplanned, organic growths with irregular street plans adjusted to the terrain: their intimate and unified architectural composition results largely from the existence of a basic repetitive element, the dwelling unit, using local materials and construction methods and determined by the social and economic structure of the population. Even the system of defence is often based on the pattern of the houses, with an outer ring of strongly constructed, connected houses constituting the town walls.

Although many districts possess distinctive vernacular architecture and building methods, certain basic features occur diffusely. Thus, compact, rectangular, storey houses (*maisons hautes*) are widely distributed and are especially characteristic of the extensive mountain areas with their pastoral economy. Animals were typically stalled on the ground floor, with human quarters above and hay and straw stored in lofts: access to the upper storey is often internal but in some areas, and especially in older buildings, is by an outside staircase. These houses may be free-standing or adjoin other houses or farm buildings in elaborate multi-cellular forms. Single-storey, linear houses and farmsteads are more typical of cultivated lowlands and plateaux. This distinction between storeyed dwellings and lower dwellings is important, but there are many intermediate types. Within individual villages, social gradations are reflected in house size and form: thus wealthier peasants might live in three-storey houses, average families in two-storey and the poor in single-storey houses.

Except in some mountain areas, timber for building purposes is generally scarce throughout the region, and in recent centuries stone has been the dominant walling material. Plaster is widely applied to the exterior of houses, sometimes concealing the basic building materials. Sod, turf and, more commonly, sun-dried bricks were widely used for walling in central Spain and in many lowland areas, such as the extensive Danubian or Pannonian plain of north-east former Yugoslavia, while reeds and straw were often used to build houses and shelters in the marshy deltas of the Mediterranean coasts. Timber construction is characteristic of the massive 'Alpine' mountain ranges that mark the northern limit of the Iberian and Italian peninsulas and extend deeply into the Balkan area. Here the oldest building technique (*blockbau*) is to construct the shell of the house with logs laid one above the other, interlocking the corners. However, there has been a gradual shift from timber to stone in these areas not only for single elements but for whole parts of the houses, beginning with the foundations. The predominant style of roof in southern Europe is ridged or pyramidical, with a low pitch. Red tiles are the main form of roof cover and have virtually replaced thatch in many areas where it was once common. In wooded areas, shingles or planks may be used as roofing materials, and stone flags or slabs of slate are employed in some stony areas. Flat, earth-covered roofs are a southerly feature found primarily in Aegean Greece and Moorish Spain, although tiled, ridged roofs spread in these areas during the 20th century.

From the 17th century onwards country houses built in polite styles proliferated as noble and bourgeois property spread out from the towns. In some rural areas superior houses are recognizably elaborations of indigenous peasant styles, but more normally they represent an introduced polite architecture informed by Renaissance classicism with its emphasis on symmetry and order, and are distinct from indigenous building traditions evolved under severe resource restraints solely to meet local peasant needs. In time, certain features of polite design were assimilated into folk styles. Baroque and Rococo decoration, for example, spread from central Europe to towns and sometimes eventually the countryside: from the mid-19th century Neo-classicism was a pervasive influence that varied in intensity from place to place. Some forms of defensive tower-houses (such as the *kule* of Albania and the *pyrgoi* of Greece), either free-standing or linked to ordinary houses, and enclosed farmsteads reflect the banditry, feuding and general insecurity that prevailed until modern times in many areas. Cave dwellings, either ancient or recent, are found widely in the countryside and in towns, especially in the south of Italy and Spain, where their frequency is explained by suitable soft rocks, which can be easily excavated, and the welcome coolness of caves in areas of high summer temperatures. Varied forms of dwelling dug into the ground and covered with straw or stone are also recorded in, for example, Albania and southern Spain.

Mediterranean landscapes contain numerous temporary dwellings and shelters once used for a wide range of purposes; some of these are remote and difficult of access, and many have disappeared or are increasingly obsolescent. They include mountain dwellings of transhumant or semi-nomadic herders often associated with animal shelters and pens; seasonal abodes of hunters and fishermen typically found on coastal islands and in swamps; and the very varied huts, shelters and watch-towers used by farmers working at a distance from their village homes. These humble structures often perpetuate archaic designs and techniques. Three basic forms are found: dry-stone huts of circular or rectangular plan roofed by a dome or vault of overlapping stones, such as the *trulli* of Apulia (see fig. 15 below), *bories* in Provence, or *petro kalives* in the Ionian islands; conical timber and straw huts with circular stone bases, generally referred to as *capanne* in the Italian peninsula and in Sardinia, where they are very numerous; and rectangular tentlike structures of reeds or straw supported on a wooden frame, such as the Andalusian *choza* or the *barraca* of the deltas of east Spain. Attempts were made to develop larger dwellings either by enlarging or linking these primitive forms, but they were generally superseded by rectangular, block-like houses, perhaps a Roman or Celtic legacy, which could be more easily extended and conveniently subdivided.

(ii) Iberian peninsula. Iberia is dominated by high mountains and plateaux, with a fundamental climatic division between the moist north-west (pluviose Spain) and the arid or semi-arid south-east (arid Spain). Relief and climate have strongly influenced the distribution and character of human settlement. With the exception of the Madrid region, dense populations are markedly peripheral, and the Meseta Central, the major plateau and core of Iberia, is on the whole barren and sparsely populated, as are the fringing mountain ranges that separate it from the sea and increase its continentality and remoteness. The deep-rootedness and prevalence of some aspects of agricultural tradition, such as transhumance, have resulted in a range of temporary residences and shelters for livestock. Farmers also use stone, straw or mud shelters when working away from the often widely separated villages. Nucleated villages are dominant throughout the Meseta, but there are many differences in settlement and house form, especially from north to south. In the northern Meseta little building stone is available, and single-storey adobe houses formed the basic vernacular, although there has been much emigration and settlement abandonment, and newer houses are in stone and storeyed. In the houses of the Cordillera Central, timber and stone are used, but in the southern Meseta low, single-storey adobe buildings are again the traditional form located in large, widely separated villages, a pattern that has its classic expression on the plains of La Mancha and Extramadura. Away from villages, dry-stone huts (*bombos*) are widely used by agricultural workers. Limestone caves are inhabited in places.

The peripheral regions of the peninsula are culturally distinct. The sparse population of the Pyrenees has traditionally lived mainly in small hamlets and in timbered, storeyed houses characteristic of mountain habitats, with all functions housed under one roof and human quarters above the animals. Rough cabins of wood or dry stone are numerous at higher altitudes, serving as shelters for shepherds and for cheese-making. The Basque territory to the west is characterized by large farmhouses of stone and abundant timberwork, with a surrounding timber balcony and mansard roof. In the eastern Pyrenees, however, the typical houses are stone-built and akin to the *masia* of neighbouring Catalonia, with rooms arranged around a patio. Galicia, in strong contrast to most of Spain, has a highly dispersed population. Two-storey houses are traditional, built of stone with projecting thatched or slated roofs to provide protection against rain. Similar houses are characteristic of northern Portugal and the Cantabrian Cordillera, regions that also share the distinctive *horreo*, a storage barn resting on pillars as protection against damp and vermin. Archaic circular or oval dwellings (*pallozas*) with large, conical thatched roofs and subdivided for animal and human accommodation are found in Galicia but are now little used, except for storage. Conical shelters of wood and straw have traditionally been widely used by pastoralists in these regions. Corbelled, dry-stone habitations, rectangular and curvilinear in plan, are also numerous here and in a broad belt stretching southwards along the border of Portugal and Spain.

Along the Levantine lowlands the most striking features are the numerous irrigated, intensively farmed and densely settled huertas. Villages here are few, and farms are characteristically scattered. The traditional dwellings of the Ebro delta and Valencia huerta are the *barracas*, with walls of wicker and dried mud and steeply pitched roofs covered with straw thatch. Most of these structures have been replaced by stone houses with thatched roofs. Further south, in Murcia and Almeria, whitewashed cubic houses appear, a legacy of the Moorish occupation. Houses with interior courtyards, flat roofs that sometimes serve as terraces, and exterior staircases occur in the large rural agglomerations of the Andalusian lowlands and of the Algarve region, the most arabicized part of Portugal. However, the common house style of the numerous agricultural labourers in these regions is a low, mud-walled, whitewashed building with a sloping red-tiled roof, simple structures that assembled together can form architectural compositions with remarkable aesthetic appeal (see fig. 14).

(iii) *West Mediterranean islands.* Each of the Balearic islands is culturally distinct. In Mallorca, the largest and most populous island, the bulk of the rural population traditionally lived in small agricultural towns, but there has been considerable secondary dispersion. The older, large farmsteads here are impressive buildings of the courtyard type, influenced by Palladian architecture. Flat-roofed 'Moorish' houses are found on the outlying islands of Ibiza and Formentera. The Balearics are also distinguished generally by a great concentration of corbelled stone buildings from many periods. In Corsica and Sardinia villages are the dominant settlement form, especially of the interior mountains, and the stone *maison haute* is the traditional house type. A large number and variety of huts and shelters are used by herders and agriculturalists, including circular and rectangular structures of corbelled stone or of wood, straw and mud. Sardinia is particularly rich in stone structures from many periods, including prehistoric towers or *nuraghi*.

(iv) *Italian peninsula.* The intricate variety of Italian vernacular architecture and rural settlement patterns is the product of a long, eventful history involving many major civilizing forces and ethnic groups interacting with a varied geology, relief and climate. Landscapes are so deeply humanized that cultural and physical traits merge. The focal position of the peninsula in the Mediterranean and its elongated form have produced marked contrasts in the north, centre and south, although in most areas there is a mingling of the basic settlement types. These include villages and hamlets of varied sizes, large farms accommodating the owner or manager and the labourers in one compact unit, and isolated family farms. Types of agriculture and land tenure strongly influence settlement systems and, in turn, house styles and the type and layout of farm buildings.

Within the extensive but lightly populated zone of the Italian Alps there are appreciable ethnic differences of house style and settlement pattern, for example between Austrian and Italian styles, but the dominant features of traditional settlement are the storeyed timber and masonry houses and the pattern of villages and hamlets inhabited by pastoralists who also made use of temporary, transhumant dwellings at different levels. The densely populated northern plain, between the Alps and the Apennines, is the only extensive lowland in Italy and is unusual in the

14. Whitewashed houses, Casares, Malaga, Spain

Mediterranean, with its long-established system of intensive commercial agriculture and large farms operated by wage labour. Large country houses (palazzi) are common features, and large independent farmsteads (*corti*) have developed in the most fertile and intensively cultivated parts of the plain, with houses for the owner and labourers being arranged with other farm buildings around a central court. These complexes often reveal the influence of sophisticated Palladian architecture. *Corti* occur singly and in groups. Moreover, they vary considerably in size and in some areas are simply single-family enterprises. The basic court form may indeed have affinities with the Roman villa: it recurs in the plain of the Roman Campania and is found in towns and cities. Straggling, linear settlements, consisting of small houses and farms aligned with roads, also occur on the northern plain. They are most closely associated with irrigation and reclamation, both ancient and modern, in the Po delta and on the Venetian plain, where houses and roads have been constructed on dry sites along the embankments. Until the late 20th century many houses in the delta area were one-roomed hovels made of straw and reeds with earth floors.

Scattered farms and small hamlets dominate the hill country of central Italy and are closely associated with the *mezzadria* system, which involves family holdings (*podere*) with mixed cultivation, including olives, vine and cereals, best worked from scattered farmsteads. This is a zone characterized by rectangular, storeyed houses of stone and brick with a tiled or slated roof, the classic 'Italic' house with the ground floor used for animals and farming functions and the living-quarters on the upper floor reached by an outside staircase and balcony. There are many local variants on the basic model: on steep slopes, for example, direct access is possible to the different levels, and the external stair and balcony are absent. Larger farms

15. Dry-stone *trullo*, Apulia, Italy

(*fattoria*) may possess a range of buildings, including a tower, which in Tuscany is often used as a dovecot. On the coastal plains of the Roman Campagna and the reclaimed Pontine Marshes and further south on the densely populated Campania, large, fortified courtyard dwellings, similar to the *corti* of the northern plain, are a fundamental settlement feature. Indeed on the Campania they cluster together to form town-like settlements. Traditionally, Apennine flocks wintered on these coastal plains, where the transhumant herdsmen lived in conical reed huts (*capanne*). Summer dwellings in the mountains were rectangular, dry-stone structures (*stazzi*) with thatched roofs.

In southern Italy and Sicily the *latifondo* system, associated with extensive cereal cultivation and sheep grazing on large estates, is marked by the concentration of tenants in large feudal villages, sometimes referred to as 'agro-towns' or 'peasant cities'. Here congested tenements were the standard accommodation. In many areas the only isolated settlements are large farms (*masseria*) that were the centres of large estates. When the *latifondo* economy began to break up through the impact of modern land reforms and other socio-economic forces, large nucleated villages became increasingly anachronistic, but they persist through physical and social inertia. Increased dispersion of the agricultural population, especially the settlement

and colonization of the previously uninhabited *latifondo*, is a common tendency throughout southern Italy.

In the Mediterranean area the greatest concentration of corbelled dry-stone huts occurs in the heel of Italy, where *trulli* have long been used as shelters by farmers, transhumant herdsmen and hunters and have also been developed into a distinctive kind of permanent dwelling (see fig. 15). Round plans have generally changed to rectangular with thinner walls, and several *trulli* joined together to form complex dwellings that combine flat and conical roofs. These striking structures are often whitewashed and the roofs tile-covered; windows are generally few and small, and the main door is arched. The key areas of development are the elevated limestone plateaux of Murgia. *Trulli* dwellings occur singly and in groups in the Apulian countryside, but they are found also in urban settings and the town of Alberobello, for example, contains whole areas of *trulli* dwellings. Often associated with *trulli* are large, ziggurat-like stone structures (*specchie*), which cover ancient burial chambers or served as watch-towers. Numerous caves, natural and man-made, are also used as dwellings in the area. In the south-west of the peninsula and in Sicily, low, whitewashed farmhouses with flat or sloping roofs reflect Moorish influences. Corbelled huts are widely found, including those built with blocks of lava on the slopes of Mt Etna.

(v) Balkan peninsula. Owing to the renowned ethnic diversity of the Balkans there is much local variety in settlement types and vernacular building traditions. However, broad regional patterns can be recognized that match the major contrasts in geology and relief. Considerable change took place in building styles in the 20th century and at varied rates in different areas. Even before industrialization and modern communications, new building materials and other innovations spread into remote areas, often diffused by itinerant masons who specialized in house building. Here, as throughout the Mediterranean area, there has been a diminution in the use of timber and a greatly increased use of either stone or bricks, with tiles tending to replace thatch and shingles as roofing material.

In the Alpine mountains of Slovenia and Croatia the villages and wooden chalets are similar to those in Austria and Switzerland. The traditional house is of two or more storeys; sometimes it is built entirely in stone, but more often the ground floor is stone and the upper walls of wooden planks. Covered wooden balconies with decorated parapets are characteristic features. Roofs are steeply inclined with big, overhanging eaves and traditionally covered with fir shingles, although tiles are also much used. In the valleys varied wooden structures are used for specialized farm functions, and on the high mountain pastures (*planina*) oval wooden huts with shingle roofs have long been constructed by transhumant herders. Towards the south-east, especially in Croatia, the typical Alpine house is progressively modified, and the turning of the gable end of the houses towards the street is a feature found widely on the Hungarian Plain to the east.

In the vast region of the Pannonian Plain, in the northeast, villages are numerous, large and frequently laid out on a grid plan imposed by Austrian and Hungarian estate owners in the 18th century after the withdrawal of the Turks. Traditional houses are single-storey, elongated structures with living quarters, barn and stable under one roof, a type ubiquitous in Eastern Europe in areas east and south of Vienna and known as a *Streckhof* (Ger.: 'extended court'). The narrow gable ends face the street, and houses are separated by narrow courtyards. A long wall with an arched gateway shuts the courtyard off from the street. This regular arrangement allows maximum concentration of accessible settlement along a single road and restricts the spread of fire. The Pannonian Plain is a treeless region, and houses are generally built with bricks and roofed with tiles. House walls are plastered and whitewashed. Sun-dried bricks were for long the main building material along with pisé (rammed clay or earth), and reed thatch was also widespread. Pile houses (*sojenica*) are found around the big Pannonian rivers, such as the Sava and Drava, where the land is subject to seasonal inundation.

In the region of the Pannonian valleys to the south of the plain, settlement pattern and village morphology vary considerably, and there is a transition from brick houses through adobe and wood to the wooden houses that are traditional in the higher, central forested regions of Bosnia and northern Serbia. Perhaps the oldest type of wooden house is a compact, oblong form made of squared logs with a steep, four-sided roof covered with shingles. Originally unicellular, with an open central hearth, this basic *blockbau* form has been expanded into more elaborate storeyed structures partially or wholly built of stone. Another traditional form is the square, single-storey house of north Serbia, made with a wooden framework filled in with clay or planks and typically possessing a four-sided, gently sloping roof, either tiled or thatched, and a prominent wooden chimney and wooden verandah. This basic layout has been retained in some modern brick-built houses.

The mountainous interior is characterized by a dispersed settlement pattern of loosely aggregated hamlets and houses (*stari vlah*) associated with large, self-contained kinship groups (*zadruga*). Around the dwellings are various outbuildings in timber, stone and wickerwork, used as sleeping sheds and animal shelters or for grain storage, hay-drying and other purposes. This primitive pattern has been modified in some areas by relief and drainage considerations, by population pressures or by defensive considerations, which have led to a more pronounced nucleation. The valleys of eastern Serbia are characterized by compact villages of the *timok* type, with an irregular plan of narrow, winding lanes and closely packed houses of stone or sun-dried mud. In the villages of the Adriatic karstland the houses are often built in a row in areas on the border of poljes, where there are springs and safety from seasonal flooding. Many peasants live in stone tenement houses in the small towns, but in the countryside houses of two storeys intermingle with the more numerous small, single-storey houses, their walls built of stone and the gently sloping roofs covered with slates, slabs of stone or rye thatch. Along the Adriatic coast concave roofing tiles are widely used, and Venetian architectural influences are discernible. The *kula*, found principally in Albania but also in surrounding upland areas such as Montenegro, southern Bosnia and Epirus, is a miniature fortress or tower house built by the wealthier members of rural society for habitation and defence in areas long afflicted by family feuding. It is constructed of stone and is usually of three storeys, with animals on the ground level and the living-quarters above, unlike the simple, single-storey houses of the bulk of the rural population.

Over much of the southern part of the former Yugoslavia and definitively in Greece, Mediterranean cultural influences prevail; isolated houses are almost unknown, and the nucleated defensive village clustered around a square is dominant. In the lowlands villages sometimes show a degree of ordered, rectilinear layout, but on hillsides they are often amorphous and sprawling. Ordinary peasant families have traditionally lived in two- or three-storey houses of unhewn stone; the ground floor is used for animals and storage, and the living-quarters (*spyti*) above, which often have a wooden balcony, are reached by an external or internal staircase. Many of the poorest class, especially on the plains, lived in primitive, single-storey, mud-walled dwellings thatched with reeds or bamboo, in which animals and humans were originally housed at opposite ends of an undivided rectangular chamber. Most of these houses are entered through a portico on the longest side, but in some areas the houses have the entrance and porch on one of the narrow sides, a form that may have some affinity with the ancient megaron. Various forms of *pyrgoi* (tower house) are found in mainland and

16. Georgios Schwartz Mansion, Ambelakia, Thessaly, Greece, 1787–98

insular Greece: some are substantial permanent residences, as on the island of Lesbos; others are attached to houses, as in parts of the Mani peninsula, and were essentially places of temporary refuge.

The turco-oriental or Turkish house appears in many areas, including southern Serbia, northern Greece and Epirus (see fig. 16). This type is characterized by its overhanging upper storey, generally a timber and wattle structure with a pitched roof, balconies and projecting windows and containing the *haremlik* or women's room; the ground-floor is stone built and almost without windows. Privacy and defence are the priorities, and a high wall usually surrounds the courtyard and garden. This house type is not only associated with the Turkish aristocracy but also served as an influential model for the impressive residences built by wealthy Greeks after the 16th century as Ottoman control progressively weakened

and growing economic contacts with western and central Europe stimulated the rise of an indigenous Greek bourgeoisie. Mountain and island communities flourished noticeably, such as Hydra and Chios in the Aegean and Makrinitza and Ambelakia on Mt Pelion. Long before independence and large-scale urbanization, rural society had developed deep class divisions, and many settlements contained lower-class houses (*laika*) and upper-class mansions (*arkhondiki*) as well as *pyrgoi*. Numerous Turkish estate villages, or *ciflics*, were established in several areas of the southern Slav lands and of Greece and are especially characteristic of the arable plains of Thessaly and Macedonia. They consisted of a compound of mud huts housing share-croppers and dominated by the square, stone tower-like residence (*konak*) of the Turkish bey, which was sometimes surrounded by a wall and bastions. These distinctive settlements have now largely disappeared.

Primitive structures in the Greek countryside include farmers' field huts and temporary residences (*kalives*) and animal shelters (*mandres*) often associated with ethnically distinct pastoral groups. These include the Vlachs of the Pindus Mountains and Rhodopian Mountains, who have long practised inverse transhumance, and the nomadic Sarakatsani, who build circular and rectangular huts of brushwood and reeds on wicker frames. Both groups are now largely sedentarized. The roughly equal distribution of flat-roofed and pitched or ridged-roofed houses is a striking feature of Greece's cultural geography. Pitched roofs are dominant on the mainland; flat roofs are essentially Aegean and insular, best developed in the Cyclades and Dodecanese, where the basic form of house is a simple, single-storey, elongated cube. The flat roof is supported by either wooden beams or corbelled stone vaults. On the Cycladic islands of Santorini, Kimolos and Andiparos, the old houses are roofed with cylindrical corbelled domes (see fig. 17). Flat, earth-covered roofs were originally used everywhere in Crete, but, as on many Aegean islands, they have been widely replaced by tiled, ridged roofs. The island is rich too in dry-stone huts used as temporary shelters, either circular corbelled structures or a rectangular, barrel-vaulted variety.

BIBLIOGRAPHY

J. Cvijic: *La Péninsule balkanique: Géographie humaine* (Paris, 1918)
Greece, Admiralty (Naval Intelligence Division) Geographical Handbook, ii (London, 1939–44)
Italy, Admiralty (Naval Intelligence Division) Geographical Handbook, ii (London, 1939–44)
Jugoslavia, Admiralty (Naval Intelligence Division) Geographical Handbook, ii (London, 1939–44)
Spain and Portugal, Admiralty (Naval Intelligence Division) Geographical Handbook, iii and iv (London, 1939–44)
G. Nangeroni: *Geografia delle dimore e degli insediamenti rurali* (Milan, 1946)
G. A. Megas: *The Greek House: Its Evolution and its Relation to the Houses of the Other Balkan Peoples* (Athens, 1951)
B. Milojevic: 'Types of Villages and Village-houses in Yugoslavia', *Professional Geographer*, v/6 (1953), pp. 13–17
V. Mossa: *Architettura domestica in Sardegna* (Cagliari, 1957)
G. Rohlfs: *Primitive Kuppelbauten in Europa* (Munich, 1957)
J. Walton: 'The Corbelled Stone Huts of Southern Europe', *Man*, lxii (1962), pp. 33–4
G. M. Houston: *The Western Mediterranean World* (London, 1964)
J. M. Wagstaff: 'Traditional Houses in Modern Greece', *Geog. Mag.*, l (1965), pp. 58–64
D. P. Branch: *Folk Architecture of the East Mediterranean* (New York, 1966)

17. Vernacular housing, Santorini, Cyclades

C. Michaelides: *Hydra: A Greek Island Town: Its Growth and Form* (Chicago, 1967)

T. Storai de Rocchi: *Bibliografica degli studi sulla casa rurale italiana* (Florence, 1968)

E. Allen: *Stone Shelters* (Cambridge, MA, 1969)

E. V. De Oliveira, F. Galliano and B. Pereira: *Construções primitivas em Portugal* (Lisbon, 1969)

M. Goldfinger: *Villages in the Sun* (New York, 1969)

J. G. Pounds: *Eastern Europe* (London, 1969)

J. Walton: 'Megalithic Building Survivals in the Balearic Islands', *Studies in Folk Life*, ed. G. Jenkins (London, 1969), pp. 35–46

G. Barbieri and L. Gambi, eds: *La casa rurale in Italia* (Florence, 1970)

G. R. Galy: 'L'Habitat de pierres sèches en Méditerranée nord-occidentale', *Méditerranée*, i/2 (1970), pp. 95–119

C. Flores: *Arquitectura popular española*, 5 vols (Madrid, 1973)

D. B. Doumanis and P. Oliver, eds: *Shelter in Greece* (Athens, 1974)

D. Vassiliadis: *To kritiko spiti* (Athens, 1976)

D. Philippides: *Greek Traditional Architecture*, 8 vols (Athens, 1983–)

D. S. Rugg: *Eastern Europe* (London and New York, 1985)

J. Caro Baroja: *De la vida rural vasca* (San Sebastian, 3/1986)

S. Lange: *La herencia románica: La casa europea de piedra* (Milan, 1989)

FRED AALEN

3. CENTRAL AND EASTERN EUROPE.

(i) Social and cultural background. (ii) Development. (iii) Building types. (iv) High-style influences.

(i) Social and cultural background. In Central and Eastern Europe there was no distinct and identifiable current of vernacular architecture before the 16th century. The architecture of the medieval period, based on a system of organized craftsmanship and international exchange of ideas, reflected the socio-cultural universalism of approach that characterized the Middle Ages. This approach of course allowed for a certain flexibility on the part of the master craftsmen and their patrons, but always within an essentially shared architectural language. A vernacular tradition can only truly be said to have come into being in the 16th century, when the architectural language became more heterogeneous. In countries that were in contact with Latin culture, the upper classes began to distance themselves culturally from the rest of the population, and a distinctly élitist type of architecture was developed to serve their needs. This process began with the Renaissance and was accompanied by a deliberate rejection of Late Gothic. Although elements of the medieval tradition persisted after this time, they were increasingly to be found only in the architecture of the lower classes, until by the end of the 19th century the medieval tradition had been abandoned even in peasant buildings. In countries less affected by Latin culture, on the other hand, such as Russia (where knowledge of Western models was very limited before the 18th century), it is possible to trace the steady development of a very different vernacular architecture, influenced primarily by Byzantine and local architectural traditions.

The truly vernacular architecture of Central and Eastern Europe can therefore be defined as an essentially middle-class phenomenon that sprang up in the gap between the élitist 'high' styles to which the Renaissance gave an impetus and the 'primitive' architecture of the lowest social classes. Gothic forms, techniques and design models continued to be used by bricklayers and carpenters associated in town guilds, who inherited the traditions of medieval builders but whose social and professional status was lowered by the emergence of architecture as a profession. These craftsmen designed and constructed buildings

essentially for the middle classes, to which they themselves belonged. They remained largely unaware of the new theory of architecture, based on the writings of Vitruvius, and if they occasionally applied non-technical rules in their work, these were usually various geometric combinations that belonged to the orally transmitted traditions of craftsmanship. Thus, when their work incorporated Renaissance, Mannerist or Baroque elements, these were usually superficial features; they never adopted the vocabulary or syntax, as it were, of these high styles.

Towards the end of the 17th century, the gap between the formalized Baroque architecture of the upper classes and the vernacular became even greater, and guild craftsmanship, already being held in lower social and professional esteem than in the medieval period, suffered as a result of the increasing influence of international models, exacerbating the social divisions within society. Vernacular architecture did, however, survive as a regional form of expression until the arrival of the Industrial Revolution. This brought with it a polarization of cultures, cosmopolitan industrialism being opposed to regional agrarianism. Peasants and others continued to use and in some cases still to produce the provincial architecture of villages and small communities, providing a final flourishing of guild craftsmanship that has assumed an importance in the cultural landscape of the 19th and 20th centuries. This building continued to combine various forms of earlier building, including elements derived from Gothic architecture, often in a simplified, reductive or even primitive form, thereby deepening the process of regionalization. Culturally isolated, however, unable to harness the great improvements in engineering and construction techniques of the Industrial Revolution or to capture the imagination of the powerful middle and upper classes, this architecture had little influence and was only a distant echo of the earlier middle-class tradition of vernacular building.

(ii) Development. Despite the shared cultural background in which it was rooted, the vernacular architecture of Eastern and Central Europe displayed great regional diversity. One reason for this was that in many communities local building traditions had already been established by the various Slavic groups who constituted the nucleus of the population in the first millennium AD. These traditions continued to be used in a variety of ways in village architecture, both in regions where wood was the predominant material (especially log structures, which showed very little development from the building techniques of the Iron Age) and in those where clay-and-stone walled structures predominated (representing to some extent a continuation of the Roman and Byzantine building traditions). At the end of the medieval period, when a true vernacular architecture began to appear, the area in which wood predominated included the Alps, the Sudeten, the Carpathians (and the land beyond them to the north) as well as all of north-eastern Europe; the clay-and-stone tradition, on the other hand, prevailed in the Danube basin and the area north of the Black Sea.

Both regions, however, were affected by the introduction from the west of brick, stone and more sophisticated uses of timber (mainly timber-frame structures but also south German log architecture), which spread through

Lower Silesia and along the Danube. The spread of this artistically and technically sophisticated architecture, which had been adopted by the Church, royalty and nobility, was partly the result of German expansion. Except in the more urbanized areas, the dissemination of the new techniques of urban craftsmanship and building was relatively limited before the 16th century. The first social group to assimilate the new influences were the more prosperous free peasants, but later others too benefited from them as landowners became responsible for the construction of housing for those tied to their land. Although in the more rural areas the old-fashioned tradition of simple wood building occasionally persisted, by the end of the medieval period it had been almost entirely superseded elsewhere by Gothic carpentry and was confined to the eastern regions, as the new influences spread from the west. This process continued as Late Gothic timber architecture and then the vernacular style that succeeded it took root throughout an area extending to the ethnic Polish–Russian border.

In the region beyond, the Ukrainian and Belarussian peasantry clung to a conservative, anti-Latin and anti-Gothic tradition, and they largely continued to do so until the mid-20th century. In this vast region, extending into Asia, Greek influence was evident, and some brick ecclesiastical buildings were occasionally built in a Byzantine style. In the early 18th century some examples of Western-style brick architecture also began to appear in the areas to the west, making the development of vernacular architecture possible, but this process was not widespread. It was only in Moscow, at the end of the 15th century, that other styles took root. Here architects summoned from Lombardy introduced a style characterized by modified Byzantine and Renaissance elements, and this was gradually disseminated throughout the Russian Empire. Timber imitations of buildings in this style were constructed, and primitive local structural techniques were very creatively adapted for the erection of unusual tower churches and the construction of massive fortresses. This Byzantine and Byzantine–Renaissance brick and timber architecture, however, while apparently formally part of the East European vernacular tradition, was in reality a direct continuation of the pre-Gothic architectural tradition.

The speed with which timber was superseded by brick and stone at the end of the Middle Ages varied from one region to another and from one period to another. In Poland, for example, at the end of the medieval period less than 1% of buildings in towns and villages were of brick, and timber and clay remained the predominant materials. In the more urbanized areas of Bohemia, Silesia and Prussia (the former Teutonic lands), on the other hand, the process kept pace with developments in Western Europe. Indeed, by the end of the 16th century in Bohemia timber had ceased to be used for churches, town houses and the residences of the nobility.

This process of development was brought to a halt at the beginning of the 17th century in all the countries involved in the Thirty Years War (1618–48). This was a period of relative peace, however, in the Polish–Lithuanian Commonwealth, which therefore began to catch up with earlier developments further south as timber at last gave way to brick and stone as the dominant materials, and vernacular housing programmes were expanded in a

process corresponding to the Great Rebuilding that took place at this time in Western Europe. In the middle of the 17th century this process was also halted by wars, and a period of general impoverishment followed, with the number of town masons decimated. The need for speedy reconstruction led to a revival of timber building, which was not only substantially cheaper than stone—and therefore better suited to the ailing economic condition—but could also make use of the unskilled workforces of the great estates. Log buildings, exhibiting varying degrees of building expertise, began once again to predominate over timber-frame structures, a process that inhibited masonry for another 80 years. Although there was a modest revival of masonry in the last quarter of the 17th century and (on a smaller scale) in the second decade of the 18th, this was restricted almost entirely to the aristocracy and nobility. A steady and enduring development did take place in brick architecture in Bohemia and Silesia in the period after the Thirty Years War, but it was not until the 1720s that this development was resumed in the Polish–Lithuanian Commonwealth.

(iii) Building types. The vernacular architecture of Eastern and Central Europe was characterized by the continued use of medieval building types, especially in the areas of housing and in buildings used for manufacture and services. The post-medieval typology was fairly uniform and limited to a few basic models and their derivatives. In areas with a higher standard of living larger buildings were constructed, and their interiors became more adapted to various specialized functions. Thus certain old types, such as tower houses, ceased to be erected, while others were continued and even developed. The latter include manor houses (which developed until the beginning of the 17th-century) and more modest town houses (until the mid-18th century). The earliest preserved timber examples date from the 17th century, but the evolution of vernacular residential architecture before this time can be observed through masonry.

Another characteristic of vernacular architecture was that, where circumstances allowed, individual types of building (whether local or imported) could be realized in different materials and at different stages of their development. They could then undergo further development or continue to be built in an unmodified, even in medieval, form. Moreover, within the framework of their functional types, they could overlap, effectively producing a vast range of hybrid examples. Some types were more permanently adopted in a given locality or region, largely due to their serial construction at the instigation of a patron. This type of standardization of stone or timber architecture often took place during rebuilding after fire damage or war devastation, or following the foundation of new towns and villages or the improvement of existing ones. It could also be the result of less pragmatic aims, such as the wish to express order, prestige, a particular artistic programme or even utopian ideas. The most commonly unified elements were façades, where an arcaded structure was favoured; the tendency towards uniformity of plans was strongest in areas of new settlement and expansion. The typology and form of such architecture usually resulted from both the needs of the investor and the professional initiative of the builder (a master mason or carpenter). The vernacular character of the architecture remained unchanged even when a wealthy and educated investor engaged an architect to design it. The same applies to service buildings with vernacular features, which were designed by engineers and architects and built in the 18th and 19th centuries in towns, villages and trade and industrial settlements founded at the initiative of great estate owners and capitalists or as state policy. Reference to the local village and town architecture was made not only by professional designers; from the end of the 18th century construction manuals also frequently included such conservative examples. Economic issues may have been the decisive factors here, but the idea of the suitability of such traditional architecture for the lower sections of society could also have derived from such concepts as the Renaissance and Baroque notion of decorum (the 'rustic style'), the Enlightenment belief in the morally healthy proximity to Nature or the Romantic idealization of peasant culture.

Regardless of its scale and function, vernacular house-types were based on pre-Gothic models. These were generally constructed on a regular, usually rectangular plan and took the form of simple cubes with massive walls of stone, clay or logs; only timber-frame walls and gables were of lighter construction. With the exception of the gently sloping roofs of the log structures (which were an archaic, disappearing type), the raftered construction and pitch of roofs were based on the Gothic tradition. Initially, gabled roofs predominated in the west and north, while hipped roofs were more common in the south; from the 17th century gambrel roofs became widespread, particularly in the Carpathian region, while from the 18th century half-hipped roofs began to predominate. Where the Gothic tradition was strong, overhanging gables were common, as were broad eaves, while in north-eastern

Slovakia the gables of chimneyless houses were given the most varied forms.

The most popular type of vernacular house was based on a plan that was three units wide, where the main room (usually with an adjacent service room) was separated by a hallway from smaller rooms. This type, adopted from central Germany during the Middle Ages, continued to be used until the 17th century by moderately affluent nobility and the clergy for their country houses. At times this type also served as a vernacular point of departure for architects designing manor houses and palaces in the high style. In its classic, late medieval version derived from the German *Wohnstallhaus*, the single-storey three-unit type of house was often also adopted by wealthy peasants, while peasants who were less wealthy often reduced the type to just the main room, hallway and a single service room. In the western reaches of Bohemia and Silesia single-storey three-unit houses were built not only in villages but also in smaller towns from as early as the beginning of the 17th century. This type of village house spread eastwards through Silesia and Poland to Russia, in line with German expansion to the north of the Karkonosze and Carpathian Mountains. In the 17th century such houses were built in East Prussia and later in many parts of Poland, particularly in the rural and industrial settlements of magnates. In the 18th century, peasant houses in Prussia and northern Poland were in most cases reduced versions of the same type, but without the service room opposite the main room and with the plan being almost a square.

Another house type also connected with German expansion was the single-storey terrace house with a wide open passageway, situated in towns or, occasionally, in densely built-up villages (see fig. 18). It was not common in northern regions of Eastern Europe. This type evolved as an adaptation of the archaic German house to the requirements of terrace building and was adopted in areas

18. Houses in Biecz, Poland, 15th–18th centuries; woodcut by Feliks Zabłocki, 63×121 mm, after an untraced drawing by Jan Matejko, *c.* 1870, from K. W. Wójcicki: *Works of Jan Matejko* (Warsaw, 1873) (Warsaw, National Museum)

where the population, despite involvement in minor craft and commercial activity, remained dependent to varying degrees on agriculture. In its rustic, pre-Gothic version this type, with only one narrow room partitioned off from the rest of the large space, survived vestigially until the end of the 19th century in German timber building in the Spiš region (Slovakia), where more sophisticated variants of it were later built. This essentially urban type of house in its Late Gothic stage of development was adopted by vernacular architecture, but the passageway was transformed into a spacious hallway, and the kitchen was located behind the main room, in the place originally occupied by an open hearth. If the house had a wide frontage a granary was occasionally built on the other side of the hallway, thus establishing a precedent for a series of service rooms. The evolution of such planning followed two basic patterns: either the main room was widened at the expense of the hallway (which was often already reduced in width by the granary) or the house was extended along the length of the plot, thus creating a plan that was three units deep.

Town houses of two or more storeys built for merchants and the urban élite represented the highest class of domestic building to be adopted from the Late Gothic by vernacular builders. The largest concentration of such buildings was in Germanized towns in the most urbanized and economically developed regions, such as Bohemia, Moravia and Silesia (see CZECH REPUBLIC, fig. 4). In the vast areas of rural Poland, where townspeople were economically and politically weak, multi-storey houses were built in significant numbers only in a few major towns. In houses of this type living-quarters were located on the upper storey. Plans remained basically unchanged throughout the later stages of development, as both the narrowness of the houses and density of building restricted the opportunities for improvement. The upper storey was either built on to an existing single-storey structure of the type described above, or the Mediterranean type of single-family house, with the living-quarters upstairs, was adopted directly. Gradually, the increasing density of population led to the subdivision of the upper storey or the construction of additional storeys, laid out like the ground-floor and intended for letting. They were reached by means of a stairwell lit from above by a lantern in the roof.

All these types of dwellings, adopted from Western Europe and frequently rooted in the architecture of the early Middle Ages, combined with influences derived from the primitive buildings of the Slavs. Throughout north-eastern Europe the latter were based on the archaic type of single-room log house with a corner hearth and stove. This type was transformed during the medieval period by the construction of a granary near to the so-called 'black' (sooty) room; the passageway linking the two was transformed into a hallway, and the granary was made into the 'white' room. This simple layout occurred independently in other regions of Central and Eastern Europe, notably in clay and stone houses in Hungary. In Belarus, and Russia, houses based on this model continued to be built using primitive log construction until the 20th century. In central and western Poland, however, they were adapted or incoporated into vernacular architecture with improved roof structures and log walls, and occasionally with the assimilation of post-Gothic decoration. Similarly, vernacular architecture influenced houses of another simple type, with a hallway flanked by a main room and a service room, the latter occasionally transformed into the 'white' room. Houses with this layout were built in both Polish and Russian villages in the Carpathian Mountains, but the majority were built in a wide belt stretching from Germany through central and eastern Poland. The older examples from this area had the entrance in the shorter side of the building, which had either broad eaves or an arcade. Such houses have their counterpart in the Greek megaron, and there is evidence that structures of this type were built on the plains of Central Europe before the arrival of the Slavs. Independently of the typology of the whole house, certain significant elements developed independently and were often combined with various house-types. The kitchen and heating appliances were particularly important. From the late Middle Ages they were often confined to the 'black kitchen', which was adopted from monastic and castle architecture. The placing of these appliances in the main room indicates a Slavic origin of the layout, while their positioning in the hallway points to a German origin. Similarly arcades, which were a typically Mediterranean feature, were adopted in the north in the late Middle Ages and subsequently became associated with every house-type.

(iv) High-style influences. From the second half of the 16th century new Italianate elements of high-style architecture began to filter into the buildings of many sections of society and were increasingly reflected in more modest architecture. In terms of spatial planning, this process primarily involved the standardization of traditional plans and elevations through the application of the classical rules of axiality and symmetry. Vernacular architecture of the nobility and patrician town houses were widely affected by this process before the mid-18th century. It only reached the more modest urban buildings in the mid-18th century, however, and the post-vernacular peasant cottages in the second half of the 19th. Specific new stylistic features were most evident in the architectural and decorative motifs, rather than in overall structure and design. From the mid-16th century the upper–middle sections of society, including the less affluent nobility, the clergy and the burghers, usually adopted Italianate designs for their increasingly numerous brick buildings. On the whole, however, this involved no more than the addition of fashionable decoration to post-medieval manors, town halls and town houses, which continued to follow traditional designs in terms of their structure and spatial layout.

Renaissance motifs in vernacular architecture were derived from a number of sources. Initially, examples were provided by élitist Italianate architecture at the royal courts of Buda, Prague and Kraków, simplified to varying degrees. These influenced both local builders and also, to some extent, north Italian bricklayers and masons, who had migrated in great numbers to Central and Eastern Europe from the second quarter of the 16th century. The latter, however, had acquired knowledge of Renaissance forms at the building sites of Lombardy and the Veneto, where they had often been employed as unskilled workers and had thus not always learnt to use the formal vocabulary correctly. Consequently, like all the local builders they drew on a wide variety of manuals, especially Sebastiano Serlio's architectural treatise. By *c.* 1600 the north Italian immigrants had absorbed the local Gothic traditions and fused them with the contemporary architectural language. In culturally peripheral regions, which Upper Hungary (now Slovakia) and Transylvania (Romania) had become on account of their political instability and the threat of Turkish expansion, further transformation of vernacular brick architecture virtually ceased until the mid-18th century. Elsewhere in the region vernacular architecture was influenced by elements of Italian Mannerism, generally through local high-style examples. In some areas, especially in Silesia and the lands of the Polish–Lithuanian Commonwealth, a number of builders looked to Netherlandish and north German examples, which were already popular with the German craftsmen living in these areas.

The masters of the Lublin Bricklayers' Guild were at the forefront of the continuous search for new means of artistic expression. Irrespective of their Italian, German or Polish origin, their vernacular work combined diverse local and imported forms, resulting in a rich and vivid artistic language that was independent of the canons of West European art. The economic and political decline of the Polish–Lithuanian Commonwealth in the second half of the 17th century disrupted and terminated the richest sequence in the development of vernacular architecture. At the same time in the Habsburg Empire, following the end of the Thirty Years War (1618–48), there was a period of splendid architectural development that also involved lower sections of society. In the 18th century, masons' guilds, no longer reinforced by Italians, began to lose their influence as an architectural community, sharing their virtual demise with that of the Ancien Régime. Thus,

master masons either merely worked to the designs of others, thus following non-vernacular models, or they simplified vernacular models to a radical degree. Nonetheless, the successive stages in the transformation of Baroque and *Zopfstil* (Austrian Baroque classicism) had a spectacular influence on the vernacular architecture of towns in Bohemia and Silesia, and later in Hungary. They also sporadically affected western Poland from the mid-18th century and, after 1772, that part of its southern region which was under the rule of the Habsburg Empire. This involved not only the Baroque treatment of gables and gates but even the addition of pilasters on façades. In Habsburg lands stone village architecture, especially that of the traditional Danube type, which was deeply rooted in the pre-Gothic period, was often decorated with corrupted Baroque forms from the late 18th century to the mid-19th.

In timber architecture, however, Late Gothic forms remained dominant for considerably longer than in brick. The vernacular architecture that succeeded Gothic is not recognizable in any timber structures from before the early 17th century, by which time the technical development of carpentry was complete and the construction of high-style Renaissance and Mannerist architecture in timber had proved completely unsuccessful. Vernacular timber architecture was hardly influenced even by Italianate decorative motifs; the Baroque proved to have a slightly greater impact, and elements of the style were adopted sporadically from the mid-18th century. From the late 17th century leading architects had begun to design manor houses and churches in timber as high-style buildings. Although Baroque in their typology and architectural vocabulary these were usually erected by carpenters who simplified the Italianate forms of detail and ornamentation and

19. Peasant houses in Chochołów, Poland, 19th century

continued to draw mainly on Gothic forms and techniques. Moreover, in the 18th century timber churches and manor houses were founded only by the minor nobility, and they were built by master carpenters who copied the earlier models of such structures without any guidance from an architect. Thus certain contemporary stylized forms, such as baluster-shaped columns or carved arcades over gates and covered walkways, reached the more modest architecture of Central and Eastern Europe through such Baroque, partly vernacular timber structures. In the mid-18th century gables with scrolled sides and decorative clapboarding were introduced following an expansion of the timber industry.

Generally, therefore, few highly qualified master carpenters came into contact with high-style architecture in the 18th century, although there were numerous carpentry workshops of lesser quality in towns and villages and at aristocratic courts throughout the Polish–Lithuanian lands. The disparate standards and forms of their work reflected the agricultural character of the economy and the under-urbanization of the country, as well as the consequent loosening of cultural ties with the West, the growing differences between town and country, the decline of urban craftsmanship and the concentration of such activity at the estates of the nobles. Despite the increasingly primitive character of the products of these workshops, however (see fig. 19), the craftsmen never returned to the archaic Slav building techniques but continued to rely on

Gothic structures as well as Renaissance and Baroque architectural forms.

BIBLIOGRAPHY
J. G. Pounds: *Eastern Europe* (London, 1969)
A. Rapoport: *House Form and Culture* (Englewood Cliffs, 1969)
V. Mencl: *Lidová architektura v Československu* [Folk architecture in Czechoslovakia] (Prague, 1980)
D. S. Rugg: *Eastern Europe* (London and New York, 1985)
A. Miłobędzki: 'Architecture in Wood: Technology, Symbolic Content, Art', *Artibus & Hist.*, x/19 (1989), pp. 177–206

ADAM MIŁOBĘDZKI

4. NORTH AMERICA. The study of vernacular architecture in North America raises particular problems and issues, since there is little consensus as to what sorts of buildings or landscapes the study embraces. Although formerly it was taken to include mainly rural folk buildings, and primarily houses and farm buildings, this is now taken to be too limited a definition, giving too much emphasis to building types and not enough to the broader questions concerning the attitudes to building of particular communities and characterizing their architectural production. However, while it may be important to stress the connection with tradition as an important element in the vernacular, the ordinary architecture of the USA and Canada cannot be related to any single long-standing or indigenous tradition.

Little colonial building was done before the late 16th century, and nothing survives from earlier than the 17th;

20. John Truman House, Sadsbury Township, Chester County, Pennsylvania, late 18th century

21. Ebenezer Wells House, Deerfield, Franklin County, Massachusetts, c. 1750

moreover, the building undertaken since this time has an extraordinary heterogeneity, relating to the building techniques and traditions of the many immigrant groups that settled across the continent, adapted to locales and materials. These diverse traditions inevitably constitute an important (and perhaps unique) area of research not only for architectural specialists but also for those interested in social, historical and other issues. Rather than attempt within the space available to discuss the whole range of traditions and approaches, therefore, this section gives a brief overview of late 20th-century approaches to the subject, by looking first at some specific issues relating to the study of the architecture associated with certain specific communities and then at perceptions of more general questions of approach and method.

(i) Diverse traditions. (ii) Historiography.

(i) Diverse traditions. The settlement architecture of the British, Germans, Dutch, Scandinavians, French, Spanish and African Americans provides a wide range of subject-matter for the student of North American vernacular architecture. Over a century of vernacular architecture documentation has shown that the colonial experience documented in the 17th and 18th centuries is anything but uniform. Regional variations, change over time, external influences, social class and local economics as well as practical exigencies all contributed to the creation of numerous permutations of architectural expression within the broader colonial context. The complexity of North America's wealth of vernacular building traditions is reflected in the architectural legacy of the middle colonies

of the USA. A building such as the John Truman House (see fig. 20) may be taken to illustrate the best of rural housing in the post-Revolutionary English-speaking settlements of the middle American colonies. In plan the house, commissioned by a Quaker family, is based on a passage extending half the depth of the house. The rear rooms include the kitchen and a narrow stair. The use of such a durable material as stone, the two-storey elevation and the multi-room plan were all exceptional qualities, however, in a countryside where a significant majority of houses were of log construction, one storey high and generally comprising a single room. It should not therefore be taken as representative; rather, it should be borne in mind that the colonial vernacular architecture of the region is made up not only of such Anglo-American building traditions but also of those of Dutch, Scandinavian and German settlers.

Even the Anglo-American traditions are far from homogeneous, as can be seen in the discernible traditions of regional English, Welsh and Scottish–Irish communities. While each group exerted an influence on the others, ranging from simple construction details to cross-cultural modifications in house plans, the colonial architectural landscape remained a composite of many building idioms. The cultural origins for building details in log construction, framing sections and fireplace placement continue to be contested by advocates of the architectural primacy of various ethnical groups. The primary consideration in this debate, however, is that the complex overlays of colonial cultures in the middle Atlantic colonies and more broadly through North America gave rise to an exceptionally diverse vernacular architecture. The three specific traditions examined here must therefore be regarded as exemplifying this diversity rather than as giving an exhaustive account of it.

(a) Anglo-American. The variety of buildings associated with Anglo-American vernacular architecture alone illustrates the diversity of American tradition. The vernacular architecture of the Anglo-American colonies historically has been divided into three broad regions: the north-east seaboard, extending from southern New England into the Canadian maritimes; the middle colonies, extending from New York south through parts of Maryland and Virginia; and the tidewater South, extending from coastal Virginia through the South Carolina and Georgia low country. The vernacular architecture in each not only is regionally distinctive but also comprehends a multiplicity of lesser local traditions, including those of other settlement groups. One key characteristic taken from each region's Anglo-American building stock underscores the historical diversity of North American vernacular architecture even within the limited context of the colonial buildings associated with the most politically powerful group.

New England studies have long focused on the characteristics associated with heavy timber-frame construction. The timber-framed houses of New England were carefully recorded and compared to English precedent in terms of house form or type and construction techniques. While some investigators contented themselves with producing catalogues of New England house-types or framing practices, others have developed an understanding of the historic culture that produced these buildings. These are represented by investigations into how British settlers ordered domestic and work space and have looked at the major plan types such as hall–parlour houses and three-bay English-style barns. More recent investigations of

New England houses place equal stress on the ways in which construction techniques or spatial arrangements maintain certain Old World characteristics even as they acquire distinctively New World details.

The Ebenezer Wells House (see fig. 21) represents the upper range, but not the best, of two-storey centre-chimney New England houses of the 18th and early 19th centuries. Regional features include the balanced symmetrical elevation juxtaposed with a central chimney and a lobby entry and stair between the chimney and front door. Although many central-chimney New England houses were built with a lean-to for service functions such as cooking, the Wells House sheltered these activities in a rear ell, which was the reused first house on the property. The amount of window glass in the Wells House was not uncommon in New England houses of this quality. Recent studies of the two-storey, central-chimney, hall-parlour houses with service sheds most closely identified with New England have revealed these dwellings as historically more exceptional than common. Parallel research suggests not only that the regionally characteristic service sheds became generally popular only towards the end of the 18th century, but also that they relate to much broader cultural attitudes regarding the integration and division of domestic work within the house and the use of furniture and architectural trim to create socially significant hierarchies within the dwelling. The most innovative work on the colonial architecture of New England now looks at buildings in the context of broader cultural systems, such as the social and political economy of landscape development and change. Thus, the vernacular architecture associated with the Anglo-American settlements of colonial New England is defined as much by the historic and cultural processes that contributed to its development, use and symbolic character as by the actual buildings.

The definition of vernacular architecture by context in North America is just as evident in the Anglo-American settlement housing of the southern colonies. In the Chesapeake Bay country of Virginia and Maryland, vernacular architecture studies have relied increasingly on archaeological data to identify historical building cycles. The great colonial plantation seats, long interpreted in terms of academic European architectural concepts, are now understood in the context of a socially stratified plantation society in transition. Equally representative of this context, however, are such buildings as Pear Valley (see fig. 22), a particularly well-built one-room house of the mid-18th century from the Chesapeake Bay region. Distinguishing features include the use of an exterior end-chimney and timber-frame construction with a brick end. The interior originally consisted of exposed and chamfered framing elements. In size (*c.* 5.0×6.5 m) the building represents the common standard for the vast majority of 18th-century residents throughout the Chesapeake and adjacent regions of the American south.

Central to understanding the historical significance of southern building periods is the architectural evidence of construction, ornament, setting and function throughout the 17th and early 18th centuries. The lack of durable construction techniques using full foundations is especially significant. Archaeology has revealed that the most common method of construction in the southern colonies

22. Pear Valley, near Machipungo, Northampton County, Virginia, mid-18th century

throughout the colonial period involved framing houses on either wooden posts set directly into the ground or on easily replaced wooden blocks. The advent and timing of durable construction (that is, construction techniques employing full foundations) have led historians to re-evaluate the social and economic development of the southern colonies. The vernacular architecture of post-in-ground houses and farm buildings is now understood in the broader context of mortality, agricultural economy, social organization, available labour and settlement ethos. Vernacular architecture in these studies is both accepted as a form of historical text, to be read in conjunction with other forms of documentary and material evidence, and viewed as an integral part of larger sets of cultural relationships of which architecture is only one component.

(b) African American. The complexity of vernacular architecture in the American South is demonstrated by the fact that a full understanding of the Anglo-American traditions requires a knowledge also of African American building traditions. African American influences on the broader body of southern vernacular architecture extended well beyond the construction of their own quarters. In southern cities before and after the American Revolution, slaves and significantly smaller numbers of free African Americans constituted the core of building trades. Far from being universally relegated to the status of untrained labourers employed at individual building sites, African Americans, both enslaved and free, were often highly accomplished builders. Ezra Waite, the British-trained contractor for the ornate townhouse (1756–9) of Miles Brewton at CHARLESTON, SC, is known to have possessed British architectural books, carved architectural trim and slaves skilled in the building trades. Slave-owners in other cities and rural areas routinely leased their skilled workers to individuals engaged in building projects. Although slaves and free African Americans were clearly employed in major building projects, their own living accommoda-tion was generally significantly meaner. Behind such southern city mansions as the Miles Brewton House or the great Virginian plantation houses of the James River Valley ranged one- and two-storey slave quarters combined with kitchens, wash houses and stables. Thus the emphasis on the cosmopolitan tastes and British building traditions celebrated in early studies of southern plantation architec-ture has given way to the recognition of a less sumptuous and ethnically more diverse vernacular architecture. The discovery and analysis of African features in buildings ranging from plantation mansions to urban quarters, the question of acculturation and ethnic identity and the issues intrinsic to racially segregated landscapes remain central to the study of African American vernacular architecture by historians, architectural historians, folklorists and an-thropologists. Examples of these features include the chimneypieces with African faces carved by Thomas Day at the Long House (1856–60), Caswell County, NC.

The study of African American building traditions in the context of southern vernacular architecture highlights several qualities that further define the field as it currently exists and the buildings that it comprehends. Vernacular architecture studies stress the dynamic, and often strained or exploitative, exchange between different social, ethnic and class groups. The design and layout of vernacular buildings provide evidence for compromises and losses in ethnic identity as well as the covert maintenance of custom associated with the forced acculturation of ethnic groups. Moreover, the study of African American vernacular architecture reveals the flow of architectural ideas ranging from construction details to decorative schema back and forth across the social spectrum. More importantly, ver-nacular buildings are seen as a type of historical text or material document providing critical evidence about the ways in which people interacted within the structured confines of prejudice and segregation.

(c) German. Although German-speaking settlers ap-peared throughout the colonies during the 18th century, they are most closely associated with the Middle Atlantic region, especially with central Pennsylvania, and western Maryland and Virginia. The building traditions of Penn-sylvania Germans were first remarked upon in the 18th century as being distinctive, and in some regards, such as household heating systems and agricultural building de-sign, worthy of emulation. Although there were several types of houses and barns erected, occupied and used by German settlers, the two most extensively studied are the three- or four-room *Flurküchen* (or entry-kitchen) house and the large multi-storey 'bank barns'. The examination of these building types has included the documentation of specific construction techniques and decorative elements in a manner consonant with the study of British, African American, Dutch and French settlement architecture.

The entry-kitchen house is organized around a large central chimney pile containing an open hearth fronting the combination entry and kitchen. A stove opening or, less often, a small hearth on the rear of the stack provides the means for heating the ground-floor parlour. The distinctive appearance of the entry-kitchen house led vernacular architecture historians to search for its Old World antecedents from the Rhenish Palatinate to Moravia in a pattern similar to the quest in East Anglia for English antecedents for New England houses. More recent studies have focused on the migration of German-speaking set-tlers within the USA and the distribution of European building forms and techniques in the larger landscape. This approach, which combines the method and theory of historical geography with architectural history, asks questions about the dynamics of ethnic migrations in the New World and the ways in which individuals and communities interacted and influenced each other in the dissemination of architectural concepts.

Later German settlements throughout the USA exhibit many of the same processual qualities. German settlements of the 19th century in Missouri, Wisconsin and Texas document parallel patterns of house form, acculturation and change over time. The distinctiveness of German-American architecture was as obvious to late 19th-century observers of the Kansas Germans as they had been to commentators in Pennsylvania a century before. As re-cently as the early 20th-century, German-speaking settlers on the plains of the USA and Canada built earthen-walled, thatched roof houses with attached barns, only to replace them within one or two generations by more popular building forms.

The two- and three-storey multi-level barns of the 19th-century Pennsylvania countryside, however, have led to different sorts of inquiries. A few of these 'bank barns' combining horse and cow stalls below and grain storage, threshing space and wagon floors above, were erected as early as the 1770s. Their general popularity, however, blossomed in the early 19th century with more acute sensibilities about the organization and reform of agricultural practice. The old questions of European antecedents, both German and English, for these buildings has given way to explorations into the process of agricultural improvement. The growing popularity of large agricultural buildings with consolidated functions paralleled the growing public debates over scientific farming and shifts in land-ownership patterns. Similar issues have been raised around other work structures, such as those used in the fisheries of Newfoundland.

(ii) Historiography. Vernacular architecture in North America, however, is more than the sum of the building traditions of the above groups and of its other myriad immigrant communities. An overall definition of the term that would apply to all communities remains elusive. While attempts to define vernacular architecture in terms of particular types of buildings have been made, the frustration inherent in the limitations of physically or stylistically defining traditional buildings has produced a second school of thought in North American studies, which defines vernacular architecture as an approach to the investigation and interpretation of commonplace buildings and environments (Wells, 1986; Carter and Herman, 1991). The range of both types of definitions is reflected in the articles printed in the *Perspectives in Vernacular Architecture* series published for the Vernacular Architecture Forum in the USA and in the proceedings of the Society for the Study of Architecture in Canada. Essays in both groups' publications have dealt with topics as diverse as Civil War military camp housing, automobile garages, adobe construction, fish merchants' houses, colonial room use, statistical studies of vanished architectural landscapes and town plans as well as investigations of regionally or ethnically defined building traditions. The authors of these studies include architectural historians, social historians, folklorists, geographers, archaeologists, anthropologists, historic preservation planners and architects, in fact all those with an interest in the design, creation and sociology of the built world. The two means for defining vernacular architecture—as a particular class of artefacts or as an approach to studying and interpreting the artefact—share the sense of traditional buildings and landscapes as both the products and agents of common usage and everyday communication. Vernacular building from this perspective, and as it is generally understood in North America, encompasses all the architecture of everyday perception and interaction.

Most studies are fundamentally regional in character. Almost all fieldwork-based studies of the built environment begin with an inventory of buildings within a given geographic area, ranging in size from a small rural community to a large multi-state or multi-province subregion. Henry Glassie, for example, recorded all the houses within a small section of the Virginia Piedmont and used the evidence of standing buildings to discuss far-reaching questions about design and cultural meaning in the built environment. John Lehr and others, in contrast, examined Ukrainian and German-Russian settler architecture across the plains of Canada in an effort to answer questions about settlement diffusion and the survival of ethnic traits in architecture. Regional studies tend to focus on questions of architectural change over time, ethnicity and acculturation, and the impact of industrialization and popular culture on established custom, all as they are reflected in the built environment.

As vague as any definition of North American vernacular architecture must be, studies of traditional buildings in the USA and Canada almost always emphasize one or more of the following elements: architectural form, construction, ornament, function and setting. The five elements clearly overlap and are unified by a concern for understanding and interpreting the historic, social and cultural context in which buildings and landscapes were created and used. Because context tends to define vernacular architecture, the best work on North American vernacular buildings attempts to integrate form, construction, ornament, function and setting elements into holistically conceived architectural histories. These include folklore studies ranging in setting from Newfoundland fishing villages or outports in the Canadian maritimes to Mormon religious settlements in the western USA, the social and architectural history of the plantation culture surrounding colonial Virginia parish churches, the spiritual ideology of the Shaker communities in New England and Kentucky (*see* SHAKERS, §1), popular culture and 19th-century domestic and agricultural reform, as well as the biography and ethnography of builders and clients.

The architectural legacies of the many immigrant groups that settled in North America as well as the promotion of popular building styles in the 19th century illustrate the ways in which form, construction, ornament, function, setting and context are represented in North American vernacular architecture and the difficulties inherent in drawing precise defined boundaries. As students of North American vernacular architecture grow increasingly sensitive to issues of ethnic and regional diversity, their emphasis on comprehending the logic and sensibility of Old World architectural values applied to New World situations remains intact. At the same time these studies recognize the development of distinctly American building traditions in terms of both the geographic movement of Americans across the larger landscape, the process of change over time represented in the architectural record of specific subregions and locales, and the interplay between innovation and established practice. The single best source introducing many of the major ethnic building groups in the USA and Canada remains Dell Upton's *America's Architectural Roots* (1986), which contains 22 descriptive entries, covering Japanese, Czech, Dutch, English, African and Danish building traditions.

BIBLIOGRAPHY

C. Carson and others: 'Impermanent Architecture in the Southern American Colonies', *Winterthur Port.*, xvi (1981), pp. 135–96
Perspectives in Vernacular Architecture (Columbia, 1982)
R. J. Lawrence: 'The Interpretation of Vernacular Architecture', *Vern. Archit.*, xiv (1983), pp. 19–28

D. Upton: 'The Power of Things: Recent Studies in American Vernacular Architecture', *Material Culture: A Research Guide*, ed. T. J. Schlereth (Lawrence, KS, 1985), pp. 57–78

D. Upton, ed.: *America's Architectural Roots: Ethnic Groups that Built America* (Washington, DC, 1986)

D. Upton and J. M. Vlach, eds: *Common Places: Readings in American Vernacular Architecture* (Athens, GA, 1986), pp. xiii–xxiv

C. Wells: 'Old Claims and New Demands: Vernacular Architecture Studies Today', *Perspectives in Vernacular Architecture*, ii (Columbia, 1986), pp. 1–10

T. Carter and B. L. Herman: 'Toward a New Architectural History', *Perspectives in Vernacular Architecture*, iv (Columbia, 1991)

BERNARD L. HERMAN

5. CENTRAL AND SOUTH AMERICA.

(i) Pre-Columbian and Hispanic models. The vernacular architecture of Central and South America is characterized by an extraordinary variety and morphological richness, reflecting with sensitivity both national and local history and moulded by diverse and subtle ethnic influences as well as by extremely wide-ranging geographical situations. While this variety and richness needs to be borne in mind, since the essence of the vernacular lies in its links with a local community, a distinctive and characteristic general feature of the vernacular architecture of Central and South America is its mixture of surviving indigenous traditions and fundamentally Spanish or Portuguese influences. On a smaller scale and again reflecting local history, there is also evidence in some regions of African and French ethnic influences and of later influences from other western European countries.

Although no examples of vernacular dwellings have survived from the Pre-Columbian period, documentary evidence—above all from Central America—provides information on the building traditions established before the time of the conquest. There exist mural and model representations, manuscript drawings and pictographic records as well as descriptions by the conquistadors and other chroniclers of the 16th century. Ceramic and stone models from Nayarit in Mexico, for example, dating from around the beginning of the Christian era, show rectangular houses, some with a single storey or where the top part of the house has been abated. Their high roofs with large eaves have such long ridges that at each end they bend inwards. Hernán Cortés, in the *Cartas de relación*, mentions dwellings made of straw and built on a masonry platform found in the warmer regions of the Mexican conquered territory. Other chroniclers from the same period write of houses made from sun-dried bricks, lime and stone, the last of these showing remarkable craftsmanship in the cutting and almost invisible joinery of the stone. The typical Aztec dwelling seems to have had very small windows and doors; many of the pictographic records of the ground-plans of dwellings—often including depictions of the area of worship, the barns and wells—provide useful information on domestic customs and family relationships.

With the domination of the Aztecs by the Spaniards and the birth of colonial architecture there began a process of cultural amalgamation. The indigenous masons, instructed by Spanish masters of works, retained their traditional knowledge while also learning new methods. From 1550, the dwellings of the conquistadors and the conquered were mixed territorially in the ancient urbanization of Tenochtitlán (now Mexico City), and thereafter all the architectural styles subsequently imported from Europe, from the Baroque to Modernism, took on a characteristically Latin American identity. Nevertheless, a vernacular architecture rooted in Pre-Columbian traditions is still produced in remote towns and isolated Indian communities, as in the single-room houses of the Chipaya in the Oruro department of Bolivia (see fig. 23).

A particularly important element in the Iberian influence was the introduction of urbanization. The orders given by Philip II in 1573 for the 'discovery, new population and pacification of the Indies' sought to impose not only a new social organization but also a new spatial structure. A process of architectural as well as religious evangelization ensued, in which the ordered layout dictated by Renaissance urban theory in Europe was imposed throughout the whole newly Hispanic territory; this has survived into

23. Circular Chipaya houses, built of earth with dried grass roofs, Department of Oruro, Bolivia

24. Calle Hatun Rumyoc, Cuzco, Peru, showing Spanish Colonial additions to Inca masonry (before 1533)

the 20th century, with a few exceptions owing to topography, throughout the whole of Castilian-speaking Latin America. However, the geometric and orthogonal layout of the towns founded or modified following Philip's decree was not in fact common throughout the Iberian peninsula, and nor was it wholly contradictory to Pre-Columbian traditions in Latin America. For example, while the central square can be traced back to its Mediterranean origins, the size of the examples built in Central and South America dates back to the time of the arrival of the conquistadors, when large public spaces already existed. Indeed, the new model city in the form of a chequer-board, with straight streets dividing blocks of buildings, with a central square of huge dimensions in which the powers of the Church and the government were united, and without a surrounding wall to impede the outward expansion of the city, can be seen as a new project for a new society, or rather a new world. This new project lent itself for many reasons to a process of architectural syncretism. Moreover, while new sacred buildings, monuments and palaces replaced existing structures, the effect was one of substitution and thus to some extent of continuity, in which the vernacular architecture of ordinary dwelling places was almost unaffected. This continuity is particularly evident in some streets in Cuzco, for example, where colonial architects added extra storeys to single-storey buildings of Inca masonry, preserving in some cases the shaded, narrow urban layout (see fig. 24).

(ii) The vernacular response. Characteristic of the surviving vernacular tradition was a reaction against the straight, wide streets of the new urban layouts. This reaction took the form of shaded, intimate interiors, protected from the new influences, as it were, by the exterior walls and often containing a patio, mirroring the Mediterranean tradition and symbolizing the mixture of cultures. Other characteristics are restricted to particular regions, reflecting the close link between vernacular architecture and the immediate environment. The huge differences in climate that can be found in the vast territory of Latin America, exacerbated by the mountainous landscape, necessarily result in an immense morphological diversity of habitat.

This diversity is further reinforced by the use of local materials, again reflecting regional climatic conditions. In the temperate regions, in towns and small cities, rows of terraced houses, usually of one storey, are predominant. Porches are common (despite the apparent reluctance of most housing to face the street), and porticos are often found around the inner patio. A huge variety of columns with their respective bases, shafts and capitals show the local peculiarities of the architecture; examples range from tree trunks joined together by ties to arcades with domes. Where the porch is absent, its place is sometimes taken by a roof with large eaves that protect the pedestrian from the sun as much as from the rain. The porticos that look on to the patios, and which are sometimes repeated at first-floor level to create half-open interior façades, form a corridor off which all the rooms lead and in which most family and social life is led. The patio itself, which is geometric in its layout and sometimes has a central fountain, is inspired much more by the plazas of a town than by a natural garden.

The shaded interiors created by these porticos and porches are frequently roofed with beams and roofing boards. The windows are very tall, with stone frames or frames in colours different from those of the façade, and are often protected by iron bars on the outside. A great variety of constructive solutions exists for roofs. They may be flat or pitched, and until the late 20th century they were made from straight slabs of concrete, covered with available raw materials, such as mud tiles or straw, according to the climatic conditions. The material used for the walls also depends on local conditions, although adobe is widely used for its thermal qualities as much in cold regions as in warmer ones. It may be smoothly inconspicuous or decoratively ostentatious, sometimes with joints of mud interspersed with stones from the river or ceramic pebbles to ensure that it is not washed away by the rain.

In the warmer and more rural regions detached dwellings are more common, each surrounded by its own small garden. These houses usually have a rectangular ground-plan, the two short sides sometimes being semicircular in shape; very occasionally the dwelling is completely circular (as on the Pacific coast of Mexico, where its origin is in the African Bautu). As is usually the case in the vernacular architecture of almost all of the vast Latin American territory, porticos are again common on either one or both sides of the longest façade, supporting an extension of the roof, or surrounding the whole house. Very occasionally houses can be found with roofs forming large eaves over the walls. Local vegetation, assembled according to varying local techniques, provides the principal building materials in these regions. Walls may be made from vertically arranged tree trunks connected by woven palm, or branches of trees may be laid horizontally and covered with mud mixed with fibres, left as they are or painted with lime; sometimes tree trunks alone may be used, roofed with hay, palm or local plants.

Most of these dwellings comprise a single multi-functional room in which, when the climate permits, the inhabitants sleep in hammocks. The solutions found for ventilation are often ingenious. Where there are no window openings, ventilation is provided by lattices made from adobe in the form of decorative patterns, by little bamboo bars and by woven liana. In certain countries and regions of Latin America the strong colouring of the vernacular architecture is remarkable and quite unlike any European examples. A notable example is a particular dark blue hue found in architectural details in the high plateaux of Mexico and used since Aztec times. Another trait common to this type of dwelling is the central role of the kitchen, in which in certain parts of Mexico the placentas of newly born babies are buried. Indeed, many of the mythical and spiritual aspects of vernacular architecture in Mexico have survived from Pre-Columbian times: the positioning of Mayan houses in the Yucatán peninsula, for example, reflected the community organization and the race of the inhabitants; although deeply affected by the orthogonal pattern imposed by the Spanish, the result was a new and organic architectural mix.

In the late 20th century the vernacular architecture of Latin America was subjected to another form of cultural domination, exercised in the name of modernity. Increasingly, examples of international modernist design took root in the capital cities and expanded towards the cities and towns of the provinces. This architecture, reflecting the modern principles of universality and supposed functionality, was incapable of being integrated into the vernacular context, since its internationalism and its hostility towards the domestic were alien to the very essence of the vernacular. Although ingenious examples of bricolage exist, making use of fragments of modern materials, such as plastics and laminates, this creativity is conditioned by poverty and can hardly be classified as vernacular. It is therefore only in minute details, such as the use of particular colours, that the vernacular tradition is visible, or else, paradoxically and with varying degrees of success, in the work of such modern architects as Luis Barragán.

BIBLIOGRAPHY
H. Cortés: *Cartas de relación* (Mexico City, 1969)
Transcripción de las ordenzas de descubrimiento de nueva población y pacificación de las Indias, dadas por Felipe II (Madrid, 1973) [facs.]
F. Vegas: *Venezuelan Vernacular* (Princeton, 1985)
G. Gasparini: *Arquitectura popular de Venezuela* (Caracas, 1986)
F. J. López Morales: *Arquitectura vernácula en México* (Mexico City, 1987)
J. A. Campos: *La arquitectura vernácula en México*, Cuadernos de arquitectura virreinal (Mexico City, 1989)
C. Aubry: *Arquitectura doméstica ecléctica en Argentina y Chile* (in preparation)

ADA DEWES, SERGIO PUENTE

6. AUSTRALASIA. European vernacular architecture in Australia owed very little to pre-existing Aboriginal building traditions, which related almost entirely to ephemeral constructions, but in New Zealand Maori construction methods were more compatible with European aspirations. The English first settled at Sydney in 1788, and the buildings that followed were generally British in concept, modified by factors of climate, locally available materials and distance from manufacturing centres. By 1836 all of what are now the states of Australia had been colonized to a greater or lesser extent (*see* AUSTRALIA, §II, 1). European settlement in New Zealand proceeded on a more tentative basis because the Maori were recognized politically, but it proceeded apace after the Treaty of Waitangi in 1840 (*see* NEW ZEALAND, §II). Despite other ethnic influences, such as that of the Germans in parts of Australia, and the French at Port Louis-Philippe (Akaroa),

New Zealand, the tone of both countries remained British. In most of New Zealand, British traditions were translated into timber, often explicitly imitating stonework, while Australia gradually developed a distinctive syndrome of elements, such as the encircling verandah and the use of corrugated iron in rural areas, the high-set house and exposed frame in tropical Queensland, and stud framing, brick veneering and Marseille tile roofing in the vernacular of the cities.

Locally available materials in Australia included: a range of stones; shells from Aboriginal middens, which were burnt for lime in coastal areas where limestone was not found; timbers, which were very hard but could be readily split; the bark of certain trees, which made a durable roofing and cladding material; some indigenous thatching substances, such as reeds and the *xanthorrhea* or grass tree; clay suitable for bricks; and a range of earths in different places suitable for the main European and Mediterranean earth-building methods. New Zealand generally had fine and much more easily worked timbers, little stone and plenty of thatching materials, but in Otago the situation was reversed because stone was available and timber was not. A range of earths were available, although, as with brick and stone, earth construction was to some extent inhibited by the prevalence of earthquakes.

In New Zealand, Maori craftsmen were actively engaged in building for the Europeans, and many of their materials and techniques, such as their *raupo* thatch roofing, passed into common use among the settlers. The most significant contribution of the Australian Aborigines was that they showed Europeans which species of tree provided useful bark, how to strip this and how to cure it. The building forms that resulted, however, owed little or nothing to Aboriginal models. By *c*. 1820 an ingenious system of roofing was developed in which the sheets were tied on to the roof and weighed down but had no fixings through them, thus avoiding the tendency for the sheets to tear apart as they shrank (see fig. 25). The same arrangement

25. Selector's hut of logs, slabs and bark, constructed without nails, Croajingalong, Gippsland, Victoria (Melbourne, State Library of Victoria, La Trobe Collection); from a photograph by Nicholas Caire, *c*. 1870

of timbers had previously been used on thatched roofs in Sumatra, but the Australian form probably evolved separately as a synthesis of elements from different European traditions of thatching, such as the longitudinal poles or *ledgers* of England and the raking poles, *stangen* or *gerten*, of Serbia and Russia.

Germans settled in South Australia in the 1840s and later spread to Western Victoria and to the Riverina of New South Wales. The goldrushes of the 1850s brought a greater mix of European races, some Americans and a considerable body of Chinese. Subsequent distinguishable ethnic minorities included Danes at Palmerston, New Zealand, from the late 1860s and in Gippsland, Victoria, from the 1870s. From *c.* 1860 the process of land selection in south-eastern Australia, by which people with little capital were enabled to establish farms, encouraged a great deal of owner-building in which vernacular traditions were often invoked. The financial depression of the 1890s gave rise to officially sponsored 'village settlements' in New South Wales and Victoria, where subsistence conditions applied, and primitive combinations of pug and timber necessarily resulted.

The fissile timbers of Australia encouraged the use of split slabs set in frames either vertically or horizontally (e.g. Dyraaba, Casino, NSW, early 19th century) and also provided shingles and palings. The European log cabin was rare, but in certain areas where there were native softwoods, small logs were set horizontally into the panels of a frame. This was done using cabbage tree palm in the first days of Sydney and on a more enduring basis with Murray pine in the vicinity of the Murray River. Combinations of timber and mud included traditional wattle and daub, which was used most in Western Australia and in Victoria. Just as in South Africa, the acacia tree became known as the 'wattle' because it could be woven in this way. The German settlers in South Australia and elsewhere used brick (e.g. Putlands Cottage, built *c.* 1840 at Paechtown, near Hahndorf, S Australia) or Dutch biscuits— stakes wound around with mud and straw—to fill the wall and ceiling panels of their framed or *fachwerk* houses. Pine and pug, a palisade of vertical timber daubed over with mud, was used later and more extensively in much the same German-influenced areas. In the mining areas of South Australia, Victoria and New South Wales a form of construction (perhaps best called pole and pug) was developed in which a frame using round trunks as verticals had light straight branches or poles nailed horizontally and fairly close together on both sides. The space between was packed with mud, and the two surfaces were daubed over to a smooth finish and in some cases plastered and ruled to look like masonry.

Sods or turfs seem to have been used to a small extent by Aboriginals in Victoria, but their more extensive use in Tasmania, Victoria, New South Wales and New Zealand is probably attributable to Irish and Scottish precedents. Apart from complete buildings of this material there were instances of its use for farm walls, planted along the top with furze or gorse in the British tradition. Even more commonly, sods were used for roofing heavily framed barns and in at least some cases were stob thatched in the Scottish manner. Cob is specifically documented only in Victoria and in New Zealand but must have been more

widely used. Pisé de terre or rammed earth appeared *c.* 1820 in Tasmania (e.g. Wanstead, Conara) and New South Wales and was specifically influenced by literary sources such as Abraham Rees's translation of François Cointeraux and by emigrants' manuals. In New Zealand, Pompallier House at Kororeka (1841–2) was built of pisé, under the supervision of the Lyonnais architect Louis Perret, who seems to have been guided by the description of pisé construction in Jean-Baptiste Rondelet's *Traité théorique*. From the 1840s pisé was being used extensively in South Australia and to some extent in Victoria; by the 1850s in Western Australia; and not long afterwards in Queensland. Adobe was used in Victoria and New South Wales, particularly in the village of Sodwalls, near Bathurst, NSW, and while its origin is debatable, it was used in at least some cases in the 1850s by miners who had been in California. It appeared in New Zealand at Wellington, where the adobe buildings were destroyed by earthquake in 1848, and it became common in Central Otago, perhaps through the influence of miners from Australia. Later still, an example in Queensland was reported to have been built by Mexican labour, while in Western Australia in the 1880s adobe was manufactured from a specifically local material, giant anthills.

Manufactured materials entered the vernacular in Australia to an unusual degree. Many of the vernacular forms depended on the cheaper nails that became available from the 1850s or on galvanized wire. Corrugated galvanized iron, although not manufactured locally until the 20th century, became ubiquitous and was especially prevalent in mining settlements. Ornamental cast iron, which gives some inner Australian suburbs a character as distinctive as that of New Orleans, had by the 1890s been rejected entirely by architects, but it remained a part of the vernacular until World War I. Once the intractability of the local hardwoods had been overcome by mechanical sawmilling, scantling could be produced in smaller standardized sizes, and the way was cleared for the evolution of the 'stud frame', a variant of the American balloon frame (*see* TIMBER STRUCTURE, §I, 2), and also for the exposed frame, lined only on the inner face, which became a characteristic of Queensland architecture. The hollow brick or brick cavity wall had been derived from England, and this was synthesized with the stud frame in the concept of brick veneer construction, which is the most distinctive aspect of the urban vernacular of the 20th century in south-eastern Australia.

Indigenous building materials played a lesser role in the 20th century. Slabs and bark continued in use in some country areas, but sod, cob and wattle and daub are no longer heard of. Various combinations of timber and pug were the norm in more remote or more depressed rural areas, especially lath and pug, a variation of pole and pug in which split or occasionally sawn laths were used. Pisé had become a particularly strong tradition in the Riverina of New South Wales, where it was later taken up by the architect Charles Horatio Macknight (*d* 1865), whose work was to be important in encouraging the revival of the technique in the 1950s and 1960s. By this time a fad of the young middle classes, pisé as well as adobe, which was revived in the same circles, could be considered as vernacular.

Between the later 1960s and 1990s the use of traditional materials such as mud brick left the province of the vernacular entirely and became the subject of technical classes and published newsletters, being taken up finally by commercial builders on a larger scale. Meanwhile the rural poor, especially in the depression from the late 1920s, had adopted forms of hut or 'humpy' construction much the same as those of many aboriginal groups, especially the use of beaten-out kerosene tins. These were used from the early 20th century not only as cladding for buildings but also for various forms of improvised 'bush' (rural) furniture. Special implements were developed for cutting and working them, and they were used on occasion in quite substantial farm buildings. A remarkable and quite large two-storey house, clad in kerosene tins by a soldier returned from World War I, has been preserved in Victoria.

BIBLIOGRAPHY

J.-B. Rondelet: *Traité théorique et pratique de l'art de bâtir* (Paris, 1802–17)

A. Rees, trans.: *The Works of Cointeraux on Rural and Economic Building* (Melbourne, 1817)

M. Lewis: *Victorian Primitive* (Melbourne, 1977)

P. Freeman: *The Woolshed: A Riverina Anthology* (Melbourne, 1980)

G. Young and others: *Lobethal 'Valley of Praise'* (Adelaide, 1983)

P. Bell: *Timber and Iron: Houses in North Queensland Mining Settlements, 1861–1920* (St Lucia, Queensland, 1984)

J. Salmond: *Old New Zealand Houses, 1800–1940* (Auckland, 1986)

J. Archer: *Building a Nation: A History of the Australian House* (Sydney, 1987)

MILES LEWIS

7. ISLAMIC LANDS. The vast region dominated by Islam since the 7th century AD is studded with the remains of the earliest built communities. Inherently these are all vernacular, and the subsequent tradition has been continuous: desolation has been due to war and natural disaster, not to abandonment. New cities arose where the old ones had stood, often with extraordinary persistence on the foundations and street lines of the earlier structures. Testimony to this long vernacular history lies in the sharp-sided tells, or artificial hills, that stud the region. The citadels of ALEPPO in Syria, Irbil in northern Iraq and Bukhara (*see* BUKHARA, §1) in Uzbekistan are dramatic examples of these ancient settlements. These tells have risen unconsciously and without deliberate command by the simple process of the continual garnering of materials into the city and their discard *in situ* as the result of decay. Differing climatic conditions, availability of materials and cultural practices have given rise to distinct regional traditions of vernacular architecture within the broad swath of land from the Atlantic Ocean to the steppes of Central Asia where Islam holds sway. The large majority of Middle Eastern towns have, at some time in their history, boasted major fortifications and rugged girdles of walls, if only in mud-brick (*see* MILITARY ARCHITECTURE AND FORTIFICATION, §IV, 2). Many of these fortifications survive, and the pattern of streets within vividly displays the containment of the city. Great ranges of other practical building work, such as mosques, madrasas, caravanserais, wind catchers and baths have evolved from need and available materials, the same constraints that produced the ordinary house. This article concentrates on regional varieties of domestic architecture; the nature of the evidence precludes uniform treatment of all regions.

For a general survey of domestic architecture in the Islamic lands *see* ISLAMIC ART, §II. For historical surveys of religious and palatial architecture *see* ISLAMIC ART, §II, and articles on specific building types, e.g. MOSQUE, MADRASA and CARAVANSERAI.

(i) Morocco and Algeria. (ii) Tunisia. (iii) Egypt. (iv) Syria and Iraq. (v) Arabia. (vi) Yemen. (vii) Anatolia and the Balkans. (viii) Iran. (ix) Western Central Asia.

(i) Morocco and Algeria. The Maghrib, or north-west Africa, is rich in regional architectural forms that vary with the geographic, cultural and historical diversity of the coastal regions along the Mediterranean and Atlantic, the Atlas Mountains and the oases of the Sahara. The study of vernacular architecture has concentrated on the spectacular defensive structures and villages of the Atlas Mountains and southern Morocco, and on the sculptural coherence of the Mzab oases of Algeria at the expense of the less distinctive and less well-preserved building traditions of the coastal plains. In the Maghrib, urban domestic architecture is also highly regionalized, although largely unstudied, except in Fez. The Mediterranean coast of Morocco and Algeria has been in the path of numerous invasions, from the Phoenicians to the French. The more accessible areas have long been under the rule of the 'Alawi sultans or Ottoman governors, and buildings have much in common with peasant architecture elsewhere in the Mediterranean. The typical house of the littoral consists of a single room built of local stone, mud-brick or rubble, flat-roofed or sloped and thatched. Wood is used for walls and roofs, depending on availability; it is also burnt to produce lime for whitewashing as protection against heavy rainfall.

Distinctive forms and settlement patterns are controlled not only by climate, resources and topography but also by the cultural and social identity of the builders. In the rugged but densely populated area of the Rif Mountains in northern Morocco, for example, houses vary in construction, plan and placement according to each tribal and linguistic group. A more recent external historical origin must be sought for the distinctive red-tiled pitched roofs of the northern villages, in areas that were settled by refugees from Spain from the 15th to the 17th century. The settlers brought with them a technique of roofing dictated by heavy snow and rainfall that, although inappropriate in their new environment, survived into the 20th century, giving such towns as Chaouén in Morocco a distinctly European aspect. A round-tiled pitched roof over dry-stone construction, a technique used in the Kabylia Mountains of north-west Algeria, is thought to have Roman antecedents, illustrated in the Classical mosaics of nearby Constantine. These houses also do not exceed a single room, divided down the middle by a bench to keep the animals on one side, and related family houses are built around a courtyard with a single entrance.

Along the Atlantic coastal plain of Morocco, less permanent, circular and conical-roofed houses (*nuwala*), built of cane and reeds covered with straw, are thought to have a sub-Saharan origin. As on the northern plains, cactus plants are grown to form wind-breaks and walls for isolated farmhouses. In some villages of the central Moroccan plains, houses or huts are arranged in circles for defensive purposes and possibly in memory of a nomadic bedouin tradition. Some neighbouring tribes of

26. *Qsar*, at Rissani, Ziz Valley, southern Morocco

the Atlantic littoral, also in the Middle Atlas and eastern Rif mountains, continue to use tents, occasionally in conjunction with buildings.

Funerary vernacular architecture consists of a cubic base surmounted by a dome (*qubba*), equipped with a mihrab and decorated with crenellations or horns at the corners. These horns or steps at the corners of flat and domed roofs are some of the few ornaments found on religious and secular buildings throughout the Maghrib, as well as in the southern Sahara and South Arabia. Their function was probably once apotropaic. The domed saint's tomb appears in towns as well as the countryside, and its form must surely originate in the royal tombs of cities in the eastern Islamic lands (*see* TOMB, §II). Building along the coast has gradually lost many of the features it shared with the more impenetrable Atlas Mountains and Sahara. Collectively built public buildings of rural areas, such as fortresses and granaries, have survived only as toponyms in northern Morocco.

The Berber villages of the Rif, Kabylia and Aurès mountains share many characteristics with those of the High Atlas and Saharan steppes. The fortified communal storehouse is the vital centre of these villages, among both sedentary and semi-nomadic people, protecting and storing food in unstable and threatened times and when nomads pastured their flocks, and functioning as market and caravanserais in peace time. Known as *agadir* in the southern and western Atlas, *tighremt* in the High Atlas and *qal'a* in the Aurès, these storehouses have immediate visual similarities with the tower houses of southern Arabia and fortified villages of Afghanistan. Although the latter examples are also fortified domestic structures, their function and plans are different. The Maghribi granaries have courtyards to house animals; a variant of the courtyard is the long narrow alley of the agriculturalist western High Atlas. In all cases there are multiple levels of small rooms,

to which families have access by climbing projecting beams and stone slabs. Built of stone in the High Atlas and Aurès, and mud in the Sahara, they have small barrel-vaulted rooms similar to those of Libyan and Tunisian granaries. The semi-sacred nature of the tribal storehouse can be expressed by the placing of a saint's tomb at the centre.

A building related in structure to the communal granary is the *qasba*, or fortified citadel and governor's residence, which existed in most Maghribi towns. In the Atlas the term refers to the large isolated structures put up by local rulers to defend mountain passes and exercise their authority over neighbouring tribes. Most of the extant *qasba*s of the Atlas were probably built in the 19th century, during the despotic expansion of the Glawa (Glaoui) tribe, which in turn destroyed many *agadir*s belonging to independent villages. The *qasba* in some form, however, has been used in the mountains at least since the reign of Mawlay Isma'il (*reg* 1672–1727), said to have built 76 *qasba*s to subdue the region. A third form is the mountain village, *qal'a* in Morocco and *qsar* in Algeria, which is used for only part of the year by mountain pastoralists. Although fortified, it has no particular plan and need not be sited on the dramatic heights selected for the two other forms.

The fortified village of the Anti-Atlas and north-west Sahara has the external appearance of, and might be mistaken for, a mountain storehouse or granary, which in turn is sometimes enclosed within its walls or placed near the village. To add to the confusion of terminology, these structures are also known as *qsur* (plural of *qsar*). These are the most distinctive buildings of this region (see fig. 26), and their plans have a formal character thought to originate in Roman or Byzantine border camps. The buttressed and tapering walls are built of pisé with unfired brick in the upper floors, elements ideally suited to the extremes of temperature in the desert. Within, the mosque, bath and other open spaces are placed near the single entrance, and contiguous houses fill the space between the square village walls and the two carefully orientated paths that meet at right angles. The houses themselves, with their narrow courtyards, thick walls and height, are well designed for the seasons of the desert oases.

Decoration is limited to the arch of the main doorway and the rich patterns of fired brickwork of the upper storey walls, which probably echo metropolitan forms. The architecture of the Tafilalt, for example, is thought to be evidence of the building tradition of Sijilmasa, one of the great medieval Saharan towns and trading posts, along with Timbuctu (Mali) and Oulata (Mauritania). The 16th-century traveller Leo Africanus wrote that after the Marinids destroyed Sijilmasa in the 14th century, its inhabitants dispersed and settled the Tafilalt. The search for origins for the mud architecture of southern Morocco in that of Sijilmasa is confounded by the impermanence of the material: the oldest standing buildings date from the 19th century, with some 18th-century ruins still in evidence.

Equally remarkable but quite different are the seven oasis towns of the Mzab Valley in central Algeria, also located in an extremely harsh environment, where survival depends on the careful regulation of agricultural and defensive building practices. The highly conservative tradition of the Kharijite heterodoxy has survived here since it took refuge in the Mzab in 1077, after the destruction of the Kharijite capital of Sédrata to the south-east. The last two Kharijite towns were founded in the 17th century. Tapering horned minarets dominate the walled towns and hills on which they are built and also act as watch-towers. A strict hierarchy is imposed on the houses, which are not allowed to surpass a certain height and are built along streets that radiate out and down from the great mosque crowning the hill. Immediately outside the towns are summer-houses in the oases, to which the Mzabites can escape in the fiercest heat. The only decorative forms in these austere towns are the simple arcades along the roads or around the market-places and the elongated horns on religious and funerary buildings, both on saints' tombs (with the characteristic conical domes of the region) or the ordinary flat-roofed tombs. The relationship of this austere tradition to the sophisticated carved stucco decoration found in the excavated houses of medieval Sedrata remains unclear.

See also ISLAMIC ART, §II, 6(iv)(b).

BIBLIOGRAPHY
Leo Africanus: *Descrittione dell'Africa* (1526); Fr. trans. by A. Epaulard as *Description de l'Afrique* (Paris, 1956)
R. Maunier: *La Construction collective de la maison en Kabylie* (Paris, 1926)
E. Blanco Izaga: *La vivienda rifeña* (Ceuta, 1930)
R. Montage: *Villages et kasbas berbères* (Paris, 1930)
H. Terrasse: *Kasbas berbères de l'Atlas et des oasis* (Paris, 1930)
E. Laoust: 'L'Habitation chez les transhumans du Maroc central', *Hespéris*, xiv (1932), pp. 115–218; xviii (1934), pp. 109–96
D. Jacques-Meunié: *Greniers citadelles au Maroc* (Paris, 1951)
A. Delpy: 'Note sur l'habitat des Ida ou Semlal, Ameln', *Cah. A. & Tech. Afrique N.*, v (1959), pp. 7–16
R. Riché: 'La Maison de l'Aurès', *Cah. A. & Tech. Afrique N.*, v (1959), pp. 30–36
D. Jacques-Meunié: *Architectures et habitats du Dadès* (Paris, 1962)
Living on the Edge of the Sahara: A Study of Traditional Forms of Habitation and Types of Settlement in Morocco, Kasba 64 Study Group (The Hague, 1973)
G. T. Peterbridge: 'Vernacular Architecture in the Maghreb', *Maghreb Rev.*, iii (1976), pp. 12–17
A. Ravereaux: *Le M'zab: Une Leçon d'architecture* (Paris, 1981)
W. J. R. Curtis: 'Type and Variation: Berber Collective Dwellings of the Northwestern Sahara', *Muqarnas*, i (1983), pp. 181–209
J. Revault, L. Golvin and A. Amahan: *Palais et demeures de Fès* (Paris, 1985)

N. ERZINI

(ii) Tunisia. Domestic architecture in Ifriqiya, the province roughly corresponding to modern Tunisia, before the period of Hafsid rule (*reg* 1228–1574) is known primarily from incomplete excavations at the sites of Raqqada (9th century) and Sabra (10th century), near Kairouan. Evidence suggests that the principles of construction changed only slightly before the 20th century: the standard arrangement was a single indirect entrance leading from the exterior to a square court surrounded by rectangular chambers. The presence of stairs suggests the existence of a second storey, but there is no evidence to confirm it. The plan evokes the memory of the antique Greco-Roman house, but the affiliation is uncertain, since these principles were well known for centuries not only throughout the Mediterranean lands but also as far as western Central Asia. Whatever the origins of the plan may be, it corresponds to an introverted conception of the family cell, visible primarily in urban domestic architecture.

In Tunis, the oldest surviving houses date from the 16th century and consist of such residences as the Dar 'Uthman or more modest private houses. One of the most characteristic is probably the Dar al-Hadri (El-Hedri). A single entrance, composed of a vestibule lined with banquettes on which the visitor is seated while waiting to be admitted, leads to a corridor with a right-angle bend for privacy. The corridor leads to a central paved court in the shape of a slightly deformed square, bordered on three sides by porticos with triple arcades resting on marble columns and capitals. Three large rooms line the sides with porticos. The largest, opposite the entrance, is the salon where the master receives his visitors. It has a door with two valves ornamented with nails and flanked by two square barred windows. An elaborately decorated central alcove is flanked by recesses, with banquette-beds at the two extremities of the antechamber. The two other rooms have only cupboards and beds. The fourth wall of the court has a stair leading to the upper floor, which has galleries on all four sides of the court; it is protected by a balustrade of turned wood, supported by columns that support the roof. From this gallery open four large rooms. An annexe composed of a small court bordered by two pitched roofs supported on two arcades on columns contains a kitchen garden, a well, latrines and storage. This is the *dwiriya* or kitchen, and from it there is access to a bath. Finally, a vast complex with a central court was used for stables and lodging servants.

Interior façades were constructed of ochre-coloured limestone quarried near Tunis. Vestibules and some principal rooms were revetted with tile, produced at Qallalin in the suburbs, and decorated with finely carved stucco. Ceilings of the rooms were supported by painted beams, while those of the alcoves of reception rooms were decorated with coffers, sculpted and painted with floral decoration (see fig. 27). Street façades were bare, except near entrances, which normally comprised a rectangular door of two valves ornamented with nails. The jambs and

27. Interior decoration, Dar el Mrabet, Tunis, 17th century

lintels were worked from stone slabs, occasionally with the addition of white and black marble, and decorated with mouldings. Some façades have consoles supporting projecting blocks, pierced by a square window with a wooden grille (*mashrabiyya*). This type of house evolved little, except for the decoration of the entrances, which followed current fashions for horseshoe arches or Italianizing motifs. Houses in other cities of Ifriqiya followed the same principles with some variation. In Kairouan, for example, loggias on the upper floor opened to the street and were protected by balustrades of turned wood. In Sfax, interior courts have a single gallery—composed of two arches on a column—on the entrance side. This is the *bortāl*, under which one finds the storerooms, latrines, well, stair, entrance to the kitchen annexe etc. In smaller cities on Cap Bon or in the Sahel, houses usually have a single ground floor.

Houses are built of stone along the coast and on the islands of Jerba and Kerkenah, although there is also a modest house (*gourbi*) made of reeds and covered with branches or with a mixture of earth and straw. The most common type of farmhouse is a family cell comprising one to four living rooms around an irregular court. The entrance passage is always indirect for privacy, and the stable adjoins the living-quarters as well as the sheds and storerooms. The rooms are often covered with barrel vaults supporting the roof. The houses of the more prosperous have a well or cistern and latrines. Elsewhere, wells or cisterns are outside the houses. Unusual housing includes the subterranean rooms in the mountains near Matmata. Carved into the clay, the chambers open on to

a court at the bottom of a vertical well. A descending gallery, with rooms for animals, leads to the interior. Near these troglodyte villages there are also villages comprised of multiple storeys of superimposed long narrow and vaulted chambers; these are the *ghorfa* of Medenine and the neighbouring villages. Earthen stairs along the façade give access to the rooms. In the Djerid, particularly at Tozeur, construction is in mud-brick, and the façades of the houses have handsome geometric patterns in the brickwork.

BIBLIOGRAPHY

A. Bernard: *Enquête sur l'habitation rurale de Tunisie* (Tunis, 1924)
S. Tlatli: *Djerbe et les djerbiens* (Tunis, 1942)
G. Marçais: *L'Architecture musulmane d'Occident* (Paris, 1954)
J. Despois: *La Tunisie orientale, sahel et basses steppes* (Paris, 1955)
J. Revault: *Palais et demeures de Tunis*, 4 vols (Paris, 1967–78)
A. Daoulatli: *Tunis sous les Hafsides* (Tunis, 1976)

LUCIEN GOLVIN

(iii) Egypt. Egypt is fortunate in its unusual wealth of material that can be used to document the history of vernacular architecture. Excavation reports document Pharaonic, Ptolemaic, Greco-Roman, Coptic and early Islamic sites, while for medieval Cairo travellers' reports, historians' accounts, documents from the Geniza—a trove of medieval papers found in a Cairo synagogue—and the archives of endowment deeds (Arab. *waqf*) supplement the monumental evidence. The excavations at Fustat have provided examples of some three dozen middle-class houses from the periods of Tulunid (*reg* 868–905) and Fatimid (*reg* 969–1171) rule. Study of these remains, together with the Geniza documents, makes it possible to identify something of the typical domestic architecture of the period. Although there was only one main entrance, a second entrance was common if the house had a wall that fronted on to another street. Unlike houses in many other Arab cities, exterior walls were provided with numerous windows, usually including a window corbelled out above the main doorway. Wooden lattices (*mashrabiyya*) screened the inhabitants from view, while permitting them to see out.

Despite the irregular contours of most of these houses, their interiors are invariably characterized by geometric regularity, insofar as this was possible. Two features have been found in every house that has been excavated: a courtyard and, on one of its sides, a unit consisting of an iwan with two adjacent rooms at its sides, fronted by a portico. In most cases, the other three sides of the courtyard show an irregular disposition of rooms, although a second iwan, with or without a portico, or, rarely, a biaxial four-iwan composition, was also known. Sometimes a pool flanked by shrubbery beds was found in the centre of the courtyard, while some enigmatic shallow gougings in the area of the porticos also could have been designed for plants. The cooling effect of the greenery was echoed in the orientation of the main iwan, which usually faced north to obtain the maximum shade in summer. The iwan clearly corresponds to the *majlis* cited in Geniza documents and to the *qā'a* mentioned in later sources as the largest living or reception room of the house. It could be on either the ground or upper floor, although the former seems, from the excavated examples, to have been more common at this period. This room would have had the most sumptuous furnishings, in which painted wooden ceilings and brightly coloured textiles—bolsters, cushions, rugs and curtains—played the major part. Occasionally the room had features that became more common from the 13th century: a *dūrqāʿa* (a lower area where one removed one's shoes) with a marble basin for a fountain, sometimes in combination with a *shādirwān* (a decorated flagstone over which water rippled) and a wind catcher or ventilation shaft above, all contributing to the coolness of the interior. The flat roofs of the houses were also used for drying clothes or fruit, or even for light wooden superstructures that could be let as individual dwellings. It has not been possible to carry out excavations at Fustat in the most densely populated areas near the Nile; perhaps for this reason no traces have been found of the multi-storey dwellings mentioned in several historical sources, which accommodated hundreds of people.

The remains of several palaces in Cairo vividly illustrate the splendour in which the principal Mamluk amirs lived. The most impressive surviving examples belonged to Bashtak (1334–9) and Qawsun (1337–8), two amirs of al-Nasir Muhammad. Their houses compete in quality and magnificence with the finest religious architecture of the Mamluks (*see* ISLAMIC ART, §II, 6(iii)(a)) and are notable for the size of their upper storeys and *qāʿa*s, which had replaced the courtyard as the focal point of the building. The *qāʿa* of Bashtak (see fig. 28) consists of two iwans facing each other across a *dūrqāʿa* bordered by an arcade of three arches. The *dūrqāʿa* rises vertiginously to an upper

28. Main *qāʿa*, palace of Bashtak, Cairo, Egypt, 1334–9

gallery shielded by lattices and to a wooden *muqarnas* roof. The *qāʿa* of Qawsun must have been even vaster, to judge by the remains of its one iwan, which is expanded on three sides by subsidiary iwans. Some idea of its proportions can be gained by the entrance to the palace with its superb MUQARNAS vault, second in height only to that of the funerary complex of Sultan Hasan (1356–62) in Cairo.

Mamluk palaces are impressive not only for their size but also for the quality of their decoration. The *qāʿa* of Tashtimur (1376–7), converted into a mosque by Khushqadam in 1486, is of relatively modest dimensions, but its fine stucco medallions and painted *muqarnas* and inscription band are the equal of work in the contemporary complex of Sultan Hasan. The inscription band encircles the whole *qāʿa*, emphasizing a horizontality unusual for the period. In addition to the enlargement of the *qāʿa*, the *maqʿad*, an open loggia on the upper storey facing the courtyard, was also increased in size during this period. The *maqʿad* of Mamay al-Sayfi (1496) is all that survives of his palace. It has five large arches, although the sources mention examples with up to fifteen.

Lower-middle-class Mamluk and Ottoman housing is represented by the *rabʿ*, a type of tenement with apartments arranged in vertical units of two or three storeys. Like the better-known *wakāla* (*see* CARAVANSERAI), they usually had shops on the group floor, but *rabʿ*s were for permanent rather than transient residents. These buildings accommodated the essential elements of courtyard houses: the *qāʿa* was retained, occupying double the height of the other rooms (although it overlooked the street rather than the interior courtyard of the buildings), while the roof, walled to obtain privacy, substituted for the courtyard. The same emphasis on verticality is found in the Ottoman houses that have survived in Rashīd (Rosetta). Although on a grander scale than the *rabʿ*s, they are similar in that they turn their backs on the small courtyards they contain and derive most of their light from the street façade. The numerous Ottoman houses of the bourgeoisie in Cairo have many of the same features as those of Fustat or, on a reduced scale, the Mamluk palaces. The reception rooms (*manzara*) are much smaller, and in consequence several could be fitted into the plan, on upper and lower storeys, facing various directions for use in different seasons. Almost invariably the *maqʿad* was reduced in scale to a double arch.

The dwellings of the urban poor are scarcely known, owing to their perishable nature and the lack of interest shown in them by historians and travellers. Jomard's account in the *Description de l'Egypte* of large courtyards or enclosures used as rubbish dumps full of huts four feet tall where crowds of the poor lived crammed together with their animals would as likely apply to the Cairo of ten centuries ago as of two. The rural architecture of Egypt is remarkable for the continuity that it shows with Pharaonic examples, although, unlike the workers' quarters discussed above, the modern examples invariably include space for animals—donkey, cow, water buffalo or chickens. The similarities are hardly surprising since the needs and materials of the poorest segments of society have not changed radically in millennia. Mud brick is still the most common building material, although those that can afford baked brick will use it to effect an upper storey and, in the

Delta, provide better protection from humidity. Two factors can be observed that differentiate rural architecture in Upper and Lower Egypt. The use of courtyards varies according to different climates; in Lower Egypt many houses do not have them, and in towns further south they tend to be larger. Vaulting is more common in the extreme south, in Nubia and in scattered settlements as far north as Esna. Except for a very few Nubian domed examples, vaulting was confined to barrel vaults over rectangular spaces. Although the inhabitants lose the advantages to be had from access to a flat roof, the scarcity of wood and the greater ventilation obtained in the hotter southern regions were undoubtedly the reasons for its popularity. It provided the inspiration for the school of modern Egyptian architects that included Ramses Wissa Wassef and HASSAN FATHY. The latter also designed houses and village communities but, perhaps because of the aversion of the rural population to living under domes, his houses have been celebrated chiefly by the urban élite.

See also EGYPT, ANCIENT, §VIII, 4.

BIBLIOGRAPHY

M. Jomard: 'Description de la ville et de la citadelle du Kaire. . .', *Description de l'Egypte, état moderne*, 2/ii (Paris, 1822), pp. 662, 696

E. W. Lane: *An Account of the Manners and Customs of the Modern Egyptians* (London, 1836/*R* 1978), pp. 15–31

V. M. Mosséri and C. Audebeau Bey: *Les Constructions rurales en Egypte* (Cairo, 1921)

J. Lozach and G. Hug: *L'Habitat rural en Egypte* (Cairo, 1930)

A. Badawy: 'La Maison mitoyenne de plan uniforme dans l'Egypte pharoanique', *Bull. Fac. A., Fouad I U.*, xvii (1953), pp. 1–58

M. Nowicka: *La Maison privée dans l'Egypte ptolémaïque*, Academia Scientarium Polona, Bibliotheca Antiqua, ix (Wroclaw, Warsaw and Cracow, 1969)

A. Lézine and A.-R. Abdul Tawab: 'Introduction à l'étude des maisons anciennes de Rosette', *An. Islam.*, x (1972), pp. 149–205

H. Jaritz: 'Notes on Nubian Architecture', *Nubians in Egypt*, ed. R. A. Fernea (Austin and London, 1973), pp. 49–60

J. Revault and B. Maury: *Palais et maisons du Caire du XIVe au XVIIIe siècle*, 3 vols (Cairo, 1975–9)

A. A. Ostrasz: 'The Archaeological Material for the Study of the Domestic Architecture at Fustat', *Afr. Bull.*, xxvi (1977), pp. 57–86

L. 'Ali Ibrahim: 'Middle-class Living Units in Mamluk Cairo', *A. & Archaeol. Res. Pap.*, xiv (1978), pp. 24–30

D. Behrens-Abouseif: 'Quelques traits de l'habitation traditionnelle dans la ville du Caire', *Actes du 2ème colloque de l'A.T.P. La Ville arabe dans l'Islam: Histoire et mutations: Carthage-Amilcar, 1979*, pp. 447–59

A. Raymond: 'The *Rab*': A Type of Collective Housing in Cairo during the Ottoman Period', *Proceedings of Seminar Four in the Series Architectural Transformations in the Islamic World, The Aga Khan Award for Architecture: Architecture as Symbol and Self-identity: Fez, 1979*, pp. 55–61

J.-C. Garcin and others: *Palais et maisons du Caire*, 2 vols (Paris, 1982–3)

S. D. Goitein: *Daily Life* (1983), iv of *A Mediterranean Society* (Berkeley, Los Angeles and London, 1967–88), pp. 150–200

M. Zakariya: *Deux palais du Caire médiévale: Waqfs et architecture* (Paris, 1983)

B. Kemp: *Ancient Egypt: Anatomy of a Civilization* (London and New York, 1989)

BERNARD O'KANE

(iv) Syria and Iraq. Many of the settlements and building types found in the region have changed little over the millennia, and great citadels such as Irbil in Iraq have been continuously inhabited for at least 10,000 years. Patterns of settlement vary enormously with the local terrain and range from the widely scattered tents and camps of the bedouin to the denser settlements of the coastal region in the west and the irrigated lands of southern Iraq, and the compact settlements of the interior plain, the deserts and the mountain villages. Local construction techniques depend on the availability of materials, the most widely used being stone and mud-brick. Sandstone, limestone and various marbles are quarried in the upland regions, and buildings in such cities as Aleppo, Damascus and Mosul are built of finely cut stone with rich architectural decoration. In villages, buildings are also constructed of stone, usually in rubble construction with cement or mud mortar. The use of baked brick is most often associated with urban construction. Mud-brick, which is cheap and has excellent thermal properties, is widely used in Iraq. Walls are often constructed with rubble stone facings up to a metre high, and wide eaves are built to protect the exposed façades of the buildings. Pisé or rammed earth is commonly used for compound and garden walls. Roofs are generally flat, constructed with poplar, date-palm, mulberry and orchard timbers and surfaced with a rolled mud finish. Brick and stone domes and vaults are built in areas with little or no timber. Two very distinctive construction techniques are also found: in northern Syria villages are roofed with stone domes in the shape of beehives, and in southern Iraq the marsh Arabs live in structures made entirely of reeds (see fig. 29).

Traditional settlements in the region are clusters of living cells woven together with a maze of winding alleys and roads, often following the lines of former garden walls. Each cell is composed of a house and yard enclosed by a wall. Enclosure is necessary for privacy, giving women their requisite inviolable domain; for security, particularly for animals, which are kept within the walls at night; and for climatic protection from sun, wind and dust. Enclosure walls are absent only in encampments of bedouin tents, around the houses of the very poor or in new construction. Houses are usually built against compound walls, generally with a southern aspect, although some houses in the extreme north of the area, as in Anatolia, are surrounded by open space within the compound walls. In mountain areas where plots are sloping, houses are built on the uphill side of the terraced compound.

29. Reed hut of the marsh Arabs, southern Iraq

Three main types of house have been used in the region since antiquity. The compact house is a rectangular building set within and usually against the wall of the yard, with typically two to nine rooms. The kitchen, latrine, bathroom, storerooms and stables may be built as individual units around the yard wall. The compound house began as a walled enclosure in which living and utility rooms are built, as required, against the walls, creating a string of rooms around a central yard or compound. Compact and compound houses are typical village forms, and when such houses are built with two storeys, the ground floor is often used for stables and storerooms. Courtyard houses have a central square or rectangular open space that acts as an outside living area. The courtyard is a designed feature with the four attendant elevations being carefully contrived and often symmetrical, with the main winter living rooms on the north wall and the summer living rooms on the south. The courtyard—an integral open-air living-room within the house—is distinguished from the yard in a compound house, which is generally irregularly shaped, randomly determined and used for agricultural as well as domestic purposes. Courtyard houses are a typical urban form and were also built by wealthier villagers and absentee landlords. Larger town houses have several courtyards, including a family courtyard, a courtyard for male guests, courtyards for different sections of the family, a brother's or son's household, as well as stable and kitchen yards.

Rooms are generally rectangular and plastered inside with mud in the villages or with lime in towns, a more expensive and fashionable material. Houses include a number of distinctive elements that might be considered typical of the domestic architecture of various areas of the Near East. These include the IWAN, a roofed space enclosed on three sides and open completely on the fourth, which faces on to a courtyard or compound. Iwans are common in the buildings of the north, where they are often built in pairs opposite each other on the north and south sides of a courtyard and covered by a brick or stone vault. In Baghdad and southern Iraq a similar type of three-walled space is known as a *tālār*, usually built with mud and timber flat roofs, often with a colonnade or pair of columns on the open side. A *riwāq* is a colonnaded space built as a gallery, verandah or loggia. In its simplest form it may support the verandah of a village house; in its more elaborate variants it may form a decorative element in the ornate façade of a palace. In Baghdad the term *tarma* is used for a colonnaded upper storey of a house, which may be built in front of an *ursi*, a room so called because of its distinctive sash window facing on to the court, made of elaborate timber lattices and often with coloured glazing. Typical of the Arab quarters in the south of the region are the rooms on the upper storey with an oriel (*shanashil*) window projecting over a street or alley. These windows are built of timber latticework shutters, metal grilles and plain and coloured glass. Often ornately decorated, they allow discreet vision out and trap cool breezes. Many houses have *sirdābs*, basements 4–5 m deep used as summer living rooms, stables and storerooms. They are ventilated by small, high windows, with metal grilles connecting them to the courtyard and also in central and southern Iraq with wind catchers (*see* WIND

CATCHER). Half basements called *nīm*s in northern Iraq are 1.5–3 m below court level and look out on to the court through large windows or colonnades. The ceilings of basements are often constructed with decorative brick patterns.

See also ISLAMIC ART, §II, 4(i)(b).

BIBLIOGRAPHY
F. Langenegger: *Die Baukunst des Iraq* (Dresden, 1911)
Conrad: 'Medieval Quṣūr', *al-Aḥdath* (1981)
J. Warren and I. Fethi: *Traditional Houses in Baghdad* (Horsham, 1982)
B. Hakim: *Arabic-Islamic Cities: Building and Planning Principles* (London and New York, 1986)
Proceedings of an International Seminar Sponsored by the Aga Khan Award for Architecture, the African Union of Architects, and the Association of Architects of Tanzania: The Architecture of Housing: Zanzibar, 1988
M. B. Behsh: *Towards Housing in Harmony with Place: Constancy and Change in the Traditional Syrian House from the Standpoint of Environmental Adaptation* (Lund, 1993)

SUSAN ROAF

(*v*) *Arabia.* The vernacular architecture of Arabia varies with region, climate and local tradition, and there are considerable differences in building styles, construction techniques and decorative techniques over this diverse region, particularly in the Yemen to the south (*see* §(vi) below). The oldest buildings seem to be no more than three or four centuries old, but archaeological and epigraphic evidence suggests that the tower houses of western Arabia and the widespread type of the courtyard house go back to very early times. Along the Tihama coast of western Arabia the main building material is coral, carved in blocks and reinforced with wooden beams laid horizontally and plastered to prevent deterioration. The same style was repeated in stone at Mecca, Ta'if and Medina in the Hijaz highlands. The best-known examples are the tall houses of Jiddah (see fig. 30), and more modest versions are found at Wajh and Qunfidhah on the coast, as well as at Hubaydah in the Yemen and SUAKIN in the Sudan, where much of the architecture was built by Hijazis. The surviving houses of Jiddah range from the impressive houses of the mercantile Nasir and Jawkhdar families to more quotidian types. Houses rise three, four and even five storeys with a single staircase shaft. Although there is no courtyard, a central shaft ventilates the interior, and numerous windows on the outer walls encourage the circulation of air in the humid and hot climate along the Red Sea. The windows are screened by carved wooden balconies or casements (*rawāshin*, much like the *mashrabiyya* of Cairo). The internal division, as in the Yemen, has lower floors for servants and women and the principal reception room on the upper floor; the enclosed staircase allows visitors to reach the upper floor without disturbing women on the intermediate floors.

Straw huts ('*ush*'*āsh*), particularly conical ones, are also common on the Tihamat coast. Women paint the plastered interior with coloured geometric decoration. Another type of residence is a single-storey pavilion-like structure with a flat roof, usually set within a courtyard and often freestanding. The *murabba*' type found at Qunfidhah has bay windows with fine woodwork and casements of the type found at Jiddah and in the Hijaz. Another type of pavilion house found at Sabya and Farasan has fine plaster carving on interiors and exteriors and carved wood. Some of the best woodwork on Farasan is said to have been imported

30. Façades of houses at Jiddah, Saudi Arabia

from India. In the highlands of the Tihamat and in the 'Asir, the houses are fortified and often built of stone, although mud courses are found in the neighbourhood of Abha and further east, towards Najran and Bishah. The stone tower houses of the south-west mountains have more in common with the highland architecture of the Yemen than with the tall houses of Jiddah and the Hijaz, although they may all derive from common antecedents. In the settlements of Jabal Fayfa' and Jabal Bani Malik, these stone houses are provided with strong circular towers and are set on rocky promontories. Ground-floor rooms are used for storage, upper rooms for social and family life. Decoration is restricted to designs in white quartz, which contrasts with the dark masonry. The tall buildings in the 'Asir have banked walls with stone slates set horizontally between the mud courses to break the erosive fall of rainwater. Interior decoration is confined to carved wooden columns and enamelled utensils in bright colours placed around the walls. Further east, the tower houses of Najran are even taller, with mud courses that curve upwards at the corners to increase stability and coloured glass windows in the finest examples. Rather different houses are built by the same method at Bishah on the western edge of Najd.

In the great central plain of Najd, where the climate is hot and dry with heavy rains in winter and spring, the principal building material is mud-brick, and the main type of town house, well represented by buildings in Riyadh,

Dir'iyah and Buraydah, consists of a two-storey structure built around a central courtyard. There are few exterior windows, and the main source of light is through the doorways facing the courtyard on the lower and upper storeys. The balcony that connects upper floor rooms is concealed by a balustrade and shades the rooms below. More modest buildings have a walled courtyard adjacent to a one- or two-storey residence, and some residential buildings are single-storey chambers built around an open courtyard and set within an enclosure wall. Exterior decoration is restrained: string courses of triangular motifs in relief break the flow of rainwater over the mud surface, and crenellations coated with hard plaster protect the summits of walls. Unlike the deeply carved doors of western and eastern Arabia, doors are lightly incised with patterns picked out in colours and burnt into the wood. The principal decoration is concentrated in the reception rooms, many of which have finely painted doors and plaster walls carved with geometric and floral motifs. In the finest examples the plaster decoration extends the full height of the wall. One of the main centres of this craft is Qaşim, but fine examples are also found at Shaqra, Sadus and Riyadh.

The traditional houses of al-Hufuf in the Ahsa' oasis of eastern Arabia depend on building traditions along the Gulf and are similar to the fine houses of Muscat and Oman. The finest houses in al-Hufuf, like those built of coral at al-Qatif on the coast, are tall structures in two or even three storeys built around a central courtyard. The building technique is especially fine: rough stone embedded in mortar and walls finished in plaster. Interior walls are elegantly coated with a hard white plaster. Door and window arches tend to be pointed, with the long sides formed by palm trunks. Entrances are distinguished by exuberant arches with lobes and ogees in carved plaster. Elegant crenellations in plaster complete the finest buildings, and carved decoration is found on interiors, but the most common feature is deeply recessed shelving, found for example at Bahrain, Dubai and in other Gulf regions. Another type of house in eastern Arabia has one or two walled storeys in a walled courtyard. Modest versions are found at al-Qatif and formerly at al-Jubayl, where each walled garden had a pavilion-like single-storey reception room. A more complex accumulation of such structures is represented by the Bayt 'Abd al-Wahhab (19th century) in Darin on Tarut Island, opposite al-Qatif, where one- or two-storey pavilions are scattered around a central courtyard. The reception rooms have open sides to take advantage of the breeze, but other rooms are enclosed for privacy. Interiors are decorated with plaster carved with lobes and ogees in the style found throughout eastern Arabia and the Gulf, and the fine wooden doors have heavily carved central panels.

BIBLIOGRAPHY
F. S. Vidal: *The Oasis of al-Hasa* (Dhahran, 1955)
G. R. D. King: 'Some Observations on the Architecture of South-west Saudi Arabia', *Archit. Assoc. Q.*, viii (1976), pp. 20–29
A. Pesce: *Jiddah: Portrait of an Arabian City* (London, 1976)
G. R. D. King: 'Traditional Architecture in Najd, Saudi Arabia', *Proc. Semin. Arab. Stud.*, vii (1977), pp. 90–100
T. Prochazka jr: 'The Architecture of the Saudi Arabian South-west', *Proc. Semin. Arab. Stud.*, vii (1977), pp. 120–33
Jedda Old and New (London, 1980)
G. R. D. King: 'Some Examples of the Secular Architecture of Najd', *Arab. Stud.*, vi (1982), pp. 113–42

T. Prochazka jr: 'Observations on the Architectural Terminology of the South-west of the Arabian Peninsula', *Arab. Stud.*, vi (1982), pp. 97–109

W. Dostal: *Ethnographic Atlas of ʿAsīr* (Vienna, 1983)

G. R. D. KING

(vi) Yemen. The environmental and social diversity of the Yemen is reflected in the variety of forms and materials used for housing in the torrid coastal plain and temperate highlands. Villages in the highlands generally have a defensive nature. Some towns, such as Rada', are built around a fortified citadel, while other villages, such as Khawlan, exploit the natural terrain, with houses forming a defensive wall on a rocky outcrop. Towns on more vulnerable sites, such as Thula, have encircling walls of mud or stone, while in the Tihamat plain rubble walls are faced with brick. The most common building materials are stone, mud and timber. Stone, either with a dressed face (*waqīs*) or the form of rubble (*shalf*), is widespread in the midlands and highlands, while mud, in the form of rammed earth (*zabūr*) or sun-dried bricks (*libn*), is common in the alluvial wadis of the eastern highlands. Timber is used throughout as a structural element for floors and roofs, but only in the Tihamat plain are entire buildings constructed of wood, combined with grass thatch. In the highlands a skilled craftsman is required for work with dressed stone, while specialist knowledge is also essential for building in mud. On the coastal plain women are responsible for decorating the interiors of thatched grass houses. In the lowlands most activities take place outdoors, and houses in the Tihamat often have fenced compounds, which enclose animal stalls, crop stores and an outdoor cooking area. In the highlands most activity is confined within the house, with stables and storage occupying the lower floors, and the seclusion of women is an important organizational consideration, particularly in urban areas.

On the coastal plain, circular or rectangular houses and other structures are formed of palm trunk frames roofed with palm thatch (*tāfi*). Further inland, circular huts are constructed of bundles of thatch (*thumām*) bound together to form walls and bent over to form a conical roof, which is then thatched. A similar technique is used in the southern Tihamat to build rectangular homes, with vertical timbers supporting the roof. Interiors of lowland houses are often smothered with mud and elaborately painted with concentric patterns, below which are hung plates, trays and baskets. The urban homes of the Tihamat also provide for outdoor living in the tropical climate. A common type has single-storey rooms with high ceilings grouped around a walled court. The modest rooms are built of lava, coral or fired brick (*yājur*), with flat roofs topped with mud. Geometric patterns are built up in brick and plaster on the interior and exterior walls. Carved hardwood doors, window screens and rafters are common and are also found in the large merchant houses of the old port of al Hudaydah. As in other areas along the Red Sea, houses have elaborately screened openings to provide both ventilation and privacy. Several floors of high-ceilinged rooms are crowned by a walled roof terrace (*kharja*), which performs the same function as the courtyard in houses in Zabid. In the foothills adjacent to the Tihamat, settlement is limited to small hamlets of low rubble houses built above the seasonal wadis.

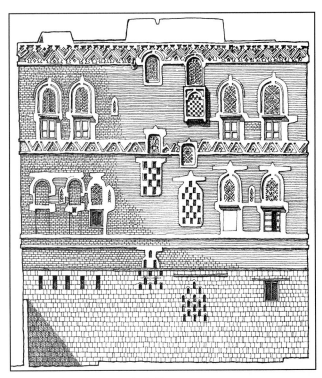

31. Façade of an urban house, San'a, Yemen

In the highlands the typical stone house is built on two or more floors. The ground floor is given over to agricultural use, and a central door also gives access to the house. Stairs lead to the upper floors, which generally have rooms of modest size, owing to the limited spans possible with available timber. Rooms are rarely limited to specific functions, and the same space might be used for eating, sleeping or conducting business. One larger space (*mafraj*), set aside for entertaining or chewing kat (qat), often has the best view. Rooms are furnished with mattresses arranged around the perimeter and cushions against the walls. The roof is the domain of women, and the kitchen is often situated on an upper floor to allow the fumes from the wood-burning stove to escape. The stonework varies in different highland regions: in the mountains of the western escarpment the scattered homesteads are built of quarried stone with a rough-dressed face and have small openings and windows topped with fanlights; on the highland plains there is more use of smooth-dressed stone, sometimes of various types to form patterned façades.

The urban house in the highlands has a ground floor of stone, while the upper storeys might be built of brick. In SAN'A baked brick is exploited to make elaborate patterns in relief on the upper floors, and coloured glass is used in tall fanlights over the windows (see fig. 31). The main rooms are extensively decorated in carved plaster. In the eastern city of Shibam in the Wadi Hadramawt, multi-storey houses are built of mud-brick, plastered and finished with lime. The town is built on a raised mound, which protects it from seasonal flooding, and has defensive walls of mud. Some of the homesteads that dot the nearby wadi have barrel vaults of mud-brick, because timber is so scarce. The austere houses in the Hadramawt have doors and windows elaborately carved in wood. In the wadis of the eastern highlands, rammed earth is common in areas with a plentiful supply of alluvial earth. The mud is sometimes mixed with straw and laid by hand on stone foundations. A rise (*midmak*) some 500 mm high is built up at a time, shaped by hand and left to dry before work begins on the next rise. The corners of the house are built up, while the rises follow an undulating pattern around the house. Ochre and white bands decorate windows and doors, and entrances are often flanked by protruding buttresses for defence. The houses of Jabal Barat, which rise up to five storeys, are built with projecting parapets around the roof to protect the mud walls from rain, while waste water runs in lime-plastered channels on the exterior face of the wall.

BIBLIOGRAPHY

H. Steffen, ed.: *Final Report of the Airphoto Interpretation Project of the Swiss Technical Co-operation Service* (Zurich, 1975)
P. Costa and E. Vicario: *Yemen: Paese di costruttori* (Milan, 1977); Eng. trans. as *Arabia Felix: A Land of Builders* (New York, 1977)
F. Veranda: *Art of Building in Yemen* (Cambridge, MA, and London, 1982)
R. B. Serjeant and R. Lewcock: *San'a': An Arabian Islamic City* (London, 1983)
L. Golvin: 'Contribution à l'étude de l'architecture de montagne en République Arabe du Yémen', *L'Arabie du sud: Histoire et civilisation*, by J. Chelhod and others, 3 vols (Paris, 1985), iii, pp. 303–28
F. Stone, ed.: *Studies on the Tihamah: The Report of the Tihamah Expedition 1982 and Related Papers* (London, 1985)

JOLYON LESLIE

(vii) Anatolia and the eastern Balkans. The vernacular architecture of Anatolia and the eastern Balkans is characterized by a single house type with common features. The ground-floor is of stone or brick; the upper storey has a timber frame with brick or stone infill (Turk. *hımış*). The lightness of the upper storey allows for numerous windows and projections. In Istanbul the timber frame is sheathed in wood; elsewhere it is plastered. The type is commonly called the 'traditional Ottoman house', for it was centred in Istanbul, the capital of the Ottoman dynasty (1281–1924) and was diffused throughout the empire, from the Balkans in the west across most of Anatolia in the east. On the hilly and chilly plateau of eastern Anatolia, the climate determined a different house type, sharing much with the type found in the Caucasus since the time of Vitruvius. In south-east Anatolia, which has a hot and arid climate, the typical house is built of fine masonry and has formal similarities to houses of Iran, Iraq and Syria. Nevertheless, even in these fringe areas the traditional Ottoman house has had some impact, and at the borders of the empire, in the Crimea, Baghdad, Yemen and Sudan, local house types known as 'Ottoman' exist but are somewhat different. Since this type of construction is subject to fire and decay, examples dating before the 19th century are rare. The origins of this type are a matter of lively speculation, with hypotheses about ethnic and national contributions abounding.

Like other house types in the Islamic lands, the Ottoman house is introverted around a courtyard or inner garden to give privacy to family life. Rarely orthogonal, the ground-floor plan follows the irregular plot. The exterior walls of the ground-floor are blind or have only a few openings, of which the most important is the courtyard or garden door, standing like a castle entrance defending the family's private world and connecting it to the street. The courtyard, with a pool, well and abundant greenery and access to storerooms, stables and cellars, is the scene of uninterrupted daily life and women's domestic activities. Wooden stairs lead from the court to the main living spaces on the upper storeys, which are often projected over the street to create orthogonal interiors. In contrast to those of the ground floor, the upper rooms have many windows, which add charm to the street fabric (see fig. 32). Houses often have two storeys and sometimes three, although single-storey houses are also known, and in many regions a mezzanine, used especially in winter, is encountered.

The most important space of the upper storeys is the *sofa* (hall), which covers at least half of the upper storey and connects individual rooms. It is used as the centre for domestic production and other home activities, including food production for winter, living, eating, recreation and sleeping (in summer). Houses may be categorized according to the location of the *sofa*: houses with an outer *sofa* are more frequent in Anatolia, and it is generally believed they were the point of origin for the evolution of houses with an inner *sofa*, characteristic of urban dwellings. In the first type, the *sofa* is orientated to the courtyard or garden, and the upper storeys are open to the exterior to take advantage of the climate. The principal element in the *sofa* is the iwan, a sort of alcove between rooms with three sides closed and one open to the *sofa*. The *köşk* or belvedere, is a separate living space projecting over the *sofa* and enlivening the court façade. The *sofa* is flanked by slightly raised living platforms (*tahtseki*, from *taht*, 'throne', and *seki*, 'platform'). In the second type, more protected from the climate and more secure, the inner *sofa* is a communal space closed to the exterior and having rooms on at least two sides. From the 19th century the *sofa* became increasingly centralized in Anatolia and the Balkans, following the style of Istanbul. Houses with centralized *sofa*s are found in the magnificent mansions of Istanbul, the waterfront houses on the Bosporus (*yalı*), and the houses of Plovdiv in the Bulgarian Renaissance style. With the integration of Western lifestyles, blind exterior walls of traditional urban houses were pierced with openings.

The rooms of the upper storeys open to the *sofa* but do not interconnect. The reception or main room (*başoda*), often located in the corner with a view over the street, is larger and more elaborately decorated. As there is no functional differentiation between the other rooms, all are similar in size and arrangement, each having a great built-in cupboard (*yüklük*) and small cubicle for ablution (*gusülhane*). Approximately one-third of the room is on the same level as the *sofa*. This space (*sekialtı*) contains the entrance, cupboard and ablution cubicle. The main space (*sekiüstü*), approximately 200–300 mm higher and separated by a balustrade, has a continuous seat (*sedir*), 200–400 mm high by 600 mm wide, along three walls. The floor is covered with a carpet and the seat furnished with cushions and pillows. Open shelves along the walls allow household items to be displayed, and some early houses have windows over these shelves. The decorated wooden ceiling is usually the most magnificent element in the

32. Typical urban house, Mudurnu, Turkey

room, complemented by wooden doors over niches and small closets in the main space. Some rooms, particularly the reception room, have a fireplace. In the Balkans, more houses have inner *sofa*s, doors connect the rooms, and the iwan and *köşk* are rare. In some houses in Bulgaria, particularly in Plovdiv, façades are decorated. With the impact of Westernization, a type of town house with neo-classical elements became more common.

BIBLIOGRAPHY

S. H. Eldem: *Türk evi plan tipleri* [Basic plans of the Turkish house] (Istanbul, 1955, 2/1968)
G. Goodwin: 'The Ottoman House', *A History of Ottoman Architecture* (London and Baltimore, 1971), pp. 428–49
Ö. Küçükerman: *Turkish House in Search of Spatial Identity* (Istanbul, 1973, 2/1985)
W. J. Eggeling: 'Hausformen in Yugoslavisch-Makedonien', *Z. Balkanologie*, (1976), pp. 12–19
E. Riza: 'La Typologie de l'habitation urbaine albanaise (XVIIIe siècle-moitié du XIXe), *Stud. Alb.*, xiv (1977), pp. 109–25
A. Bammer: *Wohnen im Vergänglichen* (Graz, 1982)
D. Kuban: 'Turk ev geleneği üzerine gözlemler' [Observations on the traditional Turkish house], *Türk ve İslâm sanatı üzerine denemeler* [Essays on Turkish and Islamic art] (Istanbul, 1982), pp. 195–209
D. Philippides: *Greek Traditional Architecture*, 2 vols (Athens, 1983)
S. H. Eldem: *Türk evi osmanlı dönemi* [Turkish houses of the Ottoman period] (Istanbul, 1984)
G. Akın: *Doğu ve güneydoğu Anadolu Ev tiplerinde anlam* [Types of construction in the houses of south and south-east Anatolia] (Istanbul, 1985)
R. Angelova: 'L'Architecture vernaculaire de la Bulgarie', *L'Architecture vernaculaire dans les Balkans* (1985)
N. Akın: *Balkanlarda osmanlı evi* [Ottoman houses in the Balkans] (Istanbul, 1987)
N. Moutsopoulos: *L'Encorbellement architectural 'Le Sachnisia': Contribution à l'étude de la maison grecque* (Thessalonika, 1988)

N. AKIN

(viii) Iran. The vernacular architecture of Iran divides into three zones: sub-tropical, mountain and plateau. On the Caspian littoral a fine tradition of reed thatching and matting for walls has been largely overtaken by the oil can. Beaten flat and usually rusted to an attractive chestnut colour, it has become the traditional roofing material just as it has in the mountains. Generously projecting eaves throw the water clear. In areas of the Elburz where there is good timber for building, pockets of a vernacular tradition reminiscent of Switzerland may survive. The vernacular of the plateau, however, is the most extensive, spectacular and 'typically Iranian'. The combination of the harsh desert climate and a severe limitation in the choice of building materials has produced a vernacular unsurpassed in providing living and working conditions that are not only tolerable but civilized. For instance, the vernacular tradition includes not only the basic requirements of shelter from the elements and a clean water supply but also provision for such luxuries as air-conditioning (*see* WIND CATCHER) or the means of making and storing ice (*see* ICE-HOUSE).

The basic building material on the plateau is mud. Timber is in short supply, and stone tends to be poor and is used chiefly for wall footings and foundations. Mud is used as cob-earth mixed with straw and water and spread by shovel in layers to form a battered wall; or as pisé, in which case little water is added and the earth is rammed. Sun-dried bricks are also made in the villages and much used. Mud with a higher clay content may be made into baked bricks. Walls other than baked brick are rendered with a mud-lime mix to improve their appearance and weathering properties. Roofs are often of brick, domed or vaulted, since there is no other way to span between the walls, unless timber or steel is available for construction. Thus the humblest building, for example an animal shelter, may have a barrel vault; a village cistern may be domed. Scarcity of timber even for the centring of arches and the support of vaults during construction has led to ingenious methods of building whereby the vaults are self-supporting during construction as well as when complete. Each brick course in a vault is tilted slightly to give support to that above. This, together with joints of thick mortar—which sets quickly in the dry atmosphere—and the speed with which the bricklayer works, give the bricks enough sticking power to stay in place until the vault is complete. (The Egyptian architect HASSAN FATHY revived this method in Egypt in the 1960s.) The brick vaults are then rendered with a mud plaster to make them waterproof, and some grander buildings are paved with baked bricks.

Flat roofs are common wherever timber is available, since they are easier to construct. Poles are laid as joists, covered with reed matting or brushwood and then with layer upon layer of mud-lime plaster up to c. 500 mm thick. Rainwater is carried clear of the walls on long wooden spouts. Mud is a very good insulator, and since walls are thick and have few openings their insulation properties are excellent, a matter of prime importance in the desert. The grave drawback of brick and cob construction in a country subject to earthquakes is their lack of tensile strength and tendency to collapse. The finish of walls, roofs and floors with the same material is not dull but has a magical effect, as the rendering transforms the most workaday building into sculpture of astonishing form. The mud, being a gentle sandy colour with its surface broken by myriad short pieces of straw, makes a restful contrast to the desert glare.

Both the plateau villages and village houses are inward-looking, an essential feature if the village is to survive the extremes of climate and gain all possible protection from the wind. Villages are mostly walled and are further protected by a buffer of trees and orchards in the surrounding irrigated fields. The street is flanked by the blank walls of houses rarely broken by windows and only where necessary by doors. The main street is sometimes partly vaulted and shaded by mulberry or pomegranate trees. The better houses focus on their individual court-yards, which are contrived to be invisible from the street door. Each has its water tank or pool and probably a tree, and thus a microclimate is created, protected from the parching wind. The use of the house is regulated by the time of day and season. Flat roofs are used for sleeping on summer nights, and the heat of the day is spent in underground rooms cooled by wind catchers. Summer evenings are passed on a raised porch (Pers. *tālār*), which catches the breeze. A range of south-facing rooms warmed by the low sun is used in winter.

BIBLIOGRAPHY
R. Rainer: *Traditional Building in Iran* (Graz, 1977)
E. Beazley and M. Harverson: *Living with the Desert: Working Buildings of the Iranian Plateau* (Warminster, 1982)

ELISABETH BEAZLEY

(ix) Western Central Asia. The earliest remains of domestic architecture in the region—apart from Palaeolithic fire marks in caves in Teshiktash, Machay etc—are communal hunting and fishing cabins of the Neolithic period in the lower reaches of the Amu River and settlements of flat-roofed structures from the Dzheytun culture in southern Turkmenistan. Square single-family houses of mud-brick with pisé floors had a fireplace to the right of the entrance and a wall altar opposite; the clay-coated walls and floors were decorated in red or black, and some walls had painted images of hoofed animals and dogs. By the Bronze Age, domestic buildings were huddled together and linked by an irregular network of streets (e.g. ALTYN TEPE); mud-brick walls were decorated with simple geometric patterns in two or three colours, and flat roofs were sometimes replaced by vaults. In ancient Khwarazm the regular contours of the town divided by a street running along the axis determined the straight network of domestic construction (e.g. Dzhanbas Kala or TOPRAK KALA), but the dominant system was that of the mansion house. These buildings—some with courtyards, some more compact in plan—were built along irrigation canals, as was typical during the medieval period. Bactrian houses in the Surkhan (Surkhab) River Basin had a courtyard and main hall decorated with murals.

In the 6th and 7th centuries AD, castles built on sloping pisé socles were erected throughout the region. Those of Khwarazm had rectangular fortified walls with a keep by the entrance, although in the largest of these castles (Yakke-Parsan) the keep was set in the middle of the courtyard. As can be seen from the well-preserved example of Great Kyz-kala (see fig. 33), the façade was decorated with closely set half-round columns to emphasize the defensive aspect, and the yard contained flat-roofed houses arranged systematically. In the Merv oasis these castles had vaulted rooms arranged in two storeys around a courtyard or domed hall, and the keep was sometimes found in the yard of a flat-roofed mansion. In the east a corridor often ran around the interior perimeter (e.g. Ak-Tepe, near Tashkent, or Aul Tepe in the Kashka River region), and the rectangular plan was elaborated in rectangular or rounded towers. In the smaller castles of Ustrushana and Tokharistan, the main hall is clearly distinguished from the surrounding mass of vaulted and flat-roofed rooms and often had four piers, carved wooden ornament and painted walls (e.g. Balalyk Tepe and Chil-khudzhra). A yard with service buildings surrounded the castle.

At PENDZHIKENT excavations have revealed the main outlines of urban domestic architecture in the 7th and 8th centuries. The residential quarters, packed within the city walls, were divided into sections by thick pisé walls. Each section had a residential and an official area. The more fashionable houses had beamed roofs, while the rest were vaulted. Reception halls with four piers were lit by an opening in the cupola; the walls were covered with multicoloured narrative murals, and the wooden elements,

33. Great Kyz-kala, Sultan-Kala, Merv, Turkmenistan, 6th–7th centuries AD

including caryatids, were carved. Pisé ramps led to the second storey, where flat-roofed rooms were used in summer. In houses without a courtyard, the entrance portico opened directly to the street. In the 11th and 12th centuries, the prevalent type of urban housing had rooms arranged around a courtyard and lighter construction with walls of mud-brick and beamed roofs (e.g. Merv, Misrian, the Buran hill), and rich wall decoration in carved stucco and painting. Excavations in OTRAR have provided a detailed picture of the situation in the late medieval period (15th–18th centuries). The town continued to be confined within the earlier boundaries, and residential plots did not exceed 100 sq. m. The one- or two-room houses had covered yards in front and storehouses behind, while a small reception room was sometimes located by the entrance. Light entered through openings in the flat roof. The houses were normally heated by fireplaces on the floor, but at Otrar hypocausts were used, and indeed this latter form of heating was found as far as the Aral Sea.

Domestic architecture in the 19th and 20th centuries can be studied through surviving structures. Local characteristics depend on natural and climatic conditions, and in towns construction was organized around yards, divided into male and female halves. Skeletal walls and flat earth roofs resting on beams predominate. Exit to the yard was effected through shuttered openings with iwan porticos. The architectural schools of the Ferghana basin, Bukhara and Khiva are notable for the organization and artistic decoration of the interiors. Local characteristics are more clearly seen in rural buildings: the reed construction of the

Amu delta, the domed houses of southern Turkmenistan and the pitched thatched roofs of southern Tajikistan. Rural mansions have tall rectangular pisé walls decorated with drawn and moulded ornament (the Samarkand *kurgons* and the *khovly* and *khauli* of the Amu River region). The survival of tradition can be seen in the central axis plan of the mansions of Khwarazm, the defensive *dinga* tower in the yards of houses in Turkmenistan, the persistence of the Otrar house in those of southern Kazakhstan, the seasonal houses of the Samarkand region cut into loess like medieval caves in southern Tajikistan, and houses with log domes in Gornyy Badakhshan. Permanent structures are often accompanied by covered felt tents of the nomads (*see* TENT, §II, 2). The Karakalpaks moved these tents in winter into a special room in the house, and a place for a tent was even set aside in the Tash-Khauli Palace in Khiva. Palace architecture always borrowed forms from ordinary dwellings, simply increasing the number of rooms and adding a grander part, as can be seen in the early medieval palaces of Pendzhikent, Bundzhikat and Varakhsha with their multi-piered throne rooms.

Rural architecture of the 6th to 8th centuries is known from the unfortified farmhouses grouped around the feudal castle (a mansion with a courtyard in the Merv region) or by the town walls (small vaulted buildings to the east of Pendzhikent). Rural accommodation in Khwarazm of the 1st to 14th centuries has been studied in some detail: construction was of clay and unfired materials, while planning varied from mansions with courtyards to compact many-roomed systems arranged in networks or along a central axis. Echoes of earlier traditions were expressed in the decorative treatment of walls, and towers were turned into pigeon towers. One particular type of settlement found between the 10th and 14th centuries was a complex of caves carved into the base of cliffs (multi-roomed, sometimes in two tiers, along the right bank of the Murgab River) or in the strata of loess (southern Tajikistan), where the ceilings imitate vaulted construction.

See also CENTRAL ASIA, §I, 2 and ISLAMIC ART, §II, 4(i)(c).

BIBLIOGRAPHY

G. A. Pugachenkova: *Puti razvitiya arkhitektury yuzhnogo Turkmenistana pory rabovladeniya i feodalizma* [The paths of development of the architecture of southern Turkmenistan in the period of slave-ownership and feudalism] (Moscow, 1958)

Ye. Ye. Narazik: *Sel'skoye zhilishche v Korezme (I–XIV vv.)* [Rural domestic architecture in Khwarazm (1st–14th centuries)] (Moscow, 1976)

K. A. Akishev, K. M. Baypakov and L. B. Yerzakovich: *Pozdnesrednekovyy Otrar* [Late medieval Otrar] (Alma Ata, 1981)

V. L. VORONINA

8. INDIAN SUBCONTINENT. It is a paradox of Indian history that, while there is very little documented history in the form of textual and archaeological evidence, there is a remarkable continuity of culture that directly relates events of 2–3000 years ago to modern beliefs and practices.

Thus individual elements of modern vernacular architecture can be traced back to the building practices of some of the earliest recorded cultures in the region. Until well into modern times, for example, the generic form of the town house throughout the Northern Indian plain remained a burnt brick structure built around a courtyard, directly fronting the street and attached to the neighbouring houses, a form traceable back to the urban architecture of the Harappan civilization that flourished on the banks of the Indus from the early 3rd to the late 2nd millennium BC. Other house-types are depicted in rock carvings, reliefs and wall paintings from the period *c.* 200 BC–AD 500 (see fig. 34).

Two types of village cottage in particular that were still being extensively built in the late 20th century can be identified from these sources: one type had thick battered mud walls and a curvilinear thatched roof with overhanging eaves, probably with a bamboo structure, while the other had timber and bamboo walls and a horseshoe-shaped, barrel-vaulted roof made of timber and bamboo and reed, leaves or thatch. There is no reason to suppose that the hundreds of other types of rural dwellings found on the Indian subcontinent—each reflecting the particularities of the local climate, materials and culture—do not have equally long ancestries.

34. Indian street scene, detail from a wall painting of the *Viśvantara Jātaka*, Cave 17, Ajanta, Maharashtra, India, *c.* late 5th century AD

35. Carved façade of a *hāvelī*, Ahmadabad, Gujarat, India

Other elements of modern practice can be traced back to prescriptions and proscriptions given in the *Vastuśāstras*, Sanskrit treatises thought mostly to have been written (or rewritten) in the second half of the 1st millennium AD. Running throughout the rules on geometry is a tension between a desire for symmetry and a fear of it. For example, a door must not be located precisely in the middle of a façade, and no two doors in a house should be exactly opposite each other. The centre of any element is considered a vulnerable point (*marmastan*), and the dictum that the doors should not be in alignment with each other is obeyed by slightly distorting the geometry. Rooms in the upper storeys should conform to those below, but alleys should not be built on both sides of a house. In South India domestic architecture based on the *Vastuśātras* remained commonplace in the late 20th century.

It is difficult, however, to trace a continuous process of development in domestic architecture from the late 1st millennium AD. Although most rural vernacular building remained virtually unaffected by subsequent cultural developments, little historical research has been undertaken in this area, and knowledge of the surviving indigenous tradition is limited only to urban houses, mainly the palaces of the nobility or of wealthy landlords and merchants. The indigenous Hindu tradition, for example, is evident in the trabeate and bracketed construction, corbelled vaults and ornamentation of the Man Mandir Palace in the fort at GWALIOR. The palace also has the deep overhanging ledges supported on brackets (*chajjās*), perforated screens (*jālī*s) and roof pavilions that remained part of the

vocabulary of domestic architecture in India until modern times. Humbler, and therefore more plausibly vernacular, examples include houses at Udaipur and Jaisalmer, most notably the lower levels of Salam Singh's *hāvelī* (18th century).

The *hāvelī* was the main urban domestic house-type until the 20th century in hundreds of cities and towns throughout the North Indian plains and as far south and west as Gujarat. Its typological importance, however, is only beginning to be realized. Although there are regional differences in the use of the term, broadly speaking the *hāvelī* refers to the ample house of a prosperous family. The house is generally attached to one of its neighbours, is invariably planned around one or more courtyards and is typically entered through an elaborate doorway, from which a crooked passageway leads to the interior. Quite humble houses also share the general arrangement of the *hāvelī* type, although the doorway may be plainer, and the courtyards may not have rooms on all four sides. There are also regional differences, principally in construction methods and materials. Hindu, Jain and Sikh houses tend to be on two or more storeys (the main floor always being one of the upper ones), with a relatively small courtyard, windows and balconies opening on to the street, especially on the upper floors (see fig. 35). Muslim homes have larger, more open courtyards but fewer and smaller rooms, and they tend to be on one floor, with the first floor partially built up. *Purdah*—the separation of the male and female areas of the home—is observed by designating the rear of the house as the women's area, while the male realm is near the entrance; some non-Muslim households with screens) and the use of steel beams in construction. The varied forms of other regional house-types can be related to the local climate, to local culture and to the availability of materials. In Gujarat, wooden *hāvelīs* with pitched roofs are common; related to these is the Maharashtran house-type known as *wada*, which has a generic form similar to that of southern Indian houses: wide-eaved, pitched-roofed buildings arranged around open courtyards and often surrounded by verandahs (*see* INDIAN, SUBCONTINENT, §III, 7(ii)(c)). In Kashmir, too, wooden houses predominate, although their plan may be less regular and more compact, with the courtyard not placed centrally. The documentation of most of these house-types is only in its infancy, and many other types remain unidentified.

Another important (if not wholly vernacular) house-type was the bungalow, so called because of its derivation

1. Vernacular trade sign for a chimney-sweep, sheet tin and wood, h. 1.17 m, late 19th century (ex-John Judkyn Memorial, Bath)

also observe *purdah* by restricting the family domain to the upper floors, with the kitchen typically on the first floor. Most *hāvelīs* have thick masonry walls and flat roofs of masonry on a stone or timber structure; both roofs and the courtyards are used as living spaces, and it is usual to sleep outside in the summer.

Despite the affinities between the *hāvelī* and the generic form of the houses of the Harappan cities, there is little documentation of the *hāvelī* as such before the 17th century. A ruin in Delhi, known as Barakhamba, which is thought by some authorities to be the house of a late 15th- or early 16th-century nobleman, has a *hāvelī*-like arrangement and may be the earliest known surviving example. More is known, however, of the evolution of the *hāvelī*-type house from the period of British influence, which led to the incorporation of Western ornamentation, the increasing use of doors to close off rooms and to shutter openings to the courtyard (previously these were hung

2. Vernacular trade sign for a gunsmith, painted fir, h. 787 mm, possibly by the Harp Alley school, London, h. 787 mm, second quarter of the 18th century (Bath, John Judkyn Memorial)

3. Vernacular trade sign for the Rising Sun Inn, painted wood, 825×680 mm, possibly by the Harp Alley school, London, 1751 (ex-John Judkyn Memorial, Bath)

from the Bengali hut. A reflection of the importance of the European cultural legacy, its development can be traced from the late 17th century, when the fledgling colonial powers (most importantly the British, but also the French and Dutch) needed to accommodate increasing numbers of soldiers and administrators in a culturally acceptable but climatically appropriate house-type. The early bungalows consisted of a square or rectangular room covered by a widely oversailing thatched roof; later a smaller room was added to each of the four corners, and the spaces between these became verandahs. It was only in the early 19th century in Bengal, however, that the bungalow was adopted as a house-type by Indians. In the course of that century two distinct types of bungalow evolved: the pitched-roofed form, having a higher central portion with clerestory windows above a columned verandah, and a grander flat-roofed version. The latter form was used by Edwin Lutyens and Herbert Baker at Delhi (*see* DELHI, §I, 8) in their plan for the new capital city.

See also INDIA, REPUBLIC OF, §II, and INDIAN SUBCONTINENT, §III.

BIBLIOGRAPHY
D. N. Shukla: *Vāstu-śāstras* (Varanasi, 1960)
A. Ray: *Villages, Towns and Secular Buildings in Ancient India* (Calcutta, 1964)
A. Rapoport: *House Form and Culture* (Englewood Cliffs, 1969)
M. Patel: *Study of Old Havelis in Gujerat* (Ahmadabad, 1981)
L. Patel: *Profiles of Built Forms: A Case Study of Nasik Houses* (Ahmadabad, 1982)
Y. R. Jain: *Havelis: A Study at Jaipur* (Ahmadabad, 1983)
A. D. King: *The Bungalow: The Production of a Global Culture* (London, 1984)
S. Prasad: *The Havelis of North India* (diss., London, Royal Coll. A., 1988)
V. S. Pramar: *Haveli: Wooden Houses and Mansions of Gujarat* (Singapore, 1989)
Bauernhof, Stadthaus, Palast: Architektur in Gujarat, Indien (exh. cat. by M. Desai, Zurich, Mus. Rietberg, 1990)

SUNAND PRASAD

Vernacular [Folk] art. Term used for works of art produced by artisans trained in a relevant skill working within a local client economy. Vernacular art is the product of traditions deeply rooted in the materials and crafts that such materials both disciplined and inspired. Work of this kind is profoundly empirical; it was created by those for whom making and designing were simultaneous activities. The grammar of this visual regional dialect depends also on structure and convention. As in language, the vernacular in the visual arts (encompassing building, painting, carving, furniture, textiles, ceramics and metalwork) exists beyond the received view of polite society. Its presence implies a relatively complex, if less than egalitarian social system. Where innovation and 'polite' details do occur in vernacular arts, they are superficial.

4. Vernacular weather vane, painted wrought iron, h. 1.45 m, from North America, 19th century (Bath, American Museum in Britain)

Vernacular art is more susceptible to definition than the all-encompassing implications of FOLK ART. Although vernacular art is almost as wide in scope as 'folk art', it is fairly closely defined in terms of its creators (rather than the response of its viewers), not so much with regard to the biographical details of an individual craftsman as in the relationships between craft traditions and the artistic and practical needs of the maker and the client. In general, the vernacular artist was, as a member of the 'client economy', beholden to the views and needs of the customer. It was a productive partnership.

The availability of art 'off the peg', which may be associated with the foundations of academies of art, is less common at the vernacular level. An 18th-century English exception was the mass production of trade signs in anticipation of their purchase. These signs (see fig. 1) and such related objects as weather vanes were made by specialist craftsmen (carvers, blacksmiths and painters), whose workshops were centred on Harp Alley in the City of London (see figs 2 and 3). In such instances, the impact on the arts (and advertising) of an emerging consumerism may be discerned. It was a development that would ultimately lead to the decline in the need for craftsmen–artists (as distinct from artist–craftsmen). The speculative production of a weather vane (see fig. 4), for example, could be more efficiently and, therefore, more cheaply achieved by factory methods to meet the conventional standards of the 'consumer society'.

A further issue concerns the possible dates within which vernacular art thrived. Is it a continuing tradition or was it destroyed by industrialization or dislocated beyond redemption by two world wars? The answer is more likely to be found through a question of greater relevance. What are the historical circumstances that permit a vernacular art to prosper? The rise of the middle classes and greater freedom for the peasantry coincided with, or was the consequence of, the Renaissance in southern Europe and the Reformation in northern Europe. It was within these circumstances that an 'instant tradition' was born, one in which secular values emerged that were nevertheless rooted in and nourished by medieval training and craftsmanship, which at a vernacular level, persisted in the post-medieval world—for example, the abundant use of painted decoration on furniture and wood-carving (see SHIP-DECORATION, fig. 3). The way in which the vernacular arts have emerged once a people has been emancipated from an overlordship, whether theocratic, aristocratic or militaristic has been examined by Kubler.

Although vernacular art is a visual language spoken outside patrician circles, it is not necessarily inimical to them. As a conservative aesthetic, it may perpetuate earlier 'high-style' features while imperceptibly producing a mutation that is original in character (for illustration see FOLK ART). These general trends are capable of moving in either direction. There are numerous examples of works that move beyond the threshold of the 'vernacular' towards the 'polite'.

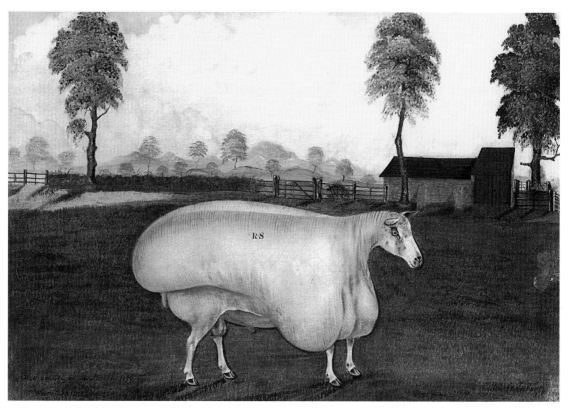

5. Vernacular painting by William Bagshaw: *White Ram*, oil on canvas, 455×665 mm, from England, 1846 (Bath, Crane Kalman Museum of Naive Art)

6. Vernacular painting attributed to William Matthew Prior: *Small Girl in a Blue Dress*, oil on canvas, 673×546 mm, from America, *c.* 1845 (Bath, American Museum in Britain)

This is not to say that vernacular art has no claim to a historical existence—it does, but as so often in the arts, it is a relative rather than an absolute term. Despite this difficulty, there is some evidence for asserting that those who worked within the disciplines of the vernacular traditions saw themselves as separate from those who obeyed the conventions implicit in academic training. The trade directories issued in a number of metropolitan centres in Britain in the 18th and 19th centuries list 'provincial' though 'polite' painters under the heading 'Artists: portrait, landscape, miniature, &c'. In contrast, the 'vernacular' artists are found under 'Painters: house, sign &c'. Such men (they were generally men) were trained in the craft of paint and are known to have produced 'easel paintings', but they saw themselves as distinct from their more academic, if less craft-trained contemporaries. Some combined other skills, such as William Bagshaw (*fl* mid-19th century; see fig. 5), who was listed in the trade directory of Rugby, Warks, England, as a 'Plumber and Glazier . . . and artist'.

In regions with small populations spread over large land masses, the specialist services of such vernacular artists and craftsmen imposed an itinerant way of life. From the 'rose painters' (*rosemaling*) of Norway to the 'face painters' of America (see fig. 6), it was only by travel that sufficient work could be found to sustain these craftsmen. In small countries with larger populations (such as Britain) this was unnecessary, and the vernacular art of such essentially urban populations may prove to be, mile for mile, more various.

The tidy compartments of the trade directories obscure the subtleties that are known to have existed. Many house

painters in extending their activities to easel-painting ultimately transferred their activities wholly to canvas and panel. Some drifted to the more academic expectations of 'provincial art' and others emerged fully into the 'polite arts'. Nevertheless, the distinctions between vernacular and polite artists (and by extension the same is true of their work) was real. That some of these artists crossed the Rubicon that separated the vernacular from the polite only reinforces the view that the history of art should, more often than is usual, reflect not one but several streams of excellence, each of which was capable of providing vital cross-fertilization for the other.

The rise in the awareness of the vernacular arts outside their point of production is an important aspect of the history of aesthetics. Perhaps one of the first, if not the first, to acknowledge publicly the importance of this level of art was William Hogarth. In 1762 Hogarth, together with Bonnell Thornton, organized an exhibition of signboard art in London, ostensibly as a persiflage of the annual exhibition of the (Royal) Society of Arts (see fig. 7). For those with the wit to see with Hogarth's eye, the exhibition evidently reflected a more serious intent. Many of the contemporary reviews are interestingly equivocal; should they see the joke or have they missed the point? The famous dinner party given in Paris in 1908 by Picasso, Georges Braque, Marie Laurencin, Guillaume Apollinaire and Gertrude Stein in honour of the painter Henri

7. Vernacular signboard art from London, from an exhibition organized by William Hogarth and Bonnell Thornton, 1762; reconstruction (Bath, John Judkyn Memorial)

8. Vernacular picture by an anonymous sailor: *H.M.S. Queen*, dyed wool, 736×895 mm, from Malta, 1851 (Bath, John Judkyn Memorial)

Rousseau was no less ambiguous. Was the dinner held in honour of a great painter or in derision of an inferior one? The answer must ultimately reside in the importance of Rousseau's work as a painter. However, it could reasonably be argued that Rousseau was a 'Sunday painter' (his full-time job was as a customs official) rather than a true vernacular artist based in a craft tradition. Rousseau was perhaps one of that new breed of non-aristocratic amateurs for whom painting was a serious recreation, a recreation that became more possible as a result of the production and sale of watercolour paint in cakes and of oil paint in tubes.

The recognition accorded to both 'vernacular artists' and 'Sunday painters' has perhaps obscured the important socio-historical differences in their origins and, therefore, in their work. It is these differences in the backgrounds of the producers (thus a 'production-based' analysis) that define their position within the history of art with more exactitude than the inherent qualities of their work (a 'reception-based' analysis; see fig. 8). Even so, it is notice-able how often in the past vernacular artists (like 'Sunday painters') and their work were first accepted without condescension by practising artists. Hogarth is a remark-ably early example of this perceptive view, but by the early

20th century he was joined by many others, including, in addition to Picasso and Braque, other European and American artists, such as Ben Nicholson and Christopher Wood, Franz Marc and Vasily Kandinsky (who published examples in the *Blaue Reiter* Almanac of 1912), Charles Sheeler and Elie Nadelman. Recognition by fellow artists was followed in due course by that of dealers, collectors and the general public.

The more recent hegemony of the art historian has been challenged by folklorists and social historians who doubt the validity of something that appeared so often to be identified retrospectively on the basis of a subjective aesthetic judgement rather than objective truths, the values of which would have been recognizable to the artists and artisans under review. These folklorists cast doubt on the validity of the historical existence of 'folk art' in ways that the greater precision of the term 'vernacular art' might have forestalled. In the absence of a serious theoretical framework, American folklorists such as Henry Glassie and social historians such as Kenneth Ames have enjoyed the freedom to apply the rigour of their respective fields of enquiry to what they perceived to be the rather lax world of 'folk art' studies as pursued by art historians.

The decline in the vernacular arts is not easily understood and inevitably varies from region to region. Industrialization is not necessarily the explanation; in certain conditions it actively encouraged the development of a vernacular art—canal boat painting and fairground carving are two British examples.

Accordingly, the explanation for the loss of vigour in the vernacular arts must be sought in more profound social circumstances. In another context ('rough music'), E. P. Thompson noted that in both rural and urban communities traditions decline in association with the weakening of dialects and regional accents and that this, in turn, may be associated with the ever decreasing importance of an oral culture.

On the basis of this hypothesis, the growth of literacy may be measured against the decline in the vernacular culture. In addition, in regions where 20th-century warfare has destroyed old communities and the pattern of life they sustained, folk traditions, and the vernacular arts associated with them, have diminished or disappeared. The naive 'art industry' of the former republics of Yugoslavia is no substitute.

In some remote areas of North America, genuine 'Sunday painters', such as Clementine Hunter (1887–1988), a black artist and native of Louisiana, retained an authentically independent vision, but artists of her kind were not working within the vernacular tradition of the craft of paint. It is a shift of circumstance acknowledged by Hemphill and Weissman, who conceded that such a phenomenon as 'folk art' produced before World War I possesses a sense of 'engagement between individual art statement and folk craft'—a vernacular art. Unlike some writers, they saw a difference between folk 'art' and folk 'arts and crafts', the latter being functional, the former being those objects of daily use decorated beyond the call of duty.

In setting aside the term 'folk art', a convincing argument may be made for stating that 'vernacular art' had, and in some remote districts retains, a real existence (see fig. 9). Ultimately, vernacular art also exists, as with the arts such things must, in the eye of the beholder. In the West this eye focuses on architecture, painting and sculpture; in the East ceramics and textiles come into greater prominence. In Roman Catholic countries religion provides both an inspiration and a theme, whereas in northern Europe and much of North America the objectives are more domestic (see figs 10 and 11).

Whatever the circumstances of their production and function, the vernacular arts raise important questions concerning the nature of art. Viewed in its historical context, vernacular art was to its maker factitive with the activities of its creation and use, a process as important as the static nature of the resulting object. In this transition from noun to verb retrospective observation from the 20th century have generally been more conscious of art than artefact.

BIBLIOGRAPHY
S. Janis: *They Taught Themselves: American Primitive Painters of the Twentieth Century* (New York, 1942)
G. A. Kubler: *The Shape of Time* (New Haven, 1962)
H. J. Hansen, ed.: *European Folk Art* (London, 1967)
H. Glassie: *Patterns in the Material Folk Culture of the Eastern United States* (Philadelphia, 1968)
R. W. Brunskill: *Illustrated Handbook of Vernacular Architecture* (London, 1971, 2/1987)
H. W. Hemphill jr and J. Weissman: *Twentieth Century American Folk Art and Artists* (New York, 1974)
J. Russell Harper: *A People's Art: Primitive, Naive, Provincial and Folk Painting in Canada* (Toronto and Buffalo, 1974)
M. Owen Jones: *The Hand Made Object and Its Maker* (Los Angeles, 1975)
J. Cuisenier: *French Folk Art* (Tokyo and New York, 1976)
R. F. Trent: *Hearts and Crowns* (New Haven, 1977)
Beyond Necessity: Art in the Folk Tradition (exh. cat. by K. L. Ames, Winterthur, DE, Du Pont Winterthur Mus., 1977)
M. Bank: *Anonymous Was a Woman* (New York, 1979)
Outsider Art (exh. cat. by V. Musgrave and R. Cardinal, ACGB, 1979)
I. M. G. Quimby and S. T. Swank, eds: *Perspectives on American Folk Art* (New York, 1980)
G. Melly: *A Tribe of One* (Yeovil, 1981)
N. McKendrick, J. Brewer and J. H. Plumb: *The Birth of a Consumer Society: The Commercialization of Eighteenth Century England* (London, 1983)
O. Bihalji-Merlin and N.-B. Tomašević, eds: *World Encyclopedia of Naive Art: A Hundred Years of Naive Art* (London, 1984)
In Another World: Outsider Art from Europe and America (exh. cat. by R. Malbert and D. Maclagan, ACGB, 1987)
P. Zora: *Folk Art* (1995), xi of *Greek Art* (Athens, 1994–6)

JAMES AYRES

9. Vernacular thatched roof decoration by Alf Wright: *Straw Eagle*, straw and wire, h. 762 mm, from England, *c.* 1976 (Bath, John Judkyn Memorial)

10. Vernacular gifts for a wedding anniversary, attributed to J. Krans, tin, life-size, from New York, *c.* 1895 (Bath, American Museum in Britain)

11. Vernacular painting on a tray: *Adam Naming the Animals*, oil on tin, 552×762 mm, second quarter of the 19th century (Bath, John Judkyn Memorial)

Vernacular furniture. *See* FURNITURE, VERNACULAR.

Verner, Frederick A(rthur) (*b* Sheridan, Ontario, 26 Feb 1836; *d* London, 6 May 1928). Canadian painter. He travelled to England in 1856 and studied at Heatherley's Academy in London. After enlisting in the 3rd Yorkshire Militia in 1858, he joined the British Legion in 1860 and fought for the liberation of Italy with Garibaldi's troops. On his return to Canada in 1862, he painted his first pictures of Native American (e.g. *Ojibway Camp, Northern Shore of Lake Huron*, 1873; Ottawa, N.G.) and began work as a photographic colourist. Although Verner was influenced by Paul Kane's paintings of Indians, his work is infused with a more romantic vision. Verner was a founder-member of the Ontario Society of Artists in 1872 and showed in their first exhibition in 1873.

Many of the details of Verner's later work of Indians would be taken from sketches that he made during a trip to North-West Angle, Lake of the Woods, near Winnipeg, to witness the signing of the North-West Angle Treaty in 1873. In 1880 Verner moved to England, perhaps to take advantage of his growing popularity in that country. He continued to paint Indian scenes, as well as scenes of the buffalo that he studied in captivity in London. His works depict a calm and tranquil world with compelling atmospheric effects (e.g. *Sunset on the Muskoka River*, 1881; Toronto, A.G. Ont.). He returned to Canada on three occasions between 1888 and 1892, travelling to Manitoba and British Columbia. He became an Associate Member of the Royal Canadian Academy in 1893 and was elected to the Royal British Colonial Society of Artists in 1905.

BIBLIOGRAPHY
J. Murray: *The Last Buffalo: The Story of Frederick Arthur Verner, Painter of the Canadian West* (Toronto, 1984)

LINDA JANSMA

Vernet. French family of artists. Antoine Vernet (1689–1753) was a prosperous artisan painter in Avignon to whom some decorated coach panels (Avignon, Mus. Calvet) are attributed. Of his three sons, (1) Joseph Vernet earned a reputation throughout Europe as a landscape and marine painter, receiving the commission from Louis XV for the series *Ports of France*. Jean-Antoine Vernet (1716–?1755) also painted seascapes, and (Antoine-)François Vernet (1730–79) was a decorative painter; their respective sons, Louis-François Vernet (1744–84) and Joseph Vernet the younger (*b* 1760; *fl* 1781–?1792), were both active in Paris as sculptors. (1) Joseph's son (2) Carle Vernet, a painter and lithographer, became known for his pictures of horses and battle scenes, though his achievement was overshadowed not only by his father's but by that of his son (3) Horace Vernet, a prolific and highly successful painter, especially of battle scenes. The family was connected by marriage to several other notable French artists, Carle becoming father-in-law of Hippolyte Lecomte and Horace that of Paul Delaroche; Carle's sister Emilie married the architect Jean-François-Thérèse Chalgrin.

BIBLIOGRAPHY
Bellier de La Chavignerie–Auvray; Bénézit; Lami; Thieme–Becker
A. Dayot: *Les Vernet: Joseph–Carle–Horace* (Paris, 1898)
P. G. Delaroche-Vernet: *Horace Vernet, Paul Delaroche et leur famille* (Paris, 1907)

(1) (Claude-)Joseph Vernet (*b* Avignon, 14 Aug 1714; *d* Paris, 4 Dec 1789). Painter.

1. Life and work. 2. Critical reception and posthumous reputation.

1. LIFE AND WORK.

(i) Early years and Rome, to 1753. Vernet probably received his first lessons in painting from his father, Antoine, who then encouraged him to move to the studio of Philippe Sauvan (1697–1792), the leading master in Avignon. Sauvan supplied altarpieces to local churches and decorative works and mythologies for grand houses in the area. After this apprenticeship Vernet worked in Aix-en-Provence with the decorative painter Jacques Viali (*fl* 1681–1745), who also painted landscapes and marine pictures. In 1731 Vernet independently produced a suite of decorative overdoors for the hôtel of the Marquise de Simiane at Aix-en-Provence; at least two of these survive (*in situ*) and are Vernet's earliest datable landscapes. These are early indications of his favoured type of subject, and Vernet would have studied works attributed to such 17th-century masters as Claude Lorrain, Gaspard Dughet and Salvator Rosa in private collections at Aix and Avignon. Three years later Joseph de Seytres, Marquis de Caumont, who had previously recommended Vernet to the Marquise de Simiane, offered to sponsor a trip to Italy. This was partly for Vernet to complete his artistic education but also to provide his sponsor with drawings of antiquities.

In the early 18th century Avignon was still papal territory; this meant that Vernet had some useful connections among influential churchmen when he arrived in Rome. He soon found himself at home in the French artistic community there, among other southerners such as Pierre Subleyras. He was allowed access to the Académie de France in Rome and was encouraged to pursue landscape studies by its Director, Nicolas Vleughels. He was also recommended to the French marine painter Adrien Manglard, who was well established in Rome and who may have taken Vernet into his studio. By 1738 Vernet was making his reputation as a marine and landscape painter, for about then he began to keep a record of his commissions. A number of these notebooks survive (Avignon, Mus. Calvet; see also Lagrange, 1864), and they reveal that his first important patron was Paul-Hippolyte, Duc de Saint-Aignan, France's Ambassador to Rome and a keen supporter of young French artists based there. The present whereabouts of the important works Vernet produced for him—recording events during the Duc's mission of 1739—is not known. Vernet's earliest known Italian works (*c.* 1737–8), such as the *Cascades at Tivoli* (Cleveland, OH, Mus. A.) or the *Rocky Landscape in Italy* (London, Dulwich Pict. Gal.), are reminiscent of Dughet and show his response to the wilder aspects of the Roman Campagna. They are more softly lit than Dughet's, however, and their superb brushwork is one of the hallmarks of Vernet's early Italian period. With them, Vernet was joining a long tradition of artists who depicted picturesque sites such as Tivoli, producing pictures for increasing numbers of visitors making the Grand Tour. These were to be Vernet's chief patrons during nearly 20 years' residence in Italy, especially the British, who virtually monopolized the Grand Tour in his day. Other patrons included Roman nobles, churchmen and French diplomats. Vernet's contacts with British visitors may have been facilitated by his marriage in 1745 to Virginia Parker, daughter of a captain in the papal navy; her father sometimes handled Vernet's business affairs. Vernet made some topographical works in Italy: a pair of views of the *Bay of Naples* (1748; Paris, Louvre) for François-Calude de Montboissier, Abbé de Canillac, French chargé d'affaires in Rome; for Elizabeth Farnese, wife of Philip V of Spain, a view of the *Villa Farnese, Caprarola* (1746; Philadelphia, PA, Mus. A.), which includes the Queen's entourage; and modest Roman views such as the *Ponte Rotto* and the *Castel S Angelo* (both Paris, Louvre). While the small-scale and refined observation of this latter pair foreshadow the open-air paintings of Corot and his generation, the larger paintings are part of a pan-European development of topography in the early 18th century, as exemplified by Canaletto's work in Venice and London or by Giovanni Battista Piranesi's Roman prints. Vernet's paintings are distinguished by their sharp observation, precise yet exquisite handling, and by the lively interest of his figures.

Imaginary landscapes and marine pictures account for the larger part of Vernet's output in Italy. The marine paintings, always set on an Italianate coast, fall into two contrasting types: calm and storm. The storm pictures vary, depicting ships either in danger or actually wrecked; the calm views are particularized by their light, atmosphere and time of day or night. The landscapes also vary in the time of day depicted, but, except for an occasional stormy scene, their weather is benign. In this way Vernet introduced variety into his art. His paintings were often conceived as pairs or sets of four; the set (1751; Rohrau, Schloss) commissioned by Aloys Thomas Raimund, Graf von Harrach, and the four ovals (1750; Russborough, Co. Wicklow) commissioned for the country seat of Joseph Leeson, later 1st Earl of Milltown, are typical. The latter show a calm, morning coastal view, a shipwreck at midday, a rosy evening harbour scene and a coastal scene by night. Through such pictures Vernet contributed to a developing sensibility in the 18th century for experiences of Nature in all its moods. Where his views were not strictly topographical representations, they strongly suggested sites on the itinerary of many a traveller through Italy: the hills and cascades of Tivoli, the harbour, lighthouses and old fortresses of Naples, or the undeveloped coastline near Naples and Rome. Vernet was the most talented of a number of landscape artists who supplied visitors to Rome with such souvenirs: Pieter van Bloemen and Andrea Locatelli provided Arcadian and pastoral landscapes, while Giovanni Paolo Panini specialized in fanciful pictures of the city or its ancient ruins. Some of Vernet's landscapes are reminiscent of the wild terrain of Rosa's work, while seaports recall those of Claude. Not only were his own works evocative of well-known sites, their allusiveness in both style and content to the works of admired Old Masters added to their appeal. In 1750, for example, a *Seaport: Sunset* (Duke of Buccleuch priv. col.) was commissioned to be painted expressly in the manner of Claude. Some works are recorded as having been commissioned 'in the manner of Salvator Rosa', while others are clearly reminiscent of Dughet. Vernet's own pictorial world is less idealized than that of Claude, and there is a sharper sense of particularized observation that the spectator can more readily explore. He skilfully combined sharp observation with a sure sense of decoration, which meant his paintings worked well in 18th-century interiors such as those at Russborough, Co. Wicklow. His pleasing effects were managed by juxtaposition of variously textured rocks, pools, cascades, leafy or blasted trees, sandy banks and so on, and above all by finding a rich diversity of brushwork with which to render them. He had a fine feeling for the medium of oil paint, so that he was enjoyed as a connoisseurs' painter.

Vernet was recognized by the Roman artistic community with his election to the Accademia di S Luca in 1743. Official recognition in his own country began when he was approved (*agréé*) by the Académie Royale in Paris on 6 August 1746, which enabled him to exhibit at the Salon for the first time that year; on 23 April 1753 he was received (*reçu*) as a full member. Exhibiting regularly at the Salon meant that Vernet's work became well known in Paris. When Abel-François Poisson de Vandières, later the Marquis de Marigny and Directeur des Bâtiments, made his educational tour of Italy in 1750, he and his party visited Vernet's studio in Rome. Very likely it was then that plans were laid for Vernet's return to France, and for his undertaking a major commission for Louis XV.

(ii) Later career, 1753–89. Vernet returned to live in France in 1753, beginning work on a series of large topographical paintings of major French commercial and military seaports. The *Ports of France* was one of the most important royal commissions of Louis XV's reign and at one level may be seen as propaganda for the French merchant and royal navies, which, ironically, were soon to take a severe beating during the Seven Years War (1756–63). If completed, the whole series would have comprised perhaps two dozen paintings, but Vernet produced only 15 (2 in Paris, Louvre; 13 on dep. Paris, Mus. Mar.). Vernet followed an official itinerary along the French coast from Antibes in the Mediterranean to Dieppe on the English Channel via Toulon, Marseille, Bandol, Sète, Bayonne, Bordeaux, Rochefort and La Rochelle. After visiting each port, he was required to report back to Marigny, explaining which views he had chosen and justifying any changes in his itinerary. Some ports merited two views (Marseille, Bayonne and Bordeaux), while Toulon needed three. At times Vernet found it difficult to reconcile the topographical requirements of his patrons with his own concern to create satisfying works of art. In 1756 there was almost acrimonious correspondence over whether he was allowed to show a storm at sea in the foreground of the *Port of Sète*; Vernet had his way, and Marigny was pleased with the result. Each painting has its own beauties, and they were well received at the Salons, where they were exhibited between 1755 and 1765. They are full of fascinating detail, for Vernet had to include all the characteristic activities of each port; this gives the pictures an almost scientific interest that is typical of the Enlightenment. He finally gave up the task and settled in Paris in 1765, the series incomplete; during the Revolution

Joseph Vernet: *Storm with a Shipwreck*, oil on canvas, 879×1381 mm, 1754 (London, Wallace Collection)

Jean-François Huë was commissioned to continue it. Vernet continued to produce variations on his well-tried themes of Italianate landscapes, calm seaports, stormy coasts, shipwrecks and moonlit harbours for the rest of his career; works such as *Storm with a Shipwreck* (London, Wallace; see fig.), bought by his patron Jean Girardot de Marigny in 1754, could equally well have been produced at a later date. In 1778 he made a trip to Switzerland with Marigny; instead of adapting his manner to fashionable depictions of Alpine scenery he chose to paint sites such as the *Falls of the Rhine at Schaffhausen* (priv. col., see 1976 exh. cat., p. 24) in the style he had formed in Italy 30 years earlier.

2. CRITICAL RECEPTION AND POSTHUMOUS REPUTATION. Vernet's international reputation had followed him from Rome to France, and to his British and French clients he added German princes and Russian nobles. From the 1760s to the 1780s no collection was deemed complete without examples of Vernet's art. He was the leading landscape and marine painter of France—even of Europe, if the newly developing (and essentially insular) school of landscape painting in Britain is discounted. Only post-Romantic prejudice led some 19th- and 20th-century commentators to criticize Vernet's repetition of subject-matter as lacking in invention or self-renewal. He was responding to market demand, though he gradually developed a slightly harder handling and colour; some discriminating connoisseurs in his own day preferred the more supple brushwork and poetic effects of light and colour of the Italian period. He was best known for his storms and shipwrecks; his grandson (3) Horace Vernet even

received a government commission for *Joseph Vernet Attached to the Mast Painting a Storm* (Avignon, Mus. Calvet). The Salon critics loved to describe the actions and gestures of the figures on seashores or doomed in wrecks, who were helpless pawns in these elemental dramas. Denis Diderot wrote eloquent commentaries on Vernet in his Salon reviews, notably in 1767. The excellence of Vernet's figure drawing and his mastery of gesture and expression brought his work close to the admired genre of history painting. Moreover, the horror of his shipwrecks gave precisely that aesthetic pleasure to be had from safe contemplation of disaster and misfortune, a topic probed in Edmund Burke's contemporaneous *Philosophical Enquiry into the Sublime and the Beautiful* (1757).

Such artists as Pierre-Jacques Volaire or Joseph Wright of Derby would develop the more sensational aspects of Vernet's art to greater extremes. Volaire was a pupil of Vernet for a time, while Wright, like many artists, knew of Vernet's work via British or perhaps Italian collections and occasionally painted a Vernet-like moonlit harbour or other Italianate coast scene. The young Scottish artist Jacob More, inspired by Vernet's *Landscape with a Waterfall* (Duke of Buccleuch priv. col), painted his *Falls of the Clyde* (Edinburgh, N.G.) before setting off in 1773 to study in Italy. The Italian Carlo Bonavia exploited Vernet's success in Italy, producing his own variations on Vernet themes during the 1750s and 1760s. These are still sometimes mistaken for works by Vernet, but Bonavia employed more open compositions and a distinctive brushwork. Around 1750 Vernet encouraged Richard Wilson to study landscape, and Wilson was to some extent influenced by his subject-matter and style. Later in Paris in 1781 Pierre-Henri de Valenciennes took Vernet's advice on painting from nature out of doors; this was to have important consequences for French landscape painting in the late 18th and early 19th centuries. Many minor artists, such as Jean Pillement or Alexandre-Jean Noël (1752–1834), the latter for a time a pupil of Vernet, occasionally produced works in his manner. Others, such as Jean-Baptiste Lallemand, worked in Rome during the 1750s and early 1760s, producing paintings in an Italianate or Vernet-like manner, whether directly inspired by him or not. Those recorded as copying works by Vernet, for instance Thomas Patch, almost inevitably produced their own Italianate works in his manner. Apart from Volaire, his chief assistant and follower was Charles-François Grenier de Lacroix. In his notebook of 1746 Vernet recorded a payment to 'Grenier' for making copies, and it seems that Vernet employed him in his studio to this end. There are paintings by Lacroix at Uppark (W. Sussex, NT), signed and dated 1751, that are precise copies of works by Vernet in the same collection and virtually indistinguishable from the originals. Excellent copies or replicas of Vernet paintings appear from time to time, but too little is known about his studio practice always to ascertain whether they are autograph or by some good copyist such as Lacroix. Among Vernet's Provençal followers was Jean Henry d'Arles (1734–84), who worked in and around Marseille producing somewhat mannered imitations of Vernet (e.g. *Shipwreck*, 1756; Marseille, Mus. B.-A.); he also executed some large-scale decorative paintings of Italianate seaports. Jean-François Huë was another follower, and perhaps had lessons from Vernet, but is chiefly remembered for his commission to take up the *Ports of France* series.

BIBLIOGRAPHY

L. Lagrange and A. de Montaiglon: 'Joseph Vernet: Pièces et notes pour servir à l'histoire de ses tableaux des *Ports de France*', *Archvs A. Fr.*, vii (1856), pp. 139–63
L. Lagrange: *Les Vernet: Joseph Vernet et la peinture au XVIIIe siècle* (Paris, 1864) [incl. Vernet's notebook of 1738]
J. Guiffrey: 'Correspondance de Joseph Vernet avec le Directeur des Bâtiments sur la collection des *Ports de France*, et avec d'autres personnes sur divers objets, 1756–87', *Nouv. Archvs A. Fr.*, 3rd ser., ix (1893), pp. 1–99
F. Ingersoll-Smouse: *Joseph Vernet: Peintre de marine*, 2 vols (Paris, 1926)
Claude-Joseph Vernet, 1714–1789 (exh. cat., ed. P. Conisbee; London, Kenwood House; rev., enlarged, Paris, Mus. Mar.; 1976)

PHILIP CONISBEE

(2) Carle [Antoine-Charles-Joseph] **Vernet** (*b* Bordeaux, 14 Aug 1758; *d* Paris, 27 Nov 1836). Painter and lithographer, son of (1) Joseph Vernet. At the age of 11 he entered the studio of Nicolas-Bernard Lépicié. His training culminated in the award of the Prix de Rome in 1782; however, his stay in Rome was terminated when he underwent a 'mystical experience' and was sent back to Paris. He was approved (*agréé*) by the Académie Royale in 1789 on presentation of the *Triumph of Aemilius Paulus* (New York, Met.). Although his sister Emilie was guillotined, none of the tragic aspects of the Revolution is apparent in his subsequent work. His wittily malicious satires of Directoire types, *Incroyables et merveilleuses* (Dayot 66), engraved in 1797, made his reputation and set the tone for most of his future aquatinted work, for example *Costumes* (1814–18; D 73). An early practitioner of lithography, he excelled in the acute, unexaggerated observation of contemporary manners, e.g. *Delpech's Print Shop* (*c.* 1818; *see* LITHOGRAPHY, fig. 5) and the *Cries of Paris* (100 plates, after 1816; D 147).

1. Carle Vernet: preparatory drawing for the *Battle of Marengo*, pencil and brown wash, 264×448 mm, 1804 (Notre Dame, IN, University of Notre Dame, Snite Museum of Art)

2. Carle Vernet: *Stag Hunt*, oil on canvas, 2.27×3.27 m, 1827 (Paris, Musée du Louvre)

In 1799 Vernet exhibited drawings of Napoleon's Italian campaign. His most famous battle painting is the huge *Battle of Marengo* (Versailles, Château), for which sketches were shown at the Salon in 1804 (see fig. 1) and 1806. Some scholars have maintained that Vernet introduced verisimilitude and strategy into contemporary battle paintings; others credit his son, (3) Horace Vernet, and still others attribute this new-found authenticity, as well as an emphasis on the infantry, to Louis-François Lejeune (1775–1848). The careers of Vernet and Lejeune in this genre are parallel, and their early attempts have remarkable stylistic similarities, featuring panoramic views of the battlefield, with very small figures and sprightly horses. The last year in which both artists exhibited contemporary battle scenes was 1824, but, whereas Lejeune's *Battle of Chiclana* has the infantry mass functioning strategically as a dynamic, thrusting wedge, Vernet's *Capture of Pamplona* (both Versailles, Château) has a static, planar row of officers stretched across the foreground, echoed by a large expanse of dull landscape.

Vernet's hunt scenes retain the picturesque charm, elegance and artificiality of the 18th century, even in such late paintings as the *Stag Hunt* (1827; Paris, Louvre; see fig. 2). His work is characterized by greater veracity when he painted from direct observation, as in *Riderless Horse Race* (1826; Avignon, Mus. Calvet), which depicts the annual event in Rome; indeed, in his own time he was known primarily as a painter of horses in full movement. He received the Légion d'honneur in 1808 and was elected

to the Institut de France in 1815. His greatest legacy was that he fostered the talents of his son and of Théodore Gericault.

BIBLIOGRAPHY

P.-A. Vieillard: *Salon de 1824* (Paris, 1825)

C. Blanc: *Histoire*, iii (Paris, 1865), pp. 1–16

A. Genevay: 'Carle Vernet', *L'Art*, viii (1877), pp. 73–83, 97–103

A. Soubies: *Les Membres de l'Académie des beaux-arts*, i (Paris, 1904), pp. 133–8

A. Dayot: *Carle Vernet* (Paris, 1925) [D] [incl. cat. rais. of works that were engraved and of his lithographs]

I. Julia: 'Antoine-Charles-Horace (called Carle) Vernet', *French Painting, 1774–1830: The Age of Revolution* (exh. cat., ed. F. Cummings and others; Paris, Grand Pal., 1975), pp. 649–51 [only significant account of Vernet in Eng.]

The Charged Image: French Lithographic Caricature, 1816–1848 (exh. cat. by B. Farwell, Santa Barbara, CA, Mus. A., 1989), pp. 169–77

(3) (Emile-Jean-)Horace Vernet (*b* Paris, 30 June 1789; *d* Paris, 17 Jan 1863). Painter, son of (2) Carle Vernet. He was born in his father's lodgings at the Palais du Louvre, where his grandfather (1) Joseph Vernet also lived; his maternal grandfather was Jean-Michel Moreau. To these antecedents and influences are ascribed the supreme ease of his public career, his almost incredible facility and his fecundity. His early training in his father's studio was supplemented by formal academic training with François-André Vincent until 1810, when he competed unsuccessfully for the Prix de Rome. He first exhibited at the Salon in 1812. In 1814 Vernet received the Légion d'honneur for the part he played in the defence of Paris, which he commemorated in the *Clichy Gate: The Defence* *of Paris, 30 March 1814* (1820; Paris, Louvre; see fig.), a spirited painting that represented a manifesto of Liberal opposition to Restoration oppression.

In 1822 the Salon jury, fearing political repercussions, refused the *Clichy Gate* and the *Battle of Jemmapes, 1792* (1821; London, N.G.), although neither painting glorifies Napoleon. In response Vernet withdrew all his paintings from the Salon, except *Joseph Vernet Attached to the Mast Painting a Storm* (Avignon, Mus. Calvet), a government commission, and opened his own 'salon', which was enthusiastically publicized by Victor-Joseph Etienne de Jouy, who equated political and artistic liberty. The public flocked to Vernet's studio, and both his reputation and his prices soared, as his account books reveal. In 1824 the government ordered two official portraits and made Vernet an Officer of the Légion d'honneur. Vernet exhibited nearly 40 paintings at the Salon, including the *Clichy Gate*, the *Battle of Montmirail, 1814* (1822) and the *Battle of Hanau, 1813* (1824; both London, N.G.), on behalf of which the Director of the Louvre, Comte Auguste de Forbin, had waged an astute campaign with the Ministère du Roi, reminding the government of the notoriety and attacks that had occurred in 1822 (Paris, Archvs N.). The range of Vernet's work exhibited at this Salon (see Jal) is vast: while such pictures as *Peace and War* (1820) and the *Veteran at Home* (1823; both London, Wallace) might appear to be simple genre paintings, their political statements are inherent in the image of the veteran being exalted, glorification of Napoleon being prohibited.

From this point Vernet's career was secure. In 1826 he was elected to the Institut de France; from 1828 to 1834 he was director of the Académie de France in Rome; and in 1835 he was appointed professor at the Ecole des Beaux-Arts, Paris, a post he held until his death. Among numerous official commissions he executed historic battle-pieces for Louis-Philippe's Galerie des Batailles at Versailles and such scenes of contemporary ceremonials and battles as *Louis-Philippe and his Sons Riding Out from the Château of Versailles* (1847) and three immense canvases of the *Siege of Constantine* (1839; all Versailles, Château).

Vernet visited Algeria several times between 1833, when he painted the *Arab Tale-teller* (London, Wallace), and 1853; his interest in the Near East seems to have focused on providing an authentic background for biblical themes (e.g. *Joseph's Coat*, 1853; London, Wallace) and on presenting the characters of the Old Testament in the guise of modern Arabs (*see* ORIENTALISM).

Vernet's technique has been described as having a 'Neo-classical porcelain finish' (Julia), but this is not his universal manner, especially in his early work, even if one discounts such sketches and drawings as the *Turkish Soldier* (1827; Paris, Ecole N. Sup. B.-A.), which has wonderful verve

Horace Vernet: *Clichy Gate: The Defence of Paris, 30 March 1814*, oil on canvas, 970×1300 mm, 1820 (Paris, Musée du Louvre)

and freedom. A carefully polished surface occurs most often in the biblical paintings after 1830, which are also his most monumentally composed works. He was notorious for the speed with which he worked. As a result the facture of such works as *Peace and War* is large, loose, almost careless; even the monumental *Charles X Entering Paris, September 30* (1824; Versailles, Château), which was completed before the Salon closed in January, is quite sketchy. Although Vernet has never been accounted a colourist, his *Brigands Surprised by Papal Troops* (1831; Baltimore, MD, Walters A.G.) is unusual in its vividness. The free brushwork of *Mazeppa and the Wolves* (1826; Avignon, Mus. Calvet) draws attention to the terrified horse.

The public was unanimous in considering Vernet one of the greatest artists of his time, and all critics stressed his journalistic approach. In the 1820s the Liberal critics, in an era when independence in art was directly linked to independence in politics, were also very laudatory. Thiers (1824) pointed out that Vernet's realism was achieved by an absence of conventions and rules: 'No subject is forbidden him, no manner of treating them is imposed on him'. Yet adverse assessments were already current before the artist's demise: Silvestre (1857) prophesied that the future would be hard on Vernet. Some of the negative assessments, such as Baudelaire's diatribe (1846), again seem related to political biases; Baudelaire detested the army, Vernet's popularity and his naturalism. By the 1980s, however, Vernet appeared to be benefiting from a general reassessment of 19th-century art, and his naturalism, which appeared as early as the 1830s (e.g. the *Duc d'Orléans Leaving the Palais Royal*, 1832; Versailles, Château), can be seen as foreshadowing that of Gustave Courbet or Edouard Manet.

BIBLIOGRAPHY
V.-J. Etienne de Jouy: *Salon d'Horace Vernet: Analyse historique et pittoresque de quarante-cinq tableaux exposés chez lui en 1822* (Paris, 1822)
A. Jal: *L'Artiste et le philosophe: Entretiens critiques sur le salon de 1824* (Paris, 1824), pp. 127–89 (127–36)
A. Thiers: *Le Globe* (8 Oct 1824), p. 47
C. Baudelaire: 'M. Horace Vernet', *Salon de 1846* (Paris, 1846); repr. in *Arts in Paris, 1845–1862* (Greenwich, CT, 1965), pp. 93–6
T. Silvestre: *Mémoire contre Horace Vernet* (Paris, 1857); rev. version in *Eclectiques et réalistes*, ii of *Les Artistes français*, ed. E. Faure (Paris, 1926), pp. 38–73
L. Lagrange: 'Horace Vernet', *Gaz. B.-A.*, 1st ser., xv (1863), pp. 297–327, 439–65
G. Levitine: '*Vernet Tied to a Mast in a Storm*: The Evolution of an Episode of Art Historical Romantic Folklore', *A. Bull.*, xlix (1967), pp. 93–100
I. Julia: 'Emile-Jean-Horace (called Horace) Vernet', *French Painting, 1774–1830: The Age of Revolution* (exh. cat., ed. F. Cummings and others; Paris, Grand Pal., 1975), pp. 611–14
Horace Vernet, 1789–1863 (exh. cat., intro. R. Rosenblum; Rome, Acad. France; Paris, Ecole N. Sup. B.-A.; 1980) [errors and lacunae in chronology, good intro.]
The Charged Image: French Lithographic Caricature, 1816–1848 (exh. cat. by B. Farwell, Santa Barbara, CA, Mus. A., 1989), pp. 178–86
DORATHEA K. BEARD

Vernis Martin. Generic term used for all types of japanning produced in France in the 18th century. It takes its name from the production of the brothers Guillaume Martin (*d* 1749) and Etienne-Simon Martin (*d* 1770), from a Parisian family of tailors, who perfected a form of

Vernis Martin bureau plat, cartonnier and encrier probably made by Jacques Dubois, green and gold lacquer on oak, 2058×717×413 mm, *c.* 1765 (London, Wallace Collection)

japanning based on copal resin (*see* LACQUER, §I, 3(iii)). The brothers were granted letters of patent on 27 November 1730, renewed on 18 February 1744, for an exclusive monopoly lasting 20 years to make 'all sorts of works in relief in the manner of Japan and China'. On 15 April 1753 a further renewal of the monopoly stated that the Martin brothers had 'brought the technique to the highest possible level of perfection'. Two younger brothers, Julien Martin (*d* 1782, and known as Martin le Jeune) and Robert Martin (1706–65), joined the business after 1748, when the factory, operating three separate workshops in Paris, was described as 'Manufacture Royale des Vernis Martin'. Guillaume Martin's son, Guillaume-Jean Martin (*b* 1743), and Etienne-Simon Martin's son, Etienne-François Martin(*d* 1771), also joined the family business. All the Martin brothers and sons, with the exception of Martin le Jeune, held the title 'Vernisseur de Roy'. Robert Martin's son, Jean-Alexandre (1739–after 1791), worked for Frederick the Great at Sanssouci and was appointed Vernisseur du Roi there in 1760. Voltaire was a client, and mentioned the elder brothers Martin twice: in *De l'Egalité des conditions* he referred to 'the gilt and varnished panels by the brothers Martin', made for Mme de Chatelet's Château de Cirey in 1738, and in *Les Tu and les vous*, he praised 'these Cabinets where the Martin have surpassed the art of China'. The technique developed by the elder brothers was so successful that it was quickly imitated by numerous makers; these imitations became generically known as *vernis Martin*. The Martin family remained active until the last decades of the 18th century.

Vernis Martin is applied in a similar manner to true lacquer. It was produced in many different colours ranging from black, red and a deep, Prussian blue (e.g. *secrétaire en pente*, *c.* 1750–60; Paris, Mus. A. Déc.) to paler or clear shades of green, lilac and yellow fashionable in the Rococo style. White *vernis Martin* often underwent a chemical reaction and could turn bright yellow (e.g. *table en chiffonnière*, *c.* 1765; Paris, Mus. Nissim de Camondo). An imitation aventurine lacquer, powdered with gold, brass or copper, was also produced (*see* LACQUER, §I, 3(iii)).

The Martin brothers not only reproduced and repaired East-Asian lacquer, but adapted the technique to the current styles in France, creating japanned panelling in the apartments of the Dauphine at Versailles (1748–9), and in the Château de Bellevue and the Hôtel d'Ormesson for Mme de Pompadour. They also lacquered such European forms as carriages, sedan chairs, furniture (see fig.), and smaller items such as fans, toilet accessories, *étuis* and snuff-boxes. The *marchand-mercier* Lazare Duvaux commissioned many items of furniture from Etienne-Simon Martin between 1755 and 1759, among them a mirror frame with gold and aventurine lacquer.

UNPUBLISHED SOURCES
Paris, Archvs N. [inventory of crown furniture (1760)]

BIBLIOGRAPHY
L. Courajod, ed.: *Livre journal de Lazare Duvaux*, 2 vols (Paris, 1873)
G. Brière: *Le Château de Versailles* (Paris, 1910)
H. Vial, A. Marcel and A. Girodie: *Les Artistes décorateurs du bois*, 2 vols (Paris, 1922)

MONIQUE RICCARDI-CUBITT

Vernon, (Charles-)Frédéric(-Victor) de (*b* Paris, 17 Nov 1858; *d* Paris, 28 Oct 1912). French medallist and sculptor. He first trained with Paulin Tasset (*b* 1839) and from 1879 with Jules-Clément Chaplain at the Ecole des Beaux-Arts in Paris. In 1887 he won the Prix de Rome for medals. In Rome he produced portrait medals of *Edgar Henri Boutry*, *Henri-Camille Danger* and *Georges Charpentier*; after his return to Paris he won a first-class medal at the Salon of 1895. He was equally successful with official commissions, such as the *Welcome to Nicholas II* (1896) and the *Mayors' Banquet* (1902), and more personal plaquettes, such as *Solidarity* (1901), *The Kiss* (1902), *Eve* (1905) and the *Communicants* (1905). In 1907 he won the medal of honour in the sculpture section of the Salon and in 1909, after Chaplain's death, he succeeded him both as a member of the Académie des Beaux-Arts and as Professor of Medal Engraving at the Ecole des Beaux-Arts. In 1908 Vernon executed a series of bas-reliefs for the French Embassy in Vienna. His later medallic portraits include *Gaston Darboux*, *Armand Gautier* and *Georges Picot* (all 1911).

BIBLIOGRAPHY
Forrer
F. Mazerolle: 'F. de Vernon', *Gaz. Numi. Fr.*, iii (1899), pp. 109–209; viii (1904), pp. 409–26
International Exhibition of Contemporary Medals (exh. cat., New York, Amer. Numi. Soc., 1911), pp. 346–55
J. Belaubre: 'Charles-Frédéric-Victor de Vernon', *Bull. Club Fr. Médaille*, xxix (1970), pp. 82–5

Vernon, Jean de (*b* 1897; *d* 1975). French sculptor and medallist. He studied in Paris at the Ecole des Arts Décoratifs and at the Ecole des Beaux-Arts. His medallic work included the *Secret of Happiness* (1936); a series of ten medals illustrating the fables of Jean de La Fontaine (1937–42); the inaugural medal for the liner *Normandie* (1945); and a medal commemorating the *Help Given by the USA to Europe* (1951). Among his other works were *Our Lady of the Wings* for Le Bourget airport and a number of ceremonial swords for members of the Académie Française.

BIBLIOGRAPHY
Catalogue général des éditions de la Monnaie de Paris, 3 vols (Paris, 1978), iii, pp. 390–93

MARK JONES

Vernon, Robert (*b* 1774; *d* London, 22 May 1849). English collector and patron. The son of a London hackneyman, he increased his modest inheritance by hiring horses to the aristocracy and gentry and to the British army during the Napoleonic wars. He began to collect in 1826 and, guided chiefly by George Jones, he concentrated on acquiring oil paintings of the British school. He bought not from dealers but from exhibition rooms, the sale room or direct from the artist: he commissioned pictures from Turner, David Roberts and William Mulready. His purchases included paintings by Richard Parkes Bonington and Augustus Wall Callcott as well as Constable, among landscapists, and works by the history painters William Etty and William Hilton. Most of his purchases were genre paintings by Charles Robert Leslie, Gilbert Stuart Newton, Thomas Webster and Daniel Maclise among others. By *c.* 1840 Vernon had resolved to leave a large part of his fortune for the relief of impoverished artists and for the establishment of fellowships. The scheme was intended to complement the provisions of Sir Francis Chantrey's will, but by mid-1847 he had decided instead to give his collection of British paintings to the nation. In 1843 he began to open his house in Pall Mall to the public for a few weeks annually, and in December 1847 Sir Charles Lock Eastlake and the Trustees of the National Gallery, London, accepted 164 works from his collection. One painting, Turner's *The Dogana, S Giorgio, Citella, from the Steps of the Dogana* (exh. 1842; London, Tate), was put on display as a representative of the gift, the first picture by Turner to enter the national collection.

After Vernon's death in 1849, his entire collection was brought together at the National Gallery. It was afterwards transferred to Marlborough House and then exhibited at the South Kensington Museum until 1869, when it was returned to Trafalgar Square. With the opening of the Tate Gallery in 1897 most of the pictures were transferred there, with some works remaining in the National Gallery and some transferred to the National Portrait Gallery. A record of the complete collection survives in the engravings after each work that were published in the *Art Journal* between 1849 and 1853. The strength of Vernon's gift lies in the survey it gives of the work of the leading Royal Academicians before the advent of Pre-Raphaelitism.

BIBLIOGRAPHY
'The Vernon Gallery', *Art-Union*, ix (1847), pp. 365–72
G. Jones: *Sir Francis Chantrey: Recollections of his Life, Practice, and Opinions* (London, 1849), pp. 206–9
V. Heath: *Vernon Heath's Recollections* (London, 1892)

ROBIN HAMLYN

Vernon, W(alter) L(iberty) (*b* High Wycombe, Bucks, 11 Aug 1846; *d* Sydney, 17 Jan 1914). Australian architect of English birth. He studied at the Royal Academy Schools and South Kensington School of Art in London and began to practise in Hastings in 1872. In 1883 he emigrated to Sydney and went into partnership (1884–9) with William Wilkinson Wardell, building many large houses in the Queen Anne style of Philip Webb and R. Norman Shaw. In 1890 Vernon was appointed New South Wales Government Architect, a post he held until his retirement in 1911. His major buildings in Sydney, the Art Gallery of New South Wales (1885–1909), the State Library (1910) and Central Railway Station (1903–6), were in the classical style, the former two buildings having Ionic porticos, while his Fisher Library (1909), University of Sydney, and Registrar-General's Office (1913) were adaptations of Perpendicular Gothic. He also designed many public buildings in the suburbs and country that were strongly influenced by Shaw and the Arts and Crafts Movement; in contrast to the classic formality adopted by his predecessor, James Barnet, these buildings were open-planned to combat harsh climatic conditions. Between 1904 and 1913 Vernon was involved in the selection of Canberra as the site for the new Australian capital and with the competition for the master-plan that was won by Walter Burley Griffin.

BIBLIOGRAPHY
D. Jones: *W. L. Vernon* (BArch thesis, Kensington, U. NSW, 1982)

PETER BRIDGES

Vernucken [Vernicke; Vernickel; Vernughen; Vernuiken; Vernuken; Vernukken; Vernuyken], **Wilhelm** (*b* Kalkar, *c.* 1540; *d* Kassel, 1607). German architect and sculptor. From 1559 he worked, at first with his father Heinrich Oych (Verneyken), on the relief ornament of fireplaces at the new Schloss Horst, Gelsenkirchen; after 1564 he worked there independently as a plasterer in the ornamentation of windows and dormers, using an Early Renaissance strapwork style.

From 1569 to 1573 Vernucken directed the building of the Doxal, a new entrance porch for the Cologne Rathaus, for which Cornelis Floris, Lambert Sudermann and Hendrik van Hasselt had submitted designs. The Council decided in favour of a 'medium-scale' (i.e. cheaper) plan, which they commissioned Vernucken to build. It is an open, two-storey hall, five bays wide and two bays deep, in a High Renaissance style; the arches of the lower arcade are rounded, but those of the upper storey are slightly pointed. The central and outer bays project slightly, the projecting entablature being supported by Corinthian columns. The profuse ornamentation of plinths, balustrades and spandrels shows Netherlandish influence. The entrance porch was altered in 1617, substantially restored between 1860 and 1893 and severely damaged in 1945. Although the details of its present form, as reconstructed in 1972, cannot be considered the work of Vernucken, it must nevertheless be placed among the finest examples of Renaissance architecture in Germany.

In 1577 Vernucken became court sculptor to Landgrave William IV of Hesse-Kassel and continued in this office under William's successor, Maurice the Learned, serving as director of the court sculptural workshop for the rest of his life. He decorated the Rittersaal of the newly built Schloss at Rotenburg an der Fulda in 1577 and its chapel in 1590. He executed stuccowork in the Güldener Saal at Schloss Kassel in 1580 and in its chapel in 1590. Both structures were destroyed in the early 19th century. Vernucken's decoration of the chapel (1586–90) at Schloss Wilhelmsburg, Schmalkalden, however, is extant. This rectangular, three-storey interior is one of the foremost Renaissance works in Germany, partly because of the harmony between its architecture and decorative elements. Three arcades are set one above the other on three sides of the chapel, with projecting orders of pilasters marking off the galleries from the main space at the two upper levels. Pilasters, archivolts, spandrels, cornices and friezes, as well as the stuccoed, three-bay groined vault, are covered with a net of fine scroll- and strapwork, with plant and animal motifs. All the ornamentation is coloured, displaying a mastery of architectural sculpture and decoration. The figures of the *Apostles* and *Evangelists* in the lunettes between the crowns of the top gallery arches and the springing of the vaults, however, are on a lower artistic level than the rest and display a certain stylistic monotony in the folds of the garments and the schematic conception of the heads, although this scarcely diminishes the overall impact of the chapel. Vernucken also designed the great display chimneypiece in the Riesensaal at Schloss Wilhelmsburg, the cast-iron panels of which consistently show his decorative skill.

Vernucken's last major scheme was the north front of the Ottoneum (1604) in Kassel, the first theatre to be built in Germany (now a museum). Even though it was altered in 1690 by Paul Du Ry, whose portico dominates the composition, it is nevertheless apparent that Vernucken had moved far from the pure Renaissance style of the Doxal in Cologne, abandoning the use of projecting bays or of the orders in columns or pilasters; instead the façade is articulated by a cornice and string courses, with scrolled gables.

The tomb of *Landgrave Philip II of Hessen-Rheinfels* (*d* 1583) in the collegiate church of St Goar provides further evidence of Vernucken's skills in figurative sculpture, although, as with the *Apostles* and *Evangelists* in the chapel at Schloss Wilhelmsburg, it is evident that he lacked his father's mastery of sculptural invention and representation of individual figures. This may be seen in three surviving fireplaces by Oych; the theme of *Christ, David and Joseph Triumphant* in the kitchen, and two, *Lot with his Daughter* and *Cain and Abel*, now in the Schloss Hugenpoet, near Düsseldorf.

BIBLIOGRAPHY
Thieme–Becker
R. Klapheck: *Die Meister von Schloss Horst im Broiche* (Berlin, 1915)
P. Kutter: 'Die Grabmäler des Landgrafen Philipp II und seiner Gemahlin in der Stiftskirche zu St. Goar', *Wallraf-Richartz-Jb.*, n.s., ii/3 (1933–4), pp. 280–88
W. Kramm: 'Die beiden ersten Kasseler Hofbildhauerwerkstätten im 16. und 17. Jahrhundert', *Marburg. Jb. Kstwiss.*, viii–ix (1936), pp. 329–90

P. Fuchs: *Das Rathaus zu Köln: Berichte u. Bilder vom Haus der Bürger in Vergangenheit und Gegenwart* (Cologne, 1973)
Denkmale in Thüringen (Weimar, 1973, rev. 2/1974)
R. Ziessler: 'Die Restaurierung des Riesensaales im Schloss Wilhemsburg in Schmalkalden', *Von Farbe und Farben* (Zürich, 1980), pp. 111–16
CAROLA WENZEL

Verny. *See* ALMATY.

Verona. Italian city in the Veneto on the River Adige *c.* 60 km west of Venice. It has substantial Roman remains, and its position at the crossing of three important trade routes gave it significant economic strength, which is reflected in numerous fine medieval buildings. From the mid-16th century Michele Sanmicheli left a lasting influence on architectural styles in the city. Verona was badly damaged in World War II, when all the bridges were blown up.

1. History and urban development. 2. Art life and organization. 3. Buildings.

1. HISTORY AND URBAN DEVELOPMENT.

(i) Before 1277. (ii) 1277–1797. (iii) After 1797.

(i) Before 1277. The pre-Roman settlement, at a fording point on the Adige, is thought to have been situated mainly on the hill of S Pietro on the left bank of the river. The Ponte Pietra (destr. 1945; rebuilt 1957–9), which is not aligned with the Roman city layout, presumably predates the Roman settlement, although it was apparently repaired in Roman and medieval times.

The Roman city was founded on the right bank of the river in the mid-1st century BC and had reached the height of its development by *c.* AD 265. Enclosed within a loop of the Adige at the foot of the hill, it was laid out on the standard grid plan, protected to the south by a brick wall divided into two sections that met at an obtuse angle. There were two further bridges, and the Forum lay on the site of the present Piazza Erbe. Of the city gates, the only surviving trace from the republican period is a brick and tufa facing in the ruins of the Porta Leoni, originally a square building flanked by two 16-sided towers. White stone blocks indicate later alterations to this gate. At the Porta dei Borsari, built in the 1st century AD (see fig. 1), the whole external façade survives, incorporating an inscription recording the rebuilding of the walls in AD 265. The twin entrances with triangular pediments are surmounted by a two-storey arcaded wall, articulated with aedicules and spiral-fluted Corinthian half-columns.

The Roman theatre was built around the end of the 1st century BC (rest. 1830–1914) on the left bank of the Adige. The cavea was built into the slope of the hill, with, above, a series of terraces leading to a temple (destr.) on the hilltop. On the other side of the city was the other great venue for spectacles, the Amphitheatre, or Arena, which can be dated to the 3rd decade AD (restored many times since the Middle Ages). The third largest antique amphitheatre in Italy, it is surrounded by an almost intact two-tier range of superimposed arches. Four bays of the original outer perimeter wall survive. The arena floor is large (73×44 m) and, together with the cavea, provides seating for over 20,000 spectators. It now hosts the annual outdoor opera season.

1. Verona, Porta dei Borsari, Roman, 1st century AD

With the advent of Christianity in the city new architectural forms were established. The remains of two Early Christian basilicas are preserved in the vicinity of the cathedral. Other such structures include the basilica of S Stefano (5th century; rebuilt in the 8th and 12th centuries), which is situated close to the Ponte Pietra. Nonetheless, following the war with the Goths in the 5th century, the city fell into a rapid decline, houses destroyed in battles being rebuilt with poorer materials, and areas formerly occupied by citizens given over to pasture and tillage.

The city recovered to some extent in the 9th century, when Archdeacon Pacificus (*d* 846) founded new churches and restored damaged old ones; but it was only from the 12th century that buildings were of a quality to leave a lasting impression on the urban topography. From 1136 to 1277 (with a brief interlude of tyranny) Verona was a commune, the Palazzo del Comune being built beside the ancient Forum from 1193 (rest. 1925), while prominent families built themselves tower-houses. The two most important architectural works of the 12th century were the cathedral (*see* §3(i) below) within the ancient centre and S Zeno Maggiore (*see* §3(ii) below) outside the walls; but other churches were built at this time (e.g. S Lorenzo (*c.* 1110), with its cylindrical western towers, S Giovanni in Valle, S Giovanni in Fonte and Santa Trinità), and this flourishing period of Romanesque architecture has left a strong imprint on the urban fabric of Verona.

(ii) 1277–1797. Under the rule of the DELLA SCALA (Scaligeri), from the accession of Alberto I della Scala (*d* 1301) in 1277 until 1387, Verona expanded to nearly six times the size of the Roman city, and it remained within these expanded limits until the end of World War I. Later fortifications followed the line of the walls erected

by Cangrande I della Scala, which enclosed large areas of land suitable for agriculture and stock raising and provided security for several important religious establishments formerly isolated in the countryside around the town, including S Giorgio in Braida and S Nazario on the left bank of the Adige, and S Zeno and Santa Trinità on the right.

The della Scala, and after them the Visconti (1387–1405), developed Verona as a military stronghold with the construction of several fortresses, such as Castelvecchio (1354–76) and the Cittadella in the plain south of the Roman city, Castel S Felice at the north end of the defensive ring, and Castel S Pietro within the Roman citadel. The della Scala also erected the first new bridge across the Adige since Roman times. This was the Ponte Nuovo, which was followed by the Ponte delle Navi and finally, for their own exclusive use, the Ponte di Castelvecchio. The della Scala remodelled the town centre, building their residences near S Maria Antica (see §3(iii) below). Next to the church they created the small private cemetery that contains the family tombs, including those of *Cangrande I*, *Mastino II* and *Cansignorio*, which have come to symbolize the artistic culture of their period of power. On the Piazza Erbe the family constructed the Casa dei Mercanti (1301; altered 17th century) and the house that in the 16th century became Casa Mazzanti.

Cansignorio della Scala (*reg* 1359–75) extended the family's residence near S Maria Antica, adding among other features the saloon and the loggia frescoed by Altichiero, and a large garden. He was also responsible for the Fountain in Piazza Erbe (1368) and the Gardello Tower (1370). Cangrande II built the Castelvecchio (now the Museo Civico), the last residence of the della Scala in Verona. Its great size, together with its distinctive battlements and the adjoining Ponte di Castelvecchio, which contributes further to the apparent scale, form an important element in the Veronese townscape.

Some large religious buildings were rebuilt during the rule of the della Scala: S Fermo Maggiore was reconstructed (*c.*1313) in Gothic form for the Franciscans under the fervent patronage of Guglielmo Castelbarco. S Maria della Scala was erected (1324) in fulfilment of a vow made by Cangrande I. The della Scala were also involved in the reconstruction of S Anastasia and the renovation of S Eufemia.

Continuous and violent civil strife of the 12th and 13th centuries must have forced the citizens to make defensive alterations to their houses, which studies indicate must have been particularly fine at that time. Following brief domination by the Carraresi and then by the Visconti, in 1405 Verona came under the sway of the Venetian Republic, and except for a few years of imperial rule (1509–16) it remained under Venetian control until 1797. This control was reflected in much of the architecture of the city. From this period, particularly in the early Renaissance, one can find Venetian architectural elements, such as the grouping of pointed arched windows.

The first important public architectural project under the Venetians was the construction (1452–66) of S Bernardino, still on Gothic lines but with some Renaissance decorative elements. The Loggia del Consiglio, begun in 1476 on the Piazza dei Signori by masons from Lombardy,

is a more complete example of Renaissance architecture. In 1517, after the brief imperial occupation of the city, Venice ordered the demolition of all the houses and churches that lay outside the town walls in order to guarantee better defences. Between 1520 and 1525 the city walls to the left of the river were rebuilt, and from 1530 MICHELE SANMICHELI was responsible for renewing the defences on the right bank, where he built a series of bastions.

In 1530 Venice ordered the Cittadella to be dismantled, and in 1535 Sanmicheli was entrusted to develop the site. A new street, the Corso Porta Nuova, was built along the moat of the Cittadella, with a gate, the Porta Nuova (1535–40; *see* CITY GATE, fig. 3). Sanmicheli also built the Porta Palio (*c.* 1547), in a style that freely re-created the forms of antiquity. After entering Porta Brà, the Corso Porta Nuova was deflected towards the Arena by Sanmicheli's Palazzo degli Honori. The stretch of Roman street between the Porta Borsari and the Arco dei Gavi was enriched by Sanmicheli's Palazzo Canossa (*c.* 1530; *see* SANMICHELI, MICHELE, fig. 1) and Palazzo Bevilacqua (before 1534; see fig. 2). These, with their full range of classical details and rich articulation, are the highpoint of Veronese Renaissance architecture. They contrast with the many painted façades, a marked feature of the city, which include those by Girolamo dai Libri at the Casa Cristani and those by Giovanni Maria Falconetto, including the Casa Trevisani-Lonardi. These fresco schemes tend to reproduce antique reliefs set against brilliantly coloured backgrounds.

The work of Sanmicheli left such an impression on Verona that much architecture in the following decades followed patterns established by him. This is particularly evident in the work of Domenico Curtoni (1556–1627), who constructed the Palazzo della Gran Guardia (1610), which has a deep ground-floor arcade supporting a richly articulated upper storey, and the foyer of the Accademia Filarmonica. Although the mature Baroque style never

2. Verona, façade of the Palazzo Bevilacqua by Michele Sanmicheli, before 1534

became a feature of the Veronese townscape, there were exceptions, notably the Palazzo Maffei (1628–68; architect unknown), which displays the full vigour of contemporary Roman Baroque architecture. This absence of the Baroque was in keeping with contemporary trends in Venice. The complementary relationship between the arts of Venice and Verona was also witnessed in the late 18th century, when Sanmicheli's Palazzo Canossa was frescoed on the interior with the *Triumphs of Hercules* (1761) by Giambattista Tiepolo.

In the 18th century Alessandro Pompei emerged from the cultural circle of Scipione Maffei as the finest architect in the city since Sanmicheli. His work established a new Neo-classical style in the city, best exemplified by major works such as the Dogana at S Fermo and the Museo Lapidario Maffeiano. His style was continued by Adriano Cristofali (1717–88), and his followers Luigi Trezza (1753–1824) and Bartolomeo Giuliari (*d* 1842). Sanmichelian influence still lingered in the work of Giuseppe Barbieri (1777–1838), among whose many contributions were the Palazzo del Municipio (1831), which is completely surrounded by an impressive range of attached giant Corinthian columns, and the Cimitero Monumentale.

(iii) After 1797. In anticipation of the Congress of Verona (1822) some important modernization projects were carried out in the city, especially the lowering of the level of Piazza Brà and the streets leading into it. After the flood of 1882 the city's aspect was decisively changed by the construction of the Adige embankments. Around the same time Basso Acquar emerged as the first industrial zone of modern Verona, and at the beginning of the 20th century the first working-class quarters rose at Porta Palio and Porto S Pancrazio.

After World War I the Ponte della Vittoria by Ettore Fagiuoli (*b* 1884) opened up a new area for expansion towards Borgo Trento, on the left bank. This and nearby Valdonega were both favoured by the middle classes, but in both cases the declared intention of building a garden city was never realized. Ettore Fagiuoli's work had a strong influence on the city's architecture from 1913 until after World War II. A typical example of his style is the Palazzo delle Poste, built on the site of the Palazzo Scaligero.

The uncontrolled building of the early post-war period was followed from the 1960s by a more conservationist policy, which attempted to recover and re-establish the architectural values of the historic centre. This trend was given added impetus through the work of Carlo Scarpa in remodelling the Castelvecchio between 1956 and 1964 as the seat of the Museo di Castelvecchio. He also designed the Banca Popolare di Verona (1974–81) on the Piazza Nogara.

BIBLIOGRAPHY

T. Sarayna: *De origine et amplitudine civitatis Veronae* (Verona, 1540)
S. Maffei: *Verona illustrata* (Verona, 1732/*R* 1975)
G. B. da Persico: *Descrizione di Verona e della sua provincia* (Verona, 1820–21/*R* 1974)
G. Biadego: *Verona* (Bergamo, 1909)
A. da Lisca: *La fortificazione di Verona dai tempi romani al 1866* (Verona, 1916)
P. Marconi: *Verona romana* (Bergamo, 1937)
E. Arslan: *L'architettura romanica veronese* (Verona, 1940)
L. Beschi: 'Verona romana: I monumenti', *Verona & Territ.*, i (1960), pp. 367–552
Michele Sanmicheli (exh. cat., ed. P. Gazzola; Verona, Pal. Canossa, 1960)
L. Franzoni: *Verona: Testimonianze archeologiche* (Verona, 1965)
L. Puppi, ed.: *Ritratto di Verona: Lineamenti di una storia urbanistica* (Verona, 1978)
L. Franzoni: 'Il collezionismo dal cinquecento all'ottocento', *Cultura e vita civile a Verona*, ed. G. P. Marchi (Verona, 1979), pp. 597–656
Verona, 1900–1960 (exh. cat., ed. F. Amendolagine, A. Sandrini and A. Vivit; Venice, Chiostro di S Fermo, 1979)
V. Jacobacci: *La piazzaforte di Verona sotto la dominazione austriaca 1814–1866* (Verona, 1980)
Palladio e Verona (exh. cat., ed. L. Magagnato; Verona, Gran Guardia, 1980)

2. ART LIFE AND ORGANIZATION. Although the date 996 has been read on the frescoes of the first layer of the Sacello dei SS Nazaro e Celso, artistic activity in medieval Verona began to flourish only in the 12th century (see fig. 3), when many architects and artists, including Nicholaus and Guglielmus at S Zeno Maggiore (*see* §3(ii) below), signed their works, indicating early recognition of the status of the artist. Only from the fuller records from the early 15th century, however, is it possible to assess the economic and social position of artists and craftsmen. The registry of births and deaths, and the records of land valuations (*Campioni d'Estimo*), the first of which dates from 1409, show that stone-carvers were generally better off than other artists such as painters; that they had many opportunities for work during the 15th century is shown by the influx of masons from Lombardy, who made up at

3. Verona, S Zeno Maggiore, bronze doors, 11th century and *c.* 1189

least a quarter of the total. The apogee of sculpture in Verona seems to have been the later Middle Ages.

Conditions for glassmakers were difficult throughout the Veneto owing to the privileged position of the glassworkers of Murano, who were protected by Venice. For similar reasons ceramicists had to yield to the dominance of Faenza. Embroiderers, however, were generally prosperous. Verona produced some excellent embroiderers, for example Paolo da Verona (*fl* c. 1470), whom Vasari praised for his scenes from the *Life of St John the Baptist*, executed in Florence for sacred vestments to a design by Antonio Pollaiuolo. Engraving and marquetry were practised by Fra' Giovanni da Verona, Fra' Vincenzo dalle Vacche (*fl* 16th century) and members of the Giolfino family.

The first numismatic collection in Verona was evidently started by the della Scala family, who were the first serious patrons of art in the city, extending patronage to Dante Alighieri as well as summoning painters to work at court, among them Giotto, ALTICHIERO and Bonino da Campione. Although in the 15th century the more peaceful conditions guaranteed by Venetian overlordship did not lead to a great flowering of architecture and public art, the influence of Venice was felt in the city. Towards the last quarter of the century, with the work on the Loggia del Consiglio, a group of fine sculptors spread the taste for sculptured decoration on portals and altars and, perhaps under the influence of Andrea Mantegna, disseminated a taste for classical values.

The city churches received much painted decoration in the 15th and 16th centuries, with work by Giovanni Badile; (S Maria della Scala; 1443–4 *see* BADILE, (1)) and, around 1500, by Domenico Morone (*see* MORONE, (1)), who executed all the important fresco commissions (e.g. S Maria in Organo, SS Nazaro e Celso) and was the main influence on the next generation of painters, including his son Francesco, Girolamo Dai Libri and the slightly younger Gian Francesco Caroto (*see* CAROTO, (1)). Paolo Veronese, who was born in the city, left one surviving work, the Bevilacqua-Lazise Altarpiece for S Fermo Maggiore (*c.* 1548; Verona, Castelvecchio), before his departure for Venice, and painted two other altarpieces in 1566 (*Martyrdom of St George*, S Giorgio Maggiore; and *Virgin and Child with SS Anthony and John*, Marogna Chapel, S Paolo), during a return visit to Verona. The leading painters later in the 16th century were Domenico Brusasorci (S Stefano; *see* BRUSASORCI, (1)) and Battista dell'Angolo del Moro (*see* ANGOLO DEL MORO, DELL', (1)), who worked with, among others, PAOLO FARINATI.

The collection of archaeological remains is documented in Verona as early as 1496, possibly linked to the presence at that time of Mantegna. In addition to the few small epigraphic collections made by craftsmen, antiquities were of interest to some noble families, but it was not until the second half of the 16th century that the collections of Mario Bevilacqua (1536–93), Agostino Giusti (1546–1615) and Girolamo Canossa (1532–91) took shape. Bevilacqua, in particular, assembled a collection of fine ancient sculpture that remained intact at the Palazzo Bevilacqua for more than two centuries until it was moved to the Glyptothek, Munich, in 1811. No less important was his art collection, for which the painter Orlando Flacco

(*b* 1530) acted as consultant. Giusti enriched the famous garden of his palazzo with a fine epigraphic collection, and Canossa's art collection was admired for its antique gems and for a picture gallery containing Raphael's *Holy Family (Madonna della Perla)* (now Madrid, Prado).

To the 17th century belong the rich painting collections of G. Pietro Curtoni and Giacomo Muselli (1697–1768); but the most complex museum project of the time was that of Lodovico Moscardo (1611–81), illustrated by him in *Note ovvero memorie del museo di L. Moscardo* (Padua, 1656, rev. Verona, 2/1672). With Moscardo the new conception of the museum as 'microcosmos' first took shape in Verona, reviving the late Renaissance image of the museum as *hospitium musarum*, which was well exemplified by the Palazzo Bevilacqua at the time of Count Mario. In the 18th century, apart from the appearance of a few new picture galleries, the main event was the foundation of the Museo Lapidario Maffeiano by SCIPIONE MAFFEI. In the 19th century more than 80 private art collections were recorded in Verona. The Castelvecchio has housed the Museo Civico since 1925.

BIBLIOGRAPHY
G. Vasari: *Vite* (1550, rev. 2/1568); ed. G. Milanesi (1878–85), iii, p. 299
A. Avena: 'L'arte vetraria in Verona', *Madonna Verona*, v (1911), pp. 112–27
A. Mazzi: 'Gli estimi e le anagrafi inedite dei pittori veronesi del secolo XV, *Madonna Verona*, vi (1912), pp. 43–60
——: 'Gli estimi e le anagrafi inedite dei miniatori e pittori veronesi del secolo XV', *Madonna Verona*, vi (1912), pp. 85–93
——: 'Gli estimi e le anagrafi dei lapicidi veronesi del secolo XV', *Madonna Verona*, vi (1912), pp. 221–8; vii (1913), pp. 25–38
A. Avena: 'Ceramisti e ceramiche in Verona nel secolo XV e nel XVI', *Madonna Verona*, x (1916), pp. 111–25
E. Arslan: *La pittura e la scultura veronesi dal secolo VIII al secolo XIII* (Milan, 1943)
P. L. Zovatto: 'Arte paleocristiana a Verona', *Verona & Territ.*, i (1960), pp. 553–613
A. M. Romanini: 'L'arte romanica', *Verona & Territ.*, ii (1964), pp. 583–777
P. L. Zovatto: 'L'arte altomedioevale', *Verona & Territ.*, ii (1964), pp. 479–582
M. T. Cuppini: 'L'arte gotica a Verona nei secoli XIV–XV', *Verona & Territ.*, iii/2 (1969), pp. 211–83
G. L. Mellini: *Scultori veronesi del trecento* (Milan, 1971)
G. P. Marchini: *Antiquari e collezioni archeologiche dell'ottocento veronese* (Verona, 1972)
G. Schweikhart: *Fassadenmalerei in Verona vom 14. bis zum 20. Jahrhundert* (Munich, 1973)
M. T. Cuppini: 'L'arte a Verona tra XV e XVI secolo', *Verona & Territ.*, iv/1 (1981), pp. 241–522
L. Rognini: *Tarsie e intagli di fra Giovanni a Santa Maria in Organo di Verona* (Verona, 1985)
Miniatura veronese del rinascimento (exh. cat., ed. G. Castiglioni and S. Marinelli; Verona, Castelvecchio, 1986)
K. Pomian: *Collectionneurs, ornateurs et curieux* (Paris, 1987)
LANFRANCO FRANZONI

3. BUILDINGS.

(i) Cathedral. (ii) S Zeno Maggiore. (iii) S Maria Antica.

(i) Cathedral. Dedicated to S Maria Matricolare, Verona Cathedral is important for its Romanesque sculpture, particularly the two porch-portals, the earlier on the south side attributed to Pelegrinus (who signed an arch, now in Verona, Castelvecchio) and the main façade portal signed by NICHOLAUS. Only the exterior walls up to the decorated cornice on the west, south and east sides belong to the Romanesque period, for the cathedral was enlarged in the 15th century. Built of fine Veronese marble ashlar, they

are crowned by a low-relief animal frieze along the cornice and around the apse window and date probably from *c.* 1120, the probable date also of the south portal. Documents mention the rebuilding of the cathedral in 1139, the period to which the main porch-portal by Nicholaus must be assigned because of its similarities to his portal of 1135 on the west front of Ferrara Cathedral.

The tympanum bears the *Virgin Enthroned* flanked by narrative reliefs of the *Adoration of the Magi* and the *Annunciation to the Shepherds.* The regal quality is reinforced by the three crowned *Theological Virtues* on the lintel. The deeply splayed jambs are articulated by prophets and the figures of *Roland* (identified by the name Durindarda inscribed on his sword) and *Oliver* from the *chanson-de-geste* on the outermost doorframe. The portal is preceded by a two-storey porch with the figures of *St John the Baptist* and *St John the Evangelist* in the spandrels and the Evangelist symbols on the soffits of the vault. It is supported by column-bearing griffins very similar to those by Nicholaus from the Porta dei Mesi at Ferrara Cathedral. The iconography relates not only to imperial traditions but also to civic justice, which was administered here, a function that these porch-portals assumed in the early communes.

BIBLIOGRAPHY

A. K. Porter: *Lombard Architecture*, iii (New Haven, 1917), pp. 466–79

D. Robb: 'Niccolò: A North Italian Sculptor of the Twelfth Century', *A. Bull.*, xii (1930), pp. 374–420

G. de Francovich: 'La corrente comasca nella scultura romanica europea, gli inizi', *Riv. Reale Ist. Archeol. & Stor. A.*, v (1935), pp. 267–305 [discusses Pelegrinus]

——: 'Contributi alla scultura romanica veronese', *Riv. Reale Ist. Archeol. & Stor. A.*, ix (1943), pp. 103–47

T. Krautheimer-Hess: 'The Original Porta dei Mesi and the Art of Niccolò', *A. Bull.*, xxvi (1944), pp. 152–74

R. Lejeune and J. Stiennon: *The Legend of Roland in the Middle Ages*, 2 vols (London, 1971)

E. Kain: *The Sculpture of Nicholaus and the Development of a North Italian Romanesque Workshop*, Dissertationen zur Kunstgeschichte, xxiv (Vienna, 1986)

C. Verzar Bornstein: *Portals and Politics in the Early Italian City-state: The Sculpture of Nicholaus in Context* (Parma, 1988)

For further bibliography *see* §§1 and 2 above.

(ii) S Zeno Maggiore. This pilgrimage church, in which the relics of the Early Christian Bishop Zeno are venerated, is one of the most unified of Romanesque ensembles, despite being rebuilt and modified throughout the 12th century. It is set at the northern edge of the town, adjacent to an old cemetery that included the legendary tomb of Pippin, King of the Lombards. The façade of the basilica is rich in stone and bronze sculpture, and the interior, with its trifoliate, late 14th-century ceiling, bears many carved capitals. The hall crypt under the raised choir is entered through a series of decorated arches, carved by Adamino di San Giorgio *c.* 1225.

The lower level of the façade was decorated by the sculptors Nicholaus and Guglielmus, whose names are recorded in several laudatory inscriptions on the sculptures. The tympanum bears an iconic image of *St Zeno* administering military orders to the cavalry and infantry of Verona, while on the lintel are scenes from his *Life*. On the south side of the doorway are *Genesis* reliefs (see fig. 4) and on the north *New Testament* scenes. The columns of the porch are supported by lions; *St John the Baptist* and *St John the Evangelist* appear on the spandrels and the *Labours of the Months* are represented on the architrave above. Scenes from the *Song of Roland* and the *Hunt of Theoderic* are set below the biblical scenes. Nicholaus was probably responsible for most of the sculpture, but the

4. Verona, S Zeno Maggiore, reliefs on south side of the west portal by Nicholaus, first half of 12th century; detail showing the Creation of animals and the Creation of Adam

New Testament scenes are signed by Guglielmus, presumably a contemporary and collaborator. The work was probably undertaken between *c.* 1120, when the architecture was completed (Quintavalle), and *c.* 1138 and may be compared to Nicholaus's work at the cathedrals of Ferrara (1135) and Verona (*c.* 1139). The portal and porch were subsequently enlarged to accommodate additional bronze panels to those of the 11th century (see fig. 3 above; for discussion and alternative dating, *see* DOOR, §II, 1(ii)). On stylistic grounds, these new bronze plaques can be attributed to Brioloto, who was responsible for the completion of the upper part of the façade *c.* 1189. This remodelling seems to have involved the reassembling of the porch-portal and the flanking narrative reliefs, and Brioloto may also have been responsible for some of the framing figures and friezes. His work on the upper part of the façade included the rose window, the figures surrounding the Wheel of Fortune and the cornice frieze.

BIBLIOGRAPHY

L. Simeoni: *La Basilica di San Zeno in Verona: Studi con nuovi documenti* (Verona, 1909)
A. K. Porter: *Lombard Architecture*, iii (New Haven, 1917), pp. 525–6
A. Boeckler: *Die Bronzetüren von Verona* (Marburg, 1931)
G. Trecca: *La facciata della Basilica di San Zeno* (Verona, 1938)
G. H. Crichton: *Romanesque Sculpture in Italy* (London, 1954)
A. da Lisca: *La Basilica di San Zenone in Verona* (Verona, 2/1956)
W. Neumann: *Studien zu den Bildfeldern der Bronzetür von San Zeno in Verona* (Frankfurt am Main, 1979)
E. M. Kain: 'An Analysis of the Marble Reliefs on the Façade of S Zeno, Verona', *A. Bull.*, lxiii (1981), pp. 358–74
A. M. Romanini, ed.: *Atti del seminario internazionale di Ferrara. Nicholaus e l'arte del suo tempo: Ferrara, 1981* [incl. articles on S Zeno Maggiore by A. Calzona, C. Verzar Bornstein and A. C. Quintavalle]

For further bibliography, *see* §§1, 2 and 3(i) above.

CHRISTINE B. VERZAR

(iii) S Maria Antica. The name suggests that this was the earliest church dedicated to the Virgin in Verona, but its existence is documented only from the 10th century. An inscription over a door (now walled up) on the north aisle records a reconsecration in 1185 by Gotfredo, Patriarch of Aquileia. A false inscription (on the interior wall of the right-hand side aisle) claims that the altar of the church was consecrated by Pope Alexander III in 1174. The bands of tufa and brick on the exterior are typical of Veronese Romanesque, and the church has an aisled nave terminating in three apses, rib vaults and a columnar arcade. Traces of a 12th-century black-and-white mosaic pavement survive in the north apse. The church was remodelled in the 17th century but restored to its original appearance in 1897.

S Maria Antica's renown lies, however, in the fine series of Gothic tombs erected by the della Scala family between 1277 and 1387 (see fig. 5). Their dynastic burial ground was established on the north side of the church, which had been chosen as their family chapel. Crowded into the churchyard and surrounded by a low wall surmounted by a fine 14th-century wrought-iron grille and statues on pillars are the tombs of *Mastino I* (*d* 1277), *Bartolomeo I* (*d* 1304), *?Cangrande II* (*d* 1359), *Alboino* (*d* 1311) or *?Bartolomeo II* (*d* 1381) and, possibly, *Alberto I* (*d* 1301). The most elaborate tombs are those of *Mastino II* (*d* 1351) and *Cansignorio* (*d* 1375). That of *Giovanni della Scala* was brought there in 1831 from S Fermo.

The only tomb located outside the enclosure is that of *Cangrande I della Scala*, who died on 22 July 1329 and was interred in the present sarcophagus some months later. Set above the door on the north flank of the church and visible from the interior through a grille, the tomb is surmounted by a canopy. The sarcophagus itself is supported by four crowned dogs, which hold the della Scala arms. In the centre, in high relief, is the *Man of Sorrows* with the *Virgin Annunciate* and the *Angel Gabriel* in quadrilobed lozenges at either side; around these, in shallow relief, are scenes of civic life and the military activities of Cangrande. Above, in a second tier, with an inscription in which the tomb appears to address the spectator in the first person, is the draped funeral bier with the recumbent effigy of Cangrande. He appears again at the summit of the roof, on horseback and in military regalia in a bold and vivid representation (original, since 1907 in Verona, Castelvecchio). A small plaque at the base of the tomb bears an inscription praising the exploits of the condottiere.

The tomb of *Cangrande I* was followed by that of *Mastino II*, which was constructed during his lifetime, between 1345 and 1350. It resembles Cangrande's tomb but is free-standing. Rectangular in plan, the tomb has two tiers of columns supporting a canopy with a truncated, pyramidal roof. The sarcophagus, set in the upper tier and visible over the perimeter grille of the churchyard, rests on eight short columns with smooth shafts and foliate capitals and is articulated by a projecting double cornice with corner colonnettes. The long sides bear two scenes, each divided into three with foliate backgrounds; unusually, they represent the *Risen Christ between St John the Baptist and a Female Saint* and *St George Presenting Mastino II to God the Father in the Presence of St Paul*. On the short sides are the *Crucifixion with the Virgin and St John*, at one end, and a symbolic figure, perhaps Fortitude or a member of the della Scala family, at the other. Above, at the corners, four angels watch over the deceased, who lies on a draped bier. The canopy has four pointed, trefoil arches surmounted by gables with, in the tympana, Genesis scenes in high relief: the *Temptation of Adam and Eve*, the *Labours of Adam and Eve*, the *Murder of Abel* and the *Drunkenness of Noah*. The four corner tabernacles, set above small pillars, contain statues of angels and saints. At the summit Mastino is again depicted, on horseback, fully armed and holding an upraised lance. The tomb stands within a rectangular enclosure formed by a marble base with railings supported by posts with four statues of Virtues.

The attribution of these two tombs remains problematic, since neither is signed. The third and most elaborate tomb, that of *Cansignorio*, was the work of Bonino da Campione and his school, as attested by the signed inscription on the east side of the base (*see* CAMPIONESI; for illustration *see* SCALA, DELLA). Like Mastino II, Cansignorio commissioned the tomb during his lifetime and was buried there in 1376, a year after his death. The free-standing monument, again two-storey, has a hexagonal plan: six columns support the slab on which the sarcophagus rests, held by nude putti. On the long sides are scenes from the Ministry of Christ: the *Woman of Samaria*, the *Raising of Lazarus*, the *Entry into Jerusalem*, the *Temptation of Christ*, *Christ and the Demoniac* and the *Miracle of the*

5. Verona, S Maria Antica, della Scala family tombs in the churchyard on the north side of the church, 1277–1387

Loaves and Fishes, while the two short sides bear the *Coronation of the Virgin* and the *St George Presenting Cansignorio to the Virgin*. The figure of Cansignorio himself lies on the cover, guarded by four angels at the head and foot of his funeral bier. The canopy has cusped arches supported by six spiral columns with heads in the spandrels. Above the cornice, in the tympana of the gables, are seated Virtues in shell niches. Interspersed with them at the angles are tabernacles containing angels holding the family coat of arms. Around the base of the tomb, set on pillars supporting the grille, are six tabernacles containing life-size statues of warrior saints: *Quirinus, Martin, Sigismund, Valentine, George* and *Louis of France*. Crowning the hexagonal, pyramidal roof is a tall plinth with the equestrian statue of *Cansignorio*, a work comparable with Bonino's statue of *Bernabò Visconti* (1364; Milan, Castello Sforzesco).

BIBLIOGRAPHY

F. De Maffei: *La chiesa di S Maria Antica: Le arche scaligere*, Le Guide, x (Verona, 1968)

Le stoffe di Cangrande: Ritrovamenti e ricerche sul trecento veronese (exh. cat., ed. L. Magagnato; Verona, Castelvecchio, 1983)

G. M. Varanini, ed.: *Gli Scaligeri, 1277–1387* (Verona, 1988)

G. L. Mellini: 'L'arca di Cansignorio di Bonino da Campione a Verona', *I maestri campionesi*, ed. R. Bossaglia and G. A. Dell'Acqua (Bergamo, 1992), pp. 173–97

MASSIMILIANO DAVID

Verona, Giovanni da. *See* GIOVANNI DA VERONA.

Verona, Guarino da. *See* GUARINO DA VERONA.

Verona, Liberale da. *See* LIBERALE DA VERONA.

Veronese, Alessandro. *See* TURCHI, ALESSANDRO.

Veronese, Bonifazio. *See* PITATI, BONIFAZIO DE'.

Veronese, Guarino. *See* GUARINO DA VERONA.

Veronese [Caliari], Paolo (*b* Verona, 1528; *d* Venice, 19 April 1588). Italian painter and draughtsman. With Titian and Tintoretto he makes up the triumvirate of great painters of the late Renaissance in Venice. He is known as a supreme colourist and for his illusionistic decorations in both fresco and oil. His large paintings of biblical feasts executed for the refectories of monasteries in Venice and Verona are especially celebrated. He also produced many altarpieces, history and mythological paintings and portraits. His compositional sketches in pen, ink and wash, figure studies in chalk, and chiaroscuro modelli and *ricordi* form a significant body of drawings. He headed a family workshop that remained active after his death (*see* CALIARI; for Veronese's adoption of this name *see* §III below).

I. Life and work. II. Working methods and technique. III. Character and personality. IV. Critical reception and posthumous reputation.

I. Life and work.

1. Verona, to 1553. 2. Venice and Verona, 1553–60. 3. Maser, Verona and Venice, 1560–73. 4. Late works, 1574–88.

1. VERONA, TO 1553.

(i) Training and first works. Paolo was the son of Gabriele, a stonecutter (whose father was also a stonecutter, from Lombardy), and Caterina. Borghini and Ridolfi named Antonio Badile IV as Veronese's master, and *Paulus eius discipulus seu Garsonus 14* is recorded as a member of Badile's household in 1541 (Verona, Archv Stato). Vasari named Giovanni Caroto as Paolo's teacher, and it is likely that training with Caroto followed the initial apprenticeship with Badile, since a 'Paulus' is no longer a member of Badile's household in 1544 (Gisolfi Pechukas, 1976, 1982).

Veronese's earliest works confirm roles for both Badile and Caroto in his training and reflect the richness of the artistic ambience of Verona during the 1540s. Verona was a Roman town and a site of antiquarian studies during the Renaissance, including a book by Caroto (1546 edn and original drgs; Verona, Bib. Civ.). Fresco cycles (*c.* 1500) by Giovanni Maria Falconetto and Domenico Morone in S Nazaro, the cathedral and the library of S Bernardino offered Veronese important examples of illusionistic cycles that intended to re-create ancient wall decoration. Paintings by Francesco Morone and Cavazzola, executed in the first two decades of the 16th century and shining with pure colours illumined by light that mimics sunlight, inspired his palette. Nicola Giolfino's decorations (*in situ*) of the 1520s in the Capella S Francesco, S Bernardino (*in situ*), were examples that successfully orchestrated architectural settings with background views, and Francesco Torbido's translation in 1534 of Giulio Romano's designs offered a powerful illusion of the *Assumption of the Virgin* in the choir of the cathedral (*in situ*). Other influences included a book of drawings by Parmigianino then in the Muselli Collection, older contemporaries of Veronese such as Domenico Brusasorci and Battista dell'Angolo del Moro, who adopted Mannerist conventions of anatomy, and Caroto, who worked in a high Renaissance style well into the 1550s (Gisolfi Pechukas, 1976, 1982).

Veronese's earliest known works are two oil sketches, similar to each other in size, technique and style, for works described by Ridolfi as 'beginnings' (Gisolfi Pechukas, 1976, 1982): the *Raising of the Daughter of Jairus* (*c.* 1546; Paris, Louvre, reserve), which is the *bozzetto* for a lost painting formerly in the Cappella degli Avanzi, S Bernardino, Verona (original stolen and replaced by a copy, 1696), and the *Virgin and Child Enthroned with SS Louis of Toulouse and John the Baptist* (*c.* 1546; Florence, Uffizi, reserve; see fig. 1), a *bozzetto* for the damaged Bevilacqua–Lazise Altarpiece (*c.* 1546; ex-S Fermo Maggiore, Verona; Verona, Castelvecchio). The surviving works show morphological similarities to Badile's documented works of the 1540s, while the clear light and colour are closer to Caroto (e.g. frescoes of archangels, 1530; S Maria in Organo, Verona). Other decipherable influences include Parmigianino's drawings, Michelangelo's *Joel* (via an engraving) and the altarpiece of *St Nicholas* (1535) by

Torbido and Battista dell'Angolo del Moro in S Fermo Maggiore.

The two oil sketches are at the centre of a group of very early works that may be dated to the late 1540s (Gisolfi Pechukas, 1982). This includes the *Magdalene Laying aside her Jewels* (London, N.G.), the *Lamentation* (Verona, Castelvecchio), the *Mystic Marriage of St Catherine* (New Haven, CT, Yale U. A.G.), the *Holy Family with the Infant John the Baptist* (Amsterdam, Rijksmus.) and the *Portrait of a Woman with her Son and Dog* (Paris, Louvre). These works share with the oil sketches their somewhat elongated figure types with mannered gestures, a simple division of foreground 'stage' and background view, a cool palette and blue skies streaked with thin white clouds, and architectural details derived from works by Sanmicheli. To this group may be added another painting of the *Mystic Marriage of St Catherine* (Tokyo, N. Mus. W.A.), datable to 1547 by the joint coat of arms.

Three modestly sized canvases for a ceiling, possibly from a palazzo in or near Verona, may date from *c.* 1550 (Gisolfi Pechukas, 1987). The allegories of *Peace* and *Hope* (Rome, Mus. Capitolino) and the *Allegory of the Arts* (Rome, Pin. Vaticana) share the *di sotto in sù* foreshortening of Veronese's subsequent ceiling decorations, but the figures are still delicately proportioned and simply clad, and the blue skies are streaked with thin clouds as in the

1. Paolo Veronese: *Virgin and Child Enthroned with SS Louis of Toulouse and John the Baptist*, oil study for the Bevilacqua–Lazise Altarpiece, 500×360 mm, *c.* 1546 (Florence, Galleria degli Uffizi, reserve)

earliest pictures. The boldness of his later series is not yet evident.

(ii) First commissions outside Verona. In 1551 Veronese's first altarpiece for a Venetian church was installed: a *Sacra conversazione* for the Giustiniani Chapel of S Francesco della Vigna. Compositionally it is a variation on Titian's Pesaro *Madonna* (1519–26; Venice, S Maria Gloriosa dei Frari) and on Badile's *Virgin and Child Enthroned with Saints* (1544; ex-Santo Spirito, Verona; Verona, Castelvecchio). St Catherine's gorgeous brocade mantle is an early example of Veronese's rich overlaying of pigments.

The surviving fresco fragments of 1551 from the Villa Soranzo (destr. 1816) by Sanmicheli (about 14; Castelfranco, Cathedral sacristy; Venice, Semin. Patriarcale; Vicenza, Mus. Civ. A. & Stor.) are not by Veronese only but by his compatriots Battista Zelotti and Anselmo Canneri as well, and close study of early descriptions, records and related drawings indicates collaboration of the three on an equal basis. Reconstruction of the decoration of the Loggia, Sala and two Camere at the villa reveals a system of feigned architecture, statuary and reliefs in monochrome, setting off 'real' landscape views and coloured figures (Schweikhart, 1971; Gisolfi Pechukas, 1987; Gisolfi, 1989–90). As in the earlier examples of Falconetto and Morone in Verona, the intent was probably to recreate ancient Roman illusionistic decorations. The large fragment of *Time and Fame* (1551; Castelfranco Cathedral sacristy) was probably the ceiling of the 'Camera C' (Crosato Larcher, 1977) and demonstrates Veronese's early mastery of *di sotto in sù* foreshortening and effects of sunlight on fabric and flesh. The tumbling figure of Fame is indebted to Giulio Romano's design of angels, executed by Torbido (1534) in the vault of the choir of Verona Cathedral. Fame's elongated proportions recall Parmigianino's figures, while the muscular Time resembles Correggio's figure of St Peter in the *Vision of St John on Patmos* (1520–23; dome fresco, S Giovanni Evangelista, Parma). In addition, Veronese's fragment of a *Putto Straddling a Baluster* (Vicenza, Mus. Civ. A. & Stor.) is close in style to Correggio's boldly foreshortened putti in the Camera S Paolo, Parma, further suggesting that Veronese had recently visited Parma.

In 1552 Cardinal Ercole Gonzaga commissioned Veronese, Domenico Brusasorci, Paolo Farinati and Battista dell'Angolo del Moro to paint altarpieces for four altars in Mantua Cathedral. Veronese's resultant *Temptations of St Anthony* (1552; Caen, Mus. B.-A.), his first fully documented commission, is unique among his early works for its warm tonality and sensuality. The softness of flesh and atmosphere must have been inspired by Correggio's canvases of similar tonality, perhaps the *Antiope* (Paris, Louvre), then in Mantua.

2. VENICE AND VERONA, 1553–60.

(i) Major decorative commissions. In 1553 Veronese moved to Venice. He had been invited by Giovanni Battista Ponchino to collaborate with him and with Giambattista Zelotti on the decoration of the Sala del Consiglio dei Dieci in the Doge's Palace (*see* VENICE, §IV, 6(ii)). The themes of the three ceilings decorated in 1553–4—the Sala del Consiglio dei Dieci, and the adjacent Stanza della Bussola and Stanza dei Tre Capi—were devised by Daniele Barbaro (Sansovino). Veronese's work predominates. In the large *Jupiter Expelling the Vices* (1553–4; Paris, Louvre), designed as the central oval for the Consiglio dei Dieci ceiling, he developed the influence of Giulio Romano. The Vices, muscular male figures who hurtle from the heavens, are sharply foreshortened though their descent, seen through the oval frame, is not as threatening as the fall of the giants in Giulio Romano's Sala dei Giganti (1530–32; Mantua, Pal. Ducale). The violent action is held in equilibrium by precise balancing and juxtaposition of forms, movements and colour areas.

The smaller oval canvas of *Youth and Age* (also known as the *Rape of Proserpina*, 1553–4; see fig. 2), in a corner of the ceiling, is an outstanding early work. The female figure of Youth is shown in brilliant sunlight beside a Michelangelesque figure of Age. The main colour areas of blue, white and gold are enhanced by judicious touches of vermilion. Ideal forms are seen in an ideal climate, in a

2. Paolo Veronese: *Youth and Age* (1553–4), oil on canvas, 2.86×1.50 m, ceiling painting in the Sala del Consiglio dei Dieci, Doge's Palace, Venice

perfect harmony of form, light and colour. The entire ceiling of the much smaller Stanza della Bussola was entrusted to Veronese. The central canvas of *St Mark and the Theological Virtues* (Paris, Louvre) recalls details of Correggio's *Assumption of the Virgin* (Parma Cathedral), but the motion is less frenzied because of Veronese's careful balancing of forms and juxtaposing of poses; the scene is characteristically suffused with bright sunlight, reflecting on luminous flesh and shiny fabric.

Zelotti painted the central panel in the Stanza dei Tre Capi, and Veronese was responsible for two smaller canvases with themes of virtue and vice, *Peace Comforting the Innocent* and the *Allegory of Nemesis* (both *in situ*). In the former the female figure of Peace or Victory is seen from behind, with a male figure in white discreetly placed below and behind her; the harmonious disposition of form and colour creates the serenity for which Veronese is celebrated. The composition is an elegant reversal of the *Allegory of Nemesis*, in which the victorious female looms over the crouching male in the foreground.

In 1555 Veronese was employed by the Veronese prior Bernardo Torlioni (*d* 1572), who was rector of S Sebastiano, Venice, from 1555 to 1572, to paint the ceiling of the church's sacristy and, in 1556, the ceiling of its nave (see Pignatti, 1966, regarding earlier monochromes). His decoration of this church in both fresco and oil continued until at least 1570. The central canvas of the sacristy ceiling represents the *Coronation of the Virgin*, and the four surrounding canvases depict the *Evangelists*. The magnificent paintings of *Esther Brought before Ahasuerus*, the *Triumph of Mordecai* and the *Coronation of Esther* on the nave ceiling show these scenes from the *Life of Esther* in *di sotto in sù* foreshortening and bright sunlight. In each of the three, background architecture is foreshortened to the extent that the receding element forms a vertical division of the composition. The *Coronation of Esther* moves furthest in a new direction. The chief change is in the more complex light: the sunlight not only illuminates different textures but dances between metal, satin and shining locks of blond hair in a rich interplay. Tea (1920) noted Veronese's use of adjacent colours, not black, to create delicate shadows that depict colour as seen in clear daylight, an observation that seems to have been inspired particularly by these ceiling pieces. It is possible that Giovanni Antonio Fasolo collaborated with Veronese on this project.

The *Feast in the House of Simon* (Turin, Gal. Sabauda), painted for the refectory of SS Nazaro and Celso in Verona, is Veronese's first surviving supper scene. Its dating is debated: Ridolfi and most later writers placed it *c*. 1559; von Hadeln (1914) suggested 1553; and Sancassani (1973–4) argued that a payment of January 1556 referred to the work as in progress. (This fits with a placement after the *Anointment of David* (Vienna, Ksthist. Mus.) and the *Presentation of Christ* (Dresden, Gemäldegal. Alte Meister), which on stylistic grounds belong to *c*. 1554 and *c*. 1555 respectively.) An architecture of Corinthian columns and acanthus frieze sets the scene in the pharisee's home. The space is rather shallow. Mary Magdalene anoints Christ's feet, while his discourse with Simon and forgiveness of her sins cause amazement among the guests. The composition is more complex than in Veronese's

earliest biblical paintings, the figures more robust and the costume richer. Ridolfi emphasized the beauty of the architectural frame and of two satyrs that must then have adorned the framework covering the now vacant upper corners of the canvas.

In 1557 Veronese was one of seven artists each of whom painted three roundels for the ceiling of the Libreria Marciana (*see* VENICE, §IV, 7(ii)), and he was awarded the gold chain for the finest tondo, his allegory of *Music*. Titian and Sansovino were judges in the contest (Ridolfi); perhaps this is why the frankly classical *Music* won. Recalling the fresh, relaxed classicism of early Titian, it stands out among the generally mannered compositions of other competitors and differs, too, from Veronese's other roundels. In *Geometry and Arithmetic* the figure types remain close to those of the S Sebastiano ceilings, the two females assuming poses that complement and reflect the frame of the roundel; in the allegory of *Honour*, however, the experiments with Mannerist devices, the elongated repoussoir figures and rather confused composition, are clearly intentional.

Around 1557 Veronese decorated in fresco the Palazzo Trevisano in Murano. This work is now damaged and partially lost, but cleaning in the early 1980s revealed landscapes in fairly good condition in the upper room, the Sala dell'Olimpo (Romano, 1981 and 1983). The illusionistic complex includes the feigned architecture, landscape 'views' and Olympian visions (in the vault) that were components of the decorations at the Villa Soranzo and in examples by Veronese's contemporaries, for instance the work of Brusasorci and the Caroto brothers at the Villa del Bene (1551) at Volargne, near Verona.

During 1558 Veronese continued decorating S Sebastiano with the frescoes of *St Sebastian Reproving Diocletian* and the *Martyrdom of St Sebastian*, which cover walls on the north and south sides of the monks' choir above the atrium of the church. Both scenes are conceived as dramas enacted on a shallow stage and are framed by ornate painted architecture, possibly executed by Veronese's brother Benedetto Caliari. The foreground space in which the action takes place is also defined by architecture, repoussoir figures directing the viewer's attention and architecture allowing room for a spacious expanse of sky as a backdrop. Also for S Sebastiano Paolo designed the organ (1558) and painted on the external shutters the *Presentation of Christ* and on the interior the *Pool of Bethseda* (1560); he designed the high altar and painted (probably in 1560) the altarpiece of *St Sebastian with the Virgin and Child and Other Saints*. The architecture of both organ and altar is rich and apparently based on Sanmicheli's style, as demonstrated, for example, in the Cappella Pellegrini of S Bernardino in Verona. Painted and actual architecture of the organ are coordinated so that, whether the shutters are open or closed, painted architecture continues the organ's exterior architecture in both perspective and vocabulary (*see* ORGAN SHUTTER, fig. 2).

(ii) Early portraits. Veronese's many portraits raise difficult problems of attribution and dating. The pendants *Giuseppe da Porto and Son* (Florence, Pitti) and *Livia da Porto Thiene and Daughter* (*c*. 1554; Baltimore, MD, Walters A.G.) are,

together with the *Portrait of a Woman with her Son and Dog* (Paris, Louvre), generally accepted as both early and authentic. The da Porto portraits are full-length, standing portraits, which suggests that Veronese knew works by Moretto or Giovanni Battista Moroni. Contemporary with these is probably the Budapest *Portrait of a Gentleman* (Mus. F.A.; see Rearick, Venice, Cini, exh. cat., 1988, and Gisolfi, 1989–90). The *Portrait of a Gentleman* (Malibu, CA, Getty Mus.), a full-length portrait of a sitter of nonchalant yet restrained elegance against an architectural setting, develops the theme of the portrait of *Giuseppe da Porto*. Gaetano Zancon (1771–1816) engraved it as a self-portrait of Veronese (see Ticozzi, 1977 exh. cat., pl. 91, p. 32) in 1802; if this identification is accepted, it suggests an early date for the painting, as the man is far less bald than the self-portrait included in the *Marriage of Cana* (1562–3; Paris, Louvre; *see* §3(ii) below), but Rearick (Washington exh. cat., 1988) gave a late date of 1578 (see Gisolfi, 1989–90, pp. 32–3).

3. MASER, VERONA AND VENICE, 1560–73. According to Ridolfi, in 1560 Veronese was invited to accompany Girolamo Grimani, Procurator of S Marco, to Rome. The greater monumentality of his work after this time, resulting from his study of antiquity and masterpieces of the High Renaissance, supports Ridolfi's dating. Smith (1977) suggested that the visit may have been arranged by Daniele Barbaro and perhaps Andrea Palladio to allow Veronese to study antique villa decoration in preparation for his commission to provide frescoes at the Villa Barbaro (now Villa Volpi) at Maser, near Treviso.

(i) Decorative frescoes: the Villa Barbaro at Maser. It seems likely that Veronese's work on the decorations for the Villa Barbaro at Maser were done *c.* 1561, after his return from Rome. Daniele Barbaro and his brother Marc'Antonio employed Palladio as architect, perhaps Alessandro Vittoria as sculptor and Veronese as painter. Undoubtedly the brothers devised the iconographical programme for the frescoes with themes that celebrate the agrarian, pastoral, cultured and Christian life (see Ackerman, 1982). The illusionistic effects are brilliantly executed in the main rooms. In the central Sala a Crociera a painted arcade of Palladian proportion and vocabulary frames landscape views *all'antica* that include ruins, travellers, animals and streams and recall Vitruvius' description of appropriate villa decoration (*On Architecture*, VII.v). The horizon of the painted landscapes coincides with that of the living landscape seen through the front window from a middle point in the room, and the feigned balustrades continue the stone balustrade framing the front window before each landscape view. Painted banners and lances rest in corners, as if casually deposited; musicians playing various instruments project from painted niches set between the arches.

3. Paolo Veronese: *Members of the Barbaro Household* (detail; *c.* 1561), fresco, Sala di Olimpo, Villa Barbaro, Maser

In each of the five rooms adjacent to the Sala a Crociera the illusion is further developed. Ceilings open up to offer views of appropriate deities and allegories; Bacchus teaches man the use of the grape in the Stanza di Bacco; other pleasures are celebrated in *Abundance* in the Stanza degli Sposi; *Faith* and *Charity* are above in the Stanza della Lucerna; and there is an allegory of *Abundance, Fortitude and Envy* in the Stanza del Cane. The celebration of the virtues and rewards of country life culminates in the vault of the main Sala di Olimpo at the end of the Crociera, where *Universal Harmony* (Lewis, 1987; Crosato, 1983) or *Divine Love* (Jackson Reist, 1985) presides, surrounded by the key residents of Olympus and deities symbolic of the four elements. The walls of each room have landscape views, feigned architectural elements carefully coordinated with real ones and feigned statuary. These views, which often evoke the atmospheric grandeur of Roman ruins, derive from prints by Hieronymus Cock (1551) and Battista Pittoni (1561), the dates of which confirm the dating of the frescoes to *c.* 1561 (Oberhuber, 1968). Humorous touches enliven every room: a dog and a cat occupy ledges in the Stanza del Cane; cleaning utensils rest on a sill in the Stanza degli Sposi. In the Stanza di Bacco vines seen in landscape views show their upper branches in lunette and cove 'windows' above; in the Stanza della Lucerna a putto seen through a ceiling oval holds a real lantern. In the Sala a Crociera and in smaller rooms visible from the main ones family members are depicted at doorways that match the actual doors (*see* ILLUSIONISM, colour pl. IV) and, in the Sala di Olimpo, Signora Giustiniani Barbaro, accompanied by a child, a servant and two pets, surveys her household from the balcony (see fig. 3). Undoubtedly Veronese and his patrons knew Pliny the elder's passage praising humour in the decorations of Spurius Tadius, which included 'splendid villas approached across marshes, men tottering and staggering along carrying women on their shoulders for a bargain, extremely wittily designed' (*Natural History* XXXV.ix.116–17).

(ii) Subject pictures and altarpieces. In 1562–3 Veronese painted the vast *Marriage at Cana* (6.69×9.90 m; Paris, Louvre), the most ambitious of his banquet scenes, for the refectory of S Giorgio Maggiore, Venice. Vasari wrote with enthusiasm of its dimensions and of its 'more than 150' figures, its 'variety of costumes' and its *'invenzione'*. At the centre of the immense activity is the silent figure of Christ, and in the right foreground are the servants, the water jars and the steward who tastes the new wine. Bride and groom are seated at the left in splendid array, while in the centre foreground a quartet performs; Boschini (1674) identified the players as Veronese (viola), Francesco Bassano (flute), Jacopo Tintoretto (violin) and Titian (bass viol). The crowded composition is made possible by a deep setting and relatively high viewpoint; this depth, the heavy grandeur of the architecture and the complexity of the composition may reflect Veronese's experience of Raphael's Stanze in the Vatican during his visit to Rome in 1560. Rosand (1973) stressed the symbolism of the lamb being carved just above Christ's head and considered the elaborate costumes to reflect contemporary theatre, and Fehl (1981) related the rich yet decorous treatment of

the subject to Pietro Aretino's *La humanità di Christo* (Venice, 1535).

In the middle of the 1560s Veronese produced a series of large subject pictures that unite noble figures and stately architecture in compositions of theatrical grandeur. These paintings form a link between the *Marriage at Cana* and the more elegantly structured banquet scenes of the early 1570s. They include the *Martyrdom of St Sebastian* and *SS Mark and Marcellianus Led to Martyrdom* (both 1565; Venice, S Sebastiano, choir), the celebrated *Mystical Marriage of St Catherine* (*c.* 1565–75; Venice, Accad.), one of Veronese's most richly painted canvases, and *Christ Preaching in the Temple* (*c.* 1565; Madrid, Prado; for debate on dating of this picture see Levey, 1960, and Gisolfi Pechukas, 1982).

In 1566 Veronese returned to Verona to marry Elena Badile, daughter of his first teacher. Two altarpieces for churches in Verona are assigned to this year, the *Martyrdom of St George* for S Giorgio Maggiore and the *Virgin and Child with SS Anthony and John* for the Marogna Chapel in S Paolo (both *in situ*). The pen sketches (Malibu, CA, Getty Mus.) for *Christ Preaching in the Temple* and the *Martyrdom of St George* exemplify Veronese's mature, rapid compositional drawings (*see* §II, 2 below).

This work culminated in the *Feast in the House of Levi* (1573; see fig. 4), which, through a series of adjustments unifying its greater width, improved on the composition of the quite similar *Supper of Gregory the Great* (1572; Vicenza, Sanctuario di Monte Berico). In both paintings the architectural setting, Palladian in proportion and detail, creates a triptych-like division of the canvas, and steps leading past the side areas direct attention to the centre. The steps resemble those leading to the raised sanctuaries sometimes found in Romanesque churches of northern Italy, thus associating the centre with the sanctuary and the table with the altar (Rosand, 1973). The lighter and more elegant composition of these later banquet scenes is achieved partly through the choice of a lower viewpoint than in the *Marriage at Cana*, so that the surface of the table is barely visible and one rhythmic line of celebrants crosses the canvas.

The *Feast in the House of Levi* was commissioned as a *Last Supper* for the refectory of SS Giovanni e Paolo in Venice. A tripartite arcade frames the whole, presenting the upper room as an open loggia with the banisters of the lateral staircases leading the eye to Christ at the centre, framed by the arch. The sacred figures are thus isolated from the wealth of incident around them but the picture nonetheless attracted the attention of the Inquisition, which sensed heresy in having 'drunken buffoons, armed Germans, dwarfs and similar scurrilities' present at the Last Supper (see Fehl, 1961, for a complete transcript of the trial). In his defence before the tribunal of the Inquisition on 28 July 1573, Veronese claimed for the painter the creative freedom of the 'poet and the madman', also pointing out that he had depicted the incidental figures and anecdotal details outside the realm of sacred elements. That his depiction conforms to ideals of decorum was reaffirmed by Fehl (1961). Yet Veronese was ordered to correct his composition, to which he ultimately responded by changing its title to *Feast in the House of Levi*, a subject

4. Paolo Veronese: *Last Supper*, renamed the *Feast in the House of Levi*, oil on canvas, 5.55×12.80 m, 1573 (Venice, Galleria dell'Accademia)

requiring 'a great company of publicans' (Luke 5:29) (Fehl and Perry, 1984).

(iii) Later portraits. A few portraits may be tentatively placed in Veronese's mature period. The tender *Portrait of a Lady* ('*La bella Nani*'; Paris, Louvre) in cool blues and silvers, which resembles the portrait of Signora Barbaro at Maser, and the three-quarter-length seated portrait of *Daniele Barbaro* (Amsterdam, Rijksmus.), shown holding an edition of Vitruvius dated 1556, were probably executed in the early 1560s. There may have followed the grander *Portrait of a Man in a Fur* (Florence, Pitti) and the *Portrait of a Man* (Rome, Gal. Colonna), their later dating suggested by a bolder brushwork and darker tonality (Gisolfi, 1989–90). It should be noted, however, that Rearick (Washington exh. cat., 1988) placed the *Portrait of a Lady* and the *Portrait of a Man in a Fur* around 1550.

Some of Veronese's finest portraits are included within major subject pictures of his maturity, such as the quartet of artists in the *Marriage at Cana*, noted above. An entire contemporary family bears witness to the *Supper at Emmaus* (*c.* 1560; Paris, Louvre); while the somewhat stiff group of family members at the right may have been executed by Benedetto, the two little girls playing with a dog in the foreground are justly famous examples of Veronese's sympathetic portrayals. The *Cuccina Family Presented to the Virgin by the Theological Virtues* is one of four canvases commissioned to decorate a room of the family palazzo on the Grand Canal (*c.* 1570–72; Dresden, Gemäldegal. Alte Meister). The sitters are sumptuously dressed, shown with gestures of affection and with the inevitable pet puppy. Veronese's most significant contributions to the art of portraiture may in fact be the skilful and sensitive group portraits incorporated in biblical and votive paintings.

4. LATE WORKS, 1574–88.

(i) Further commissions for the Doge's Palace. Directly after the fire in the Doge's Palace in 1574, Veronese received payments towards the cost of paintings he was to do for the Sala del Collegio (Zorzi, 1953; Schulz, 1968). The ceiling celebrates the Venetian State and her relationship to Ecclesia, the central canvases showing *Venice Enthroned with Justice and Peace, Mars and Neptune* and the *Old Testament Sacrifice and the Eucharist* (for discussion of the iconography see Sinding-Larsen, 1974 and 1988), while the smaller surrounding canvases represent allegories of the *Virtues*. These allegorical figures and scenes are set in the heavens and viewed through a rich gilded wood framework. The *di sotto in sù* perspective and the palette recall the Consiglio dei Dieci ceiling but with the bright daylight effect of Veronese's pieces in the earlier decorations modified: the angle of light is lower, and the pink reflections suggest an afternoon rather than a midday light. It is generally thought that Benedetto Caliari assisted his brother in the Sala del Collegio, but the conception is certainly Paolo's. The wall painting over the tribunal representing an *Allegory of the Battle of Lepanto*, with Christ at the centre (Sinding-Larsen, 1974), and the flanking monochrome niche figures of *St Sebastian* and *St Justine* are also Veronese's, executed, probably with Benedetto, *c.* 1581.

In 1579–82, after the fire of 1577 in the Doge's Palace, a competition was held to select an artist to execute the huge *Paradise* in the Sala del Maggior Consiglio. Veronese and Francesco Bassano (ii) were awarded the commission jointly, presumably in 1582, but the piece had not been executed when Veronese died in 1588 and Tintoretto (always resourceful in these matters) obtained the commission. De Tolnay (1970) argued that Tintoretto's painting is based to some extent on the original oil sketches (Veronese's: Lille, Mus. B.-A.; on this issue see also Schulz, 1980, and Sinding-Larsen, 1984). Between 1579 and 1582 Veronese and his assistants (particularly Benedetto) executed the large ceiling canvas of the *Triumph of Venice* above the ducal throne in the same Sala (*see* VENICE, fig. 25). He prepared the complex vision with *di sotto in sù* foreshortening, rich architecture and ebullient figures in a beautifully executed modello in pen with white highlighting on brown paper (Harewood House, W. Yorks; see Cocke, 1984, no. 88). Here Veronese went beyond his earlier ceiling decorations: the motion, excitement and activity are used to convey uplifting emotion, as in Baroque art.

(ii) Other mythological paintings. New directions and a more complex development are seen in Veronese's works of the 1580s. The *Triumph of Venice* is proto-Baroque, and this direction was developed ultimately by Giambattista Tiepolo (*see* §IV, 3 below). Related to this are such late mythological works as the *Choice of Hercules*, the *Allegory of Wisdom and Strength* (both *c.* 1580; New York, Frick) and *Mars and Venus* (*c.* 1580; New York, Met.). As with the contemporary *Rape of Europa* (Venice, Doge's Pal., Anticollegio), the sunny palette of the Doge's Palace ceiling paintings is still operative, the light is still full and the shadows delicate, but the paintings show a new richness of detail, as in the worldly objects cast at the feet of Wisdom, and sumptuous treatment of drapery.

(iii) Other religious works. A more radical change is evident in Veronese's late religious works. Here he abandoned for

5. Paolo Veronese: *Miracle of St Pantaleon*, oil on canvas, 2.27×1.60 m, 1587 (Venice, S Pantalon)

the first time since the *Temptations of St Anthony* (1552) the sunny palette and clear light learnt and adapted from artists of Verona. In a series of depictions of the Pietà and in his last altarpiece, the *Miracle of St Pantaleon* (see fig. 5), he experimented with chiaroscuro effects to heighten pathos. Perhaps the most powerful of these is the *Dead Christ with the Virgin and an Angel* (*c.* 1581; St Petersburg, Hermitage; x-rays show the head of a second angel on the left), originally executed for the church of SS Giovanni e Paolo, Venice, and recorded there by Borghini in 1584. As in other late religious works, Veronese has substituted nocturnal light for his usual daylight. A pale light, which could be moonlight, enters from the right and gently highlights the angel's blond ringlets and rose drapery, the Virgin's head and Christ's knee, hand and loincloth. The setting is reduced to a piece of drapery beneath Christ, and the viewer is asked to meditate on his sacrifice. Veronese's repetition of this emotional theme may reflect the instruction of the Council of Trent that religious art should inspire piety. In pursuing this more profound religious feeling, Veronese dispensed with the decorative richness of his secular pieces. He did not abandon his lifelong research on the interaction of light and colour; rather he progressed to a new phase, the study of nocturnal light.

Several other versions of the Pietà exist, usually assigned to the 1580s, and assistance from Veronese's shop has been suggested in each case. They include the *Dead Christ with Two Angels* (Berlin, Gemäldegal.; Boston, MA, Mus. F.A.) and two versions of the *Dead Christ with an Angel and a Donor* (Switzerland, priv. col.; Houston, TX, Mus. F.A.; see Pignatti, 1984). The surviving late altarpiece that matches the St Petersburg Pietà in quality and character is not thematically related. In the *Miracle of St Pantaleon* (1587; Venice, S Pantalon; see fig. 5), commissioned by Bartolommeo Borghi, who is shown in the picture supporting the sick child, the masterful brushwork, nocturnal setting and 'moonlight' entering from the right recur. The red-rose drapery of the saint is the primary colour and this reflects the pale light, through a brilliant use of lead white blending in highlights and red lakes for shadows.

II. Working methods and technique.

1. PAINTINGS. Veronese's working methods were first described by Boschini (1660), whose account mentions specific materials: orpiment; red lead; *giallolino* (probably lead-tin yellow) and lakes. Analysis of pigment from Veronese's work has confirmed use of these materials and shown the use of all the other finest pigments then available in Venice—ultramarine, azurite, malachite, verdigris, litharge, realgar, vermilion, carbon black and lead white. In addition, it is clear that Veronese used, particularly in fresco, all the earth colours and ochres. Tests show that his medium for paintings on canvas was linseed oil and/or walnut oil (Mills and White, 1978, 1981 and 1983).

Study by Lazzarini (1983 and 1984) of paint layers in works executed in oil on canvas shows that Veronese consistently used a preparation of gesso and animal glue, thinly applied. Boschini described him as first laying out the composition, applying the middle tones for each area, then adding shadows and highlights. The cross-sections of paint samples show, as Lazzarini stressed, a complex variety of practice. In a few cases traces of burnt ochre or carbon black under the paint layers indicate the remains of a drawing (see Spezzani, 1992). Sometimes there is a thin layer of priming above the preparation, but not always. Some areas, such as sky, may show only the preparation, a thin layer of pigment, and varnish. Other areas, particularly of brocades and other types of drapery, may show preparation, four or five or even six layers of pigment, and varnish. Boschini's assertion that Veronese favoured the use of red lakes to shadow draperies seems well supported: red lakes appear regularly in complex samples from draperies and are sometimes mixed with other pigments, such as lead white or ultramarine and lead white. Plesters (1966) noted that pure ultramarine was sometimes used as a glaze; Lazzarini (1983) published a cross-section from Veronese's Giustiniani Altarpiece illustrating this. Lazzarini emphasized Veronese's liking for malachite and azurite; samples from the *Feast in the House of Levi* show azurite used to model malachite, with yellow lead and white lead mixed for highlighting (Lazzarini and Scire, 1984). In Veronese's fresco painting the 'cream' of slaked lime is used for highlighting (see Lazzarini and Nepi Scire, 1984). Sometimes the pigment below it, still wet, was allowed to 'bleed' into the highlight. (See also *Paolo Veronese: Restauri*, 1988 exh. cat.)

2. DRAWINGS AND OIL SKETCHES. Veronese used both drawings and oil sketches in preparing paintings; it seems that drawings were also made in his shop to record completed compositions. The inventory of the house of the *eredi di Paolo Veronese* mentions a small chest full of pictorial drawings (*disegni pittoreschi*) and oil sketches (*dipinti in carta*) (Gattinoni, 1914). At least three kinds of preparatory drawing are known. Chiaroscuro drawings on tinted paper include the *Temptation of St Anthony* (1552; Paris, Louvre), which has been associated with the altarpiece for Mantua Cathedral (Rosand, 1966). Black chalk studies, heightened with white, for individual figures include those for the allegorical figures on the ceiling of the Sala del Collegio in the Doge's Palace (London, BM; Paris, Louvre; Rotterdam, Mus. Boymans–van Beuningen). There are also many compositional sketches in pen or pen and wash. In these spontaneous drawings, such as the sheet of studies (*c.* 1566; Malibu, CA, Getty Mus.; see fig. 6) for the *Martyrdom of St George* (Verona, S Giorgio Maggiore), Veronese experimented with swiftly drawn figures and groupings, often patterning an entire sheet with searching studies. In the late drawings, such as the sheet of studies (1587; Paris, Louvre) for the *Miracle of St Pantaleon*, his touch is yet lighter and freer. In the very early instance of the Bevilacqua–Lazise Altarpiece, two preparatory works survive, both the chiaroscuro drawing and the oil sketch. Comparison of the compositions with the surviving altarpiece shows that the oil sketch was the penultimate work (Gisolfi Pechukas, 1982). This suggests a logical progression, from preliminary sketches to finished chiaroscuro drawing to oil sketch to painting; as it is the only known instance in which both a chiaroscuro drawing and an oil sketch survive for an extant painting, it is not clear that this elaborate process was always followed.

6. Paolo Veronese: *Studies for the Martyrdom of St George*, pen and brown ink and brown wash, 289×229 mm, 1566 (Malibu, CA, J. Paul Getty Museum)

There are examples of preparatory works of all types from all phases of Veronese's career.

Chiaroscuro drawings seem to have been used in Veronese's workshop not only as modelli, but as *ricordi* of works completed (Tietze and Tietze-Conrat, 1944). The function of several such drawings is disputed and a clear sorting remains to be done. The questions raised in regard to authorship of chiaroscuro drawings of lesser quality are related to unsolved matters regarding workshop practice.

3. WORKSHOP. Veronese ran a large family workshop in Venice, employing his brother Benedetto Caliari and his own sons Carlo and Gabriele (*see* CALIARI) as well as various other assistants and apprentices, including his nephew Alvise dal Friso (1559–1611) and Francesco Montemezzano (1540–1602). Benedetto's assistance is first documented in 1556 at S Sebastiano (Pignatti, 1966, p. 124) and is thought to have been considerable at Maser in 1561. Given their age, the earliest possible date for Veronese's sons joining the workshop is 1580. The degree of workshop participation in individual works both before and after 1580 is, however, often a matter of dispute. Crosato Larcher (1967, 1969 and 1977) made significant contributions in identifying the hands of Benedetto, Carlo and Gabriele, but many, particularly late, works are clearly collaborative or are of disputed attribution. Furthermore, Veronese's family continued to produce works in his manner under the label *Haeredes Pauli* after his death. These works made use of existing drawings, stock figural

types and typical compositions by the master. Thus the definition of a work by Veronese can vary: sometimes it is entirely by the master's hand; in other cases there is some workshop participation; in others the design may be by Veronese but the execution largely by assistants; in works signed *Haeredes Pauli* the entire execution is by others possibly following or 'recycling' Paolo's preparatory studies. Unsurprisingly, there is much disagreement about the degree of Veronese's authorship in many works and those where several versions of the same composition exist. Works by associates and copyists further confuse questions of attribution.

III. Character and personality.

The picture given by early sources is appealing but not detailed. Vasari (2/1568) emphasized Veronese's youth and early success in Venice, implying that he was considered precocious. Borghini (1584) drew attention to Veronese's fame, his humble origins and his financial success, aspects that are celebrated at greater length by Ridolfi (1648), who also described his important patrons and quoted some 'memorable sayings' attributed to Veronese:

> that it was impossible to judge paintings well without a good knowledge of the art; that the ability to paint was a gift from heaven and that to try to paint without natural talent was to sow seed in the waves; that the most worthy qualities in an artist were simplicity and modesty; and that saints and angels must be painted by excellent artists since they should arouse wonder and emotion.

The same sayings are quoted by Boschini (1674), who also commented that Veronese had a 'noble and open character, as is shown in his work; he dressed with dignity and bore himself as a great lord', adding that there were no scandals about Paolo. Boschini also reported that Veronese liked to go to the Piazza S Marco to observe the exotic clothing of foreigners from all parts of the world, especially the Armenians, from whom he got ideas for his vestments, turbans and 'Persian' shoes. Documentary evidence is purely factual and provides little concerning Paolo's personality. Contracts and statements about money are brief and to the point, indicating a businesslike and straightforward approach. His financial success itself shows a talent for administering business, while a couple of letters from the late 1580s show a real humanity and warmth. His testimony before the Inquisition in 1573, besides demonstrating a practical ability to deal appropriately with others and to protect himself, bears witness to his standing as a man of faith. Ridolfi and Boschini reported that Veronese died after catching a cold in an Eastertide procession, and both writers used this to give him a virtuous end. Ridolfi praised his character as trustworthy, caring and circumspect and stressed that he instructed his children in the faith and in moral discipline. According to the sayings attributed to Veronese, he recognized his gifts as God-given. He also made the most of these gifts, sharing his success with his family and frankly enjoying his well-being. The portrait of a sane and life-loving artist is consistent with the harmony and richness of Paolo's art.

Veronese's adoption of the name Caliari might, like his love of finery, be considered vain. Fiocco (1928) pointed out that the name was adopted, and Trecca (1940) noted that it belonged to a noble family in Contrada S Paolo of Verona. It was used by Paolo and his family only after he had achieved success in Venice. Trecca's review of documents indicates that the name first appears in a contract of 1555 for the *Transfiguration* at Montagnana (*in situ*), where Veronese is referred to as 'Mis. Paulo Caliaro Veronese' but signs himself *Paullo veronese*. The use of Caliari in signatures seems to begin around 1575.

IV. Critical reception and posthumous reputation.

1. VASARI, RIDOLFI AND OTHER EARLY SOURCES. Veronese's commissions, from church and state, rulers and nobility, Venetians and foreigners, attest to his recognition and fame during his lifetime. Vasari praised his work at Soranzo for its *disegno*, the *Feast in the House of Simon* for its 'life-like portraits and unusual perspectives . . . two dogs so fine that they seemed alive . . . and further away some excellently painted cripples', the ceiling of S Sebastiano as a 'most rare' work and other works there as 'most praiseworthy'. He ended his account with a description of the *Musica* on the Libreria Marciana ceiling, using Veronese's winning of the gold chain to illustrate his youthful achievement of success. Borghini said that Veronese's works were 'much praised by everyone' and that Paolo did not 'cease to work with great profit to painting'.

Ridolfi's *Meraviglie dell'arte* includes a long biography of Veronese and a catalogue of his works. The account begins with a homage to painting as the mirror 'in which all the works of the Creator can be seen in brief', and proceeds to describe Paolo as one of the most illustrious painters of the 'modern era' and to praise Verona for its antiquities, its fine site and for having produced this renowned artist. The initial emphasis on naturalism and on the significance of Veronese's birthplace is supplemented in descriptions of paintings by praise of colour, particularly of vestments, and of perspective. Ridolfi especially admired Veronese's *Youth and Age* and quoted Palma Giovane as saying 'in that case Paolo reached the highest degree of perfection, drawing together the most learned ancient style with the nobility of his own'. In summing up the merits of Veronese's art, Ridolfi modified the creed of naturalism with which he began, saying that painters must depart from the defects of nature and that Veronese painted nature 'più bella'. Beyond this approval of idealization Ridolfi stressed that Veronese had profited by practising 'the Venetian manner, which has given light to every painter improving the way of colouring'. Boschini, in *La carta del navegar pitoresco* (1660), praised Veronese's intellect, invention, colour, drawing and brushwork. Other writers of the 16th and 17th centuries admired his work for the prized qualities of *disegno*, *invenzione* and *colorito*.

2. LATER WRITERS AND CRITICS. Joshua Reynolds, being essentially opposed to Venetian *invenzioni*, attacked Veronese's art as 'ornamental' or decorative:

> Such as suppose that the great stile might happily be blended with the ornamental, that the simple, grave and majestic dignity of Raffaelle could unite with the glow and bustle of a Paulo, or Tintoret, are totally mistaken . . . . The subjects of the Venetian painters are mostly such as give them an opportunity of introducing a great number of figures; such as feasts, marriages, and processions, publick martyrdoms, or

miracles. I can easily conceive that Paul Veronese, if he were asked, would say that no subject was proper for an historical picture, but such as admitted at least forty figures; for in less a number, he would assert, there could be no opportunity of the painter's shewing his art in composition, his dexterity of managing and disposing the masses of light and groups of figures, and of introducing a variety of Eastern dresses and characters in their rich stuffs.

John Ruskin was more kindly disposed towards Veronese's naturalism and humour. After praising Veronese's dogs, particularly in the *Supper at Emmaus* (*c.* 1560; Paris, Louvre), he added, 'Neither Titian nor Velasquez ever jest; and though Veronese jests gracefully and tenderly, he never for an instant oversteps the absolute facts of nature'. Berenson emphasized that 'Paolo was the product of four or five generations of Veronese painters' and wrote of his 'cheerfulness, his frank and joyous worldliness' (1894). Over 60 years later he wrote a broader appreciation:

> When I contemplate Veronese's paintings, I experience a satisfaction so full and perfect that I feel seized by it in all of my being, in my senses, my feelings, my intellect, and then, all things considered, I love him at least as much as I love any other painter who has ever painted (Ojetti and others, 1960).

In his initial emphasis on Veronese's origins and in his later appreciation of Paolo's intellect, Berenson anticipated the emphasis in later scholarship on the artist's training and on structure and meaning in his art.

3. INFLUENCE. Prints after Veronese were executed during his lifetime by Agostino Carracci, including one after the *Mystic Marriage of St Catherine* (see Ticozzi, 1977 exh. cat., pl. 5, pp. 11 and 63). His influence on Annibale Carracci is apparent in such works as the latter's San Lodovico Altarpiece (*c.* 1588; Bologna, Pin. N.). Peter Paul Rubens, Anthony van Dyck, Mattia Preti, Pietro da Cortona and Luca Giordano are among the many other 17th-century artists stylistically indebted to Veronese; those who made prints after him include Nicolas Cochin, Giuseppe Maria Mitelli, Valentin Le Febre (1642–80/81) and Charlotte Catherine Patin (*b* 1660). Andrea Zucchi (1679–1740) was one of Veronese's chief engravers in the 18th century (see Ticozzi, 1977). The artist for whom his example was crucial, however, was Giambattista Tiepolo. Tiepolo re-created Veronese in a late Baroque mode: the clearly recognizable models are lightened, the palette is whitened, figures become less dominant, clouds more so, the illusion more unified. The oeuvre is parallel: altarpieces, ceiling decorations, frescoed villas and supper scenes. While Reynolds deplored Veronese's 'decorative' art, he considered that Tiepolo used it with understanding, high originality and appropriately brilliant technique to provide the last great chapter of Venetian painting.

In 1797 Napoleon's agents took some of Veronese's finest works to Paris. The presence in the Louvre of major works of the highest quality by Paolo is important in the history of French art. Delacroix's journals and correspondence include repeated musings on Veronese, and in a letter of 1859, he observed, 'There is a man who makes simple that which we are always being told is impossible—Paul Veronese. In my view he is probably the only one to have grasped the secrets of Nature' (A. Joubin, ed.:

Correspondance générale d'Eugène Delacroix, Paris, 1936–8, iv, p. 94). Not surprisingly, John Rewald's *History of Impressionism* (New York, 1961, pp. 76 and 462) records Henri Fantin-Latour's and Berthe Morisot's copying of Veronese in the Louvre and Auguste Renoir's admiration of his work in Venice.

UNPUBLISHED SOURCES

Verona, Archv Stato [census inf. and wills]

BIBLIOGRAPHY

EARLY SOURCES

P. Pino: *Dialogo della pittura* (Venice, 1548)
G. Vasari: *Vite* (1550, rev. 2/1568); ed. G. Milanesi (1878–85), vi, pp. 369–74
A. Guisconi [pseud. of F. Sansovino]: *Tutte le cose notabili e belle che sono in Venetia* (Venice, 1556)
L. Dolce: *Dialogo della pittura* (Venice, 1557); ed. M. Roskill in *Dolce's 'Aretino' and Venetian Art Theory of the Cinquecento* (New York, 1968)
F. Sansovino: *Venetia città nobilissima e singolare* (Venice, 1581)
R. Borghini: *Il Riposo* (Venice, 1584), pp. 561–3
C. Ridolfi: *Meraviglie* (1648); ed. D. von Hadeln (1914–24), i, pp. 296–352
M. Boschini: *La carta del navegar pitoresco* (Venice, 1660); ed. A. Pallucchini (Venice, 1966) [incl. the 'Breve instruzione' of *Le ricche miniere...* (Venice, 1674)]
——: *Le ricche miniere della pittura veneziana* (Venice, 1674); ed. A. M. Zanetti as *Descrizione di tutte le pubbliche pitture della città di Venezia o sia rinnovazione delle ricche miniere dal 1674* (Venice, 1733)
B. dal Pozzo: *Le vite de' pittori, scultori e architetti veronesi* (Verona, 1718), pp. 77–114
E. A. Cicogna: *Delle iscrizioni veneziane*, 6 vols (Venice, 1824–53), iv, p. 128
P. Caliari: *Paolo Veronese: Sua vita e sue opere* (Rome, 1888)
G. Biadego: *Di Giambettino Cignaroli pittore veronese: Notizie e documenti* (Venice, 1890)
D. Zannandreis: *Le vite dei pittori, scultori, ed architetti veronesi* (Verona, 1890), pp. 161–77

GENERAL

J. Reynolds: *Discourses on Art* (London, 1778/R New York, 1961)
J. Ruskin: *Modern Painters*, v (New York, 1886)
B. Berenson: *Venetian Painters of the Renaissance* (1894), in *Italian Painters of the Renaissance* (London, 1952)
G. Ludwig and others: 'Archivalische Beiträge zur Geschichte der venezianischen Kunst', *It. Forsch. Ksthist. Inst. Florenz* (Berlin, 1911), iv, pp. 139–45
D. von Hadeln: *Venezianische Zeichnungen der Spätrenaissance* (Berlin, 1926), pp. 26–32
H. Tietze and E. Tietze-Conrat: *Drawings of the Venetian Painters in the Fifteenth and Sixteenth Centuries*, 2 vols (New York, 1944)
B. Berenson: *Venetian School* (1957), i, pp. 129–39
L. Crosato: *Gli affreschi nelle ville venete del cinquecento* (Treviso, 1962)
J. Schulz: *Venetian Painted Ceilings of the Renaissance* (Berkeley, 1968)
S. J. Freedberg: *Painting in Italy, 1500–1600*, Pelican Hist. A. (Harmondsworth, 1971)
S. Sinding-Larsen: *Christ in the Council Hall: Studies in the Religious Iconography of the Venetian Republic* (Rome, 1974)
W. R. Rearick: *Maestri veneti del cinquecento*, Biblioteca di Disegni VI (Florence, 1980)
Da Tiziano a El Greco per la storia del manierismo a Venezia, 1540–1590 (exh. cat., ed. R. Pallucchini; Venice, Doge's Pal., 1981)
J. Ackerman: 'The Geopolitics of Venetian Architecture in the Time of Titian', *Titian: His World and his Legacy*, ed. D. Rosand (New York, 1982), pp. 41–7
P. Spezzani: *Riflettoscopia e indagine non distruttive: Pittura e grafica* (Milan, 1992)

MONOGRAPHS AND EXHIBITION CATALOGUES

P. Osmond: *Paolo Veronese: His Career and Work* (London, 1927)
G. Fiocco: *Paolo Veronese* (Bologna, 1928, 2/1934)
D. von Hadeln: *Paolo Veronese* (MS.; before 1935); ed. G. Schweikhart (Florence, 1978)
Mostra di Paolo Veronese: Catalogo delle opere (exh. cat., Venice, Ca' Giustinian, 1939)
R. Pallucchini: *Veronese* (Bergamo, 1940)
G. Trecca: *Paolo Veronese e Verona* (Verona, 1940)
L. Vertova: *Veronese* (Milan, 1953)

T. Pignatti: *Le pitture di Paolo Veronese nella chiesa di San Sebastiano in Venezia* (Milan, 1966)

R. Marini: *L'opera completa del Veronese*, foreword by G. Piovene (Milan, 1968)

T. Pignatti: *Veronese*, 2 vols (Venice, 1976) [with catalogue raisonné, comprehensive bibliography and excellent plates]

Paolo Veronese e i suoi incisori (exh. cat., ed. P. Ticozzi; Venice, Correr, 1977)

Palladio e la maniera (exh. cat., ed. V. Sgarbi and others; Vicenza, Santa Corona, 1980)

Palladio e Verona (exh. cat., ed. L. Magagnato and others; Verona, Pal. Gran Guardia, 1980)

K. Badt: *Paolo Veronese* (Cologne, 1981)

R. Cocke: *Veronese's Drawings* (Ithaca, NY, 1984)

R. Pallucchini: *Veronese* (Milan, 1984)

The Art of Paolo Veronese, 1528–1588 (exh. cat., ed. W. R. Rearick; Washington, N.G.A., 1988)

Paolo Veronese: Disegni e dipinti (exh. cat., ed. W. R. Rearick and others; Venice, Fond. Cini, 1988)

Paolo Veronese: Restauri (exh. cat., ed. G. Nepi Sciré and others; Venice, Accad. Pitt. & Scul., 1988) [*Quaderni della Soprintendenza ai beni artistici e storici di Venezia XV: Venezia 1988*]

Veronese e Verona (exh. cat., ed. S. Marinelli and others; Verona, Castelvecchio, 1988)

F. Pedrocco and T. Pignatti: *Veronese catalogo completo* (Florence, 1991, rev. Venice, 2/1995)

Les Noces de Cana de Véronèse: Une Oeuvre et sa restauration (exh. cat., Paris, Louvre, 1992–3)

SPECIALIST STUDIES

G. Biadego: 'Intorno a Paolo Veronese: Note biografiche', *Atti Ist. Ven. Sci., Lett. & A.*, lvii (1898–9), pp. 99–111

D. von Hadeln: 'Wann ist Paolo Veronese geboren?' *Kunstchronik*, n. s., xxii (1910–11), pp. 257–60

A. Bevilacqua-Lasize: 'Un quadro di autore controverso al museo civico di Verona', *Madonna Verona*, v (1911), pp. 106–11

G. Gattinoni: *Inventario di una casa veneziana del secolo XVII (la casa degli eccellenti Caliari eredi di Paolo Veronese)* (Mestre, 1914)

D. von Hadeln: 'Veronese und Zelotti', *Jb. Kön.-Preuss. Kstsamml.*, xxxv (1914), pp. 168–220; xxxvi (1915), pp. 97–128

E. Tea: 'Il cromatismo di Paolo Veronese', *L'Arte*, xxiii (1920), pp. 59–75

T. Borenius: 'A Group of Drawings by Paul Veronese', *Burl. Mag.*, xxxviii (1921), pp. 54–9

D. von Hadeln: 'Drawings by Paul Veronese', *Burl. Mag.*, xlvii (1925), pp. 298–304

A. M. Brizio: 'Nota per una definizione critica dello stile di Paolo Veronese: I', *L'Arte*, xxix (1926), pp. 213–42

L. Coletti: 'Paesi di Paolo Veronese', *Dedalo*, vi (1926), pp. 377–410

G. Fiocco: 'Paolo Veronese und Farinati', *Jb. Ksthist. Samml. Wien*, i (1926), pp. 123–6

D. von Hadeln: 'Some Portraits by Paolo Veronese', *AIA J.*, xv (1927), pp. 239–52

A. M. Brizio: 'Nota per una definizione critica dello stile di Paolo Veronese: II', *L'Arte*, xxxi (1928), pp. 1–10

——: 'Rileggendo Vasari', *Emporium*, lxxxix (1939), pp. 123–30

R. Gallo: 'Per la datazione delle opere del Veronese', *Emporium*, lxxxix (1939), pp. 145–52

E. Arslan: 'Nota su Veronese e Zelotti', *Belle A.*, i (1948), pp. 227–45

R. Brenzoni: *La prima opera di Paolo Veronese: 'La suocera di Pietro (Simeone)' del 1546 e la sua singolare vicenda* (Verona, 1953)

G. Zorzi: 'Nuove rivelazioni sulla ricostruzione … del Palazzo Ducale', *A. Ven.*, vii (1953), pp. 123–51

U. Moussalli: 'Le Processus d'élaboration et de création dans les grands ateliers vénitiens du XVIIème siècle, notamment chez Véronèse', *Venezia e l'Europa: Atti del XVIII Congresso internazionale di storia dell'arte: Venezia, 1955*, pp. 285–8

E. Tea: 'Paolo Veronese e il teatro', *Venezia e l'Europa: Atti del XVIII Congresso internazionale di storia dell'arte: Venezia, 1955*, pp. 262–4

S. Beguin: 'La Fille de Jaire de Véronèse au Musée du Louvre', *Rev. des A.*, vii (1957), pp. 165–9

R. Brenzoni: 'Architetti e scultori dei laghi lombardi a Verona', *Arte e artisti dei laghi lombardi*, ed. E. Arslan, 2 vols (Como, 1959–64), i, pp. 89–130

A. M. Brizio: 'La pittura di Paolo Veronese in rapporto con l'opera del Sanmicheli e del Palladio', *Boll. Cent. Int. Stud. Archit. Andrea Palladio*, ii (1960), pp. 19–25

C. Gould: 'An Early Dated Veronese and Veronese's Early Work', *Burl. Mag.*, cii (1960), p. 489 [letter]

M. Levey: 'An Early Dated Veronese and Veronese's Early Work', *Burl. Mag.*, cii (1960), pp. 107–11; see also C. Gould, ibid., p. 489

P. Ojetti and others: *Palladio, Vittoria e Veronese a Maser* (Milan, 1960)

P. Fehl: 'Veronese and the Inquisition: A Study of the Subject Matter of the So-called *Feast in the House of Levi*', *Gaz. B.-A.*, 6th ser., lviii (1961), pp. 325–54

T. Pignatti: *Le pitture di Paolo Veronese nella chiesa di San Sebastiano in Venezia* (Milan, 1966)

J. Plesters: 'Ultramarine Blue, Natural and Artificial', *Stud. Conserv.*, xi (1966), pp. 62–91

D. Rosand: 'An Early Chiaroscuro Drawing by P. Veronese', *Burl. Mag.*, cviii (1966), pp. 421–2

L. Crosato Larcher: 'Per Carletto Caliari', *A. Ven.*, xxi (1967), pp. 108–24

A. Caiani: 'Un palazzo veronese a Murano: Note e aggiunte', *A. Ven.*, xxii (1968), pp. 47–59

L. Magagnato: 'I collaboratori veronesi di Andrea Palladio', *Boll. Cent. Int. Stud. Archit. Andrea Palladio*, x (1968), pp. 170–87

K. Oberhuber: 'Hieronymus Cock, Battista Pittoni and Paolo Veronese in Villa Maser', *Munuscula Discipulorum: Kunsthistorische Studien Hans Kauffmann zum 70. Geburtstag* (Berlin, 1968), pp. 207–25

——: 'Gli affreschi di Paolo Veronese nella Villa Barbaro', *Boll. Cent. Int. Stud. Archit. Andrea Palladio*, x (1968), pp. 188–202

J. Schulz: 'Le fonti di Paolo Veronese come decoratore', *Boll. Cent. Int. Stud. Archit. Andrea Palladio*, x (1968), pp. 241–54

L. Crosato Larcher: 'Note su Benedetto Caliari', *A. Ven.*, xxiii (1969), pp. 115–30

N. Ivanoff: 'La tematica degli affreschi di Maser', *A. Ven.*, xxxiv (1970), pp. 210–13

M. Kahr: 'The Meaning of Veronese's Paintings in the Church of San Sebastiano in Venice', *J. Warb. & Court. Inst.*, xxxiii (1970), pp. 235–47

C. de Tolnay: 'Il *Paradiso* del Tintoretto, note sull'interpretazione della tela in Palazzo Ducale', *A. Ven.*, xxiv (1970), pp. 103–10

A. Ballarin: 'Considerazioni su una mostra di disegni veronesi del "500"', *A. Ven.*, xxv (1971), pp. 92–118

R. Cocke: 'An Early Drawing by Paolo Veronese', *Burl. Mag.*, cxiii (1971), pp. 726–33

G. Schweikhart: 'Paolo Veronese in der Villa Soranza', *Mitt. Ksthist. Inst. Florenz*, xv (1971), pp. 187–206

R. Cocke: 'A Preparatory Drawing for the "Triumph of Mordecai" in S Sebastiano Venice', *Burl. Mag.*, cxiv (1972), pp. 322–5

——: 'Veronese and Daniele Barbaro: The Decoration of Villa Maser', *J. Warb. & Court. Inst.*, xxxv (1972), pp. 226–46

D. Rosand: 'Theatre and Structure in the Art of Paolo Veronese', *A. Bull.*, lv (1973), pp. 217–39; rev. in *Painting in Cinquecento Venice* (New Haven, 1982), pp. 145–81

G. Sancassani: 'Un autografo di Paolo Veronese per la cena in casa di Simone fariseo', *Atti & Mem. Accad. Verona*, xxv (1973–4), p. 85

M. Monteverdi: 'Ipotesi su un modello di Paolo Veronese', *Crit. A.*, xx/138 (1974), pp. 33–8

P. Ticozzi: 'Le incisioni da opere del Veronese nel Museo Correr', *Boll. Mus. Civ. Ven.*, xx (1975), pp. 6–62, figs 1–180

D. Gisolfi Pechukas: *The Youth of Veronese* (diss., U. Chicago, 1976)

W. R. Rearick: *Tiziano e il disegno veneziano del suo tempo* (Florence, 1976), pp. 157–62

R. Cocke: 'Three Fragments from the Villa Soranza', *Mitt. Ksthist. Inst. Florenz*, xxi (1977), pp. 211–18

L. Crosato Larcher: 'Nuovi contributi per la decorazione della Soranza', *A. Ven.*, xxxi (1977), pp. 72–9

R. Smith: 'A Matter of Choice: Veronese, Palladio and Barbaro', *A. Ven.*, xxxi (1977), pp. 60–62

J. Mills and R. White: 'Organic Analysis in the Arts: Some Further Paint Medium Analyses', *N.G. Tech. Bull.*, ii (1978), pp. 71–6

J. Thornton: *Renaissance Color Theory and Some Paintings by Veronese* (diss., U. Pittsburgh, 1979)

R. Cocke: 'The Development of Veronese's Critical Reputation', *A. Ven.*, xxxiv (1980), pp. 96–111

J. Schulz: 'Tintoretto and the First Competition for the Ducal Palace Paradise', *A. Ven.*, xxxiv (1980), pp. 112–26

P. Fehl: 'Veronese's Decorum: Notes on the *Marriage at Cana*', *Art, the Ape of Nature: Studies in Honor of H. W. Janson* (New York, 1981)

J. Mills and R. White: 'Analyses of Paint Media', *N.G. Tech. Bull.*, v (1981), pp. 66–8

S. Romano: 'I paesaggi di Paolo Veronese in Palazzo Trevisan', *A. Ven.*, xxxv (1981), pp. 150–51

L. Crosato Larcher: 'Considerazioni sul programma iconografico di Maser', *Mitt. Ksthist. Inst. Florenz*, xxvi/1 (1982), pp. 211–56

D. Gisolfi Pechukas: 'Two Oil Sketches and the Youth of Veronese', *A. Bull.*, lxiv (1982), pp. 388–413

R. Bacou: 'Ten Unpublished Drawings by Veronese Recently Acquired by the Cabinet des Dessins du Louvre', *Master Drgs*, xxi (1983), pp. 255–62, pls 1–10

L. Lazzarini: 'Il colore nei pittori veneziani tra il 1480 e il 1580', *Boll. A.* (1983), suppl., pp. 135–44

J. Mills and R. White: 'Analyses of Paint Media', *N.G. Tech. Bull.*, vi (1983), pp. 65–7

S. Romano: 'Gli affreschi di Paolo Veronese', *Boll. A.* (1983), suppl., pp. 119–32

P. Fehl and M. Perry: 'Painting and the Inquisition at Venice: Three Forgotten Files', *Interpretazioni veneziane: Studi di storia dell'arte in onore di Michelangelo Muraro* (Venice, 1984)

L. Lazzarini and G. Nepi Scirè: 'Il restauro del Convito in Casa di Levi di Paolo Veronese', *Quad. Sopr. Beni A. & Stor. Venezia*, xi (1984) [whole issue]

T. Pignatti: 'Una nuova *Pietà* di Paolo Veronese', *A. Ven.*, xxxviii (1984), pp. 146–8

S. Sinding-Larsen: 'The Paradise Controversy: A Note on Argumentation', *Interpretazione veneziana, studio di storia dell'arte in onore di Michelangelo Muraro*, ed. D. Rosand (Venice, 1984)

I. Jackson Reist: 'Divine Love and Veronese's Frescoes at the Villa Barbaro', *A. Bull.*, lxvi (1985), pp. 614–35

D. Gisolfi Pechukas: 'Veronese and his Collaborators at La Soranza', *Artibus & Hist.*, xv (1987), pp. 67–108

D. Lewis: 'Classical Texts and Mystical Meanings: Daniele Barbaro's Program for the Villa Maser', *Festschrift für Erik Forssman zum 70. Geburtstag* (Hildesheim, 1987), pp. 289–307, 531–4

D. Gisolfi Pechukas: 'Paolo Veronese e i suoi primi collaboratori', *Nuovi studi su Paolo Veronese: Convegno internazionale di studi: Venezia, 1988*, pp. 25–35

S. Sinding-Larsen: 'Paolo Veronese tra rituale e narrativo: Note a proposito di un disegno per il Palazzo Ducale', *Nuovi studi su Paolo Veronese: Convegno internazionale di studi: Venezia, 1988*, pp. 36–41

D. Gisolfi: '"L'anno veronesiano" and Some Questions about Early Veronese and his Circle', *A. Ven.*, xliii (1989–90), pp. 30–42

——: 'A New Early Veronese in Tokyo', *Burl. Mag.* (Nov 1995), pp. 742–6

DIANA GISOLFI

Veronesi, Luigi (*b* Milan, 28 May 1908). Italian photographer, painter and designer. He studied with the painter Carmelo Violante and the critic Raffaello Giolli (1889–1945) in 1924. At the beginning of the 1930s he was in Paris, where he frequented the atelier of Fernand Léger and was involved with avant-garde art circles, particularly the group Abstraction-Création, of which he was a member. He also followed closely the activities of the Bauhaus, especially the graphic designs and systematic colour experimentation of László Moholy-Nagy. Veronesi undertook similar explorations as part of his ongoing scientific and aesthetic research.

From his youth photography was an important part of Veronesi's activity, beginning with the innovative abstract photograms and continuing with the conventional photography he sometimes used in graphic and publicity design. In 1932 he exhibited his first abstract works in the Galleria Il Milione in Milan; they were in stark contrast to the art of the Fascist regime then in vogue. Veronesi also worked on both experimental and scientific films. As a photographer he explored a variety of photographic techniques, including photograms, solarization and photomontage, always with a view to exploiting the creative and expressive potential of the medium. He was particularly interested in the interpenetration of forms, making rigorous geometrical compositions from single transparent elements.

PHOTOGRAPHIC PUBLICATIONS
Quaderno di geometria, text L. Sinisgalli (Milan, 1936)
Fotogrammi e fotografie (Turin, 1983)

BIBLIOGRAPHY
G. Ballo: *Arte italiana dal futurismo a oggi* (Rome, 1958)
O. Patani: *Veronesi* (Milan, 1960)
Aspetti del primo astrattismo italiano, 1930–1940 (exh. cat. by L. Caramel, Monza, 1969)
P. Fossati, ed.: *Luigi Veronesi* (Parma, 1975)

ITALO ZANNIER

Verreries de Sainte-Anne. *See* BACCARAT.

Verrio, Antonio (*b* Lecce, ?1639; *d* Hampton Court, London, 15 June 1707). Italian painter, active in England. His first patrons were the Jesuits, for whom he worked in his native Lecce and in Naples. He is then said to have spent some years travelling through Italy to France, where he settled in Toulouse. By 1671 he was in Paris, where he met Charles II's ambassador Ralph Montagu, later 1st Duke of Montagu, who invited him to England. Verrio first worked for Henry Bennet, 1st Earl of Arlington, but he was soon in the employ of the King, for whom he painted an easel picture, *Charles II's Sea Triumph* (*c.* 1673–5; London, Hampton Court, Royal Col.), before being entrusted with the decoration of the state rooms at Windsor Castle (1675–*c.* 1684), which were being rebuilt by the architect Hugh May. In this scheme, full-blooded Baroque interior decoration of the sort that had developed in Italy and France was introduced to England by the combined efforts of May, Verrio and the carver Grinling Gibbons. The main theme was the glorification of Charles II. Verrio's illusionistically painted ceilings were of two basic types, some imitating plasterwork set with pictures and some painted to look as if open to the sky, beyond a feigned parapet. Only three ceilings now survive: they are the King's Dining Room, the Queen's Presence Chamber and the Queen's Audience Chamber. Most of the Baroque interiors at Windsor were destroyed in the 1820s and are now known only from written accounts and illustrations, principally those done for W. H. Pyne's *Royal Residences*, but Verrio contributed to more than 20 rooms, two of which, the Royal Chapel and St George's Hall (both destr.), were entirely painted. The Windsor scheme was the greatest undertaking of his career, occupying him and a team of assistants, including Nicolas de Largillière *c.* 1675–9, for nine years. In 1684 he was appointed Principal Painter to the King.

After the death of Charles II in 1685, Verrio continued to work for his successor, James II, but during the Revolution of 1688 he abruptly left the court. The reason, according to Vertue, was that he 'was so angry with the government that he refus'd to work for King William'. His principal patron in the years that followed was John Cecil, 5th Earl of Exeter, for whom he decorated a suite of rooms (*c.* 1688–98) at Burghley House, Cambs, where Laguerre was also employed. Verrio's work there culminated in the Heaven Room, a completely painted illusionistic interior illustrating the capture of Mars and Venus in Vulcan's net (see fig.). The framework is a painted

Antonio Verrio: the Heaven Room, Burghley House, Cambridgeshire, c. 1688–98

colonnade, recalling the lost St George's Hall at Windsor, but this scheme is conceived in a spirit of fun, and Verrio's light-hearted manner is well expressed in the lively figures weaving through it. Verrio himself was clearly a convivial character, and stories of his escapades abound. Hidden jokes and caricature portraits of individuals appear frequently in his work.

From c. 1700 to 1702, Verrio was back in royal service, working in the new state apartments at Hampton Court Palace, where he was able to forget his political scruples for long enough to paint the King's Staircase with a complicated allegory in celebration of the Protestant succession, honouring King William and pouring scorn on his Stuart predecessors. After painting the Queen's Drawing Room at Hampton Court for Queen Anne, Verrio's eyesight failed, and he retired on a handsome royal pension.

After his death Verrio's reputation collapsed. The destruction of some of his most important work and the repeated restoration of much that survives make it difficult to assess his talents. Yet even if the quality of his detail never matched the theatrical grandeur of his designs, their powerful impact helped to establish the vogue for Baroque decoration in England.

BIBLIOGRAPHY

W. H. Pyne: *The History of the Royal Residences*, ii (London, 1819)
'The Note-books of George Vertue', *Walpole Soc.*, xx (1932), p. 132
E. Wind: 'Julian the Apostate at Hampton Court', *J. Warb. & Court. Inst.*, iii (1939), pp. 127–37
E. Waterhouse: *Painting in Britain, 1530–1790*, Pelican Hist. A. (Harmondsworth, 1953, 4/1978), pp. 125–6
M. Whinney and O. Millar: *English Art, 1625–1714*, Oxford Hist. Eng. A. (Oxford, 1957), pp. 295–302
E. Croft-Murray: *Decorative Painting in England, 1557–1837* (London, 1962–70), i, pp. 50–60
H. M. Colvin, ed.: *The History of the King's Works* (London, 1963–82), v, pp. 321–6
K. Downes: *English Baroque Architecture* (London, 1966), pp. 18–22

NICOLA SMITH

Verrocchio, Andrea del [Andrea di Michele di Francesco Cioni] (*b* Florence, 1435; *d* Venice, ?30 June 1488). Italian sculptor, painter, draughtsman and goldsmith. He was the leading sculptor in Florence in the second half of the 15th century, and his highly successful workshop, in which Leonardo da Vinci trained, had a far-reaching impact on younger generations. A wide range of patrons, including the Medici family, the Venetian State and the city council of Pistoia, commissioned works from him. Exceptionally versatile, Verrocchio was talented both as a sculptor—of monumental bronzes, silver figurines and marble reliefs—

and as a painter of altarpieces. He was inspired by the contemporary interest in the Antique and in the study of nature, yet, approaching almost every project as a new challenge, developed new conceptions that often defied both traditional aesthetics and conventional techniques. His fountains, portrait busts and equestrian sculpture are indebted to an iconographic tradition rooted in the early 15th century and yet they are transformed by his original outlook. His funerary ensembles are unique, so that, despite the great admiration they inspired, they had no imitators. Though a highly important artist in his own right, Verrocchio has often had the misfortune of being seen as in the shadow of his pupil Leonardo.

I. Life and work. II. Working methods and technique. III. Character and personality. IV. Critical reception and posthumous reputation.

I. Life and work.

1. Sculpture. 2. Painting.

1. SCULPTURE.

(i) Training and early career, before c. 1477. (ii) Mature and late works, c. 1477 and after.

(i) Training and early career, before c. 1477. The son of a brickmaker, Michele di Francesco Cioni (d 1452), Verrocchio is mentioned first in 1452, when a record of a court case indicates that he was arrested and then fully acquitted for accidentally killing a woolworker by the name of Antonio di Domenico. He is next documented as the pupil of Antonio di Giovanni Dei (1406–?1480), in whose workshop on the Via Vacchereccia in Florence he worked from 1453 to 1456. Dei was a member of a large family that owned and managed several busy goldsmiths' workshops, but he did not actually practise as a goldsmith. A successful businessman, he was able to secure his pupils profitable commissions and help launch their careers. Andrea subsequently became associated with another family of goldsmiths, headed by Francesco di Luca Verrocchio and his son Giuliano Verrocchio, from whom he seems to have taken his name. His training as a sculptor in marble remains highly controversial, although two early sources, Il codice dell'Anonimo Gaddiano [Magliabechiano] and Il libro di Antonio Billi, state that he was involved in the execution of Desiderio da Settignano's tomb of Carlo Marsuppini (d 1453; Florence, Santa Croce; see DESIDERIO DA SETTIGNANO, fig. 1), and it has also been suggested that he worked in the studio of Antonio Rossellino and Bernardo Rossellino in the early 1460s (Seymour).

As a metalworker, Verrocchio was a member of the goldsmiths' guild, apparently from the late 1450s, but in his first surviving catasto return in 1457 he noted that commissions for bronze artefacts were scarce, and he appears to have been determined to widen his activities and to vie for profitable undertakings in architecture and painting. In 1461, with Desiderio da Settignano, Giuliano da Maiano and Giovannini di Meuccio di Contaldino (fl 1442–73), he competed unsuccessfully for the commission for the chapel of the Madonna della Tavola (destr.) at Orvieto Cathedral. From the outset of his career he also embarked on prestigious projects in various media for influential patrons. Between 1465 and 1467 he designed the tomb of Cosimo de' Medici (Florence, S Lorenzo) in stone and brass, and towards 1466 he was awarded the

commission for the bronze group of the Incredulity of Thomas (Florence, Orsanmichele; see fig. 1). In 1468 he received partial payment for a monumental bronze candlestick for the Palazzo della Signoria, Florence (Amsterdam, Rijksmus.). In the same year the Florentine Cathedral workshop commissioned him to execute the copper ball for the lantern of Florence Cathedral (erected 1471; destr. 1600), and, probably in 1469 (Covi, 1981 and 1983), he made a visit to Venice and Treviso to purchase copper for this project. He enrolled in the sculptors' guild in 1469 and in the painters' guild in 1472.

The monumental bronze group of over life-size figures of Christ and St Thomas in the Incredulity of Thomas and the marble and bronze tomb of Piero I and Giovanni de' Medici (completed 1472; Florence, S Lorenzo, Old Sacristy; see fig. 2) are the most original of Verrocchio's early documented works, and both reveal the influence of his experience of Venetian art. The Incredulity of Thomas was commissioned by the Tribunale di Mercanzia to replace Donatello's St Louis of Toulouse (1423; Florence, Mus. Opera Santa Croce) in a niche on the exterior east wall of Orsanmichele, and the choice of Verrocchio to contribute to the sculptural decoration of a building already enriched by works of the great early Renaissance sculptors suggests his growing prestige. The challenge of creating a dramatic ensemble rather than sculpting single figures of one or two of the guild's patron saints encouraged him to take an original approach. In a composition inspired (Covi, 1983) by a mosaic of the Incredulity of Thomas (c. 1200; Venice,

1. Andrea del Verrocchio: Incredulity of Thomas, bronze, h. 2.30 m, c. 1466–83 (Florence, Orsanmichele)

2. Andrea del Verrocchio: tomb of *Piero I and Giovanni de' Medici*, marble, porphyry, serpentine and bronze, h. 4.50 m, completed 1472 (Florence, S Lorenzo, Old Sacristy)

Old Sacristy at S Lorenzo. Presenting two equal views on both sides, it is a free-standing double funerary monument, unprecedented in its use of secular imagery. Its exceptional artistic effect depends on the geometrical contrast between the severity of its main components and the naturalistic richness of the varied ornament. Thus the simple white marble base is juxtaposed with the sumptuous red porphyry sarcophagus with green serpentine medallions. The smooth, polished surfaces of these structures, in turn, contrast with the swirling, rugged shapes of the decorative elements underneath, between, on and above them: bronze tortoises below the base, bronze lions' feet connecting the base and the sarcophagus, bronze acanthus leaves in the corners of the latter, and a screen of bronze interlacing ropes filling the entire space between the tomb and the arch itself. The animal and plant forms, including those carved in marble on the intrados, are so filled with life and motion that they animate the whole ensemble.

Two of Verrocchio's free-standing bronze sculptures, ordered by the Medici family probably in the late 1460s or early 1470s, deserve special mention: the *Putto with a Dolphin* (Florence, Pal. Vecchio) and *David* (Florence, Bargello; see fig. 3). They were described by Verrocchio's brother Tommaso (*b* 1441) in the inventory he made (1496) of the works Andrea executed for the Medici (Fabriczy, 1895). Both were conceived as dainty statuettes, despite their medium size (670 mm and 1.26 m respectively), and they epitomize Verrocchio's critical and interpretative approach to the ideals and forms of Classical antiquity. The *Putto with a Dolphin*, a rotating fountain figure apparently exhibited in the Villa Medici at Careggi during the 15th century, represents a boy, with a dolphin clutched to his chest, balancing on his left leg and turning his head to the right. Verrocchio here re-created a theme well known in Roman art yet with a new quality of realism and movement. The serpentine pose, so characteristic in the Baroque but rare in the Renaissance, promotes a sense of continuous breathtaking motion and allows the spectator to view the statue from multiple viewpoints. Verrocchio's originality is most apparent in his portrayal of the putto's delight at being able to control his playful swerve. His apparent sudden awareness of his own strength complements the suddenness of his twisting motion and lends the image a quality of truthfulness to life, which the artist counterbalances against his Classical sources.

Where the design of the *Putto with a Dolphin* presented Verrocchio with the opportunity to pay tribute to and try to outdo a popular antique image, that of *David* offered him the chance to challenge Donatello's celebrated bronze of the same subject (Florence, Bargello; *see* STATUE, fig. 1). Verrocchio's invocation both of the Classical models that influenced Donatello and of Donatello's *David* itself is evident in the dignified countenance of his frontal figure. Standing in a contrappostal pose, his left arm on his waist, the *David* carries on the tradition of a distant and near past. However, more concrete and accurate, it represents a totally novel approach. Instead of showing, as had Donatello, a heroic nude embodying general ideals of beauty, grace and youth, he portrayed a given young hero whose tight leather tunic reveals a bony but taut torso.

S Marco), he placed the figure of Christ in the middle of the frame on an elevated step and that of the apostle outside and below it to the left. Such an alignment allowed him to retain the prescribed sizes of the figures without overcrowding the relatively narrow space allotted to them. More interestingly, it enabled him to stage the emotionally charged encounter between the two on a diagonal and thereby create a dynamic instead of a static picture. Compositionally and dramatically, the axis of the scene is the wound that Christ exposes with his upraised arm, on one side, and his hand, which holds open the tear in the garment, on the other. St Thomas's tentatively outstretched right hand and his intense gaze lead the spectator towards this focal-point and into the niche. The figures form a united and balanced picture, although the figure of Christ was cast several years before that of St Thomas, which was completed only in 1483. Christ's draperies are sharper and less flowing than those of St Thomas, the facial features more elongated and the posture less graceful.

Even more unusual is Verrocchio's tomb of *Piero I and Giovanni de' Medici*, with its equally unusual location in the arched opening that connects the chapel of the Madonna (formerly the chapel of the Sacrament) and the

3. Andrea del Verrocchio: *David*, bronze, h. 1.26 m, *c. 1475* (Florence, Museo Nazionale di Bargello)

models, Verrocchio undertook to carve the marble cenotaph for *Cardinal Niccolò Forteguerri* (Pistoia Cathedral) for the cathedral workshop at Pistoia. His relationship with the authorities was difficult and may have caused the lengthy delays that resulted in the monument remaining unfinished at his death. From the start of the project there was tension: although Verrocchio's model was preferred, his request for 350 florins was considered too high so the committee reopened negotiations with Piero del Pollaiuolo, who had also competed. It was only after the intervention of Lorenzo de' Medici in 1478 that the job was reassigned to Verrocchio.

The *Forteguerri* cenotaph displays the only extant monumental figure designed by Verrocchio in marble. The work is now much altered, yet its original appearance can be deduced from a terracotta model (London, V&A), probably by Verrocchio, for the complete monument. This presents Christ in majesty within a mandorla, carried by four wingless angels, in the upper part, and, below, Niccolò Forteguerri (*d* 1473), surrounded by a triangle of the three cardinal virtues: Faith, Hope and Charity. Its iconographical and formal schema are traditional. They recall both Maso di Banco's painting above the tomb of *Bettino Bardi* (Florence, Santa Croce) and Nanni di Banco's relief above the Porta dell Mandorla (completed 1421; Florence Cathedral). Verrocchio's originality lies in the composition's greater unity and naturalism (Passavant). The figures are no longer differentiated by size, and they are so animated as to create a sense of dynamism that is most noticeable in the four angels, who seem to lift and support a heavy mandorla. In the completed monument, seven of the nine figures exhibited in the lunette framework—Christ, the four angels supporting the mandorla, and Faith and Hope—are recorded as having been carved in Verrocchio's workshop. The work was completed by Lorenzetto Lotti and Giovanni Francesco Rustici and then in 1753 disastrously given a Baroque character by Gaetano Masoni.

On 27 July 1477 Verrocchio was commissioned by the Guild of the Cloth Refiners, which supervised works at the Florentine Baptistery, to execute a silver relief of the *Beheading of St John the Baptist* for the silver altar in the Baptistery (Florence, Mus. Opera Duomo; *see* ITALY, fig. 90). He had won the commission in a contest in which Antonio del Pollaiuolo also participated, Verrocchio submitting two models, Pollaiuolo three. Verrocchio was subsequently also assigned the task of casting some of the silver figurines for the altar itself. The relief, which is on the right side of the antependium of the altar, is Verrocchio's only extant work in silver on such a small scale (310×420 mm). It is also the only surviving sculptural project that he carried out in two different techniques: low relief for the architectural background and modelling in the round for the human figures. The commission itself was unique in the artist's career in that it had been planned as a collaborative enterprise; it was part of a larger programme, and four storiated reliefs for the dossal of the altar were also intended. The scene of the beheading is set in an L-shaped courtyard formed by a palace wall, articulated by closed-in arches. At the centre is the executioner, naked except for a loin cloth and seen from the back, who raises his arms as if about to inflict the final fatal blow

Depicting a dramatic moment, he thus replaced Donatello's languorous and passive figure with an audacious conqueror, with a trace of a supercilious smile. The finely crafted statue is distinguished by a wealth of surface details: the corkscrew curls that crown the young face, the skin-tight tunic with its decorative borders and fringes, the thin ribs and firm stomach showing through the fabric, the bulging veins of the right arm, and the pleats formed by the sweeping movement of the hips.

A terracotta relief of the *Virgin and Child* (Florence, Bargello) was probably designed by Verrocchio in the mid-1470s and is close in style to the bronze *Putto with a Dolphin*. It is the only relief of this subject whose attribution to Verrocchio is unanimous. Influenced by similar images by Filippo Lippi and Alesso Baldovinetti, it is distinguished by the liveliness of the handling and the sweetness of the mood.

(ii) Mature and late works, c. 1477 and after. In 1477, after a contest in which he and three other sculptors submitted

with his sword. To the left, kneeling on the ground, is the bearded figure of the saint and three agitated young Roman soldiers, one of whom is carrying the salver. To the right are two other witnesses, one attempting to prevent the violent death and one trying to hasten it. Angrily facing one another, they seem ready to fight. Verrocchio stressed the theatricality of this climactic episode. Focusing the viewer's attention on the muscular body of the executioner, he strove to draw it then to the various other protagonists and to their reactions to him: fright, horror and rage. Verrocchio's concern with the dramatic content of the scene is reflected in the different hand gestures and facial expressions, and yet he pays no less attention to other anatomical features: every aspect of the body, for instance John's veined left arm and the executioner's taut ribcage, is meticulously detailed.

Of equally small size and delicate proportions are two undocumented works in terracotta that have been acknowledged, almost unanimously, as products of Verrocchio's maturity: the damaged relief of the *Lamentation* (290×430 mm; ex-Kaiser-Friedrich Mus., Berlin, destr., see Adorno, fig. 119) and the free-standing statuette of the *Sleeping Youth* (360×580 mm; Berlin, Bodemus.). The former seems to have been prepared as an independent artefact and not as a full-scale model for a bronze. It may have been intended as part of the cenotaph for *Niccolò Forteguerri* or of the monument to a Venetian doge (untraced) that Vasari mentioned. Verrocchio's authorship of the relief has been accepted by scholars on the basis of the monumentality of the composition, the emotional undercurrent of the scene, and the fine and detailed way in which the figures' bodies, clothes and faces are delineated. Christ's pathetically lifeless head, touched by Mary's sorrowful, aged face, crowns a pyramidal construction at the bottom of which are the grieving Magdalene and Nicodemus, kneeling on either side. They are framed by mourning figures who extend the triangle into a rectangle, and, with varied poses, enrich the seemingly simple composition. The multiple folds of the draperies reinforce the subtle complexity of forms, emphasizing the illusion of three-dimensionality and also echoing the agitated state of the mourners.

The precision and finish of the *Lamentation* also distinguishes the *Sleeping Youth*. The sculpture was inspired by that of the Hellenistic *Dying Gaul* (Roman copy, ?1st century BC; Rome, Mus. Capitolino), yet it was also studied from life and shows a specific state of mind. The boy, recumbent and asleep, may represent both innocence and relaxation. His smooth face, firm chest and bony limbs are the attributes of his tender years, while his closed eyes, the head leaning on the right arm, the dreamy face, and the drooping hands invoke an atmosphere of withdrawal and tranquillity. It is not clear whether the figure was destined to form part of a sculptural group, and it has been suggested that it was prepared as a model for the young soldier in the *Resurrection* (Florence, Bargello), a polychrome terracotta relief associated either with Verrocchio or his workshop.

Verrocchio also undertook two commissions for life-size portrait busts, one in marble and one in terracotta. The marble *Woman Holding Flowers* (Florence, Bargello; *see* ITALY, fig. 51) is almost unanimously recognized as an

authentic work from the late 1470s. Its format, a half-figure bust, including arms and hands, was unusual at that date and recalls that of a specific type of antique statue used to depict Roman officials. It enabled the artist to endow his subject with a regal stance and demeanour and to show aristocratic hands with long, elegant fingers. Of special note is the hair with its side-curled ends, the faint trace of a smile and the finely detailed clinging dress, tied at the waist. A similarly impressive personality emanates from the terracotta portrait bust of *Giuliano de' Medici* (Washington, DC, N.G.A.), perhaps the one listed in Tommaso's inventory of 1496. A debt to Classical statues is apparent in the forceful tilt of the head with its arrogant mien. Its indebtedness to Renaissance ideals may be visible in the realism with which the artist delineated each physiognomic trait.

Vasari recorded that in the late 1470s Verrocchio designed the sepulchral monument of *Francesca Tornabuoni* (destr.) for the church of S Maria sopra Minerva, Rome. A marble relief of a birth and death scene (Florence, Bargello) has been associated with this tomb, but neither this association nor the attribution of the relief are certain. From the close of the 1470s until his death, Verrocchio devoted most of his time and energy to the planning and casting of the colossal bronze monument to *Bartolomeo Colleoni* (Venice, Campo SS Giovanni e Paolo; see fig. 4). The condottiere Colleoni had bequeathed part of his wealth to the Venetian state, with the provision that a bronze equestrian statue should be erected to his memory. Alessandro Leopardi and Bartolommeo Bellani (?1400–?1492), who had collaborated with Donatello on the

4. Andrea del Verrocchio: monument to *Bartolomeo Colleoni* (*c.* 1479–92), bronze, h. 3.95 m, Campo SS Giovanni e Paolo, Venice

monument to *Gattamelata* (1447–53; Padua, Piazza del Santo; for illustration *see* DONATELLO, fig. 3), took part in the competition for the commission, for which Verrocchio prepared a true-to-life, life-size wooden model covered with black leather. Verrocchio was awarded the commission in 1480, and probably in 1486 went to Venice to supervise the statue's execution.

The monument crowned Verrocchio's career and is the most forceful of 15th-century equestrian monuments. Inspired more by Venetian precedents than by Florentine counterparts, it is a realistic depiction of a contemporary and ferocious condottiere, not the idealized representation of a military commander that is seen in the Roman *Marcus Aurelius* (2nd century AD; Rome, Piazza del Campidoglio; *see* ROME, ANCIENT, fig. 61) and in Donatello's *Gattamelata*. It also differs from these famous representations in being, typically for Verrocchio, an animated rather than a static group. The conception of the rider and horse is based on Andrea del Castagno's fresco of *Niccolò da Tolentino* (1456; Florence Cathedral; *see* ANDREA DEL CASTAGNO, fig. 4) and on the unattributed early 15th-century equestrian monument to *Paolo Savelli* (*d* 1405) (Venice, S Maria dei Frari). Yet one of the horse's forelegs is freed from any support, and its head is turned to the left. The resulting contrapposto movement, echoed by that of the rider, accentuates the forward thrust of the two figures, which, united, seem to embody the notion of unyielding, domineering strength, a quality also expressed by their facial expressions. In 1488 Leopardi was commissioned to cast the sculpture, and it was erected in 1494. On his death Verrocchio seems to have been working on a fountain ordered by Matthias Corvinus, King of Hungary.

2. PAINTING. Verrocchio's work as a painter continues to raise problems of attribution; his *Virgin and Child with SS John the Baptist and Donatus* in the Donato de' Medici Chapel of Pistoia Cathedral (*see* LORENZO DI CREDI, fig. 1) is his only extant documented painting, and was the product of a collaboration with Lorenzo di Credi. However, Verrocchio had ambitions as a painter early in his career. In 1468 he designed a decorative pennant (untraced) for Lorenzo de' Medici, and in 1469 competed unsuccessfully with Antonio del Pollaiuolo, Piero del Pollaiuolo and Sandro Botticelli for the painting of the *Virtues* at the Università dei Mercatanti in Florence. An undocumented half-length *Virgin and Child* (*c.* 1468; Berlin, Bodemus.) may be dated to this early period. A small work (720×530 mm), it is, nonetheless, a monumental image in which the two voluminous figures, seen in three-quarter profiles, fill most of the picture plane and are set against a landscape background. These figures are placed on opposing diagonals that meet in the centre, where the Virgin's left hand holds the infant's right foot, and are echoed by the distant hill behind the Virgin, and a steeper cliff in the middle ground behind Christ. Verrocchio's sculptural approach to the figures gives them an imposing grandeur: as if carved in the round, they form the shape of a rising pyramid that looks more solid and dense than the distant mountains. Light and shade enhance the illusion of plasticity. Yet the picture is tender in feeling, with the Virgin and Christ bound together by expression

and gesture in a moment of rare intimacy. In mood it is reminiscent of the terracotta relief of the *Virgin and Child* from the mid-1470s.

In 1474 Verrocchio made another tournament standard, this time for Giuliano de' Medici; a triangular-shaped drawing in silverpoint and bistre (Florence, Uffizi) of a reclining female and a putto in a flowery meadow may be a preparatory sketch for this commission. Verrocchio's most famous painting, the altarpiece of the *Baptism* (Florence, Uffizi; see fig. 5), was probably begun in the mid-1470s and was painted for S Salvi, Florence. It is the first large altarpiece in Florence to represent the scene, which had previously been the subject of sculptural and pictorial cycles and predellas. Its symmetrically balanced composition is traditional, with the figure of the Baptist on the right and those of the two attending angels on the left, flanking the centrally placed figure of Christ. Yet Verrocchio's image is nonetheless highly original. Christ and St John seem to move forward and face each other from opposite directions, thus forming a sculptural entity that is as impressive and imposing as the *Incredulity of Thomas* at Orsanmichele. They appear to be completely self-absorbed and self-contained, as if oblivious to the presence of the angels, the sound of water and the birds. The bond that unites them at the very moment of baptism accentuates their prominence and their concentrated expressions create a sense of tension that heightens the viewers' experience of the sacredness of this instant. Apparently in the 1480s areas of the picture, which include the angel seen in profile, much of the landscape, and Christ's face, were changed, repainted or added by the young Leonardo da Vinci.

5. Andrea del Verrocchio: *Baptism*, tempera on panel, 1.77×1.51 m, *c.* 1475–85 (Florence, Galleria degli Uffizi); some alterations possibly made by Leonardo da Vinci

6. Andrea del Verrocchio: *Tobias and the Angel*, tempera on panel, 840×660 mm, late 1470s (London, National Gallery)

Tobias and the Angel (London, N.G.; see fig. 6) is accepted by most critics as an autograph painting from the late 1470s. Depicting the young Tobias, accompanied by Raphael, on his journey home, the picture focuses on the figures' energetic surge as they advance from right to left towards the forefront, and their closeness as they walk arm in arm, their gazes almost locked together. Most remarkable, however, is the physical beauty that they seem to embody. It permeates their delicate faces, their elegantly colourful clothes, their graceful stride and gestures. Raphael's walk, his stretched left leg, and bent right arm are those of a ballet dancer. The landscape background is more detailed than that of the *Virgin and Child*. Sharper and perhaps harsher at the same time, it includes sections of rivers and fortresses, which extend far below the protagonists whose upper bodies are thus silhouetted against the sky.

Verrocchio's inclination to aggrandize the human figure at the expense of the background does not appear to typify the paintings completed later in his life. In the documented altarpiece of the *Virgin and Child with SS John the Baptist and Donatus* (Pistoia Cathedral), commissioned in 1474 by Bishop Donato de' Medici and executed almost entirely by Lorenzo di Credi, the different elements—protagonists, architecture and scenery—acquire a balance that is lacking in the *Baptism*, the *Virgin and Child* and *Tobias and the Angel*. They are interrelated in size and proportions to create a unity where no detail, no matter how important, overshadows another. The composition consists of three spatial tiers, beginning with the plane close to the spectator where the saints are seen standing, proceeding through an elaborate throne in which the Virgin and the infant are seated in mid-ground, and ending with a rich view of mountains, forests and winding paths at the back. Within a triangular alignment that brings the figures together both formally and emotionally, a series of subtle relationships emerges. St Donatus, on the right, gazes at St John the Baptist, on the left, who looks at us while pointing his finger at the Christ Child. The seated mother and infant draw our attention back to the standing saints. Whereas the Virgin's legs project towards St Donatus, her face turns to St John the Baptist, who appears to gain more prominence as the infant's blessing is directed at him as well. Regular and irregular forms blend into a harmonious whole. The severe lines that define the architecture in horizontal and vertical parallels contrast with the undulating lines that separate the landscape from the sky. Likewise, the harsh and angular surface of the marble is juxtaposed with the soft texture and round shapes of the leaves and flowers.

Other pictures associated with Verrocchio, the attributions of which remain controversial, include paintings of the *Virgin and Child* in the National Gallery of Art, Edinburgh (the Ruskin *Madonna*), the National Gallery, London, the Metropolitan Museum of Art, New York, and the Städelsches Kunstinstitut, Frankfurt am Main.

II. Working methods and technique.

1. SCULPTURAL TECHNIQUES AND USE OF PREPARATORY STUDIES. Vasari praised Verrocchio's versatility as goldsmith, sculptor and painter. Nevertheless, his contemporaries seem to have valued him most for his ingenuity and technical ability as a metal-caster and an engineer. The contract for the gilt copper ball to crown the lantern of Florence Cathedral laid down that he was to supervise the purchase of metal in Venice and perhaps to study methods of hammering it in Treviso and Pordenone. The ball was hammered into shape and gilded by the mercury process.

As a goldsmith and silversmith, Verrocchio used an assemblage technique, a method favoured in the 14th century. The silver *Beheading of St John the Baptist* contains many separately cast elements; the kneeling saint, his executioners and the soldiers. He also used the same process for his larger-scale statues, casting different parts of free-standing statues and reliefs separately. The *David* was cast in two sections: the figure of the hero and the severed head of Goliath; the figures were extensively chiselled after casting. In the group in the *Incredulity of Thomas* Verrocchio did not cast those sections that were not intended to be seen: the figures of Christ and St Thomas have no back, and in this they follow Donatello's *St Louis of Toulouse*. However, he paid particular attention to the parts of the hands that are exposed to the viewer. For the drapery in the *Putto with a Dolphin* he used cloth dipped into hot wax and arranged on the wax figure, a technique also used by Donatello in his *Judith and Holofernes* (Florence, Piazza della Signoria) (Cannon-Brookes).

Verrocchio was equally skilled in a variety of media and often approached one medium as he would another. His training as a goldsmith reveals itself in his love of polychromy, and the tomb of *Cosimo de' Medici* in white marble and red and green porphyry is distinguished by the richness and colour of the materials. This was developed in the tomb of *Piero I and Giovanni de' Medici*, where the combination of a variety of coloured stones with bronze decoration is strikingly original. This work has frequently been likened to a jewel box or reliquary. In Verrocchio's multifaceted art small or medium works sometimes acquire the characteristics of monumental projects while many of his large productions exhibit the traits of small artefacts. His bronze *David*, finely and precisely detailed, has the quality of a small and precious object, admired more for its delicacy than for its dramatic impact. It suggests Verrocchio's skill as goldsmith first and sculptor second. His mastery as a marble carver is revealed in the only documented examples of his work in this medium, the faces of Christ and Faith on the *Forteguerri* monument; here the surfaces attain a degree of softness that distinguishes them from the shiny hardness characteristic of many contemporary reliefs and statues (Seymour).

The preparatory work for sculpture that was produced in Verrocchio's workshop included *bozzetti* in wax or clay, terracotta modelli and drawings; *bozzetti* were also used to win contracts from prospective clients. It is not always clear whether Verrocchio's terracottas were intended as independent works or as modelli; a marble relief of the *Virgin and Child* (Florence, Bargello) is a studio variant of the terracotta relief in the same museum. Vasari described how Verrocchio, using a special plaster, cast moulds of natural forms such as hands, feet, knees, legs, arms and torsos in order to study them at length. Few drawings by Verrocchio survive, but he was a fine draughtsman, and a pen-and-ink sheet with *Studies of a Child* (Paris, Louvre) is vivid and spontaneous. He also made a group of delicately modelled black chalk cartoons of heads, which were pricked for transfer and were intended for panel paintings; these include the *Head of a Woman* (Oxford, Christ Church), the *Head of an Angel* (Florence, Uffizi) and another *Head of an Angel* (Berlin, Kupferstichkab.); Vasari mentioned a group of drawings of women's heads by Verrocchio that he owned and that had influenced Leonardo. Drapery studies acquired a new importance in Verrocchio's studio; Vasari described how Leonardo made clay models of figures, draping them with rags dipped in plaster, and then drew them on prepared linen, in brown or black and white, a practice that was adopted by several artists associated with Verrocchio's studio (Popham).

2. WORKSHOP. Verrocchio, whose diligence is frequently praised by Vasari, was outstandingly successful in maintaining an independent firm, which branched out into two studios: one in Florence and one in Venice. His prosperous Florentine studio was strikingly self-sufficient, and, unlike Antonio del Pollaiuolo, who collaborated with various goldsmiths' firms on the Via Vacchereccia, and Donatello, who had managed two sculptors' workshops with Michelozzo, he remained the sole proprietor of his multifaceted studio. The only joint enterprise in which he participated was for the silver altar of the Baptistery. His involvement in public art activities in co-operation with other masters was limited as well: in 1468 he served on the committee that appraised Giovanni di Bartolommeo's

and Bartolomeo di Fruosino's contributions to the casting of the base for the ball of the cathedral lantern. In 1473 he was a member of a committee that evaluated the marble pulpit (Prato Cathedral) of Antonio Rossellino and Mino da Fiesole.

Verrocchio's studio included Perugino, Francesco di Simone Ferrucci, Agnolo di Polo, Giovanni Francesco Rustici, Leonardo da Vinci and Lorenzo di Credi. Within his firm Verrocchio gave considerable latitude to his artists. During his second stay in Venice in the 1480s, he allowed Lorenzo di Credi, who was never granted the rank and privileges of an associate, to take full responsibility for his working facilities near the Opera del Duomo, Florence. It was probably at that time that the latter executed the altarpiece *Virgin and Child with SS John the Baptist and Donatus*, and Leonardo da Vinci retouched and overpainted the altarpiece of the *Baptism*. Verrocchio's will of 1488 made Lorenzo an heir and executor, in place of the former's brother Tommaso, and attests to Verrocchio's wish that Lorenzo complete all the projects left unfinished at his death and take care of his affairs and of some of his relatives. It is clear that the younger man did indeed regard himself as a veritable companion and family member of his master. Rather than bury Verrocchio in the church of the Madonna dell'Orto in Venice, Lorenzo took it on himself to transfer the body to Florence and lay it to rest at the Cioni family vault at S Ambrogio, as the artist had requested.

As was common practice in the 15th century, Verrocchio hired specialized artisans, who did not become part of his regular workforce, for the execution of special engineering feats. When the gilt copper ball for the lantern of Florence Cathedral had been completed he is reported to have enlisted the services of three stonecutters, Lucca di Piero, Salvestro di Paolo di Stefano and Giovanni di Tomé. During the design of the bronze equestrian monument to *Bartolomeo Colleoni*, he is known to have engaged the assistance of a woodcutter by the name of Francesco di Giovanni. Giovanni di Andrea di Domenico, a goldsmith who was chosen by Lorenzo di Credi as the most likely candidate to conclude the casting of this colossal statue, may also have been one of the craftsmen whom Verrocchio employed on a temporary basis.

III. Character and personality.

The scant information about Verrocchio's personal life in the primary sources often relates to untypical events. For example, the record of the court case in 1452, following Verrocchio's accidental killing of a woolworker, contrasts with the more general picture of an apparently uneventful, if busy, life. The assumption that this private man was a homosexual—denied by Cruttwell but supported by Seymour—cannot be verified and largely originates from his relation with the young Leonardo. Three tax declarations from 1457, 1470, and 1480 suggest that Verrocchio devoted himself almost entirely to his art. Without a family of his own, his only concern was with his stepmother, Mona Nannina, his younger brother Tommaso, and later with the latter's unmarried daughters as well as with other unmarried nieces. A document dated 5 November 1490—a tribunal action in litigation involving Tommaso and

Lorenzo di Credi—includes a list of articles left in Verrocchio's Florentine workshop: a lute, an Italian Bible, Franco Sacchetti's *Cento novelle*, Petrarch's *Trionfi* and Ovid's *Heroides*, and these attest to his intellectual pursuits. That Verrocchio was indeed a musician, or a lover of music, is confirmed by Vasari. Though his interests were varied, he was primarily a practical man and left no theoretical works. Unlike many of his fellow artists, Verrocchio did not take part in the public life of Florence and neither did he aspire to better his social standing. Despite his originality as an artist, he essentially appears as a master craftsman who plied his trade within the closed circle of his workshop. Seemingly as uninterested in wealth as he was in fame, he did not seek to develop his practice into a prosperous business establishment and made no investments in real estate, as did several of his competitors.

IV. Critical reception and posthumous reputation.

Although Verrocchio has always been considered one of the most renowned artists in 15th-century Florence, his achievements have been underestimated. He has been branded by posterity as Leonardo da Vinci's master, and the constant comparison of his style with that of his illustrious apprentice has impeded an accurate evaluation of his art. In his own lifetime, however, Verrocchio was a celebrated artist. In 1476 his bronze *David* was purchased from the Medici by the powerful members of the Florentine Signoria, for no less than 150 florins. They chose to exhibit it on the landing of the staircase in front of the Sala del Orologio in the Palazzo della Signoria (now the Palazzo Vecchio). Verrocchio's terracotta models were also prized, and in 1483 the same influential officers bought, for 40 ducats and 200 denari, the model that the artist had made of the figure of *St Thomas* for the bronze *Incredulity of Thomas* from the Tribunale di Mercanzia so as 'not to allow the sketch and source of so beautiful a work be damaged and perish' (Pope-Hennessy). Documents indicate that they decided to place this figure in the council chamber of the Università de' Mercantanti. Verrocchio's high reputation in the 1480s is also suggested by his influence on other artists; Perugino quoted the pose and gesture of Verrocchio's St Thomas in one of the apostles in his fresco *Christ Giving the Keys to St Peter* (Rome, Vatican, Sistine Chapel; *see* PERUGINO, fig. 1), as did Filippino Lippi in the *Virgin Enthroned with SS John the Baptist, Bernard, Victor and Zenobius* (completed 1486; Florence, Uffizi; *see* LIPPI, (2), fig. 1). Many copies of his sculptures were made, among them terracotta portrait busts of *Lorenzo de' Medici* (Boston, MA, Mus. F.A.; Washington, DC, N.G.A.) and of young boys (London, V&A; Berlin, Bodemus.) or stucco reliefs of the *Virgin and Child* (Oberlin Coll., OH, Allen Mem. A. Mus.).

Nonetheless, Vasari's admiration for Verrocchio was tempered by his description of his style as 'rather harsh and somewhat coarse'. Since Vasari, there has been a growing tendency to compare him unfavourably not only with Leonardo but also with Donatello and his contemporary Antonio del Pollaiuolo. Thus Hartt described Pollaiuolo's style as 'easy' and 'vivacious', but Verrocchio's as 'more solemn' and 'clumsier'. Even those art historians of the 20th century who have crusaded on Verrocchio's

behalf are not immune to this tendency. While emphasizing the versatility and novelty of his creations, Cruttwell praised him, above all, as the organizer of a workshop where greater and more gifted artists trained. Covi, while focusing on the important lessons that he had learnt in Venice, saw him as 'one of the earliest essential links in the transmission' to Florence of Venetian ideals. Because Verrocchio failed to complete several of his major projects and collaborated extensively with other artists, some scholars have tended to rob him of any independent contribution. His works are often divided into two categories: those recognized as superior and thus ascribed, at least in part, to Leonardo da Vinci, and those viewed as inferior or inadequate and thereby attributed to Lorenzo di Credi or to less skilled followers. Seymour attempted to destroy the idea of Verrocchio as a mere 'hyphen' or 'hinge' between two ages and two artistic centres. Nonetheless, an unbiased evaluation of Verrocchio's achievements remains to be made.

BIBLIOGRAPHY

EARLY SOURCES

P. Gauricus: *De sculptura* (Florence, 1504)
F. Albertini: *Memoriale di molte statue e pitture di Florentia* (Florence, 1510)
G. Vasari: *Vite* (1550; rev. 2/1568); ed. G. Milanesi (1878–85)
C. Frey, ed.: *Il libro di Antonio Billi esistente in due copie nella Biblioteca nazionale di Firenze* (Berlin, 1892)
C. von Fabriczy: 'Il codice dell'Anonimo Gaddiano [Magliabechiano] nella Biblioteca nazionale di Firenze', *Archv Stor. It.*, ser. 5, xii (1893), pp. 15–94, 275–334; repr. (Farnborough, 1969)
——: 'Andrea del Verrocchio ai servizi dei Medici', *Archv Stor. A.*, ser. 2, i (1895), pp. 163–76 [reprints of 1496 inventory made by Tommaso, with annotations]

GENERAL

EWA
J. Pope-Hennessy: *Italian Renaissance Sculpture* (Oxford, 1958, rev. 3/1986), pls 76–85, pp. 293–9 [with annotated bibliog.]
F. Hartt: *A History of Italian Renaissance Art: Painting, Sculpture, Architecture* (London, 1970, rev. 2/1987), p. 319

MONOGRAPHS

M. Cruttwell: *Verrocchio* (London, 1904) [includes documents]
L. Planiscig: *Andrea del Verrocchio* (Vienna, 1941)
G. Passavant: *Verrocchio: Sculptures, Paintings and Drawings* (London, 1969)
C. Seymour jr: *The Sculpture of Verrocchio* (Greenwich, CT, 1971)
P. Adorno: *Il Verrocchio* (Florence, 1991) [with bibliog.]

VERROCCHIO AND LEONARDO

J. Thiis: *Leonardo da Vinci: The Florentine Years of Leonardo and Verrocchio* (London, 1913)
W. R. Valentiner: 'Leonardo as Verrocchio's Co-worker', *A. Bull.*, xii (1930), pp. 43–89
E. Möller: 'Leonardo e il Verrocchio: Quattro rilievi di capitani antichi lavorati per Re Mattia Corvino', *Rac. Vinc.*, xiv (1930–34), pp. 3–38
A. Bertini: 'L'arte del Verrocchio', *L'Arte*, xxxviii (1935), pp. 433–73
W. R. Valentiner: 'Two Terracotta Reliefs by Leonardo', *A. Q.*, vii (1944), pp. 2–22
A. E. Popham: *The Drawings of Leonardo da Vinci* (New York, 1945)
W. R. Valentiner: 'On Leonardo's Relation to Verrocchio', *Studies of Italian Renaissance Sculpture* (New York, 1950), pp. 113–78
G. Scaglia: 'Leonardo's Non-inverted Writing and Verrocchio's Measured Drawing of a Horse', *A. Bull.*, lxiv/1 (1982), pp. 32–44

SPECIALIST STUDIES

H. Mackowsky: 'Das Lavabo in San Lorenzo zu Florenz', *Jb. Kön.-Preuss. Kstsamml.*, xvii (1896), pp. 239–44
C. Gamba: 'Una terracotta del Verrocchio a Careggi', *L'Arte*, vii (1904), pp. 59–61
C. Sachs: *Das Tabernakel mit Andreas del Verrocchio Thomasgruppe an Or San Michele zu Florenz* (Strasbourg, 1904)
C. Gamba: 'La Risurrezione di Andrea Verrocchio al Bargello', *Boll. A.*, xxv (1931–2), pp. 193–8

C. Kennedy, P. Bacci and E. Wildner: *The Unfinished Monument by Andrea del Verrocchio to the Cardinal Niccolò Forteguerri at Pistoia* (Northampton, MA, 1932)

L. Planiscig: 'Andrea del Verrocchios Alexander-Relief', *Jb. Ksthist. Samml. Wien*, vii (1933), pp. 89–96

W. R. Valentiner: 'Verrocchio's Lost Candlestick', *Burl. Mag.*, lxii (1933), pp. 228–32

E. Moller: 'Verrocchio's Last Drawing', *Burl. Mag.*, lxvi (1935), pp. 192–5

A. Lipinsky: 'Das Antependium des Baptisteriums zu Florenz', *Münster*, ix/5–6 (1956), pp. 133–45

C. A. Isermeyer: *Verrocchio und Leopardi: Das Reiterdenkmal des Colleoni* (Stuttgart, 1963)

D. A. Covi: 'Four New Documents Concerning Andrea del Verrocchio', *A. Bull.*, xlviii/1 (1966), pp. 97–103 [excellent documentary analysis]

G. Passavant: 'Beobachtungen am Silberaltar des Florentiner Baptisteriums', *Pantheon*, xxiv (1966), pp. 10–23

J. G. Phillips: 'The Lady with the Primroses', *Bull. Met.*, xxvii (1969), pp. 385–95

F. Cannon-Brookes: 'Verrocchio Problems', *Apollo*, xcix (1974), pp. 8–19

J. Clearfield: 'The Tomb of Cosimo de' Medici in San Lorenzo', *Rutgers A. Rev.*, ii (1981), pp. 13–30

D. A. Covi: 'Verrocchio and the Palla of the Duomo', *Art, the Ape of Nature: Studies in Honor of H. W. Janson*, ed. M. Barasch and L. Freeman Sandler (New York, 1981), pp. 151–69

——: 'Verrocchio in Venice', *A. Bull.*, lxv/2 (1983), pp. 253–73

S. Bule, ed.: *Verrocchio and Late Quattrocento Sculpture* (Florence, 1992)

L. Dolcini, ed.: *Verrocchio's Christ and St Thomas: A Masterpiece of Sculpture from Renaissance Florence* (New York, 1992)

A. Butterfield: *The Major Sculptures of Verrocchio* (diss., New York, U., 1992)

YAEL EVEN

Verrue, Jeanne-Baptiste d'Albert de Luynes, Comtesse de (*b* Paris, 18 Jan 1670; *d* Paris, 18 Nov 1736). French collector. The mistress of Victor-Amadeus II, Duke of Savoy (*see* SAVOY, §II(11)), she created in Paris one of the most celebrated private collections of paintings, books and decorative arts of the first half of the 18th century. In 1683 she married Manfredo Ignazio di Scaglia, Conte di Verrua and titular head of one of the most prominent court families in Turin. She became the acknowledged mistress of the Duke *c.* 1685, and in 1690 her husband, whose position had become intolerable, abandoned Turin and settled in France.

For 15 years Mme de Verrue was at the centre of her lover's entourage, and during this period she assembled her first collection, about which very little is known. During this period she bore the Duke two children, a son, and a daughter, Vittoria Francesca, who subsequently married (1714) Victor-Amadeus I, Prince of Carignano (1690–1741), one of the most fervent collectors of paintings in Paris during the 1720s and 1730s.

For reasons that remain unclear, Mme de Verrue decided to abandon the Duke and fled in disguise to a convent in Paris (1699). The precipitousness of her flight precluded her carrying any of her collections with her, but the Duke, who retained and legitimized their children, quickly re-established contact with her and sent on some of her possessions, perhaps the collection of medals, which Mme de Verrue subsequently sold to Elisabeth-Charlotte, Duchesse d'Orléans (*see* ORLÉANS, House of, (2)).

The death of the Conte di Verrua in 1704 transformed the status of Mme de Verrue from adulterous cast-off to respectable widow and enabled her to establish residence in the Rue du Cherche-Midi and at Meudon, where she assembled a group of close friends, many of them also collectors, and where she housed her collections. She continued to purchase property adjacent to her *hôtel particulier* to provide more space for her acquisitions, and much of the decoration of her house was entrusted to Louis Boullogne (ii), who also acted as an artistic adviser and an agent.

Much of the richness of Mme de Verrue's second collection derived from her expenditure on the decorative arts, including clocks by Thomas Tompion (1639–1713) and rock-crystal chandeliers by Thomas-Joachim Hébert, along with a library of some 15,000 to 18,000 volumes. As so much of her library has disappeared and remains unattributed to specific artists, it has been unjustly neglected in favour of the better documented collection of over 400 paintings. Mme de Verrue has habitually been presented as an 'advanced' collector, with pioneering purchases in Spanish 17th-century genre pieces, Dutch and Flemish cabinet pictures and the works of contemporary French artists. The importance of such a collection was increased because of the number of people who may have been influenced by it to collect or to commission in the same vein, and because such artists as Antoine Watteau may have used it as a source of inspiration for their own work.

Only an imperfect knowledge of the collection of paintings can be formed from two extant documents: Mme de Verrue's will and the catalogue of her sale. Some individual masterpieces were present: van Dyck's full-length portrait of *Le Roi à la chasse* (*c.* 1635; Paris, Louvre) and Claude Lorrain's *Landscape with Aeneas at Delos* (1672; London, N.G.). There were a greater number of Flemish and Dutch genre and landscape pictures by Bril, the Teniers family, Nicolaes Berchem, Caspar Netscher and Philips Wouwerman (e.g. the *Horse Fair*, 1660s; London, Wallace) and such 17th-century Spanish genre scenes as Bartolomé Esteban Murillo's *Peasant Boy Leaning on a Sill* (London, N.G.) and *Young Girl with Flowers* (London, Dulwich Pict. Gal.). She also owned paintings by François Lemoyne, Nicolas Lancret, Jean-Baptiste Oudry and Jean-Baptiste Pater, some of whom may well have visited her collections.

Mme de Verrue's interest in primarily highly refined cabinet painting of either a gallant or genre nature was largely a phenomenon of private collecting, and a romanticized account of her career is given in *La Dame de volupté* by Alexandre Dumas and celebrated in the nostalgic cult of *ancien régime douceur de vivre* extolled by Edmond and Jules DE GONCOURT. In more practical terms her sale helped to create a precedent for auctions of cabinets of pictures which had become famous in their own time, and may have influenced the decision of her daughter, the Princess of Carignano, to organize the sale of her late husband's equally prestigious collection in 1741. The Verrue and Carignano sales, separated by only four years, served as models for the dispersion of other princely collections at public sales.

BIBLIOGRAPHY

G. de Léris: *La Comtesse de Verrue et la cour de Victor-Amédée II de Savoie* (Paris, 1881)

B. Scott: 'The Comtesse de Verrue: A Lover of Dutch and Flemish Art', *Apollo*, xcvii (1973), pp. 20–24

ROBERT ORESKO

Versailles. Town and château in France, 20 km south-west of Paris. A hunting-lodge built for King Louis XIII in 1623 was rebuilt with extensive gardens from 1631. Under King Louis XIV it became the main royal residence and the seat of the French government from 1682. The château was enlarged in two main phases, first by Louis Le Vau from 1668, then, from 1678, by Jules Hardouin Mansart. The interior decorations were carried out under the supervision of the Premier Peintre du Roi, Charles Le Brun.

The gardens at Versailles, laid out by André Le Nôtre, with a programme of sculptures directed by Le Brun, were designed to complement the château: their solar imagery (*see* §2 below) was directly related to the image of Louis XIV as the Roi Soleil (Sun King). Further altered by Louis XV, Versailles was one of the most resplendent European palaces of the 18th century, a symbol of French royal power and an exemplar for contemporary monarchs.

In 1668 Louis XIV bought adjacent land where he built the Grand Trianon (*see* §3 below), initially a pavilion, rebuilt in 1687 as a château set in its own large gardens. The Petit Trianon (*see* §4 below) was built as a pavilion in these gardens by Louis XV from 1761 to 1768. From 1774 Queen Marie-Antoinette rearranged and developed the gardens, building the Hameau (Hamlet).

1. Château. 2. Gardens. 3. Grand Trianon. 4. Petit Trianon.

1. Château.

(i) 1623–77. (ii) After 1677.

(i) 1623–77. At the beginning of the 17th century Versailles was a small village, located in an undulating, wooded region about 10 km from the royal château of Saint-Germain-en-Laye. In 1623 Louis XIII, an enthusiastic hunter, acquired land in the district and a hunting-lodge was built for him, a modest, two-storey building, with three ranges of apartments, and surrounded by a moat. The King first stayed there in 1624. As he gradually spent more time on his Versailles estate, the hunting-lodge soon became too small, and in 1631 Philibert Le Roy demolished it and built in its place a château of brick and stone. Between 1631 and 1634 the principal range of apartments, flanked by two square blocks, was built at the back of the courtyard, followed by the north and south wings, the courtyard being enclosed by an arcaded portico (see fig. 1). During the same period the King purchased surrounding land, and a garden was laid out by Jacques Boyceau and Jacques de Nemours (1591–1637).

The young Louis XIV first visited Versailles in 1651, but the château was too small to receive the royal family and the accompanying nobility, and from 1661 Louis

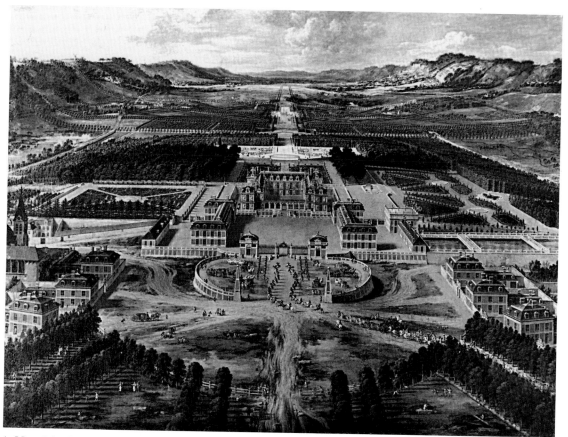

1. *View of the Château, Gardens and Park of Versailles from the East* by Pierre Patel (i), 1668 (Versailles, Musée National du Château de Versailles et de Trianon)

began to have the building enlarged by Louis Le Vau (*see* LE VAU, (1)). Two wings were built in the forecourt, one for kitchens and domestic accommodation, the other for stables. During the same period the King commissioned André Le Nôtre to design new gardens (*see* §2 below). Le Vau proposed in 1668 a plan which preserved the original château at the centre, surrounding it by an *enveloppe*, which entirely screened it from the garden side but left it visible from the courtyard. The new building, the *enveloppe*, was in white ashlar. The north wing, reserved for the King, contained the Appartement des Bains on the ground floor, the Grand Appartement on the first floor and private apartments around the Cour de Marbre. The south wing, a long block of 25 bays, contained the apartments of the Queen, her children and the King's brother, Philippe I, Duc d'Orléans. On the garden side a terrace paved in marble at first-floor level separated the apartments of the King and Queen. Between 1671 and 1679 two additional wings to the north and south of the *cour d'honneur* were built to house ministers and their departments.

The palace interiors were fitted up in the 1670s while building works continued: the apartments of the King and Queen were decorated in marbles of various colours, and the ceiling paintings were entrusted to CHARLES LE BRUN and his team; the Escalier des Ambassadeurs to the north and the Escalier de la Reine to the south gave imposing access to the Grands Appartements. At this time the King's suite comprised six rooms: guardroom, antechamber, bedchamber and three offices. The rooms were panelled with marble, some of them were hung with richly embroidered silks and filled with sumptuous furniture.

(ii) After 1677. The enlargement of the château was a constant preoccupation of Louis XIV, and in 1678 Jules Hardouin Mansart (*see* MANSART, (2)) was put in charge of extensive building works, which gave the palace of Versailles its definitive appearance. New wings, the Ailes du Nord and du Midi, were added north and south of the main block; the Galerie des Glaces replaced the first-floor terrace, with Le Vau's projecting blocks turned into the Salon de la Guerre (see fig. 2) at one end and the Salon de la Paix at the other. To accommodate the services, the Grandes and Petites Ecuries were built opposite the château, together with the Grand Commun. The works continued until 1686–7, employing a vast number of artists and craftsmen. The King regularly inspected progress in the company of Hardouin Mansart, Le Nôtre and Le Brun. The exterior, in a style of elegant classicism, has an arcaded, rusticated ground floor, supporting a main floor with round-headed windows divided by pilasters; the attic storey is crowned by a balustrade bearing sculptured trophies.

In May 1682 Versailles became the king's official residence and the seat of government. The Grand Appartement was converted to an apartment of state; the salons of Diana, Venus, Mars, Mercury and Apollo were used for concerts, games and refreshments. The Galerie des Glaces, with an arcade of 17 mirrors facing the windows looking on to the gardens, had a vault 73 m long, decorated with a scheme of allegorical paintings by Le Brun proclaiming the achievements of Louis and of France between 1661 and 1678. This was the most privileged part

of Versailles, where the courtiers might observe the monarch proceeding to mass or to receptions from his private apartments, located directly behind the Galerie des Glaces, around the inner Court, the Cour de Marbre, in the old part of the château. At the end of his reign this suite consisted of a guardroom, two antechambers (one of which was the 'Oeil de Boeuf'), his bedchamber (*see* FRANCE, fig. 45), the Cabinet du Conseil and a series of salons and small galleries in which he kept collections of paintings and *objets d'art*. (These salons and galleries were to be radically altered during the reign of Louis XV.) The last building erected during Louis XIV's reign was the Chapel (*see* MANSART, (2), fig. 4), begun in 1699 to plans prepared by Hardouin Mansart and finished by Robert de Cotte. It was dedicated in 1710, five years before the King's death.

Louis XV at first lived in Paris and Vincennes and took up residence at Versailles only in 1722. He respected the earlier work, leaving unchanged the exterior of the château and the Grands Appartements. From 1738, however, he greatly altered the cabinets of Louis XIV on the north side of the Cour de Marbre. New salons were created to form a more intimate suite, decorated with magnificent white and gold panelling by Jacques Verberckt and Anges-Jacques Gabriel. In the same part of the palace the King had a suite of small, richly decorated and furnished private rooms built around an interior courtyard known as the Cour des Cerfs, reached by interior staircases. Since the King's large family was accommodated in the palace, the Appartement des Bains was replaced by suites of rooms fitted out for his children and their households.

There was, however, no large theatre: temporary auditoria had been set up as circumstance demanded, notably (until its demolition in 1752) on the landing of the Escalier des Ambassadeurs. Gabriel had been involved in plans for an opera house as early as 1748, but the Opéra was finally built at the end of the Aile du Nord for the marriage of the Dauphin (the future Louis XVI) to Marie-Antoinette, Archduchess of Austria, in 1770. In 1771 Gabriel made plans to rebuild in stone the façades of the buildings round the Cour Royale on the city side, to harmonize them with Hardouin Mansart's work on the garden side. This 'grand dessein' was suspended by financial difficulties at the end of the reign, and only the interior wing on the north side was redone. Louis XVI, succeeeding in 1774, showed the same respect for the work of Louis XIV and made only a few changes to his inner apartments.

In October 1789 Louis XVI and the royal family were forced to leave Versailles under pressure from the revolutionary Parisian crowd. Versailles, abandoned during the revolutionary period, was stripped of most of its furniture, which was auctioned in 1793 and 1794, and the building slowly deteriorated. Some restoration work was undertaken by Napoleon I in 1810 and by Louis XVIII in 1820, but the main effort to protect it was not begun until the reign of Louis-Philippe, who as early as 1833 was determined to create at Versailles a museum dedicated to 'Toutes les Gloires de la France'. Major works were implemented. The Ailes du Nord and du Midi were converted into museum galleries housing extensive collections of 17th-, 18th- and 19th-century paintings and sculpture. Some of the work undertaken in this period was

2. Versailles, Salon de la Guerre, interior view showing a plaster relief of the *Triumph of Louis XIV* by Antoine Coyzevox, *c.* 1681–3

spectacular: the Galerie des Batailles on the first floor of the Aile du Midi was 120 m long and decorated with 33 pictures illustrating the greatest French military victories, from Tolbiac (496) to Wagram (1809); the Salles des Croisades, evoking the medieval crusades to the Holy Land; the Salles d'Afrique, which recalled the conquest of north Africa in the reign of Louis-Philippe himself. The new museum and the old royal apartments within the main central block opened in 1837.

Since then the Musée National du Château de Versailles has maintained these two aspects: the Galeries Historiques comprising the Musée de l'Histoire de France, and the royal and princely apartments in the central part of the palace, which have been restored and refurbished in successive campaigns since they were opened.

2. GARDENS. In 1661, when Louis XIV began to enlarge the château of Versailles, the surrounding grounds were in a rudimentary state, although some avenues had been laid out and box-edged flower-beds placed round the château in the 1630s under the direction of Jacques Boyceau and Jacques de Nemours (1591–1637). The King

acquired further land (at the end of his reign the estate extended over 2473 ha, now reduced to 815 ha) and had gardens designed and laid out by ANDRÉ LE NÔTRE which would harmonize with Le Vau's new building (*see* GARDEN, fig. 2). Louis paid the greatest attention to the design of the gardens, visiting them daily whenever at Versailles; in 1689 he even wrote a kind of guidebook for visitors, *Manière de montrer les jardins de Versailles*, revised several times until 1705.

The grounds still retain the general structure of Le Nôtre's layout: a principal east–west axis flanked by parallel secondary axes north and south, and intersected by four north–south avenues. In the grid squares thus defined, Le Nôtre, succeeded by Jules Hardouin Mansart, installed groves (*bosquets*) and fountains.

The east–west axis ran from the terrace of the château via the Parterre d'Eau, with the bronze allegorical statues of the rivers of France, the Latone steps, the Parterre de Latone and the Tapis Vert walk, to the Bassin du Char d'Apollon at the beginning of the 1560 m Grand Canal (1667–90; *see* FOUNTAIN, fig. 6). On the south side, the gardens terminated with the Pièce d'Eau des Suisses (1679–84), which extended the Parterre de l'Orangerie towards the château, and the Orangery built 1684–6 by Hardouin Mansart under the Parterre du Midi. To the north the gardens slope down to the Bassin de Neptune by way of the Parterre du Nord, the Pyramide fountain and the Allée d'Eau. Some bosquets survive to evoke the splendour of Louis XIV's grounds: on the south, the Salle de Bal (or Bosquet des Rocailles) by Le Nôtre (1680–83) and the Colonnade, built by Hardouin Mansart (1685); and to the north, the Bosquet d'Encelade (1674–6) and the Bosquet des Dômes (1675), both by Le Nôtre.

The excavation, setting out and decoration of the bosquets and the numerous modifications lasted nearly 40 years. One of the essential elements of the gardens was the waterworks: the prominence of water and the diversity of its use excited the admiration of contemporaries but involved the king in extensive engineering works to draw it from the rivers Seine and Eure; for example, the construction in 1681 of the 'Machine de Marly', 14 waterwheels designed to pump the 6000 cubic metres that were daily required to operate the fountains.

The sculpted decoration of the gardens was undertaken at the same time. The decorative theme was often inspired by solar myth and so connected to the person of the Roi Soleil, as, for instance, the Bassins des Saisons and the 24 statues commissioned by Jean Baptiste Colbert in 1674 (the 'Grande Commande') and inspired by the *Iconologia* of Cesare Ripa. The first sculptures in gilded or painted lead were replaced by statues of white marble, either copies of antiques or works carved under the direction of Charles Le Brun. It was not until *c.* 1684 that the first sculptures cast in bronze by the Keller brothers, Johan Jacob (1635–1700) and Balthasar (1638–1702), appeared in the grounds. These carvings, which made the gardens of Versailles the largest contemporary open-air museum of sculpture, are the work of sculptors from the Académie Royale de Peinture et de Sculpture, such artists as François Girardon, ETIENNE LE HONGRE, Martin Desjardins, Gaspard and Balthazard Marsy and ANTOINE COYZEVOX.

Louis XV and Louis XVI made few changes to the gardens of the château. During the former's reign Anges-Jacques Gabriel altered the layout of the Bassin de Neptune, created by Le Nôtre, and set up the lead sculptures by Edme Bouchardon, Jean-Baptiste Lemoyne (ii) and Lambert-Sigisbert and Nicolas-Sébastien Adam (*see* ADAM (ii), (2) and (3)). Louis XVI replanted the grounds in 1774–6, too many old trees having died. A few of the original bosquets were removed and some altered: the Bains d'Apollon north of the Parterre de Latone, which was altered to an *anglo-chinois* style (*see* CHINOISERIE) after a design by Hubert Robert, and at the south edge of the grounds the Labyrinthe was replaced by the modest Jardin de la Reine. Abandoned after 1789, the grounds were partially restored under Louis XVIII between 1816 and 1824, and restoration and replanting are still continuing.

3. GRAND TRIANON. In 1668 Louis XIV bought Trianon, next to the Versailles estate, and commissioned Louis Le Vau to build him a house there. The pavilion, finished in 1670 and decorated with white and blue tiles much like Delftware, became known as the 'Trianon de Porcelaine'. Its gardens, designed by Michel Le Bouteux (*d* 1688/9), a nephew of André Le Nôtre, became famous for the beauty, variety and scent of their flowers. Le Vau's pavilion deteriorated rapidly, and in 1687 the King appealed to Jules Hardouin Mansart to replace it with a château of white stone and pink marble (see fig. 3). The work was completed in a few months, supervised very closely by the King.

The building consists of two L-shaped single-storey wings, linked by a marble peristyle with piers of Languedoc and Campanian marble. The façades are articulated by Languedoc marble pilasters. The building has a low-pitched roof, the parapets punctuated with vases, trophies and stone statues (destr.). The main courtyard, enclosed by a wrought-iron grille, gives access to the peristyle and thence to the gardens, which were enlarged by Le Nôtre and Le Bouteux in 1687.

The south wing contains the suite occupied by Louis XIV between 1691 and 1703, and, from 1810, by Empress Marie-Louise (*d* 1847) on her rare visits to Trianon. The salons, overlooking the garden, include the Salon des Glaces, the Bedchamber, the antechamber of the Chapel (the altar set in an alcove at the back of the room, enclosed by a double door), and finally, the first antechamber, which opens on to the peristyle.

The north wing comprises two parallel series of apartments. On the garden side, a suite of rooms used by Louis XIV until 1691 became in the 19th century the reception salons. Behind them, looking east over the Jardin du Roi, is a suite with smaller rooms occupied during Louis XIV's reign by Madame de Maintenon, and which Napoleon I fitted out as a private apartment, comprising an antechamber, a study, a bathroom, a bedchamber and a dining room.

The north wing leads to the wing known as Trianon-sous-Bois through a gallery decorated with paintings commissioned by Louis XIV from Jean Cotelle II and Etienne Allegrain, which depict the principal groves and gardens of Versailles and Trianon. The chapel created by

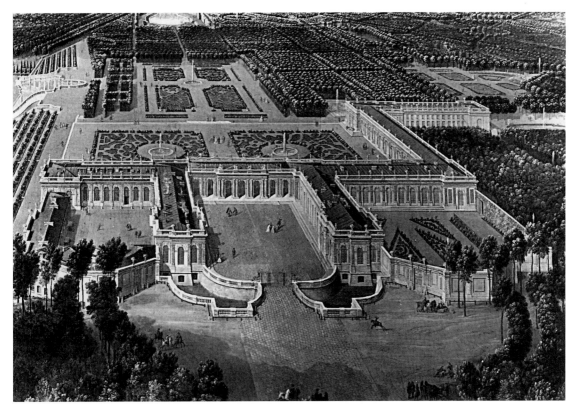

3. Versailles, Grand Trianon, by Jules Hardouin Mansart, 1687; perspective view by Jean-Baptiste Martin I, *c.* 1724 (Versailles, Musée National du Château de Versailles et de Trianon)

Louis-Philippe on the site of Louis XIV's former billiard room stands at the junction of the two wings. The Trianon-sous-Bois wing is built in stone without marble veneer and consists of a main storey with an attic.

The gardens of the Grand Trianon have largely preserved the layout designed in 1667–8. They lie along an east–west axis leading from the peristyle, with a high parterre with two pools, dropping to the low parterre, which leads to the large Bassin du Plat-Fond or Miroir. When the Grand Trianon itself was built, the plans for the garden were entrusted to Le Nôtre, then, at his death in 1700, to Hardouin Mansart, who finished planting the bosquets. From that time the garden developed northwards in a formal sequence comprising the Buffet d'Eau, the Jardin des Marronniers, the Amphithéâtre des Antiques and many 'Salles Vertes'. At the end of the Trianon-sous-Bois wing the Jardin de Laocöon leads back to the former Jardin des Sources (destr. 1776) and the Jardin du Roi. The sculptural decoration of the Trianon gardens was installed by Hardouin Mansart from 1704: the sculptures for the water-basins are mostly reused from the Bassins des Saisons in the grounds of Versailles.

Towards the end of the 18th century, the Trianon gardens were neglected in favour of Marie-Antoinette's works at the Petit Trianon (*see* §4 below), and they were further modified during alterations made to the château under the Empire. Two guard houses were built at the entrance to the grounds and near the old Jardin des Sources a small bridge spanned a ha-ha. It now connects the grounds of the Grand and Petit Trianons.

Louis XIV used Trianon as a private retreat and held festivities, concerts and suppers for selected guests. His successors were less interested in the château. Its furniture was sold at the Revolution, but from 1805 Napoleon I had it restored and entirely refurnished. Louis-Philippe, in the image of his ancestor Louis XIV, came to Trianon often with his family. In the restoration of the château between 1962 and 1966 the mural decorations were restored to their 17th-century state, while the furniture is on the whole that of the Empire period.

4. PETIT TRIANON. In 1749 Louis XV extended the Trianon gardens towards the north-east, installing a farm, 'la nouvelle ménagerie', which included a superb botanic garden; a second botanic garden located near the château was organized by Bernard de Jussieu (1699–1777). In 1761, on the advice of the Marquise de Pompadour, the King commissioned Anges-Jacques Gabriel to build a pavilion within the Trianon gardens. Built from 1762 to 1768, the five-bay façades of white stone are articulated by fluted Corinthian columns and pilasters. The building has a basement, main floor and attic storey, but the basement is properly visible only on the side facing the botanical garden (see fig. 4), leaving the salons themselves at courtyard level.

Following his accession in 1774, Louis XVI gave the Petit Trianon and its grounds to Marie-Antoinette, who,

4. Versailles, Petit Trianon, garden façade, by Anges-Jacques Gabriel, 1762–8

following Louis XV, created a seven-room apartment on the main floor. The mezzanine and attic accommodated several of the Queen's intimates. It was the rearrangement of the gardens that engaged the Queen's full attention (*see also* GARDEN, §VIII, 4(ii) and fig. 47). She drew on the advice of both her architect Richard Mique and an enlightened amateur, the Comte de Caraman (1727–1807). These gardens were laid out in the *anglo-chinois* style: artificial hills, grottoes, rivers and lakes were created, with sinuous footpaths winding among them, revealing in their twists and turns the many charming buildings commissioned by the Queen. Near the Pavillon Français (built by Gabriel for Louis XV in 1750 and decorated by Jacques Verbeckt) was concealed the Théâtre de la Reine (1780, by Mique) where the Queen staged entertainments: the actors and spectators were members of the royal family or their close friends. A small Belvédère (built by Mique in 1778–80, decorated by Jean-Jacques Lagrenée and Le Riche) overlooked the Grotto and the Petit Lac; and on an island in the 'river' stands the Temple de l'Amour, built in 1778 by Mique, with Joseph Deschamps (*c.* 1743–88).

Marie-Antoinette's garden was extended by the Hameau (Hamlet), a group of 12 peasant houses made of cob and roofed with tiles or thatch, built by Mique from 1783 to 1785: they include the Moulin with its waterwheel, the Boudoir, the Réchauffoir, the Maison du Billard connected to the Maison de la Reine by a wooden gallery, the Colombier, the Maison du Garde, the Tour de Marlborough and the Laiterie de Propreté. The Grange, which served as a ballroom, and the Laiterie de Préparation have disappeared.

In 1805 Napoleon, charmed by the Petit Trianon, ordered it to be restored and had the Hameau fitted out for Empress Marie-Louise. In 1837, Louis-Philippe, having completed the transformation of Versailles into a historical museum, restored the two châteaux at Trianon and their gardens. In 1867, the year of the Exposition Universelle in Paris, Empress Eugénie (1826–1920) assembled at the Petit Trianon a collection of objects recalling the memory of Marie-Antoinette and her family. The interior of the Petit Trianon has been restored to its state in 1774–89.

See also MAISON DU ROI, §I.

BIBLIOGRAPHY
Souchal
Louis XIV: *Manière de montrer les jardins de Versailles*, ed. S. Hoog (Paris, 1982)
A. Félibien: *Description sommaire du Château de Versailles* (Paris, 1674)
P. de Nolhac: *Versailles inconnu, les petits cabinets de Louis XV* (Paris, 1925)
——: *La Création de Versailles* (Paris, 1925)
——: *Versailles: Résidence de Louis XIV* (Paris, 1925)
——: *Versailles au 18 siècle* (Paris, 1926)
——: *Trianon* (Paris, 1927)
P. Francastel: *La Sculpture de Versailles: Essai sur les origines et l'évolution du goût français classique* (Paris, 1930/R 1970)
P. de Nolhac: *L'Art à Versailles* (Paris, 1930)
F. Kimball: *The Creation of the Rococo* (Philadelphia, 1943; rev. New York, 1980)
L. Hautecoeur: *Louis XIV, Roi-Soleil* (Paris, 1953) [symbolism of Versailles]
C. Pinatel: *Les Statues antiques des jardins de Versailles* (Paris, 1963) [with cat. rais.]
A. Schnapper: *Tableaux pour le Trianon de marbre 1688–1714* (Paris, 1967)
A. Marie: *La Naissance de Versailles* (Paris, 1968)
B. Jestaz: 'Le Trianon de marbre ou Louis XIV architecte', *Gaz. B.-A.*, n. s. 5, lxxiv (1969), pp. 259–86
W. Vitzthum and S. Hoog: *Charles Le Brun à Versailles: La Galerie des Glaces* (Paris, 1969)
A. Marie: *Mansart à Versailles* (Paris, 1972)
——: *Versailles au temps de Louis XIV* (Paris, 1976)
D. Gallet-Guerne and C. Baulez: *Versailles, dessins d'architecture de la Direction générale des bâtiments du roi* (Paris, 1983)
A. Marie: *Versailles au temps de Louis XV* (Paris, 1984)
P. Verlet: *Versailles* (Paris, 1985)
G. Weber: *French Fountains during the Reign of Louis XIV* (London, 1985)
G. Walton: *Louis XIV's Versailles* (London, 1986) [with critical bibliog.]
SIMONE HOOG

Verschaffelt, von. Family of artists of Flemish origin, active in France, Italy and, most notably, in Germany. They practised as sculptors and architects from the early 18th century to the early 19th.

BIBLIOGRAPHY
B. Grotkamp-Schepers: 'Die kurpfälzische Zeichnungsakademie in Mannheim', *Barock in Baden-Württemberg* (exh. cat., Karlsruhe, Bad. Landesmus., 1981), pp. 241–51
L'Angelo e la città (exh. cat., Rome, Castel Sant'Angelo, 1987–8)

(1) Peter Anton von Verschaffelt (*b* Ghent, 8 May 1710; *d* Mannheim, 5 April 1793). Sculptor and architect. After training as a sculptor under his uncle Pieter de Sutter (1647–1723), in 1732–3 he worked in Paris with Edme Bouchardon and until 1736 was a pupil at the Académie Royale. In 1737 he went to Rome, where he studied Classical sculpture and the paintings of Raphael and the Carracci family. From *c.* 1739 he executed his first independent sculptural works, and 'Pietro il Fiammingo', as Verschaffelt was subsequently known in Rome, gained important patrons, including Pope Benedict XIV, for whom he created such works as statues of *St John the Evangelist* (*c.* 1744; e.g. Rome, Santa Croce in Gerusalemme) and *St Paul* (1746; Bologna, S Pietro), two *Putti with Garlands* (1741–2; *in situ*) for the façade of S Maria Maggiore, a *Putto with Tiara* (1748; *in situ*) for Ancona Cathedral, as well as portrait busts and statues of the Pope. His most famous Roman work, the *Archangel Michael* (1752; Rome, Castel S Angelo) was cast in bronze by

Francesco Giardoni (1692–1757). After a brief visit to London in 1752, Verschaffelt became court sculptor to Charles Theodore, Elector Palatine (and Elector of Bavaria from 1777), in Mannheim, for whom he created works of sculpture and architecture reflecting both French neo-Baroque and Roman-inspired classical styles. Among the best-known of his Mannheim works were portrait busts and statues of *Charles Theodor* and his wife *Elisabeth Augusta* (examples in Munich, Bayer. Nmus. and Residenzmus.; Speyer, Hist. Mus. Pfalz; Mannheim, Schloss; Ghent, Mus. S. Kst.) and sculptural decoration for the Jesuit church in Mannheim (1754–60; *in situ*) and Schloss Benrath, near Düsseldorf (c. 1760–75; *in situ*). He was also responsible for the erection and decoration of the Palais Bretzenheim (1782–8) in Mannheim. Verschaffelt consolidated his fame far beyond Mannheim, especially with the foundation of the Mannheim Zeichnungsakademie and its Antikensaal (dispersed 1803), an important collection of plaster casts of the most famous ancient sculptures.

BIBLIOGRAPHY

P. A. v. Verschaffelt: *Zeichnungen im Reiss-Museum* (exh. cat., ed. I. Gesche; Mannheim, Städt. Reiss-Mus., 1976)

G. Krämer: *Die römisch-barocke Stilkomponente im Werk P. A. v. Verschaffelts* (diss., U. Heidelberg, 1978)

W. Schiering: 'Der Mannheimer Antikensaal', *Glyptothek München* (exh. cat., ed. K. Vierneisel and G. Leinz; Munich, Glyp.; 1980), pp. 322–6

Klassizismus in Bayern, Schwaben und Franken: Architekturzeichnungen, 1775–1825 (exh. cat., Munich, Stadtmus. and Tech. U., 1980), pp. 15, 255, 368, 370, 372; figs 97/3–8

E. Hofmann: *P. A. v. Verschaffelt: Hofbildhauer des Kurfürsten Carl Theodor in Mannheim* (diss., U. Heidelberg, 1982)

Der Antikensaal in der Mannheimer Zeichnungsakademie, 1769–1803 (exh. cat., Mannheim, Altertver., 1984)

(2) Maximilian Joseph von Verschaffelt (*b* Mannheim, 1754; *d* Vienna, 1818). Architect, sculptor and draughtsman, son of (1) Peter Anton von Verschaffelt. Initially he studied under his father, but after they quarrelled he continued his education at the Académie Royale in Paris (1780–81) and in Rome (1782–93), where he also worked as a sculptors' assistant and eked out a living by producing architectural watercolours for art lovers on the Grand Tour. Anna Amalia, Duchess of Saxe-Weimar, who was in Italy from 1788 to 1790, employed him as a draughtsman and architect, drawing Classical architecture in Rome and the Campagna (examples in Weimar, Schlossmus. and Schloss Tiefurt) and decorating the Villa Malta (1789), which she rented in Rome. (The decoration has since been moved to the Schloss Tiefurt in Weimar.) In 1793 Verschaffelt accepted the position of architectural and horticultural director in Munich, where he was entrusted with designing the layout of the Englischer Garten, realization of which was carried through by Friedrich Ludwig von Sckell in 1804. In 1799 Verschaffelt completed exact architectural drawings of the Munich Residenz (Munich, Bayer. Hauptstaatsarchv), for which he designed extensions, including two identical, longitudinally oval two-storey chapels, one Catholic, one Protestant, alongside each other. His designs, which were in the style of Roman buildings of the High Baroque in the spirit of Bernini and Borromini, and the modern façade in the Empire style, did not accord with the wishes of the Elector's wife, and Verschaffelt therefore left the Munich court and went to Vienna, where he entered the service of Prince Miklós Esterházy II (*see* ESTERHÁZY, §I(4)).

BIBLIOGRAPHY

Klassizismus in Bayern, Schwaben und Franken: Architekturzeichnungen 1775–1825 (exh. cat., Munich, Stadtmus. and Tech. U., 1980), pp. 17, 137, 142, 144, 177

INGRID SATTEL BERNARDINI

Verschoten, Floris. *See* SCHOOTEN, FLORIS VAN.

Verschuur, Wouterus (*b* Amsterdam, 11 June 1812; *d* Vorden, 4 July 1874). Dutch painter, draughtsman and lithographer. The son of an Amsterdam jeweller, he learnt to paint from, among others, the landscape and cattle painters Pieter Gerardus van Os and Cornelis Steffelaar (1797–1861). His talent was noted at an early age: his competition entries in 1831 and 1832 at the Felix Meritis Society in Amsterdam won gold medals. In 1833 he was appointed a member of the Akademie voor Beeldende Kunsten and of the Koninklijk Nederlands Instituut in Amsterdam. In 1839 he joined the artists' society, Arti et Amicitiae. He worked in Amsterdam from 1846 to 1857 and 1869 to 1874, residing also in The Hague, Doorn (1842), Brussels (1867) and Haarlem (1858–68).

Verschuur specialized in stable interiors and landscapes; his beach views are also particularly striking. However, his favourite subject was the horse, which he was able to depict in a particularly convincing manner (e.g. *Horses in the Meadow in Gusty Weather*; Amsterdam, Rijksmus.). From 1840, he gradually made a name for himself with work of this kind. In 1839 *Halfway House* (untraced) was particularly well received by contemporary critics. Verschuur also attracted attention from abroad: one of his entries in the Exposition Universelle in Paris in 1855 was acquired by Napoleon III. Around 1860 Verschuur was at the height of his fame, but despite his success in France, he seems not to have been attracted by foreign travel.

Although Verschuur became particularly concerned with the direct study of nature in later life, he does not appear to have considered realism of great importance to his work. With his animal paintings—generally of horses, although dogs were also a favoured subject (e.g. *Dogs Resting in Front of a Hearth*; Amsterdam, Fodor Mus.)—he belonged to the last generation of Dutch Romantic painters, for whom the masters of the 17th century were a great example; the paintings of Philips Wouwerman were the dominant influence on his style. Among Verschuur's best paintings are *Stable Interior with Horses* (Amsterdam, Hist. Mus.), *Incident from the Ten-day Campaign against the Rebellious Belgians, August 1831* (Amsterdam, Rijksmus.) and a *Horse Fair* (Haarlem, Frans Halsmus.). He sometimes collaborated with other artists, notably Cornelis Springer. Of Verschuur's many students, Anton Mauve was undoubtedly the most important. Although Mauve worked in Verschuur's studio for only a few months in 1858, he adopted his motif of draughthorses and oxen in such paintings as *Homeward Bound* (1875; priv. col.).

BIBLIOGRAPHY

Scheen

W. Laanstra: *Cornelis Springer, 1817–1891* (Utrecht, 1984)

G. JANSEN

Verso. Wrong, back or reverse side of a flat, double-sided object, such as a drawing. The term also refers to the left-hand page of a book or manuscript. The related term REVERSE is used for the back of a medal or coin that carries the subordinate design.

☐

Verspronck, Jan [Johannes] **(Cornelisz.)** (*b* Haarlem, ?1606–9; *d* Haarlem, *bur* 30 June 1662). Dutch painter. He was the son of the Haarlem painter Cornelis Engelsz. (*c.* 1575–1650) and was born not in 1597, as was formerly believed, but about ten years later. He was probably apprenticed to his father and possibly also for a period to Frans Hals. In 1632 he joined the Guild of St Luke in Haarlem, where he continued to paint until his death.

Of the approximately 100 works by him to have survived, most are portraits, with the exception of a few genre paintings, such as *Guardroom with Officer and Soldiers* (*c.* 1640; Jerusalem, Israel Mus.), and a *Still-life with Loaf, Fish and Onions* (*c.* 1640; the Netherlands, priv. col., see Ekkart, 1979, no. 27), his only known still-life. His earliest known portraits date from 1634 and are closely related in composition and in the poses of his subjects to works by Hals, but the brushwork is less free and the portrayal of the sitters more static. Verspronck's style developed only slightly over a period of about 25 years. At the beginning of his career he evolved for his portraits a number of standard compositional forms, which he continued to use for many years with only slight variations. The only development in the early works is in the background of his portraits, which became an important element for displaying the effects of light and dark; there is usually a light area close to the right side of the figure, which gradually darkens across the picture. Among the best examples from his early work are the pendant portraits of *Anthonie Charles de Liedekerke* and *Willemina van Braekel* (both 1637; Haarlem, Frans Halsmus.).

The most productive period for Verspronck was between 1640 and 1643, when he painted the group portraits of the *Governesses of the St Elisabeth Hospital* (1641; Haarlem, Frans Halsmus.) and of the *Governesses of the Orphanage* (1642; Haarlem, Frans Halsmus.) and more than 20 individual portraits, including his best-known painting, *Girl in Blue* (1641; Amsterdam, Rijksmus.; see fig.). Most of these are either head-and-shoulder or half-length portraits, but there are also some impressive three-quarter-length pieces, such as *Portrait of a Man* (1641; Louisville, KY, Speed A. Mus.) and its pendant *Portrait of a Woman* (1642; priv. col., see Ekkart, 1979, nos 38 and 41).

The portraits painted between 1644 and 1650, of which several examples can usually be dated in each year, do not differ greatly in composition from the early ones. From *c.* 1650, however, Verspronck usually portrayed his models seated. Among the best examples from this later period are the portraits of *Eduard Wallis* and his wife *Maria van Strijp* (both 1652; priv. col., on loan to Amsterdam, Rijksmus.). In some other works after 1650 he used a broader style of painting. In his final years he appears to have painted very little.

Verspronck was an isolated figure in the art circles of 17th-century Haarlem and must have led a withdrawn

Jan Verspronck: *Girl in Blue*, oil on canvas, 830×665 mm, 1641 (Amsterdam, Rijksmuseum)

existence. He was a bachelor and initially lived with his parents, later moving into a residence of his own, with one brother and an unmarried sister. Through his painting he attained some affluence. His patrons, as far as can be identified from his portraits, were Haarlem citizens or people closely connected with the town, suggesting that he worked exclusively in that area. Among his models are representatives of the ruling Calvinist patriarchy but also members of the many well-to-do Catholic families of Haarlem. Verspronck himself was probably a Catholic. His significance lies in the original way in which he took the compositions of Hals as a starting-point and developed a personal, sober and quiet style of portrait painting, combining a fairly meticulous technique with a subdued range of colours, mainly white, black, grey and brown. No pupils are known.

BIBLIOGRAPHY

R. E. O. Ekkart: *Johannes Cornelisz. Verspronck: Leven en werken van een Haarlems portretschilder uit de 17-de eeuw* (Haarlem, 1979) [incl. cat. rais. and illus. of all works; with Eng. summary]

——: 'Johannes Verspronck: Een Haarlemse portretschilder uit de zeventiende eeuw', *Antiek*, xiv (1979–80), pp. 105–16

RUDOLF E. O. EKKART

Verster, Floris (Henric) (*b* Leiden, 9 June 1861; *d* Leiden, 12 Jan 1927). Dutch painter. He trained first at the Ars Aemula Naturae school in Leiden under George Hendrik Breitner, then at The Hague Academie (1879–82) and the Brussels Académie (1882). In Leiden in 1882 he started painting landscapes in the style of the Hague school. From 1882 to 1892 he shared a studio in Leiden with the still-life painter Menso Kamerlingh Onnes (1860–1925), who was to become his brother-in-law. Influenced by Onnes and such French realists as Antoine Vollon and Théodule Ribot, in 1885 he turned to painting still-lifes in a mildly Impressionist style that by 1888–9 often attained monumental formats, as in *Peonies* (1.35×2.00 m, 1889; Amsterdam, Stedel. Mus.). He submitted some of these to exhibitions, where their reception was mixed; artists including Breitner, H. W. Mesdag and Jacob Maris were enthusiastic, but the critics quite often were not. He participated in a few exhibitions abroad, notably from 1890 to 1894 in Munich and in 1891 with Les XX in Brussels.

In 1891 Verster started experimenting by observing his compositions through sheets of green or blue coloured glass. His work became increasingly unnaturalistic as a result (e.g. *Flowers in a Conservatory*, 1891; Leiden, Stedel. Mus. Lakenhal). In 1890 he had met the poet Albert Verwey (1865–1937) and the artist Jan Toorop; Verwey's poems and Toorop's crayon drawings of 1891–4 were a particular source of inspiration. Verster's crayon drawings were not Symbolist, like Toorop's, but an attempt to get closer to nature. They date mainly from 1893 to 1899 and tend to be close-up views of flowers, trees and other plants, minutely rendered (e.g. *Eucalyptus*, 1896; Leiden, Stedel. Mus. Lakenhal). The critics deplored his decision to give up painting large still-lifes in oil, but he had no problem in selling such drawings. They are perhaps his most significant contribution to Dutch art.

By 1900 Verster's period of experimentation was at an end and for the rest of his life he painted still-lifes, mostly of flowers (e.g. *Still-life with Camellias*, 1916; Rotterdam, Boymans–van Beuningen), and an occasional portrait. His later paintings are much smaller than those of 1886–9. He used a more realistic technique, sometimes remarkably detailed, recalling his crayon drawings, but occasionally much broader and indebted to the palette knife. Verster's first solo exhibition was held, with considerable success, in the Rotterdamsche Kunstkring in 1904. His death in 1927 was followed by commemorative exhibitions in that year in Leiden (Stedel. Mus. Lakenhal) and Utrecht (Cent. Mus.), and in 1929 in The Hague (Pulchri Studio).

BIBLIOGRAPHY
W. Scherjon and others: *Floris Verster* (Utrecht, 1928) [fully illus. cat. rais.]

A. M. Hammacher: *Floris Verster* (Amsterdam, n.d.)

Floris Verster (exh. cat., intro. A. Montens; Leiden, Stedel. Mus. Lakenhal, 1986)

A. Montens, ed.: 'Aantekeningen van Jenny Kamerlingh Onnes over Floris Verster' [Notes by Jenny Kamerlingh Onnes about Floris Verster], *Jong Holland*, ii (1986), pp. 42–54, 60

The Age of van Gogh: Dutch Painting 1880–1895 (exh. cat., ed. R. Bionda and C. Blotkamp; Glasgow, Burrell Col., 1990; Amsterdam, Rijksmus. van Gogh; 1991)

MAARTEN WURFBAIN

Verstolk van Soelen, Baron **Jan Gijsbert** (*b* Rotterdam, 1776; *d* Soelen, nr Tiel, 1845). Dutch diplomat and collector. He studied law in Göttingen and Kiel. After the annexation of the Netherlands by France in 1810, he became prefect of the province of Friesland, and four years later, when the Netherlands became an independent kingdom, he was appointed ambassador to Russia. He spent several years there and then took up the post of Minister of Foreign Affairs at The Hague, which he held until his retirement in 1841. From then onwards he devoted himself entirely to collecting, an activity he had begun in 1823. Verstolk collected mainly prints and drawings but also assembled an equally impressive group of 17th-century Dutch paintings. His print collection included one of the finest groups of Rembrandt etchings ever put together. The core of this group consisted of five volumes of etchings by Rembrandt and his students purchased for 8150 florins from the sale of Graf Moritz von Fries on 21 June 1824. At the same sale Verstolk acquired three volumes of prints by Dürer for 2000 florins. He added to his collection of Rembrandt etchings, which included a rare impression of the '*Hundred Guilder Print*' (*c.* 1643–9; B. 74) on Japanese paper, from the sale of Thomas Wilson in London on 8 March 1830, as well as those of the 1st Duke of Buckingham and Chandos in 1834, A. P. F. Robert-Dumesnil in 1836 and the Chevalier Claussin (1766–1844) in 1844. Verstolk also had prints by other Dutch artists, such as Lucas van Leyden, Adriaen van Ostade, Jacob van Ruisdael, Hendrick Goltzius, Jonas Suyderhoef and Cornelis Visscher, as well as some by French and Italian artists, among them Claude, Robert Nanteuil and Francesco Bartolozzi. The collection was renowned for the many rare states and exceptionally fine impressions it included.

Verstolk's collection of drawings paralleled that of the prints, comprising mainly works by 17th-century Dutch artists. Among his drawings by Rembrandt were portraits of *Jan Six* and *Anslo* and a landscape. He also possessed drawings by Rembrandt's pupils, including Ferdinand Bol, Gerbrand van den Eeckhout, Samuel van Hoogstraten, Nicolaes Maes, Arent de Gelder and Lambert Doomer, and landscapes by Aelbert Cuyp, Nicholaes Berchem, Simon de Vlieger and van Ruisdael. Flemish artists were also represented, for example Rubens (e.g. the *Crucifixion*) and Anthony van Dyck (e.g. a portrait of *Jan Breughel*). In his will, Verstolk offered all or part of the collection to the city of Rotterdam in lieu of estate tax owed by his heirs. The city refused, however, and the collection, including his library (sold 12 Oct 1846), was dispersed. The collection of paintings was bought for £24,000 by a group of three English collectors, Thomas George Baring (1826–1904), later 1st Earl of Northbrook, Samuel Jones Loyd, 1st Baron Overstone, and Bingham Mildmay; much of it passed to the descendants of Lord Northbrook (East Stratton House, East Stratton, Hants) and Lord Overstone (Lockinge House, Oxon), while Mildmay's share was sold in 1894. The drawings were auctioned in Amsterdam on 22 March 1847, the prints on 28 June 1847 and 26 October 1847. The remains of the collection, inherited by Verstolk's sister, Baroness A. H. E. van Pallandt van Klarenbeek (1786–1866), were sold in Amsterdam on 4–7 November 1867.

BIBLIOGRAPHY
F. Lugt: *Marques* (1921), no. 2490

JANE SHOAF TURNER

Vertue [Vartu; Vertu]. English family of architects. The first documented member is Adam Vertue (*fl* 1475–85), who worked in royal service at Westminster Abbey and, from 1477 to 1485, at Eltham Palace, where he made carvings for 11 chimneys. His sons (1) Robert Vertue I and (2) William Vertue worked both for the king and for other patrons. Robert Vertue II (*fl* 1506–55), the son of Robert I, is mentioned in his father's will and should probably be equated with the master mason of Evesham Abbey (until the Dissolution in 1539), where the fan vault of the Lichfield Chapel reveals knowledge of the work of Robert I and William.

(1) Robert Vertue I (*d* Dec 1506). His early career can be traced through the muniments of Westminster Abbey, where he progressed from junior mason in 1475—breaking his service from 1480—to complete his training in 1482-3. He continued to work there until 1490. He may have been appointed King's Master Mason by 1487, but, after leaving Westminster, his next documented commission was at Greenwich, where he oversaw Henry VII's substantial rebuilding programme from 1500. In 1501 Vertue received £100 for the construction of a new tower at the Tower of London. In the same year, in partnership with his brother (2) William Vertue, he was hired by Bishop Oliver King (*d* 1503), a royal favourite, to design a new church for Bath Abbey. The building they created conformed to the contemporary style of royal chapels, with minimal aisles, turrets borrowed from St Stephen's Chapel (partly destr.) at the Palace of Westminster, and fan vaulting, which the brothers intended to rival any in England or France. Robert may have designed the Christ Church gate (1502) at Canterbury, a royal commission that has the vertical panelling and angel friezes seen in other buildings of the Windsor–Westminster workshops.

(2) William Vertue (*fl* 1501; *d* March 1527). Brother of (1) Robert Vertue I. He is first documented as a master mason when he joined his brother at Bath. Thereafter his output in the royal service was prolific. Possibly at Windsor from 1502, he was the second recorded architect in charge at St George's Chapel, completing the nave and vaulting the choir, nave and crossing (*see* WINDSOR CASTLE, §1). The west window, with its 95 tracery panels, contains an image of a mason believed to be Vertue. William may have taken charge of the work on Henry VII's Chapel at Westminster Abbey at the deaths of Robert I and Robert Janyns (ii) in 1506. He visited Cambridge between 1507 and 1509 to advise on the vaulting of King's College Chapel, vaulted the Lady chapel (1511–14) at Windsor Castle and built a gallery connecting it with St George's Chapel. At the Tower of London he may have designed the new Perpendicular chapel of St Peter ad Vincula after a fire destroyed the old one in 1512. There was further work in the royal service at Woking Palace (1515), Surrey, and Eton College (1516–21). During this time he also designed the first two-storey range of buildings for Corpus Christi College (1512–18) in Oxford. Resigning from royal service in 1519, he accepted, together with Henry Redman, a joint commission from Henry VIII and, the following year, helped prepare royal apartments for the Field of Cloth of Gold at Calais. The cloister (*c.* 1526–9) and chapel adjoining St Stephen's Chapel have been attributed to him on stylistic grounds.

BIBLIOGRAPHY
Harvey
H. M. Colvin, ed.: *1485–1660* (1975–82), iii and iv of *The History of the King's Works* (London, 1963–82)
F. Woodman: *The Architectural History of Canterbury Cathedral* (London, 1981)
C. Wilson: *The Gothic Cathedral: The Architecture of the Great Church, 1130–1530* (London, 1990)

Vertue, George (*b* London, 17 Nov 1684; *d* London, 24 July 1756). English writer, engraver and antiquary. Born to Catholic parents, he first trained (*c.* 1698–1701) under an unknown French engraver, after which he was apprenticed to Michael van der Gught (1660–1725) until 1709. Vertue was an early member of Godfrey Kneller's Academy of Painting and Drawing in Great Queen Street (1711–*c.* 1720), London, where he drew from life, and the Rose and Crown Club, to which numerous artists and patrons belonged. From 1726 he also attended the meetings in London of the Virtuosi of St Luke. In 1717 he was appointed engraver to the Society of Antiquaries, contributing to its *Vetusta monumenta*. He was also employed by Oxford University to engrave plates for its annual *Almanacks* and contributed to a number of illustrated works, including Aubrey de la Motraye's *Travels through Europe, Asia, and into Parts of Africa* (1723), Thomas Salmon's *The Chronological Historian* (1723), Alexander Pope's edition of *The Works of Shakespeare* (1725) and Paul de Rapin Toyras's *History of England* (1732–47). By the mid-1730s he was considered to be one of the best reproductive engravers. A number of his engravings were made after portraits and tomb effigies of historical persons, for example his series of nine 'Historical Prints' from paintings of the Tudor period, which he commenced in 1740; later portrait heads include *Thomas Sackville, 1st Earl of Dorset* and the philosopher *John Locke* for Thomas Birch's *The Heads of Illustrious Persons of Great Britain* (London, 1747), a collaborative effort with the engraver Jacobus Houbraken. Vertue was also known for his enthusiastic participation in the artists' clubs and private academies into which English artists were channelling their growing sense of national identity and ambitions for self-improvement. Extant portraits of Vertue made around this time include that by Jonathan Richardson the elder (1733; London, N.P.G.); he is also represented in Gawen Hamilton's well-known group portrait of a *Club of Artists* (1735; London, N.P.G.).

Vertue also enjoyed a reputation as an antiquary, having a strong interest in the artistic and cultural history of Britain. This aspect of his career was encouraged by friendships with such patrons and scholars as Heneage Finch, 5th Earl of Winchelsea (*d* 1726), and John Talman (respectively president and director of the Society of Antiquaries). In the course of his research, Vertue toured country houses and examined private collections in the company of Robert Stephens (1665–1732), the Historiographer Royal, and the antiquary and collector Henry Hare, 3rd Baron Coleraine (1693–1749). Vertue's greatest encouragement, however, came from Edward Harley, 2nd Earl of Oxford, whom he first met in 1724. The circle patronized by Harley included numerous writers, among them the poet Alexander Pope, and scholars engaged in investigating various aspects of British history; in this invigorating atmosphere Vertue's notes towards 'Musaeum', his national history of the arts, began to take shape. For this he amassed information from aged artists and active contemporaries, traced or catalogued collections extant or dispersed and gathered information on medieval and later art and monuments. Harley's death in 1741 was a major setback for Vertue's project, although one part of it, an art monograph on the engraver *Wenzel Hollar*, was published in 1745. From 1749 Vertue was employed by Frederick, Prince of Wales, to catalogue the royal collections, and under Frederick's patronage new projects were formulated, including one scheme to set up an academy and drawing school, another to catalogue additional collections and a third to complete the 'Musaeum'. None had been realized by 1751 when Frederick died suddenly, dashing Vertue's hopes.

Following Vertue's own death five years after that of his royal patron, most of his 'Note-books' were purchased at auction in 1757 by Horace Walpole (*see* WALPOLE, (2)), later 4th Earl of Orford, who obtained additional material the next year from Vertue's widow. Walpole quickly published *A Catalogue and Description of King Charles the First's Collection of Pictures* (1757), *A Catalogue of the Collection of Pictures Belonging to James the Second* (1758) and *A Catalogue of the Curious Collection of Pictures of George Villiers, Duke of Buckingham* (1758), all of which Vertue had begun compiling under Frederick's patronage. But Walpole's largest undertaking was to turn Vertue's manuscript 'Note-books', which included details on hundreds of English and immigrant painters, engravers, sculptors, medallists and architects, into the works in five volumes published at his Strawberry Hill press as the *Anecdotes of Painting in England* (4 vols, 1762–71) and the *Catalogue of Engravers* (1763). Walpole took as a model Vasari's *Vite*; but this was a model of art history that Vertue had criticized and challenged, especially in his 'Description of the Monument of Edward the Confessor', himself conceiving a more complex historical work. In fact, his 'Musaeum', contrary to Walpole's *Anecdotes*, anticipates a new type of historical account—the national history of the arts and the sciences—which developed fully later during the 18th century and at the beginning of the 19th, in such works as Gerolamo Tiraboschi's *Storia della letteratura italiana* (1772–95) and Luigi Lanzi's *Storia pittorica d'Italia* (1792–1809). Following Walpole's own death in 1797, Vertue's 'Note-books' eventually passed to the collector Dawson Turner in or after 1848. At the Turner sale in 1859 they were acquired by the British Museum and are now in the British Library, London.

WRITINGS

A Description of the Works of the Ingenious Delineator and Engraver Wenceslaus Hollar, with Some Account of his Life (London, 1745)
Medals, Coins, Great-Seals, Impressions, from the Elaborate Works of Thomas Simon (London, 1753, rev. 1780)
'A Description of the Monument of Edward the Confessor', *Archaeologia* [Soc. Antiqua. London], i (1770), pp. 35–42 [written in 1736]
A Description of Nine Historical Prints, Representing Kings, Queens, Princes &c of the Tudor Family (London, 1776)
'The Note-books of George Vertue', *Walpole Soc.*, xviii (1930), xx (1932), xxii (1934), xxiv (1936), xxvi (1938), xxix (1942) [index], xxx (1950)

BIBLIOGRAPHY

DNB
T. Birch: *The Heads of Illustrious Persons of Great Britain* (London, 1747–52/*R* 1756, 1813) [engravings by Vertue and J. Houbraken]
H. Walpole: 'Life of Mr George Vertue', *Anecdotes of Painting in England* (1762–71); ed. R. N. Wornum (1849), iii, pp. 988–1007
J. Dobai: 'George Vertue', *Die Kunstliteratur des Klassizismus und der Romantik in England* (Bern, 1974–84), i, pp. 846–66
I. Bignamini: 'George Vertue: Art Historian', *Walpole Soc.*, liv (1988)

ILARIA BIGNAMINI

Verulamium. *See* ST ALBANS, §1(i).

Verveer, Salomon Leonardus (*b* The Hague, 30 Nov 1813; *d* The Hague, 5 Jan 1876). Dutch painter. He was a pupil of Bartholomeus Johannes van Hove and also studied at the Koninklijke Academie van Beeldende Kunsten in The Hague. He travelled to Germany and France, producing several views of the French coast and a *Townscape near Koblenz* (1835; Wassenaar, Leslie Smith Gal.). His earlier work, with its preference for reddish colouring, strikingly fantastic approach to architecture and pronounced contrasts between light and dark, is Romantic in tone, for example in an *Imaginary View Based on the Kolksluis, Amsterdam* (1839; Amsterdam, Rijksmus.). Verveer is chiefly known for his townscapes, often set in Jewish districts (e.g. *Jewish Town Scene*, 1851; Delden, Twickel Castle, van Heeckeren priv. col.). However he also painted riverscapes, such as *River in Stormy Weather* (1846; Enschede, Rijksmus. Twenthe). Some of his later works, such as *On the Lookout* (1871; Haarlem, Teylers Mus.), have a rather lighter touch; the same progression is found in his charcoal sketches. But Impressionism, which appeared in the Netherlands in the third quarter of the century, left few traces on Verveer; his works from those years, such as *Torenstraat in Scheveningen after the Rain* (1872; Amsterdam, Stedel. Mus.), continued to feature detailed coastal subjects.

BIBLIOGRAPHY

Scheen
J. Gram: 'Salomon Leonardus Verveer', *Elsevier's Geïllus. Mdschr.*, xix (1900), pp. 289–302

ANNEMIEKE HOOGENBOOM

Vervloet, Frans (*b* Mechelen, 28 Jan 1795; *d* Venice, 11 March 1872). Flemish painter and lithographer. In 1809 he began to study at the Akademie voor Schone Kunsten in Mechelen and was also given instruction by his brother J. J. Vervloet (1790–1869), a genre and portrait painter. During this early period he produced both genre pieces and copies after Old Masters (including Peter Paul Rubens), although he concentrated mostly on architectural painting, for example the *Installation of Archbishop F.-A. de Méan at Mechelen* (1817; Rome, A. and F. Di Castro priv. col.). Following the great success of this painting, he devoted himself from 1817 to paintings of church interiors.

In 1822 Vervloet was awarded a two-year scholarship by the Maatschappij ter Bevordering van de Schone Kunsten (Society for the Advancement of the Fine Arts) of Brussels to study in Rome. He drew Roman views (e.g. Naples, Mus. N. S Martino), for which he often made meticulous preparatory sketches in his diary. Vervloet's new interest in landscape was also probably due to his numerous trips to the Campagna with members of the foreign artists' colony in Rome. His work around 1823 strongly resembles the architectonically balanced landscapes of the Dutch painter Joseph Augustus Knip. In 1824 Vervloet travelled to Naples, where he became friends with the founder of the SCUOLA DI POSILLIPO, A. Sminck Pitloo; Vervloet was one of the protagonists of this school, whose sketchy brushwork and clear-toned palette gave an entirely new impetus to landscape painting.

Vervloet's most productive years were during the period from 1820 to 1830. In 1854 he settled permanently in Venice after having made a number of trips through Europe. His work developed from the lively style of the Roman and Neapolitan period (e.g. *View of Monte Cavallo, Rome*, 1827; Rome, priv. col., see 1985–6 exh. cat., p. 329) into a somewhat drier manner in his Venetian years.

UNPUBLISHED SOURCES
Venice, Correr [Vervloet's four-volume diary]

BIBLIOGRAPHY
G. Lorenzetti: 'Vedute di Venezia: Disegni di Francis Vervloet, pittore fiammingo al Museo Correr', *A. Ven.*, iv (1947), pp. 288–90
S. Sulzberger: 'François Vervloet (1795–1872)', *Oud-Holland*, lviii (1953), pp. 242–5
M. Pittaluga: 'Note su Francis Vervloet e la sua "Vie"', *Ant. Viva*, ix (1970), pp. 26–39
D. Coekelberghs: 'A propos de *L'Installation de l'archevêque F.-A. de Méan à Malines en 1817*, tableau inédit de François Vervloet', *Rev. Archéologues & Historiens A. Louvain*, v (1972), pp. 132–47
——: *Les Peintres belges à Rome de 1700 à 1830* (Brussels, 1976)
Autour du néo-classicisme en Belgique, 1770–1830 (exh. cat., ed. D. Coekelberghs and P. Loze; Brussels, Mus. Ixelles, 1985–6), pp. 328–35

FRANSJE KUYVENHOVEN

Vervoort, Michiel. *See* VOORT, MICHIEL VAN DER, I.

Verwée, Alfred (Jacques) (*b* Sint-Joost-ten-Node, 23 May 1838; *d* Brussels, 15 Sept 1895). Belgian painter. After training as a land surveyor, he entered the studio of F.-C. Deweirdt (1795–1855) in Brussels, aged 16. His father, Louis Pierre Verwée (1807–77), a provincial painter of romantic genre scenes and himself a pupil of Eugène Verboeckhoven, also advised him. In 1857 Verwée first exhibited at the Brussels Salon, showing an animal painting; throughout his life he continued to paint animal scenes. After meeting such artists as Antoine-Louis Barye, Edouard Manet and the Barbizon painters Théodore Rousseau and Narcisse Diaz in Paris in 1864, his style became increasingly realistic. He returned to Brussels in 1868, where he became a founder-member of the Société Libre des Beaux-Arts, a group of young artists including Louis Dubois, Louis Artan and Edouard Huberti who espoused *plein-air* painting. *Landscape with Cows* (1868; The Hague, Rijksmus. Mesdag) is a good example of an early cattle piece painted from nature.

In the late 1870s Verwée's moderate Realism was replaced by a grand vision of Flemish outdoor life, with well-fed cattle grazing on fertile land. Among his best mature works are a number of large Impressionist landscapes with cattle, painted in the environs of Knokke, where for many years Verwée worked in summer. The animals in these paintings are usually depicted with almost photographic exactitude while the surrounding landscape is rendered freely; for example, *Fight between Young Bulls* (1883; Ghent, Mus. S. Kst.) and *Out in the Beautiful Fields of Flanders* (1884; Brussels, Mus. A. Mod.). Verwée's skill as an Impressionist and *plein-air* painter is also evident in his many smaller landscapes and studies (e.g. *Sky with Dark Clouds*, Brussels, Mus. A. Mod.).

BIBLIOGRAPHY
Oeuvres d'Alfred Verwée (exh. cat. by C. Lemmonier, Brussels, Mus. A. Mod., 1896)
G. Vanzype: *Alfred Verwée* (Brussels, 1933)

Alfred Verwee en Knokke (exh. cat. by J. Van den Heuvel, Knokke, Town Hall, 1976)
Het landschap in de Belgische kunst, 1830–1914 (exh. cat. by R. Hoozee and M. Tahon-Vanroose, Ghent, Mus. S. Kst., 1980), pp. 149–53

SASKIA DE BODT

Verwilghen, Raphaël (*b* Roeselare, 12 March 1885; *d* Brussels, 24 Oct 1963). Belgian engineer and urban planner. He graduated from the Université Catholique de Louvain in 1908 and joined the Ministry of Public Works (1913) as a public highways inspector; here he became increasingly aware of the rudimentary state of urban-planning legislation. He also worked with Josef Stübben, an urban planner from Berlin, and the internationalist Paul Otlet (1868–1944). Verwilghen was one of the first planners to promote the development of comprehensive urban-planning legislation in Belgium. Together with Fernand Bodson he founded the technical urban-planning reviews *Tekhné* (1912–13), *Art et technique* (1913–14) and, after World War I, *La Cité* (1919–35). He was sent to England (1914–16) by the Ministry to study the development of garden cities and suburbs and immediately on his return recommended that they be adopted in the reconstruction of the country. He taught at the Ecole d'Art Public in Paris (*c.* 1916–18). He became Director at the Office des Régions Devastées (1919–23) and planned several garden cities in the region of the Yser River (1919–21) and the Batavia complex in Roeselare (1919; with Fernand Bodson and Antoine Pompe).

Disillusioned with the politics of reconstruction, Verwilghen left the public service in 1923 to pursue a private career in association with Jean-Jules Eggericx. Major projects included preliminary planning studies (1929–30) for the Bukavu and Uvira territories in the Belgian Congo (now Zaire) and participation in the competition (1933) to plan the left bank of Antwerp. He also worked on the Belgian pavilion at the Exposition Internationale des Arts et Techniques dans la Vie Moderne in Paris (1937; with Eggericx and Henry Van de Velde). In 1929 he had succeeded Louis Van der Swaelmen as Professor of Urban Planning at the Institut Supérieur des Arts Décoratifs in Brussels, remaining there until 1943. During World War II, he prepared a draft bill to create general urban-planning legislation for the whole country for the Commissariat Général à la Reconstruction (1940–44); this was not put into effect until 1969.

BIBLIOGRAPHY
P. L. Flouquet: 'Raphaël Verwilghen: Ingénieur, architecte, urbaniste, humaniste', *La Maison*, ii (1964), pp. 39–45
Guide de l'architecture des années 25 à Bruxelles (Brussels, 1983, rev. 1986), p. 49

HERVÉ PAINDAVEINE

Ver Wilt [Verwilt], Domenicus (*fl c.* 1544–*c.* 1566). Flemish painter and tapestry designer, active in Sweden. He was made a master of the Guild of St Luke in Antwerp in 1544 and worked in Sweden from 1556 to 1566. He executed decorations (1558–61) at Kalmar Slott in Småland and designed the cartoons for the monumental tapestries (1561–9; e.g. Stockholm, Kun. Slott) depicting the earliest mythical kings of Sweden and their history, as related by the historian Johannes Magnus, which were influenced by the Brussels tapestry style. A fine portrait of

King Erik XIV (*c.* 1561; Stockholm, Nmus.), in the style of Antonis Mor, is also probably by Ver Wilt.

BIBLIOGRAPHY

SVKL

K. E. Steneberg: *Vasarenässansens porträttkonst* [Vasa Renaissance portrait painting] (Stockholm, 1935)

TORBJÖRN FULTON

Vesali. *See* VAISHALI.

Vesalius, Andreas [Wesel, Andries van] (*b* Brussels, 31 Dec 1514; *d* Zacynthus, Venice Repub. [now Greece], ?June 1564). Flemish scientist and writer. He was a pioneer and reformer of the study of anatomy. In 1537 he was appointed professor of anatomy at the University of Padua, where his lectures were well received, attracting large audiences. His *De humani corporis fabrica* [On the fabric of the human body], published when he was still only 28, marked a new era in anatomical illustration and knowledge (*see* BOOK ILLUSTRATION, fig. 2). The *Fabrica*, as it is known, and its companion volume, the *Epitome*, were the accomplishment of four years' work. The woodcut illustrations in the *Fabrica* represent the first published attempts at accurate ANATOMICAL STUDIES, with partially dissected figures set in landscapes (30 years earlier Leonardo da Vinci had produced similar studies but none was printed in book form). The identity of the artists who illustrated the *Fabrica* is not known, though various names have occasionally been suggested. As early as the mid-16th century the designs were ascribed to Titian; however he may have been over 60 when the *Fabrica* was published, and although he may have taken an interest in these anatomical plates, he is no longer thought to have designed them. In the 19th century it was found that Titian's pupil JAN STEVEN VAN CALCAR was responsible for some of the illustrations. Calcar may also have painted the Titianesque portrait of *Vesalius* (St Petersburg, Hermitage).

WRITINGS

De humani corporis fabrica, 7 vols (Basle, 1543)
Epitome (Basle, 1543)

BIBLIOGRAPHY

L. Choulant: *Geschichte und Bibliographie der anatomischen Abbildung* (Leipzig, 1852; Eng. trans. M. Frank, New York, 1920, 3/1962)
J. M. Ball: *Andreas Vesalius: The Reformer of Anatomy* (St Louis, 1910)
J. B. Sanders and C. D. O'Malley: *The Illustrations from the Works of Andreas Vesalius* (Cleveland and New York, 1950/*R* 1973)
C. Singer and E. A. Underwood: *A Short History of Medicine* (Oxford, 1962), pp. 90–95, 242–3
C. D. O'Malley: *Andreas Vesalius of Brussels, 1514–1564* (Los Angeles, 1964)
J. P. Arcieri: *Leonardo da Vinci and Andreas Vesalius in Anatomical Studies* (New York, 1965)
P. H. Muir and P. Amelung: *Printing and the Mind of Man* (Munich, 1983), pp. 33, 71, 73

ANNE DARLINGTON

Vesme, Alessandro Baudi di [Alexandre de] (*b* Turin, 23 May 1854; *d* Turin, 27 Aug 1923). Italian archivist and writer. He worked first as an archivist in the Regia Pinacoteca, Turin, then as its Director (1895–1923). He supervised the expansion and reorganization of the galleries (1893–8) according to the latest museological theories, arranging the paintings by nationalities and schools, rather than subject. Embodying his research, his catalogue of the picture gallery's paintings was published in 1899. Di Vesme led a scholar's life, compiling in hand-written notes a vast amount of material on prints in Turin's picture gallery and private collections and on native and foreign artists who worked in Piedmont. His *Le Peintre-graveur italien* (1906), a sequel to Adam von Bartsch's catalogue of printmakers, catalogues the work of numerous Italian artists omitted by Bartsch. Possibly most important for the catalogue of the large oeuvre of Stefano della Bella but now superseded by later catalogues of the prints of Canaletto and the Tiepolos, it is still useful for the many minor artists included. Death denied Vesme the retirement years he intended to devote to the publication of his findings, but the four posthumous volumes of the *Schede Vesme* (1963–82) became the specialist's primary tool for studies pertinent to the history of art in Savoy, encompassing all earlier sources.

WRITINGS

Catalogo della Regia Pinacoteca di Torino (Turin, 1899, 2/1909)
Le Peintre-graveur italien: Ouvrage faisant suite au Peintre-graveur de Bartsch (Milan, 1906)
Francesco Bartolozzi: Catalogue des estampes et notice biographique, entièrement réformés et complétés d'une étude critique par A. Calabi (Milan, 1928)
Schede Vesme: L'arte in Piemonte, 4 vols (Turin, 1963–82) [incl. biog. and bibliog.; articles by Vesme in periodicals are listed in iv, pp. xvii–xviii]
Stefano della Bella: Catalogue Raisonné (New York, 1971)

PHYLLIS DEARBORN MASSAR

Vesnin. Russian family of architects and urban planners. The brothers Leonid Aleksandrovich Vesnin (*b* Nizhny Novgorod, 10 Dec 1880; *d* Moscow, 8 Oct 1933), Viktor Aleksandrovich Vesnin (*b* Yur'evets, 9 April 1882; *d* Moscow, 17 Sept 1950) and Aleksandr Aleksandrovich Vesnin (*b* Yur'evets, 16 May 1883; *d* Moscow, 7 Nov 1959) worked independently on occasion but are best known for their collaborative projects. After the Revolution of 1917 they had a central role in formulating and developing Constructivism, which became the dominant form of architectural Modernism in the USSR in the 1920s. Aleksandr Vesnin, the most active and innovative of the brothers, also had a significant early career as a painter and theatre designer.

1. EARLY WORK, BEFORE 1924. The Vesnins received their secondary education at the Practical Academy of Commercial Sciences, Moscow, but while Leonid completed his architectural training at the Academy of Fine Arts in St Petersburg, Viktor and Aleksandr attended the Institute of Civil Engineering, St Petersburg, where emphasis was laid on the technical aspects of architecture. Their studies were interrupted due to the authorities closing the Institute, and they did not graduate until 1912, spending some of the intervening time working as assistants for established architects, such as Illarion Ivanovshits, Roman Klein and O. R. Munts, with whom they collaborated on the Romanesque Revival Post Office (1911), Myasnitskaya Square, Moscow. Aleksandr also studied painting (1909–11) with the impressionist artists Yan Tsionglinksy in St Petersburg and Konstantin Yuon in Moscow, and worked (1912–13) in Vladimir Tatlin's studio, the Tower, where he met Lyubov' Popova, Nadezhda Udal'tsova and other avant-garde artists. By this time he was experimenting with Cubism in numerous sketches of female nudes. In 1913–14 Viktor and Aleksandr visited Italy, where they studied the work of Palladio. This interest in classicism is reflected in their design of the

Sirotkin House (1914–16) in Nizhniy Novgorod, for which Aleksandr painted a classical ceiling fresco (1915). At the same time they worked in other styles, notably a vernacular Russian idiom for the church (1913) at Katunki. In 1916 Aleksandr joined the army for a year, and for a period the careers of the brothers followed separate paths, with Viktor emerging as the sole architect of the Dynamo Stock Company Building (1917), Moscow, in a stripped, functional style, and Aleksandr concentrating on painting. By 1917 he was producing such abstract works as *Study of Planes* (1917; Samara, City A. Mus.), inspired by Malevich's Suprematism. Later he introduced stronger structural and spatial tensions into works collectively titled *Structures of Coloured Space with Lines of Force* and characterized by linear rhythms and more complex intersections of planes. Viktor and Aleksandr collaborated again on the May Day decorations (1918) for the Red Square, Moscow, and all three brothers were involved in designing a base for a wooden monument in Red Square to *Karl Marx* (1919).

Around 1920 Aleksandr became involved in stage design, producing sets and costumes for various productions by A. Y. Tairov (1885–1950) at the Kamernyy Theatre, Moscow, including Racine's *Phèdre* in 1922 and, the following year, G. K. Chesterton's *The Man who Was Thursday*. The colourful sets and costumes for *Phèdre* reflected the interest in intersecting volumes and lines encountered in his paintings of this period, while in complete contrast the set for *The Man who Was Thursday* was an asymmetrical, industrially inspired, skeletal construction, with platforms, stairs, lifts, moving wheels and a screen for graphics. It was composed of separate units, including a diagonal stair or ramp, open-work tower and rostrum, which could be used in various combinations. The costumes were caricatures of contemporary Western dress.

From 1921 to 1924 Aleksandr was a professor of painting at the VkhUTEMAS (Rus.: Higher (State) Artistic and Technical Workshops), where he also taught colour construction on the basic course with Lyubov' Popova. In 1921 he also joined the newly founded INKHUK (Rus.: Institute of Artistic Culture), Moscow, a forum for the discussion of avant-garde theories of art. The institute was associated with such Constructivist painters as Aleksandr Rodchenko, Varvara Stepanova and Aleksey Gan (1889–c. 1940), who were themselves influenced by Malevich and Tatlin. Among the central concerns of the Constructivists were the breaking down of the pictorial image into its constituent elements and the forging of links with the technological culture of the new Soviet society. Aleksandr Vesnin sought to extend these concerns to architecture in a paper given to Inkhuk in 1922, in which he emphasized the importance of studying the basic plastic elements, such as material, colour, plane, line and texture, and of designing on the bases of economy and the principles of contemporary technology to 'organize man's consciousness'.

One of the first buildings to manifest the principles that became associated with architectural Constructivism was the Vesnins' competition design (1922–3; unexecuted) for the Palace of Labour, Moscow. Intended to serve as a congress hall, museum, theatre and restaurant, their building was to house two auditoria, with capacities respectively of 8000 and 2500. The design related structurally and stylistically to the stage design for *The Man who Was Thursday*, as well as to designs for the Khodynka Field festival, Moscow. It comprised a large elliptical amphitheatre and a rectangular sixteen-storey block, joined at seventh-storey level by a substantial bridge structure housing the smaller hall intended for the sessions of the Mossoviet. The two auditoria could be combined for special functions, providing seating for *c.* 10,000. The volumes were functionally derived, and to emphasize the technical functionalism of the Palace, it was to be built in reinforced concrete with the visible skeletal frame articulating the exterior, in a manner similar to Gropius's unexecuted design of 1922 for the *Chicago Tribune* Tower. The heaviness of the framework contrasts with the open network of metal radio masts, wires and cables on the roof.

2. LATER WORK, FROM 1924. The Constructivist principles manifested in the Vesnins' design for the Palace of Labour were expressed most memorably in their unexecuted project for the *Leningrad Pravda* Building (1924; see fig.), Moscow. They designed a five-storey building, to be contained on a 6 sq. m plot, in metal, glass and reinforced concrete that was intended, in accordance with the brief, 'to express the productive and busy nature of this building in its façade'. The ground-floor included the hall and a newspaper stand, while other floors housed a reading-room, an editorial room and offices. The exterior clearly displayed the lifts and features associated with 20th-century urban life, such as signboards, advertisements, clocks, loudspeakers and radio masts. These features were also used in the design (1924; unexecuted) for the Arcos Building, Moscow, where the reinforced-concrete frame used in the Palace of Labour project was combined with an extensive use of glass, as in the *Leningrad Pravda* Building, although the result was a rather less exciting design.

In 1924 Aleksandr also designed the cover for Moisey Ginzburg's *Stili epokha*, which established the theoretical foundations for architectural Constructivism. In 1925 he and Ginzburg founded OSA (Rus.: Union of Contemporary Architects) and began to co-edit its journal *Sovremennaya arkhitektura*, which promoted a Constructivist approach. Leonid and Viktor also became active members of OSA and were involved in developing the 'functional method' and exploring its practical application. In their Lenin Library competition design (1928) for Moscow, the Vesnins provided for a complex in which the reading-room, store and offices were, as separate functional volumes, housed in almost separate buildings. The site of the Univermag or department store (1928) at Krasnaya Presnaya, Moscow, was surrounded by other buildings, and the emphasis is not on the definition of volumes but on the wall of glass supported by the reinforced-concrete frame. At the same time the brothers collaborated with Nikolay Kolli and Georgy Orlov on the Dneprostroi hydroelectric and industrial complex (1927–32) on the Dnepr River, a project that became a symbol of the First Five-Year Plan.

Aleksandr and Viktor were both concerned with evolving new building types and tackled the question of socialist urban planning and advocated smaller urban units of functions, and Kuznetsk (1929–30), where the administrative, cultural and commercial centres were differentiated and the communal housing complexes were planned for 1100 and 2100 people.

The official demand for more traditional values in architecture that emerged in the early 1930s was expressed in the Vesnins' competition project for the Palace of Soviets, Moscow, which in its four versions became increasingly compact and monumental. However, after the death of Leonid Vesnin, Viktor and Aleksandr, with Moisey Ginzburg, publicly expressed their dislike of this return to historicism. The Vesnins continued to resist the return to traditionalism throughout the 1930s, as in their competition entries for the Nemirovich-Danchenko Theatre (1933) and for The Peoples' Commissariat of Heavy Industry (1935–6), both in Moscow. Although the final version of the latter included monumental statues and colonnades, the basic structure of concrete and glass was austerely undecorative. The Palace of Culture (1931–7) for the Proletarsky district of Moscow was influenced by Le Corbusier's spatial ideas, and various functional spaces, such as corridors, stairways, foyers and halls, were integrated to create a sense of spatial fluidity and a fusion of interior and exterior space.

Aleksandr and Viktor taught at the Institute of Architecture, Moscow (1930–36), and directed the architecture studio of Mossoviet, then that of the Commissariat for Heavy Industry and Ministry of Petroleum (1933–55). In the 1930s and 1940s Viktor played an important role in organizing the Union of Soviet Architects and served as secretary of the Union (1937–49). Viktor was the first president of the All Union Academy of Architecture (1939–49), of which Aleksandr was also a member from 1933. With their lack of success in gaining commissions, especially after World War II, Aleksandr increasingly returned to drawing and painting, in a very personal figurative style.

BIBLIOGRAPHY

A. Kopp: *Town and Revolution: Soviet Architecture and City Planning* (London, 1967)
A. Chinyakov: *Brat'ya Vesninyi* [The Vesnin brothers] (Moscow, 1970)
C. Lodder: 'Constructivist Theatre as a Laboratory for an Architectural Aesthetic', *Archit. Assoc. Q.*, xi/2, 1979, pp. 24–35
K. P. Zygas: 'Cubo-Futurism and the Vesnins' Palace of Labor', *The Avant-garde in Russia, 1910–1930: New Perspectives* (Cambridge, MA, 1980), pp. 110–17
A. Kopp: *Constructivist Architecture in the USSR* (London, 1985)
S. O. Khan-Magomedov: *Alexandr Vesnin and Russian Constructivism* (London, 1986)

For further bibliography *see* CONSTRUCTIVISM, §1.

CHRISTINA LODDER

Vesontio. *See* BESANÇON.

Vespasian [Titus Flavius Vespasianus], Emperor (*b* Reate [now Rieti], 17 Nov AD 9; *reg* AD 69–79; *d* Cutilia, 4 June AD 79). Roman ruler and patron. By the death of Nero (AD 68) he had largely subdued Judea; he was acclaimed emperor by the troops in the civil war that followed. As Suetonius aptly expressed it (*Vespasian* viii), Vespasian wished not only to give stability to the state but also to embellish it. That aim was fully expressed in the grandiose building programme that he carried out, mainly in Rome. He enlarged the enclosure of the *pomerium* (city precinct)

Aleksandr, Viktor and Leonid Vesnin: project (unexecuted) for the offices of the *Leningrad Pravda*, 1924 (Moscow, A. V. Shchusev State Research and Scientific Museum of Russian Architecture)

40,000–50,000, attached to an industrial centre. They also emphasized their preference for large communal housing units over small, believing that 'the collective way of life is possible only if one leads a communal life with a large number of people in constant communication'. Such ideas were implemented in their projects for Stalingrad (now Volgograd; 1929–30), in which they produced housing complexes for 3200 and 2600 people, located around a single city centre combining academic and administrative and made it uniform with that of the new customs barrier; he straightened the course of the Tiber and repaired roads and aqueducts; he rebuilt the Temple of the Deified Claudius (after AD 70), which had been destroyed by Nero, and that of Jupiter Optimus Maximus on the Capitol (rededicated AD 75); and he restored the stage-building of the Theatre of Marcellus. Between AD 71 and 75 the splendid Templum Pacis (*see* ROME, §V, 2) was built on the site of the old public market to commemorate the victory in Judea. The temple was connected to the Imperial Fora, to which it formed an appendix on the south-east side, and was surrounded by a monumental porticoed square resembling a forum, although only at the end of the Empire was it called the Forum Pacis. In the early years of his reign Vespasian also began the construction of the Colosseum (*see* ROME, §V, 6), a huge amphitheatre in the valley between the Palatine, Esquiline and Caelian hills that had formerly been the centre of Nero's Domus Aurea. While still unfinished—Vespasian may have been responsible only for the first two orders of arches—the Colosseum was given its first dedication by the emperor before his death. The building was completed by Titus (*reg* AD 79–81), who inaugurated it for the second time in AD 80, and later decorated under Domitian (*reg* AD 81–96).

BIBLIOGRAPHY
P. H. von Blanckenhagen: *Flavische Architektur und ihre Dekoration: Untersucht am Nervaforum* (Berlin, 1940)
G. Cozzo: *Il Colosseo* (Rome, 1971)

LUCA LEONCINI

Vespasiano da Bisticci (*b* ?Florence, *c.* 1421; *bur* Florence, July 1498). Italian bookseller, stationer (*cartolaio*) and writer. He was one of six children of Filippo (*d* 1426), a wool chandler, the eldest of whom, Jacopo (*d* 1468), became a successful doctor after partnering Bernardo Cennini (*b* 1415) as a goldsmith until *c.* 1446. Vespasiano himself recorded that he had no formal education in Latin; by 1434 he was already working for the stationer and binder Michele Guarducci, whose double shop was on the corner of the Via del Proconsolo, the centre of the Florentine book trade, opposite the Palazzo del Podestà (now the Bargello). Humanists such as Niccolò Niccoli, the avid book collector, frequented the shop and encouraged Vespasiano in his studies. By the 1440s he was acting as a bookseller in his own right, although he did not become a partner in the shop until shortly before Guarducci's death in 1451. He exploited the commercial possibilities of manuscripts, especially of the classics and the Church Fathers, written and decorated in the new 'humanistic' style developed in Florence by Niccoli, Poggio Bracciolini and their circle. This was the result of having seen how much demand there had been for such books among the dignitaries and scholars who had assembled in Florence from all over Europe for the Council of Reunion between 1439 and 1443.

Vespasiano made his first known independent sale of a book in 1442, to Pietro Donato, Bishop of Padua; by 1444 he was organizing the transcription of Classical and other texts for the visiting Englishman William Gray, Bishop of Ely, and in 1445–6 Cosimo il Vecchio de' Medici entrusted him with important commissions for purchasing and binding books for the new library of S Marco. By 1446 he was being praised by Girolamo Aliotti, Abbot of SS Fiora e Lucilla at Arezzo, for his remarkable bibliographical knowledge, which shows that he had a more than local reputation. In the 1450s and early 1460s Vespasiano produced a great many luxury books in the new style for Cosimo's sons Piero and Giovanni and also worked for Alfonso I, King of Sicily and Naples, as well as for many lesser clients from Florence and outside. In the early 1460s, at Cosimo's request, he undertook to provide a new library for the Badia of San Domenico di Fiesole. The surviving accounts and manuscripts show that between April 1462 and June 1464 he provided at least 111 manuscripts, most but not all of them newly copied. Vespasiano's most important client for bespoke manuscripts in his later years was Federigo II da Montefeltro, Count and later Duke of Urbino. Vespasiano advised Federigo on the formation of his library and provided a large proportion, running into several hundreds, of the manuscripts that were newly produced for it between about 1465 and 1480. The most famous of these is the two-volume Urbino Bible (Rome, Vatican, Bib. Apostolica, MSS Urb. lat. 1–2), copied in humanistic script, completed in June 1478 by the French scribe Hughes de Comminelles and illuminated by a galaxy of the finest contemporary Florentine illuminators, led by Francesco d'Antonio del Chierico.

Vespasiano also produced copies of texts for which there was a heavy demand—Latin Classical and patristic texts, Greek texts in new humanist translations and works by contemporary humanists, especially Leonardo Bruni—to be sold ready-made in his shop to casual customers (a novelty at this time). These manuscripts were generally copied in humanistic script and given comparatively simple 'white-vine' decoration, sometimes including painted wreaths left blank in which the eventual purchaser could have his own arms painted. When one of these manuscripts was sold to a foreign client, such as the French cleric Jean Jouffroy or the Englishman Robert Flemmyng, Proctor of the King of England at the Roman curia, Vespasiano had one of his scribes (rarely the original scribe of the manuscript) write in a note saying that Vespasiano had produced it. These advertisements, anticipating printers' colophons, have been found in 14 manuscripts. Numerous other manuscripts have notes by owners recording their purchase from Vespasiano and several times, as in the Urbino Bible, scribes state that they were working for him. Most of the leading Florentine scribes and illuminators of his day worked for Vespasiano at one time or another as independent artisans, on a piece-work basis.

With the introduction of printing into Italy in 1465 Vespasiano's trade was particularly badly affected, especially since he apparently refused to sell printed books, unlike most of his Florentine contemporaries. Thus, probably late in 1478, soon after the Urbino Bible had been completed, he gave up his shop and withdrew to the family villa at Antella outside Florence to start a new career as a writer. In 1480 he referred to writing as 'a new thing to me and alien to my profession' but from then on he wrote steadily. The bulk of his best-known work, now generally known as the *Vite di uomini illustri*, was apparently composed over a number of years in the 1480s but was not published until the 19th century. There is one main manuscript (Bologna, Bib. U., MS. 1452), with many autograph additions and corrections, but there are also numerous small presentation manuscripts containing selections of lives sent by Vespasiano to such friends as Filippo Strozzi (the latest of these dates from *c.* 1497), or important single lives, such as the *Vita* of Federigo da Montefeltro, presented to his son Guidobaldo, Duke of Urbino, and the *Vita* of Vespasiano's great friend and mentor Giannozzo Manetti (1396–1459). The *Vite* are in Italian and Vespasiano repeatedly claimed only to be providing material for others to use in more formal lives in Latin. They are in essence reminiscences of his friends and former clients, ranging from King Alfonso I and Pope Nicholas V through cardinals, bishops and distinguished clerics to eminent and not so eminent Florentines. The writing is lively and disorganized, prejudiced and full of anecdotes but the text also includes valuable facts that have often been substantiated from other sources. Vespasiano was noted among his friends as a collector of the latest news. His Florentine *Vite* and other evidence show that he was a supporter of the *via di mezzo* ('the middle way') and that despite his great debt to and affection for Cosimo il Vecchio de' Medici he was very unhappy with developments under Cosimo's successors.

WRITINGS

Vite di uomini illustri (1480s; Bologna, Bib. U., MS. 1452); ed. A. Greco (Florence, 1970); Eng. trans. by W. G. Waters and E. Waters as *Renaissance Princes, Popes and Prelates: The Vespasiano Memoirs* (London, 1926/*R* New York, 1963)

BIBLIOGRAPHY

G. M. Cagni: *Vespasiano da Bisticci e il suo epistolario*, Temi e testi, xv (Rome, 1969)

A. Garzelli: *La bibbia di Federico da Montefeltro* (Rome, 1977)

A. C. de la Mare: 'New Research on Humanistic Scribes in Florence', *Miniatura fiorentina del rinascimento*, ed. A. Garzelli, i (Florence, 1985), pp. 395–600 [lists Vespasiano's MSS]

——: 'Vespasiano da Bisticci e i copisti fiorentini di Federico', *Federico di Montefeltro: La cultura*, ed. G. Cerboni Baiardi, G. Chittolini and P. Floriani, Europa delle corti. Biblioteca del Cinquecento, xxx (Rome, 1986), pp. 81–96

A. C. DE LA MARE

Vespasian Psalter. Illuminated manuscript (255×180 mm; London, BL, Cotton MS. Vesp. A. I) now dated variously between the 720s and the 760s. The monk Thomas of Elmham described this Psalter among the books kept on the high altar of St Augustine's Abbey, Canterbury, in his *Libri missi a Gregorio ad Augustinum* (Cambridge, Trinity Hall, MS. 1) of *c.* 1414–18; he believed it to have been presented to the abbey by the founder. It is one of the earliest Psalters to arrange the Psalms in eight liturgical divisions to aid recitation over the week. Psalms 26 and 52 have historiated initials, with scenes of *David and Jonathan Shaking Hands* (fol. 31*r*) and *David Fighting the Lion* (fol. 53*r*) respectively, and the lost Beatus initial of Psalm 1 may have contained a scene of *Samuel Anointing David*. This is not an ancient practice, and only Bede's *Historia ecclesia* (St Petersburg, Rus. N. Pub. Lib., MS. Q. v. I. 18) from Wearmouth/Jarrow has historiated initials that could be earlier. The frontispiece (now fol. 30*v*, before Psalm 26) depicts King David playing the lyre between two scribes who write on a scroll and a wax diptych; in the same space four men play wind instruments while two others dance. The ornamentation and script suggest that the Psalter was produced in southern England, and it can be compared with other manuscripts thought to have been made at Canterbury, such as the Codex Aureus (*c.* 750; Stockholm, Kun. Bib., MS. A. 135) and the Canterbury Bible fragments (late 8th century; London, BL, MS. Royal I. E. VI; Canterbury, Cathedral Archvs & Lib. & City Rec. Office, Additional MS. 16). Their decoration seems to have common Early Christian prototypes. The stocky figures, broad areas of drapery and thick lines of articulation in the Psalter also suggest Italian intermediaries, while motifs such as confronted beasts and heraldically displayed birds (especially on the frontispiece) may be adapted from either Coptic or Byzantine textiles. The framing device and composition of the frontispiece resemble the 9th-century Byzantine Khludov Psalter (Moscow, Hist. Mus., MS. 129. D), and both may ultimately derive from a common Early Christian source. An almost identical lyre to that carried by David was found in the Sutton Hoo ship burial (625 or later; London, BM), indicating that contemporary as well as ancient sources were used.

BIBLIOGRAPHY

D. H. Wright: *The Vespasian Psalter*, Early English Manuscripts in Facsimile, xiv (Copenhagen, 1967)

J. J. G. Alexander: *Insular Manuscripts of the 6th to 9th Century* (London, 1978) [bibliog.]

M. A. MICHAEL

Vespignani, Virgilio [Virginio] (*b* Rome, 12 Feb 1808; *d* Rome, 4 Dec 1882). Italian architect. As a young draughtsman he contributed illustrations to books popularizing Roman archaeology, such as Edward Dodwell's *I sette colli di Roma* (London, 1829). Vespignani trained under LUIGI POLETTI and worked with him (1837–69) on the reconstruction of S Paolo fuori le mura, continuing the work on Poletti's death. Three sides of the great quadriporticus were finished (1893) to his designs after his own death. A favourite of Pope Pius IX (*reg* 1846–78), he benefited from the many papal commissions generated during his reign. He applied historical revival styles to his work, for instance in his Madonna dell'Archetto Chapel (1851) in the Via di S Marcello, and the Confessio (1864) in S Maria Maggiore, both in Rome. Three early works were public monuments in Rome, including the new façade of the Porta Pia (1852–68), an eclectic work with elements borrowed from the Arch of Titus. In contrast, his Porta S Pancrazio (1857) and the entrance and cemetery chapel of S Maria della Misericordia in the Campo Verano are formal and restrained. Other commissions in Rome followed, including the restoration of the 17th-century S Carlo ai Catinari (1861), the tabernacle of the high altar (after 1863) in S Maria in Trastevere, and the restoration of S Lorenzo fuori le mura (1864–70; with G. B. de Rossi). On the Medieval Revival apse of S Giovanni in Laterano (1874–84) and the church of S Tommaso di Canterbury (1888), he collaborated with his son Francesco Vespignani (1842–99), who finished them after his father's death. The Serra all'Orto Botanico (1855) in glass and cast iron, his monument to Pope Pius IX in the Vatican, and his theatres in Viterbo (1855) and Orvieto indicate the wide-ranging knowledge of materials and styles required of architects in mid-19th-century Rome. He was city architect to Rome, a member of the pontifical commission on antiquities and President of the Accademia di S Luca.

BIBLIOGRAPHY

Portoghesi; Thieme–Becker

C. L. V. Meeks; *Italian Architecture, 1750–1914* (New Haven and London, 1966), pp. 121, 251

R. Jodice: *L'architettura del ferro d'Italia* (Rome, 1985), pp. 175, 176, 178

GRETCHEN G. FOX

Vespinis. *See* WESPIN.

Vespucci. Italian family of merchants and patrons. The family originally came from Peretola, moving to Florence during the 14th century. They settled in the parish of S Lucia a Ognissanti, where they grew rich through trade and financial dealing. According to Vasari, at the end of the 15th century and in the first half of the 16th the Vespucci distinguished themselves as patrons. Simone Vespucci (*c.* 1438–1500), the Podestà of Monte S Savino, sponsored Andrea Sansovino at the beginning of his career, bringing him to Florence and providing for his artistic education. In his house near the Ponte Vecchio he had a collection of Sansovino's drawings and modelli. The family also had a large house in Via de' Servi, bought in 1499 by Guidantonio Vespucci (1434–1501; not Giovanni Vespucci, as Vasari says), who commissioned decorations for his new rooms from Piero di Cosimo and Botticelli, an artist closely associated with the Vespucci. Piero di Cosimo painted Bacchanalian scenes with 'fauns, satyrs, woodland gods and putti and bacchanti' (Vasari). These works may perhaps be identified as the *Discovery of Honey* (Worcester, MA, A. Mus.) and the *Misfortunes of Silenus* (Cambridge, MA, Fogg). Botticelli painted 'very lively and beautiful figures' (Vasari), perhaps the scenes from the *Life of Virginia* (Bergamo, Gal. Accad. Carrara) and the scenes from the *Life of Lucrezia* (Boston, MA, Isabella Stewart Gardner Mus.).

For the Vespucci Chapel in the church of the Ognissanti, Domenico Ghirlandaio and Davide Ghirlandaio painted the fresco of the *Madonna of Mercy* (*c.* 1470–71), which includes members of the Vespucci family. Among them is Amerigo Vespucci (1451–1512), the famous explorer, who, according to Vasari, also appears in a drawing by Leonardo. In the same church Botticelli painted *St Augustine in his Study* (1480), and some scholars believe that it was Giorgio Antonio Vespucci (1434–after 1499), the tutor of Lorenzo di Pierfrancesco de' Medici, who procured for Botticelli the commission of the *Primavera* (*c.* 1478; Florence, Uffizi; *see* BOTTICELI, SANDRO, fig. 2). Tradition has it that Simonetta Vespucci (1453–75), who married Marco di Piero Vespucci *c.* 1468, served as a model for the *Primavera* and for other works by the painter. Niccolò Vespucci (1474–*c.* 1535), the Cavaliere of Rhodes, was a man of culture and an art patron. In his house near the Ponte Vecchio he was host to Ludovico Ariosto and later also to the young Vasari, whose artistic career he afterwards continued to sponsor. Niccolò was painted by Giulio Romano in one of the frescoes in the Sala di Costantino in the Vatican Palace, Rome.

BIBLIOGRAPHY

G. Vasari: *Vite* (1550, rev. 2/1568); ed. G. Milanesi (1878–85), iii, pp. 255, 311–12; iv, pp. 26, 141; v, pp. 510, 530; vii, p. 7

A. M. Bandini: *Vite di Amerigo Vespucci* (Florence, 1898), pp. 2–14, 67–94

R. Langton Douglas: 'The Contemporary Portraits of Amerigo Vespucci', *Burl. Mag.*, lxxxiv (1944), pp. 34–56

——: *Piero di Cosimo* (Chicago, 1946)

G. Arciniegas: 'Come nacque la Primavera', *Confer. Assoc. Cult. It.*, x (1963)

C. Rosselli del Turco: *I Vespucci* (Florence, 1985)

DONATELLA PEGAZZANO

Vessanagara. *See* BESNAGAR.

Vestier, Antoine (*b* Avallon, Yonne, 28 April 1740; *d* Paris, 24 Dec 1824). French painter. After seeing Vestier's *Ascension* in the principal church of Avallon, a local notable, Philippe-Louis de Chastellux (1726–87), funded the painter's journey to Paris, where he entered the studio of Jean-Baptiste Marie Pierre. He was also taught the technique of enamel painting by his future father-in-law, Antoine Révérand (*d* before 1764), and he worked in Paris as a painter of portrait miniatures in enamels. He gained few commissions until after 1766, however, when he became the painter of the powerful d'Hozier family. In 1774 he exhibited at the Salon of the Académie de St Luc, and in 1776 he went to London, where he probably knew Philippe-Jacques de Loutherbourg and possibly Thomas Gainsborough.

Vestier returned to Paris by late 1777, but his career did not flourish until 1782, when he exhibited at the Salon de la Correspondance. He was approved (*agréé*) by the Académie Royale de Peinture et de Sculpture in 1785 and received (*reçu*) the following year on presentation of his portraits of the painters *Nicolas-Guy Brenet* (Versailles, Château) and *Gabriel-François Doyen* (Paris, Louvre). From 1785 to 1791 he exhibited regularly at the Salon, where he enjoyed considerable critical acclaim. He had by this time virtually ceased painting miniatures (of which there are examples in Paris at the Louvre and the Musée Carnavalet) to concentrate on easel painting, drawing his clients from the nobility and the upper bourgeoisie. He also portrayed actors and musicians and, frequently, members of his own family, including *Mme Vestier with a Child and a Dog* (1787; Paris, Louvre).

Vestier's portrait of *Jean-Henri Masers, Chevalier de Latude before the Bastille* (Paris, Carnavalet) was one of the few works exhibited at the 1789 Salon that may be directly associated with the French Revolution. He was, however, soon among the many artists for whom the Revolution meant economic distress, as his traditional clientele evaporated. He did not exhibit again until 1795 and in 1796 was given lodgings at the Louvre, but complained about the inadequacy of his rooms—as a result of which for a few years he painted only miniatures. In 1806 the government refused for a second time to build him a studio at the Sorbonne, where he had moved in 1802. Following this he painted nothing for the rest of his life.

In his years of prosperity Vestier was regarded highly, both for the psychological and physiological truth of his portraits, and for the rendering of still-life accessories and costume. His portrait of *Jean-Henri Riesener* (1786; Versailles, Château) is a particularly fine example of this. His works are often well composed, with harmonious colours, and give his sitters considerable presence. The better ones are far from formulaic. His three-quarter-length portrait of *Fusilier Jean Theurel* (1788; Tours, Mus. B.-A.) has a simplicity and directness that contrast with the more rhetorical and elaborate *Latude*. His success was partly due to careful preparation and technique: unusually, he prepared his own linseed oil and date-marked his pigments to ensure their freshness. He sometimes used pastel. He rarely worked outside the genre of portraiture.

BIBLIOGRAPHY

A. -M. Passez: *Antoine Vestier, 1740–1824* (Paris, 1989)

HUMPHREY WINE

Vestments, ecclesiastical. Garments and items used by the clergy.

1. Pre-Reformation. 2. Post-Reformation.

1. PRE-REFORMATION. The form of ecclesiastical vestments in the Early Christian period and during the Middle Ages is known largely from works of art rather than extant objects. Textiles are susceptible to decay with time, and although a number of vestments survive from the 14th and 15th centuries, few survive from the earlier centuries, when vestment forms were developing. Visual information is provided by mosaics, wall, panel and manuscript paintings, ivories, illuminated manuscripts and above all from tomb sculpture and sepulchral brasses.

Such evidence is abundant from the 6th century, but from the earliest years of the development of vesture for the rituals of the church it is largely lacking. It can generally be concluded, however, that most Christian vestments were derived from late Roman secular dress. It is unlikely that the ritual garments of the Jewish levitical priesthood had much influence on this early development, although this cannot be completely excluded. In the Middle Ages, when it was of importance to explain the symbolic function of vestments, writers frequently linked the Christian vestments with those described in the Old Testament for Aaron and the priests of the Old Law. Such medieval interpretations have clouded the issue as to whether any aspect of Christian vesture did originate in Jewish forms.

As vestments developed for Christian rituals they became differentiated according to the rank of the clergy and the liturgical function. For the lower orders, such as that of acolyte, the vestments were nothing more than the basic undergarments of the higher clergy. In contrast, episcopal vesture in its fullest late medieval development incorporated every one of the garments worn by the clergy of rank below the bishop, as though the bishop's authority over the lower ranks were symbolized by his wearing their characteristic vestments. In the Early Christian period and the earlier years of the Middle Ages there was less hierarchic distinction, and even acolytes may in those years have worn certain vestments that later became restricted to the higher orders of the clergy. An extreme case would be the fanon, a special form of amice, which was worn by lower ranks of the clergy in the early Middle Ages but by the end of the Middle Ages became restricted to the pope alone. Another factor is that there were regional variations in vesture for the various ranks of clergy, and also variations in practice between the religious orders. Certain unusual garments such as the rationale, an alternative to the pallium, were restricted to a few dioceses, as also were special forms of the mitre. In the 14th century, for example, the Archbishops of Benevento still wore a mitre, which was of a conical form resembling the papal tiara.

The basic division of vestments are between those for the mass and those for the Divine Office and processions. Most of the undergarments, used for all these functions, are discussed first.

(i) Undergarments. (ii) Mass vestments. (iii) Office and processional vestments.

(i) Undergarments. These were worn by all orders of the secular clergy. For the religious orders their particular form of habits also served as undergarments to vestments when these were required for the celebration of mass or for festal celebration of the Office.

Alb. White, linen, long-sleeved garment like a full-length vest worn over the cassock for the mass under the chasuble and for the priest officiating at the Office under the cope. It originated from an undergarment of the Roman period. Those medieval writers who argued for continuity from Jewish vesture thought it to be the descendant of the linen ephod of the levitical priesthood. In some regions it was worn by all serving at the altar for both the mass and the Office. In others it was restricted to the orders of subdeacon upwards, the lesser orders wearing the surplice or cotta. In some dioceses and religious orders on major feast days the whole community of a particular church would wear albs, just as on the very greatest feast days they would all wear copes. In the early Middle Ages it was sometimes ornamented with vertical coloured bands. In the later Middle Ages it was more extensively decorated on the sleeves, on the back and front of the upper section and on the lower hem with embroidered square rectangular bands called apparels.

Amice. Rectangular piece of linen with two strings or tapes attached. It originated from the Roman *amictus*, a form of hood-scarf to protect outer garments. It is placed over the head in the manner of a hood and the two strings are crossed over the chest and tied around the waist. After the alb is put on, the amice is pulled back from the head to rest around the neck in the manner of a scarf. During the later Middle Ages, perhaps in some regions as early as the 10th century, a rectangular apparel was placed on the amice such that it would form a sort of collar at the back of the neck. It was worn by all clergy of the higher orders when celebrating mass.

Cassock. Full-length, long-sleeved coat with buttons up the front from neck to foot, worn with a belt or girdle. It was frequently lined with fur in the colder regions of northern Europe, giving rise to the name pelliceum. From the 14th century it had a collar. It is a garment that could be worn outside of the church as well as being an undergarment for liturgical functions.

Cincture. Girdle tied around the waist of the alb; it could be embroidered.

Fanon. Ornamented or embroidered form of amice worn over the alb. It is circular with a round hole in the centre so that it can be placed over the head and extends just over the top of the shoulders to fall in a semicircle in front and at the back in the manner of a short cape. Until the 12th century it was worn in certain places by several orders of the clergy, but in the later centuries it became restricted to the pope alone.

Girdle. See *Cincture* above.

Rochet. Another garment that originated as a variant of the alb but with tighter sleeves, no belt, and in its developed form reaching to just below the knee. It was in some cases in the Early Middle Ages worn over the alb by priests and bishops. By the 13th century it became restricted to higher prelates, bishops, cardinals and certain religious orders (e.g. some of the regular canons). The rochet could be worn as a non-liturgical garment outside church at secular functions where the higher clergy were present.

Subcinctorium. Small girdle looped over the cincture hanging down at the side. It was perhaps first used for bishops in France and later became part of the vesture of the pope and higher prelates elsewhere. Its function is unclear, but it may originally have served a purpose in securing the stole in place; it was not, however, widely used.

Surplice. White linen full vest with wide sleeves falling some way below the waist and worn over the cassock, hence its name superpelliceum. In some regions it was called a cotta and had narrower and shorter sleeves. It originated as a short form of the alb and was later used as an alternative to the alb for the lower orders of the clergy and as a choir vestment.

(ii) Mass vestments. Most of the undergarments, as they were appropriate to the rank of the clergy, would be worn under the vestments specific to the sacred ministers involved in the celebration of mass: the sub-deacon, the deacon and the priest or bishop. These vestments denoted their rank and came to be so specified in the rites of ordination.

Chasuble. Vestment for the priest celebrant at mass (see fig. 1; see also GERMANY, fig. 79, and GOTHIC, fig. 115). It is in the form of a closed cloak with a hole for the head and is derived from the Roman penula. Early chasubles were made from a semicircular piece of fabric. During the Middle Ages they became less full as segments were cut away so that when folded they would appear conical rather than as a quarter-circle. In the late 15th century and the early 16th they became even more restricted in size as pieces were cut out of the sides to allow freer movement of the arms. This was probably a practical development in view of the excessive weight of the heavily embroidered and jewelled form of this vestment in the late Middle Ages. When celebrant at mass, the bishop wore the chasuble over the dalmatic and tunicle.

Dalmatic. Similar in shape to the tunicle, this was the mass vestment for the deacon and was worn beneath the chasuble by the bishop. It orginated from a ceremonial garment worn by high officials, consuls and emperors in Late Antiquity. It began as a longer garment but was shortened to the knee. Like the tunicle it was decorated with orphreys (embroidered strips of ornament; see fig. 2 below), tassels and fringes and had slits up the side. In the early Middle Ages dalmatics were white with coloured decorative bands. In the 12th century they became fully coloured to match the colour of the chasuble according to the liturgical feast or season.

Maniple. Wide, short strip of ornamented coloured fabric worn hanging over the left wrist and secured by a clasp. It probably originated as a form of towel or handkerchief, but in the Middle Ages it served no functional purpose. In the early Middle Ages it was used by most ranks of the clergy, but by the 10th century its use was restricted to the ranks of subdeacon upwards.

Orarium. See *Stole* below.

Pallium. Form of white, woollen scarf ornamented with black crosses, worn over the chasuble and made of a thin strip of fabric hanging over the shoulders and forming a Y shape over the chest and back. It was first restricted to bishops and from the 8th century was exclusive to archbishops except in very exceptional cases. In the same period it came to be conferred only by the pope himself.

Rationale. Version of the pallium worn in the same way over the chasuble in certain dioceses in Germany, Eastern Europe and the patriarchate of Aquileia (where it was worn under the pallium as an additional vestment). The rationale is usually H-shaped with a very broad, horizontal bar with a hole in the centre so that it can be placed over the head, and with the two verticals of the H covering the

1. Chasuble, linen embroidered with silk, 1.23×0.73 mm, made in the convent of Göss, near Leoben, Austria, mid-13th century (Vienna, Österreichisches Museum für Angewandte Kunst)

shoulders and falling over the chest and back. An alternative form was of two Y shapes meeting at the edge of the shoulder. It was heavily ornamented, sometimes with gold and silver.

Stole. This is essentially a coloured scarf worn over the alb, formed of a long, wide band of fabric long enough to extend to the ankles (*see* ANGLO-SAXON ART, fig. 15). It probably originated from the insignia of a Roman consul and was a mark of rank. In the early days of the Church it was worn by subdeacons, but it later became restricted to deacons and priests. The deacon wore it over the left shoulder and not around the neck. The priest wore it around the neck, and in later centuries it was crossed over his chest and secured in that position by the cincture. The stole was also worn by the priest for certain sacramental functions and offices other than mass, namely for the sacraments of baptism, penance, marriage and extreme unction, for the churching of women after childbirth and for the burial service.

Tunicle. Tunic resembling a long, full vest with wide, short sleeves of coloured or embroidered fabric reaching to the knees. The embroidery sometimes takes the form of orphreys and frequently has tassels and fringes at its edges. In the later centuries slits were introduced in the sides to the point where the sleeves begin. In the early Middle Ages a simple tunicle was worn even by acolytes, but it later became restricted to subdeacons. Bishops in full mass vestments wore the tunicle below the dalmatic and chasuble. In such pontifical vesture the tunicle was usually slightly longer than the dalmatic.

(iii) Office and processional vestments.

Almuce. Cloak with a hood, often partly of fur or fur-lined, which was of variable length; some were only in the form of a shoulder cape, others fell to below the waist. It was a choir garment worn over the cassock and surplice or alb and originated primarily to provide extra warmth.

Biretta. Cap, initially little more than an enlarged skullcap, first used in choir but later also at mass when processing and when seated. In the 14th and 15th centuries it became higher and was strengthened by stiff ridges. The colour varied according to rank.

Cappa magna. Voluminous, circular, purple or red cloak, having a large hood attached and with a hole for the head, worn by higher prelates, bishops and cardinals. In view of its size the cappa magna at the back trailed on the ground, and the front had to be partly draped over one arm to allow free movement of the feet. This very full form did not develop until the 14th century.

Chimere. Cloak with slits for the arms and buttons fastening the front, falling to just below the knee. It was worn over the cassock and surplice or rochet. It was essentially a cloak for use outdoors and not strictly speaking a vestment for liturgical use. It was most frequently worn by higher prelates, bishops and other higher prelates and was either purple or red.

Comb. Ivory combs carved with ornament or figure scenes were used ceremonially in the vesting of a bishop before mass.

2. Mitre and cope with morse, orphreys and hood as worn by *St Martin* (left), detail from *Canon Bernardinus de Salviatis and Three Saints* by Gerard David, 1.03×0.95 m, 1501 (London, National Gallery)

Cope. This is in the form of a semicircle worn as an open cloak, which has to be fastened at the neck by a morse (pectorale) of embroidery or metal (see fig. 2). Its origin as a cloak is evident from the small, non-functional hood that hangs over the garment at the back of the neck. It is often referred to as a pluviale, a garment providing protection from the rain, which designates its original purpose as an outdoor garment without a liturgical function. The cope was used for processions on great feasts and before the Sunday High Mass, and also for the priests officiating in the Office. Simpler forms of choir copes were used by the leaders of the choir (cantors) and by canons and monks in choir on major feast days. It was also used for the marriage and burial services, the former taking place in the Middle Ages at the church porch and the latter of course being another open-air liturgical ceremony. Of all vestments the cope received the richest ornamentation, its large size allowing artists scope for elaborate designs. The embroidered copes of OPUS AN-GLICANUM, for example, attained a peak of luxury and artistic brilliance of technique and design seldom excelled in the history of costume (*see* GOTHIC, fig. 113).

Crosier. Staff carried by the bishop at mass and in processions as the symbol of his pastoral office. From its earliest examples it had the form of a shepherd's crook with a hook at the top, although this soon became stylized into spiral shapes. For further information *see* CROSIER.

Gloves. From the 10th century bishops wore ornamented gloves as a vestment. They were usually decorated with a prominent jewelled or embroidered circular ornament on the front side.

Gremiale. Square piece of embroidered cloth placed over the bishop's lap when seated at mass. It perhaps originated to serve the practical function of protecting his richly embroidered chasuble from being soiled by his hands.

Humeral veil. Silken shawl that covered the shoulders and most of the upper part of the body. It was worn over the chasuble or cope when the Host in the pyx or monstrance was carried in procession and by the subdeacon over the tunicle when carrying the paten at High Mass. This vestment would be used, for example, in the procession on the feast of Corpus Christi.

Mitre. Bishops wore distinctive headgear from the earliest days of the Church. The first forms of the mitre were conical or helmet-like in form, a shape that persisted in the papal tiara. In the 12th century the mitre was given 'horns' and by the early 13th century developed into the established form of two attached spherical triangles. The two strips of fabric (lappets) that hang from the back or sides may have once had some practical function for attaching the mitre (see fig. 2 above).

Mozzetta. Fur and velvet cape with a hood, fastened in the front with buttons and falling to below the elbow. It was red or purple and was worn by bishops, cardinals and the pope. It can be considered as a form of the almuce for higher prelates.

Ring. Prominent jewelled ring that was worn by bishops, cardinals and abbots. The use of the ring probably originated from the custom of using the engraved design on the jewel or stone as a seal to authenticate documents. It thus represented the authority of the bishop.

Shoes and stockings. Special embroidered stockings (buskins) and shoes (sandals) were part of a bishop's vesture. The shoes, although called sandals, were of cloth that covered the whole foot and had a leather sole.

Skullcap. Small cap covering the tonsure, black for priests and red or purple for higher prelates. At mass it was removed at the beginning of the canon prayer.

Sudarium. Piece of silk attached to the knob of a crosier so that when carried it absorbed the sweat of the bishop's hands and assisted his grip on the staff.

Tiara. Form of mitre worn by the pope, which developed from the early conical helmet form of the mitre. In the 11th century a crown-like band was introduced to encircle the base to signify the pope's temporal authority. In the 13th century Pope Gregory IX and Pope Boniface VIII had first one and then two crowns. By 1300 the tiara had reached the form it was to have for the remainder of the Middle Ages.

See also EARLY CHRISTIAN AND BYZANTINE ART, §VII, 3(ii); ANGLO-SAXON ART, §VIII; ROMANESQUE, §X; and GOTHIC, §IX.

BIBLIOGRAPHY

EWA: 'Liturgical and Ritual Objects'; *LM*: 'Kamm'; *RDK*: 'Albe', 'Almutie', 'Amikt', 'Aurifrisium', 'Birett', 'Bischofshandschuhe', 'Bischofsschuhe', 'Cappa Magna', 'Dalmatik', 'Fano', 'Farbe, liturgisch'
F. Bock: *Geschichte der liturgischen Gewänder des Mittelalters*, 3 vols (Bonn, 1859–71)
W. B. Marriott: *Vestiarium Christianum* (London, 1868)
M. H. Bloxam: *Companion to the Principles of Gothic Ecclesiastical Architecture, Being a Brief Account of the Vestments* (London, 1882)
L. de Farcy: *La Broderie du XIe siècle jusqu'à nos jours d'après des spécimens anciens et les anciens inventaires*, 3 vols (Angers, 1890–1900)
O. J. Reichel: *English Liturgical Vestments in the Thirteenth Century* (London, 1895)
R. A. S. Macalister: *Ecclesiastical Vestments* (London, 1896)
H. Druitt: *A Manual of Costume as Illustrated on Monumental Brasses* (London, 1906; *R* Bath, 1970)
J. Braun: *Die liturgische Gewandung in Occident und Orient* (Freiburg im Breisgau, 1907)
F. Cabrol and H. Leclercq: *Dictionnaire d'archéologie chrétienne et de liturgie* (Paris, 1907–53)
J. Braun: *Handbuch der Paramentik* (Freiburg im Breisgau, 1912)
C. Enlart: *Le Costume*, iii of *Manuel d'archéologie française* (Paris, 1916), pp. 318–42, 367–88
W. St John Hope and E. G. C. F. Atchley: *English Liturgical Colours* (London, 1918)
H. J. Clayton: *The Ornaments of the Ministers as Shown on English Monumental Brasses*, Alcuin Club Collections, xxii (1919)
H. Norris: *Church Vestments* (London, 1949)
P. Salmon: *Etude sur les insignes du pontif dans le rite romain* (Rome, 1955)
J. Hayward: 'Sacred Vestments as they Developed in the Middle Ages', *Bull. Met.*, xxix (1971), pp. 299–309
B. Sirch: *Der Ursprung der bischöflichen Mitra und päpstlichen Tiara* (St Ottilien, 1975)
G. B. Ladner: 'Der Ursprung und die mittelalterliche Entwicklung der päpstlichen Tiara', *Festschrift R. Hampe* (Mainz, 1979), pp. 449–81
R. E. Reynolds: 'Image and Text: The Liturgy of Clerical Ordination in Early Medieval Art', *Gesta*, xxii (1983), pp. 27–38
J. Mayo: *A History of Ecclesiastical Dress* (London, 1984)

NIGEL J. MORGAN

2. POST-REFORMATION. The strong demand for reform in the Church during the first half of the 16th century, based principally on the thinking of Martin Luther and John Calvin (1509–64), led not only to sharp doctrinal division in the Church but also to unprecedented changes in liturgical practice in those areas that adopted the new ideas: all ceremony was to be obliterated from church services, as well as all artefacts made of costly materials, especially those showing representations of the saints and other holy figures, which were thought to encourage idolatry.

These stringent prohibitions meant that the mass vestments ceased to be used in much of northern Europe, including England. In countries faithful to the Roman Catholic Church, however, ceremonial remained unchanged and the use of the vestments continued. Makers looked increasingly to fine, brocaded silks produced by the developing Italian, and later French, industries to provide a sumptuous effect, although as the 16th century progressed the silks themselves became less dramatic in style, and embroidery was confined to orphreys.

An important innovation in 16th-century embroidery was the use of fashionable Renaissance motifs and ornament derived from newly discovered late Classical models (e.g. chasuble, *c.* 1550–75; Florence, Mus. Opera Duomo). This decoration, which lent itself especially well to gold embroidery, was composed of vases filled with formalized foliage, scrolls and strapwork and, in the vertical arrangements known as candelabrum, was particularly suitable for the narrow orphrey bands (e.g. of late 16th century; Paris, Mus. Cluny). Only the masks and satyrs that were a feature of the style in secular use were omitted from the vestments.

There was also a gradual decline during this period in figure embroidery, which had hitherto been all important. Although a few leading artists continued to accept commissions for designs for major vestment sets, the increasing rarity of elaborate biblical scenes was partly due to the fact that the social status of artists changed during the 16th century, and they became less willing to design for embroidery and other crafts. Where figure embroidery did exist, it was usually used to depict individual saints, very often shown half-length and framed in roundels, in accordance with the strongly classicizing mood. The sophisticated technique of *or nué* (gold shaded with colour), which had been developed by Flemish workers in the 15th century, continued to be used for ornament and figures, although less frequently.

Particularly fine vestments were made in Spain from the late 16th century to the 17th, using rich brocaded velvets and elaborate gold embroidery in the Renaissance style. Spanish embroiderers also developed special techniques for figure embroideries, which used gold thread more economically (*see* SPAIN, §XI, 3).

Throughout the 17th and 18th centuries vestments became more closely related to the decorative as opposed to the fine arts. Decoration followed successively the Baroque, Rococo and Neo-classical styles. By the end of the 17th century the counter-offensive of the Roman Catholic Church against the reformed churches entered a second phase, moving from the early austerities of the Council of Trent (1545–63) to a deliberate policy of attracting congregations with light, colour and ceremony, in contrast to the stark surroundings of Calvinism. During this period an enormous number of vestments was made, especially in southern Germany and Central Europe, to complement the many churches built or redecorated in the flamboyant Baroque style (*see* AUSTRIA, fig. 41). The mood of the Baroque in both silk-weaving and embroidery was expressed above all in floral decoration, influenced by the royal gardens created in France for the purpose of growing exotic plants, and by the rich, formal compositions of the Dutch flower painters (e.g. chasuble, *c.* 1700; Vienna, Osterreich. Mus. Angewandte Kst; see fig. 3).

Woven silks remained exceedingly important in the making of vestments, especially the newly flamboyant designs created by the silk-weavers in Lyon during the early 18th century (*see* LYON, §3(ii)). Silks were also woven to designs specifically intended for church use. The woven pattern would often be further enriched with decorative gold and floral embroidery, while illustrative scenes became increasingly unusual. The *or nué* technique was by this time completely abandoned, and both flowers and the rare figure subjects were carried out in glossy coloured silks in the flat technique sometimes called needle-painting. Embroiderers using gold employed a rich variety of techniques and threads. Baroque patterns remained popular with vestment makers well into the 18th century. The graceful, asymmetrical Rococo style was more often found in woven silks than in church embroidery.

During this period, although the medieval church rules for the use of different coloured vestments for different seasons were still theoretically in force, the emphasis was no longer on the rich crimsons of the Renaissance. Multi-coloured brocading or embroidery on a white satin ground

3. Chasuble, linen and silk, embroidered with silk and couched gold and silver threads 1.0×0.7 m, made in the convent of the Ursulines, Vienna, *c.* 1700 (Vienna, Österreichisches Museum für Angewandte Kunst)

was probably the most popular style, largely because of the increase in the number of feasts of the Virgin, for which white was mandatory, but vestments were made in almost any light and cheerful colour. The cutting back of the medieval chasuble shape, which by the 15th century had resulted in a straight chasuble in northern countries, was by this time complete, and for at least 250 years all chasubles were made approximately the width of the wearer's shoulders.

After a period when another wave of Church reform and the antagonism engendered by the French Revolution and Napoleonic Wars (1802–15) discouraged expenditure on elaborate ritual, vestments that were a continuation of late 18th-century styles were still made for the Roman Catholic Church in the southern European countries. Some 19th-century trends become clear, such as a thinning or paring down of the design, with a marked increase in the popular motifs of wheat ears and grapes and a revival of figure embroidery. Since the fashionable dress materials of the early 19th century were too lightweight to be suitable for church vestments, many more silks were woven specially for church use, often incorporating these motifs as well as such symbols as the cross and the IHS monogram. A very high technical standard of gold embroidery persisted in some areas, but vestments were even made in the popular wool cross-stitch known as Berlin woolwork.

In the Roman Catholic areas of northern Europe (the Netherlands, Belgium and the Lower Rhine) during the second half of the 19th century vestment makers began to look back to the Middle Ages, reintroducing the 'Gothic' chasuble, which in this case was not in fact the medieval bell chasuble but the partly cut-back 16th-century version. With this shape of chasuble came a revival of the medieval Y-shaped orphrey and figure embroidery, especially of standing figures of saints set in architectural arcading in the medieval style. There was also a return to the medieval colour canon with strong 'liturgical' colours. By the end of the 19th century silk-weavers in the leading centres were copying medieval and Renaissance designs, which were widely used for vestments. The Church in Italy, which had been the last to adopt the straight chasuble, did not return to the so-called Gothic shape until after World War II.

In England the Ecclesiologists, and later a second generation of Tractarian leaders, directed their efforts to reintroducing the mass vestments, which had not been seen since the end of Elizabeth I's reign. They also wished to turn the Anglican Church back to medieval practice, modelled on what the exponents of this reform felt to be the 'best' period of English architecture and worship, that is the 13th and 14th centuries (see GOTHIC REVIVAL). The 16th century version of the medieval chasuble shape was actually reintroduced in England before it reappeared elsewhere in Europe. Architects and church furnishers were aware that English embroidery had been outstanding in the Middle Ages, but they were unsure of what they were reproducing, and the technical expertise was at first unavailable to them. As a result some very individual vestments and altar furnishings were made, based for the most part on motifs used in English church embroidery of the late 15th century and markedly different from their European counterparts. By the end of the century convents and various embroidery groups as well as the church furnishers were producing highly expert embroidery.

During the early 20th century and the period between the two World Wars there was a considerable reduction everywhere in richly decorated vestments, probably because of the increasing cost of professional hand embroidery and a reluctance to spend lavishly on display in the church. Church furnishers at this time relied heavily on orphreys of woven braids, often in the Y-shaped format on a neo-Gothic chasuble; the straight chasuble was frequently decorated with a narrow braid cross on the back. After World War II there developed a school of embroidery designers working for the Church in England in a completely modern idiom, a trend that has not been seriously rivalled in the rest of Europe.

For bibliography see §1 above.

PAULINE JOHNSTONE

Vestner, Georg Wilhelm (b Schweinfurt, 1 Sept 1677; d Nuremberg, 1 Dec 1740). German medallist. Having been apprenticed to his father as a gingerbread baker, he studied drawing and sculpture at the Akademie in Nuremberg. He then spent several years travelling in the Netherlands, England and Switzerland, where he was employed for about a year (1701) by the Bishop of Chur at the local mint. Settling in Nuremberg in 1704, he joined the guild of gingerbread bakers as a master but also became a die-cutter at the mint. The first medal that can be securely attributed to him (Bernheimer, no. 2) dates from 1710 and is signed with a V. In the following two years Vestner executed 34 medals commemorating the coronation of the Holy Roman Emperor Charles VI in Frankfurt and in Bratislava (Ger. Pressburg) and the homage ceremony in Nuremberg. In 1712 he cut the dies for 96 medals (Bernheimer, nos 523–618) in a series of 250 papal portraits issued by Caspar Gottlieb Lauffer (1674–1745). In 1728 Vestner received a privilege from Charles VI that permitted him to strike medals and protected them from imitation; only a few German medallists were prolific enough to need such a privilege. A large number of Vestner's medals commemorating military events, peace treaties or important events in the life of the imperial family were intended for sale to collectors. A series of portrait medals depicting the delegates who had concluded the Peace of Westphalia in 1648 was left uncompleted after 44 medals (Bernheimer, nos 479–522) had been struck. As well as these, he produced numerous portrait medals on commission from Princes of the Church and royal personages as well as private individuals.

Vestner's son Andreas Vestner (b Nuremberg, 5 Sept 1707; d Nuremberg, 12 March 1754) was trained as a die-cutter in his father's workshop and cut his first medal die when he was only thirteen. His first medal (Bernheimer, no. 189), signed AV and commemorating the coronation of Louis XV of France at Reims, appeared in 1722. In 1726 he became his father's partner and also joined him as a die-cutter at the Nuremberg mint. Andreas adopted his father's style so closely that most of the medals produced in the Vestner workshop between 1720 and 1740 cannot be definitely ascribed to either father or son. Andreas renewed the imperial privilege granted to his father in 1738 and 1748. Their combined oeuvre consists of more than 600 medals, as well as coin dies; nearly 150 design sketches survive (e.g. Berlin, Kstbib. & Mus.).

BIBLIOGRAPHY

Forrer; Thieme–Becker
J. H. Lochner: *Sammlung merkwürdiger Medaillen*, iv (Nuremberg, 1740)
C. Thon: 'Medaillenentwürfe von Georg Wilhelm und Andreas Vestner', *Z. Dt. Ver. Kstwiss.*, xxxvi (1982), pp. 49–77
F. Bernheimer: *Georg Wilhelm Vestner und Andreas Vestner: Zwei Nürnberger Medailleure* (Munich, 1984)
G. Dethlefs: 'Lauffer contra Vestner: Zur Medaillenprägung in Nürnberg, 1714–1732', *Münster. Numi. Ztg*, xix (1989), pp. 9–11; xx (1990), pp. 4–7

HERMANN MAUÉ

Vestry. See SACRISTY.

Veth, Jan Pieter (b Dordrecht, 18 May 1864; d Amsterdam, 1 July 1925). Dutch painter, graphic artist, poet and critic. He was trained by August Allebé at the Amsterdam Rijksacademie. The circle of Allebé's pupils with whom he associated, including George Hendrik Breitner, Willem Witsen and Jacobus van Looy, were known as the 'Amsterdam school' and were closely linked with the literary world. In 1885 Veth became involved with the avant-garde periodical *De Nieuwe Gids*. The reviews he wrote for it advocated an individualistic aestheticism which is not, however, manifested in his own paintings of this period; the rather naive realism of the portrait of his sisters

Cornelia, Clara and Johanna Veth (1884–5; Amsterdam, Rijksmus.) is typical. The unforced portrait of the poet *Albert Verwey* (1865–1937) of 1885 (Amsterdam, Stedel. Mus.), dominated by blue-green and grey colours, is nearer to an assertion of mood. Around 1886 Veth attempted landscape painting under the tutelage of Anton Mauve, with whom he went on study trips in the countryside. Drawings and etchings of subjects from peasant life date from this time. Some of Veth's etchings, including *Wrecks*, were done for the Nederlandse Etsclub (Dutch etching club), an organization that he helped to run in 1885.

In 1888 Veth, settling in Baarn, painted the strongly analytic portrait of the painter *Frans Lebret* (1820–1909; Dordrecht, Dordrechts Mus.) and decided once and for all to devote himself to portraiture. The elegance attempted in his landscape work subsequently found expression in his poetry. Veth's style and choice of subject-matter as a painter were in keeping with the changes in painting around 1890 that he had comprehensively defended as a critic. At this time he coined the term *gemeenschapskunst* ('communal art') in a discussion of murals painted by his friend Antoon Derkinderen, and the 'New Art' of the 1890s, in reaction to the individualism of the previous decade, placed greater emphasis on its own social function. In terms of style, this signified a shift from colour to line that is evident in the many lithographic portraits of well-known contemporaries made by Veth for various periodicals between 1891 and 1898. The portrait of the painter *Jacob Maris* (1891) still has a painterly tendency, while later lithographs, such as those of the writer *Lodewijk van Deyssel* (1864–1952) (dated 1893) and the museum director *Wilhelm von Bode* (dated 1898) are more crisply drawn. These portraits were sometimes regarded as caricatures because of the very full, unflattering characterization. Veth often depicted subjects in everyday surroundings in order to allow their personalities to project themselves clearly, as in the drawing and lithograph of the German politician *August Bebel* (1840–1913) (dated 1896; The Hague, Gemeentemus.). Meticulous technical care enhances the penetrating character analyses in Veth's numerous painted portraits; his accentuated interest in line can be seen in oils such as the portrait of the director of the Rijksacademie in Amsterdam, *Anton Derkinderen* (1915; Dordrecht, Dordrechts Mus.). Veth also portrayed humble people: the drawing of *Heintje, a Girl from Gooi* (1891; Dordrecht, Dordrechts Mus.) and *Karen* (1892; Otterlo, Kröller-Müller) are good examples of a concern with the relationship between country people and nature that began about 1890. The etched portrait of the fisherman *Jan Schaap* (1892; Amsterdam, Rjksmus.) and the pen drawing of *Louw the Gardener* (1895; Dordrecht, Dordrechts Mus.) reveal Veth's debts to Holbein and Dürer.

BIBLIOGRAPHY
J. Huizinga: *Leven en werk van Jan Veth* (Haarlem, 1927)
A. J. Vervoorn: 'Het graphisch werk van Jan Veth', *Antiek*, 16 (1981), pp. 11–22, 255–64
F. Bijl de Vroe: *De schilder Jan Veth, 1864–1925: Chroniquer van een bewogen tijdperk* (Amsterdam and Brussels, 1987)
The Age of van Gogh: Dutch Painting, 1880–1895 (exh. cat., ed. R. Bionda and others; Glasgow, Burrell Col.; Amsterdam, Rijksmus. van Gogh; 1990)

ANNEMIEKE HOOGENBOOM

Vetraio [Vetraro], il . *See* BEMBO, (3).

Vetri, Domenico (di Polo di Angelo) de' [Domenico di Polo] (*b* Florence, *c.* 1480; *d* Florence, *c.* 1547). Italian medallist and gem-engraver. Vasari stated that he was a disciple of the gem-engraver Giovanni delle Corniole (*c.* 1470–*c.* 1516), and it is known that he studied the same craft with Pier Maria Serbaldi da Pescia, whose atelier he entered in 1501. He appears to have spent his entire career as court medallist for Alessandro de' Medici (1510–37), 1st Duke of Florence from 1531 (e.g. 1534; Pollard, nos 321–2) and Cosimo I de' Medici (1519–74), Duke of Florence from 1537 and Grand Duke of Tuscany from 1569 (e.g. Pollard, nos 327–32). None of his works is signed, but a group of medals and several cameos and gems (e.g. *Head of Hercules*, Florence, Uffizi) have been attributed to him after having been separated by de la Tour from the work of Francesco dal Prato. His medal showing a figure of *Florence* (Pollard, nos 332–32a) and, for Cosimo, another with the sign of *Capricorn* (1537; Pollard, no. 330) on the reverse serve as a basis for the attribution of others. All of de' Vetri's medals were originally struck, either in bronze or silver, and are between 29 and 44 mm in diameter. In most of his surviving medals of the Medici he established an official portrait and varied it with several interchangeable reverses, most commonly an allegorical figure derived directly from ancient Greek and Roman coinage. His portraits have the precision of the gem-cutter, but are not dry and lifeless, unlike many mint-struck pieces, and the reverses are well-balanced and delicate, though somewhat limited in invention.

BIBLIOGRAPHY
Forrer
H. de la Tour: 'Domenico di Polo, médailleur et graveur sur pierres fines du duc Alexandre de Médicis', *Procès-verbaux et mémoires, Congrès international de numismatique: Paris, 1900*, pp. 382–99
C. Johnson: 'Ancora sul "Corpus" di medaglie di Cosimo I de Medici', *Medaglia*, 14 (1977), pp. 7–28
K. Langedijk: *The Portraits of the Medici* (Florence, 1981), pp. 233–40, 495–500
G. Pollard: *Italian Renaissance Medals in the Museo Nazionale del Bargello*, ii (Florence, 1985), pp. 647–72

STEPHEN K. SCHER

Vetulonia [Etrus. Vetluna]. Site of an Etruscan city, now a village, on a hilltop *c.* 18 km north-west of Grosseto, Italy. In ancient times the city overlooked Lake Prilius, as did nearby Rusellae. There are few excavated remains: a main street *c.* 3 m wide, crossed obliquely by two smaller roads, has been uncovered. The buildings were small, crowded mud-brick or stone structures, as at Veii and San Giovenale. The city walls (?6th century BC) can be traced, as can the remains of a 3rd-century BC temple. Most information about ancient Vetulonia comes, however, from its necropoleis. The Early Iron Age is characterized by cremation burials and repositories containing many imported artefacts. Indigenous metalwork and small-scale three-dimensional sculpture is represented in this and the following Orientalizing period by some fine bronze figurines, decorated vase stands and other objects (*see also* ETRUSCAN, §VI, 2(i)). In the 7th century BC many circle-tombs were constructed: these have one or more trenches for inhumation enclosed by a circle of stone slabs (e.g. the Tomb of the Leader). From the circle-tombs have come rich finds of Oriental, Greek and Sardinian artefacts, as well as much native Etruscan work in gold and bronze.

The finds of pottery are unexceptional by comparison. Towards the end of the 7th century BC these tombs were succeeded by monumental stone chamber tombs of corbelled construction. A circular tholos design with a central supporting pillar (e.g. the Pietrera Tomb; *c.* 650–*c.* 630 BC) was later replaced by tombs on a rectangular plan. All three types were surmounted by earthern tumuli. The sandstone sculpture from the Pietrera Tomb represents some of the earliest monumental sculpture discovered in Europe (*see also* ETRUSCAN, §III, 3). The sequence of burials at Vetulonia apparently ceased at some time during the 6th century BC, and it has been conjectured that the city was conquered or destroyed by Rusellae at this time. In Roman times it was absorbed into the tribal territory of Scaptia. Vetulonia is recorded as having assisted the Latins in overthrowing the Etruscan fifth king of Rome, Tarquinius Priscus (*reg* 616–579 BC), and may also have provided Rome with its insignia of the fasces: the axe is shown brandished by the warrior Avile Feluske on an Archaic Vetulonian stele.

BIBLIOGRAPHY
A. Talocchini: 'La città e la necropoli di Vetulonia secondo i nuovi scavi, 1959–1962', *Stud. Etrus.*, xxxi (1963), pp. 435–58
G. Camporeale: *I commerci di Vetulonia in età orientalizzante* (Florence, 1969)

MARCO RENDELI

Vever, Henri (*b* Metz, 1854; *d* 1942). French jeweller and collector. Vever directed the family jewellery business, begun in Metz by his grandfather Pierre-Paul Vever (*d* 1853). After the capture of Metz in the Franco-Prussian War (1871), the family moved to Luxembourg and then Paris, where the Maison Vever became well established on the Rue de la Paix, winning the Grand Prix of the universal expositions in 1889 and 1900 and becoming a leader in the Art Nouveau movement. Vever gave an important group of Art Nouveau works to the Musée des Arts Décoratifs, Paris. His early interest in contemporary French painting led him to assemble a large and important group of works by Corot, Sisley, Renoir and Monet, of which he sold the majority (Paris, Gal. Georges Petit, 1897) to concentrate on Japanese and Islamic art. Vever had begun to collect Japanese prints in the 1880s and in 1892 joined the distinguished private group Les Amis de l'Art Japonais. In the 1920s through the dealer Sadajirō Yamanaka he sold several thousand Japanese prints to KŌJIRŌ MATSUKATA, which formed the basis of the Matsuka collection (now Tokyo, N. Mus.). During World War II Vever's huge collections were placed in storage not to re-emerge until the 1970s. The Japanese works were dispersed at several spectacular sales at Sotheby's, and the Islamic material—comprising nearly 500 manuscripts, bindings and single folios—was acquired by the Sackler Gallery, Washington, DC, in 1986.

BIBLIOGRAPHY
J. Hillier: *Japanese Prints and Drawings from the Vever Collection* (London, 1975)
G. D. Lowry with S. Nemazee: *A Jeweler's Eye: Islamic Arts of the Book from the Vever Collection* (Washington, DC, 1988)
G. D. Lowry and others: *An Annotated and Illustrated Checklist of the Vever Collection* (Washington, DC, 1988)

MILO C. BEACH

Vewicke [Waywike; Wewoke], **Maynard** [Maynerd; Meynnart; Mynour] (*fl* 1502–25). Painter, probably of Netherlandish origin, active in England. He enjoyed a long career at the courts of Henry VII and Henry VIII and is one of the few painters of pictures of this period in England whose existence is securely documented, although none of his works appears to survive. A reference in 1502 to a 'Mynour, the Inglis payntour', records that the painter had brought portraits of Henry VII, his queen and two of their children to James IV of Scotland; he remained in Scotland until 1503. It is not known whether these portraits were the work of Maynard himself. Again, a payment to him of 20s. recorded in the royal accounts in March 1505 for pictures need not have been for his own work. That Maynard was probably of Netherlandish origin is shown by a payment of 40s. in April 1506 to 'Maynard Waywike Duchman', although in 1511 he was called a Frenchman. In that year Maynard undertook to produce designs for the tomb effigy of Henry VII's mother *Lady Margaret Beaufort* (London, Westminster Abbey), which were carried out by the Italian sculptor Pietro Torrigiani in 1511–12, as well as providing posthumous portraits of her, including one stated in her executors' accounts to be in Christ's College, Cambridge. A full-length portrait of *Lady Margaret Beaufort* survives there, but there is no provable connection with the payments to Vewicke. He is documented as living in the parish of All Hallows, London, in 1523. In a payment to him in September 1525 in Henry VIII's accounts he is named as 'olde maynerd wewoke paynter' and received 100s. as his half-year's wages.

BIBLIOGRAPHY
R. F. Scott: 'On the Contracts for the Tomb of the Lady Margaret Beaufort, Countess of Richmond and Derby', *Archaeologia*, lxvi (1915), pp. 365–76
R. Strong: *Tudor and Jacobean Portraits*, i (London, 1969), pp. 18–21
L. Campbell: *The Early Flemish Pictures in the Collection of Her Majesty the Queen* (Cambridge, 1985), pp. xv, xix

SUSAN FOISTER

Vexillum [Vexilloid Standard]. *See under* FLAGS AND STANDARDS.

Veyrier, Christophe (*b* Trets, 25 June 1637; *d* Toulon, 10 June 1689). French sculptor and stuccoist. He was the most prominent member of a large family of sculptors and architects active in Provence in the second half of the 17th century; the most notable other members were his brothers Louis I (*c.* 1629–after 1697), François (1634–1707) and Joseph (1641–77); among the later generations were Louis I's son Thomas (1658–1736), architect of the Carmelite church at Aix-en-Provence (begun 1693), and François's son Lazare V (1659–after 1710), the probable sculptor of the delicate marble relief of the *Raising of Lazarus* on the high altar of Aix Cathedral.

Christophe Veyrier is referred to in 1663 in documents in Genoa as a *maître esculpteur*; he was trained in Rome in 1668–9 and from 1670 worked for the Eglise des Minimes in Toulon. Four years later he married a niece of the sculptor Pierre Puget. In 1680 Veyrier was working in Aix, where he sculpted eight stucco figures (destr.) for the triumphal arch erected for the ceremonial entry to the city of Louis-Joseph, Duc de Vendôme. By 1682 he was employed in the Toulon Arsenal workshop under Puget, whom he replaced four years later on his master's departure, but none of Veyrier's ship decorations appears to have survived. His bronze replicas of antique works, his statues of *Lysimachus*, *Jason* and *Samson* as well as others made after Gianlorenzo Bernini's works (commissioned by Louis XIV) are also untraced. The extant works he produced at Aix in the 1680s include the marble statue of the *Dying Achilles* (1683; London, V&A) and the marble relief of *Alexander and Darius* (1688; Stowe, Bucks); related to the former's elaborate contrapposto pose is his *Marsyas* (New York, Met.) and a drawing (Aix-en-Provence, Mus. Vieil-Aix) of the untraced *Milo of Croton*. The forceful realism that Veyrier exploited for his portrait busts is well exemplified in that of the *Marquis Jean Deydé* (marble, 1685–6; New York, Met.), originally part of his tomb in Montpellier Cathedral, and those of *Admiral Jean Gabaret* (marble; Paris, Louvre) and *Pierre Puget* (terracotta; Aix-en-Provence, Mus. Granet). Other works are in various museums in Aix-en-Provence and Marseille, the best of which are a monumental marble *Faun* and its pendant *Muse* (Marseille, Mus. B.-A.). Veyrier's figures are generally distinguished by the virtuosity of their surface treatment and by a vitality and elegance that prefigure the Rococo style.

Under Puget's direction Veyrier also worked on his master's monumental *Perseus Freeing Alexander* and—probably from a model by Puget—executed the marble group of *Alexander Victorious* (both Paris, Louvre) as well as the *Abduction of Helen by Paris* (Genoa, Pal. Rosso) and a *Virgin and Child* (Marseille, Mus. Vieux-Marseille). Securely attributed works by Veyrier for church patrons include the marble and stucco furnishings for the Corpus Domini Chapel of Toulon Cathedral (*c.* 1682) and the marble altar of the Annunciation in the church of Ste Marie-de-Nazareth, Trets (begun 1686).

BIBLIOGRAPHY

L. Lagrange: *Pierre Puget: Peintre, sculpteur, architecte et décorateur de vaisseaux* (Paris, 1868)
C. Ginoux: 'Christophe Veyrier, élève et collaborateur de Puget', *Nouv. Archvs A. Fr.*, 3rd ser., ii (1886), pp. 264–5
——: 'Christophe Veyrier, sculpteur provençal', *Nouv. Archvs A. Fr.*, 3rd ser., v (1889), pp. 120–23
——: 'Les Sculpteurs Levray, Langueneux, Turreau, Veyrier, Turreau dit Toro, Maucord, maîtres décorateurs de vaisseaux au port de Toulon (1639–1761)', *Réun. Soc. B.-A. Dépt.* (1890), pp. 19–32
J. Pope-Hennessy: 'A Statue by Veyrier', 'A Relief by Veyrier at Stowe', *Burl. Mag.*, lxxxix (1947), pp. 22, 135
K. Herding: *Pierre Puget: Das bildnerische Werk* (Berlin, 1970) [many pls]
J. Boyer: *L'Architecture religieuse de l'époque classique à Aix-en-Provence* (Aix-en-Provence, 1972), pp. 72, 104, 331
J.-J. Gloton: *Renaissance et baroque à Aix-en-Provence: Recherches sur la culture architecturale dans le midi de la France de la fin du 15e au début du 18e siècle*, Bibliothèques des écoles françaises d'Athènes et de Rome (Rome, 1975)
La Peinture en Provence au XVIIe siècle (exh. cat., Marseille, Mus. B.-A., 1978), pp. 156–8
K. Herding: 'Les Veyrier, une famille de sculpteurs provençaux à l'époque de Louis XIV', *Archvs A. Fr.*, n. s., xxx (1989), pp. 73–124
Pierre Puget, peintre, sculpteur, architecte 1620–1694 (exh. cat., Marseille, Cent. Vieille Charité, 1994)

KLAUS HERDING

Vézelay, Paule [Watson-Williams, Marjorie] (*b* Bristol, 14 May 1892; *d* London, 20 March 1984). English painter and printmaker. She studied from 1909 to 1912 at Bristol School of Art and from 1912 to 1914 at the London School of Art under the *Punch* draughtsman George Belcher (1875–1947). She first became known as a book illustrator and printmaker, producing mainly lithographs and wood-engravings. Her mature work as a painter followed her first visit to Paris (1920), when she began to paint in a simplified, Post-Impressionist style. Her subject-matter included scenes with people gathered together in restaurants or theatres, for example *In a Theatre* (1928; ex-artist's priv. col., see 1983 exh. cat., p. 30). In 1926 she settled in Paris and adopted the name Paule Vézelay.

From 1929 to 1932 she lived with André Masson. Her work began in 1929 to be abstract, with lines and shapes floating in a cloudy, atmospheric space, as in *Curves and Circles* (1930; London, Tate), although she also painted a few Masson-like semi-Surrealist compositions. In 1934, partly through friendship with Arp, she joined the Abstraction-Création group, and most of her later paintings such as *Forms on Grey* (1935; London, Tate) were more classical, with clear-cut forms, sometimes like vases, against a uniform background. Her most original contributions to the abstract movement, however, were probably the *Lines in Space* that she began in 1936: shallow wooden boxes with a spatial network of threads or curving wires, for example *Lines in Space No. 16* (1951; Basle, Kstmus.). Vézelay returned to England in 1939, shortly after the outbreak of war, and spent her later years in London, working in growing isolation until her work was rediscovered at the end of her life.

BIBLIOGRAPHY

Paule Vézelay (exh. cat., ed. R. Alley; London, Tate, 1983)
Paule Vézelay: Paintings and Constructions (exh. cat., ed. R. Alley; London, Annely Juda F.A., 1987)

RONALD ALLEY

Vézelay, Ste Madeleine. Former Cluniac abbey and pilgrimage church in Burgundy, France. Founded in the mid-9th century by Girart de Roussillon, initially as a convent for women, it was dependent on Cluny Abbey by 1058. Vézelay's prosperity in the 11th and 12th centuries was based on its possession of the putative relics of St Mary Magdalene; the abbey declined from the late 13th century, however, and in 1537 the Benedictines were replaced by secular canons.

1. ARCHITECTURE. Pilgrimage to the disputed relics at Vézelay was stimulated in 1103, when Pope Paschal II (*reg* 1099–1118) acknowledged their authenticity. It has been speculated that a dedication in the following year applied to a choir and transept constructed under Abbot Artaud (*reg* 1096–1106), a theory supported by traces of the west side of an early 12th-century crossing. A serious fire in 1120 appears to have necessitated the rebuilding of the nave, although the transept and choir, which may have suffered little damage, were retained. Abbot Renaud de Semur (*reg* 1106–28), a nephew of St Hugh of Cluny (*reg* 1049–1109), was styled on his tomb 'abbot and restorer [*reparator*] of the monastery of Vézelay'. The ten-bay nave was probably constructed from west to east. It has a two-storey elevation consisting of a round-headed main arcade carried by cruciform piers with addorsed half-columns and a simple clerestory (see fig. 1). Both the main vessel (h. 18.5 m) and aisles were groin-vaulted. The polychrome

1. Vézelay, Ste Madeleine, interior looking east, nave begun c. 1120

masonry of the transverse arches, employing various limestones from local quarries, is visually striking and may derive from Spanish sources (e.g. the Mezquita, Córdoba). Only the fluted pilasters that carry the formerets of the vaults reflect the influence of the third church at Cluny Abbey ('Cluny III'); rather, the nave design seems to emulate Anzy-le-Duc Priory (see ROMANESQUE, §II, 5(i)). The consecration of a chapel at Vézelay in 1131 by Pope Innocent II (reg 1130–43) does not necessarily refer to Ste Madeleine, although the nave was probably completed during the 1130s. A narthex with galleries to the north, east and south was added during the 1140s, a time of great prosperity for Vézelay: here Bernard of Clairvaux preached the Second Crusade in 1146. The east gallery, or chapel of St Michael, was blessed by Archbishop Hugh of Rouen between 1146 and 1152. The narthex, three bays long and three wide, is groin-vaulted throughout, except for the east gallery, which has rib vaults. The six-bay chapter house and the dormitory were rebuilt c. 1160–65. The reconstruction of the east end, initiated by Abbot Girard d'Arcy (reg 1171–98), was probably not completed until the 13th century. The chevet, raised above the crypt and preceded by shallowly projecting transepts and two aisled straight bays, comprises an ambulatory with five radiating chapels. The design reflects the influence of the choir of Saint-Denis Abbey, and the architect may have come from the Ile-de-France. The three-storey elevation has a main arcade of pointed arches on columnar piers, a gallery with twin openings and a clerestory. It is debated whether the flying buttresses formed part of the original design. In the

13th century a south tower was added to the west façade (a north tower was planned but never built), and a large central window inserted with five lancets adorned with statues; a tower was also added to the south transept. In 1819 the collapse of the façade tower, which had been struck by lightning, damaged the gable and narthex vaults. The restoration of Ste Madeleine under the auspices of EUGÈNE-EMMANUEL VIOLLET-LE-DUC began in 1840.

2. SCULPTURE.

(i) Nave. There are more than 100 capitals in the nave, most of which are carved from a fine white or pinkish limestone from the quarry of Champ-Rotard, Coutarnoux. Under Viollet-le-Duc, François Michel Pascal (1810–82) replaced a number of capitals with copies and restored others with plaster (originals mostly Vézelay, Dépôt Lapidaire Abbaye). As at Autun Cathedral, the capitals are not obviously arranged according to a single programme, but Old Testament scenes predominate. The New Testament scenes include *Dives and Lazarus* and the *Suicide of Judas*, while the *Mystic Mill* capital is thought to show the relationship between the Old Testament and the New. Scenes from the Life of Christ are conspicuously absent, but several capitals relate episodes from saints' lives, among them St Benedict and the hermit saints Paul and Anthony. At least two figured capitals have Classical sources: the *Rape of Ganymede* and the *Education of Achilles*. The remaining capitals reveal great diversity of sources and include *Libra* and *Gemini*; *Summer* and *Winter*; a duel; and a basilisk, grasshopper and two pelicans. The capital usually identified as *Gathering Honey* probably represents the Four Winds: the wattled, conical objects held by the central figures are bellows, not beehives. Together with the *Four Rivers of Paradise*, it is among the capitals that may reflect the influence of the hemicycle capitals of Cluny (see CLUNIAC ORDER, §III, 2).

Stylistically, the capitals are less uniform than the roughly contemporary ensemble at Autun. Six of the nine sculptors identified by Salet at Vézelay worked in the nave. Although this might imply some stylistic diversity, the sculptors were probably active simultaneously and belonged to a single large workshop. Several capitals, including the *Mystic Mill*, have been attributed to the Master of the Tympanum. Other sculpture in the nave includes the formerets and the hood moulds of the main arcade, decorated with foliate and nebule mouldings, and the string courses separating the two storeys, which bear rosettes in drilled medallions. A number of bases, which vary considerably in profile, are carved with animal, floral and foliate designs. At the apex of the south arch of the third bay is a crowned, seated female figure probably representing Ecclesia. She holds a model of a church and a banner and is framed by a medallion inscribed 'I am smoky now but after this I shall be beautiful'.

(ii) West portal of the nave. Three portals lead from the narthex into the nave and side aisles. It has been suggested that the central portal incorporates a change of design: Salet thought that the upper embrasures were added to heighten the portal when the decision was taken to build the narthex, while Beutler suggested, less convincingly, that the original design was narrower, with a dove in the centre of the tympanum instead of the figure of Christ. Neither argument can be substantiated, however, and the design of the portal must be regarded as homogeneous (*see* FRANCE, fig. 32; see also fig. 2). The tympanum (w. 9.25 m) is composed of nine blocks. In the centre an imposing *Christ* is enthroned sideways in a mandorla. His draperies are characterized by multiple parallel folds that curve over his limbs and torso and are drawn into tight swirls on his right thigh and left knee; the hems are dramatically wind-blown. This graphic style is often compared with that of the wall paintings at Berzé-la-Ville. Christ stretches his arms to left and right, and rays emanate from his fingers on to the heads of the Apostles, gathered in groups of six on either side of the tympanum. Around this scene, eight wedge-shaped compartments are carved with different races, both real and mythological, such as the dog-headed Cynocephali. On the lintel are two processions, which include a group with a sacrificial bull and pygmies, and large figures of *SS Peter and Paul* to right of centre, overlapping the tympanum. The centre of the lintel itself is overlapped by the trumeau figure of *St John the Baptist*, which may originally have been surmounted by a smaller carving. John, addorsed to a fluted half-column, technically foreshadows the column statues of Early Gothic portals (*see* COLUMN STATUE). He carries a large medallion once carved with the Lamb of God. The latter and several heads on the portal, including that of St John the Baptist, were destroyed in 1793. At the same level are six animated Apostles, two on the sides of the trumeau and four, conversing in pairs, on the upper embrasures.

2. Vézelay, Ste Madeleine, central nave portal, detail of tympanum depicting *Christ*, limestone, *c.* 1125

SS Peter and Paul on the right, represented for the third time on this doorway, are carved from brownish limestone from Tharoiseau rather than the reddish limestone of the rest of the portal sculpture. The extension of the figured programme on to the embrasures represents an innovation in portal design. There are two archivolts: the outer is carved with foliage and the inner with medallions bearing the *Signs of the Zodiac* and the *Labours of the Months*, as at Autun. The capitals of the upper embrasures are foliate, but those of the lower probably represent the *Expulsion of Adam and Eve*, as well as a faun hunting a fabulous bird, the *Sacrifice of Saul* and the *Anointing of David*. The iconography of the portal is controversial, but it seems to combine Christ's Mission to the Apostles to preach the Gospel to the peoples of the world with the gift of the Holy Spirit at Pentecost, which enabled them to speak in tongues. It has also been suggested that the programme referred to the Crusades (Katzenellenbogen).

The tympanum of the smaller, north doorway bears *Christ Appearing to the Apostles*, with the *Journey to Emmaus*, the *Supper at Emmaus* and the *Apostles Returning to Jerusalem* on the lintel below. The archivolts are carved with deeply undercut foliage; the doorpost capitals bear angels fighting demons and the outer capitals, carried by fluted pilasters, are carved with a basilisk and *Two Tones of Plain-chant*. The south doorway has the same design. On the tympanum is the *Adoration of the Magi*, and on the lintel the *Annunciation*, *Visitation*, *Annunciation to the Shepherds* and the *Nativity*. One of the angels on the doorpost capitals carries a trumpet and the other a banner; the outer capitals represent *Ulysses and the Sirens* and a faun hunting a demon. These lateral doorways are stylistically related to the central portal; the entire ensemble can be attributed to sculptors from Cluny III and dated *c.* 1125–35.

(iii) Narthex. The narthex capitals, carved in the 1140s, bear a range of subjects similar to those in the nave and sometimes repeat them. Viollet-le-Duc's restoration was more extreme here than in the nave, retaining only one original capital in the narthex galleries, the *Story of Tobias*. According to Salet, most of the figured capitals were carved by two sculptors, with a further two artists carving only one and three capitals respectively.

(iv) West façade. The three west façade portals were badly damaged during the Revolution and drastically restored by Viollet-le-Duc. The tympanum and lintel of the central doorway, respectively representing the *Last Judgement* and *St Mary Magdalene*, cannot be regarded as a faithful reproduction of what was there originally: the original tympanum (Vézelay, Dépôt Lapidaire Abbaye) retains only a fragment of its carved surface, a piece of drapery close in style to the sculpture of Autun. Grivot and Zarnecki also attributed a gable fragment (Vézelay, Dépôt Lapidaire Abbaye) to Gislebertus, who they suggested was employed at Vézelay in the early 1120s to carve sculpture for the narthex doorways, which was later relocated to the exterior façade.

BIBLIOGRAPHY

J. Banchereau: 'Travaux d'apiculture sur un chapiteau de Vézelay', *Bull. Mnmtl.*, lxxvii (1913), pp. 403–11

A. Katzenellenbogen: 'The Central Tympanum at Vézelay: Its Encyclopaedic Meaning and its Relation to the First Crusade', *A. Bull.*, xxvi (1944), pp. 141–51

F. Salet: 'Vézelay', *Bull. Soc. N. Antiqua. France* (1945), pp. 62–9; (1946), p. 262; (1947), pp. 267–8

——: *La Madeleine de Vézelay* (Melun, 1948)

D. Grivot and G. Zarnecki: *Gislebertus, Sculptor of Autun* (London, 1961, rev. 1965)

C. Beutler: 'Das Tympanon zu Vézelay: Programm, Planwechsel und Datierung', *Wallraf-Richartz-Jb.*, xxix (1967), pp. 7–30

M. Taylor: 'The Pentecost at Vézelay', *Gesta*, xix (1980), pp. 9–15

L. Saulnier: 'La Madeleine de Vézelay: Le Chantier de restauration de Viollet-le-Duc', *Actes du 52 congrès de l'Association bourguignonne des sociétés savantes: Vézelay, Avallon et Château Chinon, 1981*, pp. 213–20

L. Saulnier and N. Stratford: *La Sculpture oubliée de Vézelay: Catalogue du Musée Lapidaire* (Paris, 1984)

KATHRYN MORRISON

Vezzi Porcelain Factory. Italian porcelain factory. In 1720 a factory manufacturing hard-paste porcelain was established in Venice under the management of Giovanni Vezzi (*b* 1687) with financial backing from his father, Francesco Vezzi (1651–1740). Included in the partnership drawn up in 1721 was the Meissen arcanist Christoph Conrad Hunger (*fl c.* 1717–*c.* 1748), whom Francesco had met in Vienna; Hunger, however, returned to Meissen in 1724. In the same year Giovanni became sole owner, but financial difficulties forced the factory to close in 1727. Fewer than 200 pieces of Vezzi porcelain, all of which are table wares, are known. The paste, made from Saxon clay, was similar to that employed at the factories of Meissen and Vienna. The colours, influenced by the early palette employed at the factory of Claudius Innocentius Du Paquier in Vienna, were chiefly brick red, bright green, lemon yellow and dark blue. Characteristic products were slim beakers and saucers, and polygonal, spherical or flattened teapots (e.g. 1725; Cardiff, N. Mus.). Decoration was moulded and painted; armorials were extensively and almost exclusively used on beakers and saucers. Sprays of flowers, chinoiseries and long-necked birds, outlined and flatly painted, were common. Some well-modelled wares with pictorial decoration of allegorical subjects have been attributed to Ludovico Ortolani on the evidence of a signed dish (London, BM), but attributions to one Duramano are unsupported.

BIBLIOGRAPHY

F. Stazzi: *Porcellane della casa eccellentissima Vezzi* (Milan, 1967)

A. Mottola Molfino: *L'arte della porcellana in Italia*, i (Milan, 1976), pp. 15–22

CLARE LE CORBEILLER

Viaduct. Long bridge consisting of several arches or spans carrying a road or railway across a valley or other low-lying ground. The word viaduct is not, unlike the related term aqueduct, of ancient origin but was coined by Humphry Repton in his *Fragments on the Theory and Practice of Landscape Gardening* (London, 1816). Structures of this kind were, however, in existence long before the 19th century, and many viaduct-type bridges were built by the Romans to maintain the level and alignment of their roads (*see* ROME, ANCIENT, §III, 3). Examples include the long viaduct near Ariccia (2nd–1st century BC) and fragments of another, of Augustan date, near Città Castellana, as well as the Ponte di Nona (1st century BC), near Rome, which still carries traffic.

At later dates before the Industrial Revolution there is occasional evidence of similar structures, whose purpose was to provide a convenient and safe route over a natural obstacle, even when a low-level crossing was feasible and probably more economic. With the development of canals and railways in the 18th century and the spread of industrialization, viaducts and aqueducts were again extensively constructed. Even a relatively modest horse railway could justify the cost of building an embankment or viaduct over low ground, and several timber viaducts were built on the Newcastle wagon-ways, while at least one was proposed for a crossing over the River Tyne.

The timber viaduct ultimately became a rarity in Great Britain, though Isambard Kingdom Brunel constructed several in Devon and Cornwall, partly because at the time he mistrusted iron railway bridges and partly because timber was more economic in the conditions. The most developed were structures of considerable elegance. The greatest builders of timber viaducts were, however, the early railway engineers in the USA, where there were many natural obstacles to overcome and timber was extremely cheap. Their 'timber-trestle' viaducts exploited the full structural potential of their material.

Early railway engineers in Europe relied on brick and masonry for viaduct construction, and viaducts became distinctive and increasingly familiar features of both rural and urban landscapes. Railway builders soon appreciated that within towns and cities the high cost of transporting soil, and the even higher cost of land, made viaducts more economical to construct than earthen embankments. As early as 1836 the London and Greenwich railway ran along a brick viaduct for virtually its whole length (6 km). Railway viaducts in urban settings, such as the one in Nîmes (at 1569 m the longest in France), also offered the possibility of exploiting the vast areas beneath their arcades as sites for shops, factories, schools and even houses, giving rise to the expression 'underneath the arches'.

Masonry viaducts were built in both the Neo-classical and neo-Gothic styles and often elaborately embellished. Brick, however, remained the preferred material, since it was cheaper, and bricklayers were far easier to train than masons. It could, however, be utilized to superb effect, as in Brunel's viaducts at Wharncliffe (see fig.) and Maidenhead. These mid-19th century viaducts were extremely well constructed: few collapsed, and most survive to carry modern loads.

Metal viaducts were not common in Britain, though they were increasingly used elsewhere. Wrought iron and cast iron were unsuitable materials, and by the time steel was available the greater part of the British railway system was finished. In other countries, however, where railway building started and finished later, steel viaducts became the norm. There are many in the USA, and in France one of the finest series in the world carries the railway through the Massif Central.

In the 20th century reinforced and pre-stressed concrete became, alongside steel, the main materials of construction. After the 1940s, however, they were used primarily for viaducts carrying major roads. The speed of road traffic brought what are essentially railway concepts to bear and eliminated the possibility of constructing steep bridges with winding approaches. Motorway viaducts

Viaduct on the Great Western Railway at Wharncliffe, near Hanwell, by Isambard Kingdom Brunel, opened 1837; coloured lithograph from J. C. Bourne: *History and Description of the Great Western Railway* (London, 1846)

epitomize the transition from 19th-century concepts of arcuate and trabeate construction to 20th-century construction methods and materials. Among the most graceful examples are those in Italy, in dramatic settings south-east of Genoa and in the Apennines.

BIBLIOGRAPHY

L. T. C. Rolt: *Isambard Kingdom Brunel* (London, 1957/R 1961)
P. Gazzola: *Ponti romani*, 2 vols (Florence, 1963)
H. J. Hopkins: *A Span of Bridges* (Newton Abbot, 1970)
B. S. Morgan: *Civil Engineering: Railways* (London, 1971)
A. G. Pugsley, ed.: *The Works of Isambard Kingdom Brunel* (London, 1976/R 1980)
D. P. Billington: *Robert Maillart's Bridges* (Princeton, 1979)
M. Prade: *Ponts et viaducs au XIXe siècle* (Poitiers, 1988)

NORMAN A. F. SMITH

Viallat, Claude (*b* Nîmes, 18 May 1936). French painter. He studied at the Ecole des Beaux-Arts in Montpellier from 1955 to 1959, and spent the following two years in national service in Algeria. Until 1960 he painted still-lifes, horses and portraits in a style reminiscent of that of Courbet. From 1962 to 1963 he studied at the Ecole des Beaux-Arts in Paris, under the French painter Raymond-Jean Legueult (*b* 1898), and during this time he discovered the work of Rauschenberg, Morris Louis and Kenneth Noland. In 1964 he began teaching at the Ecole des Arts Décoratifs in Nice, where he remained for three years. By this time he had begun producing the repeated pattern works using mainly primary colours, which formed the basis of all his later works, such as *Untitled* (1968; Paris, Pompidou).

In 1966 Viallat had his first one-man show at the Galerie A in Nice, and in 1967 he moved to Limoges to take up a professorship at the Ecole des Beaux-Arts there. His first works using knotted rope, sometimes painted, were made in 1969, for example *Net* (1970; Paris, Pompidou). Also in 1969 he was one of the founders of the Supports-Surfaces group. The group first exhibited in that year in the Ecole Spéciale d'Architecture in Paris, and Viallat continued to exhibit with the group until June 1971, although he had formally withdrawn in May 1971. His later work is in much the same style as the earlier abstract patterns, although there are some examples, such as *Bâche* (1978; Paris, Pompidou), that are larger and painted on unframed coarse canvas, using a greater variety of colours in separate panels. From 1979 he lived and worked in Nîmes, where he was Director of the Ecole des Beaux-Arts from 1979 to 1985.

BIBLIOGRAPHY

Claude Viallat (exh. cat. by J. L. Froment, Bordeaux, Cent. A. Plast. Contemp., 1980)
Viallat (exh. cat. by B. Ceysson and others, Paris, Pompidou, 1982)
Claude Viallat (exh. cat. by D. Dobbels and others, Nîmes, Mus. A. Contemp., 1988–9)

□

Viana [**Vianna**]**, Eduardo (Afonso)** (*b* Lisbon, 28 Nov 1881; *d* Lisbon, 22 Feb 1967). Portuguese painter. He studied in Paris from 1905 with Jean-Paul Laurens and at the *académies libres*, painting naturalistic landscapes and still-lifes. At the outbreak of World War I he returned to Lisbon with his friend Amadeo de Souza-Cardoso and other compatriots. In 1915–16 he lived and worked in Vila do Conde with the Orphist painters Robert and Sonia Delaunay and was intrigued by their experiments in simultaneity. In the painting *In Revolt* (?1916; Oporto, Mus. N. A. Mod.) motifs of Portuguese popular life are translated into intersecting coloured arcs. But his real inclination was towards naturalism, and in 1917 these arcs were made to correspond to real objects. His last work to evoke Orphism was also a homage to Portuguese modernism: *K4: The Blue Square* (?1917; Lisbon, Mus. Gulbenkian) depicts Almada Negreiros's book of the same title and is dedicated to Amadeo.

Viana's works of the 1920s, for example *Nude* (1925; Lisbon, Mus. Gulbenkian), reflect his attraction both to the structure of Cézanne's paintings and to the sensuality of Derain's. In 1924 two of his landscapes were hung alongside works of contemporaries in the café A Brasileira, then the favoured haunt of Lisbon intellectuals. After organizing the first Autumn Exhibition for the Sociedade Nacional de Belas Artes in 1925, Viana lived in Paris (1925–30) and Brussels (1930–40), returning to Lisbon in 1940. Hardly any work from this period abroad is known to have survived. From 1940 onwards he concentrated increasingly on quiet still-lifes. While the forms became increasingly simplified, the plasticity of the volumes continued to be emphasized. Viana won wide acclaim nationally and was elected to the Portuguese Academia de Belas Artes in 1958.

BIBLIOGRAPHY
J.-A. França: *Eduardo Viana* (Lisbon, 1969)
——: *A arte em Portugal no século XX* (Lisbon, 1974, rev. 1985)
RUTH ROSENGARTEN

Viana, Fábrica de. *See* FÁBRICA DE VIANA.

Vianelli [Viennelly], Achille (*b* Porto Maurizio di Imperia, 31 Dec 1803; *d* Benevento, 2 April 1894). Italian painter and printmaker. In 1819 he moved to Naples where, together with Giacinto Gigante, he frequented the studios of Wolfgang Huber and Antonio Sminck Pitloo. He was taught to use the 'camera lucida', and his early work was tied to the panoramic tradition, using techniques similar to those of Raffaele Carelli (1818–1900). He soon abandoned oil painting and an obsession for formal perfection in favour of the watercolour and sepia works with which he made his name, gradually assuming a freer and almost impressionistic painterly style. Typical views include *Bay of Naples* (tempera; Florence, Uffizi) and the *Madonna del Soccorso at Forio d'Ischia* (watercolour, 1893; Benevento, Mus. Sannio). His interiors are typified by an evocative use of diffused light and shadow, as in the early *Grotto of the Donn'Anna Palace* (1825; Naples, Mus. N. S Martino) and also in *Interior of Salerno Cathedral* (1841; Naples, Accad. B.A.).

Although he chose to live in Benevento, Vianelli continued to travel between Rome, Paris and various parts of Campania, which he explored with his sketchbooks, documenting the views and monuments. In 1850 he opened a school of painting in the cloisters of S Sofia in Benevento. His incisive and rapid style was also employed in several figure and costume studies, influenced by Bartolomeo Pinelli, for example in a series of aquatints entitled *Scene popolari di Napoli* (1831). He also provided some of the illustrations for the *Viaggio pittorico nel Regno delle due Sicilie* (Naples, 1833) and illustrated *Napoli e le sue vicinanze* (Naples, 1845). He was a member of the Scuola di Posillipo, and was related by marriage to the artists Giacinto Gigante and Teodoro Witting (1793–1860).

BIBLIOGRAPHY
Thieme–Becker
Achille Vianelli (exh. cat., Benevento, Mus. Sannio, 1954)
G. Doria: *De Achille Vianelli e delle sue scene napoletane* (Naples, 1955)
A. Barricelli: 'Achille Vianelli e la Scuola di Posillipo', *Napoli Nob.*, viii (1969), pp. 119–29
S. Ortolani: *Giacinto Gigante e la pittura di paesaggio a Napoli e in Italia dal '600 all '800* (Naples, 1970)
Inediti di Achille Vianelli (exh. cat. by E. Galasso, Benevento, Mus. Sannio, 1983)
MARIANTONIETTA PICONE PETRUSA

Vianen, van. Dutch family of gold- and silversmiths. They were responsible for the evolution and dissemination of the AURICULAR STYLE, which flourished in the Netherlands during the first quarter of the 17th century. This style was originally confined to embossed ornament and

Adam van Vianen: silver-gilt ewer, h. 225 mm, 1614 (Amsterdam, Rijksmuseum)

consisted of an amorphous repertory of fleshy scrolls and lobe-like forms.

(1) Adam van Vianen (*b* ?Utrecht, 1569; *d* ?Utrecht, 1627). He probably trained in the workshop of the goldsmith Bruno Ellardsz. van Leydenberch and was associated with such leading artists of his day as Hendrick Goltzius and Pieter Lastman. In contrast to his brother, (2) Paulus van Vianen, Adam never travelled far from his home town. In his youth he is known to have trained as an engraver, and at least two portraits and a map of Utrecht by him survive (see 1984–5 exh. cat., nos 81, 124), but it was in the modelling and embossing of silver that he excelled.

Adam's earliest known work in silver is a standing cup (1594; St Petersburg, Hermitage); this is a vessel of standard Mannerist form, individual only in the use of a highly pictorial, embossed frieze around the centre. From this point he gradually explored the possibilities of the auricular style; in 1610 Paulus visited Utrecht, and it was probably then that the two brothers exchanged ideas on the subject. Certainly their experimentation with the style seems to have followed parallel lines, appearing first as a tentative border decoration and evolving into a fully developed decorative style soon after 1610. Adam took it to its extreme in the extraordinary silver-gilt ewer commissioned by the Amsterdam guild of silversmiths in memory of Paulus (1614; Amsterdam, Rijksmus.; see fig.). In this piece, raised from a single sheet of silver, Adam entirely broke away from Renaissance conventions of design and produced a strikingly original work that is largely abstract and completely sculptural in its conception. It is indicative of the fame of both brothers that the Amsterdam guild—with whom Paulus had no recorded association—should have wished to commemorate him and that it should have chosen to give the commission to a goldsmith from Utrecht rather than to one of its own members. The ewer soon acquired a fame of its own and appears as a still-life element in many paintings of the period (e.g. *see* EECKHOUT, GERBRAND VAN DEN, fig. 1).

(2) Paulus van Vianen (*b* Utrecht, *c.* 1570; *d* Prague, 1613). Brother of (1) Adam van Vianen. He was the most successful and in many ways the most versatile of the family. About 1580 he was apprenticed to Bruno Ellardsz. van Leydenberch and subsequently seems to have worked for his brother Cornelis Ellardsz. van Leydenberch. During the 1590s he embarked on a series of foreign travels and appointments that appear to have ensured his absence from the Netherlands for most of the rest of his life. After travelling to France, he was employed from 1596 to 1601 at the courts of the Dukes of Bavaria, William V and Maximilian I, in Munich. From 1601 to 1603, he was in the service of the Archbishop of Salzburg, Wolf Dietrich von Raitenau. Both these courts were famous for their lavish patronage of goldsmiths and jewellers. His most important appointment, however, was in 1603 when he became Kammergoldschmied to Emperor Rudolf II in Prague, a position he retained until the end of his life. There he was associated with such other outstanding artists in the Emperor's service as Hans von Aachen, Adriaen de Vries and Caspar Lehmann.

It was under the Emperor's patronage that most of Paulus's finest surviving works were made, for example a gold-mounted, jasper ewer of 1608 (Vienna, Ksthist. Mus.) and a ewer and dish embossed with *Diana and Actaeon* (1613; Amsterdam, Rijksmus.; see fig.). His embossed

Paulus van Vianen: embossed silver ewer, h. 339 mm, and dish, 410×520 mm, depicting *Diana and Actaeon*, 1613 (Amsterdam, Rijksmuseum)

plaquettes were particularly famous: they have a sophistication of modelling and a suggestion of aerial perspective through the subtle variations in relief that is unsurpassed. Unlike most contemporary embossed plaquettes—many of which were made in south Germany and the Netherlands to decorate the centre of tazze—these were often based on his own sketches drawn from nature. Rather than being conceived as decorative adjuncts, his plaquettes often appear to have been made as independent works of art and are usually signed with his initials in monogram. His exceptional skills were recognized at the time: he was paid an unusually high salary by Rudolf II, and Joachim von Sandrart in the *Teutsche Academie*, the best source of information on Paulus, said that '. . . with hammer alone he could paint whole pictures'. His skills as a draughtsman are evident both in his drawings and in his plaquettes, but, while he is recorded also as a painter, no pictures that may be attributed to him have survived.

(3) Christiaen van Vianen (*b* ?Utrecht, *c*. 1600; *d* ?Utrecht, 1667). Son of (1) Adam van Vianen. He was apprenticed to his father in 1616 and became a master in 1628, after Adam's death. By 1632 he was in the service of Charles I in London, and his most important commission was a service of altar plate (destr.) for St George's Chapel in Windsor Castle. His royal commissions have all been destroyed, but there are several extant pieces made for Algernon Percy, 10th Earl of Northumberland. His most outstanding surviving piece, made for an unknown patron, is his dolphin dish, signed and dated 1636 (London, V&A).

Christiaen remained faithful to the fully evolved style of his father, and there is little to distinguish the works made at different stages of his long career. In 1643, during the English Civil War, he returned to Utrecht. About 1650 he published *Constighe modellen*, which contains many of his father's sculptural silver designs. He returned to London in 1660 and was employed as court goldsmith to Charles II. On this occasion he formed a partnership with Michiel de Bruyen van Berendrecht (*c*. 1608–?1670) and was succeeded as court goldsmith by his son-in-law John Cooqus (*c*. 1630–97).

BIBLIOGRAPHY

J. von Sandrart: *Teutsche Academie* (1675–9); ed. A. R. Peltzer (1925)

Zeldzaam zilver mit de gouden eeuw: De Utrechtse edelsmeden van Vianen (exh. cat., Utrecht, Cent. Mus., 1984–5)

TIMOTHY SCHRODER

Viani. Italian family of painters.

(1) Giovanni Maria Viani (*b* Bologna, 11 Sept 1636; *d* Bologna, 1700). He was a pupil of Flaminio Torri, and his first paintings (datable to *c*. 1650) suggest the art of Reni, absorbed through a study of Cantarini. Under the influence of Lorenzo Pasinelli, a colleague of his in Torri's workshop, his forms gained solidity, but the mood of his paintings remained elegiac. This development is evident in two works in the Santuario della Madonna di S Luca in Bologna: *Mary Magdalene* and the altarpiece of *St Pius V with the Polish Ambassador*, which was probably painted in the same early period. The first documents relating to the artist and his first securely attributed works come from 1677: *St Roch* (Bologna, SS Vitale e Agricola) and the four

frescoed lunettes in the portico of S Maria dei Servi, representing miraculous episodes of the life of S Filippo Benizi: *Preaching to the Council of Lyon*, *Healing of the Sick*, *Succoured by Angels in the Desert* and *Ascending to Heaven*. The canvas of *St Benedict with the Peasants* (signed and dated 1689; Bologna, S Michele in Bosco) is a copy of the lost fresco painted by Reni in the cloister of the same church. It forms a pair with *St Bernard Tolomei Restores a Builder to Life* (1693). One of Viani's most interesting pictures is *Diana and Endymion* (1680s; Turin, Accad. Albertina), which shows a refined handling of colour. In the 1690s he produced *St Andrew* (Ozzano dell'Emilia, S Andrea), a work that demonstrates his individual interpretation of the Carracci school. His latest dated works are the two large ovals depicting the *Virgin Appearing to St Ignatius* and *Christ Appearing to St Ignatius* (1696) in the church of S Bartolomeo, Modena.

BIBLIOGRAPHY

G. Foglia and G. Morganti: 'Giovanni Maria Viani', *Paragone*, xxix/345 (1978), pp. 45–53

C. Volpe: 'In margine alla ricerca su G. M. Viani', *Paragone*, xxx/347 (1979), pp. 55–8

M. Gregori and E. Schleier, eds: *La pittura in Italia: Il seicento* (Bologna, 1989) [with bibliog., incl. early sources]

MATILDE AMATURO

(2) Domenico Maria Viani (*b* Bologna, 11 Dec 1668; *d* Bologna, 1 Oct 1711). Painter, son of (1) Giovanni Maria Viani. He trained with his father and in 1691 he made a visit to Venice, which, though lasting less than a year, was of enduring importance. Viani was profoundly influenced by the great masters of the 16th century, notably Tintoretto and Veronese, and by his contemporaries, especially the *tenebrosi* Antonio Zanchi and Antonio Molinari. During the 1690s he worked principally for the Servite Fathers, first in Bologna, where he frescoed one of the lunettes in the portico of their church on the Strada Maggiore, and later at Imola, where he made a number of paintings (most untraced). In about 1700 he painted a large altarpiece of the *Miracle of St Anthony of Padua* for the church of S Spirito at Bergamo (*in situ*), shortly after which he returned to Bologna. His main work there was *Christ at the Pool of Bethsaida* (1701–5; Piacenza, Coll. Alberoni), probably commissioned by Cardinal Ferdinando d'Adda, papal legate to Bologna. This imposing picture shows well the muscularity and turbulent movement of Viani's forms, combining the academic Bolognese tradition of the Carracci and Guercino with the expressive colour of the Venetians. Viani also undertook secular commissions, including a *Jupiter and Ceres* for the Marchese Ratta, of which a copy was made for Cardinal d'Adda (versions, Vienna, Ksthist. Mus.; St Petersburg, Hermitage). In 1705 he developed a malignant illness, probably tuberculosis, which prevented him from working. His last painting, *St Pellegrino Laziosi* (Bologna, Chiesa dei Serviti, Priory), was completed by his pupil Pier Francesco Cavazza (1677–1733).

BIBLIOGRAPHY

H. Voss: 'Domenico Maria Viani', *A. Ven.*, viii (1954), pp. 284–8

D. C. Miller: 'Viani, Graziani and Monti: Contributions to the Bolognese Settecento', *A. Ant. & Mod.*, vii (1964), pp. 97–100

R. Roli: *Pittura bolognese, 1650–1800: Dal Cignani ai Gandolfi* (Bologna, 1977), pp. 100–101

P. Zampetti, ed.: Il seicento (1987), iv of *I pittori bergamaschi dal XIII al XIX secolo* (Bergamo, 1983–7), pp. 141–2, 169

Viani, Alberto (*b* Quistello, nr Mantua, 26 March 1906; *d* 1989). Italian sculptor, etcher and draughtsman. He studied sculpture at the Accademia di Belle Arti in Venice and from 1944 to 1947 was assistant to Arturo Martini, whom he succeeded as Professor of Sculpture. In 1946 he was a founder-member with Renato Birolli and others of the Nuova Secessione Artistica Italiana, an association of artists embracing new trends that was soon renamed FRONTE NUOVO DELLE ARTI.

Viani's early works such as *Female Torso* (1948; New York, MOMA) reflect Martini's influence in the rounded simplification of the human form and the attenuation of the limbs. In the early 1950s, influenced by the simplified smoothness and tactile forms favoured by Hans Arp and Constantin Brancusi, he turned to a more abstract idiom in works such as *Caryatid* (1951; marble version, Venice, Ca' Pesaro; bronze version, Trieste, Mus. Civ. Revoltella). One of his most abstract works, *The Dance* (marble, 1963; see exh. cat., no. 40), was made for Renato Birolli's tomb; it represents the movement of a figure as three rounded forms in a Y shape, with one continuous edge. In later works he emphasized the apparent independence of forms from gravity, as in the series of *Bathers* (1972–5; e.g. *Large Bather*, 1972; see exh. cat., no. 47), but usually maintaining a clear derivation from human anatomy.

BIBLIOGRAPHY
S. Bettini: *L'ultima metafora di Alberto Viani* (Vicenza, 1966)
——: *Alberto Viani* (Venice, 1976)
Alberto Viani (exh. cat., Bergamo, Gal. Lorenzelli, 1976)
                                                    KENNETH G. HAY

Viani [Vianini], **Antonio Maria** (*b* Cremona; *fl* 1582; *d* ?Mantua, 1632–5). Italian architect and painter. Zaist noted that Viani was a pupil of Giulio Campi and mentioned his earliest recorded work, a painting in Cremona, signed and dated 1582 (untraced). Viani moved to Munich in 1586 to work at the court of William V, Duke of Bavaria (*reg* 1579–98), where he participated in the decoration of the Residenz (*see* MUNICH, §IV, 2). His work there, at the Antiquarium and the Grottenhof, was badly damaged during World War II. He executed a number of canvases for the Jesuit church of St Michael under the direction of Friedrich Sustris and Pieter Candid, including the *Glorification of the Name of Jesus* (*in situ*). Viani's artistic personality was influenced by the northern European and Italian Mannerist traditions represented in Bavaria.

From 1592 Viani passed into the service of Vincenzo I Gonzaga, 4th Duke of Mantua, and he played a role of primary artistic importance in Mantua for the next 40 years. His painting and architecture brought together a network of artistic influences that had developed in the 16th century between Mantua, Cremona and Bavaria and drew their common inspiration from the work of Giulio Romano. At the Gonzaga court Viani worked increasingly as an architect. In 1595, after the departure of Giuseppe Dattaro (*d* 1619), Viani became Prefetto delle Fabbriche Ducali and exercised near-absolute control over Mantuan architecture until the arrival of Nicolo Sebregondi in 1613. During Vincenzo's reign Viani constructed new apartments for the Duke and his Duchess, Eleonora de' Medici (1567–1611), in the area of the Corte Vecchia and the Castello of the Palazzo Ducale. In contrast to the earlier rooms within the palazzo, these represented a new conception of space, achieved by increasing the dimensions of the rooms and creating long and spectacular galleries. Between 1595 and 1600 he also built the crypt of S Andrea, in the form of a Greek cross, which was intended to become the Pantheon of the Gonzaga dynasty.

In the last years of the 16th century Viani designed a sumptuous palazzo (now Palazzo di Giustizia; completed 1604) for Giovanni Battista Guerrieri Gonzaga, an official at the Gonzaga court. The monumental dimensions of the building, which stands out in the small urban scale of Mantua, are enhanced by the theatrical arrangement of the façade. The traditional composition of a rusticated lower storey and an architectural order on the first floor is reinterpreted through the transformation of the vertical supports into herms, with Ionic capitals placed on top of gigantic, deformed human figures, a Mannerist motif formerly confined to gardens and decorative details. Here it takes on giant proportions and becomes an element of primary importance in an urban residence. The main staircase, with its various flights contained within a single unified space, seems to be contemporary with the façade and was the first of several such theatrical staircases in Mantua. The ceilings of some rooms are decorated with stuccowork that imitates, with many variations, the sequence of grotesque supports on the front of the building. The most original touches may be seen in the so-called Sala del Cinghiale Calidonio, where vegetable and animal motifs are fused together on scrolls of fluid and sinuous outline. Viani also set into the ceiling painted panels, which illustrate mythological stories.

The convent (partially destr. 1930) and church (1608–13) of S Orsola, built for Margherita Gonzaga (*d* 1618), widow of Alfonso II d'Este, Duke of Ferrara, had their origins in a design by Viani. They were conceived as both a political and a religious centre, being the permanent residence of the ambitious duchess. The octagonal church is screened by the façade, articulated with Corinthian columns, which runs parallel to the road. Niches set in the interior walls of the church are employed to create two superimposed registers of arches divided by pilasters, and the architectural elements are schematized to the point of becoming abstract.

Although Viani was the foremost architect in Mantua, as a painter he encountered the open rivalry of Ippolito Andreasi and Teodoro Ghisi. Furthermore, in the early 17th century he was overshadowed, as were the other employees of the Gonzaga court, by the presence—albeit temporary—of Rubens and Frans Pourbus II. Viani's main painting opportunities came from outside the Gonzaga court, including a series of altarpieces for Mantua Cathedral and various local churches, for example a *St Michael the Archangel Attacking Lucifer* (*c*. 1594; Mantua, Pal. Ducale) for S Agnese, Mantua. His awareness of trends in late Mannerist painting is revealed not only through his compositional skills but also through his silhouetted effects, transparent colours, gestures and handling of drapery. The decoration of the Cappella di S Stefano in S Andrea, commissioned by Tullio Petrozzani (1538–1609), together with his work at Mantua Cathedral, were among his most demanding works. At the chapel Viani painted an altarpiece of the *Crucifixion with the Virgin, St Michael*

Antonio Maria Viani: ceiling of the fourth room of the Appartamento delle Metamorfosi, Palazzo Ducale, Mantua, c. 1613–20

and St Stephen as well as the two adjoining frescoes of the *Dispute of St Stephen* and *Martyrdom of St Stephen*. In the apse of the cathedral Viani depicted the *Holy Trinity with the Virgin and Angels Carrying Instruments of the Passion*. The angels have a painterly freedom not found in figures in the dome and transepts. While successive attributions suggest that Viani designed the dome and transept paintings, they were actually executed by Andreasi and Ghisi.

Under Ferdinando Gonzaga, 6th Duke of Mantua, Viani maintained his official position at court but his authority was reduced owing to the presence of Sebregondi and Domenico Fetti (1613–22). Viani was responsible for the design of the Appartamento delle Metamorfosi (*c.* 1613–20; see fig.) in the Palazzo Ducale. The four rooms, which housed the Duke's eclectic natural-history collection, were decorated with stucco similar to that at the Palazzo Guerrieri Gonzaga. The wooden frame commissioned by the Società del Santissimo Sangue di Cristo for the Cappella dell'Immacolata in S Andrea is of 1616–19. The large structure brings together such characteristic themes of Viani as broken and curled pediments and an aedicule supported by corbels. In 1619 Viani painted an altarpiece of *St Ursula and St Margaret in Glory with the Trinity* (Mantua, Pal. Ducale) for S Orsola.

The serious political and economic crisis that developed after the death of Ferdinando Gonzaga slowed down Viani's artistic activity, which probably ended after the sack of Mantua in 1630.

BIBLIOGRAPHY

G. B. Zaist: *Notizie istoriche de' pittori, scultori ed architetti cremonesi*, ii (Cremona, 1774/*R* 1976), pp. 63–8

G. B. Intra: 'Il monastero di S Orsola in Mantova', *Archv Stor. Lombardo*, n. s. 2, ii (1895), pp. 166–85; as booklet (Mantua, 1902/*R* 1976)

K. Steinbart: 'Die niederländischen Hofmaler der bayrischen Herzöge', *Marburg. Jb. Kstwiss.*, iv (1928), pp. 89–164

E. Marani: 'Il Viani e la vigilia del "sacco"', *Mantova: Le arti* (1965), iii of *Mantova: La storia, le lettere, le arti* (Mantua, 1960–65), pp. 161–75

C. Perina: 'Antonio Maria Viani pittore', *Mantova: Le arti* (1965), iii of *Mantova: La storia, le lettere, le arti* (Mantua, 1960–65), pp. 422–36

M. Delaini Raspadori: 'Antonio Maria Viani pittore: Considerazioni sugli affreschi del coro della cattedrale di Mantova e della cappella Petrozzani in Sant'Andrea', *Civiltà Mant.*, vi (1972), pp. 50–79

P. Carpeggiani: 'Il crepuscolo dell'architettura manierista a Mantova: Antonio Maria Viani e il palazzo dei Gonzaga di Vescovato', *Ant. Viva*, iv (1973), pp. 56–70

D. Francini and others: *La scienza a corte: Collezionismo eclettico, natura e immagine a Mantova fra rinascimento e manierismo* (Rome, 1979), pp. 127–84

G. Pastore: 'Antonio Maria Viani: L'ancona lignea nella basilica di Sant'Andrea e le cappelle laterali della cattedrale', *Civiltà Mant.*, n. s. 5 (1984), pp. 53–66

C. Tellini Perina: 'Committenze mantovane di Antonio Maria Viani', *Quad. Pal. Te*, ii (1985), pp. 69–71
——: 'Nel segno dell'unicorno: La cappella Petrozzani in Sant'Andrea in Mantova', *Quad. Pal. Te*, iv (1986), pp. 15–24

AMEDEO BELLUZZI

Viani, Lorenzo (*b* Viareggio, 1 Nov 1882; *d* Lido di Roma, 2 Nov 1936). Italian painter, printmaker and writer. He grew up in Viareggio surrounded by poverty and misery and as a young man he became a member of the local anarchist group. After a brief attendance at the Scuole d'Arte in Lucca and Florence he began to paint systematically under the guidance of Plinio Nomellini; during that time he got to know the work of the sculptor Constantin Meunier, of the painter Eugène Laermans and of other artists involved in exposing social problems. At the Venice Biennale of 1907 he exhibited some drawings that combined elements from the analytical work of Giovanni Fattori and the distortions of satire and caricature. Viani strengthened his relationship with international anarcho-socialism, immersed himself in populist literature and studied revolutionary political essays. At the beginning of 1908 Viani went to Paris, where he met other political and humanitarian activists. In the run-down studio complex LA RUCHE, to which he returned in the winter of 1908–9 and again towards the end of 1911, he experienced extreme poverty and degradation. In the art galleries in Paris, however, he discovered the formal freedom of works by the Fauvists and the Expressionists, which he then assimilated into a personal style that found expression in *Lady with Chrysanthemum* (1911; Modena, priv. col., see 1986 exh. cat., no. 10) and in the series of drawings *To the Glory of War!* (Prato, Gal. A. Mod. Farsetti).

Embittered by the indifference of the Parisian environment, Viani returned to Viareggio in 1912 and continued studying the works of his favourite artists (in particular Laermans) that were exhibited at the Venice Biennale and the Rome Secession. His figurative style gradually matured and he painted men and women marked by poverty and grief, without descending into the sentimentalism of, for example, Jean Richepin (whose poems about tramps Viani admired) or into the programmatic forms of some art that professed social concern. The images from this period, more restrained in gesture and tone, are emotionally expressive and representative of vague realities: the sailors, anarchists, widows and tramps, as in, for example, the *Two Wayfarers* (1912–15; Arezzo priv. col., see 1986 exh. cat., no. 33), do not convey any special message, beyond their concern for their subject-matter. While he was developing this measured 'miserabilismo' style Viani discovered the formal synthesis, stillness and timelessness of early Tuscan painting and adapted its content: in the vast *Blessing of Those who Died at Sea* (2×4 m, 1914; Viareggio, Comune) and *Plague at Lucca* (2×4 m, 1914; Viareggio, priv. col., see 1986 exh. cat., no. 38) the protagonists are no longer saints and biblical characters, but ordinary people trapped in suffering.

Prior to World War I, Viani devoted himself to woodcuts, producing images of expressive clarity, for example *Poor People* (*c*. 1913/15; Geneva, Guelfi priv. col., see Cardellini Signorini, 1975, no. 72); he later concentrated on images of war that never became nationalism or mere reportage. New encounters led him to study the figurative experiments of the avant-garde; between 1918 and 1920 he combined Futurist fragmentation with the geometrical synthesis of his friend Alberto Magri (*b* 1880). At the end of the war Viani married a teacher, Giulia Georgetti, and settled down to family life. He discovered a capacity for highly effective, coloured narrative, devoting himself to his autobiography, and recalled his Parisian experiences in a novel that occupied him for three years (*Parigi*, Milan, 1925). At the same time, by resorting to his earlier drawings and to memory, he produced some intense images of Parisian life, in which spectral and hallucinatory figures seem flattened by a heavy leaden sky and others move like aliens in spaces pregnant with silence and desolation. In the large final painting *Paris: At the Inn of the Poor* (1.92×6.68 m, *c*. 1927; Camaiore, Lucca, Socci priv. col., see 1986 exh. cat., no. 47, pp. 88–93) Viani also rediscovered the cloisonné line of the Nabis. But the work is mostly impressive for its pathos and the clarity of its characterization of unfortunates, those 'forgotten by God', from La Ruche and from his homeland. During these years Viani left the anarcho-socialists and joined the fascist ranks: editors and periodicals requested new articles from him, and his economic situation improved. He did not, however, adapt to the painting style of the regime but remained the painter of the poor and those on the fringes of society, even if, at times, the intensity of the expression is weakened by the repetition of the same motif. Between 1925 and 1930 Viani produced some unconventional Futurist designs and wrote his best novels (including *Angiò uomo d'acqua*, Milan, 1928, and *Ritorno alla patria*, Milan, 1929), inspired by the war and the life of the coastal folk and seafarers. In 1927 he worked with the sculptor Domenico Rambelli (1886–1972) on the *Monument to the Fallen* in Viareggio and during a stay in Bagni di Lucca made an ironic study of the lifestyle of the middle classes. Until the end of his life Viani continued to paint seafarers, outsiders and people tested by grief and pain; his portraits of typical characters from the Viareggio coast are filled with a strong sense of their superiority and interdependence. In the series of drawings and paintings inspired by the lunatics of Nozzano (Lucca) and by the mentally ill (for example the oil painting *La clinica*, 1933–5; Lucca, Lebolle priv. col., see 1986 exh. cat., no. 74) he attenuated the chromatic violence and resorted to essential gestures in order to evoke the hallucinatory atmosphere of the hospitals and the desolation of the inmates. A number of more serene seascapes and rural scenes belong to his late works; here, man is reconciled with nature, as in *Georgica* (1931; Venice, Ca' Pesaro). He was painting various aspects of life by the sea when he died. He left a collection of poems, which was published as *La polla nel pantano* (Rome, 1954).

BIBLIOGRAPHY
Augustea, xv/4 (1936) [issue devoted to Viani]
A. Parronchi: 'Lorenzo Viani', *XXV Biennale di Venezia* (exh. cat., Venice, Biennale, 1950), pp. 126–9
Lorenzo Viani (exh. cat. by F. Bellonzi, N. Ponente and E. Francia, Rome, Pal. Barberini, 1955)
E. Francia, R. Cortepassi: *Lorenzo Viani* (Florence, 1958)
Mostra antologica di Lorenzo Viani (exh. cat. by F. Solmi and others, Bologna, Mus. Civ., 1973)
I. Cardellini Signorini: *Lorenzo Viani: Disegni e xilografie* (Florence, 1975)
——: *Lorenzo Viani* (Florence, 1978)

Lorenzo Viani (exh. cat. by C. L. Ragghianti, M. Rosi and P. C. Santini, Viareggio, Pal. Paolina, 1982)
Alla gloria della guerra! (exh. cat. by M. De Micheli and P. Pacini, Milan, Gal. A. Mod. Farsetti, 1984)
Lorenzo Viani (exh. cat. by F. Bellonzi, M. De Micheli and P. Pacini, Rome, Pal. Braschi; Viareggio, Pal. Paolina; 1986)

PIERO PACINI

Viatiensis. *See* BAEZA.

Viator. *See* PÉLERIN, JEAN.

Vicente, Gil (*b* Guimarães, *c.* 1465–70; *d* Lisbon, *c.* 1536–7). Portuguese writer, designer and goldsmith. He was active from 1502 to 1536 in the service of Queen Eleanor, Manuel I and John III as a playwright, goldsmith, musician, stage designer and actor. It is known, on the evidence of the King's will, that in 1503 Manuel I entrusted to Vicente the gold from Quiloa that Vasco da Gama (*c.* 1460–1524) had brought as tribute from his second voyage to India and commissioned Vicente to make the Belém Monstrance (1506; Lisbon, Mus. N. A. Ant.; see fig.) for the monastery of the Jerónimos at Belém. It is the only surviving example of his work as goldsmith and is one of the best examples of gold- and silverwork in the MANUELINE STYLE.

At the end of the 19th century, however, there was controversy as to whether the playwright could be identified as the creator of the Belém Monstrance. Documents of the period refer to a 'Gil Vicente' without further identification, and biographical details of the poet are not easy to establish. Analysis of the work of the dramatist, however, reveals a profound knowledge of the goldsmith's craft in the use of over 150 technical terms that would probably not have been familiar to a layman.

In 1509 Manuel I named 'Gil Vicente, goldsmith to the Queen my sister' the superintendent of all work in gold and silver for the three most important religious houses in Portugal, then in course of construction or renovation: the monastery of the Jerónimos at Belém, the hospital of Todos-os-Santos in Lisbon and Tomar Monastery. In 1512 Vicente was elected the representative of his guild in the Casa dos Vinte e Quatro (Office of Trades). His status was increased when, in 1513, the King named him Mestre da Balança (Master of the Scales) in the Casa de Moeda (Mint) in Lisbon. In the margin of this royal charter a note reads *Gil Vicente trovador e Mestre da Balança* ('Gil Vicente, poet and Master of the Scales'), important evidence for the identification of the playwright and goldsmith as the same person. In 1517 Vicente renounced by sale his post at the Casa de Moeda, and the document of this transfer is the last relating to him.

BIBLIOGRAPHY

Fr J. de Belém: *Chronica seráfica da Santa Provincia dos Algarves*, iii (Lisbon, 1755)
T. Braga: *Gil Vicente ourives e Gil Vicente poeta* (Coimbra, 1916)
Q. Veloso: *Gil Vicente, poeta e ourives* (Lisbon, 1938)
A. B. Freire: *Gil Vicente: Trovador, Mestre de Balança* (Lisbon, 1944)
A. C. de Sousa: *Provas de história genealógica da Casa Real Portuguêsa*, II/i (Coimbra, 1947)
J. F. Tomé: *Duas fases da vida de Gil Vicente: Subsídios para a sua identificação* (Lisbon, 1947)

MARIA LEONOR D'OREY

Vicentelo de Leca, Miguel Mañara. *See* MAÑARA VICENTELO DE LECA, MIGUEL.

Gil Vicente: Belém Monstrance, gold and enamel, h. 830 mm, 1506 (Lisbon, Museu Nacional de Arte Antiga)

Vicentino [Michieli], **Andrea** (*b* Vicenza, ?1542; *d* Venice, ?1617). Italian painter. He probably trained in Vicenza with Giambattista Maganza (*c.* 1509–86). His mature style, however, was largely dependent on his subsequent experience of the dominant stylistic idioms at Venice in the later 16th century. Those of Paolo Veronese, Jacopo Tintoretto, Jacopo Bassano and Palma Giovane were particularly influential. He arrived in Venice in the mid-1570s and registered in the Venetian painters' guild in 1583. In this period he assisted Tintoretto at the Doge's

Palace in Venice, making significant contributions to the ceiling decorations in the Sala del Senato and Sala dello Scrutinio. In the latter, he painted a replacement for Tintoretto's Battle of Lepanto (destr. 1577), displaying considerable skill in his organization of a crowded composition through an all-dominant chiaroscuro. His style is closely dependent on Tintoretto, but his technique remains more literal, and his forms have a heavy, static quality closer to Veronese. Vicentino's proven ability as a history painter subsequently won him further important state commissions. Paintings such as the *Arrival of Henry III at Venice* (*c.* 1593; Venice, Doge's Pal., Sala delle Quattro Porte) had an important documentary value for Vicentino's patrons, as a kind of visual proof that the event actually had occurred. He was also active as a religious painter, both at Venice and on the mainland. Such altarpieces as the *Madonna of the Rosary* (1590s; Treviso Cathedral), *God the Father with Three Theological Virtues* (1598; Gambarare) and *St Charles Borromeo* (*c.* 1605; Mestre) confirm that he played an important role in the renovation of provincial altars in accordance with the requirements of the Counter-Reformation. His style in this context is more closely dependent on the visionary luminism of the late styles of Tintoretto and Jacopo Bassano.

BIBLIOGRAPHY

C. Ridolfi: *Meraviglie* (1648); ed. D. von Hadeln (1914–24), i, pp. 147–9
Palladio e la Maniera (exh. cat. by V. Sgarbi, Vicenza, S Corona, 1980), pp. 130–35
P. Fantelli: 'Andrea Vicentino', *Da Tiziano a El Greco* (exh. cat., ed. R. Pallucchini; Venice, Doge's Pal., 1981), pp. 234–5
La pittura in Italia: Il cinquecento, ed. G. Briganti (Milan, 1983), pp. 135, 190, 205, 214, 772

THOMAS NICHOLS

Vicentino, (Giuseppe) Niccolò (*b* Vicenza; *fl c.* 1540–*c.* 1550). Italian woodcutter and printer. He signed five chiaroscuro woodcuts, each after a different artist and all undated. Probably the earliest is a two-block woodcut of *Hercules and the Lion* (B. 119, 17) after Giulio Romano. *Cloelia* (B. 96, 5) after Maturino (*d* ?1528) or Giulio Romano, in three blocks, is still rather crudely cut and registered, and probably the next chronologically. A very cursive, elegant line manifests itself in subsequent works, such as *Ajax and Agamemnon* (B. 99,9) after Polidoro da Caravaggio, the *Sacra Conversazione with St Catherine* (B. 64, 23) after a design attributed to Camillo Boccaccino and *Christ Healing the Lepers* (B. 39, 15) after Parmigianino. An unsigned *Adoration of the Magi* (B. 30, 3) and *The Cardinal and the Doctor* (B. 144,6) can also reasonably be ascribed to him. His hand is doubtless one of several discernible in a large group of anonymous chiaroscuros based on designs by Parmigianino that may represent the products of a workshop supervised by Vicentino. Vasari related how Parmigianino had certain chiaroscuros cut by Antonio da Trento, and that many other designs were printed after the painter's death by 'Joannicolo Vicentino'. A group of ten small anonymous two-block chiaroscuros after silverpoint drawings by Parmigianino (Chatsworth, Derbys; Windsor Castle, Royal Lib.; Florence, Uffizi) as well as the *Twelve Apostles* (B. 69, 1–70, 12), in which two cutting hands are visible, are presumably part of this output, along with about a dozen more anonymous

chiaroscuros. That Vicentino had a workshop is further suggested by the fact that a large number of the Parmigianino drawings related to the chiaroscuros remained together and that Andrea Andreani seems to have acquired many of the blocks and reprinted them later in the 16th century.

BIBLIOGRAPHY

G. Vasari: *Vite* (1550, rev. 2/1568); ed. G. Milanesi (1878–85), v, p. 421
A. von Bartsch: *Le Peintre-graveur* (1803–21), xii
C. Karpinski: *Italian Chiaroscuro Woodcuts*, 48 [XII] of *The Illustrated Bartsch*, ed. W. Strauss (New York, 1983), pp. 26–7, 41, 85, 144, 150, 154, 182, 189

JAN JOHNSON

Vicentino, Pasqualino. *See* ROSSI, PASQUALE.

Vicentino, Valerio. *See* BELLI, VALERIO.

Vicenza. Italian city, capital of the province of the same name. It is situated in the Veneto at the foot of Monte Berico *c.* 65 km west of Venice. The city (population *c.* 115,000) is best known as the home of Andrea Palladio, and it contains many examples of his work, including, just outside the city, the influential Villa Rotonda (begun 1565).

1. History and urban development. 2. Villa Rotonda.

1. HISTORY AND URBAN DEVELOPMENT. The history of Vicenza dates back to the Palaeo-Venetian culture associated with the ancient Euganean city of Este. Around the 1st millennium BC the first small settlement was established on the low alluvial hills where the River Astico, flowing from the north, joined the meandering course of the Retrone, which flowed from the south-west. This topography determined the future direction of Vicenza's urban development. At that time the Astico, which followed the course of the present Astichello, silted up to the north to form a huge lake, the Lacus Pusterlae; it is recalled in the name Laghetto given to the suburb that gradually grew up in the middle of the ancient basin. Palaeo-Venetian remains include numerous small bronze plates (*laminae*; 4th–2nd century BC), which were discovered in the excavation (1960) of a sanctuary between the present Corso Palladio and Piazzetta S Giacomo, at the highest point of the early settlement. In this period, when Este had entered its final decline, the future city of Vicenza gradually consolidated its autonomy, only to be absorbed by the irresistible expansion of Rome in the mid-2nd century BC: situated on the Via Postumia, which also passed through Piacenza, Cremona and Verona, the settlement formed a link in the chain of communication between Genoa and the eastern outpost of Aquilea.

The Veicentinos are first mentioned in a Latin inscription of 135 BC, and between the last republican phase and the 2nd century AD the settlement was referred to as Vicetia. Later, in the 3rd and 4th centuries AD, this name alternated indiscriminately with Vicentia, by which it became exclusively known in the 5th century. From *c.* 200 to *c.* 150 BC Roman Vicenza was a small town limited to the hilltops, centred on the typical perpendicular axes of the *cardo* running north–south (now Contrà Porti del Monte and Contrà Pescheria) and the *decumanus* running east–west (now Corso Andrea Palladio), incorporating the urban section of the Via Postumia. In 89 BC Vicenza

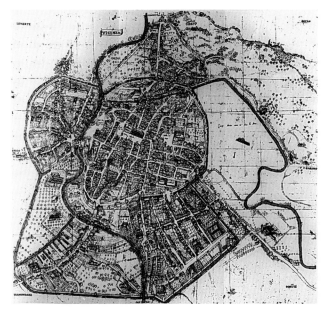

1. Vicenza, perspective plan known as the *Pianta Angelica*, pen and ink, 1.3×1.4 m, 1580 (Rome, Biblioteca Angelica)

obtained its *ius latii*, and in 49 BC it became a *municipium*. By then the settlement had increased in size; its limits were marked to the west by the present Porta Castello, to the north by the intersection of Contrà Porti-Apolloni and Pedemuro S Biagio, to the east by the apse of S Corona and to the south by the intersection of Contrà Pescheria and S Paolo. On the north, east and south-east sides the city relied for security on the Astico and the Retrone rivers and on its elevated position above the surrounding countryside; only on the west and south-west is there any evidence of walls. Immediately beyond the perimeter, which followed the topography in a circular direction around the summit, three bridges spanned the rivers. One of these, across the Astico (early 1st century AD; later the Ponte degli Angeli), carried the Via Postumia. Of the two bridges over the Retrone, that to the south (1st century AD; later the Ponte S Paolo) led to the Berga quarter, while the other linked the south-eastern and south-western quarters of the town.

Rome left an indelible mark on Vicenza, especially in the street layout, which has never been substantially altered and which determined the city's development. Inside the perimeter, minor *cardines* and *decumani* subdivided the settlement into a precise rectangular grid. In 1954 a large three-branched covered passageway (cryptoporticus) was discovered under the new presbytery of the cathedral. Traces of Roman roads in that area had been known for a long time, and stone tablets and fragments of mosaic pavements had also been found there. Subsequent excavations under Palazzo Trissino-Baston (now the Residenza Municipale) have revealed the forum, adjacent to the *decumanus* on the south side. Other remains include those of a huge aqueduct at Lobia and of a theatre (1st–2nd century AD) in the Berga quarter, both of which were well known to the humanists of Vicenza and which Palladio studied in 1540–50.

In the 5th and 6th centuries Vicenza was devastated by successive barbarian raids and invasions by Lombards, Franks and Huns. More complete fortifications were built in the 10th and 11th centuries, which respected and expanded the original Roman plan of the city. The expansion was not extensive, however, taking in only the areas immediately adjacent, including the lowlands of the Isola to the east, as far as the banks of the Bacchiglione, and the quarter surrounding the Berga Theatre across the Retrone. Thus, the medieval radial scheme was grafted on to the ancient grid system. Today the walls are reduced to a few fragments, but the ring appears intact in the perspective map of Vicenza (the *Pianta Angelica*; Rome, Bib. Angelica; see fig. 1), made in 1580. Its route corresponded to the present Contrà Pedemuro S Biagio, Contrà delle Barche and Contrà Mura Pallamio.

Within the walls little trace remains of private buildings, an exception being the Torri dei Loschi (much altered), but the tower houses of noble families must have dominated the ordinary modest dwellings. In the 12th and 13th centuries work on two important neighbouring projects began in the centre of Vicenza: the construction of the cathedral and the Palazzo del Podestà, housing the seats of civil power. These lined the south side of the Piazza Maggiore (now Piazza dei Signori), which gradually became the new centre of the city, replacing the ancient forum. Around it were built the headquarters of the mendicant orders: the Dominicans on the east, the Eremitani in S Michele on the south and the Franciscans in S Lorenzo on the north. The urban plan, acquired by the beginning of the second millennium, was subsequently identified with the city as such; later peripheral developments were defined only as suburbs.

After the stable period of Paduan rule, the dynamic Scaligeri became rulers of Vicenza (1311–87). The eastern gate leading towards Verona was fortified with a strengthened Castello (1343), and the Scaligeri began to reorganize the expanded city, including the suburbs. A new ring of walls (*c.* 1365–81) was added to the old walls, which were left intact. The suburb of S Pietro, to the north-east, developed along the roads coming from Treviso (Porta S Lucia), Padua (Porta Padova) and Casale (Porta di Camarzo), collectively crossing the Bacchiglione at the Ponte degli Angeli. The south-eastern district of Berga began to develop beyond Porta Lupia. To the north-west, the Porta Nuova district was free of any limiting preconditions. Between the tower of Porta Castello, the stronghold of the Rocchetta, Porta Nuova and Porta Santa Croce, regular blocks were built following a broad orthogonal grid of streets, anticipating humanistic preferences.

Within the city centre, however, the Scaligeri contented themselves with enriching the churches of the mendicant orders with splendid works. They founded only S Maria dei Servi (1322) in Piazza Biade and the little church of S Antonio (1361), attached to the hospice of the same name next to the cathedral. S Ambrogio in Portanuova was altered (1384), although the more ambitious abbey of S Agostino (1323–57) remained relatively untouched. Few significant changes were made, either, during the period of Visconti rule (1387–1404); in 1387 the small church of S Vincenzo was begun on the north side of the Piazza dei

Signori. Vague Lombard influences are also evident in a few fragments of buildings.

The four centuries of peace (1404–1797), however, that Venetian rule granted Vicenza proved exceptionally fruitful. From *c.* 1435–40, after a necessary phase of adjustment, the quality of building, both public and private, began to improve. The streets were adorned with residences, built in the Gothic style in clear imitation of Venice, beginning in the Barche quarter along the Bacchiglione, its river port in direct contact with ships arriving from Venice. The cultural influence of Venice was stronger and the results more striking than in any other city of the Veneto. The façades were decorated with polychrome frescoes, and the capitals of the pilasters on the mullioned windows were frequently gilded. Over the city towered the great Palazzo della Ragione (*c.* 1450–60), created by reconstructing and uniting the old Palazzo Vetus and Palazzo Communis. The walls were clad in marble, and at the north-eastern corner rose the 82 m Torre di Piazza.

Apart from rebuilding the cathedral (mid-15th century) and works at S Maria in Foro and the oratory of S Cristoforo for the church of S Chiara (*c.* 1450) in the Berga district, there was little in the way of ecclesiastical architecture during this period. Little was done, either, to the city's fortifications; in fact, they subsequently remained more or less as established by the Scaligeri, apart from minor alterations to Porta Monte in order to enclose better the Berga district, and the addition of Porta S Bartolo (1435). The latter was an isolated outpost of the fortifications (see fig. 2) of the Pusterla quarter, which were never completed despite the commands (1508–9) of Bartolomeo d'Alviano. The emphasis on secular building in Vicenza continued throughout the 16th century, helped by the stay in the city of Pietro Lombardo from *c.* 1467 to 1474, when competent workshops were set up in Pedemuro S Biagio by skilled Lombard craftsmen, notably Bernardino da Milano (1477–1504), Tommaso da Milano (1475–1510), Tommaso's son Rocco da Vicenza (*fl* 1494–1526) and Giacomo da Porlezza.

An important role was played by the architect Lorenzo da Bologna, evidently a follower of Leon Battista Alberti, who was in Vicenza from 1476 to 1489. Under his influence the rules of Renaissance architecture were grafted on to Late Gothic schemes in the city, for example Palazzo Arnaldi-Tretti and Palazzo Negri de' Salvi, and new architectural solutions were tried, for example Palazzo Thiene (*c.* 1489; *see* LORENZO DA BOLOGNA) in Contrà Porti by Lorenzo himself. Old houses were embellished with elegant portals in response to the new fashion, which found exuberant expression in the altars of churches, for example the Garzadori altar in S Corona. A typical case is the altar (destr. 19th century) of S Bortolo, which began to be updated in 1447; it incorporated local sculpture by the Pedemuro workshops and paintings by BARTOLOMEO MONTAGNA and his followers.

In the 16th century Vicenza's tenacious aspiration towards civic perfection, encouraged by the cultural leadership of GIANGIORGIO TRISSINO, took a decisive turn with the revival of classicism. In fact it was through Trissino's patronage that this tendency was consolidated, thanks to the professional skills of Andrea di Pietro della Gondola, who in 1523–4 moved from Padua to the

2. Vicenza, view from the slopes of Monte Berico showing the fortifications; detail from an altarpiece by Marcello Fogelino: *Madonna of the Stars*, oil on canvas, *c.* 1525 (Vicenza, S Corona)

3. *View of Vicenza* from the Slope of Monte Berico by Cristoforo dall'Acqua, etching, 0.31×1.02 m, after 1780 (Vicenza, Biblioteca Bertoliana)

workshop of the Pedemuro craftsmen of Vicenza, and who from 1538–40 worked independently under the name Palladio, which was bestowed on him by Trissino (*see* PALLADIO, ANDREA). Palladio's structures 'alla Romana', erected to celebrate the entrance into the city of Bishop Ridolfi in September 1543, were in anticipation of the ideal Vicenza; after only a few minor experiments, the style passed from the status of ephemeral decoration to that of permanent construction. In addition to the loggias around the Palazzo della Ragione (also known as the Basilica; 1548; *see* PALLADIO, ANDREA, fig. 3) and the Loggia del Capitaniato (early 1570s), both public buildings, Palladio undertook many important projects for private clients, to be fitted into the urban fabric of the city in the course of four decades, along with lesser but similar initiatives (*see* PALLADIO, ANDREA, figs 2 and 6). The intention was to set up a masterfully varied series of model examples of classical orthodoxy, without altering the rectangular Roman street plan. Though strikingly successful, the results of this comprehensive programme were only partial. Nevertheless, while the ideal city was never actually built, the vision was realized in the Teatro Olimpico (1580), designed by Palladio for the Accademia Olimpica. There, the ideal city was represented in the scenery created by Vincenzo Scamozzi for the opening performance (*Oedipus rex*; 1585), which presented, in the guise of Boiotian Thebes, the dream of Vicenza. It thus had the character of a paradigm, and therefore the stage set was not dismantled after the event but was permanently preserved (*see* THEATRE, fig. 4).

In the early 17th century architecture in Vicenza was characterized by the rational, severe work of Scamozzi and his followers, their pared, essential style appropriate both to the simpler residences of a threatened aristocracy and to the Counter-Reformation austerity of the many oratories and the unadorned structures of the hospices, made necessary by the increasing turbulence of the period. In these austere times the work of Scamozzi's pupil Baldassare Longhena was accepted, though much subdued, but that by the illustrious Guarino Guarini (ii) was rejected; his Aracoeli (1672) was relegated to a position outside the city walls, while his church of S Gaetano (1675) was considered unsuitable for the main street.

With the return of greater stability at the end of the 17th century there was a revival of interest in Palladio. In the sanctuary of Monte Berico (1688–1703) by Carlo Borella (1675–1707), a specific Palladian design, not executed by Palladio himself, was adopted and emphasized. Francesco Muttoni, who was in Vicenza from 1696, proposed for the Palazzo Velo Vettore (begun 1706; for illustration *see* MUTTONI, FRANCESCO) an openly Baroque interpretation of Palladio's Palazzo Chiericati. From Muttoni there spread in Vicenza an architectural vocabulary that linked Palladio's imagination and sensitivity to space, amid late Baroque and Rococo influences, with an airy scenographic tendency (see fig. 3) that was utterly in keeping with the decorative schemes of Giandomenico Tiepolo, for example at Palazzo Valmarana and Villa Valmarana (both 1757; for illustration *see* TIEPOLO, (2)).

In Muttoni's later work, however, including the Portici (1741), the covered way linking the new Monte Berico sanctuary with the city, preparing the way for the upgrading of the Campo Marzio district, he was already preaching a doctrine of dry functionality. By the middle of the 18th century, in fact, the dawn of the Enlightenment was signalling a new turn, the major developments of which were described by Domenico Cerato in *Scuola di architettura civile pratica* (1750). A critical reassessment of Palladio was already under way, manifested in S Gaetano (1721–30) by Gerolamo Frigimelica (1653–1732), in the repeated interventions (1730–48) of the measured clarity of Giorgio Massari, and in the sharp purism of Enea Arnaldi (1716–94). Against such a background the talent of Ottavio Bertotti Scamozzi reached its peak: he published a detailed critical edition of Palladio's *I quattro libri dell'architettura* (1776–83), in opposition to the pioneering one of Muttoni, which emphasized the differences between Palladio's actual buildings and the corresponding drawings of them in Palladio's treatise.

Following this phase of Neo-classicism, Palladio's popularity led to the development of Palladianism, a style derived from Palladio's vocabulary, in which, despite the changed times, the interrupted dream of the ideal city was finally to be realized. Examples of this approach include the interior loggias of Palazzo Cordellina (begun 1776) by Ottone Calderari and the four-sided portico in rusticated reddish stone of the Cimitero Maggiore (begun 1818) by

Bartolomeo Malacarne. By the middle of the 19th century, however, Giovanni Miglioranza (1798–1861) introduced new developments, manifested in the Palazzo Gualdo-Giacometti (1838), the Romantic Caffè Moresco (1838) and the Gothic Revival façade (1860–61) of the old church of Monte Berico. Thereafter, architecture in Vicenza became 'receptive to moderate eclectic tendencies, for example the Renaissance Revival style, derived from the work of Giulio Romano, of the Palazzina Zamberlan-Farina (1899). The Art Nouveau and Secession styles were used at the turn of the century by architects involved in the peripheral expansion of the city, notably in the residential quarter of Vicenza Nuova and the working-class quarter of S Francesco Nuovo. The city was heavily bombed in World War II, causing much damage to the centre, including to the cathedral, which has since been rebuilt.

BIBLIOGRAPHY

G. Mantese: *Memorie storiche della chiesa vicentina*, 5 vols (Vicenza, 1952–82)
F. Barbieri, R. Cevese and L. Magagnato: *Guida di Vicenza* (Vicenza, 1953, rev. 1956)
E. Arslan: *Catalogo delle cose d'arte e di antichità d'Italia: Vicenza: Le chiese* (Rome, 1956)
Illuministi e Neoclassici a Vicenza (Vicenza, 1972), pp. xi–xvi
E. Franzina: *Vicenza: Storia di una città, 1404–1866* (Vicenza, 1980)
F. Barbieri: *Vicenza: Storia di una avventura urbana* (Milan, 1982)
——: *Vicenza, città di palazzi* (Milan, 1987)
Storia di Vicenza, 3 vols (Vicenza, 1987–90)

FRANCO BARBIERI

2. VILLA ROTONDA. South-east of Vicenza is the famous suburban villa (also known as the Villa Rotunda, Villa Almerico-Valmarana or Villa Capra) that was designed by Andrea Palladio (*see* PALLADIO, ANDREA, fig. 5) for Cardinal Paolo Almerico, a Referendary to Pope Pius IV. Almerico and his father had purchased land in the area of the Valle Silenzio from 1533, and circumstantial evidence suggests building of the villa was begun in 1565–6. The interior decoration was under way in the 1570s, although the villa was not fully completed at the time of Palladio's death in 1580.

The villa is attractively located in the countryside outside Vicenza, but Palladio nonetheless included the villa among his designs for city palazzi. He described the site in terms of the charm of the landscape and its vistas

> upon a gently sloping hilltop flanked on one side by the navigable Bacchiglione River, from the other it is surrounded by other pleasant hills which resemble a large theatre . . . . Therefore, because it enjoys beautiful vistas from every side, some of which are near by, others more distant, others that reach the horizon, loggias have been made on all four façades.

This setting is usually considered the determining element of the quadrilateral symmetry that characterizes the design of the villa.

The interior rooms of the villa are arranged around a central two-storey rotunda. The villa is remarkable for its four identical façades, marked by pedimented porticos and flights of steps leading up from the ground-level. The whole unit is surmounted by a low stepped dome, a form usually associated with antique or religious architecture and introduced by Palladio to villa design here for the first time. The dome was executed to Palladio's design by

Vincenzo Scamozzi, who claimed to have completed the building after Palladio's death. The main north-west entrance is accentuated by the addition of two statues on the pedestals flanking the approach staircase. Palladio named Vincenzo Rubini (*fl* 1550–60) as the sculptor responsible. Figures on the angles of the pediments on all fronts were added by Giovanni Battista Albanese in 1606. The regularity of the design of the villa represents a fulfilment of Palladio's theories of ideal form and proportion, even though he had already prepared a similar plan for the unexecuted Villa Trissino at Meledo. The villa as built differs from the illustration in Palladio's *I quattro libri dell'architettura* in both plan and elevation: the central vault is lower, windows and doors have been given frames, and the four passages leading to the central rotunda are not all of equal width.

The interior rooms of the main floor contain stucco chimney-pieces, elegant stucco cornices and compartmented ceilings incorporating large figurative frescoes with small-scale grotesques (*c.* 1599–1600) attributed to Anselmo Cavera, Alessandro Maganza and his son. Figural stuccowork is attributed to Ottaviano Ridolfi (*fl* 1567–92) and Agostino Rubini. The walls of the four axial halls leading to the central rotunda were frescoed *c.* 1695–1705 by Louis Dorigny.

The unusual planning of the villa together with its representation in *I quattro libri* have made it one of the most famous villas ever built. Consequently, it has provided a source for many imitations, notably Vicenzo Scamozzi's Rocca Pisana (1576), Lonigo (*see* SCAMOZZI, (2), fig. 1), and, in England, Colen Campbell's Mereworth Castle (1722), Kent, and Chiswick House (1725), near London, by Richard Boyle, 3rd Earl of Burlington (*see* BOYLE, (2), fig. 3).

BIBLIOGRAPHY

C. Rowe: 'The Mathematics of the Ideal Villa: Palladio and Le Corbusier', *Archit. Rev.* [London], ci (1947), pp. 101–4; repr. with addendum in C. Rowe: *The Mathematics of the Ideal Villa and Other Essays* (Cambridge, MA, 1976), pp. 1–27
W. Lotz: 'La Rotonda: Edificio civile con cupola', *Boll. Cent. Int. Stud. Archit. Andrea Palladio*, iv (1962), pp. 69–73; Eng. trans. in W. Lotz: *Studies in Italian Renaissance Architecture* (Cambridge, MA, 1977), pp. 190–96
J. Ackerman: *Palladio's Villas* (Locust Valley, NY, 1967), pp. 68–72
C. A. Isermeyer: 'Die Villa Rotonda von Palladio', *Z. Kstgesch.* (1967), pp. 207–21
C. Semenzato: *La Rotonda di Andrea Palladio*, Corpus Palladianum, i (Vicenza, 1968; Eng. trans., 1969)
C. M. Sicca: 'La fortuna della Rotonda', *La Rotonda: Novum corpus Palladianum* (Milan, 1988), pp. 169–204

CAROLYN KOLB

Viciebsk [Rus. Vitebsk]. Belarusian town in the north-eastern part of the country near the confluence of the rivers Western Dźvina (Dvina) and Vićba (Vit'ba). It was first mentioned in 1021; from the 14th century it was incorporated in Lithuania and Poland and from 1772 it was part of Russia (later USSR) until Belarusian independence in 1991. The oldest architectural monument is the church of the Annunciation (12th century; rebuilt), a rare example of Old Russian architecture in the western lands. In the late 18th century and the 19th the Baroque style gave way to Neo-classicism. Notable buildings include the

Jesuit college (1716), the Basilian and Bernardine monasteries (1735–55), the Neo-classical governor's palace (before 1772) and the town hall (1775); there is an obelisk commemorating the defeat of Napoleon's army near Viciebsk (1912; by Ivan A. Fomin). Before the Revolution of 1917 the Orthodox brotherhood was the most important cultural determinant. Other important monuments include the Marakŭ (Markov) Monastery (16–17th century), the cathedral of the Assumption (mid-17th century) and the Iljinskaja (Il'inskaya) Church (17th century).

In 1871 the first Belarusian art and archaeology exhibition was organized in Viciebsk. This was followed in 1894 by the founding of a Museum of Antiquity. In 1892 Yury Pen, who had studied at the Academy of Arts in St Petersburg, opened the first art studio school in Belarus' in Viciebsk. It functioned until 1918. There, in 1906, Marc Chagall, a native of the city, received his first artistic training. After the Revolution in 1917 Chagall became Commissar of Art in Viciebsk and its region (1918–20), with responsibility for the local museum, art school and theatre productions. The first director of the school was Mstislav Dobuzhinsky, its teachers including Chagall, Pen, Jean Pougny and Kseniya Boguslavskaya. The school, which became an important centre for the Russian avant-garde, was quickly reorganized into the Vitebsk Institute for Art and Industry and then UNOVIS, with changes in staff and teaching methods reflecting the shift towards the avant-garde (Kazimir Malevich, El Lissitzky and Vera Yermolayeva). However, by 1923 it was once again reformed into an art and technological college, and its importance as an institution of innovation rapidly diminished.

Viciebsk was reconstructed on an overall plan in 1945–7 after severe damage in World War II. Local historical and archaeological objects are exhibited in the Regional Museum of Local History in the former town hall.

BIBLIOGRAPHY
T. I. Chernyavskaya: *Vitebsk* (Minsk, 1977)

L. N. DROBOV

Vicitra. *See* BICHITR.

Vico, Enea (*b* Parma, 29 Jan 1523; *d* Ferrara, 18 Aug 1567). Italian engraver. He trained in Parma and by 1541 was in Rome, where he became a pupil of Tommaso Barlacchi (*fl* 1527–42). In 1541–2, in collaboration with Barlacchi, he produced his first work, a series of 24 engravings with grotesque decorations in imitation of antique paintings (B. 467–90). In Rome, Vico was also influenced by the printmakers Agostino dei Musi, Antonio Salamanca and, above all, Marcantonio Raimondi. Vasari recorded that in 1546, following a short period in Florence, where he made engravings for Grand Duke Cosimo I de' Medici after works by Michelangelo, Vico applied to live in Venice. He remained there until 1563, when he was summoned to the court of Alfonso II d'Este, Duke of Ferrara, where he lived until his death.

About 500 prints by Vico are recorded. Notable among his single engravings are those based on Michelangelo's *Leda and the Swan* (B. 26) and on his *Judith and Holofernes* (1546; B. 1) and the *Prophet Isaiah* (B. 11) from the frescoes in the Sistine Chapel (Rome, Vatican). Many of his prints

Enea Vico: *Column of Antonius and a Roman Obelisk*, engraving, 536×324 mm, 1567 (Vienna, Graphische Sammlung Albertina)

are after Raphael, including those of the *Annunciation* (B. 2), *Entombment* (1543; B. 7), *Lamentation* (1548; B. 8), *Tarquinius and Lucretia* (B. 15) and the *Toilet of Venus* (1546; B. 19). He also made engravings after Parmigianino, for example *Lucretia* (B. 17), *Mars and Venus* (B. 21, 27), *Woman Spinning* (B. 39) and *Proserpina Turning Ascalaphus into an Owl* (B. 45), as well as after Raimondi (B. 4, 6, 16, 36, 37), Titian (B. 3), Perino del Vaga (B. 25, 38, 46), Rosso Fiorentino (B. 30) and Francesco Primaticcio (B. 31; *see* ITALY, fig. 110). Vico's engravings of the *Academy of Baccio Bandinelli* (B. 49), showing a group of artists working by candle-light, was based on a work by Bandinelli, and his *Rhinoceros* (1548; B. 47) on one by Albrecht Dürer (*see* ANIMAL SUBJECTS, fig. 1). Series of engravings by Vico include 42 allegorical figures after Francesco Salviati (B. 50–91), 8 depictions of ancient Greek philosophers (B. 92–9) and 99 of ethnic costumes (B. 134–232). Among his portraits, that of *Cosimo I de' Medici, Grand Duke of Tuscany* (B. 239), the two of *Henry II, King of France* (B. 247, 250) and the two of *Charles V, Holy Roman Emperor* (B. 251, 255) are particularly noteworthy; the *Army of Charles V Crossing the Elbe* (B. 18) is a tumultuous, oval landscape with a great number of figures, surrounded by allegorical female forms and animals.

Vico's interest in antiquity, particularly medals and engraved gems, made him important as a scholar. He made prints of antique statues in the collection of Cardinal

Andrea delle Valle in Rome in 1541 (B. 42–4). He produced 85 prints after ancient medals in *Le imagini con tutti i riversi trovati et le vite degli Imperatori tratte dalle medaglie e dalle historie degli antichi* (1548, 2/1554; B. 322–406) and 63 portraits of empresses in its companion volume, *Augustarum imagines* (1557, 2/1558; B. 257–319). In 1560 he made ten prints with medals of *Julius Caesar* (B. 407–16), and in 1567 an engraving of the *Column of Antonius and a Roman Obelisk* (Vienna, Albertina; see fig.). His *Ex antiquis cameorum et gemmae delineata* consists of 34 prints after antique gems and cameos (B. 100–133); he also made engravings of antique friezes (B. 455–66), candlesticks (B. 491–4), vases (B. 420–33) and trophies (B. 434–49). Vico's work is of inestimable value for identifying ancient works of art, particularly gems and cameos.

BIBLIOGRAPHY

Thieme–Becker

G. Vasari: *Vite* (1550, rev. 2/1568); ed. G. Milanesi (1878–85), v, pp. 427–31

A. von Bartsch: *Le Peintre-graveur*, xv (1813), pp. 273–370 [B.]

J. D. Passavant: *Le Peintre-graveur*, vi (Leipzig, 1864), pp. 121–4

Fortuna di Michelangelo nell'incisione (exh. cat., ed. M. Rotili; Benevento, Mus. Sannio, 1964), pp. 62–4, fig. 16

Mostra di stampe popolari venete del '500 (exh. cat., ed. A. Omodeo; Florence, Uffizi, 1965), pp. 46–7, no. 41 (1–24); p. 57, figs 35–42

E. Lemburg-Ruppelt: 'Der Berliner Cameo des Dioskurides und die Quellen', *Röm. Mitt.*, xci (1984), pp. 89–113

O. J. Neverov: 'La serie dei "Cammei e gemme antichi" di Enea Vico e i suoi modelli', *Prospettiva* [Florence], xxxvii (1984), pp. 22–32

C. HÖPER

Vico, Giambattista (*b* Naples, 23 June 1668; *d* Naples, 20 Jan 1744). Italian philosopher, jurist and social theorist. He was the son of a bookseller and educated in Jesuit schools and at the University of Naples. He served as a tutor for nine years to the sons of the Rocca family at Vatolla but otherwise never left Naples. In 1699 he won a competition for the Chair of Rhetoric at Naples University and held this post until his retirement in 1741, but he was compelled to supplement his salary of 100 scudi a year by private tutoring. In 1735 he was appointed historiographer to the new Bourbon king Charles VII (later Charles III of Spain).

Vico's greatest work is his *Scienza nuova* (1725), in which he tried to establish a consistent pattern in the origin and development of human institutions. A subsidiary theme that emerged from his speculations was a cyclical theory of history, in which all nations are regarded collectively as diverse aspects of a single unity. According to Vico the history of man constantly moves through three stages, the divine, the heroic and the human. Examples of the divine age are Eden and ancient Egypt, where religion arose, inspired by terror of the unknown, and family life was organized. The heroic age is an aristocratic period, with wars and duels; the human age produces cities, laws and civil obedience. Patrician tyranny provokes the masses to revolt; democratic equality is then established under a republic, the excesses of which give rise to an empire. This in its turn becomes corrupt and declines into barbarism. After a *ricorso* or period of reflux, the cycle begins again. The achievements of the previous civilized epoch are nearly all lost, until the voice of God is heard once more. The reconstructive process then starts up, with a little of the previous advance retained.

Just as human institutions change, so does human nature. 'The earliest men first felt without articulating, then articulated the wonder and emotions of their souls, and finally reflected with a pure mind.' The confused perception, or *analogon rationis*, that precedes clear thought reacts passionately to the immediate sense of things, and in so doing creates art, in words and signs. The independence of fantasy from intellect is thereby demonstrated, as is the non-rational, intuitive and lyrical, yet cosmic and universal, nature of works of art.

Vico's concept of art arising from a zone of imprecise thought is analogous to the postulate of Gottfried Wilhelm von Leibniz (1646–1716) that (in contrast to the teaching of René Descartes) obscure and confused forms of cognition form part of a continuum of consciousness, and that the products of art might thus be obscure yet distinct, hence lying midway between sense and intellect.

Many of Vico's insights into primitive society and the development of institutions anticipate in a remarkable manner the conclusions of later scholars, but his work was not appreciated outside Italy till the 19th century.

WRITINGS

De nostri temporis studiorum ratione [On the study methods of our time] (Naples, 1709; Eng. trans., Indianapolis, 1965)

De antiquissima Italorum sapientia [On ancient Italian wisdom] (Naples, 1710)

La scienza nuova (Naples, 1725, 2/1730, 3/1744; Eng. trans., Ithaca, NY, 1968)

Autobiografia (Naples, 1728/9; Eng. trans., Ithaca, NY, 1963)

BIBLIOGRAPHY

B. Croce: *La filosofia di Giambattista Vico* (Bari, 1911; Eng. trans., London, 1913)

H. P. Adams: *The Life and Writings of Giambattista Vico* (London, 1935)

A. R. Caponigri: *Time and Idea: The Theory of History in Giambattista Vico* (Notre Dame, IN, 1968)

R. Manson: *The Theory of Knowledge of Giambattista Vico* (Hamden, CT, 1969)

L. Pompa: *Vico: A Study of the 'New Science'* (Cambridge, 1975)

I. Berlin: *Vico and Herder: Two Studies in the History of Ideas* (London, 1976)

□

Victor III. *See* DESIDERIUS.

Victor-Amadeus I, 12th Duke of Savoy. *See* SAVOY, §II(4).

Victor-Amadeus II, King of Sardinia [King of Sicily]. *See* SAVOY, §II(11).

Victor-Amadeus III, King of Sardinia. *See* SAVOY, §II(13).

Victor-Emanuel II, King of Italy. *See* SAVOY, §II(14).

Victoria. Canadian city and port, the provincial capital of British Columbia. It is situated on the Pacific coastline of Canada, on the southern point of Vancouver Island, *c.* 100 km south of the city of Vancouver. It was established by the Hudson's Bay Company in 1843, becoming capital of the Crown Colony of Vancouver Island in 1849, of the Colony of British Columbia in 1866 and of the province after confederation with Canada in 1871. The forts and farms built under Hudson's Bay Company rule reflected the 18th-century conservative Neo-classical aesthetic, for example at the Craigflower farm complex, subsequently preserved as a national historic site. During the colonial period, British military surveyors and topographers introduced watercolour painting, a tradition now best represented in the collection of the Public Archives of British Columbia. As a trading centre, however, Victoria also maintained maritime connections with many native tribal groups during this period, and the collecting of West Coast native art soon became popular, leading eventually to the founding of the Royal British Columbia Museum in 1886. There were also continuous links with Asia, and Victoria became the port of entry for Chinese workers attracted by the gold rushes of the 1850s and 1890s, and by the construction of the Canadian Pacific Railway in the 1880s. A large Chinese community was established in a district that became known for its distinctive 'Tong' society buildings.

The gold rushes of the late 19th century contributed a frontier boom-town flavour to Victoria, with buildings being garnished with Italianate cast-iron and fretwork detailing, manufactured in the foundries of San Francisco and Victoria. Of the early architects, the Englishman John Teague (1833–1902) worked first as an engineer for the British naval base; the Scotsman John Wright (1830–1915) worked on colonial government projects and later established one of the larger architectural practices in San Francisco. In the 1890s, however, the completion of the Canadian Pacific Railway, a decline in American immigration and an upsurge in British settlement marked a significant shift in cultural focus. The architectural practices of SAMUEL MACLURE and FRANCIS MAWSON RATTENBURY combined American construction practices with the English Arts and Crafts aesthetic to achieve a highly distinctive form of local expression. Buildings, gardens and landscape designs were resolved in a powerful artistic formula, particularly in Government House (1901–3; destr. 1957), the one building co-designed by the two men. Maclure and Rattenbury dominated the local Five Sisters' school of architecture, whose members were influential into the 1940s. From its base in Victoria the Arts and Crafts design vocabulary was used throughout the province for c. 50 years, mainly by the Public Works Department in schools, hospitals, court houses and government offices. Collections documenting this British influence are housed in the Maltwood Art Museum and Gallery (est. 1962) at the University of Victoria. In 1909 the Vancouver Island Arts and Crafts Society was founded. Members included the Canadian Expressionist painter EMILY CARR, the Italian Secessionist sculptor Charles Marega (d 1939), the silversmith W. H. Carmichael (1892–1954) and the anthropologist and museum curator William Newcombe (1884–1960), as well as the architect Maclure. Other artists who exhibited later with the society included Canadian watercolourists, such as Charles John Collings (1848–1931) and R. Mackie Fripp (1858–1917) of Vancouver, the Canadian Pacific Railway painters T. Mower Martin (1838–1934) and Frederic Bell-Smith (1846–1923), and the painter of British Columbian scenes George Southwell (1865–1961). The Emily Carr Art Gallery (est. 1977) is devoted exclusively to the work of Carr and her circle. The society's exhibitions and lectures gave rise to numerous civic institutions, including the first School of Handicraft and Design (est. 1913) and the Art Gallery of Greater Victoria (est. 1944), and prompted notable civic beautification initiatives. The internationally renowned Burchart's Gardens had been established in 1905 by Robert Burchart and Jenny Burchart, and by 1913 distinguished landscape designers were at work as proponents of the City Beautiful Movement, including Thomas Mawson (1861–1933), the Olmsted brothers (see OLMSTED, FREDERICK LAW) and the Boston firm Brett and Hall.

During the 1930s Victoria became a favourite location for Hollywood film makers, and this brief period of international contact heralded a flirtation with Art Deco and *Style moderne* architecture from such firms as S. Patrick Birley (1904–62) and W. F. K. Gardiner (1884–1966). However, in the late 1940s and 1950s a Californian variant of the International Style became dominant in the practices of John Di Castri (b 1924), John Wade (b 1914), Peter Cotton (1918–78) and Alan Hodgeson (b 1928). With the planner Rod Clack (b 1921) this group collaborated in introducing contemporary American West Coast design principles in the project for the restoration and development of Centennial Square (1963–5). This was combined with a major urban heritage conservation scheme for Old Town, the first of its kind in Canada. After World War II Victoria's artistic community was invigorated by the arrival of several European painters, among them the German Expressionist Herbert Siebner (b 1925), the Dane James Gordanee (b 1933) and the Englishman Don Harvey (b 1930). Craftsmen were also attracted to the area, for example German potters Jan Grove (b 1930) and Helga Grove (b 1927), the English-trained ceramicist Robin Hopper (b 1939) and the Chinese–Canadian potter and painter Wayne Ngan (b 1937). The Royal British Columbian Museum began its native carving programme (1953) under Chief MUNGO MARTIN and later Tony Hunt (b 1942), stimulating a revival of West Coast native art. The museum's extensive natural history collections also gave rise to a school of realist painters of wildlife, including James Fenwick Lansdowne (b 1937).

BIBLIOGRAPHY

M. Segger and D. Franklin: *Victoria: A Primer for Regional History in Architecture* (New York, 1979)
T. Reksten: *More English than the English: A Very Social History of Victoria* (Victoria, BC, 1986)
M. Segger: *In Search of Appropriate Form: The Buildings of Samuel Maclure* (Victoria, BC, 1986)

MARTIN SEGGER

Victoria, Queen of Great Britain and Empress of India. *See* HANOVER, (6).

Victoria, Queen of Prussia and Empress of Germany. *See* HOHENZOLLERN, (15).

Victorian style. Term used to describe the fine and decorative art and architecture produced within the British Empire during the reign of Queen Victoria (1837–1901). It is sometimes applied to contemporary work elsewhere. The period is conventionally divided into early Victorian (1837–c. 1850, but often taken to have begun in 1831, after the end of the Regency period), high Victorian (c. 1850–c. 1870) and late Victorian (c. 1870–1901).

Although the GOTHIC REVIVAL, the predominant style of the early and high Victorian periods, has come to be identified as the Victorian style, during this time of rapid social change and aesthetic uncertainty—when works of art were created, reproduced, criticized and collected and buildings designed and erected, in unprecedented quantity—no one style was ever universally accepted; indeed, much late Victorian work, notably that produced by the AESTHETIC MOVEMENT and the ARTS AND CRAFTS MOVEMENT, is actively 'anti-Victorian' in spirit and form, for example the severely geometrical tableware designed by Christopher Dresser for Elkington & Co.

When faced with a challenge, Victorian designers showed themselves capable of achieving superb clarity, as exemplified by the Crystal Palace (destr.) designed by Joseph Paxton for the Great Exhibition of 1851 in London and the New Palace of Westminster designed and partially carried out (1835–60) by Charles Barry. Frequently, however, they felt circumscribed by historical precedent and the difficulties of answering to a committee, which resulted in a confused compromise and the indifferent application of poorly mass-produced details copied from such pattern-books as *Grammar of Ornament* (1856) by Owen Jones. No such timidity marked the Victorians' wholesale restoration of earlier buildings. Ponderousness (combined with fine workmanship) characterizes the furniture produced specifically for public exhibition, while the pieces created by William Morris and his followers represent a reaction to exaggerated ornamentation.

The seriousness with which A. W. N. Pugin reinterpreted Gothic contrasts with the triviality of much Victorian genre painting. Portrait photographers and the Pre-Raphaelite painters (*see* PRE-RAPHAELITISM) sought a new realism. The work of this group of artists is now held by many to epitomize Victorian style. They sought liberation from their immediate artistic past in the use of pure colour; such architects as William Butterfield and William Burges explored the possibilities of polychromy, as did the sculptor John Gibson with the *Tinted Venus* (1851–6; Liverpool, Walker A.G.; for illustration *see* GIBSON, JOHN (i)). Victorian architecture, as well as painting and sculpture, was most widely appreciated in monochrome engraving, which the illustrators of the 1860s raised to new expressive heights, as in *The Graphic*.

The central hall of Wallington Hall, Northumb. (NT), brings together many of the features that typify the Victorian style. In 1853–4 the architect John Dobson roofed over an open courtyard to create a more welcoming domestic interior. The first-floor balustrade was copied from an illustration to Ruskin's *The Stones of Venice* (1851–3). William Bell Scott was commissioned to paint eight scenes celebrating the history of Northumberland (*Building the Roman Wall*) and local heroism (*Grace Darling Rescuing the Men of Forfarshire*) and industry (*Iron and Coal on Tyneside in the 19th Century*). The artist took great trouble to include authentic detail and underlined the narrative with dramatic gesture and texts placed above. Ruskin helped to paint the elaborate flowers and foliage on the pilasters, exhibiting the truth to nature that he professed in his writings. The sculpture is ideal (*Mother and Child*, marble, 1856–7, by Thomas Woolner, symbolizing Civilization), literary (plaster maquette for *Paolo and Francesca*, exh. 1851, by Alexander Monro, the subject taken from Dante's *Inferno*) and commemorative (profile medallions of Tennyson and Robert Browning by Munro);

all these works are *in situ*. The furniture, like many Victorian pieces intended for everyday use, was based on 18th-century prototypes.

For much of the 20th century the Victorian style—antipathetic to the Modern Movement—was out of favour. The foundation of the Victorian Society in London in 1958 marked growing scholarly interest shown by Nikolaus Pevsner and others in the diverse achievements of the period.

BIBLIOGRAPHY
J. Steegman: *Consort of Taste* (London, 1950); rev. as *Victorian Taste* (Cambridge, 1970)
Vict. Stud. (1957–) [with annual bibliog.]
J. Gloag: *Victorian Taste* (London, 1962/R 1972)
N. Pevsner: *Victorian and After* (1968), ii of *Studies in Art, Architecture and Design* (London, 1968)
M. Girouard: *The Victorian Country House* (Oxford, 1971, rev. 1979)
Victorian and Edwardian Decorative Art: The Handley-Read Collection (exh. cat., ed. S. Jervis; London, RA, 1972)
P. Conrad: *The Victorian Treasure-house* (London, 1973)
H. J. Dyos and M. Wolff, eds: *The Victorian City*, 2 vols (London, 1973)
R. Dixon and S. Muthesius: *Victorian Architecture* (London, 1978)
Great Victorian Pictures (exh. cat. by R. Treble, London, RA, 1978)
B. Read: *Victorian Sculpture* (London, 1982)
S. Jervis: *High Victorian Design* (Woodbridge, 1983)

OLIVER GARNETT

Victorica, Miguel Carlos (*b* Buenos Aires, 4 Jan 1884; *d* Buenos Aires, 9 Feb 1955). Argentine painter. He studied under the Italian painter Ottorino Pugnaloni and then at the Escuela de la Asociación Estímulo de Bellas Artes in Buenos Aires under Angel Della Valle, Eduardo Sívori, Reinaldo Giudici (1853–1921) and Ernesto de la Cárcova. A travel grant in 1911 enabled him to move to Paris, where he lived for seven years. He studied under Louis Désiré Lucas (*b* 1869), from which one can deduce that his artistic education was above all academic, and he was influenced first by the work of Eugène Carrière and later by Fauvism.

Victorica returned to Buenos Aires in 1917 and like other painters set up his studio in the Riachuelo district near the harbour. Although he had previously relied on an impasto technique and earth colours, from 1918 he gradually adopted freer and more expressive methods, as in his oil painting *Nude* (1923; Buenos Aires, Mus. N. B.A.). From 1940 the sensitive use of tone and materials became essential characteristics of his painting, as in *Bohemian Kitchen* (1941; Buenos Aires, Mus. N. B.A.). His work, in giving predominance to colour in defiance of the constrictions of drawing and contour, prefigured the development in Argentina of a form of gestural abstraction using stains of colour. He worked in both oils and pastels and produced landscapes, portraits, still-lifes and scenes of local customs.

BIBLIOGRAPHY
J. E. Payró: *Veintidós pintores: Facetas del arte argentino* (Buenos Aires, 1944), pp. 75–83 [illus.]
S. Blum: *Victorica* (Buenos Aires, 1980)

NELLY PERAZZO

Victorine Canons. Religious order of canons regular following the Rule of St Augustine (*see* AUGUSTINIAN CANONS, §1). In 1109 William of Champeaux (*c.* 1070–1121) opened a monastic school at St Victor in Paris, surrounding himself with pious and learned disciples to live as canons regular; this was to form the core of the abbey of St Victor, formally founded in 1113. The foundation had royal support from Louis VI (*reg* 1108–37) and was given papal approval in 1114 by Paschal II (*reg* 1099–1118). During the time of the first abbot, Gilduin (1113–55), the house of St Victor became the head of a Congregation, and its customal, the *Liber ordinis*, was drawn up; this laid down the Congregation's variant of the Augustinian Rule, which was to influence other houses of canons regular.

The Victorines did not work outside the order but lived a communal life, cut off from society by their lifestyle and dress. The rule emphasized austerity and uniformity. The Canons' habit consisted of a white robe with a rochet on their soutane and a black cloak. Within their houses there was particular emphasis on silence, and an elaborate sign language developed.

The importance of the Victorine congregation as a scholastic centre in the 12th century was out of all proportion to its small size. It provided a base for scholars, and many continental bishops were members. The Victorines never had many houses. Early foundations included St Genovefa (1148), Paris, and the house in Senlis; in England Victorine houses included Wigmore Abbey (Hereford & Worcs) and the royal foundation of St Augustine in Bristol (now the cathedral; *see* BRISTOL, §4); in Ireland St Thomas's Abbey (1177), Dublin, founded by Henry II (*reg* 1154–89), and some daughter houses. Their heyday was in the 12th century, when the many distinguished scholars included Hugh of St Victor (*d* 1142), Richard of St Victor (*d* 1173) and Adam of St Victor (*d* 1180s). A miniature from a 13th-century copy of Hugh's treatise *De arca morali* (Oxford, Bodleian Lib., MS. Laud Misc. 409, fol. 3*v*) shows Hugh teaching his fellow Victorines; this sums up the popular image of their scholastic traditions.

BIBLIOGRAPHY

E. Martene: *De antiquis ecclesie ritibus*, iii (Venice, 1788), pp. 251–3

P. Heylot: *Dictionnaire des ordres religieux* (Paris, 1850)

H. F. Berry: 'On the Use of Signs in the Ancient Monasteries with Reference to a Code Used by the Victorine Canons at St Thomas' Abbey, Dublin', *J. Royal Soc. Antiqua. Ireland*, xxii (1892), pp. 108–23

M. J. Heimbucher: *Die Orden und Kongregationen der katholischen Kirche*, i (Paderborn, 1896–7, rev. 3/1933–4), pp. 413–16

F. Bonard: *Histoire de l'abbaye royale et de l'ordre des chanoines réguliers de St Victor de Paris*, 2 vols (Paris, 1904–7)

J. C. Dickinson: *The Origins of the Austin Canons and their Introduction into England* (London, 1950)

VIRGINIA DAVIS

Víctor Manuel (García) (*b* Havana, Oct 31 1897; *d* Havana, 1 Feb 1969). Cuban painter. He is generally considered to be the initiator of modernism in Cuba. From 1910 he studied at the Academia de S Alejandro in Havana and taught elementary drawing there until 1925, when he went to Paris. There he formed part of the Latin American artistic and literary Grupo de Montparnasse and abandoned academic painting. On his return to Cuba in 1927 he participated in the Asociación de Pintores y Escultores exhibition in Havana, which marked the official beginning of modern painting in Cuba. As a teacher and avant-garde painter he had a considerable influence on painters of his own and succeeding generations.

Víctor Manuel reconciled Parisian modernism with traditional Cuban themes and elements in order to create works that were at once culturally specific and cosmopolitan. *Tropical Gypsy* (1927; Havana, Mus. N. B.A.) is his best-known painting, referring to Gauguin and modern European art while seeking to portray a national icon: the *guajiro* or peasant. Víctor Manuel remained obsessed with the depiction of this Cuban ideal type throughout his career, and many of his paintings are thus variations on one theme. He also painted bucolic landscapes, romantic couples, portraits and Havana street scenes (e.g. *Street Scene*, 1936; Havana, Mus. N. B.A.). Almost all these works contain idealized images that have a lyrical, dreamlike quality.

BIBLIOGRAPHY

G. Pérez-Cisneros: 'Víctor Manuel y la pintura cubana contemporánea', *U. La Habana*, 1 (1941), pp. 208–30

Víctor Manuel (exh. cat., Havana, Museo N. B.A., 1969)

Origins of Modern Cuban Painting (exh. cat., ed. J. A. Martínez; Miami, FL, Frances Wolfson A.G., 1982)

Víctor Manuel: Un innovador en la pintura cubana (exh. cat., ed. R. Viera; Miami, FL, Cub. Mus. A. & Cult., 1982)

J. A. Martínez: *Cuban Art and National Identity: The Vanguardia Painters, 1927–1950* (Gainesville, 1994)

GIULIO V. BLANC

Victors [Victoors], **Jan** (*b* Amsterdam, *bapt* 13 June 1619; *d* East Indies [now Indonesia], after Jan 1676). Dutch painter. He was half-brother to the bird painter Jacobus Victors (?1640–1705) and the noted Delft potter Victor Victors (*b* 1638). About 150 oil paintings by Jan Victors, comprising portraits, genre scenes and historical subjects on both canvas and panel, have been catalogued. No signed or securely attributable drawing by him is known. Although his training is undocumented, Victors has long been considered a member of the school of Rembrandt in Amsterdam. His paintings of 1640–70 show many formal and thematic interrelationships with Rembrandt and his documented pupils of the 1630s: Govaert Flinck, Ferdinand Bol and Gerbrandt van den Eeckhout. Certain archaisms of Victors's style—his peculiarly ponderous figure types, marked linearity, emphatic gestures and generally cluttered compositions—show the direct influence of Pieter Lastman and Claes Moeyaert. His interest in the art of manual rhetoric and the theatre is shown by the arrested histrionics of his figures and their exotic costumes and accessories.

During his early years (1640–45) Victors established a firmly controlled manner of figure painting in his portraits and historical scenes. Such works as the *Young Woman at an Open Window* (1640; Paris, Louvre; see fig.) and the *Capture of Samson* (Brunswick, Herzog Anton Ulrich-Mus.) show a linear definition of form, sturdy three-dimensional figures and strong Baroque lighting. However, Victors's middle years were his most productive, and from 1646 to 1655 he produced his most accomplished works. His light-filled compositions became increasingly vibrant and frequently included more subsidiary figures, animated gestures, agitated drapery and atmospheric effects, for example in the monumental *Jacob Seeking the Forgiveness of Esau* (1652; Indianapolis, IN, Mus. A.). From 1646 Victors expanded his thematic repertory to include genre subjects depicting a variety of rustic types and provincial activities. Affinities with the genre production of Jan

Miense Molenaer, Govaert Camphuyzen and Hendrick Sorgh are apparent in such works as *The Dentist* (1654; Amsterdam, Hist. Mus.), *Scene outside a Dutch Farm* (1650; Copenhagen, Stat. Mus. Kst) and the *Greengrocer at the Sign of 'de Buyskool'* (1654; Amsterdam, Rijksmus.).

After the mid-1650s Victors became less prolific, eventually abandoning painting to become a *ziekentrooster* ('comforter of the sick') in the service of the Dutch East India Company. His late work is generally less polished. The *Portrait of a Family in Oriental Dress* (1670; sold London, Sotheby's, 14 Dec 1977, lot 111), Victors's last dated work, shows a marked tendency towards stylization and harshness. Figure proportions are more elongated (though not more attenuated), modelling is darker and more opaque, colours more garish and the definition of space less logical, in keeping with the contemporary Dutch vogue for mannered aesthetics and schematization.

Victors is last documented in Amsterdam in January 1676. Shortly thereafter he departed for the East Indies and is reported to have died there of unspecified causes. A son, Victor Victors (*b* 16 Sept 1653), had travelled to the East and was recorded in Australia in 1696–7 as a *ziekentrooster*, draughtsman and cartographer with the Dutch East India Company.

BIBLIOGRAPHY
Bénézit; Thieme–Becker; Wurzbach
F. D. O. Obreen: *Archief voor Nederlandsche kunstgeschiedenis*, 7 vols (Rotterdam, 1877–90/ *R* Utrecht, 1971), ii, pp. 282–3
A. D. de Vries: 'Biografische aanteekeningen', *Oud-Holland*, iv (1886), pp. 217–24
A. Bredius: *Künstler-inventare*, VI/ii (The Hague, 1916), pp. 596–600; XIII/vii (The Hague, 1921), pp. 255–6
H. Gerson: 'Jan Victors', *Ksthist. Meded.*, iii (1948), pp. 19–22
M. Haraszti-Takács: 'Les Tableaux de Jan Victors dans les collections de Budapest', *Bull. Mus. Hong. B.-A.*, xx (1962), pp. 61–70
E. Zafran: 'Jan Victors and the Bible', *Israel Mus. News*, xii (1977), pp. 92–118
D. Miller: 'Jan Victors: An Old Testament Subject in the Indianapolis Museum of Art', *Perceptions*, ii (1982), pp. 23–9
——: *Jan Victors (1619–76)* (diss., Newark, U. DE, 1985)
——: '*Ruth and Naomi* of 1653: An Unpublished Painting by Jan Victors', *Mercury*, ii (1985), pp. 19–28
V. Manuth: *Ikonografische Studien zu den Historien des Alten Testaments drei Rembrandt und seiner frühen Amsterdamer Schule* (diss., Berlin, Freie U., 1987)
W. Sumowski: *Gemälde der Rembrandt-Schüler*, iv (Landau, 1989), pp. 2589–2722
——: *Drawings of the Rembrandt School*, x (New York, 1990)
D. Miller: 'The World of Calvin in the Art of Jan Victors', *Ksthist. Tidskr.*, lxi/3 (1992), pp. 99–105

DEBRA MILLER

Victory of Samothrace. *See* NIKE OF SAMOTHRACE.

Vicús. Pre-Columbian site near Chulucanas, Morropon Province, in the far north of Peru. It was the centre of a culture that flourished *c.* 500 BC–*c.* AD 500. In the 1960s grave robbers found cemeteries containing deep shaft and chamber tombs on the hill of Vicús and at neighbouring sites. Further architectural remains discovered in 1987 included a large ceremonial structure with four terraces and a central asymmetrical ramp. Just to the north of this is a large complex of terraces with houses. Although these structures lack associated pottery, their proximity to the main Vicús cemetery suggests that they date to the same period.

Jan Victors: *Young Woman at an Open Window*, oil on canvas, 930×780 mm, 1640 (Paris, Musée du Louvre)

It was the cemeteries that yielded the large quantities of fine pottery and metal artefacts for which the site is known. Many of these were in a purely local style, termed Classic Vicús, Vicús-Vicús or simply Vicús. Reflecting the site's location in a transitional zone between the Central and Northern Andes, this style was strongly influenced by neighbouring cultures. Some ceramics from the same area show close similarities to phases 1 and 2 of the MOCHE style and are known as Moche–Vicús. Sawyer argued that there was GALLINAZO-style influence on Classic Vicús ceramics, and also that some elements of the CHORRERA style of southern Ecuador can be seen in Vicús pottery. Although Vicús ceramics appear childlike and disproportionate, their simplicity is attractive, and, while the range of forms and designs is limited, the small core of basic themes is enriched by various treatments that modify dimensions and combinations.

Most Vicús pottery was made by modelling with thick paste. Many non-functional vessels have two separate chambers joined by a horizontal tube and a curved strap handle (see fig.), a form also found in Gallinazo- and Chorrera-style pottery. The body of each chamber has a lenticular form which is semi-globular or drum-shaped. The base is flat or slightly convex. Most pots have a conical spout, sometimes much enlarged at the base and joined by a bridge to either the front chamber or the front of the pot itself. Many vessels have a whistle, with up to 12 air holes.

Vicús potters showed human beings in a highly stylized form, with a simple incision for the mouth, a prominent

Vicús, pottery vessel with figures of musicians, h. 172 mm, *c.* 500 BC–*c.* AD 400 (Lima, Museo del Banco Central de Reserva)

aquiline nose, a small forehead, huge ears, and lozenge-shaped 'coffee bean' eyes resembling those on some Chorrera anthropomorphic pots. The arms are thin, un-articulated and sometimes completely omitted. Only rarely are the face and body modelled anatomically. Men are shown wearing a small hat or turban, which is sometimes adorned with human heads or animal skins, possibly indicating warrior or shamanic status, or both. Both male and female headgear has a 'screw-thread' design. Many figures of both sexes have pierced ears for earrings but only a few have their noses pierced to take ornaments. Some wear collars of trophy-heads, possibly shrunken. There are numerous pots showing both heterosexual and homosexual erotic acts. Zoomorphic vessels are common, but display no true realism. While much artistic effort was devoted to modelling the animals' heads, their feet were replaced by stumps, and birds' wings were reduced to mere protuberances. The modelled heads often show felines with oversize teeth, but these cannot be classified by species.

A common decorative technique is negative painting, in which a dark painted background is used to create a linear design in the natural colour of the exposed fired clay. Some pots have positive painting repeating the same designs. On others, white paint is superimposed on red, black and cream. The most common designs include series of discs, dots inside circles, parallel lines, wavy lines, volutes, S shapes and zigzag triangles. Some design areas may be polished.

In 1969 about 700 metal artefacts were discovered in a cemetery at Loma Negra, near Vicús. The finds included nose ornaments, finials, pendants and a series of unique cut-out discs and crescentic plaques. Most were made of sheet copper with a gold or silver surface. The commonest decorative motifs represent such themes as the 'Fanged Being', the crested, dragon-like 'Moon Animal' and myth-ical creatures with human or snake bodies. These figures feature in scenes showing the capture of prisoners, human sacrifices, condors pecking bodies and trophy-heads. The style is Moche with a strong Vicús element, suggesting that the pieces were made either by Moche artisans working in the Vicús area or by Vicús craftsmen strongly influenced by Moche iconography.

BIBLIOGRAPHY

H. Horkheimer: *Vicús* (Piura, 1965)
R. Larco Hoyle: *La cerámica de Vicús* (Lima, 1965)
A. R. Sawyer: *Mastercraftsmen of Ancient Peru* (New York, 1968)
K. O. Bruhns: 'The Moon Animal in Northern Peruvian Art and Culture', *Ñawpa Pacha*, xiv (1976), pp. 21–40
F. Kauffman Doig: *Manual de arqueología peruana* (Lima, 1980)
J. C. Marcos and R. P. Zaldumbide: *Tesoros del Ecuador antiguo* (Barcelona, 1984)
K. Makowski Hanula: 'Preliminary Report of the First Season of the "Subproyecto Vicús"', *Willay*, xxvi/xxvii (1987–8), pp. 21–2
W. M. Bray: 'Stylistic and Aesthetic Developments in Peruvian Metal-work', *Sweat of the Sun: Gold of Peru/Oro del Perú*, ed. H. Coutts (Edinburgh, 1990), pp. 15–23
S. Purin and others: *Inca Peru*, 2 vols (Brussels, 1990)

GEORGE BANKES

Vida, Gheza (*b* Baia Mare, 28 Feb 1913; *d* Baia Mare, 11 May 1980). Romanian sculptor. From childhood he was attracted to wood-carving, and from 1928 to 1931 he was self-taught. He then studied (1931–5) under the painter Sándor Ziffer (1880–1962). Vida made his début in 1937 at the *Expoziţia artiştilor băimăreni* (exhibition of the artists of Baia Mare), with works carved in wood, including *Mineri* (h. 500 mm; Cluj-Napoca, priv. col.) and *Peasant Tied to the Stake* (h. 500 mm; Bucharest, priv. col.); these were further to inspire him in his researches into the mining communities of Maramures Province and their myths and rites. In 1938–9 he participated in the Spanish Civil War as a volunteer with the International Brigades attached to the Republican army. While interned in the camps at Saint-Cyprien and Gurs in France (1939–41), he made a series of linocuts based on life in the camp. After returning to Baia Mare, he studied at the Art Academy in Budapest (1942–4) under Jenö Bori. His sculptures from this period, all in wood, include *A Child Eating* (400×350 mm, 1942; Iaşi, priv. col., see Mihalache, p. 16) and *Dancer* (450×250 mm, 1943; Bucharest, City Council): these were made in a vigorous, almost primitive manner, with expressive chisel marks. His next works (from 1947) were larger and more dynamic (e.g. *Alpenhorn Blower* (1.28×1.33 m, 1947; Cluj-Napoca, Mus. A.) and were unaffected by the dogmatism of Socialist Realism, unlike such later works as *The Rest* (420×880 mm, 1957; Bucharest, N. Mus. A.) and *Village Carnival* (2.52×0.80 m, 1963; Baia Mare, Maramures Distr. Mus.). In 1970–73 Vida created a number of works, including *Rain* (h. 2.3 m; Baia Mare, Maramures Distr. Mus.), the *Peasants' Monument* (1972) at Mosei, Maramures province, and a series of totem-poles that conveyed his fascination with the cultures of the Pacific Islands and American Indians.

BIBLIOGRAPHY

M. Mihalache: *Vida Gheza* (Bucharest, 1965)
G. I. Bodea: *Vida, Artist Militant* (Cluj, 1980)
R. Sorban: *Gheza Vida* (Bucharest, 1981) [with bibliog.]

GHEORGHE VIDA

Vidal, Emeric Essex (*b* Brentford, Middx, 29 March 1791; *d* Brighton, 7 May 1861). English draughtsman and painter active in Brazil, Uruguay and Argentina. He joined the Royal Navy when he was 15. On his travels to the Baltic region, the Cape of Good Hope, St Helena, the West Indies, North America and South America he was prompted to apply his skill as a draughtsman and watercolourist to the production of local views. While staying in Brazil and Río de la Plata from May 1816 to September 1818 he produced watercolours depicting the exuberant vegetation of Brazilian landscapes and the regions surrounding Montevideo and Buenos Aires. He also recorded numerous views of Buenos Aires, its port and neighbouring villages, and its inhabitants: travelling salesmen, gauchos, soldiers and scenes of peasant customs. These include *The Cabildo, Buenos Aires, from under the Arch of the Market Plaza* (Oct 1817), and 25 hand-coloured aquatints after his illustrations were published by Rudolf Ackermann in monthly booklets as *Picturesque Illustrations of Buenos Ayres and Montevideo* (London, 1820; copy annotated by Vidal, Buenos Aires, Mus. Mun. A. Plást. Sívori), all depicting outdoor scenes accompanied by Vidal's written commentary. Drawn from nature, they

show characteristic scenes and customs of Buenos Aires and also document local dress in faithful detail.

Although Vidal protested about the liberties taken by the publisher in the production of the prints in his absence, they give a revealing and almost complete picture of Buenos Aires *c.* 1820. Vidal travelled again to Brazil and Río de la Plata in 1828–9, painting numerous works in Brazil but only one in Montevideo and two in Buenos Aires. His aquatints were used for a long time by publishers to illustrate accounts of travel in those regions.

BIBLIOGRAPHY

A. González Garaño: *Acuarelas inéditas de Vidal: Buenos Aires en 1816, 1817 y 1819* (Buenos Aires, 1931)
Emeric Essex Vidal: Su vida y su obra (exh. cat. by A. González Garaño, Buenos Aires, Asoc. Amigos A., 1933)
Acuarelas inéditas sobre Río de Janeiro (Buenos Aires, 1961) [24 lithographs executed in France]

Vidal, Miguel Angel (*b* Buenos Aires, 27 July 1928). Argentine painter and sculptor. Basing his work on the rigorous structural application of the straight line as his basic unit, he was one of the main creators in the late 1950s of a style of painting called ARTE GENERATIVO. Tending to work in series to which he gave titles such as *Dynamic Structures, Displacements, Integrations, Radiations, Fugues* and *Reflections*, he revealed his inexhaustible inventiveness in elaborating his fundamental system, for example in *Homage to Albers* (1965; Buenos Aires, Mus. A. Mod.), in which he acknowledged his debt to a pioneer of geometric abstraction, Josef Albers.

Vidal favoured strong centrifugal and centripetal tensions and often made his lines converge on a point in bundles, generating luminous irradiant foci and superimposed meshes that create fleeting sensations, as in *First Vision* (1968; New York, Guggenheim). By concentrating on the luminous energy of the lines and the poetic suggestiveness of space within a severely restricted geometric vocabulary, he was, by the 1980s, creating work that was almost mystical in tone. He applied these principles not only to paintings but also to sculptures made of plastic and metal, some of them using boxlike forms and systems of modular development.

BIBLIOGRAPHY

C. Córdoba Iturburu: *80 años de pintura argentina* (Buenos Aires, 1978), p. 185
I. Picovano: 'Arte generativo: Eduardo MacEntyre, 1929; Miguel Angel Vidal, 1928' in *Arte argentino contemporáneo* (Madrid, 1979), pp. 175–9

NELLY PERAZZO

Video art. Term used to describe art that uses both the apparatus and processes of television and video. It can take many forms: recordings that are broadcast, viewed in galleries or other venues, or distributed as tapes or discs; sculptural installations, which may incorporate one or more television receivers or monitors, displaying 'live' or recorded images and sound; and performances in which video representations are included. Occasionally, artists have devised events to be broadcast 'live' by cable, terrestrial or satellite transmission. Before video production facilities were available, some artists used television receivers and programmes as raw material, which they modified or placed in unexpected contexts. In 1959 the German artist Wolf Vostell included working television sets in three-dimensional collage works. In the same year NAM JUNE PAIK began to experiment with broadcast pictures distorted by magnets. He acquired video recording equipment in 1965, after moving to New York, and began to produce tapes, performances and multi-monitor installations (e.g. *Moon is the Oldest TV*, 1965, reworked 1976 and 1985; Paris, Pompidou). Paik is generally acknowledged to be the single most important figure in the emergence of video art, but he was not alone in grasping the artistic potential of electronic media. Several American independent film makers, including Stan Vanderbeek (*b* 1927) and Scott Bartlett (*b* 1943), made use of video processes to develop new kinds of imagery, although the end result was usually a projected film. Others, such as Steina and Woody Vasulka, used electronic skills to produce elaborate transformations of television camera images on videotape.

By 1969, when the Howard Wise Gallery, New York, presented the landmark exhibition *TV as a Creative Medium*, a fascination with electronic effects and complex imagery had been joined by other concerns. With the rise of CONCEPTUAL ART, many artists who explored relationships between themselves, the physical world and other people used video as a convenient medium for recording events. Bruce Nauman employed both film and video for his explorations of the relationship between the body and the spaces of the room and screen, while William Wegman brought the form of the television comedy sketch into the service of his own distinctive sensibility. Terry Fox (*b* 1943) used household objects in close-up in *Children's Tapes* (1974) in order to enact tiny melodramas demonstrating the laws of physics. Some artists engaged themselves with the specific qualities of video and the equipment involved, such as the camera, microphone and monitor. Joan Jonas made performance tapes in which the properties of video were made to interact with her own activity in front of the camera. *Organic Honey's Vertical Roll* (1972) features the insistent rhythmic jump of her image on a 'wrongly' adjusted monitor.

In Europe, until *c.* 1970, when video recorders became available outside commercial and scientific institutions, artists' concern with video was largely either theoretical and speculative or dependent on broadcast television as a foil and means of production. In the former Federal Republic of Germany, Gerry Schum (*d* 1974) developed the notion of a 'Gallery on TV', in which avant-garde artists could present their work in purely televisual terms, free from the distractions of physical artefacts or of programme narration or interpretation. The artists performed or directed activity for the camera, keeping in mind the eventual context of the television screen, creating not a film about the artist but a work by him or her. Schum produced two 'TV Gallery' compilations, *Land Art* (1968) and *Identifications* (1969). In 1970 he established the Videogalerie Schum in Düsseldorf, where he made and sold video-art tapes. In 1971 David Hall's *Seven TV Pieces* appeared on Scottish Television, interrupting regular programmes without announcement or explanation. In each, the filmed event emphasized the physical presence of the television set with which it was viewed, as when the set appeared to fill with water, which then drained away at a totally unexpected angle. In subsequent video installations and tapes, Hall drew attention to the illusory nature of television images, placing video art in confrontation with broadcast television.

In the 1970s a number of artists in Europe and the USA shared a commitment to video art as an autonomous form, rather than as documentation or a source of abstract

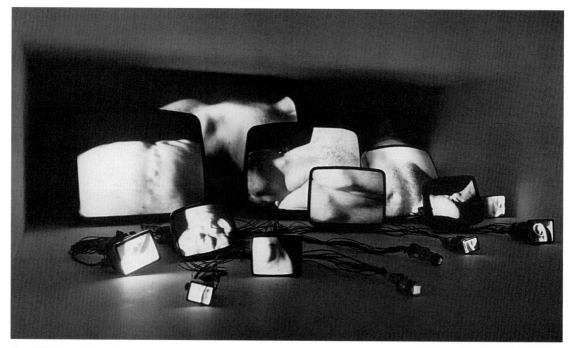

Gary Hill: *Inasmuch as It Is Always Already Taking Place*, 16-channel video/sound installation at the Museum of Modern Art, Oxford, 1990

imagery. An aesthetic evolved associated with conceptual art, which was concerned with ideas as well as images: it was characterized by real rather than edited timescales and by the use of closed-circuit, multi-monitor installations. This tendency, typified by the installation of DAN GRAHAM, was prominent in the exhibitions *Projekt '74* at Cologne; *The Video Show* (1975) at the Serpentine Gallery, London; a show at the Tate Gallery, London (1976); and at the Kassel *Documenta* of 1977.

In the late 1970s work by Bill Viola (*b* 1951), Kit Fitzgerald and John Sanborn suggested a reaction against the self-referential tendency, accompanied by an advance in video production techniques. Their tapes often deployed broadcast facilities provided by television companies and demonstrated a sophistication in the montage of image and sound that would become standard during the next decade. Dara Birnbaum, with her use of edited fragments of 'found' television material combined with rock music soundtracks, influenced the later British genre of 'Scratch Video', a style made popular by George Barber and the Duvet Brothers and quickly appropriated by directors of television programmes and popular music videos.

During the 1980s video art established its own context of production, exhibition and criticism, with organizations emerging in North America and western Europe to support and promote 'video culture'. Television producers began to buy and commission work from artists, and specialist venues, festivals, courses and workshops for video proliferated. Many artists made work addressing social, sexual and racial issues, renewing links with what survived of the 'community video' movement of the 1970s. By 1990 video installations had featured in several large international exhibitions and were a familiar presence in galleries and museums, assuming fresh authority through the work of such artists as Gary Hill (see fig.) and MARIE-JO LAFONTAINE. Artists making single-screen work exhibited increasingly on television, and the medium of video was merging with that of the computer. Video art, no longer novel nor wholly dependent on a gallery context, had become part of an increasingly elaborate network of electronic communication.

See also EXPERIMENTAL FILM.

BIBLIOGRAPHY

Video Art (exh. cat. by D. Antin and others, Philadelphia, U. PA, Inst. Contemp. A., and elsewhere; 1975)
D. Hall, ed.: *Studio Int.* (May–June 1976) [special issue on video art]
I. Schneider and B. Korot, eds: *Video Art: An Anthology* (New York and London, 1976)
Het lumineuze beeld: The Luminous Image (exh. cat. by D. Mignot, Amsterdam, Stedel. Mus., 1984)
J. G. Hanhardt, ed.: *Video Culture: A Critical Investigation* (New York, 1986)
R. Payant, ed.: *Vidéo*, Artextes (Montreal, 1986)
W. Herzogenrath and E. Decker, eds: *Video-Skulptur: Retrospektiv und aktuell, 1963–1989* (Cologne, 1989)
D. Hall and S. J. Fifer, eds: *Illuminating Video: An Essential Guide to Video Art* (New York, 1990)

MICK HARTNEY

Vidisha. *See* BESNAGAR.

Vidolenghi, Leonardo (*b* Marzano, Pavia; *fl* 1446–1501). Italian painter. In 1462 he witnessed a document in Pavia concerning Vincenzo Foppa. The only work attributable with certainty to Vidolenghi is a fresco on a pilaster representing the *Virgin and Child with SS Lucius and Lucy* in the church of S Maria del Carmine, Pavia; signed and dated 1463, it shows that he had become at least partly familiar with Foppa's artistic innovations. It testifies not only to the strength of his Pavian background but also to his contacts with the stained-glass masters of Milan and Pavia. This is confirmed by a document of 1463, probably concerning the execution of a window, which mentions a previous commission that he undertook with Bassiano Benlafaremo (*fl* 1463–71), for the church of S Tecla (later S Agostino), Genoa. In spite of this definite link with Liguria, scholars have tended to reject the identification of Vidolenghi with the Leonardo da Pavia who signed and dated the *Virgin and Child with Saints* (1466; Genoa, Pal. Bianco), a work that is still clearly related to the Late Gothic culture of Bonifacio Bembo and other Lombard painters of the period. Before 1476 Vidolenghi painted a *Maestà* (untraced) for the church of S Giorgio de' Catassi, Pavia. In 1490 he was among the group of various artists called to Milan to decorate the Sala della Balla of the Castello Sforzesco for the wedding (1491) of Ludovico Sforza, Duke of Milan, and Beatrice d'Este. Tanzi attributed to Vidolenghi the *Virgin and Child with SS Julius and Anthony Abbot* (Pavia, S Maria del Carmine) and the frescoed polyptych on the inside wall of the façade of S Pietro in Ciel d'Oro, Pavia.

BIBLIOGRAPHY

C. J. Ffoulkes and R. Maiocchi: *Vincenzo Foppa of Brescia, Founder of the Lombard School: His Life and Work* (London and New York, 1909), pp. 21–2, 37–8, 239–40, 256
F. Malaguzzi Valeri: 'Maestri minori lombardi del quattrocento', *Ant. Viva*, xi (1911), pp. 199–200
R. Maiocchi: *Codice diplomatico di Pavia dall'anno 1330 all'anno 1550*, 2 vols (Pavia, 1937–49)
F. Mazzini: *Affreschi lombardi del quattrocento* (Milan, 1965), pp. 450–51
M. Tanzi: 'Da Vincenzo Foppa al Maestro delle Storie di Sant'Agnese (1458–1527)', *Pittura a Pavia dal romanico al settecento*, ed. M. Gregori (Milan, 1988), pp. 76–7

VITTORIO NATALE

Vidor, Emil (*b* Pest [now Budapest], 27 March 1867; *d* Budapest, 8 July 1952). Hungarian architect. He began his university studies in Budapest in 1887, then in 1890 he went to the Akademie der Bildenden Künste, Munich, to study with Friedrich von Thiersch and H. Schmidt and in 1891 finished his studies under Johannes Otzen at the Technische Hochschule, Berlin. In 1894 he opened his own office in Budapest. In his many villas and residential blocks and in his factories and tombs he did not establish an enduring, individual style, but his works are characterized by bold façades and fastidious execution. The Romantic Vidor Villa (1901), Gorky Avenue, Budapest, with large structural and decorative elements of wood, is influenced by Scandinavian, particularly Norwegian, architecture. The stone façade is decorated with foliate ornament, and the roof is covered with glazed tiles. On the façade of the Egger Villa (1902), Gorky Avenue, Budapest, he unified the proportions of the closed and open elements with simple Viennese Secession lines and masses. The guttering is crowned with an ornamental dragon. More exceptional and original is the Bedő Building (1903), Honvéd Street, Budapest, inspired by the Art

Nouveau architecture of Emile André at Nancy. The five-axialed asymmetric façade consists of two contrasting treatments. The apertures and curved wall fillets on one side reveal a continuous upward movement and end in circular forms at the roof, from which they jut outwards in an organic, natural development. The architectural elements on the other side, with each level of the building in a different material, run upwards in tiers, becoming progressively less natural and more finished and ending in curved forms, as on the other side. Trees, flowers and fruits in maiolica decorate the façade and the entrance door has foliate ornamented wrought-iron work. Vidor also built an English-influenced villa at Kemenes Street, Budapest, and a vernacular-influenced building (1913), Endre Ady Street, Budapest. Such late works as the shop (1927–8), 24 Váci Street, Budapest, show the influence of Modernist architecture.

UNPUBLISHED SOURCES

Budapest, Loránd Eötvös U., Dept. A. Hist. [MS. of F. Bor: *Vidor Emil múépítész* [Emil Vidor architect] (1984)]

F. BOR

Vie et Lumière. *See under* LUMINISM (ii).

Viehweger, Hermann. *See under* LOSSOW & VIEHWEGER.

Vieira, Alvaro Siza. *See* SIZA VIEIRA, ALVARO.

Vieira, Custódio (*fl* 1728–46; *d* before Feb 1747). Portuguese architect. He worked first as a naval carpenter, then became a military engineer before rapidly climbing the hierarchy within the field of official architecture. He was highly regarded as Royal Architect (from 1734), if not prominent as an original designer; his expertise lay in the organization and execution of the large-scale building works undertaken by King John V. Vieira's first recorded work is the Palace of Vendas Novas, near Évora, built in 1728 for John V in celebration of the alliance of Spain and Portugal through the intermarriage of the Braganza and Bourbon royal families. The initial sketches for the palace were by an unknown hand, possibly either Antonio Canevari or João Frederico Ludovice, although the execution was by Vieira. It was built in an incredibly short space of time—from April 1728 to January 1729; work proceeded 24 hours a day, with 2000 workmen, lit at night by 10,000 faggots. The undistinguished building is a severely plain rectangular volume in rendered brickwork 100 m long, with a porticoed front facing south across an enormous parade ground. It suffered much damage during its later use as an artillery school in 1864.

In 1729 Vieira became supervisor of the construction of the Palace of Mafra, begun in 1717 by Ludovice. Under pressure from the King, work there also proceeded quickly: the church was consecrated in 1730, although Vieira continued work there until 1736. Vieira's work earned him the life-long enmity of Ludovice, who had no sympathy with Portuguese taste in decoration. In 1736 Vieira took over from the engineer Manuel da Maia the direction of the construction of the aqueduct of Águas Livres (1729–48) in Lisbon. This was part of the ambitious plan of civic improvements to Lisbon carried out by John V and was intended to bring a free supply of fresh water to Lisbon from hills over 18 km away. Vieira is credited

with the design of the most spectacular section, that across the Alcantara Valley in Lisbon, where it reached its maximum height of 65 m. The 14 arches, pointed like Gothic arches for structural reasons, reveal his background as an engineer. It was recognized as one of the great building achievements of 18th-century Europe. It survived the earthquake of 1755 and still functions.

In 1733 Vieira took charge of building works on the old Moorish Castelo de S Jorge in Lisbon, and the following year he succeeded João Antunes as Royal Architect as well as Francisco Tinoco da Silva (*fl* from 1683, *d* 1730) as Master at the Aulas dos Paços da Ribeira, the school in Lisbon for the apprenticeship of young architects. He also became Master of Works at Cintra and other royal palaces and at the monastery of Batalha. In 1743 he became architect for the Military Orders of Santiago and S Bento de Avis.

BIBLIOGRAPHY

F. Sousa Viterbo: *Dicionário histórico e documental dos architectos, engenheiros e construtores portugueses ou a serviço de Portugal*, iii (Lisbon, 1922)
A. de Carvalho: *D. João V e a arte do seu tempo*, ii (Lisbon, 1962)
R. C. Smith: *The Art of Portugal, 1500–1800* (London, 1968)
T. Espanca: *Distrito de Évora*, Inventário Artístico de Portugal, viii (Lisbon, 1975)
J. F. Pereira and P. Pereira: *Dicionário de arte barroca em Portugal* (Lisbon, 1989)

ZILAH QUEZADO DECKKER

Vieira, Domingos [o Escuro] (*b c.* 1600; *d c.* 1678). Portuguese painter. He was a portraitist who painted Portuguese society at the time of the Restoration of independence, 1640–50, and was appointed court painter to Peter II, Regent from 1668, although the appointment is undocumented. His portraits show great power in the psychological presentation of his sitters, conveying the restrained and austere values of 17th-century Portugal with an aristocratic dignity emphasized by figures that are sharply outlined against black backgrounds. The subjects show few attributes of rank and are depicted with finely modelled heads standing out strongly from the dark grounds, painted with vibrant whites and creams. The full-length figures of Diego de Velázquez are suggested by Vieira's portraits, and their dominating feature is their naturalism and the application of tenebrist effects. However, they have none of the subtleties of Velázquez, and Vieira's portraits follow the more traditional line of Portuguese portraiture, showing dignity without display, austere colour and solemn attitudes. Vieira was aware of contemporary Spanish portraiture but chose to concentrate on human tendencies that were characteristically more Portuguese and to give a specific picture of Portuguese society on the eve of the Restoration of the monarchy. He used fluid brushwork in which ashy and white tones have a surprising vibrancy and brilliance and in which the play of chiaroscuro effects is moderated to underline the impact of the pose.

The portraits of *Lopo Furtado de Mendonça* (signed and dated 1635) and of his wife, *Doña Isabel de Moura* (both Lisbon, Mus. N. A. Ant.), were originally full-length. During 1635 or 1636 he portrayed other members of the same Almada family, including *Doña Filipa de Melo* and *Doña Maria Antónia de Melo* (Lisbon, Mus. N. A. Ant.), two sisters of Doña Isabel de Moura. He also painted the vigorous portrait of *Dr Gonçalo de Sousa de Macedo* (see exh. cat., pl. 20) and of his wife *Doña Magarida Moreira* (1635–50; Portugal, Sousa de Macedo Freitas Branco priv. col., see dos Santos, pl. xvii). Attributed to Vieira is the portrait of *Dom Miguel de Almeida, Fourth Count of Abrantes* (*c.* 1635–50; Lisbon, Dir. Geral Fazenda Pub.); he was Chamberlain to John IV's Queen, Louise de Gusmão, and is shown with the cross of the Military Order of Christ emblazoned on his great black cape.

BIBLIOGRAPHY
A. C. Pinto: 'Domingos Vieira e não Domingos Barbosa', *Bol. Mus. N. A. Ant.*, ii/6 (1942), pp. 64–94
Personagens portuguesas do século XVII (exh. cat., Lisbon, Acad. B.A., 1942)
R. dos Santos: 'A pintura portuguesa no século XVII', *Conferências de arte* (Lisbon, 1943), pp. 37–56
J.-A. França: *O retrato na arte portuguesa* (Lisbon, 1983)

VITOR SERRÃO

Vieira, Jacinto (*b* Braga, *c.* 1700; *d* Braga, *c.* 1760). Portuguese sculptor. He was trained at Braga which, since the end of the 16th century, had replaced Coimbra as principal supplier of religious sculpture. Between 1723 and 1725 he carved an important series of statues for the Convent of S Maria, Arouca, in northern Portugal; each was 2 m high and made of stone, not wood as was customary in this region. He did not adopt the Baroque style here but retained the spirit of monastic art in the tradition of the 17th century. This series depicts female saints of the Cistercian and Benedictine Orders, together with Queen St Mafalda, patron of the Convent of S Maria, Arouca. It was placed in niches high on the walls of the nave and choir of the convent church. The figures are posed, with slightly twisted torsos. The stylized folds of their habits fall tightly against their bodies, slightly undulating as if blown by the wind, and their shoulder-length veils stand out in sharp contrast. The faces reveal the artist's preoccupation with carving variety and giving expression to each statue. Vieira also carved a kneeling *Virgin of the Annunciation* in the same church.

BIBLIOGRAPHY
R. dos Santos: 'Estatuária das monjas de Arouca' [Statues of the nuns at Arouca], *A. Ontem & Hoje*, 1 (1948), pp. 3–17
R. dos Santas: *A escultura em Portugal*, 2 vols (Lisbon, 1950–51)

PEDRO DIAS

Vieira, Jorge (Ricardo da Conceição) (*b* Lisbon, 1922). Portuguese sculptor. His early caricature figures have certain affinities with Surrealism in their aggressive humour. In the early 1950s the artist spent a year at the Slade School of Fine Art in London supervised by Reg Butler and Henry Moore. The bronze maquette he submitted to the competition in London for the *Monument to an Unknown Political Prisoner* won him a prize in 1953. At about that time he began working in terracotta, the medium he subsequently favoured. There are many similarities with 'primitive' sculpture: the earth colours; the rounded, stylized forms; the emphasis given to certain parts of the body (such as the feet, buttocks or head) and the mythological overtones present in the fusion of human and animal forms. Nevertheless, the works are pervaded by a sense of irony and humour. Vieira taught at the Escola Superior de Belas Artes in Lisbon.

BIBLIOGRAPHY
Jorge Vieira (exh. cat., Oporto, Gal. Nasoni, 1986)

RUTH ROSENGARTEN

Vieira da Silva(, Marie-Hélène) [Maria-Elena] (*b* Lisbon, 13 June 1908; *d* 6 March 1992). French painter of Portuguese birth. She arrived in Paris in 1928. She was impressed by the chequered tablecloths of the Bonnard paintings on display at the Galerie Petit, which influenced her later work; it was, however, sculpture that she first studied, with Emile-Antoine Bourdelle and then with Charles Despiau. In 1929 she began engraving in S. W. Hayter's Atelier 17 and started to design carpets for Dolly Chareau's Art Deco interiors. The influence of Joaquín Torres García, whose work was exhibited at the Galerie Pierre Loeb in 1932, was also crucial. She exhibited in 1933 and 1937 with the Galerie Jeanne Bucher, finally achieving a distinctive style in which the diamonds and squares of Portuguese *azulejos* combine with metaphors of chessboards and card games (e.g. *Chess Game*, 1943; Paris, Pompidou). Receding perspectives create an impression of vertiginous, imploding spaces that progressively absorb and annihilate the human element.

Before and during World War II Vieira da Silva's subject-matter became increasingly political in works such as *Flags* (1939; Düsseldorf, Kstsamml. Nordrhein-Westfalen), *Disaster (War)* (1941–2; Paris, priv. col., see Lassaigne and Weelen, p. 128) and *Liberation of Paris* (1945; Paris, priv. col., see Lassaigne and Weelen, p. 132). She had fled with her husband, the Hungarian painter Arpad Szènes, first to Portugal and then to Rio de Janeiro, where the couple mixed with the Brazilian intelligentsia. Returning to Paris, she exhibited in 1947, 1949 and 1951 at the Galerie Jeanne Bucher. Both her greyish palette and choice of motif, which deliberately echoed the French Impressionists, affiliated her work with the *paysagisme abstrait* of Jean Bazaine and Alfred Manessier. However, more dramatic structural motifs recalled the designs of Gustave Eiffel and of Piranesi. Vieira da Silva had first read Franz Kafka in 1936 and subjects such as *Library* (1949; Paris, Pompidou), used as a metaphor of alienation, were considered topically existential in the post-war circle around Jean-Paul Sartre. Parallels have been drawn between Sartre's concept of *nausée*, the labyrinths and mazes of the writer Jorge Luis Borges and Vieira da Silva's work.

Vieira da Silva was one of the most celebrated painters in Paris after World War II. In 1952 she painted a stage curtain for Arthur Adamov's *La Parodie*, and she often worked with the poet René Char. She collaborated with sculptor Germaine Richier, painting shield-like backgrounds for Richier's bronze figures. A retrospective at the Musée National d'Art Moderne, Paris, in 1969–70, which toured to Rotterdam, Oslo, Basle and Lisbon, marked the height of her fame. From 1970 many of her works were realized as tapestries.

BIBLIOGRAPHY
Vieira da Silva (exh. cat., preface W. Schmalenbach; Hannover, Kestner-Ges., 1958)
Vieira da Silva (exh. cat., preface J. Lassaigne; Grenoble, Mus. Peint. & Sculp.; Turin, Gal. Civ. A. Mod.; 1964)
Vieira da Silva (exh. cat., Paris, Mus. N. A. Mod.; Rotterdam, Mus. Boymans–van Beuningen; Oslo, Fond. Sonia Henie & Niels Onstads; Basle, Ksthalle; rev. Lisbon, Fund. Gulbenkian; 1969–70)

D. Vallier: *Vieira da Silva* (Paris, 1971)
Vieira da Silva: Pinturas a tempera, 1929–77 (exh. cat., Lisbon, Fund. Gulbenkian, 1977)
J. Lassaigne and G. Weelen: *Vieira da Silva* (Paris, 1978)

SARAH WILSON

Vieira de Magalhães, Mário. *See* PORTO, SEVERIANO.

Vieira Lusitano [Vieira de Matos], **Francisco** (*b* Lisbon, 4 Oct 1699; *d* Lisbon, 13 Aug 1783). Portuguese painter, draughtsman and etcher. He was the leading painter of the 18th century in Portugal. His mature work is in the 17th-century Italian late Baroque manner, which he had absorbed during his studies in Rome and transmitted into the late 18th century in Portugal. He readily found patronage from John V, who was developing closer cultural and political links with Rome and profiting from the newly discovered Brazilian gold.

Vieira Lusitano first went to Rome in 1712 as the protégé of Rodrigo Aires de Sá e Meneses, Marquês de Fontes e Abrantes, the Portuguese Ambassador Extraordinary to the Holy See. He studied under Benedetto Luti (1666–1724), a follower of Carlo Maratti, and the more Rococo Francesco Trevisani. It was in Rome that he acquired his nickname 'Lusitano'. After his return to Lisbon in 1719, he became a member of the Irmandade de S Lucas (Brotherhood of St Luke) and received commissions from John V, for a panel of the *Holy Sacrament* (1720) for the Easter procession in Lisbon, and for a series for the church of the Patriarch attached to the royal palace of Paço da Ribeira (destr. 1755). He also executed two panels for the chapel of S António in the church of S Roque, Lisbon, the *Vision of St Anthony* and *St Anthony Preaching to the Fish* (both 1720). These works are more spontaneous in execution and lighter in tone than his mature works.

During these years Vieira Lusitano married in secret a young noblewoman who was then sequestered in a convent by her family. To secure her release, Vieira Lusitano went to Rome again in 1722 with the intention of appealing to the Pope, and remained there until 1728. His appeal was unsuccessful, but he distinguished himself as an artist and was elected a member of the Accademia di S Luca. He made nine illustrations for the *Compendio delle vite de santi orefici ed argentieri* (Rome, 1727) by Liborio Caglieri, engraved by Carlo Gregori in 1727, and several others for the *Canon missae pontificalis* (Rome, 1743), a copy of which was sent to S Roque, Lisbon.

On his return to Lisbon, Vieira Lusitano managed to release his wife from the convent, although the following year he was shot and gravely wounded by one of her brothers. The brother was exiled, but Vieira Lusitano considered it prudent to hide in the monastery of the Paulistas, S Catarina, in Lisbon. There, he painted the series *The Hermits*, the *Feeding of the Five Thousand* and the *Sermon on the Mount* (all 1730–31; *in situ*) and the panel of the *Holy Family* (1730; Mafra, Pal. N.) for the monastery of Mafra. The works in the *Hermits* series show expressive figures rendered with rather sombre colours in strong chiaroscuro. Unhappy with the commissions he had received at Mafra in comparison with his contemporaries Pierre-Antoine Quillard, who had arrived in Lisbon in 1726, and Inácio de Oliveira Bernardes, he decided, in

1733, to return to Rome. However, he had got no further than Seville when he was summoned by John V to return to Lisbon to succeed the recently deceased Quillard as royal painter. He remained at the royal palace of Mafra until 1774.

The important works from this period mark the high-point of Vieira Lusitano's career, although many from the first half were lost in the earthquake in Lisbon in 1755. Among those destroyed were *The Apostles*, the *Road to Calvary*, the *Crucifixion* and others in the church of the Patriarch; the ceiling painting of the *Capture of Lisbon from the Moors* in the church of the Mártires; the ceiling painting of *Perseus* in the Galveias Palace; and portraits of the royal family. His works after 1755 include *Our Lady of the Immaculate Conception*, *St Francisco de Paula*, the *Holy Family* and *St Anthony* (all *c.* 1765; Lisbon, S Francisco de Paula), and the altarpiece of *St Augustine Stamping out Heresy* (*c.* 1760; Lisbon, Mus. N. A. Ant.). The painting of the *Virgin and Child with Saints* (*c.* 1760; Lisbon, Mus. N. A. Ant.; see fig.) is typical of his developed style, incorporating dark tones, warm colours and rather static figures within a dynamic composition. Of his late works, the *Rest on the Flight into Egypt* (1770; Lisbon, Mus. N. A. Ant; *see* PORTUGAL, fig. 7) is particularly important. From 1753 he assisted the Italian sculptor Alessandro Giusti at the school for artists, sculptors and architects that the latter directed at Mafra.

Vieira Lusitano was also distinguished as a draughtsman and etcher. Several sketchbooks are in the Museu Nacional de Arte Antiga, Lisbon, including one of studies for the destroyed royal portraits, and in the Biblioteca Pública e Arquivo, Évora. He was considered the foremost etcher

Francisco Vieira Lusitano: *Virgin and Child with Saints* (detail), oil on canvas, *c.* 1760 (Lisbon, Museu Nacional de Arte Antiga)

of the period; *Coronis Fleeing from Neptune* (1724), for instance, shows exemplary command of the technique, with a luminosity of surface and conviction of composition often lacking in his paintings. His autobiographical poem *O insigne pintor e leal esposo* (1780) remains an invaluable source of information about his life and contemporary conditions. In the year of its publication he became the first director of the short-lived Academy of the Nude in Lisbon.

WRITINGS
O insigne pintor e leal esposo (Lisbon, 1780)

BIBLIOGRAPHY
L. Xavier da Costa: *Francisco Vieira Lusitano, poeta e abridor de águasfortes* (Lisbon, 1926, rev. Coimbra, 1929)
——: *As belas artes plásticas em Portugal durante o século XVIII* (Lisbon, 1934)
J. Ferrão: *Vieira Lusitano* (Lisbon, 1956)
F. de Pamplona: *Dicionário de pintores e escultores portugueses*, iv (Lisbon, 1959)
R. dos Santos: *Oito séculos de arte portuguesa*, i (Lisbon, 1964)
R. C. Smith: *The Art of Portugal, 1500–1800* (London, 1968)
J. F. Pereira and P. Pereira: *Dicionário de arte barroca em Portugal* (Lisbon, 1989)

ZILAH QUEZADO DECKKER

Vieira Portuense [Vieira 'o Portuense'], **Francisco** (*b* Oporto, 13 May 1765; *d* Funchal, Madeira, 2 May 1805).

Portuguese painter. He was the son of the painter Domingos Francisco Vieira (*d* 1804), with whom he attended the Oporto studio of the French artist Jean Pillement. He moved to Lisbon in 1787 to take drawing lessons and two years later left for Rome, on a bursary from a group of mainly British merchants from Oporto. In Rome he studied with Domenico Corvi, became a member of the Accademia di S Luca and in 1791 set up his own studio, receiving the patronage of the Portuguese ambassador, João de Almeida e Mello e Castro, and Alexandre de Sousa Holstein, father of the 1st Duque de Palmela. The canvases he returned to Portugal, for instance *St John the Baptist* (1791; Oporto, N. Mus. Soares dos Reis) and *St Augustine, St Ambrose, St Jerome* and *St Gregory* (1792–3; Faro, Museu Mun.), show the influence of Corvi. At this time Vieira developed a rapid, synthesizing draughtsmanship while copying or drawing from nature, though the invention of figures caused him greater difficulty (sketchbooks, Lisbon, Mus. N. A. Ant.). In Italy he also began to study classical composition, as exemplified in the work of Poussin and the Carracci. His painting was subsequently characterized by the submission of colour to line.

In Rome Vieira was introduced to Angelica Kauffman and through her to Neo-classical taste and British painting, but it was when he moved to Parma in 1793 that he began

Francisco Vieira Portuense: *Jupiter and Leda*, 1798 (Lisbon, Museu Nacional de Arte Antigua)

to part with the Italian tradition. In Parma he joined the Accademia Regia in 1794 and lived under the protection of the ducal family. Most of his portraits of its members have been lost, but a three-quarter-length portrait of the duchess *Maria Amalia* (perhaps the *Portrait of a Lady at the Court of Parma*, sold Lisbon, Gal. Dinastia, 26 June 1973, fig. 62) shows the influence of British portrait painting. In Parma Vieira also became a friend of the printer Giambattista Bodoni, who later published editions of his drawings after Correggio (1800) and after other painters from Parma (1809).

In 1796 Vieira returned to Rome, where he met the British painter Guy Head, and visited Naples, meeting Sir William Hamilton; he then set out for London, travelling through German cities for a year, in order to join his patron Mello e Castro, who was then ambassador in Britain. His arrival in London in October 1797 marked an important stage in his career. He became a friend of the engraver Francesco Bartolozzi, marrying the widow of one of his pupils, and through Bartolozzi and Mello e Castro was able to exhibit at the Royal Academy in 1798 and 1799. His exhibits there included his finest canvases: *Jupiter and Leda* (1798; Lisbon, Mus. N. A. Ant.; see fig.), a reinterpretation, influenced by Francesco Albani, of a painting on the same theme (Hovingham Hall, N. Yorks) sometimes attributed to Poussin; *Edward I and Eleanor of Castile in Palestine* (1798; Oporto, Brit. Factory House), a romanticized and more balanced adaptation of Kauffman's treatment of the subject, known to Vieira through an engraving of 1780 by William Wynne Ryland; the *Oath of Viriatus* (untraced; engraving, see de Passos, p. 42); and the *Flight of Margaret of Anjou* (1768; Oporto, N. Mus. Soares dos Reis). The last three works appealed to the contemporary taste for *exempla virtutis*.

Other works by Vieira from this period treat Portuguese historical scenes, for example his most important work, *Filipa de Vilhena Presenting Arms to her Sons* (priv. col., see França, i, p. 96), which is Neo-classical in composition and background and draws on the work of Kauffman and of Gavin Hamilton, and the fine series of oil sketches (Lisbon, Mus. N. A. Ant.) illustrating Camões's epic *Os Lusiadas*. As in most of his work, Vieira's figures in these compositions tend to remain separate, often appearing small and isolated within the landscape. While in London Vieira also made drawings for engraving, such as *Napoleon Dissolving the National Assembly, 18 Brumaire 1799* (U. Oporto, Fac. Ciênc.).

In November 1801 Vieira returned to Portugal to become director of the Upper Douro Wine Company's art school in Oporto. In 1802 he was appointed court painter, together with Domingos António Sequeira. He worked on the decoration of the Ajuda Palace in Lisbon and also painted portraits (e.g. *Guilherme Archer*, Lisbon, Mus. N. A. Ant.), religious subjects (*St Anthony Preaching to the Fish*, Sesimbra, priv. col., see Varela Gomes, 1987 diss., fig. 185) and bucolic landscapes (Alpiarça, Casa-Mus. Relvas) for private patrons. A series showing scenes from 16th-century Portuguese history, painted for the regent, Prince John, later disappeared in Brazil. Vieira fell ill and in 1805 left mainland Portugal for Madeira, where he died. The troubled times through which he lived prevented his work from making an impact on subsequent Portuguese painting: he remains the country's only notable Neo-classical painter.

BIBLIOGRAPHY

E. Soares: *Vieira Portuense na obra gravada de Bartolozzi* (Oporto, 1948)
C. de Passos: *Vieira Portuense* (Oporto, 1953)
J. Couto: 'Artistas portugueses em Italia nos fins do séc. XVIII: Francisco Vieira, o Portuense', *Bol. Mus. N. A. Ant.*, ii/4 (1953), pp. 21–45
J.-A. França: *A arte em Portugal no século XIX*, (Lisbon, 1966); i; ii, pp. 350, 358
P. Varela Gomes: 'A história, a composição e a pose em Vieira Portuense: Sobre o quadro *D. Filipa de Vilhena armando os seus filhos cavaleiros*', *Prelo*, xi (1986), pp. 67–78
——: 'Mitologia e naturalismo em Vieira Portuense: Sobre a tela *Júpiter e Leda*', *Prelo*, xiv (1987), pp. 47–59
——: 'Correntes do neo-classicismo europeu na pintura portuguesa do século XVIII', *Portugal e Espanha entre a Europa e Além-Mar: IV simpósio luso-espanhol de história da arte: Coimbra, 1987*
——: *A obra de Vieira Portuense no contexto europeu* (diss., Lisbon New U., 1987)
A. Rui Marques de Araujo: *Experiência da natureza e sensibilidade pré-romântica em Portugal: Temas de pintura e seu consumo, 1780–1825* (diss., U. Oporto, 1991)

PAULO VARELA GOMES

Vieira Serrão, Domingos (*b* Tomar, *c.* 1570; *d* Tomar 1632). Portuguese painter. Of aristocratic origin, he was the son of a knight of the royal house. He was court painter to Philip III of Portugal (Philip IV of Spain), and he worked mostly at the courts of Lisbon and Madrid, though he also carried out commissions in Coimbra. In collaboration with Simão Rodrigues he worked on large fresco compositions at the church of the monastery of Anunciada (subject unknown; 1608; destr. 1755) and on the *Allegory of Charity* (1613; destr. 1750) on the ceiling of the church of the Hospital Real of Todos-os-Santos. Also lost is the fresco decoration of *c.* 1630 painted for the Buen Retiro in Madrid.

In 1602 Vieira Serrão was, with Simão Rodrigues and others, a founder-member of the Irmandade de S Lucas (the painters' guild of Lisbon). His frescoes (1592–1600) at the Rotunda of the Convent of Christ, Tomar, reveal his apprenticeship in the Roman Mannerist tradition, most notably in the allegorical frescoes of *Faith* and *Charity* and the Michelangelesque *Resurrection* on the great arch of the Rotunda. In such works as the nine panels (including *Christ Carrying the Cross*, *Calvary*, the *Agony in the Garden*, the *Visitation* and the *Last Supper*; all *c.* 1600) for the mother church and chapels of the Misericordia at Tancos (dispersed); the five panels with scenes from the *Life of Christ* (including *Christ at the Column*, *Calvary* and the *Deposition*; all *c.* 1600) for the Hermitage of Nossa Senhora do Vale at Torres Novas (*in situ*); and the elegant *Rest on the Flight into Egypt* (*c.* 1605) painted for the church at Dornes (*in situ*), hints of the late Italianate style are softened with suggestions of the style of Federico Barocci.

In the altarpieces executed in collaboration with Simão Rodrigues—that for the monastery of Santa Cruz (1611; sacristy, church of Carmo, Coimbra), the six surviving panels that allude to the worship of the True Cross, and the altarpiece for the University Chapel, Coimbra (1612–13; *in situ*), with panels depicting the *Adoration of the Shepherds*, the *Adoration of the Magi*, the *Resurrection*, *Christ Appearing to the Virgin* and the *Last Supper*—the scale of the composition and the robust poses of the figures express the Mannerist style with great clarity; some of the details by Vieira Serrão reveal his greater interest in naturalism.

Vieira Serrão may have organized the programmes for the decoration of the city for the state visit of Philip III to Lisbon in 1619, together with Amaro do Vale. He drew a *Panorama of the City of Lisbon*, showing the arrival of the King, which was engraved as a frontispiece by Jan Schorkens for the official account by João Baptista Lavanha (1622).

BIBLIOGRAPHY

J. B. Lavanha: *Viagem da catholica real magestade del rey d. Filipe III* (Madrid and Lisbon, 1622)
A. de Gusmão: *Simão Rodrigues e seus colaboradores* (Lisbon, 1957), pp. 10–12
D. L. Markl and V. Serrão: 'Os tectos maneiristas do Hospital Real de Todos-os-Santos e os seus autores' [The Mannerist ceilings at the Royal Hospital of Todos-os-Santos and their authors], offprint of *Bol. Cult. Assembl. Distr. Lisboa* (1980)
V. Serrão: *A pintura maneirista em Portugal* (Lisbon, 1982), pp. 92–5
——: *A pintura maneirista em Portugal* (exh. cat., Lisbon, 1995)

VITOR SERRÃO

Viel (de Saint-Meaux), Charles-François (*b* Paris, 12 June 1745; *d* Paris, 1 Jan 1819). French architect and writer. He studied architecture under Jean-François-Thérèse Chalgrin and became Inspector of Works at the Collège de France and the church of St Sulpice, Paris, from 1755 to 1780. His own practice, however, was concerned almost entirely with the construction of hospitals, hospices and related buildings. His best-known building is the Hôpital de St Jacques-du-Haut-Pas, better known as the Hôpital Cochin (1780–82), Paris. The giant doorway in the central projection, flanked by colossal Tuscan columns, recalls the paradoxes of Etienne-Louis Boullée and Claude-Nicolas Ledoux, whom he was later to criticize with venom. Among Viel's many other works are the Corn Exchange (1780) at Corbeil, the Hôpital La Rochefoucauld (1781) in the Avenue d'Orléans, Paris, which was supervised by Jean-Jacques Huvé (1742–1808), the Hôtel de la Pitié (1785–91) and the buildings of the Mont-de-Piété in the Rue des Francs-Bourgeois, and the Hôtel Dieu, which included individual ventilation shafts for each sick-bay. Viel was also an indefatigable polemicist, especially in the years after the Revolution when his architectural commissions declined. His unusually conservative preferences, developed towards the end of the century in contrast to his earlier 'revolutionary' stance, can be seen in *La Décadence de l'architecture à la fin du XVIIIe siècle* (1800), his best-known treatise, and in his biography of Chalgrin. In these he argues vigorously against modern technology, engineering and rationalism, which he felt were undermining the classicism in the architecture of his contemporaries.

WRITINGS

Lettres sur l'architecture des anciens et celle des modernes (Paris, 1787)
Principes de l'ordonnance et de la construction des bâtiments (Paris, 1797)
La Décadence de l'architecture à la fin du XVIIIe siècle (Paris, 1800)
Notice nécrologique sur J.-F.-T. Chalgrin (Paris, 1814)
De la chute imminente de la science de la construction des bâtiments en France (Paris, 1818)

BIBLIOGRAPHY

Thieme–Becker
L. Hautecoeur: *Architecture classique*, iv (1952), pp. 166–9, 315
E. Kaufmann: 'Three Revolutionary Architects', *Trans. Amer. Philos. Soc.*, n. s., xlii–xliii (1952), pp. 431–564

P. de Montclos: 'Charles-François Viel, architecte de l'hôpital général de Jean-Louis Viel de Saint-Meaux, peintre et avocat au Parlement de Paris', *Bull. Soc. Hist. A. Fr.* (1966), pp. 257–69
J.-R. Mantion: 'La Solution symbolique: Les Lettres sur l'architecture de Viel de Saint-Meaux', *VRBI*, ix (Brussels, 1984), pp. xlvi–lviii
A. Picon: *Architectes et ingénieurs au siècle des lumières* (Marseille, 1988), pp. 233, 243

Vien, Joseph-Marie, Comte (*b* Montpellier, 18 June 1716; *d* Paris, 27 March 1809). French painter, draughtsman and engraver. He was one of the earliest French painters to work in the Neo-classical style, and although his own work veered uncertainly between that style and the Baroque, Vien was a decisive influence on some of the foremost artists of the heroic phase of Neo-classicism, notably Jacques-Louis David, Jean-François-Pierre Peyron, Joseph-Benoît Suvée and Jean-Baptiste Regnault, all of whom he taught. Both his wife, Marie-Thérèse Reboul (1738–1805), and Joseph-Marie Vien *fils* (1762–1848) were artists: Marie-Thérèse exhibited at the Salon in 1757–67; Joseph-Marie *fils* earned his living as a portrait painter and engraver.

1. Early career, to 1775. 2. Later career, 1775–1809.

1. EARLY CAREER, TO 1775. After spending his youth in various forms of employment, including work as a painter of faience and as an assistant to the artist Jacques Giral, Vien travelled to Paris and entered the studio of Charles-Joseph Natoire in 1740. Three years later he won the Prix de Rome and in 1744 went to the Académie de France in Rome. His participation in the energetic reappraisal of form, technique and purpose taking place in French art from the mid-1740s onwards is well demonstrated by paintings executed before and during his time in Italy. These include the *Sleeping Hermit* (1750, exh. Salon 1753; Paris, Louvre), *Lot and his Daughters* (Le Havre, Mus. B.-A.) with its pendant, *Susanna and the Elders* (Nantes, Mus. B.-A.), and the first six panels of his cycle on the *Life of St Martha* (Tarascon, Bouches-du-Rhone, Ste Marthe). Vien's conflicting attractions to classicism and to the Baroque began early. Although he closely studied the works of Raphael and Michelangelo, he was also attracted to the Bolognese painters of the first half of the 17th century, whose special interest in nature and the Antique he shared. In Rome he played a part in the Académie's contribution to the Carnival celebrations of 1748, making drawings (Paris, Louvre) and etchings (e.g. Paris, Bib. N.) of its procession. Among his portraits of these years is that of his fellow student *Louis-Joseph Le Lorrain Disguised as an Oriental Queen* (Paris, Petit Pal.).

Vien returned to France in 1750. Having failed in his first attempt at election to the Académie Royale with his *St Jerome* (1750; La Fère, Mus. Jeanne d'Aboville), he succeeded in 1751 with the *Embarkation of St Martha*, the seventh panel in his Tarascon cycle; there was some criticism, however, that it relied too heavily on Italian Baroque models. Some of Vien's work of the 1750s shows clearly his desire to return French painting to the mould of its classical period; Nicolas Poussin, Sébastien Bourdon and Charles Le Brun became his models. Royal patronage helped, and in 1752 he received a commission through the Bâtiments du Roi for three works for the church at

Crécy, a village then in the domains of Mme de Pompadour. In 1754–6 he painted a set of austere classical allegories for the Danish Count Adam Gottlob Moltke (Copenhagen, Amalienborg). Although happy to accept Danish patronage, he refused an invitation to become court painter in Copenhagen to Frederick V. Vien preferred to remain in France and advance his career there. In 1757 (the year he married) he was commissioned to paint a tapestry cartoon of *Proserpina Decorating a Statue of Ceres* for the Gobelins manufactory, and in 1759 he was made a professor at the Académie. He submitted to the Salon of 1759 a gloomy and heavily Baroque religious work, the *Pool of Bethesda* (Marseille, Mus. B.-A.), reminiscent of his earlier style. His other submission, a *Supper at Emmaus*, was painted for the Benedictine monastery of Bonne Nouvelle at Orléans. His early enthusiasm for the Baroque had surfaced again. Two years later, however, his *SS Germanus and Geneviève* (exh. Salon 1761) won him extremely favourable notices, especially from Denis Diderot, who wrote of the painting: 'This is not the manner of Rubens, nor is it the style of the Italian school, this is truth itself, which belongs to all ages and all countries' (*Salons*, i, p. 120).

Under the influence of the Comte de Caylus, whose antiquarian interests had been intensified by the excavations at Herculaneum, Vien had submitted to the Salon of 1755 a picture of *Minerva* (St Petersburg, Hermitage) painted using the wax encaustic process. Such efforts to return to a highly serious classical tradition were impeded not only by his own inclinations towards the Baroque but by the fashionable taste of his contemporaries for Neoclassicism. This resulted in a great deal of mediocre, modishly classicizing work: his *morceau de réception* for the Académie, *Daedalus and Icarus* (1754; Paris, Ecole N. Sup. B.-A.), and successive works exhibited at the Salons of 1761 and 1763—the *Corinthian Maid* (untraced, engraved by Jean-Jacques Flipart), the *Virtuous Athenian Girl* (Strasbourg, Mus. B.-A.), *Sacrifice to Venus* and *Sacrifice to Ceres* (untraced, engraved by Jacques-Firmin Beauvarlet) and *Glycera: The Flowerseller* (Troyes, Mus. B.-A. & Archéol.). In these pictures, the last four of which were painted for Marie-Thérèse Geoffrin, young women in Grecian costume pose in a variety of undemanding actions before altars, urns, vases and tripods in 'antique' interior or outdoor settings. Rather than a true return to the ideals of Poussin and Raphael, they simply represent a facet of 18th-century Salon taste. Nevertheless one work

1. Joseph-Marie Vien: *Cupid Seller*, oil on canvas, 1.17×1.40 m, 1763 (Fontainebleau, Musée National du Château de Fontainebleau)

in this vein, the *Cupid Seller* (1763; Fontainebleau, Château; see fig. 1), is one of Vien's most successful, attractive and poetically expressive pictures. It is closely modelled on a Roman painting unearthed at Gragnano near Naples in 1759 (see also the engraving by Giovanni Battista Nolli in *Le pitture antiche d'Ercolano*, Naples, 1762, iii, pl. vii); in this picture Vien achieved a perfect balance between the contemporary taste for delicacy in art and his own classicizing ideals. The setting, composition and costume are all unashamedly classical, as is the frank simplicity of its emotional character.

The sureness of this poetic quality did not survive Vien's transition to large-scale history painting, which was his next experiment. *Marcus Aurelius Distributing Alms* (Amiens, Mus. Picardie), one of four works commissioned in 1764 for the Château of Choisy, near Paris, is clumsily composed, weakly drawn and lacking in any kind of poetic content, despite its attention to line, form, costume and classical detail. When exhibited at the Salon of 1765, it elicited Diderot's displeasure (see Seznec and Adhémar, ii, pp. 87–9). Two years later, however, Vien's *St Denis Preaching the Faith in France* (Paris, St Roch) met with greater success. While not expressing the emotional force of Gabriel-François Doyen's richly Baroque *St Geneviève and the Miracle of the Victims of Burning-sickness* (Paris, St Roch), the painting with which it shared centre stage at the Salon of 1767, Vien's *St Denis* achieved the calm, spare monumentality towards which he had been working since his return from Italy. Like the *Cupid Seller*, it displays many of the trappings of antiquity: St Denis preaches from the steps of a temple portico, while behind him are the ramparts and buildings of Poussin's classical backgrounds. Its strength, however, comes from the unadorned simplicity with which the scene is represented, from the conviction that emanates from St Denis and from the rapt expressions and attitudes of his audience. The picture's companion piece at the Salon, *Caesar Landing at Cadiz* (Warsaw, N. Mus.), was regarded as a failure.

In 1769 Vien exhibited the *Inauguration of the Equestrian Statue of Louis XV* (untraced; oil sketch, Paris, Carnavalet), painted for the Paris Hôtel de Ville. It was widely criticized for the poor quality of its portraits and draughtsmanship and for its lack of inspiration in conveying any sense of the occasion. Vien's reversion to a simple, classical composition is evident in the bas-relief effect he sought for the cavalcade of horsemen trooping in front of Edme Bouchardon's statue of the King, newly erected in the Place Louis XV, Paris. Many of the same concerns are displayed in the set of four decorative pictures—the *Progress of Love in the Hearts of Young Girls*—which he painted in 1773–4 to replace Jean-Honoré Fragonard's rejected *Pursuit of Love* series (New York, Frick) for the pavilion at Mme Du Barry's château at Louveciennes. These works, the *Oath of Feminine Friendship*, the *Temple of Hymen* (both Chambéry, Préfecture), the *Meeting with Cupid* (Paris, Louvre) and the *Crowning of the Lovers* (Paris, Louvre; see fig. 2), echo the one-, two- and three-figure compositions of the early 1760s in their attempt to recapture the simple, Neo-classical 'look' that had proved so successful a decade before—then avant-garde, but by this date the height of fashion.

2. Joseph-Marie Vien: *Crowning of the Lovers*, oil on canvas, 3.35×2.02 m, 1773 (Paris, Musée du Louvre)

2. LATER CAREER, 1775–1809. In addition to his elevated position at the Académie, Vien was now also active as director of the Ecole des Elèves Protégés (from 1771). In 1775 he returned to Rome to take up the post of director of the Académie de France, taking with him his pupil Jacques-Louis David. Imminent departure did not prevent Vien from exhibiting a few pictures at the Salon that year, including *St Thibault*, for the new chapel at the Grand Trianon, Versailles, painted in response to the developing vogue for scenes of medieval France. Its figures are wooden, its composition is clumsy, and the work has remained in obscurity on deposit at the Château of Versailles ever since it was painted. During his six-year tenure in Rome, Vien reorganized and reinvigorated the teaching of students while also promoting the cause of Neo-classicism. On his return he embarked on a series of works on subjects from Homer's *Iliad*, exhibiting *Briseis Led from the Tent of Achilles* (Angers, Mus. B.-A.) at the Salon of 1781. Although his teaching had some influence on pupils such as David and Peyron, Vien's Italian sojourn had done little for his own artistic abilities, and critics

continued to stress that depictions of strong passions were beyond his skills. Unabashed, he continued in his pursuit of the monumental and the Antique, submitting picture after picture on Homeric subjects to the biennial Salons. A Crown commission began in 1783 with *Priam Leaving to Beg Achilles for the Return of the Body of Hector* (exh. 1785; Algiers, Mus. N. B.-A.) and continued with the *Return of Priam* (Angers, Mus. B.-A.) and the *Farewell of Hector and Andromache* (exh. 1787; Epinal, Mus. Dépt. Vosges & Mus. Int. Imagerie).

Vien's standing with the Académie in Paris, already high, increased until 1789 when, on the death of Jean-Baptiste-Marie Pierre, he was appointed Premier Peintre du Roi. This triumph was short-lived. Protected during the Revolutionary upheavals by his pupil David, whose portrait he painted (Angers, Mus. B.-A.), Vien did not exhibit at the Salon after 1793, preferring to bask in the reflected glory of former pupils. He was ennobled by Napoleon in 1808, and his final undertaking was the compilation of his *Mémoires*.

Vien made two important contributions to the development of French painting in the 18th century. First was his unshakeable belief in the study of the Antique: this was the ultimate reason for his attachment to the work of Raphael, Michelangelo, the Carracci family and Nicolas Poussin. No matter that his attempts at emulation were often little more than mildly titillating fancy pieces in the antique mode. Strongly influenced in his formation by these models, Vien was also the first French artist of his century to embrace the Neo-classical ideal. When he vacillated towards the Baroque, despite perseverance he largely failed. Lack of technical ability and, more often, lack of conceptual vision hampered him. Gradually the fervour and energy of his youth were replaced by intellectualism, coldness and isolation. Vien's teaching and his absolute insistence on study from the life constituted his second contribution. In life study he found the only viable basis for all art, and it was precisely for lack of it that French painting had become so artificial by the mid-1740s. Notwithstanding the demonstrable limitations of his own artistic vision, Vien practised what he preached.

BIBLIOGRAPHY

J. Le Breton: *Notice historique sur la vie et les ouvrages de M. Vien* (Paris, 1809)

F. Aubert: 'Joseph-Marie Vien', *Gaz. B.-A.*, xxii (1867), pp. 180–90, 282–94, 493–507; xxiii (1867), pp. 175–87, 297–310, 470–82

J. Seznec and J. Adhémar, eds: *Salons de Diderot 1759–1781*, 4 vols (Oxford, 1957–67)

P. Rosenberg: 'Une Esquisse de J.-M. Vien: *Loth et ses filles*', *Rev. Louvre* (1968), pp. 208–11

T. W. Gaehtgens: 'J.-M. Vien et les peintres de la Légende de Sainte Marthe', *Rev. A.* [Paris], xxiii (1974), pp. 64–9

The Age of Louis XV: French Painting, 1710–1774 (exh. cat., ed. P. Rosenberg; Toledo, OH, Mus. A.; Chicago, IL, A. Inst.; Ottawa, N.G.; 1975–6)

T. W. Gaehtgens: 'Deux tableaux de J.-M. Vien récemment acquis par les musées de Brest et de Lille', *Rev. Louvre*, 5–6 (1976), pp. 371–8

D. Rice: *The Fire of the Ancients: The Encaustic Painting Revival, 1775 to 1812* (diss., New Haven, Yale U., 1979)

T. W. Gaehtgens: 'Oeuvres de Vien', *Catalogue de la Donation Baderou, Musée des Beaux-Arts, Rouen* (1980), pp. 75–80

C. Gendre: 'Esquisses de Collin de Vermont et de J.-M. Vien', *Rev. Louvre* (1983), pp. 399–403

Diderot et l'art de Boucher à David: Les Salons, 1759–1781 (exh. cat., ed. M.-C. Sahut and N. Volle; Paris, Hôtel de la Monnaie, 1984–5), pp. 410–28

T. W. Gaehtgens: 'Vien, vers un nouveau style', *Conn. A.*, 446 (1989), pp. 87–98

JOSHUA DRAPKIN

Vienna [Ger. Wien; anc. Vindobona]. Capital of Austria and one of the nine states within the federal republic. The city (pop. *c.* 1.53 million) lies at the confluence of the rivers Wien and Danube in north-east Austria, next to the foothills of the Alps and near the edge of the Carpathians. Vienna was once the capital and residence of the German kings and Holy Roman Emperors, the Austrian emperors and, from 1867 to 1918, the Austro-Hungarian monarchy. Its history is linked with that of the Habsburg family (*see* HABSBURG, §I) under whose rule it became one of the most important centres of the Baroque and Rococo in northern Europe. The city, which has a rich musical heritage, also contains some of the most important art collections in Europe.

I. History. II. Urban development. III. Art life and organization. IV. Centre of production. V. Buildings.

I. History.

Vienna's first recorded name, Vindobona, is probably of Celtic origin; it was also the name of a Roman military camp located at the centre of the present city and established in the reign of Emperor Augustus (*reg* 30 BC–AD 14) as a frontier fortification. Emperor Marcus Aurelius died there after a military expedition in AD 180. After the fall of the Roman Empire, the area was ruled by Goths, Huns and Lombards. The abandoned Roman camp served as a refuge for the surviving civilian population, and gradually an important reloading point grew up there at the crossing of land trade routes with the navigable Danube. The first Christian church was probably constructed in the 4th or 5th century (*see* §II, 1 below). In the 6th century the Avars conquered the whole region, which was settled at the same time by Slavs. Charlemagne established a border county at Vienna at the end of the 8th century, and in the Salzburg Chronicle (881), which records a war against the Hungarians, the town was referred to as Wenia. In 976 members of the Frankish Babenberg family became the margraves (and later dukes) of Austria, and they transferred their residence into the town in the mid-12th century. The flourishing trading settlement was first called a *civitas* in 1137, when a new parish church, the Stephanskirche, was founded. A greatly enlarged area was walled at the end of the 12th century (see fig. 1) and, under the rule of the last Babenberg dukes, the politically stabilized city achieved a major economic and cultural flowering.

In 1246 Austria passed through marriage to the Bohemian king Přemysl Ottakar II and then, after the Battle of Dürnkrut (1278), to the German king Rudolf I of Habsburg (*reg* 1273–91). Rudolf made the Babenberg inheritance a fief of his sons, and Vienna became the seat of the Habsburg dynasty until 1918. The city acquired the typical structure of a medieval trading town with a rich patriciate, its artistic centre based on the masons' lodge associated with the Stephanskirche (now Stephansdom; *see* §§III, 1 and V, 1(i) below). Art was also cultivated by the monastic communities who settled in Vienna, especially the Irish Benedictines from the mid-12th century, and later the

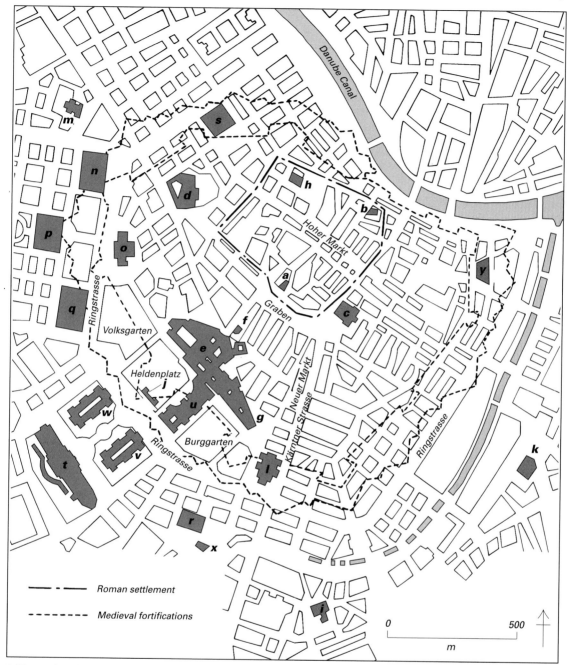

1. Vienna, plan of inner city: (a) Peterskirche; (b) Ruprechtskirche; (c) Stephansdom; (d) Schottenkirche; (e) Schweizerhof and Hofburg; (f) Michaelerkirche; (g) Augustinian church; (h) Maria am Gestade; (i) Karlskirche; (j) Burgtor; (k) Mint; (l) Staatsoper; (m) Votivkirche; (n) Universität; (o) Burgtheater; (p) Rathaus; (q) Parlament; (r) Akademie der Bildenden Künste; (s) Börse; (t) Messepalast; (u) Neue Burg; (v) Kunsthistorisches Museum; (w) Naturhistorisches Museum; (x) Secession Building; (y) Postsparkasse

Dominicans, Minorites and others (*see* §II, 1 below). Duke Rudolf IV (the Founder; *see* HABSBURG, §I(1)) founded the university (1365) and enlarged the Stephanskirche in an attempt to raise it to cathedral status, although ecclesiastical independence from Passau and an autonomous bishopric were not achieved until 1469.

In 1437, after a long interruption, a Habsburg was again elected German king, and this title (or that of Holy Roman Emperor) was held by the family almost continuously until the end of the Empire in 1806. Vienna thus became the imperial capital, even though it was situated at the edge of the Empire. The territorial expansion of the Habsburgs through a skilful marriage policy in the 15th and 16th centuries, which included acquisition of Burgundy, the Netherlands and Spain as well as Bohemia and Hungary, shifted trade to the west and for a time caused an economic recession in Vienna, while the expansion of the Ottoman empire resulted in an unsuccessful siege of the city in 1529. At about this time the city was dominated by Protestants, in opposition to the ruling Catholic Habsburgs; religious conflict intensified after the arrival of the Jesuits in 1551 and the revival of the old monastic communities. The victory of the Counter-Reformation after the Thirty Years War (1618–48), which resulted in an exodus of Protestants from the city, led to a boom in building activity in the 17th century. The more consistent presence of the ruler and his court became an increasingly dominant factor in the city's development, while burgher circles declined in importance.

The population was decimated by plague in 1679, and in 1683 the city was again unsuccessfully besieged by Turkish forces. Victory was followed by a major economic and cultural flowering in Vienna, and it became one of the most important Baroque capitals of Europe (see §II, 2 below); an archbishopric was established there in 1723. During the political and economic consolidation that followed the end of the Seven Years War (1756–1763), there was a late flourish of Rococo in Vienna; this was followed by a period of social reform under Emperor Joseph II (reg 1765–90). In 1805 and 1809 Vienna was occupied by Napoleon, under whose pressure the Holy Roman Empire disintegrated; the city remained the capital of the new Austrian empire that was created from the Habsburg patrimonial lands. The period following the Congress of Vienna (1814–15) was an age of conservatism and political repression, which led in 1848 to an open revolt of citizens and students. This was severely suppressed, although Vienna obtained the right of self-government by elected representatives. In the second half of the 19th century Vienna's renewed economic prosperity resulted in the city's expansion and the construction of its famous Ringstrasse (see §II, 3 and fig. 5 below). Unresolved social tensions remained, however, and were aggravated by national conflicts within the dual Austro-Hungarian monarchy established in 1867, which collapsed after World War I.

In 1918, when the Republic of Austria was founded, Vienna—one of the largest cities in Europe in 1910 with a population of c. 2.1 million—became the capital of a small state with barely 6.5 million. This led to new conflicts that made possible the annexation of Austria by Germany in 1938. Badly damaged in World War II, Vienna was subsequently divided into four zones controlled by France, the United Kingdom, the USA and the USSR. Full sovereignty was restored under the Austrian State Treaty of 1955, and Vienna regained its political and cultural prestige as the capital of a neutral state. It subsequently became known as a conference centre of world rank and the seat of several international organizations, including the Organization of Petroleum-Exporting Countries, the International Atomic Energy Agency and the United Nations Industrial Development Organization. After the opening of the United Nations Organization city (UNO-Stadt) in 1979, Vienna became the third most important city of the United Nations after New York and Geneva.

BIBLIOGRAPHY
Österreichische Kunsttopographie, ii (Vienna, 1908); xiv (Vienna, 1914); xv (Vienna, 1916); xxiii (Vienna, 1931); xli (Vienna, 1974); xliv (Vienna, 1980)
H. Tietze: *Wien: Kultur, Kunst, Geschichte* (Vienna and Leipzig, 1931)
K. Oettinger: *Das Werden Wiens* (Vienna, 1951)
E. Zöllner: *Geschichte Österreichs*, 2 vols (Munich, 1961)
Geschichte der bildenden Kunst in Wien, 3 vols (Vienna, 1970–73)
F. Czeike: *Das Grosse Groner Wien-Lexikon* (Vienna, Munich and Zurich, 1974)
Wien um 1900: Kunst und Kultur (Vienna, 1985)
Stadt-Chronik Wiens (Vienna and Munich, 1986)
MARIA PÖTZL-MALIKOVA

II. Urban development.

1. Before c. 1500. 2. c. 1500–c. 1800. 3. c. 1800–1918. 4. After 1918.

1. BEFORE c. 1500. The Roman legionary camp of Vindobona was established on a gravel terrace on the south bank of the Danube (the northern frontier of the Roman Empire), near the mouth of the River Wien. It was destroyed c. AD 400, although its walls survived. Subsequently, development focused on two areas within the old walls: immediately within the south gate around the Peterskirche (see fig. 1a), and, on account of the proximity of the Danube trading post, around the Ruprechtskirche (1b). The Peterskirche was traditionally founded by Charlemagne during his campaign of AD 792 against the Avars, but excavated remains of pre-Romanesque walls and the low floor level of the old Peterskirche, seven steps below the present Baroque church (see §2 below), suggest that there was an Early Christian church on the site, probably aisleless, with a narrower semicircular apse to the south. The unusual south orientation indicates that the structure included Roman walling, which must still have been visible at the time. The Ruprechtskirche, near the former 'Berghof' (a castle-like nobleman's house), is recorded in Jans Enikel's *Fürstenbuch* (c. 1280) as the oldest parish church in Vienna. Wolfgang Lazius's chronicle *Vienna Austriae* (1546) cites the unauthenticated tradition that the church was founded by the Salzburg missionaries Cunald and Gisalrich in 740. The unvaulted nave and the west tower with paired, round-arched windows survive from the Romanesque building. The apse was rebuilt in the Early Gothic style after the city fire of 1276; the southern rib-vaulted aisle was probably added in the mid-14th century.

By the 12th century Vienna was a flourishing town spreading beyond the former Roman fort. At that time the Wipplingerstrasse formed the main axis of the city, its orientation related to the new trade route from Bavaria to Hungary. The foundation charter of the Stephanskirche (1137; now Stephansdom; 1c), situated east of the ancient wall, subordinated to it all the consecrated churches of the city; originally the parish church of Vienna, then the cathedral (see §V, 1 below), it became the ecclesiastical centre of the city. A crypt beneath the former cemetery church was excavated in 1973 some 12 m beneath the present Stephansplatz. It had six niches with pointed arches, rib mouldings and wall paintings that indicate a date in the second quarter of the 13th century, but the dedication to SS Rupert and Virgil, who were connected with Salzburg, suggests an earlier origin. The oldest monastery in Vienna, founded in 1155 by Henry II Jasomirgott (reg 1141–71) near his newly established court and settled with Irish–Scottish Benedictine monks from Regensburg, also stood outside the original walls, to the west. The abbey church (Schottenkirche; 1d) was completed *c.* 1190, with a westwork, transept and crossing tower (rebuilt 17th and 19th centuries). Parts of the south aisle have been uncovered in a chapel south of the Baroque presbytery. The transverse arches and groined cross-vaults rest on massive engaged piers and corner responds, which rise from bases with the mouldings running through them.

In the 12th century large sections of the Roman walls were still standing, as well as Roman ruins and tombs outside the town, and Roman stone was frequently used in medieval construction, especially at the Stephanskirche. At the end of the 12th century, however, the growth of the town necessitated the building of new fortifications enclosing an area about three times the size of the former Roman camp. These defined the extent of the inner city until 1858. The Kärntner Strasse was also laid out as an important trade route to Italy. Initial development of the newly walled area continued until about 1230: the earlier fortifications were razed and spacious market-places, which became important focal points, were created: the Hoher Markt, Graben and Neuer Markt. The Graben followed the south boundary of the ancient Roman settlement. The medieval castle that forms the basis of the

Schweizerhof (1e; *see* §V, 5(i) below) in the south-western corner of the city was probably founded as an integral part of the new fortifications during the lifetime of the Babenberg duke Leopold VI (*reg* 1198–1230). It was square, with corner towers, and Přemysl Ottakar II, King of Bohemia (*reg* 1253–78), played a major part in its enlargement. The Late Romanesque Michaelerkirche (founded *c.* 1220; 1f; *see* §V, 4 below), which served as the first royal church, is an important survival from this period.

The new mendicant orders (Ger. *Minoriten*), who settled inside the new town walls of Vienna in the 1220s, produced an ascetic architecture that contrasted strongly with the stylistic richness of the Stephanskirche masons' lodge. The enlargement of the late 13th-century, two-aisled Minoritenkirche (completed 1251) was begun by the wife of Frederick II the Fair (*reg* 1298–1330), Elisabeth (*d* 1330), who added the Ludwig Chapel in the 1320s. Formerly, this was believed to be the long choir of the older church (now excavated), but it is now identified with the northern aisle of the later, three-aisled hall church, begun in 1339 under Albert II (*reg* 1298–1358). The tympanum of the present north portal, which depicts the enthroned Virgin with the donors Frederick and Elisabeth, originally formed

2. Vienna, the medieval townscape from the south, *c.* 1470; detail from the *Flight into Egypt* by the Master of the Vienna Schottenstift, panel, from the altarpiece of the Schottenkirche, *c.* 1469–75 (Vienna, Schottenkirche, Stiftsgalerie)

a part of the Ludwig Chapel. The three western portals, the centre and south of which are sculptured, were built *c.* 1350. The new work at the Minoritenkirche was influenced by the hall choir of the Stephanskirche (consecrated 1340); the Minorite workshop in turn later worked on the Herzogsportalen of the Gothic nave, at the Stephanskirche (begun 1359).

The first three-aisled hall church for a mendicant order in Vienna was the Augustinian church (1g), near the Hofburg, built from 1330 by the Augustinian Friars. At its consecration in 1349, the massive building, which shows German influence, was probably unfinished: the seven-sided choir with a star vault better fits a date at the turn of the century. The Georgskapelle (consecrated 1341), intended as the chapter house of the Augustinians and as the meeting place for the Knights of St George, is a delicate two-aisled building with two choirs and sculpted bosses. It still retains the elegant shafted piers that also occurred in the Augustinerkirche before it was altered in the early Baroque period and then re-gothicized in 1784. The 13th-century churches of the Johannites (now Malteserkirche) and the Teutonic Order (Deutschordenskirche St Elisabeth) are aisleless; alterations to the latter *c.* 1720 by Anton Erhard Martinelli make it an interesting example of 18th-century Viennese Gothic. The former Carmelite church (now Kirche am Hof), built *c.* 1400, is the most powerful Austrian example of a three-aisled mendicant church with a long choir. Although there are later alterations, it retains its original octagonal nave piers.

The stylistically richer masons' lodge of the Stephanskirche also influenced, or was directly involved in, the building of Maria am Gestade (1h; *see* §V, 3 below) and the Hofburgkapelle (consecrated 1449; *see* §V, 5(i) below), which was based on the Sainte-Chapelle in Paris. Vienna's architectural symbol, the Stephansturm (south tower of the Stephansdom), was completed in 1433; at 137 m it was then the tallest structure in German-speaking Europe (see fig. 2; *see also* §V, 1(i) and fig. 13 below). In the Middle Ages there were many domestic chapels, among them that of the old Rathaus (Town Hall) dating from the 14th century. An additional subsidiary chapel with an early Renaissance portal was added *c.* 1520. The present chapel of the Lower Austrian Landhaus (formerly the entrance hall) has a vault (*c.* 1515) attributed to Anton Pilgram. Other vaulted rooms in the Landhaus, which was built from 1513 onwards, have survived as examples of Viennese secular architecture of the Late Gothic period.

BIBLIOGRAPHY

R. K. Donin: *Die Bettelordenskirchen in Österreich* (Baden bei Wien, 1935)
——: *Geschichte der bildenden Kunst in Wien*, 2 vols (Vienna, 1944–55)
K. Oettinger: *Das Werden Wiens* (Vienna, 1951)
W. Buchowiecki: *Die gotischen Kirchen Österreichs* (Vienna, 1952)
Romanische Kunst in Österreich (exh. cat., Krems-Stein, Minoritenkirche, 1964)
Gotik in Österreich (exh. cat., Krems-Stein, Minoritenkirche, 1967)
A. Klaar: *Die Siedlungsformen Wiens*, Wiener Geschichtsbücher, viii (Vienna and Hamburg, 1971)
R. Feuchtmüller: *Vom frühen Mittelalter bis zur Gegenwart* (1972), i of *Kunst in Österreich*, 2 vols (Vienna, Hannover and Basle, 1972–3)
Wien im Mittelalter (exh. cat., ed. H. Bisanz and others; Vienna, Hist. Mus., 1975–6)
R. Perger and W. Brauneis: *Die mittelalterlichen Kirchen und Klöster Wiens*, Wiener Geschichtsbücher, xix–xx (Vienna and Hamburg, 1977)
R. Wagner-Rieger: 'Bildende Kunst: Architektur', *Der Zeit der frühen Habsburger: Dome und Klöster, 1279–1379* (exh. cat., Wiener Neustadt, Stadtmus., 1979), pp. 103–26
——: *Mittelalterliche Architektur in Österreich* (Vienna, 1988)
G. Brucher: *Gotische Baukunst in Österreich* (Salzburg, 1990)
M. Parucki: 'Überraschende Erkenntnisse an der Wiener Minoritenkirche: Eigentliche Ludwigskapelle wieder entdeckt', *Österreich. Z. Kst & Dkmlpf.*, xlvii/1–2 (1993), pp. 10–14
——: *Die Wiener Minoritenkirche* (Vienna, Cologne and Weimar, in preparation)
For further bibliography *see* §V, 1(i), 3, 4 and 5(i) below.

MARLENE STRAUSS-ZYKAN

2. *c.* 1500–*c.* 1800. At the end of the Middle Ages Vienna was the largest and most important city in the Holy Roman Empire, with a population of some 60,000–80,000 inhabitants. A fire in 1525 and the Ottoman siege of 1529, however, resulted in the city being badly damaged, its suburbs being deliberately destroyed to form a defensive glacis outside the city walls. After the siege Ferdinand (later Ferdinand I), brother of the Emperor Charles V, decreed that the old walls should be replaced by modern fortifications, and from 1532 Italian and German engineers directed by Hermes Schallautzer constructed a circle of bastions and outworks along the walls, creating one of the most powerful fortresses in western Europe. Its characteristic star shape (see fig. 3) was recorded by Bonifaz Wolmut and Augustin Hirschvogel in 1547, in the first accurately calculated plans based on a trigonometric survey.

Ferdinand also decreed that the Glacis, the area of suburbs immediately outside the walls that had been destroyed, should not be rebuilt but left as a gap between 100 and 450 m wide around the city to provide a clear field of fire from the new fortifications in any future siege. This strategic measure determined the way in which the nucleus of Vienna and its suburbs developed during the next 400 years. Constricted by its circle of walls, the central city plan, established in the high Middle Ages, hardly altered during this period; instead, the centre grew continually in height, while the suburbs, *c.* 1.5 km from the centre along the radial routes into the city, developed either as summer residences or as independent villages of tradesmen or craftsmen.

Vienna's role as the residence of the Holy Roman Emperor under Ferdinand I (*reg* 1558–64) and his son Maximilian II (*reg* 1564–76) led to the enlargement of the Hofburg as a modern Renaissance palace (*see* §V, 5(i) below), with the first water-supply established in 1552 from the springs to the west of the Vienna Woods. Access to the Prater, the imperial hunting-grounds to the east of the city in the wide flood-plain along the Danube, was opened up by means of a long, straight avenue that was a pioneering feat of surveying. Maximilian II (*see* HABSBURG, §I(8)) built the large Renaissance summer residence (1569–76) known as the Neugebäude (*see* AUSTRIA, fig. 4), with a pheasantry, deer-park, orangery and fountains; he also bought the Katterburg hunting-lodge to the west of the city (later rebuilt as the imperial palace of Schönbrunn (*see* §V, 7(i) below). The nobles followed the Emperor's example; many urban palaces were built in Vienna, with 115 completed by the mid-16th century; summer residences were built on the outskirts of the city and in the surrounding areas. The city council, however, ceased to

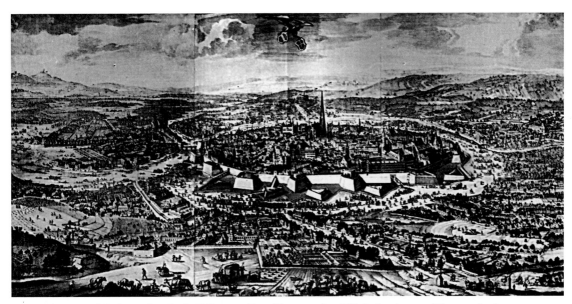

3. *View of Vienna and the Surrounding Area* by Folbert van Alten-Allen, engraving, 1683 (before the second Ottoman siege)

play an important role in urban development following Ferdinand's new city charter of 1526, which considerably reduced civic autonomy, and the first systematic attempt to pave the city streets did not get under way until 1558.

Towards the end of the 16th century the imperial court was moved to Prague under Emperor Rudolf II (*reg* 1576–1612). Following its return to Vienna under Rudolf's successors, Matthias and Ferdinand II, numerous Baroque alterations were made to the city, which until then had remained predominantly medieval. As part of the Counter-Reformation, many new churches were built, including the Capuchin church (1622–32), beneath which is the imperial burial vault (Kaisergruft); the Jesuit church (1627–31); and the Dominican church (1631–4), which replaced a 13th-century building. The end of the Thirty Years War (1648), marking the triumph of the Counter-Reformation, was followed by further development in the suburbs, which were enhanced by a large number of early Baroque monasteries and churches. The increasingly powerful nobility continued to build palaces on the outskirts of the city, mainly employing Italian architects such as members of the Carlone (ii), Tencala, Allio (*see* ALLIO, §§2(ii) and 4(iv)), Martinelli and Zuccalli families. Together with some 600 urban palaces existing at this time, many of which were also in the new Baroque style, they were recorded in the drawings of Wilhelm Prämer (1637–1716). The imperial Hofburg was also modernized and extended; the first opera house was built in 1659 (destr.), and Vienna became a centre of Italian opera and festivity.

This period of growth was dramatically interrupted in 1683 by the second Ottoman siege of Vienna, which the Turks called the 'golden apple'. Once more the suburbs were destroyed to deny cover to the enemy, and by the time the Turkish army was finally routed, the whole urban area had been laid waste. A strong economic upturn and building boom followed victory over the Ottomans, affecting not only the imperial residence and its increasing

bureaucracy, but also church, nobility and townspeople. Within a short period the city was transformed into a Baroque imperial capital, one of the most brilliant cities of Europe. Monumental church façades were created in the narrow streets, huge Baroque palaces were built and entire streetscapes were transformed into richly articulated and decorated festive buildings. The Linienwall, a line of ramparts beyond the suburbs, was built in 1704 as an outer defence on the initiative of Prince Eugene of Savoy, who had commanded many battles against the Turks. While the city centre remained constricted by its fortifications, the suburbs, protected by the Linienwall, became the main showplace for late Baroque display. The nobility and the upper bourgeoisie built magnificent summer residences there, on the rising land overlooking the city, with gardens and water displays. Surviving examples include the Belvedere (*see* §V, 6 below), Schwarzenberg, Liechtenstein, Auersperg, Trautson and Schönborn palaces, as well as such imperial summer residences as Schönbrunn (*see* §V, 7(i) below), Augarten and Favorita.

In the city itself large-scale works were carried out at the Hofburg (*see* §V, 5(i) below). The Peterskirche was rebuilt (1702–33) as an oval Baroque church to a design by Gabriele Montani; its distinctive porch was added in 1751–3 by Andreas Altomonte. Following an outbreak of plague in 1713 the Karlskirche (1716–37; see fig. 1i above) was built by Johann Bernhard Fischer von Erlach just outside the south-east corner of the city walls; its remarkable design reflects its intended purpose as a dynastic monument to the Habsburg imperial house (*see* §V, 2 below). This period of euphoric building activity was made possible not least by the presence in Vienna of such outstanding Italian-trained architects as Fischer von Erlach and his son Joseph Emanuel (*see* FISCHER VON ERLACH) and JOHANN LUKAS VON HILDEBRANDT, as well as Italian-born architects including DOMENICO MARTINELLI and

4. *View of Vienna from the Belvedere* by Bernardo Bellotto, oil on canvas, 1.35×2.13 m, 1759–60 (Vienna, Kunsthistorisches Museum)

ANTONIO BEDUZZI, assisted by a host of fine artists and craftsmen (*see* §III, 2 below).

This much admired Baroque city, with its magnificent suburbs, was very precisely recorded, first by Leander Anguissola (1652–1720) and Jakob Marinoni (1676–1755) in 1706; then in a large volume of engravings giving detailed views by Salomon Kleiner; and finally a bird's-eye view of 1769–77 by Joseph Daniel Huber. The elegance of the city can also be seen in the painting by Bellotto (see fig. 4).

In the reigns of Maria-Theresa (*see* HABSBURG, §I(21)) and her French husband Emperor Francis I (*reg* 1745–65), several French artists and architects came to Vienna, including Jean-Nicolas Jadot de Ville-Issey, who designed the Alte Universität (1753–7; now Akademie der Wissenschaften) in the eastern part of the city and worked at Schönbrunn (*see* §V, 7(ii) below). Throughout the 18th century the city continued to be hemmed in by its fortifications and to be separated from the suburbs by the open space of the Glacis. The suburbs, however, were becoming increasingly urbanized as the large Baroque gardens of the nobility were successively subdivided into lots and built over. Thus densely structured and highly populated residential and industrial areas developed, to form a large conurbation, the population of which was *c.* 175,000 in 1754 and *c.* 250,000 by 1800. This increase in population in turn led to a new upturn in trade and industry; a porcelain factory, the second oldest in Europe, was founded (*see* §IV, 3 below), as well as such institutions as the Ingenieurakademie (1717; later the Technische Hochschule), the oldest such establishment in continental

Europe; the Orientalische Kompanie (1719); and the Börse (Stock Exchange; 1771).

To moderate the social tensions accompanying this rapid growth, numerous humanitarian buildings were constructed, including an orphanage (1745; rebuilt 1768), a deaf-and-dumb institute (1779) and the Allgemeines Krankenhaus (General Hospital; 1783–4) in the north-west of the city. The latter was a vast complex commissioned by Joseph II (*reg* 1765–90); together with the Josephinum (military surgical academy) built by Isidore Canevale in 1783–5 (*see* AUSTRIA, fig. 7), it founded Vienna's reputation as a medical centre. To service these institutions, a large waterworks was installed in 1798. Joseph II also contributed to the leisure and recreation of the population by opening the Prater, the imperial hunting-grounds, to the public in 1766 and the park of the Augartenschloss in 1775. At the same time the Praterstern, a large public square and meeting-point of eight straight avenues, including the Praterstrasse, was laid out, opening up the northern part of the city that had for centuries been neglected and subject to the periodic flooding of the undrained meadows along the Danube. The Glacis, the broad area between the city fortifications and the suburbs that had been kept free of buildings since the first Ottoman siege of 1529, was improved and given a regular shape by the creation of promenades and places of refreshment and relaxation. By the end of the 18th century Vienna was the largest capital in central Europe, as well as the most important politically, economically and culturally.

BIBLIOGRAPHY

S. Kleiner: *Wunderwürdiges Kriegs- und Siegs-Lager des unvergleichlichen Heldens oder eigentliche Vor- und Abbildungen der Hoff- Lust- und Garten-Gebäude*, 10 vols (Vienna, 1731–40/*R* Dortmund, 1980)

M. Eisler: *Historischer Atlas des Wiener Stadtbildes* (Vienna, 1919)

H. Sedelmayr: 'Das Werden des Wiener Stadtbildes', *Epochen und Werke*, ii (Vienna and Munich, 1960), pp. 257ff

E. Vancsa: 'Wien', *Kunstwerk Stadt: Österreichische Stadt- und Ortsdenkmale* (Salzburg and Vienna, 1988), pp. 413–44 [with add. bibliog.]

For further bibliography see §§III, 2 and V, 2, 5(i), 6 and 7 below.]

3. *c.* 1800–1918. The development of Vienna during the early 19th century was shaped by its confrontation with Napoleon. During Napoleon's second occupation of the city in 1809 the old bastions were blown up, thus anticipating the later razing of the old city fortifications (1858), which by then were militarily useless, and their replacement by a layout that, for the first time since the Middle Ages, was of relevance to the urban design of the city centre. On the site of the bastion opposite the west front of the Hofburg the Heldenplatz was laid out (1819–23), with the Burgtor (see fig. 1j above) completed by Pietro Nobile in 1824 (*see* AUSTRIA, fig. 8; *see also* §V, 5(i) below); adjoining it to the north is the Volksgarten (1819–23) with Nobile's Theseustempel (1820–23), a modified copy of the Theseion in Athens, built to house Antonio Canova's monumental *Theseus and the Centaur* (now Vienna, Ksthist. Mus.).

After the final overthrow of Napoleon, Vienna enjoyed a new boom. In 1809 industrial development in the centre of the city had been prohibited; together with the massive growth of the population, which more than doubled to *c.* 600,000 by mid-century, this increased demand for space both in the former inner suburbs and in the outer suburbs beyond the Linienwall. The economic and industrial boom was reinforced by the founding of numerous institutions, including the Nationalbank (1815) and the Handelskammer (Chamber of Commerce; 1848), and new technologies were applied to the servicing of what was by then a metropolis. The first gasworks was installed in 1828, followed by a large waterworks and a general telegraph service in the 1840s. Public transport was improved by the construction of the first steam-powered railways (1837 and 1841), and numerous bridges were built over the branch of the Danube that passed through the city.

The rapid restructuring of the suburbs after 1817, when a first plan for the expansion of the city was produced, gave rise to the introduction of a land-registry and the institution of the Hofbaurat (Imperial Board of Works) to regulate the building boom. The most important urban achievement of this period was the creation of a more regular and attractive frontage to the inner suburbs facing the city by the erection of monumental public and private buildings among the existing Baroque churches and palaces; such new buildings included the Polytechnikum (1816–18; later extended) by Joseph Schemerl von Leytenbach (1752–1837); the prison (1831–9) by Johann Fischer; the Neo-classical Hauptmünzamt (Mint; 1835–8; 1k above) by Paul Eduard Sprenger; the Militärgeographisches Institut (1840–42) by Franz von Mayern (1799–1889) and the Finanzlandesdirektion (State Finance Board; 1844–7) also by Sprenger.

The revolution of 1848 marked the beginning of a new era of bourgeois liberalism during the long reign of Emperor Francis-Joseph (*see* HABSBURG-LORRAINE, (2)), when the city took its final step towards becoming a modern metropolis. The Hofbaurat was abolished, and

the first buildings erected in the newly fashionable historicist styles were the new parish church at Altlerchenfeld (1848–50; consecrated 1861), Vienna, by JOHANN GEORG MÜLLER, where the Nazarenes played a special part in supplying the furnishings (*see* §III, 3 below), and the Arsenal (1849–55), an imposing military complex in a castellated style that included Vienna's first museum, the Heeresmuseum (now the Heeresgeschichtliches Museum), built in a neo-Byzantine style. This was a collaboration between Theophilus Hansen (*see* HANSEN, (2)) and VAN DER NÜLL & SICCARDSBURG, who later carried out much work in Vienna (see below). It was above all the productive capacity of the large brickworks founded by Alois Miesbach and Heinrich Drasche in 1819 that later shaped the building activity of the entire period.

The outstanding project of the period in terms of both urban and architectural design was the construction of the Ringstrasse. In 1857 the Emperor issued a contract to demolish the old city walls and in their place to lay out a monumental street that would not only provide a link between the city and the suburbs but would also enhance the amenities and image of the imperial residence and capital. After an international competition, a project based on the ideas of LUDWIG FÖRSTER was approved; it envisaged a double avenue 57 m wide and 4 km long encircling the inner city, partly in polygonal form, along which the most important cultural and administrative buildings of the empire were to be arranged (see fig. 1 above). Demolition of the walls, levelling of the Glacis and new construction began in 1858, and the street was ceremonially opened in 1865, although construction of the buildings continued until the beginning of the 20th century. A series of monumental structures in a variety of styles, including Greek Revival, Renaissance Revival and Gothic Revival, surrounded by squares and parks, gives this imperial *via triumphalis* its character (see fig. 5). Notable buildings include the Staatsoper (1861–9; 1l) by Van der Nüll & Siccardsburg; the Votivkirche (1856–79; 1m) and Universität (1873–84; 1n) by HEINRICH VON FERSTEL; the Burgtheater (1874–88; 1o; *see* SEMPER, GOTTFRIED, fig. 2) by Gottfried Semper and KARL HASENAUER; the Rathaus (1872–83; 1p) by FRIEDRICH VON SCHMIDT; and the Akademie der Bildenden Künste (1872–7; 1r), Parlament (1873–83; 1q; for illustration *see* HANSEN, (2)) and Börse (1871–7; 1s) by Theophilus Hansen. The centrepiece of the project was the 'Kaiserforum', a monumental group of buildings planned as an extension of the Hofburg and incorporating the earlier Burgtor and the former imperial stables, the Messepalast (1721–5; 1t). Designed by Semper and Hasenauer, the Kaiserforum was only partially executed with the Neue Burg (1u; *see* §V, 5(i) below) and two large court museums, the Kunsthistorisches Museum (1v) and Naturhistorisches Museum (from 1872; 1w; *see* AUSTRIA, fig. 8). An abundance of private buildings and palaces, mostly in the idiom of the 'New Viennese Renaissance', was also erected on the 700 m-wide site in a grid pattern of blocks, making a major contribution to its unified and self-contained character. The Ringstrasse was one of the largest and most important urban planning achievements of the 19th century and, together with Haussmann's rationalization of Paris, one of the most original.

5. Vienna, western section of the Ringstrasse showing the Rathauspark, 1860s–1880s; photograph showing the Votivkirche and the Universität (upper left); the Rathaus (centre left); the Burgtheater (centre right); the Parlament (lower right)

Economic and technological developments resulted in a rapid expansion of the outer areas of the city; the inner suburbs had been incorporated in the 1850s, the outer suburbs were absorbed (1890–92) and the areas beyond the Danube in 1904, so that by *c.* 1900 Vienna had become the fifth largest city in the world, with a population of about 1.8 million. Numerous large projects were undertaken to rationalize the city's traffic systems and to provide adequate services. For example, the course of the Danube, previously split into numerous branches, was regularized in 1869–81 and a large canal network connected to it; a second large ring-road, the Gürtelstrasse, was built in the 1890s on the site of the Linienwall around the former inner suburbs; the railway system was extended; and two large waterworks, with aqueducts leading from the mountains, were built from 1879. At the same time, the piecemeal development of the Vienna Woods, which were threatened by the city's expansion, was forbidden, pushing industrial estates out to the plains beyond the Danube and to the southern edge of the city. The boom in trade, industry and crafts induced the city fathers to hold a world fair in 1873, for which the Rotunda was built with what was then the largest space ever covered by a single-span roof.

The end of the 19th century and the beginning of the 20th in Vienna were marked by the development of the Vienna Secession and a pioneering new style of architecture, as seen in the Secession Building (1898; 1x) by JOSEPH MARIA OLBRICH (*see* AUSTRIA, fig. 9; *see also* §III, 4 below). At the centre of the search for new directions in architecture was Otto Wagner, who taught at the Akademie der Bildenden Künste and helped create an international reputation for Viennese architecture of this period. His major urban projects (*see* WAGNER, OTTO, figs 1 and 2; *see also* TILE, fig. 10) included several remarkable municipal railway-station buildings that resulted from his largely unexecuted urban plan of 1893, and the Postsparkasse (1904–12; 1y) in the city, with a monumental glazed hall incorporating aluminium, a newly developed material. Further moves towards Modernism were made by Josef Hoffman, for example his Purkersdorf Sanatorium (1903–5; *see* HOFFMAN, JOSEF, fig. 1) at Hietzing, in the western suburbs. Vienna's most radical early modern buildings, however, were produced by Adolf Loos, who was critical of the ornament used by Secession architects: his Looshaus (1910; *see* LOOS, ADOLF, fig. 1) in the Michaelerplatz, Vienna, opposite the Hofburg, fully anticipated Functionalist work of the 1920s and 1930s.

BIBLIOGRAPHY
P. Kortz: *Wien am Anfang des XX. Jahrhunderts*, 2 vols (Vienna, 1905–6)
R. Wagner-Rieger, ed.: *Die Wiener Ringstrasse: Bild einer Epoche* (Vienna and Cologne, 1969–)
——: *Wiens Architektur im 19. Jahrhundert* (Vienna, 1970)
H. Andics: *Gründezeit: Das schwarzgelbe Wien bis 1867* (Vienna and Munich, 1981)
C. E. Schorske: *Wien: Geist und Gesellschaft im Fin de Siècle* (Frankfurt am Main, 1982)
H. Andics: *Ringstrassenzeit: Wien 1867 bis 1887. Luegen Aufstieg* (Vienna and Munich, 1983)
F. Borsi and E. Godoli: *Wiener Bauten der Jahrhundertwende* (Stuttgart, 1985)

Vienna, 1900: Art, Architecture and Design (exh. cat., ed. K. Varnedos; New York, MOMA, 1986)

I. Ackerl: *Die Chronik Wiens* (Dortmund, 1988)

4. AFTER 1918. Following the collapse of the Austro-Hungarian monarchy and its empire in 1918, Vienna suddenly became the oversized capital of a small republic, crowded with war refugees and cut off from the economic and financial sources of its former empire. The Vienna International Fair of trade and industry (1921) gave new impetus to the economic life of the city, however, and after Vienna had been proclaimed a federal province in 1922, the city government was able to initiate an unparalleled public housing programme in which 60,000 units were to be built in ten years. Much admired in Europe, this programme alleviated the most acute housing problems and gave a stimulus to employment and the economy. The design of the new buildings, which were conceived as infill in the inner city and as large estates on the outskirts, culminated in the distinctive 'Vienna superblock', for example the Seitz-Hof (1926–33), Florisdorf, by Hubert Gessner (1871–1943); the Karl-Marx-Hof (1928–30; see fig. 6) by KARL EHN; and the Friedrich-Engels-Hof (1930–33), Brigittenau, by Rudolf Perco (1884–1942). Associated amenities were provided by the government: they included swimming-pools, for example Amalienbad (1923–6), Favoriten, by Karl Schmalhofer and Otto Nadel, one of the largest in Europe; leisure centres, including one on the Höhenstrasse (1936), overlooking the city; and sports facilities, such as the Prater Stadium seating 65,000 spectators (later extended), built by Erich Otto Schweitzer in 1929–31 on the site of the Vienna International Fair. A model housing estate, the Werkbund-Siedlung (1930–32) in the south-western suburb of Hietzing, was the most important Austrian manifestation of the Modern Movement; there, under the direction of Josef Frank, a variety of architects including Josef Hoffman, Adolf Loos, Gerrit Rietveld, André Lurçat and Hugo Häring constructed a series of family houses that were intended to demonstrate a new way of living. Other building activity of this period was constrained by financial limitations; the only structure to affect the appearance of the city was its first high-rise building, the Hochhaus Herrengasse (1931–2), erected by Siegfried Theiss and Hans Jaksch, with stepped upper floors.

Six huge concrete anti-aircraft defence towers erected in pairs in the city in the early 1940s by Friedrich Tamms remain as evidence of World War II, in which Vienna suffered heavy damage. Reconstruction and new housing programmes were carried out during the ten years of Allied occupation, and the reopening of the Vienna International Fair provided a fresh economic impetus. With the post-war division of Europe, Vienna lay at the edge of the Iron Curtain; as the bridge between west and east, it shared in the economic boom of western Europe. The city expanded with new satellite towns and industrial districts, especially beyond the Danube and to the south, and this resulted in the construction of new transport systems, with motorways to the west, south and around the city. Public transport was extended by the development of the S- and U-Bahn (high-speed municipal railway and underground; from 1968); associated new buildings included the Schottenring underground station (begun 1978 by Wilhelm Holzbauer and others), a large modular structure of curved, painted steel profiles. Service infrastructure was also modernized, and a new central market was established to the south. A vast new general hospital was built to the west of the city, as well as new specialist facilities (e.g. Meidling Rehabilitation Centre, 1965–7, by GUSTAV PEICHL), while older service buildings were renovated. Numerous shopping centres were opened, including one of the largest complexes in Europe: Shopping-City-Süd (begun late 1970s) on the southern edge of the

6. Vienna, Karl-Marx-Hof, Döbling, by Karl Ehn, 1928–30

city. At the same time many innovative smaller projects were carried out in the inner city in the 1970s and 1980s, including several shops by HANS HOLLEIN and CO-OP HIMMELBLAU; the Law Faculty Building (1969–83) by Ernst Hiesmayr, a late Modern steel-and-glass structure; and the Haas Haus commercial complex (completed 1991), a Post-modern design by Hans Hollein.

Late 20th-century planning projects concentrated mainly on consolidating the areas north of the Danube (Donaustadt) and tying the urban structure more closely to the main river channel, with the creation of new residential, office and business facilities. The basis for this development was provided by the large-scale project to achieve flood protection (completed 1987), in which a second Danube channel was cut parallel with the main river, creating a long (20 km) narrow island that, together with the adjacent river-bank, was developed into a gigantic leisure and recreation centre providing 40 km of beach within the metropolis. Marking Vienna's role as the third official city of the United Nations is the Y-shaped International Style UNO-Stadt (1970–79; by Johann Staber) built at Donaupark, just across the river.

BIBLIOGRAPHY

H. L. Mikoletsky: *Österreich im 20. Jahrhundert* (Vienna, 1962)
O. Uhl: *Moderne Architektur in Wien: Von Otto Wagner bis heute* (Vienna and Munich, 1966)
Bauen in Österreich: Die Fortführung einer grossen Tradition (Vienna and Munich, 1983)
J. G. Gsteu and others, eds: *Architektur in Wien*, 2 vols (Munich and Vienna, 1984)
A. Janik and S. Toulmin: *Wittgensteins Wien* (Munich and Vienna, 1984)
H. Weihsmann: *Das rote Wien: Sozialdemokratische Architektur und Sozialpolitik, 1919–1934* (Vienna, 1985)
E. Vancsa: 'Die Gross-Stadt als Denkmal: Beispiel Wien', *Österreich. Z. Kst & Dkmlpf.*, xliii/1–2 (1989), pp. 1–6
F. Achleitner: *Wien 1–12 Bezirk* (1990), III/i of *Österreichische Architektur im 20. Jahrhundert* (Vienna, 1980–)

ECKART VANCSA

III. Art life and organization.

1. Before *c.* 1500. 2. *c.* 1500–*c.* 1800. 3. *c.* 1800–1896. 4. 1897 and after.

1. BEFORE *c.* 1500. Evidence of artistic activity in Vienna before *c.* 1300 is largely confined to scattered survivals in church decoration, such as the carved wooden crucifix (1170s) in the Melkerhof Chapel of the Ruprechtskirche, which is the earliest surviving sculpture in the city. Romanesque styles lingered well into the 13th century, as can be seen in the stained glass of the same church, which is still in the ZACKENSTIL and is related to manuscript illuminations that may be Viennese. Romanesque architectural sculpture survives at the Michaelerkirche (*see* §V, 4 below) and the Stephanskirche (*see* §V, 1(ii) below); a stone lion from the Romanesque Schottenkirche is in the Germanisches Nationalmuseum, Nuremberg. Wall painters were active in the Stephanskirche from the mid-13th century and at the Michaelerkirche at the end of the century.

From 1300 onwards there is more surviving evidence, and lines of development emerge. Artists working in Vienna were familiar with developments elsewhere in Europe and may have come from there. Direct French influence is apparent in some monumental works in the emerging Gothic style, such as the life-size *Virgin Enthroned* at Klosterneuburg Abbey; the same sculptor may have made the tomb of *Blanche of Valois* (*d* 1304; Vienna, Minoritenkirche), the wife of Duke Rudolf III of Habsburg (*reg* 1298–1307). Following on from these are the statues in the north and middle choirs of the Stephanskirche, which are closely related to Upper Rhenish art. There also seems to have been some artistic interchange with Regensburg, evidence of which is the small tympanum relief attached to the north portal of the Minoritenkirche and probably carved by a Regensburg sculptor. French influence appears again in the early 14th-century devotional image of the 'Dienstbotenmadonna' in the Stephanskirche, which has particularly graceful lines, but the majestic, powerful statue of the *Virgin* from the Dominikanerkirche in Vienna (now Vienna, Salesianerinnenkirche) is derived from Franconian models. The wooden reliefs from the Stephanskirche (mostly in Vienna, Hist. Mus. and Dom- & Diözmus.), probably from the choir-screen and dated 1340, are in a style related to the Upper Rhine Valley.

The magnificent remodelling of NICHOLAS OF VERDUN's Klosterneuburg pulpit in 1331 to form, with the addition of ten new enamel plaques, the present winged altarpiece shows that Vienna was a centre of both early Gothic panel painting and goldsmithing. The elegant figure style, which owes most to western European sources, continued in the panel painting of a *Passion* altarpiece at Klosterneuburg Abbey, wall paintings in the Michaelerkirche, Vienna, and the embroidered altar frontals donated by the Habsburg Duke Albert II (*reg* 1335–58) to the abbeys of Königsfelden in the Aargau (Berne, Hist. Mus.; *see* AUSTRIA, §XI, 1(i)) and Gaming in Lower Austria. The glass painters of the choir at the Stephanskirche modelled their earliest, mid-14th-century, monumental figure style on the Rhenish-influenced older group of choir statues, but models from the Ile-de-France and Normandy seem to have influenced the somewhat later, more refined cycle of Apostle figures in the south choir and also the reliefs and statues in the west portals of the Minoritenkirche. Viennese painters were next responsible for the earliest windows in the choir of Maria am Gestade (*see* §V, 3 below) and later made the glass in the choir of Maria Strassengel in Styria. No stained glass has survived from *c.* 1360 until the late 1380s, when the ducal workshop began to produce the Habsburg windows for one of the Herzogskapellen in the Stephanskirche. The workshop did not work only for the court; it supplied many churches in Austria until *c.* 1430.

Court influence on sculpture was apparent during the mid-14th century in the Minoritenkirche, where Albert II is depicted as donor in the *Crucifixion* relief. At the same time an Italian-trained sculptor made the elegant statues in the Michaelerkirche. The dynastic programme of sculptures made for the Stephanskirche by another ducal workshop (see fig. 7; *see also* §V, 1(ii) below) in the reign of Rudolf IV (*reg* 1358–65) provides important evidence of the contribution that Vienna made to the development of the *Schöner Stil* of Gothic sculpture from the late 14th century.

The Stephanskirche masons' lodge was not, however, exclusively a princely enterprise; it was the city that appointed the Kirchenmeister, the official who carried out

7. Vienna, Stephansdom, south portal of the nave, figures of *Rudolf IV* and an *Armsbearer*, *c*. 1360–65

all the legal transactions for the workshop and paid the workmen. Individual annual accounts of the Kirchenmeister survive (Vienna, Stadt- & Landesarchv and Diözarchv) from the 15th century onwards and give a greater insight into the organization and activity of the lodge. The standing of the Viennese lodge was confirmed in the Regensburg Ordnance of 1459 (*see* MASON (i), §III, 2), which placed it among the leading German lodges. The masons' lodges were the starting point for the formation of a cooperative, which stood apart from civic craft organization and transcended localities. From the 14th century the Viennese craftsmen joined in fraternities (also called *Zechen*), which, led by an elected Zechmeister, served to represent their common interests, foster devotion and undertake welfare work. The masons' *Zeche* was alleged to have existed since time immemorial, but the joiners received their own rule only in 1436. The earliest rule of the St Lucaszeche, the union of painters, glaziers, gilders, illuminators and other craftsmen, was drawn up in 1396 and the MASTERPIECE was introduced by 1410 at the latest. The goldsmiths had been given a rule by Albert III (*reg* 1358–95) as early as 1366.

The influence of Bohemia on Viennese painting is suggested by the anonymous portrait of *Rudolf IV* (*c*. 1360–65; Vienna, Dom- & Diözmus.) and a cycle of

secular paintings (*c*. 1400) in a house in the Tuchlauben. There is unbroken evidence of book illumination closely connected to the court from *c*. 1385 to *c*. 1485, with names of individual illuminators. In 15th-century panel painting, however, recorded names have not been linked satisfactorily with surviving works, but there seems to have been a large workshop, active *c*. 1410–*c*. 1440, whose leading representative is the MASTER OF THE ST LAMBERT VOTIVE ALTARPIECE (*see* MASTERS, ANONYMOUS, AND MONOGRAMMISTS, §I). The *Schöner Stil* of the workshop changed to a more realistic style looking back to Bohemian art of the 1370s. Among named artists, JAKOB KASCHAUER ran a large workshop, the styles of which suggest that conservative painters worked alongside more progressive sculptors.

Netherlandish influence appeared in Viennese painting *c*. 1440 in the work of the MASTER OF THE ALBRECHT ALTAR (*see* MASTERS, ANONYMOUS, AND MONOGRAMMISTS, §I), and it prevailed in the second half of the 15th century, in the great altarpiece of Maria am Gestade (*see* §V, 3 below) and the altarpiece by the MASTER OF THE VIENNA SCHOTTENSTIFT (Vienna, Schottenkirche, Stiftsgal.; *see* MASTERS, ANONYMOUS, AND MONOGRAMMISTS, §I), several panels of which depict the topography of Vienna (see fig. 2 above).

Of decisive importance for the development of sculpture in Vienna was the summoning from Strasbourg in 1467 of NICOLAUS GERHAERT by Emperor Frederick III, to make his tomb in the Stephanskirche. This work is one of the high points of Late Gothic sculpture. Gerhaert had many followers, whose work includes the fine cycle of statues of the early 1480s in the Hofburgkapelle (*see* §V, 5(i) below).

Around 1500 Vienna was the focus for a new generation of artists, the Danube school (*see* §2 below). The city was then a centre of humanism, fostered by Emperor Maximilian I, with its own book-printers' workshop. The new forms of the Renaissance were also gradually accepted, although in the charming stone monuments in the Stephansdom they were combined with a Late Gothic figure style.

BIBLIOGRAPHY

K. Uhlirz: *Die Rechnungen des Kirchenmeisteramtes von St. Stephan zu Wien*, 2 vols (Vienna, 1901–2)

——: 'Das Gewerbe, 1208–1527', *Jb. Ver. Gesch. Stadt Wien*, ii/2 (1905), pp. 592–740

O. Pächt: *Österreichische Tafelmalerei der Gotik* (Augsburg, 1929)

W. Buchowiecki: 'Geschichte der Malerei in Wien', *Jb. Ver. Gesch. Stadt Wien*, n. s., vii/2 (1955), pp. 1–42

A. Stange: *Deutsche Malerei der Gotik*, ix (Munich and Berlin, 1961)

E. Frodl-Kraft: *Die mittelalterlichen Glasgemälde in Wien*, Corp. Vitrearum Med. Aevi: Österreich, i (Graz, Vienna and Cologne, 1962)

Die Kunst der Donauschule, 1490–1540 (exh. cat., St Florian Abbey and Linz, Oberösterreich. Landesmus., 1965)

G. Schmidt: 'Die österreichische Kreuztragungstafel in der Huntington Library', *Österreich. Z. Kst & Dkmlpf.*, xx/1 (1966), pp. 1–15

K. Ginhart: 'Die gotische Bildnerei in Wien', *Jb. Ver. Gesch. Stadt Wien*, n. s., vii/1 (1970), pp. 1–81

E. Baum: *Katalog des Museums mittelalterlicher österreichischer Kunst* (1971), i of *Österreichische Galerie Wien* (Vienna, 1971–)

A. Berger-Fix: 'Das Wimpassinger Kreuz und seine Einordnung in die Kunst des 13. Jahrhunderts', *Wien. Jb. Kstgesch.*, xxxiii (1980), pp. 31–81

E.-M. Höhle, O. Pausch and R. Perger: 'Die Neidhart-Fresken im Haus Tuchlauben 19 in Wien: Zum Fund profaner Wandmalereien der Zeit um 1400', *Österreich. Z. Kst & Dkmlpf.*, xxxvi (1982), pp. 110–49

E. Lanc: *Die mittelalterlichen Wandmalereien in Wien und Niederösterreich* (1983), i of *Corpus der mittelalterlichen Wandmalereien Österreichs* (Vienna, 1983–)

G. Schmidt: 'Die Wiener Buchmalerei des 15. Jahrhunderts', *Kstgesch. Ges. Berlin*, n. s., xxxiii (1984–5), pp. 10–12

For further bibliography *see* §§II, 1 above and V, 1(ii), 3, 4 and 5(i) below.

MARLENE STRAUSS-ZYKAN

2. *c.* 1500–*c.* 1800. During the reign of Emperor Maximilian I (*reg* 1493–1519; *see* HABSBURG, §I(3)), Vienna occupied an equivocal position. Although the Emperor reinforced the city's standing as the capital of the newly developing Habsburg empire, making it a centre of humanist education and summoning scholars to teach and take up senior posts at the imperial court, he did not make it his personal residence, denying it the princely patronage of the arts this would have entailed. Consequently both the Hofburg and many of the churches in Vienna fell into a poor state of repair, and when Maximilian sought a suitable site for his own tomb, no church in Vienna was considered worthy of the distinction; his close links with Innsbruck, which was then economically stronger than Vienna and better placed geographically, explain why his monumental tomb was eventually located in the Hofkirche there. The few works of art of any real significance produced in Vienna at the beginning of the 16th century were made by foreign artists. ANTON PILGRAM, a sculptor from the Upper Rhine, made an organ base and a magnificent stone pulpit with rich figural decoration for the Stephansdom. Members of the DANUBE SCHOOL, including Lucas Cranach (i), also spent time in the city. During Cranach's stay (*c.* 1500–03), he painted members of the university, for example the humanist scholar *Dr Johannes Cuspinian* (*c.* 1502–3; Winterthur, Samml. Oskar Reinhart).

Further decline in artistic life in Vienna occurred under Charles V, who spent barely any time in the city and during whose reign a devastating fire and the first Ottoman siege took place. When Ferdinand I (*see* HABSBURG, §I(6)) succeeded as emperor in 1558, however, and chose to remain resident in the city where he had already directed important reconstruction works (*see* §II, 2 above), he encouraged Italian architects and artists such as PIETRO FERABOSCO, Jacopo Strada (*see* STRADA, (1)) and GIUSEPPE ARCIMBOLDO to settle in Vienna, beginning over two centuries of Italian domination of the arts in the city. Strada was employed by Ferdinand and his son Maximilian II (*see* HABSBURG, §I(8)) as a general artistic adviser. Closely involved with all artistic activities at the court, Strada had curatorial responsibilities for the imperial works of art, including the Kunst- and Wunderkammer of Maximilian—the first Habsburg to establish an art collection and cabinet in his residence; this was the precursor of the imperial collections.

During the imperial court's removal to Prague under Rudolf II (*reg* 1576–1612; *see* HABSBURG, §I(10)), Vienna once more dwindled into provincialism. The predominant influence on the creative arts in the city in the mid-16th to mid-17th centuries was the Counter-Reformation (*see* §§I and II, 2 above), and the churches and monasteries built during this period accounted for the most important commissions for artists and sculptors. The Jesuits, called to Vienna in 1551, also played a particularly important role

8. Paul Strudel: *Emperor Leopold I*, Lasa marble, h. 860 mm, *c.* 1696 (Vienna, Kunsthistorisches Museum)

in education. At this time there were about 20 painters in Vienna who were full members of the St Lucaszeche (*see* §1 above) and they were regularly checked to ensure that they were using only pictorial themes sanctioned by the Church.

The imperial court returned to Vienna under the emperors Matthias and Ferdinand II (*see* HABSBURG, §I(12) and (16)), Matthias bringing a large part of Rudolf's collections with him. The Thirty Years War (1618–48) limited artistic and cultural life, although a strong Italian influence remained. One of the few significant Austrian artists working in Vienna at this period was Tobias Pock of Konstanz, who painted the *Martyrdom of St Stephen* (1640–47; Vienna, Stephansdom) for the high altar in the cathedral. The marble Mariensäule Am Hof (1647) was one of the few major sculptures of the period, commissioned from Johann Jacob Pock by Ferdinand III. A bronze copy (1664–7), with a plinth by Carlo Carlone and Carlo Antonio Canevale, stands in the square. A later column, the Dreifaltigkeitssäule ('Pestsäule'; 1687–93) in the Graben, was commissioned by Leopold I as a memorial to the plague epidemic of 1679; a masterpiece of Viennese early Baroque sculpture, it was a collaborative work by MATHIAS RAUCHMILLER, Paul Strudel (*see* STRUDEL, (1)), Lodovico Ottavio Burnacini and Johann Bernhard Fischer von Erlach (for further discussion and illustration *see* BURNACINI, LODOVICO).

Nevertheless, local artistic standards remained low. During the 17th century painters and sculptors were tied to guild rules like craftsmen or tradesmen. Only a small number of artists enjoyed the privilege of freedom granted by the court, which meant that they were answerable only to the court for the quality of their work; they sometimes shared this distinction with 300–500 other 'special artists' such as glass-cutters, hatters and gunsmiths. The training of artists along guild lines was correspondingly poor, and the work they produced was far lower in quality than elsewhere in Europe. To overcome these problems Peter Strudel (*see* STRUDEL, (2)) founded the Kaiserliche Akademie in 1692 with the objective of promoting the arts. It was based on the Académie Royale in Paris, but despite state support (from 1705) Strudel was unable to make a commercial success of the venture, and it closed after his death in 1714. The idea was revived in 1725 with the founding of the Akademie der Maler, Bildhauer und Baukünstler by Jacob van Schuppen (1670–1754), who trained as a painter in Paris. This institution subsequently played a leading role in training artists, enrolling *c.* 200 pupils a year, to the great annoyance of the old painters' guild, which opposed the categorization of artists as 'academic' or 'popular'.

Baroque Vienna, which flourished after the Ottoman siege of 1683, was characterized above all by the construction of lavish churches and palaces (*see* §II, 2 above),

particularly those designed by Johann Bernhard Fischer von Erlach and Johann Lukas von Hildebrandt, both of whom studied in Rome. As court sculptor (from 1696), Paul Strudel produced several important portrait works for the Habsburgs at this time (see fig. 8), including the series of life-size marble statues in the Hofbibliothek (*see* §V, 5(i) below). Nevertheless, for the artistic work associated with the new Baroque buildings, particularly such palaces as the Belvedere and Schönbrunn (*see* §V, 6 and 7 below), patrons at first continued to turn to Italian painters and sculptors. ANDREA POZZO from Rome created the superb ceiling frescoes in the Universitätskirche (1703–4) and Palais Liechtenstein (1704–9), introducing *trompe l'oeil* painting to Vienna for the first time. Francesco Solimena of Naples painted frescoes in the Upper Belvedere and altar pictures for Prince Eugene of Savoy in the early 1720s; and the sculptors Lorenzo Mattielli (1678–1748) and GIOVANNI GIULIANI supplied statuary for palaces, churches and monasteries.

In the early 18th century, however, Austrian painters and sculptors began to obtain more important commissions, notably JOHANN MICHAEL ROTTMAYR, who had trained in Italy and whose paintings made an important contribution to Fischer von Erlach's concept of a Baroque *Gesamtkunstwerk*. Other important artists active at this time in Vienna were Martino Altomonte (*see* ALTOMONTE, (1)), who assisted in Strudel's academy and whose work

9. Martin van Meytens II: *Theatre Performance in the Redoutensaal*, from the *Wedding of Joseph II* series, 1760–80 (Vienna, Schloss Schönbrunn)

included frescoes in the Marmorsaal (1716) of the Lower Belvedere; and Daniel Gran, who painted the frescoes in the Hofbibliothek (1726–30; for illustration *see* GRAN, DANIEL). Paul Troger worked mostly outside Vienna but had a considerable influence on the artistic life of the city as a professor at the Akademie. By far the most outstanding and influential sculptor in 18th-century Vienna was Georg Raphael Donner, whose masterpiece in Vienna was the Providentia Fountain (1739), commissioned by the city authorities for the Neuer Markt (replica *in situ*; original now Vienna, Belvedere; for illustration *see* DONNER, (1)). In the mid-18th century Franz Anton Maulbertsch, a pupil of Troger, produced frescoes glorifying the Catholic Church in a final upsurge of Counter-Reformation ideals, and Franz Xaver Messerschmidt produced sculptures (e.g. *Empress Maria-Theresa* and the *Emperor Francis I*, 1764–6; Vienna, Belvedere) that were completely within the Baroque tradition at a time when French influences were beginning to prevail (see below).

An increased interest in collecting was also a feature of Baroque Vienna, in which a nobleman's rank could be measured by the value of his art collection. A great many collections of paintings were created, principally those of Prince Eugene of Savoy (*see* SAVOY, (10)) and the Princes of Liechtenstein, following the example of the imperial collection. This was based largely on the works collected in the mid-17th century by Archduke Leopold William (*see* HABSBURG, §I(18)). Its national importance was recognized by Emperor Charles VI, an outstanding patron of the arts (*see* HABSBURG, §I(20)), who in 1728 allocated new space within the Hofburg to his art treasures; the ceremonial act of handing over the inventory to him was considered so important that Solimena was commissioned to record it (Vienna, Ksthist. Mus.). The imperial collections were later transferred by Joseph II to the Belvedere and opened to the general public in 1781.

French influences were introduced to Vienna on the accession of Empress Maria-Theresa (*see* HABSBURG, §I(21)) and her French husband, Francis I (*reg* 1745–65), who brought to Vienna many French scholars, artists and architects; this process was encouraged by the marriage of their daughter Marie-Antoinette to the future Louis XVI of France. Gradually the Italian supremacy in Viennese artistic life, particularly in the applied arts, began to be challenged. French pattern sheets and engravings of ornament were imported, and a change of style to Neoclassicism began to appear. The State Chancellor Prince WENZEL ANTON KAUNITZ-RIETBERG was a Francophile and noted patron of the arts who encouraged the amalgamation of several institutions in Vienna to form the new Akademie der Bildenden Künste (1772). One of the more important figures in the artistic life of Vienna at this time was Martin van Meytens II (*see* MEIJTENS, (4)), who was involved with the Akademie and was also responsible for several works portraying events and ceremonies at court (see fig. 9). An important collection of graphic art, the Graphische Sammlung Albertina, was also formed at this time by Duke Albert of Saxe-Teschen (*see* WETTIN, (9)). Towards the end of the century, however, there was a general decline in artistic patronage following the suppression of the Jesuits (1773) and other monastic communities

under Joseph II, although this was the period of a unique musical flowering in Vienna.

BIBLIOGRAPHY

H. Tietze: *Wien: Kultur, Kunst, Geschichte* (Vienna and Leipzig, 1931)
Klassizismus in Wien: Architektur und Plastik (exh. cat., Vienna, Hist. Mus., 1978)
E. Baum: *Katalog des Österreichischen Barockmuseums im unteren Belvedere in Wien*, 2 vols (Vienna, 1980)
Maria Theresia und ihre Zeit (exh. cat., Vienna, Schloss Schönbrunn, 1980)
F. Matsche: *Die Kunst in Dienst der Staatsidee Kaiser Karls VI.: Ikonographie, Ikonologie und Programmatik des 'Kaiserstils'*, 2 vols (Berlin, 1981)

For further bibliography *see* §V, 2, 5(i), 6 and 7 below.

BARBARA WILD

3. *c.* 1800–1896. The leading representative of the classicism regarded as modern in Vienna about 1800 was the painter Heinrich Friedrich Füger, director of the Akademie der Bildenden Künste and from 1806 director of the imperial picture gallery. Franz Anton Zauner held a similarly dominant position in sculpture. The young Romantics came increasingly into conflict with them, and in 1809 a small group formed the Lukasbund (Guild of St Luke; *see* NAZARENES, §1) with the aim of achieving a renewal of religious art based on the models of Albrecht Dürer and the early Italian Renaissance. Although this artists' association, the first of modern times in German lands, moved to Rome in 1810, it continued to be influential in Vienna. The decoration of the parish church at Altlerchenfeld (begun 1848), under the overall direction of the painter Joseph von Führich, was an important late work by artists of this persuasion in Vienna.

The period between 1815 and 1848 in Vienna is usually associated with the concept of BIEDERMEIER, which denotes above all a certain intimate attitude to life. The most important activities for Biedermeier painters were landscape painting, using motifs from the immediate environment; portraiture, especially family portraits; and genre painting, depicting everyday life. Flower and miniature painting, mainly for portrait purposes, also flourished. History painting, promoted by the state to propagate nationalist and patriotic ideas, played a more subordinate role than in France. Josef Franz Danhauser (*see* DANHAUSER, (2)), Peter Fendi and FERDINAND GEORG WALDMÜLLER are regarded as the main representatives of Viennese Biedermeier painting. Waldmüller, professor at the Akademie and art reformer, broke new ground in Austrian art as an advocate of realism. He painted the Vienna Woods and the Prater (see fig. 10) as well as the bourgeoisie and regarded direct observation of nature as paramount. Friedrich von Amerling gained prominence as a portrait painter of the élite, while Thomas Ender was highly regarded as a landscape painter; Friedrich Gauermann won public favour with his paintings of animals in a landscape setting. Rudolf Alt, the most important Austrian watercolour painter, became a faithful chronicler of his home city, Vienna, capturing the atmosphere of its moods and changes in the course of his long life (for illustration *see* ALT, RUDOLF). Together with the political and social withdrawal into the private sphere that was characteristic of Biedermeier, Viennese decorative arts attained an extraordinary level of quality at this time, attested by exquisite objects in glass, porcelain and silver as well as furniture (*see* §IV, 1 below); collectively this art is summed up as 'Alt-Wiener Kunst'.

10. Ferdinand Georg Waldmüller: *Prater Landscape*, 1830s (Vienna, Belvedere)

The second half of the 19th century, following the revolution of 1848 and often referred to as the Francis-Joseph era, was characterized by a variety of styles, although it set its stamp in a unique manner on the appearance of Vienna. The flowering of historicism had its origins in architecture, the often individualistic eclecticism of which was taken over by all other genres. In conjunction with the building of the Ringstrasse in Vienna (from 1858; *see* §II, 3 above), a prestigious, monumental style emerged in painting and sculpture that fused with the so-called Ringstrasse architecture to form a unity that critics often refer to as a kind of *Gesamtkunstwerk*. The sculptors ANTON DOMINIK FERNKORN, KASPAR CLEMENS ZUMBUSCH and VICTOR TILGNER in particular benefited from this general development and the rampant cult of the monument (*see* AUSTRIA, §IV, 4 and fig. 22). HANS MAKART, a native of Salzburg, established himself as the uncontested prince of painting for the new imperial buildings of the Ringstrasse. His sumptuous large-format paintings, which use intoxicating colours, influenced a whole era. Makart's success was financed by the new plutocracy, who owed their wealth to trade and industry and were intent on aping the lifestyle of the aristocracy.

Other approaches can be seen, for example in the idiosyncratic work of the Viennese artist Anton Romako, which is now regarded as an important forerunner of Austrian Expressionism; in 1876, however, at the time of his return to Vienna after almost 20 years in Rome, his work was highly unpopular. August von Pettenkofen, Emil

Jakob Schindler (1842–92), Carl Moll and Olga Wisinger-Florian were among the best exponents of a kind of painting that, independently of French *plein-air* painting, was often concerned with analogous problems relating to the conveyance of an impression of mood. If these painters found their thematically modest motifs in their local surroundings, the group of Orientalist painters, including Leopold Carl Müller (1834–92), sought the bright sunlight of Egypt to brighten their palettes.

Viennese art life in the 19th century was shaped in a general way by the emancipation of artists from institutionalized ties to traditional patrons, the Church and the nobility. At the same time the Akademie der Bildenden Künste, through various changes to its statutes in the first half of the 19th century, became, under the protection of the Chancellor, Prince Metternich, the highest authority in all artistic matters, including the care of monuments, state art purchases and exhibitions. After 1849, with the establishment of an education ministry, the academy's activities were confined to teaching, although it was not until 1872 that it was granted college status. In the meantime, the setting up of the arts and crafts schools and the Graphische Lehr- und Versuchanstalt meant that the academy's monopoly was already at an end. As the art market developed, many new art collections emerged, some with middle-class owners. The great princely galleries were opened to the public, including the unique collection of graphic art at the Albertina (1822). When the newly built Kunsthistorisches Museum on the Ringstrasse was opened in 1891, it was possible for the rich collections of the Habsburg imperial family to be shown under one roof for the first time, although parts of the collections, such as those in the Belvedere, had previously been accessible. The Vienna Museum für Kunst und Industrie, founded in 1864 on the model of the Victoria and Albert Museum in London, was the first decorative arts museum on the European continent. The driving force behind this educational institute for industry, crafts, artists and the public was the art scholar Rudolf Eitelberger von Edelberg (1817–85), who was the first president of the newly created Kunsthistorisches Institut of the Universität in Vienna. At the Kunstgewerbeschule attached to the museum many artists who became important for the history of Viennese art received their first training. In 1861 the Genossenschaft Bildender Künstler Wiens was created from two older artists' associations. Its exhibition hall and meeting rooms, the Künstlerhaus on the Karlsplatz, built by the artists on their own initiative and opened in 1868, was the first building of its kind in the German lands. The almost official character it acquired, as a professional body representing all visual artists, was, however, disrupted by the split between its members that led to the foundation of the Vienna Secession in 1897.

BIBLIOGRAPHY

L. Hevesi: *Österreichische Kunst im 19. Jahrhundert* (Leipzig, 1903)
W. Krause: *Die Plastik der Wiener Ringstrasse: Von der Spätromantik bis zur Wende um 1900* (1980), ix of *Die Wiener Ringstrasse: Bild einer Epoche*, ed. R. Wagner-Rieger (Vienna and Cologne, 1969–)
C. E. Schorske: *Fin-de-siècle Vienna* (New York, 1980)
W. Kitlitschka: *Die Malerei der Wiener Ringstrasse* (1981), x of *Die Wiener Ringstrasse: Bild einer Epoche*, ed. R. Wagner-Rieger (Vienna and Cologne, 1969–)
W. Koschatzky: *Österreichische Aquarellmalerei, 1750–1900* (Vienna, 1987)
Bürgersinn und Aufbegehren: Biedermeier und Vormärz in Wien, 1815–1848 (exh. cat., Vienna, Hist. Mus., 1987)

4. 1897 AND AFTER. The founding of the Vienna Secession in 1897 can be regarded as one of the most decisive breaks in Viennese art history. Established by GUSTAV KLIMT, CARL MOLL and others in opposition to the official Künstlerhaus (*see* SECESSION, §3), it advocated a modernism that, after the bombast of historicism, could face international competition (see fig. 11). The Secession exhibition building (1897–8; *see* AUSTRIA, fig. 9) by Joseph Maria Olbrich, still used for its original purpose in the late 20th century, had a flexible interior structure, with pictures clearly arranged on well-lit white walls; the Secession thus broke new ground in the presentation of art and pointed the way for modern gallery design (*see* MUSEUM, §II, 2). The real flowering of the Secession came in the years 1897–1905; its activity was crucial for introducing contemporary foreign art to Vienna, not only by inviting foreign artists to exhibit but also by purchasing their work. However, the latent conflict between the Naturalists under the painter Josef Engelhart (1864–1941) and the so-called Stylists under Klimt split the Secession, and in 1905 Klimt and his party left the association.

Klimt, who was especially indebted to his native Vienna in artistic terms, created an unmistakable synthesis of subtle colourism and ornamentation, and he was recognized even during his lifetime as the leading exponent of Austrian *Jugendstil* painting (*see* ART NOUVEAU, §6).

11. Gustav Klimt: poster for the First Secession Exhibition, original version, coloured lithograph, 970×700 mm, 1898 (Vienna, Historisches Museum)

Younger artists, although influenced by the aestheticism of the Viennese *Jugendstil*, turned towards Expressionism. Of these, EGON SCHIELE developed a highly personal style combining psychological perception with a fascination for erotic subject-matter. At the same time the painter, printmaker and poet OSKAR KOKOSCHKA was gaining his first successes in Vienna with visionary works that showed an expressive social commitment. These artists made a remarkable contribution to world art, although others, including MAX OPPENHEIMER and ALBERT PARIS VON GÜTERSLOH, also accounted for Vienna's extraordinary artistic strength between 1905 and 1914. The uncompromising work of RICHARD GERSTL is to be seen in the same experimental context as Arnold Schoenberg's twelve-tone music.

Other artists' associations followed the Secession in Vienna. Of these the HAGENBUND, founded in 1900, was by 1914 the most important; in it painters, printmakers and sculptors came together, including Franz Barwig (1868–1931) and Oskar Laske. As a characteristic outcome of the cross-fertilization of painting and commercial art, the decorative arts underwent a period of great development in Viennese *Jugendstil*. The most committed organization in this regard was the WIENER WERKSTÄTTE, founded in 1903 by JOSEF HOFFMANN, KOLO MOSER and the industrialist Fritz Wärndorfer (*b* 1868). Designers and craftsmen created a rich and diverse range of flawless products, which aimed to balance elegance with utility and respect for materials (*see* §IV, 2 and 3 below). The enterprise finally foundered on its financial dependence on a liberal upper bourgeoisie that disappeared after World War I.

The year 1918 marked not only a political turning-point but also an artistic one with the deaths of Klimt, Schiele, Moser and Wagner. Kokoschka had moved to Dresden in 1917. The huge political and economic problems that followed the dissolution of the monarchy are reflected in the fate of the great Viennese art collections, many of which (e.g. the Czernin, Figdor, Lanckoronski and Schönborn collections) were dispersed or greatly reduced by sales in the 1920s and 1930s. The rich imperial collections passed to the Republic of Austria and were incorporated into a reorganized group of museums in Vienna. In the Belvedere was created the Österreichische Galerie, comprising the Österreichisches Barockmuseum (opened 1923), the Galerie des 19. Jahrhunderts (1924) and the Moderne Galerie (1927); it was completed by the opening of the Museum Mittelalterlicher Kunst (1953) to form the equivalent of a national gallery.

The promotion of art by the state, which had gradually replaced court patronage in the 19th century, was unable to provide adequate support for the economically hard-pressed artistic community in the 1920s, and consequently there was a corresponding growth in the importance of the artists' unions. Georg Ehrlich, Joseph Floch (1895–1977), Carry Hauser (1895–1985) and Franz Lerch (1895–1977) continued the work of the Hagenbund, which supported both Expressionism and critical realism associated with German Neue Sachlichkeit; the Hagenbund's influence later declined, however, and it was closed in 1938. In a general atmosphere of resignation and a return to classical values, Viennese artistic circles were unreceptive to French influences, such as Cubism. Although a number of artists forged links with international Constructivism associated with Lajos Kassák, who in 1920 transferred his periodical *MA* to Vienna, abstraction remained the exception, and it was the developments from Secessionism that dominated Viennese art, particularly seen in the expressionist work of Gütersloh and Herbert Boeckl. After the fertile and innovative tendencies and achievements of the period directly after the collapse of the monarchy, Viennese art of the 1930s went into decline, while the 1920s and 1930s also marked the gradual decline of Vienna's dominance over Austrian art, which began to flourish independently in the provinces.

The annexation of Austria by Germany in 1938 brought about a compulsory political conformity of art in terms of form, content and the organization of institutions. Art was deployed directly to project Fascist concepts and images and, as in Germany, modernism was ridiculed and banned. In 1939 the exhibition of ENTARTETE KUNST (Degenerate Art) was shown at the Künstlerhaus in Vienna, having already been seen in the larger German cities. Nazi policies resulted in Vienna losing a large number of important artists, art historians (*see* AUSTRIA, §XVII) and gallery owners. After the war, artists sought a way out of the vacuum created by Nazi isolation. Young artists began to grope towards international trends in art and to react against the realism previously imposed by the state. The mediating work of the French occupying power in Vienna made Paris a centre of interest, with the result that

Surrealism and abstract art began to exert a decisive influence. Among exiles returning to Vienna in 1945 was the sculptor FRITZ WOTRUBA, who became a professor at the Akademie. There he continued along the path towards abstraction that he had taken before the war, producing archaically conceived block figures that became ever more architectural (*see* AUSTRIA, fig. 23). His strong artistic personality captivated a generation of young artists, making the figurative element one of the constants of Austrian sculpture. The sculptor, designer and draughtsman Walter Pichler became a leading figure in Viennese art life in the 1960s, dealing intensively with architectonic problems in his work.

A truly experimental avant-garde re-emerged above all in painting in the post-war years, partly shaped by Herbert Boeckl, who became rector of the Akademie der Bildenden Künste after 1945. Maintaining a link to his rich body of inter-war work, he continued traditions of Austrian painting in its expressive use of colour. Gütersloh is regarded, alongside Wotruba and Boeckl, as the third great patriarch of post-war Viennese art. The Viennese school of PHANTASTISCHER REALISMUS developed around him, with Arik Brauer, Ernst Fuchs, Rudolf Hausner, Wolfgang Hutter (*b* 1928) and Anton Lehmden (*b* 1929). Their painting, starting with technical perfection and the study of Old Masters, mingled objectivity with surreal alienation. This extremist enclave of object-related painting stood in diametric opposition to the abstract art of the time. *Art informel* was advocated from the 1960s by Boeckl's pupil Maria Lassnig, in whose master class at the Akademie painting and film were interwoven, by Oswald Oberhuber (*b* 1931), who, by his spontaneity, subsequently sought to reject all the dictates of a consistent style, and in particular by Arnulf Rainer.

Other developments in the 1960s included the controversial AKTIONISMUS, which Otto Muehl, Hermann Nitsch, Günter Brus, Rudolf Schwarzkogler and Adolf Frohner (*b* 1934) developed from the concept of the Happening. With its social critique aiming at emancipation from conventional constraints, it is regarded as Austria's contribution to the revolutionary events of 1968. One outcome was the enshrining of the freedom of art in the Austrian constitution in 1983. The work of such painters as Christian Ludwig Attersee should be seen in the context of the international return to expressive-figurative painting and the revival of panel painting. This is more apparent with members of the 'Neue Wilden', who dominated the debate on art in the 1980s: Siegfried Anzinger (*b* 1953), Erwin Bohatsch (*b* 1951), Alois Mosbacher (*b* 1954) and Hubert Schmalix (*b* 1952).

The two most important artists' associations after 1945, both formed in 1946, were the 'Kreis' (disbanded 1980), and the 'Art-Club', of which Gütersloh was president; the latter saw itself as a union of the avant-garde and was officially dissolved in 1960. The most important exhibition venues in the post-war years were the Galerie Würthle, with a programme of pioneering modernists, and the Galerie Nächst St Stephan, where the avant-garde of the 1950s gathered around the Catholic priest Otto Mauer. In 1959 the Historisches Museum was opened in the Karlsplatz; in 1962 the newly founded Museum des 20. Jahrhunderts was opened in the Schweizergarten, and in 1979 the Museum Moderner Kunst was opened in the former Palais Liechtenstein, with a national and international exhibition policy. The 1980s and 1990s were marked by the development of a positive social role for art. This can be seen in the strenuous state promotion of art, the costly adaptation of old museums and the building of new ones, numerous exhibitions, flourishing international cooperation between galleries and the emergence of banks and insurance companies as art sponsors.

BIBLIOGRAPHY

W. Hofmann: *Moderne Malerei in Österreich* (Vienna, 1965)
C. Pack: *Moderne Graphik in Österreich* (Vienna, 1969)
P. Vergo: *Art in Vienna, 1898–1918: Klimt, Kokoschka, Schiele and their Contemporaries* (London, 1975)
W. Schmied: *Nach Klimt: Schriften zur Kunst in Österreich* (Salzburg, 1979)
H. Sterk, ed.: *Die Kunst der 70er Jahre in Österreich* (Vienna and Munich, 1980)
K. Sotriffer, ed.: *Der Kunst ihrer Freiheit: Wege der österreichischen Moderne von 1880 bis zur Gegenwart* (Vienna, 1984)
Traum und Wirklichkeit Wien, 1870–1930 (exh. cat., Vienna, Museen Stadt, 1985)
Die Wiener Secession: Die Vereinigung bildender Künstler, 1897–1985 (Vienna, 1985)
G. Fliedl: *Kunst und Lehre am Beginn der Moderne: Die Wiener Kunstgewerbeschule, 1897–1918* (Vienna, 1986)
Vienna 1900: Art, Architecture and Design (exh. cat., ed. K. Varnedos; New York, MOMA, 1986)
E. Patka, ed.: *Kunst: Anspruch und Gegenstand: Von der Kunstgewerbeschule zur Hochschule für angewandte Kunst im Wien, 1918–1991* (Vienna, 1991)
C. Bertsch and M. Neuwirth: *Die ungewisse Hoffnung: Österreichische Malerei und Graphik zwischen 1918 und 1938* (Salzburg, 1993)

G. TOBIAS NATTER

IV. Centre of production.

1. Furniture. 2. Metalwork. 3. Porcelain.

1. FURNITURE. There is evidence from the 13th century that in Vienna the joiner existed as a category of craftsman distinct from the carpenter, and about 1380 the name *Tischler* came into use for the former. In 1408 a guild of joiners was established, which in 1436 was granted its first statute by the municipal authorities. In the mid-15th century there were 12 master joiners in Vienna, compared to 32 carpenters. After Archduke Ferdinand II's attempt in 1547 to grant master craftsmen freedom from guild control had failed, Maximilian I introduced a new statute in 1573. The only works to survive from the 16th century are pieces (Vienna, Niederösterreich. Landesmus.) by the court joiner GEORG HAAS.

In 1638 Emperor Ferdinand III renewed the statutes governing the craft; during the same period, however, the guild limited the number of master joiners practising within the city boundaries to 20 and in the suburbs to 1. In 1718 there were 25 master joiners in Vienna and 59 in the suburbs; this reflects the increase in population after the wars against the Turks had ended. Besides the craftsmen belonging to the guild, there were others with a court dispensation working in the service of Emperor Charles VI. In 1725, in the general statute governing craftsmen, which became effective in 1737, the Emperor established *Dekretiste* (craftsmen licensed by decree), who had served their apprenticeship but could not become master craftsmen (generally because they were Protestants). By the mid-18th century there were 277 of these as compared to 78 master joiners. While the court and the Church had been the most important sources of commissions until the 17th century, the increase in secular building activity following the Turkish wars led to commissions for furnishing the houses of noblemen. Their taste and patronage became increasingly influential, as illustrated by the projects initiated by Prince Eugene of Savoy. The court at Vienna during the reign of Maria-Theresa and her successor, Joseph II, however, gave little encouragement to cabinetmaking.

After the Napoleonic Wars and the Congress of Vienna (1814–15), Viennese craftsmanship experienced a revival. With the BIEDERMEIER style, furniture workshops developed a repertory of forms independent of English and French models. Technical innovations, including the introduction of shellac polish and spiral springs, and such official measures promoting furniture-making as the establishment of the Fabrikproduktenkabinett and the polytechnic institute won Austrian furniture an international reputation. At that time, beside the middle-class trained craftsman, there emerged the wealthy, privileged furniture-maker, for example Josef Ulrich Danhauser (*see* DANHAUSER, (1)); and in the 1840s, as the Biedermeier style gave way to historicism, MICHAEL THONET took the first steps towards industrialization with his bentwood chairs. The Great Exhibition in London of 1851 gave Viennese furniture manufacturers their first opportunity to present their products to an international public: CARL LEISTLER, Thonet and AUGUST KITSCHELT were among the exhibitors.

The foundation of the Österreichisches Museum für Kunst und Industrie in 1864 and of an associated school in 1867 led to reform in the arts and crafts. The aim was to counter the reduction in quality that resulted from industrial methods of production and to encourage architects to contribute to creating high standards of design. A new set of requirements for middle-class customers had to be met, and large furnishing and decorating firms came into existence, including those of Friedrich Otto Schmidt, Bernhard Ludwig (1834–97) and FRANZ SCHÖNTHALER. As a reaction to historicism, adherents of Viennese modernism around 1900 called for design 'appropriate to the times' for utilitarian objects. Leading artists and architects, including Otto Wagner, Josef Hoffmann and Kolo Moser (who founded the Wiener Werkstätte in 1903), designed bentwood and wickerwork furniture; Gebrüder Thonet, J. & J. KOHN and the Prag-Rudniker Co. were firms that specialized in products of this type. Furniture in the *Jugendstil* (Art Nouveau style) was developed and had an international following. After World War I it became necessary to create a style of furniture appropriate to the new types of building, including apartment blocks. In 1925 JOSEF FRANK and OSKAR STRNAD founded the furniture store Haus und Garten, establishing principles of design that, lacking the dogmatism of international Modernism, were still upheld after World War II.

BIBLIOGRAPHY

S. Jaray: 'Die Möbelindustrie', *Die Grossindustrie Österreichs* (Vienna, 1898), pp. 307–10
M. Zweig: *Wiener Bürgermöbel aus Theresianischer und Josefinischer Zeit* (Vienna, 1921)
——: *Zweites Rokoko* (Vienna, 1924)
M. Poch-Kalous: *Das Wiener Kunsthandwerk seit der Renaissance*, ii of *Geschichte der bildenden Kunst der Stadt Wien* (Vienna, 1955)

H. Zatschek: *550 Jahre jung: Die Geschichte eines Handwerks* (Vienna, 1958)

C. Witt-Dörring: *Die Möbelkunst am Wiener Hof zur Zeit Maria Theresias, 1740–1780* (diss., U. Vienna, 1978)

Neues Wohnen: Wiener Innenraumgestaltung, 1918–1938 (exh. cat. by G. Egger and H. Egger, Vienna, Österreich. Mus. Angewandte Kst, 1980)

V. J. Behal: *Möbel des Jugendstils: Sammlung des Österreichischen Museums für angewandte Kunst* (Munich, 1981)

E. B. Ottillinger: *Das Wiener Möbel des Historismus: Formgebungstheorie und Stiltendenzen* (diss., U. Vienna, 1986)

G. Koller: *Die Radikalisierung der Phantasie: Design aus Österreich* (Salzburg and Vienna, 1987)

Wien Möbel (exh. cat., ed. H. T. Amanshauser; Vienna, Sezession; Paris, Ecole Spéciale Archit.; Helsinki, Mus. Applied A.; 1989–90)

EVA B. OTTILLINGER

2. METALWORK. The pewterers' guild of Vienna was established in 1368 and formally incorporated by ordinances in 1430, but pewtermaking in the city remained relatively unimportant until the 16th century. More than 30 pewterers are known to have been active in Vienna in the 17th century and over 50 in the 18th. In the 19th century the number rose to more than 70, but this may have been the result of more accurate record-keeping rather than an increase in the number of pewterers. Copper, brass and bronze items were manufactured in the city from the Middle Ages but only on a small scale until the 19th century, when numerous factories producing luxury bronze items were established. The Wiener Werkstätte, created in 1903 as a cooperative workshop, aimed to produce handmade, aesthetically pleasing domestic objects. Its craftsmen, who included Josef Hoffmann, Josef Gočár and Kolo Moser, made lamps, chandeliers and vases in bronze, brass and copper (e.g. brass vase by Moser, 1903–4; Vienna, Österreich. Mus. Angewandte Kst; for illustration *see* WIENER WERKSTÄTTE).

A goldsmiths' guild was established in Vienna in 1366. From the medieval period Viennese silver was stamped with a town mark, a date and subsequently a quality mark. Much of the gold- and silverwork produced in Vienna in the 18th century followed the prevalent European styles. Silver in the rectilinear Art Nouveau style was also produced in the early 20th century by the Wiener Werkstätte.

PETER HORNSBY

3. PORCELAIN. After the establishment near Dresden of the Meissen Porcelain Factory (1710) it was possible to produce hard-paste porcelain in Europe for the first time. Despite efforts to guard the secret of its manufacture, Claudius Innocentius Du Paquier (*d* 1751) succeeded in acquainting himself with the production technique by studying books written by missionaries from China and bribing Meissen employees who knew the secret formula. In 1717 he acquired the services of the Meissen arcanist Christoph Conrad Hunger (*fl c.* 1717–48) and applied for permission to found a porcelain factory in Vienna; the second porcelain factory in Europe was therefore built in Rossau, Vienna, in 1718. The following year Du Paquier employed Samuel Stölzel, also an arcanist from Meissen. Both he and Hunger, however, left Vienna in 1720 as the enterprise was not a commercial success. When Stölzel left he destroyed many models, which was financially detrimental to the factory. Unfortunately Du Paquier's efforts to increase demand for his porcelain were unsuccessful, and the factory was left deeply in debt. Additionally, the factory was unable to produce the pure-white porcelain achieved at Meissen and instead created a paste with a glaze that often blistered. Output consisted mainly of tableware and vessels, which were decorated with chinoiseries and later *Bandelwerk* (interlacing bands). The main colours used were purple, black and gold.

Due to increasing debts the factory was bought by Empress Maria-Theresa in 1744 and styled the Kaiserliche Porzellanmanufactur. From 1745 Karl Franz Xaver Mayerhofer von Grünbühel took over the running of the factory and introduced the striped shield as a factory mark. As a result of the discovery of deposits of kaolin (china-clay) in Schmöllnitz and the use of clays from Passau the factory was able to produce a finer, white porcelain paste from 1749. As such workers from Meissen as Christian Busch, Johann Gottfried Klinger (1711–81), Samuel Hitzig and Philipp Ernst Schindler (1695–1765) were employed in Vienna, Meissen forms were adopted during the first half of the 18th century; Viennese porcelain, however, differed in the use of gentler hues for figure painting and a preference for light-brown, violet and yellow. Following the pattern of Meissen, wares were no longer decorated in the Baroque style but in the elegant, dainty, Rococo style. Scrolling, rocaille decoration was used on all types of wares and figure bases and became a distinguishing feature of Viennese porcelain from 1750 to 1760. Mythological themes were supplanted by amorous scenes. The factory was soon able to outstrip Meissen by expanding its exports and in the second half of the 18th century followed the Neo-classical style emanating from the factory of Sèvres in France (*see* AUSTRIA, fig. 34).

Under the management of Conrad Sörgel von Sorgenthal (*d* 1805) who was Director from 1784 until 1805, the factory reached its economic and artistic peak. By 1799 there were 500 employees at the factory (in 1744 there had been just 20), including 150 painters. Production included everyday tableware and luxury Neo-classical services in a variety of colours painted with miniatures. The use of russet and raised gilding was characteristic of Viennese wares. In place of the figures of amorous couples, typical of the Rococo, classically inspired biscuit figures were made. The factory's most important sculptor and modeller was Antonio Grassi (1755–1807), who was in charge of the sculpture department from 1784. His work mainly consisted of figures of heroes from antiquity and portrait busts (e.g. *Joseph II*, 1789; Vienna, Ksthist. Mus.).

In 1806 Matthias Niedermayr, the son of the first master modeller, Johann Josef Niedermayr (*d* 1784), took over from Sorgenthal. He had worked in the business from 1771 and, because of his familiarity with the organization, was able to keep the factory going throughout the vicissitudes of the Napoleonic Wars (1803–15). He could not, however, prevent its decline, which was accelerated by the loss of supplies of raw materials and the increasing competition from Bohemia. By the time Benjamin von Scholtz took over the business in 1827 the factory's workforce had fallen to 257. Andreas Baumgartner became Director in 1833 followed by Franz, Freiherr von Leitner, in 1842 and Alexander Löwe (1808–95) in 1856. During its final years (1862–4) the factory was run by Alois Auer

12. Porcelain coffee-service designed by Josef Hoffmann for the Wiener Porzellanfabrik Augarten, h. 180 mm (coffeepot), c. 1928 (Vienna, Österreichisches Museum für Angewandte Kunst)

Ritter von Welsbach; his attempts to turn it into an art institute and prototype factory were, however, unsuccessful. Emperor Francis-Joseph's decision to shut down the business was announced on 22 August 1864.

After the factory closed a number of smaller enterprises were established. The company of Wahliss continued the traditions of the Kaiserliche Porzellanmanufactur by taking over their models and successfully manufacturing (from 1894) similar wares. The collaboration between the Vienna Secessionists and the firm of Josef Böckh (1879–1933) in Vienna (est. 1828), which had founded a painting workshop in 1893, gave new impetus to ceramic creativity. This firm worked to designs by Josef Hoffmann, Kolo Moser and particularly Moser's pupils. The most successful commercial firm at this time was the Goldscheider'sche Porzellan-Manufaktur und Majolika-Fabrik opened in 1885 by FRIEDRICH GOLDSCHEIDER from Plzeň.

The formation in 1906 of Wiener Keramik by Michael Powolny and Bertold Löffler marked the beginning of a new era in Viennese ceramics. In contrast to the soft colours and hues used on earlier porcelain figures, strong colours and contrasting black and white were employed. The establishment was dissolved in 1913 and merged with the Kunstlerische Werkstätte Franz und Emilie Schleiss in GMUNDEN to become the Vereinigte Wiener und Gmundener Keramik. In 1917 the Wiener Werkstätte founded a ceramics department; about 1920 the studios known as 'Karau', 'Candida' and 'Keramos Invalidengesellschaft' were also started. In 1922 the Wiener Porzellanfabrik Augarten began production; in addition to producing many new lines it also took over models produced at the imperial factory. Such Viennese artists as Hoffmann, Otto Prutscher and Vally Wieselthier designed table-services

(see fig. 12) and other wares for the factory, which continued production in the late 20th century. Studio potters working in the 1960s in Vienna included Kurt Ohnsorg, Alfred Seidl and Kurt Spurey.

BIBLIOGRAPHY

G. W. Ware: *Deutsches und österreichisches Porzellan* (Frankfurt am Main, n.d.)
J. von Falke: *Die K. K. Wiener Porzellanfabrik: Ihre Geschichte und die Sammlungen ihrer Arbeiten* (Vienna, 1887)
W. Mrazek: 'Die Wiener Porzellanmanufaktur', *Barock in Österreich*, ed. F. Grimschitz (Vienna, Hannover and Berne, 1962), pp. 91–5
——: 'Wiener Porzellan', *Biedermeier in Österreich*, ed. R. Feuchtmüller (Vienna, Hannover and Berne, 1963), pp. 80–91
W. Neuwirth: 'Wiener Keramik', *Historismus-Jugendstil-Art Deco* (Brunswick, 1974)

GABRIELE RAMSAUER

V. Buildings.

1. Stephansdom. 2. Karlskirche. 3. Maria am Gestade. 4. Michaelerkirche. 5. Hofburg. 6. Belvedere. 7. Schönbrunn.

1. STEPHANSDOM. From the time of its foundation in the 12th century, the Stephanskirche, which became a cathedral in 1469, played an important role in church politics, reinforcing ecclesiastical power in the eastern region of the vast diocese of Passau; later it became a dynastic shrine and the symbol of a self-confident burgher class. Of the Romanesque parish church only the west towers, the west portal (the so-called Riesentor) and west gallery remain, but the Gothic structure is one of the most remarkable examples of a hall church. Its south tower, the Stephansturm ('Steffel'; see fig. 13), was the tallest spire (h. 137 m) in German-speaking Europe on completion in 1433.

13. Vienna, Stephansdom, view from the south-west, begun *c.* 1137

(i) Architecture. (ii) Sculpture.

(i) Architecture.

(a) 1137–c. 1300. Construction of the first church must have begun after 1137 when an agreement was concluded between the Babenberg duke Leopold IV (*reg* 1136–41) and Bishop Reginmar of Passau concerning church property in Vienna; the consecration by Bishop Reginbert in 1147, when the probably unfinished building was still outside the town walls, may be related to preparations for the Second Crusade. The original church was a basilica 83 m long, with transepts (see fig. 14); excavations in 1970 revealed that the west towers, the lower storeys of which date from the 12th century, were linked by a projecting central part, which seems to be the origin of the 13th-century porch (renewed 1500). Two inscriptions at the west end of the church state that Roman stone was used in the construction. The original west front probably resembled the Romanesque west front of Passau Cathedral, as recorded in engravings.

Evidence of a 13th-century remodelling of the Stephanskirche was revealed in excavations following World War II, but it did not appear to alter the shape and area of the ground-plan. More important changes seem to have resulted from the long stay in Vienna of Emperor Frederick II in 1237 and the subsequent presence of his representative, Bishop Ekbert of Bamberg. The Emperor probably commissioned the unusually large west gallery and Riesentor (*see* (ii) below), and probably by the middle

of the 13th century the west gallery was prepared as a shrine for the ruling dynasty, as evidenced by the Founders' fresco on the north wall. Remodelling at the west end of the church was the occasion for a general restoration and vaulting of the whole, but work was interrupted by a devastating town fire in 1258. The restored and completed building was reconsecrated in 1263. A stylistic transition to Early Gothic is apparent in the west gallery, while the architectural decoration, particularly the chevron ornament, on the west portal and the round windows in the west towers are Romanesque. Possible prototypes for the octagonal upper storeys of the west towers (Heidentürme) are the Hahnentürme of Freiburg im Breisgau Cathedral (first third of the 13th century) and the slightly later towers on the westwork of Mainz Cathedral.

(b) After c. *1300.* Under the Habsburg king Albert I (*reg* 1298–1308) the site for enlarging the Stephanskirche was acquired in 1304. However, control of the church fabric had, since the reign of Přemysl Ottakar II of Bohemia, been held by the citizens of Vienna, and the office of master of the church was established in the municipal constitution in 1334; the influence of the burghers on the building history should therefore not be underestimated. These factors combined to create a new

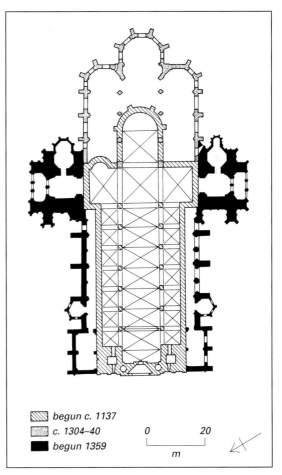

	begun c. 1137
	c. 1304–40
	begun 1359

0   20
m

14. Vienna, Stephansdom, plan, begun *c.* 1137

form of building: the first hall choir with three apses in the south German region. The hall church had been pioneered in Austria in the 13th century by the Cistercian and mendicant orders, which were strongly supported by the Habsburgs, and possible models for the Stephanskirche were the three-aisled hall choirs at the Cistercian Heiligenkreuz Abbey and the Dominican convent (destr.) at Tulin, both of which had a straight east end. The aisled choir with staggered apses at Regensburg Cathedral was an important preliminary stage. At the Stephanskirche, where the aisles are almost the same width as the nave, the prominent arcade arches and projecting central apse emphasize the longitudinal axis in a manner associated more with the basilica than the hall church. The fourth bay of the nave, linking the central and subsidiary apses, is longer, with a sexpartite vault. With its three chapel-like spaces, the choir can be regarded as a monumental version of local parish church forms. The different shapes of the engaged and free-standing piers with pear-shaped and cylindrical shafts indicate a change in plan during construction. The rood loft separating the Gothic choir from the Romanesque transepts was completed before the consecration of the choir in 1340 and can be reconstructed from documentary sources. A large proportion of the furnishings, including pier statues, stained glass and altars, must also have been completed by that time.

Under Rudolf IV (the Founder; see HABSBURG, §I(1)), the Stephanskirche became the focus of dynastic ambition, and the foundation stone for further extensions was laid by Rudolf in 1359. His aim of creating a collegiate foundation independent of the bishops of Passau was realized in 1365, but it was Rudolf's thwarted ambition to raise the Stephanskirche to cathedral status that determined the complex design of the new work (see fig. 14): two towers on the line of the Romanesque transepts; new nave walls in line with the choir; and the addition to the Romanesque west end of lateral two-storey chapels, known as the Herzogskapellen (Ducal Chapels) because of their special relationship to the ruling dynasty. The nave gables had not only a structural purpose but also referred to the pointed crown that Rudolf had assumed as a mark of sovereignty, as seen in his statues in the church (see fig. 7 above). The paired windows in the aisle walls and upper part of the Herzogskapellen derive from a local tradition. In 1446 HANS PUCHSPAUM was commissioned to vault the church, and he deviated from the original intentions for the interior by introducing stellar net vaults with curved ribs. The western part of the church, where the nave is slightly higher than the aisles, is distinguished from the choir by its richer decoration, with figure sculpture on the piers (*see* §(ii) below). An inscription indicates that the organ pedestal is by ANTON PILGRAM; the pulpit is attributed to the same master.

According to a 15th-century chronicle, work on the Stephansturm (1359–1433) had to be dismantled in 1407 to the point at which Duke Rudolf's first master had stopped work, because later masters had deviated from the original plan. The creator of the overall design of the Rudolfine work has been identified, probably incorrectly, as Michael of Wiener-Neustadt. Surviving drawings show that a shorter tower had been envisaged, but there was a change of plan *c.* 1400 under Master Wenczla from Prague

(perhaps to be identified with Wenzel Parler the elder) and his successor Peter Prachatitz (*d* 1429). Even before Wenczla's arrival in Vienna, forms from the Parler workshop in Prague were freely interpreted in the south tower porch and its eastward projection, the Katharinenkapelle (completed by 1396), which has a pendent boss. The new work began above this chapel, and stylistic details in the buttresses correspond closely to the unfinished south tower of Prague Cathedral. The Stephansturm has four storeys, including the octagonal spire, which was renewed in the 19th century; Prachatitz integrated the overall design by taking up the existing gable motif and adapting it in the upper storeys. A regular, pointed silhouette is produced by the buttresses, pinnacles and traceried gables.

Although the project for the north tower (Adlerturm) was contemporary with the Rudolfine work, it was not begun until 1450 during the reign of Frederick III (*reg* 1440–93), when the steeply pitched roof was covered with yellow, green and black tiles in a highly distinctive chevron pattern. By this time the wisdom of matching the south tower was already being doubted, and the north tower was never completed; a Renaissance cupola was added in 1556. The imperial double-headed eagle on the roof of the choir dates from a restoration in 1831. The whole building was heavily restored during the 1850s and again after damage in World War II.

For further illustration *see* ALT, RUDOLF.

BIBLIOGRAPHY

H. Tietze: *Geschichte und Beschreibung des St Stephansdomes in Wien* (1931), xxiii of *Österreichische Kunsttopographie* (Vienna, 1907–)
R. K. Donin: *Der Wiener Stephansdom und seine Geschichte* (Vienna, 1946, rev. 1952)
A. Kieslinger: *Die Steine von St Stephan* (Vienna, 1949)
W. Buchowiecki: *Die gotischen Kirchen Österreichs* (Vienna, 1952), pp. 253–5, 266–8
——: 'Die Baukunst der Gotik in Wien', *Geschichte der bildenden Kunst in Wien: Gotik* (Vienna, 1955), pp. 9–68
J. Zykan: *Die Stephanskirche* (Vienna, 1962)
R. Bachleitner: *Der Wiener Dom* (Vienna, 1966)
V. Flieder: *Franz Loidl, Stephansdom, Zerstörung und Wiederaufbau: Chronik und Dokumentation*, iii (diss., U. Vienna, 1967)
M. Zykan: 'Zur Baugeschichte der Stephanskirche in Wien', *Gotik in Österreich* (exh. cat., ed. H. Kühnel and others; Krems, Minoritenkirche, 1967), pp. 406–14
——: *Der Hochturm von St Stephan in Wien* (diss., U. Vienna, 1967)
R. Perger: 'Die Baumeister des Wiener Stephansdomes im Spätmittelalter', *Wien. Jb. Kstgesch.*, xxiii (1970), pp. 66–107
M. Zykan: 'Zur Baugeschichte des Hochturmes von St Stephan', *Wien. Jb. Kstgesch.*, xxiii (1970), pp. 28–65
R. Feuchtmüller: *Der Wiener Stephansdom* (Vienna, 1978)
M. Zykan: 'Der Stephansdom', *Wien. Geschb.*, xxvi–xxvii (1981)
Vídeňská Gotika: Sochy, sklomalby a architektonická plastika z domu Sv. Štepána ve Vídni [The Gothic in Vienna: Statuary, glass-painting and architectural sculpture from the Stephansdom in Vienna] (exh. cat., Prague, 1992)
E. Baucher: 'Aktuelle Bauforschung in St Stephan in Wien', *Österreich. Z. Kst & Dkmlpf.*, xlvii (1993)
H. W. Muller and others: 'Gesteinbestand in der Bausubstanz der Westfassade und des Albertinischen Chores von St Stephan', *Österreich. Z. Kst & Dkmlpf.*, xlvii (1993)
R. Koch: 'Ergebnisse der Bauuntersuchungen der Westfassade von St Stephan 1992/3', *Österreich. Z. Kst & Dkmlpf.*, xlvii (1993)
——: 'Vorbericht zu den Bauuntersuchungen im südlichen Heidenturm von St Stephan', *Österreich. Z. Kst & Dkmlpf.*, xlvii (1993)
G. Seebach: 'Baugeschichtliche Untersuchungen am Hallenchor von St Stephan zu Wien', *Österreich. Z. Kst & Dkmlpf.*, xlvii (1993)

R. Koch: 'Bauarchäologische Anmerkungen zur ersten romanischen Westfassade von St Stephan in Wien', *Aachen. Ksthl.*, 60 (1994), pp. 173–84

For further bibliography *see* §II, 1 above.

(ii) Sculpture. The sculptural decoration of the Riesentor and its porch poses problems, for these parts of the building underwent later alterations and a renovation around 1500. There are stylistic connections with sculptures, particularly the Gnadenpforte and the screens of the Georgenchor, at Bamberg Cathedral (*see* BAMBERG, §2(ii)). The iconography of the tympanum relief with *Christ in Majesty Borne by Angels* (*c.* 1237) can be related to that on the Marktportal of Mainz Cathedral.

The choir is decorated with statuary cycles (no longer complete) corresponding to the patrons of the three aisles. The stylistic sources for the Marian programme of the pier statues in the north choir and the representatives of the *Communion of Saints* in the middle choir are to be found mainly in the Upper Rhine region, with which the Habsburgs had many connections. The slightly later *Apostle* cycle in the south choir, however, with its more refined detail, seems to be influenced by French models, although the figured corbels and bosses are closer to the style of the earlier cycles.

The sculptures in the Fürstenportale (Princes' Doors) of the nave and on the west wall of the Herzogskapellen show strong court influence and, together with the tomb of *Rudolf the Founder*, are attributed to the Viennese ducal workshop. Besides local workmen, the workshop included masons and sculptors from south German PARLER lodges including that of Nuremberg, but the Parler component did not dominate, and the Vienna workshop developed its own character. A 'courtly' refinement detectable in the princes' statues, the founder's tomb and the *Conversion of St Paul* on the south portal of the nave can be explained only by the influence of western European art.

The rich sculptural decoration of the nave piers was made possible by the donations of citizens in the mid-15th century, but there is no recognizable overall iconographic programme. The major late medieval work, the marble tomb of *Emperor Frederick III* in the south choir, begun by NICOLAUS GERHAERT but finished only in 1513, represents the new self-assured generation of artists who were sensitive to the influences of humanism and the Italian Renaissance. These can also be seen in the self-portraits of the sculptor ANTON PILGRAM on the base of the organ and the pulpit, and in the many early Renaissance monuments dating from the second decade of the 16th century.

See also §III, 1 and fig. 7 above.

BIBLIOGRAPHY

K. Oettinger: *Anton Pilgram und die Bildhauer von St Stephan* (Vienna, 1951)

E. Doberer: 'Der plastische Schmuck am Vorbau des Riesentores', *Erlang. Forsch.*, xx (1967), p. 353ff [Festschrift Karl Oettinger]

E. Hertlein: 'In Friderici Imperatoris incolumitate salus Imperii consistit: Antike und mittelalterliche Herrscher-Auffassungen am Grabmal Friedrichs III in Wien', *Jb. Ksthist. Samml. Wien*, lxxxi (1985), pp. 33–102

G. Schmidt: 'Die Wiener "Herzogswerkstatt" und die Kunst Nordwesteuropas', *Gotische Bildwerke und ihre Meister*, ed. G. Schmidt (Vienna, Cologne and Weimar, 1992), pp. 142–75

——: 'Zur Wiener Plastik des Schönen Stils', *Gotische Bildwerke und ihre Meister*, ed. G. Schmidt (Vienna, Cologne and Weimar, 1992), pp. 101–13

R. Kohn: 'Eine bisher unbekannte Grabinschrift des Niclas Gerhaert von Leyden (+ 1473)', *Wien. Geschbl.*, xlviii/3 (1993), pp. 164–70

A. Salinger: 'Kunsthistorische Aspekte zum Grabmal des Kaiser Friedrichs III. im Wiener Stephansdom', *Wien. Geschbl.*, xlviii/3 (1993), pp. 129–163

MARLENE STRAUSS-ZYKAN

2. KARLSKIRCHE. During the plague epidemic of 1713, Emperor Charles VI vowed to build a church dedicated to St Carlo Borromeo, the plague saint. The Emperor made this monumentally conceived votive building an affair of state, to which all Habsburg lands had to contribute financially. Johann Bernhard Fischer von Erlach's design, with an oval plan behind a wide façade, was adopted in preference to those (untraced) of Johann Lukas von Hildebrandt and Ferdinando Galli-Bibiena. The church was begun in 1716 and completed in 1737 (*see* AUSTRIA, fig. 6); Joseph Emanuel Fischer von Erlach continued the work after his father's death in 1723 and was probably responsible for changes in the executed work (notably the increase in the height of the drum) from the design shown in Johann Bernhard's engravings in his *Entwurf einer historischen Architektur* (Vienna, 1721; iv, pp. 12–15) and the foundation medal struck in 1716 by Daniel Warou (1674–1729).

The façade of the Karlskirche, intended to be viewed from a distance, faces the Hofburg. Its Corinthian portico, flanked by two colossal columns and two gateway tower pavilions, is dominated by the tall oval drum and dome rising behind it. Fischer von Erlach's original achievement was to integrate the monumental columns into the façade, in which elements of French classicism and Roman Baroque are combined. The terminal pavilions are stylistically linked to François Mansart's Minorite church (1657) in Paris, although the passageways through the pavilions, unusual in a church façade, perhaps derive from Bernini's design for St Peter's, Rome. The projecting temple-front portico recalls the Pantheon in Rome, and in this context the two colossal columns of the Karlskirche should be seen as an appropriation of the triumphal columns of Trajan and Marcus Aurelius in Rome, symbolizing imperial aspirations. The main sources of information on the multi-layered symbolism of the Karlskirche are the writings of Karl Gustav Heraeus, who probably drew up the iconological programme (for further discussion *see* FISCHER VON ERLACH, (1)).

In the juxtaposition of the portico, tower pavilions and tall dome, Fischer von Erlach was inspired by a competition for the Accademia di S Luca, Rome, 30 years before, which he knew from his studies in Italy. The pavilions are crowned by statues of *Faith* and *Hope*, while *Charity* is personified by the figure of St Carlo Borromeo by Johann Stanetti on the pediment of the portico. The relief in the pediment, also by Stanetti, shows the cessation of the plague at the intercession of the saint, and scenes from the life of the saint are depicted on the colossal columns in spiral bands of relief by Johann Christoph Mader (1697–1761), Johann Baptist Staub and Jakob Christoph Schletterer (1699–1744). The crowns and imperial eagles surmounting the columns underline the dynastic pretensions of the building; at the same time the crowns in combination with the cross on the lantern of the dome are emblems of temporal and spiritual rule in a building in which the

Emperor is identified by name with the saint. Fischer von Erlach envisaged severe classical coffering for the interior decoration rather than frescoes, but in view of the building's symbolic significance, Johann Michael Rottmayr was subsequently commissioned to decorate the dome and transepts with frescoes (1725–29). Their theme, the glorification of St Carlo Borromeo, relates to the foundation of the church.

BIBLIOGRAPHY

L. Popelka: 'Studien zur Wiener Karlskirche', *Alte & Neue Kst*, iv (1955), pp. 75–132
H. Sedlmayr: 'Die Schauseite der Karlskirche zu Wien', *Epochen und Werke: Gesammelte Schriften zur Kunstgeschichte*, ii (Vienna, 1960), pp. 174–86
F. D. Fergusson: 'St Charles Church, Vienna: The Iconography of its Architecture', *J. Soc. Archit. Historians*, xxix/4 (1970), pp. 318–26
H. Lorenz: 'Das Lustgartengebäude Fischers von Erlach: Variationen eines architektonischen Themas', *Wien. Jb. Kstgesch.*, xxxii (1979), pp. 75–6

S. TRÄGER

3. MARIA AM GESTADE [Maria Stiegen]. Belonging to the Redemptorist Order since 1820, this aisleless church of the 14th and early 15th centuries is situated on a steep slope that originally directly overlooked a branch of the River Danube. Nothing remains of an earlier 12th-century Romanesque church, one of the oldest in Vienna. The present choir was built in the second third of the 14th century with three square bays and a five-sided apse and is reminiscent of large chapels in Lower Austria. The south double portal dates from *c*. 1350. Around 1360 the interior was furnished with pier statues, of which an *Annunciation* group and two Magi from a Marian cycle have survived in the church. Of high artistic quality, they represent a link between the somewhat earlier sculptures of the portals of the Minoritenkirche and the Fürstenportale of the Stephansdom. The stained glass of the chancel was made between the 1340s and the end of the 14th century; the surviving pieces have been reset in three windows in the chancel. In 1394 the Duke's architect MICHAEL CHNAB laid the foundation stone for the nave, which is narrower and off-axis and has a heptagonal tower and three chapels on its eastern bays. Patronage, which had been held by the ducal steward Hans von Liechtenstein, passed to the sovereign in 1395 and to the bishops of Passau in 1409. After Michael's death (*c*. 1404) building was continued by masons from the lodge at the Stephanskirche. An inscription records the completion of the nave in 1414, but work on the tower, which is surmounted by a slender perforated lantern, continued until *c*. 1430. Domical forms are also found in the baldacchinos on the two nave portals and the stellar net vaulting of the nave, which is lit by double windows. Two windows have stained glass dating from *c*. 1420–30. Two painted panels survive from a large winged altar of *c*. 1460, showing the *Annunciation* and *Coronation of the Virgin*, with scenes of the *Passion* on the back.

BIBLIOGRAPHY

A. Kosegarten: 'Die Chorstatuen der Kirche Maria am Gestade in Wien', *Österreich. Z. Kst & Dkmlpf.*, xvii/1 (1963), pp. 1–12
M. Zykan: 'Zur Identifizierung eines gotischen Gewölberisses in den Wiener Sammlungen', *Mitt. Ges. Vergl. Kstforsch. Wien*, xxv/3 (1973), pp. 13–20
P. Crossley: 'Wells, the West Country and Central European Late Gothic', *Medieval Art and Architecture at Wells and Glastonbury. British Archaeological Association Conference Transactions: Wells, 1978*, pp. 81–109

For further bibliography *see* §§II, 1 and III, 1 above.

4. MICHAELERKIRCHE. Founded *c*. 1220 as a court parish church by Duke Leopold VI (*reg* 1198–1230), it is a well-preserved Late Romanesque church with a Gothic extension of the chancel (before *c*. 1350) and other chapels added later. A Baroque porch by Antonio Beduzzi was added in 1724 and a Neo-classical façade by Ernest Koch towards the end of the 18th century. The church was built from east to west. It has a Late Romanesque rectangular chancel, a transept and a five-bay nave and aisles, in which the Early Gothic proportions of one aisle bay to each nave bay were adopted. A Romanesque door with splayed jambs and the *Agnus Dei* in the tympanum has been revealed in the north transept. Another door in a late Romanesque style was found in the second bay of the northern aisle. The semi-circular tympanum shows the *crux gemmata* on a triumphal column under a three-lobed arch surrounded by vine foliage. The archivolts of the west portal, preserved behind the Baroque porch, are Early Gothic in style. The exterior of the building has typical Romanesque architectural sculpture: hanging arches at two levels and figurative motifs on the slopes of the corner buttresses of the transept. In the interior the ornament of the corbels and capitals changes from Romanesque foliage and zoomorphic forms in the eastern parts to Early Gothic capitals with leaf buds and foliage motifs in the western bays of the nave. The building was completed *c*. 1250 with a west gallery, but the west tower was begun soon after the city fire of 1276, as can be seen by the architectural forms and the wall paintings in the tower chapel in the walled-off, westernmost bay of the south transept. The octagonal upper storeys of the tower were not built until after the city fire of 1327. The three chancel chapels are arranged in echelon and were closed off by a Gothic rood loft with nine arches. In the south chapel, founded 1350, are important figured bosses and pier statues. The wall paintings on the triumphal arches of the chapels are of the same period. The apse of the main choir was remodelled in 1782, with a relief stucco of the *Fall of the Angels* by Karl Georg Merville depicted over the vaults and walls; the centrepiece of the Neo-classical high altar is an icon of the Virgin (Hodegetria), which has been venerated in the church since 1673, when it was brought from Candia (now Herakleion) in Crete.

BIBLIOGRAPHY

A. Kieslinger: 'Der Bau von St Michael in Wien und seine Geschichte', *Jb. Ver. Gesch. Stadt Wien*, x (1952–3), pp. 1–74
O. Demus: 'Der Meister der Michaeler Plastiken', *Österreich. Z. Kst & Dkmlpf.*, vii/1–2 (1953), pp. 1–9
H. Lorenz: 'Ergänzungen zur Baugeschichte der Wiener Michaelerkirche', *Österreich. Z. Kst & Dkmlpf.*, xxxvi/3–4 (1982), pp. 99–109
St Michael: Stadtpfarrkirche und Künstlerpfarre von Wien, 1288–1988 (exh. cat., Vienna, Hist. Mus., 1988)
W. G. Rizzi: 'Zur Instandsetzung und Präsentation des romanischen Querhausportals der Wiener Michaelerkirche', *Österreich. Z. Kst. & Dkmlpf.*, xliv/1–2 (1990), pp. 70–71
M. Schwarz: 'Ein neuentdecktes Tympanon-Relief in der Wiener Michaelerkirche', *Österreich. Z. Kst. & Dkmlpf.*, xliv/1–2 (1990), pp. 67–9
Der Michaelerplatz in Wien: Seine städtebauliche und architektonische Entwicklung (exh. cat. by R. Bösel and C. Benedik, Vienna, Kultkreis Looshaus and Albertina, 1992), pp. 36–49

For further bibliography *see* §§II, 1 and III, 1 above.

MARLENE STRAUSS-ZYKAN

5. HOFBURG. The former residence of the Habsburg family (from the end of the 13th century), the Holy Roman

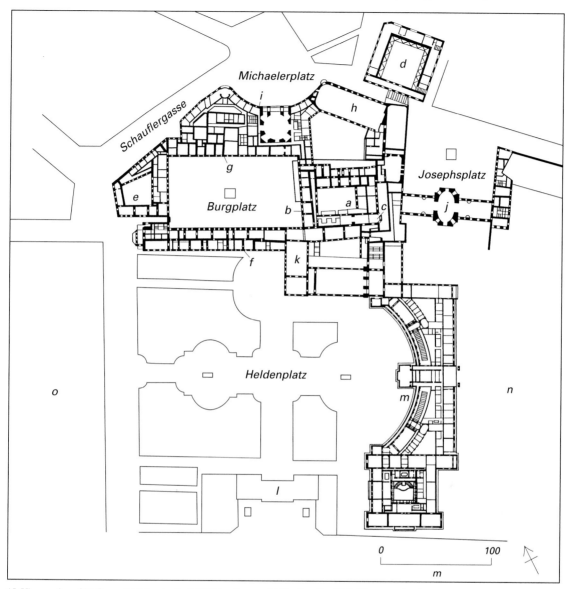

15. Vienna, plan of Hofburg: (a) Schweizerhof; (b) Schweizertor; (c) Burgkapelle; (d) Stallburg; (e) Amalienburg; (f) Leopoldinischer Trakt; (g) Reichskanzleitrakt; (h) Winterreitschule; (i) Michaelerfront; (j) Hofbibliothek; (k) Zeremoniensaal; (l) Burgtor; (m) Neue Burg; (n) Burggarten; (o) Volksgarten

Emperors (almost continually from 1452 to 1806) and the Austrian emperors (until 1918). The Hofburg is an extensive, irregular complex of buildings of varying dates in the south-western part of the inner city. From the 15th century it housed parts of the administration of the Habsburg empire and from the 17th century some imperial offices. It now accommodates the Apartment of the State President, some public institutions, a congress centre and important museums. Its main components (see fig. 15) include the Schweizerhof (Schweizertrakt; 13th century); Stallburg and Amalienburg (16th century); Leopoldinischer Trakt (17th century); Reichskanzleitrakt, Winterreitschule and Hofbibliothek (18th century); and the Heldenplatz, Burgtor, Neue Burg and Michaelerfront (19th century).

(i) Architecture. (ii) Schatzkammer.

(i) Architecture. The Schweizerhof (Schweizertrakt; 15a), at the centre of the Hofburg complex, is an approximately square structure first documented in 1275. Originally a part of the medieval fortifications of the town (*see* §II, 1 above), it was flanked by four corner towers and a gate tower and was surrounded by a castle moat, now partially filled in. Extensive alterations (1533–68) determined its present appearance: the façades were accentuated by simple Renaissance windows, the inner courtyard was given ground-floor arcades (subsequently bricked up), the rooms were replanned and most were decorated with ceiling paintings by Pietro Ferabosco, who may also have decorated the richly embellished Schweizertor (15b;

c. 1552–3; *see* AUSTRIA, fig. 3). In the mid-18th century narrow internal staircases were built, the Botschafterstiege (Ambassadors' Staircase) projecting into the courtyard, and on the opposite side the Säulenstiege (Column Staircase), which until 1988 led to the Schatzkammer (Imperial Treasury; *see* §(ii) below), were constructed to plans by Jean-Nicolas Jadot de Ville-Issey, and the imperial rooms were redecorated in the late Baroque style. In the southeast corner of the Schweizerhof is the Burgkapelle (15c), first mentioned in 1296 and rebuilt 1447–9. Embellished with tracery, it originally had two floors; in the upper hall, which has three bays, net vaults and a five-sided apse, are 13 noteworthy Late Gothic figures of saints surmounted by baldacchinos, which are the work of followers of Nicolaus Gerhaert. After a Baroque remodelling in the 17th and 18th centuries, the interior was restored in the Gothic style in 1802.

The quadrangular Stallburg (15d; 1558–69) was built, perhaps by Ferabosco or Jacopo Strada, as a separate residence for Emperor Maximilian II. Isolated from the rest of the Hofburg complex by the Reitschulgasse, it can be reached from it only by a footbridge. It is the most important Renaissance building in Vienna. In contrast to the unadorned outer walls, the inner courtyard is surrounded by three-storey arcades. The ground floor has been used since 1565 as stables, while the imperial picture gallery was displayed from 1721 to 1778 in the upper rooms designed by Claude Le Fort du Plessy.

The Amalienburg (15e) at the north-west end of the Burgplatz ('Franzensplatz') was built in 1575–7 as a self-contained residence for the Habsburg archdukes. It was remodelled in 1581 by Ferabosco and was the first building in the complex with an articulation that determined its visual impact. The interplay between the windows and asymmetrically placed portal and its decorative rustication and cornices together make it one of the most important buildings of Austrian Mannerism. In 1712 its proportions and articulation were substantially altered by the addition of a mezzanine floor. The interior was remodelled by Nikolaus Pacassi from 1765 and then frescoed by Johann Wenzel Bergl.

The Leopoldinischer Trakt (15f) was built (1660–67) for Emperor Leopold I by Philiberto Luchese to replace a sentry walk on the city wall between the Schweizertrakt and the Amalienburg. Although articulating elements are omitted from the Burgplatz front of this long residential wing, the even sequence of vertically linked windows and shallow pilasters on the outer façade is a typical device used on prestigious buildings in Austria and Bohemia in the second half of the 17th century. Soon after its completion the new wing was destroyed by fire; it was rebuilt (1668–81) by Giovanni Pietro Tencala to the old designs but with a mezzanine floor added. In 1699, for the marriage of the Archduke Joseph (later Joseph I) the royal apartments on the first floor were decorated with 148 ceiling paintings (now Vienna, Ksthist. Mus.) by Peter Strudel (*see* STRUDEL, (2)); they constitute the largest surviving decorative cycle of the Austrian Baroque (*see also* AUSTRIA, fig. 26).

The Burgplatz has existed since the 16th century; surrounded by the Schweizertrakt, Leopoldinischer Trakt,

Amalienburg and the administrative building of the Hofkammer and Reichskanzlei (former imperial chancelleries), it was used as an arena for tournaments and theatrical performances and now contains the monument (completed 1846) to *Emperor Francis I* by Pompeo Marchesi. In 1723 Johann Lukas von Hildebrandt was commissioned by the imperial chancellor Prince-Archbishop Lothar Franz von Schönborn to rebuild the Reichskanzlei; his simple façade on the Schauflergasse, facing the city, and the arrangement of the interior have survived, although many rooms were subsequently remodelled, including the imperial state rooms. These so-called Kaiserappartements of Emperor Francis Joseph (*reg* 1848–1916), which retain his furnishings, are very richly decorated with 17th-century Brussels tapestries and murals executed by Johann Wenzel Bergl and PETER KRAFFT in the 18th and 19th centuries.

The Reichskanzleitrakt (15g), occupying the entire north side of the Burgplatz, was completed for Emperor Charles VI by Joseph Emanuel Fischer von Erlach, who succeeded Hildebrandt in 1726 (*see* FISCHER VON ERLACH, (2)). He demolished Hildebrandt's original Burgplatz façade and erected a new frontage dominated by flat surfaces accentuated by three projections. The façade is articulated by giant pilasters and richly embellished with sculpture; the four statues on the two side gateways, representing the *Labours of Hercules*, are by Lorenzo Mattielli (1678–1748).

The Winterreitschule (15h; now the Spanish Riding School) and half the Durchfahrtsrondell, the opening between the Burgplatz and the Michaelerfront on the city side, were executed to Joseph Emanuel Fischer von Erlach's competition design (1727–9) following Hildebrandt's overall rebuilding plan for the Hofburg of 1724–5. The plain street façade of the Winterreitschule (1729–35) is characterized by a high, rusticated ground floor below giant pilasters framing blank panels; in contrast, on the side facing the Michaelerplatz, a rounded corner is emphasized by recessed free-standing columns and a small cupola. The severe, monochrome riding hall takes up the whole interior; its striking effect is produced mainly by monumental free-standing colonnades on each side, with balustrades supporting viewing galleries above, and by the enormous scale of the flat white ceiling with stucco coffering. The remainder of the Michaelerfront (15i) was completed only in 1889–93 by Ferdinand Kirschner (1821–96) in keeping with Fischer von Erlach's plan, after demolition of the Hoftheater (?1741; façade by Pacassi, 1764). At the centre of the new concave frontage (for illustration *see* FISCHER VON ERLACH, (2)) is the Michaelertor, a triumphal arch articulated with columns like the Winterreitschule and crowned by a tall dome above the Durchfahrtsrondell; it is flanked by two curved wings, one adjoining the Winterreitschule and the other having a matching termination, with rounded, colonnaded corners and cupola. Against the façade are two monumental neo-Baroque wall fountains adorned with figures symbolizing *Austria's Power at Sea* (1895; by Rudolf Weyr) and *Austria's Power on Land* (1897; by Edmund Hellmer).

The Hofbibliothek (15j; now part of the Österreichische Nationalbibliothek) was built in 1722–36 to plans by Johann Bernhard Fischer von Erlach and completed by his son Joseph Emanuel. It was conceived as a detached building on the south side of the Josephsplatz and was aligned to Johann Bernhard's Hofstallungen (1718–23; now Messepalast), the imperial stables built just outside the walls. The flat, pilastered façade of the library is dominated by the projecting central oval of the Prunksaal (Hall of State), its dome expressed externally in angular roof forms. A masterpiece of the Viennese Baroque, the Prunksaal (see fig. 16) is two storeys in height and contains eight marble statues of Habsburg emperors by Peter and Paul Strudel (*see* STRUDEL). The original interior was later modified; Daniel Gran's ceiling fresco of the *Apotheosis of Emperor Charles VI* (1726–30; for further discussion and illustration *see* GRAN, DANIEL) was also altered by Franz Anton Maulbertsch. The Josephsplatz, containing an equestrian bronze statue (1790–1806) of *Emperor Joseph II* by FRANZ ANTON ZAUNER, was given shape with two further wings (1769-76) by Nikolaus Pacassi and Franz Anton Hillebrandt, adopting the articulation of the library.

The Volksgarten (15o) was laid out in 1819–23, when Ludwig von Remy (1776–1851) also laid out the Heldenplatz, with two equestrian statues added in 1860 and 1865 (for illustration *see* FERNKORN, ANTON DOMINIK). Between the Leopoldinischer Trakt and the Schweizerhof, facing the Heldenplatz, is the large, Neo-classical Zeremoniensaal (15k; completed 1807; now a congress centre) by Louis Joseph Montoyer. Opposite is the fortified Burgtor (15l), built in revolutionary Neo-classical style (*see* AUSTRIA, fig. 8) to commemorate the Battle of the Nations (1813). It was begun in 1821 by Luigi Cagnola and completed by Peter Nobile in 1824.

16. Vienna, Hofburg, Prunksaal of the Hofbibliothek, by Johann Bernhard Fischer von Erlach and Joseph Emanuel Fischer von Erlach, 1722–36

The Neue Burg (15m), the final stage of the construction of the Hofburg, was begun in 1881 to plans by Gottfried Semper and KARL HASENAUER as one wing of the projected 'Kaiserforum' (*see* §II, 3 above); it was completed by Friedrich Ohmann and Ludwig Baumann (1853–1935) in 1913, when plans for the other wing were abandoned on the order of Emperor Francis-Joseph. It has a broad semicircular frontage to the Heldenplatz, with a high rusticated ground floor and an upper floor in the form of a loggia with paired, free-standing columns. The rear façade, articulated by giant half-columns above the rustication and with an exterior staircase, faces the Burggarten (15n; 1818) by Ludwig von Remy, with a glasshouse (1901) by Ludwig Baumann. The Neue Burg now houses the Ephesos Museum, sections of the Kunsthistorisches Museum and the Museum für Völkerkunde.

BIBLIOGRAPHY

M. Dreger: *Baugeschichte der K. K. Hofburg in Wien bis zum XIX. Jahrhundert* (1914), xiv of *Österreichische Kunsttopographie* (Vienna, 1907–)
A. Lhotsky: 'Die Baugeschichte der Museen und der Neuen Burg', *Festschrift des Kunsthistorischen Museums*, i (Vienna, 1941)
H. Sedlmayr: *Johann Bernhard Fischer von Erlach* (Vienna and Munich, 1956, 2/1976)
W. Buchowiecki: *Die Hofbibliothek in Wien* (Vienna, 1957)
B. Grimschitz: *Johann Lukas von Hildebrandt* (Vienna and Munich, 1959)
T. Zacharias: *Joseph Emanuel Fischer von Erlach* (Vienna and Munich, 1960)
H. Kühnel: 'Die Hofburg', *Wien. Geschb.*, v (1971)
E. Fichtenau: 'Die Hofburgkapelle in Wien: Der Zyklus des Wandpfeilerfiguren', *Österreich. Z. Kst & Dkmlpf.*, xxxii (1978), pp. 21–4
M. Zykan: 'Die Hofburgkapelle in Wien: Zur Baugeschichte und den historischen Restaurierungen', *Österreich. Z. Kst & Dkmlpf.*, xxxii (1978), pp. 1–20
E. Springer: *Geschichte und Kulturleben der Wiener Ringstrasse* (Wiesbaden, 1979), ii of *Die Wiener Ringstrasse: Bild einer Epoche*, ed. R. Wagner-Rieger (Vienna and Cologne, 1969–)
F. Matsche: *Die Kunst im Dienste der Staatsidee Kaiser Karls VI.: Ikonographie, Ikonologie und Programmatik des 'Kaiserstils'*, 2 vols (Berlin and New York, 1981)
C. Benedik: *Die Wiener Hofburg unter Kaiser Karl VI.: Probleme herrschaftlichen Bauens im Barock* (diss., U. Vienna, 1989)
R. Bösel and C. Benedik: *Der Michaelerplatz in Wien: Seine städtbauliche und architektonische Entwicklung* (Vienna, 1991)
M. Koller: *Die Brüder Strudel: Hofkünstler und Gründer der Wiener Kunstakademie* (Innsbruck, 1993)
S. Kraser-Florian: 'Pompeo Marchesis Kaiser-Franz-Denkmal in Wien: Die kunstpolitischen Beziehungen des Kaiserhofes zu Lombardo Venetien, 1814–1848', *Archv & Forsch.*, xx (1993), pp. 202–39

CHRISTIAN BENEDIK

(ii) Schatzkammer. The treasures, both secular and ecclesiastical, in the Schatzkammer (Imperial Treasury) formed part of the private collection of the Habsburgs that originated in the *Kunst- und Wunderkammer* of the Renaissance period. The present collection substantially corresponds to the exhibition of 1891, after many items from the treasure were moved to the department of sculpture and decorative arts in the newly built Kunsthistorisches Museum in Vienna, which administers the Schatzkammer.

Two items once regarded as the Habsburgs' most valuable possessions are the huge agate bowl (4th century AD) from Trier and the 'Ainkhürn' (Unicorn), of narwhal tusk, both thought to have miraculous powers. According to 18th-century reports, the agate bowl was taken from Constantinople (now Istanbul) by the Crusaders after the conquest in 1204 and came into Habsburg possession via

Charles the Bold and the Burgundian inheritance. The Ainkhürn was given to Ferdinand I in 1540.

The oldest and most venerable jewels in the Schatzkammer are the coronation insignia of the Holy Roman Empire. The Imperial Crown was probably made for Otto I c. 955–62 in Mainz (see SAXONY, (1)). In 1024 a new arch was fitted for Conrad II (reg 1024–39). The magnificently illuminated Coronation Gospels (late 8th century; see CAROLINGIAN ART, §IV, 3 and fig. 7; see also GERMANY, fig. 14) originated at Charlemagne's court at Aachen, while the richly decorated St Stephen burse reliquary (c. 830) dates to the reign of Louis the Pious (reg 813–40; see CAROLINGIAN ART, §V). Other items of the insignia and regalia of the Holy Roman Empire include the lavishly decorated Imperial Cross (c. 1024), the so-called Sabre of Charlemagne (9th or 10th century), the St Maurice Sword (c. 1200) and the Imperial Orb (last quarter of the 12th century). The magnificent silk coronation robes of the Holy Roman Emperors include the mantle made in Palermo in 1133–4 for Roger II Hauteville, which bears an Arabic inscription (see ISLAMIC ART, §VI, 2(i)(c) and fig. 183).

The crown made for Rudolf II in Prague in 1602 by the Antwerp goldsmith Jan Vermeyen (1559–1608) combines its three components, the circlet of lilies, the arch and the mitre, in an unusual way, replacing the material of the mitre with gold reliefs depicting figural scenes. The set is completed by a sceptre and an orb (1612–15), made in Prague by Andreas Osenbruck (fl 1612–17) for Rudolf's successor, Matthias. After the dissolution of the Holy Roman Empire and the foundation of the Austrian empire (1804), Francis II (reg 1792–1806) chose Rudolf's crown to be the symbol of the new state.

After the death of the last Burgundian ruler, Charles the Bold, in 1477, the Habsburgs became heir not only to Burgundy but also to the Order of the Golden Fleece, although the treasure of the Order was kept in Brussels until 1794, when it was transferred to Vienna, away from the advancing French army. The magnificent silk vestments of the Order (second and third quarters of the 15th century) reflect the styles of contemporary Netherlandish artists, the Master of Flémalle, Rogier van der Weyden and Hugo van der Goes (see EMBROIDERY, colour pl. II, fig. 2). Among the French artefacts acquired after the fall of Napoleon is the cradle made in 1811 by Jean-Baptiste-Claude Odiot and Pierre-Philippe Thomire for the King of Rome, son of Napoleon and Marie Louise of Austria.

The Schatzkammer's rich selection of ecclesiastical works of art, paraments and jewels dating from the Middle Ages to the 19th century is a result of the merging of the treasure of the Burgkapelle with the imperial store of liturgical vessels, crucifixes, votive gifts, reliquaries, busts of saints and small domestic altars.

BIBLIOGRAPHY

J. von Schlosser: *Die Schatzkammer des Allerhöchsten Kaiserhauses in Wien* (Vienna, 1918)

H. Fillitz: *Die Schatzkammer in Wien: Symbole abendländischen Kaisertums* (Salzburg, 1986)

R. Bauer and others: *Weltliche und geistliche Schatzkammer: Bildführer des Kunsthistorischen Museums* (Salzburg, 1987)

Trésors de la Toison d'Or (exh. cat., ed. H. Fillitz; Brussels, Pal. B.-A., 1987)

BARBARA WILD

6. BELVEDERE. Garden palace of Prince Eugene of Savoy, comprising two separate buildings constructed in 1714–24 by Johann Lukas von Hildebrandt. It is the grandest of the garden palaces surrounding the inner city beyond the Glacis that were built for the aristocracy and upper bourgeoisie from the late 17th century (see §II, 2 above). Some of these are mere garden houses, but some are quite substantial, and the Belvedere is in size and function almost a *residenz*. Prince Eugene began buying plots of land in 1693 at a prestigious site south of the city: the elaborate Palais Schwarzenberg (begun 1697; by Hildebrandt) lies to the west and the Salesian Convent (founded 1717; by Donato-Felice Allio (ii)) to the east. The site, where the first garden was laid out c. 1700, was a narrow and very long strip of land sloping upwards to the south. Hildebrandt was involved from at least 1702, and the city plan of 1706 by Leander Anguissola and Jakob Marinoni shows a palace at the foot of the slope. Occupying the whole width of the site, it had a small courtyard with curved wings to the street and either an oval or semicircular main hall facing the garden, reminiscent of work by Johann Bernhard Fischer von Erlach, who designed Prince Eugene's city palace (begun 1696), later completed by Hildebrandt.

As executed in 1714–16, however, the Lower Belvedere has straight wings around a courtyard towards the street and a single-storey flat façade of 35 bays facing the garden. The general appearance is that of an orangery, and indeed only the central pavilion and the west wing contain living rooms, with two orangeries of eleven bays each flanking the central pavilion. The orangery façades are very simply decorated with banded walls and pilaster-strips between the windows; the central pavilion has Corinthian pilasters and more elaborate window frames. The three central bays rise through two storeys and contain the main hall, which was frescoed in 1716 by Martino Altomonte, who painted the figurative parts, and Marcantonio Chiarini (1652–1730), who executed the architectural parts.

In 1717 after the completion of the Lower Belvedere, the Bavarian court landscape designer Dominique Girard, a pupil of André Le Nôtre, was invited to design the garden. He divided the long strip into three rectangular areas, with trees and fountains next to the Lower Belvedere and two partly sunk parterres beyond. The central axis is a visual one only and the way up is by ramps on either side of the parterres, making use of the sloping ground. The garden sculpture is by Lorenzo Mattielli (1678–1748) and his workshop; the iron railings of c. 1725 are among the most important examples of the period in Austria (see AUSTRIA, fig. 39).

The point at which the Upper Belvedere, a second building higher up the hill, was first conceived cannot be determined as the Prince's archives have disappeared. To have a building at the other end of the garden to close the vista was quite customary in Vienna, but these were nearly always small and often transparent. The idea of a hilltop palace was the basis of an unexecuted design of 1688 by Fischer von Erlach for the emperor's palace at Schönbrunn (see §7(i) below), and it is perhaps significant that Prince Eugene took up the idea and had it executed by Fischer von Erlach's rival, Hildebrandt. Building started in 1721 and must have been completed in the very short time of

17. Vienna, Upper Belvedere, entrance façade, by Johann Lukas von Hildebrandt, 1714–24

two years. Seen from the garden, the north façade of the Upper Belvedere is a long, single range of 29 bays articulated as a series of seven pavilions; the large octagonal one at the centre has a mansard roof, and pairs of small octagonal pavilions (for which see CABINET (i), §1) at either end are domed. This design owes much to the French system of linked pavilions, as seen in the Tuileries, Paris, although the very rich and decorative treatment of the walls clearly indicates Hildebrandt's personal style. Although the parts appear as pavilions on the roofline, they are firmly tied together by horizontal cornices and entablatures; the architectural ornament, including pilasters, capitals and window surrounds, becomes richer towards the centre.

Because of the sloping ground, the entrance façade (see fig. 17) on the south side of the Upper Belvedere has a semi-basement instead of a ground floor and the building thus appears to be even longer. In the centre is a single-storey loggia giving direct access to the staircase that leads up in paired flights to the Festsaal on the first floor and down to the sala terrena, where atlantids support the roof vaults (for illustration see SALA TERRENA). The sala terrena has an almost possessive view over Vienna, the symbolic importance of which can be measured by both the silhouette carefully included in Saloman Kleiner's view of the sala terrena and a painting by Bernardo Bellotto made from roughly that viewpoint. The interiors are partly lost, but what remains gives an idea of the Prince's rather heavy and sumptuous taste. The director of the interior decoration was recorded as Claude Le Fort du Plessy (by Kleiner and otherwise unknown); most of the artists came from Italy and included Antonio Beduzzi, Gaetano Fanti (1687–1759), GIACOMO DEL PO and Carlo Carlone. There were also paintings by Francesco Solimena and Giuseppe Maria Crespi, and stucco by Santin Norbert de Bossi.

The Belvedere must have been an ideal commission: an imposing building and garden of princely dimensions fit for the most important person in the empire after the emperor himself, and a client who was often absent, with few personal needs and no family, and with hardly any financial limitations. Although the prince's archives are lost, the Belvedere is one of the best documented of all Baroque buildings through the set of 140 prints published by Salomon Kleiner. In 1752 Prince Eugene's heirs sold the Belvedere to the crown and in 1779 its park was opened to the public. From 1781 to 1891 it housed the imperial picture gallery (see MUSEUM, §I and fig. 2), and after 1923 it housed important collections of the Österreichische Galerie (see §III, 4 above).

BIBLIOGRAPHY
S. Kleiner: Wunderwürdiges Kriegs- und Siegs-Lager des unvergleichlichen Heldens unserer Zeiten oder eigentliche Vor- und Abbildungen der Hoff-Lust- und Garten-Gebäude, 10 vols (Vienna, 1731–40/R Dortmund, 1980)
B. Grimschitz: Johann Lukas von Hildebrandt (Vienna and Munich, 1959)
'Prinz Eugen und sein Belvedere', Mitt. Österreich. Gal. (1963) [special issue]
H. and G. Aurenhammer: Salomon Kleiner: Das Belvedere zu Wien, 2 vols (Graz, 1969) [facs. of Kleiner with commentary]
E. Leitner: 'Zum Gartenpalais des Prinzen Eugen am Rennweg: Grundankäufe und Planungsgeschichte', Österreich. Z. Kst & Dkmlpf., xxxx (1986), pp. 20-28
Prinz Eugen und das barocke Österreich (exh. cat., Schlosshof, Schloss and Niederweiden, Schloss, 1986)

JARL KREMEIER

7. SCHÖNBRUNN. Formerly the imperial summer residence, Schloss Schönbrunn and gardens to the southwest of Vienna, near the River Wien, together form one of the most important creations of Viennese art in the 18th century. Despite its apparent unity of style, the complex incorporates various structural changes resulting from its long history and reflects the continuing development of the concept of the Gesamtkunstwerk. After World

War I the palace became a museum; it was restored after damage in World War II.

(i) Palace. The property was originally the Katterburg, an imperial hunting lodge that was destroyed in the Turkish siege of 1683. In 1688–90, possibly in connection with the coronation in 1690 of the Archduke Joseph (later Emperor Joseph I) as King of Rome, Johann Bernhard Fischer von Erlach (*see* FISCHER VON ERLACH, (1)) was commissioned by Emperor Leopold I to draw up plans for a monumental imperial hunting lodge to be erected on the hill where the Gloriette, a garden pavilion, now stands; these plans appear in his *Entwurff einer historischen Architektur* (Vienna, 1721). The projected hilltop site for this work of triumphal architecture, with elaborate terraces and cascades, reflects the Renaissance ideas absorbed by Fischer von Erlach during his stay in Italy *c.* 1671–87. Individual elements of the gigantic building, intended to eclipse Versailles, were influenced by several 17th-century architects, including Pietro da Cortona, Bernini, Louis Le Vau and Jules Hardouin Mansart, but there is no doubt that Fischer von Erlach's eclecticism was also intended to recall some legendary buildings of antiquity.

The building actually constructed in 1696–1700 looked, however, quite unlike the first utopian project. Probably for financial reasons, the architect had to forgo the hilltop site and the splendid approach, although the building's function was raised from that of hunting lodge to imperial residence. For this reason two separate courtyard blocks to accommodate the imperial household were added adjacent to each end of the main building. French and Italian models were again used in the second project (also published by Fischer von Erlach), notably Louis Le Vau's project for the garden façade at Versailles. Little has survived of the interior decoration of this first phase of building, except for Sebastiano Ricci's ceiling painting *Allegory of the Princely Virtues* in the stair hall (formerly the dining-room).

On the death of Joseph I (1711), Schloss Schönbrunn became the residence of his widow, Wilhelmina Amalia, and it was then bought by Emperor Charles VI. Remodelling and modernization began in 1743, when the young Empress Maria-Theresa ordered that the building, one of her favourite residences, should be repaired and enlarged to accommodate the imperial household in comfort. Nikolaus Pacassi was given this commission (1743–9) under the direction of Gundacker Ludwig Joseph, Graf von Althann. The internal arrangement of the palace was substantially changed. Pacassi removed Fischer von Erlach's two-storey hall occupying the full depth of the palace and replaced it with two parallel galleries running the length of the central block, the Grosse Galerie, whose windows open on to the main courtyard to the north, and the Kleine Galerie, which has associated circular and oval cabinets and whose windows lead into the garden. These new rooms are leading works of Austrian Rococo architecture. Pacassi replaced Fischer's circular staircase with a terrace and two S-shaped stairs and opened up a new driveway beneath the terrace giving access to the garden. A mezzanine floor was inserted in the side wings, the central five bays were given an attached portico, and the stable-buildings were connected to the main block (*corps de logis*) by a colonnade to create a huge entrance court. In the north-west corner of the main courtyard the Schlosstheater was built, which was later (1766–7) redecorated by JOHANN FERDINAND VON HOHENBERG.

Most of the important parts of the Rococo decoration of the palace from the reign of Maria-Theresa (1740–80) have survived. GREGORIO GUGLIELMI's frescoes in the galleries (partly reconstructed after World War II) depict the power of the House of Austria in war and peace. Of the same date are the paintings in the Ceremonial Hall of the wedding of Archduke Joseph (later Joseph II) to Isabella of Parma (see fig. 9 above). They were later supplemented by paintings of state events in neighbouring rooms. Chinoiserie also played an important part: the two Chinese cabinets, the Vieux-Laque-Zimmer, with a marquetry floor and black lacquer panels, and the Millionenzimmer, with Persian and Mughul miniatures, are examples of the Rococo Orientalism richly represented in Schönbrunn (for further discussion and illustration *see* AUSTRIA, §V, 2 and fig. 25). A new, intimate style of living, which in some respects anticipated the early 19th-century Austrian Biedermeier (*see* §III, 3 above), was realized here between 1760 and 1775; the Porzellanzimmer, Miniaturenkabinett and Schreibzimmer are good examples. The fashion for the Picturesque also found its way into the palace: the landscape rooms by Joseph Rosa (1726–1805), with romantic views of wild mountains, and by Johann Wenzel Bergl, with exotic, tropical motifs, show a desire to break out of the ceremonial framework of the Baroque.

Between 1817 and 1819 the palace façades were modernized by Johann Aman (1765–1834). Working in a Neoclassical spirit, he wanted to improve the balance and unity between the various parts of the building; he extended the pilasters up to the main, continuous entablature and removed the Rococo decoration on the garden side. The delicate blue tint of the exterior was changed to ochre, the 'Schönbrunn yellow'. The last phase of renovation of the palace interior took place under Emperor Francis-Joseph; a restoration from 1869 removed much of the early 19th-century alterations, replacing them with neo-Baroque copies of the original 18th-century work.

(ii) Gardens. Fischer von Erlach's ideas on the layout of the gardens were largely undeveloped in his first project, the ramps, grottoes and cascades of which followed outdated ideas on landscape design from the Mannerist villas of Italy. In the second project the garden was divided into monotonous box-edged borders, with a small belvedere planned for the hilltop. The layout executed *c.* 1705 by the landscape gardener Jean Trehet (*fl* 1688–1723) only partly followed Fischer von Erlach's scheme, and unfortunately no plan of the garden from this period has survived. From later documents and illustrations it can be concluded that some of the existing compartments of the ornamental shrubbery near the palace date back to Trehet's work.

The present arrangement of the garden between the palace and the hilltop was laid out in the 1750s and features long avenues of trees clipped to form tall hedges flanking the parterre. It is based on the ideas of the State Chancellor, Prince Wenzel Anton Kaunitz-Rietberg, who was especially interested in the French taste; the diagonal avenues

18. *View of the Garden Front of Schloss Schönbrunn* by Bernardo Bellotto, oil on canvas, 1.34×2.38 m, 1759 (Vienna, Kunsthistorisches Museum)

and the diverse shapes of the areas of ornamental shrubbery are in the manner of Jacques-François Blondel. An important part of the work was carried out by artists from Lorraine who came to Vienna with Maria-Theresa's husband Emperor Francis I (*see* §III, 2 above): Jean-Nicolas Jadot de Ville-Issey built the Tiergarten (Menagerie; 1751) and the Grosse Orangerie (1755); the surveyor and engineer Jean-Baptiste Bréquin de Demange probably laid out the system of paths; the landscape gardener Louis Ferdinand de Nesle (*d* 1756) may have designed the Kammergärten. Adriaen van Steckhoven (*fl* 1753–66) from the Netherlands laid out the so-called Holländischer Garten (1753), where the Emperor could indulge his keen interest in botany. Pacassi also played a part, with trellis designs and the new garden staircase to the palace. A painting by Bernardo Bellotto gives a vivid picture of the garden at that time (see fig. 18).

The sculptural decoration for the garden and the Gloriette on the hilltop to the south were added only in the 1770s. The Gloriette (1773–5) is an open arcaded belvedere designed by Hohenberg as a pantheon and viewing point; obelisks were erected (1777) as an allusion to dynastic glory; the artificial Roman Ruin (1778) was a monument to recovery from natural disaster; and an extensive historical and mythological programme was devised for the numerous statues produced at this time by the workshop of CHRISTIAN FRIEDRICH WILHELM BEYER. The lavish Rococo decoration of the main parterre was simplified in a Neo-classical manner by the landscape gardener Franz Boos about 1780, although the crowning feature remained Beyer's Fountain of Neptune. In the second quarter of the 19th century the Holländischer Garten was replaced by the new Botanical Garden, and in 1880–82 an imposing iron-and-glass Grosses Palmenhaus

(l. 114 m) was built by Franz Xaver Segenschmied, based on English models. The cultivation of rare botanical specimens at Schönbrunn has enjoyed a worldwide reputation since the 18th century.

BIBLIOGRAPHY
E. M. Kronfeld: *Park und Garten von Schönbrunn* (Vienna, 1923)
H. Sedlmayr: *Johann Bernhard Fischer von Erlach* (Vienna and Munich, 1956, 2/1976)
O. Raschauer: *Schönbrunn, eine denkmalkundliche Darstellung seiner Baugeschichte: Der Schlossbau Kaiser Josephs I.* Studien zur Österreichischen Kunstgeschichte, ii (1960)
J. Glaser: *Schönbrunner Chronik: Versuch einer bau- und wohngeschichtlichen Dokumentation über vier Jahrhunderte, 1569–1969* (Vienna, 1969)
H. Aurenhammer: *J. B. Fischer von Erlach* (London, 1973)
G. Hajós: *Schönbrunn* (Vienna and Hamburg, 1973)

GÉZA HAJÓS

Vienna Genesis. Byzantine illuminated manuscript (Vienna, Österreich. Nbib., cod. theol. gr. 31), attributed to the 6th century AD. Since the late 19th century it has been one of the most intensely studied Byzantine manuscripts. Only a fragment of the original survives, consisting of 24 single leaves of purple-dyed parchment, varying in size between 307×250 mm and 333×270 mm. Each page is divided approximately in half, with the biblical text of Genesis written entirely in silver in the upper part, and an accompanying miniature (48 in total) in the lower part (*see* BIBLE, fig. 1). The number of lines of text, and the script's size and density, vary from page to page, according to the requirements of the miniatures; parts of the biblical text were omitted altogether. Gerstinger's reconstruction of the manuscript as running to 96 folios, with 192 miniatures, has been generally accepted.

The Vienna Genesis was once held to be the oldest surviving illustrated biblical manuscript, and early scholars such as Wickhoff and von Hartel believed that its principal

Vienna Genesis: *Joseph Tempted by Potiphar's Wife*, 155×245 mm; miniature on purple-dyed parchment, 6th century AD (Vienna, Österreichische Nationalbibliothek, cod. theol. gr. 31, p. 31)

importance lay in the light it could throw on the origins of Bible illustration (still a controversial subject). Furthermore, its presence in Vienna made it of special interest to art historians of the so-called 'Vienna School' (e.g. Gerstinger). The identification of different hands in the work, both masters and assistants, and the characterization of them as the 'Miniaturist', 'Colourist' and 'Illusionist(s)', may be considered typical of this period.

More recent study has focused on attempts to explain the content, rather than the style of the miniatures. Parallels for some of the many extra-biblical elements to be found in the illustrations have been traced in Jewish written sources. For example, the scene of *Joseph Tempted by Potiphar's Wife* (see fig.) is continued at the right in the upper register by the bathing of a child, and a soothsayer, and in the lower by further figures of women and children. None of this is biblical, and while some is found in Jewish legends, much remains unexplained. The potential audience for a magnificent picture book of this sort, the images of which appear simple only on a cursory inspection, remains puzzling.

BIBLIOGRAPHY

W. Ritter von Hartel and F. Wickhoff: *Die Wiener Genesis* (Vienna, 1895)
H. Gerstinger: *Die Wiener Genesis* (Vienna, 1931)
P. Buberl and H. Gerstinger: *Der Wiener Dioskurides und die Wiener Genesis* (1937), i of *Die byzantinische Handschriften*, 2 vols (Leipzig, 1937–8)
O. Mazal: *Kommentar zur Wiener Genesis: Faksimile-Ausgabe der Codex theol. gr. 31 der Österreichische Nationalbibliothek in Wien* (Frankfurt am Main, 1980)

JOHN LOWDEN

Vienna Sketchbook [Lodgebook of Wolfgang Rixner and Jerg Reiter]. Volume of 292 pages (152×208 mm; Vienna, Albertina, Cim Kasten, Fach 6 no. 55) of architectural drawings by Wolfgang Rixner (*c.* 1445–1515) and Jerg Reiter (*c.* 1540–99 or 1608), executed on paper. Rixner worked in the Stuttgart area, and his entries cover the years *c.* 1467–1500. Reiter's entries, which are written in Franconian dialect and can be dated up to 1599, indicate that he came from Zeil am Main, near Bamberg. The sketchbook contains plans of 83 vaults, 27 traceries, 26 decorative and sculptural motifs and 39 theoretical problems, as well as stairs, templates, machinery and gables. An accompanying text gives technical information concerning measurements and proportions and also some medical advice. Rixner's drawings show that as late as the 15th century the relatively simple system of modular multiplication, or the addition of elements, was used for the construction of minor structures and decorative details. Designs based on the square or equilateral triangle and their derivatives were still employed in the Rixner sketchbook, although concealed by numerous ornamental refinements. The manuscript appears to have been used as a LODGEBOOK, handed down from one master to another.

BIBLIOGRAPHY

F. Bucher: 'Medieval Architectural Design Methods, 800–1560', *Gesta*, xi/2 (1973), pp. 37–51

——: *Architector: The Lodge Books and Sketchbooks of Medieval Architects*, i (New York, 1979), p. v

Les Bâtisseurs des cathédrales gothiques (exh. cat., ed. R. Recht; Strasbourg, Musées Ville, 1989), pp. 282–3

□

Vienne [Lat. Vienna]. City in Isère, France, situated on the left bank of the River Rhône, 28 km south of Lyon. Before the Roman Conquest it was the chief town of the Allobroges, a Gallic tribe, but it first prospered as a *colonia* founded by Julius Caesar in the 1st century BC. The most impressive remains from Gallo-Roman Vienna (*see* §1 below) are the Temple of Augustus and Livia, the Theatre, the odeion and the sites of Ste Colombe and St Romain-en-Gal, suburbs of modern Vienne on the right bank that provide evidence for its early commercial activities. Christianity was established in Vienne during the 2nd century, and in the 4th the town became the seat of an archbishopric that encompassed the entire province. The archbishops exercised a high degree of secular authority throughout the Middle Ages. Vienne was capital of the Kingdom of Burgundy from 413 until it fell into the hands of the Franks in 534. It was capital of the Kingdom of Arles from 875 to 1032, before being attached to Dauphiné, then part of the Empire. In 1023 the bishops of Vienne assumed the title of 'counts' and in 1119 'Primates of Gaul'. It was at the Council of Vienne in 1311–12 that Pope Clement V suppressed the Order of the Knights Templar. Three important medieval churches survive: St Pierre, St André-le-Bas and the former cathedral of St Maurice (*see* §2(i) below); the 13th-century Château de la Bâtie was demolished by Cardinal de Richelieu. After Vienne returned to the French Kingdom in 1450, its ecclesiastical and political significance declined as that of Lyon increased. During the Wars of Religion (1562) many buildings were damaged, and in 1801 (Concordat) the archbishopric was suppressed to be engulfed by that of Grenoble. The main industries around modern Vienne are mechanical engineering, textiles and tanning.

KATHRYN MORRISON

1. VIENNA. The Temple of Augustus and Livia (late 1st century BC), dedicated originally to Rome and Augustus, is nearly intact, owing to its later adaptation as a church. Thoroughly Classical in appearance, it resembles the slightly earlier Temple of Venus Genetrix in the Forum of Caesar in Rome in being peripteral *sine postico* (i.e. with columns on three sides only), with six columns on the front, and six columns and two pilasters engaged to short spur walls along the sides. The porch is unusually deep. The main theatre was also built during the period (30 BC– AD 14) and is the second largest in Gaul (that at Autun is the largest). The *cavea* (auditorium) is partly terraced into the hillside, partly vaulted, and still retains the portico round the top, with a small temple in the middle, as in the Theatre of Pompey in Rome (1st century BC). The lowest four of the forty-six tiers of seats were of white marble, and the *orchestra* had pink and yellow marble paving. The *scaenae frons* is an early example of the arrangement standard in the western provinces, of a central door projecting from a curved exedra, and doors to each side set in rectangular niches (*see* THEATRE, §II). The facing wall of the stage had alternating curved and rectangular niches and a frieze (*in situ*; partly reconstructed) showing Dionysus and various animals.

In Hadrian's reign (AD 117–38) an odeion was built against the opposite hillside to the south, seating about 3000 spectators. The structure is poorly preserved, but remains of marble flooring and sculpture have been found. Another theatre (mid-1st century AD) was associated with a temple (first half of 1st century AD; later modified) identified from sculpture and inscriptions as that of Cybele. Adjoining underground rooms with pools and passageways presumably served for cult ritual. Near the river, 'L'Aiguille', a stone pyramid on a four-way arch, 23.35 m high, once stood on the turning-point in the circus. On the right bank of the river at St Romain-en-Gal, excavations are revealing a residential quarter with at least 12 peristyle houses, mainly dating from the 2nd century AD.

BIBLIOGRAPHY

Stillwell

J. Formigé: *Le Théâtre romain de Vienne* (Vienne, 1950)

A. Pelletier: *Vienne antique* (Roanne, 1982)

T. F. C. BLAGG

2. BUILDINGS.

(i) St Maurice. The former cathedral of St Maurice, like the church of St André-le-Bas (*see* §(ii) below), is richly decorated with sculpture, especially figured capitals. It was rebuilt in the Gothic period (with a finely sculptured west doorway of the 15th century), but retains seven bays of its Romanesque nave. There are no firm dates, although a building campaign was undertaken by Archbishop Leger between 1030 and 1070 and a consecration by Pope Paschal II is recorded in 1107. This has led some scholars to date the church to the late 11th century and the early 12th and to compare it with the third abbey church at Cluny ('Cluny III') in Burgundy. Although the structure does show Burgundian influences these probably reflect post-Cluny III monuments such as Autun Cathedral, which would suggest a date for St Maurice in the second quarter of the 12th century. It has also been argued that St Maurice was constructed at the same time as St André, in the middle years of the 12th century, because of their close sculptural and architectural links. It is clear, however, that no individual artist worked in both places and the view that St Maurice was started and finished before St André remains persuasive, although it is unlikely that the two buildings are widely separate in date. The capitals in St Maurice are both foliate and historiated, including Old Testament and allegorical subjects. The figure style, like the architecture, derives from Burgundy and may be compared with sculpture from Autun and St Andoche, Saulieu. The nave was built from east to west, and in the later bays the style increasingly shows similarities to that found at St André.

(ii) St André-le-Bas. Although much smaller than St Maurice, the former monastic church of St André is largely intact and is dated 1152 on an inscription placed at the base of one of the nave piers, which also gives the name of the master mason, Willelmus Martini. It was built in a single campaign and probably completed by 1160.

St André has numerous features in common with St Maurice, including the use of fluted pilasters, similar moulding profiles and decorative details such as the use of framing aedicules on historiated capitals. Despite their shared repertory, however, the work in St André is much more accomplished. The capitals are among the best examples of Romanesque sculpture adapted to this small and restricted form, and the style has a confidence and a competence missing in the rather stilted capitals of St Maurice. The figures are full of motion, with swirling drapery and expressive faces. In some instances, such as the story of Samson, the same subject is represented in both churches and the figure styles can be directly compared. Such comparisons tend to confirm both an earlier date for the work at St Maurice and a much higher quality of artist at St André.

The Vienne sculptures, especially those from St André, may be seen as the centre of a middle Rhône school, which was the channel through which Burgundian influences passed to Provence. Most immediately, the St André capitals may be connected with the white marble capitals from the destroyed cloister of Notre-Dame-des-Doms at Avignon, and here the links are so close that it is uncertain from which direction the influence came. There were close ecclesiastical ties between the two cities, and it may well be that the Vienne style developed from that of Avignon. There are also connections between Vienne and sculpture from St Gilles-du-Gard Abbey, but once again the direction of influence is uncertain. The style of the middle Rhône school is reflected much further afield, notably in the Latin Kingdom of Jerusalem, where the capitals in the north transept of the Church of the Holy Sepulchre, Jerusalem, can be directly related to work in both these Vienne churches. Other, more enigmatic links exist with the splendid sculptures from the Crusader church in Nazareth.

BIBLIOGRAPHY

E. Abrand: '*L'Eglise et le cloître de St André-le-Bas à Vienne*' (Lyon, 1951)
J. Vallery-Radot: 'L'Ancienne Cathédrale St Maurice de Vienne', *Bull. Mnmt.*, cx (1952), pp. 297–362
F. Salet: 'L'Ancienne Cathédrale St Maurice de Vienne', *Congr. Archéol. France*, cxxx (1972), pp. 508–53
R. Weinberger: 'St Maurice and St André-le-Bas at Vienne: Dynamics of Artistic Exchange at Two Romanesque Workshops', *Gesta*, xxiii/2 (1984), pp. 75–86

ALAN BORG

(iii) St Pierre. The former Benedictine abbey church of St Pierre is now a museum, housing many fragments of Gallo-Roman and Early Christian art. In the Roman period the site, between the city walls and the Rhône, was occupied by an important cemetery. Excavations conducted from 1861 to 1864 revealed that the foundations of the apse and lateral walls belonged to a basilica erected in the cemetery in the 4th century. The church was rebuilt in the 6th century, when the monastery was founded by St Leonien. The renewed external facings of the north, south and west walls, characterized by *petit appareil* with projecting joints, are usually attributed to this Merovingian reconstruction. The interior of the church is thought to have been divided into three aisles by two files of re-used Roman columns carrying arcades. A 9th- or 10th-century rebuilding, perhaps necessitated by the 8th-century Arab incursions and the seizure of Vienne by the Carolingians in 882, involved attaching a veneer of two superimposed tiers of arcading, incorporating re-used Roman columns and capitals, as well as Carolingian capitals, to the inner faces of the lateral walls and apse. The present nave arcade, consisting of very high square piers, is surmounted by triple openings which do not seem to have corresponded to a tribune: this work was probably carried out in the 11th century (see fig.).

In the 11th and 12th centuries the monastery prospered. The major Romanesque addition was the west tower, with three storeys above a barrel-vaulted porch. Each of the upper storeys has three openings to east and west and two to north and south; those on the top storey are twinned. The arches are either round- or trefoil-headed. The purpose of the two walls projecting forwards from the extremities of the west tower face, with which they are bonded, remains enigmatic. The tympanum above the west door, inside the tower, is decorated with stone and terracotta elements describing a cross flanked by two triangles and surmounted by the Hand of God. This is reminiscent of 12th-century decorated masonry in the Auvergne and Velay, such as St Austremoine, Issoire, although similar work occurs closer to Vienne, at St Martin-d'Ainay, Lyon. The south doorway has octagonal colonnettes carrying historiated capitals: on the left is a figure securely mounted on horseback and inscribed HUMILITAS; on the right a figure tumbling from his horse is identified as SUPERBIA. In the middle of the tympanum is a seated figure of St Peter holding the key of Paradise. In his drapery flat plate folds characteristic of Burgundian sculpture are combined with smooth areas ornamented by curling ridges, which probably derive from the pinch-fold conventions of Languedoc (e.g. St Sernin, Toulouse).

Vienne, St Pierre, interior looking east, ?11th century

Statues of Apostles in the north porch of St Maurice and figural capitals inside St André-le-Bas, carved in the same style, date this group of sculpture to the middle or third quarter of the 12th century. There is evidence that the walls of St Pierre were decorated with Romanesque frescoes, but the only substantial remains belong to a figure of St John in one of the north wall arcades.

BIBLIOGRAPHY

J. Formigé: 'L'Abbaye de Saint-Pierre', *Congr. Archéol. France*, lxxxvi (1923), pp. 77–94

KATHRYN MORRISON

Viennelly, Achille. *See* VIANELLI, ACHILLE.

Vientiane. Capital city of Laos. It lies on the north bank of the Mekong River, close to the Thai border. Before the establishment of the kingdom of Lan Xang in 1353, the Vientiane region had been in contact with the civilizations of the Chao Phraya Basin, at first that of Mon Dvaravati, as is shown, for example, by the Buddha of Ban Thalat (8th–9th century AD; *see* LAOS, §§II, 1(i) and III, 1; THAILAND, §§II, 1(i) and IV, 1) and in the 12th century that of the Khmer kingdom of Angkor, whence the Stele of the Hospitals, which dates from the reign of the Khmer king Jayavarman VII (*reg* 1181–*c.* 1220) and was found at Say Fong. The ancient name of Vientiane was Vieng Xan-Vieng Kham ('Sandalwood citadel, golden citadel'). In 1563 King Setthathirath (*reg* 1548–71) established his capital at Vientiane, and the first major edifices date from his reign. They include the Royal Palace, Vat Ho Phra Kaeo (built for the Phra Kaeo or Emerald Buddha brought from Chiang Mai), as well as the palladium of the kingdom, the Buddha image known as Phra Bang that was brought there from Luang Prabang, and That Luang (a great stupa constructed 2 km from the city to house a relic of the Buddha). (*See* LAOS, §II, 1(ii)(a).)

During the reign of King Souligna Vongsa (*reg* 1637–94) Vientiane flourished, as contemporary accounts by G. van Wuysthoff and the Jesuit Giovanni-Maria Leria show (see Sion). The partition of Laos in 1707–13 and the ensuing struggles against the Thais of Ayutthaya interrupted Vientiane's development, which resumed at the start of the 19th century. King Chao Anu (*reg* 1805–28) built Vat Sisaket in 1818 and restored the Royal Palace. But, after the Thai invasion of 1827 and the deportation of some of its population, the city's monuments fell into disrepair. In 1872 the Ho pillaged the city and brought down the That Luang spire; only Vat Sisaket was spared destruction. At the end of the century the city was rebuilt once again, and the That Luang spire was reconstructed according to the 1867 drawing by L. Delaporte (see Garnier, iii, pl. 21). The old sanctuaries have been restored as far as possible to their original condition, in particular Vat Xan, Vat Ong Teu and Vat Ho Phra Kaeo, while the library at Vat In Peng has retained its attractive stucco decoration. But Vat Sisaket is the only monastery that remains in its original state, rising in the middle of a courtyard surrounded by cloisters and sheltering numerous statues of the Buddha (15th–19th century); its small library is in the Burmese style. Vat Ho Phra Kaeo, which is temporarily a museum, has works of Khmer origin (including the Stele of the Hospitals and others, influenced by the art of the Chao Phraya Basin, such as the Ban

Thalat Buddha), as well as an interesting collection of Lao pieces, notably some colossal Buddhas in bronze dating from the 17th and 18th centuries.

BIBLIOGRAPHY

F. Garnier: *Voyage d'exploration en Indochine* (Paris, 1885)
G. Sion: 'Voyage au Laos du Père Léria, 1642–1648', *Bull. Amis Laos*, iii (1970), pp. 51–8
J.-C. Lejosne: *Le Voyage de Gerrit van Wuysthoff et de ses assistants au Laos (1641–1642)* (Metz, 1993)

MADELEINE GITEAU

Vierendeel [Meunier], **(Jules-)Arthur** (*b* Leuven, 10 April 1852; *d* Ukkel, 8 Nov 1940). Belgian engineer and writer. In 1874 he obtained a diploma in engineering from the Ecoles Spéciales de Génie Civil, des Arts et Manufactures et des Mines of the Catholic University of Leuven. From 1876 to 1885 he was employed by the steel manufacturers Ateliers de La Louvière. In 1885 he was appointed Chief Engineer and Director of Technical Services of the province of West Flanders. From 1889 to 1935 he taught at the Ecoles Spéciales in Leuven. His *Cours de stabilité des constructions* (1889) was a major reference in construction technology for almost half a century. In 1896 he received the Prix du Roi for his *Construction architecturale en fer, fonte et acier* (published in instalments between 1897 and 1902). In 1896 he developed a girder with upper and lower beams and rigidly connected vertical members, not braced by diagonal members. The Vierendeel girder was successfully applied in bridge construction (*see* BRIDGE, §2(iii)). The first Vierendeel bridge was built of steel, over the River Leie in Avelgem in 1902 (*see* IRON AND STEEL, §§I and II, 1).

WRITINGS

Etude sur les ressorts à spirale, plane et conique et les ressorts à hélice (Brussels, 1886)
Cours de stabilité des constructions (Leuven, 1889)
L'Architecture métallique au XIXème siècle et l'Exposition de 1889 à Paris (Brussels, 1890)
Le Pont de mille mètres (Leuven, 1896)
Les Ponts architecturaux en métal (Leuven, 1896)
La Construction architecturale en fer, fonte et acier (Leuven, Brussels and Paris, 1897–1902)
Le Pont système Vierendeel (Leuven, 1898)
Esquisse d'une histoire de la technique, 2 vols (Leuven, 1921)

BNB

BIBLIOGRAPHY

J. Timmerman: 'Arthur Vierendeel (1852–1940): Een biografie', *Arthur Vierendeel (1852–1940). Hoofdingenieur–Directeur Provinciale Technische Dienst West-Vlaanderen, Hoogleraar Katolieke Universiteit Leuven* (Bruges, 1989)

LUC VERPOEST

Vieri, Ugolino di. *See* UGOLINO DI VIERI.

Viertaler, Barthlmä. *See* FIRTHALER, BARTHLMÄ.

Viervant, Leendert, II (*b* Arnhem, *bapt* 5 March 1752; *d* Amsterdam, *bur* 16 Feb 1802). Dutch architect. His father, Hendrik (1718–81), who was the brother-in-law of Jacob Otten-Husly, and his uncle Anthony (1720–75) were town carpenters. Anthony's son Roelof Roelofs (1755–1819) and Leendert moved early to Amsterdam, and Leendert probably trained there at his uncle Husly's studio. In 1768 he became master mason in Amsterdam. During the years 1772 and 1776 he was involved as a mason in the construction of the town hall of Weesp, which was designed by Husly. He was much influenced by his uncle and also by contemporary professional literature. His own considerable capabilities as an architect can be seen in his design (1779) for the library and the museum room of Teyler's Institute, Haarlem. The oval hall has two floors and is entirely panelled. The ground-floor employs an order of coupled pilasters into which the doors of arched entrances and cupboards are set. The floors are separated by a circular balcony. On the first floor the entablature runs over panels, between which bookcases and doors are fitted; overdoors feature medallions with heads of philosophers. The light comes in through a rooflight over the high, stuccoed ceiling. Between 1785 and 1787 Viervant built the Teylers' almshouses in Haarlem. The single-storey front extension is in a simple Neo-classical style. The portico, which carries the pediment, opens into the courtyard—a motif not used in the Netherlands during that period—Viervant, like Husly and Johannes Franciscus Giudici, interpreted the Louis XVI style in his own individual way.

BIBLIOGRAPHY

C. C. G. Quarles van Ufford: *Catalogus van overwegend Amsterdamse architectuur- en decoratieontwerpen uit de achttiende eeuw* [Catalogue of predominantly Amsterdam architectural and decorative designs from the 18th century] (diss., Rijksuniv. Utrecht, 1972)

J. R. Termolen: 'De Teylers Stichting te Haarlem en haar achtiende eeuwse stichtingsgebouwen' [The Teylers Foundation in Haarlem and its 18th-century foundation buildings], *Teyler 1778–1978: Studies en Bijdragen naar aanleiding van het tweede eeuwfeest* [Teyler 1778–1978: studies and contributions to mark its bicentenary] (Haarlem, 1978)

PAUL H. REM

Vierzehnheiligen. Pilgrimage church overlooking the River Main, near Banz, Franconia, Germany. The original chapel was built in 1457 on the site where, in the 1440s, a young shepherd had had visions of the 14 helper saints. According to medieval legend, the helper saints acted as intercessors in times of plague and epidemics. The chapel became an increasingly popular place of pilgrimage, and in 1735 the abbot Stephan Mösinger of the Cistercian monastery at Langheim proposed a larger and more imposing building. Projects were submitted several years later. Gottfried Heinrich Krohne's plan of 1739 was for a centralized church extended by a small choir where the shrine was to be placed, an impractical design that would not have accommodated processions or provided enough space for visitors to view the shrine. Another proposal of 1737 by Johann Jakob Michael Küchel, who had worked under Balthasar Neumann at Bamberg, placed the shrine beneath a vast dome flanked by spacious transepts.

In 1742 Neumann proposed two versions of a basilica on a Latin cross plan, one with half columns attached to slender piers supporting a balcony and a second, similar project with free-standing columns between the nave and aisles but with no balcony. In both, the shrine of the 14 helper saints was to stand in the crossing beneath a pendentive dome. Neumann also produced a further plan to satisfy his own architectural preferences, in which he transformed the interior of the Latin cross basilica into a curvilinear space: the nave contained a single, longitudinal oval with engaged columns, the crossing a circle with four free-standing paired columns, the arms of the transepts were partial ovals (again with engaged columns) and the

choir was treated as a smaller transverse oval marked by pilasters.

Friedrich Karl von Schönborn, Prince–Bishop of Bamberg and Würzburg, who was Neumann's most important patron during the 1730s and 1740s, accepted Neumann's more conventional design for a Latin cross basilica, but the abbot insisted on Krohne supervising construction. The foundations were shifted to the east by Krohne, thereby displacing the shrine, and Neumann initially refused to participate further in the project but was eventually persuaded to take it over entirely. Returning to his earlier curvilinear design, and influenced by his church in the Würzburg Residenz (1730–43), Neumann placed three longitudinal ovals within the basilica in a line from entrance to choir. The first oval pushes out the façade of the church, resulting externally in a convex central bay; tall flanking towers are crowned with small onion domes and lanterns. Inside, the oval continues into the depth of the church, marked by two free-standing piers. The second and largest of the three ovals is defined by half columns attached to slender piers; it stands entirely free within the space and contains the shrine (see fig.). The third oval, similar in size to the first, curves from the crossing into the masonry of the choir. Large airy vaults rise above the ovals. Neumann maintained their integrity and completeness by separating them from one another by means of two small ovals in the nave and by the domed cylinders of the transept arms. Although the rectilinear outer shell of the church is that of a conventional basilica on a Latin cross plan, Neumann transformed the interior into an undulating unity. The difference between outside and inside is most dramatic at the crossing, which in a conventional basilica would be marked by a dome. At Vierzehnheiligen, however, it is nothing more than the tangent of the two ovals of the nave and choir and the two cylinders of the transept arms, where the three-dimensional transverse arches that rise from the crossing piers bend and touch each other. Instead of the usual high dome at the crossing, the vaulting dips down to its lowest level at the point where the width of the church, at the transepts, and the sense of space are greatest.

Neumann placed two tiers of windows above and below the balcony in the nave; a third higher tier penetrates the bottom half of the vaults. The whole interior, set in motion by the curvilinear elements, is filled with light. The effect is augmented by the use of colour. The predominant impression is one of pink and grey, but a range of colours is used, restored to the original in 1956–9 and again in an extensive restoration of 1977–90. The marbled columns, pilasters and vaulting stucco are in matt yellow, light green, grey and pink agate, contrasting with the alabaster white walls. Other stuccowork is a delicate greyish blue with gold and ochre, and the ribs of the vaulting are in ochre, giving the impression that gold thread has been worked through it. Despite the long axis extending from the entrance to the altar, the largest oval, containing the shrine, centralizes and unifies the space. In 1762 Küchel designed the shrine, which was executed by Johann Michael Feichtmayer and Johann Georg Üblher. This monumental structure, which dominates the interior, is a baldacchino supported by Rococo volutes extending up to a shallower dome. Statues of the 14 helper saints are placed on

Vierzehnheiligen pilgrimage church by Balthasar Neumann, begun 1742; view looking east towards the altar with the shrine of 14 helper saints

pedestals on the low wall surrounding the shrine and on various projections and niches. The shrine is crowned by a figure of the *Christ Child in Glory*. Küchel also completed the church in 1772 after Neumann's death but flattened the vaults. Giuseppe Appiani frescoed the main vaults with scenes commemorating the shepherd's vision of the 14 helper saints together with scenes from the Old and New Testaments. The frescoes were renewed in the recent restoration.

BIBLIOGRAPHY
R. Teufel: *Vierzehnheiligen* (Lichtenfels, 2/1957)
F. Oswald: 'Zur Vorgeschichte der Wallfahrtskirche Vierzehnheiligen bis zum Jahre 1743', *97. Bericht des historischen Vereins für die Pflege der Geschichte des ehemaligen Fürstbistums: Bamberg, 1961*
E. Emmerling and others, eds: *Die Restaurierung der Wallfahrtskirche Vierzehnheiligen* (Munich, 1990)

CHRISTIAN F. OTTO

Vietnam, Socialist Republic of. Country on the east coast of the Indo-Chinese peninsula. It is bordered by China to the north and by Cambodia and Laos to the west (see fig. 1). The capital is Hanoi, and other population centres are Ho Chi Minh City (formerly Saigon) and HUE. Vietnam's present frontiers date from 1802, when it was unified after almost 200 years of disunity (*see* §I, 2 below). In 1954 the country was partitioned, with the Communist north being separated from the American-backed south, but it was reunified in 1976 as the Socialist Republic of Vietnam.

I. Introduction. II. Architecture. III. Sculpture. IV. Painting and graphic arts. V. Ceramics. VI. Other arts. VII. Art education.

I. Introduction.

1. Geography, peoples and languages. 2. History. 3. Religion, iconography and subject-matter.

1. GEOGRAPHY, PEOPLES AND LANGUAGES. Vietnam stretches more than 1800 km from the mountainous plateau on the border with Yunnan Province, China, to the tropical delta of the Mekong River in the south, one of the great rice-growing areas of Asia. The backbone of this long thin country comprises the central mountains of the Annam Cordillera. Major settlement has generally been confined to the narrow strip of coastal lowlands, especially the wide valleys of the Song Hong (Red River) and Song Da (Black River). The country's climate is governed by

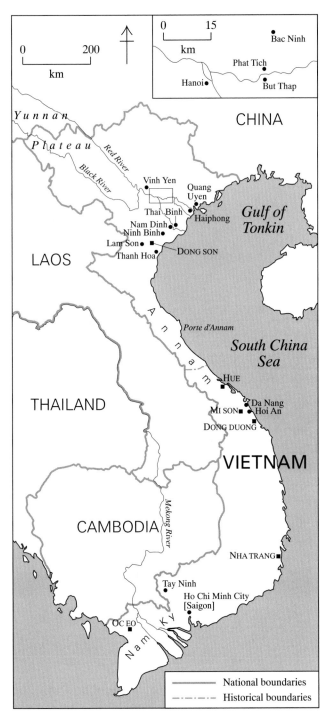

1. Map of Vietnam; those sites with separate entries in this dictionary are distinguished by CROSS-REFERENCE TYPE

Chinese and 7% highland peoples also known as 'Montagnards'. The highland peoples may be classified according to linguistic family into three groups: the Mon-Khmer or Austro-Asiatic language group, including the Katus, Stiengs and Maas; the Malayo-Polynesian or Austronesian language group, including the Jarais and Rhadés; and the Sino-Tibetan language group, including the Thais. These peoples live in the mountains of the Annam Cordillera, practising shifting cultivation, and are often despised by the lowland Vietnamese. The official language of the country is Vietnamese, but French and Chinese are also spoken.

BIBLIOGRAPHY
C. A. Fisher: *South-east Asia: A Social, Economic and Political Geography* (London, 1964)

PHILIP STOTT

2. HISTORY. The earliest people in the area that makes up the modern state of Vietnam of whom there is any record are the Yue people, who in the 1st millennium BC were widely spread along the east coasts of the Asian mainland. The Yue Nam or southern Yue lived in the provinces of Guangdong, part of Guangxi and the delta of the Red River and are the ancestors of the modern Vietnamese. To the south of the Red River were the Chams (*see* CHAMPA, §I, 1), who from the late 1st century AD were settled on the coastal plain between Da Nang and Porte d'Annam in what had formerly been the Chinese commandery of Rinan ('South of the Sun'). From the 3rd century BC the Chinese began to expand southward and gradually absorbed the Yue kingdoms, until in 111 BC the Han emperor Wudi finally conquered the Yue Nam in the Red River delta, which thus became the southernmost limit of the Chinese empire. There was little Chinese immigration into this new province, but a thoroughgoing Chinese administration was firmly established. In AD 39 there was a revolt against Chinese rule led by the sisters Trung Trac and Trung Nhi. This was suppressed in AD 43, but the sisters became national heroines and have remained so into modern times. Their story is depicted in innumerable popular paintings, prints and images.

In 543 the first independent Vietnamese dynasty was founded by the Earlier Ly, but in 589 China again imposed control over Vietnam. Under the Tang dynasty (618–907), the country was renamed Annam (Viet. An Nam, 'the Pacified South'), and the Vietnamese became deeply imbued with Chinese culture. After the collapse of the Tang, the Vietnamese seized the opportunity to set up another kingdom under the Ngo (939–54) and Dinh (968–80) dynasties. From that time until the French conquest in the late 19th century, Vietnam, except for another brief period of Chinese rule between 1407 and 1428, retained its independence. Nevertheless Chinese suzerainty continued to be recognized: ratification of the succession of each new Vietnamese ruler was sought, the official calendar of the reigning Chinese dynasty was used and tribute missions were sent regularly to the imperial court. Under the Dinh and their successors the Earlier Le (980–1010), the Later Ly (1010–1225) and the Tran (1225–1400), the southward drive of the Vietnamese began in earnest. By 1069 all the Cham lands as far as the 17th parallel had been annexed (see fig. 2), and by 1471 the Cham kingdom had been virtually obliterated. By the mid-15th century

monsoons, and the seasons are much more marked in the north than in the south. Vietnam is rich in reserves of coal, oil and iron ore, but its economic development at the end of the 20th century continued to be hampered by problems of integration. The population in the 1990s was *c.* 53 million, of whom 87% were ethnic Vietnamese, 6%

the Khmers, having been forced by a Thai invasion to abandon Angkor, had established themselves rather precariously on the lower Mekong, where their presence helped to strengthen the influence of Buddhism among the mainly peasant population.

By the mid-16th century the Later Le dynasty (1418–1802) had passed its zenith, and two rival official families, the Trinh and the Nguyen, dominated the court. The Trinh had greater power in Hanoi, and in 1558 they rid themselves of their Nguyen rivals by contriving the appointment of the head of the Nguyen family as viceroy of the south, where he created what was effectively a new state centred on Hue. By the end of the 17th century the Nguyen had all but annihilated the Chams in the south of the country and, by taking Saigon in 1691, had acquired control of the Mekong delta. The Nguyen admitted both Vietnamese settlers and Chinese refugees from Manchu rule into the delta region, and some of the latter founded Cholon, a Chinese sister city of Saigon.

In 1535 the first Portuguese ship reached the Vietnamese coast, and in the following year the first Dutch trading post was established at Qui Nam in the south. Christian missionaries, most of them French Jesuits, soon followed, and one of these, Alexandre de Rhodes, who arrived in 1651, is credited with the invention of *quoc ngu*, an alphabetic version of Vietnamese, originally devised for the purpose of translating religious works. As a result of the introduction of *quoc ngu*, Christianity soon spread to the north of the country, while *quoc ngu* itself spread rapidly among the people, who had hitherto been largely illiterate, and far beyond the circle of Christian converts. The Confucian official and land-owning class viewed this development with alarm, seeing it as a threat to their authority and an attempt by the missionaries to supplant their sinicized culture by a European Christian culture. There was also an increase in commercial activity, which led to the emergence of a new merchant class, another development viewed with alarm by the Confucian ruling class, who despised commerce. Strife continued between north and south throughout the 17th century and early 18th, and hindered economic development. In 1773 the Tay Son (Western Mountains) rebellion broke out against the ruling Nguyen family, and by 1783 the rebels had captured Hanoi. The rebellion was eventually put down by Nguyen Anh, assisted by a group of French officers, but not before it had brought about the adoption of *quoc ngu* as the official language, an increase in the influence of both Buddhism and Catholicism at the expense of Confucianism, and an upsurge of Vietnamese national sentiment.

Nguyen Anh reigned as Emperor Gia Long at Hue over a reunited Vietnam from 1802 to 1820. Despite owing his throne to French assistance, he reinforced the Chinese character of his rule, imposing a strongly anti-Western and anti-Catholic regime, marked by rigid centralization, the enforcement of the Chinese examination system for the civil service and emphasis on Confucian learning, combined with restrictions on Buddhism, and overt hostility towards Christianity. He colonized the delta region by the introduction of farmer–soldier colonies along the borders with Cambodia and in the sparsely inhabited lands along the lower Mekong. These settlers were later to offer fierce

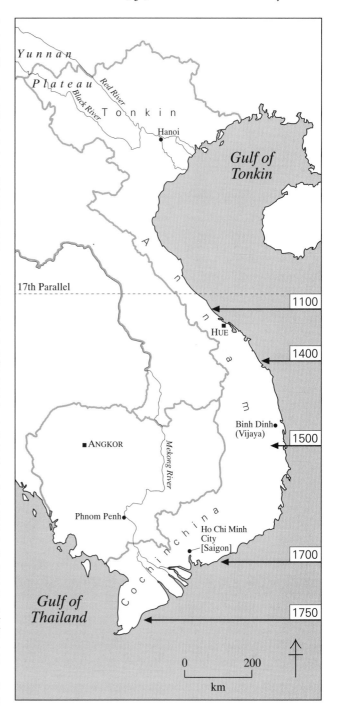

2. Map of Vietnam showing chronological movement south; those sites with separate entries in this dictionary are distinguished by CROSS-REFERENCE TYPE

resistance to the French conquest. Gia Long's three successors, Minh Mang (*reg* 1820–41), Thieu Tri (*reg* 1841–7) and Tu Duc (*reg* 1848–83), were all strict Confucians and admirers of Chinese culture and continued Gia Long's anti-Western and anti-Catholic policies. They nevertheless succumbed by degrees to French encroachments on their power and independence. In 1859 the French captured

Saigon and from there gradually extended control by forcible annexation, first over the delta region up to the Cambodian frontier and then over the rest of Vietnam. By a series of treaties between 1862 and 1884, a French protectorate was imposed over Nam Ky (Cochinchina), Annam and Tonkin. In 1887 the Union Indochinoise was created, bringing together Cambodia, Cochinchina, Annam and Tonkin under the direct authority of a civilian governor-general and reducing the emperor at Hue to little more than a ceremonial figurehead.

The colonial administration did carry out a number of ambitious public works projects and established research institutes, such as the Ecole Française d'Extrême-Orient, but it was chiefly concerned with economic exploitation. In the mid-20th century Nguyen Ai Quoc, later named Ho Chi Minh (1882–1969), began an anti-colonial campaign and founded the Indochinese Communist Party. His rebel Viet Minh forces eventually defeated the French in 1954 at the Battle of Dien Bien Phu, leading to the partition of the country: the Democratic Republic of Vietnam was established in the north, at Hanoi, and an American-backed government in the south, at Saigon. Ho Chi Minh's National Liberation Front (the Viet Cong) continued to fight against Western influence, and in 1976 Vietnam was reunited under Communist rule. After this and subsequent wars with Cambodia (1978) and China (1979), many Vietnamese left the country for political or economic reasons, and in the 1980s Vietnam was one of the poorest nations in the world. In the 1990s, however, economic reforms were made, and a programme of development was begun.

BIBLIOGRAPHY

G. Coedès: *Les Etats hindouisés d'Indochine et d'Indonésie* (Hanoi, 1944, 2/1963, rev. Paris, 3/1964); Eng. trans. by S. B. Cowing as *The Indianized States of South-east Asia* (Honolulu, 1958)

Le Thanh Khoi: *Le Viet-Nam: Histoire et civilisation* (Paris, 1955)

G. Coedès: *Les Peuples de la péninsule indochinoise* (Paris, 1962); Eng. trans. by H. M. Wright as *The Making of South-east Asia* (London, 1966)

L. Chesneaux: *Le Vietnam: Etude de politique et d'histoire* (Paris, 1968)

L. Bezacier: *Le Viet-Nam: De la préhistoire à la fin de l'occupation chinoise*, ii of *L'Asie du Sud-Est*, ed. G. Coedès and J. Boisselier (Paris, 1972)

C. P. Fitzgerald: *The Southern Expansion of the Chinese People* (New York, 1972, rev. Bangkok and Cheney, 1993)

R. P. Turner: *Vietnamese Communism: Its Origins and Development* (Stanford, 1975)

Huynh Kim Khanh: *Vietnamese Communism, 1925–1945* (Ithaca and London, 1982)

P.-Y. Manguin: 'Les Nguyen, Macau et le Portugal: Aspects politiques et commerciaux d'une relation privilégiée en mer de Chine, 1773–1802', *Ecole Fr. Extrême-Orient*, cxxxiv (Paris, 1984)

Nguyen The Anh: 'The Vietnamese Monarchy under French Colonial Rule, 1884–1945', *Mod. Asian Stud.*, xix/1 (1985), pp. 147–62

NORA TAYLOR,   JOHN VILLIERS

3. RELIGION, ICONOGRAPHY AND SUBJECT-MATTER. Religion in Vietnam is a fusion of many beliefs, and Vietnamese rituals and customs derive from many different religions and philosophies. The motifs used in Vietnamese art should therefore be interpreted in accordance with the geographical or artistic context in which they occur. The most important religions are Buddhism, Daoism, Confucianism and Christianity, but there are also many popular animistic beliefs and superstitions. Buddhism was introduced to the Vietnamese in the 2nd century AD by two different routes: Mahayana Buddhism (Viet. *Dai Thua* or *Bac Tong*), the predominant religion

of Vietnam, was brought by Chinese monks from the north, while Theravada Buddhism (*Tieu Thua* or *Nam Tong*) was brought from the south by Indian pilgrims and is practised mostly by Khmers who inhabit the Mekong delta. The largest Mahayana sect in Vietnam is *Thien* (Chin. *Chan*; Jap. *Zen*), which is also known as the Meditation School. The Pure Land School (*Dao Trang*), which is the second largest school, is practised mainly in the south. Because of the emphasis in Mahayana Buddhism on the different manifestations of the Buddha and the importance of the many *bodhisattvas* (*bo tat*), Buddhist iconography of Vietnam is rich and varied (*see also* BUDDHISM, §II). Among the most frequently found images are those of Amitabha Buddha (*A Di Da*), Shakyamuni (*Thich Ca Mau Ni*), the historical Buddha, and the Maitreya Buddha (*Di Lac*), the Buddha of the future, as well as the *bodhisattvas* Avalokiteshvara (*Quan The Am Bo Tat*) and Manjushri (*Van Thu*).

DAOISM embraces both the philosophy of the Chinese sage Lao zi (*c.* 570–490 BC), which emphasizes contemplation and simplicity, and the popular religion that evolved from it. Chinese and Vietnamese annals indicate that it was probably introduced into Vietnam during the late Han period in the late 2nd and early 3rd centuries. Perhaps because of the daunting complexities of Daoist beliefs there are very few Daoist temples in Vietnam, but principles associated with Daoism, such as the concept of *yin* and *yang* (Viet. *am* and *duong*), are integral to Vietnamese cosmology. Images of Daoist deities often occur in Buddhist temples together with Buddhist images. They include *Ngoc Hoang* (the Jade Emperor) and *Thien Hau Thanh Mau* (Queen of Heaven). In Daoist cosmology these two deities rule over the spirit world, especially the deified ancestors and heroes. Many Vietnamese magical beliefs are derived from Daoism.

CONFUCIANISM deeply penetrated Vietnam during the millennium of Chinese domination. The notion that the emperor is the mediator between heaven and earth is central to Confucianism, as is the virtue of filial piety and obedience that extends to the obedience a nation owes its ruler. Confucian principles have also contributed to the great value attached to education and literacy in Vietnam and have been used to uphold a rigid social hierarchy based on class, gender and generation. Since Confucianism is primarily a social and political philosophy and has no deities, there is no explicitly Confucian iconography. However, allusions to certain aspects of Confucian ethics are present in the architectural design of Confucian temples. For example, many plant motifs, such as bamboo and chrysanthemum, are understood as symbols of such Confucian virtues as steadfastness and endurance and may therefore be considered as instances of Confucian iconography.

Christianity was first introduced into Vietnam in the 16th century by Roman Catholic missionaries from Portugal and Spain. In the 17th century the French Jesuits established their missions in the country. Protestantism was not introduced until the 20th century, first during the French colonial period and later by American missions during the American War in the 1960s and 1970s. Most of the Catholic architecture dates from the 19th century, and cathedrals and churches in Vietnam contain statues of saints, the Virgin and the Crucifixion similar to those found in churches in the West. Some churches have replaced the stained-glass windows destroyed during the American war with glass depicting local legends or popular motifs.

Ancestor worship, which pre-dates the advent of Confucianism in Vietnam, is widely practised. It is based on the belief that the soul lives on after death to protect its descendants. The souls of the dead are believed to exert a strong influence on the living, and if sufficient homage is not paid to them, they are doomed to become eternal wanderers, haunting the living. The Vietnamese worship the spirits of their ancestors regularly and every household has a shrine to one or more deceased family member; special ceremonies are performed on the anniversary of the ancestor's death. Caodai is an indigenous Vietnamese sect founded in 1926 at Tay Ninh near Saigon. It seeks to fuse the secular and religious philosophies of East and West and includes elements of Buddhism, Confucianism, Daoism, Christianity, Hinduism and Islam, as well as the worship of a variety of saints and heroes, from different cultures, including Joan of Arc, Victor Hugo and Lenin. Most of its early followers were officials in the French administration. In line with the eclecticism of its philosophy, Caodai boasts one of the more spectacular religious structures in southern Vietnam, the Great Temple of Caodai in Tay Ninh. The temple is built on nine levels, which represent the nine steps to heaven. Each level is marked by a pair of columns with multi-coloured dragons supporting a dome, which represents the heavens. Under the dome is a giant star-speckled blue globe with the 'Divine Eye' on it. This Divine Eye, which is simply a round object with a giant pupil, is the supreme symbol of Caodai. In front of the globe there are seven chairs reserved for the Caodai pope, the leaders of the three branches of Caodai (who wear yellow, blue and red robes respectively) and the three readers of the books of the Caodai canon. On either side there is a pulpit resembling the minbars found in mosques. A mural in the entrance hall depicts the 'Third Alliance between God and Man', in which the Chinese revolutionary leader Sun Yat Sen holds an inkstone, while the Vietnamese poet Nguyen Binh Khiem and Victor Hugo write 'God and Humanity' and 'Love and Justice' in Chinese and French. There are numerous other Caodai temples throughout Vietnam, but, apart from all possessing the Divine Eye, they are sparingly decorated and are much less garish than the temple at Tay Ninh.

BIBLIOGRAPHY

Nguyen Van Huyen: *La Civilisation annamite* (Hanoi, 1944)
L. Cadière: *Croyances et pratiques religieuses des Annamites*, 3 vols (Saigon and Paris, 1944–57)
P. Huard and M. Durand: *Connaissance du Viet-Nam* (Paris, 1954)
Phan Ke Binh: *Moeurs et coutumes du Vietnam* (Paris, 1975)
Thich Thien An: *Buddhism and Zen in Vietnam* (Rutland, VT, and Tokyo, 1975)
Nguyen Hu'u Tan: *La Vie quotidienne dans le Vietnam d'autrefois* (Brussels, 1983)
P. Rutledge: *The Role of Religion in Ethnic Self Identity: A Vietnamese Community* (Lanham, 1985)
G. M. Oury: *Le Vietnam des martyrs et des saints* (Paris, 1988)

NORA TAYLOR

II. Architecture.

Houses with curved roofs and standing on piles are depicted on drums from the Dong Son culture. The existence in modern times of houses on stilts in the Vietnamese highlands and of Buddhist temples with curved roofs may therefore indicate that these architectural elements were present in the Red River delta before the arrival of influences from outside the region.

While the domestic architecture of the area now covered by Vietnam may have autochthonous origins, however, the sources of the religious architecture are more complex. It is generally thought that early religious buildings were mostly made of timber, and that this accounts for the fact that there are so few extant examples of early architecture in Vietnam. Many temples suffered in the country's humid climate and needed frequent reconstruction. Some scholars attribute the variety of temple styles in Vietnam to the fact that temples were seldom renovated but were entirely rebuilt, and not necessarily following the plan of the temple they replaced.

1. Religious and formal. 2. Domestic. 3. Urban planning.

1. RELIGIOUS AND FORMAL.

(i) Temples. (ii) Tombs. (iii) Churches and government buildings.

(i) Temples. Owing to the wide variety of religious beliefs and practices in Vietnam and the frequent rebuilding of many temples over the course of the centuries, the history of Vietnam's religious architecture is of great complexity, and it is difficult to characterize different periods and styles. Auspicious dates and geomancy have always been important considerations in the construction of temples, although the canons of the different religions are also followed. Like the spiritual life of the Vietnamese people, their religious architecture is a combination of many elements and it is informed by an assortment of religious iconographies (*see* §I, 3 above). These elements reveal influences derived not only from elsewhere in South-east Asia and from China but also from local autochthonous sources.

(a) Buddhist. (b) Confucian.

(a) Buddhist. The oldest Buddhist temple (*chua*) in Vietnam is thought to be the Dau Temple complex, although the existing monument may not be exactly the same as the original one. The complex was founded when Buddhism first arrived in Vietnam in the 2nd century AD. It was visited in the 6th century by the Indian monk Vinitaruci who came from China to establish a Dhyana sect in Vietnam. It was rebuilt in the 14th century. The Dau complex is situated *c.* 35 km north of Hanoi in Ha Bac Province, and it comprises four temples: Phap Van (Dharma Cloud), Phap Vu (Dharma Rain), Phap Loi (Dharma Thunder) and Phap Dien (Dharma Lightning). The best-known of these is Phap Van, which has a U-shaped plan. The main building faces a lake and has eight columns on its façade. In front of the building is a courtyard containing the Hoa Phong tower, which is made of brick and has three (originally nine) storeys. The roof of the structure is curved and has simple decoration. The date of the Hoa Phong tower is unclear. It bears an

inscription dated 1737, but this is probably the date of its restoration. The annals of the Dai Viet mention the renovation of the Dau Temple but make no mention of the Hoa Phong tower. The foot of the tower is square, each side measuring 7 m. The first storey has four arches. The tower has a bell that dates from 1793 and a brass gong cast in 1817. Most of the statues and stelae date from the 19th century and only a stone statue of a sheep to the left of the tower is believed to date from the original period of construction.

The rulers of the Later Ly dynasty (1010–1225) were fervent Buddhists, and many temples were built under their patronage, ranging from the most simple to the most complex. The Ly architects introduced certain technical innovations, such as the use of stone, superimposed trusses, beams and half-columns, as well as the use of eaves decorated with terracotta symbols, and both Cham and Chinese influences are discernible in their buildings.

The One-pillar or Lotus Temple in Hanoi was first built in AD 1049 and subsequently renovated in the 12th, 19th and 20th centuries. It is a small square building only 4.2×4.2 m resting on a single octagonal stone column 1.2 m in diameter. Unlike the Dau Temple, the Lotus Temple rises vertically, supported by a truss system consisting of eight huge beams leaning diagonally on the stone column so as to intersect with the suspended vertical columns at the ends of the beams (see fig. 3). These columns virtually form the building frame. The Lotus Temple is the earliest extant example of a Vietnamese building with decorative motifs in terracotta along the roof ridges. According to legend, King Ly Thai Tong (*reg* 1028–54) had a dream in which he saw the *bodhisattva* Avalokiteshvara seated on the lotus seat and inviting him

3. One-pillar Temple (Lotus Temple), Hanoi, *c.* 1050; restored

to ascend it. This was considered to be an auspicious omen, and a monk named Thien The advised him to build a temple, set a stone pillar on the earth and make a lotus seat on top of it like that he had seen in his dream. The monks would then walk round the temple praying for the King's longevity. For this reason the temple is also sometimes called Dien Huu meaning 'to prolong life'. In 1105 King Ly Nhan Tong (*reg* 1072–1127) ordered a pond to be dug round the stone pillar, which it beautifully reflects. Although alterations have been made to the temple several times since then, it retains its unique structure in the shape of a lotus flower.

The original building of the Phat Tich ('Vestiges of the Buddha') or Van Phuc Temple, 28 km north of Hanoi in Bac Ninh Province, no longer exists. All that remains is an inscription on the foundation tile, which says that it was erected by the third emperor of the Later Ly dynasty, Ly Thanh Tong (*reg* 1054–72). The only architectural vestige from this period is the three-stepped foundation built against the side of the mountain. The foundations are rectangular (*c.* 60×33 m) and edged on the outside with stone blocks. Several sculptures dating from the Later Ly period have survived at Phat Tich, including ten stone statues of animals including lions, elephants, buffaloes and horses. Each is nearly 2 m high and lying on a lotus pedestal, and each is carved from a single block of stone. In the middle of the temple there is a statue of the Buddha, 1.85 m high. The pedestal and the lotus leaves of the seat are carved with dragon and flower patterns typical of Ly-period sculpture. Some of the sculpted reliefs on the Phat Tich Temple clearly show the influence of Cham art (*see* §III, 1(i) below).

The Thay or Master Temple (*c.* 11th century AD) is located at the foot of Mt Sai Son in Ha Tay Province, *c.* 25 km south of Hanoi. In front of the temple, which has been restored several times, there is a large lake called Dragon Lake (Long Chieu), in the middle of which stands a small pavilion for water puppet performances. At the sides of the temple there are two covered bridges built in 1602. One bridge links the temple to a structure on the lake, while the other leads to a footpath up the mountain. The temple complex consists of three long parallel buildings. The central building is reserved for the worship of the Buddha. The upper building is dedicated to the various reincarnations of the monk Tu Dao Hanh (*d* 1117), the main cult figure at several temples in northern Vietnam, and contains at its centre a large stone pedestal with various carvings, such as dragons, flowers and, at each corner, *garuda*s (creatures in Hindu mythology: part bird, part human). The pedestal is the only part of the temple dating from the Later Ly dynasty. In front of it is a statue of Tu Dao Hanh wearing a lotus-shaped hat and crossing his hands on his chest, a gesture signifying enlightenment.

Unlike the Phat Tich Temple, of which only the foundations survive, the Binh Son Temple, in Vinh Yen, north-west of Hanoi, retains its original stupa. The date of its construction is uncertain, but it probably belongs to the Later Ly period. It is very modest in size, being only 15 m high and 4×4 m at the base. The stupa has a hollow interior. Along the edge of the roof there are sculpted motifs of oak and vine leaves. The eaves are decorated with a pattern of leaves of the *bodhi* or *bo* tree (*Ficus religiosa*), the tree under which the Buddha is believed to have found enlightenment. The construction of the temple without mortar suggests Cham influence, as do the sculptural details. However, whereas the Chams usually carved decorative motifs directly on the surface of the stone, the Vietnamese designed the motifs in advance and then made moulds to replicate the pattern more effectively. There are several similar stupas in Ninh Binh, Ha Nam, Bac Ninh and Vinh Yen provinces with a variety of decorative motifs such as chrysanthemums, *garuda*s (a motif perhaps also borrowed from the Chams) and dancers.

Under the Tran dynasty (1225–1400) Vietnam enjoyed a period of political stability and independence, and Buddhism again prospered. King Tran Nhan Tong (*reg* 1278–93) founded the Bamboo Grove sect of Zen Buddhism (Viet. *Thien*), and during his rule many of the old Ly *chua* were restored and new ones built. The most renowned of the latter are the Pho Minh, But Thap, Huong Tich *chua* and a monastery built on Mt Yen Tu in Nghe Tinh Province, which consists of *c.* 20 buildings stretching out over a distance of *c.* 30 km from the foot of the mountain. The Pho Minh or Thap Temple (*c.* 1262) is located *c.* 5 km north of Nam Dinh City. Its tower, which is 17 m high and has 14 storeys, has been preserved relatively intact. Many of the bricks used in its construction bear the date of 1305. The foundation and first storey are made of stone, and the remaining upper storeys of brick. The first storey is set on a stone platform, which bears low-relief stone carvings of flowers, leaves, waves and cloud rolls as does the first storey itself. The external walls of the upper storeys are decorated with dragon motifs. The other buildings in the temple complex include a vestibule, an incense-burning hall, and an upper sanctuary. The doors are made of iron-wood. Behind the upper sanctuary and separated from it by a small courtyard is a long building with 11 compartments. The five middle compartments are reserved for ceremonies performed by the patriarch; three compartments on the left constitute the monks' quarters, while on the right are three prayer halls.

Under the Later Le dynasty (1428–1802) political turmoil and warfare with the Chinese in the north and the Chams in the south caused the destruction of many temples built under the Later Ly and the Tran. However, in spite of this several large temples were built, although they were architecturally less innovative than in previous periods, and art historians are inclined to regard the Later Le dynasty as artistically merely a continuation of the Tran period. The Keo Temple, located in Thai Binh Province, is one of the largest Buddhist temples in Vietnam. The date of construction of the original temple is obscure. Some scholars have suggested that it was built in the 14th century, others that it dates from the 12th century and was constructed under the supervision of the Zen master Khong Lo. In 1611 a flood occurred in the area where the original temple was built, as a result of which a part of the population moved to Ha Nam Ninh Province, where they built another temple, which they called the Lower Keo Temple. Another part of the population moved to the left bank of the Red River, where they constructed a third temple, which they called the Upper Keo Temple. This is the one that is most often referred to as Keo Temple and

4. The Lotus Tower, But Thap (Ninh Phuc) Temple, Ha Bac Province, *c.* 17th century

is the example cited here. According to a stele found *in situ*, it was begun in 1630 and completed in 1632. It was restored several times in the 17th and 18th centuries and again in 1941, in a programme undertaken by the Ecole Française d'Extrême-Orient. The temple complex covers an area of *c.* 58,000 sq. m and comprises a variety of buildings. There are two gateways, each with three wooden doors, which date from the 17th century and are still intact. The temple gate leads to the sanctuary of the Buddha consisting of three buildings, the middle one containing the Buddha images. Behind the sanctuary is a shrine devoted to the cult of Khong Lo. Beyond a small yard is a bell-tower, 11 m high with a three-tiered roof. The second storey contains a bronze bell cast in 1686.

The But Thap or Ninh Phuc Temple (see fig. 4) in Ha Bac Province was built in the 17th century and still retains many of its original features. It consists of ten buildings lying along an axis more than 100 m long. A three-door gate leads to a two-storey bell tower with eight roofs. An incense-burning hall links the vestibule to the Great Hall, which lies on a foundation more than 1 m high. In the middle of the Hall there are three Buddha statues and two

5. Tay Phuong Temple, Ha Tay Province, *c.* 17th century

wooden altars, all dating from the 17th century. On the sides of the hall there are several other statues, one of which is a famous Avalokiteshvara with 1000 eyes and 1000 arms, which dates from 1656 (see fig. 11 below). There are several towers in the vicinity of the temple, the most impressive of which is the stone tower of Bao Nghiem, which has five storeys and is more than 13 m high. Behind the temple there is another five-storey stone tower called Ton Duc tower, which is 10 m high. Inside the tower there is a statue of Minh Hanh, the second temple patriarch, and on the faces are inscriptions dating from the 17th and 18th centuries, which relate the stories of Minh Hanh and Princess Ngoc Duyen and of land donated to the temple.

With some 80 statues and low-relief carvings adorning every building, the Tay Phuong Temple (see fig. 5) is considered to be an important source of Vietnamese sculpture. The temple dates from the 17th century but has been reconstructed many times. It has been suggested that the present building may date from 1794, owing to its similarity in style with the Kim Lien Temple in Hanoi, which is known to have been built in 1792. It is located in the commune of Thach Xa in Ha Tay Province on a hill 50 m high, and it is reached by 237 steps paved with laterite. The temple complex consists of three long, parallel buildings: the hall, the central temple and the inner chamber. Each building has a two-tier tiled roof ending in a pronounced curve. The walls are built entirely of red bricks without any plaster or paint, and the round windows are decorated with symbols representing the Buddhist principles of being and non-being. The tiles on the upper tier of the roof have engravings in the shape of *bodhi* leaves, while those on the lower tier are square and decorated in five colours. The wooden columns that support the roof stand on stone pedestals carved in the form of lotus petals. Many of the wooden surfaces of the temple, including beams and parts of the roof frame, are decorated with low-relief carving. The temple is, however, most famous for its statuary (*see* §III, 1(ii) below).

(b) Confucian. Traditionally each provincial capital in Vietnam had a Temple of Literature (*van mieu*) dedicated to Confucius in honour of scholars and men of letters. The most important of these is the Van Mieu in Hanoi, which is often referred to as 'Vietnam's first university', and is said to have been founded in 1070 by Ly Thanh Tong (*reg* 1054–72). However, it appears that it was not built until after the advent to power in 1428 of the Later Le dynasty, which promoted Confucianism. Nonetheless, a shrine to Confucius is believed to have been built on the site in the 12th century. The temple has a rectangular ground-plan and is surrounded by walls made of large red bricks. The interior of the temple consists of five symmetrical courtyards divided by walls. The central pathway, which leads through the Great Portico into the temple complex dividing it into two symmetrical halves, is flanked by grassy areas, ponds and trees. On the wall between the Great Portico and the main doorway there is a brickwork dragon, a symbol associated with the title of *tien si* ('doctorate') and thus with men of learning. The Great Portico, a double-roofed structure, may have been built in the Later Le dynasty (1428–1802). It opens on to a

6. Khue Van Cac Pavilion (1805; restored), leading to the Courtyard of the Stelae at the Van Mieu (Temple of Literature), Hanoi, 15th century

courtyard, which is joined to a second courtyard by the Dai Trung Mon ('Great Middle Gate') and two small doors called Thanh Duc ('Accomplished Virtue') and Dat Tai ('Attained Talent').

The central pathway leads to the main group of buildings in the temple complex. This is the Khue Van Cac Pavilion (see fig. 6), built in 1805 and dedicated to Literature. The pavilion is seen by scholars as an expression of the male and female principles of *yin* and *yang*, the lower roof symbolizing *yin* and the upper *yang*. The pavilion is flanked by two small doors called Suc Van ('Crystallization of Scholars') and Bi Van ('Magnificence of Letters'). The Khue Van Cac gives on to the Courtyard of the Stelae, in the centre of which there is a square pond called the Thien Quang Tinh ('Well of Heavenly Clarity'). To the right and left there are 82 stelae standing on stone tortoises and bearing the names of over 1000 *tien si* (scholars) who had passed the royal examinations, one stele for each examination year. The oldest dates from 1442 and the most recent from 1779. According to historical records 117 examinations were held during this period, so over 30 stelae are missing.

The fourth courtyard is entered through a triple portico called Dai Thanh Mon ('Gate of the Great Synthesis'). On either side of this are two small doors called Kim Thanh ('Golden Sound') and Ngoc Chan ('Object of Jade') giving access to the side buildings. These were traditionally reserved for the 72 disciples of Confucius. Stretching across the yard is the vast Van Mieu proper, also known as the Dai Bai Duong ('Great House of Ceremonies'). Built in the Later Le period, it consists of a roof supported by two parallel walls. The main decorative motifs are clouds, chrysanthemums, phoenixes, dragons, sacred fruit and lotuses. The phoenix symbolizes the intellectual élite, the clouds, knowledge, and the moon flanked by two guardians, the balance between opposing elements or *yin* and *yang*. A statue of Confucius stands in the sanctuary adjoining the Great House of Ceremonies. Behind the sanctuary there is a fifth courtyard containing buildings dedicated to the cult of the parents and disciples of Confucius and known as Khai Thanh.

(ii) Tombs. Few traces of Vietnamese secular funerary architecture remain from before the 15th century. The tomb of Dinh Tien Hoang (*reg* 968–79) at Hoa Lu, a rectangular stone construction, is of modern date, and the ruined tombs of the Later Le dynasty (1428–1802) at Lam Son are therefore the earliest unaltered examples of Vietnamese royal funerary art. These are situated within a complex that includes a temple and a series of pavilions built on a terraced slope and connected to the tumulus of the founder of the dynasty, Le Thai To (*reg* 1428–33), by a spirit road. This is flanked with statues of humans and lions, elephants and other animals. In its layout and the style of the sculptures, the Lam Son spirit road is a clear imitation of the Ming dynasty (1368–1644) spirit roads in Beijing and Nanjing (*see* CHINA, §III, 3).

The tombs of the emperors of the Nguyen dynasty (1802–1954) at Hue differ from each other in details of style but are all built on a similar plan consisting of five parts: a stele pavilion in which the virtues of the deceased emperor are recorded on marble tablets; a sepulchre where the emperor's remains are buried; an Honour Courtyard, which is paved with bricks and has stone statues of elephants, horses and members of the mandarinate along the sides; a lotus pond surrounded by frangipani and pine trees; and a temple for the worship of the emperor and empress. The temple contains two altars, with a cabinet in front of each containing the emperor's personal effects, such as his tea and betel tray and his cigarette case, or precious belongings, such as rare books and gifts from abroad.

The tomb of the first Nguyen emperor, Gia Long (*reg* 1802–20), extends along a horizontal axis, without a surrounding wall. It was built between 1814 and 1820 and is located in the hills 16 km from the centre of Hue on the Ta Trach River, the upper reaches of the Perfume River. The tomb of the emperor Minh Mang (*reg* 1820–41) is located on the northern bank of the Perfume River, 12 km from Hue, and is perhaps the most impressive of the imperial tombs, partly because of the harmony achieved between the architecture and the natural environment. The different sections of the tomb complex are disposed in such a way as to give the illusion of linking the finite world to the infinite heavens.

7. Tomb of the emperor Tu Duc, Hue, mid-19th century

The emperor Thieu Tri (*reg* 1841–7) did not build his tomb in his lifetime but instead requested on his deathbed that his tomb be economical and convenient. His mausoleum is located in a low-lying area 7 km south-west of Hue and was built in a style similar to that of the tomb of Minh Mang. The tomb of Tu Duc (*reg* 1848–83) is located on the right bank of the Perfume River, 5 km from Hue. It was designed to function as a palace to be used before Tu Duc's death as well as a tomb (see fig. 7). Tu Duc was gifted in literature and art, and his residence is often likened to a poetic park rather than a place of worship. He also had a reputation for opulence and included a building for the performance of the traditional opera *hat boi* (*see* §VI, 8 below) in his plan. His extravagance is displayed in the abundance of ponds, trees and flowering plants. The stele pavilion contains the largest stele in Vietnam, which weighs 20 tons.

The tomb of Khai Dinh (*reg* 1916–25) is in the French neo-classical style and is built of concrete. The three iron doors leading to the mausoleum were specially commissioned from France. The mausoleum of Ho Chi Minh (see fig. 8) in Hanoi is the most important tomb built since the abolition of the monarchy. Opened in 1975, it is a massive marble structure modelled on the mausoleum of Lenin in Moscow.

The burial places of monks are quite different from those of rulers and their families, and are always marked by a stupa. In most cases the stupa is quadrilateral, one notable exception being the stupa commemorating the monk Chuyet Cong attached to the Ninh Phuc Temple at But Thap, which is octagonal. In some instances there is also a statue of the monk, for example the statue of Minh Hanh in the stupa of Trach Lan in Thanh Hoa. From the 18th century brick was used in place of stone in the construction of the stupas, and the number of storeys decreased.

(iii) Churches and government buildings. Most of Vietnam's large cities have churches, the majority of which were built in the 19th century. The largest is in Phat Diem in north Vietnam and combines European and Vietnamese architectural elements. The Cathedral of Notre-Dame in Saigon, built in 1880 (spires added 1900), is made of red brick and

9. Great Church, Hanoi, west front, 1883

has many elements that are Romanesque in inspiration, such as the rounded arches. However, the decorative brick latticework in the roundels represents an assimilation of local style. The Great Church in Hanoi (see fig. 9), built in 1883, has pointed arches and other Gothic features.

During the colonial period many important government buildings and official residences were built, the most impressive being the Imperial City palace complex at HUE, which is modelled on the Imperial City in Beijing. Most colonial buildings, however, were based on French models, adapted to suit the local climate and environment. At first French architects were employed to design the buildings, but later local designers were trained to do this. Elements of Vietnamese design, such as the colour of the walls, the use of local tiles, ceramic floors, slightly curved roofs and large gateways, were incorporated in the colonial buildings in both Saigon (now Ho Chi Minh City) and Hanoi.

With the establishment of the Socialist Republic of Vietnam in 1976 after nearly 25 years of war, funds for reconstruction were extremely scarce, and only a few modern monuments were erected in the decades that followed to replace those that had been destroyed. Among the more noteworthy of these new buildings are the Cultural Palace in Hanoi, the Presidential Palace in Ho Chi Minh City and the Thang Loi Hotel in Hanoi. In the late 20th century Vietnamese architects sought to preserve some traditional features, for example in the design of

8. Mausoleum of Ho Chi Minh, Hanoi, 1975

roofs, balconies and large doorways, and in architectural decoration, while making use of non-traditional materials such as concrete and marble.

BIBLIOGRAPHY
H. Orband: 'Les Tombeaux des Nguyen', *Bull. Ecole Fr. Extrême-Orient*, xiv/7 (1914) [whole issue]
H. Gourdon: *L'Art de l'Annam* (Toulouse, 1932)
L. Bezacier: 'Note sur un tombeau de bronze à Phat-tich', *Bull. Inst. Indochinois pour l'Etude de l'Homme*, iv/1–2 (1941)
——: 'Le Panthéon des pagodes bouddhiques du Tonkin', *Bull. Soc. Etud. Indochin.*, xiii/3 (1943), pp. 29–68
——: 'Les Sépultures royales de la dynastie des Le Postérieurs', *Bull. Ecole Fr. Extrême-Orient*, xliv/1 (1951)
L. Bezacier: *L'Art vietnamien* (Paris, 1954)
B. P. Groslier: *Indochine: Carrefour des arts* (Paris, 1961)
Art and Archaeology of Vietnam: Asian Crossroads of Cultures (exh. cat., Washington DC, Smithsonian Inst., 1961)
J. Auboyer and others: 'Vietnam', *Oriental Art: A Handbook of Styles and Form* (London, 1979), pp. 335–62
G. Wright: *The Politics of Design in French Colonial Urbanism* (Chicago, 1991)
D. Hung and Mai Ung: *Hue: Monuments of an Ancient Capital* (Hanoi, 1993)
H. V. Tan: *Buddhist Temples in Vietnam* (Hanoi, 1993)

NGUYEN QUYNH, NORA TAYLOR

2. DOMESTIC. In the Bronze Age, houses in many parts of South-east Asia were raised on piles. However, this type of building and the techniques employed in its construction have almost entirely disappeared in Vietnam except among some of the highland peoples. Unlike most domestic architecture in South-east Asia, the modern urban Vietnamese house is built directly on the ground or on a slightly raised earth bank and usually consists of several structures arranged on two or three sides of a courtyard (see fig. 10). The total surface covered may be as much as 250 sq m, but the house proper, without the annexes, covers only half of this area and is therefore comparable in size to houses in Laos and Cambodia. The structure has two independent elements: wooden columns supporting the roof and a stone wall surrounding the complex. The builders have to take into account certain religious and cosmological considerations, such as geomancy and the symbolic meaning of numbers. The figure 8, for example, is traditionally written in Vietnamese with a character that also denotes 'danger' and so has to be avoided; however, the figure 4 is written with a character denoting 'peace' and so is held to be a desirable measurement. The kitchen is located in one of the annexes, but the rice store is included in the main house, entirely enclosed in the south-west corner, at the opposite end to the women's quarters. The roof beams are decorated with carved geometric patterns or vegetal motifs, and these constitute the only decoration on the inside. The main façade consists of a stone wall into which wooden frames are inserted for the windows and doors; these slide sideways and are very soberly decorated.

In mountain areas, especially close to the border with Yunnan Province, China, dwellings consist of a single rectangular structure perched on the hillside and supported by piles. These houses are not as large as those on the plains, covering only 75 sq m. They shelter not only the members of the family but also their domestic animals. Sometimes two families join together to build two dwellings under a single roof; in this case, the house can cover

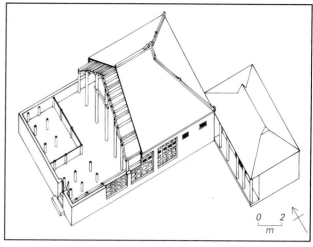

10. House at Di Luan, near Quang Tri; axonometric projection

an area of up to 120 sq m. The rooms for human occupation are arranged on either side of a central corridor with the area for the animals at the far end of the building. There is no decoration, but the beamwork is visible on the interior. Sometimes the central part has a ceiling, and the upper storey is used as a loft.

BIBLIOGRAPHY
C. Robequain: *Le Thanh Hoa* (Paris, 1928)
P. Gourou: *Esquisse d'une étude de l'habitation annamite* (Paris, 1936)

J. DUMARÇAY

3. URBAN PLANNING. The most important example of urban planning is probably HUE, which became the imperial city of Vietnam under Gia Long (*reg* 1802–20). However, Saigon (now Ho Chi Minh City) and Hanoi provide further significant models of planning from around the same time. The city of Phien An in Saigon was built at the end of the 18th century according to the designs of Oliver de Puymanel (1767–1800), one of the French officers who had assisted in the defeat of the Tay Son rebellion. De Puymanel's plan was modelled on the work of the 19th-century French urban planner Sébastien Leprestre de Vauban, who had designed fortifications for a number of European towns, including Strasbourg. The plan of Phien An consisted basically of a square aligned with the four cardinal points, with a triangular spur at each corner. The city was built as a citadel to withstand severe attacks and had a double wall *c.* 5 m high either side of a deep moat. There were two large entrances, one on the east and the other on the west, but only the east entrance was used. At the centre of the city, on precisely the same spot where Saigon Cathedral now stands, was the emperor's palace flanked by lesser palaces for other members of the imperial family.

The modern city of Hanoi was built between 1802 and 1816 according to the same basic plan as Phien An. The outer walls of the citadel form a regular pentagon and are separated by a deep moat from the inner walls, which form a square. At the centre of the citadel is the Royal Pavilion, which contains the Celestial Hall, where the emperor held audience. This consists of a small walled complex with four gateways, the most important of which faces south; it is surrounded by government buildings. The city of Hanoi stretches a long way beyond the citadel and is enclosed by a long, irregular wall with 17 city gates, each of which is composed of a triple arch surmounted by a watch-tower and parapets.

NGUYEN QUYNH

III. Sculpture.

1. Religious and formal. 2. Vernacular.

1. RELIGIOUS AND FORMAL. The earliest sculptural objects found in Vietnam belong to the Dong Son culture (see §VI, 4 below). Since the prehistoric period the development of sculpture in Vietnam has been integrally linked to the spread of Buddhism from its first introduction in the 2nd century AD. Indeed, the most important periods in the history of Vietnamese sculpture correspond with the two major flowerings of Vietnamese Buddhism, the first of which took place during the so-called Dai La period in the 8th and 9th centuries AD and the second during the Later Ly (1010–1225) and Tran (1225–1400) periods. The majority of Vietnamese sculptures are images of figures from the Buddhist pantheon or of individual Buddhist monks. These images were made for individual temples, which in matters of patronage functioned as autonomous institutions, and for that reason the stylistic development of Vietnamese sculpture does not follow a strict chronology. The oldest remaining sculptures in Vietnam are made of stone (see STONE, colour pl. IX, fig. 2): as a result of the combined effects of the humid climate and warfare, much Vietnamese wooden sculpture has been destroyed.

(i) Before 1428. The Sino-Vietnamese sculpture of the Dai La style, named after the capital of the Chinese province of Annam (Chin. An Nan) at Dai La, near Hanoi, is regarded as the finest produced in Vietnam. Characterized by a fusion of Chinese and Cham styles, it continued after the collapse of the Chinese protectorate in AD 939, when the capital was moved to Co Loa, and into the Later Ly period (1010–1225). The sculpted stone pillars at the Van Phuc Temple at Phat Tich, Bac Ninh Province, which are believed to have come from a stupa built on the site in the 9th century AD by General Gao Pian, Chinese governor of Annam, are fine examples of the Dai La style. While the dominant style of these sculptures is Chinese, there are also elements that clearly reflect Cham and Indian influences. For example, the *kinnara* (a mythical creature with a human head and the body of a bird) is reminiscent of Cham sculpture in its disposition, especially the drum suspended from its neck (see fig. 11). The *lokapala* (a guardian of the four cardinal points) is the earliest known sculpture in Vietnam to display Indian influence, apparent in the posture of the hips and the decorative details on the robe, although the leggings belong to the Chinese tradition. At the base of the columns there are low-relief carvings depicting figures among plants, which in their composition recall the sculptures from the caves of Yungang and Longmen in China. The carved corner *garuda*s (mythical creatures with the head and wings of a bird and a human torso and legs) in the vault are, by contrast, clearly of Cham inspiration. At the Van Phuc Temple there are also

11. Sandstone *kinnara*, h. *c.* 450 mm, from the Van Phuc Temple at Phat Tich, Bac Ninh Province, 9th–11th centuries (Hanoi, History Museum)

terracotta mouldings from a later stupa built of brick in 1057. The decoration is characteristic of this later period and is composed of such motifs as etiolated dragons and stylized clouds and leaves, carved in a delicate and sinuous style.

The Van Phuc Temple also contains one of the oldest and largest statues of Amitabha Buddha. Dating from the 11th century, it demonstrates a combination of Chinese and Cham artistic styles. Cham influence can be seen in the rhythmic, slender and symmetrical body, and in the large eyes, high nose and thick lips. The lotus base and drapery, by contrast, reflect the Chinese Buddhist tradition.

In the sculpture of the Tran period (1225–1400) the same themes and motifs appear, but the style is generally less refined, and the monuments are more massive in scale. There are numerous stone figures of animals on tombs of the Tran dynasty, such as the leopard on the tomb of Duke Tran Thu Do, which is supple and full of vitality. The tomb of King Tran Hien Tong (*reg* 1329–41) is adorned with a number of statues, including one of a reclining water buffalo and another of a dog in a relaxed and natural pose. This liking for representations of animals seems characteristic of the kings of the Tran dynasty and illustrates well the skill of Vietnamese artists of this period at naturalistic sculpture.

stylized fashion than in the Dai La period. The style of the stone sculptures in front of the dynastic temple of the Dinh dynasty (AD 968–80), which date from c. 1610, shows a further development and accentuation of the style used at Lam Son.

At the same time the sculptures commissioned by Buddhist temples, many of them made of wood and covered with polychrome lacquer, have stylistic features peculiar to each individual temple. For example, at the But Thap (Ninh Phuc) Temple, which was restored under two Chinese monks, Chuyet Cong and his successor, Minh Mang, the sculpture shows the influence both of the Sino-Vietnamese Dai La style and of Chinese sculpture of the Tang (618–907) and Song (960–1279) periods. The But Thap Temple has many portrait sculptures of monks and nobles and also houses the statue of the *bodhisattva* Avalokiteshvara (Viet. Quan Am) with 1000 eyes and 1000 arms, one of the most celebrated of all Vietnamese sculptures. The figure, which is 3.6 m high, is made of wood covered in red lacquer and gold and is seated on a lotus platform, which in turn is supported by the scaly hands and head of a dragon emerging from waves carved on the top of a square pedestal (see fig. 12). Twenty-eight

12. Polychromed lacquer Avalokiteshvara (Viet. Quan Am) with 1000 eyes and 1000 arms, h. 3.6 m, But Thap (Ninh Phuc) Temple, Ha Bac Province, 1656

(ii) 1428–1802. The rulers of the Later Le dynasty actively promoted Confucianism and so, unlike their Tran predecessors, did not patronize Buddhist sculpture. With commerce beginning to thrive in the villages, however, statues and carvings continued to be executed in many communities, and a rich variety of vernacular styles arose. The tendency towards localization and fragmentation that characterizes the history of Vietnamese sculpture thus became even more pronounced in this period. Furthermore, from the 16th century the authority of the Later Le dynasty was progressively undermined by the power of the Trinh and Nguyen families, and as a result stylistic uniformity was still further eroded. The formal sculpture commissioned by the early rulers of the Later Le dynasty show strong influences of the style of the Ming period in China (1386–1644). For example, on the stone sculptures from the tomb of Le Thai To (*reg* 1428–33) at Lam Son, which dates from 1433, such decorative motifs as the lotus and chrysanthemum are treated in a markedly more

13. Carved wooden temple ornament, Hang Kenh Temple, Haiphong, c. 18th century

arms, each in a different gesture (*mudrā*), radiate from the shoulders while the remaining arms form a nimbus behind the figure. In the palm of each hand there is an eye. Avalokiteshvara wears a headdress surmounted by eight hands arranged in three rows with a small Amitabha Buddha at the apex. Built at about the same time as But Thap, the Tay Phuong Temple is also notable for its rich sculptural decoration, which includes 80 statues and low-relief carvings. Among the portrait statues is a vigorous representation of the monk Mahacadiop, who was a blacksmith in his youth. Generally, the portrait sculpture at Tay Phuong is remarkable both for its grace and vitality and for its psychological depth. The carved wooden temple ornaments from Hang Kenh Temple at Haiphong, which date from the end of the 18th century, are remarkable for the repeated use of the vertical tongue-shaped motif, which appears in the guise of dragons' beards, birds' feathers and leaves on plants (see fig. 13). In style they recall the motifs found on carved wooden panels from the temple at Vinh Yen, which date from the 13th to the 15th century, and these in turn reflect the influence of the stylized flame-shaped nimbus on Chinese Buddhist sculptures of the Tang period.

(iii) From 1802. Most of the rulers of the Nguyen dynasty (1802–1954) consciously imitated the art of the Chinese Qing dynasty (1644–1911), as may be seen in the way the city of HUE was constructed to replicate the Forbidden City in Beijing. Temples and shrines continued to be decorated with lacquered wood statues of the Buddha and of monks, executed in a style similar to that of the 18th century. However, the emperor Khai Dinh (*reg* 1916–25) rejected the Chinese tradition and adopted the European neo-classical style. This is apparent in the sculptural decoration of his tomb, which was built in 1925 (see §II, 1(ii) above). The foundation in 1925 of the Ecole des Beaux-Arts de l'Indochine de Hanoi (*see* §VII below) also introduced Western techniques, such as bronze-casting, and traditional Buddhist themes were abandoned as sculptors experimented with more modern subjects and even abstraction. Under Communist rule in the second half of the 20th century, huge statues in the Socialist Realist style of workers, peasants and soldiers were erected to the glory of the revolution (see fig. 14). In 1986 the policy of *doi moi* ('renovation') was introduced, and sculptors were able to produce more intimate works, although the poverty of the country was such that the use of expensive media, such as bronze, was restricted. Among the most important Vietnamese sculptors of the 20th century is Le Cong Thanh (*b* 1931). His vast stone sculpture *Victory* at Nui Thanh, commissioned to celebrate the defeat of the Americans, was completed in 1985 and epitomizes the Socialist Realist style. However, after 1986 Le Cong Thanh began to produce sculptures of a very different style, influenced by the western European tradition, as well as by the Cham sculptures of his native Da Nang.

BIBLIOGRAPHY
L. Bezacier: *L'Art du Vietnam* (Paris, 1955)
B. P. Groslier: *Indochine: Carrefour des arts* (Paris, 1961)
Art and Archaeology of Vietnam (exh. cat., Washington, DC, 1961)
J. Hejzlar: *The Art of Vietnam* (London, New York, Sydney and Toronto, 1973)

NORA TAYLOR

2. VERNACULAR. Vietnamese communal houses (*dinh*) are traditionally adorned with carvings on the pillars, beams and other support structures. In the 16th century this sculpture was confined to simple line carvings; by the 17th century, however, it had evolved into high-relief sculpture depicting scenes from village life, such as women carrying babies and girls bathing in lotus ponds. By the 19th century the carving had reverted, however, to a more sober, more two-dimensional and purely decorative style. Recurrent motifs include dragon heads, carved on beam-ends, and dragon tails, carved on the tops of pillars. Roof tops may feature a pair of dragons on either side of a sun or moon.

Many of the highland peoples, notably the Rhadés, Jarais and Bahnars, carve wooden figures, chiefly for the adornment of tombs. Common subjects include men and women standing together or embracing, and a squatting nude man with elbows on his knees and with his hands

14. Nguyen Hai: *Female Revolutionary Fighter*, plaster version, h. 1.50 m, *c.* 1979 (Hanoi, National Museum of Fine Arts)

framing his face in a pose of contemplation. Monkeys and turtles are popular motifs, as are egrets and peacocks, both carved to convey a certain hauteur. Contemporary events are also recorded by the carvers, and so, for example, sculptures executed in the late 1940s and early 1950s include figures of French soldiers identifiable by their facial features, their manner of saluting and their casquettes. During the American War carvings were produced depicting American Special Forces soldiers wearing berets (sometimes tinted green), jet bombers and cargo aircraft. In the highlands most men and some women smoke pipes. Some pipes are fashioned out of bamboo roots, and these are identifiable by their knotty bowls. Others are made from bamboo stalks and have bowls incised with geometric designs highlighted with black dye. Pipes carved of hardwood often have elegantly curved stems and deep bowls, round which copper wire has been inlaid. Some smokers choose to carve their pipe bowls with swirling designs, while others prefer more whimsical motifs, such as human heads or elephants. In the late 20th century bullet cartridges have sometimes been used to give the stem of the pipe a dull gold appearance and also to provide a practical mouthpiece.

BIBLIOGRAPHY

G. C. Hickey: *Sons of the Mountains: Ethnohistory of the Vietnamese Central Highlands to 1954* (New Haven, 1982)

GERALD HICKEY, NORA TAYLOR

IV. Painting and graphic arts.

The pictorial arts produced before the 20th century were principally village crafts. The two principal traditional forms are woodblock prints and lacquer painting, but other forms include mosaics made with broken ceramics (rather than with glass), decorative panels and small paintings attached to doors. The subjects include Buddhist and Daoist themes, heroic episodes from history and literature, and important events in village life, such as the procession of the mandarins returning after passing the civil service examination (see fig. 15).

Although painting was regarded as one of the Confucian 'three perfections' (Chin. *san jue*)—the others being calligraphy and poetry—and was taught at the Van Mieu, the Confucian 'university', Vietnamese scholar–officials appear in most periods to have devoted themselves to literature rather than painting. Those paintings that have survived from before the 20th century are mainly confined to a few murals and portraits in ink and watercolours on silk of monks and members of the royal family. The status of painting was greatly raised, however, by French colonization in the 19th century.

1. Traditional. 2. Western-influenced.

1. TRADITIONAL.

(i) Woodblock prints. Two of the main traditional centres for the production of woodblock prints are the village of Dong Ho, in Ha Bac Province, near Hanoi, and the Hang Tron-Hang Non quarter of Hanoi itself. The production of woodblock prints in Dong Ho dates from the 15th or 16th century. The medium was created by the Nguyen Dang family, and the techniques that they used were still employed at the end of the 20th century. The pictures are

15. *Return of the Civil Servant* (detail), colour on paper, h. 1.75 m, *c.* 14th–15th centuries (Hanoi, Museum of the Revolution)

made on rice paper and coloured with mineral and plant extracts, with names such as *hoa hoe* ('day-lily yellow'), *hoa hien* ('rose pink'), *cham* ('metallic blue-grey'), *soi* ('yam brown'), *diep* ('sea-shell white'). The design is created by superimposing colours on to one another and then finally printing the black lines. The subjects depicted in the prints have changed very little over the years and consist of emblems of luck and happiness, motifs from the lunar calendar, such as chickens and pigs (see fig. 16), illustrations of popular myths, scenes from village festivals, and historical figures, such as the Trung sisters (*see* §I, 2 above). In the second half of the 20th century, scenes from the wars against France (1946–54) and the USA (1964–76) were used as subjects. In the 1990s only two artists in the village of Dong Ho were still making woodblock prints. The Le Van family on Hang Trong Street, Hanoi, began making a different kind of woodblock print in the 17th century. On Hang Trong prints, the black lines are printed

16. Woodblock print of New Year pig motif from Dong Ho village, Ha Bac Province, c. 17th century (private collection)

first and the colours added later. They are more elegant in style than the Dong Ho prints, the lines are finer and the drawings more refined. They bear the mark of an élite urban culture, whereas Dong Ho prints are the product of village folk art traditions.

BIBLIOGRAPHY
P. Rawson: *The Art of Southeast Asia* (London, 1967)

NORA TAYLOR

(ii) Lacquer. Lacquer is extracted from *Rhus vernicifera* (Viet. *son*), a plant native to Son Tay Province in the north of Vietnam. Lacquer trees have also been planted in the south, but the quality of the northern lacquer is held to be superior. Once the dark, thick liquid has been extracted it is processed and stored ready for use. Because of its viscosity, it is applied with a piece of wood rather than a brush. Lacquer painting is executed on a wooden panel covered with canvas, which is glued to the panel with the *son* itself. Next, the surface of the panel is primed with up to three coats of lacquer and allowed to rest for a few weeks. A design is then transferred on to the surface of the panel and painted with black, brown or other coloured lacquer. Sometimes it is inlaid with pieces of eggshell and mother-of-pearl. The desired space is hollowed out and *son* is again used to glue the pieces into place. When the painting is finished, a final coat of lacquer is applied, and the picture is then allowed to rest for a few weeks before being polished. This is done by wetting the surface and smoothing it with sandpaper to achieve a brilliant lustre. Gold leaf is sometimes employed to enhance the brilliance.

The earliest known lacquer dates from the Later Le period (1428–1802), when it was used on domestic furniture and inscribed wooden panels for Buddhist temples. During the French colonial period and especially with the establishment of the Ecole des Beaux-Arts de l'Indochine de Hanoi in 1925, lacquerwork was encouraged and both the quality of the raw materials and the technique improved. Many Vietnamese lacquer objects such as screens, paintings and pieces of furniture were exported to France, but lacquer furniture is inclined to crack when exposed to a drier atmosphere, so that, except for lacquer painting, the international market for lacquer is limited. In the late 20th century Vietnamese artists have had access to a wide range of pigments for lacquer painting, notably green and red. These have been incorporated into their work, resulting in a more varied and expressive, if less traditional, effect. Among the notable exponents of the medium is Nguyen Gia Tri (*b* 1908), who painted traditional images of girls among flowers.

See also LACQUER, §I, 1.

NGUYEN QUYNH

2. WESTERN-INFLUENCED. With the colonization of Vietnam by the French in the 19th century, the status of painting was gradually redefined. In 1886 a painting class was opened by the French authorities in Hanoi. Among the early painters to work in a Western style and using oil paints were Thang Tran Phanh and Le Huy Mien, who is believed to have been the first Vietnamese painter to study in France. Further impetus was given to the spread of Western influence with the foundation in 1925 of the Ecole des Beaux-Arts de l'Indochine in Hanoi (*see also* §VII below). Formal instruction in the techniques of Western painting was made central to the school's curriculum, and Vietnamese painters began to be exposed to such European movements as Fauvism, Cubism and Surrealism, and to experiment with Western forms, such as portraits and scenes of everyday life. Among this generation of painters were To Ngoc Van (1906–54), Le Pho (*b* 1907), Mai Trang Thu (1906–80) and Tran Van Can (1910–54). These artists also sought artistic effects of texture and space to which oil was more suited than the traditional media of lacquer or watercolour on silk: such paintings as Tran Van Can's portrait of *Little Thuy* (1943; Hanoi, N. Mus. F.A.), for example, use oil to seek to convey a psychological depth. Eventually, however, a debate developed between those Vietnamese painters who advocated a more purely aesthetic approach and those who believed that art was inherently political and should serve a social purpose.

Growing discontent with French colonialism around the middle of the century and subsequent political developments had a far-reaching effect on Vietnamese painting. In 1950 the Resistance Fine Arts College was established in Viet Bac, in Thai Nguyen Province, with Nguyen Tu Nghiem (*b* 1922) among the teachers. Artists associated with the resistance movement—such as Luong Xuan Nhi (*b* 1913), Pham Van Don (*b* 1918) and Duong Bich Lien (1923–88)—moved into the forested mountain regions or into the southern region of Ca Mau and depicted mainly military subjects relating to the resistance; however, some painters associated with the movement—such as Mai Van Hien (*b* 1923) and Nguyen Si Ngoc (1918–90)—preferred to create lyrical works idealizing their country, as seen in Hien's famous painting *Meeting* (1954; Hanoi, N. Mus. F.A.) and Ngoc's *Shift Relay* (1962; Hanoi, N. Mus. F.A.). With the partition of the country in 1954, two distinct schools of painting evolved. In North Vietnam, Ho Chi Minh (1882–1969) called for art 'to reflect the reality of our everyday life' and, in common with other revolutionary leaders of the time, such as Mao Zedong in China, explicitly gave art a social purpose, the service of the revolution. This led to the adoption of a Socialist Realist style as dominant as that in the USSR or China. French influence on art in Vietnam was seen by some as entirely negative, and such artists as Le Van He, Le Pho and Nguyen Tu Nghiem (*b* 1922) sought to 'rediscover' Vietnam's pre-colonial artistic heritage. There were some dissident voices, however. In 1955–7 a movement known as Aesthetic Humanism developed, focused on two journals, *Giai pham* ('Aesthetic works') and *Nhan van* ('Humanism'). Among those who participated in the movement and contributed to these journals were the painters Van Cao (*b* 1923), Bui Xuan Phai (1921–88), Duong Bich Lien and Nguyen Sang (1923–88), who called for artistic freedom and an end to political corruption. The leader of the movement, however, the poet Tran Dan, was imprisoned in 1960, and Bui Xuan Phai was dismissed from his teaching post at the Hanoi College of Fine Arts. In the 1960s and early 1970s, during the American War, many soldiers produced paintings and sketches of the everyday realities of guerrilla warfare. The revolutionary artist Do Thi Ninh (*b* 1947) was particularly notable for her sketches of soldiers, some of which she later used as the bases for larger paintings.

In South Vietnam, the Gia Dinh School of Fine Arts was established in 1955, and this was followed two years later by the Hue School of Fine Arts. Western, and particularly French, art remained popular, and French art books were sold by the government at subsidized prices. International exhibitions were also held, such as the International Fine Arts Exhibition held in 1962 in the Tao Dan Garden in Saigon (now Ho Chi Minh City), and in 1966 an independent group of artists—the Young Painters' Organization—was formed with the aim of encouraging Vietnamese painters to aspire to an international status. The most notable painters in the south during this period were: Trinh Cung (*b* 1939) and Nguyen Trung (*b* 1939), both from Saigon; Hoang Dang Nhuan (*b* 1940) and Buu Chi (*b* 1948), both from Hue; and Ta Ty (*b* 1920), and Nguyen Gia Tri (1908–93), who had both studied in the north and moved to Saigon after independence in 1954. Characteristic of these painters were works inspired by the French Impressionists, executed in watercolour on silk, oil or lacquer, and depicting riverscapes and boating scenes. Many artists also produced abstract works.

After the end of the American War some of the painters who had been prominent in the south were forbidden to paint or were sent to re-education camps. Gradually, however, a more lenient attitude prevailed. From 1978 painters were allowed to sell their works openly, and in 1986 the policy of *doi moi* (renovation) was introduced, relaxing political control of art and culture. In the late 20th century three painters were especially prominent. Bui Xuan Phai (1921–88), who had graduated from the Ecole des Beaux-Arts de l'Indochine de Hanoi in 1945 and taught at the Hanoi College of Fine Arts until his dismissal, painted simple street scenes (see fig. 17) as well as a number of portraits. His output was prolific, and he was particularly popular for his simple but subtle approach to his subject-matter, combined with his wit and his obvious love for his country. Nguyen Tu Nghiem, who had also studied at the Ecole des Beaux-Arts in Hanoi in the early 1940s, took his themes from traditional mythology and folk art and

17. Bui Xuan Phai: *Hanoi Street*, oil on canvas, 500×750 mm (Singapore, Mr and Mrs William G. Hooks private collection)

18. Nguyen Tu Nghiem: *Ancient Dance*, gouache on paper, 450×640 mm, 1965 (Hong Kong, private collection)

music, although stylistically his work is highly innovative, using flat planes and simple lines. The resulting works are full of vitality and boldness (see fig. 18), and comparisons have often been made between Nguyen's work, with its application of modernist styles to a traditional context, and that of Picasso. Nguyen Sang depicted revolutionary themes but also produced lyrical scenes of village life, creating a form of patriotic art that was neither crude in its realism nor mawkish in its romanticism.

BIBLIOGRAPHY

J. Hejzlar: *The Art of Vietnam* (London, New York, Sydney and Toronto, 1973)
N. Quan: *Vietnamese Plastic Arts* (Hanoi, 1987)
D. Thuong and others: *Bui Xuan Phai* (Hanoi, 1991)
Uncorked Soul: Contemporary Art from Vietnam (exh. cat. by J. Hantover, Hong Kong, Plum Blossom Gal., 1991)
The Art of Vietnam (exh. cat., London, Roy Miles Gal., 1994)

NORA TAYLOR

V. Ceramics.

The ceramic tradition of Vietnam began in the 1st century AD. Formerly, 'Annamese' was a collective term assigned to all ceramics made in Vietnam but it is obsolete as a geographical designation, and 'Vietnamese' is therefore the preferred name for these wares. In 1986 six kiln sites were identified by the Vietnamese. These finds include kilns near Hanoi, where two kilns have been excavated, Thanh Hoa Province (the early centuries AD to the 18th or later), Dai La (1st–19th centuries), Quang Uyen (16th century), Hue and Bat Trang and Nam Sach on the Red River (15th–17th centuries).

Unglazed earthenwares were found in tombs of the Han period (1st–3rd centuries AD). They are high-fired ceremonial wares with a reddish body. The kilns for these wares are in Thanh Hoa Province. Glazed stonewares were being made in Vietnam by the 3rd century. Early vessels are heavily potted with a whitish body and a cream-coloured glaze that often has greenish tinges. Shapes with tripod legs and appliqué handles recall metal forms. They include basins, bowls, censers, jars and vases decorated with incised bands. Characteristic of these early glazed wares are an iridescent tinge to the glaze and a dark green colour in areas where the glaze has accumulated.

Although Chinese influence is evident in the technology, shapes and designs of Vietnamese ceramics, a distinctive and individual Vietnamese style emerged between the 11th century and the 13th. Several unique types of ceramics appeared during this period.

1. PRE-EXPORT WARES. Among the earliest pre-export ceramics are brown-and-white incised wares. Shapes include urns, basins and squat jars. A typical example is a tall cylindrical urn with a row of modelled lotus petals on the rim of the mouth. The decoration of this type of ware is a striking combination of a dark design highlighted against a light background. First, a design was carved on to the body of the vessel. Horizontal bands delineate the decoration. Common motifs are floral and leaf scrolls, lotus and chrysanthemum blossoms, cloud forms, figures,

long-tailed birds, fish and other animals. Next, a brown glaze was applied to the decorated area. Finally, a thin clear glaze, often with a greenish tinge, was applied over the entire piece. White-glazed wares with modelled decoration were produced in the 11th and 12th centuries. A stem bowl with overlapping bands of carved and modelled lotus leaves is representative of this group. Production of brown monochromes probably began in the 12th century. Covered urns, small jars, beakers and bowls with a chocolate base are typical of these wares. Cream monochromes date from the 13th century and consist of dishes and bowls with carved or moulded geometric designs. The glaze is uneven, darkening in thicker areas, and often has a greenish tinge. Celadons emerged in the 12th or 13th century. Heavily potted bowls with carved footrings are typical. The dark green glaze is thick and opaque. Distinctive characteristics of many pieces in this group are a brown slip on the base and a ring of spur marks or an unglazed stacking ring in the centre of the interior. Celadon saucers, bowls, cups and jars with an apple-green copper glaze are among the most attractive Vietnamese wares. The earliest underglaze-decorated ceramics appeared in the early 14th century. They are painted with iron oxide and covered with a clear glaze. The body is fine-grained and greyish. The forms are small and include bowls, saucers, beakers and jars. The primary design is a sketchy floral spray in the centre enclosed by a band and a debased classic scroll around the rim. Popular motifs are sunbursts and stylized flowers such as chrysanthemums with a stem, leaves and blossoms. The glaze is often straw-coloured or has greenish tinges. Guangdong wares made in southern China have been identified as providing the model for this type.

2. EARLY EXPORT WARES. The materials, potting methods, shapes and designs of these early ceramics led to the emergence of certain distinctive and persistent characteristics. The most readily identifiable feature is a whitish, or sometimes greyish, body. The texture is always hard and fine. Another feature is a dark 'chocolate' base that became common on 14th-century wares. On 15th- and 16th-century examples the colour is a lighter brown, and brushstrokes are visible. The early monochromes and underglaze-iron decorated wares were the first types to be exported. They have been found in other parts of Southeast Asia from the late 13th century or early 14th. The range of shapes expanded to include small bowls, dishes, covered boxes, small jars and small gourd-shaped ewers and bottles. Carved footrings are characteristic, and glazed bases and footrings bevelled on the interior are common on later pieces.

3. BLUE-AND-WHITE WARES. As the demand increased, new types of ceramics developed. Foremost among these were underglaze blue-and-white wares. The dating of this class of ware is keyed to a bottle in the Topkapı Palace Museum in Istanbul, which has an inscription and a date of AD 1450 on the shoulder. Production of blue-and-white wares in Vietnam may have started as early as the second half of the 14th century. At this time the potting and decoration of such wares was similar to that of earlier iron-decorated wares. The apex of artistic

19. Underglaze blue-and-white dish decorated with a chrysanthemum spray, diam. 360 mm, 15th century (private collection)

achievement in the production of blue-and-white wares was the mid-15th century, and the major export markets for them were in South-east Asia. The shapes and designs closely resemble Chinese wares of the same period. Shapes include bottles, jars, dishes, plates, bowls, covered boxes, *kendi* and small jars. Popular central designs are floral, lotus scrolls and fish swimming among water plants. Lappets of lotus petals commonly surround the base and shoulder of such round forms as jars and vases. A typical 15th-century piece is a large dish with a broad base (see fig. 19). The central design is a chrysanthemum spray surrounded by a band of waves. Six flowers joined by scrolling foliage are evenly spaced around the well of the dish. A classic scroll on the rim and lotus petals on the exterior complete the decoration. Overglaze enamels appeared in the 15th century and became increasingly popular. Sometimes they were used in combination with underglaze blue-and-white. Red, green and yellow were the most common colours of these enamels. Circular boxes with a domed cover were commonly made for export to South-east Asia. Panels extending over both the body and cover contain geometric or floral designs outlined in underglaze blue and filled in with red and green enamels. A unique group of blue-and-white tiles for architectural decoration was seemingly made exclusively for the East Javanese kingdom of Majapahit in the 15th century. These tiles are thickly potted and cruciform, octagonal, rectangular or circular in shape. They are decorated with underglaze blue or moulded relief patterns.

Blue-and-white wares from the 17th and 18th centuries are thickly potted and characteristically have large dimensions. The glaze is creamish with dark-veined crazing. A typical example is a dragon jar with four lug-shaped handles evenly spaced around the shoulder. Decoration includes two large dragons chasing a flaming pearl on the body and lappets of lotus petals around the shoulder and base. In the 19th century '*bleu de Hué*' wares appeared, characterized by their small forms and delicate designs. Tea sets and small dishes decorated with landscapes and often with poems written in Vietnamese characters are representative. Modern kilns making underglaze blue-and-white wares are at Bat Trang, in southern Vietnam. They produce utilitarian bowls and dishes decorated with a fish medallion.

4. LATER DOMESTIC WARES. Wares made for religious purposes appeared in the 15th century and continued to be important until the 18th century. The most common shapes are elaborately modelled incense burners or altar vases with appliqué dragons. They were made in blue and white, unglazed stoneware, white monochrome and red and green enamels.

BIBLIOGRAPHY

Okada Seiichi: *Annam toji zukan* [Annamese ceramics] (Tokyo, 1954)
Ceramic Art of Southeast Asia (exh. cat.; intro. W. Willetts; Singapore, N. Mus., 1971)
R. M. Brown: *The Ceramics of South-east Asia: Their Dating and Identification* (Kuala Lumpur, 1977, 2/Singapore, 1988)
Vietnamese Ceramics (exh. cat., ed. C. M. Young, M. Dupoizat and E. W. Lane; Singapore, N. Mus., 1982)
Important Annamese Ceramics: The Mr and Mrs Robert P. Piccus Collection (sale cat., London, Christie's, 7 December 1984)
J. Guy: *Oriental Trade Ceramics in South-east Asia: Ninth to Sixteenth Centuries* (Singapore, 1988)
——: *Ceramic Traditions of South-east Asia* (Singapore, 1989)
J. Stevenson: 'Vietnamese Ceramics: An Introduction to Ly and Tran Monochromes', *A. Asia*, xxi/3 (1991)

DAWN F. ROONEY

VI. Other arts.

1. Coins. 2. Dress. 3. Jewellery and body adornment. 4. Metalwork. 5. Mother-of-pearl inlay. 6. Musical instruments. 7. Textiles. 8. Theatre.

1. COINS. The first local Vietnamese cash coins were minted by Dinh Bo Lang (*reg* 968–79), founder of the Dinh dynasty (AD 968–80). Although smaller and lighter than the Chinese coins on which they were modelled, the first Vietnamese cash issues (Viet. *tien* or *van*; called *sapèques* by the French) were produced according to Chinese manufacturing techniques and design principles: they have a square hole in the centre and a four-character inscription and were cast from a copper alloy (and occasionally from zinc) in a two-piece mould. Unlike their Chinese models, these early *tien* are inscribed with the name of the issuing dynasty on the reverse.

A mint was established in the capital, Hoa Lu, Ninh Binh Province, during the Earlier Le dynasty (980–1010). The first Earlier Le coins were issued in the reign of Le Dai Hanh (*reg* 980–1005). Vietnamese cash was next minted under the Later Ly dynasty (1010–1225) between *c.* 1010 and 1055. This was followed by a cessation of mint activity until the 1120s, reportedly owing to the import of enormous quantities of lightweight cash minted illegally in China. Under the Tran dynasty (1225–1400), a zinc coinage was issued in 1323, an indication of the scarcity of copper in the 14th century. Indeed, before the establishment of the Later Le dynasty (1428–1802), the emission of cash coins was sporadic, probably as a result of the vagaries of Vietnamese metal production. From 1428 to the early 20th century there was almost continuous minting in Vietnam

both by rulers and by rebel leaders, such as the Tay Son. Large quantities of gold and silver ingots (rectangular and circular in form) were minted throughout the 19th century. Multiple cash pieces, up to the 60 *van* denomination, were also made between 1848–83.

Under the French, a special coinage was struck for Conchin China from 1879 to 1885, consisting of a bronze 1 cent piece, silver 10, 20 and 50 cent coins and the piastre. A zinc cash coinage was struck for Tonkin in 1905.

Independent Vietnam issued its own coinage in 1945, a 20 *xu* coin, 5 *hao*, 1 and 2 *dong*, all in aluminium, the larger denominations featuring the portrait of Ho Chi Minh. In 1958 North Vietnam issued a series of aluminium 1, 2 and 5 *xu* coins, followed in 1976 by similar coins for use in occupied South Vietnam. South Vietnam had its own coinage beginning in 1953.

BIBLIOGRAPHY

J. Novak: *A Working Aid for Collectors of Annamese Coins* (Long View, WA, n.d.)
E. Toda: 'Annam and its Minor Currency', *J. N. China Branch Royal Asiat. Soc.*, xvii (1882), pp. 41–220
J. Whitmore: 'Vietnam and the Monetary Flow of Eastern Asia, Thirteenth to Eighteenth Centuries', *Precious Metals in the Late Medieval and Early Modern Worlds*, ed. S. F. Richards (Durham, NC, 1983), pp. 363–93
F. Thierry: *Catalogue des monnaies vietnamiennes* (Paris, 1987)

ROBERT S. WICKS

2. DRESS. Daily wear both for men and women consists of a short tunic slit at the sides from the waist to the hem. The men's tunic is loose and unfitted, but the women's is fitted and is worn unbuttoned, disclosing a breast-cloth underneath. Men wear trousers, and women wear black or brown skirts. Men's formal dress consists of a dark blue or black robe worn over a white under-robe. Women's formal dress consists of between one and three robes, or even more, depending on the weather. Bright or light colours are worn underneath, while the outer robes are darker and *c.* 10 mm shorter. When thin silk or *the* is used, the different colours of the under-robes can be seen through the outer robes. Collars, sleeves, flaps and hems discreetly show the fine stitches of the under-robes. Together with the laces of the breast-cloth, the flaps of the tunic, which are left open or tied in a loose knot, create a harmonious effect of line, colour and form against the black background of the skirt.

Traditionally, both men's and women's tunics and robes have a collar with five lobes or lappets in the shape of a lotus leaf which are buttoned on the right from the collar to the shoulder. In some cases one lappet is left out and the garment is buttoned down the front: men's robes always have five lappets.

In the 1930s the painter Cat Tuong (1915–46) created a new style of women's robe, the *ao dai*. Based on the classical Vietnamese five-lappet robe, the *ao dai* does not have the lotus-leaf collar and is fully buttoned so that the breast-cloth is not visible. The *ao dai* can be made in any colour and any material but is always worn with white trousers instead of a dark skirt. In the 20th century Western-style clothes, such as suits worn with shirt and tie, have become increasingly common in Vietnam.

Traditionally, Vietnamese men wear their hair in a chignon, which rests above the nape of the neck, and is bound with a purple turban (*nhien*) fastened at the forehead, with the left side folded over the right side at an oblique angle. Women part their hair in the middle from

20. Traditional Vietnamese women's dress

the forehead to the crown of the head and wrap a black or brown velvet band around the head, leaving the hair long on both sides. Footwear includes plain wooden clogs or leather sandals for men and clogs or slippers with curved toes and painted a glossy black for women. A conical palm-leaf hat is commonly worn. There is also a special hat that is worn by women, with a broad brim (diam. *c.* 700 mm), which is flat or concave on top. Inside there is a pad to secure the hat on to the head. The strap fastening the hat consists of many plaited black threads with loose fringes: these are draped over the shoulders while the wearer holds the strap in one hand (see fig. 20).

PHAN NGỌC KHUÊ

3. JEWELLERY AND BODY ADORNMENT. Jewellery in Vietnam is made from a variety of materials, notably gold, silver, jade, mother-of-pearl, ivory, tortoiseshell and wood. These materials are used to make pendants, rings, necklaces, earrings and small boxes to hold betel ingredients or tobacco. Pendants, rings and boxes are often carved with motifs drawn from the traditional Chinese iconography of symbols for good luck, prosperity, happiness and longevity, such as bats, dragons, chrysanthemum flowers, lotuses, phoenixes and turtles. Among the highland peoples of Vietnam, men and women wear simple metal bracelets, which in some cases indicate social relationships. Stieng and Maa women wear ivory earplugs and rows of anklets, which indicate degrees of wealth. Lat women distend their ear lobes with large ivory rings, and the Monoms have nail-like earrings. Stieng, Maa and Katu men wear their hair long and for ceremonial occasions arrange it in an elaborate coiffure held in place with metal combs and barrettes and decorated with feathers. The Katus are unique in having tattoos on the forehead, chest, arms, wrists and legs. These are relatively elaborate and incorporate motifs such as sunbursts, dancing women, stylized monkeys, Greek crosses and swastikas.

BIBLIOGRAPHY
J. Boulbet: 'Modes et techniques du pays Maa', *Bull. Soc. Etud. Indochin.*, xxxix/2 (1964), pp. 169–287

PHAN NGỌC KHUÊ, GERALD HICKEY

4. METALWORK. Archaeological excavations at Dong Son and other sites have revealed the existence of a Bronze Age culture in the Red River delta that dates from the 6th century BC. A variety of bronze objects belonging to the DONG SON civilization have been uncovered, including some of the famous kettledrums and musical instruments, statues, jewellery, weapons, such as poniards, battle-axes, lances, pickheads, spearheads and arrows, and utensils, such as jars, basins, vases, lamps (see fig. 21), ploughshares, hoe blades and water scoops. The Dong Son bronzes were cast, and from the evidence of clay moulds discovered at Lang Ca, a Dong Son site in Vinh Phu Province on the flood plain of the Red River north-west of Hanoi, it would appear that the section-mould technique was used (*see* CHINA, §VI, 2(iii)). The ornamentation on the bronze drums is characteristically linear, consisting of curves, S-shaped lines, parallel straight lines, triangles and concentric circles. Motifs include dancing figures with large feathered headdresses, warriors, peasants beating drums, pounding rice and slaying buffaloes. There are scenes of women cooking in houses with curved roofs. There are oarsmen in curved boats with helms in the shape of a dragon's or bird's head and a fish-tail stern. The curved and straight-bladed axes are adorned with motifs similar to those found on the drums, such as dancing figures, warriors, oarsmen and several types of birds and animals. Dagger handles are especially elaborate in design.

Under Chinese domination (208 BC–AD 939), Vietnamese bronzes developed in a way that paralleled trends in Chinese metalwork. After the collapse of the Han dynasty in AD 220, bronze was increasingly used in both countries to make functional objects, such as teapots, lamps and bells for buffaloes. Bronze and silver also began to be used for palace roofs. With the adoption of Buddhism as the official religion by the Later Ly dynasty (AD 1010–1225), the use of bronze was greatly encouraged; a large number of ceremonial objects, such as ritual bells, were made, and in the 15th and 16th centuries a number of flasks in the shape of animals, such as horses and elephants.

21. Lamp-holder, bronze, *c.* 330 mm, Dong Son, from Tomb 3, Lach Truong, *c.* 1st century BC–1st century AD (Hanoi, National Museum of Fine Arts)

In their soft, rounded contours and suggestion of playfulness, they show traces of Indian or Khmer influence. In 1836 the Nguyen Emperor Minh Mang (*reg* 1820–41) commissioned the casting of nine large bronze incense burners, each dedicated to a different ruler of his dynasty. The incense burners, which are located within the Imperial City at Hue, are 1.90 m high and weigh between 2 and 3 tonnes each. They are all the same shape but differ in the details of their handles, legs and rims. The decoration of each is unique and incorporates 17 figures. Altogether there are 162 images in low relief of the sun, mountains, rivers, plants and animals. There are also motifs symbolizing unification, prosperity and longevity, themes central to the Confucian values promoted by the Nguyen dynasty in imitation of the contemporary Qing emperors in China. Indeed, the commissioning of these bronzes seems to have been undertaken with the same intention as the Chinese practice of invoking archaistic vessels reminiscent of the ritual bronzes of the Shang dynasty (*c.* 1600–*c.* 1050 BC) as symbols of legitimacy and authority (*see* CHINA, §VI, 1(i)).

Chinese visitors to the early Funan kingdom (AD 100–500) south-east of the Mekong delta noted silver rings, bracelets and utensils. It can therefore be assumed that silver smithing was well established in Vietnam by the time the French arrived in the late 19th century, but its uses may have been altered by the demands of the colonial residents. Silver boxes probably became popular from the early part of the 20th century. Motifs and designs are influenced by Chinese symbolism (*see* §3 above), but the technique is closely related to Thai and Cambodian methods of silver smithing. Silver is present in small amounts in conjunction with other minerals in Vietnam. It is neither the purest nor the richest form of silver, but most silver objects and jewellery come from silver mined and worked in the country.

BIBLIOGRAPHY

V. Goloubew: 'L'Age du bronze au Tonkin et dans le Nord-Annam', *Bull. Ecole Fr. Extrême-Orient*, xxix (1929), pp. 1–46

J. Hejzlar: *The Art of Vietnam* (London, 1973)

S. Fraser-Lu: *Silverware of Southeast Asia* (Singapore, 1989)

C. Higham: *The Archaeology of Mainland Southeast Asia: From 10,000 BC to the Fall of Angkor* (Cambridge, 1989/R 1991)

Pham Huy Thong and others, eds: *Dong Son Drums in Vietnam*, (Hanoi, 1990)

PHAN NGỌC KHUÊ, NORA TAYLOR

5. MOTHER-OF-PEARL INLAY. Vietnam has a strong tradition of mother-of-pearl inlay on paintings, furniture and decorative objects. Mother-of-pearl is also an important component of lacquer paintings and lacquer objects (*see* §IV, 1(ii) above). It is believed that the technique was introduced by a craftsman named Nguyen Kim, who lived in the region of the Red River delta during the reign of Le Hien Tong (*reg* 1740–86). In the 19th and 20th centuries a considerable quantity of furniture inlaid with mother-of-pearl was exported to Europe.

The decorative effect of the inlay lies chiefly in the contrast between the pale, shimmering mother-of-pearl and the dark, luminous wood. The colour of mother-of-pearl varies; in Vietnamese work a pinkish tone is generally preferred. The designs are usually floral or geometric. For furniture, the wood must be hard, durable and supple so that it does not split: chinaberry, sandalwood, teak, poon, casuarina and limewood are all used. It is common practice to soak the wood in limewater (i.e. slaked calcium oxide), thereby darkening it until it attains a colour known as 'Tonkinese sindora'. Mother-of-pearl is first extracted with a hammer and chisel from the inside of spiral and cone-shaped shells of marine or freshwater origin. It is then cut into strips, washed and polished. It is cut according to a pattern drawn on paper and polished and filed to achieve a perfect fit. It is then placed on the wood and outlined with a sharp metal needle. The pattern is hollowed out of the wood with a knife and chisel, and the mother-of-pearl is inlaid into the settings, which are often lined with lacquer putty as an adhesive. Sometimes the mother-of-pearl is engraved. The whole object is then polished to a high lustre. In some pieces ivory or tortoise-shell is used instead of mother-of-pearl.

BIBLIOGRAPHY

J. Hejzlar: *The Art of Vietnam* (London, New York, Sydney and Toronto, 1973)

6. MUSICAL INSTRUMENTS. Vietnam has a rich heritage of bamboo, wooden and metal musical instruments, including chimes, bells, drums, scrapers, whistles, zithers and lutes. Some are simple in design, while others are elegant and highly adorned. Gourds and coconut-shells are also used. While some features of these instruments are indigenous or show Indian or South-east Asian influences, notably that of Champa, the principal influence is Chinese, and decoration is frequently Chinese in inspiration, with dragons, whirling floral shapes, and lacquer and mother-of-pearl inlay. Ancient instruments include the *khan da*, a Vietnamese lithophone dated to *c.* 3000 BC. It consists of 11 flat slabs of stone, graded according to size, which were probably suspended on a frame and played with wooden hammers. The quality of the stone-carving and the accuracy of pitch are remarkable (e.g. Paris, Mus. Homme). A similar instrument, the bamboo *to rung*, is still played today in Darlac, the same region of southern Vietnam as that where the ancient lithophone was found. Still popular among the Sedang mountain people of southern Vietnam is the ancient hydraulic orchestra of clappers and stone chimes, activated by water. The famous DONG SON bronze kettle drums have been found throughout South-east Asia but are believed by some scholars to have originated in Vietnam. They are sometimes decorated with depictions of other musical instruments, including conch trumpets, wooden clappers, kettle gongs and mouth-organs, and of the drums themselves. They were clearly of ritual importance and similar bronze drums were still used in ceremonies in Than Hoa Province as late as the 1940s. Similar drums are also used by the Lolo, Muong and Khmou peoples.

The classical Vietnamese orchestral ensemble includes many kinds of percussion instrument used to sound the beginning and end of verses in court ceremonial hymns. One such instrument is the *bien chung*, a vertical wooden frame from which rows of bells are suspended. A 24-bell *bien chung* can be seen in the Imperial City at Hue. The *p'a tchong* is a large single bell suspended from a metal link forged in the shape of two dragons. An unusual percussion instrument is the *ngu*, a rectangular-based wooden scraper in the shape of a tiger. Stringed instruments include the *dan bau*, a monochord with a gourd sound-box, and different types of lute and zither. The latter include the simple 7-string *cam*, the *dan tranh*, a zither with 16 or 17 strings, and the *sat*, a lavishly lacquered and gilded 50-string instrument. Of the wind instruments double-headed flutes, panpipes, whistles and mouth-organs are still played. Examples of the more ornate court instruments can be seen in the Hanoi History Museum in Hanoi and the History Museum in Ho Chi Minh City. In the 20th century these court instruments declined in importance while the mandolin, guitar and violin grew in popularity. In rural and mountain regions many simple traditional instruments are still used. The Horniman Museum and Library, London, has a small collection of traditional Vietnamese instruments.

BIBLIOGRAPHY
New Oxford History of Music, i (London, 1957), pp. 180–89
Tran Van Khe: *La Musique vietnamienne traditionelle* (Paris, 1962)
——: *Viet-Nam* (Paris, 1967)
Pham Duy: *Musics of Vietnam* (Carbondale, 1975)
Dao Trong Tu, Huy Tran and Tu Ngoc: *Essays on Vietnamese Music* (Hanoi, 1984)
C. Higham: *The Archaeology of Mainland Southeast Asia: From 10,000 BC to the Fall of Angkor* (Cambridge, 1989), pp. 200–03

MIRANDA BRUCE-MITFORD

7. TEXTILES.

(i) Ethnic Vietnamese. The ethnic Vietnamese use cotton and a wide variety of silk fibres to weave traditional textiles. Chemical fibres and wool are also imported for industrial textile production and carpet-weaving. The silks include *soi* (floss silk), *dui* (tusser or wild silk), *nhieu* (silk crepe), *luot* (thin black silk), *la* (gossamer silk), *gam* (brocade) and *voc* (fine silk decorated with glossy, brocaded flowers). Undyed silk is ivory white or yellowish, and the Vietnamese traditionally use a range of vegetable dyes, such as yam for brown, sophora seeds for yellow, indigo leaves for blue, tropical almond leaves for black, brazil-wood for bright red. Cochineal is used for scarlet, deep red and purple. From the beginning of the 20th century chemical dyestuffs were imported in increasing quantities and gave a greater variety of colours, but these were no match for the colours obtained from the natural dyes in depth, subtlety and warmth. Except for *gam* and *voc*, in which some six or seven colours are used in the weaving, most Vietnamese silks are woven with undyed yarn.

The traditional handloom for weaving cloth 200 mm, 430 mm or 500 mm in width, is still commonly used, but modern looms, which can weave cloth 700 mm to 900 mm wide, are increasingly employed. Twisted threads are woven to create *sa tron* (plain gauze), a fabric with a surface as fine as the wing of a dragonfly. Twisted thread is woven with plain thread to create *sa hoa* (flowered gauze with decorative geometrical patterns). *Van* silks, which traditionally come from Van Phuc village, Ha Son Binh Province, have raised woven patterns, such as sprays of mulberry flowers, stylized roses, peach blossom, tagetes, lotuses, lozenges, coins, fans, baskets of flowers and traditional musical instruments. The four holy animals, namely the dragon, phoenix, tortoise and unicorn, and the word *tho* ('long life') also occur. *Van* is popular for clothing because it is warm in winter and cool in summer (see fig. 22). *Nhieu* is made by using twisted silk threads and by two-way twisting weaving to create fine twisted

22. *Van* silk, from Van Phuc village textile mill, Ha Son Binh Province

23. Jarai Arap woven fabric from Vietnam, with motifs of M-16 automatic rifles, helicopter gunships, American soldiers and a reconnaissance helicopter flanked by two Chinook cargo helicopters

and wavy lines on the surface of the cloth, like undulating waves on a lake. *The* is made by weaving three lines of plain silk, followed by one twisted line, thus creating regular horizontal stripes. In *gam* (brocade) and *voc* (fine silk with flower patterns) the flowers are raised and glossy, as if embroidered on to the background. Sometimes it is brocaded with gold and silver threads.

PHAN NGOC KHUÊ

(ii) Highland peoples. Almost all highland women weave, using backstrap looms and in some instances locally produced cotton and dyes. The main colours are rich shades of red, blue and yellow contrasted with black, white and grey. Highland textiles are woven to be made into both flat untailored garments such as women's skirts, loincloths, mantles and slings for carrying infants, and also tailored garments including women's blouses and men's shirts (with and without sleeves). These textiles tend to be patterned primarily with simple warp stripes. Among some groups the stripes may be augmented with bands patterned with supplementary wefts. The textiles of the Maa people have long been highly prized for their elegance. In the past the Maas traded cloth with the lowland Chams and sent it, along with precious ivory and tortoiseshell, as tribute to the Cham kings. Maa geometric designs are made up of motifs with such names as 'kapok flower', 'crossbow-arrow feathers', 'tiger dimples', 'tiger teeth', 'leech's mouth' and 'buffalo paunch'. Maa weavers also weave pictorial

motifs such as gibbons with raised arms, rice wine jars (an index of wealth), peacocks and chickens. In the 1950s the highland weavers interspersed traditional motifs with stylized aircraft, telegraph poles, soldiers saluting, horses and European-style houses. The Jarai Arap weave stylized deer, fish, lizards, hunting scenes, people farming rice, and rice wine jars. During the war with the USA they added what one weaver described as 'the things we see around us', which included various types of helicopters (sometimes with structural details), jet bombers, American soldiers and M-16 automatic rifles (see fig. 23).

BIBLIOGRAPHY

J. Boulbet: 'Modes et techniques du pays Maa', *Bull. Soc. Etud. Indochin.*, xxxiv/2 (1964), pp. 169–287

GERALD HICKEY

8. THEATRE. There are numerous different forms of theatre in Vietnam. The two types of opera, both derived from Chinese opera, are *hat bo* and *hat cheo*. *Hat bo*, also known as *hat tuong*, is the more formal and was formerly only performed at court and in the houses of officials. *Hat cheo* is a simpler and more popular form, using everyday language and often dealing with satirical themes. *Cai luong* is a modern form of theatre that originated in the south in the early 20th century and is strongly influenced by the French tradition. There is also *kich* or *kich noi*, a type of performance that is spoken rather than sung and, like *cai luong*, is derived from French models.

In addition to conventional puppetry (*roi can*), there is water puppetry (*mua noi ruoc*), which is unique to Vietnam, although it is believed that a similar type of show formerly existed in China. Of these forms of theatre, opera and water puppet shows are the most important.

(i) Opera. The Chinese theatrical tradition on which the two forms of traditional Vietnamese opera, *hat bo* and *hat cheo*, are based is believed to have been introduced into Vietnam during the Yuan period (1279–1368), when there was a great flowering of the dramatic arts in China. Although both have some specifically Vietnamese features, notably the style of the singing, generally they remain heavily influenced by Chinese opera (*see* CHINA, §XIII, 25(ii)). The costumes and facial painting are borrowed from the Chinese, and the colours have the same symbolic meanings. In *hat bo* there are *c*. 40 different costumes, all full length, long-sleeved robes made of multi-coloured silk and usually embroidered. On all except the costumes of military characters, a piece of white silk is attached to the end of the sleeve (Chin. *shuixiu*). The gown (*bao*) worn by officials of high rank is coloured red, yellow or purple, and that worn by those of lower rank is blue or black. A square with an embroidered design is attached to the breast. The ceremonial dress of officials (*mang bao*) is made of ten-coloured silk and has an embroidered design of a dragon with four toes (only the dragon on the emperor's robe has five toes). The ceremonial dress for women of high birth (*nu mang bao*) is the same as the *mang bao* except that it lacks the embroidered dragon. Warriors wear either the *mang bao*, if they are of high rank, or the *binh kim giap*, a leather coat covered with round, iron mirrors as protection against arrows. People of low rank, such as servants and farmers, wear simple clothing with little adornment.

The symbolism of the different colours used for facial paint is the same as in Chinese opera: red denotes loyalty and devotion; purple a lesser degree of loyalty; black good character; blue arrogance and aggression; yellow a lesser degree of arrogance; green an unstable character; and orange and grey old age. Male characters wear black silk boots: if they are officials, their boots will have high soles; if they are warriors they will also be embroidered; other male characters wear low-soled boots. Women of high birth wear little embroidered shoes for their bound feet, while other women may wear either embroidered or unembroidered shoes.

The hats also indicate the social status of the character. They are made of papier mâché or cloth and are adorned with trinkets or feathers. The shape of the hat is the most important consideration, and the symbolism of the colours is not the same as that of the costume and facial painting.

BIBLIOGRAPHY
K. D. Huynh: *Hat Boi: Théâtre traditionnel de Vietnam* (Saigon, 1970)
W. Idema and S. H. West: *Chinese Theatre, 1100–1450: A Source Book* (Wiesbaden, 1982)
J. O. Miettinen: *Classical Dance and Theatre in South-east Asia* (Singapore, 1992)

(ii) Water puppets. Although water puppets (*mua noi ruoc*) are now unique to Vietnam, this kind of puppetry probably originated in China, where as early as the 3rd century AD puppets are known to have been operated by a hydraulic system. The puppets were placed in streams in the imperial palace and set in motion by the flowing water, performing elaborate dance movements and acrobatics. In the 8th century a type of water puppetry called *shuiguilei* came into use in China, and this was probably the immediate forerunner of the Vietnamese *mua noi ruoc*. An account of a *shuiguilei* performance given in 1147 shows that it was remarkably similar to modern Vietnamese *mua noi ruoc*. The first Vietnamese account of a water puppet show records a performance given on a river in 1121 in honour of Ly Nhon Ton (*reg* 1072–1127). Water puppets disappeared from China during the 17th and early 18th centuries, but they remained popular in the relatively isolated rural areas of northern Vietnam.

The puppets have an average height of *c*. 400 mm, with a few exceptions for important characters, such as *Teu*, the jester, who is *c*. 800 mm high, and they are mainly made out of light wood, or sometimes out of cloth. They are carved by members of the group of puppeteers (*phuong hoi*) or by independent artists. The puppets have crude, fixed, but expressive features. The costumes are carved directly on the wooden body and, like the head, are painted in bright colours. The arms of the puppets are movable, but the legs are fixed. Many characters appear in water puppet dramas, including farmers, fishermen, warriors, acrobats, dancers, immortals and a multitude of animals such as birds, fish, snakes and dragons. The most important puppet is *Teu*, who presents the performance and in some villages is worshipped as a deity, although a few groups do not include him in their performances. He is a smiling, chubby young man, who represents the Vietnamese peasant. He wears a simple waistcoat over his bare chest and a loincloth. Each puppet group has its own techniques for manipulating the puppets, but certain common principles apply. The legs of the puppets are fixed on a floater, which is connected to a bamboo rod 2 to 3 m long. Using strings that run through the rod and floater, the puppeteer is able to move the arms and, with some puppets, the head. In some cases long sticks instead

24. *Mua noi ruoc* (water puppets)

of wires are used to move the arms. During the performance the floater and bamboo rod remained submerged in the muddy water and are thus invisible to the audience. Performances take place in the afternoon or evening in the open air in a pond. Some temples have especially created ponds for *mua noi ruoc*, while others use inundated rice paddies near by. The performances are given during traditional Vietnamese and Buddhist festivals and in order to commemorate national heroes. Before a performance a beautiful water pavilion (*buong tro*), made of wood or bamboo, is erected on the pond. Inside, the players, who are hidden from view by a bamboo curtain, stand up to their chests in the water and manipulate the puppets. The audience is seated round the pond. The orchestra, consisting of three to five musicians, is situated to one side of the performance area. The performance consists of 20 to 30 short scenes from a repertory of *c.* 200, which includes heroic episodes from Vietnamese history and religious themes, such as the *mua Tien*, dances of four or eight immortals. The effect of the performance (see fig. 24) lies in the spectacular combination of water, colourful puppets, action and variety rather than in the dialogue or elaborate gestures.

BIBLIOGRAPHY

K. D. Sun: *Kuileixi kaoyuan* [Research into the origin of the puppet theatre] (Shanghai, 1952)
Song Ban: *The Vietnamese Theatre* (Hanoi, 1960)
S. To: *Nghe thuat mua noi ruoc* [The art of water puppets] (Hanoi, 1976)
Asian Puppets: Wall of the World (exh. cat., Los Angeles, UCLA, Mus. Cult. Hist., 1976)
Tran Van Khe: *Marionettes sur eau du Vietnam* (Paris, 1984)

ROBIN RUIZENDAAL

VII. Art education.

Before the French established the Ecole des Beaux-Arts de l'Indochine de Hanoi in 1925, there had been no formal art education in Vietnam. In accordance with the Confucian values that permeated Vietnamese society, people who made a living by producing works of art were held in low esteem. However, painting, which was classified along with poetry and calligraphy as one of the Confucian 'Three Perfections', was deemed to be a suitable leisure pursuit for a scholar–official and was therefore taught at the Van Mieu ('Temple of Literature'), founded during the Later Ly dynasty (1010–1225). Buddhist monasteries were the most important centres for the teaching of architecture and sculpture, while the popular arts, notably woodblock printing, were transmitted from father to son: daughters, whose loyalty was transferred to the husband's family on marriage, were excluded from the teaching process so as to keep the skills within the family. In the early 20th century, the Confucian education system was abolished and replaced by the French system. Music and painting thus became part of the school curriculum, and many of the graduates of the Ecole des Beaux-Arts de l'Indochine de Hanoi became art teachers in schools and colleges.

The Ecole des Beaux-Arts de l'Indochine de Hanoi was founded with the aim of training artists both in Vietnamese arts, such as lacquer painting, and in Western techniques, notably linear perspective, and although it was only active for 20 years it was highly influential. Victor Tardieu (*b* 1867), the founding Director, intended the school to be a 'scientific institution' that would form a bridge between modern and traditional, Western and Vietnamese. However, his successor, the sculptor Evariste Jonchère, took a more condescending view of traditional Vietnamese art and antagonized many students. During partition (1954–76), art education was carried out in different ways in the two halves of Vietnam. In South Vietnam, at the Gia Dinh School of Fine Arts and the Hue School of Fine Arts, established in 1955 and 1957 respectively, strong links with the French artistic tradition were retained, and artists were encouraged to produce work in such Western styles as Cubism. In the North by contrast there was a strong interest in rediscovering ancient Vietnamese artistic traditions. The party maintained a firm control over art, and artists were schooled in Socialist Realism and propagandist styles. With the policy of *doi moi* ('renovation') from 1986 the government relaxed its control over personal expression, and the teaching of art became correspondingly less political. The modern Hanoi Art School retains many of the teaching methods introduced by Victor Tardieu, which were borrowed in the first instance from the Ecole des Beaux-Arts in Paris. The curriculum is demanding, with classes in life drawing, composition and perspective as well as sculpture, woodblock printing and lacquerwork.

BIBLIOGRAPHY

N. Thu, L. Q. Bas and others: *L'Ecole supérieure des beaux-arts de Hanoi, 1925–1990* (Hanoi, 1990)

NORA TAYLOR, NGUYEN QUYNH

Vigarani, Gaspare (*b* Reggio Emilia, 19 Feb 1588; *d* Modena, 9 Sept 1663). Italian architect, stage designer and engineer. He is first noted in 1618 and again in 1619 as a designer of theatrical effects for church festivities in Reggio Emilia. In 1631 he moved to Modena, where he worked on the city fortifications for Francesco I d'Este (ii), Duke of Modena, for whom he also built a garden casino (1633–4; modified 18th century) and, later, the villa of Pentetorri (1652; destr.). In 1635 he became Engineer and General Superintendent of Buildings for the Duke, and in 1636 he began work on Modena's pentagonal citadel. He also supervised the decorations for court festivities, which involved the construction of ephemeral architecture. Vigarani was in addition a successful designer of theatres, building those at Reggio Emilia (1637), Carpi (1640) and the Teatro della Speltà (1654–6), Modena (all destr.). In 1659 he was summoned to Paris to design the decorations for the wedding of King Louis XIV. Vigarani's theatre at the Tuileries, the Salle des Machines (1659–62; destr.; *see* THEATRE, §III, 3(ii)(b)), designed with his sons Carlo Vigarani and Lodovico Vigarani, appears to have been a development of Giovanni Battista Aleotti's Teatro Farnese (1618–28), Parma, which prefigured the bell-shaped plan. Though criticized by Bernini for being too long and narrow, Vigarani's theatre had a circulation corridor around the hall that later became a standard feature of theatre design. His taste for ephemeral structures and his experience as a theatre designer are evident in his churches in Reggio Emilia and Modena. The group of three churches of SS Girolamo e Vitale (begun 1646), Reggio Emilio, contains a Holy Sepulchre in the crypt, above which is a *scala sancta* and a pantheon for the urns of eight martyrs. His skills as a stage designer are particularly apparent in the rotunda, with its whirl of twisted columns, statues in niches and precious incrustations. Even more theatrical is his design for S Giorgio (1649), Modena; this has a Greek-cross plan enriched by a complex play of free-standing columns framing numerous angular views that seem to anticipate the stage effects of Giuseppe Galli-Bibiena. His son Carlo Vigarani (1622–1713) subsequently became an important stage designer at the court of Louis XIV and worked on the theatre at Versailles.

UNPUBLISHED SOURCES

Modena, Bib. Estense [*Regole sicure, e geometriche per fare le fortezze, con un trattato della chiromanzia di me Gasparo Vigarani da Modona architetto, ed ingegnere*, MS. ?1646–8]

BIBLIOGRAPHY

G. Tiraboschi: *Biblioteca modenese*, 6 vols (Modena, 1781–6), i, p. 153; v, p. 388
A. G. Messori Roncaglia: *Documenti e notizie sulle opere di Gaspare Vigarani* (Modena, 1879)
G. Rouchès: *Inventaire des lettres et papiers manuscrits de Gaspare, Carlo e Lodovico Vigarani* (Paris, 1913)
B. Adorni: 'La chiesa come il teatro: Due architetture di Gaspare Vigarani', *Barocco romano e barocco italiano*, ed. M. Fagiolo and M. L. Madonna (Rome, 1985), pp. 234–50 [see also articles by C. Conforti and E. Garbero Zorzi]

BRUNO ADORNI

Vigarny [Viguerny; Biguerny; Bigarne; de Borgoña], **Felipe** (*b* diocese of Langres, *c.* 1475; *d* Toledo, 10 Nov 1542). Burgundian sculptor and architect, active in Spain. In July 1498 he arrived in Burgos, where he produced three panel reliefs in Briviesca stone (found in the quarries in Burgos) for the retrochoir of the cathedral, including the *Road to Calvary*. This project is often considered the first Renaissance work in Spain because of the obvious influence of Italian art of the Quattrocento in the grouping and rigidity of the figures. With Andrés de Nájera, a local sculptor, Vigarny was also engaged to make the choir-stalls for the cathedral and to undertake other minor architectural projects there. His reputation reached Toledo, where Cardinal Francisco Jiménez de Cisneros, of whom he later carved a beautiful alabaster medallion (*c.* 1518; Madrid, U. Complutense), secured him a position working under Enrique Egas and Pedro Gumiel on the main altarpiece of Toledo Cathedral. Under their direction, and in the company of the many other Spanish artists employed on the carving and gilding of the large larchwood altarpiece (1503–5), Vigarny's work absorbed the Spanish tendency towards realism and complex Gothic draperies, as can also be seen on his altarpieces for the chapel of Salamanca University (1503–5) and for the Capilla Mayor of Palencia Cathedral (1505). The Italian influence was again in evidence in other works.

Vigarny won further commissions throughout Castile, such as that for the altarpiece of S Anna, Cervera de Pisuerga (1513), and the porch of S Tomas, Haro (1516). In 1519 in Saragossa he formed a financial partnership with Alonso Berruguete, who had recently arrived from Italy, and carved the tomb of *Chancellor Selvagio* for the monastery of S Engracia in Saragossa (fragments, Saragossa, Mus. Zaragoza). This contact may have led him to Granada, where he made the altarpiece of the *SS John* (1519) in the Capilla Real.

Vigarny returned to Burgos in the early 1520s and with Diego de Siloé, recently returned from Italy, worked on the altarpiece for the chapel of the Condestables (1523–5) in Burgos Cathedral; he probably executed the figures of the High Priest and the expressive Prophetess Anne to the right of the central scene of the *Presentation in the Temple*. Here he also carved the tomb of the 1st Condestable, *Pedro Fernandez de Velasco*, and his wife, *Doña Mencia de Mendoza, Condesa de Haro* (Carrara marble and jasper, 1524–7). The recumbent effigies have strongly characterized features and minutely detailed draperies. In 1524 Vigarny was also working on the altarpiece (now in Cardeñuela de Riopico, Burgos, parish church) in the cathedral's chapel of the Presentación and on the tomb of *Gonzalo Diez de Lerma* there. The exquisite alabaster high relief of *St Ildefonsus Receiving the Chasuble from the Virgin* outside the Pilar Chapel in Toledo Cathedral also dates from this period (see fig.). At this time Vigarny may have worked on the tomb of the *3rd Condestable of Medina del Pomar*, the tomb of *Alonso de Burgos* (destr.) for the college of S Gregorio, Valladolid, and that of *Pedro Manso* (Oña, S Salvador).

In 1539 Vigarny and Berruguete were awarded a commission for choir-stalls for Toledo Cathedral. Vigarny made the 35 stalls on the right; with their wooden backs and finely worked alabaster canopy panels depicting figures in restful poses, they compare well with Berruguete's stalls on the left. Vigarny was probably also responsible for the design of the tomb of the *Bishop of Calahorra* (Madrid, Mus. Arqueol. N.), which was completed by his son, Gregorio Vigarny (?1513–55; usually known as Gregorio Pardo), with Esteban Jamete in 1539–40, for the tombs of the Avellaneda family in the ruined monastery of La

Felipe Vigarny: *St Ildefonsus Receiving the Chasuble from the Virgin*, alabaster relief, 1524–7 (Toledo Cathedral)

Espeja, near Valladolid, and for the choir-stalls and altarpiece of S Clemente el Real in Toledo.

BIBLIOGRAPHY

Ceán Bermúdez; Thieme–Becker

J. Agapito Revilla: 'El colegio de San Gregorio de Valladolid', *Museum* [Barcelona], i (1911), pp. 314–42

J. Dominguez Bordona: 'Felipe Vigarni: Resumen de los datos hasta a ora conocidos', *Bol. Soc. Esp. Excurs.*, xxii/4 (1914), pp. 269–74

E. Tormo: 'Algo más sobre Vigarni, primer escultor de renacimiento en Castilla', *Bol. Soc. Esp. Excurs.*, xxii/4 (1914), pp. 275–95

F. Perez Sedano and M. R. Zarco de Valle, eds: *Datos documentales ineditos para la historia del arte español*, 2 vols (Madrid, 1914–16)

M. Gómez Moreno: 'Felipe Bigarny y Alonso Berruguete', *Archv Esp. A. & Arqueol.*, i (1925), pp. 262–7

F. J. Sánchez Cantón: 'Los sepulcros de Espeja', *Archv Esp. A. & Arqueol.*, ix (1933), pp. 117–25

J. M. Azcárate: *Escultura del siglo XVI*, A. Hisp., xiii (Madrid, 1958)

I. Cadinanos: 'La iglesia de Valpuesta y su retablo obra de Felipe Vigarny', *Archv Esp. A.*, lii (1979), pp. 186–94

M. Estella: 'Los artistas realizadas en Santo Domingo el Real y otros monumentos madrileños del siglo XVI', *An. Inst. Estud. Madril.*, xvii (1980), pp. 11–21

I. Cadinanos: 'Felipe Vigarny, Alonso Berruguete y los sepulcros de los Condestables de Burgos', *Archv Esp. A.*, lvi (1983), pp. 341–54

M. J. Redondo Cantera: 'El sepulcro del IV Condestable de Castilla', *Bol. Semin. Estud. A. & Arqueol.*, (1984), pp. 261–71

Juan de Flandes (exh. cat. by I. Vandevivere, Madrid, Prado, 1986)

J. Superbiola Martinez: 'Felipe de Borgoña, autor del retablo mayor de la Capilla Real de Granada', *Bol. A. U. Málaga*, xiii–xiv (1992–3), pp. 391–4

M. A. Castillo Oreja: 'La selección del encargo: Felipe Vigarny en las empresas artísticas de Cisneros', *Homenaje al Profesor Antonio Bonet Correa*, ii (Madrid, 1994), pp. 789–805

MARGARITA ESTELLA

Vigas, Oswaldo (*b* Valencia, Carabobo, 4 Aug 1926). Venezuelan painter, potter and sculptor. He started painting around 1942. His work was initially abstract but it became figurative with surrealistic elements, as in *The Tetragramist* (1943) and *Composition* (1943–4; both artist's col.). He attended the Escuela de Artes Plásticas y Aplicadas in Caracas irregularly from 1948 to 1951. In 1949 he joined the Taller Libre de Arte, an avant-garde group, active between 1948 and 1952, that sought to explore Venezuelan historical and cultural roots. His interest in Pre-Columbian Venezuelan cultures influenced his subsequent work. From 1952 to 1964 he lived in Paris, where he studied at the Ecole des Beaux-Arts and frequented the studio of Marcel Joudon. Later Vigas produced both pottery and sculpture, in addition to paintings.

BIBLIOGRAPHY

G. Diehl: *Oswaldo Vigas* (Caracas, 1990)

ANA TAPIAS

Vigée Le Brun [Vigée-Le Brun; Vigée-Lebrun], **Elisabeth-Louise** [Louise-Elisabeth] (*b* Paris, 16 April 1755; *d* Paris, 30 March 1842). French painter. She earned an international reputation for her stylish portrayals of royalty and aristocratic society in France and throughout Europe during the period 1775–1825; before the outbreak of the French Revolution she was closely associated with Marie-Antoinette and the taste of the Ancien Régime. After 1789 she continued her highly lucrative career abroad, enjoying celebrity as one of the most successful portrait painters of her era. Her memoirs provide an intimate account of the life of a woman artist working in the orbit of the French court in the late 18th century.

1. France, 1755–89. 2. Europe and France, 1789–1842.

1. FRANCE, 1755–89. Elisabeth-Louise Vigée Le Brun was the daughter of Louis Vigée (1715–67), a pastellist who specialized in portraits. She studied with P. Davesne (*fl* 1764–96) and Gabriel Briard (1729–77), and by copying Old Masters. In addition, she received encouragement and advice from Joseph Vernet. By the age of 15 she had already developed a modest clientele for her portraits; on 25 October 1774 she became a member of the Académie de St Luc. On 11 January 1776 she married the art dealer Jean-Baptiste Le Brun; she exhibited her work at the Hôtel de Lubert, their house in Paris, and the salons that she held there provided her with important contacts.

The list that Vigée Le Brun kept of her paintings documents the increasingly high social status of her sitters. Her ceremonial portrait of *Charles-Henri-Othon, Prince of Nassau* (1776; Indianapolis, IN, Mus. A.) employed the traditional appointments, idealized interior setting and elegant stance that had been used by earlier 18th-century portrait painters such as Louis Tocqué to convey the sitter's nobility. In that same year she received her first royal commissions, portraits of one of the brothers of Louis XVI. A trip to the Netherlands and Flanders in 1781 deepened her admiration for Rubens, whose technical practices she began to emulate, switching from canvas supports to panel and experimenting with a warmer range of colours and the use of multiple, thin layers of transparent or translucent paint. Her *Self-portrait in a Straw Hat* (1782; priv. col.) was based directly on Rubens's portrait of *Susanna Fourment* ('*Le Chapeau de Paille*', *c.* 1622–5; London, N.G.). In this work Vigée Le Brun introduced a note of informality that she later used to advantage in portraying fashionable aristocratic demeanour, particularly of women. In such works as the *Duchesse de Polignac* (1783; Waddesdon Manor, Bucks, NT), who is portrayed standing at a piano, and the elegant portrait of two friends, the *Marquise de Pezay and the Marquise de Rougé with her Sons* (see fig. 1), she employed delicately animated poses, expressive faces and fashionable dress to convey the refinement and grace of Ancien Régime society. Through her smooth handling of the paint in areas of drapery she conveyed the substance of different materials without being excessively naturalistic. In contrast, details like lace edging or embroidery were carefully observed, yet loosely painted, adding visual interest to the work. The faces were finely modelled, with vitality imparted to the skin tones through a delicate layering of colour, especially in the shadows. Vigée Le Brun's contemporaries noted her characteristic preference for striking colour combinations; for example she would accent deep midnight blues in either clothing or background with vermilion or orange areas. In the 1780s she began to employ thin, openly brushed monochromatic backgrounds, similar to those seen in Jacques-Louis David's portraits from the 1790s, and this novel treatment heightened the vitality of the subjects' faces. Some of the exoticism of her female sitters derives from the original costumes and headdresses that she herself often designed or concocted (e.g. *Catherine, Countess Skavronsky*, 1790; Paris, Mus. Jacquemart-André). Vigée Le Brun's awareness of her female subjects' affectations, and her ability to flatter them, can be gauged

1. Elisabeth-Louise Vigée Le Brun: *Marquise de Pezay and the Marquise de Rougé with her Sons*, oil on canvas, 1.23×1.56 m, 1787 (Washington, DC, National Gallery of Art)

from the contrasting directness and intensity of her portraits of men, such as that of *Hubert Robert* (1788; Paris, Louvre) or of *Alexander Charles Emmanuel de Crussol-Florensac* (1787; New York, Met.).

In 1788 Vigée Le Brun was first granted favour and patronage by Marie-Antoinette. Until 1783 she exhibited her work—portraits, self-portraits and allegories of the arts—at the Académie de St Luc and the Salon de la Correspondence, the only venues then available to her. Vernet, whose portrait she painted in 1778 (Paris, Louvre), proposed her admission to the Académie Royale, but Jean-Baptiste Pierre, Premier Peintre du Roi, objected on the grounds that her husband was a dealer; and it was only through royal intervention that she was admitted to membership of the Académie on 31 May 1783, the same day as her rival Adélaïde Labille-Guiard. They filled the two remaining places of the four allotted to women. Vigée Le Brun's *morceau de réception*, *Peace Bringing Back Plenty* (1780; Paris, Louvre) was a history painting, demonstrating her ambition to be considered as one of the highest class of painter. She painted some 30 portraits of Marie-Antoinette, varying in attire and bearing. One of 1783 that portrayed the Queen 'en gaulle', in a simple gauzy dress (Darmstadt, Princess von Hessen & bei Rehin priv. col.)

was criticized as indecorous, and was replaced during the 1783 Salon by another portrait (untraced) that featured a more formal gown. In 1785 Vigée Le Brun received an official commission for a portrait of *Marie-Antoinette and her Children* (1787; Versailles, Château), which was intended to counter the increasing criticism of the Queen as frivolous and wayward; by depicting her surrounded by her affectionate children, Vigée Le Brun portrayed Marie-Antoinette as a devoted, virtuous mother and wife. The painting's overall pomp and splendour presented a dignified image of Marie-Antoinette as sovereign, in direct contrast to Adolf Ulric Wertmüller's vacuous image (1785 Salon; Stockholm, Nmus.) of the Queen strolling with her children in the gardens of Versailles. The politically sensitive nature of this image may be gauged from the artist's decision to withhold the painting from the opening days of the 1787 Salon. For such work she was paid considerably more than her contemporaries, even the history painters, and this ability to command extraordinary fees persisted throughout her career. Until 1791 she exhibited regularly at the annual Salon, and critics were generally complimentary; but because of her association with Marie-Antoinette, she became early in 1789 the victim of a slanderous press campaign. Distressed by these attacks on her private life and by the increasingly violent progress of the Revolution, in October 1789 she left France with Jeanne-Julie-Louise Le Brun (1780–1819), her only child, for what were to be 12 years of exile and travel.

2. EUROPE AND FRANCE, 1789–1842. Vigée Le Brun's first destination was Italy, where she stayed until 1793, moving in court circles in Turin, Rome, and particularly Naples, which was ruled by Ferdinand I (1751–1825), married to Marie-Antoinette's sister Caroline (1752–1814). There Vigée Le Brun painted portraits of many English tourists, such as *Frederick Augustus Hervey, 4th Earl of Bristol* (1790; Ickworth, Suffolk, NT). She also visited Florence and Venice. In Florence in 1790 she contributed to the celebrated grand-ducal collection of artists' self-portraits in the Uffizi a *Self-portrait* (*in situ*) that is a quintessential image of a painter at work at an easel, wearing an informal bonnet and holding a palette and a fistful of brushes; at the same time the artist signalled her femininity through the careful depiction of her elaborate ruffled lace collar and the colourful accent of her sash. When this portrait was exhibited in Rome in the same year, it was rapturously received, and earned Vigée Le Brun election to the Accademia di S Luca. In other self-portraits she addressed her role as a tender mother; thus in two portrayals of *Madame Vigée Le Brun and her Daughter* (1786 and 1789; both Paris, Louvre; see fig. 2)

2. Elisabeth-Louise Vigée Le Brun: *Madame Vigée Le Brun and her Daughter*, oil on canvas, 1.30×0.94 m, 1789 (Paris, Musée du Louvre)

she is seen embracing her little girl; in the latter version both are in Grecian dress.

There followed invitations to Vienna (1793–4) and then Prague, Dresden and Berlin. In each city Vigée Le Brun received numerous commissions from a noble clientele. From 1795 to 1801 she lived in St Petersburg except for a five-month stay in Moscow beginning in October 1800. Even though the Empress Catherine II found fault with her work, Vigée Le Brun prospered, painting for members of the imperial family and for the Russian nobility (e.g. *Catherine, Countess Skavronsky*, 1796; Paris, Louvre). In 1800 she became an honorary associate of the St Petersburg Academy. During that period she modernized her repertory to include portraits set in romantic landscape, suggesting the pleasure of solitude in natural settings, popularized by the writings of Jean-Jacques Rousseau; examples of such works are *Countess Potocka* (1791; Fort Worth, TX, Kimbell A. Mus.) and *Countess Bucquoi* (1793; Minneapolis, MN, Inst. A.). Although many of Vigée Le Brun's Russian works either repeated or were reminiscent of her earlier compositions—her oeuvre in general being complicated by a large number of copies, replicas and imitations—a number of the portraits displayed a new intensity and spareness very much in keeping with the Romantic era's emphasis on the individual. In these, solitary figures in relatively modest attire gaze directly at the viewer. Placed against subtly modulated plain backdrops, they convey intelligence or personality (e.g. *Countess Golovin*, 1797–1800; U. Birmingham, Barber Inst.).

After Vigée Le Brun's departure from France her name had been placed on the list of émigrés, whose citizenship was thereby revoked and property confiscated. Her husband tried to defend her, publishing in 1793 a pamphlet entitled *Précis historique de la vie de la Citoyenne Le Brun*, but he was forced to divorce her in 1794, on pain of forfeiting their possessions. In 1799 fellow artists circulated a petition, which was granted the following year, requesting that her name be removed from the list of émigrés. Once her citizenship had been restored, Vigée Le Brun returned to France, initially for a brief period preceded by a six-month stay in Berlin. She spent 1802 in France, working on paintings begun during her Russian period. Saddened by the post-revolutionary atmosphere, she then moved to London (1803–5), where her list of clients for portraits included the poet Lord Byron and the Prince of Wales (later George IV). In the summer of 1805 she returned to France for good, except for brief trips in 1807 and 1808 to Switzerland, where she visited Mme de Staël, whose portrait she painted (Geneva, Mus. A. & Hist.). After 1809 Vigée Le Brun divided her time between Paris and a country house in Louveciennes, and once more began to hold popular salons; her husband died in 1813 and her daughter in 1819. She continued to paint, though sporadically, sending works to the Salons of 1817 and 1824. In 1829 she produced a short manuscript autobiography for a friend, Princess Natalie Kourakin, and in 1834–5, with the aid of her nieces and friends, she expanded her recollections into *Souvenirs*.

WRITINGS

Souvenirs de Madame Louise-Elisabeth Vigée Le Brun, 3 vols (Paris, 1835–7); Eng. trans. as *Memoirs of Elisabeth Vigée-Le Brun* (Bloomington and London, 1989) [numerous other editions and translations]

BIBLIOGRAPHY

P. de Nolhac: *Madame Vigée-Le Brun: Peintre de la reine Marie-Antoinette, 1755–1842* (Paris, 1908)

A. Blum: *Madame Vigée-Lebrun: Peintre des grandes dames du XVIIIe siècle* (Paris, 1919)

L. Nikolenko: 'The Russian Portraits of Mme Vigée Le Brun', *Gaz. B.-A.*, n.s. 5, lxx (1967), pp. 91–120

J. Baillio: 'Le Dossier d'une oeuvre d'actualité politique: Marie-Antoinette et ses enfants par Mme Vigée Le Brun', *L'Oeil* (1981), no. 308, pp. 34–41, 74–5; no. 310, pp. 53–60, 90–91

——: *Elisabeth Louise Vigée Le Brun, 1755–1842* (exh. cat., Fort Worth, TX, Kimbell A. Mus., 1982) [includes an appendix with documents, among them excerpts from the scandalous press reports of 1789 as well as Jean-Baptiste Le Brun's pamphlet of 1793]

W. Chadwick: *Women, Art and Society* (New York, 1990)

KATHLEEN NICHOLSON

Vigeland, Gustav (Adolf) (*b* Mandal, 11 April 1869; *d* Oslo, 12 March 1943). Norwegian sculptor, printmaker and draughtsman. He was regarded in the late 20th century as the most gifted sculptor in Norway. He created *c.* 1600 sculptures, thousands of drawings and 420 woodcuts, and designs for artefacts. He was influenced by current stylistic tendencies and moved from Neo-classicism, naturalism and Impressionism towards more classical and monumental forms. Most of his work is housed in Oslo in the Nasjonalgalleri, the Vigeland-Museum and the Vigeland-Parken.

Vigeland's father, Elisus Thorsen, was a furniture-maker, and Vigeland grew up in a craftsman's milieu. With his evident talent for wood-carving, he was sent to Kristiania (now Oslo), where he was apprenticed to the wood-carver and sculptor Torsten Christensen Fladmoe (1831–86) from 1884 to 1886. At the same time he attended evening classes in draughtsmanship at the Kongelige Tegneskole. When his father died, he went home to help on the farm. At the age of 19 he returned to Kristiania where he had a difficult time, but he eventually received help and guidance from the sculptor Brynjulf Bergslien and attended evening classes in life drawing and modelling at the Kongelige Tegneskole. In autumn 1889 Vigeland made his début at the National Art Exhibition in Kristiania with a Neo-classical statuette, *Hagar and Ishmael* (Oslo, Vigeland-Mus.), a small group that demonstrates his early admiration for the Danish sculptor Bertel Thorvaldsen. In late 1889 he became pupil and assistant to the sculptor Mathias Skeibrok (1851–96) for one year. Vigeland's talent was soon recognized, and several stipends enabled him to travel. From 1891 he spent a year in Hermann Vilhelm Bissen's studio where he modelled his first lifesize group, *The Accursed* (also known as *Cain*; versions in Oslo, N.G. and Vigeland-Mus.): the main figure is an old, fleeing, guilt-ridden man, rendered with stark realism and energy of movement.

Vigeland stayed in Paris in 1893 and paid several visits to the studio of Auguste Rodin, whose unconventional depictions of human emotions and passions became influential. His first erotic groups in a hasty, impressionistic form date from this year. An echo of Rodin's *Gates of Hell* is evident in the large relief *Hell* (version, 1894, destr.; bronze version, 1897, Oslo, N.G.), although its static composition and severe form of the lean human figures clearly differ stylistically from Rodin. In 1895 and 1896 he travelled to Italy: besides the work of Donatello and Michelangelo, the Classical Greek sculpture and the simple

Gustav Vigeland: *Man Embracing Woman*, bronze, h. 1.29 m, 1905 (Oslo, Nasjonalgalleri)

severity of ancient Egyptian art also enraptured him. Lack of money forced him to take on commissions for sculptures in Gothic style for the restoration of Trondheim Cathedral (gargoyles and biblical figures, 1898–1902).

During the first decade of the 20th century Vigeland produced a large number of portrait busts of prominent Norwegian intellectuals and artists, such as the dramatist *Henrik Ibsen* (marble, 1903; Oslo, N.G.), showing his ability for psychological analysis. He also created several monuments, the earliest to the mathematician *Niels Henrik Abel* (bronze, h. 4 m, 1902–5), which was unveiled in 1908 on a ridge in the Slottspark in Oslo. Avoiding a conventional portrait statue, he made a symbolic group, a tribute to genius itself: an idealized young, naked man stands on the backs of two male figures, swooping downwards. Also unconventional is the statue of a naked *Beethoven* (bronze, 1906; Oslo, Vigelund-Mus.). Other monuments are more traditional, realistic figures, but imbued with personal expression and a distinctive mood. Also in this period he created several versions of *Man Embracing Woman* (smaller versions, 1894 and 1897, Oslo, N.G.; life-size version, 1905, Oslo, N.G.; see fig.).

After the turn of the century Vigeland continued to explore the theme of the relationship between man and woman in groups of natural size; *c.* 1910 he abandoned a detailed, naturalistic rendering in favour of a simpler, more unified form. This tendency culminated a few years later when he began to experiment with various kinds of stone and focused on mass and volume, evidently influenced by contemporary trends in European art. The time-consuming carving process, however, he left to professional artisans. Many of the works derived from earlier creations, revealing a continuity in spite of the apparent break with an earlier style.

Vigeland produced his first woodcuts in 1915, using his earlier wood-carving skills. The cut varies from broad, black contours to thin and elegant white lines. His earliest woodcuts include *Two Kneeling Angry Men Facing Each Other* (Hennum, p. 80), its rough style reflecting the influence of German Expressionism. In later years coastal landscapes predominated, and when he introduced animals and nude human figures into the harsh countryside, he seemed to depict a primordial world far removed from civilization.

In 1921 Vigeland entered into a unique contract with the Kommune of Kristiania, which agreed to give him a regular salary and to build a studio to be turned into a museum after his death. In return, all the works in his possession, as well as the original models of sculptures he would create in the future, would go to the city. Vigeland's major achievement was his sculpture park (Vigeland-Parken) in Oslo (for an illustration of a work in Vigeland-Parken *see* NORWAY, fig. 10), which developed gradually over a 40-year period. In 1924, after many years of debate, it was decided that the park should be laid out near his studio, centred on a large fountain, with a central group of six giants carrying a bowl of water. On the parapets stand 20 groups of 2-m high trees, combined with figures of all ages, the *Cycle of Life* (bronze, 1907–14), emphasizing the profound connection between man and nature. The principal theme is repeated in 60 reliefs around the basin wall.

In a series of 36 granite groups placed in rows on a circular stair (1913–36), Vigeland concentrated on fundamental human relationships but using totally different forms. Voluminous figures rest heavily on the plinths, conveying a sense of the primeval and showing the influence of contemporary predilection for primitive vitality. *The Monolith*, a granite column (h. 7 m) almost covered by colossal figures of all ages, is placed on top of the stairs; rising upwards, the figures break out from the earthbound life cycle of the granite groups below. A move towards more classical form is seen in 58 single figures and groups on the parapets of a bridge crossing the Frogner ponds, rhythmically displayed in static posture and dynamic movement. The motifs are once more man's different ages and essential relationships, such as parents and children, man and woman (bronze, 1926–33). The park, of around 80 acres, was designed in French formal style by Vigeland himself; he also designed the numerous wrought-iron gates in the park, which were executed in his own smithy (*see also* NORWAY, fig. 10).

Vigeland's younger brother Emanuel Vigeland (1875–1948) became a painter, mainly of frescoes and glass. Emanuel's son Per Vigeland (1904–68) studied at his father's academy of glass painting (1919–22) and also undertook church decorations.

NKL

BIBLIOGRAPHY

S. Przybyszewski: *Auf den Wegen der Seele* (Berlin, 1897)

J. Maier-Graefe: *Entwicklungsgeschichte der modernen Kunst*, iii (Stuttgart, 1904)
H. Maryon: *Modern Sculpture* (London, 1933)
H. P. Lødrup: *Gustav Vigeland* (Oslo, 1944)
A. Durban: *Gustav Vigeland* (Oslo, 1945)
A. Brenna and S. Tschudi-Madsen: *Vigelands fontenerelieffer: En kronologisk og stilanalytisk undersøkelse* [Vigeland's fountain reliefs: a chronological and stylistic investigation] (Oslo, 1953)
R. Stang: *Gustav Vigeland: The Sculptor and his Works* (Oslo, 1965)
N. Cabot Hale and D. Finn: *Embrace of Life: The Sculpture of Gustav Vigeland: The Cycle of Life, a Photographic Essay* (New York, 1968)
B. Wennberg: *French and Scandinavian Sculpture in the Nineteenth Century* (Stockholm, 1978)
M. Lange and N. Messel: *Nasjonal vekst* [National growth] (1981), v of *Norges kunsthistorie*, ed. K. Berg and others (Oslo, 1981–3)
K. Nakao: *Gustav Vigeland* (Tokyo, 1982)
T. Wikborg: *Gustav Vigeland: Mennesket og kunstneren* [Gustav Vigeland: the man and the artist] (Oslo, 1983)
R. Ginsberg: *Gustav Vigeland: A Case Study in Art and Culture* (University Park, PA, 1984)
G. Hennum: *Gustav Vigeland i svart og hvitt* [Gustav Vigeland in black and white] (Kristiansand, 1985)
T. Wikborg: *Gustav Vigeland: His Art and Sculpture Park* (Oslo, 1990)

INGEBORG WIKBORG

Vigh, Tamás (*b* Csillaghegy, 28 Feb 1926). Hungarian sculptor and medallist. He studied (1946–51) under Béni Ferenczy at the Fine Arts College (Képzőművészeti Főiskola) in Budapest. His early works reveal Ferenczy's influence but in later works he also remained faithful to the principles of his teacher. In the mid-1950s Vigh developed his own unique style. His brooding sculpture was indebted to, and drew upon, European sculpture; it was concerned with the essence of things and followed a logical and organic path. His familiarity with the properties of rolled sheet metals—copper, aluminium etc—played a decisive role in his development, as he explored ways of working these metals into moulded sculptures and medallions. The first work in this new style was his memorial plaque (*in situ*) to the writer *Gyula Krúdy* (lead, 1958) on the corner of Krúdy Gyula Street and József Boulevard in Budapest. The sculpture, besides depicting the writer and the atmosphere of his work, can be read as a visually stimulating play of forms and planes and a balance of tensions in an assured design. It also embodies the most typical characteristics to be found in Vigh's larger, later works: great simplicity and a synthetic design pared down to its barest essentials. The sheet metals express a carefully thought-out idea by being moulded in such a way as to avoid breaking up the planes. Although Vigh consciously avoids intimacy and the expression of emotion, his monumental works are full of human content. Some of his more exceptional works are *Sower* (stone, 2.4×4.4 m, 1964; Debrecen, Agric. Coll.), *Horn-players* (copper sheet metal relief, 7 m, 1964–7; Budapest, Post Office Engin. Inst.), *People of the Alföld* (bronze, 1967; Budapest, N.G.) and *Town Founder* (bronze and stone, 7 m, 1980; Esztergom, Castle Gate). His memorial to *Attila József* (bronze, 1991; Pécs, Union Lib.) is an unusual composition in which he successfully expressed both the ambiguous fate of the 20th-century poet, and the attitudes of 20th-century man. He also executed a number of portrait busts: for example copies of the bust of the poet *Sándor Petőfi* (bronze, 1970; Budapest, Margaret Island) were erected in Bolivia (*c.* 1973; La Paz, Petofi Square) and the German Democratic Republic (1976; Weimar, Goethepark). Vigh is also credited with reviving medallion art in Hungary; an example of his work in this genre is a medal (bronze, 1961; Budapest, Hung. N. Acad. Sci.) for the Hungarian National Academy of Sciences (Magyar Tudományos Akadémia).

BIBLIOGRAPHY

G. Rózsa: *Négy portré: A Munkácsy-díj nemzedéke* [Four portraits: the Munkácsy Prize generation] (Budapest, 1977), pp. 77–90

Vigh Tamás (exh. cat. by L. Németh, Tihany, Mus., 1977)

Vigh Tamás (exh. cat. by L. Vekerdi, Budapest, A. Hall, 1982)

L. Vekerdi: *Vigh Tamás* (Budapest, 1983) [first complete study of his work]

I. Rozgonyi: *Párbeszéd a müvekkel: Interjuk, 1955–1981* [Dialogue with art: interviews, 1955–81], Hungarian Academy of Sciences Art Historical Research Group (Budapest, 1988), pp. 278–84

S. KONTHA

Vignali, Jacopo (*b* Pratovecchio, 5 Sept 1592; *d* Florence, 3 Aug 1664). Italian painter. At an early age he entered the studio of Matteo Rosselli in Florence, and his first works, *Virgin and Saints* (1616; Florence, S Brigida, Santuario della Madonna del Sasso) and the ceiling painting *Love of the Fatherland* (1616; Florence, Casa Buonarroti), were influenced by Rosselli and Ludovico Cigoli. In 1616 he enrolled at the Accademia del Disegno in Florence, becoming an academician in 1622. In the 1620s he moved away from Rosselli's influence and developed a style distinguished by dramatic light effects, rich colour and painterly technique and by the expression of deep emotion. The decade opened with the *Investiture of St Benedict* (1620; Florence, Semin. Maggiore), one of a series of works painted in honour of St Benedict for the Confraternità di S Benedetto Bianco, to which Vignali had belonged since 1614. Having learnt the technique of fresco painting from Rosselli, he also began to work in that medium and was involved in the decoration of the Casa Buonarroti through-

Jacopo Vignali: *St Cecilia*, oil on canvas, 1.40×1.45 m, early 1620s (Dublin, National Gallery of Ireland)

out the decade, the ceiling fresco *Jacob's Dream* dating from 1621. In 1622–3 he also contributed to important fresco cycles for the Medici at the Casino Mediceo di San Marco in Florence, and at the Villa del Poggio Imperiale just outside the city.

Of Vignali's easel paintings of the 1620s, *St Cecilia* (early 1620s; Dublin, N.G.; see fig.) reveals the influence of Orazio Gentileschi, while the figures in the lyrical genre scene *May Day Offering* (Rome, Pal. Corsini) are indebted to the elegant groups found in the work of Jacques Callot and Filippo Napoletano. Vignali's interest in dramatic light effects culminated in *Christ Showing his Wounds to St Bernard* (1623; Florence, SS Simone e Giuda) and *St Peter Caring for St Agatha* (Florence, Depositi Gal.), both close to the art of Rutilio Manetti. In *Cyparissus* (priv. col., see 1986 exh. cat., i, p. 251), an intensely poetic treatment of a rare theme from Ovid, Vignali approached the style of Guercino. After visiting Rome in 1625, in the late 1620s he became influenced by the austere art of Domenico Passignano and Francesco Curradi, as shown by the deeply emotional *Agony in the Garden* (1626; Castellina, S Lucia). This was followed by the more richly coloured *Circumcision* (1627; San Casciano, Chiesa della Misericordia) and the altarpiece, the *Mystical Communion of the Blessed Clara* (1629; Florence, S Spirito), inspired by Giovanni Lanfranco's treatment of saintly ecstasy.

The early 1630s were a particularly productive period for Vignali, and several works, such as the *Virgin and Saints* (1631; Badia di Ripoli, Abbazia), may be associated with the plagues of 1630–33. In 1632 he decorated the Bonsi Chapel in SS Michele e Gaetano, Florence, where he painted the ceiling frescoes, two lunettes with the *Martyrdom of St Lucretia* and the *Domine quo vadis?*, and a lateral canvas of the *Vision of Constantine*. In 1636 Cardinal Carlo de' Medici commissioned a cabinet painting on a chivalrous theme, *Ruggiero Found by Leone and Melissa* (Florence, Pitti), and in the early 1640s the Arazzeria Medicea commissioned cartoons (untraced) for the four tapestries (Florence, Pal. Medici–Riccardi) of the *Seasons*. The new monumentality of the latter works is also evident in two lateral canvases, *St Mary Magdalene* and *St Margaret* (Florence, SS Annunziata, Accolti Chapel), and in the *Liberation of Souls from Purgatory* (1642; Florence, SS Michele e Gaetano), where the painterly freedom of Guercino is united with the soft *sfumato* and blue background of Francesco Furini. A similar monumentality also characterizes paintings of this period for private patrons, such as *David and Abigail* (Camigliano, Villa Torrigiani Colonna).

Later in the 1640s an increasingly dark and meditative tone distinguishes Vignali's works, as in the *Death of St Anthony Abbot* (Montughi, rectory of S Martino). His mature masterpiece is the *Martyrdom of St Lucy* (1649; Florence, SS Annunziata), which reveals the influence of Salvator Rosa and Felice Ficherelli. Towards the end of his life his work declined, although the late *Virgin with SS Anthony of Padua and St Liborius* (Florence, S Jacopo Sopr'Arno) retains distinction. His most famous pupil was Carlo Dolci, who was deeply affected by the intense religiosity of such works as the *Agony in the Garden*.

BIBLIOGRAPHY

S. B. Bartolozzi: *Vita di Jacopo Vignali, pittor fiorentino* (Florence, 1753)

C. Del Bravo: 'Per Jacopo Vignali', *Paragone*, cxxxv (1961), pp. 28–42

Jacopo Vignali, 1592–1664 (exh. cat. by C. Del Bravo, Florence, Uffizi, 1964)

G. Ewald: 'Opere sconosciute di Jacopo Vignali', *Ant. Viva*, iii/7–8 (1964), pp. 7–27

F. Mastropierro: *Jacopo Vignali, pittore nella Firenze del seicento* (Milan, 1973)

P. Bigongiari: 'Jacopo Vignali e la poetica degli affetti', *Il caso e il caos, I: Il seicento fiorentino tra Galileo e il 'recitar cantando'* (Milan, 1974/*R* Florence, 1982), pp. 77–82

G. Cantelli: *Repertorio della pittura fiorentina del seicento* (Fiesole, 1983), pp. 141–4

Il seicento fiorentino: Arte a Firenze da Ferdinando I a Cosimo III, 3 vols (exh. cat., ed. G. Guidi and others; Florence, Pal. Strozzi, 1986–7)

GIOVANNI PAGLIARULO

Vignay, Jean. *See under* MASTERS, ANONYMOUS, AND MONOGRAMMISTS, §III: MASTER I♡V.

Vigne, Antoine de la. *See* WYNGAERDE, ANTHONIS VAN DEN.

Vigne, de. *See* DE VIGNE.

Vignelli. Italian designers, active in the USA. Massimo Vignelli (*b* Milan, 10 Jan 1931) attended the Accademia di Belle Arti di Brera, Milan (1948–50), the Politecnico, Milan (1950–53), and the School of Architecture, University of Venice (1953–7). He chiefly worked on product and graphic design and corporate identity programmes. In the mid-1950s, while still a student, he designed a series of lighting fixtures for the Venini S.p.A. of Murano, most notably the 'Fungo' table lamp (1955; e.g. New York, Cooper-Hewitt Mus.), an original concept in striped glass in which the swelling lampshade and conical base form an integrated unit.

Between 1957 and 1960 he travelled and studied in the USA. In 1957 he married Lella [Elena] Vignelli [née Valle] (*b* Udine, Friuli-Venezia Giulia, 1936). She studied at the School of Architecture, Massachusetts Institute of Technology, Cambridge (1955–8), and worked as a junior designer (1959–60) for Skidmore, Owings & Merrill before returning to Italy and graduating in architecture at the University of Venice (1962). She specialized in interiors, furniture, exhibition display and office and household objects. At a time when small, energetic design studios were being set up in major manufacturing centres around Italy, they established the Lella and Massimo Vignelli Office of Design and Architecture, Milan (1960–64), designing office accessories, domestic products, furniture and graphics (e.g. poster for the 32nd Venice Biennale by Massimo Vignelli, 1964; New York, MOMA).

In 1965 they moved to Chicago where they founded Unimark International (1965–71), specializing in corporate graphics. Massimo Vignelli's novel use of the Helvetica typeface encouraged its widespread use in the USA. They worked with geometric forms: cubes, pyramids, cylinders and spheres. Their product design was balanced and functional, as exemplified in their line of stacking dinnerware (1964–7) for Heller Designs Inc., New York, made from moulded melamine in a range of brilliant colours (e.g. New York, MOMA). They believed that a designer should be able to produce anything 'from a spoon to the city' and executed wide-ranging design programmes, from environmental planning to tableware and packaging, displaying an unusual versatility in a period of specialization. They became known for dynamic corporate and advertising graphics that made frequent use of oversized single letters or words. In the 1960s and early 1970s they designed the corporate identity programmes for American Airlines, Knoll International and the Lancia and Ford Motor companies, as well as logos, signs and packaging for such New York department stores as Bloomingdales, Barney's and Saks Fifth Avenue.

In 1971 they established a larger operation, Vignelli Associates (from 1978 Vignelli Designs) in New York, fulfilling their initial aim of bringing contemporary Italian design and technology to the USA. Their product and furniture designs reveal a refined, almost Minimalist taste (e.g. bar set, sterling silver, made by San Lorenzo S.p.A., Milan, c. 1971; Philadelphia, PA, Mus. A.). In furniture design they favoured the use of wood, leather, plastics, marble, stone and glass, for example in the 'Metafore' (1979) and 'Tara' (1980) lines of tables (e.g. 'Metafore I' coffee-table, glass and stone, made by Casigliani, Italy, 1979; Munich, Bayer. NMus. Neue Samml.) and the 'Handkerchief Chair' (1982–7; Munich, Bayer. NMus. Neue Samml.) for Knoll International, New York, a shell-moulded, reinforced-plastic stacking chair on thin metal legs. Their award-winning designs were exhibited internationally, and in 1981 the Parsons School of Design, New York, devoted an exhibition to their work.

During the 1980s the Vignellis brought their rigorous high-styling to a series of outstanding, Post-modern interiors for showrooms, offices and art galleries. Their penthouse offices (1985) on 10th Avenue, Manhattan, featured walls and doors covered with hand-waxed squares of lead sheet, room dividers of corrugated steel and furniture of sand-blasted glass and industrial steel tubing finished in gold leaf. They redesigned many magazine formats and commercial and institutional sign systems in the USA and Europe, including signs for the New York subway and the Washington, DC, Metro.

BIBLIOGRAPHY

R. Poynor: 'Mission America', *Designers' J.*, 33 (Jan 1988), pp. 46–50 [profile of Vignellis]

G. Celant and others: *Design: Vignelli* (New York, 1990)

☐

Vignerod Du Plessis, Louis-François Armand de. *See* RICHELIEU, (2).

Vignette [Fr.: 'small vine']. Ornamental or pictorial illustration on the title-page (title-vignette) or at the beginning or end of chapters or other divisions of a book (head- or tail-piece), reproduced in any of the standard printing techniques. The term, originally used to describe a design of vine-leaves and tendrils, has also been used to refer to an illustration not enclosed in a border or squared off at the edges but shading away.

The origins of the vignette are obscure, but it is thought to have developed from manuscript decoration marking textual divisions. The earliest examples are from the 15th century: either printers' devices placed on the title-page or incorporated on the colophon leaf at the end of the

Vignette of *Thomas Bewick*, 80×62 mm, after a painting by William Nicholson; from Thomas Bewick and John Bewick: *Select Fables* (Newcastle upon Tyne, 1820)

book or symmetrical arrangements of typographic ornaments used to fill unwanted white space. In the 17th century there was increasing sophistication in the use of vignettes, with artists beginning to borrow from the symbolism of emblem books and providing decoration that occasionally even reflected the contents of a book.

The use of the vignette as decoration and illustration reached its apogee in the 18th century, notably in Italy and France. In Venice, which was the largest publishing centre in Italy, such publishers as Giambattista Albrizzi (*fl* 1745–60), Giambattista Pasquali (*fl* 1740) and Antonio Zatta (*fl* 1757–69) commissioned painters (Giambattista Tiepolo, Giovanni Battista Piazzetta, Antonio Visentini and Francesco Bartolozzi, among others) to produce work often executed as charming vignettes by a school of engravers, the most important of whom were Marco Alvise Pitteri, Giovanni Cattini, Francesco Zucchi (1692–1764), Cristoforo dall'Aqua (1734–87) and Antonio Baratti. Their masterpieces are probably Piazzetta's editions of the works of Torquato Tasso and Jacques Bénigne Bossuet (1627–1704), published (1745; 1736–58) by Albrizzi.

A wealth of illustrated texts was produced in France during the Rococo period, and at least three masterpieces feature the vignette as an extremely important element in the book. The first, an edition of Boccaccio's *Decameron* (Paris, 1757), was engraved under the direction of Gravelot from designs by him, François Boucher, Charles-Nicolas

Cochin (ii) and Charles Eisen. The second, *Contes et nouvelles en vers* (the 'Fermiers generaux' edition; Paris, 1762) by Jean de la Fontaine (1621–95) includes 57 fine vignettes by Pierre-Phillipe Choffard. The third, *Fables ou allegories philosophiques* (Paris, 1773) by Claude Joseph Donat (1734–80), contains 199 vignettes from Clement-Pierre Marillier's designs.

In the late 18th century and early 19th, Thomas Bewick (the Newcastle-based pioneer of wood-engraving) and his brother John Bewick (1760–95) produced some fine vignettes: some are straightforward illustrations (e.g. *History of British Birds and . . . Quadrupeds*; Newcastle upon Tyne, 1797–1804), while others are of a more emblematic nature (e.g. *Select Fables*; Newcastle upon Tyne, 1820; see fig.).

The gift books of the 1830s to 1860s continued this tradition, but with notable exceptions such as the *Poems* (London, 1857) of Alfred, Lord Tennyson, published by Edward Moxon (1801–58), and the best of Myles Birket Foster's work, the spontaneity of much of the earlier work was replaced by a degree of banality that reflected the increasing move towards the relegation of the engraver from artist to artisan. In the 20th century there was a revival of interest in the use of the vignette by some artist–illustrators in France and Germany, and Rex Whistler in Britain produced some whimsical reminders of the best 18th-century French work.

BIBLIOGRAPHY
H. Cohen: *Guide de l'amateur de livres à gravures du XVIIIe siècle* (Paris, 1870, rev. as 2 vols, Paris, 6/1912)
——: *Guide de l'amateur de livres à vignette du XVIIIe siècle* (Paris, 1870)
D. C. Thomson: *The Life and Works of Thomas Bewick* (London, 1882)
H. M. Cundall: *Birket Foster* (London, 1906)
G. Morazzoni: *Il libro illustrato veneziano del settecento* (Milan, 1943)
M. Lanckoronska: *Die venezianische Buchgraphik des XVIII. Jahrhunderts* (Hamburg, 1950)
L. Whistler and R. Fuller: *The Work of Rex Whistler* (London, 1960)

ADAM LANGLANDS

Vignola, Jacopo [Giacomo] **(Barozzi da)** (*b* Vignola, 1 Oct 1507; *d* Rome, 7 July 1573). Italian painter, architect and theorist. Following three decades of diversified and mainly collaborative artistic activity, he emerged in the 1550s as the leading architect in Rome after Michelangelo and was in papal service for over three decades. His masterpieces (notably the Villa Farnese at Caprarola and the church of Il Gesù in Rome) were produced as house architect to the wealthy and powerful Farnese family. In an era of experimental and sometimes dramatically personal styles, his palaces, villas and churches manifested a cool and methodically reductive classicism that became a model of orthodoxy for a generation of architects during the Counter-Reformation. His *Regola delli cinque ordini d'architettura* (1562), a concise illustrated tract on the five orders (see fig. 1), enjoyed immense popular and academic success throughout Europe and was the most influential book on classical architecture until the advent of Modernism.

1. Life and work. 2. The treatises.

1. LIFE AND WORK.

(i) Early work, before 1543. (ii) Bologna, 1543–*c*. 1549. (iii) Late work, after *c*. 1549.

(i) Early work, before 1543. Vignola was born to a family of artisans: although the occupation of his father Bartolomeo is unknown, one brother, Guarnerio (*b c*. 1510; *d* before 1 Sept 1564), was a painter while another, Giovanni Angelo (*fl c*. 1550–?1570) was, apparently, a stone-carver. According to his earliest biographers Giorgio Vasari and Ignazio Danti, Jacopo was sent as a youth to Bologna, where he was apprenticed to an unnamed painter. Poorly taught, he was unable to win much success in painting and so turned to the study of architecture and perspective. This change of direction may have been encouraged by the example of the painter–architects Baldassare Peruzzi and Sebastiano Serlio, both of whom were in Bologna during the early 1520s and profoundly affected Vignola's architectural thought. Indeed, he seems to have worked for Peruzzi, for his name appears on a list of assistants on the back of an undated drawing by the older master (Florence, Uffizi, MS. A., fol. 104*v*). It is possible that Vignola executed architectural designs at this time (the dovecote of the Villa Isolani at Minerbio, nr Bologna, 1536, may be his work), but the only sure evidence of his activity comes from the pictorial arts. For Francesco Guicciardini, Papal Governor of Bologna (1482–1540), he produced perspectival compositions, which Fra Damiano Zambelli da Bergamo (1480–1549) translated into coloured wood intarsia panels, such as the *Finding of Moses*

1. Jacopo Vignola: Doric capital and entablature from the Theatre of Marcellus (13 or 11 BC), Rome; from his treatise *Regola delli cinque ordini d'architettura* (Rome, 1562), pl. XIII

(1534; New York, Met.). Vignola was married c. 1530. He had three sons, Bartolomeo Barozzi (b Bologna, 1532), Giacinto Barozzi (b ?Bologna, c. 1534; d after 1 July 1584), who became an architect and theorist, and assisted his father in numerous projects, and Luigi Barozzi (b Bologna, 1535).

In the late 1530s Vignola moved to Rome, where he supported his family as a painter and draughtsman in a series of collaborative enterprises that brought him significant architectural experience. In November 1538 he is recorded in the Vatican as a painter of furniture and banners in association with the Ferrarese architect Jacopo Melighino, who was a favourite of Paul III. Melighino worked with Antonio da Sangallo the younger at St Peter's and elsewhere, and Vasari states that Vignola assisted him as a designer. In February 1541 he collaborated with Perino del Vaga on the construction and decoration of theatre sets for a performance of Niccolò Machiavelli's *Clizia* at the Palazzo Farnese. About this time Vignola became involved with the Accademia della Virtù, a private society of intellectuals led by Claudio Tolomei, which planned to publish a definitive annotated and illustrated edition of Vitruvius. The Accademia, Vasari reported, employed Vignola 'to measure thoroughly all of the antiquities of Rome'. Although this ambitious project never came to fruition, its impact on the artist was substantial for not only did it engage him in a systematic study of ancient architectural remains and expose him to a thoroughly up-to-date critical reading of Vitruvius, it also introduced him to a circle of influential patrons. At the age of 33 the provincial painter was qualified to receive major architectural assignments and in March 1541 Paul III appointed him architect of the basilica of S Petronio in Bologna.

Before taking up this post, however, Vignola fulfilled obligations that he had undertaken with Francesco Primaticcio for Francis I, King of France. In 1540 Primaticcio was commissioned to produce bronze copies of famous antique Roman statues to decorate the fountains and gardens of the royal château of Fontainebleau. He engaged Vignola to supervise the making of plaster moulds of ten works in the papal collection of the Belvedere. In the summer of 1541 Vignola travelled to France where, receiving a monthly stipend of 20 livres, he helped to direct the casting operation until its completion in 1543. Only five of the bronzes survive—the *Apollo Belvedere*, *Ariadne*, *Knidian Venus*, *Commodus as Hercules* and the *Laokoon* (Fontainebleau, Château). The royal account books refer to Vignola as a painter and Danti stated that he furnished Primaticcio with perspective designs for pictorial decorations at Fontainebleau, although no convincing attributions have been made. Similarly, Vasari claimed that Vignola was taken to France to assist with architectural projects, but his achievements there remain a matter of conjecture.

(ii) Bologna, 1543–c. 1549. In September 1543 Vignola presented himself to the Fabbricieri (Board of Trustees) of S Petronio in Bologna and became architect of the civic basilica (*see* BOLOGNA, §IV, 2). He shared the position with Jacopo Ranuzzi (d 1549), an undistinguished local architect who had political backing: from the outset there

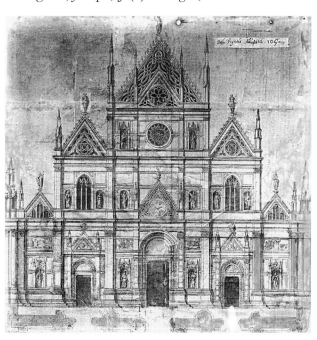

2. Jacopo Vignola: proposed design for the façade of S Petronio, Bologna, pen and ink, 1544 (Bologna, Museo di San Petronio)

were bitter hostilities between the two men. The principal task at this time was to decorate the façade in stylistic harmony with the Gothic church. On 17 December 1543 Vignola submitted a lengthy critique of earlier designs, including Ranuzzi's, and the following year he drafted his own proposal, of which two variations are known (Bologna, Mus. S Petronio). His project (see fig. 2) insists on the Classical orders as an indispensable element of architectural composition. The façade is treated as a flat plane articulated by a grid of Corinthian pilasters and entablatures corresponding to the widths and heights of the interior chapels, aisles and nave. Overtly Gothic elements, such as pointed arch windows, gables with tracery and pinnacles, are rigorously subordinated to Vitruvian logic. He presented his façade drawings to Paul III during one of several visits to Rome in 1545 and, according to Danti, they received a written commendation from Giulio Romano. Nevertheless, his project was not endorsed by the Fabbricieri and Ranuzzi's criticism compelled Vignola to compose a detailed defence on 1 February 1547. Within days Alessandro Manzuoli, an associate of the now defunct Accademia della Virtù in Rome, recommended Vignola's talents in a letter (Parma, Archv Stato) to Pier Luigi Farnese, 1st Duke of Parma and Piacenza, with the lament that 'such a fine mind may be lost if not kept continuously exercised'.

Frustrated at S Petronio, Vignola took on a variety of private and public commissions in Bologna during the late 1540s. The eccentric Palazzo Bocchi, begun in 1545 but altered within a decade and never finished, is ascribed to him by Danti with the observation that he was 'following the disposition [*l'humore*] of the patron'. The philosopher and humanist Achille Bocchi (1488–1562) intended the building as the practical and emblematic home of a private academy. For the façade (the initial design of which is recorded in an engraving, 1545; priv. col., see Schmidt, p. 84), Bocchi produced a sculptural programme as well as the unusual selection of inscriptions in Hebrew (Psalm 120:2) and Latin (Horace: *Epistles* I:i). He undoubtedly encouraged the slightly incongruous mixture of architectural motifs derived from Sangallo, Serlio and Giulio Romano. In 1547 Vignola built an innovative columnar portal in the courtyard of the Palazzo Comunale and a bridge (destr.) over the River Samoggia on the Via Emilia. The bridge, known from a drawing submitted to the municipal authorities (Bologna, Archv Stato), had piers pierced by round openings, like that of the Ponte Sisto in Rome, and three arches shaped inventively as half-ovals. On 5 May 1548 he signed a contract for the rehabilitation of the Canale Navile, the navigable waterway connecting Bologna with the River Po. This important and successful piece of civil engineering entailed the excavation of c. 6 km of channel between Bologna and the village of Corticella; he constructed three locks, one of which was elliptical, and laid out the urban port.

Vignola was awarded Bolognese citizenship on 1 February 1549 but soon he had little reason to remain in the city. In July the Fabbricieri began to pressure him to relinquish his post at S Petronio and in November the death of Paul III deprived him of papal support. Vasari claimed, moreover, that Vignola was very poorly rewarded for his work on the Canale Navile. It is little wonder that around this time he welcomed the patronage of Cardinal Marcello Cervini (later Pope Marcellus II; *reg* 1555),

another former member of the Accademia della Virtù, for whom he produced a set of working drawings (Berlin, Kstbib.) for a fortified villa (not executed) featuring a circular courtyard. Towards the end of 1549 or in early 1550 Vignola left Bologna for Rome.

(iii) Late work, after c. *1549.*

(a) Papal commissions. (b) Farnese family commissions.

(a) Papal commissions. Vignola settled permanently in Rome and soon entered papal service. His first major work was the Villa Giulia (Villa di Papa Giulio; 1551–5) or, more precisely, its casino (see fig. 3). Located above the Via Flaminia just outside the Porta del Popolo, the villa suburbana consists of a small U-shaped palace, the casino, to which is attached a rectangular walled garden court terminating in a loggia and a sunken neo-antique nymphaeum. The complex was built for Julius III and apparently conceived by Vasari in consultation with Michelangelo in the winter of 1550; Vignola is recorded at work there from February 1551 until March 1555. From a lost master-plan attributable to him it is known that two arcaded wings were to have extended laterally from the casino and the garden court was to have been lozenge-shaped. These remarkable features were discarded soon after construction began and in 1552 Bartolomeo Ammanati was commissioned to redesign much of the court and nymphaeum. Apart from assisting in hydraulic work for the fountains, Vignola was concerned only with the construction and decoration of the casino. The building's

3. Jacopo Vignola: façade of the Villa Giulia, Rome, 1551–5

two-storey façade was innovative for its rational integration of all parts into an expressive unit. Divided vertically into thirds by pilasters—rusticated Tuscan below, Composite above—the façade is dominated physically and symbolically by the centre, where the arched entrance portal is framed by engaged columns and by niches in a variation of the triumphal arch motif. This motif is repeated on the *piano nobile* by a central balcony, suitable for papal appearances, flanked by niche-windows. The entrance leads to an elegant Corinthian room that gives on to the barrel-vaulted, semicircular arcade embracing the garden court. The court façade is dominated by pilasters, with the Composite order carried over from the front on the *piano nobile*, and the Ionic order on the ground floor in triumphal arches derived from Bramante's upper Belvedere court in the Vatican. Two colonnades in a minor order with flat entablatures inserted between the triumphal arch units subtend long rectangular fields for painted decoration.

The little church of S Andrea (1551–3) on the Via Flaminia was also commissioned by Julius III. Free from collaborative constraints, in S Andrea Vignola realized a work with powerful theoretical implications. In terms of scale and function it is little more than a wayside chapel for pilgrims, but like Brunelleschi's Pazzi Chapel, Florence (from 1442), or Bramante's Tempietto (Rome, ?1502), S Andrea addressed the practical and intellectual concerns of an epoch. The church is rectangular in plan with a projecting altar room opposite the entrance. The interior walls are subdivided by Corinthian pilasters, above which rise warped pendentives carrying an oval cornice and dome. By effectively uniting an oblong space focused on the altar with a dome that extends over the entire nave, Vignola succeeded in reconciling the traditional liturgical demand for axiality with the humanistic ideal of centrality. S Andrea was the first church to employ an oval dome, a feature that won great favour in the 17th century. The façade, which ingeniously recalls the Pantheon in Rome, has Corinthian pilasters, disposed outwardly in diminishing intervals in order to accentuate the centre, carrying a pediment set into a flat wall of brick before an oval drum capped by a stepped dome.

As papal architect Vignola received commissions for diverse projects in Rome and the Papal States. In 1552 he directed construction inside the Vatican Palace. He provided plans for the Castellina, Norcia (1554–64), a diminutive but finely executed square fortress with angle bastions. It was probably for Julius III that Vignola developed a highly original project (not executed) for the church of S Giovanni dei Fiorentini in Rome. Known only from drawings by other artists, it centred on an oval nave ringed by a continuous aisle with shallow radiating chapels. Fronted on the street by a porch, the exterior had Doric half columns, an attic with 12 obelisks and buttresses surrounding a high fenestrated drum, and a ribbed oval cupola crowned by an ornate, windowless lantern. Considered within the long planning history of this building, involving Jacopo Sansovino, Antonio da Sangallo, Baldassare Peruzzi and Michelangelo, Vignola's plans represent a unique synthetic response to the problem of longitudinal versus centralized designs.

After the death of Julius III in 1555, Vignola worked in Perugia, where he designed a chapel (destr.) for the church of S Francesco and advised on Vincenzo Danti's bronze portrait statue of *Julius III* (1555; Perugia Cathedral). Ignazio Danti credits Vignola with buildings for Marchese Ascanio della Corgna in the Umbrian towns of Castiglione del Lago and Città della Pieve. The pontificate of Marcellus II was too brief to occasion building commissions, but Vignola's creative energies were exploited extensively by Pius IV. On the death of Michelangelo, Pius IV appointed Vignola as fellow architect of St Peter's with Pirro Ligorio, whose early departure left Vignola in charge from 1567. His attention was focused on the execution of Michelangelo's plans and virtually none of the present basilica was actually conceived by him (*see* ROME, §V, 14(ii)(a)).

During the 1560s Vignola was prolific as a church designer in Latium and Rome. Just outside Capránica di Sutri he built the church of S Maria del Piano (1559–65) with a simple box-like exterior and a pedimented Ionic façade. Until its partial collapse and reconstruction in the 17th century, the nave was oblong, with a cube of space covered by a cupola at the centre and exedrae at either end. He also planned the small parish churches of Mazzano Romano (*c.* 1567; destr. after World War II) and S Lorenzo, Sant'Oreste al Soratte (1568), which has an aisleless vaulted Doric nave with side chapels. For the collegiate church at Fara in Sabina he produced the elegant marble tabernacle (1563) in the form of a domed peripteral tempietto. Elsewhere he provided a fountain model for Viterbo (1566) and dispensed drawings and expertise for work on the communal palaces of Rieti (1563), Cittaducale (1569), Velletri (1572) and Camerino (1573). At the Vatican he laid out a conclave chapel in the Belvedere (1559 or 1565) and probably built the chapel of St Pius V in the Torre Pia (1566–72), both on oval plans. The most inventive and influential of these modest ecclesiastical structures was the confraternal church of S Anna dei Palafrenieri (1565–76) at the Vatican. Vignola's son Giacinto directed construction there from 1565 to 1574. The plan puts an oval nave within a rectangular shell, reserving the four residual corner spaces for service functions. Eight embedded columns with alternating wide and narrow intercolumniations encircle the central space. Here Vignola resolutely abandoned the High Renaissance preference for simple, geometrical shapes and the ideal of providing legible mutual relationships between interior and exterior. Although it was only vaulted in the 18th century, S Anna must be counted as an inspirational model for the dynamic centralized churches of such early Baroque masters as Gianlorenzo Bernini, Francesco Borromini and Carlo Rainaldi. In June 1572 Vignola presented Gregory XIII with a master-plan for the church of the Escorial (Spain), incorporating ideas from Galeazzo Alessi, Pellegrino Tibaldi, Andrea Palladio and others. The scheme was forwarded to Philip II, King of Spain.

(b) Farnese family commissions. While in papal service, Vignola was also principal architect to Cardinal Ranuccio Farnese and Cardinal Alessandro Farnese, the grandsons of Paul III. Between May 1550 and March 1552 he supervised the construction of the monumental tomb of *Paul III* designed by Guglielmo della Porta. At the same

time Cardinal Ranuccio, as the principal occupant of the unfinished Palazzo Farnese, employed Vignola to direct construction there. His responsibilities at the great palace centred mainly on the execution of plans by Michelangelo, but over the next two decades he made significant contributions to the appearance of the interior by designing doorframes, fireplaces, wooden ceilings and furniture, including the so-called Farnese Table (*c.* 1560; New York, Met.). Cardinal Alessandro provided Vignola with his greatest commissions, beginning at Caprarola, a small hill town *c.* 55 km north-west of Rome. This was a Farnese fiefdom overlooked by an unfinished pentagonal fortress with bastions built by Antonio da Sangallo the younger and Baldassarre Peruzzi during the early 1520s. Preparations for new construction were under way by May 1557 and within a year Vignola drew up a definitive project for a grand residential villa (*see* CAPRAROLA, VILLA FARNESE, and fig.). Begun in April 1559, he supervised its construction closely until the end of 1564 and then intermittently until his death, by when it was substantially complete.

The Villa Farnese at Caprarola is Vignola's greatest achievement, testifying to the full range of his talent as an urban planner, engineer, architect and painter. From the start he conceived the villa in scenic and symbolic terms. For visibility and traffic a long straight street on axis with the main entrance was cut through the medieval town. From the street the approach continues by way of semicircular ramps to a trapezoidal piazza and then by flights of stairs, ending with a drawbridge before a rusticated Doric portal. For those arriving by carriage or on horseback Vignola provided smooth access by excavating a tunnel from the piazza through the pre-existing scarp and into a circular turning space beneath the central courtyard. Ascent to the upper floors is facilitated by a large and comfortable spiral staircase with paired Doric columns inspired by Bramante's ramp staircase in the Cortile del Belvedere at the Vatican. The functional transformation of a military stronghold into a grand summer residence thus began below ground. On the exterior, however, motifs of fortification were made to serve the image of neo-feudal princely power: the arrowhead bastions remained in place, their tops converted into open-air *piano nobile* terraces, on which stand the three upper floors of the pentagonal palazzo, its corner bays projecting slightly to embrace an austere grid of pilasters, Ionic for the *piano nobile* where they enclose the arches of a formerly open gallery, and Composite for two short upper floors reserved for servants and retainers. Directly behind the implacable façades Vignola orchestrated on the main floor a sequence of a dozen spacious rectangular staterooms and a circular chapel, set in a space that is the counterpart to the staircase, most of which was lavishly decorated with frescoes by Taddeo Zuccaro (*see* ZUCCARO, (1)), Federico Zuccaro, Jacopo Bertoia and others. Vignola himself was responsible for the architectural perspectives adorning the ground-floor Sala di Giove.

The most extraordinary feature of the Villa Farnese is the perfectly round interior courtyard. This form had been considered for Caprarola by Sangallo and it had been used by Vignola himself in his Villa Cervini project, but such examples fail to anticipate the consummate power of this solution. The absolute geometry of the circle is in stark

contrast to the shifting, ambiguous prospects of the pentagonal exterior. Keyed to the five wings and corners by ten bays of superimposed arches, the cylindrical elevation has rusticated piers on the ground floor and paired Ionic half columns on the *piano nobile*. The scheme characteristically draws on and deftly conjoins two authoritative designs in Rome by Bramante—the Palazzo Caprini (House of Raphael; destr.) and the upper Belvedere court façades in the Vatican.

While at Caprarola, Vignola was called in as a consultant regarding the Palazzo Farnese at Piacenza, begun in 1558 or 1559 by Francesco Paciotto for Ottavio Farnese, 2nd Duke of Parma and Piacenza, and his wife, Margaret of Parma. Wresting control from Paciotto, Vignola presented an elaborate revised project that was accepted in 1561; construction proceeded to his orders until 1568, when it was abandoned for lack of funds. Despite efforts to finish the palace in the late 1580s, it remains an immense torso encompassing only about one-third of its intended site (112×88 m). The most compelling legacy of Vignola's work at Piacenza is a series of drawings (Parma, Archv Stato; Windsor Castle, Royal Lib.), many by his son Giacinto who assisted him there in 1561. It is apparent from these that Vignola wished the building to serve as a fortress (with scarped basement, moat, drawbridge and tower), an urban palace (with central arcaded courtyard, two grand staircases and a three-storey main façade containing more than 100 windows) and a villa suburbana (with open loggias facing extensive rear garden). For the courtyard at the heart of this ambitious project, Vignola planned a permanent neo-antique theatre with a semi-oval *cavea* (Lat.: 'auditorium') set into the south-west range and open to the sky. As a self-sustaining structure in brick and stone, the design is derived from Vitruvius and the ruins of Classical Rome rather than Raphael's hillside amphitheatre for the Villa Madama, Rome (1518). As such, it represents a significant conceptual advance in the evolution of the modern European theatre. During his visit to Piacenza in 1564 Vignola made drawings for other works, including the compact Palazzo Radini Tedeschi, Piacenza (now Palazzo Malvicini, Fontana; priv. col., see Adorni), which was only partly completed to his intentions, and the imposing Facciata dei Banchi, Bologna (see fig. 4), his most important essay in urban renovation. Stretching some 96 m across the east side of the Piazza Maggiore, this façade of tall Composite pilasters, heavy unbroken entablature and a high attic masks the 15 bays and two incoming streets of a low Gothic portico. In one masterful stroke Vignola unified, reproportioned and modernized the large civic square.

The commission for Il Gesù, Rome (1568–75), Vignola's most ambitious and influential church, came from Cardinal Alessandro Farnese, who underwrote the cost of its construction for the Society of Jesus. Farnese stipulated that the church must have a single vaulted nave with side chapels. Vignola's response was in part conditioned by his project of S Maria in Traspontina, Rome (1566; not executed), and perhaps by S Maria degli Angeli, Assisi (1568), which Danti said he laid out. These are Latin-cross churches with a nave and two aisles, relatively shallow transepts and domed crossings. At Il Gesù the elimination of side aisles allowed for enlarged lateral chapels and a

4. Jacopo Vignola: Facciata dei Banchi, Bologna, 1565

broader nave that turns the cupola into a highly visible culminating element. The innovative plan brought these ecclesiastically differentiated parts into unprecedented visual and spatial unity. Overall cohesion was enhanced by lining the interior with paired Composite pilasters without pedestals and a continuous belt-like entablature. Lowered entrance arches rendered the six nave chapels unobtrusive; above their flattened oval vaults are screened-off galleries. Under Vignola's direction, Il Gesù was constructed to the height of the main entablature; the barrel vault of the nave and the dome were built later, and higher than he had intended, by Giacomo della Porta. In the following decades, Il Gesù profoundly influenced the Roman church designs of della Porta, Martino I Longhi (i) and Carlo Maderno, while as the home church of the Jesuit Order it became a prototype for countless churches world-wide. Vignola's initial façade project for Il Gesù (see ROME, fig. 49), recorded in the foundation medal of 1568, features giant Corinthian pilasters topped by a high pedimented attic with obelisks. The emphatically horizontalizing design follows from his S Maria in Traspontina project and from the façade he built at S Maria dell'Orto, Rome (1564–7). In these a single order of pilasters masks the entire width of the church and, with the central entrance accentuated by columns, the higher nave is covered as a subordinate element. Such a conception failed to please Cardinal Farnese, whose munificence the façade was to celebrate, and in 1570 Vignola produced a more elaborate second design that acknowledged the authority of traditional Roman double-order aedicular schemes. In 1571 this design was rejected and Cardinal Farnese turned

from his architect of 20 years to award the commission to a younger man, Giacomo della Porta (see ROME, fig. 50).

Notwithstanding the setback at Il Gesù, Vignola was productive in his final years. Cardinal Farnese continued to employ him at Caprarola where, as well as work at the villa itself, he furnished projects for road works (1571), town houses (1571) and a hospital (1572). In addition, he worked on the Palazzo Comunale at Grotte di Castro (1568; see la vita e le opere) and submitted plans for fortresses at Isola Farnese (1567 and 1569) and Montalto di Castro (1570). He also visited important country estates, among them the Villa Gambara, Bagnaia (now Villa Lante, 1568, see GARDEN, fig. 1), Villa Tuscolana, Frascati (now Villa Vecchia; 1569) and Castel Gandolfo (1570), although the extent of his involvement at these locations is unclear.

When Vignola died the artists of Rome honoured him with a burial in the Pantheon. He left no workshop and, having been poorly equipped by nature for success as a building entrepreneur, much less a courtier, he had acquired neither wealth nor high social rank. Solitary and hard-working, proud but unpretentious, he had devoted himself wholly to the discipline of building well according to exacting architectural principles. His legacy was a handful of monuments, many begun or finished by others, that provided rich rewards for architects willing to study them, and a small corpus of powerful theoretical writings accessible to all.

2. THE TREATISES. Vignola wrote two books. The *Regola delli cinque ordini d'architettura* is undated but may be assigned to 1562 on the evidence of a letter (Parma,

Archv Stato) from his son Giacinto dated 12 June of that year offering a copy to Ottavio Farnese. The extremely rare first edition consists of 32 single-sided folio engravings, a title-page with a portrait of *Vignola*, a 10-year copyright from Pius IV, a dedication to Cardinal Alessandro Farnese with an introductory epistle and 29 illustrations of the five orders, including the Salomonic column and a cornice design. Almost immediately eight of the principal plates were reworked to provide the names of architectural components. For a second edition Vignola seems to have prepared five additional illustrations of four portals and a fireplace executed for the Farnese family; whether he oversaw their publication is not known. In subsequent editions by others the copyright page is invariably replaced by a synoptic illustration of the five columns. The *Regola* is neither a humanistic introduction to architecture nor a simple pattern-book. Intended for 'those who may have had some introduction in art', its narrowly focused argument is supremely graphic, the text being reduced to brief captions. It was the first book to demonstrate a universal method (or rule) for proportioning each of the five orders, including all component parts, according to a module equal to the radius of the column. Moreover, the ratios between the heights of pedestal, column and entablature in each order remain the same (4:12:3), facilitating the application of columnar decoration to any given elevation. The system is fundamentally empirical and arbitrary in that it is not derived from pure mathematics or archaeological fact: the forms of Vignola's orders have been taken directly from esteemed Classical examples, but various details within them have been adjusted to fit the rule (*see* ARCHITECTURAL PROPORTION, §II). The extraordinary success of the *Regola* was due to the clarity and precision of Vignola's system, the impeccable illustrations and the folio format, which rendered the book useful to workmen. A recent bibliography enumerates more than 500 editions, including translations in ten languages (Bassi and Marini, 1985). Of these, nearly all served as academic textbooks, which partly explains how the treatise and its author came to be widely thought of as fundamentally pedantic. Vignola's second book, *Le due regole della prospettiva pratica* (Rome, 1583), was published posthumously by Ignazio Danti, who prefaced it with a biography of the architect. Again Vignola's text is spare, consisting only of a series of succinct statements demonstrating the two principal methods (rules) of Renaissance perspective: Albertian artificial perspective (*costruzione legittima*) and the distance-point method. Although it broke no new ground, *Le due regole* became the definitive statement on Renaissance perspective, thanks in part to the long and learned commentary added by Danti.

WRITINGS

Regola delli cinque ordini d'architettura (Rome, 1562); ed. E. Bassi and P. Marini, *Trattati di architettura*, v/2 (Milan, 1985)
I. Danti, ed.: *Le due regole della prospettiva pratica . . . con i comentarij del R. P. M. Egnatio Danti* (Rome, 1583) [with biog. of Vignola by Danti]

BIBLIOGRAPHY

Macmillan Enc. Architects; Thieme–Becker; *DBI*
G. Vasari: *Vite* (1550, rev. 2/1568); ed. G. Milanesi (1878–85), v, p. 432; vii, pp. 105–8, 130, 407
H. Willich: *Giacomo Barozzi da Vignola* (Strasbourg, 1906)
Memorie e studi intorno a Jacopo Barozzi pubblicati nel IV centenario della nascità: Vignola, 1908
G. Giovannoni: *Saggi sulla architettura del rinascimento* (Milan, 1931, rev. 1935)
W. Lotz: 'Vignola: Zeichnungen', *Jb. Preuss. Kstsamml.*, lix (1938), pp. 97–115
——: *Vignola: Studien* (Würzburg, 1939)
J. Coolidge: 'Vignola's Character and Achievement', *J. Soc. Archit. Historians*, ix/4 (1950), pp. 10–14
W. Lotz: 'Die ovalen Kirchenräume des Cinquecento', *Röm. Jb. Kstgesch.*, vii (1955), pp. 9–99
M. Walcher Casotti: *Il Vignola*, 2 vols (Trieste, 1960)
M. Lewine: 'Vignola's Church of Sant'Anna de' Palafrenieri in Rome', *A. Bull.*, xxxxvii (1965), pp. 199–229
P. Dreyer: 'Beiträge zur Planungsgeschichte des Palazzo Farnese in Piacenza', *Jb. Berlin. Mus.*, vii (1966), pp. 160–203
J. K. Schmidt: 'Zu Vignolas Palazzo Bocchi in Bologna', *Mitt. Ksthist. Inst. Florenz*, 13 (1967), pp. 83–94
T. Falk: 'Studien zur Topographie und Geschichte der Villa Giulia in Rom', *Röm. Jb. Kstgesch.*, xiii (1971), pp. 101–78
W. Lotz and L. H. Heydenreich: *Architecture in Italy, 1400–1600*, Pelican Hist. A. (Harmondsworth, 1974)
C. Thoenes: 'Vignola e il teatro Farnese a Piacenza', *Boll. Cent. Int. Stud. Archit. Andrea Palladio*, xvi (1974), pp. 243–56
La vita e le opere di Jacopo Barozzi da Vignola, 1507–1573, nel quarto centenario della morte: Vignola, 1974 [good illus., bibliog.]
K. Schwager: 'Ein Ovalkirchen-Entwurf Vignolas für San Giovanni dei Fiorentini', *Festschrift für Georg Scheja* (Sigmaringen, 1975), pp. 151–78
R. J. Tuttle: 'A New Attribution to Vignola: A Doric Portal of 1547 in the Palazzo Comunale in Bologna', *Röm. Jb. Kstgesch.*, xvi (1976), pp. 207–20
K. Schwager: 'La chiesa del Gesù del Vignola', *Boll. Cent. Int. Stud. Archit. Andrea Palladio*, xix (1977), pp. 251–71
E. Kieven: 'Eine Vignola-Zeichnung für S Maria in Traspontina', *Röm. Jb. Kstgesch.*, xix (1981), pp. 245–7
W. Lotz: *Studies in Italian Renaissance Architecture* (Cambridge, MA, 1981)
B. Adorni: *L'architettura farnesiana a Piacenza, 1545–1600* (Parma, 1982)
C. Thoenes: 'Vignolas "Regola delli cinque ordini"', *Röm. Jb. Kstgesch.*, xx (1983), pp. 345–76
P. Dreyer: 'Vignolas Planungen für eine befestigte Villa Cervini', *Röm. Jb. Kstgesch.*, xxi (1984), pp. 365–96
C. Thoenes: 'Versuch über Architektur und Gesellschaft im Werk Vignolas', *Krit. Ber.*, xv/3–4 (1987), pp. 5–19
R. J. Tuttle: 'Vignola's Facciata dei Banchi in Bologna', *J. Soc. Archit. Historians*, lii (1993), pp. 68–87

RICHARD J. TUTTLE

Vignon, Alexandre-Pierre (*b* Lagny, 5 Oct 1763; *d* Paris, 21 May 1828). French architect and writer. He studied with Julien-David Le Roy and was a protégé of the Baron de Breteuil. Unlike many of his colleagues, he had a productive career during the revolutionary era, being appointed in 1789 Inspecteur du Casernement for the Paris National Guard and in 1790 architect to the Arsenal. In 1793 he was appointed Inspecteur général des Bâtiments de la République and supervised the installation of the Imprimerie Nationale in the Hôtel de la Vrillière. The exact nature of his relationship with Claude-Nicolas Ledoux is unknown, although he was certainly influenced by him; moreover, he apparently intended to complete Ledoux's *L'Architecture considérée sous le rapport de l'art, des moeurs et de la législation* (Paris, 1804) and was executor of his will. From 1806 Vignon concentrated on completing the Madeleine, a church that had remained unfinished since the days of the *ancien régime*. In several pamphlets he had suggested using the site for the Tribunat, or the Bourse, the Tribunal de Commerce and the Banque de France. In 1806 Napoleon ordered that a Temple de la Gloire should be erected there and Claude-Etienne Beaumont (1757–1811) emerged as winner of the limited competition (1807), but he was superseded by Vignon on

Napoleon's orders. He designed a vast peripteral Corinthian temple, with a single huge, barrel-vaulted interior, to form a counterpart to the distant Chambre des Députés by Bernard Poyet. Building work, however, never started; in 1815, Louis XVIII contemplated using the site for the Chapelle expiatoire dedicated to Louis XVI and another competition was held (1816), to which Vignon contributed. The enterprise was judged too expensive and it was decided to build the Madeleine as a parish church. Vignon retained the commission using his designs of 1807, subject to modifications, which included roofing the nave with three domes. The masonry of the exterior was virtually finished by 1828 when Vignon died, and the completion of the interior (1828–42) was supervised by Jean-Jacques Huvé (1783–1852).

WRITINGS
Observations sur le palais que doit occuper le Tribunat (Paris, n.d.)
Mémoire à l'appui d'un projet pour placer conformément aux intentions de S. M., la Bourse, le Tribunal de Commerce et la Banque de France dans les constructions de la nouvelle église de la Madeleine (Paris, 1806)
Mémoire à l'appui d'un projet pour utiliser les constructions de la Madeleine et les transformer en un Temple consacré par S. M. l'Empereur à la gloire des armées françaises (Paris, 1807)
Monuments commémoratifs projetés en l'honneur de Louis XVI et de sa famille (Paris, 1816)

BIBLIOGRAPHY
G. Vauthier: 'Pierre Vignon et l'église de la Madeleine', *Bull. Soc. Hist. A. Fr.* (1910), pp. 380–422
F. Boyer: 'Note sur les architectes Jacques-Pierre Gisors, Charles Percier, Pierre Vignon', *Bull. Soc. Hist. A. Fr.* (1933), pp. 258–69
A. Krieger: *La Madeleine* (Paris, 1938)
L. Hautecoeur: *Architecture classique*, v (1953), pp. 204–7; vi (1955), pp. 17–19
A. Engbring-Strysch: *Die Madeleine-Kirche in Paris* (diss., U. Bochum, 1986)

WERNER SZAMBIEN

Vignon, Claude (*b* Tours, 19 May 1593; *d* Paris, 10 May 1670). French painter, printmaker and illustrator. Born into a prosperous family in Tours, he received his early training in Paris, probably in Jacob Bunel's studio. In 1609–10 he travelled to Rome; although his presence there is recorded only in 1618–20, he was probably based there throughout that decade, becoming a member of the community of young French artists that included Simon Vouet and Valentin de Boullogne. They were all predominantly influenced by the art of Caravaggio and of his most direct follower Bartolomeo Manfredi. Vignon's severe half-length figures (*St Paul*, Turin, Gal. Sabauda; *Four Church Fathers*, on loan to Cambridge, Fitzwilliam), executed possibly even earlier than 1615, are in a Caravaggesque style, as are his paintings of singers, musicians and drinkers (e.g. the *Young Singer*, Paris, Louvre), although the latter group owes more to the style of contemporary genre painting. However, Vignon was already showing an interest in new artistic experiments, the origins of which were northern, Venetian and Mannerist. His sensitivity to the splendid colouring of Venice and to the art of Jacques Bellange, Georges Lallemand and Jacques Callot is manifest in his *Martyrdom of St Matthew* (1617; Arras, Mus. B.-A.), a work with striking references to Caravaggio's painting of the same subject (Rome, S Luigi dei Francesi), and still more so in his *Adoration of the Magi* (1619; Dayton, OH, A. Inst.), which also shows clear links with the art of several precursors of Rembrandt, including

Adam Elsheimer, Pieter Lastman, Jakob Pynas and particularly Leonard Bramer. Towards the end of his time in Rome, Vignon was awarded first prize in a painting competition organized by Cardinal Lodovico Ludovisi, for what became his most famous painting, the *Wedding at Cana* (1621–3; Potsdam, destr. 1945; see Pacht Bassani, pl. 23).

By January 1623 Vignon had returned to Paris, where he married Charlotte, daughter of the engraver Thomas de Leu. He soon achieved success at Louis XIII's court, for which he produced paintings and undertook travels as an art adviser. He worked for ecclesiastical patrons too and before 1638 executed four 'Mays', the prestigious altarpieces commissioned annually for Notre-Dame Cathedral by the Paris goldsmiths' guild. He had a growing reputation with private clients and was an important business associate of the print publisher and art dealer François Langlois. During the 1620s Vignon was highly productive, and it is possible to follow closely his development in a sequence of dated works. He vacillated between several styles. *Christ among the Doctors* (1623; Grenoble, Mus. B.-A.) and *St Jerome* (1626; Stockholm, Nmus.) are still strongly marked by the influence of Caravaggio. The *Circumcision* (1627; Lyon, Mus. B.-A.) and *Assumption of the Virgin* (1629; La Flèche, Sarthe, St Thomas) are more reserved and static, while the *Transfiguration* (1624; Châtillon-Coligny, Notre-Dame) and the *Triumph of St Ignatius* (1628; Orléans, Mus. B.-A.) have a more dramatic, Baroque impulse. *Solomon and the Queen of Sheba* (1624; Paris, Louvre), which is considered a crucial work (see Sterling), shows a taste for the exotic and for theatrical arrangement and is notable for its thick, encrusted impasto, shot through with golden highlights, and for its unusual combination of colours; it further develops the multiple influences already present in the *Adoration of the Magi*.

Chronological landmarks are much rarer between 1630 and 1656, the date of Vignon's last known work. However, the surviving paintings from these years, as well as those known only from engravings or drawings, are abundant. This confirms the almost legendary reputation for speed and prolificness that Vignon enjoyed among his contemporaries and suggests that his position in Paris remained undiminished even after Vouet's return to France in 1627. While he was passed over for the great decorative schemes of the day, most of which went to Philippe de Champaigne or to Vouet and his collaborators, Vignon nevertheless continued to enjoy the protection of Cardinal Richelieu (for whom he worked on the Palais Cardinal), of Louis XIII and of others in court circles. His work was still in demand for churches and monasteries all over France, and he was highly admired in the rarefied intellectual and artistic circle of the Hôtel de Rambouillet, particularly by Anne, Duchesse de Longueville (1619–79), for whom he decorated the gallery (destr.) at the Château of Thorigny between 1651 and 1653. A proliferation of styles continued to be typical of his art. Although primarily associated with the elegant and mannered quality of the *Queen of Sheba*, he produced a large number of pictures of a more intimate kind, designed for display in the rooms of private collectors, such as *Darius and his Family before Alexander* (1633 or 1635; priv. col., see London, Heim Gal. cat., 1979, pl.

32) and the *Continence of Scipio* (*c.* 1639; untraced, see Pacht Bassani, 1976, pl. 32). A much more serious and simplified language, which recalls the tradition of the Italian masters of the Counter-Reformation, characterizes most of Vignon's great religious compositions, such as his *St Mamert at the Feet of Christ on the Cross* (1635–42; Orléans, Mus. B.-A.) and the *Resurrection* (1635; Toulouse, Mus. Augustins). His final paintings depend on effects of blended colour, theatrical lighting and poses of great pathos, as in the *Ascension* (1650; Paris, St Nicolas-des-Champs) and the *Death of Cleopatra* (*c.* 1650; Rennes, Mus. B.-A. & Archéol.; see fig.). Vignon entered the Académie Royale in 1651. His abundant and eclectic production did indeed include facile works, partly executed by his studio, but also, even in his most productive period, works of high quality.

Throughout his career Vignon was active as an etcher, producing such works as the *Two Lovers* (after Vouet, 1618; Robert-Dumesnil, no. 26), *St Peter and St Paul Entombed* (1620; RD 19), the *Martyrdom of St Catherine* (1627) and *St Philip Baptizing Queen Candace's Eunuch* (1638). He also had reproductive engravings made by Gilles Rousselet, Abraham Bosse and Jean Couvay, among others, from his drawings, as in the suites of *Sibylles* (*c.* 1635), the *Sept sages de Grèce* (1639–40), the *Quatre monarchies* (1644–5) and the *Femmes fortes* (1647). From the end of the 1630s he also became one of the illustrators most sought after by the writers of the Précieux circle, such as Desmarets de Saint-Sorlin (*Ariane*, 1639), Madeleine de Scudéry (*Ibrahim*, 1641) and Jean Chapelain (*La Pucelle d'Orléans*, 1656).

Vignon had 34 children by his two marriages (he married his second wife, Geneviève Ballard, in 1644). The following three were active as painters: Claude François Vignon

Claude Vignon: *Death of Cleopatra*, oil on canvas, *c.* 1650 (Rennes, Musée des Beaux-Arts et d'Archéologie)

(1633–1703), who became a member of the Académie Royale in 1667, when he presented his *Hercules Striking down Ignorance and Vice in the Presence of Minerva* (Paris, Louvre); Philippe Vignon (1638–1701), who became a member of the Académie in 1687 and was best known as a portrait painter—his *morceau de réception* is of the sculptor *Philippe de Buyster* (Paris, Louvre); and Charlotte Vignon (*b* 1639), who was a flower painter.

BIBLIOGRAPHY

A. P. F. Robert-Dumesnil: *Le Peintre-graveur français*, viii (1844), pp. 148–57 [RD]

Guillet de Saint-Georges: 'Claude Vignon', *Mémoires inédits*, ed. L. Dussieux and others, i (Paris, 1854), pp. 269–79

C. Sterling: 'Un Précurseur français de Rembrandt: Claude Vignon', *Gaz. B.-A.*, 6th ser., xii (1934), pp. 123–36

W. Fischer: 'Claude Vignon', *Ned. Ksthist. Jb.*, xiii (1962), pp. 105–48; xiv (1963), pp. 137–82

J. Thuillier: *La Peinture française de Fouquet à Poussin* (Geneva, 1963), pp. 168–76

P. Rosenberg: 'Nouvelles acquisitions, Musée du Louvre: Un tableau de Claude Vignon', *Rev. Louvre*, 1 (1968), pp. 37–44

Valentin et les caravagesques français (exh. cat., ed. A. Bréjon de Lavergnée and J.-P. Cuzin; Paris, Grand Pal., 1974), pp. 185–201, 254

P. Pacht Bassani: 'Claude Vignon', *Stor. A.*, 28 (1976), pp. 259–83

France in the Golden Age: Seventeenth-century French Paintings in American Collections (exh. cat. by P. Rosenberg, New York, Met.; Paris, Grand Pal.; 1982), pp. 331–3, 374–5

C. Wright: *The French Painters of the Seventeenth Century* (London, 1985), pp. 57–9, 269–71

PAOLA PACHT BASSANI

Vignory, Comte de. *See* ORRY, PHILIBERT.

Vigny, Pierre de (*b* Saumur, 30 May 1690; *d* 1772). French architect and writer. He joined the offices of the Bâtiments du Roi in Paris under the direction of Robert de Cotte. In 1721 he accepted the offer of a journey to the Levant, which was intended to enable him to design a new palace for Monsieur de Bonnac, the French Ambassador, in Constantinople (now Istanbul). De Vigny suggested that the former Capuchin monastery on the Petra heights be preserved and that new extensions be added to it, designing a covered gallery leading to a T-shaped building overlooking the poor neighbourhood of Tophana. This new residence, designed with façades of imposing simplicity, would have commanded an exceptional view over the Bosphorus, the Seraglio Point and the Golden Horn. In the event, however, Monsieur de Bonnac was able to rebuild only the gateway. The embassy was not rebuilt until 1775. When he left Turkey, de Vigny went to Italy, where he took the opportunity to see and admire not only the work of Michelangelo and Antonio da Sangallo (ii) but also that of Francesco Borromini.

De Vigny returned to France in 1722, after an absence of 16 months. Although circumstances had forced his clients to postpone the building of the embassy in Constantinople, the regent, Philippe, Duc d'Orléans, and the Comte de Toulouse expressed their satisfaction with his work, and this enabled him to be elected to membership of the Académie Royale d'Architecture in Paris. De Vigny became architect to Louis XV and divided his efforts between Versailles and his private clients. He designed decorative work for two churches in Saumur, Notre-Dame de Nantilly and St Pierre, and also worked on projects in Meaux and Valenciennes during the same period.

The level of architectural activity in the Bâtiments du Roi was given new impetus by the return of Louis XV to Versailles in 1723. At the same time, de Vigny took over some of de Cotte's commissions as the latter was then 67 years old. Around 1726 de Vigny was thus in a position to build the Hôtel de Chenizot on the Ile Saint-Louis in Paris. This residence is noteworthy for the two chimeras supporting the balcony over the entrance gateway, and his approach here expressed his rejection of classical discipline. De Vigny designed the buildings of the Cour du Dragon (1728–32; destr. 1925) in the neighbourhood of Saint-Germain-des-Prés, Paris, for the banker and collector Antoine Crozat. Paul-Ambroise Slodtz executed a dragon (now in Paris, Louvre) to decorate the balcony set into the monumental gateway facing the Rue de l'Egout.

During the 1740s de Vigny supervised work at several different sites. He executed decorative work in the apartments of the Duc de Chevreuse in the Hôtel de Luynes, built the stables of the Bodyguards at Coulommiers and designed the church of St Martin du Tertre in the Valois as well as a considerable number of buildings in Paris, including 42 Rue François Miron. He also carried out some major work on Reims Cathedral. De Vigny's most significant project was the general hospital (1738) at Lille, a coldly elegant edifice, which he designed with a number of imposing buildings. However, he was able to execute only three quarters of his original, ambitious project. From 1755 he also worked on a new urban plan for the city of Nantes.

De Vigny was a cultivated architect and a brilliant figure in society. He was a member of several learned societies including the Société des Arts et Sciences, Paris. During a trip to England in 1741, when he was the guest of Hans Sloane, de Vigny also became a member of the Royal Society in London. He built up a handsome collection of paintings, objets d'art and other works in his house on the Rue Neuve St Eustache (now Rue d'Aboukir) and on his estate at Panchien in Touraine. The most original summary of de Vigny's ideas was his *Dissertation sur l'architecture* (1752), which he submitted as part of his application to the Royal Society. In this work he deplored the practice of following only classical models. His commendation of a wider and more exotic field from which to draw architectural inspiration anticipates the historicism of the 19th century.

WRITINGS
Dissertation sur l'architecture (Paris, 1752)

BIBLIOGRAPHY
M. Gallet: 'L'Architecte Pierre de Vigny, 1690–1772: Ses constructions, son esthétique', *Gaz. B.-A.* (Nov 1973)

GÉRARD ROUSSET CHARNY

Viiralt [Viiral't; Wiiralt], **Eduard** (*b* Robidetsa estate, St Petersburg province, 20 March 1898; *d* Paris, 8 Jan 1954). Estonian graphic artist. He studied in Tallinn at the college of art and design (1915–19), at the Pallas Art School (1919–22 and 1923–4) in Tartu under Anton Starkopf (1889–1966) and Georg Kind (1897–1945), and at the Akademie, Dresdon (1923–4), under Selmer Werner (1864–1953). He concentrated on sculpture and printmaking, later devoting himself to graphic art. From 1925 to 1938 he lived mostly in Paris. Viiralt's early work bears the stamp of late German Expressionism, but he later assimilated various Parisian influences, the most important of which was Surrealism. In engravings, lithographs and monotypes of the mid- to late 1920s, grotesquely drawn, fantastic and erotic images predominate; they are connected with the symbol of the contemporary megalopolis as the centre of entertainment and vice. The large-format prints *Hell* (etching and engraving, 1930–32), *Cabaret* (etching and engraving, 1931) and *The Preacher* (lithograph, 1932; all Tallinn, A. Mus.) were executed with a technical virtuosity that marked the culmination of this visionary period. Towards the mid-1930s his work shows clarity and harmony in everyday portraits of children and friends, nudes and landscapes, as in *Landscape near Paris* (etching, 1937; Tallin, A. Mus. Estonia), and in animal subjects (e.g. *Lying Tiger*, softground etching, 1937; Tallinn, A. Mus.). A profound humanity characterizes the drawings and prints based on impressions of a journey to Morocco in 1938. In the same year Viiralt returned to Estonia, where he created works symbolic of the country's past, present and cultural traditions (e.g. *Kristjan Raud*, drypoint print, 1937; Tallinn, A. Mus.). In 1944 he was invited to mount a solo exhibition in Vienna and, after a brief stay in Sweden, he settled again in Paris in 1946. His late work is characterized by a sense of spiritual fatigue and often of doom and isolation. Firmly contoured lines and broad gradations disappear from the vocabulary of the late engravings and a painterly texture and the modelling of form by dots take their place.

BIBLIOGRAPHY
Eduard Viiralt: Mälestusteos [Eduard Viiralt: in memoriam] (Lund, 1955)
O. Kangilaski, ed.: *Eduard Viiralt* (Tallinn, 1959)
M. Levin, ed.: *Eduard Viiralt* (Tallinn, 1985) [preface in Rus., Eng., Fr. and Ger.]

B. M. BERNSHTEIN

Vijayanagara. Kingdom that controlled portions of south India from 1336 to 1565. It was established by two brothers, Harihara and Bukka, as the TUGHLUQ dynasty abandoned its expansionist policy in south India. Originally sent to restore Sultanate authority, the brothers broke away and formed their own dynasty, Harihara being crowned at HAMPI in 1336. A royal enclave known as Vijayanagara was established near Hampi and gave its name to the new kingdom. Vijayanagara became a flourishing city in the 14th century as its territorial holdings rapidly expanded to the east and west coasts of the peninsula. The HOYSALA dynasty was conquered in 1346 and the Muslim Sultanate of Madurai overturned by 1370. Embassies were sent by Bukka (*reg* 1344–77) to China, and European visitors began to arrive in the 15th century. The Italian traveller Nicolo Conti, for example, visited Vijayanagara in 1420 and left a vivid description. Vijayanagara was in conflict with the Portuguese and the BAHMANI kingdom to the north. Krishna Deva Raya (*reg* 1509–27), the most famous ruler of Vijayanagara, was able to maintain a balance of power owing, in part, to a weakened Bahmani dynasty. The *Amuktamalyada*, a diary of Krishna Deva Raya, is a remarkable document of the period. The dynasties that emerged when the Bahmani kingdom was dismembered (principally QUTB SHAHI, 'ADIL SHAHI and 'Imad Shahi) formed a confederacy and in the Battle of

Talikota (1565) effectively destroyed Vijayanagara as a major power.

For a discussion of the monuments of the royal capital, Vijayanagara, *see* HAMPI.

BIBLIOGRAPHY

R. Sewell: *A Forgotten Empire* (London, 1900)
S. K. Aiyangar: *South India and her Muhammadan Invaders* (Madras, 1921)
H. Heras: *The Aravidu Dynasty of Vijayanagara* (Madras, 1927)
B. A. Saletore: *Social and Political Life in the Vijayanagara Empire* (Madras, 1934)
T. V. Mahalingam: *Administrative and Social Life under Vijayanagar* (Madras, 1940/R Paris, 1969–75)
S. K. Aiyangar: *Sources of Vijayanagara History* (Madras, 1946)
T. V. Mahalingam: *Economic Life in the Vijayanagar Empire* (Madras, 1952)
D. Devakunjari: *Hampi* (New Delhi, 1970)
G. Michell and V. Filliozat, eds: *Splendours of the Vijayanagara Empire: Hampi* (Bombay, 1981)
M. S. Nagaraja Rao, ed.: *Vijayanagara: Progress of Research*, 2 vols (Mysore, 1983–5)
J. M. Fritz, G. Michell and M. S. Nagaraja Rao: *Where Kings and Gods Meet: The Royal Centre at Vijayanagara* (Tucson, 1984)

J. MARR

Vijayapura. *See* BIJAPUR.

Vik, Ingebrigt (*b* Øystese, Hardanger, 5 March 1867; *d* Øystese, 23 March 1927). Norwegian sculptor. He began carving wood as a child at his father's furniture workshop in Hardanger. Around 1881 he was apprenticed to the wood-carver Sjur Utne in Hardanger and in 1882–4 to the carver Hans J. Johannessen (1851–1932) in Bergen. At the same time Vik attended evening classes at the technical school. For the next two years he worked with the carver Sophus Petersen (*c.* 1837–1904) in Copenhagen, where he entered the Kunstakademi in 1885. From 1888 to 1892 he worked again in Copenhagen, where he assisted the sculptor Hans Christian Petersen (1835–1919), resuming his studies at the Kunstakademi in 1889. Back in Bergen, Vik established himself as an independent carver, making ivory reliefs and modelling small terracotta figures in a naturalistic style. After a visit to the Exposition Universelle in Paris in 1900 he modelled the bronze *Worker* (1901; Bergen, Billedgal.), which reveals the influence of Constantin Meunier.

In 1902 Vik won first prize in the competition for the Abel Monument in Kristiania (now Oslo), although Gustav Vigeland was later chosen to execute it. The prize was, nevertheless, a great incentive, and thanks to a State travel scholarship Vik managed to train as a sculptor. He lived from 1902 to 1905 in Paris, where he studied for a short time at the Académie Colarossi and with the sculptor Jean-Antoine Injalbert. He derived more profit, however, from visits to the art collections of the Louvre and other museums. His work also attests to the influence of Auguste Rodin and other contemporaries there. Vik hired his own studio and model in Paris. The bronze *Old Woman* (1904; Oslo, N.G., and Bergen, Billedgal.) shows Vik's increasingly penetrating characterization. Its undulating forms and their effects of light and shadow reveal the impact of Impressionism. *Seated Young Girl* (1904; Oslo, N.G.), executed in a simplified naturalistic form, was awarded an honourable mention at the Salon that year. It depicts a naked young girl at the age of puberty, in smoothly polished marble, sitting on a cubic plinth of coarser

structure. A slightly stooped attitude in the upper body, and her serious face, present an attractive expression of her shy thoughts. The sculpture attests to Vik's concern with the depiction of character, particularly of the young. In 1905 Vik won another first prize in a competition but again lost the commission to Gustav Vigeland. A bequest, however, gave him the opportunity to study Classical and Renaissance art in German and Italian collections in the autumn of 1906.

From 1907 to 1910 Vik again lived in Paris, and thereafter in Kristiania until 1918. In these years he created a number of single figures, mostly of young women and children, as well as groups with adults and children, marked by simple, taut forms. The bronze *Youth* (1913; Oslo, N.G., and Bergen, Theat. Park) is regarded as his masterpiece and is the figure that most clearly reveals the influence of Greek sculpture. A naked young man in melancholy mood leans over in a relaxed pose, his body turned slightly to the side, with the weight on one leg and his hands on his back. This has been interpreted as an expression of the sculptor's own feelings; Vik, an introvert, was disappointed by the number of times he had been passed over. Vik finally got the recognition he deserved only with the unveiling in 1917 in the Bergen City Park of the bronze monument to the composer *Edvard Grieg*. He was, however, by that time a partial invalid and he moved back to his home parish. In his last years he could only make smaller works. Before his death Vik willed his sculptures to the Øystese Young People's Society on the condition that a home for the collection was built. The Vik Museum was opened in 1934.

NKL
BIBLIOGRAPHY

A. Nygård Nilssen: 'Ingebrigt Vik', *Kst & Kult.*, xv (1928), pp. 99–116
A. S. Hals, ed.: *Nasjonalgalleriet: Katalog over skulptur og kunstindustri* (Oslo, 1952)
O. Rønning Johannesen, ed.: *Maleri og skulptur: Bergen Billedgalleri* (Bergen, 1963)
A. Brenna: *Billedhuggeren Ingebrigt Vik* [The sculptor Ingebrigt Vik] (Bergen, 1967)
O. Parmann: *Norwegian Sculpture* (Oslo, 1969) [Eng. and Ger. text]
M. Lange and N. Messel: *Nasjonal vekst* [National growth] (1981), v of *Norges kunsthistorie*, ed. K. Berg and others (Oslo, 1981–3), pp. 367–71, 406

INGEBORG WIKBORG

Viking art. Art produced in Scandinavia and in Scandinavian settlements overseas between the second half of the 8th century AD and the early 12th. Few Scandinavians, however, were strictly 'Vikings', for the old Norse noun *víkingr* means sea-pirate or raider. Ornamental motifs, of animals in particular, dominate the extant examples of Scandinavian art throughout this period, and as such the study of Viking art concentrates largely on their evolution.

I. Introduction. II. Decorative arts. III. Architecture. IV. Historiography.

I. Introduction.

1. GEOGRAPHY AND SETTLEMENT HISTORY. In the Viking era Denmark included the modern southern Swedish provinces of Skåne, Halland and Blekinge, and its southern frontier extended to the base of the Jutland peninsula, close to the River Eider. Sweden, whose western province of Bohuslän was a Norwegian possession, was

thus orientated towards the Baltic. Indeed, Swedes had begun to settle in Finland and elsewhere to the east before the Viking period. Across the north of Scandinavia was the territory of the Saami (Lapps), with their separate artistic traditions. The Viking period, however, was one of overseas expansion. Scandinavian settlements were established to the east in Russia and to the west in Britain and Ireland, as well as in Normandy. The Faroes and Iceland were populated from Scandinavia, and Greenland was settled in the late 10th century, with outlying communities established briefly in North America. In the Viking period there was a growth and consolidation of royal powers, including control over Scandinavia's first towns, with their newly developed opportunities for urban craftsmen. It was also the period when Scandinavia was converted to Christianity, which introduced its own artistic traditions (both Western and Eastern), special requirements and new patronage. Scandinavian overseas activities, whether raiding, trading or settlement, also opened up the native artistic tradition to new stylistic influences.

2. SURVIVING ART FORMS. The main corpus of surviving material consists of applied art in the form of ornamental metalwork, including personal ornaments and mounts for weapons and horse harnesses. Most such items come from pagan burials of the early and middle Viking periods (from the late 8th century to the mid-10th), but grave goods decline in number with the spread of Christianity. In the late Viking period (*c.* AD 950–1100) the sequence of decorated metalwork is continued by ornaments found in coin-dated hoards and recovered from urban excavations. The preservation of organic materials in some towns adds carvings in wood and bone to the objects available for study, but in general the knowledge of artistic production in Viking Scandinavia is incomplete because of the non-survival of wooden sculpture, painted wood and textiles. The quality of what has been lost is

indicated by the outstanding carvings from the Oseberg ship-burial (*c.* 850; *see* §II, 1(iii) below) and on the Urnes Stave church (11th century; *see* §II, 1(viii) below). Apart from the remarkable group of 'picture stones' of the early Viking period on Gotland, stone sculpture is unknown in Viking art before the late period, when the royal stone erected at Jelling by the newly converted King Harald seems to have set a new fashion. Stone memorials had, however, been adopted earlier by Scandinavian converts in the west, most notably in northern England and on the Isle of Man. As knowledge of Viking architecture is based on excavated remains rather than on standing structures, it is difficult to be precise about the appearance of buildings (*see* §III below).

3. STYLISTIC CHRONOLOGY. The majority of Viking art styles—Oseberg, Borre, Jelling and Mammen—are named after grave finds, although the relevant artefacts are not necessarily the most typical or important examples of the style as a whole (for stylistic characteristics *see* §II, 1 below). A Norwegian geological term has been adopted for the Ringerike style, and the Urnes style is named after Stave church carvings referred to above. Although there are inevitable overlaps in period fashions, and the situation is further complicated by the practice of mass-producing jewellery by casting from existing pieces, the styles coincide roughly with the following periods:

Early Viking period: Style III: E and F; Oseberg style
Middle Viking period: Borre style; Jelling style
Late Viking period: Mammen style; Ringerike style; Urnes style; Urnes-Romanesque style

Relative chronology, from typology and find associations, must remain the basis for dating most of the material, although such modern techniques as dendrochronology, where they are applicable, are permitting a firmer absolute chronology.

1. Three gilt-bronze harness-mounts from a set of 22 (from left to right), (a) 50×33 mm, (b) 56×35 mm, (c) 50×28 mm, from Broa, Gotland, Sweden, late 8th century AD (Stockholm, Statens Historiska Museum)

2. Oseberg-style oval brooch (detail), silver, 63×103 mm, from Gimmeland, Hordaland, Norway, early 9th century AD (Universitetet i Bergen, Historisk Museum)

BIBLIOGRAPHY

S. Grieg: *Vikingetidens skattefund* [Viking period treasure], Universitetets Oldsaksamling, Skrifter, ii (Oslo, 1929)
P. Paulsen: *Studien zur Wikingerkultur* (Neumünster, 1933)
J. Petersen: *British Antiquities of the Viking Period Found in Norway*, ed. H. Shetelig, Viking Antiquities, v (Oslo, 1940)
H. Arbman: *Birka*, i: *Die Gräber*, 2 vols (Uppsala, 1940–43)
H. Shetelig, ed.: *Viking Antiquities*, 6 vols (Oslo, 1940–54)
R. Skovmand: 'De danske skattefund fra vikingetid og den ældste middelalder indtil omkring 1150' [Danish treasure hoards from the Viking period and the earlier Middle Ages until *c.* 1150], *Aab. Nord. Oldknd. & Hist.* (1942), pp. 1–275
H. Shetelig: *Arkeologi, historie, kunst, kultur: Mindre avhandlinger utgitt til syttiårsdagen, 25 juni 1947* [Archaeology, history, art, culture: lesser dissertations published for his 70th birthday, 25 June 1947] (Bergen, 1947) [collected articles]

3. Borre-style trefoil brooch, silver, w. 62 mm, from Vangsnes, Sogn og Fjordane, Norway, late 9th century AD (Universitetet i Bergen, Historisk Museum)

W. Holmqvist: 'Viking Art in the Eleventh Century', *Acta Archaeol.* [Copenhagen], xxii (1951), pp. 1–56
H. Christiansson: *Sydskandinavisk stil* [The south Scandinavian style] (Uppsala, 1959)
D. M. Wilson and O. Klindt-Jensen: *Viking Art* (London, 1966, rev. 1980)
C. Forsberg: 'Östergötlands vikingatida skattfynd' [Viking period treasures discovered in Östergötland], *Tor*, xii (1967–8), pp. 12–37
Sveagold und Wikingerschmuck (exh. cat., Mainz, Röm.–Ger. Zentmus., 1968)
P. G. Foote and D. M. Wilson: *The Viking Achievement* (London, 1970)
B. Hårdh: *Wikingerzeitliche Depotfunde aus Südschweden*, 2 vols (Lund, 1976)
J. Graham-Campbell: *Viking Artefacts: A Select Catalogue* (London, 1980)
——: *The Viking World* (London, 1980)
J. Graham-Campbell and D. Kidd: *The Vikings* (London, 1980)
M. Bencard, ed.: *Ribe Excavations, 1970–76*, i (Esbjerg, 1981–)
S. H. Fuglesang: 'Early Viking Art', *Acta Archaeol. & A. Hist. Pertinentia*, ii (1982), pp. 125–73
E. Roesdahl: *Viking Age Denmark* (London, 1982)
G. Arwidsson, ed.: *Birka*, II/i: *Systematische Analysen der Gräberfunde* (Stockholm, 1984)
E. Roesdahl: *The Vikings* (London, 1991)
M. Iverson, ed.: *Mammen: Grav, Kunst og Samfund i Vikingetid* [Mammen: grave, art and society in Viking times], Jysk Arkaeologiske Selskabs Skrifter, 28 (Århus, 1991) [incl. S. H. Fuglesang: 'The Axehead from Mammen and the Mammen Style', pp. 83–107]

For further bibliography see JELLING, OSEBERG, RINGERIKE and URNES.

JAMES GRAHAM-CAMPBELL

II. Decorative arts.

1. Stylistic and chronological survey. 2. Iconography and subject-matter. 3. Manufacture and workshops. 4. Regional survey.

1. STYLISTIC AND CHRONOLOGICAL SURVEY. Animal motifs, which have a continuous tradition in Scandinavian ornament throughout the Viking period, are the most important source for stylistic classification. Such classification is aided by specific diagnostic elements, for example the ribbon interlace of the middle Viking Borre style and the plant motifs of the late Viking Mammen and Ringerike styles.

(i) Style III: E. (ii) Style III: F. (iii) Oseberg style. (iv) Borre style. (v) Jelling style. (vi) Mammen style. (vii) Ringerike style. (viii) Urnes style. (ix) Urnes-Romanesque.

(i) Style III:E. This dates approximately from the second half of the 8th century to the early 9th and corresponds to the late phase of the third style identified by Bernhard Salin in *Die altgermanische Tierornamentik* (1904), a study of animal motifs between *c.* 500 and *c.* 800. The style is typified by ribbon-shaped animals with swelling and tapering bodies, frequently slit with wide openings and with a marked contraction separating two ballooning hips (see fig. 1a). Very elongated limbs and lappets make up open loops that entwine and surround the bodies. Surface patterning and frond-like terminals contribute to a restless effect. The same workshops that used style III:E animals also employed designs of semi-naturalistic animals and birds copied from west European, probably late Merovingian, models. In most cases they are stylized with the same swelling lines, slit bodies and entwining elements (1b). Another motif that was introduced at this stage is the gripping beast (1c), which is always rendered as a solid entity (juxtaposed to the style III:E manner of other motifs) and probably originated in the small, squirrel-like animals that appear in Anglo-Saxon scrolls.

The conglomeration of motifs and forms of this phase—a time of eclecticism, variety and innovation, which probably reflects an increase in trade with western Europe in the second half of the 8th century—is sometimes referred to as 'Broa style' because of the find of a set of 22 gilt-bronze harness-mounts at Broa, on Gotland, Sweden (Stockholm, Stat. Hist. Mus.; see fig. 1). The other major finds of this period are the typologically earliest carvings from Oseberg (those of the Academician and the Ship's Master). Important types of jewellery include disc-on-bow and oval brooches. The continuation of style III:E into the early 9th century is suggested by the Oseberg carvings, the occurrence of oval brooches in the style at Birka, Sweden, and the association of disc-on-bow brooches with metalwork looted from the British Isles in some Norwegian graves. The evidence of the Oseberg carvings also indicates the prominent role played by style III:E in shaping the Oseberg style.

(ii) Style III:F. This dates to the second half of the 8th century and is confined to Denmark, particularly to Jutland and Zealand. It was clearly adapted from Anglo-Carolingian work of the 'Tassilo-chalice style' (*see* CAROLINGIAN ART, §V) and is distinguished by almost abstract designs of animals with broad, irregular hips, short bodies and heads shown mostly in profile. Transverse striation is frequent, and outlines are incised. The compositions form carpet patterns within rectilinear panels. Only 12 pieces of characteristic style III:F survive, but they represent several types of metalwork, which suggests that the style was employed more generally in Denmark.

(iii) Oseberg style. This style is named after the site of the OSEBERG ship-burial in southern Norway, dated by dendochronology to 834, which contained a rich variety of wood-carving. While some of the carvings can be classified as style III:E, the work of the Baroque Master exemplifies the new style (for illustration *see* OSEBERG). The motifs are developed forms of the semi-naturalistic and gripping animal types introduced in style III:E, while ribbon-shaped animals play a subdued role. The innovations are mainly formal: compositions with motifs of equal size and compositional value disposed in a carpet-pattern manner; the suppression of open loops; a preference for squat animal types; and the plasticity of a graded relief, creating new plays of light and shade.

There is considerable variety within the Oseberg style, and it must have been employed throughout Scandinavia. Some types of oval brooch, in particular the new equal-armed brooch, reflect the personal manner of their originators, for example the brooch from Gimmeland, Hordaland, Norway (U. Bergen, Hist. Mus.; see fig. 2). Most surviving specimens, however, are attributable to copyists. Probably as a result of mass production, metalwork of the advanced stages of the Oseberg style tends to a flatter relief, but the play of light and shade is maintained through the deep grooving of the animals and small, free-standing mammals riveted to the surface of some types of brooch. Foreign influences have not been identified for the Oseberg style proper, but there are some indications of Anglo-Saxon influence on metalwork attributable to the same chronological phase. The pair of semi-naturalistic animals occupying the main panel of a new type of oval brooch is best explained against the background of the Anglo-Saxon tradition for this motif, and the squat proportions and angular outlines that were innovations in Scandinavian animal art in the second half of the 9th century are comparable to formal elements in the Anglo-Saxon Trewhiddle style.

(iv) Borre style. It was developed before the last quarter of the 9th century, and its mature phase is probably datable to the last quarter of the 9th century to the mid-10th. The most common type of animal motif is a mixture of ribbon-shaped and gripping beast, frontally rendered, with polygonal hips, four legs, a ribbon body often composed as a circle or pretzel and a triangular fronted head; one example of this is the brooch from Vangsnes, Sogn og Fjordane,

4. Gilt-bronze harness-mounts, h. 40 mm (largest), from Borre, Vestfold, Norway, late 9th century AD–early 10th (Oslo, Universitetets Oldsaksamlingen)

5. Mass-produced oval brooch, detail showing highly stylized animals of unclassified style, bronze, l. 109 mm, from Ärentuna, Uppland, Sweden, late 9th century AD (Stockholm, Statens Historiska Museum)

Norway (U. Bergen, Hist. Mus.; see fig. 3). This animal is an indigenous innovation, while novel types of angular, semi-naturalistic mammals seem to have been based on European models. Almost equally important are the ribbon motifs, of which the ring chain and the pretzel knot are especially common. They often have animal-headed terminals, for example on mounts from Borre, Vestfold, Norway (Oslo, U. Oldsaksaml.; see fig. 4). The extensive use of ribbon motifs may be due to European influence, but the peculiar types of interlace and knotwork appear to

6. Cup with engraved frieze of animals, silver, gold and niello, h. 42 mm, from the royal burial mound at Jelling, Jutland, Denmark, c. AD 925–50 (Copenhagen, Nationalmuseum)

be Scandinavian inventions. Plant motifs were copied from west European metalwork. The acanthus leaf was used mainly on cast trefoil and tongue-shaped brooches, indicating that the motif was adopted following the conversion of looted Frankish sword mounts into brooches. The leaf motifs normally retain the character of copies and appear to have been used for only a short time, probably c. 900. The full vine is rare, but it survives on trefoil brooches both in the form of very high-quality copies and transformed into a Scandinavian idiom. The pair of spirals, of either Anglo-Saxon or Carolingian origin, was used for both cast and filigree work, notably on trefoil brooches and various types of pendants. Unlike the acanthus and vine, the spirals were included in the Scandinavian ornamental repertory and continued into the 11th century.

The Borre style arrangement of animals and ribbons is dominated by equilateral shapes in static and repetitive compositions, with a preference for geometrical forms and the use of contrasts (e.g. juxtaposing circles and squares, or a grooved animal body with highly polished head and legs). New types of jewellery, notably pendants, trefoil brooches and circular brooches, were decorated with Borre-style ornament, while most types of oval brooch have animal motifs that are not immediately classifiable (e.g. the panel on a brooch from Ärentuna, Uppland, Sweden; Stockholm, Stat. Hist. Mus.; see fig. 5).

The Borre style is the earliest Scandinavian style to have been produced in the Viking settlements in Iceland, England and Russia. This indicates that it had been developed in the Scandinavian homelands before the last quarter of the 9th century. The earliest Scandinavian coin-dated hoard with decorated metalwork, deposited c. 925 at Vester Vedsted, Denmark, contains a Borre-style animal; further hoards with Borre-style ornaments were deposited c. 940 and 950. Anglo-Scandinavian stone-carving in Yorkshire apparently started c. 900 and is decorated in the Borre and Jelling styles. Historical inference suggests a dating after 910 for Anglo-Scandinavian stone-carving in the Borre style in Cumbria, while the Borre-style stone crosses on the Isle of Man are probably later than the Cumbrian ones.

(v) Jelling style. The only style to be classified by a motif alone, Jelling overlaps both the Borre and the Mammen styles. The term denotes a group of ribbon- and S-shaped animals and is usually dated to the mid-10th century. The point of departure is an engraved frieze on a small silver, gold and niello cup found in the royal burial mound at JELLING, Jutland, Denmark. It shows two elongated S-shaped animals in profile, intertwined in diagonal symmetry with bodies of even width without hips (Copenhagen, Nmus; see fig. 6). While Borre types might curve the animal body into an asymmetrical loop or pretzel, Jelling-style loops are open and animal hips subdued or absent. Some metalwork of the Jelling style has ribbon-shaped animals with slit bodies, suggesting either a tradition or, more probably, a revival of the slit animal type of style III:E. When Jelling-type animals are associated with Borre ornaments, the latter are normally attributable to an advanced stage of the Borre style, for example in the Gokstad grave, Norway, and the hoard from Vårby in Södermanland, Sweden, deposited *c.* 940. Other dating indications are supplied by the Jelling cup, which was found in the North Mound started in 958-9, and by the fragment of a very fine stone slab found in York in a mid-10th-century level.

(vi) Mammen style. Of similar importance to style III:E, this innovative phase is named after an inlaid axehead (Copenhagen, Nmus.) from Mammen, Jutland, Denmark, and is assumed to have flourished in the second half of the 10th century. The semi-naturalistic lion and bird based on west European prototypes emerged as new motifs, and the older Scandinavian snake was revitalized and given a new prominence.

The plant scroll was also introduced from either Anglo-Saxon art or from sources elsewhere in Europe, but unlike what happened in the Borre phase it was translated into a Scandinavian style rather than remaining a mere copy (see fig. 7). Formal characteristics include the use of one or two large motifs that fill a panel by abrupt twists and turns; the asymmetrical composition of scrolls; ornament lines that widen abruptly into panel-like shapes; and wavy and frequently dented outlines. The latest innovations in mass-produced bronze ornaments took place in the Jelling style, and although such ornaments were presumably still made and worn, innovation now seems to have occurred in new groups of monuments, such as decorated memorial stones, bone-carving and engraved and filigreed silver.

7. Mammen-style Crucifixion scene entwined by a scroll, from King Harald's memorial stone (side C) at Jelling, Jutland, Denmark, *c.* AD 960–85

The large memorial stone erected by King Harald at Jelling (see fig. 7; for further illustration *see* JELLING) can be dated to the 960s both by its inscription and by plausible inference from German annals on the conversion of the Danes. It is unique as a ruler's monument and seems to have begun the fashion for decorating runic memorials in Denmark and subsequently on the Scandinavian peninsula. The confrontation of lion and snake in battle may likewise be the earliest instance of this iconography in Scandinavia; certainly there is no surviving antecedent, and it was widely influential on animal representations throughout the 11th century. The Crucifixion entwined by a scroll is the only Viking example of this iconography and must have had a west European vine-entwined Crucifixion as its model. Aside from the inlaid axehead from Mammen, which came from a grave dated dendrochronologically to the winter of 970–71, further finds include two silver brooches from the hoard deposited *c.* 950 at Skaill, Orkney (Edinburgh, N. Mus. Ant.), and simple wood-carvings from the lowest level of medieval Trondheim (U. Trondheim, Mus.), as well as bone-carving and metalwork of very high artistic quality from undatable contexts. The geographical extent of the style, particularly of its plant motifs, remains conjectural.

(vii) Ringerike style. Used in the 11th century, the RINGE-RIKE style continued to employ Mammen-style animal motifs with some alterations. The main innovations lie in the handling of plant motifs and composition schemes, which indicate influence from Anglo-Saxon and Ottonian ornament. The fully developed Ringerike style is exemplified by the memorial stone at Vang Church, Oppland, Norway (see fig. 8): a double scroll with stems in strict axiality; asymmetrically placed groups of short and intertwined tendrils; and a rosette-shaped cross composed of alternating broad lobes with thin tendrils. Above the scroll, a walking lion and a small spiral with short offshoots along the outline emphasize the additive character of the full composition. The use of both Anglo-Saxon and Ottonian composition schemes—respectively the alternation of tendril and lobe, and groups of short intertwined tendrils—indicates that the Ringerike style was created in a Danish centre or centres, under the auspices of the nascent Church organization. The spread of the style throughout Scandinavia and to southern England and Dublin followed both the Church and the traditional lines of copying and trading. It was used, for example, for the vegetal frieze on the wooden panels from Flatatunga, Iceland (Reykjavík, N. Mus.), the fragments of which are the oldest surviving church decoration in Scandinavia. It also occurs both with and without Christian connotations on memorial stones in Norway and Sweden, on metal vanes and on plain wooden objects recovered from the lower 11th-century levels in the medieval towns of Trondheim and Oslo, Norway, and Lund, Skåne, Sweden. Dating is further confirmed by two coin-dated hoards, deposited *c.* 1025 and 1035, and by two Anglo-Saxon psalters of the second quarter of the century that contain Ringerike-style elements (Cambridge, U. Lib., MS. Ff.I.23; Rome, Bib. Vaticana, MS. Reg. Lat.13). The latest datable specimens are of the third quarter of the 11th century and show influence of the Urnes style.

8. Ringerike-style memorial stone at Vang Church, Oppland, Norway, c. 1000–1050

(viii) Urnes style. Taking its name from carvings on the Stave church at URNES in Sogn, Norway, the Urnes style, from the second quarter of the 11th century, is the latest Viking style proper. In contrast to the Mammen and Ringerike styles, the Urnes repertory is dominated by extremely stylized mammals (some of them lions), ribbon-shaped animals and snakes. The winged dragon makes its first Scandinavian appearance on some Upplandic memorial stones of the second quarter of the 11th century. Equal-armed crosses were used frequently on Swedish memorials. Some vegetal motifs were continued from the Ringerike style, particularly the single scroll and the union knot, but they were transformed into the Urnes idiom. Urnes-style designs are characterized by an underlying aim for unity. Typically, a design has only two contrasting line widths; animal heads and feet are reduced to mere elongated terminals; figure-of-eight and multi-loop compositions form an open and asymmetrical network of circular shapes; and larger animals frequently exhibit a gradual swelling and tapering of the body (e.g. the memorial stone at Sundby, Uppland, Sweden; see fig. 9).

The most impressive monuments are the runic memorials in Sweden, with more than 1100 stones in Uppland forming the centre of both quality and quantity; but the style is found throughout Scandinavia, and neither the area of origin nor the possible influences from elsewhere in Europe have been determined. Some Urnes-style metalwork was produced in England, but by far the greater impact was made in Ireland, where the main Urnes-style elements were applied in the revitalization of Irish art in the late 11th century and the 12th. The earliest phase of the Urnes style in Scandinavia is datable to the second quarter of the 11th century, mainly on the basis of runic memorials that mention the taking of danegeld in England under Knut the Great (latest payment, 1018) and one coin-dated hoard deposited c. 1050. These datings have been confirmed by several Urnes-style carvings from Oslo (Oslo, U. Oldsaksaml.) in levels datable to c. 1050–1100.

Like the Ringerike style, the Urnes idiom is intimately connected with church buildings and Christian monuments. Among the most important fragments of church ornament are the 11th-century doorway, post, planks and gables incorporated in the present mid-12th-century church at Urnes. Most of the Upplandic memorials carry a cross or a Christian inscription, or both. Secular objects

9. Urnes-style memorial stone at Sundby, Uppland, Sweden, c. 1050–1100

10. Urnes-Romanesque-style wooden bench, l. 2.14 m, from Kungsåra Church, Västmanland, Sweden, c. 1100–1150 (Stockholm, Statens Historiska Museum)

decorated in the Urnes style include weapons, a new type of animal-shaped brooches and wood-carving from medieval towns.

(ix) Urnes-Romanesque. A transitional, late 11th-century style, Urnes-Romanesque retains some Urnes motifs, notably the ribbon-shaped animal and the snake. The main impact of the Urnes tradition lies in the form: the contrast of two line widths, multi-loop compositions, sinuous swelling and tapering of animals and scrolls (e.g. the wooden bench from Kungsåra Church, Västmanland, Sweden; Stockholm, Stat. Hist. Mus.; see fig. 10). Most of the motifs and stylistic elements in Urnes-Romanesque were, however, imported from western Europe. The Romanesque type of winged dragon was introduced and became a staple element alongside the full set of Romanesque animal symbols, scrolls and leafwork. The Urnes-Romanesque phase is found throughout Scandinavia and is more heterogeneous than the Urnes style, with more local schools and with purely Romanesque ornament being produced at the same time. The scant dating indications in Scandinavia include excavated levels of c. 1100–1175 in Oslo. There was a parallel development in Ireland in the first half of the 12th century, which, to judge from the donor inscriptions, had no ethnic connections with the population of the Norse towns. Similar transitional monuments in England are few in number, and their motifs are restricted.

2. ICONOGRAPHY AND SUBJECT-MATTER.

(i) Ornament. (ii) Narrative.

(i) Ornament.

(a) Animals. (b) Masks and human figures. (c) Plant motifs. (d) Geometric and ribbon motifs.

(a) Animals. On the whole, Scandinavian animal ornament seems to follow the norm of most medieval ornament: its character is mainly decorative, and although specific motifs in particular contexts were probably intended as symbols, no general rules can be inferred. In the absence of written evidence, any case for symbolic interpretation must be based on the study of animal species, the ornamental function of the motif and the frequency, dating and origin of each separate animal type. The most common animal types in late Viking art are the lion (or four-legged beasts derived from it), the ribbon-shaped animal and the snake. Birds (mostly eagles, ravens and hawks) occur more sporadically.

Only the ribbon-shaped animal can be found throughout the Viking period, but even this was neither consistently popular nor morphologically unchanged. During the Oseberg and Borre styles of the 9th century and the early 10th, the ribbon-shaped animal was used sparsely, and its shape was refashioned in accordance with that of the gripping beast. The motif was renewed with the Jelling style, but it became of major importance only with the 11th-century Urnes style, possibly owing to its morphological similarity to the dragon, which was gradually gaining importance in contemporary animal art elsewhere in Europe. Other animal motifs appeared for only limited periods. The horse disappeared from Scandinavian ornament c. 800. The eagle, introduced from western Europe and dropped before the Viking period proper, appeared again only with the Mammen style in the mid-10th century.

The snake, which made its first appearance in Scandinavia on the Gallehus horns of c. 400 (untraced) in a narrative, symbolic context, is found in the 9th century as the spiralled prow of the Oseberg ship, a form that was continued in Borre-style sets of animal-shaped pendants. Scholarly interest has concentrated on the fight between the lion and the snake, probably introduced as an emblematic type with King Harald's memorial stone at Jelling. The meaning of the confrontation between the lion and the snake is uncertain. On the Jelling stone, the representation may be interpreted in two ways: if the animals are seen in context with the Crucifixion on the other side of the stone, the interpretation can be based on biblical and exegetical texts, for example Psalm 91 (and commentaries) or the Lion of Judah; if, however, the lion and snake are interpreted from the accompanying inscription, which sets forth Harald's political and military achievements, an honorific symbolism probably connected with the secular insignia of European rulers may be assumed. Either way, the animals on the Jelling stone must reflect contemporary west European ideas.

The lion and snake fight does not seem to have been adopted on other memorials of the late 10th century and the early 11th. The lion is used separately or alternatively with a cross, a mask or a ship on some memorials in Skåne, in Västergötland, Sweden, and at Vang, Norway (see fig. 8 above), but the gilt vane from Källunge, Gotland (Visby, Gotlands Fornsal), where a military or aristocratic meaning is likely, is the only surviving testimony to a tradition of the fight motif in this period. It was only with the Urnes style, of the second quarter of the 11th century onwards, that the motif became more widespread, occurring both on several memorial stones in Uppland, Sweden, on Urnes Church (where a Christian significance may be presumed) and on some animal-shaped brooches. The animal fight on these monuments must be interpreted according to the different contexts of the motif. It is probably theological or exegetical on a church, and may be Christian, secularly honorific and eschatological on memorials. It is also significant that, irrespective of context, most Urnes-style monuments show animals and snakes intertwined decoratively rather than as opponents in battle.

The semi-naturalistic mammals of style III:E recur to some extent in the Oseberg carvings and as details on some oval brooches. In metalwork of the Oseberg phase, however, other animal types were more common. The plastically modelled, semi-naturalistic animals on early types of oval brooch (see fig. 2 above) were retained but gave rise to more stylized versions (see fig. 5 above). Neither in their original state nor in subsequent adaptations are they shown as fighting; they are catlike creatures rendered either separately in panels or as pairs in playful postures. The related gripping beast is rendered in separate panels (see fig. 1c above), as pairs and, in some instances, in carpet-pattern compositions. The gripping pose appears not to connote fighting but to be mainly a means of linking the animals to each other and to the framework. Moreover, the typological merging of the gripping beast, originally from western Europe, with its plastic, catlike cousin of the same origin, and of both with the indigenous ribbon-shaped animal, does not suggest symbolic overtones for any of these motifs. A pair of semi-naturalistic animals, confronted or addorsed, was used for the main panel of most types of oval brooch in the 9th and 10th centuries

(see fig. 5 above). The motif is often assumed to originate in Anglo-Saxon art, although Scandinavian precursors in style III:E do occur (for example in the Oseberg carvings). Again, nothing in this motif suggests a peculiarly Scandinavian symbolism.

In changing stylistic form, the originally west European gripping beast and semi-naturalistic animal types dominated Scandinavian ornament throughout the 9th century and well into the 10th. The hybrid gripping and ribbon beast of the Borre style, especially, was used indiscriminately on harness-mounts, horse collars, sword chapes, women's pendants and brooches (see fig. 3 above). Most of the animals from style III:E through to the Borre style are mild-mannered grotesques, often humorous in appearance. The types are so varied and adopted from so many Christian sources that they are unlikely to reflect any inherent Scandinavian symbolism.

It is a striking fact that during the period when the Viking onslaught on the rest of Europe was at its most intense, the characteristic types of Scandinavian animal motifs were neither ferocious nor fighting. Animals whose ferocity can be deduced from stance, expression, open jaws etc are surprisingly few. They are restricted in use to c. 600–750 and to the late Viking styles (c. 950–1100); that is to say, to periods when the influence of continental western Europe was pronounced. The animal-head posts in Oseberg do have the open jaws and prominent teeth suggestive of ferocity, but these may have had an apotropaic function; their close morphological similarities to animal-head terminals of European furniture depicted in 10th and 11th-century manuscripts suggest a common north European usage.

(b) Masks and human figures. The mask, both human and animal, occurs throughout Viking art, used most frequently for terminals but also incorporated in compositions with other motifs. It is a staple element of some types of equal-armed brooches: early and ornate types frequently have anthropomorphic masks at the end of each arm, while the mass-produced type most common in the 10th century has animal masks. For the purpose of terminals, human and animal masks seem to be interchangeable, suggesting either that they did not carry any specific meaning or that they had an identical symbolic function. Masks appear to proliferate towards and after 900. The oval brooches exemplify this: although practically all oval brooch types were created with only semi-naturalistic and gripping beast motifs, on the most popular 9th-century type a mask was substituted for the main pair of animals on late varieties, while on the most common 10th-century type the animals in the top panels were exchanged for the mask of a bearded man. The increasing importance of the human mask is further indicated by its occasional use as a separate motif on memorial stones from the Mammen style onwards, as well as in metalwork and bone-carving. In contrast to Romanesque grotesque masks, Viking masks are rendered in a fairly straightforward manner with all features intact, including both eyes. Clearly the mask, especially the human mask, was important in mid- and late Viking iconography, but there are no good Scandinavian indications for its interpretation.

The full human figure occurs only very sporadically in ornament, but there are some interesting examples. Surrounded by ribbon loops of style III:E, the figure of a man is repeated four times on a small group of Norwegian oval brooches from c. 800 (U. Trondheim, Mus.). A similar man is shown on the runner of Shetelig's sledge in Oseberg (Oslo, Vikingskipshuset), and another is shown entwined with a Mammen-style scroll on a bone plaque recovered from the River Thames (London, BM). A fragmentary wood-carving from Tune, Norway (Oslo, U. Oldsaksaml.), shows a number of small standing men bound tightly together by Borre-style knots, and a painted wood-carving from the royal grave at Jelling, Jutland (Copenhagen, Nmus.), presumably from a piece of furniture, has a single profile man. The meaning of such figures is obscure and, considering the different contexts, probably not identical. The surviving instances indicate that the motif was ornamental rather than narrative and belonged more to the repertory of carving than to that of metalwork.

Women make only one known appearance on standard jewellery. On a piece found on Karmøy, Norway (Stavanger, Arkeol. Mus.), a local smith of the mid-9th century substituted four nude women for the animals normally found on a type of brooch used throughout Scandinavia. This seems to be the only surviving instance of nude women in Viking art, and whether they should be interpreted as a fertility symbol or simply as a piece of playfulness remains uncertain. The profile of a fully dressed woman used as a terminal on some types of 10th-century silver toilet implements is apparently culled from narrative art; the same type is used both as a Valkyrie on the Gotlandic picture stones c. 800 (see fig. 11) and on votive gold plaques (see §(ii)(c) below). In its ornamental function, the figure may have carried narrative overtones.

(c) Plant motifs. The scroll may probably be interpreted as the Christian vine when, for example, it entwines Christ on the Jelling stone (see fig. 7 above) or forms the stem of a cross, as on the Vang stone (see fig. 8 above). Whether the plant motifs above the row of saints on the panels from Flatatunga, Iceland (Reykjavík, N. Mus.), should be taken as a similar symbol remains uncertain. In most other contexts, for example on late Viking jewellery, weapons and vanes, the scrolls correspond to normal European types and usage, and symbolical overtones are unlikely.

(d) Geometric and ribbon motifs. Some geometric and ribbon motifs have occasionally been interpreted as symbols. In early Viking art, the cross recurs in various functions: frequently forming a framework (e.g. the Broa harness-mounts, see fig. 1 above; on some oval brooches of style III:E; and on Shetelig's sledge in Oseberg (Oslo, Vikingskipshuset), but even as a motif of surface patterning ('Carolingian' animal-head post in Oseberg; Oslo, Vikingskipshuset) and as a geometrical motif (two types of oval brooches; see fig. 5 above). Although they may have originated as copies of west European models, there seems to be no reason to attribute a Christian significance to these late 8th- and early 9th-century cross shapes. They were used for only a short period and were put to various, but always secondary, ornamental uses. The cross began to be used as a Christian symbol in Scandinavia in the

10th century, surviving mainly in pendant crosses, and as a clearly Christian symbol on memorial stones of the 11th century.

Among the ribbon motifs, the triquetra has been interpreted as a symbol when it occurs in Romanesque and Christian Viking contexts. The motif has a fairly long tradition in Scandinavia, however, and from the Oseberg style onwards it was normally used to fill triangular panels in all types of ornamented work; its ornamental context in Viking art argues against a general symbolic interpretation and suggests that its function should be studied more systematically before conclusions are drawn. A similar case is the two-loop union knot, which was introduced in the Borre style from Carolingian or Anglo-Saxon ornament. It was used as a secondary motif to tie together two tangential ornament lines, and this function was retained when the motif was reintroduced in the 11th-century Ringerike style, this time affixed with an Ottonian-type offshoot. In the subsequent Urnes style, the union knot was occasionally given greater prominence, but its function remained the same. Only on a small group of Jutish 12th-century churches does it occur as a separate motif in the tympanum. Neither the west European nor the Scandinavian history of the motif substantiates its interpretation as a Tree of Life or cross substitute.

(ii) Narrative. Pictorial narrative art in the Viking period is known largely through monuments and from descriptions contained in skaldic poetry. Though haphazard, this source material shows that the pictorial arts must have been far more important than is commonly supposed.

(a) Monuments. (b) Literary descriptions. (c) Other forms.

(a) Monuments. The incidence of decorated memorial stones shows strong regional and chronological variations. Figure scenes dominate the group of Gotlandic picture stones of the late 8th century and the early 9th, and a similar iconography is found on one contemporary stone in Sparlösa, Västergötland, Sweden. There is then a hiatus for decorated stones until King Harald's memorial at Jelling of c. 960–85, which seems to have set the fashion for the decoration of memorial stones in the late Viking period. This fashion must have spread to Skåne, Västergötland and Södermanland in Sweden and to some areas of southern Norway, all of which preserve decorated memorials from the first half of the 11th century. The great production of Swedish Urnes-style memorials began only in the second quarter of that century, however, and even there the fashion lasted only two or three generations. Late Viking memorials are dominated by animal motifs, but the narrative scenes that were included are of interest for understanding the iconography in the period of conversion to Christianity.

The most consistent group of monuments is that of the memorial stones in Gotland of the late 8th century and early 9th. Their iconography seems to have a mainly eschatological content: most of the surviving stones have a dominating representation of a ship and a rider, which has been interpreted as the journey of the deceased to Valhalla (see fig. 11), while some have heroic battle scenes that are presumably also eschatological because afterlife in Valhalla was contingent on death in battle. On a few stones, the representation of a woman in a carriage may signify the deceased's journey to the afterlife. The parallels between what is depicted on the Gotland stones and the actual burials containing a boat or a carriage, with or without horses, are suggestive.

Most memorial stones have additional mythological and heroic scenes. Some can be interpreted in the light of later, written traditions and include both Scandinavian myths, such as Thor's fishing expedition, and Germanic subjects such as Wieland the Smith. A fairly large number of scenes cannot be interpreted with certainty, however. An example of this is the memorial from Alskog Tjängvide, Gotland (c. 800; Stockholm, Stat. Hist. Mus.; see fig. 11); in the lower panel the ship is manned by warriors, while in the upper the rider (in this case on Odin's eight-legged horse, Sleipnir) is received by a woman who has reasonably been identified as a Valkyrie. The building at the upper left is normally taken to represent Valhalla. A man and a woman below the building have not been identified, while two men in the upper right are interpreted either as belonging to a mythical/heroic scene or as taking part in the battle fought daily among the heroes of Valhalla.

Comparatively few memorial stones of the 11th century have pictures, but those that do show a great iconographical variety of Christian, secular and pagan scenes. The Gotlandic stone-carvers revived the memorial types of their ancestors. Most of these late Viking stones have only animal or plant motifs based on current Upplandic memorials, but a few repeat the early Viking pictures of

11. Memorial stone from Alskog Tjängvide, Gotland, Sweden, c.AD 800 (Stockholm, Statens Historiska Museum)

warriors (Sanda I), a rider (Bosarve), and a carriage (Levide), which probably copy the early Viking representations, and one (Hablingbo) repeats the ship and the rider, though on separate sides of the stone. Although there is no indication that the revival of monument types and iconography had any lasting influence on Gotlandic art, these stones are interesting as the only fairly definite example of an indigenous revival in Viking art.

The image of a boat is also used below a lion on the stone at Tullstorp, Skåne, indicating that the symbolism of the journey was not confined to the Gotlandic memorials. More important among the pagan monuments, however, is the stone at Altuna, Uppland, Sweden, which has Thor's fishing expedition below a rider. Such outspokenly pagan iconography is very unusual among the 11th-century Upplandic memorials, which are normally Christian (c. 64% bear a cross and 26% a Christian invocation).

The hunt is a secular theme that was carved from widely different prototypes on memorials at Balingsta, Uppland, Sweden (see fig. 12), and Alstad, Norway. The picture of a rider below a bird on some Upplandic stones may be either an abbreviated hunt or an echo of the early Viking journey theme. The hunt reflected the social standing and manly virtues of the deceased and may have had eschatological overtones. The earliest extant examples occur on the Isle of Man in the second half of the 10th century.

Among Christian motifs, the Adoration of the Magi on the memorial from Dynna, Norway (Oslo, U. Oldsaksaml.), is unique, and the transposition of the scene into a Scandinavian style has affected the iconography to some extent. Christian pictures are, however, extremely rare on the memorials: most of the Upplandic stones simply incorporate a cross among the animal motifs (see fig. 9 above). The usual European identification of the vine with the Church suggests that the vine-entwined Jelling Crucifixion reflects the victorious Church in a new province.

The dominance of ornament over narrative images on 11th-century memorial stones is reflected in the figure style and the setting of narrative scenes. The possible symbolism of ornamental motifs has been discussed above. Here the function of the motifs seems to have been primarily ornamental. In this, Scandinavian art followed a trend current in western Europe since the late 10th century, where book illumination, for example, shows the increasing importance of ornamental elements. The predominance of ornamental motifs in 11th-century Scandinavian memorial stones may also reflect the artistic situation following the conversion to Christianity. The pagan scenes that were still used or revived were the group least influenced by ornamentalization, probably because they represent the last crop of an established pictorial tradition. It must have taken time before new iconographical types of Christian content became generally available. The diversity of secular, heroic and Christian pictures on memorial stones may reflect this iconographically unsettled situation, and ornamental motifs hallowed by the inclusion of a cross or Christian invocation may have filled an iconographical hiatus.

(b) Literary descriptions. Heroic scenes painted on shields and rendered in textile, painting or carving on the interiors of halls are described in some skaldic poems. The

earliest of these that survives, written by Bragi Boddason in the first half of the 9th century, enumerates the scenes painted on a shield: Thor's fishing expedition; Gefion ploughing Denmark from Skåne; Sorle and Hamde killing Jormunrek; and the battle of the Haddings. There is no obvious relationship between these motifs, which convey the highlights of apparently completely disparate tales. This corresponds to the manner of rendering narrative scenes on the slightly earlier Gotlandic stones. A common Germanic tradition for this type of composition is indicated by its similarity to the Anglo-Saxon Franks' Casket (London, BM; *see* ANGLO-SAXON ART, fig. 13). Surviving Scandinavian monuments and poems demonstrate the existence of an established pagan and heroic iconography, which must have formed a tradition quite distinct from the decorative arts. This is corroborated by the style of the pictures; each scene, even when now unidentifiable, is rendered with stylized but not ornamentalized figures and must have been easily recognizable to an educated Scandinavian of the 9th century.

Further skaldic poems preserved from the 9th and 10th centuries describe other mythological pictures, for example Thor with his goats, Thor fighting the Midgard serpent, Odin's horse and the abduction of Idunn. The latest such poem, by Ulfr Uggason, dates from *c.* 985 and describes the pagan pictures in the new hall built by Olafr Pái in Iceland. These included the cremation of Balder, Loki and Heimdall competing at swimming and Thor's fishing expedition. In the 11th century skaldic poems describing pictures concentrate on the Sigurd saga. Chronologically this corresponds to the acceptance of Christianity, and there may be a direct connection. Sigurd was a hero, not a pagan god, and his story presumably lacked the overtones of pagan religion that pervaded many earlier representations. The Sigurd saga was used not only in the commemorative arts. According to the skald Þorfinnr Munnr (*d* 1030) it was used to decorate the tent of the Norwegian king St Olaf II Haraldsson, and Illuga Bryndælaskald described it slightly later in the hall of King Harald III Hardraade.

(c) Other forms. From Oseberg there are two carved narrative scenes on the cart. On the right long side, set in a frieze of ribbon-shaped animals, is a scene of a man and woman confronting a rider. The rendering is ambiguous, and no definite interpretation has been attempted. On the front of the cart is a man attacked by snakes and beasts in a very disorganized composition where ornament and narrative appear to mingle; the story of Gunner in the snake pit has been tentatively suggested.

The pre-Viking tradition of minute golden repoussé plaques continued into the 10th century. They were presumably votive offerings because they are too fragile to have served a practical function and are often found in groups. The iconography shows either a man or a woman on separate plaques, or a confronted couple. The latter type is the most common in the Viking age. The single figures have not been identified, but the couple is often interpreted as Gerd and Freyr and the iconography as a fertility symbol. The discovery of hundreds of such plaques in one location on the island of Bornholm, however, may cause older theories to be revised.

12. Memorial stone showing hunting scene, Balingsta, Uppland, Sweden, *c.* 1025–75

Two fragments of textile from Norway suggest that the journey theme may not have been exclusive to the commemorative arts. The fragment from Tune, Østfold, shows a large ship beside two zones of men and women. The fragmentary state of the piece makes interpretation impossible, but the similarity of the iconography to the Gotlandic stones should be noted. The earlier 9th-century tapestry from Oseberg (Oslo, Vikingskipshuset) has a large composition of warriors, women, horses and carts in what has been interpreted as a procession, but the lack of comparative material and the relative smallness of the surviving pieces make assertions tenuous.

No pictures from the middle Viking period survive in Scandinavia, but there are some unstudied Norse scenes in stone-carvings in Cumbria, England, and the Isle of Man, and more evidence could perhaps be found in 10th-century skaldic poems. Among the pictures should be noted the traditional Scandinavian iconography of Thor's fishing expedition on a stone at Gosforth Church, Cumbria, and the combination of the mythical, pagan Ragnarök and the Crucifixion on the elaborate cross at the same church. On the Manx crosses scenes from the Sigurd saga and secular hunting scenes may be noted. Neither theme survives from Scandinavia until the 11th century (*see* §(b) above).

From the 10th century onwards silver pectoral crosses bear scenes of the Crucifixion. They sometimes betray ornament-makers who stylized the rendering in the Borre (Birka, Sweden, grave 660), Ringerike (Trondheim, Norway) and Urnes styles (encolpium from Gåtebo, Sweden; Stockholm, Nmus.). Mostly, however, and with the exception of a Christ with bound arms from Lilla Klintegård,

13. Memorial carving on rock, showing scenes from the Sigurd Saga, Ramsundsberget, Södermanland, Sweden, *c*. 1000–1050

Gotland (Stockholm, Nmus.), they belong to contemporary west European types.

The panels from Flatatunga, Iceland, are probably the vestiges of the earliest extant Scandinavian church decoration. The scant remains, a row of haloed men below a panel of Ringerike-style leafwork, are too fragmentary for an iconographical identification. An 11th-century carving of the Sigurd story on a rock at Ramsundsberget, Södermanland, Sweden, shows the narrative unfolding through a pictorial sequence (see fig. 13), a principle as yet undocumented in earlier Scandinavian art.

Small bronze or bone statuettes of seated men are found occasionally, the datable examples being of the 11th century. An ithyphallic figure from Rällinge in Södermanland (Stockholm, Nmus.) is sometimes taken to be a miniature copy of a cult statue of the fertility god Freyr, mentioned by Adam of Bremen as being in the temple of Uppsala. Other statuettes of bearded men are interpreted variously as Thor or Odin. They are sometimes regarded as amulets on the strength of two 13th-century saga texts, which mention 9th- and 10th-century worship of amulets of Freyr and Thor respectively. There is little foundation for such theories, however, and the function of the statuettes remains uncertain. Those of bone may have been gaming-pieces.

3. MANUFACTURE AND WORKSHOPS.

(i) Metalwork. Surviving material demonstrates several personal styles and levels of proficiency in the making of cast ornaments. Studies of Scandinavian oval brooches have shown that mass production was achieved by alternating positive models, probably of wax (but not lost wax), with negative moulds of clay. Some of this copying must have been done by making casts from existing brooches, but visual copying must also have been fairly extensive. Studies of the peculiarly Gotlandic types of brooch have increased understanding of both the copying process and the fairly small number of craftsmen needed to meet a community's demand for metal ornaments. Excavations in Ribe, Denmark, have revealed extensive

workshop remains and thrown light on the seasonal workshops of ornament-makers who manufactured oval brooches as well as other cast metalwork. Isolated fragments of casting moulds have been found also at such trading centres as Hedeby in Jutland, Birka in Sweden and Paviken on Gotland, as well as at more peripheral sites such as Ytre Moa in western Norway.

The study of filigree ornament has shown how motifs and techniques were copied simultaneously from foreign prototypes and subsequently adapted in Scandinavian ornament. Metal relief blanks for the repoussé work that formed the base for filigree have been found in Hedeby and Mammen in Jutland, Malmö in Scania, Sigtuna and Tängbro in Uppland, Sweden, and York, England. They bear witness to the widespread manufacture of the more common types of filigree ornament and include an unusual type from Mammen, which has not survived in the hoards. What was evidently a silversmith's purse lost in the harbour of Hedeby in the mid-10th century (Schleswig, Schleswig-Holstein. Landesmus.) contained around 40 relief blanks, demonstrating the variety of types that could be manufactured by one man. Work by gold- and silversmiths is of consistently high quality; cast metalwork varies markedly from the highly proficient to the artistically amateurish, although even locally made brooches of deficient draughtsmanship are technically well cast.

There are no good indications of the structure of a workshop or the number of men employed, but internal evidence shows both that craft was taught and that cast ornaments were produced by three different groups of artists: designers, who invented or innovated types and ornamental motifs; craftsmen, who mass-produced such new types by copying; and local artisans, who may also have been all-round smiths. The seasonal workshop in Ribe and the purse with blanks from Hedeby are proof of skilled itinerant craftsmen. Evidence of the local copyists, who are likely to have been stationary, is seen in low-quality work, personal vagaries of draughtsmanship and the restricted geographical distribution of objects.

(ii) Wood-carving. Like metalworkers, wood-carvers must have been trained, but conclusions are tenuous because of the lack of surviving material. Clear differences in quality among the wood-carvings from 11th-century Trondheim have been seen as reflecting the work of both professional craftsmen and amateurs. The Oseberg find of the first half of the 9th century is unique in containing a great number of carvings from several hands, but it is uncertain whether they are the work of more or less contemporary craftsmen or whether their styles diverge because of chronological differences. The ornament of one type of oval brooch that was fairly widely copied and survives in approximately 100 examples can be linked to the Baroque Master in Oseberg, but this is so far the only instance of metal ornament coming close to surviving wood-carving. The general stylistic similarities between pieces of wood-carving and cast metalwork do suggest an interrelationship between the two crafts, however, and the technique of carving an original wax model for casting is very similar to wood-carving.

(iii) Stone-carving. The Upplandic memorial stones in Sweden give some indications of the practice of 11th-century rune-masters. Some of the stones have several signatures. When the verb *raða* occasionally occurs in this context, it has been interpreted as denoting a master overseeing apprentices or assistants. The noun *lið* (group) has been interpreted as a workshop or 'school'. A division of labour is occasionally attested, but only outside Uppland, for example on the stone sarcophagus from Eskilstuna, Södermanland, Sweden (Stockholm, Stat. Hist. Mus.), where one man made the monument and another the runic inscription.

The itinerant activity of the Upplandic rune-masters is exemplified by Åsmund Kåreson, whose signature appears alone on thirteen memorials and with other signatures on six others. Fifteen unsigned memorials can be attributed to him with a high degree of certainty, and sixteen more with reasonable probability. The signed memorials cover a large north–south tract of Uppland into Gästrikland, with a cluster around Uppsala and adjacent areas. Although Åsmund's memorials are palaeographically consistent, the ornament varies both in motif and individual style. There is some correlation between the geographical grouping of these stones and the ornament employed on them, which may suggest that Åsmund was the itinerant master who oversaw the shaping of the memorial and carved the inscription, while the ornament was executed by assistants under his supervision. Other rune-masters in Uppland, especially Balle and Fot, signed memorials with more homogeneous decoration.

(iv) Royal 'schools'. On the basis of artistic quality, specific style and the royal contexts of finds, clear evidence of royal 'schools' in Scandinavia has yet to emerge. The identification of the woman's grave at Oseberg as royal may be doubted, and in any case the wood-carvings there vary considerably in quality and style. The Borre grave, Norway, which probably is royal, was furnished with harness-mounts of a homogeneous style (see fig. 4 above) but not of a quality to set them apart from other contemporary ornaments. Likewise, the meagre remains from the royal grave at Jelling are not significantly distinct from contemporary Danish chieftains' graves. Yet it is in Denmark that a consistently high quality of workmanship, combined with traditional elements and innovative designs, suggests, if not a 'court school', then at least workshops specializing in royal and aristocratic clients. Chieftains' graves at Ladby, Lejre, Mammen and Søllested, for example, as well as King Harald's memorial stone at Jelling, indicate a 10th-century milieu in which the arts played a consciously accepted role. It must be emphasized, however, that the great majority of surviving ornaments from all areas of Scandinavia are of mass-produced types for the yeomanry and merchant classes.

BIBLIOGRAPHY

STYLES, ICONOGRAPHY AND SUBJECT-MATTER

S. Müller: 'Dyreornamentiken i Norden: Dens oprindelse, udvikling, og forhold til samtidige stilarter: En archæologisk undersøgelse' [Animal ornament in the North: its origin, development and connection with contemporary style: an archaeological investigation], *Aab. Nord. Oldknd. & Hist.* (1880), pp. 185–405

B. Salin: *Die altgermanische Tierornamentik* (Stockholm, 1904, rev. 2/1935)

H. Shetelig: *Osebergfundet* [The Oseberg find], iii (Christiania, 1920)

A. Bugge: 'The Golden Vanes of Viking Ships: A Discussion on a Recent Find at Källunge Church, Gotland', *Acta Archaeol.* [Copenhagen], ii (1931), pp. 160–84

R. Wittkower: 'Eagle and Serpent: A Study in the Migration of Symbols', *J. Warb. Inst.*, ii (1938–9), pp. 293–325

O. Almgren: 'Resan till Valhall' [Journey to Valhalla], *Uppländsk bygd* [Buildings in Uppland] (1940), pp. 29–37

O. von Friesen and B. Almgren: *Sparlösastenen* [Stones in Sparlösa] (Stockholm, 1940)

S. Lindqvist: *Gotlands Bildsteine*, 2 vols (Uppsala, 1941–2)

G. Gjessing: 'Hesten i förhistorisk kunst og kultus' [The horse in prehistoric art and culture], *Viking*, vii (1943), pp. 5–144

G. Haseloff: 'Zum Ursprung des nordischen Greiftierstils', *Festschrift für Gustav Schwantes* (Neumünster, 1951), pp. 202–11

M. Strömberg: 'Schwertortbänder mit Vogelmotiven aus der Wikingerzeit', *Meddel. Lunds U. Hist. Mus.* (1951), pp. 99–121

K. Eldjárn: 'Carved Panels from Flatatunga, Iceland', *Acta Archaeol.* [Copenhagen], xxiv (1953), pp. 81–101

B. Almgren: *Bronsnycklar och djurornamentik* [Bronze keys and animal ornament] (Uppsala, 1955)

J. Brøndsted: 'Thors fiskeri' [Thor's fishery], *Nmus. Arbejdsmk.* (1955), pp. 92–104

H. Lie: 'Billedbeskrivende dikt' [Narrative poems], *Kulturhistorisk leksikon for nordisk middelalder*, ed. J. Danstrup and others (Copenhagen, 1956), cols 542–5

T. Ramskou: 'Stil F: En skitse' [Style F: a sketch], *Aab. Nord. Oldknd. & Hist.* (1963), pp. 100–18

E. Bakka: 'Eit gravfunn frå Fosse i Meland, Hordaland, og det arkeologiske periodeskiljet mellom merovingartid og vikingtid' [A grave discovery from Fosse in Meland, Hordaland, and the archaeological transition period from the Merovingian to the Viking era], *Fin. Fornminnesfören. Tidskr.*, lxxv (1973), pp. 9–17

L. Buisson: *Der Bildstein Ardre VIII auf Gotland: Göttermythen, Heldensagen und Jenseitsglauben der Germanen im 8. Jahrhundert n. Chr.*, Abhandlungen der Akademie der Wissenschaften in Göttingen (Göttingen, 1976)

L. Karlsson: *Romansk träornamentik i Sverige* [Romanesque wood ornament in Sweden] (Klippan, 1976)

M. Blindheim: 'A Norwegian Eleventh-century Picture Stone: The Journey of the Magi to Bethlehem', *J. Brit. Archaeol. Assoc.*, cxxx (1977), pp. 145–56

S. H. Fuglesang: 'Crucifixion Iconography in Viking Scandinavia', *Proceedings of the Eighth Viking Congress: Århus, 1977*, pp. 73–94

S. Margeson: 'The Völsung Legend in Medieval Art', *Proceedings of the Fourth International Symposium at Odense University. Medieval Iconography and Narrative: Odense, 1979*, pp. 183–211

S. H. Fuglesang: *Some Aspects of the Ringerike Style: A Phase of 11th Century Scandinavian Art*, Medieval Scandinavia, Supplements, i (Odense, 1980)

M. Blindheim: 'The Gilded Viking Ship Vanes', *The Vikings*, ed. R. T. Furrell (London, 1981), pp. 116–27

S. H. Fuglesang: 'Stylistic Groups in Late Viking and Early Romanesque Art', *Acta Archaeol. & A. Hist. Pertinentia*, i (1981), pp. 79–125

L. Karlsson: 'Sløjfemotivet i Sverige under missionsskedet' [Bow motifs in Sweden in the missionary period], *Romanske stenarbejder*, ed. J. Vellev, i (Århus, 1981), pp. 91–118

E. Nylén and J. P. Lamm: *Bildsteine auf Gotland* (Neumünster, 1981)

S. H. Fuglesang: 'Woodcarving from Oslo and Trondheim and Some Reflections on Period Styles', *Festskrift til Thorleif Sjøvold* (Oslo, 1984), pp. 93–108

G. Haseloff: 'Stand der Forschung: Stilgeschichte Völkerwanderungs- und Merowingerzeit', *Festskrift til Thorleif Sjøvold* (Oslo, 1984), pp. 109–124

H. Roth, ed.: *Zum Problem der Deutung frühmittelalterlicher Bildinhalte* (Sigmaringen, 1986) [incl. K. Düwel: 'Zur Ikonographie und Ikonologie der Sigurddarstellungen', pp. 221–71; D. Ellmers: 'Schiffsdarstellungen auf skandinavischen Grabsteinen', pp. 341–72; S. H. Fuglesang: 'Ikonographie der skandinavischen Runensteine der jüngeren Wikingerzeit', pp. 183–210]

MANUFACTURE AND WORKSHOPS

J. Roosval: *Die Steinmeister Gotlands* (Stockholm, 1918)

J. Petersen: *Vikingetidens smykker* [Viking age jewellery] (Stavanger, 1928)

M. Rydbeck: *Skånes stenmästare före 1200* [Stonemasons in Skåne before 1200] (Lund, 1936)

G. Arwidsson: *Vendelstile, Email und Glas im 7.-8. Jahrhundert* (Uppsala, 1942)

C. Blindheim: 'En amulett av rav' [An amulet made of amber], *U. Oldsaksaml. Åb.* (1959), pp. 78–90

I. Zachrisson: 'De ovala spännbucklornas tillverkningssätt' [Oval buckle manufacturing methods], *Tor*, vi (1960), pp. 207–38

——: 'Smedsfyndet från Smiss' [Blacksmith finds from Smiss], *Tor*, viii (1962), pp. 201–28

E. Bakka: 'Some English Decorated Metal Objects Found in Norwegian Viking Graves', *U. Bergen Åb.* (1963), pp. 3–66

W. Holmqvist: *Övergångstidens metallkonst* [Metal art in the transitional period] (Stockholm, 1963)

A. Oldeberg: *Metalteknik under vikingatid och medeltid* [Metalworking techniques during the Viking and medieval periods] (Stockholm, 1966)

T. Capelle: *Der Metallschmuck von Haithabu* (Neumünster, 1968)

M. Bencard: 'Wikingerzeitliches Handwerk in Ribe: Eine Übersicht', *Acta Archaeol.* [Copenhagen], il (1978), pp. 113–38

W. Duczko: 'Vikingatida silversmycken i Mora-skatten: Den icke-monetära delen av en nyupptäckt silverskatt från Dalarna' [Viking silver jewellery in the Mora treasure: the non-monetary part of a newly discovered silver treasure hoard from Dalarna], *Tor*, xviii (1978–9), pp. 311–57

A. S. Gräslund: 'Vikingatidens örslevar: Ursprung och funktion' [Viking-period ear ladles: origins and function], *Tor*, xviii (1978–9), pp. 295–310

K. Schietzel and O. Crumlin-Pedersen: 'Havnen i Hedeby' [The harbour of Hedeby], *Skalk*, 3 (1980), pp. 4–10

D. M. Wilson and M. L. Caygill, eds: *Economic Aspects of the Viking Age*, BM Occasional Papers, xxx (London, 1981) [incl. articles by S. H. Fuglesang: 'Woodcarvers, Professionals and Amateurs in Eleventh-century Trondheim', pp. 21–6; I. Jansson: 'Economic Aspects of Fine Metalworking in Viking Scandinavia', pp. 1–19]

A. Andersson: *Medieval Drinking Bowls of Silver Found in Sweden* (Stockholm, 1983)

A. Carlsson: *Djurhuvudformiga spännen och gotländsk vikingatid* [Animal head clasps and the Viking period in Gotland] (Stockholm, 1983)

L. Thunmark-Nylén: *Vikingatida dosspännen: Teknisk stratigrafi och verkstadsgruppering* [Box buckles from the Viking period: technical stratigraphy and workshop groups] (Uppsala, 1983)

W. Duczko: *The Filigree and Granulation Work of the Viking Period*, Birka, v (Stockholm, 1985)

I. Jansson: *Ovala spännbucklor* (Uppsala, 1985)

E. Wamers: *Insularer Metallschmuck in wikingerzeitlichen Gräbern*, Offa-Bücher, lvi (Neumünster, 1985)

S. H. Fuglesang: 'The Personal Touch: On the Identification of Workshops', *Proceedings of the Tenth Viking Congress: Oslo, 1987*, pp. 219–30

RUNES

Sveriges runinskrifter [Swedish rune inscriptions] (Stockholm, 1900–)

O. von Friesen: 'Historiska runinskrifter' [Historical rune inscriptions], *Fornvännen* (1909), pp. 57–85 [part I]; (1911), pp. 105–25 [part II]

E. Brate: *Svenska runristare* [Swedish rune carvings] (Stockholm, 1925)

L. Jacobsen and E. Moltke: *Danmarks runeindskrifter* [Denmark's rune inscriptions], 2 vols (Copenhagen, 1940–41)

Norges innskrifter med de yngre runer [Norway's inscriptions with later runes], i–v (Oslo, 1941–60)

E. Wessén: *Historiska runinskrifter* [Historical rune inscriptions] (Stockholm, 1960)

S. B. F. Jansson: *The Runes of Sweden* (Stockholm, 1962)

D. Strömbäck: *The Epiphany in Runic Art: The Dynna and the Sika Stones* (London, 1970) [Dorothea Coke Memorial Lecture, University College, London, May 1969]

C. W. Thompson: *Studies in Upplandic Runography* (Austin, 1975)

OTHER SPECIALIST STUDIES

K. Friis Johansen: 'Solvskatten fra Terslev' [Treasure from Terslev], *Aab. Nord. Oldknd. & Hist.*, ii (1912), pp. 189–263

B. Salin: 'Fyndet från Broa i Halla, Gotland' [Finds from Broa in Halla, Gotland], *Fornvännen* (1922), pp. 189–206

B. Hougen: 'Studier i Gokstadfunnet' [Studies of the Gokstad finds], *U. Oldsaksaml. Åb.*, v (1931–2), pp. 74–112

S. Curman: 'Kirstna gravmonument från 1000-talet funna i Vreta kloster' [Kirstna tomb monument from the 10th century found in Vreta cloister], *Arkeologiska studier tillägnade H. K. H. Kronprins Gustaf Adolf* (Stockholm, 1932), pp. 141–51

P. Paulsen: *Der Goldschatz von Hiddensee* (Leipzig, 1936)

J. Brøndsted: 'Danish Inhumation Graves of the Viking Period', *Acta Archaeol.* [Copenhagen], vii (1938), pp. 81–228

P. Olsén: *Die Saxe von Valsgärde I* (Uppsala, 1945)

M. Stenberger: *Die Schatzfunde Gotlands der Wikingerzeit*, 2 vols (Stockholm and Lund, 1947–58)

M. Mackeprang: *Jydske granitportaler* [Granite portals from Jutland] (Copenhagen, 1948)

K. Eldjárn: *Kuml og haugfé úr heiðnum sið á Íslandi* [Burials and gravegoods from heathen times in Iceland] (Reykjavík, 1956)

D. M. Wilson: 'The Fejø Cup', *Acta Archaeol.* [Copenhagen], xxxi (1960), pp. 147–73

B. Arrhenius: 'Vikingatida miniatyrer' [Miniatures from the Viking era], *Tor*, vii (1961), pp. 139–64

A. W. Mårtensson: 'Aus dem frühmittelalterlichen Lund: Ein Stock und eine Spange', *Res medievales Ragnar Blomqvist oblata* (Lund, 1968), pp. 217–27

J. Ypey: 'Fundstücke mit anglo-karolingischer Tierornamentik in den niederländischen Sammlungen', *Ber. Amersfoort*, xviii (1968), pp. 175–91

I. Hägg: 'Die wikingerzeitliche Frauentracht von Birka: Einige Bemerkungen zur Hemdform', *Tor*, xiii (1969), pp. 13–25

I. Jansson: 'Wikingerschmuck und Münzdatierung', *Tor*, xiii (1969), pp. 26–64

E. Roesdahl: *Fyrkat*, ii (Copenhagen, 1977)

M. Müller-Wille: 'Frühmittelalterliche Prunkgräber im südlichen Skandinavien', *Bonn. Jb.*, clxxviii (1978), pp. 633–52

E. Wamers: 'Ein karolingischer Prunkbeschlag aus dem Römisch-Germanischen Museum, Köln', *Z. Archäol. Mittelalters*, ix (1981), pp. 91–128

M. Müller-Wille: 'Königsgrab und Königsgrabkirche: Funde und Befunde im frühgeschichtlichen und mittelalterlichen Europa', *Ber. Röm.-Ger. Komm.*, lxiii (1982), pp. 349–412

M. Iversen and J. Vallev: 'Kammergravens alder' [The date of the burial chambers], *Skalk*, 6 (1986), pp. 3–8

S. Jensen: 'Det ældste Ribe, og vikingetidens begyndelse' [Early Ribe, and the beginning of the Viking period], *Femte tværfaglige vikingesymposium: Århus, 1986*, pp. 7–22

4. REGIONAL SURVEY. Viking art varies by region as well as by period. The following survey examines the Scandinavian tradition (treated in detail above) to the east of the Baltic and in the British Isles, and the cross-influences sustained and exerted by Viking art between these regions and beyond.

(i) The Scandinavian tradition. (ii) East of the Baltic. (iii) The British Isles. (iv) Influences.

(i) The Scandinavian tradition. Several constant strands can be distinguished in the Scandinavian tradition of Viking art, despite the indigenous inventions and foreign borrowings that led to periodic rejuvenation. Animal motifs were preferred. Although only the ribbon-shaped animal can be followed throughout Viking art, all new motifs were zoomorphic until the second half of the 9th century. Animals continued to dominate the repertory even with

the addition of ribbon and plant motifs in the 9th to 11th centuries. The reproduction of jewellery through casting, which evidently played an important role in the fine arts economy, helped to prolong particular motifs beyond periods of fashion. The use of such formal elements as the double contour can be documented continuously through the Ringerike style. The patterning of surfaces underwent changes of motifs and techniques, but the principle remained constant from style III:E to the Mammen style. All such elements of style and of craftsmen's procedures and training contribute to the impression that Viking art in Scandinavia developed smoothly, despite important innovations.

SIGNE HORN FUGLESANG

(ii) East of the Baltic. Since time immemorial there have been close contacts between the peoples of the Baltic coasts, and settlements with strong Scandinavian elements were established on the eastern shores, for example Grobinya in Latvia, as early as the 7th century AD. In the latter half of the 8th century Scandinavians started to travel by boat along rivers deep into eastern Europe, a movement that in the 9th to 11th centuries took them as far as the Byzantine Empire and the Caliphate. The most easterly Scandinavian relic to be discovered is a decorated sword chape from the 10th century found at Danilovka near Kamyshin on the lower Volga, while the runes and Urnes-style decoration from the 11th century carved on a marble lion (now in Venice) in the harbour of Peiraeus are the most southerly.

Many Scandinavians settled among the Finno-Ugrians, Balts and Slavs in those parts of eastern Europe that were incorporated into the Russian empire in the 9th to 10th centuries. Many were active as traders and warriors, and a few reached high positions in society. The Riurikid princes of Kiev, for example, were of Scandinavian ancestry. The largest group of undoubtedly Scandinavian finds in the area of Old Russia consists of women's bronze jewellery from the 9th to 10th centuries, with such mass-produced

types as oval, equal-armed, trefoil and circular brooches. There are also finds of high-quality jewellery, for example the silver brooches and pendants in the Gnyozdovo hoard and the magnificent silver brooch from Yelets (St Petersburg, Hermitage), as well as examples of men's jewellery and works of bone, antler and wood from the same period. In addition, many decorated Scandinavian weapons from the 10th and 11th centuries have been found in Russia and the Ukraine. A number of unfinished Scandinavian bronze ornaments of the 9th and 10th centuries found at Staraya Ladoga and Ryurikovo Gorodishche near Novgorod and moulds from Gnyozdovo indicate that Scandinavian craftsmen were active among the immigrants. The Scandinavian jewellery found in Russia shows, however, few differences from specimens found in Scandinavia. This, with other facts, suggests that the Scandinavian settlers were fairly quickly assimilated, although new groups of warriors and traders continued to arrive from Scandinavia up to the end of the Viking period.

The artistic connections between Scandinavia and eastern Europe are much less conspicuous than those between Scandinavia and western Europe. The reason for this must be partly that, as Germanic peoples, the Scandinavians were ethnically closer to many western peoples, with such shared traditions as myths, heroic legends and the use of animal ornament. Scandinavian influences for certain types of jewellery and ornamental designs can be noted among the Finno-Ugrian and Baltic peoples on the eastern side of the Baltic, but similar influences are found only rarely in the art of the western Slavs south of the Baltic. They are also comparatively rare in the Russian kingdom, the basis of whose art and culture was a blend of Islamic, nomadic and Byzantine influences, with indigenous eastern European elements. Scandinavian elements can, however, be found. Graves of the 10th-century military class (which included Scandinavians) often contain weapons and other objects of Scandinavian character. An example is a chamber grave from Shestovitsa, Ukraine, with saddle mounts

14. Battle-axe showing a snake pierced by a sword, iron overlaid with silver plates and gold foil, l. 146 mm, probably from Bilyarsk, Tatar Republic, Russia, 11th or 12th century (Moscow, State Historical Museum)

of antler decorated in the Mammen style. An 11th-century sword from Foshchevataya, Ukraine, has a bronze grip with Urnes-style animal ornaments and eastern floral ornaments (and a Slavic inscription on the blade). The magnificent battle-axe probably from Bilyarsk, Tatar Republic (Moscow, State Hist. Mus.; see fig. 14), is inlaid with distinctly eastern ornaments but also with the figure of a snake pierced by a sword, a design that shows both in motif and style close connections with illustrations of the legend of Sigurd the dragon-slayer on 11th-century rune-stones in eastern Sweden.

Eastern influences do not appear in Scandinavian art until the late Viking period. Slavic, above all Russian, granulation was adopted in Gotlandic gold and silver jewellery (e.g. in Stockholm, Stat. Hist. Mus.) in the 11th to 12th centuries. An eastern origin has been suggested, but also strongly questioned, for certain floral elements in Ringerike and related works of art from the 11th century. Floral decoration of Islamic character can be seen on, among other things, mounts for belts of an Islamic-nomadic type, which became much used and also produced in Old Russia and in the countries on both the eastern and western sides of the Baltic in the 11th to 12th centuries. A number of churches on Gotland were decorated with paintings in Russian-Byzantine style in the 12th century. Further research is necessary for a closer evaluation of a possible direct eastern influence on the Urnes-Romanesque style.

BIBLIOGRAPHY

T. J. Arne: *La Suède et l'Orient: Etudes archéologiques sur les relations de la Suède et de l'Orient pendant l'âge des vikings*, Archives d'Etudes Orientales, viii (Uppsala, 1914)

——: 'Skandinavische Holzkammergräber aus der Wikingerzeit in der Ukraine', *Acta Archaeol.* [Copenhagen], ii (1931), pp. 285–302

B. Nerman: *Grobin-Seeburg* (Stockholm, 1958)

H. Arbman: 'Skandinavisches Handwerk in Russland zur Wikingerzeit', *Meddel. Lunds U. Hist. Mus.* (1959), pp. 110–35

A. N. Kirpichnikov: *Drevnerusskoye oruzhiye* [Old Russian Weapons], i–iii, Arkheologiya SSSR (Moscow, 1966)

J. J. Żak: *'Importy' skandynawskie na ziemiach zachodniosłowiańskich od IX do XI wieku* [Scandinavian 'imports' in the west Slav countries from the 9th to the 11th century], Prace Komisji Archeologicznej, vii/1–3 (Poznań, 1967)

D. A. Avdusin: 'Smolensk and the Varangians According to the Archaeological Data', *Norw. Archaeol. Rev.*, ii (1969), pp. 52–62 [comments by various authors in *Norw. Archaeol. Rev.*, iii (1970), pp. 113–15; 115–17; iv/2 (1971), pp. 65–8; vi/1 (1973), pp. 1–4, 4–9, 10–13]

E. Kivikoski: *Die Eisenzeit Finnlands: Bildwerk und Text* (Helsinki, 1973)

G. F. Korzukhina: 'Nekotoryye nakhodki bronzoliteynogo dela v Ladoge' [Some bronze-casting finds in Ladoge], *Kratkiye Soobshcheniya Instituta Arkheologii* [Short reports of the Institute of Archaeology], cxxv (1973), pp. 35–40

I. Jansson: 'Ett rembeslag av orientalisk typ funnet på Island: Vikingatidens orientaliska bälten och deras eurasiska sammanhang' [A strap mount of oriental type found in Iceland: the oriental belts of the Viking period and their Eurasian context], *Tor*, xvii (1975–7), pp. 383–420

D. I. Blifel'd: *Davn'orus'ki pam'yatki Shestovitsi* [The old Russian antiquities of Shestovitsa] (Kiev, 1977)

Actes du colloque d'Upsal. Les Pays du Nord et Byzance: Uppsala, 1979

O. I. Davidan: 'Bronzoliteynoye delo v Ladoge' [Bronze-casting in Ladoga], *Arkheologicheskiy Sbornik* [Archaeological collection], xxi (1980), pp. 59–67

V. Ginters: *Tracht und Schmuck in Birka und im ostbaltischen Raum: Eine vergleichende Studie*, Antikvariskt arkiv, lxx (Stockholm, 1981)

W. Duczko: 'Slaviskt och gotländskt smide i ädla metaller' [Slavic and Gotlandic jewellery in precious metals], *Gutar och vikingar* (Stockholm, 1983), pp. 329–56

P.-L. Lehtosalo-Hilander: 'Viking Age Spear Heads in Finland', *Society and Trade in the Baltic during the Viking Age*, Acta Visbyensia, vii (Visby, 1985), pp. 237–50

I. Jansson: 'Communications between Scandinavia and Eastern Europe in the Viking Age: The Archaeological Evidence', *Untersuchungen zu Handel und Verkehr der vor- und frühgeschichtlichen Zeit in Mittel- und Nordeuropa*, iv: *Der Handel der Karolinger- und Wikingerzeit*, Abhandlungen der Akademie der Wissenschaften in Göttingen (Göttingen, 1987), pp. 773–807

Oldenburg–Wolin–Staraja Ladoga–Nowgorod–Kiev: Internationale Fachkonferenz: Kiel, 1987

Die Kontakte zwischen Ostbaltikum und Skandinavien im frühen Mittelalter: Internationale Konferenz: Riga, 1990

From Viking to Crusader: The Scandinavians and Europe, 800–1200 (exh. cat., Paris; Berlin; Copenhagen; 1992–3)

INGMAR JANSSON

(iii) The British Isles. Viking art was introduced into the British Isles as a result of Scandinavian settlement during the 9th century, following the Viking raids that had begun in the late 8th. In Scotland Scandinavian settlement was widespread in the northern and western islands and also on the north-east mainland (Caithness and Sutherland), whereas in Ireland the Vikings were restricted to coastal bases, some of which (most notably Dublin) developed into flourishing towns during the 10th century. In the late 9th century the Vikings took control of the Isle of Man, where Scandinavian taste became established, as well as in north-west England, where settlement began *c.* 900. North-eastern and eastern England were conquered by the Danes in the 870s; the most important of the subsequent Danelaw territories was the Kingdom of York, which prospered under Scandinavian rule until recovered by the English in the mid-10th century. England, however, experienced a second Viking age during the first half of the 11th century, when it was conquered and ruled by Danish kings.

This chronology of events helps to explain a number of factors governing the distribution and development of Viking art in the British Isles. For instance, the only examples of early Viking period art in the western Viking world are ornamented objects introduced directly from Scandinavia by their owners, found, for example, as grave goods in the pagan burials of the early raiders and first settlers (e.g. a sword from Reading, Berks, with gripping-beast ornament on its hilt; Oxford, Ashmolean). Early Viking art had no impact in either Britain or Ireland, and it was the mid-Viking Borre and Jelling styles that were the first to be introduced into the settlement areas by Scandinavian-trained craftsmen, only to be rapidly assimilated by the indigenous traditions of Insular art. The Danish dynasty in 11th-century England brought the Ringerike style into fashion, followed by the Urnes style, both of which developed distinctively Insular variants, notably in southern England and in Ireland.

(a) England. Anglo-Scandinavian art flourished from the late 9th century to the mid-10th in the areas of intensive Scandinavian settlement in northern and eastern England, based on interaction between the Borre and Jelling styles and native Anglo-Saxon art. The new styles were developed by artist/craftsmen in such metropolitan centres as York, to be copied in the rural hinterland.

In the Anglo-Scandinavian version of the Borre style, the animal motifs are mainly absent, but the S-shaped,

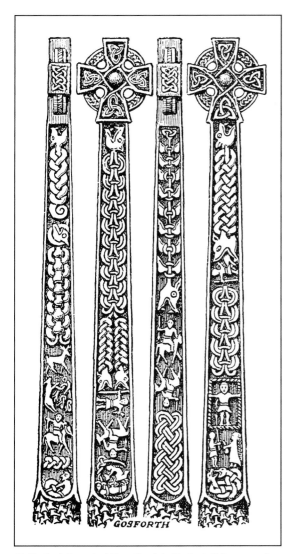

15. Gosforth Cross, h. 4.42 m, Cumbria, England, 10th century; from W. G. Collingwood: *Northumbrian Crosses of the Pre-Norman Age* (London, 1927), fig. 184

connections of Norse settlers with the Celtic West. Representations of the Norse myths were also introduced, as on the Gosforth Cross in Cumbria.

The Gosforth Cross (see fig. 15), with its richly carved, tapering shaft and ringed head, stands to a full height of 4.42 m. The decorative use of the Borre-style ring-chain motif dates this monument to the first half of the 10th century. Its complex iconography links scenes from the Scandinavian mythological concept of Ragnarök (the doom of the pagan gods) with the Crucifixion (the end of one world and the beginning of a new). This is the work of a master craftsman with an original mind whose hand can be recognized on at least three other monuments at Gosforth, of a quality unmatched elsewhere in north-west England.

Whereas in the 9th and 10th centuries Scandinavian influences were limited to the areas of Scandinavian settlement, chiefly in the north, in the 11th century the Ringerike style was most popular in the south, among the followers of Knut the Great. The grave-slab from St Paul's churchyard in London (London, Mus. London), with its Scandinavian runic inscription down the side, represents the finest manifestation of purely Scandinavian, Viking period art in the British Isles, the magnificent animal-ornament being attributable to the 'classic' phase of the Ringerike style (for illustration *see* RINGERIKE). Its importance is enhanced by the survival of much of the original scheme of highly coloured paintwork that once covered all the carving. The Urnes style in turn became established in the south, where its English version can be seen, for example, in sculpture at Jevington Church in Sussex or in the metalwork of the Pitney brooch from Somerset (London, BM) with its characteristically interlaced zoomorphic ornament executed in openwork. There is growing evidence, however, of a Midlands school of English Urnes, and in the north the most remarkable piece of metalwork ornamented in the style is, surprisingly, the crosier from a Norman bishop's tomb in Durham (Durham, Cathedral Treasury).

(b) Ireland. The restricted nature of Scandinavian settlement in Ireland was noted above, but of their emergent urban centres (including Limerick and Cork) only Dublin has been extensively excavated. Many aspects of the manufacturing industries and associated artistic production of Dublin from the 10th century to the 12th have been revealed, with good preservation of carved wood. The most remarkable body of evidence for Dublin's artistic output at this period is, however, in the form of 'motif-pieces', which in themselves belong to a native Irish craft tradition. 'Motif-pieces' are generally small pieces of bone or stone bearing panels of ornament, often unfinished. They provide a unique opportunity for the study of early medieval artistic practices as they include both craftsmen's working designs and apprentices' learning attempts, as well as leisure sketches. Those of the middle Viking period lack truly Scandinavian patterns, the nearest being the occasional use of Insular versions of the Borre-style 'ring-chain'. In the late period, however, strong Ringerike and Urnes influences can be detected, the Scandinavian motifs being reworked according to indigenous Irish principles of ornamentation. Irish designs are generally distinguishable from contemporary mainstream

ribbon-animal of the Jelling style was developed in Yorkshire into distinctive 'beast-chains'. The main innovation for the Scandinavian settlers was the adoption of stone sculpture, borrowed from Christian Anglo-Saxon art. They learnt from Anglo-Saxon sculptors not only the skills of stone-carving but also the techniques for laying out ornament (the use of gridding and of templates). The Scandinavian impact, however, was to shift the art of stone sculpture from the hands of the Church into more widespread lay patronage, introducing a new secular iconography that included depictions of Viking warriors themselves, as on Cross B in Middleton Church, N. Yorks. Other innovations in the north of England in this period were the invention of the distinctive 'hogback' form of house-shaped monument, based on Anglian shrine-tombs, and the introduction of the ring-headed cross through the

16. St Patrick's Bell-shrine, by Condulig Ua hInmainen and sons, gilt-bronze with gold filigree, silver, glass and hardstones, h. 267 mm, 1094–1105 (Dublin, National Museum of Ireland)

Scandinavian art by a general stiffness and a tendency towards symmetry, with repetition of identical forms.

The Irish versions of the Ringerike and Urnes styles had a widespread popularity in the late 11th century and the early 12th, having been introduced perhaps by way of Dublin's contacts with southern England, rather than directly from Scandinavia. They were employed, for instance, for the decoration of major pieces of ecclesiastical metalwork. Those in the Irish Urnes style include the Cross of Cong (c. 1123; Dublin, N. Mus.) and the shrines of St Manchan (Boher Church, Co. Offaly), St Lachtin's Arm and St Patrick's Bell (both Dublin, N. Mus.; see fig. 16). Their elaborate ornament represents a unique late Urnes phase that developed along different lines from the transitional Urnes-Romanesque of the Scandinavian homelands.

(c) The Isle of Man. Viking-period sculpture on the Isle of Man takes the form of small crosses and cross-slabs, largely of 10th-century date. The earliest are those with an Insular version of the Borre-style ring-chain motif (compare the Gosforth Cross), including the signed work of Gautr, who boasted in runes on a cross-slab at Kirk Michael that he had 'made this and all in Man'. His work, as well as that of his successors, is only Scandinavian in part, although there are depictions from Norse myths and legends, including the earliest definite Sigurd iconography

in Viking art. Two crosses at Braddan display elaborate Jelling/Mammen-style animal ornament, with tendril extensions, of a type most closely paralleled on some magnificent silver brooches that form part of a hoard deposited c. 950 at Skaill in Orkney. The Skaill brooches (Edinburgh, Royal Mus. Scotland) would thus seem to have an Irish Sea, most probably Manx, origin (at least for their craftsman), for nothing to match their artistic quality is to be found in Scandinavian Scotland.

(d) Scotland. There is little evidence, other than in the form of imported standard ornaments of early to mid-Viking date, for the presence of Scandinavian artistic taste in Scotland; certainly no workshops have been identified. From the late Viking period there are some pieces with ornament displaying Scandinavian affinities, the most important being a unique cross-slab at Dòid Mhàiri on Islay, but even this shows no more than superficial Ringerike-style influence in its tendril decoration. There was no equivalent fashion among the Scandinavian settlers in Scotland for carved stone monuments to match those of the Isle of Man or of northern England. The Scottish hogbacks, for instance, are mainly of so late a form that they should no longer be taken as indicative of Scandinavian taste. The lack of impact of Viking art in Scotland (or at any rate the difficulty in perceiving it) is partly explained by the pattern of dispersed rural settlements (few of which have been excavated) with no urban centres, such as York or Dublin, to provide equivalent concentrations of wealth and the associated scope for artistic patronage and development.

BIBLIOGRAPHY

P. M. C. Kermode: Manx Crosses (London, 1907)

W. G. Collingwood: Northumbrian Crosses of the Pre-Norman Age (London, 1927)

H. Shetelig: 'The Norse Style of Ornamentation in the Viking Settlements', Acta Archaeol. [Copenhagen], xix (1948), pp. 69–113

T. D. Kendrick: Late Saxon and Viking Art (London, 1949)

F. Henry: Irish Art during the Viking Invasions, 800–1020 AD (London, 1967)

——: Irish Art during the Romanesque Period, 1020–1170 AD (London, 1970)

D. M. Wilson: 'The Borre Style in the British Isles', Minjar og Menntir, ed. B. Vilhjalmsson (Reykjavik, 1976), pp. 502–9

J. T. Lang, ed.: Anglo-Saxon and Viking Age Sculpture, Brit. Archaeol. Rep., xlix (Oxford, 1978)

U. O'Meadhra: Early Christian, Viking and Romanesque Art: Motif-pieces from Ireland, i–ii (Stockholm, 1979–87)

R. N. Bailey: Viking Age Sculpture in Northern England (London, 1980)

C. Fell and others, eds: The Viking Age in the Isle of Man (London, 1983)

M. Ryan, ed.: Treasures of Ireland: Irish Art, 3000 BC–1500 AD (Dublin, 1983)

J. T. Lang: 'The Hogback: A Viking Colonial Monument', Anglo-Saxon Stud. Archaeol. & Hist., iii (1984), pp. 85–176

D. M. Wilson: Anglo-Saxon Art from the Seventh Century to the Norman Conquest (London, 1984)

S. H. Fuglesang: 'The Relationship between Scandinavian and English Art from the Late Eighth to the Mid-twelfth Century', Sources of Anglo-Saxon Culture, ed. P. E. Szarmach, Studies in Medieval Culture, xx (Kalamazoo, 1986), pp. 203–41

J. T. Lang: 'The Distinctiveness of Viking Colonial Art', Sources of Anglo-Saxon Culture, ed. P. E. Szarmach, Studies in Medieval Culture, xx (Kalamazoo, 1986), pp. 243–60

J. Graham-Campbell: 'From Scandinavia to the Irish Sea: Viking Art Reviewed', Ireland and Insular Art, AD 500–1200, ed. M. Ryan (Dublin, 1987), pp. 144–52

R. N. Bailey and R. Cramp: Cumberland, Westmorland and Lancashire North-of-the-Sands, British Academy Corpus of Anglo-Saxon Stone Sculpture, ii (Oxford, 1988)

J. T. Lang: *Viking-age Decorated Wood: A Study of its Ornament and Style*, Medieval Dublin Excavations, 1962–81, Series B, i (Dublin, 1988)

R. Hall: *Viking Age Archaeology in Britain and Ireland* (Princes Risborough, 1990)

J. Lang: *York and Eastern Yorkshire*, British Academy Corpus of Anglo-Saxon Sculpture, iii (Oxford, 1991)

From Viking to Crusader: The Scandinavians and Europe, 800–1200 (exh. cat., ed. E. Roesdahl and D. M. Wilson; Paris, Grand. Pal.; Berlin, Altes Mus.; Copenhagen, Nmus.; 1992–3)

JAMES GRAHAM-CAMPBELL

(iv) Influences. Several theories of foreign influence on Viking ornament have been proposed, but they have been invalidated or modified by new finds and the use of more systematic morphological and chronological methods. The theory that Irish art had a decisive influence on Viking art in the 9th century and the early 10th is no longer relevant. Always badly founded, the idea that Islamic motifs provided an immediate and decisive source for Scandinavian animal art is now completely invalid. It is no longer accepted that the 'Carolingian lion' was a source for the gripping beast, and the notion that the Jelling, Mammen, Ringerike and Urnes styles were developed in England is unacceptable for both chronological and morphological reasons.

Four groups of criteria help to identify foreign influences in Viking art: techniques, typology of objects, ornament motifs and style. Some information on ornament may be gleaned from the technical and typological criteria; the use of silver filigree, for instance, which began in the 9th century but gained wider currency only with the Borre and Jelling styles, was based on west European techniques, and the spiral and volute motifs were probably introduced through silversmiths. Niello inlay, especially fashionable in the Borre style, probably reflects Anglo-Saxon models. The copying of Carolingian trefoil mounts as Scandinavian women's brooches introduced the motifs of acanthus leaf and vine scroll, although neither motif had a lasting influence on Scandinavian art.

Some motifs borrowed from abroad were short-lived or of only local importance, such as the Anglo-Carolingian animals of style III:F or the acanthus and vine of the Borre style. Others were absorbed into the Scandinavian workshop tradition and contributed to subsequent developments. The gripping beast, for example, was only one of many borrowed motifs in style III:E of the late 8th century, but it was translated into several stylistic varieties and exercised a decisive influence on Scandinavian art throughout the 9th century and well into the 10th. Some of the plant motifs introduced in the Ringerike phase were used throughout the Urnes style and into the early Romanesque, notably the single scroll and the union knot. The lion, which was introduced into the Mammen style, went on into the Urnes of the second half of the 11th century. The most important phases of loans from Europe were marked by the introduction of semi-naturalistic mammals, birds and gripping beast in style III:E and of the lion, bird and plants in the Mammen style of the mid-10th century.

Many foreign motifs were transferred to objects of Scandinavian type. The plastically rendered beasts, probably of the same Anglo-Saxon origin as the gripping beast, formed the favourite motif on a large group of early Viking oval brooches (see fig. 2 above). Such brooches were produced in Ribe, Jutland, for example, where coins suggest a late 8th-century date for this addition to the Viking repertory of ornamental fauna. The gripping beast proper occurs in numerous contexts on both traditional and innovative cast metalwork of the late 8th century and the 9th (see fig. 1c above). Ringerike scrolls of the 11th century were used on objects ranging from weapons, brooches and memorial stones to household implements, although in works of high quality the motifs reflect the vocabulary of ornament in mainstream Europe.

Types of object copied from abroad could be decorated with Scandinavian motifs. Although some trefoil brooches retain the foliate motifs of their Carolingian prototypes, by far the greater number bear animals and ribbons of the contemporary Borre style (see fig. 3 above). The 10th-century circular filigree brooches probably depend on continental disc brooches; in a few instances they have scroll motifs, but most are decorated with Borre-style knots or Jelling-style animals.

This pattern of loans, transfers and Scandinavian adaptations of motifs suggests that foreign motifs that gained a wider currency were copied from contemporary west European ornament and not put together haphazardly from loot of mixed origins; that copying of foreign motifs and objects was intermittent, presumably undertaken by innovative craftsmen working in, among other places, trading centres; and that although direct copying did occur, considerable artistic ingenuity was usually exercised in first-hand copying and in the early stages of stylistic adaptation. After the initial stage, mass-produced copies and local adaptations secured both the dissemination and, in some cases, the longevity of the originally foreign motifs.

It is more difficult to identify stylistic influences, partly because the copying of motifs does not always coincide with changes of style. For instance, the gripping beasts occurring in style III:E ornament on the disc-on-bow brooches of the late 8th century are flattish animals with low relief of flat planes. Similarly, the semi-naturalistic beasts of this phase are chip-carved and rendered according to the formal concepts of style III:E. Thus it is not simply the presence of the motifs in themselves that leads to the plastic relief and rich variety of composition in the Oseberg style. Conversely, the Baroque Master of the Oseberg carvings used all the fashionable elements of a plastic style, but without applying modern animal types to any appreciable degree. The plasticity of high, modelled relief in its early Scandinavian stage survives mainly on the early types of oval brooches, used for playful animals of foreign origin (see fig. 2 above). These animal types correspond to those of Anglo-Saxon animals, which have been suggested as the models for the gripping beasts (Haseloff, 1951). Indeed, if the dating of the workshops in Ribe, Denmark, which produced such brooches, is upheld as being in the second half of the 8th century, England is the only area in northern Europe that could have provided the stylistic prototypes. It may be assumed that this plastic style was applied at some stage to all types of Scandinavian motifs, and that the Baroque Master represents this phase of hybridization. The development can be glimpsed to some extent from oval and equal-armed brooches, but gaps in the surviving material prevent a satisfactory reconstruction.

The relationship between the foreign and the indigenous in motifs and style is discernible more easily in late Viking art. In the Mammen style, probably from the mid-10th century, the west European motifs of lion, bird and plants were introduced. These animal motifs, and most of the plants, are rendered in a style that is partly traditional and partly indigenous innovation. In the Ringerike phase, starting *c.* 1000, the same motifs were continued; the animals underwent only marginal stylistic changes, while the plant motifs received some new details and, more importantly, were composed according to contemporary west European stylistic conventions. In the Urnes style, starting in the second quarter of the 11th century, the number of European motifs transmitted through the Ringerike style was reduced while new ones, including the winged dragon, were adopted, and all were transformed into the new Scandinavian idiom. Thus in the course of approximately three generations there were three different variations on the themes of motif/style, foreign/indigenous and tradition/innovation. There is no reason to suppose that the process was less complicated for early and mid-Viking art.

Viking art seems never to have made any impact in France and Germany. This fact is of some importance in assessing the origins of Romanesque animal ornament, which has been connected at times with the Scandinavian Viking styles. The Romanesque seems to have originated as a Mediterranean style of ornament, with motifs of Classical and Byzantine origin. Its transalpine form was enriched with ornaments of local French, Salian and Anglo-Norman invention, possibly reflecting local secular ornament to some extent. It was this conglomerate phase that was introduced to Scandinavia in the 12th century, apparently from several European sources. There is no evidence that Scandinavian animal motifs influenced the formative phases of the Romanesque, and the indigenous tradition of Viking art influenced the Romanesque in Scandinavia only to a very limited degree. Viking and Romanesque animal ornament must be seen as distinct art forms, differing in origin, motifs, style, application and content.

For bibliography *see* §§I and II, 3 above.

SIGNE HORN FUGLESANG

III. Architecture.

Apart from the few wooden Stave churches from the end of the Viking period that are still preserved in Norway, the evidence for Viking architecture comes from excavations, so for the most part only the ground-plans of buildings are known, and only very occasionally can the superstructure of buildings be reconstructed with confidence. This is particularly true of roof construction and cladding, but it is even difficult to estimate the height of walls, the position of windows and the structure of doors etc. Knowledge of Viking-age buildings is therefore partial. The buildings dealt with in this survey are domestic, mostly built of wood but less commonly of stone, turf or a combination of all three materials.

1. ANTECEDENTS. The building traditions inherited by the Vikings in Scandinavia and developed by them during the three centuries from *c.* 800 were derived from the rural buildings of their predecessors in north-west Europe (*see* PREHISTORIC EUROPE, §VI, 2). The aisled halls of the Low Countries and north Germany were a feature of earlier farming settlements (*c.* 300 BC–AD 800). They were rectangular in shape and could be up to 40 m long, although their width, determined by the size of timbers available for spanning the buildings, was seldom more than 5.5 m. Choice of building materials was limited by the local availability of raw materials, and the structural elements were normally oak posts to support the roof and hazel wattle for wall panels. The buildings were divided longitudinally into three aisles by two rows of paired posts to carry the weight of the roof, and the interior was transversely partitioned into a dwelling area with central hearth and a cattle byre. The byre was further divided into cattle stalls, which occupied the aisles. Good examples of this characteristic pre-Viking type have been found at Feddersen Wierde, Germany, and numerous other sites. By *c.* AD 300 these buildings were supplemented by *Grubenhäuser* ('sunken featured buildings'), which served as outhouses for storage and craft activities. Their floors lay about a metre below the ground surface, and they had very low walls and a tentlike roof above ground. In areas where stone was available the walls of the aisled halls were built of unmortared boulders, usually in a shell-wall technique using rubble and turf as the inner fill, but the longitudinal tripartite division was maintained. Such buildings are known from Norway and the islands of Öland and Gotland.

2. SCANDINAVIA.

(i) Rural. Towards the end of the pre-Viking period there is evidence of a change in the arrangement of the aisled halls. The double row of internal roof supports began to be replaced by strong posts in the walls, which were capable of supporting the roof when supplemented by external buttress posts sloping up to meet the wall heads (e.g. Elisenhof, Germany). This gave a larger unobstructed area within the buildings and was to evolve into the 'typical' Viking house. Excavations at many rural sites in Jutland have shown that aisled halls still continued to be built, but increasingly with a building type that had curved long walls, straight gables and buttresses. The division between dwelling area and cattle byre also disappeared, and buildings became more specialized in their functions. Thus, at such sites as Vorbasse, Jutland, dwellings and cattle byres were separate buildings. The buildings with curved long walls reached the peak of their development in the 10th-century fortresses of Denmark (e.g. Aggersborg, Fyrkat, Nonnebakken and Trelleborg), where they were laid out with apparently military precision. Each building was divided transversely into three with a room at each gable end and a hall with hearth occupying the central three-fifths of the floor area. In some cases the central hall was provided with benches running the length of the walls for sitting and sleeping. Full-scale reconstructions of these buildings have been erected at Trelleborg and Fyrkat. Both have stave-built walls and roofs clad with

17. Reconstruction of a 10th-century bow-sided building at the Viking fortress of Fyrkat, Denmark

shingles, but they differ in that the Trelleborg reconstruction has an external verandah whereas that at Fyrkat has sloping buttress posts (see fig. 17). The difference between the two shows clearly the difficulty of reconstructing buildings even from identical archaeological evidence.

The sunken-featured buildings of the pre-Viking period continued to be constructed during the Viking age, both on rural sites where they remained ancillary to halls and on temporarily occupied market centres (e.g. Löddeköpinge, Sweden) where they seem to have been the only type of building. They are also known from the earliest towns in Scandinavia.

(ii) Urban. The beginning of the Viking period in Scandinavia coincided with the foundation of the first towns in the area. New types of building developed in response to the particular needs of urban communities where agriculture was of only minimal importance. Smaller buildings, providing living space and perhaps a storage or workshop area, became more common, the best example of this being at the Viking town of Hedeby. The typical 9th-century building there is rectangular and divided into three areas, the central room being the dwelling, with a hearth in the middle and benches along each side wall. There may have been some type of loft. The walls were built of wattle and daub and were not load-bearing, the external sloping posts being used to counteract the thrust of the roof. A full-scale building at Moesgård (Prehist. Mus.) is one of the few examples recovered by archaeological means that can be reconstructed with confidence. When it was destroyed by fire one gable wall collapsed in its entirety and was preserved beneath later layers; thus its true height is known and also that it had a tiny window.

Other Viking towns in Scandinavia seem to have had more 'rural' buildings. The town of Ribe, Denmark, contemporary with Hedeby, seems to have had only sunken-featured buildings, as did the 10th-century town of Århus, Denmark. Other urban settlements (e.g. Kaupang, Norway; Viborg, Denmark; Lund, Sweden) had the long, bow-sided buildings seen on rural settlements. All these buildings differed from their rural counterparts by being purely dwellings or workshops; in the Viking town there seems to have been no provision for animals or storage of agricultural produce.

3. ELSEWHERE. Remains of Viking settlements have been discovered in all areas of colonization, and excavations have revealed adaptations of the traditional Viking methods of house-building in response to local environmental and cultural conditions. Rural buildings from the Viking period are best known from north Britain, Iceland and Greenland. At Jarlshof on Shetland a cluster of stone- and turf-walled buildings of traditional Viking form is known, and on Iceland many farmsteads from the earliest phases of Viking colonization have been excavated. On Shetland local stone and turf were used to build the low walls of the farmhouses, and on Iceland turf was used almost exclusively. The first buildings on Iceland were halls with turf walls, about 2 m thick, lined on the inside with wattle panelling. They usually consisted of a single room, with a central hearth and benches along each long wall. At a slightly later stage additional rooms were added as wings to the main hall. The best-known example of this Icelandic form is the farmstead of Stöng, which has been reconstructed on site, full-scale and using traditional materials. In Greenland the construction of wings went one stage further, with the development of the 'centralized house' consisting of many small rooms, all interconnected beneath the same roof. Although securely based on Scandinavian prototypes, the buildings in the Atlantic isles developed in response to the environment of their respective areas, particularly the availability of building materials and the harsh climate.

Towns also developed under Viking influence in the areas of colonization. In Ireland a densely occupied site grew up as the core of the present city of Dublin. Here the characteristic buildings were small and rectangular with wattle walls, rounded corners and a central hearth. Like the urban buildings in Scandinavia, they were specialized dwellings or workshops. The Dublin buildings, however, differed in their basic construction from Scandinavian examples and may owe something to native Irish traditions. The same divergence from Scandinavian urban buildings can be seen in England at York, where a number of 10th-century town houses have been excavated at Coppergate. Wattle-walled rectangular buildings are known from the early 10th-century phase, but they were superseded a little later in the century by substantial semi-basement structures, the walls of which were lined with heavy horizontal oak timbers. Their superstructures have not been preserved, but they were probably little more than 2 m high, with their roofs protruding only slightly above ground level. Although these buildings are so far unique to York, they have some similarities with buildings known from 10th-century towns elsewhere in England and could represent a mixture of Viking and Anglo-Saxon traditions.

BIBLIOGRAPHY

M. Stenberger: *Forntider gårdar i Island* [Early farms in Iceland] (Uppsala, 1943)
——: *Vallhagar: A Migration Period Settlement on Gotland, Sweden* (Copenhagen, 1955)
E. L. Nielsen: 'Pedersstraede i Viborg' [Peter Street in Viborg], *Kuml* (1968), pp. 23–110
A. Bantelmann: *Die frühgeschichtliche Marschensiedlung beim Elisenhof in Eiderstedt* (Frankfurt, 1975)
C. Blindheim: 'Kaupang by the Viks Fjord in Vestfold', *Archaeological Contributions to the Early History of Urban Communities in Norway* (Oslo, 1975), pp. 125–75
T. Ohlsson: 'The Löddeköpinge Investigation, i: The Settlement at Vikhögsvagen', *Meddel. Lunds U. Hist. Mus.* (1975–6), pp. 58–161
A. W. Mårtensson: *Uppgrävt förflutet för PKbanken i Lund: En investering i arkeologi* [The past disinterred for the PK bank in Lund: an investment in archaeology], Archaeologia Lundensia, vii (Lund, 1976)
H. Schmidt and O. Olsen: *Fyrkat: En jysk vikingeborg* [Fyrkat: a Viking fortress in Jutland], Nordiske Fortidsminder Series B, iii (Copenhagen, 1977)
H. J. Madsen: 'Introduction to Viking Århus', *Proceedings of the Eighth Viking Congress: Edinburgh, 1981*, pp. 69–72
K. Schietzel: *Stand der siedlungsarchäologischen Forschung in Haithabu: Ergebnisse und Probleme*, Berichte die Ausgrabungen in Haithabu, xvi (Neumünster, 1981)
H. Schmidt: 'Viking Houses in Denmark', *Economic Aspects of the Viking Age*, ed. D. M. Wilson and M. L. Caygill (London, 1981), pp. 51–3
S. Hvass: 'Viking Age Villages in Denmark: New Investigations', *Society and Trade in the Baltic during the Viking Age*, Acta Visbyensia, viii (Visby, 1983), pp. 211–28
H. Murray: *Viking and Early Medieval Buildings in Dublin*, Brit. Archaeol. Rep., cxix (Oxford, 1983)
W. Haarnagel and P. Schmidt: 'Siedlungen', *Archäologische und naturwissenschaftliche Untersuchungen an Siedlungen im deutschen Küstengebiet*, ed. G. Kossack (Weinheim, 1984), pp. 166–244
R. Hall: 'A Late Pre-conquest Building Tradition', *Archaeological Papers from York Presented to M. W. Barley* (York, 1984), pp. 71–7
B. Stoklund: 'Building Traditions in the Northern World', *The Northern and Western Isles in the Viking World* (Edinburgh, 1984), pp. 96–115
E. Roesdahl: 'Vikingernes Aggersborg' [The Vikings' Aggersborg], *Aggersborg gennem 1000 år: Fra vikingeborg til slaegtsgård* [Aggersborg for 1000 years: from Viking fortress to family farm] (Copenhagen, 1986), pp. 53–95

HELEN CLARKE

IV. Historiography.

Following introductory work on Viking art by Sophus Müller (1880), the principles that pervaded the field for much of the 20th century were those of Bernhard Salin. In his classic study of animal motifs between *c.* 500 and *c.* 800, *Die altgermanische Tierornamentik* (1904), Salin analysed specific motifs to distinguish three typological divisions. Only gradually have stylistic criteria gained in importance. A significant step in the direction of stylistic analysis was the work of Haakon Shetelig (1920) in publishing the Oseberg discoveries. Shetelig demonstrated how Salin's Style III continued into the Viking period, and he established the relative sequence of the subsequent style phases. These phases have been recognized and used by other scholars, although often with varying terminology. In 1955 Bertil Almgren attempted a new analytical approach by studying the shape and flow of the curves used by Viking artists in constructing their patterns. This has not ousted the traditional comparative methods, although it was taken up in part by H. Christiansson, whose book *Sydskandinavisk stil* [The south Scandanavian style] (1959) also contains a summary of changing ideas on Viking art. In their general survey *Viking Art* (1966; reissued with minor revision in 1980), David Wilson and Ole Klindt-Jensen used 'the tried analytical and comparative methods of our predecessors'. Their work can be said to have laid the modern basis for the systematic characterization of Viking art and to have established its chronological framework. It was Signe Horn Fuglesang, however, who developed and applied in a variety of works (especially in 1980, 1981, 1982 and 1991) a more formal methodology, particularly for late Viking art. In this field she has established successfully the more precise kind of definitions still needed for the earlier style phases.

For bibliography see §§I and II, 3 above.

JAMES GRAHAM-CAMPBELL

Vikramashila. *See* ANTICHAK.

Vikrampur. Site of a ruined city 25 km south of Dhaka, Bangladesh. Most of the city, which was situated between the Dhaleswari and Padma rivers, has been lost through erosion and floods. Rampal and neighbouring villages mark its original location.

Located in the ancient region of Vanga, Vikrampur was an important city in the 10th–13th centuries during the rule of the Chandra, Sena and Deva dynasties. The Senas made it their capital when they were forced to withdraw to south-eastern Bengal under pressure from the sultans of Delhi in the early 13th century. Vikrampur itself came under Muslim rule at the end of the 13th century. A broad ditch is all that remains of the Ballal Bari, the fortified palace of the Senas. There are several ruined temples in the area, and many stone and wooden images have been unearthed. These include a 4 m-long wooden column carved with human and animal figures (Dhaka, N. Mus.) recovered from a ruined temple in the village of North Kazi Kasba. In Rampal village, about 2 km north-west of Ballal Bari, is the mosque of Baba Adam Shahid (named after a pioneer Muslim preacher) dated by inscription to AH 888 (1483). This Jami' mosque was constructed for

Malik Kafur, a courtier of the sultan of Bengal Fath Shah (*reg* 1481–7). It is a brick-built, six-domed building in the pre-Mughal style of Bengal, with a curved cornice, terra-cotta ornamentation and multiple mihrabs (*see* INDIAN SUBCONTINENT, §III, 6(ii)(d)). Adjacent to the mosque is the shrine of Baba Adam Shahid, who was, according to local lore, martyred by Vallalsena, the ruling Hindu king. A bridge at Mirkadim and a mosque at Kazi Kasba date from the Mughal period, but both have lost their original character owing to extensive repairs.

BIBLIOGRAPHY

R. C. Majumdar, ed.: *Hindu Period*, i of *History of Bengal* (Dhaka, 1943/*R* 1963)

A. H. Dani: *Dacca* (Dhaka, 1962)

A. M. Chowdhury: *Dynastic History of Bengal* (Dhaka, 1967)

A. K. M. Zakaria: *Bangladesher Pratna Ṣampad* [The archaeological treasures of Bangladesh] (Dhaka, 1984)

PERWEEN HASAN

Vila, Joaquín Vayreda y. *See* VAYREDA Y VILA, JOAQUÍN.

Vilaça, Frei **José de Santo António Ferreira** (*b* Braga, 18 Dec 1731; *d* Tibães, 30 Aug 1808). Portuguese designer, wood-carver, sculptor and architect.

1. LIFE AND WORK. His godfather, the Reverend Constantino da Cunha Soto Maior (*d* 1757), was treasurer of the Cathedral of Braga, and one of his brothers, João de Araújo Ferreira Vilaça (*b* 1720), was clerk to the Vicar General of Vila Real in Trás-os-Montes. Frei José's early training was with his father, Custódio Ferreira, a skilled carpenter. In November 1754 Frei José signed his first contract to carve the retable of the high altar of the church of the convent of S Clara, Amarante. From 1757 he worked at Tibães, near Braga, the headquarters of the Benedictine Order in Portugal, where, with José de Álvares de Araújo, he collaborated on carving the magnificent *talha* (carved and gilded wood) designed for the church of S Martinho by André Ribeiro Soares da Silva. The work began with the high altar, for which Frei José carved the statues of SS Martinho, Bento and Escolástica, and the whole scheme, one of the finest in Portugal, was subsequently completed in 1784 after his designs including that for the organ.

On 5 January 1758 Frei José entered the Benedictine Order at Tibães, taking his vows on 2 April 1759. After 1764 he worked at other Benedictine monasteries in northern Portugal, as well as at others outside the Order. He disseminated the Braga style of carving throughout the region, strengthening and refining the type of plastic Rococo compositions at Tibães. In his late years Frei José worked increasingly only as a designer of wood-carving. In 1796 he returned to his monastery at Tibães and in 1798 became the schoolmaster there. In March 1809, two years after the French invasion of Portugal, the monks of Tibães were forced to abandon their monastery when Maréchal Soult occupied Braga. Frei José, who died in August of that year, was buried in the main cloister of Tibães.

2. WRITINGS AND SOURCES. Frei José left a diary, his *Livro de rezam*, begun in 1759, which is a fascinating and detailed account of monastic life in the 18th century. It recorded his activity in architecture, stone sculpture, furniture and ironwork as well as in wood-carving. He noted the artistic sources that were fundamental to his development and that his library contained numerous books on Baroque and Rococo architecture and related subjects. This library included Andrea Pozzo's *Perspectiva pictorum et architectorum* (Rome, 1693–1700), as well as many works published in Paris in the second half of the 17th century, with several by Jacques-François Blondel, such as *De la distribution des maisons* (Paris, 1738). He also recorded the presence in the library at Tibães of the engravings of Juste-Aurèle Meissonier, dated between 1725 and 1735, and those of the Augsburg school, principally by Franz Xaver Habermann of 1740–50, which were also important sources of influence on him, as well as on other leading figures of the Braga school.

3. DESIGN AND WOOD-CARVING. The output of Frei José as carver and designer (*riscador de entalha*) was immense, and the quality of his work correspondingly high. His place in the history of wood-carving in Portugal, one of the principal expressions of Portuguese Baroque, is unique in that he created all the designs, from each unit to the whole gilded church interior, making possible a complete unified scheme in which the single design elements are related. He designed the retables, as well as organ cases, pulpits, window frames and pelmets, choir-stalls, religious images and richly carved furniture.

The work of Frei José can be identified in three phases. The style of the first period (1758–68) is the most monumental and is based on the interpretation by André Soares da Silva of decorative motifs in Augsburg engravings. It is characterized by the complete gilding of surfaces with only the occasional use of white paint for details. Asymmetry is a constant element, and among his favourite forms are foliage; the motif of running water, derived from French Rococo sources; and volutes, often in the form of shells terminating in a shape resembling an undulating flame. These are seen at Tibães in the *talha* that he designed for the choir in the chancel with its door-frame (see fig.) and magnificent stalls and benches (1760–63), the table (*credência*; 1761; *in situ*) placed before the high altar, and the Abbot's Chair (1761; *in situ*). The chancel was completed in 1764, with the window frames and pelmets and door frames all designed by Frei José. His richly carved and gilded picture frames in the sacristy of Tibães are documented in 1763. Other works from this first period include his documented designs for the retable of the high altar (1764–6) and the two lateral retables (1764–6) of the church of Nossa Senhora dos Remédios, Lamego; the retable of the high altar (1764–7) of the church of the Benedictine monastery of Refóios de Basto; the four lateral retables (1767–70) of the church of the Benedictine monastery of S Tirso; the two collateral retables and four lateral retables (all 1767–80) for the church of the monastery at Refóios de Basto; and the retable of the high altar (1770–73) of the monastery church of S Maria at Pombeiro de Ribavizela, Felgueiras, which is one of his finest works.

The second period of Frei José's activity, from about 1768 to 1780, is characterized by a more symmetrical and linear style, one of greater elegance and fluidity, which includes the use of polychrome paint to simulate marble

Frei José de Santo António Ferreira Vilaça: doorframe, chancel, S Martinho, Tibães, near Braga

as well as large mouldings made of carved and gilded wood. There is greater use of smooth interlacing lines, and the decorative elements include chamfered pedestals, foliage, flowers, husks, vases of flowers and palm fronds occasionally combined with olive branches. Documented works of this period include the high altar (1775–7) of Santa Cruz, Braga, and the two lateral retables (1777–80) at the monastery of S Maria, Pombeiro, where he also designed the magnificent pulpits (1776–7) based on an engraving by Habermann of c. 1750.

Frei José's work produced between 1780 and 1790 is less interesting aesthetically and combines elements of Neo-classicism with Rococo forms. Among his most classical designs are the retable of the high altar and the lateral retables (all 1780–83) for the church of S João Baptista, Pendorada, Marco de Canaveses. Other works of this period include the retable (1783) for the chapel of the Abbot at the monastery of Tibães; and the retable of the high altar (1783–6) for the monastery church of S Salvador, Paços de Sousa.

4. ARCHITECTURE, STUCCO AND IRONWORK. Frei José's work as an architect includes the portals (1762) of the chapels in the main cloister at the monastery of Tibães, and the library (1767–73) at the monastery of S Tirso, where he also designed the wrought-iron railings in the church (1773–6). He designed the terrace (1777–80) in front of the entrance to the church and the new wings (1780–81) of the monastery at Refóios de Basto; the portal (1780–86) of the Quinta de Franco at the Singeverga Monastery; the chancel (1780–86) of the church of the monastery of Paços de Sousa; and the chapel and cell of the Abbot at the monastery of Tibães, where he also

designed the stucco-work on the ceiling and the carved retable (all 1783–4). His other architectural works include the chapter house (1783–6) of the monastery of S Tirso, where between 1773 and 1776 he had designed the wrought-iron screens in the church. At the monastery of Tibães he carried out remodelling work on the chapter house and designed the stone staircase in the garden of the abbot (all 1785–6). He designed the façade (1793–8) of the church of S Martinho at the monastery of Couto de Cucujães, Oliveira de Azemeis. He also designed the stucco decoration on the vault of the nave and chancel of the church of the S Casa da Misericórdia, Guimarães, which was carried out between 1775 and 1778.

WRITINGS
Braga, Bib. Pub. [*Livro de rezam do irmão fr. José de Santo António Vilaça, natural de Braga do terreiro de S. Lazaro*; part published in Smith, 1972]

BIBLIOGRAPHY
R. C. Smith: *Frei José de Santo António Ferreira Vilaça, escultor beneditino do século XVIII*, 2 vols (Lisbon, 1972)

NATÁLIA MARINHO FERREIRA ALVES

Viladomat y Manalt, Antonio (*b* Barcelona, 12 April 1678; *d* Barcelona, 19 Jan 1755). Spanish Catalan painter. He was the most significant figure in Catalan painting from the end of the 17th century to the first half of the 18th. He trained with P. B. Savall and J. B. Perramón in Barcelona. The arrival of the Archduke Charles (later Charles VI) of Austria in Barcelona in 1703 as a pretender to the throne during the War of the Spanish Succession (1702–13), accompanied by such Italian artists as Ferdinando Galli-Bibiena, acquainted Viladomat y Manalt with artistic trends in Italy. He experienced problems with the artists' guild in Barcelona because of his refusal to participate in the traditional work system. Despite this, his workshop–academy became a centre for the training of numerous painters, sculptors and engravers. Viladomat y Manalt was principally a religious painter, and his oil paintings include *Christ Appearing to St Ignatius of Loyola* (*c*. 1711–20; Barcelona, Jesuit Convent) and *St Augustine and the Holy Family* (Madrid, Prado). He also painted such murals as the tempera *Angels with the Sudarium* (*c*. 1727; Mataró, S María, Capilla de los Dolores), but most of the others have disappeared. He painted an extensive series of monastic and evangelical works, in which his revival of compositions characteristic of the Spanish Golden Age is apparent. Examples include the *Stigmatization of St Francis* (*c*. 1724; Barcelona, Mus. A. Catalunya), part of a cycle of paintings on the life of St Francis commissioned for the cloister of the convent of S Francisco de Asís in Barcelona. His late Baroque style is related to the severe and realistic trend in Spanish painting in the early 17th century. Some interesting profane allegories by the artist are extant, notably the series *Four Seasons* (*c*. 1720–30; Barcelona, Mus. A. Catalunya), which consists of landscapes with genre scenes. Several of the still-lifes by Viladomat y Manalt such as the realistic *Still-life with Dead Turkey* (Barcelona, Mus. A. Catalunya), which has strong contrasts of light, bear an affinity with Neapolitan painting of the last decades of the 17th century.

BIBLIOGRAPHY
S. Alcolea: *La pintura en Barcelona durante el siglo XVIII* (Barcelona, 1969)

JUAN J. LUNA

Vilalobos, Manuel Pinto de (*b* Oporto, *c.* 1665; *d* Viana do Castelo, *bur* 18 Dec 1734). Portuguese architect, military engineer and writer. Born into a family of converted Jews who had fled from Évora and settled in Oporto, he studied in 1682–3 at the school of military fortification, the Aula de Fortificação e Arquitectura Militar in Lisbon under Francisco Pimentel. In 1684 he was posted to the Minho province as engineering assistant in the inspectorate (Vedoria) at Viana do Castelo, where he received additional practical and theoretical experience from the French engineer Michel Lescole (*fl c.* 1653–1701), whose teaching was recognized in 1701 by the foundation of the Aula de Fortificação in Viana do Castelo. Vilalobos rose to be a colonel *c.* 1715 and was principally responsible for the maintenance and extension of the defences of northeastern Portugal that had been created as a result of the War of Restoration (concluded 1640) against Spain. In this capacity his most important work was the ramparts of Valença, following plans left by Lescole, in which he made pioneering use in Portugal of innovations devised by Sebastien Leprestre de Vauban. He drew up plans (1691) for the straw warehouses of Viana do Castelo and for the barracks (1698) of the Corpo da Guarda of Oporto. He also carried out an extensive programme of public works, including studies of the navigability of the rivers Lima (1684) and Douro (1689–91), the building of the quays of Viana do Castelo (*c.* 1698–*c.* 1718) and the construction of the Matosinhos mole.

As architect to the Archbishops of Braga, Vilalobos was responsible for many of their considerable works of patronage. In particular, between 1704 and 1726 and under Rodrigo de Moura Teles (1644–1728), he was involved in the alterations to Braga Cathedral and the rebuilding there of the chapel of S Pedro de Rates; the construction of the prison and of the first church of the Sanctuary of Bom Jesús do Monte, outside Braga, with its curious circular plan; the design of the parish church at Ponte da Barca; various works in the parish of Viana do Castelo and the Pias and Mazedo churches; and the restoration of many monasteries and convents under the jurisdiction of the Archbishops. The Misericórdia in Viana do Castelo, begun in 1716 under Vilalobos's direction, shows some of the features characteristic of his work: the use of decorative surface effects in stone, such as rustication on the exterior, the treatment of the interior with extensive panels of narrative tiles and retables made of *talha*, carved and gilded wood.

The economic prosperity of Viana do Castelo, which was due to its sea trade with Brazil and northern Europe, led to an important urban revival in which Vilalobos played a leading part. His design for the Casa da Vedoria (1689–91) shows a combination of triangular pediments and a Vitruvian juxtaposition of the classical orders. He also designed the house of the Lobo da Cunha family, the imposing palace of Canon Felgueiras Lima (1725), and, on a smaller scale and with Mannerist echoes, the houses for Gonçalo de Barros and Félix Barreto da Gama, all in Viana do Castelo. In rebuilding the Casa da Cerreira (1691–1705), he retained 16th-century elements and created a façade, the complex organization of which is decidedly revivalist in spirit and may derive from Serlio and his methods of 'restoring old houses' (Book VII). In addition to his work as an architect and military engineer, Vilalobos was a designer of works in *talha* (e.g. the Tree of Jesse in the parish church of Caminha), as well as being active as a writer and translator. This range of abilities indicates the quality of training received by 17th-century Portuguese military engineers and their importance in the development of Portuguese art.

BIBLIOGRAPHY

R. Moreira: 'Do rigor teórico á urgência prática: a arquitectura militar', *História da arte em Portugal*, viii (Lisbon, 1986), pp. 67–85

M. Soromenho: *Manuel Pinto Vilalobos: Da engenharia militar á arquitectura* (diss., Lisbon, U. Nova, 1991)

MIGUEL SOROMENHO

Vilamajó, Julio (*b* Montevideo, 1 July 1894; *d* Montevideo, 11 April 1948). Uruguayan architect, teacher and writer. He qualified as an architect in 1915 and two years later began teaching architecture. From 1921 to 1924 he was in Europe on a university scholarship and was exposed to Hispano-Islamic culture. This influenced the houses that he designed between 1925 and 1927 and one that he built for himself in 1930; the latter displays a combination of Modern Movement principles, Florentine Renaissance architecture (seen in the overall shaping of masses and the decorative treatment of the façades), and Vilamajó's fondness for the Islamic tradition, which is evident in his handling of vegetation, light and water and in the subtle gradation of external spaces. Despite his receptiveness to a variety of influences, he created some highly original works, notably the annexe to the Americana Café (1914), Montevideo; the Facultad de Ingeniería (begun 1937), Universidad de Montevideo; and the Villa Serrana resort centre (completed 1948) *c.* 140 km north of Montevideo. The geometrical clarity of the Americana Café, the severity of its proportions and the dark grey and sepia tones achieved by Vilamajó's use of ceramic cladding are reminiscent of the work of Joaquín Torres García. The Facultad de Ingeniería surprises by the systematic use of exposed reinforced concrete and the bold treatment of openings, volumes and surfaces. Its most striking feature is the convincing resolution of the problems posed by the site, which was uneven and near a low-density residential area, a public park and the Río de la Plata estuary. Its elevated setting and mass make the work a landmark. At Villa Serrana, Vilamajó planned an irregular distribution of houses and a layout of zigzag roads that follow the contours to preserve the natural features of the area. He formulated guidelines concerning the construction of private houses, which limited the materials used to local stone, wood and brick, to be painted within a fixed range of colours (ochres, browns and reds). The houses had to have sloping, thatched roofs supported on simple structures built using roughly hewn poles of eucalyptus wood. Vilamajó also designed a parador (Ventorrillo de la Buena Vista) and a hotel (Mesón de las Cañas), which were completed soon after his death. Both reveal the freshness and confidence with which he combined foreign influences and specifically local traditions in his use of materials and building techniques.

WRITINGS

'Estudios regionales para Punta del Este', *Diario 'El Dia'* (18 Aug 1943)

BIBLIOGRAPHY

'Dibujos de Julio Vilamajó', *Montevideo U. Arquit. Rev.*, vi (1965)

A. Lucchini: *Julio Vilamajó: Su arquitectura* (Montevideo, 1970)

M. Arana: 'Julio Vilamajó ante la arquitectura y el medio', *Nuestra Arquit.*, 1 (1980), pp. 34–41

M. Arana and L. Garabelli: *Arquitectura renovadora en Montevideo, 1915–1940* (Montevideo, 1991)

MARIANO ARANA

Vilanova, João B. Artigas. *See* ARTIGAS, JOÃO B. VILANOVA.

Vilar, Antonio Ubaldo (*b* La Plata, 16 May 1889; *d* Buenos Aires, 7 April 1966). Argentine engineer and architect. He graduated as a civil engineer from the Universidad de Buenos Aires in 1914 and then worked for an oil company in Patagonia (1918–20) and, throughout the 1920s, as a land surveyor. He helped with the studies for Le Corbusier's master-plan *Les Grands Travaux de Buenos Aires* (1929; unexecuted). Vilar subsequently established a large practice in collaboration with his brother Carlos Vilar, and he was among the early proponents of Rationalism and internationalism in Argentina. His early works include a minimal housing system first used at the former premises of the Hindu Club (1931; destr.) at Don Torcuato in Buenos Aires province; several large blocks of flats, such as those for the Nordiska Kompaniet (1935; altered) and those on the Avenida Libertador (1935), both in Buenos Aires; the Banco Holandés Unido (1935; altered), Buenos Aires; and a series of private houses at San Isidro, the most notable (1938) of which, on the corner of Roque Sáenz Peña and Rivera Indarte, boasts a unique curved façade that echoes Le Corbusier's 'white' period. Vilar also designed the Hospital Policial Bartolomé Churruca (1938–42; with others), Buenos Aires, but he is perhaps most widely known for his work as chief designer for the Automóvil Club Argentina. With a team that included Hector Morixe, Arnoldo Jacobs, Rafael Gimenez and Abelardo José Falamir, Vilar designed the Club's graphics and standard equipment as well as its headquarters building (1940–43) on the Avenida Libertador, Buenos Aires, and out-stations throughout the country. His later buildings tend towards an incipient classicism but are marked by high-quality construction, usually executed in such materials as granite and marble.

BIBLIOGRAPHY

M. Scarone: *Antonio Vilar* (Buenos Aires, 1975)

S. Borghini, H. Salama and J. Solsona: *1930–1950: Arquitectura moderna en Buenos Aires* (Buenos Aires, 1987), pp. 38–42, 46–50, 70–74, 97–107

LUDOVICO C. KOPPMANN

Vilar, Manuel (*b* Barcelona, 15 Nov 1812; *d* Mexico City, 25 Nov 1860). Catalan sculptor and teacher, active in Mexico. He studied at the Escuela de Nobles Artes in Barcelona under Damián Campeny and from 1834 on a scholarship in Rome under Antonio Solá at the Accademia di S Luca. He also attended the studios of Bertel Thorvaldsen and Pietro Tenerani in Rome. He adhered to the aesthetic doctrines of purism, and professed an admiration for the Italian 'primitives' of the 13th to 15th centuries. In 1846, with his friend Pelegrín Clavé, Vilar accepted the Mexican government's invitation to reorganize the departments of sculpture and painting at the Academia de S Carlos in Mexico City. They restructured the curriculum, and between 1849 and 1881 mounted regular art exhibitions, to which teachers, students and artists independent of the academy contributed their works. The interest generated raised art criticism in Mexico to a professional level.

Vilar was an excellent teacher, solicitous of his pupils at a period of economic and political instability hardly favourable to the practice of sculpture. He also acted as an agent, advising the academy about the acquisition of works and securing commissions for his students. His personal output was also prolific, although limited by lack of means. His pieces were moulded in plaster until the end of the 19th century and early 20th, when his reputation ensured that the more monumental works were cast in bronze. For example, his bronze statue of *Christopher Columbus* (1892) stands in the Plaza de Buenavista, Mexico City, while the plaster cast version (1858) is in the collection of the city's Museo Nacional de Arte. A notable work on a religious theme, *St Carlo Borromeo Protecting a Child* (1858; Mexico City, Mus. S Carlos), also allegorizes the paternalistic nature of the academy. He also explored themes of national history, in works such as *Moctezuma [Motecuhzuma] II* (1850; Mexico City, Mus. N. A.). He fulfilled various commissions for monuments to *Augustín de Iturbide*, who helped consolidate Mexican independence in 1821.

WRITINGS

S. Moreno, ed.: *Copiador de cartas y diario particular* (Mexico City, 1979)

BIBLIOGRAPHY

S. Moreno: *El escultor Manuel Vilar* (Mexico City, 1969)

FAUSTO RAMÍREZ

Vila Rica. *See* OURO PRÉTO.

Vilas Boas, Frei **Manuel (do) Cenáculo** (*b* Lisbon, 1724; *d* Évora, 1814). Portuguese archbishop, politician, collector and scholar. Of humble origin, he became a Franciscan friar and rose to be Provincial of the Order in 1768. He was a prestigious figure in Portuguese intellectual and cultural circles and was particularly associated with the education reforms of Sebastian Carvalho e Mello, 1st Marquês de Pombal, on whose recommendation he was made tutor to the Infante Dom José and was successively appointed President of the Real Mesa Censória (the state board of censorship) in 1770 and of the Junta da Providência Literária (committee for the reform of higher education) in 1772; in the latter capacity he collaborated in the reform of the University of Coimbra.

Cenáculo was the first Bishop of Beja (1770–1802), where he founded the Museu Pacense (1791), one of the first in the country, based on his own collection of antiquities, medals and coins. He was Archbishop of Évora from 1802 until his death and was present throughout the sack of the city by Napoleon's troops in July 1808, during which his collections were severely depleted.

Cenáculo's principal activity as a collector involved books and coins, as is recorded in his vast correspondence preserved in the Biblioteca Pública, Évora, which he founded in 1805. His numerous agents abroad informed him of the availability of books and *objets d'art*. He developed an early interest in paintings, and his collection in the archiepiscopal palace at Évora contained about 600 items at the time of his death. On his orders the collection was put on public display in the recently founded Livraria Eclesiástica e Pública in 1805. Important among the works of art exhibited on that occasion were the Flemish panels of the *Life of the Virgin* (*c.* 1500; artist unknown, Évora, Mus. Évora) from the earlier chancel of Évora Cathedral, which had been removed in 1718 when the chancel was rebuilt; these panels were restored by the Archbishop. Italian artists were prominently represented, the result of taste formed when he visited Rome in 1750 to attend a Chapter General of his Order. A detailed diary of this journey and of the strong impression made by Italy upon Cenáculo was kept by his travelling companion, Frei Joaquim de S José. Almost all the collection, catalogued in 1814 at his death, passed to the present Museu de Évora and consisted for the most part of paintings of religious subjects, landscapes, genre scenes, still-lifes and portraits of historical figures, friends of the collector and unknown persons.

Three of the most important works in the Museu de Évora known to have belonged to Cenáculo are the *Portrait of a Man* by Adriaen de Vries, *Skating on the Ice* by Hendrick Avercamp and *Allegory* or *Cogito mori* by David Teniers II. Portuguese art was strongly represented, and Cenáculo also commissioned several works from contemporary Portuguese artists such as the sculptor Joaquim Machado do Castro, who sent him some drawings (?Évora, Bib. Púb. & Arquiv.) connected with the equestrian statue of *Joseph I* (1775), and Francisco Vieira de Matlos, from whom in 1770 he commissioned an *Allegory of the Arts and Virtues* (1770; untraced). Cenáculo also owned drawings by Vieira de Matlos, of which 44 of high quality in red chalk survive (MSS, Évora, Mus. Évora). Cenáculo's library entered the Évora Biblioteca Pública and the Academia das Sciencias, Lisbon.

UNPUBLISHED SOURCES
Évora, Bib. Púb. & Arquiv. [*Diario do R. mo. P. M. D. Fr. Joaquim de S José na Jornada ao Capo Geral de Roma em 1750*]

BIBLIOGRAPHY
Catálogo da correspondência dirigida a D. Frei Manuel do Cenáculo Vilas Boas (Évora, 1944–56)
J. A. Gomes Machado: *Um coleccionador portugués do século das luzes: D. Frei Manuel do Cenáculo Vilas Boas, Arcebispo de Évora* (Lisbon, 1987)
JOSÉ ALBERTO GOMES MACHADO

Vilatobà, Joan (*b* Sabadell, nr Barcelona, 1878; *d* Sabadell, 1954). Spanish photographer. His eagerness to assimilate the European aesthetic currents that had not reached Barcelona led him to travel in France and Germany. In Paris he came into contact with Symbolist painting, which was to leave a profound impression on his work. On returning from his travels in 1901, he settled permanently in Sabadell, where he opened a studio that later became famous. His sophisticated nudes, the baroque quality of his compositions and his allegorical subjects make him one of the foremost representatives of Spanish Pictorialism.

BIBLIOGRAPHY
Idas y Chaos: Aspectos de las vanguardias fotográficas en España (exh. cat., J. Fontcuberta; Madrid, Salas Picasso; New York, Int. Cent. Phot., 1984–6)
MARTA GILI

Vila Viçosa. Town in Alto Alentejo, Portugal. Formerly the seat of the ducal family of Braganza, Vila Viçosa is situated in an extensive plain bounded on the west by the foothills of the Serra de Ossa and set in landscape dotted with olive trees, which give it a Mediterranean appearance. The rivers that cross the plain and the marble quarried in the region, which has provided material to decorate its buildings, contribute to its traditional description as cool and beautiful. In 1988 it had 4800 inhabitants.

Vila Viçosa was settled by Celts from Gaul *c.* 500 BC and then by the Romans in 153 BC, when Lucius Munmius, *praetor* of Hispania Ulterior, founded a votive temple to Proserpina (now the hermitage church of S Tiago). The numerous Roman remains in the Alentejo region date from this occupation. Later (after AD 711) the Muslims occupied Vila Viçosa, calling it Al-Karacha, and the present village of Bugios, south of the town, bears traces of their occupation, which ended in 1217 in the reign of Alfonso II (1211–23) with the Christian Reconquest. The town's first privilege dates from 1270, renewed in 1512 by Manuel I (*reg* 1495–1521).

Because of its strategic importance on the frontier with Spain, Vila Viçosa was walled by Diniz (*reg* 1279–1325) in 1297 and by Ferdinand (*reg* 1367–83). It passed into the lordship of Nuno Álvares Pereira (1360–1431), Constable of Portugal, and thence to his grandson, Fernando, 1st Marquês de Vila Viçosa in 1455, subsequently 2nd Duque de Braganza in 1461, who made it his permanent residence.

The nucleus of medieval Vila Viçosa developed on a rectangular plan within the walls. The bastioned castle (Paço da Alcaçova) above the town was occupied by the early Duques de Braganza until after 1501. In that year Jaime de Braganza (*see* BRAGANZA, (1)), the 4th Duque, began the new Ducal Palace, incorporating the fashionable Luso-Moorish style to the north-east. The expansion of the town thus took place in this direction and, with the enlargement of the ducal Court, developed into a network of streets in straight parallel lines running north and south in a regular Renaissance pattern. Vila Viçosa continued to grow from the 16th century until the mid-17th, the period of its greatest importance. The Braganzas were the leading Portuguese noble family, and their patronage increased the town's wealth and artistic patrimony and its prestige and renown as a centre of humanist culture and learning, especially under Teotónio de Braganza (*see* BRAGANZA, (2)). A university was founded there in 1560, and the ducal deer-park (the Tapada), celebrated in verse by Lope de Vega (1562–1635), was enlarged.

The Terreiro do Paço, the palace square, was completed on the south side by the Convento das Chagas, intended as the mausoleum of the Duquesas de Braganza, with a fine single-aisled church (1529) lined with *azulejos* (1626) and an elegant Mannerist cloister with high arcades. To the east stands the Agostinhos church, founded in 1267 but rebuilt in 1635 as a ducal pantheon by the future John IV (founder of the Braganza royal dynasty; *reg* 1640–56); it is one of the largest and most noble of Portuguese churches built in the Plain style (*estilo chão*).

The extensive classical façade of the Ducal Palace (1583–1601), 110 m long, was influenced by Italian models combined with regional characteristics; it was designed by Nicolau de Frias, who made alterations to the earlier building of 1501. The palace (*see* PORTUGAL, fig. 12) is now a museum and houses the important library and archive of the House of Braganza, instituted in 1933 in accordance with the will of Manuel II, the last King of Portugal (*reg* 1908–10; *d* in exile in London, 1932). This library of early Portuguese books was collected by Manuel II during his period in England.

The growth of Vila Viçosa from the 16th century onwards was carefully controlled; one product of this was the Praça Nova (with a fine fountain of 1587) containing the Misericórdia Hospital and adjacent church (1563) with a Serlian portal. To the west is the church of S Bartolomeu (1636–98), formerly a Jesuit college. On the south side is the Câmara Municipal (Town Hall; 1754–7), a late Baroque building designed by José Francisco de Abreu, who also designed the Sanctuary of Nossa Senhora da Lapa. Close by is the Convento da Santa Cruz (1530), which now houses the Museu de Arte Sacra. A programme of development in 1940 destroyed some 16th-century streets, and at this time the Praça Nova was doubled in size. As a result the historic centre lost something of its earlier plan and character.

BIBLIOGRAPHY
J. Espanca: *Compêndio de notícias de Vila Viçosa* (Redondo, 1892)
R. dos Santos: 'Vila Viçosa', *Guia de Portugal* (Lisbon, 1927)
T. Espanca: *Inventário artístico de Portugal: Distrito de Évora, zona sul* (Lisbon, 1978)

For further bibliographies *see* BRAGANZA, (1) and (2).

JOSÉ TEIXEIRA

Vile, William (*b* ?Somerset, *c*. 1700; *d* London, 22 Aug 1767). English cabinetmaker. He is first mentioned in a letter written to George Selwyn on 10 August 1749 on behalf of William Hallett sr (*c*. 1707–81), who may have been his master. Several break-front secrétaires (e.g. London, V&A; Portsmouth, City Mus. & A.G.), formerly belonging to the 3rd Duke of Buckingham, with broken pediments and doors ornamented with carved oval wreaths, at one time regarded as the hallmark of the Vile workshop, have recently been reattributed to Hallett or at least to Vile operating under Hallett's influence. No documented furniture by Vile has survived before the partnership he formed with JOHN COBB in 1751.

In partnership with Cobb, Vile provided furniture for many houses, including Croome Court, Worcs, Normanton Park, Leics, Woburn Abbey, Beds, Uppark, W. Sussex, and The Vyne, Hants. Work for Croome Court began in 1757 and included 'a Handsome Comode Chest of Drawers . . . , a Good Mahogy [sic] Library Table', a large amount of seating, a spectacular pair of console-tables, pier-glasses (1761; Leeds, Temple Newsam House) and a library bookcase (London, V&A). Other patrons included Jacob Bouverie, 1st Viscount Folkestone, at Longford Castle, Wilts, Sir Lawrence Dundas and the 4th Duke of Devonshire.

Vile also enjoyed royal patronage, recorded in the Great Wardrobe accounts. For Queen Charlotte he invoiced a jewel-cabinet and bureau-cabinet in 1761 and a 'very handsome mahogany bookcase' in 1762. These survive in the British Royal Collection. Two mahogany medal-cabinets, originally part of a 'Grand Medal Case' made in 1761 for George III, are in the Victoria and Albert Museum, London, and the Metropolitan Museum of Art, New York. The furniture that Vile & Cobb provided for the 2nd Earl of Buckinghamshire when he was appointed Ambassador

to the Court of Russia at St Petersburg in 1762 is also recorded in the Great Wardrobe accounts.

Vile's work includes some of the finest pieces of English Rococo furniture. It tends to be richly ornamented with carving, in particular wreaths, foliate sprays, latticework and sunbursts, and it sometimes incorporates such architectural elements as columns and pediments. He retired in 1764, and Cobb continued to operate the business.

BIBLIOGRAPHY
D. Shrub: 'The Vile Problem', *V&A Mus. Bull.*, i/4 (1965), pp. 26–35
G. Beard and C. Gilbert, eds: *Dictionary of English Furniture Makers, 1660–1840* (Leeds, 1986)
G. W. Beard: 'Vile and Cobb: Eighteenth-century London Furniture Makers', *Antiques*, cxxxvii (1990), pp. 1394–405

JAMES YORKE

Villa. Type of house, originally built as a country retreat for a wealthy patron; the term later applied also to smaller detached suburban or urban houses in garden settings. In ancient Rome the Latin word *villa* referred to a house in the country as opposed to a town house (*aedes*); the term *villa suburbana* was commonly applied to a house close to but outside a town. Some Roman villas were luxury retreats but these were not typical; the great majority were farms (*villae rusticae*) or the centres of landed estates, where the residence was known as a *villa urbana*, and even the most palatial examples were likely to have an agricultural base. After the fall of the Roman Empire, the villa virtually disappeared as a building type until the revival of economic prosperity and security in the early Renaissance period, when the word villa usually applied to a country estate or semi-rural retreat, the equivalent of the *villa suburbana*. Until *c*. 1700 the use of the term villa was confined to Italy, but during the 18th century it spread to other European countries, and by 1800 it referred to any relatively small detached house built for wealthy patrons. In the 19th century there was a vast expansion in the use of the term throughout Western Europe and, to a lesser extent, in other parts of the world subject to European influence. During this period it generally denoted a middle-class suburban house, a country residence without a great landed estate, or a pleasure house in a resort. By the middle of the 20th century few new houses of any architectural pretension outside Italy were called villas, but in the wider sense of the word, meaning a moderately sized house in a garden setting and particularly in the context of a holiday resort, villas continued to be built in ever-increasing numbers, in both Europe and the rest of the world. Indeed, the idea of the villa residence can be seen as one of the most characteristic and widespread aspirations of the modern Western man.

See also CHÂTEAU and MAISON DE PLAISANCE.

JOHN PERCIVAL, GEOFFREY C. TYACK

I. Roman, before *c*. AD 450. II. Renaissance and Baroque, *c*. 1400–*c*. 1700. III. *c*. 1700–*c*. 1800. IV. After *c*. 1800.

I. Roman, before c. AD 450.

Villas appeared in Italy from the 2nd century BC and were the product of increasing wealth as a result of Rome's recently acquired empire. In Italy the term villa implied a dwelling with at least a minimum level of comfort—a house rather than a hut—and in archaeological terms it is applied to an establishment that was 'integrated into the social and economic organization of the Roman world' (see Rivet). Ownership of land was a measure of social standing and even a determinant of political power, and the villa, along with the estate it controlled, was as much a status symbol as a financial investment. A villa owner might have been a country gentleman or a simple farmer, but he might also have been active in the political and social life of his local town, or even of Rome itself. His villa, whether his primary residence or a refuge from more public activities, would have been seen not only as a facility on which wealth could be spent but as itself a source of wealth through the working of its lands.

With the expansion of the empire, the villa began to appear in the provinces and became one of the primary indicators of Romanization, along with Roman dress and the Latin language. Like other such indicators, it was not so much imposed as eagerly adopted, being a symbol of status for the prosperous Gaulish, African and British, as it had earlier been for Italians. The frequency with which villas succeeded pre-Roman dwellings on the same sites, for example Mayen, Germany, and Lockleys, Herts, England, is a clear indication that Romanized natives rather than Roman immigrants, even in the earliest stages, were mainly responsible for their construction. Even the large villas in such an area as the Somme basin of northern France appeared so early and are so obviously related to pre-Roman settlement types that they too must be seen as in this sense 'native' rather than 'Roman'. Thus, in the provinces, as in Italy, the 'origin' of the villa is to be seen primarily in economic, and only secondarily in cultural, terms: it arose at a point when the economy of a region and of individuals within it enabled it to do so. It is 'Roman' in the sense that the economic conditions that brought it into existence were the result of Roman rule, and it was defined by these conditions as much as by cultural pressures and influences. Consequently, the adoption of the villa as a building type did not everywhere involve the wholesale adoption of Italian style and design. The characteristic Italian house, looking inwards to a colonnaded courtyard, although relatively common in Spain or southern France, gave way increasingly to the equally characteristic 'corridor' house of northern regions, such as Britain, Belgium and the Rhineland. Although within an agricultural economy the role of the villa was also most commonly agricultural, this did not by any means preclude comfort and, in many cases, luxury on a lavish scale.

1. History and development. 2. Decoration. 3. Theory and archaeology.

1. HISTORY AND DEVELOPMENT. Of the early Roman villas in Italy, that of San Rocco at Francolise, Campania, is a typical example. Begun *c.* 100–90 BC as a modest house with adjoining farm buildings, it was remodelled *c.* 50 BC and again *c.* 30 BC, by which time it had become an impressive residence (see fig. 1). Its numerous rooms, coordinated with each other and with those of earlier phases, were grouped around a central peristyle, and most were provided with mosaic pavements. Vitruvian principles of symmetry are evident in its overall design, and

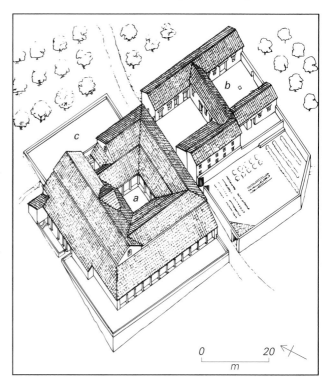

1. San Rocco Villa, Francolise, Campania, after final remodelling *c.* 30 BC; axonometric reconstruction drawing showing (a) *villa urbana*, (b) *villa rustica*, (c) water tank

attention was given to its setting within the landscape and to its appearance when approached from various directions. Adjoining it, although clearly distinguished from it, was the working farm (in Vitruvian terms the *villa rustica* (1b) as opposed to the *villa urbana* (1a)), which included water cisterns (1c), a tile kiln and olive-press, and which, like the residence, was carefully planned and constructed. Such a villa might have been owned by a wealthy farming family, the head of which perhaps had business interests or local government duties in the nearby town; alternatively, it might have served as a country retreat and source of income for someone whose primary concerns were in business or politics. Examples of the latter are common in the writings of Cicero and Pliny the younger: at Laurentum, near Ostia, was a house to which Pliny devoted an entire (and celebrated) letter (*Letters* II.17; *see* PLINY, (2)). Laurentum was more splendid than San Rocco and was not untypical of such houses: those along the coast, particularly around the Bay of Naples, were seized on by moralists and satirists as examples of unnecessary extravagance. What is striking, however, about Pliny's references to his many properties (and this is true also of Cicero) is that he rarely lost sight of their working aspects. Houses built solely for pleasure were the exception rather than the norm.

In the provinces of the Roman Empire the villa usually appeared within a generation or so of the imposition of Roman rule, as a product of the Roman Peace. It was partly introduced by expatriate Italians but was more commonly adopted by the local wealthy, eager to adopt the trappings (and benefits) of a Romanized lifestyle. Partly for this reason and partly for reasons of climate or varying social traditions, the villa evolved differently from region to region; an examination of the many examples where reasonably complete plans are available shows that their variety and diversity are as striking as any common pattern. In size alone they range from what were little more than cottages to some that are more accurately described as palaces, for example Chiragan in south-west France, which had a residential block covering more than 2.5 ha. A number of standard types within a broadly evolving framework can nevertheless be identified, if only as a helpful and convenient means of classification and comparison with the many examples that must be regarded as exceptional.

The basic type of Roman villa, known in Britain as the 'corridor' villa and in continental Europe (more accurately) as the *Portikusvilla* or villa *à galerie-façade*, consisted of a range of rooms fronted by a portico or verandah (not a corridor) with a lean-to roof, at each end of which were symmetrical wing rooms (e.g. Mayen, Germany, and Gadebridge Park, Herts, England). This plan was developed by elongation, producing an impressive façade (e.g. Hosté, Belgium); by adding a portico at both front and rear (e.g. Hambleden, Bucks, England); or by extending the wing rooms into further ranges of rooms (e.g. Witcombe, Glos, England, and Weitersbach, Germany). This last development led logically to the full 'courtyard' villa (e.g. North Leigh, Oxon, England), and to the double courtyards common in continental Europe (e.g. Estrées-sur-Noye, France) and occurring also in Britain (e.g. Bignor, W. Sussex). These last examples are in some respects similar to San Rocco, comprising a *villa urbana* and *villa rustica*, but determined by a different evolutionary process. Not all sites went through all or part of this sequence of development, although in many cases where the plan seems initially to fall outside the sequence altogether, it is possible, by separating the building phases, to discover one or more of the familiar types. Sometimes, however, other more significant features are discovered. The early phases of the Mayen villa retained the large, central, communal room represented by the original hut, and the same is true of numerous sites both in Europe and in Britain. The persistence of pre-Roman social patterns thus implied is also suggested by other features, perhaps even by ground-plans, which occasionally suggest occupancy by extended rather than nuclear families. The extent to which, in the provinces, the villa was wholly 'Roman' has already been considered above; further detailed study of the arrangement of rooms at individual sites may reveal how much, or how little, is implied by the adoption of such Roman amenities as hypocausts, mosaic pavements and baths.

The history of Roman villas is that of the Empire itself, in the sense that they begin and end with it and reflect its rises and falls in prosperity. Houses are known to have been built or extended during periods of economic decline, however, or abandoned at times of prosperity, for reasons that are particular and unconnected with national or regional developments. Nevertheless, the broad patterns are clear. In terms of numbers, wealth and quality of design and construction, the villa reached a peak in the Severan and Antonine periods of the late 2nd century AD. In the 3rd century it fell prey to the common pressures of economic decline and barbarian invasions, and in the 4th century it was part of the partial recovery achieved under Diocletian and Constantine the Great. In some regions, notably Britain, the recovery led to even greater prosperity than before, resulting not only in a resurgence of villas, with major sites appearing for the first time, but in a decisive shift in prosperity towards the west and away from the original area of settlement. Elsewhere, however, villas were less well built and maintained than they had been at the height of the Empire and were less ostentatious. During the collapse of the Empire in the late 4th century AD and the early 5th, the majority were destroyed or abandoned, although some of the larger ones, for example that of Sidonius Apollinaris at Avitacum, near Clermont Ferrand, France, were able to survive under Gothic rule. By then, however, there were signs that their character was changing: large reception areas suggest a more public role than earlier, some were at least partially fortified, and some certainly were the property of Goths or Burgundians. The term villa, as initially defined, was by this time becoming less appropriate.

See also ROME, ANCIENT, §II, 1(i)(c).

2. DECORATION. Although rural in location and function, in residential terms the villa tended to duplicate the amenities and follow the fashions of town houses. The use of the term *villa urbana* to denote the residential as distinct from the working part of the establishment is itself an indication that it was seen as a little bit of the town in the country. Bath suites and central heating were common to both, as were mosaic pavements, painted interior walls and ornamental gardens. The use of particular architectural features and ornamental motifs was concurrent in both the town and country, and there is no evidence that in the latter they were stylistically inferior, indicating the homogeneous nature of Roman society and its economy.

In terms of decoration, mosaics provide the most distinctive illustration of a villa's internal appearance, as well as being a feature most likely to have survived intact (*see* MOSAIC, §II). Although no figures survive to indicate their relative cost, they certainly represented a major expense and were thus indications of status as well as expressions of confidence. Their designs, whether mythical, religious or genre (see fig. 2), were chosen with care and reveal the beliefs and attitudes of their owners (*see* ROME, ANCIENT, fig. 92). The better-quality examples are the work of skilled craftsmen, and studies in Britain, France and North Africa have gone some way towards identifying the products, if not of individuals, at least of workshops, situated presumably in the towns, their workers sent out on a journeyman basis as required (*see* ROME, ANCIENT, §VI, 1(i)). As well as such standard designs as the Orpheus mosaics favoured by the 'Corinian school' around Cirencester, Glos, England, there are recurring ornamental motifs, which suggest the use (and perhaps the exchange) of pattern books. There is also evidence of more local, amateur work, for example the pavements at Rudston, Yorks, England.

2. Villa mosaic from Tabarka, Tunisia, late 4th century–early 5th century AD

Similar to mosaic in technique and overall effect was *opus sectile*, the use of thin slabs of marble of different kinds, laid like tiles to form a decorative pattern for floors or, more frequently, walls. Examples of this work are known from houses of the wealthy in Pompeii (*see* POMPEII, §V) and Ostia (*see* OSTIA, §2), although at sites outside Italy, where buildings have tended to survive, at best, only at ground-level, remains are limited to scattered fragments. The effect, presumably, was primarily one of pattern and colour, the aim perhaps being to provide a suitable background against which to set off furniture or sculpture and to indicate, through the variety and wide-spread origins of the materials, something of the owner's wealth and standing.

A more common form of decoration, and certainly one more readily available, was painted plaster. The most complete examples are from town houses in Italy (e.g. the House of the Vettii and the Villa of the Mysteries, both at Pompeii), where it is possible to identify and date a whole series of styles and fashions; elsewhere it is a matter of piecing together small and badly damaged pieces. Nevertheless, some remarkable reconstructions have been achieved, and, for the western provinces of the Empire at least, the broad outlines of technique, design and dating are reasonably well established (*see* WALL PAINTING, §I, 2(iv) and fig. 2). Walls were prepared by applying layers of plaster, finishing with a fine skin on which the ground colours were painted while it was still wet. More detailed decoration, if required, was applied later, the colours being mixed with gum or another binding agent. A common practice was to divide the walls into a series of panels at

eye-level and to use these as the setting for the main designs. Below them, to a height of up to a metre, was a kind of dado running round the room, decorated either with simple geometric designs or with an overall pattern; this was often flecked or mottled to imitate marble. The main panels sometimes bore simple geometric or curvilinear motifs, but they could also include leaf designs or simple patterns of flowers, birds or fishes (*see also* WALL PAINTING, colour pl. I, fig. 2). Human figures were less common but are found at various sites in Britain and Europe, usually within a simple rustic setting. The walls above the main panels were often left blank or painted in a single colour, but there is evidence to suggest decorated ceilings. There can be little doubt that painting in the Roman period achieved high levels of both technique and design.

Exterior decoration of Roman villas is something of which little is known, although it seems not to have been much used. Nevertheless, the external appearance of the villa was considered important: the symmetry that was so striking a feature of villa design is itself evidence of this, as is the care that was taken in the siting of houses to provide both a pleasing approach and agreeable vistas from inside. It is known from Roman writers (e.g. Varro, *De re rustica* IV.v.9) that gardens were an important part of the villa, as indeed were landscaped parks; the latter were influenced by Hellenistic *paradeisoi*, and the late Republican word for a gardener, *topiarius*, is also Greek. It is clear also from ground-plans that the provision of gardens was a major consideration. In the 'double court-yard' villa, for example, which was common in Gaul, Spain and elsewhere, the inner court adjacent to the main residential block lent itself to such treatment, and it is normally so depicted in reconstruction drawings. For the detailed design and layout of such gardens, however, surviving evidence relates to town houses, especially at Pompeii. Depictions of gardens in wall paintings suggest that they tended to be formal, with trees and flowers laid out in patterns around fountains or statues; this is further borne out by archaeological exploration, for example at the House of Diomedes or that of Loreius Tibertinus, Pompeii. The extent to which such evidence is relevant to country gardens, particularly outside Italy, is unclear. The garden at Pliny the younger's Laurentine villa (*see* PLINY, (2)) contained shrubs and trees, including fruit trees, but no further detail is provided, except that it was a pleasant place in which to walk or work (*see* GARDEN, §II, 4). Outside Italy, information is limited to an occasional reference, indicating merely that a garden existed (e.g. Sidonius Apollinaris, *Epistles* II.2). For evidence relating to the villa garden in Britain, almost the only archaeological material is from FISHBOURNE Palace, W. Sussex, where indications again suggest a formal layout.

3. THEORY AND ARCHAEOLOGY. In early excavations of villas in the 18th century and much of the 19th, attention was directed primarily to their residential aspects and to such amenities as bath suites. What attracted the antiquary and the wider public were such indications of wealth and civilization as hypocausts and mosaics; villa sites were also seen as sources of coins, pottery and other objects for museums and private collections. Reports, when published, tended to concentrate on such findings almost exclusively, with detailed drawings and long descriptions of the most striking items. Plans were usually incomplete and were included, if at all, to indicate in which rooms particular discoveries were made. Much space was devoted to the identification of individual rooms and the day-to-day activities within them, which, like their inhabitants, were assumed to be 'Roman' rather than 'native'; the description by Pliny of Laurentum, the technical works of Cato or Varro, or details of Pompeian town houses, were thus assumed to be wholly relevant as guides to the interpretation of a site. The 19th-century reports on Chedworth, Glos, England, are typical examples of such an approach.

In the 19th century, Roman villas tended to be studied individually; the task of the archaeologist was to describe the example, label it and, if possible, display it in the same way as he would an item in a museum. Similarities might be adduced, mosaics or hypocausts compared with others from the region or from Italy, and the dimensions of rooms recorded and similarly compared. As sites were explored in greater numbers and with greater thoroughness, attention gradually turned to the overall layout and design of villas, examples being classified according to type, consideration being given to materials and methods of construction, and attempts being made to visualize a site in its living state. Only in the early decades of the 20th century did this essentially antiquarian approach give way to one that was more historical. Questions of dating, at first mainly by coins and later by pottery and other objects, assumed greater importance, and villas were seen as having evolved and developed rather than being static entities.

Excavations began to extend beyond the residential and into the working areas; occasionally, as at Köln-Müngersdorf, Germany, a whole farmyard would be explored. Scholars turned to regional studies and to questions of distribution and settlement: a striking early example is L. Joulin's study (1901) of Chiragan in south-west France, which not only related the villa to other sites in the area but attempted to determine its internal economy, with calculations of such factors as crop yields and working and residential populations. In the later 20th century the development of new survey techniques, particularly air photography, drew attention once again away from individual villas towards their economic and social context; the aerial reconnaissance by Roger Agache, carried out in the Somme basin during the 1950s and 1960s and revealing several hundred villas within a varied archaeological landscape, is one of the more impressive examples. Nevertheless, work on individual sites continues, as does the study of architectural and decorative features, notably mosaics.

See also TIVOLI, §2(i); CAPREAE; PIAZZA ARMERINA; SETTEFINESTRE; SIRMIONE; and SPLIT, §1.

BIBLIOGRAPHY
G. E. Fox: 'The Roman Villa at Chedworth, Gloucestershire', *Archaeol. J.*, xxxxiv (1887), pp. 322–36
L. Joulin: *Les Etablissements gallo-romains de la plaise de Martres-Tolosanes* (Paris, 1901)
Receuil général des mosaïques de la Gaule (Paris, 1957–) [supplements to *Gallia*]
P. Grimal: *Les Jardins romains* (Paris, 1969)
A. L. F. Rivet: *The Roman Villa in Britain* (London, 1969)
A. Boethius and J. B. Ward-Perkins: *Etruscan and Roman Architecture*, Pelican Hist. A. (Harmondsworth, 1970)
R. Agache and B. Bréart: *Atlas d'archéologie aérienne de Picardie* (Amiens, 1975)
A. G. McKay: *Houses, Villas and Palaces in the Roman World* (London, 1975)
J. Percival: *The Roman Villa* (London, 1976, rev. 2/1988)
R. Agache: *La Somme pré-romaine et romaine* (Amiens, 1978)
D. S. Neal: *Roman Mosaics in Britain* (London, 1981)
M. A. Cotton and G. P. R.Métraux: *The San Rocco Villa at Francolise* (London, 1985)
H. Mielsch: *Die römische Villa* (Munich, 1987)

JOHN PERCIVAL

II. Renaissance and Baroque, *c. 1400–c. 1700.*

The revival of the villa in 15th-century Italy was anticipated by changing social habits that can be traced back to much earlier times. These included the custom, common to royalty and the feudal aristocracy, of retreating on occasion to a hunting-lodge (e.g. the CASTEL DEL MONTE owned by Frederick II, Holy Roman Emperor, in Apulia); the idea of temporary seclusion in a monastery; and, above all, the practice of *villegiatura*—the voluntary withdrawal from cities to avoid the summer heat. As feudal power declined and mercantile fortunes grew in the 13th century, prosperous townspeople had begun to invest money in land and to build houses on their newly acquired farms or vineyards. By the mid-15th century the powerful Strozzi family, for example, had no fewer than 32 houses in the Florentine countryside. As well as enabling their owners to enjoy the delights of *villegiatura*, these rural residences could be used as retreats in time of plague, as centres for the collection and distribution of agricultural produce (especially important under the increasingly widespread sharecropping system), as places of intellectual and physical refreshment and as residences for different members of an extended family.

The term villa was not widely used until the 15th century; it usually implied not only the house (the casino) but also its surroundings, including gardens, farm buildings, housing for the farmworkers, and the agricultural estate. Many villas were situated deep in the countryside, although within reach of a city—which explains their absence in much of southern Italy. During the 16th century in such areas as Lombardy and the Veneto, where there was an active programme of land reclamation encouraged by the State, villa building was carried out in conjunction with a programme of agricultural improvement. Other villas built at this time conformed more closely to the pattern of the ancient Roman *villa suburbana*: a detached house amid gardens built close to a city (sometimes even within its walls) and serving either as the full-time residence of a wealthy individual or as a pleasure house for a pope or prince—rarely, if ever, slept in except by important visitors before they made a triumphal entry into a city. By the 16th century rich merchants, noblemen and princes had begun to lavish as much attention on their rural houses as on their urban palazzi, using them as status symbols and for extravagant entertainment, including theatrical performances; several villas, especially those near Rome, were also used to house collections of antique sculpture. By the early 18th century many rural villas, even in the Veneto, had become little more than holiday homes, their outbuildings given over to housing guests. Villas thus gradually lost their former connection with farming and became increasingly indistinguishable from the country residences of the north European nobility that they so strongly influenced.

1. History and development. 2. Decoration. 3. Literature and theory. 4. Italian influences abroad.

1. HISTORY AND DEVELOPMENT. The villa emerged as a social phenomenon long before it acquired an architectural character of its own. For most of the 15th century there was little to distinguish a villa from a farmhouse or semi-fortified palazzo. For example, Cosimo de' Medici's villas at Careggi (remodelled 1434–1450s), Caffagiolo and Il Trebbio (both 1420s) were all built around courtyards and retain towers or machicolation, either from earlier buildings on the site or deliberately added by their architect, MICHELOZZO DI BARTOLOMEO, as an assertion of quasi-feudal authority. The villa known as La Sforzesca (1480–86) at Vigevano in Lombardy was placed behind high walls, while the early 16th-century Villa Giustinian (now the Villa Ciani-Bassetti) at Roncade in the Veneto, probably by Tullio Lombardo, was set in a farm courtyard surrounded by crenellated walls and entered through a formidable gate-house, as was the Palazzo Rossi (after 1482) at Pontecchio near Bologna.

For those villa owners who lacked seigneurial pretensions, more modest houses sufficed. In the 15th century villas were usually smaller and plainer than urban palazzi, and in such houses as the mid-15th century casino built by Cardinal Bessarion on the Appian Way, just within the walls of Rome, or Filippo Strozzi the elder's villa (1483–6) at Santuccio, near Florence (an enlargement of an earlier

building), the most striking architectural feature is an arcaded upstairs loggia leading from the main reception room or *sala*. In the relatively modest hipped-roofed villa (*c.* 1460) built for Giovanni de' Medici at Fiesole, attributed to Michelozzo, much of the ground floor is taken up by a loggia leading directly into the terraced gardens, which concealed cellars, stables and wine-presses. There are loggias on both floors of the Villa Porto-Colleoni (1441–53; now Villa Thiene) at Thiene, near Vicenza, where the block containing the *sala* is enclosed between two castellated towers. This tripartite arrangement of a loggia and *sala* (often bisecting the house) flanked by minor rooms remained an important feature of the planning of many villas. Loggias were in effect semi-outdoor rooms designed to allow the owner and his guests to enjoy the shade and breezes and to survey the walled garden, which was often planted with fruit trees and might contain a lake or fishponds. Sometimes a loggia for outdoor dining was built in the garden itself, for example the round-arched late-15th century loggia (*in situ*) at the otherwise destroyed villa of Caterina Cornaro (*see* CORNARO, (2)) at Altivole, near Treviso. Thus feudal magnificence gradually gave way to a delight in the pleasures of nature.

The architecture of Classical antiquity had little effect on the overall design of Italian villas until the last years of the 15th century. Little was known about the layout of ancient Roman villas, apart from what could be gleaned from such literary accounts as Pliny the younger's *Letters* (*see* §I, 1 above) and the remains of Hadrian's palatial villa at Tivoli (then unexcavated); there was total ignorance about the external appearance of these buildings. When architects and their patrons first seriously turned their attention to the creation of a villa *all'antica*, the emphasis was therefore on the evocation of classicism through symmetrical planning, careful detailing and appropriate proportions, rather than the strict imitation of ancient models. The first villa to be designed throughout on the new principles was that begun in 1485 by Lorenzo de' Medici to the designs of Giuliano da Sangallo (see fig. 3; *see also* POGGIO A CAIANO, VILLA MEDICI and SANGALLO, DA, (1), §1(ii)); it was symmetrically laid out and proportioned according to simple mathematical ratios, with a loggia treated as a temple-front *in antis* at the centre of the entrance front—the first appearance of this feature in Renaissance villa architecture.

Italian Renaissance villas are of three main types: those built around courtyards, those in which the house consists of a main block with wings, and those with the accommodation fitted into a single compact block. All these plans have medieval precedents. An early example of the courtyard villa is the house (begun 1487; destr.) built for Ferdinand I, King of Naples, at Poggio Reale, probably to the designs of Giuliano da Maiano (*see* MAIANO, DA, (1)). Its courtyard was colonnaded, as in an ancient Roman villa, and there were low towers at the corners—a motif borrowed 200 years later by William Kent at Holkham Hall, Norfolk, England. The second, far more common, plan was employed in the house now known as the Villa Farnesina in Rome, built *c.* 1505–10 by Pope Julius II's banker, Agostino Chigi, to the designs of Baldassare Peruzzi (*see* PERUZZI, (1), fig. 1). The internal layout is less rigorously symmetrical than at Poggio a Caiano, but

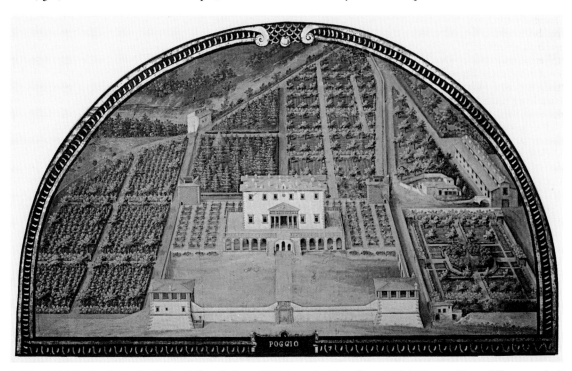

3. Villa Medici, Poggio a Caiano, by Giuliano da Sangallo, begun 1485; lunette by Giusto Utens, 1598–9 (Florence, Museo di Firenze com'era)

the façades (originally painted with frescoes) are meticulously proportioned, with a Tuscan pilaster order on each floor, a stucco frieze under a hipped roof and an arched loggia between the two wings on the garden side. The third, compact type of plan was used in the smaller and slightly later Villa Lante on the Janiculum, Rome, built to the designs of Raphael and Giulio Romano for an official in the court of Pope Leo X (*see* GIULIO ROMANO); this attractive building provided a prototype for countless smaller villas until the 19th century.

The influence of antiquity first began to affect the surroundings of the Italian villa in the early 16th century. In 1504 Pope Julius II employed Bramante to add a courtyard in imitation of an ancient Roman garden in front of the Belvedere, a pleasure house built by Innocent VIII close to the Vatican in 1487 (*see* ROME, §V, 14(iii)(a); *see also* BRAMANTE, DONATO, §I, 3(ii)(a)). The terraced Cortile del Belvedere was flanked by arcades housing the Pope's important collection of Classical statuary and terminated in a theatre-like semicircular exedra. At the Villa Madama near Rome (begun *c.* 1518, not completed), Raphael made an even more ambitious attempt to re-create a villa of the type described by Pliny the younger, with a large circular courtyard, a formal garden containing an outdoor theatre, nymphaeum and grotto, and a small grove to the rear. In its highly artificial mingling of plantations and water the villa garden thus became a poetic extension of the house.

Raphael and his followers brought a new element of monumentality to villa architecture. The vaulted garden loggia (*see* RAPHAEL, fig. 9) at the Villa Madama was intended to recapture the vanished grandeur of ancient Roman buildings, as was the new building (1530s) at the

Villa Imperiale, Pesaro, by Girolamo Genga (for illustration *see* GENGA, (1); *see also* PESARO, §3). In the Palazzo del Te (1525–35) at Mantua, Giulio Romano went even further in the evocation of antiquity by following the Roman model of four single-storey ranges of building around a courtyard. From the outside there is an effect of massive rusticity, with an extensive use of the Doric order, heavily emphasized keystones and voussoirs, and massive blocks of masonry (*see* GIULIO ROMANO, fig. 3; *see also* ORDERS, ARCHITECTURAL, fig. 6), while within there is a series of profusely decorated rooms with frescoes of writhing, lascivious gods and goddesses. A monumental loggia similar to that at the Villa Madama (where Giulio Romano had worked) leads from the courtyard into the garden, the focal point of which is a massive exedra. The spirit of artifice so evident in the Palazzo del Te reached its apogee in a group of mid-16th-century villas built by popes and members of the great papal families in and around Rome. The Villa Giulia (1551–5; *see* VIGNOLA, JACOPO, fig. 3), erected for Julius III to the designs of Vignola, Bartolomeo Ammanati and other architects, presents a reticent face to the outside world, but the garden front of the casino is semicircular and faces a screen beyond which lies a sunken nymphaeum. A similar contrast exists at the Villa Medici on the Pincian Hill, Rome, remodelled in 1576–86 by Ammanati for Cardinal Ferdinando de' Medici, who owned a notable sculpture collection; here the garden front is decorated with stucco embellishments and antique reliefs (see fig. 4). The most spectacular Roman villa of this period is the massive pentagonal Villa Farnese (*see* CAPRAROLA, VILLA FARNESE), begun to the designs of Vignola in 1559. This is a Renaissance equivalent of the medieval *castello*: a centre of territorial power dominating its surroundings. It was built on foundations intended for a fortified castle, and behind its forbiddingly monumental façades are suites of ceremonial rooms designed for the formal entertainment of large numbers of guests, with a circular courtyard in the centre; a smaller, private casino with its own garden, including a water cascade, was built 400 m away to allow the quiet seclusion traditionally associated with villa life.

The gardens of late 16th-century Roman villas were among the most ambitious and inventive ever created (*see* GARDEN, §VIII, 3(i)). At the Villa d'Este (begun 1560; *see* TIVOLI, §3) they spread in terraces down the hillside from the relatively plain house and owe much of their effect to the copious use of fountains and the play of water designed by Pirro Ligorio, who had been employed by Ippolito II d'Este (ii) to excavate the ruins of Hadrian's Villa a short distance away. The garden of the Villa Lante (begun *c.* 1568; *see* BAGNAIA, VILLA LANTE), attributed to Vignola, is arranged as a series of parterres down the hillside, with the most elaborate in front of the two residential pavilions (*see* GARDEN, fig. 1); at the Villa Aldobrandini, Frascati, begun for Cardinal Pietro Aldobrandini by Giacomo della Porta in 1601 and completed by Carlo Maderno, a cascade runs down from the hillside to a semicircular water-theatre (*see* FRASCATI, fig. 1) in front of the house and a more secluded 'secret garden' to the side.

The influence of Roman-style villas soon spread to other parts of Italy. In Genoa and its surroundings, the Umbrian-born Galeazzo Alessi designed several suburban villas for the wealthy mercantile élite of the Republic, for example the Villa Giustiniani (1548; now Villa Cambiaso; *see* ALESSI, GALEAZZO, fig. 1) and the Villa Pallavicino (*c.* 1555; see fig. 5), set among terraced gardens that take full advantage of the hilly topography of the area (*see* ALESSI, GALEAZZO, §2(iii)). The façades of these compact, beautifully proportioned buildings represent a more sculptural and ornamental development of the Farnesina type. The Venetian villa also achieved prominence in the mid-16th century as the nobility of the Veneto began to develop their estates on the mainland. Here the architecture owed much to the spread of High Renaissance ideas by the humanists Alvise Cornaro, designer of the Villa dei Vescovi (late 1530s) near Padua, and Giangiorgio Trissino, who designed a villa at Cricoli, near Vicenza, for his own use. Trissino later patronized Andrea Palladio, who became one of the most accomplished, and certainly the most famous, of all Italian villa architects. The Venetians believed that they, alone among all the Italians, had never submitted to the barbarians and were in consequence the true heirs of the Romans: Palladio's villas embody this attractive myth in a powerfully monumental form. His first villas (e.g. the Villa Godi at Lonedo, 1537–42; *see* PALLADIO, ANDREA, fig. 1) represent a refinement and

4. Villa Medici, Rome, remodelled by Bartolomeo Ammanati for Cardinal Ferdinando de' Medici, 1576–86

5. Villa Pallavicino, Genoa, by Galeazzo Alessi, *c.* 1555

regularization of the local vernacular tradition and are notable chiefly for their simple balanced porportions and symmetrical plans. Farm buildings, including stables, *barchesse* (barns with attached arcades) and dovecots, are successfully incorporated into the layout, and the main rooms are placed over a basement that (sometimes together with the top floor) is given over to storage space and service quarters. After he had been to Rome at Trissino's expense in 1541, Palladio began to incorporate elements taken from the architecture of antiquity, notably the porticoed temple-front, either engaged (e.g. Villa Barbaro, 1549–58; for illustration *see* MASER, VILLA BARBARO); projecting (e.g. Villa Foscari at Malcontenta, late 1550s); *in antis* (e.g. Villa Badoer, *c.* 1556–60, at Fratta Polesine; see fig. 6); or two-storey (e.g. Villa Cornaro, early 1550s, at Piombino Dese; *see* PALLADIO, ANDREA, fig. 4). Since the main rooms were usually placed on the *piano nobile*, the opportunity was taken to give nobility to the composition by the provision of a broad temple-like flight of steps leading up to the portico; this effect was often heightened (e.g. Villa Barbaro and Villa Emo Fanzolo, late 1550s) by linking the farm buildings to the main block by arcaded loggias. Palladio showed equal dexterity in the internal layout of his villas. The plans are usually square and compact, with a central axis containing a *sala* approached through a vestibule or *entrata* and flanked by

smaller rooms of varying shapes, sometimes influenced by Palladio's study of the ruined baths of ancient Rome. The *sala*—the formal focus of the house—could be rectangular or cruciform (e.g. Villa Barbaro and Villa Foscari) or even circular, as in the most famous of all his villas, the Villa Rotonda (begun *c.* 1565–6; *see* VICENZA, §2). Placed on a hilltop just outside Vicenza, the Villa Rotonda has porticos on each of its four fronts and a dome crowning the whole composition (*see* PALLADIO, ANDREA, fig. 5); this arrangement inspired Scamozzi at Rocca Pisani (1576), near Lonigo (*see* SCAMOZZI, (2), fig. 1), and continued to influence villa architects until the 20th century.

In the 17th century much larger villas were often built at the centres of rural estates. They drew on the architectural language of the Baroque, and their separate elements of house, interiors and gardens were usually integrated within a single unified concept. The planning of many of these houses followed that of the Villa Aldobrandini, Frascati—a plain rectangular building with a central *sala* running across the shorter axis and residential apartments for important guests on either side. Houses of this kind, with sumptuous reception rooms, spacious gardens and large complexes of ancillary buildings—sometimes even including a market-place—continued to be built into the 18th century (e.g. Villa Arconati at Castellazzo, Lombardy, by Giovanni Ruggieri; Villa Manin, 1738, at Passariano in

6. Villa Badoer, Fratta Polesine, by Andrea Palladio, *c.* 1556–60

the Veneto by Giovanni Ziborghi). The social habits that encouraged the building of smaller villas also spread in the 17th century and the early 18th to areas where few such houses had been built in the past. In the countryside around Lucca merchants began investing money in land in the 16th century, but the villas were rebuilt on a much grander scale in the early 17th century, the architecture reflecting that of 16th-century Rome, with gardens of comparable magnificence (e.g. Villa Garzoni, *c.* 1652, Collodi, nr Lucca). Villa building also spread to Sicily at the end of the 17th century, and it was in the region of Palermo, and especially at Bagheria, a favoured spot for *villegiatura*, that the Italian Baroque villa reached its final flowering. The Villa Palagonia (begun 1705) by Tommaso Maria Napoli (1655–1725) and the Villa Valguernera (1709–39) have a profusion of curved façades and extravagantly complex external staircases. Some of these features are also found in contemporary Piedmontese villas, notably in the palatial hunting villa at Stupinigi, built to the designs of Filippo Juvarra in 1729. A simpler strain in villa design persisted in Tuscany (e.g. Villa Cetinale, *c.* 1680, nr Siena, by Carlo Fontana (iv)) and in the Veneto, where quantities of moderately sized estates remained, the owners of which continued to be attracted to the arcadian *villa rustica* ideal. Here, compact villas of the type established by Palladio and Scamozzi continued to be built until well into the 18th century, when there was something of a Palladian revival (e.g. Villa Cordellina, 1735–60, by Giorgio Massari).

2. DECORATION. The rooms in 15th-century villas were relatively lightly furnished. Pictures and tapestries were more commonly found in urban palazzi than in villas, where the main embellishment took the form of frescoed walls. There are still remnants of frescoes by well-known late 15th-century artists in villas near Florence, for example those by Antonio del Pollaiuolo in the Villa della Gallina at Arcetri, which show dancing nudes against a background, as in antique vase painting, and those by Filippino Lippi inside the loggia of the Villa Medici at Poggio a Caiano. Fresco decoration remained the most significant feature of villa interiors until the 18th century. As in ancient Roman villas, the subjects of these frescoes are an indication of their owners' cultural interests and way of life: frescoes (1471) in the Palazzo di Schifanoia at Ferrara by Francesco del Cossa, for example, glorify the court of Borso d'Este (ii), Duke of Ferrara, and the astrological influences that allegedly governed it. Myth was frequently employed to reinforce the grandeur of the owner and his family, for example in the *sala* at Poggio a Caiano (decorated by Pontormo in the 16th century) and in the interiors of the Villa d'Este at Tivoli, where frescoes of the legend of Hercules are used to glorify the family. In the much smaller Villa Poiana (*c.* 1550), near Vicenza, Palladio's *sala* is decorated with figures of Roman military heroes in an attempt to give it the character of an atrium.

The evocation of a Classical Golden Age, free from mundane concerns, became a constant preoccupation from the late 15th century. The superb frescoes of the story of Cupid and Psyche and of the legend of Galatea (by Raphael and others) at the Villa Farnesina, Rome, were carefully chosen to underline the building's function as a pleasure house, far removed in character from the more austere humanist retreats of the 15th century. The decorative scheme was modelled to some extent on the descriptions of Pliny the younger's villas in his *Letters* and thus included *trompe l'oeil* landscape painting, especially in the main garden loggia and in the upstairs *sala delle prospettive*; here the intention was to blend the interior of the house with the garden, itself an artificial retreat set apart from everyday concerns. Landscapes by Dosso Dossi, some of them seen through pergolas supported by caryatids, also appear in the original building at the Villa Imperiale, Pesaro.

With increasing archaeological knowledge of such ancient Roman interiors as the Domus Aurea of Nero, Rome, *grottesche* began to be incorporated (*see* ROME, §V, 5; *see also* GROTESQUE). In the garden loggia of the Villa Madama, for example, the iconographical scheme includes representations of the *Seasons* and the *Elements*, along with scenes from Ovid, whose *Metamorphoses* remained a popular source for villa decoration throughout the 16th and early 17th centuries (e.g. Domenichino's frescoes, 1616–18, from the Villa Aldobrandini, Frascati; four panels *in situ*; six in London, N.G.). As well as mythological themes, the internal decoration of late 16th-century villas sometimes included representations of scenes of villa life, for example those by Giovanni Antonio Fasolo (*c.* 1570) in the Villa Caldogne near Vicenza. Veronese's famous frescoes in Palladio's Villa Barbaro at Maser constitute a quasi-Virgilian celebration of rural life in general (*see* ILLUSIONISM, colour pl. IV), a theme that continued until the 18th century (*see* §III below).

Fresco painting in 17th-century villas usually covered not only the walls but also the ceilings of rooms, as in the work by Guercino (1621–3) in the Villa Ludovisi, Rome. This approach created an effect of fantasy and illusion that greatly influenced the designers of domestic interiors throughout Europe. The sense of unreality was sometimes heightened (e.g. in the Villa Garzoni at Collodi, nr Lucca) by the inclusion of *trompe l'oeil* architecture, a practice known as *quadratura*. Stucco also began to be more widely employed, especially in ceilings, reaching its period of greatest popularity in the early 18th century. Impressive furniture, intended as a permanent fixture, was introduced into the guest and private apartments on either side of the central *sala*, much of it elaborately carved and gilded, along with mirrors and elaborate draperies and bed hangings, all arranged in a formal fashion. Thus the decoration of villas, like the architecture, lost its early simplicity and became virtually indistinguishable from that of urban *palazzi*.

3. LITERATURE AND THEORY. Vitruvius, the only ancient Roman writer on architecture whose writings have survived, had little to say about the design of country residences. The main literary influence from antiquity came from descriptions of villas—notably those by Pliny the younger of his villas at Laurentum and Tusculum—and from such writers as Cato and Virgil who dealt with aspects of rural life and husbandry; they helped to establish a mythology of villa life in which the wise man deliberately sought relief for limited periods in the countryside from the pressures of the city. This Classical literary tradition, celebrated in such works as the HYPNEROTOMACHIA POLIPHILI (Venice, 1499), played a powerful part in encouraging both the growth and the eventual architectural form of the Italian Renaissance villa. The first Italian writer to discuss the architecture and planning of villas was Leon Battista Alberti. In his *De re aedificatoria* (written *c.* 1452; pubd Florence, 1485; V.xiv–xviii; IX.ii–iv) Alberti gave advice on the design of country and suburban villas. Ideally both should be placed on hills, to enable the owners to enjoy the benefits of fresh air in the hot Italian summer climate, to command the view and to be visible to strangers. Villas should be more festive in their architectural and decorative character than town houses; their general appearance should be welcoming, and battlements and fortifications were not appropriate. There should be a central courtyard (*sinus*), which could be covered over. The reception rooms should be of varying shapes and sizes, but their proportions, like those of the architectural elevations, should be related to one another and to the canonic, often mathematical, proportions of ancient buildings. Loggias were appropriate, both close to the house and in the gardens, which might themselves be embellished with vases, grottoes, vines and clipped trees. The interiors could be decorated with statuary and pictures of heroic deeds or, in houses intended purely for the pursuit of pleasure, with landscapes and scenes of country sports. Alberti's account anticipates in certain respects the Italian Renaissance villa as it actually developed in the late 15th century and the 16th.

The first architectural treatise to provide plans and elevations of villas was by Sebastiano Serlio. In his unpublished 'Sixth Book' and in the seventh book of his *Architettura* (Venice, 1584) he included several of his own designs for houses in the country, some of them of a highly unusual character (e.g. one shaped like a cross); in his third book he also publicized such notable recent buildings as the Villa Madama. Serlio's influence was matched and even surpassed by that of Palladio, whose comments (II.xii–xiii) in his *Quattro libri dell' architettura* (Venice, 1570) on the siting and design of villas (based on his own very successful practice of villa architecture) supplemented, without contradicting, those of Alberti a century earlier. Palladio stressed the importance of running water in the vicinity of a villa and recommended sites either on hills or close to navigable rivers. The architect should integrate farm buildings and storage space into the overall design and should arrange housing for the farmer and labourers close to the gates. In general the architecture of a rural villa (in contrast to that of a *villa suburbana* or town house) should be plain and simple, but dignity and grandeur could be imparted to the exterior by the inclusion of a temple-front, which Palladio believed (II.xvi) might have been a feature of the houses of the ancients, as it was of their temples and public buildings. Inside, the main architectural emphasis should be on the *sala*, which, since it was used 'for entertainments, banquets, weddings and similar recreations. . .should be much bigger than the other [rooms]'. These ideas were developed by Scamozzi in Book 3 of his *Idea dell'architettura universale* (Venice, 1615). He emphasized that the building of villas would encourage landowners to visit their estates more often, which would result in greater profit. He also produced designs for villas of varying size. Some were compactly planned, but others, described as 'onorevoli' or even 'magnifiche', were supplied with accommodation as plentiful as that in urban palaces: these anticipate some of the huge villas that were subsequently erected both in 17th-century Italy and 18th-century England.

4. ITALIAN INFLUENCES ABROAD. The social circumstances that encouraged the emergence of the villa in Renaissance Italy did not appear in other parts of Europe until the 16th century. In much of northern Europe economic and political power remained, to a far greater extent than in Italy, based in the countryside, and for a long time the evolution of domestic design owed little to Italian examples. Italian influence penetrated to the rest of Europe in two ways: through travel and through the publication of accounts of visits to Italy. Michel de Montaigne in the 16th century and John Evelyn in the 17th century are only two of the many *cognoscenti* who wrote long and detailed descriptions of the more important Italian villas and their gardens. Serlio spent the years from 1541 to 1554 in France, and Inigo Jones visited Italy at least twice before embarking on his career as the 'British Vitruvius'. The works of Serlio, Palladio and Scamozzi were widely collected outside Italy, and the publication of the *Palazzi di Genova* (Antwerp, 1622) under Peter Paul Rubens's name was specifically aimed at a north-European readership, the preface emphasizing that the houses illustrated were 'suited rather to the largish families of private gentlemen than to the court of an absolute prince'.

In some respects the villa in northern Europe has a prototype in the medieval park lodge, but a consciously humanistic motivation began to emerge in early 16th-century France. Charles VIII, King of France, lived in the Poggio Reale villa near Naples in 1494–5, and the influence of Italy can perhaps be detected in the planning and symmetrical layout, if not the architecture, of the château of Chambord (begun 1519), owned by Francis I, King of France. There is a stronger Italian influence in the château of Ancy-le-Franc (Yonne), built to Serlio's designs c. 1546 around a courtyard, with four corner towers reminiscent of Poggio Reale (which Serlio had illustrated in Book III of his treatise), and in Philibert de L'Orme's château of Anet (1547). Italian ideas also lay to some extent behind the design of Wollaton Hall, Notts, England, built under the supervision of the master mason Robert Smythson from 1580 (for illustration *see* SMYTHSON). This startlingly original house is placed on a hilltop, like a villa, and has corner towers adorned with Mannerist devices culled from contemporary Flemish pattern books. The plan, however, is more compact than that of Ancy-le-Franc: the courtyard was replaced by a lofty central hall (following a variant design of the Poggio Reale villa) and a room above it, from which the owner could view the gardens and surrounding countryside. Similarly, the plan of the nearby Hardwick Hall, with the hall placed across the main axis like an Italian *sala*, is very close to that of Palladio's Villa Valmarana at Lisiera, illustrated in the *Quattro libri*; the plans of some early 17th-century Polish houses (e.g. Villa Czermierniki; Villa Wala Justowka, nr Kraków) may be derived from the same source.

In the late 16th century and the early 17th, several English country gentlemen built small villa-like houses for retirement and contemplation close to their main residences. One example is the cross-shaped house known as Lyveden New Bield, Northants, begun by the Catholic recusant Sir Thomas Tresham (?1543–1605) in 1594 with assistance from Robert Stickells, a master mason in Queen Elizabeth's Office of Works but never completed. The shape and iconography of this strange building owe much to Tresham's religious beliefs, but he may also have been influenced by the design for a cross-shaped villa in Book VII of Serlio's treatise. Italian Renaissance influence is even more evident in the lavish internal decoration (including hooded chimney-pieces taken from Serlio's Book IV) of the Little Castle at Bolsover, Derbys, a castellated villa built in c. 1612–21 to John Smythson's designs on the site of the keep of a medieval castle, away from the main reception rooms of the house. Albeit much larger, King Philip IV of Spain's El Buen Retiro (1630s; *see* MADRID, §IV, 1) was a response to a similar impulse for meditative retirement, and his hunting-lodge, the 'Casa de la Zarzuela' in the grounds of the Pardo Palace (by Juan Gómez de Mora (i), 1634–8), had the compactness and classical proportions associated with Italian villa design.

In the 16th century and early 17th, merchants and noblemen began to build villas near the edges of Dutch and English cities. In London, the villages of Kensington and, later, of Hampstead, became favoured locations for a version of *villegiatura*, anticipating their later development as middle-class suburbs. Here noblemen built substantial houses with elaborate gardens *all'italiana* (e.g. Holland House, Kensington) but with very little agricultural land. Merchants' houses were also built alongside canals near Amsterdam and Utrecht. The influence of the Italian villa on the planning and external appearance of smaller houses in England, France and Holland increased during the early 17th century. Elevations became more disciplined, plans more symmetrical and the overt or covert influence of the Classical orders more obvious; this is evident in the château of Balleroy (c. 1626) in Calvados, France, by François Mansart, in the Mauritshuis (from 1633) at The Hague, by Peter Post and Jacob van Campen and at Huis ten Bosch (1628; *see* THE HAGUE, §IV, 3), as well as at Thorpe Hall (c. 1653), Northants, by Peter Mills. In each of these houses Italian ideas, many of them derived from Palladio, Scamozzi and the *Palazzi di Genova*, are combined with features taken from local building traditions. The influence of Italy was more apparent in the houses of the English court architect Inigo Jones and his pupil John Webb (i). One of Jones's elevations of c. 1619 for a house at Newmarket, Cambs, is very close to a villa design by Scamozzi, whom he had met in Italy in 1615 and from whom he purchased some of Palladio's drawings. In the Queen's House (*see* GREENWICH, §1), begun 1615 but not completed until 1638—by which time the original design had been altered—Jones built what was then the most Italianate house in northern Europe. The unusual plan owes some of its features to the Villa Medici at Poggio a Caiano, while the internal and external proportions follow the precepts of Alberti; there is even, on the park side, an open loggia on the first floor. At Gunnersbury House (1658–63; destr.; *see* fig. 7), which was a suburban villa near London built for a rich lawyer,

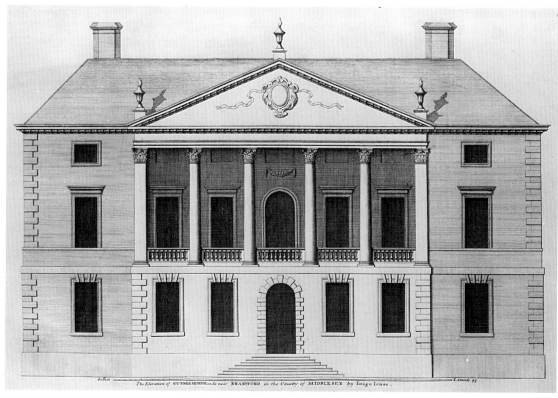

7. Gunnersbury House, Middlesex, by John Webb (i), 1658–63 (destr.); from Colen Campbell: *Vitruvius Britannicus,* i (London, 1715)

and at Amesbury (*c.* 1661), Wilts, John Webb (i) incorporated temple porticos after the fashion of Palladio and Scamozzi within the context of regular, compact façades and symmetrical, logical internal planning. These houses had little immediate influence in the francophile atmosphere of late 17th-century England, but with the Palladian revival of the early 18th century they were widely publicized and made a profound contribution to the development of the villa both in Britain and in North America. There was also a growth of Italian influence in English garden design in the late 17th century. Inigo Jones's former patron Thomas Howard, Earl of Arundel, referred in 1646 to his 'Darling *Villa*' at Albury, Surrey, and some 20 years later John Evelyn designed a terraced garden there for his grandson. Similar Italianate gardens were created at Powis Castle in Wales and at Cliveden, Bucks, the last of which reminded Evelyn of Frascati. Italian influence increased in the early 18th century and played a significant part in the evolution of the landscape garden, England's most important contribution to the visual arts during that era.

BIBLIOGRAPHY

G. Masson: *Italian Villas and Palaces* (London, 1959)
——: *Italian Gardens* (London, 1961)
J. Ackerman: *Sources of the Renaissance Villa*, Studies in Western Art, ii (Princeton, 1963)
I. Barsali: *La villa a Lucca* (Rome, 1964)
G. L. Tomasi: *Le ville di Palermo* (Palermo, 1965)
C. L. Frank: *The Villas of Frascati* (London, 1966)
E. de Negri and others: *Le ville genovesi* (Genoa, 1967)
L. Heydenreich and others: 'La villa: Genesi e Sviluppi', *Boll. Cent. Int. Stud. Archit. Andrea Palladio*, xi (1969)
G. Cuppini and A. M. Matteucci: *Ville del bolognese* (Bologna, 1969)
H. Acton: *Tuscan Villas* (London, 1973)
P. E. Foster: *A Study of Lorenzo de' Medici's Villa at Poggio a Caiano* (diss., New Haven, CT, Yale U., 1974)
R. Palluchini and others: *Gli affreschi nelle ville venete* (Venice, 1978)
M. N. Rosenfeld, ed.: *Sebastiano Serlio on Domestic Architecture* (Cambridge, MA, and London, 1978)
D. Coffin: *The Villa in the Life of Renaissance Rome* (Princeton, 1979)
J. Dixon Hunt: *Garden and Grove* (London, 1986)
A. R. Lillie: *Florentine Villas in the Fifteenth Century: A Study of the Strozzi and Sassetti Country Properties* (diss., U. London, 1986)
M. Muraro: *Venetian Villas* (New York, 1986)
J. Ackerman: *The Villa* (London, 1990)
P. Holberton: *Palladio's Villas: Life in the Renaissance Countryside* (London, 1990)
P. Thornton: *The Italian Renaissance Interior: 1400–1600* (London, 1991)
P. van der Ree, G. Schmienk and G. Steenbergen: *Italian Villas and Gardens* (Amsterdam, 1992)

III. c. 1700–c. 1800.

During the 18th century the popularity of the villa increased substantially, and by *c.* 1800 the use of the term had spread from Italy to other European countries, notably Britain, Ireland and Germany. This reflected a growing attachment to the classical ideal of a harmonious relationship between the civic and pastoral virtues, not only among the nobility of Europe but also among the increasingly wealthy and numerous middle classes. As the 18th century progressed, the design of villas engaged the creative energies of an increasing number of Europe's most talented architects and led to changes in domestic design, the effects of which lasted into the 20th century.

In 18th-century Italy the word villa continued to be used to describe substantial country houses built by noblemen, for example Villa Nazionale Già Pisani (1735–40) at Stra by FRANCESCO MARIA PRETI, decorated by Giambattista Tiepolo (*see* STRA, VILLA NAZIONALE GIÀ PISANI). Wherever social habits favoured *villegiatura* (temporary summer residence outside the city), the *villa suburbana* remained popular; the Villa Albani (1755–62; *see* ROME, §V, 27), built on the edge of Rome by CARLO MARCHIONNI to house Cardinal Alessandro Albani's collection of antique statuary, forms part of a tradition of the *villa suburbana* that goes back to the Renaissance. Villas were built near other large cities, too, for example Palermo and Genoa; common to all was the close relationship of the house to its garden setting, with which it forms a coherent aesthetic whole (*see* §II, 1 and 2 above). The theme of rural life was also an important element in the decoration of such villas as the Villa Valmarana 'ai Nani' at Vicenza, where Giandomenico Tiepolo's frescoes in the detached guest wing (1757; for illustration *see* TIEPOLO, (2)) hover on the edge of realism and form a striking contrast to the rooms in the main villa; there, Tiepolo's father, Giambattista Tiepolo, painted an equally impressive series of mythologies and subjects from the poetry of Torquato Tasso.

Outside Italy the term villa first achieved wide currency in early 18th-century Britain (*see* ENGLAND, §II, 4). The meaning of the word was ambiguous, but in general the connotations were aristocratic, the term being applied to the second home of a nobleman in the vicinity of London, or to a small country house designed on strict Renaissance principles. In the early 18th century the Palladian villa served as a model for several widely publicized English country houses by COLEN CAMPBELL, for example STOURHEAD (1721–4), Wilts, and Mereworth (*c.* 1723), Kent (*see* PALLADIANISM, fig. 2), both of which have compact square plans and façades incorporating formal entrance porticos. Compact villa-like houses were also built in Scotland, albeit with a less slavish adherence to Palladian models, for example Mavisbank (1723–39; largely destr. 1793), Lothian, by William Adam. The Palladian villa also served as the model for a group of houses built by noblemen and men of letters as secondary homes in the Thames valley to the west of London, including the 'poetical villa' of ALEXANDER POPE at Twickenham (rebuilt from 1720 with the assistance of James Gibbs; destr.); Marble Hill House (1724–9; see fig. 8), Twickenham, by Roger Morris and Henry Herbert, later 9th Earl of Pembroke; and CHISWICK HOUSE (1725–9), designed by its owner, Richard Boyle, 3rd Earl of Burlington (*see* BOYLE, (2)), as a compact and virtually self-contained extension to an older building. Each of these houses was placed in a carefully contrived garden setting designed to evoke, sometimes on a miniature scale, the villas of Horace and Pliny the younger, as described by Burlington's protégé Robert Castell (*d* 1729) in his *Villas of the Ancients Illustrated* (London, 1728).

The innovations of Campbell, Gibbs and Lord Burlington's circle were widely publicized and were included in such books as *Lectures on Architecture* (London, 1734) by Robert Morris (*c.* 1702–54). The neo-Palladian villa was adopted in Ireland in the 1730s, for example at Bellamont Forest (1729), Co. Cavan, by EDWARD LOVETT PEARCE, and later in North America, for example at MONTICELLO

8. Marble Hill House, Twickenham, Middlesex, by Roger Morris and Henry Herbert, later 9th Earl of Pembroke, 1724–9

(1700–1809), Charlottesville, VA, which was designed and built by THOMAS JEFFERSON as his own residence.

In England the squareness of Palladian models began to be broken up from the 1750s with the introduction of canted bay windows, as at Asgill House (1761–4), Richmond, Surrey, by Robert Taylor. At the same time internal planning was transformed by arranging the rooms around a central top-lit staircase, as at Taylor's Harleyford Manor (1755), Bucks. More significantly, the Palladian idea of placing the *piano nobile* over a rusticated lower storey was dispensed with, and the main rooms came to be placed at ground-level (e.g. Duddingston House (1763), near Edinburgh, by William Chambers). These innovations were incorporated into the growing number of moderately sized detached houses built by merchants, industrialists and professional men around the edges of British towns in the later years of the 18th century. To cater for this market, designs for villas of varied character were included in new pattern books, including *Original Designs in Architecture, Consisting of Plans, etc., for Villas, Mansions, Town Houses, etc.* (London, 1779–80) by James Lewis (*c.* 1751–1820), John Soane's *Sketches in Architecture* (London, 1793), John Plaw's *Rural Architecture* (London, 1785) and *Sketches for Country Houses, Villas and Rural Dwellings* (London, 1800).

The idea of the moderately sized residence also became fashionable in France in the later 18th century. Such houses were in part the response of sophisticated aristocrats to the growing interest in a simple life lived in harmony with nature, for example Mme de Pompadour's Petit Trianon (1762–8) at Versailles (*see* VERSAILLES, §4 and fig. 4) by Anges-Jacques Gabriel and the Château de Bagatelle (1777) in the Bois de Boulogne, Paris, by François-Joseph Bélanger, and in part the response to the increasing desire of merchants and financiers to acquire and adorn small estates in the vicinity of large towns. Such pattern books as *Recueil élémentaire d'architecture* (Paris, 1757–68 and 1772–80) by JEAN-FRANÇOIS DE NEUF-FORGE contained designs for houses of a size and character that were intended to appeal to such clients, although the word villa was rarely used to describe them.

In the German-speaking countries of Europe some compactly planned houses of a villa character were built in the early part of the 18th century, including Villa Portheim (1725–7) in Prague, designed by Kilian Ignaz Dietzenhofer as his own residence. With the growing taste for Neo-classical simplicity that marked the second part of the century, plain houses with simple exteriors and compact plans became increasingly popular, and as the enthusiasm for Italy and Classical antiquities spread towards the end of the century, they were increasingly described as villas, for example Villa Hamilton (1790s), a pavilion with Pompeian decoration that was built in the grounds of Schloss Wörlitz, Saxony. Under German influence this type of house spread to Eastern Europe (e.g. Villa Natolin, 1780–82, nr Warsaw) and by the end of the century German merchants and professional men were following their French and English counterparts in establishing villa residences on the edges of towns, a process that continued throughout the 19th century.

BIBLIOGRAPHY

J. Summerson: 'The Classical Country House in 18th-century England', *J. Royal Soc. A.*, cvii (1959), pp. 539–88

C. Connolly and J. Zerobe: *Les Pavillons: French Pavilions of the Eighteenth Century* (London, 1962)

M. Binney: 'The Villas of Sir Robert Taylor', *Country Life*, cxlii (6 July 1967), pp. 17–21; (13 July 1967), pp. 78–82

A. Blunt and T. Benton: 'The Villas of Palermo and Bagheria', *Sicilian Baroque* (London, 1968), pp. 39–43

M. Craig: *Classic Irish Houses of the Middle Size* (London, 1976)

M. R. Brownell: *Alexander Pope and the Arts of Georgian England* (Oxford, 1978)

A. Braham: *The Architecture of the French Enlightenment* (London, 1980)

J. Archer: *The Literature of British Domestic Architecture, 1715–1842* (Cambridge, MA, 1985)

J. Macaulay: *The Classical Country House in Scotland, 1600–1800* (London, 1987)

G. Worsley: 'Jewels in a Rich Coronet', *Country Life*, clxxxvii (14 Oct 1993), pp. 68–71

IV. After c. 1800.

In the 19th century there was a vast expansion in the use of the term villa, although it never had a very precise meaning, its use varying according to both time and place. Generally, however, it denoted a middle-class suburban house, a country residence without a great landed estate attached, or a pleasure house in a resort. The popularity of the villa resulted from a growth of middle-class wealth and a search for the sylvan benefits of *rus in urbe*, and as the people who could afford such benefits increased in number, the word was applied to houses further down the social scale. The main innovation in 19th-century villa design was the advent of irregular planning and picturesquely composed exteriors. This development occurred first in England, where the Picturesque aesthetic had originated, epitomized, for example, by Horace Walpole's Strawberry Hill (begun 1750), Twickenham, near London, an irregularly planned Gothic villa (*see* WALPOLE, (2) and fig. 3). Designs for irregular villas began to appear soon after 1800 in such pattern books as *Architectural Sketches for Cottages, Rural Dwellings and Villas* (London, 1805)

by Robert Lugar (*c.* 1773–1855), J. B. Papworth's *Rural Residences* (London, 1818; see fig. 9), *Designs for Ornamental Villas* (London, 1825–7) by Peter Frederick Robinson (1776–1858) and John Claudius Loudon's *Encyclopedia of Cottage, Farm and Villa Architecture* (London, 1833). John Nash was the first major architect to specialize in the design of such houses; examples include Cronkhill (*c.* 1802), Salop (*see* NASH, JOHN, fig. 1), and Park Village (begun 1825), Regent's Park, London, where he laid out one of the first of many planned suburban developments of picturesque villas (*see* NASH, JOHN, §2(ii)).

The use of irregular planning defied the belief that villas could be built only in the classical style. In the ensuing stylistic confusion two main trends can be detected. The first was towards the revival of Gothic and vernacular models. The English house in the latter taste was often called a COTTAGE ORNÉ, and from this engaging type of building stemmed many later developments, in the USA as well as in Europe. The second major trend derived from the irregular 'mixed Renaissance' style advocated in Richard Payne Knight's *Analytical Inquiry into the Principles of Taste* (London, 1805; *see* PICTURESQUE) and employed at Deepdene (1818–19 and 1823; destr.), Dorking, Surrey, England, which was designed by the connoisseur Thomas Hope (*see* HOPE, (1)) with the assistance of William Atkinson. This style owed much to a study of the fanciful buildings included in the backgrounds of 16th- and 17th-century French and Italian paintings, examples of which were conveniently collected in *On the Landscape Architecture of the Great Painters of Italy* (London, 1828) by Gilbert Laing Meason. Many of the details, meanwhile, particularly the ubiquitous towers, loggias and overhanging eaves, were derived from the vernacular buildings in Tuscany and the Roman Campagna that formed the subjects of such books as *Villa Rustica* (London, 1832, 2/1848) by Charles Parker (1799–1881). Because of its Italian associations, this style came to be regarded as especially appropriate for villas; it was widely employed by Charles Barry (*see* BARRY, (1)) and also by ALEXANDER THOMSON in the vicinity of Glasgow in the 1850s and 1860s.

Asymmetrical villas appeared on the Continent of Europe in such buildings as the Casino Valadier (1809–13) on the Pincio Hill, Rome, designed by Giuseppe Valadier, but it was in Germany, and above all in Prussia, that the adoption of the Italianate villa reached its apogee. Villas for middle-class owners were built in large numbers on the edges of such cities as Hamburg in the early 19th century. Most of these buildings were designed along regular, symmetrical, Neo-classical lines, but as interest in the architecture of the Renaissance increased, a more ornamental approach became fashionable, as at the Villa Rosa (1838–9; destr.), Dresden, by Gottfried Semper. The irregular Italianate villa was introduced into Germany by Karl Friedrich Schinkel in his alterations (begun 1824) to Schloss Glienecke, Potsdam, and in the remodelling (1829–33) of the nearby Hofgärtnerei at Charlottenhof. The eclectic and picturesque style of these villas was taken up by Schinkel's pupil LUDWIG PERSIUS in a number of impressive houses built in Potsdam in the 1830s and 1840s, including his own residence, the Villa Keller (1837), the designs for which were published in 1843. Friedrich von Gärtner's neo-Pompeian house, built in 1842–6 for

Ludwig I, King of Bavaria (*reg* 1825–48), at Aschaffenburg, near Munich, is in a similar taste, and such houses were built in large numbers in Germany until the 1860s, some of them on a massive scale. By then, however, the word villa was also being applied to moderately sized houses in all manner of styles: classical, Gothic and, most startlingly, in the picturesquely eclectic manner of the English *cottage orné*, for example Villa Ende (1864), Berlin, by Hermann Ende of Ende & Böckmann.

The villa was less popular in early 19th-century France than in Britain or Germany. The French middle classes were more reluctant than their British or German counterparts to flee to the suburbs, although by the 1860s villas, often used as second homes by the Parisian bourgeoisie, were being built in such places as Passy and Auteuil, as well as in and around the growing resorts of the Normandy coast and the Mediterranean. Villas in a variety of styles, ranging from the Classical to the Gothic Revival, were illustrated in such books as César-Denis Daly's *L'Architecture privée du XIXème siècle sous Napoléon III* (Paris, 1864) and Eugène-Emmanuel Viollet-le-Duc's *Habitations modernes* (Paris, 1875), and their stylistic variety—generally agreed to be a characteristic of the villa as a building type—contributed to the architectural experimentation of the *fin de siècle*.

The villa was as popular in the USA and Australia as it was in Europe. JOHN NOTMAN, for example, designed Riverside, an Italianate house for Bishop G. W. Duane at Burlington, NJ, in 1839 (destr. 1961), and the style was widely employed by a number of leading American architects in the 1840s and 1850s, especially in the vicinity of the towns of the eastern states and in the burgeoning coastal resorts. It spread throughout the country with the help of pattern books, notably A. J. Downing's *Cottage Residences* (New York, 1842; rev. as *Architecture of Country Houses*, New York, 1850) and Calvert Vaux's *Villas and Cottages* (New York, 1857). As in Britain and Germany, the idea of the villa as an individually designed suburban or resort house in its own garden proved immensely successful, but in the later 19th century Italian models were gradually discarded in favour of neo-vernacular motifs, which were handled by the best architects with an originality, especially in planning, unparalleled elsewhere. At the same time the word villa became less widely used, and by the turn of the century it was generally applied only to houses built in Renaissance styles, often by wealthy art lovers as occasional summer retreats.

With the spread of middle-class values, beginning in England, it was perhaps inevitable that the word villa would lose its exclusive connotations. In the years after the Napoleonic Wars (1803–15), estates of semi-detached villas were laid out around the edges of London and other towns, and by the middle of the 19th century former villages such as Holloway and Hackney were being engulfed by small semi-detached villas and terraces of houses with exiguous gardens designed by speculative builders and inhabited by City clerks. The growth of railway transport aided this process, and throughout the most developed parts of Europe, as well as in the USA and Australia, communities of villa residences near suburban railway stations were commonplace by the end of the century, for example Villenkolonie Friedenau (*c.* 1880),

9. Villa designed as the residence of an artist; from J. B. Papworth: *Rural Residences* (London, 1818), pl. 17

Berlin. With the development of such villa estates for the lower middle classes in Britain in the last third of the 19th century, merchants and financiers retreated to new and more socially exclusive suburban communities further away from the city centres, if not deep in the countryside; in these the term villa was never applied, being almost a term of abuse, signifying a speculatively built house that sheltered a life of stultifying social conformity.

The social downgrading of the word villa was less marked in the rest of Europe, where the single-family suburban house was never as common as in England or the USA. Instead, the word, as applied to a detached house for a wealthy and often art-loving owner, enjoyed something of a revival at the turn of the century. Many of the most original Art Nouveau houses were called villas, especially in France (e.g. Villa Majorelle, 1898–1900, at Nancy by Henri Sauvage), in the Netherlands (e.g. Villa Carel Henny, 1898, in The Hague, by H. P. Berlage) and above all in Italy and the German-speaking countries (e.g. Villa Ruggieri, 1902–7, at Pesaro, by Giuseppe Brega, and Villa Florio all'Olivuzzo, 1899–1902, Palermo, by Ernesto Basile). These houses were built for patrons similar to those of Charles Rennie Mackintosh in Scotland, C. F. A. Voysey in England and Frank Lloyd Wright in the USA, all of whom adapted the forms of the past, often in a highly original and creative way, to the needs of the present.

Many of the earliest manifestations of the Modern Movement were in the design of villas for wealthy middle-class patrons. Some of the best-known buildings of the Viennese Secession were villas, including the two houses (1886 and 1912) in Vienna built by Otto Wagner for his own use and based, in his own words, on the 'beauty of fundamental geometric forms'. The Steiner House (1910) by Adolf Loos in Vienna and the Schröder House (1924)

10. Villa Savoye, Poissy-sur-Seine, by Le Corbusier, 1929–31

by GERRIT RIETVELD in Utrecht are among the major buildings of the Modern Movement, while the early careers of Le Corbusier and Ludwig Mies van der Rohe were largely taken up with the design of villas. Le Corbusier's first house was the Villa Fallet (1906–7) at La Chaux-de-Fonds, Switzerland, and in a series of villas culminating in the Villa Savoye (1929–31; see fig. 10) at Poissy-sur-Seine, near Paris, he endeavoured to create a 20th-century equivalent of the Renaissance villa, based on mathematical proportions and harmoniously related to its natural surroundings, while using an architectural vocabulary that owes nothing to earlier decorative precedents (*see* LE CORBUSIER, §I).

Villas in the style of the Modern Movement continued to be built in Europe between the two world wars, for example Villa Mairea (1938), Finland, by Alvar Aalto (*see* AALTO, ALVAR). After World War II, however, although villas in the broadest sense of the term were built in larger numbers than ever before, large individual private houses were not thought to reflect the spirit of the age and correspondingly received relatively little attention from architects. Outside Italy the word villa dropped out of general use except to describe a second or holiday home, often a converted vernacular building. Buildings that were consciously modelled on villas of the past, for example the J. Paul Getty Museum (1974) at Malibu, CA, modelled on Hadrian's Villa at Tivoli, were at that time generally regarded as egregious architectural freaks. But the construction of a group of villas (1987–93) designed on 18th-century principles by Quinlan Terry in Regent's Park, London, suggests that the idea of the villa as a distinct building type remains capable of renewal.

BIBLIOGRAPHY

Villas on the Hudson: A Collection of Photo Lithographs of Thirty-one Country Residences (New York, 1860/*R* 1977)

H. Muthesius: *Das englische Haus*, 3 vols (Berlin, 1904–5, rev. 2/1908–11; Eng. trans., London, 1979, rev. 2/1987)

R. P. Fleetwood Hasketh: 'Ludwig Persius of Potsdam', *Architect's J.*, lxviii (1928), pp. 77–87, 113–20

C. Rowe: 'The Mathematics of the Ideal Villa', *Archit. Rev.* [London], ci (1947), pp. 101–4

J. Summerson: 'The London Suburban Villa', *Archit. Rev.* [London], civ (Aug 1948), pp. 63–72

V. Scully: 'American Villas', *Archit. Rev.* [London], cxv (March 1954), pp. 169–77

R. Aloi: *Ville in Italia* (Milan, 1960)

T. R. Slater: 'Family, Society and the Ornamental Villa on the Fringes of English Country Towns', *J. Hist. Geog.*, iv/2 (1978), pp. 129–44

F. Russell, ed.: *Art Nouveau Architecture* (London, 1979)

I. Wagner, B. Wagner and D. Prunier: 'La Ville d'hiver: Ville de la forêt', *La Ville d'hiver d'Arcachon* (Paris, 1983), pp. 111–223

T. Benton: *Les Villas de Le Corbusier, 1920–1930* (Paris, 1984; Eng. trans., New Haven and London, 1988)

D. J. Olson: *The City as a Work of Art* (New Haven and London, 1986)

W. Brönner: *Die bürgerliche Villa in Deutschland, 1830–1890* (Düsseldorf, 1987)

D. Cruickshank: 'Villas of Variety', *Architect's J.*, clxxxv (1987), pp. 12–13

A. Saint: 'The Growth of the Suburbs', *London: World City, 1800–1840*, ed. C. Fox (New Haven and London, 1992), pp. 72–6

GEOFFREY C. TYACK

Villa, Edoardo (*b* Bergamo, 31 May 1915). South African sculptor of Italian birth. He was studying sculpture in Milan when he was conscripted into the army at the outbreak of World War II. In 1940 he was captured in North Africa and sent to a prisoner of war camp in South Africa. After the war, Villa made South Africa his home. From conventional heads and figures of the 1940s, he moved progressively through stylized figuration to structural abstraction. Yet even in his most abstract work, there are constant allusions to human themes, in terms of structure, posture, attitudes, relationships and circumstances. Villa's style developed significantly in the 1950s, when the influence of the aggressive forms of the African environment led him to create his first constructed works, using abstract elements cut from sheets and rods of steel. His achievement was recognized by awards at the São

Paulo Biennales of 1957 and 1959. Notable commissioned works include *Africa* (6.75 m, 1959; Pretoria, ISCOR).

Villa alternated between organic modelling and the more mechanistic medium of welded steel, between flowing monolithic volumes and aggressive intersecting planes. He generally worked in series, while exploring variations on a particular formal theme in one medium at a time. His incorporation of die-cast machine parts into his work led logically to monumental robotic figures in the 1960s. In the 1970s he produced a series of poetic, coloured, tubular-steel figurations, including *Orange Involvement* (h. 4.85 m, 1974; Johannesburg, Rand Afrik. U.), followed by a powerful series of abstract figure groups, which culminated in the dramatic *Confrontation* (h. 4.2 m, 1979; Johannesburg, Lifegro Head Office).

BIBLIOGRAPHY
E. P. Engel, ed.: *Edoardo Villa: Sculpture* (Johannesburg, 1980)
A. von Maltitz: *Edoardo Villa* (diss., Johannesburg, Rand Afrik. U., 1987)
E. Berman: *Art & Artists of South Africa* (Johannesburg, 1993)
ESMÉ BERMAN

Villa, José Moreno. *See* MORENO VILLA, JOSÉ.

Villa Barbaro, Maser. *See* MASER, VILLA BARBARO.

Villabrille y Ron, Juan Alonso (*b* Argul, Asturias, 1663; *d* Madrid, after 1728). Spanish sculptor. He moved to Madrid in 1686 and probably worked initially with Pedro Alonso de los Rios (*fl* late 17th century). By 1687, however, he had set up his own workshop. His first known work is the polychromed wooden head of *St Paul*, signed and dated 1707 (Valladolid, Mus. N. Escul.; *see* SPAIN, fig. 22). The accomplished realism of this piece, in particular the swirling carving of the beard, is characteristic of Villabrille's style. Other documented works are the wooden statue of *St John the Baptist* (*c.* 1717) in Badajoz Cathedral, two stone statues on the Toledo Bridge in Madrid, *St Isidore* and *St Mary de la Cabeza*, an official commission of 1723 and the stone statue of *St Ferdinand* (1726) in the portal of the Madrid Hospice of St Ferdinand (now Madrid, Mus. Mun.). Luis Salvador Carmona, who was at this time apprenticed to Villabrille, assisted him on the three stone pieces. Other works attributed to Villabrille on the basis of style include a figure group of the *Virgin with SS Joachim and Anne* (Valladolid, Mus. N. Escul.), the *Prophet Elias* (Dublin, N.G.) and a *Calvary* group and statues of the *Virgin*, *St Joachim* and *St Anne* (all *c.* 1721–7; Pravia, Colegiata), all in polychromed wood. The Baroque naturalism of Villabrille's work recalls Gregorio Fernández, while the spiralling movement of his figures anticipates the vibrancy of his pupil Luis Salvador Carmona.

BIBLIOGRAPHY
Ceán Bermúdez
E. Marcos Vallaure: 'Juan Alonso Villabrille y Ron, escultor asturiano', *Bol. Semin. Estud. A. & Arqueol.*, xxxvi (1970), pp. 147–58
——: 'Juan Alonso Villabrille y Ron o Juan Ron', *Bol. Semin. Estud. A. & Arqueol.*, xl–xli (1975), pp. 403–14
G. A. Ramallo Asensio: 'Aportaciones a la obra de Juan Alonso Villabrille y Ron, escultor asturiano', *Archv Esp. A.*, ccxiii–ccxvi (1981), pp. 211–20
J. J. Martín González: *Escultura barroca en España, 1600–1770* (Madrid, 1983), pp. 375–8
MARJORIE TRUSTED

Villach, Friedrich of. *See* FRIEDRICH OF VILLACH.

Villach, Thomas Artula von. *See* ARTULA VON VILLACH, THOMAS.

Villafora, Antonio Maria da. *See* ANTONIO MARIA DA VILLAFORA.

Villafranca (y Malagón), Pedro de (*b* Alcolea de Calatrava, Cíudad Real, *c.* 1615; *d* Madrid, 27 July 1684). Spanish printmaker and painter. About 1630–35 he probably trained as a painter in Madrid under Vicente Carducho. However, he began to favour engraving and may have studied it with Pedro Perret. As a painter he was of minor importance. Among his few surviving works are a portrait of *Philip IV* (*c.* 1657; Madrid, Prado) and the *Holy Trinity Appearing to St Augustine* (*c.* 1658; Pamplona, Agustinas Recoletas), both rendered somewhat stiffly. The altarpiece of the *Canonization of St Thomas of Villanueva* (*c.* 1660), painted for S Felipe el Real, Madrid, is no longer extant. In 1677, with Claudio Coello, he restored the Sala de Batallas at the Escorial. His engravings, more than 150 done between 1637 and 1684, have a very precise technique that was the result of a careful use of the burin. He made good use of his own compositions but also engraved works after such contemporaries as Coello, Francisco Fernández (1605–46), Velázquez, Francisco de Solís and Juan de Arellano. His series of the *Cartilla de principios de dibujo del cuerpo humano* (1637–8), consisting of 21 plates printed on 13 sheets, reveals his desire to use the human body as a tool for teaching. In 1654 he was nominated Grabador del Rey to Philip IV. In addition to engraving numerous frontispieces and portraits, he produced prints for Fray Francisco de los Santos's *Descripción breve del Real Monasterio de S Lorenzo de El Escorial* (Madrid, 1657) and he did 45 illustrations (1666) for the book of the funeral rites of Philip IV. In his engraved works he slowly adopted a fully fledged Baroque style.

PRINTS
Cartilla de principios de dibujo del cuerpo humano (1637–8)
Fray Francisco de los Santos: *Descripción breve del Real Monasterio de S Lorenzo de El Escorial* (Madrid, 1657)

BIBLIOGRAPHY
A. Gallego Gallego: *Historia del grabado en España* (Madrid, 1979), pp. 170–77
E. Paez Rios: *Repertorio* (1981–3)
J. L. Barrio Moya: 'Pedro de Villafranca y Malagón, pintor y grabador manchego del siglo XVII', *Cuad. Estud. Manchegos*, 13 (1982), pp. 107–22
F. Collar de Cáceres: 'Un retablo de Pedro de Villafranca', *Cuad. Estud. Manchegos*, 18 (1987), pp. 173–86
ISMAEL GUTIÉRREZ PASTOR

Villagrán (García), José (*b* Mexico City, 22 Sept 1901; *d* Mexico City, 10 June 1982). Mexican architect, teacher and theorist. He graduated in 1923 from the Academia de S Carlos, Mexico City. There his teachers, many of whose professional careers had coincided with the dictatorial regime (1876–1910) of General Porfirio Díaz, emphasized the virtues of nationalism and modernity in architecture. At the time of Villagrán's graduation, however, the Mexican Revolution had just ended, and the great transformation of the country's social life was just beginning, in which architecture was to play an important part through the provision of an infrastructure of schools and hospitals as well as low-cost housing. It was in the medical field that

Villagrán began his career, designing the Instituto de Higiene y Granja Sanitaria (1925–7) in Mexico City, which in the shape of its isolated pavilions represented a break with the architecture of the past. The hospital was also carefully planned to meet the specific clinical demands of the medical advisers who acted as architectural consultants. The result was a synthesis of the aesthetic and the functional that was emblematic of the 'integralism' of the Modernist architecture of the time, of which Villagrán became the undisputed leader.

Villagrán continued to find hospital design a fertile area as his career developed in the 1930s and 1940s. Works from this period include: the Hospital para Tuberculosos (1929–36) in Huipulco, a suburb of Mexico City; the Instituto Nacional de Cardiología (1937–44), designed in collaboration with the distinguished cardiologist Ignacio Chávez; the Pabellón de Cirugía (1941); and the Hospital Manuel Gea González (1943–7). In all of these he overcame severe limitations in terms of economic resources to produce works notable for their breadth of outlook. These buildings are also all examples of Villagrán's gradual transition from compositions dominated by rhythm and symmetry to a more harmonious approach, in which the essential element was the asymmetrical combination of volumes and spaces. His projects were not limited to designs for hospitals, however. He designed his own house and the La Palma office building (both 1935), both in Mexico City, and the Escuela de Arquitectura y Museo de Arte (1951; in collaboration with Alfonso Liceaga and Xavier García Lascurain) at the city's Ciudad Universitaria. In the last-named, carefully proportioned areas of unadorned brickwork alternate with large areas of glazing in metal frames. In the 1950s and 1960s he also collaborated with a number of architects (including Gabriel García del Valle, José Antonio Mendizabal, Ricardo Legorreta and Raúl Gutiérrez) on a number of office buildings (e.g. for the Ford Motor Company, 1963) and hotels (e.g. Hotel Maria Isabel, early 1960s), all in Mexico City.

Villagrán was perhaps as important for his teaching and theoretical work, however, as for his executed designs. He taught at the Academia de S Carlos from 1923 until 1957, was a Director of the Universidad Nacional Autónoma de México from 1953 to 1970, where he was Professor of Theory of Architecture at the Escuela Nacional de Arquitectura. To all his students (who included Enrique del Moral, Juan O'Gorman and Enrique Yañez) he emphasized the need for 'Mexican solutions to genuinely Mexican problems' and the importance of a complete mastery of construction techniques, since they should plan only what they knew to be practically possible. While the modernity and nationalism extolled by his own teachers had been worthwhile aims, these could, he believed, be achieved only by remaining faithful to national habits and customs. An essential element in his architectural theory, derived from these beliefs, was the idea of 'architectural sincerity', derived from a commitment to national character, modernity, regionalism and beauty.

WRITINGS

Panorama de 50 años de arquitectura mexicana contemporánea (Mexico City, 1950)
Meditaciones ante un crisis formal de la arquitectura (Mexico City, 1962)

Apuntes para un estudio (Monterrey, 1963)
Esencia de lo arquitectónico (Mexico City, 1971)

BIBLIOGRAPHY

A. T. Arai: 'José Villagrán García: Pilar de la arquitectura contemporánea de México', *Arquit. México* (1955)
R. Vargas: *José Villagrán y la escuela mexicana de arquitectura* (Mexico City, 1987)
R. Vargas Salguero: *Teoría de la arquitectura* (Mexico City, 1987)

RAMÓN VARGAS

Villahermosa, Duque de. *See* GURREA Y ARAGÓN, (1).

Villajos, Agustín Ortiz de. *See* ORTIZ DE VILLAJOS, AGUSTÍN.

Villalba, Darío (*b* San Sebastián, 22 Feb 1939). Spanish painter. He began studying law and philosophy in Madrid but devoted himself to painting from 1956. He trained for four years at the Escuela de Bellas Artes de San Fernando in Madrid, continuing at the studio of André Lhote in Paris in 1958 and at Harvard University, Cambridge, MA, in 1963. After working in an abstract idiom he turned to figurative painting. In 1968 he began a series of paintings entitled *Encapsulated Figures* (exh. Venice Biennale, 1970), representing human beings imprisoned in plastic materials. These evolved into thematically related series incorporating reworked photographs and photographs retouched with brushstrokes, such as *Redemption Series* (1975; priv. col.; see 1976 exh. cat., fig. 19).

From 1977 Villalba painted a series of large black monochrome pictures with a heavy and even texture (e.g. *Anti-resonant Painting*, 2×1.6 m, 1979; see 1983 exh. cat., p. 40), and from 1980 he executed abstract collages combining reworked photographs with painted elements, as in *Transit* (triptych, 2×4.8 m, 1980; priv. col.; see 1983 exh. cat., pp. 50–51). He was awarded the Premio Nacional de Artes Plásticas by the Spanish Ministry of Culture in 1983.

BIBLIOGRAPHY

Darío Villalba: Rétrospective, 1972–1976 (exh. cat., ed. K. J. Geirlandt; Brussels, Pal. B.-A., 1976)
Darío Villalba: Obra reciente, 1980–1983 (exh. cat., essays by E. de Vicente and F. Calvo Serraller; Madrid, Bib. N., 1983)

PALOMA ALARCÓ CANOSA

Villalón, Cristóbal de (*b* ?Cuenca de Campos; *d* after 1558). Spanish writer. He studied at the universities of Alcalá, Valladolid and Salamanca and became a member of the circle of followers of Erasmus around Emperor Charles V. He visited France, England, Flanders and Italy and, after a stay in Constantinople, travelled through Greece and the Ionic Islands. Among his most interesting books are *Siguesa la tragedia de Mirrha* (1536), *Prouechoso tractado de cambios y contrataciones de mercaderes y reprouacion de usura* (1541) and *Gramática castellana* (1558). His most important work, however, is *Ingeniosa comparación entre lo antiguo y lo presente* (1539), which is composed in the characteristic Renaissance form of a dialogue. In this Villalón eruditely defended the modernity of his age, his understanding of which was moulded by his knowledge of the Spanish Renaissance—that is, the Plateresque or early Renaissance. Although Villalón praised Classical antiquity, using a broad range of criteria he considered that this had been surpassed in modern times, a period that he judged to have begun with the Gothic and to have continued with the Renaissance. The works that he considered superior to those of the Greeks and Romans were buildings with Gothic or early Renaissance tendencies, such as the Hospital de los Reyes Catolicós (1501–11), Santiago de Compostela, S Marcos (rebuilt 1513–49), León, the Colegio de Santa Cruz (1487), Valladolid, the cathedrals of Toledo (begun *c.* 1220), León (begun 1258) and Seville (1401–1506), the Catedral Nueva (begun 1513), Salamanca; and work by such artists as Alonso Berruguete, the Villalpando family, the de Siloe family and Felipe Vigarny.

WRITINGS

Siguesa la tragedia de Mirrha (Medina del Campo, 1536)
Ingeniosa comparación entre lo antiguo y lo presente (Valladolid, 1539, rev. Madrid, 1898)
Prouechoso tractado de cambios y contrataciones de mercaderes y reprouacion de usura (Valladolid, 1541)
Gramática castellana (Antwerp, 1558)

BIBLIOGRAPHY

L. Torres Campos y Balbas: 'Cristóbal de Villalón y su "Ingeniosa comparación"', *Bol. Soc. Castell. Escurs.*, vii (1915–16)
J. J. Kincaid: *Cristóbal de Villalón* (New York, 1973)
J. A. Gaya Nuño: *Historia de la crítica de arte en España* (Madrid, 1975)
J. Rivera: *Teoría e historia de la intervención en monumentos españoles hasta el romanticismo* (Valladolid, 1989)

JAVIER RIVERA

Villalpando, Cristobal de (*b* Mexico City, *c.* 1644; *d* Mexico City, 1714). Mexican painter. He worked in a decorative Baroque style, based on the primacy of light and colour over accuracy of form. In 1675 he painted the altarpiece of the church of S Rosa de Lima, Huaquechula, Puebla, and subsequently worked until 1681 on the altarpiece of the church of S Rosa de Lima, Azcapotzalco. On several occasions between 1683 and 1686 he produced paintings for Mexico City Cathedral, including the *Apotheosis of St Michael*, the *Woman of the Apocalypse*, the *Church Militant and Triumphant* and the *Triumph of the Eucharist* (all *in situ*). In 1686 he worked on the triumphal arch dedicated to the Conde de la Monclova, Melchor Portocarrero and Lasso de la Vega. This was followed by the *Apotheosis of the Eucharist* in the Cúpula de los Reyes, Puebla Cathedral, and a new version of the *Church Militant and Triumphant* for Guadalajara Cathedral. In 1691 Villalpando painted a series on the *Life of St Francis* for the Franciscan monastery of Antigua, Guatemala, and in 1710 a series on the *Life of St Ignatius Loyola* for the Jesuits at Tepotzotlán. Other works by Villalpando include the *Flagellation*, *St Teresa*, *St John of the Cross*, the *Betrothal of the Virgin*, the *Entombment*, the *Agony in the Garden*, the *Presentation of the Virgin* (Mexico City, Monastery S María de los Angeles), another version of the *Entombment*, the *Annunciation*, the *Nativity* and the *Flight into Egypt* (all Mexico City, Pin. Virreinal).

BIBLIOGRAPHY

J. Fernandez: 'Composiciones barrocas de pinturas coloniales', *An. Inst. Invest. Estét.*, xxviii (1958)
F. Maza: *Cristóbal de Villalpando* (Mexico City, 1964)
M. Toussaint: *Pintura colonial en México* (Mexico City, 1965)
E. Marco Dorta: *Arte en America y Filipinas*, A. Hisp., xxi (Madrid, 1973)
S. Sebastian, J. de Mesa and T. Gisbert: *Arte iberoamericano desde la colonización a la independencia* (Madrid, 1985)

MARIA CONCEPCIÓN GARCÍA SÁIZ

Villalpando, Francisco de (*b* Villalpando, Zamora, *c.* 1510; *d* Toledo, before 2 July 1561). Spanish metalworker, architect and writer. He came from a family of artists, his brothers being the architects and stuccoists Juan (*c.* 1505–after 1563) and Jerónimo (*c.* 1505–before 1561) del Corral de Villalpando and the wrought-iron worker Ruy Díez del Corral. Later, the architect Gaspar de Vega (*d* 1576) became his brother-in-law. Villalpando must have been trained by his family, and he may have travelled to Italy between 1533 and 1537. In 1540 he was living in Valladolid; there he came into contact with Cardinal Juan Pardo de Tavera, who took him to Toledo and commissioned him to execute the ironwork (1541–8) for the chancel of the cathedral. Villalpando also worked for the college of San Ildefonso de Alcalá de Henares, where he executed the ironwork for some of the library windows (1542–6). He settled, however, in Toledo and carried out his most important creations as a metalworker for the cathedral there: the pulpits (1543–52) in iron and bronze, the ironwork of the main altar in the choir (1551), the Lion Gate (1551/6–64) and the high altar (1556–63). He was helped in much of this work by his brother Ruy. Villalpando also executed a number of minor works for the Tavera Hospital and, outside Toledo, was commissioned by Francisco de los Cobos to execute the ironwork (1555–63) for the church of Salvador de Ubeda. As a craftsman in wrought iron, Villalpando combined a feeling for the accumulation of elements (following the family decorative tradition) with a rigorous organization of verticals and horizontals in his work. He introduced a new vocabulary based on Sebastiano Serlio's repertory, together with personal innovations in the rhythmic alternation of balusters.

As an architect, Villalpando's first commission was to supervise the building of the courtyard (1550) and staircase (1552) of the Alcázar, Toledo, to designs by Alonso de Covarrubias, making some minor alterations to the final design of the large and imposing staircase. Under Covarrubias's orders, Villalpando designed and built the gateway of the Colegio de Infantes (1555), Toledo, a sculptural work in the manner of Serlio. Villalpando also designed and supervised the construction of the house (1558; destr.) in Toledo of the Royal Secretary Diego de Vargas; while working from a basic design by Luis de Vega, he made use of Serlio's treatise, designing the courtyard with a repeated motif exactly as in Serlio's work. In 1559 he designed the vestibule gates for the Hospital de Santa Cruz de Toledo. Villalpando was an architectural innovator in his own right, although he generally followed Covarrubias's unornamented line, articulating surface areas with rusticated finishes and introducing the human figure into his gateways in the form of caryatids. His style, which combined elements from the richly decorative Castilian tradition with innovative classicizing motifs from Serlio's published works, and he exerted a considerable influence on Castilian architecture during the second half of the 16th century. Equally influential was Villalpando's work as a translator of Serlio's treatise. He appears to have translated Books I and II, although they were not published, but his translations of Books III and IV were published in Toledo in 1552, signed by Villalpando as 'architect' and dedicated to Prince Philip (later Philip II of

Spain); work would thus have predated 1548. Despite a few errors in the translation, this work implied a genuine revolution in Spanish architectural practice. Villalpando remained faithful to the Italian, adding no more than a dedication, a prologue and a few explanatory notes. He chose, however, to replace Serlio's technical and conceptual terms with a summary of Vitruvian terms and their Castilian equivalents, which his readers would more easily understand.

WRITINGS

trans.: S. Serlio: *Regole generale di architettura* (Venice, 1537) and *Delle antichità* (Venice, 1540) as *Tercer y quarto libro de architectura de Sebastian Serlio boloñes: En los quales se trata de las maneras de como se pueden adornar los hedificios con los exemplos de las antiguedades* (Toledo, 1552, 2/1563, 3/1573); ed. G. Kubler (Madrid, 1977)

BIBLIOGRAPHY

E. Llaguno y Amírola: *Noticias de los arquitectos y arquitectura de España desde su restauración*, 4 vols (Madrid, 1829; R/1977)
F. Pérez Sedano: *Datos documentales inéditos para la historia del arte español, notas del archivo de la Catedral de Toledo* (Madrid, 1914)
M. R. Zarco del Valle: *Datos documentales para la historia del arte español: Documentos de la Catedral de Toledo*, 2 vols (Madrid, 1916)
F. Rivera Recio: 'El Cardenal Tavera y los maestros de rejas de la Catedral de Toledo', *Bol. Real Acad. B. A. & Cienc. Hist.*, xxv (1947), pp. 1–14
F. Chueca Goitia: *Arquitectura del siglo XVI*, A. Hisp. (Madrid, 1953)
F. de Olaguer-Feliú Alonso: *Las rejas de la Catedral de Toledo* (Toledo, 1980)
A. Gallego de Miguel: *Rejería castellana: Valladolid* (Valladolid, 1982)
F. Marías: *La arquitectura del renacimiento en Toledo (1541–1631)*, 4 vols (Toledo and Madrid, 1983–6)

FERNANDO MARÍAS

Villalpando, Juan Bautista (*b* Córdoba, 1552; *d* Rome, 1608). Spanish architect, writer and theorist. He claimed that he owed his education to Philip II (although exactly how is not clear), that he studied mathematics and that his master was Juan de Herrera, the royal architect of the Escorial. It was probably at the Jesuit College in Baeza *c.* 1583 that Villalpando met Jerónimo del Prado (1547–95), theologian, sculptor and architect, with whom he undertook a detailed reconstruction of Solomon's Temple and a full commentary on the prophecy of Ezekiel. Villalpando believed that only by translating Ezechiel's vision into terms of real architecture could its mystical significance be understood. The form and proportions of the Temple, inspired by God and therefore perfect, provided an insight into the perfection of the City of God. He argued that the compatibility that he had demonstrated between Christian revelation and the culture of Classical antiquity was not coincidental; Classical architecture itself ultimately derived from the architecture of King Solomon. After fierce disagreement between the authors, volume one of *In Ezechielem explanationes et apparatus urbis ac templi Hierosolymitani* appeared in 1596, after del Prado's death, and the next two volumes were published in 1604. Villalpando was a practical architect as well as a hermetic theoretician. He was one of a small group of Jesuit architects who established the unadorned building style of the Order in Spain. Among other buildings, he directed the completion of the Jesuit church in Córdoba (1578) and designed the main portal of Baeza Cathedral (1585), like an austere retable, and, most important, the College of S Hermenegildo in Seville (1587), all in a severe, Classical style.

WRITINGS

with J. del Prado: *In Ezechielem explanationes et apparatus urbis ac templi Hierosolymitani*, 3 vols (Rome, 1596–1604)

BIBLIOGRAPHY

R. Taylor: 'Hermetism and Mystical Architecture in the Society of Jesus', *Baroque Art: The Jesuit Contribution*, ed. R. Wittkower and I. Jaffe (New York, 1972), pp. 63–97

HELEN M. HILLS

Villamediana, Conde de Oñate y de. *See* OÑATE Y DE VILLAMEDIANA, Conde de.

Villamena, Francesco (*b* Assisi, 1564; *d* Rome, 7 July 1624). Italian engraver. According to tradition, he was a pupil of Cornelis Cort, whose engravings he copied, and was associated in his youth with Agostino Carracci. He made few original engravings but reproduced designs of artists including Raphael, Paolo Veronese, Federico Barocci, Girolamo Muziano and Giulio Romano. His output also included frontispieces and book illustrations. Closely related to such northern late adherents of Mannerism as Hendrick Goltzius and Jacques Bellange, he employed an elegant and expressive calligraphic style with perfect control of the burin. In addition to religious and historical subjects, he executed portraits, notably a series of genre figures (Rome, Gab. N. Stampe). In 1594 he executed a series of engravings illustrating scenes from the *Life of St Francis*. His oeuvre comprised at least one hundred plates.

BIBLIOGRAPHY

K. Oberhuber: *Renaissance in Italien. 16. Jahrhundert* (Vienna, 1966), pp. 31, 208–10
A. Grelle: 'Francesco Villamena', *Claude Mellan, gli anni romani* (exh. cat., ed. S. Bonsignori; Rome, G.N.A. Ant., 1989–90), pp. 128–43

FRANÇOISE JESTAZ

Villandrando, Rodrigo de (*fl* 1608; *d* Madrid, 1622). Spanish painter. He was a pupil and collaborator of Juan Pantoja de la Cruz (whose will he witnessed in 1608) and was a portrait painter at the court of Philip III, an honour that he shared with Bartolomé González and Pedro Antonio Vidal (*fl* 1599–1617). In June 1621, in recognition of his merits, Philip IV nominated him Ugier de Cámara, a court position that Velázquez later obtained and that Eugenio Cajés asked for repeatedly without success. He held this post for only a short time, for in December 1622 it was noted that he had already died in Madrid, possibly at a young age, as in June of that year he had been admitted to the studio of Pedro García as an apprentice for six years. Few of his works survive. In the unpublished *Inventorio del Alcázar de Madrid* (1636; Madrid, Bib. Pal. Real) six portraits of members of the royal family are mentioned as hanging in the Galería del Mediodía. Their costumes, accessories and poses are precisely described, and they depicted *Philip III*, his queen *Margaret of Austria* (*d* 1611), Philip III's son *Philip with the Dwarf Solplillo* and his wife *Elizabeth of Bourbon*, and two other of Philip III's children, the *Infanta Doña Maria of Hungary* and the *Infante Cardenal Don Fernando*. The portrait of *Philip III* is described as depicting the sitter with blackened weapons and with his hand, carrying a baton, over a globe. It can therefore be identified as the work in the convent of the Descalzas Reales in Madrid, which is similar to one (1617; Madrid, Prado) by Vidal. The portraits of *Philip with the Dwarf Solplillo* and his wife *Elizabeth of Bourbon* are both in the Prado, and the latter is shown in the white dress she wore in 1619 on her arrival in Lisbon on a visit to Portugal. Through the distinctive red-and-white tiling shown in them, the portraits of the *Infanta Doña Maria of Hungary* and the *Infante Cardenal Don Fernando* can be identified with those in the Monasterio de la Encarnación in Madrid. As Philip IV became king on 21 March 1621, the whole series was probably painted *c.* 1620–21. There are two other signed portraits by Villandrando: *Philip III Wearing Court Costume* (Madrid, Convento Encarnación) and *Margaret of Austria* (Madrid, Convent of the Descalzas Reales). Sentenach mentioned another portrait of *An Old Man* (priv. col., see Sentenach, p. 50). All of Villandrando's portraits show an extreme fidelity to the representation of accessories. A detailed description of the attributes of royalty or particular rank makes the sitter's social position evident, but little attention is given to an accurate depiction of anatomy.

BIBLIOGRAPHY

N. Sentenach: *La pintura en Madrid desde sus orígenes hasta el siglo XIX* (Madrid, 1907), pp. 50–51

J. López Rey: 'Muerte de Villandrando y fortuna de Velázquez', *A. Esp.*, xxv (1968–9), pp. 1–4

ISMAEL GUTIÉRREZ PASTOR

Villandry. French château and garden in the département of Indre-et-Loire, 17 km south-west of Tours. In 1906 Dr Joachim Carvallo (1869–1936) purchased the 12th-century château. He intended to restore the grounds in the style of a 16th-century French garden; despite its axial alignment and symmetrical plan, however, his work (completed *c.* 1924) does not represent a historical reconstruction. He planned the garden as a series of three terraces set at right-angles to the château, which is located in the lower north-east corner of the grounds. Water for the garden is supplied by an ornamental pool at the highest level; this flows into a canal across the garden and encircles the château by means of a reconstructed moat. The canal divides the site and provides a vertical axis, whereas the two avenues bisecting it create east–west axes that further distinguish the different levels of the garden. As Woodbridge (1978) pointed out, in contrast to an ideal Renaissance design, which would have been based on symmetry and closure, the alignment of Carvallo's garden, with its expanding horizontal and vertical axes, exposes its 20th-century conception.

At the lowest level of the garden, to the west of the château, is an ornamental kitchen-garden, consisting of nine symmetrical squares. Each square has a distinctive geometric pattern outlined in box and is planted twice annually with seasonal vegetables. West of the kitchen-garden is a medicinal herb-garden of three rings on a north–south axis. Carvallo's choice and placement of plants was inspired by the colours of the vegetables themselves, their rate of maturity and seasonal changes. Above the kitchen-garden (to the south) are three ornamental squares broadly inspired by the engraved *parterres de broderie* published in *Les Plus Excellents Bastiments de France* (1576–9) by Jacques Androuet Du Cerceau I. This terrace forms an L-shape that is divided by the canal, but it is visually and thematically linked with the *jardin d'ornement* immediately adjoining the south front of the château. Both areas are planted in abstract shapes of yew and box, enclosing flower-beds. Four of the ornamental box and yew parterres are meant to symbolize the traditional four moods of love. These designs have no direct roots in the 16th-century French garden tradition, but rather they express the general concept of emblematic and allegorical representation. To the west of the ornamental pool that defines the southern border lies a small *bosquet* and a labyrinth.

Carvallo's garden at Villandry remains a spectacular testament to his personal commitment to the ideals of the 16th-century garden and its contribution to the evolution of the French formal garden. It is administered by the Carvallo family and is open to the public.

BIBLIOGRAPHY

K. Woodbridge: 'Dr Carvallo and the Absolute', *Gdn Hist.*, vi/2 (1978), pp. 46–68

M. d'Estienne d'Orves-Carvallo: *The Villandry Gardens* (1983)

—: *Villandry and its Gardens* (1983)

K. Woodbridge: *Princely Gardens: The Origins and Development of the French Formal Style* (London, 1986), pp. 286–8

SUSAN B. TAYLOR

Villani, Filippo (*b* Villa di S Procolo, nr Florence, *c.* 1325; *d* Florence, *c.* 1405). Italian historian, lawyer and administrator. He was Chancellor of the Commune of Perugia from 1376 to 1381. He gave public lectures (1401–4) on Dante in Florence and wrote a Latin commentary on *Inferno* i. After the death of his father, Matteo Villani (*fl c.* 1285–1363), he added a volume covering the year 1364 to the *Cronica*, a work that his uncle, Giovanni Villani (*fl c.* 1275–1348), was planning, which would re-count history from the fall of the Tower of Babel to his own time. Filippo also wrote the *Liber de origine Florentinae et eiusdem famosis civibus* (1375–1404), which contains the biographies of many eminent Florentines, including painters. In it he claimed that 13th- and 14th-century Florentine painters had resuscitated the art of ancient Greece and Rome, starting with Cimabue, who, like the Ancients, imitated nature in a way forgotten for many centuries. Cimabue was followed by Giotto, who, according to Villani, enjoyed poetry and history. Villani argued that Giotto did not merely equal the painters of antiquity but surpassed them in talent, restoring painting to its former dignity; he listed among the artist's work the *Navicella* mosaic in St Peter's, Rome, and a portrait of *Dante* (Florence, Bargello). Villani discussed three of Giotto's students, describing Maso di Stefano (1324–56) as a delicate and graceful painter, excelled by Stefano Fiorentino as an imitator of nature, and Taddeo Gaddi, whom he compared to Dimokratis (*b* 460–457 BC).

WRITINGS

with G. Villani and M. Villani: *Cronica* (MS.; 1333–64); ed. A. Racheli (Trieste, 1857–8)

Liber de origine Florentinae et eiusdem famosis civibus (MS.; 1375–1404); ed. G. C. Galletti (Florence, 1847)

BIBLIOGRAPHY

N. Sapegno: *Storia letteraria del trecento*, ii (Milan, 1963)

E. Cecchi and N. Sapegno, eds: *Storia della letteratura italiana: Il trecento*, ii (Milan, 1965)

P. Bondanella and J. Conaway Bondanella, eds: *The Macmillan Dictionary of Italian Literature* (London, 1979)

DORIS FLETCHER

Villanova de São Pedro. Site of Copper Age settlement 7 km north-west of Cartaxo in the Tagus Valley, Portugal, dated to *c.* 3500–*c.* 2200 BC. Among the important features of the site are its fortifications, evidence of the development of copper metallurgy and the range of exotic goods found there, including Bell Beaker pottery, stone plaques and idols, decorated bone vessels and North African ivory (Barcelona, Mus. Arqueol.; Madrid, Mus. Arqueol. N.; Oxford, Ashmolean). The site was discovered in 1936 and successive excavations were undertaken by Afonso do Paço and Eugénio Jalhay between 1937 and 1950 and continued by do Paço until 1961. Occupying a flat, narrow promontory, the settlement was protected on three sides by steep slopes, and on the fourth by a series of manmade fortifications. Although the relative dates of these fortifications have not been established, three main construction phases have been identified in the innermost part of the site. Characterized by a lack of fortification, the earliest phase had a wide, rock-cut ditch and a domed pottery kiln measuring 5 m in diameter. The next phase was represented by the erection of a massive stone rampart 4–5 m thick forming an irregular, square-shaped enclosure measuring *c.* 25×25 m on the inside. It was studded with ten semicircular bastions on the exterior and there were traces of pits and structures within. Following an episode of disuse and/or destruction, this enclosure was rebuilt in a third and final building phase. Some bastions were retained, while others were incorporated into the newly constructed rampart, which was up to 7 m thick in places. A second, roughly concentric, line of fortification, measuring *c.* 80 m in diameter with at least two bastions, was constructed *c.* 20 m to the north-west. A further 20 m to the north-west, in the outermost line of fortification, measuring *c.* 100 m in diameter, are the remains of what may have been the entrance. Characteristic artefacts of the site include horn-shaped clay spit supports and fine tulip-shaped ceramic vessels decorated with wide, shallow grooves (*copos*) in the pre-enclosure phase and decorated clay plaques, concave-based arrowheads, Maritime Beakers and a variety of copper tools and weapons in the later enclosure phase.

For further discussion of the art and architecture of Neolithic Europe *see* PREHISTORIC EUROPE, §IV.

BIBLIOGRAPHY

B. Blance: *Die Anfänge der Metallurgie auf der iberischen Halbinsel*, Studien zu den Anfängen der Metallurgie, iv (Berlin, 1971), pp. 59–65

H. N. Savory: 'The Cultural Sequence at Vila Nova de S Pedro: A Study of the Section Cut through the Innermost Rampart of the Chalcolithic Castro in 1959', *Madrid. Mitt.*, xiii (1972), pp. 23–37

CLAY MATHERS

Villanovan. Early culture of the European Iron Age that flourished in northern Italy, central Italy and Campania in the 8th and 9th centuries BC, continuing in northern Italy until the 6th century BC (*see also* PREHISTORIC EUROPE, §VI). It is named after the small town of Villanova, just east of Bologna, where the first series of finds were made, and is of particular importance for its role in the development of the ETRUSCAN civilization.

Ancient graves were discovered at Villanova in 1853 during agricultural work on the estate of Count G. Gozzadini, who immediately undertook a systematic excavation of the site. By 1855, 179 cremation urns and 14 inhumations had been uncovered. Over half the cinerary urns had been buried in pits in the ground without any special protection and were often simply covered by a stone slab. In many other cases—particularly burials with several accompanying vessels—the grave had been lined with pebbles or stone slabs. In two instances the urn was placed inside a large clay vessel (*dolium*), and in a number of cases the burial plot had been marked by stones. A few years after these excavations, extended cemeteries of similar urn graves were discovered within the town of Bologna, establishing the locality as the most important centre of 'Villanovan' culture north of the Apennines, and it was these cemeteries that proved to be the principal source for defining the nature of this culture. The fact that the burial zones dated from different periods led to a preliminary chronological categorization based on various areas of Bologna, in which the phases of S Vitale, Benacci I, Benacci II and Arnoaldi were distinguished. In the 1950s these categories were defined with greater precision as covering the period from the 9th century BC to the mid-6th and named Villanovan I–IV. These phases were followed by the Certosa period, which belonged to the fully developed Etruscan civilization of the late 6th century BC and the 5th. Other finds in the city included several clusters of round huts distributed throughout the old part of the town and a tremendous hoard of bronze objects weighing over 1.4 tonnes unearthed near the church of S Francesco. Most of the finds are in the Museo Civico Archeologica, Bologna.

Similar cemeteries were also found to the south of the Apennine region in ancient Etruria and in the area around Capua and Salerno. These, too, contained mainly urn graves, which were either hollowed out of the rock or enclosed by stones, depending on the geology of the location. Inhumation graves were also increasingly evident, the ratio between the two types of burial varying between regions. However, these necropoleis essentially belong only to the 9th and 8th centuries BC; the most important collections of finds are in the Museo Archeologico in Florence and the Museo Nazionale di Villa Giulia in Rome. The grave areas are found close to settlements, most of which occupy the sites of later Etruscan towns, a continuity of location that demonstrates with particular clarity that the transition from the Villanovan culture to the Orientalizing phase of the Etruscan civilization was accomplished without interruption. However, the characteristics that define Villanovan culture lasted longer around Bologna than in Etruria, and there seem to have been only loose connections with the latter. Some direct adaptations of Orientalizing motifs have been found around Bologna, for example on some stone monuments. Despite this divergent cultural development, the use of the Etruscan language in the Bologna area as early as the 7th century BC is attested by finds of graffiti on vessels.

Apart from its burial practices, Villanovan culture is distinguished by finds of certain types of material. The pottery is especially notable and includes double-coned cinerary urns, covered either with a dish or with a helmet-shaped lid, and house-shaped urns (*see* ETRUSCAN, figs 9 and 18). Various other types of vessel accompanied burials in increasing quantities as time progressed. They were decorated with geometric designs, produced by scratching and stamping, or with tin pieces or bronze nails. Only during the Villanovan IV phase in Bologna (7th century BC and early 6th) did painted pottery and figurative stamp-patterns become common. In richer graves the pottery was often replaced by bronze vessels, and female burials of the 9th and 8th centuries BC also contained jewellery—bronze fibulae (often decorated with glass beads), pendants and bracelets—as well as spinning whorls and distaffs. Male burials often included fibulae, needles, razors and such weapons as helmets, swords, spears and axes. Large metal belts were mainly found in women's graves, but horse trappings were common in the burials of both sexes. Some graves contained small clay models of carts and horses, perhaps intended to serve as a substitute for the real items; similar models decorate clay vessels (see fig.). Rudimentary scenic depictions are found engraved on sheet-bronze objects, but symbolic signs—either engraved or modelled—are more frequent and commonly represent whole aquatic birds or parts of them, sometimes combined with sun or horse motifs.

BIBLIOGRAPHY

H. Müller-Karpe: *Beiträge zur Chronologie der Urnenfelderzeit nördlich und südlich der Alpen* (Berlin, 1959)

H. Hencken: *Tarquinia, Villanovans and Early Etruscans*, 2 vols (Cambridge, MA, 1968)

K. Kilian: *Früheisenzeitliche Funde aus der Südostnekropole von Sala Consilina (Provinz Salerno): Archäologische Forschungen in Lukanien III* (Heidelberg, 1970)

M. Zuffa: 'La civiltà villanoviana', *Popoli e civiltà dell'Italia antica*, v, ed. M. Pallottino (Rome, 1976), pp. 197–363

La necropoli villanoviana di Ca' dell'Orbo a Villanova di Castenaso: Problemi del popolamento dal IX al VI secolo a.C. (exh. cat., Bologna, Mus. Civ. Archeol., 1979)

Dalla stanza delle antichità al Museo Civico: Storia della formazione del Museo Civico Archeologico di Bologna, a cura di Ch. Morigi Govi e G. Sassatelli (Bologna, 1984)

Civiltà degli Etruschi (exh. cat., ed. M. Cristofani; Florence, Mus. Archeol., 1985) [extensive bibliog.]

La formazione della città in Emilia Romagna: Prime esperienze urbane attraverso le nuove scoperte archeologiche (exh. cat., ed. G. Bermond Montanari; Bologna, Mus. Civ. Archeol., 1988)

G. Bartoloni: *La cultura villanoviana: All'inizio della storia etrusca* (Rome, 1989)

O.-H. FREY

Villanueva. Spanish family of architects. The sculptor Juan de Villanueva (1681–1765) had two sons, (1) Diego de Villanueva and (2) Juan de Villanueva, both of whom worked in a Neo-classical idiom. Diego was an erudite rather than a practical architect, his career being a succession of frustrated artistic projects. Nevertheless, he was instrumental in reshaping architectural taste in 18th-century Spain. His more successful brother Juan was one of the foremost Neo-classical architects in Spain. His most famous work is the Museo del Prado, Madrid, originally the Academia de Ciencias, which he designed in 1787.

(1) Diego de Villanueva (*b* Madrid, 12 Nov 1715; *d* Madrid, 23 May 1774). He learnt drawing and modelling with his father and completed his architectural education with a study of mathematics and classics. Highly inquisitive and independent, he reacted against the lingering Baroque and Churrigueresque architecture in favour of the new Neo-classical ideas coming mainly from France. At the same time he was one of the first to return to the Spanish classical tradition of Juan de Herrera. He collaborated with

Villanovan clay askos in the form of a horned animal with an armed horseman on top, h. 177 mm, from Benacci grave 525, Bologna, 8th century BC (Bologna, Museo Civico)

his father on the making of the Churrigueresque main altar (1745) for Coria Cathedral. From 1746, having renounced a scholarship to study architecture in Rome, he worked until 1754 as one of Giovanni Battista Sacchetti's draughtsmen at the Royal Palace in Madrid. A notebook of his from this period, *Libro de diferentes pensamientos, unos inventados y otros delineados, por Don Diego de Villanueva, año 1754*, contains some of his best inventions as well as many decorative motifs, reflecting his excellent drawing ability. His remodelling (1756) of the interior of the convent church of the Descalzas Reales, Madrid, derives stylistically from the work of Filippo Juvarra. The old convent features in a series of architectural views drawn by Villanueva and engraved by Juan Minguet (*b* 1737) in 1757, which are an example of early Romantic taste in Spain.

Villanueva's ideas as a critic and theorist of architecture are expressed in his *Colección de papeles críticos* (1766), a criticism of both Churrigueresque and Rococo principles. This shows the influence of arguments found in Marc-Antoine, Abbé Laugier's essay on rationalist architecture, 'Essai sur l'architecture' (1753), in Charles-Nicolas Cochin the younger's anti-Rococo satire, 'Supplication aux orfèvres' (1754) and in Francesco Algarotti's essay 'Saggio sopra l'architettura' (1757). Villanueva believed he had a mission to sweep away the false doctrine of ornamentation by strengthening the professional and humanist training of the architect and encouraging a study of the forms of antiquity. His intransigent character led him into open conflict in the 1760s at the Real Academia de S Fernando, Madrid, where he taught architecture and perspective from 1752. His belief in the need for a teachable system involved him in a polemic in 1762 with the Director of Architecture, Ventura Rodríguez, whose art was considered reactionary by Villanueva and his brother (2) Juan de Villanueva. They clashed again in 1769 over technical aspects of the construction of S Francisco el Grande, Madrid (begun 1761). From 1773 Villanueva was in charge of the remodelling of the Palacio Goyeneche, Madrid, which was to house the Real Academia. The building had been begun by José Benito de Churriguera in 1724, and Villanueva's design for the façade was seen as a triumph for Neoclassicism. The last years of his life were soured by the dispute over S Francisco el Grande and the Real Academia's rejection of his teaching course on architecture, his lifelong work.

WRITINGS

Colección de papeles críticos (Valencia, 1766)

BIBLIOGRAPHY

E. Llaguno y Amirola: *Noticias* (1829), iv, pp. 269–71
F. Chueca and C. de Miguel: *La vida y las obras del arquitecto Juan de Villanueva* (Madrid, 1949) [with Eng. summary]
G. Kubler and M. Soria: *Art and Architecture in Spain and Portugal and their American Dominions, 1500–1800*, Pelican Hist. A. (Harmondsworth, 1959), pp. 49–51

☐

(2) Juan de Villanueva (*b* Madrid, 15 Sept 1739; *d* Madrid, 22 Aug 1811). Brother of (1) Diego de Villanueva.

1. Before 1781. 2. 1781 and after.

1. BEFORE 1781. Like others of his generation, he trained in the official style of the Real Academia de San Fernando in Madrid, where between 1754 and 1757 he won first prize in the three examinations for which he entered. In 1758, through the Academia, he was awarded a scholarship to study in Rome. His work there included drawings (untraced) of the Arch of Titus in Rome, of the Temple of Vesta at Tivoli and of the temples of Jupiter Stator and Jupiter Tonans. These drawings were sent to the Academia as proof of his progress. His time in Rome was undoubtedly enriched by contact with artists of other nationalities visiting the city.

Villanueva returned to Madrid in 1766 and shortly afterwards set out for Andalusia at the instigation of the Academia. With Juan Pedro Arnal (*b* 1735), he acted as assistant to José de Hermosilla (*d* 1776), making sketches of the principal Islamic monuments. The drawings of the mosque at Cordoba and the Alhambra in Granada were later published in *Antigüedades árabes de España* (Madrid, 1804). On completion of this commission he was appointed Académico de Mérito.

In 1768 the Hieronymite Order of the monastery of the Escorial appointed Villanueva its architect, and soon afterwards he was placed in charge of work on the royal palace (*see* ESCORIAL, §2). This brought him into direct contact with the architecture of Juan Bautista de Toledo and Juan de Herrera. The town houses built by Villanueva for the French consul and the Marqués de Campo Villar reveal Italianate leanings, while the Casa de Infantes (1771) and, later, a third service building, the Casa de Oficios (1785), show him adapting his style to the sober architecture of Herrera. The Casa de Infantes, opposite the main west façade of the monastery and built to house the staff of the infantes, forms a large rectangle, with five inner courtyards and two staircases, one at each rear corner. The Casa de Oficios, at right angles to an earlier service building, has three inner courtyards and a central staircase.

Villanueva's finest early works are his two casinos at the Escorial. The Casita de Abajo (or del Príncipe; built 1771–5 and 1781–5), designed for the Prince of Asturias, later Charles IV (*see* BOURBON, §II(6)), is a compact building, with an entrance in the form of a tetrastyle Doric portico, in front of which Villanueva laid out a small Baroque garden. Ten years later he enlarged the building by adding two large reception rooms at the rear, transforming the ground plan from a rectangle to a T shape. He also planned a new garden on three levels, finished off by a broad semicircular area, on to which the new reception rooms gave through a portico *in antis*. The Casita de Arriba (1771–3), made for the Infante Gabriel (1752–88), is square in plan with several rooms around a domed central room. It reveals Villanueva's interest in the villas of Andrea Palladio, in particular the Villa Rotonda, Vicenza (begun *c.* 1565/6). With the entrance flanked by columns, this little house also has interesting gardens, on two levels, with spectacular views of the Escorial.

Villanueva's earliest ecclesiastical works, the sacristy (1770) and the chapel of the Venerable Palafox (1772) in the cathedral of Burgo de Osma, Soria, carried out at the same time as his work at the Escorial, reveal the influence of Ventura Rodríguez and, in the chapel, of Palladio. In 1773 Villanueva began work at the ARANJUEZ PALACE. There he built the Casa de Infantes in the Plaza de S Antonio, in which, as at the Escorial, he adapted his style to the architecture of the service buildings designed by Herrera.

2. 1781 AND AFTER. In 1781, probably as a consequence of his having been appointed Arquitecto del Príncipe y de los Infantes, Villanueva enlarged the Guadiana riverbed for the creation of an irrigation canal in La Mancha. This was a commission from the Infante Gabriel, holder of the Orden Militar de S Juan de Jerusalem, to which order the lands belonged. This project included the construction of the new town of La Magdalena, near Argamasilla de Alba, Ciudad Real, comprising two rows of dwellings for labourers and a small church with a porch, as well as, in Ruidera, the conversion of some flour mills and a fulling mill into powder mills.

In 1784 the Prince of Asturias commissioned Villanueva to build a new casino for the royal palace of El Pardo, near Madrid. The Casita del Príncipe displays an eminently mature and individual architectural style. Its ground-plan is constructed around two orthogonal axes. The shorter, longitudinal one is fronted by a portico and consists of two rooms, one circular within a square and the other rectangular. The transverse area, perpendicular to the former and much more substantial, consists of two rectangular wings, with two pavilions at the ends, which are also rectangular, their longer sides parallel to the axial line. Built in stone and brick, the Casita has five simple, geometric and contrasting parts. Its rear façade, now the main one, opens on to a garden combined with orchard, laid out on different levels.

It was probably also in 1784 that Villanueva produced the plan for the eastern sector of the Jardín del Príncipe at the Aranjuez Palace. This includes the pond, the Estanque de los Peces (or Estanque de los Chinescos), one of the first examples of landscape gardening in Spain.

On it, he built two pavilions, one a temple in the Greek style, reminiscent of the Temple de l'Amour in the garden of the Petit Trianon at the château of Versailles, and the other a Chinese kiosk, close in style to buildings by William Chambers. This area of the garden also includes the Casita del Labrador, with which Villanueva was involved from *c.* 1795. This was enlarged and remodelled by Isidro González Velázquez in 1803.

In 1785 Villanueva was appointed honorary director of architecture at the Academia and in 1786 Arquitecto Mayor de Madrid y de sus Fuentes. His activity in this period was mainly connected with the court in Madrid, principally through his work in the area of the Paseo del Prado in the eastern part of the city. Here he collaborated in the creation of the Jardín Botánico, where he constructed hot-houses and a botany classroom, as well as the propylaeum for the side entrance, now known as the Puerta de Murillo. He is also credited with simplifying the ornate Baroque garden laid out by Francisco Sabbatini. The formal grid arrangement on several levels adopted by Villanueva has something of the character of a Renaissance garden.

Undoubtedly Villanueva's most ambitious and important work is the Museo del Prado (see fig. 1), a building originally designed as the Academia de Ciencias to accommodate several scientific institutions. Its conversion into an art museum was ordered by Ferdinand VII after his restoration to the throne in 1814. Villanueva's first design, drawn up in 1785, comprised three rectangular blocks, the largest being the central one, with two connecting blocks. The side facing the Paseo del Prado was to have a circular colonnade serving as a covered passage; this was eliminated in the final design of 1787. The Academia de Ciencias was to occupy the ground-floor. As executed, it has an entrance to the south, facing the Jardín Botánico,

over which there is a Corinthian peristyle with inner areas for study. The upper floor, conceived as a wide, continuous gallery, was for the Museo Nacional de Historia Natural, the entrance to which was to the north in the form of an Ionic two-columned portico; transversally, along the axis of the building, was a huge main lecture hall, the Aula Magna, also with separate access to the Paseo del Prado. This inner spatial autonomy was extended to the outside in the form of five juxtaposed blocks: the central unit, planned as the large meeting hall, terminates in an exedra, which was never completed. This makes up the longitudinal axis of the building. It opens on to the Paseo del Prado through a large six-columned Doric portico. Two extended rectangular blocks, with a continuous Ionic colonnade on the upper level, link the prominent central block with the two end units, approximately square in dimensions, their façades facing north and south.

Constructed of stone and brick, the building displays principles seen in Villanueva's work at the casino at El Pardo. It is laid out on two perpendicular axes, of which the transverse is much the more powerful, with an interior consisting of an unbroken horizontal space, varied according to floor, capable of fulfilling the differing requirements of the academy and the museum. This great space is uninterrupted by the central classroom and yet from outside appears as distinct though contiguous blocks. This represents a departure from the principle of unity inherent in the Baroque façade.

In 1789, as municipal architect of Madrid, Villanueva built a gallery of Tuscan columns on one side of the Ayuntamiento, and he was also involved in the designs for the reconstruction of the Plaza Mayor after a fire in 1790. In addition he built several houses, including that of the

1. Juan de Villanueva: Museo del Prado (formerly the Academia de Ciencias), Madrid, designed 1787

2. Juan de Villanueva: Observatorio Astronómico, Madrid, begun 1790

Marquis del Llano in the Calle la Luna (1775), houses in the Calle de Hortaleza and the sober Nuevo Rezado building (1789) in the Calle de León, now the Real Academia de la Historia. He was also responsible for the festive external decoration (*ornato*) of the palaces of the Condesa de Benavente and the Duque de Alba, both in the Calle de Alcalá, in celebration of Charles IV's accession to the throne in 1788.

Although Villanueva executed few ecclesiastical works, he did build the oratory of Caballero de Gracia (1789), in Madrid, for which he adopted a basilican plan. In this he was influenced by trends in contemporary French architecture, although the narrow site obliged him to dispense with the side aisles. The result is a wide space, with Corinthian colonnades along the walls, under a coffered barrel vault. The façade, completed by Custodio Moreno (1780–1854), has a portico *in antis* with Ionic columns, a large window, a pediment and two small towers, clearly echoing Palladio. He used this composition again in his unrealized design (1791) for the monastery of S Fernando, also in Madrid.

In 1790 Villanueva began construction of the Observatorio Astronómico (see fig. 2), another of the buildings testifying to the atmosphere of enlightenment in Madrid in the second half of the 18th century. It is on S Blas hill, close to the Paseo del Prado and his Academia de Ciencias, on land that belonged to the Real Sitio of Buen Retiro. Simplifying two earlier designs, Villanueva devised a cruciform plan with a large octagonal central space, which served as a vestibule, and rises to a rotunda of 16 Ionic columns. The vestibule linked the instrument and research rooms at the side and in the rear block, access to the latter being through a six-column Corinthian façade without a pediment.

In 1792 Villanueva was appointed Director General of the Academia de S Fernando. In 1793 he created the great staircase leading to the royal apartments at the monastery of the Escorial. In 1798 he was appointed Arquitecto Mayor de las Reales Obras, an appointment that was

confirmed in 1809 by Joseph Bonaparte, who had been created King of Spain in 1808. Perhaps his most important late works are those associated with his position as municipal architect; among these are the design for the Teatro del Príncipe, now the Teatro Español (1804), and the creation of the Cementerio General del Norte (1804), at the end of the Calle de S Bernardo, near the Puerta de Fuencarral. The latter is a late consequence of the royal decree of 1787 enforcing the establishment of cemeteries on the outskirts of cities. Its square plan is made up of several courtyards lined with rows of superimposed niches. The central chapel is of Palladian inspiration, the portico employing the Paestum order. Flanking the cupola that covers it are two small towers.

BIBLIOGRAPHY

F. Chueca Goitía: 'Los arquitectos neoclásicos y sus ideas estéticas', *Rev. Ideas Estét.*, 2 (1943); also in *Varia neoclásica* (Madrid, 1983), pp. 129–52

——: 'Sobre la arquitectura religiosa en el siglo XVIII y las obras de Burgo de Osma', *Archv Esp. A.*, xxii (1949), pp. 287–315

F. Chueca Goitía and C. de Miguel: *La vida y las obras del arquitecto Juan de Villanueva* (Madrid, 1949)

F. Chueca Goitía: *El Museo del Prado* (Madrid, 1952)

G. Kubler: *Arquitectura de los siglos XVII y XVIII*, A. Hisp., xiv (Madrid, 1957)

A. Fernández Alba: *El observatorio astronómico de Madrid* (Madrid, 1979)

J. J. Junquera: *La decoración y el mobiliario de los palacios de Carlos IV* (Madrid, 1979)

P. Navascués: 'Arquitectura', *Del Neoclasicismo al Modernismo* (1980), v of *Historia del arte hispánico* (Madrid, 1978–80), pp. 3–146

A. Rumeu de Armas: *Origen y fundación del Museo del Prado* (Madrid, 1980)

Juan de Villanueva, arquitecto (1739–1811) (exh. cat., Madrid, Mus. Mun., 1982)

C. Añón, S. Castroviejo and A. Fernández Alba: *Real Jardín Botánico de Madrid: Pabellón de invernáculos* (Madrid, 1983)

F. Chueca Goitía: *Varia neoclásica* (Madrid, 1983)

C. Sambricio: 'El ideal historicista en la obra de Juan de Villanueva', *La arquitectura española de la ilustración* (Madrid, 1986), pp. 233–60

P. Navascués: *La formación de la arquitectura neoclásica* (1987), xxxi de *Historia de España*, ed. R. Menéndez Pidal (Madrid, 1987), pp. 567–717

C. Saguar Quer: 'La última obra de Juan de Villanueva: El cementerio General del Norte de Madrid', *Goya*, 196 (1987), pp. 213–21

P. Moleón Gavilanes: *La arquitectura de Juan de Villanueva: El proceso del proyecto* (Madrid, 1988)

AURORA RABANAL YUS

Villanueva, Carlos Raúl (*b* Croydon, Surrey, 30 May 1900; *d* Caracas, 16 Aug 1975). Venezuelan architect and teacher. His father, Carlos Antonio Villanueva, was a diplomat and author of several history books about South America. His mother, Paulina Astoul de Villanueva, was French and was his link with the culture and life of Europe, where he spent his early life. In 1920 he began to study architecture with Gabriel Héraud at the Ecole des Beaux-Arts, Paris, from which he graduated in 1928; he then went on to study at the Institut d'Urbanisme, University of Paris. In 1929 he returned to Venezuela and settled in Caracas, where he established his own architectural practice. This long stay in Europe marked his professional and personal life; his subsequent approach to architecture was inspired by his European background, and he even spoke his mother tongue, Spanish, with a strong French accent. At the same time, however, he was deeply interested in both the traditional architecture of Venezuela and its constraints, such as the brilliant light and tropical climate.

From 1929 to 1939 Villanueva was Director of Buildings at the Ministry of Public Works in Caracas. His early works included the bullring (1931) in Maracay, where a traditional arcaded form was expressed with a skeletal concrete structure, and a group of buildings in Caracas begun in 1935: the Museo de Los Caobos (now the Museo de Bellas Artes), the Museo de Bellas Artes and the Museo de Ciencias Naturales. This museum complex is characterized by a series of indoor–outdoor rooms; one of its main features is the way in which it utilizes the strong light contrasts of the climate. Other buildings of this period include the prize-winning Venezuelan Pavilion at the Exposition Internationale des Arts et Techniques dans la Vie Moderne, Paris (1937; with Luis Malaussena), and the Escuela Gran Colombia (1939), Caracas, which reveals the influence of the Paris school of architecture.

In 1940 Villanueva won a competition organized by the Banco Obrero, an institution that provided low-cost housing, for the redevelopment of El Silencio, a working-class quarter in the centre of Caracas. Here he produced a series of buildings linked by a continuous arcade at street-level and grouped around a central plaza, revealing a concern for the quality of the human environment that became characteristic of all his work. He remained consultant architect to the Banco Obrero until 1960. Another low-cost housing project of this period responded to traditional residential patterns: the General Rafael Urdaneta development (1943–4), Maracaibo, a mixture of single-family houses and low-rise blocks of flats, was planned concentrically around urban amenity centres and public spaces, and the buildings made full use of natural ventilation techniques. He developed these principles in several housing projects subsequently built in Caracas, such as the Fransico de Miranda and Coche developments (1946–7); Ciudad Tablitas and El Paraiso (with Carlos Celis Cepero and Manuel Mijares), both begun in 1951; and 23 de Enero (1955–7; with José Manuel Mijares, Carlos Brando and José Hoffman). The last two projects are considered among the best low- to middle-income housing complexes in Venezuela. Set in a hillside landscape, the mixture of low- and high-rise blocks allows much of the natural environment to be retained and makes full use of the cool breezes found above ground-level.

In 1944–5 Villanueva began work on perhaps his best-known project, the Ciudad Universitaria, Caracas (see fig.), producing a master-plan and the first building for the department of medicine. Construction continued on the project until its completion in 1959, with Villanueva designing a large number of separate faculty buildings, auditorium and library. A feature of the exposed concrete structure is the use of precast lattice panels that produce brilliant patterns of sunlight and shade as well as promoting the flow of air. The entire complex is set in landscaped gardens connected by covered walkways and plazas incorporating works of art. The integration of architecture, painting and sculpture in the Ciudad Universitaria is one of its principal characteristics; for Villanueva this symbolized the understanding of common goals as well as the compromise between different modes of expression. He included works by Alexander Calder, Victor Vasarely,

Carlos Raúl Villanueva: foyer of Aula Magna (auditorium), Ciudad Universitaria, Caracas, 1952

Antoine Pevsner, Baltasar Lobo, Hans Arp, Fernand Léger and Henri Laurens, as well as important Venezuelan artists such as Mateo Manaure, Armando Barrios, Oswaldo Vigas, Víctor Valera, Francisco Narváez and Carlos Gonzalez Bogen. The result is a truly beautiful university campus, with halls and shady plazas strewn with works of art and interspersed with spacious gardens. Another notable building designed by Villanueva at the Ciudad Universitaria is the Olympic stadium (1950–52), an elegant structure of slender concrete columns and cantilevered beams. He became the founding Professor of Architecture at the university in 1944.

Later works by Villanueva include the Fundación La Salle office building (1961–4), Caracas; the Venezuelan Pavilion (1967; with E. Trujillo) for Expo '67 in Montreal, in which he placed a *Penetrable* by the artist Jesús Soto; the Museo Jesús Soto (1970–73) in Ciudad Bolívar; and the new building for the Museo de Bellas Artes (begun 1972), Caracas. He received many national and international honours and awards, including the Premio Nacional de Arquitectura (1963) for his work on the university campus in Caracas. He was a founder and President of the Sociedad de Arquitectos de Venezuela and the Consejo Nacional de Protección de Monumentos Historicos, which reflected his continuing interest in the historical architecture of Venezuela. Villanueva's development of a lyrical and structurally dynamic version of Modernism, adapted to the environment and traditions of Venezuela, had a lasting influence on younger architects of the region.

WRITINGS
La Caracas de ayer y de hoy, su arquitectura colonial y la reurbanización de El Silencio (Paris, 1950)
Caracas en tres tiempos (Caracas, 1966)

BIBLIOGRAPHY
A. Granados Valdes: *Guía obras de arte de la Ciudad Universitaria* (Caracas, n.d.)
A. Bloc: 'Cité Universitaire de Caracas: Essai d'intégration des arts au centre culturel', *Archit. Aujourd'hui*, 55 (1954), pp. 52–61
S. Moholy-Nagy: *Carlos Raúl Villanueva and the Architecture of Venezuela* (New York, 1964)
'Three Cubes of Colour: The Venezuelan Pavilion at Expo '67', *Archit. Forum*, cxxvii/2 (1967), pp. 58–9
F. Bullrich: *New Directions in Latin American Architecture* (London and New York, 1969), pp. 73–82
G. Gasparini and J. P. Posani: *Caracas a través de su arquitectura* (Caracas, 1969)
J. P. Posani and M. Suzuki: *Carlos Raúl Villanueva* (Tokyo, 1970)
D. Bayón and P. Gasparini: *Panorámica de la arquitectura latino-americana* (Barcelona, 1977; Eng. trans., New York, 1979), pp. 214–31
J. P. Posani: *The Architectural Works of Villanueva* (Caracas, 1985)
BÉLGICA RODRÍGUEZ

Villanueva, Emilio (*b* La Paz, 28 Nov 1884; *d* La Paz, 14 May 1970). Bolivian engineer–architect and planner. He qualified as an engineer in Chile in 1907, pursued an academic career to become Dean of the Faculty of Science and Rector of the Universidad Boliviana Mayor de 'San Andrés', La Paz, and served as Minister for Education after World War I. In 1943 he founded the School of Architecture in the Universidad de La Paz, the first in Bolivia other than the short-lived school begun by Philippe Bertrés and José Núñez del Prado in the 1830s. Brought up in the aura of French academicism, Villanueva produced buildings in the 1920s and 1930s in that style; the Banco Central de Bolivia (1926), La Paz, is an example.

Buildings such as his Alcaldía Municipal (1925), La Paz, with its 17th-century French influence, and the Hospital General (1916–25), in the Miraflores district of La Paz, however, show greater eclecticism. Thereafter Villanueva worked towards a national architecture based on the ancient Pre-Columbian culture of Tiahuanaco, of which the monolithic architecture and characteristic sculpture inspired his Stadium in La Paz (1942; destr., see Mesa, pp. 40–41) and influenced the form and structure of his building for the Universidad Boliviana Mayor de 'San Andrés' (1940–8), La Paz. As an urban planner he was responsible for planning Mariscal Santa Cruz (1945), the principal avenue of the city of La Paz along the bed of the River Choqueyapu, and prepared a development plan (1927) for the Miraflores district of the city.

WRITINGS
Urbanismo: Esquema de la evolución urbana en Europa y América (La Paz, 1943)
Urbanística: Práctica y técnica (La Paz, 1967)

BIBLIOGRAPHY
C. Mesa: *Emilio Villanueva: Hacia una arquitectura nacional* (La Paz, 1984)
TERESA GISBERT

Villanueva, Jerónimo de (*b* 1594; *d* 1653). Spanish patron. From an Aragonese family of Jewish origin, he was one of the foremost members of the coterie surrounding Gaspar de Guzmán y Pimentel, Conde de Olivares, and in 1620 he became Protonotario de la Corona de Aragón. In 1626 he was appointed a Secretaría de Estado and in 1627 he was in charge of the King's privy expenditure, secretly taking control of matters relating to the Aragonese kingdom and probably also those of Catalonia. When Olivares was disgraced in 1643, Villanueva was tried by the Inquisition. Like all those linked with Olivares, Villanueva was fond of luxury and pleasure. He played an important part in the construction of the royal palace of Buen Retiro in Madrid, spending large sums on presents for the King, which were intended to adorn the royal apartments. Outstanding among these were the series of tapestries (untraced) depicting the goddess Diana, purchased in 1633, and the 12 silver lions for the Salón de Reinos (destr. 1643), executed by the silversmith Juan Calvo for 24,000 ducats. Most significant was the foundation by Villanueva of the Benedictine convent of S Plácido (1641–61) in Madrid. In the 1640s fundamental rebuilding of the convent and, in particular, of the church was begun, which Villanueva did not see completed before his death.

BIBLIOGRAPHY
G. Marañón: *El Conde-Duque de Olivares: La pasión de mandar* (Madrid, 1936, rev. 3/1952)
J. Brown and J. H. Elliot: *A Palace for a King: The Buen Retiro and the Court of Philip IV* (New Haven and London, 1980)
MARÍA TERESA DABRIO GONZÁLEZ

Villa Orsini. *See* BOMARZO, SACRO BOSCO.

Villaplana & Piñón. Spanish Catalan architectural partnership, formed in 1968 by Albert Villaplana (*b* Barcelona, 1933) and Helio Piñón (*b* Onda, Valencia, 1942). Both architects graduated in 1966 from the Escuela de Arquitectura de Barcelona, where they were later appointed professors, of Design and of Elements of Composition respectively. They developed an architectural style more in sympathy with the avant-garde in the plastic arts, architecture and construction than with the empiricism that dominated Barcelona's artistic climate in the 1960s and 1970s. Their approach to the logic of Constructivist geometry and their search for a certain monumental quality in all their projects did not depend on a literal recovery of past architectural languages but on an economical, subtle and intellectualized elaboration that took into account the site, the formal logic of the city and a sense of contingency adapted to the demands of well-constructed and solid building. Villaplana & Piñón's building designs for Huesca County Council (1974) and for the colleges of architects of Seville (1975), Barcelona (1976), Valencia (1977) and Murcia (1978) show a refreshing tendency to approach the site without banal contextualism but with the support of a geometrical rigour that is at once strict and free. Their most influential designs, however, have been those for public places, such as the S Esteban park in Murcia (1977), the Plaza de la Constitución in Lérida (1982), the Plaza de la Constitución in Gerona (1982), the Parc de l'Escorxador in Barcelona (1981), the Plaza dels Paîsos Catalans (1981–3) and Besós park (1982–7), both in Barcelona. In all these works, the feeling of the public place is rendered without the mystification of historical architectural languages but

instead with the search for an order that does not annul the confusion and diversity of the modern city.

BIBLIOGRAPHY

Albert Villaplana—Helio Piñón (Barcelona, 1986); review in *El Croquis*, xxviii (1987)

IGNASI DE SOLÀ-MORALES

Villard de Honnecourt [Wilars dehonecort; Vilars dehoncort] (*b* ?Honnecourt-sur-l'Escaut, nr Cambrai, Picardy; *fl c.* 1220–40). French draughtsman. He is known only through a portfolio of some 250 drawings (*see* HUMAN PROPORTION, fig. 2), about one-sixth of which are of architectural monuments (Paris, Bib. N. MS. Fr. 19093). His fame is due to the uniqueness of these drawings and to the 19th-century claim that he 'erected churches throughout the length and breadth of Christendom' (Mâle, Eng. trans., p. 55). However, there is no proof that he designed or built any church anywhere.

1. LIFE AND WORK. In his portfolio, Villard said nothing of his occupation and claimed not a single artistic creation of any type. He may not have been an architect or a professional craftsman but merely an inquisitive layman who travelled widely, recording some of the things he saw during his travels. The claim that Villard was educated in the Cistercian monastic school at Vaucelles is

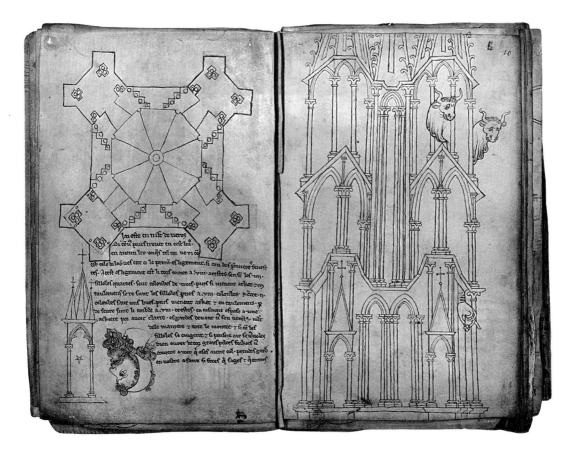

1. Villard de Honnecourt: plan and elevation of a tower, Laon Cathedral, leadpoint, pen and ink on parchment, *c.* 1220–40 (Paris, Bibliothèque Nationale, MS. fr. 19093, fols 9*v* and 10*r*)

unsubstantiated, and the tradition that he knew Latin is suspect: the one Latin word attributed to him, LEO (fols 24r and 24v), is probably an addition of 1533 to the portfolio.

When Villard made his drawings is unknown, but nothing he drew can be securely dated after c. 1240; thus he may have been active in the 1220s and 1230s. If he actually visited the monuments he drew, rather than basing his drawings on other drawings, he visited the cathedrals of Cambrai, Chartres, Laon (see fig. 1), Meaux, Reims and the abbey of Vaucelles in France; the cathedral of Lausanne in Switzerland; and the abbey of Pilis in Hungary. Villard eventually decided to make his drawings available to an unspecified audience and inscribed certain of them, or had them inscribed, in the Picard dialect of Old French, with some central French forms used consistently. These inscriptions vary in nature, some being explanations (e.g. fol. 6r: 'Of such appearance was the sepulchre of a Saracen I saw one time'), others being instructions (e.g. fol. 30r: 'If you wish to make the strong device one calls a catapult, pay attention here'). Villard addressed his 'book' to a general readership, saying of fol. 1v that it contained 'sound advice on the techniques of masonry and on the devices of carpentry. . .and the techniques of representation, its features as the discipline of geometry commands and instructs it'.

2. THE PORTFOLIO.

(i) Contents. The portfolio consists of thirty-three parchment leaves (average 230–40×150–60 mm) arranged into seven gatherings in a brown pigskin wallet, possibly their original container. Variations in sizes and textures suggest that Villard acquired the leaves individually at different times. While the portfolio was in Villard's possession, and even when it left his hands, the leaves were not stitched together, nor to the portfolio itself. The gatherings and the individual folios and bifolios are essentially as Villard arranged and left them.

The maximum number of leaves that can be proved to be lost from the portfolio is thirteen, with the possible loss of two additional leaves. Eight leaves have been lost since the 15th century, and the other five to seven leaves disappeared earlier. No leaves have been lost since the late 18th century. The contents of two lost leaves can be identified: drawings of Cambrai Cathedral and a drawing of a catapult.

Villard's drawings and inscriptions fall into ten subject categories: (i) animals, (ii) architecture, (iii) carpentry, (iv) church furnishings, (v) geometry, (vi) human figures, (vii) masonry, (viii) mechanical devices, (ix) recipes or formulae and (x) surveying. The number of palimpsests in the portfolio indicates that at times he had no blank surfaces on which to draw, so he had to erase one drawing to make another or had to juxtapose drawings of unrelated subjects on individual sheets.

Villard was at his best rendering drapery and small objects, and his treatment of the nude male figure after antique models (fols 6r, 11v, 22r and 29v) are among his more interesting drawings. Without exception, his architectural drawings vary from the actual buildings themselves. While he may have attempted to modify or

2. Villard de Honnecourt: *Humility* (detail), leadpoint, pen and ink on parchment, c. 1220–40 (Paris, Bibliothèque Nationale, MS. Fr. 19093, fol. 3v)

'modernize' the buildings he saw, his architectural drawings suggest he understood very little about architectural design, stereotomy or construction.

Villard's drawing technique was fairly complex, especially when he drew drapery. The preliminary drawing was done in leadpoint, contour first, then content. This contour was reinforced with a light sepia wash. This completed most of his figure drawings, but some (e.g. fol. 3v) he took several stages further, first by a dark inking of contours and drapery folds, then by using leadpoint to shade drapery folds (see fig. 2). For his architectural drawings, Villard employed pin-prick compass, straightedge and circular templates.

(ii) History and significance. The Villard portfolio belonged to the Félibien family by 1600 and passed from this family to the Parisian monastery of St Germain-des-Prés. In 1795 it became part of the French national collections. The Villard drawings were first published in the mid-19th century during the height of the Gothic Revival movement. His architectural drawings, although they comprise only about 16% of the total, attracted the greatest attention, leading writers to conclude that he was an architect. This assumption was based on a fundamental error: the stereotomical formulae on fols 20r and 20v were taken as proof that Villard was a trained mason; it was not discovered until 1901 that these drawings and their inscriptions were by a later hand.

The claim that the Villard portfolio is an encyclopedia of architectural knowledge that reveals the secret of stereotomical practices of the Gothic period is untenable. Moreover, there is no proof that Villard left his drawings to a north French building lodge, nor that they ever served as a shop manual (*Bauhüttenbuch*). It has been plausibly proposed that they survived not for their utilitarian value but for their unique antiquarian appeal. The most that can be accurately claimed is that the portfolio of drawings of Villard de Honnecourt records in visual form the multitude of interests of an intelligent, well-travelled 13th-century Picard, possibly made for mnemonic use as a model book.

See also VITRUVIUS, §3(i).

BIBLIOGRAPHY

J.-B.-A. Lassus: *Album de Villard de Honnecourt, architecte du XIIIe siècle: Manuscrit publié en facsimilé* (Paris, 1858/*R* 1976)

R. Willis: *Facsimile of the Sketchbook of Wilars de Honecort* (London, 1859) [trans. of Lassus with additional commentary]

E. Mâle: *L'Art religieux du XIIIe siècle en France* (Paris, 1898; Eng. trans., New York, 1948)

H. O[mont]: *Album de Villard de Honnecourt, architecte du XIIIe siècle* (Paris, [1906] [best pubd illus.]

H. Hahnloser: *Villard de Honnecourt: Kritische Gesamtausgabe des Bauhüttenbuches MS. Fr. 19093 der Pariser Nationalbibliothek* (Vienna, 1935, Graz, 2/1972)

T. Bowie: *The Sketchbook of Villard de Honnecourt* (Bloomington, 1959, 3/1968)

R. Branner: 'Gothic Architecture', *J. Soc. Archit. Hist.*, xxxii (1973), pp. 327–33

F. Bucher: '[The Lodge Book of] Villard de Honnecourt', *Architector: The Lodge Books and Sketchbooks of Medieval Architects*, i (New York, 1979), pp. 15–193 [personal interpretation]

C. F. Barnes jr: *Villard de Honnecourt, the Artist and his Drawings: A Critical Bibliography* (Boston, 1982) [with annotated bibliog. for the period 1666–1981]

C. Meckseper: 'Über die Fünfeckkonstruktion bei Villard de Honnecourt und im späten Mittelalter', *Architectura* [Berlin], xiii (1983), pp. 31–40

M. Terrenoire: 'Le Carnet de Villard de Honnecourt: Culture orale, culture savante?', *Artistes, artisans et production artistique au moyen âge: Rapports provisoires du colloque international: Rennes 1983*, i, pp. 374–421

P. Verdier: 'La "Sépouture d'un Sarrazin" de Villard de Honnecourt', *J. Sav.* (1983), pp. 219–28

J. Adam and P. Varène: 'La Scie hydraulique de Villard de Honnecourt et sa place dans l'histoire des techniques', *Bull. Mnmt.*, cxliii (1985), pp. 317–32

C. F. Barnes jr and L. Shelby: 'The Preliminary Drawing for Villard de Honnecourt's "Sepulchre of a Saracen"', *Gesta*, xxv/1 (1986), pp. 135–8

A. Erlande-Brandenburg and others: *Carnet de Villard de Honnecourt* (Paris, 1986)

C. F. Barnes jr: 'A Note on the Bibliographic Terminology in the Portfolio of Villard de Honnecourt (Paris, Bib. N., MS. Fr. 19093)', *Manuscripta*, xxxi (1987), pp. 71–6

R. Branner: 'An Unknown Gothic(?) Drawing from Saint-Quentin', *Gesta*, xxvi/2 (1987), pp. 151–2

C. F. Barnes jr and L. Shelby: 'The Codicology of the Portfolio of Villard de Honnecourt (Paris, Bib. N., MS. Fr. 19093)', *Scriptorium*, xlii (1988), pp. 20–48

C. F. Barnes jr: 'Le "Problème" Villard de Honnecourt', *Les Bâtisseurs des cathédrales gothiques* (Strasbourg, 1989), pp. 209–23

R. Bechmann: *Villard de Honnecourt: La Pensée technique au XIIIe siècle et sa communication* (Paris, 1991)

CARL F. BARNES JR

Villasana, José María (*b* Veracruz, 1848; *d* Tacubaya, Mexico City, 14 Feb 1904). Mexican illustrator and lithographer. He began his career in 1869, making prints for the weekly *La ilustración potosina* in San Luis Potosí. He collaborated with Alejandro Casarín and Jesús Alamilla on illustrations using engravings coloured with pen for the novel *Ensalada de pollos* by José Tomás de Cuéllar. In these the use of a schematic design accentuated the appearance of the figures portrayed. He created caricatures (1872–3) for *La orquesta* and other periodicals, but he established his reputation with caricatures (1874–6) of government figures for the weekly *Hijo Ahuizote*. Villasana was a member of the political party of President Porfirio Díaz and in 1880 published ferocious caricatures of Díaz's opponents in *El coyote emplumado*. He was co-publisher in 1883, with Ireneo Paz, of *La patria ilustrada* and in 1888 he founded his own weekly, *México y sus costumbres*; in both periodicals he published his own caricatures of public figures. In 1896 Díaz's government honoured him with a seat in the Chamber of Deputies. His last works were published in *El mundo ilustrado*, on which he collaborated from 1897.

BIBLIOGRAPHY

M. Toussaint: *La litografía en México en el siglo XIX* (Mexico City, 1934)

R. Carrasco: *La caricatura en México* (Mexico City, 1953)

C. Díaz y de Ovando: 'El grabado comercial en la segunda mitad del siglo XIX', *Hist. A. Mex.*, 85–6 (1982)

AÍDA SIERRA TORRES

Villate, Pierre [Malebouche] (*fl* 1451–95). French painter. Born in the diocese of Limoges, he is first mentioned in Avignon in 1451. His two sons Laurent Villate and François Villate were also painters. He is cited as *magister* and associate of ENGUERRAND QUARTON in a contract for an altarpiece in Avignon in 1452. He is last mentioned on 14 March 1495 when he stood surety for his son Laurent.

Judging by the number and importance of his commissions, Villate was one of the most renowned artists of his time in Provence. He received several commissions for stained-glass windows, including those for La Madeleine, Avignon, for the episcopal palace of Jean de Mareuil, Archbishop of Uzès (1467), for the chapel of the Archbishop of Aix (1469) and for Avignon town hall (1492); he also carried out various decorations for the entry into Avignon of the legate Charles de Bourbon in 1473.

Most of the surviving documents relate to altarpieces, however. On 16 February 1452 Villate and Enguerrand Quarton were commissioned to execute an altarpiece of the *Madonna of Mercy* for the chapel of Pierre Cadard, Seigneur du Thor, in the Chapelle St Pierre-de-Luxembourg near the Celestine church in Avignon; and two years later Villate received the commission for a *Calvary* altarpiece for Pierre Cadard's chapel in Notre-Dame-des-Doms in Avignon. Other commissions for altarpieces include those for the Friars Preachers in Avignon (1458), for the Dominican convent in Marseille (1459), for St Symphorien in Cabrière (1462), from Jacques Forbin of Marseille (1462), for the Celestine church in Avignon (1464), from a cobbler of Avignon (1466) and for the Dominican church in Marseille (1471). Villate also received payments for altarpieces for a chapel near Notre-Dame-la-Principale in Avignon (1473) and from Nicolas de Mari, Prior of Bagnière in the diocese of Nîmes (1486).

With the exception of the panel commissioned in 1452 by Pierre Cadard, none of these works has survived. Depicting the *Madonna of Mercy with SS John the Baptist and John the Evangelist* (0.66×1.87 m; Chantilly, Mus. Condé; predella untraced) on a gold ground, the altarpiece is generally attributed to Enguerrand Quarton on the grounds of its similarities to documented works by him; the association between Quarton and Villate was therefore perhaps only of legal character. The *Pietà of Villeneuve-lès-Avignon* (1.63×2.18 m; Paris, Louvre), formerly attributed to Villate, is also now generally accepted as Quarton's work. Villate's hand may, however, be recognizable in *St Bernardino of Siena and Two Donors* (370×680 mm; Marseille, Mus. Grobet-Labadié) and in a series of manuscripts, painted *c.* 1470–80, that show familiarity with the style of Quarton (Avril), including a Book of Hours of Angers use (Oxford, Bodleian Lib., MS. Gough liturg. II), a Book of Hours of Nantes use (England, priv. col.) and a Book of Hours of uncertain use (Weimar, Thüring. Landsbib., MS. Qu. 57). Sterling has also attributed to Villate one, and possibly two, illuminations added *c.* 1470–80 to the Boucicaut Hours (Paris, Mus. Jacquemart-André, MS. 2, fol. 241 and probably fol. 242; *see* MASTERS, ANONYMOUS, AND MONOGRAMMISTS, §I: BOUCICAUT MASTER); Villate did in fact appear as a witness to a document signed by Jean III le Meingre de Boucicaut in Avignon in March 1479.

BIBLIOGRAPHY

Abbé H. Requin: 'Documents inédits sur les peintres, peintres-verriers et enlumineurs d'Avignon au XVe siècle', *Réun. Soc. B.-A. Dépt.* (1889), pp. 118–217

P. Durrieu: 'La Vierge de Miséricorde d'Enguerrand Charonton et Pierre Villate au Musée Condé', *Gaz. B.-A.*, xxxii (1904), pp. 5–12

L. H. Labande: *Les Primitifs français: Peintres et peintres-verriers de la Provence occidentale* (Marseille, 1932), pp. 104–7, 176

P. Pansier: *Les Peintres d'Avignon aux XIVe et XVe siècles: Biographies et documents* (Avignon, 1934), pp. 228–53

C. Sterling: 'L'Auteur de la "Pietà" d'Avignon: Enguerrand Quarton (Charreton)', *Bull. Soc. N. Antiqua. France* (1959), pp. 213–23

F. Avril: 'Pour l'enluminure provençale, Enguerrand Quarton, peintre de manuscrits', *Rev. A.*, 35 (1977), pp. 9–40

C. Sterling: 'Une Oeuvre de Pierre Villate enfin retrouvée', *Chron. Mérid.*, i (1981), pp. 3–14

Les Manuscrits à peintures en France, 1440-1520 (exh. cat., Paris, Bib. N., 1993–4), pp. 242–3

DOMINIQUE THIÉBAUT

Villavicencio, Antonio (*b* La Plata [now Sucre], 1822; *d* Sucre, after 1888). Bolivian painter. It is possible he was taught painting by Manuel Ugalde. He went to France to improve his skills, and in 1856 he was in Paris. His known works date from 1844 to 1866. He was active mainly in Sucre, although he also worked in Potosí and La Paz. He painted in various genres but his work mainly consists of official portraits of presidents and national and regional dignitaries such as *Simon Bolívar* (U. Sucre, Mus. Charcas), *General José Ballivián* (1844; La Paz, Alcaldía) and *Mariano Melgarejo* (1866; Potosí, Mus. N. Casa Moneda). Villavicencio's style was sober and academic, but his portraits, landscapes and allegories have documentary value as a record of painting in the country after the long period of Mestizo art.

BIBLIOGRAPHY

M. Chacón Torres: *Pintores del siglo XIX*, Bib. A. & Cult. Boliv.: A. & Artistas (La Paz, 1963)

P. Querejazu: *La pintura boliviana del siglo XX* (Milan, 1989)

PEDRO QUEREJAZU

Villavicencio, Pedro Núñez de. *See* NÚÑEZ DE VILLA-VICENCIO, PEDRO.

Villecocq, de. *See* VULCOP, DE.

Villegas, Armando (*b* Pomabamba, Ancash, 1928). Peruvian painter, active in Colombia. He studied at the Escuela Nacional de Bellas Artes in Lima until 1950 and then at the fine arts faculty of the Universidad Nacional de Colombia in Bogotá, where he then settled. His work was initially figurative, but it developed towards a more abstract style, blending references to Pre-Columbian textile art and colonial art in largely monochromatic, textured paintings. Figurative elements later re-emerged in symbolic, Baroque-inspired compositions that evoke the works of Lucas Cranach, Dürer or Niklaus Deutsch, and in drawings that similarly look to European rather than Andean traditions (e.g. *Knight of the Thistle*, 1978; priv. col.; see Fraser and Baddeley, pl. 14). In the 1980s his work increasingly contained mythological and symbolic elements (e.g. *Masked Nobleman*, 1986; priv. col.; see Fraser and Baddeley, p. 76).

BIBLIOGRAPHY

J. A. de Lavalle and W. Lang: *Pintura contemporánea*, Colección arte y tesoros del Perú, ii (Lima, 1976), pp. 164–7

V. Fraser and O. Baddeley: *Drawing the Line: Art and Cultural Identity in Contemporary Latin America* (London, 1989), pp. 75–6

W. IAIN MACKAY

Villegas Marmolejo, Pedro de (*b* Seville, 1519; *d* Seville, 1596). Spanish painter and sculptor. He became the leading painter in Seville during the 1560s and 1570s and the head of a successful workshop, which, as well as satisfying local commissions, sold a large part of its production to Spanish America. He was a learned man and a friend of the humanist and theologian Benito Arias Montano. His work was academic and, lacking a strong individuality, was dependent on Flemish, German and Italian models available through drawings and engravings as well as the paintings of such foreign masters working in Seville as Peeter de Kempeneer. In the *Visitation* (1566; Seville Cathedral), the central scene of his notable altarpiece, the spatial treatment, the figure grouping and the use of soft, diffuse colours show Mannerist influence. Flemish and Mannerist traits appear in the donor portraits in the predella: their strong characterization and psychological insight reveal Villegas Marmolejo to have been an excellent portrait painter. In such later paintings as the *Holy Family with the Infant St John* (*c.* 1585; Seville, S Lorenzo) and the *Virgin of Redemption* (1590; Seville, S Vicente), the influence of Raphael is stronger. Set in an unreal space, floating in the clouds, the *Virgin of Redemption* departs compositionally from earlier Renaissance models (e.g. the *Virgin of the Rose* by Alejo Fernández 1520–30; Triana, nr Seville, S Ana) and prepares the way for such depictions of the Virgin as those of Bartolomé Esteban Murillo and other 17th-century Sevillian painters. Villegas Marmolejo was also a sculptor, producing such works as *Christ on the Cross* (1581) for the monastery of San Miguel de los Angeles, Sanlúcar la Mayor, Seville, although none of his sculptures is extant.

BIBLIOGRAPHY

F. Pacheco: *Arte* (1649); ed. F. Sánchez Cantón (1956), i, pp. I, XXVIII, 19, 36, 167

J. M. Serrera: *Pedro de Villegas Marmolejo* (Seville, 1976)

J. Brown: *The Golden Age of Painting in Spain* (New Haven and London, 1991), p. 118

Villeneuve, Julien Vallou de. *See* VALLOU DE VILLENEUVE, JULIEN.

Villeneuve-lès-Avignon. French town in the Vaucluse département, situated in the hills of Avignon near the River Rhône, with a population of *c.* 9500. Successive generations of French kings planned to develop the city of Avignon as a military stronghold. In 1293 Philip IV cleared the site for a 'ville neuve' (new town) on the west bank of the river near the Pont St Bénézet, which connected it to Avignon on the east bank. He also constructed the Tour Philippe le Bel (1293–1307; altered *c.* 1360). In the second half of the 14th century John II and Charles V constructed the Fort St André (1350–64; partly destr.; *see* GATE-HOUSE, fig. 1) on a site on Mont Andaon commanding the city, which had originally been the location of a Benedictine abbey. The fort served as a symbol of State power rivalling the Palace of the Popes in Avignon itself (*see* AVIGNON, §3(ii)(a)). During the period that Avignon was a papal seat (1309–78) luxurious cardinals' residences (termed 'Livrées') lined the streets of Villeneuve-lès-Avignon and the town flourished. Such

buildings as the Charterhouse (*see* §1 below), established in 1356, and the former collegiate church of Notre-Dame (*see* GOTHIC, §VII, 5), begun in 1333, survive. In 1868 the Musée de l'Hospice was established in a 17th-century hospice, and its collection was taken over by the Pierre du Luxembourg Museum (now Musée Municipal), preserving, among other works, the *Coronation of the Virgin by the Holy Trinity* (1453–4) by Enguerrand Quarton, *Christ among the Doctors* (1649) by Nicolas Mignard and the *Visitation* (*c.* 1644–6) by Philippe de Champaigne (*see* AVIGNON, §2).

BIBLIOGRAPHY

L.-H. Labande: *Le Palais des Papes et les monuments d'Avignon au XIVe siècle*, 2 vols (Marseille, 1925)

F. Benoit: *Villeneuve-lès-Avignon* (Paris, 1930)

1. CHARTERHOUSE. The Carthusian monastery was established in 1356; in 1352 the area had been presented as a personal domain to Etienne Aubert, Cardinal of Ostia and future Pope Innocent VI (*reg* 1352–62). The original establishment housed 11 monks, and was also known as La Chartreuse du Val de Bénédiction. Following the construction of Bonpas in 1320, the Charterhouse was established as the seventh foundation of the Order in Provence. Because the foundation received material and spiritual patronage from Avignon popes, the French kings, many cardinals and powerful aristocrats, it was able to achieve prosperity despite the general turmoil of the later Middle Ages. In the 16th century it became one of the

Villeneuve-lès-Avignon, Charterhouse, *Virgin and Child Adored by Innocent VI*, fresco from the *Life of Christ* (1354–5) by Matteo Giovanetti in the chapel of Innocent VI

most important Carthusian monasteries. At the Revolution, however, it was completely destroyed, partitioned and sold (1793–4). At the same time the monastery's documents, treasures and works of art were lost.

The monastery church is a single-nave structure, probably completed in 1372. The south aisle has chapels dedicated to the early Carthusian saints Bruno and Michael and to the Holy Trinity. The last, which is located at the east end, contains the tomb of Innocent VI: a white marble effigy lies on top of the plinth, covered by a splendid Gothic canopy. It was praised as a model of funerary art in the area around Avignon in the second half of the 14th century. Also, in 1453 Jean de Montagnac (d 1477), canon of St Agricol, Avignon, and Chapellein of the Carthusian church, commissioned on behalf of the Carthusian Order ENGUERRAND QUARTON to paint the *Coronation of the Virgin by the Holy Trinity* (see above) for the altar in the chapel of the Holy Trinity.

The monastery has three cloisters. The largest, the Cloître du Cimetière, was rebuilt in the 18th century, but the original monks' cells survive. In the south-west corner of the cloister is the small private chapel of Innocent VI. The *Canopy of Heaven*, illustrated on the walls and ceiling, was supervised by MATTEO GIOVANETTI, who was also in charge of decoration at the Palace of the Popes. The walls were decorated with frescoes, taking as their theme the *Life of St John the Baptist* and *Life of Christ* (1354–5; see fig.). The Cloître St Jean was built in 1372 by Pierre Selva de Montirac, Cardinal of Pamplona, the second founder of the monastery and nephew of Innocent VI. The monks' cells in this cloister were destroyed during the French Revolution; but the buildings around the 18th-century Fontaine St Jean are now the residence of the monks.

BIBLIOGRAPHY
J.-P. Aniel: *La Chartreuse de Villeneuve-lès-Avignon* (Rennes, 1982)
M. Laclotte and D. Thiébaut: *L'Ecole d'Avignon* (Paris, 1983), pp. 184–93
P. Amargier and others: *Chartreuses de Provence* (Aix-en-Provence, 1988)
Actes du Xe colloque international d'histoire et de spiritualité cartusiennes: Les Chartreux et l'art, XIVe–XVIIIe siècle: Paris, 1989
J. Gardner: *The Tomb and the Tiara. Curial Tomb Sculpture in Rome and Avignon in the Later Middle Ages* (Oxford, 1992)

YOSHIAKI NISHINO

Villeroi [Villeroy]. French noble family of administrators and patrons. Their political stronghold was Lyon and its surrounding districts, and the power they wielded in that region gave it an important role in French politics, which significantly affected artistic activity there. Nicolas de Neufville, Maréchal de Villeroi (1592–1685), became Governor of Lyon and its region in 1642. He became Marshal of France in 1646 and Duke in 1651; Anne of Austria (1601–66), Queen-Dowager and Regent during the minority of Louis XIV, appointed Villeroi the young King's governor. He exercised power in Lyon chiefly through his brother Camille de Neufville de Villeroi, Archbishop of Lyon (1606–86), who acted as his deputy, in which capacity he initiated the construction by Simon Maupin (fl 1623–55; d 1668) and the decoration of a new Hôtel de Ville (1646–69). The Archbishop also supervised in 1658 the reception of the Spanish envoys coming to arrange the

marriage between Louis XIV and the Infanta Maria-Theresa (1638–83). As part of the celebrations, a spectacular mock sea-battle representing *Jason's Capture of the Golden Fleece*—an allegory of Louis XIV's 'conquest' of Spain—was performed before an audience that included the King and his mother, Cardinal Mazarin and the French court. During their stay in Lyon the royal guests attended a ballet at the Théâtre des Jésuites and also visited the site of the unfinished, splendidly ornate Hôtel de Ville. The theme of both the ballet and the decoration of the new building was 'the eternal glory of Lyon'. The allegorical schemes were planned by a brilliant young Jesuit, Claude-François Ménestrier, and carried out by Thomas Blanchet; these two were also responsible for the temporary decorations celebrating the King's visit.

In 1660 Blanchet and Ménestrier were responsible for decorations for the *Réjouissances de la Paix*; in 1664 for two triumphal arches welcoming Cardinal Flavio Chigi; and in 1666 for jubilee celebrations. Blanchet also undertook the decoration of the Villeroi family's château of Ombreval. During Jean-Baptiste Colbert's ministry part of the park of Ombreval was reserved for a manufactory, planned by Blanchet, of 'Bologna silks', which was intended to rival the silk manufacture of Italy. Finally, Blanchet designed the funerary monument of *Nicolas de Villeroi* in a chapel of the Carmelite convent in Lyon that the family had endowed. During the French Revolution the Ombreval estate became the property of the nation; the château, now the Hôtel de Ville of Neuville-sur-Saône, has lost all its sculptures and decorations, except for the marble nymphaeum in the park.

BIBLIOGRAPHY
G. Dargent: 'La Famille d'Halincourt de Neuville de Villeroy', *L'Art baroque à Lyon; Actes du colloque: Lyon, 1972*, pp. 10–23
L. Galactéros-de Boissier: 'Ombreval et la Damette: Deux "maisons des champs" lyonnaises au XVIIe siècle', *Rev. Marseille*, 109 (1977), pp. 165–75 [from special issue devoted to congress report *La Qualité de la vie au XVIIe siècle*]

LUCIE GALACTÉROS-DE BOISSIER

Villeroy & Boch. German ceramics and glass manufacturers. In 1748 François Boch (1695–1754) founded a small factory for the production of faience fine (a lead-glazed earthenware) at Audun-le-Tiche in the Meurthe-et-Moselle region of France, near Luxembourg. In 1766 a second factory was opened at Septfontaines in Luxembourg, and more diversified wares were produced. In the early 19th century Boch's son Jean-François Boch (1735–1817) visited England to study ceramic techniques, which led to the introduction of transfer-printing at the factory. In 1809 Boch founded a factory for the production of creamware at the monastery of Mettlach. In 1787 another earthenware factory had been started at Vaudrevanges-Wallerfangen, Luxembourg, by Nicolas Villeroy (1759–1843). Under the direction of the Englishman John Leigh this also produced faience fine decorated with enamelled and transfer-printed flowers and views. Pierced wares and Neo-classical vases, influenced by wares from the Leeds factory, were also made. In 1836 the two factories merged to become Villeroy & Boch, and manufacture centred on Vaudrevanges and Mettlach. A new, unglazed stoneware was introduced in 1842, with white figures on a coloured background, emulating Wedgwood's 'Jasper' ware. In 1851 the joint company acquired the porcelain factory at Tournai, which it maintained until 1871. Other factories acquired included those in Schramberg (1883) and Torgau (1926). The company was very successful after World War II thanks to an imaginative design policy. In the 1950s such geometric patterns with bright colours as 'Kaleidoscope' showed the influence of Paul Klee. In the 1960s ethnic influences were evident in such patterns as the Mexican-inspired 'Acapulco', with colourful, stylized trees and birds. Later patterns incorporated *faux naïf* landscape and Art Nouveau revivals. The centre of control is at Mettlach, although there are factories also in Belgium, France and Luxembourg.

BIBLIOGRAPHY
T. Thomas: *Die Rolle der beiden Familien Boch und Villeroy in 18. und 19. Jahrhundert* (Saarbrücken, 1974)
Villeroy et Boch (exh. cat. by A. Fay-Halle, Sèvres, Mus. N. Cér., 1985)
M. Hayot: 'Septfontaines et la manufacture de Villeroy et Boch', *L'Oeil*, 369 (1986), pp. 38–45
BRUCE TATTERSALL

Villiers, George, 1st Duke of Buckingham (*b* Brooksby, Leics, 28 Aug 1592; *d* Portsmouth, 23 Aug 1628). English politician, collector and patron. As a young man he travelled abroad, although he never visited Italy. Nonetheless, he quickly developed an eye for pictures. As he was the principal dispenser of political patronage, owing to his position as the favourite of James I, King of England and Scotland, his tastes were formed by those fellow aristocrats and English diplomats resident in Italy and the Low Countries who were his suitors, as well as by artists employed in his household. Thomas Howard, 2nd Earl of Arundel, also played an important role in developing Villiers's taste: he may have presented Villiers with Anthony van Dyck's *Continence of Scipio* (Oxford, Christ Church Pict. Gal.), probably executed after van Dyck arrived in England in 1620. Arundel owned a famous collection of antiquities, and visits to his galleries at Arundel House, London, motivated Villiers to follow his example. Even so, when in 1624 Villiers instructed the English Ambassador in Constantinople (now Istanbul) to buy him statues, his request was for graceful pieces, rather than Arundel's 'misshapen stones'. Villiers's credo provides a means to understanding his patronage and collecting: the sumptuous, the magnificent and the extravagant were what really appealed to him; hence his collection was unique in England, both for the refined quality of its antiquities and for the pictures by Tintoretto, Jacopo Bassano, Veronese and Rubens.

Relations between Villiers and Arundel became increasingly strained, reaching breaking-point in May 1623, when Buckingham was elevated to a dukedom. Villiers, however, had been looking elsewhere for advice about collecting. Before 1621 he had instructed Balthazar Gerbier 'to chose for him rarities, books, medals, marble statues, and pictures'. In 1621 Gerbier went to Italy, where, among other paintings, he bought 'a great piece...of Pilatus': Titian's *Ecce homo* (Vienna, Ksthist. Mus.). In 1624 Gerbier was in France, writing to Villiers that 'I never could have thought that they had so many rare things', and where he bought a *Danaë* by Tintoretto (Lyon, Mus. B.-A.) and Titian's *Georges d'Armagnac and his Secretary* (Alnwick Castle, Northumb.). Later that year he informed Villiers,

'out of all the amateurs and princes and kings there is not one who has collected in forty years as many pictures as Your Excellency has collected in five.' Gerbier was productive in his acquisitions because Villiers's confidence in his own taste had been immeasurably strengthened by a visit to Spain in 1623, when he had taken Prince Charles (later Charles I) to Madrid. Both visited the Habsburg collections there, rich in works by Venetian artists. In Valladolid Charles was presented with Giambologna's *Cain and Abel* (probably *Samson Slaying a Philistine*; London, V&A), which he later gave Villiers, who used it as the centrepiece for a fountain at his London home, York House.

Villiers's main London residence was York House (destr.). Of the improvements he commissioned there, only the Water-gate survives, now separated by Victoria Embankment and Embankment Gardens from the Thames. In addition to York House, he had lodgings at Whitehall Palace (1619–21; destr.), London, designed by Inigo Jones. Villiers bought Wallingford House (destr.), Westminster, in addition to having a grand residence at Chelsea (destr.), once the home of Sir Thomas More. In the country he owned Burley-on-the-Hill (destr.) in Rutland and New Hall, Essex, part of which survives.

New Hall was acquired in 1622 for £20,000, and it was reported soon after that Inigo Jones had begun alterations 'according to the modern fashion', which included work on a gallery, armoury, stables and a chapel, though no drawings by Jones specifically connected with the house survive. However, there are two by him of designs (London, RIBA) for an Italianate gateway. At New Hall Villiers was able to indulge his taste for garden design, and he employed Cornelius Drebbel (1572–1634), who had formerly worked for Emperor Rudolf II in Prague. In the autumn of 1624 Drebbel was paid £20 'for his pains about the waterworks', and he may have designed the gazebos in the four angles of the west privy garden and the octagonal banqueting house to the south—perhaps that mysterious building in the background of the portrait of *George Villiers, 1st Duke of Buckingham* (1626; Euston Hall, Suffolk) by Daniel Mijtens I. Drebbel was joined at New Hall by John Tradescant (i), who entered Villiers's service in 1624. Besides advising Villiers on his grounds, Tradescant also created a cabinet of natural curiosities at York House, in the spirit of the Habsburg *Wunderkammer*.

In 1625 Villiers was in Paris, where he had his last great artistic encounter in meeting Rubens, from whom he commissioned a portrait (destr.) of himself as Lord High Admiral for £500. This painting was in the idiom of Baroque equestrian portraiture, suggesting that the taste and aspirations of the English court had become identified with those of the rulers of Catholic Europe. As a consequence, Villiers acquired Rubens's collection of his own paintings, and 32 had arrived at York House, at a reputed cost of £10,000, by 1627.

An inventory of the pictures that Villiers kept at York House, dated 11 May 1635, contains 330 items. It records 26 by Bassano, 22 by Tintoretto, 20 by Veronese, 19 by Titian, 11 by Andrea del Sarto, 2 by Correggio, 1 by Giorgione, 1 by Leonardo da Vinci and 1 by Raphael. In addition, besides those by Rubens there were a significant number of works by contemporaries, including a copy of

Caravaggio's *Martyrdom of St Peter* and paintings by Guido Reni, Gerrit van Honthorst, Domenico Fetti, Orazio Gentileschi and others. The most splendid monument to Villiers's munificence, however, is his own tomb in Westminster Abbey, London, by Hubert Le Sueur.

BIBLIOGRAPHY

R. Davies: 'An Inventory of the Duke of Buckingham's Pictures etc. at York House in 1635', *Burl. Mag.*, x (1906–7), pp. 376–82
R. Lockyer: *Buckingham* (London, 1981)
D. Howarth: *Lord Arundel and his Circle* (New Haven, 1985)

DAVID HOWARTH

Villoldo, Isidro (*b* ?Avila, *c*. 1500; *d* Seville, before 26 May 1556). Spanish sculptor. His activity was centred on Ávila, where he established a personal Mannerist style, influenced by Alonso Berruguete, but tempered by an excellent technique and with an additional Italian influence. In 1538 Villoldo was paid for a model of the choir-stalls for Avila Cathedral and in 1544 he helped to complete them. In 1539 he was described as an *'oficial'* of Berruguete in connection with work on the choir in Toledo Cathedral, where he also worked in 1543. Between 1546 and 1549 he carved the alabaster retable, dedicated to S Segundo, in the crossing of Ávila Cathedral. The alabaster retable in the sacristy of the same cathedral, on which he collaborated (1551–5) with Juan de Frias, has a fine *Flagellation* group on the central panel and a high relief of the *Ecce homo* framed by curtains. In 1553 Villoldo signed a contract with the Carthusian monastery of the Cuevas, Seville, for statues on their retable, which were only partly executed (fragments *in situ*). The value of the retable in wood of *St Antolin*, in Ávila Cathedral, was assessed in 1557, after his death.

BIBLIOGRAPHY

M. M. Zarco del Valle: *Documentos inéditos para la historia de las bellas artes en España* (Madrid, 1870), p. 397
J. Marti Monso: *Estudios histórico-artísticos relativos a Valladolid, basados en la investigación de archivos* (Valladolid and Madrid, 1898–1901)
M. E. Gómez Moreno: 'Isidro Villoldo, escultor', *Bol. Semin. Estud. A. & Arqueol. U. Valladolid*, 8 (1941–2), pp. 139–51
J. M. Parado del Olmo: *Los escultores seguidores de Berruguete en Ávila* (Ávila, 1981), pp. 191–233 [incl. illus.]
J. M. Palomero Paramo: *El retablo sevillano del renacimiento, 1560–1625* (Seville, 1983), pp. 126–8

MARGARITA ESTELLA

Villon, Jacques [Duchamp, Gaston] (*b* Damville, Eure, 31 July 1875; *d* Puteaux, nr Paris, 9 June 1963). French painter, printmaker and illustrator. The oldest of three brothers who became major 20th-century artists, including Raymond Duchamp-Villon and Marcel Duchamp, he learnt engraving at the age of 16 from his maternal grandfather, Emile-Frédéric Nicolle (1830–94), a shipbroker who was also a much appreciated amateur artist. In January 1894, having completed his studies at the Lycée Corneille in Rouen, he was sent to study at the Faculty of Law of the University of Paris, but within a year he was devoting most of his time to art, already contributing lithographs to Parisian illustrated newspapers such as *Assiette au beurre*. At this time he chose his pseudonym: Jack (subsequently Jacques) in homage to Alphonse Daudet's novel *Jack* (1876) and Villon in appreciation of the 15th-century French poet François Villon; soon afterwards this new surname was combined with the family name by Raymond. Marcel Duchamp and their sister

Suzanne Duchamp (1889–1963), also a painter, retained the original name. Villon's work as a humorous illustrator dominated the first ten years of his career, but from 1899 he also began to make serious prints, exhibiting some for the first time in 1901 at the Société Nationale des Beaux-Arts in Paris. By 1903 he had sufficient reputation in Paris to be an organizer of the first Salon d'Automne. He consciously began to expand his media in 1904, studying painting at the Académie Julian and working in a Neo-Impressionist manner. His printmaking style, formerly influencd by Toulouse-Lautrec, moved towards the fashionable elegance of Paul César Helleu.

In large part to make a break with his dependence on commercial illustration, Villon in 1906 moved to Puteaux, a suburb of Paris, where his brother Raymond and František Kupka became close neighbours. Devoting increasingly more time to painting and independent printmaking, he ceased entirely to make satirical cartoons by 1910 and in that year moved definitively from an expressionistic drawing style to an interest in volumes and planar structure; this shift is evident in a series of three prints (one drypoint and two etchings) entitled *Renée* (1911; see 1989 exh. cat., pp. 71–3) and in a dramatic portrait of *Raymond Duchamp-Villon* (1911; Paris, Pompidou). At this time he and his brothers became friendly with Albert Gleizes, Jean Metzinger, Henri Le Fauconnier, Fernand Léger and Robert Delaunay, who in showing their work together at the Salon des Indépéndants in 1911 had caused a furore as proponents of CUBISM. The circle of artists who made regular visits to Villon and Duchamp-Villon (*see* PUTEAUX GROUP) expanded rapidly, and many of them made contributions to the Maison Cubiste displayed at the Salon d'Automne in 1912, an attempt to extend the innovations of Cubism into the realm of life through architecture and the decorative arts, spearheaded by Duchamp-Villon and the French painter André Mare (1885–1932). Villon designed a tea service (priv. col., see 1976 exh. cat., pp. 51–2) for this complex. The same group of artists formed the core of an exhibition held in October 1912 entitled *Salon de la Section d'Or* (*see* SECTION D'OR (ii)), the widest manifestation of artists touched by Cubism. The term was bestowed by Villon, who had been reading the writings of Leonardo da Vinci, and it suggests the respect for proportion and harmonic structure that now characterized his art; unlike colleagues such as Juan Gris and Metzinger, however, Villon at that time did not regularly employ the formula of the golden section as a structure for all his compositions.

Villon's art and reputation were in full flower at the outbreak of World War I in 1914. By 1916 he was transferred from an infantry regiment serving at the front to a camouflage unit at Amiens. There is reason to believe that the two years during which he worked at camouflage caused him to study colour theory, especially M. A. Rosenstiehl's *Traité de la couleur* (Paris, 1913). A new and systematic use of colour is visible in the austere and pure abstract paintings produced by Villon just after the war. In works such as *Nobility* (1920), *Joy* (1921; both priv. col., see 1976 exh. cat., pp. 98–9 and 102) and the *Colour Perspective* series (e.g. *Colour Perspective*, 1921; New

York, Guggenheim; see fig.) Villon expanded his compositional approach. This now involved careful preparation and systematic distortion derived from the techniques of the etcher, including reversals and rotations, with the experience he had gained through camouflage of the deceptions of colour. Villon insisted that a visual idea be incorporated into a canvas from its moment of origin, with the object only as a starting-point and its forms represented by planes adjusted to the proportions of the picture. Along with Gleizes, he was one of the few French artists who explored abstraction during the early 1920s, for example in *The Jockey* (1924; New Haven, CT, Yale U. A.G.), but again the thrust of his painting activity was interrupted. The Bernheim-Jeune gallery in Paris, prompted by a group of their exhibiting artists who knew of Villon's skill as a printmaker, approached him with the idea of making a series of reproductive prints after established modern artists such as Manet, Renoir, Cézanne, Matisse, Picasso, Braque, André Derain, Vlaminck, Raoul Dufy and Bonnard. Between 1922 and 1930 Villon made about 40 such colour aquatints, at first fulfilling the requests of the gallery but after 1927 asserting his own choices; these included family members Marcel Duchamp, Suzanne Duchamp and his former brother-in-law Jean Crotti and friends such as Gleizes, Metzinger and Mare.

In the summer months, when not harnessed to the Bernheim-Jeune project, Villon continued to work for himself. He concentrated especially on drawing, working from life (e.g. *Seated Woman*, pencil, *c.* 1931; priv. col., see 1976 exh. cat., p. 124) from the sculptures of Duchamp-Villon (who had died in 1918), or from motifs he had developed much earlier. During these years he brought to perfection the fluid graphic style most associated with his drypoints and etchings, a linear grid formed by a dense network of energetic diagonals intersecting with varying degrees of light intensity, depending on the addition or subtraction of verticals and horizontals. *Papers on a Table* (1931; Paris, Bib. N.) is a notable example of this style, which was a considerable influence on contemporary European artists ranging from Giorgio Morandi to Marcel Gromaire. Villon returned to painting in another burst of activity during the early 1930s. Prodded by Gleizes, he took part in the activities of ABSTRACTION-CRÉATION; although these works were all derived from subjects that had their origins in common visual experience, the emphasis on planar construction against which Villon played off apparently free linear motifs produced the most lyrical abstract paintings of his entire career. These pictures are carefully governed by systems of mathematical proportion in accord with highly generalized titles, such as *Architecture* (1931), *Gaiety* (1932) and *Space* (1932; all priv. col., see 1976 exh. cat., pp. 132, 133, 135), which he reserved for the most ambitious of his accomplishments.

Jacques Villon: *Colour Perspective*, oil on canvas, 543×727 mm, 1921 (New York, Solomon R. Guggenheim Museum)

Shortly before his death, Villon recalled the 1930s as a time in which he worked in almost complete isolation, ignored or regarded as a marginal figure. He spent most of World War II living in the country, either at the home of André Mare's wife in Bernay or at the farm of her daughter, Mme Mare-Vené, at La Brunié in the Tarn. Having become interested in landscape only in the mid-1930s during a trip to Provence, Villon now alternated intimate pictures of farm life (e.g. *Kitchen-garden at La Brunié*, 1941; Cleveland, OH, Mus. A.) with abstract and sometimes grandiose landscapes based on a synthesis of the entire high plateau region from Toulouse to Albi. In painting the *Bridge at Beaugency* (1944; Paul Mellon priv. col., see 1976 exh. cat., p. 152) he evoked a traditional musical round ('Orléans, Beaugency, Notre Dame de Bercy') familiar to all French children. Works such as the *Three Orders* (1944; Richmond, VA Mus. F. A.), while consistent with his interest as a Cubist in subjects with epic resonance, assumed a special significance after World War II because they showed a resilient French past in spite of the Occupation. Louis Carré took Villon into his gallery in Paris, giving him his first one-man show since 1934. Villon very quickly re-established his reputation and his influence on a younger generation. He won numerous prizes during this period: the Grand Prix de la Gravure at the Exposition Internationale in Lugano (1949); first prize at the Carnegie International in Pittsburgh (1950); Grand Prize for painting at the Venice Biennale (1956); and the Grand Prize for painting at the Exposition Internationale in Brussels (1958). In the course of a long and productive life, Villon illustrated or contributed original prints to 27 books, of which only two, *Architectures* (Paris, 1921) by Louis Süe and André Mare and *Poésies* (Paris, 1937) by Pierre Corrard, appeared before World War II. His editions of Paul Valéry's French translation of Virgil, the *Bucoliques* (Paris, 1955), and Jean Cocteau's French translation of Hesiod, *Les Travaux et les jours* (Paris, 1962), and François Villon's *Grand Testament* (Paris, 1963) are among the most admired of his later illustrated books. In 1963, the year of his death, he was elected Grand Officier de la Légion d'honneur.

BIBLIOGRAPHY

J. Auberty and C. Pérussaux: *Jacques Villon: Catalogue de son oeuvre gravé* (Paris, 1950)

Jacques Villon: Exposition du centenaire (exh. cat., ed. H. Lassalle and O. Popovitch; Rouen, Mus. B.-A.; Paris, Grand Pal.; 1975)

Jacques Villon (exh. cat., ed. D. Robbins; Cambridge, MA, Fogg, 1976) [contains complete bibliog. and list of exhibitions to 1975]

C. de Ginestet and C. Pouillon: *Jacques Villon: Les Estampes et les illustrations* (Paris, 1979) [cat. rais.]

Jacques Villon, 1875–1963 (exh. cat. by D. Vallier and Y. Kroby, Morlaix, Mus. Jacobins, 1988)

Jacques Villon: L'Oeuvre gravé (exh. cat. by D. Tonneau-Ryckelynck and P. Cabanne, Gravelines, Mus. Arsenale; Lyon, Mus. Imprimerie & Banque; 1989)

For further bibliography *see* ABSTRACTION-CRÉATION; CUBISM; PUTEAUX GROUP; and SECTION D'OR (ii).

DANIEL ROBBINS

Vilnius [Ger. Wilna; Pol. Wilno; Rus. Vilno, Vil'nyus]. Capital of Lithuania, situated on the River Vilnya. Since becoming the capital of the Grand Duchy in 1323 its political fortunes have mainly followed those of Lithuania as a whole. Throughout its history Vilnius has been the artistic capital of LITHUANIA; despite its position on Europe's east–west cultural divide, from the late 16th century to the mid-20th its dominant Polish population brought it under the powerful influence of Latin culture. In two periods in particular, the Late Gothic and Rococo, the art of Vilnius developed a strong regional character, but at other times, notably in the 17th century, it absorbed outside influences, particularly from Italy, in their purer forms. Although the city flourished on trade with neighbouring countries and the Baltic, it was cut off from the main world trade routes; after rapid growth in the 17th century it stagnated at the turn of the 19th, leaving it with a rather underdeveloped industrial base.

By the 13th century Vilnius was a sizeable settlement around the adjoining Upper and Lower castles, where the cathedral was built after Lithuania adopted Roman Catholicism in 1387. Receiving its charter the same year, the town developed to an irregular plan. Between 1503 and 1512 fortifications were built (modernized after 1600); fragments are preserved in the Ostra Brama gate, the chapel of which became the focus of Catholic sentiment in Lithuania. Medieval art in the city is represented by architecture and only from the early 16th century, when brick Gothic styles arrived via Danzig (now Gdańsk), Königsberg (now Kaliningrad) and Kaunas. *Backsteingotik* was transformed into an expressive style of 'broken', angular, crystalline forms and fluting, intermingled with 'soft' forms in a Byzantine tradition. The former style prevailed in Catholic churches, such as St Anne's (completed after 1500); the latter appears in a few Orthodox churches, which combine a Gothic aisled hall with a Byzantine cross-in-square scheme (e.g. Holy Trinity, 1516). This eventually predominated, and by the 17th century it had evolved into the decorative post-Renaissance style adopted by general builders throughout the Polish–Lithuanian state and seen at Vilnius in, for example, the church of St Michael (completed 1627).

Already by the mid-16th century, however, Vilnius had become the northern outpost of Italian art brought by way of Kraków. Tuscan Renaissance forms were introduced to the Lower Castle by such architects as BERNARDINO ZANOBI DE GIANOTSI and Giovanni Cini (*fl* 1519–65; reconstruction of the cathedral, 1534–57; church of SS Anna and Barbara, 1551; palaces), but only tombstones survive (Vilnius Cathedral). The Counter-Reformation activity of the Jesuits, who took over the university (founded 1579), contributed to the appearance in Vilnius of a scaled-down version of Il Gesù, Rome (*see* ROME, §V, 16), in St Casimir's Church (1604–16). After Kraków and Warsaw the city became the most important centre outside Italy of early Baroque in the style of Carlo Maderno, reflected especially in the work of CONSTANTE TENCALLA (Vilnius Cathedral, St Casimir's Chapel, 1634–6; Discalced Carmelites' Church, 1634–53). Tomb designs by Giovanni Battista Gisleni were executed by Giovanni Battista Rossi (wall tomb of *Bishop Jerzy Tyszkiewicz*, 1654; Vilnius Cathedral).

After the Russian invasion (1654–61), fully developed Baroque styles flourished in Vilnius, but the real transformation occurred after the fire of 1737, when Rococo churches in numbers almost to rival Bavaria were built all round the city. The style, mainly Czech/Silesian in origin, emphasized lightness, dynamism and elegance, exemplified in the façades and crowns of the towers that were added to conventionally planned buildings. The illusionistic scenographic models of Andrea Pozzo and Ferdinando Galli-Bibena inspired the interiors, where groups of piers and stucco altars of different size formed an autonomous micro-architectural design within the rigidly shaped confines (e.g. Jesuit church of St John, 1738–62, by Jan Krzystof Glaubitz; Dominican church, 1749–60, by Father Ludwik Hryncewicz).

The late 18th century and the early 19th were dominated by varieties of Neo-classicism, the conventional secular architecture being mostly the work of architects from the university, while Wawrzyniec Guciewicz introduced a rough version of French Neo-classicism (town hall, 1781–3; cathedral reconstruction, from 1783), which reappeared after the onset of Russian rule in 1795 in the form derived from St Petersburg (Governor's Palace, 1816–20, by Vasily Stasov). Neo-classicism was also brought from Warsaw by the Rome-trained sculptors of King Stanislas II Poniatowski, primarily Tommaso Righi (1727–1802; statues in the cathedral) and André Lebrun (1737–1811), who became Professor of Sculpture in 1797. At the same time the chair of painting went to Franciszek Smuglewicz, who founded the Vilnius school, which specialized in classical themes and portraits, the latter verging on Romanticism (as, for example, in the work of Walenty Wańkowicz).

After 1830 art in Vilnius ceased to flourish. Although there was an important phase between 1925 and 1939, associated with the work of the academic painters Ferdynand Ruszczyc, Zbigniew Pronaszko and Ludomir Ślendziński, architecture, in turn Historicist, Eclectic, Art Nouveau and Modernist, was undistinguished.

BIBLIOGRAPHY

P. Weber: *Wilna: Eine vergessene Kunststätte* (Jena, 1917)
J. Remer: *Wilno* (Poznań, 1934)
J. Kłos: *Wilno: Przewodnik krajoznawczy* [Vilnius: a touring guide] (Wilno, 1937)
M. Morelowski: *Zarysy syntetyczne sztuki Wileńskiej od gotyku do neoklasycyzmu* [A general outline of art in the Vilnius region from Gothic to Neo-classicism] (Wilno, 1939)
——: *Znaczenie baroku Wileńskiego XVIII stulecia* [The significance of 18th-century Vilnius Baroque] (Wilno, 1940)
Vilniaus architektūra (Vilnius, 1985)

ADAM MIŁOBĘDZKI

Vilt, Tibor (*b* Budapest, 15 Dec 1905; *d* Budapest, 13 Aug 1983). Hungarian sculptor, husband of the sculptor ERZSÉBET SCHAÁR. He studied in Budapest at the School of Applied Arts (1922–5) and the College of Fine Arts (1925–6). From 1929 to 1931 he was a Hungarian Academy scholar in Rome. He maintained close relations with socialist artists between 1931 and 1934, and his early work developed almost entirely in this milieu. As an artist he constantly experimented and was receptive to new trends. His *Self-portrait* (wood, 1926; Budapest, priv. col., see Sík, p. 68), for example, combines Art Deco stylishness with the realist concentration of Egyptian sculpture.

Vilt's early portraits are generally sensitive and perceptive depictions of the model, while other works display an expressiveness that from World War II onwards came to dominate his oeuvre (e.g. *Loneliness*, bronze, 1944; Budapest, N.G.). The expressive form occasionally, however, gives way to more grotesque, even tragic elements, as in

The Cage (bronze, 1949; Budapest, Kiscelli Mus.). His public commissions, for example the statue of *Electricity* (1956–60; Tiszalök), show a strength and self-assurance. In the later 1960s he produced 'built-up' tectonic statues, while around 1970 he produced a series of compositions, made from sheets of glass, entitled *Music* (Budapest, priv. col., see Sík, p. 39). One of his last works, *Man-eater* (plaster, 1982; Budapest, priv. col., see Sík, p. 56), is derived from Goya.

BIBLIOGRAPHY

I. Ártinger: 'Vilt Tibor szobrai' [The sculptures of Tibor Vilt], *Magyar Művészet* (1938), pp. 302–11
J. Cassou and P. Kovács: *Vilt Tibor* (Budapest, 1972)
Művészet (1977), no. 10 [special commemorative issue]
C. Sík: *Vilt Tibor* (Budapest, 1985)

S. KONTHA

Vil'yams [Williams], **Pyotr (Vladimirovich)** (*b* Moscow, 30 April 1902; *d* Moscow, 1 Dec 1947). Russian stage designer and painter. He studied in the studio of Vasily Nikitich Meshkov (1868–1946) during the 1910s and at Vkhutemas in Moscow under Pyotr Konchalovsky and Konstantin Korovin from 1918 to 1923. He was one of the leading members of the Society of Easel Painters from 1925 to 1929. He originally worked as a painter and illustrated children's books; from 1929 he worked as a stage designer. As a painter he was noted for his portraits (e.g. of the director *Konstantin Stanislavsky*, 1933; St Petersburg, Rus. Mus.) and other works painted in a bold, energetic style with expressionistic overtones (e.g. *Woman at a Window*, 1930s; St Petersburg, Rus. Mus.).

Vil'yams's stage designs included Mikhail Bulgakov's *Molière* (1936) for MKhAT (the Moscow Art Theatre), Giuseppe Verdi's *La Traviata* (1934; Moscow, Bakhrushin Cent. Theat. Mus.) for the Nemirovich-Danchenko Music Theatre, Moscow, and Nikolay Gogol's *Government Inspector* (1939) for the Vakhtangov Theatre, Moscow. From 1937 he was a designer, and from 1941 to 1947 Principal Designer, at the Bol'shoy Theatre, Moscow, where he designed operas and ballets (e.g. Gioacchino Rossini's *William Tell*, 1942, and Sergey Prokofiev's *Cinderella*, 1945; both Moscow, Bol'shoy Theat. Mus.). As a stage designer Vil'yams made use of various media and techniques, successfully combining three-dimensional scenery and painted panels. He used gauze, with both transparent and opaque work, in order to create an effect of spaciousness in his landscape sets. He had a subtle sense of the specific differences between different theatrical genres. His work was outstanding for its historical authenticity, employment of painterly skill, refined use of colour and expressive spatial arrangements.

BIBLIOGRAPHY

F. Ya. Syrkina: *P. V. Vil'yams* (Moscow, 1933)
T. Klyuyeva: *P. V. Vil'yams* (Moscow, 1956)
V. V. Vanslov: *Izobrazitel'noye iskusstvo i muzikal'nyy teatr* [Fine art and the musical theatre] (Moscow, 1963)
A. Yu. Sidorov: *P. Vil'yams: Zhivopis', stsenografiya* [P. Vil'yams: painting, stage designs] (Moscow, 1980)

V. V. VANSLOV

Vimercate, Tomasino da. *See* TOMASINO DA VIMERCATE.

Vinaccia, Gian Domenico (*b* Massalubrense, Naples, 13 March 1625; *d* Naples, ?July 1695). Italian sculptor, silversmith and architect. He was a pupil and collaborator of Dionisio Lazzari. His independent activity in and around Naples dates from 1661, when he carved the wooden choir-stalls in the church of S Pietro ad Aram, Naples. His first sculptures are the bronze statue of *St Francis Xavier* (1664; Naples Cathedral, Cappella del Tesoro) and the silver *Christ* (1670; Naples, Santa Trinità dei Pellegrini), which reveal a relative freedom from the Baroque tradition. Like other Neapolitan artists, Vinaccia retained an ambiguity between traditional and archaic forms and more modern stylistic elements.

Vinaccia is better known for his decorative stucco work in the vault of the oratory of Nobili, near the Gesù Nuovo (1682), and in the Congregazione dell'Immacolata, near the Gesù Vecchio (1691). He also produced silver liturgical objects such as crucifixes, candelabra, reliquaries and frames for altar-cards. The large silver antependium for the altar of the Cappella del Tesoro in Naples Cathedral is his most important work, and the representation of the *Translation of the Relics of St Januarius* on the altar (1692–5; *see* NAPLES, fig. 7) is a sort of adaptation in high relief of the painterly manner of Luca Giordano. The connection between Vinaccia and Giordano is confirmed by the execution of a large salt-cellar (untraced; see de Dominici) for the Duca di Laurenzano, after a design by Giordano; this was decorated with allegorical figures and crowned by the figure of Time, being held back by Glory and Eternity, who are building the Temple of Eternity.

Vinaccia's work as an architect was limited to plans for the chapel of S Agostino in S Giuseppe dei Ruffi, Naples, and for altars of polychrome marble and *pietra dura* in the same church (1682) and in S Maria di Monteoliveto (*c.* 1690), executed by Pietro and Bartolomeo Ghetti (*fl* 1645–90).

BIBLIOGRAPHY

B. de Dominici: *Vite* (1742–5), iii, pp. 163–5
E. Catello: 'G. D. Vinaccia e il paliotto di San Gennaro', *Napoli Nob.*, xviii (1979), pp. 121–32
A. Nava Cellini: *La scultura del '600* (Turin, 1982), pp. 136, 226–7
Civiltà del seicento a Napoli (exh. cat., ed. S. Cassani; Naples, Capodimonte, 1984), pp. 223–7
E. Catello: 'Marmi, bronzi, argenti e stucchi', *Seicento napoletano*, ed. R. Pane (Milan, 1984), pp. 357–9
C. G. Borrelli: 'Alcune opere di Gian Domenico Vinaccia per le chiese dei Jesuiti', *Barocco napoletano* (Rome, 1992), pp. 671–84 [pap. from the confer. 'Centri, e periferie del barocco', Naples, 1987]

ORESTE FERRARI

Vinache, Jean-Joseph (*b* ?Paris, 1696; *d* Paris, 1 Dec 1754). French sculptor. He seems to have been the son of the leading bronze-founder Joseph Vinache (1653–after 1717) and perhaps trained with Antoine Coyzevox. His technical skill led to a summons to Dresden from Augustus II of Poland, Elector of Saxony, to complete an equestrian statue of the King left unfinished at the death of François Coudray (1678–1727). A model in gilt plaster (Dresden, Skulpsamml.) and a bronze reduction (Dresden, Grünes Gewölbe) preserve the design of this scheme: the King is shown in Roman armour on a rearing horse, stabilized by a massive tail. The concept was inspired by Bernini's equestrian statue of *Louis XIV* (Versailles, Château) and the widely diffused small bronzes of Jean-Baptiste Gobert

(*d* after 1723). Vinache executed numerous other works for Augustus and also made copies after the Antique.

On his return to Paris, Vinache was approved (*agréé*) by the Académie Royale in 1736 and received (*reçu*) as a full member in 1741 with the marble group *Hercules Enchained by Cupid* (Paris, Louvre). This charming subject, later reproduced in marble and bronze versions, is a skilful if slightly academic contrast of the childish and the mature human body. Vinache had shown two other male nudes at the Salon of 1738: *Marsyas Striving to Break his Bonds* and *St Jerome* (both untraced). Of the many works in terracotta that he modelled throughout his careers, few are traceable, of which one is his statuette of *Apollo* (Paris, Louvre). Such gallant and fashionable subjects as *Cupid Stung by a Bee* (exh. Salon 1742) and *Fidelity* (exh. Salon 1746) were intended for private collectors.

Vinache also worked on large-scale sculptures for the Bâtiments du Roi. At the Salon of 1743 he exhibited a project (untraced) for a competition for the tomb of *Cardinal de Fleury*. In 1746 he completed a bronze low relief of the *Death of St Teresa* for the chapel at the château of Versailles (*in situ*), showing clear discomfort with the specialized technique of this form. The group of *Faith Striking down Idolatry* (plaster, 1745; Paris, St Paul–St Louis), a moderated version of Jean-Baptiste Théodon's group of 1699 in Il Gesù, Rome, is more convincing.

Vinache received both royal and private commissions from Charles-François-Paul Le Normand de Tournehem, uncle of Mme de Pompadour and Directeur des Bâtiments du Roi from 1745 to 1751, though the private commissions are untraced. In 1746, for instance, Vinache showed at the Salon the terracotta sketch model for a marble statue of *Aurora* (marble version, Paris, priv. col.) intended for the gardens at Versailles. Another royal commission was a marble group of *Children Playing with Flowers* (Paris, Louvre), a Rococo work in the tradition best represented by Jacques Sarazin's *Children with a Goat* (Paris, Louvre), which Vinache restored and copied. Both the *Aurora* and the *Children Playing with Flowers* were finished by Nicolas-François Gillet after Vinache's death.

Vinache was dismissed as a mediocre talent by such influential connoisseurs as Pierre-Jean Mariette and Louis Petit de Bachaumont, yet despite the evident lack of individuality in his relief sculpture and his religious and allegorical statuary, his work is a good reflection of the Rococo taste of the circle of Mme de Pompadour and demonstrates the high level of competence reached by middle-ranking French sculptors in the 18th century.

BIBLIOGRAPHY

Lami
G. Servières: 'Les Artistes français à la cour de Saxe au XVIIIème siècle', *Gaz. B.-A.*, 4th ser., ii (1911), pp. 126–8
M. Furcy-Raynaud, ed.: 'Inventaire des sculptures exécutées au XVIIIème siècle pour la direction des Bâtiments du Roi', *Archvs A. Fr.*, n.s., xiv (1927), pp. 363–78
L. Réau: *Histoire de l'expansion de l'art français: Belgique et Hollande–Suisse–Allemagne et Autriche–Bohême et Hongrie* (Paris, 1928), p. 168
W. Holzhausen: 'Ledafiguren i Albertinum i Dresden og J. J. Vinache', *Kstmus. Årsskr.* (1935), pp. 145–51
Nouvelles acquisitions du département des sculptures (1980–1983), Musée du Louvre (Paris, 1984), no. 20, pp. 62–3 [entry by G. Bresc-Bautier]

GUILHEM SCHERF

Vinãs, Antonio de las. *See* WYNGAERDE, ANTHONIS VAN DEN.

Vinatea Reinoso, Jorge (*b* Arequipa, 22 April 1900; *d* Arequipa, 15 July 1931). Peruvian painter and illustrator. He first exhibited in Arequipa in 1917 after leaving school, and in 1918 he went to Lima, where he was influenced most notably by the work of the Peruvian painter Daniel Hernández, who from 1919 to 1924 taught him at the Escuela Nacional de Bellas Artes, along with the Spanish painter Manuel Piqueras Cotolí. After working as an art critic for the newspaper *El comercio* and contributing as a caricaturist to the magazines *Mundial* and *Variedades*, in 1925 he began teaching at the Escuela Nacional. Vinatea Reinoso's caricatures were rarely rebellious or anarchic, but reflected the gentle satire typical of the work of PANCHO FIERRO. His painting, which pioneered Peruvian Indigenism, was influenced by the work of the French Impressionists and by the other leading Indigenist painter, JOSÉ SABOGAL, although Vinatea Reinoso used more complex perspectives and structures than many Indigenists. His colours were generally subdued and were applied with fragmentary brushstrokes, giving a somewhat unfinished appearance to his works (e.g. *Church Interior, Cuzco*, 1930; Lima, Mus. Banco Cent. Reserva).

BIBLIOGRAPHY
C. Gálvez: 'Un caricaturista arequipeño', *Fanal*, xxii/81 (1967), pp. 10–13
J. Villacorta Paredes: *Pintores peruanos de la República* (Lima, 1971), pp. 60–69
Jorge Vinatea Reinoso (exh. cat. by J. M. Ugarte Eléspuru, Lima, Mus. A. It., 1980)

W. IAIN MACKAY

Vinča. Site of prehistoric settlement on the right bank of the River Danube, east of Belgrade, Serbia. It flourished during the 6th–4th millennia BC. Vinča is the type site of the Vinča culture, which extended throughout Serbia and part of western Romania. A major agricultural settlement, it has yielded evidence of the development of Neolithic crafts, especially pottery and fired clay figurines (*see also* PREHISTORIC EUROPE, §IV). It was partially excavated by Milan Vasić in 1908–12, 1924 and 1928–32, and the material recovered is in the National Museum, Belgrade, and in the Faculty of Archaeology, Belgrade University. The large mound is over 10 m high and comprises a 2 m-deep base-level of STARČEVO culture occupation debris, overlain by *c.* 7 m of Vinča culture deposits, dating from the 6th–5th millennia BC. Vasić suggested four main phases of development (A–D), sometimes simplified into Early or Vinča–Turdaş and Late or Vinča–Pločnik.

The site yielded a range of distinctive dark handmade pottery, which contrasts with contemporary painted styles elsewhere in the Balkans. It was decorated with fluting and channelling, burnished and fired under reducing conditions. Forms were varied, ranging from bowls and footed bowls, shallow dishes and handled pear-shaped jars to globular and biconical vessels. Like other Balkan Neolithic sites, Vinča produced anthropomorphic figurines (see fig.). Vinča culture figurines have a distinctive style, and the site itself is notable for having yielded over 2000 examples. These mostly comprised small fired clay figurines, rarely over 150 mm high. The subjects are generally shown standing or seated, although in some Early pieces they are shown in a semi-reclining position. The sex is often unclear, although both females and males

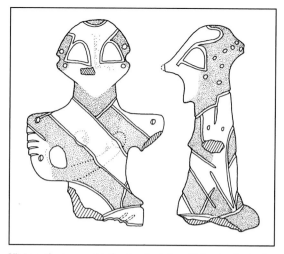

Vinča, anthropomorphic figurine, fired clay with bands of red paint, h. 300 mm, Neolithic period, 6th millennium BC (Belgrade, University of Belgrade, Faculty of Archaeology); front and side views

are represented. The figurines are schematized, with flat torsos, short arms and closed legs; in Late Vinča examples the body treatment is more natural and dress is sometimes represented. Early figurines have more triangular faces, Late pieces more rounded or polygonal. Face treatment is distinctive: blank, sometimes bulging, eyes are outlined by incised decoration, there is generally no mouth and Late Vinča examples have protruding noses. The incised diagonal decoration, supplemented in Late examples with white encrustation and bands of red paint, are also distinctive. Small lids in the form of human or animal faces and clay bucrania (bulls' heads) are decorated in a similar style. The figurines are usually interpreted as cult objects—some archaeologists have interpreted the various figures as specific deities—and religious or ritual practice may have been one of the important activities at the site. Stone industry included the working of imported obsidian, and copperworking was also practised.

BIBLIOGRAPHY
M. Vasić: *Preistoriska Vinča* [Prehistoric Vinča], i–iv (Belgrade, 1932–6)
J. Chapman: *The Vinča Culture of South-east Europe* (Oxford, 1981)
M. Gimbutas: *The Goddesses and Gods of Old Europe* (London, 1982)

ALASDAIR WHITTLE

Vincennes. Château and park in east Paris, France.

1. CHÂTEAU. Begun as a hunting-lodge in 1162, the château was enlarged by Philip II Augustus (*reg* 1180–1223) in 1183 and by Louis IX in 1248 and was one of the favourite residences of the Capet dynasty. The donjon, begun by Philip VI (*reg* 1328–50) in 1337 and completed 1370, is a square building (h. 54 m) with cylindrical corner towers: it follows the design of that of the Temple (1306; destr.) in Paris. It was surrounded by an outer wall with a *chemin-de-ronde* and a gate-house, in which was the king's study. Charles V wished to establish a royal city here, almost a prototype of Versailles. He built the curtain wall with nine large towers capable of lodging 2000 people. The area enclosed by the moat measured 334×175 m. Raymond du Temple was Charles V's architect, although

Charles probably contributed to the design. The donjon has six storeys: the kitchens were at the bottom, the next two storeys were reserved for the king, the fourth storey for the treasury, the fifth for officers of the household, and the top storey for soldiers.

The Sainte-Chapelle (from 1379; for illustration *see* SAINTE-CHAPELLE) was left unfinished by Charles V and Charles VI and completed by Francis I and Henry II. Philibert de L'Orme managed to copy the original style almost exactly. In 1550 a choir-screen was ordered from the sculptor Jehan de la Gente and choir-stalls (destr. 1789–99) to house 84 canons and choristers were commissioned from Francisque de Carpy (*fl* 1531–58). On either side of the sanctuary are the private chapels of the king and queen, each with a fireplace. The Queen's Chapel contains the monument to *Louis Antoine Henri de Bourbon, Prince Conde, Duc d'Enghien* (marble, 1816–22) by Louis-Pierre Deseine.

In 1653 Cardinal Jules Mazarin became governor of Vincennes and employed Louis Le Vau to build two symmetrical blocks either side of the south entrance, one pavilion each for the king and queen (*see* LE VAU, (1), §3). Le Vau also designed the monumental south entrance. Philippe de Champaigne and Michel Dorigny were responsible for the interior paintings (from 1659; largely destr.). These two buildings are forerunners of the Louis XIV style. Vincennes also provided Jean-Baptiste Colbert the elder with his first experience of building administration (1654–61).

BIBLIOGRAPHY

E. Lemarchand: *Le Château Royal de Vincennes dès son origine à nos jours* (Paris, 1907)
F. de Fossa: *Le Château historique de Vincennes à travers les âges*, 2 vols (Paris, 1908)
M. Pradel de Lamase: *Vincennes* (Paris, 1932)
J. Cordey: 'Colbert, Le Vau et la construction du Château de Vincennes', *Gaz. B.-A.*, ix (1933), pp. 273–93
A. Erlande-Brandenburg: 'Aspects du mécénat de Charles V: La Sculpture décorative', *Bull. Mnmtl*, cxxx (1972), pp. 303–29
I. Dunlop: *Royal Palaces of France* (London, 1985)
J. Mesqui: *Les Demeures seigneuriales*, ii of *Ile-de-France gothique*, Les Monuments de la France gothique (Paris, 1988), pp. 332–61

IAN DUNLOP

2. CENTRE OF PORCELAIN PRODUCTION. In 1740 a workshop was established in disused premises at the royal château of Vincennes by a small group of workers from Chantilly. The factory was directed by Claude-Humbert Gérin (1705–50), a former carpenter who had discovered the secret of producing a soft-paste porcelain (a non-kaolin, frit porcelain) of dazzling whiteness. In 1741 Philibert Orry, Comte de Vignory, Contrôleur-Général des Finances, who was anxious to avoid capital leaving France for the purchase of porcelain from East Asia and Meissen, gave the factory a loan of 10,000 livres from the Royal Treasury on the strength of this highly promising invention (the pastes produced in the factories at Saint-Cloud and Chantilly having proved unsatisfactory). The factory was soon financed by the Intendant des Finances, Jean-Henri-Louis Orry de Fulvy (1703–1751), half-brother of the Comte, which enabled new workers to be employed. In July 1745 Orry de Fulvy obtained a royal privilege, which reserved for the factory the right to 'make porcelain in the Saxe manner . . . painted and gilded with human

figures' and also to produce sculptures and flowers. At this time, however, only the paste and glaze had been perfected; it was not until 1746 that the firing of the body was mastered and only two years later that the kiln for firing enamels was introduced. Also in 1748, the factory acquired the process of preparing and applying gold from Brother Hippolyte, a Benedictine monk; this was subsequently a major characteristic of the enterprise and created a sufficient range of opaque colours to enable miniatures to be painted in the style of Meissen. Little is known about the items produced during these early years, although small objects that required simple modelling, such as boxes, pommels for walking-sticks and possibly porcelain flowers in imitation of real ones, were produced.

The privilege Orry de Fulvy had obtained enabled him to bring together in 1745 a group of shareholders under the name of Charles Adam (Orry de Fulvy's *valet de chambre*). Repeated appeals for funds, soon encouraged by royal gifts, led to the factory's rapid development: the number of workers increased from 16 in 1741 to 24 in August 1745 and 63 in 1749, and production began to diversify. The most lucrative line was that of porcelain flowers, which the *marchands-merciers* would attach to bronze stalks to create bouquets (e.g. 1749; Dresden, Porzellansamml.). These were sometimes placed in vases or were used to embellish ornamental pieces in gilt bronze, lacquer or porcelain. Developments in other areas included single figures or groups usually covered only with a transparent glaze and such useful wares as beakers, various pots, pots-pourri and vases encrusted with relief flowers. At first, Meissen wares constituted the main source of inspiration. The decoration comprised stylized flowers or animated landscapes, around the body or set in geometric reserves. A new development began in 1748 with the arrival at the factory of the goldsmith Jean-Claude Chambellan Duplessis (*see* DUPLESSIS), who was soon responsible for all new forms, including the first figures inspired by the work of François Boucher.

The transition to an entirely original style was accelerated by the appointment, in 1752, of JEAN-JACQUES BACHELIER as artistic director. One of his first tasks was probably to change the engravings used as models by the decorators: 17th-century designs were abandoned in favour of contemporary ones. The death of Orry de Fulvy in May 1751 provoked a crisis, which led to royal intervention and the appointment of the chemist Jean Hellot (1685–1766) to improve and record the pastes. The factory was, however, running into debt. The stockholders dissolved the company in 1752, and a new company, a quarter of which was acquired by Louis XV, was established in the name of Eloy Brichard. Despite these upheavals, the factory continued to develop.

The fashion for porcelain flowers painted in natural colours suddenly ceased in 1751–2, and the figures changed completely. In place of figures intended to decorate furniture or mantelpieces, isolated or grouped in pairs, the factory began to produce figures intended to adorn tables. It was probably the need to obtain similar copies from good moulds that led to the production of biscuit (unglazed) porcelain, one of the most important inventions of the factory. The range of items produced was also greatly expanded to include dinner-services (e.g. tureen

Vincennes soft-paste porcelain tureen and dish, h. of tureen 130 mm, *c.* 1749–53 (New York, Metropolitan Museum of Art)

and dish, *c.* 1749–53; New York, Met.; see fig.), tea-services, ornamental items and vases with increasingly rich and bold decoration. Bachelier introduced such new motifs as children *à la Boucher* or fantastic birds and sprays of naturalistic or imaginary flowers in clear, bright colours; and landscapes began to be better placed in relation to the curves of the forms. Bachelier's most important innovation came about in 1751, when he introduced coloured grounds inspired by East Asian wares, probably via Meissen. Previously, yellow was the only ground colour possible and was probably used even before the death of Orry de Fulvy. At first, it was used to surround landscapes in the style of Meissen and later with polychrome birds and children *en camaïeu bleu*. The inventory made after the death of Orry de Fulvy mentions trial pieces with green and violet grounds, but it took more time to master the technique of spraying the powdered colour on a mordant. An uneven blue, highlighted with gilding, seems to date from 1752, a light violet ground appeared in 1753 and in the same year the first green grounds were noted, although green was in regular use only after 1756. In 1753 a turquoise blue called *bleu céleste* was discovered and was immediately used on the table-service delivered to Louis XV between 1753 and 1755 (Duke of Buccleuch priv. col.).

Once coloured grounds could be successfully achieved, entirely new decorative schemes were possible: reserves of delicate, symmetrical curves, with gilt frames of extraordinary richness, enclose 'bat-wing' motifs, trellis-work and foliage from which issue animals, trees and garlands of flowers and palms. Paralleling these innovations, sales rocketed; wares had initially been reserved for dealers and a few privileged customers, including the Marquise de Pompadour, and it was only *c.* 1751 that a shop was opened in Paris for the general public. From that moment the court flocked to buy these luxury products. Foreign, especially English, customers were also attracted. In 1756 the factory, which by then employed more than 200 highly specialized workers, was transferred to buildings specially built at Sèvres, which was ideally situated between Paris and Versailles (*see* SÈVRES PORCELAIN FACTORY). In the same year Louis XV presented a table-service, decorated with a green ground, flowers and fruit, to Christian VII, King of Denmark (Copenhagen, Kon. Saml.). The magnificent and numerous services made at Vincennes not only served political ambitions but also illustrated and advertised the splendours of French art of the period.

BIBLIOGRAPHY
Porcelaines de Vincennes: Les Origines de Sèvres (exh. cat. by T. Préaud and A. Faÿ-Hallé, Paris, Grand Pal., 1977–8)
T. Préaud and A. d'Albis: *La Porcelaine de Vincennes* (Paris, 1991)

A. Sassoon: *The J. Paul Getty Museum: Vincennes and Sèvres Porcelain: The Catalogue of the Collection* (Malibu, 1991)

TAMARA PRÉAUD

Vincent, François-André (*b* Paris, 30 Dec 1746; *d* Paris, 3 or 4 Aug 1816). French painter and draughtsman. He was one of the principal innovators in French art of the 1770s and 1780s, in the field of both Neo-classical subjects and themes from national history. Despite the fact that he worked in a variety of styles, his sense of purpose appears to have been coherent at a time of profound change. His stylistic sources lay in the art of Classical antiquity and such masters as Raphael, the great Bolognese painters of the 17th century and Charles Le Brun; yet he also studied reality in a quasi-documentary way. His work, too often confused with that of Jean-Honoré Fragonard, Jacques-Louis David or Louis-Léopold Boilly, is of a high standard, even though the completed paintings do not always uphold the promise of energy of his drawings and oil sketches.

1. TRAINING AND YEARS IN ITALY, TO 1775. He was the son of the miniature painter François-Elie Vincent (1708–90), who was perhaps his first teacher. He then studied in Joseph-Marie Vien's studio at the Académie Royale de Peinture et de Sculpture, Paris. A brilliant pupil, he won the Prix de Rome in 1768 with the painting *Germanicus Quelling a Revolt* (Paris, Ecole N. Sup. B.-A.), which is nearer to François Boucher than to Vien in style. Until July 1771 he was a pupil at the Ecole Royale des Elèves Protégés. Among his pictures of this period is a *Self-portrait in Spanish Costume* (Grasse, Mus. Fragonard), which shows the influence of Fragonard's *figures de fantaisie*.

The time Vincent spent at the Académie de France in Rome, from summer 1771 to autumn 1775, was crucial to his development. He produced many drawings in various styles and techniques of antiquities, landscapes, nudes and after the Old Masters (e.g. Orléans, Mus. B.-A.; Paris, Fond. Custodia, Inst. Néer.; Vienna, Albertina), as well as caricatures of his fellow students (e.g. Montpellier, Mus. Atger; Paris, Carnavalet). Paintings of this period include portraits, both formal (e.g. *Monseigneur Ruffo*, 1775; Naples, Mus. N. S Martino) and informal (e.g. *Jean-Pierre Houel*, 1772; Rouen, Mus. B.-A.). During the months in which Fragonard was in Rome and Naples (December 1773 to June 1774) Vincent produced paintings that are particularly close in style to his: the portrait of Fragonard's travelling companion *Jacques-Onésyme Bergeret de Grancourt* (Besançon, Mus. B.-A. & Archéol.) is an example; the two artists' drawings are also very similar, for example four red chalk drawings, two by Fragonard, two by Vincent, depicting young girls (Besançon, Mus. B.-A. & Archéol. and Bib. Mun.).

2. ANCIEN RÉGIME CAREER, 1775–*c*. 1790. Vincent returned to France in October 1775, staying for a time at Marseille, where he painted a triple portrait of himself with the architect Pierre Rousseau (1751–1810) and the painter van Wyck (1775; Paris, Louvre; see fig.). He was approved (*agréé*) by the Académie Royale in May 1777 on presenting a painting of *St Jerome* (Montpellier, Mus. Fabre), which shows the influence of Guercino. He exhibited 15 paintings at the Salon of that year, including the pendants

Socrates and Alcibiades and *Belisarius* (both Montpellier, Mus. Fabre), Neo-classical themes depicted in a realistic, neo-Bolognese style. His *President Molé and the Insurgents* (Paris, Pal. Bourbon), a large, colourful and dramatic scene from French history, was a tremendous success at the 1779 Salon. In 1782 he was received (*reçu*) as a full member of the Académie Royale with the *Abduction of Oreithyia by Boreas* (Chambéry, Préfecture). He exhibited regularly at the Salon, showing large canvases on religious themes such as *Christ at the Pool of Bethesda* (1783; Rouen, La Madeleine), and in particular exemplary themes from Greek and Roman history, such as the *Intervention of the Sabine Women* (1781; Angers, Mus. B.-A.) and *Paetus and Aria* (1785; Amiens, Mus. Picardie). One of Vincent's recognized specialities both before and after the *Molé* was his 'national' subject-matter, in which he was a precursor of the painters of the Louis-Philippe period. Among his works of this kind is a set of six tapestry cartoons based on the *Life of Henry IV* (1783–7; Fontainebleau, Château, and Paris, Louvre).

3. THE FRENCH REVOLUTION AND LATER CAREER, FROM *c*. 1790. In 1790 Vincent replaced Charles-Nicolas Cochin (ii) as Garde des Dessins du Roi, and in 1792 he became a professor at the Académie Royale just before its dissolution. He was also on the committees set up to organize and administer the new museum established in the Palais du Louvre, but he had to resign in October 1793, shortly after its inauguration. In 1794 his painting *Heroine of St Minier* (untraced) won the second prize in the 'Competition of the year II', designed to commemorate 'the most glorious periods of the French Revolution', and his *William Tell Tipping over Gessler's Boat* (Toulouse, Mus. Augustins), commissioned by the state in 1791, was exhibited at the 1795 Salon. He painted an increasing number of portraits from the 1790s. Sober and warm, they were generally half-lengths, such as that of *Mme Justine Boyer-Fonfrède and her Son* (1796; Paris, Louvre).

Vincent continued to be innovative in his choice of subject-matter: as with the Rousseauist *Agriculture Lesson* (Bordeaux, Mus. B.-A.), shown at the Salon of 1798, which illustrates the father of a family teaching his young son how to steer a plough; and the proto-Romantic *Melancholy* (Malmaison, Château N.), exhibited at the Salon of 1801, which depicts a young girl draped in white, in a cemetery at night. A commission in 1800 for a huge painting of the *Battle of the Pyramids* was never finished, though there are numerous drawings as well as painted sketches in the Musée du Louvre and at the château of Versailles. With a few exceptions—the *Allegory of the Liberation of the Slaves of Algiers* (1806; Kassel, Neue Gal.), for instance—Vincent's last years as a painter were largely devoted to portraiture. Though his health was not good, he spent much time teaching, and his studio was, with those of David and Jean-Baptiste Regnault, the most popular in Paris. He painted family portraits, among them *Jean-Baptiste Boyer-Fonfrède with his Wife and Son* (1801; Versailles, Château), as well as portraits of writers, including *Antoine-Vincent Arnault* (1801) and *François Andrieux* (1815; both Versailles, Château), and of artists, such as that of the engraver *Charles-Clément Bervic* (1813; priv. col.). He continued to produce a large number of drawings

François-André Vincent: *Self-portrait with Pierre Rousseau and van Wyck*, oil on canvas, 810×980 mm, 1775 (Paris, Musée du Louvre)

in varied techniques, including some striking pen caricatures of his colleagues during meetings of the Institut, which he joined in 1795 (e.g. Rouen, Mus. B.-A.). In 1800 he married Adélaïde Labille-Guiard, his lifelong companion, but she died in 1803. He received the Légion d'honneur in 1805.

BIBLIOGRAPHY

H. Lemonnier: 'Notes sur le peintre Vincent', *Gaz. B.-A.*, n. s. 2, xxxii (1904), pp. 287–98

French Painting 1774–1830: The Age of Revolution (exh. cat. by J.-P. Cuzin; Paris, Grand Pal.; Detroit, MI, Inst. A.; New York, Met.; 1975), pp. 661–6

J.-P. Cuzin: 'De Fragonard à Vincent', *Bull. Soc. Hist. A. Fr.* (1981), pp. 103–24

——: *François-André Vincent, 1746–1816*, Cahiers du dessin français, 4 (Paris, 1988)

JEAN-PIERRE CUZIN

Vincent, George (*bapt* Norwich, 27 June 1796; *d* Bath, April 1832). English painter. He was the son of James Vincent, a weaver and shawl manufacturer in Norwich. George Vincent exhibited his first pictures with the Norwich Society of Artists in 1811 and by 1812 had probably received tuition from John Crome, as both his entries that year were described as 'after Crome'. He became the most original of Crome's pupils, first exhibiting at the Royal Academy in 1814. In January 1816 he accompanied John Berney Crome (1794–1842) to Paris and the following year moved to London. He may have visited Scotland in the summer of 1819; he exhibited Scottish views throughout the rest of his career. He was well patronized in London and lionized in Norwich, which he visited for John Crome's funeral in 1821.

In 1822 Vincent married a woman thought at the time to be a wealthy heiress. However, from letters, now in the British Library, where he recounted the story of his later career to his friend William Davey, it appears he was badly in debt, suffered from poor health and as a result of his debts was sent to the Fleet prison in December 1824; he complained, 'I can paint small pictures here, but not any of size'. He was released in February 1827 and continued to exhibit his work in London and Norwich. In 1832 the Society of British Artists exhibited a selection of his works at its winter exhibition. Although the quality of his work was not consistent, a number of his grandest compositions, for example *A Distant View of Pevensey Bay, the Landing Place of King William the Conqueror* (1824; Norwich, Castle Mus.), place him in the forefront of British artists exhibiting in the 1820s.

BIBLIOGRAPHY

W. F. Dickes: *The Norwich School of Painting* (Norwich, 1905)

A. W. Moore: *The Norwich School of Artists* (Norwich, 1985), pp. 33–4, 42–6

For further bibliography *see* NORWICH, §2.

ANDREW W. MOORE

Vincentius [Vincencius; Winceciu] **Cibiniensis** (*fl* 1500–30). Transylvanian painter. His early works were influenced by the style of Lucas Cranach the elder, the sources for which may have reached him through the artists' workshops of the northern Carpathian Mountains. He was mentioned for the first time in 1500 in a list of taxes for the town of Sibiu (now in Romania), being recorded as Vincens Moler. In 1508, with his father-in-law, the sculptor Simon (*fl* 1470–1508), he executed a polyptych for the altar of the church in Jidvei (now in the Evangelical church of Tătirlaua). His later works show influences from Renaissance art in their rich and vivid colouring, careful distribution of light and modelling of nudes with accentuated musculature. These works include an altarpiece of *St Thomas* for the church in Mojna, the central panel being signed and dated 1521. The pinnacle gables (now Cincu, Evangelical Church) show scenes of the *Incredulity of Thomas* and *St Christopher Crossing the River with Christ*; the composition of the latter appears to have been based on engravings by Dürer. The 14 saints on the predella have also been attributed to Vincentius. He also painted the altarpiece of the *Baptism* for the church in Cisnădie (1525), with the predella depicting scenes from the life of *St Severus*, the pinnacle panel of the altar *St Michael Weighing the Soul of a Dying Man* (both Sibiu, Brukenthal Mus.; the central and side panels are in Bratislava, Slovak, N.G.). Attributed to Vincentius too is the *Last Supper* (1525–30; central panel and wings, Mediaş Evangelical Church; predella, Sibiu, Brukenthal Mus.). A date of 1522 and his signature appear on a fragment of the *Resurrection* from a mural painting in the Reformed church at Ocna Sibiului.

BIBLIOGRAPHY

V. Roth: 'Der Hermannstädter Maler Vincencius', *Korrbl. Ver. Siebenbürg. Landesknd.*, xxxvii (1914)

——: 'Siebenbürgische Altäre', *Stud. Dt. Kstgesch.*, 192 (1916), pp. 40–41, 136–53

V. Vătăşianu: *Istoria artei feudale în ţările romăne* [The history of feudal art in the Romanian countries], i (Bucharest, 1959), pp. 797–800

I. Dancu: *Die Kirchenburg in Cisnădie* (Bucharest, 1970), p. 26

E. Antoni: *Die Grosschenker Kirchenburg* (Bucharest, 1982), pp. 30–35

V. Drăguţ: *Arta romănească* [Romanian art], i (Bucharest, 1982), pp. 303–4

SUZANA MORE HEITEL

Vincenzo da Treviso. *See* DESTRE, VINCENZO DALLE.

Vincenzo di Biagio. *See* CATENA, VINCENZO.

Vinci, Leonardo da. *See* LEONARDO DA VINCI.

Vinci, Pierino da. *See* PIERINO DA VINCI.

Vincidor, Tommaso (di Andrea) [il Bologna] (*b* Bologna; *d* Breda, 1534–6). Italian painter. He is first mentioned in a document drafted in Rome in 1517. According to Vasari, he was a pupil of Raphael and was among the artists who worked with him on the frescoes in the Vatican Logge. In 1520 he travelled to Flanders, carrying a letter of recommendation from Pope Leo X, to prepare cartoons for tapestries—to be woven in Brussels—for the Sala di Costantino and the Sala del Concistoro in the Vatican. In Flanders he met Dürer, who mentioned him in his *Journal of Travels in the Low Countries* (travels made between 1520 and 1521). Vincidor made a portrait of Dürer (untraced; copy by Willem van Haecht II, Antwerp, Rubenshuis). On the basis of the written descriptions of the tapestry cartoons for the Sala di Costantino that Vincidor sent Leo X in 1521, the following works have been firmly attributed to him: the drawings of *Playing Putti* (Munich, Staatl. Graph. Samml.) and the *Adoration of the Shepherds with Leo X Kneeling* (Paris, Louvre), in which the figures of the putti, surrounded by animals and festoons of flowers and fruit, are clearly derived from Raphael, although other elements would seem to owe more to Dürer. The *Playing Putti* theme is reproduced in a suite of four prints (1532) by the MASTER OF THE DIE (*see* MASTERS, ANONYMOUS, AND MONOGRAMMISTS, §I). Vincidor's hand has been identified in the panel (transferred to canvas) of the *Circumcision* (Paris, Louvre) and in some of the frescoed scenes in the Vatican Logge, including the *Meeting of Jacob and Rachel*. Some fragments of tapestry cartoons for the Sala del Concistoro have also been attributed to Vincidor, including those depicting the *Feet and Head of a Warrior* and a *Head of a Woman* (Oxford, Ashmolean). He is mentioned in 1534 in a register of the Castle of Breda, where he was working for Hendrik III of Nassau-Breda. According to the same account he was dead by 1536.

BIBLIOGRAPHY

F. Filippini: 'Tommaso Vincidor da Bologna, scolaro di Raffaello e amico del Dürer', *Boll. A.*, viii/7 (1929), pp. 309–24

N. Dacos: 'Tommaso Vincidor: Un Elève de Raphaël aux Pays-Bas', *Relations artistiques entre Pays-Bas et l'Italie à la Renaissance: Etudes dédiées à Suzanne Sulzberger* (Brussels and Rome, 1980), pp. 61–99 [with full bibliog.]

ANNA MARIA FERRARI

Vinckboons [Vingboons]. Dutch family of artists of Flemish origin. Philip Vinckboons (*d* 1601) painted watercolours on canvas (*waterschilderijen*)—an art form practised mainly in Mechelen, which he taught to his son (1) David Vinckboons, later active as a painter, draughtsman and printmaker. The Vinckboons household moved to Antwerp *c.* 1580. The religious wars in the southern Netherlands probably occasioned their subsequent move to Middelburg *c.* 1586 and finally to Amsterdam, where Philip was registered as a citizen in 1591. Five of David's sons were artists, the most important being (2) Philips Vingboons, an architect renowned for his work in and around Amsterdam, where he built houses for affluent merchants and members of the patrician class. Johannes Vingboons (1616/17–1670) was a mapmaker and engraver who worked with his brother Philips on the two volumes illustrating Philips's architectural designs. Justus Vingboons (1620/21–1698) was also an architect, whose outstanding work was the monumental double house (1660–62) in Amsterdam for the brothers Louys and Hendrick Trip, a magnificent example of Dutch Classicism in the style of Jacob van Campen.

(1) David Vinckboons (*b* Mechelen, 1576; *d* Amsterdam, before 12 Jan 1633). Painter, draughtsman and printmaker. He does not appear to have had any teacher

David Vinckboons: *Jew's Harp Seller*, oil on panel, 302×420 mm, 1614 (Brussels, Musée d'Art Ancien)

other than his father. Although the influence of Gillis van Coninxloo III (who lived in Amsterdam from 1595) is unmistakable in his work, van Mander mentioned nothing about a definite period as a pupil. In 1602 David Vinckboons married Agneta van Loon, daughter of a notary from Leeuwarden; they had ten children. In 1611 David bought a house on the Antoniebreestraat in Amsterdam. His widow, who appeared before the Amsterdam orphanage committee on 12 January 1633, and some of his children continued to live there after his death.

1. PAINTINGS. David Vinckboons's paintings comprise landscapes, often with many small figures, peasant scenes, courtly companies, biblical scenes with numerous small figures and a few history pieces with large figures. The earliest dated work is from 1602, the latest from 1629. In his early wooded landscapes (e.g. *Wood with Hunting Scene*, 1602; ex-E. Perman priv. col., Stockholm, see Gossens, 1954, p. 21), Vinckboons was completely inspired by van Coninxloo's example. In a large panel such as the *Flemish Kermis* (1610; Brussels, Mus. A. Anc.) the high horizon and accumulation of architectural elements also recall the work of Pieter Bruegel the elder and Hans Bol. Similarly unimaginable without Bruegel's example are Vinckboons's fantastic landscapes with meadows, peopled by innumerable tiny figures and representing a biblical episode (e.g. the *Large Crucifixion*, 1611; Munich, Alte. Pin.). He also continued Bruegel's tradition of peasant

scenes (e.g. the *Jew's Harp Seller*, 1614; Brussels, Mus. A. Anc.; see fig.). Such paintings form an important link between the work of Bruegel and that of such Dutch artists as Adriaen and Isaack van Ostade. Vinckboons made an entirely personal contribution to the peasant genre with his series entitled *Peasant Sorrows* (various series are known, not only as paintings and drawings but also as prints). These portray the tense relationship between the local people and the Spanish soldiers during the Revolt of the Netherlands, particularly in the period preceding the Twelve-Year Truce (1609–21). Such scenes were probably regarded as counterparts to the many pamphlets that appeared concerning the forthcoming Truce. Of greater significance for the development of Dutch painting in the first decades of the 17th century, however, are Vinckboons's paintings of fashionably attired groups entertaining themselves with food, drink and flirtation in country-house landscapes (e.g. *Merry Company*, c. 1610; Amsterdam, Rijksmuseum). Country-house parties by Willem Buytewech, Esaias van de Velde and Dirck Hals were directly influenced by Vinckboons's models. Some large figural history-pieces occupy a separate place in Vinckboons's oeuvre that is difficult to define (e.g. *Hercules, Nessus and Deianeira*, 1612; Vienna, Ksthist. Mus.).

2. DRAWINGS AND PRINTS. Vinckboons's drawings are more numerous than his paintings. Wegner and Pée catalogued 83 autograph drawings, and the total number

is now estimated at *c.* 90. There must originally have been many more, given the many engravings after lost designs by Vinckboons. Nearly all the drawings are executed in pen and brown ink with a wash of grey, brown and sometimes yellow, green and blue. An exception is the *Jew's Harp Seller* (*c.* 1608; Amsterdam, Rijksmus.), an earlier version of the painted composition; it is drawn in pen and ink only, in a style that imitates an engraving. Vinckboons's earliest dated drawing is a large *Landscape with the Healing of the Blind* (1601; Amsterdam, Rijksmus.), which belongs to a group of six landscapes with biblical subjects, all engraved by Johannes van Londerseel. The *Large Kermis* (1602; Copenhagen, Stat. Mus. Kst, engraved by Nicolaes de Bruyn and later by Boetius Bolswert) and the *Party in a Park* (*c.* 1602–4; USA, priv. col.; engraved by de Bruyn) are among the most spectacular of the young Vinckboons's drawings. One subject to which he repeatedly turned in his drawings is that of the *Birdsnester* (e.g. *c.* 1604–6, Amsterdam, Rijksmus.; *c.* 1606–7, Brussels, Bib. Royale Albert 1er; *c.* 1607–8, Stuttgart, Staatsgal.), derived from Pieter Bruegel's model. Vinckboons also supplied drawings for print series, such as the four drawings of the *Story of the Prodigal Son* (London, BM; engraved by Claes Jansz. Visscher I, 1608) and the twelve *Hunting Scenes* (Berlin, Kupferstichkab.; engraved by Pieter Serwouters (1586–1657) and Visscher in 1612). Vinckboons also executed designs for decorations on a number of maps, including those for world maps by Willem Jansz. Blaeu (1605), Petrus Planicus (1607) and Jodocus Hondius I (*c.* 1611). Vinckboons designed many book illustrations although none of the drawings survives; there are prints after his drawings in such works as Daniel Hensius's *Nederduytsche poemata* (1616), J. van Heemskerck's *Ovidius' minne-kunst, gepast op d' Amsterdamsc[h]e vrijagien met noch andere minne-dichten ende mengel-dichten* (1622) and G. A. Bredero's *Boertigh, Amoreus, en aendachtig grood lied-boeck* ('Amorous, humorous and religious songbook'; 1622).

Vinckboons also designed one of the stained-glass windows in Amsterdam's Zuiderkerk (removed before 1658), for which the drawing of *Moses and the Burning Bush*, possibly dating from *c.* 1609, survives (Amsterdam, Rijksmus.). Two drawings assumed to be designs for wall hangings are the *Continence of Scipio* (Windsor Castle, Berks, Royal Lib.) and *Quintus Fabius Cunctator Meeting his Son on Foot* (*c.* 1609–10; left half, New York, Pierpont Morgan Lib., right half, Amsterdam, Rijksmus.). After *c.* 1610 Vinckboons's drawing style became looser, the design less rigid and the characterization more spirited. Far fewer works are preserved from the years after 1610; the *Triumph of Frederick Henry* (*c.* 1629; New York, Met.; print by an unknown engraver) is typical of his later style. No Dutch artist of the early 17th century had as many drawings made into prints as David Vinckboons. Apart from the artists already named, Simon Frisius, Hessel Gerritsz. (1581–1632), Jacob Matham, Salomon Savery (1594–1665) and Jan van de Velde II engraved after his designs. Vinckboons executed a few prints himself, only three of which are known: the *Annunciation to the Shepherds* (drawing, 1604; Amsterdam, Rijksmus.), a *Beggar Woman with Two Children* (1604) and the *Bagpipe-player with a Child under a Tree* (1606).

BIBLIOGRAPHY
Hollstein: *Dut. & Flem.;* Thieme–Becker
K. van Mander: *Schilder-boeck* ([1603]–1604), fols 299*r–v*
I. H. van Eeghen: 'De familie Vinckboons–Vingboons', *Oud-Holland*, lxvii (1952), pp. 217–32
K. Gossens: *David Vinckboons* (Antwerp and The Hague, 1954/*R* Soest, 1977)
——: 'Nog meer over David Vinckboons', *Jb.: Kon. Mus. S. Kst.* (1966), pp. 59–106
W. Wegner and H. Pée: 'Die Zeichnungen des David Vinckboons', *Münch. Jb. Bild. Kst.*, n. s. 2, xxxi (1980), pp. 35–128
Printmaking in the Age of Rembrandt (exh. cat. by C. S. Ackley, Boston, MA, Mus. F.A.; St Louis, MO, A. Mus.; 1980–81), pp. 39–41
The Age of Bruegel: Netherlandish Drawings in the Sixteenth Century (exh. cat. by J. O. Hand and others, Washington, DC, N.G.A.; New York, Pierpont Morgan Lib.; 1986–7), pp. 298–302
M. Schapelhouman: *Netherlandish Drawings circa 1600 in the Rijksmuseum* (The Hague, 1987), pp. 152–71
S. K. Bennett: 'Drawings by David Vinckboons as Models for Ornamenting Bible Maps', *Hoogsteder–Naumann Mercury*, x (1989), pp. 15–25
J. F. Heijbroek and M. Schapelhouman, eds: *Kunst in kaart: Decoratieve aspecten van de cartografie* (Utrecht, 1989), pp. 65–70
J. E. Huisken and F. Lammertse, eds: *Het kunstbedrijf van de familie Vingboons* (Maarssen, 1989)
S. K. Bennett: *Art on Netherlandish Maps, 1585–1685: Themes and Sources* (diss., Baltimore, MD, Johns Hopkins U., 1990), pp. 192–211
MARIJN SCHAPELHOUMAN

(2) Philips Vingboons (*b* Amsterdam, 1607–8; *d* Amsterdam, 1678). Architect, son of (1) David Vinckboons. He probably trained as a painter and engraver in his father's studio, but nothing is known about his architectural training. During his career, the greater part of Vingboons's commissions came from the wealthy Roman Catholic merchants of Amsterdam, who asked him to design their town and country residences. Vingboons's marriage in 1645 into a distinguished Catholic family may have contributed to an increase in these commissions. In Amsterdam, his designs for houses were limited by the narrow canal-side sites, which measured approximately 7.35×28.3 m, and by the necessity for tall, narrow façades. Vingboons experimented with the use of a strictly classical vocabulary of form on narrow as well as broad façades. In a few cases he dropped the use of pilasters for articulation and restricted himself to pediments above the windows and at the top. When he did use pilasters, he often applied a tier to each storey but in other cases ran the pilasters all the way up. Flat and rusticated façades also occur in a number of his designs but are found in only a few of his executed works.

Vingboons's first canal house was at Herengracht 168 (1638; now Amsterdam, Theatmus.), where he introduced a new solution for the treatment of a narrow façade: the problem of how to incorporate classical architectural features into a compressed façade with a triangular top had existed in the Netherlands since the beginning of the Renaissance. Vingboons's solution was to place a pediment on a raised central bay, with a scroll or volute capping the bay on either side. This is called a *halsgevel* or neck façade (*see* GABLE, DECORATIVE). Apart from pediments over the windows (later removed), he kept the façade completely flat. Vingboons's façade at the house for Daniel Soyhier (1639; see fig.) is handled in a more sculptural way: the side bays are framed by two tiers of pilasters and crowned with a pediment. At the top of the elevation a subdivision is contrived by introducing a smaller step at the base of the neck. This is called a raised neck façade.

Philips Vingboons: façade of the Daniel Soyhier House, Amsterdam, 1639; from his *Gronden en afbeeldsels* (1688) (Amsterdam, Rijksmuseum), pl. 18

Vingboons was inspired by the older tradition of the stepped gable with scrollwork in the style of Hendrick de Keyser I. Scrollwork reappears on the façade of the Soyhier House in the form of stone scrolls. The symmetry of this façade is emphasized by the centrally placed entrance, which was later moved to the right-hand bay. With broader façades Vingboons often used the aedicula motif on the top storey. It is a characteristic feature of his style that this classical detail should be regarded only as decoration, and, although prominently placed, it does not coincide with a main part of the interior. In other cases the pediment of

this central part was replaced by a balustrade. Both types also appear in the designs for country houses.

Vingboons also designed both town and country residences in the style of the Mauritshuis in The Hague (for illustration *see* CAMPEN, JACOB VAN); his finest examples of this austere pilaster style with a pediment over the central bay are the house for Ioan Poppen (Amsterdam, 1642) and a design (*c.* 1640; unexecuted) for Vredenburgh Manor in the Beemster. Both Vingboons and Pieter Post were invited by the patron Frederick Alewijn to submit plans for Vredenburgh, and although Post's work was selected, he probably made use of one of the other architect's designs. In his later work, Vingboons created façades in a more sober style. For example, the house for Joseph Deutz (Amsterdam, 1672) is horizontally grooved, and the ornamentation is restricted to sculptural decoration on the balcony above the entrance. The theme of an austere, soberly decorated façade was subsequently developed further in the Netherlands by Adriaen Dorsman. Vingboons's scheme (*c.* 1643) for Amsterdam Town Hall is worth special mention. The design for the façade is hardly controlled or regulated; most notable are the domed corner pavilions and the four massive pilasters of the central bay, crowned with a pediment. The plan is one of the first monumental and symmetrical designs in the northern Netherlands. The rooms are grouped around a gallery surrounding a courtyard. These three motifs—a gallery, a courtyard and a hall on the central axis—were adopted by Jacob van Campen, whose design of *c.* 1648 was implemented (*see* TOWN HALL, fig. 3). One of the most important architects during the period of Dutch classicism, Vingboons continues to be remembered above all for the façade type he created, examples of which can be found not only in Amsterdam but also in many other parts of the Netherlands (e.g. Dordrecht, Middelburg, Kampen, Zwolle and Deventer). He is also known for the two volumes of plans and engravings of his designs and was the first Dutch architect to publish his own work.

WRITINGS

Gronden en afbeeldsels der voornaemste gebouwen von alle die Philips Vingboons geoordinet heeft [Plans and illustrations of the most important buildings designed by Philips Vingboons], 2 vols (Amsterdam, 1648–74/R 1674–1715)

BIBLIOGRAPHY

Macmillan Enc. Architects; Thieme–Becker

F. A. J. Vermeulen: *Handboek tot de geschiedenis der Nederlandsche bouwkunst* [History of Dutch architecture], iii (The Hague, 1941)

I. H. van Eeghen: 'De familie Vinckboons—Vingboons', *Oud-Holland*, lxvii (1952), pp. 217–32

S. J. Fockema Andreae and others: *Duizend jaar bouwen in Nederland* [Thousand years of Dutch architecture], ii (Amsterdam, 1957)

W. Kuyper: *Dutch Classicist Architecture* (Delft, 1980)

R. Meischke and H. E. Reeser: *Het Trippenhuis te Amsterdam* [The Trippenhuis in Amsterdam] (Amsterdam, 1983)

PAUL H. REM

Vinckenbrinck, Albert Jansz. (*b* Spaarndam, *c.* 1604; *d* Amsterdam, after 20 Aug 1664, before 12 Feb 1665). Dutch sculptor. He was probably apprenticed to his father, Jan Albertsz. Vinckenbrinck, a cabinetmaker. Most of his surviving works are small objects in box-wood, though he is said also to have worked in mother-of-pearl and ivory. His most famous work is the richly decorated oak pulpit (*c.* 1646–9) in the Nieuwe Kerk in Amsterdam. The high reliefs on the six sides of the pulpit represent the *Acts of Mercy*: these panels are flanked by personifications of the *Virtues*. The pulpit is signed and dated in a number of places. For the Oude Doolhof (Old Labyrinth) in Amsterdam he produced a *David and Goliath with Shield-bearer* (*c.* 1648; Amsterdam, Hist. Mus.) and a fountain with the figure of *Bacchus*; the latter is known only from a print by Pieter Holsteyn II (*c.* 1614–83).

Vinckenbrinck's small pieces in box-wood include *Adam and Eve* (Hamburg, Mus. Kst & Gew.); the *Rat-poison Seller* (Amsterdam, Rijksmus.); two skulls (Amsterdam, Rijksmus.; Amsterdam, Hist. Mus.); three reliefs depicting *Job on the Dungheap* (e.g. Amsterdam, Rijksmus.; Leiden, Stedel. Mus. Lakenhal; priv. col.); and a *Crucifixion* (sold London, Christie's, 4 July 1989, lot 60). The J. Paul Getty Museum, Malibu, CA, has three reliefs in fruit-wood on an Augsburg cabinet: two ovals depicting *Cleopatra* and *Lucretia* and a small door with *Christ and the Woman of Samaria*. Vinckenbrinck produced portrait medallions of an *Unknown Man* (Amsterdam, Rijksmus.; Berlin, Bodemus.; Paris, Louvre) and *Philip the Good* (Amsterdam, Hist. Mus.). All these works are marked with his monogram, AVB or ALVB. His famous box-wood apple opens to show the *Seven Acts of Mercy* (sold Cologne, Lempertsz, 28 Sept 1941, lot 586, fig. 586). Vinckenbrinck also made a small oak copy (Amsterdam, Rijksmus.) of Hendrik de Keyser I's bronze statue of *Erasmus* (Rotterdam, Grote Kerkplein). Two terracotta figures, representing a *Hurdy-gurdy Player* and a *Beggar Woman with Two Children* (both Loosdrecht, Kasteel-Mus. Sypesteyn), after prints by Jacques Callot, bear the monogram AV but may have been made by Albert's son, Abraham Vinckenbrinck (1639–86); two other sons, Jan Vinckenbrinck (*b* 1631) and Hendrik Vinckenbrinck, also became sculptors. Albert Jansz. possibly also designed the title-page for Petrus Wittewrongel's *Oeconomia Christiana ofte Christelicke Huyshoudinge* (Amsterdam, 1661). Numerous works by him are detailed in an inventory drawn up after his death. He is known primarily for his detailed and intricately cut relief; larger figures by his hand tend to be somewhat clumsy. He is depicted in a print by Pieter Holsteyn II (Amsterdam, Rijksmus.; Hollstein: *Dut. & Flem.*, no. 30).

BIBLIOGRAPHY
D. Franken Dan: 'Albert Jansz. Vinckenbrinck', *Oud-Holland*, v (1887), pp. 73–92
T. H. Lunsiningh Scheurleer: 'Nieuws over den Amsterdamschen beeldhouwer Albert Vinckenbrinck', *Oudhdkend. Jb.*, xiii (1946), pp. 29–33
J. Leuwenberg and W. Halsema-Kubes: *Beeldhouwkunst in het Rijksmuseum: Catalogus* (The Hague and Amsterdam, 1973), pp. 192–5, 462
W. Halsema-Kubes: 'Kleinplastiek van Albert Jansz. Vinckenbrinck', *Bull. Rijksmus.*, xxxix (1991), pp. 414–25

WILHELMINA HALSEMA-KUBES

Vinçotte, Thomas (*b* Borgerhout [now in Antwerp], 8 Jan 1850; *d* Brussels, 25 March 1925). Belgian sculptor. He studied under Guillaume Geefs and Louis-Eugène Simonis in Brussels between 1866 and 1874, and then under Pierre-Jules Cavelier in Paris, where he produced his first sculpture, *Giotto* (Brussels, Mus. A. Mod.). In 1877 he went to Florence for two years. On his return to Belgium, he rapidly received many official commissions, including two allegorical groups for the railway station at Leuven and the statue of the *Surgeon Palfijn* in Kortrijk.

After 1881, as sculptor to the court, he was commissioned to make many portrait busts in marble, including those of *Leopold II* and *Maria-Henrietta* (both 1881; Brussels, Mus. A. Mod.), which in their classical treatment are reminiscent of Italian Renaissance sculpture.

Vinçotte executed several open-air monuments to specific individuals, such as the monument to the sculptor *Gilles Lambert Godecharle* (1881), erected in the Parc-Royal in Brussels, and the statue of the Flemish patriot *François Agneessens* (1889) in the Place Agneessens, Brussels. In more ambitious works, Vinçotte revealed his skill in manipulating contrasts in size and shape within a sculpted group; this is especially clear in the bronze group of the *Horse-tamer* (1885) in the Avenue Emile de Mot, Brussels. Vinçotte's skill in more restrained works is seen in the marble low relief *Music* (1880), which he carved for the façade of the Musée d'Art Ancien, and in *Belgium between Commerce and Industry* (1910) for the pediment of the Palais-Royal, both in Brussels. At the end of his career, in collaboration with Jules Lagae (1862–1931), he executed the *Quadriga* above the triumphal arch in the Palais du Cinquantenaire, Brussels.

BIBLIOGRAPHY
BNB
P. Lambotte and A. Goffin: *Thomas Vinçotte et son oeuvre* (Brussels, 1912)
M. Devigne: *Thomas Vinçotte: Les Grands Belges* (Turnhout, 1919)
H. Lettens: 'Vinçotte, Thomas', *La Sculpture belge au 19ème siècle* (exh. cat., Brussels, Gén. de Banque, 1990), pp. 605–9

RICHARD KERREMANS

Vindobona. *See* VIENNA.

Vingles, Jean de (*b* Lyon, 1498; *d* ?France, *c.* 1552). French printmaker. He was the son of a Lyonnais printer and an important illustrator and designer of engraved decoration. He was active throughout Spain from 1534, when his signature I. D. V. began to appear on woodcuts the style of which was still imbued with the Gothic tradition of Provence. In 1547 in Saragossa he signed a contract with the calligrapher and writer Juan de Iciar, for whom he illustrated the frontispieces of several works including *Recopilación intitulada, orthographia practica* (Saragossa, 1548), which contains a fine portrait of the author. They also collaborated on *Arte subtilisima por la qual se enseña a escrivir perfectamente* (Saragossa, 1550). From 1552 he was active in Pau in the south of France. His engravings for the borders of books, frontispieces and coats of arms were very popular and his work was widely disseminated and used in the mid-16th century. His style was Italianate rather than Germanic, but he made use of models by Holbein in his designs for initial letters.

BIBLIOGRAPHY
G. K. Nagler: *Die Monogrammisten und diejenigen . . .* (Munich, 1858–79)
H. Thomas: *Juan de Vingles, ilustrador de libros del siglo XVI* (Valencia, 1949)
J. Ainaud de Lasarte: 'Grabado', *A. Hisp.*, xviii, (Madrid, 1958), pp. 243–320
A. Gallego: *Historia del grabado en España* (Madrid, 1979), pp. 95–9
B. Garcia Vega: *El grabado del libro español: siglos XV–XVI–XVII* (Valladolid, 1984)

BLANCA GARCÍA VEGA

XX, Les [Vingt, Les; Fr.: 'The Twenty']. Belgian exhibition society. It was founded on 28 October 1883 in Brussels and held annual shows there between 1884 and

1893. The group was formed by 11 artists dissatisfied with the conservative policies of the organization L'Essor: Frantz Charlet (*b* 1862), Paul Dubois (ii), James Ensor, Alfred William Finch, Charles Goethals (?1853–85), Fernand Khnopff, Darío de Regoyos, Théo Van Rysselberghe, Willy Schlobach (*b* 1864), Guillaume Van Strydonck (1861–1937) and Rodolphe Wytsman (1860–1927). They invited an additional nine members—Achille Chainaye (1862–1915), Jean Delvin (*b* 1853), Jef Lambeaux, Périclès Pantazis, Frans Simons (1855–1919), Gustave Vanaise (1854–1902), Piet Verhaert (1852–1908), Théodore Verstraete (1850–1907) and Guillaume Vogels—thereby fixing their number at 20. In contrast to L'Essor, Les XX had neither a president nor governing committee but was run by its secretary, Octave Maus, who organized the exhibitions. Maus, in turn, secured the aid of his friend, fellow lawyer and co-founder of the Belgian periodical *L'Art moderne* (1881–1914), Edmond Picard (1836–1924). Through Picard, *L'Art moderne* provided Les XX with a strong theoretical defence against hostile critics and members of the public attending the Salon. Maus and Picard identified the Academy and the Salon system as their principal foes and symbols of the status quo. With his inflammatory rhetoric, Picard intentionally created enemies both within and ouside Les XX. His attacks on established tradition drew the hostility of critics, and the resulting hostile press frightened some members of the society. By 1887 conservative artists Lambeaux, Verhaert, Verstraete, Simons, Delvin and Vanaise had fled from Les XX, some under direct pressure from Maus and Picard. Les XX replaced them with members more sympathetic to its cause: Anna Boch (1848–1926), Guillaume Charlier, Henry De Groux, Georges Lemmen, George Minne, Robert Picard (*b* 1870), Auguste Rodin, Félicien Rops, Paul Signac, Jan Toorop, Henry Van de Velde and Isidore Verheyden. Over its ten-year history Les XX actually included 32 members.

From the outset, Les XX brought an international dimension to its exhibitions by inviting non-Belgians to exhibit. With the help of Van Rysselberghe and the writer and critic Emile Verhaeren, Maus sought out important emerging artists from Europe and the USA: Whistler, Sargent, Odilon Redon, Cézanne, Monet, Renoir, Toulouse-Lautrec, Seurat, Signac, Rodin and Walter Crane were among those invited. In all, 126 *invités* showed at Les XX's exhibitions, an eclectic group that reflected various styles including Realism, Impressionism, Neo-Impressionism, Symbolism, Art Nouveau and, in the final years, the growing interest in the decorative arts. A healthy interaction between original members and those invited to exhibit often resulted in close ties between avant-garde circles in Brussels, London and Paris. The repeated participation of Seurat and his circle at Les XX led to the creation of a Belgian Neo-Impressionist school. The early influence of William Morris and Walter Crane stimulated a strong Belgian response to the English Arts and Crafts Movement. Filtered through Finch, Lemmen and Van de Velde, this in turn swept through Paris and, eventually, Austria and Germany. Khnopff, Xavier Mellery, Minne, Rops and Toorop developed a local response to French Symbolism. Les XX emphasized all the arts, including music and literature. It strove to present a unified avant-garde front

by hosting concerts of the latest music of Claude Debussy, Ernest Chausson and Gabriel Fauré, and lectures by Stéphane Mallarmé, Théodore de Wyzewa and Paul Verlaine. To underline this artistic interrelationship, these events were held during the exhibitions in the Palais des Beaux-Arts, Brussels. After ten years of successfully defending and defining the avant-garde in Europe, Les XX voted for its own dissolution. It gave way to the LIBRE ESTHÉTIQUE, the brainchild of Maus, who continued his role as impresario and defender of a jury-free, independent society that offered an alternative to the academic Salon. The example of Les XX encouraged similar experiments outside Belgium and was a model for a number of 20th-century art movements. Les XXX in Paris, Die XI in Berlin and the Vienna Secession each consciously adopted some of Les XX's policies.

BIBLIOGRAPHY

M. O. Maus: *Trente années de lutte pour l'art* (Brussels, 1926/*R* 1980)
Le Groupe des XX et son temps (exh. cat. by F.-C. Legrand, Brussels, Mus. Royaux B.-A., 1962)
J. Block: 'Les XX: Forum of the Avant-garde', *Belgian Art, 1880–1914* (exh. cat., New York, Brooklyn Mus., 1980), pp. 17–40
Les XX: Catalogue des dix expositions annuelles (Brussels, 1981) [reprint of original cats 1884–93]
J. Block: 'What's in a Name? The Origins of "Les XX"', *Mus. Royaux B.-A. Belgique: Bull.*, n.s., xxx–xxxiii/1–3 (1981–4), pp. 135–42
——: *Les XX and Belgian Avant-gardism, 1868–1894* (Ann Arbor, 1984)
S. Canning: *Le Cercle des XX* (Antwerp, 1989)
Les XX and the Belgian Avant-garde: Prints, Drawings and Books, ca. 1890 (exh. cat., ed. S. H. Goddard; Lawrence, U. KS, Spencer Mus. A., 1992) [essays by J. Block and others]
J. Block: 'Les XX and La Libre Esthétique: Belgium's Laboratories for New Ideas', *Impressionism to Symbolism: The Belgian Avant-garde, 1880–1900* (exh. cat., London, RA, 1994)

JANE BLOCK

Viniziano, Sebastiano. *See* SEBASTIANO DEL PIOMBO.

Vinkeles, Reinier (*b* Amsterdam, 12 Jan 1741; *d* Amsterdam, 30 Jan 1816). Dutch draughtsman and engraver. He studied for some ten years with Jan Punt. Vinkeles was a member of four foreign academies and joined the Amsterdam Stadstekenacademie (City Drawing School) in 1762, becoming one of its directors as early as 1765. The same year he travelled to Brabant with Jurriaan Andriessen and Izaak Schmidt. In 1770 Vinkeles left for Paris, where he studied with Jacques-Philippe Lebas and also met the Dutch artists Hermanus Numan and Izaak de Wit (1744–1809). A year later, Vinkeles was back in Amsterdam, where he worked on innumerable stage and book illustrations, historical prints, topographical scenes (e.g. *Corner House at Lime Market*, 1765; Amsterdam, Gemeente Archf), engraved portraits, copies after paintings etc. The same year, he was invited by Catherine the Great of Russia to become director of the St Petersburg Academy of Arts but refused. Vinkeles's oeuvre is estimated at over 3000 prints; while his enormous productivity may sometimes have led to superficiality, he was able, at his best (during the 1770s and 1780s), to maintain great spontaneity in his work. Among his best-known works are the engravings after well-known Old Masters for the *Vignettes of Theatre Poetry* by N. S. Winter and L. W. van Merken (1774, 1776).

Vinkeles had a busy studio, which employed among others his sons Abraham Vinkeles (1790–after 1864) and

Johannes Vinkeles (1783–1803). His most important students were Jacob Ernst Marcus, Abraham Hulk (1751–1817), Jacobus Millies (1767–1813) and Daniël Vrijdag (1765–1822).

BIBLIOGRAPHY

J. Knoef: 'Het grafisch oeuvre van Reinier Vinkeles', *Elsevier's Geillus. Mdschr.*, xliii (1933), pp. 374–83
Dutch Masterpieces from the Eighteenth Century: Paintings and Drawings, 1700–1800 (exh. cat. by E. R. Mandle and J. W. Niemeijer, Minneapolis, MN, Inst. A.; Toledo, OH, Mus. A.; Philadelphia, PA, Mus. A.; 1971–2), pp. 108–9
G. Jansen: 'De brieven van Reinier Vinkeles aan Volkert van der Plaats', *Amstelodamum*, lxxvii (1985), pp. 107–21
Hollandse aquarellen uit de 18de eeuw (exh. cat. by J. W. Niemeijer, Amsterdam, Rijksmus., 1990–91), pp. 152–3

TON GEERTS

Vinne, van der. Dutch family of artists. They were Mennonites from Haarlem, and about ten members of the family practised as artists during the 17th and 18th centuries. Some members of the family were also employed in the manufacture and sale of textiles. (1) Vincent Laurensz. van der Vinne is best known for his travel diaries and sketches. It is possible that some of the drawings attributed to him are by his son Laurens Vincentsz. van der Vinne (1658–1729), whose brothers (2) Jan Vincentsz. van der Vinne and Izaak Vincentsz. van der Vinne (1665–1740) were also artists. Three of Laurens's children worked as painters and engravers: Vincent Laurensz. van der Vinne (1686–1742), Jacob Laurensz. van der Vinne (1688–1737) and Jan Laurensz. van der Vinne (1699–1753). In the next generation Jacob's son Laurens Jacobsz. van der Vinne (1712–42) became a flower painter, and two of Jan's children, Jan Jansz. van der Vinne (1734–1805) and Vincent Jansz. van der Vinne (1736–1811), seem to have been the last artists active in the family.

(1) Vincent Laurensz. van der Vinne (*b* Haarlem, 11 Oct 1628; *d* Haarlem, 26 July 1702). Painter and draughtsman. After initial training at a weaving mill, he spent nine months when he was 18 as the pupil of Frans Hals (who later painted his portrait *c*. 1655–60; Toronto, A.G. Ont.), and in 1649 he joined the Haarlem Guild of St Luke. From 1652 to 1655 van der Vinne travelled through Germany, Switzerland and France, accompanied some of the time by Guillam Dubois (*c*. 1610–80), Dirck Helmbreker and Cornelis Bega. During the trip van der Vinne kept an illustrated diary of his travels and on his return worked this up in a second volume, copying his drawings and adding topographical prints by Matthäus Merian the elder and Jean Boisseau. He also filled a sketchbook with Rhineland landscapes (Haarlem, Gemeentearchf). The year after he returned from this trip he married Anneke Jansdr de Gaver (*d* Feb 1668), and six months after her death he married Catalijntje Boekaert. Besides the drawings from his 1652–5 travels, he produced a number of townscapes in pen and ink with grey wash, some on a journey through the Netherlands in 1680. He also made drawings in black and red chalk depicting the city gates of Haarlem and ruins found in the surrounding countryside. He received commissions for ceiling paintings, signboards, landscapes, portraits and other works, but his known painted work is confined to a few *vanitas* still-lifes (e.g.

Vanitas Still-life with a Print of Charles I of England, after 1649; Paris, Louvre).

UNPUBLISHED SOURCES

Haarlem, Gemeentearchf, Stell. 21D/171–2 and Stell. 21D/231 [van der Vinne's MS. travel diaries and Rhineland sketchbook]

BIBLIOGRAPHY

E. Caljé-van den Berg: 'Haarlemse stadspoorten door Vincent Jansz. van der Vinne', *Miscellanea I. Q. van Regteren Altena* (Amsterdam, 1969), pp. 162–3
——: 'Vincent van der Vinnes Eindrücke in Köln, 1652–1653', *Wallraf-Richartz-Jb.*, xxxv (1973), pp. 281–308
B. C. Sliggers: *Dagelijckse aentekeningen van Vincent Laurensz. van der Vinne: Reisjournaal van een Haarlems schilder, 1652–1655* [Daily notes by Vincent Laurensz. van der Vinne: the travel diary of a Haarlem painter, 1652–1655] (Haarlem, 1979)
B. C. Sliggers and D. F. Goudriaan: 'De Haarlemse kunstenaars-familie van der Vinne', *Jb. Cent. Bureau. Geneal.*, xli (1987), pp. 149–207

B. C. SLIGGERS

(2) Jan Vincentsz. van der Vinne [des Nageoires] (*b* Haarlem, 3 Feb 1663; *d* Haarlem, 1 March 1721). Painter, draughtsman and etcher, son of (1) Vincent Laurensz. van der Vinne. He trained under his father and Jan van Huchtenburg (1647–1733). In 1686 he travelled to England, where he produced drawings as well as paintings in the manner of van Huchtenburg that were much sought after. While there, he was friendly with the painter Jan Wyck. In 1688 Jan van der Vinne returned to Haarlem, where he lived with his brother Izaak, an engraver and book dealer. On his return Jan was principally engaged in the manufacture of silks, although he continued to paint, draw and etch. He was also active as a dealer.

The subjects of Jan's drawings include views of identifiable places in England and landscapes with hunting scenes or travellers on foot or on horseback. The majority depict small, doll-like figures among stylized clumps of trees set against a hilly background. Examples can be found in museums in Amsterdam (Rijksmus.), Brussels (Mus. A. Anc.), Haarlem (Teylers Mus.), Hamburg (Ksthalle), Leiden (Rijksuniv., Prentenkab.), London (BM and Courtauld Inst. Gals), Paris (Ecole N. B.-A.) and Rotterdam (Mus. Boymans–van Beuningen), among others.

The current whereabouts of any of his paintings are not known, although a number of works are described and illustrated in the literature: Bryan noted that 'Wainscot panels by him are occasionally to be found in old houses'; Terey discussed a *Deer Hunt* (ex-Friedrich priv. col., Budapest) and a *Rest from the Hunt* (ex-Hermitage, St Petersburg); and a *Departure for the Hunt* was formerly on the London art market (ex-Terry Engell Gal., 1963, no. 36). All three paintings are apparently signed and measure *c*. 380×490 mm. A signed *Hunting Scene* with a distant view of Windsor Castle, possibly one of a pair, was once in Packington Hall, Warwicks. This material suggests that the artist's paintings share the same subject-matter as his drawings. Van der Vinne is occasionally called 'des Nageoires', on account of the signature on his series of etched *Views of Savoy*. In style and subject, these are comparable to his other work, but there is no evidence that he ever visited Savoy.

BIBLIOGRAPHY

Hollstein: *Dut. & Flem.*; Thieme–Becker
M. Bryan: *A Biographical and Critical Dictionary of Painters and Engravers* (London, 1858)

G. von Térey: 'Ein *Jagdstück* des Jan van der Vinne', *Oud-Holland*, xli (1923–4), pp. 63–7

G. Krämer: 'Handzeichnungen aus den graphischen Sammlungen des Museums für Kunst und Gewerbe', *Jb. Hamburg. Kstsamml.*, xvi (1971), p. 65

Drawing in England from Hilliard to Hogarth (exh. cat. by L. Stainton and C. White, London, BM, 1987)

E. CALJÉ-VAN DEN BERG

Viñolesco style. *See* ESTILO DESORNAMENTADO.

Vint, Tõnis (*b* Tallinn, 1942). Estonian printmaker. He was a design student at the Estonian SSR State Art Institute in Tallinn (1962–7) when he first came to prominence as the leader and theorist of ANK '64, a group of nonconformist student artists, formed in response to the suffocating conditions of Soviet culture. In his flat, Vint held seminars on modern art and a broad range of theoretical interests, from oriental philosophy to Jungian archetypal theory and semiotics. These private gatherings incurred the wrath of officials, who harassed Vint and limited his professional opportunities. Nevertheless, as editor of *Kunst*, Estonia's principal art publication, Vint played a countervailing role against officialdom. He encouraged a rediscovery of the indigenous avant-garde, particularly the ESTONIAN ARTISTS' GROUP, which profoundly inspired his contemporary, LEONHARD LAPIN. Vint's own work from the 1970s was typically spare and geometric, with the occasional addition of erotic female motifs in the style of Aubrey Beardsley. A folio of erotic minimalist images was inexplicably accepted for publication in *Noorus*, a youth magazine, as a result of which the printer was forced to tear out the 36,000 offending nudes by hand. The lithograph *Room 1* (1973; New Brunswick, NJ, Rutgers U., Zimmerli A. Mus.) is one such image, albeit prim by modern Western standards. That a graphic artist occupied such a central, catalytic role in Estonian culture indicates not only Vint's talent and erudition but also the privileged status of graphic art in Soviet-era Estonia, as it dominated and influenced graphic trends throughout the USSR. Furthermore, Vint's expertise in Baltic folklore was an inspiration to his Latvian contemporaries, with whom he co-produced a film about Latvian folk ornament.

BIBLIOGRAPHY

E. Sepp: 'Estonia: Art as Metaphor of its Time', *Baltic Art during the Brezhnev Era: Nonconformist Art in Estonia, Latvia and Lithuania* (exh. cat., Toronto, John B. Aird Gal., 1992), pp. 11–14

MARK ALLEN SVEDE

Viola, Domenico (*b* Naples, *c.* 1610–20; *d* Naples, 1696). Italian painter. He was a pupil of both Andrea Vaccaro and Mattia Preti, although de Dominici claims that no trace of either of his teachers appeared in Viola's work, which he finds to be 'without choice details or noble countenances'. In 1634 Viola became a member of the Accademia di S Luca in Rome and worked in that city in the late 1630s, though he was otherwise active mainly in Naples. His most ambitious work was the decoration (*in situ*; damaged) of the Neapolitan church of S Antonio Abate, where he depicted, with great freedom of brushwork, stories from the *Legend of St Anthony Abbot* and other hermit scenes. In the style of these decorations he attempted to imitate Mattia Preti's chiaroscuro and grandiosity. De Dominici states that Viola enjoyed painting nocturnal scenes reminiscent of Matthias Stomer, such as the *Denial of St Peter* (priv. col., see Spinosa, pl. 873). Some genre works have been attributed to Viola (Spinosa), and many of his drawings are preserved in the Uffizi, Florence.

BIBLIOGRAPHY

Bolaffi; Thieme–Becker

B. de Dominici: *Vite* (1742–5), iii, pp. 351–2

L. Salazar: 'La chiesa di S Antonio Abate', *Napoli Nob.*, xiv/3 (1905), pp. 51–2

N. Spinosa, ed.: *La pittura napoletana del '600* (Milan, 1984) [illustrations]

ALEXANDRA HERZ

Viola, Giovanni Battista (*b* Bologna, 6 May 1576; *d* Rome, 10 Aug 1622). Italian painter. He was the first known Italian to work exclusively as a landscape painter. According to Malvasia, he arrived in Rome as a young man with Francesco Albani, who joined Annibale Carracci's studio there in 1601. He is recorded working with Albani and Domenichino on the frescoed decoration of the Palazzo Giustiniani–Odescalchi, Bassano di Sutri, in 1610, and was living in Albani's house in Rome in 1612. In 1617 he assisted Domenichino with ten landscape frescoes depicting scenes from the *Life of Apollo* for the Villa Aldobrandini, Frascati ($2\frac{1}{2}$ *in situ*; $7\frac{1}{2}$ London, N.G.). His fresco *Landscape with Travellers* (1621–2) in the Camerino dei Paesi in the *casino* of the Villa Ludovisi, Rome, forms part of a decorative scheme to which Domenichino, Paul Bril and Guercino also contributed. On the basis of these frescoes and of works listed under his name in 17th-century inventories, including the *Landscape with the Death of Absolom* (*c.* 1600; Paris, Louvre), Spear (1980) attributed a coherent body of works to Viola. His work is characterized by a predominantly cool colour scheme with dark, blue-green water and dark green and brown trees, bushes and ground. His figure drawing is awkward, and the figures tend to stand in the foreground, with exotically shaped mountains in the distance. Spatial recession is achieved through contrasting bands of light and dark tones. Sometimes the paintings illustrate common biblical or mythological subjects, as in the *Landscape with St John the Baptist Preaching* (Cambridge, Fitzwilliam; see Spear, fig. 36), but more typically they show fishing or hunting scenes. Although he evidently helped to popularize the Bolognese landscape idiom, which foreshadows the ideal landscapes of Claude Lorrain and Nicolas Poussin, he was quickly forgotten after his death. His paintings have been confused with those of other artists, particularly Domenichino.

BIBLIOGRAPHY

Thieme–Becker

G. Baglione: *Vite* (1642); ed. V. Mariani (1935), p. 173

C. C. Malvasia: *Felsine pittrice* (1678); ed. F. Zanotti (Bologna, 1841), ii, pp. 89–92

F. Baldinucci: *Notizie* (1681–1728); ed. F. Ranalli (1845–7), iii, pp. 359–61

L. Salerno: *Pittori di paesaggio del seicento a Roma* (Rome, 1976), i, pp. 98–9; iii, pp. 1098–9

R. E. Spear: 'A Forgotten Landscape Painter: Giovanni Battista Viola', *Burl. Mag.*, cxx (1980), pp. 298–313 [with bibliog.]

A. Sutherland Harris: *Landscape Painting in Rome, 1595–1675* (New York, 1985), pp. 282–9

ANN SUTHERLAND HARRIS

Viola Zanini, Giuseppe [Gioseffe] (*b* Padua, ?1575–80; *d* Padua, 1631). Italian theorist, architect, cartographer and painter. He was trained by his father Giulio, city architect of Padua, and at the school of Vincenzo Dotto (1572–1629), a Paduan cosmographer and architect in the Palladian tradition. Despite his vast and genuine erudition, Viola Zanini never held an important post and was beset with financial difficulties throughout his life. He worked as an architect and, by necessity, as a painter of architectural perspectives; none of his work has survived, however, apart from the Palazzo Cumano in Padua (1628–31; now Liceo Ippolito Nievo), which is generally attributed to him. His town plan of Padua, drawn in 1599, was widely imitated, and his treatise on architecture (1629) brought him fame. The organization of topics seems to have been influenced in particular by Leon Battista Alberti's *De re aedificatoria*, while its architectural forms were inspired by Vitruvius and the writings and buildings of Andrea Palladio. Viola Zanini's work differed from these sources, however, in omitting all considerations of urban planning, ethics and aesthetics. Dry, schematic in content and limited in its aspirations, his work reflects the transition from Renaissance expository writing to the purely technical works that began to appear in the 17th century.

WRITINGS

Della architettura di Gioseffe Viola Zanini padovano, pittore ed architetto, 2 vols (Padua, 1629/*R* 1678)

BIBLIOGRAPHY

Thieme–Becker

F. Cessi: 'Giuseppe Viola Zanini, architetto padovano del XVII secolo', *Padova & Prov.*, ix (1963), no. 3, pp. 7–14; no. 4, pp. 8–13

G. Bresciani Alvarez: 'Chiesa dello Spirito Santo', *Padova: Basiliche e chiese*, ed. C. Bellinati and L. Puppi (Vicenza, 1975), ii, pp. 341–2

G. Mazzi: 'Iconografia di Padova ai tempi del Cornaro', *Alvise Cornaro e il suo tempo* (exh. cat., ed. L. Puppi; Padua, Loggia Cornaro, 1980), pp. 178–94, 232–52

A. Bellini: 'G. Viola Zanini, pittore di prospettive e trattatista di architettura', *Padova & Prov.*, xxvii/3 (1981), pp. 3–16

F. Bernabei: 'Cultura artistica e critica d'arte', *Stor. Cult. Ven.*, iv/1 (1983), pp. 549–74

DONATA BATTILOTTI

Viollet-le-Duc, Eugène-Emmanuel (*b* Paris, 27 Jan 1814; *d* Lausanne, 17 Sept 1879). French architect, restorer, designer and writer. He is one of the few architects whose name is known to the general public in France, although his fame as a restorer of medieval buildings is often accompanied by a somewhat unflattering critical judgement: a restoration 'à la Viollet-le-Duc' is usually understood to be abusive in terms of the original work and is often confused with the type of eclectic architecture that he himself particularly disliked. Through his published writings, particularly his *Dictionnaire raisonné de l'architecture française du XIe au XVIe siècle* (1854–68), he made a substantial contribution to contemporary knowledge of medieval buildings. In addition, his writings and theories had an enormous impact on attitudes to restoration (*see* ARCHITECTURAL CONSERVATION AND RESTORATION) and on contemporary design, not only for the Gothic Revival movement but also in the development of rationalism, providing an important stimulus to new movements in architecture both in France and abroad (*see* §4 below).

1. Architectural career. 2. Restoration theories and work. 3. Decorative arts. 4. Writings.

1. ARCHITECTURAL CAREER. He was born into an enlightened upper middle-class family; his father was Sous-Contrôleur des Services for the Palais des Tuileries, and his maternal uncle Etienne-Jean Delécluze, who lived with them, had studied painting with Jacques-Louis David and frequented the liberal artistic and literary circles of his time. Among those who visited Viollet-le-Duc's home was Prosper Mérimée (1803–70), who later played an important role in his career. Viollet-le-Duc decided very early to embark on an architectural career, but he refused to train at the Ecole des Beaux-Arts, believing that the essential skills were acquired in an architect's office. Thus he spent time with Jean-Jacques-Marie Huvé (1783–1852), a family friend who had completed the Madeleine in Paris, and in particular with François-René Leclère. Travel was also an accepted part of the education of a young man, and between 1831 and 1836 Viollet-le-Duc visited the Auvergne, Provence, Normandy, the châteaux of the Loire, the Pyrenees and Languedoc. In 1834 he married and began teaching at the Ecole de Dessin, and in 1836 he set out for Italy, where he was later joined by his wife Elisabeth and his brother Adolphe. He spent six months in Rome, toured Sicily on foot and also visited Naples and Venice. On his return to Paris in 1837, he recommenced his courses at the Ecole de Dessin, and between 1837 and 1844 he contributed 249 drawings to the *Voyages pittoresques et romantiques dans l'ancienne France* (Paris, 1820–78), an important topographical–architectural survey by Isidore-Justin-Séverin Taylor, Charles Nodier (1783–1844) and Alphonse de Cailleux.

In 1838 Viollet-le-Duc was appointed auditor to the Conseil des Bâtiments Civils under Leclère, its Inspecteur Général. One of the two principal government institutions concerned with buildings (with the Commission des Monuments Historiques), the Conseil supervised all work on buildings belonging to the State and destined for use by a government department, as well as projects over a certain value in local communities. All important restoration plans regarding monuments of national importance, for example Notre-Dame, Paris, and Saint-Denis Abbey, thus passed before it. Viollet-le-Duc worked for the Conseil on the construction of the Hôtel des Archives du Royaume in Paris and in 1839 was sent to Narbonne to study a project for completing the cathedral. The Commission des Monuments Historiques, composed of archaeologists, scholars and architects, was responsible for distributing grants intended for the restoration of architectural monuments, and in 1840 Prosper Mérimée, Inspecteur Général des Monuments Historiques, proposed that Viollet-le-Duc be made responsible for the restoration of STE MADELEINE, VÉZELAY. Viollet-le-Duc was also appointed to work with Jean-Baptiste-Antoine Lassus on the restoration of the Sainte-Chapelle (*see* PARIS, §V, 2), and in 1844 Lassus and Viollet-le-Duc won an open competition for the restoration of Notre-Dame in Paris (*see* PARIS, §V, 1(i)). Thereafter, Viollet-le-Duc was involved in many restoration projects: some of the most important were carried out at Saint-Denis (from 1846; *see* SAINT-DENIS ABBEY, §V); the ramparts at CARCASSONNE (from 1849) and Avignon (1860–68); the cathedrals of Amiens (1849–75), Reims (1861–73) and Clermont-Ferrand (from 1862); the church at Poissy (1852–65); and the Salle Synodale (1855–65) at Sens (see fig. 1).

Closely associated with officials in power during the July Monarchy (1830–48), Viollet-le-Duc was introduced about 1852 to the imperial court circles of Napoleon III by Mérimée, who had known the Empress Eugénie before her marriage. Despite his own liberal convictions, Viollet-le-Duc participated in court life and the organization of its celebrations, such as the decorations in Notre-Dame for the baptism (1856) of the Prince Imperial. The emperor also entrusted him with the restoration (1857–70) of the château of Pierrefonds, Oise, in order to create a private residence, and four years later asked him to build a monument (1862–5) to *Napoleon I* at Ajaccio, Corsica. New buildings designed by Viollet-le-Duc included several houses, for example the Maison Courmont (1846–8) at 22 Rue de Berlin (now 28 Rue de Liège), Maison Milon (1857–60) at 15 Rue de Douai and his own house (1862–3) at 68 Rue Condorcet, all in Paris. His châteaux included Ambrières-les-Vallées (1857–65) in the Mayenne and La Flachère (1862–74) near Saint-Verand (Rhône), and he built three churches in accordance with his theories: St Gimer (1854–9) at Carcassonne, Aillant-sur-Tholon (1861–5) in the Yonne and St Denis-de-l'Estrée (1864–6) at Saint-Denis. In 1853 he was appointed Inspecteur Général des Edifices Diocésains.

Viollet-le-Duc learnt his profession as architect and restorer through practical experience. Acquired through direct contact with medieval buildings, this experience not only influenced his theories on their construction (*see* §2 below) but also contributed to his definition of the characteristics of a 'modern' architecture. Like Lassus, Viollet-le-Duc was devoted to the study of the past, a study that was simultaneously erudite, archaeological and scientific in its approach. However, while Lassus sought to combine the most ingenious medieval solutions in order to create model churches, Viollet-le-Duc analysed the supposed mechanism at the heart of medieval construction—explained at length in his *Dictionnaire raisonné de l'architecture* (1854–68; *see* §4 below)—in order to evolve new solutions and establish the basis of a modern Gothic style.

Despite his vehement attacks on eclecticism, Viollet-le-Duc only just managed to avoid it himself. In his restoration of the cathedral at Clermont-Ferrand, for example, his project for the west façade borrowed the rose-window design from the south transept of Chartres Cathedral and the octafoil design from the tall, twin-light windows in the nave aisles of Amiens Cathedral, while the scene of the *Last Judgement* in the tympanum is similar to that of St Urbain at Troyes. Yet for Viollet-le-Duc the universality of the Gothic style was based on its constructional and rational values, and he perceived an intimate compatibility between the 13th and 19th centuries. He subsequently became a more outspoken critic of eclecticism and worked on the creation of an architecture that constituted a pertinent response to the requirements of new building types, using modern materials. In this respect he seems to have been more interested in the construction of new village churches on a modest budget than in taking part in the great competitions organized for the construction of major new cathedrals such as that at Marseille (1852). His churches at Carcassonne, Aillant-sur-Tholon or Saint-Denis may appear rather disappointing in terms of 'correct' construction techniques, but they reflect his concern to satisfy the needs of contemporary society, as did his plans

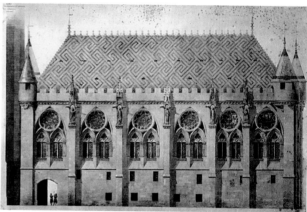

1. Eugène-Emmanuel Viollet-le-Duc: Salle Synodale at Sens before and after proposed restoration, watercolour, 455×650 mm and 650×983 mm, 1851 (Paris, Centre de Recherche sur les Monuments Historiques)

for rental housing, the gardener's house for the Maison Sabatier (1860–63) at Pierrefonds and his own villa La Vedette (1874–8; destr.) at Lausanne, where he spent increasing amounts of time.

Viollet-le-Duc was extraordinarily prolific. His day began at 6 a.m. and ended at midnight. He organized not only his own work but also that of his subordinates, yet he welcomed anyone who required advice or information and was a prodigious correspondent. He also continued his teaching ventures: for a short time from 1857 he ran an atelier, where one of his most devoted pupils was ANATOLE DE BAUDOT, and in 1863 he was appointed a professor at the newly reorganized Ecole des Beaux-Arts (*see* FRANCE, §XV). Although he resigned the following year, the course he evolved for his teaching formed the basis of his *Entretiens sur l'architecture* (1863–72; *see* §4 below). The defeat of France (1870) in the Franco-Prussian War and the events of the Paris Commune in 1871, however, affected him deeply. Although he agreed to restore (1873–6) Lausanne Cathedral at the request of the city authorities he resigned from his post as Inspecteur Général des Edifices Diocésains in 1874 and thereafter spent his time completing projects in hand, notably Pierrefonds, Carcassonne and the château d'Eu (1862–79) for the Orléans family. He also dedicated himself to matters of hygiene and public health and he served as a municipal councillor in Paris from 1874 until his death.

2. RESTORATION THEORIES AND WORK. The French Revolution, which resulted in damage to many medieval buildings, had broken the continuity of skills handed down among master masons and stonecutters, and until Viollet-le-Duc turned his attention to the subject, the usual method of restoring historic buildings was to dismantle their damaged parts and then reassemble them in hypothetical reconstructions. An understanding of the structural principles of medieval architecture had also been lost, placing monuments in even greater danger, while the use of iron bars to support buildings acted to the detriment of their aesthetic qualities, as did the reinforcement of piers by encasing them in masonry. It was in this context that Viollet-le-Duc was appointed by the Commission des Monuments Historiques to undertake the restoration of Ste Madeleine at Vézelay.

(i) Aesthetics and style. Viollet-le-Duc gave a clear definition of his understanding of restoration in his Dictionnaire raisonné de l'architecture: 'Restoration: both the word and the activity itself are modern. To restore a building is not to repair or rebuild it, but to re-establish its original state which must, at a certain moment in time, have existed.' In achieving this objective Viollet-le-Duc had the advantage of skills acquired from the new science of archaeology, and he knew that the initial step was to carry out a critical examination of the building; in this respect he was enthusiastic about the use of photography in recording the existing state of a building. The drawings that accompanied his schemes for restoration projects (see fig. 1) highlighted the structure and gave the correct value to the profiles of mouldings, while taking into account all the architectural aspects of the building. There is, however, a marked difference between the evocative power of the drawings and the dry style of the restorations themselves, which were interpreted on site by less expert hands and with imperfect restoration methods. In some cases this dry style has been attributed to the introduction of industrialized methods to the building trade.

Description and classification, the key words of the 1830s, established the 'style' or typology of a building, which Viollet-le-Duc considered should determine its restoration, both in appearance and structurally. The claim of the Monuments Historiques that restoration should conform to the original building, however, contradicted the desire to re-establish a unity of style that had been changed over the centuries. Viollet-le-Duc sought to analyse and resolve this contradiction, and in buildings that had been repaired several times he considered that individual circumstances should determine whether to attempt to re-create an original coherence of style or to reproduce the building with its subsequent modifications. In his restoration of Ste Madeleine at Vézelay, for example, Viollet-le-Duc replaced four bays of 13th-century pointed groin vaults with 12th-century style domical groin vaults in order to give a sense of unity to the nave, although he preserved the vault in the bay nearest the choir as an example of the later style. His justification for this alteration was that the later vaults, which had themselves

replaced earlier work, were in danger of collapse and needed to be rebuilt anyway and that it was better to replace them in the earlier style to match the rest of the building. Had the later vaults been of exceptional beauty, however, he would not have destroyed them simply to restore the original unity of the nave. Nevertheless, the affirmation of style at the expense of the individuality of a building, in a period when overall knowledge was still far from complete, the chronology of significant buildings approximate and the number of publications limited, could only result in simplifications that have rightly been criticized; they were not unique to Viollet-le-Duc, however, but reflected prevailing attitudes to restoration.

Louis Vitet and Mérimée, the first Inspecteurs Généraux des Monuments Historiques, forcefully affirmed that restoration should give preference to structure over decoration, but monumental sculpture was considered an integral part of the structure, being an essential complement to the architecture. Indeed, the churches and cathedrals mutilated during the Revolution had lost with their decoration a large part of their evocative and didactic power. This led Viollet-le-Duc to substitute new work for those parts that were incomplete, damaged or missing, for example at Notre-Dame (see PARIS, §V, 1(ii)), Amiens Cathedral and Ste Madeleine, Vézelay. At both Vézelay, where the old sculpture was removed to the museum (Vézelay, Dépôt Lapidaire Abbaye), and Notre-Dame, where some of the medieval heads (Paris, Mus. Cluny) from the Gallery of Kings were discovered in 1977, it is possible to compare the originals with the 19th-century copies. It can be seen that, despite efforts to imitate the medieval spirit, the later work clearly belongs to its own period.

Viollet-le-Duc's theories served to improve public understanding of medieval architecture and its restoration, even though his methods were subsequently much contested. His decision to substitute new work for old has undoubtedly attracted the most criticism: Auguste Rodin and Achille Carlier, for example, both considered that restoration by alteration was an unacceptable falsification.

(ii) Structure, construction and materials. The real contribution of Viollet-le-Duc was the attention he paid not only to the appearance of a building but also to its structure. He regarded every aspect of Gothic architecture as a function of its structure rather than free imagination; this concept of medieval functionalism was reflected in the dynamics of Gothic structure, in which the thrusts of the pointed arches and ribs supporting the stone vaults were counter-balanced by interior piers and arcades and by exterior buttresses, flying buttresses and pinnacles. The emphasis placed on the structure of the building in the initial study played an essential role in Viollet-le-Duc's restoration work. In their preparatory report on the restoration of Notre-Dame in Paris, he and Lassus stated that the replacements for damaged elements should be identical, both in materials and in function, to the original, and this extended even to the reproduction of a defective solution. By the time he was considering restoration in his Dictionnaire raisonné de l'architecture, however, Viollet-le-Duc's attitude had changed and he wrote that the replacement of each part should be in better materials, using better and more refined methods. He seems to have adopted this approach from about 1860 in work on St Sernin, Toulouse, where he removed the 15th-century roof, reduced the walls to their original height and covered the apsidal chapels with stone slabs, both in order to reinstate the original proportions and, above all, to make the building watertight.

Viollet-le-Duc's awareness of his responsibility as an architect–builder increased over the years. He always remembered how François Debret's use of heavy stone to rebuild the spire of the north tower at Saint-Denis Abbey had nearly caused the façade and tower to collapse in 1846, and he knew that the principal objective of the restorer was to secure the stability of the building. After many years of experience he came to believe that it was dangerous to reproduce a defective design if the structural safety of a building was thereby compromised.

The third criterion for the authenticity of a restoration was the use of materials consistent with those originally employed. This rule was subject to exceptions, particularly when there were difficulties in finding the identical stone. Viollet-le-Duc sometimes used materials that he considered superior but that subsequently proved disappointing. His own work at Vézelay and St Sernin, for example, later needed restoration. His early assertion that damaged material should be replaced only by something similar was later slightly modified. Initially the use of cast iron, as in the new spire (1829–75) at Rouen Cathedral by Jean-Antoine Alavoine, was considered a sacrilege, but towards the end of the century, as the architects of the Monuments Historiques gave wider approval to new materials, its use was accepted, particularly in roof structures, to avoid the risk of fire. Although Viollet-le-Duc, in his *Entretiens* (*see* §4 below), enthusiastically promoted the use of iron, he himself never used it in any of his significant works. He did, however, use iron tie-bars in some of his restoration work (e.g. above the vaults of Notre-Dame, Paris).

3. DECORATIVE ARTS. Viollet-le-Duc saw the architect as a conductor, orchestrating and coordinating the work of other artists in the way he believed that medieval master masons had directed sculptors, painters and goldsmiths, thus ensuring the unity of their buildings. Like William Morris in England, he argued for a total art work (*Gesamtkunstwerk*), and in accordance with these principles he worked on the decoration, fittings and furnishings of restored buildings (see fig. 2) and those he designed himself. In his *Histoire d'une maison* (1873) he even proposed wallpaper designs. In all these areas he developed theories in parallel with his projects, thus providing material for his dictionaries of architecture and furniture.

The revival of interest in Gothic architecture was accompanied by renewed interest in stained glass (*see* STAINED GLASS, §II, 2); indeed, research into the chemical composition of medieval glass and studies of the iconography and successive styles of windows became major preoccupations of the period. The chapter on stained glass in Viollet-le-Duc's *Dictionnaire du mobilier* (1858–75) attacked the art of painting on glass (*vitrail tableau*), which was considered a technique alien to the spirit of medieval stained glass; instead he supported the use of coloured glass, directly inspired by the techniques, composition and

2. Eugène-Emmanuel Viollet-le-Duc: chimney-piece in the Emperor's Bedchamber, château of Pierrefonds, late 1860s; from *Le Château de Pierrefonds* (Paris, 1875), pl. xi

colours of 13th-century stained glass. Between 1840 and 1847 Viollet-le-Duc collaborated on the production of stained glass at the Sèvres Porcelain Factory. Its work at that period was destined for the windows of the Orléans funerary chapel at Dreux. Viollet-le-Duc was first responsible for providing designs (1840–43) for the borders and upper parts of the four apse windows, where the figures were by Achille Devéria and M. Ziegler. He then adapted the 12 cartoons of saints commissioned in 1843–4 from Ingres for the transepts. His designs were broadly inspired by Flamboyant sculpture, relatively freely executed and thus quite different from 13th-century models; they can be compared to the frames with which he surrounded his drawings for the *Voyages pittoresques*.

Medieval church furnishings, especially church plate, had not survived the *ancien régime* in large quantities. Many further losses during the Revolution, combined with the radical reorganization of the Roman Catholic Church in France, justified the creation of a new type of liturgical furnishing, for which there was a large government budget under the Second Empire. The new works were commissioned in two styles: Neo-classical and, from the 1840s, Gothic Revival, which became well established during the second half of the 19th century, inspired by that golden period of the French Middle Ages, the 13th century. Viollet-le-Duc was a leader of the Gothic style. His

3. Eugène-Emmanuel Viollet-le-Duc: design for the reliquary of the Holy Nail, watercolour, 396×329 mm, c. 1865 (Paris, Centre de Recherche sur les Monuments Historiques)

personal vision was set forth at length in the *Dictionnaire du mobilier*: while inspiration came from medieval models, the objects created should be beautiful and modern in that their forms should correspond to their uses and functions. He designed the best pieces in the treasury of Notre-Dame, Paris: the candelabra and the Easter candle, the reliquaries of the Sacred Thorn, the True Cross and the Holy Nail (see fig. 3) are remarkable creations that incorporate plant and animal forms and are closer to the work of Gustave Doré than to their 13th-century prototypes.

Viollet-le-Duc was interested in manufacturing techniques and the possibilities offered by prefabrication, which would allow a reduction in cost and make certain pieces more widely available. His determination to understand the Middle Ages in all its aspects, and to restore the framework of everyday life as well as the architecture of the period, led him to study secular furniture, and he collected designs from original sources, including medieval manuscripts. As with goldsmithing, he studied furniture production techniques and freely used constructions and forms inspired by the past but reinterpreted for the modern world. He favoured the use of natural wood, particularly a light oak, and he rejected any kind of dissimulation by paint or gilding. Great importance was given to plant motifs in his works, and certain benches, chairs and armchairs for Pierrefonds have been considered as precursors of Art Nouveau.

4. WRITINGS. Viollet-le-Duc is perhaps best known for his literary works, which show his didactic approach

and profound scholarship. In 1845 he began to express his ideas in the periodical *Annales archéologiques*, and in 1854 he began publication of his *Dictionnaire raisonné de l'architecture*, which embodies all his knowledge and experience of medieval buildings. This was followed from 1858 by his highly influential *Entretiens sur l'architecture* and *Dictionnaire du mobilier*, the latter containing sections on goldsmiths' work, musical instruments, games, tools, clothes, jewellery and armour as well as furniture. Viollet-le-Duc's sketches and drawings perfectly complemented his writings (for illustrations *see* CURTAIN WALL (i) and TAS-DE-CHARGE). In his *Histoire d'un dessinateur* (1879) he explained the important role he assigned to the skill of drawing and recommended its practice as a training in reflection and a means of acquiring knowledge. His virtuosity as a draughtsman far surpassed the skills of most contemporaries, although the translation of his drawings into engravings did not fully convey the nervous quality of his hand.

Demonstrating his interest in politics, Viollet-le-Duc also published numerous articles in political journals, and towards the end of his life he produced more popular works: these included *Histoire d'un hôtel de ville et d'une cathédrale* (1878), in which he developed current theories on the secularization of power during the 18th century, and *Histoire d'une maison*. These later works reflected his belief that architects should respond to the needs of modern life in the 19th century and that a dynamic, lucid and efficient society could be created through the use of a modern architecture. The range of his knowledge is emphasized by two other publications, *Le Massif du Mont Blanc* (Paris, 1876) and *L'Art russe: Ses origines, ses éléments constitutifs, son apogée, son avenir* (Paris, 1877).

Viollet-le-Duc's interest in the potential of new materials to create a new architecture was given an important place in his *Entretiens* (nos 12, 13 and 18). Iron offered particular innovations, including the construction of a skeletal framework that allowed large areas of transparent wall, as in Gothic architecture, and designs of various hypothetical iron structures were included. Viollet-le-Duc also proposed solutions using iron to a variety of structural problems, for example the transfer of lateral thrusts from a traditional vault into vertical thrusts with iron ties (see fig. 4). Aware of the characteristics of each material, he suggested different uses for wrought iron and cast iron. He also made a distinction between public buildings, which should be conceived to last several centuries and should thus be built in stone or brick, and more ephemeral buildings that were better suited to iron, such as private houses, where a metal frame could replace a traditional timber frame.

Viollet-le-Duc was the most brilliant representative of the rationalist school in France. He trained an entire generation of architects, the most famous being Anatole de Baudot, who was the first to use reinforced concrete in the restoration of historic monuments. Viollet-le-Duc's influence was exerted primarily through his *Dictionnaire raisonné de l'architecture* and *Entretiens*, both in France and abroad. Victor Horta, Antoni Gaudí and Louis Sullivan all cited the *Entretiens* among the works that influenced their conception of architecture.

For further illustrations *see* PINNACLE; GARGOYLE; and MASONRY, figs 6 and 8.

UNPUBLISHED SOURCES

Paris, Cent. Rech. Mnmts Hist. [drgs]
Paris, Archvs Mnmts Hist. [drgs]

WRITINGS

Dictionnaire raisonné de l'architecture française du XIe au XVIe siècle, 10 vols (Paris, 1854–68)
Dictionnaire raisonné du mobilier français de l'époque carolingienne à la renaissance, 6 vols (Paris, 1858–75)
Entretiens sur l'architecture, 2 vols (Paris, 1863–72); Eng. trans. (London, 1959)
Histoire d'une maison (Paris, 1873)
Histoire d'une forteresse (Paris, 1874)
with F. Narjoux: *Habitations modernes*, 2 vols (Paris, 1875–7/*R* 1979)
Histoire d'un hôtel de ville et d'une cathédrale (Paris, 1878)
Histoire d'un dessinateur (Paris, 1879)

BIBLIOGRAPHY

C. Sauvageot: *Viollet-le-Duc et son oeuvre dessiné* (Paris, 1880)
E. L. Viollet-le-Duc: *Lettres inédites de Viollet-le-Duc recueillies et annotées par son fils* (Paris, 1902)
P. Gout: 'Viollet-le-Duc: Sa vie, son oeuvre, sa doctrine', *Rev. A. Chrét.* (1914) [suppl. 3]
C. Bricarelli: *Eugène Viollet-le-Duc e il rifioramento degli medioevali nel secolo XIX* (Rome, 1915), pp. 565–75, 697–717
G. H. West: 'Eugène-Emmanuel Viollet-le-Duc, Royal Gold Medallist 1864', *RIBA J.*, xxviii (1920–21), pp. 25–31
P. Abraham: *Viollet-le-Duc et le rationalisme médiéval* (Paris, 1934)
A. Nava: 'La teoria di Viollet-le-Duc e l'architettura funzionale', *Crit. A.*, viii (1949), pp. 59–65, 230–41
J. Summerson: 'Viollet-le-Duc and the Rational Point of View', *Heavenly Mansions* (London, 1949), pp. 135–58
R. Middleton: *Viollet-le-Duc and the Rational Gothic Tradition* (diss., U. Cambridge, 1958)
M. Besset: 'Viollet-le-Duc: Seine Stellung zur Geschichte', *Historismus und bildende Kunst*, ed. L. Grote (Munich, 1965), pp. 43–58
Eugène Viollet-le-Duc, 1814–1879 (exh. cat. by P.-M. Auzas, Paris, Hôtel de Sully, 1965)
Mnmts Hist. France, n. s., xi (Jan–June 1965) [issue devoted to Viollet-le-Duc]
N. Pevsner: *Ruskin and Viollet-le-Duc: Englishness and Frenchness in the Appreciation of Gothic Architecture* (London, 1969)
G. Viollet-le-Duc, ed.: *E. Viollet-le-Duc: Lettres d'Italie, 1836–1837, adressées à sa famille* (Paris, 1971)
——, ed.: *Viollet-le-Duc: Voyage aux Pyrénées, 1833: Lettres à son père et journal de route: Dessins, lavis et aquarelles de l'auteur* (Paris, 1972)
R. Middleton: 'Viollet-le-Duc's Academic Ventures and the *Entretiens sur l'architecture*', *Gottfried Semper und die Mitte des 19. Jahrhunderts*, ed. A. M. Vogt, C. Reble and M. Frohlich (Basle, 1976)
R. Mark: 'Robert Willis, Viollet-le-Duc and the Structural Approach to Gothic Architecture', *L'Architectura*, 1 (1977), pp. 52–64
P. Boudon, H. Damisch and P. Deshayes: *Analyse du Dictionnaire raisonné de l'architecture française du XI siècle par E. Viollet-le-Duc* (Paris, 1978)
L. Grodecki: *Pierrefonds* (Paris, 1979)
Viollet-le-Duc au château d'Eu (exh. cat. by M. Bailleux-Delbecq, Eu, Mus. Louis-Philippe, 1979)
Viollet-le-Duc: Centenaire de sa mort à Lausanne (exh. cat., Lausanne, Mus. Hist., 1979)
'Viollet-le-Duc e il restauro dei monumenti', *Restauro*, xlvii–xlix (1980), pp. 3–291
Viollet-le-Duc (exh. cat., ed. B. Foucart and others; Paris, Grand Pal., 1980) [incl. extensive bibliog. and list of sources]
Le Voyage d'Italie d'Eugène Viollet-le-Duc (exh. cat. by J. J. Aillagon, G. Viollet-le-Duc and M. Vernes, Paris, Ecole N. Sup. B.-A., 1980)
L. MacClintock: 'Monumentality versus Suitability: Viollet-le-Duc's Saint-Gimer at Carcassonne', *J. Soc. Archit. Historians*, xl/3 (1981), pp. 218–35
L. Saulnier: 'La Madeleine de Vézelay: Le Chantier de restauration de Viollet-le-Duc', *Actes du 52 congrès association bourguignonne soc. savantes: Vézelay, 1981*, pp. 213–20
B. Foucart, ed.: *L'Eclectisme raisonné* (Paris, 1984)
——: 'Viollet-le-Duc et la restauration', *Les Lieux de mémoire: La Nation*, ii (Paris, 1986), pp. 613–49
Viollet-le-Duc: Architect, Artist, Master of Historic Preservation (exh. cat. by F. Bercé and B. Foucart, Trust of Museum Exhibitions, Washington, DC, N. Bldg Mus., 1988)

4. Eugène-Emmanuel Viollet-le-Duc: *Maçonnerie*; from his *Entretiens sur l'architecture* (Paris, 1865), pl. xxii

M. Bressani: 'Notes on Viollet-le-Duc's Philosophy of History: Dialectics and Technology', *J. Soc. Archit. Historians*, xlviii/4 (1989), pp. 327–50
O. Foucard: 'La Restauration de Saint-Germain de Toulouse de 1860 à 1862: 29 nouveaux documents iconographiques signés Viollet-le-Duc et Esquié', *Bull. Mnmtl*, cxxxxvii/4 (1989), pp. 333–4
F. Very: 'Eugène Viollet-le-Duc, Pol Abraham et Victor Sabouret', *J. Hist. Archit.*, 2 (1989), pp. 23–31
Viollet-le-Duc et la montagne (exh. cat. by P. A. Frey and L. Grenier, Paris, 1993)

FRANÇOISE BERCÉ

Vionoja, Veikko (*b* Ullava, Ostrobothnia, western Finland, 30 Oct 1909). Finnish painter, draughtsman and engraver. As a youth he painted the altarpiece of the local church; only later, in 1936–8, did he study at the Drawing School of the Finnish Arts Association, Helsinki (later the Academy of Art). His career was interrupted by World War II and its aftermath, during which he concentrated on drawing, not becoming productive as a painter until the 1950s. Vionoja's work remained faithful to the village life and landscapes of his childhood and youth. During the 1950s his paintings were still relatively expressive and relied on heavy colour tones. At this time he also tried his hand at illustration, for which he produced a wealth of busy, lively charcoal drawings. A number of books appeared with illustrations by Vionoja, for example Lauri

Simonsuuri's *Kansa tarinoi* ('Folk tales'; Porvoo, 1950) and Oskari Tokoi's *Lapsuuteni muistoja* ('My childhood memories'; Kokkola, 1953).

Vionoja's style matured during the 1960s. The subdued expressionism of his early works gradually gave way to a new, increasingly minimalist vision, which persisted through the following decades. While the themes of his work remained the same, he moved towards a more abstract expression. For him the technical problems of painting were as important as the subject-matter. He made expert use of colour, and the dark, hazy tones of his paintings are reminiscent of old Ostrobothnian woven rugs (*ryijy*) and peasant carpentry. The composition of his paintings is clean and structured, often Cubist in style, and the surface is worked in order to make the detailing appear silhouette-like against a subdued background. An essential feature of his paintings is their atmosphere of tranquillity, whether they depict a brilliant summer's day, dusky evening or the approach of a storm (*Keskikangas Farmyard*, 1975; Tampere, Hildén A. Mus.). In later work the poetic effects of light increasingly dominated his art. Vionoja also painted a number of portraits, the best-known being that of the former President of Finland, *Urho Kekkonen* (1975), though portraits of country people are more in tune with Vionoja's artistic vision. In addition he produced several monumental paintings, such as altarpieces and murals, which are, similarly, realist-based romantic works. In his countless drawings, paintings and, from the 1970s, lithographs, Vionoja preserved a picture of the life and landscape of Ostrobothnia in earlier decades (*Windmill*, charcoal, 1979; Helsinki, priv. col., see Peltola, p. 243).

BIBLIOGRAPHY

L. Peltola: *Vionoja: Piirustuksia/Teckningar/Drawings* (Helsinki, 1981) [Fin., Swed., Eng. text]
M. Niiniluoto: *Veikko Vionoja: Talvisotapiirustuksia* [Veikko Vionoja: drawings of the winter war] (Helsinki, 1982)
Vionoja—Taiteilijan vuosikymmenet [Vionoja—the artist by decade] (exh. cat., texts S. Niinivaara and J. Tanttu; Helsinki, A. Exh. Hall; Turku, A. Mus.; Vaasa, Pohjanmaan Mus.; 1982)
P. Suhonen: *Veikko Vionoja: Maalauksia/Målningar/Paintings, 1935–1984* (Helsinki, 1984) [Fin., Swed., Eng. text]

LEENA PELTOLA

Vipper, Boris (Robertovich) (*b* Moscow, 16 April 1888: *d* Moscow, 24 Jan 1967). Russian art historian. He studied art history at Moscow University (1906–11) under Nikolay Romanov (1867–1948) and Vladimir Mal'mberg (1860–1921), then travelled abroad, studying in museums and libraries in Germany, Italy and Holland; he also painted in private studios in Munich and Moscow (1911–13). In 1913 he became curator of the picture gallery at the Rumyantsev Museum in Moscow; in 1915 he began lecturing at Moscow University, and in 1918 he became a professor there. He moved to Riga, Latvia, in 1924 and taught art history at the Latvian Academy of Arts and at the Latvian University (1924–41). He headed the art history faculty at the Central-Asian University, Tashkent, Uzbekistan (1941–3), returning to teach at Moscow University (1943–54). At the same time he worked in the Pushkin Museum of Fine Arts (from 1943). His lectures and writings relate mainly to the Renaissance, Mannerism and Baroque, although he also dealt with ancient Greek art and taught in other periods and areas. His most important and most typical works are overviews of national schools during a particular—albeit wide—period, notably his books on Italian art of the 16th to 18th centuries and on Dutch 17th-century art. Vipper also turned his attention to Russian and Latvian art. His methodology was initially influenced by HEINRICH WÖLFFLIN's interest in form, while later he put increasing emphasis on the general outlook of the artist himself and the society in which he lived. In the 1930s Vipper paid particular attention to national elements in art and his late works were influenced by a sociological approach. Occasionally he submitted to the official Marxist sociology of art, but dogmatic generalizations were balanced by specific analysis of the works of art themselves.

WRITINGS

Latvijas māksla baroka laikmetā [Latvian art in the Baroque period] (Riga, 1937; Eng. trans., Riga, 1939)
L'Art letton: Essai de synthèse (Riga, 1940)
Stanovleniya realizma v gollandskoy zhivopisi XVII veka [The establishment of realism in Dutch 17th-century painting] (Moscow, 1957)
Ocherki gollandskoy zhivopisi epokhi rastsveta (1640–1670) [Studies of Dutch painting during its heyday (1640–1670)] (Moscow, 1962)
Problema realizma v ital'yanskoy zhivopisi XVII–XVIII vekov [The question of realism in Italian painting of the 17th and 18th centuries] (Moscow 1966)
Ital'yanskiy Renessans XIII–XVI veka: Kurs lektsiy po istorii izobrazitel'nogo iskusstva i arkhitektury [The Italian Renaissance of the 13th to 16th centuries: lecture course on the history of fine art and architecture] (Moscow, 1977)
Arkhitektura russkogo barokko [Russian Baroque architecture] (Moscow, 1978)

EDUARDS KLAVINS

Virasoro, Alejandro (*b* Buenos Aires, 1892; *d* Buenos Aires, 1978). Argentine architect. From the age of 15 he attended the school of architecture set up in 1901 by Alejandro Christophersen in the Universidad de Buenos Aires, where his final projects revealed a challenge to prevailing academic attitudes that continued throughout a successful professional career. Virasoro acknowledged the influence upon his work of Léon Bakst's stage designs for the Diaghilev ballet, which visited Buenos Aires after World War I, and of Matila Ghyka's early books on the theories of mathematical proportion: *Esthétique des proportions* (Paris, 1927) and *Le Nombre d'or* (Paris, 1931). In line with the populist reforms of the 1920s, Virasoro adopted high standards of performance and provided good facilities for employees in his design and construction organization, for which he adopted the motto *Viribus Unitis*. Although the change to right-wing government in 1930 caused the collapse of Virasoro's practice, he is regarded as one of the pioneers of the Modern Movement in Latin America and of prefabricated housing in particular. His approach to modernism was through Art Deco, for example in his own house (1925) at calle Agüero, Buenos Aires, and in La Equitativa del Plata (1929), which has been criticized for excessive use of the square in its decoration. Virasoro also built a number of non-rhetorical urban buildings in Buenos Aires, such as the Banco El Hogar Argentino (1926), calle B. Mitre, and the Casa del Teatro (1927), Avenida Santa Fé. Perhaps most notable, however, were his early contributions to social housing, using prefabricated components to achieve simple geometrical forms, as in La Continental housing development (1929) at Banfield, Buenos Aires Province.

BIBLIOGRAPHY
F. Bullrich: *Arquitectura argentina contemporánea* (Buenos Aires, 1963)
J. M. Peña and J. Martini: *Alejandro Virasoro* (Buenos Aires, 1969)

LUDOVICO C. KOPPMANN

Virgin Islands. *See under* ANTILLES, LESSER.

Virsaladze, Simon (Bagratovich) (*b* Tiflis [now Tbilisi], 13 Jan 1909). Georgian stage designer. He studied at the Tbilisi Academy of Arts under Iosif Sharleman' (1880–1957), at the Higher Artistic and Technical Institute (Vkhutein, formerly Vkhutemas) under Isaak Rabinovich (1894–1961) and Nisson Shifrin (1892–1961) and at the Leningrad (now St Petersburg) Academy of Arts under Mikhail Bobyshov (1885–1964). He started working in the theatre in 1927, and from 1932 to 1936 he was the principal designer of the Paliashvili Theatre of Opera and Ballet in Tbilisi, for which he also designed productions in later years. His best works at this theatre were his stagings of the ballets *Serdtse gor* ('Heart of the hills'; 1936) with music by Andrey Balanchivadze and *Othello* (1957) with music by Aleksey Machavariani. From 1937 Virsaladze worked for the Kirov Theatre of Opera and Ballet in Leningrad; from 1940 to 1941 and from 1945 to 1962 he was the theatre's Principal Designer. Among the best productions he staged there were operas—Mozart's *Don Giovanni* (1956), Rossini's *Barber of Seville* (1958) and Wagner's *Lohengrin* (1962)—and ballets: *Laurensiya* (1959) with music by Aleksandr Kreyn, *Raymonda* by Glazunov (1948), Tchaikovsky's *Swan Lake* (1950), *Sleeping Beauty* (1952) and *The Nutcracker* (1954), Prokofiev's *Skaz o kammenom tsvetke* ('Tale of the stone flower'; 1957) and Melikov's *Legenda o lyubvi* ('Legend of love'; 1961). He also staged productions at Tbilisi's Mardzhanishvili and Rustaveli Drama Theatres in 1941–5, at the Leningrad Maly Theatre of Opera and Ballet in Leningrad in 1940–55, and individual productions at theatres in Baku and Novosibirsk. He designed costumes for many of the Georgian National Dance Ensemble's programmes and for the films *Hamlet* and *King Lear* by Grigory Kozintsev (1905–73).

From 1957 Virsaladze worked almost exclusively with the choreographer Yury Grigorovich (*b* 1927), designing all the latter's ballets at the Bol'shoy Theatre in Moscow: these included works by Tchaikovsky, Glazunov, Prokofiev, Melikov, as well as Khatchaturian's *Spartacus* (1968), Andrey Eshpay's *Angara* (1976) and Shostakovich's *Golden Age* (1985). Here, Virsaladze created completely new versions of works he had already staged, corresponding to Grigorovich's production concepts. Virsaladze achieved great success as a designer of ballets in the USSR and abroad, in particular in partnership with Grigorovich. A romantic elation, an emotional intensity and a thorough exposure of the theme (especially of tragic themes) are characteristic of his designs. Virsaladze is noted for his profound understanding of the specific requirements of designing for the ballet. His work is further distinguished by its harmony of colouring, its receptiveness to the music, its skilful combination of costume and scenery into a single unity, and its use of generalized forms that underline the meaning of the production.

BIBLIOGRAPHY
V. V. Vanslov: *Simon Virsaladze* (Moscow, 1969)

V. V. VANSLOV

Virtaler, Barthlmä. *See* FIRTHALER, BARTHLMÄ.

Visala. *See* UJJAIN.

Visby. Town on the island of Gotland, Sweden. One of the best-preserved medieval towns in northern Europe, surrounded by a high wall (l. 3.5 km) built of limestone with 27 surviving towers, Visby was an important port and market-place in the Viking period. During the early Middle Ages the town became increasingly important as a commercial centre in the Baltic region. In 1161 Visby became a free port as a result of a treaty with Henry the Lion, Duke of Saxony (*reg* 1142–80). The consequent sharp rise in the immigration of German merchants resulted in the rapid development of the town, which became one of the Hanseatic League's most important city ports. During the Middle Ages about half the population was German. Owing to antagonism between the merchants in Visby and the trading peasants in the rest of Gotland—which in 1288 led to civil war—the wall was started towards the middle of the 13th century without the Swedish king's knowledge, and completed by about 1300 (see fig.).

Increasing trade during the first half of the 14th century made Gotland and Visby affluent, but towards the middle of the century the lively building activity and expansion of Visby seem to have slackened, primarily because of the Black Death in 1349–50, which drastically reduced the town's population, and the conquest of Gotland and a ransom demand exacted in 1361 by the Danish king Valdemar IV (*reg* 1340–75). The town never fully recovered. The shift in the Hanseatic League's trade routes along the German and Baltic coast meant that Visby was no longer the centre of Baltic trade, and during the 15th century the decline became even more marked. Building activity had completely stopped, except for the construction of the castle in Visborg, which was totally destroyed two centuries later. In 1525 Lübeck forces stormed Visby

Visby, curtain wall, mid-13th century to early 14th

and burnt down large sections of it. After the Reformation in the 1530s, the monasteries were closed, and of the many churches only St Maria (originally the German merchants' church and now the cathedral) was saved from decay. Several churches stood as burnt-out ruins and were never rebuilt but plundered for their building materials, especially in the 18th century. By 1645, when the island was recovered by Sweden, Visby had lost its commercial significance. The town revived somewhat during the 19th century with the establishment of industries and the construction of the railway.

Inside the wall the medieval town plan survives, with narrow streets and tall step-gabled houses. The oldest surviving building is the Gunpowder Tower (Kruttornet), also known as the Lamb's Tower (Lammets torn), a 12th-century castellated tower that originally defended the harbour. Along Strandgatan are several medieval merchants' houses with high stepped-gables facing the street. The best-preserved is the so-called Old Pharmacy (Gamla Apoteket), dating from the 13th century.

During the Middle Ages Visby had numerous churches, of which two lay just outside the walls. Three were monastic, and two were hospital churches, one of which, St Göran, was situated north of the city walls. Visby had more churches than any other town in medieval Sweden, probably because several were so-called factory churches, mainly intended for the foreign traders with trading establishments in the town, notably the Germans, Danes and Russians; the Russians were said to have had two churches in Visby. The only medieval church still in use is St Maria. Building began at the end of the 12th century, and the Romanesque basilica was consecrated in 1225. During the late 13th century it was extended and converted to a hall church following Westphalian models. In the 14th century a large Gothic chapel was added on the south side.

Three monasteries were established during the 13th and 14th centuries. The remains of the conventual buildings attached to the Dominican church of St Nicholas lie underground to the north of the church itself, which dates mainly from the 13th century (the choir is 14th-century). One of the largest and most remarkable church ruins in Visby is that of the Franciscan church of St Katarina, with remains of its conventual buildings to the south. The church was probably built just after the monks' arrival in Visby in 1233, but its present appearance dates mainly from the 14th century. It was completed in 1412. The excavated traces of the town's third monastery, a Cistercian convent founded in 1246, are situated just outside the city walls on the east side.

The most interesting church plan in Visby is that of the church of the Holy Spirit, probably dating from the first half of the 13th century. It has a two-storey octagonal nave and an apse concealed in the flat end wall of the choir. The groin vaults of the lower storey rest on four octagonal piers. This type of church is reminiscent of the Palatine chapel at Aachen (see AACHEN, §2(ii)(a)). The so-called Russian church and the church of St Lars show Byzantine influences. The former, now in ruins, is a small Romanesque building with an apse linked to an almost square nave. It may have served as the Russian merchants' church. The Greek-cross plan of St Lars was based on centrally planned Byzantine churches.

BIBLIOGRAPHY

E. Eckhoff and O. Janse: *Visby stadsmur*, 2 vols (Stockholm, 1922–36)
G. Svahnström: *Visby under 1000 år* (Stockholm, 1984)
H. Yrving: *Visby: Hansestad på Gotland* (Stockholm, 1986)

ERLAND LAGERLÖF

Viscardi, Giovanni Antonio (*bapt* San Vittore, nr Roveredo, Grisons, 27 Dec 1645; *bur* Munich, 9 Sept 1713). Swiss–Italian builder and architect, active in Germany. His father, Bartolomeo Viscardi (1599–1654), was summoned to Munich by Elector Maximilian I of Bavaria in 1630 and worked in the Innviertel area and in Lower Bavaria from 1634. Giovanni Antonio completed his apprenticeship in the building trade, at that time strongly influenced by Italian architectural models, in the Swiss canton of Grisons. He is first mentioned in documents in connection with the construction in 1674 of the pilgrimage church at Altötting, Lower Bavaria, where he acted as clerk of works for Enrico Zuccalli. It must have been on Zuccalli's recommendation that Viscardi eventually went to Munich in 1677. In 1678 he was appointed court master mason and in 1685 court architect. His first years in office were taken up with small-scale but varied duties for the court building office, but he was ousted in 1689 after disputes with Zuccalli and had to make his way as an independent architect until 1702.

Viscardi then emerged as a building contractor employing up to 150 journeymen and clerks of works from both Switzerland and Bavaria. He dominated building activity in Munich and a large surrounding area, proving himself a notable church architect. After he had designed extensive monastic buildings for the Cistercian abbey of Fürstenfeld (built 1691–9 by Martin Guneztrhainer (*d* 1699), a master mason from Munich), he had a three-year term of office as architect to the Theatine Order in Munich. The Jesuits there commissioned him to extend their college and build an assembly hall, and he also did work for the nobility and the upper middle classes. From *c*. 1700 he built various summer residences and country houses in Munich and the surrounding area. Although few of these have survived, they exerted a considerable influence on suburban secular architecture in Bavaria during the late Baroque period. The former Premonstratensian monastery church at Neustift (now the parish church of SS Peter and Paul, Freising) had a basilica-type plan designed by Viscardi and built by Giovanni Giacomo Maffioli (*d* 1721) in 1700–21 (later altered). The façade was flat and articulated by pilasters, while the interior was of the wall buttress type (*Wandpfeilerkirche*), with no galleries but otherwise deeply modelled. The rebuilding (1700–02) of the Jesuit church of St Salvator, Augsburg, was followed by designs for the former Cistercian abbey church of Maria Himmelfahrt in Fürstenfeld, where Viscardi produced another variation of the type of construction used at Neustift, with internal wall pillars displaying pairs of engaged columns. There are two tiers of galleries above the side chapels, the lower one very narrow; the transverse vaults above them are almost as high as the crown of the nave vault. Building was halted in 1705 and not resumed until 1717, to new designs by Johann Georg Ettenhofer (1668–1741).

Viscardi's pilgrimage church of Mariahilf in Freystadt, Upper Palatinate, built between 1700 and 1710, has a ground-plan in the form of a Greek cross. Viscardi started from the central plan typical of the Roman High Baroque that he had learnt from Zuccalli and his design for the pilgrimage church at Altötting and combined this with the local building tradition. He developed an arcaded octagonal space covered with a dome, which served as a model for 18th-century Bavarian country churches. The salient features of the interior of the Mariahilf are the dominating vault of the dome and the contrast between the powerfully three-dimensional emphasis created by the wall pillars and the smooth, unarticulated planarity of the external walls. After his reinstatement as court architect to Elector Maximilian II Emanuel of Bavaria in 1702, Viscardi was put in charge of the large building schemes at Schloss Schleissheim and Schloss Nymphenburg in Munich. Although Bavaria was under imperial Austrian administration, he became chief court architect in 1706, after Zuccalli's dismissal. His last years were filled with official duties and work as an expert consultant in the court building service. The Bürgersaalkirche (1709–11; destr. 1944; rest.), Munich, was the result of collaboration with Johann Andreas Wolff, court painter in Munich. Viscardi's Dreifaltigkeitskirche (1711–18), Munich, is another notable example of the complex spatial organization that he had achieved in his church at Freystadt, on a reduced scale but in a more concentrated form. In its organization of space it represents the transition from Italian Baroque to Bavarian Late Baroque. The large frescoes in the dome and the altar structures contribute substantially to the spatial impression. The two-storey façade of the Dreifaltigkeitskirche has a superelevated middle section that juts out in the form of a bay, with columns marking the points of return of the strongly vertical components of the façade, an innovative solution that heralded the Rococo style in southern Germany. This entrance bay is echoed internally by an apse at the back of the deep choir, which leads off from a square nave roofed by a dome on pendentives, broken by four windows above a circular cornice. The transepts are stubby and flat-ended.

Most of Viscardi's work comprises simple functional buildings in the typical style of a master builder from the Grisons, with a feeling for simple cubic masses composed of a unified type of wall surface with flat articulation. He was adept at adjusting to the indigenous Bavarian style and was important not only for the development of centrally planned religious buildings in Bavaria but also for the formation of a sound building trade.

BIBLIOGRAPHY

M. Hauttmann: *Geschichte der kirchlichen Baukunst in Bayern, Schwaben und Franken, 1550–1780* (Munich, 1921)

A. M. Zendralli: *Graubündner Baumeister und Stukkatoren in deutschen Landen zur Barock- und Rokokozeit* (Zurich, 1930)

N. Lieb: *Münchner Barockbaumeister* (Munich, 1941)

A. M. Zendralli: *I Viscardi di San Vittore: Edili, magistrati e mercenari* (Poschiavo, 1954)

K.-L. Lippert: *Giovanni Antonio Viscardi (1634–1713): Studien zur Entwicklung der barocken Kirchenbaukunst in Bayern* (Munich, 1969)

N. Lieb: *München: Die Geschichte seiner Kunst* (Munich, 1971, 2/1977)

N. Lieb and H. -J. Sauermost, eds: *Münchens Kirchen* (Munich, 1973)

M. Pfister: *Baumeister aus Graubünden: Wegbereiter des Barock* (Chur, 1993)

SABINE HEYM

Viscardi [Viscardo], **Girolamo** [Gerolamo] (*b* Laino, nr Lugano, 1467; *d* ?Genoa, after Feb 1522). Italian sculptor. He spent four years working for the sculptor Antonio della Porta. From 1497 to 1501 he collaborated with Giovanni d'Aria (*fl c.* 1490–*c.* 1508) and his brother Michele d'Aria (*fl c.* 1466–*c.* 1502) on the marble tomb of the brothers *Agostino and Giovanni Adorno* in S Gerolamo in Quarto, Genoa (fragments *in situ*). As a result of the French occupation of Genoa (1499–1508), he received a number of important commissions from French patrons and was therefore instrumental in introducing the Italian Renaissance style into France. There is, however, no evidence that he himself ever visited France. In 1502 Louis XII commissioned a tomb in honour of his ancestors the Dukes of Orléans from Viscardi and Michele d'Aria in association with the Florentines Donato Benti and Benedetto da Rovezzano. The marble monument, now in the abbey church of Saint-Denis, was originally set up in 1504 in the Celestine Church (destr.), Paris; it combines a typically Italianate base in the form of a sarcophagus surrounded by small statues of apostles in niches with a more French style for the four reclining figures of *Louis, Duke of Orléans* (1372–1407), his wife *Valentina Visconti* (1366–1408) and two of their sons, *Charles, Duke of Orléans* (1391–1465) and *Philippe, Comte de Vertus* (1396–1420). In 1507 and 1508 Antoine Bohier (*c.* 1460–1519), Abbot of Fécamp, who had accompanied Louis XII to Italy, commissioned from Viscardi an altar, a tabernacle, a reliquary and two statues of saints (all marble); though damaged, these remain at the abbey church of La Trinité, Fécamp. Kruft, who attributed to Viscardi the carved screen of the Adorno chapel in S Giuliano d'Albaro, Genoa, suggested that the stone screens enclosing the chapels around the choir at La Trinité were executed by French craftsmen at Rouen to designs by Viscardi. Blunt, however, considered the Renaissance detailing to be more Italianate than French, endorsing the view that they must have been executed by Italian workmen in Normandy. Viscardi is documented in Genoa until at least 1522, working at the Palazzo Spinola in 1516 and at the churches of S Lorenzo and S Domenico. With the possible exception of a marble tabernacle from the latter (fragment, London, V&A), attributed to him by Kruft, none of this later work is known.

BIBLIOGRAPHY

P. Vitry: *Michel Colombe et la sculpture française de son temps* (Paris, 1901)

A. Blunt: *Art and Architecture in France, 1500–1700*, Pelican Hist. A. (Harmondsworth, 1953, rev. 6/1982)

H. W. Kruft: 'Gerolamo Viscardi: Ein genuesischer Bildhauer der Renaissance', *Mitt. Ksthist. Inst. Florenz*, xv (1971), pp. 273–88

Le Roi, la sculpture et la mort: Gisants et tombeaux de la basilique de Saint-Denis (exh. cat. by A. Erlande-Brandenburg and others, Saint-Denis, Maison Cult., 1976)

PHILIPPE ROUILLARD

Visch, Henk (*b* Eindhoven, 18 Sept 1950). Dutch sculptor and draughtsman. He trained at the Koninklijke Academie voor Kunst en Vormgeving in 's Hertogenbosch between 1968 and 1973. Initially he made drawings, but in 1981 he put together his first exhibition of installations, entitled *Getimmerde tekeningen* ('Drawings in carpentry') at the Apollohuis, Eindhoven. His work is partly based on a personal mythology created in drawings and executed in installations. The mannequin-like figures, for example *Untitled* (wood and cloth, 1983; Amsterdam, Stedel. Mus.), and objects are constructed from natural materials such as wood, feathers, paper and hair. Particularly characteristic is the delicate balance and the treatment of the surfaces of his sculptures. Another part of his work comprises geometric constructions in the form of such structures as footbridges (e.g. *Untitled*, 1980; Otterlo, Kröller–Müller) or pylons, or crystal shapes. These works are partly influenced by Ludwig Wittgenstein's philosophy of language. Among Visch's monumental commissions is the installation (1985) at the Paradiso youth centre, Amsterdam, consisting of two prisms, a clock on the roof and a diamond-shaped stone in front of the entrance, carried out in collaboration with John Kormeling.

For illustration *see* NETHERLANDS, THE, fig. 32.

BIBLIOGRAPHY

Henk Visch: Skulpturen, 1980–1986 (exh. cat., Nordhorn, Städt. Gal., 1987)
Henk Visch (exh. cat., Venice, Biennale, Dut. Pav., 1988)

JOHN STEEN

Vischer. German family of brass founders, or redsmiths (*Rotschmiede*), and artists. They were active in Nuremberg from the mid-15th century until the second half of the 16th. Their foundry near the Pegnitz River, referred to as 'der Vischerhütte', was the most important in Germany during this period. The Vischers worked exclusively in brass, preferred in Nuremberg for both sculpture and church furnishings, as opposed to bronze, which was mostly restricted to the casting of bells. (1) Hermann Vischer (i) and his son (2) Peter Vischer (i) made large furnishings and tomb monuments commissioned for churches as far away as Breslau (now Wrocław), Kraków and Posen (now Poznan). Peter (i) had five sons, (3) Hermann Vischer (ii), (4) Peter Vischer (ii), (5) Hans Vischer, Jacob Vischer and Paulus Vischer (*d* Mainz, 1531), the first two of whom predeceased their father. The foundry presumably continued until the death in 1592 of Hans's son, (6) Georg Vischer. Since the casting workshop as a whole or the master in charge were nearly always credited with any completed work, clear delineations within the cooperative effort and of the roles played by younger family members are often elusive. Current opinion, however, tends to describe the first two Vischers as primarily brass-casters, while their descendants are recognized also to have been the creators of models to be cast and as inventive artists.

The commissions of the Vischerhütte before the 16th century were exclusively Late Gothic in style, whereas later productions abandoned this in favour of a Renaissance style. This second Vischer style evidences a new preoccupation with humanistic subjects. While large-scale works continued to be provided through the fourth decade of the 16th century, the Vischers expanded the scope of their production to include important smaller objects. Intended for specific individuals with humanistic tastes, these included portrait medals, plaquettes and inkpots. Johann Neudörfer, Germany's first biographer of artists (1547), provided much valuable information about the Vischers' activities and interests.

(1) Hermann Vischer (i) (*fl* 1453; *bur* Nuremberg, 13 Jan 1488). Brass founder. He was listed as a redsmith in the Nuremberg council's rolls for 1453. He probably emigrated from northern Germany, rather than from the Netherlands, as some have thought, and established his own foundry in the imperial city. The large baptismal font (see fig.) is an expertly cast and precisely finished work that reflects the lost wood model executed by an unknown carver. The credit for the final product is clear from the inscription: *Meister Hermann Vischer zu Nurbeg*. The interlocked ogee and cusped arches of the central support, the clustered piers, the sturdy buttresses, the rampant escutcheon bearing lions, the stocky and heavily draped Apostle figures and the large, swelling foliage motifs are combined in a composition that is at once dramatic and monumental.

Under Hermann (i)'s direction the workshop produced from the late 1450s a series of highly finished tomb monuments for the cathedrals of Bamberg, Wrocław, Meissen, Merseberg and Poznań. Based on wood models by anonymous carvers, these imposing works are entirely Late Gothic in both composition and detail. The last commission cast while Hermann (i) was still alive, the life-size, standing tomb figure in full Gothic armour of *Otto IV of Henneberg* (*c.* 1487–8; Römhild, Marienkirche), has often been credited to Peter (i). The model, also by an unknown artist, was probably carved in wood.

1. Hermann Vischer (i): baptismal font, brass, 1457 (Wittenberg, St Marien)

(2) Peter Vischer (i) (*b* Nuremberg, *c.* 1460; *d* Nuremberg, 7 Jan 1529). Brass founder, son of (1) Hermann Vischer (i). After his father's death, Peter (i) was permitted by the Nuremberg city council to head the family brass-casting foundry, which had already become one of the most prominent foundries in Germany. He was registered as a redsmith in 1489. The elegant brass candelabra (Nuremberg, St Lorenz), cast after a wood model made by a woodturner, has traditionally been regarded as his masterpiece (in the medieval sense).

The authorship of the designs and models associated with Peter (i) continues to be debated. His collection of 300 'Altfränkisch pild' has often been presumed to include old wooden sculptures or models, although another suggestion is that these were Roman coins (Holst). A large pen-and-ink drawing on sheets of parchment (1488; h. 1750 mm; Vienna, Akad. Bild. Kst) is entirely Late Gothic and delineates the first idea for the Sebaldus Tomb (Nuremberg, St Sebaldus; *see* (3) and (4) below). This design is now considered to be by another Nuremberg artist, perhaps SIMON LAINBERGER or Adam Kraft. Lainberger may have collaborated with Peter (i) when both were at the Palatine court in Heidelberg in 1494. According to Neudörfer, Kraft was a lifelong friend of Peter (i).

One of the earliest casting projects undertaken by Peter (i) was the *Kneeling Man with a Branch* (1490; Munich, Bayer. Nmus.; see fig.). Kraft may have supplied the wax model for this powerful example of Late Gothic naturalism. Rather than being in the act of breaking the branch, as is often thought, the figure was to have used it to steady the heavy weight intended for his right shoulder (had the context been completed); this could have been a font, pulpit or sacrament house. The *Kneeling Man* may be seen as an allegory glorifying applied ability and masterly craft.

Another early project of Peter (i)'s workshop was the large tomb of *Archbishop Ernst von Sachsen* (1495; Magdeburg Cathedral), with a massive effigy of the Archbishop, an intricate Gothic canopy and a dated inscription on the lid mentioning Peter Vischer. The sides are punctuated with large panels with coats of arms beneath ogee arches and tracery, alternating with 14 statuettes of Apostles and saints under individual openwork canopies. While the authorship of the lost graphic design remains in question, it is presumed that Simon Lainberger may at least have provided some of the wood models for the statuettes. A second cast from the original model of one of these, *St Maurice* (h. 575 mm; Nuremberg, Ger. Nmus.), was made *c.* 1507 as an ornament for the courtyard fountain of the Imhoff family house, the gift of Peter (i) to his friend Peter Imhoff.

Peter (i) continued to oversee other important commissions, both engraved and in relief, for the cathedrals at Merseberg (1490), Wrocław (1496), Poznan (1498) and Bamberg (1506), and for the abbey church at Ellwangen. The Sebaldus Tomb in Nuremberg and the free-standing, life-size statues of *King Arthur* and *Theodoric* for the tomb of *Emperor Maximilian I* (Innsbruck, Hofkirche) followed in 1507–19 and 1513, respectively. The latter sculptures, with their easy contrapposto and convincing sense of arrested movement, display a new freedom in the rendering of the human figure, despite the rich ornamentation and complex elements of each figure's armour. One may sense

Peter Vischer (i): *Kneeling Man with a Branch*, brass, h. 360 mm, 1490 (Munich, Bayerisches Nationalmuseum)

here the partial influence of the ideals of the Venetian Renaissance sculptors and of Albrecht Dürer.

Peter (i)'s sons, especially Hermann (ii) and Peter (ii), figured more prominently in the artistic output of the workshop after 1510. It was, however, Peter (i) who in 1512 received the original commission for the large brass screen (mostly destr.) for the Fugger funerary chapel in St Anna, Augsburg. According to the Nuremberg humanist Pankratz Bernhaupt, called Schwenter (1481–1555), work on the screen began *c.* 1515 (Meller; Wuttke). Hermann (ii) probably provided the designs and many of the models for this vast project, but the screen was abandoned after difficulties with the Fugger heirs and Hermann (ii)'s premature death. Ownership of the completed parts and models was assumed by the Vischer workshop on 2 August 1529.

(3) Hermann Vischer (ii) (*b* Nuremberg, *c.* 1486; *d* ?Nuremberg, 1 Jan 1517). Brass-caster, sculptor and draughtsman, son of (2) Peter Vischer (i). Neudörfer praised Hermann (ii) for his skill in casting, inscribing, tracery and portraiture, ranking him in importance with Peter (i). He was also a sculptor of models and a superior draughtsman. Efforts to distinguish the work of the son from that of the father, made difficult by the family workshop system, have been founded primarily on stylistic distinctions, including references to the paintings and graphics of Dürer, and the presumption that Hermann (ii) himself provided some of the designs and wood models for the early commissions credited to him in Kraków, Meissen and Römhild. His early tomb-plate of *Piotr Kmita* (*d* 1505; Kraków, Wawel Cathedral) presents a low-relief

Hermann Vischer (ii): Lunette relief with the arms of the German emperor Charles IV and a scene of fighting centaurs, 0.90×1.90 m, modelled *c.* 1515–16, cast in brass by Hans Vischer 1535–40 (Annecy, Musée Léon Matès); from the Fugger Screen (most sections melted down after 1806)

effigy of the deceased in full armour in a stance that recalls Dürer's *St Eustace* from the Paumgärtner Altarpiece (*c.* 1502; Munich, Alte Pin.) and anticipates the statue of *King Arthur* for the Maximilian monument (*see* (2) above).

The effigies in relief on the lid of the tomb-chest of *Elizabeth and Hermann VIII of Henneberg* (Römhild, Marienkirche), cast from a wood model of *c.* 1507–12, are freely based on Dürer's pen-and-ink design for a tomb slab (Oxford, Christ Church). The relief has a freshness, simplicity and subtlety in the balance of the two figures, the distinction of the figural masses from the background, the contrasts of soft/hard and patterned textures, and the pensive facial expressions. Other portions of this tomb are more conservative, such as the small statuettes, also cast from wood models, that stand on short, double columns round the tomb-chest.

A large statuette depicting a pilgrim saint (h. 660 mm; Vienna, Ksthist. Mus.) has long been attributed to Hermann (ii), partly on the basis of its relationship to some of the smaller statuettes on the Römhild tomb-chest. The creator of the original wood model, however, whether Hermann (ii) or not, was certainly a remarkably gifted sculptor who, while retaining an entirely Gothic style, gave his sculpture an extraordinary sense of balance, repose and conviction in the definition of mass and weight. By placing the figure's right leg in frontal view and the left leg behind it, in profile, the artist depicted a kind of contrapposto position, but not in the classical sense, for the equal weight on both legs precludes this. The saint stands with quiet dignity, his head tipped sideways and eyes lowered towards the missing attribute formerly held in the right hand.

In 1515, after the death of his wife, Hermann (ii) visited Siena and Rome. The impact of this trip was specifically felt in his architectural design and sculptural invention. Architectural drawings (Paris, Louvre), including the severely classical but unexecuted designs for the Sebaldus Tomb as well as those for the reconstruction of the exterior of St Peter's choir of Bamberg Cathedral, show a skilled adaptation of Italian Renaissance architecture. This change in architectural style is not evident, however, in the revised and executed upper portion of the Sebaldus Tomb (*see* (2) above and (4) below), which has often been attributed to him. Here the canopy—a kind of heavenly Jerusalem—takes the form of three openwork cupolas constructed of a complex mixture of Romanesque and Gothic detail with stepped piers, flying buttresses, cusped

pinnacles, domed chapels and pointed and rounded arches. The anti-Classical intricacy of these interlocking elements suggests either that this portion of the Sebaldus Tomb must have been designed before Hermann's visit to Italy in 1515 or that the attribution to him is incorrect.

After his return to Nuremberg, Hermann must have concentrated on the overall design and many of the models for major portions of the Fugger Screen (*see* (2) above). The screen, even as it was later erected in the Great Hall of the Nuremberg Rathaus, must have closely followed Hermann's Renaissance scheme. The appearance of the Nuremberg version, which was dismantled in 1806 and mostly melted down soon after, is known from 17th- and 18th-century paintings and engravings—for example an engraving (*c.* 1715; Nuremberg, Städt. Graph. Samml.) by Johann Adam Delsenbach (1687–1765). It comprised a colonnade of eight columns, a decorated architrave and a geometrically patterned grille. A tall, open triple arcade with an architrave and decorated pediment was placed above the central, arched doorway, whereas the two flanking rectangular doors, which contained a continuation of the grillework, were surmounted by decorated lunettes. The details of the screen are depicted in a series of sketches (Nuremberg, Ger. Nmus.) made by Karl Haller von Hallerstein just before the sale and demolition; these provide convincing evidence that the screen was decorated on both sides. From these drawings and the two extant lunette reliefs (see fig.) and two sections of the friezes (l. 2.85 m; all Annecy, Mus. Léon Marès), it is possible to attribute to Hermann (ii) the models for all four sides of the lunettes and the extant frieze with acanthus rinceaux and two battling male nudes in the centre. These attributions derive in part from details that reveal traces of his earlier experience as a carver of wood models for tombs.

Most importantly, the screen reliefs demonstrate again that Hermann (ii)'s excursion to Italy had a marked impact on his work. Building upon his already considerable facility to render convincingly figural mass, decorative detail and composition, he was especially receptive to Italian Renaissance modifications of these elements. His evident intelligence and taste as chief designer and main sculptor of the models should have been well matched to meeting the Fugger family's humanistic requirements, but the endeavour was short-lived, as Hermann died less than two years after the actual work began. Yet even with the ensuing adaptation of the project and its subsequent destruction, the screen is still regarded as one of the pre-eminent humanistic achievements in Renaissance art north of the Alps.

(4) Peter Vischer (ii) (*b* Nuremberg, 1487; *d* Nuremberg, 1528). Brass-caster, sculptor and draughtsman, son of (2) Peter Vischer (i). He was intrigued with certain ideas from the Classical world and the Italian Renaissance, probably from the very beginning of his activity as an artist and craftsman in the Vischerhütte. His responsibility for several portrait medals would support this. (His father may have owned a large collection of ancient Roman coins.) In addition, his medallic self-portrait in profile (1509; Paris, Bib. N. Cab. Médailles), which was produced using the lost-wax technique, is a direct reflection of 15th-century Italian medallic style and technique. His clearest statement in a Renaissance style and perspective is the epitaph of *Provost Anton Kress* (*d* 1513; h. *c.* 1050 mm without inscription; Nuremberg, St Lorenz). This low relief shows the provost kneeling in profile before an altar set within a chapel framed by a coffered barrel vault and round arch supported on decorated pilasters. Two plump, winged putti cling to the outer edge of the arch.

Peter (ii)'s greatest contributions, however, were made for the Sebaldus Tomb (Nuremberg, St Sebaldus; *see* (3) above and NUREMBERG, fig. 6), including countless wax models for many, if not all, of the figures that peopled this complex monument (see fig.). The intention of the original commission by the Nuremberg Council was to provide a large, brass, tabernacle-like cage to protect the relics of the patron saint contained in the shrine, a sloped-roof coffin of silver and silver-gilt over wood, dating from 1391–7. The 1488 drawing (*see* (2) above), or the wooden model (destr.) made after it, provided the fundamental idea: the cage concept, the protective series of 12 Apostles and the reliefs on the base with episodes of the life of the saint. Peter (i) was commissioned to reactivate the project in 1507 and directed work on the tomb until its completion

Peter Vischer (ii) (with Peter Vischer (i)): Sebaldus Tomb, brass, 1507–12 and 1514–19 (Nuremberg, St Sebaldus)

in 1519; an interruption from 1512 to 1514 may have been the result of a shortage of funds or the simultaneous commission from Emperor Maximilian I for work on his tomb-monument (Innsbruck, Hofkirche). The striking changes in the Sebaldus project included a reduction in the height of the canopy, the use of snails and dolphins to support the whole structure, the rich amalgam of Romanesque, Gothic and Renaissance architectural detail, and the dark patination throughout. The multitude of figures, large and small, scattered about the base and within the canopy, were newly invented by Peter (ii) and reflect the style and technique of the great Paduan master of the small bronze statuette, Andrea Riccio. The mythological, allegorical, biblical and other subjects include the *Four Heroes of Antiquity*, the *Cardinal Virtues*, planets, tritons, sirens, putti, small dogs, harpy candle brackets and Old Testament prophets. Originally modelled in wax, these figures convey a rare animation, expressiveness and, in certain instances, humour.

Also attributed to Peter (ii) are the almost hidden low reliefs about the inner base, which depict episodes from the *Life of St Sebaldus*. Retaining the Late Gothic style, they are masterpieces of dramatic simplicity, subtle poetry and poignancy. Standing near by, at each end of the base, are two statuettes also in the Late Gothic style rendered with an expressive naturalism: one depicts the haggard old saint as a pilgrim holding a model of the church, while the other represents the sculptor's father, Peter (i). Portrayed in his leather apron and cap and holding the tools of his craft, the subject of this statuette may be allied, in its interpretation of the dignity of a master of a fine craft, with the *Kneeling Man* (Munich, Bayer. Nmus.), cast in the Vischerhütte in 1490, and Adam Kraft's stone self-portrait beneath his sacrament house (1493; Nuremberg, St Lorenz).

The tall statuettes of the *Apostles* (h. *c.* 540 mm), each standing above thin colonnettes at mid-level around the perimeter of the complex, are perhaps Peter (ii)'s most sublime works. These figures are a remarkable melding of earlier Gothic elements with the easy contrapposto stances of the Italian Renaissance. Their proportions may derive simultaneously from a direct perception of Italian art and familiarity with Dürer's reworking of ancient theories of proportion. The *Apostles*' draperies may also owe a debt to Dürer's drapery studies, such as his preparatory drawing of an *Apostle* (1508; h. 240 m,; Berlin, Kupferstichkab.) for the Heller Altarpiece (destr.).

Peter (ii)'s visit to Italy in 1507–8 (probably his first) must have greatly enhanced his ability to model in wax and cast easily using the lost-wax technique: his *Apostles* were probably produced shortly after this trip. Following a presumed second visit (1512–14), his style became noticeably more Paduan and closer to that of Riccio, and the subjects betray a greater attention to humanist thought.

Peter (ii)'s drawings are figurative and didactic in their use of myth and allegory. His knowledge of Latin and his friendship with the humanist Schwenter may help to explain the narrative accuracy of these drawings. Peter (ii)'s pen-and-ink illustrations of Ovid's *Metamorphoses*, dated 1514, are sensitive interpretations of the stories of *Scylla* and of *Orpheus and Eurydice* (Nuremberg, Ger. Nmus.). He also illustrated Schwenter's *Histori Herculis*

(1515; Berlin, Kupferstichkab.) and Boccaccio's *Decameron* (Paris, Louvre; Würzburg, Ubib.). One of Peter's allegorical drawings depicts the *Triumphs of the Reformation* (1524; Weimar, Goethe-Nmus. Frauenplan).

Related to the humanist tenor of Peter (ii)'s drawings are several plaquettes and small containers, each cast in brass in the lost-wax technique. Three of them bear the Vischer family mark: two fish impaled on an arrow. The plaquettes depicting *Orpheus and Eurydice* (*c.* 1516; h. 163 mm, Hamburg, Mus. Kst & Gew.; h. 194 mm, Washington, DC, N.G.A.) are remarkable for their great economy of detail, subtlety in both modelling and movement, and keen restraint in composition. The sculptor conveys through them an elegaic mood while representing the most touching moment in Ovid's retelling of the Greek myth. Two inkpots (*c.* 1516, h. 167 mm; 1525, h. 193 mm; both Oxford, Ashmolean), each with a female nude, have been shown to be allegories expanding on the Vischer family motto, VITAM NON MORTEM RECOGITA ('Reflect on life, not death'). The enlarged meaning embodies the admonition to reflect upon eternal life (in the Christian sense), not death, vanity and earthly fortunes (Wuttke, 1965). Both inkpots, as well as another depicting *Adam and Eve* (*c.* 1520; h. 146 mm; Cleveland, OH, Mus. A.), recall not only Peter (ii)'s own smaller figures on the Sebaldus Tomb but also the small bronzes of the Paduan Renaissance, most notably those of Riccio, reflecting the latter's figural proportions, surfaces and technique. Peter's inkpots, like his plaquettes, may have been made for one of his aspiring humanist friends in Nuremberg, such as Sebald Schreyer (1446–1520), a patron and close associate of the Vischer family.

The epitaph of *Cardinal Albrecht von Brandenburg* (1525; Aschaffenburg, SS Peter und Alexander) and the wall tomb of *Elector Frederick III* (1527; Wittenberg, Schlosskirche), each inscribed by Peter (i) as head of the workshop, are clearly Renaissance in their form and ornament. The massive portrait of Frederick is particularly powerful in its intensity of facial expression. The high finish and contrast between the smooth and engraved surfaces reflect back to the Late Gothic monuments also produced under the direction of Peter (i). The Elector's tomb has the further distinction of being Peter (ii)'s official masterpiece as approved by the Nuremberg council in 1527, an honour that allowed him to be recognized as a master (redsmith) in the brass-casting craft. Up to then he had worked as an assistant or journeyman for his father.

(5) Hans Vischer (*b* Nuremberg, *c.* 1489; *d* Leipzig, 8 Sept 1550). Sculptor, draughtsman and brass-caster, son of (2) Peter Vischer (i). He assumed the direction of the family workshop in 1529 following the deaths of Peter (ii) and Peter (i). He is credited with several works in a rather vapid Renaissance style, such as the two epitaphs of 1521 of *Henning Goden* (Erfurt Cathedral; Wittenberg, Schlosskirche). The double tomb of *Electors Joachim I and John Cicero* (1530; Berlin Cathedral), however, is a particularly imposing work, featuring a formidable frontal effigy of John Cicero on the upper level of this two-tiered ensemble. In 1534 Hans was responsible for the cast of the figure of *St Wenceslas*, its supporting base, canopy and candlestick in Prague Cathedral. The wood model for the statue of *St*

Wenceslas (Nuremberg, Ger. Nmus.) was probably by Hans Peisser. About 1534 Hans Vischer also provided the screen and candelabra for the Sigismund Chapel in Wawel Cathedral, Kraków, and completed the wall tomb of *Elector John* (Wittenberg, Schlosskirche); in the latter Hans emulated the more powerful tomb relief of *Elector Frederick III* cast by his brother for the same church.

Particularly important was Hans's salvage work commissioned in 1536 by the Nuremberg Council to complete the abandoned Fugger screen exactly after the old 'model' ('*gerissenes Muster*'). Owing to financial difficulties, Hans did not finish the project for four years. In adopting Hermann (ii)'s models for the lunettes, Hans had to replace the Fugger arms with those of Nuremberg. He was also forced to supply some entirely new models, such as that for the extant frieze with sea centaurs (ichthyocentaurs), battling men, and women and children fleeing through a river (Annecy, Mus. Léon Marès). This relief, however, lacks the sophistication, vigorous movement, elegance of line and balanced composition evident in Hermann (ii)'s earlier reliefs. Hans does not seem to have benefited from a sojourn in Italy and showed a limited ability in assimilating Renaissance freedoms of figural movement and proportion. His classicism, despite a dependence on Italian engravings, is diminished; the heads are too small for the oversized and neckless bodies, and the movement, always parallel to the plane of the relief, is abrupt and lacks the involved, twisting forms that were used so effectively by Hermann (ii).

(6) Georg Vischer (*b c.* 1520; *d* 1592). Brass-caster, son of (5) Hans Vischer. Little is known about his life and artistic output. The allegorical inkpot (h. 176 mm; Berlin, Skulpgal., 810), bearing the artist's initials (G.F.) and date (1547) inscribed on the underside of the base, represents an iconographic variation of the two inkpots by his uncle, (4) Peter Vischer (ii). The style of Georg's inkpot also derives in part from Peter (ii)'s figural proportions and the spatial relationships established between figure, base, vase and skull. Yet Georg's nude female lacks the older Vischer's subtle modelling and conception of organic mass. By contrast, Georg's sharp, angled lines and planes, coupled with an over-simplified treatment of the limbs, are likely manifestations of his lesser talent, rather than deliberate artistic choices. This is further demonstrated in his small brass figure groups, some of which are signed (Florence, Bargello; Moscow, Pushkin Mus. F.A.; Nuremberg, Ger. Nmus.). This awkwardness is, perhaps, an extension of the weaknesses seen in his father's frieze for the screen erected in the Nuremberg Rathaus.

BIBLIOGRAPHY

Thieme–Becker

G. W. K. Lochner, ed.: *Des Johann Neudörfer Schreib- und Rechenmeisters zu Nürnberg Nachrichten von Künstlern und Werkleuten daselbst aus dem Jahre 1547, nebst der Fortsetzung des Andreas Gulden*, Quellenschr. Kstgesch. & Ksttech., x (Vienna, 1875)

A. Mayer: *Die Genreplastik an Peter Vischers Sebaldusgrab* (Leipzig, 1911)

A. Feulner: *Peter Vischers Sebaldusgrab in Nürnberg* (Munich, 1924)

S. Meller: *Peter Vischer der Ältere und seine Werkstatt* (Leipzig, 1925)

E. F. Bange: 'Die künstlerische Bedeutung Peter Vischers des Älteren', *Jb. Preuss. Kstsamml.*, 1 (1929), pp. 167–82

R. Berliner: 'Peter Vischer: Problem', *Münch. Jb. Bild. Kst*, n. s., viii (1931), pp. 133–55

N. von Holst: 'Kunstkammer oder Wunderstube', *Kunstchronik*, ii (1949), pp. 222–3

T. Müller: 'Der sogenannte Astbrecher des älteren Peter Vischer', *Wiss. Z. Karl-Marx-U. Leipzig*, v (1955–6), pp. 223–7

D. Wuttke: 'Die Handschriften-Zeugnisse über das Wirken der Vischer nebst kritischen Bemerkungen zu ihrer Auswertung', *Z. Kstgesch.*, xxii (1959), pp. 324–36

K. Pechstein: *Beiträge zur Geschichte der Vischerhütte in Nürnberg* (diss., Berlin, Freie U., 1962)

H. Stafski: *Der jüngere Peter Vischer* (Nuremberg, 1962)

G. von Osten: 'Über Peter Vischers törichten Bauern und den Beginn der Renaissance in Nürnberg', *Anz. Ger. Nmus.* (1963), pp. 71–83

E. Meyer: 'Hermann Vischer und sein Sohn Peter Vischer der Ältere', *Z. Dt. Ver. Kstwiss.*, 19 (1965), pp. 97–116

D. Wuttke: 'Vitam non mortem recogita: Zum angeblichen Grabepitaph für Peter Vischer den Jüngeren', *Forsch. & Fortschr.*, xxxix (1965), pp. 144–6

——: 'Theodoricus Ulsenius als Quelle für das Epigramm auf den Orpheus-Eurydike-Plaketten Peter Vischers des Jüngeren', *Z. Dt. Ver. Kstwiss.*, 20 (1966), pp. 143–6

——: 'Methodisch-Kritisches zu Forschungen über Peter Vischer den Älteren und seine Söhne', *Archv Kultgesch.*, xlix (1967), pp. 208–61

K. Pilz: *Das Sebaldusgrabmal im Ostchor der St.-Sebaldus-Kirche in Nürnberg: Ein Messingguss aus der Giesshütte der Vischer* (Nuremberg, 1970)

H. Stafski: 'Der künstlerische Messingguss im 15. und 16. Jahrhundert', *Nürnberg: Geschichte einer europäischen Stadt*, ed. G. Pfeiffer (Munich, 1971), pp. 229–35

K. Riederer: 'Die Zusammensetzung deutscher Renaissancestatuetten aus Kupferlegierungen', *Z. Dt. Ver. Kstwiss.*, 36 (1982), pp. 42–8

Gothic and Renaissance Art in Nuremberg, 1300–1550 (exh. cat., New York, Met.; Nuremberg, Ger. Nmus.; 1986), nos 97, 183–5, 187–90, 192–200, 202, 233 [entries by H. Maué, R. Schoch, W. D. Wixom]

W. D. Wixom: 'Some Italian Sources for the Decoration of the Rathaus Screen in Nuremberg', *Festschrift für Gerhard Bott zum 60. Geburtstag* (Darmstadt, 1987), pp. 53–69

F. J. Worstbrock and F. Anzelewsky: *Apologia Postarum: Die Schwenter-Handschrift M.S. lat. fol. 335 der Staatsbibliothek Preussischer Kulturbesitz zu Berlin* (Wiesbaden, 1987)

K. Pechstein: 'Hans Peisser: Modellschnitzer für Hans Vischer und Pankraz Labenwolf: Studien zur süddeutschen Renaissanceplastik, iii', *Anz. Ger. Nmus.* (1990), pp. 113–20

WILLIAM D. WIXOM

Visconti (i). Italian dynasty of rulers and patrons. As Lords and later Dukes of Milan, they dominated the politics of northern Italy from the mid-14th century to the mid-15th, when the related SFORZA dynasty succeeded to the duchy. From 1311 Matteo I Visconti (*d* 1322) held the joint offices of Captain General and Imperial Vicar of Milan and gained control of most of western Lombardy. In 1327 his son Galeazzo I Visconti (*reg* 1322–8) was expelled from Milan by Ludwig of Bavaria. Galeazzo's son (1) Azzo Visconti recovered the Imperial Vicariate in 1329 and subsequently regained control of the surrounding cities. Azzo was succeeded by his uncles Lucchino Visconti (*reg* 1339–49) and Giovanni Visconti, Archbishop of Milan (*reg* 1349–54). In 1349 the heirs of Matteo I the Great were granted the perpetual hereditary right to the title Lord of Milan. This provided surety for the position of the family but did not prevent rivalry and dispute between different family members. A balance was kept by exile, occasional murder and various agreed divisions of responsibility. After the death of Archbishop Giovanni, the lordship of Milan passed to three of his nephews; when one of them, Matteo II (*reg* 1354–5), died in 1355, the rule of the Milanese state was divided between his brothers, (2) Bernabò Visconti and (3) Galeazzo II Visconti, with only Milan held in common. In 1385 (4) Gian Galeazzo Visconti, son of Galeazzo II, captured and overthrew his uncle, Bernabò, to assume sole rule of the dominions of Milan. In 1395 Gian Galeazzo was created Duke of Milan.

The title and rule of the city was inherited by his sons Galeazzo Maria Visconti (*reg* 1402–12) and (5) Filippo Maria Visconti, the last Visconti ruler of Milan. With the fall of the Ambrosian Republic (1447–50), the rule and dukedom of Milan went to FRANCESCO SFORZA I, husband of Filippo Maria's illegitimate daughter. In the 16th century members of a collateral branch of the family, (6) Prospero Visconti and (7) Pirro Visconti, also contributed as patrons to Milan's art life.

(1) Azzo(ne) Visconti, Lord of Milan (*b* 1302; *reg* 1328–39). The public and private buildings erected during the relative political stability of Azzo's rule were possibly the greatest fruits of Visconti patronage. Citadels were built in subject cities, the walls of Milan were rebuilt and extended, towers were erected by the town gates, and aqueducts and fountains were constructed to bring water to the citizens. These projects were praised by contemporary chroniclers not only for their practical advantage but also for their ornament. Azzo was responsible for the employment in Milan of the Tuscan artists Giotto and GIOVANNI DI BALDUCCIO, whose influence had a fundamental effect on the development of Lombard painting and sculpture. In public works Azzo had himself explicitly visually identified with the government of the city. For example, the sides of the rebuilt campanile of S Maria Maggiore (destr.), the Winter cathedral of Milan, were to be decorated with the emblems of the districts of the city, the church, the empire, the Visconti, and, on the side facing S Tecla (destr.), the Summer cathedral, there was to be a figure of Azzo on a gilded horse. The frieze around the sarcophagus of the tomb of *Azzo Visconti* (erected *c.* 1339; see below) by the workshop of Giovanni di Balduccio shows Azzo receiving the Imperial Vicariate from Ludwig of Bavaria under the protection of St Ambrose, patron saint of Milan; they are flanked by kneeling personifications of the subject cities of Lombardy and their patron saints.

The writer who provided the fullest account of the transformation of Milan in these years was a Dominican, Galvanno Fiamma (or Flamma), who was chaplain and adviser to Azzo's uncle, Archbishop Giovanni. Under the year 1335 in his chronicle of Milan Fiamma described in elaborate detail the two most magnificent structures built by Azzo: a chapel in honour of the Virgin (now S Gottardo in Corte) and the palace (mostly destr.) that adjoined it. The outstanding features of the chapel included pictures in gold and blue of wonderful workmanship, jewelled metalwork screens, miraculous windows, a paved floor, pulpits of ivory, altars decorated with gold and silver, and porphyry vessels. Fiamma emphasized the richness and great value of the works, along with their aesthetic and decorative excellence. Worthy of even greater wonder than the chapel was the adjacent palace, with a multistorey tower, all the rooms of which were adorned with paintings. The palace included an aviary and menagerie with a lion, bears, monkey, baboon and ostrich, fountains with fish and a garden with a lake. One painting in a great hall near the birdcage was singled out for particular attention and praised for a beauty and subtle artifice unmatched in the whole world. It has been convincingly argued that this painting, which showed Vainglory with Aeneas, Attila,

Hector, Hercules, Charlemagne and Azzo himself, was produced by Giotto when the Florentine government sent him to serve the Lord of Milan in the mid-1330s. As well as describing the buildings and their decoration, Fiamma gave an account of Azzo's purpose in erecting them. Using quotations from Aristotle, Fiamma justified Azzo's lavish artistic and architectural patronage as a display of magnificence appropriate to a ruler and as an expression of the invincible power of a prince, and deemed Azzo a benefactor of his community who served both the common good and God.

The campanile of S Gottardo in Corte, decorated with small marble columns thought so delightful by Fiamma, no longer has either the metal angel with the banner of the Visconti arms or the clock that struck the hours; the interior of the chapel has lost almost all of its original decoration. Even Azzo's tomb, erected there shortly after his death, was dismantled and only partially reconstructed. Only a few arches and window embrasures incorporated into the Palazzo Reale survive from Azzo's palace. Subsequent Visconti lords built many palaces and castles but, with one exception, neither surviving monuments nor literary accounts reveal a discrimination or a sophisticated political motivation equalling those attributed by Fiamma to Azzo.

(2) Bernabò Visconti, Lord of Milan (*b* 1323; *reg* 1354–85; *d* Dec 1385). Cousin of (1) Azzo. Little has survived of the most ambitious buildings erected for Bernabò and his wife, Regina della Scala (*d* 1384), in and around Milan. The castle at Pandino (begun *c.* 1379) is one of the best preserved of the Visconti castles of the 14th century and retains intact much of its original, largely heraldic, fresco decoration, but nothing remains of Bernabò's principal residence in Milan, the Castello di Porta Romana (1358). The latter was in the parish of S Giovanni in Conca (mostly destr.), the church that served as a mausoleum for Bernabò and his family. The apse contained his funeral monument: a sarcophagus (1380–85) with sides carved in high relief, supported on 12 columns and surmounted by an earlier equestrian statue of *Bernabò Visconti* (*c.* 1363) by Bonino da Campione (both Milan, Castello Sforzesco; *see* CAMPIONESI). This massive and imposing statue showing Bernabò in armour and accompanied by Fortitude and Wisdom was in the apse of S Giovanni in Conca from 1363.

Bernabò's reputation for brutality has encouraged the tendency to underestimate his interest in literature and learning. Two illuminated manuscripts are known that were certainly made for him, however, and letters (Mantua, Archv Stato) show that members of his family and court borrowed books from the Gonzaga lords in Mantua in order to have them copied. One of Bernabò's manuscripts, a copy of *Guiron le courtois* (*c.* 1370; Paris, Bib. N., MS. nouv. acq. fr. 5243; *see* MASTERS, ANONYMOUS, AND MONOGRAMMISTS, §I: MASTER OF THE GUIRON LE COURTOIS), is one of the masterpieces of Italian manuscript illumination. Bernabò's interest in Arthurian romance can be inferred not only from his ownership of this manuscript but also from the names he gave to several of his illegitimate children: Palomede, Lionella, Lancelotto, Sagramoro, Ginevra and Isotta. The other manuscript made

for Bernabò is Alfodhol da Merengi's *Liber iudiciorum et consiliorum* (Paris, Bib. N., MS. Lat. 7323).

(3) Galeazzo II Visconti, Lord of Milan (*reg* 1354–78; *d* Pavia, 4 Aug 1378). Brother of (2) Bernabò. Galeazzo II was an enthusiastic builder, but his role in shaping Milan was apparently more remarkable for the buildings that he tore down than for those he put up. Pietro Azario, writing in 1362, recorded that having inherited all but one of the houses of his Visconti predecessors, Galeazzo demolished them, leaving only Azzo's chapel (now S Gottardo in Corte), an ancient tower and one wing of a palace. Azario assessed that the destroyed houses, with their adornments, paintings and fountains, could not have been rebuilt for 300,000 florins. This account, however, antedated Galeazzo's move from Milan to Pavia and the construction there of a castle that was described by Petrarch in a letter (14 Dec 1363 or 1366) to Giovanni Boccaccio ('Epistolae rerum senilium', in *Librorum Francisci Petrarche annotatio impressorum* (Venice, 1501)) as 'the most noble production of modern art'.

Pavia had been independent of the Milanese state for 50 years when it was conquered in 1359. The vast and beautiful fortified palace that Galeazzo began building within four months of taking the city gave visual expression to his control. The castle (begun 1360), though the most magnificent example, conformed to a general pattern that was followed for other Visconti castles of the 14th century: it had a square ground-plan, with a large central court and a tower at each corner. The four sides were surmounted with battlements and had elegant and elaborate loggias above arcades on their inner faces, while the exterior walls were pierced with large windows. The arches and embrasures were embellished with terracotta mouldings or architectonic decoration and columns of pale stone contrasted with the red brick mass. Galeazzo intended the interior to be equally splendid: Venetian tapestry-weavers were employed, the Bolognese artists Andrea de' Bartoli, Jacopino and Pietro de' Papazoni travelled to work there, and, there being insufficient painters locally, Galeazzo asked Guido Gonzaga to send all the painters of Mantua. Galeazzo also asked Guido for advice, carvers, plants for the park and even decorative livestock. From 1365 the castle was Galeazzo's principal residence, and the elegance and refinement of the building were matched by the lifestyle of its inhabitants, making Pavia a prototype Renaissance court.

(4) Gian Galeazzo [Giangaleazzo] Visconti, Lord and then 1st Duke of Milan (*b* 15 Oct 1351; *reg* 1378–1402; *d* 3 Sept 1402). Son of (3) Galeazzo II. Gian Galeazzo was the most politically successful of all the Visconti; he joined the lands that he inherited from his father with those of his uncle Bernabò and, by the time of his death, had so extended his control of northern and central Italy that he was feared to be on the point of conquering Florence. There has been a tendency to attribute to him a commensurate importance as a patron of the arts. The rebuilding of Milan Cathedral (*see* MILAN, §IV, 1(i)(a)) began after he had gained control of the city; its vast scale has been regarded as a consequence of its being a tyrant's church, and its Gothic style and the use of northern artists have been seen as the result of the dynastic links of the Visconti family. The evidence does not conform with this interpretation. Gian Galeazzo supported the project to rebuild the cathedral and pledged donations and granted the cathedral works marble from the quarries of Candoglio, but he was neither the principal benefactor nor the instigator of the rebuilding, and does not appear to have had any determining role or even interest in the design of the church. His known acts of patronage, for example the carved marble altarpiece (Milan, S Eustorgio) that he gave to the Dominicans, are conventional and relatively modest.

Even after he had control of Milan, the castle built by his father in Pavia remained Gian Galeazzo's principal residence. As his court and administration expanded, he extended and modified the buildings that he had inherited. He continued the decoration of this Pavia castle and turned, as his father had, to Mantua for competent artists: in September 1380 he asked Ludovico Gonzaga (reg 1369–82) to send four or six painters skilled at making figures and animals, as he wished to have rooms of the castle painted with scenes of the hunt and other figures. The Gonzaga apparently provided the Visconti with both the role model and the means for aristocratic patronage on several occasions. The Certosa di Pavia (begun 1396; see PAVIA, §2(i)) was to include his family mausoleum in the same way as the Charterhouse of Champmol (founded 1383), Dijon, served Gian Galeazzo's brother-in-law Philip the Bold, Duke of Burgundy. Both monasteries were for 24 monks, double the usual number. Bernardo da Venezia (fl 1391–1403) was initially appointed architect, but three leading designers of Milan Cathedral, Giovannino de Grassi, Giacomo da Campione and Marco da Carona (d 1405), advised on the project. Contrasting Gian Galeazzo to his predecessors, Paolo Giovio wrote that he had 'built no building of even a little magnificence save the Certosa'. Although Gian Galeazzo had written of his intention to build a monastery that would not have its like in the world, at his death only the monks' cells were much above ground-level. The financial demands of his armies and his political expansionism were of higher priority. His involvement diminished, and by 1401 he had invested the prior of the monastery with complete authority for the building works.

By the end of Gian Galeazzo's life the library at Pavia numbered almost 1000 manuscripts and was as large as any princely library in Europe; yet very few of the books had been commissioned for the Duke, even as gifts. During the final two decades of his life a distinctive school of illumination, producing luxury manuscripts, became established in Milan, but the Visconti Psalter–Hours (Florence, Bib. N. Cent., MSS Banco Rari 397 and Landau Finaly 22) begun by Giovannino de Grassi (see GRASSI, (1)) is the only such work known to have been intended for his use. Gian Galeazzo was studious and learned, and the library of Pavia was open to the scholars and writers attracted to his court. It is likely that he valued his books for their content rather than for their artistic value.

By the time that Gian Galeazzo had unified the Milanese state his family had been established as rulers and identified with Milan for almost a century. He undertook a prince's customary display of lavishness, for example the trousseau that his daughter took to France, but in general his artistic and architectural patronage was neither innovative nor extravagant. Instead, he used other more direct and effective means to influence his contemporaries and secure his State.

BIBLIOGRAPHY

G. Fiamma: *Opusculum de rebus gestis ab Azone, Luchino ed Iohanne Vicecomitibus ab anno MCCCXXVIII usque ad annum MCCCXLII* (after 1342), Rerum Italicarum Scriptores, xii/4 (Bologna, 1938)

P. Azario: *Liber gestorum in Lombardia* (c. 1362), Rerum Italicarum Scriptores, xvi/4 (Bologna, 1939)

P. Giovio: *Vite duodecim vicecomitum mediolani principum* (Paris, 1549)

C. Magenta: *I Visconti e gli Sforza nel castello di Pavia e loro attinenze con la Certosa e la storia cittadina*, 2 vols (Milan, 1883)

L. Beltrami: *La Certosa di Pavia* (Milan, 1891, rev. 3/1924)

E. Pellegrin: *La Bibliothèque des Visconti et des Sforza ducs de Milan au XVe siècle* (Paris, 1955); *Supplément* (Florence, 1969)

L. Green: 'Galvano Fiamma, Azzone Visconti and the Revival of the Classical Theory of Magnificence', *J. Warb. & Court. Inst.*, liii (1990), pp. 98–113

K. Sutton: 'Milanese Luxury Books: The Patronage of Bernabò Visconti', *Apollo*, cxxxiv (1991), pp. 322–6

——: 'Giangaleazzo Visconti as Patron: A Prayerbook Illuminated by Pietro da Pavia', *Apollo*, cxxxvii (1993), pp. 89–96

E. Welch: *Art and Authority in Renaissance Milan* [in preparation]

KAY SUTTON

(5) Filippo Maria Visconti, 3rd Duke of Milan (b 23 Sept 1392; reg 1412–47; d Milan, 14 Aug 1447). Son of (4) Gian Galeazzo Visconti. Filippo Maria became Duke of Milan after his brother's assassination. His long career was devoted to the reconstruction of the Visconti dominions in Lombardy, and numerous wars with Venice and Naples punctuated his reign. He was known as an eccentric recluse who rarely left his fortified castle in Milan. Nevertheless, he maintained a large court and supported numerous humanist writers, in particular Pier Candido Decembrio and Francesco Filelfo. His early patronage followed that of his father, supporting the construction of Milan Cathedral and the Certosa di Pavia. A statue by Jacopino da Tradate (fl 1401–25) of *Pope Martin V* (1421; Milan, Mus. Duomo), who consecrated the high altar of the cathedral in 1418, is traditionally thought to have been commissioned by Filippo Maria. In 1431 the Duke corresponded with the painter Pisanello concerning an unidentified and unfinished work of art. In 1440 the artist appeared before the Duke, this time, however, as a prisoner of war captured in Verona. A portrait drawing (Paris, Louvre, Cabinet des Dessins, no. 2482) and Pisanello's medal of *Filippo Maria Visconti* (Paris, Bib. N.) are usually associated with this period. A lost fresco cycle in the castle at Pavia, mentioned by the architect and writer Cesare Cesariano in 1512, was probably also painted at this time. It may have represented images of women playing games and was possibly the iconographic source for the fresco of the *Giuochi Borromei* in the Palazzo Borromeo, Milan.

The greater part of the works made for Filippo Maria that have survived are small-scale and seem to have been for his personal use. The Duke was reported to have paid his secretary, Marziano da Tortona, 1500 scudi for tarot cards painted with images of gods and animals. These cannot be identified, but a set of cards (New Haven, CT, Yale U., Beinecke Lib.) displaying Visconti imprese and coins with Filippo Maria's monogram (examples, London, BM) has survived. In 1426 the Duke had ordered an unusually detailed inventory to be compiled of the library in the castle at Pavia, and he subsequently became an important collector of manuscripts. There are dedication miniatures showing the Duke in Galassio da Correggio's *Historia Angliae* (Paris, Bib. N., MS. lat. 6041) and a translation of Suetonius' *Vitae imperatorum* (Paris, Bib. N., MS. it. 131), both attributed to the MASTER OF THE VITAE IMPERATORUM (*see* MASTERS, ANONYMOUS, AND MONOGRAMMISTS, §I). His most impressive commission, however, was the continuation by Belbello da Pavia of an illuminated Book of Hours (Florence, Bib. N., Landau Finaly 22; for illustration *see* BELBELLO DA PAVIA) begun by the de Grassi for Gian Galeazzo Visconti. According to Pier Candido Decembrio's biography of Filippo Maria, the Duke carried out some large-scale building in Milan, such as the enlargement and decoration of his fortress. During the three years of the Ambrosian republic that followed the Duke's death, however, the castle was sacked and much of the Visconti heritage destroyed, rendering a full assessment of Filippo Maria's patronage impossible.

BIBLIOGRAPHY

P. C. Decembrio: *Vita di Filippo Maria Visconti* (Milan, 1625); trans., ed. E. Bartolini (Milan, 1983)
G. Biscaro: 'Pisanus pictor alla corte di Filippo Maria Visconti nel 1440', *Archv. Stor. Lombardo*, n. s. 3, xv (1901), pp. 171–4
E. Pellegrin: *La Bibliothèque des Visconti et des Sforza, ducs de Milan au 15ème siècle* (Paris, 1955)
F. Cognasso: *I Visconti* (Varese, 1966)
M. Meiss and E. W. Kirsch: *The Visconti Hours* (London, 1972)
A. Cadei: *Belbello, miniatore lombardo: Artisti del libro alla corte dei Visconti* (Rome, 1976)
G. Mulazzani: *I tarocchi viscontei e Bonifacio Bembo: Il mazzo di Yale* (Milan, 1981)
A. Cadei: *Studi di miniatura lombarda: Giovannino de Grassi e Belbello da Pavia* (Rome, 1984)
E. S. Welch: *Secular Fresco Painting at the Court of Galeazzo Maria Sforza* (diss., U. London, 1987)

E. SAMUELS WELCH

(6) Prospero Visconti (*b* ?Milan, 1543–4; *d* Tortona, before 10 March 1592). A member of a collateral branch of the former ruling dynasty of Milan, he was among the most prominent figures in Milanese cultural life in the late 16th century. He was a respected scholar, interested in ancient and modern history and in languages, including Greek and Hebrew, and a poet in both Latin and Italian. From a poem by the Lombard writer Bernardino Baldini (1515–1600/01), which praises Visconti's mastery of both the historian's pen and the sculptor's chisel, it would appear that he was also an amateur sculptor. His interests and his particular concern with the local history of Milan and Lombardy were reflected in his library, which included manuscripts written on lime-tree bark (*tiglia*) in a medieval Lombard dialect. He had a notable collection of Classical antiquities, including an extensive series of medals. The library and the collection were housed in his palace in Via Lanzone, Milan, which was built *c.* 1589–91 by the architect and engineer Giuseppe Meda (*d* 1599). Visconti also acted as art agent in Milan for William V, Duke of Bavaria, and his wife Renée of Lorraine. During the 1570s he regularly supplied the Duke with antique gems and statuary, paintings, carved and painted portraits of Italian cardinals and Spanish governors of Milan, armour, inventions for jousts and tournaments, vases, crystalware and such curiosities as a rare conch shell, as well as musical scores and political news from Italy.

BIBLIOGRAPHY

G. Borsieri: *La nobiltà di Milano di P. Morigi ... il supplimento in questa nova impressione del Sig. Girolamo Borsieri* (Milan, 1619)
F. Picinelli: *Ateneo dei letterati milanesi* (Milan, 1670)
H. Simonsfeld, ed.: 'Mailander Briefe zur bayerischen und allgemeinen Geschichte des 16. Jahrhunderts', *Hist. Kl. Kön. Bayer. Akad. Wiss.*, xxii (1902), pp. 231–575
G. Treccani degli Alfieri, ed.: *Stor. Milano*, x (Milan, 1957)

(7) Conte **Pirro Visconti** (*d* Milan, before 1619). A member of the former ruling dynasty of Milan, his sympathies with the Spanish government of the day were reflected in the award to him of the Spanish Order of S Giacomo. His interest in art is evident from the dedication to him by the artist and art critic Giovanni Paolo Lomazzo of his *Poésie* (Milan, 1589). As a patron, Visconti was responsible for bringing the Procaccini family of artists from Bologna to Milan, having met Camillo Procaccini in Bologna *c.* 1580 and invited him first to Rome and then to Milan. Camillo worked on Visconti's estate at Lainate, north of Milan, providing mosaic decoration (1585–9) for a building that adjoined a grand fountain (destr.), which Visconti had commissioned, perhaps from Francesco Brambilla the younger. A contemporary, Girolamo Borsieri, described the fountain as one of the wonders of the world and also commented that Visconti possessed a collection of paintings that, though not large, was 'exquisite'. It included Correggio's *Agony in the Garden* (*c.* 1555; London, V&A), which Visconti bought for 400 scudi and later sold to the Governor of Milan for 750 doppie (Lomazzo). Pirro's son Fabio Visconti inherited most of the collection.

BIBLIOGRAPHY

G. P. Lomazzo: *Idea del tempio della pittura* (Milan, 1590); ed. R. Klein, 2 vols (Florence, 1974)
G. Borsieri: *La nobiltà di Milano di P. Morigi ... il supplimento in questa nova impressione del Sig. Girolamo Borsieri* (Milan, 1619), pp. 69–70
G. Melzi d'Eril: 'Federico Borromeo e Cesare Monti: Collezionisti milanesi', *Stor. A.*, xv–xvi (1972), pp. 293–306
Lombard Paintings, c. 1595–c. 1630: The Age of Federico Borromeo (exh. cat., ed. P. Cannon-Brookes; Birmingham, Mus. & A.G., 1974)

JANET SOUTHORN

Visconti (ii). Italian family of antiquarians and museum directors.

(1) Giovanni Battista Visconti (*b* Vernazza, Liguria, 26 Dec 1722; *d* Rome, 2 Sept 1784). Visconti was raised in a scholarly family, came to Rome at the age of 14 and joined the circle of Johann Joachim Winckelmann after 1750. After Winckelmann's death, Visconti succeeded him (1768) as Commissioner of Antiquities, an office first held by Raphael. He found favour in the enlightened pontificate of Clement XIV (*reg* 1769–75), under the patronage of the papal treasurer Giovanni Angelo Braschi, who helped to inspire and found the Vatican Museo Clementino (1770) and subsequently, as Pius VI (*reg* 1775–1800), enlarged it into the Museo Pio-Clementino. Visconti helped Braschi to direct purchases, excavations, restorations and displays for the new museum, enlisting artists, dealers and entrepreneurs in the thriving antiquities industry in Rome. He effected the purchase of major works from the Mattei, Barberini, Verospi, Altemps and other local collections, to prevent their export and to maintain Rome's superiority as a Mecca of antiquarianism during the contemporary craze for ancient sculptures. In 1782 Visconti began the publication of a new kind of illustrated catalogue, with a detailed essay on each of the Vatican sculptures. His more famous son and assistant in publication, (2) Ennio Quirino Visconti, completed the subsequent volumes of the series while Commissioner of Antiquities, continuing Visconti's zeal and scholarly methods. Another son, Filippo Aurelio Visconti, also worked in the Louvre, served as Commissioner of Antiquities and published the Vatican Chiaramonti antiquities (1808) with G. A. Guattani. Visconti's objectivity, precision and learning led the way to modern professionalism in archaeological scholarship and museology.

WRITINGS
Il Museo Pio Clementino descritto, ii–vii (Rome, 1784–1807)
ed., with T. B. Emeric-David and others: *Le Musée français: Recueil complet des tableaux, statues et bas-reliefs qui composent la collection nationale*, 4 vols (Paris, 1803–9) [sculptural text in vols iii and iv]

SEYMOUR HOWARD

(2) Ennio Quirino Visconti (*b* Rome, 1 Nov 1751; *d* Paris, 7 Feb 1818). Scholar and antiquarian, son of (1) Giovanni Battista Visconti. He was educated by his father, whom he assisted in the compilation of the first volume (Rome, 1782) of the catalogue of the Museo Pio-Clementino. He prepared the other six volumes himself (Rome, 1784–1807). His theoretical and methodical leanings were of fundamental importance for the history of antiquity and art historiography of the period, and he played a decisive role in the debate on the restoration of antique sculpture through his support for interpretative repair. Using his broad knowledge, he would identify the antique model of a particular fragment and from that its precise iconographic and stylistic appearance; once the model had been established, it was then possible to proceed towards restoration of the statue. For other works, reconstruction was unnecessary. For example, for the Belvedere *Torso* (Rome, Vatican, Mus. Pio-Clementino) it was sufficient to put forward the hypothesis that it came from a group including Hercules and Omphales to inspire the Neoclassical sculptor John Flaxman to create a work on this theme, *Hercules and Hebe* (1792; London, U. Coll., Slade Sch. F.A.). Visconti's move to Paris in 1799 and the prestigious commissions that followed, including the directorship of the Musée Napoléon (now Musée du Louvre), brought to the fore his gifts as a historian. This is borne out by the explanatory notices on the exhibits and by his notes on sculpture in the last two volumes of the catalogue of the Musée Français.

WRITINGS
Il Museo Pio Clementino descritto, ii–vii (Rome, 1784–1807)
ed. with T.-B. Emeric-David and others: *Le Musée français: Recueil complet des tableaux, statues et bas-reliefs qui composent la collection nationale*, 4 vols (Paris, 1803–9) [sculptural text in vols iii and iv]

BIBLIOGRAPHY
G. Sforza: 'Ennio Quirino Visconti e la sua famiglia', *Atti Soc. Ligure Stor. Patria*, li (1923)
S. Howard: 'An Antiquarian Handlist and Beginnings of the Pio-Clementino', *18th C. Stud.*, vii (1973), pp. 40–61
D. Gallo: 'Ennio Quirino Visconti e il restauro della scultura antica fra settecento e ottocento', *Thorvaldsen, l'ambiente, l'influsso, il mito*, ed. P. Kragenlund and M. Nykjaer (Rome, 1991), pp. 101–22
——: 'Les Visconti de Rome', *Visconti, 1791–1853* (Paris, 1991), pp. 48–59

FRANCESCA CAPPELLETTI

(3) Louis-Tullius-Joachim [Ludovico Tullio Giacomo] **Visconti** (*b* Rome, 11 Feb 1791; *d* Paris, 29 Dec 1853). Architect, son of (2) Ennio Quirino Visconti, active in France. He accompanied his father from Rome to Paris in 1798 and became a French citizen in 1799. He entered the Ecole Spéciale d'Architecture in Paris in 1808 as a student of Charles Percier and remained there until 1817. After working from 1822 to 1824 under François-Hippolyte Destailleur on the Ministère des Finances in Paris (completed 1832; destr. 1871), Visconti became the architect in 1825 of the Bibliothèque Royale (now the Bibliothèque Nationale) in Paris, for which he designed numerous unrealized projects and where he was succeeded by Henri Labrouste. Around this time he also began designing several increasingly ornate public fountains in Paris, such as the Gaillon Fountain (1824–8), the Louvois Fountain (1835–9) and the Molière Fountain (1841–3). In 1840 he was commissioned to design the decorations for the ceremonial return to Paris of the ashes of Napoleon I, and the following year he won the competition to design the tomb of *Napoleon*. Built between 1843 and 1853, this open circular crypt in the Dôme des Invalides in Paris centres on Napoleon's porphyry sarcophagus. In 1852 Napoleon III named Visconti the architect of the palaces of the Louvre (replacing Félix-Jacques Duban) and the Tuileries in Paris. Visconti's project for the new Louvre, with six pavilions extending west from the old Louvre in two wings on either side of the Cour du Pavillon, was redesigned after his death by Hector-Martin Lefuel, yet his scheme was definitive in two ways. First, he subtly disguised the lack of alignment between the Louvre and the Tuileries by introducing a large open space between them, and second, he based his design on the Renaissance pavilions of the old Louvre rather than on the Baroque east façade by Claude Perrault. Visconti's two wings helped unify the immense complex by echoing the pavilions of the old Louvre and Tuileries, and they established the French Renaissance as the stylistic model for the residence of Napoleon III. Visconti was elected to the Académie des Beaux-Arts in 1853.

BIBLIOGRAPHY
Bauchal
A. Lance: *Dictionnaire des architectes français*, 2 vols (Paris, 1872)
V. Baltard: *L'Ecole de Percier* (Paris, 1873) [transcription of lecture given at the Académie des Beaux-Arts]
G. Sforza: *Ennio Quirino Visconti e la sua famiglia*, Atti della società ligure di storia patria (Genoa, 1923)
L. Hautecoeur: *Histoire de l'architecture classique en France* (1943–57)
The Second Empire: Art in France under Napoleon III (exh. cat., Philadelphia, PA, Mus. A., 1978), pp. 72–3
J.-C. Daufresne: *Louvre et Tuileries: Architectures de papier* (Paris, 1987)
F. Hamon and C. MacCallum, eds: *Louis Visconti, 1791–1853* (Paris, 1991)

CHRISTOPHER MEAD

Visconti, Eliseu (d'Angelo) (*b* Salerno, 30 July 1866; *d* Rio de Janeiro, 15 Oct 1944). Brazilian painter and decorative artist. He was taken as an infant from Italy to Rio de Janeiro. In 1884 he began studying in Rio de Janeiro at the Academia Imperial das Belas Artes and the Liceu Imperial de Artes e Ofícios under Victor Meirelles de Lima, Henrique Bernardelli (1837–1946) and Rodolfo Amoedo (1857–1941). He was active in efforts to eliminate the academy's rigid academic discipline. He went to Paris in 1892 and attended the Ecole des Beaux-Arts and the

Ecole des Arts Décoratifs, where he was taught by Eugène-Samuel Grasset. At the 1900 Exposition Universelle in Paris Visconti won a silver medal for the paintings *Youth* (1898) and *Dance of the Wood Nymphs* (1899; both Rio de Janeiro, Mus. N. B.A.). Following the Pre-Raphaelites, his main influences were Botticelli and other painters of the Italian Renaissance, but he was also affected by Grasset and Art Nouveau. On his return to Brazil, among the works exhibited in 1901 in Rio de Janeiro were a series of ceramic objects with Brazilian floral motifs and designs for postage stamps. His florid style began to give way to Impressionism in the stage curtain, circular ceiling panel and proscenium frieze he executed for the Rio de Janeiro Teatro Municipal (1906–7; *in situ*). In 1906 he became director of painting at the Escola Nacional de Belas Artes in Rio de Janeiro.

In 1923 Visconti decorated the hall of the Conselho Municipal in Rio de Janeiro (*in situ*), and in 1924 he painted the panel the *Signing of the First Republican Constitution* (*in situ*) for the Palácio Tiradentes, also in Rio. At the end of his life, continuing to paint in an Impressionist style, he carried out a series of joyful family portraits and luminous landscapes of the mountain region of Teresópolis, near Rio.

BIBLIOGRAPHY
Pontual
F. Barata: *Eliseu Visconti e seu tempo* (Rio de Janeiro, 1944)
J. M. dos Reis Júnior: *História da pintura no Brasil* (São Paulo, 1944)
P. M. Bardi: *The Arts in Brazil* (Milan, 1956)
Art of Latin America since Independence (exh. cat. by S. L. Catlin and T. Grieder, New Haven, Yale U. A.G.; Austin, U. TX, Huntington A.G.; San Francisco, Mus. A.; La Jolla, A. Cent.; 1966)
Q. Campofiorito: *História da pintura brasileira no século XIX* (Rio de Janeiro, 1983)
Eliseu Visconti e a arte decorativa (exh. cat. by I. Arestizabal, Rio de Janeiro, Solar Grandjean de Montigny, 1983)

ROBERTO PONTUAL

Visegrád. Ruined castle, palace and medieval city near Esztergom on the River Danube in the county of Pest, north of Budapest, Hungary. A Roman castrum was built as a *limes* (boundary) fort in the first half of the 4th century AD on the summit of the steep hill known as Sibrik; remains of walls and of towers with an irregular pentagonal plan survive. On the eastern edge of the castrum, a modest longitudinal stone building was erected at the beginning of the 11th century as the residence of the count of Pilis. The aisleless church of the early medieval castle, decorated with contemporary wall paintings (various animals in roundels), has been excavated outside the castrum, as has another in a settlement on the north slope of the hill. The first reference to *civitas Wsagrad* dates from 1002. Next to the settlement stood a Basilian monastery founded by Andrew I (*reg* 1046–60) with palmette-decorated imposts of the second half of the 11th century.

After the Mongol invasion (1241–2), King Béla IV (*reg* 1235–70) built a new fortress for the royal family (1251–9). A massive hexagonal residential tower, called the Solomon Tower, was connected to the water-tower on the Danube below and to the upper castle above by a wall strengthened with towers. At the same time the King built at the top of the steep rocky hill a pentagonal tower (Ger. *Bergfried*) with adjoining walls surrounding a triangular courtyard.

During the 14th century the settlement gradually developed into a town, and *c.* 1316 King Charles of Anjou (*reg* 1309–42) began to build the new royal palace between the castle hill and the Danube. It was far advanced in 1335 when it was used for the meeting at which the kings of Hungary, Poland and Bohemia, with the Grand Master of the Teutonic Order, formed an alliance against the Duke of Austria. Between 1342 and 1355 Louis the Great (*reg* 1342–82) extended the palace on a regular ground-plan. The wings, with several storeys, and the three courtyards were arranged in five terraces on the sloping terrain. The fine Gothic complex of buildings had a very animated and picturesque appearance, an effect heightened by the building of the fine, hall-like chapel on the third terrace between the palaces of the King and Queen. The regular construction of the palace suggests Italian connections, easily explained by the Neapolitan origins of the Angevin kings. This Italian source is also evident in three fountains built in the 1360s: a small fountain (destr.) by the outer wall of the complex, an octagonal fountain (destr.) in the lower cloister, and a quadrangular wall fountain in the triangular court of the fourth terrace. The last two were surrounded by slender columns bearing canopies supported by pointed arches. The first resembled monastic cloister fountains, while the other is in the unusual form of a canopied tomb, the canopy bearing the arms of Anjou.

After a serious fire *c.* 1400, the palace was considerably extended by King Sigismund of Luxembourg (*reg* 1387–1437), with the development of the lower court with pier arcades, the series of niches in the cloister on the second terrace and the south entrance to this cloister, also furnished with niches for seating, and the final arrangement of the third terrace. Sigismund also extended the fortifications in the lower and upper castles. The well-preserved pentagonal eastern gate-tower, the curtain wall and the system of rock-hewn trenches are clear evidence of large-scale building activity. By the 14th and 15th centuries a city with two communities, one German, the other Hungarian, also developed around the castle, where the aristocrats built stone houses. A few of these are known from excavations, as are the remains of the two parish churches, but there is only documentary evidence for other buildings and a Franciscan friary.

The palace was the favourite residence of King Matthias Corvinus (*reg* 1458–90), who inaugurated the last great building period. His earliest work is thought to be the so-called Lion Fountain, built in 1473 in the same place and using the same construction as the wall fountain of Louis of Anjou, which he demolished, perhaps owing to its out-of-date subject-matter. The fountain is of local red marble and supported by five lions. The outer surfaces of the baldacchino rest on slender columns and bear the arms of the subject lands. The interior of the fountain was decorated with family arms, stressing the noble origins of the ruler, and culminated in the ceiling of the baldacchino, which bears the Corvinus (Hunyadi) arms with the date. The iconography glorifies Matthias Corvinus as the ruler of the lands named and as scion of the glorious Hunyadi and Szilágyi families. Matthias's taste for heraldic decoration also appears in the sequences of coats of arms on the Renaissance fountain in the lower terrace courtyard and on the western gate-tower, which is presumed to have followed the model of the chapel façade of Emperor Frederick III's palace at Wiener Neustadt.

In the 1480s the court workshop, its Silesian connections apparent in both style and masons' marks, was again active at the palace. The cloister on the second terrace was given an arcade with a star-shaped net vault (1484). In the centre of the court the King replaced the Angevin fountain with an octagonal Renaissance one, built in red marble, surmounted by a figure of Hercules. The quadrangular passage above the court had stone balusters and fluted colonnettes, which already show the gradual advance of the new style. On the fourth terrace a sauna bath was built and plumbed into the excellent water system.

Excavations have revealed many objects of furniture and decoration, which give an accurate picture of the high level of court life. In his *Hungaria* the humanist Nicolaus Olahus, a friend of Erasmus of Rotterdam, gave a detailed eye-witness account of its wonderful situation and construction, with many details about the palace as it was before the Turkish invasion of 1543.

During Turkish rule the buildings decayed, and on the liberation of the country at the end of the 17th century the ruins gradually disappeared. Restoration started after 1871, with work to uncover the upper castle, and the residential tower was restored by Frigyes Schulek. In 1934 János Schulek discovered the palace. Archaeological investigations gained momentum after World War II and have been accompanied by continuous restoration work.

BIBLIOGRAPHY

D. Dercsényi, M. Héjj and G. Rózsa: *Visegrád: Pest megye műemlékei* [Visegrád: the monuments of the county of Pest], ii (Budapest, 1958), pp. 397–479
J. Balogh: *A művészet Mátyás király udvarában* [Art at the court of King Matthias], 2 vols (Budapest, 1966), i, pp. 205–51; ii, pp. 151–98, 252–73
M. Héjj: *The Royal Castle in Visegrád* (Budapest, 1970)
Matthias Corinus und die Renaissance in Ungarn, 1458–1541 (exh. cat., Schallaburg, Schloss, 1982), pp. 376–93

GÉZA ENTZ

Visentin, Giovanni. *See* DEMIO, GIOVANNI.

Visentini, Antonio (*b* Venice, 21 Nov 1688; *d* Venice, 26 June 1782). Italian painter, engraver, architect and theorist. He trained with Giovanni Antonio Pellegrini and was first mentioned as a painter in 1711. Visentini first earned fame with a volume of his drawings engraved by Vicenzo Mariotti (*d* 1734) as *Iconographia della Ducal Basilica dell'Evangelista di S Marco* (Venice, 1726). His own work as an engraver dates from the end of the 1720s, when he was commissioned by Joseph Smith, with whom he had been in contact since 1717, to produce engravings of Canaletto's views of Venice; they were published in *Prospectus magni canalis Venetiarum* (Venice, 1735). An enlarged version was published by Giambattista Pasquali (*fl* 1730–90) as *Urbis Venetiarum prospectus celebriores* (Venice, 1742–54). From 1735 to the 1750s Visentini worked as an engraver for Pasquali and also undertook commissions from Giovanni Poleni for the printing-house of the seminary at Padua. Vignettes and illustrations by his hand are to be found in many publications, such as *Utriusque thesauri antiquitatum Romanorum Graecorumque nova supplementa* (Venice, 1737), *Raccolta di vari schizi de ornati* (Venice, 1747) and the first printed edition of Teofilo Gallaccini's *Trattato sopra gli errori degli architetti* (Venice, 1767).

Visentini was a leading exponent of the capriccio genre. In 1726 he was appointed Prior of the Collegio dei Pittori, and from 1733 he was paid for paintings for the Stanza di Tesoro (destr.) in the Doge's Palace. About 1740 he painted eight architectural fantasies in the Palazzo Contarini, Venice (Venice, priv. col.); these reflect his ideas on contemporary architecture, which were derived from antiquity and the works of Palladio. In 1744 Francesco Algarotti commissioned two paintings of Palladio's S Francesco della Vigna and Il Redentore. The interest in Palladio's architecture shown by Algarotti and Smith also led the latter to commission a series of overdoors (1745–6) from Canaletto, Visentini and Francesco Zuccarelli. The 11 paintings, with architecture by Visentini and figures by Zuccarelli, show various English Palladian buildings, based on illustrations in Colen Campbell's *Vitruvius Britannicus* (London, 1715–25) and William Kent's *The Designs of Inigo Jones* (London, 1727), from which was derived *Mr Benson's House at Wilbury and Chiswick Temple* (1746; U. Würzburg; Wagner-Mus.).

Visentini first worked as an architect in 1731, when he embellished Smith's villa (destr.) at Momigliano. In 1755, also for Smith, he modernized the Palazzetto Balbi on the Grand Canal, Venice. The façades of an apartment building (1736) for the Michiel family and the Palazzo Giusti (1766) are distinguished by a sparing use of ornamentation, but they do not fully represent the architectural ideas of Visentini or Smith. The clarification and dissemination of these ideas was reserved for Visentini's writings. His first theoretical work, *Libro di architettura*, was produced as early as 1733 and incorporated Rococo-influenced drawings executed by Pier Antonio Morelli after Visentini's ideas. In contrast, Visentini's later writings (e.g. Venice, Correr, Cod. Cicogna 3658) are imbued with neo-Palladian and anti-Baroque ideas. Common to these not very original but highly didactic texts, some in verse form, is a critique of infringements of architectural rules, using Jacopo Vignola as the sole source of architectural information. The *Soda e reale architettura* regularly mentioned by Visentini is not defined. His ideas are best gleaned from his architectural criticism and references to the necessity of studying the works of Palladio and, above all, of antiquity. With the help of the pupils in his workshop, Visentini produced numerous drawings, mostly of ancient buildings but some of contemporary ones, that served to disseminate exemplary architecture and were intended for sale to interested foreigners. He was a founder-member of the Accademia in 1755 and was proposed as teacher of architectural perspective there in 1764 but was able to take up the post only in 1772.

UNPUBLISHED SOURCES

Venice, Correr, coll. A. Iv.72 [1733; *Libro di architettura e sue annotationi con archi, intercolumni, portici e logge, e sue piante, facciate, profili, e spaccati …*]
Venice, Correr, MS. Cicogna 3656 [*Il Contro-Rusconi ó sia l'esame sopra l'architettura di Giovantonio Rusconi*]
Venice, Correr, MS. Cicogna 3658 [*c.* 1761; *Trattato delli cinque ordini dell'architettura et anco della prospettiva, posto in versi; Delle osservazioni sopra le fabbriche di Andrea Palladio; Il parallelo dell'architettura virtuosa a confronto dell'ignoranza ó sia l'ardir scoretto e vizioso; L'esame che fa l'architettura alli muratori, marangoni, e tagliapietra*]

Rome, Vatican, Bib. Apostolica, MS. Vat. lat. 8482 [c. 1764; *L'introduzione della soda e reale architettura e prospettiva*]

WRITINGS

Osservazioni di Antonio Visentini . . . che servono di continuazione al trattato di Teofilo Gallaccini sopra gli errori degli architetti (Venice, 1771)

BIBLIOGRAPHY

P. A. Orlandi: *Abecedario pittorico* (Bologna, 1704); rev. P. Guarienti (Venice, 1753), p. 80
A. Blunt: 'A Neo-Palladian Programme Executed by Visentini and Zuccarelli for Consul Smith', *Burl. Mag.*, c (1958), pp. 283–4
E. Bassi: *Architettura del sei e settecento a Venezia* (Naples, 1962), pp. 358–74
F. Vivian: 'Joseph Smith, Antonio Visentini e il movimento neoclassico', *Boll. Cent. Int. Stud. Archit. Andrea Palladio*, v (1963), pp. 340–58
D. Succi: *Venezia nella felicità illuminata delle acqueforti di Antonio Visentini* (Treviso, 1984)
Canaletto & Visentini: Venezia & Londra (exh. cat., ed. D. Succi; Venice, Ca' Pesaro, 1986)
A. Delnieri: 'Antonio Visentini', *Capricci veneziani del settecento* (Turin, 1988), pp. 223–51

ANJA BUSCHOW OECHSLIN

Viseu. Portuguese city and provincial capital of Beira Alta in the north of the country, with a population in the late 20th century of *c.* 21,000. Situated on a hill dominating an important intersection of Roman roads traversing the whole of the western Iberian Peninsula, Viseu emerged from two distinct original centres: one derived from a megalithic hill settlement on the summit, traces of which remain in tomb sites in the surrounding country (*see* PREHISTORIC EUROPE, §IV, 3(i)), while the other developed at the foot of the hill in the last stages of Roman expansion from the 2nd century AD; the centre of this settlement was established on an octagonal plan with the traditional Roman arrangement of a *cardo* with *decumani*. Under the Swabians and the Visigoths, Viseu was of some importance: in a reference dating from 569 it is described as the seat of a diocese with a cathedral dedicated to S Maria, but the town underwent a relative decline in the 10th and 11th centuries. The first phase of important work on the new cathedral was conducted under Count Henrique between 1100 and 1112. Alterations were made during the 13th and 14th centuries, which resulted in the definitive Latin-cross ground-plan and a Gothic south portal, the capitals of which are carved with figures of beasts in the Romanesque style. In the 14th century the pre-Roman walls of the city and those erected in the 11th century were replaced by a new ring, begun under John I (*reg* 1385–1433) and completed under Alfonso V (*reg* 1438–81). This imposed an effective limit on urban growth, concentrating the organization of space within the walls, with houses following the contours of the hill.

During the 16th century Bishop Diogo Ortiz de Vilhegas was responsible for alterations and restorations (completed in 1513) at the cathedral that profoundly altered its appearance, with Manueline knotted-cable vaulting being used in the nave and aisles (*see* MANUELINE STYLE). Although Viseu did not achieve the importance of other Portuguese cities—according to a census in 1527 it had only 2340 inhabitants—it was nevertheless significant at this time for the activities of Miguel da Silva (*see* SILVA, (2)), who was bishop from 1525 to 1539. He was familiar with the humanism of the papal court, where he had acted as ambassador, and he brought back with him the Italian architect Francesco da Cremona, who had trained in the workshop of St Peter's and from whom he commissioned (1544) the choir and cloister for the cathedral. Da Silva also concerned himself with the surroundings of the cathedral and constructed a wide loggia at right angles to it, while outside the city he built for his small court of humanists the ambitious Paço do Fontelo, in the style of an Italian palace. This was decorated by, among other artists, the painter VASCO FERNANDES, who had also worked on the restoration of the cathedral, painting a magnificent retable of 14 panels (1501–6; dispersed). As his fame spread, 'O Grão Vasco' ('the great Vasco') transformed Viseu into an important artistic centre that furnished many of the religious houses in the province of Beira Alta.

The exuberant decoration, particularly of windows, of the many surviving Manueline houses in Viseu bears witness to the development of the city. The decoration of the 'Casa de Dom Duarte', for example, is divided by an elegant columnette and framed by twisted columns and a decorative band of fleurons, clearly identifiable with Late Gothic architectural schemes. During the late 16th century and the 17th the monumental centre of the modern city was established. To the side of the cathedral the Paço dos Três Escalões (now the Museu de Grão Vasco) was built in 1593, initially to house the clergy and later altered as the bishop's palace. Between 1635 and 1648 the Salamancan architect Juan Moreno designed and built a new façade (see fig.) for the cathedral, after that built by Diogo Ortiz de Vilhegas had collapsed. Moreno's portal, in a sober Mannerist style, has three storeys surmounted by a pediment and niches for decorative statuary, in which the influence of contemporary retables is evident.

A revival in urban Viseu occurred in the late 18th century. In 1775 the Misericórdia Church was begun by ANTÓNIO DA COSTA FARO to plans by the city architect António Mendes Coutinho; with its elegant windows, curving pediments and a massive, finely carved doorway with rocaille decoration, it is a grandly theatrical composition. The city was beginning to expand, and the Rococo

Viseu Cathedral, façade (1635–48) by Juan Moreno

churches of the Franciscan Tertiaries (*c.* 1768; with its octagonal chancel) and the Third Order of Carmelites (1734–8; substantially altered in the late 18th century) are outside its established boundary. The old streets were enlivened in the late 19th century by the mansions of the counts of Prime and Treixedos, with their long façades aligned along the medieval lanes and characteristically dymamic fenestration of the *fin-de-siècle*. In the 20th century new residential areas for the wealthy began to extend to the north, east and west, often absorbing small rural communities on the borders of the old city.

BIBLIOGRAPHY

A. Girão: *Viseu: Estudo de uma aglomeração urbana* (Coimbra, 1925)
A. de Lucena e Vale: *Viseu monumental e artístico* (Viseu, 1969)
A. Correia: *Viseu* (Lisbon, 1989)

MIGUEL SOROMENHO

Vishnudasa. *See* BISHAN DAS.

Vishnyakov, Ivan (Yakovlevich) (*b* Moscow, 1699; *d* St Petersburg, 19 Aug 1761). Russian painter. He trained at the Admiralty College under Vasily Gruzinets (1667–1739) and in 1727 joined the staff of the Office of Buildings with the rank of apprentice, working for a time under Louis Caravaque (1684–1754). In 1739 he became a Master and head of the Office's department of paintings. He contributed to the monumental and decorative works, which he also supervised, in the palaces and churches of St Petersburg and environs, Moscow and Kiev, and in the decoration of triumphal arches in Moscow and St Petersburg.

Vishnyakov's portraits are of especial interest, reflecting the general problems in Russian 18th-century art of the transition of Russian painting from medieval to modern times, but the combination of new and traditional features produces an effect of originality rather than contradiction. In, for example, the companion portraits of the *Yakovlevs*, husband and wife (*c.* 1756; both St Petersburg, Hermitage), and of the *Tishinins* (1755; both Rybinsk, Mus. Hist. A.) he made use of the decorative possibilities of representational art and treated his subjects with delicacy and refinement. Vishnyakov's treatment of children is particularly appealing, as in the portraits of *Sarah Fermor* (1749) and *William Fermor* (late 1750s; both St Petersburg, Rus. Mus.) and of *Fyodor Golitsyn* (1760; Moscow, Tret'yakov Gal.).

BIBLIOGRAPHY

N. Moleva and E. Belyutin: *Zhivopisnykh del mastera: Kantselyariya ot stroyeniy i russkaya zhivopis' pervoy poloviny XVIII veka* [Masters of painting: the Office of Buildings and Russian painting in the first half of the 18th century] (Moscow, 1965)
T. V. Il'ina: *I. Ya. Vishnyakov: Zhizn' i tvorchestvo* [I. Ya. Vishnyakov: life and work] (Moscow, 1979)
——: 'Mesto I. Ya. Vishnyakova v russkom iskusstve XVIII veka' [I. Ya. Vishnyakov's place in 18th-century Russian painting], *Russkoye iskusstvo vtoroy poloviny XVIII–pervoy poloviny XIX veka: Materialy i issledovaniya* [Russian art in the second half of the 18th century and the first half of the 19th: materials and research], ed. T. V. Alekseyeva (Moscow, 1979), pp. 145–54

ANDREY A. KAREV

Visigothic art. Term applied to any object made by the Visigoths during their migrations across Europe from the 1st to the 8th century AD.

1. ORIGINS AND AQUITAINE. The Visigoths were a Germanic tribe first mentioned by Pliny the elder in the 1st century AD as living along the western shores of the Baltic Sea. They gradually moved south and east until the 4th century. Emperor Aurelian (*reg* AD 270–75) conceded Dacia to them, and the Visigoths were converted to Arian Christianity in this region; in 341 Ulfilas, an Arian bishop and monk, was appointed to the Goths. Later in the 4th century pressures on the peoples living to the north and east of the Visigoths caused them to move south of the

1. Visigothic votive crown of King Recceswinth, gold and precious stones, d. 200 mm, mid-7th century AD (Madrid, Museo Arqueológico Nacional)

River Danube and into the Roman Empire. Eventually their leader, Alaric, led them to Italy in 401, and their sack of Rome in 410 horrified the inhabitants of the Empire and caused much self-recrimination; it was to explain the event that St Augustine wrote *The City of God*. By 419 the Visigoths had become *foederati*, legal allies of Rome, and were assigned the province of Aquitaine in return for its defence, establishing their capital at Toulouse. The Visigoths replaced Roman officials and took over governmental property along with its functions.

Until then the art of the Visigoths had consisted mainly of elements of personal adornment: belt buckles, fibulae (dress pins) and horse trappings. These were used as grave goods and have been found from central Europe to Spain. A pair of eagle fibulae (Baltimore, MD, Walters A.G.) was found at Terra de Barros in Spain. Because of their large size and fine workmanship they are among the most beautiful of surviving barbarian personal effects: they are covered in cloisonné gems, rock crystal and white, blue, red and green stones.

The Visigoths held Toulouse until 508, when Clovis, the Catholic King of the Franks, defeated them and they retired to Spain, which they had gradually infiltrated, invited at first by the local population who used them as mercenaries. Although nothing Visigothic survives in Toulouse, an engraving published in 1727 shows the church of Notre-Dame-de-la-Daurade (*see* TOULOUSE, §2(ii)), which was built under the Visigoths and pulled down in 1761. It was an ovoid octagonal brick building with a cloister vault and covered with gold mosaics, which gave the church its nickname. The church may have served as a palace chapel, as similar buildings had been erected for imperial Roman courts. Whatever its original function, the building type and its decoration place it in the late 5th century and recall in general the layout of S Vitale, Ravenna (*see* RAVENNA, §2(vii)); they show how completely the Visigoths had adapted themselves to Roman precedents.

2. IBERIAN PENINSULA. The Museo de los Concilios y de la Cultura Visigoda at Toledo, the Visigothic capital of Spain from 568 to 712, has an important collection of architectural sculpture; and there are also examples of fibulae and other personal ornaments in other provincial museums and in the Museo Arqueológico Nacional in Madrid. There is displayed the votive crown of King Recceswinth (*reg* 649–72; see fig. 1), which hangs on golden chains suspended by a floral element surmounted by a finial of rock crystal. The crown itself is a flat band or sheet of gold bordered by cloisonné gems with a series of openwork 'X's the height of the band, creating small fields for gems mounted in simple, deep bezels, so that the stones, mostly aquamarines and pearls, stand up from the background. Hanging from this are rectangles of emeralds and crystals held by strips of gold with aquamarine pendants. It is one of the supreme examples of medieval metalwork. The use of votive crowns is well attested in mosaics (e.g. Ravenna, S Apollinare Nuovo), and they are also depicted in the canon tables of gospel books. The upper chain consists of pointed openwork, lozenge-shaped motifs. These can be shown to have been used in Italy as ornament from at least the mid-4th century, as in the so-called Chronograph of 354 (destr.; known from copies). Thus, the Crown of Recceswinth, though Visigothic, follows directly in the Early Christian artistic tradition.

Another surviving votive offering by Recceswinth is a small church, S Juan Bautista, at Baños de Cerrato, in the province of Palencia. As the name implies, Baños was once a Roman establishment where people sought cures from the waters. The King, healed of some malady, fulfilled his vow of building a church on this spot, appropriately to St John the Baptist. It is a low ashlar building with a three-aisled nave and originally three square-ended chapels with barrel vaults; the outer apses have been destroyed. The building is now devoid of all church trappings. Enlivening the arch over the small entrance porch is some carved decoration, an even-armed cross in a circle from which descend traditional chip-carved motifs, in which the flat planes of the carving meet at sharp angles. Chip-carving was not an invention of the Visigoths, but they

2. Quintanilla de las Viñas, Visigothic church of S Maria, marble relief of Christ, two angels and the sun, 8th century AD

seem to have favoured it, at least in the 7th-century monuments. The same type of decoration can be seen along the extrados of the main apse arch, and the technique was used for the nave capitals. Derived from the Early Christian interpretation of the Corinthian order, they are smaller in scale than their prototypes, the acanthus leaves are less three-dimensional in appearance, and they are much more 'colouristic', dependent on light rather than on surface modelling to create form.

No illuminated manuscripts survive from the Visigothic period nor are there any monumental paintings, unless those at the baptistery at Manresa in Catalonia may be considered as Visigothic and not Early Christian.

Several churches in northern Spain, possibly of the 8th century, might be considered Visigothic. The most interesting is the partial ruin of S Maria at Quintanilla de las Viñas near Burgos. The transept and square sanctuary of the church still stand, but the nave and the rest of the building are gone. It now has a timber truss roof. The stone is grey-blue with streaks of dark orange. Inside are several pieces of relief carving, each with representations of Christ, the Virgin Mary or angels and the sun (see fig. 2). Some of these marble slabs serve as impost blocks for the columns and capitals of the east wall. On the exterior of the east end are two carved string courses (see fig. 3), carrying motifs that are traditional in an Early Christian sense, clearly recognizable and, though flatly carved, still reminiscent of vine trails and clusters. Decorative interlace is almost absent from Visigothic art in contrast to its great popularity in the rest of Europe.

The carving on the interior slabs is in a style that may be found at this time over a wide area: Italy and France in sculpture, Ireland and northern England in manuscript illumination. On the slab with Christ and two angels, the third dimension has been completely abandoned in favour of a strictly linear interpretation; the background is completely flat. The design is asymmetrical: the angel to Christ's right occupies more space than his counterpart on the left, even though he is shown with only one wing. The wing is replaced by a hand holding an even-armed cross. Christ is carved strictly frontally and also holds a cross in his right hand. His halo is but a rope twisted around his head. The angel on the left touches the halo with his left hand and with his right Christ's shoulder. The angel's garment brushes the field of the design at the bottom left; his wing remains parallel to the top left border, while the wing of the angel to the right touches the border along its length, and his garment floats above the bottom right border. The sculptor was working intentionally rather than incompetently, consciously avoiding any sense of the Classical tradition. He even varied the width of the two fillets used as a moulding around the edges, giving a rough or unfinished look to the plaque.

S Pedro de la Nave, Zamora, is possibly of a similar date to Quintanilla de las Viñas. This small church has a set of historiated capitals, among the earliest examples in the Middle Ages. The decorative elements on the impost blocks are similar to those found on the exterior apse wall of Quintanilla de las Viñas, and the style of the historiated scenes has the same characteristics as the carvings at Quintanilla.

3. Quintanilla de las Viñas, Visigothic church of S Maria, exterior decoration of apse (detail), 8th century AD

In 711 a few aristocratic Visigoths invited the Arabs across the Straits of Gibraltar to come to their assistance. Experiencing little military opposition in the Iberian peninsula, the Moors gradually took over the kingdom and forced the Visigoths into the north, where, protected by precipitous mountains and far from the centres of Islamic power, the small kingdom with its capital at Oviedo in the Asturias was never taken by the Arabs. Although the Visigoths withdrew to Oviedo (see OVIEDO, §1), scholars have avoided describing as Visigothic the remarkable 9th-century monuments there, which nevertheless must recall the much more magnificent monuments at the lost capital of Toledo.

BIBLIOGRAPHY
Dom J. Martin: *La Religion des Gaulois* (Paris, 1727)
H. Schlunk: *Arte visigodo*, A. Hisp., ii (Madrid, 1947) [with bibliog.]
J. Hubert, J. Porcher and W. F. Volbach: *Europe in the Dark Ages* (London, 1969) [with bibliog.]
A. Arbeiter, S. Noak-Haley and O. K. Werkmeister: 'The Kingdom of the Asturias and Mozarabic Spain', *The Art of Medieval Spain, AD 500–1200* (exh. cat., New York, Met., 1993)
M. Jenkins: 'Visigothic Spain', *The Art of Medieval Spain, AD 500–1200* (exh. cat., New York, Met., 1993)

CARL D. SHEPPARD

Vismara, Gaspare (*d* 1651). Italian sculptor. He headed a Milanese family that produced two generations of sculptors and painters, including his sons, Domenico Vismara (*fl* 1640–45) and Francesco Vismara. He came under the influence of Gian Andrea Biffi, one of the many sculptors engaged in decorating Milan Cathedral. By 1610 Vismara was listed among them and he continued to work there for most of his life. His marble sculptures and his bas-reliefs of saints and other religious figures may be found throughout the cathedral, all executed in the late Mannerist style favoured by Biffi and many other 17th-century Milanese sculptors. Examples include his statues of *St Peter* and *St Paul* (1612). He carved a group of angels for the ornamentation of the chapel of the Madonna dell'Albero, in collaboration with his brother Giuseppe Vismara, Gian Pietro Lasagna (*d* 1658) and Marc'Antonio Prestinari (*d* 1621). A brief hiatus in Gaspare's career occurred after 1621, owing to the plague, but payment records indicate that he had resumed his work by the mid-1620s. His most famous piece, the marble bas-relief

Creation of Eve (1629–35; terracotta model, Milan, Mus. Duomo), was one of five relief panels based on designs by Cerano (Giovanni Battista Crespi) and placed in the portals of the cathedral's main entrance. Crespi's designs displeased Vismara, but he executed them as required. In 1631 Vismara became chief of sculptural production for the cathedral, a position he held until his death. His reputation derives primarily from his long association with the cathedral, but he occasionally created sculptures for other sites as well. For S Paolo, Milan, he provided a bas-relief of the *Conversion of St Paul.*

BIBLIOGRAPHY
R. Wittkower: *Art and Architecture in Italy 1600–1750*, Pelican Hist. A. (Harmondsworth, 1958, rev. 3/1982)
J. Pope-Hennessy: *Catalogue of Italian Sculpture in the Victoria and Albert Museum*, ii (London, 1964)
'Il Duomo di Milano', *Dizionario storico artistico e religioso*, ed. A. Majo (Milan, 1986)

Viṣṇupura. *see* BISHNUPUR.

Viso del Marqués. Palace of the nobility near Ciudad Real, La Mancha, Spain. The site was acquired in 1539 by Álvaro de Bazán el Viejo. It was inherited by his son Álvaro de Bazán y Guzmán (1526–88), 1st Marqués de Santa Cruz, who built the family palace. Construction had probably begun by 1562, when a contract was drawn up for the roofs and ceilings of the front section and its towers. The ground-plan of the palace is almost square, with four towers, a vestibule with triple access to the rectangular courtyard and an imperial staircase with five flights that occupied the breadth of the courtyard; the whole plan is derived from that used by Alonso Covarrubias in the rebuilding of the Alcázar of Toledo (1536–52). It is possible that either Covarrubias or his pupil Enrique Egas the younger (*c.* 1500–*c.* 1565), who was active in the neighbouring town of Almagro, may have assisted in the original design of the palace. The project was modified, however, when the Genoese Giovanni Battista Castello el Bergamasco was put under contract (*see* CASTELLO (i), (1)). From 1567 to 1569 he was assisted by members of the Italian Olamosquin family. The intervention of the Italians resulted in the remodelling of the courtyard, with Doric and Ionic pilasters adjoining pillars with arches (see fig.), a new formula in Spain (but related to the contemporary Patio de los Evangelistas at the ESCORIAL) and of the staircase (where the open stairwell was closed by the introduction of the chapel on the second floor). The entire interior was now decorated with stucco and frescoes, as was, most probably, the exterior façade (decoration destr.). Further modifications, such as the addition of the present portal (*c.* 1778) by Juan Pedro Arnal (1735–1805) took place in the 18th century as part of the restoration work carried out after the Lisbon earthquake of 1755.

The architecture of the Viso del Marqués combines in a perfectly integrated manner the most advanced tendencies of the Spanish Renaissance of the mid-16th century with novel Genoese elements in the tradition of Galeazzo Alessi. The interior mural decoration is characteristic of that initiated by Philip II and his court in palace architecture. Its type is represented in the Alcázar of Madrid and in the palaces of El Pardo (carried out by Philip II), of the

Viso del Marqués, near Ciudad Real, begun *c.* 1562, courtyard

Mendoza-Infantado at Guadalajara or in the frescoes of the palace in Alba Tormes, Salamanca (both restored in the second half of the 16th century). At the Viso del Marqués the decoration, with its evident Genoese character, was probably designed by Castello—although it is only documented from 1578 to 1586—and was carried out by his sons Niccolò Castello and Fabrizio Castello, by Cesare Arbasia and, above all, by the Peroli family of painters from Crema. All these artists were of limited talent, but the impact of the decoration is in the ornamental ensemble rather than in the detail.

The decorative scheme constitutes an extensive programme, the style and iconography of which have not been studied in depth; it represents the glorification of the Marqués de Santa Cruz and his family and his personal virtues and naval triumphs. This is done through images drawn from Classical mythology, from biblical and ancient Roman sources and contemporary history, and it is completed by two statues on the staircase of the Marqués de Santa Cruz, of *Neptune* and *Mars.* Various rooms are devoted to such mythological deities as Neptune, Danaë, Proserpina and Venus and Adonis, who often have either allegorical or political significance. Such allusions are also seen in the decoration of the vaults and walls of the staircase, which show episodes from the *Labours of Hercules.* The frescoes of the patio galleries depict military and naval victories associated with the Marqués, views of Spanish cities and of allied and hostile countries, and contemporary figures, such as the Emperor Charles V. Other rooms depict portraits of the Marqués's ancestors, the victories of his grandfather Francisco de Bazán, and the Marqués's own most notable triumphs, such as the Battle of Lepanto (1571). The overall scheme is completed by fine marble and slate fireplaces. The Viso del Marqués constitutes the best-preserved example of a Spanish Renaissance palace in the age of Philip II.

BIBLIOGRAPHY

E. Llaguno y Amírola: *Noticias de los arquitectos y arquitectura de España desde su restauración*, 4 vols (Madrid, 1829/*R* Madrid, 1977)
P. Alcalá Galiano: *El palacio del Marqués de Santa Cruz en el Viso* (Madrid, 1888)
D. Angulo: 'La mitología y el arte español del Renacimiento', *Bol. Real Acad. Hist.*, cxxx (1952), pp. 63–209
F. Chueca Goitia: *Arquitectura del siglo XVI*, A. Hisp., xi (1953)
J. F. Guillén y Tato: *El palacio del Viso del Marqués* (Madrid, 1971)
T. de Antonio Sanz: *El palacio de Viso del Marqués y sus pinturas* (diss., Madrid, U. Complutense, 1972)
C. Wilkinson: 'Il Bergamasco e il Palazzo a Viso del Marqués', *Galeazzo Alessi e l'architettura del cinquecento* (Genoa, 1974)
——: 'The Escorial and the Invention of the Imperial Staircase', *A. Bull.*, lvii (1975), pp. 65–90
S. Sebastián: *Arte y humanismo* (Madrid, 1978)
T. de Antonio Sanz: 'Pinturas mitológicas en el zaguán del palacio de Viso del Marqués', *Miscelánea de arte* (Madrid, 1982)
A. Bustamante and F. Marías: 'La estela de El Viso del Marqués: Esteban Perolli', *Archv Esp. A*, lvi/218 (1982), pp. 173–85
R. López Torrijos: *La mitología en la pintura española del Siglo de Oro* (Madrid, 1985)

FERNANDO MARÍAS

Vispré, François-Xavier [Saverino] (*b* ?Besançon, *c.* 1730; *d* London, after 1789). French painter, pastellist and engraver, active in England and Ireland. As a young man in Paris he engraved portraits in mezzotint, among them those of *Louis XV*, the *Dauphin* and other members of the French royal family. A portrait made in 1761 of the painter and draughtsman *Charles Eisen* (e.g. London, BM) shows Vispré's eye for the delicate detail of soft drapery and lace, and his effective use of a very dark background to highlight his sitter's face. It is not known exactly when he first settled in London, but by 1760 he was established as a painter of portraits, miniatures and small genre scenes. He exhibited regularly until 1783 with the Society of Artists, where his work attracted the attention of Horace Walpole, who several times commented upon the prettiness of his miniatures and pastel drawings of young women. In 1764 Vispré exhibited his first experimental attempt at painting on glass, a speciality that his brother Victor Vispré (*fl* 1736–78) was to develop in his still-lifes of fruit. In 1774 François-Xavier is known to have produced aquatints, among the earliest made in England. He continued to engrave portraits, after drawings by Philippe-Jacques de Loutherbourg, Annibale Carracci and other artists, notably those of the *Chevalier d'Eon* (1765) and of *Pastor Fido* (exh. 1774).

Vispré had been elected a Fellow of the Society of Artists in 1771; he moved to Dublin in 1776 but was back in London by the end of the decade. In 1788 and 1789 he exhibited portraits at the Royal Academy, but there is no record of him after this date. Among his pastels are the *Musician's Family* (Dijon, Mus. B.-A.) and a charming portrait of *John Farr* (Oxford, Ashmolean), who is depicted reclining on a sofa reading a volume of Horace.

BIBLIOGRAPHY

Waterhouse: *18th C.*
A. Graves: *The Society of Artists of Great Britain, 1760–1791; The Free Society of Artists, 1761–1783: A Complete Dictionary of Contributors and their Work* (London, 1907)
P. Brune: *Dictionnaire des artistes et ouvriers d'art de la France: Franche-Comté* (Paris, 1912)
English Portrait Drawings and Miniatures (exh. cat. by P. Noon, New Haven, CT, Yale, Cent. Brit. A., 1979)

LOUISE GOVIER

Visscher, Claes Jansz. (*b* Amsterdam, 1587; *d* Amsterdam, 19 June 1652). Dutch draughtsman, printmaker and publisher. His father was a ship's carpenter. Visscher's master is unknown, although Constantijn Huygens the elder suggested that Jacques de Gheyn the younger taught him to etch. Visscher is recorded as an engraver in Amsterdam in 1608, and his early engravings, from 1605 onwards, consist entirely of reproductive prints after the designs of Flemish artists, in particular David Vinckboons, who settled in Amsterdam in 1602. In the second decade of the 17th century Visscher etched and published landscapes of a strong local character, of both real and imaginary views, to the designs of young Dutch draughtsmen such as Jan and Esaias van de Velde (i) and Willem Buytewech. These proved extremely popular and formed the basis of Visscher's early success as a publisher. He became the most important Amsterdam print publisher, specializing in portraits, landscapes and maps, the elaborate borders of which were often to his own designs. He himself etched more than 200 plates.

Visscher's unquestioned importance as a publisher of prints and maps has tended to overshadow his contribution as a draughtsman to the early development of landscape in the Netherlands. Few of his drawings are dated, but etchings made after some of them by Visscher and published by him *c.* 1611–12 in a series known as *Pleasant Places around Haarlem* show how advanced a draughtsman he was by this date. A number of these sheets, almost certainly drawn from life, are on similar paper, are of similar size and may have come from a single sketchbook. Several are dated 1607 or 1608, some years before the earliest works of the van de Veldes or Willem Buytewech, thus putting Visscher at the forefront of the development of Dutch landscape art.

Visscher's earliest drawings, such as the *View of the Bergevaerderscamer* (1608; Amsterdam, Gemeente Archf) and the *View of Houtewael* (*c.* 1608; Newton, MA, Maida and George Abrams priv. col., see 1991–2 exh. cat., no. 22), are simply executed in pen and brown ink over black chalk. Slightly later sheets, such as the *Study of a Farm* and the *View of a Village*, both of similar dimensions (both *c.* 1610; Paris, Fond. Custodia, Inst. Néer; see fig.), incorporate brown wash. In handling, they are clearly influenced by David Vinckboons, particularly in the use of wash, by Jacques de Gheyn and by the landscape drawings of the Haarlem Mannerist artists Hendrick Goltzius and Jacob Matham. In composition, however, they are much more advanced than the work of these artists, and a likely source of inspiration is the set of 14 prints called *Multifarium casularum . . .*, showing views in a village engraved after drawings by the Master of the Small Landscapes and published by Hieronymus Cock in 1559. Their realistic

Claes Jansz. Visscher: *View of a Village*, pen and brown ink and brown wash, over black chalk, 107×162 mm, *c.* 1610 (Paris, Fondation Custodia, Institut Néerlandais)

treatment of the subject-matter and the approach to the composition, with a low horizon and limited reliance on framing elements, prefigure Visscher's early drawings. Visscher was undoubtedly well aware of these prints (which he took to be after designs by Pieter Bruegel the elder), since he engraved and published an extensively revised edition of them in 1612. Visscher's later drawings, none of which is dated, do not differ much in style from his early work, although he appears to have used a greater variety of washes, perhaps initially under the influence of Jan van de Velde. Ater the second decade of the 17th century, he seems to have made few if any drawings, perhaps as a result of the demands that his increasingly successful business was making on his time. After his death, the firm continued to flourish under his son, Nicolaes Visscher (1618–1709).

BIBLIOGRAPHY

Hollstein: *Dut. & Flem.*: 'Cock, Hieronymous'
J. G. van Gelder: *Jan van de Velde* (The Hague, 1933), pp. 25–30
M. Simon: *Claes Jansz. Visscher* (diss., U. Fribourg, 1958)
Landscape in Perspective: Drawings by Rembrandt and his Contemporaries (exh. cat. by F. J. Duparc, Cambridge, MA, Sackler Mus.; Montreal, Mus. F.A.; 1988), pp. 221–3
Seventeenth-century Dutch Drawings: A Selection from the Maida and George Abrams Collection (exh. cat. by W. W. Robinson, Amsterdam, Rijksmus.; Vienna, Albertina; New York, Pierpont Morgan Lib.; Cambridge, MA, Fogg; 1991–2), pp. 62–3

GEORGE GORDON

Visscher, Cornelis (de) (*b* ?Haarlem, ?1629; *d* Amsterdam, *bur* 16 Jan 1658). Dutch engraver and draughtsman.

He was one of the most important and productive Dutch portrait draughtsmen and engravers of the 17th century, despite his short lifetime. He was probably a pupil of the Haarlem painter and engraver Pieter Soutman. In 1649–50 he made numerous portrait engravings for several print series published and supervised by Soutman. He was probably Soutman's principal collaborator during this period, although the quantity of prints produced suggests that he was not the only one. After 1650 Visscher apparently set up independently. In 1653 he joined the Haarlem Guild of St Luke, but he must have moved to Amsterdam shortly thereafter.

Between 1651 and 1658 Visscher made dozens of engravings of biblical and historical subjects, genre scenes and landscapes, both after his own designs and after past and present masters (e.g. *see* LAER, PIETER VAN, fig. 1). Most impressive, however, are his attractive and accomplished portrait engravings, most to his own designs. He was also of particular importance as a portrait draughtsman, as is apparent from his numerous independent portrait drawings in black chalk (e.g. many in Vienna, Albertina, and Berlin, Kupferstichkab.). He also made excellent detailed animal studies. His drawings show parallels with the work of such Haarlem artists as Jan de Bray and Leendert van der Cooghen, who used chalk to draw in a comparable style, with regular horizontal hatching. His younger brothers Jan Visscher (*b* ?Amsterdam or Haarlem, *c.* 1636; *d* after 1692) and Lambert Visscher (*b* ?Amsterdam or Haarlem, 1633; *d* ?Florence, after 1690) also worked as portrait draughtsmen and engravers.

BIBLIOGRAPHY
Hollstein: *Dut. & Flem.*
J. Wussin: *Cornelis Visscher: Verzeichnis seiner Kupferstiche* (Leipzig, 1865)
E. Bock and J. Rosenberg: *Die Zeichnungen niederländischer Meister im Kupferstichkabinett zu Berlin* (Berlin, 1930)
Dutch Figure Drawings from the Seventeenth Century (exh. cat. by P. Schatborn, Amsterdam, Rijksmus.; Washington, DC, N.G.A.; 1981–2), pp. 100–01, nos 97–8

RUDOLF E. O. EKKART

Visser, Carel (Nicolaas) (*b* Papendrecht, 3 May 1928). Dutch sculptor, collagist and draughtsman. He produced his first geometric constructions, such as *Double Stepped Pyramid* (untraced; see Blotkamp, pl. 22), which is noticeably influenced by Constantin Brancusi, in 1948. From 1948 to 1949 he studied architecture at the Technische Hogeschool in Delft. Between 1949 and 1951 he trained at the Koninklijke Academie voor Beeldende Kunsten in The Hague, where he also taught from 1958 to 1962. In 1951 he travelled to London and Paris, visiting Brancusi, and became interested in the work of Alberto Giacometti. Influenced by Julio González and Pablo Picasso, from the late 1940s he made welded constructions in iron, usually representing plants and animals, such as *Dying Horse* (h. 1.5 m, 1949; Otterlo, Kröller-Müller). In 1952 he submitted work to the open-air exhibition in Sonsbeek Park, Arnhem. His first one-man exhibition was held at the Kunsthandel Martinet in Amsterdam in 1954.

In the mid-1950s Visser explored the concepts of the work of De Stijl artists. He applied their principles of composition but at the same time sought more dynamic expression in his work. In 1958 he received a commission for the Exposition Universelle in Brussels. Between 1958 and 1962 his work evolved from figurative to abstract-geometric, although it retained its source of inspiration, seen, for example, in the *Double Form* series of 1957–8, which derived from a reflection of a stylized figure of a bird (e.g. Amsterdam, Stedel. Mus.). From 1963 he taught at the Ateliers 63 in Haarlem.

The repetition of geometric shapes is particularly noticeable in Visser's work from the period 1963–8: welded, irregular piles of iron components, which sometimes drop down from the base. In the year that he participated in the Venice Biennale (1968) his work became more regular, and he started to use such materials as aluminium. In 1969–70 he started to construct installations of steel plates joined with leather. The use of organic material led to the use of *objets trouvés*. This stylistic change was prompted by his response to the Vietnam War (1954–75) and to the apparent failure of technology in opposition to human factors.

From 1971 until 1976 Visser composed his installations from a number of pieces of folded sheet-steel, which were piled up or placed on top of or alongside each other. From 1972–3 he made *c.* ten to twelve installations a year. He made collages from 1974 by colouring paper black with a pencil and pasting on to this such natural *objets trouvés* as peacock and turkey feathers, hair, egg and mussel shells, knots of sheep's wool, as well as labels from cigar boxes, bottles and photographic reproductions of famous works by Brancusi, Hans Arp, Piero Manzoni, Rembrandt and Pieter Saenredam.

After 1977 Visser incorporated recognizable motifs from nature and architecture, such as crested waves and capitals from Greek temples, as part of a stylized imitation of reality. He bent rather than folded the steelplate. After 1978, however, the sculptures regained their object character and for a period the influence of Surrealism was evident in his work. He no longer used iron as the sole material, but added organic elements that he collected both on travels and at home. His *Walking Stick* series (1978–9) consists of walking sticks from the British Rail lost property department in London (e.g. *Spanish Fork*, 0.3×1.6×0.3 m, 1979; Otterlo, Kröller-Müller), combined with natural materials such as sheep's wool and cows' horns from his farmhouse in Rijswijk in the province of Gelderland. In the 1980s Visser made installations in a variety of materials, including cardboard, iron, sand, glass and even car tyres, for example *Charlie I* and *II* (1.2×4.0×4.0 m, 1985), which represents his son's dog. He also constructed rafts and farming carts, and in 1985 he exhibited jewellery.

BIBLIOGRAPHY
Carel Visser, papierbeelden (exh. cat., Amsterdam, Stedel. Mus., 1978)
Carel Visser: Werken, 1975–1985 (exh. cat., Rotterdam, Boymans–van Beuningen, 1985)
Carel Visser, beelder 1975–1985 (exh. cat., Rotterdam, Boymans–van Beuningen, 1986)
C. Blotkamp: *Carel Visser* (Utrecht, 1989) [with bibliog.]

JOHN STEEN

Visser, Martin (*b* Papendrecht, 1922). Dutch furniture designer, collector and patron. Having originally trained as an architectural draughtsman, he became one of the most important furniture designers in the Netherlands after World War II. From 1947 he worked as a buyer, salesman and designer in the furniture department of the Bijenkorf store in Amsterdam. From 1955 to 1974 he designed for the furniture manufacturer 't Spectrum in Bergeijk. Visser's utilitarian concept of furniture was tempered by his interest in craftsmanship and his desire to produce unique works. Until 1955 he designed simple, well-constructed wooden furniture, using mostly natural pine. About 1955 he and his wife, Mia, moved into a house in Bergeijk, which had been designed and built for them by Gerrit Rietveld, and which they filled with furniture designed by Visser and his colleagues. In 1959 they began seriously to collect art by contemporary artists and enlarged their house with the addition of a gallery designed by Aldo van Eyck. Although their early acquisitions were works by artists of the Cobra group, the strength of their collection was Nouveau Réalisme and Minimalism. The collection included works by Christo, Sol LeWitt, Robert Morris (ii), Dan Flavin, Carl André and Robert Indiana, many of whom stayed at the Vissers' home, a popular centre for American and European artists.

Between 1968 and 1984 there were three major exhibitions of objects from the Vissers' collection. Works are also on long-term loan to the Stedelijk Van Abbemuseum in Eindhoven and to the Centrum voor Kunst en Cultuur in Ghent. The couple donated Christo's *Barrel Structure 1968–1977* to the Rijksmuseum Kröller-Müller in Otterlo. In later years Visser served as both critic and curator of exhibitions of contemporary art.

WRITINGS

Benne Premsela: Onder andern (exh. cat., Amsterdam, Stedel. Mus., 1981) [essay by Visser]

BIBLIOGRAPHY

Hans Polak, Martin Visser, Kho Liang Ie (exh. cat., Amsterdam, Stedel. Mus., 1961)

Zeichnen/Bezeichnen: Zeichnungen aus der Sammlung Mia und Martin Visser, Bergeyk, mit Beiträgen aus der Sammlung Geert Jan Visser, Antwerpen (exh. cat., Basle, Kstmus., 1976)

Kleine Arena: Drawings and Sculptures from the Collection Adri, Martin and Geertjan Visser (exh. cat., ed. T. van Kooten; Otterlo, Kröller-Müller, 1984)

G. Vreeburg: 'De meubelkunst van Martin Visser', *Jong Holland*, i/2 (1985), pp. 38–55, 64

Vista Alegre Factory. *See* FÁBRICA DA VISTA ALEGRE.

Vital Brazil, Álvaro (*b* São Paulo, 1 Feb 1909). Brazilian architect. He studied in Rio de Janeiro, graduating as a civil engineer from the Escola Politécnica and as an architect from the Escola Nacional de Belas Artes (1933), where he participated in the reforms of 1931–2 when Lúcio Costa introduced Modernist teachers; this exposed him to the teachings of Le Corbusier and his rationalist approach to Modernism. Until 1936 he worked with Adhemar Marinho (*b* 1911), and they designed the Esther building (1936) in São Paulo, which is considered to be the first free-standing modern building in the city. It was also the first multi-use building in São Paulo, comprising ten floors of shops, offices and flats as well as an underground car park. Conceived in accordance with Le Corbusier's principles, it combined a new structural system of pilotis and open-plan floors with a sculptural sense of the building's volume, its four façades articulated in a manner reminiscent of Art Deco. A member of CIAM, Vital Brazil worked as a Modernist architect for 50 years, particularly in Rio de Janeiro, adopting an extremely elegant, rational style with great simplicity and clarity of structure: for example the Vital Brazil Institute (1941), Niteroi, a scientific laboratory building named after his father, a famous scientist, was a long, white block raised on pilotis with small windows on the exposed side and full glazing on the other, its crisp appearance expressing the building's use. He won first prize at the first São Paulo Biennale (1951) with his design for the Clemente Faria bank building in Belo Horizonte, a triangular-shaped building with an elegant design incorporating horizontal bands of vertical *brises-soleil* on one façade. His work during the 1960s and 1970s includes the apartment block in Rua Timbiras (1961), and the Banca da Lavoura de Minas Gerais (1963), both in Belo Horizonte, the house in Rua Constantino Menelau, Cabo Frio (1961), and the house for Tiso Vital Brazil, Rua Alves Mota, Guaratinguetá (1972).

WRITINGS

50 anos de arquitetura (São Paulo, 1986)

BIBLIOGRAPHY

H. E. Mindlin: *Modern Architecture in Brazil* (Amsterdam and Rio de Janeiro, 1956)

C. A. C. Lemos: *Arquitetura brasileira* (São Paulo, 1979)

A. Xavier, C. Lemos and E. Corona: *Arquitetura moderna paulistana* (São Paulo, 1983)

CARLOS A. C. LEMOS

Vitale, Filippo (*b* Naples, *c.* 1585; *d* Naples, 1650). Italian painter. Little is revealed about his life and work in the early sources, yet artistic and family links with Annella (Diana) de Rosa (*b* 1602), Pacecco, Giovanni Dò, Aniello Falcone and Agostino Beltrano have been identified. In the early years of the 17th century his contact with the workshop of Carlo Sellitto is recorded. His first documented works form part of a cycle of canvases (after 1617; badly damaged) for the ceiling of the church of the Annunziata at Capua, to which he contributed the *Nativity*, the *Pentecost*, the *Circumcision* and the *Annunciation*.

In this period, when Vitale's late 16th-century style was only superficially modified by a Caravaggesque treatment of light, he also produced *SS Nicholas, Januarius and Severus* (Naples, S Nicola alle Sacramentine) and the *Holy Family* (Naples, S Maria delle Grazie at Caponapoli). The monogrammed *Lament of Adam and Eve over the Body of Abel* (priv. col.) reveals a more profound response to Caravaggio, perhaps stimulated by Sellitto, while the monogrammed *Guardian Angel* (Naples, Pietà dei Turchini) suggests his response to the naturalism of Jusepe de Ribera. Other works, including the *Virgin Giving the Rosary to St Charles Borromeo in the Presence of St Dominic* (Naples, S Domenico Maggiore), the large canvas with *St Anthony of Padua Interceding for Naples* (*c.* 1635; Naples, Congrega di S Antonio in S Lorenzo Maggiore), the signed *Deposition* (*c.* 1645; Naples, S Mara Regina Coeli) and paintings in which throughout his career he collaborated with his stepson, Pacecco de Rosa, reveal that in his mature years Vitale adopted the classicist style of Massimo Stanzione and Domenichino.

BIBLIOGRAPHY

Painting in Naples from Caravaggio to Giordano (exh. cat., ed. C. Whitfield and J. Martineau; London, RA, 1982), pp. 263–4

Civiltà del seicento a Napoli (exh. cat., ed. S. Cresani; Naples, Capodimonte, 1984–5), i, pp. 181, 498–504

N. Spinosa: *La pittura napoletana del '600* (Milano, 1984), figs 877–84

G. De Vito: 'Un contributo per Filippo Vitale', *Ricerche sul '600 napoletano*, ed. G. De Vito (Milan, 1987), pp. 105–43

RICCARDO LATTUADA

Vitale da Bologna [Vidalino di Aymo de Equis] (*b* before 1309; *d* between 1359 and 1361). Italian painter.

1. LIFE AND WORK. The earliest documentary references to Vitale concern S Francesco, Bologna, where he was paid for decorating a chapel in 1330 and where he witnessed deeds in 1334. He was probably born before 1309, since he would have been at least 25 to act as a witness. The earliest works attributed to him are the frescoes of standing saints and *Abraham and the Blessed Souls* (Bologna, S Martino), which show a strong Riminese influence in the cool, wine-red and olive tones and lean, high-cheeked faces. Vitale's work continued to reflect Riminese iconography and features, particularly the vivid characterizations associated with Pietro da Rimini, but his style became less dependent upon these sources. He was paid for paintings in a chapel and the guests' refectory of S Francesco in 1340. The *Last Supper* from the refectory (detached; Bologna, Pin. N.) retains the cool pinks and rows of standing saints of the S Martino frescoes, but the modelling of the figures is richer and more expressive. The long table and symmetrical architecture are inspired by Giotto's frescoes in the Bardi Chapel, Santa Croce,

Florence (*see* GIOTTO, fig. 7), and the radical transformation in Vitale's style, which set him apart from his Bolognese contemporaries, was partly due to Giotto's influence. Above all, however, his style was influenced by the Master of the Triumph of Death at Pisa. The lively gestures, the loose modelling and lime-green and vermilion palette of Bolognese illuminators, particularly the Illustratore, also began to influence Vitale. Bolognese illumination provided a repertory of genre observation that undoubtedly affected his wide range of iconographic innovations. These varied influences can be seen in the uneven but lively quality of the *Crucifixion* (*c.* 1335–40; Philadelphia, PA, Mus. A.). Vitale's work is also often compared to that of Sienese painters. There is no substantial evidence of direct influence but his use of dramatic facial types reminiscent of Pietro Lorenzetti and a decorative richness akin to Simone Martini's painting suggest that he knew their work.

A fresco fragment of the *Virgin Embroidering Christ's Tunic* (*c.* 1340; priv. col., on dep. Bologna, Pin. N.) introduces a new subject, which combines domestic realism with Passion symbolism and includes richly patterned fabrics. The stylized posture of the Virgin becomes typical of a series of paintings of the Virgin and Child, of which the *Madonna dei Denti* (Bologna, Pal. Davia–Bargellini) is the most important. Signed, and dated 1345 according to D'Agincourt, it was painted for the oratory of the Virgin, Mezzaratta, Bologna, probably forming a polyptych with panels including *St Peter and a Pilgrim* and *SS Anthony and James* (Bologna, Pal. Com.). The composition and the structure of Mary's throne are derived directly from the polyptych (Bologna, Pin. N.) by Giotto and painted for the neighbouring church of S Maria degli Angeli, but the space is abstracted by the backcloth that envelops the back of the throne. Mary's face is stylized and simple, contrasting with the lively characterization of the tiny donor figures below.

The *Annunciation* and *Nativity* frescoes (Bologna, Pin. N.) from the west wall of S Apollonia, Mezzaratta, probably of similar date, are composed within a definite space compressed by the high viewpoint and flattened perspective to emphasize the geometry of the crib and shed and the related sweeping movements of a choir of angels. Similar qualities underlie the construction of the narratives from a dismembered polyptych of the *Miracles of St Anthony of Padua* (Bologna, Pin. N.), notable also for the precocious depiction of dense woods and meadows, a delicate Gothic fountain and a range of special light effects including fire and ball lightning.

The *St George and the Dragon* (see fig.), probably dating from the earlier 1340s, is signed on the horse with an anagram similar to Bolognese lawyers' marks. Its blue ground and the mosaic-like border suggest that it was part of a cupboard or tabernacle. St George's anatomically impossible swastika-like pose, his flying coat-tails and rearing horse contrast with the serene princess abruptly cut off by the hillside.

In 1349 Vitale frescoed the presbytery of Udine Cathedral. All but the lowest frescoes are lost, but they can be reconstructed from copies in the presbytery of Spilimbergo Cathedral, a small fresco from a house in Udine (Udine, Mus. Città) and a fine panel by Vitale himself of the

Vitale da Bologna: *St George and the Dragon*, tempera on panel, 880×700 mm, *c.* 1340–45 (Bologna, Pinacoteca Nazionale)

Crucifixion (Madrid, Mus. Thyssen-Bornemisza) with soldiers attacking the Jews and gambling for Christ's tunic. Above the frescoed *Crucifixion* was a *Coronation of the Virgin* set under a pavilion, a motif widely used by Vitale's Friulian followers and later by Piero della Francesca, to show Mary as Queen of Heaven and Tabernacle of the Lord. These frescoes were very dramatic; a calmer mood prevails in the *Life of St Nicholas* in the adjacent chapel at Udine. The *Funeral of St Nicholas* owes an obvious debt to Giotto's *Funeral of St Francis* in the Bardi Chapel of Santa Croce, Florence, both in composition and architectural setting. The St Nicholas scenes strongly influenced frescoes at Breg pri Preddvoru, Slovenia, *c.* 1400.

Vitale frescoed the apse of the Early Christian basilica of S Maria, Pomposa, with a deliberately archaic *Christ in Majesty* surrounded by an exquisite choir of angels and fashionably dressed virgins; the majestic compositions of the *Life of St Eustace* below are ruined by damp. The main works of the last ten years of Vitale's career were the frescoes of the apsidal chapels of S Maria dei Servi, Bologna, of which fragments of the *Doctors of the Church*, the *Lives of the Virgin and St Mary Magdalene*, signed again with a monogram on a horse, and a late *Trinity* in the north chapel survive. A parishioner of the church, Vitale is last recorded here in 1359.

A polyptych for S Salvatore, Bologna, dated by the contract of 1353, exemplifies Vitale's late work; set in a luxuriant Venetian frame, the paintings are more calmly composed, the figures smaller in scale and set further into the picture space. The central *Coronation* is enhanced by the exquisite patterns incised into delicate varnishes of the vestments. Probably dating from the same period are the signed *Virgin and Child* (Rome, Pin. Vaticana) in which the Virgin appears as a vision to the Flagellants of Ferrara, a diptych showing the *Adoration of the Magi* (Edinburgh, N.G.) remarkable for its naturalistic hedgerows and exotic horsemen, and a *Pietà* (Florence, Fond. Longhi).

2. TECHNIQUE. Whether in fresco or on panel Vitale consistently used a more fluid medium than his Tuscan contemporaries, and his brushstrokes are broader and more painterly. The fine brushstrokes following the form are a deliberate exception made to suit the iconic nature of some of his Virgins, and both techniques are often found together. His use of dense shadows was perhaps inspired by Byzantine or Venetian painting. The frescoes of S Maria dei Servi, Bologna, appear to be finished with oil glazes and fixatives.

The parallel pleats and cool tones of Riminese art disappear from Vitale's draperies *c.* 1340 to be replaced by exuberant folds and richer colour. Vitale's pigments are less pure, and probably cheaper, than those of Tuscan artists, but more subtle in hue. Elaborate stamped patterns decorate the haloes and the borders of the gold ground in his panel painting. A comparable use of incisions and *pastiglia* appears in his frescoes. His frames became increasingly like their Venetian models.

3. INFLUENCE. Vitale was probably the most widely influential north Italian artist of the 14th century. His impact was due partly to his assimilation of the legacy of Bolognese illumination combined with his mastery of the expressive and decorative techniques of fresco and tempera, but also to the large workshops that he established in Bologna, Udine and Pomposa. His work was reflected for some 70 years throughout north-east Italy, the eastern Alps and the Kingdom of Hungary. The nave of Pomposa, the cathedrals of Spilimbergo, Trent, Trieste, Venzone and Gurk, the churches of Hermagor and Neuhaus-an-der-Gail (Kärnten) and Breg pri Preddvoru (Slovenia) provide notable examples of his followers' work. His greatest pupil Tomaso da Modena developed his iconographical and technical ideas even further. Andrea da Bologna and Cristoforo di Jacopo Biondi perpetuated his style in Bologna. Although Andrea Bartoli and Simone dei Crocefissi changed the character of local painting in the 1360s, their own technique and iconography also owed much to Vitale.

BIBLIOGRAPHY

C. C. Malvasia: *Le pitture di Bologna* (Bologna, 1686); ed. A. Emiliani (Bologna, 1969)
S. D'Agincourt: *Histoire de l'art par les monuments* (Paris, 1811–20)
F. Filippini and G. Zucchini: *Miniatori e pittori a Bologna: Documenti dei secoli XIII e XIV* (Florence, 1947), pp. 230–35
C. Gnudi: *Vitale da Bologna* (Milan, 1962)
C. Quintavalle: *Vitale da Bologna*, Maestri Colore (Milan, 1966)
Primo convegno internazionale di storia dell'arte sul tema 'La pittura trecentesca in Friuli e i rapporti con la cultura figurativa delle regioni confinanti': Udine, 1970
R. Longhi: *Lavori in Valpadana*, Opera Completa, vi (Florence, 1973)
S. Skerl Del Conte: 'Vitale da Bologna e il Duomo di Udine', *A. Friuli, A. Trieste*, i (1975), pp. 15–34
F. Arcangeli: *Pitture bolognese del '300* (Bologna, 1978)
R. Gibbs: 'A Group of Trecento Bolognese Painters Active in the Veneto', *Burl. Mag.*, cxxiv (1981), pp. 77–86
L. Lodi: 'Note sulla decorazione punzonata di dipinti su tavola di area emiliana', *Mus. Ferrar.: Boll. Annu.*, xi (1981), pp. 9–208
R. D'Amico and M. Medica: *Vitale da Bologna* (Bologna, 1986)
R. Gibbs: *Tomaso da Modena: Painting in Emilia and the March of Treviso 1340–1380* (Cambridge, 1988) [bibliog.]
G. Gnudi and P. Casadio: *Itinerari di Vitale da Bologna: Affreschi a Udine e a Pomposa* (Bologna, 1990)

ROBERT GIBBS

Vitali [Vitale], **Alessandro** (*b* Urbino, 1580; *d* Urbino, 4 July 1630). Italian painter. He was a favoured pupil of Federico Barocci and as early as 1598 Francesco Maria II della Rovere, Duke of Urbino, commissioned him to execute copies of his teacher's work. The Duke paid him 30 scudi for a *Nativity* and 12 scudi for a painting of *St Francis of Assisi* (both untraced). In 1603 the council of the town of Urbino decided to commission Vitali, rather than Barocci, to paint the *Gathering of Manna* (untraced) for the chapel of the Sacrament in the cathedral. Vitali remained in Barocci's workshop, the latter often adding his own touch to pictures by his protégé. Not surprisingly Vitali's style of drawing and use of harmonies of yellows, reds and blues are very close to those of his master. However, like other pupils, he failed to rival Barocci as an artist. Vitali's *Virgin and Child between a Saint and an Angel* in the parish church of Cavallino (Urbino) was based on Barocci's *Martyrdom of St Sebastian* (1558–60) in Urbino Cathedral, but its awkward composition, with the figure of the donor clumsily placed in the right foreground, gives the picture an arid quality. After Barocci's death (1612) information on his pupils becomes scarcer. Possibly Vitali's last work was the *Birth of the Virgin* in S Simpliciano, Milan, a work that presents a harder and cooler version of the Baroque style.

BIBLIOGRAPHY

Mostra di opere d'arte restaurate (exh. cat., Urbino, 1966)
Mostra di opere d'arte restaurate (exh. cat., Urbino, 1970), pp. 160–63
Pittori nelle Marche tra '500 e '600: Aspetti dell'ultimo Manierismo (exh. cat. by L. Arcangeli and others, Urbino, Pal. Ducale, 1979), pp. 12–18

RENATE MÖLLER

Vitali, Ivan (Petrovich) [Giovanni] (*b* St Petersburg, 1794; *d* St Petersburg, 15 July 1855). Russian sculptor. He came from a family of Italian craftsmen who had worked in Russia for many years. He trained in the workshop of Agostino Triscorni (1761–1824) in St Petersburg and from 1818 he was head of the Moscow branch of this workshop. Among Vitali's works from this period in Moscow are the decorative sculpture (stone, 1820–25) for the Council of Guardians (Opekunsky Soviet) building (part *in situ*), a sculpture group (stone, 1829–30) on the pediment of the Technical Academy (now Bauman Higher Technical Academy) and another (stone, 1830–35; Moscow, Shchusev Res. & Sci. Mus. Rus. Arch.) on the pediment of the Sirotsky Institute, the fountain (bronze, 1835) on Teatral'naya Square, and the funerary monuments to *P. A. Beketov* (bronze, 1823) and *I. I. Baryshnikov* (marble, 1834; both Moscow, Shchusev Res. & Sci. Mus. Rus. Arch.). In 1840 Vitali received the title of academician.

In 1841 Vitali returned to St Petersburg, where he produced many sculptures for St Isaac's Cathedral, notably the compositions for the western and southern pediments, *St Isaac Blessing the Emperor Theodosius* and the *Adoration of the Magi* (bronze, 1841–4). The sculptures for the cathedral are in a classical style but executed with a realism that is characteristic of Vitali's later work. Among the other works of the sculptor are the monument to *Paul I* in front of the palace at Gatchina (zinc, 1850; copy, 1872; Peter & Paul Fortress), a statue of *Venus* (marble, 1852; St Petersburg, Rus. Mus.) and a large number of portrait busts, for example of *Aleksandr S. Pushkin* (plaster, 1837), the painter *Vasily K. Shebuyev* (plaster, 1840; both St Petersburg, Rus. Mus.) and *Aleksandr A. Dolgoruky* (marble, 1844; Moscow, Tret'yakov Gal.).

BIBLIOGRAPHY

T. V. Yakirina and N. V. Odnoralov: *Vitali, 1794–1855* (Leningrad, 1960)

SERGEY ANDROSSOV

Vitberg, Aleksandr (Lavrent'yevitch) (*b* St Petersburg, 1787; *d* St Petersburg, 1855). Russian painter and architect. He studied at the St Petersburg Academy of Arts (1802–7) under Grigory Ugryumov, for whom he later worked as an assistant (1807–12). His work, which shows his teacher's influence, explores biblical, mythological and historical themes, as in the *Killing of Patriarch Germogen* the *St Peter Released from Prison*, for which he was made an academician (1815). His landscapes and particularly his portraits are in the Romantic style. In 1813, inspired by a competition to build a church in Moscow to commemorate Russia's deliverance from the French invasion, he retrained as an architect and submitted the winning entry. Work on Vitberg's design for the church of Christ the Redeemer (Khram Khrista Spasitelya) began in 1825, but was abandoned the following year. The victim of an intrigue, he was disgraced and exiled to Vyatka. His work in the town includes the monumental gates (1836) for the Alexander Garden and the Alexander Nevsky Cathedral (1839–48). Eventually proved innocent, he returned to Moscow in 1840. He continued to work as an architect for the remaining years of his life, but died in obscurity and poverty.

BIBLIOGRAPHY

Y. S. Moskalets: *Vitberg v Vyatke* [Vitberg in Vyatka] (Kirov, 1975)

Y. I. Kirichenko: 'Aleksandr Lavrent'yevitch Vitberg', *Arkhit. SSSR*, vi (1987)

Y. Skopin: 'Arkhitekturnaya deyatel'nost A. Vitberg v Vyatke' [The architectural work of Vitberg in Vyatka], *Arkhit. SSSR*, vi (1987)

YE. I. KIRICHENKO

Vitebsk. *See* VICIEBSK.

Viterbese, il. *See* ROMANELLI, GIOVANNI FRANCESCO.

Viterbo. Italian city in Lazio, between the Cimino Mountains and the valley of the River Tiber. A provincial capital, episcopal see and university town, it was the seat of the popes in the 13th century. Despite heavy bombardment in World War II (1944), the medieval fabric is largely preserved, although there has been considerable restoration. Several churches have been stripped of their later accretions and restored to their original form.

An Etruscan and then a Roman settlement, the site was fortified in AD 773 by the Lombard leader Desiderius (*reg* 756–74), taken by the Franks and ceded by them to the Church in 787. It was established as a commune in 1095, when the town walls were begun; with the creation of the bishopric in 1192 Viterbo became the principal rival of Rome in the region. From the early 13th century it was dominated by two rival families, the Guelph Gatti and the Ghibelline Tignosi. In 1257 Pope Alexander IV (*reg* 1254–61), in conflict with both the Empire and the Roman aristocracy, moved to Viterbo, which became the official papal residence until the death of Nicholas III in 1280. The riots following the election of Martin IV (*reg* 1281–5) led to the excommunication of the city and the departure of the papal court. This hastened the decline of the commune, which gradually became subject to Rome. Some members of the Vico family resisted, but Giovanni Vico was defeated in 1354 by the papal legate Cardinal Gil Alvarez Carrillo de Albornoz (1310–67), after which the city lost its autonomy. Viterbo was annexed to the Italian state in 1870.

The most significant urban and artistic development in the city occurred between the foundation of the commune and the 16th century. Lombard architects are recorded as early as 1090, their presence reflected in the style of the principal Romanesque churches, which have plain, round-headed columnar arcades, small clerestory windows, three parallel eastern apses and wooden roofs: examples include S Silvestro (now Il Gesù), S Giovanni in Zoccoli and S Maria Nuova. The 9th-century church of S Sisto was vaulted in the 13th century, perhaps under Burgundian influence from the nearby Cistercian abbey of S Martino al Cimino. The cathedral of S Lorenzo, built in the 11th century on the site of the Etruscan acropolis, has been restored to its original Romanesque stonework.

Gothic styles were introduced to the area in the flurry of building following the establishment of the papal residence, culminating in the Palazzo Papale (now the bishop's house; see fig.), built 1257–66, and the slightly later attached Loggia, which is related in style to the upper church of S Francesco, Assisi. In 1236 building had begun at S Francesco, the architectural style of which shows influence from S Martino al Cimino; but its significance lies in its tombs of both the nobility and popes, in particular those of *Clement IV* (*d* 1268) by PIETRO DI ODERISIO, which combines a Gothic gabled canopy with Cosmati mosaic decoration, and *Adrian V* (after 1276), for a long time attributed to ARNOLFO DI CAMBIO. Of greater importance is the civic architecture, in particular the Palazzo del Podestà (1247) and the Fontana Grande (1206–79), the first of a series of public fountains. Two characteristic house types became widespread, that with a ground-floor loggia and the so-called *profferli*, with an external staircase. The latter are most common in the S Pellegrino quarter and were the predecessors of the tower houses, of which 12 survive.

The building of the Rocca d'Albornoz after 1354 effectively signalled the start of the post-communal era in Viterbo. The 15th-century palazzi built by such members of the Roman patriciate as the Chigi and Farnese families foreshadowed the opulent villas in the rural environs, of which JACOPO VIGNOLA was to be the principal architect, as at the Villa Farnese (1557–84) at Caprarola. Vignola designed the Palazzo Chigi (after 1562) at Soriano, the Villa Lante (1556–78) at Bagnaia and influenced the unique Sacro Bosco, the garden below Bomarzo created from 1552 for Pier Francesco Orsini (*d* 1585; *see* BOMARZO, SACRO BOSCO). In the suburbs of Viterbo is the Renaissance church of S Maria della Quercia, completed in 1525;

Viterbo, Palazzo Papale, 1257–66

the three terracotta lunettes (1507–8) on the portals are by Andrea della Robbia.

Paintings in S Maria Nuova, such as those of Matteo Giovannetti, show that in 14th-century Viterbo artists were under the influence of Siena; but the work of FRANCESCO D'ANTONIO DA VITERBO and Antonio da Viterbo (*c.* 1450–*c.* 1480) in the 15th century shows contact with the art of Umbria–Tuscany. This later trend is particularly evident in the frescoes (1469) by Lorenzo da Viterbo (?1437–after 1476) in the Cappella Mazzatosta in S Maria della Verità. In the 16th century, however, with the magnificent *Pietà* (1517) and *Flagellation* (1524–5; both Viterbo, Mus. Civ.) of SEBASTIANO DEL PIOMBO, painters in Viterbo increasingly looked to Rome.

BIBLIOGRAPHY
C. Pinzi: *I principali monumenti di Viterbo* (Viterbo, 1911)
V. Scriattoli: *Viterbo nei suoi monumenti* (Rome, 1920)
A. Gottardi: *Viterbo nel duecento* (Viterbo, 1955)
I. Faldi: *I pittori viterbesi* (Rome, 1972)
A. M. Corbo: 'Chiese e artisti viterbesi nella prima metà del secolo XV', *Commentari*, i–iii (1977), pp. 162–71
B. Barbini and P. Petrassi: *Il Palazzo dei Priori a Viterbo* (Rome, 1983)
Il quattrocento a Viterbo (exh. cat. by R. Cannata and C. Strinati, Viterbo, Mus. Civ., 1983)

GIUSEPPE PINNA

Viterbo, Francesco d'Antonio (Zacchi) da. *See* FRANCESCO D'ANTONIO DA VITERBO.

Viterbo, Francisco Sousa. *See* SOUSA VITERBO, FRANCISCO.

Viterbo, Matteo Giovanetti da. *See* GIOVANETTI, MATTEO.

Viterbo, Pier Francesco da. *See* PIER FRANCESCO DA VITERBO.

Viteri, Oswaldo (*b* Ambato, 8 Oct 1931). Ecuadorean painter and draughtsman. He studied architecture at the Universidad Central del Ecuador, Quito. In 1960 he won the Gran Premio at the Salón Mariano Aguilera with the work *Man, House and Moon* (Quito, Mus. Municipal Alberto Mena Caamaño), with which he expressed an ongoing attempt to come to terms with the past and with the history of South America, as well as a desire to move beyond the anecdotal language of some Ecuadorean art. There followed a brief 'Pre-Columbian' phase during which he sought mestizo symbols for his painting. By the mid-1960s his work was abstract, and by 1970 he had moved on to assemblage and a rejection of previous pictorial language, producing compositions of rag dolls, old cement bags and the gold borders of ecclesiastical vestments and other elements redolent of Latin America's colonial past. In the 1970s he continued to use rag dolls coupled with other textures, for example in *We Are*

Wanderers of the Night and of Suffering (1979; Quito, artist's col.). Viteri's conceptually based art sought to universalize from a mestizo perspective Andean and characteristic local themes, such as isolation, in a highly contemporary language that helped rejuvenate Ecuadorean art.

BIBLIOGRAPHY
Viteri (exh. cat., Madrid, Club Int. Prensa, 1969)
M. Traba: *Dos décadas vulnerables en las artes plásticas latinoamericanas, 1950–1970* (Mexico City, 1973), p. 43
H. Rodríguez Castelo: 'Viteri', *Rev. Diners*, 14 (1982), pp. 54–8
—: *Viteri* (Bogotá, 1992)

CECILIA SUÁREZ

Vitéz [Witéz], Cardinal **Johannes** [János] (*b c.* 1408; *d* 1472). Hungarian prelate and patron. He studied in Vienna and became a notary at the Buda court of Sigismund, King of Hungary and Bohemia and Holy Roman Emperor. He was appointed Bishop of Varad in 1445, royal chancellor in 1453 and in 1465 became Archbishop of Esztergom and primate of Hungary. Vitéz must have visited Italy and is known to have been closely connected with many of the most prominent Italian humanists, including Pope Pius II. He was instrumental in developing a highly esteemed humanist culture in Hungary and possessed a remarkable library. He planned to establish a university at Esztergom based on that of Bologna, although the site was eventually moved to Posonia (Bratislava). Later he had the 13th-century archbishop's palace at Esztergom remodelled in the style of an Italian Renaissance palace. It was razed during the Turkish wars of the 16th and 17th centuries, but the excavations of 1934–8 revealed foundations and sections of the palace, including the remains of extensive fresco decoration. In the archbishop's study were wall paintings of allegorical female figures representing the *Four Cardinal Virtues*, painted in the Florentine manner of *c.* 1450, probably by a follower of Fra Filippo Lippi. They stand on a foreshortened marble pavement beneath an arcade on piers with engaged columns carrying an architrave. There is evidence that the vaults were decorated with the *Triumph of the Seven Planets*, with the *Signs of the Zodiac* on the archivolt. Both the architecture and the scheme correspond to ideas set out in the writings of such Italian theorists as Leon Battista Alberti and Antonio Filarete. Vitéz probably owned texts by Alberti and Filarete, but in any case these were available in the Corvina library in Buda.

BIBLIOGRAPHY
Z. Nagy: 'Ricerche cosmologiche nella corte umanistica di Giovanni Vitéz', *Rapporti veneto-ungheresi all'epoca del rinascimento*, ed. T. Klaniczay (Budapest, 1975), pp. 65–93
M. Prokopp: 'Italian Renaissance Frescoes in the Castle of the Hungarian Archbishop at Esztergom', *Renaissance Studies in Honor of Craig Hugh Smyth*, ii (Florence, 1985), pp. 365–82

☐

Viti. *See* FIJI.

Viti, Timoteo (*b* Urbino, 1469; *d* Urbino, 1523). Italian painter. According to Vasari and Malvasia, he was apprenticed to Francesco Francia in Bologna between 1490 and 1495. While there is no documentary proof of this, constant aspects of Viti's style would seem to confirm an apprenticeship in Bologna. In 1503 he was in Urbino, painting the banners of Cesare Borgia, then lord of the city. In 1504 the Montefeltro returned to Urbino, and the young painter, together with Girolamo Genga, was commissioned by Bishop Arrivabene to decorate the chapel of S Martino in the cathedral. This cycle included a central panel by Viti, stylistically indebted to Perugino, showing *SS Thomas Becket and Martin Worshipped by Bishop Arrivabene and Duke Guidobaldo da Montefeltro* (Urbino, Pal. Ducale). Similar in style and probably from this period is the *Virgin and Child with Two Saints* (ex-Urbino Cathedral; Milan, Brera). Also painted for the cathedral was *Mary Magdalene* (1508; Urbino, Pal. Ducale). For the Tempietto delle Muse of the Palazzo Montefeltro, Viti painted the *Muse Thalia with Apollo* (Florence, Gal. Corsini), a composition that originally included two other figures. Around 1511, perhaps during a visit to Rome, he saw works by Raphael, which for a while had a strong influence on him, as can be seen in the large altarpiece of *Christ Appearing to Mary Magdalene, SS Michael the Archangel and Anthony Abbot* (*c.* 1512) for the church of S Angelo Minore in Cagli (Pesaro). In later works (e.g. the *Annunciation with SS John and Sebastian*; Milan, Brera), he rejected Raphael's influence and looked back to the art of the late 15th century. In his last works (e.g. the *Mary Magdalene*, 1521; Gubbio Cathedral) his style became heavier, perhaps because of the increasing intervention of pupils.

BIBLIOGRAPHY
G. Vasari: *Vite* (1550, rev. 2/1568); ed. G. Milanesi (1878–85), iv, pp. 492–9
C. C. Malvasia: *Felsina pittrice* (1678); ed. G. Zanotti (1841), i, pp. 54–5
L. Pungileoni: *Elogio a Timoteo Viti* (Urbino, 1835)
Urbino e le Marche prima e dopo Raffaello (exh. cat., ed. M. G. C. Duprè dal Poggetto and P. dal Poggetto; Urbino, Pal. Ducale, 1983), pp. 157–8, 279–85, 315–20 [with bibliog.]
L. Arcangeli: 'Viti, Timoteo', *La pittura in Italia: Il cinquecento*, ed. G. Briganti, ii (Milan, 1987, rev. 1988), pp. 864–5 [with bibliog.]

MARCO CARMINATI

Vitoni, Ventura di Andrea (*b* Pistoia, 1442; *d* ?Pistoia, 1522). Italian architect and sculptor. He is first recorded as a master carpenter at Pistoia Cathedral in 1464. In 1473 he began a long association with the nunnery of S Giovanni Battista, Pistoia, where he worked until about 1485. In around 1483 the abbess founded another nunnery in Pistoia, dedicated to S Chiara, and Vitoni worked there for many years, most notably on the church. The work shows strong Florentine influences, which are combined with Vitoni's own skills, demonstrated in the building's attractive proportions. Owing to the restricted site, he designed an aisleless nave with a coffered ceiling and a dome at the east end; circular windows in the drum show Brunelleschi's influence. The church was completed in 1498, and Vitoni began work on the adjacent cloisters in the same year. He returned to S Giovanni Battista at about this time, where the church itself was rebuilt after 1500. Here the central space is octagonal, and the cupola owes much to Brunelleschi's Pazzi Chapel in Florence, even down to the detailing of the radiating ribs. The upper orders of the interior again recall Brunelleschi; they are finely worked but rather fussily detailed. The octagon is dated 1513 on the trabeation.

In 1492 Giuliano da Sangallo won a competition for the new church of S Maria dell'Umiltà and asked Vitoni to prepare a wooden model. Sangallo's other commitments prevented him from building the church himself, and the work was executed by Vitoni, who made several visits to Florence to discuss progress with Sangallo. The building (see fig.) owes much more to Vitoni, however, and is perhaps his most important work. Construction began in 1495 and was completed by *c.* 1509. Vitoni was strongly influenced by Michelozzo's S Maria delle Grazie, Pistoia, itself based on the Pazzi Chapel. Spatially, Vitoni was influenced by Sangallo's sacristy at Santo Spirito, Florence, together with its vestibule by Cronaca. Yet overall Vitoni lacked the clear vision of Michelozzo and Sangallo's precision of detailing. The church is an unusual structure, consisting of a spacious rectangular atrium and an octagonal nave, with a niche for the altar. The atrium has a coffered barrel vault, with a frieze and other details of pinkish marble. The octagon itself has four superimposed orders, the lowest in the form of an open arcade. All the detailing is in *pietra serena* (grey limestone), with white plastered walls. The scale is monumental, reminiscent of Romanesque baptisteries rather than the intimate refinement of the Pazzi Chapel. Much of the detailing, though, is crowded and awkwardly resolved, particularly in the altar niche, which cuts arbitrarily into the perforation of the second order windows.

Several other works in Pistoia are associated with Vitoni. His interventions at the cathedral were confined to the remodelling of the entrance portico, including the vaulting, decorated *c.* 1505 by Andrea della Robbia. Another later work was the little oratory of the Crocefisso della Morte, completed just before 1500. Two other secular works can be attributed to him with certainty; one is the Palazzo Comunale, where he rebuilt the main entrance doorway,

and the other is the Palazzo Panciatichi, built for his close friend Gualtieri Panciatichi. His last important commission was at the Ospedale del Ceppo, where he built a new portico in the form of a spacious, attractive colonnade across the face of the older building. It was completed in 1514 and decorated by Giovanni della Robbia, with characteristic tondi as well as a bold, continuous frieze of coloured terracotta.

Vitoni was effectively Pistoia's city architect for several decades. Although in some examples his designs are elegant (notably the Ospedale del Ceppo and S Chiara), elsewhere his work shows a certain lack of refinement and an inability to appreciate fully the classical restraint of his Florentine mentors. Nevertheless, Vitoni, almost alone, introduced Renaissance architecture to Pistoia.

BIBLIOGRAPHY
Venturi
H. Strack: *Central- und Kuppelkirchen der Renaissance in Italien* (Berlin, 1882)
C. Stegman and H. von Geymüller: *Die Architektur der Renaissance in Toskana*, 10 vols (Munich, 1890–1908)
O. H. Giglioli: *Pistoia nelle sue opere d'arte* (Florence, 1904)
G. Marchini: *Giuliano da Sangallo* (Florence, 1942)
Ventura Vitoni e il rinascimento a Pistoia (exh. cat., ed. M. C. Buscioni; Pistoia, Mus. Civ., 1977)
Pistoia: Una città nello stato mediceo (exh. cat., Pistoia, Fortezza S Barbara, 1980)
N. Andreini Galli: *Ville pistoiese* (Lucca, 1989)

Ventura di Andrea Vitoni: interior of S Maria dell'Umiltà, Pistoia, 1495–*c.* 1509

Vitoria [Basque: Gasteiz]. Spanish city, capital of the province of Alava, with a population of *c.* 210,000. It can be divided in two parts: the upper old quarter, perhaps of Visigothic origin, occupies an extended slope that is ellipsoid in shape, with its longest axis running from north to south; while the surrounding modern industrial town extends to the south and is at a considerably lower level. The 14th-century Gothic S Maria, a cathedral since 1862, is at the north central part of the old quarter and contains a magnificent doorway (*c.* 1400) in the vaulted west portico. The elliptical shape of the old town is flanked by the churches of S Miguel (14th century), with a very fine Baroque retable by Gregorio Fernández (1624–32), and S Vicente (15th century; tower 1865). The 14th-century S Pedro at the west side of the old town contains a fine carved Gothic portal. The modern part of Vitoria begins at the Plaza de la Virgen Blanca, which leads to the Plaza Mayor (1791), and then through broad straight streets to the Plaza de los Fueros (1980). In this area is the monumental new cathedral begun in 1906 by Julián de Apraiz and Javier de Luque in Gothic Revival style with crypt, five naves and a double apse. The Museo Provincial de Alava has a noted collection of 15th- and 16th-century triptychs and altarpieces from local churches dating from the 16th century; outstanding among its paintings is a *Virgin of the Immaculate Conception* (1645–52) by Alonso Cano.

BIBLIOGRAPHY
Catálogo monumental de la provincia de Alava
J. M. Azcarate: *Monumentos españoles: Alava* (Madrid, 1953)
GERMÁN RAMALLO ASENSIO

Vitozzi, Ascanio (*b* ?Baschi, nr Orvieto, 1539; *d* Turin, 23 Oct 1615). Italian architect and engineer.

1. EARLY WORK AND CIVIL ARCHITECTURE. He probably trained in Orvieto, which was then part of the Papal States and where Antonio da Sangallo (ii) had been active. About 1559 Vitozzi moved to Rome, where he increased his experience of civil and hydraulic engineering. He took part in the Battle of Lepanto and fought as a captain in Portugal in 1580 for Philip II of Spain. In October 1584 he entered the service of Charles-Emanuel I, 11th Duke of Savoy, who appointed him overall superintendent of the fortresses of Provence. In this capacity he worked on the defences of Cannes, Grasse and Antibes and was later active in Val di Susa (1596–7), Savoy (1598) and Monferrato (1605–15). On his arrival in Turin, however, Vitozzi was also required to fulfil the role of architect and was thereby instrumental in bringing the Baroque to Piedmont. The starting-point for his transformation of the city into an adequate seat for the new Duke was his design for the new Palazzo Ducale. Although replaced in the 17th century by a design by Amedeo di Castellamonte, it is known that Vitozzi's building surrounded a courtyard with Doric half-columns applied to pilasters. Behind the palace the royal garden extended to an elegant pavilion constructed on a bastion of the city. The forms originate from a central Italian tradition and are based on examples by Antonio da Sangallo (ii) and Jacopo Vignola.

The new palace led to the transformation of the entire surrounding area, and Vitozzi was also responsible for the initial designs for the chapel of the Holy Shroud (1612) and the link between the cathedral and the palace. He planned to open up a regular rectangular piazza in front of the palace by a corridor link to the old Castello degli Acaja (now Palazzo Madama), which was given a new façade, probably articulated by giant pilaster strips. For the rest of the square, Vitozzi planned a uniform façade in a simple, elegant style derived from early 16th-century Roman models. It had a series of porticoed buildings (1606–12), the two upper storeys articulated by simple windows with triangular or segmental pediments on the first floor. From 1587 a new road was also planned, leading from the piazza to the castle of Mirafiori (now the Via Roma) as the first stage of the future enlargement of the city, although work did not begin on it until 1615. Vitozzi's use of continuous, uniform street layouts was fundamental in influencing subsequent developments in 17th-century Turin.

2. RELIGIOUS ARCHITECTURE. Vitozzi also designed several churches, mostly in Turin. The Capuchin church of the Madonna del Monte (begun 1583), set on a hill on the far side of the River Po, was intended as the terminal point of a devotional trail of chapels planned by the Milanese engineer Giacomo Soldati (fl 1561–1600). A square plan with four projecting apses of different sizes emphasizes the principal axis on the line of the entrance. The tension of these forms is reflected on the exterior by tall pilaster strips and blind windows with pediments or frames that create a vertical emphasis, ultimately stopped off by a heavy cornice. Above this, the drum prepares the eye for the formerly spheroidal dome. The same vertical emphasis is present in the interior, where the square base is transformed into an octagon by rounded angles opening

Ascanio Vitozzi: sanctuary of the Madonna, Vicoforte, begun 1596

into niches, a feature that accentuates the thrust of the central nucleus. This solution represents a reworking of Renaissance centralized plans while emphasizing tension and dynamic counterpoint in both plan and elevation. Also on a central plan is the church of the Santa Trinità, built from 1583 on the present Via Garibaldi. The circular nave plan gives on to a rectangular secondary space opposite the entrance, which houses the high altar. The compositional rhythm of the interior (which also has two other altars in concave openings) is based on the triangle symbolic of the Holy Trinity. Above the cylindrical nave and separated by a pronounced cornice, a circular drum with rectangular windows rises to a tall dome with a small lantern, adding vertical emphasis to the building. The rhythmical relationships of the structure and the original tension of the various elements (in particular the pilaster strips) remain visible despite successive redecorations.

Vitozzi's Corpus Domini (completed by 1507) in Turin was one of the first churches to be erected in Piedmont on the nuclear model of Il Gesù, Rome. It has a single nave and three side chapels on each long wall; these communicate with the chancel, covered by an almost flat elliptical dome. The façade has two superimposed orders and a crowning pediment; this gives three-dimensional emphasis to the structure, which, with the articulated design of the mouldings, highlights the tension and dynamism of the wall surface. This idea was used by Vitozzi throughout his period in Turin.

In 1596 Vitozzi began work on the sanctuary of the Madonna at Vicoforte, near Mondovi (see fig.), commissioned by Charles-Emanuel I as a family mausoleum. Elliptically planned, it has deep chapels built into the thickness of the wall and entrances featuring elegant Serlian motifs. The grandly arched chapels animate the interior without disturbing the general profile. Vitozzi's design culminated in an elliptical but not very high dome, its external profile masked by four bell-towers flanking the ends of the oval. The present dome, by Francesco Gallo, dates from 1729–33, but those parts of the nave erected under Vitozzi's supervision show great attention to the pilasters, cornices and decorative details. Vitozzi also planned other residential buildings to create a piazza around the basilica, but these plans were never executed.

See also TURIN, §I, 1.

BIBLIOGRAPHY
N. Carboneri: *Ascanio Vitozzi: Un architetto tra manierismo e barocco* (Rome, 1966)
A. Scotti: *Ascanio Vitozzi: Ingegnere ducale a Torino* (Florence, 1969)

AURORA SCOTTI TOSINI

Vitruvius (*fl* later 1st century BC). Roman architect, engineer and writer, renowned for his treatise in ten books, *On Architecture* (Lat. *De architectura*), the only text on architectural theory and practice to have survived from Classical antiquity.

1. Life and work. 2. *On Architecture*. 3. Influence.

1. LIFE AND WORK. Vitruvius is known in the earliest manuscripts of *On Architecture* only by this name, a *nomen gentilicium* or clan name. By his own testimony (I. Preface), he was already an older man at the time he dedicated his treatise to the Emperor Augustus (?27 or 14 BC). He had earlier served Augustus' adoptive father, Julius Caesar, as a siege engineer, and at some time after Caesar's death (44 BC) he entered the service of Octavian (after 27 BC called Augustus). He enjoyed Octavian's continued patronage on the recommendation of the latter's sister, Octavia, a fact that suggests a period of service under her second husband, the triumvir Mark Antony. In addition to having sufficient education and leisure to engage in writing, Vitruvius clearly had first-hand knowledge of several areas of his subject. As might be expected, he was familiar with siege engines and made remarkable application of the study of music to the tuning of catapults. His treatment of architecture proper suggests greater experience of private, domestic building than of religious or secular public works, although Frontinus (*De aquaeductibus* XXV.1–2) indicated that Vitruvius worked under Agrippa in the construction of baths and aqueducts in the Campus Martius at Rome.

There is little external evidence concerning Vitruvius. The basilica that he allegedly built at Fano, north of Ancona (*On Architecture* V.i.6), has not been identified, and no inscription bearing his name has been discovered there. *On Architecture* is itself cited only a few times in other Classical sources. Its author is almost always named simply Vitruvius, although in the 4th century AD Faventius, who produced a condensed version of the work, gave the cognomen or family name 'Pol[l]io'. The name 'Vitruvius Pollio' has become traditional but remains unsubstantiated by contemporary documents. Vitruvius has also been identified by P. Thielscher (see Pauly–Wissowa, 1961, pp. 427–89) with L. Vitruvius Mamurra, possibly the Mamurra from Formia who was Julius Caesar's chief engineer

in Gaul. The name M. Vitruvius Mamurra has been found in a Roman inscription from Africa, and the *nomen gentilicium* Vitruvius occurs in Formia. Vitruvius or his literary executors may have dropped the cognomen Mamurra for good reasons: the contemporary poet Catullus had libelled Mamurra in a particularly scurrilous manner (e.g. *Poems* 29, 41, 43, 57, 94). Moreover, the same Mamurra had also acquired a reputation for extravagance by being the first person in Rome to cover whole walls of his house with marble veneer. While this theory of Vitruvius' identity has not won general acceptance, it might account for his intimate familiarity with the domestic architecture and building materials of Campania and perhaps explain his confident defence of magnificence in private architecture. It might also provide a means of connecting Vitruvius with such eminent men of letters of Julius Caesar's time as Lucretius, Cicero and Varro, each of whose ideas find resonance in his work.

2. 'ON ARCHITECTURE'.

(i) The text. (ii) The ten books.

(i) The text. On Architecture is a didactic treatise on the subject of architecture in all its branches as understood in Classical antiquity. Vitruvius' claim to represent accurately the theory and practice of ancient Greek and Roman architecture has been challenged by modern scholars, but his influence on later architects and students of Classical architectural styles, particularly in the Italian Renaissance and in northern Europe and America in early modern times, has been enormous (*see* §3 below). A revival of scholarly interest in Vitruvius' treatise, with several international colloquia during the 1980s, may also reflect renewed interest in Classical styles among architects, and an important new edition of the text, with French translation and commentary, has been undertaken.

The text of *On Architecture* presents two main obstacles. The first involves the corruptions of and lacunae in the original text that accumulated in the course of its transmission from antiquity. These are inevitably numerous, since Vitruvius' work abounds in technical terms and exotic proper names. As a consequence, there are considerable differences, even between the texts of modern printed editions. The two most popular English translations, for example (Morgan and Granger), differ significantly, being based on different Latin texts. A further problem concerns the illustrations. *On Architecture* was originally 'published' in parallel columns on papyrus scrolls, one scroll for each of its ten books, and the illustrations essential to the content of the treatise were either simple drawings inserted into the text or more elaborate figures appended to it. In most cases these illustrations did not survive the process of manuscript copying. Since the publication of the earliest printed editions, editors have needed either to reconstruct the drawings as indicated by the text or to find illustrations appropriate to otherwise obscure passages. Hence, the exact nature of Vitruvius' influence on architects from the Renaissance onwards often relates to specific printed editions.

The second obstacle stems from Vitruvius' literary style, which ranges from the laconic to the bombastic, often without full control of either. Vitruvius' stylistic shortcomings have often obscured his meaning, in terms both of detail and of broader questions. It has, for example, often been noted that the matter and the organization of the individual books vary greatly. For this reason *On Architecture* has been considered by its severest critics as nothing more than a compendium composed by an embittered, unsuccessful and unemployed architect. Perhaps anticipating such criticism, Vitruvius spoke in his own defence in the Preface to Book VII (all quoted passages are from Morgan's translation): 'From their commentaries [of earlier authors] I have gathered what I saw was useful for the present subject, and formed it into one complete treatise, and this principally because I saw that many books in this field had been published by the Greeks, but very few indeed by our countrymen.'

The overall organization of the treatise reflects the division of architecture into three parts: Books I–VIII deal with *aedificatio*, the science of building; Book IX with *gnomonice*, the art of making sundials; and Book X with *machinatio* or mechanics. The preface of each of the books is designed as a literary introduction, sometimes anecdotal, sometimes expository, to the more technical material presented in the particular book.

(ii) The ten books. The Preface to Book I dedicates *On Architecture* to the Emperor Augustus, thus indicating a date of 17 BC or later. Vitruvius avowed his thanks for Augustus' patronage and his hope of educating him concerning the discipline of architecture. Elsewhere in *On Architecture* there is evidence that Vitruvius was writing for a readership of other knowledgeable patrons and for professional architects themselves. It was Vitruvius' contemporary M. Terrentius Varro (116–27 BC) who seems to have been the first Roman to raise the study of architecture to the level of the Liberal Arts, dedicating a book to it in his encyclopedic *Disciplinarum libri*. Vitruvius' work was no doubt, in addition to its other claims, intended to raise the social status of the profession (*see also* ROME, ANCIENT, §I, 3).

The first chapter of Book I defines a broad range of subjects appropriate to the education of the architect: he should be literate, able to draw and have a knowledge of geometry, optics, arithmetic, history, philosophy (including physics), music, medicine, law and astronomy. Though he should be educated in all the arts, the architect must not be expected to excel in each. Here Vitruvius made an important distinction between practice and theory, stating that the arts were each dualities composed of the work itself (*opus*) and its theoretical dimension (*ratiocinatio*). For the architect, the theory of architecture should suffice. However, despite the great influence that Vitruvius' treatise was to have over architectural design, it does not accord practice (*fabrica*) and theory the usual relation to one another found in dualist systems. Theory is presented not as a preparatory basis for the work in the form of design, but rather as a way of explaining or justifying the effect produced by the work. Hence, the importance of theory lies in the relation of the architect to his patron, and the treatise provides the means of appreciating the subject for those who are not professional architects.

In the second chapter the fundamental principles of both architectural practice and theory are laid out. These are: Order (*ordinatio*), Arrangement (*dispositio*), Eurhythmy (*eurythmia*), Symmetry (*symmetria*), Propriety (*decor* or *decorum*) and Economy (*distributio*). It has been noted (see Watzinger) that the six fundamental principles of architecture listed by Vitruvius actually consist of three distinct concepts, each divided into pairs according to the opposition of artistic practice and theory, or 'process' and 'product'. These are: Order/Symmetry; Arrangement/Eurhythmy; and Economy/Propriety. Certain phrases demonstrate that Vitruvius conceived of the design process as essentially synthetic, consisting of different components and their 'adjustment[s] according to quantity'. Products, on the other hand, he saw as unities subject to analysis, 'fashioned with quality'. Hence, Order is 'an adjustment according to quantity' by which the whole is constructed, whereas Symmetry, the 'proper arrangement between members of the work', is its qualitative result. Arrangement is the quantitative 'putting of things in their proper places', and Eurhythmy its qualitative result. Finally, Economy involves the architect's quantitative consideration of the appropriateness of the site and what the client can afford, and Propriety is the quality that results. Of the six principles, Propriety alone receives further analysis, being divided into three parts: religious custom or prescription (*statio*), social usage or habit (*consuetudo*) and natural causes (*natura*) (*see also* ORDERS, ARCHITECTURAL, §§I, 2(i)(b) and II, 2). If this passage constitutes Vitruvius' theory of architecture (see Watzinger), his exposition leaves much to be desired. Nevertheless, the application of these principles elsewhere in his treatise is more or less consistent, indicating that, whatever the source of the theory, Vitruvius made it his own. In any case, Vitruvius' discussion is an important source for the study of ancient architectural theory (*see also* GREECE, ANCIENT, §II, 3).

The remainder of Book I deals with the selection of the site for a city and its buildings. The site itself should be healthy, with a temperate balance of the four Empedoclean elements of moisture, heat, air and earth. Having ascertained that the city can be supplied by roads, rivers or sea ports, the architect should lay out encircling walls and towers. Then, setting up a gnomon in the centre of the site, he should determine from the sun's course the cardinal directions and sources of the eight winds. The text provides sufficient detail here for the illustration to be reconstructed (see fig. 1). Having determined the cardinal directions, the architect can lay out streets and alleys. Book I ends with a discussion of the proper sites for the forum and for the temples (*see also* ROME, ANCIENT, §III, 2).

Book II is devoted to the materials used in construction. This book shows Vitruvius at his most original and for this reason seems to break the continuity between Book I and Book III, so that some scholars have considered it to be a later, ill-fitting addition. It presents a thorough attempt to relate materials used in building to their occurrence in nature and also views human technology as a product of man's natural inclination to learn through imitation. Like his contemporary Lucretius, Vitruvius was, therefore, inclined to discover the authority for current practices in the remote, natural origins of human culture. For example, the control of fire and the society of the hearth preceded

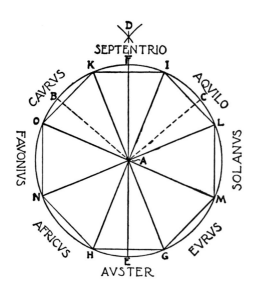

1. Vitruvius: design for a sundial (gnomon), to be used in determining the optimum site for a city; from his *Ten Books on Architecture*, translated by M. H. Morgan (Cambridge, MA, 1914), Bk I, p. 30

even the development of language, a fact that lends antiquity and dignity to the profession of architecture.

In discussing the methods of building masonry walls with a concrete core, Vitruvius distinguished two types, one faced with irregular stones laid in an irregular pattern (*opus incertum*), the other employing regular wedges laid in a reticulate pattern (*opus reticulatum*) (*see* ROME, ANCIENT, fig. 16). In a passage that has received much attention from archaeologists, Vitruvius preferred the more ancient *opus incertum* to the contemporary *opus reticulatum*. In declaring his allegiance to the 'Ancients' he explained the contemporary preference for *opus reticulatum* as an aesthetic rather than a structural choice. While archaeology has verified Vitruvius' relative chronology, it has also confirmed the impression that he may have been a pious antiquarian out of touch with the reasoning behind contemporary practice. Economics rather than aesthetics probably dictated the choice of *opus reticulatum*, especially since walls of both types were normally faced with stucco or marble. Furthermore, Vitruvius' misgivings about the structural properties of *opus reticulatum* do not seem to be borne out in surviving examples.

Current practices occasionally won the approval of this conservative author, however. One passage in Book II (II.viii.17) gives an invaluable glimpse of contemporary Roman multistorey city housing:

> In these tall piles reared with piers of stone, walls of burnt brick, and partitions of rubble work, and provided with floor after floor, the upper storeys can be partitioned off into rooms to very great advantage. The accommodations within the city wall being thus multiplied as a result of the many floors high in the air, the Roman people easily find excellent places in which to live.

Given Vitruvius' evident approval of this type of construction, his conservatism cannot be simply regarded as indiscriminate.

Books III and IV are both concerned with temple architecture. Book III begins with a discussion of Symmetry in temples and in the human body, and the first chapter contains the famous passage constructing the ideally proportioned 'Vitruvian Man' (see fig. 2). In resuming the discussion of the organization of architecture according to type and returning to theory, Book III appears to continue from Book I rather than from Book II. It proceeds to a classification of temples according to plan and to a discussion of the *eustyle*, or 'well-proportioned' elevation. Vitruvius acknowledged the source for his ideas here to be the 2nd-century BC Greek architect HERMOGENES, and this has led many commentators to infer that he followed Hermogenes closely in his treatment of the Ionic order, which in retrospect (III.v.15) he declares to have been the subject of Book III.

Accordingly, Book IV contains a discussion of material not treated by Hermogenes: the Corinthian and Doric orders, and the rules for Etruscan temples (*see also* ETRUSCAN, §II and ORDERS, ARCHITECTURAL, §I, 1 and 2(i)). Vitruvius' treatment of the Doric order (IV.iii) begins with the observation that the 'Ancients', among whom he numbers Hermogenes and PYTHEOS, considered this order unsuitable for temples because of such inherent design problems as the uneven spacing of triglyphs at the corners of a Doric building. Given Vitruvius' earlier discussion of ideal, *eustyle* proportion in the Ionic order, his treatment of Doric proportions is perfunctory, though informative. It covers the subject of such Doric refinements as curvature on the stylobate and entasis, which are considered necessary to correct optical illusions and are therefore subject to the general principle of Symmetry. Chapter seven briefly deals with the construction of an Etruscan temple using modular measurements and chapter eight is devoted to circular temples and other variations, as determined by Decorum (IV.viii.6): 'For we must not build temples according to the same rules to all gods alike, since the performance of the sacred rites varies with the various gods.'

Book V deals with the remaining public building types: fora, basilicas, theatres, baths and palaestrae. It concludes with a brief discussion of harbours, breakwaters and shipyards. The treatment of fora begins by contrasting the Greek agora with the Roman forum, the latter requiring two-storey buildings with wider intercolumniations, thanks to the custom of staging gladiatorial combats in the forum. In treating basilicas and their proportions in general, Vitruvius gave specific dimensions for his own (unlocated) building at Fano. The discussion of theatres again distinguishes between the Roman type and the Greek; both descriptions follow a treatment of harmonics based on the theories of Aristoxenos (*fl c.* 300 BC) and the amplification of the voice by means of bronze vessels. In the designs for both Roman and Greek theatres Vitruvius employed a circle containing a 12-sided polygon to determine the relation of the *orchestra* to the *cavea* (auditorium) and the stage building (*see also* THEATRE, §II). In the Roman figure four equilateral triangles are inscribed within the circle, 'as the astrologers do in a figure of the twelve signs of the zodiac, when they are making computations from the musical harmony of the stars', and each fifth point is connected (representing the diapason). In the Greek figure

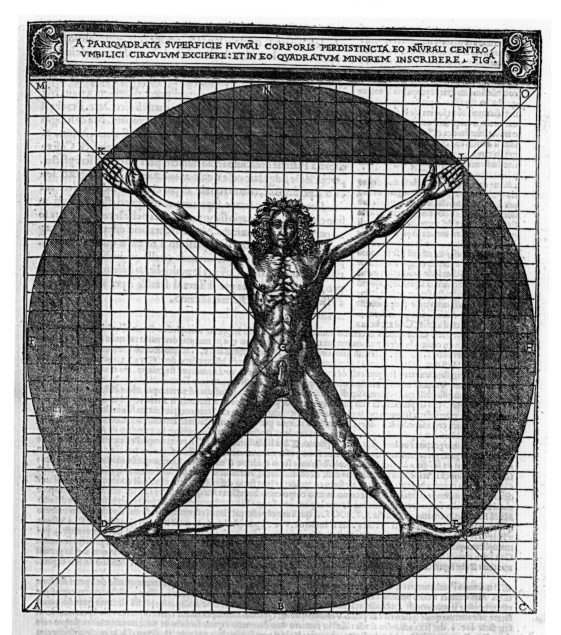

2. Vitruvius: 'Vitruvian Man'; from C. Cesariano: *Di Lucio Vitruvio Pollione de architectura libri dece* (Como, 1521)

three squares are inscribed: each fourth point is connected (the diatesseron). Excavation has shown that many ancient Greek theatres were designed according to the principle given by Vitruvius, but no Roman theatres have as yet been found conforming to this scheme. The passage is thus better understood as an attempt to propose new architectural principles than as evidence of Vitruvius' lack of knowledge of current practice.

Book VI is concerned with such private building types as the Roman town house (*domus*) and farm house (*villa*), and the Greek house, though a treatment of the luxury villa is noticeably absent. The material evidence from excavations at Pompeii and elsewhere in Italy has confirmed Vitruvius' account of the design of both *domus* and *villa* types, and the arrangement and proportioning of rooms of the grand houses from Pompeii conform closely to his rules. This is important evidence that he was intimately familiar with Italian domestic design as it had evolved from the 3rd–1st centuries BC. Appealing to the principle of Decorum, Vitruvius justified building on a grand scale for the houses of prominent public figures. In contrast with moralists who condemned contemporary luxury as vanity, Vitruvius noted the many public uses such houses afforded, as places for public meetings, private trials and judgements, and other functions.

Book VII addresses the interior decoration of houses, including floors, stuccoed walls and frescoes. In addition to its valuable information concerning contemporary practice, Book VII is notable for Vitruvius' historical summary of representational wall painting (VII.v.1–4) and his tirade against the decadence of the current fashion for the grotesque (VII.v.3–4). As well as providing an important document for post-Classical arguments in favour of the natural as opposed to the imaginary in art, this passage has also been important for the classification and dating of Pompeian wall painting.

Book VIII is devoted to hydrology and hydraulics and is essentially both a continuation of the study of building on certain sites and a transition to the last two books, which deal with the construction of water clocks and sundials (IX) and with mechanics (X). In addition to the ways of locating good water, Book VIII deals with aqueducts, wells and cisterns. Although Vitruvius provided technical specifications for constructing water systems with lead pipes, he strongly recommended against the use of lead for health reasons (VIII.vi.10–11). The extensive Introduction to Book IX concerns the workings of the heavens, and this book as a whole is extremely important for the history of ancient mathematics. Book X, on the subject of mechanics and ballistics, is perhaps the closest of all the books to Vitruvius' own area of expertise as a military engineer. Yet the extended treatment of mechanical advantage was also no doubt a subject of the greatest importance to contemporary civil architects and builders.

On Architecture is important both for the history of architecture and its theory, thanks to Vitruvius' conscientious habit of citing his sources; although he wrote as a historian, he had the viewpoint of a practising architect. Much has been written in criticism of Vitruvius as a historical source, but a better understanding of the biographical evidence (*see* §1 above) now promises to improve his reputation.

See also ROME, ANCIENT, §II, 3(ii) and ARCHITECTURAL PROPORTION, §1.

WRITINGS

M. H. Morgan, trans.: *The Ten Books on Architecture* (Cambridge, MA, 1914/*R* New York, 1960)

F. Granger, ed. and trans.: *On Architecture*, 2 vols (London and Cambridge, MA, 1931, 1934) [ed. from Harleian MS. 2767]

S. Ferri, ed.: *Vitruvio: Architettura, dai libri I–VII* (Rome, 1960) [with commentary]

C. Fensterbusch, ed. and trans.: *Vitruvii: De architectura libri decem* (Berlin, 1964) [with Ger. trans.]

J. Soubiran, ed. and trans.: *Vitruve: De l'architecture, Livre IX* (Paris, 1969) [with Fr. trans. and commentary]

L. Callebat, ed. and trans.: *Vitruve: De l'architecture, Livre VIII* (Paris, 1973) [with Fr. trans. and commentary]

L. Callebat and P. Fleury, eds and trans.: *Vitruve: De l'architecture, Livre X* (Paris, 1986) [with Fr. trans. and commentary]

P. Fleury, ed. and trans.: *Vitruve: De l'architecture, Livre I* (Paris, 1990) [with Fr. trans. and commentary]

BIBLIOGRAPHY

Macmillan Enc. Architects; Pauly–Wissowa

C. Watzinger: 'Vitruvstudien', *Rhein. Mus. Philol.*, lxiv (1909), pp. 203–23

A. Boethius: 'Vitruvius and the Roman Architecture of his Age', *Dragma M. P. Nilson dedicatum* (Lund, 1939), pp. 114–43

P. Ruffel and J. Soubiran: 'Vitruve ou Mamurra?', *Pallas*, xi (1962), pp. 123–79

P. Gros: 'Vitruve: L'Architecture et sa théorie à la lumière des études récentes', *Aufstieg und Niedergang der römischen Welt*, ii (Berlin, 1982), pp. 659–95

Vitruv-Kolloquium des deutschen Archäologen-Verbandes: Darmstadt, 1982

L. Callebat and others, eds: *Vitruve, De architectura: Concordance*, 2 vols (Hildesheim, Zurich and New York, 1984)

H. Knell: *Vitruvs Architekturtheorie: Versuch einer Interpretation* (Darmstadt, 1985)

Munus non Ingratum: Proceedings of the International Symposium on Vitruvius' 'De architectura' and the Hellenistic and Republican Architecture: Leiden, 1989

EUGENE DWYER

3. INFLUENCE.

(i) Middle Ages. (ii) Renaissance and after.

(i) Middle Ages. There has been a persistent belief that Vitruvius was unknown throughout the Middle Ages because the 'rediscovery' of his treatise by such humanist scholars as Boccaccio and Poggio Bracciolini played an important part in launching Italian Renaissance architecture. This inference is, however, fallacious, except in the limited sense that he appears to have been virtually unknown in Italy owing to the precarious circumstances of the survival and transmission of his text. It has been demonstrated that most if not all of the surviving manuscripts of Vitruvius can be traced back to a Carolingian text (London, BL, Harleian MS. 2767) written *c.* AD 800, either in the palace scriptorium itself or somewhere close at hand. Where the model came from is unknown. It used to be thought that the Harleian MS. was Anglo-Saxon, made in Northumbria a century earlier. This went hand in hand with the theory that a single unwanted copy of Vitruvius found its way from the Vivarium, Flavius Magnus Aurelius Cassiodorus' monastery in Calabria or from some other Italian library to Northumbria in the late 7th century, when Benedict Biscop and Ceolfrith were searching Italy for books to fill the libraries of their own newly founded monasteries. It was also supposed that Alcuin (*c.* 735–804), who spent his early years in the north of England, brought another single copy with him when he took up his position as director of cultural affairs at the Carolingian court. Although this theory is now only an

unverified speculation, it remains attractive because it explains why Vitruvius' writings virtually disappeared from Italy at an early date and why the centre from which all the early medieval manuscripts seem to have been disseminated was located in the Carolingian heartland. On the other hand, the crucial copy may have reached the Carolingian court directly from Italy. No extant English copy is earlier than the 12th century and the English tradition, centred on the abbey of St Augustine, Canterbury, cannot be pursued back before the 10th century. An archetype in Anglo-Saxon script has nevertheless been postulated for the Harleian MS.

More than 80 medieval manuscripts of *On Architecture* are known to exist, some of them illustrated (e.g. Sélestat, Bib. Com., MS. 17, first half of the 10th century; and Paris, Bib. N., MS. lat. 7227, 10th–11th century). The Paris example includes a diagram illustrating the ratio of the side to the diagonal of a square. The diagram was contemporary with the text, but it is impossible to say whether it represents the interests of architects in geometry or of mathematicians in architecture. Despite this number of copies, however, it is seldom possible to be sure of their location at any particular time. It is known that there were copies at Reichenau in Germany, St Gall Abbey in Switzerland, Cluny Abbey in France, and Canterbury and Oxford in England, all of them places where Vitruvius' theories could have had some influence on medieval buildings. But there is no guarantee that these books were read, nor that anyone who read them was in a position to influence architectural practice.

There is, however, evidence that some medieval architects knew about Vitruvius. Carolingian interest was not antiquarian but was centred on the hope that attention to what he said would improve the quality of architecture. Alcuin may have pressed Vitruvius into the hands of men such as EINHARD, who were responsible for actually commissioning buildings. Thus Einhard pedantically insisted that the bricks for his church at Seligenstadt (built 831–40) should conform to sizes favoured at Rome and quoted by Vitruvius. The problem was how to put Vitruvius to good use. From a medieval point of view there was a serious impediment: Vitruvius did not discuss churches. He expanded at length about temples, but no one in the Middle Ages was emancipated enough to think that churches could be built in the form of temples, even though on occasion they were prepared to adapt existing temples to serve as churches. The nearest Vitruvius came to describing anything that resembled what the Middle Ages understood by a church was in his account of basilicas (V.i.4–5). Most of what he had to say on that subject was not idiosyncratic enough for a Vitruvian basilica to be easily distinguished from an Early Christian church, although a reading of Vitruvius might well have reinforced the Carolingian prejudice in favour of Early Christian models for new churches. By way of a pendant to his general account of basilicas, however, Vitruvius added a description (V.i.6) of the basilica (unlocated) that he built at Fano, in which he apparently varied his own recommendations by linking the aisles and upper galleries with an order of giant columns. This description may have alerted medieval attention to the possibilities of the giant order. On the rare occasions when it was used to embellish

Carolingian buildings with imperial connotations, such as the chapel and hall of the palace at Aachen, the debt to Vitruvius is not obvious. In the 11th century, however, churches were built on the fringes of Burgundy and in the west of England (e.g. St Germain, Auxerre, and Tewkesbury Abbey) where both the shapes and dimensions of the structures conform to the text of Vitruvius with sufficient precision to give substance to speculation (see Kidson 1981; for further discussion *see* ORDERS, ARCHITECTURAL, §II, 2).

Another sign that Vitruvius may have been studied by medieval readers with a taste for architecture is the possible medieval use of entasis: in the infirmary of Canterbury Cathedral and at Oxford Cathedral—both places where copies of Vitruvius may have been within reach at the time of building—bulges, tapering and subtle curves on the profiles of columns have been detected and these can be recognized as efforts to produce the effect of entasis. Other explanations are also possible, however, and entasis 'seeing' in the medieval context may be wishful thinking on the part of modern scholars.

Although the evidence is modest in quantity and restricted in distribution, it would not have been surprising if Vitruvius had been discovered by the 12th-century renaissance as he was by that of the 15th. When Hugh of St Victor compiled his *Didascalicon de studii legendi* in Paris in the 1120s, on the eve of the invention of Gothic, he listed Vitruvius as the authority to be read on the subject of architecture; after that, however, apart from a passing comment by Thomas Aquinas, references to Vitruvius seem to have disappeared until the Italians rediscovered him. Why Vitruvius apparently failed to live up to Hugh's expectations raises some very interesting questions. It is possible that Vitruvius remained the property of the literate classes in medieval society, and that his disappearance from the scene represented a closing of the ranks by professional masons, who did not read Classical texts and resented the interference of the dilettanti who did. Medieval architects were not schoolmen; architecture was classified as one of the manual arts, and those who practised it learnt their trade by long years of apprenticeship. By the time Gothic was invented, they were in a position to squeeze out the educated busybodies among the clergy. But there is more to it than that. During the 12th century ancient authorities were sought in every field of technical and cultural activity, and architecture is quite extraordinary in being the odd man out, not only in not following a Classical authority but in ostensibly rejecting the one that was to hand. This is where a second obstacle appears. It may be suspected that Vitruvius was not adopted in the 12th century because he had nothing of value to say about vaults, which had by then become the central issue in architecture, both technically and symbolically. Even so, the completeness of his rejection suggests not only that Vitruvius was found wanting but that Gothic architects knew that he had been found wanting on the same grounds in antiquity as well. They could not have known Heron of Alexandria's treatise on vaults (1st century AD), but they could well have known that there had been such a treatise.

Perhaps the most important thing about Vitruvius for the Middle Ages was that he kept alive the notion that architecture was a subject that could be written about. Within the normal limits of medieval experience this was very nearly a contradiction in terms, and it staked the claim of architecture to be ranked among the liberal arts. In this respect no medieval architect even tried to emulate Vitruvius. That particular challenge was taken up only by Alberti (*see* §(ii)(a) below). But Vitruvius' example was not entirely ignored: it is just possible that Villard de Honnecourt had Vitruvius in mind when he compiled his notebook (*c.* 1220–40). Villard was not an ordinary architect, if he was an architect at all. His curiosity at least matched the range of interests Vitruvius thought an architect ought to have; and in certain respects the correspondence between them is close enough to invite close attention. A comparison of the machines that they felt obliged to include in their writings will make the point clear: both were fascinated by clocks, automata, waterworks, hoisting gear and military engines. This may be a coincidence, but the fact that Villard's machines are close to the realm of fantasy, whereas those of Vitruvius presumably worked, suggests that Villard was trying to follow a model that made exceptional demands on his mechanical virtuosity. If so, Villard kept alive the Vitruvian ideal of the accomplished practical man, which resurfaced in the *uomi universali* of the Italian Renaissance.

BIBLIOGRAPHY

B. Bischoff: 'Die wiedergefundenen Schlussblätter des Vitruvius Harleianus', *Philol. Wochschr.*, v (1942)
L. A. Ciapponi: 'Il "De architectura" di Vitruvio nel primo umanesimo (dal MS. Bodl. Auct. F. S.7)', *Italia Med. & Uman.*, iii (1960), pp. 59-99
B. Bischoff: 'Die Überlieferung der technischen Literatur', *Artigianato e tecnica nella società dell'alto medioevo occidentale*, i (Spoleto, 1971), pp. 267-96
L. D. Reynolds, ed.: *Texts and Transmission: A Survey of the Latin Classics* (Oxford, 1983), pp. 440-44
P. Kidson: The Abbey Church of St Mary at Tewkesbury in the Eleventh and Twelfth Centuries, *Medieval Art and Architecture at Gloucester and Tewkesbury: Conference Transactions of the British Archaeological Association for 1981* (London, 1985), pp. 12-14

PETER KIDSON

(ii) Renaissance and after.

(a) c. 1350–c. 1500. In spite of the relatively wide circulation of *On Architecture* north of the Alps in the medieval period (*see* §(i) above), until about the middle of the 14th century there was apparently just one copy in the Italian peninsula, in the library of Montecassino. Shortly after 1350 Petrarch brought a copy from France and showed it to Boccaccio and other literary friends, so it became known in northern Italy and in Florence (see Ciapponi, 1960). Thus, long before Poggio Bracciolini 'rediscovered' the treatise at St Gall in 1416, a favourable climate existed for a new interest in the Vitruvian text.

In the 15th century, almost 15 centuries after it was written, *On Architecture* increasingly began to affect architectural practice in a way it had never done before, enjoying a uniquely delayed influence. The new humanist interest in Greek and Latin writings obviously extended to Vitruvius. In addition, the admiration for the unsurpassed architecture of the ancient Romans encouraged the belief that there was a lost body of knowledge, a set of principles and laws according to which ancient architecture had been created that could be found in Vitruvius' treatise—the only

one that survived from the whole Greco-Roman world, and one written by an architect. Moreover, basing architecture on a set of rules meant giving this discipline a scientific dignity on a par with the liberal arts, lifting it from the artisanal sphere and giving architects the higher social position to which they had aspired at least since the time of Filippo Brunelleschi in the early 15th century. At first Vitruvius' treatise seemed to hold great promise for the humanists. As few architects had a literary education, however, the Latin language, the obscurity of the text (corrupted by successive manuscript transcriptions) and the loss of the original illustrations made it inaccessible to most of them. Even those who could read the treatise found inconsistencies in the most interesting part, the section on the orders in books III and IV, which made it hard to apply in practice.

Alberti was the first humanist to study architectural theories. Initially, perhaps in 1440 at the suggestion of Lionello d'Este (i), Marchese of Ferrara, he may have planned to write a commentary on *On Architecture*. Soon, however, he became dissatisfied with the obscurities and imprecisions of the ancient text and began a work of his own, *De re aedificatoria* (Florence, 1485), which he finished in 1452 (*see* ALBERTI, LEON BATTISTA). Alberti criticized Vitruvius' language and also his notion of the encyclopedic education necessary for architects, but he nonetheless adopted several elements from *On Architecture* in his own work. Some were purely formal, such as the division into ten books and the use of many of the same headings, though in a different order. He also followed Vitruvius' indications to reconstruct the types of ancient buildings. In particular, he proposed a plan for a house with a courtyard inspired by the *domus*, showing a comprehension of that type of dwelling that long remained unequalled. Drawing on Vitruvius' books III and IV, he described the various kinds of columns, including the 'Italic' (later known as the Composite), which was not mentioned by Vitruvius; Alberti thus laid the basis for the Renaissance system of orders that became canonical in the following century (*see* §(b) below). He also used the Latin treatise to interpret the variety of evidence provided by ancient architecture itself; and he was the first to expound, first in writing and then in actual practice, the project of enriching Vitruvius' descriptions with the analysis of monuments.

It is possible (though unproven) that, even before Alberti, Brunelleschi had read *On Architecture* and that in studying ancient Roman monuments his knowledge of the treatise helped him to distinguish the various types of columns. In fact, in using well-defined Corinthian and Ionic capitals with fragments of trabeation, Brunelleschi indicated that he had an idea of two essential aspects of the orders described by Vitruvius: the distinction of the types of columns and the trilithic system. In this sense he can be considered the first of the Vitruvian architects.

The first attempts to create houses based on the types described in *On Architecture* may have been almost as early. Initially, it seems, only the names of the principal parts of the *domus* were used; but later efforts were made to make the plans conform to Vitruvian types. For example, in 1432 Francesco Pizzolpasso (documented after that date as owning a codex of Vitruvius) used the word 'atrium' for the entrance hall of a palazzo built in the 1420s for Cardinal Branda Castiglione Olona near Varese (see Morresi, 1986; Onians, 1988); and in the Este villa of Belriguardo, near Ferrara, finished in 1435, the elevation remains Gothic while the plan seems inspired by the Vitruvian description of the Greek house (see Kehl, 1992). The type of palazzo with a court surrounded by porticos, the Renaissance equivalent of the *domus* that later became common, was then unusual. In fact, in the 1450s Flavio Biondo (*Roma triumphans*), describing the form of the ancient Roman house, cites as modern examples the palace of Bernabò Visconti in Milan and the cloisters of convents, which he thought had preserved the ancient form of the *domus* because such dwellings had often been converted to house the original monasteries of religious orders.

In the second half of the 15th century, perhaps thanks to Alberti's criticisms, the spread of *On Architecture* increased. It was circulated in many manuscript copies (see fig. 3), held in the libraries of the most important courts and owned by great patrons and literary men of all kinds, including philologists (e.g. Ermolao Barbaro and Angelo Poliziano), authors of treatises on government (e.g. Francesco Patrizi of Siena) and, less frequently, cultured architects interested in architectural theory. During the years when Alberti was writing *De re aedificatoria*, Lorenzo Ghiberti, who owned a copy of *On Architecture*, inserted in his *Commentarii* passages from his own translation of it. A copy made by Buonaccorso Ghiberti in his *Zibaldone* of other parts translated by Lorenzo shows that he was seeking information on types of temples, orders and their proportions, the *domus* and its rooms—subjects for which Vitruvius was studied throughout the Renaissance. FILARETE, in his treatise finished in 1464, referred to Book III of *On Architecture* for the proportions of the human figure and the temple, and introduced a chapter on the analogy between architecture and the human body, in which he combined elements of Vitruvius' exposition

3. *Vitruvius* (holding stonecutting tools); decorated initial from a manuscript copy of *On Architecture*, Book I (Eton, Berks, Eton College Library, MS. 137, fol. 1*r*)

with Greek and Christian sources. In his unpublished writings of the mid-1480s Francesco di Giorgio Martini further extended the significance of Vitruvius' analogies as a basis for justifying proportions. He used a passage from Vitruvius on the human body as a model of proportion, the theme of man as microcosm and the anecdote of Dinocrates, to propose a correspondence between the human body and cities, forts and castles, and—recalling medieval allegories—between the human body, plants, and sections of churches.

Francesco di Giorgio Martini was one of the first architects to produce an extensive translation of *On Architecture*. First, with the help of humanist friends, he translated selected passages to use in the first edition of his own treatises; then (mid-1480s) he made a translation of almost the whole work, one of the first to survive. With his numerous descriptions of ancient monuments he began the long process of comparing Vitruvius' writings with the realities of Roman architecture, and his exposition of the typology of houses and of the orders was inspired by Vitruvius. One of Francesco di Giorgio's most obvious misunderstandings—he confused Doric and Ionic capitals—shows how difficult it still was for an architect to connect Vitruvius' descriptions with the forms of ancient architecture. In the same period (1488) Giuliano da Sangallo, assisted by no less a literate architectural dilettante than Lorenzo de' Medici, took his inspiration from Vitruvius' description of the *domus* in designing a palace for Ferdinand I of Naples, attempting to recreate a plan in the antique style. He also proposed, for the first time, the interpretation of the atrium as a hall in basilican form (see Biermann, 1970). Giuliano, who evidently read Latin and knew Alberti's treatise as well as *On Architecture*, enriched the application of the Vitruvian orders, making use again of the Tuscan order in the courtyard of the Palazzo Scala, and giving a new importance to the Ionic (at Poggio a Caiano and Cestello), which was formerly confined to secondary positions (see Tönnesmann, 1983; Guillaume, 1988, pp. 135–50). The difficulty of the text, however, still made the treatise inaccessible to most architects.

In most of the manuscript copies of *On Architecture* made in Italy in the second half of the 15th century (the Vatican library alone has more than a dozen), copious marginal notes give clues to the culture and interests of those who were reading it. The notes, almost always in Latin, concern not only geographical and historical curiosities but also the vocabulary of ancient architecture—especially the types of dwellings, the orders and their rules of proportion. Now and then sketches appear in the margins, mostly referring to the scientific, astronomical and geometrical topics rather than the specifically architectural ones. It would appear that very few skilled draughtsmen were reading the treatise. The work of two or three generations of humanists and architectural scholars was needed before architects could make more than sporadic use of the text.

The first printed edition of *On Architecture*, with emendations, was produced by a philologist, Sulpizio da Veroli, between 1486 and 1492. The initiative came from the circle of Cardinal Raffaele Riario, who was especially interested in Vitruvius' treatment of the theatre. In the same climate, the façade of the Cardinal's Roman palazzo (*c.* 1485–*c.* 1511), later called the Palazzo della Cancelleria (*see* ROME, §V, 23(i)), was clad with Travertine slabs—a direct evocation of the *opus isodomum*, the most admired ancient stonework described by Vitruvius.

(b) After c. 1500. In the 16th century Vitruvius' treatise became more comprehensible thanks to the work of Fra Giovanni Giocondo, who, after more than two decades of preparation, published the first abundantly illustrated edition (Venice, 1511). A humanist philologist who knew Latin and Greek, he was at the same time an architect and student of ancient architecture and of Latin and Greek texts on scientific disciplines. For his edition of Vitruvius he drew on his knowledge in all these areas (rarely united in one person) and put what he learnt from ancient texts to immediate use in his own architectural work, for example in the building of the Pont Nôtre-Dame in Paris (see Ciapponi, 1984). Fra Giocondo's emendations to the text, sometimes conjectural, are for the most part still accepted by modern scholarship; and his drawings, reproduced as woodcuts, created a precedent for illustrated treatises on architecture in the following decades (for illustration *see* GIOCONDO, GIOVANNI). They gave readers considerable help in understanding the text and they clarified the architectural orders so that errors like Francesco di Giorgio's became impossible. Less useful in making the treatise correctly comprehensible was the first translation into the vernacular (Como, 1521) by the Lombard architect CESARE CESARIANO. Like that of Fra Giocondo, this edition was illustrated (see fig. 2 above), and it was provided with a full commentary. Though the comments are learned, the figures are often inspired less by Classical architecture than by the *all'antica* architecture of 15th-century northern Italy. One of the main merits of this translation is its graphic reconstruction of the types of dwellings, for which the author used Alberti's treatise (without citing it) and his own knowledge of courtyard houses in various northern Italian cities of Roman foundation.

In Rome Vitruvius' treatise had a direct influence on architectural practice from the early 16th century, especially on the development of a vocabulary based on the system of orders. Bramante, drawing on Vitruvius' text, which he knew from his Milanese period, as well as on Alberti and on his direct observation of ancient structures, used the complete Doric order in the Tempietto (after 1502) at S Pietro in Montorio, Rome, and in the spiral stairway of the Cortile del Belvedere (*c.* 1512) in the Vatican he placed in orderly sequence the types of columns—Tuscan, Doric, Ionic and Composite, which was not then clearly distinguished from the Corinthian (*see* BRAMANTE, DONATO, figs 4 and 5). In the second decade of the 16th century Raphael, in particular, gave greater importance to the Ionic order. Antonio da Sangallo (ii) showed an early tendency to follow the Vitruvian text more rigidly, even in the canons of proportionality. The standard system of orders, which was elaborated first in the Roman architecture of the first part of the 16th century, was later codified in the treatises of SEBASTIANO SERLIO (1537), JACOPO VIGNOLA (1562) and Andrea Palladio (1570), and remained for centuries the foundation

of Western architectural language (*see* ORDERS, ARCHITECTURAL, especially §I, 2(iii) and fig. 5). This was not taken entirely from Vitruvius, however. The Corinthian style was partly invented by 16th-century architects on the basis of examination of Roman monuments; the Composite order was first described by Alberti; and even the Tuscan, to which Vitruvius devoted only a few summary remarks, was partly re-created by Renaissance architects. Certain fundamental concepts are nevertheless obviously Vitruvian: trabeation, the numerical proportioning of elements, their definition by set types and the meanings associated with each type of column could not have been arrived at through the mere study of ancient monuments without reference to the text of Vitruvius.

At the same time the generation after Bramante, especially Antonio da Sangallo (ii), tended to draw inspiration from Vitruvius' description of Roman and Greek houses not only in the generic reference to the type of house with a courtyard, but also in trying (as Palladio did later) to re-create the principal parts of the *domus* (at times in accordance with distorted restorations). Thus in the Palazzo Farnese (1514–16) and some other palace schemes, Antonio reintroduced an atrium in the form of a basilican hall from Fra Giocondo's version of the Vitruvian *domus*; the same type of atrium reappeared in Raphael's plans for the Villa Madama (1518), Rome; and Giulio Romano built one in the Palazzo del Te (from 1526), Mantua, as did Michele Sanmicheli in the Palazzo Grimani (1556), Venice.

Antonio da Sangallo (ii) and his brother Battista da Sangallo thought of themselves as true Vitruvians and were so judged by their contemporaries. They owned the principal editions of *On Architecture*, which they both tried to translate (when he died in 1548 the latter had almost finished an illustrated translation, which he intended to publish), and they used Vitruvian theory to criticize the work of other architects, from Raphael's plan for St Peter's (*c.* 1529) to Michelangelo's cornice for the Palazzo Farnese (1546). According to the explicit testimony of his brother, Antonio wanted to follow the 'rule of Vitruvius' in the Palazzo Farnese. For him, following the rule meant drawing on the plans described in the treatise to re-create the *domus*, villas and theatres for modern use and aiming to adopt Vitruvius' syntax and proportions in the use of the orders. He tried to establish types of details (especially in the 1530s and 1540s) by translating the appropriate passages of *On Architecture* into drawings, with many misunderstandings and some adaptations to ideas taken from ancient architecture. He also sought to interpret and extend the Vitruvian principle of truth and naturalness of the architectural elements (see Guillaume, 1988, p. 52). His whole approach was singularly consonant with Vitruvius' prescriptive aims.

At the same time Antonio da Sangallo (ii) and his assistants, as well as others, were directly studying ancient architecture to compare the reality with the precepts of Vitruvius, and to fill the gaps in the treatise with what could be learned from analysis of the monuments. Very soon the systematic analysis of these structures, surveyed and restored through the medium of scale drawings along lines proposed by Raphael (*c.* 1519), showed how ill-founded was the naive, *a priori* notion (expressed by Antonio in the preface to his own translation of Vitruvius) that Roman architecture of the Imperial age, being later than Vitruvius, necessarily followed his precepts. In fact most of the time, for example in defining a type of archaic Ionic base, Vitruvius referred to models remote in time and space, using the writings of Greek theorists rather than contemporary Roman practice.

There were different reactions to the contradictions between the descriptions of Vitruvius and the reality of ancient buildings. Raphael, when he was appointed architect for St Peter's in 1514, read Vitruvius in an Italian translation made at his request by Marco Fabio Calvo. In it he found 'great light, but not enough of it' and drew freely on ideas derived from ancient architecture. Baldassare Peruzzi observed that ancient buildings offered a great variety of solutions and that those described by Vitruvius were not always the best; he used his own judgement in the choice of elements. Serlio, in book III of his treatise (1540) tried to follow Vitruvius dogmatically in studying ancient architecture to distinguish the positive aspects from those to be condemned. Antonio da Sangallo sometimes tried to eliminate contradictions by bending his interpretation of the text to fit what he saw in the ancient monuments.

The Accademia della Virtù, a private society of intellectuals, was more critical and flexible in its approach. In its programme of Vitruvian studies (1542) it proposed to compare ancient monuments and their details with the rules in *On Architecture* and wherever there was divergence to seek the particular reasons for it. To this end Vignola was engaged to do scale drawings of Roman monuments. The academy's programme marked the high point of research on Vitruvius and closely related studies of ancient architecture in 16th-century Rome. The group, led by Claudio Tolomei, intended to prepare and publish 17 works on *On Architecture* and antiquarian studies: the corrected Latin text, a translation, a set of illustrations much fuller than that of Fra Giocondo, lexicons and various accessory materials, and annotated surveys of monuments. Because the project lacked financial backing, however, they managed only to organize a series of weekly meetings in which each member of the group in turn read his commentary on one part of the treatise. It took three or four years to complete the study of the whole work. This initiative recalls other early experiences of collective teaching or study of architectural theory based on the reading of Vitruvius: Fra Giocondo's public lectures on *On Architecture*, given in Paris at the beginning of the century, in which he supplemented his comments with drawings, and the group readings organized by Michelangelo and Giovan Francesco da Sangallo, together with other artists and *letterati*, in Florence in 1520.

The only direct printed results of Tolomei's grand programme were the *Annotationes* to Vitruvius by the humanist and philologist GUILLAUME PHILANDER. This was published in Rome in 1544 and in Paris the next year, and was reprinted several times. It was the first commentary on Vitruvius by a non-Italian; the only (very partial) forerunner was the *Medidas del Romano* by DIEGO DE SAGREDO, a condensed summary of details of the orders, first printed in 1526 in Toledo. Philander became interested in architectural theories as a pupil of Serlio in Venice; later, in Rome, he took part in the meetings of Tolomei's

academy. While his commentary covered all ten books of *On Architecture*, it only partly realized the academy's programme of making the text more accessible to architects and artists without Latin. His interest was concentrated on the orders; these were explained with simple drawings of whole orders and details of each, with a glossary placed carefully alongside the relevant passages of the text. For the sake of completeness on this subject Philander inserted a long excursus of his own on the orders, in which he summarized Serlio's treatment of that subject. This commentary, the first Renaissance treatise on architecture published by a Frenchman, disseminated beyond the Alps not only its author's interpretation of the Latin treatise, but also the application of the orders by Bramante and his successors, from which Serlio had taken his inspiration. The illustrations encouraged the use of fixed types for each of the elements of the orders: for example, Ionic bases of the type described by Vitruvius appear more often in late 16th-century architecture in France than in Italy, especially Rome, where the comparison between Vitruvius and the variety of ancient examples led architects to doubt and criticize the Latin text and to choose other solutions.

In the first printed French translation of *On Architecture*, made by Jean Martin (Paris, 1547), and the first German one, by Gualtherus Rivius (Nuremberg, 1548), the interpretation and illustration of the Latin text was often inspired by the drawings and comments of Fra Giocondo and Cesariano, and sometimes by illustrations from Serlio's treatise. The study of Vitruvius, which became obligatory for anyone interested in ancient architecture, was thus increasingly linked with the study of the theories and practices of Italian Renaissance architecture. Francisco de Hollanda, in *Da pintura antigua*, declared a wish to follow Vitruvius but in fact used Serlio's more accessible, free interpretation of the Latin treatise (see Deswarte, p. 254). In Spain, while Diego de Sagredo's *Medidas del Romano* was reprinted numerous times, an annotated translation of *On Architecture* prepared by Lazaro de Velasco between 1554 and 1564 remained unpublished (see Bustamante and Marías). Velasco criticized Cesariano and favoured the text of Fra Giocondo. He followed Serlio in adapting Vitruvius' treatise to modern Christian uses. Only in 1582 was his work first published in Spain by M. de Urrea, while Juan de Herrera set the ideas of Vitruvius in a different philosophical context from the original one, and El Greco criticized Vitruvius' principles while accepting his morphological code.

Meanwhile in Venice Daniele Barbaro, with the help of Palladio for the main illustrations, had prepared his own annotated translation of *On Architecture*, published in 1556 (see fig. 4). Thanks to his scientific education, Barbaro, who tackled all the ten books of the treatise with equal interpretative zeal, produced the first printed translation showing a full comprehension of the Latin text (*see* BARBARO, (1)). His version was unrivalled for a couple of centuries, until the 18th-century version of Galiani. Basing himself on Barbaro's translation, Palladio continued the attempt begun in the previous century to recreate *all'antica* types of palazzi, villas and theatres derived from Vitruvian descriptions (*see* THEATRE, §III, 2(i)(b)). To the revival of the atrium of the *domus* he added, both in theory and

4. Illustration printed opposite the opening text page of D. Barbaro: *I dieci libri dell'architettura di M. Vitruvio* (Venice, 1556)

practice, that of the hall with four columns (see Wittkower). Vignola's contemporary *Regola delli cinque ordini d'architettura* (Rome, 1562), based on a study of ancient monuments that resulted from Vignola's involvement with the Accademia della Virtù, has little connection with the precepts of Vitruvius, however: only for the Tuscan order does the author mention having referred to *On Architecture*, for lack of ancient examples. But the result of Vignola's work, a simple rule drawing together a long series of relationships between the elements of the five orders, is close to the spirit if not the letter of Vitruvius.

After the publication of Vignola's *Regola* and Palladio's *I quattro libri dell'architettura* (Venice, 1570), Vitruvius' treatise lost its pre-eminent position by comparison with new standard works annotated with examples of ancient or modern architecture. At the same time the founding of the design academies reduced its importance as an introduction to architectural theory. Interest in Vitruvius revived later, however, in all the periods of renascent classicism, especially in the 18th century with Galiani's translation. The reading of Vitruvius' treatise was then heavily influenced by the interpretations given by Renaissance architects and literary men.

See also TREATISE, §I.

BIBLIOGRAPHY

EARLY SOURCES

G. Giocondo: *M. Vitruvius, per iucundum solito castigatior factus, cum figuris et tabula, ut iam legi et intellegi possit* (Venice, 1511)
C. Cesariano: *Di Lucio Vitruvio Pollione de architectura libri dece traducti de Latino in Vulgare* (Como, 1521); ed. F. Piel, with intro. by C. H. Krinsky (Munich, 1969)
D. de Sagredo: *Medidas del romano* (Toledo, 1526); ed. F. Marías and A. Bustamante (Madrid, 1986)
G. Philander: *In decem libros M. Vitruvii Pollionis de architectura annotationes* (Rome, 1544)
D. Barbaro: *I dieci libri dell'architettura di M. Vitruvio* (Venice, 1556); ed. M. Tafuri (Milan, 1987)
G. Poleni: *Exercitationes vitruvianae primae* (Padua, 1739)

GENERAL

E. Forsmann: *Dorisch, Ionisch, Korintisch: Studien über das Gebrauch der Säulenordnungen in der Architektur des 16.–18. Jahrhunderts* (Stockholm, 1961)
R. Wittkower: *Architectural Principles in the Age of Humanism* (London, 1962)
R. Weiss: *The Renaissance Discovery of Classical Italy* (Oxford, 1969, rev. 1988)
A. Tönnesmann: *Der Palazzo Gondi in Florenz* (Worms, 1983)
J. Onians: *Bearers of Meaning: The Classical Orders in Antiquity, the Middle Ages and the Renaissance* (Princeton, 1988)

SPECIALIST STUDIES

F. Pellati: 'Vitruvio nel medio evo e nel rinascimento', *Boll. Reale Ist. Archeol. & Stor. A.*, v/4–5 (1932), pp. 111–18
——: 'Vitruvio e il Brunelleschi', *Rinascita*, ii (1939), pp. 343–65
H. Koch: *Vom Nachleben des Vitruv* (Baden Baden, 1951)
P. G. Hamberg: 'G. B. da Sangallo detto il Gobbo e Vitruvio con particolare riferimento all'atrio di palazzo Farnese a Roma e all'antico castello reale di Stoccolma', *Palladio*, viii (1958), pp. 15–21
L. A. Ciapponi: 'Il *De architectura* di Vitruvio nel primo umanesimo', *Italia Med. & Uman.*, iii (1960), pp. 59–99
R. Krautheimer: 'Alberti and Vitruvius', *Acts of the 20th International Congress of the History of Art: New York, 1961*, ii, pp. 42–53
C. H. Krinsky: 'Seventy-eight Vitruvius Manuscripts', *J. Warb. & Court. Inst.*, xxx (1967), pp. 36–70
H. Biermann: 'Das Palastmodell Giuliano da Sangallos für Ferdinand I, König von Neapel', *Wien. Jb. Kstgesch.*, xxiii (1970), pp. 154–95
J. Onians: 'Alberti and φιλδρετε : A Study in their Sources', *J. Warb. & Court. Inst.*, xxxiv (1971), pp. 96–114
P. N. Pagliara: 'L'attività edilizia di Antonio da Sangallo il giovane: Il confronto tra gli studi sull'antico e la letteratura vitruviana', *Controspazio*, iv/7 (1972), pp. 19–55
V. Juřen: 'Fra Giovanni Giocondo et le début des études vitruviennes en France', *Rinascimento*, 2nd ser., xiv (1974), pp. 101–15
V. Fontana and P. Morachiello: *Vitruvio e Raffaello: Il 'De architectura' di Vitruvio nella traduzione inedita di Fabio Calvo ravennate* (Rome, 1975)
L. A. Ciapponi: 'Vitruvius', *Catalogus translationum et commentariorum*, ed. F. E. Cranz (Washington, DC, 1976), iii, pp. 399–409
C. Thoenes: 'Spezie e ordine di colonne nell'architettura del Brunelleschi', *Filippo Brunelleschi: La sua opera e il suo tempo: Convegno internazionale di studi: Firenze, 1977*, ii, pp. 459–69
L. Cervera Vera: *El codice de Vitruvio hasta sus primeras versiones impresas* (Madrid, 1978)
V. Juřen: 'Politien et Vitruve (Note sur le MS. Lat. 7382 de la Bibliothèque nationale)', *Rinascimento*, 2nd ser., xviii (1978), pp. 285–92
L. Marcucci: 'Regesto cronologico e critico' and 'Giovanni Sulpicio e la prima edizione del *De architectura* di Vitruvio', *Stud. & Doc. Archit.*, viii (1978), pp. 29–184, 185–95
M. Tafuri: 'Cesare Cesariano e gli studi vitruviani del quattrocento', *Scritti rinascimentali di architettura* (Milan, 1978), pp. 388–92
L. Vagnetti: 'Per una coscienza vitruviana', *Stud. & Doc. Archit.*, viii (1978), pp. 15–24
G. Scaglia: 'A Translation of Vitruvius and Copies of Late Antique Drawings in Buonaccorso Ghiberti's "Zibaldone"', *Trans. Amer. Philos. Soc.*, lxix (1979), pp. 3–30
S. Deswarte: 'Francisco de Hollanda et les études vitruviennes en Italie', *A introdução da arte da renascença na península ibérica: Actas do simpósio international: Coimbra 1981*, pp. 227–80
F. P. Fiore: 'Cultura settentrionale e influssi albertiani nelle architetture vitruviane di Cesare Cesariano', *A. Lombarda*, 64 (1983), pp. 43–52
L. A. Ciapponi: 'Fra Giocondo da Verona and his Edition of Vitruvius', *J. Warb. & Court. Inst.*, xlvii (1984), pp. 72–86

A. Bustamante and F. Marías: 'La Révolution classique: De Vitruve à l'Escorial', *Rev. A.*, 70 (1985), pp. 29–40

F. P. Fiore: 'La traduzione di Vitruvio di Francesco di Giorgio', *Archit.: Stor. & Doc.*, i (1985)

G. Scaglia, ed.: *Il Vitruvio magliabechiano di Francesco di Giorgio Martini* (Florence, 1985)

M. Morresi: 'Pier Candido Decembrio, Francesco Pizzolpasso e Vitruvio', *Ric. Stor. A.*, 28–9 (1986), pp. 217–23

P. N. Pagliara: 'Vitruvio da testo a canone', *Memoria dell'antico nell'arte italiana*, ed. S. Settis, iii (Turin, 1986), pp. 3–85

A. Cerutti Fusco: 'La restituzione grafica di teatri antichi nei primi decenni del cinquecento: Interesse antiquario, studi vitruviani e "inventioni"', *Saggi in onore di Guglielmo De Angelis d'Ossat*, ed. S. Benedetti and G. M. Mariani (Rome, 1987), pp. 301–12

F. Zöllner: *Vitruvs Proportionsfigur: Quellenkritische Studien zur Kunstliteratur: 15. und 16. Jahrhunderts* (Worms, 1987)

J. Guillaume, ed.: *Les Traités d'architecture de la Renaissance* (Paris, 1988) [relevant essays: pp. 49–59, 135–50, 179–206, 207–26, 307ff]

P. Kehl: 'Belriguardo, una villa principesca nel hinterland di Ferrara', *C.E.S.R. XXe colloque d'histoire de l'architecture: Tours, 1992*

PIER NICOLA PAGLIARA

Vitry, Paul (*b* Paris, 11 Nov 1872; *d* Paris, 7 April 1941). French art historian and writer. He was educated at the Sorbonne and went on to become a pupil of Louis Courajod and André Michel at the Ecole du Louvre. His numerous writings are principally devoted to French sculpture, especially cathedral statuary. His dissertation on Michel Colombe, published in 1901, was followed by other studies of medieval sculpture, of early Renaissance sculpture in Touraine and of such masters of the 17th, 18th and 19th centuries as Jean-Antoine Houdon, Joseph Chinard, Antoine-Louis Barye, Jean-Baptiste Carpeaux, François Rude and, among his own contemporaries, Albert Bartholomé and Emile-Antoine Bourdelle. Having joined the staff of the Musée du Louvre in 1897, he became head of the sculpture department in 1920. In 1906 he founded the review *Musées et monuments de France*, which he directed until 1939. He was also active as an exhibition organizer and as a professor at the Ecole des Arts Décoratifs (1901–20), at the Ecole du Louvre (1920–39) and at the Université Libre in Brussels (1934–9).

WRITINGS

Michel Colombe et la sculpture française de son temps (Paris, 1901)

Tours et les châteaux de Touraine (Paris, 1905)

with G. Brière: *L'Eglise de Saint Denis et ses tombeaux* (Paris, 1908)

Jean Goujon (Paris, 1908)

Le Musée de Tours (Paris, 1911)

Carpeaux (Paris, 1912)

Le Château de Maisons-Laffitte (Paris, 1912)

Hôtels et maisons de la Renaissance française, 3 vols (Paris, 1912–13)

ed.: *L'Art en Europe et en Amérique au XIXe siècle et au début du XXe* (1913–26), viii/1–3 of *Histoire de l'art depuis les premiers temps chrétiens jusqu'à nos jours*, 18 vols, ed. A. Michel (Paris, 1905–29) [also contributed the following essays: 'L'Architecture de la Renaissance en France', iv/2, pp. 491–571; 'La Sculpture dans les Pays-Bas au XVe et au XVIe siècle', v/1, pp. 313–34; 'La Sculpture en France de 1789 à 1850', viii/1, pp. 45–76]

La Cathédrale de Reims, 2 vols (Paris, 1915–19)

Henri Lebasque (Paris, 1928)

La Sculpture française au temps de Saint-Louis (Paris, 1929)

La Sculpture française classique de Jean Goujon à Rodin (Paris, 1934)

Les Chefs d'oeuvre de l'art français à l'Exposition internationale de 1937: La Sculpture française du XIIe au XVIe siècle, du XVIe au XIXe siècle, 2 vols (Paris, 1937)

BIBLIOGRAPHY

F. Salet: *Paul Vitry, 1872–1941* (Paris, 1951) [with list of writings comp. L. Vitry and G. Hubert]

GÉRARD HUBERT

Vittone, Bernardo Antonio (*b* Turin, 1702; *d* Turin, 19 Oct 1770). Italian architect and writer. He was the last of the three great masters of Piedmontese Baroque, and he achieved a reconciliation of the ideas of his predecessors Guarino Guarini and Filippo Juvarra in developing an architecture of immense creativity, particularly for churches. Vittone was the only one of the three to be born in Piedmont; most of his work was built outside Turin, however, and it remains generally less well known than that of Guarini and Juvarra.

1. Early life and work, before *c*. 1755. 2. Late work and writings, *c*. 1755 and after.

1. EARLY LIFE AND WORK, BEFORE *c*. 1755. He came from a family of small merchants, and his introduction to architecture probably came from his uncle, the architect Gian Giacomo Plantery (1680–1756). His first works were minor: the high altar (*c*. 1730; attrib.) in the sanctuary of S Ignazio (1725), Lanzo, a small church perhaps designed by Plantery; a wall (1730; destr.) separating the courtyard from the garden at Guarini's unfinished Palazzo Carignano, Turin; and the parish church of S Maria della Neve (1730; consecrated 1739), Pecetto, a simple, barrel-vaulted church with side chapels. In 1731 Vittone went to Rome to study, and in 1732 he won first prize in the Concorso Clementino at the Accademia di S Luca with a project for a fortified town with a harbour. Although this scheme, like most of his designs done in Rome, is generally of an academic Roman Baroque character, the design of its four centralized Greek-cross churches and the spatial complexity of their corner chapels indicates that by then he was familiar with the work of both Guarini and Juvarra. Vittone referred to Juvarra as his 'maestro' (Vittone, 1760, p. 285) and may have worked with him in Turin before going to Rome; Juvarra's late work in Turin, then under construction, made a strong impression on Vittone, apparent particularly in his sketches showing the effects of light and shade without surface decoration. Vittone continued his studies in Rome under the sponsorship of Charles-Emanuel III, King of Sardinia and 17th Duke of Savoy, and he was invited by Cardinal Alessandro Albani, the King's representative at the papal court, to study his collection of architectural books and drawings. Vittone's two volumes of sketches from this period (Paris, Mus. A. Déc.) reveal an appreciation of the work of Carlo Fontana (see FONTANA (v), (1)) and of the *Entwurf einer historischen Architektur* (1721) by Johann Bernhard Fischer von Erlach, who had himself studied in Rome under Fontana. Vittone's election to the Accademia was confirmed with his presentation of a design for a Temple of Moses in 1733, just before he returned to Turin.

Vittone returned to Turin with a recommendation from Cardinal Albani, but he did not enjoy royal patronage as this was a time of restraint in Piedmont because of the War of the Polish Succession (1733–6). He was occupied instead from 1735 with editing Guarini's treatise *Architettura civile*, published in 1737 by the Theatine Order, perhaps at the instigation of Vittone himself, and this must have increased his interest in Guarini's work. After Juvarra's death in 1736 Vittone received a few official commissions, mainly for works of a charitable nature, including the Collegio delle Provincie (begun 1738), Turin; the Ospedale di Carità (begun 1739), Casale Monferrato; and the Ricovero dei Catecumeni (*c.* 1740), Pinerolo. These incorporated careful planning and often austere elevations, showing the influence of Juvarra; the Ospedale di Carità has a rusticated portico and a courtyard featuring arches flanked by trabeated openings, a system used by Plantery at the Palazzo Saluzzo-Paesano (1715–22), Turin. When royal building work began again in earnest after 1740, Vittone lost favour to Benedetto Innocente Alfieri, who became the royal architect. Vittone instead found extensive patronage from the small parishes in and around Turin, for whom he built more than thirty churches, three town halls and other projects.

From the first, Vittone's churches reveal a mastery of the themes that occupied him for the rest of his life: geometric forms, double structures derived from Juvarra, and complex domes derived from Guarini. These features are all present in the sanctuary of S Maria della Visitazione (1738), Vallinotto, near Carignano. Its plain, undulating exterior walls and three-tiered elevation (see fig. 1) reflect the interior arrangement: a series of segmental chapels surrounding the hexagonal plan, and an inner structure of pilasters supporting arches and a triple-layered dome and lantern above. The design of the complex dome (see fig. 2(left)) is a structural *tour de force*. Its lower level is formed by a network of intersecting ribs clearly inspired by Guarini's dome at S Lorenzo, Turin (*see* GUARINI, GUARINO, fig. 1); the ribs are strongly lit by large windows in the middle level of the elevation, from which light is also directed down into the central space and into the chapels through oval apertures in their vaults—an arrangement reminiscent of Juvarra's Chiesa del Carmine (*see*

1. Bernardo Vittone: S Maria della Visitazione, Vallinotto, near Carignano, 1738

JUVARRA, FILIPPO). Through the central hexagon of the ribs can be seen the second shell of the dome, which is not lit, and through its central opening in turn can be seen the third shell, which is lit by circular windows in the upper level of the walls, concealed from the interior. Surmounting the whole is the cupola of the lantern, lit by small windows and visible through the opening in the uppermost shell of the dome. Vittone intended the entire arrangement to be seen as a symbol of the hierarchy of heaven, emphasized by the rich decoration on the soffit of each layer of the dome that culminates with the Holy Trinity in the lantern.

Vittone's design for Vallinotto also illustrates other themes that he developed consistently in his work, notably the vertical integration of elements from the body of the church through the piers to the ribs of the vaulting, omitting the separating entablature or cornice ring above the piers that is seen in Guarini's domes. In Vittone's later work the boundaries were dissolved by windows merging drum and dome and by hollowed-out pendentives. Stripped interior decoration, more classical in character than Guarini's High Baroque colours, was used to heighten the effects of concealed illumination. The exterior form, closely following the internal arrangement, gives a characteristic complexity to the building, while the plain stuccoed walls provide a powerful presence in the Piedmontese landscape. Vittone's buildings were generally constructed of brick and stucco to reduce costs as complex stereotomy was not required.

Vallinotto represents the initial stage of Vittone's development; he subsequently worked with smoother surfaces in his domes in place of the network of ribs, but he continued to develop complex geometrical shells and concealed light sources. This can be seen in S Chiara (1741–2), Bra, perhaps the masterpiece of his early work. Planned as a quatrefoil, it has a central circular space inscribed by four piers linked by curved arches that open into four surrounding oval chapels with galleries above. The dome is again a double structure: over the central space is an inner domical vault (see fig. 2(right)), deeply cut away by the arches over the galleries, and with ornate openings revealing the frescoes of the outer dome beyond; skylights in each segment of the outer dome provide light to the frescoes and to the galleries below, while the central openings provide light from the main lantern above. The stucco surfaces of the inner vault are washed in delicate pale green and ochre, giving it a strongly Rococo character and emphasizing the effects of the lighting. The restrained exterior, mostly in unadorned brickwork, contrasts with and emphasizes the effect of the interior.

Vittone's subsequent experiments with the form of pendentives revealed his interest in unifying the composition of the interior and in the achievement of a luminous centre by means of concealed lighting. At S Bernardino (1740–44), Chieri, he was commissioned to reconstruct the façade and upper parts of a plain, Greek-cross church that had already been begun by another architect when the dome collapsed, damaging the façade. Above the arches of the crossing Vittone placed a circular gallery of eight slender piers supporting an octagonal ribbed dome. The external wall of the gallery undulates, following the line of the crossing at the corners but projecting out over

2. Bernardo Vittone: (left) dome of S Maria della Visitazione, Vallinotto, 1738; (right) dome of S Chiara, Bra, 1741–2

the chapels; these are lit through apertures in their vaults by windows in the gallery wall above. The most innovative aspect of this design is the piercing of the pendentives with small apertures, marked by gilded rays, and the overall effect is of a solid dome resting on an open, pierced structure. The façade of the church was completed only in 1792, greatly modified by Vittone's assistant Mario Ludovico Quarini (1736–*c.* 1800).

More extreme variations can be seen in Vittone's design for the church of the Albergo di Carità (1744–9), Carignano, where the pendentives are eroded by inverted semi-domes, which continue as concave semicircular bays through the cornice ring and drum, terminating in groins in the central domical vault. At S Chiara (*c.* 1750; restored 1967), Vercelli, Vittone placed a hexagonal vault over an undulating base, with alternate concave and convex chapels. The parish church of the Assunta (1750), Grignasco, has a similar plan, but the domical vault springs directly from the inner circle of columns, with large, fan-shaped windows below each segment of the vault, above the arches of the chapel openings. In the sanctuary of S Maria di Piazza (1751–4), Turin, the upper parts of the pendentives are scooped out to introduce light to the vault and to make them appear continuous with the drum, a device possibly derived from Francesco Borromini's S Ivo della Sapienza, Rome. These developments culminated in Santa Croce (1755), Villanova Mondovì, where the four arches of the crossing appear to support pairs of 'brackets' from which spring the eight ribs of the star-shaped vault, while the pendentives of the crossing are hollowed out in the corners between each pair; windows surround the base of the vault, four in the corner pendentives and four between the paired 'brackets'.

2. LATE WORK AND WRITINGS, *c.* 1755 AND AFTER. Vittone's success resulted in more important commissions for churches and palaces. Such churches as S Salvatore (1755), Borgomasino, S Michele (1758), Rivarolo-Canavese, and the Assunta (1761), Riva di Chieri, however,

were more restrained than his earlier work—perhaps reflecting the growing influence of Neo-classicism—with pendentives broken to reveal corner windows extended up from square plans. For buildings in rural contexts Vittone was usually content to let the exterior form express the interior design, which frequently resulted in convex main façades; in an urban context, however, such as S Michele, he added a screen to give continuity to the street, recalling at a more modest scale the design of Borromini's S Agnese in Piazza Navona, Rome. Just before his death Vittone received a commission to build the parish church of S Benigno, Canavese; the construction of a simple longitudinal project, based on Vittone's design, was begun under Quarini in 1771. Vittone also built town halls at Bra (?1740–50), Montanaro (1769) and Chieri (1770), and the Collegio dei Gesuiti (*c.* 1769), Turin. The Municipio at Bra has a plain façade relieved by a recessed convex central bay, recalling Guarini's Palazzo Carignano, Turin (*see* GUARINI, GUARINO, fig. 4). Vittone's designs (1746) for the façade of Milan Cathedral were Gothic in style, which he deemed appropriate for the project (see Vittone, 1766, pls XLVI, XLVII).

Vittone published two treatises: *Istruzioni elementari* (1760) and *Istruzioni diverse* (1766). The former mainly concerns the architectural orders and the latter his own works. Among the few buildings by other architects that he included were Jacopo Vignola's Palazzo Farnese, Rome, and Bernini's Scala Regia at the Vatican, from which he derived a project for a staircase (see Vittone, 1766, pl. XV). Athough Vittone doubtless derived his knowledge of projective geometry from Guarini's *Architettura civile*, he did not include it in his own treatises. Some of his vaults, however, for example the project for a parish church at Spigno (pl. LXI), seem to spring directly from illustrations in *Architettura civile* (see Guarini, pl. XXVIII, fig. 2). Vittone's emphasis in these treatises on musical proportion in architecture, continuing an important Renaissance concept, was considered old-fashioned and a retreat from

Guarini's more empirical approach, and it helped to isolate Vittone from later generations of architects. Further volumes he planned were never realized, and on his death many copies of his publications were left unsold. His treatises were rejected by contemporary critics, and in the revival of classicism his brilliant, individual work was largely forgotten until the 20th century.

UNPUBLISHED SOURCES

Turin, Bib. Reale [MS. of 'L'architetto civile', 1760]
Paris, Mus. A. Déc. [2 vols of drgs]

WRITINGS

ed.: G. Guarini: *Architettura civile* (Turin, 1737/*R* Farnborough, 1964); ed. B. Tavassi La Greca (Milan, 1968)
Istruzioni elementari per indirizzo dei giovani allo studio dell'architettura civile (Lugano, 1760)
Istruzioni diverse concernenti l'officio dell'architetto civile (Lugano, 1766)

BIBLIOGRAPHY

E. Olivero: *Le opere di Bernardo Antonio Vittone, architetto piemontese del secolo XVIII* (Turin, 1920)
A. E. Brinckmann: *Theatrum Novum Pedemontii* (Düsseldorf, 1931)
V. Golzio: 'L'architetto Bernardo Antonio Vittone urbanista', *Atti del X congresso di storia dell'architettura: Torino, 1957*, pp. 101–12
R. Wittkower: *Art and Architecture in Italy, 1600–1750*, Pelican Hist. A. (Harmondsworth, 1958, rev. 1991)
H. A. Millon: 'Alcune osservazioni sulle opere giovanili di Bernardo Antonio Vittone', *Boll. Soc. Piemont. Archeol. & B.A.*, xii–xiii (1958–9), pp. 144–53
——: 'Vittone', *Arch. Rev.* [London], cxxxii (1962), pp. 95–104
P. Portoghesi: 'La chiesa di Santa Chiara a Brà nell'opera di B. A. Vittone', *Quad. Ist. Stor. Archit.*, liv (1962), pp. 1–22
N. Carboneri: 'Appunti sul Vittone', *Quad. Ist. Stor. Archit.*, lv (1963), pp. 59–74
P. Portoghesi: 'La parocchiale di Grignasco nell'opera di B. A. Vittone', *Archit. Cron. & Stor.*, viii (1963), pp. 772–9
——: *Bernardo Vittone, un architetto tra illuminismo e rococo* (Rome, 1966)
W. Oechslin: 'Un tempio di Mosè, i disegni offerti da Bernardo Vittone all'Accademia di San Luca nel 1733', *Boll. A.*, lii (1967), pp. 167–73
R. Pommer: *Eighteenth-century Architecture in Piedmont: The Open Structures of Juvarra, Alfieri and Vittone* (New York, 1967)
L. Quaglino Palmucci: 'Églises Saint Bernardin de Chieri et Sainte Claire de Verceil', *Congr. Archéol. France*, cxxix (1971), pp. 387–403
C. Norberg-Schulz: *Late Baroque and Rococo Architecture*, Hist. World Archit. (Milan, 1972; Eng. trans., London, 1979, rev. 1986)
W. Oechslin: *Bildungsgut und Antikenrezeption im frühen Settecento in Rom: Studien zum römischen Aufenthalt Bernardo Antonio Vittone* (Zurich, 1972)
V. Viale, ed.: *Bernardo Vittone e la disputa fra classicismo e barocco nel settecento*, 2 vols (Turin, 1972)
M. Kiene: 'Die italienischen Universitätspaläste des 17. und 18. Jahrhunderts: Das Turiner Kollegium', *Röm. Jb. Kstgesch.*, xxv (1989), pp. 363–8   □

Vittore di Matteo. *See* BELLINIANO, VITTORE.

Vittoria, Alessandro (*b* Trent, ?1525; *d* Venice, 27 May 1608). Italian sculptor, stuccoist and architect. He was a pupil and collaborator of Jacopo Sansovino and in the second half of the 16th century became one of the most important sculptors active in Venice. He was by temperament more of a modeller than a carver, and his stuccos, bronzes and terracottas are characterized by a verve and warmth that his work in marble tends to lack. His fluent, innovative and expressive style is in many ways opposed to Sansovino's thoughtful, classicizing, High Renaissance idiom. Vittoria's portrait sculpture is particularly fine. In his altars and funerary monuments he gradually evolved a dynamic relationship between sculptural and architectural elements that was more fully explored by artists of the Baroque. Comparatively little is known of Vittoria's work

as an architect. Although he is known to have been active also as a painter, none of his paintings has been identified. His workshop was clearly extensive. His principal collaborators were his nephews Agostino Rubini (*b c.* 1560; *d* before 1595) and Vigilio Rubini (*b c.* 1558; *d* after 1608), sons of his sister Margherita and the Vicentine sculptor Lorenzo Rubini (*fl* 1550–68), and a third nephew, Andrea dell'Aquila (*b c.* 1565; *d* after 1608).

1. Life and work. 2. Working methods and technique.

1. LIFE AND WORK.

(i) Training and early years, to *c.* 1560. (ii) The 1560s and 1570s. (iii) Later works, from *c.* 1580. (iv) Bronze statuettes.

(i) Training and early years, to c. *1560.* Alessandro was the son of Vigilio Vittoria, a tailor in Trent. It is likely, given the correspondences between his early works and those of the Paduan sculptors Vincenzo and Giovanni Girolamo Grandi, that he trained with them during their time in Trent (1534–42). In July 1543 he went to Venice, where he lived, with only two interruptions, for the rest of his life. There he entered the workshop of Jacopo Sansovino and soon assisted him with two great projects in bronze for S Marco: the door of the sacristy and the figurated reliefs for the singing-galleries to right and left of the choir. The overt emotionality of these works was the most significant influence on Vittoria's development as an artist.

Vittoria continued to work for Sansovino during the 1540s but by 1550 was an independent master. His earliest known sculpture, the marble statuette of *St John the Baptist* (h. *c.* 600 mm; Venice, S Zaccaria, right-hand stoop), dates from that year. It was originally commissioned by the monks of S Geremia, Venice, but payment was never fully made, and Vittoria bought it back in 1565. It remained in his possession until he died, and his will of 1608 included 'my little St John' as a bequest to the nuns of S Zaccaria. The *St John* occupies a key position in Vittoria's career. The figure is conceived within a closed silhouette and steps slightly forward in the act of baptism. The skin is stretched taut over the gaunt body, so that each bone and muscle protrudes. As in later works, the drapery patterns are clear and simple; the particularized features of the face foreshadow Vittoria's calling as a portraitist. The exploration of a highly emotional state of being—in this case of the saint's asceticism—remained a constant feature of Vittoria's artistic approach, as did his preference for small-scale figures: in an age dominated by Michelangelesque gigantism, Vittoria's most personal creations tended to be statuettes and under life-size figures.

After finishing the *St John* and carving some decorative figures for Sansovino's Libreria di S Marco, Venice, Vittoria returned to Trent, most likely attracted by the possibilities for work occasioned by the convening of the Council of Trent. In April 1551 he was paid for work on decorations (destr.) for the triumphal entry into the city by the future Philip II of Spain. By December 1551 he was in Vicenza, where he remained until early 1553. Around this time he and Sansovino had a bitter falling-out. The exact reasons for this remain obscure, but it seems Vittoria had tried to take away an important commission from Sansovino in 1552, and it would not be surprising if the quarrel arose from rivalry between the former pupil and his master.

Vittoria's main project in Vicenza was the stucco decoration of rooms in Andrea Palladio's Palazzo Thiene (now Banca Popolare), where the ceilings chart the development of his decorative idiom. The earlier ones, while rich and vigorous, merely follow and articulate the architectural layout. But in the Sala degli Dei the ceiling was conceived as one large high relief, and the cartouches, garlands and figures are not only more imaginative and graceful but powerful sculptural presences in their own right. This was probably the first programme in Italy to be carried out in strapwork, while the busts of Roman historical characters in the Sala dei Principi mark the first appearance of the portrait bust in Vittoria's work. It was also at this time that he made a series of portrait medals, including two of the writer *Pietro Aretino* (both lead; Munich, Staatl. Münzsamml.).

It was as a result of Aretino's mediation that in early 1553 Vittoria was reconciled with Sansovino, and by May of that year he was back in Venice. The two large caryatids known as the *Feminone* (1553–5), at the entrance to the Libreria Sansoviniana, were carried out with a good deal of studio assistance; they were Vittoria's first essay in large-scale stone sculpture and are not among his most successful works. As Sansovino's closest collaborator during the 1550s, he worked on a number of projects in Venice that were headed by Sansovino, including the bronze statue of *Tommaso Rangone* (1556–7) over the portal of S Giuliano; the marble *Pietà* (1557–8) in the lunette of the Venier tomb in S Salvatore; and, most important, the stuccos (1556; 1559–60) over the monumental staircase of the Libreria Sansoviniana and those (1557–9) over the Scala d'Oro (*see* VENICE, fig. 7) in the Doge's Palace. These sumptuous decorations further extend the principles applied in the Palazzo Thiene: the vaults over the staircases are treated as sculpture, with the result that the frescoes, which in both cases are by Battista Franco, are overwhelmed by the massive stuccos surrounding them. The Scala d'Oro was the ceremonial entrance to the palace, and Vittoria's stuccos display the richness and splendour of the Venetian state. The panels, with svelte, elongated figures in elegant contrapposto, also reveal his assimilation of a vocabulary formed by Central Italian Mannerists such as Parmigianino; he continued to refine and experiment with figures in contrapposto throughout his career. He acquired Parmigianino's *Self-portrait in a Convex Mirror* (Vienna, Ksthist. Mus.) in 1560 and also bought drawings by Parmigianino in 1558 and 1581.

Vittoria's independent projects of the 1550s include four stone statues (1555–8) on the tomb of *Alessandro Contarini* in S Antonio, Padua; the *Mercury* (stone, 1558–9) on the Piazzetta façade of the Doge's Palace, Venice; a stone *Angel* (commissioned 1555; Verona, Pal. Vescovile, courtyard); and the marble bust of *Giovanni Battista Ferretti* (1557; Paris, Louvre; mid-18th-century copy *in situ*) for his tomb in S Stefano, Venice. Meanwhile he continued his association with Palladio at the Villa Pisani (now Villa Placco) in Montagnana, where he executed stucco statues of the *Four Seasons* (1554–5; *in situ*).

(ii) The 1560s and 1570s. The 1560s marked the start of the period during which Vittoria reached full artistic maturity. His marble portrait busts of *Benedetto Manzini* for S Geminiano (now Ca' d'Oro), Venice (*in situ*), and the procurator *Marc'Antonio Grimani* (Venice, S Sebastiano) date from 1560–61. The sitters are shown full of energy and movement, forceful and alert, in their cross-movements of shoulders, heads and glances manifesting Vittoria's concern for contrapposto and the *figura serpentinata*. The bust of *Grimani*, placed on the left-hand wall of his family chapel, is accompanied by small marble statues of *St Anthony Abbot* and *St Mark* (both completed 1561), in niches to either side of the altar; together, they form Vittoria's first altarpiece. In November 1561 Vittoria was commissioned to work on the altar in the Montefeltro chapel, S Francesco della Vigna, Venice. Carved of Rovigo stone, the statues of *St Anthony Abbot*, *St Sebastian* and *St Roch* (completed by 1564; *in situ*) show him in full command as a sculptor of life-size figures. He was not, however, responsible for their architectural setting. Other projects of this decade include the two marble caryatids (terracotta model of right-hand caryatid, Padua, Liviano), eventually placed on Vittoria's tomb in S Zaccaria, Venice; a stone statue of *St Thomas* (Venice, Semin. Patriarcale) with the features of Tommaso Rangone, who commissioned it for the portal of the convent of S Sepolcro, Venice; a marble bust of *Priamo da Lezze*, placed on the family monument in S Maria Assunta (the Gesuiti), Venice, in the 1580s; and a marble bust of *Niccolò Massa* (Venice, Ateneo Veneto) for S Domenico di Castello, Venice.

Vittoria's most ambitious undertaking of the 1560s, however, was the altar of the *Zane Family* in S Maria Gloriosa dei Frari (the Frari), Venice. This was described by Vasari in the second edition of the *Vite* and must therefore have been under way by 1566–8; Vasari's testimony resulted in the long-held belief that it was complete by 1568, but Leithe-Jasper (1963) showed that the centrepiece of the work, a marble, over life-size *St Jerome*, was not begun until at least 1570. The complex originally consisted of a large stucco relief of the *Assumption of the Virgin*, set above five large statues of saints, one of which was of marble and in the round, the other four of stucco and in varying degrees of relief. The altar was dismantled in the mid-18th century by the monks of the Frari, and only the architectural frame of the altar, two angels on top of the pediment, two of the stucco figures and the central marble *St Jerome* survive. This is a serious loss, representing as it does Vittoria's first attempt to set up dynamic relationships between the various components of an altar, a theme he would further explore in the 1570s and 1580s.

The *St Jerome* of the altarpiece bears the features of Giulio Contarini (*c.* 1500-1580), whose marble bust and tomb monument (1570–72; *in situ*) Vittoria executed for S Maria del Giglio, Venice. In 1569 Contarini had bought a house in the Calle della Pietà for Vittoria; he lived there for the rest of his life. Vittoria responded to his patron's generosity by carving one of his finest portraits, also the prototype for most of his later sepulchral monuments (including his own): a bust set above an inscribed commemorative plaque, flanked by caryatids or putti.

During 1574 Vittoria paid Andrea Palladio's son Marcantonio (*c.* 1538–after 1600) for work on the four great

1. Alessandro Vittoria: *Ottaviano Grimani*, marble, 1570s (Berlin, Skulpturen-galerie mit Frühchristlich-Byzantinischer Sammlung)

stucco *Evangelists* set into the inner façade of S Giorgio Maggiore, Venice, which was designed by Palladio himself. These statues formed the earliest component of the decoration of the church, and their spiralling, ecstatic rhythms show the increased expressiveness and poetic quality of Vittoria's figural language at this time. Despite this, however, he was not successful in his attempt to be awarded the commission for the high altar of the church, losing out to his younger competitor Gerolamo Campagna. During the 1570s he supervised the decoration of the Rosary chapel in SS Giovanni e Paolo.

It was during the 1570s that Vittoria brought his portrait style close to perfection. From the busts of *Contarini* and *Giuseppe Grimani* (marble, 1573; Venice, S Giuseppe di Castello) to that of *Tommaso Rangone* (bronze, *c.* 1575; Venice, Ateneo Veneto) for S Geminiano, Venice (Vittoria's only bronze bust), there is a steady progression in which the size and breadth of the torso are increased, the contrapposto of head and torso is more intense and complex, and the richness of chiaroscuro contrasts is deeper. The busts also increase in expressive power, for example those of *Ottaviano Grimani* (marble; Berlin, Skulpgal.; *see* fig. 1), *Orsato Giustiniani* (marble; Padua, Mus. Civ.) and *Sebastiano Venier* (marble; Venice, Doge's Pal.).

In 1576 Vittoria was at work on the altar for the Scuola di S Fantin (now the Ateneo Veneto), Venice, the major element of which was the marble *St Jerome* (now Venice, SS Giovanni e Paolo); in September that year he fled to

Vicenza to avoid the plague but completed the work after his return to Venice (by April 1577). This later *St Jerome*—kneeling and exhausted from his penances, a strong contrast with the heroic stance of the saint in the Frari altar—reveals an increasing pathos in Vittoria's work, as well as a change in his sculptural technique to a less detailed, more astringent manner.

In 1579 two of the most prominent statues in Venice were executed by his workshop to Vittoria's design: the stone *Justice* and *Venice* set over the great windows on the western and southern façades of the Doge's Palace. The marble statues of *Faith*, *Charity* and the *Risen Christ* (Brescia, Mus. Civ. Cristiano) for the tomb monument of *Bishop Domenico Bollani* in S Maria Rotondo, Brescia, must also have been substantially complete by 1579, the year of Bollani's death. Although *Faith* and *Charity* seem largely to be products of the workshop, the *Risen Christ* is autograph. (The monument was ruined in 1708 when a tower of the church collapsed; *Faith* and *Charity* survived intact, but the *Christ* is now without arms or legs.) From the early 1580s onwards Vittoria left more and more tasks to his workshop.

(iii) Later works, from c. 1580. In 1581 Vittoria paid his nephew and assistant Andrea dell'Aquila for carving the stone *Christ* over the entrance to the Frari, an indication of the increasing role of the workshop. Nonetheless Vittoria produced some of his greatest works during the 1580s, including a second altar for the Scuola di S Fantin. Probably dating from the first half of the decade, it depicts the *Crucifixion*, for which Vittoria supplied bronzes of the *Virgin* and *St John* (Venice, SS Giovanni e Paolo), each a little over 1 m high. Weighed down by the heavy folds of her robes but even more by her grief, the sorrowing *Virgin* has her hands clasped tightly together as she stares downward, providing a counterbalance to the figure of *St John*, who is portrayed with his arms spread wide and his neck strained upwards to gaze at Christ.

Between 1578 and 1583 Vittoria and his workshop were also engaged on two projects at S Giuliano, Venice, where in the 1570s he had succeeded Sansovino as architect in charge of rebuilding the church. In 1583 Vittoria paid Ottaviano Ridolfi (*fl*1567–92) for executing to his design the stucco decorations of the ceiling of the chapel of the Sacrament. Although the two small bronzed terracotta figures of the *Virgin* and *St John* in the side niches of the altar of this chapel have been attributed to Vittoria, Davis (1985) showed that they are signed by Agostino Rubini.

During this period Vittoria devoted his personal attention to another altar in the church, that of the Merciai (the grocers' guild; see fig. 2). The architecture, which consists of an elaborately carved altar table decorated with reliefs and herms surmounted by an aedicular structure of paired Corinthian columns supporting a complex broken segmental pediment, was designed by him and built by Francesco Smeraldi (*c* 1540-1614); Vittoria executed the lateral statues of *St Catherine of Alexandria* and *Daniel* (marble; completed 1584). At Vittoria's instigation, Palma Giovane painted the *Assumption of the Virgin* above the altar. This design constitutes one of Vittoria's finest achievements. The statues are not set into niches, as are those of S Francesco della Vigna or the Frari, but stand

2. Alessandro Vittoria and Francesco Smeraldi: altar of the Merciai, showing Vittoria's statues of *St Catherine of Alexandria* and *Daniel*, marble, h. 1.3 m, completed 1584 (Venice, S Giuliano)

suddenly to gaze directly at him; above, two groups of angels play in clouds as a tiny dove descends towards the Virgin. The great height of the relief contrasts powerfully with the smooth background, a contrast emphasized by the turbulent draperies and clouds.

The terracotta bust of *Doge Nicolò da Ponte* (Venice, Semin. Patriarcale; see fig. 3), perhaps Vittoria's greatest portrait, was made around 1584 for S Maria della Carità, Venice. In being his only depiction of a doge in ducal regalia, his only half-length and by far his largest portrait, it sums up Vittoria's aims as a portraitist, the foremost of which was to bring to the sitter a sense of movement. He used one of his favourite devices, an asymmetrical base, so that the Doge seems to lean towards the right, the direction in which he looks. This effect, counterbalanced by the way his shoulders recede in depth to the left, is further enforced by the contrasting drapery patterns on the robe: the folds are flat and vertical on the right, but deeply cut and diagonal on the left. The huge scale of the portrait is enhanced by the depth with which the torso projects in front and to either side of the socle. In the face, below the Doge's wrinkled flesh, every bone and muscle is apparent. Da Ponte, who was in his 90s when the bust was modelled, is shown vigorous and alert, old but wise.

After 1585, the autograph production of portrait busts declined sharply. While those of *Pietro Zen* (terracotta, *c.* 1585; Venice, Semin. Patriarcale) and *Giovanni Donà* (marble, after 1585; Venice, Ca' d'Oro), executed for SS Giovanni e Paolo, Venice, are by Vittoria himself, the busts of *Giovanni Battista Peranda* (marble, 1586; Murano,

free from the double columns behind them. Inward-turning, in contrapposto poses, they are shown looking upwards as if drawn towards the scene depicted in Palma's painting. The result is a new synthesis between the painting, sculpture and architecture of an altar that was widely developed in the Baroque art of the 17th century.

In 1583–4 Vittoria oversaw the execution of the two *Angels* and the *Virgin* that crown the pediment of the Scuola di S Fantin. He also designed the façade of the Scuola, providing the two-storey structure with a strongly sculptural effect achieved through the alternation of projecting and recessive elements: windows surmounted by deeply carved pediments supported by colonettes are framed by projecting units composed of a pair of columns separated by a shallow niche. Vittoria's experience as a stuccoist no doubt influenced his striving after such effects of relief and chiaroscuro. Around this time the marble and stone monument to the *Lezze* family in the Gesuiti, Venice, was under construction; its close resemblance to the Scuola makes its attribution to Vittoria quite likely, particularly as the Palazzo Balbi, built between 1582 and 1590 under Vittoria's supervision, features similar, though reduced, effects.

The so-called Pala Fugger (early 1580s; Chicago, IL, A. Inst.), a bronze relief of the *Annunciation* made for Johann Fugger, a member of the famous German banking family, was inspired by Titian's painting of the same subject (Venice, S Salvatore). The composition is simple: Gabriel rushes in from the left as the Virgin, kneeling, turns

3. Alessandro Vittoria: *Doge Nicolò da Ponte*, terracotta, 1.00×0.78 m, *c.* 1584 (Venice, Seminario Patriarcale)

S Maria degli Angeli) for S Sepolcro, Venice, *Vincenzo Morosini* (marble, 1588; Venice, S Giorgio Maggiore) and *Tommaso Contarini* (marble, mid-1580s; Venice, Madonna dell'Orto) are by the workshop.

Although the altar Vittoria designed for the Scuola dei Luganegheri (the guild of sausage-makers) in S Salvatore is usually dated to 1600, it more likely dates from *c*. 1590. In the composition and placing of the marble statues of *St Sebastian* and *St Roch*, Vittoria continued the affective relationship between architecture and sculpture begun at the altar of the Merciai in S Giuliano. The figure of *St Sebastian*, writhing in pain against the column behind him, is one of the most moving in all Venetian sculpture.

In 1591 the death of his second wife, Veronica Lazzarini (whom he had married in 1567), caused Vittoria to restrict his activities still further. For the marble busts of *Alvise Tiepolo* (1594; Venice, S Antonin), *Lorenzo Cappello* (*c*. 1595; Trent, Castello Buonconsiglio) and *Domenico Duodo* (1596; Venice, Ca' d'Oro), for example, only a standard torso was used in each case. From 1602 to 1605 Vittoria oversaw the work on his tomb monument in S Zaccaria, Venice, which was largely carried out by his nephews Vigilio Rubini and Andrea dell'Aquila, to whom he bequeathed his drawings, models and tools.

(iv) Bronze statuettes. Vittoria's bronze statuettes, although an important aspect of his output, have never been thoroughly studied, with the result that basic problems of attribution and chronology persist. They include some of his most beautiful works and demonstrate how medium affects aesthetic: unlike the marble statues, which tend to command only one main viewpoint and which always reflect the shape of the original block of stone, the bronzes are more overtly three-dimensional. *St John the Baptist* (Venice, S Francesco della Vigna), for instance, steps and leans forward as his shoulders twist in opposite directions from his hips and his raised right arm stretches above and behind him. Similarly, the opposed torsion between the head and right arm of *Neptune* (London, V&A) gives to the body a spiralling motion that continues through the arched neck of the attendant seahorse and on to the back of the statuette. The compositional movement is fully three-dimensional, and the figure is designed to be viewed from many angles. Other bronze statuettes securely attributable to Vittoria are *Jupiter* (1560s; Ecouen, Mus. Ren.), *St Sebastian* (1566; New York, Met.), *Winter* (*c*. 1585; Vienna, Ksthist. Mus.) and *Diana* and *Apollo* (Berlin, Skulpgal.).

2. WORKING METHODS AND TECHNIQUE. Although Vittoria made many references to drawings in his wills, not one has been securely identified, so that little is known about his working procedure. It is reasonable to assume that he followed the standard practice of first making sketches and then working up clay, wax or terracotta models, before beginning the actual carving. One terracotta model (Padua, Liviano) survives—that for the right caryatid on Vittoria's own tomb in S Zaccaria. Although the terracotta portraits are usually described as full-scale models for marble versions, they are much more likely to be independent works, produced to meet a demand. They also demonstrate that 16th-century Venetian patrons were willing to commission in a humble medium, in order to enjoy brilliant artistic effects.

BIBLIOGRAPHY

G. Vasari: *Vite* (1550, rev. 2/1568); ed. G. Milanesi (1878–85), vii, pp. 518–20
T. Temanza: *Vite dei più celebri architetti e scultori veneziani* (Venice, 1778/*R* 1966), pp. 475–98
R. Predelli: 'Le memorie e le carte di Alessandro Vittoria', *Archv Trent.*, xxiii (1908), pp. 8–74, 129–265 [Vittoria's account book and other source material; Venice, Archv Stato]
L. Planiscig: *Venezianische Bildhauer der Renaissance* (Vienna, 1921), pp. 435–524
G. Gerola: 'Nuovi documenti veneziani su Alessandro Vittoria', *Atti Ist. Ven. Sci., Lett. & A.*, lxxxiv/2 (1924–5), pp. 339–59
V. Moschini: 'Aspetti del gusto artistico del Vittoria', *Riv. Mens. Città Venezia*, xiii (1934), pp. 125–40
A. Venturi: *Storia* (1901–40), xiii, pp. 64–179
M. Leithe-Jasper: *Alessandro Vittoria: Beiträge zu einer Analyse des Stils seiner figürlichen Plastiken unter besonderer Berücksichtigung der Beziehungen zur gleichzeitigen Malerei in Venedig* (diss., U. Vienna, 1963)
J. Pope-Hennessy: *Italian High Renaissance and Baroque Sculpture* (1963, 2/1970), iii of *Introduction to Italian Sculpture* (Oxford, 1955–63)
C. Semenzato: 'Il Vittoria', *Rinascimento europeo e rinascimento veneziano*, ed. V. Branca (1967), iii of *Civiltà europea e civiltà veneziana* (Venice, 1963–73), pp. 275–80
C. Davis: 'Shapes of Mourning: Sculpture by Alessandro Vittoria, Agostino Rubini, and Others', *Renaissance Studies in Honour of Craig Hugh Smyth*, ii (Florence, 1985), pp. 163–71
T. Martin: 'Grimani Patronage in S Giuseppe di Castello: Veronese, Vittoria and Smeraldi', *Burl. Mag.*, cxxxiii (1991), pp. 825-33

THOMAS MARTIN

Vittorino da Feltre [Vittore da Rambaldoni] (*b* Feltre, 1378–9; *d* Mantua, 1446). Italian scholar, teacher and writer. He left Feltre in 1396 and enrolled at the Faculty of Arts at Padua University. While there he was influenced by many of his contemporaries and teachers, especially Pier Paolo Vergerio (1370–1444), whose *De Ingenibus Moribus* (1392) upheld Latin as an integral part of higher education, and who introduced Vittorino to the writings of Quintilian and Cicero. In 1415, disillusioned at the decline in standards and the absence of the teaching of Greek, Vittorino left Padua and went to teach Latin for his friend Guarino da Verona (1370–1460), who was running a school in Venice. In return Guarino taught Vittorino Greek. In 1420 Vittorino went briefly to Padua, but his continued dissatisfaction with university life led him to consider a monastic career until, in 1423, he accepted the invitation of Gianfrancesco Gonzaga, 1st Marchese of Mantua, to be tutor to his children. Vittorino was given a house in the grounds of the Castello S Giorgio, which he named La Casa Giocosa. There he was able to practise his ideals of education, teaching poor children free of charge and uniting Classical and Christian ideas into a coherent educational system, which included even the students' diet. Physical exercise and the seven liberal arts formed the basis of the curriculum and Latin was always spoken as an aid to pronunciation and understanding. Vittorino's personality dominated his educational ideals. His reputation for scholarship and integrity attracted patrons and enhanced their standing. He also prepared subsequent generations of Gonzaga patrons for the ideas of such men as Alberti and Andrea Mantegna. Vittorino's writings have not survived, but much was written about him by his contemporaries and pupils.

BIBLIOGRAPHY
V. da Bisticci: *Vite di uomini illustri del secolo XV* (n.p., *c.* 1490); Eng. trans. by W. George and E. Waters as *The Vespasiano Memoirs* (London, 1926/*R* New York, 1963)
W. H. Woodward: *Studies in Education: The Age of the Renaissance, 1400–1600* (n.p., 1906/*R* New York, 1965)
——: *Vittorino da Feltre and Other Humanist Educators: Essays and Versions. An Introduction to the History of Classical Education* (Cambridge, 1921/*R* New York, 1963)
Vittorino da Feltre nel 5 centenario della sua morte (Feltre, 1946)
N. Giannette, ed.: *Vittorino da Feltre e la sua scuola: Umanesimo, pedagogia, arti. Atti del convegno: Venezia 1979* (Florence, 1981)

DANA ARNOLD

Vittorio Amedeo, 12th Duke of Savoy. *See* SAVOY, §II(4).

Vittorio Amedeo II, King of Sardinia [King of Sicily]. *See* SAVOY, §II(11).

Vittorio Amedeo III, King of Sardinia. *See* SAVOY, §II(13).

Vittorio Emanuele II, King of Italy. *See* SAVOY, §II(14).

Vitullo, Sesostris (*b* Buenos Aires, 6 Sept 1899; *d* Paris, 16 May 1953). Argentine sculptor active in France. He studied at the Escuela Nacional de Bellas Artes in Buenos Aires before moving in 1925 to Paris, where he studied under Emile-Antoine Bourdelle. Living a tragic bohemian existence and feeling a strong nostalgia for Latin America, he returned incessantly to the theme of the gaucho, as in *Gaucho in the Bough* (grey granite, 1951; Buenos Aires, Mus. A. Mod.), and sought also to conjure the landscape of Argentina—with its light, its wind and the contours of the Andes—in sculptures such as *Totem Patagonia* (wood, 1951; Buenos Aires, Mus. A. Mod.).

Basing his stark and violently contrasting intersecting planes on a close analysis of natural forms, Vitullo arrived at a symbolic visual language by which the horizontality of the pampa and the verticality of the mountains are equated with masculine and feminine archetypes. He carved a variety of materials, notably oak, marble, granite and other stone.

BIBLIOGRAPHY
Vitullo sculpteur argentin (exh. cat., intro. B. Dorival; Paris, Mus. N. A. Mod., 1952) [45 works, 1940–52]
Vitullo au Musée Bourdelle et dans les grandes collections (exh. cat., intro. M. Dufet; Paris, Mus. Bourdelle, 1981)

NELLY PERAZZO

Viva, Angelo (*b* Naples, 1747; *d* Naples, 27 Feb 1837). Italian sculptor. About 1758 he studied at the Accademia di Disegno in Naples. He was later a follower of the sculptor Giuseppe Sanmartino, becoming one of his most noted pupils. Nevertheless, the exclusive role assumed by Luigi Vanvitelli, even in the production of statuary, did not permit the participation of Viva, or of other Neapolitan sculptors even more gifted, on the important building and decoration of the royal palace at Caserta then in progress. His prolific work, produced in a career of more than 50 years, was frequently monotonous. He did not succeed in developing beyond a well-mannered decorativeness, derived from the period in which he had been trained. His work often fell into a formal lack of precision and, especially in the larger pieces, he did not succeed in overcoming a dry echo of the Antique. With the exception of the *Angels Bearing Torches* for the high altar of S Paolo Maggiore in Naples, executed in 1776 to the designs of Ferdinando Fuga, and of the vigorous images of *Sobriety* and *Modesty*, executed in stucco in 1781 for the Neapolitan church of the Annunziata, his work is somewhat facile.

In 1778 Viva completed the high altar for the Neapolitan church of S Maria di Portosalvo, where in 1806 he added the two sculptures depicting *St Peter* and *St Paul*. In 1779 he executed the *Faith* and *Hope* for Lecce Cathedral, commissioned by the Bishop Sozi-Carafa, and in which he was assisted by his brother Giacomo. In 1780 he was commissioned to make the *Four Evangelists* for the Neapolitan church of S Giovanni dei Pappacoda, which were finished some years later. In 1798 he was paid for the enormous group in stucco depicting the *Trinity*, placed in the arch between the presbytery and the oratory in the church of the Pellegrini in Naples. To the last years of the 18th century can be assigned two figures wearing veils: a *Virtue* (Naples, Mus. N. S Martino) and an *Allegory* (Pignataro Maggiore, nr Caserta, Chiesa Madre), which can be linked stylistically to the *Allegories* made by Viva in 1786 for the altar of S Giorgio Maggiore in Naples. The sculptor also executed a number of portraits for funeral monuments: in 1779 that of *Francesca Maria Spinelli de Cardenas* (Naples, S Caterina a Formello), in 1787 that of *Baldassarre Cito* (Naples, S Chiara), in 1790 that of *Giovan Battista Albertino* (Naples, SS Severino e Sossio) and in 1799 that of *Cardinal Giuseppe Maria Zurlo* (Naples, S Paolo Maggiore). Viva was also a restorer of ancient marbles. In addition certain monograms recently discovered confirm his activity as the modeller of figures in nativity scenes. In 1806 he presented a petition to Joseph Bonaparte, King of Naples, to become the sculpture teacher at the Accademia di Belle Arti in Naples but was unsuccessful.

BIBLIOGRAPHY
Thieme–Becker
C. Padiglione: *La biblioteca del Museo Nazionale della Certosa di S Martino ed i suoi manoscritti* (Naples, 1876)
G. Borrelli: *Il presepe napoletano* (Rome, 1970)
C. Garzya: *Interni neoclassici a Napoli* (Naples, 1978)
E. Catello: 'Il presepe alla mostra della Civiltà del settecento a Napoli', *Napoli Nob.*, 3rd ser., xix (1980), pp. 117–26
T. Fittipaldi: *La scultura napoletana del '700* (Naples, 1980)
E. Catello: 'Scultura napoletana del settecento in Puglia', *Napoli Nob.*, 3rd ser., xx (1981), pp. 39–48

GIAN GIOTTO BORRELLI

Vivaceta Rupio, Fermín (*b* Santiago, Chile, 1829; *d* Valparaíso, 1890). Chilean architect. His father was unknown and his mother a humble washerwoman who made great efforts in order to educate her son. He began working for a cabinetmaker at the age of 13 and then joined a drawing class for craftsmen at the Instituto Nacional, Santiago. There were few professional architects in Chile at that time, and he was commissioned at the age of 18 to design the Casa de Orates building. Vivaceta joined the first architecture class of the Frenchman Claude François Brunet-Debaines (1788–1855), who had been contracted by the Chilean government. His fellow pupil Ricardo Brown and he were the first architects to be trained in Chile. As a result of Vivaceta's assiduity and determination, he was selected by Brunet-Debaines to complete outstanding works when the contract expired. Working in the 19th-century Neo-classical tradition, with some gestures towards the neo-Gothic, Vivaceta rebuilt the towers of several Santiago churches, and built several private houses and the church and convent of Carmen Alto. He contributed to repairs to the cathedral of Santiago and collaborated with Brunet-Debaines on plans for the Portal Tagle, Casa McClure and the Iglesia de la Veracruz (1852) and with Lucien Ambrose Hénault (1790–1880) on the Universidad de Chile (1863; for illustration *see* SANTIAGO DE CHILE), all in Santiago. Outstanding in his social work for labourers and artisans, in 1862 he founded the first mutual benefit society in Chile, the Unión de Artesanos and also the Escuela Nocturna de Artesanos to provide training in the trades and to foster a spirit of fraternity.

BIBLIOGRAPHY

E. Pereira Salas: *La arquitectura chilena en el siglo XIX* (Santiago, n.d.)
R. A. Méndez Brignardello: *La construcción de la arquitectura: Chile, 1500–1970* (Santiago, 1983)

RAMÓN MÉNDEZ ALFONSO

Vivant-Denon, Dominique. *See* DENON, VIVANT.

Vivar, Juan Correa de. *See* CORREA DE VIVAR, JUAN.

Vivares, François [Francis] (*b* St Jean-du-Bruel, Aveyron, 11 July 1708; *d* London, 26 Nov 1780). French engraver and print publisher, active in England. He is considered to be one of the founders of the English school of landscape engraving. A Huguenot, he came to London in 1711 and learnt engraving with Joseph Wagner (1706–80). His earliest dated print is from 1739. He helped introduce the Rococo style into England as an engraver or publisher of ornament books *c*. 1740–60, for example his engraved plates for William De la Cour's *First Book of Ornament* (1741). Many of his landscape prints were after paintings by French and Dutch Old Masters, beginning with 11 plates for Arthur Pond's *Italian Landscapes* project (1741–6; London, BM), a 44-plate survey of the works of Gaspard Dughet and Claude Lorrain in British collections. Typical of his mature work is the print after Claude, *Great Annual Sacrifice at the Temple of Apollo on the Island of Delos* (1764; London, V&A; Vivarez, no. 3). He also engraved landscapes by English contemporaries and visiting foreign artists, for example Gainsborough (v 41, 42, 89) and Francesco Zuccarelli (v 55, 56). In 1743 he engraved one of Francis Hayman's Vauxhall Garden supper-box paintings, *The Fortune Teller, or Casting the Coffee Grounds*. At this time he began a working partnership with the painter Thomas Smith of Derby (*fl* 1743; *d* 1767), which resulted in 23 prints, Vivares's largest group after a single artist, most dating from the 1740s. Their *View of the Upper Works at Coalbrookdale* and *South West Prospect of Coalbrookdale* (both 1758; London, Sci. Mus.) are the earliest surviving depictions of the most important site of the Industrial Revolution. In 1749 Vivares opened a print shop in Soho. In 1753 he published *A View in Craven, Yorkshire* and *A View of Amazing Rock in Craven, Yorkshire* (London, V&A) after his own designs, but he seems never to have repeated the experiment. In the 1750s and 1760s he engraved and published decorative borders for use in print rooms, in which prints surrounded by printed borders were stuck directly on to the walls. He exhibited landscape prints after Claude and Vernet with the Society of Artists of Great Britain in 1766 and 1768. At the time of his death he was working on a print of Claude's *The Enchanted Castle* (etching, London, V&A; v 6), later completed by William Wollett. The Fitzwilliam Museum, Cambridge, holds two albums (compiled *c*. 1812) of Vivares's work.

On François Vivares's death his son and pupil Thomas Vivares (*c*. 1735–1805) carried on his business. In 1764 Thomas won a prize from the Society of Arts for two engravings and went on to engrave plates for Robert and James Adam's *Works in Architecture* (1773, v 9; 1779). He exhibited paintings at the Royal Academy in the 1780s, and *Six Landscapes from Nature* (1800; London, V&A) were drawn and engraved by him.

BIBLIOGRAPHY

H. Vivarez: *Pro domo mea: Un Artiste graveur au XVIIIe siècle, François Vivares* (Lille, 1904) [with oeuvre catalogues for F. Vivares and T. Vivares] [v]
T. F. Friedman: 'Two Eighteenth-century Catalogues of Ornamental Pattern Books', *Furn. Hist.*, xi (1975), pp. 66–75 [reprints *A Catalogue of Prints Ingraved by Francis Vivares* from *c*. 1760]
L. Lippincott: *Selling Art in Georgian London: The Rise of Arthur Pond* (London and New Haven, 1983)
S. Lambert: *The Image Multiplied: Five Centuries of Reproductions of Paintings and Drawings* (London, 1987) [discusses print rooms and illustrates Vivares's etched borders]
C. Archer: 'Festoons of Flowers...For Fitting Up Print Rooms', *Apollo*, cxxx (1989), pp. 386–91
E. Miller: 'Landscape Prints by Francis Vivares', *Prt Q.*, ix(1992), pp. 272–81

ELIZABETH MILLER

Vivar y de Mendoza, Rodrigo Diaz de. *See under* MENDOZA.

Vivarini. Italian family of painters. Descended from a family of glassworkers active in Murano, (1) Antonio Vivarini became prominent in Venetian painting *c*. 1440, producing many joint works with his brother-in-law GIOVANNI D'ALEMAGNA. Antonio also often collaborated with his younger brother (2) Bartolomeo Vivarini, and the family dynasty remained important until the death of Antonio's son (3) Alvise Vivarini.

Giovanni d'Alemagna must, as his various signatures show, have been of German origin, but he was completely integrated into the family workshop, and attempts by earlier art historians to attribute to him supposedly German elements in his joint works with Antonio seem misjudged. The question of northern influence on the works is not resolved. Giovanni's name often appears before that of Antonio in documents and signatures and his role in the workshop was surely an important one.

A major part of the workshop's production was of tiered polyptychs in elaborately carved Gothic frames made by a number of different wood-carvers but of similar design. Developed by Antonio and Giovanni, these were, in the 1440s, very fashionable in Venice, but the market for them continued in various provincial centres under Venetian influence—the Marches, Puglia and to a lesser extent Istria—until the 1470s, and in these areas the Vivarini workshop enjoyed a virtual monopoly, producing a large number of works, many of low quality and probably entirely by studio assistants. In the late 1480s and the

1490s Bartolomeo opened up a new market for such works in the small centres around Bergamo.

This element of mass-production should not obscure the creative originality of the family. Each had, at least for a while, a substantial degree of success in Venice and the Veneto. There are also certain iconographic and stylistic habits which continue across the shifts in style and make the fact that a work is by the Vivarini as apparent to a 20th-century viewer as it would have been to the client who commissioned it. Comparison with the Bellini family reveals that the Vivarini were less innovative both stylistically and iconographically.

BIBLIOGRAPHY
Thieme–Becker
J. Crowe and G. Cavalcaselle: *A History of Painting in North Italy*, i (London, 1871, rev. T. Borenius, 2/1912), pp. 17–71 [with Borenius's notes, good for basic research]
L. Testi: *Storia della pittura veneziana*, ii (Bergamo, 1915) [Antonio and Bartolomeo only; out of date but, in the absence of monographs, still useful for both artists]
R. Longhi: *Viatico per cinque secoli di pittura veneziana* (Florence, 1946), pp. 8–10 [perceptive notes on all three artists]
V. Moschini: *I Vivarini* (Milan, 1946)
B. Berenson: *Venetian School*, i (London, 1957), pp. 195–203 [not always reliable in distinguishing the late work of Antonio from Bartolomeo]
R. Pallucchini: 'I Vivarini', *Saggi & Mem. Stor. A.*, iv (1962) [whole issue, standard work with a cat. and a corpus of plates for all three artists]
F. Zeri: 'Antonio e Bartolomeo Vivarini: Il polittico del 1451 già in San Francesco a Padova', *Ant. Viva.*, xiv/4 (1975), pp. 3–10

(1) Antonio Vivarini (da Murano) (*fl* Venice, 1440; *d* between 1476 and 24 April 1484). Because of the collective nature of much Vivarini workshop activity, connoisseurs have remained unusually confused about Antonio's work, and attributions, particularly as regards his late work, are often misleading. After Giovanni d'Alemagna's death in 1450, Antonio probably continued to produce independent works but also collaborated with (2) Bartolomeo; from *c.* 1460 he ran the workshop alone.

1. EARLY WORK AND COLLABORATION WITH GIOVANNI D'ALEMAGNA, 1440–50. Antonio's first work, a signed polyptych (1440; Parenzo, S Eufrasiana), reveals the originality of his style *vis-à-vis* the Venetian Gothic of the preceding decades. The saints, who flank the Virgin and a Man of Sorrows on two tiers, are still Gothic in their generalized types but are fully realized as solids in space. The linear rhythms of Gothic art are almost entirely absent, and the Virgin in particular is conceived, with almost Byzantine frontality, as a simple, cone-like solid, complementing the plain apsidal architecture of the throne on which she sits. This style, which Longhi compared with Masolino's, is already a long way from the lyricism and decorative linearity of Jacobello del Fiore, but its origins are not easy to determine. Longhi's comparison is useful insofar as it situates Antonio in relation to the fully fledged Renaissance style of, for example, Masaccio or Donatello; nothing is known of Masolino's work in the Veneto, so his actual influence, if any, cannot be quantified.

Antonio's collaboration with Giovanni d'Alemagna is first recorded in 1441, and between then and Giovanni's death in 1450 they executed a series of major commissions in Venice and Padua which are probably the most original Venetian paintings of the decade. These works are so homogeneous in style that it is as fruitless as it is alien to their workshop practice to try to distinguish their hands.

However, the signature 'Johannes' on a *St Jerome* (1444; Baltimore, MD, Walters A.G.) provides a basis for considering Giovanni's own style, which was flatter and more decorative than that of Antonio and without his overriding drive towards three-dimensional form. On this basis it is probably right to associate with Antonio the more realistic tendencies in their joint style and with Giovanni the more decorative tendencies. This is in no way to diminish Giovanni's share or the leading role he played in the workshop itself, as it must have been in large part to their decorative splendour that their Venetian works of the 1440s owed their success.

This can be seen in the three reliquary altars (1443) executed for the Benedictine convent of S Zaccaria, Venice (now the chapel of S Tarasio attached to the rebuilt church), which, with Castagno's apse frescoes of the year before, remain *in situ*. The commission, because of the convent's ceremonial connections with the Doge, was one of major importance. The altars, which are signed by their carvers as well, are Gothic complexes of great elaboration in which decorative and narrative carvings play as important a part as the paintings. The painted saints are of exceptional richness, the bright colours of their robes enhanced by damasked surfaces in stamped gold and embossed accessories in gilded gesso. However, they are not formally subsumed into the decorative rhythms of the altarpiece as a whole. Each panel opens up a consistent space behind the frame, and within it the saints are presented as palpable, three-dimensional presences, consistently illuminated by a real light. They are represented as if standing on plinths, an honorific device common in sculpture but in Venetian painting peculiar to the Vivarini circle, but they do so in such a relaxed way that their human reality is paradoxically enhanced. They are still types rather than individuals, but the clear purpose of the style is to present them as physical presences to the worshipper. A similar intention is evident in the *Coronation of the Virgin* (1444; Venice, S Pantalon), where the vault of heaven is conceived as a semicircular apse crowded with, and made up from, figures.

In the great tripartite canvas for the Scuola della Carità (3.44×4.77 m, 1446; Venice, Accad.; for illustration *see* VENICE, fig. 30) the Virgin and Child, accompanied by the four fathers of the Church, are set in a unified space, half throne, half crenellated courtyard, enthroned in the former Sala dell'Albergo immediately above the heads of the governors of the Scuola. The Virgin is of a more courtly type than the figure in the Parenzo Polyptych, probably a result of the demands of the Scuola rather than of stylistic development, and a particular feature is the extensive use of yellow paint hatched with black to simulate gold fictively. This skill, which appears to have been specific to the Vivarini workshop, may well have been invented by them and is perhaps associated with Giovanni, as it largely disappeared after his death. Its cheapness in comparison with gold leaf must have been an important factor in enabling the Vivarini to create in the 1440s works that embody the aristocratic values of the neighbouring north Italian courts in a manner economically as well as stylistically satisfactory to Venetian patrons.

The stylistic range of the joint workshop, even within a single work, was, however, considerable, and different types of commission produced different results. In the polyptych for the Franciscan Observants at Padua (1447; Prague, N.G.; see fig.) the saints, who flank a central *Nativity*, still stand on plinths but they are more active and individualized than in the more courtly Venetian works. *St Bartholomew*, with his firm, natural stance and toga-like robe is directly influenced by Castagno's saints on the vault of S Tarasio. The realism and humanity of these figures suggest a considerable understanding of the values of Tuscan 15th-century art, while by contrast the flatter and more decorative style of the central *Nativity*, like a comparable *Adoration of the Magi* (Berlin, Gemäldegal.), is close to the decorative Late Gothic style. These two works may well have been influenced by German art.

Other narrative scenes of the *Life of St Monica*, the fragments of an altar from S Stefano, Venice, signed by the brothers-in-law (dispersed, panels in Detroit, MI, Inst. A.; Venice, Accad.), show a more straightforward narrative style, anecdotal in the Venetian tradition, with simple, empirically constructed settings. There is no concern with linear perspective or with the innovative, complex narrative modes found in Jacopo Bellini's sketchbooks. In four elaborate scenes of female martyrdoms (two in Bergamo,

Gal. Accad. Carrara; Bassano del Grappa, Mus. Civ.; New York, Met.) *all'antica* details are prominent. These details are in the style of a Late Gothic sketchbook and were probably demanded by the patron. The scenes are very decorative, the bright colours of the buildings negating the perspective.

In 1447 Antonio Vivarini and Giovanni d'Alemagna registered in the Paduan painters' guild, and in 1448 they were commissioned by the heirs of Antonio Ovetari to paint half of his chapel in the Eremitani, Padua, alongside Niccolò Pizzolo and Mantegna. In the event, only the vault of the chapel was executed (destr. 1945), and it included elaborate foliated decoration in simulated gold; the Evangelists demonstrated the same physical and human values as the saints in the Prague Polyptych, and the nude angels were related to similar figures painted by Castagno on the S Tarasio vault. Nonetheless, the vault as a whole must have looked out of date in comparison with Mantegna's scenes on the walls. On Giovanni d'Alemagna's death, Antonio Vivarini abandoned the commission and returned to Venice, where he executed a number of polyptychs in collaboration with Bartolomeo (*see* §(2) below).

Antonio Vivarini and Giovanni d'Alemagna: polyptych with the *Nativity* and *Saints*, tempera, centre panel 1.31×0.60 m, side panels 1.14×0.31 m, 1447 (Prague, National Gallery)

2. AFTER 1450. Alongside his extensive work with Bartolomeo, Antonio probably executed a number of independent works just before or after Giovanni's death. Among these is the small-scale polyptych for the Benedictine abbey of Praglia in the Euganean hills (?c. 1448; Milan, Brera) where the *Virgin and Child* are softened and humanized variants of the much earlier figures in the Parenzo Polyptych and the saints are of great dignity, each embodying in pose and expression his own kind of authority.

This style is continued on a grand scale in the nearly life-size *St Peter* and *St Paul* who formed, with a *St Ursula and her Virgins* (all Brescia, Nuo. Semin. Dioc.), part of a polyptych for a church in Brescia. Usually dated early, these panels are more likely to be from the 1450s, as the saints are close to another pair (Prague, N.G.) which probably formed part of the high altarpiece of S Francesco in Padua signed by the brothers in 1451, and show Antonio's own style at its most mature. The figures stand directly on the ground without plinths; gold is used only in the background and for a limited number of suitable details; and the colours, strong in the male saints and soft for the virgins, are gently modelled by a palpable light which explores texture as well as form. In the *St Ursula* scene, the virgins, clustering around the saint, disappear one behind another into the distance until only the tops of their heads show, a device of considerable optical subtlety which suggests their numbers—11,000 according to the legend. This sophisticated style cannot easily be categorized as either Gothic or Renaissance, but exists between the two. Antonio's means belong optically and psychologically to a new age but his ends are still directed primarily towards devotion.

That in the mid-1450s Antonio was still held in high esteem in Venice is shown by the commission of 1456, apparently without Bartolomeo, to paint a high altar for the church of the Carità. This is lost, unless the *Virgin and Child Enthroned* (Milan, Mus. Poldi Pezzoli), surely of this period, was its centre. The exquisite and intimate *Virgin and Child* (Venice, Accad.) is also best dated at this time.

This style was continued, with an increasing sharpness of outline, in the elegant male saints on the lower tier of a polyptych (Rome, Vatican, Pin.) for the Confraternity of St Anthony Abbot at Pesaro, signed and dated by Antonio in 1464. The figures on the upper tier of the polyptych are, however, by a different and inferior hand; the distinction is important, because this hand seems also to have executed all the surviving parts of the last dated work from Antonio's studio, the polyptych for S Maria Vetere, Andria, of 1467 (dispersed; panels in Bari, Pin. Prov.; Andria, S Maria Vetere). Unfortunately, this work has been taken as a measure for Antonio's last style and a number of inferior workshop pieces, for example *SS John the Baptist and Augustine* (Venice, Accad.), have wrongly been seen as representative of his own late work. Conversely, others of higher quality have been wrongly attributed to Bartolomeo (Steer, 1982).

BIBLIOGRAPHY

G. Fogolari: 'La chiesa di Sta Maria della Carità di Venezia: Documenti inediti di Bartolomeo Bon, di Antonio Vivarini, di Ercole del Fiore e di altri artisti', *Archv Ven.-Trident.*, v (1924), pp. 77–9

R. Longhi: 'Una eventualità relativa a una Madonna di Antonio Vivarini', *Paragone*, xi/123 (1960), pp. 32–3

F. d'Arcais: *Antonio Vivarini* (Milan, 1966)

F. Zeri: 'Un "San Gerolamo" firmato di Giovanni d'Alemagna', *Studi di storia dell'arte in onore di Antonio Morassi* (Venice, 1971), pp. 40–49

J. Steer: *Alvise Vivarini: His Art and Influence* (Cambridge, 1982) [monograph with cat. of accepted and rejected works; full pls]; review by J. Fletcher in *Burl. Mag.*, cxxv (1983), pp. 99–101, and by A. de Nicolo Salamazò in *A. Ven.*, xxxix (1985), pp. 41–6

(2) Bartolomeo Vivarini (*fl* Venice, *c.* 1440; *d* after 1500). Brother of (1) Antonio Vivarini. The date of 1432, sometimes given for his birth, is derived from an inscription, almost certainly faked, on an inferior *Virgin and Child* (ex-Hugh Lane col., untraced). Bartolomeo was still alive in 1500 when he judged an altarpiece in S Marco, Venice (Paoletti, 1893), with his brother and the Bellini.

Bartolomeo's style was, from the beginning, distinct from that of his brother. He appears to have been trained in Padua in the orbit of Squarcione, probably in the late 1440s. Line, wiry and in his later works omnipresent, dominated his conception of form, which never showed Antonio's sense of physical substance and became increasingly schematic.

Bartolomeo emerged in 1450 when he signed jointly with Antonio a large-scale polyptych (Bologna, Pin. N.) for the Certosa di Bologna, a commission of some importance as it was given by Nicholas V in honour of Cardinal Albergati. A second joint polyptych, dated 1451 (fragments Prague, N.G.), was for the high altar of the Observant Franciscans in Padua. It is always assumed that Bartolomeo joined the family workshop because of Giovanni d'Alemagna's death, but, given the importance of these commissions, concurrent with the Ovetari frescoes, it is likely that a third partner would have been needed.

While it is probably impossible to distinguish the hands of the brothers in the Bologna Polyptych, since they may both have worked on the same figure and at least one studio hand is also involved, the type of the central *Virgin and Child*, with the Child asleep on the Virgin's lap and her hands joined over him in prayer, is repeated by Bartolomeo in several depictions of the Virgin in the following decade. From the very beginning, therefore, Bartolomeo's role in the production of such polyptychs would seem to have been substantial, even dominant.

Most of these polyptychs were done for provincial sites in the Marches and Puglia and vary greatly in quality; those in Osimo (Pal. Mun.) and Corridonia (Mus. Coll. SS Pietro & Paolo), for example, are probably entirely by assistants. The brothers' last jointly signed and dated work (1458; Arbe, S Eufemia) is typical of the genre. The dominant hand is again that of Bartolomeo, who seems to have painted both the central *St Bernardino* and the *Virgin and Child* above. At the sides, a continuous ground plane unites the saints, except where, as with St Christopher, tradition demanded a miniature landscape. The background is still gold.

Bartolomeo's first dated independent work is the *St Giovanni Capistrano* (1459; Paris, Louvre) and thereafter his practice seems to have developed rapidly. During the 1460s and 1470s he was regularly employed on commissions in Venice itself, almost all of them for altarpieces. In 1467 he was commissioned with Andrea da Murano to paint two canvases (destr.) for the Scuola di S Marco, but this is the only occasion in which he is recorded tackling this kind of work and it is evident that his subject-matter was limited; there are no portraits and no signs in his works of humanist or intellectual interests.

Nevertheless, from 1464 until the late 1470s Bartolomeo enjoyed great success in Venice, painting a series of works for major altars in the Certosa di S Andrea, the Frari and SS Giovanni e Paolo, often under the patronage of leading Venetian families such as the Morosini and the Corner, as well as producing smaller but high-quality works for the *scuole piccole* and for parish churches. In these, Bartolomeo brought the Vivarini altarpiece up to date, gradually replacing Gothic frames with Renaissance ones and sometimes gold backgrounds with sky. This last development is by no means consistent, however, and it was surely partly to his adaptability that Bartolomeo owed his success. At this period he had cornered the market for altarpieces in Venice, apparently excluding even the Bellini, before Giovanni's triptych for the church of the Frari (1488; *in situ*).

Bartolomeo also continued to work in the Marches and Puglia. The *Virgin and Child Enthroned with Four Saints* (1476; Bari, S Nicola) updates the arrangement of Antonio's tripartite canvas for the Scuola della Carità, placing the figures in a crenellated courtyard with an evening sky behind and setting the whole in a Renaissance frame. The reference to Antonio's work is unmistakable, and it is a nice point whether Bartolomeo was simply copying his brother or fulfilling a patron's demand for a similar kind of work.

The saints in Bartolomeo's best altarpieces are more psychologically intense than those of his brother and strongly characterized as contrasting types. Contemplative rather than dramatic, they nonetheless give out a sense of nervous interior life, which adds a new dimension to the devotional ends they are designed to serve. This is apparent in the Ca' Morosini Polyptych (1464; Venice, Accad.), in which the delicately outlined and subtly coloured *St John the Baptist* (see fig.) is an example of Bartolomeo's work at its most refined.

This style is developed to produce the powerful saints in the works of the 1470s, who, often seen from a low viewpoint, tower over the worshipper. Examples are the surviving figures from the polyptych of *St Augustine* (1473; Venice, SS Giovanni e Paolo)—which, particularly in the way they are lit, reveal the influence of Giovanni Bellini's *St Vincent Ferrer* altarpiece in the same church—and the paired saints in the *St Mark* triptych (1474; Venice, Frari). Although still in a Late Gothic frame, this shows Bartolomeo's style at its most advanced, with St Mark seated on an early Renaissance throne, angels with swags and the diagonally grouped saints standing out against the sky and set in a continuous space. These saints are psychologically alive and their common mood gives unity to the altarpiece.

By contrast, in the polyptych for the Arte dei Tagliapietra (1477; Venice, Accad.), the saints, although strongly characterized and on a continuous ground plane, are still placed in separate compartments against a gold ground. Local colour is also strong and one guesses that Bartolomeo was responding to the demands of the stonecutters for a traditional polyptych in bright colours.

Bartolomeo Vivarini: *St John the Baptist*, tempera on panel, 1.08×0.36 m, from the Ca' Morosini Polyptych, 1464 (Venice, Galleria dell'Accademia)

During the mid-1470s, the period of his greatest success, Bartolomeo also painted an important and original *Sacra conversazione* (1475; ex-Certosa di Padua; Lussingrande, S Antonio Abate) in which saints and angels, with God the Father above, surround the Virgin and Child set in a landscape. The style of this work appears, perhaps because of its Paduan provenance, to be more linear than in the Venetian altarpieces and the relationship between Bartolomeo and Crivelli is at its strongest. During the 1480s, however, Bartolomeo's works became increasingly linear and schematic and their quality declined, coinciding with a decline in his Venetian practice. He developed a new area of patronage in the small towns and villages around Bergamo, which vied with one another in the scale and splendour of the altarpieces that they commissioned from him (see Griffiths). The last Bergamask altarpieces (e.g. Bergamo, Gal. Accad. Carrara; Milan, Bib. Ambrosiana) are, for all their gilded splendour, distressingly arid; even the colours have lost their edge.

As well as altarpieces, Bartolomeo painted a large number of pictures of the Virgin and Child, mostly, after an initial Paduan phase, very like each other. He also painted a few smaller devotional images, such as the small *Sacra conversazione* (1465; Naples, Capodimonte) in which the Virgin is seated on a Renaissance-style throne and courtly elements from Giovanni d'Alemagna and Antonio are fused with Paduan features. It was perhaps, given its comparatively small scale, for private devotion.

BIBLIOGRAPHY

P. Paoletti: *L'architettura e la scultura del rinascimento in Venezia* (Venice, 1893), pp. 105, 107

A. Griffiths: *Bartolomeo Vivarini* (MA thesis, Courtauld Inst., U. London, 1976) [useful on patronage, the market for Vivarini paintings outside Venice and frame makers]

(3) Alvise [Luigi] **Vivarini** (*b* 1442–53; *d* 1503–05). Son of (1) Antonio Vivarini. He is first mentioned in the wills of his mother in 1457 and 1458. He emerged as an independent artist in 1476 when he was enrolled in the Scuola della Carità, Venice, and signed a polyptych (Urbino, Pal. Ducale) for the Franciscans of Montefiorentino in the Marches. In 1488, conscious of the family prestige, he petitioned to work alongside the Bellini in the Sala del Gran Consiglio of the Doge's Palace. He was allotted three canvases, but at his death two were incomplete and one only begun. Vasari mentioned these historical scenes (destr. 1577) and also referred to him as the 'unhappy Vivarini', confirming an impression, conveyed in documents, that he became ill in his last years. Perhaps for this reason he died poor and in debt.

Alvise's artistic personality was more pronounced than that of his uncle. He was aware of the work of the more advanced artists, particularly sculptors, and strove to keep his own art up to date. His style was formed under the influence of both his uncle and his father, but from the first he learnt from the work of Giovanni Bellini. There are, however, no literary references to him (Fletcher, 1983) and no known humanist connections such as the Bellini family enjoyed. In the Montefiorentino Polyptych, which has a traditional Vivarini Gothic frame, the Virgin with the Child sleeping on her lap are types taken directly from his uncle. However, they are realized with a sense of substance as solid forms in space. As in Giovanni Bellini's *St Vincent Ferrer* altarpiece (Venice, SS Giovanni e Paolo), light is reflected back from the smooth surfaces of the forms and acts as a spiritual metaphor. The saints, particularly St John, are informed by a new principle of dramatic expression conveyed through movement.

Alvise's range was more extensive than that of his father and uncle. The tiny *St Jerome* (Washington, DC, N.G.A.) is a personal variation on a Bellinesque invention, the saint in a landscape with an emotive light effect, and landscape also plays an important part in his *Christ Carrying the Cross* (Venice, SS Giovanni e Paolo), probably a banner, in which a full-length Christ pathetically drags his cross through an arid landscape. Alvise also contributed, with Giovanni Bellini and Lazzaro Bastiani, to the narrative scenes decorating the Scuola di S Girolamo; his canvas known only from a tiny engraving suggests that he made a significant contribution to the development of such painting (Steer, 1982, p. 112).

In the 1480s Alvise responded strongly to the influence of Antonello da Messina, as can be seen in his *Virgin and Child Enthroned* (1483; Barletta, S Andrea). The linear qualities of the 1470s have been replaced by a broader, more volumetric style, in which light alone defines and models the forms, simplifying them as in Antonello's works to shining solids of great purity. Through this formal perfection, the traditional image is given for the worshipper a fresh spiritual meaning.

During the same decade Alvise made important contributions to the *Sacra conversazione*. In his first treatment of the subject, for S Francesco, Treviso (1480; Venice, Accad.), the horizontal format and the enclosed interior space are in the family tradition, but Alvise's understanding of Renaissance principles is apparent in the certainty of

1. Alvise Vivarini: *Risen Christ*, tempera on panel, 1.45×0.76 m, 1498 (Venice, S Giovanni in Bragora)

the spatial construction and the sculptural grouping of the figures, who exist with absolute assurance as solids in space. Their quiet gestures—the hands were studied from life on a sheet of drawings (Paris, Fond. Custodia, Inst. Néer.)—give a muted eloquence to the scene, and an evening light endows it with a poetic quality. The essence of the subject, the intersection of the human and divine in a moment of contemplation, is perfectly realized.

Alvise's second treatment of the subject was a full-scale, round-topped altarpiece of the *Virgin and Child Enthroned with Saints* (Berlin, Kaiser-Friedrich Mus., destr.) for S Maria dei Battuti, Belluno. The architectural setting was continuous with the frame of the painting and stylistically close to Codussi's architecture. From a rediscovered list (Lucco) it can probably be dated 1486, but whether in enthroning the Madonna under a golden dome it followed the form of Antonello's lost S Cassiano Altar or was a pioneering work remains unresolved. It also shows the influence of the wall tombs of Pietro Lombardo and Antonio Rizzo.

Alvise does not appear to have worked much in Venice before 1488, but from the 1490s on he received varied and important commissions, taking part, as did Cima, in the refurbishing of S Giovanni in Bragora, painting a banner for the Scuola di S Marco and beginning a large-scale altarpiece in the Frari (*in situ*) for the Milanese *scuola*, completed after his death by Basaiti.

Alvise's *Risen Christ* (1498; Venice, S Giovanni in Bragora; see fig. 1) is a fine example of his late work, showing an increasing use of movement as a means of dramatic expression; one notes the spiralling upward movement of Christ and the terrified flight of the soldiers. The signed and dated *Virgin and Child with SS Jerome, Mary Magdalene and a Saint Bishop* (1500; Amiens, Mus. Picardie), formerly attributed to Marco Basaiti by Berenson, shows a contemplative subject being turned into a dramatic dialogue. In these moves towards a more dynamic and dramatic style he anticipated the artists of the early 16th century, although how far he actually influenced them, as argued by Steer (1982), remains a matter of debate. Berenson's high opinion of Alvise's significance was based on the attribution to him of a *St Giustina* (Milan, Bagatti-Valsecchi priv. col.), which is by Giovanni Bellini. However, Gilbert's (1956) view that the original qualities in his late works were due to assistants, notably Jacopo dei Barberi, is misjudged.

Alvise also practised as a portrait painter, closely following Antonello da Messina, although with a more forthright approach to both appearance and personality. A *Portrait of a Middle-aged Man* (1497; London, N.G.; see fig. 2) develops the static portrait bust familiar in Messina's work by showing the sitter's hand and emphasizing the turn of the body. In this it prepares the way for the more dynamic portraiture of the 16th century.

BIBLIOGRAPHY

G. Vasari: *Vite* (1550, rev. 2/1568); ed. G. Milanesi (1878–85), iii, pp. 158–9

B. Berenson: *Lorenzo Lotto: An Essay in Constructive Art Criticism* (London, 1895, rev. 2/1905) [important historiographically but out of date]

C. Gilbert: 'Alvise e compagni', *Scritti in onore di Lionello Venturi*, i (Rome, 1956), pp. 277–308 [presents a view of Alvise's late work challenged by Steer, 1982]

J. Steer: 'Some Influences from Alvise Vivarini in the Art of Giorgione', *Burl. Mag.*, ciii (1961), pp. 220–25 [controversial]

R. Longhi: 'Ritorni e progressi su Alvise', *Paragone*, xx/1 (1969), pp. 38–42 [new attributions to Alvise; some questioned by Steer, 1982]

F. Zeri: 'Primazie di Alvise Vivarini', *Ant. Viva*, xiv/2 (1975), pp. 3–8

——: 'Aggiunta ad Alvise Vivarini', *Ant. Viva*, xv/1 (1976), pp. 3–5

M. Lucco: 'Due problemi antonelliani', *Antol. B.A.*, iii (1979), pp. 27–33 [attribution to Alvise of an *Assumption of the Virgin* at Noale]

P. Humfrey: 'Cima da Conegliano, Sebastiano Mariani and Alvise Vivarini at the East End of S Giovanni in Bragora', *A. Bull.*, xxxiv (1980), pp. 350–63

J. Steer: *Alvise Vivarini: His Art and Influence* (Cambridge, 1982) [monograph with cat. of accepted and rejected works; full plates]; review by J. Fletcher in *Burl. Mag.*, cxxv (1983), pp. 99–101, and by A. de Nicolo Salmazò in *A. Ven.*, xxxvii (1983), pp. 248–50

P. Humfrey: 'The Life of St Jerome Cycle from the Scuola di San Gerolamo in Cannaregio', *A. Ven.*, xxxix (1985), pp. 41–6

JOHN STEER

2. Alvise Vivarini: *Portrait of a Middle-aged Man*, oil on panel, 622×470 mm, 1497 (London, National Gallery)

Viviani, Antonio [il Sordo] (*b* Urbino, 1560; *d* Urbino, 6 Dec 1620). Italian painter. He was a pupil of Federico Barocci and is first documented in 1581 in connection with his part in the decoration of the oratory of the SS Annunciata in Urbino. From 1585 to 1590 he went to Rome with his master to assist in painting the fresco decorations commissioned by Pope Sixtus V, in the Vatican Library, the Lateran Palace and the Scala Santa. He achieved some fame through the commission he received from Cardinal Cesare Baronio (1538–1607) to execute the frescoes in the chapel of St Barbara in S Gregorio Magno, Rome. These were finished after Viviani had visited Genoa to paint two altarpieces (untraced) in 1604. Around 1614 he moved back to Urbino and worked in the Marches until his death, for instance in Urbino Cathedral (*Annunciation*, *Crucifixion*), Ancona (*Virgin with Saints*, S Ciriaco) and Fabriano (*Annunciation*, oratory of the Gonfalone). Viviani imitated the style of his master Barocci and sometimes made complete copies (e.g. *Annunciation*, Nancy, Mus. B.-A.), though even here his considerable talent is evident. He sensitively interpreted Barocci's art and used a gentle, elegant style, though he sometimes destroyed the tonal balance of his works by placing pale, retiring colours next to strong dissonant ones. He had a brother, Ludovico Viviani (*d* 1649), who was also a painter.

BIBLIOGRAPHY
Thieme–Becker
Restauri nelle Marche (exh. cat., ed. P. Torrito; Urbino, Pal. Ducale, 1973)
A. Costamagna: 'Antonio Viviani, detto il sordo di Urbino', *Annu. Ist. Stor. A.*, (1974), pp. 237–303

RENATE MÖLLER

Vivien, Joseph (*b* Lyon, 1657; *d* Bonn, 5 Dec 1734). French painter and pastellist, active in Germany. He trained in Paris in 1672 with the painter François Bonnemers (1638–89), also attending the Académie Royale, where his oil painting the *Punishment of Adam and Eve* (untraced) won a second prize in 1678. Only in 1698 was he received (*reçu*) at the Académie, as a pastellist, on presentation of portraits of the sculptor *François Girardon* and of the architect *Robert de Cotte* (both Paris, Louvre; *see* PASTEL, fig. 1). Having been commissioned to execute a pastel *Self-portrait* (Florence, Uffizi) by Maximilian II Emanuel, Elector of Bavaria, in 1699, the following year he was appointed the Elector's principal court painter (*see* WITTELSBACH). He henceforth divided his time between Paris, the Elector's courts at Brussels and Munich, and the court of Maximilian Emanuel's son, Clemens August, Elector of Cologne, at Bonn.

In 1700 Vivien executed, presumably in Brussels, the first of a series of imposing portraits of Maximilian II Emanuel and his family. Like the portraits of *Girardon* and *de Cotte*, Vivien's first portrait of the Elector (pastel; Paris, Louvre) is very much in the formal spirit of the portraiture of the age of Louis XIV, as exemplified in the paintings of Hyacinthe Rigaud, which must have been Vivien's main inspiration. In 1701 the Elector returned to Munich, but from 1704 to 1715 he was in exile, first in the Netherlands and later in France. To mark his return to Munich in 1715, Vivien painted his most ambitious work, the oil painting *Maximilian II Emanuel Reunited with his Family* (1715–33; Munich, Alte Pin.), a work that combines portraiture with history painting. Apart from such formal works, Vivien also produced more intimate portraits in oils, including a late *Self-portrait* (1730; Munich, Alte Pin.), in which the artist's features and direct gaze are depicted with great realism, and portraits of the writer *François de la Mothe Fénelon* (*c.* 1713; Munich, Alte Pin.) and of *Clemens August, Elector of Cologne* (*c.* 1722; Brühl, Schloss Falkenlust). The latter, which depicts the sitter in a flowered robe and holding a cup of chocolate, adumbrates the easy informality of the Rococo portrait. Many of Vivien's portraits were engraved. In the generation between Robert Nanteuil and Rosalba Carriera he was the most important exponent of the art of the pastel portrait.

BIBLIOGRAPHY
H. Börsch-Supan: 'Joseph Vivien als Hofmaler der Wittelsbacher', *Münch. Jb. Bild. Kst*, 3rd ser., xiv (1963), pp. 129–212 [with cat.]
G. Monnier: *Pastels: XVIIe et XVIIIe siècles*, Paris, Louvre cat. (Paris, 1972), nos 14–20
J. J. Luna: 'Dos retratos al pastel de Vivien', *Archv Esp. A.*, l (1977), pp. 153–6

CATHRIN KLINGSÖHR-LE ROY

Vivin, Louis (*b* Hadol, nr Epinal, 27 July 1861; *d* Paris, 28 May 1936). French painter. He moved in 1880 to Paris, where he worked as an inspector for the French postal service. He led a calm and ordered existence, living for 47 years at the same lodgings in Montmartre and painting and drawing regularly, having been interested in art from an early age. On his retirement in 1923 he devoted himself full time to painting. Vivin's early works, often melancholy in mood, were landscapes and scenes of his native countryside, painted from memory and often with narrative elements. In visits to the Louvre he admired the detail of Meissonier's paintings, which he emulated in his own work by reference to sketches, illustrations, postcards and other ephemera. This extraordinary clutter, intertwining his life and art, astonished Wilhelm Uhde, who championed Vivin's paintings after seeing them exhibited in the open air at the foot of the Sacré-Coeur during the Foire aux Croûtes in 1925. Vivin's first one-man exhibition, at the Galerie des Quatre Chemins, was organized by Uhde in 1927.

The exclusive subject-matter of Vivin's later paintings, such as *Versailles* (undated; Paris, Möring priv. col., see Bihalji-Marin, p. 63), consisted of meticulously detailed buildings tirelessly recorded as accumulations of building blocks or paving stones in a flat, graphic style. Space is suggested not by means of perspective but by subdivisions of the surface into registers or receding planes, as in medieval paintings. In the 1930s he specialized in paintings of Parisian architectural landmarks such as Notre-Dame, the Palais de Justice, the Louvre, the Sacré-Coeur and the Moulin Rouge, in which he went even further in eliminating both changes of light and the movement of milling crowds; empty, almost monochromatic and based on the systematic repetition of a single element, they reflect the solitude, monotony and resignation of Vivin's daily life. Far from being exercises in realism, his paintings were thus metaphors of his introspective temperament. Inclusion of his works in the exhibition *Les Maîtres populaires de la réalité*, held in Paris in 1937, signalled the growth of his posthumous reputation. He is represented by 15 paintings in the Centre Pompidou in Paris.

BIBLIOGRAPHY
Les Maîtres populaires de la réalité (exh. cat., Paris, Salle Royale, 1937)
W. Uhde: *Fünf primitive Meister: Rousseau, Vivin, Bombois, Bauchant, Séraphine* (Zurich, 1947)
A. Jakovsky: *Louis Vivin, peintre de Paris* (Paris, 1953)
Bauchant, Bombois, Séraphine, Vivin (exh. cat., Basle, Ksthalle, 1956)
O. Bihalji-Marin: *Das naive Bild der Welt* (Cologne, 1959; Eng. trans. as *Modern Primitives: Masters of Naïve Paintings*, New York, 1959/R London, 1961)
Vivin: His Paris (exh. cat., New York, Perls Gals, 1971)
For further bibliography *see* NAIVE ART.

NADINE POUILLON

Vivio dell'Aquila, Giacomo (*b* L'Aquila; *fl* 1588–90). Italian priest, jurist and wax modeller. As a student in

Rome he became proficient in modelling lifelike reliefs in coloured wax on slate. His only recorded work (1588; untraced) was a model of Michelangelo's *Last Judgement* (1536–41; Rome, Vatican, Sistine Chapel), which was presented to Pope Sixtus V. According to Vivio's published description, there were 146 images set in a frame reminiscent of the Sistine Chapel Ceiling. The work comprised Old and New Testaments scenes, with prophets, sibyls, saints and Christian heroes, including Charlemagne, Christopher Columbus (1451–1506) and Philip II, King of Spain; the central field had a portrait of *Michelangelo* and Vivio included a self-portrait at one end. The work was much admired in its day: it earned its inventor Roman citizenship and the Roman Senate considered buying it for display on the Capitol.

WRITINGS

Discorso sopra la mirabil opera di basso rilievo di cera stuccata con colori scolpita in pietra negra colle storie del Vecchio e del Nuovo Testamento (Rome, 1590)

BIBLIOGRAPHY

S. Massonio: *Memorie degli uomini celebri dell'Aquila* (L'Aquila, 1594), p. 152

G. Pansa: 'Giacomo Vivio dell'Aquila e i suoi bassi rilievi in cera stuccata', *L'Arte*, ix (1906), pp. 449–52

R. Lightbown: 'Le cere artistiche del cinquecento', *A. Illus.*, iii (1970), pp. 46–56

JANET SOUTHORN

Vivonne d'Angennes, Catherine de, Marquise de Rambouillet. *See* RAMBOUILLET.

Vix. Site of burial mound near the Iron Age settlement of Mont Lassois in the Côte d'Or département, France. The

Vix, bronze krater, h. 1.64 m, *c.* 500 BC (Châtillon-sur-Seine, Musée Archéologique)

tumulus of Vix has been dated by its contents to *c.* 500 BC. It was excavated in 1953 by René Joffroy after part of its stonework was revealed during agricultural activity. Originally 42 m in diameter and 5–6 m high, the circular mound of stone covered a timber-lined grave dug into the ground and slightly trapezoidal in shape (3.10×2.75 m). Changes to the water-level of the River Seine had rendered the grave partly waterlogged, hampering excavation; nevertheless, it was possible to plan carefully its spectacular contents (all works mentioned in this article, except the harness and the cloth edged with roundels, are in Châtillon-sur-Seine, Mus. Archéol.).

The burial was of a woman aged 30–35, found lying on her back across the remains of a four-wheeled vehicle. The wheels had been removed and propped against the east wall of the chamber, and the metal decorations from the vehicle, the harness and a goad (?or sceptre) lay scattered over the eastern half of the chamber. The whole of this area, including the corpse, appears to have been covered with a cloth edged with roundels, from which pigments seen on the floor during excavation may have come. The woman wore, or was buried with, a considerable amount of jewellery, comprising bronze leg-rings, a bronze torque (heavy neck-ring) found in the waist region, three bracelets of schist and two of amber, a necklace of stone and amber beads and seven brooches (five of bronze and two of iron), some with gold, amber or coral inlay. The most spectacular personal ornament was a gold ring, found around the skull and originally described as a diadem but now generally considered to be a torque. This ring weighs 480 g and is slightly oval in shape, ending in lions' feet with highly decorated globular terminals. A little gold figure of Pegasus adorns the joining-point of each terminal and lion's foot. Without exact parallel anywhere, this piece is thought by some to be of Iberian manufacture, while others believe it to have been eastern European in origin.

In the western half of the grave was the astonishing collection of imported luxury objects that has made it famous. The north-western corner contained an enormous, highly decorated bronze krater (see fig.), 1.64 m high, weighing 208.6 kg and with a capacity of 1200 litres. The heavy handles with gorgons' heads measure 0.5 m high and weigh 45 kg. The neck is decorated with a frieze of small chariots with drivers and teams of four horses, accompanied by foot soldiers. During restoration it was discovered that each of the 23 elements in the frieze had a Greek letter or sign scratched on the back, with a corresponding sign on the neck, so that each piece could be mounted in the right place. The krater had a bowl-like cover with a female statuette in the centre. It was probably made in workshops in Sparta and Tarento (anc. Taras), but it is not known how it was transported to central France. There was also a silver bowl, a bronze beaked wine flagon and two Attic cups, one plain black and one of Black-figure ware.

BIBLIOGRAPHY

R. Joffroy: *Le Trésor de Vix* (Vendôme, 1954)

——: *L'Oppidum de Vix et la civilisation halstattienne finale dans l'est de la France* (Paris, 1960)

SARA CHAMPION

Vizivàros. *See under* BUDAPEST, §I, 2.

Vkhutemas [Vysshiye (Gosudarstvennyye) Khudozhest-venno-Tekhnicheskiye Masterskiye; Rus.: Higher (State) Artistic and Technical Workshops]. Soviet school of art and architecture, active in Moscow from 1920 to 1930. It was established by state decree on 29 November 1920, on the basis of the first and second State Free Art Studios (Svomas), which had themselves been set up in December 1918 by fusing the old Moscow School of Painting, Sculpture and Architecture with the Stroganov School of Applied Art. The Vkhutemas was conceived explicitly as 'a specialized educational institution for advanced artistic and technical training, created to train highly qualified master artists for industry, as well as instructors and directors of professional and technical education'. Official concerns reflected contemporary artistic discussions on the role of art in the new society and its participation in industrial production; this was called 'production art', although the term covered a wide range of approaches, from applied and decorative art to the emerging concept of design promoted by the First Working Group of Constructivists, who were committed to the fusion of the artistic, ideological and industrial (see CONSTRUCTIVISM, §1). These various attitudes were reflected in the composition and teaching of the school.

The history of the Vkhutemas corresponds to the tenures of its three directors. From 1920 to 1923, under Yefim Ravdel', the staff and teaching inherited from the State Free Art Studios were adapted to the new task of industrial design. The government reform in higher education of 1923 led to a revision of the teaching programmes, and under Vladimir Favorsky (from 1923 to 1926) workshops undertook commissions from external bodies to establish more concrete links with industry. Pavel Novitsky (1888–1971), Director from 1926 to 1930, reorganized the school in 1927–8 into a more narrowly industrial and technological training institute. The artistic content of courses was reduced, new statutes were drawn up and the name changed to the Vkhutein (Higher (State) Artistic and Technical Institute).

Originally there were seven faculties: Painting, Sculpture, Textiles, Ceramics, Architecture, Woodwork and Metalwork; but in 1926 Woodwork and Metalwork were amalgamated. Although the relative lengths of the overall training and the introductory or Basic Course altered under the various directors, the Basic Course remained fundamental to the ideas behind the school's teaching. Originally highly open to change and dedicated to a 'new synthetic art', it employed various innovative artists to teach its five disciplines: Lyubov' Popova (Colour), Aleksandr Osmyorkin and German Fyodorov (Form and Colour), Aleksandr Drevin (Form, Colour and Plane), Ivan Klyun (Colour and the Plane or Suprematism) and Aleksandr Rodchenko (Construction). By 1922 the disciplines were reduced to four: Colour Construction (Aleksandr Vesnin and Popova), Spatial Construction (Nikolai Ladovsky, Nikolay Dokuchayev and Vladimir Krinsky), Graphic Construction (Rodchenko, Viktor Kiselyov and Ivan Yefimovy) and Volumetric Construction (Anton Lavinsky). By 1923 these were reorganized into three areas: Plane and Colour, Volume and Space, and Space and Volume. In 1929 the categories became Space, Volume, Colour and Graphics. Inevitably the detailed content

and exercises of the courses changed but all were rigorously analytical.

The Woodwork and Metalwork Faculty (Dermetfak) was the most Constructivist in orientation. Its staff included Rodchenko, Gustav Klucis, Lavinsky, Vladimir Tatlin and El Lissitzky, and its students were trained as 'engineer–artists': designers capable of devising interiors for clubs, transport centres, trains and buses, as well as producing smaller objects such as light fittings. Its products combined an economic use of materials with multi-functional capacities, typified by the designs by Boris Zemlianitsyn (b ?1897) for a cupboard the door of which came down to form a table (see Lodder, pl. 4.25) and for a fold-away chair (see RUSSIA, fig. 39).

The Architecture Faculty was the leading architectural school in Russia during the 1920s and contained both Rationalist and Constructivist contingents. The Rationalists (members of ASNOVA, the Association of New Architects) Ladovsky, Krinsky and Dokuchayev were responsible for the first two years of the course, concerned with the aesthetic and formal problems of contemporary architecture. The Constructivists of OSA (the Association of Contemporary Architects) Moisey Ginzburg and the Vesnin brothers (Aleksandr, Leonid and Viktor) taught the final two years, promoting a functional method that involved analysing the political, social and economic factors of the architectural brief and that was intended to minimize the individualistic and aesthetic factors in the design process. A third grouping was established in 1922 by Konstantin Mel'nikov and Il'ya Golosov to occupy a central position between the innovators and the more traditional members of staff, such as Ivan Zholtovsky.

The Painting Faculty initially included major avant-garde figures such as Klyun, Rodchenko, Popova, Aleksandr Vesnin and Vladimir Baranoff-Rosiné, but by 1923 it was orientated towards more figurative aesthetic concerns, with teachers such as David Shterenberg, Robert Fal'k, Drevin, Il'ya Mashkov and Nadezhda Udal'tsova. Its graduates included artists such as Aleksandr Deyneka and Yury Pimenov. The Sculpture Faculty also moved from experimentation with Cubism in 1920 to figurative and monumental work by 1923 under teachers such as Sergey Konyonkov and Ivan Yefimov. The Graphics Faculty, divided into lithography, engraving and book-printing departments, included former members of the avant-garde such as Pyotr Miturich and Lev Bruni, as well as more conventional artists, for instance Favorsky, Novitsky and Ignaty Nivinsky. The Textiles and Ceramics faculties were more orientated towards production. Textiles was divided into weaving and printing departments, but both produced essentially figurative designs using mechanical and industrial elements. Although Varvara Stepanova taught there between 1924 and 1925, she does not seem to have been able to introduce her innovative ideas involving the relation of textile design to function and clothing design. The Ceramics Faculty established a close relationship with the Dulevsky factory, where many students acquired practical experience of industrial processes and where many graduates, such as Aleksey Sotnikov (b 1904) and Sergei Kozhin, were ultimately employed. Tatlin worked in the faculty (1927–30) producing designs for tableware, which were based on an appreciation of natural forms and the organic quality of the materials.

In 1930 the school closed, and the various departments formed the basis for, or were absorbed into, existing specialist institutes.

BIBLIOGRAPHY

S. O. Chan-Magomedov: *Pioniere der sowjetischen Architektur* (Dresden, 1983); Eng. trans. as S. O. Khan-Magomedov: *Pioneers of Soviet Architecture* (London, 1987)
C. Lodder: *Russian Constructivism* (New Haven, 1983)
S. O. Khan-Magomedov: *Rodchenko: The Complete Work* (London, 1986)

CHRISTINA LODDER

Vlad, Ion (*b* Feteşti, 24 May 1900; *d* Paris, 30 Jan 1992). Romanian sculptor. He studied sculpture at the Fine Art School in Bucharest under Cornel Medrea (1939–44). In 1945 Vlad made his début at the Official Salon in Bucharest, winning the prestigious Simu prize. In 1946, at his first one-man exhibition in Bucharest, he showed himself to be a sensitive portrayer of the human figure with his haunting image of the painter *Ştefan Luchian*. His early work showed the influence of Emile-Antoine Bourdelle and Brancusi, but Vlad gradually developed his own creative identity. He concentrated on depicting human beings in portrait busts and statuary. His best-known works include the statue of *Brancusi* (1949; Bucharest), portrayed in a simplified, vigorous and almost geometrical style, and that of the writer *Ion Creangă* (1950; Bucharest), in which generous planes depict a rural physicality and debonair nature. Vlad's statue of the composer *Georges Enescu* (bronze, h. 3m, 1955; Bîrlad), is restrained and almost Classical in its modelling, yet the figure appears to have an air of hesitancy. He also sculpted torsos, low- and high-relief murals (e.g. low relief, Bucharest Opera House façade; travertine, 10×6 m) and open-air monuments. In 1964 he received the state prize for sculpture and in the same year moved to Paris, where he was exposed to a great deal of modern art that had never been exhibited in Romania. His style remained largely unaffected by this experience, and his last work, the bronze statue of the Romanian poet *Mihail Eminescu*, erected in the Latin Quarter of Paris in 1989, shows a characteristic penetration and technical skill. Vlad was a professor at the Institute of Architecture, Bucharest (1960–64), and at the Centre Américain in Paris (1969–72); he was also a visiting professor at the Sorbonne, Paris, in 1975.

BIBLIOGRAPHY

M. Mihalache: *Ion Vlad* (Bucharest, 1966)
I. Jianou and others: *Ion Vlad* (Paris, 1991)

AUREL BOGDANESCU

Vladimir, Prince of Kiev (*b c.* AD 965; *reg c.* 980–1015; *d* Berestovo, 1015, *fd* 15 July). Prince and saint. He was a descendant of Varangian (Scandinavian) adventurers who had established themselves as rulers in the Land of Rus' and gradually coalesced with their Slav subjects to form a single people. The two most important centres of this vast and ill-defined territory, Novgorod and Kiev, both lay on the great trade route 'from the Varangians to the Greeks' that passed through the country. No works of art or architecture survive from the period of Vladimir's reign but it was of crucial importance in determining the

subsequent development of Russian art. His most significant act, traditionally dated to AD 988, was his adoption of Christianity as the official religion of the country. Contact with Constantinople had already ensured significant Christian influence; Vladimir's grandmother, St Olga (*reg* 945–64), had herself been a convert, but it took several generations for the new religion to become completely established. In Vladimir's time Christianity seems to have been primarily the religion of the upper classes. The local pre-Christian culture gradually lost its status, while the ruling classes deliberately copied Byzantine patterns. Vladimir's baptismal name was that of the reigning emperor, Basil II (*reg* 976–1025), and the wooden cathedrals dedicated to St Sophia in Novgorod and (almost certainly) Kiev (both destr.) were evidently built in imitation of Hagia Sophia in Constantinople. Byzantine traditions of ecclesiastical architecture, monumental arts, icon painting and book production were adopted as authoritative in the Land of Rus'. Local artists learnt quickly from the Byzantine masters who worked there, and Rus' became, culturally speaking, part of the Byzantine commonwealth, although so remote from its artistic and intellectual centres that much of Russian art, for example the icons of the Novgorod school, has its own distinctive character.

See also KIEV, §1(i).

BIBLIOGRAPHY

D. Obolensky: *The Byzantine Commonwealth* (London, 1974)
A. Poppe: *The Rise of Christian Russia* (London, 1982)

R. M. CLEMINSON

Vladimirescu, Wanda Sachelarie-. *See* SACHELARIE-VLADIMIRESCU, WANDA.

Vladimir–Suzdal'. Principality in north-eastern Rus' (now part of Russia), which flourished from the mid-12th century to the Tatar-Mongol invasion of 1238. The region, also known as Suzdal'skaya Zemlya, lies between the Volga and Oka rivers, and the cities of Vladimir (*see* §1 below), Suzdal' (*see* §2 below) and ROSTOV controlled the trade routes from Asia and the Caucasus. The riches provided by this trade, employing fleets of boats on the Klyaz'ma and Oka rivers, leading to the Volga, and by agriculture enabled the princes of Vladimir–Suzdal' to maintain an extensive building programme that made the principality one of the most important centres of architectural activity in Rus' (*see* RUSSIA, §III, 1(ii)(a)). In the 15th century the descendants of the princes of Vladimir–Suzdal', by now rulers of Muscovy, were still able to look back on the architecture of the earlier principality as the true custodian of the traditions of Rus'.

1. Vladimir. 2. Suzdal'.

1. VLADIMIR. Vladimir lies on the River Klyaz'ma, 200 km east of Moscow. From the 12th century until the 14th, when it was incorporated into Muscovy, it was the capital of the principality and the most important urban centre in Rus'.

(*i*) *History and urban development.* A Finno-Ugric settlement was established on the hill that dominates the wide flood-plain of the Klyaz'ma during the 1st millennium AD. Slavic migrants from the lands of the Krivichi of Smolensk

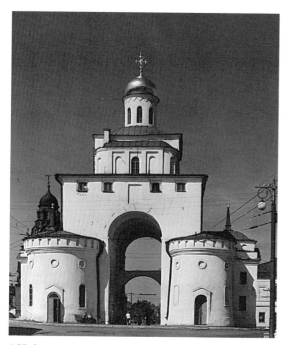

1. Vladimir, Golden Gates, 1164, rebuilt 15th and 17th centuries; the round towers are 18th-century additions

the Dormition (Uspensky; 1158–60; rebuilt 1185–9; *see* §(ii) below), within the area of Monomakh's original fortress, were also built in Andrey's reign. His main residence was a fortified limestone palace complex (begun 1158) at Bogolyubovo, 8 km north of the town. The only surviving sections of the palace, where he was assassinated in 1175, are an entrance gate and a stair-tower. The church of the Protective Veil of the Virgin (Pokrov Bogoroditsy; 1166; see fig. 2), built 1 km from Bogolyubovo beside the River Nerl', is a particularly well-preserved structure arranged around four piers, with three apses and a single dome.

Medieval Vladimir assumed its definitive appearance as the power of the Great Princes strengthened under Vsevolod (*reg* 1176–1212). Most of the buildings, including the churches and monasteries as well as the houses, were constructed in wood; a chronicler stated that 32 churches were burnt down in the fire of 1185. The town was an elongated triangle bounded by the Klyaz'ma and Lybed' rivers, and divided into three walled districts: the New Town in the west, Monomakh's Town (or the Middle Town) in the centre, and the Vetchanoy Town in the east. The New Town had four gate-towers: the Golden and Irina Gates to the West, the Copper Gates to the north,

and the Slavs of Novgorod arrived in the 10th century, attracted by the economic advantages of the region's geographical location. The forests along the fringes of Kievan Rus', known as the Zalessky Territory, abounded with fur-bearing animals, the numerous lakes and rivers were suitable for fishing, the flood-plains permitted live-stock rearing and, most importantly, Vladimir stood near the Opol'ye, a wide tract of unforested, cultivable land, rare in Rus'.

In the 11th century the region came into the possession of Prince Vsevolod I Yaroslavich (*reg* 1078–93). His son, Prince Vladimir II Monomakh (*reg* 1113–25), built a strong fortress bearing his name in 1108. Its layout, surrounded by an earthen rampart (h. *c*. 10 m; l. 2.5 km) topped by a palisade, was determined by the steep sides of the hill and the riverbanks. Settlements sprang up to the east and west of the fortress, and in 1157 Prince Andrey I Bogolyubsky (*reg* 1157–75) transferred the capital of Rus' from Kiev to Vladimir. From 1158 to 1165 the earthern ramparts were rapidly extended to enclose the new areas of the town as well as the fortress, which became the heart of the settlement. Gate-towers were placed on the approaches to the town. The stone Golden (Zolotyye) Gates (1158–64; rebuilt 15th and 17th centuries; see fig. 1) is the only survivor and a rare example of Russian 12th-century defensive architecture. The two massive limestone piers support a light tufa vault, above which a church is raised on a platform. The oak gates were plated with gilded copper, emphasizing its role as the main triumphal en-trance to the capital. The round buttresses either side of the gateway were erected in the 18th century when the town walls were demolished. The palace church of the Saviour (Spassky; 1164; rebuilt 1778) and the cathedral of

2. Vladimir, church of the Protective Veil of the Virgin, 1166

through which ran the road to Suzdal', and an entrance near the Klyaz'ma. An east–west thoroughfare cut across the length of Vladimir. Entering through the Golden Gates, a traveller from Kiev would see to the south the palaces (destr.) of Yury Dolgoruky and Andrey, with the churches of St George (1129; rebuilt 1784) and the Saviour, respectively. North of the Golden Gates stood the Princess (Knyagigin) Convent with a stone cathedral dedicated to the Dormition (1200–01; rebuilt 15th–16th centuries; rest. late 1940s). The palaces and the convent were surrounded by walls that made each a small citadel within the stronghold of the town. The Middle Town was reached through the Trading (Torgovyye) Gates, south of which lay the main inner citadel (Detinets), surrounded by white-stone walls. Within stood the palace of Vsevolod (destr.), the bishop's palace (destr.), the Nativity (Rozhdestvensky) Monastery (1191–6) and Vladimir's two largest churches, the cathedrals of the Dormition (see §(ii) below and fig. 3) and St Demetrius (Dmitry; 1194–7; see §(iii) below and ROMANESQUE, fig. 22). In the northern part of the Middle Town, next to the citadel walls, there was a wide market-place and, beyond, shops, warehouses and merchants' houses. The Ivanovsky Gates in the east wall of the Middle Town led into the Vetchanoy Town, where the craftsmen and merchants lived; all the buildings here were wooden. At the east end of the main thoroughfare stood the Silver Gates, which led to Bogolyubovo.

Vladimir suffered heavy damage in 1238, when it was sacked by Tatar-Mongol forces, and never recovered its former glory. Until the 15th century, however, it retained its moral eminence as the custodian of the traditions of Rus'. The cathedral of the Dormition served as the model

3. Vladimir, cathedral of the Dormition, founded 1158, rebuilt 1185–9

for the cathedral of the Dormition (1326–7) in the Moscow Kremlin (see MOSCOW, §IV, 1(ii)), while Prince Dmitry Donskoy (reg 1359–89) undertook a careful restoration of the cathedral of St Dmitry in 1380. Vladimir's population declined to a fraction of its earlier size and no further stone buildings were erected until the founding of a few small churches in the mid-17th century and the 18th, including those dedicated to the Virgin (Bogoroditsa; 1649), St Nicholas in Galei (1735) and the Ascension (Vorneseniye; 1742). The replanning of the town at the end of the 18th century did not greatly change its ancient layout, but many buildings and the fortress walls were demolished. A square was laid out in front of the cathedrals of St Dmitry and the Dormition, surrounded by the Provincial Administration buildings (1785), the Governor's Palace (1808), the Nobles' Assembly (1826) and other buildings. The reconstruction of the town has been undertaken with due concern for the preservation of its ancient monuments, which are administered by the Vladimir–Suzdal' Museum of Art History and Architecture. Between 1947 and 1965 extensive areas were laid out with residential quarters, streets, squares and public gardens. Among the more recent buildings of interest is the theatre (1970s), which has sculptural decoration in white stone.

(ii) Cathedral of the Dormition. The foundations of the cathedral of the Dormition were laid on the highest point of Monomakh's Town in 1158. This was the largest building in 12th-century Vladimir and emphasized the new state's desire for independence from Kiev and release from its spiritual authority. According to the chronicles, craftsmen were brought from many lands to work here; these may have included architects from Poland or Germany. It was so severely damaged in the fire of 1185, however, that it is difficult to ascertain its original appearance. Walls with connecting arches (1185–9) were built all round the surviving structure so that it was in effect encased in Vsevolod's new cathedral. The upper part of this large, complexly structured edifice rests on the six piers of the old building, above which a lofty dome covers the well-lit crossing. Large openings were inserted into the walls of the earlier building, so as to transform what was left into supports for the two-storey galleries that surrounded it to the north, west and south. This gave the resulting building an almost square plan, with five longitudinal aisles and five transverse divisions, to which were added three massive eastern apses. Two smaller domes were placed above the east ends of the north and south galleries, producing a three-domed plan rarely encountered in early Russian architecture.

The exterior decoration of the cathedral, which relies almost entirely upon the placing of architectural elements rather than on sculpture, corresponds to the division of its interior. Each façade was divided into five arched sections by slim, clustered demi-columns, reminiscent of Gothic influence. The overall impression, however, emphasized by the round-headed arches, is not at all Gothic but one of repose, balance and strength. This impression is intensified by the encircling corbel table on decorative colonnettes, which divides the façade almost in half. The massiveness of the masonry is brought out by deep, recessed portals and windows framed by multi-stepped, arched surrounds.

The interior is renowned for its wall paintings, including fragments showing prophets and two peacocks (1160) that originally decorated the exterior north wall of the first cathedral. There are also prophets, Church Fathers and ornamental decoration (1189) on the west wall and early 13th-century fragments in the south gallery. In 1408 the cathedral was painted anew by ANDREY RUBLYOV, with the assistance of DANIIL CHORNY and pupils. The surviving *Last Judgement* beneath the west gallery, presented without any sense of severity or menace, is a complex composition distinguished by the same softness of form, elegance of line and tranquil radiance that can be found in other 15th-century paintings following Russia's recovery from the Tatar invasions. Rublyov and Daniil Chorny also painted icons (some now in Moscow, Tret'yakov Gal.; St Petersburg, Rus. Mus.) for the iconostasis, which was dismantled in 1773. Until 1395 the cathedral housed the celebrated miracle-working icon of the *Virgin of Vladimir* (Moscow, Tret'yakov Gal.; *see* UKRAINE, §III, 1(ii)).

(iii) Cathedral of St Dmitry. The cathedral that Vsevolod built from 1194 to 1197 in the courtyard of his palace in Middle Town is considerably smaller than the cathedral of the Dormition. It belongs to a series of churches with four piers and a single dome that was widespread in the 12th century, but the solemn splendour of its architecture and sculptural decoration were intended to reflect the greatness of the Prince of Vladimir. The cathedral displays a singularly harmonious appearance. Each façade is divided into three arched sections by pilasters and tall, narrow windows pierce the upper parts of the walls. The lowest section of the walls, to above the level of the portals, is devoid of sculptural decoration. Above this, however, separated by a band of carved figures set between colonnettes, the windows are surrounded by densely packed figural relief carvings. The lavishly decorated drum of the dome then appears as though an embroidered veil had been flung over the whole building.

The iconography of the façade expresses the mythological world known to the Russian people in the 12th century in a great 'poem in sculpture', drawing upon Christian stories, memories of ancient times, including the *Apotheosis of Alexander the Great*, and contemporary political ideas, with a representation of the Prince himself. Over the three façades there are only 46 sculptures of martyrs and the patron saints of the princely dynasty of Vladimir that are directly Christian in character. Animals, however, appear 243 times and birds more than 250 times: lions, wolves, griffins, eagles and doves abound. The conceptual focus on each façade is a figure of *King Solomon*, whose image holds sway over a fantastic world of animals, birds, monsters, galloping horsemen and saints, intertwined with imaginary plants, reflecting the 12th-century legend that Solomon was the ruler of the world of plants, animals and demons. There was little sculpture inside the cathedral, which was covered with wall paintings: fragments of a *Last Judgement* were uncovered on the vault above the west entrance and the adjacent vaults and arches in 1918–20.

2. SUZDAL'. One of the oldest settlements in north-eastern Rus', Suzdal' lies on the River Kamenka, 40 km north of Vladimir, in the middle of the fertile plain of the Opol'ye. It was briefly the capital of the state founded in 1125 by Prince Yury I Dolgoruky and its ecclesiastical influence long outlasted the decline of its secular power.

(i) History and urban development. Suzdal' is first mentioned in 1024, but a settlement had been established earlier. In the late 11th century and the early 12th Prince Vladimir II Monomakh erected a fortress with three gate-towers within a bend in the river. Inside the ramparts of this kremlin complex (*see* §(ii) below), the large brick cathedral of the Dormition stood next to the prince's palace (both destr.). An extensive semicircular suburb, where the artisans lived, adjoined the kremlin to the east, protected by earthen ramparts and, beyond, the River Gremyachka and a moat. On opposite sides of the river on the south side of the town were the monasteries of St Demetrius (11th century) and SS Cosmas and Damian (12th century). Suzdal' grew in importance about 1200 under Vsevolod (*reg* 1176–1212) and Yury II (*reg* 1212–38), who strengthened the fortifications. The cathedral of the Dormition was demolished and replaced on the same site by the stone cathedral of the Birth of the Virgin (Rozhdestvensky; 1222–5). Suzdal' was stormed by the Tatar-Mongols in 1238, but had already recovered from its devastation by the mid-13th century. As the power of the princes waned, apart from a brief resurgence in the 14th century, the ecclesiastical authorities assumed an increasingly important role in the ordering of the town. The plan of the town and the surrounding area was now largely determined by the position of the monastic complexes, which remain the principal influence on the appearance of Suzdal', forming citadels around which building was concentrated (*see* §(iii) below). Some stand on the massive natural rampart of the meandering Kamenka's higher bank, some were surrounded by level fields that stretched far from the town, while others hide in hollows. The town never spread beyond the vicinity of the monasteries.

In 1392 Suzdal' became part of the Grand Principality of Moscow. Although it lost its political and economic power, it remained an important religious centre, symbolized by the archbishops' occupation of what had been the prince's palace in the kremlin. In the 16th century there were more than 50 places of worship serving a mere 414 dwellings, including 14 churches within the ramparts of the artisans' suburb alone in 1573. The town grew in the 17th and 18th centuries, but the ratio of ecclesiastical buildings to secular remained, with the erection of dozens of new parish churches. Most of these have survived, including the churches of the Emperor Constantine (Tsarevokonstantinovskaya; 1707), St John the Baptist (1720), the adjoining churches of the Entry into Jerusalem (Vkhodo-Iyerusalimskaya; 1707) and Good Friday (Pyatnitskaya; 1772), the Resurrection (Voskresenskoye; 1732) and St Antipas (1745). These are of a similar design, comprising a small central cube with a single dome, a wide eastern apse and, usually, a tall belfry with a tent roof of slightly concave outline placed alongside the main body of the church or above the entrance. Subsidiary chapels were often built along the sides. The high artistic standards evident in these churches demonstrate the survival of old Russian building traditions into the 18th century.

The town was little affected by replanning in the 18th century and its ancient layout was preserved, arranged along a main north–south thoroughfare to the east of the kremlin. In 1806–11 an arcade was built on the market-place, midway along the main street. A lofty bell-tower (1813–19; h. 60 m) was added to the street front of the monastery of the Deposition of the Robe (Rizopolo-zhensky) to commemorate the victory over Napoleon. Since then no important buildings have been erected in the historic part of the town, which has preserved the originality and deep-rooted traditions of Russian urban planning. The town's architectural monuments and mu-seums are under the care of the Vladimir-Suzdal' Museum of Art History and Architecture.

(ii) Kremlin. The ramparts of the kremlin were originally 10 m high, topped by a wooden palisade and towers. The east side was protected by a moat (w. 35 m). Excavations in the 1930s and 1940s revealed the plan of Monomakh's cathedral (*see* §(i) above). The large, somewhat elongated cathedral of the Birth of the Virgin, which replaced it in 1222–5, originally had three domes, but this was increased to five in the 16th century (*see* RUSSIA, fig. 2). The roof rests on six massive piers, as in the earlier building, and there are three eastern apses. The cathedral is entered through a galleried narthex at the west. The main structure consists of irregular tufa slabs, which give a picturesque wall surface, while the decorative elements, such as the pilasters and belts of colonnettes, were painstakingly hewn from limestone, lending the building a sophistication typical of the Vladimir school of the 12th and 13th centuries. The façades, however, are simpler in composi-tion than those on the cathedrals of the Dormition and St Dmitry (*see* §1(ii) and (iii) above), and the decorative elements do not correspond exactly to the building's internal articulation.

The cathedral's interior was richly decorated with col-oured, glazed floor-tiles and wall paintings (1233), of which fragments remain. The south and west portals were adorned with gilded copper panels engraved with New Testament scenes, a rare surviving example of Russian applied art of the 13th century. Major alterations to the cathedral's structure were made in later centuries. The roof collapsed in 1445, and the walls were demolished to half their height in 1528 and rebuilt in brick (1530). The ancient slit windows were widened in the 17th century and the original helmet-shaped domes were replaced by immense onion domes; the present domes were erected in 1750. An octagonal bell-tower (1635) was built to the south of the cathedral. The interior of the cathedral was redecorated in 1635–6 with monumental, austere wall paintings, distinguished by their restrained use of colour, and a simple, severe iconostasis.

The earliest surviving sections of the Archbishop's Palace (completed 1707) date from the 15th century. This is an intricate complex, south of the cathedral, and consists of interconnecting buildings of differing heights, with galleried porches and an assortment of doorway and window styles that makes it particularly picturesque. The main formal apartment, the vaulted Cross Chamber

(13×26 m), is of particular interest. Also within the kremlin are the churches of the Dormition (17th century) and St Nicholas (1720–39).

(iii) Monasteries. All the monastic complexes built between the 11th and 15th centuries were of wood and no examples have survived. The monasteries of St Demetrius and SS Cosmas and Damian (*see* §(i) above) were joined by five more in the 13th century: the monasteries of the Deposi-tion of the Robe (1207), the Trinity (Troitsky) and St Alexander (1240) were founded north of the town on the higher bank of the Kamenka, the Presentation of the Virgin to the south and St Basil to the west. In the 14th century the monastery of the Saviour and St Euthymius (Spas-Yefimyersky; 1352) and the convent of the Protec-tive Veil of the Virgin (Pokrovsky; 1364) were built on opposite sides of the Kamenka, north of the town.

The monasteries reached the peak of their power in the 16th and 17th centuries, enriched by numerous gifts from the rulers and nobility of Muscovy. The most important of the many monumental stone buildings erected at this time, most of which survive, are in the convent of the Protective Veil of the Virgin, and in the monasteries of the Saviour and St Euthymius and the Deposition of the Robe. The convent of the Protective Veil stands amid extensive meadows on the flood-plain, surrounded by low whitewashed walls with some ten octagonal turrets (16th–17th centuries), some of which have retained their massive stone tent roofs (17th century; see fig. 4). The main entrance, the Holy Gates, is in the south wall and above is the elegant church of the Annunciation (Blagoveshche-niye; 1518), which has three well-proportioned domes and is decorated with *zakomary* around its roof-line. The cathedral of the Protective Veil (1510–14), at the centre of the complex, has four internal piers and three massive eastern apses. This structure is raised on a high basement that was used as the burial vault for nuns of noble birth. A covered arcade runs around three sides, leaving only the apses exposed. The upper walls above the arcade terminate on each side in three ogee arches. The whole edifice, a splendid example of 16th-century Russian ecclesiastical architecture, is crowned by a huge central dome, with two smaller domes over side chapels. The lower part of a massive, free-standing, octagonal bell-tower, the first of an imposing series built by the 16th-century tsars, was begun in 1515; its decorative tent roof was added in the 17th century. The bell-tower was linked to the cathedral's arcade by a bridge-like, enclosed stone passage in the 18th century. The plan of the convent largely dates from the first half of the 16th century, its rapid development explained by the confinement here of Solomoniya Sabur-tova (*d* 1542), the unloved first wife of Vasily III (*reg* 1505–33). Other buildings in the convent include the church of the Conception (Zachat'yevskaya), a large refectory (1551) and a stone kitchen and administrative offices (16th century). The cells were mostly wooden and stood along the walls.

The monastery of the Saviour and St Euthymius towers above the convent of the Protective Veil on the opposite bank. It forms a mighty fortress with high brick walls and 12 enormous towers. The monumentality of the rectan-gular entrance tower (h. 22 m), which dominates the

4. Suzdal', convent of the Protective Veil of the Virgin, 16th–17th centuries

monastery's skyline, is emphasized by the low arch and the extremely rich decorative carving, resembling lacework, that covers the entire upper section. The other towers are lower and less embellished, and not even the churches exceed its height. The entrance arch leads to a narrow courtyard and another gate cut through the lower level of the church of the Annunciation (before 1628). Beyond, in the centre of the monastery, is the cathedral of the Transfiguration (Spas-Preobrazheniya; 1594), somewhat squat in appearance, with a wide central drum and five immense onion domes (18th–19th centuries). The bell-tower (early 16th century) to the east was extended in the 17th century with a three-bay arcaded belfry. The church of the Assumption (Uspenskaya; 1526) has one of the earliest examples of a tent roof. To the north-east are the cell blocks (17th–18th centuries) and the infirmary, with the adjoining church of St Nicholas (1664).

The first stone church in the monastery of the Deposition of the Robe was built in the first half of the 16th century. The monastery's striking and unified appearance, however, only developed from the late 17th century, when the wooden walls were replaced in stone. The main entrance, the Holy Gates (1688), has an asymmetric design with two arches of unequal size. The main structure is covered in patterned brickwork and surmounted by two close-set, high octagonal tent roofs carried on flat-sided, polyhedral drums, reflecting the joyful decorativeness characteristic of late 17th-century Russian architecture. The monastery's cathedral of the Holy Trinity (1700; destr.) had a richly carved façade and a graceful, tent-roofed bell-tower.

BIBLIOGRAPHY

V. Georgiyevsky: 'Suzdal'skiy Rizopolozhensky monastyr' [The monastery of the Deposition of the Robe in Suzdal'], *Trudy Vladimirskoy Uchonoy Arkhv Kom.*, ii (1900), pp. 87–190

Suzdal' i yego dostoprimechatel'nosti [Suzdal' and its monuments] (Moscow, 1912)

F. Halle: *Die Bauplastik von Wladimir-Ssusdal* (Berlin, 1929)

A. Varganov: 'K arkhitekturnoy istorii Suzdal'skogo sobora' [On the architectural history of Suzdal' Cathedral], *Kratkoye Soobshcheniye Inst. Istor. Mat. Kul't.*, xi (1945), pp. 99–106

G. H. Hamilton: *The Art and Architecture of Russia*, Pelican Hist. A. (Harmondsworth, 1954, 3/1983)

N. Voronin: *Zodchestvo severo-vostochnoy Rusi, XII–XV vekov* [The architecture of north-east Rus', 12th–15th centuries], 2 vols (Moscow, 1961–2)

Y. Karavayeva: 'Gradostoitel'noye razvitiye Suzdalya' [The urban-planning development of Suzdal'], *Issledovaniya Istor. Arkhit.*, i (1964), pp. 147–81

Y. Karavayeva and A. A. Shennikov: 'Suzdal' v 1700 g.' [Suzdal' in 1700], *Arkhit. Nasledstvo*, xviii (1969), pp. 61–6

G. K. Vagner: *Skul'ptura drevney Rusi: XII vek: Vladimir* [The sculpture of ancient Rus': 12th century: Vladimir] (Moscow, 1969)

——: *Suzdal'* (Moscow, 1969)

A. Varganov: *Suzdal', Yaroslavl'* (Moscow, 1971)

N. Voronin: *Vladimir, Bogolyubovo, Suzdal'* (Moscow, 1974)

D. O. SCHVIDKOVSKY

Vladislav II, King of Bohemia and Hungary. *See* JAGIELLON, (1).

Vlaminck, Maurice de (*b* Paris, 5 April 1876; *d* Rueil-la-Gadelière, Eure-et-Loir, 7 Oct 1958). French painter, printmaker, draughtsman and writer. His nature, character, tastes and way of life were in perfect harmony with the freedom, daring and violence of his painting. He was brought up in a musical environment: his father, of Flemish origin, was a violin teacher and his mother, from Lorraine, was a piano teacher. He studied music himself to quite a high standard and later played the double-bass (and sometimes the bass drum, a source of considerable pleasure) in his regimental band. His family had come to live at Le Vésinet near Paris, and he spent his childhood both there and later at Chatou on the Seine. From 1892 he began to take an interest in painting, though he worked as a mechanic and became a racing cyclist.

Maurice de Vlaminck: *Red Trees*, oil on canvas, 650×810 mm, 1906 (Paris, Pompidou, Musée National d'Art Moderne)

After his first marriage (to Suzanne Berly) Vlaminck gave up cycling and returned to music. He gave violin lessons and played the violin in popular orchestras and café-concerts in Paris. He also made his début as a journalist in the late 19th century and wrote articles for anarchist papers such as *Le Libertaire*. From 1900 to 1901, when he was called up for military service, he shared a studio at Chatou with André Derain. Self-taught, Vlaminck was still in search of a style in his first canvases, but his violence of expression was already apparent in works such as the *Bar Counter* (1900; Avignon, Mus. Calvet) or the portrait of *Père Bouju* (1900; Paris, Pompidou). Freeing colour from its purely descriptive function, Vlaminck used broad, turbulent brushstrokes in a kind of proto-Expressionism but very quickly graduated to the Fauvist style that he practised from 1904 to 1907.

Vlaminck's first exhibited works were in a group show at the Berthe Weill gallery, Paris, in 1904, followed by four canvases at the 1905 Salon des Indépendants and eight paintings in the Salon d'Automne that same year. It was in the last exhibition that he and other artists, including Matisse and Derain, were derisively labelled 'Fauves' ('wild beasts'; *see* FAUVISM). Similarities in the work produced during these years by Derain and Vlaminck in particular were not coincidental, since they had shared the same studio and often painted scenes depicting their immediate surroundings, as in Vlaminck's *Houses at Chatou* (*c*. 1905–6; Chicago, IL, A. Inst.; for illustration *see* FAUVISM). Vlaminck's boldest paintings of the period include the *Portrait of Derain* (1905; Mexico City, J. Gelman priv. col., see 1976 exh. cat., p. 48), in which the face is vermilion, the *Restaurant de la Machine at Bougival* (*c*. 1905; Paris, Mus. d'Orsay), the *Bateaux-lavoirs* (1905; Paris, priv. col., see Muller, p. 72) and the *Red Trees* (1906; Paris, Pompidou; see fig.).

The impact on Vlaminck of the van Gogh exhibition of 1901 at the Bernheim-Jeune gallery, Paris, where he was introduced to Matisse by Derain, was succeeded in 1907 by that of the Cézanne retrospective at the Salon d'Automne. In response to these stimuli, Vlaminck's exuberant use of colour gave way to a concern with structure, and at the same time he developed a dramatic view of landscape that was to remain a hallmark of his work. Although his Cézanne-influenced period continued only to *c*. 1910, it included a series of excellent canvases that included such works as *Factory Chimney at Puteaux* (Chartres, Mus. B.-A.), *Still-life with Pitcher* and the *Seine Seen from Bougival* (priv. col.).

Vlaminck remained consistently hostile to the most avant-garde movement in contemporary French art, Cubism, in spite of the fact that its roots were also in the work of Cézanne. Instead he developed a more naturalistic treatment of landscape, retaining his vigorous style but using more austere colours. Ambroise Vollard, who bought all the paintings in Vlaminck's studio in 1906 and organized his first exhibition the following year, had the idea of sending him to England in 1911. Vlaminck returned with some beautiful landscapes, such as *Southampton* (1911; Pully, Switzerland, priv. col., see Selz, p. 26) and *Tower Bridge* (1911; New York, priv. col., see Selz, p. 31). In 1913 he spent some time in Martigues with Derain, worked on the Côte d'Azur and painted the *Old Port of Marseille* (1913; New York, priv. col., see Selz, p. 32) under one of the gloomy skies of which he was so fond.

From 1917 at Valmondois, where he bought a house, Vlaminck painted canvases that summarized his whole way of seeing. They show his favourite subjects under a violent light: a road, a few houses, trees tossed in the wind. The same country roads appear repeatedly in his paintings, executed in Ile-de-France and later in the Perche region. He consistently accentuated their lyrical character, loading his skies with the threat of a storm or a tempest. It is in its dramatic representation of nature that Vlaminck's painting of the period can be characterized as landscape Expressionism, evident also in its equally vehement use of gouache and watercolour, but the repetition of the same effects eventually became somewhat theatrical and melodramatic. He also painted some handsome portraits, notably *Self-portrait* (1912; priv. col., see Selz, p. 28) and *M. Itasse* or *Cher Ami* (1924; Paris, Roudinesco priv. col., see Selz, p. 47). Among his most characteristic late canvases painted after the move to his country house 'La Tourillière' in Rueil-la-Gadelière, Eure-et-Loir, are *Sunset in the Forêt de Sénonches* (1938; Paris, priv. col., see Selz, p. 91), *Harvest in the Storm* (1946; Paris, priv. col., see Selz, p. 82) and the *Red Tractor* (1956; Zurich, priv. col., see Selz, p. 83).

Vlaminck continued writing while working as a painter. By the beginning of the century he had published three novels in collaboration with Fernand Sernada. These were followed by some 20 works—novels, poems and reminiscences—of which the most noteworthy are *Tournant dangereux* (Paris, 1929; Eng. trans., 1961), *Le Ventre ouvert* (Paris, 1937), *Portraits avant décès* (Paris, 1943) and *Paysages et personnages* (Paris, 1953). He also illustrated with drawings, woodcuts, etchings and lithographs more than 20 books, including *Les Hommes abandonnés* (Paris, 1927) by Georges Duhamel, *Le Diable au corps* (Paris, 1926) by Raymond Radiguet and works by other writers such as Julien Green and Marcel Aymé, in addition to books that he himself had written.

BIBLIOGRAPHY

F. Carco: *Vlaminck* (Paris, 1920)
G. Duhamel: *Maurice de Vlaminck* (Paris, 1927)
P. MacOrlan: *Vlaminck: Peintures 1900–1945* (Paris, 1945)
A. Derain: *Lettres à Vlaminck* (Paris, 1955)
M. Sauvage: *Vlaminck: Sa vie et son message* (Geneva, 1956)
J. Selz: *Vlaminck* (Paris, 1963)
J. E. Muller: *Fauvism* (New York, 1967)
The 'Wild Beasts': Fauvism and its Affinities (exh. cat. by J. Elderfield, New York, MOMA; San Francisco, MOMA; Fort Worth, Kimbell A. Mus.; 1976)
Vlaminck (exh. cat., Paris, Gal. Présidence, 1987)

For further bibliography see FAUVISM.

JEAN SELZ

Vlasiu, Ion (*b* Lechinţa, 6 May 1908). Romanian sculptor, painter and teacher. He studied in 1928–31 at the Academy of Fine Arts in Cluj under Romul Ladea. In 1933, together with a group of young writers and artists in Cluj, he edited the only issue of the avant-garde magazine *Herald*. In 1937 he stayed for a year in Paris, where in April 1938 he had a one-man exhibition at the Galerie Contemporaine and exhibited paintings and sculptures at the Salon des Tuileries. He also wrote there the autobiographical novel *Am plecat din sat*, the first work in a cycle in which he narrated the stages of his formation as man and artist. In the early 1940s he became interested in the simple geometry of peasant art, which he incorporated in his sculpture and painting (*Bride*, albabaster, h. 0.5 m, 1957; Bucharest, N. Mus. A.). He preferred carving in wood or stone, not only as a technical challenge but also for their primeval associations. He also produced portrait busts (*Portrait of a Student*, bronze; Cluj-Napoca, A. Mus.) and terracotta reliefs (some with a religious theme) in wide planes with brusque interstices. His style was constantly evolving, and while a tendency towards allusive abstract shapes with symbolic meanings is evident, for example, both in the early *Rhythms* series (1933) and in the much later *Ghosts of War* series (1965–70), his sculptures of fretwork from the 1980s were coloured and figurative. Vlasiu also executed several monuments commemorating events or memorable figures in Romanian history and culture, such as *Horia, Cloşca and Crişan* (bronze, h. 4.5 m, 1975; Cluj-Napoca), and the three allegorical female figures of the Union Monument (bronze, h. *c* 4.5 m, 1975; Blaj). He was a professor at the Academy of Fine Arts in Timişoara (1938) and between 1965 and 1968 chief editor of *Arta*.

WRITINGS
Am plecat din sat [I left the village] (Bucharest, 1957)

BIBLIOGRAPHY
D. Grigorescu: *Ion Vlasiu* (Bucharest, 1970)
I. Frunzetti: *Ion Vlasiu* (Cluj, 1973)
C. Demetrescu: *Ion Vlasiu* (Bucharest, 1984)

IOANA VLASIU

Vlasov, Aleksandr (Vasil'yevich) (*b* Bol'shaya Kosha, Tver' Province, 1 Nov 1900; *d* Moscow, 25 Sept 1962). Russian architect and urban planner. From 1918 to 1928 he studied in the architectural faculty of the Vkhutemas (Higher Artistic and Technical Workshops), Moscow, and he was a founder-member in 1929 of VOPRA (All-Russian Society of Proletarian Architects). His unexecuted design (1931–4) for the KOMVUZ (Communist University) in the Lenin Hills, Moscow, a grandiose neo-classical fantasy, demonstrated his grasp of large-scale projects, but the exaggerated design of the vast theatre (1931–40) in Ivanov led to essential alterations during construction. From 1934 he led the design of facilities in Gor'ky Park in Moscow, and the development of services and the planting of trees and gardens in the city's suburbs. He also designed the architectural parts of the Krymsky Bridge (1936–8), Moscow. In the late 1930s Vlasov became interested in the fantastic architecture depicted in the frescoes at Pompeii, which influenced the complex of buildings of the Central Soviet of Unions (1938–58), Leninsky Prospect, Moscow, and motifs from the baths at Pompeii were used in the interiors (1939–40) of the Central House of Architects, Moscow. From 1944 to 1950 he was chief architect of Kiev, with responsibilities for the general plan of reconstruction and for the construction of the principal street, the Kreshchatik, where the use of its natural site to provide views across the city balances the excess of eclectic decoration in the buildings.

From 1950 to 1955 he was chief architect of Moscow, with responsibility for the construction of the southwestern district of the city, with a population of 250,000. The elements of this vast plan, which in spite of its scale avoids monotony, are a precise network of roads, combined with massive well-organized spaces half-enclosed by the groups of residential blocks. He also designed, with Igor' Rozhin, N. N. Ullas (b 1914) and A. F. Khryakov (1903–76), the Central Lenin Stadium (1955–7), Luzhniki, Moscow, and his competition design (1957; unexecuted) for the Palace of Soviets, Moscow, influenced the standard design of large public buildings throughout the USSR. From 1960 to 1962 Vlasov was head of the Union of Soviet Architects.

BIBLIOGRAPHY

A. Andreyev and Yu. Yaralov: 'Aleksandr Vlasov', *Sov. Arkhit.*, xvi (1964), pp. 89–102

A. V. IKONNIKOV

Nicolas Vleughels: *Apelles Painting Campaspe*, oil on canvas, 1.25×0.97 m, 1716 (Paris, Musée du Louvre)

Vleughels [Wleughels], **Nicolas** (b Paris, 6 Dec 1668; d Rome, 11 Dec 1737). French painter, administrator and teacher of Flemish origin. He trained with his father Philippe Vleughels (?1620–94), a Flemish painter who had moved to Paris in 1642; he was also a pupil of Pierre Mignard I. In 1694 he came second in the Prix de Rome competition with *Lot and his Daughters Leaving Sodom* (untraced); despite repeated attempts, he failed to win the first prize. He became a close friend of Watteau and was, like him, greatly influenced by Flemish painting, notably that of Rubens. In 1704 Vleughels travelled to Italy at his own expense. From his base in Rome he made trips to Venice (1707–9) and Modena (1712–14) and was much influenced by the work of the Venetian colourists, particularly Veronese, whose works he copied (drawings Paris, Louvre, Cab. Dessins). In 1716, back in Paris, he was approved (*agréé*) by the Académie Royale and in the same year was received (*reçu*) on presentation of *Apelles Painting Campaspe* (Paris, Louvre; see fig.) as his *morceau de réception*. The influence of Veronese can be seen in the preparatory studies in oil and pastel for his paintings of this period, such as the *Studies of a Woman's Legs* (Paris, Louvre) for the figure of Campaspe. His close relationship to Watteau's *fêtes galantes* can be seen in the *Abduction of Helen* (c. 1716; New York, priv. col., see Conisbee, fig. 66).

In 1724 Vleughels was appointed Director, jointly with Charles Poërson, of the Académie de France in Rome; on Poërson's death in 1725 he became sole Director, remaining in this post until his own death. Through his efforts, the Académie moved in 1725 from its cramped lodgings in the Palazzo Capranica to the spacious Palazzo Mancini on the Corso (where it remained until 1803). In the same year he was elected a member of the Accademia di S Luca, and the following year he was ennobled. In 1731 he married Marie-Thérèse Gosset, a sister-in-law of Giovanni Paolo Panini. His own work from the Roman years consisted largely of religious paintings, including two for Louis XV: *David and Abigail* and *Solomon and the Queen of Sheba* (1728–9; both untraced). Such works as the *Visitation* and the *Holy Family* (both 1729; St Petersburg, Hermitage) show clearly the direct influence of Rubens and the Venetian colourists. He also made a series of six small paintings (two of which are in New York, Suida-Manning priv. col.) of Roman women in various costumes; in these he studied the play of light on a single picturesque figure. They were engraved by Edmé Jeaurat (1688–1738) in 1734 (see Hercenberg, nos 123–7).

Vleughels was an outstanding administrator and teacher; his pupils included Michel-François Dandré-Bardon, Charles-Joseph Natoire, Pierre Subleyras and Carle Vanloo. He allowed the students great freedom of choice because 'one cannot contain genius'. He also encouraged them to accompany him on expeditions to the Roman Campagna to sketch from nature; however, none of his own landscape drawings has yet been securely identified. During the 1730s he worked on a translation of Ludovico Dolce's *Dialogo della Pittura*, which appeared in a bilingual edition in 1735.

BIBLIOGRAPHY

G. Campori: *Lettere artistiche inedite* (Modena, 1866/R Bologna, 1975), pp. 152–79

A. de Montaiglon and J. Guiffrey, eds: *Correspondance des directeurs de l'Académie de France à Rome avec les surintendants des bâtiments*, vi–ix (1896–9)

H. Lapauze: *Histoire de l'Académie de France à Rome*, i (Paris, 1924), pp. 181–213

P. Rosenberg: 'A propos de Nicolas Vleughels', *Pantheon*, xxxi (1973), pp. 143–53

B. Hercenberg: *Nicolas Vleughels: Peintre et directeur de l'Académie de France à Rome, 1668–1737* (Paris, 1975); review by P. Conisbee in *Burl. Mag.*, cxviii (1976), pp. 868–71

Les Collections du Comte d'Orsay: Dessins du Musée du Louvre (exh. cat. by J.-F. Méjanès, Paris, Louvre, 1983), pp. 83–4, 100–04, 177–81

O. Michel: 'Nicolas Vleughels (1668–1737): Relations et collections', *Archvs A. Fr.*, xxvi (1984), pp. 165–76

Vlieger, Simon (Jacobsz.) de (*b* Rotterdam, *c.* 1600–01; *d* Weesp, March 1653). Dutch painter, draughtsman, etcher and stained-glass designer. He was one of the leading marine and landscape artists of the Dutch school and decisively influenced the direction of Dutch marine art during the 1630s and 1640s. His late works anticipated the shift from the monochrome or tonal phase of Dutch marine art to the more classical style of Jan van de Cappelle and Willem van de Velde the younger (*see* MARINE PAINTING). Although de Vlieger's reputation rests chiefly on his marine paintings, he was also a notable draughtsman and etcher.

De Vlieger moved from his native Rotterdam, where he married Anna Gerridts van Willige on 10 January 1627, to Delft in early 1634 and became a member of the Guild of St Luke there on 18 October that same year. In December 1637 he bought a house in Rotterdam from the painter Cryn Hendricksz. Volmaryn (1604–45) for 900 guilders; as part of this transaction, de Vlieger agreed to deliver each month for a stipulated period paintings with a total value of 31 guilders. He was still living in Delft on 12 March 1638, but by 19 July he was resident in Amsterdam where he became a citizen on 5 January 1643. He may have been attracted to Amsterdam by the commission to provide two designs for the festivities associated with Marie de' Medici's entry into Amsterdam on 31 August 1638; etchings by Salomon Savery (1594–1665) after de Vlieger's designs appear in C. Barlaeus: *Medicea hospes* (Amsterdam, 1638; Hollstein: *Dut. & Flem.*, xxiv, no. 144e–g). De Vlieger fulfilled commissions for tapestry designs from the city magistrates of Delft (1640 and 1641) and in 1642 received the commission to paint the organ shutters (destr. 1788) for the St-Laurenskerk, Rotterdam, for which he received the substantial payment of 2000 guilders on 7 January 1645. Presumably he resided in Rotterdam at least sporadically during these years, but in September 1644 he sold his house there. Early in 1648 he received the prestigious commission to design some stained-glass windows for the Nieuwe Kerk in Amsterdam, for which he was paid 6000 guilders by the city. On 16 May 1648 he appeared as a witness in Amsterdam on behalf of Willem van de Velde the elder, giving his age as about 47. On 13 January 1649 de Vlieger bought a house in Weesp, a small town near Amsterdam.

Although de Vlieger's early training is undocumented, his paintings of the 1620s and 1630s show the strong influence of the marine painter Jan Porcellis. By the 1640s, for his mature marine pictures, he had transformed Porcellis's monochrome palette into a transparent silvery tonality. De Vlieger also appears to have been familiar with Adam Willaerts's rugged coastal scenes from the 1620s, and he developed this motif in his depictions of such subjects in calm and stormy weather. De Vlieger's versatility as an artist is evident from the wide variety of his marine subjects, which constitute the vast majority of

1. Simon de Vlieger: *Dutch Herring Fleet*, oil on panel, 702×1238 mm, *c.* 1650–53 (Budapest, Museum of Fine Arts)

2. Simon de Vlieger: *Goats before a Shed*, black chalk, 251×290 mm, 163[3] (Berlin, Kupferstichkabinett)

his paintings. He depicted the open ocean and the estuaries of the Dutch Republic in calm and breezy weather (characteristic examples in Copenhagen, Stat. Mus. Kst; London, N.G.; Paris, Fond. Custodia, Inst. Néer.; Rotterdam, Mus. Boymans–van Beuningen; and Vienna, Akad. Bild. Kst). The imaginary coastal scenes inspired by Willaerts represent Dutch fleets approaching a rugged coast in calm weather (four such pictures in London, N. Mar. Mus., and another in Montreal, priv. col., see 1987–8 exh. cat., no. 113) or use such rocky terrain as an awesome setting for shipwrecks in stormy weather. Late in his career de Vlieger represented parades in which many different vessels are crowded together as part of official ceremonial arrivals of important dignitaries (e.g. 1649; Vienna, Ksthist. Mus.). Among de Vlieger's most ambitious paintings are those depicting shipping scenes before distant cities in cloudy weather (e.g. 1651; Cambridge, Fitzwilliam; and Schwerin, Staatl. Mus.). As early as 1633 de Vlieger produced beach scenes (e.g. London, N. Mar. Mus.) in which he refined the monochrome palette of Jan

Porcellis. Late in his career, possibly in response to Jan van de Cappelle, de Vlieger's colours became brighter and more blond. An outstanding example of his late manner is the large panel painting of a *Dutch Herring Fleet* (Budapest, Mus. F.A.; see fig. 1). De Vlieger only rarely represented naval battles or religious subjects (e.g. *Christ in the Storm on the Sea of Galilee*, c. 1638; Oakly Park, Ludlow, Salop; see 1980–81 exh. cat., no. 74). Like Jan van Goyen, de Vlieger occasionally depicted sail-boats and larger ships in thunderstorms.

De Vlieger was also a landscape artist of note. His few surviving forest subjects (e.g. *Landscape with Hunters*, Budapest, Mus. F.A.) are a significant contribution to the genre and anticipate the work of Jacob van Ruisdael and Meindert Hobbema. Paralleling these rare landscape paintings are de Vlieger's numerous large chalk representations of wooded landscapes, often on blue paper (e.g. Berlin, Kupferstichkab.; Groningen, Groninger Mus.; Paris, Fond. Custodia, Inst. Néer.; and Rotterdam, Mus. Boymans–van Beuningen). He also produced splendid marine drawings of two types: ships along rocky coasts in calm weather (e.g. Cambridge, Fitzwilliam; Vienna, Albertina) or ships in Dutch estuaries (e.g. Amsterdam, Rijksmus.). In addition, he drew townscapes and large-scale topographical subjects, which rank among the finest examples in this specialized category (e.g. Boston, Abrams priv. col., see 1991–2 exh. cat., nos. 36–7; and Leiden, Rijksuniv. Prentenkab.). His sympathetic depiction of animals is manifest in his large signed drawing of *Goats before a Shed* (Berlin, Kupferstichkab.; see fig. 2). De Vlieger also produced 20 etchings, ranging from landscapes and beach scenes to a series of 10 prints representing various types of domesticated animals.

A number of younger marine painters were influenced by de Vlieger, the most prominent of whom were Jan van de Cappelle, Hendrik Dubbels and Willem van de Velde the younger. Arnold Houbraken asserted that Willem van de Velde the younger was de Vlieger's pupil *c.* 1648. This list has been enlarged (Bol) to include Hendrick van Anthonissen (1606–after 1660), Arnoldus van Anthonissen (*fl* 1662–9), Willem van Diest (1610–after 1663), Claes Claesz. Wou (*c.* 1592–1665), Henrick Staets (*c.* 1558–1631), Pieter Mulier the elder (*c.* 1615–1670), Abraham van Beyeren and two marine painters active in Rotterdam, Hendrick Martensz. Sorgh (1611–70) and Jacob Adriensz. Bellevois (*c.* 1621–after 1672). Although de Vlieger's exact relationship to Jan van de Cappelle remains unclear, the fact that van de Cappelle possessed so many paintings and more than 1300 drawings by him suggests that he was able to secure much of this material *en bloc* from de Vlieger's estate. De Vlieger's daughter Cornelia married the painter Paulus van Hillegaert II (1631–58).

BIBLIOGRAPHY

Hollstein: *Dut. & Flem.*
A. Houbraken: *De groote schouburgh* (1718–21), ii, p. 325
P. Haverkorn van Rijsewijk: 'Simon Jacobsz. de Vlieger', *Oud-Holland*, ix (1891), pp. 221–4; ix (1893), pp. 229–35
F. C. Willis: *Die niederländische Marinemalerei* (Leipzig, 1911), pp. 44–50
A. Bredius: *Künstler-Inventare*, i (The Hague, 1915), pp. 356–8; iv (The Hague, 1916), p. 1643
Catalogue of Old Foreign Paintings, Copenhagen, Stat. Mus. Kst cat. (Copenhagen, 1951), pp. 346–8
H. Gerson and W. Godison: *Catalogue of Paintings, I: Dutch and Flemish*, Cambridge, Fitzwilliam cat. (Cambridge, 1960), pp. 136–8
J. Kelch: *Studien zu Simon de Vlieger als Marinemaler* (diss., U. Berlin, 1971)
L. J. Bol: *Die holländische Marinemalerei des 17. Jahrhunderts* (Brunswick, 1973), pp. 176–90
Gods, Saints and Heroes: Dutch Painting in the Age of Rembrandt (exh. cat., ed. A. Blankert; Washington, DC, N.G.A.; Detroit, MI, Inst. A.; Amsterdam, Rijksmus.; 1980–81), pp. 260–61
R. Ruurs: '"Even If It Is Not Architecture": Perspective Drawings by Simon de Vlieger and Willem van de Velde the Younger', *Simiolus*, xiii (1983), pp. 189–200
Masters of Seventeenth-century Dutch Landscape Painting (exh. cat. by P. Sutton, Amsterdam, Rijksmus.; Boston, MA, Mus. F.A.; Philadelphia, PA, Mus. A.; 1987–8), pp. 511–15
Mirror of Empire: Dutch Marine Art of the Seventeenth Century (exh. cat. by G. Keyes, Minneapolis, MN, Inst. A.; Toledo, OH, Mus. A.; Los Angeles, CA, Co. Mus. A.; 1990–91), pp. 184–91, 263–4
Seventeenth-century Dutch Drawings: A Selection from the Maida and George Abrams Collection (exh. cat. by W. W. Robinson, Amsterdam, Rijksmus.; Vienna, Albertina; New York, Pierpont Morgan Lib.; Cambridge, MA, Fogg; 1991–2), pp. 90–93

GEORGE S. KEYES

Vliet, Hendrick (Cornelisz.) van (*b* Delft, 1611–12; *d* Delft, *bur* 28 Oct 1675). Dutch painter. He is the only living artist discussed in Dirck van Bleyswijck's contemporary description of Delft, where he is said to have studied with his uncle, the portrait painter Willem van Vliet (?1583/4–1642), and then with Michiel van Mierevelt. From 1632 to *c.* 1650 van Vliet practised portraiture in a conservative South Holland style (e.g. *Portrait of a Woman*, 1650; Amsterdam, Rijksmus.). Around 1651 he turned to painting interior views of actual churches, mostly the Oude Kerk or the Nieuwe Kerk in Delft. His earliest known dated architectural picture, the *Pieterskerk in Leiden* (1652; Brunswick, Herzog Anton Ulrich-Mus.), is one of about 20 paintings representing churches in Leiden, Haarlem and Dutch towns other than Delft.

Van Vliet followed the example of Gerrit Houckgeest, whose portraits of Delft church interiors and their tomb monuments both met and stimulated a demand for such pictures. Like his contemporary Emanuel de Witte, van Vliet adopted Houckgeest's 'two-point' perspective scheme, in which the architecture ascends high in the foreground and recedes obliquely to the sides. However, van Vliet did not emulate Houckgeest's goal of fidelity to the architecture, and in such characteristic works as the Pieterskerk pictures (another, of 1653, is in Sarasota, FL, Ringling Mus. A.), the *Oude Kerk in Delft* (1654; Amsterdam, Rijksmus.) and the *Oude Kerk in Delft* (*c.* 1658–60; The Hague, Mauritshuis) he arbitrarily increased the apparent depth of the view and the viewer's distance from the picture plane. The columns are stretched vertically and are frequently placed at will, as are epitaphs, hatchments, pulpits and occasionally tombs. During the 1650s and early 1660s van Vliet frequently employed a painted archway, a *trompe l'oeil* curtain or both devices together to enhance the illusionistic space of his church interiors, which was complemented by his concentration on the cracked, rubbed, porous texture of the stone and a suggestion of damp atmosphere. Van Vliet's palette is often cooler than either Houckgeest's or de Witte's, favouring greenish tones and pervasive shadows penetrated by thin shafts of sunlight.

After the 1650s van Vliet's style could be stiff or careless, as in the numerous small pictures hastily produced in his later years. His distinctive figures, as well as his inclusion of dogs and such favourite motifs as groups of children and freshly dug graves, help to separate van Vliet's unsigned paintings from those by followers such as Cornelis de Man (1621–1706).

BIBLIOGRAPHY

H. Jantzen: *Das niederländische Architekturbild* (Leipzig, 1910)
W. A. Liedtke: *Architectural Painting in Delft: Gerard Houckgeest, Hendrick van Vliet, Emanuel de Witte* (Doornspijk, 1982)

WALTER LIEDTKE

Vliet, Jan Joris van (*b* Delft or Leiden, *c.* 1610; *d* after 1635). Dutch draughtsman and etcher. He owes his reputation to the fact that from *c.* 1629 he worked for Rembrandt in Leiden for a few years and again after Rembrandt moved to Amsterdam in 1631. However, it is uncertain whether van Vliet also moved to Amsterdam. He was not Rembrandt's pupil but an independent etcher, who also made etchings after his own designs. He collaborated with Rembrandt in preparing his painted compositions as prints and also copied etchings by Rembrandt. In addition, van Vliet made etchings after works by other artists, for example *Susanna and the Elders* (Hollstein, no. 53) after a painting by Jan Lievens (untraced). Van Vliet's etchings after his own designs were done during the same period he was working for Rembrandt, and these works he signed. Some are thematically derived from Rembrandt, such as the series of *Beggars* (1635), a subject etched by Rembrandt *c.* 1630 (B. 138, 150, 160, 162–7, 171, 173–5, 179, 183). Van Vliet's principal subjects were drawn from everyday life and depicted peasants, card-players, craftspeople and brothel scenes. However, his work lacks the humorous force of comparable works by such artists as Adriaen van Ostade, Jan Miense Molenaer and Cornelis Dusart. While van Vliet's early work is dependent on Rembrandt's style, the later etchings are divided between a much rougher manner and a strongly simplified technique, for example the series of *Tradesmen* (1635; B. 32–49). Van Vliet's career seems to have been a short one, as his last dated work is from 1635. A number of drawings and paintings have been attributed to him, but these are doubtful.

BIBLIOGRAPHY
Hollstein: *Dut. & Flem.*; Thieme–Becker
A. von Bartsch: *Catalogue raisonné de toutes les estampes qui forment l'oeuvre de Rembrandt et ceux de ses principaux imitateurs* (Vienna, 1797) [B.]
W. Fraenger: *Der junge Rembrandt, I: Johann Georg van Vliet und Rembrandt* (Heidelberg, 1920)
A. Hämmerle: *Handwerke und Künste: Ein Zyklus in 18 Radierungen von Jan Joris van Vliet (1610–1635)* (Munich, 1925)
K. Bauch: *Der frühe Rembrandt und seine Zeit* (Berlin, 1960), pp. 228–30
W. Sumowski: *Drawings of the Rembrandt School*, x (New York, 1990)
Delft Antiques Fair, cat. (Delft, 1990), pp. 129–35
NETTY VAN DE KAMP

Vliete, Gillis van den [Egidio Fiammingho; Egidio da Malines; Egidio della Riviera; Gilles de Rivière] (*b*? Mechelen; *d* Rome, *bur* 4 Sept 1602). Flemish sculptor, active in Italy. He is first recorded in Rome in 1567, when he was said to be a native of Mechelen. He was involved in the restoration of antique sculpture and collaborated on a number of monumental works with Nicolas Mostaert (*d* 1601–4), a sculptor from Arras. His style is typically Northern Renaissance in its heavily pleated draperies, uniform faces and interest in detail. It is best exemplified in the marble reliefs for the tomb of *Charles Frederick, Duke of Cleves* (with Mostaert, 1576–9) in the German church of S Maria dell' Anima, Rome; though overloaded, these compositions gain depth from a decentralized perspective. In the same church is the funerary monument of *Cardinal Andreas Habsburg* (marble, *c.* 1600), also a collaborative work with Mostaert.

BIBLIOGRAPHY
BNB; *NKL*; Thieme–Becker
G. K. Nagler: *Neues allgemeines Künstlerlexicon*, xiii (Munich, 1843), p. 217
IRIS KOCKELBERGH

Vlugt, Leendert Cornelis van der. *See under* BRINKMAN.

Vluten, Guillaume (*d* before 1445). Netherlandish sculptor. He was active in Paris during the second quarter of the 15th century. Between *c.* 1435 and 1442 he carved the tomb of *Anne of Burgundy, Duchess of Bedford* (1404–32), on commission from her brother Philip the Good (*see* BURGUNDY, (3)), for the monastery church of the Célestins, Paris. A drawing in the Gaignières Collection (Paris, Bib. N.) shows the monument as it appeared in the late 17th century. The tomb originally included seven weepers, one of which has been convincingly identified as representing *Philip the Good*. Only the white marble effigy of the Duchess, placed on its original slab of black Mosan marble, has survived (Paris, Louvre). Despite Vluten's probably Flemish origins, the effigy follows a long tradition of Parisian tomb sculpture. Notable for its youthful idealization of features and precisely defined details of costume, it is the artist's only known work. Vluten's work represents a conservative current in French sculpture.

BIBLIOGRAPHY
A. de Laborde: *Preuves* (1851), ii of *Les Ducs de Bourgogne: Etude sur les lettres, les arts et l'industrie pendant le XVe siècle et plus particulièrement dans les Pays-Bas et le duché de Bourgogne* (Paris, 1849–52), pp. vi–ix, 215
C. Dehaisnes: *Inventaire sommaire des archives départementales antérieures à 1790: Archives civiles, série B, Chambre des comptes de Lille*, iv (Lille, 1881), pp. 164, 187, 193–5
M. Aubert: *Moyen âge* (1950), i of *Catalogue des sculptures du moyen âge, de la renaissance et des temps modernes*, Paris, Louvre cat. (Paris, 1950–), pp. 196–7
J. C. Smith: 'The Tomb of Anne of Burgundy, Duchess of Bedford, in the Musée du Louvre', *Gesta*, xxiii (1984), pp. 39–50
J. STEYAERT

Vlyndt, Paul, II. *See* FLINDT, PAUL, II.

Voerman, Jan (*b* Kampen, nr Zwolle, 25 Jan 1857; *d* Hattem, nr Zwolle, 25 March 1941). Dutch painter. Between 1870 and 1875 he studied during the evenings at the Kampen art school, from 1876 to 1883 at the Amsterdam Academy, and from 1880 to 1881 at the Antwerp Academy. He became friendly with the writers and painters of the 'Eighties Movement' (Tachtigers) in Amsterdam, and from 1883 he painted interiors and street scenes from the Jewish quarter of Amsterdam in contrasting light and dark tones, in a precise style that was indebted to his academic education (e.g. the *Widow at the Second-hand Dealer, c.* 1884; priv. col., see Wagner, pl. 3). Around 1885 he produced more individual flower-pieces and landscapes with cattle near Amsterdam and Kampen; the landscapes, in white, deep blue and rich green, had a more spontaneous and emotional character than his earlier work, seen for example in *Cattle in the Meadows (at Hattem)* (1885–6; Amsterdam, Stedel. Mus.).

About 1887 Voerman adopted the Impressionist brushstroke, the figures in his townscapes becoming merely colour patches in his compositions and his palette less fresh. He also studied watercolour technique intensively at this period. In 1889 he married Anna Verkade and settled in Hattem. In his flower-pieces and landscapes between 1891 and 1896 he sought a purer means of artistic expression in planes of unmixed and opaque colour and simplified form, for example in *Grazing Cows at Hattem* (*c.* 1891–6; priv. col., see Wagner, pl. III). In 1896 he returned to producing more atmospheric landscapes and naturalistic colour, and from 1905 the glazes of his oil paintings had the transparency of watercolour (e.g. *Moors with Puddles in the Rain* (1911–18; Otterlo, Kröller-Müller). In colours varying from pale grey, blue and green to dark blue, dark green and orange, he captured the changing mood of the Dutch river landscape, expressing both tranquillity and an intense emotionalism reminiscent of Turner (e.g. *View of Hattem*, 1925–8; priv. col., see Wagner, pl. VI).

BIBLIOGRAPHY
A. Wagner: *Jan Voerman: IJsselschilder* (Wageningen, 1977, rev. Zwolle, 1991)
L. Boudewijns and Henk van Ulsen: *Broeden op een wolk: Jan Voerman, schilder 1857–1941* (Veenendaal, 1987)

ANNA WAGNER

Vöge [Voege], **Wilhelm** (*b* Bremen, 17 Feb 1868; *d* Ballenstedt, 30 Dec 1952). German art historian. A contemporary of Emile Mâle and Bernard Berenson, his relative obscurity compared to other art historians of his generation has been explained by his early and complete retirement from public life and the difficulties of translating his writings, which are both densely written and poetically sensitive. When he was 18 he wrote, 'How one descends to the sources . . . is the secret of all scientific history'; his approach was to remain that of a scientist, making an objective study of his subject from all points of view.

Vöge graduated from Leipzig University in 1886 and began work on his doctorate at Bonn in 1887, bringing together a group of Ottonian manuscripts and for the first time propounding a study of them as 'a body of material and sketches serving the transmission of motifs'. Turning to the study of sculpture after visiting Strasbourg he published his study of the west portal (the *portail royal*) of Chartres Cathedral in 1894. This work evinces the depth of his response to the sense of movement in Gothic sculpture and their carvers' relationship to the natural world. Following a prolonged tour of Italy, which resulted in *Raphael und Donatello* (Strasbourg, 1896), he went to Berlin in 1897 to work as an assistant to Wilhelm Bode. After ten years they quarrelled over a promotion, however, and in 1908 Vöge took up the chair of art history at the Albert-Ludwigs-Universität in Freiburg im Breisgau. His efforts made it one of the best regarded faculties in Germany, and he assembled a library and photographic archive. One of the students he supervised was the young Erwin Panofsky, who took his doctorate under Vöge in 1914 and was to remain one of his closest friends.

World War I precipitated a nervous crisis, and in 1916 Vöge retired at the age of 48. After a long period of silence he published a study of Nikolaus Hagenauer in 1930. At the outbreak of World War II in 1939 he was working in retirement at Ballenstedt on a book about Jörg Syrlin the elder, which at its much postponed publication in 1950 was hailed as his masterwork, not least by Panofsky, who called it 'a book which comes closest to the often postulated ideal of a total history of art'.

WRITINGS
'Eine deutsche Malerschule um die Wende des ersten Jahrtausends', *Wdt. Z. Gesch. & Kst* (1891) [suppl. vii]
Die Anfänge des monumentalen Stiles im Mittelalter (Strasbourg, 1894)
Raphael und Donatello (Strasbourg, 1896)
Die deutsche Plastik des 13. Jahrhunderts (Berlin, 1905)
Niclas Hagnower (Freiburg im Breisgau, 1931)
Jörg Syrlin der Ältere und seine Bildwerke, 2 vols (Berlin, 1950)

BIBLIOGRAPHY
C. G. Heise: *Wilhelm Vöge: Zum Gedächtnis* (Freiburg im Breisgau, 1968)
E. Panofsky: 'Wilhelm Vöge: A Biographical Memoir', *A. J.* [New York], xxviii/1 (1968), pp. 27–37

JACQUELINE COLLISS HARVEY

Vogel (i). German family of stuccoists. (1) Johann Jakob Vogel was assisted by his son (2) Franz Jakob Vogel in several projects at Bamberg. Another son, Andreas Vogel

(married 1734), is believed to be the stuccoist AV who in 1763 worked on the decoration of the Fliesensaal of the Residenz in Ansbach. Their relationship to Johann Caspar Vogel (*fl* 1690–1718, perhaps a brother of (1) Johann Jakob Vogel), Heinrich Vogel (*d* 20 March 1759) and Christoph Vogel (*d* 1770), stuccoists in the Bamberg region, is not clearly established.

(1) Johann Jakob Vogel (*b* before 1660; *d* Bamberg, 6 May 1727). He was one of the most outstanding German late Baroque decorators. Around 1688 he developed an individual style of decoration with distinctive, delicately articulated acanthus leaves that suggests that he was trained in the Wessobrunn schoool of plasterers. Examples of decorative schemes in this style (*Laubwerk*) are the interiors of St Stephan and the Residenz in Bamberg, the latter being Vogel's main project from this period. The style of ribbonwork adopted for his decoration (1711–13) of the Obere Pfarrkirche, Bamberg, is influenced by the engravings of Paul Decker the elder, in particular the first volume of the *Fürstlicher Baumeister* (1711). Vogel worked mainly to his own designs, and sometimes also acted as a contractor. Outside Bamberg, important work by him includes the church at Freienfels (*c.* 1700), the monastery and church at Banz (1702–9 and 1714), churches at Forchheim (1719–20), Dormitz (1723–4) and Memmelsdorf (1708), as well as stuccoed ceilings at various mansions or castles, including those in Seehof (from *c.* 1690), Eyrichshof, Greifenstein near Heiligenstadt (*c.* 1692) and Gailbach (from 1695).

(2) Franz Jakob Vogel (*b* Bamberg, *bapt* 23 July 1698; *d* ?Bamberg, 7 June 1770). Son of (1) Johann Jakob Vogel. He was a pupil of his father, whom he was assisting at St Michael's church in Bamberg by the 1720s. There are examples of his early ribbonwork decoration in churches at Tiefenstürmig, Sambach, Hirschaid and Schlüsselfeld. His masterpiece is the stuccowork in the pilgrimage church of Gössweinstein (1733–5), where in the vaulting of the choir and the nave, the soffits of the window and door frames and in the tower chapels he employed a personal variation on the French Régence style, richly interspersed with figure motifs. He collaborated with his brother-in-law Martin Walter (*c.* 1687–1763) and Johann Peter Benkert (1709–69) on the high altar for Gössweinstein, which has a large number of stucco figures. In the mid-1740s Vogel began using rocaille shapes. Works of this period include the ceiling of the hall at Bamberg Rathaus and the banqueting hall at Schloss Seehof, with reliefs based on themes from antiquity, including *Apollo and Daphne*, *Diana and Actaeon* and *Pan and Syrinx*. He was also a talented draughtsman, as his design (*c.* 1745; Bamberg, Staatsbib.) for the Virgin altar in St Martin's church in Bamberg demonstrates. Vogel was a master of sculpture in stucco, moving from the most delicate low relief to work in the round with a total sureness of touch.

BIBLIOGRAPHY
K. Sitzmann: *Künstler und Kunsthandwerk in Oberfranken* (Kulmbach, 1983), pp. 162–5

ERICH SCHNEIDER

Vogel (ii). German family of painters. The portrait painter (1) Christian Leberecht Vogel, although known primarily for his studies of children, also wrote several books on art theory. Among his pupils was his son (2) Carl Christian Vogel von Vogelstein, a portrait painter who also produced works on religious and literary themes.

(1) Christian Leberecht Vogel (*b* Dresden, 6 April 1759; *d* Dresden, 11 April 1816). Painter, draughtsman and art theoretician. He studied with Johann Eleazar Schenau (1737–1806) in Dresden and at the Dresden Akademie. From 1780 he worked for the Saxon nobility in the Muldenland, including (until 1804) Friedrich Magnus, Graf von Solms, at Schloss Wildenfels, near Zwickau. He not only painted portraits of his employers, but also taught their children drawing. His portraits of children were especially popular, eg. the *Master's Sons* (1793; Coburg, Schloss). He exhibited in Dresden and in 1800 became a member of the Dresden Akademie, where he was appointed professor in 1814. Because his works have been largely in private ownership, his extensive oeuvre is not completely known. His portraits, transitional between Enlightenment Rococo and classicist Romanticism, have a somewhat sentimental, genre quality. Their emotive transfiguration of childhood is thoroughly bourgeois and anticipates the intimacy of Biedermeier art. The technical quality of his work is exceptionally high, being based on the traditions of the Dresden school.

WRITINGS
Ideen über die Schönheitslehre in Hinsicht auf sichtbare Gegenstände überhaupt und auf bildende Kunst insbesondere (Dresden, 1812)

BIBLIOGRAPHY
O. E. Schmidt: 'Dresdener Kunst vor 100 Jahren', *Walderburger Schr.*, viii (1928)
——: *Fürst Otto Carl Friedrich von Schönburg und die Seinen* (Leipzig, 1931), pp. 53–78
H. J. Neidhardt: *Die Malerei der Romantik in Dresden* (Wiesbaden, 1976), pp. 323, 375

VOLKER HELAS

(2) Carl Christian Vogel von Vogelstein (*b* Wildenfels, 26 June 1788; *d* Munich, 4 March 1868). Painter, son of (1) Christian Leberecht Vogel. He first trained with his father and from 1804 attended the Dresden Akademie where he began to attract attention as a skilled portrait painter. He was employed as a drawing instructor in the home of Baron von Löwenstern and in 1808 accompanied the Baron's family to St Petersburg, where he worked as a portrait painter until 1812. In Russia he amassed a collection of his own sketches of celebrated men. These drawings were in the form of medallion portraits, the earlier ones in chalk, the later ones in fine pencil. He subsequently travelled widely in Europe to make additions to his collection, which eventually numbered 700 drawings (Dresden, Kupferstichkab.).

From 1813 to 1820 Vogelstein lived in Rome where he studied Italian 14th- and 15th-century painting and was closely affiliated with the circle of the Lukasbrüder (Nazarenes). He completed portraits there of several artists, including the Danish sculptor *Bertel Thorvaldsen* (1815; Copenhagen, Thorvaldsens Mus.). On his return to Dresden in 1820 he became a professor at the Akademie and in 1824 was appointed court painter. In this capacity he decorated the Banquet Hall in Schloss Pillnitz with eight tempera paintings of *Allegories of the Arts* (1822), and for the chapel he provided ten frescoes representing scenes

from the *Life of the Virgin* (1830). In both projects he emulated the Italian murals painted by the Lukasbrüder and was one of the first artists to bring this style of mural painting to Dresden.

Both contemporary and posthumous opinion have esteemed Vogelstein's portraiture more highly than the rest of his oeuvre. In his portraits he combined psychological penetration of character with a candid naturalness. He often showed his sitters at work or surrounded by attributes of their professions, as in his well-known painting *David d'Anger Sculpting the Bust of Ludwig Tieck* (1834; Leipzig, Mus. Bild. Kst.). This work is typical of Vogelstein's style with its pronounced contours, precise detailing, enamel surfaces and the exquisite colouring for which he was celebrated. The picture is set in his studio and shows the painter, with his small son looking on, recording the scene before him: Tieck seated in front of the sculptor at work on the bust, surrounded by Dresden artist friends and accompanied by his daughter Dorothy. As with most of Vogelstein's portraits, this work is characteristic of Biedermeier painting in its fusion of genre and portraiture and its combination of bourgeois intimacy, busy productivity and domesticity.

Vogelstein showed more Romantic tendencies in his many paintings based on literary themes from Dante Alighieri and Johann Wolfgang von Goethe. During his second visit to Rome in 1842–4, he painted the polyptych *Dante in Relation to the 'Divine Comedy'*, containing a central panel showing Dante seated at the grave of Beatrice, surrounded by 11 small paintings illustrating scenes from the poet's life. His later works included several altarpieces and many portraits. He also completed a pendant (1847–52) to the *Dante* polyptych which depicted scenes from Goethe's *Faust*. He was increasingly active as a graphic artist and published *Die Hauptmomente von Goethes Faust, Dantes Divina Comedia und Virgils Aeneas* (Munich, 1861). In 1853 Vogelstein moved to Munich where he remained until his death, with the exception of a third trip to Italy in 1856–7.

BIBLIOGRAPHY
A. Raczynski: *Geschichte der neueren deutschen Kunst*, iii (Berlin, 1841), pp. 218–19
F. von Boetticher: *Malerwerke des neunzehnten Jahrhunderts* (Dresden, 1891–1901/*R* Hofheim am Taunus, 1974), pp. 937–40
F. Noack: *Das Deutschtum in Rom* (Berlin, 1927)
Kunst in Sachsen vor hundert Jahren (exh. cat., Dresden, Sächs. Kstver., 1928)
E. Sigismund: 'Der Dresdner Graff des 19. Jahrhunderts', *Dresdn. Nachr.*, xxix (1939), p. 7
H. J. Neidhardt: *Die Malerei der Romantik in Dresden* (Leipzig, 1976), pp. 236–8, 326–8

MARSHA L. MORTON

Vogel, David (*bapt* Zurich, 12 Feb 1744; *bur* Zurich, 10 Dec 1808). Swiss architect. After training as a mason (1759–62) with his father Heinrich, then presiding officer of the Zurich Masons' Guild, he undertook further study in Rome (1763–5), moving in the circle of Johann Joachim Winckelmann and meeting artists on scholarships to the city. There are records of his contacts with Giovanni Battista Casanova, Giovanni Stern (1734–94) and possibly Jacques Gondoin. From this period large-scale, measured drawings of ancient and Renaissance buildings survive (Zurich, Zentbib., MS. Escher vom Glas 188.6). After returning to Zurich, Vogel passed his master's examination (1766) and carried out some small-scale buildings (Rorbas, vicarage, 1773; Embrach, Protestant church, 1779–80). Of special interest are his neo-Romanesque and neo-Gothic projects (1780; not executed) for the Gross-Münster in Zurich. According to a fragmentary manuscript entitled *Geschichte der englischen Kunst* (1790; untraced), Vogel was engaged from *c.* 1770 in writing a history of architecture. A sympathizer with the French Revolution, Vogel went to Paris in 1793 and lived there for five years, associating with the architects Claude-Nicolas Ledoux, Jacques-Denis Antoine and Charles Percier, among others. From 1798 he was again in Switzerland, where he was made head of the Ministry of Works of the Helvetian Republic (1798–1803). Connected with this appointment are the unexecuted projects for converting the Zunfthaus 'zur Zimmerleuten' (Carpenters' Guildhall) in Zurich and the Kloster Maria-Hilf, Lucerne, into a National-Palast or parliament building. He also produced proposals for reorganizing the building industry and cultural policy in Switzerland (MS., Berne, Schweizer. Bundesarchv, Bd. 1482).

Vogel's technical interests are most apparent in his projects for the Rhine Bridge at Eglisau (1806), while his theoretical interests are revealed in the contents of his personal library, which contained more than 300 books on architectural subjects; many of these survive (printed auction catalogue, Zurich, 1808). However, although he was among the best-trained architects in Switzerland in the 18th century, Vogel's practical skill did not match his theoretical knowledge, so that his few built works do not reflect his real importance.

BIBLIOGRAPHY

H. Blümner: *Winckelmanns Briefe an seine Zürcher Freunde* (Freiburg, 1882)
H. Hoffmann: 'Die klassizistische Baukunst in Zürich', *Mitt. Antiqua. Ges. Zürich*, xxxi (1930), pp. 9–14
B. Carl: *Klassizismus* (Zurich, 1963)
G. Germann: *Der protestantische Kirchenbau in der Schweiz: Von der Reformation bis zur Romantik* (Zurich, 1963), pp. 124–9
H. M. Gubler: 'Der Zürcher Architekt David Vogel (1744–1808): Zu seinen Architekturstudien in Rom, 1763–1765', *Unsere Kstdkml.*, xxv (1974), pp. 281–94
——: 'Brückenmacher gegen Brückenbaumeister: David Vogels Kampf um eine kunstgerechte Eglisauer Rheinbrücke', *Turicum*, ii (1981), pp. 43–9

HANS MARTIN GUBLER

Vogel, Jean Philippe (*b* The Hague, 9 Jan 1871; *d* Oegstgeest, 10 April 1958). Dutch archaeologist and linguist. He initially studied Dutch literature in Amsterdam (1890) but specialized in Sanskrit in his thesis (1897). After a year of private lecturing (1898–9) on Indian literature at the University of Amsterdam, in 1900 he went to India to study Sanskrit further and to visit the Hindu and Muslim monuments. The British archaeologist Sir Aurel Stein, whom he met in Kashmir, recommended that the Indian Government appoint Vogel as Archaeological Surveyor. From 1901 to 1913 Vogel undertook surveys, first of the Muslim monuments and the Hindu antiquities and inscriptions in the Punjab; later, transferred to Uttar Pradesh, he was in charge of the early Hindu and Buddhist monuments and participated in excavations. In 1914 Vogel was appointed professor in Sanskrit and Archaeology at Leiden University. He was one of the founders of the archaeological Kern Institute in 1925 and the supervisor of 12 volumes of the *Annual Bibliography of Indian Archaeology* edited by the Kern Institute from 1926 onwards.

BIBLIOGRAPHY

Kok Wie Lim: *J. Orient. Res.*, xxvii (1957–8), pp. 17–47 [with annotated bibliog.]

H. I. R. HINZLER

Vogel, (Georg) Ludwig (*b* Zurich, 10 July 1788; *d* Zurich, 20 Aug 1879). Swiss painter. He served an apprenticeship as a pastry-cook, simultaneously training as an artist under Samuel Scheurmann (1770–1844) and Johann Pfenninger (1765–1825) in Aarau (1802–3) and from 1804 with Henry Fuseli and Konrad Gessner in Zurich. In 1807 he set out on a study tour in Switzerland, visiting the Bernese Oberland, the Valais and Ticino: the subsequent exhibition was so successful that he was able to give up baking and devote himself entirely to painting. In 1808 he went to the Akademie der Bildenden Künste in Vienna, where he studied under Lorenz Schönberger (1768–1847). With his friends Friedrich Overbeck and Franz Pforr he was a founder-member of the Lukasbund (*see* NAZARENES), a student group whose formation was precipitated by the temporary closure of the Akademie early in 1809. The group looked back to early German and Italian Renaissance painting in its search for artistic sincerity, and when in 1810 Vogel travelled to Rome with Overbeck and Pforr, he turned his back definitively on academicism. As well as his work within the Lukasbund circle, the main influences on him in Rome were Bertel Thorvaldsen, Joseph Anton Koch and Peter Cornelius. In 1813 he returned to Zurich for good after a second visit to Italy. Occasional painting trips took him to the Black Forest (1820), Paris (1822), Stuttgart (1824) and Munich, where he also took part in exhibitions (1830 and 1832). Most of his pictures treat historical subjects from Swiss history (*Battle of Grandson 1476*, 1836; Berne, Kstmus.); very popular in his lifetime, they were often reproduced and widely disseminated.

BIBLIOGRAPHY

Bénézit; Kstgesch. Schweiz; Thieme–Becker

CHRISTINA STEINHOFF

Vogel, Sebestyén Antal (*b* Pest, ?1779; *d* Pest, 14 June 1837). Hungarian furniture manufacturer. He learnt his craft in Pest and then spent two years abroad, mainly in Vienna. Bypassing the traditional division of labour determined by the guilds, he opened the first comprehensive furniture factory in Hungary in Pest in 1805, employing designers, carpenters, gilders, turners, bronze-founders, upholsterers and glassmakers in a single location; 130 craftsmen were involved by 1816. Vogel established distribution warehouses in several towns throughout Hungary. In addition to his own designs, he used French, English and Viennese designs for his furniture and introduced an element of Egyptian Revival influence into his decoration. After 1818 he used moulded composition ornaments, instead of bronze mounts, to produce less expensive pieces that became widely popular. The factory also created entire decorative schemes, including the interiors of the New German Theatre (1811; destr.), the

National Casino (1827–30; destr.), both in Pest, and the pulpit and clergy stalls (*in situ*) in the Protestant Reformed church of Debrecen. The firm closed after Vogel's death.

BIBLIOGRAPHY
M. Zlinszkyné Sternegg: 'Az első magyar "butorgyárnok" Vogel Sebestyén Antal' [The first Hungarian furniture manufacturer Vogel Sebestyén Antal], *Művészettörténeti Tanulmányok* (1957), pp. 153–218

FERENC BATÁRI

Vogel, Zygmunt [pseud. Ptaszek] (*b* Warsaw, 15 June 1764; *d* Warsaw, 20 April 1826). Polish painter, printmaker and teacher. He trained as a master builder and then from 1780 studied under André Lebrun (1737–1811) in the school of painting at the Royal Castle in Warsaw, as well as under Jakub Monaldi and Simon Bogumił Zug. In 1785 Vogel produced several watercolour copies of *vedute* of Warsaw by Bernardo Bellotto, which laid the foundations of his future career. He also became Bellotto's first successor in the field of *veduta* painting. From 1785 Vogel painted over 100 *vedute* of the capital and its environs (e.g. *Panoramic View of Warsaw from Praga*, 1816; St Petersburg, Rus. Mus.), many of which, because of their detail and precision, were later used to reconstruct monuments destroyed during World War II. From 1787 until 1800, on the recommendation of Stanislav II Poniatowski, who appointed him his Government Illustrator, and later, on his own initiative, Vogel made several trips around Poland, painting views of castles and their ruins, and of large and small towns mainly in the Wisła River basin. From 1794 Vogel painted many landscapes in the King's summer residence at Łazienki Palace near Warsaw. In addition to his royal commissions, Vogel painted several series of landscapes for wealthy families, recording the appearance of their palaces and parks, which were modelled on famous English landscape parks and gardens. He painted mainly in watercolour, but occasionally in India ink and sepia. He was also active as a printmaker, undertaking an edition of etchings of an enormous series of drawings entitled *Zbiór widoków sławniejszych pamiątek narodowych* ('A collection of views of the more famous national relics'), whose first and only series—of 20 views by Jan Zachariasz Frey (1769–1829)—appeared in Warsaw in 1806. From 1800 Vogel was mainly occupied with teaching, culminating with his appointment in 1817 to the chair of perspective at the Fine Arts Department of the University of Warsaw. From 1810 he executed several state commissions for military and other forms of architecture. Vogel's paintings expressed the new patriotic and romantic themes that characterized a nation striving for a sense of identity. The largest collection of his watercolours is housed in the National Museum in Warsaw and the Drawing Room of the University of Warsaw Library.

BIBLIOGRAPHY
E. Rastawiecki: *Słownik malarzów polskich tudzież obcych w Polsce osiadłych lub czasowo w niej przebywających* [Dictionary of Polish and foreign artists resident in and visiting Poland], 3 vols (Warsaw, 1850–71), iii, pp. 10–14
K. Sroczyńska: *Zygmunt Vogel rysownik gabinetowy Stanisława Augusta* [Zygmunt Vogel: official illustrator to Stanislav Augustus] (Wrocław, 1969)
——: *Podróże malownicze Zygmunta Vogla* [The painted travels of Zygmunt Vogel] (Warsaw, 1980)
——: *Warszawa Zygmunta Vogla* [Zygmunt Vogel's Warsaw] (exh. cat., Warsaw, Pałacyk Gal., 1981)

KRYSTYNA SROCZYŃSKA

Vogeler, (Johann) Heinrich (*b* Bremen, 12 Dec 1872; *d* nr Karaganda, Kazakh SSR, [now Kazakhstan], 14 June 1942). German painter, printmaker and architect. He studied from 1890 to 1893 in Düsseldorf. In 1895 he bought the Barkenhoff in Worpswede, near Bremen. Soon afterwards, with colleagues from the WORPSWEDE COLONY, including Fritz Mackensen, Fritz Overbeck (1869–1909), Hans am Ende (1864–1918) and Otto Modersohn (1865–1943), he exhibited successfully at the Glaspalast in Munich. He provided illustrations for the periodical *Die Insel*, and undertook the interior decoration of the Güldenkammer in Bremen. In 1906 he visited Ceylon (now Sri Lanka) for convalescence and in 1909 he went to England to study the principles of the garden city movement. He served in the German army in World War I, his writing of a pacifist letter to the Emperor in January 1918 prompting an official inquiry into his state of mental health. In 1919 he founded the Arbeitsgemeinschaft Barkenhoff in Worpswede, in an unsuccessful attempt to create an Arbeitsschule and a utopian community. From 1920 to 1926 he painted the Barkenhoff-Diele, the hall at Barkenhoff, with scenes from the revolutionary political struggle.

In 1923 Vogeler made his first journey to the USSR, when he painted such works as *The Kremlin* (1923; New Haven, CT, Yale U. A.G.). After co-founding the ARBKD (Association of Revolutionary Painters and Sculptors in Germany) he made a new attempt to create a commune, this time at Fontana Martina near Ascona, Switzerland. His political views, allied to his ability as an architect, led him to work in Russia in 1931 for the Union Committee for the Standardization of Building and to exhibit his new work in Moscow (1932). He undertook propaganda work on the cotton farms in Kazakhstan and in 1935 became artistic manager of an exhibition of the International Red Aid in Moscow. Following criticism that his paintings were too complex, he turned to social realism, producing portraits of *Lotte Loebinger* and *Heinrich Greif* (1938; Berlin, Alte N.G.) and making dolls for the German collectivist theatre in Odessa. After the German invasion of the USSR in 1941 he produced anti-Fascist pamphlets and spoke on Radio Moscow, but because of his German nationality he was evacuated to Kazakhstan, where, under difficult conditions, he worked on his memoirs and wrote more pamphlets.

WRITINGS
Reise durch Russland (Dresden, 1925/*R* 1974)
Werden: Erinnerungen mit Lebenszeugnissen aus den Jahren 1923–1942 (Berlin, 1989)

BIBLIOGRAPHY
K.-R. Schütze: *Heinrich Vogeler: Leben und architektonisches Werk* (diss., Berlin, 1980)
H. H. Rief: *Heinrich Vogeler: Das graphische Werk* (Lilienthal, 1983)
Heinrich Vogeler: Kunstwerke, Gebrauchsgegenstände, Dokumente (exh. cat., Berlin, 1983)

KARL-ROBERT SCHÜTZE

Vogelgesang, Klaus (*b* Radebeul, 27 April 1945). German painter. He grew up in Gronau, Westphalia, but in 1965 he moved to Berlin, where he studied until 1969 at the Akademie für Grafik, Druck und Werbung. After his studies he worked as a freelance artist. In 1972 he founded the group Aspekt with other representatives of Critical Realism (*see* BERLIN, §II, 5). During 1976 he was in Rome as a scholar at the Villa Massimo. Having painted in watercolour and produced line drawings verging on caricatures with heightened outlines, he began *c.* 1970 to work on compositions that were small at first but already pictorial. The inner spaces of his figures were filled with modulations of light and shade; the accessories had brilliant likeness and perfect detail, lending his work, which almost exclusively comprised pencil and crayon drawings, an illusory effect.

After 1974–5 the format of Vogelgesang's work grew considerably, culminating in the enormous *Metropolis Triptych* (1.96×4.50 m, 1977; Bonn, Samml. BRD). As well as alluding to the work of Otto Dix, in the triptych he adopted the technique of photomontage from the Dadaists. He combined contradictory or apparently disconnected pictures, such as photographs from magazines and advertising posters, into an organic whole, using drawing to imbue it with a visually superior meaning. The persons and objects depicted are symbols or signs, and a subtle demand for changes in society.

BIBLIOGRAPHY

Klaus Vogelgesang, 1969–1982 (exh. cat., W. Berlin, Staatl. Ksthalle, 1982)

DOMINIK BARTMANN

Vogelherd. Cave site in Kreis Heidenheim, Germany. It has yielded one of the earliest and best-executed assemblages of art objects of the Upper Palaeolithic period (*c.* 40,000–*c.* 10,000 BP; *see also* PREHISTORIC EUROPE, §II). Excavated in 1931 by Gustav Riek, Vogelherd has the longest known stratigraphic sequence in south-western Germany, having yielded Middle Palaeolithic, Micoquian, Mousterian, Aurignacian, Magdalenian and Early Neolithic stone tool assemblages. The most important in terms of the number of artefacts and bones recovered are the Aurignacian levels, which also yielded human skeletal remains belonging to the earliest known specimens of *Homo sapiens sapiens* in the region. The rich fauna comprised mammoths, horses, reindeer, rhinoceroses, red deer, cattle, chamois, wolves, foxes and lions. Radiocarbon dates for these levels range from *c.* 32,000 BP to *c.* 27,000 BP. During this period stone artefacts were produced on the terrace outside the cave, and many tools have been found in the interior, where most of the antler and bone artefacts were concentrated around a large hearth belonging to level V; almost all the art objects in the cave were also found in a single location, suggesting an intentional cache. The art material recovered from the site is exhibited by the university library, Tübingen, and the Altes Schloss, Württembergisches Landesmuseum, Stuttgart.

An area for working mammoth ivory was discovered at the south-western entrance of the cave, and all but one of the figurines found at Vogelherd were carved from this material. Pieces from lower level V are fully sculptured, while upper level V also contained flat pieces and low reliefs. The construction scheme of the figurines is based on the body, to which shortened legs and a detailed head have been added. Mammoths, lions, a horse, a bison and a human figure have been identified. The horse is one of the most beautiful and expressive figurines; it has a long

curved neck—a posture adopted by stallions to appear larger (*see* PREHISTORIC EUROPE, fig. 11). Two of the lion figures have aggressive postures, indicated by the backward-pointing ears. Four figurines pierced between the legs are pendants, as is the single bone specimen, a bone with a low-relief carving of a mammoth, used to retouch stone tools. Differences in size and design point to a variety of functions (*see* PREHISTORIC EUROPE, §II, 3).

BIBLIOGRAPHY

G. Riek: *Die Eiszeitjägerstation am Vogelherd* (Tübingen, 1934)

J. Hahn: 'Kraft und Aggression', *Archaeologica Venatoria* (Tübingen, 1986)

JOACHIM HAHN

Vogels, Guillaume (*b* Brussels, 9 June 1836; *d* Ixelles [now in Brussels], 9 Jan 1896). Belgian painter. He first worked as a house painter, running his own painting and decorating business from 1855 on. Although he was essentially self-taught, he appears to have been influenced by Périclès Pantazis, whom he employed in his business. He began exhibiting his work in 1874, and in 1878 he joined the group La Chrysalide; he was a founder-member of Les XX (*see* ⟨VINGT⟩, LES), later took part in La Libre Esthétique and exhibited regularly in the Cercle Artistique and in 1881 at the Salon in Paris. Vogels was particularly indebted to the work of landscape painters working in Tervuren, near Brussels, such as Hippolyte Boulenger, and he used a broad technique similar to that of Louis Artan but even more daring; many of his paintings were executed not with brushes but with a palette knife. *Foul Weather* (exh. 1885; Brussels, Musées Royaux B.-A.) is an outstanding example of his direct, free and spontaneous use of paint to represent landscape and effects of light, which influenced the early work of James Ensor and anticipated such 20th-century styles as Fauvism and Tachism.

BIBLIOGRAPHY

Vogels (exh. cat., Brussels, Mus. Ixelles, 1968)

Belgian Art, 1880–1914 (exh. cat., New York, Brooklyn Mus., 1980)

FRANCINE-CLAIRE LEGRAND

Voghelarius, Livinus [Vogeleer, Lieven de] (*fl* 1551–68). Flemish painter, active in England. He was presumably the painter Lieven de Vogeleer who became a freeman of the Antwerp Guild of St Luke in 1551, but is known by only one work, the *Memorial of Lord Darnley* (Edinburgh, Pal. Holyroodhouse, Royal Col.), commissioned in London in January 1568 by Darnley's parents, Matthew and Margaret Stewart, 4th or 12th Earl and Countess of Lennox. It is a 'revenge' picture, of a type specifically Scottish and without parallel in England, and the iconography has been worked out with extreme care. Ten Latin and three English inscriptions emphasize the message: that the murder at Kirk o'Field of Henry Stewart, Lord Darnley, in February 1567 must be avenged and that the murderer Bothwell and his associates acted with the consent of Darnley's wife, Mary Queen of Scots. The effigy of Darnley is represented in armour lying on an elaborate sarcophagus before an altar, on the step of which is the signature *Livinus Voghelarius*. In the middle foreground kneels the infant James VI (future James I of England), a scroll issuing from his mouth praying God to avenge his father's innocent blood, and to the right kneel his grandparents and uncle Charles with similar scrolls. In the lower left corner is an inset picture showing Mary surrendering to the confederate lords of Scotland at Carberry in June 1567, with Bothwell—whom she had married in May—riding away in the distance; the landscape is Flemish in character. Some of the more offensive inscriptions about Mary have been obliterated, perhaps when James I began the rehabilitation of his mother's memory; they can be reconstructed from a version at Goodwood House, W. Sussex.

BIBLIOGRAPHY
E. Waterhouse: *Painting in Britain, 1530–1790*, Pelican Hist. A. (Harmondsworth, 1953, 4/1978), pp. 48–9
O. Millar: *The Tudor, Stuart and Early Georgian Pictures in the Royal Collection*, i (London, 1963), pp. 75–7
Painting in Scotland, 1570–1650 (exh. cat. by D. Thomson, Edinburgh, N.P.G., 1975)

MARY EDMOND

Vogt, Christian (*b* Basle, 12 April 1946). Swiss photographer. He studied photography at the Gewerbeschule, Basle (1964–7). After being apprenticed to American photographer Will McBride in Munich, he opened his own studio in Basle in 1970. From 1972 he worked for various magazines, such as *Du*, *Camera*, *Time-Life* and *Playboy*. His photographs were created in clearly defined phases, such as his 'blue period' with tinted prints (1973–5) or the 'frame' series (1975) of photographs in which a rectangular frame photographed inside the field of view became the parameter for a picture within a picture (e.g. *Without Title*, 1975; Basle, Antikenmus.). His best-known series of erotic self-presentations of women, with a wooden crate as a prop (1979–81), explored a similar principle. His photographs often implied reflections on the photograph itself, on its subject, its selection and the relationship between what was shown and what was left out.

PHOTOGRAPHIC PUBLICATIONS
In Camera, 82 Images by 52 Women (Basle, 1982)
Fotografische Notizen und notierte Zufälle (Basle, 1984)
Katzenschattenhase (Basel, 1988)

BIBLIOGRAPHY
M. Pellerin: *Masterpieces of Erotic Photography* (London, 1972, 2/1977)

REINHOLD MISSELBECK

Vogtherr. German family of artists. (1) Heinrich Vogtherr (i) trained and, for a while, collaborated with his son (2) Heinrich Vogtherr (ii), largely in the execution of woodcuts, for which both are best known.

BIBLIOGRAPHY
F. Vogtherr: *Geschichte der Familie Vogtherr (v. Vogtsberg) im Lichte des Kulturlebens* (Ansbach, 1908)
H. Röttinger: 'Die beiden Vogtherr', *Jb. Kstwiss.* (1927), pp. 164–84
L. Schneeman: 'Pieter Brueghel the Elder and the Vogtherrs: Some Sources of Influence', *Z. Kstgesch.*, xlix (1986), pp. 29–40

(1) Heinrich Vogtherr (i) (*b* Dillingen an der Donau, 1490; *d* Vienna, 1556). Woodcutter, draughtsman, etcher, painter, writer and publisher. Although he wrote and printed several medical books and became an eye specialist, his main career was as an artist. He may have received his training in the workshop of Hans Burgkmair I in Augsburg and may have spent some time as a journeyman with Hans Schäufelein I. By 1513 he had returned to Dillingen. A *Self-portrait* (1518; see Geisberg, no. 1348) is signed HSD, a monogram reading 'Henricus Satrapitanus Dilinganus' (Gr. *satrapes*, Ger. *Vogt*: 'deputy'); Satrapitanus was the

name he later used as an author. From 1522 he lived in Wimpfen an der Neckar, as documented by a woodcut of *Christ as Redeemer* (1522), signed 'Hainricus Vogtherr Maler zu Wimpffen', and by frescoes of the *Annunciation* and *Last Judgement* (Wimpfen, St Mary; rest. 1869). In 1525 he moved to Strassburg (Strasbourg), where he became a citizen and member of the guild the following year. In 1536 he began a printing business, publishing chiefly medical works, some written by himself. Collaboration with the Zurich printer Christoph Froschauer (*fl* 1519; *d* 1566) documents his presence in that city and in the late 1540s he may have been in Augsburg, where his son had lived since 1541. In 1550 he was called to Vienna as painter and eye specialist at the court of the future Holy Roman Emperor Ferdinand I.

The work for which Vogtherr is now best known is his *Kunstbüchlein* (Strasbourg, 1537; copy in Wolfenbüttel, Herzog August-Bib.), the first printed model-book for artists. In the introduction, although sympathetic to many of Luther's causes, he bewailed the fate of art and artists in German lands since the Reformation. It was for the benefit of artists, especially those unable to travel, that he had compiled what he called a catalogue of all the strange and most difficult pieces that an artist must know how to draw. The book follows the traditional pattern book of late medieval workshop practices: there are pages with fantastic heads and headgear (see fig.), with hands and feet in various attitudes, and with armour, weapons and

Heinrich Vogtherr (i): *Nine Female Heads*, woodcut from his *Kunstbüchlein* (Strasbourg, 1537)

ornaments. The book was produced with the assistance of his son Heinrich Vogtherr (ii), whose name and portrait medallion appear on the title page alongside those of his father.

Although Vogtherr produced some remarkable works, his output is characterized by its vigour, technical skill and diversity of subject-matter rather than any artistic originality. He remained indebted to Burgkmair and the Augsburg school throughout his career. Little is known of his paintings, and he is now remembered chiefly for his woodcuts and a few drawings. His subject-matter encompassed the entire spectrum of 16th-century popular iconography: biblical and devotional subjects, genre and satirical scenes, allegories, battles, festivals, images of torture and death, portraits, ornaments, coats of arms and printers' marks, maps, astrological signs and freaks of nature, such as an abnormal rabbit (1532; Geisberg, no. 1439), a giant ear of wheat (1542; Geisberg, no. 1441) and portrait of *Margarete Weiss* (1542; Geisberg, no. 1436), a twelve-year old girl who had not eaten or drunk for three years. Images are often accompanied by texts, in broadsheet manner, mostly written by the artist himself. The *Carrying of the Cross* (1527; Geisberg, nos 1424, 1425), printed on eight woodblocks, is one of the largest German woodcuts (951×665 mm). The map of Greece by Nikolaus Sophianus, drawn and cut by Vogtherr and printed by Johannes Oporinus (1507–68) in Basle in 1544, has been described as one of the most beautiful woodcuts of the mid-16th century. His *Allegory of Hope* (1545; Geisberg, no. 1429) is remarkable for the genre-like scenes surrounding the central personification of Spes (Hope). It has been suggested that Pieter Bruegel I was inspired by the design as well as the accompanying poem when he drew his *Allegory of Hope* (1559–60; Hollstein: *Dut. & Flem.*, no. 133) for the engraved series of the *Seven Virtues*. Vogtherr also designed the title pages and illustrations for books.

BIBLIOGRAPHY

H. Koegler: 'Erster Versuch eines Kataloges der Holzschnitte Heinrich Vogtherrs des Älteren', *Anz. Schweiz. Alterknd.*, xxii (1920), pp. 61–5

M. Geisberg: *Der deutsche Einblatt Holzschnitt in der ersten Hälfte des 16. Jahrhunderts* (Munich, 1924–30); Eng. trans. as *The German Single Leaf Woodcut, 1500–1550*, rev. and ed. W. L. Strauss (New York, 1974)

J. Bergström: 'The Iconological Origins of Spes by Pieter Bruegel the Elder', *Ned. Ksthist. Jb.*, vii (1956), pp. 53–63

J. Funke: *Beiträge zum graphischen Werk Heinrich Vogtherrs des Älteren* (diss., U. Berlin, 1967)

G. Werner: *Nützliche Anweisungen zur Zeichenkunst: Illustrierte Lehr- und Vorlagenbücher*, Nuremberg, Ger. Nmus. cat. (Nuremberg, 1980)

Die Renaissance im deutschen Südwesten zwischen Reformation und Dreissigjährigem Krieg (exh. cat. by H. Appuhn and others, Heidelberg, Schloss, 1986), i, p. 304

F. Muller: 'Heinrich Vogtherr der Ältere (1490–1556): Aspekte seines Lebens und Werkes', *Jb. Hist. Ver. Dillingen*, xcii (1990), pp. 173–276

——: *Heinrich Vogtherr l'Ancien (1490–1556): Un Artiste entre Renaissance et Réforme* (diss., Strasbourg, 1990)

——: 'Heinrich Vogtherr d. Ä.', *Jb. Hist. Ver. Dillingen*, xciii (1991), pp. 9–19

KRISTIN LOHSE BELKIN

(2) Heinrich Vogtherr (ii) (*b* Dillingen an der Donau, 1513; *d* Vienna, 1568). Painter and woodcutter, son of (1) Heinrich Vogtherr (i). He may have spent his childhood with his father, travelling between such towns as Augsburg (1518–22) and Wimpfen (1522–5), and certainly served his apprenticeship and journeyman years with him. In late 1525 or early 1526 he went with his father to Strassburg (Strasbourg), where he was granted citizenship on 17 May 1526. The first evidence of his collaboration with his father in his workshop and presumably also his printing works comes from his later days in Strasbourg (1536–40); the precise extent of this collaboration has not yet been established, but his first *Self-portrait* appears in the form of a medallion on the title page of his father's *Kunstbüchlein* (Strasbourg, 1537). His marriage to Sybilla Steinmaier of Augsburg enabled him to settle there, gain acceptance as a master in the guild of painters on 28 March 1541 and obtain a work permit for the imperial city. His activities probably extended to painting frescoes and producing woodcuts with religious and secular themes as well as bookplates and coats of arms. Some of his woodcuts were built up in several parts to create large formats, such as the *Resurrection* (Geisberg, nos 1462, 1463) and the *Death of the Just Man and the Unjust Man* (Geisberg, nos 1466, 1467); some were after drawings by other artists, including Dürer, Hans Schäufelein (i) and Hans Burgkmair I. In 1541 he presented Christinus Spiegel to the Augsburg painters' guild as his apprentice, in 1543 Jeremias Wirsing and in 1549 Anthoni Jörg Breu, son of Jörg Breu (ii).

From 1554 Heinrich Vogtherr (ii), though still a citizen of Augsburg, was documented in book-keeping accounts relating to works for the Viennese court. His subsidiary commissions included simple panels (1556), designs for coins (1560), pictures for banners for a shooting match, contributions towards the triumphal arch for the Holy Roman Emperor Ferdinand I (1563), as well as the imperial coat of arms for the Emperor's funeral, and paintings (1564). There is documentary evidence of other work while he was in Vienna: woodcuts, dated pen drawings (e.g. the *Risen Christ*, 1563) and oil paintings. The clarification of earlier confusions and mistaken attributions has resulted in his work being somewhat overshadowed by that of his father, with some justification, but his allegorical work influenced even an artist of the calibre of Pieter Bruegel I.

BIBLIOGRAPHY

ADB; Thieme–Becker

P. von Stetten: *Kunst-, Gewerbe- und Handwerksgeschichte des Reichstags Augsburg*, i (Augsburg, 1779), p. 279

M. Geisberg: *Der deutsche Einblatt Holzschnitt in der ersten Hälfte des 16. Jahrhunderts* (Munich, 1924–30); Eng. trans. as *The German Single Leaf Woodcut, 1500–1550*, rev. and ed. W. L. Strauss (New York, 1974)

Augsburger Renaissance (exh. cat., Augsburg, Schaezlerpal., 1955)

Augsburger Stadtlexikon (Augsburg, 1985), p. 394

F. Kobler: 'Ein Retabel des 16. Jahrhunderts mit Holzschnitten im Diözesanmuseum zu Klagenfurt', *Jb. Zentinst. Kstgesch.*, iii (1987), pp. 253–63

JOSEF MANČAL

Vogt [Voigt] **von Wierandt, Caspar** (*b* Dresden; *d* Aug 1560). German master builder. He was appointed master of fortifications by Maurice, Elector of Saxony (*reg* 1547–53) and originally produced mainly plans for defensive works. The plans for Schloss Moritzburg (1542–6) near Dresden, a rectangular *corps de logis* (30×15 m) surrounded by an outer wall with circular corner towers, can probably be ascribed to Vogt. In 1545–55 extensive fortifications in Dresden and Leipzig were built to his plans. His most important commission, however, was the remodelling and extension of the Dresdner Schloss. The conversion of the late medieval complex to an imposing Renaissance palace began under Elector Maurice in 1543, and many Italian artists were engaged to decorate it. It was the first time in central German architecture that the remodelling of a palace had started from an overall design while incorporating the medieval buildings. The scheme is usually attributed to Vogt, but all that can be proved is that he directed the building work; whether the design is also his has not been proven with certainty. Vogt's last important project was for an armoury in Dresden, which was completed in 1563.

BIBLIOGRAPHY

Thieme–Becker
C. Gurlitt: 'Das königliche Schloss in Dresden und seine Erbauer: Ein Beitrag der Geschichte der Renaissance in Sachsen', *Mitt. Kön.-Sächs. Altertver.*, xxviii (1878), pp. 1–58
H.-R. Hitchcock: *German Renaissance Architecture* (Princeton, 1981), pp. 104–6
Das Dresdner Schloss: Monument sächsischer Geschichte und Kultur (exh. cat., Dresden, Schloss Moritzburg, 2/1989), p. 51

S. TRÄGER

Vogüé, (Charles-Jean-)Melchior de (*b* Paris, 18 Oct 1829; *d* Paris, 10 Nov 1916). French archaeologist and diplomat. He initially worked as a diplomat in Petrograd (now St Petersburg) in 1850, but he soon resigned and from 1853 to 1854 travelled around Greece, Turkey, Syria and Palestine, where he collected material for his work on Christian buildings. In 1861 he was sent to Cyprus by the historian Ernest Renan, with William Henry Waddington (1826–94), the epigrapher, and Edmond-Clément-Marie-Louise Duthoit, the architect, in order to explore the island systematically and organize large-scale excavations. Vogüé and Waddington continued their research in Syria and Jerusalem in 1862, enabling Vogüé to publish a detailed study of the Temple of Jerusalem two years later. Following Waddington's departure in late 1862, Vogüé stayed a little longer in the East with Duthoit, exploring central Syria and Hawrān; this trip provided him with the material for the three-volume *Syrie centrale*. From 1868 Vogüé was a free member of the Académie des Inscriptions et Belles-Lettres, and he was involved in producing the *Corpus inscriptionum semiticarum*. In 1869 he travelled to Palestine again, before returning to diplomacy as ambassador, first in Istanbul (1871), then in Vienna (1875); he resigned in 1879. He was elected a member of the Académie Française in 1901 and returned to Jerusalem for the last time in 1911.

WRITINGS

Les Eglises de la Terre Sainte (Paris, 1860)
Le Temple de Jérusalem: Essai sur la topographie de la Ville Sainte (Paris, 1864)
Syrie centrale, 3 vols (Paris, 1865–77)
Mélanges d'archéologie orientale (Paris, 1868)
Jérusalem hier et aujourd'hui (Paris, 1912)

BIBLIOGRAPHY

R. Cagnat: 'Notice sur la vie et les travaux de M. le Marquis de Vogüé', *Acad. Inscr. & B.-Lett.: C. R. Séances* (1918), pp. 443–73

PASCALE LINANT DE BELLEFONDS

Voigt, Carl Friedrich (*b* Berlin, 6 Oct 1800; *d* Trieste, 13 Oct 1874). German medallist and gem-engraver. He trained as an engraver in Berlin with the founder and engraver Friedrich Vollgold (*b c*. 1790) and also with the medallist Leonhard Posch. From 1820 to 1825 he worked at the minting works of Gottfried Bernhard Loos (1773–

1843) in Berlin. He then travelled to London, where he worked at the Royal Mint under Benedetto Pistrucci, and from there via Paris and Milan to Rome, where his career was furthered by Bertel Thorvaldsen. From 1830 onwards he worked as chief medallist at the Royal Mint in Munich, an office that he held until he moved once again to Rome in 1857. Voigt was a very prolific engraver and his work is among the best of the 19th century. Among the Bavarian coins, special mention should be made of the series of Geschichtstaler (historical thalers) showing the head of Ludwig I of Bavaria on the obverse of every coin and some important event from Bavarian history on the reverse. In Rome Voigt cut several dies for the Papal Mint. His numerous portrait medals reflect his contacts with the ruling houses of Germany, as well as with major artists of his day, such as Thorvaldsen, Peter Cornelius, Ludwig von Schwanthaler and Jakob Rauch. The models for his medals, executed in wax, are in the Accademia Nazionale di S Luca in Rome.

BIBLIOGRAPHY

Forrer; Thieme–Becker

HERMANN MAUÉ

Voigtel, (Karl Eduard) Richard (*b* Magdeburg, 31 May 1829; *d* Cologne, 28 Sept 1902). German architect. He attended the Domgymnasium at Magdeburg (1838–47) and in 1848 passed the qualifying examination as a surveyor, after which he worked in that capacity in Saxony. From 1849 to 1851 he studied at the Bauakademie in Berlin and went to Paris on a scholarship (1851). During the next year he was active under Friedrich Hitzig in Berlin and made designs for the surroundings of Magdeburg Cathedral and the bridge over the Vistula at Dirschau (now Tczew, Poland). In 1852 and 1853 he directed several road-building projects near Posen (now Poznań) and Bromberg (now Bydgoszcz, both in Poland), and designed two church buildings for Murzyno (now Murzynno) and Kruswice (now Kruszwica, both in Poland). Later he was active in the Rhineland, initially with road-building near Cologne, and was engaged by J. Schopen to direct the restoration of the Appellhof (1854–5) in Cologne.

The cathedral architect Friedrich Ernst Zwirner took notice of his works in this city and, in 1855, after Voigtel had qualified as an architect, made him his deputy for the cathedral works. Voigtel had not only risen from the status of craftsman but also had a solid academic training. He began by calculating the system of buttresses and the load capacity of the pillars at the crossing; one result of this was his abandonment of a crossing tower in favour of a ridge-turret (completed 1862). After Zwirner's death (1862), he became cathedral architect; in this capacity, in 1869 he was appointed Baurat, in 1873 Regierungsbaurat and in 1880 Geheimer Oberbaurat. Under his direction the nave and transepts were vaulted (1863) and the 600-year-old choir wall was removed so that the western side and the choir were finally united. The west façade with its twin towers (completed 1880) must be regarded as Voigtel's main achievement. His portrait appears as a console figure on the north tower, which he executed from almost ground level up. He endeavoured to conform to the original medieval elevation (rediscovered in 1814), but this was not wholly possible. In 1870, together with the cathedral sculptor Peter Fuchs, he built the flight of steps and Petrusbrunnen ('Drüggen Pitter') outside the east end of the cathedral, which had needed lengthy planning and negotiations with the city. Only part of the original plan was executed. It had a lasting influence throughout Germany in favour of decorating the immediate vicinity of Gothic Revival church buildings with areas of greenery and flights of steps, as Schinkel had picturesquely anticipated in his cathedral visions of the early 19th century.

After the cathedral was completed in 1880, Voigtel devoted himself for the next 20 years to the decoration of the entrance and roof. He designed the Kaiserglocke (1876; called 'Gloriosa'; melted down 1918). Besides cathedral works he also designed the chapter house (executed 1866) and continued some restoration works begun by Zwirner, such as the Minoritenkirche in Cologne and the Romanesque church of St Peter (1862–3) at Sinzig (Ahrweiler district); in the latter case the main emphasis was on securing the vaulting and removing the church's baroque character. Two plans by Voigtel are known for the restoration of the Catholic parish church of St Servatius at Siegburg (executed 1864–9). Voigtel was also active as a prize judge and consultant for the extension of Ulm Minster. Less charismatic than Zwirner, he is regarded as a strict Gothic Revivalist. He was a brilliant organizer and one of the first curators of monuments who could defend his views from an academically assured basis.

BIBLIOGRAPHY

P. Clemen, ed.: *Der Dom zu Köln* (1937), VI/iii of *Die Kunstdenkmäler der Rheinprovinz* (Düsseldorf, 1908–)

'Zum 50. Todestag des Dombaumeisters Richard Voigtel', *Köln. Dombl.* (1952), pp. 133–4

H. Rode: 'Der Werdegang des Dombaumeisters Richard Voigtel', *Köln. Dombl.* (1963), pp. 157–8

W. Weyres and A. Mann: *Handbuch zur rheinischen Baukunst des 19. Jahrhunderts, 1800 bis 1880* (Cologne, 1968), p. 107

J. Schulze: *Kirchenbauten des 19. Jahrhunderts im alten Siegkreis* (Cologne, 1977), pp. 145–6, 211

Der Kölner Dom im Jahrhundert seiner Vollendung, 2 vols (exh. cat., ed. H. Borger; Cologne, Joseph-Haubrich-Ksthalle., 1980) [many pls]

J. Breuer: *Die Kölner Domumgebung als Spiegel der Domrezeption im 19. Jahrhundert* (Cologne, 1981)

MICHAEL BOLLÉ

Voigt von Wierandt, Caspar. *See* VOGT VON WIERANDT, CASPAR.

Vois [Voijs; Voys], **Arie** [Adriaen; Ary] **de** (*b* Utrecht, 1630–35; *d* Leiden, July 1680, *bur* Oegstgeest, 11 July 1680). Dutch painter. He was the son of Alewijn de Vois from Utrecht, who was appointed organist of the St Pieterskerk, Leiden, in 1635. Arie received his first training in Utrecht from Nicolaus Knüpfer (*c.* 1603–55), who also taught Jan Steen. He then studied in Leiden with Abraham van den Tempel, who lived there between 1648 and 1660. De Vois joined the Leiden Guild of St Luke on 16 October 1653 and paid his dues until 1677, serving as headman in 1664–5 and dean in 1662–4 and 1667–8. Houbraken's remark that he turned idle after marrying a wealthy woman is belied by the large number of paintings he produced, both surviving and mentioned in inventories and sale catalogues, and by the fact that his wife, Maria van der Vecht, whom he married on 5 February 1656, was not rich.

Among de Vois's works are numerous history paintings (e.g. *Dido and Aeneas*; Leiden, Stedel. Mus. Lakenhal) in the small size favoured by the LEIDEN 'FINE' PAINTERS, some genre scenes (e.g. *Woman Peeling a Lemon*; Paris, Louvre) and portraits (e.g. *Self-portrait as a Hunter*; The Hague, Mauritshuis). He was highly regarded in his day and well thought of throughout the 18th and 19th centuries. Some of his paintings were later falsely attributed to Frans van Mieris (i), whose style was very similar (see Naumann, i, pp. 144–5; ii, nos B1, C3, C11). De Vois's work also influenced the young Willem van Mieris.

BIBLIOGRAPHY

A. Houbraken: *De groote schouburgh* (1718–21), iii, p. 163

B. J. A. Renckens: 'Drie zelfportretten van Arie de Vois', *Oud-Holland*, lxv (1950), pp. 160–62

F. W. Robinson: *Gabriel Metsu* (New York, 1974), pp. 22, 28, 30, 48, 76, 78, 82

O. Naumann: *Frans van Mieris the Elder*, 2 vols (Doornspijk, 1981), i, pp. 37, 64, 67–8, 139, 144–5; ii, nos 16, 18, 54, 96

De Hollandse fijnschilders (exh. cat. by P. Hecht, Amsterdam, Rijksmus., 1989), nos 49–54

MAARTEN WURFBAIN

Voit, August von (*b* Wassertrüdingen, 17 Feb 1801; *d* Munich, 17 Dec 1870). German architect. He studied (1822–3) at the Akademie in Munich under Friedrich von Gärtner and afterwards made study trips to Italy and France. He began working in his father's practice, where his first building was the Protestant Friedhofskirche (1825–6) in Augsburg. After mainly administrative work as Landbau-Kondukteur (1827–31) in Amberg, he became Zivilbauinspektor (1832–41) in Speyer, which gave him his first opportunity to produce major works of his own. He built numerous churches, including the parish church of St Michael (1839–41) at Homburg and others at Ludwigshafen (Lutherkirche, 1858–64; destr. 1943), Speyer (St Ludwig, 1834–6) and Weissenhorn in Bavaria (Stadtpfarrkirche, 1864–9), all influenced by the *Rundbogenstil* of von Gärtner. In 1841 Ludwig I, King of Bavaria, appointed Voit professor of architecture at the Munich Akademie. Commissioned directly by the King, he produced the Glasmalerei-Anstalt (1843–6; destr. 1945) in Luisenstrasse, a cubic building almost free of ornamentation, reminiscent of Schinkel's Bauakademie, Berlin. In 1846–54, Voit built the Neue Pinakothek (conceived 1843; destr. 1945; rebuilt by Alexander Freiherr von Branca in 1975–81) in Munich to house a collection of 19th-century art, with an exterior made particularly striking by a large fresco cycle (destr. 1945) by Wilhelm Kaulbach (*see* KAULBACH, (1)). After von Gärtner's death in 1847, Voit succeeded him as Oberbaurat, retaining the office in the two subsequent reigns of Maximilian II (*reg* 1848–64) and Ludwig II (*reg* 1864–86). Apart from copious administrative work the post involved the supervision of numerous public building projects in Bavaria, which allowed Voit to exert substantial influence on the architectural developments of his time. As part of his duties he designed a number of prisons for Bavarian cities, including Nuremberg (1864–7) and Munich (1866–70), whose novel conception, with individual cells for the inmates, remained valid until the 20th century. Voit's most important building during the reign of Maximilian II was the Glaspalast (1853–4; destr. 1931) in Munich, modelled on the Crystal

Palace, London, by Joseph Paxton, and likewise constructed entirely of glass, timber and iron. It first housed industrial exhibitions and festivities, followed by regular art exhibitions from 1886. In 1851–3 Voit built a winter garden for Maximilian II, followed (1860–67) by conservatories in the botanic garden, Munich. A project for a palace (1863–4) at Feldafing on the Starnberger See remained unrealized due to Maximilian's death. Finally, Voit constructed a winter garden (1866–8; destr. 1897) on the roof of the Residenz in Munich for Ludwig II; its size and its fabulous furnishings made it world famous. As architectural fashions changed in the 1860s, when the strict reserve of the Romanesque Revival style gave way to the more picturesque and animated Gothic and Renaissance Revivals, Voit's architecture was considered outdated and irrelevant.

BIBLIOGRAPHY

E. Roth: *Der Glaspalast in München* (Munich, 1971)

W. Mittlmeier: *Die Neue Pinakothek in München, 1843–1854* (Munich, 1977)

H. J. Kotzur: *Forschungen zum Leben und Werk des Architekten August von Voit* (diss., U. Heidelberg, 1978)

V. Hütsch: *Der Münchner Glaspalast, 1854–1931* (Munich, 1981)

Romantik und Restauration: Architektur in Bayern zur Zeit Ludwigs I, 1825–1848 (exh. cat., ed. W. Nerdinger; Munich, Stadtmus., 1987)

J. Meissner: 'Das Landauer Bezirksgefängnis oder, die Schwierigkeiten im Umgang mit einem "Stein des Anstosses"', *Dt. Kst- & Dkmlpf.*, xxxxvi/2 (1988), pp. 138–45

DIETRICH NEUMANN

Volaire, Pierre-Jacques (*b* Toulon, 30 April 1729; *d* Italy, *c.* 1790–1800). French painter. He was born into a family of artists in Toulon: his grandfather Jean (*c.* 1660–1721) was a decorator of naval vessels and painter of religious works; his father, Jacques Volaire (1685–1768), was official painter of Toulon between 1729 and 1766 and in 1745 was commissioned to paint a large *Glory of the Holy Sacrament* (Toulon Cathedral); his uncle François-Alexis (1699–1775) was also a painter, and his cousin Marie-Anne (1730–1806) was a portrait painter. In 1755 Volaire is documented (as '*le fils*') working on the restoration of paintings in Toulon Cathedral. In September 1754 Joseph Vernet arrived in Toulon. He was painting a series of topographical views of the major French seaports for Louis XV. Almost certainly Vernet took on Volaire as an assistant in 1754 or 1755, although this is not documented until 1759. Volaire's role in the series of ports is unknown; it may have been merely mechanical, but he could have provided expert knowledge of the military port of Toulon and French naval life. From his master Volaire learned a sharp sense of observation, a lively technique and care in the design and lighting of a painting. He was Vernet's most inventive follower, not content to copy his master's well-tried formulae but prepared to adapt to new aesthetic criteria.

By 1764 Volaire was in Rome, where he worked until the end of the decade, producing landscapes and seascapes

Pierre-Jacques Volaire: *Shipwreck*, oil on canvas, 0.99×1.36 m, 1765 (Stockholm, Nationalmuseum)

in the manner of Vernet, such as *Landscape with a Waterfall* (Toulon, Mus. A.) and *Shipwreck* (1765; Stockholm, Nmus.; see fig.). These Roman works are close to Vernet in theme and style, although Volaire liked to depict his figures in lively silhouettes against the light; his figure types are generally heavier and more clumsily modelled than those of Vernet.

Volaire moved to Naples, probably in 1769, and remained there during the 1770s and 1780s. In 1770 he painted a fine pair of large pictures, *Marine with Fishermen* and *Seaport by Moonlight* (both Compiègne, Château). The latter is based on the coast near Naples, with the town silhouetted in the middle distance. Night scenes such as this became Volaire's speciality. He used vivid contrasts of cool moonlight and warm fires with figures depicted as lively silhouettes against light. His last known signed and dated work, *Nocturnal Marine at Naples* (1784; Naples, Pal. Reale), is another variation on this theme.

Probably the eruption of Mount Vesuvius in 1771 turned Volaire's attention to the theme of volcanic eruption. Several paintings of the event are inscribed as representing this particular eruption, for example the *Eruption of Vesuvius* (1771; Nantes, Mus. B.-A.), and there are many others dating from the 1770s and 1780s. One painting of the 1771 eruption was engraved for Abbé Richard de Saint-Non, to appear in his *Voyage pittoresque, ou description des Royaumes de Naples et de Sicile* (1781; i, pl. 32), and it is possible that Saint-Non commissioned the painting and turned Volaire's interest that way. Saint-Non also published Volaire's *View of Solfatara, near Pozzuoli* (ii, pl. 19), probably the painting now in the Marquess of Hertford's collection at Ragley Hall, Warwicks, one of Volaire's few topographical works whose subject is not Vesuvius.

Volaire developed a European reputation for his scenes of volcanic eruption. The collector Bergeret de Grancourt commissioned a huge *Eruption of Vesuvius* (Nègrepelisse, Château), having been guided up Vesuvius by the artist in 1774. The paintings of Vesuvius can be interpreted in two ways: they reflect the contemporary fashionable scientific interest in volcanoes in both France and England, and they take the depiction of horrific drama a stage further than the works of Vernet, almost to the point of being illustrations complementary to Edmund Burke's theories of the Sublime. For all his international success, Volaire had no official recognition in France. He exhibited in Paris only three times, at the Salon de la Correspondance (1779, 1783, 1786), and he was a corresponding member of the Académie in Marseille. Aided by his important patron Bailli de Breteuil, he tried in 1786 to persuade the French Crown to buy one of his paintings of the eruption of Vesuvius, but the Direction des Bâtiments was more interested in acquiring important Old Master paintings to display in the Grande Galerie of the Louvre. The work of a contemporary landscape painter, especially one as sensationalist as Volaire, was not considered sufficiently dignified at a time when the authorities were trying to elevate French taste.

BIBLIOGRAPHY
M. C. Picone: 'Volaire', *Antol. B.A.*, v (1978), pp. 24–48

PHILIP CONISBEE

Volaterrano, il. *See* MAFFEI, RAFFAELE.

Volcii. *See* VULCI.

Volgograd [formerly Tsaritsin; Stalingrad]. Russian city on the Lower Volga. In 1925 Tsaritsin was renamed in honour of Stalin, but in 1961 its name was changed to Volgograd. Its existence is first mentioned in *c.* 1555; its wooden buildings were surrounded by a parallelogram of wooden walls with 12 towers and ditches. Only four churches, built between 1664 and 1771, were of stone. In 1820 a regular plan was drawn up for the settlement, which began to develop rapidly in the second half of the 19th century, when Tsaritsin became a major trading and industrial centre. The centre of the town consisted of residential and public buildings in Neo-classical, neo-Renaissance and neo-Baroque styles. The Kazan' cathedral (1903; rest. 1948) was built in neo-Byzantine style. During the early Soviet period the city grew quickly. In 1929–30 a new plan was drawn up by the Vesnin brothers, based on Nikolay Milyutin's idea of a linear town and on the concept of a town as an agglomeration of several settlements. An architectural style was developed here combining Constructivist compositional ideas with a generalized treatment of the Neo-classical heritage. The city was virtually destroyed during the Battle of Stalingrad (1942–3). In 1945 work began on its reconstruction following the overall plan by VASILY SIMBIRTSEV. A monumental esplanade was built through the city along the Alley of Heroes. Buildings continued to be constructed in the Neo-classical style until the 1960s; thereafter, numerous prefabricated structures were built. The sculptor YEVGENY VUCHETICH and the architect Yakov Belopol'sky built a grandiose memorial ensemble (1963–7; see fig.) dedicated to the

Volgograd, monument to the *Heroes of the Battle of Stalingrad* by Yevgeny Vuchetich and Yakov Belopol'sky, 1963–7

Battle of Stalingrad. The Museum of Fine Arts houses a collection of Russian 19th- and 20th-century art.

BIBLIOGRAPHY

F. Chekalin: *Saratovskoye Povolzh'ye s drevneyshikh vremyon do kontsa XVIII v.* [The Volga area around Saratov from ancient times to the end of the 18th century] (Saratov, 1892)

A. Yeremenko: *Stalingrad* (Moscow, 1951)

V. Antonov: *Volgograd* (Moscow, 1985)

P. Gundyrin: *Puteshestviye po Volgogradu* [A journey around Volgograd] (Volgograd, 1987)

D. O. SHVIDKOVSKY

Volkmann, Artur (Joseph Wilhelm) (*b* Leipzig, 28 Aug 1851; *d* Geislingen, 13 Nov 1941). German sculptor, painter, draughtsman, lithographer and writer. He studied at the Akademie in Dresden (1870–73) and then joined the studio of Albert Wolff in Berlin. In 1876 a scholarship allowed him to travel to Rome, where he resided for the next seven years. There he befriended other German artists and was influenced by the painter Hans Reinhard von Marées who introduced him to neo-classicism. In the 1880s he produced some of his best works (e.g. a bronze group of *Ganymede* and a female bust, both Berlin, Neue N.G.). He also began to produce polychrome sculptures, including terracotta busts and marble figures and reliefs. After a brief stay in Berlin and Leipzig, from 1885 to 1910 he was again in Rome, and from 1885 he shared a studio with the German sculptor Louis Tuaillon. Both were interested in horses, and these became an important theme in Volkmann's sculptural and graphic repertory, leading to such works as the sculpture *Rider* (bronze, 1920; Frankfurt am Main, Städel. Kstinst.). He also produced drawings, mostly in pen and ink, and a series of lithographs. Some twenty of his drawings, *Aus der Kriegszeit gegen Kriegsleid* (Jena, 1917), were published by the Red Cross in Heidelberg. Most of his graphic work was published under the title *Künstlerischer Wandschmuck* by Breitkopf & Härtel in Leipzig. Volkmann's paintings were mostly executed in tempera and inspired by classical themes, as in *Lion Hunt* (see von Wasielewski, fig. 10).

WRITINGS

Vom Sehen und Gestalten (Jena, 1912)

BIBLIOGRAPHY

Thieme–Becker

W. von Wasielewski: *Artur Volkmann: Eine Einführung in sein Werk* (Munich and Leipzig, 1908)

W. Grzimek: *Deutsche Bildhauer des 20. Jahrhunderts: Leben, Schulen, Wirkung* (Munich, 1969), pp. 10, 21, 30–31, 238

HANNELORE HÄGELE

Volkov, Aleksandr (Nikolayevich) (*b* Skobelev [now Fergana], 19 Aug 1886; *d* Tashkent, 17 Dec 1957). Russian painter and draughtsman, active in Uzbekistan. He trained at the St Petersburg Academy of Arts (1908–10) under Vladimir Makovsky and at the Kiev Art School (1912–16) under Fyodor Krichevsky (1879–1947), then moved to Tashkent. Characteristic of Volkov's early work are Art Nouveau features, as in *Persian Woman* (Moscow, Mus. Orient. A.). The influence of Cubism is combined with the ornamental flatness of Central Asian art in the *Eastern Primitive* series (1918–20; Moscow, Mus. Orient. A. and artist's family's col.). His monumental generalization of form and powerful colour harmonies, at times transformed into semi-abstract, futuristic rhythms, as in *Caravan I* (1922–3; Moscow, Tret'yakov Gal.), attained a special

symbolic significance in the *Pomegranate Teahouse* (1924; Moscow, Tret'yakov Gal.), the artist's best-known work. In Volkov's hands scenes of rural labour typical of Socialist Realism (e.g. *Girls with Cotton*, 1932; Moscow, Tret'yakov Gal.) achieve a dignity comparable to that of the Mexican muralists. In later years Volkov's work became more intimate, while retaining its power of expression and freshness of colour, as in *By the Irrigation Canal (Evening)* (1946–56; Moscow, artist's family's col.). Volkov was also a talented draughtsman and watercolourist. He taught at the Tashkent Art School and was one of the founders of the new Central Asian painting, which brought together Islamic traditions and current European stylistic elements.

BIBLIOGRAPHY

M. I. Zemskaya: *Aleksandr Volkov: Master 'Granatovoy chaykhany'* [Aleksandr Volkov: painter of the *Pomegranate Teahouse*] (Moscow, 1975)

R. Kh. Taktash: *A. N. Volkov Al'bum* (Tashkent, 1982)

M. B. Myasina and N. V. Apchinskaya, eds.: *A. Volkov i ego ucheniki* [A. Volkov and his pupils] (exh. cat., Moscow, 1987)

M. N. SOKOLOV

Vollard, Ambroise (*b* St-Denis, Réunion, *c.* 1867; *d* Paris, 19 Feb 1939). French art dealer and publisher. He was the most notable contemporary art dealer of his generation in France, as well as an innovative publisher of prints and illustrated books. Brought up in Réunion, he arrived in Paris *c.* 1890 as a law student and soon started buying and selling prints and drawings for his own pleasure. After a period working at L'Union Artistique for Alphonse Dumas, an established dealer, he set up on his own and in 1894 opened a small gallery near the Opéra on the Rue Laffitte, then the centre of the Paris art trade.

Vollard made his first major impact as a dealer in 1895 when he organized Cézanne's first one-man exhibition. Over the next ten years he built up, at relatively low cost, a large stock of paintings by Cézanne, which eventually provided him with enormous profits. Concurrently he acquired work by van Gogh, Gauguin, Bonnard, Denis, Redon, Vuillard, Derain, Rouault, Vlaminck, Rousseau, Picasso, Maillol and Matisse, as well as by more established artists such as Degas and Renoir. Vollard kept his gallery on a modest scale. It was his practice to buy paintings outright from artists, and he often purchased the contents of their studios *en bloc*. Works acquired in this way appear often to have been kept in reserve for years, unseen until Vollard considered it opportune to put them on the market. Although he was respected and liked by the artists he supported, this method of promotion had disadvantages for them. Georges Rouault, for instance, whose studio Vollard bought up in 1913, suffered from the fact that his paintings were rarely exhibited, and hence little known, in the 1920s and 1930s.

Vollard began his career at a time when printmaking had been successfully revived as an original art form. He edited two mixed albums of prints in 1896–7 and several portfolios of prints by individual artists, including Vuillard's set of colour lithographs, *Landscapes and Interiors* (1899). After 1900 the print boom subsided, and although he continued to publish prints he henceforth turned his attention to the illustrated book. His first books date from 1900–04, and by commissioning artists (mainly from the Nabi circle) rather than illustrators and liberating them from the traditional subservience of image to text, he created almost single-handed the genre of the 'fine art' book (see LIVRE D'ARTISTE), later taken up by Daniel-Henry Kahnweiler, Albert Skira, Tériade and others. The masterpiece of this group is Verlaine's *Parallèlement* (1900), illustrated with lithographs by Bonnard.

After 1915, helped by increasing profits from his picture stock, Vollard launched over 40 publishing projects with artists, of which many remained incomplete at his death. His choice of authors and artists ranged from Virgil to Baudelaire, and from Emile Bernard to Picasso, who illustrated Balzac's *Chef d'oeuvre inconnu* (1931), one of Vollard's greatest publishing achievements. Rouault occupied a special place, working for Vollard almost continuously throughout the 1920s and 1930s. Of the seven publications they planned together, only three were completed in Vollard's lifetime: *Les Réincarnations du Père Ubu* (1925), for which he provided his own satirical text, with aquatints by Rouault; André Suarès's *Passion* (1939), with Rouault's etchings; and *Cirque de l'étoile filante* (1938), which was both written and illustrated by Rouault (see ROUAULT, GEORGES). Among Vollard's other writings are his studies, serious if anecdotal, of the three older masters he had known—Cézanne, Degas and Renoir. His memoirs provide an amusing account of the foibles of the art world, particularly of the cupidity and ignorance of other collectors. Vollard commissioned portraits of himself from many of the artists he admired, including Cézanne (1899; Paris, Petit Pal.), Renoir (1908; U. London, Courtauld Inst.) and Picasso (1909; Moscow, Pushkin Mus. F.A.). His distinctive, burly figure was memorably recorded in the 1930s in a series of photographs by Brassaï, and his wry, secretive nature is summed up in an etching by Bonnard of 1914, showing Vollard with his cat (see F. Bouvet, *Bonnard, l'oeuvre gravé: Catalogue complet*, Paris, 1981, pl. 89).

WRITINGS

Paul Cézanne (Paris, 1915)
La Vie et l'oeuvre de A. Renoir (Paris, 1919)
Degas (Paris, 1924)
Les Réincarnations du Père Ubu (Paris, 1925)
'Comment je devins éditeur', *A. Vivant* (15 Dec 1929)
Sainte Monique (Paris, 1930)
Souvenirs d'un marchand de tableaux (Paris, 1936); Eng. trans. as *Recollections of a Picture Dealer* (London, 1936/R 1978)
En écoutant Cézanne, Degas, Renoir (Paris, 1938)

BIBLIOGRAPHY

J. Guenne: 'La Vérité sur Vollard', *Cah. B.-Lett.*, i/3 (May 1944)
Schenkung Vollard (exh. cat., Winterthur, Kstmus., 1949)
M. Dormoy: *Souvenirs et portraits d'amis* (Paris, 1963)
D. W. Druick: 'Cézanne, Vollard and Lithography: The Ottawa Maquette for the *Large Bathers* Colour Lithograph', *Bull. N.G. Canada*, xix (1972), pp. 1–35
Ambroise Vollard, Editeur: Prints, Books, Bronzes (exh. cat. by U. E. Johnson, New York, MOMA, 1977)
J. Russell: 'Out of Nowhere he Became the Top Art Dealer in Paris', *Smithsonian*, xviii/4 (1977–8), pp. 68–95
F. Chapon: 'Ambroise Vollard: Editeur', *Gaz. B.-A.*, 6th ser., xciv (1979), pp. 33–47; xcv (1980), pp. 25–38

MALCOLM GEE

Vollon, Antoine (*b* Lyon, 20 April 1833; *d* Paris, 27 Aug 1900). French painter. Having worked for a maker of enamelled metalwork and an engraver, Vollon attended the Ecole des Beaux-Arts in Lyon (1850–52), where he won awards in printmaking. He subsequently copied 18th-century paintings for industrial design. He had begun to concentrate on his own work by 1858 and joined a group of Romantic artists based in Lyon, including Francis Verney (1833–96), Fleury Chenu (1833–75), Joseph Ravier (1832–78) and Joseph and Jean Antoine Bail. In 1859 Vollon moved to Paris, where he met the realist painters François Bonvin and Théodule Ribot, who encouraged him to paint genre and still-life scenes. Until 1863 he earned government stipends for copying pictures in the Louvre (e.g. Ribera's *Adoration of the Shepherds*); that year he exhibited at the Salon des Refusés. He achieved public recognition in 1864 after his genre piece *Kitchen Interior* (untraced), one of two paintings accepted at the official Salon, was purchased by the state. In 1865 he earned a Salon medal for *Interior of a Kitchen* (Nantes, Mus. B.-A.), a genre scene inspired by Chardin and 17th-century Dutch art. Vollon was best known for his still-lifes, in which he frequently depicted objects stored in his studio. Painted in a vigorous style, these range in palette from pastels to vibrant reds. In the rich colouring and sumptuous effects of *Curiosities* (Lunéville, Mus. Lunéville) Vollon demonstrated his love of metallic surfaces, armour and elegant porcelains. He exhibited at the Salon until 1880 and was admitted to the Académie des Beaux-Arts in 1897. His son Antoine (1865–1945), who worked under the name Alexis Vollon, painted genre scenes and still-lifes and exhibited at the Salon from 1885. He won a few awards but did not achieve the success of his father.

BIBLIOGRAPHY

E. Martin: *Antoine Vollon: Peintre, 1833–1900* (Marseille, 1923)
G. P. Weisberg: 'A Still Life by Antoine Vollon, Painter of Two Traditions', *Bull. Detroit Inst. A.*, lvi/4 (1978), pp. 222–9
The Realist Tradition: French Painting and Drawing, 1830–1900 (exh. cat., ed. G. P. Weisberg; Cleveland, OH, Mus. A.; New York, Brooklyn Mus.; St Louis, MO, A. Mus.; Glasgow, A.G. & Mus.; 1980), pp. 311–12

GABRIEL P. WEISBERG

Vologda. Russian town *c.* 500 km north-east of Moscow. It was well sited both strategically and for trade, since it is near the confluence of the rivers Sukhona and Dvina and is not far from the White Sea and the rivers Kama and Volga. It was first recorded in 1147, and excavations have shown that in the 12th century it was already a medium-sized town. Until the 11th century north-eastern Russia was inhabited by Finnish tribes, but by the 12th century the rich northern forests had been appropriated by the citizens of Novgorod. When, at the end of the 15th century, Vologda was annexed by the Moscow principality, it had become a large, fortified town. From the 16th century its importance as a major trading and political centre increased through trade with England, Holland and other European countries. In 1565 the construction of a stone fortress was begun, the walls of which must have marked the boundary of the kremlin in the new town centre. A wooden palace was built for the visiting tsars, and canals were dug around the fortress.

The white stone cathedral of St Sophia (originally known as the cathedral of the Dormition; 1568–70) is a rectangle with semicircular apses. The exterior walls are divided horizontally by a roll moulding and two ledges and vertically by arched bays but are almost without decoration.

There are two recessed portals, and the west door is fronted by a monumental porch. Five large drums topped by glittering cupolas crown the mass. The interior is decorated with paintings (1686–8) executed in a technique often used in Russian monumental painting at the time, combining fresco with later work in tempera. The walls and piers are divided into horizontal bands and painted with figural scenes of various thematic cycles. The effect is of a unified whole closely related to the architecture. Near the cathedral was the residence of the bishops of Vologda. The Prilutsky Monastery, founded on the outskirts of Vologda in 1371, is dominated by the massive five-domed cathedral of the Saviour (1537–42).

With the foundation of St Petersburg and the introduction of new water routes in the 18th century, Vologda lost its trading and political significance. In the late 17th century and the 18th, however, several stone churches in the Baroque style were erected, such as those of the Protective Veil of the Mother of God (Pokrov; 1710), the Feast of the Purification (Sreteniye; 1731–5) and St John the Baptist (*c.* 1710), in which wall paintings are preserved. The most intensive period of construction was in the late 18th century and first quarter of the 19th. Many Neo-classical buildings date to this period, among them the stone church of Varlaam Khutynsky (1780), the house of the merchant Kolychev and the Fair Hall. The town was built primarily of wood, however, and parts of it still provide an example of an Old Russian town in which the majority of the buildings were richly decorated with wood-carving. The Vologda Art Gallery houses work by regional artists, and there is also a local history museum.

Vologda is known for its bobbin lace; the trade here began in the early 19th century (most surviving examples date from this period or later), but the origins of Russian folk lace-making are centuries older. Bobbin lace was probably introduced into the region in the 17th century. In Vologda lace the division into pattern and ground is executed with great precision. Large, expressive ornamental forms appear to be drawn with an unbroken white line on a mesh ground formed of transparent hexahedrons, circles and squares. Bed valances are a particularly common form, decorated with stylized plant motifs worked as continuous clothwork tapes with 'wheat-ear' and decorative mesh fillings; the supporting mesh is worked round the pattern in a separate process. The products are memorable for their rhythmic patterns and delicate openwork. The range of goods produced by present-day local associations includes machine-made lace by the yard, napkins, tablecloths, bedspreads and scarves, which are exhibited outside Russia.

BIBLIOGRAPHY
G. Lukomsky: *Vologda i yeyo starina* [Vologda and its past] (St Petersburg, 1914)
Vologodskoye kruzhevo [Vologda lace], intro. I. P. Rabotnova (Moscow, 1960)
G. Vzdornov: *Vologda* (Leningrad, 1978)
G. Bocharov and V. Vygolov: *Vologda, Kirillov, Ferapontovo, Belozersk* (Moscow, 1979)
V. Faleyeva: *Russkoye pletyonoye kruzhevo* [Russian woven lace] (Leningrad, 1983; Eng. trans., Leningrad, 1986)

N. N. TOMSKAYA

Volos. *See* IOLKOS.

Voloshin, Maksimilian (Aleksandrovich) (*b* Kiev, 16 May 1877; *d* Koktebel', Crimea, 31 July 1932). Russian painter, poet, theorist and critic of Ukrainian birth. He travelled extensively in Europe between 1899 and 1914 and for several years lived in Paris. From 1917 he lived mainly at Koktebel'. He was a self-taught artist; his talent was soon recognized and he exhibited with the World of Art (Mir Iskusstva) group. He was a Symbolist, re-creating in his watercolours a mythological image of the Crimea. The watercolours are often accompanied by a verse commentary. 'The Voloshin House' was a gathering place for artists and poets and still houses Voloshin's large library, together with a photoarchive and his letters. He wrote for the magazines *Vesy*, *Zolotoye Runo*, *Rus'* and *Apollon*, publishing articles on Vasily Surikov, Konstanin Bogayevsky, Martiros Saryan, Anna Golubkina, Mikhail Nesterov and Claude Monet. His main theoretical work on painting is 'Skelet zhivopisi'. He suggests that painting consists of 'basic colour combinations', that creativity is 'the ability to control the subconscious' and that 'the brain of man is like a book in which the whole of the history of the world is written, most brilliantly embodied in dreams'. He added that 'artists are the eyes of humanity; they reveal images that no one has seen before'.

WRITINGS
'Skelet zhivopisi' [The skeleton of painting], *Vesy*, no. 11 (1904)
Liki tvorchestva [The faces of creation] (Leningrad, 1989)

BIBLIOGRAPHY
R. I. Popova, ed.: *M. Voloshin: Khudozhnik* [M. Voloshin: artist] (Moscow, 1976)

V. S. TURCHIN

Volpaia. Italian family of clockmakers, astronomers and architects. Lorenzo di Benvenuto Volpaia (*b* Florence, 1446; *d* 1512) made his reputation in Florence as a clockmaker. In 1490–94 he constructed a public clock for the Palazzo Comunale and from 1500 to 1511 he was the official in charge of its regular maintenance and repair. In 1497 he began constructing a clock for the cathedral and in 1511 he also renewed that in the Torre del Saggio in the Mercato Vecchio. In about 1510 he made a complex planisphere, a clock which also indicated the movements of the planets, for the Capitani di Parte della Signoria. Various other works were undertaken to improve the clock of the Palazzo Comunale, and Lorenzo was assisted by his son Camillo di Lorenzo Volpaia (*d* 1560), who was primarily an astronomer; later Camillo's son Girolamo took over this responsibility. Morelli identified Lorenzo and his sons as the authors of a number of surviving drawings for other mechanical devices and inventions, and Lorenzo has also been associated with Alesso Baldovinetti's frescoes (destr. 1760) in the Gianfigliazzi Chapel at Santa Trinita, Florence.

Of Lorenzo's sons, Benvenuto di Lorenzo Volpaia (*b* Florence, 1486; *d* 1550) is the most prominent. He was trained by his father as a clockmaker, although his later career seems to have included architecture, surveying and map-making, at which he excelled, according to Vasari. He worked with his brother Fruosino di Lorenzo Volpaia (*fl* 1532; *d* Frankfurt) for a time. In 1521 Benvenuto became the official in charge of the clock in the Mercato Nuovo and in 1549 renewed that in the Servite nunnery of SS Annunziata. In 1529, in association with Niccolò

Tribolo, a prominent figure at the Medici court, he executed what was perhaps his most intriguing work. He was commissioned by Pope Clement VII to prepare a model of Florence, to be used as a source of information for Clement in the forthcoming conflict between the Imperial army and the Medici. It was to be a three-dimensional model, based on accurate surveys which themselves took several months. The heights of all the city's towers were measured, as well as the elevations of the surrounding hills, for a distance of one mile around the city. The cupola of the cathedral was used as the datum or focus for the survey. To reduce its weight, the completed model was made of cork, and all of the features were accurately carved to scale. The overall size was four braccia (about 2.4 m) square, and it was in several pieces. When complete, it was smuggled out of the city and taken to Perugia. The Pope made constant use of the model during the ensuing ten-month siege of the city by the Imperial army, thus closely following the military events. In 1531 Benvenuto became superintendent of the Belvedere fortress, where he became an associate of Michelangelo.

BIBLIOGRAPHY

G. Vasari: *Vite* (1550, rev. 2/1568); ed. G. Milanesi (1878–85)

J. Morelli: *Codici manoscritti volgari della Libreria Naniana* (Venice, 1776)

U. Dorini: 'L'Orologio dei pianeti di Lorenzo di Volpaia', *Riv. A.*, vi (1909), pp. 137–44

Volpato, Giovanni (*b* Angarano di Bassano, 30 March 1740; *d* Rome, 22 Sept 1803). Italian engraver. In 1760 he entered the famous copperplate printworks of Giambattista Remondini in Bassano and, under the guidance of Antonio Baratti, learnt the art of engraving and etching. During this early period he engraved, signing himself Jean Renard, four *Rustic Capricci* after Giovanni Battista Piazzetta, the *Four Parts of the World* after Jacopo Amigoni, the *Four Ages of Man* after Andrea Zucchi and the portrait of *Giambattista Morgagni*. On the invitation of Francesco Bartolozzi, who had noted his talent during a visit to Bassano, he moved to Venice in 1762 and was thus able to refine his technique while maintaining his connection with the Remondini concern as a technical consultant and commercial adviser.

In Venice, Volpato engraved four landscapes after Francesco Zuccarelli, six landscapes after Marco Ricci, four religious scenes after Amigoni, the *Four Seasons* and six *Flemish Scenes* after Francesco Maggiotto, as well as various portraits, including those of the *Doge Foscarini*, the *Procurator Pisani* (after Bartolozzi) and the *Procurator Calbo* (after Francesco Canal). After Bartolozzi's departure for England (1764), Volpato collaborated more frequently with Francesco Maggiotto, after whose drawings he produced a pleasant series of ten prints showing itinerant occupations (e.g. *Tooth-drawer*, *Juggler*, *Puppeteer*), published by Nicolò Cavalli. In 1769 he went to Parma to work with other artists on the 36 plates illustrating the celebrations held for Ferdinand of Bourbon's marriage to Maria-Amalia of Habsburg-Lorraine. In the same year he made an engraving of the funerary monument to *Conte Francesco Algarotti*, designed by Carlo Bianconi (1732–1802) and erected in the Camposanto, Pisa. On his return to Venice he began engraving the plates for *Paesti quod Posidoniam etiam dixere Rudera* (Rome, 1784), which includes a frontispiece representing the *Apotheosis of Charles II*, from a drawing by Giovanni Battista Tiepolo.

In 1772 Volpato moved to Rome to make reproductions of Raphael's frescoes in the Vatican Loggie and the following year engraved the portrait of *Clement XIV on Horseback*. In 1773 Gavin Hamilton's *Schola italica picturae*, to which Volpato had contributed eight plates after Leonardo, Raphael, Polidoro, Correggio, Veronese and Caravaggio, was published. The works he produced during the Roman period are characterized by a cold and academic technical virtuosity and are mostly reproductions of works by the great masters of previous centuries, for example Raphael, Michelangelo, Poussin, Claude, the Carracci and by Giovanni Paolo Panini (various views of Rome and a large panorama engraved on three plates).

Volpato opened a porcelain factory in 1786 in Rome, in the Via Pudenziana (this was later taken over by his son Giuseppe). In the same year, in collaboration with Raphael Morghen and Costanzo Angelini, he published in Rome the *Principi del disegno tratti dalle più eccellenti statue antiche*. He gave impetus to a flourishing school of engraving in which Morghen himself, Domenico Cunego, Giovanni Folo (1764–1836), Pietro Fontana (1762–1837) and others were formed.

BIBLIOGRAPHY

Thieme–Becker

G. Verci: *Notizie intorno alla vita e alle opere de' pittori, scultori e intagliatori della città di Bassano* (Venice, 1775), pp. 300–09

G. Baseggio: *Della pittura e dell'intaglio in rame in Bassano* (Bassano, 1847), pp. 42–8

C. Le Blanc: *Manuel de l'amateur d'estampes* (Paris, 1854–90), iv, pp. 151–4

G. A. Moschini: *Dell'incisione in Venezia* (Venice, 1924), pp. 134–6

P. M. Tua: 'Un incisore veneto del secolo XVIII: Giovanni Volpato', *Riv. Venezia*, xiii (1934), pp. 421–30

C. A. Petrucci: *Catalogo generale delle stampe tratte dai rami incisi posseduti dalla Calcografia nazionale* (Rome, 1953), pp. 127–9

Da Carlevarijs ai Tiepolo: Incisori veneti e friulani del settecento (exh. cat. by D. Succi, Venice, Correr; Gorizia, Mus. Prov. Pal. Attems; 1983), pp. 427–31

DARIO SUCCI

Volpato [Volpati], **Giovanni Battista** (*b* Bassano del Grappa, 1633; *d* Bassano del Grappa, 1706). Italian painter and writer. He was at the centre of a 17th-century revival of the art of Jacopo Bassano and established the division of Jacopo's stylistic evolution into four periods, prizing most highly the works of the 1540s. In 1671 Volpato executed a series of canvases for the church of S Daniele at Lamon and the portrait of the *Podesta Boldù Seated in Council* (Feltre, Mus. Civ.). The latter is, unusually, free of the influence of Bassano; its refined style is closer to that of Nicolas Régnier. In 1672 Volpato decorated the Chapel of the Holy Sacrament in Feltre Cathedral with a series of canvases (*in situ*): the *Annunciation*, *God the Father*, the *Nativity*, the *Adoration of the Magi*, the *Last Supper* and a *Glory with Angels*. He was paid for these, secretly, by the bishop, Bartolommeo Gera, with two canvases by Bassano, stolen from the villages of Tomo and Rasai: the *Virgin and Child Enthroned, with SS James and John* and the *Virgin Enthroned, with SS Martin and Anthony Abbot* (both Munich, Alte Pin.). Copies of these by Volpato were substituted but the fraud was discovered and in 1686 Volpato was tried and found guilty. Other works by Volpato include the decoration of the vault of Bassano

Cathedral in 1689 with the *Assumption of the Virgin*, *Martyrdom of St Clement* and *St Bassian*, as well as a contribution to the decoration of the Villa Rezzonico, Bassano, and two works painted in Venice: a *Pentecost* and an *Adoration of the Shepherds* (both *c.* 1687; Venice, S Maria del Giglio). Volpato's writings are kept, largely unpublished, at the Biblioteca Comunale at Bassano del Grappa.

UNPUBLISHED SOURCES

Bassano del Grappa, Bib. Com. [*Alcuni dialoghi della verità pittoresca* (1670–85); *Trattato de' muscoli e moti* (1700); *Dimostrazione figurata sopra la testa dell'uomo* (1704)]

WRITINGS

Il vagante corriero a curiosi che si dilettano di pittura (Vicenza, 1685)
Baseggio, ed.: *Del preparare tele, colori ed altro . . . aspettante all' pittura* (Bassano, 1847)

BIBLIOGRAPHY

G. B. Verci: *Notizie intorno alla vita e alle opere de' pittori, scultori, intagliatori della città di Bassano* (Venice, 1775)
E. Bordignon Favero: '*La natura pittrice' di Giovanni Battista Volpato* (Padua, 1978)
——: *Il processo per furto e falso contro G. B. Volpato pittore del '600* (Padua, 1979)
——: 'La *Pentecoste* di G. B. Volpato e il *Lume serrato* di Jacopo Bassano', *Atti & Mem. Accad. Patavina Sci., Lett. & A.* (1980–81), pp. 78–107
S. Claut: 'Giambattista Volpato', *Arte del '600 nel Bellunese* (exh. cat., ed. M. Lucco; Belluno, Pal. Crepadona, 1981)
R. Pallucchini: *La pittura veneziana del seicento* (Milan, 1981)
S. Claut: 'L'attività feltrine di Giambattista Volpato', *A. Ven.*, xxxvii (1983), pp. 187–93
M. Gregori and E. Schleier, eds: *La pittura in Italia: Il seicento*, 2 vols (Milan, 1988, rev. 1989)
E. Bordignon Favero: 'Il rinnovamento seicentesco del Duomo di Bassano e il soffitto di Giovan Battista Volpato. Note storico-artistiche e ritrovamenti d'archivio', *Arte Doc.*, iii (1992), pp. 204–17

SERGIO CLAUT

Volpe [Fox], Vincent [Vicenzo] (*b* Naples; *d* London, Nov–Dec 1536). Italian decorative and heraldic painter, active in England. He was one of the first Italian artists employed by Henry VIII, and in 1513 he was granted an annuity of £20—twice what his contemporary John Brown (*d* 1532) would be paid as Serjeant Painter. In that year he also received £30 for banners and streamers for seven ships, and in 1514 he was paid the very large sum of £112 19s. 8d. for similar decorative work for the new ship *Henry Grace à Dieu*; the receipt (London, BL, Stowe MS. 146, fol. 124) is made out to 'Vincent Fox' and is signed 'Vicenzo Volpe'. He was sent to Antwerp as 'the King's painter' in 1520, presumably to make decorative preparations for the Field of the Cloth of Gold when Henry met Francis I at Guisnes. In 1527 he was paid £13 for 13 weeks' work at Greenwich Palace, London, for festivities to mark an Anglo-French treaty. He received £15 3s. 12d. for 'trimming' the royal barge in 1530. In 1530 he was paid £3 10s. for a 'plat', or topographical drawing, of Rye and Hastings and may have done a bird's-eye view of Dover harbour on parchment in pen and ink tinted with watercolour. In 1534 he provided a New Year gift to the King. For a time Volpe lived in the London parish of St Martin Outwich before settling in St Andrew Undershaft, a parish then popular with immigrant artists.

BIBLIOGRAPHY

E. Auerbach: 'Vincent Volpe, the King's Painter', *Burl. Mag.*, xcii (1950), pp. 222–7
——: *Tudor Artists* (London, 1954), pp. 8, 11–13, 38, 140–41, 157, 176, 181, 190, 193

MARY EDMOND

Volpedo, Giuseppe Pellizza da. *See* PELLIZZA DA VOLPEDO, GIUSEPPE.

Volpi, Alfredo (*b* Lucca, 14 April 1896; *d* São Paulo, ?30 May 1988). Brazilian painter. He was taken as an infant to São Paulo by his Italian parents. He began painting in 1914 after working as a painter-decorator. In the 1930s he was involved in the modernist groups active in São Paulo, including the Família Artística Paulista; he held his first one-man exhibition at the Itá Gallery, São Paulo, in 1944. He became involved in the Concrete art movement in Brazil and took part in Concrete art exhibitions in São Paulo and Rio de Janeiro in 1956 and 1957.

Until the mid-1940s Volpi painted landscapes and figures in a rough, realistic manner, already revealing his strong attraction for the picturesque and popular aspects of the subjects. Between 1945 and 1950 he painted seascapes and groups of houses along the Itanhaem littoral, but after 1950 he established his characteristic vocabulary of soft and sensual brushstrokes and simple schematized shapes with a limited range of motifs such as popular façades, church arches, flags, sails and masts; examples include *Night Façade* (1955; U. São Paulo, Mus. A. Contemp.; see fig.). In the 1970s these motifs gradually

Alfredo Volpi: *Night Façade*, tempera on canvas, 1.15×0.73 m, 1955 (Universidade de São Paulo, Museu de Arte Contemporânea)

evolved into abstract geometrical paintings with contrasting ranges of colour, as in *Kinetic Composition* (1970; São Paulo, Mus. A. Mod.). In 1951 he painted a panel for the church of Cristo Operário (São Paulo), which he followed with frescoes for the chapel of Our Lady of Fátima (1958) and for the Palácio dos Arcos (1966) in Brasília.

BIBLIOGRAPHY

J. A. França: 'Volpi', *Aujourd'hui*, 46 (1964)

Alfredo Volpi (exh. cat., ed. A. Amaral; Rio de Janeiro, Mus. A. Mod., 1972)

T. Spanudis: *Volpi* (Rio de Janeiro, 1975)

A. Amaral, ed.: *Projeto construtivo brasileiro na arte, 1950–1962* (São Paulo, 1977)

R. Pontual: *Cinco mestres brasileiros: Pintores construtivistas* (Rio de Janeiro, 1977)

O. T. Araújo: *Dois estudos sobre Volpi* (Rio de Janeiro, 1986)

Volpi: 90 anos (exh. cat. by O. T. Araújo, São Paulo, Mus. A. Mod., 1986)

ROBERTO PONTUAL

Volsinii Veteres. *See* ORVIETO, §1.

Volterra [Etrus. Velathri; Lat. Volaterrae]. Italian city in Tuscany, *c.* 55 km south-west of Florence and *c.* 28 km east of the Tyrrhenian port of Vada. It is situated on a steep outcrop overlooking the valleys of the rivers Era and Cècina and strategically controlling the north–south routes of the Val d'Elsa. A centre of Villanovan culture in the 9th–7th centuries BC, it became one of the most powerful Etruscan principalities in the 7th century BC (*see* §1 below). In the Middle Ages control of Volterra was disputed between Siena, Pisa and Florence, the last finally conquering the city in the war over the acquisition of the alum mines in 1472. Volterra remained under Florentine control until the unification of Italy in 1861. Within the 13th- and 15th-century walls the city has largely retained its medieval appearance, but the *balze* (chasms in the clayey soil on which it was built) have caused the disappearance of both Etruscan monuments and of the older medieval churches. Its alabaster workings, traceable to Etruscan times, were revived in 1791 by Marcello Inghirami. Artists born in Volterra include the painters Daniele Ricciardelli, called Daniele da Volterra, and Baldassare Franceschini, called il Volterrano.

ALESSANDRA ANSELMI

1. VELATHRI. The northernmost city of the Etruscan twelve-city league, it occupied the site of modern Volterra but at its height was far more extensive. Velathri grew from Villanovan settlements, although evidence is sparse before the 7th century BC, and it did not begin to emerge as an important city until the second half of the 6th century BC. This phase was completed by the construction of city walls, enclosing an area of *c.* 10 ha, during the 5th century BC. Finds of architectural terracottas from large temples (Volterra, Mus. Etrus. Guaranacci) also date from the 5th century BC. The city's greatest period of development, however, occurred between the 4th and 2nd centuries BC, when it came to dominate an extensive territory in what is now central Tuscany. Volterran Red-figure pottery was widely distributed in Italy, and production of alabaster funerary urns began in the mid-3rd century BC. The latter are the most characteristic artefacts from Hellenistic Volterra and reflect the practice of replacing the sarcophagi and stone beds of earlier Etruscan rock-cut tombs with numerous ash urns ranged around a single chamber (e.g. the Inghirami Tomb, early 2nd century BC; reconstructed in Florence, Mus. Archeol.). The prosperity of Hellenistic Volterra is evinced by the extended city walls, *c.* 7 km in length and enclosing 116 ha, and the issues of coinage by the city mint (*see also* ETRUSCAN, §VII, 1). Monumental buildings were constructed on the acropolis, and the necropoleis contain large family tombs from this period.

The decline of the ancient city begins to be evident from the second half of the 2nd century BC. Volaterrae sided with the consul Gaius Marius (*c.* 157–86 BC) in the Civil War that broke out in 102 BC and was besieged for two years (82–80 BC), finally capitulating to Sulla (*c.* 138–78 BC) and losing Roman citizenship. The aristocracy, however, remained sufficiently prosperous to erect several large public monuments during the 1st century BC, including the theatre dedicated by Cecina Severus, of which parts of the *cavea* and *scena* remain. From this time onwards the decline of the ancient city was gradual but continuous, counteracted only by the presence of a flourishing Christian community.

BIBLIOGRAPHY

E. Fiumi: 'Volterra', *Not. Scavi Ant.* (1972), pp. 52–136

M. Cristofani: 'Volterra', *Not. Scavi Ant.* (1973) [suppl. 1]

E. Fiumi: *Volterra etrusca e romana* (Pisa, 1976)

MARCO RENDELI

2. LATER HISTORY. After the fall of the Roman Empire, Volterra fell under the domination of the Lombards and the Franks. It had become a bishopric in the 5th century AD, and in the 11th and 12th centuries imperial privileges reinforced the power of the bishop alongside that of the count; the bishopric became hereditary with the Pannochieschi family (1150–1239). The commune, which had its own consuls from 1150 and a podestà from 1193, succeeded in affirming its authority only in the 13th century, but in 1348 the tyrannical signoria of Ottaviano Belforte was imposed. Florentine support for the commune ended in a definitive seizure of power in 1361, and, despite important attempts at rebellion (for example that of 1472), Volterra's fortunes were linked with those of Florence until Italian unification.

The first recorded medieval buildings are the Early Christian churches dedicated to the city's patron saints, SS Clemente, Giusto and Ottaviano, but they have all vanished in the subsidence caused by the *balze*. The present aspect of Volterra is characterized by its 12th- and 13th-century buildings in the grey limestone *pietra panchina*: the urban centre is concentrated on the Piazza dei Priori (1208–57), with the Torre del Podestà, the Palazzo Pretorio and the bishop's palace. Adjoining this square is the Piazza di S Giovanni, which contains the earliest surviving building, the cathedral (consecrated 1120), which, together with the octagonal baptistery, was built in Pisan Romanesque style. The medieval core of Volterra was much smaller than the extensive Etruscan town, and in the 13th century a new 2 km circuit of walls was built inside the line of the Etruscan walls, although the latter were not abandoned. Domestic architecture of the medieval period is characterized by tower-houses (e.g. that of the Buonparenti), built in groups for defence and later converted to private homes.

In the 15th century palazzi were built, including the Pilastri-Bargiotti, Biondi, Campani, Incontri and Contugi (now Ricciarelli), and the churches of S Lino, S Pietro in Selci and S Girolamo. The Palazzo Solaini (now Minucci), attributed to Antonio da Sangallo (i), and the façade of the Palazzo Viti, attributed to Bartolommeo Ammanati, date from the 16th century. From then on, however, activity centred on rebuilding and redecorating existing structures rather than on constructing new buildings. Characteristic features of the palazzi are small windows for children beneath the main ones.

When the city was retaken by Florence in 1472, Lorenzo de' Medici extended the defences by joining the Rocca Vecchia to the Rocca Nuova. The former, founded 1342–3, has a trapezoidal plan with a semi-elliptical tower in the centre; the Rocca Nuova is square, with angle towers. They were linked by a double curtain wall, and their dominant position at the top of the town has defined its subsequent appearance.

Volterra did not develop an independent artistic tradition, and its considerable artistic patrimony consists mainly of works by outsiders, notably from Pisa, Siena and Florence, each of which exerted their influence in succession: Pisa from the 11th to the 13th century, Siena in the 14th and Florence from the second half of the 15th century. Finds from the Etruscan period are preserved at the Museo Etrusco Guarnacci, while the Museo Diocesano di Arte Sacra, founded in 1936, displays works from the 12th to the 19th centuries. The Galleria Pittorica, founded in 1905, is located in the Palazzo Minucci–Solaini.

BIBLIOGRAPHY

C. Ricci: *Volterra* (Bergamo, 1905)
E. Carli: *Volterra nel medioevo e nel rinascimento* (Pisa, 1979)
F. Lessi and U. Bavani: *Arte a Volterra* (Pisa, 1980)
Momenti dell'arte a Volterra (exh. cat., ed. M. Burresi and A. Caleca; Volterra, Pal. Minucci–Solaini, 1981)
E. Fiumi: *Volterra e S Gimignano nel medioevo*, ed. G. Pinto (Siena, 1983)

ALESSANDRA ANSELMI

Volterra, Daniele da. *See* DANIELE DA VOLTERRA.

Volterra, Francesco da [Capriani, Francesco] (*b* Volterra, 1535; *d* Rome, 15 Sept 1594). Italian architect. He started as a *falegname* (It.: 'joiner') and developed his career as an architect mainly in Rome; he was recorded there in 1559. He continued the late Renaissance manner of Giacomo da Vignola; Giacomo della Porta regarded him as among the foremost architects of his time. He became a member of the Accademia di San Luca in 1594. He was seldom able to complete his commissions, however, which all passed to Carlo Moderno after his death. His first architectural commissions came from Cesare Gonzaga in 1563–64, for alterations to the Galleria in the Palazzo Ducale, Mantua, and to the Palazzo Ducale, Palazzo della Comunità, and cathedral of S Pietro, Guastalla (all altered), and improvements to the town plan. He returned to Rome in 1570 to work for Cardinal d'Este; he has been credited with the design of the Fontana del Dragone at the Villa d'Este, Tivoli. His connections with the Gonzagas gave him invaluable access to the Curia; although he was recommended for court architect at Mantua in 1583, he preferred to remain in Rome. Volterra left Rome only in

1580 to renovate the cathedral in Volterra, to which he added an elaborately carved ceiling.

The church of S Giacomo degli Incurabili, Rome, also commissioned by Cardinal Antonio Maria Salviati, is da Volterra's most important and influential work; he employed an oval plan (long axis *c.* 25.5 m, short axis *c.* 18.7 m) in a major ecclesiastical building, which may have been a development of designs for oval churches by Vignola, particularly for S Andrea (1554). A series of drawings (1590; Stockholm, Nmus.; 1595–6; Vienna, Albertina) shows the development from a conventional rectangular plan to a longitudinal oval with transepts and then to the final unified oval plan surrounded by chapels. The double pilasters that originally articulated the side chapels gave way to single pilasters, emphasizing the longitudinal axis, and the exterior underwent a similar change, the articulated side façades being replaced by unadorned and unarticulated walls to form a simple shell for the interior. The façade to the Via del Corso followed Vignola's unexecuted design (1568) for Il Gesù, Rome, of a two-storey façade constrained by volutes. Da Volterra gave it a resolutely vertical emphasis, with modest volutes; he reduced it to a flat plane framed with pilasters and with engaged columns to the entrance portico. Maderno completed the vaulting and the façade, and the church was consecrated in 1602. This new design became a model for oval churches in the 17th and 18th centuries.

Salviati also commissioned da Volterra to build a palazzo (1592–8; destr. 1659) in the Piazza Collegio Romano, Rome. The block (33.5 m long, 26.8 m deep) had a three storey façade; the courtyard (18.8 sq. m) had loggias and a fountain. The design of the Salviati Chapel (1600) in S Georgio, with a polychromatic marble interior, is usually attributed to da Volterra but was executed after his death and may therefore have been significantly altered by Maderno. Volterra also executed various projects for Cardinal Nicola Caetani: a funerary monument in the basilica of Loreto, Marches, statuary and the entrance portal for the Ninfa gardens, Rome (destr.), and the palace at Cisterna, Latium (altered), all in 1578. The unexecuted project for the Palazzo all'Orso (1581; Florence, Uffizi) for Cardinal Enrico Caetani followed the design of the Palazzo Farnese (1541–46; Antonio Sangallo II); the plain three-storey façade was relieved only by a projecting balcony over the main entrance, similar to that of the Palazzo Salviati alla Lungara by Antonio da Sangallo II. The Caetani Chapel (*c.* 1590) in the church of S Pudenziana had an oval sail vault over a rectangular plan with a polychrome marble interior; it was finished by Maderno in 1601.

Other works in Rome designed by da Volterra include the convent and church of S Chiara a Casa Pia (1582; destr. 1883), which had a plain pilastered façade similar to S Giacomo degli Incurabili; the rebuilding (1585–91) of the church of the Orfanelli, S Maria in Aquiro; the new convent of S Susanna (1587–96; destr.); and the Ospizio di S Luigi dei Francesi (1588; destr. 1798). Volterra also supervised the execution of the nave and four chapels (1591–4) of Giacomo della Porta's design for S Andrea della Valle. Later works were finished and modified by Maderno: the convent (1588–91) and church (1591) of S Silvestro in Capite (destr.), which had a barrel-vaulted nave and oval dome; the Palazzo Lancelotti (begun 1591, finished 1621) built for Cardinal Scipio Lancelotti (1527–98); and the Lancelotti Chapel (1594; destr. 1640s) in S Giovanni in Laterano.

BIBLIOGRAPHY
H. Hibbard: *Carlo Maderno and Roman Architecture, 1580–1630*, Stud. Archit., x (London, 1971)
L. H. Heydenreich and W. Lotz: *Architecture in Italy, 1400–1600*, Pelican Hist. A. (Harmondsworth, 1974)
A. C. Beccarini: 'La cappella Caetani nella basilica di Santa Pudenziana in Roma', *Quad. Ist. Stor. Archit.*, 25 (1975), pp. 143–58
M. Tafuri: 'Francesco Capriani', IXX (1976), pp. 189–95
S. Benedetti and G. Zander: *L'arte in Roma nel secolo XVI*, Storia di Roma, xxix/1 (Bologna, 1990)
L. Marcucci: *Francesco da Volterra: Un protagonista dell'architettura post-tridentina* (Rome, 1991)

ZILAH QUEZADO DECKKER

Volterrano, il. *See* FRANCESCHINI, BALDASSARRE.

Voltri, Nicolò da. *See* NICOLÒ DA VOLTRI.

Volubilis [Arab. Walīla]. Roman site in Morocco, 20 km north of Meknès. The town was inhabited from the 3rd century BC by a Libyophoenician (mixed Berber and Carthaginian) population. It grew rapidly in the mid-1st century AD when it became a *municipium* (free town) of the Roman province of Mauretania Tingitana. Abandoned by the Romans in AD 280–85, Volubilis was briefly the capital of the Islamic Idrisid dynasty at the end of the 8th century AD. A forum was built during the reign of Nero (AD 54–68), and by the end of the 1st century AD several *insulae* (apartment blocks) had been laid out around it. In the later 2nd century AD the urban grid was extended to the north-east, and a 3–km circuit of walls was built (AD 168–9) enclosing an area of around 40 ha. The forum was completely reconstructed at the time of Septimius Severus (*reg* AD 193–211), and a basilica was built with twin apses and rows of two-tiered columns dividing it into nave and aisles, as at Leptis Magna. Opposite is an imposing capitolium approached by a high staircase, and near by is the Arch of Caracalla (AD 216–17). A large number of impressive peristyle houses have been uncovered at Volubilis (2nd and 3rd centuries AD), with fountains and polychrome mosaic pavements. These include the House of Orpheus, with its circular mosaic of *Orpheus Charming the Animals with his Music*; the so-called Palace of Gordian, a huge complex with a street façade of 15 Ionic columns; and the House of the Cortège of Venus, with mosaics depicting *Diana Bathing* and *Hylas Attacked by the Nymphs*. Several fine bronzes were found on the site, notably the busts of Cato the Younger and King Juba II (both ?1st century AD; Rabat, Mus. Ant.).

BIBLIOGRAPHY
R. Thouvenot: *Volubilis* (Paris, 1949)
R. Etienne: *Le Quartier nord-est de Volubilis* (Paris, 1960)
A. Luquet: *Volubilis* (Tangier, 1972)

F. B. SEAR

Volute [from Lat. *voluta*: 'scroll']. Decorative architectural motif in the form of a coiled scroll, used especially on Classical capitals (*see* CAPITAL and ORDERS, ARCHITECTURAL, figs 1 and 3).

Volute krater. Ancient pottery form, used as a mixing bowl (*see* GREECE, ANCIENT, figs 71(ii)e and 97).

□

von. For German, Austrian and Swiss proper names consisting of a given name or names followed by this prefix and another part or parts, *see under* the part of the name following the prefix; for tripartite surnames, *see under* the first part of the surname.

Voogd, Hendrik (*b* Amsterdam, *bapt* 10 July 1768; *d* Rome, 4 Sept 1839). Dutch painter and printmaker, active in Italy. He studied from 1783 at the Stadstekenakademie in Amsterdam and subsequently with the wallpaper painter Jurriaan Andriessen. The financial aid of the Amsterdam art collector D. Versteegh (1751–1822) enabled him to depart in 1788 for Rome to obtain further training in landscape painting. Voogd's works from his first Roman years are primarily drawings with coloured wash in the typical late 18th-century linear style; an expressive example is *River Landscape near Narni* (1789; Haarlem, Teylers Mus.). Owing to the absence of Dutch colleagues in Rome, Voogd spent much of his time with the Franco-Flemish and German artists' colonies there. Internationally famous landscape painters, such as Nicolas-Didier Boguet, Johann Christian Reinhart and Johann Martin von Rohden, were among his close friends, and the work of the last, in particular, is often mistaken for that of Voogd. It is apparent, from one of the infrequent letters that Voogd sent to Versteegh in the Netherlands, that he made numerous drawings of Rome and its environs (Tivoli, Lake Albano, Castel Gandolfo, Lake Nemi etc). Some of these drawings, executed mostly in pencil and black chalk, consist of motifs taken directly from nature, such as trees and rocks; others portray views. Both categories are represented in Amsterdam (Hist. Mus. and Rijksmus.). Voogd claimed that his great exemplar, in addition to nature, was Claude Lorrain; from shortly after 1800 he was named the 'Dutch Claude Lorrain'. Although this nickname is somewhat exaggerated, it does indicate that Voogd's style had developed between 1795 and 1805 from an austere draughtsman-like manner into something far more picturesque. Examples illustrating this development include his *Italian Landscape with Umbrella Pines* of 1795 (Amsterdam, Rijksmus.) and two Italian landscapes (priv. col.) from 1802 and 1803. However, Voogd never completely abandoned his Netherlandish heritage: he was fascinated by unusual lighting effects and luxuriant foliage (e.g. 1804; Leipzig, Mus. Bild. Kst.) and from 1806 onwards was fond of drawing animals, particularly cattle (1806; Hamburg, Ksthalle). Italian cattle began to feature prominently in his drawings (see fig.) and paintings (1817; Bassano del Grappa, Mus. Civ.; and 1829; Heino, Hannema–De Stuers Fund.).

Voogd's lithographs, dating from 1818 and 1823, are among the earliest examples of this technique by a Dutch artist and were probably intended to satisfy the great demand for souvenirs in the years 1815–20 by travellers on the Grand Tour. Except for a few classicizing etchings (Amsterdam, Rijksmus.) and a series of eight engravings after Claude Lorrain, Poussin, Gaspard Dughet and Herman van Swanevelt (Rome, Calcografia N.), all of which

Hendrik Voogd: *Study of an Italian Bull* (*recto*), black chalk, 226×309 mm, *c.* 1815 (Hoofddorp, private collection)

were made around 1800, no other prints by Voogd have survived.

Voogd composed his paintings in a traditional manner. For his lithographs, wash drawings and oil paintings, he first made preparatory studies (whether or not based on his own observations), sometimes also preceded by a preliminary sketch. For the figures of cattle, he made separate preparatory sketches. These studies were meticulously copied, sometimes as reversed mirror images. He occasionally recycled his own motifs, by combining them in different groupings. This mechanical approach may have been due to his position as an established artist. No coloured drawings dating from after 1800 have survived; there are only oil paintings, for which he demanded extremely high prices. His new-found freedom as an artist of international reputation is probably also the reason why he never returned to the Netherlands, except for a single visit in 1828. Voogd deliberately turned down requests to provide biographical information. He never married and left no children. Around 1820 his success began to wane: Nagler described Voogd in 1850 as old-fashioned, and his obituary makes it clear that he was a completely forgotten artist at the time of his death. Interest in this early Dutch Romantic was only reawakened in 1959, with the rediscovery of about 200 drawings.

BIBLIOGRAPHY

Scheen

G. K. Nagler: *Neues allgemeines Künstler-Lexicon*, xx (Linz, 1850/*R* 1913)

A. Bredius: 'De schilder Hendrik Voogd en zijn maecenas', *Meded. Ned. Hist. Inst. Rome*, n. s. 2, vi (1936), pp. 111–19

C. J. de Bruyn Kops: 'Hendrik Voogd: Nederlands landschapschilder te Rome (1768–1839)', *Ned. Ksthist. Jb.*, xxi (1970), pp. 319–69

Reizen naar Rome: Italië als leerschool voor Nederlandse kunstenaars omstreeks 1800 [Journeys to Rome: Italy as a school for Dutch artists around 1800] (exh. cat., Haarlem, Teylers Mus.; Rome, Ist. Oland.; 1984) [with It. trans.]

F. Kuyvenhoven: 'Lady Devonshire, an English Maecenas in Post-Napoleonic Rome: Her Publication of Virgil's Aeneid and Hendrik Voogd's Contribution to it', *Meded. Ned. Inst. Rome*, n. s. 11, xlvi (1985), pp. 145–54

——: 'De Leidse collectie tekeningen en grafiek van Hendrik Voogd' [The Leiden collection of drawings and engravings by Hendrik Voogd], *Leids Ksthist. Jb.*, iv (1987), pp. 269–87 [with Eng. summary]

FRANSJE KUYVENHOVEN

Voorhelm Schneevogt, C. G. *See* SCHNEEVOGT, C. G. VOORHELM.

Voort [Vervoort], **Michiel van der, I** (*b* Antwerp, 3 Jan 1667; *d* Antwerp, 6 Dec 1737). Flemish sculptor. He was possibly an apprentice of Jan Cosyns but later moved to the studio of Pieter Scheemakers the elder and became a master in the Antwerp Guild of St Luke in 1690. Between 1690 and 1693 he travelled in Italy, visiting Rome and Naples. In 1700 he married Elisabeth Verberckt (aunt of the sculptor Jacques Verberckt), and they had five children, one of whom, Michiel van der Voort II (1704–after 1777), was also a sculptor and painter. The majority of his commissions were for religious works, generally church furnishings in various materials. His memorial statues were classical and simple, and he drew on the knowledge he had acquired in Rome of Hellenistic statues. Other influences were Michelangelo and Rubens. The memorial to *Humbert Guilliebmus de Precipiano, Bishop of Mechelen* (1709; Mechelen Cathedral) is traditional in design, but the marble figure of the Bishop is a penetrating portrait. The tomb of the Bishop's brother, *General Prosper de Precipiano* (marble, 1709), is in the same church, and its base is a vast stele combined with an allegorical figure and a portrait bust of de Precipiano. The use of the stele was subsequently adopted with enthusiasm by other Flemish sculptors.

Van der Voort had a decided inclination for the depiction of flora and fauna, and the pulpit originally erected in the Abbey of St Bernard near Antwerp in 1713 (now Antwerp Cathedral) is a riot of plants and animals sculpted in a most realistic manner. In 1720 he executed one of his finest reliefs, the *Elevation of the Cross* (Antwerp, St-Jacobskerk). The design is taken from Rubens's painting of the same subject (Antwerp Cathedral), but depth is created by overlapping figures placed before a background landscape and in the way the figures lean out of the relief.

Van der Voort's most exuberant work is the pulpit carved in 1721 for the abbey of Leliendael (now in Mechelen Cathedral). This pulpit is akin to a free-standing landscape, and its dramatic representation of the *Conversion of St Norbert* depicts the saint thrown from his horse beneath a small mountain adorned with trees, animals and figures that emerge from the background of rough-hewn rocks and detract from the function of the pulpit. He also produced secular works, particularly of such mythological subjects as *Andromeda* (marble, 1746; Antwerp, Huis Osterrieth).

BIBLIOGRAPHY

Thieme–Becker

J. Immerzeel: *De levens en werken der Hollandsche en Vlaamsche kunstschilders, beeldhouwers, graveurs en bouwmeesters* [The life and work of Dutch and Flemish painters, sculptors, engravers and architects] (Amsterdam, 1843), iii, p. 189

M. E. Tralbaut: 'Die preekstoelen van Michiel van der Voort de Oude [The pulpits of Michiel van der Voort the elder], *Gent. Bijdr. Kstgesch.*, x (1944), pp. 233–65

——: *De amors en putti, serafijnen an cherubijnen van Michiel van der Voort de Oude* [The amors and putti, seraphim and cherubim of Michiel van der Voort the elder] (Antwerp and Utrecht, 1946)

——: *Michiel van der Voort de Oude als dierenbeeldhouwer* [Michiel van der Voort the elder as a sculptor of animals] (Antwerp and Utrecht, 1946)

——: *De Antwerpse 'meester-constbeldthouwer' Michiel van der Voort de Oude* [The Antwerp master-sculptor Michiel van der Voort the elder] (Brussels, 1949; rev. Antwerp, 1950)

La Sculpture au siècle de Rubens (exh. cat., Brussels, Musées Royaux B.-A., 1977), pp. 219–42

IRIS KOCKELBERGH

Vopra [Vsesoyuznoye Ob'yedineniye Assotsiatsii Proletarskikh Arkhitektorov; Rus.: All-Union Alliance of Associations of Proletarian Architects]. Russian architectural group, active from 1929 to 1932. It was one of several 'proletarian' cultural organizations that came into being in every branch of art in the late 1920s and served to criticize Constructivism and the avant-garde from the viewpoint of proletarian class ideology. Organizations particularly attacked by Vopra were OSA (Association of contemporary architects) for its Constructivism, ASNOVA (Association of new architects) for its rationalist formalism, and MAO (Moscow architectural society) for its eclecticism and stylizations. Vopra's chairman was the art historian Ivan Matsa (1893–1974), while other prominent members included the architects Karo Alabyan (1897–1959), Vasily Simbirtsev, Arkady Mordvinov (1896–1964), Aleksandr Vlasov, Gevork Kochar (1901–73), Abram Zaslavsky (1899–1962) and Viktor Baburov (1903–77), many of whom were recent graduates from Vkhutein (Higher (state) artistic technical institute; *see* VKHUTEMAS), Moscow. In its Declaration published in *Stroitel'stvo Moskvy* in 1929, Vopra denounced the Constructivists for their 'mechanical approach' and proclaimed that 'the new proletarian architecture must develop its theory and practice on the basis of an application of the method of dialectical materialism', which was to be combined with critical use of historical experience and the latest technological achievements. Disseminating its ideas through the unofficial organ *Sovetskaya arkhitektura* ('Soviet architecture'), it also sought to consolidate young Communist Party members who were architects on the grounds of Marxist–Leninist theory and the 'Party general line'. By 1930 Vopra had 49 members in its Moscow section and had also organized branches in the Ukraine, Georgia, Armenia, Leningrad (now St Petersburg) and Tomsk. Teams of architects from the organization took part in many open competitions in 1930 and 1931, for example that for the Palace of Soviets, Moscow. Although its members were able to realize very little during the Vopra period, not least because this was abruptly curtailed in 1932 with the dissolution of the group and the foundation of the all-embracing Union of Soviet Architects, many went on to assume dominant positions in the latter and as a result became successful Soviet architects.

BIBLIOGRAPHY

'Deklaratsiya vserossiyskogo obshchestva proletarskikh arkhitektorov' [Declaration of the All-Russian Society of Proletarian Architects], *Stroitel'stvo Moskvy*, viii (1929), pp. 25–6
Iz istorii sovetskoy arkhitektury, 1926–1933 [From the history of Soviet architecture, 1926–1933] (Moscow, 1984)
A. V. Ikonnikov: *Russian Architecture of the Soviet Period* (Moscow, 1988)

JEREMY HOWARD

Voragine, Jacobus de. *See* JACOPO DA VORAGINE.

Vordemberge-Gildewart, Friedrich (*b* Osnabrück, 1899; *d* Ulm, 1962). Dutch painter of German birth. After serving a joinery apprenticeship he started to study interior design and architecture in 1919 at the Kunstgewerbeschule and Technische Hochschule in Hannover. From 1922 he assisted with architectural reliefs in the studio of his teacher Ludwig Vierthaler (*b* 1875), and in 1923–4 he produced radical picture-constructions, in which he included stereometric elements and the tools of the designer, as in *Construction No. 8* (see fig.). He combined these applied parts of the picture with a flat-surfaced geometric painting. In his choice of colours he did not stick to any restrictive formula, and even his early works are rich in graduated colours.

Vordemberge-Gildewart quickly attracted critical attention, particularly after he took part in the first exhibition of the Kestner-Gesellschaft in Hannover (1924). Through Schwitters he met Arp and also Theo van Doesburg, who accepted Vordemberge-Gildewart into the De Stijl group. Van Doesburg found him a ready ally in the development of a dynamic variant of Neo-plasticism, which they called 'Elementarism'. In 1927 van Doesburg published pictures by Vordemberge-Gildewart in the magazine *De Stijl* in order to explain his pictorial ideas, and tried to persuade him to become involved in joint propaganda activity. During this period Vordemberge-Gildewart often reduced the content of his pictures to diagonally chequered geometric picture forms, predominantly in shades of grey, ranging from white to black, and sometimes with a splash of red, as in *Composition No. 31* (1927; The Hague, Gemeentemus.). However, in the late 1920s he introduced multi-layered interpenetrations of form in his pictures, and in 1931–2 came up with form-constellations, which gave a clear view through to the picture surface, as in *Composition No. 73* (1932; Hannover, Sprengel Mus.).

In 1927 Vordemberge-Gildewart combined with Schwitters, Carl Buchheister, Rudolf Jahns (*b* 1896) and César Domela to form the group known as Die Abstrakten Hannover, and he was also a founder-member of the Ring Neue Werbegestalter, an association instigated by Schwitters that included typographical designers. From 1924 until late in life Vordemberge-Gildewart produced remarkable

Friedrich Vordemberge-Gildewart: *Construction No. 8*, oil on wood with T-square, 650×850 mm, 1924 (Berlin, Neue Nationalgalerie)

typographical work alongside his art. After a first one-man show at the Galerie Pavolozky in Paris in 1929, he participated in the first function organized by the Cercle et Carré group in the following year, and in 1932 became a founder-member of Abstraction-Création. Foreign contacts enabled him to keep on exhibiting when the Nazis' rise to power threatened free artistic expression. He showed his work successfully in 1934 in Rome and Milan, where it appealed to the Futurists.

Vordemberge-Gildewart and his wife Ilse Leda hoped to escape political persecution by moving to Berlin in 1936, but this proved to be a mistaken assumption; after a spell in Switzerland he moved to Amsterdam in 1938. There he was helped by Willem Sandberg and Hans Jaffé of the Stedelijk Museum, and given commissions by the printer and publisher Frans Duwaer. This tided him over the difficult period of the Occupation in the Netherlands. He painted in secret, producing pictures that were especially light and free, with celebratory pictorial ideas and well-balanced constellations of linear triangular forms with inserted and applied coloured pieces, as in *Composition No. 122* (1941; Cologne, Mus. Ludwig). In the preface to the first monograph of Vordemberge-Gildewart's work in 1949 Arp commented that the paintings, in their purity, provide a counter-image to the chaotic confusion of the period.

After a series of particularly lightly constructed and coloured rod compositions around 1950, Vordemberge-Gildewart started to produce more compact arrangements, increasingly based on verticals and horizontals and with stronger colouring, as in *Composition No. 176* (1949; Eindhoven, Stedel. Van Abbemus.). He also had the opportunity of using his pictorial ideas publicly in the creation of show window displays in the Bijenkorf department stores in Amsterdam, The Hague and Rotterdam (1950), just as quotations from his own work were becoming accepted as a possible basis for typographic creativity (for example in wrappers for the magazine *Forum*). His work once more achieved international recognition at the second São Paulo Biennale in 1953, and also through its inclusion in retrospectives of the pioneering achievements of the 1920s and 1930s.

In 1954 Vordemberge-Gildewart, who had been awarded Dutch citizenship after the war, accepted Max Bill's invitation to work at the newly founded Hochschule für Gestaltung in Ulm as the head of the Department of Visual Communication. From Ulm he strengthened his contacts with the representatives of Concrete art in Switzerland, developing close ties with Richard Paul Lohse in particular. In his pictures vertical banded arrangements now predominated, fitting into an arithmetically worked-out picture plan. However, he did not abandon his fondness for powerful colours, interruptions, small inserted forms and imaginary diagonal relationships, as in *Composition No. 215* (1961; Ingolstadt, Stadtmus.).

WRITINGS
Vordemberge-Gildewart: Époque néerlandaise (Amsterdam, 1949) [preface by Hans Arp]

BIBLIOGRAPHY
R. P. Lohse, ed.: *Vordemberge-Gildewart: A Visual Biography* (Teufen, 1959)
H. L. C. Jaffé: *Vordemberge-Gildewart: Mensch und Werk* (Cologne, 1971)
D. Helms, ed.: *Friedrich Vordemberge-Gildewart: Schriften und Vorträge* (St Gall, 1976)
W. Rotzler: *Vordemberge-Gildewart* (St Gall, 1979)
D. Helms, ed.: *Vordemberge-Gildewart: The Complete Works* (Munich, 1990)
Friedrich Vordemberge-Gildewart: Typographie und Werbegestaltung (exh. cat., ed. D. Helms and V. Rattemeyer; Wiesbaden, Mus. Wiesbaden, 1990)
Friedrich Vordemberge-Gildewart: Baugestaltung (exh. cat., ed. D. Helms; Wiesbaden, Mus. Wiesbaden, 1993)
Typographie kann unter Umständer Kunst sein (exh. cat., ed. D. Helms; 1993)

DIETRICH HELMS

Vorkink & Wormser. Dutch architectural partnership formed *c.* 1905 by Pieter Vorkink (*b* Amsterdam, 1878; *d* Ede, 1960) and Jacobus Wormser (*b* Amsterdam, 1878; *d* Amersfoort, 1935). Vorkink trained at the Industrieschool van de Maatschappij voor de Werkende Stand, and Wormser at the Quellinusschool, Amsterdam, and both worked for a period in H. P. Berlage's office. One of their first works was an expansion plan for the local authorities of Watergraafsmeer. Part of this plan formed the basis of the Watergraafsmeer garden suburb, also known as Betondorp (Concrete Village). The partnership was mainly concerned with residential buildings in Velzen, Hilversum, Breukelen and elsewhere, including variations on the theme of terrace housing. Their villa designs in the Amsterdam school style are more interesting: Reigersnest (1918–20) at Oostvoorne, with gardener's house and summerhouse on the dunes, is the most controversial. Vorkink & Wormser also designed the interior (still intact). With its fanciful, organic forms, the whole scheme is one of the finest examples of AMSTERDAM SCHOOL style. The ironware shop Gunters and Meuser (1918), on the corner of Prinsengracht and Egelantiersgracht, Amsterdam, is also in this style. The country house (1924) at Santpoort is less spectacular. The unexecuted plan (1920) for a country house at Hulshorst directly recalls the cross-section of a snail's shell. After the partnership was dissolved in 1925, Vorkink became director of the School voor Bouwkunde, Versierende Kunsten en Ambachten in Haarlem. He did not build much more, but his *strokenbouw* (parallel-built, high rise blocks, constructed to provide maximum internal light), built in 1937 on the Louise de Colignystraat, Amsterdam, show that his architectural outlook had shifted entirely in favour of Functionalism. Wormser, who during the partnership had some commissions on which he worked alone, built little more after its break-up.

BIBLIOGRAPHY
G. Fanelli: *Architettura moderna in Olanda, 1900–1940* (Florence, 1968; Dut. trans., with abridged Eng. text, The Hague, 1978)
The Amsterdam School (exh. cat., ed. W. de Wit; New York, Cooper-Hewitt Mus., 1983)
M. Casciato: *De Amsterdamse School* (Rotterdam, 1991)
E. Mattie: *The Amsterdam School* (Amsterdam, 1991)

E. MATTIE, M. DE MOOR

Voroneţ. Monastery in north Moldavia, Romania. It is famous for its church of St George, built in 1488 by Voivode Stephen III (*reg* 1457–1504). A typical Moldavian church of the 15th to 17th century with a layout suitable for the celebration of the Orthodox liturgy (*see* ROMANIA, §II), it combines a large rectangular narthex and Serbian trefoil plan with a Moldavian system of arches and pendentives supporting the tall cylindrical drum and dome over the nave. Two external buttresses are placed between the middle and lateral apses, while the portals and windows are of Gothic design. The wall paintings (1488–96) in the sanctuary and nave follow a Byzantine iconographic programme (*see* ROMANIA, §III, 1 and fig. 5); they are sober and robust in character and include a portrait of the founder and his family on the west wall of the nave, in a votive composition often found in Moldavia. The narthex was painted in 1552.

In the 16th century (before 1547) Metropolitan Grigorie Roşca commissioned the construction of an outer narthex, the interior of which was painted with the *Menologion*. He is also associated with the paintings that cover the church's façades. The most renowned composition is the *Last Judgement* on the western wall. On the apse and other walls are an *All Saints*, a *Tree of Jesse*, scenes from *Genesis*, and the *Life of St John the New* from Suceava and the *Life of St George*, the patron of Moldavia. These works by anonymous painters are exceptional for their elegant drawing, their colourful palette set against a ground of lapis lazuli, the clarity of their composition and the skilful combination of fresco and secco techniques. The church also contains some of the oldest and finest carved wooden ecclesiastical furniture in Moldavia (16th century; *see* ROMANIA, §IV).

BIBLIOGRAPHY

N. Stoicescu: *Repertoriul bibliografic al localităţilor şi monumentelor medievale din Moldova* [Bibliographical index of medieval localities and monuments in Moldavia] (Bucharest, 1974), pp. 920–25

V. Drăguţ: *Pictura murală din Moldova, sec. XV–XVI* [Mural painting in Moldavia, XV–XVI centuries] (Bucharest, 1982)

TEREZA-IRENE SINIGALIA

Voronikhin, Andrey (Nikiforovich) (*b* Novoye Usol'e in Perm', 27 Oct 1759; *d* St Petersburg, 5 March 1814). Russian architect. His mother was a serf on one of the estates of Count Aleksandr Sergeyevich Stroganov, who is generally considered to have been his father, and who certainly took a great interest in his education. Stroganov sent Voronikhin to study painting in Moscow (1777–9), where he is said to have participated in frescoing the refectory vestibule at the Trinity-Sergius Monastery (1778). While in Moscow, he developed an interest in architecture and came to the notice of Vasily Bazhenov and Matvey Kazakov, the two most distinguished Russian architects of the day. At their prompting, Stroganov enrolled Voronikhin in the St Petersburg Academy of Fine Arts. In 1786 he was sent abroad and, before leaving Russia, was given his freedom. He travelled to Switzerland and France, where he studied under Charles de Wailly, returning to Russia on the outbreak of the French Revolution.

In St Petersburg, Voronikhin was employed by Count Stroganov to design new interiors for his palace on the Nevsky Prospekt, a masterpiece by Bartolomeo Francesco Rastrelli which had been damaged by fire. The most interesting rooms, which survive intact but lack their original collections, are the picture gallery and the mineral cabinet, where geological specimens from Stroganov's vast estates in the Urals were displayed. The picture gallery is barrel-vaulted over its long central tract, with bays at the end prefaced by pairs of Ionic columns supporting an entablature. Voronikhov also designed a Neo-classical dacha (1796–8) for the Stroganov family, where a rusticated base provides a piquant contrast to the light, open loggia above it. Further commissions followed for work at other Stroganov country houses: at Bratsevo near Moscow, at Marino and at Prince Galitsin's house at Gorodnaya (1798). The décor throughout is in the early Neo-classical style—refined, complex and elegant with a tendency to cuboid volumes and a wealth of columns and colonnades.

Voronikhin's success in these commissions and his evident flair were a source of gratification to Count Stroganov, who succeeded in 1797 in getting him elected a member of the St Petersburg Academy of Fine Arts. In 1800 Voronikhin was granted the title of architect and began teaching architecture at the Academy. He was made professor in 1802, senior professor and head of the Department of Architecture in 1811. The greatest prize, however, that Stroganov was able to secure for his protégé was the commission to build a new cathedral in honour of the miraculous icon of the Virgin of Kazan' (Kazan' Cathedral, 1801–11; see fig.), which the Count's friend Emperor Paul I (*reg* 1796–1801) was proposing to erect in St Petersburg. A scheme had already been drawn up by Giacomo Quarenghi, but this was now abandoned. The Emperor wanted the architect to recreate St Peter's, Rome, by the side of the Nevsky Prospekt. To ensure that ritual orientation was preserved, Voronikhin sited his Latin cross plan—itself unusual for an Orthodox church—parallel to the Prospekt, its east end facing towards the Yekaterininsky (now Griboyedov) Canal. Two Bernini colonnades, each of 136 Corinthian columns, were planned to reach out from the north and south transept entrances; only one, towards the Nevsky, was actually built. A third colonnade was likewise planned, but not executed, leading into the real main entrance on the west front. Inside, the nave, transepts and chancel are flanked by double rows of granite columns, with gilt bronze bases and capitals, which support a coffered barrel vault via a deep entablature. Voronikhin's colonnade (unlike Bernini's) is the same height as the cathedral and its portico, which are brought down to the level of the adjacent buildings, thus promoting their integration into the urban grain; the transparency of the colonnade (whose columns repeat the rhythm and spacing of those inside) contrasts with the walls of the ambient buildings and their even grid of fenestration. Despite the cathedral's Roman overtones, many details, including the exiguous crossing piers supporting the drum and its iron dome, together with the general proportions, recall the Panthéon in Paris.

Voronikhin's other great building in St Petersburg is the Institute of Mines (1811) on St Basil's Island (the Vasil'evsky Ostrov). Its 12-columned Doric portico, based on the Temple of Poseidon at Paestum, helps to create a ceremonial entrance to the capital from the sea. The heroic size of the portico is mediated to the human scale via the two groups of sculpture in front, which form an integral part of the composition. Other schemes of Voronikhin's include the Ministry of Crown Domains on the Palace Embankment (1807, rebuilt), the church in the Court Ministry on the Fontanka Canal (1813) and the completion of interiors at the Winter Palace. Voronikhin joined

Andrey Voronikhin: Kazan' Cathedral, St Petersburg, 1801–11; chromolithograph published by Lemercier from a drawing by Jules Arnout, second half of the 19th century (Paris, Bibliothèque Nationale)

Vincenzo Brenna's team at the palace in Pavlovsk (1803–14), where remodelling was in progress after damage by fire: he designed the Egyptian vestibule, the grand staircase and the lantern room. The 'lantern' is a bay window with a domed and coffered ceiling supported on an Ionic colonnade. Voronikhin also designed much of the furniture at Pavlovsk, including the chairs with arms formed from gryphon's wings. In the park he worked on the dairy farm, the ice house and the beautiful Rose Pavilion.

In his last years Voronikhin worked a great deal on the plans for St Isaac's Cathedral, the memorial column for the Patriotic War and the church of Christ the Saviour in Moscow. He also created a design for a Tatar town house in the Oriental style, showing new trends in architecture. His interiors, always designed to complement the furniture, reveal both grandiosity and comfort (low soft divans, designs for banquettes, mirrors and tables; for an example of his furniture see ST PETERSBURG, fig. 9). He was one of the first Russian artists to begin to design stone items decorated with metal and to use cut glass. An extensive graphic legacy shows that Voronikhin, an outstanding master of Russian Neo-classicism, was also a brilliant draughtsman with perfect command of Indian ink and watercolours.

BIBLIOGRAPHY

V. A. Panov: *Arkhitektor A. N. Voronikhin* [The architect A. N. Voronikhin] (Moscow, 1937)

G. G. Grimm: *A. N. Voronikhin: Chertezhi i risunki* [A. N. Voronikhin: drafts and drawings] (Moscow, 1952)

D. E. Arkin: *Zakharov i Voronikhin* [Zakharov and Voronikhin] (Moscow, 1953)

A. S. Terekhin: *Arkhitektor Andrey Voronikhin* [The architect Andrey Voronikhin] (Perm', 1968)

V. G. Lisovsky: *Andrey Voronikhin* (Lenizdat, 1971)

YE. I. KIRICHENKO

Voronin, Nikolay (Nikolayevich) (*b* Vladimir, 13 Dec 1904; *d* Moscow, 4 April 1976). Russian archaeologist and art historian. He graduated from the history department at Leningrad (now St Petersburg) State University in 1926. From 1928 to 1931 he was a postgraduate student and then joined the staff of the State Academy for the History of Material Culture. In 1934 he published his thesis on the history of Russian architecture in the 16th and 17th centuries. He became a doctor of historical sciences in 1944 and a professor in 1946. He directed excavations in the Old Russian cities of Yaroslavl', Rostov, Vladimir, Suzdal', Pereyaslavl'-Zalessky, Staritsa, Murom and Grodno and, as a result of the excavations in Bogolyubovo (1943–54), the remains of a 12th-century palace complex were discovered. He was particularly interested in the synthesis of Romanesque and Byzantine influences in Old Russian architecture; he also revealed the decisive influence of Vladimir and Suzdal' on the architecture of the state of Muscovy. From 1962 he conducted research into the architecture and painting of medieval Smolensk.

WRITINGS

Vladimir, Bogolyubovo, Suzdal', Yuryev-Polsky (Moscow, 1958; Eng. trans., Moscow, 1971)

Zodchestvo Severo-Vostochnoy Rusi [The architecture of north-eastern Rus'], 2 vols (Moscow, 1961–2)

Smolenskaya zhivopis' 12–13 vv. [Smolensk painting of the 12th and 13th centuries] (Moscow, 1977)

with P. A. Rappoport: *Zodchestvo Smolenska XII–XIII vv.* [The architecture of Smolensk in the 12th and 13th centuries] (Leningrad, 1979)

BIBLIOGRAPHY

G. K. Vagner: *Nikolay Nikolayevich Voronin: Kul'tura drevney Rusi* [Nikolay Nikolayevich Voronin: the culture of Old Rus'] (Moscow, 1966) [bibliog.]

——: *Nikolay Nikolayevich Voronin: Srednevekovaya Rus'* [Nikolay Nikolayevich Voronin: medieval Rus'] (Moscow, 1976) [bibliog.]

V. YA. PETRUKHIN

Vorsterman. Dutch family of artists, active in Flanders. They came from Zaltbommel, Gelderland, but their exact relationship is difficult to establish. (1) Lucas Vorsterman (i) was one of the finest engravers of the work of Rubens, although his career with the latter ended early and with great acrimony. His son (2) Lucas Vorsterman (ii) was also an engraver but lacked his father's talent. The painter Otto Vorsterman (married 1632) may have been a relative, for Lucas Vorsterman the elder engraved his painting of a *Youth Playing a Flute* (Hymans, no. 132). It is possible that Otto Vorsterman was the father of JAN VORSTERMAN, whose career as a landscape and topographical painter took him to France and England.

(1) Lucas Vorsterman (i) (*b* Zaltbommel, 1595; *d* Antwerp, 1675). Engraver and art dealer. He began to practise as an engraver when he was only 12 years old. He joined Rubens's studio *c.* 1617–18 and in 1620 became a master. Rubens clearly took on the sensitive young Vorsterman with a view to training him to reproduce his paintings, having realized the potential profits to be made from reproductive engravings of his work. Vorsterman's talent doubtless encouraged Rubens to intensify and guarantee his production of engravings by attaining exclusive licences in France, the northern Netherlands and the southern Spanish Netherlands. It is possible that the young Anthony van Dyck provided drawings after Rubens's paintings for the engravings by Vorsterman (Bellori), although some have been attributed to Vorsterman himself or to the studio of Rubens. Under Rubens' guidance, Vorsterman developed his burin technique in the period 1618–20, using a complex method of building up numerous layers of lines of varying thicknesses in order to do full justice to the colouring in Rubens's paintings. Vorsterman was able to reproduce the expressiveness and nobility of Rubens's figures in a way that virtually no other engraver equalled. His best engravings from this early period include ten large works from 1620 (e.g. *Adoration of the Shepherds*, Hymans, nos 6, 7, and the *Deposition*, Hymans, no. 34; *see* ANTWERP, fig. 5) and a further five dated 1621 (e.g. *Adoration of the Magi*, Hymans, no. 9; see fig.; and the *Tribute Money*, Hymans, no. 13).

That Rubens was a godparent to Vorsterman's eldest son indicates a friendly relationship between the two artists. However, Vorsterman had a difficult nature, with enormous ambition, and he felt that he was being exploited by Rubens. The conflict between the two artists seems to have begun in the early 1620s, with the engraver demanding privileges and dedicative inscriptions on the engravings for himself. Thus the *Fall of the Angels* (1621; Hymans, no. 84) and the commemorative engraving of *Gen. Charles de Longueval, Duc de Bucquoy* (Hymans, no. 184) bear

dedicative inscriptions by Vorsterman. Held discovered a verse with Vorsterman's monogram carved into Rubens's own oil sketch (St Petersburg, Hermitage) for the latter engraving; in this, the engraver complains of the suffering caused by the execution of the work. From early 1622 Vorsterman almost entirely abandoned his work for Rubens, including several plates that had already been begun or were almost complete; among these was the large engraving of the *Battle of the Amazons* (Hymans, no. 92; Rubens's painting, Munich, Alte Pin.), consisting of six plates, which was first issued in 1623. In April 1622 Vorsterman made an attempt on Rubens's life. In July he was granted a licence to produce engravings by the Infante Isabella Clara Eugenia, Governor of the southern Netherlands. Meanwhile, friends of Rubens had to appeal to the Infanta for his protection, and by 1624 the relationship between the two men had so broken down that Vorsterman moved to England. There he was employed by Charles I, Thomas Howard, 2nd Earl of Arundel, and the Earl of Pembroke to reproduce paintings and drawings from their collections (after Raphael, Holbein and others). He also supplied portrait engravings, some of which were taken from his own drawings (e.g. *George Villiers, 1st Duke of Buckingham*, Hymans, no. 142; drawing, 1624; London, B.M.).

Vorsterman returned to Antwerp *c.* 1630, perhaps following a trip to Paris. He made engravings from paintings by van Dyck and supplied 28 portrait engravings for the latter's *Iconographie* (e.g. *Charles de Mallery*, Hymans, no.186). In these works Vorsterman enriched his soft,

Lucas Vorsterman (i): *Adoration of the Magi*, engraving, 571×435 mm, 1621 (Cologne, Wallrafs-Richartz-Museum); after an altarpiece by Rubens in St Jans, Mechlin

tonal technique in a style that was stronger in contrasts and powerfully graphic. Van Dyck became a godfather to Vorsterman's daughter Antonia (*bapt* 10 May 1631) and drew, etched and painted his portrait (drawing, Cambridge, Fitzwilliam; for van Dyck's etched portrait of Vorsterman, *see* BELGIUM, fig. 17; painting, Lisbon, Mus. N. A. Ant.). Vorsterman made further engravings from works by Old Masters as well as contemporary artists, such as Hendrik van Balen, Adriaen Brouwer, Abraham van Diepenbeek, Jacob Jordaens, Erasmus Quellinus and Gerard Seghers. His four plates for a series of twelve antique marble busts, although issued by Rubens in 1638 (Hymans, nos 102, 103, 105, 106), actually date from his period in Rubens's studio. Vorsterman's best pupils were the other outstanding engravers after Rubens, Paulus Pontius, Hans Witdoeck and Marinus van der Goes (1639–after 1644). From the mid-1650s Vorsterman's production of engravings began to dwindle. According to a note by Erasmus Quellinus, he finally lost his sight, became impoverished and suffered from deep depression.

(2) Lucas Vorsterman (ii) (*bapt* Antwerp, 27 May 1624; *d* Antwerp, 1666). Engraver, son of (1) Lucas Vorsterman (i). He was his father's pupil and became a master in 1651/2. He produced engravings after Anthony van Dyck, Jacob Jordaens, Rubens and Cornelius Schut, as well as landscapes after Jan Peeters (1624–80). His works show little skill in draughtsmanship and are mechanical in execution. He supplied numerous reproductive engravings for David Teniers the younger's *Theatrum pictorium* (Antwerp, 1658), an illustrated catalogue of the Italian pictures in Archduke Leopold William's collection.

BIBLIOGRAPHY

Hollstein: Dut. & Flem; Würzbach

G. P. Bellori: *Vite* (1672); ed. E. Borea (1976), p. 254

J. von Sandrart: *Teutsche Academie* (1675–9); ed. A. R. Peltzer (1925), pp. 243–4

E. Dutuit: *Manuel de l'amateur d'estampes* (Paris, 1885/*R* Amsterdam, 1972), iv, pp. 21–274

T. Levin: 'Handschriftliche Bemerkungen von Erasmus Quellinus', *Z. Bild. Kst.*, xxiii (1888), pp. 171–2

H. Hymans: *Lucas Vorsterman (1595–1675) et son oeuvre gravé* (Brussels, 1893/*R* Amsterdam, 1972)

A. Rosenberg: *Die Rubensstecher* (Vienna, 1893), pp. 37–66

M. Rooses and C. Ruelens: *Correspondance de Rubens (Codex Diplomaticus Rubenianus)*, ii (Antwerp, 1898)

F. van den Wijngaert: *Inventaris der Rubeniaansche prentkunst* (Antwerp, 1940), pp. 9–13, 100–05

H. Vey: *Die Zeichnungen Anton van Dycks* (Brussels, 1962), pp. 32–5

J. S. Held: 'Rubens and Vorsterman', *A. Q.*, xxxii (1969), pp. 111–29

K. Renger: 'Planänderungen in Rubensstichen', *Z. Kstgesch.*, xxxvii (1974), pp. 2–5

——: 'Rubens dedit dedicavitque', *Jb. Berlin. Mus.*, xvi (1974), pp. 124, 134–40, 145, 165, 168

Rubens e l'incisione (exh. cat. by D. Bodart, Rome, Villa Farnesina, 1977), pp. 67–81, 154–5

J. Pohlen: *Untersuchungen zur Reproduktionsgraphik der Rubenswerkstatt* (Munich, 1985), pp. 46–70, 244–82

M. van der Meulen: *Rubens' Copies after the Antique*, Corpus Rubenianum, xxxiii/2 (1993), nos 108, 111, 115, 117

HELLA ROBELS

Vorsterman [Vorstermanns, Vosterman], **Jan** [Johannes] (*b* Bommel, *c*. 1643; *d* Bommel, after 1685). Dutch painter. He was the son of a portrait painter and was apprenticed in Utrecht to Herman Saftleven (II), whose work he imitated and occasionally even surpassed in quality. Vorsterman himself was master to Jan Soukens (*fl* 1678–1725). After his training, Vorsterman led a spendthrift life in Paris. He returned to Utrecht, but in 1672, when the French occupied the city, he fled to Nijmegen and is known to have bought works of art in various Dutch cities for the French commander François Gaston, Marquis de Béthune (1638–93). Vorsterman went to England before 1678, the date when his *View of Althorp* (Althorp House, Northants) was seen by John Evelyn. Vorsterman stayed at the court of Charles II, for whom he executed an overmantel painting for Whitehall Palace (destr.) and a *View of Stirling Castle* with figures by Jan Wyck. Probably the two artists went to Scotland together to paint this picture. Vorsterman asked £200 for his overmantel painting, in anticipation of which he incurred so many debts that he was imprisoned; he begged the King in vain to set him free. Eventually he was released through the help of friends who lent him money. He was taken to Constantinople (now Istanbul) by Sir William Soames, envoy of James II, *c*. 1685, in order to draw antiquities. Soames died on the way. It is possible that Vorsterman rejoined the Marquis de Béthune in Poland. Besides those works mentioned, his oeuvre, which is well executed and was much appreciated by his contemporaries, includes various mountain and river landscapes.

BIBLIOGRAPHY

Thieme–Becker

C. Kramm: *De levens en werken der Hollandsche en Vlaamsche kunstschilders, beeldhouwers, graveurs en bouwmeesters van den vroegsten tot op onzen tijd* [The lives and works of Dutch and Flemish painters, sculptors, engravers and architects from the earliest times until the present], 6 vols (Amsterdam, 1857–64), vi, p. 1792 [this bk mentions an engr. from 1661 included in C. de Cock van Kerkwijck's *Pest-Basiliscus* (s'Hertogenbosch, 1686); acc. to the foreword, the prt was made by Vorsterman, but on inspection neither the ref. nor the engr. seems to be in the work mentioned]

O. Millar: *The Tudor, Stuart and Early Georgian Pictures in the Collection of Her Majesty the Queen* (London, 1963)

INGEBORG WORM

Vorticism. British artistic and literary movement, founded in 1914 by the editor of *Blast* magazine, Wyndham Lewis, and members of the REBEL ART CENTRE. It encompassed not only painting, drawing and printmaking but also the sculpture of Henri Gaudier-Brzeska and Jacob Epstein and the photographs of Alvin Langdon Coburn. Notable literary allies were Ezra Pound, who coined the term Vorticism early in 1914, and T. S. Eliot. T. E. Hulme's articles in *The New Age* helped to create a climate favourable to the reception of Vorticist ideas.

The arrival of Vorticism was announced, with great gusto and militant defiance, in a manifesto published in the first issue of *Blast* magazine, which also included work by Edward Wadsworth, Frederick Etchells, William Roberts and Jacob Epstein. Dated June 1914 but issued a month later, this puce-covered journal set out to demonstrate the vigour of an audacious new movement in British art. Vorticism was seen by Lewis as an independent alternative to Cubism, Futurism and Expressionism. With the help of Pound, Gaudier-Brzeska and others, he used the opening manifesto pages of *Blast* to launch an uninhibited attack on a wide range of targets. Britain was blasted first 'from politeness', and its climate cursed 'for its sins and infections, dismal symbol, set round our bodies, of effeminate lout within'. The Vorticists wanted to oust all lingering traces of the Victorian age, liberating their country from what they saw as the stultifying legacy of the past. In giant black letters, *Blast*'s inventive typography roared: 'Blast years 1837 to 1900.' Using humour 'like a bomb' to ridicule British inertia, which was preventing any realization that a new century demanded a bracing and innovative art, *Blast* cried, 'We are Primitive Mercenaries in the Modern World . . . a movement towards art and imagination could burst up here, from this lump of compressed life, with more force than anywhere else.'

Ezra Pound declared in *Blast* that 'the vortex is the point of maximum energy. It represents, in mechanics, the greatest efficiency. We use the words "greatest efficiency" in the precise sense—as they would be used in a text book of Mechanics.' Wyndham Lewis put it another way when he recommended that a friend should think 'at once of a whirlpool. At the heart of the whirlpool is a great silent place where all the energy is concentrated. And there, at the point of concentration, is the Vorticist' (D. Goldring: *South Lodge* (London, 1943), p. 65). The 'stillness' of Lewis's definition is significant. It sets Vorticism up in adamant opposition to Italian Futurism, although the British movement owed a considerable debt to Filippo Tommaso Marinetti for inspiring the exuberant typography of *Blast* and for realizing the importance of making art interpret the rapidly changing character of the modern world. The Vorticists wanted to place the machine age at the very centre of their work, and *Blast* proposed that they fill their art with 'the forms of machinery, factories, new and vaster buildings, bridges and works'. They criticized the Futurists for making their paintings 'too "picturesque", melodramatic and spectacular, besides being undigested and naturalistic to a fault'. They also abhorred the rhapsodic romanticism of the Italian movement and rejected the Futurists' emphasis on blurred movement in their attempts to depict the sensation of speed. Lewis and his allies sought clarity of definition, enclosing their forms with strong contours that often gave Vorticist pictures an almost sculptural solidity (e.g. Wyndham Lewis, *Workshop*, *c.* 1914–15; London, Tate; and William Roberts, *Study for Two-step*, 1915; London, BM). The containing line was a crucial element in Vorticism; even when the compositions took on an explosive force that threatened to burst the bounds of the picture-frame, the harsh lucidity of Vorticist design ensured that order prevailed. Exhilaration was an important part of their art, and Pound emphasized that the vortex itself was 'a radiant node or cluster . . . from which, and through which, and into which, ideas are constantly rushing'.

Familiarity with the results of the Industrial Revolution made the Vorticists view the machine world with far less eager excitement than the Futurists. Their undoubted involvement with the age of mechanization was coupled with an awareness of its darker side. There is a curious innocence about Marinetti's admiration for the racing automobile, whereas Lewis saw the machine-age metropolis as an 'iron jungle', a severe and ferocious place where city dwellers were dehumanized and diminished, as exemplified in *The Crowd* (*c.* 1915; London, Tate). Vorticist

Vorticist drawing by Edward Wadsworth: *Enclosure*, gouache, ink and pencil on paper, 710×547 mm, 1915 (Houston, Museum of Fine Arts)

images possess a cool, clear-cut consciousness of the impersonal harshness of the 20th-century world, and in this respect they prophesy the destructive machine power that became so horrifyingly evident in World War I.

The onset of war meant that the Vorticists had very little time in which to implement the bold artistic programme they had outlined in *Blast*. But from 1914 to 1916 they did manage to produce an impressive range of images, which substantiated their claim to revitalize British art. Seven members of the movement contributed to the main section of the June 1915 Vorticist Exhibition at the Doré Gallery, London: Jessica Dismorr, Frederick Etchells, Lewis, Gaudier-Brzeska, William Roberts, Helen Saunders (1885–1963) and Edward Wadsworth, who exhibited *Enclosure* (see fig.). Several other artists were included in another section called 'Those Invited To Show', including Lawrence Atkinson, David Bomberg, Jacob Kramer (1892–1962) and the British Futurist Christopher Nevinson. Jacob Epstein was not represented but did have his drawings reproduced in *Blast*. Sculptures such as *Rock Drill* (1913–16) and *Doves* (1913; both London, Tate) show his affinity with the Vorticists' preoccupations. In July 1915 the second issue of *Blast* appeared, a 'War Number' with an appropriately harsh monochrome cover bearing Lewis's grim drawing *Before Antwerp*, and containing reproductions of works such as Helen Saunders's *Atlantic City* (untraced, see *Blast*, 2 (1915), p. 57). However, with the death of Gaudier-Brzeska in the war and most of the other Vorticists away on active service, British Vorticism found itself overwhelmed by the conflict raging in Europe.

Pound tried to keep the spirit of the movement alive in London by writing supportive articles, publishing *Gaudier-Brzeska: A Memoir* (London, 1916) and encouraging Alvin Langdon Coburn's ingenious attempts to develop a form of abstract photography called Vortography. He also persuaded the New York collector John Quinn to purchase Vorticist works in considerable quantities and eventually to stage a Vorticist exhibition at the Penguin Club in New York in January 1917. When Lewis returned from the trenches, he hoped to revivify the Vorticist spirit, planning a third issue of *Blast* and regaining contact with old allies. But the whole context of pre-war experimentation had been dispersed by the destructive power of mechanized warfare, which persuaded most of the former Vorticists to pursue more representational directions thereafter. By 1920 even Lewis was obliged to admit that the movement was dead.

WRITINGS
P. Wyndham Lewis, ed.: *Blast*, 1 (1914) [facs., Santa Barbara, 1981]
E. Pound: 'Vorticism', *Fortnightly Rev.* (1 Sept 1914), pp. 46–71
P. Wyndham Lewis, ed.: *Blast*, 2 (1915) [facs., Santa Barbara, 1981]

BIBLIOGRAPHY
J. Thrall Soby: *Contemporary Painters* (New York, 1948)
W. C. Wees: *Vorticism and the English Avant-garde* (Toronto and Manchester, 1972)
Vorticism and its Allies (exh. cat. by R. Cork, London, Hayward Gal., 1974)
R. Cork: *Vorticism and Abstract Art in the First Machine Age*, 2 vols (London, 1975–6)
——: 'What Was Vorticism?', *Wyndham Lewis*, ed. J. Farrington (London, 1980), pp. 23–9
——: 'Vorticism', *Futurismo & futurismi* (exh. cat., ed. P. Hulten; Venice, Pal. Grassi, 1986)
                                          RICHARD CORK

Vos, de (i). Flemish family of artists. The family, who moved from Hulst to Antwerp in 1596, must have come from a strong artistic background. Three brothers, (1) Cornelis de Vos, Jan de Vos (*c.* 1588–1627) and (2) Paul de Vos, became painters, beginning their training as apprentices to the relatively unimportant Antwerp painter and guilder David Remeeus (1559–1626) in 1599, 1601 and 1605 respectively. In 1611 their eldest sister Margaretha married Frans Snyders, the animal painter and assistant of Rubens. Cornelis also married into an artistic family, wedding Susanna Cock in 1617, a half-sister of the landscape painter Jan Wildens. Of their six children, one son, Jan-Baptist de Vos (1619–79), trained as a painter under his father. Simon de Vos, another pupil of Cornelis, seems not to have been related to the family.

BIBLIOGRAPHY
Cornelis de Vos and Paulus de Vos: Schilders van Hulst (exh. cat., Hulst, Stadhuis, 1960)

(1) Cornelis de Vos (*b* Hulst, *c.* 1584; *d* Antwerp, 9 May 1651). Painter and art dealer. He was one of Antwerp's most prominent portrait painters between 1620 and 1635, especially after Anthony van Dyck's departure from the city in 1621.

1. Life and work. 2. Working methods and technique.

1. LIFE AND WORK.

(i) Before 1620. After only five years of apprenticeship, Cornelis became a 'master's assistant' in the Remeeus workshop. On 29 April 1604 he asked the Antwerp city council to grant him a travel document that would enable him to improve his skills elsewhere; whether he undertook the journey is uncertain. By 1608 he was living in Antwerp, where he became a master in the Guild of St Luke. In 1613 he painted a *Whitsuntide Celebration* for the church of Onze-Lieve-Vrouw in Nieuwerkerken in eastern Flanders (*in situ*), the composition of which is derived from a work by Marten de Vos (no relation). On 23 September 1616 Cornelis, described by then as a dealer, became a citizen of Antwerp. About 1617, together with Rubens, Jordaens and van Dyck, he was involved in painting the cycle of the *Garland of Roses* for the church of St Paul in Antwerp. The earliest evidence of his activity as a portrait painter comes from 1618, when he was paid by the society of rhetoricians De Olijftak (Flem.: 'The Olive Branch') for a portrait of their 'Prince', *Balthasar Charles*. At the beginning of 1619 de Vos asked the city council for permission to visit the Paris market of St-Germain; he was appointed dean of the Antwerp Guild of St Luke the same year.

De Vos's early works show a conventional use of forms and a traditional sense of solidity. His religious paintings were structured in a variety of ways, but are characterized by the theatrical placement of the figures, the lack of a three dimensional setting and the use of local colour. The same qualities, though with a more limited palette, are found in the portraits executed before 1620, for example the *Portrait of a Family* (Brunswick, Herzog Anton-Ulrich-Mus.). The heads are placed on a level within the picture plane and the figures appear divorced from the background.

(ii) 1620–25. In the early 1620s de Vos began to achieve considerable success with his attractively coloured and well-balanced portraits, for example that of *Abraham Grapheus* (1620; Antwerp, Kon. Mus. S. Kst.). The strength of this portrait lies in the plasticity of the well-lit face, modelled with broad strokes. Rough sketches of the head of the same model by Jordaens and van Dyck may have influenced de Vos to treat the face more freely. De Vos's early style is also characterized by the detailed, meticulous and decorative representation of interiors. These add colour to, and provide a context for, his portraits. This can be clearly seen in the *Artist's Family* (1621; Brussels, Mus. A. Anc.). The compositions are always well balanced, and gestures are often used to emphasize the relationship between the sitters, particularly in the touching portraits of children. Cornelis was also inspired by the formal portraits of van Dyck, particularly the latter's portrait of his sister *Margaretha Snyders-de Vos* (*c.* 1620–21; New York, Frick), which Cornelis copied with few alterations in numerous portraits, for example the *Portrait of a Lady* (*c.* 1622; London, Wallace; see fig. 1). In 1623 de Vos is mentioned more than once as a 'picture merchant'.

From *c.* 1624 compositional changes occur in de Vos's portraits, which begin to have opened-up backgrounds and distant views of scenery, as in the portrait of *Antonia van Eversdyck-Canis* (1624; Madrid, Thyssen-Bornemisza Col.). De Vos then applied these compositional changes to religious and allegorical pictures of the period, such as the *Mystic Marriage of St Catherine* (Antwerp, priv. col., see Greindl, 1944, pl. 84) and the *Vanitas Allegory* (Brunswick, Herzog Anton-Ulrich-Mus.). A number of well-modelled figures, generally shown before an ornamented architectural screen, dominate the compositions.

(iii) 1626–30. From *c.* 1626, in addition to individual portraits, Cornelis began to paint more large-scale family portraits, skilfully using variations on standard compositional formulae. These group portraits, for example the *Portrait of a Family* (Würzburg, Mainfränk. Mus.), are set out of doors with a view of a French-style garden in the background, in an attempt to adapt them to Baroque tastes. That the market for his pictures was expanding can be seen from a documented commission from 1627 for six royal portraits, of *Philip IV of Spain*, *Archduke Albert* and *Isabella*, *Henry III of France*, *Henry IV* and his wife, *Marie de' Medici* (all untraced), which were executed partly by his workshop and intended for export to Spain. Van Dyck's return to Antwerp in 1627 gave a new impetus to de Vos's art and inspired him to paint several full-length portraits, in which scenery came to play a significant role (e.g. *Maria-Anna Schotten*, *c.* 1628; Boston, MA, Mus. F. A.). De Vos maintained good relations with his native city and in 1628 donated a rare townscape, his *View of the City of Hulst* (Hulst, Town Hall).

De Vos's reputation both as a portrait and history painter was enhanced by his epitaph painting of *St Norbert Receiving the Sacred Host and Church Vessels after the Heresy of Tankelin*, with donor portraits of the Snoek-van Utrecht family (1630; Antwerp, Kon. Mus. S. Kst.), which originally hung in Antwerp's abbey of St Michael. By 1630 the artist was producing more biblical scenes and history paintings. The subjects became more complicated, the number of characters increased and the composition broadened in order to include several episodes side by side. The *Worship of Solomon* (Moscow, Pushkin Mus. F.A.) and the *Continence of Scipio* (Nancy, Mus. B.-A.) can both be assigned to the period *c.* 1626 to *c.* 1630. For his religious subjects de Vos drew on the examples of colleagues; for example his *Raising of the Cross* (1626) in the church of St Amelberga at Wechelderzande (Antwerp) is a version, with few changes, of the same composition painted by Gerard Seghers for the Jesuit church in Antwerp. In all these works the unpronounced musculature, the black, wide-open eyes and the vague profiles of the figures emerge as consistent stylistic features. The artist's few genre pieces, of which *The Card-players* (Stockholm, Nmus.) is a good example, also date from the second half of the 1620s.

(iv) 1631–6. In this period de Vos continued to paint in two contrasting portrait styles. The first is exemplified by works from the beginning of the decade, such as his monumental *Portrait of a Family* (1631; Antwerp, Kon. Mus. S. Kst.) and *Anton Reyniers and his Family* (1631; Philadelphia, PA, Mus. A.), both of which are remarkable for their reuse of older prototypes. In the early 1630s he also painted several versions of the *Adoration of the Magi*, using Rubens's composition of the same subject as an example. Various biblical scenes and history pieces can also be attributed, on stylistic grounds, to this period. In these, as in his earlier portraits, the landscape background plays a more important role. Distant vistas are combined

1. Cornelis de Vos: *Portrait of a Lady*, oil on canvas, 1235×924 mm, *c.* 1622 (London, Wallace Collection)

with a lavish display of still-life objects in the foreground, as in the *Apotheosis of Agriculture* (Rotterdam, Mus. Boymans–van Beuningen; see fig. 2), the *Noli me tangere* (priv. col., see Müller Hofstede, pls 2–3) and the *Sacrifice of Isaac* (ex-T. Hartner priv. col., Nuremberg, see Vlieghe, pl. 12).

The number of individual portraits by de Vos seems to have declined drastically in the early 1630s, but life-size family portraits occupied him again from *c.* 1634; in these, unlike the monumental family portraits of *c.* 1631, he experimented with innovative arrangements, as in the *Famille à la promenade* (St Petersburg, Hermitage), which may be a self-portrait with his family. At the end of 1634 the Antwerp city council commissioned de Vos and Jacob Jordaens to work on the decoration of the Philippus Arch, one of the triumphal arches to be erected on the occasion of the entrance of the Cardinal–Infante Ferdinand in 1635. De Vos's task consisted mainly of painting two sets of six royal portraits that were designed, and later retouched, by Rubens (eight survive, including *Archduke Albert* and *Archduchess Isabella*; both Brussels, Mus. A. Anc.). Approximately two years later (*c.* 1636–8) de Vos was Rubens's assistant while the latter decorated Philip IV's hunting-lodge near Madrid, the Torre de la Parada. There are three mythological scenes made after modelli by Rubens that are signed by de Vos (all Madrid, Prado).

2. Cornelis de Vos: *Apotheosis of Agriculture*, oil on canvas, 1.76×2.45 m, early 1630s (Rotterdam, Museum Boymans–van Beuningen)

Stylistically these works accord well with his own history paintings of the early 1630s and show little direct influence from Rubens.

(v) 1637–51. After the collaboration on these two Rubens projects, de Vos's creativity declined considerably. The number of works surviving from his late period is small; their technical quality seldom equals his earlier work and a stylistic impoverishment is characteristic of everything he produced after 1635. His portraits became uninspired repetitions of outdated compositional formulae. The figures he painted were less sturdy, and their anatomy often ill conceived. Furthermore, the stereotyping of faces is pushed to extremes. Yet his reputation as a portrait painter after 1640 was still sufficient for him to receive in 1644 an important commission to paint the group portrait of the board of governors of the Antwerp militia company; the appearance of this work (destr. 18th century) is preserved in a preparatory oil sketch (England, priv. col.) that shows de Vos still capable of achieving remarkable portrait effects through varied modelling and well-balanced spatial organization.

2. WORKING METHODS AND TECHNIQUE. In de Vos's earliest paintings subtle effects are worked into the details by means of a technique that is largely descriptive: the well-defined contours and the thick impasto of the brushwork lend an enamel-like gloss to the surface.

Vermilion red and olive green are among the most prominent colours. From *c.* 1624 there is an alteration in his brush technique, which gradually became more fluid and transparent. Individual strokes of the brush can be readily distinguished and are used to model the various forms and shapes, creating a softened effect without sharp outlines and similar to that of pastel drawings. The brushstrokes are both freer and more schematic, resulting in more tactile effects, especially in the sketchy rendering of costumes. De Vos may have adopted this quicker and more fluent style for practical reasons, as a result of the growing number of commissions he received in the course of the 1620s. The pastel-like brush technique of the early 1620s was replaced in the second half of the decade by a new firmness of form and a more precise rendering of details. The effect is intensified by numerous highlights on the drapery, intended to heighten even more the sense of tactility.

While de Vos's exposure in the late 1630s to Rubens's designs for the Torre de la Parada may not have influenced his style, it did influence his technique. The paint surface shows a flakier and more hesitant stroke, seen particularly in the rendering of the skin, which appears leathery and wrinkled. The same hesitant brushstroke and dry treatment can be found in de Vos's portraits, such as *Portrait of a Man* (1640; Rotterdam, Mus. Boymans–van Beuningen), which features a stereotyped silhouette against a plain background.

Drawings by de Vos are rare. Those that have been attributed to him are chalk studies of heads, mostly of children (e.g. Paris, Louvre; Oxford, Christ Church; Leiden, Prentenkab. Rijksuniv.). Only one such drawing (ex-Deiker priv. col., Kassel) can be connected directly with a painting, the portrait of the *Artist's Two Daughters* (*c.* 1622; Berlin, Gemäldegal.).

Cornelis often collaborated with colleagues who specialized in a particular genre, a common practice in Antwerp studios at this time. On several occasions he painted figures in still-lifes by his brother-in-law Frans Snyders, for example the *Fish Market* (Vienna, Ksthist. Mus.). For the fruit, animals, silver plate and armour in his own work, Cornelis depended on Snyders (e.g. *Diogenes*; ex-art market, Amsterdam; see Vlieghe, pl. 9) and his own brother Paul (e.g. *Triumph of a Hero*; Rome, Vatican, Pin.). The picturesque little landscapes that enrich many of his compositions were painted by Jan Wildens, for example the *Portrait of a Married Couple* (1629; ex-Kaiser-Friedrich Mus., Berlin; destr.) or *Vertumnus and Pomona* (Paris, Louvre). Very little is known about the artists who worked in de Vos's workshop. Between 1615 and 1642 he was training at least nine pupils apart from his son Jan-Baptist, of whom only Simon de Vos and Jan Cossiers were to become well-known painters.

BIBLIOGRAPHY

J. Muls: *Cornelis de Vos: Schilder van Hulst* (Antwerp, 1933)
E. Greindl: 'Einige besondere Wesenszüge der Bildnisse des Cornelis de Vos', *Pantheon*, xxiii (1939), pp. 109–14
——: *Corneille de Vos: Portraitiste flamand (1584–1651)* (Brussels, 1944)
A. Czobor: 'An Oil Sketch by Cornelis de Vos', *Burl. Mag.*, cix (1967), pp. 351–5
J. Müller Hofstede: 'Drei neue Historienbilder des Cornelis de Vos', *Ned. Ksthist. Jb.*, xxiii (1972), pp. 291–302
H. Vlieghe: 'Oelskizzen von Cornelis de Vos', *Beiträge zur Geschichte der Oelskizze vom 16. bis zum 18. Jahrhundert* (Brunswick, 1984), pp. 59–70
M. Díaz Padrón: 'Nuevas pinturas de Cornelio de Vos identificadas en colecciones españolas y extranjeras', *Archv. Esp. A.*, ccxxxiv (1986), pp. 121–46
K. Van der Stighelen: 'The Provenance and Impact of Anthony van Dyck's Portraits of *Frans Snyders* and *Margaretha de Vos* in the Frick Collection', *Hoogsteder–Naumann Mercury*, v (1987), pp. 37–47
——: 'Cornelis de Vos as a Draughtsman', *Master Drgs*, xxvii (1989), pp. 322–40
——: *De portretten van Cornelis Vos (1584/5–1651): Een kritische catalogus* (Brussels, 1990)
The Age of Rubens (exh. cat., ed. P. C. Sutton; Boston, Mus. F.A.; Toledo, Mus. A.; 1993–4)

KATLIJNE VAN DER STIGHELEN

(2) Paul [Paulus] **de Vos** (*b* Hulst, 1591–2 or 9 Dec 1595; *d* Antwerp, 30 June 1678). Painter and draughtsman, brother of (1) Cornelis de Vos. Paul is perhaps best described as a gifted follower of his brother-in-law Snyders rather than as a truly original artist. Like Snyders, he specialized in still-lifes, animal and hunting scenes, generally on a large scale, and his works were in demand in the same aristocratic circles.

1. LIFE AND WORK. In September 1670 and October 1672 the artist himself testified to be 78 and 'about 80' years old, suggesting that he was born earlier (Duverger) than, as traditionally stated, on 9 Dec 1595 (Manneback). Before studying with Remeeus, Paul was briefly, in 1604, a pupil of Denys van Hove (*fl* 1604). He became a master only in 1620, possibly because he worked for some time

for his brother-in-law. From then onwards, he is cited in the guild archives almost every year until 1664–5, when he paid his death debt in advance. Only two pupils of his are listed: Alexander Daems in the guild year 1627–8 and Lanselot van Dalen in 1636–7. Paul had ten children by his wife Isabella Waerbeek (*d* 27 Aug 1660), a notary's daughter, whom he married on 15 Nov 1624; one of the children, Peter Paul, was baptized in 1628, with Rubens as godfather. Paul de Vos seems to have been fairly well off: he bought a house in 1638, owned rents on various other houses and, at his death, had a sizeable collection of paintings (inventory drawn up on 5 July 1678, sold at auction later the same year).

De Vos's output was apparently enormous: besides large paintings on canvas, there are also a few surviving drawings and oil sketches. He often signed his paintings but never dated them. It is thus difficult to establish a precise chronology. His earliest work closely resembles that of Snyders, in terms of subject-matter, composition and individual motifs; and this influence remained noticeable for some time, though increasingly de Vos began to develop his own style: he preferred a somewhat chaotic composition, full of turbulent and abrupt movement. The anatomy of his animals is less tightly designed, and he exceeded even Snyders in the amount of gruesome detail. His colours are warmer and keyed to a yellowish–brownish middle tone; his brushwork is broader. These characteristics are already clear in the 1630s—his best documented period (see fig.)—and are fully worked out later on, but are also latent in several somewhat quieter compositions that are more reminiscent of Snyders and thus to be dated earlier in his career. In his scenes of pantries, quarreling dogs, birds' concerts, hunts and fighting animals, Paul de Vos followed close on the heels of Snyders, but he also enriched this iconographic tradition with scenes of fighting cats and horses attacked by wolves.

As was common practice in Flanders in the 17th century, Paul de Vos often collaborated with other painters, calling on them for staffage or landscape backgrounds and himself contributing the animals or still-life elements to their compositions. The first documentary reference to work by Paul de Vos is from 1626, when Rubens is recorded as owing him 310 florins. This may have been for paintings Rubens had bought from de Vos—three are mentioned in Rubens's collection after his death—or to his collaboration in some of Rubens's works. On a sheet in de Vos's sketchbook (Amsterdam, Rijksmus.), he noted 'I Paul de Vos have worked for Rubens six days', and in the catalogue of Rubens's collection there is one such collaborative painting listed. The works now recognized as joint efforts by Rubens (or his studio) and Paul de Vos are hunting scenes, in which de Vos contributed the animals, and allegories of war, in which he painted the armour. He must have made a name for himself in this speciality, since the inventory (1659) of Archduke Leopold William attributes the armour in a *Virgin and Child with Saints* (Laxenburg, Parish Church) by Gerard Seghers to de Vos. (Jan Davidsz. de Heem and David Teniers (ii) also contributed to this same painting.) Paul de Vos seems more than once to have assisted Thomas Willeboirts Bosschaert (*c.* 1613–54; e.g. *Flora*, ex-Schloss Charlottenburg, Berlin), and a payment from Frederick Henry of Orange Nassau in 1648 to

Paul de Vos: *Deer Hunt*, oil on canvas, 2.17×3.47 cm, *c.* 1633–7 (Brussels, Musée d'Art Ancien)

Willeboirts, de Vos and Adriaen van Utrecht may be associated with such a collaboration. Less frequently de Vos worked with Erasmus Quellinus (i) (e.g. *Aeolus* and *Vulcan*; both Madrid, Prado) and Anthony van Dyck (e.g. the *Rest on the Flight into Egypt*; St Petersburg, Hermitage). For the backgrounds in his own paintings, de Vos usually relied on the assistance of the landscape painter Jan Wildens.

2. PATRONS AND COLLECTORS. From 1633 to 1640 Charles-Philip, Duc d'Arenberg, then resident at Madrid, commissioned at least 36 paintings with birds, hunts and fables from Paul de Vos, and although he is not explicitly mentioned in documents concerning the decoration of Philip IV's hunting lodge near Madrid, the Torre de la Parada, it appears that many of the animal paintings for which Snyders was contracted were actually executed (and signed) by de Vos. (The visit of the Cardinal-Infante Ferdinand, the King's brother, to the artist's studio may have had something to do with this commission (Papebrochius).) Works by de Vos were also found in other palaces of the Spanish king, such as the Alcázar and the Buen Retiro in Madrid. Another important Spanish patron was the 1st Marqués de Leganés, in whose inventory of 1655 at least 16 paintings by de Vos were included, 14 of them having already figured in that of 1642. Eight further hunts by de Vos were owned by Luis Méndez de Haro y Guzmán, 6th Marqués de Carpio (or by his son Gaspar, Marqués de Eliche; now Madrid, Pal. de Liria, Alba priv. col.). Later, in 1728, another four hunting scenes were recorded in the possession of José Francisco Sarmiento, Conde de Salvatierra. According to de Bie, Emperor Ferdinand III also collected his work; in any case his brother, Archduke Leopold William owned a few of his paintings. In Antwerp too his paintings were avidly acquired and are recorded in the collections of J. Snellinck (1638), J. R. van de Wouwer (1645), S. Willemsen (1657), G. Caillet (1659), J. B. Borrekens (1668), J. de Mont (1686), J. C. de Witte (1688) and J. B. Anthoine (1691). The Antwerp dealer Gisbert van Colen sold three important works of his to Maximilian II Emanuel of Bavaria in 1698, and among the 18th-century collectors with important holding of paintings by Paul de Vos were Karl-Heinrich, Graf von Hoym (1732), Heinrich, Graf von Brühl (acquired in 1769 by Catherine II of Russia and still in the Hermitage, St Petersburg) and Count Czernin (Prague, *c.* 1720–30).

Despite this noticeable success during his lifetime, de Vos has long been neglected in the literature. Only de Bie, Palomino, Houtbraken, Descamps and Mariette mention him. His re-emergence as one of the important Flemish animal and still-life painters of the 17th century is due to Rooses, Oldenbourg and Glück, and especially to Manneback, and, more recently, Robels.

BIBLIOGRAPHY

BNB; Thieme–Becker; Wurzbach

C. de Bie: *Het gulden cabinet* (1661), pp. 236–7

A. A. Palomino de Castro y Valasco: *Museo pictórico* (1715–24), i, p. 152; iii, p. 155

A. Houbraken: *De groote schouburgh* (1718–21), i, p. 291

J.-B. Descamps: *La Vie des peintres flamands, allemands et hollandais*, 4 vols (Paris, 1753–64), ii, p. 43

D. Papebrochius: *Annales Antverpienses ab urbe condita ad annum MDCC*, ed. F. H. Mertens and E. Buschmann (Antwerp, 1848), v, pp. 223–4

C. V[osmaer]: 'De ordinantie-boeken van Prins Frederik Hendrik, over de jaren 1637–1650' *Kunstchronyk*, n. s. 2 (1861), pp. 37–40

P. Rombouts and T. Van Lerius: *De liggeren en andere historische archieven der Antwerpsche Sint-Lucasgilde*, 2 vols (Antwerp, 1864–76/*R* Amsterdam, 1961)

M. Rooses: *Geschiedenis der Antwerpsche schilderschool* (Antwerp, 1879), pp. 401–2

[J. Pichon]: *Vie de Charles-Henry, Comte de Hoym* (Paris, 1880), ii, pp. 80–81, 87

A. Berger: 'Inventar der Kunstsammlung des Erzherzogs Leopold Wilhelm von Österreich', *Jb. Ksthist. Samml. Allhöch. Ksrhaus.*, i (1883), pp. cxx, cxxii

F. J. Van den Branden: *Geschiedenis der Antwerpsche schilderschool*, 2 vols (Antwerp, 1883), ii, pp. 679–83 [still the most detailed biog.]

M. Rooses: 'Staat van goederen in het sterfhuis van Isabella Brant' [List of property taken in the house in mourning belonging to Isabella Brandt], *Rubens-Bull.*, iv (1895), p. 180 [inventory taken after the death of Rubens]

F. Donnet: 'Van Dyck inconnu', *Bull. Acad. Royale Archéol. Belgique* (1898–1901), pp. 392–3

A. Somof: *Ecoles néerlandaises et allemandes*, ii of *Ermitage impérial: Catalogue de la galerie des tableaux*, St Petersburg, Hermitage cat. (St Petersburg, 1901), nos 1328–32

A. M. de Barcia: *Catálogo de la colección de pinturas del excmo sr. Duque de Berwick y de Alba* (1911), pp. 196–7, 247, 252, 256–7 [inc. the Méndez de Haro inv.]

R. Oldenbourg: *Die flämische Malerei des XVII. Jahrhunderts* (Berlin, 1918, rev. 1922), pp. 192–3

J. Denucé: *Kunstuitvoer in de 17e eeuw te Antwerpen: De firma Forchoudt*, Bronnen voor de geschiedenis van de Vlaamse kunst [Sources for the history of Flemish art], i (Antwerp, 1930), p. 27

——: *De Antwerpsche 'Konstkamers': Inventarissen van kunstverzamelingen te Antwerpen in de 16e en 17e eeuwen*, Bronnen voor de geschiedenis van de Vlaamse kunst, ii (Antwerp, 1932)

G. Glück: *Rubens, Van Dyck und ihr Kreis* (Vienna, 1933), pp. 360–62

A. J. J. van Delen: *Catalogue des dessins anciens, écoles flamande et hollandaise: Cabinet des Estampes de la Ville d'Anvers*, 2 vols (Brussels, 1938), pp. 82–4

J. Denucé: *Na Peter Pauwel Rubens: Documenten uit de kunsthandel te Antwerpen in de 17e eeuw van Matthijs Musson*, Bronnen voor de geschiedenis van de Vlaamse kunst, v (Antwerp, 1949), pp. 40, 143, 190

M. Manneback: 'Paul de Vos et François Snyders', *Miscellanea Leo van Puyvelde* (Brussels, 1949), pp. 147–52

H. Funk: 'Frans Snyders oder Paul de Vos?', *Edwin Redslob zum 70. Geburtstag* (Berlin, 1954), pp. 316–20

E. Greindl: *Les Peintres flamands de nature morte au XVIIe siècle* (Brussels, 1956, rev. 1983), pp. 94–5, 387

H. Gerson and E. H. ter Kuile: *Art and Architecture in Belgium, 1600–1800*, Pelican Hist. A. (Harmondsworth, 1960), p. 160

J. López Navio: 'La gran colección de pinturas del Marqués de Leganés', *Anlct. Calasanct.*, viii (1962), pp. 259–330, nos 99–101, 197–9, 202–4, 233, 235, 237, 323, 365, 1320–21

Le Siècle de Rubens (exh. cat., Brussels, Musées Royaux B.-A., 1965), pp. 283–5 [by M. Manneback]

G. Heinz: 'Studien über Jan van den Hoecke und die Malerei der Niederländer in Wien', *Jb. Ksthist. Samml. Wien*, lxiii (1967), pp. 109–64 (115, 143)

A. P. de Mirimonde: 'La Musique dans les allégories de l'amour, II: Eros', *Gaz. B.-A.*, lxix (1967), pp. 319–49 (325–6)

S. Alpers: *The Decoration of the Torre de la Parada*, Corpus Rubenianum Ludwig Burchard, ix (Brussels, 1971), pp. 101, 119–21, 203–5

E. Duverger: 'De moeilijkheden van Abraham van Diepenbeeck met de Antwerpse Sint-Lukasgilde', *Jb. Kon. Mus. S. Kst. Antwerpen* (1972), pp. 239–62 (248, 252, 258–9, 260–61)

M. Díaz Padrón: *Escuela flamenca siglo XVIII*, 2 vols (1975), i of *Museo del Prado, Catálogo de pinturas* (Madrid, 1975–), pp. 431–40

U. Krempel: 'Max Emanuel als Gemäldesammler', *Kurfürst Max Emanuel. Bayern und Europa um 1700, I: Zur Geschichte des Max-Emanuel-Zeit* (exh. cat., Schleissheim, Altes Schloss, 1976), pp. 221–38

M.-L. Hairs: *Dans le sillage de Rubens: Les Peintres d'histoire anversois au XVIIe siècle* (Liège, 1977), p. 17

M. Crawford Volk: 'New Light on a Seventeenth-century Collector: The Marqués of Leganés', *A. Bull.*, lxii (1980), pp. 256–68

J. Brown and J. H. Elliott: *A Palace for a King: The Buen Retiro and the Court of Philip IV* (New Haven and London, 1980, rev. 1986), p. 131

K. J. Müllenmeister: *Tierdarstellungen in Werken niederländischen Künstler N-Z* (Bremen, 1981), iii of *Meer und Land im Licht des 17. Jahrhunderts*, pp. 91–3

A. Balis: 'Fabeluitbeeldingen in de 17de-eeuwse Vlaamse schilderkunst', *Zoom op zoo: Antwerp Zoo Focusing on Arts and Sciences*, ed. C. Kruyfhooft (Antwerp, 1985), pp. 259–75

——: *Rubens: Hunting Scenes*, Corpus Rubenianum Ludwig Burchard, xviii/2 (London, 1986)

H. Robels: *Frans Snyders: Stilleben- und Tiermaler, 1579–1657* (Munich, 1989) [list of ptgs and drgs wrongly attrib. to Snyders but by Paul de Vos]

ARNOUT BALIS

Vos, de (ii). Dutch family of collectors, patrons and businessmen. Three generations of family members, all named Jacob de Vos, were active in the family insurance business, while avidly pursuing collecting and the promotion of the arts in their spare time.

(1) Jacob de Vos (*b* 1735; *d* Amsterdam, 1833). He formed a small but impressive collection of Old Master paintings, mostly of the Dutch school. His collection of drawings was more ambitious, rivalling the groups assembled by his contemporaries Cornelis Ploos van Amstel and the Goll van Franckenstein family. It contained drawings by Italian, French and German artists, but, like his paintings cabinet, was dominated by the work of 17th-century Dutch masters. The long-lived collector never married, and on his death his collections were sold at auction in Amsterdam, the paintings in July 1833, the drawings from 30 October 1833. The drawings fetched high prices, the most expensive item being a large, finished watercolour by Adriaen van Ostade of *Peasants Playing Gallet outside an Inn* (London, BM), bought on behalf of Baron Jan Gijsbert Verstolk van Soelen.

(2) Jacob de Vos Wzn [Willemszoon] (*b* Amsterdam, 1774; *d* Amsterdam, 1844). Nephew of (1) Jacob de Vos. A competent amateur draughtsman, he purchased a number of drawings from the sale of his uncle, including van Ostade's preliminary pen-and-ink study for *Peasants Playing Gallet outside an Inn* (Amsterdam, Rijksmus.). It is not clear, however, to what extent he added to this collection. More is known of his activities as a supporter of the arts. He served as secretary of the fourth class of the Koninklijk Nederlandsch Instituut van Wetenschappen, Letterkunde en Schoone Kunsten, Amsterdam, and was vice-chairman of the governing body of the Koninklijke Academie van Beeldende Kunsten, where he campaigned for the establishment of a course of training for printmakers. A fluent public speaker and noted art critic, he was also a great advocate of contemporary French history painting and singled out for praise such artists as Paul Delaroche. On his death, Jacob Wzn's art collection passed to his son (3) Jacob de Vos Jbzn.

(3) Jacob de Vos Jbzn [Jacobszoon] (*b* Amsterdam, 28 March 1803; *d* Amsterdam, 8 July 1878). Son of (2) Jacob de Vos Wzn. Having inherited his father's collection, he went on to develop as keen a passion for collecting as that of his great-uncle. Like both his ancestors, Jacob Jbzn concentrated on acquiring drawings, mostly by 17th-century Dutch artists, building up the last great collection of this type in the Netherlands. He owned over 50 sheets by Rembrandt, including the artist's copy (Berlin, Kupferstichkab.) after Leonardo's *Last Supper* and a *View of the Amstel* on parchment (Amsterdam, Rijksmus.), as well as drawings by Hendrick Avercamp, Aelbert Cuyp, Hendrick

Goltzius, Rubens, Leonardo and Claude, among many others. There were also paintings, watercolours and drawings by contemporary artists, such as Constant Troyon, Delacroix, Johannes Bosboom, Rosa Bonheur and William Bouguereau.

Like his father, Jacob Jbzn did much to promote cultural education and the preservation of the national heritage. In 1850 he too became a member of the governing body of the Koninklijke Academie van Beeldende Kunsten, where he helped to organize exhibitions of contemporary art. Three years later he became a member of the governing body of the Rijksmuseum and in 1858 was a co-founder of the Koninklijk Oudheidkundig Genootschap. He was involved in several other art societies and institutions, such as the Felix Meritis Society (to which he belonged from the age of 15) and the art academy in Antwerp (of which he was an honorary member). De Vos helped save for the Rijksmuseum the superb collection of paintings bequeathed to the city of Amsterdam by the banker Adriaen van der Hoop (1778–1854); the city was unable to pay the inheritance tax, and the collection, which included Rembrandt's *Jewish Bride* (Amsterdam, Rijksmus.), would have been lost had it not been for the efforts of de Vos and a few other wealthy collectors.

Jacob Jbzn also shared his father's enthusiasm for history painting. To encourage interest in this neglected genre, he commissioned 30 young contemporary artists to fill a garden pavilion at the back of his house at Herengracht 130 with works of art illustrating the *History of the Netherlands*. The gallery comprised 253 oil sketches and 10 statuettes, divided into 10 series (each covering a particular period). Part of the gallery opened in March 1854, not to the general public but only to other artists and to potential clients who, it was hoped, would commission finished versions of the paintings from the aspiring artists.

De Vos's marriage in 1830 to Abrahamine Henriette Wurfbain (1808–83) remained childless, and on his death the collection, except for the history gallery, was sold at auction on 22–4 May 1883. A group of his friends and fellow collectors raised 50,000 florins to purchase drawings from the sale; they acquired 494 of the 1350 sheets offered (including a few drawings by Rembrandt) and presented these in his honour to the Rijksprentenkabinet. Shortly thereafter, they established the Vereniging Rembrandt, a charitable society that helps Dutch museums buy important works of art. (It is the oldest organization of its kind in the world.) De Vos's widow donated the history gallery to another society, the Artis et Amicitiae, but following staff changes and a gradual loss of interest in the objects, it was sold *en bloc* to a London dealer in 1895. Another group of Dutch collectors bought it back and presented it to the Stedelijk Museum (now Amsterdam, Hist. Mus.).

BIBLIOGRAPHY

F. Lugt: *Marques* (1921), no. 1450

I. H. van Eeghen: 'Die familie de Vos: Kerk, kunst en zaken', *Doopsgezinde Bijdr.*, vi (1980), pp. 124–36

Het beste bewaard: Een Amsterdamse verzameling en het ontstaan van de Vereniging Rembrandt (exh. cat. by M. Schapelhouman, Amsterdam, Rijksmus., 1983)

Helden van het vaderland: Onze geschiedenis in 19de-eeuwse taferelen verbeeld: De historische galerij van Jacob de Vos Jacobszoon, 1850–1863 (exh. cat., ed. D. Carasso; Amsterdam, Hist. Mus., 1991–2)

JANE SHOAF TURNER

Vos, Marten [Maarten; Maerten] **de**, the elder (*b* Antwerp, 1532; *d* Antwerp, 4 Dec, *bur* 7 Dec 1603). Flemish painter and draughtsman. Together with the brothers Ambrosius Francken I and Frans Francken I, he ranks among the most important painters of altarpieces in Antwerp during the 1590s. Due, in part, to the Counter-Reformation, there was a renewed demand for altarpieces to replace those lost during iconoclastic riots in 1566 or the reformist movement of 1581. De Vos produced works for, among others, the Old Crossbowmen, the Brabant Coiners, the Antonites, the wine merchants and the Guild of St Luke. The importance of these works would seem to suggest that, after the deaths of Pieter Bruegel I in 1569 and Frans Floris in 1570, de Vos was considered, with some justification, the most important figure painter in Antwerp before Rubens. He was also a prolific draughtsman, especially during the first half of the 1580s, when the Calvinists were in power in Antwerp. During this period he provided numerous designs for print publishers, such as Peeter Baltens, Frans van Beusecom, the widow of Hieronymus Cock, Adriaen Collaert, Phillip Galle, Willem van Haecht, Eduard van Hoeswinkel, Gerard de Jode, Hans van Luyck and Johannes Baptista Vrints. This increased activity is probably indicative of the economic recession and a dwindling market for paintings (especially of religious themes). A total of some 1600 prints were produced after designs by de Vos, an output three times that of Maarten van Heemskerck. De Vos's drawings have been praised (see Mielke) for their lively, industrious and generally positive character, frequently with romantic Italianate landscapes in the background. His obvious proficiency is counterbalanced, however, by a degree of routine formularization.

1. Life. 2. Work.

1. LIFE. Marten was one of four children of the painter Pieter de Vos the elder (*b* Leiden, 1490; *d* Antwerp, *bur* 18 Nov 1566) and his wife, Anna de Heer, and it is assumed that he was first apprenticed to his father. A supposed apprenticeship to Frans Floris is not supported by documents. Two letters from Scipio Fabius to Abraham Ortelius (16 June 1561 and 14 April 1565) suggest that Pieter Bruegel the elder and Marten de Vos either travelled together to Italy, perhaps in mid-1552 (Zweite), or spent time together in southern Europe, but neither hypothesis can be proved. Van Mander claimed that de Vos visited Rome as well as Venice, where, according to Carlo Ridolfi, he studied with Jacopo Tintoretto. It is also assumed that de Vos spent time in Florence.

In 1558 de Vos was enrolled as a master in the Antwerp Guild of St Luke. He may have returned to Antwerp earlier if the date of 1556—which, however, has been restored—on a *Portrait of a Woman* (Washington, DC, Mrs. Harlan Fiske Stone priv. col., in 1952, see Zweite, no. 108) is accurate. Five daughters and three sons were born to de Vos and his wife, Joanna Le Boucq (*b*

Valenciennes), whom he married in 1560. On 18 September 1566 he made his first will; in 1571 and 1572 he was Dean of the Guild of St Luke. Van Mander recorded de Vos's successful attempt to prevent the Antwerp magistrates from allowing the sale of Quinten Metsys's *St John* altarpiece (1508–11; Antwerp, Kon. Mus. S. Kst.) to Queen Elizabeth I of England; van Mander reported this as having occurred in 1577, but the actual date of de Vos's intervention was 1581. De Vos was documented as a Lutheran as of 1584, but by the following year he had apparently adapted to the prevailing Catholicism: he chose to remain in Antwerp, forgoing the general amnesty granted by Alessandro Farnese, Duke of Parma, that would have enabled him to leave Antwerp without hindrance within four years from August 1585. Except for a short stay in Ghent in the summer of 1589 for a tax assessment of a *Last Judgement* by Raphael Coxie, de Vos, as far as is known, spent the rest of his career in Antwerp. A second journey to Italy, posited to explain Venetian influences in a few later works, was rejected by Zweite.

In his second will of 10 October 1603, de Vos bequeathed his painting equipment, drawings and the like to his sons Daniel de Vos (1568–1605) and Marten de Vos the younger (1576–1613). His daughter Sybilla was left a dowry of 1000 guilders. Daniel became a master of the Guild in 1596 and registered a student in 1600. He is documented as having collaborated with his father in painting the lids of harpsichords, but none of his work has survived, nor has any by Marten the younger, who may have continued his father's workshop in 1605–6; additional evidence for this is that he was already registering students with the Guild before gaining his mastery in 1607. From 1564 to 1599 the elder Marten de Vos himself registered 11 students with the Guild: Balten Vlierden (1564), Wenzel Coebergher (1573), Hans Snyers (1575), Merten Boly (1577), Jaeckes Keerel (1577), Jan Adriansen Cnottaert (1584), Peeter Goutsteen (1588), Hans Cnottaert (1594), Hans van Alten (1595), Hans de La Torte (1595) and Abraham van Lievendale (1599)—of whom only Coebergher is well known today.

2. WORK. Neither the paintings nor the drawings of de Vos exhibit any startling stylistic evolution. He assembled his compositions from separate motifs and figures, revealing himself to be an eclectic artist, who was variously indebted to one or more of the Italian painters Veronese, Tintoretto and Michelangelo, as well as to Flemish painters such as the Master of the Prodigal Son, Pieter Aertsen, and the Romanists Lambert Lombard, Frans Floris and Michiel Coxie. Most of the works, however, are dated, showing, for instance, that during the period 1562–72 his output was devoted entirely to painting while in the 1580s he concentrated largely on designs for prints and book illustrations. Two groups of works previously thought to date from his early career have been removed from his oeuvre: the so-called Marten de Vos Sketchbook (*c.* 1560; Amsterdam, Rijksmus.)—with copies of earlier drawings of Classical works of art—has been rejected by Netto-Bol on grounds of both style and content and relegated to the circle of Frans Floris. A second body of discredited early works consists of paintings now assigned to a pseudo-de Vos, who has been tentatively associated by Zweite (p. 64,

and 'Zweifelhaft', nos 2–3) with de Vos's brother, Pieter de Vos the younger (*d*?1567).

(i) Paintings. Among the earliest works is a series of light panels illustrating the *Life of Rebecca* (1562–3), of which six survive (all Rouen, Mus. B.-A.). The *Resurrection* (1564; priv. col., see Zweite, no. 12) exhibits the more flowing style that characterizes paintings of this decade. Two patrons can be identified for commissions dating from the latter part of the 1560s. For the dining room of the Calvinist merchant Gilles Hooftman, de Vos produced five panels with episodes from the *Life of St Paul*, three of which survive (Zweite, nos 14–16; see also the marriage portrait of 1570, Zweite, no. 111). This commission represented a significant breakthrough to an important segment of the élite of Antwerp; it resulted from a recommendation by Ortelius, and the project was suggested by Johannes Radermacher. De Vos's painting of *St Paul on Malta* (Paris, Louvre) includes many portraits of people who were part of Hooftman's social circle as 'witnesses' of the biblical scene. A self-portrait is included in a similar *portrait historié*, which was painted for a member of Hooftman's immediate family, Pieter Panhuys: dated 1575, the picture of *Moses Showing the Tablets of Law to the Israelites* (The Hague, Mauritshuis, on loan to the Catharijnenconvent, Utrecht; see fig. 1) belongs to a period when Calvinists in Antwerp were refused entry to churches or houses of prayer. It is an important work because of its unusual clarity and richly nuanced colouring. Characteristic features include the egg-shaped heads of the female figures and the high degree of detail within an overall composition that is summary in effect.

De Vos's other known patron in Antwerp in the late 1560s was Duke William of Brunswick-Luneburg, for whose palace chapel in Celle he provided a Lutheran scheme of decoration (*c.* 1569–72; *in situ*; see CELLE, §2). Of the 76 paintings, 24 are by de Vos; only the altar wing of the *Crucifixion* is signed in full and dated 1569. Others may be by a member of de Vos's workshop after his designs, as well as by a few anonymous artists. Dating from the year in which the Celle decoration was completed is a group of six animal studies (Schwerin, Staatl. Mus., Mainz, Landesmus.), which were probably commissioned by John Albert I, Duke of Mecklenburg-Schwerin (*reg* 1503–76).

De Vos's definitive breakthrough as a painter of altarpieces for the domestic market in Antwerp soon followed in 1574, with the triptych of the *Doubting St Thomas* for the Furriers' guild (Antwerp, Kon. Mus. S. Kst.), in which the monumental figures have a vigour of modelling and detail unprecedented in his earlier work. Despite the fact that de Vos's sympathies seem initially to have been with the Calvinists and Lutherans, he was able to secure a 'Catholic' commission of this type, and he received many such commissions in the 1590s and the early years of the 17th century. Among the altarpieces for other guilds and religious orders are the *Triumphant Christ* (1590) for the Old Crossbowmen, the *Temptation of St Anthony* (1594) for the Antonites, *St Luke Painting the Virgin* (1602) for the Guild of St Luke (all Antwerp, Kon. Mus. S. Kst.) and the *Marriage at Cana* (1597; Antwerp Cathedral) for the wine merchants.

1. Marten de Vos: *Moses Showing the Tablets of Law to the Israelites*, oil on panel, 1.52×2.38 m, 1575 (The Hague, Koninklijk Kabinet van Schilderijen 'Mauritshuis', on loan to Utrecht, Het Catharijnenconvent)

In these late altarpieces de Vos tended to recall the work of earlier Flemish masters, such as Maarten van Heemskerck and, in the case of the *St Luke Painting the Virgin*, Quinten Metsys. There is also a tendency in this period to soften the colours into a more tonal palette, related to that of Otto van Veen and Ambrosius Francken. However, the persistent influence of Tintoretto still characterizes late works, such as the *Marriage at Cana*. If the two paintings dated with certainty to 1602 (Zweite, nos 106–7) had not been associated with that date, they no doubt would have been placed with pictures from the 1570s. Constancy of style also typifies de Vos.

(ii) Drawings. Most of de Vos's 500 known drawings were designs for prints and were engraved by the best reproductive printmakers, including Adriaen Collaert, Hans Collaert II, Hendrick Goltzius, Pieter de Jode (i), Aegidius Sadeler I, Jan Sadeler I (for illustration *see* SADELER, (1)) and Raphael Sadeler and the Wierix brothers. Another important engraver for de Vos in the 1590s was Crispijn de Passe the elder, who was working in Germany at the time. The earliest known drawings by de Vos date from 1573, such as the *Trinity* (Vienna, Albertina), of which the engraving after it by Philip Galle (1574; B. 56) was already copied in the same year by Petrus Valck (Hollstein, no. 1). A second drawing from 1573 is the *Pax et Justitia* (Brussels, Bib. Royale Albert 1er), which was made into a print by Jan Wierix.

In 1578–9 de Vos furnished designs for a series of seven prints to be made by one of the Wierix brothers (Mauquoy-Hendrickx, nos 1656–62) illustrating the taking and dismantling of the fortifications of Antwerp by the troops of Willem of Orange in August 1577.

A rare piece of evidence for the communication between draughtsman and printmaker is provided by the written instructions for the engraver Aegidius Sadeler on a drawing of *Samuel Anointing David* (New York, Pierpont Morgan Lib.; see fig. 2). The drawing is in an album of 24 drawings by de Vos, 16 of which are for Sadeler's series of the *Story of David* (*c.* 1581–3; Hollstein, nos 2–17). Dating from roughly the same period is de Vos's work as a draughtsman for the illustrated Bible *Thesaurus veteris et novi testamenti* published in 1585 by Gerard de Jode. The degree to which de Vos's style left its mark on this edition can be seen in numbers: of the *c.* 300 prints, 78 are after drawings by de Vos, and some 90 pages more are by masters who were strongly influenced by de Vos (Jan Snellinck, Ambrosius Francken I and Hans Collaert II). The export of this illustrated Bible by de Jode, as well as a revised edition circulated by the 17th-century Amsterdam publisher Claes Jansz. Visscher and later by his sons, made de Vos's illustrations, more than his paintings, familiar throughout Europe.

De Vos's eight small roundel designs (all Antwerp, Mus. Plantin–Moretus) for the border of the *Abrahami patriarchae peregrinatio et vita*, Ortelius's biblical map of 1586, are exceptional: no other map decorations have

2. Marten de Vos: *Samuel Anointing David*, pen and brown ink, grey-brown wash, heightened with white, 189×289 mm, *c.* 1581 (New York, Pierpont Morgan Library)

come to light. During the early 1590s the draughtsmen Bernardino Passeri and the Florentine Jesuit Gian Battista Fiammeri (1530–1609) were given preference over de Vos for the production of the important missionary text by Hieronymus Natalis (1507–80), the *Evangelicae historiae Imagines* (1593); only 6 of the 152 illustrations are after de Vos (engraved by the Wierix brothers; see Mauquoy-Hendrickx, nos 1989, 1993, 2019, 2041 and 2043). In 1594, with Ambrosius Francken, de Vos worked on the designs for the allegorical decorations for the Triumphal Entry into Antwerp of Archduke Ernst of Austria. The programme was organized as a whole by the municipal secretary, Jan Boghe; 70 of de Vos's designs have survived (Antwerp, Mus. Plantin–Moretus; Amsterdam, Rijksmus.).

BIBLIOGRAPHY

Hollstein: *Dut. & Flem.*
A. von Bartsch: *Le Peintre-graveur* (1803–21) [B.]
A. Reinsch: *Die Zeichnungen des Marten de Vos* (diss., Tübingen, Eberhard-Karls-U., 1967)
R.-A. d'Hulst: 'Over enkele tekeningen van Maarten de Vos', *Miscellanea Jozef Duverger*, ii (Ghent, 1968), pp. 505–18
H. Mielke: 'Antwerpener Graphik in der 2. Hälfte des 16. Jahrhunderts: Der *Thesaurus veteris et novi testamenti* des Gerard de Jode (1585) und seine Künstler', *Z. Kstgesch.*, xxxviii (1975), pp. 29–83
M. M. L. Netto-Bol: *The So-called Maarten de Vos Sketchbook of Drawings after the Antique*, Kunsthistorische Studiën van het Nederlands Instituut te Rome, iv (The Hague, 1976)
M. Mauquoy-Hendrickx: *Les Estampes des Wierix*, 4 vols (Brussels, 1978–83)
J. V. Shoaf: 'A Seventeenth-century Album of Drawings by Marten de Vos', *Master Drgs*, xviii (1980), pp. 237–52
A. Zweite: *Marten de Vos als Maler* (Berlin, 1980)
C. Dittrich: 'Stichvorlagen bei Marten de Vos', *Jb. Staatl. Kstsamml. Dresden* (1988), pp. 29–38
S. K. Bennett: 'Drawings by Maerten de Vos: Designs to Ornament an Ortelius Map', *Hoogsteder-Naumann Mercury*, xi (1990), pp. 4–13

CHRISTIAAN SCHUCKMAN

Vos, Simon de (*b* Antwerp, 20 Oct 1603; *d* Antwerp, 15 Oct 1676). Flemish painter. In 1615 he became a pupil of Cornelis de Vos (no relation), with whom Jan Cossiers may have been a fellow-apprentice. By 1620 de Vos was a master in the Antwerp Guild of St Luke. For the next eight years he may either have worked in Rubens's studio or have travelled abroad (Martin). The latter is more likely in view of the similarities between de Vos's oeuvre and that of Johann Liss, who was in Rome and Venice at that time. This hypothesis is supported by the italianizing characteristics evident in de Vos's early work. Vlieghe (1988) attributed the *Portrait of Three Men* (1626; Paris, Louvre) to de Vos and identified the sitters as Jan Cossiers, Simon de Vos and ?Johan Geerlof; if this is correct, de Vos would have painted it in Aix-en-Provence. (De Vos and Cossiers may already have met in Rome between 1624 and 1626.) According to Vlieghe, the iconography of the picture is consonant with the genre works of the Bentveughels (members of the Schildersbent, a confraternity of northern artists working in Rome).

De Vos married a sister of the painter Adriaen van Utrecht in 1626 and between 1629 and 1642 took two pupils in his studio in Antwerp, where he worked for most

Simon de Vos: *The Fortune-teller*, oil on copper, 444×620 mm, 1639 (Antwerp, Koninklijk Museum voor Schone Kunsten)

of his life. Among the artists with whom he collaborated were Alexander Adriaenssen and Frans Snyders.

De Vos began his career in a rather traditional manner, executing cabinet pictures of genre scenes, including various merry companies and group portraits. Most of these have dense, unbalanced, Mannerist compositions, often constructed pyramidally. Elegant, often exotic, doll-like figures strike Mannerist poses; they have plump faces, rather prominent eyes, heavy eyebrows, full lips and untidy hair. The settings are lightly sketched in and de Vos's colours are rich and often gaudy. His style is related to that of Frans Francken (ii) and Liss, whose influence is evident in the Caravaggesque treatment of the merry company scenes. Outdoor scenes generally show wide landscapes with a high horizon, with unconnected groups of figures giving the works a feeling of incoherence. Paintings of this period include the *Marriage at Cana* (1624; Antwerp, Rockoxhuis), the *Seven Acts of Mercy* (1635; Warsaw, N. Mus.), *The Fortune-teller* (1639; Antwerp, Kon. Mus. S. Kst.; see fig.) and the pendants *David and Abigail* and *Solomon and the Queen of Sheba* (both 1641; St Petersburg, Hermitage).

After *c.* 1640 de Vos painted mainly religious and history pieces, favouring works with a more spiritual and Christian character. The compositions of these larger works adopt the same structural formulae as the small-scale scenes and thus also lack balance and authority. The figures are large and clumsy, although the putti and playing children add an air of life to what are otherwise works in a forced, fanciful and very sentimental style. In these later years, the influence of Rubens, Claude Vignon and van Dyck became sharper. Paintings of this period include a 12-part series from *Genesis* (1635–44; Seville Cathedral and elsewhere), the *Adoration of the Magi* (1643; Salzburg, Residenzgal.) and the *Martyrdom of St Peter* (1648; Antwerp, Kon. Mus. S. Kst.). The *Genesis* paintings contain a large number of animals, suggesting that Simon de Vos, like his namesake Paul de Vos, was perhaps also a specialist in that field.

Simon de Vos is known to have supplied paintings to the Forchout family firm of dealers and also to have worked for the dealer Chrysostoom van Immerseel. His standing among his contemporaries is indicated by the fact that Rubens owned a painting by him; de Vos's portrait (1635; Antwerp, Kon. Mus. S. Kst.) was painted by Abraham de Vries (*c.* 1590–1650 or 1662), and a print of it was included in Anthony van Dyck's *Iconography* (Antwerp, *c.* 1632–44).

BIBLIOGRAPHY

Thieme–Becker; Wurzbach

P. D'Arschot: 'Tableaux peu connus conservés au Brabant, I', *Rev. Belge Archéol. & Hist. A./Belge Tijdschr. Oudhdknde & Kstgesch.*, xiii/4 (1942), pp. 269–70

F.-C. Legrand: *Les Peintres flamands de genre au XVIIème siècle* (Brussels, 1963), pp. 57–62

M. Díaz Padrón: 'Simon de Vos en la catedral de Sevilla', *Archv Esp. A.*, xxlvii/192 (1975), pp. 397–402

J. Michalkowa: 'Les Tableaux de Simon de Vos dans les collections polonaises', *Bull. Mus. N. Varsovie/Biul. Muz. N. Warszaw.*, xvii (1977), pp. 1–21

Le Siècle de Rubens dans les collections publiques françaises (exh. cat. by J. Foucart, Paris, Grand Pal., 1977–8), pp. 255–6, no. 213

Het aards paradijs [The earthly paradise] (exh. cat. by A. Balis, Antwerp, Zoo, 1982), pp. 100, 102

G. Martin: 'Two Newly Attributed Works by Simon de Vos', *Rubens en zijn tijd: Bijdragen aangeboden aan R.-A. d'Hulst* (Antwerp, 1985), pp. 201–5

R. Klessmann: 'Eine *Bussende Magdalena* von Simon de Vos in Braunschweig', *Niederdt. Beitr. Kstgesch.*, xxv (1986), pp. 69–78

H. Vlieghe: '*Fecit Simon Cossiers Gerelof:* Een zeventiende-eeuws kunstenaarshommage', *Cultuurgeschiedenis in de Nederlanden van de Renaissance naar de romantiek* (Leuven and Amersfoort, 1986), pp. 371–7

——: 'A propos d'un *Portrait de trois hommes* par Simon de Vos (1603–1676) au Louvre', *Rev. Louvre*, xxxviii/1 (1988), pp. 37–8

CHRISTINE VAN MULDERS

Vosmaer, Carel (*b* The Hague, 20 March 1826; *d* Territet, Switzerland, 12 June 1888). Dutch writer and art historian. He studied law in Leiden from 1849 to 1850 and practised from 1853 until he resigned in 1873. In his retirement he devoted himself exclusively to literature, and from 1850 until *c.* 1880, due largely to Vosmaer, The Hague rivalled Amsterdam as the main literary and cultural centre of the Netherlands. In 1858 he co-founded the periodical *De tijdstroom* ('The stream of time'), which he edited until 1859, and in 1860 he co-founded the authoritative cultural periodical *De Nederlandsche spectator* (until 1888), which later merged with *De tijdstroom.* In addition, he wrote articles for *De Nederlandsche spectator.* From 1874 to 1876 he was editor of the *Kunstkronijk.*

In 1856 Vosmaer published *Een studie over het schoone in de kunst*, which was an idealistic study of the concept of beauty in art, written in the manner of Plato. In 1863 he published *Rembrandt Harmensz. van Rijn: Ses Précurseurs et ses années d'apprentissage* and in 1868 *Rembrandt Harmensz. van Rijn: Sa Vie et ses oeuvres.* Conversations between artists about art play an important role in one of Vosmaer's best-known books, *Amazone* (The Hague, 1880). His great love for the Classics is manifest in his translations of the *Iliad* (The Hague, 1879–80) and the *Odyssey* (The Hague, 1888). The first in the 24-part series *Onze hedendaagsche schilders* (The Hague) appeared in 1881 and the last in 1885; these contained short, well-researched and documented lives of such contemporary artists as H. W. Mesdag, Willem Roelofs, August Allebé, Johannes Bosboom, Lawrence Alma-Tadema, Charles Rochussen, Jacob Maris, Jozef Israels and Jan Hendrik Weissenbruch.

WRITINGS

Rembrandt Harmensz. van Rijn: Ses Précurseurs et ses années d'apprentissage (The Hague, 1863)

Een studie over het schoone in de kunst (Amsterdam, 1856)

De schilderschool (Haarlem, 1868)

Rembrandt Harmensz. van Rijn: Sa Vie et ses oeuvres (Amsterdam, 1856

Onze hedendaagsche schilders, 2 vols (The Hague, 1881–5)

Over kunst, schetsen en studieen (Leiden, 1882)

BIBLIOGRAPHY

F. L. Bastet: *Mr Carel Vosmaer: Zijn achtergronden, zijn reizen, zijn tijdgenoten, zijn invloed* [Mr Carel Vosmaer: his background, his travels, his contemporaries, his influence] (The Hague, 1967); repr. as *Met Carel Vosmaer op reis* (Amsterdam, 1989)

R. Borger: *Drei Klassizisten: Alma Tadema, Ebers, Vosmaer* (Leiden, 1983)

M. C. van Leeuwen-Canneman: *Inventaris van het archief van de familie Vosmaer, 17de–20ste eeuw* (The Hague, 1988) [cat. of the holdings in The Hague, Gemeentearchf]

F. L. Bastet and J. F. Heybroek, eds: *De verzameling van Carel Vosmaer (1826–1888)* (The Hague, 1989)

N. Maas, F. L. Bastet and J. F. Heybroek: *De literaire wereld van Carel Vosmaer: Een documentaire* (The Hague, 1989) [with extensive bibliog.]

W. F. Rappard: 'Enige niet uitgegeven brieven van Willem Roelofs aan Carel Vosmaer' [Some unpublished letters from Willem Roelofs and Carel Vosmaer], *Oud-Holland*, civ (1990), pp. 173–85

WILLEM FREDERIK RAPPARD

Voss, Hermann (*b* Lüneburg, 30 July 1884; *d* Munich, 28 April 1969). German art historian. He studied at the University of Heidelberg, where he took as the subject of his thesis the work of the 16th-century painter Wolfgang Huber and the origins of the Danube school. Of critical importance to his development as an art historian was his first visit to Italy, during which he identified the statue of *St Rock* in the tribune of the church of SS Annunziata in Florence as being by Veit Stoss; his article on this subject (1908) was his first important publication. In 1910 he followed up his interest in the Danube school with his study of *Albrecht Altdorfer und Wolf Huber*. Although he was deeply appreciative of the great Italian Renaissance artists, especially Michelangelo, Voss set himself the task of exploring the work of the then lesser-known Italian artists of the late 16th and the 17th centuries, publishing the results of his research in two pioneering studies in 1920 and 1924.

Voss worked for many years as curator of the Kaiser Friedrich Museum (now the Bodemuseum), Berlin; but with the rise of National Socialism in the 1930s he found this prominent public post untenable. His application in 1934 to settle in Britain was refused, on the grounds that he was not actually suffering persecution; he then accepted the modest position of Director of the Museum Wiesbaden. However, on the death of Hans Posse in 1942, he accepted the directorship of the Dresden Gemäldegalerie Alte Meister, with additional responsibility for planning a gallery in Linz. While in Dresden, Voss was primarily concerned with protecting his gallery's collections from war damage. After Germany's surrender in 1945 he moved to Munich, where he remained for the rest of his life.

Voss's interest as a student in the relatively unresearched field of late medieval German painting was an early indication of the independence of approach that, together with his visual sensitivity and forthright style of writing, became one of his principal characteristics as art historian. His broad interests also embraced French art: his article on Georges de La Tour (1915) was the beginning of the long process of rediscovery of that then almost forgotten artist. In 1953–4 he also published a major essay on Boucher. Late in life Voss published a study of the work of the Baroque painter Johann Heinrich Schönfeld; his most influential work, however, was in the field of Italian art.

WRITINGS

Der Ursprung des Donaustils (Leipzig, 1905)
'Zwei unbekannte Werke des Veit Stosz in florentiner Kirchen', *Jb. Kön.-Preuss. Kstsamml.*, xxix (1908), pp. 20–29
Albrecht Altdorfer und Wolf Huber: Meister der Graphik (Leipzig, 1910)
'Georges du Mesnil de la Tour', *Archv Kstgesch.*, ii/3–4 (1915)
Die Malerei der Spätrenaissance in Rom und Florenz (Berlin, 1920)
Die Malerei des Barock (Berlin, 1924)
'Boucher's Early Development', *Burl. Mag.*, xcv (1953), pp. 81–93; xcvi (1954), pp. 206–10
Johann Heinrich Schönfeld (Biberach an den Riss, 1964)

BIBLIOGRAPHY

G. Fiocco and others: *Hommage à Hermann Voss* (Strasbourg, 1966) [incl. complete list of Voss's pubns to 1965]
G. Ewald: 'Hermann Voss' [obituary], *Burl. Mag.*, cxii (1970), pp. 540–41

JANET SOUTHORN

Vostell, Wolf (*b* Leverkusen, nr Cologne, 14 Oct 1932). German painter, sculptor, décollagist, video artist and performance artist. He studied typography and lithography from 1950 to 1954 in Cologne and Wuppertal and painting at the Ecole des Beaux-Arts in Paris (1955–7) and at the Kunstakademie in Düsseldorf (1957–8). Much of his early work centred on *décollage*, a word that he found in the newspaper *Le Figaro* (6 Sept 1954), where it described the simultaneous take-off and crash of an airliner. Like certain artists associated with Nouveau Réalisme he made recourse to the technique of that name (*see* DÉCOLLAGE) in works such as *Coca Cola* (1961; Cologne, Mus. Ludwig), but he also explored the term's dialectical implications of destruction and creation; by emphasizing the syllabic division of dé-coll/age, he underscored the destruction and recombination of material through time.

While working in the late 1950s as a layout artist for a Cologne pacifist magazine, Vostell daily sorted through hundreds of 20th-century photographs of war crimes, violence and pornography. Identifying destruction and sexuality as the great themes of the period, he realized that these subjects had been most powerfully depicted in television, newspaper and magazine images. He developed a technique of applying chemicals to photographs so as to erase and distort highly recognizable mass-media images, as in *Marilyn Monroe 2* (1963; Cologne, Wolfgang Hahn priv. col.; see *Wolf Vostell: dé-coll/agen, 1954–69*, p. 51). In removing the slick media surface he sought the viewer's active participation in deciphering new relationships. In later works such as *Miss America* (1968; Cologne, Mus. Ludwig), in which a picture of the model Jean Shrimpton is juxtaposed with an infamous photograph by Eddie Adams of an atrocity in Vietnam, he used screenprinting to bring together images from different sources in order to demonstrate their connections, in this case between violence and eroticism.

Vostell used similar methods in live performances (which he called dé-coll/age Happenings), sculptures and multimedia installations. A member of FLUXUS and one of the first Europeans to produce Happenings, he created events that commented starkly on technology and consumerism so as to convey a highly politicized view of the underlying tragedy of contemporary social conditions and values. He created video installations, such as an automobile implanted with more than a dozen televisions. Vostell collaborated with other artists and writers, wrote theoretical essays and composed music. From 1962 to 1969 he edited *Dé-coll/age: Bulletin der aktuellen Ideen*, an international anthology devoted primarily to Happenings and Fluxus art. In the late 1970s he established the Museo Vostell in Malpartida de Cáceres, Spain, to exhibit his work along with that of other Fluxus artists.

WRITINGS

with J. Becker: *Happenings, Flux, Pop Art, Nouveau Réalisme* (Cologne, 1965)
Miss Vietnam and Texts of Other Happenings (San Francisco, 1969)
Wolf Vostell: dé-coll/agen, 1954–69 (Berlin, 1969)

BIBLIOGRAPHY

R. Wick: *Vostell soziologisch* (Bonn, 1969)
Wolf Vostell: Zeichnungen, 1952–1976 (exh. cat., Dortmund, Mus. Ostwall; Hannover, Kestner-Ges.; Barcelona, Cent. Miró; 1977)
Wolf Vostell: dé-coll/agen, Verwischungen, Schichtenbilder, Bleibilder, Objektbilder, 1955–1979 (exh. cat., Brunswick, Kstver., 1980) [incl. interview by W. Schmied]
Vostell Fluxus Zug: Das Mobile Museum Vostell (Wuppertal, 1981)

Vostell und Berlin: Leben und Werk, 1971–1981 (exh. cat., text W. Schmied, W. Berlin, daad gal., 1982)

KRISTINE STILES

Vosterman, Jan. *See* VORSTERMAN, JAN.

Vouet, Simon (*b* Paris, 8 Jan 1590; *bur* Paris, 1 July 1649). French painter and draughtsman. Although at the time regarded as one of the leading French painters of the first half of the 17th century, he is now known more for his influence on French painting than for his actual oeuvre. He made his reputation in Italy, where he executed numerous portraits for aristocratic patrons and was commissioned for religious subjects. Although the early Italian works show the influence of Caravaggio, his work was subsequently modified by the Baroque style of such painters as Lanfranco and the influence of the Venetian use of light and colour. When he was summoned back to France by Louis XIII in 1627 he thus brought with him an Italian idiom hitherto unknown in France that revitalized French painting (*see* FRANCE, §III, 3). His style became highly popular among Parisian aristocrats who saw in Vouet a painter capable of decorating their hôtels and châteaux in a manner that would rival the palazzi of their Italian counterparts. He quickly established a large workshop through which passed many of the leading French painters of the mid-17th century. There followed numerous commissions for allegorical works, religious subjects and decorative paintings for royal residences and the burgeoning hôtels and châteaux in and around Paris.

The schemes introduced a new type of illusionistic decoration with steep perspective that influenced a generation of decorative painters. Few of his canvases are signed and dated and many of his decorative schemes have been destroyed; precise attribution is made more difficult because of his prolific output and his extensive use of his workshop to fulfil his numerous commissions. Although much of his oeuvre has been lost, it is known from the work of such distinguished engravers as Claude Mellan and Michel Dorigny, who reproduced and circulated his work.

1. Early years and Italy, 1590–mid-1627. 2. Paris, late 1627–49.

1. EARLY YEARS AND ITALY, 1590–MID-1627. Little is known of his early life, except for the fact that his father, Laurent Vouet (*b c.* 1553–8), was a Parisian painter. Félibien records that he travelled to England at the age of 14 to 'make the portrait of a Lady of quality', and left for Constantinople in 1611, under the auspices of the King's Ambassador, in order to execute the portrait of a 'Grand Seigneur'. It was thus his talent as a portrait painter that brought him recognition. In 1612 he left Constantinople for Venice and by 1614 he was in Rome, where he received a pension from the French crown and enjoyed the protrection and patronage of the Barberini family. He rapidly established a reputation and received numerous commissions from ecclesiastical and aristocratic patrons, among them Cassiano dal Pozzo, Vincenzo Giustianini, Paolo Giordano Orsini and the Doria family, whom he

1. Simon Vouet: *Birth of the Virgin*, oil on canvas, 2.24×3.33 m, *c.* 1620 (Rome, S Francesco a Ripa)

depicted in such portraits as that of *Gian Carlo Doria* (Paris, Louvre).

Vouet became part of the Caravaggist movement (*see* CARAVAGGIO, MICHELANGELO MERISA DA, §IV, 1), which flowered in the 1620s and involved artists of all nationalities working in Rome. He worked on such themes as *Judith with the Head of Holofernes* (Vienna, Ksthist. Mus.), *David with the Head of Goliath* (Genoa, Pal. Bianco), *The Fortune-teller* (Ottawa, N.G.) and *St Jerome and the Angel* (Washington, DC, N.G.A.). The presentation of life-size figures on a plain background, the dramatic contrasts of light, the realistic anatomical studies drawn from life and the lack of any attempt to achieve a decorative layout were part of the language of Caravaggio. Several of Vouet's great religious works executed for churches in Rome, such as the *Temptation of St Francis* (Rome, S Lorenzo in Lucina), also show the influence of Caravaggio in their presentation of effects of light and their use of a restricted palette of blacks, browns and whites. He also continued to work in a personal style, and was familiar not only with the great examples of the first and second schools of Fontainebleau but also with the great Venetian artists of the 16th century. *The Fortune-teller*, for example, is a fine illustration of a Caravaggesque genre scene but its burlesque treatment is quite alien to the Caravaggesque spirit.

Vouet also travelled in Italy. In 1621 he was in Genoa, where he painted portraits of *Marcantonio Doria* (Paris, Louvre) and *Donna Isabella Appiana, Princess of Piombino* (lost). He was impressed by the *Circumcision* (1606) by Rubens in Sant'Ambrogio, Genoa, and saw the work of the great artists of Bologna. He also saw such northern artists as Gerrit van Honthorst, and such contemporary Italian painters as Giovanni Lanfranco, Bartolomeo Manfredi, Orazio Borgianni, Bernardo Strozzi (1581–1644), Orazio Gentileschi and Artemisia Gentileschi.

His letters express his admiration of fine collections and his eagerness to explore Piacenza, Parma, Bologna and Florence, which he probably visited on his way back to Rome. During the years in Italy Vouet executed numerous portraits, with broad brushstrokes, in which the model is captured from life, the mouth slightly open and the head and shoulders turned towards the spectator, e.g. *?Self-portrait* (Arles, Mus. Réattu), *Portrait of a Young Man* (Paris, Louvre) and *Portrait of a Bravo* (Brunswick, Herzog Anton Ulrich-Mus.). He produced a considerable number of religious paintings: *Circumcision* (1622; Naples, Sant'Angelo a Segno), the *Appearance of the Virgin to St Bruno* (?1626; Naples, Mus. N. S Martino), the *Apotheosis of St Theodore* (Dresden, Alte Pin.) for the Scuola di San Teodoro, Venice, *Birth of the Virgin* (*c.* 1620; Rome, S Francesco a Ripa; see fig. 1), the *Clothing of St Francis* and the *Temptation of St Francis* (both 1624; Rome, S Lorenzo in Lucina, Alaleoni Chapel). In the *Birth of the Virgin*, the dramatic side lighting that makes the figures stand out against the dark background, the *di sotto* viewpoint, the plastic appearance of the figures and the gravity of the faces all reflect Vouet's thoughtful contemplation of Caravaggio's work, making this painting an exceptional piece from his Roman period. The linked series of gestures, the fullness of the draperies, the delicacy of the colour harmony and the care taken to achieve an elegant effect

2. Simon Vouet: *Study for a Figure of Intellect*, black chalk with white highlights, 430×267 mm, *c.* 1645 (Paris, Musée du Louvre)

were already characteristic of Vouet's work, which, at this period, still retained a breath of lyricism.

The *Clothing of St Francis* commissioned by Paolo Alaleone represents another stage in Vouet's development. Although the presentation of the characters' psychological reactions recalls Caravaggio, the attention paid to the narrative does not, and the decorative arrangement and lighting contrasts recall the artists of Bologna and Lanfranco. Vouet subsequently often adopted the decorative option seen here, setting his scene on a staircase with a background of columns, and this colour palette grew lighter. The *Temptation of St Francis* was a daring and singular work; commissioned for a church, in its dancing figure of a courtesan and its candlelit illumination it recalls the work of Honthorst, and the highly realistic treatment of detail is one of the lasting influences of his stay in Italy. Much of his Roman oeuvre was engraved by Claude Vignon, Johann Freidrich Greuter (*c.* 1600–60) and Claude Mellan.

Vouet's advice to Mellan was 'to draw and to set this study above all others'; it is therefore certain that he continued to develop his drawing skills in Italy. Very few of his drawings from his Italian period have survived, however, although numerous drawings from his Parisian period (e.g. *Study for a Figure of Intellect*; see fig. 2), mainly executed in black chalk highlighted with white, show a considerable debt to Italian draughtsmen, in particular

Annibale Carracci, Domenichino and some of the Genoese artists. The study (Reims, Mus. St-Denis) for part of the *Allegory of the House of Savoy*, engraved by Mellan, and *St Peter Healing the Sick with his Shadow* (Princeton U., NJ, A. Mus) are among the few extant Italian drawings. The second, executed in wash over an outline in black chalk, is of particular interest as it appears to refer to a prestigious commission for an altar painting for St Peter's in Rome. The election of Urban VIII in 1623 helped to promote Vouet's position, and he was commissioned for a painting on the subject of St Peter healing the sick. This subject was, however, abandoned in 1625 in favour of the *Adoration of the Cross, with St Francis, St Anthony of Padua and St John Chrysostom*. The painting, intended for the Canon Choir chapel behind Michelangelo's *Pietà*, was destroyed during the 18th century. Documents indicate that Vouet had already executed drawings on the St Peter subject.

In 1624 Vouet was elected President of the Accademia di S Luca, in 1626 he married Virginia da Vezzo (*b c.* 1607) and, having received a pension from Louis XIII for several years, he seemed ready to follow an entirely Italian career. In 1627, however, he was recalled by the King, who wished to have a painter at court who would be capable of realizing the ambitious projects for the royal residences. Vouet visited Venice on his way back to France and the Venetian influence—clear colouring and the mastery of large-scale composition—impregnated his Parisian oeuvre. *Time Vanquished by Venus, Love and Hope* (Madrid,

Prado), which he had painted in Rome in 1627, foreshadowed his new interest in Venice and the privileged role of colour, moving figures, wind-blown draperies, light colouring and landscape background.

2. PARIS, LATE 1627–49. Vouet reached Paris in late November 1627. He became Premier Peintre du Roi at a time when new fortunes were amassing and there was a revival in construction. He worked for the King on numerous projects. He executed cartoons (untraced) for an *Old Testament* series of tapestries that remain in the Louvre (*see* FRANCE, fig. 92), rich compositions, in which he deployed large numbers of figures in vast landscapes or architectural decors, known from six scenes engraved (1665) by François Tortebat (1616–90). The tapestries were highly coloured and had unusual wide, handsome borders embellished with fruits, flowers and putti. In the presence of the King, and at his express request, he made pastel drawings of the ladies and gentlemen of the court, of which some 60 examples have recently been found (divided among various French collections; see Brejon, 1982). For these simple, sober but lively images, in which the model seems vividly present, Vouet used pastels of different colours to create an entirely new version of the typical contemporary court portrait executed in three colours by such Parisian artists as members of the Dumontiers family. He also executed numerous paintings for such royal residences as the Château Neuf de Saint-Germain-en-Laye (destr. 1777; the *Four Cardinal Virtues*;

3. Simon Vouet: *Diana at Rest*, oil on canvas, 1.02×1.41 m, 1637 (London, Hampton Court, Royal Collection)

now Versailles, Salon de Mars) the château of Fontaine-bleau (*The Four Elements*; lost; engraved by Michel Dorigny, 1644) and the Palais Royal where, for Anne of Austria, he executed the *Allegory of Prudence* (Montpellier, Mus. Fabre) and the *Assumption of the Virgin* (Reims, Mus. St-Denis).

As well as royal commissions Vouet also received commissions from statesmen, politicians and wealthy art lovers, all of whom wished to decorate their hôtels in Paris and their châteaux in the surrounding area. Vouet quickly organized a large studio, and was eagerly approached by young painters wishing to extend their training and study drawing. Virginia da Vezzo, Vouet's Italian wife, also taught a drawing course for women. The decorative schemes he and his assistants executed extended to and occupied the ceilings, in the Italian style. Engravings by Michel Lasne, Pierre Daret, Michel Dorigny and, later, François Tortebat have made it possible to reconstruct these schemes, many of which were destroyed. Of the 14 mythological subjects on the gallery ceiling in the Château de Chilly, executed *c.* 1630–31 for the Marquis d'Effiat, Surintendant des Finances, the *Meeting of the Gods* is lost, but *Sunrise* and *Moonrise*, reproduced in engravings by Dorigny (*see* DORIGNY, (1)), document Vouet's sense of composition and his mastery of lighting effects. He remained faithful to the typical ceiling *trompe l'oeil* in which the figures are shown *di sotto in sù* with striking foreshortening. Early sources and archive texts mention several other decorative schemes executed in châteaux in the Paris area, such as those of Chessy (a series of *Rinaldo and Armida*, 1631; Paris, priv. col.) and, notably, Wideville, where Vouet provided fresco decorations (*Parnassus* and *Nymph and River God, in situ*) for the nymphaeum. For the hôtel of CLAUDE DE BULLION, Vouet painted 24 scenes from the *Story of Ulysses* for the upper gallery, thus renewing his links with the great epic narrative works of the 16th century. Only eight scenes from the set are known from tapestries (Cheverny, Château). Vouet's most ambitious decorative scheme was that in the chapel of the Hôtel Séguier (destr.) for the Chancellor PIERRE SÉGUIER. It consisted of an astonishing *Adoration of the Magi* (destr.; engraving by Dorigny, 1638) accompanied by a long retinue in which Vouet used powerful *trompe l'oeil* effects to suggest architectural elements and space. A *Crucifixion* (*c.* 1635; Lyon, Mus. B.-A.) was situated over the altar and accompanied by 22 compositions fitted into the chapel's panelling. The allegorical language of the library decor (engraved 1640) referred to Séguier's intellectual and artistic interests of which the prestigious library was by no means the only example. The decor of the hôtel's lower gallery showed 12 mythological compositions (engraved 1651), which alluded to the important events of the reign of Louis XIII (Sauval). These decorative schemes, whether from the beginning or the end of Vouet's Parisian career, are elaborate, highly decorative and animated by a spirit of great lyricism. He was equally at ease with simpler and more poetical motifs such as *Diana at Rest* (1637; London, Hampton Court, Royal Col., see fig. 3), a painting probably done for Charles I and sent by Vouet to the English court. He multiplied his draperies and splashes of colour, demonstrating his mastery of the human figure studied from life, embellished by a pearly treatment of the flesh and

4. Simon Vouet: *Adoration of the Divine Name by Four Saints*, oil on canvas, 2.65×1.76 m, *c.* 1645–9 (Paris, St Merry)

attention to detail. The paintings of *c.* 1630–31 for the Galerie des Hommes Illustres in the Palais Cardinal (now Palais Royal), on which he worked with Philippe de Champaigne, were more uneven, and the contribution of the studio can be clearly seen. Although Vouet did not seem to take particular care with the depiction of these historical figures, Cardinal Richelieu was satisfied and commissioned a *Nativity* (lost; engraving by Dorigny, 1638) for the chapel of the château of Rueil and an altarpiece for the Jesuit Novitiate, the *Presentation in the Temple* (1641; Paris, Louvre; *see* FRANCE, fig. 20). Vouet also provided drawings for paintings to be executed in the *cabinets* of the château of Richelieu.

The religious congregations and orders also commissioned Vouet. Examples include *St Carlo Borromeo Offering his Life to God* (*c.* late 1630s; Brussels, Mus. A. Anc.) for the Congrégation de la Doctrine Chrétienne in Paris, *Adoration of the Divine Name by Four Saints* (Paris, St-Merry; see fig. 4), the altarpiece of the *Martyrdom of St Eustache and his Family* (lower section; Paris, St Eustache) and the *Apotheosis of St Eustache and his Family* (upper section; Nantes, Mus. B.-A.) and *Rest on the Flight into Egypt* (1640; Grenoble, Mus. B.-A.) for the Achères chapel in the church of the Feuillants, Paris. Dorigny's engravings reproduced paintings executed for the Minims, the Jesuits and the Carmelites. Apart from the *Last Supper* (Loreto,

Pal. Apostolico) and the *Assumption* (Paris, St Nicolas-des-Champs), works executed just after his return from Italy in which there is still a latent suggestion of Caravaggio's luminism and of Rubens's figures, his religious paintings showed no further stylistic development during the last two decades of his career. Vouet retained his sense of monumental format, with realistic and powerful figures shown in movement and *da sotto in sù* and with the Baroque influence of Lanfranco. The pictorial language of his religious works was the same as that of his secular paintings; his altarpieces were treated with identical dynamism, and the figures of his great works, scientifically composed, were linked like great splashes of colour, forming images appropriate to the wishes of the faithful and the congregations who were then undergoing a spiritual revival in Paris. Subsequently, however, Vouet's use of a restricted vocabulary and his interchangeable secular and religious worlds have been criticized. His work has been labelled decorative, without regard for his audacious combinations of colour, the rich effects of his brushwork and his mastery of space, perspective and large surfaces. An artist who, apart from his religious works, limited his subject-matter to mythology and allegory, without recourse to the Classical world or to contemporary history, Vouet was in fact a great decorator; and in the first half of the 17th century, such a description was an accolade.

BIBLIOGRAPHY

H. Sauval: *Histoire et recherches des antiquités de la Ville de Paris* [*c*. 1655–70] (Paris, 1724)
A. Félibien: *Entretiens* (1666–8) [esp. 7th *Entretiien*]
W. R. Crelly: *The Painting of Simon Vouet* (New Haven, 1962) [with cat. rais.]
G. Dargent and J. Thuiller: 'Simon Vouet en Italie: Essai de catalogue critique', *Saggi & Mem. Stor. A.*, iv (1965), pp. 27–63
Valentin et les caravagesques français (exh. cat. by J. P. Cuzin and A. Brejon, Paris, Grand Pal., 1974)
B. Brejon de Lavergnée: 'Simon Vouet à Milan en 1621: Une Lettre inédite de l'artiste français', *Rev. A.*, l (1980), pp. 58–64
B. Brejon: 'Some New Pastels by Simon Vouet: Portraits of the Court of Louis XIII', *Burl. Mag.*, cxxiv/956 (1982), pp. 689–93
——: *Catalogue des dessins de Simon Vouet* (Paris, 1986)
J. P. Cuzin: 'Un Chef d'oeuvre avorté de Simon Vouet: *Le Saint Pierre et les malades* commandé pour Saint-Pierre de Rome', *Etudes offertes à André Chastel* (Rome and Paris, 1987), pp. 359–70
Vouet (exh. cat. by J. Thuiller, B. Brejon de Lavergnée and D. Lavalle, Paris, Grand Pal., 1990–91)

BARBARA BREJON

Vouni. Site on the north coast of Cyprus, *c*. 8 km northeast of Lefka. Here the extensive remains of a 5th-century BC palace, a complete plan of which was recovered (*see* CYPRUS, §II, 2(iii) and fig. 7), were excavated by the Swedish Cyprus Expedition in 1928–9. The reception rooms of the original palace (Vouni I; first half of the 5th century BC) were arranged around a central square court surrounded on three sides by a portico. On the fourth side, at the south-west, a magnificent flight of stairs led to the palace's main entrance with its flanking state apartments. The strict axiality in the arrangement of the court and the entrance block is to be noted. Service wings to the south contained living-rooms, baths, kitchens and storerooms. During a rebuilding in the later 5th century BC (Vouni II) a second court, flanked by a number of storerooms and other apartments, was added to the southeast, and the main entrance block was walled up. A new main entrance was devised, which followed a winding route into the courtyard by way of rooms in the northwest corner of the court. The palace shows the influence of contemporary Near Eastern architecture (*see* CYPRUS, §II, 1(iii) and 2(iii)), and it is reasonable to assume that it belonged to the rulers of the nearby kingdom of Soli. The hypothesis that Vouni II represents a 'Hellenized' rebuilding scheme (*see* CYPRUS, §II, 2(iii)) is based on a number of untenable assumptions. The buildings were finally destroyed in the early 4th century BC.

BIBLIOGRAPHY

E. Gjerstad and others: *Finds and Results of the Excavations in Cyprus, 1927–1931* (1937), iii of *The Swedish Cyprus Expedition* (Stockholm, 1934–)
F. G. Maier: 'Factoids in Ancient History: The Case of Fifth-century Cyprus', *J. Hell. Stud.*, cv (1985), pp. 32–9

FRANZ GEORG MAIER

Voussoir. Wedge-shaped stone in an arch (*see* ARCH, fig. 1i and MASONRY, §III).

Voyer, Marquis de [Marc-René d'Argenson, Vicomte de Paulmy] (*b* 20 Sept 1722; *d* Les Ormes, Saint-Martin, Vendée, 16 Sept 1782). French soldier, patron and collector. He is usually referred to as the Marquis de Voyer to distinguish him from his cousin, the bibliophile Marquis de Paulmy (1722–87). A connoisseur of fine art, he possessed a collection of paintings, among which were works by contemporary French artists and the 17th-century Dutch painter Nicolaes Berchem. He also collected medals, Classical works of art and objects of natural history. The collection was dispersed rather quickly in order for him to pay off huge debts accumulated through his passion for architecture. In Paris he lived in the Hôtel de Voyer, which he had redecorated (1762–70) in splendour by the architect CHARLES DE WAILLY, whose patron he became. He also employed Jean-Honoré Fragonard, Jean-Jacques Lagrenée and Augustin Pajou, who produced a unique decorative ensemble; it was famous for its ceilings by Charles-Antoine Coypel and Louis-Jacques Durameau. The house was destroyed in 1916 by the Banque de France. Its décor, stored at Asnière, is still awaiting refitting. A free associate of the Académie Royale and patron of the Académie de St Luc, the Marquis de Voyer played an active part in the cultural life of his times. He had the family château of Les Ormes refurbished (1769–78) by de Wailly in collaboration with Pascal Lenot, a young local architect, and he retired there to lead a 'philosophical' life.

WRITINGS
Journal et mémoires du Marquis d'Argenson, ed. E. J. B. Rathery, 9 vols (Paris, 1859–67)

BIBLIOGRAPHY
DBF
Charles de Wailly: Peintre architecte dans l'Europe des Lumières (exh. cat., ed. P. Mosser and D. Rabreau; Paris, Hôtel de Sully, 1979), pp. 43–5
B. Pons: *Grands décors français, 1650–1800* (Dijon, 1994), p. 277

ANNE LECLAIR

Voyez. French family of engravers. Nicolas-Joseph Voyez (*b* Abbeville, 1742; *d* Paris, 1806) studied in Abbeville with Jacques-Firmin Beauvarlet, one of the engravers who were helping, through reproductive engravings, to popularize Netherlandish Baroque paintings in France. Both

Nicolas-Joseph and his brother François Voyez (*b* Abbeville, 1746; *d* Paris, 1805) engraved portraits and genre scenes after such contemporary French painters as Jean-Baptiste Greuze, François Boucher and Charles Eisen. Problems of attribution arise with prints signed *Voyez Sculp.*, since they could be by either brother, or the result of a collaboration between them.

BIBLIOGRAPHY

Portalis–Beraldi; Thieme–Becker

V. Atwater: *A Catalogue and Analysis of Eighteenth-century French Prints after Netherlandish Baroque Paintings* (diss., Seattle, U. WA, 1988)

VIVIAN ATWATER

Voÿgh, Jacob. *See* FACHT, JACOB.

Voysey, C(harles) F(rancis) A(nnesley) (*b* Hessle, nr Hull, 28 May 1857; *d* Winchester, Hants, 12 Feb 1941). English architect and designer. Although his importance and his influence on his contemporaries has long been recognized, his reputation rests on an oeuvre that is limited in both quantity and scope. He is chiefly remembered for a small number of country houses (*c.* 1890–1910) that are neither large nor grand and for the fittings (and often the furniture, wallpaper and textiles) that he put into them. What is remarkable about these houses is that they are independent of past styles to an extent revolutionary at the time, and yet they breathe the spirit of vernacular tradition.

1. Life and work. 2. Style.

1. LIFE AND WORK.

(i) Early life. He was the son of a Yorkshire clergyman, the Rev. Charles Voysey, who was expelled from the Church of England for denying the doctrine of Everlasting Hell. The family moved to London in 1871, where his father founded the Theistic Church. In 1874 Voysey was articled for five years to the architect J. P. Seddon, with whom he subsequently remained a further year as chief assistant. From Seddon Voysey learnt the 'Gothic' principles of design first propounded by A. W. N. Pugin: elevations should grow naturally out of the requirements of the plan and only 'honest' construction should be used. Seddon and Voysey both believed in following these principles of design without slavishly copying Gothic styles. But, however freely Seddon interpreted the Gothic styles, his work remained discernibly Gothic, whereas Voysey's mature work eliminated all trace of period styles. Voysey followed Seddon in believing, like Pugin, that it was the business of an architect to make designs not only for buildings but also for the allied crafts. In 1879 Voysey spent a brief period as assistant to the architect H. Saxon Snell (1830–1904), and from 1880 to 1881 he worked as an assistant in the office of George Devey, who was a follower of his father's Theistic Church. There he gained valuable site experience, and would have encountered Devey's skill as a watercolourist and his considerable knowledge of English vernacular architecture. In 1881 or early 1882 Voysey set up his own practice in London.

(ii) Architecture. Voysey's architectural practice began slowly, with small alterations and surveys; a number of unexecuted designs from these early years were published and reveal the influence of both Seddon and Devey. In 1888 he obtained his first architectural commission, for The Cottage (addition by Voysey, 1900) at Bishop's Itchington, Warwicks. The Cottage was built of thin, buttressed brickwork, roughcast and painted cream. This form of construction was chosen by Voysey because it was cheap, but in his hands it became an aesthetic end in itself, as he skilfully juxtaposed the solid and void, light and shadow, of the clean-cut forms. Other 19th-century architects, including Devey, had built country cottages in a simple vernacular style with whitened roughcast for estate workers, parsons and schoolmasters. For 1888, The Cottage was unusual not only for being entirely roughcast but also for its simplicity and informality, which were revolutionary in a gentleman's house.

Walnut Tree Farm (1890) at Castlemorton, near Malvern, Hereford & Worcester, and a house at Bedford Park (1891), Chiswick, London, have certain novel features that became characteristic of Voysey's designs. Walnut Tree Farm shows for the first time the lively colouring that was to become typical of his houses: whitened roughcast, bright green exterior woodwork, over-size, bright green water-butts, bright green tubs of bay trees and bright red curtains at the windows. At Bedford Park the innovation consisted in very simplified classical or Queen Anne details, a slate roof and practical metal frames and stone surrounds of the windows.

In 1893 Voysey obtained his first commission for a relatively expensive house, Perrycroft, at Colwall, near Malvern. From then until *c.* 1910 Voysey received a steady stream of architectural commissions; most were simple, white country or suburban houses with low, spreading lines, for which he became famous. He introduced some mannered, even eccentric, classical detailing into two fairly expensive houses in Surrey, designed in 1897: New Place, near Haslemere, and Norney, near Shackleford. But there was a return to simplicity at Broadleys and Moorcrag, the lakeside houses near Windermere that he designed in 1898.

Between *c.* 1900 and *c.* 1910 Voysey obtained a series of commissions that gave him the opportunity to design complete houses, including every detail of the interiors, not only fixtures, but also moveable furniture, carpets, curtains and wall coverings. The Orchard, Chorleywood, Herts, designed for himself and his wife in 1899, was the first such house. In 1901 came The Pastures at North Luffenham (see fig. 1); in 1905 Hollymount, near Beaconsfield, Bucks, and The Homestead at Frinton-on-Sea, Essex. An interior design carried out in London was Garden Corner (1906) on the Chelsea Embankment. In the typical Voysey interior the low ceilings and deep friezes were white; the woodwork was unpolished oak, if possible, or cheaper deal painted white. Colours in furnishings, tiled fireplaces and wall and floor coverings were soft and light, for example delicate greens and heathery purples, with a few bright accents of red and turquoise. There was no clutter in a Voysey interior: furniture was sparse and the use of pattern in wallpapers, carpets and metalwork was sparing.

From *c.* 1910 Voysey's architectural practice declined, largely because he was out of sympathy with the new fashion for classical forms. He reacted against this by introducing details of Gothic origin into his work. In 1909 he used a pointed arch in the porch of Brooke End at

1. C. F. A. Voysey: design for The Pastures, North Luffenham, pen and ink, 300×440 mm, 1901 (London, British Architectural Library, Royal Institute of British Architects)

Henley-in-Arden, Warwicks, and in the same year he built a miniature courtyard house in Tudor Gothic style at Combe Down, near Bath. Unexecuted designs of 1914 for larger houses have eccentric courtyard plans, pointed arches, crenellations and towers.

Voysey obtained commissions only occasionally for buildings other than country or suburban houses, but when he did he displayed considerable versatility. On the restricted site of his Bedford Park house he abandoned his usual horizontal planning and built a 'tower house'. The two brick-faced terrace houses (1891) that he built in Hans Road, Knightsbridge, London, display great ingenuity in the arrangement of plan and section. The Sanderson wallpaper factory (1901) in Chiswick is severely functional in form and faced with white-glazed bricks. However, for the fitting out of the offices of the Essex and Suffolk Equitable Insurance Company (designed c. 1906–9), Capel House, New Broad Street, London, he considered a degree of expensive decoration to be appropriate.

(iii) Furniture and pattern designs. Voysey's designs in the field of applied art included furniture, wallpapers, fabrics, carpets, tiles, metalwork, ceramics and graphic design (best examples in London, V&A; U. Manchester, Whitworth A.G.). Sometimes he designed artefacts specially for his own buildings, and sometimes he sold designs to manufacturers for wider use.

Voysey's development as a furniture designer corresponded to his development as an architect, and by c. 1895 he had evolved a definitive personal style. His furniture conformed, with a few exceptions, to this style until c. 1910, when he began to introduce greater elaboration, including Gothic motifs, into his designs. The simple elegance of Voysey's furniture from the period c. 1895–1910 was achieved by relying on the innate beauty of high quality materials, especially unpolished oak, and by eschewing complicated decoration in favour of a careful balance of the vertical and horizontal elements in a design. The vertical elements were often emphasized by tapering the vertical supports from a square to an octagonal section and by carrying corner supports up above the functionally necessary height; the horizontal elements were often emphasized by simply moulded cornices, by circular caps on the tops of corner supports (a motif borrowed from A. H. Mackmurdo) and by long strap-hinges made of unpolished bronze.

Voysey was a distinguished designer of flat patterns for wallpapers, fabrics, carpets and tiles (see fig. 2). It was A. H. Mackmurdo who first introduced him to the techniques of wallpaper design, and some of Voysey's early pattern designs incorporated more restrained versions of the swirling motifs beloved by Mackmurdo and the CENTURY GUILD OF ARTISTS. Voysey sold his first wallpaper design in 1883; by the late 1880s his reputation as a wallpaper designer was established at home and abroad,

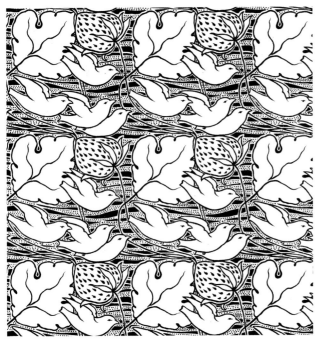

2. C. F. A. Voysey: machine-printed cotton for Newman, Smith & Newman, 1897 (London, Victoria and Albert Museum)

and he was still selling pattern designs in 1930. His career as a pattern designer was thus longer and more prolific than his career as an architect. But it was also complementary to his architectural career, because selling patterns supplemented his income in the lean years of his architectural practice, before *c.* 1895 and after *c.* 1910.

Many of Voysey's pattern designs rely for their effect on rhythmically contrasted shapes consisting of areas of flat, clear colour, usually bounded by dark or pale outlines. This is in the tradition of oriental design praised by Victorian reformers of design, such as Owen Jones and Matthew Digby Wyatt. In Voysey's work stylized natural forms, especially plants and birds, often represent the positive shapes, and areas of background form the contrasting negative shapes. This skilful juxtaposition can also be seen in his handling of the solids and voids in his designs for two-dimensional metalwork, such as ventilator grilles and hinges. Some of Voysey's pattern designs after *c.* 1900 consist of motifs placed in comparative isolation against a light ground. The use of scale is arbitrary, giving an effect of naive charm reminiscent of medieval illuminations and tapestries. The later designs are generally smaller and more delicately coloured than the designs of the 1880s and 1890s.

2. STYLE. Voysey's mature work exhibits a remarkable degree of consistency. In a single-minded way he worked out the simplest solutions to individual functional and visual problems according to his principles of fitness for purpose and truth to materials. He then re-used these solutions over a period of years, albeit sometimes modified or elaborated, as he saw no reason for gratuitous innovation. The same consistency can be seen in the way that,

having worked out his personal repertory of shapes and forms, Voysey was happy to re-use them even in different media. For example, the same corner buttresses appear on a chest of drawers as on buildings; a clock is given the same ogee cap as a stable block; the same flat pattern is used in a wooden stair balustrade as appears in the bronze fitting of a cabinet; and the heart appears everywhere from chairbacks to letter-boxes.

Voysey's work cannot be satisfactorily squeezed into any one art-historical compartment. Voysey belonged to the Arts and Crafts Movement to the extent that he followed Ruskin in believing in the moral value of handwork, but he did not turn his back on the machine, nor did he always insist on the use of local materials. And although he was careful to ensure high standards of craftsmanship in the execution of his designs, unlike A. W. N. Pugin or C. R. Ashbee he never set up his own workshops. The attenuated elegance of some of Voysey's metalwork and furniture and the swirling forms of his early pattern designs have been linked with the origins of Art Nouveau although Voysey himself did not approve of Art Nouveau, which he considered exaggerated and unnatural. He has also been linked with the Modern Movement because of his use of simple, white forms, and undoubtedly his work, which was widely published abroad, did influence the European avant-garde. But when in the 1930s he was acclaimed as a pioneer of the Modern Movement, he was indignant that such a self-consciously revolutionary movement, which rejected the traditional values in which he believed, should be connected with his work in any way.

WRITINGS

Reason as a Basis of Art (London, 1906)
T. Raffles Davison, ed.: 'Ideas in Things', *The Arts Connected with Building* (London, 1909), pp. 103–37
'Patriotism in Architecture', *Archit. Assoc. J.*, xxviii (1912), pp. 21–5
Individuality (London, 1915)
The Work of C. F. A. Voysey (exh. cat., intro. C. F. A. Voysey; London, Batsford Gal., 1931)

BIBLIOGRAPHY

N. Pevsner: *Pioneers of the Modern Movement* (London, 1936); rev. as *Pioneers of Modern Design* (Harmondsworth, 1960, rev. 1975)
J. Brandon-Jones: *C. F. A. Voysey: A Memoir* (London, 1957/R New York, 1977) [Archit. Assoc. pamphlet]
——: 'C. F. A. Voysey', *Victorian Architecture*, ed. P. Ferriday (London, 1963), pp. 267–87
D. Gebhard: *Charles F. A. Voysey: Architect* (Los Angeles, 1975) [incl. some of Voysey's writings]
J. Symonds: *RIBA Drawings Collection: C. F. A. Voysey* (Farnborough, 1976) [incl. extensive bibliog.]
C. F. A. Voysey: Architect and Designer, 1857–1941 (exh. cat., ed. J. Brandon-Jones; Brighton, Royal Pav., 1978) [applied art well illus.]
D. Simpson: *C. F. A. Voysey: An Architect of Individuality* (London, 1979) [well illus.]

J. HESELTINE

Vrancx [Vranckx], **Sebastiaen** [Sebastian; Sébastien] (*bapt* Antwerp, 22 Jan 1573; *d* Antwerp, 19 May 1647). Flemish painter and draughtsman. He is best known for his depictions of battle scenes (*see* BATTLE PICTURES AND MILITARY SCENES) and was probably the first artist in the northern or southern Netherlands to attempt this subject-matter.

1. EARLY WORKS, BEFORE *c.* 1611. He was the son of Jan Vrancx and Barbara Coutereau. Van Mander's claim that he trained as a painter with Adam van Noort seems

possible but is unconfirmed. Vrancx's earliest known work, a drawing (1594; Frankfurt am Main, Städel. Kstinst.), is closely related to the Antwerp scrollwork decorations of Cornelis Floris and Cornelis Bos. The next drawings and paintings were executed during Vrancx's stay in Italy (*c*. 1596–1601) and show strong parallels with the early style of Paul Bril, who was working in Rome, and of Jan Breughel I. Typical examples are the *Massacre of the Innocents* and its pendant *Crossing the Red Sea* (both 1600; Parma, G.N.; on dep. Rome, Pal. Montecitorio); they reveal a liking for anecdotal detail and for colourfully dressed figures who move in a decorative, but conventional landscape. These features remained characteristic of his style throughout his career. The vividly gesticulating figures and the clumsy trees, which look as if they are made of marzipan, were used only in this early period, before the guild year 1600–01, when Vrancx became a free master.

Early in his career Vrancx, who later joined a civic guard company, began to paint the small-scale cavalry scenes for which he was to become well known. Notable is his untraced *Battle between Lekkerbeetje and Bréauté on the Heath of Vught* (1601), of which numerous versions survive, including an incorrectly attributed copy (Antwerp, Kon. Mus. S. Kst.). Over half his oeuvre is devoted to this subject-matter, and, apart from Jan Snellinck, Vrancx was the principal artist to introduce the subject of cavalry battles to the Netherlands: in the southern Netherlands he was followed by Pieter Meulener (1602–54) and Jacques van der Wijhen (*b c*. 1588) and in France by Adam-Frans van der Meulen, who was a pupil of Pieter Snayers, himself a pupil of Vrancx. In the northern Netherlands Vrancx's influence can be seen clearly in the work of Esaias van de Velde and Pauwels van Hillegaert (1595/6–1640). Vrancx's cavalry scenes remained conservative, comparable with those by Antonio Tempesta.

Between *c*. 1602 and *c*. 1611 Vrancx produced his first treatments of palace architecture borrowed from Hans Vredeman de Vries (*see* ARCHITECTURAL PICTURES, §2), with groups of distinguished people enjoying themselves, and a moralizing undertone. The print after Vrancx by Jacob Matham of the *Parable of Lazarus and the Rich Man* (1606; Hollstein, xi, p. 220) is a good example, in which Vrancx organized the space according to a rigid central perspective (a recurring feature in subsequent works); another, later, example is his *Interior of the Jesuit Church in Antwerp* (Vienna, Ksthist. Mus.). He also applied this principle to landscape painting: his *Avenue with Trees and a Country House* (Hamburg, Ksthalle; wrongly attributed to Adriaen van de Venne) is echoed in Meindert Hobbema's famous *Avenue at Middelharnis* (1689; London, N.G.). Vrancx's trees are taller and less clumsy than before.

In 1610 Vrancx became a member of the Fraternity of SS Peter and Paul, a select society whose members included Peter Paul Rubens. In the guild year 1611–12 he was an associate dean and in the following year chief dean of Antwerp's Guild of St Luke. In 1612 he married Maria Pamphi, daughter of an art dealer and sister-in-law of the painter Tobias Verhaecht, who later became his daughter's godfather.

2. MATURE WORKS, FROM *c*. 1611. Not until the next stage in Vrancx's stylistic development, *c*. 1611–25, did his landscapes and the figures in them show the clear-cut and determined handling of form characteristic of his mature style. He achieved greater control of the representation of space and of large and more complex groups of figures. In this respect, such paintings as the *Siege of Ostend Seen from the Spanish Camp* (1618; ex-Lord Aldenham priv. col. see *Vlaamse kunst uit Brits bezit*, exh. cat., Bruges, 1956, fig. 41) and the *Festival of the 'Hail-cross' at Ekeren*

Sebastian Vrancx: *Festival of the 'Hail-cross' at Ekeren*, oil on wood, 565×1193 mm, 1622 (Munich, Alte Pinakothek)

(1622; Munich, Alte Pin.; see fig.) are high-points in his oeuvre.

Vrancx's subjects also encompass allegorical scenes, such as the Months and the Seasons, and religious and mythological subjects, which he presented as genre scenes with the emphasis on narrative detail. He was a member of the Antwerp chamber of rhetoricians, the Violieren (stocks), which had ties with the Guild of St Luke, and produced paintings for them in addition to his literary involvement (see Keersmaekers). From *c.* 1625 to 1647 Vrancx gave greater emphasis to the space than the figures in his paintings. A refinement, which originated *c.* 1620 in the 'aristocratic' characterization of horses, became a feature of the whole image, while the painting of trees became more 'woolly'. Vrancx continued painting until the end of his life; his final works exchange strength for gracefulness.

Vrancx often collaborated with other painters, providing staffage for Josse de Momper (e.g. *Wild Boar Hunt*, Amsterdam, Rijksmus.), Jan Breughel I (e.g. *Raid on a Convoy*, Vienna, Ksthist. Mus.), Tobias Verhaecht (e.g. *Hunting Adventure of Emperor Maximilian I*, Brussels, Mus. A. Anc.), Alexander Keirinck (e.g. *Landscape with Chasing Horsemen*, Darmstadt, Hess. Landesmus.), Jan van Balen (1611–54) and Frans Francken II together (e.g. *Rebus Arms* for the Violieren, 1618; Antwerp, Kon. Mus. S. Kst., on dep. Antwerp, Etnog. Mus.) and Pieter Neeffs (i) (e.g. *Church Interior*, 1613; Brussels, Mus. A. Anc.). Whenever he worked with other artists, Vrancx provided the figures. However, he usually painted the landscapes in his own works himself, with typically decorative foliage.

BIBLIOGRAPHY

Hollstein: *Dut. & Flem.*; Thieme–Becker; Wurzbach
K. van Mander: *Schilder-boeck* ([1603]–1604), fol. 295*v*
F. C. Legrand: 'Un *Combat de cavaliers* par Sébastien Vrancx', *Bul. Kon. Mus. Royaux B.-A. Belgique*, i (1952), pp. 95–102
J. Grauls: 'Het spreekwoordenschilderij van Sebastiaen Vrancx', *Bull. Kon. Mus. Royaux. B-A. Belgique*, ix (1960), pp. 107–64
M. H. Takacs: 'Un Tableau de Sébastien Vrancx à la Galerie des maîtres anciens', *Bull. Mus. N. Hongrois B.-A.*, xviii (1961), pp. 51–62
F. C. Legrand: *Les Peintres flamands de genre au XVIIe siècle* (Paris and Brussels, 1963), pp. 189–201 [good illus.]
A. Thijs: 'Het Hagelkruisfeest te Ekeren (1622) door S. Vrancx in de Alte Pinakothek te München', *Jb. Kon. Mus. S. Kst.* (1974), pp. 187–98
J. Vander Auwera: *Sebastiaen Vrancx (1573–1647): Een monografische benadering* (thesis, Ghent, Rijksuniv., 1979)
——: 'Sebastiaen Vrancx (1573–1647) en zijn samenwerking met Jan I Breughel (1568–1625)', *Jb. Kon. Mus. S. Kst.* (1981), pp. 135–51
A. A. Keersmaekers: 'De schilder Sebastiaen Vrancx (1573–1647) als rederijker', *Jb. Kon. Mus. S. Kst.* (1982), pp. 165–86
L. Wood Ruby: 'Sebastiaen Vrancx as Illustrator of Virgil's *Aeneid*', *Master Drgs*, xxviii/1 (1990), pp. 54–73
The Age of Rubens (exh. cat., ed. P. C. Sutton; Boston, Mus. F.A.; Toledo, Mus. A.; 1993–4), pp. 465–8

JOOST VANDER AUWERA

Vrangel', Nikolay (Nikolayevich), Baron (*b* Kiev province, 2 July 1880; *d* Warsaw, 15 July 1915). Russian art historian. One of the founders of Russian art history, in 1902, despite his youth and inexperience, he organized and compiled the catalogue for a retrospective exhibition of Russian portraits in the St Petersburg Academy of Sciences. This event proved one of the first penetrating visual assessments of 18th- and early 19th-century Russian culture. His role in the organization of exhibitions was fundamental: through his efforts the first Russian solo

exhibitions were held (of Orest Kiprensky and Aleksey Venetsianov, both in 1911, at the Russian Museum in St Petersburg), for which he wrote and compiled the catalogues, as well as the important exhibition *One Hundred Years of French Art, 1812–1912* (St Petersburg, 1912). In 1904 he published the first catalogue of the painting and sculpture in the Russian Museum of Tsar Alexander III. In 1907 he joined the editorial board of the new magazine *Staryye gody* ('Bygone years'), in which he published many important articles, including a pioneering study of Russian miniatures (Oct 1909) and his influential research into the influence of foreign artists working in Russia in the post-Petrine era (July–Sept 1911). He also became a director of the new Museum of Old Petersburg (from 1909); a founder-member of the Society for the Protection and Preservation in Russia of Monuments of Art and Antiquity (from 1909), in which one of his activities, in collaboration with Mstislav Dobuzhinsky and Sergey Sudeykin, was the revival of Russian folk plays and *balagan* (fair-booth acts); a critic for and co-editor with Sergey Makovsky of the Symbolist arts periodical *Apollon* (1910–12); and the author of the only pre-revolutionary comprehensive survey of Russian sculpture.

WRITINGS

Podrobnyy illustrirovanyy katalog vystavki russkoy portretnoy zhivopisi za 150 let (1700–1850) [A detailed illustrated catalogue of an exhibition of 150 years of Russian portraiture (1700–1850)] (St Petersburg, 1902)
Russkiy muzey imperatora Aleksandra III: Zhivopis' i skul'ptura [The Russian Museum of Emperor Alexander III: painting and sculpture], 2 vols (St Petersburg, 1904)
Katalog starinnykh proizvedeniy iskusstva, khranyashchikhsya v Imp. Akademii khudozhestv [Catalogue of antique works of art in the Imperial Academy of Art] (St Petersburg, 1908)
Aleksey Gavriilovich Venetsianov v chastnykh sobraniyakh [Aleksey Gavriilovich Venetsianov in private collections] (St Petersburg, 1911)
Istoriya skul'ptury [The history of sculpture] (1911), v of *Istoriya russkogo iskusstva* [History of Russian art], ed. I. Grabar' (Moscow, 1910–15)
Orest Adamovich Kiprensky v chastnykh sobraniyakh [Kiprensky in private collections] (St Petersburg, 1911)

BIBLIOGRAPHY

A. N. Benois and others: *Venok Vrangelyu* [A wreath for Vrangel'] (Petrograd, 1916)

JEREMY HOWARD, SERGEY KUZNETSOV

Vredeman de Vries, Hans [Jan] [Frisio, Johan] (*b* Leeuwarden, 1527; *d* ?Antwerp, ?1606). Dutch designer, architect and painter, active in the southern Netherlands and throughout the Holy Roman Empire. Though an artist of many talents, it was through his engravings that he most influenced his contemporaries. The distribution of his works by the publishers of Antwerp made him one of the leading and best-known exponents of Mannerist decoration and the instigator of a new urban vision in northern and central Europe.

1. LIFE. He first studied drawing in his native Leeuwarden in Friesland for five years with Reijer Gerritsz., a glass painter from Amsterdam, who moved to Leuven *c.* 1544. Vredeman de Vries then spent two years in Kampen, before moving to Mechelen, where he learnt to paint in watercolour on canvas, a technique typical of that town. In 1549 he assisted Pieter Coecke van Aelst on the decoration of the triumphal arches constructed for the ceremonial entry into Antwerp of Charles V and his son, the future Philip II. On Vredeman de Vries's return to

Friesland, he was briefly in Kollum, where he is reported to have applied himself 'night and day' to copying the works of Sebastiano Serlio and Vitruvius from editions published and translated by Coecke van Aelst. Vredeman de Vries returned to Mechelen to stay with the painter and art dealer Claude I Dorici [Dorizy, de Roisy] (*fl* 1536–65), who asked him to complete a perspective painting by Cornelis van Vianen left unfinished at his death. It was this that first stimulated Vredeman de Vries's great interest in perspective.

Vredeman de Vries probably married in Mechelen: his wife was Johanna van Muysen, possibly a sister of the painter and sculptor Gielis van Muysen (*fl c.* 1560); he then settled in Antwerp, perhaps in 1561. After his first wife's death, he married Sara van der Elsmaer on 10 February 1566; she was the daughter of the sculptor Wouter van der Elsmaer (*fl* 1533–86). They had at least three sons, two of whom became architectural draughtsmen and painters and collaborated with their father: Saloman Vredeman de Vries (1556–1604) and Paul Vredeman de Vries (1567–after 1630).

In 1570 Hans set up in only five days a triumphal arch for the passage of Queen Anne of Austria, wife of Philip II, through Antwerp. Then, in July of that year, he left Antwerp with his family to escape religious persecution. He lived for a number of years in Aachen, then in Liège, before returning to Antwerp in 1575. In 1582 one P. Leys commissioned him to decorate the triumphal arches and floats for the ceremonial entry of Francis, Duke of Anjou (known through engravings sometimes attributed to Vredeman de Vries himself). After the fall of Antwerp in 1585, he left the city for good and went to Wolfenbüttel at the invitation of Julius, Duke of Brunswick (*reg* 1568–89). In 1591 Vredeman de Vries settled in Hamburg, whence he was called to Danzig (now Gdańsk) to carry out decorations at the Polish court and town hall. From Danzig he went to Prague, where his son Paul decorated a ceiling and the reception rooms of Emperor Rudolf II's castle. Finally, on the advice of Gillis Congnet, he left Hamburg for Amsterdam and finally settled in The Hague.

2. WORK.

(i) Designs. During the 1550s Vredeman de Vries began to produce architectural and ornamental designs for engraved series; these were invariably engraved by others. The few dozen surviving original drawings by him (Berlin, Kstbib. & Mus.; Vienna, Albertina; Leeuwarden, Prov. Bib. Friesland) represent only a small part of his oeuvre. Over a period of 33 years (from 1555 to 1587) he published in Antwerp with Hieronymus Cock, Gerard de Jode (i) and Phillip Galle a total of 27 volumes with 483 engravings after his designs. While living in The Hague, he published with Hendrik I Hondius (ii) a two-part work entitled *Perspective id est celeberrima ars inspicient is* (1604–5), presenting the synthesis of his knowledge in 74 engravings, and the architectural treatise *Architectura* (1606), to which his son Paul contributed some of the 31 engravings. All these collections were composed of models intended for practising artisans, painters and architects. Most of the works were printed in several editions, both during the author's lifetime and after his death.

1. Hans Vredeman de Vries (after): *Perspective View of Antwerp*, engraving, *c.* 1560; pl. I of *Scenographiae, sive perspectivae* (Antwerp, 1560) (Brussels, Bibliothèque Royale Albert 1er)

Vredeman de Vries also produced numerous series of designs for scrolls, grotesques (*see* GROTESQUE, fig. 2), vases and trophies. For artists who had never been to Italy, these engravings provided a vast repertory of antique motifs and grotesques in the style of Raphael and could be adapted to every medium from goldsmithing to tapestry; extraordinarily, Vredeman de Vries appears never to have visited Italy himself. The Mannerist fantasy of his engravings was in tune with the taste of the day; their rich inventiveness anticipates Baroque decoration, and his work stands on the borderline between the two styles.

It was, above all, the collections of his engravings devoted to architecture and perspective that were the most widely disseminated and most frequently reprinted. These include the *Scenographiae, sive perspectivae* (1560/reprinted 1563 and enlarged 1601 as *Variae architecturae formae*; see fig. 1); three series of models of the five architectural orders, Doric and Ionic (1565), Corinthian and Composite (1565) and Tuscan (1578), reprinted together in 1581, with a second undated edition; a series of caryatids (*c.* 1565); the *Architectura oder Bauung der Antiquen aus dem Vitruvius*, which had eight pages of text and was published in 1577 in three versions, German, Dutch and French (all retaining the German title), and reprinted in Dutch and French in 1581, 1597, 1598 and 1615; *Perspective. . .*, published in The Hague (1604–5) and reproduced in the *Oeuvres mathématiques traitans de la géométrie, perspective. . .* by Samuel Marolois, which reached 12 editions between 1612 and 1651; and *Architectura* (1606), which was reprinted ten times between 1607 and 1662 (for illustration of gable designs from *Architectura*, *see* GABLE, DECORATIVE).

Linked to these architectural collections are several series dealing with more precise themes: one on cenotaphs (1563 and two undated reprints); two on fountains and wells (1568 and 1573); two on gardens including the *Hortorum . . . formae* (1583) and one on models for carpenters, the *Differents pourtraicts de menuiserie. . .* (*c.* 1585).

Through his engravings, Vredeman de Vries put the work of Vitruvius within the reach of all and initiated the art of perspective, addressing such particular problems as stairwells, high towers and views from a high or low position. Moreover, his examples suggested an architectural and urban ideal that spread through the Netherlands in the 17th century, to Germany, central Europe and even to England. This ideal is embodied in buildings with well differentiated storeys, often extensively open by means of porticos and galleries, by columns articulating the cross beams, voluted consoles supporting string courses and cornices; and balustrades concealing the roofline and often bearing obelisques supported on four spheres. His style of town planning is represented by spacious, regular plans, with the main thoroughfare bordered by arcades that form a ground-floor gallery below solid structures above. The theatrical effect is further accentuated by the presence of water courses, fountains or terraced waterfalls. The town of WOLFENBÜTTEL provides an example of this urban ideal.

(ii) Architecture. Vredeman de Vries was, above all, a designer and architectural theorist, and his actual building achievements were few and on a quite modest scale. In Antwerp, he is attributed with the belvedere (1565–7) erected below the van Straelen House in Korte St Annastraat and with the rebuilding of the gable (1578) of the House of the Four Winds in Gildenkamerstraat. The town archives have monogrammed plans of the abaci for the restoration of the citadel (destr.). At Wolfenbüttel, where Vredeman de Vries's theories visibly influenced the organization of the town, the only building directly attributed to him is the chancellery.

(iii) Paintings. Vredeman de Vries's curiosity about the optical effects of perspective led him from an early stage to create *trompe l'oeil* wall paintings, none of which survive. Some idea of this aspect of his work can be gained from the few copies (Antwerp, Gemeente Archv) of the wall paintings that decorated the council room of the Antwerp Stadhuis.

Very little is known of his easel painting. At the beginning of his career, Vredeman de Vries painted architectural settings for other artists, as in Michiel Coxcie's *Circumcision* (Mechelen, St Romboutskathedraal). An invoice issued by the 17th-century Antwerp merchants Forchoudt records 'perspectives painted by Vredeman and figures by Maarten van Cleve', and it is likely that Vredeman de Vries contributed to other collaborative projects

2. Hans and Paul Vredeman de Vries: *Palace Scene with Figures Strolling*, oil on canvas, 1.37×1.74 m, 1596 (Vienna, Kunsthistorisches Museum)

of this nature, which were quite common. He also collaborated with his son Paul (see fig. 2).

The paintings entirely by his hand and reliably dated were nearly all executed during the last period of his life. The *Return of Antwerp to the Rule of Philip II* (1586; Antwerp, Stadsarchf) commemorates the fall of the city in 1585; a triptych of the *Redemption* (1590; Wolfenbüttel, Hauptkirche) was painted for the cenotaph of the Duke of Brunswick; *Orpheus Charming the Animals* (1596) for the court of Gdańsk (Artus Court; destr. World War II). All these works were official commissions, bearing witness to the reputation acquired by the artist.

See also ARCHITECTURAL PICTURES, §2.

PRINTS

No complete catalogue of the many editions of Vredeman de Vries's prints is available, and it is recognized that the following list cannot therefore be comprehensive.

Multarum variarum'que protractionum (Compartimenta vulgus pictorum vocat) (Antwerp, Gerard de Jode, 1555); facs. edn (Brussels, 1870)

Variarum protractionum (vulgo Compartimenta vocant) (Antwerp, Gerard de Jode, 1555); facs. edn (Brussels, 1870)

Untitled series of three scrollwork cartouches (Antwerp, Hieronymus Cock, c. 1555–7)

Scenographiae, sive perspectivae (ut aedificia, hoc modo ad opticam excitata) (Antwerp, Hieronymus Cock, 1560, 2/1563; enlarged as *Variae architecturae formae* (Antwerp, 1601); facs. edns (Brussels, 1877, and Amsterdam, 1979)

Untitled series of oval architectural views (Antwerp, Hieronymus Cock, c. 1560–62)

Untitled series of grotesque cartouches (Antwerp, Hieronymus Cock, c. 1560–63)

Untitled series of perspectival architectural views (Antwerp, Hieronymus Cock, 1562)

Pictores, statuarii, architecti … uarias caenotaphiorum … (Antwerp, Hieronymus Cock, 1563, 2/[n.d.], 3/[n.d.])

Untitled series of ornamental trapezoids (Antwerp, Hieronymus Cock, 1564–5)

Den eersten boeck, ghemaect opde twee colomnen Dorica en Ionica (Antwerp, Hieronymus Cock, 1565)

Das ander Buech, gemacht auff die zway Colonnen, Corinthia und Composita (Antwerp, Hieronymus Cock, 1565, 2/1578)

Caryatidum (vulgus termas vocat) sive athlantidum (Antwerp, Gerard de Jode, c. 1565); facs. edn (Brussels, 1870)

Grottesco in diverse manieren (Antwerp, Gerard de Jode, c. 1565, 2/1612); facs. edn (Brussels, 1870)

Icones duodecim Caesarum Roma (Antwerp, Gerard de Jode, c. 1565–9)

Quantum forma Fugax (Antwerp, Hieronymus Cock, 1566)

Artis perspectivae plurium generum elegantissimae formulae, multigenis fontibus (Nijmegen, Gerard de Jode, 1568, 2/The Hague, 1604, 3/Amsterdam, 1633; Fr. trans., Leiden, 1604; Ger. trans., Amsterdam, 1628)

Exercitatio alphabetica nova et utilissima (Antwerp, Christoph Plantin, 1569)

Panoplia seu armamentarium ac ornamenta (Antwerp, Gerard de Jode, 1572, 2/1585)

Deorum dearumque capita ex vetustis numismatibus (Antwerp, Phillip Galle, 1573)

Untitled series with putti and fountains (Antwerp, Phillip Galle, 1573)

Architectura oder Bauung der Antiquen aus dem Vitruvius (Antwerp, Gerard de Jode, 1577, 2/1581, 3/1597, 4/1598, 5/1615) [1st edn pubd in Ger., Dut. and Fr.; later edns in Dut. and Fr.]

Theatrum vitae humanae (Antwerp, Petrus Balt, 1577)

De orden Tuschana (Antwerp, 1578, 2/[n.d.])

La Ioyeuse & Magnifique Entree de Monsigneur Francoys, fils de France … d'Anvers (Antwerp, Christoph Plantin, 1582)

Hortorum viridariorumque elegantes et multiplicis formae (Antwerp, Phillip Galle, 1583, 2/c. 1600, 3/1615, 4/1635, 5/1655); facs. edn (Amsterdam, 1980)

Differents pourtraicts de menuiserie asçauoir portaux (Antwerp, Phillip Galle, c. 1585); repr. as *Verscheyden schrynwerck als portalen* (Amsterdam, C. J. Visscher, 1630, 2/1658); facs. edn (Brussels, 1869)

Untitled series of gardens (Antwerp, Phillip Galle, 1587, 2/c. 1600, 3/1635); facs. edn (Amsterdam, 1980)

Untitled series of gardens after Pieter van der Borcht (Antwerp, Phillip Galle, c. 1590)

Amphitheatrum sapientiae aeternae solius verae ([n.p.], 1602)

Perspective id est celeberrima ars inspicient is, pt 1 (The Hague, Hendrick Hondius, 1604)

Perspective id est celeberrima ars inspicient is, pt 2 (Leiden, Hendrick Hondius, 1605)

Architectura: Die hooghe en vermaerde conste bestaende in vijf manieren van edifitien (The Hague, Hendrick Hondius, 1606, 2/1607, 11/1662)

BIBLIOGRAPHY

Thieme–Becker
K. van Mander: *Schilder-boeck* ([1603]–1604), fols 265r–267r
C. H. Peters: *Hans Vredeman de Vries: Het leven en de werken van de Nederlandsche kunstenaar* (The Hague, 1895)
F. Thöne: 'Hans Vredeman de Vries in Wolfenbüttel', *Braunschweig. Jb.*, xli (1960), pp. 47–68
F. Blockmans: 'Hans Vredeman de Vries te Antwerpen', *Rev. Antwerp.*, viii/1 (April 1962), pp. 20–42
F. Thöne: 'Werke des Hans Vredeman de Vries in Wolfenbüttel', *Pantheon*, xx (1962), pp. 248–55, 335–6
E. Iwanoyko: *Gdański okres Hansa Vredemana de Vries* [Hans Vredemana de Vries' Gdańsk period] (Poznań, 1963)
H. Mielke: *Hans Vredeman de Vries* (diss., Berlin, Freie U., 1967)
U. M. Schneede: 'Interieurs von Hans und Paul Vredeman', *Ned. Ksthist. Jb.*, xviii (1967), pp. 125–66
J. Ehrman: 'Hans Vredeman de Vries (Leeuwarden 1527–Anvers 1606)', *Gaz. B.-A.*, n. s. 5, xciii (1979), pp. 13–26
Hans Vredeman de Vries, 1526–ca. 1606 (exh. cat., The Hague, Rijksmus. Meermanno-Westreenianum; Leeuwarden, Gemeentelijk Mus. Het Princessehof; 1979)
T. DaCosta Kaufmann: *The School of Prague: Painting at the Court of Rudolf II* (Chicago and London, 1988), pp. 287–91
M. van de Winckel: 'Hans Vredeman de Vries', *Les Traités d'architecture de la Renaissance*, ed. J. Guillaume (Paris, 1988), pp. 453–8

MADELEINE VAN DE WINCKEL

Vredis, Judocus [Jodocus] [Pelsers, Joest] (*b* Vreden, *c*. 1473–4; *d* Marienburg, nr Dülmen, 16 Dec 1540). German sculptor. In 1493 he entered the Carthusian monastery of Marienburg, becoming procurator in 1506 and prior in 1531. He presumably learnt his skills in the pottery town of Vreden, Westphalia. He produced devotional pictures and house altars as low reliefs completely in the tradition of the Utrecht 'picture bakers' or 'picture makers' using white pipeclay and fired hollow moulds (*see* NETHERLANDS, THE, §VII, 1). He signed most of his works *Judocus Vredis* or *F*[rater] *Judocus Vredis Cartus*[iensis]. His subject-matter was strictly limited: the Virgin as the Queen of Heaven, the Holy Trinity, the Annunciation, the Crucifixion, the virgin martyrs—SS Catherine of Alexandria, Barbara, Margaret and Dorothy—and also SS Anne and Mary Magdalene. He mainly worked from drawings by Master E.S. and Israhel van Meckenem (ii), elaborately decorating the figures formed in the mould and modelling them while the clay was soft using stencils, small metal stamps and punches. He embellished the hems of robes and headgear and added attributes, inscriptions, flowers, leaves and fruit. Most of his surviving work is in the Westfälisches Landesmuseum and the Cathedral Treasury in Münster.

BIBLIOGRAPHY

Thieme–Becker
B. Meier: 'Judocus Vredis und die Utrechter Bilderbäcker', *Z. Westfalen*, vii (1915), pp. 105–34
T. Rensing: 'Über das Leben des Jodocus Vredis', *Z. Westfalen*, xxv (1940), pp. 37–8
J. Leeuwenberg: 'Die Ausstrahlung Utrechter Tonplastik', *Festschrift Theodor Müller* (Munich, 1965), pp. 151–66
C. Göllmann: *Die Kartause in Weddern bei Dülmen* (Coesfeld, 1975)

G. Jászai: 'Aspekte der monastischen Kunst in Westfalen', *Monastisches Westfalen: Klöster und Stifte, 800–1800* (exh. cat., ed. G. Jászai; Münster, Westfäl. Landesmus., 1982), pp. 237–86
H. Arnold: 'Judocus Vredis', *Imagination des Unsichtbaren: 1200 Jahre bildende Kunst im Bistum Münster*, ii (exh. cat., ed. G. Jászai; Münster, Westfäl. Landesmus., 1993), pp. 451–7

GÉZA JÁSZAI

Vrel, Jacobus (*fl* 1654–?1670). Dutch painter. Some 38 paintings, depicting domestic interiors, street scenes and a church interior, have been attributed to this enigmatic artist. Four copies after his works are possibly autograph; one drawing has also been ascribed to him. Over half of Vrel's paintings are signed or bear traces of signatures that were altered to read *Johannes Vermeer* or *Pieter de Hooch*, with whose paintings Vrel's work was often confused. Indeed, Theophile Thoré discussed Vermeer as a townscape painter largely on the basis of works that were actually by Vrel.

Vrel has been associated on stylistic grounds with the Delft school of painters in the circle of de Hooch and Vermeer, but this has been questioned since his *Woman at a Window* (1654; Vienna, Ksthist. Mus.) predates comparable works by these two artists. There is also no firm basis for believing he worked in Delft. His name does not appear in the Delft archives and his seemingly naive style would be unusual in an artist working in a major Dutch city. Certain architectural elements in his street scenes may indicate that he worked in an outlying area such as Friesland, Flanders or the lower Rhineland. However, there is reason to believe that Vrel had ties with a major art centre. The *Woman at a Window* and two other paintings by Vrel are listed in Archduke Leopold Wilhelm's inventory (1659), which suggests that they were available in one of the cities visited by the Archduke's agent and curator David Teniers (ii). It also indicates that Vrel's paintings were highly regarded during his lifetime.

Vrel's interiors show an affinity to the schools of Amsterdam and Delft, but his narrow, cramped street scenes in vertical format, probably painted later in his career, are paralleled in works by Haarlem artists. The townscape painter Gerrit Berckheyde occasionally used a similar vertical format for his street views. A painting by Nicolaes Hals (1628–86), *Grote Houtstraat* (Haarlem, Frans Halsmus.), is even closer to Vrel's work in composition, tonality and the type of figures depicted.

Vrel's style is remarkable for its clear and controlled simplicity. He rejected the traditional Dutch detailed description of surfaces in favour of the depiction of lofty spaces, which often convey an eerie feeling of emptiness. Typical of his quiet domestic scenes is an *Interior* (Detroit, MI, Inst. A.), set in a high, bare room where a mother is absorbed in combing the hair of a child whose face is hidden in her lap; another child looks through a doorway, out of the painting, to the world beyond. Equally unusual is the total anonymity of Vrel's street scenes, which depict unremarkable back streets and their ordinary inhabitants. In the *Street Scene* (date barely legible, ?1670; Hartford, CT, Wadsworth Atheneum) both social and commercial exchange are absent. The bakery, which appears repeatedly in Vrel's works, attracts no customers; the baker watches from a window high above the shop and a sign announces that the house is to let. A pair of Capuchin monks

disappearing into a chapel adds to the sense of mystery and silence.

BIBLIOGRAPHY
T. Thoré: 'Van der Meer de Delft', *Gaz. B.-A.*, xxi (1866), pp. 458–70
C. Brière-Misme: 'Un "Intimiste" hollandais: Jacob Vrel', *Rev. A. Anc. & Mod.*, lxviii (1935), pp. 97–114, 157–72
G. Regnier: 'Jacob Vrel, un Vermeer du pauvre', *Gaz. B.-A.*, n.s. 6, lxxi (1968), pp. 269–82
Masters of Seventeenth-century Dutch Genre Painting (exh. cat., ed. P. C. Sutton; Philadelphia, Mus. A.; W. Berlin, Gemäldegal.; London, RA; 1984), pp. 352–4
E. A. Honig: 'Looking in(to) Jacob Vrel', *Yale J. Crit.*, iii/1 (1989)

ELIZABETH ALICE HONIG

Vrelant [Vredeland; Vredelant; Vreeland; Vreelant; Vreland; Vreyland; Vreylant; ?Wielant; ?Wyelant]**, Willem** [Guillaume; Willam] **(Backer van) (de, du)** (*b* Utrecht; *fl* 1449; *d* Bruges, 1481). Netherlandish illuminator. He is considered one of the most influential illuminators working in Bruges during the third quarter of the 15th century. Despite this, there is no consensus about attributions to Vrelant, his studio or imitators. He is not known to have had any pupils, and the documentary evidence for studio works is slight; on the other hand, the different artistic levels of the works attributed to this artist and his followers are very marked.

Vrelant was born in Utrecht, the son of Jacob, and was registered there in 1449 as a citizen and illuminator. Among the manuscripts ascribed to his period in Utrecht is the Montfort Hours (Vienna, Österreich. Nbib., Cod. s.n. 12878), on which Vrelant collaborated with the Master of Catherine of Cleves. The manuscript is dated to *c.* 1450 on codicological grounds and because of its immature style. Another early work is the Hours of Isabella the Catholic (Madrid, Pal. Real), on which he collaborated with the Master of Arsenal 575, whose activities (*c.* 1450) have been distinguished from Vrelant's oeuvre (Farquhar; Pächt, 1983).

Vrelant moved to Bruges before 1454, from which date he was an active and prominent member of the Bruges Guild of St John the Evangelist; his annual contributions to the guild are recorded until his death, with one gap from 1456 to 1459/61. Records cite him as a citizen of Bruges from 1456. The numerous Books of Hours that comprise the best-known part of Vrelant's work in Bruges account for the popularity of his style there. Only a few of these, however, can be attributed to Vrelant himself (e.g. Malibu, CA, Getty Mus., MS. Ludwig IX.8; see fig.; and Vienna, Österreich. Nbib., Cod. 1987), while others in his style were made for the Spanish market (e.g. Chicago, IL, Newberry Lib., MS. 39; Brussels, Bib. Albert 1er, MSS IV. 35 and IV. 375; Vienna, Österreich. Nbib., Cod. s.n. 13243). Several important manuscripts can be dated to this period: Vincent of Beauvais's *Le Miroir historial* (Paris, Bib. N., MS. fr. 308–II), executed *c.* 1455 for Louis de Gruuthuse; a copy of the *Traité sur la salutation angélique* (Brussels, Bib. Royale Albert 1er, MS. 9270) dated 1461, with just one fine miniature of the *Annunciation* (fol. 2*v*); the Breviary of Philip the Good (Brussels, Bib. Royale Albert 1er, MSS 9026 and 9511), which has two portraits of the Duke and must be dated before 1467. The latter is a complex work, the illumination of which is derived in part from Jean Le Tavernier, while the borders seem French.

Another commission from Philip the Good is possibly documented. In 1468 a payment was recorded to 'Guillaume Wyelant', a name subsequently identified with Vrelant. The 60 miniatures in the second part of the *Chronicles of Hainault* (Brussels, Bib. Royale Albert 1er, MS. 9243) were executed by Wyelant on commission for Philip the Good, Duke of Burgundy, and completed for his son Charles the Bold. Farquhar explained the variant spelling of the artist's name as a copyist's mistake. Pächt, Jenni and Thoss (1983) cited the great influence of the illuminator of these miniatures on manuscript painting in Bruges as well as his relations with the Burgundian court. For von Euw and Plotzek the stylistic similarity of the *Chronicles* with the earlier, Montfort Hours, is direct evidence for accepting the identification with Vrelant. The *Chronicles* are thus regarded as the highpoint of his style. His only work documented with certainty, however, is a *Life of Christ* (destr.); records show that he illuminated this manuscript in 1469 and was also responsible for finishing the binding. Surviving works from this later period include the Missal of Cardinal Ferry of Clugny (Siena, Bib. Com. Intronati, MS. X.V.I), with a frontispiece of the *Cardinal Kneeling before the Virgin* (c. 1473). Together with three other leading Bruges illuminators, Vrelant also worked c. 1475–80 on the lavish Hours of Mary of Burgundy (Vienna, Österreich. Nbib., Cod. 1857). From 1481 the Bruges guild records show payments for memorial masses, suggesting that Vrelant must have died by this date. His widow continued his work until her death in 1494. Thereafter there are citations of the work of Betkin Vrelant, probably a daughter.

Distinguishing Vrelant's personal style is made difficult by the numerous imitations of it in the Bruges milieu. It is characterized by a sober and yet elegant manner, combined with a use of intense colours. The motionless figures have expressionless faces, blushing cheeks and thick lips, and drapery folds are highlighted in gold. Interiors are often set in a half-open building with a view out to a landscape; thin pillars determine the rhythm of the space, which is completed by vaults and tiled floors decorated with letters. Much attention is given to the landscape, in which winding rivers and whimsically drawn paths connect the various levels—generally steeply rising clumps of rocks, groups of trees and towns silhouetted on the horizon. The style of Vrelant's borders is adopted from Bruges manuscripts: the basis is flowering acanthus with curling, blue and gold leaves, to which he added small, delicate details, for example a leaping white stag with golden antlers or one lady crowning another. He also painted borders with gold and grey acanthus. His surviving manuscripts reveal that Vrelant also worked in grisaille, partly combined with colour: for example the copy of Leonardo Bruni's *De primo bello punica* (Brussels, Bib. Royale Albert 1er, MS. 10777), Christine de Pisan's *L'Epistre d'Othéa* (Erlangen, Ubib., MS. 2361) and a *Life of St Catherine* (Paris, Bib. N., MS. fr. 6449).

Vrelant's compositions are modelled on the work of such south Netherlanders as Jan van Eyck and the Limbourg brothers, who were known in Utrecht as well as in Bruges. Van Eyck's *Holy Face* (untraced) was the

Willem Vrelant: *St John the Evangelist*; miniature from a Book of Hours, 255×172 mm, Bruges, *c.* 1460 (Malibu, CA, J. Paul Getty Museum, MS. Ludwig IX. 8, fol. 45*r*)

source used by Vrelant and his followers to illustrate the prayer 'Salve sancta facies' in Books of Hours (e.g. Vienna, Österreich. Nbib., Cods 1987 and s.n. 13243; Baltimore, MD, Walters A.G., MS. W. 220; Munich, Bayer. Staatsbib., Cod. gall. 40; and Madrid, Bib. N., MS. Vit 24-2). Vrelant must have also known Hans Memling, as he contributed between 1477 and 1479 to the payment for Memling's triptych, commissioned by the Guild of St John the Evangelist for Eekhout Abbey, which included portraits of Vrelant and his wife. Although Weale identified this work as the *Panorama with Scenes from the Passion* (Turin, Gal. Sabauda), this was challenged, and Farquhar suggested that the couple's portraits appear on the surviving wings of a *Crucifixion* (New York, Pierpont Morgan Lib.).

BIBLIOGRAPHY

Thieme–Becker

W. H. J. Weale: 'Documents inédits sur les enlumineurs de Bruges', *Le Beffroi*, ii (1864–5), pp. 301–2; iv (1872–3), pp. 111–19, 233–337

P. Durrieu: *La Miniature flamande au temps de la cour de Bourgogne, 1415–1530* (Paris, 1921), pp. 20–21, 52–4, pls xi–xiv

F. Winkler: *Die flämische Buchmalerei des XV. und XVI. Jahrhunderts* (Leipzig, 1925, rev. with addenda by G. Dogaer, Amsterdam, 1978), pp. 70–74, pls 35–7

V. Leroquais: *Le Bréviaire de Philippe le Bon* (Brussels, 1929)

C. Gaspar and F. Lyna: *Philippe le Bon et ses beaux livres* (Brussels, 1942), p. 30, pls xxvi–xxviii

Le Siècle d'or de la miniature flamande: Le Mécénat de Philippe le Bon (exh. cat. by L. M. J. Delaissé, Brussels, Bib. Royale Albert 1er; Amsterdam, Rijksmus.; 1959), nos 100–10, 122–6, 129, 131–3, 137–42, 149, 224–5, pl. 46

F. Unterkircher and A. de Schrijver: *Gebetbuch Karls des Kühnen vel potius Stundenbuch der Maria von Burgund*, Codices selecti, xiv (Graz, 1969) [facs. and commentary]

'The Vrelant Atelier', *French and Flemish Illuminated Manuscripts from Chicago Collections* (exh. cat., Chicago, IL, Newberry Lib., 1969), nos 5–9

O. Pächt, U. Jenni and D. Thoss: *Die illuminierten Handschriften der Österreichischen Nationalbibliothek: Holländische Schule* (Vienna, 1975), pp. 24–36, figs 39–62, pl. iii [Montfort Hours]

J. D. Farquhar: *Creation and Imitation: The Work of a Fifteenth-century Manuscript Illuminator*, Nova University Studies in the Humanities, i (Fort Lauderdale, 1976)

A. von Euw and J. M. Plotzek: *Die Handschriften der Sammlung Ludwig*, ii (Cologne, 1982), pp. 142–59, pls 139–214 [identification prob. pp. 122–4, 152–4]

O. Pächt, U. Jenni and D. Thoss: *Die illuminierten Handschriften der Österreichischen Nationalbibliothek: Flämische Schule*, i (Vienna, 1983), pp. 85–103 [identification prob. pp. 90–91]; ii (Vienna, 1990), pp. 69–85, pl. x, figs 102–50 [Hours of Mary of Burgundy]

G. Dogaer: *Flemish Miniature Painting in the 15th and 16th Centuries* (Amsterdam, 1987), pp. 99–105, figs 54–9 [list of attrib. MSS]

Flämische Buchmalerei: Handschriftenschätze aus dem Burgunderreich (exh. cat., ed. D. Thoss; Vienna, Österreich. Nbib., 1987), nos 7–9, 16, figs 4, 7–9, 36–7, 39

K. van der Horst: *Illuminated and Decorated Medieval Manuscripts in the University Library, Utrecht: An Illustrated Catalogue* (Maarssen, 1989), p. x

M. Smeyers and B. Cardon: 'Utrecht and Bruges: South and North "Boundless" Relations in the 15th Century', *Masters and Miniatures. Proceedings of the Congress on Medieval Manuscript Illumination in the Northern Netherlands: Utrecht, 1989*, pp. 89–108 [99–104]

J. M. Caswell: 'Two Manuscripts from the Chroniques II Workshop: *Chroniques de Hainaut*, Volume II and Morgan-Mâcon Golden Legend', *Rev. Belge Archéol. & Hist.*, lxii (1993), pp. 17–45

B. Bousmanne: *Prolégomènes à la constitution et à l'interprétation d'un corpus des manuscrits attribués au groupe Vrelant: Un Aspect de l'enluminure dans les Pays-Bas méridionaux au XVe siècle* (diss., Leuven, U. Catholique, 1994)

D. PROSKE-VAN HEERDT

Vretblad, Maud (*b* Fröson, Jämtlant, 10 Aug 1942). Swedish architect. She received a degree in architecture in 1970 from the Royal Institute of Technology, Stockholm. She undertook additional studies in social science (1972–3) and also at the Royal Academy of Fine Arts School of Architecture, Stockholm. From the mid-1970s she was an associate of the architectural firm Berg Arkitektkontor AB in Stockholm. Her built works include factories, industrial workshops and corporate offices. She has also renovated several buildings. Vretblad's work combines a clean, flowing, essentially Modernist geometry with inviting open spaces, such as covered internal courtyards. In her renovation and redevelopment (1986) of the Bryggmastaren complex in central Stockholm for example, glass-enclosed office spaces look down into a courtyard restaurant. The glazed roof allows for vast amounts of natural light, while providing protection from the harsh outer climate. With this project, which converted an old public building for new use, she made a significant contribution to the regeneration of Stockholm's city centre. Similar concepts appear in the headquarters (1988) of Linjeflyg, Sweden's domestic airline, at Arlanda Airport, Stockholm. Offices face either outward, with views of the Arlanda forests, or inward to the central courtyard. Even the inner offices have a connection with the natural environment, provided by pivoting windows bringing in reflections of sky and natural light from the glass roof of the courtyard. Such considerations reflect Vretblad's basic philosophy, which is concerned with the way in which occupants will experience and use a building. She therefore designed 'from the inside outwards, starting from the individual's need to function in the company of others'.

WRITINGS
'Målargarten 1', *Arkitektur* [Stockholm], lxxxv/10 (1985), pp. 18–22 [Bryggmastaren complex; Eng. summary p. 45]

BIBLIOGRAPHY
C. Lorenz: *Women in Architecture: A Contemporary Perspective* (New York, 1990)

Vriendt, de. *See* FLORIS.

Vries [Fries], **Adriaen** [Adrian] **de** (*b* The Hague, *c.* 1545; *d* Prague, *bur* 15 Dec 1626). Dutch sculptor and draughtsman, active in Italy and central Europe. He is particularly associated with the court of Rudolf II, Holy Roman Emperor, in Prague, to which he carried the sophisticated Florentine Mannerist court style of Giambologna. Baldinucci recorded de Vries as a collaborator with Giambologna in Florence. There is documentary evidence of his presence there in 1581 and 1585; from 1586 until 1588 he worked with Pompeo Leoni in Milan on the high altarpiece for the Escorial; in 1588 there is mention of him as a court sculptor in Turin. However, his first documented independent work is the over life-size bronze group of *Mercury and Psyche* (1593; Paris, Louvre) produced for Rudolf II, a work that owes much in composition and style to similar two-figure groups by Giambologna.

From 1595 to 1602 de Vries worked in Augsburg, where he produced the works for which, apart from the *Mercury and Psyche* group, he is probably best known: the bronze Mercury Fountain (1599) and the bronze Hercules Fountain (1597–1602), both of which are in Maximilianstrasse in Augsburg. Typologically, the more ornately executed Hercules Fountain represents a development of late 16th-century Florentine fountain designs. He probably returned to Prague before its inauguration and in 1601 was appointed Kammerbildhauer. At this period he seems to have produced mainly small-scale works in bronze, although he is known to have modelled stucco or terracotta sculptures (destr.) for the Emperor's new apartments in the Hradčin.

Among de Vries's most important works were two bronze portrait busts of *Rudolf II*. That of 1603 (Vienna, Ksthist. Mus.) depicts him heroically at half-length, in Roman armour. The bust is raised on an allegorical socle with figures of Mercury, Jupiter, an eagle and a ram. The bust of 1607 (Vienna, Schatzkammer) is short-fronted. There is also a profile portrait relief of the Emperor dating from 1609 (London, V&A). Two fine bronze allegorical reliefs characteristic of the iconography of Rudolfian court art are the *Allegory on the Turkish War in Hungary* (*c.* 1603; Vienna, Ksthist. Mus.) and *Rudolf II as Patron of the Arts and the Sciences* (1609; Windsor Castle, Berks, Royal Col.). Such works reveal stylistic and thematic similarities with works by the Prague court painters; indeed, the *Turkish War* was modelled after designs by Hans von Aachen.

Adriaen de Vries: *Laokoon and his Sons*, bronze, h. 1.72 m, 1623 (Stockholm, Drottningholm Slott)

During Rudolf II's lifetime, other than works for the Emperor himself, de Vries apparently executed sculpture only for members of the immediate circle of Imperial advisers. Among these works were an equestrian statue of *Duke Henry Julius of Brunswick-Wölfenbüttel* (ex-Herzog Anton Ulrich-Mus., Brunswick; untraced since 1945) and a statue of *Christ* (Warsaw, N. Mus.) for the funerary monument of the Imperial Councillor *Adam Hannewaldt*. For Prince Charles of Liechtenstein, de Vries produced an almost life-size bronze seated statue of *Christ* with legs crossed and hands clasped in prayer (1607), and a bronze statue of *St Sebastian* in expressive contrapposto (c. 1616; both Vaduz, Samml. Liechtenstein). A bronze bust of *Christian II of Saxony* (1603; Dresden, Skulpsamml.) was given by the Emperor as a present to the young Elector.

After Rudolf II's death in 1612, de Vries became a member of Emperor Matthias's household but is not known to have received any commissions; when the Imperial court moved to Vienna, he stayed in Prague. In the following years he worked for foreign patrons. In 1615–17 he designed and executed a large fountain, recalling both the Hercules Fountain in Augsburg and Bartolomeo Ammanati's Neptune Fountain of 1575 in Florence, for Frederiksborg Slot in Denmark. In 1659 the

sculptures of which it was composed were taken to Sweden as spoils of war (now Stockholm, Drottningholms Slott, and Stockholm, Nmus.; replica of 1888, Hillerød, Frederiksborg Slot).

De Vries had earlier produced an iconographically and formally very interesting bronze font (1615) for the newly built Stadtkirche (1611–15) of Bückeburg, commissioned by Ernst, Graf von Schaumburg-Lippe. For the mausoleum that Graf Ernst had erected in Stadthagen after designs by Giovanni Maria Nosseni, de Vries executed a large monument on the theme of the Resurrection. He also produced two almost life-size sculptures: *Venus and Adonis* (1621) and *Rape of a Sabine Woman* (1621; both Berlin, Bodemus.).

De Vries's last great patron was Graf Albrecht von Wallenstein. Between 1623 and 1626 he produced a bronze fountain and a series of statues and groups for the grounds of the Wallenstein (now Valdštejn) Palace in Prague, plundered by the Swedes in 1648. The fountain was a simplified replica of the Neptune Fountain at Frederiksborg Palace. Among the garden sculptures, the bronze group *Laokoon and his Sons* (Stockholm, Drottningsholm Slott; see fig.) is especially interesting: by transforming the essentially relief-like composition of his antique prototype (Rome, Vatican, Mus. Pio-Clementino), de Vries produced one of the most convincing multi-viewpoint sculptures of Mannerism. Among his last works is a bronze statue of *Hercules* (c. 1625–6; Prague, N.G., Convent of St George), a theme he had earlier treated in drawings (e.g. c. 1615, Dresden, Kupferstichkab.; Prague, N.G., Kinsky Pal.).

BIBLIOGRAPHY

F. Baldinucci: *Notizie* (1681–1728); ed. F. Ranalli, ii (1846), p. 580
A. Ilg: 'Adrian de Fries', *Jb. Ksthist. Samml. Allhöch. Ksrhaus.*, i (1883), pp. 118–48
C. Buchwald: 'Adriaen de Vries', *Beitr. Kstgesch.*, n. s., xxv (1899)
E. V. Strohmer: 'Bemerkungen zu den Werken des Adriaen de Vries', *N. Mus. Årsbok* (1947–8), pp. 93–138
E. B. Cahn: 'Adriaen de Vries und seine kirchlichen Bronzekunstwerke in Schaumburg', *Schaumburg. Stud.*, xv (1966)
L. O. Larsson: *Adrian de Vries* (Vienna, 1967)
E. Zimmermann: 'Herkules, Deianeira und Nessus: Eine Bronzeskulptur des Adriaen de Vries im badischen Landesmuseum', *Jb. Staatl. Kstsamml. Baden-Württemberg*, vi (1969), pp. 55–78
T. DaCosta Kaufmann: 'Empire Triumphant: Notes on an Imperial Allegory by Adrian de Vries', *Stud. Hist. A.*, viii (1978), pp. 63–75
L. O. Larsson: 'Die niederländischen und deutschen Schüler Giambolognas', *Giambologna: Ein Wendepunkt der europäischen Plastik* (exh. cat., ed. C. Avery, A. Radcliffe and M. Leithe Jasper; Vienna, Ksthist. Mus., 1978), pp. 57–62
——: 'Bildhauerkunst und Plastik am Hofe Kaiser Rudolfs II', *Leids Ksthist. Jb.*, i (1982), pp. 211–35
——: 'Die Brunnen auf Schloss Frederiksborg', *Leids Ksthist. Jb.*, ii (1984), pp. 25–36
Z. Waźbiński: 'Adriano de Vries e Domenico Portigiani: Un contributo alla collaborazione fra scultore e fonditore intorno al 1588', *Scritti di storia dell'arte in onore di Roberto Salvini* (Florence, 1984), pp. 449–53
L. O. Larsson: 'Bildhauerkunst und Plastik aus Hofe Rudolfs II', *Prag um 1600: Kunst und Kultur am Hofe Rudolfs II* (exh. cat., ed. J. Schultze; Essen, Villa Hugel, 1988), pp. 127–38; nos 56–69, 81–7
R. Mulcahy: 'Adriaen de Vries and Pompeo Leoni: The High Altarpiece of El Escorial', *Apollo*, cxxxix (Feb 1994)

LARS OLOF LARSSON

Vries, Simon de. *See* FRISIUS, SIMON.

Vriesendorp, Madelon. *See under* OFFICE FOR METRO-POLITAN ARCHITECTURE.

Vrindavan [Brindaban; anc. Vṛndāvana]. Sacred town in Uttar Pradesh, India. Located on the River Yamuna 9 km north of Mathura, Vrindavan is considered to be the place where the god Krishna gambolled with the milkmaids (*gopīs*). The poet Jayadeva (12th century AD) immortalized these exploits in his Sanskrit lyric *Gitagovinda*, but it was not until the Vaishnava reformer Chaitanya (1485–1527) visited Vrindavan that it began to emerge as a stronghold of the Vaishnava movement. None of the monuments pre-dates the 16th century. The Govinda Deva Temple was built, according to inscription, by Raja Man Singh Kachchhwaha (*reg* 1590–1614) of Amer in 1590. Only the hall remains, the sanctum having been pulled down in the time of the Mughal emperor Aurangzeb (*reg* 1658–1707). Constructed of red sandstone, the hall has projecting porches, notable for their elaborate brackets, on two storeys. The exterior walls, devoid of sculpture, are articulated with courses of mouldings. The interior is spanned by arches and a dome recalling contemporary Mughal architecture. The 16th-century Madana Mohana Temple stands on the mound called Dvadashaditya Tila. It consists of a hall and an octagonal spire (h. *c.* 20 m). A second, more ornate, tower was added later (1821), and the building was restored in the 19th century (see Growse). East of the Madana Mohana is the Ashta Sakhi Temple with its prominent spire. Krishna is enshrined there with Radha and eight consorts (*sakhīs*). The Gopinath Temple corresponds both in style and dimensions to the Madana Mohana Temple and has a similar shrine attached to the south side. The Jugal Kishor Temple (1627) is notable for its doorways, with eaves supported on eight closely set brackets carved in the form of elephants. Krishna is shown within supporting Govardhana Hill. Of the later monuments, the finest is the 17th-century Banke Bihari Temple, Banke Bihari (Krishna) being the most famous deity of Vrindavan. Also of note are the Krishna Chandrama Temple, built *c.* 1810 by Lala Babu (*b* ?1780), and the Rangnath or Rang Ji Temple (1845–51).

BIBLIOGRAPHY
F. S. Growse: *Mathura: A District Memoir* (Mathura, 1874/*R* New Delhi, 1979)
A. W. Entwistle: *Braj: Centre of Krishna Pilgrimage* (Groningen, 1987)
R. K. Das: *Temples of Vrindavan* (Delhi, 1990)

G. BHATTACHARYA

Vrizakis, Theodoros. *See* VRYZAKES, THEODOROS.

Vroom. Dutch family of artists. Cornelis Hendricksz. Vroom the elder was a sculptor and ceramic artist, and his brother Frederick Vroom I (*d* 1593) was city architect in Danzig (now Gdańsk). Cornelis's son (1) Hendrick Vroom initiated the Dutch 17th-century tradition of MARINE PAINTING. His three sons—(2) Cornelis Vroom the younger, (3) Frederick Vroom II and Jacob Vroom I—all became painters, as did his grandson Jacob Vroom II (*d* 1700), the son of (2) Cornelis Vroom.

(1) Hendrick (Cornelisz.) Vroom (*b* Haarlem, *c.* 1563; *bur* Haarlem, 2 Feb 1640). Painter and draughtsman. By his own account, he received his early training in Delft, home of his mother's family. Van Mander reports that Hendrick's stepfather, like his father a ceramic artist, forced him to work as a decorator of ceramic vessels, which caused the young artist to leave home and embark on extensive travels in Spain and Italy. After working for ecclesiastical patrons in Florence and Rome, he was employed for at least two years (*c.* 1585–7) by Cardinal Ferdinando de' Medici, who in October 1587 succeeded Francesco I as Grand Duke of Tuscany. Ferdinando's keen interest in ships and the navy seems to have been a determining factor in Vroom's choice of subject-matter. According to Lanzi, he was known in Rome as 'Lo Spagnolo' (since he had arrived there from Spain). Among his earliest works may be a group of marine paintings attributed to him (Rome, Villa Colonna). His friendship in Rome with Paul Bril, mentioned by van Mander, had no effect on Hendrick's painting style, but Bril's influence is discernible in a group of landscape drawings (Russell, figs 105–11), apparently produced in the Rhône region of France, where the artist stopped on his return journey from Italy.

Vroom was back in Haarlem by 1590, when he purchased a house on 28 April, shortly before marrying Joosje Cornelisse. After their marriage the young couple went to stay in Danzig with Hendrick's uncle Frederick Vroom, who was the town architect. There Hendrick made paintings (untraced) for the Danzig Jesuits. After returning to Haarlem in 1591, around which time his first son, (2) Cornelis, was born, Hendrick sailed to Portugal, where he survived a shipwreck. He sold pictures of the event and of other marine subjects in Lisbon and Setubal. Two paintings of sea battles (Lisbon, Mus. N.A. Ant.; Portugal, priv. col.) probably belong to that period (Santos).

When Vroom subsequently settled in Haarlem, his reputation as an expert painter of ships was well established. His first commission of international importance was to design a series of tapestries, illustrating the crucial English victory in 1588 over the Spanish Armada, for the English Lord High Admiral, Charles, 2nd Baron Howard of Effingham (1536–1624). The magnificent set of ten huge tapestries, woven by Frans Spiering (*c.* 1550–1630) in Delft from 1592 to 1595, hung in the House of Lords from 1650 until 1834, when it was destroyed along with the Parliament buildings by fire. (It is known from an 18th-century engraved series by John Pine (1690–1756).) A similar set of six tapestries, commemorating the victories at sea of the Dutch over the Spanish (1572–4), was commissioned from Vroom by the States of Zeeland. It is known as the 'Middelburg Tapestries' and, except for the first hanging, which was woven by Spierings, was made by Hendrick de Maecht between 1595 and 1603 and hung on the walls of the great chamber of the abbey of Middelburg (now Zeeuws Mus.; *in situ*).

Vroom's return to Haarlem coincided with an unprecedented increase in shipping in the Netherlands, for both military and commercial purposes: the northern provinces achieved political independence through superior seamanship, while simultaneously undertaking voyages of discovery that brought them great commercial gain. Vroom, the only expert marine painter available, was called on to paint mementos of Dutch ships before they sailed to faraway lands, or after they had returned home laden with treasures

1. Hendrick Vroom: *Arrival of Frederick V, Elector Palatine, with his Wife, Elizabeth Stuart, at Flushing, May 1613*, oil on canvas, 2.03×4.09 m, 1623 (Haarlem, Frans Halsmuseum)

from the Indies or Brazil. His first known painting of a festive gathering in honour of Dutch ships is *Ships in Dordrecht Harbour* (1594; destr. 1945; see Russell, fig. 122). Such paintings secured Vroom's exemption from military duty by a decree of the burgomasters of Haarlem dated 7 February 1594. On 28 January 1597 he was also exempted for life from any administrative duties in the Guild of St Luke. The *Return to Amsterdam of the Second Expedition to the East Indies, 19 July 1599* (Amsterdam, Rijksmus.) was painted to commemorate the spectacular success of the new Compagnie van Verre, predecessor to the Dutch East India Company (founded 1602). Other paintings celebrated Dutch and English victories at sea, for example the *Seventh Day of the Battle of the Armada* (1600–01; Innsbruck, Tirol. Landesmus.), which Vroom produced on his return from a visit to Lord Howard in London.

From the 1590s Vroom produced paintings and drawings illustrating the most important events in Dutch naval history, including such masterpieces as the *Battle of Cadiz, 1596* and its pendant, the *Great Sea Storm* (both English priv. col., see Russell, figs 136 and 135), known from many reproductions. The battle scene, with accurate details of ships, flags and manoeuvres, is juxtaposed with a dramatic rendering of the ocean in a storm, with monster fish and a whale threatening a Dutch ship that is skilfully steering through all these dangers. This painting probably symbolizes the 'Ship of State' and in a wider sense Dutch statesmanship prevailing over the stormy seas of warfare with Spain. Excursions into this 16th-century type of symbolism are rare in Vroom's work and usually confined to his drawings.

Supported throughout his long career by the municipalities and the Admiralty, the Dutch East India Company and individuals concerned with shipping, Vroom portrayed almost every coastal city in the northern Netherlands and many minor and major engagements at sea.

Outstanding in the first category, which often included ceremonial gatherings of ships, is the *Arrival of Frederick V, Elector Palatine, with his Wife, Elizabeth Stuart, at Flushing, May 1613* (1623; Haarlem, Frans Halsmus.; see fig. 1). This, one of Vroom's best works, is one of a group of retrospective historical paintings. In 1629, reviving the theme of the 'Middelburg Tapestries', he painted the *Battle between Dutch and Spanish Ships on the Haarlemmermeer, 26 May 1571* (Amsterdam, Rijksmus.). Apart from these officially commissioned works, he painted 'portraits' of individual ships, such as *Dutch Ship off a Rock with Castle* (1626; London, N. Mar. Mus.), and many beach scenes, often featuring the coast at Scheveningen.

Vroom was a pioneer in marine painting and, as such, had to find his own stylistic means of representing ships in harbour or on the open sea. His characteristic approach was already apparent in the early *Ships in Dordrecht Harbour* (1594), which incorporates many features that were adopted and refined by later generations of Dutch marine painters, notably Jan Porcellis. A diagonal strip of foreshore with figure groups sets off alternating zones of brightly lit and shaded water, animated by a breeze that fills the ships' sails and makes the flags flutter. Tiny coastal profiles mark the far horizon; light vibrates from the ships' hulls and sails. Ship outlines are crisp while the atmosphere softens the background, merging water and sky in the distance. Having found this way of representing ships in their natural setting, he introduced few stylistic changes. Occasionally he varied the height of the horizon: raising it in the *Seventh Day of the Battle of the Armada* to allow a panoramic view of ships engaged in battle, lowering it to give an almost eye-level view and to emphasize the sky in *The Mauritius and Other East Indiamen Sailing out of the Marsdiep* (Amsterdam, Rijksmus.). He used this lower horizon, which was a new compositional feature in Dutch painting, most frequently in beach scenes and views of harbour cities seen across water with relatively little

2. Hendrick Vroom: *Beach Scene*, pen and ink, 129×83 mm (London, Victoria and Albert Museum)

shipping, such as *View of Hoorn* (*c.* 1622; Hoorn, West-fries. Mus.) and *View of Haarlem* (*c.* 1625; Haarlem, Frans Halsmus.). Occasionally it occurs in 'portraits' of single ships. He was also a pioneer in presenting meticulous observations of water, clouds and weather conditions, for which van Mander praised him. Dutch 17th-century landscape painting has its roots in his realistic depiction of ships, convincingly moving in the wind with clouds drifting in the same direction.

Vroom was also a skilful and individualistic draughts-man. While his views along the Rhône, which are land-scapes rather than seascapes, recall the manner of Bril, his studies of beaches with fisherfolk and small craft are entirely original. He appears to have been the first artist to sketch such motifs from life. In his drawings he also experimented more boldly than in his paintings with a low horizon, having huge clouded skies over a narrow strip of water or coastline (e.g. two *Marine Studies, verso* and *recto, c.* 1600; Amsterdam, Rijksmus.; and *Beach Scene*, London, V&A; see fig. 2). Etchings made from his drawings by other artists anticipated and clearly stimulated the pro-nounced emphasis on skies found in Dutch landscape and marine painting later in the 17th century. His most famous drawing is the large *Landing at Philippine, 1600* (Rotter-dam, Boymans–van Beuningen), which realistically por-trays the countless vessels assembled by Prince Maurice near the Flemish border. For this he chose a long, horizontal format and a very high skyline, reminiscent of the tapestry designs, to accommodate the ships against the panoramic views of the territory in the background. Prints after this drawing were presented to the Dutch towns and the States General, which rewarded the painter handsomely.

Vroom's paintings and drawings were always in great demand and were highly priced. He had a large studio and many followers, among them Aert Anthonisz. (*b* 1579), Cornelis Verbeeck (1590–1631/5), Cornelis Claesz. van Wieringen and Abraham de Verwer (*d* 1650). Houbraken's remark that Jan Porcellis was a student is, however, unfounded.

(2) Cornelis (Hendricksz.) Vroom the younger (*b* Haarlem, *c.* 1591; *bur* Haarlem, 16 Sept 1661). Painter and draughtsman, son of (1) Hendrick Vroom. He studied with his father and collaborated with him on the painting *Dutch Ships Ramming Spanish Galleys off the Flemish Coast* (1617; Amsterdam, Rijksmus.); Cornelis provided the fig-ures and the background. Only one signed marine painting by Cornelis is known, the *Spanish Men-of-War Engaging Barbary Corsairs* (1615; London, N. Mar. Mus.). The *Battle of Lepanto* (Ham House, Surrey, NT) is unsigned but plausibly attributed to him. By *c.* 1620 he seems to have abandoned marine painting and joined the group of young Haarlem artists whose drawings pioneered a new realistic landscape style. Jan and Esaias van de Velde and Willem Buytewech strongly influenced Cornelis's drawings and early landscape paintings, which are also reminiscent of Adam Elsheimer's arcadian scenes, known in the

Netherlands through Hendrick Goudt's popular engravings. The first known dated landscape painting, *River View with Boating* (1622; London, F. Paynhurst priv. col., see Keyes, fig. 23), anticipates the river-shore landscapes of Salomon van Ruysdael. Other paintings and drawings feature wooded scenes and panoramic views of dunes and countryside. The panoramas, with their simple horizontal division of sky and ground, recall the compositional structure of many of Hendrick Vroom's marines, including the diagonal foreground repoussoir, which now sets off a brightly lit expanse of fields in place of the water surface, as in the drawing *Country House before an Inland Sea* (New Haven, CT, Yale U. A.G.). Cornelis's late paintings, such as *Edge of a Forest* (1651; Copenhagen, Stat. Mus. Kst) and *Forest View with Cattle* (late 1650s; Rotterdam, Mus. Boymans–van Beuningen), show a great affinity with Jacob van Ruisdael's wooded scenes. The contact between the two artists was mutually beneficial: Vroom's early work, particularly the drawings, played an important part in van Ruisdael's development.

Cornelis Vroom emerged from the stimulating milieu of early marine painting to become one of the most influential artists of the first phase of Dutch 17th-century landscape painting. His training and early work no doubt account for his masterly treatment of light: even in his dense forest scenes he achieved an all-pervading luminosity that distinguishes them from the prototypes by Gillis van Coninxloo and other earlier painters of wooded landscapes.

(3) Frederick (Hendricksz.) Vroom II (*b* Haarlem, *c*. 1600; *d* Haarlem, 16 Sept 1667).

Painter and draughtsman, son of (1) Hendrick Vroom. He seems to have worked with his father longer than did Cornelis. However, no marine painting or drawing signed by him has ever been found. The only extant signed painting is his *Self-portrait* (Darmstadt, Hess. Landesmus.). Inventories made after his death list marine paintings by him and also still-lifes, landscapes and portraits. The large painting of the *Return of Prince Charles and the Duke of Buckingham from Spain, 5 October 1623* (London, N. Mar. Mus.; smaller version, Hampton Court, Royal. Col.) and a group of drawings (e.g. *Two Marine Studies*, Paris, Fond. Custodia, Inst. Néer.) are tentatively attributed to Frederick.

BIBLIOGRAPHY

K. van Mander: *Schilder-boeck* ([1603]–1604)

A. Bredius: 'Bijdragen tot de levensgeschiedenis van Hendrick Goltzius', *Oud-Holland*, xxxii (1914), pp. 137–8

——: *Künstler Inventare, Urkunden zur Geschichte der holländischen Künstler des 16., 17. und 18. Jahrhunderts* (The Hague, 1915–22), v–vii, x–xiv

L. R. Santos: 'Hendrick Vroom en Portugal', *Bol. Mus. N.A. Ant.*, i/4 (1949), pp. 207–8

L. J. Bol: *Die holländische Marinemalerei des 17. Jahrhunderts* (Brunswick, 1973)

G. Keyes: *Cornelis Vroom* (Alphen aan den Rijn, 1975); review by P. Biesboer in *Simiolus*, x/3–4 (1978–9) [the review points out that several attributions, particularly of drawings, have not been accepted by other scholars]

M. Russell: *Visions of the Sea: Hendrick C. Vroom and the Origins of Dutch Marine Painting* (Leiden, 1983)

——: 'Seascape into Landscape', *Dutch Landscape: The Early Years* (exh. cat., London, N.G., 1986)

MARGARITA RUSSELL

Vroutos, Georgios (*b* Athens, 23 June 1843; *d* Athens, Dec 1908). Greek sculptor. He studied at the School of Fine Arts in Athens and at the Accademia di S Luca in Rome. His works were based on classical academic principles, except perhaps for the controversial *Spirit of Copernicus* (1877; Athens, N.G.), which was greatly criticized for its unorthodox composition. Influenced by the school of Canova (Vroutos's Athenian studio was full of plaster copies and photographs of Canova's works), his sculpture remained conservatively classicist throughout his career, both in his funerary monuments (e.g. tomb of *Papadakis*, 1881; Athens, First Cemetery) and his lighter genre sculptures (e.g. *Eros Breaking his Bow*, *c*. 1900; Athens, Záppeion). Vroutos taught sculpture at the School of Fine Arts and was also involved in the restoration of ancient Greek sculpture.

BIBLIOGRAPHY

S. Lydakes: *E ellenes glyptes* [The Greek sculptors] (Athens, 1981), pp. 60–63, 297

C. Christou and M. Koumvakali-Anastasiadi: *Modern Greek Sculpture, 1800–1940* (Athens, 1982), pp. 51–2, 178–80

EVITA ARAPOGLOU

Vrubel', Mikhail (Aleksandrovich) (*b* Omsk, 5 March 1856; *d* St Petersburg, 1 April 1910). Russian painter and draughtsman. He was a pioneer of modernism, and his highly innovative technique broke with the traditions of the Academy of Arts in St Petersburg, where he had been a brilliant student; at the same time he felt dissociated from the social consciousness of The Wanderers. He remained a lonely figure in Russian art, but he was the only one of his generation who successfully achieved the monumentality for which so many painters were aiming.

As a boy Vrubel', whose health was frail and who had a nervous disposition, showed considerable talent for music and drawing. He finished school in Odessa and enlisted in the law faculty of the University of St Petersburg, where he successfully completed his training in 1880. In the same year he entered the Academy of Arts, St Petersburg, where his exceptional talent was appreciated by both his teachers and his fellow students, particularly Valentin Serov. Under the influence of Pavel Chistyakov (1832–1919), an inspired teacher who insisted on representing the structure as opposed simply to the surface of the object depicted, the creative method of Vrubel' began to develop: his portrait drawings of the period show the structure of the human face as facets of a cut diamond.

In 1883 Vrubel' was recommended to go to Kiev to take part in the restoration of the 12th-century church of St Cyril under the guidance of Professor Adrian Prakhov. This commission was crucial for his later development. Not only was it there that he created his masterpieces of religious painting (he was entrusted with the additional icons required for the iconostasis of St Cyril), but there too he fully developed his own style. In the Byzantine mosaics of St Sofia in Kiev and later in San Marco in Venice, he found the same divided colours and surfaces that had already fascinated him in St Petersburg in the watercolours he had seen by Mariano Fortuny y Marsal. As the originality of his work grew, however, so too did the hostility of the art establishment. His designs for the decoration of Vladimir Cathedral in Kiev (four variants of the *Lamentation*, the *Resurrection* and an *Angel with Candle and Censer*; all Kiev, Mus. Rus. A.), which were to be

Mikhail Vrubel': *Demon (Seated)*, oil on canvas, 1.14×2.11 m, 1890 (Moscow, Tret'yakov Gallery)

another religious masterpiece, were rejected, and he was allowed only to paint the ornamentation of the cathedral ambulatory. It was also in Kiev that he showed the first signs of mental illness.

In 1889 Vrubel' moved to Moscow, where the range of his activities widened considerably thanks to the enlightened support of Savva Mamontov, the most important Russian patron of the time. Vrubel' contributed stage designs to Mamontov's private opera, and music and opera—particularly the operas of Rimsky-Korsakov, with their themes from folklore—became central in his work. Vrubel''s monumental style was ideally suited to wall decoration for the new Art Nouveau houses in Moscow: he painted *Venice* (St Petersburg, Rus. Mus.), *Spain* and a triptych with the *Judgement of Paris* (both Moscow, Tret'yakov Gal.) for the house of E. D. Dunker in 1893–4 and around the same time three panels, *Morning*, *Noon* and *Evening*, for the house of S. T. Morozov at 17 Spiridonovka (now Aleksey Tolstoy Street; *in situ*).

The most dramatic event in Vrubel''s life occurred in 1896, when the jury rejected two huge canvases, *Mikula Selyaninovich* (St Petersburg, Rus. Mus.) and *Pelléas and Mélisande* (untraced), commissioned as decoration for the art pavilion of the Great Exhibition in Nizhny Novgorod. Mamontov, defying public opinion and pressure from the government, built his own pavilion, where the pictures were shown and created a great public scandal. Critics of all persuasions attacked Vrubel' for his 'decadent' style. The subject that was most congenial to Vrubel''s art was the image of the Demon, inspired by the hero of Mikhail Lermontov's poem 'Demon', an epitome of rejection and loneliness. Through the years this image took more tragic and pictorially abstract forms in Vrubel''s work, as for example in the paintings *Demon (Seated)* (1890; Moscow,

Tret'yakov Gal., see fig.), *Demon Flying* (1899; St Petersburg, Rus. Mus.) and *Demon Downcast* (1902; Moscow, Tret'yakov Gal.) and in the illustrations for the complete edition of Lermontov published in 1890–91 (original sketches in Moscow, Tret'yakov Gal.).

In 1896 Vrubel' married the leading soprano of Mamontov's opera, Nadezhda Zabela, and his portraits of her are his most inspired works, both in their lyricism and in the subtlety of their colours, for example *Nadezhda Zabela-Vrubel' in an Empire-style Summer Dress* (1898; Moscow, Tret'yakov Gal.) and *Zabela-Vrubel' against Birch Trees* (1904; St Petersburg, Rus. Mus.). The latter portrait was painted after a period of insanity, which darkened the last years of his life. Between attacks Vrubel' continued to work in oils, pastels and gouache. As well as portraits, he executed a number of flower studies (e.g. *Campanulas*, 1904; Moscow, Tret'yakov Gal.), until he became blind in 1906. By the time of his death, Vrubel' was considered an artist of great importance, although the next generation of avant-garde artists moved in a different direction.

WRITINGS
M. Vrubel': Pisma k sestre [M. Vrubel': letters to his sister] (Leningrad, 1929)
Ye. P. Gomberg-Verzhbinskaya and Zh. N. Podkopayeva, eds: *Vrubel': Perepiska; vospominaniya o khudozhnike* [Vrubel': correspondence; reminiscences about the artist] (Moscow, 1963, rev. 2/1976)

BIBLIOGRAPHY
S. Y. Yaremich: *Mikhail Aleksandrovich Vrubel'* (Moscow, 1911)
Y. Yevdokimov: *M. A. Vrubel'* (Moscow, 1925)
M. A. Vrubel' (exh. cat., Kiev, Mus. Rus. A., 1956)
Vystavka M. A. Vrubelya [An exhibition of M. A. Vrubel'] (exh. cat., intro. Ye. V. Zhuravleva; Moscow, Tret'yakov Gal., 1956)
Vystavka proizvedeniy M. A. Vrubelya [An exhibition of the works of M. A. Vrubel'] (exh. cat., intro. Zh. N. Pruzhan; St Petersburg, Rus. Mus., 1956)
Ye. V. Zhuravleva: *Mikhail Aleksandrovich Vrubel'* (Moscow, 1958)
Ye. P. Gomberg-Verzhbinskaya: *Vrubel'* (Moscow, 1959)
S. Druzhinin: *Mikhail Aleksandrovich Vrubel'* (Moscow, 1961)

A. Yagodovskaya: *Mikhail Aleksandrovich Vrubel'* (Leningrad, 1966)

A. A. Fyodorov-Davidov: *Mikhail Aleksandrovich Vrubel', 1856–1910* (Moscow, 1968)

V. Zh. Rakitin: *Mikhail Vrubel'* (Moscow, 1971)

N. M. Tarabukin: *Mikhail Aleksandrovich Vrubel'* (Moscow, 1974)

S. G. Kaplanova: *Vrubel'* (Leningrad, 1975)

A. Todebsky-Pritchard: *The Art of Mikhail Vrubel' (1856–1910)* (Ann Arbor, 1982)

P. K. Suzdalev: *Vrubel'* (Moscow, 1984)

M. I. Guerman: *M. A. Vrubel'* (Leningrad, 1985)

P. K. Suzdalev: *Vrubel'* (Moscow, 1988)

M. I. German, Gayduk and others: *Mikhail Vrubel': Zhivopis', grafika, knizhnaya illustratsiya i prikladnoye iskusstvo* [Mikhail Vrubel': painting, graphic art, book illustration and applied art] (Moscow, 1989)

N. A. Dmitriyeva: *Vrubel'* (Moscow, 1990)

P. K. Suzdalev: *Vrubel' i Lermontov* (Moscow, 1991)

LARISSA HASKELL

Vryzakes [Vrizakis], **Theodoros** (*b* Thebes, 1814 or 1819; *d* Munich, 7 Dec 1878). Greek painter. He was one of the first to study at the Akademie der Bildenden Künste in Munich. The son of a freedom fighter who was hanged by the Turks, he concentrated on subjects related to the Greek War of Independence (1821–32), such as the *Camp of Karaïskaki at Kastella* (1855; Athens, N.G.). His painting is mixed in style and uneven in quality. In history subjects and portraits alike he often exhausted himself in the delineation of external features, without reaching the essence of the events or the soul of his sitters. However, despite his sentimental and rhetorical tendencies, he managed to depict the heroic character of the period.

BIBLIOGRAPHY

A. Vakalopoulos: 'Theodoros Vryzakes', *Oi ellenes zographoi* [The Greek painters], ed. S. Lydakes and A. Karakatsane, i (Athens, 1974), pp. 62–99

ALKIS CHARALAMPIDIS

Vuchetich, Yevgeny (Viktorovich) (*b* Yekaterinoslav [now Dnepropetrovsk], 28 Dec 1908; *d* Moscow, 12 April 1974). Russian sculptor. He studied at art school in Rostov-on-Don (1921–30) and at the Academy of Arts in Leningrad (now St Petersburg; 1931–3). From 1939 to 1941 he was artistic manager of the experimental construction workshops of the Palace of Soviets in Moscow. He was on active service in World War II, and in 1943 he joined the M. B. Grekov Studio of Military Artists in Moscow.

Vuchetich's works are distinguished by their academic romanticism, lofty pathos and dramatic grandeur. The monument to Soviet soldiers who fell in the battles against Fascism (bronze and granite, 1946–9; Berlin, Treptower Park; architect Yakov Belopol'sky (1916–91)) covers an area over 120 sq. m, and the entrance to the area is formed by two semicircular piazzas with monumental single arches. Placed centrally to the avenue is the sculpture *The Motherland*, which depicts symbolically a mother bearing both the loss of her children and the burdens of war. The main entrance is formed by two enormous lowered banners of red granite, next to which are two bronze genuflecting soldiers holding machine-guns. From the main entrance a panorama opens up off the cemetery, and along the central axis of the parterre in the direction of the main monument are five communal graves. Along both sides of these are eight light-grey stone sarcophagi, with carved bas-reliefs. The centre of the memorial is marked by a 13 m high bronze figure of a soldier, on a high artificial mound, with his left arm around a small girl and his right hand holding a lowered sword, having cut through a Fascist swastika. Inside the base is a memorial room, with a wall mosaic depicting the peoples of Europe laying wreaths on the graves of soldiers.

Between 1963 and 1967 Vuchetich led a team of sculptors (with architects Belopol'sky and others) constructing a grandiose monument to the heroes of the Battle of Stalingrad on the Mamayev burial ground in Volgograd. This reinforced concrete monument, terraced along the slope of the burial ground, successively reveals in sculptural compositions, reliefs and inscriptions the themes of courage, determination, grief and victory, as well as patriotic exploits. It comprises an entrance composition, *The Memory of the Generations*, which depicts people of different generations bringing a wreath to the grave of the fallen heroes, an avenue of pyramidal poplars leading to the first square, in the centre of which is a 12 m high figure of a sub-machine gunner, surrounded by a pool, and ruined walls adjoining the square, on which are figures and faces of defenders of the town and depictions of life at the front. The Square of the Heroes contains an enormous water garden and sculptural compositions relating military exploits. It is bounded by a wall over 100 m long, in the form of an unfurled banner. Granite steps lead into the Hall of Military Glory decorated with gold smalti and 34 red banners with the surnames of 7200 fallen soldiers. It also contains an enormous marble hand with the Eternal Flame. In the Square of Grief, the main sculpture represents a mother bending over a dead soldier. The whole monument is crowned by a 52 m-high sculpture of *The Motherland* raising her punishment sword in anger, calling her sons to the battle with Fascism (for illustration *see* VOLGOGRAD).

Vuchetich was also the author of the monument to the founder of the Soviet secret police (the Cheka), Felix Dzerzhinsky, in Moscow (bronze and granite, 1958; destr. 1991 as a symbol of despotism), and of numerous portrait busts (e.g. General I. D. Chernyakhorsky; bronze and granite, 1945; Moscow, Tret'yakov Gal.) suffused with pompous 'ancient Roman' majesty. His allegorical sculpture *We Shall Beat our Swords into Ploughshares* (bronze, 1957), a gift from the then Soviet government, was erected in front of the UN building in New York.

The most famous Russian official sculptor of the mid-20th century, Vuchetich embodied the principles of Socialist Realism.

BIBLIOGRAPHY

A. V. Paramonov: *Ye. V. Vuchetich* (Moscow, 1952)

F. F. Shakmagonov: *Yevgeny Vuchetich: Portret khudoznika* [Yevgeny Vuchetich: portrait of the artist] (Moscow, 1970)

A. S. Fedorov: *Ye. V. Vuchetich* (Moscow, 1972)

A. V. PARAMONOV

Vuez, Arnould de (*b* Hautpoint, 17 Oct 1644; *d* Lille, 18 June 1720). French painter. He trained in Paris as a pupil of Claude François (Frère Luc). In 1660 he left for Italy to complete his artistic education in Venice and Rome, where he copied the works of Raphael in particular. On his return to Paris he obtained a stipend from Louis XIV thanks to Charles Le Brun, whom he assisted at the château of Versailles. After a duel, however, he was obliged to take refuge in Constantinople (now Istanbul). He apparently accompanied Charles-Henri-François-Olivier, Marquis de Nointel, French ambassador to the Porte, around the Orient *c.* 1670–79. In 1681, after his return to Paris, he was received (*reçu*) as a member of the Académie Royale de Peinture et de Sculpture on presentation of his *Allegory of the Marriage of the Dauphin* (Paris, Louvre). In 1693 he executed the *Incredulity of St Thomas*, the altarpiece (or 'May') commissioned each year by the goldsmiths' corporation for Notre-Dame, Paris. The success of his *Presentation of the Virgin in the Temple* commissioned the previous year by François-Michel Le Tellier, Marquis de Louvois, for a religious foundation in Lille led him to settle in that city. He was a prolific painter much in demand in French Flanders and produced a number of large religious compositions for the churches and convents of Lille, Douai and Cambrai. The Musée des Beaux-Arts in Lille preserves a representative selection of his mature works, including *St Bonaventura Preaching* and *St Augustine Healing the Sick*. In these paintings Vuez succeeded in creating an able and personal synthesis of the influences of Raphael, Le Brun and Rubens.

BIBLIOGRAPHY
Thieme–Becker
A. Delobel: *Notice ayant trait à Arnould de Vuez, peintre historique et magistrat de Lille* (Lille, 1868)
L. Gonse: 'Musée de Lille: Ecole française', *Gaz. B.-A.*, n. s. 1, ix (1874), p. 143
L. Quarré-Reybourbon: *Arnould de Vuez, peintre lillois, 1644–1720* (Lille, 1904)
L. Quinchon: *Arnould de Vuez* (diss., U. Lille III, 1984)
ANNIE SCOTTEZ-DE WAMBRECHIES

Vuibert, Rémy (*b* Réthel, Ardennes, *c.* 1600; *d* Moulins, Allier, *bur* 19 Sept 1652). French painter and engraver. André de Félibien and Florent Le Comte mention him as a student of Simon Vouet. Until 1638 Vuibert stayed in Rome, where he became familiar with Caravaggism and classicism. He was a friend of Nicolas Poussin, as attested by some of the letters that Poussin wrote to Paul Fréart de Chantelou; on his return to France, Vuibert collaborated from 1641, under Poussin's direction, on decorative projects in the Grande Galerie of the Louvre. Paintings sometimes attributed to him include the *Death of St Cecilia* (Montpellier, Mus. Fabre) and the *Death of Lucretia* (Troyes, Mus. B.-A. & Archéol.). However, the only paintings confidently attributed to Vuibert are those depicting the *Life of the Virgin* (1650–52) on the ceiling of the liturgical choir of the former convent of the Visitation (now the Lycée Banville), Moulins.

Vuibert engraved *Christ Healing the Possessed Man* (1639) and the *Presentation in the Temple* (1640) after his own paintings. His engravings of the work of other artists include *St Andrew* (1629) after Francesco Du Quesnoy; the *Judgement of Solomon, Adam and Eve*, and *Apollo and Marsyas* after Raphael; *St Michael Overcoming Satan* (1635) after Guido Reni; and the *Martyrdom of St Andrew* after Domenichino.

Vuibert was also the author of a design (Princeton U., NJ, A. Mus.) for a painted decoration for the gallery and vestibule of the château of Tanlay, Yonne, commissioned by Michel Particelli, Sieur d'Hémery (*c.* 1595–1650), Contrôleur Général des Finances. In the contract of 15 February 1646 Vuibert is described as 'Peintre Ordinaire

du Roi' and as living in Paris at the Palais des Tuileries. The company he kept, the choice of artists whose works he engraved and the grandeur and elegance of his style mark him out as an artist of classical tendencies.

BIBLIOGRAPHY
A. P. F. Robert-Dumesnil: *Le Peintre-graveur français* (1853–71)
C. Le Blanc: *Manuel de l'amateur d'estampes*, iv (1889), pp. 163–4
J. Thuillier: 'Pour un peintre oublié: Rémy Vuibert', *Paragone*, ix/97 (1958), pp. 22–41, pls 16–26
Vouet (exh. cat. by J. Thuillier, B. Brejon de Lavergnée and D. Lavalle, Paris, Grand Pal., 1990), p. 47
ALEXANDRA SKLIAR-PIGUET

Vuillard, Edouard (*b* Cuiseaux, Saône-et-Loire, 11 Nov 1868; *d* La Baule, nr Saint-Nazaire, 21 June 1940). French painter, draughtsman and printmaker.

1. Life and work. 2. Working methods and technique. 3. Character and personality. 4. Critical reception and posthumous reputation.

1. LIFE AND WORK.

(i) Early work, to 1900. (ii) 1900–14. (iii) 1915–40.

(i) Early work, to 1900. He was brought up in Paris in modest circumstances, and his home life was closely involved with his mother's and elder sister's dressmaking work. He attended the Lycée Condorcet where his contemporaries included the musician Pierre Hermant and the writer Pierre Véber, as well as Maurice Denis. His closest friend was Ker-Xavier Roussel, and, on leaving school in 1885, Roussel encouraged Vuillard to join him at the studio of the painter Diogène Maillart (1840–1926), where they received the rudiments of artistic training. Vuillard began to frequent the Louvre and soon determined on an artistic career, breaking the family tradition of a career in the army.

In March 1886 Vuillard entered the Académie Julian where he was taught by Tony Robert-Fleury, and on his third attempt in July 1887 he passed the entrance examination to the Ecole des Beaux-Arts. He was taught by Jean-Léon Gérôme for a brief period of about six weeks in 1888, but his studies at the Ecole appear to have been spasmodic. In 1888 Vuillard began to keep a journal in which he made sketches of works he was studying in the Louvre and noted ideas about future paintings. From these sketches and from his earliest-known studies in oil, it is clear that Vuillard was drawn to the realistic study of still-life and domestic interiors. He was particularly attracted to the 17th-century Dutch artists and to the works of Chardin in La Caze collection.

In 1889 Vuillard was persuaded by Maurice Denis to join a small dissident group of art students that had formed within the Académie Julian around Paul Sérusier and that referred to itself as the brotherhood of NABIS. Sérusier had communicated to his fellow students his knowledge of SYNTHETISM following his contact with Gauguin in Brittany. By means of a small landscape painted under Gauguin's instructions, known as *The Talisman* (Paris, Mus. d'Orsay; for illustration *see* SÉRUSIER, PAUL), Sérusier demonstrated the Synthetist method of painting; this entailed a reliance on memory and imagination rather than direct observation, and the application of forms and colours reduced to their simplest as equivalents to sensations and emotions received from nature. At first Vuillard was reluctant to accept the idea that the painter should not seek to reproduce realistically what he saw, although during 1890 he made his first bold experiments in Synthetist painting.

Vuillard painted these experimental works, usually based on a subject from his immediate environment, on small pieces of board. The earliest were painted in bright, often arbitrary colours with the subject reduced to its essential components; tones and hues were combined and balanced to produce a dense pattern-like surface. By 1892 he was using a more muted palette and had turned to family themes. *La Causette* (Edinburgh, N.G. Mod. A.; see fig. 1), which depicts his mother and sister seated in an interior, is typical of this phase: painted predominantly in browns, it conveys the strong aura of mystery characteristic of much of Vuillard's early work. Like other Nabi artists, especially Denis and Bonnard, Vuillard was influenced by the simplification and emphasis on expressive contour of 19th-century Japanese woodcuts. The theatre was an important stimulus on his choice of subjects and his predilection for muted and mysterious light effects. He was courted early on by such theatrical patrons as the actor Coquelin Cadet and by the theatre director André Antoine. His closest friend in the theatre was, however, the young actor–manager Aurélien Lugné-Poe who was largely responsible, through Paul Fort's Théâtre d'Art and later through his own company L'Oeuvre, for introducing Symbolist drama to Paris. Vuillard not only attended many of the latter's rehearsals and performances of plays by Maeterlinck, Ibsen, Strindberg and others but often painted scenery and designed costumes and programmes. Vuillard was a founder-member of Lugné-Poe's Théâtre de l'Oeuvre, which opened in 1893. With other members of the Nabi group, Vuillard had exhibited small-scale works at the Le Barc de Boutteville gallery. Later in the 1890s he showed work at Ambroise Vollard's; in 1897 the latter commissioned him to produce a series of colour lithographs on the theme *Landscape and Interiors* (1899; New York, MOMA).

An important factor in Vuillard's development as a painter in the 1890s was his association with the *Revue Blanche* and his friendship with its editors, the Natanson brothers. The editor-in-chief and art critic was Thadée Natanson, and he and his wife, Misia (a frequent model during these years), became close friends of Vuillard. In 1892 Vuillard received a commission to paint panels (Paris, Desmarais priv. col.) for Paul Desmarais, a cousin of the Natansons; this was followed by a major decorative commission in 1894 from the wealthiest of the Natanson

1. Edouard Vuillard: *La Causette*, oil on canvas, 324×413 mm, *c.* 1892 (Edinburgh, National Gallery of Modern Art)

2. Edouard Vuillard: (left) *The Interrogation*, (right) *Little Girls Playing*, distemper on canvas, 2145×880 mm and 2145×940 mm, two of the nine panels of *Public Gardens*, 1894 (Paris, Musée d'Orsay)

brothers, Alexandre, to paint nine panels for the dining-room of a grand mansion on the Avenue du Bois. Vuillard chose the theme of *Public Gardens* and produced an amalgam and imaginative reconstruction of his observations in the Tuileries or the Bois de Boulogne, for example *Little Girls Playing* and *The Interrogation* (both Paris, Mus. d'Orsay; see fig. 2), and the figures of nannies seated gossiping while overseeing their charges. Although planned as a decorative ensemble, the panels were later dispersed, and the eight that survive (one was lost during World War II) are now housed in different museums (five panels, Paris, Mus. d'Orsay; Cleveland, OH, Mus. A.; Houston, TX, Mus. F.A.; Brussels, Mus. A. Mod.). In 1896 Vuillard was commissioned by Dr Henri Vaquez to paint four panels for a library, *Figures and Interiors* (Paris, Petit Pal.), and further important decorative commissions followed: two panels in 1898 for the novelist Jean Schopfer, *Figures in the Garden of Le Relais, Villeneuve-sur-Yonne* (priv. col., see 1954 exh. cat., pp. 66–7), and two in 1899 for Adam Natanson, *Landscapes—Ile-de-France* (Chicago, IL, A. Inst.; Pasadena, CA, Norton Simon Mus.).

(ii) 1900–14. In the early years of the 20th century Vuillard began to show work at the Parisian gallery of the Bernheim-Jeune family and was later contracted to them. Lucy Hessel, wife of Jos Hessel, a partner in the firm, became a close friend, confidante and model, and Vuillard's time was spent increasingly in the Hessels' entourage, which included successful actors and playwrights as well as wealthy business people. Under his new commercial arrangements, Vuillard was encouraged to produce a wider range of work, landscapes and portraits as well as the decorative panels and small interiors typical of the 1890s.

He found a new delight in landscape studies at this period, most of which were inspired by the seaside holidays in Normandy and Brittany that he spent with the Hessels. Work was plentiful, and he was commissioned to paint more decorative panels for private clients: between 1908 and 1910 he produced a series of eight views of *Streets of Paris* (New York, Guggenheim; priv. col.), acquired by the playwright Henry Bernstein, and between 1911 and 1913 an extensive decorative scheme for the vast seaside villa of the Bernheim-Jeune family at Villers-sur-Mer. In 1912 Vuillard received his first commission for a public building, a series of decorations in Paris on theatrical themes to ornament the foyer of the Comédie des Champs-Elysées, a theatre within the new Théâtre des Champs-Elysées (inaugurated in 1913). The two principal panels represent *Classical Comedy* (a scene from Molière's *Le Malade imaginaire*) and *Modern Comedy* (a scene from Tristan Bernard's *Le Petit Café*).

Portraiture became an increasingly dominant aspect of Vuillard's work, and he found no shortage of sitters; many were fashionable members of the beau monde, others were intimate friends and professional associates. One of his most striking portraits of these years, *Théodore Duret in his Study* (1912; Washington, DC, N.G.A.), typifies Vuillard's broad strategy, probably influenced by the theories of the late 19th-century Realist critic Edmond Duranty. He effectively amalgamated the role of portrait painter with that of painter of interiors, portraying his models in domestic settings characteristic of them and often, in the process, extending the psychological penetration of the portrait. In the case of Duret, the writer is shown in his study, surrounded by the books and papers that are the tools of his profession and by other paintings and portraits acquired over the years. Whereas during his Nabi phase Vuillard had simplified and pared down his vision to a flattened pattern and had frequently attracted criticism for imprecision, from *c.* 1900 he treated space in a more three-dimensional way. Typically he set his model well back into the picture space and in some instances lavished almost as much attention on the familiar objects and minutiae that make up the interior setting as on the distinguishing features of his sitter.

(iii) 1915–40. Vuillard's established patterns of work were little affected by World War I. In 1914 he was called up to serve briefly as a railway look-out near Paris. He later served as a war artist, sketching soldiers on the front line at Gérardmer and producing a large painting recording the *Interrogation of the Prisoner* (1917; Paris, Mus. Hist. Contemp.). In 1916 he was commissioned by Thadée Natanson, director of the Lazare-Lévy munitions factory in Lyon, to record in two panels (Troyes, Mus. A. Mod.), as part of a decorative scheme, the assembly-line work at the factory. When hostilities ceased, Vuillard concentrated mainly on portraiture, still undertaking decorative commissions occasionally. The last of his major schemes for a private client was the series *At the Louvre* (1921–2; priv. col., see Thomson, pls 125-7), four panels and two overdoors inspired by different aspects of the Louvre's collections. These were destined for the house of a Swiss friend whom Vuillard had met during the war. It is the

only example of the artist's private decorative schemes to remain intact, although not *in situ*.

Between 1923 and 1937 Vuillard painted four important portraits of his closest artist friends, all former members of the Nabi group: Roussel, Denis, Bonnard and Maillol, each of whom is shown at work in characteristic manner. The four portraits were shown at the Exposition Internationale of 1937 and bought with full-scale studies by the City of Paris (Paris, Petit Pal.). In the same year Vuillard painted a decorative panel, again on the theme of Comedy, for the inauguration of the Théâtre de Chaillot in Paris. The panel depicts characters from Shakespeare and Molière, in a bucolic setting inspired by the park of the Château des Clayes, the Hessels' country home near Versailles. A final major project was an enormous mural (*in situ*) for the new League of Nations building in Geneva, the Palais des Nations, an ambitious and courageous undertaking but, given the traditional allegorical theme, scarcely one that Vuillard was ideally equipped to execute. He sought inspiration in the art of the past, particularly that of Eustache Le Sueur, an artist he had long admired. Vuillard was elected to the Institut de France in 1937, a mark of his country's esteem, and in 1938 a major retrospective, selected by the artist's friend Claude Roger-Marx, was held at the Pavillon de Marsan in Paris. Ill and severely distressed by the fall of France, Vuillard fled occupied Paris.

2. WORKING METHODS AND TECHNIQUE. At the outset of his career Vuillard worked in conventional media, usually oil on canvas, exploiting the luminous qualities of oil paint in a series of tonal still-lifes. In experimenting with the ideas of his Nabi friends, however, and in emphasizing the flat decorative qualities of his painting, he began to use cardboard, a more solid absorbent base, and cultivated a matt surface, using very dry oil paint and often allowing the light buff or grey colour of the ground to play a vital part in the establishment of relationships of colour and tone. Many of his early Nabi studies were subsequently varnished by others, a practice Vuillard avoided, thereby losing much of their intended muted texture. Around 1890 his drawing style underwent a similar reductive process to his painting, and for a time he deployed simple shapes and strong silhouette-like or cloisonnist outlines.

In a number of his paintings of the mid-1890s, Vuillard's interest in the patterns and textures of fabrics, wallpapers and carpets and his avoidance of indications of depth produced a dense overall effect and spatial ambiguity. Good examples of such an effect are *Large Interior with Six Figures* (1897; Zurich, Ksthaus) and *Misia and Vallotton in the Dining-room, Rue Saint Florentin* (New York, William Kelly Simpson priv. col., see fig. 3). After the turn of the century, however, possibly as a result of his working increasingly from photographs, he returned to a more conventional use of perspective and lightened his palette, concentrating in an almost impressionistic manner on luminosity. His later drawing style became more nervously linear, and when working on a portrait, for example, he patiently built up a dossier of sketches recording fragments and details that were incorporated into the whole at the final stage.

Vuillard is recognized as an artist of great technical expertise. For most of his career, in preference to oil, he used the difficult medium of distemper or *peinture à la colle*, a water-based medium mixed with glue that dried quickly and left a matt, opaque surface. He had first used distemper in scenery painting in the early 1890s and found its properties suitable for his large decorative panels. After *c.* 1900 most of Vuillard's painting in all genres was done in this medium. Because of distemper's rapid drying time, he was able to build up layer upon layer of paint, so that certain areas of his canvases are thickly encrusted while others are less worked. Over time the distemper has generally hardened. In cases where Vuillard had left insufficient time for the drying process, mixed up a faulty balance of glue and pigment or, as frequently happened with his decorative panels, reworked a canvas after an interval, his paintings have suffered damage from cracking and flaking and pose problems of conservation. For drawing Vuillard particularly favoured pastel after 1900 and again he made full use of the subtle delicacy of this difficult medium.

3. CHARACTER AND PERSONALITY. Vuillard was a likeable man who inspired affection in those close to him. He was of a reserved and quiet rather than extrovert personality, though capable of expressing pent-up emotion in sudden violent outbursts. He was suspicious of some of the more flamboyant of his contemporaries, such as Gauguin, preferring to associate himself with the achievements of such artists as Monet, Degas or Puvis de Chavannes. He weighed his words carefully and thought deeply about his art, as can be seen from his exchange of letters with his theoretically minded friend Maurice Denis in 1898, published in Denis's *Journal*. Beset by moral scruples, he frequently agonized over his personal conduct, as is revealed in his journal. Although Vuillard was a bachelor and lived with his mother until her death in 1928, he was very much a part of the Roussel family, lovingly watching and recording the development of their children. He also evidently enjoyed the company of women and had several close female friends; Lucy Hessel, his 'dragon' as his mother referred to her, played a particularly influential role in his life. Women and children were the main inspirations for his figure paintings; indeed Vuillard was somewhat puzzled to note this personal predilection in his diary of 1894, quizzing himself on why he tended to envisage men only as sources for comic images while seeing women as sources of beauty.

Despite the successes later in his career, he continued to live modestly; from 1908 he occupied a succession of apartments overlooking Place Vintimille (now Place Adolphe-Max), a quiet residential square near the Montmartre cemetery. Vuillard's interiors, approached from a realist perspective, are a faithful and telling record both of his own private circumstances and of the changing styles of living in the period during which he worked. Some critics feel that his art was detrimentally affected by his introduction through the Hessels and their *grand bourgeois* friends to a world of ease, prosperity and sometimes vulgar ostentation; they argue that the essence of his work lay in its sensitivity to the scrubbed, frugal interiors of the Parisian *petite bourgeoisie*, settings associated with the

3. Edouard Vuillard: *Misia and Vallotton in the Dining-room, Rue Saint Florentin*, oil on cardboard, 721×514 mm, c. 1899 (New York, William Kelly Simpson private collection)

artist's mother. In his diary of 1893, Vuillard asked himself the question: 'Why is it in the familiar places that the mind and the sensibility find the greatest degree of genuine novelty?' In his later portrait work Vuillard was notorious for changing and omitting nothing, recording the most trivial of details and the most garish of colour combinations. While occasionally the paintings may seem over-elaborated and uninspired as a result, he was also capable of approaching an irksome commission with an ironic or at least mischievous eye by which he achieved a telling picture.

4. CRITICAL RECEPTION AND POSTHUMOUS REPUTATION. Although when first exhibited at Le Barc de Boutteville's gallery the works of the Nabi group as a whole were considered outrageous, daub-like and incomprehensible by many critics, Vuillard tended to escape the worst attacks and was quickly singled out for praise by such critics as Roger Marx, Thadée Natanson and Léon-Paul Fargue. In the climate of Symbolism, Vuillard's ability to infuse a mundane subject with an atmosphere of mystery had a special appeal. He was much admired for his abundant natural talents by such contemporary artists as Denis, Signac and Sickert. Vuillard, however, also found a sympathetic audience among writers: he was admired by the poet Stéphane Mallarmé, and his large-scale decorations, exhibited at the Salon d'Automne of 1905, were highly praised by André Gide. Seen against the gathering momentum of developments in 20th-century art for which he felt little sympathy (Fauvism, Cubism and Surrealism), Vuillard's style seemed to settle as a kind of latter-day Impressionism, and he became accepted as an independent member of the establishment. By the 1920s he could be accused of conservatism by the more avant-garde critics of the day, such as André Lhote, who chided him for the superficiality of attending to modish material details in his portraits and interiors. By the time of his 1938 retrospective, the critic Claude Roger-Marx (the exhibition selector) was of the opinion that Vuillard's early works, before he was inundated with commissions for demanding clients, had been his greatest achievements. This preference for the early experimental work, a syndrome of modernist criticism, affects the work of many artists who, like Vuillard, made the transition from the avant-garde to the establishment.

Given his particular sensitivity to the study of everyday life, of domestic interiors and their inhabitants, Vuillard has frequently been categorized as an *intimiste*, belonging to the realist domestic tradition in painting that had its roots in the Netherlands in the 17th century and that was carried forward in France by such artists as Watteau, Chardin and Corot. Since Vuillard's death, his qualities as a colourist and an experimenter in tone have continued to be celebrated. The mysterious magic of his early interiors continues to hold the widest appeal, while his considerable achievements in the sphere of decorative painting are beginning to be more fully appreciated.

UNPUBLISHED SOURCES

Journal, 48 vols, Paris, Institut de France

BIBLIOGRAPHY
MONOGRAPHS

J. Salomon: *Vuillard, témoignage* (Paris, 1945)
A. Chastel: *Vuillard, 1868–1940* (Paris, 1946)
C. Roger-Marx: *Vuillard: His Life and Work* (London, 1946)
——: *L'Oeuvre gravé de Vuillard* (Paris, 1948)
J. Salomon: *Auprès de Vuillard* (Paris, 1953)
——: *Vuillard admiré* (Lausanne, 1961)
S. Preston: *Vuillard* (New York, 1971/ R London, 1985) [good pls]
L. Oakley: *Edouard Vuillard* (New York, 1981)
B. Thomson: *Vuillard* (Oxford, 1988) [good pls; contains new inf. about the artist's life and work based on extracts from the artist's j.]
G. Gloom: *E. Vuillard: Painter-Decorator: Patrons and Projects, 1892–1912* (London, 1993)

SPECIALIST STUDIES

A. Chastel: 'Vuillard et Mallarmé', *La Nef* (26 Jan 1947), pp. 13–25
J. Salomon and A. Vaillant: 'Vuillard et son Kodak', *L'Oeil*, 100 (1963), pp. 14–25, 61
R. Bacou: 'Décors d'appartements au temps des Nabis', *A. France*, iv (1964), pp. 190–205
J. Dugdale: 'Vuillard the Decorator', *Apollo*, lxxxi/36 (1965), pp. 94–101; lxxxvi/68 (1967), pp. 272–7
M. Kozloff: 'Four Short Essays on Vuillard', *Artforum*, x/4 (1971), pp. 64–71
G. Mauner: 'Vuillard's Mother and Sister Paintings and the Symbolist Theatre', *Artscanada*, xxviii/162–3 (1971–2), pp. 124–6
C. Frèches-Thory: '*Jardins publics* de Vuillard', *Rev. Louvre*, 4 (1979), pp. 305–12
J. Wilson Bareau: 'Edouard Vuillard et les princes Bibesco', *Rev. A.* [Paris] (1986), pp. 37–46

EXHIBITION CATALOGUES

Exposition E. Vuillard (exh. cat., ed. C. Roger-Marx; Paris, Mus. A. Déc., 1938)
Edouard Vuillard (exh. cat., ed. A. Carnduff-Ritchie; New York, MOMA, 1954/R 1969)
Bonnard, Vuillard et les Nabis (1888–1903) (exh. cat., Paris, Mus. N. A. Mod., 1955)
Edouard Vuillard, Ker-Xavier Roussel (exh. cat., ed. P. Georgel; Paris, Mus. Orangerie, 1968) [good illus.]
Vuillard (exh. cat., ed. J. Russell; Toronto, A.G. Ont.; San Francisco, CA Pal. Legion of Honor; Chicago, IL, A. Inst.; 1971; rev. with intro. by J. Russell and extracts from important sel. texts by Vuillard's contemps, London, 1971)
Vuillard Interiors (exh. cat., ed. G. Shackelford and E. Easton; Houston, TX, Mus. F.A.; Washington, DC, Phillips Col.; 1989)
Vuillard (exh. cat., ed. B. Thomson; London, S. Bank Cent., 1991)

BELINDA THOMSON

Vukanović, Beta (*b* Bamberg, 18 April 1872; *d* Belgrade, 1972). Serbian painter of German birth. At first she studied painting at the Kunstgewerbeschule in Munich. She also worked with Anton Ažbé. From 1898 she lived mostly in Belgrade. Her earliest works reflected the influence of *plein-air* painting in Munich, which changed to Impressionism before World War I. Her later style was predominantly realistic; she painted many pictures of the Serbian landscape and its people. She was the originator of Serbian artistic caricature and left around 500 humorous portraits of contemporaries from the social and cultural scene in Belgrade.

BIBLIOGRAPHY

Beta Vukanović: Retrospective Exhibition (exh. cat., text B. Kovačević; Belgrade A. Pav., 1958)
Motivi Bete Vukanović [The motifs of Beta Vukanović] (exh. cat., text P. Vasić; Belgrade, Cult. Cent. Gal., 1966)

JURE MIKUŽ

Vulci [Etrus. Velc; Gr. Olkion; Lat. Volcii]. Site of Etruscan city near Montalto di Castro, Italy. It occupies a tufa plateau overlooking the lower reaches of the River Fiora *c.* 120 km north-west of Rome and *c.* 15 km inland from its ancient port, Regisvilla, on the Tyrrhenian coast. Vulci was a member of the Etruscan 12-city league but is seldom mentioned in ancient sources, and most evidence relating to its pre-Roman history consists of finds from its surrounding necropoleis. Already a substantial settlement by the Late Bronze Age, Vulci flourished during the 9th and 8th centuries BC as a metalworking centre, and the earliest imports of Near Eastern and Sardinian artefacts date from this time. From around 630 BC Vulci experienced remarkable prosperity and productivity. There were copious imports of Greek and Near Eastern artefacts which, together with the arrival of immigrant craftsmen, stimulated the establishment of local fine pottery workshops. In the 6th century BC there was prolific production of Etrusco-Corinthian and Black-figure pottery (*see also* ETRUSCAN, §IV). Some of the earliest Etruscan sculpture in stone also comes from Vulci. Notable examples include the animals or monsters intended as tomb guardians (e.g. the *Centaur*; *c*. 590 BC; Rome, Villa Giulia) and the standing female figure from the Isis Tomb (*see* ETRUSCAN, §III and fig. 15), all carved from nenfro, the local volcanic stone. Later, Vulci was once again primarily a metalworking centre, with workshops specializing in candelabra, rod tripods (*see* ETRUSCAN, fig. 32) and engraved mirrors.

Apart from the substructure of a huge temple (36×25 m), little now remains of the Etruscan city: a few stretches of the city wall, in which there were at least four gates, are visible. The necropoleis surrounding the city contain some large family chamber tombs of the Archaic period, including the Cucumella tumulus, the Isis Tomb and the Tomb of the Sun and Moon. Between *c*. 550 and *c*. 450 BC Attic Greek pottery was imported to Vulci on a scale and of a quality unparalleled elsewhere in Etruria. When modern excavations of the tombs began in the early 19th century, many thousands of examples were found. The second half of the 5th century BC was apparently a period of crisis, but elaborate later tombs (e.g. the François Tomb and the Tomb of the Inscriptions) testify to revived prosperity. The François Tomb contains some of the finest Etruscan wall paintings (*c*. 330 BC; Rome, Villa Albani), with scenes from Greek mythology and Etruscan history and daily life (*see also* ETRUSCAN, §V and fig. 28). A slow but marked decline began in 280 BC with the defeat of Vulci by Rome and the subsequent loss of almost all its territory. The city survived through the Republican and Imperial periods, but like other Etruscan cities near the coast Vulci was affected by the advent of malaria, and its demise came during the 8th century AD when the bishopric of the area was transferred to Montalto di Castro.

BIBLIOGRAPHY
A. Hus: *Vulci étrusque et étrusco-romaine* (Paris, 1971)
Atti del X convegno di studi etruschi ed italici: Firenze, 1977
G. Riccioni: 'Vulci: A Topographical and Cultural Survey', *Italy before the Romans*, ed. D. Ridgway and F. R. Ridgway (London, 1979), pp. 241–76

MARCO RENDELI

Vulcop [Villecocq; Wilcop; Wulcob], **de.** Family of painters, probably of Netherlandish origin, active in France.

(1) Conrad de Vulcop (*fl* 1446–59). The earliest reference to him is as a painter in the service of King Charles VII of France in 1446. Between 1448 and 1459 he is mentioned with the official title 'painter to the King'. He appears to have collaborated closely with his brother (2) Henri de Vulcop, since in 1454 he provided gold and colours to enable Henri to carry out his work. No surviving work can be associated with him. He was not among the painters responsible for the decorations for the obsequies of Charles VII in 1461.

(2) Henri de Vulcop (*fl* 1454; *d* before 1479). Brother of (1) Conrad de Vulcop. He was possibly the younger of the two brothers and is first documented in Paris in 1454 working for Queen Mary of Anjou, wife of Charles VII of France. He was charged with illuminating the miniatures in Books of Hours and other books for the Queen. He seems to have continued in her employment, working at Tours and Chinon, until her death in 1463. Henri then entered the service of Charles, Duc de Berry, and settled in Bourges. No signed or documented work by Henri is known, but he may tentatively be identified with the MASTER OF COËTIVY (*see* MASTERS, ANONYMOUS, AND MONOGRAMMISTS, §I), whose activities included panel painting, manuscript illumination and tapestry design.

BIBLIOGRAPHY
P. Durrieu: 'Les Heures de Coëtivy à la bibliothèque de Vienne', *Bull. Soc. N. Antiqua. France* (1921), pp. 301–17
N. Reynaud: 'La Résurrection de Lazare et le Maître de Coëtivy', *Rev. Louvre*, xv (1965), pp. 171–82
——: 'Un Peintre français cartonnier de tapisseries au XVe siècle: Henri de Vulcop', *Rev. A.*, xxii (1973), pp. 6–21
C. Sterling: *La Peinture médiévale à Paris, 1300–1500*, 2 vols (Paris, 1987)

THOMAS TOLLEY

Vurnik, Ivan (*b* Radovljica, 1 June 1884; *d* Radovljica, 1971). Slovene architect, goldsmith, designer and teacher. He studied in Vienna at the Technische Hochschule under Karl Mayreder and Karl Kőnig (1841–1915) and at the Akademie der Bildenden Künste under Otto Wagner. After spending some time in Rome, Vurnik joined Wagner's studio and in 1912–15 took part in the construction of the new wing of the Hofburg, Vienna. In 1920 he became a professor at the Technical Faculty in Ljubljana. In his early work he was preoccupied with a romantic formalism, combining associations from the Slovene vernacular with the Vienna Secession style; this is seen in the articulated façades and polychromatic elements of his Industrial Bank (1922) and SOKOL headquarters (1923–5), both in Ljubljana. He produced several other buildings during this period, after 1925 adopting a more Functionalist approach influenced by the Bauhaus and Le Corbusier (e.g. the beach resort (1932) at Radovljica and his project (1934; unexecuted) for the University Library in Ljubljana). Vurnik was also active in urban planning and the restoration of historic monuments, and he was a goldsmith and graphic artist. His designs included a baldacchino in St Peter's, Ljubljana; elaborate casings for church organs in Dovje and Žiri; the war memorial in Bohinjska Bela, near Jesenice; tabernacles for churches in Ribnica and Radovljica; and numerous chalices, monstrances and flags. Vurnik also wrote on contemporary architectural issues. Together with Jože Plečnik, he played a major role in Slovene architecture between the wars.

WRITINGS

Vseučiliška knjižnica ljubljanska [Collected Ljubljana ntbks] (Ljubljana, 1934)

BIBLIOGRAPHY

M. Mušič: 'Ob sedamdesetletnici profesorja Ivana Vurnika' [On the occasion of the 70th birthday of Professor Ivan Vurnik], *Arhitekt*, xiv (1954), pp. 4–7

F. Šijanec: *Sodobna slovenska likovna umetnost* [Contemporary Slovenian fine art] (Maribor, 1961)

PAUL TVRTKOVIĆ

Vyborg [Fin. Viipuri; Swed. Viborg]. City in the Russian Federation *c.* 170 km west of St Petersburg on the northern shore of the Gulf of Finland. It was part of the Finnish portion of Sweden until the Peace of Nystad (1712), when it was surrendered to Russia. In 1810 it became part of the newly created Grand Duchy of Finland, within the Russian empire, and from 1917 it was part of independent Finland. In 1944, however, it was captured by the USSR (now the Russian Federation).

Archaeological evidence suggests that there was a settlement on the site from the 10th century AD, and written evidence shows that it was a trading centre patronized by the Swedes even before the Swedish crusade to the area in 1293 and the building of the castle on the hill at Vyborg shortly afterwards. The late 13th-century castle is a square, turreted granite stronghold that reflects Romanesque influences. It was expanded between 1442 and 1448 into a rectangular structure (50×44 m), with storage and living-quarters in the north, south and east wings. The town itself was eventually built along a broad promontory to the east of the hill, with the earliest settlements probably functioning as dependants of the castle (see fig.). The harbour lying slightly further east, on the island of Björkö, belonged to the Russian principality of Novgorod, the neighbouring power to the east.

With the Nöteborg peace treaty of 1323 between Sweden and Novgorod, Vyborg became the administrative centre of the section of the Karelian province that fell to Sweden, but, probably owing to its exposed position on the eastern border, its inhabitants had to wait until 1403 to enjoy the privileges of Vyborg's new status as an independent town with two mayors or chief magistrates and a council. Before then they were considered to be servants of the castle. A river ran down the centre of the promontory on which the castle was built. The main street, Kungsgata, followed the river, with, directly to the south, a square with the town hall and guildhall (some remains exist of both buildings). The main church (the cathedral from 1554) also stood near this square. Built in the late 15th century and consecrated in 1494, it had a nave and aisles. It is now a ruin without vaults. Another square lay at the western end of the street, on the river bank, with a bridge leading off westwards to the oldest highway in Finland, the great coastal road to Turku.

Probably owing to Vyborg's position on the eastern frontier of the Roman Catholic world, both the main mendicant orders founded houses here, with papal permission. A Dominican convent was established in 1392, followed in 1403 by the Franciscans, but it was unusual for both orders to be present in the smaller Nordic towns. In addition, Vyborg had an almshouse for the elderly and handicapped (the House of the Holy Spirit) and a leper hospital, established with papal permission in 1475. The

Vyborg, view from the west, showing the castle (late 13th century) and the medieval town; from a photograph taken *c.* 1930

Muscovite conquest of Novgorod in 1478 meant the end of the 150-year peace between Russia and Sweden, and in the late 1470s Vyborg became the only town in Finland to have a city wall. The wall stretched straight across the cape and continued slightly westwards along both the northern and southern shores. There were about ten towers, both round and square, and according to 18th-century sources the wall was about 'three fathoms high' (5.5 m). The wall was torn up gradually in the 18th and 19th centuries, but two towers survive, one from the 1470s, the other from 1547–50.

The City Library (1927–35; badly damaged in 1940–41) by Alvar Aalto was an outstanding example of 20th-century architecture, in which the problem of lighting in the reading-rooms was solved by an imaginative system of skylights and portholes, while the lecture hall had a ceiling of interwoven red pine that created a subtly undulating surface intended to diffuse sound (*see* ACOUSTICS).

BIBLIOGRAPHY

J. W. Ruuth: *Viborgs stads historia* [The history of Vyborg], i (Helsinki, 1906)

J. W. Ruuth and R. Rosin: *Viipurin kaupungin historia* [The history of Vyborg], i (Helsinki, 1982)

CARL JACOB GARDBERG

Vyner, Lady **Mary.** *See under* GREY.

Vyšší Brod Abbey [Ger. Hohenfurth]. Cistercian monastery in the southern Czech Republic, *c.* 20 km south of Ceský Krumlov. The abbey was founded in 1259 by Vok of Rožmberk (*d* 1262), a leading nobleman at the court of the Přemysls. In 1258 he had asked the general chapter of the Cistercian Order to visit the site intended for the new monastery, to which he had already given the first endowment. On 23 May 1259 the Bishop of Prague, Bishop John III of Dražice, confirmed the monastery in the grant of rights of patronage to the churches at Rožmitál and Přídolí, and on 1 June he confirmed the grant in full to Vok at Vyšší Brod. At the same time the church (or probably its foundation level) was consecrated.

The site of the abbey is on the upper reaches of the River Vltava, at the edge of the Rožmberk domains on the border between Bohemia and Austria, and close to the old road from Linz to Prague. This evidently caused the abbey to be colonized by monks from Wilhering Abbey, near Linz. On 17 July 1264 King Přemysl Ottokar II confirmed the foundation. After the death of Vok of Rožmberk, Vyšší Brod became the Rožmberk family burial church. With the death of the patron, however, building work was held up, and it was not until the 1270s that Jindřich, Lord of Rožmberk (*reg* 1262–1310), gave further endowments. In 1277 he and his brother Vítek granted several villages to the abbey, and in 1278 he arranged for an annual payment of ten talents until the building was completed. In 1281 Jindřich gave a further eight villages. In 1292–3 the high cost of completing the church led to the issue of indulgences to those who contributed to its building and furnishing; indulgences issued in July 1293 concerned payment for the chandeliers, and that year the church was finally consecrated.

The oldest and, from the architectural point of view, most interesting part of the monastic ensemble is the choir and transept of the church, and the east range of conventual buildings, an integrated structure of inventive design from the 1280s. The plan of the church, dedicated to the Assumption of the Virgin, derives from the so-called Clairvaux II or Bernardine type of Cistercian plan: a central high choir flanked by a pair of low side chapels opening into the transept, which projects one bay beyond the nave aisles (see fig.). Compared with the earlier plan, however, the choir has a polygonal apse, and the side chapels have attractive triangular apses. On the exterior the main apse is articulated by flat buttresses and double windows with continuous mouldings, and tracery in the Amiens Cathedral style of open cinquefoil and trefoil. Inside, the choir still has 'classical' grouped shafts, which also replace the triumphal arch and articulate the transept walls. In the side chapels, however, the vault ribs are corbelled into consoles decorated with double rows of abstract, geometric leaf patterns, similar to those in the chapel of the Guardian Angels at the Cistercian abbey of Zlatá Koruna. Outside, built into the north wall of the north side apse, is a spiral staircase, reached from inside through a door with the Rožmberk emblem in its tympanum, leading to the Rožmberk family tribune above the side chapels, a unique instance of a family gallery in a monastic church.

Abutting the south transept is the rib-vaulted sacristy, which is probably the earliest of the conventual buildings. The tympanum of the sacristy portal has a complex iconographic programme of vine leaves (symbolizing the Lord as the vine) with two foxes' heads, and the hand of God at the top. The archivolt is ornamented with stylized

Vyšší Brod Abbey, view from the east, founded 1259

foliage that is most closely paralleled by that in the Elisabethkirche at Marburg.

The chapter house, south of the sacristy, has the same stylistic elements as the eastern parts of the church. Its entrance has as simple a profile as that of the sacristy portal, and the mouldings of the window jambs have undulating profiles, as in the transept chapels. The chapter house has a central column with four major and four minor shafts, rising from a polygonal pedestal decorated with small gables. The tall cup-shaped capitals have two layers of crisply cut foliage. The vault ribs, however, do not correspond to the shafting: only four ribs spring from the centre, to meet others corbelled in to the side walls, forming a tri-radial pattern (as in the transept chapels), which is one of the first examples in Bohemia. The window tracery, patterns of teardrops and rosettes, is as correspondingly free as the vaulting. The designer of these earliest parts of the monastic buildings drew his inspiration from French High Gothic architecture, which he freely enriched with post-classical elements.

About 1320 the design of the church was altered: the basilican nave was abandoned in favour of a hall design with the walls articulated by polygonal supports and wide four-light windows with curvilinear tracery. The piers do not belong to a single campaign. About 1330 the lower parts of the four eastern pairs were built in the form of irregular octagons, the crossing piers being fluted. The two western piers were built c. 1340–50, the upper parts of all the existing piers were completed, and the nave was vaulted with quadripartite rib vaults. The completion of the church can be associated with Petr of Rožmberk (d 1347) who is regarded as the second founder of the monastery. The bays next to the crossing are also 14th-century work, the oldest being the north transept (c. 1350). There followed the vaulting of the choir straight bay with spur consoles, while in the south transept there are Czech bases. Finally the western arm was vaulted (1380). In 1422 the church was burnt down by the Hussites. Most of the subsequent restoration was undertaken in the 19th century.

UNPUBLISHED SOURCES

Prague, State Inst. Care & Protection Nature [V. Mencl: *Klášterní a opatský kostel P. Marie ve Vyšším Brodě* [The monastic and abbey church of the Virgin Mary at Vyšší Brod] (1968)]

BIBLIOGRAPHY

M. Pangerl: *Urkundenbuch des Cistercienserstiftes B. Mariae V. zu Hohenfurt in Böhmen*, Fontes rerum austriacarum, ii/23 (Vienna, 1865)

V. Mencl: 'Podunajská reforma gotické katedrály' [Danubian modifications to the Gothic cathedral], *Umění*, xvii (1969), pp. 301–34

V. Všetečka: *Příspěvek k opoznání nejstarších stavebních dějin vyšebrodského kláštera* [Contribution regarding the history of the oldest buildings at Vyšší Brod Abbey] (diss., Prague, Charles U., 1973)

J. Kutham: *Počátky a rozmach gotické architektury v jižních Čechách: K problematice cisterciácké stavební tvorby* [Beginnings and flowering of Gothic architecture in southern Bohemia: on the problems of Cistercian architecture] (Prague, 1983), pp. 220–63

P. Crossley: *Gothic Architecture in the Reign of Kasimir the Great* (Kraków, 1985)

H. SOUKUPOVÁ

Waagen, Gustav Friedrich (*b* Hamburg, 11 Feb 1794; *d* Copenhagen, 15 July 1868). German art historian and museum director. His father was the painter Friedrich Ludwig Waagen (1750–1822), and his uncle was the poet Ludwig Tieck. He volunteered for the Napoleonic campaign of 1813–14 and after his return from the war attended lectures at the university of Breslau (now Wrocław, Poland). He then devoted himself to studying art, visiting galleries in Germany, the Netherlands and Italy. He attracted attention with a pamphlet on *Über Hubert und Johann van Eyck* (1822), which led to his appointment as director of the new Altes Museum in Berlin in 1832.

He wrote *Kunstwerke und Künstler in England und Paris* (Berlin, 1837–9) after trips to England and Paris, and this became the basis of the more significant *The Treasures of Art in Great Britain* (London, 1854–7) translated from the German by Lady Elizabeth Eastlake. One volume of this work, *Galleries and Cabinets of Art in Great Britain*, mentions over 9000 pictures and, although written in the form of a travel diary, is invaluable for locating works of art in private collections and providing a picture of the state of connoisseurship in Victorian England. Waagen was greatly respected in England and gave evidence on more than one occasion to select committees of the House of Commons. The evidence he gave to the select committee of 1835–6, which was examining ways of popularizing the study of art and design, revealed Waagen to be deeply committed to the arts and to public access to them, and it displayed his expertise as a curator of art.

Waagen's evidence provided a sketch of a coherent national gallery policy; he was emphatic that centralization of all national works in a centre of excellence in a capital city was a mistake, and he urged the proliferation of regional centres around a great national collection. He also made trenchant comments on art education, speaking of the time when artists were also craftsmen and when young would-be artists were apprenticed to masters to learn their craft. He contrasted this with teaching in academies, which he thought led to art produced according to cold general rules and to the elevation of the mediocre at the expense of innovation. Waagen shared this reaction to Neoclassicism with Johann Wolfgang von Goethe, Gotthold Ephraim Lessing and Johann Gottfried Herder. He was committed to the need to 'educate the eye of the people', to be achieved by carefully thought-out exhibitions using historical arrangements, supplemented by short catalogues and lectures, with Sunday opening of galleries (this being the day when workers were free to attend). He also favoured entry fees on the grounds that people gave more attention to what had been paid for. He recommended state purchase of major works and advocated the employment of artists to undertake the decoration of public buildings, such as the new House of Commons in London.

Waagen also gave evidence to the select committee of 1850, which was investigating the accommodation offered by the National Gallery in London and the best ways of preserving and exhibiting works of art. Waagen drew attention to the greater deterioration of pictures in London compared to Berlin, which was entirely due to London's polluted atmosphere; he thought it was impossible to preserve pictures in central London and recommended the location of the new gallery in Kensington. He also gave advice on the lighting and grouping of pictures in galleries (*see* DISPLAY OF ART, §II, 3(iii)). As in his evidence to the committee of 1835, Waagen's wish to make art available to all was apparent; he thought that although the uneducated might not be capable of appreciation, they could enjoy and contemplate works of art.

In 1844 Waagen had been appointed professor of art history at the University of Berlin, and in 1861 he went to St Petersburg to advise on the arrangement and classification of pictures in the imperial collection. On his return to Germany in 1864 he published *Die Gemäldesammlung in der Kaiserlichen Eremitage zu St Petersburg* (1864). His other works include *Handbuch der deutschen und niederländischen Malerschulen* (1862), *Die vornehmsten Kunstdenkmäler in Wien* (1866–7) and essays on Rubens, Mantegna and Signorelli.

WRITINGS
Über Hubert und Johann van Eyck (Breslau, 1822)
Kunstwerke und Künstler in England und Paris (Berlin, 1837–9; Eng. trans. London, 1838)
The Treasures of Art in Great Britain, 4 vols (London, 1854–7)
Handbuch der deutschen und niederländischen Malerschulen (Stuttgart, 1862)
Die Gemäldesammlung in der kaiserlichen Eremitage zu St Petersburg (Munich, 1864)
Die vornehmsten Kunstdenkmäler in Wien, 2 vols (Vienna, 1866–7)
A. Woltmann, ed.: *Kleine Schriften* (Berlin, 1875)

BIBLIOGRAPHY
A. Graves: *Summary of an Index to Waagen* (London, 1912)

COLIN LYAS

Wąchock Abbey. Cistercian abbey in Poland, dedicated to the Virgin Mary and St Florian. The abbey was founded in 1179 by Bishop Gedko of Kraków as the third daughter house of Morimond to be established in Little Poland after Jędrzejów (1140–49) and Sulejów (1177). The site, in the valley of the River Kamienna, lay on an important trade route linking Russia with the Baltic Sea; contrary to Cistercian habit, the monks settled in a densely populated area.

Excavations on the monastic site unexpectedly revealed sections of a large, late 11th-century ducal residence of stone, probably built for Prince Vladislav I Herman (1079–1102) and his wife Judyta Maria Salicka, sister of Emperor Henry IV. The residence, with the surrounding lands, was donated *c.* 1124 to the diocese of Kraków, which presented it to the Cistercians arriving from France in 1179. At the same time, probably at the founder's expense, the old residence was adapted to meet the monks' requirements. Evidence suggests that the first abbey church was built in stone on the site of the residence and made use of its building materials.

In the 13th century the Cistercians replaced the existing buildings with a complex conforming closely to the Order's traditions. The basilican church is 41.17 m long internally and consists of a four-bay aisled nave, a transept and a square-ended choir flanked by rectangular side chapels. The nave is now 12.53 m high and has quadripartite rib vaulting supported by cruciform piers, which are strengthened by projecting half-columns with carved capitals and semi-conical corbels. Of the original east cloister range only the chapter house (see fig.), with a vault supported by four columns, a cell, a passageway and a monks' hall with a vault supported by a single pier remain in their original form. The only other surviving element is a hall

Wąchock Abbey, chapter house, interior looking south-west, 13th century

refectory occupying the central part of the south range. The remaining parts of the cloister and the monastic complex have been either destroyed or rebuilt in modern times: the monks' gate, a guest-house, an infirmary, surrounding walls and outhouses.

In addition to the rooms already mentioned, the east range had a sacristy, a large two-aisled dormitory, a novices' hall and latrines with a sewage system built of stone. Above the sacristy were the abbot's room and an archive. In the south range there was a kitchen, its vault supported by a single pier, and a similarly vaulted warming-room with a heat distribution system closely modelled on Roman steam baths. It heated the monks' refectory and dormitory, the monks' hall, a room above the warming-room and the novices' hall. The west range had a two-aisled cellar, a passageway, a dispensary and the lay brothers' hall refectory and hall dormitory. The quadripartite ribbed vaulting has survived in the chapter house, monks' hall and refectory, although it existed elsewhere. The passageways, stairways and the cell had barrel vaults, while the cloister, the lay brothers' dormitory, the archive and the abbot's room had open tie-beam roofs. Most of the construction used ashlar selected from varieties of local sandstone, giving a characteristic red and white band effect. Some of the vaults, as in the church and the monks' refectory, were built of brick. Corbels, keystones, the bases and capitals of columns and the friezes in the church, chapter house, refectory and probably once in the cloister have rich sculpture with zoomorphic, figurative, geometric and plant motifs. There were multicoloured glazed ceramic tile floors in the church and other buildings, while the monastic buildings had a glazed ceramic tile roof. Contemporary wall paintings survive in the chapter house, refectory and cloister with geometric, figural and plant motifs. Numerous fragments of 13th-century stained glass have been excavated on the site of the glassworks.

A brief signature carved on the church façade indicates that the designer of the 13th-century monastic complex was the architect Simon. Probably a Cistercian lay brother, he was in charge of a large workshop, the other work of which includes three Cistercian monasteries (Koprzywnica, similarly signed Simon, Sulejów and Jędrzejów) and at least ten collegiate and parish churches in the vicinity of the monastic establishments. Numerous masons' marks and other identification marks indicate that nearly all of Simon's craftsmen were laymen. Evidence suggests that all the workmen of the team operating in Little Poland between 1218 and 1239 were Italians and that Simon was a Tuscan who had gained his professional experience in the artistic circle at Casamari Abbey (Lazio). He is often identified with a master of the same name who was mentioned in 1239 as one of those in charge of the building of S Galgano Monastery in Tuscany.

The abbey was partially destroyed, losing the church's lead roof, during a Mongol invasion in 1259; the abbot's palace was built and the cloister transformed in the first half of the 16th century, and there was a fundamental reconstruction of the cloister ranges and surrounding buildings after fire damage caused by Tartars (*c.* 1636) and Hungarians (1656). The church interior was partially modernized in 1764, but the abbey was devastated after the closure in 1819. Restoration work continued into the

20th century, with conservation carried out between the two world wars and after World War II. Wąchock was returned to the Cistercians in 1951.

BIBLIOGRAPHY

W. Łuszczkiewicz: 'Romańska architektura w Wąchocku: Kościół i reszty cysterskiego klasztoru' [Romanesque architecture in Wąchock: the church and other remains of the Cistercian abbey], *Sprawozdania Komisji Historii Sztuki* [Proceedings of the Commission for the History of Art], v (1892), pp. 49–71

M. Niwiński: *Opactwo cystersow w Wąchocku: Fundacja i dzieje uposażenia do końca wieków średnich* [The Cistercian abbey at Wąchock: its foundation and endowments to the end of the Middle Ages] (Kraków, 1930)

Z. Świechowski and J. Zachwatowicz: 'L'Architecture cistercienne en Pologne et ses liens avec la France', *Biul. Hist. Sztuki* [Bulletin of the history of art], xx (1958), pp. 139–73

K. Białoskórska: 'L'Abbaye cistercienne de Wąchock', *Cah. Civilis. Méd.*, v (1962), pp. 335–50

——: 'Polish Cistercian Architecture and its Contacts with Italy', *Gesta*, iv (1965), pp. 14–22

——: 'Wąchocka rezydencja książęca: Nieznany episod z dziejow Polski wczesnopiastowskiej' [The Wąchock ducal residence: a little-known episode in the history of early Piast Poland], *Biul. Hist. Sztuki* [Bulletin of the history of art], xli (1979), pp. 135–78

——: '*Cum muros eius quadro consumasset lapide*: Contribution à l'histoire de la fondation de l'abbaye de Wąchock', *Mélanges à la mémoire du père Anselme Dimier*, iii (Pupillin, 1982), pp. 195–204

G. Labuda: 'W sprawie osoby fundatora i daty powstania najstarszych (przedcysterskich) budowli sakralno-pałacowych w Wąchocku' [On the identity of the founder and the date of foundation of the earliest (pre-Cistercian) religious-palatial buildings in Wąchock], *Biul. Hist. Sztuki* [Bulletin of the history of art], xlv (1983), pp. 251–5

K. Białoskórska: 'Wąchocki skarb brakteatów: Przyczynek do dziejów mennictwa kościelnego w Polsce w XIII stuleciu' [The Wąchock hoard of bracteates: a contribution to the history of church coinage in 13th-century Poland], *Wiadomości Numi.* [Numismatic news], xxix (1989), pp. 166–90

KRYSTYNA BIAŁOSKÓRSKA

Wachsmann, Konrad (Ludwig) (*b* Frankfurt an der Oder, 16 May 1901; *d* Los Angeles, CA, 25 Nov 1980). American architect of German birth. He began his career in 1917 as an apprentice cabinetmaker and carpenter, and, already a skilled craftsman, he undertook more formal academic studies at the Kunstgewerbeschule in Berlin in 1922. During 1923–4 he studied under Heinrich Tessenow at the Hochschule der Bildenden Künste in Dresden, and the following year he was a 'master student' under Hans Poelzig at the Akademie der Künste in Berlin. Through Poelzig in 1926 he went to work in Niesky, Silesia, at Christoph and Unmack, then probably the largest manufacturer of prefabricated wooden buildings in Europe; for the first time he experienced the potential of the industrial production of buildings, which he described as a 'revelation'. In 1929, on the strength of a commission to design a house for the scientist Albert Einstein at Caputh (see Wachsmann, 1930, p. 95), he resigned his position as chief designer at Christoph and Unmack to set up private practice in Berlin; this was, however, unsuccessful because of the Depression.

In 1932 Wachsmann won the Prix de Rome and took up residence at the German Academy in Rome, but Adolf Hitler's accession to power the following year forced Wachsmann, as a Jew, to leave. He practised architecture on a modest scale in Rome, worked in Spain and travelled throughout Europe, photographing architectural monuments for guidebooks. It was on one such mission in Split, Croatia, that he met WALTER GROPIUS for the first time.

In 1938, anxious about the growing Italian–German alliance, he went to France, an ill-timed move that led to his internment as a German when World War II began in 1939. Largely through the efforts of Gropius and Einstein, both by then in the USA, he was released and finally joined Gropius in Lincoln, MA, in 1941 as a house guest and professional collaborator. In 1942 he moved to New York and was instrumental in setting up the General Panel Corporation, to develop, manufacture and market the 'Packaged House', a prefabricated housing system that he and Gropius had jointly designed. This venture, technically impeccable but financially disastrous, was to consume a great deal of Wachsmann's time and creative energy until its final collapse in 1952. In the same period, however, he perfected his Mobilar Structural System (1942), a lightweight steel space-frame of great ingenuity and elegance, which was the forerunner of his tubular steel system for the construction of aircraft hangars, undertaken for the US Air Force in 1951. Significant later projects included unbuilt designs for a steel skyscraper and port development for Genoa (1961–3, see Ward, pl. 11) and a high-tension cable structure for the Civic Center in California City, CA (1966–71).

Central to all Wachsmann's work was the development of industrially produced repetitive modular units, such as enclosing panels and structural tubes, and the devising of universal jointing systems and connections of ever-increasing sophistication to maximize the combination of these units. These designs were motivated by Wachsmann's passionate belief in the potential of technology, illuminated by imagination and a radiant aesthetic sense, and presented in highly finished drawings. Most of his proposals were prototypical rather than specific, often carried out as research and development projects together with his students, first at the Illinois Institute of Technology in Chicago, where he was the Director of Advanced Building Research (1949–56), and later at the University of Southern California, Los Angeles (1965–72), where he remained as Professor Emeritus.

WRITINGS

Holzhausbau (Berlin, 1930)
'Machine Energy: The Technique of our Time', *Building for Modern Man*, ed. T. H. Creighton (Princeton, 1949), pp. 46–8
Wendepunkt im Bauen (Wiesbaden, 1959); Eng. trans. as *The Turning Point of Building* (New York, 1961)

BIBLIOGRAPHY

D. Travers, ed.: 'The Work of Konrad Wachsmann', *A. & Archit.*, lxxxiv/5 (1967), pp. 6–29
Konrad Wachsmann—50 Years of Life and Work: Towards Industrialized Building (exh. cat., Los Angeles, UCLA 1971); review by R. Ward jr in *Amer. Inst. Architects J.*, lvii/3 (1972), pp. 33–42
G. Herbert: *The Dream of the Factory-made House: Walter Gropius and Konrad Wachsmann* (Cambridge, MA, 1984)
M. Grüning: *Der Wachsmann-Report: Auskunfte eines Architekten* (Berlin, 1985)
R. Ward, S. Cruz and E. Wang: *The Complete Project Works of Konrad Wachsmann, May 16, 1901–November 25, 1980* (in preparation)

GILBERT HERBERT

Wächter, (Georg Friedrich) Eberhard (*b* Balingen, nr Tübingen, 29 Feb 1762; *d* Stuttgart, 14 Aug 1852). German painter. He was one of the leading figures of German Neo-classicism and a precursor of the Nazarenes. From 1781 to 1784 he trained as an artist at the Karlsschule in Stuttgart and worked on his own in Mannheim. In 1785 he went to Paris, where he studied with Jean-Baptiste Regnault until 1792. From either 1792 or 1793 to 1798 he lived in Rome and was influenced by Asmus Jakob Carstens's strict formal language and tendency to monumentalize. He was also impressed with Classical art and the work of Italian painters of the 13th and 14th centuries. He created his most original works in Rome, among them *Job and his Friends* (begun 1793 or 1794, completed 1824; Stuttgart, Staatsgal.). His choice of a biblical subject and his flat relief-like space accounts for his subsequent popularity with the Nazarene painters. In 1796 he married Franziska Bandini and converted to Catholicism. In 1808 he returned to Stuttgart but soon moved to Vienna, where he taught at the Akademie der Bildenden Künste and particularly influenced such pupils as Franz Pforr and Friedrich Overbeck. It was probably his nostalgia for all aspects of Rome that encouraged the future Nazarenes to go there themselves. His paintings executed after his departure from Italy rarely rise above the mediocre. They were done in a more conventionally classicist style and show his obvious lack of technical ability. However, *Ship of Life* (version v, *c.* 1825; Stuttgart, priv. col.; see Köster, 1966, fig. 3) is thought to have inspired Ludwig Richter (who in 1826 visited Wächter in his studio) to paint his well-known *Crossing the River at the Schreckenstein bei Aussig* (1837; Dresden, Gemäldegal. Neue Meister). Many of Wächter's compositions deal with pictorial concerns central to 19th-century art; Köster calls them 'building-blocks to later pictorial ideas' (Köster, 1966, p. 249).

BIBLIOGRAPHY

P. Köster: 'Wächters *Lebensschiff* und Richters *Überfahrt am Schreckenstein*', *Z. Kstgesch.*, xxix (1966), pp. 241–9

——: *Eberhard Wächter (1762–1852): Ein Maler des deutschen Klassizismus* (Bonn, 1968)

H. von Einem: *Deutsche Malerei des Klassizismus und der Romantik, 1760 bis 1840* (Munich, 1978), pp. 55–6, 124, 180

□

Wackenroder, Wilhelm (Heinrich) (*b* Berlin, 13 July 1773; *d* Berlin, 13 Feb 1798). German writer. He was trained in law but devoted most of his time to music, poetry and the visual arts. In these pursuits he received guidance and support from Karl Philipp Moritz, Johann Friedrich Reichardt (1752–1814), Erduin Julius Koch (1764–1834) and, above all, Ludwig Tieck, with whom he travelled to Wörlitz, Dessau, Halle, Leipzig, Meissen and Dresden in the autumn of 1792. The following spring Tieck and Wackenroder both entered the university at Erlangen, from where they explored Nuremberg, Banz, Bamberg and the pilgrimage church of Vierzehnheiligen. Later in 1793 they transferred to the Georg-August-Universität in Göttingen, where Wackenroder was introduced to art history by Johann Dominicus Fiorillo. While at Göttingen the friends planned a trip to Italy, where Tieck intended to pursue his poetry and Wackenroder his music. The trip was never realized, however, and in the autumn of 1794 Wackenroder was called back to legal work in Berlin by his father. In 1796 an essay by Wackenroder on Albrecht Dürer appeared in Reichardt's periodical *Deutschland*. The following year, more of Wackenroder's essays on art and music, along with additions by Tieck, were published anonymously as *Herzenser-giessungen eines kunstliebenden Klosterbruders*. The success

of this publication did not release Wackenroder from his legal work, and it was only after his death that several of his last essays were incorporated by Tieck in the *Phantasien über die Kunst, für Freunde der Kunst* (1799).

The *Herzensergiessungen*, one of the seminal works of early Romanticism, attracted considerable attention on its publication. In it Wackenroder offered a new understanding of art and the artist, emphasizing inspiration, tolerance and the role of nature and art as revelations of the divine. Drawing on the theories of Johann Gottfried Herder, Johann Georg Hamann and Moritz as well as on the writings of Joachim von Sandrart and Giorgio Vasari, few of these ideas were new. The originality lies in the synthesis, passion and pietistic enthusiasm, challenging contemporary notions of objective aesthetic standards with their emphasis on rational and classical norms. In Wackenroder's view rationality was an inadequate foundation for either the creation or the appreciation of art, both of which depended on enthusiasm and imagination. Moreover, these qualities, while sufficient for the appreciation of art, were inadequate for true creativity. The latter depended on inspiration, which blossomed only under divine illumination. Wackenroder's ideal artists, Raphael and Dürer, are depicted as simple, devout individuals, sensitive to the divine and fortunate to work within a sympathetic and pious culture. In contrast, Joseph Berglinger, Wackenroder's loosely autobiographical modern artist and protagonist of one of the essays, is presented as imbued with enthusiasm but creatively constrained by his deficiencies of character and by the materialistic society in which he works.

Though Wackenroder has been associated with Romantic medievalism, his writings are dominated by Renaissance artists, especially Raphael, Dürer, Leonardo, Francesco Francia and Michelangelo. He promoted medievalism only indirectly, by advocating the toleration of personal and national variations in artistic production and appreciation. By challenging the prerogatives of classical art within rationalist criticism Wackenroder fuelled German interest in a national art and fostered medievalism, but his own tastes remained quite conventionally rooted in the work of early 16th-century masters.

WRITINGS

The editions by A. Gillies (Eng. trans., Oxford, 1948) and by M. H. Schubert (Eng. trans., University Park and London, 1971) of the second item below and of Wackenroder's contributions to the third both contain substantial introductions.

'Ehrengedächtnis unsers ehrwürdigen Ahnherrn Albrecht Dürers, von einem kunstliebenden Klosterbruder', *Deutschland*, iii (1796), pp. 59–73

with L. Tieck: *Herzensergiessungen eines kunstliebenden Klosterbruders* (Berlin, 1797)

——: *Phantasien über die Kunst, für Freunde der Kunst* (Hamburg, 1799)

L. Tieck, ed.: *Phantasien über die Kunst, von einem kunstliebenden Klosterbruder* (1814, 2/1818, 3/1917)

H. Höhn, ed.: *Werke und Briefe von Wilhelm Heinrich Wackenroder* (Berlin, 1938, rev. 1984)

——: *Wilhelm Heinrich Wackenroder: Reisebriefe* (Berlin, 1938)

BIBLIOGRAPHY

ADB

W. D. Robson-Scott: 'Wackenroder and the Middle Ages', *Mod. Lang. Rev.*, l (1955), pp. 156–67

H. Lippuner: *Wackenroder/Tieck und die bildende Kunst: Grundlegung der romantischen Aesthetik* (Zurich, 1965)

M. Bollacher: *Wackenroder und die Kunstauffassung der frühen Romantik* (Darmstadt, 1983)

J. Ellis: *Joseph Berglinger in Perspective* (Berne, 1985)

M. Barasch: *Modern Theories of Art: From Winckelmann to Baudelaire* (New York, 1990), pp. 293–303

ROBERT E. MCVAUGH

Wackerbarth, Christoph August von (*b* Kogel, nr Ratzeburg, 22 March 1662; *d* Dresden, 14 Aug 1734). German diplomat, building administrator and patron. He came from the old aristocracy of Lower Saxony. In 1685 he was summoned to the court in Dresden of John-George III, Elector of Saxony and King of Poland (*reg* 1680–91), where he trained under Wolf Caspar von Klengel in the science of building and fortifications. His studies took him as far as the Peloponnese and twice to Rome (1691 and 1695). Elector Frederick-Augustus I appointed him to succeed Johann Georg Starke in 1695 as chief supervisor of civil buildings, and in 1697 he became general superintendent of military and civil building and of all academies in Saxony and Poland. He reorganized the state building office, enabling it to function with improved effectiveness. In 1705 Wackerbarth was promoted to the rank of Reichsgraf, and from 1718, as governor of Dresden, he was also in charge of private building there. Under his direction building regulations were issued in 1720 that remained in force until 1827; it was to their aesthetic and health provisions that Dresden owed much of its beauty. Although it is unlikely that Wackerbarth was a practising architect, he played an important role in recognizing and fostering the talents of the architects in his charge, including Mathäus Daniel Pöppelmann, Zacharias Longuelune, Johann Christoph Knöffel, Georg Bähr, Johann Gottfried Fehre (*c.* 1685–*c.* 1753) and Johann Georg Schmidt. Among the projects in Dresden constructed under his direction was the government building (1718; destr. 1728). In 1719 he began work on the castle and park at Grosssedlitz, near Pirna, and in 1723 he initiated the building of the Ritterakademie (destr.) at Dresden Neustadt. This building, together with his own home, Wackerbarths Ruhe, at Radebeul, near Dresden, and the rebuilding (1728) of Schloss Zabeltitz at Riesa, which he also owned, involved Knöffel, to whom Wackerbarth gave particular support. Wackerbarth also bought works of art in Italy, Vienna and Leipzig, for the Elector's collection and his own, and arranged the nuptial festivities for the heir to the throne (later Frederick-Augustus II) in 1719.

BIBLIOGRAPHY

Thieme–Becker

Frigander: *Leben und Taten des Welt-berühmten General-Feld-Marschalls Grafens von Wackerbarth* (1738)

F. Löffler: *Das alte Dresden* (Dresden, 1956)

Barock in Dresden (exh. cat., Essen, Villa Hügel, 1986)

VOLKER HELAS

Wackernagel, Martin (*b* Basle, 2 Jan 1881; *d* Begnins, nr Geneva, 14 Jan 1962). Swiss art historian. He completed his doctorate under Heinrich Wölfflin in Berlin in 1905 and during his subsequent assistantship at the Istituto Storico Germanico, Rome, wrote *Die Plastik des XI. und XII. Jahrhunderts in Apulien.* He taught art history in Halle and Leipzig before accepting a professorship (1920) at the University of Münster, where he taught until 1948.

Wackernagel pioneered the study of art in relation to a particular historical and social context, specifically that of Renaissance Florence. His *Der Lebensraum des Künstlers in der florentinischen Renaissance* (1938) set an imposing precedent for similar studies that proliferated later in the 20th century. In sections on commissions and functions of art, patronage and the life, working conditions and social status of artists, the book provides detailed, carefully documented information on the Florentine artistic setting from *c.* 1420 to 1530, including descriptive reconstructions of the original locations of many works. He focused on great projects such as the cathedral, baptistery and Palazzo Vecchio and on smaller undertakings for individual churches, convents and private homes; on the demands and taste of such individual patrons as the Medici and such corporate ones as the city government, the guilds and the religious orders. He assembled data on artists as individuals and as a group: their work and business practices, professional organization, social life and personalities, as well as their relationship to the contemporary art market. His aim was not to expound a theory so much as to create a detailed, panoramic image of Renaissance Florence as a successful nurturing environment for flourishing artistic production. In this he was influenced by the work of Hippolyte Taine and his concept of the influential milieu; Jacob Burckhardt (especially his studies on Renaissance collectors and on commissions grouped by type and function); and Aby Warburg, who in his studies of Florentine Renaissance art first drew attention to the impact of demand and the requirements of the patron. Eugène Müntz's surveys of Renaissance art may also have been models as well as sources.

Wackernagel outlined his approach in *Vier Aufsätze über geschichtliche und gegenwärtige Faktoren des Kunstlebens* and his article 'Der Lebensraum der bildenden Kunst in älterer und gegenwärtiger Zeit'. There he discussed his term 'Lebensraum' (with a usage quite distinct from Hitler's) as 'the whole complex of economic-material, social and cultural ... preconditions that in any way affected the existence and activity of the artist'. His interest in the close relationship of art to daily life in the past had its counterpart in an intense involvement with art and artists of his own time. He directed art associations and organized exhibitions, competitions and festivals. Like his wife, Ilse von Stach, a poet and playwright whom he married in 1911, he was a convert to Roman Catholicism (1921). He regarded religious art as an area where the alienation he perceived between modern artists and the public might be overcome. His essays on contemporary church art demonstrate his conviction that churches, which still needed the artist to produce works for a particular destination and purpose, could foster modern art of high quality and relevance to its audience; and he saw valuable examples of this in the ecclesiastical projects that had called forth much of the greatest Florentine Renaissance art.

Resolutely apolitical, Wackernagel avoided theoretical generalizations about the impact of social conditions or class on an artist's style. He sought instead to show how the many purposes for which art was considered necessary, the consequent widespread demand, and the patrons' openness to artistic innovation made possible the scope and brilliance of Florentine art. His hope was that a fuller awareness of these conditions might benefit the artists and public of his own time. His interests also included Apulian Romanesque sculpture, German Baroque architecture, the writings of Erasmus and the works of Cézanne and Manet. At the end of his life he was at work on a manuscript on 19th-century Italian painting.

WRITINGS

Die Plastik des XI. und XII. Jahrhunderts in Apulien (Leipzig, 1911)
Die Baukunst des 17. und 18. Jahrhunderts, II. Baukunst des 17. und 18. Jahrhunderts in den germanischen Ländern (Berlin and Neubabelsberg, 1915, rev. Potsdam, n.d.)
ed. and trans. G. Vasari: *Le vite de' più eccellenti pittori, scultori, ed architettori* (Florence, 1568) as *Die Lebensbeschreibungen der berühmtesten Architekten, Bildhauer und Maler* (Strasbourg, 1916) [first half of vol. 1]
'Die Kunst der Kirche', *Hochland*, xvii/2 (1920), pp. 88–93
'Der Lebensraum der bildenden Kunst in älterer und gegenwärtiger Zeit', *Schweiz. Rundschau*, xxxv (1935–6), pp. 42–55
Vier Aufsätze über geschichtliche und gegenwärtige Faktoren des Kunstlebens (Wattenscheid, 1936); review by U. Middeldorf in *A. Bull.*, xx (1938), pp. 123–4
Der Lebensraum des Künstlers in der florentinischen Renaissance (Leipzig, 1938), trans. A. Luchs: *The World of the Florentine Renaissance Artist* (Princeton, 1981) [see esp. intro., pp. xi–xxx]; review by U. Middeldorf in *A. Bull.*, xxi (1939), pp. 298–300
'Von Stiftertum in der kirchlichen Kunst', *Hochland*, xxxv/2 (1938), pp. 476–87
'Der ideale Landsitz eines christlichen Humanisten in der Renaissance', *Festgabe für Alois Fuchs zum 70. Geburtstag* (Paderborn, 1950), pp. 159–71

BIBLIOGRAPHY

I. von Stach: *Der Petrus-Segen* (Münster, 1940)
Festschrift Martin Wackernagel zum 75. Geburtstag (Cologne, 1958), pp. 212–16 [bibliog. to 1957]
G. Fiensch: 'Erinnerungen an Martin Wackernagel', *Westfalen: Hft. Gesch., Kst & Vlksknd.*, lix (1981), pp. 93–6

ALISON LUCHS

Wadsworth, Daniel (*b* Middletown, CT, 8 Aug 1771; *d* Hartford, CT, 28 July 1848). American patron and collector. The son of Hartford's wealthiest merchant and financier, Wadsworth led the retired and somewhat eccentric life of a *rentier*. He dabbled in architecture and achieved a moderate competence in landscape drawing. Wadsworth collected art in a desultory manner, buying original paintings and copies from John Trumbull (his wife's uncle) and commissioning works from Thomas Sully, Alvan Fisher, Chauncey B. Ives and Robert Ball Hughes (1806–68). His preference was for landscape painting, his interest no doubt stimulated by his purchase in 1805 of a spectacular country estate, Monte Video, overlooking Hartford. He was an early and fervent supporter of Thomas Cole, commissioning seven paintings from the artist between 1826 and 1828 including *White Mountain Scenery*, *St John the Baptist in the Wilderness*, *Last of the Mohicans* and *View of Monte Video* (all Hartford, CT, Wadsworth Atheneum).

Wadsworth is remembered primarily as the founder of the first public art museum in the USA. Conceived in 1841, the Wadsworth Atheneum opened in 1844 in a Gothic Revival building designed by Ithiel Town and Alexander Jackson Davis. Wadsworth commissioned works from Cole and Frederic Edwin Church for the fledgling institution and bequeathed to it his own collection.

BIBLIOGRAPHY

Daniel Wadsworth, Patron of the Arts (exh. cat. by R. Saunders and H. Raye, Hartford, CT, Wadsworth Atheneum, 1981)

B. J. McNulty, ed.: *The Correspondence of Thomas Cole and Daniel Wadsworth* (Hartford, 1983)

ALAN WALLACH

Wadsworth, Edward (*b* Cleckheaton, W. Yorks, 29 Oct 1889; *d* London, 21 June 1949). English painter. He was raised in a northern industrial environment that was to appear with great forcefulness in his Vorticist work. He studied engineering in Munich from 1906 to 1907 and, like many other Vorticists (*see* VORTICISM), Wadsworth's interest in the machine showed itself at an early age. He also studied art at the Knirr School in Munich in his spare time, before attending Bradford School of Art; he then studied through a scholarship at the Slade School of Art (1908–12) in London. Early paintings like *Harrogate Corporation Brickworks* (1908; untraced) show a growing interest in industrial subjects. Under the impact of the Post-Impressionists, he turned for a while to portraiture, beach scenes and still-lifes. His work was included in the final month of the Second Post-Impressionist Exhibition held at the Grafton Galleries in 1912, and in the summer of the same year he joined the Omega Workshops, although his alliance with Roger Fry was short-lived. Wadsworth's new friendship with Wyndham Lewis led to an abrupt departure from Omega in October, when several of his works were included in Frank Rutter's Post-Impressionist and Futurist exhibitions at the Doré Gallery in London. His painting *L'Omnibus* (*c.* 1913; untraced; see 1974 exh. cat., no. 12) announced his involvement with motorized themes that clearly derived from Futurism.

Wadsworth was a member of the committee that organized a dinner in honour of Filippo Tommaso Marinetti at the Florence Restaurant, London, in 1913, but he shared Lewis's growing reservations about the Italian movement. Although paintings of *c.* 1913 like *Radiation* (1913–14; untraced; see 1974 exh. cat., no. 15) and *March* (1913–14; untraced; see 1974 exh. cat., no. 13) show his interest in machine-age subjects, Wadsworth was also fascinated by Vasily Kandinsky's writings and published a translation of them in the first issue of *Blast*. By that time he had become one of Lewis's associates, joining the activities at the Rebel Art Centre and reproducing several of his works in *Blast*. They include *Cape of Good Hope* (1914; untraced; see 1974 exh. cat., no. 19), which uses an aerial viewpoint to present an austere yet dynamic vision of dockland with moored ships. Wadsworth found great excitement in maritime themes throughout his life, and *Blast* shared his enthusiasm. The manifestos blessed 'ALL PORTS', praising their 'scooped out basins' and 'heavy insect dredgers' as well as the 'SHIPS which switchback on Blue, Green and Red SEAS all around the PINK EARTH-BALL'.

Wadsworth was equally interested in the new vision of the world opened up by air travel. He may have taken a trip in an aeroplane himself during this period, and he was certainly inspired by the images to be found in aerial photographs. His painting *A Short Flight* (1914; untraced; see 1974 exh. cat., no. 22) celebrates the exhilaration of air travel. Since so many of his paintings of the Vorticist period have been lost, woodcuts provide a valuable insight into his approach; in his extended series he often looks down on northern industrial centres from far above. This dizzying new perspective enabled him to organize his forms in a remarkably abstract way, even though he retained reference to factory chimneys, railway lines and striped fields.

After contributing to the Vorticist Exhibition of June 1915 at the Doré Gallery and reproducing more work in the second issue of *Blast*, Wadsworth served in the Royal Naval Volunteer Reserve on the island of Mudros until invalided out in 1917. Although Ezra Pound contrasted his work with Lewis's, arguing that they stood for 'turbulent energy: repose. Anger: placidity and so on', Wadsworth was the painter most closely allied to him in the Vorticist period. Their relationship did not continue for long after the war. Wadsworth's vast painting of *Dazzleships in Drydock at Liverpool* (3×2.4 m; 1919; Ottawa, N.G.) heralded his return to a more representational way of seeing. Industrial subjects formed the focus of his dramatic *Black Country* series, which he exhibited in a one-man show at the Leicester Galleries and published as a collection with an introduction by Arnold Bennett in the same year (London, 1920).

Maritime themes were his principal subjects in the following period. They led him, at first, in the direction of a more straightforward naturalism, exemplified at its most limpid and structurally compact in the *Cattewater, Plymouth Sound* (1923; Mr & Mrs T. W. Southern priv. col.; see 1974 exh. cat., no. 44). A strain of Surrealist unease and expectancy gradually entered Wadsworth's work, most notably in mysterious still-life compositions like *Regalia* (1928; London, Tate). He corresponded with Giorgio de Chirico about their shared interest in reviving the tempera medium, although his increasingly meticulous attitude towards technique did not prevent him from taking interest in avant-garde developments during the 1930s.

Wadsworth travelled widely and contributed to the Parisian journal *Abstraction-Création*. He also became a founder-member of UNIT ONE, a group dedicated to promoting the spirit of renewal in British art between the wars. He was selected for the Venice Biennale in 1940 and became an ARA in 1943.

BIBLIOGRAPHY

Edward Wadsworth, Early Woodcuts (exh. cat., intro. R. Cork; London, Christopher Drake Ltd, 1973)

Edward Wadsworth, 1889–1949: Paintings, Drawings, Prints (exh. cat. by M. Glazebrook, London, Colnaghi's, 1974)

Edward Wadsworth: Paintings and Drawings from the 1920s (exh. cat. by M. Glazebrook, London, Mayor Gal., 1982)

For further bibliography *see* VORTICISM.

RICHARD CORK

Wael, de. Flemish family of artists and dealers, active in Italy. The brothers (1) Lucas de Wael and (2) Cornelis de Wael were the sons of the painter Jan Baptist (Hans) de Wael I (1558–1633), from whom they learnt to paint. They both went to Italy *c.* 1610 and by 1613 had settled in Genoa. There Cornelis founded the Cenacolo Fiammingo, where he trained many young painters. Their circle of expatriate Flemings included Anthony van Dyck, who lived with them for a time and painted a double portrait of them (*c.* 1627; Rome, Mus. Capitolino). Cornelis received commissions from Italian churches but is best known for his military pieces, harbour views and *bambocciante* or low-life subjects, whereas Lucas made a name for himself as a landscape painter. (3) Jan Baptist de Wael II is primarily known as an etcher; he may also have worked in Italy.

(1) Lucas [Luca] **de Wael** (*b* Antwerp, 3 March 1591; *d* Antwerp, 25 Oct 1661). Painter. After studying with his father, he became a pupil of Jan Breughel the elder. In many of Lucas's paintings the figures were added by Cornelis; Lucas, in turn, painted the landscapes in Cornelis's battle scenes and harbour views. The only painting inscribed with the name 'LUCAS DE WAEL' is the so-called *Piazza di Spagna* (New York, Dr Collins priv. col.), depicting a popular scene somewhere in Rome. According to Suida the inscription must be the artist's signature, whereas Biavati suggested that it could also be a reference to the particular event represented. The work shows a certain resemblance to Sinibaldo Scorza's *Piazza di Pasquino* (Rome, Pal. Corsini) and follows the style of Pieter van Laer's *bambocciate*. In 1628 Lucas de Wael returned to Antwerp.

BIBLIOGRAPHY

W. Suida: 'L'unica opera firmata di Luca de Wael', *Paragone*, ix (1958), pp. 72–4

G. Biavati: 'Paesaggio con figure: Problemi di collaborazione tra paesisti e figuristi', *Boll. Civ. Mus. Genov.*, i (1979), pp. 101–3

(2) Cornelis [Corneille] **de Wael** (*b* Antwerp, 7 Sept 1592; *d* Rome, 21 April 1667). Painter, draughtsman and dealer, brother of (1) Lucas de Wael. Documentary evidence suggests that he may have collaborated with van Dyck; he may also have worked with the Italian landscape painter Giovanni Battista Vicino (*fl c.* 1650), since, according to Biavati, various landscapes by Vicino have figures in them by either de Wael or a painter from his circle. During visits to Rome, Cornelis came into contact with the Schildersbent, the confraternity of northern artists there, and in 1627 he was recorded in the documents of Rome's Guild of St Luke. He moved there from Genoa in 1656, following an outbreak of the plague.

The only signed painting by Cornelis de Wael is the *Horsemen at Rest* (ex-Kstsamml. Stadt, Königsberg), which makes it difficult to determine the stylistic development in his work. Nevertheless, in order to trace some stylistic evolution, Baldass compared de Wael's *Crossing of the Red Sea* (Vienna, Ksthist. Mus.; see fig.), apparently attributed on good grounds to Cornelis in the inventory of Archduke Leopold William, with the *Meeting of Jacob and Esau* (ex-Gal. Otto Schatzker, Vienna). In both paintings the main motif is formed by a procession; they are also similar in technique, and form and colour are applied directly with the brush.

In the *Jacob and Esau* there are still traces of late Mannerism, notably in the arrangement of the figures and in the way their movements are rendered; the overall impression, however, is of a painting in the Baroque style. Cornelis achieved this effect by paying less attention to details and by painting in a loose manner, with short, broad brushstrokes. His colours, moreover, unite the figures with the surrounding landscape. In his landscapes especially, the style comes very close to that of Rubens and his followers. It is likely, therefore, that de Wael revisited Flanders *c.* 1620. In contrast to the *Jacob and*

Cornelis de Wael: *Crossing of the Red Sea*, oil on canvas laid down on panel, 750×1215 mm, *c.* 1630 (Vienna, Kunsthistorisches Museum)

Esau, the *Crossing of the Red Sea* has no Mannerist elements whatsoever. The theme and basic composition of this painting derive from a print by Jacques Callot, published in Paris in 1629. Compared with the *Jacob and Esau*, the colour is brighter, more cheerful and cooler in tone, closer, in fact, to Italian Baroque painting. The harmony of turbulent figure groups against a variegated sky also characterized the work of such artists as Salvator Rosa in the 1630s. Certain details in the *Crossing of the Red Sea* are, moreover, reminiscent of the genre and animal scenes by Cornelis's Genoese colleague Castiglione.

Cornelis de Wael's drawings are more direct in style than his paintings. Many are either signed or inscribed. A series of drawings of military subjects has survived (London, BM), the graphic style of which recurs in various paintings attributed to him, including *Looting the Village* and the *Military Camp* (both Brunswick, Herzog Anton Ulrich-Mus.). The typically broad composition of these works is close to that of Pieter de Meulener (1602–54) and Adam Frans van der Meulen, but their static quality owes something to the work of Sebastiaen Vrancx.

There are also some portraits by Cornelis (e.g. a pen-and-ink drawing of a *Young Man Standing*, Rome, Gab. N. Stampe) in the style of van Dyck. De Wael may also have designed a series of tapestries showing the *History of Meleager* (Vienna, E. Pollak priv. col.); the name 'C. DE WAEL' was woven into these tapestries. Among the patrons of the artist was Philip III of Spain.

BIBLIOGRAPHY

M. Vaes: 'Corneille de Wael', *Bull. Inst. Hist. Belge Rome* (1925), p. 204

H. Fischel: 'Eine Gobelinserie des Cornelis de Wael', *Belvedere*, x (1931), pp. 210–13

L. Baldass: 'Two Biblical Histories by Cornelis de Wael', *A. Q.*, xx (1957), pp. 265–74

O. Grosso: 'Appunti sull'arte di C. De Wael', *Liguria*, xxvi (1959), p. 11

F. C. Legrand: *Les Peintres flamands de genre au XVIIe siècle* (Brussels, 1963), pp. 209–11

G. Biavati: 'Paesaggio con figure: Problemi di collaborazione tra paesisti e figuristi', *Boll. Mus. Civ. Genov.*, i (1979), pp. 101–3

G. Fusconi and S. P. Valentino Rodino: 'Note in margine ad una schedatura: I desegni del Fondo Corsini nel Gabinetto Nazionale delle Stampe', *Boll. A.*, lxvii (1982), pp. 94–5

Flemish Drawings in the Age of Rubens (exh. cat. by A.-M. Logan, Wellesley Coll., MA, Davis Mus. & Cult. Cent.)

(3) Jan Baptist de Wael II (*b* Antwerp, 25 July 1632; *d* ?after 1669). Etcher and painter. Son or nephew of (2) Cornelis de Wael. In 1658 he etched the series of the *Story of the Prodigal Son* (e.g. *Return of the Prodigal Son*, B. 16) after drawings by Cornelis de Wael. There is also an etched series of *Figures with Animals* (B. 1–14) with Italianate peasants reminiscent of *bambocciate*, which may also support the suggestion that Jan Baptist was in Genoa *c.* 1658 and that in 1669 he was in Rome. Among the only known paintings attributed to him is the *Two Drinkers in a Tavern* (Nantes, Mus. B.-A.).

BIBLIOGRAPHY

Thieme–Becker

O. Nauman: *Netherlandish Artists* (1980), 6 [V/1] of *The Illustrated Bartsch*, ed. W. Strauss (New York, 1978–) [B.]

C. Levesque: *Netherlandish Artists, Commentary* (1986), 6C [V/1] of *The Illustrated Bartsch*, ed. W. Strauss (New York, 1978–) [B.]

JETTY E. VAN DER STERRE

Waele, Jan [Iennin; Janin; Jennyn] **de.** *See* GOSSART, JAN.

Wagemaker, Jaap (Adriaan Barend) (*b* Haarlem, 6 Jan 1906; *d* Amsterdam, 26 Jan 1972). Dutch painter and sculptor. He trained from 1920 in the decorative arts department of the School voor Bouwkunde, Versierende

Kunsten en Kunstambachten in Haarlem. He was self-taught as a painter. In his early work the influences of Constant, Permeke and Herman Kruyder are noticeable. He made regular trips to Paris, in the company of Piet van Egmond (1889–1965), and in 1946 he moved to Amsterdam. His discovery of the work of matter painters Jean Dubuffet, Jean Fautrier, Wols and Alberto Burri led him to adopt matter painting in 1955. He had an exhibition at Galerie le Canard in Amsterdam and participated in a group exhibition at the Stedelijk Museum in Amsterdam in 1957.

During 1958 Wagemaker stayed in Paris for four months at the Rue Santeuil, where Karel Appel, Corneille and Bram Bogart had a studio. He started to take photographs of walls, dry landscapes and strange rock formations. The titles of his reliefs and assemblages of organic and industrial waste are direct references to topographic situations, which set an imaginative process in motion. He also made scrapbooks with memorabilia from his numerous travels and produced sculptures. In 1958 he started to collect ethnographics. In 1958 and 1962 he submitted work to the *Junger Westen* exhibition in Recklinghausen. He met German matter painters, such as Emil Schumacher and K. F. Dahmen. In 1966 his first retrospective exhibition took place in Bochum.

BIBLIOGRAPHY
Jaap Wagemaker (exh. cat., Amsterdam, Stedel. Mus., 1967)
D. Wagemaker-van der Meer and others: *Jaap Wagemaker* (Vlaardingen, n.d.)

JOHN STEEN

Wagemans Maastricht b.v. Dutch furniture company. It was established in Maastricht in 1890 by Jules Wagemans (1866–1943), a wallpaper hanger and upholsterer. In 1920 his son Henricus Wagemans (1892–1948) succeeded him and began to produce armchairs, adopting the brand name Artifort in 1927. The earliest models, heavy pieces of upholstered furniture in traditional styles, enjoyed a reputation for solidity and good craftsmanship. In the 1930s the firm also made furniture by such well-known interior designers as Paul Bromberg.

After World War II, H. J. J. (Harry) Wagemans (*b* 1921), eldest son of Henricus and director from 1948 to 1986, installed high-pressure moulding machinery, which resulted in plainer designs. During the 1950s Theo Ruth (1915–71) was responsible for new designs (e.g. Armchair 1001 'Congo', 1952), and Artifort's reputation for craftsmanship was enhanced by the production of furniture for the Swedish company Dux. Although the firm soon became one of the leading furniture manufacturers in Holland, it lacked a clearly identifiable style. This was remedied by the Dutch designer LIANG IE KHO, who, from 1958 until his death in 1975, created the restrained, classic image that became characteristic of Artifort furniture. Within a few years the firm had achieved an international reputation due to progressive design policies, the recruitment of both Dutch and foreign designers and the striking exhibition stands organized by Kho. Other designers also created very successful products for the firm: the colourful 'seat sculptures' by Pierre Paulin (*b* 1927), who worked for Artifort from 1959 (e.g. Chair 577; New York, MOMA), and the interlocking system furniture

devised by Geoffrey D. Harcourt (*b* 1935), whose connection with Artifort began in 1962. Their seat furniture can be seen in museums in Holland and elsewhere and in offices and major airports (e.g. Kho's bench seating Series 720, Amsterdam, Schiphol Airport; Harcourt's Chair 042, Tokyo, Narita Airport). Since 1986, under the direction of Harry's son Henri-Jean Wagemans (*b* 1948), various young designers have worked on a new collection of 'timeless' pieces, as much for the home as for the projects market—an area in which Artifort International has become widely respected.

BIBLIOGRAPHY
H. Wagemans: 'Design en zitmeubelproductie bij Wagemans b.v.' [Design and production of seating furniture at Wagemans Ltd], *Ontwerpen voor de industrie, 1* [Industrial designs, 1], ed. I. Szénássy (Groningen, 1982), pp. 116–17
F. Huygen and M. von Krefelt: 'Artifort, de nieuwe koers van een oud bedrijf' [Artifort, an old firm setting a new course], *Items*, xx (1986), pp. 14–21
P. Vöge and B. Westerveld: *Stoelen: Nederlandse Ontwerpen, 1945–1985* [Chairs: Dutch designs, 1945–1985] (Amsterdam, 1986)
G. Staal and H. Wolters, eds: *Holland in vorm/Dutch Design, 1945–1987* (The Hague, 1987), pp. 141–65
E. Jamin, L. Schwenke and S. Weijnen: *Artifort* (Rotterdam, 1990)

MONIQUE D. J. M. TEUNISSEN

Wagenfeld, Wilhelm (*b* Bremen, 15 April 1900). German industrial designer and printmaker. He began his artistic training as an apprentice in the design office of a Bremen silverware factory (1914–18) and attended lessons in script and drawing at the local Kunstgewerbeschule (1916–19). A grant enabled him to continue his studies at the famous Zeichenakademie in Hanau (1919–22), where he received a varied training including silversmithing, engraving, design and modelling. The graphic works that he produced in 1920–23 were probably made during a short stay in Bremen and at the Worpswede artists' colony; they are mostly woodcuts and engravings with religious themes, for example *Death and the Virgin* (woodcut, 1921; Bremen, Focke-Mus.), motifs from everyday life and the world of work. These are mostly in a brittle style, expressing themes of destruction, hunger, pain, suffering and death. By 1923 the themes became more optimistic and were depicted with a soft voluminosity.

In 1923 Wagenfeld entered the metal workshop of the Weimar Bauhaus, where he worked under László Moholy-Nagy. He submitted a gravy-boat for his apprenticeship examinations in 1923. His time at the Bauhaus was the beginning of a long and fruitful period as a designer and model-maker of industrially-produced consumer goods that made him famous worldwide. In 1923–4, in collaboration with Karl J. Jucker, he created the famous Bauhaus table-lamp, with hemispherical frosted-glass shade, glass stem and base, which has continued to be reproduced since the first models were made (Berlin, Tiergarten, Kstgewmus., 1983, 73; 1972, 46). Its construction and design, aimed at industrial production, demonstrated the spirit of the industry-oriented second Bauhaus phase (from *c.* 1925).

From 1926 to 1930 Wagenfeld became an assistant in the metal workshop of the Staatliche Bauhochschule in Weimar. He worked mostly on models of lamps and household objects such as bowls and kettles for various companies (including the Bau- und Wohnungskunst

GmbH, Weimar). After the closure of the school (1930), the Finance Ministry of Thüringen commissioned him to improve the quality of glass production by the glass-blowers in the Thüringer Wald. Wagenfeld's committed attempts to do this failed owing to the lack of cooperation of those involved. A year later he held a professorship at the Staatliche Kunsthochschule in Berlin (1931–5), also working at the Schott & Gen. glassworks in Jena (1931–5). Under his artistic direction the company produced many household containers made of heat-resistant glass, for example the Wagenfeld tea service (1930–34), which retained its popularity owing to its elegance (Berlin, Tiergarten, Kstgewmus., 1975, 44; 1986, 9). The functional and unpretentious beauty of these Jena glass products was influential on other manufacturers.

One of Wagenfeld's most successful posts was as artistic director (1935–44) of the Vereinigte Lausitzer Glaswerke (VLG) in Weisswasser. With his team of colleagues, which included such people as Heinrich Löffelhardt (1901–79) and Hermann Gretsch (1895–1950), he produced high-quality functional glassware sold under the name of Rautenglas. He also carried out decisive improvements in the field of compressed glass, an important result of which is the Kubusgeschirr storage ware (1938), rectangular stackable containers of various sizes (Berlin, Tiergarten, Kstgewmus., 1981, 108; see INDUSTRIAL DESIGN, fig. 7).

World War II brought Wagenfeld's career at VLG to an end. After military service and a period as a prisoner in the USSR (1944–5), he went to Dresden (1946), before spending two years in Berlin (1947–9), where his posts included a professorship at the Hochschule für Bildende Künste. From 1949 he was based in Stuttgart. After a brief period as an industrial design consultant (1949–50), Wagenfeld devoted himself exclusively to independent work as a designer and model-maker in manufacturing industry, working from 1954 to 1978 in his own workshop with a small team of colleagues. He also worked for a number of firms including WMF/Geislingen (hollow stainless steel and silverware, cutlery, glass containers), Peill & Putzler/Düren (drinking glasses and lamps), Lindner GmbH/Bamberg (lamps) and Joh. Buchsteiner/Gingen Fils (plastic ware). He designed services and other consumer products for the porcelain industry (Rosenthal AG/Selb; Fürstenberg/Weser).

Wagenfeld discussed his aims and experiences in a large number of publications. His work was not concerned with selective improvements but with generally raising the level of quality of industrial consumer items, a task that would have been impossible without the equally important contribution of those involved in the production process. Walter Gropius described Wagenfeld's work as a consistent application of the ideas of the Werkbund and the Bauhaus in his emphasis on socially responsible work. His designs are characterized by their functionalism and unobtrusive beauty and by being reworked several times.

WRITINGS
Wesen und Gestalt der Dinge um uns (Potsdam, 1948)

BIBLIOGRAPHY
Wilhelm Wagenfeld: 50 Jahre Mitarbeit in Fabriken (exh. cat. by B. Klesse and others, Cologne, Kstgewmus., 1973)

Täglich in der Hand: Industrieformen von Wilhelm Wagenfeld aus sechs Jahrzehnten (exh. cat., ed. B. Manske and G. Scholz; Bremen, Focke-Mus., 1987)

FREYA PROBST

Wagenfeldt, Otto (*b* Hamburg, *c.* 1610; *d* Hamburg, 1671). German painter. Although probably self-taught, he was influenced by Netherlandish art, particularly that of Rembrandt. He worked in Hamburg, where he married the widow of the painter Jacob Schlepkau (*fl* 1622; *d* 1636) in 1639, becoming a citizen and a master in the painters' guild. In 1649 he painted 53 busts of Roman emperors, for the frieze in the Great Hall of the Rathaus, and in 1650 the ceiling of the old city library in the former Johanniskloster. The 26 paintings by Wagenfeldt surviving in a cycle of the *Life of Christ* (1650–51; ex-Jakobikirche, Hamburg; some on loan to Hamburg, Ksthalle) are among the few examples of Protestant Baroque church painting in North Germany and show Wagenfeldt's interest in the early Rembrandt. Other surviving works include *Solomon Serving the Idols* (1664; U. Göttingen Kstsamml.) and the *Bird's Nest* (1661; Hamburg, Ksthalle), formerly attributed to Mattias Scheits, which shows the influence of Jacob Jordaens in its depiction of children. Avoiding extravagance, Wagenfeldt concentrated the picture on a narrow scene, capturing the children's curiosity and joy in discovering the nest, with a warm use of colour.

BIBLIOGRAPHY
H. Röver: *Die hamburgischen Maler Otto Wagenfeldt und Joachim Luhn und ihre Schulen* (diss., U. Hamburg, 1926)
B. Bushart: *Deutsche Malerei des Barock* (Königstein im Taunus, 1967), pp. 18, 51
A. Hentzen, ed.: *Hamburger Kunsthalle, Meisterwerke der Gemäldegalerie* (Cologne, 1969), p. 455, ill. 114–15
G. Adriani: *Deutsche Malerei im 17. Jahrhundert* (Cologne, 1977), pp. 129–30, ill. 122–4
G. Unverfehrt: *Sammlung der Universität Göttingen. Die niederländischen Gemälde. Mit einem Verzeichnis der Bilder anderer Schulen* (Göttingen, 1987), no. and ill. A 88

C. HÖPER

Wägmann [Wegmann], **Jakob** (*b* Lucerne, 16 Aug 1586; *d c.* 1656). Swiss stained-glass maker. He probably trained with his father, the painter and stained-glass artist Hans Heinrich Wägmann (1557–*c.* 1628), who had moved to Lucerne from Zurich in 1582. Jakob Wägmann worked mainly for the Lucerne town council, producing numerous stained-glass pictures, mainly church windows but also such secular works as discs as collector's items for private individuals. His first known work is a disc (1610) with the coat of arms of Ritter W. Am Ryn. His other works included a cycle of glass panels for Rathausen monastery (after 1612; two in Zurich, Schweizer. Landesmus.), a sequence of 29 scenes from the *Life of the Virgin* and the *Passion* for the convent of St Anna in Bruch (1619–24; now Gerlisberg, Convent of St Anna) and a series of 19 stained-glass pictures (1654–5; Lucerne, Hofkirche St Leodegard) for the pilgrimage chapel in the Hergiswald. Wägmann is regarded as Lucerne's last great representative of the art of stained glass.

BIBLIOGRAPHY
SKL; Thieme–Becker
H. Lehmann: *Geschichte der Luzerner Glasmalerei von den Anfängen bis zu Beginn des 18. Jahrhunderts* (Lucerne, 1941), pp. 166–71
Künstler von der Antike bis zur Gegenwart, xxxv (Leipzig, 1942), pp. 17–18

F. Thöne: 'Hans Heinrich Wägmann als Zeichner', *Schweiz. Inst. Kstwiss. Jber. & Jb.* (1966), pp. 108–53
J. Schneider: *Glasgemälde: Katalog der Sammlung des Schweizerischen Landesmuseums Zürich*, ii (Stäfa, 1970), p. 491

F. FORTER

Wagmüller, Michael (*b* Karthaus Prüll, nr Regensburg, 14 April 1839; *d* Munich, 26 Dec 1881). German sculptor and painter. He trained at the Munich Akademie der Bildenden Künste, where he soon turned against the basically Neo-classicist attitudes of his teacher Max von Widnmann and turned to naturalism, following the example of Reinhold Begas. After establishing a studio of his own in 1860, he received few commissions for sculpture and turned his hand to genre painting instead. Between 1868 and 1874 he exhibited paintings at the Royal Academy in London. However, he went on to achieve wide recognition through commissions from Ludwig II and from the Munich Akademie, which made him an honorary member in 1872.

Wagmüller is considered the most important Munich representative of naturalistic sculpture; he left a substantial body of work, which displays both a knowledge of antique sculpture and scrupulous attention to living models. Even in his most mature works Wagmüller emphasized the painterly values of light and shade and rich detail, as well as clear formal construction. This combination is exemplified by his own tomb at the cemetery in Old Schwabing, a sarcophagus decorated with sphinxes supporting a seated female figure holding a child. In contrast, the decorative figures in Baroque garb modelled for Ludwig II at Schloss Linderhof and Schloss Herrenchiemsee show only cursory naturalistic modelling. His best works were his many portraits, the most outstanding of which is the statue of *Baron Justus von Liebig* on the Maximiliansplatz in Munich. Completed posthumously by Wilhelm von Rümann, it shows the famous chemist sitting in his gown with crossed legs looking up thoughtfully from a book. Wagmüller was favoured to succeed Joseph Knabl (1819–1881) as professor of sculpture at the Munich Akademie but died before the appointment could be made.

BIBLIOGRAPHY

ADB; Thieme–Becker
A. Heilmeyer: *Die Plastik des 19. Jahrhunderts in München* (Munich, 1931)
G. Finckh: '"Plastisch, das heisst antik, zu denken . . ." Die Bildhauerei an der Münchner Akademie und der Klassizismus von Roman Anton Boos (1733–1810) bis Adolf von Hildebrand (1849–1921)', *Tradition und Widerspruch: 175 Jahre Kunstakademie München*, ed. T. Zacharias (Munich, 1985)

CLEMENTINE SCHACK VON WITTENAU

Wagner. German family of artists.

(1) Johann Peter (Alexander) Wagner (*b* Obertheres, Unterfranken, *bapt* 26 Feb 1730; *d* Würzburg, 7 Jan 1809). Sculptor. He first trained with his father, the sculptor Johann Thomas Wagner (*b* 1691). In 1747 he travelled to Vienna, where he probably worked first for another Johann Wagner (*fl c.* 1731–48) and then for Balthasar Ferdinand Moll. After travelling in southern Germany, Wagner settled in Mannheim, where he worked for either Paul Egell or Augustin Egell (1731–85). At some time before 1756 he entered the workshop of Johann Wolfgang von der Auwera, court sculptor to the Prince–Bishop of Würzburg. Following his master's death in 1756, Wagner married in 1759 his widow, Maria Cordula Curé (*d* 1764), daughter of Claude Curé (*d* 1745), an earlier court sculptor, and took over the joint-management of the workshop with her brother-in-law, Lukas von der Auwera (*d* 1766). He received his first court commission, for a console table (untraced; drawing in Würzburg, U. Mus.), in 1759. In 1760 he executed an altar for the Augustinerkirche in Würzburg, as well as a high altar with a canopy and a baptismal font for the Stadtpfarrkirche of St Maria and St Regiswindis at Gerolzhofen, Schweinfurt. Between 1763 and 1766 he collaborated with Lukas von der Auwera on his Baroque Vierröhren Fountain (Würzburg, facing the Rathaus), for which he carved the figures. In 1766 he sculpted a *Crucifixion* group for the church in Kürnach; a year later he began work on the figures for the approach to the Wallfahrtskirche Mariae Heimsuchung (known as the 'Käppele') in Würzburg. He produced 14 groups, each of four to six figures, representing the *Stations of the Cross*; numerous journeymen were required for this large project, which was completed in 1775. The series of groups shows stylistic development between the earlier and later groups.

In the 1770s Wagner worked on the first two of four large commissions for Adam Friedrich von Seinsheim, Prince–Bishop of Würzburg, whose court sculptor he became in December 1771. He decorated the interior and exterior staircases of the Residenz in Würzburg with stone carvings of figures and putti, and he executed a group of *Pluto and Proserpina* for the gardens. For the park at Schloss Veitshöchheim he produced a group of the *Rape of Europa*, as well as sculptural decorations (destr. 1790s) for the staircase. Throughout this period he continued to execute altars, pulpits and statues of saints for numerous Franconian churches. The demand for Wagner's work was so great that some of the designs, such as the choir-stalls decorated with alabaster reliefs for the Klosterkirche at Ebrach, Oberfranken, were repeated by his workshop for the Augustine monastery at Triefenstein, which also commissioned wood statues for the altars.

Wagner ran a large and prolific workshop to fulfil the demands of both his ecclesiastical and his secular patrons. He worked chiefly in the Rococo style, assimilating it to the Franconian tradition of ornamentation, until his appointment as court sculptor, when he began to adopt a more classicizing manner; in 1790 he executed a wholly classicizing marble life-size *Virgin* for the Jesuit college in Würzburg. Towards the end of his career he returned to Rococo. His working method was to produce sketches, detailed drawings and clay *bozzetti*, which served him as conceptual models rather than as miniature versions to be translated exactly into wood, stone or marble. Collections of his models and drawings, as well as *bozzetti* by his master Auwera and his predecessor Curé, are held by the Mainfränkisches Museum and several other museums in Würzburg.

BIBLIOGRAPHY

Thieme–Becker
H.-P. Trenschel: 'Die Bozzetti-Sammlung des Mainfränkischen Museums Würzburg', *Die Weltkunst*, xlii (1972), p. 830
——: 'Zur Rolle der Vorstudien bei Johann Wolfgang von der Auwera und Johann Peter Wagner', *Entwurf und Ausführung in der europäischen Barockplastik: Beiträge zum internationalen Kolloquium des Bayerischen Nationalmuseums und des Zentralinstituts für Kunstgeschichte: München, 1985*

HANNELORE HÄGELE

(2) (Johann) Martin von Wagner (*b* Würzburg, 24 June 1777; *d* Rome, 8 Aug 1858). Painter, sculptor and collector, son of (1) Johann Peter Wagner. His early training in sculpture was in his father's studio in Würzburg, but in 1797 he went to Vienna to study painting with Heinrich Füger at the Akademie der Bildenden Künste. He also studied in Paris in 1803–4 under David. In 1803 he won a competition, advertised by Goethe and the Weimarer Kunstfreunden, with the drawing *Ulysses and Polyphemus* (untraced). In 1804 he went to Rome, where he spent the greater part of his life. While there he executed his outstanding painting, the *Greeks in Council outside Troy* (1807; U. Würzburg, Wagner-Mus.). In 1808 he met Crown Prince Ludwig of Bavaria (later Ludwig I), who put him in charge of the Villa Malta and appointed him his art agent in Rome. Wagner's most important purchases for Ludwig were the fragments of sculptures from Aegina (5th century BC; Munich, Glyp.), which were later restored by Bertel Thorvaldsen. Several of Wagner's own designs secured him a significant place among artists of German Klassizismus: the *Arts Protected by Athena* (1818) on the pediment of Leo von Klenze's Glyptothek in Munich, the frieze (1822–37) representing the history of pre-Christian Germany for the Walhalla, near Regensburg, and the idea for *Bavaria* (from 1841) on the Siegestor in Munich. He left his fortune and his extensive private collection of paintings, prints, sculptures and plaster casts to the Universität Würzburg, which named its museum after its generous benefactor.

BIBLIOGRAPHY
W. von Pölnitz: *Ludwig I und Johann Martin von Wagner* (Munich, 1929)
Martin von Wagner: Gemälde, Handzeichnungen (exh. cat., Würzburg, U. Würzburg, Wagner-Mus., 1977)

SEPP KERN

Wagner, Joseph (*b* ?Thaldorf, Württemburg, 1706; *d* Venice, 1780). German engraver and print publisher, active in Italy. The pupil of Jacopo Amigoni, he was one of the leading mid-18th-century reproductive engravers active in Venice. As well as publishing engravings after such leading painters as Canaletto, he also worked on a two-volume set of engravings, *Delle antiche statue greche e romane* (1740–43), based on drawings of Classical statuary in Venice by Anton Maria Zanetti (i) and Anton Maria Zanetti (ii). His workshop included such engravers as Francesco Bartolozzi and Antonio Baratti. ☐

Wagner, Leonhard ['Wirstlin'] (*b* Schwabmünchen, nr Augsburg, 1453–4; *d* Augsburg, 1 Jan 1522). German calligrapher. From 1472 he was a Benedictine monk at SS Ulrich and Afra in Augsburg. He worked as a scribe on liturgical manuscripts from at least 1480. According to his own notes (*Conscriptiones*, 1494; Augsburg, Staats- & Stadtbib.) and the history of the monastery, he completed in all over 50 manuscripts, including commissions outside his Augsburg monastery, some being illuminated by important miniaturists. For Emperor Maximilian, a patron of his monastery, he produced the *Vita Sancti Simperti* (1492; Munich, Bayer. Staatsbib.), with some illustrations by Hans Holbein I. On journeys—to St Gall, among other places, where he could study medieval manuscripts—he

taught calligraphy. His most famous calligraphic work is the *Proba centum scripturarum* (after 1509; Augsburg, Bischöf. Ordinariat), a pattern book of 100 medieval (*lettera antica*) and contemporary (*lettera moderna*) scripts, some invented by Leonhard himself. His portrait was drawn several times by Hans Holbein I (e.g. Berlin, Kupferstichkab.).

Konrad Wagner (*d* 1496), a monk in the same monastery, is often mentioned in connection with Leonhard Wagner but was not related to him. Around 1490 he illuminated several liturgical works containing calligraphy by Leonhard.

BIBLIOGRAPHY
Thieme–Becker
C. Wehmer: *Leonhard Wagners Proba Centum Scripturarum* (Leipzig, 1963) [facs.]
O. Pächt: *Vita Sancti Simperti* (Berlin, 1964)
W. Pötzl: 'Der Kalligraph Leonhard Wagner aus Schwabmünchen', *Jber. Heimatver. Landkreis Augsburg* (1973)

TILMAN FALK

Wagner, Martin (*b* Königsberg [now Kaliningrad, Russian Federation], 5 Nov 1885; *d* Cambridge, MA, 28 April 1957). German architect, urban planner and theorist, active also in the USA. After brief apprenticeships in the studio of Hermann Muthesius in Berlin (1908–9) and with Fritz Schumacher in Hamburg (1911), he was appointed director of urban planning at Rüstringen (now Wilhelmshaven), where he remained until 1914, producing his first examples of municipal architecture. From 1918 to 1920 he was chief planner at Schöneberg, a suburb of Berlin. Here he designed the Siedlung Lindenhof housing estate (1918–19; destr. 1944). Wagner's principal interest was in producing low-cost housing provided with the social and hygienic requisites lacking in the speculative building typical of large 19th-century cities. This preoccupation led him to assist in the establishment of cooperative building ventures funded by trades unions, such as the Bauhütte Berlin (1919), the Verband Sozialer Baubetriebe (1920–24) and the Deutsche Gesellschaft zur Förderung des Wohnungsbaus (Dewog). As director of the latter's branch in Berlin, the Gemeinnützige Heimstätten AG (Gehag), Wagner initiated the construction of the Hufeisensiedlung (1925–7; by Bruno Taut; *see* BERLIN, fig. 5), the first of the large-scale residential developments with subsidized rents, known as the Grossiedlungen, which were built in Berlin between 1925 and 1931.

In 1926 Wagner was appointed leader of the planning department and building control office of Berlin. In this capacity he planned the transformation of the city to adapt it to the needs of an expanding metropolis, particularly with regard to increased traffic demands, and began to propound his theory of constantly evolving, 'dynamic' town planning. Unlike his predecessor, Ludwig Hoffmann, however, he had little interest in the aesthetics of architecture and designed almost nothing himself. Interpreting his role as that of a manager of a large industry, he planned projects that were intended to be economically productive for the city, such as the office development (1928–31; by Peter Behrens) at Alexanderplatz and the Exhibition and Fair Ground (1930; with Hans Poelzig) at Charlottenburg. The large functional lido (1929–30; with Richard Emmerisch), Wannsee, expressed the possibility of rationally organized leisure for workers. Following the failure, however, of his Chapman Plan (1927) for a large residential quarter south of Schöneberg, Wagner was directly involved with residential building only through the Stadtplanungsamt, of which he was director. In this capacity he oversaw the construction of Siemensstadt, a Grossiedlung produced collaboratively between 1927 and 1931 by members of the modernist architectural group Der Ring, to which Wagner also belonged.

The political and economic crisis of Germany in the early 1930s effectively prevented the further implementation of Wagner's plans for Berlin. His constant drive to reduce costs, which included experiments with prefabrication of buildings and supporting large cost-effective developments such as the Grossiedlungen, led him into conflict with the Social Democratic Party, from which he resigned in 1931. In 1933 he was dismissed as leader of the planning department and building control office by the Nazis. He went to Turkey in 1935, where he was engaged in urban planning in Istanbul and after 1937 in Ankara, and in 1938 to the USA, where he taught at Harvard University, Cambridge, MA. He continued to propound the theory of 'dynamic' urban planning, particularly in his book *Wirtschaftlicher Städtebau*. In this he advanced the view that architecture, unlike painting, has no right of continuance once its practical function has been exhausted, and it must not be allowed to prevent the urban planner from realizing the modern city. The latter should be regarded as an economic enterprise to be managed in such a way as to increase its general economic productivity, thus improving the well-being of all its inhabitants. After World War II he tried unsuccessfully to return to Germany. Remaining in the USA, he was critical of the West German rebuilding programme for its neglect of such issues as low-cost housing in favour of what he considered to be a spurious modernity, exemplified by the replanning (1957) of the Hansa district of West Berlin.

WRITINGS

Die Sozialisierung der Baubetriebe (Berlin, 1919)
Alte oder neue Bauwirtschaft (Berlin, 1923)
Probleme der Baukostenverbilligung (Berlin, 1924)
Die städtebauliche Probleme der Grossstadt (Berlin, 1929)
Das wachsende Haus (Berlin and Leipzig, 1932)
'American Versus German City Planning', *J. Land Pub. Utility Econ.*, xxii/4 (1946), pp. 321–38
Wirtschaftlicher Städtebau (Stuttgart, 1951)
Potemkin in Westberlin (Berlin, 1957)

BIBLIOGRAPHY

L. Scarpa: *Martin Wagner e Berlino: Casa e città nella Repubblica di Weimar* (Rome, 1983)
Martin Wagner, 1885–1957: Wohnungsbau und Weltstadtplanung: Die Rationalisierung des Glücks (exh. cat., ed. K. Homann, M. Kieren and L. Scarpa; Berlin, Akad. Kst., 1985)
L. Scarpa: 'Martin Wagner', *Baumeister, Architekten, Stadtplanen: Biographien zur baulichen Entwicklung Berlins*, ed. W. Ribbe and W. Schäche (Berlin, 1990), pp. 453–66

LUDOVICA SCARPA

Wagner, Otto (Colomann) (*b* Penzing, nr Vienna, 13 July 1841; *d* Vienna, 11 April 1918). Austrian architect, urban planner, designer, teacher and writer. He was one of the most important architects of the 19th and 20th centuries—in 1911 Adolf Loos called him 'the greatest architect in the world'—and a key figure in the development of 20th-century European architecture. His work, spread over more than half a century, embodies the transition from mid-19th-century historicism to the earliest expressions of 20th-century Modernism. Wagner was an influential teacher and theorist, and in addition to his executed work he designed and published more than 100 ambitious schemes, the last volume of his *Einige Skizzen* being published posthumously in 1922; this long series of often fantastic but always highly pragmatic and carefully thought out projects included urban plans, museums, academies, parliament buildings and public monuments.

1. Training and work, before 1894. 2. 1894 and after.

1. TRAINING AND WORK, BEFORE 1894. After studying at the Technische Hochschule in Vienna from 1857 to 1860 and spending a short period at the Bauakademie in Berlin, where he became familiar with the work of Karl Friedrich Schinkel, Wagner studied from 1860 to 1863 at the Akademie der Bildenden Künste, Vienna, with Eduard van der Null and August Sicard von Siccardsburg, the architects of the Opera House on the Ringstrasse, Vienna, a building Wagner greatly admired throughout his life and regarded as a direct precursor of his own work. He also worked for a short time in the studio of Ludwig Förster and, in 1867, as a master builder for Theophilus Hansen; both Förster and Hansen had earlier been responsible, with Wagner's energetic mother, for the rebuilding (1847–8) of Wagner's family home in the Göttweihergasse after the early death of his father (1846). This played an extremely important role in his life as his first encounter with architecture. From 1869 Wagner was an attentive and critical observer of Gottfried Semper's contribution to the urban development of Vienna at the height of the Ringstrasse project (1857–85), and he went on to develop the conceptual and artistic influences absorbed from all these teachers into an oeuvre of creative work and teaching that laid the foundations of the Secession in the 1890s.

Far from being eclectic, Wagner's earliest executed works display an inner unity deriving from the use of a common basic form underlying the planning and detailed design; the outwardly Moorish-style Orthodox Synagogue (1868), Budapest, for example, is based on the octagon, which is reflected in the façade towers and details, the shape of the hall and windows, and even the candlesticks and candelabra. During the 1870s he designed and built speculatively the first of a career-long series of 13 large residential blocks, all modelled to a greater or lesser extent on his family home and each of which Wagner lived in briefly until the next had been built. Those at Schottenring 23 (1877) and Stadiongasse 6–8 (1882) are typical examples, with rusticated lower floors and trabeated openings; the former has an ornate iron balcony to the three central rooms of the second floor.

In 1879 Wagner received his first official commission from the city of Vienna: a temporary pavilion opposite the Burgtor on the Ringstrasse, from which the royal party could view the procession to celebrate the emperor's silver wedding. This was followed by the gigantic 'Artibus' project (1880; unexecuted), which transformed Semper's Hofburg plans into an idealized arts district linking Johann Bernhard Fischer von Erlach's Karlskirche with Semper's Kaiserforum, then under construction. This scheme formed the basis of all the later projects of Wagner and his students. Other significant early works included the tomb for his parents (1881); the competition-winning Giro und Kassenverein (1880; unexecuted); and the Länderbank (1882–4), the external appearance of which could have held its own among the Functionalist works of the 1920s. During this period Wagner was developing an approach based upon the integration of decoration with underlying forms related to building function rather than prescribed styles, which enabled him to develop flexible spatial planning systems that became common practice only decades later. Wagner's work was much influenced by the tenets and practice of Van der Nüll, who believed that in a 'rational modern architecture' of the future traditional forms would be preserved by modernization, and of Semper, who held that the separation of form and ornament was inimical to good design (see Semper: *Der Stil in den technischen und tektonischen Künsten*, Frankfurt and Munich, 1860–63). In 1889 Wagner published the first volume of his *Einige Skizzen*, in the preface of which he used the terms utilitarian and future style (*Nutzstil* and *Zukunftsstil*) to replace direct historicist references. He believed that, on the one hand, new techniques had to be brought into an artistic synthesis with the rapidly growing cities to control piecemeal urban proliferation and, on the other hand, architecture had to be freed from the influence of eclecticism, and artistic tradition preserved and reinvigorated through modernization. Throughout his career Wagner spoke repeatedly of 'Zweck-Konstruktion-Poesie' (Vitruvius' utilitas-firmitas-venustas), arguing that they

should be the guiding principles of the new architecture. However, his early plans for urban redevelopment in Budapest and Vienna, breath-taking in their scope, foundered when the stock market collapsed in 1873, but a more mature scheme eventually won a competition for a general regulatory plan for Vienna in 1893.

2. 1894 AND AFTER. In 1894, following his competition success, Wagner was commissioned to design the buildings and installations for the 45 km-long Stadtbahn in Vienna, for which he developed one of the most important unified schemes for an urban transport system (completed 1901). Several lines were planned to link the city with its suburbs; the scheme eventually also encompassed flood regulation and embankment development of the Donaukanal. Joseph Maria Olbrich, who entered Wagner's office in 1894, also worked on the project, which involved some 36 stations (see fig. 1), abutments, cuttings, open tunnels, 15 bridges and viaducts, in addition to platform buildings, signal boxes and the gamut of associated furnishings and equipment. The remarkable consistency in the designs, carried out in iron, stone and brickwork, indicates that Wagner maintained close personal control of the whole project. After the systematic and artistic exploration of the Doric column in the Stadtbahn and of the form of the great Sphinx in the floodgates at Nußdorf, *Jugendstil* played a very minor role in the work of Wagner and his pupils.

Also in 1894 Wagner was appointed professor at the Akademie der Bildenden Künste in succession to Karl

1. Otto Wagner: Karlsplatz Stadtbahn, Vienna, 1897

2. Otto Wagner: banking hall, Postsparkasse, Vienna, 1904 (modified 1980s)

Hasenauer, thus initiating the Wagnerschule. In 1896 his principal theoretical work, *Moderne Architektur*, was published: he deplored the division of architecture into 'styles', which he called an 'edifice of madness' that needed to be demolished, and he called for an architecture based upon the requirements of modern living, simplified expression of structure and the materials of construction. These ideas helped to create the intellectual climate that led to the foundation (1897) of the Vienna Secession (*see* SECESSION, §3), with Olbrich, his assistant, and Josef Hoffman, one of his students, as founder-members. For the second exhibition of the Secession in 1898 Wagner contributed designs for a new academy, a church and a modern art gallery. In 1898 he also produced a scheme for the conversion and extension of Semper's Hofburg and two more residential blocks at Linke Wienzeile 38–40, including the Majolika Haus (*see* TILE, fig. 10); the form of this crisp, flat, six-storey urban façade, with its positive cornice and iron balconies to the lower two storeys, is reminiscent of Schinkel's work: Wagner covered the façade in faience with flat, flowing patterns in pinks, blues and greens—only the ten lions' heads immediately below cornice level are in relief. Wagner joined the Secession the following year to the dismay of the establishment, which branded him an enemy of the official culture.

Wagner's late projects from 1903 radically continued the transformation of the work of Schinkel, Van der Nüll and Semper, as seen in his two master buildings: the sanatorium church of St Leopold (1903–7), Steinhof, and the Postsparkasse (1903–12), both in Vienna. The church is built on a Greek-cross plan and is surmounted by a steel-framed semicircular dome with a tall drum on an octagon. The domed ceiling within is carried on a gilded steel mesh. A modified Roman Doric order is expressed in four giant columns that pierce the projected transom of the entrance arch, to be crowned by bronze statuary below a deep, coffered cornice outlining the shallow narthex, transepts and sanctuary. The design for the Postsparkasse, one of his best-known works, won a competition (1903) and is based on a logical trapezoidal plan with a banking hall at its centre. The six-storey entrance façade, surmounted by a simple *Sezessionstil* pergola flanked by winged figures, has large windows set in walls faced with white marble with aluminium fixings. The central space of the banking hall (see fig. 2; modified 1980s) had a glass vault of stilted elliptical section carried on riveted steel columns, and a floor with glass lenses to light the basement below; aluminium ventilation bollards ranged around the wall added to the illusion of an industrial aesthetic. The bank owed its atmospheric effect to the impression of silver light produced by glass, aluminium and marble. One of the earliest icons of the Modern Movement, it is contemporary with Frank Lloyd Wright's Larkin Building, pre-dates Peter Behrens's Turbinenfabrik in Berlin by several years and marks the achievement of Van der Nüll's concept of a tradition-driven modern architecture of the future.

Wagner built one or two other urban buildings, such as the residential block on the corner of Neustiftgasse and Doblergasse (1909), its upper four storeys with simple undecorated surfaces and window openings and its ground and first floor with black tiles applied in stripes and rectangles. In 1886 Wagner had built his first villa at Hütteldorf, near Vienna. The second Villa Wagner (1912), on the Hüttelburgstrasse, was built on an asymmetrical, rectilinear plan and has a band of coloured, rectangular tiles in a counterchange pattern. Wagner's ideas and his attacks on his contemporaries made him enemies in the establishment. Despite international acclaim for his work, therefore, the last 20 years of his life were filled with unpleasant conflicts and defeats, and other major projects remained unrealized: the competition design (1905) for the Peace Palace at the Hague; the House of Glory (1907), probably intended for San Francisco; a portrait gallery and manuscript museum; competition designs for the War Ministry (1908), Technisches Museum (1909) and the university library (1910); the beautiful projects for the Stadtmuseum (five different designs, 1900–12); and a new urban plan for Vienna (1911), designed to accommodate large numbers of new inhabitants in what was envisaged as the central metropolis of Europe for the 20th century.

Wagner's influence continued to be seen in the work of architects who had studied at the celebrated Wagnerschule (1894–1914), including Leopold Baur, Karl Ehn, Josef Hoffmann and Emil Hoppe in Vienna and others in the provinces, for example Mauriz Balzarek in Linz. Olbrich graduated under Hasenauer but owed much to his work with Wagner. The school's influence was also carried abroad, for example in the work of Jan Kotěra, Josef Chochol, Pavel Janák and Jože Plečnik in Prague, Viktor Kovačič in Zagreb and Rudolph Schindler in the USA.

WRITINGS

Einige Skizzen: Projekte und ausgeführte Bauten, 4 vols (Vienna, 1889–1922); Eng. trans. by E. V. Humphreys (New York, 1987)
Moderne Architektur (Vienna, 1896, rev. 2/1902); Eng. trans. by H. F. Mallgrave (Santa Monica, CA, 1988)
Die Baukunst unserer Zeit (Vienna, 1913)

BIBLIOGRAPHY

H. Geretsegger and M. Peintner: *Otto Wagner, 1841–1918; Unbegrenzte Grosstadt: Beginn der modernen Architektur* (Salzburg, 1964, 3/1983)
O. A. Graf: *Die vergessene Wagnerschule* (Vienna, 1969)
R. Weissenberger: *Die Wiener Sezession* (Vienna, 1972)
M. Pozzetto: *La scuola di Wagner, 1894–1912* (Trieste, 1979)
P. Asenbaum, P. Haiko, H. Lachmayer and R. Zettl: *Otto Wagner: Möbel und Innenräume* (Salzburg, 1984)
O. A. Graf: *Otto Wagner*, 5 vols (Vienna, 1985–)
V. H. Pintaric: *Vienna 1900: The Architecture of Otto Wagner* (London, 1989)
R. Trevisol: *Otto Wagner*, Guide all'architettura moderna (Bari, 1990)
H. F. Mallgrave, ed.: *Otto Wagner: Reflections on the Raiment of Modernity* (Santa Monica, CA, 1993)

Wagner, (Wilhelm) Richard (*b* Leipzig, 22 May 1813; *d* Venice, 13 Feb 1883). German composer and writer.

Though his writings are not primarily concerned with the visual arts, they contain interesting general aesthetic theories. In his crucial essay *Das Kunstwerk der Zukunft* (1849) Wagner made the first use of the term GESAMTKUNSTWERK. In this work he called for a unification of all the arts in a manner that had not been experienced since the days of ancient Greece, and his main preoccupation was with the interrelationship of words and music. For Wagner art was a natural, necessary product of uncorrupted man and as much a product of the unconscious as the conscious mind. He divided art into two broad categories: the human arts, which derive directly from man, and, on the other hand, those arts that are created by man from the materials of nature. With regard to the former, which are generated by bodily motion and rhythm, he spoke of the 'three purely human arts' of music, poetry and dance. The latter category contains the arts of architecture, sculpture and painting, to all of which he ascribed a merely secondary role. Their proper task is to be found in support of drama. Thus architecture was to provide the necessary stage-set for the artwork of the future, sculpture should be employed in the service of architecture, and landscape painting should be used to create a natural backdrop in stage scenery. Under the influence of Schopenhauer's philosophy, Wagner later modified his theories, and in *Beethoven* (1870) he gave music a dominant role over all the other arts. Despite this unflattering hierarchy, the idea of the *Gesamtkunstwerk* provided an important stimulus for visual artists from the 19th century onwards.

Though not, therefore, given great prominence in his theories, the visual arts played a vital role in Wagner's life and creative processes. His stepfather, the actor and painter Ludwig Geyer (1779–1821), encouraged him to take up painting. In his autobiography, *Mein Leben*, Wagner wrote of his early enthusiasm for art, blaming a tedious drawing master for his failure to progress. Several of his closest friends as an adult were painters, notably the portrait painter Ernst Kietz (1815–92), whom he offered to adopt in 1858, and Paul von Joukovsky, who lived with Wagner and his second wife Cosima Wagner (1837–1930) for the last three years of the composer's life. During his residence (1839–41) in Paris, Wagner's acquaintances included Gustave Doré and Friedrich Pecht. In 1882 he met Renoir in Palermo, and in their conversations the word 'Impressionism' was first used as a term applied to music. Wagner also sat to him for his portrait (Paris, Mus. d'Orsay).

The visual arts inspired various of Wagner's writings and compositions. He claimed that *Das Kunstwerk der Zukunft*, although written in Zurich, was conceived in a café in Paris while gazing at wallpaper with depictions of scenes from Classical mythology. These images made him recall a watercolour that he had seen in Leipzig in his youth, *Dionysus and the Muses of Apollo* by Bonaventura Genelli. In his autobiography he wrote that the impetus to compose the music for his comic masterpiece *Die Meistersinger von Nürnberg* (1861–2) was provided by Titian's *Assumption of the Virgin* (1518; Venice, S Maria Gloriosa dei Frari), which he saw on a visit to Venice in November 1861. His writings about music itself are replete with painterly metaphors; for example he compared his orchestration of *Parsifal* (1876–82) to Titian's use of paint.

Wagner's contribution to the history of stage design was immense. In his own theatre at Bayreuth (now the Bayreuth Festspielhaus) he eliminated the boxes, left the auditorium in darkness throughout the performance and introduced a double proscenium and sunken orchestra pit. For the performance of *Der Ring des Nibelungen* in 1876 Cosima Wagner tried, but failed, to engage Arnold Böcklin to design the sets. Josef Hoffmann (1831–1904), who fulfilled the task, provided cluttered decoration, whereas the composer sought mythic simplicity.

WRITINGS

Beethoven (Leipzig, 1870)
W. A. Ellis, ed. and trans.: *Richard Wagner's Prose Works*, 8 vols (London, 1892–9; i, rev. 2/1895; ii, rev. 2/1900) [contains *Das Kunstwerk der Zukunft*, 1849]
M. Gregor-Dellin, ed.: *Richard Wagner: Mein Leben* (Munich, 1963); Eng. trans. by A. Gray (Cambridge, 1983)
A. Goldman and E. Sprinchorn, eds: *Wagner on Music and Drama: A Selection from Richard Wagner's Prose Works*; Eng. trans. by H. Ashton Ellis (London, 1970)
D. Borchmeyer, ed.: *Dichtungen und Schriften* (Frankfurt am Main, 1983)

BIBLIOGRAPHY
Grove 6
W. Schuh: *Renoir und Wagner* (Stuttgart, 1959)
J. M. Stein: *Richard Wagner and the Synthesis of the Arts* (Detroit, 1960/R Westport, 1973)
J. Deathridge and C. Dahlhaus: *Wagner*, The New Grove Composer Biography Series (London and New York, 1984)
B. Millington, ed.: *The Wagner Compendium* (London, 1992)

SIMON BANKS

Wagner, Veit (*d* 1516–20). German sculptor. In 1492 he worked for St George's Church, Haguenau, Alsace, and in 1495 he became a citizen of Strasbourg. The large quantities of wood and stone sculptures that were produced suggest that he had a large workshop.

Little of Wagner's documented work survives, but his style can be seen in the unpainted limewood reliefs of *SS Peter and Maternus* from the high altar of St-Pierre-le-Vieux, Strasbourg (1.91×1.58 m, destr. 1749; ex-church of the Confession d'Augsbourg, parish of St Pierre-le-Vieux). According to the contract recorded by Bebel in 1669, the altar was finished in 1500–01. It was 3.2 m high and unpainted. An early 18th-century description states that the shrine (central panel) contained the *Coronation of the Virgin with Saints*.

The main characteristic of Wagner's style is the combination of the Late Gothic tradition in landscape, drapery, pose and gesture with the new demands of the early 16th century, so that the generally balanced type of figure favoured by the previous generation of artists is offset by individualized heads with strongly introspective facial expressions.

Wagner's other documented works have been destroyed. They include wooden sculptures for the organ (1492), an altar of the Virgin (1496), the pulpit and two crucifixes (1503 and 1504) for St George's, Haguenau, as well as an altar panel for the Spitalkirche in Baden-Baden. Many works have been attributed to Wagner: the most important are the *Mount of Olives* (1498; Strasbourg Cathedral) for St Thomas, Strasbourg, an altar panel for Bergheim (Colmar, Mus. Unterlinden), the busts of *SS Egidius and Benedict*, which are probably from the high altar of St Pierre-le-Vieux, Strasbourg (Mulhouse, Mus.

Hist.), and the *Head of a Dead Christ* (Selestat, Bib. Human.).

BIBLIOGRAPHY
Thieme–Becker
B. Bebel: *Antiquitates Germaniae primae et in hoc argentoratensis ecclesiae evangelicae* (Strasbourg, 1669), p. 39
L. Pfleger: 'Der Veit-Wagner-Altar in der Alt-St Peters-Kirche zu Strassburg', *Archv Elsäss. Kstgesch.*, iii (1928), p. 341
W. Pinder: *Die deutsche Plastik vom ausgehenden Mittelalter bis zum Ende der Renaissance* (Potsdam, 1929), p. 411
T. Müller: *Sculpture in the Netherlands, Germany, France and Spain, 1400–1500*, Pelican Hist. A. (Harmondsworth, 1966), p. 170
A.-M. Burg: 'Le Retable dit "du Jugement dernier" à l'église St-Georges de Haguenau', *Cah. Alsac. Archéol., A. & Hist.*, xi (1967), pp. 49–54
Spätgotik am Oberrhein, 1450–1530 (exh. cat., ed. E. Zimmermann and others; Karlsruhe, Bad. Landesmus., 1970), pp. 179–82
M. Baxandall: *The Limewood Sculptors of Renaissance Germany* (New Haven and London, 1980), p. 279
R. Recht: 'Nicolaus de Leyde et la sculpture à Strasbourg (1460–1525)', *Pays Elsace*, 142 (1987), pp. 284–97, 385–90, figs 326–52 [supplement to no. 142]

VINCENT MAYR

Wagner-Rieger [née Rieger], **Renate** (*b* Vienna, 21 Jan 1921; *d* Vienna, 11 Dec 1980). Austrian architectural and art historian and writer. She studied art history from 1942 at the Universität, Vienna, where she began her academic career in 1945 as a Student Assistant. After a nine-year assistantship she was appointed Lecturer in 1956 and in the same year married the historian Walter Wagner. Her main interests lay in the field of European architecture and Austrian art. She first gained international attention in the mid-1950s through her extensive research on Early Gothic architecture in Italy; her paper on historicism, presented to the International Congress of Art History in Bonn (1964), was the first of her important contributions to this developing branch of research. Her classifications of 19th-century art and her guiding insights into the work of the period have since been widely accepted. In 1964 she was appointed Associate Professor at the Universität, Vienna, and she became Director of the Forschungsunternehmen Wiener Ringstrasse, editing 11 volumes of the institute's journal. In the last years of her life she joined the editorial staff of the *Zeitschrift für Kunstgeschichte*. She was appointed Professor of Austrian Art History in 1971. She was one of the leading architectural historians of her time and was well known even to the lay public; she was a distinguished teacher and author on major historical subjects and contributor to dictionaries and encyclopedias. Her outstanding ability to impart the very essence of medieval and modern topics made her books and studies models of scholarly approach within the Viennese school of art history.

WRITINGS

Die italienische Baukunst zu Beginn der Gotik, 2 vols (Graz, 1956–7)
'Der Historismus in der Wiener Architektur des 19. Jahrhunderts', *Stil und Überlieferung in der Kunst des Abendlandes. Akten des XXI. internationalen Kongresses für Kunstgeschichte: Bonn, 1964*, 1, pp. 240–48
'Architektur', *Das Mittelalter: I*, ed. H. Fillitz, Propyläen-Kstgesch., v (Berlin, 1969), pp. 170–230
Wiens Architektur im 19. Jahrhundert (Vienna, 1970)
with G. Egger: *Geschichte der Architektur in Wien*, Gesch. Stadt Wien, n. s. vii/3 (Vienna, 1973)
Historismus und Schlossbau, ed. with W. Kraus (Munich, 1975)
with M. Reissbergen: *Theophil von Hansen* (Vienna, 1980)
A. Rosenauer, ed.: *Mittelalterliche Architektur in Österreich* (St Pölten, 1988, rev. 2/1991)

BIBLIOGRAPHY
H. Fillitz, P. Haiko and W. Krause, eds: *Renate Wagner-Rieger* (Wiesbaden, 1981) [contains an almost complete list of writings]
G. Schmidt: 'Renate Wagner-Rieger', *Z. Kstgesch.*, xliv (1981), pp. 196–8

WALTER KRAUSE

Wahl [du Wahl], **Johann** [Johan] **Soloman** (*b* Chemnitz, 1689; *d* Copenhagen, 5 Dec 1765). German painter. He trained (1705–11) in Leipzig under the painter David Hoyer (1670–1720); in this studio he probably came into contact with Jan Kupecký, whose assistants, burdened with work during a visit to Leipzig, had appealed to Hoyer for help. Kupecký's influence remained discernible in Wahl's palette and style. After travelling for some years in Germany he settled in Hamburg, where, as well as painting the local nobility, he began his long connection with the Danish royal family. In 1721 he painted an informal portrait (Hillerød, Frederiksborg Slot) of the Danish painter *Hendrick Krock* (1671–1738) and subsequently executed for the Danish royal family several portraits (1723–4), all of which were despatched from Hamburg. In 1727 Wahl was appointed court painter to Frederick IV (*reg* 1699–1730). Inspired by Hyacinthe Rigaud's portraits of Louis XIV of France, Wahl depicted *Frederick IV* (Schleswig, Schleswig-Holsteinisches Landesmus.) in the grandiose image of a military commander. After the accession to the throne of Christian VI (*reg* 1730–1746) Wahl moved to Copenhagen, where he continued in the royal service, producing numerous portraits in a formal southern German Baroque style. Among these works was a portrait of *Ferdinand Anton Dannesiold Laurivegen* (1738; Hillerød, Frederiksborg Slot), painted on copper; this may have been similar in style to the (untraced) miniatures that Wahl is said to have painted.

In 1737 Wahl was appointed curator of the royal art collections, while also working as a restorer of paintings. He initiated a catalogue of the royal collection and donated to it a number of works from his own large art and book collection. His *Self-portrait* (1755; Copenhagen, Stat. Mus. Kst) is a remarkably relaxed yet imposing portrait, far removed from the pompous chilliness of his official portraiture, while its colours are still reminiscent of Kupecký's work. Wahl's failure to modernize his palette and his compositions, in spite of encouragement from Marcus Tuscher, his son-in-law, enabled young painters such as Carl Gustaf Pilo to capture his market with a lighter-toned Rococo portrait style.

DBL

BIBLIOGRAPHY
E. Lassen, ed.: *Dansk Kunst Historie, Billedkunst og Skulptur: Rigets maend lader sig male, 1500–1750* [History of Danish art, painting and sculpture: portraits of statesmen, 1500–1750] (Copenhagen, 1973), pp. 398–406

ANTONIA BOSTRÖM

Wahlberg, (Herman) Alfred (Leonard) (*b* Stockholm, 13 Feb 1834; *d* Tranås, 4 Oct 1906). Swedish painter. He received some tuition in drawing at the Royal Academy of Arts in Stockholm, although he was never formally enrolled as a student. In 1857 he went to Düsseldorf where he was a student of Hans Fredrik Gude. *Swedish Landscape, Kolmården* (1866; Stockholm, Nmus.) is representative of Wahlberg's Düsseldorf period. After a journey to the Netherlands and Belgium he returned to Stockholm in 1862 and became a member of the circle of artists around Karl XV.

In 1866 Wahlberg went to Paris, where he was to live for most of his life, and achieved great success. He held exhibitions and was awarded numerous prizes at the Salon for his Barbizon-inspired paintings, such as *Moonlit Landscape* (1870; Stockholm, Nmus.), which made his reputation in France. Wahlberg's successes in Paris and the paintings he sent home, together with his summer travels in Sweden, contributed greatly to the reorientation that took place in Swedish landscape painting during the 1870s and 1880s away from the influence of the Düsseldorf school towards that of Paris. Wahlberg also applied *plein-air* painting techniques to Swedish themes and thereby presented a new image of his homeland, at the same time as he continued with romantic moonlight themes. Forest subjects were common during the 1870s and, in the following decade, themes from the Riviera, in which he used a technique and palette influenced by Impressionism (e.g. *Grebbestad Harbour*, *c.* 1885; Stockholm, Nmus.). Wahlberg's landscapes exemplify the process of transition between tradition and regeneration in late 19th-century Swedish painting.

BIBLIOGRAPHY
J. K. Janzon: *Alfred Wahlberg* (Stockholm, 1909)
Alfred Wahlberg (exh. cat. by T. Hedberg, Stockholm, Svensk-Frankas Kstauktioner, 1928)
G. Nordensvan: *Svensk konst och svenska konstnärer i det 19 århundradet* [Swedish art and Swedish artists in the 19th century], ii (Stockholm, 1928), pp. 125–7, 293–4
A. Strindberg: 'Herman Alfred Leonard Wahlberg', *Före Röda rummet: Strindberg ungdomsjournalistik i urval* [Before 'The Red Room': selections from the journalism of Strindberg's youth], ed. T. Eklund (Stockholm, 1946)

TORSTEN GUNNARSSON

Wahlman, Lars Israel (*b* Hedemora, Dalecarlia, 17 April 1870; *d* 1952). Swedish architect. He studied under Isak Gustaf Clason at the Kungliga Tekniska Högskolan (Royal Institute of Technology) in Stockholm (1889–93) and in Clason's studio. With him he designed Hjularöd (1895), a romantic brick castle in Scania. His personal style was developed from the influence of the British Arts and Crafts Movement, the work of M. H. Baillie Scott and *Jugendstil*. He became a leading exponent of National Romanticism. Manorial and villa projects dominate his early work. Tjolöholm Castle (1897–1906) is a baronial country house in granite, with exquisite interiors. For his own home, Villa Tallom (1904) at Stocksund, he developed the jointed log-timber style of his native province, Dalecarlia. With the winning entry for Engelbrekt Church (1906) in Stockholm, however, he entered the field of ecclesiastical architecture, which was his main concern thereafter.

Completed in 1912, the church rises from a terraced rocky site as a cluster of brick volumes with high-pitched tiled roofs and a tall side tower terminated by an openwork wrought-iron crown. The broad nave with a high timber roof is crossed by vaulted transepts formed by sequences of parabolic arches; arches of this type also separate the nave and the crossing. Characteristic features are the linear chiselling of the granite on the lower walls, both externally and internally, and the similar rustic treatment of woodwork and painting. The small Gustavus

Adolphus Chapel (1907) at Lützen in Germany, built of a local sandstone, is in a more romantic vein. Wahlman's later churches, for example those at Sandviken, Nynäshamn, Tranås and Östersund, include more traditionalist features such as stellar vaulting. St Margaret's (1925) in Oslo combines this with classicist elements, while the Roman Catholic St Bridget's (1928) in Norrköping is more Italianate. Wahlman also did restoration work. Interior decoration, furnishings, woodwork and metalwork always play an integral part in Wahlman's designs, and he was a highly artistic draughtsman in pencil, charcoal and watercolour. His planning also encompassed landscaping, for example the garden at Tjolöholm and the terraced hill around Engelbrekt Church. A major work in this field is Slottskogsvallen sports ground (1919–27) in Göteborg, which includes a classicist arena in wood. Wahlman taught at the Kungliga Tekniska Högskolan, Stockholm, from 1905 and was appointed professor in 1912.

BIBLIOGRAPHY
S. I. Lind, ed.: *Verk av L. I. Wahlman* (Stockholm, 1950)
H. O. Andersson and F. Bedoire: *Swedish Architecture Drawings, 1640–1970/Svensk arkitektur ritningar* (Stockholm, 1986) [bilingual text]

Wah-Pah-Nah-Yah. *See* WEST, RICHARD.

Wailly, Charles de (*b* Paris, 9 Nov 1730; *d* Paris, 2 Nov 1798). French architect, designer and urban planner. As one of the pre-eminent architects of the second half of the 18th century, he enjoyed an international reputation, and his practice embraced architecture, the decorative arts, urban planning and teaching. His oeuvre is characterized by an eclectic, dramatic personal style informed by the study of antiquity and the architecture of Baroque Rome and Genoa.

1. Training in Paris and Rome, to 1757. 2. Commissions in France and abroad, from 1757. 3. Critical reception.

1. TRAINING IN PARIS AND ROME, TO 1757. The son of a cloth merchant whose family was originally from Amiens, de Wailly began his architectural training in Paris in the offices of Jean-Laurent Legeay and Jacques-François Blondel. He studied at Blondel's Ecole des Arts from 1748 to 1752, when he won the Prix de Rome of the Académie Royale d'Architecture. De Wailly received permission to share his scholarship to the Académie de France in Rome with his friend Pierre-Louis Moreau-Desproux, who had been placed third in the competition. The two travelled in Italy from the autumn of 1754 to early 1757.

In Rome de Wailly joined the international community of artists that included Giovanni Battista Piranesi, Hubert Robert and Robert Adam. With Moreau-Desproux and Marie-Joseph Peyre, he conducted excavations and made restoration studies of the baths of Diocletian and Caracalla. De Wailly gave equal attention to the monuments of the late 16th century and the 17th and developed a profound admiration for the work of Gianlorenzo Bernini. In June 1757 he was elected to the Accademia Clementina in Bologna.

2. COMMISSIONS IN FRANCE AND ABROAD, FROM 1757. On his return to Paris in 1757, de Wailly encountered an architectural climate depressed by the Seven Years War (1756–63), with royal commissions virtually at a standstill. He sought to establish a private practice through exhibitions of drawings and a variety of modest commissions. He designed interiors and furnishings in the fashionable *Goût grec* style and worked in the studio of the stage designer Giovanni Servandoni. De Wailly admitted students to his own atelier in 1759 and continued to offer private instruction throughout his career. Among his pupils were Bernard Poyet, Antoine-Marie Peyre and a number of foreigners, including Heinrich Christoph Jussow from Germany and Vasily Bazhenov from Russia. De Wailly received support from several powerful patrons, notably the Marquis de Voyer and the Marquis de Marigny, the Directeur-Général des Bâtiments, Jardins, Arts, Académies et Manufactures du Roi. In 1767 Marigny appointed de Wailly directly to the first class of the Académie Royale d'Architecture. The action circumvented long-established procedures and provoked a serious rift between the administrator and the academicians but did not damage de Wailly's personal standing among his peers. His appointment to the Académie opened the way for royal commissions and enhanced his prestige in the private market.

(i) *Residential architecture.* De Wailly was an inventive designer who delighted in textural and spatial effects. On the exteriors of his buildings he frequently contrasted porticos of smooth, free-standing columns with rusticated walls. Elaborate staircases, circular and oval rooms, and spaces expanded by screens of columns and the reflections of opposing mirrors are hallmarks of his interiors. His decorative schemes were structured by the architectural orders and richly embellished with sculpture and stuccowork.

De Wailly's first major residential commission was to modernize the Parisian town house of the Marquis de Voyer, which had been built in 1704 by Germain Boffrand on the eastern edge of the Palais-Royal gardens. The transformation of the Hôtel de Voyer (1762–70; destr. 1916) retained little more than the shell of Boffrand's building. On the exterior de Wailly lowered the pitch of the roof to give the house a more cubic mass, refaced the façades with rustication and added an Ionic, tetrastyle portico derived from Julien-David Le Roy's engravings of the Erechtheion (see Wiebenson, pl. 31) in Athens, published in *Les Ruines des plus beaux monuments de la Grèce* (Paris, 1758). The interior made similar references to antiquity, such as the series of caryatids sculpted by Augustin Pajou installed in the dining-room. As the hôtel neared completion, de Wailly undertook a similarly extensive reconstruction of another d'Argenson family property, the Château des Ormes (1769–78; remodelled), Châtellerault, Vienne.

In 1763 Jean-Philippe Fyot de La Marche, the Premier Président of the Parlement of Burgundy, whose family was allied to that of d'Argenson, commissioned de Wailly to design a country house dedicated to Apollo and the Muses. The Château de Montmusard (1764–9; partially destr.; see fig. 1), Dijon, was a compact block articulated as one storey. The principal elements of its plan were two circular forms on the central axis that projected from the front and the rear of the block: an open-air colonnade,

1. Charles de Wailly: Château de Montmusard, Dijon, 1764–9 (partially destr.); from a painting by Jean-Baptiste Lallemand, oil on canvas, 0.89×1.18 m (Dijon, Musée des Beaux-Arts)

termed the 'Odeum' or 'Temple d'Apollon', and a domed 'Salon des Muses'. The private and public apartments occupied opposite sides within the block. In 1773 de Wailly repeated this scheme in a project (unexecuted) for a country house for Catherine II, Empress of Russia.

During the 1770s and 1780s de Wailly was much in demand for his buildings and his drawings, and he travelled to Italy, Belgium, Germany and England; he received numerous residential commissions in France and abroad. Among his Parisian works were a house on the Rue de Richelieu for Mme Denis (Voltaire's niece), which was noted for its double-flight suspended staircase (1774–8; destr.), and adjacent houses he built for himself and Pajou on the Rue de la Pépinière (now the Rue de la Boétie; 1776–8; destr.). His own house featured a remarkable entry sequence, composed of a tetrastyle portico set directly on the street, a dark passageway lined with primitive-looking columns inspired by the Greek temples at Paestum and a top-lit, double-height, circular stairwell.

Outside Paris de Wailly designed garden pavilions for the château of the Marquis de Marigny at Ménars (1768–72), near Blois. Another client, the Comte de Seneffe, a connoisseur of the arts from the Austrian Low Countries (now Belgium), acted as the intermediary for commissions in the regions of Brussels and Antwerp. Among these were garden pavilions for the Duc d'Ursel at Hingene (1782; built 1790–92), near Antwerp, and for the Herzog von Saxe-Teschen at Laeken (1782), near Brussels. For Seneffe himself, de Wailly made plans for the gardens of his estate at Rivierenhof (1779–80), near Antwerp, and built a theatre on his estate at Seneffe (1780), Hainaut.

In Germany Ludwig IX, Landgrave of Hesse (*reg* 1768–90), commissioned projects from de Wailly for palaces at Kassel (1783) and Wilhelmshöhe (1785), but none was realized. De Wailly's most acclaimed work outside France was his renovation of the salon (1771–3; destr.) of the Palazzo Spinola (now Palazzo Campanella) in Genoa, built by Galeazzo Alessi in 1552. Windows and mirrors dissolved the walls of the room, leaving a polychrome framework of Corinthian columns and ribs adorned with caryatids and atlantids supporting a low dome. De Wailly exhibited his drawings for the palazzo at the Salon of 1773 in Paris and published them in a supplement (1777; see vol. 5, 'Architecture, Sallon Spinola', pls 1–4) of Diderot's and d'Alembert's *Encyclopédie* (1751–6). His designs are typically drawn in perspective and emphasize the character of the building through the use of chiaroscuro, colour and animation.

(ii) Religious buildings. De Wailly built one complete religious building, the chapel of the Reposoir (1769; destr.)

at Versailles. His initial plans called for a domed, circular nave encased by a simple, rectangular block preceded by a tholos-like portico. The juxtaposition of the circular form of the tholos and the cube was a recurrent theme in his work, appearing in such different building types as this chapel, residences such as Montmusard, and theatres (projects of 1769 for the Comédie-Française, Paris). The final design for the chapel, however, replaced the tholos with a simpler portico composed of four piers and a pediment. In Paris de Wailly built a crypt beneath the choir of St Leu–St Gilles (c. 1780). At St Sulpice he remodelled the chapel of the Virgin (1777) and designed a pulpit (1788) dramatically suspended by staircases between two piers of the nave.

(iii) Theatres and urban plans. De Wailly was one of a number of French architects, including Jacques-Germain Soufflot, Pierre Patte and Victor Louis, who sought to improve the design of theatres in the later 18th century. They addressed technical and aesthetic matters regarding stage equipment, sight-lines, acoustics, circulation, fire safety and the appropriate imagery for public theatres, which had become symbols of civic prosperity and sophistication.

In 1767 the Marquis de Marigny appointed de Wailly to the team of architects working under Anges-Jacques Gabriel on the Opéra at the château of Versailles (1770) and commissioned him, along with Marie-Joseph Peyre, to design a new theatre in Paris for the Comédie-Française (1767–82; known as the Théâtre de l'Odéon from 1797, now Théâtre de France). The theatre was to be built on the site of the old Hôtel Condé, near the Palais du Luxembourg, and financed by the development of unused portions of the site. Delays incurred by shortages of funds and a changing cast of royal administrative personnel forced numerous design revisions and prolonged construction for 15 years.

The new theatre of the Comédie-Française was a striking contrast to the company's previous home, designed by François d'Orbay in 1691. Whereas the old theatre was barely distinguished from the neighbouring town houses, the new Comédie was a monumental, free-standing block with a temple front. Inside, de Wailly and Peyre provided grand staircases and lobbies as settings for the public spectacle of seeing and being seen, as well as the necessary support facilities for the on-stage entertainment. A drawing of the vestibule and staircase (1771; Paris, Louvre; see fig. 2), submitted as his *morceau de réception* for the Académie Royale de Peinture et de Sculpture, has a deep, dramatically lit pictorial space populated by figures in ancient dress, who reinforce the Neo-classical architecture and the ancient roots of the theatre as an important civic institution. The nearly circular shape of the auditorium, a departure from the deep U-shape of the older theatre, was chosen for its regularity and to bring the audience closer to the stage. Other innovations included the provision of seating throughout the stalls and the subordination of the individual boxes to a unifying scheme of continuous balconies set against a frame of pilasters.

Following the completion of the Comédie-Française, de Wailly was called on to design other theatres in Paris. He submitted projects for a new Opéra (1781–98) and a Théâtre des Arts (1798), and he remodelled the interior

2. Charles de Wailly: *Vestibule and Staircase for the Entrance Hall of the Comédie-Française, Paris*, pen and ink with wash and gouache highlights, 380×620 mm, 1771 (Paris, Musée du Louvre)

of the Comédie Italienne (1783). Abroad, he made projects for the Théâtre de la Monnaie (1785–91) in Brussels and built an elegant little theatre (1780) in the grounds of the Château de Seneffe (1780).

De Wailly's brief for the Comédie-Française included the design of its urban setting. He located the theatre at the head of a semicircular *place* (Place de l'Odéon) that enhanced the monumental appearance of the theatre and provided space for the carriages of the patrons. Buildings with plain, uniform façades (1778–85) lined the *place*, and arcades (destr.) serving as *portes-cochères* linked the theatre with adjacent cafés. New streets led from the *place* into the neighbouring quarters.

De Wailly's subsequent projects in Paris and Brussels display similar attention to the integration of the theatre into the fabric of the city. He also addressed broader issues of urban planning. Like Patte and other contemporary observers of the city, de Wailly advocated the use of master-plans that treated the city as a system of monumental and utilitarian components linked by an efficient street system. In 1779 the Crown commissioned him to design the new town of Port-Vendres (1779–83) on the Mediterranean coast. During the late 1780s he worked on proposals for the embellishment of Paris that culminated with a plan exhibited at the Salon of 1789 and contributions to the Plan des Artistes of 1793.

3. CRITICAL RECEPTION. De Wailly's success as an architect was due to his formidable artistic talents and to skilful self-promotion. A brilliant draughtsman, he became the first architect to be elected to the Académie Royale de Peinture et de Sculpture in 1771. His bravura renderings and *vedute*, such as the dramatic night view of the Capitol in Rome (Vienna, Albertina), were popular with foreign as well as French collectors. He was comfortable with bourgeois and noble clients alike, and these diplomatic skills served him well during the turbulent years of the French Revolution. He sat on numerous artistic and scientific committees, including the Commission du Plan des Artistes (1793), and made proposals for remodelling the Louvre (1793) and for the embellishment of Paris (1789–93). In 1795 he became a founder-member of the Institut de France.

BIBLIOGRAPHY

Diderot–d'Alembert

L. Hautecoeur: *Architecture classique*, iii–v (1950–53) [esp. vol. iv, pp. 232–42]

S. Pressouyre: 'Un Ensemble néo-classique à Port-Vendres', *Mnmts Hist. France*, iv (1963), pp. 199–222

D. Wiebenson: *Sources of Greek Revival Architecture* (London, 1969)

D. Rabreau and M. Gallet: 'La Chaire de Saint-Sulpice: Sa création par Charles de Wailly et l'exemple du Bernin en France à la fin de l'Ancien Régime', *Bull. Soc. Hist. Paris & Ile-de-France* (1971), pp. 115–39

Piranèse et les français, 1740–1790 (exh. cat., ed. G. Brunel; Rome, Acad. France; Dijon, Mus. B.-A.; Paris, Hôtel Sully; 1976)

Y. Beauvalot: 'Un Château extraordinaire à Dijon: Le Château de Montmusard', *Cah. Vieux-Dijon*, vi (1978)

X. Duquenne: *Le Château de Seneffe* (Brussels, 1978)

Charles de Wailly: Peintre architecte dans l'Europe des lumières (exh. cat., ed. M. Mosser and D. Rabreau; Paris, Hôtel Sully, 1979)

A. Braham: *Architecture of the French Enlightenment* (Berkeley and London, 1980)

R. Middleton and D. Watkin: *Neoclassical and 19th-century Architecture* (New York and London, 1980)

RICHARD CLEARY

Wainewright, Thomas Griffiths (*b* Richmond, Surrey, ?4 Oct 1794; *d* Hobart, Tasmania, 17 Aug 1847). Australian painter and writer of English birth. He first achieved notice as an art critic and essayist for the *London Magazine* (1820–23) under a variety of pseudonyms. His circle of acquaintances included Charles Lamb, William Hazlitt and Thomas De Quincey. Between 1821 and 1825 he exhibited six paintings on literary subjects at the Royal Academy, London (and probably drawings, since he preferred to work on paper). A wash drawing of amorous couples in a landscape (early 1820s; London, BM) is reminiscent of Fuseli, whom he described as 'the God of his worship'.

In his writings and manner, Wainewright affected the style of the dilettante; he was reputed to be a poisoner and embezzler. In 1837 he was tried for forgery and transported to Hobart in Tasmania (then Van Diemen's Land) where in the next ten years, despite his convict status and poor health, he made an important contribution to the early art of Australia. He was, with Thomas Bock (1790–1855), the most skilful convict portrait draughtsman in Hobart in the mid-19th century. Apart from a group of small imaginary pencil drawings, Wainewright's Australian works were all portrait drawings, usually half-length and executed in pencil with watercolour wash. His elegant elongation of his subjects and poised line owed much to the style of English portrait painters such as Thomas Lawrence, who was among the artists he most admired. Most of Wainewright's Australian works have deteriorated considerably, but well-preserved examples are the *Cutmear Twins, Jane and Lucy* (*c.* 1842, pencil and watercolour; Canberra, N.G.) and *Sir Alfred Stephen* (*c.* 1838, pencil; Hobart, Allport Lib. & Mus. F.A.).

WRITINGS

W. C. Hazlitt, ed.: *Essays and Criticisms* (London, 1880)

BIBLIOGRAPHY

J. Curling: *Janus Weathercock* (London, 1938)

R. Crossland: *Wainewright in Tasmania* (Melbourne, 1954)

E. Buscombe: *Artists of Early Australia and their Portraits* (Sydney, 1978), pp. 167–72, 328–39

J. Kerr, ed.: *The Dictionary of Australian Artists* (Melbourne, 1992)

ANDREW SAYERS

Waitere, Tene (*b* Mangamuka, nr Kaitaia, 1854; *d* Rotorua, Sept 1931). New Zealand Maori wood-carver. He went to Rotorua with his mother when he was a few years old, following her capture and forced removal to North Auckland. He grew up at Ruato on Lake Rotoiti among his own people of Ngati Tarawhai, who were celebrated wood-carvers and canoe builders. He learnt the art of wood-carving in the 1870s from his skilled older relatives, Anaha Te Rahui (1822–1913) and Wero Taroi (*fl* 1850–80), but by this time large carved war canoes had become obsolete, being replaced by fully carved meeting-houses as the focus of tribal pride and prestige. Waitere assisted his older relatives on the large carved houses that many tribes in various parts of North Island were commissioning from Ngati Tarawhai; the houses on which he worked include Tiki-a-Tamamutu (1878) at Taupo, Uenuku-mai-Rarotonga (1875) at Maketu and Tuhoromatakaka (1909) at Whakarewarewa. He also became a prolific carver for the Rotorua tourist market, executing large commissions for the New Zealand Government Tourist Department.

While working for these European patrons he experimented with naturalism, perspective elements and narrative scenes illustrating local tribal legends. Rauru meetinghouse (1898–9, Hamburg, Mus. Vlkerknd.), largely carved by Waitere, was a product of this patronage.

BIBLIOGRAPHY

R. Neich: 'The Maori Carving Art of Tene Waitere: Traditionalist and Innovator', *A. NZ.*, 57 (Summer 1990–91), pp. 73–9

ROGER NEICH

Wakabayashi, Isamu (*b* Tokyo, 9 Jan 1936). Japanese sculptor and printmaker. He graduated from the sculpture section of the Tokyo National University of Fine Arts and Music in 1959. In the same year he had his first exhibition at the Mitsugi Gallery, Tokyo, of various wood and steel sculptures. After graduating he worked until 1961 as an assistant instructor in the sculpture section of the University. From 1960 until 1966 he exhibited every year in the Nikaten (Tokyo, Met. A. Mus.), the exhibition of the Nikakai (Second Division Society). In 1962 he won the Gold Award at the 47th Nikaten. In 1968 he exhibited a work entitled *Steam Exhaled from a Dog* (steel, h. 740 mm, 1968; Kamakura, Mus. Mod. A.), which was awarded the Kamakura Museum of Modern Art Prize at the first Gendai Chōkoku Ten (Contemporary Sculpture Exhibition), Kobe, Suma Detached Palace Garden. The following year his sculpture *Opacity: Low Altitude* (lead, paper, wood, steel, 245×1680×720 mm, 1969; Tokyo, N. Mus. Mod. A.) was awarded the National Museum of Modern Art of Tokyo's Prize at the ninth Gendai Nihon Bijutsu Ten (Contemporary Art Exhibition of Japan) at the Tokyo Metropolitan Art Museum. From 1973 to 1974 he lived in Paris. In 1975 he became an associate professor at Musashino Art University. In 1985 he created a garden at the Museum of Modern Art, Seibu Takanawa, Karuizawa. An exhibition of his sculptures, drawings and prints was held in 1990 at the Machida City Museum of Graphic Arts.

BIBLIOGRAPHY

Wakabayashi Isamu Ten [An exhibition of the works of Isamu Wakabayashi] (exh. cat., essay by M. Ichikawa; Tokyo, N. Mus. Mod. A., 1987)

Wakabayashi Isamu: 1986.10–1988.2 (exh. cat., essay by M. Ichikawa and S. Gotō; Kitakyūshū City, Mun. Mus. A., 1988)

YASUYOSHI SAITO

Wakakusadera. *See* HŌRYŪJI.

Wakelin, Roland (Shakespeare) (*b* Greytown, New Zealand, 17 April 1887; *d* Sydney, 28 May 1971). Australian painter of New Zealand birth. He moved to Sydney in 1912, having studied painting part-time at the Wellington Technical College and having exhibited at the New Zealand Academy of Fine Arts. In 1913 he enrolled in classes at the Royal Art Society of New South Wales, where he studied life drawing in the evenings under Anthony Dattilo Rubbo (1870–1955) and Norman Carter (1875–1963) for three years. On Saturday afternoons he painted with Dattilo Rubbo. In 1913 he was also introduced to modern art through one of Dattilo Rubbo's pupils, Norah Simpson (1895–1974). She had studied under the Camden Town painters in London and had seen the paintings of Paul Cézanne, Paul Gauguin, Henri Matisse and Pablo Picasso in Paris, reproductions of which she showed to Wakelin.

In the same year he saw an exhibition of work by Emanuel Phillips Fox, whose lively brushwork enhanced a more formal kind of Impressionism than had been seen before in Sydney; the exhibition and Simpson's revelations inspired him to develop his modern painting style. He also worked for the Federal Land Tax Office until the beginning of World War I and from 1916 as a commercial artist with Smith & Julius.

In this period Wakelin painted some of the most experimental works in Australia, breaking the picture space into touches of bold colour, and culminating in his colour-music paintings, or 'synchromies', for example *Synchromy in Orange Major* (oil on cardboard, 1919; Sydney, A.G. NSW), exhibited with similar works by Roy de Maistre in 1919. His use of the term suggests that he was aware of the American movement known as Synchromism. In this year Wakelin and de Maistre also painted, but did not exhibit, some of the first truly abstract paintings in Australia. Wakelin did not, however, abandon his sense of reality. In many of his works he achieves a harmony of composition and the perceived world; his painting *Down the Hills to Berry's Bay* (1916; Sydney, A.G. NSW) has a vibrancy of colour and arabesque movement that anticipate the abstract works. The artist's appreciation of the light, colour and atmosphere of the subject is similarly conveyed.

In 1922 Wakelin went to London where he stayed for three years. When he returned to Sydney his painting was heavily influenced by that of Cézanne, for example *In the Luxembourg Gardens No. 1* (1924; Sydney, A.G. NSW); he worked as a commercial artist with O'Brien Publicity Co. until 1941. After the early 1930s colour took on a new sonority. His subject-matter became romantic but the composition of his pictures weakened, and his work did not develop significantly after this time.

BIBLIOGRAPHY

Roland Wakelin (exh. cat., intro. D. Dundas; Sydney, A.G. NSW, 1967)

L. Walton: *The Art of Roland Wakelin* (Sydney, 1987)

BARRY PEARCE

Wakil, Abdel Wahed el- (*b* Cairo, 7 Aug 1943). Egyptian architect. He graduated from Ain-Shams University in Cairo in 1965. Between 1965 and 1970 he lectured at the university whilst studying and working with his mentor Hassan Fathy, the well-known proponent of indigenous architecture. In 1971 he went into private practice, eventually establishing offices in Cairo, Jiddah and Ashford, Kent. From 1993 he was based in Miami, Florida. He acted as an adviser to the Ministry of Tourism in Egypt (1972) and as consultant to UNESCO (1979–80). In 1980 he won the Aga Khan Award for Architecture for the Halawa house in Agamy, Egypt, completed in 1975. The two-storey house was built around a courtyard, and the articulation of space was handled with great sensitivity and simplicity. Openings in the white walls filter light to the interior through carved wooden screens (Arab. *mashrabiyya*s), and much of the courtyard remains in shadow, staying cool during the heat of the day. From this small vacation house El-Wakil went on to design larger houses such as the spectacular Al Sulaiman Palace in Jiddah, which uses the same principles but on a more lavish and larger scale. For a short time the architect toyed with other expressions of form but quickly returned to his exploration of tradition. El-Wakil's most convincing designs have been those for mosques (for illustration *see* SAUDI ARABIA) in Saudi Arabia. His Island Mosque, in gleaming white along the water's edge off the Corniche in Jiddah, is a design inspired by architecture of the Mamluk period (*see* ISLAMIC ART, §II, 6(iii)(a)). Together with other works such as the Harithy (1986) and Azizeyah (1988) mosques in Jiddah, it makes an important contribution to one genre of contemporary mosque design. His work continued to draw heavily on the traditional architectures of Egypt and the Middle East, largely to the exclusion of other modern influences.

BIBLIOGRAPHY
'El-Wakil's Buildings in the Middle East', *Mimar: Archit. Dev.*, 1 (1981), pp. 46–61
R. Holod with D. Rastorfer, eds: *Architecture and Community: Building in the Islamic World Today* (Millerton, NY, 1983), pp. 109–18
C. Abel: 'Works of El-Wakil', *Archit. Rev.* [London], clxxx/1077 (1986), pp. 52–60
L. Steil, ed.: 'Tradition and Architecture', *Archit. Des.*, lvii/5–6 (1987), pp. 49–52

HASAN-UDDIN KHAN

Walbaum [Walbom; Waldpaum; Wallbaum], **Matthias** [Matthäus; Matthes] (*b* Kiel, *c*. 1554; *d* Augsburg, 10 Jan 1632). German goldsmith. With his extensive surviving oeuvre of around 80 authenticated works, he is one of the most renowned goldsmiths of Augsburg. Embossed and cast-silver and silver-gilt reliefs, plaquettes and ornamental mountings, applied to small pieces of ebony furniture, were a speciality of his workshop. He mostly produced devotional and ecclesiastical objects, especially small altarpieces and reliquaries, for predominantly Catholic patrons (he himself was a Protestant). Less numerous are such secular luxury items as ornamental cabinets and jewellery caskets and, still fewer, examples of silver sculpture (e.g. automaton table decorations).

In 1569 Walbaum began a six-year apprenticeship under the goldsmith Hans von Tegelen I (master in 1546) in Lübeck, and from before 1579 he worked as a journeyman for at least five Augsburg goldsmiths, including Isaak Sal (master *c*. 1580–1612). He sometimes worked illegally, as was the case when he executed work for the Bavarian ducal court, commissioned by the court artist Jörg Bernhart (*fl* 1572–1612). Despite being punished more than once by the municipal authorities for breaking the rules of the Augsburg goldsmiths' craft, Walbaum became a master craftsman in 1590 and married into a socially successful circle of Augsburg goldsmiths. Walbaum's tax payments reflect the growth of his fortune and the flourishing state of his workshop. By 1600 he was paying eight gulden, double what he paid in 1594, and by 1620 (after a second lucrative marriage to a goldsmith's widow) his tax amounted to over 37 gulden.

Throughout Walbaum's career his connections with a court clientele were important for his professional advancement. He built on early links with Duke William V of Bavaria: a solid silver and silver-gilt writing case (Munich, Residenz) is associated with his residence at the Munich court in 1594; in 1605 he restored some of the court's ecclesiastical silver, while in the same year two ducal remunerations refer to small altarpieces; and an ebony writing case (London, BM), which nearly repeats

the decoration of the Munich prototype, has been supposed to be that for which, together with a mirror frame (untraced), he was paid 700 gulden by the Bavarian court in 1609.

By around 1600 the Walbaum workshop had supplied the Habsburg courts as well: two pairs of miniature altars (h. 400 mm; Vienna, Schatzkam.) must have been made in the period 1596–1608 for the Archduke Matthias. They are representative of two common types in Walbaum's production of small altars: both are mounted on high socles, like monstrances, and the silver, partly gilded, decoration, made of many small pieces and predominantly cast, constitutes a montage of frequently repeated and fully interchangeable ornamental and figurative motifs. The first type, a winged altarpiece with a predella niche, opens to reveal miniature paintings. These bear a variety of monograms; Walbaum's supposed collaboration in such works with the Augsburg miniaturist Anton Mozart is controversial. The second, wingless type has a panel with a semicircular top displaying a central embossed silver relief. In Viennese examples, this is of *Mary Queen of Heaven*, the prototype for which was an altar painting by the Munich court painter Pieter Candid (*c*. 1591–2; Augsburg, SS Ulrich and Afra). Walbaum used the same relief composition at least nine times, as in a pax board of the same overall design, dated 1606 (Überlingen Minster, Treasury). In this type the silver picture is sometimes replaced with a display repository for relics. The somewhat bizarre and spiky appearance of all these works is due to a decorative style that is often thought typical of Walbaum: a profusion of Mannerist ornament, including pierced scrollwork, open-cast strapwork, grotesque and floral motifs, combined with tiny figures, plays across the ebony bodies, rendering bronze contours indistinct. Equally characteristic of the workshop, however, are methods of decoration that respect or even accentuate architectonic structures. The ebony surfaces of caskets, cabinets and retable frames, for instance, could be organized rhythmically by appliqué silver openwork lattices alternating with cast plaquettes, or covered with a 'net' of sawn-out silver fretwork.

The most important example of the 'spiky' decorative style, and one of the highest quality pieces in his oeuvre, is the Borghese Altar (h. 1.05 m; Rome, Gal. Borghese; see fig.), produced *c*. 1613 for the private chapel of Cardinal Scipione Borghese, at his newly built villa. Made of ebony and silver, partly gilded, it rises in four stages above a mensa-like pedestal. The central panel is of the embossed silver *Mary Queen of Heaven* type, while above it exhibits a *Pietà* relief of a pattern also found elsewhere in Walbaum's work. A series of smaller and more modest altars is related to the Borghese Altar through their architectonic structure. Their comparatively roughly executed silver mounts are here subordinated to the schematic organization of the tier units and show an almost stereotypical use of figurative and ornamental motifs. A few of these are components of a shrine casket with leaved doors, the inner surfaces of which are adorned with miniature paintings and silver fittings (e.g. Budapest, Mus. Applied A.).

A monumental retable made by Walbaum for the cathedral church of the Prince–Bishop of Eichstätt, Konrad von Gemmingen (*reg* 1595–1612), which was partially completed in 1611, is no longer extant. Written sources

Matthias Walbaum: Borghese Altar, ebony, silver and parcel gilt, h. 1.05 m, *c.* 1613 (Rome, Galleria Borghese)

in this piece, unique among the Walbaum altars, he drew on the workshop repertory, employing the familiar *Mary Queen of Heaven* relief composition on the highest stage. The only surviving communion cup from the Walbaum production (Zeil, Upper Swabia, Castle Church) is dated 1611 and bears silver reliefs of a pattern employed by other workshops as well as Walbaum's.

In the years 1611–16 Walbaum was involved in one of the most spectacular collaborative projects undertaken by Augsburg artists. This was the sumptuous cabinet (destr. 1945; *see* AUGSBURG, fig. 3) made under the direction of the art dealer PHILIPP HAINHOFER for Philip, Duke of Pomerania-Stettin. Walbaum cast the crowning silver sculptural Parnassus group, figures of the eight muses on the mouldings as well as the griffins with shields that served as the feet of the cabinet. The wooden models for sculpture on the cabinet were carved by the sculptor Caspar Meneller from designs provided by the painter Hans Rottenhammer I and the goldsmith Christoph Lencker (master 1584). This is the only case in Walbaum's oeuvre where it has been possible to document with certainty the various individual artists involved in the evolution of a work. It is known, however, that one of his finest reliefs the *Adoration of the Shepherds*, set into the centre of an ebony and silver altar (*c.* 1600–05; Milan, Castello Sforzesco), derives from a drawing by Rottenhammer that was also used by other Augsburg goldsmiths for similar reliefs and that relief compositions of the *Last Supper* and the *Washing of Christ's Feet*, used a number of times by Walbaum (e.g. Florence, Pitti), were taken from engraved models by Cornelis Cort.

Among the last works of the Walbaum workshop is a silver relief of the *Crucifixion* (from 1627 at the latest; Augsburg, SS Ulrich and Afra), originally the central image of a small reliquary altar. Its Italian-derived composition had been taken up around 1600 by several Augsburg goldsmiths. For four decades from 1590 Walbaum's master's mark (a small tree in a shield) represented one of the most productive goldsmith's workshops in Augsburg. His personal contribution to this large oeuvre is difficult to assess, for the master's mark guarantees merely the quality of the metal, not that the work is a product of the master's hand. The works bearing Walbaum's mark are variable in quality, ranging from artistically superior and technically elaborate one-off pieces to mass-produced articles. Certain object-types, figurative compositions and ornamental components were reproduced in identical or nearly identical forms of greater or lesser refinement of workmanship, and even royal commissions were characterized by features of serial production. Walbaum's achievement, both as artist and businessman, lies primarily in the richly varied decoration of small altars, cabinets and caskets. He has also been credited with the invention of the automaton drinking cup type with *Diana and the Deer* (e.g. Berlin, Tiergarten, Kstgewmus.), which other Augsburg goldsmiths later took up. In such three-dimensional works, as well as in his best relief compositions, Walbaum also proved himself a gifted sculptor. He was not, however, the equal of other leading Augsburg goldsmiths of his time, both in terms of his financial success and the esteem in which he was held by contemporaries. Nevertheless, he did display exceptional entrepreneurial abilities: the large

describe its embossed silver relief panels, on to which separately worked components, some almost in the round, were screwed into place. This elaborate technique connects it with the largest (h. 2.35 m) and finest surviving sacred work by Walbaum—the Christian IV Altar, in Frederiksborg Castle, Denmark. Datable to around 1610–15 on the basis of its Augsburg hallmark, the altar, which employed an iconological programme dedicated to the Virgin, is known, somewhat surprisingly, to have been in the oratory of the Protestant Danish King by 1646 at the latest. Even output of his workshop and its versatility in accommodating a socially disparate clientele suggest that he was able to establish a highly productive and economically efficient organization of the manufacturing process, with collaborators both within and without his own workshop.

BIBLIOGRAPHY

M. Gradowski: 'Mateusz Wallbaum i jego prace w Polsce' [Matthäus Wallbaum: his work in Poland], *Sarmatia Artistica: Festschrift für T. Tomkiewicz* (Warsaw, 1968), pp. 83–93

R. Löwe: *Die Augsburger Goldschmiedewerkstatt des Matthias Walbaum* (Munich, 1975)

H. Seling: *Die Kunst der Augsburger Goldschmiede, 1529–1868*, 3 vols (Munich, 1980) [numerous illus.]; suppl. to vol. 3 (Munich,1994), p. 26

Welt im Umbruch: Augsburg zwischen Renaissance und Barock (exh. cat., Augsburg, Rathaus, 1980), ii, pp. 393–8, 471, 511–14

J. M. Fritz: 'Ein Messkelch von Matthäus Wallbaum aus dem Jahre 1611', *Studien zum europäischen Kunsthandwerk: Festschrift Yvonne Hackenbroch* (Munich, 1983), pp. 155–63

D. Alfter: *Die Geschichte des Augsburger Kabinettschranks* (Augsburg, 1986)

L. Seelig: 'Die Diana: Trinkspiele', *Der heilige Georg im Kampf mit dem Drachen: Ein Augsburger Trinkspiel der Spätrenaissance*, Munich, Bayer. Nmus. Bildführer, xii (Munich, 1987)

Kunsthistorisches Museum Wien: Weltliche und Geistliche Schatzkammer, Bildführer (Vienna, 1987), pp. 260–63

H. Tait: *Catalogue of the Waddesdon Bequest in the British Museum* (London, BM, 1988), ii, pp. 190–201 [good illus.]

Silber und Gold: Augsburger Goldschmiedekunst für die Höfe Europas, 2 vols (exh. cat., Munich, Bayer. NMus., 1994), i, pp. 22, 25, 156, XXVII; ii, pp. 257–60, 282–5, 290–92, 603 [good illus.]

MARION HAGENMANN-BISCHOFF

Walcot, William [Valkot, V.F.] (*b* Lustdorf, nr Odessa, Russia, 10 March 1874; *d* Hurstpierpoint, W. Sussex, 21 May 1943). English draughtsman printmaker, architect and painter of Russian birth. At the age of 17 he began to study architecture under Louis Benois (*b* 1856) at the Imperial Academy of Art, St Petersburg. He continued his studies in Paris at the Ecole des Beaux-Arts and the Atelier Redon and then practised briefly as an architect in Moscow where he designed the Hotel Metropole (1898). Subsequently he visited Rome and then London where he settled in 1907. In London he was first employed as a draughtsman by the South African-born architect Eustace Frere (1863–1944), and Walcot himself designed one London building: 61 St James's Street (1933). His main architectural activity however was that of a freelance draughtsman, producing presentation watercolour drawings for architects to show to their clients and to exhibit at the Royal Academy summer exhibitions. He soon became the most celebrated architectural draughtsman in England and remained so throughout the 1920s and 1930s, evolving an inimitable impressionistic style that enhanced the scale and drama of the buildings he depicted and developing a mastery of technique, especially in watercolour and gouache. His drawings are characterized by their richness of colour and use of foreground figures, which fade away at the foot, giving his compositions a sense of movement and atmosphere. Walcot was employed to make drawings of their projected buildings by many of the leading architects of his day, notably Edwin Lutyens, for whom he made the presentation drawings of Viceroy's House, New Delhi (exh. London RA May 1914, before being despatched to India), Herbert Baker and Aston Webb.

Walcot also became well known as a printmaker, employing a mixture of techniques including etching, drypoint and aquatint, both separately and on the same plate. His subjects were mostly Classical scenes and buildings, and he specialized in imaginative reconstructions of ancient buildings and in architectural fantasies (that showed, however, scholarly archaeological knowledge) based on Egyptian, Babylonian, Greek and Roman models and on biblical themes. The influence of Piranesi's etchings was evident. The Fine Art Society sent him to Venice and Rome, the resulting watercolours being exhibited in London in 1909. He held another successful exhibition in Edinburgh in 1919. In the same year the publishers H. C. Dickins issued a folio volume of his watercolours and etchings. He was elected to the Royal Society of British Artists in 1913, an associate of the Royal Society of Painter-Etchers and Engravers in 1916 and a Fellow of the RIBA in 1922. He was also an associate of the British School at Rome. Walcot's career was at the height of its success in the late 1930s, when he was working from studios in London, Oxford and Rome, but it collapsed with the outbreak of World War II, leading to his suicide in 1943.

BIBLIOGRAPHY

Architectural Watercolours and Etchings of William Walcot, intro. R. Blomfield (London, 1919)

M. C. Salaman: *William Walcot RE*, Modern Masters of Etching (London and New York, 1927)

William Walcot (exh. cat., London, F.A. Soc., 1974)

G. Stamp: *The Great Perspectivists* (London, 1982)

Art of the Architect: Treasures from the RIBA's Collections (exh. cat. by J. Lever and M. Richardson, London, RIBA, 1984)

J. M. RICHARDS

Walcourt, Hugo de. *See* HUGO D'OIGNIES.

Waldalgesheim. Iron Age site on the edge of the Hunsrück-Eifel in the Mainz–Bingen district, Germany. Found by chance in 1869 (*see also* PREHISTORIC EUROPE, §VI, 2(iii)), the burial mound was originally thought to be a double burial. In fact this mound, the latest by at least a generation of the rich chieftains' graves of the Rhineland, contained the burial of a woman. Among the artefacts in the grave was a spouted, swollen-bellied bronze flagon, perhaps an heirloom. The flagon has a bearded head on the handle attachment, a horse on the lid and four bands of finely punched compass-based plant decoration in the Early style of CELTIC ART around the body. There was also an Italic bell situla (wine bucket), probably of Tarentine origin, dated to *c.* 380–370 or, more likely, *c.* 340–320 BC. The grave also contained a gold neck-ring, three gold arm-rings, bronze and lignite ornaments (*see* CELTIC ART, fig. 4) and a large number of horse trappings and chariot fittings. Most of these are decorated in the Continuous Vegetal style of 4th-century BC Celtic art, also termed the Waldalgesheim style. This style is not otherwise found in similar barrow graves, nor elsewhere in Rhineland Germany, though it can be seen in artefacts from contemporary flat grave cemeteries in southern Germany, Italy, Switzerland, France, Hungary and into the Balkans. The decoration of the neck-ring contains small stars, similar to those found on the situla. This suggests that Waldalgesheim may be the last resting place of an immigrant bride from one of the newer, possibly Italian, centres of Celtic power, who brought with her imported goods or craftsmen. The pieces probably date not from the earliest development of the style but from *c.* 325 BC. Both Paul

Jacobsthal and Edward Jope postulated the existence of a single 'Waldalgesheim Master' responsible for all the metalwork; but Jurgen Driehaus has shown on technical grounds that at least four and perhaps eight different workers were involved, and he doubts whether the objects even came from the same workshop.

BIBLIOGRAPHY

P. Jacobsthal: *Early Celtic Art* (Oxford, 1944/*R* 1969), pp. 10–12, 135, 141–3
J. Driehaus: 'Zum Grabfund von Waldalgesheim', *Hamburg. Beit. Archäol.*, i (1971), pp. 100–13
E. M. Jope: 'The Waldalgesheim Master', *The European Community in Later Prehistory: Studies in Honour of C. F. C. Hawkes* (London, 1971), pp. 165–80
G. Zahlhaas: 'Der Bronzeeimer von Waldalgesheim', *Hamburg. Beit. Archäol.*, i (1971), pp. 115–30
W. Schiering: 'Zeitstellen und Herkunft der Bronzesitula von Waldalgesheim', *Hamburg. Beit. Archäol.*, v (1975), pp. 77–97
M. Lenerz-de Wilde: 'Zur Verzierung der Röhrenkanne aus dem Fürstengrab von Waldalgesheim', *Archäol. Korrbl.*, ix (1979), pp. 313–16

J. V. S. MEGAW, M. RUTH MEGAW

Waldeck, Johann Friedrich (Maximilian), Graf von [Jean Frédéric Waldeck, Comte de] (*b* Prague, 17 March 1766; *d* Paris, 30 April 1875). French painter and printmaker of German–Bohemian origin, active in Mexico. After studying in Paris under Jacques-Louis David, Pierre-Paul Prud'hon and Joseph-Marie Vien he travelled to Chile and then to Mexico, where he was employed by an English mining company in Tlalpujahua to draw machinery to be used in extracting minerals. He became more interested, however, in drawing archaeological ruins. While in Mexico he declined the offer of two posts: that of directing the first lithographic press in 1826, shortly before its installation by the government, and the presidency of the Academia de S Carlos in Mexico City. He did, however, publish *Colección de antigüedades que existen en el Museo Nacional*.

Waldeck continued to publish his illustrations after returning to Europe, where he settled in Paris. In 1866 he was involved in a polemic in the newspapers with Eugène-Emmanuel Viollet-le-Duc over the merits of using photography as archaeological evidence.

WRITINGS

Colección de antigüedades que existen en el Museo Nacional (Mexico City, 1827) *Voyage pittoresque et archéologique dans la province d'Yucatan (Amérique Centrale), pendant les années 1834 et 1836* (Paris, 1838)
Monuments anciens du Mexique, Palenque et autres ruines de l'ancienne civilization du Mexique, text by C. E. Brasseur de Bourbourg (Paris, 1866)

BIBLIOGRAPHY

R. L. Brunhouse: *In Search of the Maya: The First Archaeologists* (Albuquerque, 1973), pp 50–83
E. Acevedo: *1781–1910* (1983), vii of *Historia social de la producción plástica de la ciudad de México*, ed. E. Uribe (Mexico City, 1987)
F. Ramírez: 'La visión europea de la américa tropical: Los artistas viajeros', *Hist. A. Mex.*, pp. 67–8

ESTHER ACEVEDO

Waldegrave, William, 1st Baron Radstock (*b* 9 July 1753; *d* London, 20 Aug 1825). English sailor and collector. A distinguished naval officer, he was elevated to the peerage in 1801 and attained the rank of admiral in 1802. He developed an interest in art during a tour of Europe between 1781 and 1783 and made his principal acquisitions in the course of the following decade. His purchases included pictures by, or then attributed to, Annibale Carracci, Correggio, Domenichino, Parmigianino, Rubens and Raphael. He was a buyer at the Orléans sale (London, 1798) and at the sale of William Young Ottley's pictures (London, 1811), acquiring at the latter Garofalo's *St Augustine with the Holy Family and St Catherine of Alexandria* (*c.* 1518; London N.G.). Later purchases included Guercino's *Angels Weeping over the Dead Christ* (*c.* 1618), Carracci's *Temptation of St Anthony* (*c.* 1597) and Domenichino's *Landscape with Tobias Laying Hold of the Fish* (*c.* 1617–18; all London, N.G.). He sold several of his pictures to Francis Egerton, 3rd Duke of Bridgewater, Frederick Howard, 5th Earl of Carlisle, and John Julius Angerstein. He was the owner of a number of Dutch paintings of high quality, among them Jacob van Ruisdael's *Ruined Castle Gateway* (*c.* 1655, London, N.G.), which failed to reach its reserve at auction (London, Phillips, 19 April 1823). A second, larger sale of his pictures was held at Christie's, London, on 12–13 May 1826. Gustav Friedrich Waagen judged the Radstock collection to have been among the most distinguished to have been assembled at the time.

BIBLIOGRAPHY

G. F. Waagen: *Treasures of Art in Great Britain*, 4 vols (London, 1854–7), i, p. 26; iv, p. 152
G. Redford: *Art Sales: A History of Sales of Pictures and other Works of Art*, 2 vols (London, 1888)
W. T. Whitley: *Art in England, 1800–1820* (Cambridge, 1928)
——: *Artists and their Friends in England, 1700–1799*, ii (London and Boston, 1928), p. 346

R. WINDSOR LISCOMBE

Walden, Herwarth (Georg Lewin) (*b* Berlin, 16 Sept 1879; *d* Saratov, Russia, 31 Oct 1941). German writer, editor and critic, active also in Russia. He attended the Königstätter Gymnasium and the Leibnizgymnasium in Berlin and studied the piano, composition and musicology under Conrad Ansorge, becoming a notable pianist. He visited Florence in 1897–8 on a Franz Liszt scholarship, subsequently working in Berlin as a pianist and composer of operas, symphonies, pantomimes, piano works and songs. His acquaintances included Arnold Schoenberg, who aroused his interest in 12-note music and the theories of the German musicologist Else Lasker-Schüler, whom Walden married. The first society founded by Walden was the Beethoven-Verein; in 1904 he founded the 'Verein für Kunst' in Berlin and then the society's publishing house, which published Schoenberg. From 1908 he was co-editor of the weekly *Morgen*; he was also joint-editor of *Der Komet* and *Nord und Süd* in 1908, and chief editor of *Der neue Weg*. On 3 March 1910 the first issue of DER STURM appeared; it was a weekly journal on culture and the arts that became an important mouthpiece for modernism and that reflected Walden's strong interest in the visual arts. Until World War I the dominant influences were Futurism, Cubism, Expressionism and the beginnings of the new socio-political tendencies in Russia; after 1918 *Der Sturm* included work by Kurt Schwitters and László Moholy-Nagy and by other artists associated with Constructivism and Dada. The first exhibition organized by Walden that featured artists connected with *Der Sturm* was mounted at the Gilka Villa, 34A Tiergartenstrasse, Berlin, in March 1912. This was the first public showing of Alexander Archipenko, Umberto Boccioni, Heinrich Campendonk,

Franz Marc, Marc Chagall, Robert Delaunay, Lyonel Feininger, Albert Gleizes, Paul Klee, Fernand Léger, Johannes Itten, August Macke, Jean Metzinger, Schwitters and the German painter Johannes Molzahn (1892–1965). In June 1913 Walden changed to the Sturm-Galerie on the Potsdamerstrasse in Berlin. The exhibitions there were held monthly and included a remarkable range of avant-garde art: in March 1912 the gallery had shown work by members of the Blaue Reiter, followed in April by the Futurists, and later by German and French Expressionists. Walden proceeded to organize the Erster Deutscher Herbstsalon, which from September to November 1913 exhibited paintings by 75 European artists. In 1916 he founded the *Sturmschule* (known as the *Sturmkunsthochschule* after 1920), offering instruction in acting, diction, painting, poetry and music; the school, which closed in 1932, had a branch in The Hague run by Jacoba van Heemskerk. In 1917 an art association called *Sturmbühne* was founded and opened next door to the Sturm-Galerie. In the 1920s and 1930s Walden became concerned with practical political work. Although he continued to supervise the activities of the gallery until its closure in 1924 and the production of the journal until it folded in 1932, his influence was less vital. In 1932 he moved to Moscow with his fourth wife, Ellen Bork, living at the Hotel Metropol. There he wrote dramas and novels and in 1936–9 edited the emigrants' journal *Das Wort* and wrote book reviews. After he was arrested in Moscow in 1941 he was imprisoned in Saratov. He was rehabilitated in 1966.

BIBLIOGRAPHY

N. Walden and L. Schreyer, eds: *Der Sturm* (Baden-Baden, 1954)
Der Sturm: Herwarth Walden und die europäische Avantgarde, Berlin 1912–1932 (exh. cat., ed. L. Reidemeister; W. Berlin, N.G., 1961)
N. Walden: *Herwarth Walden: Ein Lebensbild* (Berlin, 1963)
Schenkung Nell Walden (exh. cat., Berne, Kstmus., 1967)
G. Brühl: *Herwarth Walden und der Sturm* (Leipzig, 1983)
M. S. Jones: *Der Sturm: A Focus of Expressionism* (Columbia, 1984)

INGRID SEVERIN

Wälder, Gyula (*b* Szombathely, 25 Feb 1884; *d* Budapest, 10 June 1944). Hungarian architect and teacher. He graduated from the Hungarian Palatine Joseph Technical University, Budapest, in 1905. After a study trip to Italy he taught at the University's Department of Ancient Architecture, where he was appointed professor in 1923. Wälder's work can be seen as contributing to a revival of Baroque architecture, which from 1920 coincided with official Hungarian cultural policy. His version of the neo-Baroque style was based more on ornamentation than on distribution of mass. Characteristic of his buildings are block symmetry, liaisons spanning several levels, rich sculptural ornamentation of the window- and doorframes and decorative wrought-iron railings. This ornamentation provides a harmonious counterpoint to the use of large volumes. Wälder was also highly skilful at adapting his buildings to the architectural environment. He received many commissions for public buildings and residential blocks during the 1920s. Outstanding among the former is the design (1927) for the Cistercian church, secondary school and monastery, Budapest. His design followed the model of south German churches, with a central projection and twin towers whose steeples rest on columns. A further two buildings with identical façades were to be linked to the church by a colonnade. However, only the secondary school was erected, in 1929, while the church was built (1939) to a much simpler design. Modernist architecture also interested Wälder, although to a lesser degree: his design contribution (1931) for Budapest's first modern residential district, with detached and semi-detached family homes, is conspicuously conservative. He also later experimented with vitrified bricks, for example in the U-shaped complex (1937), Madách Square, Budapest, where the decoration and arrangement of the façade again have a historical feeling.

BIBLIOGRAPHY

E. Ybl: 'Wälder újabb épületei' [Wälder's latest buildings], *Magyar Építőművészet*, xxxvi/9–12 (1937), pp. 1–32
A. Bardon: 'Gyula Wälder', *Szépművészet*, v (1944), p. 244

FERENC VADAS

Waldmann, Kaspar (*b* Innsbruck, 15 July 1657; *d* Innsbruck, 18 November 1720). Austrian painter. After studying with his father, Michael Waldmann I (*c.* 1605–58), he learnt fresco-painting from Egid and Johann Paul Schor in Innsbruck. He may have travelled to Italy during his journeyman years but from 1684 is recorded as a citizen of Innsbruck. He married a rich brewer's daughter and was appointed to the city council in 1692. The same year he finished an altarpiece for Brixlegg Pfarrkirche, *St Anthony with the Infant Jesus, and SS Erasmus and Maximilian* (now Innsbruck, Tirol. Landesmus.). Taking the ideas of Egid Schor as his starting point, Waldmann here moves from an originally sharply delineated approach to freer compositions. This closeness to Late Baroque conventions of form is evident in Waldmann's altarpiece for the Servitenkloster in Rattenberg, *St Nicholas of Tolentino Kissing the Wounds of Christ* (1700; Innsbruck, Tirol. Landesmus.).

BIBLIOGRAPHY

E. Egg: *Kunst in Tirol*, ii (Innsbruck, Vienna, Munich, 1972), pp. 172, 174
J. Ringler: *Die barocke Tafelmalerei in Tirol* (Innsbruck, 1973), i, pp. 67–8; ii, nos 35–9
Barock in Innsbruck (exh. cat. by E. Egg and G. Amann, Innsbruck, Tirol. Landesmus., 1980), pp. 32, 56, 71, 127

HANNES ETZLSTORFER

Waldmüller, Ferdinand Georg (*b* Vienna, 15 Jan 1793; *d* Helmstreitmühle in der Hinterbrühl, nr Baden, 23 Aug 1865). Austrian painter. He received sporadic art lessons of varying quality in Vienna between 1807 and 1820, first under Zinther and then with Johann Baptist Lampi, Hubert Maurer (1738–1818), Josef Lange (1751–1831) and Wilhelm Johann Nepomuk Schödlberger (1799–1853) at the Akademie der Bildenden Künste. After 1811 he made a meagre living painting miniatures and giving art lessons. Perhaps more significant than this haphazard formal training was Waldmüller's extensive copying after the Old Masters at the court and municipal art galleries of Vienna, mostly between 1817 and 1821. His copy of Jusepe de Ribera's *Martyrdom of St Andrew* (1821; Vienna, Gemäldegal. Akad. Bild. Kst.) is an example of his accomplished technique. However, commissions for copies barely enabled him to support himself.

In 1822 Waldmüller made his début at the Vienna Akademie exhibition with five original paintings. Three years later he made his first trip to Italy, and in 1827 he visited Dresden, Munich and Frankfurt. Throughout this period his main source of income derived from portraiture. An opportune court commission for a half-length portrait of *Emperor Francis I* (two versions, both 1827; Vienna, Hypotheken & Creditinst.; Vienna, Hist. Mus.) assured a steady stream of similar work. During the following 15 years his output was dominated by the portraits that have come to be seen as typical expressions of Austrian Biedermeier. These pictures celebrate the refinement, elegance, material luxury and settled tranquillity that were valued by both the middle class and the aristocrats of Vienna. Waldmüller's treatment of his sitters is direct and unrhetorical; their frontal poses convey a sense of comfortable self-assurance, warmth, charm and natural aplomb. He painted in a highly naturalistic style abjuring academic panache and studio artifice, although he did use classical compositions. The plain, neutral backgrounds, vibrant palette and extreme precision of texture and detail in his portraits generate a feeling of personal dignity and of timeless human values. This style of portraiture allowed the artist to use his talent to the full, while satisfying the expectations of his clients. The *Publisher and Engraver François Haury* (1834; Vienna, Belvedere) is a characteristic example. The powerful near frontal pose projects

dependability and self-confidence, while the unvarnished naturalism of expression suggests integrity and strength of character. Waldmüller's numerous portraits of older women, such as *Frau Josefine Schaumburg* (1834; Vienna, Belvedere), are fashionably elegant, dignified and charming.

Waldmüller also specialized in flower paintings. While these are acutely observed, lush and effulgent, it was as a landscape painter that he staked out a special place in the evolution of 19th-century art. From the 1830s he began to make *plein-air* sketches in the city parks and woods around Vienna. These Prater landscapes, his most important contribution to the European avant-garde, combine naturalistic settings, precise detail and lighting and a brilliant, luminous palette (e.g. *Prater Landscape*; Vienna, Belvedere; see VIENNA, fig. 10), their almost sculptured chiaroscuro anticipating by some 30 years the Italian Macchiaioli.

In 1829 Waldmüller became professor at the Vienna Akademie. His relationship with the institution was stormy—at one point his pay was suspended and reinstated only after the personal intervention of the Emperor—largely because of his unyielding radical opposition to the methods of teaching practised at the Akademie; he went

Ferdinand Georg Waldmüller: *Collecting Brushwood in the Vienna Woods*, oil on panel, 620×770 mm, 1855 (Vienna, Belvedere, Österreichische Galerie)

so far as to recommend that it should be abolished. His own writings on art were at the forefront of European Realism and were uncompromising in their pursuit of naturalism. He wrote ten publications on the need for academic reform, the three most important of which were *Das Bedürfniss eines zweckmässigeren Unterrichtes in der Malerei und plastischen Kunst* (Vienna, 1846), *Vorschläge zur Reform der Österreichischkaiserlichen Akademie der bildenden Kunst* (Vienna, 1849) and *Andeutungen zur Belebung der vaterländischen bildenden Kunst* (Vienna, 1857). All aroused great hostility with their caustic tone and caused him great personal hardship. To improve sagging financial fortunes by selling his works abroad, in 1856 he accepted an invitation to Philadelphia but got only as far as London, where he sold all the 31 paintings he had taken along before returning home via Paris.

From *c.* 1840 the emphasis of Waldmüller's work shifted dramatically as he developed an interest in genre paintings or *Sittenbilder*. These depictions of Austrian peasant life are often seen as his most important and characteristic works. His scenes of festivals, courtship and family gatherings are specifically Biedermeier variations of the peasant genre scene. There is, however, a conflict between his progressive style and technique—the naturalistic emphasis on individual appearance and realist detail and his use of vibrant outdoor lighting that almost anticipates early Impressionism—and the sentimental idealism of subject-matter that resulted from his grounding in the 18th-century tradition of such artists as Greuze and Chardin. *Collecting Brushwood in the Vienna Woods* (1855; Vienna, Belvedere; see fig.), the *Return from the Annual Parish Fair* (*c.* 1860; Berlin, Alte N.G.), *Early Spring in the Vienna Woods* (*c.* 1861; Munich, Neue Pin.) and *Rosenzeit* ('Youth and blossom time', *c.* 1862; Vienna, Hist. Mus.) all espouse social tranquillity and the rightness of the order of things. But their structural disunity—the divergence of style and content—is palpable. This has contributed to critical views of the *Sittenbilder* as staged sermons on the virtues of an imaginary country life that gloss over the reality of deep and widespread poverty, ignorance, dehumanizing toil and moral degradation. Nevertheless, these paintings contributed to the lasting popularity of Waldmüller in his native country as well as abroad. He is widely regarded as one of the greatest Austrian painters of the 19th century and the leading figure in the circle of such outstanding Viennese Naturalists as Friedrich von Amerling, Jose Danhauser and Peter Fendi. He worked quickly, finishing his paintings within days or a few weeks, thus producing a colossal body of work of some 1016 paintings. His last years were marred by faltering eyesight, which accounts for the choppy brushstrokes that give his late works a superficial resemblance to Impressionist paintings (e.g. *Coming back to Life*, 1865; Wuppertal, Von der Heydt-Mus.).

WRITINGS
Das Bedürfniss eines zweckmässigeren Unterrichtes in der Malerei und plastischen Kunst (Vienna, 1846)
Vorschläge zur Reform der österreichisch-kaiserlichen Akademie der bildenden Kunst (Vienna, 1849)
Andeutungen zur Belebung der vaterländischen bildenden Kunst (Vienna, 1857)

BIBLIOGRAPHY
Int. Dict. A. & Artists
A. Roessler and G. Pisko: *Ferdinand Georg Waldmüller* (Vienna, 1908)
K. K. Eberlein: *Ferdinand Georg Waldmüller: Das Werk des Malers* (Berlin, 1938)
B. Grimschitz: *Ferdinand Georg Waldmüller* (Salzburg, 1957) [with catalogue raisonné by B. Grimschitz and E. Richter]
F. Novotny: *Painting and Sculpture in Europe, 1780–1880* (Harmondsworth, 1970)
R. Bisanz: *The René von Schleinitz Collection of the Milwaukee Art Center: Major Schools of German Nineteenth-century Popular Painting* (Milwaukee, WI, A. Mus., 1980), pp. 258ff

RUDOLF M. BISANZ

Waldner, Hans (*b* Ravensburg; *d* 1573). German cabinetmaker, active in Austria. His first recorded work is the choir-stalls (1562–5) of the Hofkirche, Innsbruck, for which he received 30 florins. From January 1566 he received correspondence from Archduke Ferdinand of Austria (*reg* 1564–95) regarding work at Schloss Ambras, Tyrol, which had just been completed, relating mainly to furnishing the chapel and room panelling. However, immediately after the Archduke's death all this woodwork was removed to Günzburg, and nothing more is known about it. His most important commission for the court was the creation of the Fürstenchor, a projecting oratory built of wood above the left choir-stalls of the Hofkirche in Innsbruck. He worked on the two south window axes, while the northern section was completed by the joiner Conrad Gottlieb between 1567 and 1571. This splendid intarsia work is an outstanding example of Renaissance craftsmanship. The doors show the influence of the Italian grotesque style and differ from the rest of the panelling in the way the ornamentation is concentrated on the middle of the intarsia section; in the other intarsia-decorated areas perspective strapwork is used. In 1568–9 Waldner may have worked for Georg Ilsung, at Schloss Tratzberg, Tyrol, where the ceiling of the Königinzimmer (*in situ*) has been tentatively attributed to him. The last work that can definitely be assigned to him is a carriage with magnificent intarsia decoration (1569–73) made for Duchess Joanna of Florence.

BIBLIOGRAPHY
H. Kreisel: *Die Kunst des deutschen Möbels*, i (Munich, 1968)
Österreichische Kunsttopographie, Innsbruck: Die Hofbauten, xxvii (Vienna, 1986)

GABRIELE RAMSAUER

Waldo, Samuel Lovett (*b* Windham, CT, 6 April 1783; *d* New York, 16 Feb 1861). American painter. After attending a country school and working on his father's farm, he decided at the age of 16 to become an artist. He took lessons from Joseph Steward (1753–1822), a retired minister who operated a portrait studio in Hartford, CT. Waldo opened his own studio in Hartford in 1803, before moving on to paint portraits in Litchfield, CT, and Charleston, SC. In 1806, bearing letters of introduction to Benjamin West and John Singleton Copley, Waldo travelled to London, where he studied at the Royal Academy. His portrait of *Mr M'Dougle* (untraced) was shown at the Royal Academy in 1808.

In January 1809 Waldo returned to America and settled in New York. By 1812 he was exhibiting frequently there and in Philadelphia. Waldo's education and period of study in Europe prepared him for a leading role in the emerging cultural life of New York. He became a director of the American Academy of the Fine Arts in 1817 and remained active in that institution even while supporting the development of its rival, the National Academy of Design. He encouraged the aspirations and efforts of younger artists, such as Charles Loring Elliott and Asher B. Durand, and he initiated a subscription to commission Thomas Lawrence's full-length portrait of *Benjamin West* (*c.* 1819; Hartford, CT, Wadsworth Atheneum). His own work from this time demonstrates a vigorous style and considerable ambition, as seen in a romantically conceived *Self-portrait* (*c.* 1817; New York, Met.) and the forceful but empathetic *Independent Beggar* (1819; Boston, MA, Athenaeum).

In 1812 Waldo accepted an apprentice, William Jewett (?1789/90–1874), who had purchased a release from his apprenticeship to a coachmaker. After Jewett had completed his apprenticeship, Waldo offered him a salary and then a partnership. The team was active in New York from about 1818 to 1854 (when Jewett retired to a farm in New Jersey), painting some of the most solid and characteristic portraits of the period. Although they produced portraits in such number as to become formulaic and monotonous, their best paintings, such as the portrait of *George Griffin* (1827; New York, NY Hist. Soc.), stand as vivid likenesses and lively characterizations. Their typical waist-length portraits combine strong modelling, broad paint handling and robust colour, and their sitters wear comfortable, genial expressions. Such later works as *Stephen Allen* (1846; New York, NY Hist. Soc.) demonstrate more ambitious compositions, elaborate settings and richer colours, although the appealing portrait of *The Knapp Children* (*c.* 1849–50; New York, Met.) betrays in its awkward composition the team's unfamiliarity with group portraiture.

In practice, it seems that Waldo determined the composition and executed the heads of portraits before turning them over to Jewett, who painted the costume and background (see, for example, the unfinished portrait of *Deliverance Mapes Waldo*, *c.* 1826; New York, Met.). Yet so closely bound are the two artists' styles that even their contemporaries admitted it was impossible to distinguish the work of one from the other. Waldo occasionally exhibited independent work after 1820 (e.g. *Mrs C. F. Lindsley*, 1844; San Francisco, de Young Mem. Mus.), although Jewett did not. (Contemporary sources indicate that Jewett was often inactive for long periods due to illness.) Waldo's successful collaboration with Jewett appears to have overshadowed and eventually consumed his individual talents and contributions; by 1820 he had settled into the predictable rewards of his portrait practice, and his later career is marked by prosperous, if uneventful, success.

BIBLIOGRAPHY

W. Dunlap: *A History of the Rise and Progress of the Arts of Design in the United States* (New York, 1834, rev. 3/1965), ii, pp. 295, 354–8; iii, p. 61

'Artist Biography: Samuel L. Waldo', *Crayon*, viii (1861), pp. 98–100

F. F. Sherman: 'Samuel L. Waldo and William Jewett, Portrait Painters', *A. America*, xviii (1930), pp. 81–6

Benjamin West and his American Students (exh. cat. by D. Evans, Washington, DC, N.P.G., 1980)

SALLY MILLS

Wale, Samuel (*b* ?Yarmouth, 25 April ?1721; *d* London, 6 Feb 1786). English draughtsman, illustrator and painter. In 1735 he was apprenticed to a goldsmith; he studied at the St Martin's Lane Academy, London, where he was influenced by Gravelot. He worked briefly as a decorative painter in partnership with Francis Hayman, presenting topographical roundels of *Christ's Hospital*, *St Thomas's Hospital* and *Greenwich Hospital* to the Foundling Hospital (all before 1748; *in situ*).

Wale was among the most prolific book illustrators of the third quarter of the 18th century, producing illustrations for over 100 publications. The fact that he did not engrave his own designs may have contributed to the enormity of his output: he usually supplied only a pen-and-ink drawing, sometimes tinted, which would then be engraved; he could also be repetitive. Around 1751 he designed a series of prints of Vauxhall Gardens, which were etched and engraved by Thomas Bowles (*b c.* 1712) and Johann Sebastian Müller (1715–*c.* 1785). *Vauxhall Gardens Showing the Grand Walk* (e.g. London, Mus. London) is one such view that shows Wale's ability to combine topographical detail with Rococo lightheartedness. His skill in narrative illustration is evident in his designs for an edition (1769) of Isaac Walton's *Compleat Angler* and in the first compilation of *The Newgate Calendar* (1773); his original drawings for the latter survive (London, BM; London, V&A; Nottingham, Castle Mus.; priv. cols).

Wale was interested in the formation of a royal academy, and he assisted his friend John Gwynn in the preparation of *Proposals for Erecting a Public Academy for Drawing and the Several Arts* (1749), to which he also contributed designs. With William Hogarth he supplied a frontispiece to the first exhibition catalogue (1761) of the Society of Artists, with whom he exhibited from 1760 to 1767. Wale was a founder-member of the Royal Academy in 1768 and its first professor of perspective. He exhibited there from 1769 to 1778, when he stopped painting because of a paralytic stroke. He was compensated by the Academy for this disability: he was given one of its first charitable contributions and was made its librarian in 1778.

BIBLIOGRAPHY

E. Edwards: *Anecdotes of Painters* (London, 1808/R 1970), pp. 116–18

H. A. Hammelmann: 'Eighteenth-century Book Illustrators: Samuel Wale', *Bk Colr*, i (1952), pp. 150–65

H. A. Hammelmann and T. S. R. Boase: *Book Illustrators in Eighteenth-century England* (New Haven and London, 1975), pp. 89–96

Rococo: Art and Design in Hogarth's England (exh. cat., ed. H. Snodin; London, V&A, 1984)

SHEARER WEST

Walenkamp, Herman J(ohannes) M(aria) (*b* Weesp, 12 Dec 1871; *d* Zandvoort, 24 Sept 1933). Dutch architect, theorist and teacher. After training at the Quellinusschool, Amsterdam, he worked in the office of P. J. H. Cuypers from 1890 as a draughtsman. In subsequent years, with his friends and colleagues K. P. C. de Bazel and J. L. Mathieu Lauweriks, he became involved with socialist and anarchist groups. His affiliation to the Theosophical Society led to a definitive break with Cuypers. As a result of his anarchist activities, Walenkamp was unable to participate when, between 1895 and 1898, de Bazel and Lauweriks formulated their theosophical theory of art and established their reputations as the leaders of *Nieuwe Kunst*. Accordingly, his reputation was overshadowed by that of his friends, although in his ideas and work he was often ahead of them and other architects. For example his designs (1895) for a library building decisively influenced H. P. Berlage's Beursgebouw (1893–1906), Amsterdam.

Between 1900 and 1915 Walenkamp was on the juries of many competitions and gave many lectures. He was editor of *Architectura* from 1902 and wrote numerous articles for it. He was a council member of Architectura et Amicitia (chairman in 1913) and taught at the most important schools of applied art: the Quellinusschool, the Kunstnijverheidsschool in Haarlem, where the Hoger Bouwkundig Onderwijs (Higher Diploma in Architecture) was partly set up by him in 1908, and on the theosophical Vahana drawing course. He was responsible for renovating numerous interiors, including Herengracht 502, Amsterdam, later the burgomaster's residence. In 1910 he and Jacob van den Bosch (1868–1948) won the Grand Prix at the Exposition Universelle et Internationale in Brussels; Walenkamp's prize was for a dining-room interior. In 1910–11 he designed what was then Amsterdam's largest public housing complex for Het Westen housing association, consisting of *c.* 800 units at Tasmanstraat, Bontekoestraat and Roggeveenstraat in the Spaardammer district. That was followed in 1915–16 by De Zaanhof in the same district, a workers' housing complex. In 1915 Walenkamp's early anarchist activities became known, and this ruined his career. He retired and lived in seclusion in Zandvoort until his death.

WRITINGS

'Enkele beschouwingen over kunstonderricht en de plaats die het bekleedt in het hedendaagsche leven', *Architectura*, xii (1906), pp. 59–60, 68

BIBLIOGRAPHY

G. Fanelli: *Architettura moderna in Olanda, 1900–1940* (Florence, 1968; Dut. trans., with abridged Eng. text, The Hague, 1978)

Architectura: Nederlandse architectuur, 1893–1918 (exh. cat., ed. M. Bock; Amsterdam, Ned. Doc. Bouwkst, 1975)

Kunstenaren der Idee: Symbolistische tendenzen in Nederland, ca. 1880–1930 (exh. cat. by C. Blotkamp and others, The Hague, Gemeentemus., 1978)

C. Blotkamp: 'The Annunciation of the New Mysticism: Dutch Symbolism and Early Abstraction', *The Spiritual in Art: Abstract Painting, 1980–1985* (Los Angeles and New York, 1986), pp. 89–111

M. Bax: 'De onbekende Walenkamp' [The unknown Walenkamp], *Jong Holland*, iv/4 (1988), pp. 2–14 [with Eng. summary]

——: 'Het 'sfeeren'systeem, 1898–1900: Berlage, van den Bosch, de Groot, Lauweriks en Walenkamp' [The 'sphere' system, 1898–1900: Berlage, van den Bosch, de Groot, Lauweriks and Walenkamp], *Jong Holland*, vi/4 (1990), pp. 17–30 [with Eng. summary]

MARTY TH. BAX

Wales [Cymru]. Region bounded by the Irish Sea to the north, St George's Channel to the west, Bristol Channel to the south and England to the east (see fig. 1). Much of the interior is comprised of hills separated by deep, narrow valleys. The highest parts are the Cambrian Mountains to the west, running north to south. The coastal areas are flatter, particularly in the south; the Isle of Anglesey and the Llŷn peninsula to the north-west are also relatively flat.

There are substantial differences of landscape and climate. The western coastal strip and the mountainous interior are exposed and are relatively poor both in their agricultural base and in material resources. The eastern part of the country, the Vale of Glamorgan in the south,

and the Vale of Clwyd in the north, are richer in natural resources and more accessible to England. The total landmass is 20,761 sq. km. The capital is CARDIFF (Caerdydd) in the south, and other important cities and towns include Swansea (Abertawe), Glams; Newport (Casnewydd), Mons; Bangor, Caerns; Merthyr Tydfil, Glams; Carmarthen (Caerfyrddin), Carms; Aberystwyth, Cards; and Wrexham (Wrecsam), Denbs.

I. Introduction. II. Architecture. III. Painting and graphic arts. IV. Sculpture. V. Interior decoration and furniture. VI. Metalwork, ceramics and glass. VII. Textiles. VIII. Patronage, collecting and dealing. IX. Museums. X. Art education.

I. Introduction.

Wales emerged as one of the remnant nations of the British Celts when the westward expansion of Germanic peoples into the British Isles ended in the 7th century AD. These Celtic origins have marked contemporary visual culture with periodic Celtic revivals and references and persist in a living indigenous language and literature. In the 16th century Wales was incorporated by the English government, leaving it a nation without a state. This condition had a decisive influence on its visual culture, as there was no urban centre of political and economic power within which patronage of the fine arts could flourish. Welsh intellectual life was scattered throughout the country and, ironically, found its most concentrated expression among expatriates in London. In the mid-18th century this already ambiguous situation was further complicated when paintings and prints of the Welsh landscape and objects from Wales's early history became highly fashionable in England.

Since academic artists were trained outside Wales until the late 19th century, the indigenous visual culture is characterized by a non-academic art and a vernacular architecture overlaid with high art patronage by some resident gentry. This situation continued until the expansion of the urban middle class began to have a significant impact in the late 18th century. That expansion coincided with industrialization in both north and south based on coal, metals and slate, which changed the culture dramatically. The population increased from under 300,000 substantially monoglot Welsh speakers in the 1530s to two and a half million speakers of both Welsh and English by 1914. This massive social change that occurred throughout the 19th century, as well as a strong identification of the new nation with Nonconformist Christianity overlaid on the older Celtic tradition, was the basis of modern Welsh nationhood.

BIBLIOGRAPHY

J. Davies: *A History of Wales* (London, 1993)

II. Architecture.

Vernacular architecture is unusually well documented and understood, reflecting its relative importance in a nation at the western edge of European high art and architectural tradition. Although from an early date military and religious building reflected influences from other parts of Europe, some domestic buildings in the vernacular manner were tied to the particular social characteristics of the nation

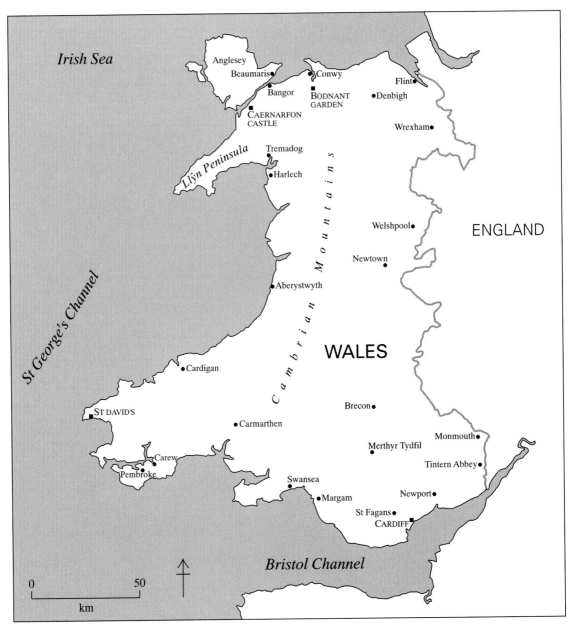

1. Map of Wales; those sites with separate entries in this dictionary are distinguished by CROSS-REFERENCE TYPE

and to geographical and climatic conditions, even into the 19th century. Nevertheless, wide regional variations substantially affected architecture. In the 19th century the standardized demands of industrial building overwhelmed many, but not all, of these regional variations.

1. Before *c.* 1600. 2. After *c.* 1600.

1. BEFORE *c.* 1600. In the period of the emergence of Wales, from the 7th century when such Roman towns as Isca (now Caerleon), Mons, fell into disrepair, some pre-Roman Celtic settlements were reoccupied. At Din Llugwy farmstead in Anglesey (Ynys Môn), substantial remains indicate that building in the emergent Wales belonged to

the general Celtic type with low stone walls and turfed roofs supported on centre-posts. Early religious buildings from the Christian Celtic period are known largely from archaeological records, since subsequent rebuildings have obscured the original layouts. Circular churchyard walls may indicate a Celtic site, sometimes of pre-Christian origin.

Ynys Seiriol, off the coast of Anglesey, was a monastic settlement where remains of buildings, possibly dating from the 7th century AD, include the outer wall, monastic cells and a chapel. A number of isolated wells of similar date survive elsewhere in Wales. Although repaired in the 18th century, the stone-walled and roofed structure over the Maenddu well, Brecon, seems likely to reflect closely the Celtic original.

In Wales, Celtic Christianity developed its own non-hierarchical and loose organization of *clas* churches (Celtic monastery churches). Visual evidence of the evolution of this type of church into the mainstream of medieval European architecture is apparent throughout the country, as at Llanbadarn Fawr, Cards, and Llantwit Major (Llanilltud Fawr), Glams, and notably at Penmon, Anglesey, where a well and a number of crosses from the Celtic period survive among buildings of a 12th-century priory church. A most unusual survival from this period is the stone shrine of St Monacella (*c.* 1160–70) at Pennant Melangell, Montgoms. At the end of the 12th century, Gerallt Cymro (*c.* 1146–*c.* 1220), Archdeacon of Brecon, reported that the Welsh 'do not erect sumptuous palaces, nor lofty stone buildings, but content themselves with small huts made of boughs of trees twisted together, constructed with little labour and expense, and sufficient to endure throughout the year'. His description was probably typical of the habitations of subsistence farmers and labourers found throughout much of the country, and traces of this building tradition—in the form of clay-walled buildings with embedded scarfed crucks, reed-thatched or turfed roofs, wickerwork fireplace hoods and partitions—were still to be found in the early 19th century in the poorest parts of Cardiganshire and Carmarthenshire. However, Gerallt Cymro's comments must be assessed in the context of contemporary descriptions of the house recorded in the Welsh law books. These describe a range of buildings and also outline the much more substantial features of the aisled hall house of the *uchelwyr* ('aristocrat'): 'his larder and his cowhouse and his barn and his kiln and the sheepcote and the pigsty and his summerhouse and his harvest-house'.

Between the first incursions by the Normans in the late 11th century and the conquest by the English king Edward I in 1282–3, about 300 military sites were constructed. They varied from wooden fortifications on earthworks to some of the largest medieval stone fortresses in Europe (*see* CASTLE, §I). Most were the work of the occupying forces, but about two dozen substantial military buildings survive, including Dolwyddelan and Dolbadarn castles (both Caerns). Dolbadarn is characterized by a single round tower. The siting of these fortifications is often spectacular, as at Criccieth, Caerns, where the castle sits on a high promontory extending into Tremadoc Bay, and at Castell y Bere, Merions, which is on a rocky outcrop; the latter was built *c.* 1221 as the main stronghold of Prince Llywelyn Fawr (*reg* 1194–1240). During the conquest, an arc of military buildings was constructed by Edward I around the heartland of Welsh resistance. Seven castles extend along the coast from Flint in the north-east to Aberystwyth in the west and were enormous undertakings. They were characterized by concentric ring construction and reached their elegant epitome in Beaumaris Castle, Anglesey (*see* MILITARY ARCHITECTURE AND FORTIFICATION, fig. 10). However, the much larger CAERNARFON CASTLE was the most important, militarily and symbolically. It is notable for its huge scale and its exterior walls of distinct bands of contrasting coloured stone copied from the city walls of Constantinople (now Istanbul).

Several of these castle sites were developed by Edward I as settlement towns and were based on French models. At Conwy, Caerns, not only the castle but also most of the enclosing town wall and street plan survive. However, the largest of all concentric castles was at Caerphilly (Caerffili), in the south. It was begun in 1271 before the completion of the conquest and, after Windsor Castle, is the largest medieval fortress in the British Isles (*see* CASTLE, fig. 8; for further information on medieval Welsh castles *see* JAMES OF ST GEORGE).

Welsh princes had developed a cooperative relationship with monastic orders in mainland Europe, in particular the Cistercians, who built substantial abbeys, from Whitland (Hendy Gwyn ar Daf), Carms, in the south-west, to Valle Crucis near Llangollen in the north-east. The abbey of Strata Florida (Ystrad Fflur), Cards, founded by the Lord Rhys and built between 1184 and 1235, became a most important centre of the indigenous culture, but the only substantial part of it to have survived is the massive west door, Romanesque in form but with triskel decoration in the Celtic tradition. In the south-east, an area dominated from an early period by the Normans, Tintern Abbey was also built by the Cistercians but was endowed from England. Under Norman domination nearly all *clas* churches were rebuilt as parish churches or cathedrals, as at Llandaff, Glams. The grandest ecclesiastical development took place at the Celtic site of St David's (Tŷ Ddewi), where a bishop's palace on a large scale was constructed primarily in the early 14th century by HENRY DE GOWER (*see* ST DAVID'S, §2 and fig. 2). Its Great Hall is on the first floor, a feature characteristic of medieval *uchelwyr* houses in the south-west. Externally, the palace is notable for its arcaded parapet and stone chequerwork pattern.

During the period of settlement, some military sites were transformed into fortified houses. Tretower Court (Tretwr), Brecs, is similar to structures in mainland Europe, being built around a courtyard with cantilevered exterior walkways at first-floor level. In contrast to the palace at St David's, its fine hall is at ground level, characteristic of most medieval Welsh hall houses. Crucktruss structures were widespread in the north and east, though with considerable regional variations. The A-frame, encased by wooden, stone or mud-built walls, extended from the ground to the roof ridge and was common both to the large houses of the *uchelwyr*, as at Bryndreinog, Radnors, and to the more modest constructs of better-off farmers. However, in the north-west the design gave way to a collar-beam truss standing on structural stone walls, as at Gloddaeth, Caerns, and in the east the English box-frame construction became more common. The earliest hall houses had no chimneys but rather an open hearth in the middle of the floor; they evolved from a single room to a multi-cellular form, initially by partition across the house at one or both ends. Most surviving hall houses are basically of this three-room type. In farmhouses—though probably at a rather later date—the tendency was for one of the end bays, beyond a through-passage across the full width of the house, to be used by the animals, giving the widespread and characteristic form of a longhouse. The Cilewent Farmhouse, reconstructed at the Welsh Folk Museum at St Fagans (Sain Ffagan), is of this type. From about the mid-15th century the fireplace began to replace the open central hearth and was initially placed on a long wall. Roof structures on hall houses occasionally developed from the aisle-truss type into the hammerbeam form as seen at Althrey, Flints, and in its full development at the earlier Cochwillan, Caerns, probably of the late 15th century, which also retains its original side fireplace. Some houses, such as Tŷ Mawr, Montgoms, evolved with combinations of cruck-truss and aisle-truss construction. The lesser gentry and farmers in the early modern period further developed the plan of the hall house, introducing upper floors and wings or small rectangular designs; such designs continued to be built by poorer rural communities into the 19th century. A later type, widespread in the poorer areas, had two units, often with outbuildings added in line but separate; this characteristic distinguishes it from the superficially similar longhouse. In Pembrokeshire, a distinct group of late medieval stone-built houses are characterized by tall, round chimneys, as at Monkton Old Hall.

Late medieval church-building generally followed developments in the rest of Europe, as seen in a notable group in the Perpendicular style in the north-east including All Saints, Gresford, St Mary's, Mold (Yr Wyddgrug), and the tower of St Giles, Wrexham (Wrecsam), added in 1506. St Beuno's, Clynnog Fawr, Caerns, incorporating the mausoleum of the Celtic saint, is of a similar date but in more restrained style.

Union with England in the 16th century resulted in a period of preference for the leading Welsh squirearchy in English public life, and such Renaissance innovations as central planning and emphasized frontages began to affect

the design of large Welsh houses, though often mixed with indigenous features; St Fagans Castle (1560–90), for example, has a fine Elizabethan frontage but retains elements of the hall house. Gate-houses, both for defence and display, were popular, as at Rhiwaedog, Caerns, and Plas Mawr (see fig. 2), a town house within the medieval walls of Conwy and built of stone, although extensive pictorial records show that wooden construction was dominant in many Welsh towns until the early 19th century. Plas Mawr shows the influence of Dutch architecture that was acquired directly from the Low Countries and was most remarkably expressed at Bachegraig (1567–8), one of two brick houses built by Richard Clough (*d* 1570) in Denbighshire. Now destroyed, it had a square plan with a central chimney.

2. AFTER *c.* 1600. As in the 16th century, the influence of English court fashion was seen in some large early 17th-century gentry houses, including the symmetrically planned Plas Teg (*c.* 1610) at Hope, Flints, and the castellated Ruperra (1626) at Llanfedw, Glams. A substantial number of fine Jacobean houses were built in the Vale of Clwyd, Flints (e.g. Nerquis Hall, 1636) and in the Vale of Glamorgan, where the three-storey porch added in 1600 to Beaupré Castle is notable. Tredegar House at Newport (Casnewydd), built *c.* 1670 in brick by the Morgan family, is by far the most splendid house of the later 17th century in Wales. Its front elevation suggests a complete new design, but the plan incorporates the medieval stone hall house facing an inner court. The interior has a magnificent gilded and painted room and sumptuous panelling.

In public building, a comparison of the half-timbered Old Market Hall in Llanidloes, Powys, built in 1609 on arches over an open space, with the stately Shirehall at Monmouth (Trefynwy), Mons, which is similar in conception but built in 1724 in a classical manner, demonstrates the change from vernacular to international sources of style. In the second half of the 18th century, the medieval fabric of most towns began to be replaced by unpretentious, yet often elegant, domestic buildings of classical character, sometimes designed by architects who, in this period, emerged as professionals distinct from builders. Urban development was graced by the occasional, more imposing, civic building, for example the Town Hall at Carmarthen (Caerfyrddin) begun in 1767. Soon after, the first of a number of small planned towns was developed at Morriston (Treforus), near Swansea (Abertawe), followed by Milford Haven, Aberdavgleddav, Pembs, in the 1790s, and Aberaeron and Tremadog, from the first decade of the 19th century. Classically inspired houses of the gentry in the 18th century, including Taliaris (*c.* 1730), near Llandeilo, Carms, and Nanteos (1739), near Aberystwyth, were Palladian in character and generally rather more severe than the Shirehall at Monmouth. Later in the century Anthony Keck (1726–97) built for the collector and patron THOMAS MANSEL TALBOT a fine villa (1773–9) at Penrice (Penrhys) and the exceptionally long and elegant Orangery (1787–90) at Margam.

The general mainstream of Neo-classical building was overlaid by the Romantic fashion for the Gothic style and the PICTURESQUE, also expressed in the fashion for landscape, for which Wales became an international focus.

2. Plas Mawr, Conwy, Caernarfonshire, exterior, *c.* 1576–95

The most important manifestation of this movement occurred at Hafod Uchtryd, near Aberystwyth, where in 1786 Thomas Johnes (1748–1816) commissioned Thomas Baldwin (1750–1820) from Bath to construct a house (destr. 1958) with Gothic fenestration, castellated parapets and pinnacles. Johnes himself added an octagonal library. The house and grounds, where Johnes contrived Picturesque combinations of wild and controlled nature, were much visited by artists and intellectuals, notably the English writer Uvedale Price, who commissioned JOHN NASH to design Castle House (*c.* 1795; destr. 1885), a triangular Gothic villa, for his summer use at Aberystwyth. John Nash's parents were Welsh, and although he was educated in England, he returned to work in Wales between 1784 and 1796, making Carmarthen his principal base. During this time he designed elegant Neo-classical villas of external simplicity but innovative internal planning; these set a new standard for Welsh architecture and were the foundation of his subsequent career in England; Ffynone (1793) and Llanerchaeron (1794; both Cards) are the most notable surviving examples. He also worked in a rustic manner, considered appropriate to the Picturesque landscape, designing, for example, the church and Gothic cottage near Llanerchaeron (both *c.* 1794).

The most unlikely exercise in Gothic construction was Trefecca, near Talgarth, Brecs, a religious community of Calvinistic Methodists that was established and probably designed from *c.* 1752 by Hywel Harris (1714–73). Methodists, in common with other Nonconformists, stressed the rationality of their beliefs and so favoured a classical style for their buildings. The earliest Nonconformist meeting-houses, either converted from barns (e.g. Capel Penrhiw, Drefach Felindre, built *c.* 1770, converted 1777; now at the Welsh Folk Museum, St Fagans) or purpose-built chapels, usually had restrained and symmetrical façades on the long wall of the single-cell rectangular building, often with two entrances (see fig. 3). In the interior, the pulpit was the focus of worship and was placed between the entrances. In larger buildings, a raised gallery looked down on the pulpit from the opposite wall, and details in the form of turned and panelled box pews were simple and restrained. In the early 19th century a Classical reference was sometimes more pronounced, most notably in the massive Doric-columned frontage of Peniel, Tremadog, Caerns, built in 1811 for the planned town. In the mid-19th century, when Nonconformism was at a peak of self-confidence, the internal arrangements of the buildings changed, the pulpit being placed against the end wall opposite the entrance façade, which was often highly ornate and was designed in classical or Gothic revival or other more exotic styles. The Anglican Church responded to the dual challenges of Welsh Nonconformism and massive population growth in the 19th century with a sudden increase in building mainly, but not exclusively, in the industrialized areas. The Church also rebuilt older foundations, so that by the end of the century all but a few medieval churches had been restored. A characteristic large example of this new building is William Butterfield's St Augustine's (1864–6), Penarth, Glams. Notable among new foundations funded privately was the Marble Church (1856), Bodelwyddan, Flints, by John Gibson (ii), and St Mark's (1896) at Brithdir, near Dolgellau, built by Henry

3. Capel Bilidu, Pentre Bach, Breconshire, exterior, *c.* 1800

Wilson in the Art Nouveau style. (For further discussion *see* NONCONFORMIST CHAPEL.)

The simplicity of the earlier chapel buildings was consistent with the mood of contemporary industrial buildings, as for example the vast ironworks (destr.) at Cyfarthfa, Merthyr Tydfil, and, on a smaller scale, the Dinorwig quarry workshops in Caernarfonshire. A more flamboyant expression of industrial confidence were the blast furnaces (destr.) at Rhymni, Glams, built in the style of Egyptian temples. Since much of the industrial development in South Wales in the 19th century occurred along steep-sided valleys, workers' housing took on a particularly distinctive quality. The Scotch Houses (*c.* 1865) at Llwynypia, Rhondda, epitomize the parallel ascending stacks of contour-following terraces that characterize the coalfield. This particular group of terraces was of better quality than many, reflecting a need to attract workers in a period of labour shortage, but attempts to improve housing for industrial workers, such as The Triangle (destr.) at Merthyr Tydfil, built between 1840 and 1852 for Anthony Hill of the Plymouth Ironworks, were generally sporadic. Housing in the Valleys was usually of local stone, but terraces in Newtown (Y Drenewydd), Montgoms, and Llanidloes, centres of the woollen industry, were built of brick. In the 20th century heavy industry gradually declined, creating few architecturally important industrial buildings. However, the Williams & Robinson Turbine Factory (1901–5) by H. B. Creswell at Queensferry, Flints, is a notable early exception, and the Dunlop Rubber Factory (1947–52) at Brynmawr, Mons, is a remarkable and dramatic exercise in ferro-concrete by OVE ARUP and the ARCHITECTS' CO-PARTNERSHIP. Public investment in what was, by the later 20th century, a depressed area, funded the INMOS Microprocessor Factory at Newport (completed 1982), designed by RICHARD ROGERS. In Cardiff, the docklands development, begun in the late 1980s, sought to rejuvenate a vast area of the city made derelict by the decline of the coal and steel industry.

The wealth of Welsh industrialists in the 19th century enabled them to build on a large scale. George Day Hawkins Pennant (1763–1840), had THOMAS HOPPER build Penrhyn Castle (*c.* 1827–40), a neo-Norman building with central heating, near Bangor, Caerns, on the strength of the slate industry. Hopper also built Margam Abbey (1830) in a similar style. In 1825 Robert Lugar (*c.* 1773–1855) built Cyfarthfa Castle for William Crawshay, an ironmaster from Merthyr Tydfil. However, all these historical exercises, though on a substantial scale, were dwarfed by the investment of John Patrick Crichton-Stuart, 3rd Marquess of Bute, in rebuilding Cardiff Castle (1868–93; for illustration of interior *see* BURGES, WILLIAM, fig. 1; *see also* CARDIFF) and the nearby Castell Coch (1875–91; *see* STUART, HOUSE OF, (2) and CASTLE, fig. 11). These architectural fantasies in medieval style, designed by William Burges, are among the most dramatic and sumptuous reactions against the Industrial Age in Europe. The inclination to Historicism and Eclecticism continued in the 20th century in the work of CLOUGH WILLIAMS-ELLIS, as seen at Llangoed Castle (1918), near Talgarth, built in Neo-Tudor style, and Portmeirion, Caerns, a harbour village built from 1926 in Italianate style.

The great wealth and importance of Cardiff (Caerdydd) at the beginning of the 19th century were expressed in the Civic Centre group of buildings in Cathays Park, begun in 1897 but not completed until 1927. The Law Courts and City Hall (both 1897–1904; for illustration *see* CARDIFF) are by LANCHESTER & RICKARDS, and the National Museum of Wales (1910; officially opened 1927) was designed by SMITH & BREWER. Perhaps the most distinguished of late 20th-century public buildings in Wales is the offices (1982) built for Gwynedd at Caernarfon, a cooperation between the County Architects' Department and Dewi Prys Thomas (1916–85), who was Principal of the Welsh School of Architecture. The building's national symbolism reflects Thomas's commitment to the indigenous culture of the nation.

BIBLIOGRAPHY
P. Smith: *Houses of the Welsh Countryside* (London, 1975)
J. B. Hilling: *The Historical Architecture of Wales* (Cardiff, 1976)

III. Painting and graphic arts.

1. BEFORE *c.* 1775. The Lichfield or Chad Gospels (second quarter of 8th century AD; Lichfield Cathedral), associated with Llandeilo Fawr, Carms, contains the only painting from before the 11th century with Welsh provenance. Although the book is incomplete, it contains portraits of St Luke and St Mark, a carpet page, and the Incarnation Initial. The finest product of the scriptorium at the *clas* church (Celtic monastery church) of Llanbadarn Fawr, Cards, is the Rhygyfarch Psalter (Dublin, Trinity Coll. Lib), illuminated in 1086 by Ieuan ap Sullen (*c.* 1060–1137). It has four carpet pages and numerous initials in the zoomorphic style and is among the very last works produced in the unbroken Celtic tradition. Medieval manuscript illumination in the Gothic manner is best represented by the 14th-century Llanbeblig Hours (Aberystwyth, N. Lib. Wales), containing seven full-page paintings including what is probably a representation of Macsen

Wledig (the Roman emperor Magnus Clemens Maximus; *reg* 383–8).

Fragmentary survivals of early wall paintings are widespread, the 15th-century depiction of the *Seven Acts of Mercy* in St Mary's, Ruabon (Rhiwabon), Denbs, being one of the most complete ecclesiastical examples. However, more remarkable is the double portrait of *Elis ap Richard and Jane Hanmer* (*c.* 1540; Althrey Hall, Flints) by an anonymous artist. Rhys Cain (*c.* 1555–1614) is known to have painted pictures, as he was criticized by a contemporary Puritan for doing so. Regrettably, his only surviving works are heraldic illustrations on pedigree rolls (e.g. *Edward Almer*, 1602; Aberystwyth, N. Lib. Wales). According to local tradition, the portrait on panel of *Sir Edward Stradling and his Wife* (St Donat's, Castle Church), signed by a painter called Byrd and dated 1590, was done in Wales, but Welsh intellectuals of this period spent much time in England and in mainland Europe and had their portraits painted there. For example, in 1568, the year after his marriage, Sir Richard Clough (*d* 1570) commissioned in the Low Countries, and possibly from Adriaen von Cronenburgh (*c.* 1525–*c.* 1604), the portrait of his wife *Katheryn of Berain* (Cardiff, N. Mus.). The double portrait of *Sir Thomas Mansell and Jane Mansell of Margam* (*c.* 1625; Cardiff, N. Mus.) is perhaps the most notable of early 17th-century examples of patronage by the gentry.

One of the first depictions of the Welsh landscape is that seen through an open window in the portrait of *Jenkyn Williams of Aberpergwm* (1627; M. Williams priv. col., see Rowan, i, p. 102) by an anonymous artist. However, the first group of paintings showing Welsh country houses in their landscape settings dates from the Restoration period (after 1660), the most sophisticated being *Troy House, Monmouth* by Hendrick Danckerts, presumably painted before the house was remodelled in 1673. The most remarkable pictures of this period are the four bird's-eye view representations (priv. col.; on loan to Newport, Gwent, Tredegar House) of *Newton House* and *Dinefwr Castle*, homes of the Rice family, near Llandeilo. The depictions of *Dinefwr Castle*, probably made by a local painter, have strong Welsh historical and legendary overtones and so may be considered among the earliest visual intimations of the mid-18th-century intellectual revival that was both the foundation of modern Welsh national identity and an important contributor to the fashion among the English for the landscape and the early culture of Wales.

From the early 1720s John Dyer (1699–1757) from Carmarthen travelled and painted widely in Wales, although most of his work is lost. RICHARD WILSON (i) painted the Welsh landscape as early as the 1740s. His *Castle of Dinas Bran from Llangollen* (New Haven, CT, Yale Cent. Brit. A.), painted for Sir WATKIN WILLIAMS-WYNN in 1770–71 after Wilson's visit to Italy (1750–*c.* 1757), echoes the national iconography of the paintings of *Dinefwr Castle*. Previously, Wilson painted portraits for Welsh patrons, particularly in the north-east, where he had family connections (e.g. *Richard Owen of Ynysmaengwyn*, *c.* 1748; Cardiff, N. Mus.). William Parry (*c.* 1742–91), trained in London by Reynolds at Williams-Wynn's expense, also painted portraits, not only among the circle of the Cymmrodorion Society in London (*see* §VIII below) but also in Wales itself. In 1774 Wilson's pupil THOMAS JONES of Pencerrig executed *The Bard* (Cardiff, N. Mus.), his only historical painting on an explicitly Welsh theme; this national image was to be further developed by Welsh artists in the 19th and 20th centuries. Jones's Welsh landscapes (e.g. *View in Radnorshire, c.* 1776; Cardiff, N. Mus.), produced both before and after his Italian visit (1776–83), and his townscapes of Naples (e.g. *Buildings in Naples*, 1782; Cardiff, N. Mus.) have an informal naturalism that is prescient of a later age.

2. AFTER *c*. 1775. The publication (1775) of Richard Wilson's later Welsh landscapes and, from 1775, the aquatints of the English painter Paul Sandby helped encourage a flood of tourists to Wales that lasted for many years; these included nearly all the important artists working in the English landscape tradition. For Turner, visiting several times between 1792 and 1799, and David Cox, whose first visit was in 1805, such experiences were important for their future development. The most important later Welsh contributors to the fashion for touring were Edward Pugh (*c.* 1761–1813), whose *Cambria Depicta* was published in London in 1816, and Hugh Hughes (1790–1863), whose *Beauties of Cambria* (London, 1823) was published as wood-engravings, an unusual medium for depicting landscape.

In the late 18th century, the growing market for portraits among the expanding middle class was occasionally exploited by workshop-trained artisans who painted mainly carts, houses, signs for shops and inns and some religious images. The finest example of portraits done in Wales in the 18th century is the series depicting servants at Erddig, Wrexham (Wrecsam), Denbs (1791–6; *in situ*), the only known paintings by John Walters (*fl* 1791–6) of Denbigh (Dinbych). They are narrative and heraldic, though not untouched by academic art. By the early 19th century it had become worthwhile for painters specializing in portraits to make tours of various Welsh towns. Hugh Hughes, whose printmaking activity obscures his origins within the artisan tradition, toured in the north-west in 1812–14, though his work reached its height later in the 1820s with the *Family of John Evans, Carmarthen, at Breakfast* (see fig. 4). The most productive of the travelling artisans was William Roos (1808–76), who painted a number of vigorous portraits of prominent intellectuals, among them *John Jones, Talhaiarn* (1850; Cardiff, N. Mus). In the absence of an academic tradition based in Wales, this new intelligentsia—in particular, poets and Nonconformist leaders—was recorded mainly by artisans. The images were widely distributed as engravings and had an important influence on national consciousness, as is reflected in the work of Robert Hughes (1811–92) of Uwchlaw'r Ffynnon, Caerns, a painter of naive portraits, who sometimes copied from them. From the early 19th century a few Welsh towns offered sufficient patronage to support resident portrait painters, notably William Watkeys (1800–73) in Swansea (Abertawe), J. F. Mullock (1818–92) in Newport (Casnewydd) and John 'Cambrian' Rowland (1819–90) in Aberystwyth and later Caernarfon. In the first half of the 19th century there was a rapid growth of publications in Welsh, with accompanying woodcuts and wood-engravings.

4. Hugh Hughes: *Family of John Evans, Carmarthen, at Breakfast*, oil on canvas, 107×710 mm, *c.* 1823 (Ambleside, private collection)

James Cope (1806–after 1842) illustrated ballads and broadsheets in an extravagant and grotesque style for the publisher John Jones of Llanrwst, Denbs.

Several painters from an artisan background later received academic training in London. Penry Williams (1800–85) was the son of a house painter in Merthyr Tydfil but worked most of his life in Rome with the sculptor John Gibson (i). Thomas Brigstocke (1809–81) from Carmarthen (Caerfyrddin), also the son of a painter and decorator, visited Italy and subsequently Egypt, where in 1847 he painted *Muhammad 'Ali Pasha* (London, Orient. Club). Thereafter, he settled in London, from where he was patronized in particular by the gentry of south Wales and where he associated with a group of expatriate intellectuals and artists who determined to introduce academic art to a public whose taste they regarded as in need of improvement. Brigstocke and his circle showed at the exhibitions of the Eisteddfod movement (1861–76), which became the main platform for the promotion of academic painting in Wales into the period of the national revival at the beginning of the 20th century. The movement reached its height in the paintings of Christopher Williams (1873–1934), which were based on the ancient literary classic the *Mabinogi* (e.g. *Branwen*, 1915; Swansea, Vivian A.G. & Mus.), and in his large-scale allegory of national revival, *Wales Awakening* (1911; Aberystwyth, N. Lib. Wales). A generation later, DAVID JONES used the same source for his works containing Welsh historical and mythological subject-matter, as seen in his much-imitated painted inscriptions and such watercolour drawings as the unfinished *Tristram and Isolde* (*c.* 1962; Cardiff, N. Mus.), though he worked in Wales only in 1924–6, the brief period of his association with the English sculptor Eric Gill at Capel y Ffin, Mons.

Unlike Christopher Williams and the painter of portraits and subjects Margaret Lindsay Williams (1888–1960), Augustus John rejected English academicism early in his career. He was ambiguous in his attachment to his native Wales but nevertheless painted landscapes there (e.g. *Llyn Treweryn*, 1912; London, Tate), particularly with JAMES DICKSON INNES from Llanelli, Carms. Landscape continued to be the main focus for Welsh painters in the 1920s and 1930s. Harry Hughes Williams (1892–1953) painted his luminous pictures almost exclusively in Anglesey (Ynys Môn), but other painters, including CEDRIC MORRIS and Edward Morland Lewis (1903–43), worked more sporadically in Wales. However, to John's irritation, Evan Walters (1893–1951) remained in Wales painting landscapes and also portraits of the mining community (e.g. *A Welsh Miner*, 1926; Swansea, Vivian A.G. & Mus.), foreshadowing a trend that reached its height in the 1950s with the formation of the Rhondda Group. Ernest Zobole (*b* 1927), its most distinguished member, remained committed to the industrial culture and landscape of the Rhondda Valley as the source of his imagery (e.g. *Ystrad and People, No. 1*, 1960; Swansea, Vivian A.G. & Mus.). Similarly, Will Roberts (*b* 1910), though not a member of the group, developed rapidly in the late 1940s as a painter whose imagery was rooted in the industrial communities of south Wales. The Polish-born artist Josef Herman lived for 11 years (1944–55) in the mining village of Ystradgunlais, which inspired a series of paintings and drawings (e.g.

Miners on the Road, 1946; London, V&A) and had an important influence on young Welsh artists. Kyffin Williams (*b* 1918) continued the tradition of painting lyrical depictions of the mountain areas (e.g. *Ogwen*, 1966; B. Richards priv. col., see Rowan, ii, p. 142), although he is also highly regarded as a portrait painter. CERI RICHARDS achieved a substantial reputation working in an international modernist idiom, occasionally painting landscape in Wales and essaying Celtic themes. Brenda Chamberlain (1912–71) came to prominence primarily through her lyrical paintings of people, the land and the sea (e.g. *Children on the Seashore*, 1950; Merthyr Tydfil, Cyfartha Castle Mus. & A.G.) but later also turned to more experimental forms to pursue her interest in the natural world. In the 1970s and 1980s a number of painters emerged who were committed to working within Wales, e.g. Shani Rees James (*b* 1953) and Iwan Bala (*b* 1956).

BIBLIOGRAPHY

E. Rowan, ed.: *Art in Wales: An Illustrated History*, 2 vols (Cardiff, 1978–85)

P. Lord: *Y Chwaer-Dduwies: Celf, Crefft a'r Eisteddfod* [The sister goddess: art, craft and the Eisteddfod] (Llandysul, 1992)

——: *Gwenllian: Essays on Visual Culture* (Llandysul, 1994)

IV. Sculpture.

Approximately 450 crosses and inscribed stones from the Christian Celtic period survive, most of them—as at Llantwit Major (Llanilltud Fawr), Margam (both Glams) and Penmon, Anglesey (Ynys Môn)—associated with the sites of *clas* churches (Celtic monastery churches). Among the largest and most richly carved with interlace panels are the late 10th-century Carew High Cross (see fig. 5) and the Nevern (Nanhyfer) Great Cross in Pembrokeshire, both of massive proportions and standing around 4 m high. The human figure is rarely depicted, but the Llanbadarn High Cross in Cardiganshire has a portrait of a bishop, presumably Padarn, who founded the *clas*.

The princely courts were obliterated following the Norman subjugation of Wales in the 11th century, but the few surviving carvings from Castell y Bere, Merions, and Degannwy, Caerns, and in particular the effigy of *Siwan* (Beaumaris, St Mary) from Llanfaes, Anglesey, commissioned by Prince Llywelyn Fawr (*reg* 1194–1240) on his wife's death in 1237, show an uncompromising modernism with little attempt to establish stylistic continuity with the earlier tradition. In the 14th and 15th centuries the *uchelwyr* ('aristocrats') substantially patronized stone-carvers in north Wales, who formed a distinctly Welsh school and whose work is characterized by such fine effigies as that of *Meurig ab Ynyr Fychan* (*c.* 1345; Dolgellau, St Mary). An individual, but unknown, hand is clearly discernible in a group of carvings that includes *St Iestyn* (Anglesey, Llaniestyn church), *St Pabo* (Anglesey, Llanbano church) and *Eva* in Bangor Cathedral, Caerns (all *c.* 1380). Evidence of the quality and particular style of medieval woodcarving is confined to the ornate rood screens of such churches as those at Llanegryn (Merions) and Patrisio (Brecs) as most figurative sculpture was destroyed by iconoclasts in the 16th century. The most notable surviving wood-carvings are the Mostyn *Christ* (*c.* 1518) in Bangor Cathedral and a *Sleeping Jesse* (late 14th century) in St Mary's, Abergavenny. Among the finest polychromed

5. Carew High Cross, Pembrokeshire, stone, h. 4 m, late 10th century

from Ruthin. He was apprenticed to Peter Roberts, a mason from London, but by 1707 had certainly returned to Wales. From 1719 he produced complex, large-scale memorials for the Myddleton family at Chirk (Y Waun), and then for their political rivals, the Wynns, at Ruabon (Rhiwabon). Subsequently, he was almost certainly responsible for the finest Baroque sculpture in Wales, the memorial to *Maurice Jones* (1702; Llanrhaeadr Llan-rhaeadr-yng-Nghinmeirch, St Dyfnog). In the later 18th century, the gentry commissioned most of the prestigious works from sculptors in England: for example, Louis-François Roubiliac executed the marble funerary memorial to *Mary Middleton* (1750; Wrexham, St Giles) and Joseph Nollekens that to *Lady Henrietta Somerset* (1773; Ruabon, St Mary), wife of Sir Watkin Williams-Wynn. Thomas Johnes (1748–1816) from Hafod Uchtryd, Cards, patronized Thomas Banks and Francis Chantrey; the monument to *Mariamne Johnes* (completed 1811), the masterpiece Johnes commissioned from Chantrey, was destroyed by fire in 1932. Nevertheless, the Welsh mason Daniel Mainwaring (*fl* 1809–31) produced monuments of fine quality in the Carmarthen area.

Although John Gibson (i) regarded himself as Welsh and was much eulogized by 19th-century intellectuals as an example to the nation, he did no public sculpture in Wales. However, in the mid-19th century there was a burst of creative activity by Welsh sculptors who were partly stimulated by his example. Although their studios were in London, they were very interested in the development of an indigenous Welsh culture. The father-figure of this group was Joseph Edwards (1814–82), born in Merthyr Tydfil, who expressed his mystical philosophy particularly in his work in shallow relief but who also produced such monumental works as *Religion* (*c*. 1872) at Cefn-coed-y-cymmer cemetery, near Merthyr Tydfil. The brothers William Lorando Jones (*c*. 1820–*c*. 1890) and Watkin D. Jones (1830–after 1861) and William Davies (1826–1901) and David Davies (1837–after 1912)—all from Merthyr Tydfil—also lived and worked in London. John Evan Thomas (1810–73) and his brother William Meredydd Thomas (1819–77) from Brecon (Aberhonddu) and Edward Davis (1813–78) from Carmarthen (Caerfyrddin) also established studios in London. William Meredydd Thomas executed the fine portrait bust of *Thomas Price, Carnhuanawc* (1848, Llandovery Coll.) shortly after he had modelled, to his brother's concept, the large bronze *Death of Tewdrig* (Cardiff, N. Mus.), the most important piece of national imagery of the mid-19th century. John Evan Thomas produced public statuary in Wales, including the monumental *Albert the Good* (1863) that dominates Castle Hill overlooking Tenby (Dinbych y Pysgod), Pembs. In the 1830s a school of naive carvers associated with the slate quarrying industry in Dyffryn Ogwen, Caerns, was at its peak. Their work is characterized by incised decoration on massive slate slab fireplaces found in the area (e.g. of *c*. 1835; Bangor, Mus. Welsh Art.).

From the mid-19th century, architectural restoration in CARDIFF (Caerdydd) had an important influence on Welsh sculpture. Milo ap Griffith (1843–97), who received his first training at Llandaff Cathedral, produced public statuary in both the idiom of NEW SCULPTURE (e.g. *Hugh Owen*, 1888; Caernarfon, Castle Square) and in a romantic

tombs is that of *Richard Herbert and Magdalene Herbert* (1600) in St Nicholas, Montgomery (Trefaldwyn). The naively carved polychromed bust of the Dean of Westminster *Gabriel Goodman* in St Peter's, Ruthin (Rhuthun), erected in his home town following his death in 1601, is a more unusual public sculpture of the same period.

The first Welsh sculptor known by name and by a significant body of work is Robert Wynne (*c*. 1655–1731) historical style (e.g. *Llywelyn Fawr*, *c.* 1880; Cardiff, N. Mus). WILLIAM GOSCOMBE JOHN, the son of a foreman carpenter working for William Burges at Cardiff Castle, became the dominant figure in Welsh art in the early 20th century. He was a prolific sculptor of portrait busts, medals and public statuary, the small bronze *Merlin and Arthur* (1902; Cardiff, N. Mus.) and the memorial to the *Writers of the National Anthem* (1930; Pontypridd, Ynysangharad Park) being among his finest works. Goscombe John also acted as an adviser for the Pantheon of National Heroes in the Marble Hall in City Hall, Cardiff. Of this group of 11 sculptures, completed in 1916, *Llywelyn ap Gruffydd* (*c.* 1914–16) by Henry Pegram (*b* 1862) became one of the most celebrated images of Welsh culture. The national imagery employed by Goscombe John in several of his medals (examples in Cardiff, N. Mus.) is part of a tradition associated with the Eisteddfod movement dating to the 18th century. This movement also promoted the elaborately carved Eisteddfod chair as a vehicle for national imagery, the most notable examples being the group of Celtic Revival chairs carved in 1917, 1919 and 1920 (priv. col., see Lord, pls 74, 75).

Ivor Roberts-Jones (*b* 1913) sculpted portraits of many distinguished Welsh people but completed only one large-scale public commission in Wales, the *Two Kings* (1983; Harlech), a bronze equestrian statue based on a theme from the *Mabinogi*. In the 1950s Jonah Jones (*b* 1919)

emerged as a leading sculptor and also as a letter-cutter, and Peter Nicholas (*b* 1934) also carried out numerous public and private commissions. Among artists born after World War II, David Nash (*b* 1945) established an international reputation for his use of rough-hewn and growing timber in site-specific works (e.g. *Table with Cubes*, 1973; Cardiff, N. Mus.).

BIBLIOGRAPHY

V. E. Nash-Williams: *The Early Christian Monuments of Wales* (Cardiff, 1950)

C. A. Gresham: *Medieval Stone Carving in North Wales* (Cardiff, 1968)

V. Interior decoration and furniture.

In the Elizabethan period the partitions of some medieval hall houses, notably Maenan, Caerns, were embellished with flamboyant plaster decoration (see fig. 6). Of Renaissance houses, Plas Mawr, Conwy (*see* §II, 1 above), is notable for its early plaster ceilings and overmantel decoration (*c.* 1576–80). However, the most remarkable interior of the period is the Long Gallery at Powis Castle, Montgoms, which has painted *trompe l'oeil* wainscoting, a plaster frieze and ceiling (1592) and a fireplace with plaster reliefs of *The Temptation* and *The Expulsion* (1593). Elsewhere in the castle, the landings and treads of some staircases are inlaid with marquetry and parquetry. Jacobean plasterwork of good quality is found at Newton House, near Llandeilo, Carms, while both Fonmon Castle, Glams, and Cresselly, Pembs, have rooms of the mid-Georgian period with delicate Rococo plaster ceilings. Between 1763 and 1773 Chirk Castle, Denbs, was remodelled, with staterooms and an entrance hall designed by Joseph Turner (*fl* 1752–85) from Hawarden, Flints. The saloon has a painted ceiling (1772–3) in the Adam style with medallions on canvas. The restoration of Cardiff Castle and Castell Coch by William Burges in the 1860s and 1870s included the provision of splendid interiors that were largely fanciful evocations of medieval domestic settings, with furniture inspired by manuscript illuminations and surviving medieval pieces (*see* BURGES, WILLIAM, fig. 1, and §II, 2 above).

Like other aspects of Welsh visual culture, furniture is characterized by a conservative tradition displaying both national and local characteristics overlaid by gentry patronage of fashionable urban design transmitted particularly through London (though in the north-west also through Dublin). Until the mid-18th century most furniture was made of locally grown oak, ash or elm. Early medieval law books list some of the furnishings and features of the interior of the houses of the *uchelwyr* ('aristocrats'), in particular 'the benches and the end-benches, and the fireback stones and the doors and the porches', but the Peniarth 22 manuscript (mid-13th century; Aberystwyth, N. Lib. Wales) clearly illustrates a chair with separate legs, as distinct from a bench or a box chair, which was most unusual for that period. Notable among surviving early pieces is a canopied buffet (*c.* 1535) carved with heraldic designs and made for Sir John Wynn (*d* 1559) from Gwydir, Caerns. In poorer areas, chairs of an ancient type made in coiled basketry of straw rope were produced into the 20th century.

In the 16th century the two-tiered court cupboard was introduced into Wales, but by the mid-17th century an extra canopy and shelf for the display of pewter and

6. Plasterwork decoration, 16th century, encasing a medieval cruck frame in the hall, looking towards the passage, at Maenan, Caernarfonshire

earthenware had been added to give the characteristic *tridarn* or three-tiered form, sometimes ornately carved and inscribed. Unlike the *tridarn*, the open-topped dresser (or 'Welsh' dresser) is not unique to Wales but became highly developed both formally and socially, characteristically displaying lustreware. By the 19th century it had become the most colourful and expressive element in both the rural and urban houses of ordinary people. Generally, in the north and east, dressers were fitted with cupboard doors on the lower section, while in the south and west, dressers were fully open with an apron.

Furniture-makers' names appear in account books from the second half of the 17th century. Provincial cabinet-makers whose work was of high quality emerged in the 18th century, notably William Owen (*c.* 1780–1831) in Haverfordwest (Hwlffordd) and David Morley (1760–1840) in Carmarthen (Caerfyrddin). They established substantial businesses that produced high-quality work to both traditional and imported fashionable designs. Cases for longcase clocks, made in substantial numbers in Welsh towns, were another common item. About 1660, a lacquer had been extracted from coal deposits in the area around Pontypool, Mons, and the manufacture of japanned tin-ware trays, baskets, tea-caddies and other items began. This work was at its best in the mid-18th century but continued for another 100 years (e.g. tea-urn, late 18th century; Cardiff, N. Mus.). During the Depression of the 1930s, unemployed people were trained in furniture man-ufacture at the Brynmawr and Clydach Valley Industries workshops (both Mons). Working to the designs of Paul Matt, and marketing the finished pieces in London, the venture achieved considerable success but ended with World War II. After the war, Christie-Tyler Ltd relocated to Bridgend where, by the late 1950s, it was the largest furniture manufacturer in Wales. In the late 1970s David Colwell (*b* 1944) set up a design studio and workshop near Caersws, Powys, where he produced a range of high-quality furniture, notably tables and chairs (examples in London, Crafts Council Gal.) that won him an international reputation.

BIBLIOGRAPHY
L. Twiston-Davies and H. J. Lloyd-Johnes: *Welsh Furniture: An Introduction* (Cardiff, 1950)

VI. Metalwork, ceramics and glass.

The blacksmith was accorded high status in Celtic society. Later, the smelting industry in the north-east produced the most remarkable examples of wrought ironwork. The brothers Robert Davies (1675–1748) and John Davies (*d* 1755), with substantial patronage from the gentry, were able to develop their work to an elaborate brilliance in the gates (1712) to Chirk Castle, Denbs, and those (*c.* 1726) for Leeswood Park (Coed-Ilai), Mold (Yr Wyddgrug). Of 20th-century smiths, David Peterson (*b* 1944) has, in his work, been particularly conscious of this ancient and distinguished tradition. Among smiths working with precious metals, Silvanus Crue (*d* 1681) of Wrexham (Wrecsam) also produced engraved brasses, notably the portrait of *Mary Mostyn* (1658; *in situ*, Llanrwst, Gwydir Chapel). In the 20th century, Harry Hall (*c.* 1890–*c.* 1950) worked at the Swansea School of Art, producing jewellery and commemorative caskets in copper, silver and enamel in

7. Ceramic plate decorated by Sarah Jane Roberts, made at the Llanelli Pottery, early 20th century (Llanelli, Llanelli Borough Council)

the Celtic Revival manner, notably that presented in 1918 to British Prime Minister David Lloyd George (Llanstumdwy, Lloyd George Mem. Mus.).

There have been important centres of ceramic production in Wales that have supplied the whole spectrum of the market, from functional domestic earthenwares for local consumption to highly sophisticated porcelain for export. The earliest attested activity at the Buckley potteries in Flintshire was in the 14th century. Later, finely made jugs and storage vessels, as well as roof-furniture, were produced there, in anticipation of the brickmaking industry that would later dominate the area. In the 18th and 19th centuries the potteries became renowned for the production of lead-glazed domestic ware with slip-trailed decoration, marketed throughout Wales. Production continued, largely unmechanized, into the 1940s. In the south, the Ewenni potteries in Glamorganshire provided a corollary to Buckley, producing a wide range of domestic ware characterized by *sgraffito* decoration. However, in the 19th century, Ewenni was known for the production of ornate wassail bowls, money-boxes and puzzle-jugs. The potteries at Swansea (Abertawe; 1764–1870) and at Nantgarw (1813–23) produced refined ceramics mainly for export, including the high-quality porcelain made by WILLIAM BILLINGSLEY, initially at Nantgarw and later at Swansea. Porcelain made at the Cambrian Pottery (est. *c.* 1767) in Swansea was distinguished by the painting and gilding of Thomas Pardoe (1770–1823), who worked there from *c.* 1795 to *c.* 1805 and subsequently at Nantgarw. Between 1810 and 1820, the best porcelain pieces produced at Swansea and Nantgarw were the equal of the highest-quality European wares. The Llanelli Pottery (1840–1921) had a varied output. Initially transfer-printed domestic ware was produced; after 1877 hand-decorated ware dominated, including characteristic floral and fruit motifs and naive paintings of cockerels by Sarah Jane Roberts (1859–1935; see fig. 7). Studio pottery in the tradition of

BERNARD LEACH began in the 1930s at John Bew's Rhondda Pottery and reached its height in a proliferation of small workshops in the 1970s, set up mostly by new residents who espoused a philosophy of simple rural living. In Rhayader, Powys, Phil Rogers (*b* 1951), who was born and trained in Wales, produced salt-glazed and reduction-fired stoneware domestic pieces, and David Frith (*b* 1940) in Denbigh continued to produce domestic and individual pieces of reduced stoneware and porcelain. Morgen Hall (*b* 1960) had a workshop in Cardiff, where she produced highly decorated domestic tableware.

In general there has not been a strong tradition of glass production in Wales. The earliest glass of fine quality dates from 1498 and is found at All Saints, Gresford, Denbs, including scenes from the *Life of the Virgin* and the *Life of St Anne*; St Dyfnog, Llanrhaeadr-yng-Nghinmeirch, Denbs, has a magnificent *Tree of Jesse* window (1533). From the early 20th century, the Swansea School of Art specialized in glassmaking, which continues to flourish.

BIBLIOGRAPHY
I. Edwards: *Y brodyr Davies: Gofaint gatiau* [The Davies brothers: gatesmiths] (Cardiff, 1977)
M. Vincintelli: *Talking Pots* (Aberystwyth, 1993)

VII. Textiles.

The production of woollen textiles has always been of great importance in a rural economy well suited to sheep husbandry. By the 14th century the large export trade in raw wool developed by 14 Cistercian monasteries was overtaken by the export of woven, but usually unfinished, friezes; this change was stimulated by technical advances, in particular water-powered fulling. The trade served the bottom of the market, and goods left Wales through seaports in the south and also through Bristol and Shrewsbury in England, where merchants developed a firm grip on the industry. In the 16th century new fabrics were developed; the most important of these was flannel (the English word is a corruption of the Welsh *gwlanen*), which dominated production into the 20th century. At first, it was probably exported undyed and unbleached.

The expansion of the trade was hamstrung by conservative attitudes to organization and technology, even in Montgomeryshire, the main centre of production, where factory organization began to develop in the late 18th century, notably at Newtown (Y Drenewydd), Welshpool (Y Trallwng) and Llanidloes (all Montgoms). However, from 1859 Pryce Jones of Newtown pioneered mail-order direct selling, which for a time helped revive the factories. In the 19th century, the Teifi Valley in Cardiganshire became another important centre of production, supplying textiles to the expanding population in the coalfields of the south.

Narrow red-and-black striped patterns, red, white and black stripes and chequered and plain patterns were characteristic designs of flannel textiles. They became associated with the patriotic efforts of Augusta Hall (1802–96) to revive the industry in Monmouthshire from the 1830s by establishing a fashion for indigenous products. The longest lasting outcome of her work was the creation of the national costume. *Carthenni*, or doublecloth bedcovers and blankets in chequered patterns, were characteristic of individual mills and were first produced in the

north but subsequently in the rest of Wales. They were of a heavier weave than the flannels, generally subdued in colour and fringed on all edges. With the increase of tourism in the mid-20th century, there was a revival in the weaving of *carthenni*, widely regarded as characteristically Welsh.

Developments in the later 20th century include the setting up of a factory (1967) in Carno, Powys, by Laura Ashley Ltd, a company producing well-known furnishing and dress fabrics sold worldwide. The Welsh-born textile designer Cefyn Burgess (*b* 1961) established a workshop at Penmaenmawr, Caerns, where he produced Jacquard-woven cloths in wool, cotton and linen, including bedcovers and blankets.

BIBLIOGRAPHY
J. G. Jenkins: *The Welsh Woollen Industry* (Cardiff, 1969)
A. Smith: *The Textiles of Wales* (London, 1987)

VIII. Patronage, collecting and dealing.

Without an urban centre in which an art market could develop, patrons before the 18th century often sought portrait commissions in England and occasionally mainland Europe. To what extent they also brought painters to Wales or made use of local artisans is difficult to determine. The outstanding early example of connoisseurship is that of Thomas Walker (*d* 1707) from Newton, Brecons, who by 1689 had acquired approximately 180 Dutch, Italian and English paintings. However, in the early 18th century, the Myddleton family at Chirk Castle, Denbs, patronized Welsh artists, including the sculptor Robert Wynne (*c.* 1655–1731; *see* §IV above) and the blacksmiths Robert Davies (1679–1748) and John Davies (*d* 1755; *see* §VI above), and the Cymmrodorion Society, established in London in 1751, provided the first national focus of patronage. The main beneficiary was Richard Wilson, whose works were bought by its first president, William Vaughan (1707–75) of Cors-y-gedol, and by his successor Sir WATKIN WILLIAMS-WYNN, as well as by several less prominent members; the portrait painter William Parry (*c.* 1742–91; *see* §III above) also benefited. As well as collecting contemporary paintings, Vaughan, Williams-Wynn and other members of the gentry kept in their houses most of the manuscript record of the Welsh-language poetry and prose tradition and generally encouraged its study by antiquaries.

Several gentry patrons, including Sir Erasmus Philipps (*d* 1743) from Picton Castle, bought works on their Grand Tour, but Sir Watkin Williams-Wynn was by far the most important 18th-century Welsh patron in the international market. When in Italy in 1768–9, he bought paintings by Old Masters, as well as works by Joseph Vernet, and commissioned new paintings from Pompeo Batoni (e.g. portrait of *Watkin Williams-Wynn, Thomas Apperley and Captain Edward Hamilton*, 1768–71/2; Cardiff, N. Mus.) and Anton Raphael Mengs. On his return to London he commissioned sculpture from Joseph Nollekens (*see* §IV above), several paintings from Reynolds (e.g. *A Meeting of the Society of the Dilettanti*, 1777–9; London, Soc. Dilettanti), bought Poussin's masterpiece *Landscape with a Snake* (1648; London, N.G.) and had Robert Adam (i) design his town house (1772–6) at 20 St James's Square,

London. However, Williams-Wynn's collection at Wynnstay, Denbs, was devastated by fire in 1858, as was the extensive collection of Thomas Johnes (1748–1816) at Hafod Uchtryd, Cards, in 1807. Johnes lost not only paintings by Old Masters and contemporary artists but also important medieval Welsh and French manuscripts. THOMAS MANSEL TALBOT, who from 1769 made several Grand Tours of Europe, was a collector, primarily of antique gems and antique and contemporary sculpture.

In the second half of the 18th century the urban middle class began to commission portraits from resident and travelling artisans. It was from this first-generation middle class that many of the intelligentsia, in particular religious leaders and literati, were drawn, and they became aware of the deficiency of national patronage. Methodist leaders and the Anglican intellectuals who had led the revival of the Eisteddfod movement provided small-scale but important commissions for Hugh Hughes (1790–1863; see §III above) and others, inspired at least in part by patriotism. The Eisteddfod itself provided an important, if rather sporadic, focus for public patronage throughout the 19th century. However, the ambitions of its art-conscious leaders were hamstrung by the absence of public buildings as receptacles for their patronage in a nation with no indigenous seat of government. Not until the later 19th century, when there was expansion in local government and developments in education (in particular the opening of the University of Wales in 1893 and various theological colleges (e.g. the Bala Theological College, founded 1837)), did public and institutional patronage become a significant factor.

The earliest entrepreneurs of visual culture were publishers of popular prints, engravings of landscapes and portraits of national figures. The most notable was Hugh Humphreys (1817–96) from Caernarfon, who sold original paintings, as well as prints and books, in his shop on Castle Square, which was probably the first commercial gallery in Wales. Humphreys's generally down-market approach reflected the change in the nature of the tourist market in the later 19th century as the country was opened up by the railways. In the 20th century patronage of the fine arts was dominated by the sisters Gwendoline Davies (1882–1951) and Margaret Davies (1884–1963) from Llandinam, Powys. Advised by Hugh Blaker (1873–1936), Curator of the Holburne of Menstrie Museum, Bath, they used their family fortune to acquire, between 1908 and the mid-1920s, approximately 200 works, consisting mainly of Old Master paintings and 19th-century French paintings and sculptures. In the 1930s they redirected their fortune into projects for the unemployed but later added to the collection before bequeathing it to the nation. Works by Monet, Manet, Renoir, Cézanne, van Gogh, Bonnard and others now form the core of the international collection in the National Museum of Wales, Cardiff (Caerdydd). They also established and financed a private press at Gregynog, Powys, the family house near Newtown (Y Drenewydd), producing books illustrated by important artists and craftsmen, among them DAVID JONES. In 1937 the Contemporary Art Society for Wales was founded with a committee led by Lord Howard de Walden (b 1912), and it has continued, on a limited scale, to buy the work of living artists. However, the Arts Council of Wales, initially a regional committee of the Arts Council of Great Britain, was by far the most important institution in the second half of the 20th century to purchase and facilitate the commissioning of contemporary art.

BIBLIOGRAPHY
B. Ford: 'Sir Watkin Williams Wynn: A Welsh Maecenas', *Apollo*, xcix (1974), pp. 435–9
E. White: *The Ladies of Gregynog* (Cardiff, 1985)

IX. Museums.

Proposals to establish a Welsh national portrait gallery in London in 1830 were never realized, and it was the Eisteddfod movement that pioneered the exhibition of collections of art, crafts and industrial products. These exhibitions, the first of which was held at the Abergavenny Eisteddfodau in Monmouthshire in the 1830s, reached their peak in 1876 at Wrexham (Wrecsam), where William Cornwallis West (1835–1917), Squire of Ruthin Castle, created what was, in effect, the first national gallery, in a purpose-made building that remained open for a year.

The National Museum of Wales received its charter in 1907. Its collections, which absorbed those of the Cardiff Museum, cover a wide range, but in the absence of a separate national gallery of art, the Art and Archaeology departments assumed a particular importance. The museum's new building by SMITH & BREWER was opened in 1927 and was substantially enlarged by John Phillips of the Alex Gordon Partnership in 1993. In the opening ceremony programme, its Council stated that 'the new Museum shall be primarily and essentially national in character. . . . Nothing should be admitted . . . which does not illustrate or elucidate Wales in some aspect or other.' In 1931 a separate department of Folk Studies was created under the direction of Iorwerth C. Peate (1901–82) with the ultimate intention of establishing an open-air museum modelled after those in Scandinavia. From 1946 one was developed at St Fagans Castle. Known as the Welsh Folk Museum, it acquired a distinguished international reputation for scholarship and display. The National Library of Wales at Aberystwyth (founded 1907) holds the second national collection of visual culture, specializing in portrait painting and topographical art, and also has the largest photographic archive in Wales.

The first regional museum was the Royal Institution of South Wales, opened in 1841 in Swansea (Abertawe). It displayed the mixed collections of art, crafts and natural history artefacts conventional for the time. The Museum and Art Gallery in Newport (Casnewydd) was opened in 1888, but the most important regional collection in Wales is in the Glynn Vivian Art Gallery and Museum in Swansea, which opened in 1911. The Mostyn Art Gallery, the first specialist art gallery in the north, was built in 1902 in Llandudno under the patronage of Augusta Mostyn. Of other regional museums and galleries, there are notable specialized collections of ceramics at the Arts Centre of the University of Wales, Aberystwyth, and of the work of the wildlife artist C. F. Tunnicliffe (1901–79) at Oriel Môn, Llangefni, Anglesey (Ynys Môn).

BIBLIOGRAPHY
P. Lord: *The Aesthetics of Relevance* (Llandysul, 1992)

X. Art education.

Until the mid-19th century, fine artists who wanted to train beyond an artisan workshop level had to study outside Wales, though they sometimes did so under the auspices of patriotic gentry. The 18th-century gentry themselves employed personal tutors, but it was not until the early 19th century that teachers of drawing and painting began to advertise in Welsh towns. The first art schools on the South Kensington model (*see* ENGLAND, §XV, 2) were established at Caernarfon and Swansea (Abertawe) in 1853 and at Cardiff (Caerdydd) in 1865. Against this background, patriotic and progressive intellectuals became much concerned with what they considered to be the deficient understanding of visual art in Wales. In response, the first substantial attempts at writing art history and criticism for the Welsh-speaking public were made from 1848 by the painter Evan Williams (1816–78). As the national revival reached its peak at the beginning of the 20th century, there was an increase in critical writing, notably by Thomas Matthews (1874–1916) from Llandybie. *Welsh Painters, Engravers and Sculptors*, the first dictionary of Welsh art, was compiled by T. Mardy Rees (1861–1953) and was published in Caernarfon in 1912.

Artists of national stature began to emerge through the state system, especially in Cardiff, at the beginning of the 20th century, but after World War I art education was dominated by the remarkable achievement of William Grant Murray (1877–1950), who developed the Swansea School of Art into an institution with an international reputation and who trained a generation of prominent Welsh painters. Dewi Prys Thomas (1916–85), the distinguished first Principal of the Welsh School of Architecture, Cardiff, had a concern for indigenous Welsh culture that went against the prevailing trend in art colleges in the 1960s and 1970s.

BIBLIOGRAPHY

T. Matthews: *Perthynas y Cain a'r Ysgol* [The relationship between art and schools] (Cardiff, 1916)

PETER LORD

Waley, Sir **Arthur (David)** (*b* Tunbridge Wells, 19 Aug 1889; *d* London, 27 June 1966). English museum curator and translator. He was the second of three sons of David Schloss, an economist and Fabian socialist, and his wife Rachel, daughter of Jacob Waley, whose name the family used from 1914. After school at Rugby (1903–6), he spent a year in France before going to Cambridge University (1907). In 1910 he abandoned Cambridge with eye problems and travelled in Europe. In 1913 he began work at the British Museum, London, in what was the new Sub-department of Oriental Prints and Drawings under Laurence Binyon. Waley had the task of indexing the works of Chinese and Japanese painters in the museum's collection, and it was at this point that he started to teach himself Chinese and Japanese. By 1916 he was having his first translations of Chinese poems privately printed; thereafter his career as a translator flourished. He continued to work at the British Museum until 1929, publishing *An Index of Chinese Artists* in 1922 and *An Introduction to the Study of Chinese Painting* in 1923. He also arranged and described the British Museum's collection of Japanese books with woodcut illustrations and its large collection of Japanese

paintings. In 1931 he published a catalogue of the paintings found by Sir Aurel Stein at the Buddhist cave temples at Dunhuang, Gansu Province, China. By this time, however, translating had become Waley's foremost concern, occupying him for the remainder of his life. Between 1925 and 1933 he published in separate parts what was his most ambitious translation, the *Genji monogatari* ('Tale of Genji'), by the 10th-century Japanese writer Murasaki Shikibu; this was published in one volume in 1935. Despite his studies, he never travelled to East Asia.

WRITINGS

An Index of Chinese Artists Represented in the Sub-department of Oriental Prints and Drawings in the British Museum (London, 1922)
An Introduction to the Study of Chinese Painting (London, 1923)
A Catalogue of Paintings Recovered from Tun-huang by Sir Aurel Stein, KCIE, Preserved in the Sub-department of Oriental Prints and Drawings in the British Museum and in the Museum of Central Asian Antiquities, Delhi (London, 1931)

BIBLIOGRAPHY

DNB
D. Hawkes: Obituary, *Asia Major*, n. s., xii/2 (1966), pp. 143–7
F. A. Johns: *A Bibliography of Arthur Waley* (New Brunswick, NJ, 1968; rev. London and Atlantic Highland, NJ, 1988)
I. Morris, ed.: *Madly Singing in the Mountains: An Appreciation and Anthology of Arthur Waley* (London, 1970)

S. J. VERNOIT

Walford, Andrew (*b* Bournemouth, 4 Dec 1942). South African potter of English birth. He moved to South Africa with his parents in 1947 and trained as a commercial artist at the Durban Art School. After a six-month sculpture course he started a pottery apprenticeship at the Walsh Marais Studio in Durban and continued his training with Sammy Liebermann (1920–84) in Johannesburg. In 1961 he took over the Walsh Marais Studio, but in 1964 he closed it and travelled to Europe, where he met such leading potters as Lucie Rie, Bernard Leach and Michael Cardew. He was invited to work at the Gustavberg factory near Stockholm and later went to Germany, where he started a pottery studio and signed a year's contract to teach at the art academy in Hamburg. In 1967 he returned to South Africa and in 1968 established a studio at N'Shongweni in Natal. In 1969 he visited Japan and befriended Shōji Hamada, who strongly influenced him. Walford produced mainly functional but individual pieces.

BIBLIOGRAPHY

F. G. E. Nilant: *Contemporary Pottery in South Africa* (Cape Town, 1963)
'Andrew Walford, Ceramicist', *Artlook*, 29 (April 1969), p. 27

A. E. DUFFEY

Walgate, C(harles) P(ercival) (*b* Beverley, Yorks, 4 Feb 1886; *d* Fish Hoek, Cape Prov., 26 April 1972). British architect, active in South Africa. In 1907 he won the National Scholarship in Architecture and went to the Architectural School of the Royal College of Art in London. In 1910 he was made a Travelling Scholar and studied in the British School in Rome. He was engaged by Herbert Baker to work on projects in London and Delhi. In 1920 he arrived in South Africa to assist J. M. Solomon (1888–1920) with plans for the new University of Cape Town, Rondebosch. In 1921 Walgate took L. A. Elsworth (1891–1971) into partnership and, in association with W. Hawke and W. N. McKinley, replanned residences (1924) and designed a tutorial building (1926–8), hall and library buildings (both 1930) for the university. His university buildings, the college chapel (1926), Rondebosch, the Zonnekus mansion (1929), Milnerton, and a hostel (1930) in Kloof Street, Cape Town, show Baker's influence in their formal classical idiom. Walgate's experiments with local materials and building traditions produced the Tea House (1924; destr. 1982), Kirstenbosch Gardens, Cape Town, with a thatched roof raised on white columns; a restaurant (1928), on top of Table Mountain, a chalet built of local stone; and the Town Hall (1940), Stellenbosch, with Cape Dutch-style fenestration. Walgate also coordinated the design of the Huguenot Monument (1943), Franschhoek. The Capitol Cinema (1932) and Plaza Cinema (1932; destr. 1970), both Cape Town, in non-vernacular style, were less successful. In 1946 he was appointed sole architect for the new Cape Town railway station. His ambitious design consisted of a huge 24-platform complex sited beneath public gardens, with multi-storey parking, a sunken forecourt and connecting subways. In 1949 most of the project was abandoned, after the change of the government; a high-rise railway office, the Paul Sauer Building, was completed in a mutilated form in 1960. Walgate was active in the School of Architecture, Cape Town, and in the promotion of the Architects' Act. He received the Bronze Medal of the Cape Provincial Institute in 1940.

UNPUBLISHED SOURCES
Cape Town, State Archvs, Accession 1659 [archvs of Cape Provincial Institute of Architects, 1937–68]
Cape Town, U. Cape Town Libs, B.C. 318 Walgate

BIBLIOGRAPHY
'C. P. Walgate', *S. Afr. Architect*, ii/8 (1940), pp. 296–7

ROMAN SOLTYNSKI

Waliszewski, Zygmunt (*b* St Petersburg, 1 Dec 1897; *d* Kraków, 5 Oct 1936). Polish painter of Russian birth. He painted and exhibited his work from a very early age. His drawings from this period show his extreme dexterity and sense of humour and parody, as in *Ingres Drawing Odalisques* (1915; K. M. Zdaniewicz priv. col.). After he settled in Poland he trained at the Academy of Fine Arts in Kraków (1921–4) under Wojciech Weiss and Józef Pankiewicz. He continued his education in Paris as one of the KAPISTS, where he was able to study the Old Masters. Freely interpreting their art he created a number of works that depicted well-known literary and mythological subjects. Scenes like feasts, shown theatrically, with Italian Renaissance stylization of costumes and architecture, were executed in quick and sketchy oil technique. Waliszewski's very individual style derived from Post-Impressionism. He applied separate touches of pure colour and made very limited use of chiaroscuro. He often modelled forms with strong contours and thick impastos, as in *Balzac* (1931; Warsaw, N. Mus.). One of his last works was *The Concert* (1935–6), a ceiling painting at the Wawel Castle in Kraków.

BIBLIOGRAPHY
J. Wolff: *Zygmunt Waliszewski* (Warsaw, 1969)
W. Waliszewska: *O Zygmuncie Waliszewskim: Wspomnienia i listy* [On Zygmunt Waliszewski: memoirs and letters] (Kraków, 1972)

ANNA BENTKOWSKA

Walker, Anthony (*b* Thirsk, Yorks, 6 March 1726; *d* London, 9 May 1765). English printmaker and draughtsman. He was apprenticed *c.* 1741 to the engraver and

printseller John Tinney (*d* 1761) and must have worked on the many topographical plates that Tinney issued. In 1747 he designed and engraved a satire entitled *The Beaux Disaster*, but much of his earlier signed work was for the book trade, taken from his own drawings. His skill as an etcher gave an unusual degree of freedom to his work. Five Shakespearian subjects designed and engraved by Walker and sold by Tinney appeared on 15 January 1754; these show Walker's great ability in handling figures, also seen in his charming groups for drawing books, such as *The Complete Drawing Book* (2nd ed.; London, 1757). In his last five years Walker was in demand as an engraver of large singly issued prints; he engraved five for John Boydell, which were published in 1763–5 and exhibited in 1763–5 at the Society of Artists. His brother William Walker (1729–93) also worked for Boydell and later collaborated as engraver and publisher with his own son John Walker (*fl c.* 1787–1802).

BIBLIOGRAPHY
DNB; Thieme–Becker
A. Graves: *The Society of Artists of Great Britain, (1760–1791); The Free Society of Artists (1761–1783)* (London, 1907), p. 271
H. Hammelmann and T. S. R. Boase: *Book Illustrators in Eighteenth-century England* (London, 1975), pp. 96–101

DAVID ALEXANDER

Walker, C(harles) Howard (*b* Boston, MA, 9 Jan 1857; *d* Boston, MA, 17 April 1936). American architect, teacher and writer. He trained (1874–9) in the office of the Boston firm Sturgis & Brigham before moving to New York City, where he organized a sketch club where he and other young men could draw in congenial surroundings. The membership included Thomas Hastings (1860–1929; later a partner in Carrère & Hastings) and Cass Gilbert, both of whom worked in the office of McKim, Mead & White. Influenced by such European-trained architects as Charles F. McKim, Walker travelled in Europe and Asia Minor (1882–3) before returning to Boston to practise. In 1883 he began lecturing on the philosophy of fine arts at the Massachusetts Institute of Technology, where he taught for the next 47 years. His buildings were comparatively few, and he was best known as a teacher and writer and also, for a period, as editor of the *Architectural Review*. As a designer, however, he cooperated with the sculptor Daniel Chester French in making bases for public sculpture and built the Charles Rollins House (1897) at 497 Commonwealth Avenue, Boston, and the Carnegie Public Library (1914), Sharon, MA. Walker took an active role in the celebrations following the World's Columbian Exhibition (1893) in Chicago and was architect-in-chief of the Great Exposition (1898) in Omaha, NE. He also designed the layout of the Louisiana Purchase International Exposition (1904) in St Louis, MO. In his last years he devoted himself to automotive design.

WRITINGS
'The Great Exposition at Omaha', *C. Illus.*, lv (1898), pp. 518–21
'Louisiana Purchase Exposition at St Louis, Missouri', *Archit. Rev.* [Boston], xi (1904), pp. 197–220
An Architectural Monograph on Some Old Houses on the Southern Coast of Maine (St Paul, MN, 1918)
The Theory of Mouldings (Cleveland, 1926)

BIBLIOGRAPHY

Macmillan Enc. Architects
G. Sheldon: *American Country Seats* (New York, 1886)
W. Emerson: Obituary, *Amer. Architect*, cxlviii (1936), p. 109

MOSETTE GLASER BRODERICK

Walker, Sir (Byron) Edmund (*b* nr Caledonia, Ont., 14 Oct 1848; *d* Toronto, 27 March 1924). Canadian banker, collector and museum founder. He joined the Canadian Bank of Commerce in 1868 and became its president in 1907. He pursued a variety of interests, including palaeontology, botany, music, literature and art. He travelled extensively in North and South America, Europe, China and Japan, looking at art and architecture and visiting museums, private collections and artists' studios. He built a modest collection, which included two views by Francesco Guardi of St Mark's, Venice (Ottawa, N.G.), and a number of Hague and Barbizon school paintings. While in New York he began to collect intaglio prints, including impressions by Rembrandt, Dürer and Whistler (Toronto, A.G. Ont.). He also assembled a superb collection of 5000 Japanese *ukiyoe* prints, which were given to the Royal Ontario Museum, Toronto.

The unrivalled leader of the museum movement in Canada, Walker founded the Art Gallery of Ontario in 1900 and the Royal Ontario Museum (both in Toronto) in 1912. As Chairman of the Advisory Arts Council of the National Gallery of Canada, Ottawa, he helped build the collection and establish the Prints and Drawings Department. Walker founded many other organizations to further the cause of the arts, education and the study of history.

UNPUBLISHED SOURCES

Walker Papers (Correspondence; dealers' invoices; journal, 1899–1924, 3 vols), Toronto, U. Toronto, Thomas Fisher Rare Book Lib.

BIBLIOGRAPHY

B. E. Walker: *Jubilee of Sir Edmund Walker* (Toronto, 1918)
N. McTavish: 'Sir Edmund Walker's Collection of Art', *Can. Mag.*, lii (1919), pp. 833–41
G. P. T. Glazebrook: *Sir Edmund Walker* (Oxford, 1933)
Sir Edmund Walker: Print Collector (exh. cat. by K. A. Jordan, Toronto, A.G. Ont., 1974)
Images of Eighteenth-century Japan: Ukiyo-e Prints from the Sir Edmund Walker Collection (exh. cat. by D. Waterhouse, Toronto, Royal Ont. Mus., 1975)
K. A. Lochnan: 'The Department of Prints and Drawings at the National Gallery: The First Hundred Years', *Artmagazine*, 48/49 (1980), pp. 24–6
——: 'The Walker Papers: Reminiscences of John Lavery and William Holman Hunt', *RACAR*, ix/1–2 (1982), pp. 133–7

KATHARINE A. LOCHNAN

Walker, Dame Ethel (*b* Edinburgh, 9 June 1861; *d* London, 2 March 1951). English painter and sculptor. Inspired to become an artist after seeing a collection of oriental art in Edinburgh, she studied in London at the Putney Art School for two years (*c*. 1883) and at the Westminster School of Art and the Slade School of Fine Art (1892–4) under Frederick Brown. On a visit to Spain in 1884 she was greatly impressed by Velázquez's blend of realism and myth, and in Paris she identified particularly with Manet and with the Impressionists. In 1898 she settled in Cheyne Walk, Chelsea, London, and established there a studio that she maintained for the rest of her life. She also painted regularly at Robin Hood's Bay, N. Yorks. The sombre tones of her early flower compositions and figures in interiors gave way to brighter, richer interpretations derived from Impressionism. In 1900 she was elected the first woman member of the New English Art Club. Her works displayed a vibrancy of colour and spontaneity of composition without any apparent interest in the scientific aspects of Impressionist colour theory. Particularly successful are her precise and uncluttered drawings and her portraits of women, such as *Vanessa* (1937; London, Tate), which often had a dominant key of brilliant colour. Much the same fullness of spirit pervades her flower-pieces, such as *Flowers in a Jug* (1935–6; London, Tate). A series of large, decorative figure paintings combined Classical themes with spiritual concerns; typical of these are the *Zone of Hate* (1914–15) and the *Zone of Love* (1930–32; both London, Tate). She also produced sculptures of these themes, which were decorative in approach and inspired by her vision of a golden age. She was elected ARA in 1940 and appointed DBE in 1943.

DNB

BIBLIOGRAPHY

Ethel Walker, Frances Hodgkins, Gwen John: A Memorial Exhibition (exh. cat., foreword by J. Rothenstein and Philip James; London, Tate, 1952)
Distinguished British Paintings, 1875–1950: An Accent on Ethel Walker (exh. cat., London, Roland, Browse & Delbanco, 1974)
Dame Ethel Walker (exh. cat., London, Blond F.A., 1979)

EMMANUEL COOPER

Walker, Fred(erick) (*b* London, 26 May 1840; *d* St Fillans, Perthshire, 4 June 1875). English painter and illustrator. He acquired his training in drawing and painting through study in the British Museum (where he copied heavily from the Antique), a short period spent in an architect's office, life classes at Leigh's school, a studentship at the Royal Academy and three years' employment as a draughtsman on wood with the commercial engraver Josiah Wood Whymper (1813–1903).

Walker was one of an exceptional band of young illustrators working during the 1860s. His drawings, reproduced as wood-engravings by artists such as Joseph Swain and the Dalziel brothers, appeared in all the influential magazines of the time, notably *Cornhill*, *Good Words*, *Once a Week* and *Punch*. Swain was the source of Walker's early and important commission for the re-drawing of Thackeray's own illustrations to *The Adventures of Philip* for the *Cornhill* (1862). Mere copying was uncongenial to Walker, but after a short time he was allowed to use his own ideas in illustrating Thackeray's story, and these brought him critical success.

Walker's career as an illustrator, which came to an end about 1865–6, was too brief for his work to show much stylistic development. Influenced initially by John Gilbert, he was never a naturally fluid draughtsman, and, although he soon became adept at composing groups of figures, he never achieved any great dramatic force. In 1871 Walker designed his famous poster for the stage adaptation of Wilkie Collins's *The Woman in White*. His dramatic image of Anne Catherick, swathed in a cloak and seen full length from behind, is generally considered the first successful modern pictorial poster and anticipates many similar designs of the 1890s. Walker himself believed that the designing of posters could become 'a most important branch of art'.

Fred Walker: *The Vagrants*, oil on canvas, 832×1264 mm, 1868 (London, Tate Gallery)

As a painter in watercolours and oils Walker began to enjoy success from about 1863 onwards. About 1862 he painted the much acclaimed watercolour *Philip in Church* (exh. OWCS, 1864; London, Tate), originally a wood-engraved illustration of Thackeray's novel. Walker employed a meticulous and heavily worked gouache technique that owed much to William Henry Hunt and Myles Birket Forster. Details of flowers and foliage were carefully stippled into thick layers of chinese white, as in *Stobhall Gardens, Perthshire* (1869; Paris, priv. col.), and were often combined with atmospherically appropriate figures, for instance the young girl in *Spring* (1864; London, V&A). Walker also occasionally supplied the figures for the paintings of his close friend and fellow illustrator, J. W. North (1842–1924).

Walker's study of the Antique as a student led him to rely on the formal conventions of antique sculpture in his oil paintings. The mower in the *Harbour of Refuge* (1872; London, Tate) is particularly indebted to Phidias, and John Ruskin described such consciously posed figures as 'galvanised-Elgin'. Other important oil paintings include *The Bathers* (exh. RA 1867; Port Sunlight, Lady Lever A.G.), which reveals the influence of Michelangelo and Puvis de Chavannes, *The Vagrants* (1868; London, Tate; see fig.) and the *Old Gate* (exh. RA 1869; London, Tate). *The Bathers* was bought by the dealer William Agnew, who was an influential supporter, and sold to William Graham, an enthusiastic patron of Walker.

To Victorian eyes Walker seemed a sincere and unsentimental observer of rustic life, and his work was often compared favourably with that of Jean-François Millet.

His paintings were considered sensitive portrayals of rural landscape and life. Walker's agreeable character and his early death from tuberculosis sustained his posthumous reputation, and he was an important influence on young British painters working in the 1870s and 1880s. But the idealized and sentimental quality of much of his work engendered subsequent critical neglect. His studio sale was held at Christie's on 17 July 1875. The most complete collection of his graphic work is in the British Museum, London, which also holds E. E. Leggatt's complete record of his oeuvre.

BIBLIOGRAPHY

DNB

C. Phillips: *Frederick Walker*, Port. Monographs A. Subjects, vi (1894)

J. G. Marks: *Life & Letters of Frederick Walker ARA* (London, 1896)

C. Black: *Frederick Walker* (London, 1902)

LEO JOHN DE FREITAS

Walker, Horatio (*b* Listowel, Ont., 12 May 1858; *d* Sainte-Pétronille, Que., 27 Sept 1938). Canadian painter and photographer. As a boy he displayed an aptitude for drawing animals and portraits. From 1873 to 1876 he was an apprentice photographer at the Notman–Fraser Studio, Toronto, and also studied drawing and painting with Robert F. Gagen (1848–1926). In 1876 he settled in Rochester, NY, working initially as a photographer. In 1877 he made a sketching tour in Quebec, visiting the Ile d'Orléans, on the St Lawrence River. From May to November 1880 he walked from Montreal to Quebec, marking the beginning of his close rapport with rural French Canadians. He also did some etching during this period, a technique he had learnt from F. Seymour Haden.

After visiting Europe in 1881, Walker's style was influenced by Jean-François Millet; he was widely acclaimed as 'the American Millet' during his lifetime. Other influences included Anton Mauve, Jacob and Willem Maris and Albert Pinkham Ryder, with whom he was acquainted.

Following the success of *Turkeys in a Cornfield* (exh. New York, N. Acad. Des., 1883; untraced), Walker moved to New York in 1885. About three years later he acquired a house at Sainte-Pétronille, on the Ile d'Orleans, moving seasonally between Canada and the USA. Newman E. Montross, his dealer for 40 years from 1883, contributed, by judicious use of photographic reproductions, to the growth of a lucrative market for Walker's paintings. By 1900 the dollar value of Walker's work was unsurpassed by that of any living North American painter. His *Oxen at the Trough* (1899) was acquired by the National Gallery of Canada, Ottawa, in 1909 for £10,000.

Walker lived in London from 1901 to 1905, winning critical acclaim at the 1901 annual exhibition of the Royal Institute of Painters in Water-Colours. Henceforth, he worked mainly in oils. Returning to Canada *c.* 1905, Walker became involved with a group of young painters in Toronto, who had formed the Canadian Art Club; in 1915 he replaced his friend Homer Watson as its President. During these years, the human figure assumed a greater role in his painting. He executed biblical and mythological themes, which included farm animals, such as the *Enchanted Sty—Circe and the Friends of Ulysses* (1908; Ottawa, N.G.).

Following World War I, Walker settled into semi-retirement. The value of his work began to decline in 1923, following the retirement of Montross. The most successful of Walker's biblical paintings, *The Prodigal Son* (1923; Quebec, Mus. Québec), reflects his gloominess at this time. He was involved in the foundation of the Quebec and Montreal Ecoles des Beaux-Arts (1921) and the Musée du Québec (1933), which owns an extensive collection of his work. At the insistence of his new dealer, Frederic Newlin Price, he returned to watercolour; however, his market dried up totally after 1933.

Walker's training as a photographer influenced his painting; his use of colour always remained essentially tonal, evocative of the grey scale. Frequent use of dramatic or selective lighting lends strength to his most successful works, notably *Ploughing—the First Gleam at Dawn* (1900; Quebec, Mus. Québec), in which the sun's rays highlight the muscular exertions of a team of oxen, straining to draw the ploughshare uphill through the frosty soil. The sky, as in many other works (e.g. *Ave Maria*, 1906; Hamilton, Ont., A.G.), recalls J. M. W. Turner, who, with Thomas Gainsborough and John Constable, had inspired Walker from the outset of his career. Walker's working method in oil, as in watercolour, was meticulous. At times, however, he displayed vigorous brushwork, especially in smaller formats (e.g. *The Wood-cutter*, 1900; Toledo, OH, Mus. A.) and oil sketches (e.g. *First Snow*; Ottawa, N.G.).

Walker's contribution to the birth of a nationalist tendency in Canadian painting has been largely overlooked, as younger artists (e.g. the Group of Seven) discredited his 'Dutch' affiliation as an inappropriate style in which to express Canadian content. Walker's approach to painting was the antithesis of modernism, but he influenced such younger artists as André Biéler (*b* 1896) and Clarence Gagnon.

BIBLIOGRAPHY

F. N. Price: *Horatio Walker* (Montreal, 1928)
Catalogue of a Retrospective Exhibition of the Work of Horatio Walker (exh. cat., Toronto, A.G. Ont., 1929)
Première exposition annuelle d'artistes canadiens: Rétrospective des oeuvres de Horatio Walker (exh. cat., Montréal, Ecole B.-A., 1929)
American Art in the Barbizon Mood (exh. cat. by P. Bermingham, Washington, DC, N. Col. F.A., 1975)
Horatio Walker, 1858–1938 (exh. cat. by D. Farr, Kingston, Ont., Queen's U., Agnes Etherington A. Cent., 1977)
Horatio Walker (exh. cat. by D. Karel, Quebec, Mus. Québec, 1986)

DAVID KAREL

Walker, John (*b* Birmingham, 12 Nov 1939). English painter and printmaker. He studied at Birmingham College of Art from 1955 to 1960 and first came to public attention at the John Moores exhibition in Liverpool in 1965, where he was awarded third prize. Typical of his large-scale paintings of that period is *Study* (acrylic and canvas collage on canvas, 2.2×3.0 m, 1965; London, Tate), in which folded and dramatically lit shapes are presented against a sprayed fencelike background. He continued looking to the American models of Abstract Expressionism and Post-painterly Abstraction in panoramic canvases such as *Barrier 3* (acrylic on canvas, 1.8×2.7 m, 1969; British Council), although he combined the insistent flatness of these sources with shapes rendered in the illusion of three dimensions.

In Walker's next series, such as *Juggernaut II* (acrylic and French chalk on canvas, 3.0×2.4 m, 1973–4; Liverpool, Walker A.G.), he reinterpreted Cubist collage on a massive scale, layering shapes of cut-out canvas painted to look like the rusting metal of the industrial vehicles alluded to in the title. As early as his *Numinous* series (1977–8) of variations on a balcony motif borrowed from Edouard Manet, Francisco de Goya and Henri Matisse, Walker increasingly referred to earlier painted images. *Red Strand Infanta II* (oil on canvas, 1981; British Council) was one of a group of canvases that made direct allusion to Velázquez and that introduced into his work illusions of deep space; from this point on, he favoured oil painting rather than acrylic.

Following a residency in Australia from 1979 to 1980, Walker was appointed Dean of Melbourne's Victoria College of the Arts in 1982. In works such as *Oceania My Dilemma III* (triptych, 1984; Los Angeles, CA, Broida Trust) he began to incorporate elements from Oceanic art such as carved masks, skull racks, painted barks and wall paintings in the bush, while continuing to work in series in an essentially modernist idiom that had much in common with international developments in Neo-Expressionist and 'New Image' painting. The changes in his painting are likewise reflected in his production as a printmaker, from the larger-scale lithographs such as the *Blackboard Print* series (1.0×0.7 m, 1973; British Council) to his later preference for the gestural surfaces and physicality of etching, for example *Oceania II* (0.4×0.4 m, 1984; see 1985 exh. cat., p. 43).

BIBLIOGRAPHY

A. Lewis: 'John Walker', *Artscribe*, 31 (1981), pp. 24–36
John Walker: Paintings from the Alba and Oceania Series, 1979–84 (exh. cat., London, Hayward Gal., 1985)

John Walker: Prints, 1976–84 (exh. cat. by M. Holloway, London, Tate, 1985)

ADRIAN LEWIS

Walker, Ralph (Thomas) (*b* 1889; *d* 1973). American architect. He was apprenticed for three years before attending Massachusetts Institute of Technology, Cambridge, MA (1909–11). In 1916 he was the winner of the Rotch Traveling Scholarship. He joined the office of McKenzie, Voorhees & Gmelin, New York, in 1919, becoming a partner in 1926 when the firm became Voorhees, Gmelin & Walker. Walker's works included the Barclay-Vesey Telephone Building (1923–6), the Western Union Building (1928–9) and the Irving Trust Building (1928–31), all skyscrapers in New York in the setback Modernist style later referred to as Art Deco. After 1939 the firm became Voorhees, Walker, Foley & Smith and produced many large projects including the Bell Telephone Laboratories (1937–49) at Murray Hill, NJ, several buildings for the World's Fair of 1939 in New York and office, laboratory and research centres for American companies. Walker was prominent in professional circles, received various honours and was president of the American Institute of Architects from 1949 to 1951. After that his reputation declined; while his Art Deco work was acclaimed, his later work was criticized for its somewhat timid Modernism.

WRITINGS

The Fly in the Amber: Comments on the Making of Architecture (New York, 1957)
Ralph Walker: Architect (New York, 1957)

BIBLIOGRAPHY

J. N. Bosserman, ed.: *Ralph Walker Bibliography* (Charlottesville, VA, 1960)

JOHN F. PILE

Walker, Robert (*b* ?1595–1610; *d* ?1659). English painter. He was the favourite painter of the Parliamentarian leaders during the Commonwealth and Protectorate (1649–58) and worked chiefly as an image-maker for Oliver Cromwell and his immediate circle. His austere and direct portraits of *John Lambert* (1619–84), *Thomas Fairfax* (1612–71) and *Henry Ireton* (1611–51) are known through engravings and copies after the originals. Copies of Walker's portraits of *Cromwell* (London, N.P.G.; and *c.* 1649, Leeds, C.A.G.) were mass-produced, and the images were also popularized through the engravings of William Faithorne. Walker had little to offer the market for fashionable portraiture, which was dominated by Lely.

There is no evidence to support the suggestion that Walker was a pupil of Anthony van Dyck, yet he relied heavily on van Dyck's portrait formulas, often using compositions, poses and colour schemes taken directly from his portraits. Walker lacked the imagination and technical ability to develop van Dyck's achievements, and his works failed to match the strong characterization and rich painterly effects found in the portraits of his Royalist counterpart, William Dobson.

Walker borrowed freely from Italian painting: his portrait of *Colonel John Hutchinson and his Son* (Milton Park, Cambs)—Hutchinson bought several works in the sale of the collection of Charles I—is a pale reflection of Titian's *Marchese Del Vasto Addressing his Troops* (Madrid, Prado).

It appears that Walker's work as a copyist of Italian masters was highly profitable. Richard Symonds recorded in his *Notebook* that Walker was paid £50 for a copy of a Titian, and the diarist John Evelyn wrote that he saw an 'excellent' copy of a Titian *Venus* in the artist's studio on 6 July 1650.

Walker's most striking portraits are those that are more personal. His *Self-portrait* (*c.* 1640–55; Oxford, Ashmolean) is an amusing and original parody of van Dyck's *Self-portrait with a Sunflower* (Duke of Westminster priv. col.). Walker depicts himself in the same pose, though he points not to a sunflower (a symbol of royal patronage) but to a sculpture of Mercury, patron of the arts. His most unusual work is the portrait of *John Evelyn* (on loan to London, N.P.G.), who sat for Walker on 1 July 1648. This intriguing piece, possibly a representation of Melancholy, shows the sitter languidly posing with a skull, a *memento mori*, and may be loosely based on a 16th-century Italian painting of the Penitent Magdalene.

BIBLIOGRAPHY

'The Note-books of George Vertue', *Walpole Soc.*, xx (Oxford, 1932), p. 142
H. Walpole: *Anecdotes of Painting in England* (1762–71), ed. R. N. Wornum (1849), pp. 421–3
C. H. Collins Baker: *Lely and the Stuart Portrait Painters*, i (London, 1912), pp. 106–10
E. Waterhouse: *Painting in Britain, 1530–1790*, Pelican Hist. A. (Harmondsworth, 1953, 4/1978), pp. 86–8
M. K. Talley: *Portrait Painting in England: Studies in the Technical Literature before 1700* (London, 1981), p. 97

JOHN SHEERAN

Walker, Roger (Nevill) (*b* Hamilton, 21 Dec 1942). New Zealand architect. He studied in Auckland where he received a degree in architecture in 1964. He worked for Michael Fowler in Wellington before opening his own practice in 1970. His instantly recognizable architecture can be described as pluralistic fantasy. He used an array of High Victorian elements: steeply pitched turrets and pyramidal roof clusters, finials, criss-cross bracing, spatial intimacy and extrusions, colour and human scale, which is juxtaposed against modernist circles, domed lightscoops, drooping lamp standards, port-hole windows, in a three-dimensional intensity. Among his best works are the Wellington Club (1969–72), the Britten House (1972–4), the Whakatane Airport (1973–4), Rainbow Springs Tourist Buildings (1976–81), Rotorua, the Hudson House (1982–3), Pukerua Bay, north of Wellington, the Tourist Hotel (1985–7), Queenstown, Centre City (1989–90), New Plymouth, the Walker House (1990–91), Thorndon, Chesterman Group Offices (1992–3), Hamilton, and the Street Farm Building (1993–4), Naike, near Huntly.

BIBLIOGRAPHY

A. Best: 'The Architecture of Ebullience', *Architects' J.*; clxviii/45 (1978), pp. 881–91
R. Walden: 'New Zealand Audacity: The Work of Roger Walker', *Archit. Rev.* [London], clxix/1008 (1981), pp. 91–7
——: 'The Romantic Rebellion of New Zealand's Roger Walker', *Transition [Austral.]*, ii/3–4 (1981), pp. 48–53
T. Nakamura: 'Works of Roger Walker', *A & U*, 151 (1983), pp. 31–7
G. Melling: *Positively Architecture: New Zealand's Roger Walker* (Dunedin, 1985)
R. Walden: 'Towards a New Zealand Identity—The Last Thirty Years', *NZ Architect*, 1 (1985), pp. 13–20

RUSSELL WALDEN

Walker, William Aiken (*b* Charleston, SC, 23 March 1838; *d* Charleston, 3 Jan 1921). American painter. Together with Richard Clague (1821–73) and Joseph Rusling Meeker (1827–89), Walker is considered to be one of the leading painters of the American South in the late 19th century. Brought up in Baltimore and Charleston, he quickly showed a talent for painting and was given his first one-man exhibition at the age of 20. In 1861 he enlisted in the Confederate army, was wounded and returned to Charleston, working as a topographical artist mapping the defence works. Walker remained in Charleston until 1868, when he returned to Baltimore. After a trip to Cuba in 1869 and some European travel in 1870 he worked in the South, primarily in New Orleans, but making an annual circuit of the tourist areas of the Carolinas and Florida. His paintings are of landscapes and still-lifes, and his most typical scenes depict the unchanging ways of the 'old South', often showing blacks working at domestic chores or out in the cotton fields as in *Cotton Plantation in the Mississippi* (1881; Mobile, AL, J. Altmayer priv. col.). His work is usually small-scale with carefully delineated forms statically arrayed across the picture plane under bright, even daylight.

BIBLIOGRAPHY

A. P. Travaioli and R. B. Toledano: *William Aiken Walker: Southern Genre Painter* (Baton Rouge, LA, 1972)
Painting in the South, 1564–1980 (exh. cat., Richmond, VA Mus. F.A., 1983), pp. 96–7, 252
Art and Artists of the South: The Robert P. Coggins Collection (exh. cat. by B. W. Chambers, Nashville, TN Botan. Gdns & F.A. Cent., 1984), pp. 44, 46–7

BRUCE W. CHAMBERS

Walkowitz, Abraham (*b* Tyumen, Russia, 28 March 1878; *d* Brooklyn, NY, 1965). American painter and etcher of Russian birth. In 1889 he emigrated with his family to New York, settling on the Lower East Side, which he took as the subject of his early work. While still at school he attended art classes in New York at the Cooper Union, the Educational Alliance and the National Academy of Design (1898–1900), developing a precise rendering of anatomical detail and systematic method of shading. His figurative work was first exhibited at the Educational Alliance in New York, where he taught from 1900 to 1906.

In 1906 Walkowitz moved to Paris, where he remained until 1907 and where he came under the influence of Matisse and Picasso, whom he met, and other avant-garde artists. He was particularly affected by the American dancer and choreographer Isadora Duncan, whom he met in 1906 and whose style of free movement transformed his approach to the figure. He drew her obsessively in later years, seeking to capture in a few strokes the essential disposition of her pure movements and gestures. The impact of Fauvism and particularly of Matisse's use of colour remained visible in the paintings produced by Walkowitz after his return to New York. He became part of the avant-garde group of artists associated with Alfred Stieglitz's gallery in New York, 291, and in 1913 exhibited ten works at the historic ARMORY SHOW in New York. He moved closer to abstraction after a second trip to Europe in 1914, but he was not one of its most radical exponents; he found modernism particularly appropriate in capturing the dynamism of New York, in paintings such as *Metropolis No. 2* (1923; Washington, DC, Hirshhorn), although he continued to employ such elements in figure compositions as late as the mid-1930s, when failing eyesight made it difficult for him to work. By the mid-1940s he stopped painting completely.

BIBLIOGRAPHY

Abraham Walkowitz, 1878–1965 (exh. cat. by M. Sewin, Salt Lake City, U. UT, Mus. F.A., 1975)
Abraham Walkowitz: Figuration, 1895–1945 (exh. cat. by K. Smith, Long Beach, CA, Mus. A., 1982)

SUSAN T. GOODMAN

Wall, Willem Hendrik van der (*b* Utrecht, 15 Oct 1716; *d* Utrecht, 1790). Dutch sculptor. He is said to have been a pupil of Jacob Cressant and of Jan Baptiste Xavery. It was not until 1764 that he enrolled as a sculptor in the painters' guild; in 1778 he became joint head of the guild. Although contemporaries spoke of him as a painter, no paintings by him are known. His earliest known sculptural work is a signed and dated terracotta group representing *Charity* (1755; Utrecht, Cent. Mus.). The Rijksmuseum in Amsterdam has a very similar *Charity*, signed and dated 1775, as well as two companion figures, *Faith* and *Hope*, dating from 1775 and 1776 respectively; it also has two small terracotta figures of *Mars* and *Neptune*, the latter signed and dated 1757. A terracotta *Justice* (London, V&A) is signed and dated 1765.

Around 1764–5 van der Wall made two life-size altar figures in wood (untraced) for the clandestine Catholic church of St Catherine in Utrecht. For the same church he made a wooden pulpit (1765) with five panels portraying *Christ* and the *Four Evangelists*; these, together with *bozzetti* for four of the panels, are owned by the Catharijneconvent Museum, Utrecht. Other works by van der Wall include a sandstone garden group of *Three Putti and a Goat* (1772; ex-art market, London); a marble figure of a *Woman with Anchor and Snake* (1778; Utrecht, Cent. Mus.); a marble *Boy with Dog* (1780; sold Berlin, H. Ball and P. Graupe, 24/25 April 1931, lot 291); and a marble *Venus on a Dolphin* (1782; Utrecht, Cent. Mus.).

On the basis of certain parallels with the children of *Charity*, a small putto cast in bronze has been attributed to van der Wall (examples Hamburg, Mus. Kst & Gew.; Utrecht, Cent. Mus.). Another attributed work is a series of *Apostles* (Langhaar, Catholic church). These large Baroque wood figures are placed on finely decorated consoles that are, like the pulpit panels in Utrecht, wholly free of Rococo elements. The Centraal Museum in Utrecht has an engraved copper plate for a vignette that occurs in P. Bondam's printed oration *De foedere trajectino* (Utrecht, 1779); this is signed *W. H. van de Wal inv. L. de Wit sculp.*

BIBLIOGRAPHY

Thieme–Becker
Catalogus van het Historisch Museum der stad: Centraal Museum Utrecht (Utrecht, 1928), no. 3754
Beeldhouwkunst: Aartsbisschoppelijk Museum [Sculpture: archiepiscopal Museum] (Utrecht, 1962), pp. 19, 157; nos 336–40
Het beeld in de Nederlandse barok [Sculpture at the time of the Dutch Baroque] (exh. cat., Utrecht, Aartsbisschoppelijk Mus., 1963), nos 72–4
J. Leeuwenberg and W. Halsema-Kubes: *Beeldhouwkunst in het Rijksmuseum: Catalogus* (The Hague and Amsterdam, 1973), nos 420–21

WILHELMINA HALSEMA-KUBES

Wall, William Guy (*b* Dublin, 1792; *d* Ireland, *c.* 1864). American painter of Irish birth. He arrived in New York in 1812 already well-trained as an artist and soon became famous for his sensitive watercolour views of the Hudson River valley and environs. Some of these watercolours were published as engravings by John Hill and his son John William Hill in the *Hudson River Portfolio* (New York, 1821–5), the first book to make Americans aware of the beauty and sublimity of their own scenery. Wall is often seen as a forerunner or early member of the HUDSON RIVER SCHOOL. Good examples of his work are the *Covered Bridge across the Sacandaga River, Hadley, New York* (1820; New York, NY Hist. Soc.) and the *View near Hudson* (1822; Yonkers, NY, Hudson River Mus.). Wall was a founder-member of the National Academy of Design, New York, and exhibited frequently at such institutions as the Pennsylvania Academy of Fine Arts, Philadelphia, and the Apollo Association, New York. He lived in America from 1812 to 1835 and again from 1856 to 1860; little is known of the years after his final return to Ireland. His son, William Archibald Wall (1820–1875), was also a landscape painter.

BIBLIOGRAPHY
D. Shelley: 'William Guy Wall and his Watercolours for the Historic *Hudson River Portfolio*', *New York Hist. Soc. Q.*, xxxi (1947), pp. 24–45
J. Howat: 'A Picturesque Site in the Catskills: Katerskill Falls as Painted by William Guy Wall', *Honolulu Acad. A. J.*, 1 (1974), pp. 16–29, 63–5

MARK W. SULLIVAN

Wallace, Richard. *See* SEYMOUR-CONWAY, (3).

Wallace, William (*fl* 1615; *d* Edinburgh, Oct 1631). Scottish architect. A prominent figure in the school of Scottish Renaissance building and design that flourished in the first half of the 17th century, he progressed from mason to become the architect responsible for some of the finest buildings of the period. First recorded working as a stone-carver on the palace block at Edinburgh Castle (1615–17), in April 1617 he was granted the post of Master Mason to the Scottish Crown; subsequent royal works he undertook in this capacity include the north wing of Linlithgow Palace, Lothian (1618–20). Wallace's talents are more apparent, however, in the private commissions attributed to him on the basis of stylistic evidence. The grand new wing for Pinkie House, Lothian, for example, begun in 1613 for Alexander Seton, 1st Earl of Dunfermline (?1555–1622), is distinguished by tall chimney-stacks, regular windows, string courses, a three-storey bay window projecting from the gable and columned buttresses. It is probable that he was also responsible for the L-shape block of Moray House, Edinburgh (begun 1618).

Between 1620 and 1627 Wallace remodelled, extended and embellished the original L-plan Winton House, Pencaitland, Lothian, for George Seton, 3rd Earl of Winton (1584–1650). A new wing was added to create a U-plan symmetry, embellished with grouped octagonal chimney-stacks as well as string courses to highlight each floor. The two ogee-capped staircase towers, one in each corner of the wing, display pilasters and heraldic carvings, with further carved detailing in the pediments and tympana above the windows. The main interiors of this wing are distinguished by their volumetric grandeur, encrusted plasterwork and gigantic carved chimney-pieces. Engravings by John Clerk (iii) and Francis Grose of the sumptuous Seton Palace, Lothian (destr. 1780s; see D. Laing, ed.: *A Series of Etchings, Chiefly of Views in Scotland*, Edinburgh, 1855, pls 50–51), and the Wrights Houses, Bruntsfield, Edinburgh (destr. 1870; see F. Grose: *The Antiquities of Scotland*, London, 1789–91, p. 39), reveal that both had tall, grouped chimney-stacks providing a focal part of the design, as well as exuberantly carved dormer windows and classical pilasters flanking the openings—features that probably justify their attribution to Wallace. His funeral monument to *John Byres of Coates* (*d* 1629) in Greyfriars Churchyard, Edinburgh, with its twin Corinthian columns supporting a broken pediment, shows a firmer command of classical detail than he had hitherto managed in his buildings.

The plan of Wallace's masterpiece of Scottish Renaissance architecture, George Heriot's Hospital (begun 1628), a school for orphans in Edinburgh, was supplied by Heriot's nephew, Walter Balcanquall, Dean of Rochester (?1586–1645), and has much in common with the general plan-forms of Scottish Renaissance buildings as well as with mid-16th-century designs by Sebastiano Serlio. The hospital consists of four equal ranges enclosing a central courtyard; at each corner is a massive rectangular tower with turreted battlements. There are entrance towers at the centre of two of the four ranges; a third displays the chapel's tall tracery window. Tooled and carved window-heads create an external richness that is complemented internally by great carved chimney-pieces. Despite the foreign influences—the Flemish strapwork and decorative detail and the Serlian plan—Wallace and William Aytoun (*d* ?1643), who took over at his death, created a building that is *sui generis*.

BIBLIOGRAPHY
Colvin
F. Grose: *The Antiquities of Scotland* (London, 1789–91)
D. MacGibbon and T. Ross: *The Castellated and Domestic Architecture of Scotland*, 5 vols (Edinburgh, 1887–92)
J. Gillespie: *Details of Scottish Domestic Architecture* (Edinburgh, 1922)
J. G. Dunbar: *Historic Architecture of Scotland* (London, 1966)
A. Rowan: 'George Heriot's Hospital, Edinburgh', *Country Life*, clvii (6 March 1975), pp. 554–7; clvii (13 March 1975), pp. 634–7
C. McWilliam: *Lothian*, Bldgs Scotland (Harmondsworth, 1978)
J. Gifford, C. McWilliam and D. Walker: *Edinburgh*, Bldgs Scotland (Harmondsworth, 1984)

CHARLES McKEAN

Wallerij, Nicholas. *See* VALLARI, NICHOLAS.

Wallgren, Carl Wilhelm. *See* VALLGREN, VILLE.

Wallis, Alfred (*b* Devonport, 8 Aug 1855; *d* Madron, Cornwall, ?29 Aug 1942). English painter, fisherman and scrap merchant. Although the exact date of Wallis's birth is doubtful, he stated in letters to Jim Ede, one of his greatest patrons, that he was born on the day of the fall of Sebastopol. He claimed to have gone to sea at the age of nine and was involved in deep-sea fishing, sometimes sailing as far as Newfoundland. About 1875 he married Susan Ward, a woman 21 years his senior, and shortly afterwards gave up deep-sea fishing to become an inshore fisherman. In 1890 he moved to St Ives, Cornwall, where he set up as a marine scrap merchant. In 1912 he retired.

His wife died in 1922, whereupon he took up painting to keep himself company, as he told Ede.

In 1928 Christopher Wood and Ben Nicholson discovered Wallis in St Ives. Both artists were already working in a primitive idiom but were further encouraged by the discovery of Wallis. His principal subjects were ships at sea and shipwrecks, especially the ships that had disappeared during his lifetime (e.g. *Two-masted Ship, c.* 1928; London, Tate). Other typical subjects were landscapes with trees and houses. His paintings rarely depict people. Nicholson described his working method as follows:

> He would cut out the top and bottom of an old cardboard box, and sometimes the four sides, into irregular shapes, using each shape as the key to the movement in a painting, and using the colour and texture of the board as the key to its colour and texture. When the painting was completed, what remained of the original board, a brown, a grey, a white or a green board, sometimes in the sky, sometimes in the sea, or perhaps in a field or a lighthouse, would be as deeply experienced as the remainder of the painting. He used very few colours, and one associates with him some lovely dark browns, shiny blacks, fierce greys, strange whites and a particularly pungent Cornish green.

Wallis also painted on objects such as jugs and jars. His informal approach appealed to many artists of this period, particularly because of the prevailing interest in children's and primitive art. He sold paintings to many patrons of the English avant-garde such as Ede, Margaret Gardiner, Geoffrey Grigson, Herbert Read, Adrian Stokes, John Summerson and Helen Sutherland. Two of his paintings were shown in the exhibition of the Seven and Five Society in March 1929.

Wallis regarded his paintings as expressions of his experiences. He was unaware of linear perspective but arranged the objects depicted in terms of relative importance, determining their sizes accordingly. Thus the principal subject of a painting would be the largest object depicted, regardless of where it stood in relation to others. While his pictorial naivety appealed in particular to Wood, his handling of materials attracted Nicholson. Furthermore, Nicholson perceived in Wallis's work a stress on the painting as an object, which was one of his own principal considerations. Wallis died in Madron Workhouse. Although his paintings have a directness and distinction of their own, his principal importance lies in his relation to the prevailing interests in English art.

BIBLIOGRAPHY

S. Berlin and B. Nicholson: 'Alfred Wallis', *Horizon*, vii (1943), pp. 41–50
S. Berlin: *Alfred Wallis: Primitive* (London, 1949)
E. Mullins: *Alfred Wallis: Cornish Primitive Painter* (London, 1967)
Alfred Wallis (exh. cat., ed. A. Bowness; London, ACGB, 1968)

JEREMY LEWISON

Wallis, Henry (*b* London, 21 Feb 1830; *d* Croydon, Surrey, 20 Dec 1916). English painter, writer and collector. He first studied at F. S. Cary's academy and in 1848 entered the Royal Academy Schools, London. He is also thought to have trained in Paris at some time in the late 1840s or early 1850s, first in Charles Gleyre's atelier and subsequently at the Ecole des Beaux-Arts. He specialized in portraits of literary figures and scenes from the lives of past writers, as in *Dr Johnson at Cave's, the Publisher* (1854; untraced). His first great success was the *Death of Chatterton* (London, Tate), which he exhibited at the Royal Academy in 1856. The impoverished late 18th-century poet Thomas Chatterton, who while still in his teens had poisoned himself in despair, was a romantic hero for many young and struggling artists in Wallis's day. He depicted the poet dead in his London garret, the floor strewn with torn fragments of manuscript and, tellingly, an empty phial near his hand. The painting was universally praised, not least by John Ruskin who described it as 'faultless and wonderful', advising visitors to 'examine it well, inch by inch'. Although Wallis was only loosely connected with the Pre-Raphaelite movement, his method and style in *Chatterton* reveal the importance of that connection: the vibrant colours and careful build-up of symbolic detail are typical Pre-Raphaelite concerns. The success of *Chatterton* was such that, when exhibited in Manchester the following year, it was protected from the jostling crowds by a policeman. It was bought by another artist, Augustus Egg.

Wallis's next success came in 1858 with the exhibition at the Royal Academy of *The Stonebreaker* (Birmingham, Mus. & A.G.). Accompanied by quotations from Tennyson's poem 'A Dirge' (1830) and Thomas Carlyle's *Sartor resartus* (1833–4), its theme was the human cost of hard labour and poverty. It showed a dead stone-breaker slumped by the roadside in a symbolically twilit landscape. Although Wallis was not the first to portray such hardships, his painting attracted much attention through its combination of shocking realism and glorious sunset. Critics disagreed about it: the *Illustrated London News* proclaimed it 'shocks the sight and offends the sense', while the *Spectator* found it 'a picture of the sacredness and solemnity which dwell in a human creature, however seared, and in death, however obscure'.

In the early 1860s Wallis was an exhibitor, along with various Pre-Raphaelites, at the Hogarth Club, London. He also continued to show history paintings, many with a literary theme, at the Royal Academy until 1877. His work was engraved for the *Art Journal*, for example *Found at Naxos* (untraced), which appeared in 1878. He was also a prolific watercolourist, exhibiting over 80 examples at the Old Water-Colour Society, to which he was elected in 1880. He travelled widely in Europe and the Near East; many of his later paintings show scenes or events apparently witnessed during the course of his travels, such as *Winnowing Corn, Capri* (1862; untraced) and a watercolour of a *Coffee Merchant, the Bazaar at Suez* (untraced), exhibited at the Old Water-Colour Society in 1887. In late life he made less impact as a painter than he did as an authority on Italian and oriental ceramics, about which during the last two decades of his life he wrote a number of books and articles, many of them illustrated by his own drawings. He also built up a huge collection of ceramics, which is now in the Victoria and Albert Museum. In the 1890s he was also involved in campaigns to preserve ancient Egyptian monuments.

WRITINGS

'The Boulag Museum', *A. J.* [London], xi (1888), pp. 103–10
'The Destruction of Egyptian Monuments', *19th C.* [London], xxviii (1890), pp. 720–32
Italian Ceramic Art: Examples of Maiolica and Mezza-maiolica Fabricated Before 1500 (London, 1897)
Egyptian Ceramic Art: The Macgregor Collection (London, 1898)

'Ancient Egyptian Ceramic Art', *19th C.* [London], xlvii (1900), pp. 308–20

The Art of the Precursors: A Study in the History of Early Italian Maiolica (London, 1901)

Italian Ceramic Art: The Maiolica Pavement Tiles of the Fifteenth Century (London, 1902)

Italian Ceramic Art: The Albarello; A Study in Early Renaissance Maiolica (London, 1904)

BIBLIOGRAPHY

A. van de Put: 'Henry Wallis, 1830–1916', *Faenza*, v (1917), pp. 33–8

The Pre-Raphaelites (exh. cat., ed. L. Parris; London, Tate, 1984)

J. Treuherz: *Hard Times: Social Realism in Victorian Art* (London, 1987), pp. 36–39

Ceramic Art of the Renaissance (exh. cat., ed. T. Wilson; London, BM, 1987)

JENNY ELKAN

Wallis, Thomas (*b* London, 22 June 1873; *d* London, 4 May 1953). English architect. He was articled to Sydney R. J. Smith (1858–1913). In 1908 Wallis set up in partnership with J. A. Bowden (1876–1949), built extensions (1908) to the Town Hall in Stoke-on-Trent and entered competitions (e.g. Marylebone Town Hall, 1911, and Port of London Authority, 1913). In 1914 he formed a new practice, Wallis, Gilbert & Partners, with the American architect Gilbert, following an approach by the American engineering company Kahncrete to promote use of reinforced concrete industrial structures. Although Gilbert never became involved in the firm, his name was retained. The actual partners included Wallis's son, Douglas T. Wallis (1901–68). Henceforth, Wallis specialized in industrial buildings in concrete characterized by a decorative architectural façade concealing the utilitarian shop floor and giving visual identity towards the road.

Wallis produced large buildings in the London suburbs and other parts of Britain, as well as France, Germany and South Africa. The façades evolved from simplified Beaux-Arts towards modernism by the early 1930s, while remaining colourful and angular. The use of projecting framing motifs and Egyptian detailing shows the influence of J. J. Burnet and Thomas Tait, as in the Firestone Factory (1929; destr.), Brentford, Middx, and the Hoover Factory (1932–5), Perivale, London. These and similar factories became notorious as examples of 'jazz–modern', although Wallis was employed by industrialists principally because of his specialized knowledge of designing for industry, and his buildings pioneered workers' welfare provision and environmental control. The British Bemberg Factory (1931), Doncaster, Yorks, lacks the usual façade, while the Daimler Hire Garage (1931), Herbrand Street, London, exploits the compositional possibilities of a spiral ramp. In 1932 Wallis built Victoria Coach Station, London, on a corner site with a tower, and this was followed by coach stations at Reigate, Windsor, Amersham, Hemel Hempstead and Hertford, which were designed to suit the rural locations.

WRITINGS

Wallis, Gilbert and Partners: *Industrial Architecture* (Geneva, 1932)

'Factories', *RIBA J.*, n. s. 2, xl (1932–3), pp. 301–12

BIBLIOGRAPHY

D. T. Wallis: 'Modern Factory Planning', *Architecture* [London], vii/38 (1929), pp. 61–73

J. J. Snowdon and R. W. Platts: 'Great West Road Style', *Archit. Rev.* [London], clvi (1974), pp. 21–7

J. Skinner: 'The Firestone Factory, 1928–1980', *Twentieth-Century Architecture*, 1 (1994), pp. 12–22

ALAN POWERS

Wallot, Paul (*b* Oppenheim am Rhein, 26 June 1841; *d* Langenschwalbach, 18 Aug 1912). German architect and teacher. He trained in Darmstadt, Hannover and Berlin and completed his architectural studies in Giessen in 1863. In 1864 he went to Berlin to work in the offices of Johann Heinrich Strack, Richard Lucae and Friedrich Hitzig, all former pupils of Karl Friedrich Schinkel and at that date the most prominent architects in Berlin. After extensive travels in England and Italy (1867–8), Wallot set up his own practice in Frankfurt am Main, where he became acquainted with Heinrich Burnitz and Alfred F. Bluntschli, who introduced him to the forms and motifs of the Italian High Renaissance. At the time, Frankfurt was in the forefront of the Renaissance Revival in Germany, and Wallot soon became one of its most competent and eloquent followers. During the 1870s and 1880s he designed a number of elegant urban houses, the models for which were the palazzi of the Italian Renaissance. Following contemporary developments, however, he used German Renaissance forms just as competently and also adopted the Baroque Revival of the 1890s. His designs had a strong emphasis on functional and practical planning. Many of his houses in Frankfurt incorporated shops on the ground-floor. Behind the rich, ornamental façades, their planning and layout were invariably orientated to the needs and requirements of the shops and offices. Together with Bluntschli, Wallot was also one of the first to allow the iron construction of the shops and offices to be revealed.

Wallot took part in a number of competitions, and his reputation became firmly established when he won first prize in the second competition (1882) for the German Reichstag building in Berlin. Commissioned to execute his design, he moved to Berlin in 1884 to oversee its construction (1884–94; destr. 1933; partly restored 1970s). His monumental Baroque Revival entry had a central dome and four corner towers (*see* GERMANY, fig. 10). As was recognized by the jury, it combined the symbolic character of the Baroque Revival with functional planning, while at the same time attempting to invoke national sentiments through medieval allusions expressed in sculpture and painted decoration. Nevertheless, the visible iron construction of the central dome and the treatment of ornament and plain surfaces already indicated a non-historical approach. The influence of the Reichstag on many large public works undertaken at the time is evident, for example, in Hamburg Railway Station (1900) and the national museum of Bucharest (1887). Wallot left Berlin amid controversy about the interior decoration of the Reichstag and took up a teaching post in Dresden, where he built the Sächsische Ständehaus (1901–6). Some of Wallot's pupils, including Gustav Halmhuber, Otto Rieth and Bruno Schmitz, formed a school of characteristically heavy, monumental architecture, mainly expressed through the many monuments to the German Empire. Highly respected as an architect and teacher, Wallot retired in 1911. He died the following year, and in 1913 the Akademie der Künste in Berlin organized a large memorial exhibition of his work.

BIBLIOGRAPHY

Thieme–Becker

W. Machowsky: *Paul Wallot und seine Schüler* (Berlin, 1912)

J. Schmädecke: *Der deutsche Reichstag* (Berlin, 1970)

K. Milde: *Neorenaissance in der deutschen Architektur des 19. Jahrhunderts* (Dresden, 1981)

V. Hammerschmidt: *Anspruch und Ausdruck in der Architektur des späten Historismus in Deutschland, 1860–1914* (Frankfurt am Main, 1985)

□

Wall painting. Painting applied to a prepared wall surface.

I. Survey of techniques. II. Conservation.

I. Survey of techniques.

1. Introduction. 2. Antiquity. 3. Asia. 4. Western.

1. INTRODUCTION. Knowledge of wall painting techniques is growing rapidly as more murals are examined scientifically and conserved. It is becoming increasingly evident that methods varied, sometimes substantially, within one region or even within the practice of one artist from project to project. Consequently, this survey must be considered provisional, especially in regard to little-explored periods and locations. Documentary sources can help to establish broad conceptions about the methods and materials of a given era, but they may be difficult to interpret and can also be unreliable. Data from the scientific examination of works *in situ* or of fragments in the laboratory are essential to refine, expand and correct these conceptions. The summary that follows represents a critical conflation of textual information, where available, with the more specific evidence from technical investigations.

At the outset, however, it is necessary to outline the various stages of a wall painting, the variations of which distinguish one technique from another. Of primary importance are the composition of the rendering or plaster ground and the method in which it is applied. Renderings may be clay-based or composed of lime plaster, to name only the two most common types. They are often applied in several coats: in the Western tradition the first, rough coat of plaster is known as the *arriccio* and the final, smooth layer(s) on which the mural is executed as the *intonaco*. When lime plaster is used, the condition of the *intonaco* layer is a factor in determining whether the work is painted *a fresco* or *a secco*: FRESCO painting is executed on a damp *intonaco*, so that the pigments are fused to the wall by the carbonation of the calcium hydroxide from the wet plaster; SECCO painting is carried out on a dry rendering with the pigments fixed by binders. Also in the case of lime plaster, a basic distinction is drawn between two different ways of applying the *intonaco* layer. In the *pontate* system, the *intonaco* is applied in broad horizontal bands that correspond roughly in height to the levels of scaffolding (It. *ponteggio*). This method is used when very large surface areas are to be painted quickly *a fresco*, or when a lot of secco work is envisioned. For a fresco painting, however, the *intonaco* can also be applied in smaller patches of varying sizes known as *giornate*. These represent the amount of work that can be painted in one day (It. *giorno*) while the plaster is fresh. The medium in which the pigments are applied is one further feature that characterizes the overall technique of the wall painting. In *buon fresco* (or true fresco) the pigments are ground in pure water and applied to a wet *intonaco* of lime plaster. For secco painting a variety of binders, including egg, glue, casein and drying oils, can be used to secure the pigments to the dry ground. Two important intermediate techniques are 'lime fresco', a fresco technique in which the pigments are ground in lime water or milk of lime to increase their opacity, and LIME SECCO, in which the pigments, similarly mixed with lime water or milk of lime, are applied to dry lime plaster that has been wetted down. The preparatory underdrawing of a wall painting, applied before the pigments, is called a SINOPIA.

2. ANTIQUITY.

(i) Prehistoric. The earliest surviving wall paintings, which date from the Upper Paleolithic period (40,000–10,000 BP), were generally produced with a limited range of earth pigments and black, usually manganese dioxide, applied by hand or brush on to the bare rock interior of caves (*see* PREHISTORIC EUROPE, §II, 2(iii)(b)). Alternatively, dry pigment was blown through a tube on to a wall surface coated with mixtures of grease, blood and urine. In the limestone cave at LASCAUX in south-western France the pigments may have become fused to the wall by the natural presence of calcium carbonate in a process of crystallization. Some Australian Aborigines continue to use similar techniques (see fig. 1). During the Neolithic period (8000–3000 BC) wall paintings began to be applied to architectural structures, and clay renderings were used for the first time, sometimes covered by a thin whitewash of plaster. In the secco paintings (*c.* 6500–5700 BC) discovered at ÇATAL HÜYÜK in Turkey, the pigments were found to include not only earth, clay and carbon colours but also haematite and azurite. Whether a binder was employed could not be ascertained.

(ii) Egypt and the Ancient Near East. In Egypt the Neolithic secco techniques were elaborated and refined (*see* EGYPT, ANCIENT, §X, 2). The rendering was composed of fine-grained silt from the banks of the Nile, containing sand, clay and a little calcium carbonate, mixed with straw or other fibrous materials. The final coats were made of gypsum plaster prepared from heated raw gypsum (calcium sulphate) and usually applied in two layers, the second finer and smoother than the first. Painting was carried out after the plaster had dried using a water-soluble binder with a gum or gelatin base. A set working procedure can be reconstructed from the tomb paintings. First the wall was divided with grid lines by snapping a cord coated with red pigment. Preliminary drawings were made in red, and then the contours were reinforced in black. The outlines were filled in with areas of flat colour and the details added on top. The Neolithic palette was enhanced by the addition of Egyptian blue, which is a copper-based frit and the earliest known artificial pigment (see colour pl. I, fig. 1).

The cultures of Mesopotamia practised a secco technique similar to that of the Egyptians, with a rendering composed of clay and chopped straw covered by a lime plaster final coat. There is some evidence, however, that fresco techniques were also employed. The paintings that decorated the palace of Yarim-Lim at TELL ATCHANA (*c.* 1800 BC) were executed on brick wall sometimes prepared first with clay and then covered with two coats of lime plaster, the first layer measuring 4–8 mm, the second

1. Wall painting being retouched by an Aboriginal artist at Mamadai, Western Australia, *c.* 1968

(of pure lime) no more than 1 mm. The murals may have been painted largely *a fresco* with secco highlights. If this is so, they constitute the earliest known fresco paintings.

(iii) Pre-Columbian Americas. Wall paintings were used extensively in Mesoamerica and the Central Andean area and were executed in both secco and fresco techniques. For illustration *see* COLOUR, colour pl. I, fig. 1, and for further discussion *see* MESOAMERICA, PRE-COLUMBIAN, §V, and SOUTH AMERICA, PRE-COLUMBIAN, §III, 4.

(iv) Greece and Rome. The wall paintings surviving from Crete and Mycenae seem to represent a tradition intermediary to those of the Ancient Near East and Greece. The exact nature of the techniques used (*see* MINOAN, §IV, 1) has aroused controversy, but recent evidence indicates that fresco techniques were known in Crete by the 2nd millennium BC and that the use of an unusually thick *intonaco*, which dried very slowly, enabled fresco painting to continue over a period of days without the necessity of a *giornate* technique. There is abundant evidence that preliminary sketches were carried out on the *intonaco* in *sinopie*. The range of pigments corresponds to the palette used in the Ancient Near East, generally comprising earth minerals with the exception of Egyptian blue.

Although little evidence of mural painting survives *in situ* from ancient Greece, the Greek traditions are reflected in Etruscan painted tombs in Italy dating from the 7th century BC to the 1st. Etruscan wall paintings exhibit a range of techniques, but the dominant method was fresco on a natural tufa wall prepared with a rough lime plaster rendering and finished by a thin lime whitewash. Preparatory sketches were engraved with a stylus in the fresh rendering and then gone over with chalk. Colours were applied in flat tones circumscribed by emphatic black contour lines.

In ancient Rome (see colour pl. I, fig. 2; *see also* ROME, ANCIENT, §V, 1(ii)) the wall was prepared with a rough *arriccio* of lime and sand on which *sinopia* sketches were often carried out. Several *intonaco* layers composed of lime and powdered marble were then applied using the *pontate* system and polished with a hard instrument to achieve shiny, transparent effects, often in imitation of marble veneers. The *pontate* were sometimes also subdivided into *giornate* following the outlines of architecture or figures. Alternatively, as in the late Fourth Style murals at the House of the Vettii in Pompeii, more complex inserted pictures could be executed after the remainder had been completed by cutting out and replacing the *intonaco* for the circumscribed areas with fresh plaster. Roman murals of this type were painted *a fresco*, but the pigments were probably mixed with lime water or milk of lime with a clay such as kaolin added. As a finishing touch, wax was applied to the surface for protection and to enhance the rich, shiny appearance. Pliny also mentioned a form of wall painting (*cretula*) carried out on dry, clay-based renderings (*Natural History* XXXV, xxxi), which suggests that more traditional secco techniques were also current.

3. ASIA. As in the Ancient Near East, the techniques used in Asia have evolved on the whole from the secco methods of the Neolithic period. In Iran, little is known of the wall paintings from early times, although a few examples have survived of frescoes painted on polished lime-based renderings in a technique reminiscent of Classical Roman works. By contrast, the large body of paintings from the Safavid period (1501–1732; *see* ISLAMIC ART, §II, 9(iii)(b)) seem to reflect traditional secco methods. A clay-based rendering would be completed by a gypsum plaster final coat and painted when dry using tempera binders, perhaps egg. Lavish gilding was applied with gum arabic.

The similar secco wall-painting tradition of India (*see* INDIAN SUBCONTINENT, §VI, 1(v)) is described in a series of Sanskrit texts dating from the 4th century AD to the 16th. According to these writings, the wall was prepared with a thick rendering composed of clay, straw or other fibrous materials and sometimes also granular matter. Then the finishing coats, made from white clay and gypsum or lime, were applied in one or more thin, smooth layers. The binders recorded include gums, resins, wax, sugars, saps and oil. Study of the surviving murals suggests, however, a technical development: from secco painting on a thin clay rendering, as found in the earliest preserved murals in Buddhist rock temples (e.g. the Jogimara Caves of the Ramgarh Hill, probably 2nd century BC), to an intermediary secco method resembling the textual descriptions, as found in Buddhist murals up until the 6th century AD (e.g. the 5th-century examples from the Gupta period in the Ajanta caves), and culminating in what may be an early form of fresco painting, involving the use of renderings composed of lime and sand. For the murals (8th–9th centuries) in the Jaina temple at Sittannavasal, near Madras, a rendering of lime and sand was covered with a thin wash of pure lime that may have been painted while wet. This method was employed for temple wall paintings as late as the 18th century. An extensive range of pigments has been identified in Indian works, including lapis lazuli from Afghanistan. However, the binding media for the secco paintings are unknown.

Another Indian fresco technique is the so-called *fresco lustro*, still practised in Rajasthan and represented earlier by the 18th-century murals of the Amer Fort, near Jaipur. The rendering, composed of slaked lime, sand, limestone and marble powder, is beaten on to the wall using a flat stick. The finishing coat, made of very fine slaked lime and casein, is then brushed on to a small area, polished and painted while wet, using a gum or glue binder. The polishing before and after painting helps to incorporate the pigments and lends a special shine to the surface.

In Central Asia and China there are many examples of Buddhist wall paintings in the major temples along the pilgrim route. They date from the 3rd century AD to the 10th and were executed in a limited variety of secco techniques (*see* CENTRAL ASIA, §II, 4) similar to those found in the early Buddhist wall paintings in India. Generally a clay and straw rendering was covered by a thin final coat of lime, gypsum or kaolin (a pure clay) applied with gum or starch, which were probably also used to bind the pigments (*see also* CHINA, §V, 2).

Nearly all the surviving wall paintings from Thailand date from the 17th century onwards. These are typically painted using gum made from tamarind seeds on dry lime-based renderings (*see* THAILAND, §VI, 1(iii)(a)). Similar techniques were employed in Burma (*see* BURMA, §V, 1(i)).

Two associated wall painting sites from Korea (*see* KOREA, §IV, 1) and Japan also merit consideration, as they may represent early examples of the fresco technique and possibly relate to contemporary work in India. These are the murals in the tombs near P'yŏngyang in Korea (5th–7th centuries AD) and the paintings in the tomb of TAKAMATSUZUKA (late 7th century) in Japan. At Takamatsuzuka the colours, applied to a very smooth lime plaster, are fused to the surface through carbonation (*see also* JAPAN, §VI, 1(i) and 3(i)(a)). However, the murals of the nearby temple of Hōryūji (*c.* AD 700; destr.) include secco work in mineral pigments on renderings of mud and sand.

4. WESTERN.

(i) *Early Christian and Byzantine.* During the Early Christian period the methods used in Roman times were continued in a much simplified form. In the catacombs, for example, fresco paintings were executed rapidly on thinner, two-layer renderings in large *pontate*. By the 5th century, however, more elaborate methods had developed. The mural techniques characteristic of the Byzantine world were recorded in a series of texts known as the *Ermeneia* ('Interpretation'). These survived in later recensions, the best known being the 'Mt Athos Painters' Guide' by DIONYSIOS OF FURNA, which was probably composed between 1730 and 1734. Examination of remaining murals affirms the reliability of Dionysios's account. The work was carried out *a fresco* on lime-based renderings to which fibrous materials had been added, following the Asian clay-based tradition. The *intonaco* was applied using the *pontate* system, and the area to be painted was then polished to draw the calcium hydroxide to the surface and ensure carbonation. Deep, lustrous tones resulted. Working within a relatively formulaic iconographic system, Byzantine artists seem usually to have omitted the *sinopia* stage and outlined their compositions on the *intonaco* layer. Colours were modelled in a series of overlays, with a unified ground tone applied first to each part of the composition, middle tones painted on top, highlights and darker shadow tones added as a third step and, finally, the contours of the picture reinforced (see colour pl. II, fig. 1). Although the Byzantine fresco tradition continued in the Balkans up until the 19th century, in Russia from the 15th century the desire to imitate icon painting led to an increased use of decorative secco effects.

(ii) Medieval. Romanesque wall painting seems to be a version of the Byzantine method, with regional variations due to the influence of local techniques that survived from the late Roman era. Lime plaster was used and the *intonaco* applied according to the *pontate* system, but the Byzantine technique of polishing was abandoned. The tradition of modelling through successive overlays continued in a simplified form, and the final layers of colour, now largely lost, seem to have been applied once the *intonaco* had dried using binders or by dampening the plaster and applying pigments in a lime medium (i.e. lime secco). In northern Europe decorative relief techniques, especially gilded stucco, became popular, and the *Zackenstil* artists of 13th-century Germany used gilding extensively.

Decorative and translucent effects achieved through secco techniques, including the use of oil as a binder, reached a peak of popularity, however, during the Gothic period (*see* GOTHIC, §IV, 4(i)). Although in Italy fresco painting remained the standard method, northern European artists strove to reproduce some of the aesthetic effects of stained glass and the decorative arts in their murals. In such projects as the Sainte-Chapelle (1239–43), Paris, artists experimented with transferring the rich techniques of panel painting to the wall. The wall surface was plastered and then treated with a white priming to enhance the luminosity of the paint layers. Painting was carried out *a secco*, and binders capable of creating translucent effects, particularly oils and varnishes, were selected. Glazing was used over opaque ground tones and metal leaf. The surfaces were also extensively gilded and encrusted with glass pieces and gemstones to maximize the decorative effect.

(iii) Renaissance. In the late 13th century and the 14th, the methods that were to be perfected during the Italian Renaissance were introduced and developed, particularly in the work of the ISAAC MASTER (*see* MASTERS, ANONYMOUS, AND MONOGRAMMISTS, §I) and Giotto and his followers. These methods are summarized below; they are described in greater detail in FRESCO.

The most widespread early Italian technique involved painting in true fresco on *giornate* with some areas completed *a secco*. The procedure is described in detail in Cennino Cennini's *Libro dell'arte* of *c.* 1390. An *arriccio* composed of one part lime to two parts sand was applied to the entire wall space and left rough to provide a tooth for the *intonaco*. Compositional drawings were sketched in charcoal on the *arriccio* and then gone over in *sinopia* with a brush. This enabled the exploration of increasingly complex pictorial conceptions including perspectival settings. The process of execution could then be mapped out and the *giornate* divisions determined. After an area had been covered by *intonaco*, the drawing would be retraced, perhaps from memory. Sketches on parchment or paper may have been used, though none survives from the 14th century. The amount of secco work varied considerably from artist to artist and even between compositions by the same artist. For instance, Giotto and his workshop painted the Arena Chapel in Padua (*c.* 1303–6) using the true fresco technique with only small additions *a secco*, but for the Peruzzi Chapel at Santa Croce in Florence (probably 1320s) the *intonaco* was applied using the *pontate*

system and painted *a secco* (*see* GIOTTO, figs 1, 5 and 8; *see also* PERSPECTIVE, colour pl. VIII, fig. 1). Secco techniques were used most extensively in Siena, as in Simone Martini's *Maestà* (1315–16; Siena, Pal. Pub.; see colour pl. II, fig. 2), painted largely in a decorative secco method reminiscent of northern European Gothic works with large amounts of glazing, gilding and distinctive haloes moulded in relief.

During the 15th century the *sinopia* was gradually replaced by other forms of transfer more suitable for the increasingly complex designs. Squared grids, described by Leon Battista Alberti, were used to enlarge and transfer small-scale studies (e.g. the face of the Virgin in Masaccio's *Trinity* (*c.* 1428); Florence, S Maria Novella). POUNCING came into use for detailed passages by the mid-15th century (see fig. 2), and by the late 15th century the technique of incising into the *intonaco* layer through the contours of a CARTOON was being employed in Florence.

In the High Renaissance period some Florentine artists experimented with the more subtle colouristic and modelling effects possible in secco work. Leonardo, in particular, painted the *Last Supper* (1495–8) at S Maria delle Grazie in Milan on a dry ground with a lead white priming layer and tempera binders, probably egg with a little drying oil. Michelangelo, in contrast, held *buon fresco* to be the most elevated technique and for the Sistine Chapel Ceiling (1508–12; Rome, Vatican; see fig. 3) employed the fresco methods developed during the 15th century. The wall paintings by Raphael and his school in the Stanza della

2. Wall painting by Andrea del Castagno: *Trinity with St Jerome* (after 1541), detail of head of St Jerome showing pounce marks from transfer of the cartoon, SS Annunziata, Florence

3. Ceiling painting by Michelangelo: *The Flood*, detail (after cleaning) revealing a snapped line and pounce marks from transfer of the cartoon, Sistine Chapel (1508–12), Vatican, Rome

Segnatura, the Stanza dell'Incendio and the Stanza d'Eliodoro at the Vatican (1509–11, 1511–14) reflect his concern to enrich the mural painting repertory with methods drawn from contemporary easel painting (*see* RAPHAEL, fig. 4). The flat, linear characteristics of fresco are replaced by more textured brushwork and surface finishes. In the Sala di Costantino (1519–20), carried out by Raphael's school, the aesthetic potential of oil painting is juxtaposed with that of fresco: allegorical figures of Justice and Comity in oil frame and contrast with fictive tapestries of Christian narratives painted *a fresco*. Such technical effects were picked up by several of the Mannerists and used in simulating different levels of reality within an image. In Venice canvas was the preferred support, and such artists as Paolo Veronese strove to imitate the textural qualities of a coarse canvas weave by working in fresco on a rougher plaster ground with more emphatic brushwork (e.g. *c.* 1561; Villa Barbaro, Maser).

(iv) Baroque and after. Although some Italian Baroque artists, including Caravaggio, worked in oil on canvases that were then fixed to the wall, in general the fresco method continued to be used with adaptations. On account of the extreme complexity of architectural settings and compositions, the stages of preparatory drawing evolved to include detailed coloured sketches and oil studies. Coloured grounds were sometimes used, and to allow for the textural effects favoured during the period the *intonaco* layer was roughened. The pigments were applied more thickly and unevenly, perhaps sometimes with the addition of lime to increase the opacity of the colours. In France a type of secco work known as marouflage was preferred. It involved painting in oil on canvas that was glued to the wall using an adhesive cement made of resin and wax or white lead in oil.

In the late 18th century the monumental style and complex perspectives of Baroque mural painting fell out of favour. Some Neo-classical artists became absorbed with discovering the technique of ancient Roman mural painting, which led to experiments with ENCAUSTIC PAINTING, while others explored various methods of secco painting. In the early 19th century, however, the Nazarenes' nostalgia for the styles and methods of the Italian Renaissance led to a somewhat rigid revival of *buon fresco* techniques (*see* NAZARENES). This was followed by an increasing scholarly interest in historic techniques (e.g. in the work of MARY PHILADELPHIA MERRIFIELD) and some imitation of them. Despite this, wall painting was usually carried out *a secco* using glue, casein or oil as binders (e.g. by THOMAS GAMBIER-PARRY) or done in marouflage: the underlying trend, which continued into the early 20th century, was to borrow the techniques of canvas painting in an effort to reproduce textural effects on the wall.

In the 1920s a revival of fresco painting took place in several countries (*see* MURAL), especially Mexico, where Diego Rivera adapted the *giornate* technique for his epic compositions. On the whole, however, fresco painting has been abandoned. More and more synthetic commercial products have been introduced for secco painting, including resins, acrylic and vinyl on a variety of supports.

II. Conservation.

Conservation treatments are geared so specifically to the unique features of each site that only certain facets of the subject permit generalizations of the kind necessary in a survey article. The basic causes of deterioration can be enumerated, however, as well as the general approaches that have been adopted to stabilize and restore wall paintings.

1. Causes of deterioration. 2. Treatment.

1. CAUSES OF DETERIORATION. Three general categories of deterioration, which often operate together, can be distinguished: they relate to environmental factors, the method in which the painting was executed and earlier conservation treatments.

(i) Environmental factors. Among the environmental factors detrimental to wall paintings moisture is the most critical, both because it is so frequently present and because it initiates several types of deterioration. The sources of moisture comprise the infiltration of water from leaking roofs and walls (or from rain and wind when the wall occupies an exposed location), moisture rising in the walls from the ground due to capillary action, the condensation of moisture from the air on cold walls and the absorption of moisture by hygroscopic materials in the mural layers.

The principal type of alteration due to moisture is caused by soluble inorganic salts, which migrate through the wall and recrystallize. These salts can originate within the components of the wall, in the soil or in the atmosphere. They can be deposited by pests, or they can result from later conservation treatments. The most damaging are the sulphates of sodium, potassium, magnesium and calcium. Such salts often crystallize on the wall painting and disfigure the surface (see fig. 4), but they can also recrystallize within the rendering and cause disintegration by expanding.

If harmful compounds are present in the air, damage takes place when water passing through the paint layer initiates chemical reactions between gases in the atmosphere and the materials of the painting. Among the natural gases, carbon dioxide, a component of the air and one of the by-products of human respiration, can cause serious damage to paintings on lime-based renderings. In the presence of water, carbon dioxide is transformed into carbonic acid, which acts on lime plaster to produce white incrustations of insoluble calcium carbonate on the surface. The detrimental effects on fresco paintings of sulphur dioxide, found in polluted urban environments, have been recognized only recently. In moist air the gas is transformed to sulphuric acid, which reacts on the lime renderings to change surface areas into calcium sulphate,

 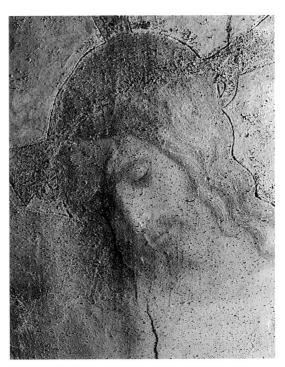

4. Wall painting by Fra Angelico: *Christ on the Cross Adored by St Dominic* (after 1442), details of the head of St Dominic (left) and the head of Christ (right) showing salts crystallized on the surface, before restoration with barium in 1973, convent of San Marco, Florence; photographs taken in raking light

a white efflorescence, with an increase in volume that results in surface disintegration.

Biological organisms, for example bacteria and moulds, flourish in damp areas on the surface of wall paintings. They appear as spots or stains, spread quickly and may cause large areas of disfigurement or colour loss. Extremes of temperature, which lead to the expansion and contraction of moisture within the mural layers, can also cause disintegration. In addition, in the presence of moisture the hues of some pigments undergo changes caused by chemical transformations. In northern European and Italian Gothic wall paintings, for example, azurite blue used for areas of sky or to depict the vault of heaven has often been transformed into its green relative, malachite.

Other environmental factors responsible for damage include wind exposure, which can lead to surface erosion, and exposure to strong light, which causes some colours to fade. The heat from isolated sources, for example candles, may damage limited areas of a painting's surface. Intermittent overall heating of churches and monuments, which alters the temperature and relative humidity, can cause damage by destroying the equilibrium between the masonry and the interior, inducing moisture exchange. In addition, surface deposits of dust can be problematic, clouding the surface and providing a site for bacterial growth.

(ii) Painting methods. Deterioration can result from the composition and method of application of any one of the layers of the painting: support, rendering or pigment layer. The support may not be strong enough to resist weathering over an extended period of time, as in the case of unbaked brick walls when the bricks are of poor quality and contain salts. Moreover, walls made of heterogeneous substances that differ in porosity and thermal conductivity, such as brick combined with stone, can cause condensation in areas of the paint surface, which leads to staining due to salts or biological organisms. Clay-based renderings tend to be very friable and extremely sensitive to moisture; they have usually been employed only in regions with very dry climates. Lime-based renderings can also be delicate, because they often absorb moisture from the air. If one component of the lime plaster is gypsum, the calcium carbonate will have a more marked tendency to be transformed into calcium sulphate when sulphur dioxide is present in polluted air. When walls are prepared for fresco painting, particular care must be taken in the choice and mixing of the lime and filler ingredients. Straw and other vegetable fibres, which are often added to ensure cohesion, also absorb moisture. The moisture provides conditions favourable to biological attack and in freezing temperatures can expand in volume, which leads to problems within the rendering and paint layers. In secco painting, on the other hand, a rendering that is too powdery may adhere poorly and cause the paint layer to flake, particularly if the binding medium used was too concentrated and contracted too much on drying.

The way in which the paint layers were applied can also in part determine the extent of deterioration. Whereas skilfully executed *buon fresco* paintings tend to be relatively resistant to deterioration because the pigment layer is fused to the lime plaster ground (*see* §I, 1 above), secco wall paintings are often more fragile. The traditional binders, which include egg, oil, glue, casein and lime, often lose their adhesive power over time, and this leads to the flaking of the paint layer. For instance, in Romanesque wall paintings that were painted in superimposed layers, typically little remains of the final modelling layers of the compositions. With the advent in the 20th century of modern secco techniques, which employ newly manufactured synthetic products in highly personal and eclectic ways, numerous conservation problems have arisen due to as yet poorly understood defects in the materials and methods.

(iii) Previous conservation treatments. Until early in the 20th century it was common to apply substances to the surface of wall paintings to heighten the colours or to improve adhesion, including varnish, oils, waxes, fats and glue. These often cause distortions in the colour balance of works. Wax, for instance, deepens the colours and creates a shine. Such substances as glue can induce cracking of the paint layers due to contraction during the drying process. Alkaline silicates have been used liberally as fixatives, but they form a cloudy veil on the surface that is very hard to remove.

2. TREATMENT. Unlike an easel painting, a wall painting is by its physical nature part of its contextual environment. Conservation is extremely complex, because the environment in which the painting is fixed is usually the principal cause of its deterioration. This fundamental problem can be approached in two contrasting ways, either by removing the wall painting from its environment through a process of detachment or by regulating the environment and then proceeding to repair the work *in situ*.

(i) Detachment. The three standard techniques of detachment developed in Italy are the *stacco*, *stacco a massello* and *strappo* methods. Of these, the *stacco* method is generally preferred as the least damaging. A soluble adhesive is applied to the surface of the mural, and pieces of gauze and hemp are laid on top. The *intonaco* is pounded to free it from the *arriccio*, and then a knife is used to separate the two plaster layers. The paint layer and *intonaco* are pulled away together from the *arriccio* and mounted on a new, inert support. The *stacco a massello* method is more radical as it involves the removal of the *arriccio* as well as the *intonaco*. To achieve this, the wall is hollowed out behind the painting to a depth of 100–200 mm. In the *strappo* technique only the thin paint layer is removed. A cloth, fixed with a soluble adhesive to the surface of the painting, is securely attached to an overhead beam, and when the adhesive has dried the paint layer is detached by slowly peeling the cloth away from the wall.

The detachment methods that were popular in the past salvaged wall paintings, but often at the expense of damage to the site or to the painting itself. *Stacco a massello*, entailing destruction of the wall behind the painting, was clearly a very hazardous approach. The *strappo* technique could be equally damaging, as the peeling process resulted in the pulverization of the enamel surface of the painting, which caused paint loss and impaired the original surface qualities of the work. The surface characteristics of the painting could also be substantially altered by the texture of the new support, particularly when a canvas layer was included.

Improvements are being made in detachment procedures to reduce the degree of resulting damage. For instance, wet adhesives, which sometimes caused staining on fragile works, have been replaced by dry paper foils, and suction plates pressed up against the surface are used to ease the painting gently from its site. Detachment has fallen out of favour and is resorted to only when less radical approaches have proved unviable.

(ii) Regulating the environment. With the aim of preserving the wall painting within its original context, most modern conservation teams strive first to alleviate, in non-destructive ways, the detrimental environmental factors acting on it. This can offer a sometimes insurmountable challenge, as the sites that wall paintings occupy were typically not designed to maintain a stable environment. The initial project is generally to identify the origin of moisture through diagnostic testing of relative humidity, temperature and moisture levels and then to eliminate its cause. A wide spectrum of solutions are in practice, geared to the specific nature of the moisture problem. Obvious remedies involve repairing leaks and covering exposed walls with overhangs or inserting protective screens. To eliminate rising damp, walls can be isolated at the bottom and sides from the source of moisture by cutting through the entire thickness of the wall low down and by inserting isolating layers. Walls may be heated to avoid condensation. For underground archaeological sites, where, over the ages, the wall paintings have reached an equilibrium with the site, sophisticated systems have been designed by engineering specialists to isolate the site climatically by controlling the temperature and humidity.

(iii) Restoration. Once the environmental causes of deterioration have been alleviated or, as a last resort, the painting has been detached from its site, restoration typically proceeds in a sequence of three stages: consolidation, cleaning and inpainting. Consolidation is carried out through the application of fixatives (*see* CONSOLIDANT). The appropriate fixative must be carefully selected after the specific problem has been diagnosed, that is to say, after it has been ascertained whether the paint layer is flaking or powdering or has lost its surface qualities, or whether the rendering has lost its cohesive strength. The conservator chooses between a wide range of traditional organic or inorganic fixatives and fixatives based on synthetic resins. One important organic fixative is barium hydroxide, which has been used successfully together with ammonium carbonate solution to correct the deterioration caused by the crystallization of calcium sulphate on the surface of frescoes.

The consolidated painting is then cleaned to remove layers of dirt and other accretions (see fig. 5). However, the extent to which these additions, whether natural or applied by man, should be removed is a subject of continuing debate. Wall paintings, although generally free from varnish, acquire a patina naturally with age as dirt particles are incorporated into the substance of the surface. Similarly, wall paintings have often acquired layers of coatings or repaintings over the centuries for reasons of

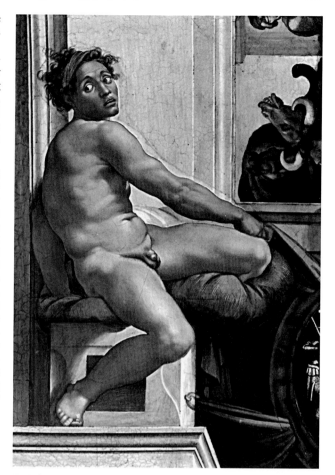

5. Ceiling painting by Michelangelo: *Ignudo*, detail photographed during cleaning; Sistine Chapel (1508–12), Vatican, Rome

taste or cult. There is a growing understanding that cleaning cannot restore a wall painting to its original state but only to the present state of the original materials, and also that every act of preservation involves subjective interpretations and judgements. After the degree of cleaning necessary has been decided, the cleaning materials and methods are selected depending on the nature of the substances to be removed and the condition and stability of the painted surfaces. The conservator makes his choice from a range of solvents, chemical agents, detergents and biological agents and begins the cleaning process on less important areas of the work, leaving the most significant and delicate regions to the end. If the painting has been the site of biological attack, disinfection and cleaning are usually carried out by washing the surface with water containing a fungicide.

The final stage in the restoration of wall paintings is the treatment of losses through inpainting. Although in the past deceptive techniques were adopted in the attempt to return wall paintings to their original glory, a number of inpainting methods are now in use that help to consolidate and unify the composition while still preserving the distinction between the original and the restorer's hand. One widely adopted technique is *tratteggio*, in which the

6. Wall painting by Giulio Romano: south wall of the *Sala dei Giganti* (1532–4), detail showing inpainting using the *tratteggio* technique, Palazzo del Te, Mantua

loss is filled with thin parallel lines of a pure hue, resolving at a distance into a neutral colour or a colour that blends in with the original (see fig. 6). Only easily soluble paints are used. Such sensitive approaches reflect the increasing awareness among conservators of the ethical implications of their treatments, as well as a great respect for the authenticity and the historical dimensions of the paintings under repair.

See also Secco, §2, and Technical examination, §VIII, 6.

BIBLIOGRAPHY

C. Cennini: *Il libro dell'arte* (*c.* 1390); Eng. trans. and notes by D. V. Thompson jr as *The Craftsman's Handbook: 'Il libro dell'arte'* (New Haven, 1933/*R* New York, 1954)

N. Heaton: 'The Mural Paintings of Knossos: An Investigation into the Method of their Production', *J. Royal Soc. A.*, lviii (1910), pp. 206–12

R. J. Gettens: 'The Materials in the Wall Paintings from Kizil in Chinese Turkestan', *Tech. Stud. Field F.A.*, vi (1937–8), pp. 281–94

R. Oertel: 'Wandmalerei und Zeichnung in Italien', *Mitt. Ksthist. Inst. Florenz*, v (1940), pp. 217–314

P. Duell and R. J. Gettens: 'A Review of the Problem of Aegean Wall Painting', *Tech. Stud. Field F.A.*, x (1941–2), pp. 178–223

L. Woolley and others: *Alalakh: An Account of the Excavations at Tell Atchana in the Hatay, 1937–1949* (Oxford, 1955), pp. 228–34

C. Wales: 'The Treatment of Wall Paintings at the Kariye Çamii', *Stud. Conserv.*, iii (1958), pp. 120–24

E. Borsook: *The Mural Painters of Tuscany from Cimabue to Andrea del Sarto* (London, 1960, rev. Oxford, 1980)

J. Mellaart: 'Excavations at Çatal Hüyük', *Anatol. Stud.*, xi (1961), pp. 159–95; xii (1962), pp. 41–65

U. Procacci: *Sinopie e affreschi* (Milan, 1961)

L. Tintori: 'Methods Used in Italy for Detaching Murals', *Recent Advances in Conservation: Contributions to the IIC Conference: Rome, 1961*, pp. 118–22

A. Lucas: *Ancient Egyptian Materials and Industries* (London, 1962)

C. Brandi: *Teoria del restauro* (Rome, 1963/*R* Turin, 1977)

L. Tintori, E. V. Sayre and L. J. Majewski: 'Studies for the Preservation of the Frescoes by Giotto in the Scrovegni Chapel at Padua', *Stud. Conserv.*, viii (1963), pp. 37–54

S. Augusti: 'Analysis of the Material and Technique of Ancient Mural Paintings', *Application of Science in Examination of Works of Art: Boston, 1965*, pp. 67–70

The Great Age of Fresco: Giotto to Pontormo (exh. cat. by M. Meiss, U. Procacci and others, New York, Met., 1968)

D. C. Winfield: 'Middle and Later Byzantine Wall Painting Methods: A Comparative Study', *Dumbarton Oaks Pap.*, xxii (1968), pp. 61–139

O. P. Agrawal: 'A Study on the Techniques of Indian Wall Paintings', *J. Ind. Mus.*, xxv–xxvi (1969–70), pp. 99–118

H. Lehmann: 'Dry Conservation of Mural Paintings', *Stud. Conserv.*, xv (1970), pp. 231–2

A. Reith: 'Maltechnik von Lascaux', *Maltechnik*, lxxvi/2 (1970), pp. 33–4

W. J. Young, ed.: *Application of Science in Examination of Works of Art, 1970* (Boston, 1973)

M. Lefèvre: 'La "Maladie verte" de Lascaux', *Stud. Conserv.*, xix (1974), pp. 126–56

M. A. S. Cameron, R. E. Jones and S. E. Philippakis: 'Analyses of Fresco Samples from Knossos', *Annu. Brit. Sch. Athens*, lxxii (1977), pp. 121–84

P. Mora, L. Mora and P. Philippot: *La Conservation des peintures murales* (Bologna, 1977; Eng. trans., London and Boston, 1984) [best survey of subject]

M. Matteini and A. Moles: 'A Preliminary Investigation of the Unusual Technique of Leonardo's Mural *The Last Supper*', *Stud. Conserv.*, xxiv (1979), pp. 125–33

Atti de XXIV congresso internazionale di storia dell'arte. La pittura nel XIV e XV secolo: Il contributo dell'analisi tecnica alla storia dell'arte: Bologna, 1979

F. Mancinelli: 'Raphael's *Coronation of Charlemagne* and its Cleaning', *Burl. Mag.*, cxxvi (1984), pp. 404–10

P. Burman, ed.: *Conservation of Wallpaintings: The International Scene* (London, 1986)

Case Studies in the Conservation of Stone and Wall Painting: Preprints of the Contributors to the Bologna Congress, 1986 (London, 1986)

'The Conservation of Wall Paintings', *Proceedings of a Symposium Organized by the Courtauld Institute of Art and the Getty Conservation Institute: London, 1987*

K. M. Wilson-Yang and G. Burns: 'The Stability of the Tomb of Nefertari, 1904–1987', *Stud. Conserv.*, xxxiv (1989), pp. 153–70

C. Danti, M. Matteini and A. Moles: *Le pitture murali: Tecniche, problemi, conservazione* (Florence, 1990) [extensive bibliog.]

CATHLEEN HOENIGER

Wallpaper. Paper, usually coloured or decorated with a hand- or machine-printed design, applied to the walls of a room.

I. Types. II. History. III. Conservation.

I. Types.

1. Painted. 2. Printed. 3. Flock.

1. PAINTED. Hand-painting as a technique in wallpaper production has been mainly used in the Western world in combination with printing processes. In the early to mid-18th century in England, France and Germany imitation Chinese wallpaper was produced by hand-colouring printed outlines, usually with gouache or tempera, or, rarely, an entire design might be hand-painted. Some engraved wallpapers printed from copper plates were also hand-coloured, either with watercolour or oil-based inks, although the latter produced flat, lustreless results compared with distemper printing. Sets of hand-painted wallpaper, in colours and grisaille, were produced as special orders in England in the 1760s for export to America, such as those ordered by Jeremiah Lee (1721–75) of Marblehead, MA, for the formal rooms of his house in the late 1760s (see Nylander, Redmond and Sander, figs 1–5, p. 7).

The lengths of paper imported into Europe from China from the late 17th century to the 19th were made up of pasted sheets up to 1.2 m wide joined together with an overlap to form lengths of over 3 m. Each sheet was a laminate of thin papers held together with starch pastes topped by a layer of white mulberry fibre paper (*mien lien*) and was probably painted with a white lead ground. Powdered mica was either mixed with the ground or dusted on to the surface, both to smooth it and to give a lustrous sheen. The outline of the design was drawn—or in some later examples printed—in black carbon ink, and inscriptions identifying individual motifs were added to aid colouring in. The outlines were then filled in using ground pigments mixed with animal glue used as gouache or tempera. Details were applied last, and coloured glazes were sometimes added to highlight such motifs as flowers or fruit. After lining with a thin bamboo paper and then a mulberry paper, the sheets were probably stretched over a drying board and then trimmed. Each length in a set of paper was numbered to show its sequence in the design. Additional sheets were supplied so that individual motifs could be cut out and used to hide joins or to enhance the design.

2. PRINTED.

(i) Hand-printing.

(a) Woodblock. Woodblock-printing is the commonest method of hand-printing wallpaper. Block cutters made up the block from a laminate of three or four woods, generally two white woods, such as pine or poplar, topped by a fine-grained fruitwood, for example apple or pear, that was more suitable both for carving and use as a printing surface. The design was carved in relief, and thin wooden wedges could be inserted to print delicate lines or dots. Small brass pitch pins were fitted into the sides of the block to help register the design on the paper.

In the 16th and 17th centuries the technique involved inking the block, which was positioned face up on the printing table, carefully placing the paper to be printed over the block and pushing a weighted roller across: the paper was then peeled off and hung up to dry. Colour was usually added, if required, using a stencil (*see* §(b) below). With the introduction of multicolour distemper printing in the mid-18th century, designs were divided up according to colour (usually by the blockmaker), and a new block was carved to print each shade. A very large repeat design that was to be printed in several colours might require two or more blocks for each colour if the repeat exceeded the width of the block (a standard 21 ins (525 mm) in Britain by the 19th century but smaller in France).

1. Woodblock-printing (left) and flocking (centre) of wallpaper in a paper-stainer's workshop, oil on canvas, 635×534 mm, *c.* 1842 (Hull, Ferens Art Gallery)

With the introduction of the wallpaper piece—a roll made up of pasted sheets—at the end of the 17th century, sizing and grounding could be done along the entire roll. First size and then a coloured ground were spread across the length and width of the roll using elongated rectangular brushes; finally, a round brush was used to give uniform coverage. Different finishes could be added: passing the paper face down through a rounded copper roller produced a very smooth finish; brushing the surface of the paper with a hand brush produced a striated effect; adding powdered mica to the ground colour gave a lustrous finish; or varnish could be applied to brighten the coloured ground. Later innovations included the *irisé*, or blended colour grounds, developed by the French firm of ZUBER & CIE from 1819.

Once sizing and grounding were completed, the roll to be printed was fixed to an iron rod at the side of the printing table. Beside this stood the colour tray, a square trough with a layer of paper scraps covered with water in the bottom, then a tight-fitting wooden frame covered with calfskin and finally another felt- or cloth-covered frame. An apprentice spread the colour to be printed on to the cloth or felt, and the block was pressed into it lightly by hand. The 'water-bed' principle of the colour tray ensured an even take-up of colour. The block was then positioned on the paper using the pitch pins and tapped with a rounded hammer to print the image clearly (see fig. 1). Any areas of insufficient colour were touched up by hand. In the 19th century a foot-operated leverage system was introduced using a weighted wooden cross lever fixed on to the back of the printing table. When the block was positioned on the paper, the lever was swung on to the batten on the back of the block and pressure applied by weights. After the paper had been printed, a system of rods and ropes carried it away to dry in festoons before another colour could be printed. Gilding could be added by printing the design in a slow-drying adhesive over which the silver leaf or bronze powder was spread.

Woodblock-printing became increasingly rare in the 20th century but continued to be used mainly for luxury wallpapers produced by such companies as ARTHUR SANDERSON and Sons Ltd, which used the original Morris & Co. blocks acquired in 1925 after the takeover of Jeffrey & Co. by the Wall Paper Manufacturers Ltd.

(b) Stencilling. In the late 17th century stencils, probably of leather or oilcloth, were used to add watercolour to woodblock-printed outlines on paper hangings (*see* STENCILLING). Registration was often poor as large brushes were used, and colours were limited. Stencils continued to be used until *c.* 1760, most notably by the French firm of PAPILLON, which refined the technique using watercolour washes and inks. Stencils were also used for large-scale flock designs, which would have required more than one woodblock to print the adhesive.

In the late 19th century stencilling was employed as a technique in its own right, principally to print friezes, most notably by SHAND KYDD LTD (see colour pl. V, fig. 2). Stencils were used both for background and motifs, although woodblocks were generally used to print the outlines, thereby concealing the stencil ties and hiding any poor registration or colour seepage from beneath the stencil plates. These were made of copper, brass or zinc (from the mid-1920s), although varnished cartridge paper was thought to produce the best results. Different types of brushes and sponges were used to produce a range of print effects, usually with water- rather than oil-based paint. By 1912 the aerograph spray painter had largely replaced these more labour-intensive techniques.

(ii) Machine-printing. The first wallpaper-printing processes to be mechanized were sizing and grounding, and by the beginning of the 19th century power-driven cylindrical brushes were replacing hand techniques. In the 1820s French manufacturers, using cylindrical rollers and the newly available continuous paper rolls, attempted to apply textile-printing techniques to wallpaper. By *c.* 1830 Zuber & Cie had succeeded in printing stripes by steam power, using brass cylinders into which parallel grooves had been cut.

In 1839 Potter & Ross of Darwen, Lancs, developed a steam-driven wallpaper-printing machine that used engraved copper rollers. By 1840 POTTER & CO. had replaced the copper rollers with wooden ones that produced much better results using distemper colours. In this 'surface-printing machine' the paper was fed around a large rotating drum. Rollers were arranged horizontally around the base of the drum, and the paper was printed as it passed over each roller in turn (see fig. 2). As in block-printing, each roller carried a different part of the design and printed in one colour, although different shades could be produced by overprinting. Potters also perfected a method of using a belt system to fill the colour tray for each roller, thus ensuring an even supply of colour.

In the early 1870s British manufacturers revived the use of copper cylinders. Etched with an intaglio design, the cylinders printed in spirit- and oil-based colours, which were resistant to water and gave a semi-washable finish to what became known as sanitary wallpaper. Intaglio printing produced delicate and detailed effects and a very smooth finish, which was often varnished for added protection. In 1884 Lightbown, Aspinall & Co., Lancs, introduced multicoloured sanitaries.

In the 1870s embossing techniques developed from the simple use of two heated metal rollers to print an imitation of silk moiré—patented in France by Isidore Leroy in 1842—to the production of much more elaborate raised designs, often incorporating gold or silver, by such companies as Paul Balin in France and Jeffrey & Co. and Woollams & Co. in England.

In 1877 a new type of wall covering, Lincrusta Walton, was invented by a British engineer, Frederick Walton. It was made from a semi-liquid linoleum-like mixture, which was forced between two metal rollers, one of which carried the design to be produced as a raised pattern. Once dry, the material hardened and could either be used plain, decorated (often once hung on the wall) or varnished. The

2. Machine-printing of wallpaper in up to 12 colours, engraving from *Scientific American* (24 July 1880)

wide range of designs that were produced included imitations of tiles, architectural ornaments and leather. The disadvantage of Lincrusta Walton was its weight, and in 1887 Thomas J. Palmer took out a patent on a similar but lighter-weight material, Anaglypta, which was launched in 1887.

In the 20th century new printing techniques applied to the mass production of wallpaper included silkscreen-printing, first used in Britain by JOHN LINE & SONS LTD (see colour pl. V, fig. 3), machine photogravure (see PRINTS, §III, 4) and flexographic printing, in which rubber rollers replace the surface-printing rollers.

3. FLOCK. The art of flocking on cloth and canvas in order to make them resemble more expensive wall coverings was known in the Middle Ages, and flocked hangings were in use in Holland in the late 16th century. By the mid- to late 17th century paper-manufacturing techniques had improved sufficiently to produce paper that was strong enough to be covered either wholly or partially with cloth clippings to imitate cut velvet or tapestries, and methods of adhering the flock to painted paper were also developed.

In the technique developed in England in the 18th century, and subsequently copied in France, the paper piece was first grounded with a watercolour wash and allowed to dry. From *c.* 1750 the ground was often block-printed in distemper colours in a diaper or other simple design prior to flocking. The design to be flocked was then stencilled or block-printed in a slow-drying adhesive, such as linseed oil mixed with litharge ground with white lead, on which the flock—wool clippings, bleached, dyed and ground to powder—was scattered by hand. The flocked paper could be compressed under a board to improve adhesion. After drying, any excess flock was

brushed off. In the 1750s two-stage grounding was perfected; after the ground had dried a varnish, made of oil of turpentine, resin and gums, and sometimes pigmented, was brushed over the piece, both to improve the adhesion of the flock and to brighten the ground. Experiments were also carried out using cotton and silk flock.

In the 19th century the process was modified. After the paper roll had been printed with adhesive, about two metres of paper at a time were laid in a flocking box—an elongated drum with a hinged lid and a base of stretched canvas (see fig. 1 above). The flock was sifted over the paper, then, with the lid closed, the base was beaten by hand from below with two sticks to align the flock fibres and ensure they settled into the adhesive. After the entire piece had been flocked, often several times to build up a raised surface, the paper was hung up to dry vertically, thereby also removing any excess flock. Additional colours were added by block-printing over the fibres. In *c.* 1877 WOOLLAMS & CO. of London introduced raised flocks, a process that combined embossing and flocking by moulding the paper under pressure with a heated die after printing. Machine techniques have involved spraying powdered flock on to paper prepared with adhesive and, in the 20th century, the electrostatic application of synthetic flock.

BIBLIOGRAPHY

R. Dossie: 'On the Manufacture of Paper Hangings', *The Handmaid to the Arts, Teaching: I. A Perfect Knowledge of the Materia Pictoria*, ii (London, 1758, 3/1796), pp. 304–16

C. Lynn: *Wallpaper in America* (New York, 1980)

C. C. Oman and J. Hamilton: *Wallpapers: A History and Illustrated Catalogue of the Collection of the Victoria and Albert Museum* (London, 1982)

F. Teynac, P. Nolot and J. D. Vivien: *Wallpaper: A History* (London, 1982)

Historic Paper Hangings from Temple Newsam and Other English Houses (exh. cat. by A. Wells-Cole, Leeds, Temple Newsam House, 1983)
A Decorative Art: 19th-Century Wallpapers from the Whitworth Art Gallery (exh. cat. by J. Banham, U. Manchester, Whitworth A.G., 1985)
R. C. Nylander, E. Redmond and P. J. Sander: *Wallpaper in New England* (Boston, 1986)

II. History.

1. Europe and North America. 2. Chinese export.

1. EUROPE AND NORTH AMERICA.

(i) Before *c.* 1800. (ii) After *c.* 1800.

(i) Before c. *1800.* The process of applying paper already printed with a repeating design to the wall has its origins in western Europe. The earliest papers may have been portable or temporary wall coverings, cheap alternatives to such costly materials as tapestry, painted cloth or leather hangings, woven textiles or, in particular, wall paintings. The earliest extant European printed wallpaper was found during restoration work in 1911, decorating the beams of a room in the Master's lodge at Christ's College, Cambridge, and has been dated *c.* 1509. Fragments of paper found in their original settings are very rare before the late 17th century; this may be a reflection of the scarcity of their use as well as the ephemeral nature of the medium. These early papers consisted of a single woodblock design, printed in black ink on individual sheets of plain paper, by printers who produced goods for a range of purposes. By the 16th century the French *dominotiers*, originally printers of popular illustrations and playing cards, were printing small-scale diaper patterns and were also producing marbled papers for binding books or decorating cased furniture. Surviving examples in England (lining-paper for Camden's deed box, 1622; Oxford, Ashmolean) indicate that papers used to line deed boxes and furniture were also applied to the wall; this was probably also the practice elsewhere in Europe. By the late 17th century colour was being introduced, either by painting the plain paper in pigment prior to printing or by stencilling in two or more colours after the outline of the design had been printed.

3. Heraldic pattern wallpaper, woodblock print in black ink, 420×572 mm, from Besford Court, Hereford & Worcs, *c.* 1550–75 (London, Victoria and Albert Museum)

The limited range of designs that survives from the 16th and 17th centuries in England (or English papers exported to America) are derived from textiles or heraldry. The floral motifs of blackwork embroidery appear in designs for paper used both for linings and to hang on the wall (e.g. 1615; Oxford, Ashmolean). Larger-scale heraldic designs imitate those found in wall paintings and cloth hangings and show the beginning of the technique of treating each sheet as separate panels of the pattern, which interconnect once seen on the wall (see fig. 3). In the late 17th century narrative scenes from outdoor life or mythology were also taken up, inspired by contemporary tapestries or illustrations. A series of late 17th-century papers found in England and the USA (e.g. 'Stag Hunt', late 17th century: U. Manchester, Whitworth A.G.; Colonial Williamsburg, VA) evidently used a common design source, which suggests that the range of available patterns was limited and was supplied by a small number of printers. Ceiling papers imitating wood effects have been found in Holland and other parts of Europe.

By the end of the 17th century the trade in papers was established in England and France, although there were still no exclusive makers of paper hangings (the English term for wallpapers used into the 19th century) or *papiers de tapisserie*. Expansion in the market was combined with technological developments. In England by the 1680s individual sheets of paper were being pasted together to form a 'piece' or roll, which became standardized to 12 yards (10.8 m) long by 21 ins (525 mm) wide. Grounding and printing were carried out over the entire piece, enabling joins to be hidden and complex designs to be printed. Jean-Michel Papillon's descriptions of the working practices of his father, Jean Papillon, a French maker of *papiers de tapisserie* who had workshops in Paris during the 17th and 18th centuries, show that in France block-printing was still carried out on individual sheets (although designs were formed over more than one sheet) or straight on to a wall already hung with unprinted paper. Such firms as Papillon used better quality paper than their predecessors and experimented with stencilling, using different types of pigment.

In England around 1680 improved paper quality and the invention of the piece enabled flock, already in use on cloth and leather hangings, to be successfully applied to paper. Early designs were often of simple scrolling foliage, but by the 1730s larger-scale and more complex designs were being produced (e.g. panel of flock wallpaper from Hurlcote Manor, Towcester, Northants, early 18th century; London, V&A). Flocked paper was able to compete with brocade, damask and cut velvet both in appearance and price: in the 1750s even an elaborate high-quality flock cost less than half the price of cut velvet. Flock was nevertheless still a luxury item. A pattern imitating a contemporary silk damask, flocked in red, was hung in the offices of the Privy Council in Whitehall, London, *c.* 1735 (see fig. 4); by the end of the 1760s this pattern had been hung in various colour-ways in the reception rooms and best bedchambers of country houses throughout Britain and at the castle of Strömsholm in Sweden. Blue, green and red were the most popular colours, and by the mid-1750s English flocks—or *papiers bleus d'Angleterre* as they were called—were both available and highly fashionable in

4. Wallpaper pattern of stylized flowers and foliage, flocked in red, 1.87×1.54 m, from the offices of the Privy Council, Whitehall, London, *c.* 1735 (London, Victoria and Albert Museum)

France, where, in 1754, the Marquise de Pompadour used them in her apartments. However, by the end of the decade Parisian manufacturers had perfected the flocking technique and were advertising *papiers veloutés* in damask designs as perfect as the English product.

Flocks dominated the luxury end of the market from *c.* 1730 to 1760. Cheaper block-prints could only be produced in two colours—a painted ground overprinted in one colour—with additional colours laboriously applied by stencil. In the early 1750s JOHN BAPTIST JACKSON set up business in London printing wallpapers in chiaroscuro (*see* PRINTS, §III, 1; *see also* WOODCUT, CHIAROSCURO) from woodblocks. Jackson used oil-based pigments to colour his designs, but the business was a failure, and by the 1760s distemper printing from woodblocks was well established in England and France. Pigment was carried in a water-based medium bound with glue, which produced thick, matt, opaque effects when printed, often with a slightly chalky appearance as whiting, in the form of chalk, was often added.

Distemper colours enabled the development of multicolour printing. Many designs were inspired by textiles and paper hangings imported from India and East Asia. The 'Indiennes' floral chintzes (*see* COTTON) were adapted for wallpapers in both England and France and spawned a wealth of designs, from sinuous curves of rich flowers and foliage, and later ribbon and lace, to simple floral sprigs and stripes. The first Chinese paper hangings

appeared in Europe in the mid-17th century (*see* §2 below); such was the demand for these novelties that block-printed and painted imitations were produced in England and France.

Although the initial development of distemper printing took place in England, it was the firm set up by JEAN-BAPTISTE RÉVEILLON just outside Paris in 1759 that exploited the technique to the full, using high-quality wove paper pasted up into rolls and fast colours developed by the firm. Designs were often printed on a blue ground using soft shades with touches of bright colour, such as a characteristic orange. The crucial element in his success was the employment of decorative artists to produce patterns for the firm. They were inspired by *toile de Jouy* textile patterns and by discoveries at Classical sites in Italy. One of the firm's best-known designs is an arabesque pattern of exotic birds, bouquets and garlands (see colour pl. IV, fig. 1). Réveillon's products were exported, particularly to the USA, and demand for them influenced the establishment of wallpaper manufactories in Germany. Linen cloth, which was treated with oil and wax before printing or painting in colours, was already being produced for the domestic market and for export in towns such as Berlin and Potsdam. By the end of the 18th century, wallpaper factories had been opened in such centres as Leipzig (e.g. by Gottfried Wilhelm, who advertised rolls of wallpaper in the latest fashion from 1775–80), Potsdam (e.g. Isaac Joel) and Kassel (J. C. Arnold, founded in 1758).

Trompe l'oeil wallpapers were also developed in the 18th century. In England the brief fashion for print rooms *c.* 1755–65 was taken up by paper stainers, including Jackson, who produced plain grounds ready printed with engravings in *trompe l'oeil* frames linked by imitation swags and ribbons. Three-dimensional representations of Gothic architectural schemes were also popular for halls and staircases. In the USA 'architectural' papers reproducing mouldings, stuccowork and other details remained popular into the 19th century.

At the beginning of the 18th century paper hangings were being sold by stationers, booksellers and general printers; by the 1790s wallpaper was being manufactured and sold by specialist firms operating from a shop or warehouse, usually with workshops attached. By *c.* 1750 there were 12 wallpaper businesses in Paris and others in provincial towns. A similar development seems to have taken place in Britain. Before the 1760s there had been no indigenous wallpaper manufacturers in America, and wallpaper had been imported from England, East Asia and France. By the 1790s American firms were established in Philadelphia (e.g. William Poyntell), Boston (e.g. J. F. Bumstead & Co.) and New York (e.g. John Rugar), often advertising the fact that members of their staff were trained in Europe. Unlike French wallpaper firms, which from 1771 were required to stamp their name at each end of a roll, British products only received a tax stamp. Duty was imposed on British-made paper hangings from 1712 to 1836, on imported papers from 1773 and on Chinese imports from 1792.

(ii) After c. 1800. During the first half of the 19th century French manufacturers were pre-eminent in wallpaper design and printing, producing elaborately block-printed

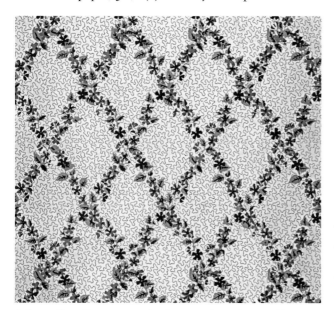

5. Ivy trellis wallpaper pattern by Potter & Co., colour machine print, 546×527 mm, 1840s (Manchester, University of Manchester, Whitworth Art Gallery)

scenic decorations and *trompe l'oeil* patterns. Scenic decorations were first exhibited by Zuber & Cie and JOSEPH DUFOUR & CIE in Paris in 1806. They were designed to form a continuous scene around the room in the manner of Chinese papers but with the addition of perspective and three-dimensional effects. The technique of using block-printing to reproduce such painterly effects had been introduced on a small scale by the firm of Albert & Robert in Paris in the 1790s, but these vast scenes could consist of up to thirty individual lengths and take two years to produce. The choice of subject was therefore conservative, often based on popular engravings or printed panoramas, and included topographical views, exotic landscapes (see colour pl. III), military campaigns and literary and mythological themes. During the 1830s designs became increasingly naturalistic, and in the 1850s and 1860s DESFOSSÉ & KARTH produced a series based on garden and landscape subjects. Cheaper and more adaptable pilaster decorations, which used vertical and horizontal borders around central panels, were developed, as were *trompe l'oeil* wallpaper imitations of such materials as draped and swagged silks and velvets, which, when joined in lengths, could imitate the effect of a wall hung with fabric. They were often hung with an elaborately printed border, using flocking, gilding and silvering to highlight details (see colour pl. IV, fig. 3).

At the same time as hand-printing techniques were being perfected, European and American manufacturers were exploring methods of machine-printing cheap wallpaper on a large scale. A small-scale version of a machine that could supply long lengths of paper had been invented by a Frenchman, Louis Robert, in 1799. His original design was developed on a large scale and produced by Henry and Sealy Fourdrinier in England in 1805, although the Excise Office did not permit its use for wallpaper printing

in Britain until 1830. Continuous paper was in use at Zuber & Cie in France by 1820, and by 1827 a Fourdrinier machine had been exported to the USA.

Attempts had been made since the late 18th century to adapt textile printing techniques to print wallpaper, but progress had been slow owing to the problems of paper, colour and power supply. The early versions of the 'surface-printing machine', patented by Potter & Co. in 1840, which printed only small repeats in a restricted range of thin colours (see fig. 5), were rapidly improved, and by 1850 up to eight colours could be printed. In 1856 the aniline dyes developed by an English chemist, W. H. Perkins, became available, and bright blues, greens and mauves began to appear in wallpaper patterns. Such firms as LIGHTBOWN, ASPINALL & CO. in England and J. C. Arnold (1752–1842) in Kassel, Germany, were producing cheap machine-prints on a huge scale by 1860, when British firms produced nine million yards of wallpaper, nearly eight times the amount that had been printed in 1834.

From 1860 to 1900 developments in manufacturing techniques were mainly in methods of creating raised or gilded surfaces. These new wall coverings, produced by such firms as PAUL BALIN in France (embossed, flocked and gilded designs), JEFFREY & CO. in London and M. H. Birge & Sons Co. in New York (both of whom produced imitation leather designs) and Woollams & Co., England, who developed embossed flocks, were partly responsible for the decline in elaborate French block-prints. Other innovations during this period included mother-of-pearl wallpaper (*Perlmuttapeten*), developed in the 1860s by Carl Herting of Einbeck, which used transparent glazes over small pieces of stamped metal that formed the central motif in a design.

In the 1870s cheaper raised wall coverings appeared in Britain in the shape of Lincrusta Walton (also manufactured in New York from 1879) and later Anaglypta. Also in the 1870s the technique of copper-roller printing using rollers etched with intaglio designs was finally applied with success to wallpaper to produce sanitary, washable papers that were being produced in multicoloured, detailed, pictorial designs by 1884 (*see* §I, 2(ii) above).

In Europe and America the wallpaper industry of the second half of the 19th century was dominated by ornate, technically elaborate products. British wallpapers were inspired by the swagged draperies, Rococo scrollwork and naturalistic flower designs of French manufacturers (see colour pl. IV, fig. 2) or machine-printed pictorial papers. The design reform movement in Britain was to change all this: three-dimensional, illusionistic effects were condemned by such critics as Charles Locke Eastlake. The architect A. W. N. Pugin had used two-dimensional motifs from medieval architecture for the papers he designed for the New Palace of Westminster, London, in 1847 (London, V&A), and his contemporary Owen Jones also designed wallpapers using small-scale, flat, geometric motifs. Jones's designs were among those printed by Jeffrey & Co., an established firm that had taken over the printing of wallpaper for Morris & Co. in 1864 after Morris's attempts to print from zinc etched plates had failed. From 1871 Jeffrey & Co. was run by Metford Warner (1843–1930), who reacted to Eastlake's criticisms by commissioning designs from him and many other prominent British architects and artists, including WALTER CRANE. Although not all these designs were commercially successful—the majority were block-printed, reaching only a limited market—they were exhibited internationally, establishing the firm as the leading manufacturer of avant-garde designs. Eastlake's criticisms were echoed by other European and American critics, who encouraged manufacturers to commission art wallpaper designs in the English style, and in the late 19th century Jeffrey & Co. opened an office in New York. The firm also introduced in 1872 the division of the wall into three horizontal sections: dado, filling and frieze. The complementary designs produced for each section could be printed up as a complete length, angled versions of which were produced for stairs. Although intended for lofty rooms or public buildings, the fashion was vigorously promoted for use in the home, and certain elements were used into the 20th century.

By the 1890s designers of the British Arts and Crafts Movement, including Walter Crane and C. F. A. Voysey, were producing deep friezes with a complementary wallpaper and abandoning the dado (see colour pl. V, fig. 1). 'Crown' decorations, in which the filling paper and frieze were incorporated in a single design, were popularized for the mass market around the turn of the century, often featuring flowering plants whose blossoms formed the frieze.

Machine-, block- and stencilling-printing methods were used on textured papers for the frieze, which by 1900 was often hung above a whitewashed wall or plain textured paper. The deep friezes produced by Shand Kydd Ltd (see colour pl. V, fig. 2) and designs by the SILVER STUDIO for Alexander Rottmann & Co., an importer and manufacturer of Japanese leather and grass papers, illustrate the range of hand-stencilling effects. Popular patterns were inspired by Art Nouveau floral motifs, such as those designed by Alphonse Mucha for French and American manufacturers and reproduced in his book *Documents decoratifs* (Paris, 1902), or scenic designs including landscapes.

Sixteen major German wallpaper manufacturers amalgamated in 1889 in order to control prices and competition more effectively. In 1899 major manufacturers in Britain followed suit and formed the Wall Paper Manufacturers Ltd. One result was a loss of avant-garde designs, which were mostly promoted by smaller firms, many of them block-printers, outside the consortium. Several of these firms, for example Jeffrey & Co., were taken over by the association.

In 1911 Paul Poiret founded the Atelier Martine, in Paris, which produced designs for decorative art including wallpapers. Its colourful, loosely drawn flower and leaf motifs (e.g. 'Poppies', *c.* 1912; Paris, Bib. Forney) were briefly popular in fashionable interiors, but when the European wallpaper industry returned to production after World War I, decorators had turned to other ways of introducing pattern into interiors. There were exceptions: during the late 1910s and early 1920s Dagobert Peche, a member of the Wiener Werkstätte, designed wallpapers based on abstract floral and plant motifs (e.g. 'Daphnis', 1924–5; Kassel, Dt. Tapetenmus.) for Austrian and German manufacturers.

In Britain the use of the frieze alone gave way to cut-out appliqué decorations for use below the picture rail and 'complete decorations' of borders, horizontal stiles and corners, which were applied to plain, textured filling papers. The designs reflected brief fashions for chinoiserie and Egyptian-inspired motifs in the 1920s. More 'modern' geometric motifs were introduced in the ubiquitous 'Autumn Tints' during the 1930s.

After World War II manufacturers concentrated on the rebuilding and modernization of machinery to cater for an expanding market. Designers such as Bent Karlby (*b* 1912) brought a distinct identity to Scandinavian wallpapers in such brightly coloured designs as the floral sprig in 'Floral Danica', produced by the Danish firm of Dahls Tapetfabrik in 1951. Later in the 1950s designs became more abstract, for example Viola Grasten's (*b* 1910) 'G String' (1953) by AB Durotapet of Sweden, based on the distorting effects of sound waves. These simple, regular, machine-printed patterns were influential on such other European producers as John Line & Sons Ltd (see colour pl. V, fig. 3). In 1949 the Wall Paper Manufacturers Ltd in Britain produced the Lancastria collection of large-scale designs, for export to the USA, for use on one wall in a room. Rotary screenprinting was first used commercially by British wallpaper firms during the 1950s, notably for the Palladio collections printed by the Lightbown, Aspinall branch of the Wall Paper Manufacturers Ltd from 1955 to 1963. In the 1960s several new techniques were introduced into mass production in Europe and America: photogravure (used extensively in Germany); flexographic printing; and the application of PVC to paper and vinyl, which enabled new pattern effects to be created.

BIBLIOGRAPHY

A. V. Sugden and J. L. Edmundson: *A History of English Wallpaper, 1509–1914* (London, 1925)

H. Clouzot and C. Follot: *Histoire du papier peint en France* (Paris, 1935)

E. A. Entwisle: *The Book of Wallpaper* (London, 1954)

——: *A Literary History of Wallpaper* (London, 1960)

B. Greysmith: *Wallpaper* (London, 1976)

C. Lynn: *Wallpaper in America from the Seventeenth Century to World War I* (New York, 1980)

O. Nouvel: *Wallpapers of France, 1800–1850* (London, 1981)

E. W. Mick: *Hauptwerke des Deutschen Tapetenmuseum in Kassel* (Tokyo, 1981), 2 vols

C. C. Oman and J. Hamilton: *Wallpapers: A History and Illustrated Catalogue of the Collection of the Victoria and Albert Museum* (London, 1982)

F. Teynac, P. Nolot and J. D. Vivien: *Wallpaper: A History* (London, 1982)

J. Hamilton: *An Introduction to Wallpaper* (London, 1983)

Historic Paper Hangings from Temple Newsam and Other English Houses (exh. cat. by A. Wells-Cole, Leeds, Temple Newsam House, 1983)

A Decorative Art: 19th-century Wallpaper in the Whitworth Art Gallery (exh. cat. by J. Banham, U. Manchester, Whitworth A.G., 1985)

R. Nylander, E. Redmond and P. J. Sander: *Wallpaper in New England* (Boston, 1986)

M. Schoeser: *Fabrics and Wallpapers: Twentieth Century* (London, 1986)

B. Jacque and O. Nouvel-Kammerer: *Le Papier peint décor d'illusion* (Barenbach, 1987)

Papiers peints panoramiques (exh. cat., ed. O. Nouvel-Kammerer; Paris, Mus. A. Dec., 1990)

E. F. Koldeweij, M. J. F. Knuijt and E. G. M. Adriaansz: *Achter het behang: 400 jaar wanddecoratie in het Nederlandse binnenhuis* (Amsterdam, 1991)

R. C. Nylander: *Wallpapers for Historic Buildings* (Washington, DC, 1992)

London Wallpapers: Their Manufacture and Use, 1690–1840 (exh. cat. by T. Rosaman, London, RIBA, 1992)

L. Hoskins, ed.: *The Papered Wall* (London, 1994)

CLARE TAYLOR

2. CHINESE EXPORT. Hand-painted Chinese wallpapers first appeared in Europe in the late 17th century. In response to the vogue for CHINOISERIE, they were made specifically for the European market in imitation of the hanging scrolls used, sometimes in a series, in the homes of the wealthy in China. The Chinese themselves did not use elaborate papers of this kind. Father Louis Le Comte, a Jesuit missionary, noted the use of scrolls in China in the 1690s but added, 'Others only whiten the Chamber, or glew Paper upon it'. Later accounts (Chambers, 1757; Anderson, 1795) indicate that plain papers were preferred.

There is little or no documentation relating to the development of the trade in Chinese wallpapers. It appears that most were imported to the West through London by the East India Company, but some were taken directly to France or the Netherlands by other agencies. None of the earliest accounts of goods imported mentions wallpaper: it seems to have been classed as a minor product and carried as 'private trade' rather than being inventoried separately. The papers were supplied in sets of 25 or 40 rolls, each approximately 3.5 m long by 1 m wide. This length suited most European interiors, but an undecorated area of background colour was usually left at the top of each sheet so that the length could be readily adapted. Each length was made up of several smaller sheets joined together, as were European wallpapers at that time.

Chinese papers with their rich, clear colours and exquisite draughtsmanship, unrivalled by the relatively crude printed papers produced in Europe in the 17th century, established a new fashion for wallpaper and were used extensively in England and France; they appeared, though less commonly, in Wales, Scotland, Ireland, Italy and Germany, as well as in the USA (examples in New York, Cooper-Hewitt Mus.; Winterthur, DE, Du Pont Winterthur Mus.). They were considered appropriate decoration for private sitting-rooms, bedrooms and, sometimes, the best apartments (e.g. the state bedrooms at Erddig, Clwyd, NT, and Nostell Priory, W. Yorks). There are frequent references in 18th-century letters and journals to 'Japan' or 'India' papers, both erroneous terms used indiscriminately for all kinds of East Asian imports.

Chinese papers were much sought after and very valuable, so they were rarely (if ever) pasted directly on to the walls. Instead, the sheets were mounted on canvas stretched over battens, which were then nailed to the walls. This method had the advantage of making these expensive papers portable so they could be moved to other rooms when redecoration or refurbishment took place. It also offered the papers some protection against damp. Consequently there are a very large number of intact examples of Chinese wallpapers in English houses.

The sheets were hung in sequence to form a continuous decoration around the room: unused and untrimmed rolls found at Penrhyn Castle, Gwynedd, NT, are marked with Chinese numbers (in the centre of the bottom *r* edge), indicating the sequence in which they should be hung to achieve a flowing design. Alternatively, but more rarely, they were framed as individual panels with a European chinoiserie border; an unusual example of this survives at Saltram House, Devon, NT (see ENGLAND, fig. 41). Spare sheets were often supplied with each set so extra birds, flowers or branches could be cut out and pasted on to the

hangings, either to cover damaged areas and disguise joins or to embellish the overall effect, since the Chinese designs were not always sufficiently ornate for Western tastes.

All known examples of Chinese wallpaper in Europe are hand-painted, though there are two examples (London, V&A, E.412, 413-1924, Oman and Hamilton, cat. no. 655; and London, V&A, E.21146-1957, Oman and Hamilton, cat. no. 676) where the outlines have been printed. Black carbon ink outlines were filled in with flat colour, gouache or tempera; flowers and fruit sometimes have coloured glazes. The papers can generally be divided into three classes, according to the design and predominant motifs. Most surviving examples are of the so-called 'bird and flower' type, in which a flowering tree on a rocky base fills each sheet, extending the length of the paper. Bamboo, irises, roses, peonies, plums and other flowering shrubs are depicted around the roots of these trees, while birds and butterflies are to be seen in the higher branches. The composition is silhouetted against a plain-coloured ground, often cream or buff but sometimes a rich blue (e.g. London, V&A, E.3674-3682-1913, Oman and Hamilton, cat. no. 657) or green and occasionally pink. The early papers were the simplest in design, but, presumably in response to the Western demand for variety, the later 18th-century papers are busier, with birdcages suspended from branches and trelliswork, ornamental pools and shrubs in porcelain vases crowding the foreground (e.g. London, V&A; see colour pl. VI).

One of the most remarkable features of the early papers is their strict botanical accuracy. Indeed all the flora and fauna depicted are identifiable species. The botanist Sir Joseph Banks noted that 'some of the plants which are common to China and Java, as bamboo, are better figured there than by the best botanical authors that I have seen'. This detailed naturalistic style, though stemming in part from the traditions of Chinese painting, was a further response to European tastes. As John Barrow observed in 1804, 'the Chinese having found that the representation of natural objects are more in request among foreigners, they pay strict attention to the subject that may be required.' In later papers, though, errors were often made, with two different kinds of flower or fruit growing from the same plant. Generally, by the late 18th century the naturalistic style was abandoned in favour of the fantastic or whimsical rendered in strident colours.

The second group of Chinese papers is dominated by human figures engaged in various activities. Recurring subjects include silk-weaving, ceramic production, the cultivation and preparation of tea and other scenes of daily life (for example at Coutts' Bank in The Strand, London, and Ramsbury Manor, Wilts). As an alternative to views of city life, a number of surviving papers represent hunting scenes. A fragment with figures on an unusually large scale shows an open-air theatrical performance (see fig. 6). In these papers the landscape is represented in accordance with Chinese pictorial conventions for space, depth and perspective. These panoramic papers were more expensive than the ubiquitous 'bird and flower' type. According to a letter in the archive at Dunster Castle, Somerset, NT, 'Indian paper representing the several stages of a Chinese manufacture—the figures very compleat and intersperst with romantick views' cost at least seven shillings a yard,

PLATE I

Wall painting

1. Wall painting of a garden, from the tomb of Nebamun, Thebes, Egypt, *c.* 1400 BC (London, British Museum)

2. Wall painting of a garden scene (detail), from the Villa of Livia, Prima Porta, late 1st century BC (Rome, Museo Nazionale Romano delle Terme)

1. Wall painting of the *Anastasis* ('Harrowing of Hell'; early 14th century), in the apse of the parekklesion of the church of Christ the Saviour in Chora, Istanbul

2. Wall painting by Simone Martini: *Maestà* (1312–15), Sala del Mappamondo, Palazzo Pubblico, Siena

PLATE III

Wallpaper

Great Indian Tiger Hunt (detail), wallpaper by Joseph Dufour & Cie, Paris, colour printed from woodblocks, 2.27×1.60 m, from the series *Views of India*, 1815 (Manchester, University of Manchester, Whitworth Art Gallery)

1. Arabesque wallpaper panel by Jean-Baptiste Réveillon, colour printed from woodblocks, from near Paris, c. 1785–8 (Paris, Musée des Arts Décoratifs)

2. Wallpaper with pattern of lace, ribbons and roses, colour printed from woodblocks on satin ground with flocking, 640×500 mm, from France, c. 1850 (Uxbridge, Arthur Sanderson & Sons Ltd)

3. Wallpaper frieze of drapery by Zuber & Cie, colour printed from woodblocks with flocking and overprinting, 490×690 mm, from Paris, 1826 (Rixheim, Musée du Papier Peint)

PLATE V   Wallpaper

1. Wallpaper design by Walter Crane, printed by Jeffrey & Co., colour printed from woodblocks, frieze of *Fruit* (right), 546×1010 mm, detail of filling of *Orange Tree* (below right), 1.57×1.06 m, from London, 1902–3 (Manchester, University of Manchester, Whitworth Art Gallery)

2. *Roma*, wallpaper frieze by William Shand Kydd, colour printed and stencilled on Japanese grasspaper, 740×1204 mm, *c.* 1900 (Manchester, University of Manchester, Whitworth Art Gallery)

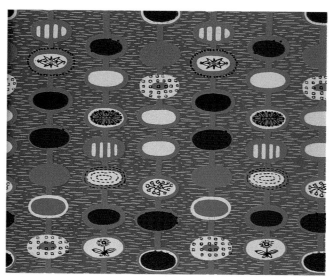

3. *Provence*, wallpaper designed by Lucienne Day, printed by John Line & Sons Ltd, colour screenprint, 200×255 mm, 1951 (London, Middlesex University, Silver Studio Collection)

Chinese export wallpaper, tempera, 2.44x1.22 m, second half of the 18th century (London, Victoria and Albert Museum)

PLATE VII   Watercolour

1. Anthony van Dyck: *Wood near a Harbour*, watercolour and gouache, over some pen and brown ink, 189×267 mm, *c.* 1635–41 (Birmingham, University of Birmingham, Barber Institute of Fine Arts)

2. Eugène Delacroix: *Woman Bathing and her Moorish Servant*, watercolour over graphite, 160×183 mm, 1832 (Cambridge, MA, Fogg Art Museum)

1. J. M. W. Turner: *The Rhine at Reichenau*, watercolour, 244×311 mm, *c.* 1841 (London, Tate Gallery)

2. Paul Klee: *Abstraction: Coloured Circles Joined by Bands of Colour*, watercolour, 117×172 mm, 1914 (Berne, Kunstmuseum, Paul Klee Stiftung)

whereas those 'representing trees, birds and flowers' could be had for four.

The third group of Chinese papers consists of a combination of the 'bird and flower' type with figures. The flowering trees fill the top three-quarters of the sheets, forming a backdrop to the lively incidents below. All papers of this kind date from the second half of the 18th century.

Unlike papers of native manufacture and imports from the Continent, the East India Company merchandise was specifically exempted from the taxes on wallpaper introduced in 1712 and 1773. It is therefore difficult to date Chinese papers precisely since they carry no tax stamp, a feature that often provides an approximate guide for dating other papers. Some are documented in decorators' accounts or family archives, but in most cases any estimate of date must be largely based on changes in style and technique, which, given the strict adherence of the artists to a limited range of models, were minimal.

By the end of the 18th century, Chinese papers were going out of fashion: Rococo taste had given way to the formality and restraint of Neo-classicism, and both English and French manufacturers were producing papers that matched the Chinese in quality. In 1792 the import tax was extended to Chinese papers. These factors combined to kill the trade completely. A brief revival in the 19th century was inspired by the chinoiserie extravaganza of the Royal Pavilion at Brighton, but the quality of the Chinese papers had by then declined.

BIBLIOGRAPHY

L. Le Comte: *Memoirs and Observations Made in a Late Journey through the Empire of China* (London, 1697), p. 160

W. Chambers: *Designs of Chinese Buildings* (London, 1757)

A. Anderson: *An Accurate Account of Lord Macartney's Embassy to China* (London, 1795)

J. Barrow: *Travels in China* (London, 1804)

J. Banks: *Journal of the Right Hon. Sir Joseph Banks, 1768–71* (London, 1896)

M. Jourdain: 'Old English Wall-papers and Wall Hangings', *Country Life*, lv (24 May 1924), pp. 835–7

C. C. Oman: 'Old Wallpapers in England: 3. Chinese Papers', *Old Furn.*, iii (1928), pp. 15–22

E. A. Entwisle: 'Painted Chinese Wallpapers', *Connoisseur*, xciii (1934), pp. 367–74

A. K. Longfield: 'Old Wallpapers in Ireland: 5. More English, Chinese and French Examples', *J. Royal Soc. Antiqua. Ireland*, lxxxvii (1957), pp. 141–6

C. C. Oman and J. Hamilton: *Wallpapers: A History and Illustrated Catalogue of the Collection of the Victoria and Albert Museum* (London, 1982)

F. Wappenschmidt: *Chinesische Tapeten für Europa: Vom Rollbild zur Bildtapete* (Berlin, 1989)

GILL SAUNDERS

III. Conservation.

The deterioration of wallpaper is caused by the inherent and external dangers common to all works of art on paper (*see* PAPER, §VI): acidity (from the paper, support, media and environment); accumulated dirt and accidental damage; extremes of temperature and humidity; biological attack; and damage caused by overexposure to light. But wallpaper is also subject to damage resulting from defects in the fabric of the building that acts as its ultimate support (see Phillips).

Many of the earliest surviving European wallpapers have been discovered on wooden beams and panels or

6. Chinese export wallpaper panel showing a theatrical performance, gouache, 3.95×1.18 m, second half of the 18th century (London, Victoria and Albert Museum)

inside cupboards and boxes. Wood acids, insects and the natural movement of the wood itself usually result in the paper becoming extremely discoloured, brittle and fragmented. Papers hung on a plaster wall have often fared better, but dampness in the wall may cause moisture staining and mould growth and contribute to insect activity, especially attack by silver-fish. Also, settlement cracks will tear the paper. Wallpaper mounted on canvas and attached to the wall with wooden battens is protected to some extent from these problems, but the acidity of the aging canvas and adhesives, combined with the continual expansion and contraction of the support (related to changes in relative humidity), can themselves cause discoloration, weakening and splitting of the paper while crumbling plaster and dust accumulates in the space behind.

Although many standard paper-conservation techniques can be applied to the preservation and restoration of wallpaper, especially in the case of unused samples and archival material, paper on the wall does call for a unique approach from the conservator. The treatment is complicated by vertical orientation and scale, interaction with the building and the difficulty of maintaining ideal environmental conditions in the historic interior. Each case has to be separately assessed, and the extent of conservation or restoration treatment required will further modify the conservator's approach. For example, in the hypothetical case of fragments, perhaps in multiple layers, of 19th-century machine-printed wallpaper, found behind panelling in a house undergoing renovation or demolition, the conservation treatment will simply involve surface-cleaning one or more repeats of the pattern and removing these from the wall for preservation in an archive. In contrast, a stateroom in a great house hung with 18th-century hand-painted Chinese wallpaper or with French *papiers peints* of the 19th century will demand much more extensive work. Treatment might then include the following stages: survey, documentation and photography; surface cleaning; consolidation of media; separation from the supports and removal of the paper from the wall; removal of such secondary supports as paper, canvas and plaster; removal of discoloration; repair and relining with compatible conservation paper and perhaps a textile; remounting and/or rehanging; and finally retouching. Meanwhile, building defects would have to be remedied and, if necessary, modifications to other decorative features of the interior carried out.

In practice, the conservator will try to preserve papers *in situ* and choose appropriate options from the following treatment stages. The initial stage is surface cleaning, which involves removing dust, soot and accretions of dirt with soft brushes, low-suction vacuum-cleaners, erasers and sponge rubbers; solvents, mainly water, can sometimes be used locally. The next stage is to consolidate flaking, powdery or fugitive pigments and media (especially common on 19th-century block-printed wallpapers), using a variety of natural and synthetic polymers applied by spray, brush or syringe. If wallpaper that is mounted or hung on plaster has to be removed (perhaps to be rehung in another room, to facilitate repairs to the building or simply for thorough conservation treatment), then removal is often effected by scalpels and spatulas inserted between the

paper and the wall. This process may be carried out while the paper is dry, or after varying degrees of moistening by spray, humidification or direct wetting intended to soften the original adhesive. The use of steam will soften less easily soluble adhesives, and if enzyme solutions are applied at the same time the structure of the adhesive can be broken down. If moisture or steam is used the paper must be surface cleaned first, otherwise any stains may become permanently fixed in the paper. Very fragmented or fragile wallpapers may have to be temporarily faced with thin tissue-paper and a reversible adhesive before removal from the wall. Wallpaper mounted on canvas can often be de-backed by removing the linings by standard methods, after releasing fixings around the edge of battens. In extreme cases, where none of the above methods is effective, the wall behind the paper may have to be dismantled. Once the wallpaper is off the wall, further conservation treatment can proceed: cleaning, the removal of old backings and supports, chemical stabilization, repair, relining and, if required, retouching. For this, standard paper-conservation techniques can be used, albeit on a larger scale than usual and with the important exception of treatment by immersion, which is rarely possible.

When the treated paper is rehung, various techniques are again possible. A choice is made according to the condition and structure of the walls and surrounding features. The conservation principle of reversibility precludes pasting the treated wallpaper directly on to a wall. Instead, the same effect can be achieved by first lining the prepared wall with a polyester fabric release layer between two layers of acid-free paper; if it is necessary at a later date to remove the wallpaper, in theory the paper support can be separated from this release layer. Alternatively the paper can be relined with a final support of a natural or synthetic textile and attached by its borders to the wall by means of wooden stretchers. An expensive but more desirable variation is to mount the conserved wallpaper on panels of acid-free honeycomb board faced with acid-free paper, or on screens constructed according to the oriental pattern, like the Japanese *karibari* board. Panels can be screwed to the wall or even secured with magnets.

Inpainting, or retouching to restore missing areas of the design, though not often practised in other fields of paper conservation, can represent a major proportion of the cost of wallpaper conservation. Various techniques of reproducing historic papers, for infills or even whole rooms, are increasingly the province of the conservator, working with artists and printers.

After conservation and restoration, wallpaper that is displayed *in situ* in a historic interior should be protected from future damage by careful building maintenance and environmental controls. Barriers and glass or perspex panels may be necessary to protect the paper from passing visitors.

BIBLIOGRAPHY

IIC Congress: Conservation within Historic Buildings: Vienna, 1980 [incl. articles by J. Hamm and P. D. Hamm, K. Jahoda and H. Rosenberger, and A. Fiedler]

M. Phillips: 'Conservation of Historic Wallpaper', *J. Amer. Inst. Conserv.*, xx/2 (1981) [issue also contains other related articles]

C. Rickman: 'Wallpaper Conservation', *UKIC Conference: Conservation Today: London, 1988*, pp. 64–70

IIC Conference: The Conservation of Far Eastern Art: Kyoto, 1988 [incl. articles by P. Webber, M. Huxtable and C. Rickman]

P. J. Kipp: 'Wallpaper Conservation', *IADA Preprints, 7th International Congress of Restorers of Graphic Art: Uppsala, 1991*

CATHERINE RICKMAN

Wall-pillar church. Type of aisleless hall church in which the thrust of the vaulting is taken by tongues of wall—wall pillars—that jut out into the building. The wall pillars assume the same function as buttresses, except that the external wall of the wall-pillar church starts at the outside face of the buttresses, which are extended in the form of tongues, so that additional space is gained internally. This form developed in the late 13th century (e.g. the choir of St Mary, Marburg, consecrated 1297) and first appeared in a fully evolved form in the mid-15th. It allowed relatively large, wide areas to be built cheaply and quickly from bricks or rubble. The spaces between the wall pillars were generally used as chapels, with the altar placed at right angles to the longitudinal axis.

The constructional principle of the wall-pillar church has its roots in the development of architecture from *c.* 1300. Thus in the chapel of St Jean in the church of St-Pierre-le-Jeune, Strasbourg, and in the north aisles of St Thomas (both 14th century), also in Strasbourg, the buttresses are built inwards. Wall pillars in the structural sense appeared in the nave buttresses extended like tongues in Salem abbey church (nave begun 1300), with chapels inserted between them. The treatment of the choir by builders in the circle of the Parler family represented a considerable step towards the creation of wall-pillar churches; such choirs can be seen at Kolín in St Bartholomew (choir, 1360–78), at Schwäbisch Gmünd in the cathedral of the Holy Cross (begun 1351; for illustration *see* SCHWÄBISCH GMÜND, CATHEDRAL OF THE HOLY CROSS) and, influenced by it, the new choir of St Lorenz in Nuremberg (*see* NUREMBERG, §IV, 2). In these buildings the wall areas separating the chapels were developed into massive supports clearly extending into the interior, and the external wall of the chapels ends flush with the outer face of these supporting walls; the structural system was confined to chapel extensions of the choir, and in that form it became widespread throughout Europe, as, for example, in Narbonne Cathedral (begun 1272; *see* NARBONNE, §1) and the choir of St Martin, Halle/Flandern (1398–1409).

The crucial breakthrough in the creation of the wall-pillar church took place in southern Germany in the mid-15th century, particularly in the bishoprics of Passau and Salzburg. Here, especially where brick buildings were widespread, the design was initially used in fairly small parish churches where the naves could be extended in this relatively inexpensive way (e.g. Asten parish church, 1453–61; Münsteuer daughter church, 1454–8, by Hans Moringer; St Michael, Altötting, consecated 1469). The wall-pillar system is found in such large buildings as the choir of St Salvator (1479–84; completed 16th century), Passau, the choir (from 1408, begun by HANS VON BURGHAUSEN and completed by Stefan Krumenauer) of the Franziskanerkirche (*see* SALZBURG, fig. 2) and the Frauenkirche, Munich (*see* MUNICH, §IV, 1). By around 1500 the wall-pillar system was widespread throughout Europe, although it was particularly prevalent in areas where brick was used for building. Examples of how widely distributed the type

was include the church of the Assumption (1517–44) at Most, Czech Republic; S Pedro (completed 1577), Soria, Spain; and the collegiate church (1526), Berlanga de Duero, Spain, by Juan Rasinas. A further development in Swabia was represented by hall-like buildings roofed over with richly reticulated, shallow, barrel vaulting (e.g. Gärtringen parish church, 1496; Schwaigern parish church, 1517–40). The church at the Benedictine monastery of Blaubeuren (1491–1500) by Peter von Koblenz (*fl* 1474–1501) and others already demonstrated the differentiation between the nave, conceived as a wall-pillar area, and an aisleless choir separated by an intermediate feature resembling a transept. In contrast with 14th-century structural prototypes, the wall-pillar system was used in Swabia exclusively for the nave, or the part of the church used by the laity; often, for example in Blaubeuren, this was so that the building of the church could be financed by donations for chapels.

The wall-pillar principle of construction is relatively safe, and structurally it encouraged the development of new spatial forms at the end of the 16th century. The Jesuit Michaelskirche (1583–97; *see* WITTELSBACH, §I(4)) in Munich was based on the structural principle of the wall-pillar church, but here additional galleries were inserted above the chapels—a feature that influenced many 17th- and 18th-century wall-pillar churches. Alternative proposals for the Jesuit church (1618–29) in Cologne, by Christoph Wamser, 'Idea bavarica I–III', were also based on the wall-pillar principle. Many subsequent buildings, such as the former Jesuit church (1631–4) and college of St Ignatius (1631) in Landshut and the Jesuit church (1680–88) in Solothurn, by Heinrich Mayer (1636–92), built relatively late under the influence of the Vorarlberg school, refer back to the Michaelskirche. Around 1600 the wall-pillar church was regarded as a typically Catholic style of building; the first design submitted by Joseph Heintz (i) for the Protestant church (1603; from 1617 the Jesuitenkirche) in Neuburg an der Donau envisaged it as a wall-pillar church, and it was rejected for that reason. Another important source of inspiration in the early 17th century came from architects from the Grisons, especially Hans Alberthal, who built the Jesuit church of the Ascension (from 1610) in Dillingen and the Jesuit church (1617–20) in Eichstätt. In its combination of a wall-pillar hall area without galleries in the nave and a hall with free-standing piers in the choir, the church of the Ascension at Dillingen served as a prototype for a group of churches built in the third quarter of the 17th century by Vorarlberg architects, tentatively grouped together by the misleadingly named 'Vorarlberg minster plan'.

After the Thirty Years War (1618–48) the wall-pillar system was widely used in southern Germany, from the Rhine Valley across to Bohemia. A number of local variations developed, and in the 18th century these were adapted by individual architects. The master masons and architects from the Bregenzer Wald used the wall-pillar system for monastery churches in particular, the first examples being Michael Thumb's pilgrimage church of St Marie (1682–95) on the Schönenberg (*see* THUMB, (1)) and the Premonstratensian abbey church (1686–90) at Obermarchtal (see fig.). The interiors of both churches are relatively high in cross-section and are characterized

Wall-pillar church by Michael Thumb: Premonstratensian abbey church, Obermarchtal, 1686–90

by the strict division of nave and choir: the nave as a wall-pillar hall with galleries, a widened nave bay without galleries forming a rudimentary transept, and the choir as a hall with free-standing piers and galleries. The individual bays of the nave and the choir are uniform in size. This pattern was widely followed in many churches in Upper Swabia, for example at the church and priory (1695–1701) in Hofen-Friedrichshafen, by Christian Thumb.

The finest formulation of the wall-pillar church type by Vorarlberg builders was at Weingarten abbey church (1715–24); the building as executed was designed substantially by Franz Beer. The wide spacing of the tongues of wall, which are pierced by large passageways, removes the narrowness and massiveness of Michael Thumb's early wall-pillar churches. The choice of vaulting forms, from the sail vault to the drummed dome, lends the bays a hierarchical development, so producing spatial and focal centres, in contrast with the spatial continuum of the early wall-pillar churches. Franz Beer varied the wall-pillar system still further in other buildings, where the combination of domes of varying widths and heights producing a sequence of wide-spanned domes was a particular feature, as at Münsterlingen monastery church (1711–27). Special forms of the wall-pillar church in designs by Vorarlberg builders occur at EINSIEDELN ABBEY and pilgrimage church (1719–26), by Caspar Moosbrugger, and St Gall Abbey church (1755–68), executed by Peter Thumb to designs by Johann Caspar Bagnato (see THUMB, (3)).

From the mid-17th century architects from the Grisons were active in Bavaria, where they constructed buildings

similar to those in their native area. Foremost among them was Lorenzo Sciasca, who built St Oswald parish church (1675; to designs by Johann Kaspar Zuccalli) at Traunstein; the abbey church (1676–8) at Herrenchiemsee, as a wall-pillar hall with galleries; the parish church of St Ägidius (1688) at Gmund am Tegernsee; and the Augustinian canons' church (1688–93) at Weyarn, where the nave is a wall-pillar hall area without galleries, and the choir is aisleless. The churches at Herrenchiemsee and Weyarn incorporated the two basic types of the wall-pillar hall combined with an aisleless choir that were adopted by most architects in Old Bavaria, for example Hans Mayr the elder (1643–1718) and Georg Zwerger II (b c. 1643–4). The buildings of Hans Mayr the younger (b 1677), Abraham Millauer (c. 1680–1758) and Wolfgang Dinzenhofer (1678–1747) revealed rather more traditional tendencies (e.g. St Martin, 1719–23, Au bei Aibling; Kössen im Tirol parish church, 1719–24; Götting parish church, 1724–5). At the same time there were also attempts to give a new interpretation to the wall-pillar system by such people as GIOVANNI ANTONIO VISCARDI, who built the Cistercian abbey church of Maria Himmelfahrt (1701–66) at Fürstenfeld, with much wider wall pillars and galleries above the clerestory windows; François de Cuvilliés I at Schäftlarn abbey church (1733–60; executed by Johann Baptist Gunetzrhainer (c. 1692–1763) and Johann Michael Fischer), which combined a centralized building and the wall-pillar hall; and JOHANN MICHAEL FISCHER at the Premonstratensian convent church (1727–40) at Osterhofen, Altenmarkt. In other buildings Fischer successfully achieved a radical resolution of the wall-pillar system.

St Michael's, Munich, influenced such buildings in Franconia and Bohemia as St Martin (1689–93) in Bamberg, by Georg Dientzenhofer and Johann Leonhard Dientzenhofer, or the pilgrimage church of Maria (1690–1702), Kulm, by Marcantonio Canevale. Basing his ideas on Guarino Guarini's unexecuted design (1679) for the Theatine church in Prague, Christoph Dientzenhofer transformed the wall-pillar system into a system of apparently intersecting cubes. To achieve this the tongues of wall no longer stood head on towards the centre of the church with a pilaster on their short end; rather, the corners were cut off, in line with the shape of the imaginary cubes, and the pilasters applied to these slanting faces, while the central axis was faced by the corner framed by the two pilasters, the point of intersection of the imaginary cubes. Dientzenhofer used this system at several churches, including St Nicholas (1703–11), Mala Strana, Prague. From c. 1710 Christoph Dientzenhofer reverted to the classic wall-pillar system, but reducing the wall pillars to relatively broad support elements that did not jut out far into the interior, as at St Klemens in the Klementinum (1710–15), Prague.

The traditional wall-pillar concept was dependent on the tongues of wall and the external wall being given equal value. At the abbey church at Weingarten, a negation of the external wall was already creeping in. In the 18th century the wall pillars were given a more powerful sculptural form and architectural structuring, while the external wall was increasingly treated as an unadorned shell. The supports and the external wall were no longer on an equal footing, and the building came to be perceived as having a double skin. This was first suggested by the different treatment of the architectural members found in Christoph Dientzenhofer's late buildings, or the centralized churches developed by Johann Michael Fischer. Kilian Ignaz Dientzenhofer created something similar in his canopy-like church interiors, including St John Nepomuk (1730–35), Prague. In the mid-18th century such architects as Dominikus Zimmermann and Balthasar Neumann resolved the system of the wall-pillar church by freeing the supports and thus the internal spatial skin from the outside wall; such works as the Würzburg court chapel (Neumann), NERESHEIM ABBEY church (see NEUMANN, BALTHASAR, fig. 3), the pilgrimage church of Steinhausen (1728–31; for illustration see ZIMMERMANN, (2)) near Schussenried and the Frauenkirche (1736–41; by Zimmermann) at Günzburg illustrate this. In the last quarter of the 18th century, under the influence of early French Neo-classical architecture, wall-pillar churches were again built in Upper Swabia; in the severity of their construction and the rejection of galleries (e.g. Rot an der Rot abbey church, from 1780) they are very close to early 17th-century buildings.

BIBLIOGRAPHY
H. Hammer: 'Die St Jakobs-Kirche in Innsbruck und die süddeutsche Wandpfeilerkirchen', Z. Dt. Ver. Kstwiss., v (1935), pp. 94–117
G. Deppen: Die Wandpfeilerkirchen des deutschen Barock unter besonderer Berücksichtigung der baukünstlerischen Nachfolge von St Michael in München (diss., U. Munich, 1953)
O. Freiermuth: 'Die Wandpfeilerkirchen im Werke Johann Michael Fischers', Das Münster, viii (1955), pp. 320–32
H. G. Franz: 'Die Wandpfeilerhalle im böhmischen Barock', Forsch. & Fortschr., xxxv (1961), pp. 87ff
——: 'Die "böhmische Wandpfeilerhalle" im 18. Jahrhundert'. Z. Ostforsch., xi (1962), pp. 625ff
H. J. Sauermost: 'Schema und Eigenbrödler: Eine Analyse der Vorarlberger Forschung', Unsere Kstdkml., xx (1969), pp. 310–21
Die Vorarlberger Barockbaumeister (exh. cat., ed. W. Oechslin; Einsiedeln and Bregenz, 1973)
H. G. Franz: Dientzenhofer und 'Hausstätter': Kirchenbaumeister in Bayern und Böhmen (Munich and Zurich, 1985), pp. 11–49

ULRICH KNAPP

Wallraf, Ferdinand Franz (b Cologne, 20 July 1748; d Cologne, 18 March 1824). German collector. The son of a master tailor, he took up teaching immediately after completing his education and became a priest in 1772. He studied science at the Universität zu Köln, graduating in 1780, and started to form a natural history collection. In 1784 he was appointed to the Chair of Botany at the university, and two years later his teaching responsibilities were extended to include natural history and aesthetics, subjects he had become interested in during the 1770s. His passion for collecting began to embrace works of art. An eminent, though controversial, figure, he was elected Rector of the university in 1793.

After the decree of secularization of 1802, a great many items of artistic interest came on to the market, and Wallraf took advantage of the situation. Between 1799 and 1804 he edited an almanac under varying titles to which he contributed poems and articles on history and painting. He was instrumental in arranging the commission for Peter Cornelius to paint frescoes, in St Quirinus at Neuss, which were based on Wallraf's proposals. Friedrich von Schlegel, who was for a time one of his colleagues, used Wallraf's collections in formulating his theories on art.

From 1801 he was in touch with the collectors Melchior Boisserée and Sulpiz Boisserée, exchanging pictures with them. In 1818 he decided to bequeath his collections to the city of Cologne. After Wallraf's death a complete inventory of his collections was made. Besides manuscripts, books and documents, he had collected 1712 pictures (notably medieval paintings of the Cologne school), 41,655 prints and drawings and 47 pieces of stained glass as well as antiquities and natural history specimens. The collection of works of art went on public display in 1827 and from 1861 was exhibited in its own building, the Wallraf-Richartz-Museum (see RICHARTZ, JOHANN HEINRICH). It includes the anonymous Crucifixion painted in Cologne c. 1330 and the centre panel of the Last Judgement (1435–40) attributed to Stefan Lochner. Other items were distributed between various institutions in Cologne.

See also COLOGNE, §III, 5.

WRITINGS
Ausgewählte Schriften (Cologne, 1861)
J. Deeters, ed.: 'Der Nachlass Ferdinand Franz Wallraf', Mitt. Stadtarchv Köln, 71 (Cologne and Vienna, 1989)

BIBLIOGRAPHY
K. Pabst: 'Ferdinand Franz Wallraf: Opportunist oder Kölner Lokalpatriot?', Gesch. Köln, xxiii (1988), pp. 159–77

JOACHIM DEETERS

Walois, Jean (fl 1411–45). Netherlandish tapestry merchant. At the time when Arras was the most important centre of production of tapestry of the highest quality, he was probably the most prominent tapestry merchant there for nearly three decades. Between 1413 and 1445 he supplied John the Fearless and Philip the Good, successive dukes of Burgundy, with many tapestries for their own use and as dynastic and diplomatic gifts. Particularly prominent among his sales were individual pieces and sets depicting hunting scenes, such as those destined for Robert Stewart, 1st Duke of Albany, in 1415, Jean, Duc de Touraine and his wife, Jacqueline of Bavaria, in 1416, Philip the Good in 1428 and Arnold, Duke of Guelders, in 1435. Comparison with other contemporary sales has suggested such subjects as a specialization or even a monopoly in Walois's trade. Inevitably (although without further evidence) his name has been associated with the four Devonshire Hunting Tapestries (London, V&A) and two further hunting tapestries (Glasgow, Burrell Col. and Minneapolis, MN, Inst. A.). His success was undoubtedly founded on the legacy of his parents, both of whom were members of highly influential and wealthy Arras families. Huart, his father (d 1413), held high civic office from 1372 to his death, and his mother Marguerite (d 1377) was the daughter of Vincent Boursette, himself a wealthy Arras tapestry merchant. Both Huart and Marguerite are named in sales of tapestry to the Duke and Duchess of Burgundy, and on the Duchess's death in 1405 they were entrusted with some of her possessions, including many tapestries.

BIBLIOGRAPHY
G. Wingfield-Digby and W. Hefford: The Devonshire Hunting Tapestries (London, 1971)
J. Lestocquoy: Deux siècles de l'histoire de la tapisserie, 1300–1500: Paris, Arras, Lille, Tournai, Bruxelles (Arras, 1978), pp. 49–56

SCOT MCKENDRICK

Walpole. English family of statesmen, patrons and collectors. (1) Robert Walpole, 1st Earl of Orford, was one of the most important political figures during the reigns of George I and George II, and his accumulated wealth enabled him to build Houghton Hall, Norfolk, and to amass an impressive collection of pictures and sculptures. His youngest son, (2) Horace Walpole (4th Earl of Orford), was one of the leading society and literary figures of the mid-18th century and the most influential supporter of the GOTHIC REVIVAL in architecture and the decorative arts at that time.

(1) Sir Robert Walpole, 1st Earl of Orford (*b* Houghton, Norfolk, 26 Aug 1676; *d* London, 18 March 1745). After attending King's College, Cambridge (1696–8), he first sat as an MP in 1701. He rapidly rose through the ranks of the Whig party, becoming Prime Minister and Chancellor of the Exchequer in 1715. He had wide-ranging financial and commercial interests and was one of the earliest advocates of free trade. He began to collect pictures in the 1720s; at first collections were formed in London, but a proportion was moved after his fall from power in 1742, the year he was elevated to the peerage as Earl of Orford, to his new country house, Houghton Hall, Norfolk. It was begun in 1722 to designs by Colen Campbell and William Kent and completed in 1735 by Thomas Ripley (*c.* 1683–1758), and it is one of the leading examples of English Palladian architecture, enhanced by the work of the sculptor John Michael Rysbrack and the Venetian stuccoist Giuseppi Artari (*d* 1769). The great bronze copy (*in situ*) of the Borghese *Gladiator* (Paris, Louvre), probably cast by Hubert Le Sueur, was the gift of Thomas Herbert, 8th Earl of Pembroke. The Picture Gallery at Houghton, originally built as a greenhouse, was fitted out with damask to display paintings removed from Downing Street in 1742.

Walpole's family helped him add to his collection through their travels abroad, among them his youngest brother, Horatio Walpole (1678–1757), later Baron Walpole of Wolterton, who was in Paris from 1723 to 1730. Unlike Walpole himself, each of his three sons made the Grand Tour, charged with the task of returning with works of art. The eldest son, Robert Walpole the younger (1700–51), later 2nd Earl of Orford, was abroad in 1722–3. His most stunning purchase was the life-size bronze version (Houghton Hall, Norfolk) of the *Laokoon* (Rome, Vatican, Cortile Belvedere), made from casts under the direction of François Girardon. Both Robert and his brother, the Hon. Edward Walpole (1706–84), had their portraits in pastel (Houghton Hall, Norfolk) executed in Paris by Rosalba Carriera. Others who helped Walpole acquire works for his collection included John Macky (*d* 1726), a spy and author of the guidebook *A Journey through England* (1714–29), who collected for him in the 1720s. The artist John Ellys (*c.* 1701–57) acted as an agent for Walpole and was rewarded with the position of Master Keeper of the Lions in the Tower of London. Walpole also bought at auction: Velázquez's *Innocent X* (Washington, DC, N.G.A.), for example, was purchased for 11 guineas in 1735 at a sale organized by the dealer Andrew Hay.

Artists whom Walpole patronized included Charles Jervas and the skilled copyist Ranelagh Barret (*fl c.* 1737–

68), for whom he provided a work-room in his house at the Treasury in Whitehall, London. Barret copied a number of works in Walpole's collection, including Anthony van Dyck's portrait of *Inigo Jones* (St Petersburg, Hermitage). One of several coups by Walpole was the purchase of the Wharton family portraits, which included 14 full-lengths by van Dyck, sold from Winchendon House, Bucks, in 1722. Walpole also commissioned the Walpole Salver (1728; London, V&A; *see* SILVER, fig. 2), engraved with his cipher, from the goldsmith Paul de Lamerie.

The richest sources for Walpole's activities as a collector are George Vertue's 'Note-books' and the catalogue of the Houghton collection, *Aedes Walpolianae*, made by his youngest son, (2) Horace Walpole. An inventory of 1736 lists 114 pictures at Houghton, while his houses in London contained many more: 149 in Downing Street, 64 in Grosvenor Street and 78 in Chelsea. After Walpole's death three sales dispersed a collection that was rich in the work of artists favoured by collectors of the period, notably Carlo Maratti, Nicolas Poussin, Guido Reni and van Dyck. The first sale (5–6 May 1748) was disguised under the name of the dealer Robert Bragge (annotated sale cat., Oxford, Bodleian Lib.); the later ones, in 1751 and 1779, were initiated by Robert Walpole's grandson George Walpole, 3rd Earl of Orford (1730–91). Many of the works of art sold in 1779, except family portraits and sculpture, were acquired by Catherine II, Empress of Russia (*see* ROMANOV, (3)).

DNB   BIBLIOGRAPHY
A. Michaelis: *Ancient Marbles in Great Britain* (Cambridge, 1882)
'The Note-books of George Vertue', *Walpole Soc.*, xviii (1930), xxii (1934), xxvi (1938), xxix (1947) [index], xxx (1955)
D. Sutton: 'Aspects of British Collecting—I', *Apollo*, cxiv (1981), pp. 282–339
Norfolk and the Grand Tour: Eighteenth-century Travellers Abroad and their Souvenirs (exh. cat. by A. W. Moore, Norwich, Castle Mus., 1985)
A. W. Moore: *Dutch and Flemish Painting in Norfolk: A History of Taste and Collecting* (London, 1988)
                                        ANDREW W. MOORE

(2) Horace [Horatio] **(William) Walpole**, 4th Earl of Orford (*b* London, 24 Sept 1717; *d* London, 2 March 1797). Antiquarian and writer, son of (1) Robert Walpole. He was educated at Eton and King's College, Cambridge. In 1739, accompanied by the poet Thomas Gray, he went on the Grand Tour, returning in 1741. From that date until 1768 he was MP for several boroughs in succession, after which, in his own words, 'arts, books, painting, architecture, antiquities and those amiable employments of a tranquil life. . .assumed an entire empire' over him. His importance for the history of English art derives from his activities as an amateur architect, collector, patron and historian.

Walpole (see fig. 1) had no training in architecture and was never a competent draughtsman, but at Strawberry Hill, a house in Twickenham, London, which he leased in 1747 and purchased two years later, he created a revolution in Gothic Revival domestic architecture. For the enlargement of Strawberry Hill he abandoned the symmetrical planning that had characterized the work of William Kent in the Gothic Revival style and also insisted on fidelity to historical precedent in the designs for furniture and interior fittings. His principal architects at the start of the building programme in 1753 were the amateurs John Chute and

1. *Horace Walpole, 4th Earl of Orford*, by John Giles Eckhardt, oil on canvas, 394×318 mm, 1754 (London, National Portrait Gallery)

Richard Bentley (1708–82), the former principally responsible for the exterior elevations, although he also designed the library (see fig. 2), but from 1766 Walpole employed professional architects: Robert Adam and James Essex. Even Adam, however, was not free to design as he wished, for Walpole selected the design that each of his architects was to follow from books of prints; this is evident throughout the interior. For external elevations Chute and Walpole depended on the model that Kent had provided at Esher Place, Surrey (1733), and on prints in Batty Langley's *Ancient Architecture Restored and Improved* (1742). Essex completed the building work at Strawberry Hill in 1776, and his design of the gateway was inspired by that of a tomb in Ely Cathedral; Thomas Gayfere built the beautiful Chapel in the Woods (1772), designed by Chute, with a stone front modelled on the screen of a tomb in Salisbury Cathedral. These two features at Strawberry Hill survive intact, and though some alterations were made to the house in the 19th century, including an added storey to its Round Tower, most of the work commissioned by Walpole has survived (see fig. 3).

Strawberry Hill became extremely well known, partly because of its proximity to London but also through Walpole's publication (1774) recording its architecture and contents; this had begun as a brief catalogue in 1760 and reached definitive form in 1784. Walpole was tireless in promoting the revival of the Gothic style in his correspondence with friends and lived to see it established in England, for example in James Wyatt's Lee Priory, Kent (1785), which Walpole described as 'a child of Strawberry, prettier than the parent'. The Gothic Revival style of the 19th century was characterized by the asymmetry of plan

and fidelity to historical precedent that Walpole had initiated at Strawberry Hill.

Walpole's art collection, recorded in his *Description* of 1774, was not marked by quality but rather by its usefulness as historical documentation. The largest and most coherent group was of prints of portraits; he was among the first collectors to organize these on the thematic principles proposed in Karl Heinrich von Heinecken's *Idée générale d'une collection complette d'estampes* (1771). Walpole's collection of Greek and Roman coins and medals was also noteworthy but was principally acquired at one sale, that of Conyers Middleton in 1744. He also had a good collection of French porcelain. Walpole was embarrassingly erratic, however, in his judgment of contemporary art, particularly where it was clouded by friendship; one friend, nevertheless, was Joshua Reynolds, who executed two portraits (1757; Ragley Hall, Warwicks; Toronto, A.G.) of Walpole as well as two group portraits of friends and family (Bristol, Mus. & A.G.; Edinburgh, N.G.).

One of Walpole's earliest publications, the *Aedes Walpolianae*, a detailed catalogue of the paintings collected by his father for Houghton Hall, Norfolk, completed in 1743 and issued four years later, is the earliest catalogue of a private collection by an English art historian. Walpole began publishing at his Strawberry Hill Press in 1757, with a reprinting of the *Odes* of his friend Thomas Gray; the illustrations by Richard Bentley for the earlier 1753 edition, commissioned by Walpole, are among the finest examples of the Rococo style in English fine art. Between 1762 and

2. *Horace Walpole in the Library at Strawberry Hill*, collotype print after the watercolour (1756) by Johann Heinrich Müntz (London, British Library)

3. Strawberry Hill, Twickenham, commissioned by Horace Walpole and remodelled in the Gothic Revival style by John Chute, Richard Bentley, Robert Adam and James Essex, 1753–76

1771 Walpole issued his four-volume *Anecdotes of Painting in England*, based on the 'Note-books' of GEORGE VER-TUE, which he had acquired after Vertue's death in 1756, but amplified by his own research. These *Anecdotes* form a major component of early source material for the historiography of the arts in England, although they are strongly shaped by Walpole's own prejudices. The fourth volume included his *History of the Modern Taste in Gardening*, reissued separately in 1785. Though it is neither comprehensive nor exact, the fluency of style of this essay and its memorable phrasing have ensured its status as the most important account of the art in 18th-century England. His other writings included the first Gothic novel, *The Castle of Otranto* (1765), a play, political memoirs, antiquarian studies and a mass of correspondence. The last forms an indispensable source for the social, political and artistic history of England in the 18th century. In 1791 Walpole succeeded as 4th Earl of Orford on the death of his nephew George Walpole, 3rd Earl; by then he was a celebrity and an object of curiosity, dividing his last years between his house in Berkeley Square, London, and Strawberry Hill. On its dispersal in 1842—in a sale (*in situ*) that lasted 32 days—his collection raised the sum of £33,000.

WRITINGS

Aedes Walpolianae, or a Description of the Collection of Pictures at Houghton Hall in Norfolk (Twickenham, 1748, dated 1747, 2/1752)
Anecdotes of Painting in England, 4 vols (Twickenham, 1762–71); rev., ed. R. N. Wornum, 3 vols (London, 1876)
Miscellaneous Antiquities (Twickenham, 1772)
A Description of the Villa of Mr Horace Walpole at Strawberry Hill (Twickenham, 1774, rev. 2/1784)
The Works of Horatio Walpole, Earl of Orford, 5 vols (London, 1798)
W. S. Lewis, ed.: *The Yale Edition of Horace Walpole's Correspondence*, 48 vols (New Haven, 1937–83)

BIBLIOGRAPHY

R. W. Ketton-Cremer: *Horace Walpole: A Biography* (London, 1940, 2/1956)
I. W. U. Chase: *Horace Walpole: Gardenist* (Princeton, 1943)
W. S. Lewis: *Horace Walpole* (New York, 1960)
W. H. Smith, ed.: *Horace Walpole: Writer, Politician, Connoisseur* (New Haven, 1967)
P. Sabor: *Horace Walpole: A Reference Guide* (Boston, 1984)
M. McCarthy: *The Origins of the Gothic Revival* (New Haven and London, 1987)

MICHAEL MCCARTHY

Wals, Goffredo [Gottfried] (*b* Cologne, *c.* 1600–95; *d* Calabria, 1638–40). German painter, draughtsman and printmaker, active in Italy. According to early sources, when very young he travelled to Naples and then worked in Rome with Agostino Tassi from 1616–17 to the end of 1618. There followed periods in Naples, in Genoa (*c.* 1630), where he taught Antonio Travi, and in Savona (1631–2). He returned to Naples, where Gaspar Roomer in 1634 owned 60 of his landscapes, and perished in an earthquake in Calabria.

Wals was well known in the 17th century, and Claude Lorrain, attracted by 'the fame of Goffredo, painter of landscapes, distant views, and architecture' (Baldinucci), is said to have studied with him for two years in Naples. Yet his art was subsequently forgotten until the 1960s, when scholars, on the basis of a signed circular etching of *River and Trees* (e.g. London, BM) and of works bearing old attributions, reconstructed his oeuvre, although its chronology remains shadowy. He favoured small circular landscapes with simple, naturalistic motifs, such as farm buildings on a riverbank, overgrown ruins in the Roman Campagna and quiet country roads. The distinction of his style, most beautifully revealed in *A Country Road by a House* (Cambridge, Fitzwilliam), lies in his sensitivity to effects of light, in his subdued palette of blues, greys and greens and in his highly sophisticated compositions, which depend on the abstract beauty of simplified shapes and patterns of light and dark. The drawing *Landscape with*

Ruins (Paris, Louvre) reveals the delicacy of his penmanship. His style was influenced by Adam Elsheimer and is close to that of Filippo Napoletano.

BIBLIOGRAPHY

R. Soprani: *Le vite de' pittori, scoltori, et architetti genovesi* (Genoa, 1674); ed. and rev. G. Ratti (Genoa, 1768), i, pp. 305, 463–4

F. Baldinucci: *Notizie* (1681–1728); ed. F. Ranalli (1845–7), iv, pp. 357ff; v, p. 89

M. Roethlisberger: 'Da Bril a Swanevelt: Tondi olandesi di paesaggio, 1600–1650', *Palatino*, xii/4 (1968), pp. 386–93

R. Hohl: 'Elsheimers Figurenzeichnungen: Stilkritik einiger Neuzuschreibungen', *Städel-Jb.*, iv (1973), p. 200

A. Sutherland Harris: 'A Drawing by Goffredo Wals', *Master Drgs*, xvi/4 (1978), pp. 399–403

M. Roethlisberger: 'Additional Works by Goffredo Wals and Claude Lorrain', *Burl. Mag.*, cxxi (1979), pp. 20–28

A. Repp: *Goffredo Wals: Zur Landschaftsmalerei zwischen Adam Elsheimer und Claude Lorrain* (Cologne, 1986) [early sources; full bibliog.; illus.]

Walser, Karl (*b* Teufen, 8 April 1877; *d* Zurich, 1943). Swiss painter, printmaker, illustrator and theatre designer. He studied with a decorative painter in Stuttgart and briefly at the Kunstgewerbeschule in Strasbourg (1902), though he was chiefly self-taught through study trips to Belgium, France, Spain, Italy and Japan, which impressed him deeply. His freely brushed, figurative style and preoccupation with such Symbolist artists as Ferdinand Hodler and Arnold Böcklin allied him with the avant-garde of his day. He was a member of the Berlin Secession, and the connections he made through the group, together with the acknowledged clarity of his stylish book illustrations, won him many commissions. In a prolific career he also produced costume and stage designs, wall frescoes and numerous prints. Later paintings showed his admiration for the flat, all-over colour planes of Cézanne. He was the brother of the writer Robert Walser (1878–1956) and illustrated a number of his books, for example *Seeland* (1919); in this the etchings are characterized by broad cross-hatching and fluid, wiry outlines.

BIBLIOGRAPHY

H. K. Roethel: *Modern German Painting* (London, 1958)

P. Paret: *The Berlin Secession* (Cambridge, MA, 1980)

Walter, Thomas U(stick) (*b* Philadelphia, PA, 4 Sept 1804; *d* Philadelphia, 30 Oct 1887). American architect. In 1818 he was apprenticed as a bricklayer to his father, the builder Joseph Walter (1782–1855), who was contracted that year to build William Strickland's Second Bank of the United States (1819–24) in Philadelphia, one of the earliest examples of Greek Revival architecture in the USA. Although no formal architectural curriculum had been established at this time, Walter's professional education followed a pattern that later became standard practice. During a six-year apprenticeship he acquainted himself with the operations of Strickland's office and learnt Euclidian geometry. After becoming a master mason in 1824, he joined his father's business, took membership in the Bricklayers' Company and enrolled in the 'Drawing School' at the Franklin Institute, Philadelphia, under the direction of John Haviland. After four years studying mathematics, physics, draughtsmanship and other subjects related to building, as well as landscape painting in watercolour, he entered Strickland's office as a draughtsman in 1828. In 1831, Walter set up his own practice, which was immediately successful. Through connections in city government he won the commission for the Philadelphia County Prison and Debtors Apartment (destr. 1967).

In 1833 Walter's design for the Girard College for Orphans in Philadelphia won the premium award in what was then the most prestigious architectural competition to have been held in the USA. To honour the French origin of the banker Stephen Girard (1750–1831), who had bequeathed £2,000,000 to build the college, Walter originally presented an impressive but naive reworking of Anges-Jacques Gabriel's two massive blocks on the north side of the Place de la Concorde, Paris, framing a third, central block. The importance of the commission and the shortcomings of Walter's design induced Nicholas Biddle (1786–1844), a financier and the principal arbiter of American taste at the time, to take on the chairmanship of the college's building committee, in which capacity he influenced Walter's final design. Having travelled in Greece, Biddle had become the leading advocate of Greek Revival architecture as an expression of the American spirit. The college remains one of the finest examples of Greek Revival architecture in the USA. It consists of a central block and associated flanking blocks. The centrepiece, known as Founder's Hall (see fig.), has three storeys, with two vestibules and four large vaulted classrooms on each floor. Under Biddle's influence, Walter radically simplified the flanking buildings and dressed Founder's Hall with a peristylar screen of giant marble Corinthian columns reminiscent of Alexandre-Pierre Vignon's La Madeleine, Paris, but with the Corinthian order closely based on the choregic monument of *Lysikrates* in Athens. Few of the interior details were Greek; indeed the functional nature of the building led Walter to visit Europe in 1838 to study educational facilities in England and buildings in Paris and Rome. The economic depression of 1841 interrupted work on the college, during which time Walter worked on the design and construction of the breakwater

Thomas U. Walter: Founder's Hall, Girard College for Orphans, Philadelphia, 1833–48

at La Guaira, Venezuela, and the college was eventually finished in 1848.

Walter established a reputation for immaculate taste, partly through his association with Biddle, to whose country house called Andalusia, near Philadelphia, he added a wing in 1831, surrounded with a Doric peristyle in the form of the Temple of Hephaestos in Athens. By 1851 he had produced hundreds of designs for simple and monumental buildings from Maine to South Carolina and as distant as Shanghai. It is not known how many of these were built, but the largest concentrations of his surviving work are in West Chester, PA (e.g. Presbyterian church, 1831–5; County Court House, 1847; and Chester County Bank), and in Virginia (e.g. First Baptist Church, Richmond, 1839; Freemason Street Baptist church and Norfolk Academy, Norfolk; and Presbyterian churches in Petersburg and Lexington). Most follow the external form of Greek temples, with or without a columned porch and without the academic emphasis that characterizes most Greek Revival buildings in Europe. Walter's principal aim was to emulate Greek thought, and he consistently relied on simplicity, regularity and restraint even when he embraced other styles. None of his Egyptian pieces survive, however, and what remains of his work in the picturesque taste, such as the Italianate Glenelg (1851), Ellicott City, MD, has been severely altered. His finest work in a Renaissance style is the small but monumental front added in 1851 to the Spruce Street Baptist church in Philadelphia, which is based on Trinità dei Monti in Rome. His neo-Gothic buildings were always basic classical volumes in schematic medieval dress.

In 1851 President Millard Fillmore (reg 1850–53) chose Walter as the architect of the extensions of the United States Capitol in Washington, DC. The new building is on a huge scale (214×107 m) and accommodates two congressional chambers and their associated offices. It is covered externally in white marble and decorated in the Greek Revival style, resulting in a stylistic marriage between a severe Neo-classicism and the late Palladianism of the original Capitol building, which was retained. The altered proportions of the building required a new dome, which was designed in 1855 and constructed during the following decade, during which the Civil War was waged, before becoming a symbol of national unity (see WASHINGTON, DC, fig. 5). It was frequently imitated in new state capitol buildings, for example at Sacramento, CA. The dome was executed entirely in cast iron, with the assistance of Montgomery C. Meigs (1816–1892), and served as a stimulus to the iron industry and the development of architectural applications of metal in America. Walter executed numerous other government and private commissions while in Washington, before retiring to Philadelphia in 1865. In 1873 he undertook to supervise the construction of John McArthur's Second Empire design for the Philadelphia City Hall (completed 1900). At the time of his death, Walter was president of the American Institute of Architects, which he helped found in 1857, after a previous unsuccessful attempt to establish such an institute in 1835. Through his lectures on the history and philosophy of architecture he was among the first to raise public taste in architectural matters in the USA.

UNPUBLISHED SOURCES
Philadelphia, PA, Athenaeum [Walter's pap. and drgs]

BIBLIOGRAPHY
W. S. Rusk: 'Thomas U. Walter and his Works', *Americana*, xxxiii (1939), pp. 151–79
T. Hamlin: *Greek Revival Architecture in America* (New York, 1944/R 1964)
T. C. Banister: 'The Genealogy of the Dome of the United States Capitol', *J. Soc. Archit. Hist.*, vii/1–2 (1948), pp. 1–31
A. A. Gilchrist: 'Girard College: An Example of the Layman's Influence on Architecture', *J. Soc. Archit. Hist.*, xvi/2 (1957), pp. 22–5
R. B. Ennis: 'Thomas U. Walter', *19th C. [New York]*, v (1979), pp. 59–60
R. W. Liscombe: 'T. U. Walter's Gifts of Drawings to the Institute of British Architects', *J. Soc. Archit. Hist.*, xxxix (1980), pp. 307–11

ROBERT B. ENNIS

Walter-Kurau, Johann. *See* VALTERS, JĀNIS TEODORS.

Walter of Hereford [de Ambresbury; Herford] (*fl* 1277; *d* 1309). English architect. He was an important royal master mason during the period when the architecture of the English court led Europe in the development from High to Late Gothic. From 1277 to 1290 he directed the construction of Edward I's Vale Royal Abbey, Cheshire, the largest Cistercian church built in Britain. In the following year he contracted with the abbot of Winchcombe, Glos, to complete the Abbey's 'new work'. In 1295 he became master mason of CAERNARFON CASTLE, a post that he held until his death. He may have designed the tomb of Edward I's mother, *Eleanor of Provence*, at Amesbury, Wilts, in 1291 (destr.). In 1304 he took part in Edward's Scottish war, directing the production of stone ammunition at the siege of Stirling Castle and fortifying Perth. The Franciscan church in the City of London (destr.), founded by Queen Margaret in 1306, is also credited to him. The subsequent destruction of most of his work inhibits our understanding of the early Decorated style, although the masonry details of Caernarfon and surviving fragments from Vale Royal indicate his importance in the early development of Decorated mouldings. The plan of the London Franciscan church, known from excavation, is regarded as the progenitor of the light-limbed, open spatial formula adopted for most major English parish churches until the Reformation. Adapted to the requirements of a preaching order, audibility and visibility, and the need to exploit a restricted urban site, its plan was a single large rectangle divided into aisles by arcades of great delicacy. There were no transepts, but the friars' choir was divided from the nave by a transverse corridor or 'walking space'. The spatial character of this remarkable design may be experienced in several early 14th-century parish churches, notably Holy Trinity, Hull (*c.* 1320), and the naves of Newark, Notts (1312), and Boston, Lincs (1309).

BIBLIOGRAPHY
Harvey
H. M. Colvin, ed.: *The History of the King's Works*, i (London, 1963), pp. 205–6, 248–57

J. M. MADDISON

Walters. American family of businessmen, collectors and patrons.

(1) William T(hompson) Walters (*b* Liverpool, PA, 23 May 1819; *d* Baltimore, MD, 21 Nov 1894). By 1850 he headed his own liquor importing business in Baltimore. He maintained that with the first five dollars he earned he bought a painting, the *Retreat from Moscow*, by E. A. Odier (1800–87). By the late 1850s he had become an influential patron, not only of such regional talents as the sculptor W. H. Rinehart (1825–74) and the painter of the Far West Alfred Jacob Miller but also of such leading American artists as Asher B. Durand, Frederic Edwin Church and John Frederick Kensett. Following his purchase of Jean-Léon Gérôme's *Duel after the Masquerade* (after 1857; Baltimore, MD, Walters A.G.) in 1859, he turned increasingly to contemporary European painting, eventually disposing of much of his earlier, American holdings. During the American Civil War (1861–5) he made a sojourn in Paris, where he met many leading French artists, with his friend and adviser GEORGE A. LUCAS serving as intermediary. Back in Baltimore after the war, he increased his fortunes through investment in banking and railways, which enabled him to continue to buy art by both academic and Barbizon artists; he had a particular passion for the *animalier* sculpture of Antoine-Louis Barye. After 1873 he began to assemble one of the first extensive collections in the USA of Chinese and Japanese ceramics and other decorative arts. Walters opened his collections to the public on a regular basis, printed handbooks and financed several major publications, including *Notes: Critical and Biographical: Collection of W. T. Walters* (Indianapolis, 1895). He also served as chairman of the acquisitions committee of the Corcoran Gallery of Art in Washington, DC, and as US Commissioner at the Weltausstellung of 1873 in Vienna.

(2) Henry Walters (*b* Baltimore, MD, 20 Sept 1848; *d* New York, 30 Nov 1931). Son of (1) William T. Walters. He succeeded his father in business. Though a resident of New York, he retained his ties with Baltimore and continued his father's practice of making the collections accessible to the public. Initially he augmented the 19th-century works with paintings by Romantic artists and the Impressionists. His aims, however, were more ambitious, and with the purchase in 1893 of some Ancient Near Eastern cylinder seals he began to widen the collection so that it would include works from all periods. In 1902 he bought the collection of Marcello Massarenti, Assistant Almoner to the Holy See under Leo XIII and Pius X, which comprised more than 1540 works, including 500 late medieval, Renaissance and Baroque paintings, numerous examples of Renaissance decorative arts and sculpture and an array of antiquities. To house these works Walters commissioned Delano & Aldrich to design a Renaissance-style building (1910) in Baltimore, with its interior modelled after Bartolomeo Bianco's Palazzo dell'Università in Genoa. Although the gallery was quickly filled, Walters's collecting continued at an unabated pace, extending into such diverse fields as incunabula and medieval manuscripts, Sasanian silver, Coptic ivories and textiles, Asiatic migration arts, Limoges enamels, maiolica and jewellery of all periods. Following his marriage in 1922, he furnished his New York residence with major examples of 18th-century French decorative arts. He served as vice-president of the Metropolitan Museum of Art and as a trustee of the New York Public Library. He was also one of the ten founders of the American Academy in Rome. He bequeathed his gallery and collections (now the Walters Art Gallery) and a portion of the income from his estate to the City of Baltimore. His New York holdings were sold at auction by his widow in 1941 and 1943.

BIBLIOGRAPHY
E. Strahan [E. Shinn]: *The Art Treasures of America, Being the Choicest Works of Art in the Public and Private Collections of America* (Philadelphia, [1886]), pp. 91–4
D. Sutton: 'Connoisseur's Haven', *Apollo*, lxxxv (1966), pp. 422–33
W. R. Johnston: *The Nineteenth Century Paintings in the Walters Art Gallery* (Baltimore, 1982)

WILLIAM R. JOHNSTON

Walters, Gordon (Frederick) (*b* Wellington, 24 Sept 1919). New Zealand painter. He trained at Wellington Technical College (1939–40). In 1946 he began his studies of Polynesian art, which led to a series of abstract paintings. He visited Europe in 1950, where he was impressed by the works of Piet Mondrian, Victor Vasarely and Auguste Herbin. He returned to Wellington in 1953. Between 1956 and 1966 he evolved the distinctive formal language of his mature style, in which elements from Maori decorative art are synthesized with European geometric abstraction. Most of the paintings he produced after 1964 are formally related through the use of the same few distinctive elements, most notably the *koru* motif, a stem with a curving bulblike termination found in Maori *moko* (tattoo patterns) and *kowhaiwhai* (patterns painted on house rafters and canoe hulls). Walters transformed the Maori prototype, which is hand-drawn and organic, into a severe geometric form constructed with precise, ruled lines and compass-drawn circular terminations, for example in *Painting No. 1* (1965; Auckland, C.A.G.). Walters used ambiguities of readings between figure and ground as well as optical effects such as dazzle and after-images to create perceptual movement and space in two-dimensional, non-illusionistic paintings. There are some affinities with the works of Giuseppe Capogrossi and Bridget Riley. Walters moved to Christchurch in 1976. His work is represented in most public collections in New Zealand, in the National Gallery, Canberra, and the Art Gallery of New South Wales, Sydney.

BIBLIOGRAPHY
E. Gombrich: *The Sense of Order: A Study in the Psychology of Decorative Art* (Oxford, 1979), p. 133
M. Dunn: *Gordon Walters* (Auckland, 1983)

MICHAEL DUNN

Walther [Walter]. German family of sculptors. They were originally from Breslau (now Wrocław, Poland), and there were many branches of the family in Silesia and Saxony. The most important members over four generations exerted a decisive influence on sculpture in Dresden between the Late Gothic and the Baroque. The first member referred to in documents is Hans Walther I (*fl* 1487–1511; *d* Steinmetz), who concluded an inheritance settlement with his brothers in 1497 in Breslau and signed a sandstone figure of *St Christopher* (1511) in the parish church of Neurode in Silesia (now Nowa Ruda, Poland). Of his two sons, (1) Christoph Walther I was the first member of the family to settle in Dresden; this branch of the family was continued by his son, Hans Walther II (1526–86). After Christoph's death in 1546, Hans II took over his workshop and received many commissions when, from 1548, Maurice, Elector of Saxony (*reg* 1547–53), converted the medieval castle in Dresden into a modern residence. Through the Italians working on the castle, Hans II was guided in the direction that was to characterize the Dresden school of sculpture for decades. As a citizen of Dresden, Hans II achieved the highest standing and the greatest prosperity of all members of the family, being a member of the council from 1561 and burgomaster, alternating for three-year periods, from 1571. His only son, Christoph Walther III (*fl c.* 1550–92), was trained as a painter and musician by his future father-in-law, Benedikt de Tola (1525–72), whom he succeeded as organist in the Elector's orchestra.

Hans I's second son, Andreas Walther I (*d c.* 1560), worked as a sculptor in Breslau. Earlier scholarship attributed several important works in Breslau to him, although this has been rejected by more recent Polish scholars; in particular, they have sharply restricted his contribution to the principal façade of the castle at Brieg (now Brzég, Poland). His second son, Andreas Walther II (*d c.* 1581), moved to Dresden, probably on account of the plague rife in Breslau at that time. His first son, (2) Christoph Walther II, had arrived in Dresden some time earlier. Christoph II followed the work of his cousin Hans II so closely when he came to Dresden that, apart from the somewhat more elegant and animated posture of his figures, their works are hardly distinguishable. Andreas II was a sculptor and gunsmith. Only some unimportant sculptures by him are known. Of Christoph II's sons, (3) Andreas Walther III, Christoph Walther IV (*fl c.* 1572–1626) and Michael Walther (*fl c.* 1574–1624) were without heirs, while (4) Sebastian Walther's only son Christoph Abraham Walther (1625–80) was the last sculptor of the family. His main work, in the High Baroque style, comprises 16 life-size figures made in Regensburg for the Stiftskirche in Lambach, Upper Austria.

(1) Christoph Walther I (*b* ?Breslau; *d* Dresden, 1546). He was the son of Hans Walther I and was probably trained in the family workshop. He received decisive impressions during his years of travel in south Germany, probably in the circle of Hans Leinberger in Landshut and also perhaps in Vienna. He is first recorded in 1518, when he produced a stone crucifix (destr.) for the churchyard of Annaberg in the Erzgebirge. The Bäcker altar, his first work for the decoration of the Annenkirche in Annaberg, probably commissioned by the bakers' guild *c.* 1515, however, is likely to have been produced even earlier. In this carved altar, which depicts the *Lamentation* in the centre panel, clear Lower Bavarian stylistic elements are prominent, and it is still entirely in the Late Gothic idiom. The Münzeraltar (1522), an altar of the Virgin that was commissioned from Christoph I by the minters' guild, also for the Annenkirche, shows features of the Renaissance both in the architectural frame and in the decoration. About this time he must have carved the 44 busts of Old Testament prophets and kings that appear as ornamental motifs on the ribs of the side-aisle vaulting of the Annenkirche. In 1524 Christoph I went to Meissen with the Annenkirche foremen, whom Duke George (*reg* 1500–39) had engaged in 1521 to complete the parts of the Albrechtsburg, the margrave's castle in Meissen, left unfinished by George's father, Albert, Elector of Saxony. During erection of the vaulting of the Wappensaal, Christoph I produced busts of escutcheon-holders at the bases of the vault ribs and executed reliefs on the balustrade of the spiral staircase of the ambulatory on the first and second storeys (*in situ*). In the reliefs of the second storey, escutcheon-holders with the insignia of the territories of the Wettin family are depicted (*in situ*). The reliefs on the first floor show scenes with a moralizing, humanist content, taken from the Old Testament and ancient mythology or history. When the work on the castle was completed, commissions, especially for tombs of the canons and the local nobility, kept the sculptor in Meissen. There, in a

Christoph Walther I: *Dance of Death*, sandstone (previously painted), h. 1.15 m, from the Georgenbau, Dresden, 1535 (Dresden, Dreikönigskirche)

field previously foreign to him, he developed the type of the architectural epitaph that was to be the main task of Dresden sculptors for the next century.

At the beginning of the 1530s Christoph was summoned by George to Dresden. For the Georgenbau, the new gatehouse between the old Residenz and the Elbtor in Dresden, which George had built from 1530 and which was the first early Renaissance building in Middle Germany, Christoph I created the sculptural decoration, based on a theological programme directed against the ideas of the Reformation. The theme of the decoration on the Elbe side was death as the result of original sin, while the other side showed the redemption of mankind through Christ's death. The building, which was altered several times after a fire in 1701, was entirely replaced from 1899 to 1901; Christoph's contribution to its sculptural decoration, on which north Italian masons were also employed, can therefore no longer be exactly delineated. He probably produced, in addition to the insignia frieze, all the large reliefs and the pediment figures, but certainly the extant friezes depicting the *Dance of Death* (1535; now Dresden, Dreikönigskirche; see fig.). Particular themes from the iconographic programme of the Georgenbau, such as the allusion to transience or such motifs as the circular reliefs with portraits of the Duke and his wife, were again taken up by Christoph I in a similar form on portals, oriels or bannisters in civic buildings in Dresden, Meissen and Oschatz.

After the completion of the Georgenbau, the emphasis in Christoph I's work shifted to the execution of tombs for the Saxon nobility. Twelve such epitaphs, produced between 1524 and 1545, are extant, with the deceased shown kneeling in prayer in a round-arched niche between pilasters and closed by an attic at the top. In the few freestanding figures that he produced in addition to tombs and architectural sculpture, the Late Gothic stylistic tradition is more clearly manifested, especially in the *Crucifixion* group commissioned (1544) by the council of Joachimsthal (now Jáchymov, Bohemia). This late work is again dominated, like the early altars in Annaberg, by the influence of Lower Bavarian Late Gothic art. Nevertheless, Christoph I is one of the very few Saxon sculptors who completed the stylistic transition to the Renaissance style.

(2) Christoph Walther II (*b* Breslau, 1534; *d* Dresden, 27 Nov 1584). Nephew of (1) Christoph Walther I. He is first recorded in the inheritance settlement of his father-in-law, the Dresden mason Matz Kramer (*d*?1561); he must have arrived in Dresden before 1560, and through his marriage he became part of a widely renowned masons' family. This connection undoubtedly made it easier for him to establish himself as an independent master and to obtain citizenship of Dresden in 1562. It can be assumed that his earliest work, the pulpit (1558; destr.) for the Johanniskirche in Zittau (Lausitz), with a carved angel as pulpit bearer and four Evangelists, was supplied from Dresden, although he was referred to in the documents as 'Christoph Walther von Breslau'.

In the 1560s, in addition to smaller epitaphs, Christoph II produced, as his first large works, the signed altar (1564) in the Liebfrauenkirche in Penig, Saxony, and the epitaph of monumental dimensions (6.58×2.95 m) erected (1567)

for *Hugo von Schönburg* in the Stadtkirche in Waldenburg, Saxony. The latter, also signed, is the most important work of Dresden sculpture of the 1560s. Like all extensive architectural altarpieces and epitaphs made by the second Walther generation in Dresden, these works show the influence of the portal of the Schlosskapelle, the outstanding classical work of Renaissance architecture in Dresden, built to the design of the Italian known as Johann (Giovanni) Maria in 1555. Christoph II adapted the Italian model in his work to suit the indigenous sense of form. A flat attic decorated in relief, which extends the whole width of the portal, sits above the architrave of the main body of the portal. In contrast, a narrow framed section with reliefwork, which only extends from the middle of the main body of the portal, can be seen in the epitaphs or altars of Christoph II (and Hans II). Above this is a pediment and sometimes an even narrower relief section. This tends to emphasize the vertical, a feature of the northern Gothic tradition, and is in contrast to Italian work. The predominance of the architecture over the small figure reliefs in the niches between the columns or on top of the pediments recalls the shapes of the German Late Gothic period.

The close ties between the cousins Hans Walther II and Christoph II led to both being commissioned in 1567 by Elector Augustus to create the tombs of the Wettin margraves in the Romanesque abbey on the Petersberg, a summit north of Halle. The ten recumbent figures on the tombs are the work of the two cousins, as is shown by the initials H W and C W on their coats of arms. The epitaphs for *Anna von Whese* and *Heinrich von Hermsdorf* in the Stadtkirche of Neustadt, near Stolpen, produced between 1579 and 1582, and the epitaph of *Nickel Pflugk* in the church in Zabeltitz, near Grossenhain, follow the same structural pattern as Christoph II's earlier work, with slight variations. All these works are closely related to those of Hans Walther II. Only a short description exists of the last altar (destr.) by Christoph II, made for the Frauenkirche, Dresden, and completed in 1584, but it would have belonged to the same type. The image sequence of the Last Supper, Crucifixion and Last Judgement, with a half-length depiction of God the Father in the pediment, was in the tradition of those on the altars by the masters of the second Walther generation in Dresden.

The strict architectural form of the late epitaphs is heavily obscured in the positive organ (1584; Dresden, Hist. Mus., destr. 1945; see fig.), the last work by Christoph II. The full-size design (Dresden, Kupferstichkab.) is signed CHRISTOPH WALTHER VON PRESSLAU BILDENHAUER ZUE DRESSDEN 1583. Under the influence of the style of Cornelis Floris, which was widely known in Germany, the architecture is submerged in a proliferation of figures and relief motifs. The use of many different types of materials (e.g. agate, alabaster, painted wood) in strongly contrasting colours contributes further to this effect. The lower part, in the form of an altar, enclosed the organ mechanism, and the shallow lectern covered the keyboard, while behind it rose the staggered altarpiece with relief images and rich decoration on both the front and back. The work might easily have been used as an altar for a chapel, but it also bore a close resemblance to the cabinets popular in the *Kunstkammer* of the period

Christoph Walther II: positive organ, painted and gilded wood, marble, alabaster, agate, serpentine and stone, h. *c.* 2.3 m, 1584 (ex-Dresden, Historisches Museum; destr. 1945)

and was in fact originally installed in the *Kunstkammer* of Elector Augustus in the Residenz, Dresden. In the relaxed attitudes of the slender caryatids shrouded in thin garments with sharp-edged folds, the sculptor attained a quality equal to the best achievements of the period. As Christoph II was ill in the last years of his life, his eldest son, Andreas Walther III, is likely to have contributed to this masterpiece.

(3) Andreas Walther III (*b* Dresden, *c.* 1560; *d* Dresden, 1596). Son of (2) Christoph Walther II. He probably trained in his father's workshop and worked there until his father's death in 1584. With him a new generation emerged whose work transcended the mannered style of the second generation of Walthers, setting against it the beginnings of a vigorous early Baroque style. He was awarded extensive contracts by the pomp-loving Elector Christian I (*reg* 1586–91) for sculptural ornamentation on the series of large buildings erected during his short reign.

For the Stallhof (1586–8; now the Johanneum) in Dresden, Andreas III supplied the figural and heraldic parts of the portals, and the horses' heads and insignia cartouches on the courtyard side of the Langer Gang. Of the portals, only the so-called Jagdportal has survived, although the figures are copies from *c.* 1900. The four allegorical figures of *Faith*, *Magnanimity*, *Strength* and *Abundance*, with animals as attributes, produced for the new main portal of the castle gatehouse, completed in 1589, are recorded only in an engraving (*Das Dresdener Schloss*, 1989, p. 41), as are the trombone-blowing genii on the corners of the roof balustrade and a figure of *Justice* surmounting the cupola. Of the sculptures on the new portal of the castle, only the frieze with lions' heads and a group of pelicans above the keystone of the portal arch have survived and display Andreas III's importance as an animal sculptor.

For the Pirnaisches Tor (before 1593) Andreas III created his most important work, culminating in two life-size equestrian statues of *Elector Christian I* on the inner and outer side of the gate of the new fortifications. In the round niches on either side of an aedicula above the central gate were figures of riders on rearing horses, while the pediments of the side gates were each surmounted by a gigantic warrior in Roman dress. This, the first monument in German art depicting a prancing horse, was erected long before the much-admired monument to *Philip IV* (begun 1634) by Pietro Tacca in Madrid. The gate was destroyed during the bombardment of Dresden by the Prussians in 1760 and is recorded only in inadequate pictures. An idea of the powerful form and Baroque movement of horse and rider is given, perhaps, by a cast-iron stove plate with a depiction of the valiant Roman soldier Marcus Curtius, for which Andreas III produced the mould as one of a series of stove plates depicting ancient battle scenes for the stove in the Stallhof, Dresden. At about the same time as the sculptures were made for the Pirnaisches Tor, Andreas III's workshop produced another work for the new fortifications. The Jungfern bastion, the north-east bastion built between 1589 and 1591, was adorned with a huge coat of arms of the elector (*c.* 6×11 m), visible from a distance. Above it was a figure of *Justice* (destr.), almost 6 m high. Three figures above the portal of the Schlosskapelle in Colditz, Saxony, may be attributed to Andreas III on stylistic grounds only. Epitaph sculpture, previously the main field for Dresden sculptors, is entirely lacking in Andreas III's oeuvre.

(4) Sebastian Walther (*b* Dresden, 1576; *d* Dresden, 1645). Son of (2) Christoph Walther II. He is the most important member of the family. It is not known with whom he trained, although it is possible that he was apprenticed to his eldest brother, Andreas III, who died at exactly the time when Christoph Walther IV took his place as an independent master and when Michael Walther and Sebastian had probably just finished their apprenticeships. Like Christoph IV and Michael, Sebastian seems to have been influenced by the work of Italian sculptors active in Saxony, by the bronze figures (1590–93) by Carlo di Cesare del Palagio in Freiberg and Dresden, and by the extensive collection of Italian sculpture owned by the Dresden-based architect Giovanni Maria Nosseni. It was, however, decisive for the further artistic development of the three brothers that Nosseni, who later always worked closely with them and engaged them to execute his commissions, clearly assisted them on their travels to Venice and Florence. Sebastian seems to have extended his study period, for he is recorded in Dresden in documents only from 1605, when he was provided with civic rights of the city, although he had married in 1601. His first signed work is a pen-and-wash drawing with a dramatic depiction of the *Fall of the Titans* (1605; Nuremberg, Ger. Nmus.).

What Christoph IV, Michael and Sebastian produced after their return diverges fundamentally from the stylistic ideas of the older generation and manifests a familiarity with Italian sculpture that could only have been acquired through a prolonged stay in Italy. In the high altar for the Sophienkirche, Dresden, commissioned to Nosseni in 1606, the collaboration of Christoph IV and Sebastian can be assumed almost with certainty. The socle relief depicting the *Last Supper* shows the hand of Sebastian by comparison with the epitaph for *Lucas Cranach the Younger* in the Stadtkirche St Marien, Wittenberg, of about the same date, which is securely attributed to him. The signature CWF below the pediment figures on the altar can be related only to Christoph IV; no sculpture has been attributed to him

with any certainty, so that the individual figures, diverging in style from the *Last Supper* relief, can be only tentatively assigned to him. If the statues of *Peter* and *Paul*, entirely in the Italian spirit, in the side niches were actually carved by Christoph IV, which can hardly be doubted, he must have been as good a sculptor as his younger brother. In the large relief depicting the *Burial of Christ* on the Cranach epitaph, the style of Sebastian is clearly discernible in the heightened movements of the figures, the very varied, strongly characterized heads and the sharp, broken folds of the garments.

Sebastian's collaboration on the mausoleum for *Prince Ernst von Schaumburg-Lippe* in Stadthagen is expressly recorded in the contract of 1608, with the condition that the three putti above the door and the sculptural parts of the architecture, with eight stucco angels, should be made 'by his own hand without the help of his brothers or anyone else'. Sebastian's next outstanding work, executed for Nosseni, was the figural part of the altar (*c.* 1611–13) of the Schlosskirche in Lichtenburg, near Prettin. In particular, the life-size statues of the apostles *Peter* and *Paul*, already in the Baroque spirit, bear witness to a figural style aiming at monumentality and expressive power. When Nosseni built his own tomb (1616; partially destr. 1945; see fig.) in the Sophienkirche, Dresden, he allocated the sculptural work to Sebastian and Sebastian's son-in-law, Zacharias Hegewald. The expressive, free-standing, life-size *Ecce homo* in the centre of the epitaph and the kneeling figures of *Nosseni* in high relief on the left-hand side and of his three wives on the other (both Dresden, Mus. Gesch.) are by Sebastian. The head of the kneeling Nosseni, conceived as a portrait, must be a faithful likeness. When Nosseni died in 1620, Sebastian succeeded him to complete the Lusthaus, which Nosseni had been erecting since 1591 on the Jungfern bastion in Dresden. With his brothers, Hegewald and his great-nephew Wolf Ernst Brohn (*c.* 1600–64), Sebastian worked on the interior decoration of the building and 20 life-size sandstone statues as figural decoration in the Grosser Saal. This splendid building, which contained Sebastian's most important works from his most creative years, was destroyed in an explosion in 1747. After 1630 archivally documented works become infrequent. In the grim period of the Thirty Years War, Sebastian and his family suffered greatly as no commissions were received and there was no money from the Elector. Despite this, Sebastian produced a joyful Christmas engraving, an alabaster relief depicting the *Annunciation to the Shepherds* (1640; Dresden, Grünes Gewölbe). This relief, with its choir of angels and rays of light from the clouds, is reminiscent of old German Christmas depictions of the Late Gothic period. It was only bought by the Elector after the artist's death.

BIBLIOGRAPHY

R. Bruck: 'Der bildnerische Schmuck am Pirnischen Tore', *Dresdn. Geschbl.*, xi (1902), pp. 98–9

W. Hentschel: 'Meissner Frührenaissance', *Mitt. Landesver. Sächs. Heimatschutz*, xviii (1929), pp. 274–85

——: 'Der Dresdner Bildhauer Sebastian Walther', *Z. Bild. Kst*, lxiv (1930), pp. 59–64

K. Bimler: *Die schlesische Renaissaneplastik* (Breslau, 1934), pp. 77–116

W. Hentschel: 'Zwei sächsische Reliefs im Grünen Gewölbe', *Jb. Staatl. Kstsamml. Dresden* (1961–2), pp. 52–65

——: 'Die Breslauer und Dresdener Bildhauerfamilie Walther zwischen Spätgotik und Barock', *Geneal. Jb.*, ii (1962), pp. 67–100

Sebastian Walther with Zacharias Hegewald: tomb of *Giovanni Maria Nosseni*, sandstone, marble and alabaster, h. 3 m, 1616 (ex-Dresden, Sophienkirche; partially destr. 1945)

——: *Dresdner Bildhauer des 16. und 17. Jahrhundert* (Weimar, 1966), pp. 27–87 [detailed bibliog.]

Dresdener Zeichnungen, 1550–1650 (exh. cat. by W. Schade, Dresden, Kupferstichkab., 1969)

Das Dresdener Schloss: Monument Sächsischer Geschichte und Kultur, Dresden, Staatl. Kstsammlungen (Dresden, 1989, 3/1992), pp. 57–67

MARTIN RAUMSCHÜSSEL

Walther, Franz Erhard (*b* Fulda, 22 July 1939). German sculptor and conceptual artist. He studied at the Werkkunstschule, Offenbach (1957–9), and at the Staatliche Hochschule für Bildende Künste, Frankfurt (1959–61). By the end of the 1950s he was already breaking away from a naturalistic style and creating works that emphasized process and materials over form, such as crosshatched drawings and composite sculptures. From 1962 to 1964 he attended the Staatliche Kunstakademie, Düsseldorf, under Karl-Otto Götz, where he was influenced by *Art informel*. In the 58 works from his *First Movement* series of 1963–9 (versions in Bonn, Städt. Kstmus., and New York, Dia A. Found.), he defined a new concept wherein the artwork was no longer autonomous but was 'completed' by interaction with the viewer. The participant was invited to don variously shaped and stitched linen 'instruments' and place part or all of their physical selves within the perimeters of the object. Between 1967 and 1971 he lived in New York, where his work was appreciated by such artists as Lawrence Weiner (*b* 1940) and Joseph Kosuth. In the 1970s Walther made works that were formally even more reductive, with titles that often referred to specific spatial situations (e.g. *Two Plinths. Four Standing-places. Two Walking-tracks*, 1975; Hamburg, Ksthalle). From the end of the 1970s his work developed a more traditional and autonomous character (e.g. *RED (with Five Flaps)*, 1982; Berlin, Alte N.G.). These were wallformations stitched out of cotton cloth, often in strong colours, which were meant to be understood as form as well as a basis for interaction. He also produced freehand drawings that clarified some of the principles inherent in his three-dimensional works, as demonstrated in his publication *Organon* (Klagenfurt, 1983).

BIBLIOGRAPHY

K. König, ed.: *Franz Erhard Walther: Objekte benutzen* (Cologne and New York, 1968)

Franz Erhard Walther: 'Ich bin die Skulptur' Wandformationen, 1978–1985 (exh. cat., Brunswick, Kstver., 1986)

Franz Erhard Walther: Zeichnungen–Werkzeichnungen, 1957–1984 (exh. cat. by A. Dückers, W. Berlin, Kupferstichkab.; W. Berlin, Preuss. Akad. Kst., Archv; 1989)

EVA MEYER-HERMANN

Walton. Scottish family of artists.

(1) E(dward) A(rthur) Walton (*b* nr Barrhead, Renfrewshire [now Strathclyde], 15 April 1860; *d* Edinburgh, 18 March 1922). Painter. He trained at the Staatliche Kunstakademie in Düsseldorf (1876–7) and Glasgow School of Art. One of the GLASGOW BOYS, he painted outdoors in the Trossachs and at Crowland, Lincs, with James Guthrie, Joseph Crawhall and George Henry. He also painted in W. Y. Macgregor's life studio in Glasgow. He joined the New English Art Club in 1887 and developed an atmospheric landscape style influenced by *plein-air* painting and by James McNeill Whistler with whom he

was friendly during his stay in London (1894–1904); *Autumn Sunshine* (1884; U. Glasgow, Hunterian A.G.) is characteristic. Walton was a regular exhibitor from 1880 in both Glasgow, at the Institute of the Fine Arts, and Edinburgh, at the Royal Scottish Academy. He was elected an Associate of the Academy in 1889 and a full member in 1905, taking an active role in its affairs after moving to Edinburgh in 1904. He concentrated after *c.* 1885 on pastel and on watercolour, which he used notably in his Helensburgh and Kensington scenes of contemporary life. From 1915 he served as President of the Royal Scottish Water Colour Society. Oil was reserved largely for portraits in a Whistlerian style, such as the *Artist's Mother* (1885; Edinburgh, N.G.). Such portraits became his chief source of income. During the late 1880s and 1890s he painted murals for the main building of the Glasgow International Exhibition of 1888 and various other buildings in the city. His only surviving decoration is *Glasgow Fair in the Fifteenth Century* (1899–1901; Glasgow, City Chambers).

BIBLIOGRAPHY

J. L. Caw: *Scottish Painting Past and Present, 1620–1908* (Edinburgh, 1908), pp. 370–73

E. A. Walton, 1860–1922 (exh. cat. by H. Weller, Edinburgh, Bourne F.A., 1981)

J. Halsby: *Scottish Watercolours, 1740–1940* (Braintree, 1986), pp. 138–41

W. Hardie: *Scottish Painting, 1837 to the Present* (London, 1976, rev. 2/1990)

For further bibliography *see* GLASGOW BOYS.

CLARE A. P. WILLSDON

(2) George Walton (*b* Glasgow, 3 June 1867; *d* 10 Dec 1933). Architect and designer, brother of (1) E. A. Walton. He was the youngest of 12 children and because of family financial difficulties became a bank clerk for the British Linen Bank in 1881. While working for the bank, he attended evening classes at the Glasgow School of Art (his only formal training), and in 1888 he set up a design and decorating business known as George Walton and Co., Ecclesiastical and House Decorators. The venture was an immediate success, and over the next ten years he redecorated numerous houses and shops in Glasgow. Wider recognition came in 1896–7, when he was commissioned to fit out Miss Catherine Cranston's Buchanan Street tea-room, Glasgow. Walton made the overall interior design for the four-storey tea-rooms, and CHARLES RENNIE MACKINTOSH provided the stencilled mural decoration.

In 1897 George Walton moved his base of operations to London, and for a short time from 1899 he had showrooms in Glasgow, York and London. He also designed furniture, glass, metalwork and textiles and, unlike the more extreme artist-craftsmen, was not averse to the mechanical reproduction of textile and carpet designs. Also in 1897 he was commissioned by the photographer George Davison (who became his most important client) to refurbish a Kodak shop in Clerkenwell Road, London. As a result he designed the interiors and fronts of a chain of Kodak shops in London, Glasgow, Brussels, Milan and Vienna, which brought him international recognition.

The period between 1897 and World War I was his most successful. He decorated numerous private residences (including the dining-room of C. F. A. Voysey's home, The Orchard, Chorleywood, Herts; 1903) and built a series of small and medium-sized houses. His best-known house is The Leys (1901), Elstree, Herts, which became a home for the elderly. The exterior, in a dull vernacular, is disappointing, but the three-storey galleried hall/billiards-room and long, narrow dining-room (which was illustrated in Hermann Muthesius's *Das englische Haus*, 1904) were supremely successful; the remarkable interior fittings, also designed by Walton, are untraced. In 1916 he joined C. F. A. Voysey as assistant architect and designer to the Central Liquor Traffic Control Board, where he stayed until 1922 surveying and furnishing about 100 public houses. Over the next few years he was in financial difficulty, receiving only a few minor commissions, but between 1926 and 1931 he made over 60 textile designs for the Morton-Sundour Fabric Co.

Muthesius identified George Walton in parallel with Charles Rennie Mackintosh as the founder of the Glasgow style. Walton's designs have the simplicity and clarity associated with that group, but they are less effete and more solid than those of Mackintosh. To some extent Walton looked back to the achievements of the Arts and Crafts Movement while at the same time moving away from their earthy, rural qualities to a more urban sophistication. Muthesius said of the work, 'He is more down-to-earth, that is the demands of pure utility are more to the fore in his work than that of the Mackintosh group, but he is nonetheless a poet from whose creations a subtle spiritual atmosphere always radiates.' Nikolaus Pevsner, excusing his omission of Walton from *Pioneers of Modern Design* (1936), went further than Muthesius: 'His designs, mainly those of 1895–1905, are amongst the most brilliant and historically significant examples of the rapid and constructive progress of Britain away from William Morris towards a new style of the new century.' Some more recent opinion is, however, less enthusiastic about his work (MacMillan, 1988).

BIBLIOGRAPHY

H. Muthesius: *Das englische Haus* (Berlin, 1904–5/*R* 1908–11; Eng. trans., London, 1987)

H. S. Goodhart-Rendell: *English Architecture since the Regency* (London, 1953)

N. Pevsner: *Studies in Art, Architecture and Design*, ii (London, 1968)

A. MacMillan: *Mackintosh and his Contemporaries*, ed. P. Nuttgens (London, 1988), p. 38

DAVID PROUT

Walton, Henry (*b* Dickleburgh; *bapt* Tivetshall St Mary, Norfolk, 5 Jan 1746; *d* London, 19 May 1813). English painter. He studied in London under Johan Zoffany *c.* 1769, after which he completed his training at the Maiden Lane Academy. It was probably Zoffany who introduced Walton to the conversation piece, a genre in which he was to specialize. The *Cricket Scene at Harrow School* (1771; priv. col., see 1963 exh. cat., no. 1) reveals Walton's debt to Zoffany, but it also shows him to be an exceptional colourist and able to compose his figures with a sense of rare warmth and intimacy. By *c.* 1778, when he painted the *Rev. Charles Tyrrell with his Family* (priv. col., see Waterhouse, p. 399), his treatment of group portraits was more cohesive and he was able to relate his figures to the landscape more successfully than he had managed in the *Cricket Scene*.

In 1776 Walton exhibited a genre subject, *Plucking the Turkey* (London, Tate), at the Royal Academy; its proximity to works by Jean-Siméon Chardin lends support to the claim by Dawson Turner (1840) that Walton visited France, where he would have seen examples by Chardin. The *Fruit Barrow* (1779; priv. col., see 1963 exh. cat., no. 14) was Walton's last exhibited canvas, in which he avoided the kind of sentimentality adopted by some of his contemporary genre painters, such as Henry Robert Morland. Walton returned to East Anglia soon after 1779, settling at Burgate in Suffolk.

Once Walton had moved away from London and public exhibitions, his originality clearly waned. The conversation piece was becoming less fashionable, although Walton's *Sir Robert and Lady Buxton and their Daughter Anne* (1786; Norwich, Castle Mus.) displays his usual elegance, and for the rest of his career he concentrated on painting single portraits. Those of *Charles, 2nd Earl Cornwallis* (*c.* 1795; Bury St Edmunds, St Edmundsbury Museums) and *A Lady of the Henniker Family* (*c.* 1800–05; priv. col., see 1963 exh. cat., no. 40) reveal a broader handling than is found in his earlier work and are reminiscent of the manner of John Opie. At this stage in his career Walton was also providing advice for collectors; he was instrumental in the formation of the collections of Richard, 7th Viscount Fitzwilliam, and Sir Thomas Proctor Beauchamp.

BIBLIOGRAPHY

Waterhouse: *18th C.*

D. Turner: *Outlines in Lithography* (Yarmouth, 1840)

Paintings by Henry Walton (1746–1813) (exh. cat., ed. M. Rajnai; Norwich, Castle Mus., 1963)

HUGH BELSEY

Wanderers [Itinerants; Rus. *Peredvizhniki*]. Russian exhibiting society, active 1870–1923. It takes its name from Tovarishchestvo Peredvizhnykh Khudozhestvennykh Vystavok: 'Association of travelling art exhibitions'. The Association grew from the earlier Artists' Cooperative Society (Artel' Khudozhnikov) founded in 1863 by a group of 14 artists, headed by Ivan Kramskoy, who had broken away from the Academy of Art, St Petersburg, in protest against its traditional style and subject-matter, wanting instead to focus on Russian art. In 1870, on the initiative of Kramskoy, Grigory Myasoyedov, Vasily Perov and Nikolay Ge, an association was founded aiming to take art to the people by means of travelling exhibitions, the first of which took place in November 1871 in the Academy of Arts, St Petersburg. In 1872 the exhibition moved to Moscow, and exhibitions were held annually from then on in Moscow and St Petersburg as well as in smaller cities. Members of the Association became known as the Wanderers.

Inspired in particular by the writings of Nikolay Chernyshevsky (1828–89), who advocated a didactic function for art, and Vladimir Stasov, the Association's intentions embodied the prevailing spirit of the period, which was both realist and critical of the political system. There was a turning away from the romantic and legendary to an emphasis on life as it was lived and as a subject for reform. Initially, the Wanderers concentrated on the exposure of contemporary evils, whether social, political or ecclesiastical, as for example in *Inspecting the Estate* (1881; Moscow, Tret'yakov Gal.) by Nikolay Kuznetsov (1850–1929), but they also produced portraits of outstanding creative personalities as well as landscapes that were among the first to show an appreciation of Russian scenery. This reformist phase soon gave way to an interest in historical subjects; during the 1880s pan-Slavism and an intense nationalism were much in evidence, not least in the illustration of legend and folk-tale. A further element in this movement was the quest for a specifically Russian portrayal of Christ (e.g. Kramskoy's *Christ in the Wilderness*, 1872; Moscow, Tret'yakov Gal.).

Many artists who did not become members contributed to the Association's travelling exhibitions, which finally included most of the country's major artists (for illustration *see* LEVITAN, ISAAK). Most Russian painters (the Association also included some sculptors among its supporters) paid token allegiance to its vaguely populist aims. The majority of the Wanderers had been trained in traditional techniques and were strongly opposed to French Impressionism; the style they adopted is generally referred to as Critical Realism. Within their own ranks they made what they considered vital innovations, such as the muted colour harmonies in the work of Vasily Surikov (as in, for example, *Men'shikov in Beryozovo*, 1883; Moscow, Tret'yakov Gal.), Mikhail Nesterov's horizontal linear compositions and the luminist landscapes of Arkhip Kuindzhi. The member of the Association with the greatest reputation was Il'ya Repin (for illustration *see* REPIN, IL'YA), whose vast and varied output covered a large range of subjects and techniques. Although the Wanderers dominated the major teaching institutions throughout Russia at the beginning of the 20th century, their reputation and influence were greatest during the 1880s. From 1932 the Wanderers were officially proclaimed predecessors of Soviet Socialist Realism, which adopted their emphasis on Realism and the importance of subject-matter.

BIBLIOGRAPHY

G. Burova, O. Gaponova and V. Rumiantseva: *Tovarishchestvo Peredvizhnykh Khudozhestvennykh Vystavok* [The association of travelling art exhibitions], 2 vols (Moscow, 1959)
E. Valkenier: *Russian Realist Art* (Ann Arbor, 1977, rev. 1991)
Peredvizhniki, intro. A. Lebedev (Leningrad, 1977, 2/1982); Eng. trans. as *The Itinerants* (London, 1982)
V. V. Andreyeva and others, eds: *Tovarishchestvo Peredvizhnykh Khudozhestvennykh Vystavok, 1869–1899: Pis'ma, dokumenty* [The association of travelling art exhibitions, 1869–1899: letters, documents], 2 vols (Moscow, 1987)

ALAN BIRD

Wandpfeilerkirche. *See* WALL-PILLAR CHURCH.

Wang (i). Chinese family of calligraphers. The Wang were one of the most prestigious families of the Eastern Jin period (AD 317–420). Since the accession of Emperor Taizong (*reg* 626–49) of the Tang period (618–907), (1) Wang Xizhi has been revered as China's greatest master of calligraphy; prior to this, (2) Wang Xianzhi, his son, was considered superior.

See also CHINA, §IV, 2(ii)(d)).

BIBLIOGRAPHY

Zhang Huaiguan: *Er Wang deng shulu* [Writings by the two Wangs] (postscript AD 760); *R* in *Fashu yaolu* (Beijing, 1984), *juan* 4
L. Ledderose: *Mi Fu and the Classical Tradition of Chinese Calligraphy* (Princeton, 1979)

(1) Wang Xizhi [Wang Hsi-chih; *zi* Shaoyi] (*b* Langye (modern Linyi), Shandong Province, AD 307; *d* 365). He developed calligraphy into a transcendent art form, which rather than simply conveying written information served as a vehicle for communication of a higher order, focusing on beauty of line and form and above all on dynamic and rhythmic flow and transmutation of energy. He nominally served the Eastern Jin court, holding various posts in the capital Jiankang (modern Nanjing, Jiangsu Province) and then becoming General of the Army on the Right (*youjun*), by which title he is sometimes known. His last position was that of governor of Guiji, Zhejiang Province.

The Tang-period critic Zhang Huaiguan noted that Wang excelled in many scripts, including cursive (*caoshu*), clerical (*lishu*), a variant of clerical known as *bafen*, a type with splayed brush tip called *feibai*, a reduced draft form of clerical (*zhangshu*) and running script (*xingshu*). Others acclaimed his regular script (*kaishu* or *zhenshu*). Wang's influence came to permeate all script types, forming the basis in approach and technique of almost every subsequent major master. However, since no original work survives, the appearance of Wang's various script types remains a matter of speculation.

Wang's most celebrated work was the *Lanting xu* ('Orchid pavilion preface'), a text of 28 columns in running script. This recounted a literary gathering of 41 persons, including Wang Xizhi and his sons, (2) Xianzhi and Huizhi, and friends at the Orchid Pavilion (Lanting) in Shanyin, near Shaoxing, Zhejiang Province, in AD 353. It was later acquired by Emperor TAIZONG (Tang period), who in total amassed over 2000 Wang specimens. The original was eventually buried with the Emperor in his tomb, Zhao ling, near Xi'an in Shaanxi Province, but he had it traced beforehand by various scribes in the Hongwen Academy and free-hand copied by Ouyang Xun and Chu Suiliang. Thus many different versions were distributed during the 7th century, some outline-and-fill tracing copies and some freer copies, and the tradition was established whereby later calligraphy was judged entirely according to the Wang-style model as reproduced in these versions. Some critics favour the Dingwu version as most closely resembling Wang Xizhi's style. This Song (960–1279) engraving, based on a Tang rubbing of Ouyang Xun's free-hand copy, survives as a rubbing (Taipei, N. Pal. Mus.). Other critics prefer the Shenlong tracing copy with half-seals (Beijing, Pal. Mus.) of the Shenlong reign era (AD 705–7), which is considered the most lively and natural.

Versions of Wang's works in regular script include the stone rubbings, *Huangting jing* ('Scripture of the Yellow Court'; Beijing, Pal. Mus.) and *Yueyi lun* ('On the power of music', AD 348; see Shimonaka, iv, pls 1–5). Tracing copies of running script works include *Sanghian tie* (Tokyo, Imp. Household Col.; *see* CHINA, fig. 87) and *Kong shizhong tie* ((Tokyo, Maeda Ikutokukai Found. Lib.), both bearing imperial seals of the Japanese Enryaku era (AD 782–805); the *Kuaixue shiqing tie* and *Fengju tie* (both Taipei, N. Pal. Mus.); and the *Xingrang tie* (Princeton U., NJ, A. Mus.). The *Da Tang sanzang shengjiao xu* ('Tripitaka' preface; Hyogo, Kurokawa Inst. Anc. Cult. Res.), on the pilgrim-monk Xuanzang, is a stone rubbing in running script, with characters collated from various Wang sources in Taizong's collection. Some 20 letters in cursive script have been collected in the *Shiqi tie*.

After retirement from office in AD 335 Wang Xizhi hired a stand-in (*daibi*), who executed most of his calligraphy, and rarely wrote himself.

BIBLIOGRAPHY

Chu Suiliang: *Jin youjun Wang Xizhi shimu* [Writings by Wang Xizhi of the Jin period] (7th century); *R* in *Fashu yaolu* (*c.* AD 847/*R* Beijing, 1984), *juan* 3

Sang Shichang: *Lanting kao* [Investigation of the *Lanting xu*] (preface 1208)

Xu Bangda: 'Tan Shenlong ben *Lanting xu*' [On the Shenlong version of the *Lanting xu*], *Wenwu* (1957), no. 1, pp. 19–20

Y. Nishikawa: 'Shinjutsu no Gyojo-jo' [On the newly discovered version of the *Xingrang tie*], *Shohin*, 142 (Aug 1963), pp. 2–39

Han Chuang: 'Hsiao I Gets the Lan-t'ing Manuscript by a Confidence Trick', *N. Pal. Mus. Bull.*, v/3 (July–Aug 1970); v/6 (Jan–Feb 1971)

R. Goepper: 'Wang Xizhi', *Die Grossen der Weltgeschichte* (Zurich, 1972), ii, pp. 598–609

Lanting lunbian [Collected papers on the *Lanting xu*] (Beijing, 1977)

Shuhuajia [Classical Chinese calligraphy and fine art], 39–40 (1981) [issues dedicated to Wang Xizhi]

(2) Wang Xianzhi [Wang Hsien-chih; *zi* Zijing] (*b* AD 344; *d* 386–8). Son of (1) Wang Xizhi. He was a child prodigy in calligraphy; he was only eight years old when he participated in his father's literary gathering at the Orchid Pavilion. He is traditionally held to have first studied his father's style and then that of Zhang Zhi (*fl c.* AD 190), who was renowned for his one-stroke, 'flying-white' calligraphy linking a column of characters in one charge of the brush. According to other commentators, he followed the style of his father's anonymous stand-in (*daibi*). Wang Xianzhi himself claimed that at the age of 24, while roaming the mountains, he received instructions in the form of a piece of writing of 579 characters, which profoundly affected his writing style. He excelled not only in various calligraphic scripts but also in the painting of animals and insects. He served, as did his father, at the Eastern Jin court, attaining the rank of Chief Councillor (*zhongshuling* or *daling*), by which title he was later frequently known.

It was only with the accession of Emperor Taizong, who was passionately devoted to the current interpretation of Wang Xizhi's style, that Wang Xianzhi lost his reputation as the greatest calligrapher who ever lived, and the more reserved mode of the elder Wang came to dominate Chinese calligraphy. Wang Xianzhi, meanwhile, has come to be associated with a calligraphic spirit of poetic and romantic abandon that has never been rivalled. His style in running script (*xingshu*) was revived and elevated during the Northern Song period (960–1127) by Mi Fu, whose many copies and interpretations of the younger Wang have provided Chinese calligraphy with a highly personal and elegantly elegiac style. Compared to calligraphy associated with the Wang Xizhi style, in which brush force is implicit, suggesting complex, internalized twists for a minimum of obvious excitement, Xianzhi's calligraphy features movements that are explicit, lighter, simpler and much more expressive, imparting a sense of untrammelled freedom. First the critic Zhang Huaiguan (first half of the 8th century) and then Mi Fu associated Xianzhi's style with the so-called 'single-stroke writing' (*yibi shu*), in

which several characters are written in one stretch without lifting the brush tip from the writing surface.

Transmitted works in tracing copies and stone-rubbings associated with Wang Xianzhi are few and contested. The best-known example in regular script (*kaishu*) is a 13-line fragment from *Luoshen fu* ('Nymph of the Luo River'; see Shimonaka, iv, pp. 90–91). Regular-script pieces in manuscript include *Zhongqiu tie* (see CHINA, fig. 91), *Dihuang tangtie* and *Equn tie* (Shimonaka, iv, pls 94–6), which have been largely ascribed to Mi Fu. A rubbing of a version of the *Shieryue tie* survives in the *Bao Jin zhai fatie* ('Bao Jin studio copybook'; Shanghai, Mun. Cttee. Cons. Cult. Relics) and a rubbing of two lines of the *Songli tie* in the *Sanxi tang fatie* (Sanxi Hall copybook; Taipei, N. Pal. Mus.).

BIBLIOGRAPHY

K. Shimonaka, ed.: *Shodō zenshū* [Complete collection of calligraphy]

L. Ledderose: 'Mi Fu yu Wang Xizhi de guanxi' [Mi Fu and Wang Xianzhi], *Gugong Jikan*, vii/2 (1972–3), pp. 71–84

Chiugoku shoren taikei [Annotated collectanea of Chinese calligraphy treatises] (Tokyo, 1977)

Bao Jin zhai fatie xuan [Selections from the Bao Jin studio copybook] (Shanghai, 1979)

Léon Long-Yien Chang and P. Miller: *Four Thousand Years of Chinese Calligraphy* (Chicago and London, 1990), pp. 288–9

JOAN STANLEY-BAKER

Wang (ii). Chinese family of artists. (1) Wang Shimin and his grandson, (2) Wang Yuanqi, were the oldest and youngest, respectively, of the Four Wangs, the founding fathers of the ORTHODOX SCHOOL of landscape painting, who consolidated DONG QICHANG's aesthetic principles into a coherent style. The other two, WANG JIAN and WANG HUI, shared the styles, artistic allegiances, backgrounds and surname of Shimin and Yuanqi but were unrelated to them. Shimin and Yuanqi belonged to a prosperous and distinguished family from Taicang, Jiangsu Province, many of whose members held eminent positions in national and local government. Among the benefits of such a background was not only the assurance of an official career, which permitted them to practise their art as amateur literati painters, but also access to the cultivated artistic circles of their time. They viewed themselves as heirs to a literati painting tradition (*see* CHINA, §V, 4(ii)) that began in the 8th century AD with Wang Wei and as such were obliged to study and absorb the styles of their predecessors; like them, too, they became not only practitioners but also connoisseurs and historical authorities. Wang Shimin had nine sons, many of whom became poet-painters and high officials.

(1) Wang Shimin [Wang Shih-min; *zi* Xunzhi; *hao* Yanke] (*b* Taicang, Jiangsu Province, 1592; *d* 1680). Painter, calligrapher and official. He travelled widely from an early age, accompanying his grandfather, Wang Xijue (1534–1611), on official missions. It was on one of these that he met the famous painter and art theorist Dong Qichang, who later tutored him in painting and calligraphy. Wang was fortunate not only in these propitious beginnings but also in being able to study at first hand works of the Song (960–1279) and Yuan (1279–1368) periods that comprised the renowned art collection of his grandfather. Among these were paintings by the four great masters of the Yuan period, Huang Gongwang, Wu Zhen, Ni Zan and Wang Meng.

From c. 1624 to 1636 Wang was at the height of his fairly brief and unremarkable official career, becoming Keeper of the Seals and then sub-director of the Court of Sacrificial Worship. Illness forced him to retire in 1636, and, though summoned later to other official posts, he remained in retirement, painting, and tending his garden. During the 1620s and 1630s, as a number of dated works testify, the artist's greatest source of inspiration was Huang Gongwang (e.g. *Landscape after Huang Gongwang*, 1638; New Haven, CT, Yale U. A.G.). Wang's teacher, Dong Qichang, was so impressed by these paintings that on one of them he wrote, in 1627: 'Mist and clouds fly by, the forest at the foot of the mountain is dark and dense. It really is a poem in images. Thirty years ago I saw this landscape; now it stands before my eyes afresh. I sit in the pavilion and wonder at this extraordinary achievement.'

Later Chinese critics, on the other hand, disparaged Wang's work, accusing the painter of being so scrupulously faithful to his models that his transcriptions were, at best, uninspired and repetitive. Certainly Wang Shimin was less original than the innovative Dong Qichang or the more varied virtuoso Wang Hui. However, as is revealed by a much later painting in the Huang manner, *Landscape in the Style of Huang Gongwang* (see fig.), Wang was able to rearrange and transform past motifs, creating a landscape of extraordinary complexity with the simplest of means. Characteristic Huang elements such as flat-topped bluffs, mountain ridges and a dividing gorge have here been reduced to a series of repeated geometric units modelled and accentuated by rows and columns of dots (Chin. *dian*). Together with underlying contour lines, they are virtually the sole constituents of the composition. In one area, equally spaced horizontal strokes serve for the progression into distance of a path; in another, they emphasize the successive conical layers of the central ridge; elsewhere, applied more wetly and thickly, they become a cluster of trees: 'Wang Shimin's paramount concern is in the brush pattern and movement, in the variation between light and dark tones of ink, rather than in the description of detail' (Whitfield, p. 40). The central mountain ridge follows the model of Huang's *Stone Cliff at the Pond of Heaven* (1341; Beijing, Pal. Mus.), but whereas in Huang's painting it begins as a mass of smaller units inclining to the right and then shifting to the left, buttressed by flat-topped precipices, in Wang's painting the ridge becomes an uninterrupted bowlike curve topped with staccato tree trunks. The intelligence of the idea is striking rather than the brilliance of the art.

The sheer number of paintings produced by Wang during a period of almost 50 years counters any notion that he relied exclusively on one model. In addition to Huang Gongwang, Wang cited in inscriptions on his paintings other masters such as Dong Yuan, Ni Zan, Juran and Mi Fu as sources for individual pictures. His inscriptions reveal that he was an accomplished calligrapher in the *bafen* ('eight-tenths') style, an elegant version of *lishu* ('clerical script'; *see* CHINA, §IV, 2(ii)).

Wang Shimin's pupils included the brilliant Wang Hui and his less illustrious friend Wu Li, as well as his own grandson (2) Wang Yuanqi. In 1677 Shimin presented

Wang Shimin: *Landscape in the Style of Huang Gongwang*, hanging scroll, ink on paper, 1.43×0.56 m, 1666 (New York, Metropolitan Museum of Art)

Yuanqi with an album of reduced copies of his own works, *The Great Revealed in the Small* (*Xiaozhong xianda*; Taipei, N. Pal. Mus.), which he had made when economic necessity had forced him to sell the original paintings. Dong Qichang's inscriptions were reproduced on the pages facing the paintings. The album, with its many works in the styles of the ancients (particularly those designated appropriate models by Dong), became an important source book for Orthodox school masters.

(2) Wang Yuanqi [Wang Yüan-ch'i; *zi* Maojing; *hao* Lutai] (*b* Taicang, Jiangsu Province, 1642; *d* 1715). Painter, art theorist and official, grandson of (1) Wang Shimin. Through Wang Shimin he inherited the teachings of the latter's tutor, the late Ming-period (1368–1644) painter DONG QICHANG. Wang thus represented the culmination of a lineage of landscape painting, loosely corresponding to the literati tradition (*see* CHINA, §V, 4(ii)), that stretched back to the 8th-century AD painter and poet Wang Wei.

Wang achieved eminence in his official career, becoming a district magistrate and a censor and, in 1712, rising to the rank of Vice-president of the Board of Revenue. He became a member of the Hanlin Academy, the highest in the hierarchy of intellectual institutions centred on the court. He was in the service of the Kangxi emperor (*reg* 1662–1722), to whom in 1700 he became adviser on the imperial art collection. His impact on the art world of the early Qing period (1644–1911) therefore went beyond the products of his brush. He was a prolific editor and theorist: from *c.* 1705 he was editor-in-chief of the *Peiwen zhai shuhuapu*, the calligraphy and painting manual of the Peiwen (Kangxi experor's) studio (published 1708), a massive compilation of excerpts from texts; he also wrote the theoretical essay *Yuchuang manbi* ('Scattered notes at a rainy window'), the most comprehensive expression of the principles and working methods of the ORTHODOX SCHOOL. Wang was equally successful as a painter and dominated the court academy during his later years.

Wang Yuanqi was artistically precocious. His grandfather is reported to have observed, on seeing one of Wang's youthful works, that the boy would surely surpass him and that he had grasped not only the form (style) of the great Yuan-period (1279–1368) landscape painter HUANG GONGWANG but also his spirit. Wang drew artistic inspiration from the works of Huang and of Dong Qichang, both of whom he regarded as significant figures in the revival and transmission of literati ideals, in so far as they had transformed the styles of the Northern Song (960–1127) landscape painters Dong Yuan and Juran.

In his own work Wang confined himself almost entirely to landscape studies, usually without figures. Details such as buildings and bridges were reduced to a minimum and conventionalized. While stylistic development can be traced in his work, his typical compositions, usually depicting hills rising above a river with trees and houses on the shore, remained constant. Underpinning his landscapes were his theories of painting as set out in the *Yuchuang manbi*. The artist should begin with an inspiration, purging himself of 'trite feelings' and imagining the general composition before applying the brush. He must establish proportions, foreground and distance, dense and sparse areas and basic tonal values well in advance of the details. The painter's purpose is not to create beautiful scenery nor to reproduce old compositions precisely, rather it is to capture the *qishi* ('dynamic force' or 'spirit-momentum', a term originally associated with calligraphy criticism; *see* CHINA, §IV, 3), transferring the concept of kinetic energy inherent in calligraphy to the larger problems of pictorial composition.

Wang Yuanqi: *Wangchuan Villa* (detail), handscroll, ink and colours on paper, 0.36×5.45 m, 1711 (New York, Metropolitan Museum of Art)

Wang used the term *longmo* ('dragon vein') to express the principal dynamic structure within a landscape. In the 17th century *longmo* referred to dragon-like (Chin. *long*) or serpentine compositional movements, built up with individual brushstrokes and connected by 'arteries' (*mo*) within these larger movements. The composition contained passages that 'opened and closed' (*kaihe*) and 'rose and fell' (*qifu*). The former clearly depicted open spaces, such as a long valley closed off at one end by a large and distant mountain; the latter could refer to a succession of hills or boulders, arranged one behind the other, the contours of which could be seen to rise and fall. The clear articulation of all these elements was the essence of a good painting. Wang believed that the painter, having mastered these principles, was capable of a creative synthesis, borrowing from the compositions of past masters but renewing and refreshing their ideas and methods. This insistence on individual creativity moved him beyond the more imitative antiquarian interests of Wang Shimin and Wang Jian, and closer to Dong Qichang's concern with 'encountering the spirit' of earlier masters.

One of his best-known landscapes is *Wangchuan Villa* (see fig.), based on an engraving of 1617 of a legendary Wang Wei composition. The scene represented the quintessential domain of the scholar–recluse. Since only copies and popular ink rubbings from stone engravings of the 8th-century composition existed, Wang was free to improvise, using Wang Wei's poems as a further source of inspiration. As he pointed out, the picture was more than a 'physical likeness by a professional painter'. The detail illustrated preserves the general appearance of the engraving, particularly the tilt of the ground-plane and the disposition of trees and hills. However, Wang created a sharp contrast between empty expanses of water and plain and the vigorously outlined and textured rock forms. The interplay between dense and open areas creates a formal rhythm that continues simultaneously back into the distance and across the picture plane. Wang's debt to Huang Gongwang is apparent in the rounded rocks piled one against the other in receding, roughly triangular configurations, and in the dry, wiry texture strokes (*cun*) defining the edges of the mountains. Intermittent cool tones for washes and dots recall the archaic Blue-and-green manner of the Tang period (AD 618–907). These are combined in places with warmer hues so that two distinct colour schemes emerge: the 'cool' manner of the Tang period and the 'warm–cool' idiom popular with literati painters from the Yuan period onwards. In his ability to work with limited conventional means, while remaining consistently original, Wang's artistic contribution represents both a summation of Orthodox theory and an escape from the occasional banality of its adherents.

Wang Yuanqi collaborated with other artists such as DAOJI (e.g. *Bamboo in Wind*, 1691, Taipei, N. Pal. Mus.) and had many followers, mostly in the court academy and among court officials; an exception was Huang Ding (1660–1730), who worked outside court circles.

BIBLIOGRAPHY

EWA: 'Wang Yüan-ch'i'

O. Sirén: *The Chinese on the Art of Painting* (Beijing, 1936), pp. 202–8

——: *Chinese Painting: Leading Masters and Principles* (London, 1956–8), v, pp. 200–11

S. Bush: '*Lung-mo, k'ai-ho,* and *ch'i-fu:* Some Implications of Wang Yuan-ch'i's Three Compositional Terms', *Orient. A.*, viii/3 (1962), pp. 120–27

R. Whitfield: *In Pursuit of Antiquity* (Princeton, 1969)

J. Cahill: *The Compelling Image: Nature and Style in Seventeenth-century Chinese Painting* (Cambridge, MA, 1982), pp. 184–96

VYVYAN BRUNST, with JAMES CAHILL

Wang, C. C. *See* WANG JIQIAN.

Wang Chen-p'eng. *See* WANG ZHENPENG.

Wang Chi-ch'ien. *See* WANG JIQIAN.

Wang Chien. *See* WANG JIAN.

Wang E [*zi* Tingzhi; *hao* Dongyuan] (*b* Fenghua, Zhejiang Province, *c.* 1462; *d c.* 1541). Chinese painter. He first studied painting in Fenghua from a minor master called Xiao Feng. At court he served in the imperial workshop known as the Renzhi dian and was much favoured by the Hongzhi emperor (*reg* 1488–1505), who, as an admirer of Ma Yuan (*see* MA, (1)), hailed Wang E as 'the Ma Yuan of our time'. The Zhengde emperor (*reg* 1506–21) honoured Wang even more highly, raising him to the rank of battalion commander in the Embroidered Uniform Guard and in 1510 presenting him with a seal. On his retirement from the court, Wang E returned to Fenghua.

Wang's *Gazing by the Railing at the Pavilion* (ink and colours on silk; *c.* 1492; Beijing, Pal. Mus.) measures 1.43×2.29 m and was perhaps once mounted as a free-standing screen; it bears imperial seals of the Hongzhi reign. The painting depicts a gentleman gazing over an expanse of water from a lakeside pavilion, accompanied by a boy servant. Wang uses Ma Yuan's idiom and typical 'one-corner' composition in a masterly fashion: trees, cliffs and distant mountains feature virtuoso brushwork and ink wash, and there are touches of colour in the finely-drawn architecture and figures. However, despite the links with Ma Yuan, the painting lacks the poetic vision essential to Southern Song painting.

Wang's greatest fame was as a landscape painter of the late ZHE SCHOOL. His contemporary Lang Yang praised him for the 'misty appearance' of his landscapes and for his accomplishment in the *pomo* ('broken ink') technique but pointed out that his trees and rocks lacked three-dimensionality. *Snowy Peaks in a High Wind* (hanging scroll, colour on silk, 1870×988 mm; Tokyo, Idemitsu Mus. A.) well illustrates the characteristics of Wang's style. Mountains are composed of large masses of rocks, with forceful, nail-like brushstrokes and strong contrasts between black crevasses and snow-covered surfaces. The painting bears a brief inscription by the painter, together with an imprint from the seal that he received from the emperor.

A more scholarly aspect of Wang's painting is revealed by the handscroll presented to the Japanese envoy Minamoto Nagaharu in 1510. Typical of the genre of Ming-period (1368–1644) 'farewell' paintings, this is simply an ink sketch of two gentlemen bidding adieu to a departing sailing boat, but it is accompanied by the inscriptions of numerous high-ranking officials and men of letters, all residents of Ningbo, Zhejiang Province, the port from which Minamoto returned to Japan.

BIBLIOGRAPHY

K. Kawakami: 'Sei Minamoto Nagahara kankoku shigakan to Ō Gaku' [The scroll of poems and paintings given to Minamoto Nagaharu as a farewell gift on his departure for home and the life and works of Wang E], *Bijutsu Kenkyū*, 221 (March 1962), pp. 1–22

K. Suzuki: 'Mindai kaigashi no kenkyū: Seppa' [A study of Ming painting: the Zhe school], *Tōyō Bunka Kenkyūjō Kiyō* (1968) [special issue], pp. 184–91

R. Whitfield: 'Some Che School Paintings in the British Museum', *Burl. Mag.*, cxiv (May 1972), pp. 285–94

J. Cahill: *Parting at the Shore: Chinese Painting of the Early and Middle Ming Dynasty, 1368–1580* (New York and Tokyo, 1978), pp. 125–6

Ming dai gongting yu Zhe pai huihua xuanji [Selection of Ming-period court and Zhe school paintings] (Beijing, 1983), pls 45–7

Zhongguo meishujia renming cidian [Dictionary of Chinese artists] (Shanghai, 1985), p. 135

Ming dai huihua [Ming painting], *Zhongguo meishu quanji: Huihuabian* [Encyclopedia of Chinese arts: painting], vi (Shanghai, 1988), pp. 60–61, pls 154–6

Circa 1492: Art in the Age of Exploration (exh. cat., ed. J. A. Levenson; Washington, DC, N.G.A., 1991), pp. 437–8

R. M. Barnhart: *Painters of the Great Ming: The Imperial Court and the Zhe School* (exh. cat., Dallas, TX, Mus. A., 1993), pp. 260–65

RODERICK WHITFIELD

Wang Fu [*zi* Mengduan; *hao* Youshi] (*b* Wuxi, Jiangsu Province, 1362; *d* Beijing, 1416). Chinese painter, calligrapher and poet. Following early promise as a painter and poet, Wang Fu passed the provincial examinations—the second stage in the civil service examination ladder—to receive his *juren* degree in 1376. He went to Nanjing soon after to take up a government post, but in 1380 was banished to the northern frontier, near Datong, Shanxi Province, as the result of alleged political activity against the Ming (1368–1644) government. For the next 20 years Wang served as a frontier guard, after which he returned to the south to paint and write. From 1403 to 1412 he worked as a calligrapher in the imperial palace at Nanjing, and in 1414 he went to Beijing to join the Central Draughting Office; he died there two years later.

Accounts of Wang's character and artistic skill have the ring of conventional formulae. It is said that he painted infrequently, while travelling and often when drunk. In spite of his reputation for eccentricity, his extant works reveal a diligent hand and serious application to his art. In his *Futionji* (1574/*R* Shanghai, 1910) Wen Zhengming wrote:

> The quality of his painting is above [mere] competence; the critics say that the artisan's [technique] and the scholar's spirit are both provided by his works. His personal quality was superior, and he was not used by his art. He would not give away even his small works to anyone whom he did not consider to be the right kind of man.

Wang Fu is best known for his landscapes and bamboo, both typical subjects of literati painters (*see* CHINA, §V, 3(iv)(a) and (vi)(a)). In painting bamboo, Wang followed the style of WU ZHEN, one of the Four Great Masters of the Yuan period (1279–1368). *Wan zhu qiu shen* ('Ten thousand bamboos in late autumn'; long handscroll, 1410; Washington, DC, Freer) is one of his best works. The plants are arranged along the length of the handscroll in a free and natural manner, thick stalks running the full height of the scroll, dark leaves clustered in a rhythmic series, sometimes at the base, sometimes at the uppermost edge.

Wang Fu's landscapes were frequently painted either to commemorate a particular event or to repay the generosity

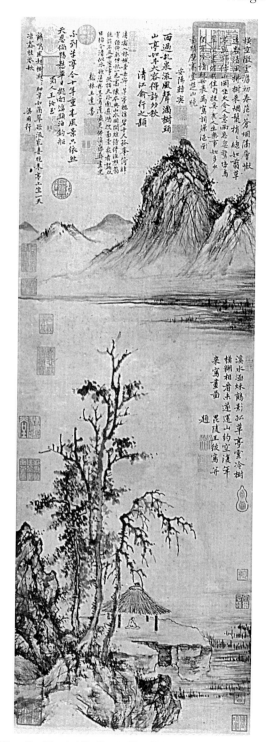

Wang Fu: *Thatched Pavilion in Mist-filled Trees*, hanging scroll, ink on paper, 1.01×0.35 m, late 14th century to early 15th (Taipei, National Palace Museum)

of a host. One such example, *River Landscape in the Manner of Ni Zan* (1401; priv. col., see Cahill, pl. 22), was a parting present for Wu Shunmin, a friend with whom

Wang had stayed. They had not met for ten years, and Wang composed a poem for the work to 'express the emotions of parting'. NI ZAN's spare, dry style is ideal for the sense of nostalgia and impending loneliness or distance one would expect on such an occasion, as well as being a tribute to his friend's sensitivity and taste.

Thatched Pavilion in Mist-filled Trees (see fig.) uses a more elaborate version of the Ni Zan style, although the composition—thatched pavilion beside tall trees in the foreground, an expanse of water and a distant range of mountains—is reduced to its essential elements, painted with an even greater economy than Ni Zan's own work. In this example, a scholar sits in the pavilion beneath three deciduous trees that have already lost leaves. The influence of HUANG GONGWANG is evident in the stringlike *cun* ('texture strokes') applied to the mountains in the background. The style and technique of the painting recall the masters of the Yuan period (1279–1368) and convey a sense of solitude. It is a brilliant variation on a theme, at once finely rendered and deeply moving. In his imitations of Yuan painters Wang Fu exemplifies the institutionalization of imitation, which was to become characteristic of literati painters of the Ming period.

DMB

BIBLIOGRAPHY

O. Sirén: *Chinese Painting: Leading Masters and Principles*, 7 vols (London and New York, 1956–8), vii, pp. 252–3
J. Cahill: *Parting at the Shore: Chinese Painting of the Early and Middle Ming Dynasty, 1368–1580* (New York and Tokyo, 1978), pp. 58–9
K. Liscomb: 'Wang Fu's Contribution to the Formation of a New Painting Style in the Ming Dynasty', *Artibus Asiae*, xlvii/1–2 (1987), pp. 39–78

VYVYAN BRUNST, with JAMES CAHILL

Wang Hsi-chih. *See* WANG (i), (1).

Wang Hsien-chi. *See* WANG (i), (2).

Wang Hui [*zi* Shigu; *hao* Gengyan Sanren] (*b* Changshu County, Jiangsu Province, 1632; *d* Changshu County, 1717). Chinese painter. He was one of the group of painters of the early Qing period (1644–1911) known as the Four Wangs; the others were Wang Shimin, Wang Jian and Wang Yuangi (*see also* ORTHODOX SCHOOL). Wang Hui came from a family of painters, and his own career began in 1651, when he was discovered by Wang Jian and became the pupil of the latter and of Wang Shimin.

WANG JIAN and Wang Shimin (*see* WANG (ii), (1)) taught landscape painting according to the methods advocated by Dong Qichang, who in his theory of a SOUTHERN SCHOOL had attempted to reconstruct the whole history of literati painting. Dong emphasized Yuan-period (1279–1368) recluse painters such as Wu Zhen and Huang Gongwang, who brought landscape painting to a pre-eminent position among the subjects preferred by the literati. Through nature, as experienced by the landscape artist, ideas on the workings of the universe were expressed, in a manner, moreover, that distinctively revealed the character of the individual.

Under the guidance of Wang Shimin and Wang Jian, Wang Hui sought to paint works that were 'transformations' of classical styles. However, whereas his masters had principally followed the brush style of the great late-Yuan masters Huang Gongwang and Wang Meng, Wang Hui developed his own transformations of the styles of virtually all the principal Song (960–1279) and Yuan masters. His creation of a 'Grand Synthesis' (*da cheng*) of Song and Yuan landscape styles was made possible by his study of the many ancient masterpieces in Wang Shimin's personal collection and his creation of a particular brush idiom for each style. Wang Shimin himself had reproduced a number of such paintings from his own collection, on a reduced scale, in the albums *Xiaozhong xianda* ('The great revealed through the small'; Taipei, N. Pal. Mus., and Shanghai Mus.), and Wang Jian imitated him. In such works, repetition of strokes not only reproduces the appearance of the older style, whether in ink monochrome or colour, on paper or silk, but also reveals the forces immanent in the landscape, which previously were hidden and grasped only through an indefinable sense of 'life-motion'. The meaning of such concepts as 'dragon-veins' (*longmo*) is conveyed with startling clarity. Certain elements in paintings are repeated, including particular kinds of trees, rocks or other natural or manmade elements of landscape. Appropriate patterns of texture strokes (*cun*) were used to distinguish one style from another. A single artist such as Wang Hui would display a variety of Song and Yuan landscape styles within the compass of a series of ten or twelve album leaves, contained within an accordion mounting (*see* ALBUM, §1), and usually concluding with a winter scene. Generally, the stylistic origin of each leaf or scene is briefly indicated in the artist's inscription; such albums must have served a useful purpose as a succinct overview of the history of Chinese painting. For some of these album series, Wang Hui cooperated with his exact contemporary YUN SHOUPING, creating a brilliant alternation of landscape and floral subjects, as in the album *Flowers and Landscapes* (1672; Taipei, N. Pal. Mus.).

Wang Hui worked for almost 30 years under the direction of the two elder Wangs, reaching his prime during the 1670s and 1680s (see fig.). Paintings such as the handscroll *Taihang shanse* ('Colours of Mt Taihang'; 1669; Princeton U., NJ, A. Mus.), with a title added by Wang Shimin, typify his achievement. He was so successful in following the classic landscape styles that some of his works were passed off as original Song or Yuan paintings; his *Travellers* (Taipei, N. Pal. Mus.), for example, was long attributed to Fan Kuan. The critical apparatus of connoisseurship originated only with the theories of Dong Qichang, and thus Wang Hui's paintings, in which concepts such as 'dragon-veins' and 'breath-force' were made visible, corresponded point for point with contemporary understanding of ancient paintings.

The deaths of Wang Jian (1677), Wang Shimin (1680) and Yun Shouping (1690) must have deprived Wang Hui of his accustomed encouragement and example. Resident in Beijing, he continued to paint prolifically for the court, but in a manner less varied than that of his earlier works. His paintings from this period reflect a preference for a manner derived from the Yuan master Wang Meng, although some titles, such as *Landscape after Yan Wengui and Juran* (long handscroll, 1713; Princeton U., NJ, A. Mus.), acknowledge a debt to earlier painters.

Wang Hui: *Fishermen's Hats and Clearing Sky in Autumn*, ink and colour on paper, 622×400 mm, 1680 (Honolulu, HI, Honolulu Academy of Arts)

Under the Kangxi emperor (*reg* 1662–1722) Wang Hui directed the team that created the great series of outsize handscroll paintings, the *Nanxun tu* ('Paintings of southern progress'; Beijing, Hist. Mus. and New York, Met.), recording imperial tours of inspection in the south, for which his long experience of organizing complex compositions with myriad details must have stood him in good stead. However, it is impossible to identify Wang's individual contribution to such collaborative works.

BIBLIOGRAPHY

In Pursuit of Antiquity: Chinese Paintings of the Ming and Ch'ing Dynasties from the Collection of Mr. and Mrs. Earl Morse (exh. cat. by R. Whitfield; Princeton U., NJ, A. Mus., 1969)
V. Contag: *Chinese Masters of the Seventeenth Century*, trans. by M. Bullock (Rutland, VT, and Tokyo, 1970)
Images of the Mind: Selections from the Edward L. Elliot Family and John B. Elliot Collections of Chinese Calligraphy and Painting at the Art Museum (exh. cat. by Wen Fong and others; Princeton U., NJ, A. Mus., 1984), pp. 179–92
Zhongguo meishujia renming cidian [Biographical dictionary of Chinese artists] (Shanghai, 1985), p. 130
The Century of Tung Ch'i-ch'ang, 1555–1636 (exh. cat., ed. Wai-kam Ho; Kansas City, MO, Nelson–Atkins Mus. A.; Los Angeles, CA, Co. Mus. A.; New York, MOMA; 1992–3)

RODERICK WHITFIELD

Wang Jian [Wang Chien; *zi* Yuanzhao, *hao* Lianzhou] (*b* Taicang, Jiangsu Province, 1598; *d* 1677). Chinese painter.

He was one of the group of painters of the early Qing period (1644–91) known as the Four Wangs; the others were Wang Shimin, Wang Hui and Wang Yuanqi. The Four Wangs are credited with establishing the principles of the ORTHODOX SCHOOL as inspired by Dong Qichang. Wang Shimin was Wang Jian's friend and, being six years senior, his mentor. Both artists came from prominent families in Taicang but were unrelated. Wang Jian was the great-grandson of the famous collector Wang Shizhen and inherited his collection of paintings. Owing to his distinguished ancestry, under the Chongzhen emperor (*reg* 1628–44), Wang Jian was appointed to the government post of Prefect of Lianzhou in Guangdong Province, from which his *hao*, 'Lianzhou', derives. He served only briefly, however, and lived the rest of his life in retirement.

Wang Jian's writings, largely in the form of inscriptions on paintings by his colleagues and protégés, such as Wang Hui, are frequently concerned with Dong Qichang's theory of the SOUTHERN SCHOOL, asserting the legitimacy of the Orthodox lineage and castigating contemporaries for their decadent artistic practices. The most serious charge levelled at 'degenerate' painters, by both Wang Jian and Wang Shimin, is that they failed to follow the old masters who form the basis for Southern school theory, particularly the Four Masters of the Yuan (1279–1368), Huang Gongwang, Wu Zhen, Ni Zan and Wang Meng. Not surprisingly, landscape albums in the styles of the old masters comprise a large part of Wang Jian's output. At his most impressive, in his early and middle periods, he was capable of a higher level of technical skill and a greater textural richness than Wang Shimin (*see* WANG (ii), (1)), but in his late period he resorted to a similar formulaic monotony. Wang Jian was one of the most 'painterly' of the early Qing masters, combining a restrained use of colour with sensitive brushwork to create landscape scenes that go beyond simple imitation of his chosen models.

Wang Jian's earliest surviving works date to the late 1640s; thereafter, he was prolific. The ten-leaf *Album of Landscapes in Old Styles* (1648; Berkeley, U. CA, A. Mus.) exemplifies his originality in reworking established motifs. The first leaf is inscribed 'in the manner of Huichong' in reference to the 11th-century monk–painter and in composition is typical of the Northern Song (960–1127) painter Zhao Lingrang; by the later part of the Ming (1368–1644) and early Qing, the styles of these two painters had been conflated. The leaf features the standard thatched hut and mist-enshrouded willows, but Wang introduces a human touch by depicting a departing guest looking back as an expression of affection for his host.

Although Wang Jian's painting became increasingly repetitive in his later period, his eye for colour and the delicacy of his brushwork remained apparent in his most engaging work. In album leaves in the style of Zhao Mengfu (*see* ZHAO, (1)), he reproduces Zhao's use of yellow–orange and warm green, a variant of the warm–cool or Gold-and-green (*jinbi*) idiom that in the Yuan period became popular with Southern school painters, and combines it with touches of blue and red on the foreground trees and bushes. A similar colour scheme appears in *White Clouds on the Xiao and Xiang Rivers, after Zhao Mengfu* (1668; see fig.). This is an outstanding example of Wang's many hanging-scroll landscapes in canonical styles,

Wang Jian: *White Clouds on the Xiao and Xiang Rivers, after Zhao Mengfu*, hanging scroll, ink and light colours on paper, 1355×625 mm, 1668 (Washington, DC, Freer Gallery of Art)

all with essentially the same composition: a river flanked by tall hills, a recession into the middle distance at one side, trees and houses, and a steep ridge rising to a central mountain. Wang notes that he once saw a Zhao Mengfu painting with the same title that 'followed completely' the style of Dong Yuan, this representing another step in the perpetuation of the Orthodox lineage. The power of Wang's work relies as much on the muscular interaction of land masses as it does on the felicity and elegance of particular brushstrokes, that is on the general conception of forms, as well as their execution. The representation of the hillside in the central portion, with its serpentine ridges and compartmentalized, jutting bluff, has only enough in

common with the natural world to allow recognition. In keeping with the Orthodox method, the composition is determined not by fidelity to the scenery of a specific locale but by a system of aesthetic formal rules governing placement and balance of landscape elements.

In essays on the painting of landscape by Dong Qichang, Zhao Zuo, Wang Yuanqi and others are allusions to the Chinese metaphysical concepts of geomancy (*fengshui*: 'wind and water'). A mountain, for example, is seen as a 'dragon in motion', with matter-energy (*qi*) coursing through it. Such ideas aid an appreciation of Wang Jian's dynamic middle-ground masses, their definition and activation of 'habitable' space, and his contrast of a still imposing peak in the distance with the nearer shore.

BIBLIOGRAPHY

Hummel: 'Wang Chien'; *EWA*: 'Wang Shih-min, Chien, Hui and Yuan-ch'i'

O. Sirén: *Chinese Painting: Leading Masters and Principles* (London, 1956–8), v, pp. 104–9

J. Cahill: 'The Orthodox Movement in Early Ch'ing Painting', *Artists and Traditions: Uses of the Past in Chinese Culture*, ed. C. F. Murck (Princeton, 1976), pp. 169–81

VYVYAN BRUNST, with JAMES CAHILL

Wang Jiqian [Wang Chi-ch'ien; C. C. Wang; *ming* Jiquan] (*b* Suzhou, Jiangsu Province, 14 Feb 1907). Chinese painter, calligrapher, collector and connoisseur, active in the USA. Wang studied Chinese painting and connoisseurship first with Gu Linshi (1865–1933) in Suzhou and subsequently with Wu Hufan (1894–1968) in Shanghai, where he gained access to major painting collections, including that of the Palace Museum. In 1947 he toured the USA and two years later settled in New York. Thereafter he did much to promote the study of Chinese painting in the USA and was often invited to lecture at universities and to advise museums and collectors. Exhibitions of his work were held in prestigious institutions in both Asia and the USA. In keeping with his study of traditional Chinese paintings, in his early work Wang followed the orthodox masters (*see* ORTHODOX SCHOOL) and continued the elegant styles of the later literati tradition (*see* CHINA, §V, 4(ii)). Living in New York put him in contact with trends in modern Western art. Finding parallels between Western abstract art and traditional Chinese painting with its emphasis on spiritual expression, from 1962 he aimed at a synthesis of the two. He experimented with new techniques, creating interesting 'accidental' textural formations without the brush, which he incorporated in his elaborate and complex artistic conception, achieving images that are monumental and overwhelming. His landscape paintings are intended to evoke thought and emotion and were referred to by him as 'mountains of the mind' or 'mind landscapes'. After 1980 he made more use of the brush, enriching his landscapes with interesting brush details and daring use of colour.

BIBLIOGRAPHY

The Landscape of C. C. Wang: Mountains of the Mind (exh. cat. by L. Katz and C. C. Wang, New York, Arthur M. Sackler Found., 1977)

A. Chang: 'The Landscape Paintings of Wang Jiqian', *Orientations*, xiv/1 (1983), pp. 26–39

J. Silbergeld: *Mind Landscapes: The Paintings of C. C. Wang* (Seattle, 1987)

MAYCHING KAO

Wang Meng [*zi* Shuming; *hao* Huanghe Shanqiao, Xiang-guang Jushi] (*b* Wuxing, Zhejiang Province, *c.* 1308; *d* 1385). Chinese landscape painter, poet and scholar–official. He is traditionally ranked as one of the Four Masters of the Yuan, with HUANG GONGWANG, NI ZAN and WU ZHEN. He was the leading figure in the development of a type of landscape that blended monumental, powerful visual presence with complex, ambiguous structures evocative of mental states and personal situations. Later generations of artists painted landscapes in imitation of Wang Meng, creating an image of his style that at times has obscured his own achievement and identity.

Wang Meng was born into an eminent family of scholars, artists and officials. His father, Wang Guoqi (1284–*c.* 1366), was a poet, calligrapher and connoisseur; his maternal uncle was the painter–official Zhao Yong, and his maternal grandfather was Zhao Mengfu, the leading painter and calligrapher of the early part of the Yuan period (1279–1368). Little is known of Wang Meng's early life except that he had a talent in poetry. Family connections were probably crucial in his securing an introduction into cultured circles. Wang moved to Mt Huanghe near Hangzhou, from which derives his literary name, Huanghe Shanqiao ('Fuel gatherer of Mt Huanghe'), and embarked on a career as a painter, perhaps in the early 1340s, although no genuine works survive from this period. He also travelled widely in nearby areas of southeastern China, including Suzhou and Wuxi (Jiangsu Province) and Songjiang (in modern Shanghai Municipality), visiting famous sites, attending literary gatherings and becoming acquainted with the leading writers and painters of the day.

Wang Meng's *Secluded Dwellings in Summer Mountains* (*c.* 1354; hanging scroll, ink on silk; Washington, DC, Freer; see fig. 1) is representative of his early style. Features suggesting the influence of Zhao Mengfu (*see* ZHAO, (1)) include the schematic river landscape composition, simplified figural and architectural details and the systematic use of 'hemp-fibre strokes' (*pima cun*) for texturing rocks and mountains, a technique associated with the 10th-century painters DONG YUAN and JURAN. The centralized, frontal composition and rich, multi-layered spatial complexity are Wang Meng's own innovations. *Fisherman-recluse at Huaqi* (vertical scroll, ink and light colours on paper; Taipei N. Pal. Mus.), probably of later date, is similar in style. Both works are preoccupied with the theme of reclusion and withdrawal, echoed in the stylistic retreat to a manner already centuries old. Wang Meng's own attitude to political engagement is difficult to ascertain. There is evidence that he was a provincial prosecutor (*liwen*) in the late Yuan period; he may have had the post as early as the 1340s, serving the Mongol rulers as did many of his maternal relatives. His withdrawal to Mt Huanghe perhaps marked a severance of that service and a response to the stirrings of military uprisings that began to affect south-eastern China at that time.

Wang Meng painted his most historically important and powerful works in the 1360s, a decade of social and political upheaval in south-east China, during which Mongol authority was displaced. He was often in Suzhou at this period—he participated in a literary gathering there in 1365, with Ni Zan, Gao Qi (1336–74), Yao Guangxiao

1. Wang Meng: *Secluded Dwellings in Summer Mountains*, hanging scroll, ink on silk, *c.* 1354 (Washington, DC, Freer Gallery of Art)

(1335–1418), Zhang Yu (1333–85) and others—and perhaps, like many cultural figures, served in the rebel administration of Zhang Shicheng (1321–67) based in the city. Issues of loyalty and affiliation, and of involvement versus withdrawal, were particularly pressing in such an environment. Though Wang's paintings of the 1360s have no overt political content, the political situation constitutes a subtext to his increasingly powerful pictorial representation of themes of reclusion. His landscapes of the mid-1360s share an exploitation of tonal contrast for dramatic effect. In reflection of 10th- and 11th-century landscape styles, especially that of Guo Xi, they have powerful, monumental mountainscape compositions and are preoccupied with the cycle of the seasons. At a time characterized by an intellectual, almost diagrammatic reworking of the past, Wang's paintings derive their individualism from the investing of monumental themes with personal expression.

Wang's *Spring Plowing at the Mouth of the Valley* (vertical scroll, ink on paper; Taipei, N. Pal. Mus.) probably dates to the early 1360s. There is a crowding of forms (to become more pronounced in later works), a soft chiaroscuro and use of the Dong Yuan–Juran 'hemp-fibre' idiom.

The ostensibly bucolic theme is tempered by hints of structural ambiguities and the somewhat disquieting constriction of pathways through the landscape. These aspects are developed in *Lofty Recluses in Summer Mountains* (1365, vertical scroll; ink and colours on silk; Beijing, Pal. Mus.), in which the breadth of the scene, the complexity of subsidiary forms and pathways, an almost total closure of the background and a dark tonal range create an effect verging on the oppressive, at odds with the theme of quiet summer seclusion. *Ge Hong Moving his Residence* probably dates to the same period. It is notable for its explicit narrative theme, that of the 4th-century AD scholar–official Ge Hong late in life, after giving up government service, wandering with his family in search of alchemical knowledge, appropriate to the sense of uprootedness felt at the end of the Yuan. There is a contrast with the images of quiet domesticity of Wang's early landscapes. In this painting the cottages nestled in a distant valley are cut off by seemingly impassable terrain, composed largely of angular and deeply undercut blocky forms unusual for the period.

Wang's most powerfully complex image of the natural world is his *Dwelling in Reclusion in the Qingbian Mountains* (see fig. 2), which reflects on many of his earlier concerns: family relationships, social and political upheaval, pictorial sources of the past and eremitic withdrawal. It depicts a site near Wang's home town of Wuxing that had been a family retreat as far back as the time of Zhao Mengfu, and it was probably done for a contemporary relative who was forced to flee from a retreat in the mountains in the military campaigns of mid-1366. The image of a shattered family refuge is portrayed in a mixed style, drawing on both the 10th-century southern style of Juran and the 11th-century northern style of GUO XI. Deliberate ambiguities of space, light and structure emphasize the idea of landscape as personal expression. *A Refined Gathering among Forests and Streams* (1367; vertical scroll; untraced) portrays, in a more unified style, an idyllic retreat set before a restrained, monumental landscape. The scene is limited to a few elements—stately pines, regularly shaped central cliffs—given impact by a consummate control of ink tone. In *Reading in Spring Mountains* (vertical scroll, ink on paper; Shanghai Mus.) a group of similar tall pines and central cliffs is enlivened by the leaning of the trees.

After Zhu Yuanzhang founded the Ming dynasty (1368–1644) and became the Hongwu emperor (*reg* 1368–98), Wang Meng served briefly as sub-prefect magistrate in Taian, Shandong Province. Literary records note that at this period he executed a painting of Mt Tai in collaboration with the artist Chen Ruyan. Wang seems to have moved to the capital, Nanjing, *c.* 1371, where his activities were focused for the rest of his life. His association with Buddhist monks in Nanjing is recorded, but no reliable dated works from the period survive. However, a cluster of stylistically related works are distinguishable from his better documented early- and middle-period works: *Forest Chamber Grotto at Juqu* (vertical scroll, ink and colours on paper; Taipei, N. Pal. Mus.), *Su'an Retreat* (vertical scroll, ink and colours on paper; New York, C. C. Wang priv. col.), *Buddhist Temple at Mt Taibo* (handscroll, ink and colours on paper; Shenyang, Liaoning Prov. Mus.) and others. Characterized by a loosening of brushwork

2. Wang Meng: *Dwelling in Reclusion in the Qingbian Mountains*, hanging scroll, ink on paper, 1410×422 mm, 1366 (Shanghai, Shanghai Museum)

and pictorial structure consistent with works of later age, they share a rich texturing of forms with dynamic curling strokes and dots, a liberal use of colour and compositions crowded with relatively small-scale forms. Many depict studios, retreats or temples, often with Buddhist or Daoist associations. They lack the seasonal overtones and spatial grandeur of earlier works, as well as clearly definable stylistic references to earlier paintings.

Wang Meng eventually fell victim to Hongwu's paranoia, as had so many of his literati associates from the south-east. It was reported that he had visited the home of the prime minister Hu Weiyong, who was executed in 1380 for allegedly taking part in a plot to assassinate the Emperor. Wang was put in prison and died there in 1385. Wang Meng was the most prominent figure in a loose grouping of painters active in the late Yuan and early Ming periods, including FANG CONGYI, CHEN RUYAN and Xu Ben (d 1378), who depicted monumental mountainscapes crowded with dynamic and textured forms strongly indebted to 10th- and 11th-century painting. Wang's version of the mode was the one most imitated by Ming (1368–1644) and Qing (1644–1911) artists.

EWA

BIBLIOGRAPHY

M. Loehr: 'Studie über Wang Mong (die datierten Werke)', *Sinica*, xiv/5 and 6 (1939), pp. 273–90

V. Contag: 'Schriftcharakteristiken in der Malerei, dargestellt an Bildern Wang Meng's und anderer Maler der Südschule', *Ostasiat. Z.*, n. s., xvii (1941), nos 1 and 2, pp. 46–61

O. Sirén: *Chinese Painting: Leading Masters and Principles* (London, 1956–8), iv, pp. 85–92

Pan Tianshou and Wang Bomin: *Huang Gongwang yu Wang Meng* (Shanghai, 1958)

Wang Jiqian and Li Lincan: 'Wang Meng di "Huaxi yuyin tu"' [Wang Meng's 'Fisherman-recluse at Huaxi'], *Gugong Jikan*, i/1 (1966), pp. 63–8; Eng. summary, pp. 23–4

C. T. Li: 'Stages of Development in Yuan Landscape Painting, Part 2', *N. Pal. Mus. Bull.*, iv/3 (1969)

Wen Zhaotong: *Yuan ji si da huajia* [The four masters of the Yuan] (Hong Kong, 1970)

Zhang Guangbin: *Yuan si da jia: Huang Gongwang, Wu Zhen, Ni Zan, Wang Meng* [The four masters of the Yuan: Huang Gongwang, Wu Zhen, Ni Zan, Wang Meng] (Taipei, 1975)

J. Cahill: *Hills beyond a River: Chinese Painting of the Yuan Dynasty (1279–1368)* (New York, 1976), pp. 120–27

R. Vinograd: *Wang Meng's 'Pien Mountains': The Landscape of Eremitism in Later Fourteenth Century Chinese Painting* (diss., Berkeley, U. CA, 1979)

Wai-kam Ho, Y. Iriya and Y. Nakada: *Kō Kōbō, Gei San, Ō Mō, Go Chin* [Huang Gongwang, Ni Zan, Wang Meng, Wu Zhen], iii of *Bunjinga suihen* [Essence of Chinese and Japanese literati painting] (Tokyo, 1979)

R. Barnhart: *Along the Border of Heaven: Sung and Yuan Paintings from the C. C. Wang Family Collection* (New York, 1983)

R. Vinograd: 'Family Properties: Personal Context and Cultural Pattern in Wang Meng's "Pien Mountains" of A.D. 1366', *A. Orient.*, xiii (1983), pp. 1–29

RICHARD VINOGRAD

Wang Mian [Wang Mien; *zi* Yuanzhang; *hao* Zhushi Shannong] (*b* Zhuji, Shaoxing District, Zhejiang Province; *d* Kuaiji, in modern Shaoxing, Zhejiang Province, 1359). Chinese poet and painter. He was the most influential master in the later *momei* ('ink-plum') tradition and the only early plum specialist with a substantial surviving oeuvre.

Born into a modest family of the gentry, Wang, like many southern Chinese scholars under the Mongol Yuan dynasty (1279–1368), was thwarted in his ambition to enter official life. He became an eccentric itinerant, winning recognition as a scholar, poet and painter but failing to obtain sustained private or political patronage. He depended on painting plum blossoms for his living. In 1348, on returning south from the capital Dadu (modern

Beijing), he predicted chaos and withdrew to Mt Jiuli. In 1359, shortly before his death, he emerged from seclusion to offer strategic advice to the rebel forces of Zhu Yuanzhang; Zhu later became the emperor Taizu (*reg* 1368–98), first ruler of the Ming dynasty (1368–1644). A problematic figure in his own time, Wang was idealized by later scholars; he remains best known for his fictional role as a paragon of virtue in the 18th-century novel *Rulin waishi* ('The scholars').

Wang was the pivotal figure in the development of the *momei* genre from classical Song (960–1279) practice to the later tradition that has endured into modern times (*see* CHINA, §V, 3(vi)(c)). He created stylized plum branches with sweeping horizontal or vertical S-curves framing poetic inscriptions, as for example *Ink Plum* (New Haven, CT, Yale U. A. G.; *see* CHINA, fig. 125). By joining pictorial and written elements in formal and expressive unity, he extended the subtlety and range of the genre and established its characteristic form. Wang's large hanging scrolls feature new heroic images of massive, battered old trees with soaring young branches in full bloom. Because of traditional associations of plum blossoms with endurance and simplicity, and in conjunction with Wang's vivid personality, such images became an emblem of integrity and survival in adversity. Wang's works became the definitive stylistic and iconographic model for later *momei* painting, and his life inspired other scholar-painters who had to turn their literati accomplishments into their means of subsistence.

Wang's paintings survive in collections in Asia and the USA, including the Cleveland Museum of Art, Cleveland, OH; the Metropolitan Museum of Art, New York; the Shanghai Museum; the National Palace Museum, Taipei; the Palace Museum, Beijing; and the Imperial Household Collection, Tokyo. His poetry is collected in his *Zhu zhai shiji* ('Poetry collection of the Bamboo Studio').

BIBLIOGRAPHY

DMB: 'Wang Mien'

O. Sirén: *Chinese Painting: Leading Masters and Principles* (London and New York, 1956–8), iv, pp. 100–02; vi, pls 118–19

Hong Rui: *Wang Mian* (Shanghai, 1962)

Li Chu-tsing: 'Problems Concerning the Life of Wang Mien, Painter of Plum Blossoms', *Renditions*, 6 (Spring 1976), pp. 111–24

Wang Te-i and others, eds: *Yuan ren zhuan ji ziliao suoyin* [Index to biographical materials of Yuan Figures] (Taipei, 1979), i, pp. 104–6

Chen Gaohua, ed.: *Yuan dai huajia shiliao* [Historical materials on painters of the Yuan period] (Shanghai, 1980), pp. 350–70

Chi Jo-hsin: 'Wang Mian yu momei hua de fazhan' [Wang Mian and the development of ink-plum painting], *Gugong Xueshu Jikan*, ii/1 (Spring 1985), pp. 37–58; ii/2, pp. 41–66; ii/3, pp. 29–51

Bones of Jade, Soul of Ice: The Flowering Plum in Chinese Art (exh. cat., ed. M. Bickford; New Haven, CT, Yale A. G., 1985), pp. 76–82, 256–7

MAGGIE BICKFORD

Wang Mien. *See* WANG MIAN.

Wang Shen [*zi* Jinqing] (*b* Taiyuan, Shanxi Province, *c*. 1046; *d* after 1110). Chinese connoisseur, collector and painter. Son-in-law of the Northern Song emperor Yingzong (*reg* 1064–8), Wang collected old and modern paintings and writings about painting, thus acquiring a good knowledge of different styles. He also exchanged ideas about classical studies and aesthetics with his friend, the eminent writer and artist SU SHI. He based his landscape paintings on two distinct modes: for the more serious and austere he used the monochrome ink style of LI CHENG, and for the grand and lavish he took up the Blue-and-green (*qinglü*) manner of Li Sixun (*see* LI, (1)). Both styles exhibited the then prevalent idea of expressing the artist's personal interpretation of nature's force and spirit. Wang frequently included tiny figures of fishermen and gentlemen in his landscapes as an indication of man's position in nature. He often portrayed misty rivers and valleys with massive mountains in the middle ground and background, and in the foreground heavy, wrinkled rocks, to which cling dry, writing pine trees. His rivers or lakes usually twist among the rocks and mountains, as for example in *Fishing Village in Light Snow* (handscroll, ink and light colours on silk, 444×2197 mm; Beijing, Pal. Mus.), though a massif sometimes rises from a wider surface of water. Streams with waterfalls rive the mountains and become mixed with clouds and mists, and trees are scattered among the rocks. The texture of the mountains is suggested by dark and light brushstrokes, whereas their contours are executed in forceful, long and short calligraphical strokes. In some of Wang's coloured paintings the blue and green colours are reduced to a minimum in order to highlight the central massif and to avoid spoiling the basic monochrome setting, as in a *Cliff Folds up in the Yan River* (452×1660 mm; Shanghai Mus.).

BIBLIOGRAPHY

O. Sirén: *Chinese Painting: Leading Masters and Principles* (London and New York, 1956–8), ii, pp. 70–71

BENT L. PEDERSEN

Wang Shih-chen. *See* WANG SHIZHEN.

Wang Shih-min. *See* WANG (ii), (1).

Wang Shimin. *See* WANG (ii), (1).

Wang Shizhen [Wang Shih-chen; *zi* Yuanmei; *hao* Fengzhou, Yanzhou Shanren] (*b* Taicang, near Suzhou, Jiangsu Province, 1526; *d* Taicang, 1590). Chinese art patron, literary critic, poet and scholar–official. Born into a wealthy, aristocratic family, Wang passed the national civil-service examinations to gain the title of *jinshi* at the early age of 21. He spent most of his life in public service, retiring temporarily from 1560 to 1567 after his father was tried and executed at the instigation of Grand Secretary YAN SONG (the feud between the families was the subject of great contemporary interest and notoriety), and again from 1570 to 1574 after his mother died. From then on he remained more or less on active duty almost until his death.

Wang is best known for his patronage of painters, but in his own day he was most celebrated for his literary achievements. He became an influential member of the *guwen* movement, which advocated a revival of the Qin (221–206 BC) and Han (206 BC–AD 220) style of literary prose. He is anecdotally attributed with authorship of the great novel *Jinping mei* ('Golden lotus') and the drama *Mingfeng ji* ('Cry of the phoenix'; *c.* 1565).

Wang's most fruitful artistic connections were with painters around Suzhou. It is certain that he himself did not paint to any significant extent, but he sponsored painters and collected paintings. Artists he supported include LU ZHI, Wen Jia, You Qiu (*fl* 1570–90) and Mo Shilong (*c.* 1538–87). Perhaps the best-known extant work associated with Wang is the topographic album painting in three parts originally by Qian Gu (1508–*c.* 1578) and completed *c.* 1575 by Zhang Fu (1546–after 1631), the *Shuicheng tu* ('Journey by water'; Taipei, N. Pal. Mus.). This records Wang's return to Beijing in 1574 along the Grand Canal and is an early precursor of a painting genre that became extremely popular in the 17th century.

Although Wang certainly accumulated an art collection, no specific catalogue was ever compiled. Most of what is known about his acquisitions and his views on painting comes from his literary contributions on the subject, in the form of dedications, rubbings, colophons, calligraphy, histories and poetry, as collected in the *Yanzhou Shanren sibu gao* ('Wang Shizhen's writings'), completed in 1576. After Wang's death, further writings were published in the *Yanzhou Shanren xu gao* ('Supplement to Wang Shizhen's writings'), edited by a grandson. It is unlikely that all the paintings he commented on or inscribed were in his possession. Indeed, he often borrowed works in order to have them copied.

In the mid-1560s, during the mourning period after his father's execution, Wang became interested in garden design and instigated the building of two gardens in Taicang, the Lizi yuan and another, later named the Yanshan yuan. The artists Qian Gu and You Qiu executed paintings to commemorate the completion of the Lizi yuan in 1565.

BIBLIOGRAPHY

DMB: 'Wang Shih-chen'

H. Lovell: *Annotated Bibliography of Chinese Painting Catalogues and Related Texts*, MI Pap. Chin. Stud., xvi (1973), pp. 17–21

L. Yuhas: 'Wang Shih-chen as Patron', *Artists and Patrons: Some Social and Economic Aspects of Chinese Painting* (Kansas City, MO, 1980), pp. 139–45

C. Clunas: *Superfluous Things: Material Culture in Early Modern China* (London, 1991)

LAURA RIVKIN

Wang Tingyun [Wang T'ing-yün; *zi* Ziduan; *hao* Huanghua Shanren] (*b* Xiongyue, Liaoning Province, 1151; *d* Beijing, 1202). Chinese painter, calligrapher and poet. A scholar–painter who perpetuated the ideals of Su Shi and his circle, he was the most prominent artist of the Jin period (1115–1234), the alien Jürchen (Ruzhen) regime in northern China. He and his circle flourished during the reign of Zhangzong (*reg* 1190–1208), the cultural high point of the Jin period. Best known for his paintings after WEN TONG of bamboo, the quintessential scholar's subject (*see* CHINA, §V, 3(vi)(c)), Wang also painted monochrome landscapes and old trees. In calligraphy, he modelled his style after MI FU and was most skilled in running script (*xingshu*). His contemporaries acclaimed him as excelling in the Three Perfections (*sanjue*) of poetry, calligraphy and painting.

Wang came from a prominent literati family, possibly non-Han, and passed the civil service examination to gain the title of *jinshi* in 1176. In 1180, under suspicion of corruption, he suspended his career as a local official and retired to study and practise self-cultivation at Huanghuashan, near Anyang in Henan Province. Recalled to office in the capital by Zhangzong, Wang was ordered to catalogue the palace collection of calligraphy and painting in 1192. Shortly afterwards he was made a compiler at the Hanlin Academy, the highest office of his career.

Wang's sole surviving work is the short handscroll entitled *Secluded Bamboo and Withered Tree* (1180s; Kyoto, Yurinkan; *see* CHINA, §V, 5(ii), fig. 136), an ink-splashed, impressionistic rendering of a pale and mossy old tree beside a dark young bamboo. The painting, in ink monochrome on paper, is richly varied in textures, tonalities and brush techniques. Wang also wrote the four large characters that constitute a frontispiece and the cursive-script inscription that follows the painting. His calligraphy is forceful but elegant, showing a natural modulation from dark, thick strokes to pale, dry ones as the brush ran out of ink. The Yuan critic Tang Hou's colophon on the scroll praises it as an exemplary piece of scholarly 'ink-play'.

On Wang Tingyun's calligraphy *see also* CHINA, §IV, 2(iv)(b).

WRITINGS
Huanghua ji [Collected writings from Huanghua]

BIBLIOGRAPHY
Tuotuo and others, eds: *Jin shi* [Standard history of the Jin dynasty] (1345); punctuated edn (Beijing, 1975), *juan* 126, pp. 2730–32
K. Shimonaka, ed.: *Shodō zenshū* [Complete collection of calligraphy], xvi (Tokyo, 1955), pp. 8, 31–2, 161–2, 174; pls 92–4
J. Cahill: *Chinese Painting* (Ascona and New York, 1960), pp. 94–6
S. Bush: 'Literati Culture under the Chin (1122–1234)', *Orient. A.*, n. s., xv (1969), pp. 103–12
Chen Gaohua, ed.: *Song Liao Jin huajia shiliao* [Material on painters of the Song, Liao and Jin periods] (Beijing, 1984), pp. 819–31

JULIA K. MURRAY

Wang Wei [*zi* Mojie] (*b* near Taiyuan, Shaanxi Province, AD 701; *d c.* 761). Chinese poet, painter and musician. One of China's greatest poets, he was also a painter at a time when relatively few men of high social position practised this art. His reputation as a painter was limited in his own time, but his unparalleled stature as a man of letters attracted the attention of scholar–official painters of subsequent periods, who celebrated Wang Wei as the founder of the literati tradition of painting (*see* CHINA, §V, 4(ii)). Born into a powerful and prestigious clan, at the age of 15 he dazzled the Tang court at Chang'an (modern Xi'an, Shaanxi Province) with his precocious skills as a poet, painter, calligrapher and musician. He passed the metropolitan examinations to receive his *jinshi* degree at the age of 20 and was appointed Assistant Secretary of Music. He ended his career with the high office of Right Assistant Director of the Department of State Affairs.

Despite his lifelong service to the court, Wang Wei continuously expressed longing for the life of the recluse, and he periodically retired to the countryside, particularly his famous estate at Wangchuan (about 47 km south of Chang'an). He was also a devout Buddhist, taking the sobriquet Mojie, which, combined with his given name Wei, recalls the great Indian Buddhist layman, Vimalakirti. The identification was significant: Vimalakirti, a man who lived in the mundane, material world with family and servants, yet maintained spiritual purity, provided the perfect model of being simultaneously engaged yet detached, a part of society yet transcending the vagaries of human existence. This same quality of detachment underlies many of Wang Wei's best poems. His juxtapositions of imagery and colours quietly capture the essence of nature's processes and suggest a glimpse into a realm of meaning beyond material substance. His fame as a poet of images that convey the ineffable, and a longstanding tradition of having painted Meng Haoran (689–740) in the act of composing a poem while riding a donkey, made

Wang Wei (attrib.): *Fu Sheng Transmitting the Classics* (detail), handscroll, ink and colours on silk, 254×447 mm, mid-8th century AD (Osaka, Municipal Museum of Art)

Wang Wei a natural focus of attention in the 11th and 12th centuries, when serious efforts were made to link poetry to painting: the poet and art theorist Su Shi declared that within Wang Wei's paintings there were poems and within his poems paintings. The professional painters at the Academy often chose evocative couplets by Wang Wei as themes to be illustrated in the small fan and album-leaf format.

Wang Wei was primarily known for his landscapes. Judging from literary descriptions, these were characterized by level scenes and distant cloudy mountains with a degree of atmospheric perspective achieved through ink-wash techniques. There was a quality of blunt awkwardness to his paintings that was presumably cultivated and was perhaps inspired by an esteem for archaism. In the early 10th century Wang Wei was praised by Jing Hao for having judiciously brought together brush and ink-wash techniques. It was not until the late 11th century, however, when the emphasis on illusionism, grandeur and rationalism in landscape painting began to fade, that Wang Wei's paintings were fully appreciated. His archaism was esteemed, and it was held not only acceptable but a mark of his superior faculties that he portrayed the seasonal impossibility of a banana plant in snow. The precipitous rise of his popularity towards the end of the Northern Song period (AD 960–1127) was accompanied by an increasing ignorance of his paintings: according to Mi Fu, many of the delicate snowscapes produced in Shu (Sichuan Province) and the Jiangnan area during the Five Dynasties period (AD 907–60) were attributed to Wang Wei. Despite the rarity of authentic paintings by Wang Wei, his reputation grew, reaching its height when DONG QICHANG formulated his theory of the Northern and Southern schools of painting and established Wang Wei as the founder of the latter.

It is questionable whether any original works by Wang Wei survive. The most famous composition associated with him is the *Wangchuan Villa* scroll, a landscape of connected vistas that mostly match the poet's renowned 20-poem cycle describing his famous country estate, but this is known only through later recensions and interpretations. Also of note are three related snowscapes, the *Feeling of Snow on the River Bank* (Kyoto, Ogawa Col; Honolulu, HI, Acad. A.; Taipei, N. Pal Mus.) The latter, though a fragment, is close to the style of the Northern Song painter Zhao Lingrang, whose snowscapes, according to Mi Fu, were related to the many anonymous paintings commonly ascribed to Wang Wei in their time. Another snowscape, entitled the *Snowy Stream* (Sirén, iii, pl. 97), a small painting now lost but apparently once in the imperial collection of the Northern Song dynasty, joins this small group to provide an idea of the late 11th-century perception of Wang Wei. The figure painting *Fu Sheng Transmitting the Classics* (see fig.) is held by some to be an authentic work by Wang Wei. It portrays the aged Confucian scholar, who escaped the persecutions of Qin Shi Huangdi (*reg* 221–210 BC) and lived into the Han period (206 BC–AD 220) to transmit his exegesis of the *Book of Documents* (*Shujing*). Although the right half of the scroll, with the person(s) to whom Fu Sheng benignly expounds

a passage from the text, is missing, the painting remains a most compassionate and touching portrait.

See also CHINA, §V, 3(iv)(a).

EWA

BIBLIOGRAPHY

Zhao Diancheng, ed.: *Wang Youcheng ji jionzhu* [Annotated edition of Wang Youcheng's collected works], 28 vols (1737)
O. Sirén: *Chinese Painting: Leading Masters and Principles*, 7 vols (London and New York, 1956–8), i, pp. 125–35; ii, p. 21; iii, pls 90–98
Wen Fong: 'Rivers and Mountains after Snow (Chiang-shan hsüeh chi): Attributed to Wang Wei (AD 699–759)', *Archvs Asian A.*, xxx (1976–7), pp. 6–33
J. Cahill: *An Index of Early Chinese Painters and Paintings* (Berkeley, 1980), pp. 23–4
M. Sullivan: *Chinese Landscape Painting in the Sui and Tang Dynasties* (Berkeley, 1980), pp. 54–65
P. Yu: *The Poetry of Wang Wei: New Translations and Commentary* (Bloomington, 1980)
M. L. Wagner: *Wang Wei* (Boston, 1981)
Shan Chou: 'Beginning with Images in the Nature Poetry of Wang Wei', *Harvard J. Asiat. Stud.*, xlii/1 (1982), pp. 117–37
Xu Bangda: *Gu shuhua wei e kao bian* [Examinations of the authenticity of ancient paintings and works of calligraphy], 4 vols (Nanjing, 1984), i, pp. 107–18; ii, pls 156–9
P. C. Sturman: 'The Donkey Rides as Icon: Li Cheng and Early Chinese Landscape Painting', *Artibus Asiae*, 55 (April 1995), pp. 1–32

PETER C. STURMAN

Wang Wu-hsieh. *See* WONG, WUCIUS.

Wang Wuxie. *See* WONG, WUCIUS.

Wang Xianzhi. *See* WANG (i), (2).

Wang Xizhi. *See* WANG (i), (1).

Wang Yuan [*zi* Ruoshui; *hao* Tanxuan] (*b* Qiantang [now Hangzhou], Zhejiang Province; *fl* 1301–50). Chinese painter. Although known as a landscape and figure painter, he was particularly noted for his paintings of birds and flowers. One of the few recorded details of his life is that when young he worked under Zhao Mengfu, a leading painter of the early Yuan period (1279–1368), who was then serving as an official under the Mongol rulers in Hangzhou. It is said that through Zhao's instructions Wang gave up the academic style that had dominated Chinese painting during the Southern Song period (1127–1279) and began to study the works of ancient masters— the method of study advocated by literati artists (who stood in opposition to the academic tradition). Of some 50 paintings attributed to Wang, only about a quarter can be securely given to him. Most of these are birds and flowers painted in monochrome black ink, with some landscape elements in the background. Typical of his style are *Two Pheasants and Other Birds among Rocks and Bamboos* (1344; Shanghai Mus.), *Two Quails and Some Birds among Rocks and Trees* (1347; Cleveland, OH, Dean Perry priv. col., see Cahill, pl. 73) and *Quails and Sparrows among Rocks and Bamboos, after Huang Quan* (Osaka, Mun. Mus. A.). All three are hanging scrolls done only in black ink, with rocks, bamboo and other plants but no further background. This type of work seems to be derived from the tradition of the 10th-century master Huang Quan. Two other hanging scrolls in ink of this type, but with deeper spatial background, are *Bird on Peach Tree* (1346; Taipei, N. Pal. Mus.) and *Pheasant under Blossoming Peach Tree* (1349; Beijing, Pal. Mus.), which show some lingering influence of the academic landscape of the Southern Song, with misty background combined with the antique spirit. His only securely attributed landscape is the *Meeting in the Pine-tree Pavilion* (hanging scroll, ink and slight colours on silk, 1347; Taipei, N. Pal. Mus.), in which the trees, rocks, pavilion and boats show that he derived aspects of his style from the 11th-century painter Guo Xi.

BIBLIOGRAPHY
J. Cahill: *Hills beyond a River: Chinese Painting of the Yuan Dynasty, 1279–1368* (New York and Tokyo, 1976), pp. 157–8
Mu Yiqin: 'Wang Yuan and his Ink Bird and Flower Paintings', *Gugong Bowuyuan Yuankan*, iv (1979), pp. 48–53
Chan Gaohua: *Yuan dai huajia shiliao* [Literary sources of Yuan period painters] (Shanghai, 1980), pp. 521–4

Wang Yüan-ch'i. *See* WANG (ii), (2).

Wang Yuanqi. *See* WANG (ii), (2).

Wang Zhenpeng [Wang Chen-p'eng; *zi* Pengmei; *hao* Guyun Chushi] (*b* Yongjiā, Zhejiang Province, *c.* 1280; *d c.* 1329). Chinese painter. He was the most famous exponent of 'boundary painting' (*jiehua*), which is characterized by precision and accuracy, especially in the depiction of architectural details, usually achieved with a ruler. He served at the Yuan court in Beijing and became known to the emperor, Renzong (*reg* 1312–21), who bestowed on him the name Guyun Chushi ('The Hermit of Lonely Clouds'). Appointed an official in the fifth rank, he served in the Imperial Library, thus having an opportunity to view many of the paintings and books in that collection, sometimes even making copies of the paintings. He painted many works of interest to the Emperor and the court, such as famous palaces of the past, well-known pavilions and buildings, activities in the court and historical and Buddhist figures, all executed in extremely fine lines without colour.

Wang's most famous work, painted for the Emperor in 1310, is the *Dragon Boat Regatta on Lake Jinming*, depicting an event in the Dragon Boat Festival during the late 11th century. The original no longer survives, but there are several copies (e.g. Taipei, N. Pal. Mus.; Beijing, Pal. Mus.; Detroit, MI, Inst. A.; priv. col., Tokyo), some by Wang and others probably by his followers. The best version (handscroll, ink on silk; New York, Met.), painted in 1323 for the Emperor's elder sister, exemplifies his refinement in the detailed depiction of palaces, pavilions, dragon boats and figures. Other significant paintings include *Baiya Playing the Qin for his Friend* (handscroll, ink on paper; Beijing, Pal. Mus.), painted in the fine line (*baimiao*) manner, and *Hariti Nursing the Infant Buddha* (handscroll, ink on silk; Boston, MA, Mus. F.A.), in the *jiehua* manner.

BIBLIOGRAPHY
O. Sirén: *Chinese Painting: Leading Masters and Principles*, iv (London, 1956–8), pp. 36–7
K. Brock: *Wang Chen-p'eng: Painter of 'Chieh-hua'* (MA thesis, Lawrence, U. KS, 1975)
Chen Gaohua: *Yuan dai huajia shiliao* [Historical materials on Yuan period painters] (Shanghai, 1980), pp. 260–65
CHU-TSING LI

Wank, Roland (Anthony) (*b* Budapest, 2 Oct 1898; *d* New Rochelle, NY, 22 April 1970). American architect of Hungarian birth. He is best known as a designer of dams for the Tennessee Valley Authority (TVA), where he tried 'to make sure that the dams look as efficient as the engineers have made them'. Throughout his career he combined an understanding of technical requirements with strong artistic sensibilities. Educated at the Fine Arts Academy, Budapest, and the Royal Technical University of Budapest, he graduated in 1922 from the Technical University of Brno, Moravia (now in Czech Republic) and designed industrial projects before emigrating to the USA in 1924. Between 1927 and 1933 he worked in New York, designing the Grand Street cooperative housing (1929) for the firm of Springsteen & Goldhammer, the Union Station (1931) in Cincinnati, OH, and the passenger railway station (1932) in Hamilton, Ont., for Fellheimer & Wagner.

As Chief Architect for the TVA from 1933 to 1944, Wank was responsible for the architectural design of 18 dams and related facilities, of which Norris Dam (1933–7) was the first. Here he initiated the use of rough, board-formed concrete to provide texture to the walls of the power-house and incorporated visitor facilities in the building and site design. The clean lines, bold massing and rugged simplicity of these dams placed TVA in the forefront of modern design. After leaving TVA, Wank worked briefly for Albert Kahn Associates, then returned to Fellheimer & Wagner (which became Wank, Adams & Slavin), where his work for the New Jersey Turnpike Authority is among his best known.

BIBLIOGRAPHY
J. Huxley: 'TVA: An Achievement of Democratic Planning', *Archit. Rev.* [London], xciii (June 1943), pp. 139–66
F. Gutheim: 'Roland Wank: 1898–1970', *Archit. Forum*, cxxxiii (Sept 1970), pp. 58–9
M. Moffett and L. Wodehouse: *Built for the People of the United States: Fifty Years of TVA Architecture* (Knoxville, 1983)
MARIAN MOFFETT

Wańkowicz, Walenty (*b* Kalużyca, nr Minsk, 14 Feb 1799; *d* Paris, 12 May 1842). Polish painter. He began his studies in 1818 at the Fine Arts Department of the University of Vilna (now Vilnius, Lithuania) under Jan Rustem (1762–1835), before studying (1825–9) under Vasily Shebuyev, Aleksey Yegorov (1776–1851) and Aleksandr Ivanov at the St Petersburg Academy of Fine Arts, where he won a gold medal. Despite his training in the classicizing style of Rustem, Wańkowicz was more influenced by Romantic painting. In Vilna and St Petersburg he became acquainted with Aleksandr Pushkin and maintained close contact with the literary and artistic circle around the great Polish Romantic poet Adam Mickiewicz, whose portrait he painted in 1827–8 (oil on canvas; Warsaw, N. Mus.). This was exhibited at the Academy of Fine Arts in St Petersburg in 1828, and its exceptional popularity encouraged Wańkowicz to make several copies of it. From 1829 to 1840 Wańkowicz lived on his family's estate in Slepianka, near Minsk. During this period he became a disciple of Andrzej Towiański, a theosophist and the founder of a mystical sect of Polish emigrés in France. His portraits of this period, for example of *Andrzej Towiański* and of *Karolina Towiańska* (both oil on canvas, 1831; Warsaw, N. Mus.), are closer to the Biedermeier style. Although primarily a portrait painter, Wańkowicz also painted religious and symbolic paintings, which propagated Towiański's ideas, as well as many compositions commemorating Napoleon, such as *Napoleon by the Fire* (oil on canvas, 1834; Warsaw, N. Mus.). In 1840 he visited Dresden and Munich before going to Paris at Mickiewicz's invitation in the autumn of 1841.

BIBLIOGRAPHY

Z. Ciechanowska: 'Malarz sprawy Walenty Wańkowicz' [Walenty Wańkowicz: the painter of the idea], *Pamiętnik Lit.* [Literary memoirs] (1948), pp. 429–75

I. Svirida: 'Valenty Vankovich v Peterburge' [Walenty Wańkowicz in St Petersburg], *Mezhslavyanskiye kulturnyye svyazi* [Interslavic cultural communications] (Moscow, 1972), pp. 182–206

Polnische Malerei von 1830 bis 1914 (exh. cat., ed. J. C. Jensen; Kiel, Christian-Albrechts U., Ksthalle; Stuttgart, Württemberg. Kstver.; Wuppertal, von der Heydt-Mus.; 1978), pp. 263–4

Nineteenth-Century Polish Painting (exh. cat., Warsaw, N. Mus.; New York, N. Acad. Des.; 1988), pp. 52–3

BARBARA BRUS-MALINOWSKA

Wanley, Humfrey (*b* Coventry, 21 March 1672; *d* London, 6 July 1726). English palaeographer and librarian. He was one of the greatest palaeographers that Britain has produced, who even as a child enjoyed transcribing manuscripts. He went to Oxford University in 1695 as a protégé of the Bishop of Lichfield and, without taking a degree, became an assistant in the Bodleian Library in 1696. Here he contributed to one of the most ambitious scholarly projects of the time: the *Catalogus manuscriptorum Angliae et Hiberniae* (1697). From 1699 to *c.* 1705 he searched out and described Anglo-Saxon manuscripts for the second volume of George Hickes's *Linguarum veterum septentrionalium, thesaurus* (1705), compiling a catalogue that was not superseded until the 1950s. Wanley's lasting fame is due to his work as the devoted and trusted librarian to Robert and Edward Harley, Earls of Oxford, whose collections of manuscripts are now in the British Library, London. He acquired for them such landmarks of art and scholarship as the Codex Aureus (Harley MS. 2788), the Book of Nunnaminster (Harley MS. 2965), the Arnstein Bible (Harley MSS 2798–9) and the Bible Historiaux (Harley MSS 3481–2). Also now in the British Library is the diary (MSS Lansdowne 771–2) he kept between March 1715 and June 1726 (with a gap from Aug 1715 to Jan 1720), recording in vivid detail his administrative duties for the Harleys. It is a most skilfully narrated and witty account. His correspondence also survives in large quantities in the British Library, the Bodleian and elsewhere: 243 out of the known total of *c.* 450 letters are printed in Heyworth.

WRITINGS

Catalogus manuscriptorum Angliae et Hiberniae, ii (Oxford, 1697), pp. 33–4, 203–6

with G. Hickes: *Linguarum veterum septentrionalium, thesaurus grammatico-criticus et archaeologicus,* ii (Oxford, 1705) [cat. of Anglo-Saxon MSS]

A Catalogue of the Harleian Collection of Manuscripts . . . (London, 1759/*R* 1808–12), i, pp. 1–656; ii, 1–690 [description of the first 2407 MSS]

C. E. Wright and R. C. Wright, ed.: *The Diary of Humfrey Wanley,* 2 vols (London, 1966)

P. L. Heyworth, ed.: *Letters of Humfrey Wanley, Palaeographer, Anglo-Saxonist, Librarian, 1672–1726, with an Appendix of Documents* (Oxford, 1989)

BIBLIOGRAPHY

DNB

C. E. Wright: 'Humfrey Wanley: Saxonist and Library Keeper', *Proc. Brit. Acad.,* xlvi (1961), pp. 99–129

ANDREW G. WATSON

Wansart, Adolphe (*b* Verviers, 18 Oct 1873; *d* Uccle, nr Brussels, 3 Oct 1954). Belgian sculptor and painter. He studied at the academies in Liège and in Brussels (1889–1893), and in 1894 he married the painter Lucie De Smet. He excelled in executing portraits, both in his paintings, which are characterized by simple lines and vivid colours, and in his work as a sculptor, to which he turned *c.* 1900. His best works, dating from after 1920, include a portrait of *My Wife with Hat* (1923; Ghent, Mus. S. Kst.) and busts of the writers *André Baillon* (bronze, 1932; Brussels, Mus. A. Mod.) and *Fernand Crommelynck* (1942; Antwerp, Kon. Mus. S. Kst.). The emphasis on structure in such works, whether modelled or assembled, makes them look like stone carvings, conveying an impression of strength also evident in works on a monumental scale, such as *Navigation* (bronze, h. 4.4 m, 1934; Brussels, Grand Pal. Centenaire), *Burgundian Period* (blue stone, h. 6 m, 1948; Liège, Pont des Arches) and *Industry and Arts* (white stone, 25×5.5 m), a bas-relief that decorates the entrance of the Palais des Fêtes in Liège. His son, Eric Wansart (*b* 1899), was also a painter.

BIBLIOGRAPHY

R. de Bendere: *Artistes d'aujourd'hui: Cécile Cauterman, Rodolphe Strebelle, Ferdinant Schirren, Adolphe Wansart* (Paris and Brussels, 1924)

H. Kerels: *Adolphe Wansart* (Antwerp, 1955)

Rétrospective du sculpteur Adolphe Wansart (exh. cat., Uccle, Cent. A., 1955)

DANIELLE DERREY-CAPON

Wantage, Lady Harriet. *See under* LOYD, SAMUEL JONES.

Wappers, (Egidius Karel) Gustaf [Gustave], Baron (*b* Antwerp, 23 Aug 1803; *d* Paris, 6 Dec 1874). Belgian painter and teacher. He studied at the Antwerp Academie under Mathieu Van Brée, from whom he gained a taste for large-scale history painting and an admiration of Peter Paul Rubens. His first subjects were strictly classical (e.g. *Regulus*, 1823) and, like Van Brée, he illustrated episodes from the life of the great Flemish painters (e.g. *Van Dyck and his Model*, 1827; Amsterdam, Rijksmus.). He also painted a few portraits (e.g. *Portrait of a Lady*, 1828; Antwerp, Kon. Mus. S. Kst.). He exhibited his first work at the Salon of 1822 in Ghent. In 1824 he went to the Netherlands to look at works by the Old Masters, and from 1826 to 1829 he lived in Paris, during which time he ceased to exhibit at the Belgian Salons. In Paris he frequented the studios of such Romantic artists as Paul Delaroche and Horace Vernet but felt intimidated by the more audacious manner of Eugène Delacroix. When he reappeared at the Salon of 1830 in Brussels, his *Sacrifice of the Burgomaster van der Werff* (Utrecht, Cent. Mus.) was received enthusiastically. Although the subject had already been treated by Van Brée, Wappers cast it in a new Romantic light that reflected his time in Paris. This appealed to his Brussels audience, but the weighty, patriotic content of the work also encouraged claims that Wappers was a genius who had rediscovered a distinctively Belgian national art. Since July of that year Paris had been in the throes of revolution, and in Brussels unrest was brewing that finally broke out in September. In this tense atmosphere it was perhaps understandable that even such a mediocre work should have been so enthusiastically misinterpreted as leading the contemporary Belgian revolt against foreign artistic influences. For the same reason

Gustaf Wappers: sketch for *Events of September 1830*, oil on canvas, 650×760 mm, *c.* 1834 (Brussels, private collection)

François-Joseph Navez, the head of the Belgian Neo-classical school and a disciple of Jacques-Louis David, was widely attacked when his *Athalia Questioning Joash* (Brussels, Mus. A. Anc.) was hung opposite Wappers's picture at the Salon of 1830 in Brussels. In the following months Wappers hardened his anti-classical stance and turned Navez (by now his sworn enemy) and his followers into objects of derision.

Wappers was appointed professor at the Antwerp Academie in 1833 and became the head of the Romantic school in Antwerp. In the same year he exhibited at the Salon a portrait of *Leopold I* (Brussels, Mus. A. Anc.) and *Christ at the Tomb* (Leuven, St Michielskerk), which confirmed his success. In comparison to the work of Van Brée, however, they reveal Wappers to have been an artist of limited talent. He enjoyed another triumph the following year at the Antwerp Salon, where he exhibited the large *Events of September 1830* (Brussels, Mus. A. Mod.). The picture was displayed to widespread acclaim throughout Belgium and in several European capitals; it marked the summit of his career. While a sketch (Brussels, priv. col.; see fig.) for this work is in a bold and spontaneous style,

the final painting is not a masterpiece. The pathos of the conflict is expressed with an awkward theatricality, and the composition is uncomfortably crowded.

In 1839 Wappers was appointed Director of the Antwerp Academie, where he trained a large number of followers, including Lawrence Alma-Tadema. He resigned in 1853 to move to Paris, where the facile effects and at times cheap eroticism of his declamatory history paintings brought him steady success. Wappers was not so much continuing a great 17th-century Flemish tradition as dutifully following Van Brée; he shared Van Brée's opportunistic streak, and his work has a similar naivety and awkwardness.

BIBLIOGRAPHY

J.-G.-A. Lutherau: *Le Baron Gustave Wappers* (Paris, 1862)
Gustaf Wappers en zijn school (exh. cat., Antwerp, Kon. Mus. S. Kst., 1976)
1770–1830: Autour du Néo-classicisme en Belgique (exh. cat., Brussels, Mus. Ixelles, 1985–6), pp. 256–8, 380

DOMINIQUE VAUTIER

Waqqas, Tell. *See* HAZOR.

Warakhshah. *See* VARAKHSHA.

Waramin. *See* VARAMIN.

Warangal. *See* HANAMKONDA AND WARANGAL.

Warburg, Aby (*b* Hamburg, 13 June 1866; *d* Hamburg, 26 Oct 1929). German art historian. His research interests ranged widely, including the art of the Renaissance, costume, festivals, medicine, astrology and magic, but his primary contribution to cultural history is the Warburg Institute.

1. LIFE AND WORK. Warburg was born into a wealthy Jewish banking family and was never obliged to seek academic employment. He trained at the University of Bonn with scholars such as Hermann Usener (1834–1905) and Karl Lamprecht (1856–1915), becoming interested in psychology, in a broad evolutionary perspective and in historical periods of transition. He continued his studies in Munich, Florence and Strasbourg, finally completing a dissertation in 1891 on how Botticelli's *Primavera* and the *Birth of Venus* demonstrate the 'afterlife of the Antique'. At this time Jacob Burckhardt's interpretation of the Renaissance as a period of emancipation from medieval values and the rise of the modern individual was being challenged by scholars such as Henry Thode, who argued for an important role for Christian influences. Warburg can be seen as siding with Burckhardt in this disagreement; but whereas Burckhardt conceived of history as progress and the Renaissance as a cultural unity within that progressive movement, Warburg interpreted the Renaissance as a period of transition and uncertainty, viewing it as if abstracted from the course of time. For Warburg history was a vital and energetic tradition, communicated through images as well as words, but these documents could best be understood by looking for their non-temporal unity. Such themes were particularly evident in his dissertation and his writings of 1907 on Francesco Sassetti's burial chapel at S Maria Novella, Florence, where he affirmed that Renaissance artists learnt how to express pathos—emotion, vitality, energy, movement—from examples of Classical art. The same church also contains an image to which his writings often return as an example of this process, the figure, dubbed by Warburg the *Nympha*, of a serving-girl with free-flowing hair and garments in Ghirlandaio's *Birth of St John the Baptist*. Because he was concerned with the expression of intense emotion, psychological interpretations for the depictions of movement, and the role of empathy (*Einfühlung*), Warburg's name has often been associated with the phrase 'pathos formula' (*Pathosformel*).

In 1895 Warburg travelled in the United States, visiting Pueblo and Navajo peoples in the south-west. His interest in Native American rituals and artefacts is evidence of his early effort to break away from the confinement of traditional art-historical studies. He was committed to the view that art must be analysed in relation to its historical context, which for him included the period's arts, literature, science and intellectual scholarship in general. Between 1897, when he married the artist Mary Hertz, and 1918 Warburg worked on a variety of problems, most of which focused on the transition of medieval to Renaissance. He identified his own time with 15th-century Florence as a period of cultural clash between the old and new. During these years he also turned to the study of astrological imagery in order to investigate the emergence of rationality from magical beliefs and practices. His interest in schemes of correspondence between macrocosm and microcosm and of relationships between the human body and the zodiac led him to collect books on cosmology.

Too old to serve in World War I, Warburg began at this time to study political propaganda and pamphlets, focusing on Martin Luther, the German Reformation and Dürer's prints. In 1918 he succumbed to severe mental illness, which confined him to nursing homes. A test of his recovery in 1923 was his ability to deliver a lecture on 'Serpent Ritual', discussing his earlier visit to the Navajo. From 1927 until his death in 1929 Warburg focused on the role of memory in civilization, constructing a picture atlas, *Mnemosyne*, consisting of 40 large canvas screens holding nearly 1000 images. It is distinguished by Warburg's passion for the interrelationships between fascinating details; his favourite saying was 'Der liebe Gott steckt im Detail' ('God dwells in minutiae'). Writing was difficult for Warburg; he preferred working with movable images that did not need to be presented as part of one grand narrative. Thus in *Mnemosyne* he tried to demonstrate through images his typology for the expression of basic emotions, not through describing an historical sequence for the appearance of particular forms, but rather by juxtaposing images under disparate categories such as human sacrifice, tragic pathos, redemption, Oriental astrology and the *Nympha*.

Warburg's scholarly work, which began with the drapery styles of Filippino Lippi and Botticelli, covered a wide range of historical and iconographical issues. His method was part of a general trend to broaden the framework for the study of objects. This commitment was especially developed later in his life, when he turned to diverse cultural materials, including postage stamps, posters, playing cards, newspaper illustrations and photographs as resources in his investigations. He studied the interaction of form and content as traditions clashed and questioned the concept of art and style as the expression of a *Zeitgeist*. Warburg was always more concerned with the individual image as a record of a particular situation rather than in the work of art *qua* art: his life work argues persuasively against theories such as those of Heinrich Wölfflin and Alois Riegl that focus on formal and autonomous developments in art history.

2. THE WARBURG INSTITUTE. In 1909 Warburg established his extensive library, the result of his book-collecting since 1886, in a house in Hamburg, and in 1914 first discussed with his assistant Fritz Saxl the possibility of turning the library into an institute. But the outbreak of World War I made this impossible. However, on Warburg's return to Hamburg in 1924 after his illness, Saxl initiated the plan for making Warburg's private library into a research institute: Die kulturwissenschaftliche Bibliothek Warburg. This was opened in 1926 but moved to London in 1933 because of the deteriorating political situation in Germany. In 1944 it was incorporated into the University of London. The extensive library consists of a systematic yet idiosyncratic collection of information on numerous

topics related to the psychology of human expression. Many 20th-century art historians and scholars have been associated with the Warburg Institute, notably Saxl, Gertrud Bing, E. H. Gombrich, Ernst Cassirer, Erwin Panofsky, Edgar Wind and Dame Frances Yates.

WRITINGS

Sandro Botticellis 'Geburt der Venus' und 'Frühling'. Eine Untersuchung über die Vorstellungen von der Antike in der italienischen Frührenaissance (Hamburg and Leipzig, 1893)
Bildniskunst und florentinisches Bürgertum. Domenico Ghirlandaio in Santa Trinita: Die Bildnisse des Lorenzo de' Medici und seiner Angehörigen (Leipzig, 1902)
'Francesco Sassettis letztwillige Verfügung', *Kunstwissenschaftliche Beiträge August Schmarson gewidmet* (Leipzig, 1907)
G. Bing, ed.: *Gesammelte Schriften*, vols 1 and 2: *Die Erneuerung der heidnischen Antike* (Leipzig and Berlin, 1932/R Nedeln, 1969)

BIBLIOGRAPHY

E. H. Gombrich: *Aby Warburg: An Intellectual Biography* (London, 1970/R New York, 1986) [with extensive bibliog.]
S. Füssel, ed.: *Mnemosyne: Beiträge zum 50. Todestag von Aby M. Warburg* (Göttingen, 1979)
D. Wuttke, ed.: *Aby Warburg: Ausgewählte Schriften und Würdigungen* (Baden-Baden, 1979) [extensive bibliog., essays by other scholars]
S. Ferretti: *Il demone della memoria* (Genoa, 1984); Eng. trans. by R. Pierce as *Cassirer, Panofsky and Warburg: Symbol, Art and History* (London and New Haven, 1989)
W. Sauerländer: 'Rescuing the Past', *New York Times Review of Books* (3 March 1988), pp. 19–22
Warburg Institute: *Summary Guide to the Photographic Collection of the Warburg Institute, University of London* (London, 1988)

DEBORAH J. HAYNES

Warchavchik, Gregori (*b* Odessa, 2 April 1896; *d* São Paulo, 27 July 1972). Brazilian architect, writer and teacher of Russian birth. He studied architecture at the University of Odessa and the Scuola Superiore di Architettura, Rome, graduating in 1920, and he worked in Rome for the classicist architect Marcello Piacentini before moving to São Paulo in 1923 and entering private practice. In 1925 he published an article that became a manifesto for modern architecture in Brazil; its emphasis on the industrialization of construction, particularly of standard components for low-cost housing, foreshadowed the theories of CIAM, of which he was a member (1929–42). Warchavchik was responsible for the first modern houses in Brazil; they were functionalist designs and included his own house (1927–8), some low-cost housing (1929) and the 'Modernistic House' (1930), all in São Paulo. The latter, built for exhibition, introduced modern architecture to a wider audience; it was a Cubist design, complete with furniture, lighting and decoration, and it also contained works by avant-garde artists such as Anita Malfatti (1896–1964), Victor Brecheret, Emiliano di Cavalcanti, Lasar Segall and Tarsila do Amaral who had participated in the earlier Semana de Arte Moderna (1922). In 1931 Warchavchik was invited to teach a new course in modern architecture at the Escola Nacional de Belas Artes, Rio de Janeiro, by Lúcio Costa who had been appointed to direct and reform the teaching there. Although the course was short-lived, it introduced the principles of avant-garde European architecture to a generation of Brazilian architects. He worked in partnership with Costa from 1931 to 1933, and with Oscar Niemeyer in their team they carried out several Functionalist projects such as the group of low-cost houses (1933) in Gamboa, Rio de Janeiro. In 1939, with João B. Vilanova Artigas, Warchavchik won second prize in a competition for the town hall, São Paulo, his first urban-scale project (unexecuted). After 1940 his work moved away from the purism of his earlier projects and began to incorporate natural materials, as in the Crespi beach house (1943), with painted timber shutters, or the Prado beach house (1946), both in Guarujá. He continued to be a regular contributor to the newspapers of Rio de Janeiro and São Paulo until 1961; these writings and his early work had a profound influence on the development of modern architecture in Brazil.

WRITINGS

'Acerca de arquitetura moderna', *Correio Manha* (1 Nov 1925)

BIBLIOGRAPHY

A. Sartoris: *Gli elementi dell'architettura funzionale* (Milan, 1931)
G. Ferraz: *Warchavchik e a introdução da nova arquitetura no Brasil, 1925 a 1940* (São Paulo, 1966)

REGINA MARIA PROSPERI MEYER

Ward. English artists.

(1) E(dward) M(atthew) Ward (*b* Pimlico, London, 14 July 1816; *d* Windsor, 15 Jan 1879). Painter. His parents encouraged his early interest in art. He was sent to a number of art schools, including that of John Cawse (1779–1862), before gaining entry to the Royal Academy Schools in 1835. He first exhibited at the Royal Academy in 1834 with *Adelphi Smith as 'Don Quixote'* (untraced). In 1836 he went abroad for further study, visiting Paris and Venice on the way to Rome, where he spent three years. His first work of any consequence was *Cimabue and Giotto* (untraced), which he sent back to the Royal Academy show of 1839. On the way back to England at the end of that year Ward visited Munich to learn the technique of modern fresco painting in order to take part in the competition to decorate the Palace of Westminster, but his cartoon, *Boadicea* (1843; untraced), was unsuccessful. However, in 1852 he was commissioned to produce eight pictures for the Palace of Westminster, on subjects drawn from the English Civil War, the best of which is the *Last Sleep of Argyll* (1860s) in the Commons Corridor of the Houses of Parliament.

From 1840 until his death, Ward was a constant exhibitor at the Royal Academy, his primary choice of venue. His first notable success there was *Dr Johnson in the Ante-room of Lord Chesterfield Waiting for an Audience, 1748* (1845; London, Tate), for which his future wife (2) Henrietta Ward modelled for the principal female character. His entry of 1856 was also particularly popular: *Marie Antoinette Parting with the Dauphin* (untraced). Elected ARA in 1847, Ward became an RA in 1855 and for the next decade was patronized by the royal family and several important collectors of mainstream taste, including Robert Vernon. Both Ward and his wife enjoyed the influential support of their friend Samuel Carter Hall, editor of the *Art Journal*.

Throughout his career Ward chose his subjects from 17th- and 18th-century English history and French history of the Revolution and First Empire, often drawn from literary sources. With immaculately smooth brushwork and a rather hot palette he emphasized the touching and melodramatic aspects of the episodes he depicted. By the late 1860s his style began to go out of fashion. From 1874 Ward suffered a nervous disorder and died in 1879, possibly by his own hand. The contents of his studio were auctioned at Christie's on 29 March 1879.

BIBLIOGRAPHY

H. W. Sweny: 'Our Living Artists: E. M. Ward RA', *Mag. A.*, i (1878), pp. 14–19

J. Dafforne: *The Life and Works of E. M. Ward* (London, 1879)

Great Victorian Pictures (exh. cat., ed. R. Treble; ACGB, 1978), pp. 84–5

(2) Henrietta (Mary Ada) Ward (*b* London, 1 June 1832; *d* London, 12 July 1924). Painter, wife of (1) E. M. Ward. She was the daughter of George Raphael Ward and the miniaturist Mary Webb (*fl* 1828–49). An indulged only child, she was encouraged in her artistic talent and received instruction at home, supplemented by attendance at Henry Sass's drawing school. She also had advice from her husband, whom she married in 1848 against her family's wishes. She made her exhibition début at the Royal Academy in 1846 with the drawing *Elizabeth Woodville Parting from the Duke of York* (priv. col., artist's family). After her marriage Ward continued to attend Sass's and also the Royal Academy Schools lectures, although they were officially closed to women. From 1850 she exhibited widely in Britain, though she sent her principal works to the Royal Academy throughout her career. She also exhibited at the Society of Female Artists, which was formed in 1857.

Ward's early subjects were domestic genre paintings, still-lifes and portraits, though it was as a painter of historical genre that she became well known in the 1860s. Her frequent Royal Academy exhibits invariably featured dramas from English or French history, usually drawn from literary sources. The protagonists were royal, aristocratic or patriotic, often a mother and child or a family. Ward's greatest success was *Palissy the Potter* (1866; Leicester, Mus. & A.G.), though her celebration of the Quaker reformer and philanthropist Elizabeth Fry, *Newgate 1818* (1876; London, Friends House), was also very popular. In 1875 and 1876 she was proposed for election to the Royal Academy despite the official ineligibility of women. After her husband's death in 1879 she started a school for the artistic education of women, patronized by royalty and the aristocracy. Of the Wards' eight children, three became artists: Leslie Ward, Flora Ward (*fl* 1872–6) and Eva Ward (*fl* 1873–80).

WRITINGS

Mrs E. M. Ward's Reminiscences, ed. E. O'Donnell (London, 1911)

Memories of Ninety Years, ed. I. G. McAllister (London, 1924); repr. in *Canvassing: Recollections by Six Victorian Women Artists*, ed. P. Gerrish Nunn (London, 1986)

BIBLIOGRAPHY

P. Gerrish Nunn: 'The Case History of a Woman Artist: Henrietta Ward', *A. Hist.*, i (1978), pp. 293–308

Great Victorian Pictures (exh. cat., ed. R. Treble; ACGB, 1978), pp. 85–6

P. Gerrish Nunn: *Victorian Women Artists* (London, 1987), pp. 132–46

PAMELA GERRISH NUNN

Ward, Basil Robert. *See under* CONNELL, WARD & LUCAS.

Ward, Edmund Fisher. *See under* GOLLINS, MELVIN, WARD.

Ward, James (*b* London, 23 Oct 1769; *d* Cheshunt, Herts, 17 Nov 1859). English painter and engraver. He was the most important animal painter of his generation. Many of his dynamic compositions depict horses, dogs or wild animals in agitated emotional states, the sense of movement being reinforced by vigorous brushwork and strong colours. With their sweeping landscapes and dramatic skies, his canvases epitomize Romanticism. Not content to excel merely as an animal painter, Ward also produced portraits, landscapes and genre and history paintings of varying quality. A prolific artist, he was a frequent exhibitor at the British Institution and at the Royal Academy, London.

Ward was trained as an engraver by his brother William Ward (1766–1826) and John Raphael Smith and was in great demand as a mezzotinter at the end of the 18th century and the beginning of the 19th when he translated into prints works by William Beechey, John Hoppner, Thomas Lawrence and others. He began working in oil around 1790. Ward's painting career is traditionally divided into two phases, with 1803 as the watershed: in the first period the influence of his brother-in-law, George Morland, is most evident, particularly in genre scenes of children and rustics (e.g. *Children Playing in a Meadow*, *c.* 1795); in the second the influence of Peter Paul Rubens dominates. In 1803 Ward painted *Bulls Fighting, with a View of St Donat's Castle in the Background* (London, V&A) in emulation of Rubens's *Autumn Landscape with a View of Het Steen* (London, N.G.), then just recently acquired by Sir George Beaumont. His unsuccessful attempt to exhibit this painting and *Liboya Serpent Seizing its Prey* (lost) at the Royal Academy resulted in a rift with that institution; however, in 1807 he was elected an ARA. While the impact of Rubens on Ward's development is well documented and was long lasting (for a late example, see *Kenilworth Castle*, 1840; New Haven, CT, Yale Cent. Brit. A.), this traditional division of Ward's career oversimplifies the diverse influences, ranging from Classical art to Old Masters and contemporary painters, that shaped his highly eclectic style.

Shortly before 1810 Ward began painting portraits of thoroughbreds and blood horses. Among major early works in this genre, *Eagle* (1809; New Haven, CT, Yale Cent. Brit. A.) established him as 'the first of English animal painters now living' (*Sporting Mag.*, 1811, p. 265). Placed in a landscape that seems to stretch to infinity, the horse exudes the power and force typical of Ward's finest animal portraits. Similar works led to his being elected an RA in 1811, and many comparable examples followed. Of special note are Napoleon's charger *Marengo* and Arthur Wellesley, 1st Duke of Wellington's *Copenhagen* (both 1824; Alnwick Castle, Northumb.). These were undoubtedly painted as pendants; with the horses symbolizing their masters, the compositions comment on the conflict that pitted France against England.

In the 1810s and early 1820s Ward produced a number of major paintings. *Gordale Scar* (?1812–14; London, Tate; see fig.), depicting a gorge in North Yorkshire, ranks as one of his most ambitious compositions. The dark brooding landscape, dominated in the right foreground by a white aboriginal bull and populated with a vast array of cattle and deer, is one of the finest visualizations of the Sublime, an aesthetic then enjoying widespread currency.

From 1815 to 1821 Ward spent much of his time painting the *Waterloo Allegory* (lost), a gigantic composition of 6.4×10.7 m commissioned by the British Institution. It was during this period that Ward suffered a number

James Ward: *Gordale Scar*, oil on canvas, 3.33×4.22 m, ?1812–14 (London, Tate Gallery)

of personal tragedies, including the deaths of his wife and a daughter. The commission was the result of Ward winning the Institution's competition for a design honouring the Duke of Wellington's victory and the final defeat of Napoleon. The study for the painting (London, Chelsea Hosp.) is clearly indebted to Rubens's *Triumph of the Eucharist over Ignorance and Blindness* (1625–7; Madrid, Prado). Ward hoped to augment the money he received from the Institution by exhibiting the work privately in London with an entrance fee, a practice used to great advantage by such contemporaries as Benjamin West and John Singleton Copley. Derivative as it was of an outmoded artistic form, the completed allegory was neither a critical nor a financial success.

Although in the 1820s Ward created such successful and provocative compositions as *The Deer-stealer* (*c.* 1823; London, Tate) and a *Day's Sport* (1826; New Haven, CT, Yale Cent. Brit. A.), he became increasingly disillusioned with the art world. In 1830 he retired to a cottage in Cheshunt, Herts, with his second wife, but he continued to exhibit regularly at the Royal Academy and the British Institution.

Many works from the last several decades of Ward's life have religious themes or contain overt moral messages; for example he used a series of 20 canvases, which ostensibly depict character and expression in horses, as a vehicle for commenting on the human condition (e.g. *Confidence* and *Disappointment*, both *c.* 1840). These are described in the catalogue of works shown by the artist in 1841 at his London residence. Ward wrote theological tracts and poetry that date mostly from this period. A stroke in 1855 ended his artistic career and forced him to seek financial assistance from the Royal Academy.

BIBLIOGRAPHY

J. Frankau: *William Ward, A.R.A., James Ward, R.A.* (London, 1904)
C. R. Grundy: *James Ward, R.A.: His Life and Works* (London, 1909)
D. Farr: *James Ward, 1769–1859* (London, 1960)
G. E. Fussell: *James Ward, R.A.: Animal Painter, 1769–1859* (London, 1974)
E. Nygren: 'James Ward's Exhibition Pictures of 1838', *A. Bull.*, lxi (1979), pp. 448–59
——: *The Art of James Ward, R.A. (1769–1859)* (Ann Arbor, 1980)
——: *James Ward's 'Gordale Scar': An Essay in the Sublime* (London, 1982)

EDWARD J. NYGREN

Ward, John Quincy Adams (*b* nr Urbana, OH, 29 June 1830; *d* New York, 1 May 1910). American sculptor. He was apprenticed to the sculptor Henry Kirke Brown in Brooklyn from 1849 to 1856 and learnt to work in clay, plaster, marble and bronze. In 1861 Ward opened his own studio in New York. His first life-size sculpture, the *Indian*

Hunter (1866; New York, Cent. Park), was based on numerous studies and first-hand observation of the Dakota Indians and convincingly depicts a sinewy Indian youth holding back his snarling dog. The sculpture's success brought Ward numerous commissions for outdoor portrait busts and statues. Among his most celebrated monuments are the equestrian statue of *Major-Gen. George H. Thomas* (1878; Washington, DC, Thomas Circle) and the grandiose monument to *James Abram Garfield* (1887; Washington, DC, The Mall).

Ward believed that American sculptors should depict American subjects, and he fostered a native school of sculpture. In works such as *George Washington* (1883; New York, Wall and Broad Streets) and his masterful *Henry Ward Beecher* (bronze, 1891; Brooklyn, NY, Cadman Plaza) he combined the grace of Classical sculpture with a straightforward naturalism and psychological intensity. His mature bronzes are also attuned to the influence of Beaux-Arts sculpture (although not so closely as the work of Daniel Chester French and Augustus Saint-Gaudens), evidenced by their heightened realism, animated surfaces and multi-figure compositions.

Ward was the first sculptor to become president of the National Academy of Design (1874) and was the National Sculpture Society's first president (1893).

BIBLIOGRAPHY

W. Walton: 'The Work of John Quincy Adams Ward, 1830–1910', *Int. Studio*, xl (1910), pp. lxxxi–lxxxviii
A. Adams: *John Quincy Adams Ward: An Appreciation* (New York, 1912)
W. Craven: *Sculpture in America* (New York, 1968, rev. Newark, 2/1984), pp. 245–57

William Wilkinson Wardell: St Patrick's Cathedral, Melbourne, begun 1858; spires redesigned by Connolly and Van Heems, completed 1939

L. I. Sharp: *John Quincy Adams Ward: Dean of American Sculpture* (Newark, 1985) [definitive monograph, excellent plates]

MICHELE COHEN

Wardell, William Wilkinson (*b* London, 27 Sept 1823; *d* Sydney, 19 Nov 1899). English architect and engineer, active in Australia. He trained as an engineer for the Commissioners of the London Sewers (1839–1843) and as an architect with W. F. East. He greatly admired A. W. N. Pugin, whose work influenced him. In 1843 he became a convert to Roman Catholicism. Between 1846 and 1858 he designed 36 Catholic Gothic Revival churches in Britain, four in an Italianate style, and numerous parsonages, convent buildings and schools. His works are characterized by elegant proportions and architectonic massiveness. St Birinus (1847), Dorchester-on-Thames, Oxon, and Our Immaculate Lady of Victories (1849–51), Clapham, London, are excellent examples of his early Decorated work. His later work in Britain is characterized by a simpler and bolder architectural exposition, in which geometric, rather than curvilinear, patterns dominate the tracery design.

In 1858 owing to ill-health Wardell sold his professional practice and emigrated to Melbourne, Australia. In December of that year he was commissioned to design St Patrick's Cathedral, Melbourne (see fig.). The cruciform composition combines English geometric Decorated Gothic with a French-inspired apse of ambulatory and chevet chapels. The massive scale was enhanced by the use of local bluestone. Work on the cathedral continued throughout Wardell's lifetime and beyond; unfortunately the elegant proportions of the original design were marred by the elongated spires added in 1937. Some 16 Catholic parish churches were also built in Victoria from his designs.

In 1859 Wardell gained the position of Inspecting Clerk-of-Works and Chief Architect for the Government of the Colony of Victoria; in 1861 he became Inspector-General of the Public Works Department (PWD) and Chief Architect, a position he held until dismissal due to a change of government. Architecture for the PWD under Wardell's direction was characterized by conservatism. He favoured an Italianate style, building simply and solidly 'so long as proper architectural effect [was] preserved' (*Victorian Papers*, 1873). He gathered around him a talented group of draughtsmen. The PWD produced a series of buildings including the Newstead Court House (1865); Post Offices in Kilmore (1861), Beechworth (1869) and St Kilda (1874); and large works such as the General Post Office (1859–67, extn 1880), Supreme Court (1873–84) and Government House (1873), Melbourne. The latter is one of Australia's finest Italianate mansions and incorporates asymmetrical accents in a balanced composition. Public and private spaces are differentiated, and the prominent tower became a significant landmark on Melbourne's skyline. In the years immediately following his dismissal, Victorian PWD architecture visibly changed, becoming more flamboyant and eclectic.

In 1878 Wardell established himself in Sydney, having already designed the city's grandest collegiate building, St John's College (1859), Sydney University, and St Mary's Cathedral (1865), which was more traditionally English in plan than St Patrick's. His mainly secular Sydney practice was dominated between 1878 and 1899 by commissions for banks, such as the ES&A, Union and Australasian; private clubs, such as the Union (1883–8; destr. 1955) and the New South Wales or NSW (1884–6); and warehouses, such as the Grafton Bond (1881–2) and Australasian Steam and Navigation Company (1883–5). In the innovative Gothic ES&A Bank (1883; now ANZ), Melbourne, he combined solid masonry with a lightness and elegance inspired by Venetian Gothic; internally he provided a sumptuous Byzantine-inspired banking chamber.

UNPUBLISHED SOURCES
Sydney, Mitchell Lib. [largest repository of Wardell's drgs; lett., bks, misc. papers]
Melbourne, Dioc. Hist. Comm. [drgs and phot relating to St Patrick's Cathedral]
Melbourne, ANZ Bank Archv [drgs and phot relating to Bank comms]

BIBLIOGRAPHY
Victorian Papers Presented to Parliament by Command, Royal Commission into the Victorian Public Works Department (Melbourne, 1873)
W. A. Ebsworth: *St Patrick's Cathedral, Melbourne* (Melbourne, 1938, rev. 1979)
P. O'Farrell, ed.: *St Mary's Cathedral, Sydney, 1821–1971* (Sydney, 1971)
U. M. de Jong: *William Wilkinson Wardell: His Life and Work* (Clayton, Victoria, 1983)
——: *From England to Australia: The Architecture of William Wilkinson Wardell, 1823–99* (PhD diss., Clayton, Victoria, Monash U., 1988)

URSULA M. DE JONG

Wardour, 8th Baron Arundell of. *See* ARUNDELL, HENRY.

Ware. American family of architects, writers and teachers.

(1) William Robert Ware (*b* Boston, MA, 1832; *d* Boston, 1915). He belonged to a Boston family that played a crucial part in the development of the architectural profession in the USA. Graduating from Harvard University (1852), Cambridge, MA, he subsequently studied civil engineering at Harvard's Lawrence Scientific School and architecture in the Boston office of Edward Clarke Cabot (1818–1901). By 1859 he was in Richard Morris Hunt's New York studio, where he was introduced to the ideas of the Ecole des Beaux-Arts, Paris, where Hunt had studied. In 1863 Ware formed a professional practice with HENRY VAN BRUNT, a companion in Hunt's studio, and the firm of Ware & Van Brunt became active in the Boston area. The partnership's most notable work, the result of a limited competition held in 1865, is the Memorial Hall (1868–80), Cambridge, MA, a High Victorian Gothic Revival monument to Harvard men who died in the Civil War (1861–5). The partnership was dissolved in 1881 when Ware moved to New York, and his only substantial commission thereafter was the American School of Classical Studies (1886–8) in Athens.

In 1865 Ware was appointed the first professor and head of the new architecture programme at the Massachusetts Institute of Technology, Cambridge. His approach to architectural education was based on the design principles of the Ecole des Beaux-Arts, which he modified to suit conditions of practice in the USA. In 1881 he was asked to found a department of architecture in the School of Mines, Columbia University, New York, providing further evidence of the debt that 19th-century American architecture owed to building and engineering. A writer and lecturer on architecture, Ware lent his sense of

professionalism to *The American Vignola* (1901), a presentation of the Classical orders, written to assist those who were unable to go to architectural school and which has remained a standard text. He was also active in professional affairs, and, as a member of the American Institute of Architects, he drew up the official rules for architectural competitions adopted by the institute. He also served on many competition juries. Ware retired in 1903.

WRITINGS
An Outline of a Course of Architectural Instruction (Boston, 1866)
'On the Condition of Architecture and of Architectural Education in the United States', *Pap. RIBA* (1866–7), pp. 81–90
Greek Ornament (Boston, 1878)
'Architecture at Columbia University', *Architect & Bldg News*, x (1881), pp. 61–2
Modern Perspective (New York, 1882, rev. 1900)
'Instruction in Architecture at the School of Mines', *Sch. Mines Q.*, x (1888), pp. 28–43
The American Vignola (New York, 1901/*R* 1977)

BIBLIOGRAPHY
Macmillan Enc. Architects
J. A. Chewning: 'William Robert Ware at MIT and Columbia', *J. Archit. Educ.*, xxxiii (1979), pp. 25–9

(2) William Rotch Ware (*b* Boston, MA, 1848; *d* Boston, 1917). Nephew of (1) William Robert Ware. He was encouraged in the study of architecture and the promotion of the architectural profession by his uncle. After studying architecture at the Massachusetts Institute of Technology, Cambridge, he worked in his uncle's firm of Ware & Van Brunt before going to Paris, where, at the Ecole des Beaux-Arts, he was a member of Joseph Auguste Emile Vaudremer's studio (1874–6). On his return to the USA he became first assistant editor and then editor (from 1880) of the *American Architect and Building News*, the first American architectural journal. The publication was as important in establishing the professional status of the architect as were architectural schools and the American Institute of Architects (founded 1857), because it spread ideas about the professional practice of architecture to those beyond academia and the AIA meetings. Ware championed the work of such architects as H. H. Richardson, Robert Swain Peabody and McKim, Mead & White, and his influence through his journal's editorials and the works he edited was considerable.

BIBLIOGRAPHY
Obituary, *Amer. Architect*, cxi (1917), pp. 273–6
C. H. Walker: Obituary, *J. Amer. Inst. Architects*, v (1917), p. 242

JUDITH S. HULL

Ware, Isaac (*b* before 1704; *d* Hampstead, London, 6 Jan 1766). English architect. He was the son of a London cordwainer and was apprenticed to Thomas Ripley (*c.* 1683–1758), Master Carpenter to the Crown, in 1721. According to a story that Ware is said to have told to the sculptor Louis-François Roubiliac, a gentleman of 'taste and fortune' spotted him as he was sketching the Banqueting House in Whitehall in chalk on the basement of the building. He had the boy educated, sent him to Italy to study architecture and on his return helped him in his career.

It is unlikely that this anonymous benefactor was Richard Boyle, 3rd Earl of Burlington, as has been suggested, and the story may point instead to Ripley's patron Sir Robert Walpole. Indeed, Ware's publication in

1735 of detailed drawings of Walpole's mansion at Houghton in Norfolk suggests that he may have acted as Ripley's assistant when his master was supervising construction there during the 1720s. The possibility of an Italian trip is supported by Ware's ability to produce, in 1738, the best English translation of Palladio's *I quattro libri dell'architettura* (1570); he also (in 1756) translated Lorenzo Sirigatti's *La pratica di prospettiva* (1596). Nonetheless, by the 1730s Ware had direct connections with the Earl of Burlington's circle. In 1730 he provided drawings for at least two of the plates for the Earl's *Fabbriche antiche disegnate da Andrea Palladio* (1730), and his own publication the *Designs of Inigo Jones and Others* utilized several unpublished drawings from the Earl's collection; moreover, he dedicated his Palladio translation to the Earl, whose assistance is acknowledged in the preface.

In 1728, at the end of his apprenticeship, Ware had joined the Office of Works as Clerk Itinerant and Draughtsman. He was subsequently made Clerk of the Works at Windsor and Greenwich before being appointed Secretary to the Board in 1736. In this capacity he pursued a career as an architectural civil servant until his death. Little is known of this aspect of his activity, and his reputation rests on a relatively small number of commissions outside the Office of Works. The principal sources of his style are illustrated by the two unexecuted schemes he prepared in 1735 for a new Mansion House for the City of London, one derived from Inigo Jones's Banqueting House, Whitehall, and the other from the Earl of Burlington's Chiswick House, London. Ware's buildings in general exemplify the well-mannered astylar Palladianism propagated by the architects of the Office of Works and are particularly close in manner to those of his more prolific colleague Henry Flitcroft. Typical examples are Clifton Hill House (1746–50), Bristol, an austerely elegant villa that had a considerable influence both in Bristol and further afield, and Amisfield House (1756–9; destr. 1928), Lothian, which was probably Scotland's finest Palladian mansion. At Wrotham Park (1754), Herts, he ingeniously synthesized Chiswick and Colen Campbell's Wanstead, Essex, prototypes of the Palladian villa and mansion respectively.

Despite his apparent conformity to Palladian norms, Ware was also a prominent member of the St Martin's Lane Academy in London, where he associated with such proponents of the Rococo as Hogarth and Roubiliac. At his finest building, Chesterfield House (1748–9; destr. 1934), Mayfair, London, he contrived a dazzling suite of rooms in an authentic French Rococo idiom that was unique for its time in England. He could also turn his hand to Gothic, as at Chicksands Priory (1750), Beds. The text of his most important publication, the compendious *Complete Body of Architecture*, makes clear his view that, having studied and assimilated the works of such past masters as Palladio and Jones, the architect must feel free to indulge the fancies of his own genius. Through its wide currency the book helped to loosen the stranglehold of Palladian orthodoxy in the 1750s and 1760s.

WRITINGS
The Designs of Inigo Jones and Others (London, 1731, 1743, 1756)
The Plans, Elevations and Sections of Houghton in Norfolk (London, 1735)
trans.: *The Four Books of Architecture: By Andrea Palladio* (London, 1738)
A Complete Body of Architecture (London, 1756, 1767, 1768)
trans.: *The Practice of Perspective from the Original Italian of Lorenzo Sirigatti with the Figures Engraved by Isaac Ware, Esq.* (London, 1756)

BIBLIOGRAPHY
Colvin
J. Summerson: *Architecture in Britain, 1530–1830*, Pelican Hist. A. (Harmondsworth, 1953, rev. 1969)
M. Girouard: 'English Art and the Rococo', *Country Life*, cxxxix (13 Jan 1966), pp. 58–61
R. White: 'Isaac Ware and Chesterfield House', *The Rococo in England* (London, 1984), pp. 175–92
ROGER WHITE

Warehouse. Building for the storage of goods, especially those in transit. In Western architecture the warehouse has a history that can be traced back to the ancient world, although this building type has also been of substantial architectural interest in other cultures. The earliest known examples are the *horrea* of Roman times. For Rome and her armies the organization of an adequate food supply was of fundamental importance. The necessary storage of corn required special conditions, and granaries had to be dry, cool, free from vermin and able to resist the considerable lateral thrust that grain exerts. Hence Roman granaries were solidly built, brick-vaulted and efficiently planned. Those at Ostia (early 2nd century AD) are particularly impressive. The Horrea Epagathiana (*c.* 145–50) is typical, with a rectangular plan and different-sized rooms opening on to a central court with a brick-piered arcade. Two staircases lead to the second floor, which has a similar arrangement of rooms, and there is an unrestored third floor. An elaborate security system guarded against pilfering. The courtyard has a cistern to collect rain water, and a black-and-white mosaic with meander patterns, a swastika, a tiger and a panther. Few warehouses of architectural significance survive from the early Middle Ages, although the great medieval tithe barns (e.g. Great Coxwell, Berks, *c.* 1250) might be considered as granaries. However, as seaborne trade increased during the late medieval period, warehouses were built in substantial numbers in the Hanseatic ports of northern Europe. Those of Bruges are the earliest, several of them dating to the 15th century, but the great flowering came in Amsterdam.

Possibly more than any other European city, Amsterdam produced a strong merchant class that regarded the warehouse as both a business necessity and a symbol of family achievement. In addition to the numerous family firms, there were great overseas trading corporations such as the Dutch East India Company. Engravings show that the early warehouses of the 15th century were half-timbered in the typical north European manner. Masonry construction was generally adopted in the 16th century, however, to avoid the danger of fire. The most influential architects were Hans Vredeman de Vries and Hendrik de Keyser, although very few individual warehouses can safely be attributed in their entirety to either man. De Vries used richly decorated gables, while de Keyser introduced various classicizing elements, such as pediments, pilasters and swags. Alongside this sophisticated tradition there also developed a plain or functional style that relied on excellent proportions and brick detailing, visible in numerous warehouses throughout Amsterdam (e.g. Prinsengracht 219–233 and Brouwersgracht 272–4). These buildings are generally five or six storeys high, with large central openings and smaller apertures on the sides. Goods were loaded and unloaded by means of a crane. Sometimes a single carved figure, such as a lion or a stag, adorns the top of the gable. The plain brick is relieved by stone trim or terracotta. Attention was also given to the design of warehouses in groups, for instance the rhythmical divisions of the façades, and the 17th- and 18th-century warehouses of Amsterdam contribute substantially to the beauty of the city. Variants of the Amsterdam form can be found in the smaller cities of the Netherlands (Hoorn, Enkhuizen, Middelburg), as well as in Ghent, Gdańsk (formerly Danzig), Lübeck and Visby.

As international trade expanded and the Industrial Revolution developed in Great Britain, large numbers of warehouses were needed, particularly in the dock areas of London and Liverpool. British designers, very few of whom were architects, emphasized the plain or functional side of the warehouse tradition. Like the earlier Dutch prototypes, these buildings were brick, five or six storeys high, and distinguished by their plainness and severity (e.g. the warehouses at Sharpness on the Gloucester and Sharpness Ship Canal). Many used the overdesigned timber frame later known in the USA as 'mill construction'. Cast iron was used with great effect by Jesse Hartley in Liverpool, most notably in the enormous Albert Dock (1839–45), which also used granite and brick in a masterpiece of fireproof construction, one of the high points in the history of industrial architecture.

The major North American contribution to the warehouse came in the late 19th century with the development in the USA and Canada of transcontinental railway networks and the emergence of the wholesaler as the pioneer of mercantile capitalism. As in 17th-century Amsterdam, the warehouse became both a business necessity and an emblem of family or corporate achievement. Thus the warehouse districts of such towns as Chicago, IL, Minneapolis, MN, St Paul, MN, Omaha, NE, and Winnipeg, Manitoba, suddenly received a large number of outstanding structures that were true civic monuments. Perhaps the most influential single building was H. H. Richardson's wholesale store for Marshall Field and Co. in Chicago (1885–7; destr. 1930; see RICHARDSON, H. H., fig. 4). Louis Sullivan adapted its general form in his Walker Warehouse of 1889, and numerous other designers followed suit. The finest remaining collection of these Richardsonian warehouses is in Winnipeg, where J. H. Cadham and John Atchison were the most important architects in the warehouse district. Their building for the great hardware merchant J. H. Ashdown (1909) is outstanding.

A radical change in structure occurred in 1906–7, when the Minneapolis engineer C. A. P. Turner built the Bovey Johnson Building using the first reinforced concrete flat slab system of construction. Although Turner's patent was disallowed in the federal courts, this new method of construction was immediately successful and was used during the next decade for thousands of American buildings. Construction was quicker and cheaper, with better storage height and much easier installation of automatic sprinkler systems. More light was also admitted, and the danger of collapse was less than with beam and girder construction. Exterior walls could be reduced to screens,

Warehouse for Deere and Co., Omaha, Nebraska, by Oscar Eckerman, 1908

and the possibility of articulation was substantial. A good example of this new type of warehouse is the enormous warehouse built in 1908 in Omaha by Oscar Eckerman for Deere and Co. (see fig.).

It was left to the Swiss engineer–architect Robert Maillart, however, to understand the true nature of the structural forces at work within the flat slab. Between his application for a patent for a 'Beamless Ceiling' in 1909 and the outbreak of World War I, Maillart built a large number of structures with his new system in cities as far apart as St Petersburg and Barcelona. However, these warehouses were of greater technical than architectural significance. The finest 20th-century European warehouses were probably those built by Lars Sonck at Katajanokka, on Helsinki harbour (1911–28). None of the leading practitioners of the International Style concentrated on warehouse design, and in any event most of the European commercial infrastructure was already in place. In the USA, Frank Lloyd Wright's warehouse for A. D. German (Richland Center, WI, 1915), while not entirely successful, is a fascinating building. Cass Gilbert's enormous supply base for the US Army (Brooklyn, NY, 1922) is also impressive. These buildings are all concrete. With the arrival of large-scale automotive transport, distribution became decentralized, and the warehouse was no longer a civic monument of the first order. It became the province of specialists in industrial architecture and package builders. While many warehouses of the late 20th century in the European and North American tradition are very advanced technologically, and many are very large, it would be difficult to claim much architectural distinction for any of them.

BIBLIOGRAPHY

M. Revesz-Alexander: *Die alten Lagerhäuser Amsterdams* (The Hague, 2/1954)

Buildings for Industry (New York, 1957)

J. M. Richards: *The Functional Tradition in Early Industrial Buildings* (London, 1958)

Q. Hughes: *Seaport: Architecture and Townscape in Liverpool* (London, 1964)

W. W. Horn and E. Born: *The Barns of the Abbey of Beaulieu at its Granges of Great Coxwell and Beaulieu St. Leonards* (Berkeley, CA, 1965)

W. L. MacDonald: *The Architecture of the Roman Empire* (New Haven and London, 1965)

G. Rickman: *Roman Granaries and Store Buildings* (Cambridge, 1971)

R. Meiggs: *Roman Ostia* (Oxford, 1973)

L. K. Eaton: 'Oscar Eckerman: Architect to Deere and Company, 1897–1942', *Racar*, iii (1977), pp. 89–99

——: 'Warehouses and Warehouse Districts in Mid-American Cities', *Urb. Hist. Rev.*, xi (June 1982), pp. 17–26

——: 'Winnipeg: The Northern Anchor of the Wholesale Trade', *Urb. Hist. Rev.*, xi (Oct 1982), pp. 17–30

LEONARD EATON

Warhol, Andy [Warhola, Andrew] (*b* Pittsburgh, PA, 6 Aug 1928; *d* New York, 22 Feb 1987). American painter, printmaker, sculptor, draughtsman, illustrator, film maker, writer and collector. After studying at the Carnegie Institute of Technology in Pittsburgh from 1945 to 1949, he moved to New York and began working as a commercial artist and illustrator for magazines and newspapers. His work of the 1950s, much of it commissioned by fashion houses, was charming and often whimsical in tone, typified by outline drawings using a delicate blotted line that gave even the originals a printed appearance; a campaign of advertisements for the shoe manufacturers I. Miller & Sons in 1955–6 (Kornbluth, pp. 113–21) was particularly admired, helping to earn him major awards from the Art Directors Club.

Warhol continued to support himself through his commercial work until at least 1963, but from 1960 he determined to establish his name as a painter. Motivated by a desire to be taken as seriously as the young artists whose work he had recently come to know and admire, especially Jasper Johns and Robert Rauschenberg, he began by painting a series of pictures based on crude advertisements and on images from comic strips. These are among the earliest examples of POP ART. The first such works, for example *Water Heater* (1960; New York, MOMA) and *Saturday's Popeye* (1960; Mainz, Landesmus.), were loosely painted in a mock-expressive style that parodied the gestural brushwork of Abstract Expressionism. Those that followed, however, such as *Before and After 3* (1962; New York, Whitney), one of several paintings based on advertisements for plastic surgery, were phrased in a deliberately inexpressive style of painting characterized by hard outlines and flat areas of colour.

In their calculated exclusion of all conventional signs of personality, in their apparent rejection of invention and in their blatant vulgarity these first Pop works were brutal and shocking, designed to offend the sensibilities of an audience accustomed to thinking of art as an intimate medium for conveying emotion. Warhol extended these concerns through techniques that gave his images a printed appearance, including the use of stencils, rubber stamps and hand-cut silkscreens, and in his choice of subject-matter. He was drawn to the shocking images of tabloid newspapers, as in *129 Die in Jet (Plane Crash)* (see fig.), to money (in a series of screenprinted paintings representing rows of dollar bills) and to the denigrated products of consumer society, including Coca-Cola bottles and tins of Campbell's Soup (e.g. *One Hundred Cans*, 1962; Buffalo, NY, Albright–Knox A.G.).

From autumn 1962 Warhol's paintings were made almost exclusively by screenprinting photographic images on to backgrounds painted either in a single colour or in

Andy Warhol: *129 Die in Jet (Plane Crash)*, acrylic on canvas, 2.54×1.83 m, 1962 (Cologne, Museum Ludwig)

flat interlocking areas that corresponded approximately to the contours of the superimposed images. In these works, executed with the help of assistants in the studio that he called The Factory, he succeeded in removing his hand even more decisively from the canvas and in challenging the concept of the unique art work by repeating the same mechanically produced image until it appeared to be drained of all meaning. Among the most successful of these were portraits of glamorous film stars such as the recently deceased Marilyn Monroe, whose masklike face acquires an iconic quality in works such as *Marilyn Diptych* (for illustration *see* POP ART), and gruesome images of car crashes and other daily disasters as seen in photographs reproduced in mass-circulation newspapers, such as *Green Disaster Ten Times* (1963; Frankfurt am Main, Mus. Mod. Kst). He also applied his ideas about art based on mass production in a witty installation of sculptures at the Stable Gallery in New York in 1964, replicating supermarket cartons to their actual size by screenprinting their designs on to blocks made of plywood (e.g. *Brillo Boxes*, 1964; Cologne, Mus. Ludwig).

During a visit to Paris for an exhibition of his work in 1965, Warhol announced his intention to retire from painting in order to devote himself to the experimental films that he had begun making in 1963. Although he continued to paint and contributed significantly to the growing interest in limited edition prints through works such as the *Marilyn* portfolio of ten screenprints published in 1967 (Feldman and Schellmann, p. 39), he became increasingly involved with other media. Films such as

Empire (black and white, 8 hours long, 1964), an unbearably prolonged shot of the Empire State Building against a darkening sky, presented his aesthetic of boredom in its most extreme and provocative form. His multi-media events under the banner of The Exploding Plastic Inevitable, which combined the live music of The Velvet Underground rock band with projections of film and light, subjected the audience to a sensory experience that combined the energy of popular culture with the concerns of performance art.

After an attempt on his life in 1968, Warhol distanced himself from the drug addicts, transvestites and other unconventional types who had formed his entourage and became associated primarily with the wealthy and fashionable members of high society. With the exception of particular series such as his portraits of Mao Zedong (e.g. *Mao*, 4.44×3.47 m, 1973; Chicago, IL, A. Inst.), a topical subject chosen at the time of President Nixon's visit to China, he concentrated in the 1970s primarily on commissioned portraits printed from enlargements of Polaroid photographs. Deprived of the glamour of an immediately recognizable public figure, these frankly commercial works, such as *Jane Lang* (1976; Seattle, WA, A. Mus.), were seen by many as the mark of his artistic decline, although the income they generated enabled Warhol to celebrate his final self-declared transformation from commercial artist to business artist.

Among the most striking works of Warhol's prolific later production are a series of 102 *Shadows* (each 1.93×1.32 m, 1979; New York, Dia A. Found.), all screen-printed from a vastly enlarged photograph of a shadow cast by a painting in his studio, which were exhibited edge-to-edge as an installation that completely surrounded the viewer's field of vision. His *Oxidation Paintings* of the late 1970s (e.g. see MOMA exh. cat., pp. 350–51), made by urinating on a surface of copper paint, were equally experimental and came close to pure abstraction; seductively beautiful in their metallic sheen, they, too, contain an element of savage parody in their reinterpretation of the principles of 'all-over' composition ascribed to the paintings of Abstract Expressionists such as Jackson Pollock.

Warhol's work regained much of its lost spirit in the 1980s, thanks in part to the support of younger artists indebted to his example. After producing a group of collaborative paintings with Francesco Clemente and the American painter Jean-Michel Basquiat (1960–88), he returned for the first time since the early 1960s to painting by hand. His last works included several hand-painted pictures on religious themes after Renaissance masters, such as the *Last Supper* (acrylic on canvas, 3.02×6.68 m, 1986; artist's estate, see MOMA exh. cat., p. 395), in which a version in outline of Leonardo's enduring interpretation of one of Christianity's most sacred events is partly obliterated by grossly enlarged logos of brand names. It is a fittingly ambiguous testament to an artist who was a devout Catholic but who maintained an equally strong reverence for the capitalist system that was so central to his subject-matter. He died as a result of complications following a routine gall-bladder operation. A service attended by more than 2000 people was held in his memory at St Patrick's Cathedral, New York.

Warhol was remembered by friends and associates as a compulsive shopper. The bulk of his extensive collection, which contained only a small amount of contemporary art amongst a great deal of jewellery and decorative art (especially Art Nouveau and Art Deco), Native American art and American folk art, was auctioned a year after his death. His published writings, characterized by the same tone of dead-pan naivety as his work, contain some of the most revealing insights into the attitudes that moulded his art. The Andy Warhol Museum, housing a large collection of his works from all periods drawn in large part from his estate, was inaugurated in Pittsburgh in May 1994.

WRITINGS
Andy Warhol's Index (New York, 1967)
A: A Novel (New York, 1968)
The Philosophy of Andy Warhol (From A to B and Back Again) (New York and London, 1975)
with B. Colacello: *Andy Warhol's Exposures* (New York and London, 1979)
with P. Hackett: *POPism: The Warhol '60s* (New York and London, 1980/R New York, 1983)
America (New York, 1985)
P. Hackett, ed.: *The Andy Warhol Diaries* (New York and London, 1989)
BIBLIOGRAPHY
Andy Warhol (exh. cat., ed. A. Warhol and others; Stockholm, Mod. Mus., 1968)
R. Crone: *Andy Warhol* (Stuttgart, 1970; Eng. trans., New York, 1970)
S. Koch: *Stargazer: Andy Warhol's World and his Films* (New York, 1973; rev. New York, 1985)
D. Whitney, ed.: *Andy Warhol: Portraits of the '70s* (New York, 1979)
C. Ratcliff: *Andy Warhol* (New York, 1983)
F. Feldman and J. Schellmann: *Andy Warhol Prints: A Catalogue Raisonné* (New York, 1985)
P. S. Smith: *Andy Warhol's Art and Films* (Ann Arbor, 1986)
J. Kornbluth: *Pre-Pop Warhol* (New York, 1988)
P. S. Smith: *Warhol: Conversations about the Artist* (Ann Arbor, 1988)
The Andy Warhol Collection, 6 vols (sale cat., New York, Sotheby's, 23 April–3 May 1988)
V. Bockris: *Warhol* (London, 1989) [biog.]
D. Bourdon: *Warhol* (New York, 1989)
Andy Warhol: A Retrospective (exh. cat., ed. K. McShine, essays K. McShine, R. Rosenblum, B. H. D. Buchloh and M. Livingstone; New York, MOMA, 1989)
'Success Is a Job in New York...' The Early Art and Business of Andy Warhol (exh. cat., ed. D. M. De Salvo, essays D. M. De Salvo, E. Lupton and J. A. Miller, and T. Fairbrother; New York U., Grey A.G.; Pittsburgh, Carnegie; 1989)
Andy Warhol, cinéma (exh. cat., ed. B. Blistène and J.-M. Bouhours; Paris, Pompidou, 1990)
Pop Muses: Images of Women by Roy Lichtenstein and Andy Warhol (exh. cat. by M. Livingstone and E. A. Busche; Tokyo, Isetan Mus. A., Shinjuku, 1991)
H. Geldzahler and R. Rosenblum: *Andy Warhol Portraits* (London, 1993)
C. Angell, A. Berman, A. C. Danto and others: *The Andy Warhol Museum* (Pittsburgh, 1994)

For further bibliography *see* POP ART.

MARCO LIVINGSTONE

Wari. *See* HUARI.

Warin [Varin], Jean (*b* Liège, *bapt* 6 Feb 1607; *d* Paris, 26 Aug 1672). French sculptor, medallist and painter. He was one of the most eminent French medallists and a sculptor of considerable reputation during the first half of the 17th century. He trained in the Liège workshop of his father, the medallist and chaser Jean Warin. By 1615 the family had left Liège, perhaps for Sedan, and by 1625 Warin was in Paris, where in 1629, having renounced his Protestantism, he took part charge of the Monnaie du Moulin during the minority of the heirs of the Olivier family, its hereditary owners. Having secured his position by marrying their widowed mother, he took charge of the studio of the Lyon mint around 1642–3, and in 1646 he was appointed Tailleur Général des Monnaies de France, to which in the following year he added the office of Contrôleur Général des Poinçons et Effigies des Monnaies de France. He became a member of the Académie Royale de Peinture et de Sculpture in 1665. In addition to designing many of the dies and stamps used for coinage and commemorative tokens, in 1635 Warin engraved the die for the seal of the Académie Française, decorated with a bust of Cardinal Richelieu (see Mazerolle, no. 208).

Warin was one of the great masters of the medal in France. Among his cast medals are portraits of *Louis XIII* and of *Cardinal Richelieu* (bronze, both 1630, M 2, 7–8), both with the same reverse depicting the chariot of victorious France. The most accomplished are the gold medal commemorating the laying of the foundation-stone of the church of the Val-de-Grâce in Paris (1645, M 60), which depicts Anne of Austria holding the young Louis XIV, and that depicting Gianlorenzo Bernini's projected design for the Louvre colonnade (gold, 1665, M 10). The obverse features a magnificent profile portrait of *Louis XIV*. Warin's struck medals in bronze are more numerous and include portraits of *Louis XIII* (1629, M 12), *Richelieu* (1631, M 13), *Anne of Austria* and *Louis XIV* (1643, M 14–15), as well as those marking the great events of the reign of Louis XIV, beginning with his consecration in 1654 (M 16). All exhibit a clarity of composition based on the study of antique sources, as well as great finesse in their execution.

Warin's earliest known sculptural work, a small gold bust of *Richelieu*, is lost, as is the plaster bust of the cardinal executed in December 1641. However, in 1643 Richelieu's niece, the Duchesse d'Aiguillon, had cast in bronze six busts, probably after Warin's plaster, four by Hubert Le Sueur and two by Henri Perlan (1597–1656), of which several survive. The best are those in the Bibliothèque Mazarine, Paris (h. 710 mm), the Musée Jacquemart-André, Paris, and in the British Royal Collection. In 1665 he executed a marble bust of *Louis XIV* (h. 800 mm; Versailles, Château). The King is represented half-length, frontally and dressed in the antique manner with a sun on his breastplate. The classicizing serenity of the composition, the severity of the characterization and the exquisite skill with which the details of clothes and armour are delineated contrast sharply with Bernini's dramatic Baroque marble bust of the King (Versailles, Château), executed in the same year.

Since Warin was essentially a modeller and chaser, it is likely that he employed a *praticien* to carve the life-size marble statue of *Louis XIV* (h. 1.94 m; Versailles, Château) that he presented to him in 1672. Something of the medallist's style is recognizable in this hieratic and static work, where the symbolic ornamentation and the intricately sculpted trophies are the focal point of a carefully balanced composition.

Warin was also active as a painter of portraits and mythological subjects, but none is known to survive. Warin's brother Claude (*fl* 1630; *d* 1654) was also a medallist and sculptor. He was active between 1630 and 1645 in England, where he executed medallic portraits of,

among others, *Hubert Le Sueur* (1635) and *Sir Thomas Bodley* (*c.* 1645). On his return to France he was successively engraver to the Lyon mint (1647–51) and Graveur Ordinaire to the city of Lyon. Jean Warin's son François (*b* after 1637; *d* after 1705) succeeded to his father's official posts but had been relieved of them all by 1681.

BIBLIOGRAPHY

C. Perrault: *Les Hommes illustres qui ont paru en France pendant ce siècle*, ii (Paris, 1700), pp. 85–6
N. Rondot: 'Claude Warin', *Rev. Numi.* (1888), pp. 121–51, 270–305
F. Mazerolle: *Jean Varin: Sa vie, sa famille, son oeuvre (1596–1672)*, 2 vols (Paris, 1932) [M; with earlier bibliog.]
——: 'La Maquette de la statue de Louis XIV par Jean Varin', *Bull. Soc. Hist. A. Fr.* (1935), pp. 272–4
F. Peny: *Jean Varin de Liège, 1607–1672* (Liège, 1947)
J. Tricou: *Médailles lyonnaises du XVe au XVIIIe siècles* (Paris, 1958)
M. Jones: *1600–1672* (1988), ii of *A Catalogue of French Medals in the British Museum* (London, 1979–)

GENEVIÈVE BRESC-BAUTIER

Warin, Quentin. *See* VARIN, QUENTIN.

Waring, John Burley (*b* Lyme Regis, Dorset, 29 June 1823; *d* Hastings, E. Sussex, 23 March 1875). British architect, designer and writer. Educated from 1836 at the Bristol branch of University College, London, he learnt watercolour drawing from Samuel Jackson (1794–1869) and was apprenticed in 1840 to the London architect Henry E. Kendall (1805–85). In 1842 he entered the Royal Academy Schools, and after a brief trip to Italy during the winter of 1843–4 he returned to England to work as a draughtsman in a series of architectural firms, including those of Ambrose Poynter (1796–1886), Laing of Birkenhead, Robert Smirke and D. Mocatta.

In 1847 Waring visited Italy and Spain to measure and draw public buildings; this resulted in a book, *Examples of Architectural Art in Italy and Spain*, containing 60 fine lithographs. He continued to publish books on architecture, including *Thirty Designs Adapted to Civic Architecture* and a study of the Miraflores monuments at Burgos. Among his unexecuted architectural designs, the drawing *Design for a Family Mansion in the Country* (London, V&A) shows an Elizabethan-style elevation and plans for the ground floor and chambers above, revealing a firm grasp of picturesque design and planning principles.

Beginning with the Great Exhibition of 1851 in London Waring was involved in organizing and publishing aspects of the major British exhibitions of industrial art and design. With Matthew Digby Wyatt, he wrote four architectural guidebooks to the courts of the Crystal Palace at Sydenham. His connections placed him within the circle of Henry Cole and the South Kensington Museum (later the Victoria and Albert Museum), and it was probably in this way that he was asked to contribute texts on Byzantine and Elizabethan ornament to Owen Jones's authoritative *The Grammar of Ornament* (London, 1856). He sold a series of drawings created in Italy in 1855 to the South Kensington Museum, later published as *The Arts Connected with Architecture Illustrated by Examples in Central Italy*.

As superintendent of ornamental art and sculpture for the Manchester Art Treasures Exhibition in 1857, Waring edited *Art Treasures of the United Kingdom*, providing a chromolithographic record of the exhibition. He played a similar role in the International Exhibition of 1862 in

London, where he was the superintendent of the architectural gallery and of the classes for furniture, earthenware, glass, goldsmiths' work, jewellery and architectural objects. During the 1860s he designed furniture for Messrs Trollope and continued to publish numerous books and pamphlets on a variety of topics.

WRITINGS

Examples of Architectural Art in Italy and Spain (London, 1850)
Thirty Designs Adapted to Civic Architecture (London, [1850])
Architectural, Sculptural and Picturesque Studies in Burgos (London, 1852)
with M. D. Wyatt: *The Byzantine and Romanesque Courts in the Crystal Palace* (London, 1854)
——: *The Italian Court in the Crystal Palace* (London, 1854)
——: *The Medieval Court in the Crystal Palace* (London, 1854)
——: *The Renaissance Court in the Crystal Palace* (London, 1854)
ed.: M. D. Wyatt: *Observations on Metallic Art* (London, 1857)
The Arts Connected with Architecture Illustrated by Examples in Central Italy (London, 1858)
Art Treasures of the United Kingdom, 2 vols (London, 1858)
Masterpieces of Industrial Art and Sculpture at the International Exhibition, 1862, 3 vols (London, 1863)
Illustrations of Architecture and Ornament (London, [1865])
Stone Monuments, Tumuli and Ornaments of Remote Ages, with Remarks on the Early Architecture of Ireland and Scotland (London, 1870)

BIBLIOGRAPHY

DNB
Illus. London News (17 June 1868), p. 633
A. J. [London] (Sept 1875), p. 279
High Victorian Design (exh. cat., ed. S. Jervis; Ottawa, N.G., 1974–5)

E. A. CHRISTENSEN

Warka. *See* URUK.

Warmond Castle. Dutch 18th-century manor house near Warmond in the province of South Holland. It was constructed on the site of fortifications dating from *c.* 1250, incorporating traces of medieval architecture. The original timber structures were replaced by buildings that were subsequently damaged by fire in the 14th, 15th and 16th centuries and rebuilt each time on the old foundations. A 16th-century drawing makes it possible to reconstruct the medieval original, when the castle consisted of a square ground-plan of four wings and four corner towers set around an interior court, the whole surrounded by a moat. The living-quarters were in the north and east wings. The massive west tower was once assumed to have been the keep, but the thickness of its walls (0.9–1.2 m) and its dimensions (7×7 m) are too small for this purpose. In 1629 the castle was given a new entrance range by Salomon de Bray, featuring pilasters and a broad pediment. The south tower, originally octagonal, was replaced by a square one after 1650. Owing to the various rebuilding projects, Warmond acquired an irregular character in the course of the centuries. In 1780 the castle was extensively rebuilt. Floor levels and the proportions of the rooms were altered, and the walls were stuccoed. Medieval remains were hidden by new walls and plasterwork; de Bray's additions disappeared.

BIBLIOGRAPHY

S. J. Fockema Andreae and others: *Ridderhoisteden en buitenplaatsen in Rijnland* [Knightly lodges and country houses in the Rhineland] (Leiden, 1952)
Het Huys te Warmont: Zijn geschiedenis en zijn bewoners [The lodge at Warmond: its history and its occupants], Nederlandse Jeugdbond ter Bestudering van de Geschiedenis [Dutch young people's group for the study of history] (Leiden, 1963)

J. M. M. KYLSTRA-WIELINGA

Warner, Olin Levi (*b* West Suffield, CT, 9 April 1844; *d* New York, 14 Aug 1896). American sculptor. Between 1869 and 1872 he studied at the Ecole des Beaux-Arts in Paris under François Jouffroy and worked as an assistant to Jean-Baptiste Carpeaux. Warner returned to New York in 1872 with a sound technical training and an intimate knowledge of the current French Beaux-Arts style but initially struggled to make a living. Portrait busts and medallions, such as his characteristically boldly modelled relief *Chief Joseph* (1889; Washington, DC, N. Mus. Amer. A.), accounted for the majority of his production; he did much to establish low-relief sculpture in America. Critical recognition came with busts of his two friends, *Daniel Cottier* (1878; New York, N. Acad. Des.) and *J. Alden Weir* (bronze, 1880; New York, Amer. Acad. A. & Lett.), and with the seated, ideal nude *Diana* (1887; New York, Met.). These works reveal his development of a personal brand of the Beaux-Arts style that combined his innate strength as a modeller with a restrained and classical sensibility.

Few in number, Warner's public monuments and architectural decorations, such as the superb *William Lloyd Garrison* (bronze, 1885; Boston, MA, Commonwealth Avenue) and the impressive bronze doors for the Library of Congress (1896; Washington, DC), which depict in elaborate allegory the transmission of human knowledge, attest the range of his abilities. Warner was a founder-member of the Society of American Artists and the National Sculpture Society. At the time of his accidental death, he was considered one of the leading American sculptors.

BIBLIOGRAPHY

W. Craven: *Sculpture in America* (Newark, 1968, rev. 1984), pp. 406–9, 419
G. Gurney: *Olin Levi Warner (1844–1896): A Catalogue Raisonné of his Sculpture and Graphic Works*, 3 vols (diss., Newark, U. DE, 1978)
P. M. Kozol: *American Figurative Sculpture in the Museum of Fine Arts, Boston* (Boston, 1986), pp. 201–3
The Beaux-Arts Medal in America (exh. cat. by B. A. Baxter, New York, Amer. Numi. Soc., 1987–8); pp. 4–5, 12, 26–7, 32–4, 47
A. Boime: 'Olin Levi Warner's Defence of the Paris Commune', *Archvs Amer. A. J.*, xxviiii (1939), nos 3/4, pp. 2–22

GEORGE GURNEY

Warpechowski, Zbigniew (*b* Volhynia, 10 Oct 1938). Polish performance artist and conceptual artist. He studied at the Faculty of Architecture at Kraków Technical University from 1956 to 1962 and at the Academy of Fine Arts, Kraków (1964–5). After 1969 he produced at intervals powerful linear semi-abstract paintings resembling three-dimensional projections on to a plane. His first performance, *Poetic Quarter Hour with Piano and Record Player* (1967; Kraków), based on an improvised poetic recitation, was transformed into verbal-jazz improvisations featuring Tomasz Stańko (1967–8). In the early 1970s Warpechowski produced a number of conceptual works bordering on performance art (e.g. a clock encased in a block of plaster of Paris, a blank tape-measure, a book-binding press with an empty plate, darkness enclosed in the palms of hands). The performances of the 1970s, such as *Liberation of Pure Usefulness* (1974), were inspired by Daoist philosophy and dealt with ideas, reality and nothingness, whereas his understanding of the creative process stemmed from the European Romantic tradition. After

1973 he compiled collections of axioms for a treatise on art, which were published at his own expense, as well as Daoist philosophical stories. Between 1978 and 1981 the cycle of performances *Champion of Golgotha* was repeated in several dozen versions. He also designed film sets.

BIBLIOGRAPHY

A. Kęińska: *Nowa sztuka: Sztuka polska w latach, 1945–1978* [New art: Polish art 1945–1978] (Warsaw, 1981)

EWA MIKINA

Warren, Sir (Frederick) Miles (*b* Christchurch, 10 May 1929). New Zealand architect. In 1946–7 he worked for Cecil Wood, from whom he gained an appreciation of the Arts and Crafts philosophy of total design, and later studied at the University of Auckland School of Architecture (1949–50). After working for the London County Council on the Roehampton Estate (1953–4), he entered private practice in Christchurch in 1955. In 1957–8 he was in partnership with G. T. Lucas (1890–1972) and from 1958 with M. E. Mahoney (*b* 1929), as Warren and Mahoney.

Warren's reputation was established with the series of flats and houses he built in Christchurch during the 1950s and early 1960s. Constructed from white-painted concrete block with fair-face concrete beams and high-pitched roofs, they combined the influences of New Brutalism and contemporary Scandinavian housing with local building traditions to form a distinctive regional style. Typical examples are the Dorset Street Flats (1959), Christchurch, and the M. B. Warren house (1961), Christchurch. The direct expression of materials, clarity of planning and respect for tradition of these works was further developed on a larger scale at Christchurch College (1965), Christchurch, and the Christchurch Town Hall (1965–72). The success of the town hall, a concert hall of international quality, established Warren as New Zealand's leading contemporary architect and brought many new commissions. The Chancery, New Zealand Embassy (1979), Washington, DC, revealed his skill in contextual design in a foreign setting, while the Michael Fowler Centre (1983), Wellington, a reworking of the Christchurch Town Hall design, exemplified the more extrovert quality that marked Warren's works of the 1980s. The Administration Building (1986–88), Christ's College, Christchurch, a historicist addition to Wood's Gothic Dining Hall that is as daring as it is accomplished, and the New Zealand High Commission (1990), New Delhi, which pays tribute to Lutyens's classicism, revealed a deepening responsiveness to historical influences. A prolific designer, Warren received a knighthood in 1985 for his contribution to New Zealand architecture.

WRITINGS

'Style in New Zealand Architecture', *NZ Architect*, iii (1978), pp. 2–15
Warren and Mahoney: Architects (Christchurch, 1989)

IAN J. LOCHHEAD

Warren, Russell (*b* Tiverton, RI, 5 Aug 1783; *d* Providence, 16 Nov 1860). American architect. Born into a family of builders, he was the first individual in Rhode Island to make the transition from architect–builder to architect. His move in 1800 to Bristol, RI, where he worked as a carpenter with his brothers, was timely: under the mercantile leadership of the De Wolf family, Bristol experienced an economic boom based on shipping and the illegal slave trade. Warren designed four large, elaborate houses for that family between 1808 and 1840; the two early ones, Hey Bonnie Hall (1808; destr.) and Linden Place (1810), gave the talented young designer an early opportunity to deal with ambitious commissions for sophisticated patrons.

By 1827, after a few years in Charleston, SC, Warren was in Providence, RI, where he was associated with Tallman & Bucklin. Warren and James C. Bucklin introduced the Greek Revival to Rhode Island with their monumental Providence Arcade (1828). By the summer of 1835 Warren was in New York and was associated with Alexander Jackson Davis. His work with Davis provided him with a variety of projects in north-east USA and led to his involvement with the short-lived American Institution of Architects, founded in 1837.

Warren returned to Providence in the late 1830s. His stature as an architect helped him to obtain important commissions in Bristol and the nearby cities of Fall River and New Bedford, MA. Many of these were sober, monumental Greek Revival structures, such as the Dr Nathan Durfee House (1840; destr.) in Fall River. He remained active into the late 1850s. His last designs, such as the Henry Lippitt house (1856) in Providence, were stylish Italianate buildings, but they lack the vigour of the many buildings he designed in the Greek Revival style.

BIBLIOGRAPHY

R. L. Alexander: *The Architecture of Russell Warren* (diss., New York U., 1952)
Buildings on Paper: Rhode Island Architectural Drawings, 1825–1945 (exh. cat., ed. W. M. Jordy and C. P. Monkhouse; Providence, RI, Brown U., Bell Gal.; Providence, RI Sch. Des., Mus. A.; Providence, RI Hist. Soc.; New York, Met.; New York, N. Acad. Des.; Washington, DC, Amer. Inst. Architects Found.; 1982)

W. McKENZIE WOODWARD

Warren & Wetmore. American architectural partnership founded in 1898 by Whitney Warren (*b* New York, 29 Jan 1864; *d* New York, 24 Jan 1943) and Charles D. Wetmore (*b* Elmira, NY, 10 June 1866; *d* New York, 8 May 1941). The partnership was formed when Wetmore, a successful lawyer, contracted Warren to design a country house. So impressed was Warren with Wetmore's contribution to the design that he persuaded him to enter into an architectural partnership. Warren entered Columbia University, New York, in 1882, but continued his studies in Paris (1885–94) at the Ecole des Beaux-Arts. On his return to New York he was employed by McKim, Mead & White. Wetmore graduated from Harvard University in 1889, receiving his law degree there in 1892. Before beginning law practice he designed three dormitories (*c.* 1890) for Harvard: Claverly and Westmorly Halls and Apley Court.

The new firm's first major recognition was winning the competition for a new club house for the New York Yacht Club, built in 1899. This building is in the rather flamboyant Beaux-Arts style that was to become the trademark of all the firm's work. Between 1899 and 1913 they designed a number of railway stations, for the New York Central, the Michigan Central, the Canadian Northern and the Erie railways. Warren & Wetmore's best-known work is the Grand Central Terminal (completed 1913) at 42nd Street and Park Avenue, New York, initially designed by Charles Reed (1858–1911) and Allen Stem (1856–1931), Warren & Wetmore were commissioned to modify the design in 1903. The major modifications were the incorporation of a French Beaux-Arts façade, and designs for the monumental, flowingly spacious interiors, which were similar in concept to those of Charles Garnier's Opéra in Paris. Indeed, Warren & Wetmore's main contribution is 'the general *parti*, or character and form of the building, as well as . . . its imagery and finesse' (Nevins, p. 16). The project was not free from controversy, however. When Reed died in 1911, Warren & Wetmore arranged with the New York Central Railroad, without consulting Stem, to take on sole responsibility for the project. Stem subsequently sued, and in 1920 he and Reed's estate were awarded £500,000.

Warren & Wetmore also designed a number of hotels, apartment houses and office buildings conceived as part of the 'Terminal City' being developed around Grand Central Station. The Biltmore Hotel (1914) at Madison Avenue and 43rd Street has a façade characterized by its overall restraint, although certain passages, such as the Beaux-Arts arcade facing the top three storeys, display extraordinarily elaborate detailing. Later office buildings include the Marshall Field Building (*c.* 1920) at 200 Madison Avenue, New York. The building is designed in receding blocks, an arrangement dictated by the zoning laws then current in New York.

A devoted francophile, Warren spent most of World War I in France. In 1920 he was commissioned to build the university library in Leuven, Belgium, which had been destroyed by the German army. An international controversy ensued over Warren's proposed inscription (executed but subsequently removed), which read 'destroyed by German fury; restored by American Generosity'. He was a founding member of the Beaux-Arts Institute of Design in New York and its director in the early 1920s. During these years he supervised architectural studies at the institute's Fontainebleau School of Fine Arts, conceived as a summer school for American students. The institute's motivation in establishing this school was the perpetuation of Beaux-Arts traditions, particularly that of the atelier. During his partnership with Warren, Wetmore was primarily responsible for the Ritz–Carlton Hotel (1911), Montreal, the Equitable Trust Company Building (1918) on Madison Avenue, New York, and the Royal Hawaiian Hotel (1927), Honolulu. After Warren retired in 1931, Wetmore was the firm's senior member until his own death.

BIBLIOGRAPHY
Macmillan Enc. Architects
G. H. Edgell: *The American Architecture of Today* (New York, 1928)
National Cyclopaedia of American Biography (New York, 1948–58), xxxiv, pp. 173–4, xlii, pp. 213–14
D. Nevins, ed.: *Grand Central Terminal: City within the City* (New York, 1982)
I. Gournay: 'Architecture at the Fontainebleau School of Fine Arts', *J. Soc. Archit. Historians*, xlv/3 (1986), pp. 270–85

☐

Warrick Fuller, Meta Vaux. *See* FULLER, META VAUX.

Warsaw [Warszawa]. Capital city of Poland and the country's cultural, academic and artistic centre, with a population of *c.* 1,600,000. It lies on the River Vistula in the Masovian Plain, east-central Poland.

I. History. II. Urban development. III. Art life and organization. IV. Centre of production. V. Buildings.

I. History.

A settlement on the site of the present-day Old Town was granted a charter at the end of the 13th century and became the main centre of the Duchy of Masovia, with *c.* 2900 inhabitants by the mid-15th century. In 1526 Masovia was incorporated into the Kingdom of Poland and, owing to its central location, Warsaw became the country's capital and the seat of the Polish kings from 1611. Warsaw flourished until the mid-17th century, and by 1655 its population had grown to *c.* 18,000; but 60% of the city was destroyed and the population fell to *c.* 6000 following the Swedish invasion of 1655–60. Warsaw was soon rebuilt but was destroyed again in the Northern War (1700–21). During the reign of Stanisław Augustus Poniatowski (1764–95) it became an important cultural centre in Europe. The population grew to *c.* 115,000, but following the third Partition of Poland (1795) the city lost its status as capital and became a provincial town. The establishment of the Congress Kingdom (1815–30) brought a short period of prosperity, but the insurrections of 1831 and 1863 limited its political importance. In the second half of the 19th century, however, Warsaw became one of the most dynamically expanding cities in Europe, and the population increased from *c.* 260,000 (1870) to *c.* 1,000,000 (1914). In 1918 Poland regained independence and Warsaw became the capital once again. During World War II 75% of the city was destroyed and *c.* 850,000 people lost their lives, but Warsaw was rebuilt after 1945 and regained its political and cultural importance.

BIBLIOGRAPHY
W. Tomkiewicz, ed.: *Straty kulturalne Warszawy* [Warsaw's cultural losses], i (Warsaw, 1948)
K. Konarski: *Warszawa w pierwszym jej stołecznym okresie* [Warsaw in its first years as capital] (Warsaw, 1970)
A. Zahorski: *Warszawa za Sasów i Stanisława Augusta* [Warsaw under the Saxon kings and Stanislav Augustus] (Warsaw, 1970)
I. Ihnatowicz: *Obyczaj wielkiej burżuazji warszawskiej w XIX wieku* [Customs of the grand bourgeoisie in Warsaw in the 19th century] (Warsaw, 1971)
A. Kersten: *Warszawa kazimierzowska, 1648–1668: Miasto, ludzie, polityka* [Warsaw under John Kasimir Vasa, 1648–1668: town, people, politics] (Warsaw, 1971)
S. Kieniewicz: *Warszawa w latach 1795–1914* [Warsaw between 1795 and 1914] (Warsaw, 1976)
S. K. Kuczyński: *Herb Warszawy* [Warsaw's emblem] (Warsaw, 1977)
A. Gieysztor and J. Durko, eds: *Warszawa: Jej dzieje i kultura* [Warsaw: its history and culture] (Warsaw, 1980)
——: *Warszawa w latach 1525–1795* [Warsaw between 1525 and 1795] (Warsaw, 1984)

II. Urban development.

1. Before 1795. 2. 1795 and after.

1. BEFORE 1795.

(i) Early growth, before *c.* 1569. (ii) Expansion, *c.* 1569–1720. (iii) Growth, 1720–94.

(i) Early growth, before c. *1569.* Warsaw grew from a fortified settlement that was exceptionally favourably situated on a high bank, above flood level, with easy access to the Vistula. There were numerous springs and

much land suitable for both urban development and cultivation in the vicinity. It is thought that the settlement was granted town rights towards the end of the 13th century, due to the efforts of a group of rich merchants, who probably arrived from Toruń. Around the beginning of the 14th century Warsaw took on the functions of earlier artisan and market settlements situated along the river; it thus established itself as a trading centre at the junction of north–south and east–west trade routes. The new town was laid out on a grid plan that was adjusted to allow for the irregularities of existing roads and, in the southern quarters, for the adjacent ducal estates. Three parallel streets (present-day Piwna, Świętojańska-Nowomiejska and Jezuicka-Krzywe Koło) ran north–south and were intersected twice at right angles (present-day Piekarska-Celna and Wąski Dunaj streets). The spatial layout included both the main Market Square and a secondary market in Dunaj Street (see fig. 1). The 14th-century buildings, including the parish church of St John the Baptist (cathedral from 1798), were constructed of timber. The town was initially surrounded by an earth rampart and a moat; brick defences, begun in 1339, eventually replaced the rampart.

The town grew in importance during the reign of Janusz I, Duke of Masovia (*reg* 1374–1429), who chose Warsaw as his permanent seat, granting it a charter under the Chełmno (Kulm) law in 1413. Work on the extension of the ducal castle resulted in changes to the layout of the town. A brick ducal residence, the Curia Maior, was built, forming the nucleus of the future Royal Castle. Two brick churches dominated the skyline: the Augustinian church of St Martin (*c.* 1380) and St John the Baptist, elevated to collegiate status and rebuilt in brick (1390–98; 1406–50). By the 15th century merchants' houses were also being built of brick, with stepped or triangular gables. Each plot had separate storage and utility space at the back, linked with the main building by a wooden porch. By the mid-16th century the population had grown to such an extent that it was necessary to increase the available living accommodation. Extensions were constructed behind existing buildings and floors added, creating three- and four-storey houses.

Development and growth in the 14th and 15th centuries prompted further expansion along the Vistula, resulting in the formation of two main suburbs. The first, in the area of present-day Freta Street to the north-west of the Old Town, had already existed at the end of the 14th century and became known as the New Town. In 1408 it was exempted from the jurisdiction of the Old Town. A second suburb, Czerskie (later renamed Krakowskie

1. Warsaw, Old Town, aerial view from the south, showing the medieval urban plan, with the main Market Square in the centre and Świętojańska Street with the cathedral, leading to Castle Square with the Royal Castle on the right

Przedmieście), developed to the south, near the Kraków Gate. It had a wide market-place flanked on its west side by a row of burgher houses, and with ducal orchards on the east side. The adjoining arable land was subdivided into strips 150 m wide at right angles to the Vistula, a pattern reflected in the later street network.

(ii) Expansion, c. 1569–1720. Following the Union of Poland and Lithuania (1569), sessions of the Sejm (parliament) were held in Warsaw. Lasting from a few weeks to several months, they were attended by thousands of nobles from all parts of the country, whom the town was obliged to provide with lodgings and other services. The town was also bound to meet the requirements of the royal court (which moved to Warsaw from 1596 to 1611), central administrative institutions and the courts of higher state officials. Such new responsibilities transformed Warsaw, prompting the construction of new palaces and mansions as well as such municipal investments as a bridge. The most significant symbol of the town's new status was the remodelled and expanded Royal Castle, the official residence of the king and headquarters of the government (*see* §V, 1 below).

The church and nobility were rapidly expanding their holdings both within the town and in the suburbs. In addition to the medieval ecclesiastical *jurydyki* (lands belonging to the church or nobility and independent of municipal jurisdiction) outside the town walls, new ones were formed on the east bank of the river. Dense urban development took place along the Krakowskie Przedmieście market in the southern suburb and, in the northern suburb, along Mostowa Street, which led to the bridge. Timber buildings were erected along the main roads leading into the town, for example present-day Nowy Świat and intersecting streets (e.g. Świętokrzyska and Chmielna). The areas to the south of Warsaw were particularly densely built up, especially in the vicinity of the church of the Holy Cross and Krakowskie Przedmieście, where the Carmelites and the Nuns of the Visitation established monastic complexes. Nearby, Vladimir IV Vasa (*reg* 1632–48) built a residence, later known as the Kazimierzowski Palace; this was followed by the palaces of Adam Kazanowski (*c.* 1599–1649), Jerzy Ossoliński (1595–1650) and Mikołaj Daniłowicz (*d* 1624). More monasteries were established in the western part of the town, for example by the Piarists and the Brigittine Order in Długa Street. The mendicant orders settled in the Freta suburb: the Dominicans (1603) in Freta Street and the Franciscans (1643) in Zakroczymska Street. New ramparts were constructed (1621–5) on account of the threat of a Turkish invasion and they hampered urban expansion for a time. The Arsenal was built (1638–43) near the ramparts, in the western part of the city.

The Renaissance did not have a great impact on Warsaw's architecture and was soon superseded by the Baroque style, which was introduced in the early 17th century, when there were two periods of increased building activity. The first was between the fire of 1607 and the epidemics of the 1620s, while the second ended with the Swedish invasion of 1655. Several dates within this period are relevant to the history of Polish architecture: around 1610 early Baroque forms based on Roman principles were developed in the design of the Royal Castle; around 1630 the detail and decoration of town houses were modernized; between 1635 and 1645 Warsaw's stately architecture flourished. By the mid-17th century almost three-quarters of the suburbs were owned by the nobility and clergy, whose estates, typically featuring a centrally situated palace, manor house or ecclesiastical buildings surrounded by gardens, were a dominant feature of the townscape. Warsaw's appearance had evolved to reflect the social structure of the Commonwealth and the function it performed as the seat of the Polish kings. The wars of 1655–8 interrupted growth. Within the span of three years Warsaw was besieged, captured and occupied by the Swedish army and their allies on three separate occasions. The Old Town was destroyed, the New Town was gutted by fire, and the suburbs were severely damaged; this was further compounded by systematic looting carried out by the invading armies.

There was a period of economic and cultural regeneration during the last four decades of the 17th century, and it was crucial to the development of Warsaw's urban planning and architecture. With the final shift of gravity away from the Old Town and the growing importance of the suburbs, Warsaw's specific character developed. The nobility and church were increasing their holdings (at the expense of the burghers) at a far greater rate than before, owing to the progressive disintegration of central authority in the Commonwealth and the increasing power of the magnates. They continued to build castles and palaces on their extensive country estates and to erect imposing and prestigious residences on privately owned land in Warsaw and its outskirts. Palaces and manors built in the 1670s and early 1680s usually followed conservative designs of the type that had been fashionable under the Vasa kings. There was greater diversity in ecclesiastical architecture, and new models had continued to develop since the mid-17th century. The oustanding architect TYLMAN VAN GAMEREN made a considerable contribution to the townscape in the late 17th century with his many churches and palaces.

The vigorous building activity of the 1680s and 1690s was followed by a period of marked decline, partly on account of the Northern War (1700–21) and the outbreak of epidemics (1708–12). Despite elaborate plans by Augustus II (*reg* 1697–1706) the first two decades of the 18th century were unremarkable in terms of both architecture and urban planning, with the exception of the work (begun 1713) on the Saxon Axis urban scheme.

(iii) Growth, 1720–94. The economic and political stability of the Commonwealth between 1720 and 1764 allowed a consolidation of the trends that shaped the town's 18th-century planning and architecture. High-ranking dignitaries continued to build and remodel their prestigious town houses in a country mansion style. At the same time Warsaw's appearance was greatly enhanced by new schemes stemming from the absolutist ambitions and aspirations of Augustus II. Although neither Augustus II nor Augustus III (*reg* 1733–63) could equal the creations of the French king Louis XIV or the Holy Roman Emperor Charles VI, they nevertheless conceived such grandiose plans and unique architectural programmes as the projects

2. Warsaw, Wilanów Palace, central block by Augustyn Locci, 1677–9, with lateral wings by Giovanni Spazzio added 1723–9

for the expansion of Ujazdów Castle and Wilanów Palace, the Royal Castle, the Saxon Axis, Marymont and Czerniaków. Few of the projects were realized, on account of financial difficulties and, it seems, the reluctance of the nobility to accept architecture that was perceived as absolutist in character. Those that were carried out—the Saxon Axis, the Ujazdów Calvary (*see* JAUCH, JOACHIM DANIEL) and Gwardia Avenue—were significant for the town's further development.

Many of the outstanding artists and craftsmen attracted to Warsaw by the Wettin court were also employed by the magnates and the Church; thus architectural and artistic standards were particularly high in the first half of the 18th century. During this period basic structural and decorative concepts in urban planning and palace architecture were French in origin and were brought to Poland from Dresden and also through direct contacts with French artistic circles. At that time the *entre cour et jardin* type of palace arrangement, known in Warsaw since the early 17th century (e.g. the Kazimierzowski and Koniecpolski palaces), became fully formulated. The principal exponent of the format was Tylman van Gameren, who adopted it in the Radziwiłł Palace in Miodowa Street and the remodelling of the Ossoliński Palace, structures that directly influenced the work of other architects active in Warsaw in the first half of the 18th century. The idea of expanding the traditional form of palace by the addition of lateral wings was introduced to Warsaw by Jan Zygmunt Deybel and Karol Fryderyk Pöppelman (*c.* 1697–1750) in their extension of the Błękitny Palace in 1726 and by Giovanni Spazzio (*d* 1726) at Wilanów Palace (see fig. 2; *see also* §V, 3 below). Ecclesiastical architecture began to dominate the townscape, becoming much more distinctive than the secular buildings. Several new churches were built in Warsaw during the first half of the 18th century, and most of the existing ones were given new façades, following traditional designs popular in 17th-century Warsaw, enriched by new elements derived from Italian and Central European church architecture of the early 18th century.

After 1764 the dynamic patronage of Stanisław II Poniatowski Augustus (*reg* 1764–95) contributed enormously to the development of Warsaw, which became a vibrant centre of cultural and scientific life and the focus of a progressive programme for national education. The process of incorporating new land progressed, and the construction of new buildings continued steadily, despite an antiquated organizational structure. Until 1791 Warsaw remained a cluster of small townlets, country-style mansions and extensive monastic complexes, all independent of the central municipal authorities. Undeveloped sites in the centre of Warsaw were systematically built up, and further development took place in all directions along the west bank of the river, and partly also along the opposite bank. Early in his reign Stanisław established the *jurydyka* of Stanisławów, which was administratively bound with Ujazdów, an estate that he had purchased from the Lubomirski family in 1764 with a view to creating a summer residence and park (*see* §V, 2 below). The remodelled Ujazdów Castle became the nucleus of the Stanislav Axis, a grandiose urban plan that significantly influenced the spatial organization of south Warsaw. Radial squares dominated the scheme, and they survive as Zbawiciela, Na Rozdrożu, Politechniki and Unii Lubelskiej squares. The design was slightly restricted by a ring of trenches (1770) built around Warsaw by the Grand Crown Marshal Stanisław Lubomirski (1719–83) owing to the threat of epidemics. Stanisław also acquired municipal land and neighbouring villages on the east bank of the Vistula, and in 1764 he purchased Targówek and a portion of Golędzinów, subsequently establishing the Royal Golędzinów *jurydyka*. In 1780 he further increased his estate on the east bank, buying land and villages from the Płock Chapter. The King presented the acquisitions to his nephew Stanisław Poniatowski, who in turn founded the Kamion *juydyka*, the nucleus of the present-day Praga district.

Despite Stanisław's efforts to turn Warsaw into a Neo-classical city, the Baroque palaces of Tylman van Gameren and tall Baroque church towers continued to dominate the skyline, although the appearance of the most prestigious streets did change significantly. The most successful Neo-classical palaces and churches were built by architects closely connected with the royal court, especially Jakub

Fontana (1710–73), DOMENICO MERLINI and JAN CHRYSTIAN KAMSETZER, as well as by such prominent architects working mainly for magnates and wealthy burghers as SZYMON BOGUMIŁ ZUG, EFRAIM SZREGER and CHRYSTIAN PIOTR AIGNER. The town's appearance was further affected in this period by the incorporation of large parks laid out in the fashionable English and French manner, while the earlier Baroque parks, including Łazienki, Natolin and Wilanów, were remodelled and expanded.

2. 1795 AND AFTER.

(i) 19th century. Various projects that significantly influenced the city's appearance were carried out during the Congress Kingdom of Poland period (1815–30). Most importantly, Warsaw's main squares were laid out; in 1823–4 the old road to the Nowa Jerozolima settlement was extended towards the Vistula, creating Jerozolimskie Avenue, one of the most important urban thoroughfares. In the 1820s several dozen municipal buildings and 419 apartment houses were built. The latter were two- or three-storey brick buildings, usually modestly decorated, with five- or seven-bay façades. The most magnificent buildings of 1815–30 were erected along the Royal Way leading from Castle Square to the Belvedere Palace, as well as along Senatorska Street and in Bankowy Square. The principal designers of this Neo-classicist architecture were Chrystian Piotr Aigner, Jakub Kubicki, Hilary Szpilowski (1753–1827) and ANTONI CORAZZI (see fig. 3).

The construction of the Citadel (1832–6) in north Warsaw halted natural development along the Vistula, and as a consequence the city's growth continued in the westerly and south-westerly directions of Ochota, Wola and Mokotów, within the boundaries of the earlier Lubomirski trenches. The construction and rapid expansion of the Warsaw railway network greatly influenced the city's economy and development and consolidated expansion along the east–west line. Between 1833 and 1864 around 2500 houses were built. New building regulations specified that internal courtyards of apartment houses should measure 9.14×9.14 m, thus defining the character of such buildings in Warsaw. In the first half of the 19th century earlier architectural styles, especially the Renaissance style, became very popular. After almost a century dominated by secular architecture, new churches began to be built and became the compositional focus of several Warsaw squares. The architect Henryk Marconi (*see* MARCONI, (1)) made the greatest contribution to the city's appearance in the 19th century, but the buildings designed by Franciszek Maria Lanci, Andrzej Gołoński (1799–1854), Alfons Kropiwnicki (1803–81) and Jan Jakub Gay are also notable.

Growth of the city's economy and population was extremely dynamic between 1863 and 1918. In the 1880s the Tsarist authorities surrounded Warsaw with a ring of forts, conclusively halting expansion; as a result all undeveloped sites within the city were systematically built up. By the second half of the 19th century the city centre had

3. Warsaw, Grand Theatre, by Antoni Corazzi, 1826–33 (destr. 1939, reconstructed 1951–65), central block of north-west façade

shifted to Marszałkowska Street and Jerozolimskie Avenue together with their intersecting streets, an area inhabited by the wealthy middle classes. Ujazdowskie Avenue and surrounding streets formed an elegant district for the aristocracy and rich bourgeoisie; most of the Jewish population inhabited the north-western area. Large industrial plants were located in the Wola, Powiśle and Praga districts, while the areas beyond the town boundaries still retained their semi-rural character. In addition to the dominant historical styles, Eclecticism became popular by the end of the 19th century. At the beginning of the 20th century Art Nouveau was briefly introduced but soon gave way to Modernism. Multi-storey apartment houses lined the major new streets and also began to be built in the historical ensemble of Krakowskie Przedmieście and Nowy Świat streets, creating aesthetic discords.

(ii) 20th century. At the turn of the 20th century, Warsaw, as a prestigious capitalist centre, needed new office and administrative buildings. These were built throughout the city centre, so that no single financial district of the type common in other European capitals developed. Not all of the new and remodelled buildings met with the approval of Warsaw's citizens, who particularly objected to the style of the Russian Orthodox Church and the Byzantine-style Staszic Palace, considering them manifestations of cultural expansion by the occupying power. Among several dozen architects active in Warsaw between 1865 and 1914, particularly high standards were achieved by Leandro Jan Marconi and Władysław Marconi (*see* MARCONI, (2) and (3)), Witold Lanci (1828–92), Józef Huss (1846–1904), Jan Kacper Heurich sr (1834–87), Julian Ankiewicz (1820–1903), JÓZEF PIUS DZIEKOŃSKI and Stefan Szyller (1857–1933), as well as the architects of the younger generation, JAN HEURICH, Karol Jankowski (1868–1928), Franciszek Lilpop (1870–1937), Tomas Oskar Sosnowski and Czesław Przybylski.

After Poland regained independence in 1918, work commenced on a new urban plan that encompassed the city's new boundaries. This ambitious project was realized only in part. The railway network was improved, and the broad Niepodległości Avenue was laid out in south Warsaw; other main roads leading out of the city were widened. Among the most important and impressive projects was the creation of Żwirki i Wigury Avenue. In all, around a thousand streets were either newly laid out or re-aligned; a large bus and tramway network was also built. Urban planners were inspired by the idea of the garden city (e.g. in the Sadyba and Żoliborz districts). A related concept developed, whereby a circular or semicircular 'square' (e.g. Narutowicza, Wilsona and Inwalidów) was situated in the centre of a district and was cut across by a major road. Residential districts, for example the Żoliborz WSM (Warsaw Housing Cooperative) Housing Estate, were designed according to the most avant-garde concepts.

Between 1918 and 1939 numerous monumental government buildings, banks, churches and apartment houses were built along the main thoroughfares. The public buildings were designed in a Modernist style that was a simplified and structurally clearer version of that current at the beginning of the 20th century. The finest examples include the National Economic Bank (1928–31) by Rudolf Świerczyński, the High Courts (1935–9) by Bohdan Pniewski, the Mint (1925–9) by Antoni Dygat (1886–1949), the Ministry for Religious Denominations and Public Enlightenment (1925–30) by Zdzisław Mączeński (1878–1961) and the Central Institute of Physical Education (1928–30) by Edgar Norwerth (1884–1950). At the same time an academic Neo-classicism was favoured by graduates of the St Petersburg Academy, including Marian Lalewicz, who designed the Agricultural Bank (1926–8) and the headquarters of the Polish State Railway (1928–30). A number of architects popularized earlier architectural styles, primarily the Baroque, as in the Stefan Batory School (1922–4) by Tadeusz Tołwiński. The 'Manorhouse' style developed from this trend; fine examples of this quest for a national style include the 'manor houses' in the Żoliborz district and in Mochnackiego and Mianowskiego streets. Warsaw architecture of the time was characterized by sound workmanship and luxurious interiors finished by expert craftsmen. From *c.* 1925 architects were inspired by the most recent achievements of the European avant-garde and developed a radically functionalist style, chiefly represented by Bohdan Lachert and Jerzy Szanajca (*see* LACHERT AND SZANAJCA), Barbara and Stanisław BRUKALSKI, JULIUSZ ŻÓRAWSKI and Julian Puterman-Sadłowski (1892–1953) and closely connected with a social programme based on the need for small apartments. Experimental designs were followed by housing estates that were among the finest achievements of the Warsaw architectural community in the period.

Warsaw was almost entirely destroyed during World War II. Work on its reconstruction commenced in January 1945 and the Office for the Reconstruction of the Capital was instituted on 14 February 1945. Two decrees were issued: Warsaw was to be rebuilt and all its land nationalized. In the first stage (1945–7) the aim was to restore the basic infrastructure and to provide housing. The most interesting housing estates of the period were those designed by Helena and Szymon Syrkus and Stanisław Brukalski's extension of the Żoliborz WSM Housing Estate. Among the most notable buildings constructed for the state administration were those by Bohdan Pniewski, for example the headquarters of the Ministry of Transport (1946–50) in Chałubińskiego Street and the new Sejm (parliament) buildings (1948–51) in Wiejska Street. The reconstruction and restoration of historical buildings was begun in the late 1940s and proceeded on a scale that was without precedent. The Old Town and New Town were entirely rebuilt along with the Krakowskie Przedmieście area, Nowy Świat, Długa, Miodowa and Senatorska streets and Ujazdowskie Avenue. The vast undertaking ended in the 1970s with the reconstruction of the Royal Castle and Ujazdów Castle, two key buildings in Warsaw's skyline.

From 1949 to 1955 the city's architecture was affected by the doctrine of Socialist Realism, the main projects being the Marszałkowska Housing Estate (1949–52), the Ministry of Agriculture Building (1951–5) in Wspólna Street and the Palace of Culture and Science (1952–5). Other architectural trends were not entirely eliminated in this period. The Central Department Store (1948–52) in Bracka Street by Zbigniew Ihnatowicz and Jerzy Romański (1909–68) is an example of functional design and clear construction. The Tenth Anniversary Stadium (1945–55) by JERZY HRYNIEWIECKI, Marek Leykam (1908–83) and Czesław Rajewski (1908–84), another clear and functional composition, has become an important element in the panorama of the east bank. Between 1957 and 1965 the first large housing estates were built, but owing to economic and technological restrictions many of the designs were conservative and schematic. Some buildings were, however, very successful, for example the Supersam (1959–62), a supermarket by J. Hryniewiecki in Puławska Street. The Trasa Łazienkowska (1971–4), a motorway 14 km long linking east and west Warsaw, the largest urban enterprise, was one of the largest investments undertaken after World War II. The north and south districts of the city are to be linked by the first line (begun 1982) of an underground train network.

BIBLIOGRAPHY

J. Bartoszewicz: *Kościoły warszawskie rzymsko-katolickie opisane pod względem historycznym* [A historical description of the Roman Catholic churches in Warsaw] (Warsaw, 1855)

O. Sosnowski: 'Powstanie, układ i cechy charakterystyczne sieci ulicznej na obszarze Wielkiej Warszawy' [The origin, layout and characteristics of the street network in Greater Warsaw], *Stud. Dziejów Sztuki Polsce*, ii (1930), pp. 1–62

J. Zachwatowicz: 'Mury obronne Warszawy i prace nad ich odsłonięciem' [Warsaw's defensive walls and work on their excavation], *Biul. Hist. Szt. & Kult.*, v/3–4 (1937), pp. 279–87 [with Fr. summary]

S. Herbst: *Ulica Marszałkowska* [Marszałkowska Street] (Warsaw, 1949)

E. Szwankowski: *Warszawa: Rozwój urbanistyczny i architektoniczny* [The urban and architectural development of Warsaw] (Warsaw, 1952)

O. Sosnowski: 'Stare Miasto w Warszawie: Odbudowa' [The reconstruction of Warsaw's Old Town], *Teka Kons.*, iv (Warsaw, 1956) [whole issue]

E. Szwankowski: *Ulice i place Warszawy* [The streets and squares of Warsaw] (Warsaw, 1963)

M. M. Drozdowski and A. Zahorski: *Dzieje Ochoty* [A history of Ochota] (Warsaw, 1970)

——: *Dzieje Pragi* [A history of Praga] (Warsaw, 1970)

A. Zahorski: *Żoliborz: Wczoraj, Dziś, Jutro* [Żoliborz: its past, present, future] (Warsaw, 1970)

M. M. Drozdowski and A. Zahorski: *Dzieje Mokotowa* [A history of Mokotów] (Warsaw, 1972)

——: *Historia Warszawy* [A history of Warsaw] (Warsaw, 1972)

——: *Dzieje Woli* [A history of Wola] (Warsaw, 1974)

——: *Dzieje Śródmieścia* [A history of Śródmieście] (Warsaw, 1975)

Ł. Heyman: *Nowy Żoliborz, 1918–1939* (New Żoliborz, 1918–1939) (Wrocław, 1976)

J. Chróścicki and A. Rottermund: *Atlas of Warsaw Architecture* (Warsaw, 1977)

A. Miłobędzki: *Architektura polska XVII wieku* [Polish architecture in the 17th century] (Warsaw, 1980)

T. S. Jaroszewski: *Księga pałaców Warszawy* [The book of Warsaw palaces] (Warsaw, 1985)

H. Faryna-Paszkiewicz: *Saska Kępa, 1918–1939* [Saska Kępa, 1918–1939] (Wrocław, 1989)

M. Kwiatkowski: *Architektura mieszkaniowa Warszawy: Od potopu szwedzkiego do powstania listopadowego* [The residential architecture of Warsaw: from 'the Swedish Deluge' to the November Insurrection] (Warsaw, 1989)

III. Art life and organization.

1. Before 1795. 2. 1795 and after.

1. BEFORE 1795.

(i) Early development, to *c.* 1600. (ii) *c.* 1600–*c.* 1740. (iii) Development, *c.* 1740–94.

(i) Early development, to c. *1600.* With the prolonged isolation of Masovia from the rest of the Polish lands, Warsaw remained cut off from the dominant artistic developments of the 14th and 15th centuries. Yet evidence shows that it already had a small artistic community. The earliest known examples of painting are the two codices dated 1449 and 1450 (both Kraków, Czartoryski Lib., MS. 1418), with Polish translations of the statutes of Kasimir III, Vladislav Jagiellon and the Dukes of Mazovia. The illustrations include such scenes as the *King and Archbishop in Majesty* and were executed in Warsaw, possibly in the workshop of the painters Piotr (*d* 1472) and his son, also Piotr (*d* 1459). No panel paintings survive from this period; the only two known examples were destroyed in 1944 (19th-century copies in the church of St Martin, Warsaw). Fragments of wall paintings, such as the *Virgin and Child Enthroned* (Warsaw, Mus. Hist. City), survive from the first half of the 16th century and are almost certainly the product of local painters, of whom there must have been a fair number by that time, as a guild of painters and glass-makers was founded in 1516. There is no evidence that sculptors were active in Warsaw before the 16th century. The small number of earlier surviving sculptures were imported; for example the Crucifix in the chapel of the Miraculous Lord Jesus, Warsaw Cathedral,

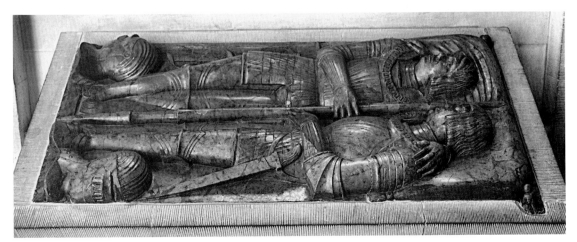

4. Bernardo Zanobi de Gianotis: tombstone of *Stanisław and Janusz III*, 1526 (Warsaw Cathedral)

was produced in Breslau (now Wrocław) at the beginning of the 16th century. A notable artist of the mid-16th century was Jan Jantas (*fl* 1537–58), whose best-known work is a polyptych (Boguszyce parish church) with a relief *Crucifixion*, signed *Joannes Jantas Fecit, Pictor Varschowiensis Anno 1558*. Sculptors belonged to either the stone-masons' or the wood-carvers' guild. Their works are largely anonymous, with the exception of Jantas, who probably ran a large painters' and wood-carvers' workshop to which several surviving pieces of sculpture from Mazovia are attributed.

A number of artists went to work in Warsaw from other towns and from abroad. The presence, for example, of Giovanni Battista Ferro of Padua (*fl* 1458; *d c.* 1460) (who had been employed by Sigismund I Jagiellon in Kraków in 1548) and the importing of such works as Joos van Cleve's *Adoration of the Magi* (Warsaw, N. Mus.) accelerated the introduction of the Renaissance. Nonetheless, most extant paintings and sculptures produced before the mid-1560s are Late Gothic in character. Interesting products of Kraków workshops include the tombstone of the last Mazovian dukes, *Stanisław and Janusz III* (1526; Warsaw Cathedral; see fig. 4) by Bernardo Zanobi de Gianotis and assistants, and that of *Mikołaj and Stanisław Wolski* (1568; Warsaw Cathedral) attributed to the workshop of Jan Michałowicz z Urzędowa. Works from the last quarter of the 16th century show a diversity of stylistic forms with strong northern Mannerist influences, as exemplified by the epitaph of *Jan Kaleński-Wilk* (ex-Warsaw Cathedral; destr. 1944). Overall, 16th-century Warsaw failed to develop into an important and independent artistic centre, although owing to frequent and prolonged visits of the royal court it attracted prominent artists from Italy, the Netherlands and Germany, as well as from other towns of the Polish–Lithuanian Commonwealth.

(ii) c. *1600–c. 1740.* From 1611 the royal court was in Warsaw permanently, and the town's artistic life developed rapidly. During the first half of the 17th century artists drew heavily on works from Kraków and Gdańsk, as well as from Italy and the Netherlands. Original designs were developed, mainly in architecture and interior decoration, and royal court painters played a major role in the latter (e.g. Tommaso Dolabella, who executed the ceiling paintings at the Royal Castle). During the reign of Vladislav IV Vasa (*reg* 1632–48), black marble from Dębniki (nr Kraków) became widely used in building and in monumental sculpture. It was frequently combined with alabaster figures and architectural details in such works as the epitaph to Sigismund III's musician *Asprilio Paceli* (*c.* 1570–1623) (*c.* 1630; Warsaw Cathedral) designed by Constante Tencalla, with sculpture by Sebastian Sala (1618–52). The fashion for this combination of materials soon spread from the Warsaw court to other parts of the country. Vladislav IV also commissioned Tencalla to design the Column of Sigismund III Vasa (1644; Castle Square). The statue of the King was made by Clemente Molli (*fl* 1635; *d c.* 1678), who was specially summoned from Bologna, and cast together with four plaques by the royal bell-founder Daniel Tym in his Warsaw workshop. The monument, unique in its time, recalled antique Roman columns supporting the statue of an emperor. It had a profound political significance as it did not merely extol royal virtues but became a symbol of the Commonwealth's sovereignty. The finest achievement of Vladislav IV's patronage is undoubtedly the decoration in the Royal

5. Giovanni Battista Gisleni: Marble Room, Royal Castle, Warsaw (1640–43; remodelled 1769–71; destr. 1939–44, reconstructed 1971–84)

6. Andreas Schlüter: relief sculpture (before 1694) on the garden façade of the Krasiński Palace, Warsaw (now the National Library), 1677–82 (damaged 1939–45, reconstructed 1948–61)

Castle's Marble Room (1640–43; see fig. 5). It was designed by Giovanni Battista Gisleni, with decorative paintings by Peter Danckerts de Rij, and was conceived to commemorate the Jagiellon and Vasa dynasties. Portrait painting was particularly important at Vladislav IV's court and was commissioned from many artists, including Danckerts de Rij, Bartolomäus Strobel II and Adolf Boy (1612–39). Warsaw became the country's leading artistic centre, due largely to the initiative of King John II (reg 1648–68) and his wife Ludwika Maria Gonzaga, who reorganized and enlarged their artistic patronage. Among the new artists they employed were the painters Francesco dei Rossi (from Rome) and Daniel Schultz II (from Gdańsk). The latter painted portraits, for example *John Kasimir with his Wife Ludwika Maria* (Gdańsk, N. Mus.), as well as such animal scenes as the *Cockerel and Chicken* (Gdańsk, N. Mus.) and religious scenes, exemplified by the picture of *St Aloysius Gonzaga at Prayer* (Warsaw, Church of the Visitation).

Under Michael Wiśniowiecki (reg 1669–73) and John Sobieski an original artistic intellectual movement and associated artistic style known as Enlightened Sarmatism developed in Warsaw. It represented a successful combination of the late Baroque style with elements derived from antiquity. The new style was greatly encouraged by Sobieski and the magnates Stanisław Herakliusz Lubomirski and Jan Dobrogost Krasiński, for several reasons. Prominent Polish magnates sought to establish their ancient pedigree and thus to distance themselves from the rest of the nobility. Furthermore, the harmony of Classical forms was particularly appealing after the turbulent years of war, while Classical imagery seemed the most suitable for glorifying higher authority. The style was developed most successfully in architecture and sculpture. The latter is exemplified by the highly original artists Andreas Schlüter, who produced sculptural decoration on the Krasiński Palace in Warsaw (see fig. 6), and Stefan Szwaner (fl c. 1686–8) whose decorative sculpture adorns the façade of Wilanów Palace. In painting, the style is best represented by the court artists, Jerzy Eleuter Szymonowicz-Siemiginowski (1660–1711) and Jan Reisner (d 1714). Martino Altomonte, a painter trained in Naples and Rome, occupied a unique position at the royal court. His Baroque artistic temperament had to be adapted to the Neo-classical taste of Sobieski. Nevertheless, at the beginning of the 18th century the style favoured by the king co-existed with pure Baroque. This found expression in rich stucco decorations, for example those at Wilanów by Józef

Szymon Bellotti (*d* 1708), and in such frescoes as the decoration of the sacristy at the church of the Immaculate Conception, Bielany, Warsaw, by Michelangelo Palloni (1637–1711/13). Following the calamitous early years of the 18th century, artistic life in Warsaw began to intensify in 1717. The city had, however, lost its role as the leading artistic centre, because the magnates had established artistic circles on their own country estates (*see* POLAND, §XI, 2). Very close ties with Warsaw were, however, maintained by Elżbieta Sieniawska (1666–1729), who purchased the Wilanów estate from the Sobieski family in 1720 and created the most important artistic centre in the country there, with leading sculptors, stuccoists (including Franciszek Fumo and Piotr Innocenty Comparetti) and painters (including Józef Rossi).

(iii) Development, c. *1740–94.* Both architecture and sculpture flourished once again from the 1740s, and Warsaw regained its pre-eminence. The most outstanding sculpture of the time was produced by JAN JERZY PLERSCH, but other works are also notable. Several major sepulchral monuments, for example the tomb of *Princess Maria Karolina de Bouillon* (neé Sobieska) (1746; Church of the Holy Sacrament), were carved in the mid-18th century and are distinguished by their refined late Baroque form. Szymon Czechowicz, who trained and worked in Rome and was active in Warsaw from 1731, is considered one of the most outstanding Polish painters of the mid-18th century. He attracted numerous pupils and followers who emulated his elegant Rococo style and interesting colouring. Through his studio and teaching activities he exerted a considerable influence on the artistic life of the capital. Many hundreds of his works, mostly on religious subjects, found eager buyers throughout the Commonwealth.

Warsaw became one of the earliest centres of Rococo in central Europe, through direct contacts with Paris. The decoration of a room in Franciszek Bieliński's palace (destr.), commissioned in 1735 from Juste-Aurèle Meissonier, is a fine example. During the reign of Stanisław II Augustus Poniatowski (*reg* 1764–95; *see* PONIATOWSKI, (1)) Warsaw emerged as a major European centre of Neo-classical art, mainly owing to the King, who was a distinguished patron and a passionate collector. He employed mainly Polish artists and craftsmen and sent them to study abroad at his own expense. He also summoned foreign artists to work for him permanently or on individual projects. The presence in Warsaw of the finest talents and the growth of collecting provided local artists with the best tutors and most representative examples of European art. Although Stanisław did not establish a true art academy as he intended, the painting and sculpture studios at the Royal Castle largely fulfilled that role (*see* POLAND, §XIV, 1). His attention was focused chiefly on his three Warsaw residences: the Royal Castle (*see* §V, 1 below), the Ujazdów Castle and Łazienki (*see* §V, 2 below). By the late 1760s Stanisław had assembled a group of artists, including the painters MARCELLO BACCIARELLI, BERNARDO BELLOTTO (to 1780) and Jan Bogumił Plersz (*see* PLERSZ, (2)), and the sculptors JAKUB MONALDI and André Le Brun (1737–1811), who worked for him for the next 30 years. The court artists also worked for other patrons, primarily members of the King's family and circle,

but also for leading Warsaw bankers. It is interesting that the art of the period lacked stylistic unity: works of the court painters and sculptors had Baroque overtones to *c.* 1770, when new forms appeared (e.g. in Bacciarelli's paintings for the Royal Castle). The Neo-classical style never entirely dominated in the work of the most important artists at the royal court, Bacciarelli and Le Brun, but it did find expression in the works of others, as for example in the decorative wall paintings of Jan Bogumił Plersch.

2. 1795 AND AFTER. Warsaw's artistic life was suppressed for over 120 years following the Third Partition of Poland in 1795; Russian policy towards Poles and Polish culture became even more hostile following several national insurrections, and Russification was introduced while all artistic activities were severely restricted. During the Congress Kingdom of Poland period (1815–31) the situation improved somewhat, and Warsaw's artists were supported by the Faculty of Fine Art at Warsaw University. The professors there, particularly Antoni Brodowski, promoted Neo-classicism; the favourite subjects included mythological and historical themes, genre scenes (especially by Aleksander Kokular; 1793–1816) and portrait painting, with Antoni Blank (1785–1844) a leading exponent (*see also* POLAND, §XIV, 2). The unveiling in 1830 of Bertel Thorvaldsen's monument to *Nicolaus Copernicus* was an important artistic event. Among the measures of oppression following the November Insurrection (1830) was the closure of Warsaw University; the art faculty's role was taken over by several private schools of painting, including those of A. Blank and A. Kokular. Major public art exhibitions were restricted, and large parts of the collections of the Royal Castle and of other institutions were removed to Russia.

The Neo-classical tradition was still current and was represented, for example, in the early work of the sculptor JÓZEF JAKUB TATARKIEWICZ. Romanticism was expressed mainly in themes from Polish history, as in the works by January Suchodolski (1797–1875). In the 1850s the first large public commissions were carried out, including Karol Marconi's painted decoration in the Land Credit Society building and the figure of *Christ Carrying the Cross* outside the church of the Holy Cross, by Andrzej Pruszyński (1836–95). The founding in 1862 of the Society for the Encouragement of Fine Arts (Towarzystwo Zachęty Sztuk Pięknych) enlivened Warsaw's artistic life, but its effects were undermined following the January Insurrection (1863). The School of Fine Arts (1844–64) was closed and replaced in 1865 by the Drawing Class, which was to prepare pupils for higher artistic education. Wojciech Gerson (see fig. 7), an outstanding painter and pedagogue, taught there (1872–96) and trained leading painters of the next generation, including Józef Chełmoński, Maksymilian Gierymski (*see* POLAND, fig. 9), Aleksander Gierymski, Józef Pankiewicz, Władysław Podkowiński and Leon Wyczółkowski. Along with the Zachęta Gallery, several private art salons opened, including those of Gracjan Unger (1853–1911) and Aleksander Krywult (*d* 1903). There were new illustrated periodicals, including the very influential *Wędrowiec* (The Wayfarer), which grouped a number of painters and critics, among them Stanisław Witkiewicz (1851–1915).

7. Wojciech Gerson: *Cemetery in the Mountains*, oil on canvas, 0.67x1.00 m, 1894 (Warsaw, National Museum)

Warsaw became the country's leading sculptural centre during the second half of the 19th century. There was great stylistic variety, ranging from realism and naturalism to the delicate Art Nouveau in the works of leading Warsaw sculptors, including Konstanty Hegel (1788/9–1876), Tomasz Oskar Sosnowski, Andrzej Pruszyński and Pius Weloński (1849–1931). In 1890 Józef Pankiewicz and Władysław Podkowiński exhibited paintings produced under the influence of Impressionism, and this date is considered a turning-point in the history of Warsaw art, although other artistic disciplines were still firmly set in academic eclecticism. The activity of artistic institutions was revived after *c.* 1900, with the opening of art salons and such associations as the Society of Friends of the Graphic Arts (Towarzystwo Przyjaciół Sztuk Graficznych; 1912). In 1904 the Warsaw School of Fine Arts opened, and its professors, who included Konrad Krzyżanowski, Ferdynand Ruszczyc, Ksawery Dunikowski and Władysław Ślewiński, set the tone for the city's artistic life. Between 1900 and 1914 Warsaw was an important centre of graphic arts, with such exponents as J. Pankiewicz and Zofia Stankiewicz (1862–1955). The periodical *Chimera* (1901–7) propagated the idea of pure aestheticism and introduced to its readers the finest paintings and works of graphic art, mainly in the Art Nouveau style. This style was popular with sculptors, among whom Wacław Szymanowski (1859–1930), who created the *Chopin* monument (1904) in Łazienki Park, was the most outstanding.

After 1918, Warsaw continued to play an important and often dominating role in the country's artistic life. The Zachęta Gallery remained the principal art salon; the Polish Art Club was also influential until 1930, when it was replaced by the Institute for the Propagation of the Arts. The National Museum was transferred to a new, larger building in 1938. These institutions were reinforced by such private art galleries as the Czesław Garliński Art Salon (1922–39), as well as by the exhibition venues of the Trade Union of Polish Artists and the Jewish Society for the Dissemination of Fine Arts. The School of Fine Arts (renamed the Academy of Fine Arts in 1932) and the Municipal School of Decorative Arts and Painting were the leading art schools; the School of Applied Graphic Arts opened in 1926. These institutions and the numerous new artistic groups transformed Polish art. The most important groups were the FORMISTS, the RHYTHM GROUP, the PRAESENS GROUP, the Colourists with Jan Cybis (1897–1972) and Józef Czapski, and Pryzmat (Prism) with Felicjan Kowarski and his students. Three more artistic groups, the FELLOWSHIP OF ST LUKE, the Szkoła Warszawska (Warsaw School) and the Loża Wolnomalarska (Freepainters' Lodge), were formed in the circle of Tadeusz Pruszkowski (1888–1942), a professor at the Academy of Fine Arts. In 1925 Władysław Skoczylas (1883–1934) and Edmund Bartłomiejczyk (1885–1950) founded Ryt (Engraving), the Association of Polish Graphic Artists.

Following the destruction of Warsaw during World War II, Kraków became the leading centre of Polish artistic life. Members of the Warszawa (Warsaw), the Polscy Artyści Niezależni (Polish Independent Artists) and Powiśle (Vistula Embankment) groups of 1945–7 continued with pre-1939 trends, while avant-garde movements were developed only by members of the Klub Młodych Artystów i Naukonków (Young Artists' and Scientists' Club), formed in 1947. From 1949 the doctrine of SOCIALIST REALISM was obligatory, and Warsaw became the command centre of all Polish artistic institutions. Independent artistic groups and small galleries were replaced with nationwide art exhibitions, held in Warsaw in 1950–54. In 1955 an exhibition organized in the Arsenal, with works by young artists including Stefan Gierowski, Jan Lebensztejn, Jerzy Tchórzewski (b 1928) and Rajmund Ziemski (b 1930), signalled a break with the doctrine (see ARSENALISTS). Soon after, they founded the first groups involved in the abstract movement: Grupa 55 (Group 55), Galeria Krzywe Koło (Crooked Circle Gallery; 1955) and Kardarz (1957). The *Sculpture in the Garden* exhibition (1957) was an important event that brought attention to a group of young sculptors (e.g. Alina Szapocznikow), whose work was related to the western European abstract and surrealist movements. In the 1960s and 1970s Warsaw lost its dominant position when many artistic centres developed in the provinces. Nevertheless, several new groups, including Rekonesans (Reconnaissance; 1964) and neo-neo (1967), were established in the capital and continued the abstract trend with the introduction of New Figuration. The metaphysical and neo-realistic current chiefly represented by Franciszek Starowiejski (b 1930) and Zdzisław Beksiński (b 1929) was also strong. Such new artistic directions as environmental art, conceptual art and happenings were promoted by independent galleries: the Contemporary Gallery (1965), Foksal (1966), Remont (1972) and Repassage (1972). Warsaw's role as an important centre of poster art increased in 1968 when the world's first Museum of Posters was founded at Wilanów. From the early 1980s the Centre of Contemporary Art, the National Museum and the Museum of the Academy of Fine Arts were the leading art institutions, organizing the most interesting exhibitions of Polish and European art.

BIBLIOGRAPHY

M. Karpowicz: *Sztuka oświeconego sarmatyzmu* [The art of enlightened Sarmatism] (Warsaw, 1970)

I. Tessaro-Kosimowa: *Historia litografii warszawskiej* [A history of Warsaw lithography] (Warsaw, 1973)

B. Grocholska and W. Pruss, eds: *Z dziejów rzemiosła warszawskiego* [On the history of craft in Warsaw] (Warsaw, 1983)

M. Karpowicz, ed.: *Sztuka Warszawy* [The art of Warsaw] (Warsaw, 1986)

——: *Sztuka Warszawy czasów Jana III* [The art of Warsaw under John III Sobieski] (Warsaw, 1987)

IV. Centre of production.

1. METALWORK. Warsaw became a notable centre of goldsmithing in the 15th century. The most prominent goldsmiths active at that time included the masters Grzegorz (fl 1425–50), Mikolaj (fl mid-15th century), Pietr (fl 1427–50), Sobek (fl 1426–50) and Jan Sowa (fl 1427–50), but it is difficult to attribute any works to them. In the 16th century the number of goldsmiths increased, and the most notable among them were Master Paweł (d 1533), Andrzej Półtorak (1505–62), who made a monstrance (1549) for the church of St Francis in Sarbiewo, near Płońsk, and a monstrance (1560) for the church in

Prażmow, near Piaseczno, Andrzej Erler, Gabriel Erler, Mikolaj Erler, to whom a silver cockerel (1552) for the City Watchman Confraternity has been attributed, and Maciej Hildebrand (fl 1571–6). The works of these goldsmiths have Gothic structures but Renaissance ornament. In 1589 the goldsmiths' guild received a charter, and at the beginning of the 17th century new Baroque styles were introduced. The most notable craftsmen at this time were Karol Libberth, Joachim Puszcz (1597–1617) and, in the second half of the 17th century, Wacław Grotko (1665–75) from Prague. Grotko's monstrance for the monastery in Częstochowa is one of the most magnificent examples of Polish Baroque silver.

In the first half of the 18th century craftsmen from Saxony and Silesia settled in Warsaw: their works combine late Baroque forms and Rococo ornament, which persisted until the late 18th century and are evident in the work (e.g. cup, 1770; London, V&A) of Jan Martin (in Warsaw 1769–91). The most prominent goldsmiths working in the Neo-classical style were Jan Jerzy Bandau (fl c. 1768–1817), who made two soup tureens (1785–8; Warsaw, N. Mus.) for the silver table service of Władysław Gurowski (1715–90), Teodor Pawłowicz (fl 1784–94), Szymon Stanecki (fl 1783–1810), Tomasz Klimaszewski (fl early 19th century), Jan Jerzy Holke (fl 1814–37), Jan Maciej Schwartz (fl late 18th century) and Samuel Gotthelf Schmidt (fl late 18th century) from Gdańsk. Their works are well proportioned and have austere decoration. In the second half of the 18th century clockmaking developed in Warsaw. The chief craftsmen in this field were Michał Gugenmus (fl mid-18th century), his son Franciszek Gugenmus (d 1820) and his grandson Antoni Gugenmus (d 1850), Jan Heckel (d before 1786), Franciszek Krantz (d 1786), his son Jan Krantz (d c. 1817), Antoni Krantz (d c. 1818), Michał Krantz (d c. 1816), Ludwik Mauryc Lilpop (fl 1854) and Franciszek Schubert (fl 1835). The last two craftsmen made clocks from imported parts.

Warsaw remained the main centre of goldsmithing in Poland throughout the 19th century, when numerous large silverware factories were established, for example those of Norblin, Karol Jerzy Lilpop (1781–1833), Józef Fraget (1797–1867), KAROL FILIP MALCZ, Kazimierz Klimaszewski and Emil Radtke. They developed industrial production of silver, and their products were sold in Poland, Russia and other European countries. The most important factory founded in the mid-19th century was that of Łopieński, which mainly produced silver services but also cast bronze sculptures and statues. At the beginning of the 19th century the style of gold- and silverware made in Warsaw derived from the French Directoire and Empire styles; later the most fashionable products followed Renaissance and Rococo forms until the Art Nouveau style was introduced at the end of the 19th century.

In the 20th century Warsaw ceased to be an important centre for silverware, and after World War II only the work of Henryk Grunwald (1904–58) was of significance.

BIBLIOGRAPHY

A. Weryho: *Warsaw Neo-classical Silverware*, Warsaw, N. Mus. cat. (Warsaw, n. d.)

2. FURNITURE. In the second half of the 18th century Warsaw became a centre of furniture production. The

workshops at the court of Stanisław II Poniatowski produced furniture designed by such royal architects as Jakub Fontana (1710–73; *see* POLAND, §VI) and Jan Chrystian Kamsetzer (e.g. throne, 1785–6; Warsaw, Royal Castle). In 1775 Prince Adam Poniński (1732–98) brought cabinetmakers from the Roentgen workshop in Neuwied, Westphalia, to Warsaw. The most notable were Andreas Simmler (1753–1810), Diercks, Neucha, Sturzig, Fries, Gersting and Johann Michael Rummer. They made mahogany furniture with English and French Neo-classical elements, sometimes combining them with neo-Gothic motifs; examples of late pieces can be found in the collections of the palaces of Wilanów, Łańcut and Łazienki in Warsaw and in the palace at Nieborów. In the late 18th century there were 198 cabinetmakers working in Warsaw; with the growth of industrialization and more efficient production the number increased to over 700 in the mid-19th century. The most distinguished workshop was that of Hans Jakub Simmler the younger (1791–1872) and Jakub Karol Simmler (1822–77). It manufactured mahogany furniture based on Renaissance patterns or combining elements from different styles; the most fashionable were the Rococo Revival suites known as 'Simmler' furniture (e.g. settee, *c.* 1840–50; Warsaw, N. Mus.). In the second half of the 19th century the largest furniture workshops were those established by Fritzki, Jaroszynski, Tarnowski and Olssen; at the beginning of the 20th century the most notable were those of Tworkowski, Karmanski, Ortwein and Zalaczyński & Herodek. In 1901 K. Szczerbinski and K. Trentowski established the first mechanized factory in Poland to produce artistic furniture, with retail outlets in Warsaw, Łódź, Moscow and St Petersburg. From 1918 to 1939 the trend towards a national style based on folk craft and culture strongly influenced Warsaw furniture production, and in 1922 Wojciech Jastrzebowski (1884–1963) opened a workshop at the Academy of Fine Arts specializing in this type of furniture. His ideas were taken up by the Artists' Cooperative 'Ład', which was established in Warsaw in 1926 and produced modern functional furniture for middle-class homes. After World War II furniture in Poland was mass-produced in state-owned factories to designs supplied by, among others, the Institute of Industrial Design in Warsaw.

BIBLIOGRAPHY

I. Huml: *Polska sztuka stosowana XX wieku* [Polish applied arts of the 20th century] (Warsaw, 1978) [with Eng. summary]
I. Grzeluk: 'Meble Simmlerowskie' [Simmler furniture], *Roc. Muz. Warszaw./Annu. Mus. N. Varsovie*, xxvi (1982), pp. 515–21

3. CERAMICS. In the second half of the 18th century Warsaw became the most important centre for ceramic production in Poland. In 1768 King Stanisław II Poniatowski charged August Moszyński (1731–86) with the organization of a royal faience factory in the Belvedere Palace. In 1770 the King signed a contract with Baron Franciszek Jozef Teodor Schütter for the production of faience, which began in 1772. The factory was unprofitable and needed regular financial support from the King, although the number of items produced reached 45,000 in 1778. Vases (*see* POLAND, fig. 19), baskets and dinner and tea services were especially popular, the most notable being a large service (Istanbul, Topkapı Mus.) consisting of 280 pieces with enamel decoration made as a gift for the Sultan of Turkey, Abdülhamid I (*reg* 1774–89). Belvedere ceramics were influenced in their forms by Japanese and Chinese porcelain and were marked with the letter B (for Belvedere) or V (for Varsovia). The factory was closed in 1780. Another faience factory, in Bielino, near Warsaw, was founded in 1779 by Karol Wolff, who was of Saxon origin. At the beginning the factory's wares hardly differed from those of the Belvedere; later they acquired more original forms and characteristics, notably the brown enamelled vases decorated with Chinese motifs (e.g. Warsaw, N. Mus.). Ceramics produced by Wolff were marked with the letter W. The factory was closed *c.* 1800.

BIBLIOGRAPHY

T. Mańkowski: 'Królewska Fabryka Farfurowa w Belwederze', *Mecenat artystyczny Stanisława Augusta* (Warsaw, 1976), pp. 171–196 [with Eng. summary]

For bibliography *see* POLAND, §VII.

V. Buildings.

1. ROYAL CASTLE. Former royal residence and seat of the government, situated between the Vistula escarpment and the Old Town, Warsaw. There is evidence of early 14th-century timber and brick buildings on the site, and towards the end of that century Janusz I, Duke of Mazovia (*reg* 1374–1429), built a splendid Gothic residence, the Curia Maior. The decoration of its red-brick façade shows links with the architecture of the Teutonic Order. The Ducal Cellar, the largest secular interior of the period to survive in Warsaw, also belongs to this phase.

In 1529 the Duchy of Mazovia was incorporated into the Polish kingdom, and the castle began to be used by the Polish kings. Its enlargement was begun in 1569 under the direction of Giovanni Battista Quadro and Giacomo Parri, for Sigismund II Jagiellon. Following the establishment of Warsaw as capital by Sigismund III Vasa, the castle underwent major changes and became the centre of political and cultural life in Poland and one of the most magnificent residences in Europe. The north, west and south wings were added (1600–19), forming a pentagon with a courtyard. The work was begun by Giacomo Rotondo and completed by Matteo Castelli, who designed the elevations in an early Roman Baroque style. He also added some north European features, noticeable, for example, in the form of the tower cupolas. The residence was typically urban in character and linked architecturally with the town.

The next important enlargement of the castle was undertaken by Augustus II and Augustus III. During the latter's reign (1733–63), Antonio Solari (1700–63) completed the late Baroque façade (*c.* 1740) overlooking the Vistula, considered one of the major architectural achievements in Poland in the first half of the 18th century. Its sculptural decoration was carved by Jan Jerzy Plersch. From 1764 the castle was greatly altered through the patronage of Stanisław II Augustus Poniatowski. The King's private apartments and the staterooms were reconstructed in 1765–86 to designs by Jakub Fontana (1710–73), DOMENICO MERLINI, Victor Louis and Jan Chrystian Kamsetzer, under the direction of the King's principal painter MARCELLO BACCIARELLI. The interior decoration is in the so-called 'Stanisław II style', characterized by a harmonious integration of architectural features with free-standing sculpture and large paintings. The most notable examples are the Old Audience Chamber, the Knights' Hall and the Great Hall or Ballroom (see fig. 8), all with particularly harmonious colour schemes.

In September 1939 the building was seriously damaged, but the greatest works of art and a large part of the interior decoration (including fireplaces, stuccowork, panelling, floors etc.) were saved and later replaced. The castle was blown up in November 1944, shortly after the Warsaw Uprising. The decision to reconstruct it was made in January 1971 and designs based on archival and photographic material were drawn up by Jan Bogusławski (1910–82). Structural work was finished in July 1974, and the whole building was complete by August 1984, although work on the Ballroom continued until July 1988. The reconstruction of the Royal Castle is considered one of the greatest achievements of conservation in the late 20th century.

BIBLIOGRAPHY

J. Lileyko: *Zamek Warszawski: Rezydencja Królewska i siedziba wiaolz Rzeczypospolitej, 1569–1763* [The Royal Castle: royal residence and seat of the Commonwealth government, 1569–1763] (Wrocław, 1984)

A. Rutkowski: *Zamek Piastów i Jagiellonów w Warszawie* [The castle of the Piasts and Jagiellons in Warsaw] (Warsaw, 1985)

S. Lorentz: *Walka o Zamek, 1939–80* [The fight for the castle, 1939–80] (Warsaw, 1986)

M. Karpowicz: *Królenski zamek Wazón w Warszawie: Wartości artystyczne* [The Royal Castle of the Vasas in Warsaw: artistic values] (Warsaw, 1988)

A. Rottermund: *Zamek Warszawski w epoce Oświecenia: Rezydencja monarsza, funkcje i freści* [Warsaw Castle in the age of the Enlightenment: monarchal residence, functions and contents] (Warsaw, 1989) [with Eng. summary]

2. ŁAZIENKI. Large park with palaces and pavilions in south Warsaw. From 1674 the land and the nearby Ujazdów Castle (1619–20) belonged to Stanisław Herakliusz Lubomirski, who built a Baroque Bath House ('Łazienka'; 1683–94) designed by TYLMAN VAN GAMEREN and situated on a small island. The building, erected on a square plan, was richly decorated with stuccos, statues and paintings; some of the original décor survives in the Bath Room and in Bacchus' Room. In 1766 King Stanisław II Augustus Poniatowski bought the estate and decided to convert the pavilion into a summer residence. Designs were drawn up by DOMENICO MERLINI, and work proceeded in four stages: a second storey was added in 1775–6; the south façade was reconstructed in 1784; the north façade (by Jan Chrystian Kamsetzer; see fig. 9), lateral wings and a belvedere were completed in 1788; and lateral pavilions with colonnades were added by Kamsetzer in 1792–3. The design was clearly influenced by such early French Neo-classical buildings as the Petit Trianon, Versailles, but links with the style of late Baroque garden pavilions can also be seen. The interiors, and especially the Ballroom (designed by Kamsetzer), are among the best produced under the patronage of Stanisław. Łazienki Palace was destroyed in 1944 and totally rebuilt after

8. Warsaw, Royal Castle, Great Hall by Domenico Merlini and Jan Chrystian Kamsetzer, 1777–81; destroyed 1944, reconstructed 1971–88

9. Warsaw, Łazienki (Palace on the Island), north façade by Jan Chrystian Kamsetzer, completed 1788

World War II. It is considered one of the most outstanding examples of Neo-classicism in Central Europe.

The King also commissioned the construction of several smaller palaces and pavilions in the park. The White House (1774–7; by D. Merlini) was influenced by the architecture of Jean-François de Neufforge. The interiors were painted by Jan Bogumił Plersz (*see* PLERSZ, (2)); the design of the Dining Room is one of the earliest Polish examples of decoration derived from ancient and Renaissance grotesque painting. The Myślewicki Palace (1775–8; by Merlini) is a characteristic example of early Polish Neo-classicism, with spatial arrangements based on the Palladian tradition and decorative motifs of interiors and façades derived from the Antique. The Old Orangery (1784–8; by Merlini) has a very well-preserved royal theatre in the east wing, with paintings by Jan Bogumił Plersch. The Amphitheatre (1790–91; by Kamsetzer) is an outstanding example of architecture inspired by austere ancient forms. The stage, situated on an island in the lake, was modelled on the Temple of Jupiter in Baalbek.

BIBLIOGRAPHY
W. Tatarkiewicz: *Łazienki Warszawskie* [The Łazienki in Warsaw] (Warsaw, 1965)
M. Kwiatkowski: *Łazienki* (Warsaw, 1972)

3. WILANÓW. Palace and park with pavilions and outbuildings, on the southern outskirts of Warsaw (see fig. 2 above). From 1677 to 1696 it was the summer residence of John Sobièski, who employed Augustyn Locci (*c.* 1640–1732) to design and build a single-storey manor (1677–9) with four projecting corner pavilions. It soon proved insufficient, and in 1681–3 one storey was added

and two galleries with towers were built. In 1686–92 another storey was added to the central part of the palace, and as a result of the expansion the building acquired the appearance of an Italian villa, topped by a belvedere on the main axis. Inside this was the largest of the rooms, the Great Hall. Inside and outside the palace was richly decorated with stuccowork, sculpture by Andreas Schlüter and Stefan Szwaner (*fl* 1686–8) and paintings by Jerzy Eleuter Szymonowicz-Siemiginowski (*c.* 1660–*c.* 1711), Jan Reisner (*d* 1714), Claude Callot (1620–87) and Michelangelo Palloni (1637–1711/12). The King's Anteroom, the Queen's Anteroom (see fig. 10), the Al Fresco Cabinet and the Mirror Cabinet have the most notable interiors. The subject-matter of the decoration was derived from mythology and ancient history and designed to glorify the monarch. In 1686–92 a second storey was added, and the towers were given tall cupolas, so that the small building gained a certain monumentality (see fig. 2 above). From 1720 Wilanów belonged to Elżbieta Sieniawska (1666–1729), who commissioned Giovanni Spazzio (*d* 1726) to add lateral wings (1723–9). The palace subsequently changed hands a number of times; it was owned in turn by King Augustus II and by Izabela Lubomirska, née Czartoryska (1736–1816), in the 18th century and by the Potocki family in the 19th. In 1805 STANISŁAW KOSTKA POTOCKI opened the palace to the public, thus forming one of the first public museums in Poland. Only minor alterations were made to the building, so that the elevations and interiors have remained largely intact. Since 1945 the palace and park have formed part of the National Museum, Warsaw.

10. Warsaw, Wilanów Palace, the Queen's Anteroom, begun c. 1681

BIBLIOGRAPHY

M. Karpowicz: *Sztuka oświeconego sarmatyzmu* [The art of enlightened Sarmatism] (Warsaw, 1970)

W. Fijałkowski: *Wilanów* (Warsaw, 1973)

W. Fijałkowski and I. Voise, eds: *Rzemiosło artystyczne i plastyka w zbiorach wilanowskich* [Art and craft in the Wilanów collection] (Warsaw, 1980)

ANDRZEJ ROTTERMUND

Wartburg, Schloss. Castle near Eisenach, Germany. It represents the claims to power and the self-assurance of the medieval landgraves of Thuringia. A centre of court culture in the 13th century—a legendary contest for the *Minnesänger*, or singers of courtly love, is supposed to have taken place in 1206–7—it was also the home from 1211 to 1227 of St Elisabeth of Hungary, wife of the Landgrave Ludwig IV. In 1262 the castle passed to the House of Wettin, and it belonged to the Electors of Saxony from 1423 to 1547. Martin Luther lived there from 1521 to 1522, translating the New Testament into German. In 1741 the castle came into the ownership of the Dukes of Saxe-Weimar and became a symbol of German history and culture, inspiring the work of Goethe, Liszt and Wagner. The *Wartburgfest* of German student fraternities took place there in 1817.

Founded by Ludwig der Springer, the castle is first mentioned in 1080. Ludwig III (1172–90) built the Landgrave's House and the residential quarters of the castle. In 1317–18 a fire seriously damaged the keep, the Landgrave's House and Heated Chamber; the chapel was built on the first floor of the Landgrave's House c. 1320. Between 1450 and 1500 defensive passages were built on the surrounding walls, and all the buildings were plastered. Much building activity is recorded between 1549 and 1630, but in the 17th and 18th centuries buildings fell into ruin and were demolished. The castle was renovated between 1838 and 1890 by Grand Duke Charles Alexander of Saxe-Weimar (*reg* 1853–1901); in 1854–5 Moritz von Schwind decorated the residence with frescoes of the legendary song contest, depicting episodes from the history of the Thuringian landgraves and scenes from the life of St Elisabeth. Between 1902 and 1906 the Elisabeth Chamber was decorated with mosaics. The castle was extensively restored from 1952 to 1966 and became a national monument (see fig.).

The castle, built on a hill, the Wartberg, was designed to control the *via regia* (royal road) between Frankfurt am Main and Breslau (now Wrocław, Poland). It is built of sandstone and tufa, on a plateau c. 140 m long. Its inner and outer baileys are separated by a ditch. The outer bailey is approached from an earthwork, across a drawbridge and through a gatehouse in the old north tower. It is bounded to the east by the curtain wall with its defensive passage, the Elisabeth Gallery. Adjoining the gatehouse on the west are the Knight's House, the Governor's House (containing the Luther Room and the Nuremberg oriel window added in 1872), the Margarethe Gallery and the Heated Chamber. A gatehouse between the Heated Chamber and the New Chamber separates the outer bailey from the inner bailey. On the east side of the inner bailey are the New Chamber and the keep (built in 1859 to replace the one demolished in 1790), the new staircase, the Landgrave's House and the Knights' Bath. On the west side stands the *Gadem* (hut), which once served as stables, arsenal and brewhouse. In between is the well. The southern end is protected by the south tower.

The earliest building in the enclosure was a dwelling between the north and south towers. Soon afterwards a keep was added, to form a three-towered castle. Remains of the earliest buildings are preserved in cellars below the Governor's House, the New Chamber and the *Gadem*; the bear cage beneath the Knights' Bath can still be identified. The nucleus of the castle is the Landgrave's House, to which the Landgrave Hermann I (1190–1217) added a third storey. The ground-plan is rectangular, with halls and square corner rooms. The groin vaults of the Elisabeth Chamber and of the Knights' Hall on the ground-floor rest on central supports; the dining hall between them has a massive beamed ceiling. Between the Knights' Hall and the dining hall a barrel-vaulted staircase leads to the first floor on which are the Landgrave's Room (originally the audience hall), the Singers' Hall and the chapel. On the second floor is the Feast or Banqueting Hall. The architectural ornament is of very high quality and is of Lower Rhenish origin, having parallels with the double chapel at Schwarzrheindorf near Bonn (third quarter of the 12th century). The side facing the courtyard, with arcaded galleries in the centre, is the show façade. The ground-floor has three pairs of double arches; the first floor has three groups of five smaller arches on paired colonnettes, while the third storey has four quadruple arcades with two twin round-arched arcades to the south. Between the two upper storeys a round-arched frieze marks the cornice of Ludwig's building; the later cornice

Schloss Wartburg, view from the south-east, begun third quarter of the 12th century; restored 1952–66

above is copied from it. As an aristocratic residence this is equal to the Hohenstaufen imperial palaces at Eger (Cheb), Goslar and Gelnhausen.

BIBLIOGRAPHY

G. Voss: *Die Wartburg* (Magdeburg, 1925)
H. C. van de Gabelentz: *Die Wartburg* (Munich, 1931, 2/1941)
J. Streisand: *Die Wartburg in der deutschen Geschichte* (Berlin, 1954)
S. Asche: *Die Wartburg: Geschichte und Gestalt* (Berlin, 1962)
W. Noth: *Die Wartburg* (Leipzig, 1967)
W. Noth and K. Beyer: *Die Wartburg: Denkmal und Museum* (Leipzig, 1989, rev. 3/1989)
J. Krauss: *Die Wiederherstellung der Wartburg im 19. Jahrhundert* (Kassel, 1990)

ERNST ULLMANN

Warwick, Earls of. *See* GREVILLE.

Waser, Anna (*bapt* Zurich, 16 Oct 1678; *d* Zurich, 20 Sept 1714). Swiss painter and etcher. She received her first lessons in Zurich, from Johannes Sulzer (1652–1717), under whose direction she painted a *Self-portrait at the Age of Twelve* (1691; Zurich, Ksthaus), in which the portrait on the easel beside her is of Sulzer. From 1692 to 1695/6 she studied with Joseph Werner II in Berne, then set up as a miniature painter in Zurich. Soon her reputation grew and earned her commissions from all over Europe, especially from Germany, England and the Netherlands. From 1699 to 1702 she was employed at the court of Solms-Braunfels, then returned to Zurich, where she continued to paint mainly allegorical and idyllic pastoral subjects (none of which survive) and miniature portraits. An elegant silverpoint drawing of the *Ideal Head of a Woman* (1711; Berlin, Altes Mus.) shows a profile drawn in the manner of antique busts but with finely delineated hair and a lively expression; it resembles contemporary French drawings. Her sister Elisabetha Waser (1683–1729) was a calligrapher and graphic artist.

BIBLIOGRAPHY

SKL; Thieme–Becker
R. Füssli: *Geschichte der besten Künstler in der Schweiz* (Zurich, 1763)

Wash. Broad area of dilute INK or transparent WATER-COLOUR applied by brush. Gradations of tone and colour can be achieved through successive applications of washes (see fig. on next page). The technique developed from medieval manuscript illumination and was used from the 14th century to give tone to pen-and-ink drawings (*see* DRAWING, figs 1, 5, 6 and 7). In watercolour painting the technique was most fully developed by the English water-colourists of the late 18th century. Washes have also been used by miniature painters on parchment or ivory since the 16th century.

RUPERT FEATHERSTONE

Washington, DC. Capital city of the USA. Founded as the permanent seat of Federal government in 1790, it is located in and around a Federal enclave, the District of Columbia (DC), at the confluence of the Potomac and Anacostia rivers, and bordered by the states of Maryland and Virginia.

I. History and urban development. II. Art life and organization. III. Buildings.

I. History and urban development.

1. Introduction. 2. The L'Enfant Plan. 3. 19th century. 4. 20th century.

1. INTRODUCTION. The city was established following years of uncertainty regarding its appropriate location. Between 1774 and 1789 the Federal government met in eight established East Coast cities, giving a distinctly itinerant character to the fledgling institution. The Constitution of the USA in 1787 provided for the permanent national capital city to consist of a Federal district not exceeding 25.9 sq km. The subsequent Residence Act of 1790 established a broad 80 km area along the Potomac River between the Eastern Branch (now the Anacostia River) and the Pennsylvania line where the President of the US might locate the new city. In the 1790 Act, the Federal government agreed to meet for the next ten years

Wash and pen-and-ink drawing by Guercino: *Four Youths Singing, with an Old Man*, 266×381 mm, *c.* 1625–30 (Windsor, Windsor Castle, Royal Library)

in Philadelphia, before moving to the new capital. In the interim, three District Commissioners were to oversee the planning of the city and the construction of the necessary buildings.

The site President Washington selected in 1791 was located on land belonging to the states of Maryland and Virginia, with the President's House approximately at mid-point and the corners of the square due north, east, south and west. The selection of the site incorporated several strategic considerations. It straddled the Piedmont Plateau and the Coastal Plain and reflected a compromise between the sectional and cultural differences of the Northern and the Southern states. The site lay just south of the point where the rivers began to fall and thus stood poised to benefit from this limitation on river traffic. The presence of the thriving port cities of Georgetown, established in 1751 in Maryland, and Alexandria, established in 1749 in Virginia, gave credence to the urban aspirations of the city's founders. President Washington's home at Mount Vernon, VA, south of Alexandria, was also a factor in the location of the Federal city. The settlements of Hamburg, now Foggy Bottom, and Carrollsburg, now the Southwest Quadrant, were plotted but remained largely undeveloped.

At the time the Federal government took up residence in the new city in 1800, the population stood at 8000. By the mid-19th century the growth of the government brought the population to 52,000. After the Civil War (1861–5) the population burgeoned to 132,000 by 1870.

By 1900 suburban development began to extend beyond the District's boundaries into Maryland and Virginia, a pattern continued into the next century. By 1950 the population had peaked at 802,000. In the decades following the mid-20th century, the residential population within the 25.9 sq. km area declined owing to the expansion of the commercial areas into older neighbourhoods and the spilling-over of residential settlement into the surrounding jurisdictions. In 1980 the population of the city numbered 638,500 within a larger metropolitan area of 3,500,000 inhabitants.

2. THE L'ENFANT PLAN. The city was designed by PIERRE-CHARLES L'ENFANT in 1791 and covered only the triangular flat basin closest to the junction of the two rivers. Its northernmost boundary was Boundary Street, now Florida Avenue. Rings of terraces, escarpments, slopes and ridges cut through by creeks and stream valleys surrounded this flat area.

The plan created by L'Enfant (see fig. 1) consisted essentially of a right-angled triangle formed by the President's House (now the White House; *see* §III, 2 below) on a small rise to the west of the ceremonial core. The short leg of the triangle ran south from the President's House through the President's Park (now the Ellipse) to an equestrian statue of George Washington (later the Washington Monument; *see* below). The long leg of the triangle linked the statue with the Capitol through a 'Grand

Avenue' (later the Mall) 122 m wide, lined with carriage drives and gardens and bordered by embassies. The Capitol (*see* §III, 1 below) was located on Jenkins' Hill, described by L'Enfant as a pedestal waiting for a monument. The hypotenuse, a road 1.6 km long, which connected the President's House and the Capitol, became Pennsylvania Avenue; it was envisaged as the commercial and social heart of the city, and lined with shops, boarding houses, hotels and playhouses. Pennsylvania Avenue did, in fact, serve as a major commercial thoroughfare for more than a century and a half.

From this central core, streets that were criss-crossed by a grid of irregularly placed roads radiated out to Boundary Street and the river frontages. This pattern allowed for the aggrandizement of certain axes, such as 8th Street, which was to be highlighted by a proposed non-sectarian National Church placed due east of the President's House. 8th Street continued south to end on the banks of the Potomac River where the site for a naval column was provided, although this was never erected. The site intended for the National Church was used for the Patent Office building (1836; now the National Portrait Gallery).

To the south, 8th Street was to be further blocked by the construction of the National Archives building (1935–

9) designed by John Russell Pope. The points in the L'Enfant Plan where the grid and radial streets met were located on strategic topographical features and were reinforced by the siting of major public buildings and parks. The points of conjunction were also visualized as development nodes, which would generate growth throughout a decentralized city.

A canal fashioned from the Tiber Creek was initially intended to transport building materials to the public building sites and, later, to generate the commercial life of the city. The canal was also envisaged as a picturesque and tranquil element in the landscape. It ran from the mouth of the Tiber, at its confluence with the Potomac River, east through a turning basin on the 8th Street axis (the site of the Central Market) to the foot of the Capitol in a Grand Cascade. From the Capitol, the canal flowed diagonally to a Civic Center containing five 'grand fountains intended with a constant spout of water', and then divided into two legs, each running into the Eastern Branch. The canal was filled in in the early 1870s and renamed Constitution Avenue on its east–west axis. The major triangle evolved as planned although the location of the Washington Monument was off-centre owing to the instability of the land for the necessary foundations. Rather than a residential Grand Avenue, the Mall gradually

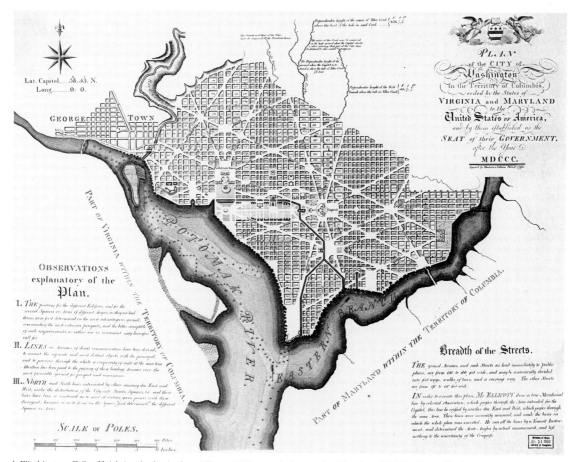

1. Washington, DC, official city plan by Andrew Ellicott, 1792, reproducing much of the plan of 1791 by Pierre-Charles L'Enfant (Washington, DC, Library of Congress)

became the sites of the Smithsonian museums, the National Gallery of Art and the Department of Agriculture building.

The essentials of the L'Enfant street system endured, although several radial avenues were straightened or eliminated soon after the plan's publication in 1792. In the District of Columbia, beyond the area covered by the L'Enfant Plan, many of the radial streets were extended, for example Massachusetts and Pennsylvania Avenues, which run to the District boundary line.

3. 19TH CENTURY. In 1800 the unfinished President's House and the Capitol figured prominently on the landscape. In between these major buildings, houses were scattered over what seemed interminable distances. The Washington Canal was built of inferior materials and was in constant need of repair. Few streets were paved and few municipal services were available.

Over the first half century, the city developed closest to the river frontages and between the President's House and the Capitol. Several major Classical Revival structures were constructed with light-coloured materials, such as marble and sandstone. The first was City Hall, designed by GEORGE HADFIELD with an Ionic order and begun in 1820; it became the focal point of the area known today as Municipal Center. The Greek Revival sandstone Treasury building of ROBERT MILLS, designed with Ionic columns, was begun in 1836 on 15th Street, one block east of the President's House. The 8th Street axis was emphasized by the location in 1836 of the Doric order Patent Office building (now the National Portrait Gallery) constructed of marble and designed by Mills. Also by Mills were the Post Office Department building (begun 1839; now the Tariff Commission), located just to the south of the Patent Office, and the great marble obelisk, the Washington Monument (1848–84).

In 1850 A. J. Downing was commissioned to prepare the first comprehensive plan for the area, which L'Enfant called the 'Grand Avenue' and is now known as the Mall. It had become a patchwork of lands, each under the jurisdiction of a separate government agency, and Downing's plan provided for a sequence of distinctive pleasure grounds linked by carriage drives and walkways. Owing to Downing's untimely death and the lack of Federal government commitment, however, only the grounds surrounding the Romanesque style Smithsonian Institution building of 1847–55 (see fig. 3 below) by JAMES RENWICK were redesigned to conform to the plan.

At the outbreak of the Civil War in 1861 Washington's settlement pattern strongly evoked L'Enfant's intentions. Much of the settlement clustered close to the White House and the Capitol and along the stretch in between, as well as along the river frontages and around the Navy Yard, which faced on to the Eastern Branch. The neat, compact pattern was changed with the introduction in the 1850s of an expanded water system originating at Great Falls, and the development of rail and streetcar lines, which led to growth beyond the city planned by L'Enfant and eventually beyond the District boundaries.

During the Civil War the capital, especially vulnerable to attack by Confederate forces owing to its proximity to Virginia, became an armed camp. Forts were sited on the circle of heights that ringed the city and new military roads were cut through from the city to the hinterland, thereby reinforcing the role of the capital as the centre of communication.

The city's brief experiment with the territorial form of government between 1871 and 1874 resulted in a vigorous programme to pave streets, construct sewers and plant trees, in the process of which Constitution Avenue was formed from the original city canal. After 1874 the Army Corps of Engineers assumed responsibility for the Federal government's public works, buildings and parks, and municipal public works fell under the jurisdiction of the Engineer Commissioner. The Corps of Engineers supervised the reclamation of the swampy Potomac Flats, which created East and West Potomac Parks, thus enlarging the monumental core south and west of the Washington Monument, the completion of which was overseen by the Corps.

Important buildings of this period include the grey granite State, War and Navy building (1871–86) west of the President's House, designed in the Second Empire style by Alfred B. Mullett, and the Library of Congress (1886–97) at the other end of Pennsylvania Avenue. Also of grey granite, the latter was designed by SMITHMEYER & PELZ in Italian Renaissance style and crowned by a copper dome. Beyond the monumental core, dense residential areas developed, such as Capitol Hill and Foggy Bottom and other areas around Logan, Scott and Dupont Circles, with whole blocks of red-brick town houses, elaborated with turrets and bay windows, and decorated with terracotta, pressed brick and cast iron.

4. 20TH CENTURY. In the 1890s proposals were developed to commemorate the centennial of the 'removal of government'. Sweeping all the proposals under a single study, the Senate Park Commission, commonly referred to as the McMillan Commission, provided a plan in 1902 (see fig. 2) that was the most comprehensive since the L'Enfant Plan. Chaired by Senator James McMillan of Michigan, the Commission included as members DANIEL H. BURNHAM, FREDERICK LAW OLMSTED, Charles McKim and AUGUSTUS SAINT-GAUDENS. The Commission proposed a kite-shaped configuration that lengthened the White House cross axis southwards to the head of the Washington Channel. Here, on a reclaimed site, the Commission proposed a Pantheon, which later became the Jefferson Memorial, and the Washington Common. The plan called for a westward extension of the Washington Monument–Capitol axis to what became the site for the Lincoln Memorial, joined to the Washington Monument by the Reflecting Pool.

Portions of the L'Enfant Plan were transformed into City-beautiful set pieces made up of groupings of monumental public buildings with adjoining plazas and formal parks. Around the White House and the Capitol, the Commission proposed the Executive Group and Legislative Group of new public buildings and the triangle formed by the Mall, Pennsylvania Avenue and 15th Street (later known as the Federal Triangle) as the location for future public buildings.

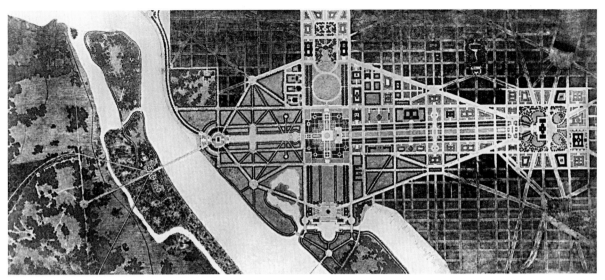

2. Washington, DC, McMillan Commission plan for the Mall, 1902 (Washington, DC, National Archives)

The McMillan Commission Plan formed a comprehensive system of regional parks, reminiscent of the metropolitan one in Boston, MA (*see* BOSTON, §I), which linked the formal open spaces of the Mall and those around major public building groupings with parkland adjoining the shores of the Potomac and the Anacostia rivers and along the stream valleys of Rock Creek, and extended as far as Mount Vernon to the south and Great Falls to the north-west. The park plan provided for a variety of functional and formal needs for open space and formed the basis of a long-term programme to acquire land. The McMillan Plan, which was institutionalized in 1910 by the Commission of Fine Arts, was implemented gradually, but its power was such that, for decades afterwards, private organizations commissioned new structures to conform to it in location and architectural style. Private individuals donated lands for parks and open spaces according to the comprehensive park proposal.

World War I led to delays in constructing new permanent office buildings and to severe shortages of space in Federal buildings in Washington. The Public Buildings Act of 1926 authorized the construction of many new Federal buildings, including those that made up the Federal Triangle. The Federal Triangle plan was conceived as an ensemble of public buildings. Each building was designed separately but conformed to an overall scheme and all were constructed of limestone. Edward H. Bennett (1874–1954) set the overall style as an 'adaptation of the eighteenth century classic'. The buildings were to be grouped around large interior courts and plazas. The first building in the group was the Commerce Building (1932) by Louis Ayers of York & Sawyer along 15th Street; the last the Federal Trade Commission (completed 1937) by Bennett at the apex of the Federal Triangle at 6th Street.

While the massive public buildings programme was underway, the residential parts of the city continued to develop outwards. The most common house form was the row or terrace house that accommodated thousands of civil servants of moderate means. The proliferation of the row house responded to advances in building technology and mass production. In the 1920s and 1930s entire complexes of row houses covering several blocks, such as Burleith and Foxhall Village, promised future occupants the advantages of harmonious 'village' surroundings. High-income families lived in houses with generous lawns, which were sited along tree-lined streets. Closer to the centre of the city, apartment houses offered an alternative form of housing.

In the early decades of the 20th century planning in Washington had been regularized, and the low-rise character of the city was reinforced in 1910 with the Heights of Buildings Act. In 1920 the first zoning ordinance was adopted. In 1924 the National Capital Park Commission was created to guide the acquisition of parklands in the District and adjoining Maryland and Virginia. Its successor agencies were given broad powers to oversee transport, subdivisions and public works as well as parks, and to prepare comprehensive plans.

The style of public buildings in this period was influenced largely by historical precedents. Built for the Episcopalian Church and designed by G. F. Bodley in collaboration with his former pupil, Henry Vaughan (1845–1917), the great Washington Cathedral was begun in 1908 on a commanding site in the north-west quadrant of Washington 122 m above the Potomac River, making it visible from many vantage points throughout the region. St James's Cathedral was constructed of Indiana limestone in a style dependent on 13th-century English cathedral Gothic. It is vaulted and contains rich sculptures and stained-glass windows. The Lincoln Memorial (1915–22) was designed by HENRY BACON and constructed of white-marble in Greek Temple Style with large Doric columns. Its setting and relationship to the Washington Memorial, the Mall and the Reflecting Pool and parkways enhances its monumentality. By the time of the Jefferson Memorial (1938–42) the classical style seemed out of date for monumental buildings. As designed by John Russell Pope, the white-marble memorial was modelled on the Pantheon in Rome, an appropriate choice for Thomas Jefferson, who admired Roman architecture and used the same model for the Rotunda at the University of Virginia.

During World War II the great increase in population led to the transformation of numerous mansions and large row houses into rooming houses. Planning efforts were thwarted by the decision to place the Department of War in the Pentagon on the Virginia side of the Potomac River rather than in the Northwest Rectangle west of the White House, an area designated as the location of future Federal government buildings. The construction of the Pentagon and the establishment of other military facilities in Virginia served as precursors to the dispersal of Federal functions into adjoining jurisdictions and to the development of a multi-centred regional city.

After the war, owing to concerns for decreasing population in the central city and the condition of housing, the city authorities focused their attention on improving older areas. Plans for urban redevelopment reached their fullest expression in the Southwest Urban Renewal Area, where much of the land was cleared and rebuilt with clusters of high-rise apartment houses, row houses and office buildings as well as a suburban-type shopping centre.

By the 1950s major buildings were designed in the style of the Modern Movement with an emphasis on clean functional lines. Important buildings of this era include Marcel Breuer's Department of Housing and Urban Development building (completed 1968), a concrete building with sweeping curves that recalled his buildings for UNESCO in Paris and for IBM in Nice; the Kennedy Center, completed in 1971 after designs by Edward Durrell Stone, a large rectangular white-marble box with cantilevered eaves supported by bronze columns; and the concrete doughnut-shaped Hirshhorn Museum (completed 1974) on the Mall designed by Gordon Bunshaft of Skidmore, Owings & Merrill. Also in the 1950s existing buildings in the older sections of the city began to receive greater protection. The charms of Georgetown were rediscovered as early as the 1930s, by which time the former port city had become a working-class area. The Old Georgetown Act of 1950 designated Georgetown a historic district and empowered the Commission of Fine Arts with review of new additions and alterations. Similar schemes were introduced for the Capitol Hill and Foggy Bottom neighbourhoods.

Planning in the 1960s was characterized by the waning of large-scale redevelopment projects and the emergence of efforts to recognize and protect the city's scenic, architectural and cultural character. As exemplified in the residential-scale Lafayette Square project across the street from the White House, President and Mrs John F. Kennedy inaugurated a renewed interest on the part of the Executive Branch in the physical appearance of the city. Mrs Lyndon B. Johnson brought her 'beautification' campaign to the capital in the form of massive plantings of flowers and trees throughout the monumental core.

The influence of historic preservation and the Post-modern preoccupation with historicism also affected new construction. During the 1950s and 1960s the expansion of the central business district west of 17th Street was marked by variations on the theme of the glass-box. By the 1970s and 1980s, as the Downtown East area became revitalized, new construction strained to break out of the glass-box formula with oversized towers, rusticated bases, marble sheathing and mansard roofs. Monumental building projects such as the pink-marble triangular East Wing (begun 1970) of the National Gallery of Art by I. M. PEI drew the fulcrum of art leadership further south away from New York City. The popularity of the Vietnam Veterans' Memorial (1982), a polished black-granite wall designed by Maya Lin, provoked many demands by other memorial organizations for a spot on the Mall. Other new developments have been influenced by the operation of the new and largely underground rail system. Areas near Metro stops became targets for high-density development, offering a mixed blessing of both convenience and radical redevelopment.

The legacy of planning and development in Washington can be seen in the surviving imprint of the L'Enfant Plan south of Florida Avenue (formerly Boundary Street) and in the placing of major public buildings and parklands according to planning precepts. Beyond the 'ideal city' are numerous patches of residential and commercial development that evolved according to the subdivision plans of developers and serve the needs of civil servants and employees of government-related businesses. While parts of Washington are comparable to similar areas in other American cities, its residential facilities—school buildings, commercial structures and recreational areas—are frequently cited as models for the nation.

BIBLIOGRAPHY

Washington: City and Capital, US Works Progress Administration (Washington, DC, 1937)

F. Gutheim: *The Potomac*, Rivers of America (New York, 1949, rev. 1974)

H. Caemmerer: *The Life of Pierre Charles L'Enfant, Planner of the City Beautiful, the City of Washington* (Washington, DC, 1950)

M. Green: *Washington, Village and Capital, 1800–1878* (Princeton, 1962)

——: *Washington, Capital City, 1879–1950* (Princeton, 1963)

J. Reps: *Monumental Washington: The Planning and Development of the Capital Center* (Princeton, 1967)

Toward a Comprehensive Landscape Plan for Washington, D.C., US National Capital Planning Commission (Washington, DC, 1967)

M. Scott: *American City Planning since 1890* (Berkeley, 1969)

F. Gutheim: *Worthy of the Nation: The History of Planning for the National Capital*, US National Capital Planning Commission (Washington, DC, 1977)

ANTOINETTE J. LEE

II. Art life and organization.

Since the designation of Washington as the permanent seat of the Federal government in 1790, the local art community has struggled to establish and maintain a sense of regional identity in a city devoted to national issues. Although generations of talented artists have lived and worked there, the District of Columbia is best known for its museums and monuments.

Early in the life of the city, artists came to the District of Columbia to paint portraits and views of the new capital and to seek government patronage, which was generous. From the first Federal building boom in the mid-19th century to the end of the New Deal era in the mid-1940s, European and American artists created or installed architectural sculpture and ornament, murals and other public works of art in and around the new Federal buildings. The building campaigns that involved the greatest number of artists were the US Capitol (*see* §III, 1 below), the Library

3. Washington, DC, original Smithsonian Institution building by James Renwick, 1847–55, with the Haupt Green garden in the foreground

of Congress and the buildings of the Federal Triangle bounded by Pennsylvania and Constitution avenues and by 6th and 15th streets.

Throughout the 19th and 20th centuries, art schools and other organizations in the city fostered a sense of community among local artists. Such accomplished painters as Charles Bird King, Joseph Wood (1778–1832) and Pietro Bonanni (1792–1825), who came to Washington in the early 19th century, offered the first private art instruction. The Washington Art Club, established in 1877, sponsored one of the earliest schools, which was active between 1879 and 1885. Other schools, now defunct, that made significant contributions to the local community were the Studio House (1933–45), affiliated with the Phillips Memorial Gallery; the Washington Workshop Center for the Arts (1943–56), which began as a recreation centre for Washington war workers and was reorganized in August 1945 as a non-profit making cooperative offering classes in painting, sculpture, ceramics, writing, music and dance; and the Institute of Contemporary Arts (1948–c. 1964) founded by the poet Robert Richman (1914–87), who came to Washington in the summer of 1947 to head the less well-known King-Smith School of Creative Arts. Inspired by Herbert Read's *Education Through Art* (1943), Richman radically redesigned the King-Smith School to support an integrated approach to the arts and named it after the Institute of Contemporary Arts in England, headed by Read. From the late 1940s until the mid-1960s the ICA sponsored exhibitions, concerts, performances, workshops, readings and lectures and operated a short-lived school for the arts (1948–51).

The oldest and most important professional art school in the District is now the Corcoran School of Art,

established in 1890 as an integral part of the Corcoran Gallery of Art. Other significant and lively schools in the area are Howard University, American University and the University of Maryland at College Park. The Washington Art Club, established in 1877, was the first formal organization of local artists devoted exclusively to art. Other local organizations followed, the most important of which were: the Art Students' League of Washington (1884); the Society of Washington Artists (1891); the Washington Watercolor Club (1896); the Fine Arts Union (c. 1899); the Washington Society of Fine Arts (1905); the Landscape Club of Washington, DC (1913); the Arts Club of Washington (1916); the Society of Washington Etchers (1934); the Artists' Guild of Washington (1941); the Washington Print Club (1964); the Washington Women's Arts Center (1975–88); and the Coalition of Washington Artists (1983).

The Smithsonian Institution, the world's largest museum complex comprising 15 museums and the National Zoo, both overshadows and enriches the local art community. Established in 1846 with funds bequeathed to the United States by the English James Smithson (1765–1829), the Smithsonian holds some 137 million artefacts and specimens in trust 'for the increase and diffusion of knowledge'. It is partially funded by the Federal Government and is dedicated to public education, national service and scholarship in the arts, science and history (see fig. 3).

Among the Smithsonian's art museums are: the Arthur M. Sackler Gallery by Jean-Paul Carlhian (*b* 1919), which opened in 1987, specializing in the artistic traditions of Asia from ancient times to the present with a focus on Chinese jades and bronzes, ancient Iranian gold and silver and Persian manuscripts; the Freer Gallery of Art (opened

1923), also a museum of Asian art with objects dating from Neolithic times to the early 20th century, which also houses works by late 19th- and early 20th-century Americans including a major collection of the works of James McNeill Whistler; the Hirshhorn Museum and Sculpture Garden, established in 1974, housing an extensive collection of modern and contemporary European and American art; the National Museum of African Art (by Jean-Paul Carlhian; opened 1987), the only museum in the United States dedicated exclusively to the collection, exhibition and study of the traditional arts of Africa south of the Sahara; the National Museum of American Art, which includes 34,000 paintings, sculptures and examples of the graphic arts, photography and folk art by American artists housed in a restored landmark, the old Patent Office building (see §I, 2 above), which it shares with the National Portrait Gallery and the Archives of American Art; the Renwick Gallery, a department of the National Museum of American Art featuring 20th-century American crafts and decorative arts; the National Portrait Gallery, where visitors can trace US history through representations of men and women who contributed to its political, military, scientific and cultural development; and the newest Smithsonian museum, the National Museum of the American Indian, dedicated to the collection, preservation, study and exhibition of the culture and history of the native peoples of the Americas, scheduled to open in Washington, DC, in 1998. (The Cooper-Hewitt National Museum of Design in New York City is also a part of the Smithsonian devoted to the study and exhibition of historical and contemporary design.)

The National Gallery of Art (1936–43, by John Russell Pope), opened in 1941 and affiliated with the Smithsonian Institution, includes the Andrew W. Mellon, Samuel H. Kress and Peter A. B. Widener and Joseph Widener collections, as well as those of European and American painting, sculpture, decorative arts and graphic arts from the 12th to the 20th centuries; European Old Master paintings; Chinese porcelain; and prints and drawings from the 15th century to the present. The National Gallery also supports the Center for Advanced Study in the Visual Arts, which sponsors research in the history of the visual arts.

Washington possesses an unparalleled wealth of libraries, special collections and research facilities for the study of art including the Smithsonian's Archives of American Art, the world's largest collection of primary source material documenting the visual arts of the United States and such national databases as the Inventory of American Sculpture and the Inventory of American Paintings at the National Museum of American Art and the Catalog of American Portraits at the National Portrait Gallery. The Sculpture Source of the International Sculpture Center has an international database and slide registry for sculptors.

The District of Columbia is the home of many privately funded museums and non-commercial galleries including the Corcoran Gallery of Art, founded in 1869, with American and European painting, sculpture, graphic arts and photography; Howard University Gallery of Art, founded in 1928, with African American and American painting, sculpture and graphic arts; the Textile Museum,

founded in 1925, with rugs and textiles from Greece, Turkey, Egypt, Islamic Spain, Portugal, Oceania and the Americas; the Phillips Collection (formerly the Phillips Memorial Gallery), founded in 1921, with 19th- and 20th-century American and European art; Dumbarton Oaks Research Library and Collection, founded in 1940 by Robert Woods and MILDRED BLISS, with Byzantine, Pre-Columbian and some European and American painting, sculpture and decorative arts, as well as rare books and manuscripts; Museum of Modern Art of Latin America, founded in 1976, with 20th-century Latin American art; the National Museum of Women in the Arts, founded in 1981, with painting, sculpture, graphic arts and decorative arts by women; and the Washington Project for the Arts, founded in 1975, one of the largest artist spaces in the United States, committed to showing the best of contemporary and experimental art in all media. Some of the more important museums and non-profit-making galleries no longer in existence are: the Museum of Modern Art Gallery of Washington (1937–9), the Barnett-Aden Gallery (1943–62), the Washington Gallery of Modern Art (1962–8) and the Museum of Temporary Art (1974–81). While the Corcoran Gallery of Art and the National Museum of American Art have acquired and exhibited the work of Washington artists, the Washington Project for the Arts is the only non-commercial gallery in Washington, DC, that has demonstrated a long-term commitment to exhibit and promote local talent.

Many national arts organizations are also based in Washington, DC, including the National Endowment for the Arts, which awards grants to museums and individual artists across the country; the United States Information Agency (USIA), which sponsors travelling exhibitions; the International Sculpture Center, which publishes the only international magazine for sculpture (Sculpture) and organizes conferences; as well as the American Association of Museums, the African-American Museum Association, the American Art Alliance and the National Artists Equity Association.

Although there were some 75 commercial galleries in Washington before 1950, the city's art market developed slowly and it was not until the late 1960s that a distinct commercial district emerged on P Street in the Dupont Circle area of north-west Washington. While the art market has never rivalled that of New York City, by the early 1990s there were more than 100 commercial galleries in the city, mostly located in the Dupont Circle area, in Georgetown, and on 7th Street downtown, and trading in contemporary painting. Auction houses included C. G. Sloan & Co., Inc., and Adam A. Weschler and Son, as well as regional branches of Sotheby's and Christie, Manson & Woods of London, UK.

While some commercial buildings in the District of Columbia have been converted to studio spaces, there is no distinctive artists' quarter. The Washington Color Painters, a school that emerged in the late 1950s, is one of the only indigenous art movement associated with the city. The artists identified with that school—Leon Berkowitz (1919–87), Gene Davis (1920–85), Thomas Downing (1928–85), Sam Gilliam, Morris Louis, Howard Merhing (b 1931), Kenneth Noland and Paul Reed (b 1919)—produced large abstract paintings by staining or pouring thinned paint. The paintings emphasized the flatness of the canvas and created a colourful environment in expressive hues. The Washington Color school represents a mere fraction of the art produced in the District of Columbia in the last four decades of the 20th century. Washington art has been an eclectic mix of styles and approaches to art, and there is no predominant style or group identity among Washington artists; indeed their diversity of individual expression is their greatest contribution to contemporary art.

BIBLIOGRAPHY

A. Cohen: *Washington Artists: A Directory*, Artists Equity Association (Washington, DC, 1972)

J. Goode: *Outdoor Sculpture of Washington, DC: A Comprehensive Historical Guide* (Washington, DC, 1974)

V. McMahan: *Washington, DC: Artists Born Before 1900: A Biographical Dictionary* (Washington, DC, 1976)

A. Consentino and H. Glassie: *The Capital Image: Painters in Washington, 1800–1915* (Washington, DC, 1983)

G. Gurney: *Sculpture and the Federal Triangle* (Washington, DC, 1985)

K. Morrison: *Art in Washington and its Afro-American Presence: 1940–1970*, Washington Project for the Arts (Washington, DC, 1985)

R. Decatur: *The Art Trade in the District of Columbia, 1929–1950* (diss., George Washington U., Washington, DC, 1986)

L. Arden and others: *Washington Art: A Guide to Galleries, Art Consultants and Museums*, Art Calendar (Great Falls, VA, 1988)

J. Cohen: 'The Old Guard: Washington Artists in the 1940s', *Mus. & A. Washington* (May/June 1988), pp. 55–71

——: 'The Making of the Color School Stars, 1950–1960', *Mus. & A. Washington* (Nov/Dec 1988), pp. 55–61, 84

L. KIRWIN

III. Buildings.

1. Capitol. 2. White House.

1. CAPITOL. Located on Jenkins' Hill and linked by the Mall to the White House, the distance between the two buildings reflects the separation of the Legislative and Executive Branches of federal government. The three distinct sections of the Capitol itself, the centre balanced by equal wings (see fig. 4), express the structure of the US Congress, with the Senate and the House of Representatives. The dome over the centre symbolizes the enduring unity of the nation. The interior of the Capitol is arranged in interlocking rooms and corridors, a product of several enlargements and rebuildings, and is decorated with architectural ornament and works of art.

The Capitol's location was fixed in the L'Enfant Plan of 1791 (*see* §I, 2 above). In 1792 the District Commissioners responsible for the implementation of the plan announced a competition for the design of the building, offering £500 and a city lot. The competition yielded at least 16 entries, but no suitable design. A few months later, the Commissioners accepted a submission by WILLIAM THORNTON and in 1793 awarded him the premium. Thornton's design called for a central section, modelled on the Panthéon in Paris, and comprising a shallow dome placed behind a seven-bay portico and above a one-storey arcade. Flanking the central section were balanced wings

4. Washington, DC, aerial view from the east in 1987, showing the main vista from the Capitol along the Mall to the Washington Monument with the Lincoln Memorial behind

with elevations of Corinthian pilasters supported by rusticated piers. Above the pilasters was a full entablature with balustrade. The overall composition was based on English Palladian architecture.

Construction on all sections of the building began in 1793. By 1796, however, difficulties associated with the transportation of the Aquia sandstone, labour shortages and the scarcity of funds limited work to the north wing. During this period three architects, Stephen Hallet (?1760–1825), George Hadfield and James Hoban, took turns superintending the construction. By 1800 the north wing was complete enough to incorporate both houses of Congress, the Supreme Court and other legislative and judicial functions.

During much of the first decade of the 19th century BENJAMIN HENRY LATROBE served as architect of the Capitol. He altered Thornton's design for the interior of the south wing by elevating the House Chamber over a floor of offices. He also built the wing's interior of brick vaults and embellished the Hall of the House with decorations inspired by Classical Greece. Once the south wing was underway, Latrobe redesigned and rebuilt the eastern half of the north wing with brick vaults and columns with capitals sculpted into the shape of corncobs and leaves.

On 24 August 1814 British forces burnt the major buildings in the city, including the Capitol. Latrobe returned to Washington to redesign and supervise the restoration of the two wings. The House Chamber was rebuilt as a semicircle. Columns in the House and Senate Chambers were modelled on the Greek orders. The Supreme Court Chamber, directly below the Senate Chamber in the north wing, was also rebuilt, with a semi-dome ceiling and archway supported by Doric columns. Demands for greater speed and economy forced Latrobe to give up the work on the Capitol in 1817 and to leave the city altogether.

Charles Bulfinch was appointed in 1818 to complete the restoration of the wings. He also oversaw the construction of the centre section and a copper-covered wooden dome. On the East Front, at the base of the dome, Luigi Persico (1791–1860) designed the sandstone pediment sculpture depicting the 'Genius of America', with America pointing to Justice and Hope. It was executed from 1825 to 1828 and was later reproduced in white Georgia marble when the East Front was extended from 1958 to 1962. The Capitol building with its grounds was completed by 1830, 37 years after it was begun.

By 1850 the entry of new states into the Union and an increase in Congressional work led to severe overcrowding. The Senate Committee on Public Buildings held a competition for the Capitol extension and, after a second informal competition, selected a design by Thomas Ustick Walter. Over the next 14 years Walter provided large wings on either end of the building connected by narrow corridors. The resulting floor plan was an amalgamation of the original section with subsequent additions. The wings were designed to harmonize with the existing building; but Walter used marble from Massachusetts and Maryland instead of the sandstone used in the original building.

In 1853 Captain MONTGOMERY MEIGS of the Corps of Engineers was placed in charge of the work and proceeded to make changes to Walter's plans for the location of the House and Senate Chambers in the new wings. Despite disagreements between Meigs and Walter, the House wing was completed in 1857 and the Senate wing in 1859. The former Senate Chamber was assigned to the Supreme Court, which occupied it until 1935, when it acquired its own building. The old House Chamber was converted into Statuary Hall to contain statues contributed by each state, representing notable citizens. The collection includes over 90 statues, mostly of politicians, religious leaders, educators and scientists.

As part of the Capitol extension the pediment on the Senate side of the East Front, 'Progress of Civilization', was designed from 1855 to 1859 by THOMAS CRAWFORD and erected in 1863. The House pediment, 'Apotheosis of Democracy' by Paul Wayland Bartlett, was unveiled much later, in 1916. The enlarged Capitol building was by the late 1850s more than double its original length and required a new dome. Designed by Walter in 1855 and fabricated of cast iron with the assistance of Meigs, the Capitol dome was modelled on those of St Paul's Cathedral, London, and St Peter's, Rome. It was completed in 1863, and a bronze 'Statue of Freedom' (1855–62) by Crawford was placed on top. CONSTANTINO BRUMIDI completed the fresco *Apotheosis of George Washington* on its inner canopy, and in 1878 he began painting the rotunda frieze, which depicted American history from the landing of Columbus to the Gold Rush (see fig. 5). The frieze was eventually completed by 1953, with the historical panorama being updated to include the Wright Brothers' flight of 1903.

In 1874 Frederick Law Olmsted designed a comprehensive landscape plan for the Capitol grounds, leading to the creation of a great marble terrace around the north, west and south elevations of the building, as well as broad open lawns, low stone walls and picturesque landscape features (see fig. 4 above).

By the early 20th century the Capitol was again overcrowded, and new office buildings were constructed around the perimeter of the grounds, following the Mc-Millan Plan's recommendation of a legislative group of public buildings. These include the Beaux-Arts Cannon House office building and the Russell Senate office building (both 1905–10) by Carrère & Hastings of New York; the Longworth House office building (1932–3) by the Allied Architects of Washington; and the most recent office building, named in honour of Senator Philip A. Hart and completed in 1982, designed by John Carl Warnecke & Associates under the direction of George M. White, Architect of the Capitol.

Although additional office buildings, a Supreme Court building and an expanded Library of Congress complex relieved the Capitol of much pressure on space, the East Front was extended by 10.1 m between 1958 and 1962 in order to correct the impression that the cast-iron dome was insufficiently supported and to provide 90 additional rooms. To commemorate the nation's bicentennial in 1981 the old House Chamber was restored, as were the old Senate Chamber and the old Supreme Court Chamber, and the restoration programme was subsequently extended to include the reconstruction of the West Front by the replacement of one-third of its sandstone façade with Indiana limestone.

5. Washington, DC, the Capitol, interior view of the dome designed in 1855 in cast iron by Thomas Ustick Walter, showing the central fresco of the *Apotheosis of George Washington* (1865) by Constantino Brumidi and the rotunda frieze (begun 1878; completed 1953) illustrating American history

BIBLIOGRAPHY
G. Brown: *History of the United States Capitol*, 2 vols (Washington, DC, 1900–03)
C. Fairman: *Art and Artists of the Capitol of the United States of America* (Washington, DC, 1927)
M. E. Campioli: 'Building the Capitol', *Building Early America*, ed. C. Peterson (Radnor, PA, 1976), pp. 202–31

2. WHITE HOUSE. Although it is best known as the residence of the US president, the White House is a complex of residential, ceremonial and office spaces, which serves as the centre of the Executive Branch. By European standards, the White House is small, but the building above ground represents only a fraction of the complete structure, which is spread over several subterranean levels and two wings.

The White House originated as the President's House in the L'Enfant Plan. It is located on a rise in the western portion of the Federal city, providing for a view of the river, and six avenues radiate from the site, reinforcing the building's central position in the city. In 1792 the City Commissioners held a competition for the design of the President's House. JAMES HOBAN won the competition with a design for a three-storey rectangular building with a projecting central section of engaged columns over a heavy base. President Washington later made several changes to the design: he extended the outer dimensions by one fifth, added the pediment ornament and called for more stone embellishments. The building was constructed of Aquia sandstone and the planned third storey was omitted. The elaborate swag above the entrance door was carved in the 1790s.

Completed in 1803, the building was the largest house in the United States. It was rebuilt under Hoban's supervision after it was burnt by British forces in 1814. In 1824 the semicircular south portico was added, consisting of Ionic columns two storeys in height carved of Seneca sandstone. From 1829 to 1830, the north portico (see fig. 6) was built, an addition that served as a *porte-cochère* and lightened the stern façade. The restoration of 1902,

6. Washington, the White House, by James Hoban, 1792–1803; view of the north elevation with the north portico addition of 1829–30

carried out according to designs prepared by Charles McKim, improved the interior layout of the rooms but left the exterior undisturbed. The building's role as a national monument was underscored during the reconstruction of the interior (1949–52) with a free-standing steel frame, undertaken during the presidency of Harry S. Truman. The Truman-era rebuilding took pains to avoid disturbing the exterior. Thus, while none of the public rooms of the house dates from the building's early years, they are finished in Federal and classical style and adorned with fine works of statuary, porcelain, paintings and period furniture.

BIBLIOGRAPHY
The White House: An Historic Guide, White House Historical Association (Washington, DC, 1962, rev. 1982)
W. Ryan and D. Guinness: *The White House: An Architectural History* (New York, 1980)
W. Seale: *The President's House*, 2 vols (Washington, DC, 1986)

ANTOINETTE J. LEE

Washington Color Painters. Group of American painters based in Washington, DC, who from the mid-1950s responded to Abstract Expressionism by producing non-gestural, totally abstract canvases that stressed the optical effects created by the interrelationships of various colours. Named retrospectively in a survey exhibition held in 1965, they worked in a number of different styles including those loosely referred to as POST-PAINTERLY ABSTRACTION, HARD-EDGE PAINTING and COLOUR FIELD PAINTING, but all used acrylic paints. One of the most influential of the painters, Morris Louis, moved in 1952 from his native Baltimore to Washington, DC, where he met several like-minded artists at the Washington Workshop for the Arts, founded by local painter Leon Berkowitz (1915–87). Following the example of Helen Frankenthaler, Louis began in the early 1950s to pour extremely thin acrylic paints directly on to unprimed canvases to produce 'stains' of overlapping, translucent colours. The work of most of his colleagues, however, and particularly that of Kenneth Noland, was characterized by hard-edged, geometric abstract forms and especially by repeating patterns, such as concentric circles and chevrons, from which Noland

produced series of works (for illustration *see* NOLAND, KENNETH). The third principal group member was Gene Davis (1920–85), a native of Washington, who began painting in 1958 and quickly developed his signature approach of narrow, vertical stripes of colour that covered the entire canvas surface from edge to edge. The other painters who participated in the exhibition of 1965 and continued to be associated with the group were Thomas Downing (*b* 1928), Howard Mehring (*b* 1931) and Paul Reed (*b* 1919).

BIBLIOGRAPHY
E. Stevens: 'The Washington Color Painters', *Arts* [New York], xl (Nov 1965), pp. 29–33
The Washington Color Painters (exh. cat., essay G. Nordland; Washington, DC, Gal. Mod. A., 1965)

NANCY G. HELLER

Wash manner [Fr. *manière de lavis*]. Term applied to a broad range of printmaking processes that attempt to imitate the effect of ink-and-wash or watercolour drawings. The printmaking plate (or plates) may be delicately worked in either AQUATINT, GOUACHE MANNER or *lavis* (and sometimes in combination) so that it has a finely textured surface that catches just enough ink to print in transparent layers of colour. Wash manner prints were produced mainly by French engravers working in the last quarter of the 18th century (e.g. JANINET, JEAN-FRAN-ÇOIS). The tools used directly on to the plate, or through an etching ground, are generally the roulettes and mattoirs developed for crayon manner (*see* ENGRAVING, fig. 1) and modifications of these (e.g. mushrooms). It is often difficult to tell precisely whether a chemical or mechanical process has been employed, though aquatint, when viewed with a magnifying glass, tends to have a more granular patterning.

BIBLIOGRAPHY
Regency to Empire: French Printmaking, 1715–1814 (exh. cat. by V. I. Carlson and J. W. Ittmann, Baltimore, MD, Mus. A.; Minneapolis, MN, Inst. A.; 1984)
A. Griffiths: 'Notes on Early Aquatint in England and France', *Prt Q.*, iv (1987), pp. 255–70

S. J. TURNER

Wąsowski, Bartłomiej Nataniel (*b* 24 Aug 1617; *d* Poznań, 4 Oct 1687). Polish Jesuit priest, teacher, architect and writer. He went on a grand tour of Italy and western Europe (1650–56) as tutor to the young Grudziński noblemen, during which he kept a diary (*Europea peregrinatio*) that includes 40 pages containing 170 annotated drawings of such subjects as buildings, sculptures, decorations and gardens that he visited for their novelty. His own work as a designer came to the fore between 1671 and 1675 when, as College Rector in Jarosław, he designed many decorations, both permanent and temporary, for church and school services and festivals. Wąsowski's most prolific period of artistic activity occurred during his rectorship (1675–8 and 1683–7) of the Jesuit college in Poznań. In connection with his mathematics and architecture course, he published *Callitectonicorum seu de pulchro architecturae* (1678), a lengthy, illustrated treatise for students and other intellectuals and lovers of architecture. He particularly emphasized aesthetic problems, examined within the context of the teachings of Vitruvius, while almost completely ignoring technical problems. The main body of the treatise is an eclectic discourse on the architectural orders and it is not until the final section that it touches upon different types of buildings, showing Wąsowski to be an admirer of Roman Baroque.

From 1677 Wąsowski designed, organized the construction and executed the stuccowork of the Jesuit church in Poznań, begun in 1651 by Tomasso Poncino, whose design he altered. By 1687 he had managed to finish the new nave, the walls of which are articulated by a colossal order of detached composite columns in red scagliola, their deeply offset segments of entablature supporting figures of saints. The columns flank a nave arcade, with windowed galleries above, which gives on to side aisles. The remainder was completed according to his design between 1696 and 1705 by Giovanni Catenazzi (*fl* 1694–1724) together with the stuccoist Adalberto Bianco (*fl* 1699–1701), and between 1727 and 1732 by Pompeo Ferrari. It was the finest church of the High Baroque in Poland and justly established Wąsowski as a member of the group of distinguished clergymen-architects of the Baroque.

UNPUBLISHED SOURCES
Kraków, Czartoryski Col. MS XVII. 3031 [*Europea peregrinatio quam perilliarum ac MMDD: Nicolai a Gruda Grudziński tunc Ustiensis, postea Golubiensis, Gryboviensis et Guzaviensis Capitanei et Sigismundi a Gruda Grudziński tunc Bolemviensis Capitanei germanorum fratrum peregrinationis comes. P. Bartholomaeus Nathanael Wąsowski S Jesu omnium opere hoc contectorum spectator Calamo manuque propria descripsit et reliquit Collegio Posnaniensis S.J. Anno a Peregrino in terris Verbo Dei 1650 ad 1656*]

WRITINGS
Callitectonicorum seu de pulchro architecturae sacrae et civilis: Compendio collectorum liber unicus in gratiam et usum matheseos auditorum in Collegio Posnaniensis Societatis Iesu de superiorum facultate Posnaniae typis eiusdem Collegii anno 1678 (Poznań, 1678); ed. and intro. J. Baranowski (Wrocław, 1975)

BIBLIOGRAPHY
J. Baranowski: *Bartłomiej Nataniel Wąsowski: Teoretyk i architekt XVII w* [Bartłomiej Nataniel Wąsowski: theorist and architect of the 17th century] (Wrocław, 1975)

ADAM MIŁOBĘDZKI

Wassenhove, Joos van (*fl c.* 1460–80). South Netherlandish painter, active also in Italy. First documented in 1460, when he matriculated in the Antwerp painters' guild, he subsequently moved to Ghent, entering the painters' guild on 6 October 1464. In 1467 he painted 40 escutcheons with the papal arms for the cathedral of St Bavo, Ghent, his only documented commission in the Netherlands. He sponsored the entry of Hugo van der Goes to the Ghent guild on 5 May 1467 and of Sanders Bening on 19 January 1469, the last date on which Joos is recorded at Ghent. He is stated, in a document of 1475, to have departed for Rome some time previously, with an advance of money from Hugo van der Goes. It is not known if Joos reached Rome, but it is generally accepted that he worked at Urbino, where early sources mention a Netherlandish painter, Giusto da Guanto (Justus of Ghent), who was responsible for the altarpiece of the *Communion of the Apostles* (Urbino, Pal. Ducale) of 1473–4. The influence of van der Goes in this work reinforces the identification of Joos van Wassenhove with Justus of Ghent.

For further discussion and bibliography *see* JUSTUS OF GHENT.

PAULA NUTTALL

Wastell, John (*fl* 1485; *d* Bury St Edmunds, *c.* 1518). English architect. He is first mentioned in 1485 at King's College, Cambridge, with Simon Clerk and the churchwardens of Saffron Walden, Essex. By 1490 he was living in Bury St Edmunds, where he took an active part in local affairs. He worked at King's Hall (now part of Trinity College), Cambridge, from 1491 to 1492 and was called Master in 1496–7. The lower section of the Great Gate dates from this period. Between *c.* 1490 and 1508 Wastell designed the central tower (Bell Harry) of Canterbury Cathedral for Archbishop John Morton, and from 1496 he was also master mason of the Cathedral. Wastell's connection with King's College Chapel probably began in 1506, when Henry VII visited the College and made a gift to 'one John Wastell, a scoler', the architect's son. Wastell was entertained often at King's throughout the 1490s, and in 1508 he became master mason for the last campaign on the chapel. He is featured in all the agreements and accounts and was clearly in sole command. In July 1515 Wastell signed the final account for the work. On 31 August 1516 Wastell agreed to make the tomb of Thomas Howard, 2nd Duke of Norfolk, in Thetford Priory (destr.), the sole reference to a monumental practice.

The tower at Canterbury Cathedral and the completion of King's College Chapel represent Wastell's most important works. Bell Harry tower was built in two campaigns; the lower lantern was intended to stand alone, and the upper belfry was added in June 1494. His compromise solution is masterful: a 70-metre profile, with sheer lines, polygonal angle turrets and a clear, two-stage elevation divided by blind tracery. The upper stage is built in brick with stone facing, providing relief for the earlier crossing piers, which were strengthened with fretted strainer arches. Wastell's design for the pinnacles was the subject of a famous correspondence between Archbishop and Prior. The interior fan vault is a forerunner of the high vault of King's College Chapel.

The work at King's College Chapel involved building the remaining elevational sections of the antechapel, providing a new design for the high vault and completing the side chapel vaults. Outside, Wastell designed the corner towers, again a compromise with the existing structure. They were raised in 1513. He also designed the porches, pinnacles and parapets.

All Wastell's known works show a clear sense of design and restrained use of ornament. In this he stands apart from his contemporaries, especially the masons of the royal workshop. In general, he avoided the ogee curve and all tendencies towards the Flamboyant, employing instead an almost puritanical severity of plain ashlar and simple openings. Fan vaults were clearly Wastell's speciality, but they too were dominated by his sense of geometric line, at the expense of decoration and fluidity.

BIBLIOGRAPHY
Harvey
H. M. Colvin: *The History of the King's Works*, iii (London, 1975)
F. Woodman: *John Wastell of Bury, Master Mason* (diss., U. London, 1978)
——: *The Architectural History of Canterbury Cathedral* (London, 1981)
——: *The Architectural History of King's College Chapel, Cambridge* (London, 1986)

FRANCIS WOODMAN

Watanabe, Hitoshi [Jin] (*b* Kyoto, Feb 1887; *d* Tokyo, 5 Sept 1973). Japanese architect. He graduated from Tokyo Imperial University in 1912 and established his own office in 1920. He was very successful as a commercial architect, but his name is generally associated with only one building, Tokyo Imperial (now National) Museum (completed in 1937). This commission was won in an open competition held in 1931, often compared to that held for the Palace of the Soviets in Moscow at almost the same time. Both took place in difficult political conditions and both resulted in the success of conservative and authoritarian projects. In striking contrast to modernist entries, such as that by Kunio Maekawa, Watanabe's design for the museum is recognized as the most representative example of a new style later known as the Imperial Crown [Roof] (*teikan yōshiki*), a mixture of elements from traditional Japanese architecture, especially heavy, tiled, curved roof forms, and bulky, monotonous, citadel-like buildings that are characteristic of totalitarian regimes throughout the world. The style of Watanabe's Imperial Museum was repeated in a number of public buildings in the 1930s, such as the Nagoya City Hall (1933) by the Nagoya City Architect's Department, reflecting the nationalism and conservatism evident in Japanese architecture at the time. Another significant work by Watanabe is the Ginza-Hattori (Seiko) Building (1932), Tokyo, which was not in the Imperial Crown style.

BIBLIOGRAPHY
'Tokyo Imperial Museum', *Kokusai Kenchiku* (June 1931)
'Tokyo Imperial Museum', *Shinkenchiku* (Jan 1938)

HAJIME YATSUKA

Watanabe Kazan [Watanabe Sadayasu; Kazan; Gūkaidō] (*b* Edo [now Tokyo], 1793; *d* Tawara [now in Aichi Prefect.], 1841). Japanese painter. He was the son of an impoverished retainer of the Miyake family, holders of the small Tawara fief. He began to study painting in his teens, having been advised that he could finance his Confucian studies through art. Kazan's first teacher was a little-known painter, Shirakawa Shizan (?1765–?1857). When Shizan dismissed him for non-payment of tuition fees, Kazan took up his studies with Kaneko Kinryō (*d* 1817), a pupil of TANI BUNCHŌ who produced bird-and-flower and animal paintings. Perhaps with an introduction from Kinryō, Kazan himself began to study under Bunchō in 1809. His talent was immediately recognized, and within a few years Kazan had pupils of his own and was adding greatly to his family's meagre stipend with profits from painting sales. In 1819 he hosted his first *shogakai*, a creative gathering of poets, calligraphers and painters.

Kazan also worked hard at acquiring an education in the Confucian classics, first under Takami Senseki (1785–1858) and later under Satō Issai (1772–1859) and Matsuzaki Kōdō (1771–1844), earning promotion to the highest levels of service in the Tawara clan. By the early 1830s he had also become interested in Western knowledge (*rangaku* or 'Dutch studies', so called because the only European trading missions then allowed in Japan came from the Netherlands). Working with the Shōshikai, a study group of *rangaku* scholars formed in the 1830s, Kazan became aware of Japan's comparative backwardness. In 1839 this group was arrested by the shogunal

Watanabe Kazan: *Ichikawa Beian*, hanging scroll, ink and colours on silk, 1.30×0.59 m, 1837 (Tokyo, Agency for Cultural Affairs)

police and falsely accused of attempting to establish an international trading colony on a formerly uninhabited island off the coast, a charge that was soon dropped. However, among Kazan's personal effects the investigating officers found two manuscripts critical of the Tokugawa shogunate's isolationist policies. He spent more than seven months in prison before being exiled to house arrest in the Tawara fief. He nearly died during the move in the snows of early 1840, and the expenses of his trial, confinement and the support of his family left him almost bankrupt. His friends and former pupils in Edo arranged a series of painting sales and forwarded the profits to Kazan, until the scheme was discovered by Tawara clan officials. In 1841, rather than shame his family and friends with the scandal, Kazan committed ritual suicide. He was officially pardoned in 1871 and in 1891 posthumously granted the Imperial Award by the Meiji government.

Much of Kazan's fame as an artist rests on a series of strikingly naturalistic portraits. Their development can be traced through many sketches and studies he made from life. His finest portraits were meticulous paintings of the literati of Edo, which were not only accurate physical likenesses but conveyed the sitters' personalities as well. Among his subjects were his own father, Confucian teachers and the calligrapher *Ichikawa Beian* (1837; Tokyo, Agy Cult. Affairs, see fig.). A long series of sketches and preparatory drawings, many still extant, preceded several differing versions of the *Portrait of Satō Issai* (e.g. Washington, DC, Freer, and Tokyo, N. Mus.). Kazan's interest in realism is also indicated by his use of such devices as the camera obscura, for example to produce a life-size image of *Ozora Buzaemon*, a giant 2.14 m tall who visited Edo in 1827 (Cleveland, OH, Mus. A.).

Kazan was an accomplished painter of landscapes in the literati style (Jap. *Nanga* or *Bunjinga*; see JAPAN, §VI, 4(vi)(d)). He is equally respected for gently lyrical studies of birds, flowers and insects. Among the finest examples is the delicate album leaf of a *Spider and Sparrow* (Tokyo, Idemitsu Mus. A.), which bears the date 1837 but which many scholars believe was actually executed during Kazan's final year of exile in Tawara, the earlier date having been inscribed as a subterfuge. Its style follows that of the Chinese Qing-period (1644–1911) master Yun Shouping, combining calligraphic brushwork to outline the bamboo leaves with areas of colour lacking an outline, in the 'boneless' (*mokkotsu*) manner, for the bird, spider and ivy leaves. His style also shows the influence of the powerful brushstroke of ICHIKAWA BEIAN. Although Kazan produced woodblock-printed illustrations for numerous books, all in collaboration with other artists, he was solely responsible for only one volume of illustrations. The *Issō hyakutai* ('A hundred forms in one sweep'), brushed in 1821, consisted entirely of figure studies (published posthumously 1879; London, BM).

BIBLIOGRAPHY
T. Suganuma: *Kazan* (Tokyo, 1962)
S. Mori: 'Watanabe Kazan', *Mori Senzō chosakushū* [Collection of writings of Mori Senzō], vi (Tokyo, 1971), pp. 5–192
M. Sugiura and others: *Watanabe Kazan* (1975), xii of *Bunjinga suihen* [Selections of literati painting], ed. J. Ishikawa and others (Tokyo, 1974–9)
B. Abiko: *Watanabe Kazan: The Man and his Times* (diss., Ann Arbor, U. MI, 1982)
Reflections of Reality in Japanese Art (exh. cat. by S. F. Lee, M. Cunningham and J. T. Ulak, Cleveland, OH, Mus. A., 1983)
Bushi to bunjin no aida: Watanabe Kazan ten [Between samurai and literati: an exhibition of Watanabe Kazan] (exh. cat., Tochigi, Prefect. Mus. F.A., 1984)

FRANK L. CHANCE

Watanabe Shikō [Shōken; Soshin] (*b* Kyoto, 1683; *d* 1755). Japanese painter. He was apparently a masterless samurai (*rōnin*) who entered the service of the aristocratic Konoe family in Kyoto in 1709. Some of his early paintings reflect his training in the academic style of the KANŌ SCHOOL, as seen in two sets of sliding doors (*fusuma*), one set depicting pine trees, the other flowers and grasses, in Konbuin in Nara. He is best known as one of the leading exponents of the decorative *Rinpa* style practised by Ogata Kōrin (see OGATA, (1)). Later works only show Kanō influence in landscape. Although some of Shikō's works clearly derive from earlier Kōrin compositions, he was never a slavish imitator. His *Kakitsubata* ('Irises'; pair of six-panel folding screens; ink and colours over gold leaf on paper; Cleveland, OH, Mus. A.) is modelled after Kōrin's treatment of the same theme (Tokyo, Nezu A. Mus.; for illustration see OGATA, (1)). Unlike Kōrin, who depicted the irises in their entirety, clustering many of them along the bottoms of the screens, Shikō dispersed them more loosely across the surface, with their tops emerging from a low-lying golden mist.

Shikō displays greater originality in other works, such as *Yoshinoyama* ('Yoshino mountains'; pair of six-panel folding screens; ink and colours over gold leaf on paper; Japan, priv. col.), in which cherry trees blossom against a background of gold and rounded green hills spattered with golden mists. Here Shikō is indebted to the anonymous Muromachi-period (1333–1568) *Nichigetsusansuibyōbu* ('Landscapes of the sun and the moon'; pair of six-panel folding screens; ink, colours, silver and gold on paper; Osaka, Kongōji), but his choice of a limited palette of colours and the repetition of simple motifs create a bold composition and an outstanding example of the *Rinpa* style (see JAPAN, §VI, 4(v)). Shikō is also important for his influence on the development of Maruyama Ōkyo, founder of the Maruyama school of naturalistic painting (see JAPAN, §VI, 4(viii)), who admired Shikō's closely observed *chōjū shashin* ('sketches of birds and animals').

BIBLIOGRAPHY
Y. Yamane: *Rinpa kaiga zenshū* [Complete collection of Rinpa paintings], 5 vols (Tokyo, 1977–80)
Exquisite Visions: Rinpa Paintings from Japan (exh. cat., ed. H. Link and S. Toru; Honolulu, HI, Acad. A., 1980)

JOAN H. O'MARA

Watch. *See under* CLOCKS AND WATCHES.

Watelet, Claude-Henri (*b* Paris, 28 Aug 1718; *d* Paris, 12 Jan 1786). French government official, writer, collector and amateur painter and engraver. He was the son of Nicolas-Robert Watelet, Receveur-général des Finances in Orléans, and in 1740 inherited his father's lucrative post, as well as the family fortune. In his youth he travelled in Germany and to Vienna, Naples and Rome; in the latter city he lodged with the Painter to the King, Jean-Baptiste Pierre. By the late 1750s Watelet's country house near Paris, Le Moulin-Joli, had become a meeting-place for intellectual society, being frequented, among others, by the Comte de Caylus, the Marquis d'Argenson, the poet Jean-François Marmontel (1723–99), the Abbé Jacques Delille (1738–1813) and the Marquise de Pompadour. With their encouragement Watelet published in 1760 *L'Art de peindre*, a long didactic poem on the principles and techniques of painting, which won him election in 1760 to the Académie Française.

In 1763 Watelet, accompanied by his mistress, Mme Marguerite Le Comte, and by his former teacher, the Abbé Copette, made a journey to Italy, where they were official guests of the King of Sardinia, the French Embassy and the Académie de France in Rome. The trip was commemorated by the publication in 1765 of *Nella venuta in Roma di Madama Le Comte, e dei' Signori Watelet e Copette*, a volume of engravings of Italian scenes by various members of the Rome Académie. The facing page of each scene bore a sonnet by the Academician Louis de Subleyras. In 1774 Watelet published his *Essai sur les jardins*, in which his formulation of his ideas on gardens reflected his own garden at Le Moulin-Joli; this book was largely responsible for the popularization in France of the informal English garden. The *Recueil de quelques ouvrages de M. Watelet* (1784) was based on various articles on fine art that he had contributed to Denis Diderot's *Encyclopédie*, while his two-volume *Dictionnaire des beaux-arts* (1788–91), completed by Pierre-Charles Lévesque and republished posthumously in 1792, was intended as a supplement to the *Encyclopédie*.

The extent of Watelet's activities as collector can be gauged from the catalogues of the sales in Paris of his collection in 1780 and posthumously in 1786. Contemporary, French art predominated: among the best of the works were paintings by Carle Vanloo, Joseph Vernet, Hubert Robert and Charles-Joseph Natoire. The collection also included a *Holy Family* by Nicolas Poussin, as well as pastels by Rosalba Carriera and numerous finished and coloured drawings of Roman monuments by Robert. In addition there were enamels, miniatures, figures and vases of marble, and scientific and musical instruments. Among the most important works was the large collection of engravings and engraved plates by Rembrandt, including examples of almost all of his work. Watelet also owned a number of rare proofs by other Old Masters, as well as many contemporary prints of high quality. Watelet was himself an amateur draughtsman, painter and, especially, engraver, producing more than 150 engravings, mostly in the style of Rembrandt.

WRITINGS
L'Art de peindre: Poëme avec des réflexions sur les différentes parties de la peinture (Paris, 1760; Amsterdam, 1761)
Essai sur les jardins (Paris, 1774)
Dictionnaire des beaux-arts, 2 vols (Paris, 1788–91; completed by P.-C. Lévesque and reprinted as *Dictionnaire des arts de peinture, sculpture et gravure*, 5 vols (Paris, 1792/*R* Geneva, 1972)

BIBLIOGRAPHY
L. Subleyras: *Nella venuta in Roma di Madama Le Comte, e dei' Signori Watelet e Copette: Componimenti poetici di Luigi Subleyras . . . colle figure in rame di Stefano della Vallee Poussin . . .* (Paris, 1764/*R* Stuttgart, 1965)
M. Henriet: 'Un Amateur d'art au XVIIIe siècle: L'Académicien Watelet', *Gaz. B.-A.*, n. s. 4, vi (1922), pp. 173–94
L. Wittmer: 'Au temps des bergerades: Gessner et Watelet', *Rev. Litt. Comp.*, ii (1922), pp. 537–77
P. Hofer: *A Visit to Rome in 1764*, Fogg Museum Picture Book 5 (Cambridge, MA, 1956)
J. de Cayeux: 'Watelet et Rembrandt', *Bull. Soc. Hist. A. Fr.* (1965), pp. 131–61 [incl. cat. of Watelet's engravings]

Watercolour [Fr. *aquarelle*; Ger. *aquarellfarbe*; It. *acquerello*; Sp. *acuarela*]. Pigment dissolved in water and bound by a colloid agent so that it adheres to the working surface when applied with the brush. The same name is used for a work of art in that medium. Watercolour may be transparent or opaque and is usually applied to paper, but sometimes also to such materials as silk or vellum. The term arises because, in varying degrees, water is always used in the largest proportion and, in the purest application of the medium, twice—both to mix pigments and to dilute the colours. This article concentrates on the use of watercolour predominantly in Europe and the United Kingdom; for further discussion *see* INDIAN SUBCONTINENT, §V, 4(ix) and ISLAMIC ART, §I, 8.

1. Materials and techniques. 2. History.

1. MATERIALS AND TECHNIQUES. The colloid matter is usually combined with the pigment, which may be made up in dry cakes or moist in tubes. More rarely, it is dissolved in water, and the brush is dipped in the solution before taking up the colour. Varieties of gum are the most common colloids, the usual being gum arabic, derived from the acacia. Pastes of flour or rice, egg yolk or white, animal size or the casein of cheese have also been used. The binding medium may also include a wetting agent such as ox-gall or a thickener such as gum tragacanth, starch or dextrin, and, nowadays, a fungicide and bacteriacide. Further agents may be added while painting; glycerin to retard the drying of the pigment, alcohol to accelerate it.

The first proper list of watercolour pigments was given in Edward Norgate's *Miniatura or the Art of Limning* (*c.* 1630), written for Sir Théodore Turquet de Mayerne and later widely circulated. Norgate listed the varieties of white, yellow, red, green, blue, brown and black—24 in all—that could be bought in apothecaries' shops for artists to grind themselves. These pigments were derived from natural materials and were to be combined with gum arabic and 'sugar candy' to ensure that they dried 'smooth and even'. Subsequent writers have refined Norgate's recipes and enlarged his range of pigments without altering the basic principles, and the process remains essentially the same today. The establishment of artists' colourmen in the large European cities (*see* COLOURMAN) and the rapid expansion of pigment choice during the 18th century did little to change working practices. Artists long preferred to grind their own colours and even now often choose to work with a basic set of about 15 pigments rather than use all the hundreds available.

The production of colours in small hard cakes, begun in England by the REEVES firm *c.* 1780, was, however, a crucial development. Portable watercolour boxes, available from the early 18th century, were readily adapted to these and developed into the boxes with pans or cakes of colour used from the 19th century onwards (*see* PAINTBOX). Tube colours, containing additional glycerine as a plasticizer, are currently preferred by most professionals. Modern pigments are generally synthetic and, being very fine-ground, produce smooth and regular washes rather than the granular effects so vigorously exploited by earlier artists; however, they are also exceptionally pure and lend themselves to a wide range of colour mixes. Colours are mixed on watercolour palettes or on china plates or saucers.

So that washes flow steadily over the paper without running out of control of the brush, the studio watercolourist generally works on an easel or drawing board inclined at an angle of 5° to 10°. The paper, first moistened and stretched, is mounted over a frame or board and held tight and smooth. If working outdoors on a large scale, the artist may use a folding easel. Brushes must be strong but pliant and should not abrade the damp paper. They should readily twist to a fine point when required (traditionally this was done in the mouth). Early Chinese painters turned to deer, fox, rabbit and even to rats' whiskers or kingfishers' beaks for appropriately fine hairs. More recently, expensive brushes have been made from red sable, more economical ones from camel-hair. Artists in the 18th and 19th centuries used broader brushes than those now preferred. Early brushes were set into quill handles; from the mid-19th century onwards these were replaced by wooden handles with nickel or aluminium fixings (*see* BRUSH).

In its pure form a watercolour is made with pigment and colloid, with water as the only vehicle, so that it is transparent. The colour sinks into the paper without completely hiding its tone. Watercolourists have always exploited their papers, sometimes choosing textured or granulous papers to retain pockets of colour, or toned papers to modify the colour values, sometimes leaving patches of paper bare to act as highlights. Pure watercolour is therefore applied over white or pale buff paper. Artists continue to prefer fine, handmade rag papers rather than machine–made varieties.

Watercolour may be applied in a broad wash, laid down with a full and well-soaked brush, or in separate brush-strokes or stipples with relatively little water. The swift application of a flat or tonally gradated wash is a fundamental skill. Additional washes may be laid over the initial one, sometimes while it is still wet. When using transparent washes, pale ones are applied first and the darker ones laid over them; each preceding wash, and the paper beneath, will contribute to the final effect. A wash may be smooth or broken. The latter effect is achieved by dragging a lightly damped brush, charged with dry or almost dry colour, on its side across the paper so that patches of pigment remain trapped in the surface recesses. To develop or alter effects, damp colour may be lifted, 'stopped' or blended by a variety of methods. Rags, blotting paper, india-rubber, bread pellets, a brush handle, penknife or finger nail have served widely to remove colour and to expose the paper. Since the medium is resoluble when dry, more radical transformations may be achieved by wiping over the entire watercolour or even holding it under a tap; other washes may then be floated over it or dabs of stronger colours run in.

Watercolour may be made opaque by the addition of a further agent. In this form it is called GOUACHE or, traditionally, bodycolour. The extra 'body' is usually Chinese white, an opaque white originally based on lead and later on oxide of zinc, which is added to all the colours. Barium sulphate or precipitated chalk may also be added to the pigments as opaque extenders. To obtain the greater opacity and flexibility required of gouache, both pigment and glycerine are used in larger proportions than for transparent watercolour. The medium is favoured by designers and illustrators, who need to achieve flat, even fields of colour, and also by miniature-painters, who appreciate its possibilities for a jewel-like texture. Although it will not leave the paper visible, gouache is often applied to toned papers. Whereas in pure watercolour, tonal gradations must be anticipated, and a dark one can only be reduced by thinning down or washing out with water,

with gouache a pale colour may be laid over a dark. Gouache can be used exclusively or combined as a heightening agent with transparent watercolour; the latter requires great skill and is rarely entirely satisfactory. Some artists prepared their paper with white gouache and then painted over it in transparent watercolour, thus producing great brilliance of tone, a result similar to that achieved by oil painters—for example the Pre-Raphaelites—when painting over a pale ground.

2. HISTORY. Painting with pigment and water goes back to antiquity and occurs throughout the world. The ancient Egyptians dipped brushes made from rush stems in water and rubbed them on cakes of ink and gum to decorate papyrus rolls. The Chinese were beginning to paint on paper by about the 9th century (although they were using other supports, e.g. silk, before this; *see* CHINA, §V). In the West, early manuscripts were illuminated with transparent washes adorning ink outlines or more elaborate applications of bodycolour or mixed media heightened with gold; the first manner led to 'stained' or 'tinted' drawing and ultimately to the modern watercolour, the second to gouache. Medieval manuscripts were also the ancestors of Turkish and Mughal miniatures, or those made in England by Nicholas Hilliard. Technically, inks are watercolours, so that the early calligraphers may be said to have practised the art, as can brush draughtsmen from East and West who have worked in monochrome or ink-based washes—the classical Chinese and Koreans or Japanese artists such as Toso Sesshū and his school, whose economy of line went far beyond anything achieved in Europe for at least a century; or, later, Rembrandt and Claude. A complete history of watercolour defined in purely technical terms would need to embrace these and many other elements, but, in practice, the term has usually been understood to apply to particular Western manifestations and mainly to the classical transparent watercolour as evolved in Europe—and especially in Britain—in the 18th century and afterwards.

(i) 16th century–mid-18th. (ii) Mid-18th century–19th. (iii) 20th century.

(i) 16th century–mid-18th. The beginnings of a coherent and autonomous tradition are generally traced to the 16th and 17th centuries in northern Europe. Albrecht Dürer's alpine studies made in 1490 and his later watercolours of animals or birds employed the medium with unprecedented richness and breadth; his landscapes (*see* DÜRER, (1), fig. 3) were unequalled in Europe. More typically, watercolour was being used as a tint for line drawings of places, people or natural history made by the growing number of itinerant draughtsmen, such as Anthonis van den Wyngaerde, who drew London, Italy, Gibraltar or the Netherlands in the 1550s and 1560s, John White, who recorded Virginia and Florida in 1585, or Jacques Le Moyne de Morgues, who drew in England and America.

Norgate's *Miniatura* discusses watercolour's use for portraiture, subject painting and 'history', as practised, for example, by Isaac Oliver and his son Peter, and landscape, recognizing the increasing recourse to the medium in the Low Countries and England. Dutch and Flemish artists of the 17th century used watercolour in their chalk, ink or bistre drawings, usually in a restrained and delicately

1. Rembrandt: *Winter Landscape*, brown wash over pen and brown ink, 66×158 mm, *c.* 1647–9 (Cambridge, MA, Fogg Art Museum)

atmospheric manner to tint outlines and imitate the colours of nature. Exceptions are the richer and denser effects achieved by Rubens and his school, especially Jordaens, who applied strong local colours over their initial washes, or the vivid monochrome wash drawings of Claude (*see* CLAUDE LORRAIN, fig. 2) or Rembrandt with their tonal abstraction or emphasis on chiaroscuro (see fig. 1). Perhaps most advanced in their handling of pure watercolour and liberation from outline were the landscapes of van Dyck (see colour pl. VII, fig. 1).

Van Dyck might stand at the head of the European tradition of landscape watercolour, Wenceslaus Hollar at that of the tinted topographical drawing. Hollar's drawings in pen, lightly washed with a limited range of descriptive colours, made in England, continental Europe (*see* HOLLAR, WENCESLAUS, fig. 1) or Morocco, correspond closely to techniques of printmaking, which he also practised. They set a pattern widely followed in England during the first half of the 18th century, though sometimes modified, as in certain works by Francis Place (for illustration *see* PLACE, FRANCIS), by a sensitive appreciation of effects of light and shade. Such artists as William Taverner and Jonathan Skelton perfected the 'stained' drawing, in which local colour is applied over shading in India ink and sometimes also worked in a range of fresh colours without monochrome under painting. By the second half of the century the method of the English topographical watercolour—often made for engraving—had become firmly established; foundations of mass and shade were laid in blue or grey washes over pencil indications, and when these were dry, local colour and appropriate heightenings in pen and ink were added to contribute a dense and intricately descriptive effect. This discipline, perfected by artists such as Edward Dayes, was the springboard for Turner and Girtin's development of their own highly individual and expressive styles.

(ii) Mid-18th century–19th. It was also in England, however, that artists had striven hardest to explore the possibilities of watercolour as a medium uniquely adapted to render light, atmosphere and the fleeting movement of nature. With greater appreciation of the qualities of the medium came also its maturity as an art in its own right. From the middle of the century Paul Sandby united a sensitive eye for pure landscape and a corresponding freedom and delicacy of technique, closest to Netherlandish prototypes, to the business of military and architectural topography (for illustration *see* SANDBY, (2)), thus earning Gainsborough's accolade of 'genius'. Alexander Cozens rendered the essence of ideal landscape or climatic effect in monochrome washes with the abstract grandeur and simplicity of East Asian artists, while his son John Robert Cozens broke away from topographical constraints to discover a lyrical style based on a limited range of tones applied directly, without underpainting (*see* COZENS, (2), fig. 1). Meanwhile Francis Towne produced no less remarkable effects through clear washes of jewel-like brilliance laid over taut and economical outlines in ink (for illustration *see* TOWNE, FRANCIS).

The bold exploration of watercolour's possibilities in 18th-century England, the sheer variety of approach, was unmatched elsewhere, giving rise to the understandable, if misleading, image of watercolour as a 'British' art form. Watercolour was widely used in continental Europe, and some artists, for instance the Frenchman Charles-Joseph Natoire in his later years, even came to prefer it to oils. Generally, however, it remained an essentially decorative medium, one that was subordinate to ink or chalk. Touches of local colour rather than broad washes remained the continental norm, and while Delacroix and Gericault produced some vivid studies, many artists in France or Germany continued well into the 19th century to practise habits that seem archaic compared to those of their British counterparts.

Gouache, on the other hand—though regarded by purists as the vulgar cousin of watercolour—reached its own perfection in continental Europe during the 18th century. Marco Ricci and later Francesco Zuccarelli mastered a type of classical landscape with ruins (*see* CAPRICCIO) that became fashionable throughout Europe and found ready followers in London. French draughtsmen were also fond of gouache, and in London it was taken up by Sandby in some large landscapes with heroic trees that were sent to exhibitions to compete with oil paintings. Painting in gouache reached its nadir in the following century in the thousands of quick and shoddy views of continental scenery—above all of the Bay of Naples—peddled to tourists, but not before it had enjoyed a splendid apotheosis (though often combined with oil or varnish) in the huge views of antiquities or beauty spots by Louis Ducros, which impressed the young Turner.

By the end of the 18th century, and chiefly in England, watercolours had broken out of their long-standing place in the cabinet or portfolio and assumed space on the exhibition wall. Grudgingly admitted to the Royal Academy in London, they came into their own with the foundation in 1804 of the Society of Painters in Watercolours (see WATERCOLOUR SOCIETIES AND SKETCHING CLUBS). Their shows encouraged the development of the large and highly finished 'exhibition watercolours', exploiting new pigments and techniques to the full, that dominated the Victorian exhibitions. At the same time, however, British watercolourists could benefit from the broad, modulated effects achieved during a brief life by Girtin

(see GIRTIN, THOMAS, fig. 2), from the vast range of technical refinements and quirks developed by Turner during his many years of devotion to the medium (see colour pl. VIII, fig. 1 and TURNER, J. M. W., fig. 5), from the subtle colour harmonies of Peter De Wint, the lyrical economy of John Sell Cotman (see COTMAN, JOHN SELL, fig. 1) or the dynamic vigour of David Cox (for illustration see COX, DAVID). If Samuel Palmer, whose early work expressed his visionary imagination through unique combinations of watercolour, gouache and other media (see fig. 2), was later obliged to adapt to convention and to propagate consensual wisdom through his activities as a drawing master—inevitable for many artists as a means of financing their careers—it is also true that invention and individuality remained abundant in English watercolour throughout the century. Certainly these qualities were very apparent to foreign observers, for example at the Paris Exposition Universelle in 1878.

In continental Europe watercolour continued to be associated with popular topography, although the gradual erosion of academic principles and hierarchies in France encouraged artists to work in a variety of media regardless of subject-matter. Richard Parkes Bonington and Delacroix painted brilliant figure subjects in watercolour (see

2. Samuel Palmer: *Pear Tree in a Walled Garden*, watercolour and gouache over brush and grey wash, 222×283 mm, *c.* 1829 (New York, Pierpont Morgan Library)

colour pl. VII, fig. 2), while Henri-Joseph Harpignies, Johan Barthold Jongkind and Jules Jacquemart anticipated the Impressionists in developing a fluent, expressive brushwork to convey sensations and to record fugitive effects. The establishment of the Société d'Aquarellistes Français in 1879 acknowledged a growing middle-class market for works in a medium more affordable than oil, and while the Impressionists were to capitalize on this demand, watercolour was clearly highly relevant to their artistic objectives. For Cézanne, it was central to his investigation of the structure of landscape (*see* CÉZANNE, PAUL, fig. 6) and still-life, used not only for preparatory work but also, by the 1880s, for exhibition subjects, while Pissarro showed a particular commitment to watercolour and gouache and advised younger artists such as Paul Signac and his own son Lucien to specialize in them. Meanwhile, high prices were paid for highly finished watercolours by Puvis de Chavannes or Gustave Moreau (*see* MOREAU, GUSTAVE, fig. 2).

(iii) 20th century. Even if the century from 1750 to 1850 was perhaps the great age of the 'amateur' watercolourist, instructed by an army of drawing masters and manuals, the medium has retained its broad appeal in the 20th century and indeed has never been more popular. Unfortunately, the sheer abundance of stylistic examples from the past has tended to depress the imaginative zeal of many later practitioners, and a sense of *déja vu* is likely to be communicated by many mainstream exhibitions. While many of the fundamental concerns of modernism—with space, form or pattern, with the flatness of the pictorial plane, with the inner life of the medium or with spontaneity and immediacy of impression and effect—may be found anticipated in the watercolours of the Romantics, the medium is less often today the vehicle for searching advances in imagery or style.

Watercolour has nonetheless continued to find fresh interpreters in the 20th century. Moreau's studies had already suggested its abstract possibilities, while the sensual works of Rodin and Klimt opened up other avenues. Vestiges of its topographical function survived, for instance in Fauvism, and for such artists as Raoul Dufy the medium's immediacy and intensity were paramount. In Germany the painters associated with the Blaue Reiter used this saturation differently. While Kandinsky made large numbers of abstract watercolours in preparation for his oils, Klee was one of the few modernists whose work was dominated by the medium, using its strong colour and intimate scale to capture a quixotic personal vision (see colour pl. VIII, fig. 2).

For artists emerging after World War I, watercolour took on different possibilities. It served utopian ends in the sketches of many abstract artists (e.g. El Lissitzky, Johannes Itten and Theo van Doesberg), but had a different function in the satirical works of George Grosz, Jules Pascin and others. In England the tradition for topographical watercolour was renewed in the visionary landscapes of Paul Nash, John Piper, David Jones and others; while Henry Moore developed an original combination of wax, ink and watercolour in his wartime *Shelter* drawings. Having been forbidden to paint by the Nazis, Emil Nolde produced secret watercolours (preferred to

oil, which could be smelt) that have a strong emotional and chromatic dependence on his native landscape. By contrast, Wols, a late associate of Surrealism, produced minute gestural abstractions, the jewel-like intensity of which was comparable to works by Klee, whom he admired. Watercolour was taken up both by Pop artists R. B. Kitaj, David Hockney and others, and by those in the 1970s who looked back to the Abstract Expressionists, such as Brice Marden and Sean Scully. The subsequent return of neo-Expressionistic figuration also favoured the fluency of watercolour, and its use by Francesco Clemente unites it with still potent non-Western (especially Indian) traditions of watercolour painting.

For information on the conservation of watercolours *see* DRAWING, §VI.

BIBLIOGRAPHY
N. Hilliard: *The Arte of Limning* (MS.; *c.* 1600); ed. R. K. H. Thornton and T. G. S. Cain (Manchester, 1981)
T. H. Fielding: *On Painting in Oil and Watercolours for Landscape and Portraits* (London, 1839)
G. Bernard: *The Theory and Practice of Landscape Painting in Water-Colours* (London, 1858)
J. L. Roget: *A History of the Old Water-Colour Society, now the Royal Society of Painters in Water-Colours* (London, 1891)
I. A. Williams: *Early English Watercolours* (London, 1952/R Bath, 1970)
M. Hardie: *Watercolour Painting in Britain*, 3 vols (London, 1967–8)
R. D. Harley: *Artists' Pigments, 1600–1835* (London, 1970)
W. Koschatzky: *Watercolour History and Technique*, trans. M. Whittall (London, 1970)
G. Reynolds: *A Concise History of Watercolours* (London, 1971)
W. Haltmann: *Meisteraquarelle des 20. Jahrhunderts* (Cologne, 1973)
T. E. Stebbins: *American Master Drawings and Watercolours: A History of Works on Paper from Colonial Times to the Present* (London and New York, 1976)
Wash and Gouache: A Study of the Development of the Materials of Watercolors (exh. cat. by M. Cohn, Cambridge, MA, Fogg, 1977)
A. Wilton: *British Watercolours, 1750–1850* (London, 1980)
M. Clarke: *The Tempting Prospect: A Social History of English Watercolours* (London, 1981)
The Art of Watercolour (exh. cat. by J. Spalding, Manchester, C.A.G., 1987)
Nature into Art: English Landscape Watercolours from the British Museum (exh. cat. by L. Stainton, London, BM; Cleveland, OH, Mus. A.; Raleigh, NC, Mus. A.; 1991)
Original Eyes: Progressive Vision in English Watercolour, 1750–1850 (exh. cat. by D. B. Brown, Liverpool, Tate, 1991)
C. Newall: *Victorian Watercolours* (London, 1992)
The Great Age of British Watercolours, 1750–1850 (exh. cat. by A. Wilton and A. Lyles, London, RA; Washington, DC, N.G.A.; 1993)

DAVID BLAYNEY BROWN

Watercolour societies and sketching clubs. With the foundation of the Royal Academy in 1768, British oil painters obtained recognition as professionals; to protect their status, they tried to maintain a division between the high art of oil painting and mere tinted drawing or watercolour, the province of drawing-masters and topographers. Watercolours were inevitably 'skied' in the Academy exhibitions, and it was thus natural that watercolour painters should eventually seek to improve their standing by forming their own professional association. During the 18th century in Britain, a number of informal groupings of artists had arisen, such as the York Virtuosi, a prominent member of which was Francis Place, or the Society of St Peter Martyr, centered on the Oxfordshire patron and painter Oldfield Bowles (1739–1810), which linked cultivated amateur artists with like-minded professionals. A later example was the United Patna and Gaya Society in India, otherwise known as the Behar School of Athens, which was founded in 1824 by Sir Charles D'Oyly (1781–1845).

Thomas Monro's 'Academy' provided a rather different meeting-place for young artists: during the 1790s Monro invited future luminaries of the British school, such as Turner and Thomas Girtin, to his London house to copy drawings from his extensive collection, for the reward of a small sum and supper. The Monro 'Academy' and the similar scheme run by Monro's next-door neighbour John Henderson (1764–1834) were undoubtedly the stimulus for the most important of the 19th-century sketching clubs, which first met, under the title of the Brothers, in May 1799. Its members, both professionals and amateurs, met once a month, when all would work at the same subject for two hours. Girtin was the club's first focus, but Turner would not join because, it is said, all sketches became the property of the host for the evening. The other members included the club's probable originator, Louis Francia, and Robert Ker Porter; around 1802 they were joined by John Sell Cotman, and soon afterwards the club reformed around the brothers John James Chalon (1778–1854) and Alfred Chalon (1780–1860), with the addition of Augustus Wall Callcott. It continued in existence until 1851, attracting many of the ablest watercolourists.

A rather similar group, established in 1830 and known as the Artists' Society or the Clipstone Street Academy, and later as the Langham Sketching Society, from its meeting places, provided models 'for the study of historic, poetic and rustic figures'. Among its members in the 1840s were Frederick Goodall, Charles Keene, Paul Falconer Poole and William James Müller. However, the first professional exhibiting body was set up only on 30 November 1804, at a meeting in the Stratford Coffee-house in Oxford Street, attended by, among others, William Sawrey Gilpin, Robert Hills, Francis Nicholson, Nicholas Pocock, William Henry Pyne, Cornelius Varley and John Varley. They formed themselves into the Society of Painters in Water-Colours (although some felt that the word 'painters' was presumptuous), and five months later opened their first exhibition, having added to their number such artists as George Barret jr (1767–1842), Joshua Cristall, John Glover and William Havell. The first annual exhibitions were so fashionable and successful that a rival Associated Artists in Water-Colours was set up in 1808; David Cox was its president in 1810. However, the fashion waned; in 1812 the Associated Artists collapsed, and between 1813 and 1820 the Society of Painters in Water-Colours admitted oil paintings. By 1820 it was once more financially possible to exclude them, and in 1831 the New Society of Painters in Water-Colours was set up (as opposed to the 'Old' Water-Colour Society). Both had associate as well as full members, and it is usual at this period to distinguish members by the letters (A)OWS, or (A)NWS after their names. In 1863 the New Society renamed itself the Institute of Painters in Water-Colours. The OWS received its Royal charter in 1881, and the Institute followed in 1887; as the RWS and the RI they continue to attract the foremost practitioners of the art.

The Royal Scottish Water-Colour Society, known as the RSW, was set up in 1878 by Sir Francis Powell (1833–1914), William McTaggart and others in emulation of the London groups; for a short time it was limited to 25 members. In the late 19th century there were sketching clubs, or art societies that encouraged drawing, in a number of Scottish towns such as Dundee, Dunfermline, Kilmarnock, Kirkcaldy, Stirling, Aberdeen and Ayr.

The Water Colour Society of Ireland originated in a local drawing society founded in 1870 by six ladies in Lismore, Co. Waterford; there is also the Ulster Watercolour Society, founded in Belfast in 1977. The American Society of Watercolour Painters, founded in 1866, now the American Watercolor Society with its headquarters in New York, had an Irishman, William Craig (1829–75), among its founders. The Canadian Society of Painters in Watercolour was first organized in 1926 and incorporated ten years later; there are similar groups in Australia and New Zealand. Although guilds of painters existed in the Netherlands and Germany from the late Middle Ages, and official academies have flourished in a number of European countries, notably France and Italy, since the 18th century, the watercolour artists of the Continent have no significant tradition of banding themselves into associations. Spain has followed the British 19th-century path most closely: the Agrupación de Acuarelistas de Catalonia was founded in Barcelona in 1865, and there are similar associations in the Basque country, Andalucía and Valencia. The Associazione Italiana Acquerellisti was founded in Milan in 1974, and the Belgian Kempische Akwarellisten dates only from 1980. There is also the Haagse Aquarellisten in the Netherlands. In 1987 the Institut Européen de l'Aquarelle was set up in Brussels. It not only exhibits the work of artist members but promotes the medium in many other ways, developing contacts with artists in other disciplines and with interested amateurs and virtuosi. In this it has some resemblance to the early informal groups in England.

BIBLIOGRAPHY

J. L. Roget: *History of the 'Old' Water-colour Society, now the Royal Society of Painters in Water-Colours* (London, 1891/*R* Woodbridge, 1972)
I. A. Williams: *Early English Watercolours* (London, 1952/*R* Bath, 1970)
M. Hardie: *Watercolour Painting in Britain*, 3 vols (London, 1967–8)
J. Hamilton: *The Sketching Society* (London, 1971)
H. L. Mallalieu: *The Dictionary of British Watercolour Artists*, 3 vols (Woodbridge, 1976–90)
——: *Understanding Watercolours* (Woodbridge, 1985)

HUON MALLALIEU

Waterford. Irish city and centre of glass production. The earliest Waterford glass factory was established in Gurteens, near Waterford, during the 1720s, and production included lead-glass drinking vessels with pedestal stems, garden glasses, vials, bottles and other green glassware. The factory was closed about 1739.

In 1783 the Waterford Glass House was established by the merchants George Penrose and William Penrose, who employed John Hill and other glassmakers from Stourbridge, England. In 1799 the factory was taken over by three partners, James Ramsey (*d c.* 1810), Jonathan Gatchell (1752–1823) and Ambrose Barcroft, who in 1802 extended the works and installed new machinery. In 1823 George Gatchell became manager, and the works remained in the family until it closed. The factory produced cut, engraved and moulded glass of excellent quality, and *c.* 1832 steam power was installed in the factory, which allowed an increase in production.

The outstanding qualities of Waterford glass are its clarity and the precise cutting. The typical early Waterford decanter is barrel-shaped, has three or four neck rings and a wide, flat, pouring lip (*see* IRELAND, fig. 21). Stoppers of Waterford production are almost invariably mushroom-shaped with a rounded knop below the stopper neck. From the cut patterns on marked Waterford decanters it would seem that popular designs included the pillar and arch embellished with fine diamonds. The numerous drawings of Waterford designs (Dublin, N. Mus.) made between 1820 and 1830 by Samuel Miller, the foreman glasscutter, show that the fashionable heavy, thick-walled style was used for tableware, embellished with wide pillar flutes, printies (depressions), hollow prisms, strawberry diamonds, star-cut bases and fan-shaped rims. The decanters of this period have perpendicular sides with broad, flat or pillared flutes or are round-bodied with variations of the diamond frieze or vertical panels.

The Waterford Glass House constantly tried to produce the variety of ware required by its customers at home and abroad. In 1849 it advertised a range of wares that included decanters, claret jugs, liqueur bottles, pickle urns, salad, celery and sugar bowls, butter-coolers, jelly-glasses and wine-glasses, and such luxury items as chandeliers, lustres, lamps, hall bells and candelabra. The firm followed the international fashions of the time and displayed heavily cut and layered glass in the Great Exhibition of 1851 in London, but in the same year the factory was forced to close for financial reasons. In 1947–9 Waterford Glass Ltd was established for the production of cut glass. In 1986 the company was amalgamated with the ceramic factory of Wedgwood to become Waterford Wedgwood.

BIBLIOGRAPHY

M. S. D. Westropp: *Irish Glass: An Account of Glass-making in Ireland from the XVIth Century to the Present Day* (London, 1920, rev. Dublin, 1978)

P. Warren: *Irish Glass: The Age of Exuberance* (London, 1970, rev. 1981)

M. Dunlevy: *Penrose Glass* (Dublin, 1989)

MAIREAD DUNLEVY

Waterford, Louisa Anne, Marchioness of [née Stuart, Louisa Anne] (*b* Paris, 14 April 1818; *d* 1891). English painter. Largely untutored, she trained herself by copying portraits and prints and famous works of art in Rome during the winter of 1836. She also executed many studies from nature. Most of her output was in watercolour, and although she was one of the best-known amateur artists of her time, she never became an accomplished painter, due probably to a combination of the demands of her aristocratic background and the lack of importance accorded to women artists, as well as her own belief that art did not have a significant impact on the world in the pursuit of goodness. In 1842 she married the 3rd Marquis of Waterford, who was killed shortly thereafter. In the early 1850s she met, and was influenced by, Ruskin, and in 1859 she moved to Ford Castle in Northumberland, where she painted a series of frescoes, *Lives of Good Children of the Bible* (1862–83), for the village school (now Lady Waterford Hall; *in situ*). These were done in distemper on paper and were then mounted on the walls.

Other paintings of religious subjects include *Sleeping Disciples* and *Christ Raising the Dead* (both London, Tate). After her death, three large retrospective exhibitions of her work were held in 1891, 1892 (both Ford) and 1910 (Carlton House Terrace, London).

BIBLIOGRAPHY

C. Stuart: *Short Sketch of the Life of Louisa, Marchioness of Waterford* (London, 1892)

A. Hare: *Two Noble Lives* (London, 1893)

M. Joicey: *The Lady Waterford Hall and its Murals* (Ford, 1983)

P. G. Nunn: *Victorian Women Artists* (London, 1987)

Waterhouse, Alfred (*b* Aigburth, Liverpool, 19 July 1830; *d* Yattendon, Berks, 22 Sept 1905). English architect, furniture designer and painter. In financial terms he was probably the most successful architect of the 19th century, and his office, of a dozen or so full-time staff, was able to produce large quantities of high-quality drawings with speed and efficiency. His skill in planning was recognized at an early stage, but appreciation of his stylistic achievement has been slower. He was influenced by Ruskin and A. W. N. Pugin, as well as by the more practical approach of George Gilbert Scott, but he developed his own approach to the composition of forms and a preference for bold simple ornament to match the increasing scale of his buildings. He did not confine himself to a single style but was adept in Gothic and, later, free Renaissance styles, and he developed a preference for the neo-Romanesque. He distinguished between carved or moulded ornament on plain stone and decorative materials such as veined marble, which he generally left unornamented. His concern for hard-wearing surface materials led him to adopt terracotta as a facing material, in which he was both a pioneer and protagonist. His sensitive handling of materials approached the aims of the Arts and Crafts Movement, but he always accepted that building was an industrial process. His buildings are characterized by sound planning and bold and picturesque outline, with particular attention given to the skyline in urban buildings.

Waterhouse was born into the well-to-do commercial world of Liverpool, and his family's Quaker background soon brought him wider contacts. He served an apprenticeship with the Quaker partnership of Richard Lane (*fl* 1821–58) and P. B. Alley in Manchester. Then, after an extended continental tour, he opened his own office in Manchester in 1854. Much of his early work was for Quaker friends and relatives and included a group of picturesque houses in the Lake District that follow the tradition of J. C. Loudon. His first buildings of note were the warehouse for Binyon & Fryer (1856; destr.), Manchester, with Ruskinian Gothic upper parts; and Hinderton Hall (1856), Cheshire, a severe Gothic house with a sophisticated plan. Success in the Manchester Assize Courts competition (1859) brought national fame for a Ruskinian building drawing on French and Italian Gothic sources. During the 1860s he was much occupied with warehouses, schools and chapels and a variety of plain but substantial middle-sized houses; but perhaps the most important buildings that furthered his career were the banks and offices, notably Alexander's & Cunliffe's Bank (1864; destr.), London, which had a convincing mixture of Gothic and Renaissance motifs. He was also responsible for a small group of Anglican churches (the best is St John Brooklands, 1860s, Manchester) that demonstrate a sure handling of space and a highly personal use of Gothic motifs.

In 1865 Waterhouse moved his office to London where he built the New University Club (1865; destr.), a bold Gothic design on a cramped and irregular site. He also competed unsuccessfully in the Law Courts competition (1867), though his design was praised for its planning. In Manchester he won the competition for the town hall (1868; *see* MANCHESTER, fig. 1, and TOWN HALL, fig. 4), with a French Gothic building on an awkward triangular site. This design demonstrates his skill in planning and his ability to meet changing requirements and still improve the architectural quality of the building. He was also responsible for the design of its furniture and fittings. Furniture design was an important part of his oeuvre; he favoured turned legs and spindles, but these were always subservient to manufacturing constraints. Two other major works of this period were the Natural History Museum (1872; see fig.), London, and Eaton Hall (1870–83; destr. 1963), Cheshire. The museum is the first example of the use of terracotta for the complete internal and external facing of a building, and it is decorated with a series of sculptures illustrating the museum's contents, all to Waterhouse's design. The rebuilding of Eaton Hall (originally a late 17th-century house remodelled in Gothic style earlier in the 19th century by William Porden) was chiefly notable for its rich and varied decoration. The house was in the

French château style, but the stables are in the half-timbered Cheshire vernacular style.

In the 1870s Waterhouse's practice was extensive. He continued to design mansions, of which the most significant is Blackmoor House (1869), Hants, in a modified Gothic style; in Oxford he produced buildings for Balliol and a new debating hall for the Union, while in Cambridge he designed buildings for the Union Society and for Jesus, Trinity Hall, Gonville and Caius, Pembroke and Girton colleges, in a range of different styles. From 1877 he was employed by the Prudential Assurance Company to build the series of offices, mostly in red brick and terracotta, that are his most characteristic contribution to commercial architecture. Apart from their dramatic skylines they are also notable for their faience interior decoration. In the 1880s Waterhouse was in great demand as an architect for institutional buildings, designing schools, hospitals and orphanages in London and north-west England, as well as the university buildings in Leeds, Liverpool and Manchester. Churches such as St Elizabeth (1880), Reddish, or Lyndhurst Road Chapel (1883), Hampstead, London, and such other buildings in London as the National Liberal Club (1883) and University College Hospital (1896) demonstrate the continued fluency of his decorative vocabulary as well as originality in planning. He was, in addition, involved in restoration, notably at St Anne's church (1887), Manchester, Jesus College Hall (1871), Cambridge, and at Staple Inn (1887), London, where, although his aim was to reconstruct for contemporary use, he was nevertheless

Alfred Waterhouse: Natural History Museum, London, 1872

amply sensitive to the existing fabric. He was a founder-member of the Society for the Protection of Ancient Buildings as well as a life trustee of Sir John Soane's Museum, London.

Waterhouse was closely involved in the developing architectural profession and served as president of the RIBA from 1888 to 1891. His tact and fairness led to his appointment as assessor for most of the major competitions in the last decades of the 19th century. As a watercolour painter he had a deserved reputation for the exciting perspectives of his designs, but he also produced many attractive topographical works. He was elected ARA in 1878 and RA in 1885. Once established as a successful architect, he bought an estate at Yattendon, Berks, and designed his own house there (1878; destr.), where his wife developed local craft workshops known as the Yattendon Guild. At the time of his death he was still liked for his personal qualities, though the style of his work was generally reckoned to be out of date.

WRITINGS
'A Short Description of the Manchester Assize Courts', *Trans. RIBA*, xv (1864–5), pp. 165–74
Courts of Justice Competition: General Description of Design (London, 1867)
'Description of the Town Hall at Manchester', *Trans. RIBA*, xxvii (1876–7), pp. 117–31
'The President's Address to Students: Colour in Architecture', *J. Proc. RIBA*, n. s. 2, vii (1890–91), pp. 121–6
'Architects', *Unwritten Laws and Ideals of Active Careers*, ed. E. H. Pitcairn (London, 1899)

BIBLIOGRAPHY
M. Girouard: 'Blackmoor House Hampshire—II: The Property of the Earl of Selbourne', *Country Life*, clvi (5 Sept 1974), pp. 614–17
S. A. Smith: 'Alfred Waterhouse: Civic Grandeur', *Seven Victorian Architects*, ed. J. Fawcett and N. Pevsner (London, 1976), pp. 102–21
M. Girouard: *Alfred Waterhouse and the Natural History Museum* (New Haven, 1981)
J. H. G. Archer: 'A Civic Achievement: The Building of Manchester Town Hall', *Trans. Lancs & Ches Antiqua. Soc.*, lxxxi (1982), pp. 3–41
S. Maltby, S. MacDonald and C. J. K. Cunningham: *Alfred Waterhouse, 1830–1905* (London, 1983) [essays]
J. H. G. Archer: 'A Classic of its Age', *Art and Architecture in Victorian Manchester*, ed. J. H. G. Archer (Manchester, 1985), pp. 127–61
C. J. K. Cunningham and P. Waterhouse: *Alfred Waterhouse: Biography of a Practice* (Oxford, 1992)

COLIN CUNNINGHAM

Waterhouse, Sir Ellis (Kirkham) (*b* Epsom, 16 Feb 1905; *d* London, 7 Sept 1985). English art historian and curator. He was educated at Marlborough College, Wilts, and New College, Oxford. In 1927 he went for two years to Princeton University, NJ, where he was Commonwealth Fund Fellow at the Graduate School and did research on El Greco. On his return he worked at the National Gallery, London (1929–32), and then as librarian at the British School in Rome (1933–6). His first book, *Baroque Painting in Rome* (1937), made valuable contributions to research in this field. During World War II he served in Athens and as Monuments and Fine Arts Officer in the Netherlands and Germany, where his activities contributed to the exposure of the forger Hans van Meegeren. Waterhouse was appointed Reader in the History of Art at Manchester University (1947), Director of the National Gallery, Scotland (1949), and Director of the Barber Institute at the University of Birmingham (1952), where he remained until his retirement in 1970. His major contributions lay in the newly serious study of British art, his *Painting in Britain,*

1530–1790 (1953) immediately becoming a standard text. He wrote a book on Gainsborough, two on Reynolds and, at the end of his life, a dictionary of British 18th-century artists. Waterhouse was an extremely generous scholar, ready to share his knowledge and his vast collection of sales catalogues. He was knighted in 1975. His notebooks and papers are at the Paul Mellon Centre for Studies in British Art, London, the Barber Institute, Birmingham, and at the John Paul Getty Museum, Malibu, CA.

WRITINGS
Baroque Painting in Rome: The Seventeenth Century (London, 1937, rev. 1976)
Reynolds (London, 1941)
Painting in Britain, 1530–1790, Pelican Hist. A. (London, 1953, rev. 4/1978)
Gainsborough (London, 1960)
Italian Baroque Painting (London, 1962)
Reynolds (London, 1973)
Dictionary of British 18th-century Painters in Oils and Crayons (Woodbridge, 1981)

BIBLIOGRAPHY
G. Robertson: Obituary, *Burl. Mag.*, cxxxviii (1986), pp. 111–13

DAVID CAST

Waterhouse, John William (*b* Rome, 6 April 1849; *d* London, 10 Feb 1917). English painter. His father was a minor English painter working in Rome. Waterhouse entered the Royal Academy Schools in London in 1870. He exhibited at the Society of British Artists from 1872 and at the Royal Academy from 1874. From 1877 to the 1880s he regularly travelled abroad, particularly to Italy. In the early 1870s he had produced a few uncharacteristic Orientalist 'keepsake' paintings, but most of his works in this period are scenes from ancient history or classical genre subjects, similar to the work of Lawrence Alma-Tadema (e.g. *Consulting the Oracle*, c. 1882; London, Tate). However, Waterhouse consistently painted on a larger scale than Alma-Tadema. His brushwork is bolder, his sunlight casts harsher shadows and his history paintings are more dramatic.

Waterhouse created a distinctive type of female beauty which dominates his work, and he was fascinated by myths of the enchantress. His favourite device was to create psychological tension between a single figure and a group, as in *Marianne* (exh. RA 1887; New York, Forbes Mag. Col.), in which the isolated heroine, condemned by her husband Herod the Great, casts back an angry final glance at him.

Waterhouse is the best known of the artists who from the 1880s revived the literary themes popularized by the Pre-Raphaelites, though he was not Pre-Raphaelite in technique. His obituary in *The Times* (12 Feb 1917) describes him as 'a kind of academic Burne-Jones . . . with less insistence on design and more on atmosphere'. The *Lady of Shalott* (exh. RA 1888; London, Tate), the first of his three paintings based on Tennyson's poem, exemplifies this tendency. The English landscape background is reduced to muted patches of colour and the foreground reeds are suggested by single brushstrokes. Richer colour and greater detail serve to emphasize the central figure. Waterhouse abandoned his earlier interest in brilliant lighting effects to concentrate on such combinations of atmosphere and decoration. His fondness for backgrounds conceived as blocks of colour and tone, as well as the broad, chunky brushwork of his draperies and accessories, ultimately derive from such European prototypes as Jules Bastien-Lepage. This style was transmitted to Waterhouse through his acquaintance with members of the Newlyn school, in particular Frank Bramley.

Waterhouse drew all the themes of his later work from literature and Greek mythology. The style he had evolved remained unchanged, although after 1900 his handling became slightly looser and his colour lighter and brighter. Pentiments suggest that he finalized his compositions on the canvas itself.

From the 1890s Waterhouse annually exhibited one multi-figured painting at the Royal Academy and single-figure paintings at the Academy or the New Gallery. He was elected ARA in 1885 and RA in 1895. Waterhouse's works were well received until the early 20th century when his style had become outdated. He received considerable support from *The Studio* magazine. Besides Sir Henry Tate, who owned three works, Waterhouse was patronized by the financier Alexander Henderson, 1st Lord Faringdon (1850–1934), who bought many paintings between 1903 and 1917 (e.g. *Lamia*; exh. RA 1905; priv. col., see Hobson, 1980, p. 93). Many of Waterhouse's works, such as *Hylas and the Nymphs* (1896; Manchester, C.A.G.) and *Ulysses and the Sirens* (1891; Melbourne, N.G. Victoria), were purchased by British provincial museums and Australian public galleries. The contents of his studio were auctioned at Christie's, London, on 23 July 1926.

BIBLIOGRAPHY
Victorian Olympians (exh. cat., ed. R. Free; Sydney, A.G. NSW, 1975)
John William Waterhouse, RA, 1849–1917 (exh. cat., ed. A. Hobson; Sheffield, Mappin A.G., 1978)
A. Hobson: *The Art and Life of J. W. Waterhouse, RA, 1849–1917* (London, 1980) [fully illus.; incl. cat. of works]

HILARY MORGAN

Waterlo [Waterloo], **Antoni** [Anthonie] (*b* Lille, *bapt* 6 May 1609; *d* Utrecht, 23 Oct 1690). Dutch painter, draughtsman and etcher. He was the son of a Flemish cloth-shearer who had fled to Amsterdam for religious reasons. In 1640 Antoni married Cathalyna van der Dorp in Amsterdam, and between 1641 and 1651 they had six children. Although he is recorded as a 'painter' in the baptismal registers of his children, his work predominantly consists of landscape drawings and etchings. His earliest known dated work is a sheet depicting a *View of the Blaauwbrug in Amsterdam* (1649; Amsterdam, Gemeente Archf).

Woodland scenery compositionally inspired by Jacob van Ruisdael and technically executed in the vein of Jan Vermeer van Haarlem II features prominently in his few paintings. There are two works signed *A. waterlo f* in public collections: *Forest Scene with a Wooden Bridge* (Gotha, Schloss Friedenstein) and *Ambush in a Wood* (Munich, Alte Pin.; see fig.). Works bearing the monogram AW may be found in private collections or on the art market. Several unsigned works have been ascribed to him, including *Landscape with Trees* (Amsterdam, Rijksmus.), *Winter Scene with Houses* (Bordeaux, Mus. B.-A.) and *Landscape with Farmhouses* (Innsbruck, Tirol. Landesmus.). Paintings ascribed to Waterlo have sometimes

Antoni Waterlo: *Ambush in a Wood*, oil on canvas, 860×770 mm (Munich, Alte Pinakothek)

turned out to be copies after his etchings (e.g. *Landscape*, Liverpool, Walker A.G.).

Waterlo was a renowned etcher in his time and there are almost 140 prints to his name, mostly forest and woodland scenes with both Dutch and Italianate motifs and usually published in series. A number of etchings of panoramic views from the Cunera Tower in Rhenen are not by Waterlo, as was originally thought, but are by Johannes Ruisscher. The inscriptions *AW ex.* indicate only that these works were published by Waterlo, though he did rework the original copperplates. In 1653 a painter of this name was given freedom of the city of Leeuwarden, but it is unclear whether this refers to the same artist.

Between 1650 and 1653 Waterlo made many topographical views of Amsterdam. These were large detailed drawings of folio size, which were not conceived as studies, but were intended for sale. During this period, Waterlo, with Jan Beerstraten and Roelant Roghman, popularized this genre. Among the best examples are views of the Binnen Amstel River (Paris, Fond. Custodia, Inst. Néer.), the Rijzenhoofd ramparts (Amsterdam, Hist. Mus.) and the Haarlem, Heiligeweg and Zaagmolen city gates (all three Amsterdam, Fodor Mus., Rijksmus. and Gemeente Archf respectively). Waterlo travelled a great deal after 1655, the year he probably made the traditional Rhine voyage. While travelling along the lower Rhine he drew large-scale landscapes of Utrecht, near Rhenen, Arnhem, Nijmegen and Cleves (e.g. Amsterdam, Rijksmus.; Edinburgh, N.G.; London, BM). His drawing of a *View of Augsburg* (Vienna, Albertina) indicates that afterwards he went south and possibly visited Italy. Some time between this trip and 1660 he toured northern Germany and Poland, recording his impressions in a sketchbook. He presumably sold the sheets of this book himself, after inscribing them with his monogram, AW. He also made large, detailed drawings of views in and around Hamburg, along the Elbe (Altona, Blankenese) in the province of Holstein, near Bergedorf and from Lüneburg east to Danzig (now Gdańsk), where he depicted, among other things, the Oliva monastery (e.g. Hamburg, Ksthalle).

In 1674 his wife died and he settled in Maarssen, a country seat near Utrecht. From about 1675 he was in regular contact with Jan Weenix, who painted the staffage in his landscapes. In 1677 he lived in Paarlenburg, a small country house outside Maarssen, where he drew a series of country houses and views of the nearby seigniory of Maarsseveen (Amsterdam, Hist. Mus. and Rijksmus.; Brussels, Mus. A. Anc.; Haarlem, Teylers Mus.; Leiden, Rijksuniv., Prentenkab.; Ottawa, N.G.; Paris, Fond. Custodia, Inst. Néer.). Waterlo is presumed to have left before 1688 for Utrecht, where he died in Job's Hospital.

BIBLIOGRAPHY

L. Stubbe and W. Stubbe: *Um 1660 auf Reisen gezeichnet: Anthonie Waterloo, 1610–1690. Ansichten aus Hamburg, Altona, Blankenese, Holstein, Bergedorf, Lüneburg und Danzig-Oliva* (Hamburg, 1983)

B. P. J. Broos: '"Anthonie Waterlo f(ecit)" in Maarsseveen', *Jb. 'Niftarlake'* (1984), pp. 18–48

B. P. J. BROOS

Watermark. Distinguishing mark incorporated into paper and visible only through transmitted light. Watermarks may include names, symbols, initials, seals and dates. They are used as a mill or papermaker's trademark, with a given mill using several different watermarks to distinguish papers of differing qualities. Before *c.* 1790 they were usually referred to as 'papermarks'.

A watermark appears as a pale pattern in the sheet when a piece of paper is held up to the light or placed over a lightbox. In handmade paper the watermark is produced during the manufacture of the sheet by the screen and by the vatman's handling of the mould (*see* PAPER, §I). The design is made of wire and set into the screen in the mould on which the sheet of paper is to be formed. The vatman dips the mould into the prepared paper pulp and then lifts it out horizontally. The screen retains the fibred pulp while allowing the water to drain away. The vatman then shakes the mould in two directions, from left to right and then from back to front, matting the fibres together. The wet pulp settles out more thinly over the wires that form the watermark design than it does over the rest of the screen, so the mark is more translucent than the sheet around it. The mould is then passed to a second workman, who turns it over and quickly releases the paper on to a piece of felt.

East Asian papers have no watermarks, nor have those of Islamic and European manufacture before the end of the 13th century. They were first used in Italy, either in Bologna in 1285 or in Fabriano in 1293. Since then they have been in common use. In the 14th century watermarks were characterized by simple designs and large wires. By 1545 the date of manufacture began to be added to the full name of the maker. When John Baskerville introduced the wove mould (*c.* 1750), the laid and chain lines of the earlier laid-paper mould were replaced by a fine brass

'Strasbourg bend' watermark (named after the arms of that city), 18th century; Beta radiograph

screen. The only prominent wires on the face of a wove mould are therefore the wires of the watermark.

Watermarks can be helpful in determining the age and origin of a piece of paper, and thus to some extent of a drawing or print on it. However, they are not an infallible guide, because if a paper was popular its mark was soon imitated by other mills. Moreover, artists have frequently had access to old paper. This makes the identification and dating of papers and works of art through watermarks extremely difficult. An additional problem is the difficulty of documenting watermarks, especially when layers of media or print on the paper surface may obscure the detail. Accuracy is necessary for specific identifications, and the most widely used method of recording a watermark is to trace the design over a lightbox. As well as the design, the chain and laid line spacing and the sewing dots where the watermark wire was attached to the mould should be noted. Other methods include transmitted light photography, low-voltage X-ray radiography and beta radiography (see fig.; *see also* TECHNICAL EXAMINATION, §§II, 3, and III, 1).

BIBLIOGRAPHY

C. M. Briquet: *Les Filigranes: Dictionnaire historique des marques du papier dès leur apparition vers 1282 jusqu'en 1600*, 4 vols (Geneva, 1907)

C. F. Cross and E. J. Bevan: *A Textbook of Paper-making* (London, 1907)

D. Hunter: *Paper-making through Eighteen Centuries* (New York, 1930)

W. A. Churchill: *Watermarks in Paper in Holland, England, France etc in the Sixteenth and Seventeenth Centuries and their Interconnections* (Amsterdam, 1935)

E. Heawood: *Watermarks Mainly of the Seventeenth and Eighteenth Centuries* (Hilversum, 1950)

G. Piccard: *Die Wasserzeichenkartei . . . im Hauptstaatsarchiv Stuttgart* (Stuttgart, 1961–) [numerous vols]

SHIRLEY MILLIDGE

Watkins, Carleton E(mmons) (*b* Oneonta, NY, 11 Nov 1829; *d* Imola, CA, 23 June 1916). American photographer. He migrated to San Francisco in the early 1850s in the wake of the gold rush. In 1854 Watkins met the daguerreotypist Robert Vance (1825–76), who hired him as a camera operator. Watkins opened his own studio in 1858 and began travelling to photograph the American West. Using a mammoth-plate camera (some views measuring as much as 560×710 mm), he photographed in Yosemite Valley from 1861 (e.g. *Panoramic View of the Yosemite Valley*, *c.* 1865; Washington, DC, Lib. Congr.). These transcendental views were praised in the early photographic journals by many writers, including Oliver Wendell Holmes (1809–94), and influenced the US Congress to make the Valley a national park. By making purposefully artistic images, Watkins became one of the best-known landscape photographers, with an international reputation.

For three decades Watkins was a very successful commercial photographer, working for government-sponsored geological surveys and for industrial clients including Las Mariposas Mines and the Central and Southern Pacific Railroads. Watkins used the commissions to travel and to produce views of landscapes in Oregon (1868), Utah (1873), Nevada (1876), Southern California and Arizona (1880), the Pacific Northwest (1882–3) and Idaho and Montana (1884–5). All of these trips yielded series of photographs sold through Watkins's San Francisco studio. He sent the best examples to exhibitions across the USA and Europe, winning prizes and maintaining a strong reputation until his eyesight began to fail in 1892. In 1906 all his negatives were lost in the San Francisco earthquake fire.

BIBLIOGRAPHY
Carleton E. Watkins: Photographer of the American West (exh. cat. by P. Palmquist, Fort Worth, TX, Amon Carter Mus.; Boston, MA, Mus. F. A.; St Louis, MO, A. Mus.; Oakland, CA, Mus.; 1983)

SHERYL CONKELTON

Watkins, Dick [Richard] (*b* Sydney, 4 May 1937). Australian painter. His formal training began at the Julian Ashton school in 1955, continuing at the National Art School in 1958 (both Sydney). An important factor in his artistic development was the period from 1959 to 1961 when he lived and travelled in Europe and the USA. In 1963 he exhibited what were probably the first hard-edge paintings executed in Australia at the Barry Stern Gallery, Sydney. His next show, however, included works painted in dramatically different styles. Thereafter he refined his very personal interpretation of a variety of styles, including more traditional modes of landscape and figuration as well as drip painting, colour-field and gestural abstraction: *Pilot* (1967; Melbourne, N.G. Victoria) shows the influence of Fernand Léger.

Watkins's often witty manipulation of styles has taken on a particular importance for a younger generation of artists interested in questioning the heroic assumptions of modernism. Watkins himself, however, evinced no interest in the theoretical issues of Post-modernism and had an intensely private personality. His works of the 1980s are in a mode of abstraction characterized by strongly linear compositional elements and astonishingly intense colours

of bright green, purple and orange, for example *A Prodigy in Search of Himself* (1980; Canberra, N.G.). Generally acrylics on canvas, the surface was quickly worked and often overpainted wet, creating areas of dense pigment contrasting with areas of unpainted canvas. It was this unique combination of compositional force and colouristic innovation that set Watkins apart from his contemporaries.

BIBLIOGRAPHY
G. Catalano: *The Years of Hope: Australian Art and Criticism, 1959–68* (Oxford, 1981), pp. 187–96
G. Gunn: 'Dick Watkins', *A. & Australia* (Summer 1983), pp. 210–16
N. Yuill: *Dick Watkins* [Biennale of São Paulo] (Sydney, 1985)

NICHOLAS BAUME

Watkins, Mary Philadelphia. *See* MERRIFIELD, MARY PHILADELPHIA.

Watling, Thomas (*b* Dumfries, 19 Sept 1762; *d* after ?1810, before 1814). Australian painter and draughtsman of Scottish birth. He was a coach painter in Glasgow in 1788, and a trade card designed by him announcing drawing lessons at 'Watling's Academy' was brought forward as evidence of his artistic abilities at his trial for forgery in Dumfries in 1789. He was sentenced to 14 years' transportation, but escaped the convict ship at Cape Town; he was eventually recaptured, and arrived at Port Jackson, New South Wales, in 1792 (*see* AUSTRALIA, §III). He was assigned to surgeon-general John White, an ardent natural history collector, who required him to depict the local topography, inhabitants, flora and fauna, for example *Turquoise Parrot* (1792; London, BM). Watling aspired to paint picturesque views of the colony and drafted a prospectus soliciting patronage from the British public, but nothing came of the project. His landscape drawings reveal only rudimentary ability, and he professed disappointment with the pictorial potential of the country. His *A Direct North General View of Sydney Cove... As it Appeared in 1794* (Sydney, Mitchell Lib.) was long accepted as the first work in oils painted in Australia, but is now believed to have been executed in Britain from drawings and watercolours made on the spot, such as *A Direct North View of Sydney Cove and Port Jackson* (London, BM). Others works were engraved to illustrate *An Account of the English Colony in New South Wales* (London, 1798) by Judge-advocate David Collins. Watling left Australia in 1797, apparently *en route* for India. In Edinburgh in 1806 further charges of forgery against him were found 'not proven'.

WRITINGS
Letters from an Exile at Botany-Bay to his Aunt in Dumfries (Penrith, 1794, rev. Sydney, 2/1967/*R* Dubbo, 1979)

BIBLIOGRAPHY
H. Gladstone: *Thomas Watling, Limner of Dumfries* (Dumfries, 1938)
T. McCormick and others: *First Views of Australia 1788–1825* (Sydney, 1987)
B. Smith and A. Wheeler, eds: *The Art of the First Fleet and Other Early Australian Drawings* (Melbourne, 1988)

ROBERT SMITH

Watson. Irish family of engravers, active in England.

(1) James Watson (*b* Dublin, *c.* 1740; *d* London, 22 May 1790). He trained in the schools of the Dublin Society and learnt mezzotint engraving in London, possibly from

James McArdell. In 1762 he began to exhibit at the Society of Arts, London, showing 19 prints in the period 1762–75, 13 of which were after Joshua Reynolds. Sixty-two of his some 200 plates were after Reynolds; these included several portraits of Reynolds's literary friends and some fine full-lengths of society beauties such as *Lady Stanhope* (Chaloner Smith, no. 135). Watson worked for a number of publishers, in particular Robert Sayer, and until 1775 occasionally published prints himself. At the end of his career Watson worked primarily for John Boydell, engraving six plates (dated 1777–88) for the Houghton Gallery. He retired as a prosperous man about 1780.

BIBLIOGRAPHY

Thieme–Becker

J. Chaloner Smith: *English Mezzotinto Portraits*, iv (London, 1900), pp. 1487–1548

G. Goodwin: *Thomas Watson* (London, 1904) [with chronological cat.]

(2) Caroline Watson (*b* London, *c.* 1760; *d* London, 10 June 1814). Daughter of (1) James Watson. In 1780 she signed a stipple print of *Isaac Watts* and was soon employed by John Boydell (e.g. *Prince William of Gloucester*, 1784, after Joshua Reynolds). In 1785 she became Engraver to Queen Charlotte (1744–1818), a keen print collector. She was particularly fitted to working after miniatures, such was the delicacy of her engraving, and some of her best prints are portraits and small subjects after Samuel Shelley (*c.* 1750–1808). She did private commissions of this kind, notably for the Bute family, and also engraved large plates, some for the Boydell Shakespeare Gallery, including the *Death of Cardinal Beaufort* (1792) after Reynolds, allegedly at his request. She was employed by William Hayley (1745–1820) on his *Life of George Romney Esq* (London, 1809), and the correspondence involved shows her as a reliable and respected professional.

BIBLIOGRAPHY

Thieme–Becker

Gentleman's Magazine, lxxxiv (1814), p. 700

G. Goodwin: *Thomas Watson* (London, 1904), pp. 73–80

G. E. Bentley: *Blake Records* (London, 1969), pp. 153–5, 160–61

DAVID ALEXANDER

Watson, Barrington (*b* Lucea, Hanover, Jamaica, 9 Dec 1931). Jamaican painter and dealer. He studied at the Royal College of Art, London, the Rijksacademie, Amsterdam, and elsewhere in Europe. He came to the forefront in the early 1960s. Together with Karl Parboosingh and Eugene Hyde he was one of the founding members of the Contemporary Jamaican Artists' Association, which gave impetus to the second generation of the Jamaican Art Movement. His approach was in essence academic and realist, with occasional modernist intrusions. He experimented with abstraction and in some works he employed a futurist analysis of movement. He is best known for his large-scale, epic depictions of Jamaican life painted in grand academic manner, such as the *Garden Party* (1976; Bank of Jamaica col.), which is a panoramic commentary on the idiosyncrasies of Jamaican society. He was also a popular portrait painter, and his finest portraits, such as the *Portrait of Valerie Bloomfield* (1962; Kingston, Inst. Jamaica, N.G.), have an intimate, immediate quality. He was also well known for his nudes and erotic scenes, painted mainly in oil and watercolour. From 1962 to 1967

he was Director of Studies at the Jamaica School of Art, Kingston.

BIBLIOGRAPHY

Jamaican Art, 1922–1982 (exh. cat. by D. Boxer, Washington, DC, Smithsonian Inst.; Kingston, Inst. Jamaica, N.G.; 1983), pp. 19, 24, 69–70

P. Archer Straw and K. Robinson: *Jamaican Art* (Kingston, 1990), pp. 57, 59, 70–73, 166–7

VEERLE POUPEYE

Watson, George (*b* nr Greenlaw, Borders, 1767; *d* Edinburgh, 24 Aug 1837). Scottish painter. He was taught by Alexander Nasmyth in Edinburgh and in the studio of Joshua Reynolds in London before 1787, after which he established himself as a professional portrait painter in Edinburgh. During the next 40 years he painted over a hundred portraits; a large number of these remain unrecorded in family hands although many were also engraved. He also produced some figure subjects, such as *A Young Female Artist* (1813; Dunrobin Castle, Highland).

Watson's work is uneven and often lacks flair. Sometimes unsuccessful with backgrounds and not always able to achieve the studied simplicity of his friend and rival Henry Raeburn, Watson was nonetheless an honest and decent chronicler of Scottish society. Among his sitters were *Sir Adam Fergusson* (*c.* 1788), the artist *David Stewart, 11th Earl of Buchan* (*c.* 1807; untraced), *Bishop George Hay* (*c.* 1807–8; untraced; copy after Watson, London, N.P.G.) and *James Durham of Largo* (*c.* 1820; St Andrews, Royal & Anc. Clubhouse). Perhaps his finest results were realized in the series that records his family—his father-in-law, the printer William Smellie (Edinburgh, N.P.G.), his wife Rebecca (Edinburgh, N.G.), himself (Edinburgh, N.P.G.), his four daughters and his son, the portrait painter William Smellie Watson (1796–1874). In 1830 Watson was elected the first president of the Scottish Academy, a post he held until his death. His nephew, John Watson Gordon, was also a portrait painter.

BIBLIOGRAPHY

DNB

J. Tonge: *The Arts of Scotland* (London, 1938), pp. 43, 54–5

D. Irwin and F. Irwin: *Scottish Painters at Home and Abroad, 1700–1900* (London, 1975)

W. T. JOHNSTON

Watson, Homer (Ransford) (*b* Doon, nr Kitchener, Ont., 14 Jan 1855; *d* Doon, 30 May 1936). Canadian painter. The son of a mill-owner, he was born in a region of rural southern Ontario, which he painted throughout his life. In 1874 he moved to Toronto to work at the Notman Photographic Studios; he also spent many hours copying paintings in the Toronto Normal School in order to improve his technique. In 1876 he visited New York, where he was impressed with the carefully composed paintings of the Hudson River school and the rural scenes of George Inness, who encouraged Watson to pursue his career. The following year he returned to Doon to work up his New York sketches into finished paintings. A work of this early period, *Landscape with River* (1878; Toronto, A.G. Ont.), is composed in bands of light and dark and shows Watson's preoccupation with the dramatic wildness of nature.

In 1878 Watson exhibited for the first time in the Ontario Society of Artists annual exhibition. Two years later he exhibited at the first Royal Canadian Academy

Show. The *Pioneer Mill* (*c.* 1879; Windsor Castle, Berks, Royal Col.), a highly romantic painting based on the landscape near his father's mill at Doon, was bought from this show by John Campbell, Marquis of Lorne (1845–1914; later 9th Duke of Argyll), Governor-General of Canada, for the Royal Collection. This sale secured Watson's early success, and in 1882 he was elected a member of the Royal Canadian Academy.

Watson continued to paint scenes of rural southern Ontario, in which moody skies, water-mills, rutted roads and farmers' carts predominated. The *Old Mill* (1886; Toronto, A.G. Ont.) depicts a rushing torrent of water, boulders, wooden fences and gnarled oak trees, the whole scene darkened by a leaden sky. This heightened response to nature's more dramatic moods earned him the nickname 'the Canadian Constable' from Oscar Wilde, who had seen some of Watson's works in Toronto in 1882. However, it was not until 1887, when he visited Britain for the first time, that he encountered Constable's paintings. He also took lessons in etching from Whistler and made a trip to France to examine the work of the Barbizon painters, with whom he felt a strong kinship.

Watson returned to Canada in 1890. The decade of the 1890s was his most successful in terms of recognition and sales. Wealthy Montreal and Toronto patrons eagerly collected his scenes of rural life, such as *Log-cutting in the Woods* (1894; Montreal, Mus. F.A.). During the 1890s a change in Watson's style can be discerned: he began to apply his paint more thickly and he heavily reworked his surfaces. His treatment became less detailed, as in his best-known work, the *Flood Gate* (1900; Ottawa, N.G.). His earlier paintings had been highly focused, often with a hallucinatory clarity of form and a strongly modelled projection, while in his later work he seems to have been tentatively responding to the techniques of the French Impressionists. Such pictures as the *River Drivers* (1914; U. Regina, Mackenzie A.G.) are painted with an almost complete lack of outline and capture changing light effects and fugitive movement at the expense of compositional clarity. The particular is sacrificed to the general effect. Watson served as president of the Royal Canadian Academy from 1918 to 1921. After the death of his wife in 1918 he painted less and became interested in spiritualism.

BIBLIOGRAPHY

M. Miller: *Homer Watson: The Man of Doon* (Toronto, 1939)
F. Page: *Homer Watson: Artist and Man* (Kitchener, 1939)
Homer Watson, RCA, 1855–1936: Paintings and Drawings (exh. cat. by J. R. Harper, Ottawa, N.G., 1963)
J. Van Every: *With Faith, Ignorance and Delight* (Kitchener, 1967)
P. Godsell: *Enjoying Canadian Painting* (Toronto, 1976), pp. 102–5

KIRK MARLOW

Watson, Musgrave Lewthwaite (*b* Carlisle, 24 Jan 1804; *d* London, 28 Oct 1847). English sculptor. After training as a solicitor in Carlisle, he moved in 1824 to London, where he met John Flaxman. He studied briefly at the Royal Academy Schools and was at the same time a pupil of Richard Sievier; but on Flaxman's advice he went to Italy, where he worked from 1825 to 1828. On his return he assisted Francis Chantrey, Sir Richard Westmacott, William Behnes and Edward Hodges Baily. They recognized Watson's talent, but he received major commissions

only from 1842. These include the colossal marble monument to the brothers *Lord Eldon and Lord Stowell* (1842; Oxford, U. Coll.), *Elizabeth I* (marble, 1844; London, Royal Exch.), *Major Francis Aglionby* (marble, 1843) and *Lord Lonsdale* (marble, 1845; both Carlisle, Assize Courts), and *John Flaxman* (marble, 1843–7; London, U. Coll.). His most successful work is the posthumously completed bronze relief, the *Battle of St Vincent*, for the *Nelson Memorial* (1850; London, Trafalgar Square). This shows Watson's emergence from stylistic dependence on Flaxman into a robust realism, anticipating John Henry Foley.

Although Watson had contemporary admirers, such as Foley and the architect Charles Robert Cockerell, lack of encouragement often meant that his sculpture did not advance beyond the plaster model stage, as in the case of his Neo-classical relief *Sleep Bearing off the Body of Sarpedon* (1844; Carlisle, Mus. & A.G.) and his witty statuette the *Jolly or Crutched Friars* (Carlisle, Mus. & A.G.). Watson's proud and quarrelsome nature during his short life perhaps deprived him of the commissions that were due to his qualities as a sculptor. In Gunnis's opinion, 'had he lived he would assuredly have been one of the greatest sculptors of the 19th century'.

Gunnis

BIBLIOGRAPHY

H. Lonsdale: *The Life and Works of Musgrave Lewthwaite Watson, Sculptor* (London, 1866)
B. Read: *Victorian Sculpture* (London, 1982), pp. 50, 209, 212

MARK STOCKER

Watson, Osmond (*b* Kingston, Jamaica, 1934). Jamaican painter. He attended the art classes of the Institute of Jamaica's Junior Centre (1948–52) and then studied at the Jamaica School of Art in Kingston (1952–8). He began to exhibit in Jamaica with some success, but decided to further his studies at St Martin's School of Art in London (1962–5). On his return to Jamaica it was clear that his work had undergone a dramatic transformation, primarily as a result of his visits to the British Museum in London and his encounters there with masterpieces of African art. These may have struck a chord within him, but it was clear in his paintings that Picasso's Cubism provided the conduit for his Africanisms. In his sculpture, particularly his delicately polychromed bas-reliefs, the influence seems to have been more direct: many seem related to Yoruba carvings in the proportions and massing of the figures. Intensely Jamaican in his subject-matter, he produced in the late 1960s and 1970s an extended series of paintings that drew their imagery from Jamaican Jonkonnu, a Christmas festival where the revellers are costumed and masked; these paintings are among his best-regarded and most popular works. Later he extended his iconography by delving into Jamaica's pre-colonial past to retrieve symbols and motifs from the lost Arawak culture. In some of these paintings of 'Arawak Vibrations', Watson skirted the brink of abstraction. The teachings of the Black Nationalist Marcus Garvey and the philosophy of the Rastafarian movement influenced him tremendously and he produced some moving images of Rastafarian and other Black subjects. He was also an obsessive painter of self-portraits, in some of which he is to be found in Rastafarian guise, as a revolutionary *Freedom Fighter*, or as a Black Christ.

BIBLIOGRAPHY

Jamaican Art, 1922–1982 (exh. cat. by D. Boxer, Washington, DC, Smithsonian Inst.; Kingston, Inst. Jamaica, N.G.; 1983)

DAVID BOXER

Watson, Peter (Victor William) (*b* Berkshire, April 1909; *d* London, 3 May 1956). English patron and collector of art. A family fortune amassed by his father, Sir William Watson, through the Maypole Dairy Co., enabled him to devote himself to supporting the arts. He was known in London, Paris and New York in the 1930s, and his friends included Pavel Tchelitchew and Cecil Beaton. A discerning patron, he encouraged young artists such as Salvador Dalí and Alberto Giacometti. He also gathered a remarkable collection of contemporary art, including works by Pablo Picasso, Giorgio De Chirico and Paul Klee, which disappeared in Paris during the Nazi occupation.

In the 1940s Watson adopted a more frugal lifestyle. During World War II his London flat became a cultural refuge for British artists and writers, whom he offered invaluable support, including John Craxton, Lucian Freud, Robert Colquhoun and Dylan Thomas, many of whom were associated with NEO-ROMANTICISM. His most important work was as proprietor and arts editor of *Horizon* magazine (London, 1940–50). Committed to internationalism, he was also a founder and benefactor of the Institute of Contemporary Arts, London, in 1948, serving on the managing committee.

BIBLIOGRAPHY

M. Sheldon: *Friends of Promise: Cyril Connolly and the World of 'Horizon'* (London, 1989)

VIRGINIA BUTTON

Watson Gordon [Watson], Sir **John** (*b* Edinburgh, 1788; *d* Edinburgh, 1 June 1864). Scottish painter. He initially trained for the army and subsequently studied with David Wilkie under John Graham (1754–1817) at the Trustees' Academy in Edinburgh. He also learnt painting from his uncle, George Watson (1767–1837), and from Henry Raeburn, a close family friend, some of whose works he copied. Early pictures depicted historical and religious subjects, but he later turned to portraiture, becoming, after Raeburn's death in 1823, the leading Edinburgh portrait painter. From 1826 he called himself Watson Gordon to distinguish himself from three other Edinburgh artists called Watson.

Stylistically, his portraits are heavily influenced by Raeburn and by Velázquez, whom Wilkie much admired; they are straightforward and direct, often displaying extremely free brushwork. His female portraits are constrained and greatly inferior to his male portraits, which are simple and sincere and show a strong grasp of character, for example *John Taylor* (1824; Edinburgh, Hon. Co. Golfers). The smaller works, usually set against plain backgrounds, are generally more successful than the large full lengths. Watson Gordon's sitters were usually Scottish and included many notable figures: *Sir Walter Scott* (Edinburgh, N.P.G.) and the physicist *Sir David Brewster* (London, N.P.G.), as well as Thomas de Quincey, Lord Cockburn and Edward, Prince of Wales. He exhibited at the Royal Academy from 1827 to 1864, and in 1850 he became President of the Royal Scottish Academy and Queen's Limner for Scotland. He was much involved in

Scottish artistic matters, and in 1872 his sister founded in his memory the Watson Gordon chair in fine art at Edinburgh University, the first such full-time post in Britain.

BIBLIOGRAPHY

DNB

R. Brydall: *Art in Scotland: Its Origin and Progress* (Edinburgh, 1889), pp. 229–32

S. Cursiter: *Scottish Art to the Close of the 19th Century* (London, 1949), pp. 69–70

F. Irwin and D. Irwin: *Scottish Painters at Home and Abroad* (London, 1975), pp. 308–10

CATHERINE WILLS

Watson-Wentworth, Charles, 2nd Marquess of Rockingham (*b* Yorkshire, 13 May 1730; *d* London, 1 July 1782). English statesman, collector and patron. He was educated at Westminster School, London, and St John's College, Cambridge. In 1748 he set out on the Grand Tour. While in Italy, he ordered copies and casts after the Antique and medals and coins to augment his existing collection; he also bought two bronze statuettes (Wentworth Woodhouse, S. Yorks) by Giambologna and an ambitious group of *Samson and the Philistines* (1749; London, V&A) by Vincenzo Foggini (*fl* 1736–55). Soon after Watson-Wentworth's return to England his father, Thomas Watson-Wentworth, 1st Marquess of Rockingham (1693–1750), died, and he became the 2nd Marquess. With James Stuart as his chief architect and adviser in the 1760s, he completed Wentworth Woodhouse, which, with a range of 183 m, was the largest house built in Britain in the 18th century. In 1762 Lord Rockingham commissioned George Stubbs to paint the first of many pictures of his racehorses, including the large *Horse Attacked by a Lion* (New Haven, CT, Yale Cent. Brit. A.; *see* STUBBS, GEORGE, fig. 1), a theme suggested by a statuette of the kind that Rockingham collected. Horace Walpole reported that the celebrated portrait of the stallion *Whistlejacket* (1762; priv. col., on loan to St Osyth Priory, Essex) was intended to have George III (painted by another artist) as its rider, but the plan was abandoned when Rockingham, having quarrelled with the King in 1762, temporarily lost his offices of state. Stubbs also painted a life-size portrait of another horse, *Scrub* (Garrowby, Earl of Halifax priv. col., see *Country Life*, cvi (1949), p. 469, fig. 10), for Rockingham, but following a dispute he withdrew it; despite this he continued to paint for Rockingham until 1776. In 1764 Lord Rockingham purchased Donatello's relief known as the Chellini *Madonna* (London, V&A). In 1765 Rockingham formed a short-lived government in opposition to John Stuart, 3rd Earl of Bute; from this period date two portraits of him by Joshua Reynolds: a full-length portrait in Garter robes (Wentworth Woodhouse, S. Yorks) and the unfinished double portrait *Lord Rockingham and his Secretary, Edmund Burke* (Cambridge, Fitzwilliam). The latter is based on the portrait in Rockingham's collection of *Thomas Wentworth, 1st Earl of Strafford, with Sir Philip Mainwaring* by Anthony van Dyck (Petworth House, W. Sussex, NT). During the 1770s the sculptor Joseph Francis Nollekens found Rockingham a sympathetic patron, whose commission of the group of the *Judgement of Paris* (Malibu, CA, Getty Mus.) represented their shared preference for antique sculpture, freely interpreted and inflected by the Florentine tradition. In Rockingham, who was one of the most interesting British collectors of sculpture, medals and coins in the 18th century, connoisseurship and patronage were united to an unusual degree.

BIBLIOGRAPHY

O. B.: 'Wentworth Woodhouse, Yorkshire: A Seat of Earl Fitzwilliam', *Country Life*, xix (31 March 1906), pp. 450–62
H. A. Tipping: 'Wentworth Woodhouse, Yorkshire: The Seat of Earl Fitzwilliam', *Country Life*, xcix (10 May 1946), pp. 854–7
H. Honour: 'English Patrons and Italian Sculptors in the First Half of the Eighteenth Century', *Connoisseur*, cxli (1958), p. 223
J. Harris: 'Wentworth Woodhouse', *Archaeol. J.*, cxxv (1968), pp. 325–7
J. Allan: 'Wentworth Woodhouse', *Archaeol. J.*, cxxxvii (1980), pp. 393–6
R. J. Hopper: 'The Second Marquis of Rockingham as a Coin Collector', *Antiqua. J.*, lxii (1982), p. 322
M. Baker: 'Giambologna, Donatello and the Sale of the Gaddi, Marucelli and Stosch Bronzes', *Städel-Jb.*, xii (1989), pp. 179–96
N. Penny: 'Lord Rockingham's Sculpture Collection and the *Judgment of Paris* by Nollekens', *Getty Mus. J.*, ixx (1991), pp. 5–34

ELIZABETH ALLEN

Watson-Williams, Marjorie. *See* VÉZELAY, PAULE.

Watteau. French family of painters and draughtsmen. (1) Antoine Watteau was one of the foremost exponents of the ROCOCO style in French painting, creating an entirely distinctive pictorial world. His nephew (2) Louis Watteau and the latter's son (3) François Watteau (both known as Watteau de Lille) were provincial painters who dominated the artistic life of Lille in the later 18th century and the early 19th.

(1) (Jean-)Antoine Watteau (*b* Valenciennes, *bapt* 10 Oct 1684; *d* Nogent-sur-Marne, nr Paris, 18 July 1721). He is best known for his invention of a new genre, the *fête galante*, a small easel painting in which elegant people are depicted in conversation or music-making in a secluded parkland setting (*see under* FÊTE CHAMPÊTRE). His particular originality lies in the generally restrained nature of the amorous exchanges of his characters, which are conveyed as much by glance as by gesture, and in his mingling of figures in contemporary dress with others in theatrical costume, thus blurring references to both time and place.

Watteau's work was widely collected during his lifetime and influenced a number of other painters in the decades following his death, especially in France and England. His drawings were particularly admired. Documented facts about Watteau's life are notoriously few, though several friends wrote about him after his death (see Champion). Of over two hundred paintings generally accepted as his work—of which many of the compositions survive only in the form of reproductive prints by others—only the *Pilgrimage to the Isle of Cythera* (1717; Paris, Louvre), his *morceau de réception* for admission to the Académie Royale, and a handful of others can be dated with reasonable certainty. Moreover, most of the titles by which his works are known were not recorded until after his death, when prints of them were published.

1. Life and work. 2. Working methods and technique. 3. Critical reception and posthumous reputation.

1. LIFE AND WORK.

(i) Early years, to c. 1708. (ii) Initial independence, c. 1708–1712. (iii) *Fêtes galantes*, 1712–17. (iv) Later works, 1718–21.

(i) Early years, to c. 1708. (It has been suggested (see Vangheluwe) that Watteau was the Antoine Watteau born in 1676, and not the Jean-Antoine Watteau born in 1684; the traditional birth date has been retained in this article.) Watteau spent his youth in Valenciennes, which until it was conquered by the French in 1678 had been part of the Spanish Netherlands. Whether his father, a roofer, wished Watteau to become a painter is a matter of dispute between his early biographers. He was apprenticed in Valenciennes, either to the painter Jacques-Albert Gérin (*c.* 1640–1702) or to the sculptor Antoine-Joseph Pater (1670–1747), the father of Watteau's only pupil, Jean-Baptiste Pater. Watteau's friend and biographer, Edmé-François Gersaint, states that the artist used all his spare time making drawings of the pedlars and quack doctors attracted to this garrison town. The generally accepted, but undocumented, date for Watteau's arrival in Paris is 1702. Only Gersaint related that Watteau's first master there was a scene painter called Métayer. The early accounts are agreed, however, that soon after Watteau's arrival in Paris he worked in a kind of picture factory, turning out small portraits and devotional paintings for an artist–dealer who sold them wholesale.

It was probably around 1705 that Watteau met Claude Gillot, who for some years had been painting scenes from the theatre, including subjects from the *commedia dell'arte*. The troupe of Italian Comedians had been expelled from the French Court and from their theatre in Paris by Louis XIV in 1697, but their stock characters, such as Harlequin, Columbine and Scaramouche, thereafter enjoyed a vogue at the informal theatres that played at the Paris fairs. It was there that Pierrot, a figure of naivety, became a popular, permanent addition to the shows. The performance of these plays contravened the official monopolies held by the Opéra and the Comédie-Française, and this, together with the satirical nature of some of these informal productions, may have given a frisson to the performances, which appealed to Watteau. No writing of the artist about his attitudes survives, but his later circle in Paris included free-thinkers such as Gersaint and Pierre-Maurice Haranger. He assisted Gillot for perhaps two or three years in the production of paintings that illustrated scenes from contemporary comedies at the fairs. The precise nature of his work for Gillot is unknown, but it possibly involved making replicas of the master's paintings or painting from his designs. Watteau absorbed from Gillot a repertory of theatrical subjects, a technique for portraying them and a taste for what Gersaint later called 'the grotesque and the comical'. His adoption of Gillot's style of drawing, with its elongated figures and sharp, quick line, and of his figural types and compositional schemes in such early paintings as *Pour garder l'honneur d'une belle* (untraced, but known through an engraving, see Dacier, Hérold and Vuaflart, no. 83) has led to confusion between their works since at least the 1730s.

Watteau and Gillot parted company around 1708; some early biographies suggest that Gillot was jealous of his pupil's ability. He had, however, introduced his assistant to Claude Audran III, a leading ornamental painter, who ran a studio providing interior decoration in the new, light style of the Arabesque and who engaged Watteau at this period, probably to paint figures. The Comte de Caylus in his life of Watteau described Audran's practice of providing an ornamental framework with blank spaces to be filled in with subjects of the patron's choice, for which purpose he employed distinguished specialists. Gersaint stated that Watteau was often left free to design the pieces he had to execute—a statement that seems confirmed by significant differences between Audran's and Watteau's drawn designs (Stockholm, Nmus.) for a *singerie* (destr.) for the château of Marly. The role gave Watteau an opportunity to learn the art of ornamental decoration in the then fashionable style and also more opportunities for his own invention. Audran was, moreover, curator of the Palais du Luxembourg, Paris, which contained Peter Paul Rubens's *Life of Marie de' Medici* cycle (1622–5; Paris, Louvre). Pierre-Jean Mariette related how the artist studied this work, which is confirmed by his numerous later borrowings of some of its individual motifs.

(ii) Initial independence, c. 1708–1712. To comply with guild regulations, Watteau would have had to work as an assistant to Audran, who was a member of the Académie de St Luc, the Paris painters' guild, rather than independently. This explains Gersaint's comment that Watteau at this time did not wish to spend the rest of his life working for someone else. Audran, on the other hand, valued Watteau highly. Gersaint's further comment to the effect that Audran paid Watteau in the proportion to which his work contributed to the overall value of the decoration suggests an arrangement in which, to satisfy guild regulations, the older artist acted as nominal contractor while the younger was left with a degree of independence in providing designs. This would explain the reports by Watteau's biographers of continued collaboration between them after Watteau's departure from Audran's studio, and how Watteau was allowed, seemingly without Audran's artistic intervention, to decorate or produce designs for furniture, illustrations and rooms. Among Watteau's designs was one for a room of the Paris *hôtel* belonging to Charles-Henry-François Olivier, Marquis de Nointel; he provided eight Arabesque panels, two of which, known as *The Cajoler* and *The Faun*, survive (priv. col., see 1984 exh. cat., p. 249). These have been variously dated between 1707 and 1712, but their elegant lightness of touch suggests a date after Watteau had left Gillot's studio, and the easy grace of the figures implies he had practised drawing from the live model; he could have got such experience at the school run by the Académie de St Luc, which opened in 1706.

One of the few documented facts about Watteau's life is that on 6 April 1709 he was among the artists chosen by the officers of the Académie Royale de Peinture et de Sculpture to compete for that year's Prix de Rome, a prize entitling the recipient to be sent to Rome at the King's expense to study the city's art and antiquities. Watteau, whose submission is untraced, won second prize but no trip to Rome. Disappointment may have been a factor in his returning to Valenciennes, probably towards the end of 1709. Gersaint related how Watteau funded the trip by selling a small military painting, the *Departure of the Troops* (untraced), for the modest sum of 60 livres to the merchant and dealer Pierre Sirois (1665–1726), who later became Gersaint's father-in-law. Sirois liked the work enough to request a pendant, *The Bivouac* (Moscow, Pushkin Mus. F.A.), for which Watteau was able to charge 200 livres.

There was further demand for military subjects when he returned to Paris, probably some time in 1710, with his pupil Jean-Baptiste Pater. Most of the small-scale military scenes he painted then depict not battle but the more mundane aspects of campaigning—soldiers in camp resting, cooking or smoking. Painting military heroics may have seemed inappropriate after recent French defeats during the War of the Spanish Succession. Watteau's quiet scenes, include figures of attractive girls and nursing mothers as well as walking wounded, seem to reflect the languor of the French troops who were, according to contemporary accounts, inadequately led and fed.

A separate enterprise of Watteau's has been variously dated to *c.* 1709–10 or *c.* 1713. This is the series of seven plates, plus frontispiece (DHV 41–8), which make up the *Figures de modes* etched by Watteau and later retouched by the engraver Henri-Simon Thomassin and published as a small book. Each plate shows a male or a female figure wearing fashionable clothes, shown in a landscape setting. After this series Watteau himself etched only two other plates; the 11 plates of his *Figures françoises et comiques* (1715 or later) were engraved by others.

(iii) Fêtes galantes, 1712–17. On 11 July 1712 the members of the Académie Royale met to choose one painter and one sculptor from among previous prizewinners to be sent to Rome. Watteau still wished to go to Italy—Gersaint noted that he wished in particular to study the colour and composition of Venetian art—but once again he was not chosen. At the following meeting (30 July) Watteau was accepted (*agréé*) following, it seems, some lobbying on his behalf by the senior Academician, Charles de La Fosse, who, according to Gersaint, had been surprised by the

1. Antoine Watteau: *Les Fêtes vénitiennes*, oil on canvas, 559×457 mm, 1716–20 (Edinburgh, National Gallery)

2. Antoine Watteau: *Les Charmes de la vie*, oil on canvas, 673×925 mm, *c.* 1717–18 (London, Wallace Collection)

quality of paintings that Watteau had left hanging anonymously at the Académie.

According to Mariette, among the paintings and drawings that Watteau had left to be judged was *Les Jaloux* (untraced; known through an engraving), which showed *commedia dell'arte* characters in a forest clearing. No scene from a specific play is shown, however, nor does it appear to be an episode from a sequential plot. Instead, costumed characters relax in a coherent setting surrounded by objects symbolic of their qualities or desires—for example the jester's sceptre lying on the grass denotes foolishness, and the satyr term standing half-hidden in the trees alludes to lust. *Les Jaloux* has a mood, contains a situation, but shows no event. As such it did not fall within any of the accepted categories of painting. Whereas it was customary for the Académie to specify the subject for an *agréé*'s *morceau de réception*, the novelty of the painting led the academicians, exceptionally, to leave the choice of subject to Watteau himself. They were to be kept waiting five years for the piece in question.

During this period Watteau produced a number of pictures in which *commedia dell'arte* figures predominate. Most of the prints made in his lifetime after his paintings were of such subjects, attesting to their popularity. In one of the later works, *Voulez-vous triompher des belles?* (or *Harlequin and Columbine*; London, Wallace), there is an ironic contrast between the lady gently listening to music with her companions on the illuminated left side of the

painting and the masked Harlequin lunging from the shadows on the right towards the breast of his Columbine. The distorted perspective that places the two groups either side of an earthbank of indeterminate depth may be taken to pose the question: what, if anything, separates virtuous love from carnal lust? The ambiguity that has been attributed to Watteau's paintings lies less in their message, the general tenor of which is usually clear, than in their shuffling of reality and fantasy. Which figures are actors, and what would such actors actually be feeling? Do they stand before a natural vista or a mere backdrop? The masterly illusions of the painted surfaces are perhaps a counterpart to the theatrical unrealities of social intercourse.

Similar questions are provoked by Watteau's *fêtes galantes*. The term denotes social gatherings of elegant people in a park setting; he concentrated on such scenes between 1714 and 1717. If, however, his *fêtes galantes* were no more than that, there would be little to distinguish them from prints of contemporary society by such as Bernard Picart. Their distinctiveness rests partly in the psychological interaction between their characters, and partly in their detachment from temporal and spatial location, mixing contemporary dress and theatrical costume in settings of suggestive ideality. These characteristics are clearly evident in *Les Fêtes vénitiennes* (1716–20; Edinburgh, N.G.; see fig. 1). As with the theatre pictures, Watteau showed situations or moods rather than events, although, like them, the situations echo a reality observable in contemporary polite society. This is explicitly acknowledged in some *fêtes galantes* in which actual people, friends such as Sirois or the painter Nicholas Vleughels, are included wearing *commedia dell'arte* costume. Indeed, alternative personae were adopted by those wealthy members of society who donned peasant costume or staged their own versions of the *commedia dell'arte* at country house gatherings outside Paris.

The *fêtes galantes* have a psychological content often identifiable through the animated statues that inhabit them or through the musical instruments played by their human participants. Thus in *La Leçon d'amour* (*c.* 1716–17; Stockholm, Nmus.) the nude statue, rising beside an adjacent dolphin (symbolizing amorous desire), signifies the awakening love of the couples making music—itself a metaphor for love. In the later *Les Charmes de la vie* (London, Wallace; see fig. 2) the central figure is a lutenist trying to tune his instrument—a metaphor for attempts to initiate gallant conversation. The lute was notoriously difficult to tune and the lutenist's difficulties have allowed another man to make his move towards the woman who waits for the music to begin. What distinguishes these paintings and most of Watteau's other *fêtes galantes* from the 17th-century Dutch and Flemish paintings of merry companies, with their similar subject-matter (e.g. works by Jan Steen, Dirck Hals, Esaias van de Velde and Willem Buytewech), is a more restrained language of gesture and emotion, the latter often conveyed by no more than a glance. The lack of specificity allows more scope for individual viewers to exercise their interpretative imagination.

If the iconographic sources of the *fêtes galantes* lie in earlier works painted in the Low Countries and in contemporary French prints and society itself, their stylistic sources are to be found in the works of Peter Paul Rubens and Venetian art. At some time after 1711 Watteau was introduced to the wealthy banker and collector Pierre Crozat. Watteau painted a series of the *Four Seasons* for the dining-room of Crozat's house in Paris, probably *c.* 1715–16 (*Spring*, untraced; *Summer*, Washington, DC, N.G.A.; *Autumn*, untraced; *Winter*, ex-château of Chenonceaux), and is recorded as living there the following year. Caylus related that among the extensive number of paintings and drawings in Crozat's collection, the artist was particularly drawn to the oil sketches of Rubens and Anthony van Dyck, and to the landscape drawings of Titian and Domenico Campagnola. Indeed, most of Watteau's surviving drawn copies after other artists are of works by Rubens or 16th-century Venetians. Rubens provided material for Watteau as a source of motifs: the achitecture of the portico in *Sous un habit de Mezzetin* (or *Sirois and his Family*; London, Wallace), for example, is copied from that in Rubens's *Garden of Love* (Madrid, Prado); the dog in Rubens's *Coronation of Marie de' Medici* (Paris, Louvre) appears in *Les Charmes de la vie* and reappears in *L'Enseigne de Gersaint* (1721; Berlin, Schloss Charlottenburg.; *see* DRESS, fig. 43). Rubens's work was also a source for practising figural relationships, as of a

3. Antoine Watteau: *Pilgrimage to the Isle of Cythera*, oil on canvas, 1.29×1.94 m, 1717 (Paris, Musée du Louvre)

Dancing Couple (Paris, Mus. A. Déc.) after the embracing pair of dancers in Rubens's *Flemish Kermesse* (Paris, Louvre) testifies. Venetian paintings provided examples of open brushwork and broken colour, while Venetian drawings gave Watteau examples of landscape composition complementary to his own studies after nature.

These influences coalesce in Watteau's *morceau de réception* for the Académie, which was finally presented on 28 August 1717, following four reminders to the artist. The *Pilgrimage to the Isle of Cythera* (Paris, Louvre; see fig. 3) was entered in the institution's minutes with a note referring to Watteau as a 'peintre des festes galantes'; the Académie thus formally recognized a new genre of painting and Watteau as its originator. At the same time it denied him the title of history painter, the highest category and the only one from which the Académie's professors could be drawn—possibly because as Charles-Antoine Coypel, the son of its then director later put it: 'The charming paintings of this gracious painter would be a bad guide for whoever wished to paint the Acts of the Apostles'. The pilgrimage to Cythera, the island of Venus, was invoked in stage works by Florent Dancourt (1700) and Houdar de la Motte (1705), and Watteau painted a straightforward theatrical treatment of the theme, the *Island of Cythera* (Frankfurt am Main, Städel. Kstinst. & Städt. Gal.), about 1709. For the *morceau de réception* he seems to have studied an engraving of the subject (*c.* 1708) by Claude Duflos, the appended verses to which speak of delightful days spent on Cythera besides 'secret nights which are worth yet more'. A contemporary association between voyaging and sensual love could, moreover, be observed in the pleasure boats that took couples from Paris down the Seine to the park of St Cloud, for short amorous adventures. Levey suggested that 'Pèlerinage à l'île de Cythère' should be translated not as 'Pilgrimage *to* the Isle of Cythera' but rather as 'Pilgrimage *on* the Isle of Cythera', for, he argued, the pilgrims are about to depart; hence the painting's wistfulness. Others deny that Watteau's paintings were conceived as logically coherent narratives in this way. The painting's theme however remains unmistakable: from the rose-garlanded term of Venus on the right to the flight of putti on the left, Watteau traces the stages of amorous discourse, from proposal to harmonious fulfilment. The painting's appeal led to a commission for a second version (Berlin, Schloss Charlottenburg), probably from the collector Jean de Jullienne.

(iv) Later works, 1718–21. After his admission (*réception*) to the Académie, Watteau seems to have painted fewer *fêtes galantes*, despite the popularity of the genre; those he did were on a larger scale. He painted some mythological subjects (e.g. the *Judgement of Paris*; Paris, Louvre; see NUDE, fig. 4) and also erotic works, some of which, according to Caylus, he arranged to have burnt shortly before he died. Among the survivors is *Lady at her Toilet* (*c.* 1718–19; London, Wallace), in which Watteau painted the female nude as an object purely for the eye, and without any pretence of moral content such as might have accompanied a portrayal of Bathsheba. The life-size representation of the *commedia dell'arte* character Pierrot, known as *Gilles* (Paris, Louvre), was painted at about the same time, possibly as a decoration for the café owned by the actor Belloni who had played this part.

Watteau's reputation in Paris, according to Jullienne, was at this point very high; by the end of 1719, however, he was in London. According to Horace Walpole, Watteau made the trip in order to consult Richard Mead, a celebrated doctor, about his tuberculosis. However Mead was also a well-known collector, and Mariette stated that the purpose of the trip was to make money; while Jullienne and Caylus described it as a symptom of the restlessness for which Watteau was notorious.

Watteau painted two pictures for Mead, *L'Amour paisible* (untraced), known only through a print (DHV 268) by Bernard Baron, and the *Italian Comedians* (Washington, DC, N.G.A.). An unusual number of compositional drawings for the *Italian Comedians* exist (for illustration *see* LIFE DRAWING). This may be an accident of survival or may suggest the particular care Watteau took with it. Unusual also is his depiction of a precise moment in time, namely the curtain-call. Like some other works of this period, for example *Iris c'est de bonne heure* (Berlin, Gemäldegal.), also believed to have been executed in London, it is finished with particular care: if, as has been suggested, the above works are portraits, this may have been to meet the demands of that genre, at least as it was understood in England.

By August 1720 Watteau had returned to Paris in poor health and went to live with Gersaint, who dealt in paintings and *objets d'art* on the Pont Notre-Dame. Gersaint related that in early 1721 Watteau suggested he should paint a shopsign, in Watteau's phrase 'to flex his fingers', and that he wanted it displayed outside the shop. Watteau's absence in England would have deprived him of the chance to exhibit his paintings at the only organized art exhibition in Paris, which took place early each June, and he had lost money in the collapse of John Law's bank in France in 1720; thus, more than an advertisement for Gersaint's shop, the resulting painting, known as *L'Enseigne de Gersaint* (1721; Berlin, Schloss Charlottenburg), which originally had an arched top to fit the space above Gersaint's shop, may be seen as Watteau's advertisement for himself, a declaration to the public that he had returned to Paris and was ready to paint again.

The view sometimes expressed, that *L'Enseigne* was Watteau's artistic testament, assumes that because he was ill the artist was aware of his imminent death. Such awareness is, however, inconsistent with the announcement of February 1721 that Crozat had engaged Watteau, among others, on a long-term project, namely to draw the paintings in famous collections in preparation for having them published in the form of engravings. If the *Enseigne* was a self-advertisement, Watteau may have been less concerned to display in it those iconographic subtleties for which he was already recognized, than to demonstrate strength in what those of a conservative taste (exemplified by Caylus) perceived as areas of weakness in his art, namely the expression of emotion and the depiction of action. The *Enseigne*, which shows the interior of the dealer's shop, was one of Watteau's few paintings that Caylus exempted from these criticisms. Action and emotion in the painting are subdued, but three factors that may have impressed Caylus are the deployment of a greater variety of pose and gesture than in earlier paintings; expressions that were less veiled and that may have been reinforced by the subject-matter of the fictive paintings on the shop's walls; and the overall balance and clarity of the composition.

2. WORKING METHODS AND TECHNIQUE. For Watteau drawing lay at the heart of the creative process, and his early biographers agreed that it was an incessant activity for him (*see* DRAWING, colour pl. I, fig. 2). Before publication of his two-volume edition of engravings of Watteau's paintings, the *Recueil Jullienne* (1735), Jullienne had published etchings of numerous of his drawings, the *Figures de différents caractères* of 1726 and 1728. Such homage to a dead artist was unprecedented in scope, although Watteau was not the first artist to have had his drawings posthumously published. Whereas contemporaries such as Caylus or Gersaint criticized Watteau's paintings for their subject-matter, lack of variety, use of a dirty palette or over-use of oil, Watteau's drawings, of which

there are large groups in London (BM) and Paris (Louvre), were the most widely admired part of his artistic production. His use of them did not accord, however, with academic practice. He seems only rarely to have made compositional studies. According to Caylus, Watteau's practice was to draw studies in a bound notebook so that he had a large number to hand, and once he had worked out his landscape background he would choose the figures that best suited it. This method of composition, which Caylus blamed for the repetition of poses in some of Watteau's paintings, explains why figures in Watteau's mature work are in some cases related to drawings that, judging from their style, were made many years earlier. For example, the man standing holding a musket in *Le Rendezvous de chasse* (*c.* 1720; London, Wallace) is derived from a drawing (Baltimore, MD, priv. col.; see 1984 exh. cat., p. 87) of some eight years earlier.

Apart from his drawing after Italian, Flemish and French painters, Watteau's biographers speak of his drawings

4. Antoine Watteau: *Seated Woman and Head-and-shoulders Study of a Woman*, red, white and black chalk on brown paper, 231×263 mm, ?1716 (Amsterdam, Rijksmuseum)

from nature—by which they mean not just landscape but studies of figures who appear to have been posed and rapid sketches of actors or of people seen in the street. He also made more worked-up studies to explore a pose, the modelling of a face or a facial expression. In the *Seated Woman and Head-and-shoulders Study of a Woman*, drawn on a single sheet (?1716; Amsterdam, Rijksmuseum; see fig. 4), Watteau seems first to have studied the general pose of his model, and then to have made a further head-and-shoulders sketch, with a slightly modified tilt of the head, in which he concentrated on her expression. The drawing was used for one of the figures in the painting *L'Assemblée galante* (untraced) engraved by Jacques-Philippe Lebas (DHV 139), and he used the figure again in a second painting, *The Family* (Switzerland, priv. col., see 1984 exh. cat., p. 379). Although he also made landscape drawings from nature—according to Caylus he was continually drawing the trees in the Jardin du Luxembourg in Paris—some of Watteau's painted landscape backgrounds were also derived from Venetian landscape drawings in Crozat's collection or, possibly, from the scenic backdrops designed *c.* 1700–02 by Jean Berain I for the Paris Opéra.

Watteau's drawing technique *aux trois crayons* was analysed by the 18th-century collector of drawings Antoine-Joseph Dézallier d'Argenville, who described how Watteau would use one, two or three coloured chalks (red, white and black, though sometimes he used two shades of red in a varient technique *aux quatre crayons*), pastel, oil colours or gouache, but never pen (for an illustration showing Watteau's chalk drawing technique *see* CHALK). Indeed, although Gillot and Audran both used pen and wash, only one pen drawing has been attributed to Watteau. He also occasionally used watercolour. Broadly speaking, he seems to have used red chalk on its own when it was a question of catching a gesture from life, but added black and/or white chalk when he required a fuller pictorial effect (as in fig. 2), although in different combinations, depending on the effect he required and in order to suggest the full chromatic range. Additionally *c.* 1718 he used graphite to pick out details. Dézallier d'Argenville well expressed what was admirable in the drawings so created (*Abrégé*, iv, p. 409): 'the freedom of the hand, the lightness of touch, a subtlety in the profiles of heads and the drawing of hair, the expressiveness of the figures and compositions, the pervasive feeling of these drawings are in collectors' eyes unmistakably characteristic of Watteau'.

3. CRITICAL RECEPTION AND POSTHUMOUS REPUTATION. A biographical notice of Watteau appeared as early as 1719, in Pellegrino Antonio Orlandi's *Abecedario pittorico*, which was published in Bologna and dedicated to Crozat. Following Watteau's death, there were several accounts by his friends: the collector and textile manufacturer Jean de Jullienne prefaced his edition of Watteau's drawings, the *Figures de différents caractères* (1726), with a brief life of the artist; Gersaint contributed an account of him to a collector's catalogue in 1744, and the Comte de Caylus gave his 'Vie de Watteau' as a lecture to the Académie Royale in 1748. Pierre-Jean Mariette's account probably also stems from first-hand acquaintance. Watteau's friend Antoine de La Rocque, writing in the *Mercure de France* shortly after the artist's death (see Champion),

spoke of the excessive prices of his paintings; Jullienne also remarked on their high price and on their dispersal among Spanish, English, German and Italian, as well as French, collections. The volume of Watteau's oeuvre over a short working career further attests to his popularity, as does the adoption of the *fête galante* genre by his one pupil, Jean-Baptiste Pater, and by other followers, including Nicolas Lancret. In the generation following his death Watteau's work was widely collected in England. Philippe Mercier, a Huguenot painter working in London from *c.* 1716 to 1736, borrowed elements of his style; Watteau's influence can also be seen in some of William Hogarth's paintings. On the other hand, the Regent Philippe, Duc d'Orléans, a notable collector, owned only one painting by Watteau (which served as a pendant to a picture by David Teniers II), while Crozat, although an admirer, possessed none of his easel pictures. Watteau's prices may only have seemed high for work in a genre deemed subordinate to history painting.

From *c.* 1750, when critics began to insist that painting should appeal to the mind as well as to the eye, the very popularity of works by or after Watteau told against him, as evidence of their appeal to a less elevated taste. It was in fact mainly pictures by artists such as François Boucher against which critics were then reacting. Boucher's assumption that gallantry could provide subject-matter even for a history painter is due, at least in part, to Watteau having created a visual language for depicting love that was socially acceptable to a wide class of people and could be adopted by artists involved in producing easel paintings, internal decorative schemes or *objets d'art*. Watteau's popularity waned as the more austere art of Neo-classicism became fashionable.

From *c.* 1830, however, the aesthetic qualities of Watteau's art once more began to find favour with collectors and painters. He is described as 'extremely fashionable' in Honoré de Balzac's novel *Le Cousin Pons* (1846). To this enthusiasm the influential essay by Edmond and Jules de Goncourt, *La Philosophie de Watteau* (1856), which they incorporated in their *L'Art du dix-huitième siècle*, added a new element, which even Watteau's admiring contemporaries had not claimed for him: intellectual respectability. The Goncourts ascribed to Watteau the insight of the Romantic poet, and hence to his art a seriousness of purpose not apparent on superficial examination. The particular quality of melancholy ascribed to Watteau's paintings by the Goncourts and subsequent writers seemed justified by references to the melancholy of the artist himself provided by his early biographers, though melancholy was a trait traditionally ascribed to those suffering from tuberculosis. It was further emphasized in the 1860s by reinterpretations of Pierrot, the *commedia dell'arte* character who appears in a number of Watteau's paintings, as a tragic rather than ribald character, and as symbolizing some essential sadness in the human condition. The interpretation of Watteau's paintings as mediators of the artist's own alleged tragic solitude continued during the following century: Panofsky identified the figure of Pierrot with the artist himself in *Gilles* and with the victimized Christ in the *Italian Comedians*. More recently, however, commentators have rightly pointed out that Watteau's nearer contemporaries saw his paintings as lighthearted:

Dézallier d'Argenville in 1745 specifically contrasted Watteau's own melancholy character with the gaiety and lively spirit of his work.

BIBLIOGRAPHY

A.-J. Dézallier d'Argenville: *Abrégé de la vie des plus fameux peintres* (1745–52, 2/1762), iv, pp. 403–10

E. de Goncourt and J. de Goncourt: *L'Art du dix-huitième siècle* (Paris, 1860, rev. 3/1880–82), i; Eng. trans. as *French Eighteenth-century Painters* (London, 1948)

P. Alfassa: 'L'Enseigne de Gersaint', *Bull. Soc. Hist. A. Fr.* (1910), pp. 126–72

P. Champion, ed.: *Notes critiques sur les vies anciennes d'Antoine Watteau* (Paris, 1921) [anthology of writings by La Rocque, Jullienne, Gersaint, Mariette, Dézallier d'Argenville, the Comte de Caylus and Coypel]

E. Dacier, J. Hérold and A. Vuaflart: *Jean de Jullienne et les graveurs de Watteau au XVIIIe siècle*, 4 vols (Paris, 1921–9) [DHV]

K. T. Parker: *The Drawings of Antoine Watteau* (London, 1931)

H. Adhémar and R. Huyghe: *Watteau, sa vie, son oeuvre* (Paris, 1950)

D. Panofsky: 'Gilles or Pierrot?', *Gaz. B.-A.*, n. s. 5, clxii (1952), pp. 319–40

K. T. Parker and J. Mathey: *Antoine Watteau: Catalogue complet de son oeuvre dessiné*, 2 vols (Paris, 1957)

J. Lévy: 'Une Vie inconnue d'Antoine Watteau', *Bull. Soc. Hist. A. Fr.* (1958), pp. 175–203

M. Levey: 'The Real Theme of Watteau's *Embarkation for Cythera*', *Burl. Mag.*, ciii (1961), pp. 180–85

A. P. de Mirimonde: 'Les Sujets musicaux chez Antoine Watteau', *Gaz. B.-A.*, n. s. 5, lviii (1961), pp. 248–88

——: 'Statues et emblèmes dans l'oeuvre de Watteau', *Rev. Louvre*, i (1962), pp. 11–20

H. Adhémar: 'L'Enseigne de Gersaint par Antoine Watteau: Aperçus nouveaux', *Bull. Lab. Mus. Louvre*, ix (1964), pp. 7–18

S. O. Simches: *Le Romantisme et le goût esthétique du XVIIIe siècle* (Paris, 1964)

E. Camesasca and P. Rosenberg: *L'opera completa di Watteau* (Milan, 1968, rev./1983); trans. by E. Camesasca and J. Sunderland as *The Complete Paintings of Watteau* (London, 1971)

R. Démoris: 'Les Fêtes galantes chez Watteau et dans le roman contemporain', *XVIIIe Siècle*, iii (1971), pp. 337–57

F. Haskell: 'The Sad Clown: Some Notes on a 19th-century Myth', *French 19th-century Painting and Literature* (Manchester, 1972)

D. Posner: *Watteau: 'A Lady at her Toilet'* (London, 1973)

O. T. Banks: *Watteau and the North: Studies in the Dutch and Flemish Baroque Influence on French Rococo Painting* (New York and London, 1977)

M. P. Eidelberg: *Watteau's Drawings: Their Use and Significance* (New York and London, 1977)

D. Posner: 'The Swinging Women of Watteau and Fragonard', *A. Bull.*, lxiv (1982), pp. 75–88

——: Antoine Watteau (London, 1984)

M. Roland-Michel: *Watteau: An Artist of the Eighteenth Century* (London and Paris, 1984)

Watteau, 1684–1721 (exh. cat. by M. M. Grasselli and P. Rosenberg; Paris, Grand Pal.; Washington, DC, N.G.A.; 1984) [extensive bibliog.]

P. Rosenberg: *Vies anciennes de Watteau* (Paris, 1985)

Watteau: Technique picturale et problèmes de restauration (Brussels, 1986)

M. M. Grasselli: *The Drawings of Antoine Watteau: Stylistic Development and Problems of Chronology* (diss., Harvard U., 1987)

F. Moureau and M. M. Grasselli, eds: *Antoine Watteau (1684–1721): Le Peintre, son temps et sa légende* (Paris and Geneva, 1987)

M. Vangheluwe: 'Watteau à Valenciennes', *Antoine Watteau (1684–1721): Le Peintre, son temps et sa légende*, ed. F. Moureau and M. M. Grasselli (Paris and Geneva, 1987), pp. 7–9

H. Wine: 'Watteau's Consumption and *L'Enseigne de Gersaint*', *Gaz. B.-A.*, 6th ser., cxv (1990), pp. 163–70

E. Munhall: *Little Notes Concerning Watteau's 'Portal of Valenciennes'* (New York, 1992)

M. Vidal: *Watteau's Painted Conversations: Art, Literature and Talk in Seventeenth- and Eighteenth-century France* (New Haven and London, 1992)

HUMPHREY WINE

(2) Louis(-Joseph) Watteau [Watteau de Lille] (*b* Valenciennes, 10 April 1731; *d* Lille, 27 Aug 1798). Nephew of (1) Antoine Watteau. He trained in Paris with Jacques Dumont, and at the Académie Royale, where in 1751 he was awarded first prize for painting. In 1755 he settled in Lille; there he became assistant teacher at the school of drawing, but was dismissed, because of what was considered a scandalous innovation, the introduction of study of the nude, as in Paris. He then returned to Valenciennes for some 15 years; around 1770 he became assistant teacher to Louis-Jean Guéret, director of the school of drawing in Lille, whom he succeeded in the post in 1778. On Watteau's initiative, an annual Salon, at which he himself exhibited regularly, was established in Lille in 1773. In 1795 he was chosen to draw up an inventory of works of art seized during the French Revolution from religious foundations and the houses of émigrés, with a view to establishing a museum.

Louis Watteau was chiefly a genre painter in the 18th-century tradition; he concentrated on pastoral scenes such as the cycle *Four Hours of the Day* (1771; Valenciennes, Mus. B.-A.) and the *Wafer Seller* and *The Fiddler* (both Lille, Mus. B.-A.), and also on landscapes such as *View of Lille from Dieu de Marcq* (Lille, Mus. B.-A.). He was, however, equally competent at religious painting (examples, Lille, St Maurice and Avesnes-sur-Helpe, St Nicolas), and in depicting current events such as *Monsieur Blanchard's Fourteenth Aerostatics Experiment at Lille* (1785; Lille, Mus. Hosp. Comtesse) and the *Proclamation in the Ruins of Lille* (1793; Lille, Mus. B.-A.). Watteau was a prolific draughtsman and an observant painter, whose works show Flemish, rather than Parisian influence, in the warmth of their colouring and their picturesque touches.

(3) François(-Louis-Joseph) Watteau [Watteau de Lille] (*b* Valenciennes, ?18 Aug 1758; *d* Lille, 1 Dec 1823). Son of (2) Louis Watteau. He was first his father's pupil at the Lille school of drawing, where in 1774 he was awarded a medal for the *Death of Socrates* (Lille, Mus. B.-A.). This success won him a municipal scholarship to study in Paris, first (1775–7) with Louis-Jacques Durameau, and then at the Académie Royale. He won a prize for drawing in 1777 and a medal in 1782, and exhibited a drawing entitled the *Garden Party* at the Exposition de la Jeunesse in 1783. On his return to Lille, he became his father's assistant in 1786, succeeding him in 1798 as principal teacher and director of the school of drawing. He also became a member of the Lille academy of art. During this period he exhibited regularly at the Lille Salon, and also at two Paris Salons, submitting two companion-pieces, *Alexander Defeating Darius* (1795) and *Alexander Defeating Porus* (1802; both Lille, Mus. B.-A.), which won him a gold medal. In 1807 Watteau became assistant curator of the Lille museum that his father had helped to establish.

It is sometimes difficult to distinguish the work of François Watteau from that of his father, whose romantic and informal manner greatly influenced him. Nevertheless, his style, in the elegance of its line and the freshness of its colouring, was closer to the French verve of Hubert Robert than to his father's Flemish-influenced style, as may be seen in François's *Minuet under an Oak* (1787; Valenciennes, Mus. B.-A.) or his *Festival at the Colosseum* (Lille, Mus. B.-A., see fig.). Despite the incomprehension of his Lille contemporaries, he pursued an independent line by inclining towards history painting; examples include

François Watteau: *Festival at the Colosseum*, oil on canvas, 750×910 mm, *c.* 1791 (Lille, Musée des Beaux-Arts)

the two battle scenes previously mentioned, as well as the *Siege of Beauvais in 1472* (Valenciennes, Mus. B.-A.).

BIBLIOGRAPHY

J. Houdoy: *Etudes artistiques* (Paris, 1878)
P. Marmottan: *Notice historique et critique sur les peintres Louis et François Watteau, dits Watteau de Lille* (Paris, 1889)
A. Mabille de Poncheville: 'Les Peintres Louis et François Watteau, dits Watteau de Lille', *Gaz. B.-A.*, n. s. 4, xiii (1926), pp. 219–30
——: 'Louis et François Watteau, dits Watteau de Lille' (Paris, 1928)
J. Vergnet-Ruiz and M. Laclotte: *Petits et grands musées de France* (Paris, 1962)

ANNIE SCOTTEZ-DE WAMBRECHIES

Wattle-and-daub. Basic construction technique using woven branches (wattle) covered with mud or plaster (daub) to make walls and to fill the areas between timbers in medieval buildings.

☐

Watts, G(eorge) F(rederic) (*b* London, 23 Feb 1817; *d* London, 1 July 1904). English painter and sculptor. Though renowned as one of the great portrait painters of the later Victorian era, he saw himself as part of the tradition of history painting. His imaginative subject paintings evolved into 'symbolical' works (see fig.) on which he intended his future reputation to rest.

The son of a poor pianoforte-maker, Watts studied informally from *c.* 1827 in the studio of the sculptor William Behnes, where he drew from casts after the Antique. Like Behnes, Watts developed facility as a portrait draughtsman, and from the age of 16 he supported himself. Although he entered the Royal Academy Schools in 1835, he found the teaching disappointing and spent little time there, later claiming his 'only teachers were the Elgin Marbles'. Throughout his life, he professed complete devotion to Pheidias; such works as *Ariadne in Naxos* (1875; London, Guildhall A.G.) reflect his knowledge of the Classical Greek wet drapery style.

Watts exhibited at the Royal Academy from 1837, sending literary subjects and portraits in oils. One early patron, Alexander Ionides, commissioned portraits of his family, as did succeeding generations (many in London, V&A). By 1840 Watts had matured as a history painter, treating serious historical subjects in the spirit of Benjamin Robert Haydon. In 1843 he won one of the three highest premiums in the first competition for decorations for the new Palace of Westminster, with his vast cartoon *Caractacus Led in Triumph through the Streets of Rome* (fragments, London, V&A). Watts was in Italy from 1843 to 1847 to

G. F. Watts: *Hope*, oil on canvas, 1.42×1.11 m, 1886; version (London, Tate Gallery)

study fresco technique; while there he painted large canvases (e.g. the *Story from Boccaccio, c.* 1845; London, Tate, on loan to Oxford, Keble Coll.), depicting scenes from Romantic literature; these show a new exploration of colour resulting from his study of Italian art. He also executed landscapes in oil (e.g. *Fiesole*, 1844–5; Compton, Watts Gal.) and portraits that include the intimate pencil drawings executed for his patron Henry Fox, 4th Baron Holland, and the full-length in the grand manner *Augusta Fitzpatrick* (1844; London, Tate).

Watts returned to London in 1847 to enter *Alfred Inciting the Saxons to Encounter the Danes at Sea* (1846–7; London, Pal. Westminster) in the fourth of the Houses of Parliament competitions, winning a first premium of £500. His efforts to consolidate his reputation at exhibitions met with mixed critical reaction. Ruskin, who once called Watts a genius, briefly tried but failed to guide his work. Watts expressed personal depression in a series of four canvases on social realist themes painted *c.* 1848–50 in a newly simplified style and sombre palette (e.g. *Found Drowned*; Compton, Watts Gal.).

From 1851 to 1875 Watts resided with Henry Thoby Prinsep and his wife, Sara, at Little Holland House in Kensington. The social circle he encountered there included Tennyson, Julia Margaret Cameron and several young Pre-Raphaelites, and provided the physically delicate and temperamentally uncertain Watts with a secure environment in which to work. In the early 1850s, due in part to contact with such luminaries, Watts began to paint a series of portraits of noted individuals of the day. These range from the restrained colour and presentation of

William Morris (*c.* 1870; London, N.P.G.) to the rich Venetian colouring of the disturbingly skeletal *Cardinal Manning* (1882; London, N.P.G.).

In the 1850s Watts finally visited Venice (1853), worked briefly in Paris (1855–6) and saw antique sculpture excavated at Bodrum in Turkey (the ancient Halicarnassus) in 1856. His relations with the Royal Academy deteriorated after the poor hanging of the *Good Samaritan* (Manchester, C.A.G.) at the exhibition of 1850. He withdrew to devote himself to what he saw as more worthy endeavours that he pursued alongside his lucrative portrait practice. Private mural commissions included frescoes for Charles Somers, 3rd Earl Somers, at 7 Carlton House Terrace in London (1854–5; London, Crown Estate Office) and a fresco and an oil (1858–62) for Henry Petty-Fitzmaurice, 3rd Marquess of Lansdowne, at Bowood House, Wilts. Public murals, in the House of Lords (the *Triumph of the Red Cross Knight* from Spenser for the Upper Waiting Hall, 1853–4), in the Great Hall at Lincoln's Inn (*Justice: A Hemicycle of Lawgivers*, completed 1860) and at St James the Less, Pimlico (1861), evince Watts's ability to work on a monumental scale. In the 1860s Watts exhibited regularly at the Academy again. Early in 1867 he was elected an ARA, followed, unusually quickly, by elevation to RA at the end of the same year.

In the late 1860s Watts turned to sculpture. The marble bust *Clytie* (1868; London, Guildhall A.G.) was a revelation to young sculptors in its freedom of movement. Tomb memorials, notably to his friend *William Kerr, 8th Marquess of Lothian* (*d* 1870; Blickling Church, Norfolk), show expressive carving. In 1870, a commission from Hugh Lupus Grosvenor, 3rd Marquess of Westminster (later 1st Duke), for a depiction of his ancestor *Hugh Lupus* as an equestrian hunter (completed 1884; Eaton Hall, Ches) inspired the equally monumental *Physical Energy* (cast, London, Kensington Gdns), which Watts worked on until the end of his life. The exaggerated musculature and dynamic pose of both horse and naked rider express in symbolic terms the energy Watts saw as characteristic of his age. Watts also executed a colossal statue of *Tennyson* for the city of Lincoln (1898–1903).

In 1865 Watts met the Manchester patron Charles Rickards, who began to buy his non-narrative symbolic paintings. It was only in 1877, with the first Grosvenor Gallery exhibition, that this side of Watts's work was triumphantly revealed to a wider audience with the appearance of the large version of *Love and Death* (U. Manchester, Whitworth A.G.). Stylistically, these works, which also include the *Eve* and *Cain* series and *Time, Death and Judgement* (completed 1886; Ottawa, N.G.), pay tribute to Watts's study of antique form and his attraction to an Italianate richness of colour and handling. They satisfied the ambition, stimulated by the Westminster competition, to paint ideas on a grand scale, and some were related to Watts's earlier vast, unrealized project for a symbolic history of mankind, the so-called House of Life.

Watts's growing stature was underlined by exhibitions in Manchester (1880) and at the Grosvenor Gallery (1881–2). More than most English artists at the time, Watts actively sought an international audience for his work, exhibiting in New York and on the Continent, and presenting paintings to museums in the USA, Canada and

France. This sustained exposure popularized contemporary English symbolic painting abroad and did much to create his enormous reputation. Watts's awareness of his own position grew as his career progressed: he built and opened a gallery at his residence in Melbury Road, London, in 1881. He presented his series of portraits of eminent men to the National Portrait Gallery in 1895 and, soon after, 23 allegorical paintings to the National Gallery of British Art (now the Tate Gallery), where they hung in their own gallery until the 1930s. Watts's status (and an indication of his personality) is underlined by his refusal of a baronetcy in 1885 and again in 1894. He accepted the new Order of Merit in 1902. In 1891 he settled at Limnerslease, in Compton, Surrey, with his second wife, Mary Fraser Tytler (1850–1938). (He had been married to the actress Ellen Terry in 1864–5.) A craftswoman in her own right, Mrs Watts set up a pottery, designing and decorating in an Art Nouveau style the Mortuary Chapel dedicated to Watts's memory. The nearby Watts Gallery contains a representative collection of his works.

BIBLIOGRAPHY
Mrs R. Barrington: *G. F. Watts: Reminiscences* (London, 1905)
G. K. Chesterton: *G. F. Watts* (London, 1905)
M. S. Watts: *George Frederic Watts: The Annals of an Artist's Life*, 3 vols (London, 1912)
G. F. Watts, 1817–1904: A Nineteenth Century Phenomenon (exh. cat. by J. Gage and C. Mullen, London, Whitechapel A.G., 1974)
W. Blunt: *'England's Michelangelo': A Biography of George Frederic Watts, O.M., R.A.* (London, 1975)
The Hall of Fame (exh. cat. by R. Ormond, London, N.P.G., 1975)
The Victorian High Renaissance (exh. cat. by A. Staley and others, Manchester, C.A.G.; Minneapolis, MN, Inst. A.; New York, Brooklyn Mus.; 1978–9)

BARBARA BRYANT

Watts, John (Cliffe) (*b* Kildare, Ireland, 7 May 1785; *d* Adelaide, 28 March 1873). Irish architect, active in Australia. He trained as an architect in Dublin and then joined the army and arrived in Australia in 1814 as a lieutenant with the 76th Regiment. Appointed aide-de-camp to Governor Lachlan Macquarie, he designed several military buildings in Sydney including a hospital (1815) on Observatory Hill, a simple Georgian building with a two-storey verandah that was later much altered, and the Lancer Barracks (1816–22), Parramatta, Australia's oldest military barracks, which has two flanking bungalows with front verandahs. He also designed twin towers (1817) for St John's in Parramatta based on a picture of Reculver Church, Kent, provided by the wife of the Governor, which survive as a characteristic example of the Gothick style in Australia. Government House, Parramatta, where he added two single storey wings connected by corridors (completed 1820; *see* AUSTRALIA, fig. 2) in the Palladian form, was possibly one of his most important works. As one of the first trained architects in Sydney, he made an important contribution to the development of colonial architecture. Watts left Australia in 1818 and took no further professional interest in architecture. In 1841 he returned to Australia and succeeded his brother Henry Watts—who had emigrated to South Australia in 1838—as Postmaster General, a post he held for 20 years.

BIBLIOGRAPHY
M. Herman: *The Early Australian Architects and their Works* (Sydney, 1954)
M. and A. Macfarlane: *John Watts, Australia's Forgotten Architect 1814–1819 and South Australia's Postmaster General 1841–1861* (Bonnells Bay, 1992)

ROBERT IRVING

Watz, Antonius (*b* Breslau [now Wrocław]; *fl* 1572; *d* 1603). Silesian stuccoist and architect, active in Sweden. His earliest work in Sweden was probably the stucco decoration (1572) in the King's Apartment at Kalmar Castle. This consists of a hunting frieze running round the walls, executed in a somewhat naive manner, and cartouches, strapwork, garlands and caryatid figures on the ceiling of the window embrasures. The decoration survives, though it was coarsely repainted in the 19th century.

Watz was occupied mainly at Uppsala Castle, where from 1573 he worked with the architect Franciscus Parr as a stuccoist. When Parr died, Watz took over as architect until the year of his death. Uppsala Castle was never completed, but both the exterior and the interior were given sumptuous stucco ornament: large-scale figures of angels, niches with shells, strapwork and heraldic devices covered the main façades. The richest stucco, however, must have been inside the chapel, a high room with three aisles, probably with a barrel vault, the walls and vault ornamented with stuccos, standing angels and large-scale reliefs. What survives of the decoration is Mannerist, apparently strongly influenced by patterns corresponding with the engravings (1593–8) of the Strasbourg artist Wendel Dietterlin, combining Late Gothic and Renaissance forms. The State Hall adjoining the chapel seems to have had stuccoed walls, though only fragmentary evidence exists, and some of the royal apartments were stuccoed. Fragments from this ruined part of the castle are in store and have not been thoroughly investigated. They suggest that the rooms were once decorated with life-size figures and various types of ornament, perhaps from a series of historical or mythological scenes.

Whereas the exterior and interior stuccos at Uppsala Castle are in fragments, the decorations in Uppsala Cathedral on the walls and vaults of the mortuary chapel of Katarina Jagellonica (1526–83), first wife of Johan III, King of Sweden, are well preserved. Probably dating from the 1590s, they were repainted in the 1890s. The decorations correspond with features from the chapel of the castle and have angels within aediculae, cartouches, strapwork and Gothic tracery. The mortuary chapel of Gustav I (*reg* 1523–60) at the east end of the cathedral (formerly the Lady chapel) had stuccos of a related design, and these, too, were probably executed by Watz and his assistants. They were removed towards the end of the 18th century (for illustrations see Dahlbergh). Watz was also associated with stuccowork (destr.) in the old castle (now the Royal Palace) in Stockholm and in Gävlehus Castle. The stucco decorations of Watz and his assistants are original in style and remarkable in quantity: Uppsala Castle must once have been one of the most richly stuccoed buildings in central and northern Europe. They belong to a period from which little stuccowork in Europe survives outside Italy.

BIBLIOGRAPHY
E. Dahlbergh: *Svecia antiqua et hodierna*, 3 vols (Stockholm, 1716, rev. 1723)
A. Hahr: 'Vasastuckaturerna på Uppsala slott', *Studier i Vasatidens konst* (Uppsala, 1920), pp. 64–82

S. Karling: 'Les Stucateurs italiens en Suède', *Società archaelogica comense arte e artisti dei laghi lombardi: Como, 1964*, ii, pp. 291–302
N. Sundquist: 'Slottskyrkan på Uppsala slott', *Uppland* (1965), pp. 13–68
——: *Willem Boy i Uppsala* (Uppsala, 1971)
T. Fulton: 'Katarina Jagellonicas kapell', *Uppsala domkyrka*, ed. Ö. Sjöholm (Uppsala, 1982), pp. 121–30
——: 'Slottet ur konstvetenskaplig aspekt', *Uppsala Slott Vasaborgen*, ed. B. Douhan (Stockholm, 1990), pp. 69–96
——: *Stuckarbeten i svenska byggnadsmiljöet från äldre Vasatid* [Stucco decoration in Swedish architectural settings of the early Vasa period] (Uppsala, 1994)

TORBJÖRN FULTON

Watzek, Hans [Johann] **(Josef)** (*b* Bilin, Bohemia [now Bílina, Czech Republic], 20 Dec 1848; *d* Vienna, 1903). Austrian photographer of Bohemian birth. He attended the Kunstakademien in Leipzig and Munich from 1866 to 1867 and taught drawing from 1873 at the Mittelschule in Komotau [now Chomutov], Bohemia, and from 1875 in Vienna. In 1890 he took his first photographs and joined the Wiener Camera-Klub, where in 1891 he met Hugo Henneberg and in 1894 Heinrich Kühn, the three becoming closely associated. In 1894 Watzek became a member of the LINKED RING. He worked first of all with platinum, then with gum prints, and from 1896 made coloured gum prints. Finally, with Heinrich Kuehn and Hugo Henneberg, he perfected the techniques of coloured gum printing and combination printing. He exhibited with Kuehn and Henneberg under the group name of Trifolium (Das Kleeblatt) from 1897 to 1903 and travelled with them in Italy, Germany and the Netherlands. From 1898 to 1902 he corresponded with Alfred Stieglitz.

Watzek wrote for a number of journals, especially the *Wiener photographische Blätter* between 1894 and 1897 (for example, the essays 'Zur Technik der künstlerischen Photographie' and 'Das Künstlerische in der Photographie', *Wien. Phot. Bl.*, 2 (1894) and 8 (1895) respectively). With his portraits and full-length figures, still-lifes and landscapes, he was one of the leading Austrian art photographers of the turn of the century.

BIBLIOGRAPHY
O. Hochreiter and T. Starl, eds: *Geschichte der Photographie in Österreich*, 2 vols (Bad Ischl, 1983)

HANS CHRISTIAN ADAM

Wauters, Emile(-Charles) (*b* Brussels, 19 Nov 1846; *d* Paris, 11 Dec 1933). Belgian painter. He trained in Brussels in the studio of the decorator Charles Albert (1821–89) and then became a pupil of Jean-François Portaels. In 1867 he spent six months in the studio of Jean-Léon Gérôme in Paris, subsequently visiting Italy and Germany. On his return to Brussels he showed his *Battle of Hastings* at the Salon of 1869 and, three years later, caused a stir with another large, dramatic historical composition, the *Insane Painter Hugo van der Goes at the Monastery of Roode* (Brussels, Mus. A. Mod.). Further success in exhibitions in Vienna, Paris, Berlin and Munich confirmed his position as a leading history painter of the time, and the city of Brussels accordingly commissioned from him two historical compositions for the Hôtel de Ville (*in situ*).

In 1880 Wauters travelled to Egypt, Spain and Morocco and, on his return to Brussels, painted a panorama of *Cairo* (untraced) for the Exposition Nationale of 1880. This work, as well as another view of *Cairo* (1881, Antwerp, Kon. Mus. S. Kst), revealed Wauters's taste for Orientalist themes, not only in the subject itself, but also in his eye for detail and the effects of light and atmosphere. Around 1883 he painted another historical subject, *Sobieski before Vienna* (6.85×7.80 m; Brussels, Mus. A. Mod.), a vast panoramic view crowded with military figures. By this time, however, he had already begun to devote himself principally to portraiture. At the Salon of 1882 in Brussels his portraits of *Mme Somzée* and of her son *Gaëtan* (both Brussels, Mus. A. Mod.) were especially admired. Wauters then went on to paint a vast number of society portraits notable for their idealized elegance and details of costume. In 1890 he settled in Paris, where he continued to make portraits such as that of *Princess Clementine of Belgium* (1905; Brussels, Mus. A. Mod.).

BIBLIOGRAPHY
Thieme–Becker
C. Lemonnier: *L'Ecole belge de peinture, 1830–1905* (Brussels, 1906)
H. Hymans: *L'Art au XVIIe et au XIXe siècle dans les Pays-Bas* (Brussels, 1921)
L'Oeuvre de Emile Wauters (exh. cat., ed. G. Vanzype; Brussels, Pal. B.-A., 1934)

RICHARD KERREMANS

Wavere, Jan van (*fl c.* 1514–1521/22). Netherlandish polychromer. The deaths of two painters named Jan Wavere are recorded in Malines in 1521 and 1522, and three early 16th-century Netherlandish carved wooden altarpieces are signed with the name Jan van Wavere. The altarpiece in the church of Jäder in Sweden bears an inscription on the border of the Virgin's robe in the carved *Nativity* scene, stating that the work was made in Mechelen in 1514 by *Jannen Van Wavere*; the name reappears with the date 1515 on the edge of the robe of a carved bishop in the uppermost of two carved altarpieces dedicated to the life of St Dymphna in the church of St Dymphna, Gheel, Belgium; the signature *I. V. Wavere* is stamped on to the small columns enclosing the central compartment of an undated carved altarpiece, originally from the church of Our Lady, Gdańsk, and now in the chapel of the Teutonic Knights, Vienna. The style of the carved sections of the three altarpieces varies widely and the painted shutters of the Jäder Altarpiece bear the signature of the Brussels painter Jan van Coninxloo II, suggesting that Jan van Wavere was neither the carver nor the artist responsible for the painted wings. The appearance of the artist's signature in conjunction with the Mechelen mark certifying the quality of the polychromy of the Vienna Altarpiece suggests instead that he was a polychromer, one of the very few during this period of sufficient reputation to sign his works. The polychromy of the carved sections of these three altarpieces has been subsequently renewed.

BIBLIOGRAPHY
F. Donnet: 'Jean Van Wavere—peintre ou sculpteur Malinois', *Bull. Cerc. Archéol., Litt. & A. Malines*, xxvi (1921), pp. 1–12
G. Van Doorslaer: 'Considérations sur l'auteur du retable de Sainte-Dymphne à Gheel', *An. Acad. Royale Archéol. Belgique*, lxxvii (1930), pp. 251–8
——: 'Marques de sculpteurs et polychromeurs malinois', *Belg. Tijdschr. Oudhdknd. & Kstgesch.*, iii (1933), pp. 160, 162, 164–5, 170–71
R. Marijnissen and M. Sawko-Michalski: 'De twee gotische retabels van Geel, een onderzoek van materiele feiten', *Bull. Inst. Royal Patrm. A.*, iii (1960), pp. 154–9, fig. 8 [Eng. summary pp. 161ff]
A. Andersson: *Medieval Wooden Sculpture in Sweden*, iii (Stockholm, 1980), pp. 201–2, fig. 128

KIM W. WOODS

Illustration Acknowledgements

We are grateful to those listed below for permission to reproduce copyright illustrative material and to those contributors who supplied photographs or helped us to obtain them. The word 'Photo:' precedes the names of large commercial or archival sources who have provided us with photographs, as well as the names of individual photographers (where known). It has generally not been used before the names of owners of works of art, such as museums and civic bodies. Every effort has been made to contact copyright holders and to credit them appropriately; we apologize to anyone who may have been omitted from the acknowledgements or cited incorrectly. Any error brought to our attention will be corrected in subsequent editions. Where illustrations have been taken from books, publication details are provided in the acknowledgements below.

Line drawings, maps, plans, chronological tables and family trees commissioned by the *Dictionary of Art* are not included in the list below. All of the maps in the dictionary were produced by Oxford Illustrators Ltd, who were also responsible for some of the line drawings. Most of the line drawings and plans, however, were drawn by one of the following artists: Diane Fortenberry, Lorraine Hodghton, Chris Miners, Amanda Patton, Mike Pringle, Jo Richards, Miranda Schofield, John Tiernan, John Wilson and Philip Winton. The chronological tables and family trees were prepared initially by Kate Boatfield and finalized by John Johnson.

Varnish Trustees of the National Gallery, London
Vasari: (1) Giorgio Vasari *1, 3, 6, 8* Photo: Archivi Alinari, Florence; *2, 5, 7* Photo: Scala, Florence; *4* Photo: © RMN, Paris; *9* Fondation Custodia, Collection Frits Lugt, Institut Néerlandais, Paris; *10* Photo: Dr J. Kliemann
Vase painters, §II: Berlin Painter Staatliche Museen zu Berlin, Preussischer Kulturbesitz
Vase painters, §II: Exekias Vatican Museums, Vatican City, Rome
Vase painters, §II: Kleophrades Painter J. Paul Getty Museum, Malibu, CA
Vasnetsov: (1) Viktor Vasnetsov Tret'yakov Gallery, Moscow
Vaudoyer: (2) Léon Vaudoyer *1* Photo: Arch. Phot. Paris/© DACS, 1996; *2* Photo: Agence Roger-Viollet, Paris
Vaudremer, Emile Photo: Arch. Phot. Paris/© DACS, 1996
Vaux-le-Vicomte Bibliothèque Nationale de France, Paris
Vecchi, Giovanni de' Photo: Gabinetto Fotografico Nazionale, Istituto Centrale per il Catalogo e la Documentazione, Rome
Vecchietta *1–2* Photo: Archivi Alinari, Florence
Vedder, Elihu Museum of Art, San Diego, CA (Gift of Elizabeth Johnson)
Veduta *1* Royal Collection, Windsor Castle/© Her Majesty Queen Elizabeth II; *2* Photo: British Architectural Library, RIBA, London
Veen, Otto van *1* Musées Royaux des Beaux-Arts de Belgique, Brussels; *2* Pierpont Morgan Library, New York
Veii Soprintendenza Archeologica per l'Etruria Meridionale, Rome
Veit, Philipp Landesmuseum, Mainz
Vela, Vincenzo Photo: Gabinetto Fotografico Nazionale, Istituto Centrale per il Catalogo e la Documentazione, Rome
Velasco, José María Instituto Nacional de Bellas Artes y Literatura, Mexico City
Velázquez, Diego *1* Board of Trustees of the Wellington Museum, London/Photo: Bridgeman Art Library, London; *2* Photo: Patrimonio Nacional, Archivo Fotográfico, Madrid; *3* Index/Photo: Bridgeman Art Library, London; *4–6, 9–10* Photo: Bridgeman Art Library, London; *7* Museo del Prado, Madrid; *8* National Gallery, London/Photo: Bridgeman Art Library, London
Velde (i): (1) Esaias van de Velde *1* Rijksmuseum Twenthe, Enschede; *2* Rijksmuseum, Amsterdam
Velde (i): (2) Jan van de Velde II Museum Boymans–van Beuningen, Rotterdam
Velde (ii): (1) Willem van de Velde I National Maritime Museum, London
Velde (ii): (2) Willem van de Velde II *1* National Maritime Museum, London; *2* Rijksmuseum, Amsterdam
Velde, Adriaen van de Syndics of the Fitzwilliam Museum, Cambridge
Veliky Ustyug Photo: Aleksandr U. Grekov
Vellert, Dirk *1* Photo: © ACL, Brussels; *2* Rijksmuseum, Amsterdam
Venda Trustees of the British Museum, London

Venegas, Francisco © Instituto Português do Património Cultural, Lisbon
Venetian empire *2* Photo: Osvaldo Böhm, Venice
Veneto-Saracenic Trustees of the British Museum, London
Venetsianov, Aleksey Photo: VAAP, Moscow
Venezuela *2* Horniman Museum, London; *3–5* South American Pictures, Woodbridge, Suffolk/Photo: Tony Morrison; *6* Asociación Venezolana, Amigos del Arte Colonial Colección, Caracas/Photo: M. Aldaca, 1981; *7* Galería de Arte Nacional, Caracas; *8* Art Museum of the Americas (OAS), Washington, DC; *9* Asociación Venezolana, Amigos del Arte Colonial Colección, Caracas
Venice *1* Museo Correr, Venice; *2* Istituto Geografico Militare Italiano, Florence; *3, 14* Photo: Anthony Kersting, London; *4* Photo: Conway Library, Courtauld Institute of Art, London; *5, 15–21, 23–25, 27, 31* Photo: Osvaldo Böhm, Venice; *6* Photo: Scala, Florence; *7–9, 20–21, 26, 28, 30* Photo: Archivi Alinari, Florence; *10* Museo Civico Medioevale, Bologna (neg. Ab2, inv. no. 1364-1365); *11* Museo Vetrario di Murano, Venice; *12* Corning Museum of Glass, Corning, NY; *13* Österreichisches Museum für Angewandte Kunst, Vienna; *22* Archivio Veneziano, Venice/Photo: Sarah Quill; *29* Board of Trustees of the Victoria and Albert Museum, London
Venne, Adriaen van de *1* Rijksmuseum, Amsterdam; *2* Trustees of the British Museum, London
Venturi, Rauch & Scott Brown Venturi, Rauch & Scott Brown/Photo: Tom Bernard
Verandah British Library, London (India Office; no. 7-183)
Vereshchagin, Vasily Photo: M.N. Sokolov
Vergara, José Photo: Ampliaciones y Reproducciones MAS, Barcelona
Vergina Photo: Ekdotiki Athenon S.A., Athens
Verhelst, Egid, I Bayerisches Nationalmuseum, Munich
Vermeer, Johannes *1* Mauritshuis, The Hague; *2* Metropolitan Museum of Art, New York (Gift of Henry G. Marquand, 1889; no. 89.15.21); *3* Foundation Johan Maurits van Nassau, Mauritshuis, The Hague; *4* Photo: Art Resource, New York; *5* Rijksmuseum, Amsterdam; *6* Kenwood House, London (Iveagh Bequest)/Photo: English Heritage Photographic Library, London
Vermeyen, Jan Cornelisz. Kunsthistorisches Museum, Vienna
Vernacular architecture *1* Photo: K. Dymock, London; *2–4* Photo: Anthony Quiney; *5–7* Photo: Gwyn Meirion-Jones; *8–9* Photo: Conway Library, Courtauld Institute of Art, London; *10* Photo: SHBO, Arnhem; *11* Photo: Jane Helliwell; *12* Photo: Jane Geddes; *13* Photo: Tim Benton, Cambridge; *14* Photo: Documan Press, Kalamazoo, MI; *15* Photo: Overseas Agenzia Fotografica, Milan; *16–17* Photo: Melissa Publishing House, Athens; *18* National Museum, Warsaw; *19* Institute of Art PAN, Warsaw (neg. no. L/42965)/Photo: Jan Swiderski; *20* Center for Historic Architecture and Engineering, University of Delaware, Newark, DE/Photo: Gabrielle M. Lanier; *21* Photo: J. Ritchie Garrison; *22* Colonial Williamsburg Foundation, Williamsburg, VA/

925

Photo: Willie Graham; *23–4* South American Pictures, Woodbridge, Suffolk/Photo: Tony Morrison; *25* La Trobe Collection, State Library of Victoria, Melbourne; *26* Photo: Jonathan M. Bloom; *27* Photo: Lucien Golvin; *28* Photo: Bernard O'Kane; *29* Robert Harding Picture Library, London/Photo: V. Southwell; *30* Photo: Robert Harding Picture Library, London; *31* Photo: Mr Jolyon Leslie; *32* Photo: N. Akin; *33* International Merv Project, London; *34* Asian Art Archives of the University of Michigan, Ann Arbor, MI; *35* Photo: Miki Desai

Vernacular art *1–3, 8, 11* Judkyn/Pratt Collection, Bath; *4, 6, 10* American Museum in Britain, Bath; *5* Museum of English Naive Art, Bath; *7* Reconstruction by James Ayres, Bath; *9* Collection James Ayres, Bath

Vernet: (1) Joseph Vernet *1* Trustees of the Wallace Collection, London

Vernet: (2) Carle Vernet *1* Snite Museum of Art, Notre Dame, IN (Purchased with funds provided by the William and Walter Klauer Fund; no. 71.9); *2* Photo: © RMN, Paris

Vernet: (3) Horace Vernet Photo: © RMN, Paris

Vernis Martin Trustees of the Wallace Collection, London

Verona *1* Photo: Anthony Kersting, London; *2–3, 5* Photo: Archivi Alinari, Florence; *4* Photo: Conway Library, Courtauld Institute of Art, London

Veronese, Paolo *1, 4–5* Photo: Gabinetto Fotografico, Soprintendenza ai Beni Artistici e Storici, Florence; *2–3* Photo: Archivi Alinari, Florence; *6* J. Paul Getty Museum, Malibu, CA

Verrio, Antonio Burghley House, Stamford

Verrocchio, Andrea del *1–3, 5* Photo: Archivi Alinari, Florence; *4* Photo: Osvaldo Böhm, Venice; *6* Trustees of the National Gallery, London

Versailles *1, 3–4* Photo: © RMN, Paris; *2* Photo: Anthony Kersting, London

Verspronck, Jan Rijksmuseum, Amsterdam

Vesnin A.V. Shchusev Research and Scientific Museum of Russian Architecture, Moscow

Vestments, ecclesiastical *1, 3* Österreichisches Museum für Angewandte Kunst, Vienna; *2* Trustees of the National Gallery, London

Vézelay, Ste Madeleine *1–2* Photo: James Austin, Cambridge

Viaduct British Library, London (no. Cup.1248.b.1)

Vianen, van: (1) Adam van Vianen Rijksmuseum, Amsterdam

Vianen, van: (2) Paulus van Vianen Rijksmuseum, Amsterdam

Viani, Antonio Maria Soprintendenza per i Beni Artistici e Storici per le Provincie di Brescia, Cremona, Mantova, Mantua

Vicente, Gil Museu Nacional de Arte Antiga, Lisbon

Vicenza *1* Biblioteca Angelica, Rome; *2* Photo: Franco Barbieri; *3* Biblioteca Civica Bertoliana, Vicenza

Vico, Enea Graphische Sammlung Albertina, Vienna

Victors, Jan Photo: © RMN, Paris

Vicús Museo del Banco Central de Reserva, Lima

Video art Donald Young Gallery, Seattle, WA

Vieira Lusitano, Francisco Arquivo Nacional de Fotografia, Lisbon

Vieira Portuense, Francisco Museu Nacional de Arte Antiga, Lisbon

Vien, Joseph-Marie *1–2* Photo: © RMN, Paris

Vienna *2–3, 6–7* Photo: Bundesdenkmalamt, Vienna; *4, 8, 11, 18* Kunsthistorisches Museum, Vienna; *5* Photo: Bildarchiv, Österreichische Nationalbibliothek, Vienna; *9* Schloss Schönbrunn, Vienna/Photo: AKG London Ltd; *10* Österreichische Galerie, Belvedere, Vienna; *12* Österreichisches Museum für Angewandte Kunst, Vienna; *13, 16–17* Photo: Bildarchiv Foto Marburg

Vienna Genesis Photo: Bildarchiv, Österreichische Nationalbibliothek, Vienna

Vienne Photo: Conway Library, Courtauld Institute of Art, London

Vierzehnheiligen Photo: Anthony Kersting, London

Vietnam *3–6, 9, 14, 16* Photo: Nora Taylor; *7* Ecole Française d'Extrême Orient, Paris/Musée Guimet, Paris; *8* © Tettoni, Cassio and Associates Pte Ltd, Singapore; *11–13, 15, 21* Photo: Werner Forman Archive, London; *17–18* Plum Blossoms (International) Ltd; *19* Photo: Christie's Images, London; *20* National Museum of Fine Arts, Hanoi; *22* Photo: Phan Ngoc Khûe; *23* Yale University Art Gallery, New Haven, CT; *24* Photo: Robert Harding Picture Library, London

Vigarny, Felipe Photo: Margarita Estella

Vigée Le Brun, Elisabeth-Louise *1* National Gallery of Art, Washington, DC (Gift of the Bay Foundation in memory of Josephine Bay Paul and Ambassador Charles Ulrick Bay); *2* Photo: © RMN, Paris

Vigeland, Gustav Nasjonalgalleriet, Oslo

Vignali, Jacopo National Gallery of Ireland, Dublin

Vignette Photo: Adam Langlands

Vignola, Jacopo *1* Photo: British Architectural Library, RIBA, London; *2–3* Photo: Archivi Alinari, Florence; *4* Overseas Agenzia Fotografica, Milan/Photo: A. Villani, Bologna

Vignon, Claude Photo: Scala, Florence

Viking art *1, 5, 9–13* Antikvarisk–Topografiska Arkivet, Stockholm; *2–3* Universitetet i Bergen, Historisk Museum, Bergen; *4, 8* Universitets Oldsaksamlingen, Oslo; *6–7* Nationalmuseum, Copenhagen; *14* Historical Museum, Moscow; *16* National Museum of Ireland, Dublin; *17* Photo: Helen Clarke

Vilaça, José de Santo António Ferreira Photo: Conway Library, Courtauld Institute of Art, London

Villa *2* Photo: Deutsches Archäologisches Institut, Rome (neg. no. 61.531); *3–4* Photo: Archivi Alinari, Florence; *5* Photo: Archivio Fotografico, Servizio Beni Culturali-Comune, Genoa; *6* Architectural Association, London/Photo: Theo Armour; *7* Photo: British Architectural Library, RIBA, London; *8* Photo: Anthony Kersting, London; *9* British Library, London (no. 61.e.16); *10* Photo: Tim Benton, Cambridge

Villanovan Museo Civico Archeologico, Bologna (no. Benacci t.525)

Villanueva: (2) Juan de Villanueva *1–2* Ampliaciones y Reproducciones MAS, Barcelona

Villanueva, Carlos Raúl South American Pictures, Woodbridge, Suffolk/Photo: Tony Morrison

Villard de Honnecourt *1–2* Bibliothèque Nationale de France, Paris

Villeneuve-lès-Avignon Photo: Yoshiaki Nishino

Villon, Jacques Solomon R. Guggenheim Foundation, New York (Gift, Estate of Katherine S. Dreier, 1953; no. FN 53.1356)/© ADAGP, Paris, and DACS, London, 1996

Vincennes Metropolitan Museum of Art, New York

Vincent, François-André Photo: © RMN, Paris

Vinckboons: (1) David Vinckboons Photo: © ACL, Brussels

Vinckboons: (2) Philips Vingboons Rijksmuseum, Amsterdam

Viollet-le-Duc, Eugène-Emmanuel *1, 3* Photo: Arch. Phot. Paris/© DACS, 1996; *2, 4* Photo: British Architectural Library, RIBA, London

Visby Photo: Erland Lagerlöf

Vischer: (1) Hermann Vischer (i) Photo: Bildarchiv Foto Marburg

Vischer: (2) Peter Vischer (i) Bayerisches Nationalmuseum, Munich

Vischer: (3) Hermann Vischer (ii) Musée Léon Marès, Château de Montrottier, Lovagny

Vischer: (4) Peter Vischer (ii) Bildstelle und Fotoarchiv, Nuremberg

Viseu Architectural Association, London

Visigothic art *1* Museo Arqueológico Nacional, Madrid; *2–3* Photo: Ampliaciones y Reproducciones MAS, Barcelona

Viso del Marqués Photo: Ampliaciones y Reproducciones MAS, Barcelona

Visscher, Claes Jansz. Fondation Custodia, Collection Frits Lugt, Institut Néerlandais, Paris

Vitale da Bologna Photo: Gabinetto Fotografico, Soprintendenza ai Beni Artistici e Storici, Bologna

Viterbo Photo: Archivi Alinari, Florence

Vitoni, Ventura di Andrea Photo: Archivi Alinari, Florence

Vitozzi, Ascanio Photo: Archivi Alinari, Florence

Vitruvius *1* British Library, London (no. 2261.f.14); *2* British Library, London (no. L.40/33); *3* Provost and Fellows, Eton College/Photo: Conway Library, Courtauld Institute of Art, London; *4* British Library, London (no. 59.f.23)

Vittone, Bernardo Antonio *1* Yale University Press Photo Library, London/Photo: © John Witt, London; *2* Yale University Press Photo Library, London/Photo: © Prof. Paolo Portoghesi

Vittoria, Alessandro *1* Staatliche Museen zu Berlin, Preussischer Kulturbesitz; *2* Photo: Osvaldo Böhm, Venice; *3* Photo: Archivi Alinari, Florence

Vivarini: (1) Antonio Vivarini National Gallery, Prague

Vivarini: (2) Bartolomeo Vivarini Gabinetto Fotografico, Soprintendenza ai Beni Artistici e Storici, Venice

Vivarini: (3) Alvise Vivarini *1* Photo: Reale Fotografia Giacomelli, Venice; *2* Trustees of the National Gallery, London

Vix Photo: Labeaune Photos, Châtillon-sur-Seine

Vladimir–Suzdal' *1–4* Photo: VAAP, Moscow

Vlaminck, Maurice de Musée National d'Art Moderne, Paris/© ADAGP, Paris, and DACS, London, 1996

Vleughels, Nicolas Photo: © RMN, Paris

Vlieger, Simon de *1* Museum of Fine Arts, Budapest; *2* Staatliche Museen zu Berlin, Preussischer Kulturbesitz

Vogtherr: (1) Heinrich Vogtherr (i) Photo: Kristin Lohse Belkin

Volaire, Pierre-Jacques Statens Konstmuseer, Stockholm

Volgograd Photo: NOVOSTI Photo Library, London

Volpi, Alfredo Museu de Arte Moderna do São Paulo

Voogd, Hendrik Photo: Fransje Kuyvenhoven

Vordemberge-Gildewart, Friedrich Staatliche Museen zu Berlin, Preussischer Kulturbesitz/Negativ Archiv, Abzug Hollenstein, Rapperswil/Photo: Bauter/© DACS, 1996

Voronikhin, Andrey Bibliothèque Nationale de France, Paris

Vorsterman: (1) Lucas Vorsterman (i) Photo: Rheinische Bildarchiv, Cologne

Vorticism Museum of Fine Arts, Houston, TX (Museum purchase with funds provided by the Brown Foundation)/© Estate of Edward Wadsworth, 1996. All rights reserved/DACS

Vos, de (i): (1) Cornelis de Vos *1* Trustees of the Wallace Collection, London; *2* Museum Boymans–van Beuningen, Rotterdam

Vos, de (i): (2) Paul de Vos Photo: © ACL, Brussels

Vos, Martende *1* Mauritshuis, The Hague; *2* Pierpont Morgan Library, New York

Vos, Simon de Koninklijk Museum voor Schone Kunsten, Antwerp

Vouet, Simon *1* Photo: Gabinetto Fotografico Nazionale, Istituto Centrale per il Catalogo e la Documentazione, Rome; *2* Photo: © RMN, Paris; *3* Royal Collection, Windsor Castle/© Her Majesty Queen Elizabeth II; *4* Photo: Giraudon, Paris

Voysey, C. F. A. *1* Photo: British Architectural Library, RIBA, London; *2* Board of Trustees of the Victoria and Albert Museum, London

Vrancx, Sebastiaen Bayerische Staatsbibliothek, Munich

Vredeman de Vries, Hans *1* Bibliothèque Royale Albert 1er, Brussels; *2* Kunsthistorisches Museum, Vienna

Vrelant, Willem J. Paul Getty Museum, Malibu, CA

Vries, Adriaen de Statens Konstmuseer, Stockholm

Vroom: (1) Hendrick Vroom *1* Frans Halsmuseum, Haarlem/Photo: Tom Haartsen; *2* Board of Trustees of the Victoria and Albert Museum, London

Vrubel', Mikhail Photo: Aurora Art Publishers, St Petersburg

Vuillard, Edouard *1* Scottish National Gallery of Modern Art, Edinburgh; *2* Photo: © RMN, Paris; *3* Brooklyn Museum, Brooklyn, NY/William Kelly Simpson/© DACS, 1996

Vyborg National Museum of Finland, Helsinki

Vyšší Brod Abbey Photo: Helena Soukupová

Wąchock Abbey Institute of Art PAN, Warsaw/Photo: Tadeusz Kazmiarski

Wael, de: (1) Cornelis de Wael Kunsthistorisches Museum, Vienna

Wagner, Otto *1–2* Photo: Bildarchiv, Österreichische Nationalbibliothek, Vienna

Wailly, Charles de *1* Musée des Beaux-Arts, Dijon; *2* Photo: © RMN, Paris

Walbaum, Matthias Photo: Gabinetto Fotografico Nazionale, Istituto Centrale per il Catalogo e la Documentazione, Rome

Waldmüller, Ferdinand Georg Österreichische Galerie im Belvedere, Vienna

Wales *2–3, 5–6* Royal Commission on the Ancient and Historical Monuments of Wales/© Crown Copyright; *4* Private collection, Ambleside; *7* Llanelli Borough Council

Walker, Fred Tate Gallery, London

Wall painting *1* Western Australian Museum, Perth; *2, 4* Photo: Gabinetto Fotografico, Soprintendenza ai Beni Artistici e Storici, Florence; *3, 5* Vatican Museums, Vatican City, Rome; *6* Consorzio

C.R.O.M.A and Consorzio Te, Mantua (from C.M. Belfanti, C. Tellini Perina and G. Basile: *I Giganti di Palazzo Te*, Mantua, 1989)

Wallpaper *1* Ferens Art Gallery, Hull City Museums, Art Galleries and Archives, Hull; *2* British Library, London (no. PP.1612.f); *3–4, 6* Board of Trustees of the Victoria and Albert Museum, London; *5* Whitworth Art Gallery, University of Manchester

Wall-pillar church Photo: Hirmer Fotoarchiv, Munich

Walpole: (2) Horace Walpole *1* National Portrait Gallery, London; *2* British Library, London (no. 10368.i.23); *3* Country Life Picture Library, London/Photo: Henson

Walter, Thomas U. Library of Congress, Washington, DC

Walther: (1) Christoph Walther I Sächsische Landesbibliothek, Dresden

Walther: (2) Christoph Walther II Sächsische Landesbibliothek, Dresden

Walther: (4) Sebastian Walther Sächsische Landesbibliothek, Dresden

Wang (ii): (1) Wang Shimin Metropolitan Museum of Art, New York (Gift of Douglas Dillon, 1980; no. 1980.426.2)

Wang (ii): (2) Wang Yuanqi Metropolitan Museum of Art, New York (Gift of Douglas Dillon, 1977; no. 1977.80)

Wang Fu National Palace Museum, Taipei

Wang Hui Honolulu Academy of Arts, Honolulu, HI (Purchase, 1955)

Wang Jian Freer Gallery of Art, Smithsonian Institution, Washington, DC (no. 56.27)

Wang Meng *1* Freer Gallery of Art, Smithsonian Institution, Washington, DC; *2* Shanghai Museum

Wang Wei Institute of Oriental Culture, University of Tokyo/Collection of the Municipal Museum, Osaka

Wappers, Gustaf Photo: Dominique Vautier

Ward, James Tate Gallery, London

Wardell, William Wilkinson Ministry of Tourism, Government of Victoria/Photo: Michael Cheshire

Warehouse Photo: Prof. Leonard K. Eaton

Warhol, Andy Rheinische Bildarchiv, Cologne/© ARS, New York, and DACS, London, 1996

Warsaw *1* Photo: Leszek Wroblewski, Warsaw; *2–4, 6, 9–10* Andrzej Voellnagel, Warsaw/Photo: Edmund Kupiecki; *5, 8* Andrzej Voellnagel, Warsaw/Photo: Edmund Kupiecki/Zbyszko i Maciej Siemaszko; *7* National Museum, Warsaw

Wartburg, Schloss Photo: Bildarchiv Foto Marburg

Wash Royal Collection, Windsor Castle/© Her Majesty Queen Elizabeth II

Washington, DC *1, 5* Library of Congress, Washington, DC; *2* National Archives, Washington, DC (neg. no. 111-SC-80718); *3* Photo: Robert Harding Picture Library, London; *4* Photo: Carol M. Highsmith Photography, Washington, DC; *6* Photo: Antoinette J. Lee

Watanabe Kazan National Museum, Kyoto. All rights reserved

Watercolour *1* Harvard University Art Museums, Cambridge, MA; *2* Pierpont Morgan Library, New York (no. 1980.37)

Waterhouse, Alfred Photo: RCHME/© Crown Copyright

Waterlo, Antoni Bayerische Staatsgemäldesammlungen, Munich

Watteau: (1) Antoine Watteau *1* National Gallery of Scotland, Edinburgh; *2* Trustees of the Wallace Collection, London; *3* Photo: © RMN, Paris; *4* Rijksmuseum, Amsterdam

Watteau: (3) François Watteau Photo: Giraudon, Paris

Watts, G. F. Tate Gallery, London